33D CONGRESS, 2d Session. } HOUSE OF REPRESENTATIVES. { Ex. Doc. No. 98.

# MORTALITY STATISTICS

OF THE

# SEVENTH CENSUS OF THE UNITED STATES,

# 1850:

EMBRACING—

I.—THE CAUSE OF DEATH,
II.—THE AGE AND SEX,
III.—THE COLOR AND CONDITION,
IV.—THE NATIVITY,
V.—THE SEASON OF DECEASE,
VI.—THE DURATION OF ILLNESS,
VII.—THE OCCUPATION,

OF THE

PERSONS REPORTED TO HAVE DIED IN THE TWELVE MONTHS PRECEDING THE FIRST OF JUNE OF THAT YEAR,

WITH

SUNDRY COMPARATIVE AND ILLUSTRATIVE TABLES.

---

BY J. D. B. DE BOW,

SUPERINTENDENT UNITED STATES CENSUS.

---

WASHINGTON:

A. O. P. NICHOLSON, PRINTER.

1855.

# LETTER

FROM

# THE SECRETARY OF THE INTERIOR,

TRANSMITTING

*The Mortality Statistics of the Seventh Census, prepared by the Superintendent of the Census, in compliance with the resolution of the House of Representatives of December* 13, 1854.

---

DECEMBER 13, 1854.

"*Resolved*, That there be printed for the use of the members of the present House of Representatives, fifteen thousand copies of that portion of the returns of the Seventh Census which relates to the Mortality Statistics of the United States, to be arranged by the Superintendent of the Census: *Provided*, The same shall be printed in royal octavo form, and not to exceed three hundred pages."

---

DEPARTMENT OF THE INTERIOR,
*Washington, November* 23, 1855.

SIR: I herewith transmit to you the Mortality Statistics of the Seventh Census, as arranged by the Superintendent of the Census, under the resolution of the House of the 13th December, 1854.

Very respectfully, your obedient servant,

R. McCLELLAND,
*Secretary.*

TO JOHN W. FORNEY,
*Clerk of the House of Representatives.*

# TABLE OF CONTENTS.



## PART I.—UNITED STATES TABLES.



## PART II.—STATE TABLES.

CENSUS OFFICE, *November* 20, 1855.

SIR: I stated in my last official report that the mortality statistics of the Census were nearly ready for publication, and subsequently, at the instance of a committee of Congress, estimated that four or five months would be necessary for their completion in the shape in which they were required by that body.

The appropriation was made on the 4th of March. You will, therefore, perceive that a delay of several months more than was anticipated has occurred, for which I assign as reasons—first, the utter impossibility of estimating very closely where such an amount and kind of material are involved; second, the peculiar experience required, limiting necessarily the clerical force; third, the state of my own health, impaired by long, close, and arduous labors upon the Quarto and Compendium, putting it out of the question for me, during several months, to exercise any personal supervision of the work My anxiety to see the volume completed has not been surpassed by your own, and to the extent of that anxiety I bear cheerful testimony.

To embrace the whole material within the compass of three hundred pages, exclusively of titles, required my constant superintendence of the press up to the present moment, and it is but fair to add, in this connexion, that the reading of proof was left entirely to the printers, the means at my disposal being inadequate to the employment of special readers, (as was done upon the tables of the Compendium,) familiar with statistics, and responsible to the office for their accuracy.

The calculations for the work were all made under my direction by persons approved for their capacity, who have been employed in the office from almost its first organization. This is the guaranty I have for their correctness; for I could not incur the expense of those frequent revisions by different sets of persons, resorted to in the report of last year, and it was plainly impossible for me to make them myself.

I believe the errors, however, will not be found more numerous nor important than are to be met with in statistical works generally; and although I know that the work is very incomplete, from the original deficiencies of the returns, and have so stated it in the introductory chapter, I am yet assured that its publication will subserve many and valuable purposes.

The Census Office, which was revived by the act calling for this report is, by its completion, again dissolved, and my duties as Superintendent of the Census, under your reappointment, are at end. I have endeavored to fulfill the trust faithfully and energetically, and, under all the circumstances, to secure the best results.

With high regard, your obedient servant,

J. D. B. DE BOW.

To Hon. R. MCCLELLAND, *Secretary of the Interior.*

# INTRODUCTORY CHAPTER.

PROGRESS OF VITAL STATISTICS—HISTORY OF IN THE UNITED STATES.—PLAN AND RESULTS OF THE VOLUME.

It is more easy to satisfy mankind of the value of any other branch of statistics than that which relates to the numbers that die in any given period, their ages, their sex, occupation, condition and nativity, and the causes which produce such deaths. The consequence is that the facts remain uncollected or unrecorded, while everybody seems busy enough, more especially in our practical, money-making country, in running after those which relate to the fluctuations of stocks, the valuation of exports and imports, the rates of taxation and the results in agriculture and manufactures, internal improvements and general commerce. The life of man is of less importance than his larder and his cloth. It was the remark of a physician, now no more, founded on severe experience, that the lawyer who saved the property of his client was always quicker, better and more cheerfully paid than the doctor who saved his life. Steamboat and railroad companies understand this well enough, for whilst they must pay heavily for destroying a bundle of merchandise, in human life they can and do wanton at pleasure.

Such being the case, it is not singular that investigations having for their object sanitary improvement are pursued slower and later in all countries than those which relate to property. They meet with greater impediments and their results are least consulted or credited. Man is the same in all ages, and this fact meets us in all.

The Romans had, indeed, their registries, in which were carefully preserved the particulars of population, as births, sex, deaths, etc., but there is no evidence, we believe, of a *regular system of registration of births, marriages and deaths* prior to that of Geneva in the middle of the sixteenth century. Subsequently, most of the European nations have followed the example of Geneva, and their results for several periods may be found elaborately given in the sixth annual report of the registrar general of England, 1847. A condensed table from this report is here presented:

| Countries. | Year. | Population. | Annual deaths. | | Annual mortality. | |
|---|---|---|---|---|---|---|
| | | | Years. | Numbers. | Per cent. | Living to 1 death. |
| England | 1841 | 15,927,867 | 1838-42 | 346,905 | 2.207 | 45 |
| France | 1841 | 34,213,929* | 1838-42 | 816,840 | 2.397 | 42 |
| Prussia | 1840 | 14,928,501 | 1838-41 | 392,349 | 2.658 | 38 |
| Austria | 1840 | 21,571,594 | 1838-42 | 651,239 | 2.995 | 33 |
| Russia | 1842 | 49,525,420 | 1842 | 1,856,183 | 3.590† | 28 |

* The population of France, according to the corrected returns, is 34,230,178.

† Corrected for the stillborn included in the 1,856,188 deaths; the stillborn have been subtracted from the deaths in Austria and Prussia; they are not included in the deaths of France, and are not registered in England.

On comparing the rate of mortality in England with the mortality of France, Prussia, Austria, and Russia, it appears to be lower in this country than in either of the four States; but it must be remembered that Scotland and Ireland are not included, no steps having hitherto been taken for registering and abstracting the births and deaths in those parts of the United Kingdom, the only countries now in Europe where it has not been deemed advisable to record and analyze such facts, with the exception, perhaps, of Hungary, Spain, Turkey, and Greece.

Parochial registration, which had been in use in England for more than two hundred years, was found so inadequate and defective that the subject was brought into Parliament in 1833 and referred to a committee, who, after thorough investigation, reported as follows:

1. That the subject is urgently important.
2. That it involves matters of great public and national interest, as well as individual satisfaction, and rights and claims to property, and deserves the attention of the humblest artizan as well as of the most philosophical and statesmanlike inquirer.
3. That the existing law is imperfect and unjust, and requires not only partial amendment but real fundamental reform.
4. That great trouble, vast expense, utter uncertainty, capricious changes, and local and general evils exist, while no means are supplied to obtain the information other countries possess and justly value, as to the state of disease, the operation of moral and physical causes on the health of the people, the progress of the population, and other matters on which accurate knowledge can scarcely be too highly appreciated or too intensely pursued.

The result of this investigation and report was an act for the registration of births, marriages and deaths in England, which, introduced by Lord John Russell, and supported by Peel, Morpeth and Bowring, passed on the 6th June, 1836. Under the operation of the act regular annual reports have been made, of which a complete series have been furnished for the use of the Census Office, the present year, through the courtesy of Mr. Graham, the registrar general. These volumes vary from 5 to 700 pages, and are issued in the most admirable style. The following table is extracted from the report for 1850, p. 14:

*Annual rate of mortality per cent. of males and females at different ages in England.*

| Years... | 1838 | 1839 | 1840 | 1841 | 1842 | 1843 | 1844 | 1845 | 1846 | 1847 | 1848 | 1849 | 1850 | Average of the 13 years 1838--50. |
|---|---|---|---|---|---|---|---|---|---|---|---|---|---|---|
| All ages. | 2.343 | 2.281 | 2.377 | 2.242 | 2.244 | 2.206 | 2.245 | 2.173 | 2.398 | 2.549 | 2.394 | 2.584 | 2.147 | 2.322 |
| 0.... | 7.041 | 7.167 | 7.542 | 6.843 | 7.048 | 6.898 | 6.984 | 6.665 | 7.760 | 7.588 | 7.401 | 7.513 | 6.695 | 7.165 |
| 5.... | .901 | .904 | 1.083 | .956 | .901 | .844 | .897 | .823 | .825 | .970 | 1.043 | 1.124 | .814 | .930 |
| 10.... | .519 | .512 | .542 | .510 | .501 | .478 | .473 | .466 | .507 | .550 | .530 | .646 | .467 | .515 |
| 15.... | .851 | .819 | .832 | .811 | .783 | .772 | .763 | .781 | .859 | .929 | .858 | .951 | .717 | .825 |
| 25.... | 1.064 | .986 | .995 | .978 | .928 | .924 | .940 | .926 | 1.025 | 1.100 | 1.026 | 1.243 | .879 | 1 001 |
| 35.... | 1.342 | 1.255 | 1.266 | 1.217 | 1.197 | 1.218 | 1.225 | 1.202 | 1.272 | 1.436 | 1.303 | 1.581 | 1.165 | 1.283 |
| 45.... | 1.949 | 1.798 | 1.796 | 1.785 | 1.733 | 1.722 | 1.750 | 1.715 | 1.800 | 2.065 | 1.864 | 2.262 | 1.716 | 1.848 |
| 55.... | 3.410 | 3.192 | 3.142 | 3.137 | 3.041 | 3.008 | 3.051 | 2.975 | 3.129 | 3.649 | 3.266 | 3.655 | 2.980 | 3.208 |
| 65.... | 6.916 | 6.421 | 6.678 | 6.482 | 6.595 | 6.578 | 6.736 | 6 491 | 6.758 | 7.696 | 6.793 | 7.244 | 6.306 | 6.746 |
| 75.... | 14.752 | 13.874 | 14.488 | 14.266 | 14.578 | 14.090 | 14.651 | 14.400 | 15.070 | 17.326 | 14.986 | 16.187 | 14.019 | 14.745 |
| 85.... | 29.745 | 27.923 | 30.242 | 29.650 | 29.438 | 28.758 | 31.716 | 30.191 | 32.214 | 35.553 | 30.622 | 29.976 | 28.555 | 30.353 |
| 95& up | 49.699 | 43.112 | 48.498 | 46.633 | 46.427 | 45.681 | 43.228 | 49.035 | 51.651 | 56.607 | 42.435 | 42.859 | 38.560 | 46.494 |

*Deaths to* 100 *females living.*

| All ages. | 2.136 | 2.094 | 2.205 | 2.085 | 2.100 | 2.048 | 2.085 | 2.013 | 2.222 | 2.381 | 2.225 | 2.447 | 2.014 | 2.158 |
|---|---|---|---|---|---|---|---|---|---|---|---|---|---|---|
| 0.... | 6.047 | 6.138 | 6.432 | 5.861 | 6.023 | 5.897 | 5.885 | 5.657 | 6.675 | 6.553 | 6.396 | 6.488 | 5.738 | 6.138 |
| 5.... | .895 | .935 | 1.113 | .963 | .925 | .848 | .902 | .800 | .813 | .951 | .997 | 1.102 | .810 | .927 |
| 10.... | .543 | .535 | .569 | .520 | .512 | .485 | .508 | .476 | .533 | .577 | .566 | .653 | .491 | .536 |
| 15.... | .854 | .848 | .868 | .842 | .830 | .784 | .810 | .815 | .870 | .919 | .878 | 1.000 | .777 | .853 |
| 25.... | 1.046 | 1.007 | 1.083 | 1.007 | 1.005 | .976 | 1.006 | .980 | 1.048 | 1.173 | 1.090 | 1.347 | .988 | 1.054 |
| 35.... | 1.313 | 1.248 | 1.269 | 1.227 | 1.229 | 1.227 | 1.200 | 1.188 | 1.242 | 1.422 | 1.301 | 1.617 | 1.169 | 1.280 |
| 45.... | 1.660 | 1.549 | 1.567 | 1.542 | 1.526 | 1.484 | 1.525 | 1.467 | 1.559 | 1.789 | 1.589 | 1.998 | 1.473 | 1.894 |
| 55.... | 2.977 | 2.730 | 2.829 | 2.740 | 2.744 | 2.692 | 2.773 | 2.668 | 2.783 | 3.226 | 2.860 | 3.355 | 2.625 | 2.846 |
| 65.... | 5.919 | 5.554 | 5.899 | 5.841 | 6.013 | 5.877 | 6.052 | 5.856 | 6.156 | 6.964 | 6.072 | 6.596 | 5.717 | 6.040 |
| 75.... | 13.281 | 12.519 | 13.541 | 13.875 | 13.084 | 13.037 | 13.494 | 13.036 | 13.794 | 15.945 | 13.604 | 14.028 | 12.684 | 13.494 |
| 85.... | 26.463 | 25.242 | 28.394 | 28.255 | 28.438 | 27.655 | 28.434 | 27.569 | 30.350 | 32.104 | 27.623 | 28.028 | 25.922 | 28.037 |
| 95& up | 41.099 | 39.915 | 46.199 | 45.907 | 42.832 | 46.679 | 44.616 | 42.036 | 52.200 | 53.230 | 46.816 | 43.323 | 42.927 | 45.214 |

The table may be read thus:—Of 100 males living of the age of 35 and under 45, 1.342 died in 1838, 1.255 in 1839, 1.217 in 1841, and so on for other years; a correction for increase of population having been made for each age at each year.

n the year 1789 Dr. Wigglesworth formed certain tables from re- ns embracing 4,893 deaths, which were in use in Massachusetts up the commencement of her registration system in 1842.

' If the diminutive number,'' says the report of 1851, '' of less than *thousand* deaths, collected without official responsibility, from a all region of country, was deemed of so much importance, of how ch more value will be the results obtained from the returns from ry section of our territory through a period of eleven years, of ut *one hundred and thirty-five thousand* deaths, observed and re- ded with more minuteness, and probably more accuracy, and certi- l to be correct by town officers whose official duties require them to form the service with as much truthful precision as possible.''

The first registration report of Massachusetts was made to the gen- l court in February, 1843, according to the act of March, 1842, d there have been published since regular reports, each more elabo- e and minute in its details, until the system in that State has come be considered very nearly perfect.

The following table from these digest the results of deaths:

| CAUSES OF DEATH. | WHOLE NO. OF DEATHS. | | PER CENTAGE OF DEATHS. | |
|---|---|---|---|---|
| | One year, 1853. | Eleven years & eight mo's ending Dec. 31, 1852. | One year, 1853. | Eleven years & eight mo's ending Dec. 31, 1852. |
| CAUSES | 20,301 | 148,024 | ............ | ............ |
| IFIED CAUSES | 19,561 | 138,451 | 100. | 100. |
| . ZYMOTIC DISEASES | 5,446 | 40,681 | 27.84 | 29.37 |
| *Sporadic diseases of,* | | | | |
| . UNCERTAIN SEAT | 2,409 | 16,862 | 12.22 | 12.17 |
| . NERVOUS ORGANS | 2,008 | 13,427 | 10.27 | 9.69 |
| . RESPIRATIVE ORGANS | 5,783 | 38,713 | 29.56 | 27.94 |
| . CIRCULATIVE ORGANS | 475 | 2,883 | 2.43 | 2.08 |
| . DIGESTIVE ORGANS | 1,191 | 8,981 | 6.09 | 6.55 |
| . URINATIVE ORGANS | 88 | 608 | .45 | .44. |
| . GENERATIVE ORGANS | 222 | 1,575 | 1.13 | 1.14 |
| . LOCOMOTIVE ORGANS | 113 | 752 | .58 | .55 |
| . INTEGUMENTIVE ORGANS | 13 | 132 | .07 | .09 |
| . OLD AGE | 997 | 8,481 | 5.10 | 6.12 |
| . VIOLENT CAUSES | 816 | 5,356 | 4.17 | 3.86 |

y this it will be noticed that the class of diseases designated as zymotics, and the diseases connected with respiratory organs, have been most fatal during the year under consideration, 57.40 per cent. of all the ths whose causes have been reported having been caused by them. This has been the case, also, in the twelve rs and eight months in which registration has been carried on in Massachusetts.

From the tenth annual report of Massachusetts we take the fol- wing:

'' As observed above, the law in this State was passed in 1842. his law was modified and improved by the act of March 16, 1844, d still further by the act of May 2, 1849. The State of New York llowed with a registration law, passed April 28, 1847, and made eir first report in April, 1848. New Jersey passed a law on the bject March, 1848, and remodelled it with improvements by the act March 19, 1851. Their report, before us, bears date of February, 52. The registration law of Connecticut passed June 24, 1848. Te have their three reports; the last is dated May, 1852. New ampshire passed a less efficient law July 7, 1849, and altered it ithout much improvement July 4, 1851.

"The act in Pennsylvania on this subject passed the legislature of that State April 14, 1851, and became a law without the signature of the governor, as certified by the proper authorities, January 12, 1852. During the last session of the legislature that body manifested their approbation of it by appropriating $4,500 to put the law into operation.

"On the 9th of January, 1852, the legislature of Kentucky passed a registration law, and the subject will come from influential sources before the next legislature of South Carolina. All of these enactments, and especially the reports that have been made in different States in compliance with them, bear an analogy to the same from our own State which had preceded them.

"This indicates not only the estimated importance of the subject as its results develop themselves, but also the confidence reposed in the system adopted by this State. The former feature, however, has the most notable point."

The federal census of 1850 furnishes the first instance of an attempt to obtain the mortality during one year in all of the States of the Union, and had there been as much care observed in the execution of the law as was taken in framing it, and in the preparation of necessary blanks, a mass of information must have resulted relating to the sanitary condition of the country, attained as yet in no other part of the world. This, however, would have been expecting too much. It was to take for granted, first, that the person, interrogated in each family, whoever he might be, with regard to its affairs, would be able to recollect whatever death had occurred in it within the period of twelve months; and, second, to give the true designation of the cause of such death. 1. One would think it not unreasonable that the facts of actual deaths would be striking and impressive enough in every household to be remembered for a much longer period than a single year, yet the returns of the marshals have only to be examined with care and deductions made from them, to satisfy the most careless observer that in the Union at large at least one-fourth of the whole number of deaths have not been reported at all. Making allowance for even this error, the United States would appear to be one of the healthiest countries of which there is any record. The varying ratios between the States, as drawn from the returns, show not so much in favor of or against the health of either, as they do, in all probability, a more or less perfect report of the marshals. Thus it is impossible to believe Mississippi a healthier State than Rhode Island, etc. For *rural* population the returns are no doubt nearer correct than they are for *urban,* and the old States are in general better reported than the new. 2. So far as the educated are in question, the assigned causes of death on the returns, may be considered sufficiently near the truth for popular purposes, though falling far short of the precision necessary in skillful scientific calculations; but among the large mass of the community vagueness and inaccuracy may naturally be expected, even where the parties are disposed to speak the truth and make the best effort to do so. The physician's certificate of the *cause* of death is the only positively reliable evidence of the fact.

The other points and particulars of inquiry, such as the age, sex, color, condition, occupation and nativities of parties, the season of decease and duration of sickness, stand upon somewhat different ground and are, from their character, no doubt as correctly answered as the inquiries of the census relating to the ages, pursuits, etc., of the living.

Upon the whole, then, and we cannot be too emphatic on the point, whilst this publication of the mortality statistics of the census is disclaimed as of authority in showing the respective pretentions to healthfulness or the degree of unhealthfulness of the several States, or of very great scientific worth in showing the *specific* causes of death, it may be considered of much value, notwithstanding, in giving with even ordinary claims to precision very minute phenomena relating to the deaths of about one-third of a million of people scattered over three millions of square miles of territory. The value of such a multitude of facts cannot but be very great, even although they do not constitute the whole of them. We are every day accustomed to draw deductions for the whole from a part, and to argue out the true and complete from the approximate and uncertain.

It may also be said in favor of the returns as published, that they constitute but a beginning, and are not, perhaps, further from the truth than were the first attempts in States having registration systems. The same improvement as in these States may be expected hereafter. The publication of this volume will stimulate investigation and lead to a better understanding of the importance of the subject.

Upon page 49 will be found the instructions to marshals under which the mortality statistics were collected. The instructions cover a wide field and are necessary to an understanding of the schedules. But a small part of the material collected can be condensed into this publication. To have issued the work in detail by towns, counties, etc., upon the formula proposed on page 110 of Compendium,* and which should have been the one, must have swelled it to 2 or 3,000 pages. The act of Congress confines it to three hundred. It became necessary then to change the formula, and condense by States and divisions of States, as will be seen particularly hereafter. The very best, it is believed, has been done that was possible under the circumstances. Those who may desire, however, to consult the material in detail, for counties, &c., necessarily prepared in the progress of

* *The formula was as follows:*

| | | Whites. | | | | | | | | | Free colored. | | Slaves. | | Married. | | Place of birth. | Occupation. | Period of sickness. | Seasons. |
|---|---|---|---|---|---|---|---|---|---|---|---|---|---|---|---|---|---|---|---|---|
| | | Native divided as males and females. | | | | | | | | Foreign. | Black. | Mulatto. | Black. | Mulatto. | White. | Free col'd. | | | | |
| Disease or cause of death. | Total number of deaths. | Birth. | Under 1 year. | 1 and under 5. | 5 and under 20. | 20 and under 50. | 50 and under 100. | 100 and upwards. | Total. | Same subdivisions of age and sex as native. | Same subdivisions as whites. | Same subdivisions as whites. | Same subdivisions as whites. | Same subdivisions as whites. | Subdivided by ages of under 20, 20 to 30, 30 to 40, 40 to 50, 50 to 70, and 70 and upwards. | Same subdivisions as whites. | Subdivided by columns for State, for New England, Middle, Southern, S. W. and N. W. States, and for England, Ireland, Scotland, Germany and other foreign countries. | Subdivided by columns for mechanical, agricultural, commercial, laborious, educational pursuits, &c.; each divided into ages, as 15 to 20, 20 to 30, &c. | Subdivided by columns for under 1 week, 1 week to 1 month, 1 month to 3 months and over 3 months. | Subdivided by columns for spring, summer, autumn and winter. |

the work, will find the manuscripts in the Census Office under the charge of the Secretary of the Interior, compiled in some cases with all of the elaboration proposed in the Compendium.

To the same cause must be attributed the very small number of cities and towns that are given in the volume, notwithstanding the figures were separated and aggregated for nearly every considerable town in the Union.

The whole of the statistics now presented are arranged with reference to—

I. *The leading Cities and Towns.* These will be found on pages 302–303 of the volume. The statistics could not be given in the same detail as those for the States, except in the instances where they are published as sections of such States, to wit, Boston, New Orleans, &c. Other tables are given, compiled from the Compendium, showing, for purposes of comparison, the ages, sex, nativities, &c., of the living population of these cities. A few facts digested from the city reports are also embraced on page 16.

II. *Sections of several States.* The sheets were prepared for all of the States, but it became necessary to select for publication from among them, so as to include States in the several great divisions of the Union. The sections are made up with reference to physical peculiarities as far as possible, such as rivers, sea-coast, lakes, mountains, &c. A table of the living population of the sections embraced will be found on page 32. The limits of the work precluded the insertion of ages, sex, &c., in the same connection, which is much to be regretted.

III. *All of the States and Territories.* Comparative tables of the living population, their ages, sex, nativity, occupation, &c., accompany these statistics.

IV. *The United States.* The United States tables are arranged somewhat differently from those of the States, as will be explained hereafter. In these the classification is adopted which is usual among vital statisticians. The formula proposed by Dr. Edward Jarvis, of Massachusetts, a distinguished authority in these matters, and to whom the Census Office is under many and great obligations, was adopted in every particular. His letter, which is given on page 45, enters minutely into the consideration of the subject.

All of the tables show, with reference to the mortality of the several States—

FIRST. *The cause of death.* This was taken, in the first instance, literally from the returns of the marshals. The list was then reduced by combining such as were evidently merely verbal differences, and about which there could be no mistake, as, for example, scarlet, scarletina, &c., fever and ague, chills, &c. A further reduction was made in some cases not so obvious by reference to the best medical authorities. The list was then ready for publication. The office did not deem it advisable to condense for the State tables to the extent recommended by Dr. Jarvis, believing it would be better to enter into greater detail. Indeed, had space admitted, the cause of death assigned in each case on the returns would have been given, although leading often to inconsistencies. It is true that causes are assigned for death which are not in their nature fatal, but these will be found in ost of the publications made by States and Cities. The condensa-ons would be proper in aggregating for the United States tables. n page 304 will be found a list of most of the causes assigned on the turns. The labors of a medical man skilled in such matters was ily necessary in these final condensations. Dr. Jarvis was, there-re, consulted, and his letter was predicated upon a list of diseases rnished him, very nearly the same as that adopted for the State bles. Had the appropriation been adequate, the States would have en shown by classes as well as by individual diseases. To have iven an aggregate table showing for each State, for each disease, all the peculiarities, as age, color, condition, must have required an xtent of space, in addition, nearly equal to that of the present volume. r. Jarvis says that he has added some diseases omitted in the list nt to him; the omission was accidental, as the terms he specified ere adopted in the office work.

*Classified and aggregate deaths in the several States.*

| STATES. | All causes. | I. Zymotic diseases. | SPORADIC. | | | | | | | | | XI. Old age. | XII. External causes. | XIII. Stillborn. | XIV. Unknown. |
|---|---|---|---|---|---|---|---|---|---|---|---|---|---|---|---|
| | | | II. Diseases of uncertain or variable seat. | III. Diseases of brain and nervous system. | IV. Diseases of respiratory organs. | V. Dis. of organs of circulation. | VI. Diseases of digestive organs. | VII. Diseases of urinary organs. | VIII. Diseases of generative org'ns and childbirth. | IX. Dis. of locomotive organs. | X. Diseases of the skin. | | | | |
| labama | 9,091 | 3,029 | 638 | 676 | 1,174 | 34 | 709 | 36 | 151 | 41 | 13 | 176 | 616 | 7 | 1,791 |
| rkansas | 3,021 | 1,358 | 122 | 144 | 396 | 6 | 254 | 5 | 62 | 13 | 2 | 89 | 132 | 7 | 481 |
| alifornia | 905 | 659 | 9 | 13 | 15 | .... | 6 | .... | ...... | 1 | 1 | 2 | 38 | .... | 161 |
| olumbia, Dist. of. | 846 | 289 | 34 | 89 | 197 | 12 | 37 | 2 | 11 | 8 | 1 | 29 | 33 | .... | 104 |
| onnecticut | 5,781 | 1,987 | 457 | 517 | 1,293 | 106 | 195 | 26 | 41 | 39 | 4 | 356 | 240 | 7 | 513 |
| elaware | 1,209 | 461 | 82 | 113 | 190 | 5 | 63 | 1 | 10 | 8 | .... | 28 | 40 | .... | 208 |
| orida | 931 | 307 | 97 | 51 | 108 | 8 | 114 | 3 | 21 | 3 | 2 | 25 | 76 | 2 | 114 |
| eorgia | 9,925 | 3,136 | 912 | 474 | 1,384 | 33 | 872 | 31 | 199 | 53 | 16 | 248 | 663 | 29 | 1,925 |
| inois | 11,759 | 5,858 | 433 | 712 | 1,799 | 32 | 411 | 41 | 167 | 60 | 11 | 107 | 332 | 4 | 1,792 |
| diana | 12,708 | 6,331 | 512 | 905 | 1,824 | 37 | 414 | 42 | 137 | 64 | 31 | 182 | 361 | 33 | 1,835 |
| wa | 2,044 | 954 | 83 | 147 | 376 | 3 | 67 | 4 | 26 | 6 | 5 | 13 | 100 | 1 | 259 |
| entucky | 15,033 | 6,895 | 852 | 878 | 2,101 | 68 | 588 | 50 | 141 | 75 | 20 | 306 | 569 | 17 | 2,473 |
| ouisiana | 11,956 | 5,999 | 521 | 861 | 1,175 | 50 | 781 | 18 | 135 | 36 | 13 | 170 | 599 | 15 | 1,578 |
| aine | 7,584 | 2,654 | 498 | 492 | 2,077 | 76 | 292 | 35 | 58 | 36 | 46 | 310 | 302 | .... | 708 |
| aryland | 9,621 | 3,345 | 496 | 855 | 1,792 | 129 | 405 | 22 | 109 | 70 | 11 | 278 | 332 | 17 | 1,760 |
| assachusetts | 19,404 | 7,189 | 1,627 | 1,296 | 4,418 | 335 | 1,065 | 59 | 209 | 85 | 66 | 792 | 657 | 24 | 1,582 |
| ichigan | 4,515 | 1,428 | 388 | 483 | 1,081 | 30 | 157 | 25 | 74 | 26 | 23 | 109 | 195 | 4 | 492 |
| ississippi | 8,721 | 3,639 | 509 | 570 | 1,091 | 45 | 732 | 21 | 130 | 38 | 9 | 126 | 601 | 10 | 1,200 |
| issouri | 12,292 | 6,832 | 447 | 649 | 1,344 | 37 | 555 | 15 | 149 | 56 | 8 | 101 | 371 | 7 | 1,721 |
| ew Hampshire | 4,231 | 1,582 | 302 | 333 | 1,072 | 89 | 140 | 21 | 30 | 27 | 2 | 279 | 146 | .... | 208 |
| ew Jersey | 6,465 | 2,512 | 431 | 667 | 1,201 | 72 | 268 | 17 | 58 | 51 | 8 | 272 | 231 | 4 | 673 |
| ew York | 45,600 | 17,976 | 3,633 | 4,492 | 8,913 | 549 | 1,906 | 182 | 358 | 262 | 68 | 1,393 | 1,633 | 51 | 4,184 |
| orth Carolina | 10,165 | 2,495 | 1,010 | 527 | 1,728 | 28 | 620 | 63 | 188 | 67 | 14 | 409 | 596 | 20 | 2,393 |
| hio | 28,957 | 16,138 | 1,265 | 1,809 | 4,025 | 137 | 836 | 92 | 221 | 119 | 29 | 506 | 707 | 6 | 3,067 |
| ennsylvania | 28,551 | 11,645 | 1,919 | 2,824 | 5,055 | 323 | 957 | 121 | 365 | 193 | 28 | 928 | 954 | 33 | 3,206 |
| hode Island | 2,241 | 780 | 164 | 222 | 572 | 31 | 60 | 2 | 15 | 10 | 7 | 97 | 101 | 17 | 163 |
| outh Carolina | 8,047 | 2,645 | 678 | 467 | 1,343 | 30 | 755 | 15 | 150 | 47 | 15 | 263 | 403 | 11 | 1,225 |
| ennessee | 11,875 | 4,524 | 733 | 628 | 1,493 | 34 | 542 | 42 | 131 | 85 | 26 | 316 | 570 | 29 | 2,720 |
| exas | 3,057 | 1,285 | 150 | 159 | 377 | 11 | 180 | 3 | 73 | 13 | 2 | 34 | 204 | 6 | 560 |
| ermont | 3,129 | 951 | 258 | 267 | 886 | 67 | 100 | 16 | 24 | 11 | 3 | 210 | 93 | 1 | 242 |
| irginia | 19,059 | 5,190 | 1,427 | 1,249 | 3,567 | 103 | 925 | 83 | 312 | 133 | 17 | 867 | 942 | 15 | 4,229 |
| Visconsin | 2,903 | 1,242 | 177 | 228 | 541 | 12 | 129 | 7 | 47 | 24 | 1 | 29 | 123 | .... | 343 |
| Territories: Minnesota | 29 | 12 | 2 | 3 | 4 | .... | 3 | .... | ...... | .... | .... | ...... | 2 | .... | 3 |
| New Mexico | 1,157 | 335 | 120 | 19 | 165 | 2 | 31 | ... | 32 | 10 | 2 | 26 | 67 | .... | 348 |
| Oregon | 47 | 23 | 1 | 2 | 6 | 1 | 4 | .... | 1 | 1 | 1 | ..... | 3 | .... | 4 |
| Utah | 239 | 149 | 10 | 12 | 35 | .... | 5 | 1 | 1 | .... | .... | 1 | 9 | .... | 16 |

Second. *Age and sex of deceased.* This table, combined with the cause of death, could not be made up more minutely. The ages were selected after consultation with leading medical writers in different parts of the Union. The results would have been more valuable had it been possible, within the space allotted, to separate the several colors, native and foreign. Tables of the living population at the several ages are also given. The following will show the aggregate number who died at each age, male and female, in the United States, arranged according to classes, and also the ratios per cent. to the total living of those ages, and to the total deaths of all ages, exclusive of unknown.

| | Under 1. | | | | 1 and under 5. | | | | 5 and under 10. | | | | 10 and under 20. | | | |
|---|---|---|---|---|---|---|---|---|---|---|---|---|---|---|---|---|
| | Males. | Ratio. | Fem'les. | Ratio. | Males. | Ratio. | Fem'les. | Ratio. | Males. | Ratio. | Fem'les. | Ratio. | Males. | Ratio. | Fem'les. | Ratio. |
| ALL CAUSES............ | 29569 | 9.29 | 24696 | 7.94 | 36349 | 2.50 | 32364 | 2.28 | 11549 | 0.70 | 10172 | 0.63 | 13760 | 0.51 | 14485 | 0.53 |
| I. Zymotic diseases.... | 10828 | 3.49 | 9236 | 2.97 | 19716 | 1.36 | 17957 | 1.27 | 6422 | 0.39 | 5856 | 0.37 | 6258 | 0.23 | 6473 | 0.24 |
| II. Diseases of uncertain or variable seat.... | 1407 | 0.44 | 1229 | 0.40 | 1797 | 0.12 | 1451 | 0.10 | 697 | 0.04 | 562 | 0.04 | 937 | 0.03 | 879 | 0.03 |
| III. Diseases of brain and nervous system.... | 3444 | 1.08 | 2635 | 0.85 | 2989 | 0.21 | 2499 | 0.18 | 879 | 0.05 | 685 | 0.04 | 982 | 0.04 | 848 | 0.03 |
| IV. Diseases of the respiratory organs.. ... | 2778 | 0.87 | 2203 | 0.71 | 3315 | 0.23 | 3018 | 0.21 | 953 | 0.06 | 984 | 0.06 | 2142 | 0.08 | 3295 | 0.12 |
| V. Dis. of the organs of circulation...... | 129 | 0.04 | 95 | 0.03 | 67 | .... | 55 | .... | 69 | .... | 59 | .... | 118 | .... | 133 | .... |
| VI. Diseases of the digestive organs...... | 1530 | 0.48 | 1284 | 0.41 | 2886 | 0.20 | 2690 | 0.19 | 531 | 0.03 | 478 | 0.03 | 407 | 0.02 | 369 | 0.01 |
| VII. Diseases of the urinary organs. ..... | 23 | 0.01 | 12 | .... | 33 | .... | 14 | .... | 21 | .... | 14 | .... | 47 | .... | 17 | .... |
| VIII. Dis. of the generati'e org'ns and childb'th | .... | .... | .... | .... | .... | .... | 5 | .... | .... | .... | .... | .... | .... | .... | 393 | 0.02 |
| IX. Diseases of the locomotive organs.... | 66 | 0.02 | 51 | 0.02 | 104 | 0.01 | 67 | 0.01 | 94 | 0.01 | 60 | .... | 198 | 0.01 | 132 | .... |
| X. Diseases of the skin.. | 55 | 0.02 | 60 | 0.02 | 44 | .... | 46 | .... | 16 | .... | 14 | .... | 19 | .... | 14 | .... |
| XI. Old age. ......... | .... | .... | .... | .... | .... | .... | .... | .... | .... | .... | .... | .... | .... | .... | .... | .... |
| XII. External causes..... | 784 | 0.25 | 783 | 0.25 | 1298 | 0.09 | 1086 | 0.07 | 785 | 0.05 | 527 | 0.03 | 1290 | 0.05 | 400 | 0.02 |
| XIII. Stillborn.......... | 217 | 0.07 | 160 | 0.05 | .... | .... | .... | .... | .... | .... | .... | .... | .... | .... | .... | .... |
| XIV. Unknown......... | 8308 | 2.61 | 6948 | 2.23 | 4100 | 0.28 | 3535 | 0.25 | 1082 | 0.07 | 933 | 0.06 | 1367 | 0.05 | 1482 | 0.06 |

| | 20 and under 50. | | | | 50 and under 80. | | | | 80 and under 100. | | | | 100 and over. | | | | Total. | | | |
|---|---|---|---|---|---|---|---|---|---|---|---|---|---|---|---|---|---|---|---|---|
| | Males. | Ralio. | Females. | Ratio. | Males. | Ratio. | Females. | Ratio. | Males. | Ratio. | Females. | Ratio. | Males. | Ratio. | Females. | Ratio. | Males. | Ratio. | Females. | Ratio. |
| ALL. | 48773 | 1.05 | 41734 | 0.97 | 26511 | 2.62 | 20840 | 2.16 | 5152 | 12.29 | 5020 | 10.64 | 173 | 16.06 | 190 | 12.85 | 172800 | 1.46 | 150045 | 1.32 |
| I. | 21483 | 0.46 | 13866 | 0.32 | 6934 | 0.68 | 5145 | 0.53 | 508 | 1.21 | 479 | 1.02 | 12 | 1.11 | 3 | 0.20 | 72476 | 0.61 | 59221 | 0.52 |
| II. | 2316 | 0.05 | 3096 | 0.07 | 2968 | 0.29 | 2829 | 0.30 | 472 | 1.13 | 347 | 0.74 | 8 | 0.74 | 11 | 0.74 | 10624 | 0.09 | 10420 | 0.09 |
| III. | 2471 | 0.05 | 1637 | 0.04 | 2234 | 0.22 | 1753 | 0.18 | 347 | 0.83 | 329 | 0.70 | 4 | 0.37 | 2 | 0.14 | 13392 | 0.11 | 10395 | 0.09 |
| IV. | 11871 | 0.26 | 12446 | 0.29 | 5952 | 0.60 | 4852 | 0.50 | 480 | 1.14 | 420 | 0.89 | 4 | 0.37 | 5 | 0.34 | 27540 | 0.23 | 27260 | 0.24 |
| V. | 437 | 0.01 | 399 | 0.01 | 512 | 0.05 | 377 | 0.04 | 59 | 0.12 | 30 | 0.06 | ... | ..... | ... | ..... | 1384 | 0.01 | 1151 | 0.01 |
| VI. | 1543 | 0.03 | 1305 | 0.03 | 1237 | 0.12 | 773 | 0.08 | 89 | 0.21 | 33 | 0.07 | 1 | 0.09 | ... | ..... | 8237 | 0.07 | 6935 | 0.06 |
| VII. | 165 | .... | 57 | .... | 509 | 0.05 | 63 | 0.01 | 118 | 0.28 | 4 | ..... | 2 | 0.19 | ... | ..... | 920 | 0.01 | 181 | .... |
| VIII. | ..... | .... | 3389 | 0.08 | ..... | .... | 49 | .... | .... | ..... | 1 | ..... | .. | ..... | ... | ..... | ...... | .... | 3842 | 0.04 |
| IX. | 286 | 0.01 | 221 | 0.01 | 268 | 0.03 | 183 | 0.02 | 21 | 0.05 | 15 | 0.03 | ... | ..... | ... | ..... | 1038 | 0.01 | 732 | 0.01 |
| X. | 76 | .... | 56 | .... | 60 | .... | 43 | .... | 9 | 0.02 | 2 | .... | ... | ..... | ... | ..... | 280 | .... | 236 | .... |
| XI. | 9 | .... | 12 | .... | 1383 | 0.14 | 1793 | 0.18 | 2571 | 6.13 | 2934 | 6.22 | 133 | 12.35 | 156 | 10.55 | 4111 | 0.04 | 4916 | 0.04 |
| XII. | 3902 | 0.09 | 612 | 0.01 | 1126 | 0.11 | 270 | 0.03 | 86 | 0.21 | 55 | 0.12 | 2 | 0.19 | 1 | 0.07 | 9315 | 0.08 | 3691 | 0.03 |
| XIII. | ..... | .... | ..... | .... | ..... | .... | ..... | .... | ... | ..... | ..... | ..... | .. | ..... | .. | ..... | 217 | .... | 160 | .... |
| XIV. | 4214 | 0.09 | 4638 | 0.11 | 3328 | 0.33 | 2710 | 0.29 | 401 | 0.96 | 371 | 0.79 | 7 | 0.65 | 12 | 0.81 | 23266 | 0.20 | 20905 | 0.19 |

*Ratio per cent. at each age to the total of all ages by classes, exclusive of unknown.*

| | Under 1. | | 1 and under 5. | | 5 and under 10. | | 10 and under 20. | | 20 and ander 50. | | 50 and under 80. | | 80 and under 100. | | 100 and over. | |
|---|---|---|---|---|---|---|---|---|---|---|---|---|---|---|---|---|
| | No. | Ratio. | No. | Ratio. | No. | Ratio. | No. | Ratio. | No. | Ratio. | No. | Ratio. | No. | Ratio. | No. | Ratio. |
| ALL CAUSES........ | 54265 | 16.80 | 68713 | 21.27 | 21721 | 6.72 | 28195 | 8.73 | 90507 | 28.02 | 47351 | 14.66 | 10172 | 3.15 | 363 | .11 |
| I............ | 20064 | 15.21 | 37673 | 28.58 | 12278 | 9.32 | 12731 | 9.66 | 35349 | 26.84 | 12079 | 9.16 | 987 | .74 | 15 | .01 |
| II............ | 2636 | 12.53 | 3248 | 15.43 | 1259 | 5.98 | 1816 | 8.63 | 5412 | 25.72 | 5797 | 27.55 | 819 | 3.89 | 19 | .09 |
| III............ | 6079 | 25.56 | 5479 | 23.03 | 1564 | 6.57 | 1830 | 7.70 | 4108 | 17.26 | 3987 | 16.76 | 676 | 2.84 | 6 | .03 |
| IV............ | 4981 | 9.09 | 6333 | 11.56 | 1937 | 3.54 | 5437 | 9.92 | 24317 | 44.36 | 10804 | 19.72 | 900 | 1.64 | 9 | .02 |
| V ............ | 224 | 8.82 | 122 | 4.82 | 128 | 5.04 | 251 | 9.90 | 836 | 33. | 889 | 35.07 | 80 | 3.16 | .... | .... |
| VI............ | 2814 | 18.55 | 5576 | 36.75 | 1009 | 6.65 | 776 | 5.11 | 2848 | 18.77 | 2010 | 13.25 | 122 | .81 | 1 | .01 |
| VII............ | 35 | 3.18 | 47 | 4.27 | 35 | 3.18 | 64 | 5.82 | 222 | 20.16 | 572 | 51.95 | 122 | 11.08 | 2 | .18 |
| VIII............ | ..... | ..... | 5 | .13 | ..... | ..... | 393 | 10.23 | 3389 | 88.21 | 49 | 1.27 | 1 | .03 | .... | .... |
| IX............ | 117 | 6.61 | 171 | 9.66 | 154 | 8.70 | 325 | 18.36 | 507 | 28.65 | 451 | 25.48 | 36 | 2.03 | .... | .... |
| X............ | 115 | 22.29 | 90 | 17.44 | 30 | 5.81 | 33 | 6.40 | 132 | 25.58 | 103 | 19.96 | 11 | 2.13 | .... | .... |
| XI............ | ..... | ..... | .... | ..... | ..... | ..... | ..... | .... | 21 | .23 | 3176 | 35.18 | 5505 | 60.98 | 289 | 3.21 |
| XII ............ | 1567 | 12.05 | 2334 | 17.94 | 1312 | 10.09 | 1690 | 13.00 | 4514 | 34.71 | 1396 | 10.74 | 141 | 1.08 | 3 | .02 |
| XIII............ | 377 | 100. | ..... | ..... | ..... | ..... | ..... | ..... | ..... | .... | ..... | ..... | ..... | ..... | .... | .... |
| XIV............ | 15256 | 34.49 | 7635 | 17.26 | 2015 | 4.55 | 2849 | 6.44 | 8.852 | 20.01 | 6038 | 13.65 | 772 | 1.75 | 19 | .05 |

THIRD. *Color and condition.* What is said in the last paragraph th reference to ages need not be repeated here; this table will be und of much value, and for comparison a table is extracted from the mpendium of the Census showing the whites, free colored, and ves, in each State, and also the blacks and mulattoes. The follow- g table is presented, showing the deaths and per cent. to the total ing of each color and condition:

| | WHITES. | | COLORED. | | | | | | | | Aggregate deaths. |
|---|---|---|---|---|---|---|---|---|---|---|---|
| | | | Slaves. | | | | Free. | | | | |
| | | | Blacks. | | Mulattoes. | | Blacks. | | Mulattoes. | | |
| | Total. | Ratio. | Total. | Ratio. | Total. | Ratio. | Total. | Ratio. | Total. | Ratio. | |
| All causes | 264601 | 1.35 | 48675 | 1.64 | 3289 | 1.33 | 4719 | 1.71 | 1739 | 1.09 | 323023 |
| I. Zymotic diseases | 112515 | 0.57 | 16088 | 0.54 | 1166 | 0.48 | 1461 | 0.53 | 583 | 0.37 | 131813 |
| I. Uncertain seat | 16915 | 0.09 | 3453 | 0.12 | 203 | 0.08 | 344 | 0.13 | 129 | 0.08 | 21044 |
| I. Nervous organs | 20435 | 0.10 | 2671 | 0.09 | 223 | 0.09 | 331 | 0.12 | 127 | 0.08 | 23787 |
| V. Respirative organs | 46131 | 0.23 | 6874 | 0.23 | 432 | 0.18 | 1053 | 0.38 | 310 | 0.20 | 54800 |
| V. Circulative organs | 2255 | 0.01 | 190 | 0.01 | 15 | ...... | 55 | 0.02 | 20 | 0.01 | 2535 |
| I. Digestive organs | 11199 | 0.06 | 3505 | 0.12 | 251 | 0.10 | 144 | 0.06 | 73 | 0.05 | 15172 |
| I. Urinary organs | 990 | ...... | 96 | ...... | 3 | ...... | 10 | ...... | 2 | ...... | 1101 |
| I. Generative organs | 3061 | 0.02 | 684 | 0.02 | 48 | 0.02 | 26 | 0.01 | 23 | 0.01 | 3842 |
| X. Locomotive organs | 1462 | 0.01 | 235 | 0.01 | 21 | 0.01 | 35 | 0.01 | 17 | 0.01 | 1770 |
| X. Integumentive organs | 456 | ...... | 52 | ...... | 3 | ...... | 4 | ...... | 1 | ...... | 516 |
| I. Old age | 7148 | 0.04 | 1552 | 0.05 | 78 | 0.03 | 198 | 0.07 | 51 | 0.03 | 9027 |
| II. External causes | 9144 | 0.05 | 3374 | 0.12 | 224 | 0.09 | 189 | 0.07 | 75 | 0.05 | 13006 |
| II. Stillborn | 314 | ...... | 52 | ...... | 4 | ...... | 3 | ...... | 4 | ...... | 377 |
| V. Unknown | 32576 | 0.17 | 9849 | 0.33 | 618 | 0.25 | 866 | 0.31 | 324 | 0.20 | 44233 |

FOURTH. *Nativity.* The returns show the exact nativity in each istance, but it was necessary to condense for the native population ccording to the several great sections of the Union, to wit, New ngland, &c. The foreign nativities are condensed even more. By ermans are meant those from all Germanic sources, viz: Prussia, ustria, Holland, &c. In the aggregate tables of the United States hose born in the State in which they died are separately given. hose born in New England in the same tables must be understood o mean those born in that section who died out of the State in which hey were born; the same for the other sections. This must be nown to fully comprehend the table. The proportion of foreign leaths to the whole foreign population of the Union shows more avorably, no doubt, than is the fact, since in all cases where the iativity was left blank and not marked, "unknown," by the marshal he party was construed to have been born in the State—this being ilways implied where the contrary was not expressed. Most valuable ables could have been given had we been able to show the ages of leceased foreigners, for it is by reference to these only that any comparative ratios of mortality, native and foreign, can be framed. There is sufficient, however, to indcate that the mortality among foreigners does not differ so widely from that of the natives as has been supposed. Several tables of nativities of the living population are included; the one below combines the mortality with nativities.

*Deaths, Native and Foreign, with Ratios to Living Population.*

| | All classes. | | | Per cent. to total deaths. | Per cent. to total livihg populat'n. | Total native deaths | Total foreign deaths. | Per cent. native, including slave. | Per ct. foreign. |
|---|---|---|---|---|---|---|---|---|---|
| | Males. | Females. | Total. | | | | | | |
| ALL CAUSES | 172800 | 150045 | 323023 | ......... | 1.393 | 288336 | 32970 | 1.377 | 1.469 |
| I. ZYMOTIC DISEASES | 72476 | 59221 | 131813 | 40.811 | .568 | 113587 | 17638 | .542 | .786 |
| SPORADIC DISEASES. | | | | | | | | | |
| II. Diseases of uncertain or variable seat | 10624 | 10420 | 21044 | 6.514 | .091 | 19427 | 1502 | .093 | .067 |
| III. Diseases of brain and nervous system | 13392 | 10395 | 23787 | 7.363 | .102 | 22184 | 1524 | .106 | .068 |
| IV. Diseases of respiratory organs | 27540 | 27260 | 54800 | 16.965 | .235 | 49551 | 5021 | .236 | .224 |
| V. Diseases of the organs of circulation | 1384 | 1151 | 2535 | .785 | .011 | 2238 | 293 | .011 | .013 |
| VI. Diseases of digestive organs | 8237 | 6935 | 15172 | 4.696 | .066 | 14203 | 931 | .068 | .042 |
| VII. Disease of urinary organs | 920 | 181 | 1101 | .344 | .005 | 996 | 97 | .005 | .004 |
| VIII. Diseases of generative organs and childbirth | ...... | 3842 | 3842 | 1.189 | .017 | 3292 | 532 | .016 | .024 |
| IX. Diseases of locomotive organs | 1038 | 732 | 1770 | .544 | .008 | 1606 | 154 | .008 | .007 |
| X. Diseases of the skin | 280 | 236 | 516 | .160 | .002 | 463 | 50 | .002 | .002 |
| XI. Old age | 4111 | 4916 | 9027 | 2.794 | .039 | 7937 | 994 | .038 | .044 |
| XII. External causes | 9315 | 3691 | 13006 | 4.026 | .056 | 11275 | 1648 | .054 | .073 |
| XIII. Stillborn | 217 | 160 | 377 | .117 | .002 | 377 | ...... | .002 | ....... |
| XIV. Unknown | 23266 | 20905 | 44233 | 13.692 | .191 | 41250 | 2586 | .196 | .115 |

FIFTH. *Occupations.* These also were necessarily classed, adopting very nearly the classification used in the Compendium of the Census. "Agriculture," and "Other Occupations," are the same in both tables; "Educational" of Mortality Report includes the "Army," "Law, Medicine, &c.," "Government Civil Service," and "Other Educational Pursuits." "Commercial" of Compendium embraces the similar head in this work, combined with "Mechanical" of that. "Sea and River Navigation," embraced with "Commercial." "Domestic Servants," included with "Labor," not "Agricultural." The table cannot show the tendency of certain pursuits to longevity, or the contrary, but only how far these pursuits are more or less exposed to the influence of certain diseases. The occupation of slaves, though given in many cases on the returns, were not taken off for publication, since no similar tables could be framed for the living slave population. The occupation of females is, for a similar reason, not given in the mortality tables.

SIXTH. *Duration of Sickness.* The periods selected are as many as could be embraced; the results are also aggregated.

SEVENTH. *Season of Decease.* It was impossible to give the months in detail; the seasons were selected after consultation with medical writers. It is obvious that these would include practically different months in different sections. In order to show the fall diseases by autumn is intended in the publication August, September, and October; winter will therefore embrace November, December, and January, &c. This is somewhat arbitrary, but no arrangement by seasons for all sections of the Union could be less so. The table annexed condenses the results and gives the appropriate ratios.

*Season of decease and duration of illness.*

| | Season of decease. | | | | | | | | Duration of sickness. | | | |
|---|---|---|---|---|---|---|---|---|---|---|---|---|
| | Spring, | Ratio. | Summer. | Ratio. | Autumn. | Ratio. | Winter. | Ratio. | Ratio under 1 week. | Ratio 1 week under 1 m'th. | Ratio 1 month under 3 m's. | Ratio 3 mo'ths and over. |
| LL CAUSES | 75538 | 23.39 | 89283 | 27.64 | 96790 | 29.96 | 56233 | 17.41 | 32.94 | 30.33 | 8.18 | 15.72 |
| I. ZYMOTIC DISEASES | 21293 | 16.15 | 40763 | 30.93 | 50567 | 38.36 | 17687 | 13.42 | 41.65 | 39.16 | 7.19 | 2.93 |
| II. Uncertain or variable seat | 5593 | 26.58 | 5775 | 27.44 | 5252 | 24.96 | 4200 | 19.96 | 12.98 | 22.38 | 13.66 | 39.84 |
| III. Brain and nervous system | 6610 | 27.79 | 6174 | 25.96 | 6123 | 25.74 | 4611 | 19.38 | 43.60 | 30.90 | 5.99 | 9.29 |
| IV. Respiratory organs | 18299 | 33.39 | 12791 | 23.34 | 11279 | 20.58 | 11858 | 21.64 | 12.01 | 25.54 | 10.44 | 42.13 |
| V. Organs of circulation | 711 | 28.05 | 671 | 26.47 | 569 | 22.44 | 567 | 22.37 | 29.51 | 22.17 | 11.40 | 23.55 |
| VI. Digestive organs | 3280 | 21.62 | 4300 | 28.84 | 4952 | 32.64 | 2487 | 16.39 | 30.89 | 35.80 | 11.52 | 13.99 |
| VII. Urinary organs | 304 | 27.61 | 277 | 25.16 | 253 | 22.98 | 258 | 23.43 | 11.17 | 32.61 | 12.16 | 34.97 |
| VIII. Generative organs, and childbirth | 1163 | 30.27 | 985 | 25.64 | 838 | 21.81 | 825 | 21.47 | 45.39 | 34.33 | 6.12 | 3.80 |
| IX. Locomotive organs | 540 | 30.51 | 451 | 25.48 | 410 | 23.16 | 356 | 20.11 | 9.72 | 24.86 | 12.26 | 44.41 |
| X. Diseases of the skin | 131 | 25.39 | 130 | 25.20 | 159 | 30.81 | 88 | 17.05 | 13.95 | 34.69 | 16.09 | 24.03 |
| XI. Old age | 2653 | 29.39 | 2217 | 24.56 | 2081 | 23.05 | 2000 | 22.16 | 14.87 | 16.92 | 7.12 | 19.03 |
| XII. External causes | 3446 | 26.50 | 3625 | 27.87 | 2875 | 22.10 | 2840 | 21 84 | 65.39 | 9.95 | 2.71 | 2.64 |
| XIII. Stillborn | 104 | 27.59 | 102 | 27.06 | 82 | 21.75 | 77 | 20.42 | ..... | ..... | ..... | ..... |
| XIV. Unknown | 11411 | 25.80 | 11022 | 24.92 | 11350 | 25.66 | 8379 | 18.94 | 32.64 | 20.74 | 7.30 | 15.89 |

The tables prepared for this work do not, as must have been expected, harmonize in all particulars with those previously published by the office in regard to the mortality returns. In such a multitude of figures differences were but natural. They do not, however, reach an amount to affect in an appreciable degree the ratios. The work was all prepared anew, and with severe revisions. The tables of the Compendium being, nevertheless, valuable and necessary for illustration, are incorporated. (See table IV., p. 37.)

Table VI., on pages 29–31, and also the table on page 11, will be found in several unimportant particulars to differ from the other tables. At the time of going to press they were not harmonized, but as the difference in no case affects the ratio the fortieth part of one per cent., it was conceived best not to reject the tables.

It ought to have been observed before, that, for condensation in the State tables, the unknown "season of decease" and "duration of sickness" are omitted, but can be always ascertained easily by deductions from the totals.

To Mr. Shattuck, of Boston, and Dr. Barton, of New Orleans, the office expresses its indebtedness for many important suggestions, and for the aid which has been derived from their invaluable Sanitary Reports.

The clerical and typographical errors discovered upon examination in the State sheets are corrected in the aggregate tables, including cases of manifest inconsistencies of disease, with age and sex, such as an adult dying of a disease of infancy, &c.

The total female slaves in Mississippi should read 2389 instead of 238, the 9 being dropped in the print. The total nativities of Massachusetts should read 1170 instead of 116.

NOTE.—Extracted from Compendium, pp. 106–107.

The following exhibits the proportion of annual deaths to the whole population of certain European countries: Norway, one in 54; Sweden, one in 41½; Russia, one in 25 92-100; Denmark, one in 40; Mecklenburg, one in 46½; Saxony, one in 34½; Wurtemburg, one in 31⅓; North Holland, one in 30 6-10; Belgium, one in 43; France, one in 39 6-10; Azores, one in 48; Genoa, one in 28 4-7.

Number and centesimal proportions of deaths of different ages that occurred in Ireland during 10 years, between June 6th, 1831, and June 6th, 1841.

Births to 1 year, 269,199, 23.38 per cent.; 2 to 5 years, 165,918, 14.41 per cent.; 6 to 10 years, 58,272, 5.06 per cent.; 11 to 20 years, 83,259, 7.23 per cent.; 21 to 30 years, 101,518, 8.82 per cent.; 31 to 40 years, 86,585, 7.52 per cent.; 41 to 50 years, 82,537, 7.17 per cent.; 51 to 60 years, 108,518, 9.43 per cent.; 61 to 70 years, 89,507, 7.77 per cent.; 71 to 80 years, 69,997, 6.08 per cent.; 81 to 90 years, 27,579, 2.40 per cent.; 91 to 100 years, 8,365, 0.73 per cent.; ages not specified, 36,120. Total, 1,187,374, 100.00 per cent.

In *Boston*, according to the report of the Sanitary Commission, the number of deaths of persons under five years of age during a period of nine years, was 11,705, being nine per cent. annually of the total population of that age; of persons aged from five to ten years, 1,312 or 1.28 per cent.; from ten to fifteen years, 633 or 0.72 per cent.; from fifteen to twenty, 738 or 0.74 per cent.; from twenty to thirty, 3,303 or 1.24 per cent.; from thirty to forty, 2,917 or 1.62 per cent.; from forty to fifty, 1,948 or 2.15 per cent.; from fifty to sixty, 1,273 or 2.97 per cent.; from sixty to seventy, 1,057 or 4.75 per cent.; from seventy to eighty, 787 or 9.78 per cent.; from eighty to ninety, 379 or 19.04 per cent.; over ninety, 75 or 29.64 per cent.; those of all ages, 26,127 or 2.53 per cent.

In *New York*, according to the annual report of the City Inspector, there were in 1853, 22,702 deaths, of which 12,230 were males and 10,472 females. Those of foreign birth were 7,104. Of the age of one year and under, there were 7,724 deaths; of one to two years, 2,942; of two to five, 2,297; of five to ten, 771; of ten to twenty, 854; of twenty to thirty, 2,441; of thirty to forty, 2,037; of forty to fifty, 1,413; of fifty to sixty, 866; of sixty to seventy, 671; of seventy to eighty, 439, of eighty to ninety, 140; of ninety to one hundred, 34; of one hundred and over, 2; ages unknown, 51. Here follows the ratio to total mortality in each decade in New York:

| Age. | 1847. | 1848. | 1849. | 1850. | 1851. | 1852. | 1853. |
|---|---|---|---|---|---|---|---|
| Birth to 10 | 1 to 1.60 | 1 to 1.45 | 1 to 1.57 | 1 to 1.55 | 1 to 1.67 | 1 to 1.86 | 1 to 1.65 |
| 10 " 20 | " 24.43 | " 24.54 | " 22.04 | " 27.00 | " 25.50 | " 26.93 | " 26.58 |
| 20 " 30 | " 8.10 | " 8.16 | " 8.16 | " 9.59 | " 8.70 | " 9.89 | " 9.30 |
| 30 " 40 | " 8.61 | " 8.60 | " 7.79 | " 10.61 | " 10.50 | " 10.78 | " 11.14 |
| 40 " 50 | " 12.34 | " 12.00 | " 10.96 | " 15.43 | " 16.54 | " 15.76 | " 16.07 |
| 50 " 60 | " 21.16 | " 19.32 | " 19.15 | " 22.64 | " 23.70 | " 24.54 | " 25.62 |
| 60 " 70 | " 26.72 | " 28.20 | " 25.89 | " 31.41 | " 35.00 | " 34.34 | " 33.83 |
| 70 " 80 | " 45.23 | " 37.12 | " 48.02 | " 56.59 | " 60.00 | " 55.88 | " 51.71 |
| 80 " 90 | " 103.18 | " 74.65 | " 105.19 | " 94.30 | " 123.25 | " 120.05 | " 162.16 |
| 90 " 100 and upwards | " 451.00 | " 469.60 | " 552.86 | " 943.00 | " 710.00 | " 600.00 | " 667.71 |
| Unknown | " 74.16 | " 111.25 | " 74.00 | " 99.25 | " 203.75 | " 175.61 | " 445.13 |

In *Philadelphia*, according to the report of the Board of Health for 1850, the total number of deaths during the year was 8,509, of whom 2,557 were under one year of age; 1,055 between one and two years; 930 between two and five; 419 between 5 and ten; 145 between ten and fifteen; 212 between fifteen and twenty; 1,649 males and 1,542 females of twenty and upwards; 460 over seventy.

In *Baltimore*, by the report of the Board of Health, there were in 1850, 4,576 deaths, of which 411 were still-born; 995 of persons under one year of age; 500 between one and two years; 414 between two and five; 174 between five and ten; 93 between ten and fifteen; 144 between fifteen and twenty; 435 between twenty and thirty; 433 between thirty and forty, 336 between forty and fifty; 195 between fifty and sixty; 207 between sixty and seventy; 152 between seventy and eighty; 59 between eighty and ninety; 21 between ninety and one hundred, and 7 above one hundred.

In *Charleston*, according to the report of the Board of Health in 1850, there were 216 deaths of white males; of white females, 158; total white, 374; black males, 225; black females, 257; total black, 482; total deaths, 856. (This was a sickly year.) Of these, 702 were native born; 125 foreign; 29 were born in other States of the Union.

*Mobile.*—The following table from Fenner's "Southern Medical Reports" gives the deaths in Mobile during the years 1844, 1845, 1846, 1847, and 1848.

| Years—Whites. | Unknown. | Under 1 year. | 1 under 10. | 10 under 20. | 20 under 30. | 30 under 40. | 40 under 50. | 50 under 60. | 60 under 70. | 70 under 80. | 80 under 90. | 90 under 100. | Over 100. | Total males. | Unknown. | Under 1 year. | 1 under 10. | 10 under 20. | 20 under 30. | 30 under 40. | 40 under 50. | 50 under 60. | 60 under 70. | 70 under 80. | 80 under 90. | 90 under 100. | Over 100. | Total females. | Total of all cases. |
|---|---|---|---|---|---|---|---|---|---|---|---|---|---|---|---|---|---|---|---|---|---|---|---|---|---|---|---|---|---|
| 1844.... | 43 | 15 | 17 | 8 | 44 | 27 | 25 | 8 | 7 | .. | .. | .. | .. | 194 | .. | .... | .... | 3 | 13 | 10 | 2 | 2 | .. | .. | .. | .. | .. | 30 | .... |
| 1845.... | 43 | 26 | 17 | 7 | 32 | 37 | 19 | 11 | 3 | .. | .. | 2 | .. | 197 | 2 | 21 | 32 | 5 | 30 | 16 | 4 | 7 | 1 | 2 | 1 | 1 | .. | 122 | .... |
| 1846.... | 13 | 39 | 22 | 13 | 46 | 41 | 33 | 7 | 4 | 3 | .. | 2 | 2 | 225 | .. | 20 | 18 | 6 | 14 | 10 | 5 | 3 | 2 | 1 | 1 | 1 | .. | 81 | .... |
| 1847.... | 29 | 46 | 22 | 10 | 49 | 64 | 37 | 19 | 5 | 2 | .. | 1 | .. | 284 | 19 | 31 | 25 | 9 | 24 | 19 | 10 | 6 | 4 | .. | .. | 1 | .. | 148 | .... |
| 1848.... | 26 | 58 | 72 | 25 | 70 | 85 | 37 | 14 | 6 | 2 | .. | 2 | .. | 397 | 3 | 49 | 60 | 14 | 14 | 18 | 3 | 3 | 2 | 2 | .. | .. | .. | 168 | .... |
| Total. | 154 | 194 | 150 | 63 | 241 | 254 | 151 | 59 | 25 | 7 | .. | 7 | 2 | 1,297 | 24 | 121 | 135 | 37 | 95 | 73 | 24 | 21 | ) | 5 | 2 | 3 | .. | 549 | .... |
| Blacks. | | | | | | | | | | | | | | | | | | | | | | | | | | | | | |
| 1844.... | 8 | .. | 15 | 2 | 2 | 5 | 2 | 5 | .. | .. | .. | .. | .. | 39 | 7 | .... | 5 | 2 | 1 | 3 | 2 | 3 | .. | .. | .. | .. | .. | 23 | 2 |
| 1845.... | 3 | 26 | 6 | 2 | 12 | 10 | 3 | 2 | 1 | 3 | .. | 3 | .. | 71 | 1 | 14 | 7 | 5 | 9 | 6 | 1 | 3 | 1 | .. | .. | 2 | .. | 49 | 4 |
| 1846.... | 1 | 28 | 19 | 6 | 8 | 7 | 4 | 8 | 6 | .. | 2 | .. | .. | 89 | 23 | 3 | 6 | 2 | 10 | 2 | 4 | 3 | 5 | 1 | 2 | .. | .. | 61 | 4 |
| 1847.... | 12 | 17 | 18 | 8 | 9 | 9 | 11 | 6 | 5 | 4 | 1 | 2 | .. | 102 | 1 | 26 | 11 | 7 | 3 | 4 | 6 | 2 | 2 | 2 | .. | .. | .. | 64 | 5 |
| 1848.... | 23 | 25 | 20 | 41 | 14 | 14 | 9 | 5 | 8 | 4 | 2 | 3 | 1 | 169 | 6 | 25 | 22 | 9 | 5 | 12 | 8 | 8 | 2 | 1 | .. | .. | .. | 98 | 8 |
| Total. | 47 | 96 | 78 | 59 | 45 | 45 | 29 | 26 | 20 | 11 | 5 | 8 | 1 | 470 | 38 | 68 | 51 | 25 | 28 | 27 | 21 | 19 | 10 | 4 | 2 | 2 | .. | 295 | 2, 6 |

In New Orleans the Board of Health reported for the year preceding June, 1850, 7,265 deaths against 3,6 reported in the Census. The following table will show the ages and color of those dying in 1849 and 1850 New Orleans. Lafayette has since been incorporated with the city. The deaths in 1850 were regularly r turned only in part. About 1,000 were mentioned by the marshal without any particulars, and were not ther fore included in the mortality table.

# UNITED STATES TABLES.

TABLE I.—*Classification of the ages of those who died during the year ending June 1, 1850—white, free colored, and slave—with the causes of death.*

| | AGES. | | | | | | | | | |
|---|---|---|---|---|---|---|---|---|---|---|
| | Under 1. | | 1 and under 5. | | 5 and under 10. | | 10 and under 20. | | 20 and under 50. | |
| | M. | F. | M. | F. | M. | F. | M. | F. | M. | F. |
| ALL CAUSES. | 29569 | 24696 | 36349 | 32364 | 11549 | 10172 | 13760 | 14435 | 48773 | 41734 |
| I. Zymotic Diseases | 10828 | 9236 | 19716 | 17957 | 6422 | 5856 | 6258 | 6473 | 21483 | 13866 |
| Sporadic Diseases. | | | | | | | | | | |
| II. Diseases of uncertain or variable seat | 1407 | 1229 | 1797 | 1451 | 697 | 562 | 937 | 879 | 2316 | 3096 |
| III. Diseases of brain and nervous system | 3444 | 2635 | 2989 | 2490 | 879 | 685 | 982 | 848 | 2471 | 1637 |
| IV. Diseases of the respiratory organs | 2778 | 2203 | 3315 | 3018 | 953 | 984 | 2142 | 3295 | 11871 | 12446 |
| V. Diseases of the organs of circulation | 129 | 95 | 67 | 55 | 69 | 59 | 118 | 133 | 437 | 399 |
| VI. Diseases of the digestive organs | 1530 | 1284 | 2886 | 2690 | 531 | 478 | 407 | 369 | 1543 | 1305 |
| VII. Diseases of the urinary organs | 23 | 12 | 33 | 14 | 21 | 14 | 47 | 17 | 165 | 57 |
| VIII. Diseases of the generative organs, and childbirth | ...... | ...... | ...... | 5 | ...... | ...... | ...... | 393 | ...... | 3389 |
| IX. Diseases of the locomotive organs | 66 | 51 | 104 | 67 | 94 | 60 | 193 | 132 | 286 | 221 |
| X. Diseases of the skin | 55 | 60 | 44 | 46 | 16 | 14 | 19 | 14 | 76 | 56 |
| XI. Old age. | ...... | ...... | ...... | ...... | ...... | ...... | ...... | ...... | 9 | 12 |
| XII. External causes | 784 | 783 | 1298 | 1036 | 785 | 527 | 1290 | 400 | 3902 | 612 |
| XIII. Stillborn | 217 | 160 | ...... | ...... | ...... | ...... | ...... | ...... | ...... | ...... |
| XIV. Unknown | 8308 | 6948 | 4100 | 3535 | 1082 | 933 | 1367 | 1482 | 4214 | 4638 |
| I.— 1. Cholera | 746 | 671 | 2244 | 2039 | 1249 | 1059 | 1611 | 1479 | 9694 | 5640 |
| 2. Cholera infantum | 1009 | 833 | 1045 | 955 | 63 | 44 | 7 | 2 | ...... | ...... |
| 3. Cholera morbus | 102 | 75 | 223 | 179 | 61 | 54 | 72 | 65 | 237 | 179 |
| 4. Croup | 2716 | 2012 | 2608 | 2326 | 439 | 407 | 52 | 50 | 25 | 32 |
| 5. Diarrhœa | 774 | 693 | 1168 | 1016 | 170 | 127 | 137 | 122 | 896 | 455 |
| 6. Dysentery | 1810 | 1501 | 4436 | 3728 | 1184 | 988 | 767 | 672 | 1710 | 1497 |
| 7. Erysipelas | 269 | 248 | 208 | 196 | 85 | 80 | 132 | 165 | 363 | 444 |
| 8. Fever | 921 | 798 | 1892 | 1741 | 914 | 827 | 1295 | 1509 | 3270 | 2594 |
| 9. Fever, intermittent | 97 | 85 | 110 | 112 | 48 | 48 | 50 | 48 | 115 | 95 |
| 10. Fever, remittent | 4 | 3 | 11 | 8 | 6 | 9 | 16 | 14 | 46 | 19 |
| 11. Fever, scarlet | 533 | 456 | 2659 | 2497 | 1163 | 1181 | 313 | 471 | 120 | 128 |
| 12. Fever, ship | 2 | 4 | 14 | 19 | 11 | 8 | 19 | 21 | 67 | 45 |
| 13. Fever, typhoid | 197 | 194 | 707 | 569 | 581 | 531 | 1432 | 1536 | 3558 | 2199 |
| 14. Fever, yellow | 2 | 1 | 2 | 6 | 4 | 3 | 51 | 20 | 565 | 92 |
| 15. Hooping cough | 1009 | 1094 | 1233 | 1426 | 155 | 207 | 39 | 46 | 23 | 25 |
| 16. Influenza | 39 | 31 | 29 | 28 | 7 | 10 | 8 | 6 | 12 | 17 |
| 17. Measles | 254 | 233 | 778 | 786 | 172 | 172 | 106 | 131 | 133 | 174 |
| 18. Small pox | 210 | 156 | 287 | 263 | 102 | 88 | 148 | 106 | 610 | 179 |
| 19. Syphilis | 5 | 8 | 6 | 6 | 1 | 1 | 2 | 8 | 39 | 39 |
| 20. Thrush | 129 | 140 | 61 | 57 | 7 | 12 | 1 | 2 | ...... | 13 |
| II.— 21. Abscess | 17 | 16 | 15 | 13 | 11 | 5 | 21 | 15 | 89 | 43 |
| 22. Cancer | 18 | 17 | 31 | 20 | 12 | 14 | 18 | 22 | 144 | 334 |
| 23. Debility | 249 | 236 | 52 | 68 | 17 | 9 | 11 | 13 | 65 | 79 |
| 24. Dropsy | 376 | 340 | 866 | 682 | 421 | 303 | 526 | 446 | 1189 | 1765 |
| 25. Gout | 3 | ...... | ...... | 1 | ...... | ...... | 2 | ...... | 6 | 3 |
| 26. Hemorrhage | 30 | 21 | 27 | 13 | 17 | 13 | 42 | 43 | 191 | 136 |
| 27. Inflammation | 400 | 291 | 370 | 320 | 94 | 84 | 125 | 123 | 257 | 334 |
| 28. Malformation | 33 | 28 | 15 | 6 | 2 | ...... | ...... | ...... | 1 | ...... |
| 29. Marasmus | 98 | 131 | 89 | 80 | 13 | 17 | 8 | 14 | 22 | 22 |
| 30. Milk sickness | 1 | ...... | 4 | 2 | 3 | 10 | 9 | 6 | 21 | 25 |
| 31. Mortification | 36 | 27 | 20 | 15 | 7 | 8 | 13 | 4 | 40 | 39 |
| 32. Rickets | 9 | 7 | 33 | 13 | 1 | ...... | 4 | 2 | ...... | 1 |
| 33. Scrofula | 120 | 103 | 259 | 204 | 90 | 89 | 149 | 173 | 219 | 230 |
| 34. Scurvy | ...... | ...... | 1 | 2 | 2 | 1 | 3 | 1 | 28 | 6 |
| 35. Tumor | 17 | 12 | 15 | 12 | 7 | 9 | 6 | 17 | 44 | 79 |
| III.— 36. Apoplexy | 12 | 12 | 18 | 14 | 11 | 7 | 40 | 44 | 323 | 265 |
| 37. Brain and nerves, disease of. | 359 | 277 | 480 | 381 | 168 | 133 | 173 | 136 | 329 | 203 |
| 38. Cephalitis | 916 | 664 | 1160 | 906 | 414 | 301 | 436 | 362 | 613 | 364 |
| 39. Chorea | ...... | 3 | 1 | 3 | 1 | 1 | 2 | 18 | 8 | 12 |
| 40. Convulsions | 1591 | 1233 | 803 | 776 | 144 | 120 | 153 | 153 | 334 | 341 |
| 41. Delirium tremens | ...... | ...... | ...... | ...... | ...... | ...... | 3 | 1 | 283 | 26 |
| 42. Epilepsy | 16 | 14 | 18 | 12 | 16 | 10 | 32 | 26 | 93 | 65 |
| 43. Hydrocephalus | 344 | 253 | 442 | 344 | 73 | 58 | 29 | 35 | 34 | 23 |

## TABLE I—Continued.

| | AGES. | | | | | | | | | |
|---|---|---|---|---|---|---|---|---|---|---|
| | Under 1. | | 1 and under 5. | | 5 and under 10. | | 10 and under 20. | | 20 and under 50. | |
| | M. | F. | M. | F. | M. | F. | M. | F. | M. | F. |
| 44. Insanity | .... | .... | 1 | .... | 1 | 1 | 7 | 5 | 95 | 60 |
| 45. Neuralgia | 4 | 1 | 12 | 4 | 14 | 14 | 14 | 13 | 57 | 46 |
| 46. Paralysis | 11 | 8 | 21 | 23 | 15 | 18 | 35 | 33 | 210 | 197 |
| 47. Tetanus | 191 | 170 | 33 | 27 | 28 | 22 | 58 | 22 | 92 | 30 |
| IV.— 48. Asthma | 16 | 9 | 19 | 16 | 3 | 4 | 7 | 6 | 48 | 35 |
| 49. Bronchitis | 543 | 456 | 464 | 442 | 85 | 82 | 73 | 127 | 317 | 309 |
| 50. Consumption | 686 | 608 | 927 | 907 | 278 | 336 | 1144 | 2335 | 8410 | 10198 |
| 51. Laryngitis | 80 | 50 | 171 | 174 | 106 | 123 | 58 | 83 | 55 | 67 |
| 52. Pleurisy | 78 | 68 | 98 | 72 | 36 | 33 | 145 | 110 | 560 | 292 |
| 53. Pneumonia | 1163 | 879 | 1363 | 1165 | 356 | 318 | 655 | 554 | 2195 | 1288 |
| 54. Quinsy | 44 | 27 | 98 | 79 | 37 | 37 | 19 | 25 | 67 | 61 |
| 55. Respiratory organs, disease of | 168 | 106 | 175 | 163 | 52 | 51 | 41 | 55 | 219 | 196 |
| V.— 56. Aneurism | .... | .... | .... | .... | .... | .... | .... | 1 | 6 | .... |
| 57. Circulatory organs, disease of | .... | .... | .... | .... | .... | .... | .... | .... | .... | .... |
| 58. Heart, disease of | 129 | 95 | 67 | 55 | 69 | 59 | 118 | 132 | 431 | 399 |
| VI.— 59. Colic | 104 | 71 | 71 | 74 | 30 | 20 | 49 | 34 | 260 | 136 |
| 60. Digestive organs, disease of | 283 | 245 | 406 | 354 | 61 | 50 | 62 | 57 | 161 | 150 |
| 61. Dirt eating | 1 | .... | 4 | 1 | 8 | 5 | 12 | 10 | 25 | 22 |
| 62. Dyspepsia | 5 | 3 | 8 | 8 | 4 | 4 | 12 | 13 | 137 | 123 |
| 63. Enteritis | 374 | 271 | 396 | 337 | 130 | 94 | 139 | 124 | 355 | 326 |
| 64. Gastritis | 19 | 15 | 11 | 17 | 8 | 6 | 7 | 13 | 44 | 70 |
| 65. Hemorroids | .... | .... | 3 | 2 | .... | .... | .... | .... | 11 | 9 |
| 66. Hernia | 14 | 9 | 6 | 6 | 5 | .... | 12 | 2 | 62 | 28 |
| 67. Jaundice | 50 | 49 | 32 | 38 | 18 | 18 | 9 | 12 | 64 | 36 |
| 68. Liver, disease of | 101 | 57 | 102 | 63 | 24 | 31 | 61 | 64 | 398 | 382 |
| 69. Peritonitis | 1 | .... | 2 | 1 | 4 | .... | 2 | 2 | 11 | 12 |
| 70. Teething | 431 | 405 | 813 | 772 | 14 | 6 | .... | .... | .... | .... |
| 71. Worms | 147 | 159 | 1032 | 1017 | 225 | 244 | 42 | 38 | 15 | 11 |
| VII.— 72. Bladder, disease of | 2 | .... | .... | .... | 1 | 1 | 5 | 2 | 10 | 4 |
| 73. Diabetes | 6 | 5 | 13 | 5 | 11 | 6 | 18 | 10 | 63 | 21 |
| 74. Gravel | 9 | 3 | 13 | 4 | 5 | 2 | 13 | .... | 40 | 12 |
| 75. Kidneys, disease of | 6 | 4 | 7 | 5 | 4 | 5 | 11 | 5 | 52 | 20 |
| VIII.— 76. Childbirth | .... | .... | .... | .... | .... | .... | .... | 319 | .... | 2778 |
| 77. Generative organs, disease of | .... | .... | .... | 5 | .... | .... | .... | 19 | .... | 144 |
| 78. Paramenia | .... | .... | .... | .... | .... | .... | .... | 2 | .... | 5 |
| 79. Puerperal fever | .... | .... | .... | .... | .... | .... | .... | 53 | .... | 462 |
| IX.— 80. Hip, disease of | 2 | .... | 10 | 2 | 8 | 2 | 9 | 6 | 9 | 2 |
| 81. Rheumatism | 11 | 9 | 24 | 22 | 42 | 32 | 98 | 64 | 167 | 119 |
| 82. Spine, disease of | 48 | 42 | 61 | 39 | 36 | 21 | 60 | 50 | 85 | 86 |
| 83. White swelling | 5 | .... | 9 | 4 | 8 | 5 | 26 | 12 | 25 | 14 |
| X.— 84. Carbuncle | .... | .... | .... | .... | .... | .... | 2 | 2 | 9 | 3 |
| 85. Fistula | .... | .... | .... | .... | .... | .... | .... | .... | 6 | 4 |
| 86. Leprosy | 1 | .... | 1 | .... | .... | .... | .... | .... | 4 | 4 |
| 87. Skin, disease of | 13 | 24 | 10 | 15 | 2 | 3 | .... | .... | 5 | 2 |
| 88. Ulcer | 41 | 36 | 33 | 31 | 14 | 11 | 17 | 12 | 52 | 43 |
| XI.— 89. Old age | .... | .... | .... | .... | .... | .... | .... | .... | 9 | 12 |
| XII.— 90. Accident | 297 | 284 | 415 | 269 | 339 | 176 | 693 | 115 | 1800 | 165 |
| 91. Accident, burned | 71 | 78 | 340 | 445 | 104 | 245 | 38 | 121 | 83 | 101 |
| 92. Accident, drowned | 8 | 9 | 235 | 105 | 260 | 54 | 428 | 103 | 887 | 97 |
| 93. Accident, scalded | 23 | 18 | 149 | 94 | 16 | 12 | 7 | .... | 21 | 2 |
| 94. Executed | .... | .... | .... | .... | .... | .... | 1 | .... | 14 | 2 |
| 95. Fracture | 1 | 1 | 3 | 1 | 5 | .... | 14 | 2 | 108 | 9 |
| 96. Frozen | 1 | .... | .... | 1 | 1 | 1 | 3 | .... | 31 | 3 |
| 97. Heat | 2 | .... | 6 | 5 | 3 | 3 | 21 | 5 | 148 | 14 |
| 98. Hydrophobia | .... | .... | 3 | 1 | 3 | 2 | 1 | 2 | 5 | 3 |
| 99. Intemperance | .... | .... | .... | .... | 1 | .... | 3 | 1 | 289 | 46 |
| 100. Lightning | .... | .... | 2 | 2 | 6 | 2 | 22 | 9 | 29 | 16 |
| 101. Mercury, effects of | .... | .... | 2 | 2 | 3 | 1 | 1 | 1 | 6 | 6 |
| 102. Murder | 4 | 2 | 3 | 1 | 3 | .... | 11 | 8 | 161 | 3 |
| 103. Poison | 23 | 20 | 57 | 43 | 32 | 26 | 26 | 20 | 70 | 53 |
| 104. Suffocation | 354 | 376 | 83 | 67 | 9 | 5 | 3 | 2 | 15 | 5 |
| 105. Suicide | .... | .... | .... | .... | .... | .... | 18 | 16 | 235 | 87 |
| XIII.—106. Stillborn | 217 | 160 | .... | .... | .... | .... | .... | .... | .... | .... |
| XIV.—107. Unknown | 8308 | 6948 | 4100 | 3535 | 1082 | 933 | 1367 | 1482 | 4214 | 4 |

# TABLE I—Continued.

| | AGES. | | | | | | | | | | |
|---|---|---|---|---|---|---|---|---|---|---|---|
| | 50 and under 80. | | 80 and under 100. | | 100 and over. | | Age unknown. | | Total. | | Aggregate deaths. |
| | M. | F. | M. | F. | M. | F. | M. | F. | M. | F. | |
| ALL CAUSES | 26511 | 20840 | 5152 | 5020 | 173 | 190 | ‡964 | 594 | 172800 | 150045 | 323,023 |
| I. ZYMOTIC DISEASES | 6934 | 5145 | 508 | 479 | 12 | 3 | *315 | 206 | 72476 | 59221 | 131,813 |
| SPORADIC DISEASES. | | | | | | | | | | | |
| II. Diseases of uncertain or variable seats | 2968 | 2829 | 472 | 347 | 8 | 11 | 22 | 16 | 10624 | 10420 | 21,044 |
| III. Diseases of brain and nervous system | 2234 | 1753 | 347 | 329 | 4 | 2 | 42 | 16 | 13392 | 10395 | 23,787 |
| IV. Diseases of the respiratory organs | 5952 | 4852 | 480 | 420 | 4 | 5 | 45 | 37 | 27540 | 27260 | 54,800 |
| V. Diseases of the organs of circulation | 512 | 377 | 50 | 30 | .... | .... | 2 | 3 | 1384 | 1151 | 2,535 |
| VI. Diseases of the digestive organs | 1237 | 773 | 89 | 33 | 1 | .... | 13 | 3 | 8237 | 6935 | 15,172 |
| VII. Diseases of the urinary organs | 509 | 63 | 118 | 4 | 2 | .... | 2 | .... | 920 | 181 | 1,101 |
| VIII. Diseases of the generative organs, and childbirth | ...... | 49 | .... | 1 | .... | .... | .... | 5 | ...... | 3842 | 3,842 |
| IX. Diseases of the locomotive organs | 268 | 183 | 21 | 15 | .... | .... | 6 | 3 | 1038 | 732 | 1,770 |
| X. Diseases of the skin | 60 | 43 | 9 | 2 | .... | .... | 1 | 1 | 280 | 236 | 516 |
| XI. Old age | 1383 | 1793 | 2571 | 2934 | 133 | 156 | 15 | 21 | 4111 | 4916 | 9,027 |
| XII. External causes | 1126 | 270 | 86 | 55 | 2 | 1 | 42 | 7 | 9315 | 3691 | 13,006 |
| XIII. Stillborn | ...... | ...... | .... | .... | .... | .... | .... | .... | 217 | 160 | 377 |
| XIV. Unknown | 3328 | 2710 | 401 | 371 | 7 | 12 | †459 | 276 | 23266 | 20905 | 44,233 |
| I.— 1. Cholera | 2706 | 1679 | 126 | 192 | 7 | .... | *192 | 146 | 18575 | 12815 | 31,506 |
| 2. Cholera infantum | ...... | ...... | .... | .... | .... | .... | 2 | .... | 2126 | 1834 | 3,960 |
| 3. Cholera morbus | 165 | 108 | 22 | 16 | 1 | .... | 6 | 3 | 889 | 679 | 1,568 |
| 4. Croup | 15 | 5 | 2 | 2 | .... | .... | 7 | 8 | 5864 | 4842 | 10,706 |
| 5. Diarrhœa | 391 | 308 | 51 | 36 | 1 | .... | 19 | 2 | 3607 | 2759 | 6,366 |
| 6. Dysentery | 879 | 1086 | 111 | 141 | 1 | .... | 30 | 15 | 10928 | 9628 | 20,556 |
| 7. Erysipelas | 293 | 245 | 28 | 35 | .... | .... | .... | .... | 1373 | 1413 | 2,786 |
| 8. Fever | 1269 | 872 | 89 | 81 | 2 | 2 | 21 | 11 | 9673 | 8435 | 18,108 |
| 9. Fever, intermittent | 66 | 65 | 12 | 9 | .... | .... | 4 | .... | 502 | 462 | 964 |
| 10. Fever, remittent | 7 | 4 | 1 | .... | .... | .... | .... | .... | 91 | 57 | 148 |
| 11. Fever, scarlet | 24 | 28 | 4 | 1 | .... | .... | 4 | 2 | 4820 | 4764 | 9,584 |
| 12. Fever, ship | 20 | 6 | 3 | 1 | .... | .... | .... | .... | 136 | 104 | 240 |
| 13. Fever, typhoid | 887 | 616 | 36 | 35 | .... | 1 | 12 | 8 | 7410 | 5689 | 13,099 |
| 14. Fever, yellow | 28 | 9 | .... | 2 | .... | .... | .... | .... | 652 | 133 | 785 |
| 15. Hooping cough | 5 | 6 | 1 | 1 | .... | .... | 7 | 3 | 2472 | 2808 | 5,280 |
| 16. Influenza | 16 | 24 | 16 | 9 | .... | .... | .... | .... | 127 | 125 | 252 |
| 17. Measles | 18 | 21 | .... | .... | .... | .... | 3 | 2 | 1464 | 1519 | 2,983 |
| 18. Small pox | 122 | 54 | 5 | 8 | .... | .... | 8 | 6 | 1492 | 860 | 2,352 |
| 19. Syphilis | 22 | 8 | 1 | .... | .... | .... | .... | .... | 76 | 70 | 146 |
| 20. Thrush | 1 | 1 | .... | .... | .... | .... | .... | .... | 199 | 225 | 424 |
| II.— 21. Abscess | 35 | 28 | 3 | .... | .... | .... | .... | .... | 191 | 120 | 311 |
| 22. Cancer | 372 | 554 | 70 | 60 | 1 | 4 | 2 | 2 | 617 | 1027 | 1,704 |
| 23. Debility | 66 | 84 | 17 | 11 | 1 | 1 | 2 | 3 | 480 | 504 | 984 |
| 24. Dropsy | 1970 | 1780 | 292 | 229 | 6 | 6 | 12 | 8 | 5658 | 5559 | 11,217 |
| 25. Gout | 28 | 5 | 1 | 1 | .... | .... | .... | .... | 40 | 10 | 50 |
| 26. Hemorrhage | 76 | 45 | 7 | 5 | .... | .... | 1 | .... | 391 | 276 | 667 |
| 27. Inflammation | 181 | 117 | 31 | 16 | .... | .... | 3 | 1 | 1461 | 1286 | 2,747 |
| 28. Malformation | ...... | ...... | .... | .... | .... | .... | .... | .... | 51 | 34 | 85 |
| 29. Marasmus | 30 | 24 | 3 | 3 | .... | .... | 1 | .... | 64 | 291 | 555 |
| 30. Milk sickness | 4 | 1 | .... | .... | .... | .... | .... | .... | 42 | 44 | 86 |
| 31. Mortification | 49 | 30 | 19 | 10 | .... | .... | .... | .. | 184 | 133 | 317 |
| 32. Rickets | ...... | ...... | 1 | .... | .... | .... | .... | | 48 | 33 | 71 |
| 33. Scrofula | 109 | 92 | 16 | 6 | .... | .... | ... | . | 962 | 898 | 1,860 |
| 34. Scurvy | 5 | 3 | .... | .... | .... | .... | | 1 | 40 | 14 | 54 |
| 35. Tumor | 43 | 66 | 3 | 6 | .... | .... | .... | .... | 135 | 201 | 336 |
| III.— 36. Apoplexy | 620 | 463 | 83 | 37 | 2 | .... | 6 | 1 | 1115 | 843 | 1,958 |
| 37. Brain and nerves, disease of. | 135 | 62 | 8 | 6 | .... | .... | 4 | 1 | 1656 | 1199 | 2,855 |
| 38. Cephalitis | 173 | 92 | 8 | 3 | .... | .... | 7 | 3 | 3727 | 2695 | 6,422 |
| 39. Chorea | ...... | 4 | .... | 1 | .... | .... | .... | .... | 12 | 42 | 54 |
| 40. Convulsions | 190 | 142 | 28 | 35 | .... | .... | 13 | 6 | 3256 | 2816 | 6,072 |

* 116, age and sex unknown are included in total whites and aggregate.
† 62, age and sex unknown are included in total whites and aggregate.
‡ 178, age and sex unknown are included in total whites and aggregate.

## TABLE I—Continued.

| | Ages. | | | | | | | | | | |
|---|---|---|---|---|---|---|---|---|---|---|---|
| | 50 and under 80. | | 80 and under 100. | | 100 & over. | | Age unknown. | | Total. | | Aggregate deaths. |
| | M. | F. | M. | F. | M. | F. | M. | F. | M. | F. | |
| 41. Delirium tremens | 72 | 2 | .... | 1 | .... | .... | 4 | 1 | 362 | 31 | 393 |
| 42. Epilepsy | 38 | 26 | 5 | 7 | .... | .... | 1 | .... | 213 | 160 | 373 |
| 43. Hydrocephalus | 20 | 12 | .... | 1 | .... | .... | 1 | .... | 943 | 731 | 1,674 |
| 44. Insanity | 68 | 51 | 4 | 3 | .... | .... | 4 | .... | 180 | 120 | 300 |
| 45. Neuralgia | 43 | 53 | 4 | 2 | .... | .... | 1 | 1 | 149 | 134 | 283 |
| 46. Paralysis | 860 | 831 | 207 | 233 | 2 | 2 | .... | 3 | 1361 | 1348 | 2,709 |
| 47. Tetanus | 15 | 5 | .... | .... | .... | .... | 1 | .... | 418 | 276 | 694 |
| IV.— 48. Asthma | 128 | 117 | 22 | 19 | .... | .... | 2 | .... | 245 | 206 | 451 |
| 49. Bronchitis | 240 | 157 | 28 | 32 | .... | 1 | 2 | 2 | 1752 | 1608 | 3,360 |
| 50. Consumption | 3761 | 3379 | 256 | 235 | 1 | 2 | 27 | 26 | 15490 | 18026 | 33,516 |
| 51. Laryngitis | 35 | 29 | 4 | 2 | 1 | .... | .... | 1 | 510 | 529 | 1,039 |
| 52. Pleurisy | 360 | 253 | 30 | 22 | 1 | 1 | 6 | 2 | 1314 | 853 | 2,167 |
| 53. Pneumonia | 1219 | 759 | 111 | 93 | 1 | 1 | 6 | 4 | 7069 | 5061 | 12,130 |
| 54. Quinsy | 38 | 25 | 4 | 1 | .... | .... | .... | .... | 307 | 255 | 562 |
| 55. Respiratory organs, disease of | 171 | 133 | 25 | 16 | .... | .... | 2 | 2 | 853 | 722 | 1,575 |
| V.— 56. Aneurism | 1 | .... | .... | .... | .... | .... | .... | .... | 7 | 1 | 8 |
| 57. Circulatory organs, disease of | .... | .... | .... | .... | .... | .... | .... | .... | .... | .... | .... |
| 58. Heart, disease of | 511 | 377 | 59 | 30 | .... | .... | 2 | 3 | 1377 | 1150 | 2,527 |
| VI.— 59. Colic | 205 | 132 | 23 | 9 | 1 | .... | 2 | .... | 745 | 476 | 1,221 |
| 60. Digestive organs, disease of | 120 | 85 | 8 | 4 | .... | .... | 3 | .... | 1104 | 945 | 2,049 |
| 61. Dirt eating | 5 | 1 | .... | .... | .... | .... | .... | .... | 55 | 39 | 94 |
| 62. Dyspepsia | 193 | 96 | 8 | 2 | .... | .... | .... | .... | 367 | 249 | 616 |
| 63. Enteritis | 220 | 97 | 14 | 7 | .... | .... | 2 | .... | 1630 | 1256 | 2,886 |
| 64. Gastritis | 29 | 30 | .... | 2 | .... | .... | .... | 1 | 118 | 154 | 272 |
| 65. Hemorroids | 25 | 7 | 1 | .... | .... | .... | .... | .... | 40 | 18 | 58 |
| 66. Hernia | 66 | 15 | 14 | 1 | .... | .... | 1 | .... | 180 | 61 | 241 |
| 67. Jaundice | 56 | 71 | 9 | 2 | .... | .... | .... | .... | 238 | 226 | 464 |
| 68. Liver, disease of | 314 | 235 | 11 | 5 | .... | .... | 2 | 1 | 1013 | 838 | 1,851 |
| 69. Peritonitis | 1 | 1 | .... | .... | .... | .... | .... | .... | 21 | 16 | 37 |
| 70. Teething | .... | .... | .... | .... | .... | .... | 2 | .... | 1260 | 1183 | 2,443 |
| 71. Worms | 3 | 3 | 1 | 1 | .... | .... | 1 | 1 | 1466 | 1474 | 2,940 |
| VII.— 72. Bladder, disease of | 23 | 2 | 9 | .... | .... | .... | .... | .... | 50 | 9 | 59 |
| 73. Diabetes | 51 | 11 | 7 | 3 | .... | .... | 1 | .... | 170 | 61 | 231 |
| 74. Gravel | 345 | 24 | 86 | .... | 2 | .... | 1 | .... | 514 | 45 | 559 |
| 75. Kidneys, disease of | 90 | 26 | 16 | 1 | .... | .... | .... | .... | 186 | 66 | 252 |
| VIII.— 76. Childbirth | .... | 15 | .... | .... | .... | .... | .... | 5 | .... | 3117 | 3,117 |
| 77. Generative organs, disease of | .... | 29 | .... | 1 | .... | .... | .... | .... | .... | 198 | 198 |
| 78. Paramenia | .... | .... | .... | .... | .... | .... | .... | .... | .... | 7 | 7 |
| 79. Puerperal fever | .... | 5 | .... | .... | .... | .... | .... | .... | .... | 520 | 520 |
| IX.— 80. Hip, disease of | 4 | 2 | .... | .... | .... | .... | 1 | .... | 43 | 14 | 57 |
| 81. Rheumatism | 214 | 145 | 19 | 13 | .... | .... | 2 | 2 | 577 | 406 | 983 |
| 82. Spine, disease of | 40 | 32 | 2 | 1 | .... | .... | 3 | 1 | 335 | 272 | 607 |
| 83. White swelling | 10 | 4 | .... | 1 | .... | .... | .... | .... | 83 | 40 | 123 |
| X.— 84. Carbuncle | 5 | 3 | 1 | .... | .... | .... | .... | .... | 17 | 8 | 25 |
| 85. Fistula | 2 | 2 | 1 | .... | .... | .... | .... | .... | 9 | 6 | 15 |
| 86. Leprosy | 1 | .... | .... | .... | .... | .... | .... | .... | 7 | 4 | 11 |
| 87. Skin, disease of | 1 | 5 | 1 | .... | .... | .... | .... | .... | 32 | 49 | 81 |
| 88. Ulcer | 51 | 33 | 6 | 2 | .... | .... | 1 | 1 | 215 | 169 | 384 |
| XI.— 89. Old age | 1383 | 1793 | 2571 | 2934 | 133 | 156 | 15 | 21 | 4111 | 4916 | 9,027 |
| XII.— 90. Accident | 521 | 140 | 54 | 37 | 1 | .... | 13 | 4 | 4133 | 1190 | 5,323 |
| 91. Accident, burned | 25 | 44 | 8 | 8 | .... | 1 | .... | 1 | 669 | 1039 | 1,708 |
| 92. Accident, drowned | 136 | 19 | 5 | .... | 1 | .... | 9 | 1 | 1969 | 388 | 2,357 |
| 93. Accident, scalded | 1 | 1 | .... | .... | .... | .... | .... | .... | 217 | 127 | 344 |
| 94. Executed | 3 | .... | 1 | .... | .... | .... | .... | .... | 19 | 2 | 21 |
| 95. Fracture | 17 | 7 | 1 | 1 | .... | .... | 1 | .... | 150 | 21 | 171 |
| 96. Frozen | 29 | 1 | 1 | 1 | .... | .... | .... | .... | 66 | 7 | 73 |
| 97. Heat | 26 | 7 | 2 | 2 | .... | .... | 8 | 1 | 211 | 37 | 248 |
| 98. Hydrophobia | 4 | 2 | .... | .... | .... | .... | .... | .... | 16 | 10 | 26 |
| 99. Intemperance | 187 | 12 | 7 | 3 | .... | .... | 9 | .... | 496 | 62 | 558 |
| 100. Lightning | 6 | .... | .... | .... | .... | .... | .... | .... | 65 | 29 | 94 |
| 101. Mercury, effects of | 1 | 3 | .... | .... | .... | .... | .... | .... | 13 | 13 | 26 |
| 102. Murder | 24 | 6 | 2 | 2 | .... | .... | 2 | .... | 210 | 17 | 227 |
| 103. Poison | 22 | 12 | .... | 1 | .... | .... | .... | .... | 230 | 175 | 405 |
| 104. Suffocation | 8 | 4 | .... | .... | .... | .... | 3 | .... | 475 | 459 | 934 |
| 105. Suicide | 116 | 12 | 5 | .... | .... | .... | 2 | .... | 376 | 115 | 491 |
| XIII.—106. Stillborn | .... | .... | .... | .... | .... | .... | .... | .... | 217 | 160 | 377 |
| XIV.—107. Unknown | 3328 | 2710 | 401 | 371 | 7 | 12 | †459 | 276 | 23266 | 20905 | 44,283 |

## UNITED STATES TABLES—Continued.

TABLE II.—*Natívities of those who died during the year ending June 1, 1850—white, free colored, and slave—with the causes of death.*

| | Born in the State in which they died. | N. England States. | Middle States. | Southern States. | Southwest'n States. | Northwest'n States. | California and Territories. | Ireland. | Germany. | Other foreign countries. | Unknown. | Aggregate deaths. |
|---|---|---|---|---|---|---|---|---|---|---|---|---|
| ALL CAUSES | 235176 | 9749 | 14373 | 16452 | 4578 | 7956 | 52 | 15784 | 8550 | 8627 | 1717 | 323,023 |
| I. ZYMOTIC DISEASES | 94585 | 2583 | 5268 | 5156 | 2128 | 3795 | 17 | 8053 | 5713 | 3872 | 638 | 131,813 |
| SPORADIC DISEASES. | | | | | | | | | | | | |
| II. Diseases of uncertain or variable seat | 15173 | 920 | 1076 | 1624 | 275 | 356 | 3 | 747 | 266 | 489 | 115 | 21,044 |
| III. Diseases of brain and nervous system | 18742 | 824 | 1041 | 911 | 243 | 420 | 3 | 718 | 276 | 530 | 79 | 23,787 |
| IV. Diseases of the respiratory organs | 38206 | 2540 | 3236 | 3223 | 784 | 1545 | 17 | 2718 | 789 | 1514 | 228 | 54,800 |
| V. Diseases of the organs of circulation | 1695 | 204 | 178 | 120 | 18 | 23 | ...... | 158 | 34 | 101 | 4 | 2,535 |
| VI. Dis. of digestive org's | 12056 | 362 | 516 | 775 | 211 | 282 | 1 | 472 | 163 | 296 | 38 | 15,172 |
| VII. Dis. of urinary org'ns | 608 | 97 | 113 | 138 | 18 | 22 | ...... | 48 | 18 | 31 | 8 | 1,101 |
| VIII. Diseases of gen'ative org's, and childb'th | 2319 | 80 | 219 | 360 | 139 | 174 | 1 | 254 | 151 | 127 | 18 | 3,842 |
| IX. Diseases of the locomotive organs | 1195 | 66 | 123 | 144 | 27 | 51 | ...... | 70 | 27 | 57 | 10 | 1,770 |
| X. Diseases of the skin | 367 | 25 | 26 | 30 | 2 | 13 | ...... | 22 | 10 | 18 | 3 | 516 |
| XI. Old age | 4939 | 1023 | 783 | 1138 | 27 | 27 | ...... | 412 | 171 | 411 | 96 | 9,027 |
| XII. External causes | 9172 | 356 | 554 | 693 | 170 | 330 | ...... | 921 | 299 | 428 | 83 | 13,006 |
| XIII. Stillborn | 377 | ...... | ...... | ...... | ...... | ...... | ...... | ...... | ...... | ...... | ...... | 377 |
| XIV. Unknown | 35742 | 664 | 1240 | 2140 | 536 | 918 | 10 | 1191 | 642 | 753 | 397 | 44,233 |
| I.— 1. Cholera | 14375 | 608 | 1932 | 1624 | 658 | 1247 | 6 | 4447 | 4276 | 1989 | 344 | 31,506 |
| 2. Ch'ra infant'm | 3795 | 21 | 35 | 20 | 13 | 28 | ...... | 23 | 8 | 16 | 1 | 3,960 |
| 3. Ch'ra morbus | 1093 | 49 | 105 | 64 | 30 | 44 | ...... | 81 | 39 | 58 | 5 | 1,568 |
| 4. Croup | 10120 | 50 | 146 | 65 | 59 | 131 | ...... | 51 | 30 | 51 | 3 | 10,706 |
| 5. Diarrhœa | 4690 | 142 | 228 | 285 | 97 | 190 | ...... | 403 | 112 | 186 | 33 | 6,366 |
| 6. Dysentery | 17074 | 545 | 676 | 325 | 81 | 315 | 2 | 871 | 240 | 398 | 29 | 20,556 |
| 7. Erysipelas | 1947 | 182 | 181 | 158 | 26 | 101 | ...... | 86 | 31 | 60 | 14 | 2,786 |
| 8. Fever | 13203 | 386 | 746 | 1165 | 512 | 666 | 6 | 516 | 424 | 404 | 80 | 18,108 |
| 9. Fever, interm't | 672 | 16 | 47 | 69 | 34 | 41 | ...... | 35 | 15 | 31 | 4 | 964 |
| 10. Fever, rem'nt | 99 | 5 | 7 | 6 | 4 | 3 | ...... | 12 | 7 | 5 | ...... | 148 |
| 11. Fever, scarlet | 8796 | 78 | 177 | 77 | 74 | 151 | ...... | 94 | 32 | 93 | 12 | 9,584 |
| 12. Fever, ship | 69 | 2 | 3 | 1 | ...... | 1 | ...... | 135 | 12 | 17 | ...... | 240 |
| 13. Fever, typhoid | 8742 | 341 | 696 | 1057 | 429 | 595 | 2 | 727 | 199 | 247 | 64 | 13,099 |
| 14. Fever, yellow | 66 | 23 | 36 | 16 | 5 | 7 | ...... | 317 | 139 | 163 | 13 | 785 |
| 15. Hooping cough | 4980 | 16 | 53 | 37 | 40 | 64 | ...... | 38 | 13 | 36 | 3 | 5,280 |
| 16. Influenza | 207 | 9 | 7 | 17 | 4 | 3 | ...... | 3 | ...... | 2 | ...... | 252 |
| 17. Measles | 2021 | 20 | 70 | 59 | 27 | 101 | 1 | 102 | 35 | 41 | 6 | 2,983 |
| 18. Small pox | 1619 | 91 | 118 | 102 | 31 | 101 | ...... | 102 | 101 | 69 | 23 | 2,352 |
| 19. Syphilis | 108 | 2 | 6 | 8 | 2 | 2 | ...... | 9 | ...... | 5 | 4 | 146 |
| 20. Thrush | 409 | 2 | 4 | 1 | 2 | 4 | ...... | 1 | ...... | 1 | ...... | 424 |
| II.—21. Abscess | 186 | 19 | 17 | 23 | 8 | 6 | ...... | 32 | 6 | 10 | 4 | 311 |
| 22. Cancer | 1022 | 172 | 119 | 183 | 18 | 26 | ...... | 79 | 21 | 52 | 12 | 1,704 |
| 23. Debility | 787 | 21 | 17 | 15 | 7 | 4 | ...... | 81 | 11 | 36 | 5 | 984 |
| 24. Dropsy | 7833 | 472 | 622 | 1101 | 178 | 186 | 1 | 338 | 163 | 257 | 66 | 11,217 |
| 25. Gout | 32 | 2 | 2 | 5 | 1 | ...... | ...... | 1 | 1 | 5 | 1 | 50 |
| 26. Hemorrhage | 430 | 28 | 47 | 64 | 12 | 21 | ...... | 25 | 16 | 20 | 4 | 667 |
| 27. Inflammation | 2170 | 112 | 134 | 90 | 24 | 86 | 1 | 93 | 18 | 67 | 2 | 2,747 |
| 28. Malformation | 83 | ...... | ...... | ...... | ...... | ...... | ...... | 1 | 1 | ...... | ...... | 85 |
| 29. Marasmus | 472 | 11 | 7 | 8 | 2 | 3 | ...... | 31 | 8 | 9 | 4 | 555 |
| 30. Milk sickness | 50 | 2 | 4 | 7 | 2 | 14 | ...... | 2 | 2 | 3 | ...... | 86 |
| 31. Mortification | 240 | 13 | 9 | 14 | 2 | 4 | 1 | 21 | 4 | 8 | 1 | 317 |
| 32. Rickets | 67 | ...... | ...... | ...... | 2 | 1 | ...... | ...... | 1 | ...... | ...... | 71 |
| 33. Scrofula | 1533 | 43 | 68 | 96 | 17 | 47 | ...... | 23 | 7 | 14 | 12 | 1,860 |
| 34. Scurvy | 30 | 1 | 7 | 5 | 1 | 3 | ...... | 1 | 2 | 3 | 1 | 54 |
| 35. Tumor | 238 | 24 | 23 | 13 | 1 | 5 | ...... | 19 | 5 | 5 | 3 | 336 |
| III.—36. Apoplexy | 1150 | 188 | 166 | 167 | 23 | 25 | ...... | 96 | 41 | 94 | 8 | 1,958 |
| 37. Brain & nerves, disease of | 2297 | 98 | 100 | 70 | 34 | 65 | ...... | 87 | 19 | 71 | 14 | 2,855 |
| 38. Cephalitis | 5372 | 100 | 219 | 187 | 84 | 168 | 1 | 124 | 58 | 101 | 8 | 6,422 |
| 39. Chorea | 46 | 1 | ...... | 2 | 3 | 1 | ...... | 1 | ...... | ...... | ...... | 54 |
| 40. Convulsions | 5377 | 93 | 125 | 107 | 48 | 72 | ...... | 97 | 53 | 86 | 14 | 6,072 |
| 41. Delirium trem. | 154 | 11 | 31 | 17 | ...... | 11 | 1 | 104 | 20 | 32 | 12 | 393 |
| 42. Epilepsy | 258 | 9 | 24 | 25 | 10 | 6 | ...... | 17 | 5 | 17 | 2 | 373 |
| 43. Hydrocephal's | 1517 | 21 | 39 | 12 | 6 | 17 | ...... | 35 | 6 | 21 | ...... | 1,674 |
| 44. Insanity | 187 | 21 | 18 | 13 | 5 | 1 | 1 | 28 | 15 | 8 | 3 | 300 |

## TABLE II—Continued.

| | Born in the State in which they died. | N. England States. | Middle States. | Southern States. | Southwest'n States. | Northwest'n States. | California and Territories. | Ireland. | Germany. | Other foreign countries. | Unknown. | Aggregate deaths. |
|---|---|---|---|---|---|---|---|---|---|---|---|---|
| 45. Neuralgia .... | 173 | 11 | 20 | 31 | 7 | 13 | ...... | 9 | 12 | 7 | ...... | 283 |
| 46. Paralysis ... | 1593 | 264 | 295 | 265 | 18 | 35 | ...... | 102 | 40 | 83 | 14 | 2,709 |
| 47. Tetanus ..... | 618 | 7 | 4 | 15 | 5 | 6 | ...... | 18 | 7 | 10 | 4 | 694 |
| IV.— 48. Asthma...... | 253 | 14 | 35 | 74 | 5 | 6 | ...... | 24 | 7 | 30 | 3 | 451 |
| 49. Bronchitis ... | 2804 | 42 | 93 | 167 | 47 | 67 | 3 | 55 | 28 | 48 | 6 | 3,360 |
| 50. Consumption. | 22353 | 1993 | 2307 | 1635 | 346 | 879 | 7 | 2120 | 597 | 1146 | 133 | 33,516 |
| 51. Laryngitis ... | 918 | 16 | 24 | 23 | 11 | 11 | ...... | 19 | 2 | 13 | 2 | 1,039 |
| 52. Pleurisy ..... | 1587 | 63 | 102 | 154 | 39 | 54 | ...... | 85 | 22 | 50 | 11 | 2,167 |
| 53. Pneumonia .. | 8689 | 336 | 575 | 1050 | 316 | 461 | 7 | 329 | 113 | 184 | 70 | 12,130 |
| 54. Quinsy ...... | 455 | 4 | 18 | 37 | 4 | 20 | ...... | 9 | 5 | 9 | 1 | 562 |
| 55. Respirat'y organs, dis. of. | 1147 | 72 | 82 | 83 | 16 | 47 | ...... | 77 | 15 | 34 | 2 | 1,575 |
| V.— 56. Aneurism .... | 3 | 1 | 1 | 1 | ...... | ...... | ...... | 1 | ...... | 1 | ...... | 8 |
| 57. Circ'latory organs, dis. of. | ...... | ...... | ...... | ...... | ...... | ...... | ...... | ...... | ...... | ...... | ...... | ...... |
| 58. Heart, dis. of. | 1692 | 203 | 177 | 119 | 18 | 23 | ...... | 157 | 34 | 100 | 4 | 2,527 |
| VI.— 59. Colic ....... | 844 | 35 | 54 | 124 | 15 | 24 | ...... | 48 | 40 | 31 | 6 | 1,221 |
| 60. Digestive organs, dis. of. | 1670 | 67 | 54 | 56 | 15 | 17 | 1 | 100 | 10 | 52 | 7 | 2,049 |
| 61. Dirt eating... | 80 | ...... | 1 | 8 | 3 | 2 | ...... | ...... | ...... | ...... | ...... | 94 |
| 62. Dyspepsia ... | 340 | 23 | 58 | 123 | 17 | 19 | ...... | 15 | 2 | 17 | 2 | 616 |
| 63. Enteritis ..... | 2281 | 75 | 114 | 125 | 33 | 53 | ...... | 105 | 38 | 53 | 9 | 2,886 |
| 64. Gastritis ..... | 170 | 4 | 16 | 32 | 5 | 18 | ...... | 16 | 4 | 7 | ...... | 272 |
| 65. Hemorrhoids. | 27 | 4 | 5 | 14 | 2 | 2 | ...... | 2 | 1 | 1 | ...... | 58 |
| 66. Hernia ... .. | 155 | 14 | 12 | 20 | 5 | 7 | ...... | 9 | 3 | 15 | 1 | 241 |
| 67. Jaundice .... | 322 | 20 | 24 | 25 | 5 | 12 | ...... | 28 | 6 | 18 | 4 | 464 |
| 68. Liver, dis. of. | 1127 | 97 | 135 | 171 | 44 | 79 | ...... | 100 | 30 | 62 | 6 | 1,851 |
| 69. Peritonitis ... | 18 | 1 | 3 | 3 | ...... | ...... | ...... | 5 | 2 | 5 | ...... | 37 |
| 70. Teething..... | 2276 | 19 | 26 | 11 | 18 | 21 | ...... | 28 | 23 | 20 | 1 | 2,443 |
| 71. Worms ...... | 2746 | 3 | 14 | 63 | 49 | 28 | ...... | 16 | 4 | 15 | 2 | 2,940 |
| VII.— 72. Bladder, dis. of | 35 | 2 | 5 | 5 | 1 | ...... | ...... | 5 | 2 | 3 | 1 | 59 |
| 73. Diabetes ..... | 138 | 24 | 20 | 14 | 4 | 6 | ...... | 12 | 7 | 6 | ...... | 231 |
| 74. Gravel....... | 279 | 48 | 67 | 100 | 10 | 9 | ...... | 20 | 6 | 14 | 6 | 559 |
| 75. Kidneys, dis. of | 156 | 23 | 21 | 19 | 3 | 7 | ...... | 11 | 3 | 8 | 1 | 252 |
| VIII.— 76. Childbirth ... | 1918 | 67 | 182 | 257 | 101 | 123 | 1 | 214 | 128 | 111 | 15 | 3,117 |
| 77. Generative organs, dis. of. | 125 | 1 | 5 | 42 | 4 | 5 | ...... | 5 | 6 | 4 | 1 | 198 |
| 78. Paramenia... | 4 | ...... | 1 | 1 | 1 | ...... | ...... | ...... | ...... | ...... | ...... | 7 |
| 79. P'rperal fever. | 272 | 12 | 31 | 60 | 33 | 46 | ...... | 35 | 17 | 12 | 2 | 520 |
| IX.— 80. Hip, dis. of .. | 44 | 5 | 2 | ...... | ...... | ...... | ...... | 3 | ...... | 3 | ...... | 57 |
| 81. Rheumatism . | 596 | 43 | 78 | 102 | 16 | 25 | ...... | 50 | 24 | 40 | 9 | 983 |
| 82. Spine, dis. of. | 460 | 17 | 40 | 29 | 7 | 21 | ...... | 17 | 3 | 12 | 1 | 607 |
| 83. White swelling | 95 | 1 | 3 | 13 | 4 | 5 | ...... | ...... | ...... | 2 | ...... | 123 |
| X.— 84. Carbuncle.... | 15 | ...... | 4 | 4 | ...... | ...... | ...... | ...... | 2 | ...... | ...... | 25 |
| 85. Fistula....... | 5 | 1 | 2 | 4 | ...... | ...... | ...... | 2 | 1 | ...... | ...... | 15 |
| 86. Leprosy...... | 5 | ...... | ...... | ...... | 1 | 2 | ...... | ...... | 1 | 2 | ...... | 11 |
| 87. Skin, dis. of .. | 72 | 2 | 2 | 1 | ...... | ...... | ...... | 1 | 2 | 1 | ...... | 81 |
| 88. Ulcer ........ | 270 | 22 | 18 | 21 | 1 | 11 | ...... | 19 | 4 | 15 | 3 | 384 |
| XI.— 89. Old age...... | 4939 | 1023 | 783 | 1138 | 27 | 27 | ...... | 412 | 171 | 411 | 96 | 9,027 |
| XII.— 90. Accident..... | 3589 | 159 | 303 | 336 | 83 | 147 | ...... | 364 | 140 | 180 | 22 | 5,323 |
| 91. Do. burned.. | 1486 | 17 | 34 | 47 | 14 | 29 | ...... | 40 | 21 | 15 | 5 | 1,708 |
| 92. Do. drowned | 1553 | 74 | 103 | 122 | 33 | 80 | ...... | 191 | 74 | 108 | 19 | 2,357 |
| 93. Do. scalded . | 300 | 4 | 5 | 4 | 2 | 6 | ...... | 10 | 2 | 9 | 2 | 344 |
| 94. Executed .... | 11 | ...... | ...... | 6 | 2 | ...... | ...... | 1 | ...... | 1 | ...... | 21 |
| 95. Fracture..... | 56 | 8 | 5 | 5 | 1 | 3 | ...... | 61 | 12 | 13 | 7 | 171 |
| 96. Frozen ...... | 42 | 2 | 2 | 10 | 1 | 3 | ...... | 6 | 2 | 3 | 2 | 73 |
| 97. Heat ........ | 71 | 6 | 4 | 6 | 1 | 2 | ...... | 116 | 21 | 19 | 2 | 248 |
| 98. Hydrophobia. | 23 | 1 | ...... | ...... | ...... | ...... | ...... | 1 | 1 | ...... | ...... | 26 |
| 99. Intemperance | 313 | 20 | 33 | 58 | 4 | 9 | ...... | 73 | 5 | 32 | 11 | 558 |
| 100. Lightning .... | 66 | ...... | 1 | 13 | 3 | 7 | ...... | 1 | 2 | 1 | ...... | 94 |
| 101. Mercury, effects of ... | 12 | ...... | 1 | 8 | 4 | ...... | ...... | ...... | ...... | 1 | ...... | 26 |
| 102. Murder ....... | 133 | 7 | 11 | 27 | 9 | 9 | ...... | 9 | 4 | 11 | 7 | 227 |
| 103. Poison........ | 317 | 9 | 14 | 18 | 9 | 19 | ...... | 12 | 2 | 3 | 2 | 405 |
| 104. Suffocation ... | 907 | 4 | 4 | 4 | 2 | 4 | ...... | 8 | ...... | 1 | ...... | 934 |
| 105. Suicide ....... | 293 | 45 | 34 | 29 | 2 | 12 | ...... | 28 | 13 | 31 | 4 | 491 |
| XIII. 106. Stillborn ...... | 377 | ...... | ...... | ...... | ...... | ...... | ...... | ...... | ...... | ...... | ...... | 377 |
| XIV. 107. Unknown ..... | 35742 | 664 | 1240 | 2140 | 536 | 918 | 10 | 1191 | 642 | 753 | 397 | 44,233 |

# UNITED STATES TABLES—Continued.

## TABLE III.—*Season of decease and duration of sickness, with causes of death.*

| | SEASON OF DECEASE. | | | | | DURATION OF SICKNESS. | | | | | |
|---|---|---|---|---|---|---|---|---|---|---|---|
| | Spring. | Summer. | Autumn. | Winter. | Unknown. | Under 1 week. | 1 week and under 1 m'th. | 1 month and under 3 m's. | 3 months and over. | Unknown. | Aggregate deaths. |
| ALL CAUSES................. | 75538 | 89283 | 96790 | 56233 | 5179 | 106412 | 97962 | 26418 | 50794 | 41437 | 323,023 |
| I. ZYMOTIC DISEASES......... | 21293 | 40763 | 50567 | 17687 | 1503 | 54901 | 51621 | 9471 | 3860 | 11960 | 131,813 |
| SPORADIC DISEASES. | | | | | | | | | | | |
| II. Diseases of uncertain or variable seat... ....... | 5593 | 5775 | 5252 | 4200 | 224 | 2731 | 4710 | 2875 | 8384 | 2344 | 21,044 |
| III. Diseases of brain and nervous system............ | 6610 | 6174 | 6123 | 4611 | 269 | 10370 | 7351 | 1426 | 2209 | 2431 | 23,787 |
| IV. Diseases of the respiratory organs................ | 18299 | 12791 | 11279 | 11858 | 573 | 6582 | 13995 | 5719 | 23087 | 5417 | 54,800 |
| V. Diseases of the organs of circulation............. | 711 | 671 | 569 | 567 | 17 | 748 | 562 | 289 | 597 | 339 | 2,535 |
| VI. Dis. of the digestive organs. | 3280 | 4300 | 4952 | 2487 | 153 | 4686 | 5432 | 1747 | 2123 | 1184 | 15,172 |
| VII. Dis. of the urinary organs. | 304 | 277 | 253 | 258 | 9 | 123 | 359 | 134 | 385 | 100 | 1,101 |
| VIII. Diseases of the generative organs, and childbirth.. | 1163 | 985 | 838 | 825 | 31 | 1744 | 1319 | 235 | 146 | 398 | 3,842 |
| IX. Diseases of the locomotive organs................ | 540 | 451 | 410 | 356 | 13 | 172 | 440 | 217 | 786 | 155 | 1,770 |
| X. Diseases of the skin... ... | 131 | 130 | 159 | 88 | 8 | 72 | 179 | 83 | 124 | 58 | 516 |
| XI. Old age.................. | 2653 | 2217 | 2081 | 2000 | 76 | 1342 | 1527 | 643 | 1718 | 3797 | 9,027 |
| XII. External causes.......... | 3446 | 3625 | 2875 | 2840 | 220 | 8504 | 1294 | 352 | 344 | 2512 | 13,006 |
| XIII. Stillborn.................. | 104 | 102 | 82 | 77 | 12 | ...... | ...... | ...... | ...... | 377 | 377 |
| XIV. Unknown................ | 11411 | 11022 | 11850 | 8379 | 2071 | 14437 | 9173 | 3227 | 7031 | 10365 | 44,238 |
| I.— 1. Cholera ............ | 1636 | 18243 | 9869 | 1427 | 331 | 24820 | 2382 | 163 | 79 | 4062 | 31,506 |
| 2. Cholera infantum... | 200 | 1453 | 2027 | 195 | 85 | 1452 | 1489 | 378 | 221 | 425 | 3,960 |
| 3. Cholera morbus..... | 159 | 495 | 737 | 123 | 54 | 855 | 489 | 48 | 33 | 143 | 1,568 |
| 4. Croup.............. | 3130 | 1972 | 2732 | 2734 | 138 | 7607 | 2159 | 195 | 106 | 639 | 10,706 |
| 5. Diarrhœa........... | 652 | 1766 | 3176 | 686 | 86 | 1465 | 2631 | 761 | 732 | 777 | 6,366 |
| 6. Dysentery.......... | 1009 | 3570 | 14254 | 1554 | 169 | 5239 | 11184 | 1587 | 656 | 1890 | 20,556 |
| 7. Erysipelas.......... | 932 | 680 | 521 | 611 | 42 | 717 | 1465 | 284 | 153 | 217 | 2,786 |
| 8. Fever............... | 3760 | 4095 | 7074 | 2912 | 267 | 3847 | 10560 | 2210 | 621 | 870 | 18,108 |
| 9. Fever, intermittent.. | 164 | 186 | 440 | 156 | 18 | 244 | 454 | 136 | 91 | 39 | 964 |
| 10. Fever, remittent..... | 16 | 33 | 70 | 28 | 1 | 22 | 88 | 13 | 1 | 24 | 148 |
| 11. Fever, scarlet....... | 3266 | 2266 | 1804 | 2195 | 53 | 4055 | 4517 | 504 | 104 | 404 | 9,584 |
| 12. Fever, ship......... | 67 | 78 | 48 | 47 | ...... | 62 | 120 | 20 | 8 | 30 | 240 |
| 13. Fever, typhoid...... | 3034 | 2488 | 4667 | 2802 | 108 | 2555 | 7539 | 1626 | 400 | 979 | 13,099 |
| 14. Fever, yellow....... | 22 | 24 | 598 | 131 | 10 | 114 | 166 | 5 | 3 | 497 | 785 |
| 15. Hooping cough...... | 1413 | 1505 | 1413 | 891 | 58 | 750 | 2703 | 1096 | 347 | 384 | 5,280 |
| 16. Influenza........... | 109 | 38 | 37 | 66 | 2 | 102 | 111 | 16 | 9 | 14 | 252 |
| 17. Measles ........... | 807 | 1212 | 605 | 329 | 30 | 553 | 1692 | 327 | 156 | 255 | 2,983 |
| 18. Small pox.......... | 807 | 505 | 308 | 710 | 22 | 342 | 1676 | 81 | 39 | 214 | 2,352 |
| 19. Syphilis ............ | 37 | 44 | 31 | 21 | 13 | 9 | 18 | 11 | 63 | 45 | 146 |
| 20. Thrush............. | 73 | 110 | 156 | 69 | 16 | 91 | 178 | 65 | 38 | 52 | 424 |
| II.— 21. Abscess ........... | 76 | 85 | 71 | 78 | 1 | 42 | 75 | 49 | 100 | 45 | 311 |
| 22. Cancer............. | 450 | 450 | 400 | 369 | 35 | 64 | 155 | 150 | 1108 | 227 | 1,704 |
| 23. Debility ............ | 211 | 290 | 278 | 195 | 10 | 211 | 163 | 108 | 222 | 280 | 984 |
| 24. Dropsy............. | 2994 | 3090 | 2726 | 2312 | 95 | 873 | 2177 | 1830 | 5323 | 1014 | 11,217 |
| 25. Gout................ | 11 | 11 | 16 | 12 | ...... | 8 | 10 | 6 | 18 | 8 | 50 |
| 26. Hemorrhage........ | 183 | 189 | 165 | 127 | 3 | 274 | 173 | 58 | 73 | 89 | 667 |
| 27. Inflammation....... | 823 | 714 | 692 | 477 | 41 | 921 | 1299 | 228 | 138 | 161 | 2,747 |
| 28. Malformation... ... | 26 | 29 | 13 | 17 | ...... | 23 | 17 | 3 | 16 | 26 | 85 |
| 29. Marasmus.......... | 120 | 151 | 194 | 86 | 4 | 52 | 97 | 87 | 130 | 189 | 555 |
| 30. Milk sickness....... | 10 | 22 | 32 | 20 | 2 | 31 | 47 | 6 | ...... | 2 | 86 |
| 31. Mortification........ | 63 | 77 | 122 | 53 | 2 | 70 | 92 | 40 | 46 | 69 | 317 |
| 32. Rickets............ | 17 | 27 | 16 | 11 | ...... | 11 | 7 | 11 | 36 | 6 | 71 |
| 33. Scrofula............ | 500 | 547 | 443 | 350 | 20 | 121 | 325 | 228 | 1001 | 185 | 1,860 |
| 34. Scurvy......... ... | 8 | 14 | 9 | 17 | 6 | 1 | 19 | 14 | 12 | 8 | 54 |
| 35. Tumor . .......... | 101 | 79 | 75 | 76 | 5 | 29 | 54 | 57 | 161 | 35 | 336 |
| III.— 36. Apoplexy ...... ... | 573 | 502 | 429 | 425 | 29 | 1301 | 187 | 37 | 87 | 346 | 1,958 |
| 37. Brain and nerves, disease of......... | 777 | 732 | 762 | 546 | 38 | 1092 | 1105 | 195 | 160 | 303 | 2,855 |
| 38. Cephalitis........... | 1709 | 1703 | 1823 | 1136 | 51 | 2473 | 3008 | 435 | 217 | 289 | 6,422 |
| 39. Chorea............. | 12 | 25 | 11 | 5 | 1 | 14 | 15 | 4 | 11 | 10 | 54 |
| 40. Convulsions ........ | 1797 | 1538 | 1531 | 1141 | 65 | 3662 | 1102 | 219 | 360 | 729 | 6,072 |
| 41. Delirium tremens... | 101 | 113 | 96 | 74 | 9 | 139 | 77 | 10 | 17 | 150 | 398 |
| 42. Epilepsy........... | 98 | 101 | 87 | 79 | 8 | 150 | 50 | 14 | 86 | 73 | 378 |
| 43. Hydrocephalus...... | 415 | 456 | 435 | 341 | 27 | 316 | 870 | 224 | 150 | 114 | 1,674 |
| 44. Insanity............ | 80 | 84 | 61 | 69 | 6 | 18 | 54 | 16 | 137 | 75 | 300 |

## TABLE III—Continued.

| | Season of decease. Spring. | Summer. | Autumn. | Winter. | Unknown. | Duration of sickness. Under 1 week. | 1 week and under 1 m'h. | 1 month and und'r 3 m'hs. | 3 months and over. | Unknown. | Aggregate deaths. |
|---|---|---|---|---|---|---|---|---|---|---|---|
| 45. Neuralgia | 67 | 75 | 78 | 63 | ...... | 34 | 95 | 32 | 107 | 15 | 283 |
| 46. Paralysis | 812 | 669 | 631 | 573 | 24 | 706 | 646 | 232 | 871 | 254 | 2,709 |
| 47. Tetanus | 169 | 176 | 179 | 159 | 11 | 465 | 142 | 8 | 6 | 78 | 694 |
| IV.— 48. Asthma | 164 | 87 | 74 | 117 | 9 | 86 | 99 | 50 | 181 | 35 | 451 |
| 49. Bronchitis | 1275 | 654 | 594 | 777 | 60 | 853 | 1402 | 379 | 483 | 243 | 3,360 |
| 50. Consumption | 9679 | 8742 | 7982 | 6800 | 313 | 1031 | 3033 | 3898 | 21511 | 4043 | 33,516 |
| 51. Laryngitis | 244 | 205 | 297 | 281 | 12 | 338 | 544 | 48 | 47 | 62 | 1,039 |
| 52. Pleurisy | 865 | 400 | 337 | 532 | 33 | 617 | 1166 | 180 | 90 | 114 | 2,167 |
| 53. Pneumonia | 5313 | 2242 | 1582 | 2859 | 134 | 3009 | 6917 | 972 | 519 | 713 | 12,130 |
| 54. Quinsy | 164 | 104 | 131 | 157 | 6 | 274 | 225 | 29 | 8 | 26 | 562 |
| 55. Respiratory organs, disease of | 595 | 357 | 282 | 335 | 6 | 374 | 609 | 163 | 248 | 181 | 1,575 |
| V.— 56. Aneurism | 3 | 1 | 4 | ...... | ...... | 2 | 1 | ...... | 3 | 2 | 8 |
| 57. Circulatory organs, disease of | ...... | ...... | ...... | ...... | ...... | ...... | ...... | ...... | ...... | ...... | ....... |
| 58. Heart, disease of | 708 | 670 | 565 | 567 | 17 | 746 | 561 | 289 | 594 | 337 | 2,527 |
| VI.— 59. Colic | 311 | 351 | 306 | 239 | 14 | 833 | 259 | 23 | 43 | 63 | 1,221 |
| 60. Dig've org'ns, dis. of. | 302 | 556 | 881 | 292 | 18 | 580 | 831 | 218 | 190 | 230 | 2,049 |
| 61. Dirt eating | 19 | 40 | 25 | 9 | 1 | 8 | 11 | 3 | 53 | 19 | 94 |
| 62. Dyspepsia | 157 | 153 | 174 | 125 | 7 | 27 | 72 | 81 | 389 | 47 | 616 |
| 63. Enteritis | 674 | 814 | 884 | 484 | 30 | 990 | 1298 | 244 | 172 | 182 | 2,886 |
| 64. Gastritis | 74 | 80 | 73 | 38 | 7 | 76 | 86 | 36 | 32 | 42 | 272 |
| 65. Hemorrhoids | 16 | 16 | 16 | 9 | 1 | 9 | 11 | 6 | 23 | 9 | 58 |
| 66. Hernia | 65 | 65 | 60 | 49 | 2 | 91 | 71 | 26 | 30 | 23 | 241 |
| 67. Jaundice | 121 | 95 | 121 | 125 | 2 | 80 | 158 | 67 | 109 | 50 | 464 |
| 68. Liver, disease of | 480 | 512 | 501 | 346 | 12 | 182 | 481 | 355 | 679 | 154 | 1,851 |
| 69. Peritonitis | 6 | 7 | 14 | 10 | ...... | 9 | 8 | 2 | 3 | 15 | 37 |
| 70. Teething | 400 | 815 | 880 | 326 | 22 | 512 | 1061 | 435 | 244 | 191 | 2,443 |
| 71. Worms | 655 | 796 | 1017 | 435 | 37 | 1289 | 1085 | 251 | 156 | 159 | 2,940 |
| VII.— 72. Bladder, disease of | 18 | 16 | 7 | 17 | 1 | 6 | 24 | 4 | 15 | 10 | 59 |
| 73. Diabetes | 57 | 54 | 64 | 52 | 4 | 30 | 67 | 22 | 82 | 30 | 231 |
| 74. Gravel | 162 | 147 | 115 | 132 | 3 | 65 | 196 | 64 | 204 | 30 | 559 |
| 75. Kidneys, disease of | 67 | 60 | 67 | 57 | 1 | 22 | 72 | 44 | 84 | 30 | 252 |
| VIII.— 76. Childbirth | 933 | 800 | 686 | 670 | 28 | 1590 | 1001 | 159 | 56 | 311 | 3,117 |
| 77. Generative organs, disease of | 50 | 55 | 57 | 34 | 2 | 22 | 50 | 24 | 72 | 30 | 198 |
| 78. Paramenia | 3 | 3 | 1 | ...... | ...... | 1 | 1 | 3 | 1 | 1 | 7 |
| 79. Puerperal fever | 177 | 127 | 94 | 121 | 1 | 131 | 267 | 49 | 17 | 56 | 520 |
| IX.— 80. Hip, disease of | 16 | 11 | 20 | 9 | 1 | 5 | 8 | 5 | 30 | 9 | 57 |
| 81. Rheumatism | 300 | 254 | 210 | 211 | 8 | 95 | 272 | 115 | 434 | 67 | 983 |
| 82. Spine, disease of | 186 | 150 | 154 | 115 | 2 | 63 | 134 | 75 | 262 | 73 | 607 |
| 83. White swelling | 38 | 36 | 26 | 21 | 2 | 9 | 26 | 22 | 60 | 6 | 123 |
| X.— 84. Carbuncle | 10 | 3 | 8 | 2 | 2 | 1 | 12 | 3 | 6 | 3 | 25 |
| 85. Fistula | 8 | 4 | 1 | 2 | ...... | ...... | 1 | 4 | 8 | 2 | 15 |
| 86. Leprosy | 6 | 2 | 2 | 1 | ...... | ...... | 1 | ...... | 6 | 4 | 11 |
| 87. Skin, disease of | 17 | 29 | 24 | 11 | ...... | 20 | 38 | 9 | 10 | 4 | 81 |
| 88. Ulcer | 90 | 92 | 124 | 72 | 6 | 51 | 127 | 67 | 94 | 45 | 384 |
| XI.— 89. Old age | 2653 | 2217 | 2081 | 2000 | 76 | 1342 | 1527 | 643 | 1718 | 3797 | 9,027 |
| XII.— 90. Accident | 1466 | 1318 | 1274 | 1183 | 82 | 3046 | 602 | 161 | 148 | 1366 | 5,323 |
| 91. Accident, burned | 620 | 283 | 259 | 505 | 41 | 956 | 319 | 79 | 41 | 313 | 1,708 |
| 92. Accident, drowned | 467 | 958 | 528 | 369 | 35 | 2357 | ...... | ...... | ...... | ...... | 2,357 |
| 93. Accident, scalded | 92 | 72 | 81 | 92 | 7 | 203 | 77 | 6 | 3 | 55 | 344 |
| 94. Executed | 5 | 6 | 8 | 2 | ...... | 21 | ...... | ...... | ...... | ...... | 21 |
| 95. Fracture | 34 | 53 | 45 | 38 | 1 | 26 | 23 | 7 | 9 | 106 | 171 |
| 96. Frozen | 30 | 2 | 2 | 37 | 2 | 37 | 3 | 2 | 3 | 28 | 73 |
| 97. Heat | 14 | 171 | 56 | 6 | 1 | 147 | 21 | 6 | 3 | 71 | 248 |
| 98. Hydrophobia | 7 | 7 | 3 | 9 | ...... | 11 | 6 | 2 | 1 | 6 | 26 |
| 99. Intemperance | 141 | 134 | 133 | 141 | 9 | 150 | 109 | 44 | 85 | 170 | 558 |
| 100. Lightning | 6 | 56 | 28 | 1 | 3 | 68 | 2 | 2 | ...... | 22 | 94 |
| 101. Mercury, effects of | 2 | 8 | 6 | 10 | ...... | 2 | 11 | 7 | 5 | 1 | 26 |
| 102. Murder | 52 | 61 | 51 | 60 | 3 | 102 | 17 | 3 | 3 | 102 | 227 |
| 103. Poison | 97 | 126 | 114 | 66 | 2 | 212 | 91 | 29 | 37 | 36 | 405 |
| 104. Suffocation | 291 | 210 | 175 | 230 | 28 | 934 | ...... | ...... | ...... | ...... | 934 |
| 105. Suicide | 122 | 160 | 112 | 91 | 6 | 232 | 13 | 4 | 6 | 236 | 491 |
| XIII.—106. Stillborn | 104 | 102 | 82 | 77 | 12 | ...... | ...... | ...... | ...... | 377 | 377 |
| XIV.—107. Unknown | 11411 | 11022 | 11350 | 8379 | 2071 | 14437 | 9173 | 3227 | 7031 | 10265 | 44,233 |

# UNITED STATES TABLES—Continued.

TABLE IV.—*Occupations of the whites and free colored who died during the year ending June 1, 1850, with the aggregate number of deaths in that year.*

| | Agricultural. | Mechanical. | Labor not specified. | Commercial. | Educational. | Other pursuits. | Ag'te deaths. |
|---|---|---|---|---|---|---|---|
| ALL CAUSES | 23468 | 12388 | 11323 | 4108 | 2374 | 1174 | 323,023 |
| I. ZYMOTIC DISEASES | 6979 | 4845 | 5461 | 1641 | 873 | 478 | 131,813 |
| SPORADIC DISEASES. | | | | | | | |
| II. Diseases of uncertain or variable seat | 2012 | 746 | 510 | 225 | 133 | 61 | 21,044 |
| III. Diseases of brain and nervous system | 1588 | 760 | 571 | 303 | 173 | 84 | 23,787 |
| IV. Diseases of the respiratory organs | 5781 | 3373 | 2251 | 1014 | 649 | 253 | 54,800 |
| V. Diseases of the organs of circulation | 289 | 177 | 99 | 82 | 45 | 18 | 2,535 |
| VI. Diseases of the digestive organs | 1061 | 408 | 276 | 131 | 109 | 37 | 15,172 |
| VII. Diseases of the urinary organs | 387 | 96 | 44 | 20 | 20 | 7 | 1,101 |
| VIII. Diseases of the generative organs, and childbirth | ........ | ........ | ........ | ........ | ........ | ........ | 3,842 |
| IX. Diseases of the locomotive organs | 227 | 86 | 72 | 22 | 24 | 6 | 1,770 |
| X. Diseases of the skin | 42 | 22 | 14 | 2 | 3 | 4 | 516 |
| XI. Old age | 1430 | 334 | 177 | 54 | 52 | 14 | 9,027 |
| XII. External causes | 1298 | 719 | 1018 | 328 | 117 | 140 | 13,006 |
| XIII. Stillborn | ........ | ........ | ........ | ........ | ........ | ........ | 377 |
| XIV. Unknown | 2374 | 822 | 830 | 286 | 176 | 72 | 44,233 |
| I.— 1. Cholera | 1615 | 2349 | 2824 | 654 | 310 | 256 | 31,506 |
| 2. Cholera infantum | 3 | 1 | 3 | ........ | 1 | ........ | 3,960 |
| 3. Cholera morbus | 126 | 72 | 68 | 28 | 11 | 6 | 1,568 |
| 4. Croup | 11 | 8 | 9 | 2 | ........ | 3 | 10,706 |
| 5. Diarrhœa | 294 | 168 | 244 | 80 | 39 | 29 | 6,366 |
| 6. Dysentery | 769 | 466 | 437 | 189 | 105 | 40 | 20,556 |
| 7. Erysipelas | 252 | 135 | 91 | 35 | 26 | 13 | 2,786 |
| 8. Fever | 1779 | 606 | 609 | 223 | 139 | 61 | 18,108 |
| 9. Fever, intermittent | 77 | 31 | 45 | 13 | 6 | 2 | 964 |
| 10. Fever, remittent | 16 | 9 | 9 | 5 | 2 | 3 | 148 |
| 11. Fever, scarlet | 57 | 23 | 26 | 4 | 7 | 2 | 9,584 |
| 12. Fever, ship | 9 | 17 | 31 | 5 | 2 | ........ | 240 |
| 13. Fever, typhoid | 1705 | 647 | 561 | 216 | 195 | 46 | 13,099 |
| 14. Fever, yellow | 24 | 133 | 294 | 105 | 5 | 3 | 785 |
| 15. Hooping cough | 11 | 4 | 1 | 1 | 4 | ........ | 5,280 |
| 16. Influenza | 20 | 5 | 1 | 2 | ........ | ........ | 252 |
| 17. Measles | 61 | 24 | 21 | 3 | 4 | 3 | 2,983 |
| 18. Small pox | 142 | 145 | 155 | 68 | 16 | 10 | 2,352 |
| 19. Syphilis | 8 | 4 | 12 | 6 | 1 | 1 | 146 |
| 20. Thrush | ........ | ........ | ........ | ........ | ........ | ........ | 424 |
| II.— 21. Abscess | 36 | 21 | 26 | 7 | 6 | 6 | 311 |
| 22. Cancer | 255 | 86 | 34 | 20 | 12 | 3 | 1,704 |
| 23. Debility | 29 | 22 | 24 | 11 | 2 | 2 | 984 |
| 24. Dropsy | 1196 | 408 | 290 | 116 | 62 | 33 | 11,217 |
| 25. Gout | 7 | 5 | 3 | 3 | 2 | ........ | 50 |
| 26. Hemorrhage | 69 | 43 | 29 | 19 | 15 | 5 | 667 |
| 27. Inflammation | 192 | 85 | 49 | 21 | 17 | 6 | 2,747 |
| 28. Malformation | ........ | ........ | 1 | ........ | ........ | ........ | 85 |
| 29. Marasmus | 10 | 8 | 11 | 6 | 2 | ........ | 555 |
| 30. Milk sickness | 22 | 1 | ........ | ........ | 2 | ........ | 86 |
| 31. Mortification | 40 | 9 | 10 | 5 | 1 | 3 | 317 |
| 32. Rickets | 1 | ........ | ........ | 1 | ........ | ........ | 71 |
| 33. Scrofula | 111 | 43 | 24 | 10 | 12 | 2 | 1,860 |
| 34. Scurvy | 11 | 4 | 2 | 2 | ........ | ........ | 54 |
| 35. Tumor | 33 | 11 | 7 | 4 | ........ | 1 | 336 |
| III.— 36. Apoplexy | 340 | 130 | 93 | 61 | 49 | 18 | 1,958 |
| 37. Brain and nerves, disease of | 126 | 82 | 57 | 41 | 27 | 6 | 2,855 |
| 38. Cephalitis | 372 | 154 | 141 | 66 | 33 | 14 | 6,422 |
| 39. Chorea | 2 | ........ | 1 | 2 | ........ | ........ | 54 |
| 40. Convulsions | 143 | 82 | 60 | 24 | 4 | 5 | 6,072 |
| 41. Delirium tremens | 31 | 60 | 75 | 27 | 3 | 12 | 393 |
| 42. Epilepsy | 24 | 14 | 13 | 7 | 6 | 4 | 373 |
| 43. Hydrocephalus | 16 | 10 | 9 | 2 | ........ | 1 | 1,674 |
| 44. Insanity | 29 | 33 | 18 | 8 | 3 | 2 | 300 |
| 45. Neuralgia | 41 | 13 | 10 | 7 | 8 | ........ | 288 |
| 46. Paralysis | 545 | 168 | 72 | 56 | 38 | 20 | 2,709 |
| 47. Tetanus | 19 | 14 | 22 | 2 | 2 | 2 | 694 |

## TABLE IV—Continued.

| | Agricultural. | Mechanical. | Labor not specified. | Commercial. | Educational. | Other pursuits. | Ag'te deaths. |
|---|---|---|---|---|---|---|---|
| IV.— 48. Asthma | 55 | 24 | 14 | 5 | 4 | 6 | 451 |
| 49. Bronchitis | 159 | 72 | 62 | 24 | 24 | ....... | 3,360 |
| 50. Consumption | 3713 | 2700 | 1661 | 808 | 479 | 194 | 33,516 |
| 51. Laryngitis | 31 | 16 | 13 | 9 | 6 | ....... | 1,039 |
| 52. Pleurisy | 293 | 114 | 130 | 33 | 8 | 6 | 2,167 |
| 53. Pneumonia | 1334 | 361 | 326 | 108 | 105 | 38 | 12,130 |
| 54. Quinsy | 47 | 10 | 8 | 5 | 5 | 3 | 562 |
| 55. Respiratory organs, disease of | 149 | 76 | 37 | 22 | 18 | 6 | 1,575 |
| V.— 56. Aneurism | 3 | 1 | 3 | ....... | ....... | ....... | 8 |
| 57. Circulatory organs, disease of | ....... | ....... | ....... | ....... | ....... | ....... | ....... |
| 58. Heart, disease of | 286 | 176 | 96 | 82 | 45 | 18 | 2,527 |
| VI.— 59. Colic | 163 | 63 | 45 | 13 | 16 | 6 | 1,221 |
| 60. Digestive organs, disease of | 77 | 42 | 40 | 13 | 14 | 4 | 2,049 |
| 61. Dirt eating | ....... | ....... | ....... | ....... | ....... | ....... | 94 |
| 62. Dyspepsia | 191 | 34 | 16 | 13 | 16 | 4 | 616 |
| 63. Enteritis | 204 | 89 | 71 | 36 | 26 | 6 | 2,886 |
| 64. Gastritis | 17 | 12 | 6 | 8 | 1 | ....... | 272 |
| 65. Hemorrhoids | 20 | 1 | 3 | ....... | ....... | 1 | 58 |
| 66. Hernia | 39 | 15 | 8 | 4 | 1 | 1 | 241 |
| 67. Jaundice | 41 | 18 | 18 | 8 | 3 | 5 | 464 |
| 68. Liver, disease of | 299 | 127 | 67 | 35 | 29 | 8 | 1,851 |
| 69. Peritonitis | 1 | 4 | 1 | 1 | 2 | 2 | 37 |
| 70. Teething | ....... | ....... | ....... | ....... | ....... | ....... | 2,443 |
| 71. Worms | 9 | 3 | 1 | ....... | 1 | ....... | 2,940 |
| VII.— 72. Bladder, disease of | 10 | 4 | 7 | 1 | ....... | 3 | 59 |
| 73. Diabetes | 58 | 12 | 6 | 4 | 5 | 1 | 231 |
| 74. Gravel | 263 | 52 | 19 | 8 | 5 | 2 | 559 |
| 75. Kidneys, disease of | 56 | 28 | 12 | 7 | 10 | 1 | 252 |
| VIII.— 76. Childbirth | ....... | ....... | ....... | ....... | ....... | ....... | 3,117 |
| 77. Generative organs, disease of | ....... | ....... | ....... | ....... | ....... | ....... | 198 |
| 78. Paramenia | ....... | ....... | ....... | ....... | ....... | ....... | 7 |
| 79. Puerperal fever | ....... | ....... | ....... | ....... | ....... | ....... | 520 |
| IX.— 80. Hip, disease of | 5 | 5 | ....... | ....... | ....... | ....... | 57 |
| 81. Rheumatism | 161 | 49 | 56 | 13 | 16 | 5 | 983 |
| 82. Spine, disease of | 45 | 27 | 13 | 7 | 4 | 1 | 607 |
| 83. White swelling | 16 | 5 | 3 | 2 | 4 | ....... | 123 |
| X.— 84. Carbuncle | 3 | 3 | 1 | 1 | 1 | 1 | 25 |
| 85. Fistula | 3 | ....... | ....... | ....... | ....... | ....... | 15 |
| 86. Leprosy | 1 | 1 | 1 | 1 | ....... | ....... | 11 |
| 87. Skin, disease of | 2 | ....... | ....... | ....... | ....... | ....... | 81 |
| 88. Ulcer | 33 | 18 | 12 | ....... | 2 | 3 | 384 |
| XI.— 89. Old age | 1430 | 334 | 177 | 54 | 52 | 14 | 9,027 |
| XII.— 90. Accident | 731 | 352 | 468 | 107 | 54 | 57 | 5,323 |
| 91. Accident, burned | 18 | 13 | 22 | 3 | 3 | 7 | 1,703 |
| 92. Accident, drowned | 168 | 138 | 216 | 160 | 23 | 41 | 2,357 |
| 93. Accident, scalded | ....... | 2 | 3 | 1 | 1 | 1 | 344 |
| 94. Executed | 2 | ....... | 2 | 1 | ....... | 1 | 21 |
| 95. Fracture | 5 | 6 | 19 | 10 | 2 | 12 | 171 |
| 96. Frozen | 16 | 6 | 13 | 1 | 1 | ....... | 73 |
| 97. Heat | 18 | 28 | 92 | 2 | 1 | 3 | 248 |
| 98. Hydrophobia | 2 | 1 | 5 | ....... | ....... | ....... | 26 |
| 99. Intemperance | 89 | 93 | 93 | 11 | 12 | 9 | 558 |
| 100. Lightning | 11 | 4 | 2 | ....... | ....... | ....... | 94 |
| 101. Mercury, effects of | 3 | ....... | 1 | 1 | ....... | ....... | 26 |
| 102. Murder | 62 | 10 | 31 | 9 | 7 | 5 | 227 |
| 103. Poison | 21 | 7 | 8 | 2 | 2 | ....... | 405 |
| 104. Suffocation | 6 | 3 | 8 | 1 | ....... | ....... | 934 |
| 105. Suicide | 146 | 56 | 35 | 19 | 11 | 4 | 491 |
| XIII.—106. Stillborn | ....... | ....... | ....... | ....... | ....... | ....... | 377 |
| XIV.—107. Unknown | 2374 | 822 | 830 | 286 | 176 | 72 | 44,283 |

## UNITED STATES TABLES—Continued.

### TABLE V.—*Sex, color and condition of those who died during the year ending June* 1, 1850, *with the causes of death.*

| | WHITES. | | | COLORED. | | | | | | | | | | | | Aggregate deaths. |
|---|---|---|---|---|---|---|---|---|---|---|---|---|---|---|---|---|
| | | | | Slaves. | | | | | | Free. | | | | | | |
| | Males. | Females. | Total. | Black. | | Mulatto. | | Total. | | Black. | | Mulat. | | Total. | | |
| | | | | M. | F. | M. | F. | Bl'k. | Mul. | M. | F. | M | F. | Bl'k | Mul. | |
| ALL CAUSES | 142496 | 21927 | 264601 | 25238 | 23437 | 1691 | 1598 | 48675 | 3289 | 2485 | 2234 | 890 | 844 | 4719 | 1739 | 323023 |
| I. Zymotic Diseases... | 62179 | 50220 | 112515 | 8597 | 7491 | 598 | 568 | 16088 | 1166 | 785 | 676 | 317 | 266 | 1461 | 583 | 131813 |
| Sporadic Diseases. | | | | | | | | | | | | | | | | |
| II. Diseases of uncertain or variable seat.. | 8602 | 8313 | 16915 | 1692 | 1761 | 82 | 121 | 3453 | 203 | 181 | 163 | 67 | 62 | 344 | 129 | 21044 |
| III. Diseases of brain and nervous system .. | 11570 | 8865 | 20435 | 1456 | 1215 | 129 | 94 | 2671 | 223 | 179 | 152 | 58 | 69 | 331 | 127 | 23787 |
| IV. Diseases of the respiratory organs.. | 23111 | 23020 | 46131 | 3532 | 3342 | 205 | 227 | 6874 | 432 | 528 | 525 | 164 | 146 | 1053 | 310 | 54800 |
| V. Diseases of the organs of circulation | 1228 | 1027 | 2255 | 110 | 80 | 4 | 11 | 190 | 15 | 31 | 24 | 11 | 9 | 55 | 20 | 2535 |
| VI. Diseases of the digestive organs.... | 6074 | 5125 | 11199 | 1908 | 1597 | 138 | 113 | 3505 | 251 | 75 | 69 | 42 | 31 | 144 | 73 | 15172 |
| VII. Diseases of the urinary organs ...... | 827 | 163 | 990 | 84 | 12 | 2 | 1 | 96 | 3 | 5 | 5 | 2 | ... | 10 | 2 | 1101 |
| VIII. Diseases of the generative organs, and childbirth........ | ...... | 3061 | 3061 | ..... | 684 | .... | 48 | 684 | 48 | .... | 26 | ... | 23 | 26 | 23 | 3842 |
| IX. Diseases of the locomotive organs ... | 856 | 606 | 1462 | 135 | 100 | 11 | 10 | 235 | 21 | 23 | 12 | 13 | 4 | 35 | 17 | 1770 |
| X. Diseases of the skin. | 242 | 214 | 456 | 35 | 17 | 1 | 2 | 52 | 3 | 2 | 2 | ... | 1 | 4 | 1 | 516 |
| XI. Old age.... ..... | 3198 | 3950 | 7148 | 763 | 789 | 46 | 32 | 1552 | 78 | 85 | 113 | 19 | 32 | 198 | 51 | 9027 |
| XII. External causes.... | 7072 | 2072 | 9144 | 1925 | 1449 | 136 | 88 | 3374 | 224 | 133 | 56 | 49 | 26 | 189 | 75 | 13006 |
| XIII. Stillborn .......... | 184 | 130 | 314 | 28 | 24 | 2 | 2 | 52 | 4 | 2 | 1 | 1 | 3 | 3 | 4 | 377 |
| XIV. Unknown .......... | 17353 | 15161 | 32576 | 4973 | 4876 | 337 | 281 | 9849 | 618 | 456 | 410 | 147 | 177 | 866 | 324 | 44233 |
| I.— 1. Cholera... ... | 15758 | 10784 | 26658 | 2272 | 1591 | 175 | 142 | 3863 | 317 | 265 | 231 | 105 | 67 | 496 | 172 | 31506 |
| 2. ..do..infantum | 1959 | 1650 | 3609 | 131 | 152 | 13 | 18 | 283 | 31 | 14 | 10 | 9 | 4 | 24 | 13 | 3960 |
| 3. ..do..morbus.. | 812 | 614 | 1426 | 49 | 50 | 6 | 4 | 99 | 10 | 19 | 10 | 3 | 1 | 29 | 4 | 1568 |
| 4. Croup ........ | 4875 | 3975 | 8850 | 887 | 758 | 56 | 51 | 1645 | 107 | 35 | 39 | 11 | 19 | 74 | 30 | 10706 |
| 5. Diarrhœa ..... | 3080 | 2292 | 5372 | 435 | 381 | 45 | 28 | 816 | 73 | 32 | 36 | 15 | 22 | 68 | 37 | 6366 |
| 6. Dysentery..... | 10296 | 9126 | 19422 | 470 | 370 | 33 | 28 | 840 | 61 | 96 | 82 | 33 | 22 | 178 | 55 | 20556 |
| 7. Erysipelas .... | 1295 | 1334 | 2629 | 58 | 53 | 6 | 8 | 111 | 14 | 11 | 11 | 3 | 7 | 22 | 10 | 2786 |
| 8. Fever......... | 7850 | 6628 | 14478 | 1578 | 1577 | 111 | 112 | 3155 | 223 | 85 | 70 | 49 | 48 | 155 | 97 | 18108 |
| 9. Fever, interm't. | 435 | 397 | 832 | 63 | 54 | 1 | 4 | 117 | 5 | 2 | 4 | 1 | 3 | 6 | 4 | 964 |
| 10. Fever, remi't .. | 78 | 50 | 128 | 12 | 5 | .... | .... | 17 | .... | 1 | 1 | ... | 1 | 2 | 1 | 148 |
| 11. Fever, scarlet . | 4494 | 4413 | 8907 | 272 | 272 | 20 | 29 | 544 | 49 | 20 | 30 | 14 | 20 | 50 | 34 | 9584 |
| 12. Fever. ship.... | 133 | 102 | 235 | ..... | 1 | .... | .... | 1 | .... | 2 | 1 | 1 | ... | 3 | 1 | 240 |
| 13. Fever, typhoid. | 5977 | 4457 | 10434 | 1262 | 1085 | 67 | 67 | 2347 | 134 | 74 | 59 | 30 | 21 | 133 | 51 | 13099 |
| 14. Fever, yellow.. | 649 | 128 | 777 | ..... | 4 | 2 | .... | 4 | 2 | .... | .... | 1 | 1 | .... | 2 | 785 |
| 15. Hooping cough | 1649 | 1897 | 3546 | 730 | 797 | 38 | 43 | 1527 | 81 | 39 | 56 | 16 | 15 | 95 | 31 | 5280 |
| 16. Influenza ..... | 98 | 97 | 195 | 24 | 25 | 2 | 2 | 49 | 4 | 2 | 1 | 1 | ... | 3 | 1 | 252 |
| 17. Measles ....... | 1221 | 1286 | 2507 | 208 | 202 | 15 | 16 | 410 | 31 | 15 | 10 | 5 | 5 | 25 | 10 | 2988 |
| 18. Small pox..... | 1327 | 784 | 2111 | 74 | 46 | 6 | 6 | 120 | 12 | 67 | 17 | 18 | 7 | 84 | 25 | 2352 |
| 19. Syphilis ....... | 49 | 34 | 83 | 22 | 26 | 1 | 4 | 48 | 5 | 4 | 5 | ... | 1 | 9 | 1 | 146 |
| 20. Thrush ....... | 144 | 172 | 316 | 50 | 42 | 1 | 6 | 92 | 7 | 2 | 3 | 2 | 2 | 5 | 4 | 424 |
| II.— 21. Abscess....... | 171 | 109 | 280 | 17 | 9 | 1 | 1 | 26 | 2 | .... | 1 | 2 | ... | 1 | 2 | 311 |
| 22. Cancer........ | 633 | 912 | 1545 | 36 | 94 | 2 | 8 | 130 | 10 | 5 | 7 | 1 | 6 | 12 | 7 | 1704 |
| 23. Debility ....... | 428 | 431 | 859 | 37 | 58 | 4 | 5 | 95 | 9 | 6 | 5 | 5 | 5 | 11 | 10 | 984 |
| 24. Dropsy ....... | 4382 | 4267 | 8649 | 1071 | 1079 | 52 | 70 | 2150 | 122 | 113 | 111 | 40 | 32 | 224 | 72 | 11217 |
| 25. Gout.......... | 38 | 8 | 46 | 1 | 2 | .... | .... | 3 | .... | ... | .... | 1 | ... | .... | 1 | 50 |
| 26. Hemorrhage .. | 314 | 208 | 522 | 61 | 63 | 4 | 3 | 124 | 7 | 10 | 1 | 2 | 1 | 11 | 3 | 667 |
| 27. Inflammation . | 1339 | 1166 | 2505 | 97 | 92 | 3 | 7 | 189 | 10 | 17 | 12 | 5 | 9 | 29 | 14 | 2747 |
| 28. Malformation.. | 36 | 23 | 59 | 15 | 11 | .... | .... | 26 | .... | .... | .... | ... | ... | .... | .... | 85 |
| 29. Marasmus..... | 238 | 259 | 497 | 20 | 28 | .... | 2 | 48 | 2 | 5 | 2 | 1 | ... | 7 | 1 | 555 |
| 30. Milk sickness.. | 41 | 44 | 85 | 1 | ..... | .... | .... | 1 | .... | ... | .... | ... | ... | .... | .... | 86 |
| 31. Mortification .. | 175 | 118 | 293 | 5 | 9 | .... | 1 | 14 | 1 | 1 | 5 | 3 | ... | 6 | 3 | 317 |
| 32. Rickets ....... | 24 | 14 | 38 | 23 | 9 | 1 | .... | 32 | 1 | .... | .... | ... | ... | .... | .... | 71 |
| 33. Scrofula....... | 636 | 563 | 1199 | 287 | 292 | 13 | 23 | 579 | 36 | 21 | 15 | 5 | 5 | 36 | 10 | 1860 |
| 34. Scurvy........ | 37 | 12 | 49 | 2 | 2 | 1 | .... | 4 | 1 | .... | .... | ... | ... | .... | .... | 54 |
| 35. Tumor ........ | 110 | 179 | 289 | 19 | 13 | 1 | 1 | 32 | 2 | 3 | 4 | 2 | 4 | 7 | 6 | 336 |
| III.— 36. Apoplexy ..... | 958 | 659 | 1617 | 127 | 149 | 8 | 12 | 276 | 20 | 16 | 14 | 6 | 9 | 30 | 15 | 1958 |
| 37. Brain & nerves, disease of... | 1459 | 1068 | 2527 | 154 | 102 | 16 | 9 | 256 | 25 | 26 | 17 | 1 | 3 | 43 | 4 | 2855 |
| 38. Cephalitis ..... | 3316 | 2368 | 5684 | 316 | 252 | 35 | 24 | 568 | 59 | 42 | 32 | 18 | 19 | 74 | 37 | 6422 |
| 39. Chorea........ | 9 | 35 | 44 | 3 | 6 | .... | .... | 9 | .... | .... | 1 | ... | ... | 1 | .... | 54 |
| 40. Convulsions... | 2702 | 2352 | 5054 | 447 | 376 | 41 | 26 | 823 | 67 | 47 | 45 | 19 | 17 | 92 | 36 | 6072 |
| 41. Delirium trem's | 349 | 28 | 377 | 7 | 1 | 1 | .... | 8 | 1 | 4 | 2 | 1 | ... | 6 | 1 | 393 |
| 42. Epilepsy ...... | 169 | 123 | 292 | 37 | 32 | 1 | 3 | 69 | 4 | 5 | 2 | 1 | ... | 7 | 1 | 373 |
| 43. Hydrocephalus | 871 | 684 | 1555 | 45 | 28 | 4 | 5 | 73 | 9 | 16 | 11 | 7 | 3 | 27 | 10 | 1674 |
| 44. Insanity ...... | 158 | 103 | 261 | 15 | 12 | 1 | 1 | 27 | 2 | 6 | 4 | ... | ... | 10 | .... | 300 |

## TABLE V—Continued.

| | WHITES. | | | COLORED. | | | | | | | | | | | | Aggregate deaths |
|---|---|---|---|---|---|---|---|---|---|---|---|---|---|---|---|---|
| | | | | Slaves. | | | | | | Free. | | | | | | |
| | | | | Black. | | Mulatto. | | Total. | | Black. | | Mulat. | | Total. | | |
| | Males. | Females. | Total. | M. | F. | M. | F. | Bl'k. | Mul. | M. | F. | M. | F. | B'k. | Mul. | |
| 45. Neuralgia.... | 140 | 123 | 263 | 9 | 8 | .... | 1 | 17 | 1 | .... | 1 | ... | 1 | 1 | 1 | 283 |
| 46. Paralysis .... | 1258 | 1225 | 2483 | 86 | 83 | 6 | 6 | 169 | 12 | 9 | 22 | 2 | 12 | 31 | 14 | 2709 |
| 47. Tetanus...... | 181 | 97 | 278 | 210 | 166 | 16 | 7 | 376 | 23 | 8 | 1 | 3 | 5 | 9 | 8 | 694 |
| IV.— 48. Asthma....... | 176 | 153 | 329 | 56 | 48 | 4 | 4 | 104 | 8 | 6 | 1 | 3 | ... | 7 | 3 | 451 |
| 49. Bronchitis.... | 1202 | 1046 | 2248 | 463 | 485 | 29 | 29 | 948 | 58 | 48 | 39 | 10 | 9 | 87 | 19 | 3369 |
| 50. Consumption.. | 14097 | 16129 | 30226 | 876 | 1271 | 65 | 124 | 2147 | 189 | 354 | 399 | 98 | 103 | 753 | 201 | 33516 |
| 51. Laryngitis.... | 427 | 449 | 876 | 75 | 74 | 3 | 2 | 149 | 5 | 4 | 3 | 1 | 1 | 7 | 2 | 1039 |
| 52. Pleurisy...... | 917 | 641 | 1558 | 319 | 179 | 19 | 7 | 498 | 26 | 37 | 21 | 22 | 5 | 58 | 27 | 2167 |
| 53. Pneumonia... | 5287 | 3769 | 9056 | 1612 | 1172 | 76 | 56 | 2784 | 132 | 67 | 48 | 27 | 21 | 110 | 48 | 12130 |
| 54. Quinsy........ | 258 | 215 | 473 | 46 | 35 | 2 | 1 | 81 | 3 | 1 | 3 | ... | 1 | 4 | 1 | 562 |
| 55. Respirat'y organs, dis. of. | 747 | 618 | 1365 | 85 | 78 | 7 | 4 | 163 | 11 | 11 | 16 | 3 | 6 | 27 | 9 | 1575 |
| V.— 56. Aneurism..... | 6 | ..... | 6 | .... | 1 | .... | .... | 1 | .... | 1 | .... | ... | ... | 1 | .... | 8 |
| 57. Circulat'y organs, dis. of. | ...... | ...... | ...... | ...... | ...... | ...... | ... | ...... | ...... | ...... | ...... | ... | ... | ...... | ...... | ...... |
| 68. Heart, dis. of.. | 1222 | 1027 | 2249 | 110 | 79 | 4 | 11 | 189 | 15 | 30 | 24 | 11 | 9 | 54 | 20 | 2527 |
| VI.— 59. Colic......... | 579 | 360 | 939 | 138 | 97 | 13 | 7 | 235 | 20 | 12 | 6 | 3 | 6 | 18 | 9 | 1221 |
| 60. Digestive organs, dis. of. | 914 | 776 | 1690 | 168 | 153 | 13 | 10 | 321 | 23 | 5 | 4 | 4 | 2 | 9 | 6 | 2049 |
| 61. Dirt eating... | 9 | 1 | 10 | 41 | 37 | 5 | 1 | 78 | 6 | .. | .... | ... | ... | .... | .... | 94 |
| 62. Dyspepsia.... | 345 | 225 | 570 | 17 | 18 | 1 | 1 | 35 | 2 | 2 | 4 | 2 | 1 | 6 | 3 | 616 |
| 63. Enteritis...... | 1349 | 1059 | 2408 | 238 | 167 | 21 | 17 | 405 | 38 | 16 | 10 | 6 | 3 | 26 | 9 | 2886 |
| 64. Gastritis...... | 97 | 133 | 230 | 17 | 16 | 2 | 2 | 33 | 4 | 2 | 3 | ... | ... | 5 | .... | 272 |
| 65. Hemorrhoids . | 33 | 16 | 49 | 6 | 1 | .... | .... | 7 | .... | .... | 1 | 1 | ... | 1 | 1 | 58 |
| 66. Hernia....... | 117 | 43 | 160 | 62 | 16 | 1 | 2 | 78 | 3 | .... | .... | ... | ... | .... | .... | 241 |
| 67. Jaundice..... | 220 | 211 | 431 | 15 | 11 | 1 | 1 | 26 | 2 | 2 | 3 | ... | ... | 5 | .... | 464 |
| 68. Liver, dis. of.. | 928 | 760 | 1688 | 69 | 63 | 5 | 2 | 132 | 7 | 7 | 12 | 4 | 1 | 19 | 5 | 1851 |
| 69. Peritonitis.... | 20 | 15 | 35 | .... | .... | .... | .... | .... | .... | 1 | .... | ... | 1 | 1 | 1 | 37 |
| 70. Teething ..... | 840 | 828 | 1668 | 372 | 303 | 20 | 23 | 675 | 43 | 17 | 16 | 11 | 13 | 33 | 24 | 2443 |
| 71. Worms........ | 623 | 698 | 1321 | 765 | 715 | 56 | 47 | 1480 | 103 | 11 | 10 | 11 | 4 | 21 | 15 | 2940 |
| VII.— 72. Bladder, dis. of | 40 | 7 | 47 | 9 | 2 | .... | .... | 11 | .... | 1 | .... | ... | ... | 1 | .... | 59 |
| 73. Diabetes...... | 161 | 57 | 218 | 7 | 2 | .... | .... | 9 | .... | 1 | 2 | 1 | ... | 3 | 1 | 231 |
| 74. Gravel........ | 455 | 41 | 496 | 55 | 3 | 1 | .... | 58 | 1 | 2 | 1 | 1 | ... | 3 | 1 | 559 |
| 75. Kidn'ys, dis. of | 171 | 58 | 229 | 13 | 5 | 1 | 1 | 18 | 2 | 1 | 2 | ... | ... | 3 | .... | 252 |
| VIII.— 76. Childbirth..... | ...... | 2501 | 2501 | ..... | 535 | .... | 38 | 535 | 38 | ... | 22 | ... | 21 | 22 | 21 | 3117 |
| 77. Generat'e organs, dis. of. | ...... | 106 | 106 | ..... | 83 | .... | 5 | 83 | 5 | .... | 4 | ... | ... | 4 | ... | 198 |
| 78. Paramenia .... | ...... | 2 | 2 | ..... | 5 | .... | .... | 5 | .... | .... | .... | ... | ... | .... | .... | 7 |
| 79. Puerper'l fev'r | ...... | 452 | 452 | ..... | 61 | .... | 5 | 61 | 5 | .... | .... | ... | 2 | .... | 2 | 520 |
| IX.— 80. Hip, disease o | 38 | 13 | 51 | 2 | ..... | .... | 1 | 2 | 1 | 2 | .... | 1 | ... | 2 | 1 | 57 |
| 81. Rheumatism.. | 482 | 321 | 803 | 70 | 65 | 6 | 7 | 135 | 13 | 13 | 10 | 6 | 3 | 23 | 9 | 983 |
| 82. Spine, dis. of.. | 274 | 241 | 515 | 48 | 26 | 4 | 2 | 74 | 6 | 7 | 2 | 2 | 1 | 9 | 3 | 607 |
| 83. White swelling | 62 | 31 | 93 | 15 | 9 | 1 | .... | 24 | 1 | 1 | .... | 1 | ... | 1 | 4 | 123 |
| X.— 84. Carbuncle.... | 15 | 8 | 23 | 2 | .... | .... | ... | 2 | .... | .... | .... | ... | ... | .... | .... | 25 |
| 85. Fistula........ | 8 | 6 | 14 | 1 | .... | .... | ... | 1 | .... | .... | .... | ... | ... | .... | .... | 15 |
| 86. Leprosy...... | 6 | 1 | 7 | 1 | 2 | .... | 1 | 3 | 1 | .... | .... | ... | ... | .... | .... | 11 |
| 87. Skin, dis. of.. | 26 | 42 | 68 | 6 | 5 | .... | 1 | 11 | 1 | .... | 1 | ... | ... | 1 | .... | 81 |
| 88. Ulcer......... | 187 | 157 | 344 | 25 | 10 | 1 | .... | 35 | 1 | 2 | 1 | ... | 1 | 3 | 1 | 384 |
| XI.— 89. Old age...... | 3198 | 3950 | 7148 | 763 | 789 | 46 | 32 | 1552 | 78 | 85 | 113 | 19 | 32 | 198 | 51 | 9027 |
| XII.— 90. Accident...... | 3307 | 702 | 4009 | 715 | 445 | 47 | 23 | 1160 | 70 | 52 | 13 | 12 | 7 | 65 | 19 | 5323 |
| 91. ..do..burned.. | 364 | 532 | 896 | 270 | 439 | 15 | 34 | 709 | 49 | 16 | 27 | 4 | 7 | 43 | 11 | 1708 |
| 92. ..do..drowned | 1546 | 285 | 1831 | 345 | 87 | 32 | 6 | 432 | 38 | 24 | 4 | 22 | 6 | 28 | 28 | 2357 |
| 93. ..do..scalded. | 203 | 116 | 319 | 6 | 9 | 4 | .... | 15 | 4 | 4 | 1 | ... | 1 | 5 | 1 | 344 |
| 94. Executed..... | 7 | 1 | 8 | 11 | 1 | 1 | .... | 12 | 1 | .... | .... | ... | ... | .... | .... | 21 |
| 95. Fracture...... | 144 | 20 | 164 | 4 | 1 | .... | .... | 5 | .... | 2 | .... | ... | ... | 2 | .... | 171 |
| 96. Frozen....... | 43 | 3 | 46 | 16 | 4 | 1 | .... | 20 | 1 | 5 | .... | 1 | ... | 5 | 1 | 73 |
| 97. Heat......... | 200 | 28 | 228 | 6 | 6 | 3 | .... | 12 | 3 | 2 | 1 | ... | 2 | 3 | 2 | 248 |
| 98. Hydrophobia.. | 14 | 7 | 21 | 1 | 3 | .... | ... | 4 | .... | .... | .... | 1 | ... | .... | 1 | 26 |
| 99. Intemperance. | 442 | 52 | 494 | 29 | 3 | 5 | .... | 32 | 5 | 15 | 6 | 5 | 1 | 21 | 6 | 558 |
| 100. Lightning..... | 36 | 18 | 54 | 28 | 11 | 1 | .... | 39 | 1 | .... | .... | ... | ... | .... | .... | 94 |
| 101. Mercury, effects of...... | 12 | 11 | 23 | 1 | 1 | .... | 1 | 2 | 1 | .... | .... | ... | ... | .... | .... | 26 |
| 102. Murder....... | 168 | 8 | 176 | 33 | 7 | 4 | 1 | 40 | 5 | 3 | 1 | 2 | ... | 4 | 2 | 227 |
| 103. Poison ....... | 141 | 108 | 249 | 81 | 64 | 3 | 3 | 145 | 6 | 4 | .... | 1 | ... | 4 | 1 | 405 |
| 104. Suffocation.... | 89 | 74 | 163 | 363 | 362 | 20 | 19 | 725 | 39 | 3 | 2 | ... | 2 | 5 | 2 | 934 |
| 105. Suicide....... | 356 | 107 | 463 | 16 | 6 | .... | 1 | 22 | 1 | 3 | 1 | 1 | ... | 4 | 1 | 491 |
| XIII.—106. Stillborn...... | 184 | 130 | 314 | 28 | 24 | 2 | 2 | 52 | 4 | 2 | 1 | 1 | 3 | 3 | 4 | 377 |
| XIV.—107. Unknown..... | 17353 | 15161 | 32576 | 4973 | 4876 | 337 | 281 | 9849 | 618 | 456 | 410 | 147 | 177 | 866 | 324 | 44238 |

# TABLE VI—*Deaths in the several States, showing the sex, color, condition, occupation, nativity, etc., etc.*

| | State. | Ages. Under 1. | | 1 and under 5. | | 5 and under 10. | | 10 and under 20. | | 20 and under 50. | | 50 and under 80. | | 80 and under 100. | | 100 and over. | | Age unknown. | | Total. | | Aggregate deaths. |
|---|---|---|---|---|---|---|---|---|---|---|---|---|---|---|---|---|---|---|---|---|---|---|
| | | M. | F. | M. | F. | M. | F. | M. | F. | M. | F. | M. | F. | M. | F. | M. | F. | M. | F. | M. | F. | |
| 1 | Alabama | 1082 | 942 | 1090 | 968 | 373 | 363 | 515 | 444 | 1065 | 1074 | 580 | 410 | 84 | 63 | 16 | 10 | 7 | 5 | 4812 | 4279 | 9,091 |
| 2 | Arkansas | 283 | 244 | 361 | 296 | 159 | 132 | 160 | 175 | 501 | 414 | 173 | 94 | 15 | 7 | 2 | 4 | ... | ... | 1654 | 1367 | 3,021 |
| 3 | California | 16 | 20 | 15 | 23 | 5 | 6 | 40 | 16 | 641 | 33 | 61 | 6 | 4 | 2 | ... | ... | 12 | 5 | 794 | 111 | 905 |
| 4 | Columbia, District of | 83 | 70 | 99 | 87 | 30 | 35 | 34 | 37 | 111 | 114 | 60 | 64 | 9 | 11 | 1 | 1 | ... | ... | 427 | 419 | 846 |
| 5 | Connecticut | 382 | 316 | 486 | 419 | 177 | 119 | 187 | 188 | 715 | 811 | 717 | 684 | 197 | 275 | 3 | ... | 60 | 45 | 2924 | 2857 | 5,781 |
| 6 | Delaware | 126 | 120 | 130 | 104 | 43 | 28 | 44 | 53 | 149 | 141 | 137 | 100 | 13 | 19 | 2 | ... | ... | ... | 644 | 565 | 1,209 |
| 7 | Florida | 81 | 68 | 133 | 118 | 37 | 38 | 53 | 43 | 129 | 102 | 59 | 45 | 11 | 10 | ... | ... | 4 | ... | 507 | 424 | 931 |
| 8 | Georgia | 1189 | 1051 | 1173 | 1020 | 350 | 290 | 508 | 535 | 1054 | 1106 | 705 | 601 | 160 | 122 | 2 | 2 | 35 | 22 | 5176 | 4749 | 9,925 |
| 9 | Illinois | 1252 | 1031 | 1314 | 1221 | 413 | 379 | 579 | 531 | 1886 | 1541 | 814 | 540 | 63 | 35 | *3 | *130 | 12 | 15 | 6336 | 5293 | 11,759 |
| 10 | Indiana | 1336 | 1023 | 1543 | 1389 | 505 | 480 | 630 | 599 | 1857 | 1628 | 878 | 607 | 116 | 92 | ... | ... | 17 | 8 | 6882 | 5826 | 12,708 |
| 11 | Iowa | 243 | 216 | 280 | 242 | 87 | 58 | 83 | 87 | 313 | 246 | 125 | 51 | 7 | 4 | ... | ... | 2 | ... | 1140 | 904 | 2,044 |
| 12 | Kentucky | 1439 | 1186 | 1588 | 1436 | 523 | 454 | 778 | 852 | 2277 | 1960 | 1118 | 932 | 210 | 188 | 9 | 8 | 46 | 34 | 7983 | 7050 | 15,033 |
| 13 | Louisiana | 709 | 576 | 1070 | 993 | 424 | 347 | 565 | 474 | 3699 | 1682 | 761 | 438 | 73 | 64 | 13 | 14 | 37 | 17 | 7351 | 4605 | 11,956 |
| 14 | Maine | 482 | 402 | 875 | 753 | 258 | 261 | 333 | 414 | 960 | 1086 | 718 | 637 | 201 | 196 | ... | ... | 5 | 3 | 3832 | 3752 | 7,584 |
| 15 | Maryland | 1027 | 867 | 1110 | 961 | 364 | 321 | 376 | 396 | 1258 | 1118 | 835 | 664 | 134 | 142 | 9 | 17 | 14 | 8 | 5127 | 4494 | 9,621 |
| 16 | Massachusetts | 1584 | 1234 | 2355 | 2063 | 609 | 485 | 487 | 744 | 2636 | 2745 | 1732 | 1568 | 457 | 530 | 2 | 5 | 116 | 52 | 9978 | 9426 | 19,404 |
| 17 | Michigan | 478 | 388 | 506 | 473 | 171 | 125 | 185 | 195 | 608 | 608 | 422 | 267 | 46 | 29 | ... | 2 | 7 | 5 | 2423 | 2092 | 4,515 |
| 18 | Mississippi | 1007 | 867 | 1159 | 1060 | 359 | 299 | 422 | 433 | 1141 | 1044 | 462 | 297 | 45 | 68 | 11 | 15 | 23 | 9 | 4629 | 4092 | 8,721 |
| 19 | Missouri | 1039 | 904 | 1298 | 1220 | 454 | 390 | 611 | 597 | 2647 | 1765 | 710 | 487 | 50 | 45 | 4 | 2 | 41 | 28 | 6854 | 5438 | 12,292 |
| 20 | New Hampshire | 272 | 191 | 401 | 356 | 105 | 132 | 139 | 222 | 466 | 608 | 492 | 467 | 161 | 214 | ... | 2 | 2 | 1 | 2038 | 2193 | 4,231 |
| 21 | New Jersey | 588 | 486 | 702 | 626 | 210 | 175 | 247 | 199 | 903 | 739 | 681 | 561 | 168 | 153 | ... | ... | 14 | 13 | 3513 | 2952 | 6,465 |
| 22 | New York | 3603 | 3043 | 5190 | 4632 | 1576 | 1429 | 1581 | 1732 | 7439 | 6208 | 4002 | 3161 | 857 | 783 | 7 | 9 | 191 | 157 | 24446 | 21154 | 45,600 |
| 23 | North Carolina | 1045 | 903 | 984 | 821 | 290 | 333 | 545 | 478 | 1192 | 1332 | 908 | 803 | 235 | 240 | 21 | 24 | 7 | 4 | 5227 | 4938 | 10,165 |
| 24 | Ohio | 2485 | 1945 | 3509 | 3164 | 1248 | 1043 | 1191 | 1307 | 4719 | 3794 | 2284 | 1589 | 340 | 269 | 4 | 5 | 38 | 23 | 15818 | 13139 | 28,957 |
| 25 | Pennsylvania | 2793 | 2241 | 3601 | 3160 | 1077 | 936 | 1038 | 997 | 3837 | 3157 | 2559 | 2010 | 525 | 465 | 6 | 1 | 96 | 52 | 15532 | 13019 | 28,551 |
| 26 | Rhode Island | 213 | 151 | 246 | 199 | 65 | 38 | 65 | 85 | 309 | 321 | 219 | 223 | 41 | 57 | ... | ... | 5 | 4 | 1163 | 1078 | 2,241 |
| 27 | South Carolina | 737 | 684 | 919 | 811 | 283 | 262 | 430 | 400 | 915 | 932 | 699 | 573 | 145 | 118 | 18 | 16 | 62 | 43 | 4208 | 3839 | 8,047 |
| 28 | Tennessee | 1378 | 1240 | 1193 | 982 | 363 | 350 | 642 | 693 | 1519 | 1583 | 889 | 667 | 183 | 215 | 6 | 3 | 56 | 13 | 6179 | 5696 | 11,875 |
| 29 | Texas | 272 | 286 | 318 | 316 | 147 | 109 | 186 | 149 | 518 | 393 | 179 | 97 | 13 | 10 | †2 | †4 | 6 | 4 | 1641 | 1368 | 3,057 |
| 30 | Vermont | 179 | 121 | 260 | 218 | 89 | 73 | 95 | 174 | 353 | 435 | 409 | 431 | 145 | 142 | 1 | 1 | 3 | ... | 1584 | 1595 | 3,129 |
| 31 | Virginia | 1722 | 1485 | 1877 | 1739 | 610 | 547 | 831 | 978 | 2305 | 2486 | 1913 | 1590 | 414 | 431 | 31 | 44 | 32 | 24 | 9735 | 9324 | 19,059 |
| 32 | Wisconsin | 329 | 294 | 426 | 355 | 93 | 90 | 108 | 123 | 445 | 358 | 166 | 99 | 6 | 9 | ... | ... | 2 | ... | 1575 | 1328 | 2,903 |
| 33 | Minnesota | 5 | 1 | 5 | 4 | 2 | 3 | 1 | ... | 5 | 1 | ... | 1 | 1 | ... | ... | ... | ... | ... | 19 | 10 | 29 |
| 34 | New Mexico | 106 | 100 | 121 | 123 | 37 | 30 | 54 | 65 | 151 | 178 | 77 | 64 | 24 | 16 | ... | 1 | 10 | ... | 580 | 577 | 1,157 |
| 35 | Oregon | 5 | ... | 7 | 4 | 2 | 1 | 2 | 1 | 14 | 7 | 2 | 2 | ... | ... | ... | ... | ... | ... | 32 | 15 | 47 |
| 36 | Utah | 18 | 12 | 27 | 26 | 11 | 10 | 16 | 15 | 34 | 34 | 23 | 10 | ... | 1 | ... | ... | 2 | ... | 131 | 108 | 239 |

* 130 whites, age and sex unknown, included in total white and aggregate.

† 48 whites, age and sex unknown, included in total white and aggregate.

# TABLE VI—Continued.

| | STATES. | SEASON OF DECEASE. | | | | | DURATION OF SICKNESS. | | | | | NATIVITIES. | | | | | | | | | | |
|---|---|---|---|---|---|---|---|---|---|---|---|---|---|---|---|---|---|---|---|---|---|---|
| | | Spring. | Summer. | Autumn. | Winter. | Unknown. | Under 1 week. | 1 week and under 1 month. | 1 month and under 3 months. | 3 months and over. | Unknown. | Born in State. | New England. | Middle. | South. | Southwest. | Northwest. | California and Territories. | Ireland. | Germany. | Other foreign countries. | Unknown. |
| 1 | Alabama | 2084 | 2229 | 2852 | 1686 | 240 | 3089 | 2905 | 824 | 1432 | 841 | 6379 | 53 | 64 | 1971 | 224 | 54 | .... | 111 | 24 | 106 | 105 |
| 2 | Arkansas | 756 | 718 | 935 | 584 | 28 | 1819 | 1031 | 232 | 330 | 109 | 1512 | 7 | 37 | 495 | 638 | 244 | 1 | 7 | 3 | 10 | 72 |
| 3 | California | 54 | 92 | 417 | 322 | 20 | 28 | 90 | 17 | 15 | 755 | 157 | 136 | 115 | 43 | 42 | 263 | 6 | 25 | 9 | 82 | 27 |
| 4 | Columbia, District of | 236 | 253 | 189 | 146 | 22 | 197 | 336 | 66 | 203 | 44 | 511 | 11 | 197 | 62 | 3 | 3 | .... | 26 | 10 | 14 | 9 |
| 5 | Connecticut | 1390 | 1162 | 2127 | 1026 | 76 | 1150 | 1388 | 429 | 947 | 1867 | 5098 | 224 | 103 | 12 | 6 | 13 | 1 | 227 | 7 | 90 | .... |
| 6 | Delaware | 273 | 380 | 345 | 209 | 2 | 366 | 359 | 118 | 186 | 180 | 1013 | 1 | 122 | 4 | .... | 2 | .... | 38 | 8 | 19 | 2 |
| 7 | Florida | 226 | 253 | 246 | 174 | 32 | 332 | 295 | 129 | 129 | 46 | 537 | 4 | 19 | 291 | 19 | 1 | .... | 12 | 5 | 30 | 13 |
| 8 | Georgia | 2559 | 2535 | 2692 | 2051 | 88 | 3876 | 3439 | 994 | 1376 | 240 | 8349 | 22 | 60 | 1254 | 33 | 4 | .... | 77 | 12 | 90 | 24 |
| 9 | Illinois | 2492 | 3333 | 3649 | 1742 | 543 | 4654 | 3806 | 850 | 1114 | 1335 | 6016 | 445 | 1204 | 630 | 416 | 1359 | 15 | 362 | 622 | 608 | 81 |
| 10 | Indiana | 2765 | 3540 | 4166 | 2039 | 198 | 4374 | 4471 | 1057 | 1066 | 1740 | 7527 | 215 | 1254 | 985 | 136 | 1770 | .... | 245 | 372 | 201 | 3 |
| 11 | Iowa | 523 | 526 | 605 | 356 | 34 | 770 | 755 | 150 | 222 | 147 | 974 | 39 | 209 | 113 | 51 | 466 | 1 | 43 | 59 | 76 | 13 |
| 12 | Kentucky | 3436 | 4942 | 4060 | 2424 | 171 | 4965 | 4772 | 1483 | 2693 | 1120 | 11292 | 45 | 551 | 1885 | 314 | 315 | .... | 193 | 222 | 144 | 72 |
| 13 | Louisiana | 2784 | 3505 | 3053 | 2514 | 100 | 4886 | 2064 | 570 | 1310 | 3126 | 6728 | 90 | 317 | 1092 | 613 | 339 | .... | 1325 | 504 | 803 | 145 |
| 14 | Maine | 1882 | 1744 | 2569 | 1334 | 55 | 1961 | 2159 | 716 | 1957 | 791 | 6721 | 535 | 16 | 2 | 4 | .... | .... | 128 | 1 | 140 | 37 |
| 15 | Maryland | 2385 | 2730 | 2561 | 1777 | 168 | 2680 | 3239 | 863 | 1939 | 900 | 8599 | 30 | 258 | 95 | 2 | 13 | .... | 270 | 248 | 102 | 4 |
| 16 | Massachusetts | 3945 | 3964 | 7645 | 3583 | 267 | 4060 | 5335 | 1346 | 3156 | 5507 | 15264 | 1170 | 195 | 36 | 27 | 14 | 1 | 2140 | 22 | 520 | 15 |
| 17 | Michigan | 1117 | 1047 | 1425 | 832 | 94 | 1534 | 1651 | 384 | 789 | 157 | 2221 | 454 | 1157 | 35 | 3 | 140 | .... | 160 | 74 | 253 | 18 |
| 18 | Mississippi | 2089 | 2371 | 2645 | 1460 | 156 | 3332 | 2342 | 565 | 1104 | 1378 | 5959 | 3 | 69 | 1522 | 715 | 161 | 2 | 33 | 16 | 45 | 198 |
| 19 | Missouri | 2160 | 5422 | 2842 | 1507 | 361 | 6227 | 3238 | 653 | 1589 | 585 | 5957 | 74 | 385 | 1037 | 546 | 1481 | 10 | 683 | 1517 | 585 | 23 |
| 20 | New Hampshire | 1013 | 990 | 1459 | 752 | 17 | 1058 | 1429 | 355 | 1160 | 229 | 3543 | 544 | 13 | 1 | .... | .... | .... | 90 | .... | 37 | 3 |
| 21 | New Jersey | 1463 | 1750 | 2175 | 1037 | 46 | 2019 | 1963 | 495 | 1087 | 901 | 5412 | 54 | 412 | 14 | 3 | 4 | 1 | 317 | 58 | 164 | 26 |
| 22 | New York | 10101 | 12444 | 14843 | 7602 | 610 | 13941 | 12795 | 3309 | 7843 | 7212 | 31664 | 3131 | 969 | 159 | 19 | 91 | 1 | 5772 | 1324 | 2162 | 308 |
| 23 | North Carolina | 2797 | 2678 | 2425 | 2097 | 168 | 2794 | 3142 | 1025 | 2090 | 1114 | 9601 | 14 | 69 | 386 | 10 | 1 | 1 | 12 | 4 | 47 | 20 |
| 24 | Ohio | 6122 | 9520 | 9010 | 4159 | 146 | 11298 | 9072 | 1855 | 3818 | 2914 | 18125 | 914 | 4029 | 1116 | 59 | 402 | .... | 977 | 2422 | 740 | 173 |
| 25 | Pennsylvania | 7649 | 7517 | 8129 | 4942 | 314 | 9284 | 20200 | 2422 | 4646 | 1999 | 23415 | 281 | 1221 | 149 | 11 | 88 | 1 | 1840 | 686 | 736 | 123 |
| 26 | Rhode Island | 473 | 520 | 817 | 420 | 11 | 397 | 466 | 144 | 477 | 757 | 1843 | 134 | 17 | .... | .... | 1 | .... | 171 | 4 | 68 | 3 |
| 27 | South Carolina | 1997 | 2057 | 2259 | 1465 | 269 | 2529 | 2750 | 740 | 1205 | 823 | 7426 | 13 | 40 | 300 | 10 | 3 | .... | 110 | 24 | 113 | 8 |
| 28 | Tennessee | 2924 | 3318 | 3039 | 2244 | 350 | 3383 | 3610 | 1343 | 1448 | 2091 | 9201 | 16 | 155 | 2166 | 24 | 179 | 2 | 72 | 20 | 37 | 3 |
| 29 | Texas | 685 | 706 | 894 | 691 | 81 | 1214 | 929 | 230 | 339 | 345 | 1377 | 18 | 58 | 471 | 617 | 178 | .... | 20 | 102 | 83 | 133 |
| 30 | Vermont | 890 | 672 | 941 | 590 | 36 | 804 | 919 | 315 | 747 | 344 | 2151 | 774 | 65 | 1 | .... | 5 | .... | 63 | 2 | 60 | 8 |
| 31 | Virginia | 5144 | 5469 | 4576 | 3608 | 322 | 5701 | 5564 | 1891 | 3820 | 2083 | 18238 | 43 | 417 | 75 | 17 | 72 | 1 | 69 | 35 | 79 | 13 |
| 32 | Wisconsin | 768 | 630 | 963 | 509 | 33 | 981 | 1030 | 248 | 445 | 199 | 1221 | 224 | 524 | 27 | 8 | 223 | 3 | 164 | 135 | 346 | 28 |
| 33 | Minnesota | 6 | 10 | 7 | 6 | .... | 11 | 13 | 3 | .... | 2 | 12 | 1 | 2 | .... | .... | 9 | .... | .... | 1 | 4 | .... |
| 34 | New Mexico | 287 | 235 | 214 | 292 | 129 | 242 | 430 | 97 | 105 | 233 | 1131 | .... | 4 | 3 | .... | 2 | .... | 2 | .... | 9 | 6 |
| 35 | Oregon | 13 | 5 | 9 | 19 | 1 | 9 | 19 | 5 | 6 | 8 | 16 | 3 | 9 | 7 | .... | 9 | .... | .... | .... | 2 | 1 |
| 36 | Utah | 56 | 97 | 30 | 52 | 4 | .... | .... | .... | .... | 239 | 59 | 25 | 38 | 13 | 10 | 69 | 1 | 2 | .... | 22 | .... |

# TABLE VI—Continued.

| | STATES. | WHITES. | | | COLORED. | | | | | | | | | | | | OCCUPATIONS. | | | | | |
|---|---|---|---|---|---|---|---|---|---|---|---|---|---|---|---|---|---|---|---|---|---|---|
| | | | | | Slaves. | | | | | | Free. | | | | | | | | | | | |
| | | | | | Black. | | Mulatto. | | Total. | | Black. | | Mulatto. | | Total. | | | | | | | |
| | | Males. | Females. | Total. | M. | F. | M. | F. | Black. | Mul. | M. | F. | M. | F. | Black. | Mul. | Agricultural. | Mechanical. | Labor not specified. | Commercial. | Educational. | Other pursuits. |
| 1 | Alabama | 2386 | 1946 | 4332 | 2287 | 2208 | 116 | 100 | 4495 | 216 | 12 | 5 | 11 | 20 | 17 | 31 | 568 | 107 | 163 | 105 | 49 | 8 |
| 2 | Arkansas | 1201 | 956 | 2157 | 390 | 367 | 59 | 43 | 757 | 102 | 1 | | 3 | 1 | 1 | 4 | 315 | 34 | 67 | 20 | 26 | 8 |
| 3 | California | 783 | 109 | 892 | 3 | | 5 | 1 | 3 | 6 | 2 | 1 | 1 | | 3 | 1 | 11 | 13 | 96 | 15 | 15 | 3 |
| 4 | Columbia, District of | 300 | 281 | 581 | 21 | 24 | 8 | 5 | 45 | 13 | 71 | 84 | 27 | 25 | 155 | 52 | 6 | 31 | 58 | 18 | 8 | 2 |
| 5 | Connecticut | 2865 | 2794 | 5659 | | | | | | | 46 | 52 | 13 | 11 | 98 | 24 | 511 | 317 | 222 | 115 | 49 | 10 |
| 6 | Delaware | 494 | 452 | 946 | 11 | 7 | 2 | 1 | 18 | 3 | 119 | 97 | 18 | 8 | 216 | 26 | 81 | 55 | 21 | 24 | 6 | 1 |
| 7 | Florida | 277 | 205 | 482 | 204 | 179 | 23 | 30 | 383 | 53 | 1 | 4 | 2 | 6 | 5 | 8 | 62 | 19 | 24 | 8 | 16 | |
| 8 | Georgia | 2512 | 2068 | 4580 | 2514 | 2558 | 123 | 109 | 5072 | 232 | 18 | 5 | 9 | 9 | 23 | 18 | 607 | 98 | 61 | 40 | 59 | 78 |
| 9 | Illinois | 6287 | 5269 | 11686 | | | | | | | 32 | 16 | 17 | 8 | 48 | 25 | 1411 | 460 | 360 | 101 | 115 | 14 |
| 10 | Indiana | 6834 | 5783 | 12617 | | | | | | | 30 | 29 | 18 | 14 | 59 | 32 | 1301 | 389 | 237 | 48 | 131 | 24 |
| 11 | Iowa | 1130 | 897 | 2027 | | | | | | | 10 | 6 | | 1 | 16 | 1 | 238 | 85 | 30 | 19 | 15 | 4 |
| 12 | Kentucky | 5734 | 4907 | 10641 | 1952 | 1842 | 202 | 197 | 3794 | 399 | 75 | 78 | 20 | 26 | 153 | 46 | 1249 | 468 | 289 | 118 | 88 | 65 |
| 13 | Louisiana | 3957 | 1950 | 5907 | 3063 | 2347 | 235 | 191 | | | 27 | 26 | 69 | 91 | | | 339 | 501 | 1139 | 311 | 69 | 34 |
| 14 | Maine | 3816 | 3733 | 7549 | | | | | | | 11 | 13 | 5 | 6 | 24 | 11 | 728 | 283 | 146 | 282 | 59 | 46 |
| 15 | Maryland | 3630 | 3180 | 6810 | 733 | 672 | 54 | 53 | 1405 | 107 | 596 | 494 | 114 | 95 | 1090 | 209 | 410 | 399 | 500 | 254 | 53 | 2 |
| 16 | Massachusetts | 9901 | 9354 | 19255 | | | | | | | 70 | 59 | 7 | 13 | 129 | 20 | 839 | 1175 | 903 | 392 | 112 | 42 |
| 17 | Michigan | 2400 | 2078 | 4478 | | | | | | | 19 | 10 | 4 | 4 | 29 | 8 | 521 | 181 | 119 | 38 | 40 | 23 |
| 18 | Mississippi | 1802 | 1549 | 3351 | 2665 | 238 | 148 | 148 | 5044 | 296 | 7 | 4 | 7 | 2 | 11 | 9 | 493 | 51 | 41 | 31 | 51 | 25 |
| 19 | Missouri | 6145 | 4728 | 10873 | 587 | 608 | 87 | 75 | 1195 | 162 | 26 | 20 | 8 | 8 | 46 | 16 | 956 | 430 | 855 | 116 | 112 | 16 |
| 20 | New Hampshire | 2085 | 2190 | 4225 | | | | | | | 3 | | | 3 | 3 | 3 | 586 | 82 | 146 | 64 | 29 | 1 |
| 21 | New Jersey | 3348 | 2818 | 6166 | 8 | 5 | | | | | 133 | 117 | 24 | 12 | 250 | 36 | 386 | 423 | 336 | 115 | 67 | 41 |
| 22 | New York | 24029 | 20765 | 44794 | | | | | | | 351 | 347 | 66 | 42 | 698 | 108 | 2971 | 2006 | 2008 | 630 | 368 | 521 |
| 23 | North Carolina | 2933 | 2706 | 5639 | 2044 | 1961 | 101 | 121 | 4005 | 222 | 63 | 64 | 86 | 87 | 127 | 173 | 925 | 144 | 146 | 49 | 58 | 21 |
| 24 | Ohio | 15590 | 12956 | 28546 | | | | | | | 129 | 123 | 99 | 60 | 252 | 159 | 2588 | 1596 | 1137 | 397 | 239 | 63 |
| 25 | Pennsylvania | 15102 | 12637 | 27739 | | | | | | | 346 | 286 | 84 | 96 | 632 | 180 | 1580 | 1755 | 1153 | 398 | 197 | 70 |
| 26 | Rhode Island | 1132 | 1044 | 2176 | | | | | | | 25 | 27 | 6 | 7 | 52 | 13 | 118 | 108 | 142 | 51 | 12 | 6 |
| 27 | South Carolina | 1544 | 1265 | 2809 | 2570 | 2481 | 65 | 50 | 5051 | 115 | 11 | 16 | 18 | 27 | 27 | 45 | 498 | 85 | 57 | 61 | 54 | 2 |
| 28 | Tennessee | 4271 | 3877 | 8148 | 1744 | 1666 | 126 | 114 | 3410 | 240 | 20 | 7 | 18 | 32 | 27 | 50 | 986 | 246 | 130 | 49 | 82 | 3 |
| 29 | Texas | 1186 | 941 | 2175 | 427 | 395 | 24 | 32 | 822 | 56 | | | 4 | | | 4 | 323 | 83 | 57 | 26 | 41 | 8 |
| 30 | Vermont | 1531 | 1592 | 3123 | | | | | | | 3 | 2 | | 1 | 5 | 1 | 467 | 132 | 92 | 33 | 36 | 3 |
| 31 | Virginia | 5027 | 4870 | 9897 | 4026 | 3724 | 317 | 333 | 7750 | 650 | 245 | 256 | 120 | 141 | 501 | 261 | 1098 | 420 | 325 | 162 | 111 | 35 |
| 32 | Wisconsin | 1561 | 1318 | 2879 | | | | | | | 1 | | 13 | 10 | 1 | 23 | 234 | 99 | 108 | 31 | 15 | 2 |
| 33 | Minnesota | 19 | 10 | 29 | | | | | | | | | | | | | 1 | 2 | | 2 | | |
| 34 | New Mexico | 580 | 577 | 1157 | | | | | | | | | | | | | 88 | 15 | 53 | 1 | 1 | 12 |
| 35 | Oregon | 32 | 15 | 47 | | | | | | | | | | | | | 9 | 3 | 1 | 1 | | |
| 36 | Utah | 131 | 107 | 238 | | | | | | | | 1 | | | 1 | | 32 | 9 | 7 | 1 | 1 | |

TABLE VII—*Table of sex, color, and condition of the living population of several States, arranged by sections,* 1850.

| Sections. | | Whites. Males. | Whites. Females. | Whites. Total. | Colored. Slaves. | Colored. Free. | Aggregate. |
|---|---|---|---|---|---|---|---|
| Georgia | Southern section | 66,886 | 65,153 | 132,039 | 118,757 | 1,139 | 251,935 |
| | Northern section | 117,531 | 113,696 | 231,227 | 96,644 | 534 | 328,405 |
| | Middle section | 81,816 | 76,490 | 158,306 | 166,281 | 1,258 | 325,845 |
| Illinois | Northern section | 168,758 | 147,899 | 316,657 | ....... | 1,053 | 317,710 |
| | Middle section | 152,161 | 145,133 | 297,294 | ....... | 942 | 298,236 |
| | Southern section | 124,625 | 107,458 | 232,083 | ....... | 3,441 | 235,524 |
| Louisiana | Northern section | 33,213 | 28,219 | 61,432 | 89,577 | 1,348 | 152,357 |
| | Southern section | 53,378 | 45,860 | 99,238 | 133,994 | 5,993 | 239,225 |
| | City section | 62,411 | 47,066 | 109,477 | 24,264 | 10,812 | 144,553 |
| Maine | Northern section | 96,631 | 86,979 | 183,610 | ....... | 114 | 183,724 |
| | Southern section | 200,114 | 198,089 | 398,203 | ....... | 1,242 | 399,445 |
| Massachusetts | Northeastern section | 140,780 | 150,578 | 291,358 | ....... | 1,325 | 292,683 |
| | Western section | 147,540 | 147,832 | 295,372 | ....... | 2,893 | 298,265 |
| | Southeastern section | 127,551 | 129,090 | 256,641 | ....... | 2,808 | 259,449 |
| | City section | 68,222 | 73,857 | 142,079 | ....... | 2,038 | 144,117 |
| Mississippi | Northwestern section | 34,774 | 30,371 | 65,145 | 78,520 | 57 | 143,722 |
| | Northeastern section | 47,801 | 43,622 | 91,423 | 53,096 | 110 | 144,629 |
| | Middle Eastern section | 29,045 | 26,644 | 55,689 | 35,173 | 37 | 90,899 |
| | Southwestern section | 34,523 | 29,969 | 64,492 | 133,244 | 537 | 198,273 |
| | Southeastern section | 10,144 | 8,825 | 18,969 | 9,845 | 189 | 29,003 |
| New Jersey | Northern section | 150,082 | 150,919 | 301,001 | 160 | 12,719 | 313,880 |
| | Southern section | 83,370 | 81,138 | 164,508 | 76 | 11,091 | 175,675 |
| New York | North'n and Lake section | 375,235 | 355,194 | 730,429 | ....... | 3,646 | 734,075 |
| | Eastern eection | 410,180 | 388,353 | 798,533 | ....... | 24,485 | 823,018 |
| | Central section | 511,066 | 506,565 | 1,017,631 | ....... | 7,123 | 1,024,754 |
| | City section | 248,008 | 253,724 | 501,732 | ....... | 13,815 | 515,547 |
| North Carolina | Eastern section | 58,010 | 58,967 | 116,977 | 103,687 | 10,368 | 231,032 |
| | Western section | 75,153 | 76,681 | 151,834 | 27,827 | 1,843 | 181,504 |
| | Northern Middle section | 87,007 | 90,743 | 177,750 | 97,362 | 10,321 | 285,433 |
| | Southern Middle section | 52,855 | 53,612 | 106,467 | 59,672 | 4,931 | 171,070 |
| Ohio | Northeast section | 184,777 | 176,628 | 361,405 | ....... | 1,270 | 362,675 |
| | Northwest section | 124,363 | 114,879 | 239,242 | ....... | 855 | 240,097 |
| | Middle East section | 172,777 | 168,860 | 341,637 | ....... | 1,957 | 343,594 |
| | Middle West section | 146,360 | 136,636 | 282,996 | ....... | 5,509 | 288,505 |
| | Southeast section | 157,961 | 151,365 | 309,326 | ....... | 7,024 | 316,350 |
| | Southwest section | 217,879 | 202,565 | 420,444 | ....... | 8,664 | 429,108 |
| Pennsylvania | Eastern section | 273,752 | 267,999 | 541,751 | ....... | 15,207 | 556,958 |
| | Western section | 343,288 | 326,526 | 669,814 | ....... | 9,668 | 679,482 |
| | Middle section | 337,738 | 319,856 | 657,594 | ....... | 8,990 | 666,584 |
| | City section | 187,956 | 201,045 | 389,001 | ....... | 19,761 | 408,762 |
| South Carolina | Eastern section | 30,183 | 29,145 | 59,328 | 142,782 | 5,152 | 207,262 |
| | Northern section | 36,254 | 35,689 | 71,943 | 104,310 | 1,955 | 178,208 |
| | Southern section | 25,690 | 25,563 | 51,253 | 70,362 | 910 | 122,525 |
| | Western section | 45,620 | 46,419 | 92,039 | 67,530 | 943 | 160,512 |
| Tennessee | Eastern section | 102,816 | 103,499 | 206,315 | 19,474 | 2,121 | 227,910 |
| | Western section | 87,158 | 82,240 | 169,398 | 83,080 | 660 | 253,138 |
| | Eastern Centre section | 76,266 | 74,336 | 150,602 | 31,158 | 1,667 | 183,427 |
| | Western Centre section | 115,995 | 114,526 | 230,521 | 105,747 | 1,974 | 338,342 |
| Texas | Northern section | 28,636 | 24,599 | 53,235 | 22,843 | 72 | 76,150 |
| | Southern section | 22,622 | 17,727 | 40,349 | 18,181 | 246 | 58,776 |
| | Central section | 33,611 | 26,839 | 60,450 | 17,137 | 79 | 77,666 |
| Virginia | Eastern section | 97,733 | 97,205 | 194,938 | 177,782 | 31,805 | 404,525 |
| | Southern section | 101,704 | 101,717 | 203,421 | 231,523 | 14,339 | 449,283 |
| | Western section | 104,005 | 97,260 | 201,265 | 8,159 | 1,374 | 210,798 |
| | Mountain section | 147,858 | 147,318 | 295,176 | 55,061 | 6,815 | 337,055 |

## TABLE VIII.—*Aggregate population of the United States by ages and sex.*

| | STATES. | AGES. Under 1. M. | Under 1. F. | 1 and under 5. M. | 1 and under 5. F. | 5 and under 10. M. | 5 and under 10. F. | 10 and under 20. M. | 10 and under 20. F. | 20 and under 50. M. | 20 and under 50. F. | 50 and under 80. M. | 50 and under 80. F. | 80 and under 100. M. | 80 and under 100. F. | 100 and over. M. | 100 and over. F. | Age unknown. M. | Age unknown. F. |
|---|---|---|---|---|---|---|---|---|---|---|---|---|---|---|---|---|---|---|---|
| 1 | Alabama | 10301 | 10074 | 55355 | 54813 | 60089 | 59300 | 97134 | 96686 | 140251 | 133466 | 27542 | 23786 | 1035 | 1028 | 78 | 85 | 58 | 42 |
| 2 | Arkansas | 3363 | 3279 | 15958 | 15556 | 16991 | 16489 | 27184 | 26191 | 40288 | 33967 | 5909 | 4419 | 120 | 128 | 15 | 9 | 18 | 13 |
| 3 | California | 149 | 124 | 843 | 785 | 1084 | 1016 | 5786 | 1724 | 74507 | 3080 | 2621 | 274 | 21 | 10 | ..... | ..... | 669 | 4 |
| 4 | Columbia, District of | 648 | 671 | 2769 | 2659 | 3316 | 3415 | 5859 | 6366 | 9876 | 11559 | 2126 | 2682 | 67 | 149 | ..... | 7 | 8 | 15 |
| 5 | Connecticut | 3925 | 3721 | 16540 | 16268 | 19726 | 19464 | 38658 | 38828 | 79944 | 79153 | 23396 | 27687 | 1813 | 1899 | 5 | 5 | 197 | 63 |
| 6 | Delaware | 1281 | 1273 | 5491 | 5408 | 6650 | 6421 | 11084 | 10758 | 17361 | 17329 | 3904 | 4172 | 142 | 191 | 8 | 6 | 89 | 19 |
| 7 | Florida | 1123 | 1113 | 6260 | 6111 | 6770 | 6610 | 9994 | 9852 | 17042 | 14999 | 3554 | 2693 | 120 | 123 | 20 | 16 | 44 | 1 |
| 8 | Georgia | 12668 | 12190 | 66006 | 63933 | 71804 | 70031 | 114621 | 115931 | 157391 | 155049 | 32249 | 30706 | 1483 | 1659 | 111 | 110 | 132 | 111 |
| 9 | Illinois | 13621 | 13060 | 58714 | 56765 | 66764 | 63884 | 106115 | 100675 | 172152 | 144518 | 29877 | 23432 | 573 | 503 | 11 | 7 | 490 | 305 |
| 10 | Indiana | 16505 | 15791 | 69066 | 66350 | 80430 | 77284 | 125167 | 121083 | 181307 | 164124 | 38174 | 30831 | 1038 | 950 | 18 | 14 | 188 | 146 |
| 11 | Iowa | 3144 | 2955 | 14320 | 13871 | 15893 | 15123 | 28168 | 22308 | 38172 | 32131 | 6216 | 4668 | 112 | 78 | ..... | 1 | 27 | 27 |
| 12 | Kentucky | 15159 | 14914 | 67938 | 65981 | 77038 | 74791 | 122594 | 121151 | 181067 | 165551 | 37048 | 35329 | 1704 | 1778 | 62 | 95 | 120 | 85 |
| 13 | Louisiana | 6007 | 6225 | 30550 | 30652 | 82993 | 82465 | 51502 | 53596 | 133721 | 104298 | 18868 | 15190 | 602 | 594 | 77 | 99 | 276 | 47 |
| 14 | Maine | 7067 | 6918 | 31561 | 30220 | 37788 | 36655 | 70012 | 68756 | 115184 | 107947 | 33444 | 33027 | 1843 | 1944 | 9 | 4 | 613 | 207 |
| 15 | Maryland | 8319 | 8163 | 34692 | 34470 | 39410 | 38859 | 66592 | 67532 | 116489 | 112860 | 25748 | 27247 | 1022 | 1482 | 42 | 89 | 9 | 9 |
| 16 | Massachusetts | 11612 | 11580 | 45869 | 44984 | 51607 | 51190 | 98806 | 104959 | 224662 | 227532 | 53341 | 61686 | 2568 | 3865 | 7 | 12 | 1045 | 189 |
| 17 | Michigan | 5501 | 5397 | 25193 | 23950 | 30560 | 29016 | 46945 | 45504 | 84397 | 70799 | 16871 | 12762 | 360 | 267 | 6 | 3 | 63 | 60 |
| 18 | Mississippi | 8083 | 8003 | 44804 | 44167 | 47701 | 46654 | 74329 | 73235 | 116253 | 105723 | 19373 | 15871 | 640 | 592 | 54 | 86 | *194 | 182 |
| 19 | Missouri | 11440 | 10891 | 47654 | 46293 | 53582 | 51594 | 84950 | 82931 | 138248 | 114512 | 21325 | 17451 | 517 | 456 | 21 | 24 | 95 | 60 |
| 20 | New Hampshire | 3074 | 3037 | 13682 | 13270 | 17409 | 16855 | 34892 | 35703 | 68726 | 65720 | 22422 | 25149 | 1481 | 1992 | 6 | 6 | 28 | 24 |
| 21 | New Jersey | 6762 | 6794 | 27746 | 27082 | 32099 | 31662 | 55186 | 55287 | 97866 | 96283 | 24529 | 25618 | 1057 | 1384 | 7 | 18 | 94 | 81 |
| 22 | New York | 38672 | 37665 | 164872 | 162221 | 190504 | 187105 | 381756 | 344224 | 680748 | 646112 | 153716 | 144746 | 6451 | 6805 | 45 | 43 | 1181 | 582 |
| 23 | North Carolina | 12605 | 12129 | 59424 | 57960 | 66331 | 65010 | 107608 | 106494 | 146011 | 154557 | 36758 | 39421 | 2002 | 2335 | 91 | 158 | 79 | 71 |
| 24 | Ohio | 28858 | 28026 | 128601 | 124841 | 147751 | 143535 | 238097 | 237884 | 384353 | 350888 | 85722 | 75867 | 3040 | 2682 | 28 | 30 | 358 | 268 |
| 25 | Pennsylvania | 32566 | 31865 | 141165 | 138901 | 160385 | 157841 | 260703 | 263837 | 461593 | 441492 | 106142 | 104672 | 3821 | 4653 | 29 | 46 | 699 | 476 |
| 26 | Rhode Island | 1777 | 1833 | 7108 | 7003 | 7786 | 7805 | 14849 | 15553 | 32453 | 33272 | 7721 | 9427 | 373 | 570 | ..... | 3 | 16 | 1 |
| 27 | South Carolina | 7840 | 7961 | 45563 | 45854 | 48353 | 48831 | 80033 | 81491 | 116410 | 122435 | 28646 | 29191 | 1872 | 1648 | 89 | 117 | 1328 | 1345 |
| 28 | Tennessee | 15212 | 14939 | 70839 | 69278 | 79601 | 78007 | 130954 | 129563 | 169146 | 170034 | 36432 | 34792 | 1766 | 1782 | 66 | 82 | 116 | 108 |
| 29 | Texas | 3142 | 3052 | 15566 | 15028 | 16671 | 15878 | 25552 | 25105 | 46056 | 35116 | 6449 | 4454 | 146 | 124 | 17 | 22 | 181 | 33 |
| 30 | Vermont | 3360 | 3234 | 15664 | 15391 | 19479 | 18674 | 36037 | 34457 | 63233 | 60279 | 20882 | 20723 | 1847 | 1312 | 5 | 5 | 26 | 12 |
| 31 | Virginia | 18062 | 18246 | 93088 | 91075 | 105643 | 102617 | 173330 | 171077 | 257989 | 251725 | 66085 | 64740 | 3326 | 3884 | 135 | 254 | 206 | 179 |
| 32 | Wisconsin | 5294 | 5130 | 20871 | 20077 | 21815 | 20464 | 32145 | 30656 | 72546 | 55551 | 11747 | 8575 | 185 | 141 | 1 | 1 | 112 | 80 |
| 33 | Territ's. Minnesota | 66 | 102 | 388 | 363 | 363 | 358 | 531 | 499 | 2178 | 958 | 185 | 79 | 5 | 2 | ..... | ..... | ..... | ..... |
| 34 | Territ's. New Mexico | 639 | 594 | 3773 | 3793 | 4402 | 4325 | 6866 | 7182 | 12698 | 11548 | 2950 | 2188 | 253 | 153 | 19 | 21 | 142 | 1 |
| 35 | Territ's. Oregon | 161 | 149 | 925 | 853 | 920 | 953 | 1414 | 1238 | 4363 | 1651 | 433 | 164 | 4 | 1 | ..... | ..... | 38 | 27 |
| 36 | Territ's. Utah | 220 | 212 | 877 | 867 | 699 | 670 | 1348 | 1359 | 2546 | 1902 | 355 | 821 | 1 | 3 | ..... | ..... | ..... | ..... |
| | Total | 818226 | 811220 | 1451234 | 1417093 | 1641407 | 1600851 | 2710796 | 2709625 | 4652177 | 4297620 | 1012660 | 964040 | 41910 | 47167 | 1077 | 1473 | 8884 | 4823 |

* 578, age and sex unknown.

## TABLE IX.—*Ages of the aggregate population of the United States.*

| STATES AND TERRITORIES. | Under 1 year. | 1 and under 5. | 5 and under 10. | 10 and under 20. | 20 and under 50. | 50 and under 80. | 80 and under 100. | 100 & up'ds. | Unk'n. |
|---|---|---|---|---|---|---|---|---|---|
| Alabama | 20,375 | 110,668 | 119,389 | 193,820 | 273,717 | 51,328 | 2,063 | 163 | 100 |
| Arkansas | 6,642 | 31,514 | 33,480 | 53,375 | 74,255 | 10,328 | 248 | 24 | 31 |
| California | 273 | 1,628 | 2,300 | 7,510 | 77,587 | 2,795 | 31 | ...... | 673 |
| Columbia, District of | 1,319 | 5,428 | 6,731 | 11,725 | 21,435 | 4,808 | 216 | 7 | 18 |
| Connecticut | 7,646 | 32,808 | 39,190 | 77,486 | 159,097 | 51,083 | 3,212 | 10 | 260 |
| Delaware | 2,554 | 10,899 | 13,071 | 21,842 | 34,690 | 8,076 | 333 | 9 | 58 |
| Florida | 2,236 | 12,371 | 13,380 | 19,846 | 33,041 | 6,247 | 243 | 36 | 45 |
| Georgia | 24,858 | 129,939 | 141,835 | 230,552 | 312,440 | 62,955 | 3,142 | 221 | 243 |
| Illinois | 26,681 | 115,479 | 130,622 | 206,790 | 316,670 | 53,309 | 1,076 | 18 | 795 |
| Indiana | 32,296 | 135,416 | 157,714 | 246,200 | 345,431 | 69,005 | 1,988 | 32 | 334 |
| Iowa | 6,099 | 28,191 | 31,016 | 45,476 | 70,303 | 10,884 | 190 | 1 | 54 |
| Kentucky | 30,073 | 133,919 | 151,829 | 243,745 | 346,618 | 72,377 | 3,482 | 157 | 205 |
| Louisiana | 12,232 | 61,202 | 65,458 | 105,098 | 238,019 | 34,058 | 1,196 | 176 | 323 |
| Maine | 13,995 | 61,781 | 74,453 | 138,768 | 223,081 | 66,471 | 3,787 | 13 | 320 |
| Maryland | 16,482 | 69,162 | 78,269 | 134,124 | 229,349 | 52,995 | 2,504 | 131 | 18 |
| Massachusetts | 23,192 | 90,853 | 102,797 | 203,765 | 451,194 | 115,027 | 6,433 | 19 | 1,234 |
| Michigan | 10,898 | 49,143 | 59,576 | 92,449 | 155,196 | 29,633 | 627 | 9 | 123 |
| Mississippi | 16,086 | 88,975 | 94,355 | 147,564 | 221,976 | 35,244 | 1,232 | 140 | 954 |
| Missouri | 23,231 | 93,947 | 105,176 | 167,881 | 252,760 | 38,776 | 973 | 45 | 155 |
| New Hampshire | 6,111 | 26,952 | 34,264 | 70,095 | 129,446 | 47,571 | 3,473 | 12 | 52 |
| New Jersey | 13,556 | 54,828 | 63,761 | 110,473 | 194,149 | 50,147 | 2,441 | 25 | 175 |
| New York | 76,337 | 327,093 | 377,605 | 675,980 | 1,326,860 | 298,462 | 13,256 | 88 | 1,713 |
| North Carolina | 24,734 | 117,384 | 131,341 | 214,097 | 300,568 | 76,179 | 4,337 | 249 | 150 |
| Ohio | 56,884 | 253,442 | 291,286 | 475,981 | 734,741 | 161,589 | 5,722 | 58 | 626 |
| Pennsylvania | 64,331 | 281,066 | 318,226 | 524,540 | 908,085 | 210,814 | 8,474 | 75 | 1,175 |
| Rhode Island | 3,610 | 14,106 | 15,591 | 30,402 | 65,725 | 17,148 | 943 | 3 | 17 |
| South Carolina | 15,801 | 91,417 | 97,184 | 161,524 | 238,845 | 57,837 | 3,020 | 206 | 2,673 |
| Tennessee | 30,151 | 140,117 | 157,608 | 260,517 | 339,180 | 71,224 | 3,548 | 148 | 224 |
| Texas | 6,194 | 30,594 | 32,549 | 50,657 | 81,172 | 10,903 | 270 | 39 | 214 |
| Vermont | 6,594 | 31,055 | 38,153 | 70,494 | 123,512 | 41,605 | 2,659 | 10 | 38 |
| Virginia | 36,308 | 184,163 | 208,260 | 344,407 | 509,714 | 130,825 | 7,210 | 389 | 385 |
| Wisconsin | 10,424 | 40,948 | 42,279 | 62,801 | 128,097 | 20,322 | 326 | 2 | 192 |
| Territories. Minnesota | 168 | 751 | 721 | 1,030 | 3,136 | 264 | 7 | ...... | ...... |
| Territories. New Mexico | 1,233 | 7,566 | 8,727 | 14,048 | 24,246 | 5,138 | 406 | 40 | 143 |
| Territories. Oregon | 310 | 1,778 | 1,873 | 2,652 | 6,014 | 597 | 5 | ...... | 65 |
| Territories. Utah | 432 | 1,744 | 1,369 | 2,707 | 4,448 | 676 | 4 | ...... | ...... |
| Total | 629,446 | 2,868,327 | 3,241,268 | 5,420,421 | 8,949,797 | 1,976,700 | 89,077 | 2,555 | 14,285 |

## TABLE X.—*Sex, color, and condition of the population of the United States,* 1850.

| States and Territories. | White. | | Free colored. | | Slave. | | Total white. | Total F. C. | Total slave. |
|---|---|---|---|---|---|---|---|---|---|
| | Male. | Female. | Male. | Female. | Male. | Female. | | | |
| Alabama | 219,483 | 207,031 | 1,056 | 1,209 | 171,804 | 171,040 | 426,514 | 2,265 | 342,844 |
| Arkansas | 85,874 | 76,315 | 314 | 294 | 23,658 | 23,442 | 162,189 | 608 | 47,100 |
| California | 84,708 | 6,927 | 872 | 90 | ........ | ........ | 91,635 | 962 | ........ |
| Columbia, Dist. of | 18,494 | 19,447 | 4,248 | 5,811 | 1,422 | 2,265 | 37,941 | 10,059 | 3,687 |
| Connecticut | 179,884 | 183,215 | 3,820 | 3,873 | ........ | ........ | 363,099 | 7,693 | ...... |
| Delaware | 35,746 | 35,423 | 9,035 | 9,038 | 1,174 | 1,116 | 71,169 | 18,073 | 2,290 |
| Florida | 25,705 | 21,498 | 418 | 514 | 19,804 | 19,506 | 47,203 | 932 | 39,310 |
| Georgia | 266,233 | 255,339 | 1,375 | 1,556 | 188,857 | 192,825 | 521,572 | 2,931 | 381,682 |
| Illinois | 445,544 | 400,490 | 2,777 | 2,659 | ........ | ........ | 846,034 | 5,436 | ....... |
| Indiana | 506,178 | 470,976 | 2,715 | 5,547 | ........ | ........ | 977,154 | 11,262 | ....... |
| Iowa | 100,887 | 90,994 | 165 | 168 | ........ | ........ | 191,881 | 333 | ....... |
| Kentucky | 392,804 | 368,609 | 4,863 | 5,148 | 105,063 | 105,918 | 761,413 | 10,011 | 210,981 |
| Louisiana | 141,243 | 114,248 | 7,479 | 9,983 | 125,874 | 118,935 | 255,491 | 17,462 | 244,809 |
| Maine | 296,745 | 285,068 | 726 | 630 | ........ | ........ | 581,813 | 1,356 | ....... |
| Maryland | 211,187 | 206,756 | 35,192 | 39,531 | 45,944 | 44,424 | 417,943 | 74,723 | 90,368 |
| Massachusetts | 484,093 | 501,357 | 4,424 | 4,640 | ........ | ........ | 985,450 | 9,064 | ....... |
| Michigan | 208,465 | 186,606 | 1,431 | 1,152 | ........ | ........ | 395,701 | 2,583 | ....... |
| Mississippi | 156,287 | 139,431 | 474 | 456 | 154,964 | 154,914 | 295,718 | 930 | 309,878 |
| Missouri | 312,987 | 279,017 | 1,361 | 1,257 | 43,484 | 43,938 | 592,004 | 2,618 | 87,422 |
| New Hampshire | 155,960 | 161,490 | 260 | 260 | ........ | ........ | 317,456 | 520 | ....... |
| New Jersey | 233,452 | 232,057 | 11,798 | 12,012 | 96 | 140 | 465,509 | 23,810 | 236 |
| New York | 1,544,489 | 1,503,836 | 23,452 | 25,617 | ........ | ........ | 3,048,325 | 49,069 | ....... |
| North Carolina | 273,025 | 280,003 | 13,298 | 14,165 | 144,581 | 143,967 | 553,028 | 27,463 | 288,548 |
| Ohio | 1,004,117 | 950,933 | 12,691 | 12,588 | ........ | ........ | 1,955,050 | 25,279 | ....... |
| Pennsylvania | 1,142,734 | 1,115,426 | 25,369 | 28,257 | ........ | ........ | 2,258,160 | 53,626 | ....... |
| Rhode Island | 70,340 | 73,535 | 1,738 | 1,932 | ........ | ........ | 143,875 | 3,670 | ....... |
| Sauth Carolina | 137,747 | 136,816 | 4,131 | 4,829 | 187,756 | 197,228 | 274,563 | 8,960 | 384,984 |
| Tennessee | 382,235 | 374,601 | 3,117 | 3,305 | 118,780 | 120,679 | 756,836 | 6,422 | 239,459 |
| Texas | 84,869 | 69,165 | 211 | 186 | 28,700 | 29,461 | 154,034 | 397 | 58,161 |
| Vermont | 159,658 | 153,744 | 375 | 343 | ........ | ........ | 313,402 | 718 | ....... |
| Virginia | 451,300 | 443,500 | 26,002 | 28,331 | 240,562 | 231,966 | 894,800 | 54,333 | 472,528 |
| Wisconsin | 164,351 | 140,405 | 365 | 270 | ........ | ........ | 304,756 | 635 | ....... |
| Territ's. Minnesota | 3,695 | 2,343 | 21 | 18 | ........ | ........ | 6,038 | 39 | ....... |
| Territ's. New Mexico | 31,725 | 29,800 | 17 | 5 | ........ | ........ | 61,525 | 22 | ....... |
| Territ's. Oregon | 8,138 | 4,949 | 120 | 87 | ........ | ........ | 13,087 | 207 | ....... |
| Territ's. Utah | 6,020 | 5,810 | 14 | 10 | 12 | 14 | 11,830 | 24 | 26 |

## TABLE XI—*Black and Mulatto population of the United States.*

| STATES AND TERRITORIES. | FREE. | | | SLAVES. | | | SLAVE AND FREE. | | RATIO OF MULATTOES TO 100 BLACKS. | | |
|---|---|---|---|---|---|---|---|---|---|---|---|
| | Blacks. | Mulat's | Total. | Blacks. | Mulat's | Total. | Blacks. | Mulat's. | Free. | Slave. | Total. |
| Alabama | 567 | 1,698 | 2,265 | 321,239 | 21,605 | 342,844 | 321,805 | 23,303 | 299.47 | 6.73 | 7.24 |
| Arkansas | 201 | 407 | 608 | 40,739 | 6,361 | 47,100 | 40,940 | 6,768 | 202.49 | 15.61 | 16.53 |
| California | 875 | 87 | 962 | ........ | ....... | .......... | 875 | 87 | 9.94 | ...... | 9.94 |
| Columbia, Dis. of | 6,783 | 3,276 | 10,059 | 2,885 | 802 | 3,687 | 9,668 | 4,078 | 48.30 | 27.80 | 42.18 |
| Connecticnt | 5,895 | 1,798 | 7,893 | ........ | ....... | .......... | 5,894 | 1,798 | 30.51 | ...... | 30.51 |
| Delaware | 16,425 | 1,648 | 18,073 | 2,207 | 83 | 2,290 | 18,632 | 1,731 | 10.03 | 3.76 | 9.29 |
| Florida | 229 | 703 | 932 | 36,288 | 3,022 | 39,310 | 36,517 | 3,725 | 306.99 | 8.33 | 10.20 |
| Georgia | 1,403 | 1,528 | 2,931 | 359,013 | 22,669 | 381,682 | 360,416 | 24,197 | 108.91 | 6.31 | 6.71 |
| Illinois | 2,930 | 2,506 | 5,436 | ........ | ....... | .......... | 2,930 | 2,506 | 85.53 | ...... | 85.53 |
| Indiana | 5,941 | 5,321 | 11,262 | ........ | ....... | .......... | 5,941 | 5,321 | 89.56 | ...... | 89.56 |
| Iowa | 178 | 155 | 333 | ........ | ....... | .......... | 178 | 155 | 87.08 | ...... | 87.08 |
| Kentucky | 7,381 | 2,630 | 10,011 | 181,252 | 29,729 | 210,981 | 188,633 | 32,359 | 35.63 | 16.40 | 17.15 |
| Louisiana | 3,379 | 14,083 | 17,462 | 224,974 | 19,835 | 244,809 | 228,353 | 33,918 | 416.78 | 8.82 | 14.85 |
| Maine | 895 | 461 | 1,356 | ........ | ....... | .......... | 895 | 461 | 51.51 | ...... | 51.51 |
| Maryland | 61,109 | 13,614 | 74,723 | 82,479 | 7,889 | 90,368 | 143,588 | 21,503 | 22.28 | 9.56 | 14.98 |
| Masschusetts | 6,724 | 2,340 | 9,064 | ........ | ....... | .......... | 6,724 | 2,340 | 34.80 | ...... | 34.80 |
| Michigan | 1,465 | 1,118 | 2,583 | ........ | ....... | .......... | 1,465 | 1,118 | 76.31 | ...... | 76.31 |
| Mississippi | 295 | 635 | 930 | 290,148 | 19,730 | 309,878 | 290,443 | 20,365 | 215.25 | 6.80 | 7.01 |
| Missouri | 1,687 | 931 | 2,618 | 74,187 | 13,235 | 87,422 | 75,874 | 14,166 | 55.19 | 7.84 | 18.67 |
| New Hampshire | 336 | 184 | 520 | ........ | ....... | .......... | 336 | 184 | 54.76 | ...... | 54.76 |
| New Jersey | 20,113 | 3,697 | 23,810 | 232 | 4 | 236 | 20,345 | 3,701 | 18.38 | 1.72 | 18.19 |
| New York | 40,930 | 8,139 | 49,069 | ........ | ....... | .......... | 40,930 | 8,139 | 19.89 | ...... | 19.89 |
| North Carolina | 10,258 | 17,205 | 27,463 | 271,733 | 16,815 | 288,548 | 281,991 | 34,020 | 167.72 | 6.19 | 12.06 |
| Ohio | 11,014 | 14,265 | 25,279 | ........ | ....... | .......... | 11,014 | 14,265 | 129.52 | ...... | 129.52 |
| Pennsylvania | 38,285 | 15,341 | 53,626 | ........ | ....... | .......... | 38,285 | 15,341 | 40.07 | ...... | 40,07 |
| Rhode Island | 2,939 | 731 | 3,670 | ........ | ....... | .......... | 2,939 | 731 | 24.87 | ...... | 24.87 |
| South Carolina | 4,588 | 4,372 | 8,960 | 372,482 | 12,502 | 384,984 | 377,070 | 16,874 | 95.29 | 3.36 | 4.48 |
| Tennessee | 2,646 | 3,776 | 6,422 | 219,103 | 20,356 | 239,459 | 221,749 | 24,132 | 142.71 | 9.29 | 10.88 |
| Texas | 140 | 257 | 397 | 50,458 | 7,703 | 58,161 | 50,598 | 7,960 | 183.57 | 15.27 | 15.73 |
| Vermont | 512 | 206 | 718 | ........ | ....... | .......... | 512 | 206 | 40.23 | ...... | 40.23 |
| Virginia | 18,857 | 35,476 | 54,333 | 428,229 | 44,299 | 472,528 | 447,086 | 79,775 | 188.13 | 10.34 | 17.84 |
| Wisconsin | 338 | 297 | 635 | ........ | ....... | .......... | 338 | 297 | 87.87 | ...... | 87.87 |
| Territories. Minnesota | 16 | 23 | 39 | ........ | ....... | .......... | 16 | 23 | 143.75 | ...... | 143.75 |
| Territories. N. Mexico | 6 | 16 | 22 | ........ | ....... | .......... | 6 | 16 | 266.67 | ...... | 266.67 |
| Territories. Oregon | 45 | 162 | 207 | ........ | ....... | .......... | 45 | 162 | 360.00 | ...... | 360.00 |
| Territories. Utah | 15 | 9 | 24 | 9 | 17 | 36 | 24 | 26 | 60.00 | 188.89 | 108.33 |
| Total | 275,400 | 159,095 | 434,495 | 2,957,657 | 246,656 | 3,204,313 | 3,233,057 | 405,751 | 58.13 | 8.34 | 12.55 |

## TABLE XII.—*Ages of the whole population of the United States.*

| Age. | Number. | Ratio. | Age. | Number. | Ratio. |
|---|---|---|---|---|---|
| Under 1 year old | 629,446 | 2.71 | 80 and under 100 | 89,077 | .39 |
| 1 and under 5 | 2,868,327 | 12.37 | 100 and over | 2,555 | .01 |
| 5 " 20 | 8,661,689 | 37.35 | Age unknown | 14,285 | .06 |
| 20 " 50 | 8,949,797 | 38.59 | | | |
| 50 " 80 | 1,976,700 | 8.52 | Aggregate population | 23,191,876 | 100.00 |

## TABLE XIII.—*Ages of the white, free colored, and slaves.*

| Age. | Whites. | | Free colored. | | Slaves. | | Aggregate. | |
|---|---|---|---|---|---|---|---|---|
| | Number. | Ratio. per ct. | Number. | Ratio per ct. | Number. | Ratio per ct. | Number. | Ratio per ct. |
| 15 years and under | 8,002,715 | 40.93 | 171,181 | 39.40 | 1,455,774 | 45.43 | 9,629,670 | 41.52 |
| Over 15 and under 60 | 10,720,175 | 54.83 | 238,859 | 54.97 | 1,630,095 | 50.87 | 12,589,129 | 54.28 |
| 60 and over | 819,871 | 4.19 | 24,169 | 5.56 | 114,752 | 3.58 | 958,792 | 4.14 |
| Unknown ages | 10,307 | .05 | 286 | .07 | 3,692 | .12 | 14,285 | .06 |
| Totals | 19,553,068 | 100.00 | 434,495 | 100.00 | 3,204,313 | 100.00 | 23,191,876 | 100.00 |
| 80 and over | 74,585 | 0.381 | 3,820 | 0.887 | 13,227 | 0.413 | 91,632 | 0.395 |
| 100 and over | 787 | 0.004 | 343 | 0.079 | 1,425 | 0.044 | 2,555 | 0.011 |

# TABLE XIV & XV.—*Nativities of white and free colored population.*

| States and Territories. | Born in the State. | | Born out of the State and in the United States. | | Born in foreign countries. | | Unknown. | | Aggregate. |
|---|---|---|---|---|---|---|---|---|---|
| Whites and colored. | Number. | Ratio. | Number. | Ratio. | Number. | Ratio. | Number. | Ratio. | |
| Alabama | 234,691 | 55.03 | 183,324 | 42.98 | 7,493 | 1.76 | 1,001 | .23 | 426,514 |
| Arkansas | 60,996 | 37.61 | 98,950 | 61.01 | 1,468 | 0.90 | 775 | .48 | 162,189 |
| California | 7,696 | 8.40 | 61,866 | 67.51 | 21,629 | 23.60 | 444 | .49 | 91,635 |
| Columbia, Dist. of | 18,375 | 48.43 | 14,620 | 38.54 | 4,913 | 12.95 | 33 | .08 | 37,941 |
| Connecticut | 284,978 | 78.49 | 39,117 | 10.77 | 38,374 | 10.57 | 630 | .17 | 363,099 |
| Delaware | 55,591 | 78.11 | 10,326 | 14.51 | 5,243 | 7.37 | 9 | .01 | 71,169 |
| Florida | 19,120 | 40.51 | 25,332 | 53.67 | 2,740 | 5.80 | 11 | .02 | 47,203 |
| Georgia | 396,298 | 75.98 | 118,268 | 22.67 | 6,452 | 1.24 | 554 | .11 | 521,572 |
| Illinois | 331,089 | 39.13 | 399,733 | 47.25 | 111,860 | 13.22 | 3,352 | .40 | 846,034 |
| Indiana | 520,583 | 53.28 | 398,695 | 40.80 | 55,537 | 5.68 | 2,339 | .24 | 977,154 |
| Iowa | 41,305 | 21.53 | 129,248 | 67.36 | 21,014 | 10.95 | 314 | .16 | 191,881 |
| Kentucky | 580,129 | 76.19 | 148,582 | 19.51 | 31,401 | 4.13 | 1,301 | .17 | 761,413 |
| Louisiana | 126,917 | 49.67 | 60,641 | 23.74 | 67,308 | 26.34 | 625 | .25 | 255,491 |
| Maine | 514,655 | 88.46 | 35,019 | 6.02 | 31,695 | 5.45 | 444 | .07 | 581,813 |
| Maryland | 326,040 | 78.01 | 40,610 | 9.72 | 51,011 | 12.20 | 282 | .07 | 417,943 |
| Massachusetts | 679,625 | 68.97 | 139,419 | 14.15 | 163,598 | 16.60 | 2,808 | .28 | 985,450 |
| Michigan | 137,637 | 34.84 | 201,586 | 51.02 | 54,593 | 13.82 | 1,255 | .32 | 395,071 |
| Mississippi | 135,501 | 45.82 | 154,946 | 52.40 | 4,782 | 1.61 | 489 | .17 | 295,718 |
| Missouri | 265,304 | 44.81 | 249,223 | 42.11 | 76,570 | 12.93 | 907 | .15 | 592,004 |
| New Hampshire | 258,132 | 81.31 | 44,925 | 14.15 | 14,257 | 4.49 | 142 | .05 | 317,456 |
| New Jersey | 361,691 | 77.70 | 43,711 | 9.39 | 59,804 | 12.85 | 303 | .06 | 465,509 |
| New York | 2,092,076 | 68.63 | 296,754 | 9.74 | 655,224 | 21.49 | 4,271 | .14 | 3,048,325 |
| North Carolina | 529,483 | 95.74 | 20,784 | 3.76 | 2,565 | 0.46 | 196 | .04 | 553,028 |
| Ohio | 1,203,490 | 61.56 | 529,208 | 27.07 | 218,099 | 11.15 | 4,253 | .22 | 1,955,050 |
| Pennsylvania | 1,787,310 | 79.15 | 165,966 | 7.35 | 303,105 | 13.42 | 1,779 | .08 | 2,258,160 |
| Rhode Island | 98,754 | 68.64 | 21,221 | 14.75 | 23,832 | 16.56 | 68 | .05 | 143,875 |
| South Carolina | 253,399 | 92.29 | 12,601 | 4.59 | 8,508 | 3.10 | 55 | .02 | 274,563 |
| Tennessee | 580,695 | 76.73 | 168,966 | 22.33 | 5,638 | 0.74 | 1,537 | .20 | 756,836 |
| Texas | 43,281 | 28.10 | 92,657 | 60.15 | 17,620 | 11.44 | 476 | .31 | 154,034 |
| Vermont | 228,489 | 72.91 | 50,894 | 16.24 | 33,688 | 10.75 | 331 | .10 | 313,402 |
| Virginia | 813,811 | 90.95 | 57,582 | 6.44 | 22,953 | 2.56 | 454 | .05 | 894,800 |
| Wisconsin | 54,312 | 17.82 | 139,166 | 45.66 | 110,471 | 36.25 | 807 | .27 | 304,756 |
| Territories: Minnesota | 1,572 | 26.04 | 2,486 | 41.17 | 2,977 | 32.74 | 3 | .05 | 6,038 |
| New Mexico | 58,404 | 94.93 | 761 | 1.24 | 1,151 | 3.49 | 209 | .34 | 61,525 |
| Oregon | 2,301 | 17.58 | 9,636 | 73.63 | 959 | 7.33 | 191 | 1.46 | 13,087 |
| Utah | 1,159 | 10.23 | 8,117 | 71.64 | 2,044 | 18.04 | 10 | .09 | 11,330 |

| States and Territories. Whites only, | Born in the State and now residing in the State. | Born in the State and now residing out of the State. | Total number born in the State, now residing in the State and in other States. | Excess received from other States. | Excess given to other States. | Number born in other States now residing in the State. | Total native population. | Native and foreign. | Total, including unknown. |
|---|---|---|---|---|---|---|---|---|---|
| Alabama | 237,542 | 83,388 | 320,930 | 99,102 | ........ | 182,490 | 420,032 | 427,670 | 428,779 |
| Arkansas | 63,206 | 10,916 | 74,122 | 86,223 | ........ | 97,139 | 160,345 | 161,973 | 162,797 |
| California | 6,602 | 96 | 6,698 | 62,912 | ........ | 63,008 | 69,610 | 91,968 | 92,597 |
| Columbia, Dist. of | 24,967 | 7,269 | 32,236 | 10,720 | ........ | 17,989 | 42,956 | 47,923 | 48,000 |
| Connecticut | 292,653 | 154,891 | 447,544 | ........ | 115,019 | 39,872 | 332,525 | 369,998 | 370,792 |
| Delaware | 72,351 | 31,965 | 104,316 | ........ | 20,348 | 11,617 | 83,968 | 89,179 | 89,242 |
| Florida | 20,563 | 4,734 | 25,297 | 20,023 | ........ | 24,757 | 45,320 | 48,077 | 48,135 |
| Georgia | 402,666 | 122,954 | 525,620 | ........ | 7,541 | 115,413 | 518,079 | 523,986 | 524,503 |
| Illinois | 343,618 | 45,889 | 389,507 | 347,424 | ........ | 393,313 | 736,931 | 847,524 | 851,470 |
| Indiana | 541,079 | 92,038 | 633,117 | 298,275 | ........ | 390,313 | 931,392 | 985,818 | 988,416 |
| Iowa | 50,380 | 6,358 | 56,738 | 113,882 | ........ | 120,240 | 170,620 | 191,852 | 192,214 |
| Kentucky | 601,764 | 257,643 | 859,407 | ........ | 118,526 | 139,117 | 740,881 | 770,070 | 771,424 |
| Louisiana | 145,474 | 14,779 | 160,253 | 45,668 | ........ | 60,447 | 205,921 | 272,334 | 272,953 |
| Maine | 517,117 | 67,193 | 584,310 | ........ | 33,181 | 34,012 | 551,129 | 582,585 | 583,169 |
| Maryland | 400,594 | 127,799 | 528,393 | ........ | 89,477 | 38,322 | 428,916 | 492,204 | 492,666 |
| Massachusetts | 695,236 | 199,582 | 894,818 | ........ | 64,752 | 134,830 | 830,066 | 990,975 | 994,514 |
| Michigan | 140,648 | 12,409 | 153,057 | 188,534 | ........ | 200,943 | 341,591 | 396,443 | 397,654 |
| Mississippi | 140,885 | 31,588 | 172,473 | 118,641 | ........ | 150,229 | 291,114 | 296,072 | 296,648 |
| Missouri | 277,604 | 37,824 | 315,428 | 205,398 | ........ | 243,222 | 520,826 | 593,300 | 594,622 |
| New Hampshire | 261,591 | 109,878 | 371,469 | ........ | 67,242 | 42,636 | 304,227 | 317,798 | 317,976 |
| New Jersey | 385,429 | 133,381 | 518,810 | ........ | 88,369 | 45,012 | 430,441 | 488,805 | 489,319 |
| New York | 2,151,196 | 547,218 | 2,698,414 | ........ | 259,118 | 288,100 | 2,439,296 | 3,091,097 | 3,097,394 |
| North Carolina | 556,248 | 283,077 | 839,325 | ........ | 261,575 | 21,502 | 577,750 | 580,274 | 580,491 |
| Ohio | 1,219,432 | 295,453 | 1,514,885 | 242,671 | ........ | 538,124 | 1,757,556 | 1,976,068 | 1,980,329 |
| Pennsylvania | 1,844,672 | 422,055 | 2,266,727 | ........ | 252,108 | 169,947 | 2,014,619 | 2,309,490 | 2,311,786 |
| Rhode Island | 102,641 | 43,300 | 145,941 | ........ | 21,642 | 21,658 | 124,299 | 147,410 | 147,545 |
| South Carolina | 262,160 | 186,479 | 448,639 | ........ | 173,826 | 12,653 | 274,813 | 283,475 | 283,523 |
| Tennessee | 585,084 | 241,606 | 826,690 | ........ | 71,035 | 170,571 | 755,655 | 761,395 | 763,258 |
| Texas | 49,160 | 2,481 | 51,641 | 85,412 | ........ | 87,893 | 137,053 | 153,827 | 154,431 |
| Vermont | 232,086 | 145,655 | 377,741 | ........ | 96,775 | 48,880 | 280,966 | 313,797 | 314,120 |
| Virginia | 872,923 | 388,059 | 1,260,982 | ........ | 334,828 | 53,231 | 926,154 | 948,548 | 949,133 |
| Wisconsin | 63,015 | 3,775 | 66,790 | 131,122 | ........ | 134,897 | 197,912 | 304,607 | 305,391 |
| Territories: Minnesota | 1,334 | 949 | 65,260 | 19,355 | ...... | 2,673 | 4,007 | 6,055 | 6,077 |
| N. Mexico | 58,421 | | | | | 840 | 59,261 | 61,324 | 61,547 |
| Oregon | 3,175 | | | | | 8,817 | 11,992 | 13,151 | 13,294 |
| Utah | 1,381 | | | | | 7,974 | 9,355 | 11,345 | 11,354 |

## TABLE XVI.—*Ratio to Total Native Population of the United States.*

| Sections. | Living in the State where born. | Per cent. | Living in the Eastern Section. | Per cent. | Living in the Middle. | Per cent. | Living in the Southern. | Per cent. | Living in the Southwest'n. | Per cent. | Living in the Northwest'rn and Territories. | Per cent. |
|---|---|---|---|---|---|---|---|---|---|---|---|---|
| Eastern ....... | 2,101,824 | 10.51 | 2,367,932 | 11.85 | 241,596 | 1.21 | 6,845 | .08 | 9,376 | .05 | 196,074 | .98 |
| Middle ........ | 4,879,209 | 24.41 | 48,781 | .24 | 5,155,698 | 25.79 | 40,857 | .20 | 27,146 | .13 | 876,414 | 4.39 |
| Southern ...... | 2,114,560 | 10.58 | 2,954 | .02 | 31,101 | .16 | 2,266,088 | 11.34 | 425,335 | 2.13 | 374,385 | 1.87 |
| Southwestern .. | 1,221,351 | 6.11 | 718 | ..... | 2,542 | .01 | 19,086 | .10 | 1,441,220 | 7.21 | 142,543 | .71 |
| Northwes'n and Territories... | 3,308,453 | 16.55 | 2,827 | .01 | 19,259 | .10 | 9,240 | .05 | 67,043 | .34 | 3,962,518 | 19.83 |

## TABLE XVII.—*Free Persons born in to those born out of each Section of the United States.*

| Sections. | Born and residing in | Ratio pr. cent. | Born in and residing out of | Ratio pr. cent. | Total born in |
|---|---|---|---|---|---|
| Eastern .................................. | 2,367,932 | 83.91 | 453,891 | 16.09 | 2,821,823 |
| Middle .................................. | 5,155,698 | 83.85 | 993,198 | 16.15 | 6,148,896 |
| Southern .................................. | 2,266,088 | 73.10 | 833,775 | 26.90 | 3,099,863 |
| Southwestern .................................. | 1,441,220 | 89.73 | 164,889 | 10.27 | 1,606,109 |
| Northwestern and Territories.................. | 3,962,518 | 97.58 | 98,369 | 2.42 | 4,060,887 |

## TABLE XVIII.—*Proportion of native to foreign born in different sections of the United States—white and free colored.*

| Sections. | Total free population—native, includ'g unknown. | Total foreign population. | Proportion of foreign to native, per ct. |
|---|---|---|---|
| Eastern.................................. | 2,421,867 | 306,249 | 12.65 |
| Middle.................................. | 5,447,733 | 1,080,674 | 19.84 |
| Southern.................................. | 2,342,255 | 43,530 | 1.86 |
| Southwestern .................................. | 1,973,581 | 105,335 | 5.34 |
| Northwestern and territories .................. | 5,557,529 | 708,860 | 12.75 |
| Total.................................. | 17,742,915 | 2,244,648 | 12.65 |

## TABLE XIX.—*Aggregate population of the United States calculated for each year from* 1790 *to* 1860.

| Years. | Aggregate. | Years. | Aggregate. | Years. | Aggregate. | Years. | Aggregate. | Years. | Aggregate. | Years. | Aggregate. |
|---|---|---|---|---|---|---|---|---|---|---|---|
| 1790.. | 3,929,827 | 1802 | 5,646,176 | 1814 | 8,117,710 | 1826 | 11,462,088 | 1838 | 16,131,087 | 1850 | 23,191,876 |
| 1791.. | 4,049,600 | 1803 | 5,824,398 | 1815 | 8,353,338 | 1827 | 11,708,013 | 1839 | 16,593,630 | 1851 | 23,873,717 |
| 1792.. | 4,173,024 | 1804 | 6,008,246 | 1816 | 8,595,806 | 1828 | 12,143,783 | 1840 | 17,069,453 | 1852 | 24,575,604 |
| 1793.. | 4,300,210 | 1805 | 6,197,897 | 1817 | 8,845,312 | 1829 | 12,499,687 | 1841 | 17,600,752 | 1853 | 25,298,126 |
| 1794.. | 4,431,272 | 1806 | 6,393,534 | 1818 | 9,102,060 | 1830 | 12,866,020 | 1842 | 18,148,589 | 1854 | 26,041,890 |
| 1795.. | 4,566,329 | 1807 | 6,595,346 | 1819 | 9,366,261 | 1831 | 13,234,931 | 1843 | 18,713,479 | 1855 | 26,807,521 |
| 1796.. | 4,705,504 | 1808 | 6,803,528 | 1820 | 9,638,131 | 1832 | 13,614,420 | 1844 | 19,295,971 | 1856 | 27,595,662 |
| 1797.. | 4,848,919 | 1809 | 7,018,282 | 1821 | 9,920,600 | 1833 | 14,004,789 | 1845 | 19,896,574 | 1857 | 28,406,974 |
| 1798.. | 4,996,705 | 1810 | 7,239,814 | 1822 | 10,211,358 | 1834 | 14,406,350 | 1846 | 20,515,871 | 1858 | 29,242,139 |
| 1799.. | 5,148,994 | 1811 | 7,449,960 | 1823 | 10,510,618 | 1835 | 14,819,425 | 1847 | 21,154,444 | 1859 | 30,101,857 |
| 1800.. | 5,305,925 | 1812 | 7,666,206 | 1824 | 10,818,659 | 1836 | 15,244,344 | 1848 | 21,812,893 | 1860 | 30,986,851 |
| 1801.. | 5,473,407 | 1813 | 7,888,729 | 1825 | 11,135,727 | 1837 | 15,681,447 | 1849 | 22,491,305 | | |

TABLE XX.—*Place of Birth of the White and Free Colored Population of the United States, 1850.*

| States and Territories. | Alabama. | Arkansas. | California. | Columbia, District of. | Connecticut. | Delaware. | Florida. | Georgia. | Illinois. | Indiana. | Iowa. | Kentucky. | Louisiana. | Maine. | Maryland. | Massachusetts | Michigan. | Mississippi. | Missouri. | N. Hampshire. | New Jersey. |
|---|---|---|---|---|---|---|---|---|---|---|---|---|---|---|---|---|---|---|---|---|---|
| Alabama | 237,542 | 91 | ..... | 66 | 612 | 73 | 1,060 | 58,997 | 114 | 93 | 7 | 2,694 | 628 | 215 | 757 | 654 | 3 | 2,852 | 158 | 151 | 271 |
| Arkansas | 11,250 | 63,206 | 6 | 49 | 121 | 51 | 38 | 6,367 | 3,276 | 2,128 | 106 | 7,428 | 1,096 | 80 | 326 | 174 | 17 | 4,463 | 5,328 | 49 | 117 |
| California | 631 | 350 | 6,602 | 86 | 1,317 | 305 | 54 | 876 | 2,722 | 2,077 | 341 | 4,690 | 929 | 2,700 | 1,164 | 4,760 | 284 | 772 | 5,890 | 904 | 1,022 |
| Columbia, Dis. of | 45 | 4 | ..... | 24,967 | 135 | 99 | 26 | 67 | 24 | 29 | 1 | 90 | 58 | 87 | 9,245 | 331 | 28 | 55 | 28 | 84 | 163 |
| Connecticut | 74 | ..... | ..... | 50 | 292,653 | 58 | 46 | 217 | 80 | 47 | 18 | 41 | 64 | 670 | 265 | 11,366 | 89 | 23 | 28 | 795 | 1,174 |
| Delaware | 4 | ..... | ..... | 28 | 50 | 72,351 | 4 | 14 | 5 | 19 | ..... | 16 | 4 | 24 | 4,360 | 113 | 12 | 6 | 8 | 31 | 1,186 |
| Florida | 2,340 | 5 | ..... | 33 | 179 | 9 | 20,563 | 11,316 | 8 | 14 | ..... | 87 | 146 | 140 | 194 | 235 | 7 | 92 | 7 | 61 | 83 |
| Georgia | 3,154 | 25 | ..... | 72 | 712 | 117 | 1,103 | 402,666 | 41 | 50 | 1 | 458 | 42 | 178 | 703 | 594 | 3 | 184 | 60 | 122 | 331 |
| Illinois | 1,335 | 727 | 3 | 226 | 6,899 | 1,397 | 23 | 1,341 | 343,618 | 30,953 | 1,511 | 49,588 | 480 | 3,693 | 6,898 | 9,230 | 2,158 | 490 | 7,228 | 4,288 | 6,848 |
| Indiana | 395 | 151 | ..... | 227 | 2,485 | 2,737 | 21 | 761 | 4,173 | 541,079 | 407 | 68,651 | 321 | 976 | 10,177 | 2,678 | 1,817 | 287 | 1,006 | 886 | 7,837 |
| Iowa | 180 | 163 | 3 | 70 | 1,090 | 439 | 51 | 119 | 7,247 | 19,925 | 50,380 | 8,994 | 133 | 713 | 1,888 | 1,251 | 521 | 138 | 3,807 | 580 | 1,199 |
| Kentucky | 792 | 271 | ..... | 176 | 448 | 507 | 30 | 892 | 1,649 | 5,898 | 59 | 601,764 | 671 | 227 | 6,470 | 665 | 59 | 657 | 1,467 | 225 | 1,249 |
| Louisiana | 7,346 | 803 | 1 | 156 | 469 | 117 | 372 | 5,917 | 401 | 414 | 28 | 2,968 | 145,474 | 816 | 1,440 | 1,620 | 68 | 10,913 | 909 | 247 | 498 |
| Maine | 6 | 6 | 2 | 28 | 460 | 36 | 24 | 24 | 38 | 5 | 1 | 14 | 21 | 517,117 | 113 | 16,535 | 19 | 16 | 11 | 13,509 | 134 |
| Maryland | 51 | 14 | 1 | 1,940 | 484 | 4,373 | 37 | 74 | 54 | 65 | 5 | 131 | 181 | 456 | 400,594 | 1,421 | 16 | 143 | 86 | 260 | 1,321 |
| Massachusetts | 71 | 10 | 7 | 196 | 15,602 | 90 | 32 | 237 | 165 | 60 | 12 | 75 | 179 | 29,507 | 744 | 695,236 | 122 | 34 | 58 | 39,592 | 778 |
| Michigan | 19 | 25 | 3 | 45 | 6,751 | 368 | 12 | 68 | 496 | 2,003 | 59 | 402 | 30 | 1,117 | 537 | 8,167 | 140,648 | 34 | 92 | 2,744 | 5,572 |
| Mississippi | 34,047 | 456 | 1 | 73 | 242 | 67 | 629 | 17,506 | 311 | 413 | 7 | 3,948 | 2,557 | 139 | 791 | 339 | 10 | 140,885 | 303 | 100 | 221 |
| Missouri | 2,067 | 2,120 | 4 | 238 | 742 | 518 | 67 | 1,254 | 10,917 | 12,752 | 1,366 | 69,694 | 746 | 311 | 4,253 | 1,103 | 295 | 638 | 277,604 | 304 | 885 |
| New Hampshire | 13 | 8 | 1 | 14 | 1,105 | 10 | 1 | 16 | 31 | 20 | 4 | 11 | 9 | 9,635 | 34 | 18,495 | 48 | 9 | 12 | 261,591 | 49 |
| New Jersey | 36 | 2 | 3 | 82 | 2,105 | 1,384 | 17 | 87 | 61 | 61 | 7 | 64 | 83 | 287 | 1,400 | 1,494 | 66 | 43 | 28 | 301 | 385,429 |
| New York | 184 | 20 | 7 | 538 | 66,101 | 899 | 135 | 510 | 605 | 415 | 70 | 369 | 563 | 4,509 | 3,953 | 55,773 | 1,921 | 164 | 173 | 14,519 | 35,319 |
| North Carolina | 131 | 1 | ..... | 28 | 272 | 96 | 54 | 844 | 23 | 67 | 3 | 141 | 14 | 68 | 635 | 261 | 2 | 57 | 33 | 26 | 174 |
| Ohio | 209 | 141 | ..... | 598 | 22,855 | 4,715 | 17 | 447 | 1,415 | 7,377 | 378 | 13,829 | 648 | 3,314 | 36,698 | 18,763 | 2,238 | 422 | 656 | 4,821 | 23,533 |
| Pennsylvania | 87 | 10 | 3 | 767 | 9,266 | 12,552 | 21 | 176 | 333 | 399 | 70 | 497 | 187 | 1,157 | 21,013 | 7,330 | 224 | 101 | 220 | 1,775 | 29,117 |
| Rhode Island | 13 | ..... | ..... | 64 | 3,976 | 50 | 22 | 68 | 15 | 11 | 9 | 19 | 21 | 768 | 365 | 11,888 | 22 | 8 | 13 | 716 | 193 |
| South Carolina | 225 | 9 | 1 | 30 | 228 | 14 | 55 | 1,504 | 6 | 11 | ..... | 73 | 30 | 68 | 320 | 407 | 2 | 60 | 3 | 39 | 182 |
| Tennessee | 6,398 | 496 | ..... | 101 | 261 | 95 | 369 | 4,863 | 872 | 769 | 30 | 12,609 | 261 | 97 | 1,554 | 331 | 7 | 2,137 | 920 | 64 | 248 |
| Texas | 12,040 | 4,693 | ..... | 35 | 369 | 61 | 365 | 7,639 | 2,855 | 1,799 | 109 | 5,478 | 4,472 | 226 | 521 | 414 | 125 | 6,545 | 5,139 | 97 | 205 |
| Vermont | 11 | 2 | ..... | 5 | 4,551 | 1 | 6 | 18 | 34 | 15 | 5 | 7 | 12 | 835 | 23 | 15,059 | 86 | 5 | 10 | 19,609 | 171 |
| Virginia | 92 | 150 | 4 | 1,184 | 556 | 542 | 26 | 193 | 126 | 288 | 37 | 2,029 | 93 | 271 | 10,328 | 1,193 | 33 | 78 | 223 | 239 | 11,447 |
| Wisconsin | 49 | 67 | ..... | 33 | 4,125 | 141 | 4 | 495 | 5,292 | 2,773 | 445 | 1,429 | 78 | 3,252 | 462 | 6,285 | 1,909 | 35 | 1,012 | 2,520 | 1,566 |
| Territories. Minnesota | 6 | 11 | 1 | 3 | 48 | 3 | ..... | 4 | 168 | 35 | 81 | 71 | 4 | 365 | 31 | 92 | 41 | ........ | 90 | 47 | 115 |
| Territories. N. Mexico | 5 | 17 | 6 | 12 | 10 | 6 | 5 | 9 | 24 | 11 | 3 | 62 | 4 | 12 | 37 | 24 | 8 | ........ | 93 | 6 | 9 |
| Territories. Oregon | 20 | 61 | 25 | 15 | 72 | 18 | 4 | 22 | 1,023 | 739 | 452 | 730 | 6 | 129 | 73 | 187 | 37 | 8 | 2,206 | 44 | 69 |
| Territories. Utah | 62 | 7 | 14 | 1 | 193 | 17 | 4 | 12 | 1,285 | 303 | 726 | 256 | 8 | 151 | 27 | 350 | 121 | 119 | 519 | 123 | 98 |
| Total | 320,930 | 74,122 | 6,698 | 32,236 | 447,544 | 104,316 | 25,297 | 525,620 | 389,507 | 633,117 | 56,738 | 859,407 | 160,253 | 584,310 | 528,393 | 894,818 | 153,057 | 172,473 | 315,428 | 371,469 | 518,810 |

## TABLE XX—Continued.

| States and Territories. | New York. | North Carolina. | Ohio. | Pennsylvania. | Rhode Island. | South Carolina. | Tennessee. | Texas. | Vermont. | Virginia. | Wisconsin. | Territories. | Ireland. | Total Great Britain and Ireland. | Prussia. | Rest of Germany. | Austria. | Holland. | Belgium. | Total native. | Total foreign. | Unknown. | Ratio per ct. of foreign born to total white and free colored population. |
|---|---|---|---|---|---|---|---|---|---|---|---|---|---|---|---|---|---|---|---|---|---|---|---|
| Alabama | 1,443 | 28,521 | 276 | 876 | 74 | 48,663 | 22,541 | 55 | 155 | 10,387 | 3 | .... | 3,639 | 5,231 | 45 | 1,068 | 33 | 1 | 4 | 420,032 | 7,638 | 1,109 | 1.78 |
| Arkansas | 537 | 8,772 | 1,051 | 702 | 36 | 4,587 | 33,807 | 336 | 82 | 4,737 | 13 | 9 | 514 | 792 | 24 | 516 | .... | 2 | 2 | 160,345 | 1,628 | 824 | 1.00 |
| California | 10,160 | 1,027 | 5,500 | 4,506 | 861 | 519 | 3,145 | 250 | 1,194 | 3,407 | 248 | 317 | 2,452 | 6,567 | 158 | 2,926 | 87 | 63 | 12 | 69,610 | 22,358 | 629 | 24.15 |
| Columbia, Dist. of | 817 | 100 | 123 | 1,164 | 23 | 100 | 58 | 7 | 48 | 4,950 | 2 | 3 | 2,373 | 3,217 | 11 | 1,404 | 3 | 4 | 14 | 42,956 | 4,967 | 77 | 10.35 |
| Connecticut | 14,416 | 95 | 400 | 1,055 | 6,890 | 116 | 13 | 20 | 1,508 | 228 | 23 | 3 | 26,689 | 33,807 | 42 | 1,671 | 20 | 19 | 2 | 332,525 | 37,473 | 794 | 10.11 |
| Delaware | 218 | 18 | 54 | 5,067 | 204 | 13 | 4 | 1 | 12 | 139 | 1 | 2 | 3,513 | 4,637 | 28 | 343 | .... | 5 | 1 | 83,968 | 5,211 | 63 | 5.84 |
| Florida | 614 | 3,537 | 53 | 240 | 66 | 4,470 | 112 | 8 | 55 | 643 | 3 | .... | 878 | 1,371 | 17 | 307 | 8 | 8 | 4 | 45,320 | 2,757 | 58 | 5.73 |
| Georgia | 1,203 | 37,522 | 46 | 642 | 138 | 52,154 | 8,211 | 28 | 186 | 7,331 | 2 | .... | 3,202 | 4,261 | 25 | 947 | 13 | 11 | 41 | 518,079 | 5,907 | 517 | 1.13 |
| Illinois | 67,180 | 13,851 | 64,219 | 37,979 | 1,051 | 4,162 | 32,303 | 63 | 11,381 | 24,697 | 1,095 | 16 | 27,786 | 51,647 | 286 | 38,160 | 65 | 220 | 33 | 736,931 | 110,593 | 3,946 | 12.99 |
| Indiana | 24,310 | 33,175 | 120,193 | 44,245 | 438 | 4,069 | 12,734 | 44 | 3,183 | 41,819 | 99 | 11 | 12,787 | 19,847 | 740 | 28,584 | 17 | 43 | 86 | 931,392 | 54,426 | 2,598 | 5.51 |
| Iowa | 8,134 | 2,589 | 30,713 | 14,744 | 256 | 676 | 4,274 | 10 | 1,645 | 7,861 | 692 | 135 | 4,885 | 9,734 | 88 | 7,152 | 13 | 1,108 | 4 | 170,620 | 21,232 | 362 | 11.05 |
| Kentucky | 2,881 | 14,279 | 9,985 | 7,491 | 226 | 3,164 | 23,623 | 71 | 277 | 54,694 | 11 | 3 | 9,466 | 13,125 | 198 | 13,607 | 12 | 38 | 27 | 740,881 | 29,189 | 1,354 | 3.78 |
| Louisiana | 5,510 | 2,923 | 1,473 | 2,493 | 239 | 4,583 | 3,352 | 864 | 283 | 3,216 | 7 | 1 | 24,266 | 29,060 | 380 | 17,507 | 156 | 112 | 115 | 205,921 | 66,413 | 619 | 24.33 |
| Maine | 973 | 27 | 68 | 201 | 410 | 31 | 6 | 9 | 1,177 | 94 | 10 | 4 | 13,871 | 16,412 | 27 | 290 | 3 | 12 | 2 | 551,129 | 31,456 | 584 | 5.39 |
| Maryland | 2,646 | 225 | 535 | 16,076 | 209 | 158 | 39 | 24 | 262 | 7,030 | 4 | 1 | 19,557 | 24,377 | 188 | 26,936 | 16 | 106 | 5 | 438,916 | 53,288 | 462 | 10.82 |
| Massachusetts | 14,483 | 196 | 593 | 1,831 | 11,414 | 224 | 25 | 10 | 17,646 | 796 | 32 | 9 | 115,917 | 137,285 | 98 | 4,319 | 10 | 138 | 36 | 830,066 | 160,909 | 3,539 | 16.18 |
| Michigan | 133,756 | 312 | 14,677 | 9,452 | 1,031 | 81 | 101 | 4 | 11,113 | 1,504 | 332 | 36 | 13,430 | 26,538 | 190 | 10,070 | 21 | 2,542 | 112 | 341,591 | 54,852 | 1,211 | 13.79 |
| Mississippi | 952 | 21,487 | 594 | 921 | 62 | 27,908 | 27,439 | 139 | 141 | 8,357 | 4 | 5 | 1,928 | 2,848 | 71 | 1,064 | 16 | 8 | 3 | 291,114 | 4,958 | 576 | 1.67 |
| Missouri | 5,040 | 17,009 | 12,737 | 8,291 | 124 | 2,919 | 44,970 | 248 | 630 | 40,777 | 123 | 80 | 14,734 | 21,338 | 697 | 44,352 | 71 | 189 | 58 | 520,846 | 72,474 | 1,322 | 12.19 |
| New Hampshire | 1,171 | 10 | 66 | 148 | 364 | 21 | 3 | 2 | 11,266 | 48 | 10 | 2 | 8,811 | 10,758 | 2 | 147 | 1 | 1 | .... | 304,227 | 13,571 | 178 | 4.27 |
| New Jersey | 20,561 | 98 | 372 | 15,014 | 264 | 141 | 21 | 6 | 280 | 628 | 15 | 1 | 31,092 | 44,898 | 57 | 10,686 | 20 | 357 | 43 | 430,441 | 58,364 | 514 | 11.93 |
| New York | 2,151,196 | 673 | 3,743 | 26,352 | 13,129 | 935 | 116 | 46 | 52,599 | 3,347 | 360 | 53 | 343,111 | 458,931 | 2,211 | 118,398 | 168 | 2,917 | 401 | 2,439,296 | 651,801 | 6,297 | 21.04 |
| North Carolina | 468 | 556,248 | 48 | 665 | 59 | 4,420 | 2,037 | 6 | 27 | 10,838 | 4 | .... | 567 | 1,980 | 19 | 344 | 2 | 4 | 1 | 577,750 | 2,524 | 217 | .43 |
| Ohio | 83,979 | 4,807 | 1,219,432 | 200,634 | 1,959 | 1,468 | 1,873 | 29 | 14,320 | 85,762 | 196 | 24 | 51,562 | 88,303 | 765 | 111,257 | 29 | 348 | 103 | 1,757,556 | 218,512 | 4,261 | 11.03 |
| Pennsylvania | 58,835 | 409 | 7,729 | 1,844,672 | 1,946 | 559 | 158 | 17 | 4,532 | 10,410 | 45 | 2 | 151,723 | 205,983 | 413 | 78,592 | 49 | 257 | 126 | 2,014,619 | 294,871 | 2,296 | 12.75 |
| Rhode Island | 2,055 | 76 | 93 | 427 | 102,641 | 57 | 4 | 4 | 459 | 191 | 6 | 40 | 15,944 | 21,434 | 5 | 230 | 1 | 12 | 2 | 124,299 | 23,111 | 135 | 15.66 |
| South Carolina | 884 | 6,173 | 23 | 362 | 97 | 262,160 | 188 | 1 | 37 | 1,621 | .... | .... | 4,051 | 5,633 | 44 | 2,180 | 11 | 9 | .... | 274,813 | 8,662 | 48 | 3.06 |
| Tennessee | 1,019 | 72,027 | 742 | 2,146 | 38 | 15,197 | 585,084 | 100 | 179 | 46,631 | 8 | 2 | 2,640 | 3,690 | 32 | 1,168 | 10 | 57 | 4 | 755,655 | 5,740 | 1,863 | .75 |
| Texas | 1,589 | 5,155 | 947 | 1,005 | 56 | 4,482 | 17,692 | 49,160 | 144 | 3,580 | 42 | 14 | 1,403 | 2,683 | 75 | 8,191 | 11 | 14 | 8 | 137,053 | 16,774 | 604 | 10.86 |
| Vermont | 7,218 | 7 | 165 | 158 | 801 | 5 | 6 | 1 | 232,086 | 21 | 32 | 1 | 15,377 | 18,025 | 6 | 218 | .... | 2 | .... | 280,966 | 32,831 | 323 | 10.45 |
| Virginia | 2,934 | 7,343 | 5,206 | 6,323 | 100 | 381 | 1,560 | 7 | 231 | 872,923 | 11 | 3 | 11,643 | 15,761 | 36 | 5,511 | 15 | 65 | 7 | 926,154 | 22,394 | 585 | 2.36 |
| Wisconsin | 68,595 | 322 | 11,402 | 9,571 | 690 | 107 | 449 | 4 | 10,157 | 1,611 | 63,015 | 26 | 21,043 | 47,841 | 3,545 | 34,519 | 61 | 1,157 | 45 | 197,912 | 106,695 | 784 | 34.94 |
| Territ's. Minnesota | 488 | 6 | 241 | 227 | 3 | 4 | 21 | ..... | 100 | 59 | 301 | *7 | 271 | 396 | 5 | 141 | 1 | 16 | 1 | 4,007 | 2,048 | 22 | 33.70 |
| Territ's. New Mexico | 101 | 13 | 34 | 97 | 1 | 18 | 25 | 46 | 8 | 77 | 1 | *56 | 292 | 365 | 14 | 215 | .... | 2 | .... | 59,261 | 2,063 | 223 | 8.35 |
| Territ's. Oregon | 618 | 201 | 653 | 337 | 20 | 34 | 402 | 15 | 111 | 469 | 10 | *7 | 196 | 518 | 1 | 155 | ... | 1 | 11 | 11,992 | 1,159 | 143 | 8.72 |
| Territ's. Utah | 1,430 | 92 | 694 | 553 | 21 | 53 | 294 | 6 | 232 | 99 | 30 | *76 | 106 | 1,519 | 6 | 50 | 3 | ..... | .... | 9,355 | 1,990 | 9 | 17.53 |

* These are the persons born out of the particular Territory in which they live, but in the other Territories. There were also in Minnesota 1,334 born in that Territory; in New Mexico 58,421 born in New Mexico; in Oregon 3,175 born in Oregon; and in Utah 1,381 born in Utah.

TABLE XXI.—*Ratio of increase of population in the great geographical divisions.*

| Census periods. | N. Engl'nd States. | Middle States. | Southern States. | Southwestern States. | Northwestern States. | California & Terr'ies. | Aggregate. |
|---|---|---|---|---|---|---|---|
| 1790—Population | 1,009,823 | 1,337,456 | 1,473,680 | 35,791 | 73,077 | .......... | 3,929,827 |
| 1800—Population | 1,233,315 | 1,820,894 | 1,865,995 | 114,452 | 271,195 | .......... | 5,805,925 |
| " Per cent. of increase | 22.13 | 36.15 | 26.62 | 219.78 | 271.11 | .......... | 35.02 |
| 1810—Population | 1,471,891 | 2,491,938 | 2,197,670 | 378,635 | 699,680 | .......... | 7,239,814 |
| " Per cent. of increase | 19.34 | 36.85 | 17.77 | 230.82 | 158.00 | .......... | 36.45 |
| 1820—Population | 1,659,808 | 3,212,983 | 2,547,936 | 793,842 | 1,423,622 | .......... | 9,638,131 |
| " Per cent. of increase | 12.77 | 28.94 | 15.94 | 109.66 | 103.47 | .......... | 33.13 |
| 1830—Population | 1,954,717 | 4,151,286 | 3,082,130 | 1,374,179 | 2,298,390 | .......... | 12,866,020 |
| " Per cent. of increase | 17.77 | 29.20 | 20.96 | 73.10 | 61.45 | .......... | 33.49 |
| 1840—Population | 2,234,822 | 5,118,076 | 3,333,483 | 2,245,602 | 4,131,370 | .......... | 17,069,453 |
| " Per cent. of increase | 14.33 | 23.29 | 8.16 | 63.41 | 79.75 | .......... | 32.67 |
| 1850—Population | 2,728,116 | 6,624,988 | 3,952,837 | 3,321,117 | 6,379,923 | 184,895 | 23,191,876 |
| " Per cent. of increase | 22.07 | 29.44 | 18.58 | 47.89 | 54.43 | .......... | 35.87 |

TABLE XXII.—*Employments of the Free Male Population of the United States over fifteen years of age—1850.*

| States and Territories. | Com'ce, trade, man'factures, mech'nic arts, and mining. | Agriculture. | Labor not agricultural. | Army. | Sea and river navigation. | Law, medicine, and divinity. | Other pursuits requiring education. | Gov'ment civil service. | Domestic servants. | Other occupations. | Total. |
|---|---|---|---|---|---|---|---|---|---|---|---|
| Alabama | 16,630 | 68,635 | 7,683 | ...... | 807 | 2,610 | 3,638 | 325 | 42 | 97 | 100,467 |
| Arkansas | 4,296 | 28,942 | 5,684 | 33 | 106 | 911 | 676 | 110 | ...... | 27 | 40,785 |
| California | 69,007 | 2,059 | 3,771 | 140 | 617 | 876 | 198 | 130 | 710 | 123 | 77,631 |
| Columbia, Dist. of. | 6,128 | 421 | 2,535 | 91 | 186 | 330 | 436 | 559 | 507 | 16 | 11,209 |
| Connecticut | 38,653 | 31,881 | 16,813 | ...... | 4,801 | 1,614 | 2,162 | 189 | 220 | 677 | 97,010 |
| Delaware | 5,633 | 7,884 | 6,663 | ...... | 743 | 251 | 581 | 124 | 69 | 113 | 22,061 |
| Florida | 2,380 | 5,977 | 2,666 | 423 | 708 | 357 | 302 | 268 | 12 | 42 | 13,135 |
| Georgia | 20,715 | 83,362 | 11,505 | 18 | 282 | 2,815 | 3,942 | 416 | 15 | 178 | 123,248 |
| Illinois | 36,232 | 141,099 | 29,788 | ...... | 1,644 | 3,307 | 2,071 | 701 | 376 | 151 | 215,359 |
| Indiana | 45,318 | 163,229 | 29,854 | ...... | 1,725 | 4,229 | 3,031 | 677 | 184 | 449 | 248,696 |
| Iowa | 9,255 | 32,779 | 5,392 | 71 | 163 | 1,077 | 425 | 103 | 10 | 40 | 49,315 |
| Kentucky | 36,598 | 115,017 | 28,413 | 204 | 1,027 | 3,811 | 4,420 | 902 | 212 | 471 | 191,075 |
| Louisiana | 32,879 | 18,659 | 15,264 | 45 | 4,263 | 1,827 | 2,444 | 811 | 508 | 488 | 77,168 |
| Maine | 38,247 | 77,082 | 26,833 | 114 | 15,649 | 2,212 | 1,727 | 419 | 232 | 196 | 162,711 |
| Maryland | 47,616 | 28,588 | 32,102 | 67 | 9,746 | 2,059 | 2,442 | 963 | 1,021 | 278 | 124,876 |
| Massachusetts | 146,002 | 55,699 | 57,942 | 73 | 19,598 | 4,702 | 5,371 | 1,566 | 1,375 | 2,972 | 295,300 |
| Michigan | 22,375 | 65,865 | 15,662 | 143 | 1,220 | 2,007 | 1,092 | 337 | 220 | 167 | 108,978 |
| Mississippi | 12,053 | 50,284 | 6,067 | ...... | 292 | 2,339 | 3,380 | 377 | 69 | 231 | 75,082 |
| Missouri | 30,098 | 65,511 | 20,326 | 305 | 2,471 | 2,893 | 3,147 | 767 | 1,458 | 1,149 | 128,175 |
| New Hampshire | 27,905 | 47,440 | 14,953 | 38 | 778 | 1,642 | 1,425 | 305 | 47 | 81 | 94,564 |
| New Jersey | 46,544 | 32,834 | 38,383 | ...... | 4,351 | 1,731 | 2,457 | 373 | 404 | 1,663 | 128,740 |
| New York | 312,697 | 313,980 | 196,613 | 1,462 | 23,243 | 14,258 | 11,104 | 4,985 | 6,324 | 3,628 | 888,294 |
| North Carolina | 20,613 | 81,982 | 28,560 | ...... | 1,659 | 2,263 | 3,447 | 570 | 46 | 247 | 139,387 |
| Ohio | 142,687 | 270,362 | 92,766 | ...... | 4,109 | 9,001 | 8,263 | 1,218 | 1,167 | 1,219 | 530,792 |
| Pennsylvania | 266,927 | 207,495 | 163,628 | 101 | 9,064 | 9,954 | 10,830 | 3,719 | 4,431 | 4,495 | 680,644 |
| Rhode Island | 21,004 | 8,482 | 9,296 | ...... | 2,033 | 556 | 881 | 176 | 774 | 269 | 43,471 |
| South Carolina | 13,205 | 41,302 | 8,151 | ...... | 346 | 1,829 | 3,161 | 372 | 149 | 84 | 68,549 |
| Tennessee | 23,432 | 118,979 | 16,559 | ...... | 258 | 3,363 | 3,589 | 705 | 10 | 345 | 168,240 |
| Texas | 7,327 | 25,299 | 6,194 | 584 | 321 | 1,368 | 996 | 677 | ...... | 90 | 42,856 |
| Vermont | 17,063 | 48,327 | 22,997 | ...... | 159 | 1,827 | 1,563 | 129 | 34 | 127 | 92,226 |
| Virginia | 52,675 | 108,364 | 48,338 | 274 | 3,263 | 4,791 | 5,622 | 1,491 | 79 | 1,978 | 226,875 |
| Wisconsin | 20,526 | 40,980 | 13,196 | 77 | 561 | 1,477 | 800 | 185 | 191 | 146 | 78,139 |
| Territories. Minnesota | 656 | 563 | 751 | 163 | 4 | 68 | 37 | 59 | 15 | 20 | 2,386 |
| Territories. New Mexico | 1,054 | 7,956 | 6,209 | 655 | 2 | 45 | 58 | 206 | 1,292 | 1 | 17,478 |
| Territories. Oregon | 1,007 | 1,704 | 511 | 289 | 130 | 99 | 48 | 40 | 40 | 6 | 3,874 |
| Territories. Utah | 828 | 1,581 | 622 | ...... | 18 | 26 | 48 | 12 | ...... | ...... | 3,185 |
| Total | 1,596,265 | 2,400,583 | 993,620 | 5,370 | 116,341 | 94,515 | 95,814 | 24,966 | 22,243 | 22,159 | 5,371,876 |

BLE XXIII.—*Nativities of the Inhabitants of the Leading Cities of the United States*—1850.

| Cities. | Born in the United States. | | | | | | | | | | | | | | | | | | | | |
|---|---|---|---|---|---|---|---|---|---|---|---|---|---|---|---|---|---|---|---|---|---|
| | In city or rest of same State. | Alabama. | Columbia, District of. | Connecticut. | Delaware. | Florida. | Georgia. | Illinois. | Indiana. | Kentucky. | Louisiana. | Maine. | Maryland. | Massachusetts. | Michigan. | Mississippi. | Missouri. | New Hampshire. | New Jersey. | New York. | N. Carolina. |
| Albany | 28738 | 1 | 2 | 553 | 13 | ... | 3 | 9 | 4 | 6 | 5 | 43 | 49 | 736 | 7 | ... | 1 | 111 | 218 | .... | 10 |
| Baltimore | 113583 | 26 | 1170 | 326 | 756 | 23 | 61 | 17 | 43 | 85 | 96 | 396 | .... | 1192 | 11 | 121 | 51 | 215 | 723 | 2037 | 126 |
| Boston | 68687 | 17 | 47 | 575 | 29 | 9 | 82 | 17 | 3 | 12 | 32 | 7689 | 191 | .... | 15 | 5 | 6 | 6628 | 118 | 1594 | 47 |
| Charleston | 16066 | 18 | 9 | 58 | 1 | 22 | 182 | .... | 4 | 10 | 11 | 19 | 119 | 227 | ... | 2 | ... | 6 | 58 | 545 | 109 |
| Chicago | 5831 | 21 | 7 | 506 | 29 | 4 | 8 | .... | 89 | 97 | 24 | 203 | 69 | 480 | 249 | 28 | 71 | 170 | 239 | 3870 | 24 |
| Cincinnati | 39322 | 52 | 127 | 527 | 215 | 1 | 105 | 147 | 1185 | 2096 | 378 | 220 | 1643 | 1079 | 87 | 189 | 126 | 225 | 1417 | 3142 | 169 |
| Detroit | 6323 | 6 | 15 | 224 | 9 | 2 | 13 | 25 | 10 | 98 | 6 | 70 | 34 | 296 | ... | 4 | 19 | 80 | 83 | 2620 | 15 |
| Hartford | 8293 | 9 | 4 | .... | 7 | 5 | 14 | 9 | 4 | 1 | 4 | 46 | 40 | 983 | 6 | 1 | 2 | 110 | 67 | 636 | 6 |
| Louisville | 16285 | 71 | 53 | 116 | 59 | 3 | 51 | 99 | 1255 | .... | 195 | 45 | 742 | 219 | 8 | 69 | 148 | 39 | 206 | 777 | 109 |
| Manchester | 9555 | ... | .... | 11 | .... | 1 | 1 | 2 | 13 | .... | ... | 197 | 1 | 1012 | ... | ... | 1 | .... | ..... | 82 | 1 |
| Memphis | 2134 | 187 | 18 | 36 | 4 | 10 | 96 | 67 | 94 | 360 | 56 | 21 | 100 | 56 | 4 | 164 | 79 | 16 | 20 | 160 | 351 |
| Milwaukie | 2641 | 1 | 1 | 263 | 14 | ... | 1 | 91 | 33 | 19 | 5 | 156 | 30 | 350 | 122 | 5 | 26 | 83 | 80 | 2281 | 3 |
| Mobile | 5507 | ... | 18 | 139 | 5 | 133 | 355 | 1 | 14 | 91 | 228 | 100 | 154 | 289 | ... | 230 | 16 | 39 | 73 | 701 | 216 |
| Nashville | 4883 | 78 | 2 | 31 | 6 | 2 | 26 | 12 | 16 | 382 | 30 | 4 | 91 | 54 | 1 | 36 | 3 | .... | 30 | 283 | 243 |
| Newark | 21477 | 4 | 12 | 533 | 31 | 1 | 16 | 12 | 2 | 7 | 16 | 46 | 111 | 277 | 9 | 2 | 1 | 45 | ..... | 3239 | 20 |
| New Haven | 13775 | 21 | 9 | .... | 13 | 15 | 92 | 6 | 6 | 15 | 34 | 79 | 57 | 551 | 5 | 12 | 8 | 35 | 270 | 1167 | 20 |
| New Orleans | 34101 | 620 | 92 | 228 | 44 | 139 | 249 | 147 | 118 | 1038 | ... | 620 | 733 | 1178 | 52 | 842 | 431 | 155 | 274 | 4086 | 214 |
| New York | 234843 | 90 | 261 | 7784 | 393 | 54 | 277 | 72 | 41 | 122 | 303 | 1432 | 1852 | 5587 | 86 | 83 | 56 | 826 | 13255 | .... | 284 |
| Philadelphia | 242681 | 55 | 394 | 829 | 8678 | 15 | 123 | 52 | 62 | 197 | 163 | 333 | 5760 | 1858 | 18 | 24 | 60 | 288 | 15570 | 4858 | 198 |
| Portland | 15110 | 5 | 15 | 43 | 8 | 1 | 6 | 7 | 1 | .... | 8 | .... | 35 | 1208 | 1 | ... | ... | 474 | 9 | 142 | 3 |
| Portsmouth | 7088 | ... | 5 | 30 | 3 | ... | 2 | .... | .... | .... | 2 | 866 | 7 | 415 | ... | ... | ... | .... | 1 | 51 | 1 |
| Providence | 24368 | 6 | 35 | 989 | 22 | 9 | 29 | 5 | 3 | 9 | 6 | 326 | 218 | 4003 | 5 | 4 | ... | 321 | 86 | 760 | 58 |
| Richmond | 14138 | 8 | 40 | 72 | 14 | 5 | 8 | .... | .... | 24 | 4 | 22 | 268 | 161 | 1 | 1 | 2 | 37 | 75 | 254 | 102 |
| St. Augustine | 1100 | 1 | .... | 33 | .... | ... | 25 | 1 | .... | 3 | 1 | 6 | 9 | 8 | ... | ... | ... | 3 | 3 | 5 | 7 |
| Savannah | 4774 | 14 | 8 | 84 | 9 | 121 | ... | .... | 2 | 5 | 6 | 25 | 49 | 100 | ... | 3 | 1 | 24 | 75 | 305 | 69 |
| St. Louis | 20321 | 82 | 109 | 325 | 79 | 10 | 73 | 1210 | 438 | 1846 | 360 | 112 | 841 | 603 | 94 | 234 | ... | 137 | 270 | 2470 | 126 |
| Washington | 19237 | 18 | .... | 122 | 66 | 23 | 60 | 23 | 26 | 78 | 23 | 79 | 7017 | 284 | 26 | 39 | 25 | 77 | 139 | 723 | 86 |
| Wilm'ton, Del | 8671 | 2 | 10 | 21 | .... | ... | 5 | 2 | 11 | 3 | 3 | 21 | 765 | 50 | ... | 1 | 2 | 10 | 525 | 100 | 10 |
| Wilm'ton, N.C | 3527 | 9 | 3 | 55 | 3 | 17 | 13 | 2 | .... | 5 | ... | 16 | 26 | 42 | ... | 1 | 1 | 2 | 8 | 97 | ... |

| Cities. | Born in the United States. | | | | | | | Foreign Born. | | | | | | | | | Aggregate. | |
|---|---|---|---|---|---|---|---|---|---|---|---|---|---|---|---|---|---|---|
| | Ohio. | Pennsylvania. | R. Island. | S. Carolina. | Tennessee. | Vermont. | Virginia. | England and Wales. | Ireland. | Scotland. | Germany. | Prussia. | Austria. | France. | Spain. | Italy. | Native.* | Foreign.* |
| Albany | 26 | 154 | 92 | 21 | 1 | 322 | 31 | 2082 | 13079 | 540 | 2875 | 1 | .... | 97 | 2 | 1 | 31162 | 16591 |
| Baltimore | 276 | 4986 | 181 | 122 | 26 | 211 | 3605 | 2133 | 12057 | 525 | 19274 | 164 | 16 | 346 | 16 | 67 | 130491 | 35492 |
| Boston | 69 | 393 | 584 | 94 | 6 | 1744 | 251 | 3213 | 35287 | 897 | 1777 | 39 | .... | 225 | 67 | 134 | 88948 | 46677 |
| Charleston | 2 | 165 | 38 | .... | 9 | 13 | 115 | 546 | 2369 | 323 | 1789 | 27 | 1 | 187 | 23 | 56 | 17809 | 4643 |
| Chicago | 390 | 545 | 46 | 5 | 18 | 456 | 119 | 1883 | 6096 | 610 | 5035 | 38 | 21 | 234 | 2 | 4 | 13693 | 15682 |
| Cincinnati | .... | 5112 | 143 | 112 | 245 | 250 | 2178 | 4135 | 14393 | 718 | 33374 | 148 | 18 | 797 | 4 | 152 | 60558 | 54541 |
| Detroit | 305 | 276 | 21 | 12 | 24 | 281 | 161 | 1245 | 3289 | 474 | 2838 | 13 | 7 | 282 | 4 | 4 | 11055 | 9927 |
| Hartford | 25 | 66 | 67 | 7 | 3 | 114 | 12 | 235 | 2188 | 58 | 271 | 12 | 13 | 27 | .... | 4 | 10551 | 2915 |
| Louisville | 1090 | 1365 | 22 | 72 | 306 | 42 | 1582 | 720 | 3105 | 162 | 7357 | 145 | 24 | 422 | 4 | 112 | 25079 | 12461 |
| Manchester | .... | 1 | 15 | .... | .... | 1343 | 8 | 182 | 1193 | 31 | ...... | .... | .... | 1 | .... | .... | 12244 | 1688 |
| Memphis | 150 | 194 | 5 | 131 | .... | 7 | 419 | 133 | 704 | 20 | 341 | 8 | 1 | 69 | 1 | 44 | 5026 | 1401 |
| Milwaukie | 334 | 314 | 35 | 16 | 4 | 225 | 42 | 1212 | 2816 | 245 | 6028 | 1243 | 16 | 129 | .... | .... | 7181 | 12782 |
| Mobile | 86 | 237 | 24 | 459 | 75 | 32 | 330 | 547 | 2009 | 205 | 513 | 22 | 17 | 303 | 144 | 65 | 9565 | 4086 |
| Nashville | 106 | 178 | 4 | 61 | .... | 8 | 608 | 137 | 421 | 70 | 193 | 15 | .... | 36 | 1 | 3 | 7185 | 948 |
| Newark | 41 | 504 | 38 | 25 | 1 | 45 | 43 | 2124 | 5564 | 265 | 3818 | 4 | 6 | 240 | 8 | .... | 26561 | 12322 |
| New Haven | 57 | 212 | 47 | 21 | 4 | 63 | 39 | 371 | 2772 | 107 | 273 | 11 | .... | 54 | .... | 3 | 16641 | 3697 |
| New Orleans | 781 | 1515 | 174 | 502 | 484 | 133 | 1232 | 2670 | 20200 | 854 | 11220 | 205 | 129 | 7522 | 1150 | 658 | 50470 | 48601 |
| New York | 499 | 5283 | 961 | 535 | 26 | 953 | 1702 | 23671 | 133730 | 7660 | 55476 | 665 | 109 | 4990 | 303 | 708 | 277752 | 235733 |
| Philadelphia | 505 | .... | 288 | 470 | 85 | 157 | 2602 | 17500 | 72312 | 3291 | 22750 | 270 | 84 | 1981 | 291 | 236 | 286346 | 121699 |
| Portland | 1 | 49 | 32 | 6 | .... | 78 | 23 | 156 | 2301 | 50 | 22 | 14 | 2 | 14 | .... | 6 | 17265 | 3512 |
| Portsmouth | 6 | 15 | 9 | 3 | 1 | 27 | 7 | 343 | 523 | 62 | 25 | 1 | .... | 6 | .... | .... | 8540 | 1179 |
| Providence | 30 | 170 | .... | 20 | 1 | 134 | 99 | 1119 | 7635 | 322 | 87 | 2 | 1 | 40 | 10 | 19 | 31755 | 9679 |
| Richmond | 12 | 206 | 9 | 43 | 11 | 16 | .... | 268 | 685 | 183 | 740 | 18 | 2 | 68 | 5 | 34 | 15541 | 2102 |
| St. Augustine | .... | 3 | 9 | 19 | 1 | 1 | 6 | 7 | 11 | 4 | 5 | .... | .... | 6 | 3 | 1 | 1244 | 56 |
| Savannah | 6 | 87 | 26 | 720 | 6 | 9 | 60 | 227 | 1555 | 60 | 383 | 3 | 7 | 37 | 13 | 15 | 6590 | 2434 |
| St. Louis | 1638 | 2684 | 45 | 73 | 380 | 176 | 1630 | 2957 | 9719 | 550 | 22340 | 231 | 13 | 682 | 36 | 101 | 36529 | 38397 |
| Washington | 114 | 1000 | 19 | 71 | 54 | 40 | 4046 | 585 | 2023 | 136 | 1246 | 10 | 1 | 69 | 22 | 49 | 33530 | 4282 |
| Wilm'ton, Del. | 15 | 1908 | 2 | 1 | 1 | 2 | 56 | 240 | 1215 | 24 | 157 | 26 | .... | 16 | 1 | .... | 12198 | 1763 |
| Wilm'ton, N.C. | 1 | 34 | 15 | 57 | .... | 1 | 89 | 33 | 63 | 14 | 72 | .... | 1 | 9 | .... | .... | 4025 | 208 |

NOTE.—Exclusive of 5 Arkansians in Baltimore, 25 in Cincinnati, 26 in Louisville, 80 in Memphis, 97 in New Orleans, and 39 in St. Louis, &c.; 4 Californians in New York; 19 Iowans in Chicago, 24 in Cincinnati, 10 in Louisville, 5 in Memphis, 6 in Milwaukie, 21 in New Orleans, 4 in New York, 7 in Philadelphia, and 77 in St. Louis; 19 Texans in Baltimore, 9 in Cincinnati, 8 in Hartford, 9 in Louisville, 10 in Mobile, 164 in New Orleans, 23 in New York, 8 in Philadelphia, 4 in Richmond, 21 in St. Louis, and 6 in Washington; 76 natives of Wisconsin in Chicago, 8 in Cincinnati, 21 in Detroit, 4 in New Haven, 28 in New York, 7 in Philadelphia, and 23 in St. Louis; 4 natives of the Territories in Louisville, 31 in New York, and 8 in Providence. Savannah cannot be defined on the returns.

* Exclusive of those unknown. The total foreign includes other countries not named in the table.

TABLE XXIV.—*Age and sex of the aggregate population in the leading cities of the United States*, 1850.

| Cities. | Sex. | Under 1 year old. | 1 and under 5. | 5 and under 10. | 10 and under 15. | 15 and under 20. | 20 and under 30. | 30 and under 40. | 40 and under 50. | 50 and under 60. | 60 and under 70. | 70 and over. | Age unknown. | Total. |
|---|---|---|---|---|---|---|---|---|---|---|---|---|---|---|
| Baltimore, | M | 2,668 | 9,108 | 9,698 | 8,261 | 7,606 | 18,588 | 13,840 | 7,186 | 3,401 | 1,533 | 762 | 1 | 82,652 |
| Md. | F | 2,619 | 9,270 | 9,941 | 9,230 | 9,481 | 18,458 | 12,359 | 7,150 | 4,265 | 2,362 | 1,265 | 2 | 86,402 |
| Charleston, | M | 240 | 1,747 | 2,345 | 2,323 | 2,032 | 4,028 | 3,333 | 2,135 | 1,139 | 585 | 317 | .... | 20,224 |
| S. C. | F | 243 | 1,744 | 2,621 | 2,576 | 2,340 | 4,209 | 3,660 | 2,296 | 1,601 | 961 | 510 | .... | 22,761 |
| Louisville, | M | 657 | 2,317 | 2,519 | 2,163 | 1,995 | 5,582 | 3,917 | 1,981 | 924 | 329 | 150 | 42 | 22,576 |
| Ky. | F | 676 | 2,226 | 2,595 | 2,342 | 2,240 | 4,533 | 2,829 | 1,660 | 890 | 402 | 187 | 38 | 20,618 |
| Memphis, | M | 142 | 446 | 479 | 501 | 389 | 1,217 | 910 | 411 | 168 | 41 | 17 | 3 | 4,724 |
| Tenn. | F | 138 | 494 | 494 | 519 | 443 | 921 | 612 | 278 | 139 | 59 | 19 | 1 | 4,117 |
| Mobile, | M | 231 | 1,012 | 1,140 | 932 | 734 | 2,307 | 2,351 | 1,114 | 454 | 155 | 88 | 2 | 10,520 |
| Ala. | F | 259 | 1,130 | 1,159 | 1,083 | 1,070 | 2,154 | 1,566 | 812 | 430 | 209 | 122 | 1 | 9,995 |
| Nashville, | M | 102 | 550 | 600 | 571 | 510 | 1,350 | 786 | 407 | 243 | 87 | 43 | 2 | 5,249 |
| Tenn. | F | 113 | 531 | 597 | 651 | 643 | 1,037 | 610 | 402 | 209 | 81 | 40 | .... | 4,916 |
| N. Orleans, incl'ing | M | 1,807 | 6,374 | 7,344 | 5,852 | 4,884 | 19,550 | 18,501 | 8,653 | 2,900 | 1,051 | 424 | 236 | 77,576 |
| Jeff. & Orle'ns par. | F | 1,873 | 6,393 | 7,259 | 6,331 | 6,845 | 16,760 | 11,540 | 5,567 | 2,520 | 1,249 | 605 | 35 | 66,977 |
| Norfolk, | M | 158 | 683 | 821 | 727 | 703 | 1,193 | 869 | 580 | 286 | 151 | 66 | .... | 6,237 |
| Va. | F | 165 | 758 | 993 | 955 | 888 | 1,536 | 1,074 | 799 | 513 | 245 | 163 | .... | 8,089 |
| Petersburg, | M | 127 | 681 | 783 | 850 | 735 | 1,247 | 986 | 722 | 344 | 156 | 99 | .... | 6,730 |
| Va. | F | 133 | 676 | 808 | 921 | 871 | 1,311 | 983 | 727 | 458 | 230 | 161 | 1 | 7,280 |
| Richmond, | M | 245 | 1,343 | 1,453 | 1,534 | 1,400 | 2,951 | 2,581 | 1,502 | 732 | 298 | 124 | 2 | 14,165 |
| Va. | F | 222 | 1,321 | 1,495 | 1,540 | 1,457 | 2,650 | 1,965 | 1,290 | 808 | 424 | 233 | .... | 13,405 |
| St. Louis, | M | 1,127 | 3,807 | 3,752 | 3,200 | 3,526 | 14,185 | 9,339 | 3,587 | 1,269 | 424 | 143 | 16 | 44,375 |
| Mo. | F | 1,013 | 3,612 | 3,807 | 3,544 | 4,052 | 8,623 | 4,919 | 2,285 | 1,048 | 457 | 118 | 7 | 33,485 |
| Washington, | M | 511 | 2,184 | 2,507 | 2,185 | 1,838 | 3,473 | 2,671 | 1,663 | 999 | 446 | 178 | 2 | 18,657 |
| D. C. | F | 525 | 2,054 | 2,614 | 2,386 | 2,465 | 4,314 | 2,926 | 1,873 | 1,174 | 627 | 344 | 15 | 21,344 |
| Wilmington. | M | 221 | 732 | 843 | 680 | 673 | 1,215 | 968 | 592 | 336 | 167 | 111 | .... | 6,538 |
| Del. | F | 209 | 712 | 847 | 719 | 886 | 1,618 | 1,059 | 640 | 397 | 216 | 138 | .... | 7,441 |
| Wilmington, | M | 85 | 446 | 427 | 441 | 329 | 697 | 545 | 296 | 146 | 67 | 36 | .... | 3,515 |
| N. C. | F | 85 | 423 | 491 | 462 | 348 | 730 | 528 | 312 | 184 | 112 | 74 | .... | 3,749 |

TABLE XXIV.—Continued.—*Age and sex of the aggregate population in the leading cities of the United States*, 1850.

| Cities. | Sex. | Under 1 year old. | 1 and under 5. | 5 and under 10. | 10 and under 15. | 15 and under 20. | 20 and under 30. | 30 and under 40. | 40 and under 50. | 50 and under 60. | 60 and under 70. | 70 and over. | Age unknown. | Total. |
|---|---|---|---|---|---|---|---|---|---|---|---|---|---|---|
| Albany, | M | 722 | 2,852 | 3,129 | 2,539 | 2,163 | 4,858 | 3,936 | 2,470 | 1,190 | 479 | 239 | 5 | 24,577 |
| N. Y. | F | 643 | 2,777 | 3,138 | 2,797 | 3,018 | 5,772 | 3,674 | 2,248 | 1,216 | 613 | 290 | 2 | 26,186 |
| Boston, | M | 1,814 | 6,278 | 6,763 | 5,955 | 6,003 | 15,377 | 11,811 | 6,555 | 2,864 | 1,285 | 501 | 568 | 65,774 |
| Mass. | F | 1,962 | 6,347 | 6,933 | 6,209 | 7,273 | 18,155 | 11,637 | 6,407 | 3,513 | 1,752 | 851 | 68 | 71,107 |
| Chicago, | M | 493 | 1,603 | 1,677 | 1,445 | 1,400 | 4,268 | 3,189 | 1,495 | 492 | 188 | 48 | 2 | 16,300 |
| Ill. | F | 483 | 1,663 | 1,759 | 1,460 | 1,437 | 3,280 | 2,063 | 892 | 410 | 170 | 41 | 5 | 13,663 |
| Cincinnati, | M | 1,910 | 6,395 | 6,603 | 5,500 | 5,219 | 15,732 | 11,019 | 5,099 | 1,939 | 1,086 | 316 | 50 | 60,868 |
| Ohio. | F | 1,847 | 6,275 | 6,346 | 5,386 | 6,309 | 13,386 | 7,693 | 3,769 | 2,068 | 1,042 | 409 | 37 | 54,567 |
| Cleveland, | M | 240 | 1,050 | 1,080 | 782 | 653 | 1,942 | 1,541 | 773 | 313 | 167 | 42 | 20 | 8,603 |
| Ohio. | F | 257 | 995 | 1,090 | 881 | 893 | 1,990 | 1,273 | 571 | 273 | 147 | 52 | 9 | 8,431 |
| Columbus, | M | 237 | 1,214 | 1,099 | 907 | 789 | 2,292 | 1,624 | 763 | 317 | 173 | 60 | .... | 9,475 |
| Ohio. | F | 234 | 1,168 | 1,120 | 852 | 942 | 2,015 | 1,127 | 464 | 271 | 158 | 56 | .... | 8,407 |
| Detroit, | M | 331 | 1,211 | 1,393 | 1,090 | 890 | 2,404 | 1,856 | 1,026 | 438 | 149 | 75 | 1 | 10,864 |
| Mich. | F | 316 | 1,187 | 1,320 | 1,094 | 1,221 | 2,317 | 1,442 | 680 | 332 | 175 | 70 | 1 | 10,155 |
| Newark, | M | 623 | 2,126 | 2,244 | 1,884 | 1,991 | 4,094 | 2,870 | 1,817 | 826 | 366 | 143 | 5 | 18,989 |
| N. J. | F | 606 | 2,132 | 2,292 | 2,030 | 2,164 | 4,457 | 2,728 | 1,775 | 942 | 518 | 255 | 5 | 19,904 |
| New York, | M | 7,402 | 25,859 | 27,518 | 22,313 | 21,946 | 63,779 | 44,940 | 23,869 | 10,468 | 4,379 | 1,591 | 42 | 254,106 |
| N. Y. | F | 7,405 | 26,490 | 27,263 | 23,612 | 28,113 | 69,588 | 40,041 | 20,866 | 10,842 | 5,536 | 2,676 | 36 | 261,441 |
| Philadelphia, Pa., | M | 5,558 | 21,493 | 24,057 | 20,337 | 18,471 | 41,562 | 30,187 | 18,705 | 9,428 | 4,433 | 1,972 | 188 | 196,391 |
| as organized 1854. | F | 5,459 | 21,252 | 23,563 | 21,369 | 23,515 | 48,247 | 29,767 | 18,560 | 10,833 | 6,098 | 3,605 | 103 | 212,371 |
| Pittsburg, | M | 709 | 2,681 | 2,799 | 2,306 | 2,320 | 5,596 | 3,503 | 2,076 | 952 | 407 | 149 | 15 | 23,513 |
| Pa. | F | 769 | 2,678 | 2,876 | 2,508 | 2,727 | 5,292 | 9,891 | 1,770 | 902 | 493 | 172 | 10 | 23,088 |
| Portland, | M | 275 | 1,037 | 1,079 | 993 | 1,034 | 2,077 | 1,478 | 1,034 | 523 | 275 | 155 | .... | 9,960 |
| Me. | F | 254 | 911 | 1,106 | 1,100 | 1,303 | 2,353 | 1,504 | 1,064 | 645 | 379 | 236 | .... | 10,855 |
| Providence, | M | 546 | 2,100 | 2,052 | 1,889 | 1,840 | 4,678 | 3,341 | 1,872 | 938 | 454 | 223 | .... | 19,933 |
| R. I. | F | 597 | 2,052 | 2,150 | 1,970 | 2,228 | 5,052 | 3,297 | 1,996 | 1,167 | 687 | 384 | .... | 21,580 |

TABLE XXV.—*Sex and condition of the population in the leading cities of the United States*, 1850.

| Cities. | Color and condition. | Sex. | Total. | Cities. | Color and condition. | Sex. | Total. | Cities. | Color and condition. | Sex. | Total. |
|---|---|---|---|---|---|---|---|---|---|---|---|
| Albany, N. Y. | White | M | 24,187 | Columbus, Ohio. | White | M | 8,848 | Pittsburg, Pa. | White | M | 22,606 |
| | | F | 25,716 | | | F | 7,757 | | | F | 22,036 |
| | Free col'd | M | 390 | | Free col'd | M | 627 | | Free col'd | M | 907 |
| | | F | 470 | | | F | 650 | | | F | 1,052 |
| | Total | M | 24,577 | | Total | M | 9,475 | | Total | M | 23,513 |
| | | F | 26,186 | | | F | 8,407 | | | F | 23,088 |
| Boston, Mass. | White | M | 64,855 | Detroit, Mich. | White | M | 10,556 | Portland, Me. | White | M | 9,755 |
| | | F | 70,027 | | | F | 9,876 | | | F | 10,665 |
| | Free col'd | M | 919 | | Free col'd | M | 308 | | Free col'd | M | 205 |
| | | F | 1,080 | | | F | 279 | | | F | 190 |
| | Total | M | 65,774 | | Total | M | 10,864 | | Total | M | 9,960 |
| | | F | 71,107 | | | F | 10,155 | | | F | 10,855 |
| Chicago, Ill. | White | M | 16,119 | Newark, N. J. | White | M | 18,446 | Providence, R. I. | White | M | 19,267 |
| | | F | 13,521 | | | F | 19,218 | | | F | 20,747 |
| | Free col'd | M | 181 | | Free col'd | M | 543 | | Free col'd | M | 666 |
| | | F | 142 | | | F | 686 | | | F | 833 |
| | Total | M | 16,300 | | Total | M | 18,989 | | Total | M | 19,933 |
| | | F | 13,663 | | | F | 19,904 | | | F | 21,580 |
| Cincinnati, Ohio. | White | M | 59,306 | New York, N. Y. | White | M | 248,008 | | | | |
| | | F | 52,892 | | | F | 253,724 | | | | |
| | Free col'd | M | 1,562 | | Free col'd | M | 6,098 | | | | |
| | | F | 1,675 | | | F | 7,717 | | | | |
| | Total | M | 60,868 | | Total | M | 254,106 | | | | |
| | | F | 54,567 | | | F | 261,441 | | | | |
| Cleveland, Ohio. | White | M | 8,499 | Philadelphia as organised 1854. | White | M | 187,956 | | | | |
| | | F | 8,311 | | | F | 201,045 | | | | |
| | Free col'd | M | 104 | | Free col'd | M | 8,435 | | | | |
| | | F | 120 | | | F | 11,326 | | | | |
| | Total | M | 8,603 | | Total | M | 196,391 | | | | |
| | | F | 8,431 | | | F | 212,371 | | | | |

TABLE XXV.—Continued.—*Sex and condition of the population in the leading cities of the United States*, 1850.

| Cities. | Color and condition. | Sex. | Total. | Cities. | Color and condition. | Sex. | Total. | Cities. | Color and condition. | Sex. | Total. |
|---|---|---|---|---|---|---|---|---|---|---|---|
| Baltimore, Md. | White | M | 70,873 | Nashville, Tenn. | White | M | 4,016 | Washington, D. C. | White | M | 14,526 |
| | | F | 69,793 | | | F | 3,610 | | | F | 15,204 |
| | Free col'd | M | 10,832 | | Free col'd | M | 256 | | Free col'd | M | 3,398 |
| | | F | 14,610 | | | F | 255 | | | F | 4,760 |
| | Slave | M | 947 | | Slave | M | 977 | | Slave | M | 733 |
| | | F | 1,999 | | | F | 1,051 | | | F | 1,380 |
| | Total. | M | 82,652 | | Total | M | 5,249 | | Total | M | 18,657 |
| | | F | 86,402 | | | F | 4,916 | | | F | 21,344 |
| Charleston, S. C. | White | M | 10,238 | Norfolk, Va. | White | M | 4,196 | Wilmington, Del. | White | M | 5,607 |
| | | F | 9,774 | | | F | 4,879 | | | F | 6,232 |
| | Free col'd | M | 1,355 | | Free col'd | M | 364 | | Free col'd | M | 931 |
| | | F | 2,086 | | | F | 592 | | | F | 1,209 |
| | Slave | M | 8,631 | | Slave | M | 1,677 | | Slave | M | .......... |
| | | F | 10,901 | | | F | 2,618 | | | F | .......... |
| | Total | M | 20,224 | | Total | M | 6,237 | | Total | M | 6,538 |
| | | F | 22,761 | | | F | 8,089 | | | F | 7,441 |
| Louisville, Ky. | White | M | 19,468 | Petersburg, Va. | White | M | 5,177 | Wilmington, N. C. | White | M | 1,795 |
| | | F | 16,756 | | | F | 3,488 | | | F | 1,786 |
| | Free col'd | M | 698 | | Free col'd | M | 1,177 | | Free col'd | M | 285 |
| | | F | 840 | | | F | 1,439 | | | F | 367 |
| | Slave | M | 2,410 | | Slave | M | 2,376 | | Slave | M | 1,435 |
| | | F | 3,022 | | | F | 2,353 | | | F | 1,596 |
| | Total | M | 22,576 | | Total | M | 6,730 | | Total | M | 3,515 |
| | | F | 20,618 | | | F | 7,280 | | | F | 3,749 |
| Memphis, Tenn. | White | M | 3,579 | Richmond, Va. | White | M | 7,783 | | | | |
| | | F | 2,776 | | | F | 7,491 | | | | |
| | Free col'd | M | 51 | | Free col'd | M | 1,075 | | | | |
| | | F | 75 | | | F | 1,294 | | | | |
| | Slave | M | 1,094 | | Slave | M | 5,307 | | | | |
| | | F | 1,266 | | | F | 4,620 | | | | |
| | Total | M | 4,724 | | Total | M | 14,165 | | | | |
| | | F | 4,117 | | | F | 13,405 | | | | |
| Mobile, Ala. | White | M | 7,022 | St. Louis, Mo. | White | M | 42,367 | | | | |
| | | F | 5,975 | | | F | 31,439 | | | | |
| | Free col'd | M | 286 | | Free col'd | M | 742 | | | | |
| | | F | 429 | | | F | 656 | | | | |
| | Slave | M | 3,212 | | Slave | M | 1,266 | | | | |
| | | F | 3,591 | | | F | 1,390 | | | | |
| | Total | M | 10,520 | | Total | M | 44,375 | | | | |
| | | F | 9,995 | | | F | 33,485 | | | | |

TABLE XXVI.—*Ages of Persons who died between June* 1, 1849, *and June* 1, 1850.

| States and Territories. | | Under 1. | 1 and under 5. | 5 and under 10. | 10 and under 15. | 15 and under 20. | 20 and under 30. | 30 and under 40. | 40 and under 50. | 50 and under 60. | 60 and under 70. | 70 and under 80. | 80 and under 90. | 90 and under 100. | 100 and upwards. |
|---|---|---|---|---|---|---|---|---|---|---|---|---|---|---|---|
| Alabama | w | 839 | 811 | 394 | 271 | 245 | 482 | 402 | 285 | 241 | 191 | 138 | 63 | 18 | 3 |
| | c | 1,184 | 1,279 | 343 | 202 | 232 | 429 | 286 | 262 | 190 | 166 | 62 | 44 | 19 | 22 |
| Arkansas | w | 390 | 453 | 212 | 106 | 134 | 264 | 224 | 168 | 96 | 67 | 30 | 13 | 1 | 2 |
| | c | 134 | 206 | 83 | 39 | 55 | 125 | 71 | 60 | 30 | 34 | 13 | 6 | 1 | 4 |
| California | w | 35 | 38 | 10 | 13 | 26 | 281 | 167 | 84 | 36 | 13 | 6 | 1 | 2 | .... |
| | c | 1 | .... | .... | .... | .... | 9 | 1 | 5 | 1 | 2 | .... | .... | .... | .... |
| Columbia, Dis. of | w | 110 | 148 | 42 | 22 | 23 | 51 | 55 | 40 | 33 | 24 | 26 | 10 | 1 | .... |
| | c | 44 | 39 | 21 | 10 | 16 | 31 | 26 | 22 | 15 | 18 | 12 | 4 | 2 | 1 |
| Connecticut | w | 684 | 905 | 282 | 138 | 223 | 591 | 487 | 423 | 406 | 479 | 490 | 390 | 79 | 5 |
| | c | 21 | 22 | 6 | 5 | 6 | 15 | 10 | 23 | 10 | 16 | 8 | 4 | .... | 1 |
| Delaware | w | 186 | 184 | 60 | 37 | 32 | 74 | 91 | 69 | 77 | 61 | 53 | 17 | 6 | .... |
| | c | 53 | 53 | 12 | 12 | 19 | 29 | 17 | 9 | 17 | 16 | 14 | 4 | 5 | 2 |
| Florida | w | 62 | 120 | 41 | 25 | 28 | 55 | 51 | 34 | 21 | 22 | 8 | 9 | 1 | 1 |
| | c | 85 | 128 | 34 | 17 | 27 | 49 | 21 | 23 | 24 | 15 | 12 | 6 | 5 | 2 |
| Georgia | w | 890 | 830 | 230 | 230 | 270 | 490 | 380 | 292 | 289 | 260 | 217 | 115 | 37 | 5 |
| | c | 1,393 | 1,330 | 296 | 238 | 330 | 466 | 315 | 252 | 199 | 234 | 132 | 76 | 49 | 43 |
| Illinois | w | 2,261 | 2,530 | 753 | 492 | 617 | 1,416 | 1,138 | 931 | 630 | 430 | 239 | 78 | 15 | 1 |
| | c | 9 | 10 | 4 | 3 | 4 | 13 | 5 | 5 | 6 | 3 | 2 | .... | 1 | .... |
| Indiana | w | 2,247 | 2,748 | 968 | 823 | 862 | 1,488 | 1,029 | 818 | 631 | 477 | 341 | 176 | 36 | 5 |
| | c | 22 | 21 | 14 | 6 | 11 | 20 | 11 | 8 | 10 | 7 | .... | 2 | 1 | .... |
| Iowa | w | 446 | 539 | 141 | 81 | 81 | 235 | 195 | 129 | 82 | 66 | 27 | 18 | .... | .... |
| | c | .... | 3 | .... | .... | .... | 1 | .... | .... | .... | .... | .... | .... | .... | .... |
| Kentucky | w | 1,743 | 2,074 | 655 | 456 | 618 | 1,359 | 1,006 | 748 | 623 | 540 | 445 | 251 | 60 | 6 |
| | c | 967 | 906 | 296 | 257 | 285 | 522 | 338 | 258 | 197 | 166 | 93 | 50 | 25 | 10 |
| Louisiana | w | 538 | 762 | 342 | 176 | 286 | 1,324 | 1,156 | 667 | 322 | 160 | 83 | 29 | 5 | 3 |
| | c | 737 | 1,302 | 435 | 279 | 326 | 851 | 778 | 535 | 320 | 237 | 90 | 62 | 38 | 25 |
| Maine | w | 910 | 1,584 | 519 | 260 | 454 | 921 | 631 | 497 | 403 | 459 | 462 | 350 | 82 | 4 |
| | c | 9 | 8 | 2 | .... | 3 | 5 | 3 | 4 | 1 | 1 | 2 | 1 | 1 | .... |
| Maryland | w | 1,536 | 1,555 | 454 | 475 | | 579 | 473 | 492 | 412 | 383 | 352 | 151 | 22 | 5 |
| | c | 554 | 575 | 209 | 277 | | 253 | 197 | 172 | 143 | 127 | 100 | 73 | 30 | 22 |
| Massachusetts | w | 2,833 | 4,380 | 1,064 | 584 | 725 | 2,203 | 1,802 | 1,309 | 1,070 | 1,138 | 1,078 | 793 | 174 | 7 |
| | c | 9 | 25 | 6 | 6 | 9 | 23 | 11 | 15 | 17 | 9 | 5 | 5 | 4 | 1 |
| Michigan | w | 851 | 995 | 293 | 177 | 198 | 493 | 408 | 312 | 280 | 227 | 165 | 61 | 8 | 2 |
| | c | 5 | 13 | 2 | 3 | 2 | 5 | 3 | 1 | 3 | .... | 1 | .... | .... | .... |
| Mississippi | w | 569 | 746 | 288 | 188 | 170 | 419 | 283 | 233 | 157 | 145 | 80 | 53 | 9 | .... |
| | c | 1,270 | 1,502 | 375 | 248 | 256 | 543 | 408 | 296 | 164 | 152 | 62 | 36 | 16 | 26 |
| Missouri | w | 1,632 | 2,179 | 750 | 465 | 564 | 1,726 | 1,366 | 891 | 562 | 363 | 187 | 53 | 16 | 6 |
| | c | 322 | 309 | 100 | 92 | 91 | 188 | 120 | 75 | 51 | 39 | 29 | 8 | 11 | 3 |
| New Hampshire | w | 450 | 760 | 240 | 146 | 202 | 466 | 333 | 282 | 275 | 299 | 389 | 318 | 63 | 2 |
| | c | 1 | 1 | 1 | 1 | .... | .... | .... | 1 | .... | .... | .... | .... | .... | .... |
| New Jersey | w | 1,040 | 1,282 | 344 | 185 | 232 | 592 | 472 | 469 | 421 | 438 | 366 | 245 | 40 | .... |
| | c | 41 | 47 | 17 | 14 | 21 | 33 | 34 | 21 | 24 | 18 | 18 | 15 | 6 | 2 |
| New York | w | 6,628 | 9,758 | 2,889 | 1,387 | 1,834 | 5,404 | 4,369 | 3,534 | 2,608 | 2,351 | 2,098 | 1,341 | 243 | 15 |
| | c | 80 | 141 | 53 | 30 | 49 | 133 | 102 | 99 | 62 | 65 | 44 | 30 | 10 | 8 |
| North Carolina | w | 853 | 743 | 366 | 276 | 309 | 636 | 502 | 513 | 326 | 417 | 354 | 206 | 54 | 11 |
| | c | 1,059 | 1,147 | 264 | 217 | 272 | 415 | 294 | 216 | 243 | 234 | 192 | 140 | 62 | 36 |
| Ohio | w | 4,363 | 6,553 | 2,252 | 1,098 | 1,327 | 3,464 | 2,753 | 2,115 | 1,523 | 1,369 | 967 | 522 | 92 | 17 |
| | c | 57 | 97 | 27 | 19 | 33 | 65 | 32 | 29 | 24 | 13 | 15 | 2 | 2 | 1 |
| Pennsylvania | w | 4,835 | 6,683 | 1,978 | 838 | 1,079 | 2,663 | 2,146 | 1,779 | 1,543 | 1,590 | 1,425 | 838 | 165 | 15 |
| | c | 142 | 178 | 52 | 35 | 44 | 102 | 79 | 78 | 55 | 42 | 23 | 20 | 5 | 2 |
| Rhode Island | w | 340 | 437 | 104 | 36 | 102 | 249 | 206 | 152 | 148 | 127 | 147 | 78 | 24 | .... |
| | c | 13 | 6 | 2 | 4 | 2 | 8 | 8 | 7 | 10 | 3 | 5 | 2 | .... | 1 |
| South Carolina | w | 325 | 466 | 209 | 142 | 154 | 356 | 254 | 226 | 187 | 203 | 160 | 91 | 19 | 3 |
| | c | 1,091 | 1,261 | 320 | 272 | 269 | 462 | 304 | 244 | 242 | 300 | 173 | 99 | 49 | 34 |
| Tennessee | w | 1,517 | 1,318 | 499 | 369 | 443 | 992 | 594 | 489 | 428 | 350 | 318 | 241 | 62 | 13 |
| | c | 1,028 | 845 | 234 | 227 | 305 | 520 | 281 | 211 | 191 | 140 | 105 | 50 | 26 | 11 |
| Texas | w | 369 | 401 | 196 | 118 | 116 | 283 | 237 | 173 | 117 | 74 | 29 | 12 | 3 | 3 |
| | c | 186 | 235 | 59 | 46 | 56 | 94 | 70 | 51 | 36 | 12 | 9 | 6 | 3 | 3 |
| Vermont | w | 300 | 479 | 162 | 89 | 178 | 329 | 240 | 208 | 233 | 278 | 330 | 245 | 46 | 2 |
| | c | 1 | 2 | .... | .... | .... | .... | 1 | 1 | 1 | 1 | .... | .... | .... | .... |
| Virginia | w | 1,457 | 1,707 | 630 | 372 | 466 | 1,062 | 899 | 764 | 632 | 683 | 643 | 355 | 90 | 24 |
| | c | 1,693 | 1,918 | 513 | 464 | 492 | 892 | 611 | 571 | 591 | 531 | 434 | 271 | 121 | 58 |
| Wisconsin | w | 645 | 770 | 183 | 90 | 139 | 310 | 266 | 206 | 118 | 92 | 62 | 15 | 1 | .... |
| | c | .... | .... | .... | .... | .... | 2 | .... | .... | .... | .... | .... | .... | .... | .... |
| Territ's. Minnesota | w | 5 | 11 | 5 | 1 | .... | 3 | 2 | 1 | .... | 1 | .... | 1 | .... | .... |
| New Mexico | w | 207 | 240 | 67 | 45 | 78 | 158 | 99 | 66 | 52 | 55 | 37 | 29 | 11 | 3 |
| Oregon | w | 5 | 11 | 3 | 2 | 1 | 9 | 9 | 3 | 2 | 2 | .... | .... | .... | .... |
| Utah | w | 41 | 49 | 19 | 8 | 18 | 28 | 22 | 20 | 17 | 11 | 5 | 1 | .... | .... |

| Ages. | White. | Colored. | Total. | Ages. | White. | Col'd. | Total. | Ages. | White. | Colored. | Total. |
|---|---|---|---|---|---|---|---|---|---|---|---|
| Under 1.. | 42,142 | 12,211 | 54,353 | 30 and 40 | 24,747 | 4,437 | 29,184 | 90 and 100 | 1,504 | 473 | 1,977 |
| 1 and 5. | 55,249 | 13,609 | 68,858 | 40 and 50 | 19,422 | 3,554 | 22,976 | Unknown | 1,330 | 317 | 1,647 |
| 5 and 10. | 17,644 | 3,780 | 21,424 | 50 and 60 | 15,001 | 2,877 | 17,878 | 100 & over | 163 | 318 | 481 |
| 10 and 15. | 10,221 | 3,023 | 13,244 | 60 and 70 | 13,845 | 2,601 | 16,446 | | | | |
| 15 and 20. | 12,234 | 3,215 | 15,449 | 70 and 80 | 11,757 | 1,655 | 13,412 | | | | |
| 20 and 30. | 31,455 | 6,303 | 37,758 | 80 and 90 | 7,169 | 1,016 | 8,185 | Aggregate. | 263,883 | 59,389 | 323,272 |

NOTE.—Average age of white deceased 25.45 yrs., colored 21.39, supposing those under 1 to have lived 6 mos., and those between 1 and 5, 3 years, &c. which is not true in point of fact, but sufficiently so for the comparison.

Free colored in Alabama 28, District of Columbia 204, Delaware 241, Florida 8, Georgia 46, Kentucky 184, Louisiana 165, Maryland 1,220, Mississippi 15, Missouri 83, New Jersey 304, North Carolina 462, South Carolina 81, Tennessee 125, Virginia 801. In Alabama 5 slaves died aged 105, 2 120; Arkansas 1 white 105, and 1 slave 110; District of Columbia 1 slave 103; Delaware 1 free colored 100, and 1 107; Georgia 1 white 105, 1 107, 3 slaves 103, 2 105, 1 120, 1 131; Michigan 1 white 103, 1 110; New Jersey 1 colored 114, 1 109; New York 1 white 102, 1 103, 1 free colored 104, 1 106, 2 110, 1 113; North Carolina 1 Indian female 140, 1 slave 120; Texas 1 slave 115.

# APPENDIX.

## LETTER FROM DR. EDWARD JARVIS, OF MASSACHUSETTS, UPON THE CLASSIFICATION OF DISEASES.

DORCHESTER, MASS., *September* 22, 1855.

DEAR SIR: I have your late favor of the 17th ult. now before me, and also the nosological nomenclature of the mortality of the United States in the year ending June, 1850.

I have examined the catalogue of diseases with very great care in all its relations. I have compared it with the established and authorized systems, and especially those adopted by the American National Medical Association and published in their Transactions for 1847, and by the Registration office of England. I have moreover submitted your papers to some of the most learned scholars and professors of medical science in New England.

In order to have this nosology of the Census the most perfect and in the best accordance with the received views of the present time, I have examined the reports of mortality of every State and city in the Union which have published their bills, and also the English and some of the Swiss reports, as well as the best writers on nosology. The result of all this inquiry, which has taken my time since the receipt of yours, I now send to you.

Your document is to be not only permanent, but also of very extensive use. It is to speak to the whole world of the diseases and mortality of the United States in the year 1849–'50; and it will be to them, for the present at least, the only authority in these matters. It is also to speak to all future ages of the deaths and their causes in this country at the present time, and perhaps it will be the only authority that will survive.

It is therefore of the utmost consequence that your statements should not only correspond exactly with the facts, but also be so clearly made that they be perfectly understood by all, and in the same way, and that the facts they represent be placed distinctly in the minds of all your readers.

For these purposes, I have made, and I propose to you to make, sundry and divers alterations in the nosological system that you sent to me, which will bring it more into harmony with the best scientific ideas of the time, and place the country, as to its mortality and the causes thereof, and you, as the historian of these matters for 1850, rightly before the world.

In doing this work, I have had much occasion to regret that you could not send me all the original returns, or, at least, a copy of all the manifold names of diseases or causes of death, which came to your office from the several districts of the Union, and also the names of the States and the counties in which they were found.

A great majority of these names of disease were to be translated into scientific and more intelligible language. It is not always easy to determine what disease a popular term represents, in what class it shall be included, and what legitimate name shall be used for it there.

Looking at the catalogue of names you sent to me, and which is condensed from the multifarious list that came to you, looking also at the explanations you have given in connection with your list, it is manifest that there is, and there must be, some latitude in this translation and interpretation, and that also there may be some difference of opinion among the various persons who examine the original returns.

Many of these popular names of diseases have only a local use and meaning, many are not even known beyond the district where they are used. It is, then, improbable that any one man, however learned in this science, could understand and interpret and arrange the whole, and yet it is very necessary that all the diseases or causes of death reported to you should be faithfully represented and described in some of the classes and by some of the terms you adopt, and that few or none should be put into the uninstructive class of the "unknown;" nor should they be published under names that will convey no ideas, or uncertain ideas, or different ideas to different persons.

I was, therefore, desirous, and in my former correspondence with you I urged, that a physician who is an accomplished medical scholar should have the supervision of this branch of your department; that he should carefully examine all the original returns, and reduce their manifold and varied language to the legitimate and recognized nomenclature, and then, whenever he should find any word of local and doubtful or unintelligible meaning, he should correspond with the best physicians of the State or region where the unknown words were found, and thus ascertain what disease they were intended to represent.

Wanting the original names, from which, perhaps, I might have made a different list from this which I now send to you, I have taken this, your translated and condensed catalogue, and made further alterations, as you will see, based, of course, on the facts therein stated.

In doing this I have omitted the names of several diseases which alone and unaccompanied are not fatal, and also several which have no distinct and specific meaning. Some of them I propose to include among the "unknown," because the disease stated gives no clue to the real cause of death. There are others among these names of disease which, although not the real cause of death, yet indicate that some disease of the same class, or of the same organ or system of organs, produced the fatal event. These I propose to include in the genus or class in general where they are found, without attempting to specify their particular nature.

I have condensed several names which are synonymous of each other.

I have exchanged several names for others which were considered as the better representatives of their diseases.

I have also added some diseases that were omitted, but which are in the systems adopted here and elsewhere, and which are the causes of considerable mortality.

In this way I have reduced the list of diseases from the one hundred and forty-eight given in your paper to one hundred and fourteen, which include all that you present, besides some others which I have added.

1, chicken pox; 2, disease of eyes; 3, herpes; 4, hives; 5, mumps; 6, onanism; 7, ringworm; 8, suppressed menses; 9, tetter; 10, vaccination; 11, fluor albus, are all omitted for the reason first stated: standing alone, they cannot safely be given as the causes of death. For yourself, and for the country, you would not take the responsibility of stating abroad that these diseases, which are not destructive elsewhere, are fatal here, nor would you state to the readers of another year or another age, that these maladies, which were harmless as to life, before and after 1850, were in that year the causes of death.

It need not be denied that these diseases did exist at the time of death, but they were merely incidents in connection with the really fatal disease, or perhaps consequences of it; they may have performed a part, at most a small part, of the destructive process, but could not have acomplished it alone.

1. *Chicken pox*, a very mild and harmless disease, yet sometimes bears so strong a resemblance to small pox as to be mistaken for it. Probably those cases which are stated to be of fatal chicken pox were really small pox, the real name, if not character, of which was mistaken. It would be proper, therefore, to put these with *diseases of the skin.*

4. *Hives*, varicella pustular or globular, (not urticaria, as in your paper,) chicken pox, or swine pox, the former may have been mistaken for small pox, and thus proved fatal. These should be in *diseases of the skin.*

*Hives*, or *bold hives*, is a name applied to croup; it is a corruption of *heaves*, descriptive of the paroxysms. If there be any evidence that croup was intended, the cases should be transferred to that.

3. *Herpes*, 7. *Ringworm*, 9. *Tetter*, are all harmless diseases, and, unless in combination with other and more serious diseases, could not be assumed as causes of death. Strictly speaking, they should be transferred to the *unknown*, yet, as they may have been mistaken for some other cutaneous disease, I propose to include these in the *diseases of the skin.*

2. *Disease of the eyes* may involve disease of the brain; but otherwise it is not fatal. It should, therefore, be included in *diseases of the brain and nervous system.*

5. *Mumps* comes under the same category as the last. It may be connected with disease of the brain, and it may coexist with other and fatal disease. It would be safer to put these cases in the *unknown.*

I am aware that the Massachusetts, New York State and city, Kentucky, and Philadelphia reports give cases of *parotitis* (mumps) as causes of death. Yet the English reports omit it, and the National Medical Association excluded it.

6. *Onanism* possibly, but not probably, was a cause of death. It wastes life and produces other disorders. Cases under this head should be put under the *unknown.*

8. *Suppression of menses* (amenorhœa) is a symptom or consequence of many other diseases. It generally happens in diseases of high excitement, as fevers, &c.; and also in diseases of waste—consumption, scrofula, and cancer, especially uterine. It may be safe to put these cases in the *diseases of the organs of generation.*

11. *Fluor Albus*, unless complicated with disease of the uterus, as inflammation, cancer, &c., is not a fatal disease. This is put in *diseases of organs of generation.*

10. *Vaccination* may have been followed by inflammation, or erysipelas, in constitutions peculiarly susceptible, which terminated fatally. These, if known, should be given as the cause of death; otherwise the cases stated to be from this cause should be in the *unknown;* but *small-pox*, certainly, should not include them.

12. *Amputation* comes nearly under the same category as vaccination. It may have been in itself fatal; yet it is probable that such event was rather the result of previous disease, for which the operation was performed; or a subsequent disease, inflammation, erysipelas, &c., which should have been stated. Wanting these facts, cases reported under this name should be in the *unknown.*

13. *Cachexia* describes nothing. It signifies merely a depraved or diseased state of the system, a low vitality. These should be in the *unknown.*

14. *Congestion* is equally untelligible and should be in the same class, the *unknown.*

15. *Congestion of the brain*, probably, is apoplexy; yet it may not be. Other affections may have been intended. It should, then, be in *diseases of the brain.*

16. *Cramp*, as ordinarily understood, is not fatal. If this was a real cause of death, and was what is called "cramp in the stomach," it was *colic;* if it was "cramp of the muscles," it was *tetanus* and should be thus arranged; otherwise in the *unknown.*

17. *Eruption* is the most vague and unsatisfactory term, meaning, at most, *disease of the skin*, to which it should probably be transferred.

18. *Brain, congestion of*, probably intended for apoplexy. Yet it may be used for other cerebral affections which are not revealed in the returns. I have placed this, therefore, in *diseases of brain and nerves.*

19. *Fever, bilious*, is a most vague and uncertain term. In some regions it seems to be used

for all sorts of fevers, and the word *bilious* for all sorts of difficulties of the digestive organs.

20. *Gastric fever* is probably intended for inflammation of the stomach. Yet it is in many places used as vaguely, in respect to fever, as the word bilious.

21. *Winter fever* is more vague than either of the last two. It may mean bilious, or typhus, or synochus.

These three, with specific names, conveys no specific idea, and should be included under the general name of *fever* without further description.

22. *Congestive fever* is merely a form or phase of *typhus*.

23. *Inflammatory fever* is a name sometimes given to cases of *typhus*.

These two are therefore included in *typhus fever*.

24. *Brain fever* is usually intended for *cephalitis*, inflammation of brain, and yet it is sometimes used for typhus fever, in which there is some cerebral irritation. It is safe, however, to call these cases *cephalitis*.

25. *Menses, excess of*, a mere menorrhagia, excess of the menstrual flux, is seldom or never fatal of itself. There is not unfrequently a great and fatal uterine hæmorrhage, growing out uterine disease, which is the true cause of the death. These cases, therefore, should be strictly referred to *uterine hæmorrhage*. But as this is generally dependent on an anterior cause, it is better to include the whole in *diseases of the organs of generation*.

*Menses, suppression of*, already referred to.

26. *Milk leg*, not in itself fatal, yet was an accompaniment of the fatal disease. I include this in *childbirth*.

The last fifteen diseases (12 to 26, inclusive) reappear in their respective genera, or classes, or in the unknown. If, however, you conclude to retain them, or any part of them, it would be well to append a note to each one, thus: *This term has an uncertain meaning, yet it is here printed as found in the original returns.* This would throw the responsibility of unscientific or unreliable statements of the causes of death where it belongs; yet it is best to be accurate, and make the corrections as proposed.

There are also many terms, which being synonyms of each other, are condensed so far as they can be. 27, canker; 28, canker rash; 29, putrid sore throat. These are but various names for *scarlet fever*, which includes them.

30. *Bronchitis;* there seems to be an error in the explanation connected with this term in your paper. It is an inflammation of the mucous membrane of the bronchial tubes in the lungs. It is, however, generally applied to the lining membrane of all the air vessels, both to those in the chest and the throat, and very commonly to those in the head.

It is not exclusively a chronic disease, but is more often acute. Neither is it exclusively a disease of adult years, for children are subject to it.

Nor, on the other, is catarrh exclusively an acute disease, or one of childhood, for it is often chronic and it comes upon persons of all ages.

The true distinction between bronchitis and catarrh, and one that was held by scientific writers is, that the former affected the lining of the bronchi, or larger air tubes *below the throat*, and the latter affected the air passages *in the head*, principally the lining of the nasal passages. But there is very little discrimination between these diseases, both names being used to designate inflammation of the mucous membrane of any of the air passages. Therefore, 31, *Catarrh*, and 32, *Catarrhal fever*, are both included in bronchitis.

31. *Chlorosis*, is included in paramenia, and strictly it should be in diseases of the generative organs.

34. *Debility;* general custom does not confine this cause of death to infancy. The bills of mortality in all the States and cities which have printed them, include deaths from debility at all ages, from infancy to 90 and over. Unless, therefore, your returns limit the deaths under this head to infancy, or you have and use the means of thus limiting the cases, your explanation will not cover the whole ground, and should be omitted. The term itself is a bad one, and amounts to but little more than the unknown.

35. *Hæmorrhoids* is a better term than piles, and includes it.

36. *Head, disease of*, is included in disease of brain, &c.

37. *Inflammation of the brain* is included in *Cephalitis;* 38, *Inflammation of the lungs*, is included in *Pneumonia;* 39, *Inflammation of the throat*, is included in *laryngitis*.

40. *Killed*, is included in *accident;* 41, *Lockjaw*, is included in *tetanus*.

42. *Lungs, disease of*, is included in *respiratory organs, disease of;* 43, *nerves, disease of*, is included in *brain and nervous system, disease of;* 44, *piles* is included in *hæmorrhoids*; 45, *premature birth* is included in *debility;* 46, *putrid sore throat* is included in *scarlet fever;* 47, *salivation* may safely be included in *effects of mercury;* 48, *stomach, disease of*, is included in *digestive organs, disease of;* 49, *summer complaint* is included in *cholera morbus;* 50, *sunstroke* is included in *heat;* 51, *throat, disease of*, in included in *bronchittis and laryngitis;* 52, *venereal* is included in *syphilis;* 53, *bowels, disease of*, is included in *digestive organs, disease of;* 54, *atrophy* is included in *marasmus* which includes *tabes mesenterica*. These terms, from 27 to 54 inclusive, excepting numbers 30, 34, and 35, are omitted in my text, and condensed with, or replaced by, others.

There are some others concerning which I have great doubts, and yet I have let them remain, mainly for want of doing better.

55. *Dirt eating*. Probably this is secondary to a morbid condition of the stomach, dyspepsia, irritation, or craving for strange things, as in certain female and, perhaps, male diseases, slate pencils are eaten, which may precede death but are not deemed its cause.

56. *Fracture*, alone in itself, is a very doubtful cause of death. The shock communicated to the system by the blow or fall that caused the fracture, may and often does produce death. Also, the subsequent conditions, inflammation, erysipelas, &c., may cause death. Sometimes one has two or more limbs broken, and these in more places than one, and death follows. In this case, it is rather the violent shock to the system than the breaking of the bone, that is the fatal cause. Yet, I have let this, and the preceding, 55, remain.

I have introduced, as you see, several terms to represent either some of yours which I have omitted, or some diseases which I have omitted, or some diseases which seem to be omitted in yours.

| These are— | They represent— |
|---|---|
| 1. *Anæmia* | *Consumption of the blood*, a common term. |
| 2. *Bones, disease of* | *Necrosis.* |
| 3. *Cephalitis* | *Inflammation of the brain*; *brain* fever. |
| 4. *Circulatory organs, disease of* | Many cases here are reported under this general class or name. |
| 5. *Cold water drinking* | A very common cause of death in summer, especially among laborers. |
| 6. *Delirium tremens* | *Mania-a-potu.* |
| 7. *Digestive organs, disease of* | *Disease of bowels; disease of stomach*, but not *tabes mesenteria.* |
| 8. *Enteritis* | *Inflammation of bowels.* |
| 9. *Gastritis* | *Inflammation of stomach.* |
| 10. *Generative organs, disease of* | *Fluor albus; disease of uterus; excessive menses;* uterine *hæmorrhage*, and perhaps *suppressed menses.* |
| 11. *Hemorrhoids* | *Piles.* |
| 12. *Joints, disease of* | Many cases are reported under this title, and I suppose you must have found such in your returns. |
| 13. *Parmenia* | Diseases of menstruation; *excessive or suppressed menses*, (if no other cause of death,) and *chlorosis.* |
| 14. *Pneumonia* | *Inflammation of lungs.* |
| 15. *Respiratory organs, disease of* | Disease of lungs. |
| 16. *Skin, disease of* | *Eruption; herpes; hives*, (if not croup;) *ringworm; tetter; chicken pox.* |

With these alterations, I have made out the list of diseases, which I now send to you on other sheets.

I have made this list according to the alphabetical arrangement, as you have done.

Yet it is better, if possible, to arrange the diseases into classes according to their natural affinities, or the affinities of their causes, or to the organs and systems in which they are found. This plan is adopted by the English Registrar General, by the American National Medical Association, and by the registration officers of Massachusetts and Kentucky, and it shows, at least, the parts or systems of the human frame which suffered, or the general character of the causes that produced the disease.

I have therefore sent you a duplicate schedule of this nosological system, arranged according to this classification.

I hope you will print the entire list of all the names of diseases, or causes of death, that you found in all the returns, with the names of the States from which they came. This will take but a few pages and will do a good service to the investigator of these things. When we prepared the nosological nomenclature for the National Medical Association, in 1847, we obtained all the names that were returned in the Massachusetts reports for several years, and those that were printed in the various States and cities, and from all other sources we could reach. In this way we obtained about eleven hundred names of diseases supposed to be fatal. These we reduced to a scientific catalogue of about one hundred and fifteen. Mr. Farr, of London, did the same for the British government. He found about a thousand popular names, which he reduced and systematised.

There never has been, and there may not be again, another opportunity, such as you now enjoy, of showing to the world the popular names of diseases which are found in the several States and thought to be fatal. Of course, you will not give numbers and tables in connection with this popular nosology, only the bare names, alphabetically arranged, with the names of the States or region where they are used, as New England, Middle, Northwest, Southern, Southwest, or if in only one or two States they should be mentioned. These would take two columns.

I hope I have not delayed you too long. I desired to let you have this earlier; but there was so much investigation needed to determine all the principles and facts that this was impossible; and I would not send you a report less perfect than such as the range of means about me would allow me to give you.*

As it is, it is at your service. Trusting that it may be followed in your book, I am, very respectfully, yours,

EDWARD JARVIS.

J. D. B. De Bow, Esq.
*Superintendent of Census, Washington, D. C.*

---

* In the Compendium of the Census, p. 121, 3d paragraph, Dr. Jarvis is made to say "certainly *for one port*," instead of "certainly for the seaports," (5th line.)

# CLASSIFICATION

OF

# DEATHS IN THE SEVERAL STATES,

EMBRACING*—

I. CAUSES OF DEATH.
II. AGE AND SEX.
III. COLOR AND CONDITION.
IV. NATIVITIES.
V. SEASON OF DECEASE.
VI. DURATION OF ILLNESS.
VII. OCCUPATIONS.—(See Aggregate Tables of the United States.)

---

* *The instructions to marshals* in taking this portion of the census were as follows:

1. Under heading 1 of schedule insert the "*name of every person who died during the year ending* 1st *June*, 1850, *whose place of abode at the time of his death was in the family*." The family in which the death occurred from disease is to be considered as having been the place of abode of the deceased. Where the death was *sudden*, or the *result of accident*, the *usual* place of abode should be given, although the death may have occurred during temporary absence and in another family.

2. Under heading 2, entitled *Age*, insert in figures opposite the name the specific age in years of each person at the last birthday. If the exact age cannot be ascertained, insert a number which shall be the nearest approximation to it. The age in years, either exact or estimated, is in all cases to be inserted. If the person be a child which was under one year old, the entry is to be made in the fractional part of a year.

3. Under heading 3, entitled *Sex*, insert the letter M for male, or F for female, opposite the name in all cases.

4. Under heading 4, entitled *Color*, in all cases where the person is *white*, leave the space blank. In all cases where the person is black, insert the letter B. If mulatto, the letter M.

5. Under heading 5, entitled "*Free or slave*," in all cases where the person is free, leave the space blank. In all cases where the person is a slave, make a letter S opposite his or her name.

6. Under heading 6, entitled *Married or widowed*. This column only applies to the free inhabitants. The spaces opposite all slaves are to be left blank. When the deceased, being a free person, has been married, and the wife, or husband, as the case may be, survived, insert (M.) When the deceased *has been* married, but left no wife, or husband, as the case may be, insert (W.) In all other cases where the deceased is unmarried, or whether it is not known whether he or she was ever married, leave the space opposite such names blank.

7. Under heading 7, entitled *Place of birth*. The marshal should ascertain the place of birth of the deceased. If unknown, he should insert "unknown." If born in the town, city, or district where the deceased died, or in a foreign country, insert the name of the State, Territory, government, or country of birth.

8. Under heading 8, entitled *Month in which the person died*, insert, in all cases, the month when the death occurred opposite the name of the deceased. Should it happen that the date is not known, insert "unknown."

9. Under heading 9, entitled *Profession, occupation, or trade*, insert the specific *profession, occupation, or trade*, which the person was known or reputed to follow. Where the deceased, being an adult, had no particular occupation, insert the word "none;" when it is unknown, insert "unknown."

10. Under heading 10, entitled *Disease or cause of death*, insert the name of disease or cause of death opposite each name. The usual name given to a disease is to be inserted. When unknown, state "unknown." Where by accident, as steamboat explosion, so state; where the death was sudden, but natural, say "sudden," and enter also the cause.

11. In column eleven state the number of days' sickness. If of long duration, insert C for chronic.

REMARKS.—At the bottom of the page is left a space for remarks, where the assistant marshal should state any particular malady which has been prevalent in his district, and any cause which may account for the same. He is desired to state the character of the water, the character of the soil or rocks, kind of timber which grows naturally, the existence of natural fertilizers, as lime, or marl, or ores, or any other facts of interest relating to mines, seasons, or any particular or unusual natural phenomena, in fine, record any interesting event or circumstance connected with the history of his region for which he may find space.

In every case where the assistant has reason to believe that a portion of the information sought to be obtained by this schedule can be *more accurately* ascertained from any reliable bills of mortality, the facts may be abstracted from such registry, according to the form of this schedule, and the same rate of compensation will be allowed as if taken by actual visitation. It is, however, only admissible to avail one's self of such information where the record is of the most reliable nature or character.

## CLASSIFICATION OF DEATHS

| | Cause of death. | AGES. | | | | | | | | | | | | | | | | | | NATIVITIES. | | | | | |
|---|---|---|---|---|---|---|---|---|---|---|---|---|---|---|---|---|---|---|---|---|---|---|---|---|---|
| | | Under 1. | | 1 and under 5. | | 5 and under 10. | | 10 and under 20. | | 20 and under 50. | | 50 and under 80. | | 80 and under 100. | | 100 & over. | | Age unknown. | | Born in State. | New England. | Middle. | South. | Southwest. | Northwest. |
| | | M. | F. | M. | F. | M. | F. | M. | F. | M. | F. | M. | F. | M | F. | M | F. | M | F. | | | | | | |
| 1 | Abscess | 1 | 1 | | | 1 | | 1 | | 2 | 2 | | | | | | | | | 4 | 1 | | 1 | 1 | |
| 2 | Accident, not specif'd | 25 | 17 | 16 | 10 | 6 | 3 | 24 | 7 | 32 | 10 | 12 | 1 | | | | | | | 117 | 1 | 3 | 35 | 1 | 1 |
| 3 | ....do...burned | 13 | 4 | 30 | 34 | 12 | 28 | 3 | 6 | 5 | 5 | 1 | 2 | | | | | | | 128 | | 1 | 13 | 1 | |
| 4 | ....do...drowned | | 1 | 6 | 2 | 4 | 1 | 15 | 1 | 32 | 6 | 5 | 2 | | | | | | | 48 | 3 | | 12 | 2 | |
| 5 | ....do...scalded | | | | 1 | | | 1 | | | | | | | | | | | | 2 | | | | | |
| 6 | ....do...shot | | | | 1 | | 1 | 2 | | 6 | 1 | 1 | | | | | | | | 7 | | | 4 | 1 | |
| 7 | Amputation | | | | | | | | | 1 | | | | | | | | | | 1 | | | | | |
| 8 | Apoplexy | | | | 1 | 2 | 1 | 2 | 2 | 7 | 12 | 12 | 8 | 2 | | | | | | 13 | 2 | 2 | 23 | 2 | |
| 9 | Asthma | | | | | | | | | 2 | 3 | 3 | 6 | | | | | | | 2 | | | 11 | 1 | |
| 10 | Bladder, disease of | | | | | | | | | | | 1 | | | | | | | | 1 | | | | | |
| 11 | Bowels.......do | 6 | 4 | 9 | 11 | | 1 | 1 | | 2 | 2 | 2 | 2 | | | | | | | 31 | | 1 | 5 | 1 | |
| 12 | Brain.......do | 3 | 2 | 6 | | 3 | 2 | 1 | | 3 | 2 | | | | | | | | | 17 | | | 4 | 1 | |
| 13 | Bronchitis | 4 | 2 | 2 | 5 | | 1 | | | 5 | 1 | | 3 | | | | | | | 17 | | | 5 | 1 | |
| 14 | Cancer | | | | | 1 | | | 1 | 3 | 6 | 7 | 10 | | | | | | | 5 | 1 | | 19 | | 1 |
| 15 | Catarrh | 13 | 17 | 10 | 8 | 3 | 1 | 1 | 5 | 4 | 14 | 4 | 3 | 2 | | | | | | 65 | | | 13 | 4 | |
| 16 | Chicken pox | | | | 1 | | | | | | | | | | | | | | | 1 | | | | | |
| 17 | Childbirth | | | | | | | | 18 | | 101 | | | | | | | | | 54 | | 1 | 54 | 6 | |
| 18 | Chlorosis | | | | | | | | | | 1 | | | | | | | | | 1 | | | | | |
| 19 | Cholera | 2 | | 4 | 4 | 5 | 1 | | 5 | 26 | 8 | 7 | 7 | | | | | | | 37 | 1 | | 27 | | |
| 20 | ...do..infantum | 9 | 6 | 14 | 13 | | | | | | | | | | | | | | | 42 | | | | | |
| 21 | ...do..morbus | | 1 | 8 | 5 | 1 | 1 | 2 | 3 | 5 | 2 | 2 | 1 | | | | | | | 23 | | | 7 | | |
| 22 | Chorea | | | | 1 | | | 1 | | 1 | 1 | | | | | | | | | 4 | | | | | |
| 23 | Colic | 5 | 2 | 2 | 3 | 2 | | 4 | 1 | 17 | 5 | 3 | 4 | 1 | 1 | | | | | 29 | 1 | 1 | 17 | 1 | |
| 24 | Congestion | | | 2 | 3 | | 3 | 2 | | 2 | 4 | 1 | | | | | | | | 12 | | | 4 | 1 | |
| 25 | ....do....bowels | | | | | | | | | | | 1 | | | | | | | | | | | 1 | | |
| 26 | ....do....brain | 4 | 2 | 7 | 3 | 3 | 1 | 7 | 3 | 8 | 3 | 2 | 4 | | | | | | | 35 | | 1 | 11 | | |
| 27 | ....do....lungs | | | | 1 | | | 2 | 1 | 1 | | 1 | | | | | | | | 4 | | | 2 | | |
| 28 | Consumption | 2 | 1 | 4 | 3 | 4 | 2 | 9 | 22 | 101 | 133 | 47 | 31 | | 3 | | | | | 109 | 5 | 9 | 178 | 23 | |
| 29 | Convulsions | 44 | 50 | 23 | 12 | 4 | 6 | 10 | 7 | 17 | 13 | 6 | 5 | | | | | | | 157 | 3 | 2 | 24 | 3 | |
| 30 | Croup | 106 | 75 | 81 | 46 | 7 | 11 | 1 | 1 | 1 | | | | | | | | | | 319 | | | 10 | | |
| 31 | Debility | | 3 | | 2 | | | | | 3 | 4 | | | | | | | | | 6 | 1 | | 1 | 1 | |
| 32 | Diabetes | | | | | | | | 2 | 1 | | 1 | | | | | | | | | | | 4 | | |
| 33 | Diarrhœa | 34 | 29 | 68 | 46 | 7 | 10 | 9 | 6 | 32 | 22 | 23 | 12 | 1 | 1 | | | | | 212 | 1 | 1 | 65 | 10 | |
| 34 | Dirt eating | | | 1 | | 1 | 2 | 3 | 4 | 3 | | 1 | | | | | | | | 10 | | | 5 | | |
| 35 | Dropsy | 6 | | 27 | 19 | 17 | 15 | 53 | 26 | 43 | 88 | 70 | 31 | 6 | 6 | | | | | 195 | 3 | 4 | 174 | 7 | |
| 36 | Dysentery | 18 | 17 | 70 | 43 | 24 | 15 | 13 | 13 | 22 | 19 | 9 | 5 | 1 | | | | | | 224 | 3 | 3 | 29 | 3 | |
| 37 | Dyspepsia | | | | 1 | | | 2 | | 8 | 4 | 8 | 2 | 1 | | | | | | 7 | | | 13 | 2 | |
| 38 | Epilepsy | | | | | | | | | 3 | 1 | | | | | | | | | 2 | | | 2 | | |
| 39 | Eruption | 2 | | 1 | | | | | | | | | | | | | | | | 3 | | | | | |
| 40 | Erysipelas | 3 | 3 | 2 | 2 | 3 | | 1 | 1 | 1 | 3 | | 3 | | | | | | | 13 | | | 8 | | |
| 41 | Executed | | | | | | | | | 2 | | | | | | | | | | 1 | | | 1 | | |
| 42 | Fever, not specified | 24 | 28 | 80 | 64 | 42 | 45 | 52 | 59 | 70 | 70 | 23 | 27 | 1 | | | | | | 431 | | | 107 | 31 | |
| 43 | ..do..bilious | 3 | 6 | 11 | 15 | 8 | 8 | 8 | 14 | 14 | 11 | 7 | 3 | | | | | | | 73 | 2 | 1 | 23 | 3 | |
| 44 | ..do..brain | 5 | 2 | 15 | 9 | 6 | 3 | 6 | 8 | 11 | 1 | 5 | 1 | | | | | | | 52 | 1 | 1 | 15 | 1 | |
| 45 | ..do..congestive | 6 | 6 | 24 | 14 | 28 | 18 | 23 | 31 | 43 | 18 | 18 | 12 | 1 | 1 | | | | | 160 | 2 | 2 | 59 | 6 | |
| 46 | ..do..inflammatory | 2 | | 1 | | 1 | 1 | 3 | 1 | 5 | 1 | | 1 | | | | | | | 8 | 1 | | 6 | | |
| 47 | ..do..intermittent | 6 | 2 | 5 | 9 | 5 | 3 | 4 | 7 | 3 | 6 | 1 | 1 | | 1 | | | | | 39 | | | 10 | 3 | |
| 48 | ..do..puerperal | | | | | | | | 3 | | 11 | | | | | | | | | 5 | | | 8 | 1 | |
| 49 | ..do..remittent | | | | | | | | | 1 | | | | | | | | | | | | | 1 | | |
| 50 | ..do..scarlet | 12 | 16 | 35 | 46 | 19 | 20 | 5 | 6 | 3 | 4 | 1 | 2 | | | | | | | 157 | | | 9 | 3 | |
| 51 | ..do..typhoid | 4 | 4 | 31 | 17 | 17 | 16 | 45 | 40 | 72 | 52 | 16 | 8 | 1 | | | | | | 224 | 1 | 3 | 70 | 12 | |
| 52 | .do..yellow | | | | | | 1 | 2 | 1 | 13 | 6 | | 1 | | | | | | | 3 | 1 | 3 | 1 | | |
| 53 | Fistula | | | | | | | | | 1 | | | | | | | | | | | | | 1 | | |
| 54 | Fracture | | | | | 1 | | | | 2 | | 2 | | | | | | | | 1 | 2 | | 1 | | |
| 55 | Frozen | | | | | | | 1 | | 2 | 1 | | | | | | | | | 2 | | | 1 | | |
| 56 | Gout | | | | | | | | | | | | 1 | | | | | | | | | | 1 | | |
| 57 | Gravel | | | | | 1 | 1 | | | 2 | | 11 | 1 | | | | | | | 2 | | | 13 | 1 | |
| 58 | Head, disease of | 4 | 3 | 1 | 1 | | | | | | | 1 | | | | | | | | 10 | | | | | |
| 59 | Heart....do | 2 | | 1 | | 1 | 1 | 3 | 3 | 8 | 7 | 5 | 3 | | | | | | | 16 | | | 12 | 1 | |
| 60 | Heat | | | | | | | | | 2 | | | | | | | | | | 1 | | | | | |
| 61 | Hemorrhage | | 1 | 1 | | 1 | 1 | | 4 | 6 | 6 | 1 | 4 | | | | | | | 13 | | | 11 | | |
| 62 | Hernia | 1 | | 1 | | | | | | 2 | | 2 | | | | | | | | 4 | | | 2 | | |
| 63 | Hip, disease of | | | | | | | 1 | | | | | | | | | | | | 1 | | | | | |
| 64 | Hives | 39 | 19 | 4 | 5 | 2 | | | | | | | | | | | | | | 68 | | | 1 | | |
| 65 | Hooping cough | 63 | 58 | 72 | 84 | 8 | 12 | 2 | 4 | | 1 | 1 | | | | | | | | 295 | | | 7 | 3 | |
| 66 | Hydrocephalus | 9 | 3 | 3 | 3 | 2 | 3 | | 1 | | 1 | | | | | | | | | 24 | | | 1 | | |
| 67 | Inflammation | 11 | 6 | 7 | 6 | 3 | 3 | 3 | 4 | 5 | 11 | 6 | 3 | | | | | | | 45 | | | 20 | 1 | |
| 68 | .....do.....bowels | 11 | 14 | 11 | 13 | 5 | 5 | 3 | 5 | 13 | 19 | 9 | 4 | 1 | | | | | | 72 | 2 | | 26 | 1 | |
| 69 | .....do.....brain | 14 | 12 | 13 | 10 | 6 | 3 | 10 | 10 | 12 | 10 | 4 | 2 | | | | | | | 82 | | 2 | 15 | 3 | |
| 70 | .....do.....stomach | 1 | 1 | | 2 | | | | 1 | | 1 | | 3 | | | | | | | 4 | | | 5 | | |
| 71 | Insanity | | | | | 1 | | | | 3 | 2 | 1 | 1 | | | | | | | 3 | | | 5 | | |
| 72 | Intemperance | | | | | | | | | 27 | 2 | 6 | | | | | | | | 4 | 3 | 1 | 8 | 1 | |
| 73 | Jaundice | 3 | | 4 | 3 | | | | 2 | 2 | 2 | 2 | 4 | | | | | | | 11 | | | 8 | 1 | |
| 74 | Kidneys, disease of | | | 1 | | | | 2 | | 8 | | 4 | | | | | | | | 4 | | 1 | 9 | | |
| 75 | Killed | 1 | | | 1 | | | | | 12 | 2 | | | | | | | | | 9 | 1 | | 4 | | |

IN THE STATE OF ALABAMA.

| NATIVITIES. | | | | | SEASON OF DECEASE. | | | | DURATION OF SICKNESS. | | | | WHITES. | | | COLORED. | | | | | | | | | |
|---|---|---|---|---|---|---|---|---|---|---|---|---|---|---|---|---|---|---|---|---|---|---|---|---|---|
| | | | | | | | | | | | | | | | | Slaves. | | | | Free. | | | | | |
| | | | | | | | | | | | | | | | | Black. | | Mulatto. | | Black. | | Mul. | | | |
| California and Territories. | Ireland. | Germany. | Other foreign countries. | Unknown. | Spring. | Summer. | Autumn. | Winter. | Under 1 week. | 1 week and under 1 month. | 1 month and under 3 months. | 3 months and over. | Males. | Females. | Total. | M. | F. | M. | F. | M. | F. | M | F. | Aggregate deaths. | |
| | | | 1 | | 2 | 3 | 1 | 2 | 2 | 4 | 1 | 1 | 3 | 2 | 5 | 1 | 1 | | | | | 1 | | 8 | 1 |
| | 1 | 1 | 3 | | 46 | 42 | 37 | 32 | 112 | 20 | 4 | 2 | 41 | 8 | 49 | 71 | 35 | 3 | 4 | | | | 1 | 163 | 2 |
| | | | | | 53 | 22 | 19 | 45 | 78 | 32 | 7 | 3 | 17 | 19 | 36 | 46 | 55 | 1 | 5 | | | | | 143 | 3 |
| | 7 | 1 | 1 | 1 | 19 | 26 | 17 | 13 | 30 | | | | 26 | 4 | 30 | 34 | 8 | 2 | | | | | 1 | 75 | 4 |
| | | | | | | | 1 | 1 | 1 | | | | | 1 | 1 | 1 | | | | | | | | 2 | 5 |
| | | | | | | 3 | 4 | 5 | 9 | 1 | 1 | | 6 | 3 | 9 | 2 | | 1 | | | | | | 12 | 6 |
| | | | | | 1 | | | | 1 | | | | | | | 1 | | | | | | | | 1 | 7 |
| | 1 | 2 | 4 | | 15 | 12 | 11 | 11 | 35 | 6 | | 3 | 16 | 10 | 26 | 8 | 13 | 1 | 1 | | | | | 49 | 8 |
| | | | | | 8 | 2 | 3 | 1 | 3 | 1 | 1 | 8 | 3 | 4 | 7 | 2 | 4 | | 1 | | | | | 14 | 9 |
| | | | | | 1 | | | | | | | 1 | | | | 1 | | | | | | | | 1 | 10 |
| | | | 2 | | 7 | 22 | 9 | 2 | 5 | 13 | 9 | 7 | 6 | 9 | 15 | 13 | 10 | | | | 1 | 1 | | 40 | 11 |
| | | | | | 6 | 6 | 6 | 4 | 7 | 10 | 3 | 1 | 6 | 3 | 9 | 10 | 2 | | 1 | | | | | 22 | 12 |
| | | | | | 5 | 5 | 9 | 4 | 8 | 8 | 1 | 6 | 7 | 5 | 12 | 4 | 7 | | | | | | | 23 | 13 |
| | | | | 2 | 8 | 10 | 7 | 3 | 2 | 1 | 4 | 21 | 7 | 11 | 18 | 3 | 6 | 1 | | | | | | 28 | 14 |
| | | | | | 24 | 13 | 16 | 30 | 25 | 36 | 6 | 13 | 17 | 12 | 29 | 19 | 36 | 1 | | | | | | 85 | 15 |
| | | | | | | | 1 | | 1 | | | | | | | | | | 1 | | | | | 1 | 16 |
| | 2 | | | 1 | 31 | 26 | 35 | 24 | 61 | 41 | 11 | 2 | | 62 | 62 | | 52 | | 5 | | | | | 119 | 17 |
| | | | | | 1 | | | | | | | | | | | | 1 | | | | | | | 1 | 18 |
| | 2 | | 1 | | 39 | 17 | 6 | 7 | 55 | 12 | 1 | | 18 | 7 | 25 | 23 | 18 | 1 | | 1 | | 1 | | 69 | 19 |
| | | | | | 4 | 21 | 13 | 3 | 8 | 21 | 8 | 3 | 13 | 11 | 24 | 10 | 6 | | 2 | | | | | 42 | 20 |
| | | | 1 | | 2 | 16 | 10 | 2 | 13 | 13 | 3 | 2 | 8 | 10 | 18 | 10 | 3 | | | | | | | 31 | 21 |
| | | | | | | 1 | 2 | 1 | | 2 | 1 | 1 | 1 | 1 | 2 | 1 | 1 | | | | | | | 4 | 22 |
| | 1 | | | | 8 | 16 | 15 | 10 | 42 | 7 | | 1 | 16 | 8 | 24 | 16 | 7 | 1 | | 1 | | | 1 | 50 | 23 |
| | | | | | 1 | 7 | 7 | 2 | 9 | 7 | | 1 | 3 | 5 | 8 | 3 | 5 | 1 | | | | | | 17 | 24 |
| | | | | | 1 | | | | | | | 1 | 1 | | 1 | | | | | | | | | 1 | 25 |
| | | | | | 6 | 10 | 29 | 2 | 30 | 14 | 1 | 1 | 20 | 13 | 33 | 11 | 3 | | | | | | | 47 | 26 |
| | | | | | 1 | 1 | 4 | | 4 | 1 | | | 3 | 1 | 4 | 1 | 1 | | | | | | | 6 | 27 |
| | 12 | 1 | 10 | 8 | 104 | 74 | 81 | 99 | 4 | 5 | 30 | 301 | 125 | 112 | 237 | 39 | 71 | 2 | 10 | | | 1 | 2 | 362 | 28 |
| | 2 | | 1 | 4 | 32 | 48 | 76 | 39 | 151 | 21 | 2 | 8 | 48 | 39 | 87 | 52 | 49 | 3 | 3 | | | 1 | 2 | 197 | 29 |
| | | | | | 90 | 72 | 85 | 76 | 226 | 75 | 10 | 2 | 86 | 64 | 150 | 96 | 66 | 14 | 3 | | | | | 329 | 30 |
| | | | 3 | | 2 | 2 | 6 | 2 | | 2 | 4 | 3 | 2 | 8 | 10 | 1 | | | | | | | 1 | 12 | 31 |
| | | | | | 1 | 2 | 1 | | | 1 | | 3 | 1 | 1 | 2 | 1 | 1 | | | | | | | 4 | 32 |
| | 8 | | 2 | | 36 | 114 | 116 | 23 | 73 | 116 | 54 | 45 | 89 | 66 | 155 | 80 | 58 | 3 | 1 | 1 | | 1 | 1 | 300 | 33 |
| | | | | | 2 | 7 | 5 | 1 | 3 | 2 | 1 | 6 | | | | 9 | 6 | | | | | | | 15 | 34 |
| | 1 | 2 | 8 | 9 | 98 | 120 | 104 | 76 | 14 | 47 | 79 | 254 | 122 | 59 | 191 | 94 | 108 | 5 | 8 | | | 1 | | 407 | 35 |
| | 2 | 1 | 3 | 1 | 28 | 115 | 90 | 32 | 69 | 157 | 25 | 14 | 91 | 72 | 163 | 62 | 39 | 4 | 1 | | | | | 269 | 36 |
| | 1 | | 1 | 1 | 7 | 5 | 7 | 6 | | 4 | 3 | 17 | 17 | 4 | 21 | 2 | 2 | | 1 | | | | | 26 | 37 |
| | | | | | 1 | | 1 | 2 | 2 | 2 | | | 1 | 1 | 2 | 2 | | | | | | | | 4 | 38 |
| | | | | | | 2 | 1 | | | 1 | 1 | 1 | | | | 3 | | | | | | | | 3 | 39 |
| | 1 | | | | 6 | 5 | 6 | 5 | 8 | 10 | 3 | 1 | 7 | 10 | 17 | 3 | 2 | | | | | | | 22 | 40 |
| | | | | | | | 2 | | | | | | | | | 2 | | | | | | | | 2 | 41 |
| | 1 | 1 | 1 | 9 | 74 | 107 | 315 | 70 | 160 | 310 | 70 | 18 | 160 | 163 | 323 | 121 | 120 | 9 | 5 | 2 | 2 | | 3 | 585 | 42 |
| | 2 | 1 | 2 | 1 | 8 | 16 | 77 | 6 | 18 | 78 | 7 | 3 | 33 | 32 | 65 | 17 | 24 | 1 | 1 | | | | | 108 | 43 |
| | 1 | | | 1 | 12 | 14 | 35 | 8 | 43 | 24 | 2 | | 27 | 16 | 43 | 20 | 7 | 1 | 1 | | | | | 72 | 44 |
| | 6 | 2 | 4 | 2 | 12 | 27 | 175 | 26 | 146 | 89 | 4 | 2 | 72 | 55 | 127 | 67 | 43 | 4 | 2 | | | | | 243 | 45 |
| | | | | | | 2 | 12 | 2 | 4 | 8 | 3 | 1 | 5 | 1 | 6 | 7 | 3 | | | | | | | 16 | 46 |
| | | | | 1 | 4 | 12 | 33 | 4 | 19 | 20 | 9 | 5 | 17 | 20 | 37 | 7 | 9 | | | | | | | 53 | 47 |
| | | | | | 6 | 3 | 4 | 1 | 2 | 6 | 4 | 2 | | 9 | 9 | | 5 | | | | | | | 14 | 48 |
| | | | | | | | 1 | | 1 | | | | 1 | | 1 | | | | | | | | | 1 | 49 |
| | | | | | 41 | 49 | 31 | 48 | 62 | 95 | 8 | 1 | 44 | 52 | 96 | 29 | 40 | 2 | 1 | | | | 1 | 169 | 50 |
| | 3 | | 1 | 7 | 76 | 74 | 102 | 65 | 32 | 225 | 52 | 6 | 94 | 61 | 155 | 89 | 75 | 3 | 1 | | | | | 323 | 51 |
| | 12 | 2 | 2 | | 2 | 1 | 10 | 11 | 15 | 9 | | | 15 | 8 | 23 | | 1 | | | | | | | 24 | 52 |
| | | | | | 1 | | | | | | 1 | | 1 | | 1 | | | | | | | | | 1 | 53 |
| | | | 1 | | | 4 | | 1 | 1 | 2 | | 1 | 5 | | 5 | | | | | | | | | 5 | 54 |
| | | | | | 1 | | | 3 | 2 | | | | | | | 3 | 1 | | | | | | | 4 | 55 |
| | | | | | | | 1 | | | | | 1 | | 1 | 1 | | | | | | | | | 1 | 56 |
| | | | | | 3 | 6 | 2 | 4 | 2 | 6 | 2 | 5 | 10 | 1 | 11 | 4 | 1 | | | | | | | 16 | 57 |
| | | | | | 1 | 5 | 2 | 1 | 1 | 5 | 1 | 2 | 2 | 3 | 5 | 4 | 1 | | | | | | | 10 | 58 |
| | 1 | | 3 | 1 | 6 | 9 | 8 | 11 | 9 | 10 | 4 | 10 | 11 | 5 | 16 | 9 | 6 | | 3 | | | | | 34 | 59 |
| | | | | | | | 2 | | 2 | | | | | | | 1 | | 1 | | | | | | 2 | 60 |
| | | | 1 | | 12 | 9 | 2 | 2 | 12 | 6 | 3 | 4 | 5 | 9 | 14 | 4 | 7 | | | | | | | 25 | 61 |
| | | | | | 1 | 3 | 1 | 1 | 2 | 2 | 2 | | 4 | | 4 | 2 | | | | | | | | 6 | 62 |
| | | | | | 1 | | | | | | | 1 | | | | 1 | | | | | | | | 1 | 63 |
| | | | | | 19 | 18 | 17 | 15 | 46 | 19 | 2 | 2 | 36 | 19 | 55 | 9 | 5 | | | | | | | 69 | 64 |
| | | | | | 87 | 68 | 78 | 65 | 47 | 169 | 53 | 20 | 51 | 55 | 106 | 94 | 102 | 1 | 2 | | | | | 305 | 65 |
| | | | | | 6 | 3 | 6 | 10 | 9 | 9 | 1 | 5 | 9 | 7 | 16 | 5 | 3 | | 1 | | | | | 25 | 66 |
| | | | | | 16 | 17 | 20 | 11 | 21 | 25 | 9 | 11 | 25 | 18 | 43 | 10 | 14 | | | | | | 1 | 68 | 67 |
| | 3 | 3 | 3 | 1 | 22 | 40 | 35 | 11 | 35 | 53 | 17 | 5 | 31 | 32 | 63 | 21 | 26 | 1 | 2 | | | | | 113 | 68 |
| | 1 | | 3 | | 19 | 38 | 30 | 19 | 44 | 47 | 8 | 4 | 30 | 30 | 60 | 26 | 17 | 3 | | | | | | 106 | 69 |
| | | | | | 1 | 4 | 3 | 1 | 2 | 5 | 1 | | 1 | 6 | 7 | | 2 | | | | | | | 9 | 70 |
| | | | | | 3 | 2 | 1 | 2 | | 3 | | 4 | 5 | 2 | 7 | | | | 1 | | | | | 8 | 71 |
| | 11 | 1 | 4 | | 6 | 5 | 12 | 12 | 2 | 5 | 5 | 18 | 28 | 2 | 30 | 4 | | 1 | | | | | | 35 | 72 |
| | 1 | | | | 3 | 6 | 6 | 7 | 4 | 5 | 2 | 9 | 8 | 10 | 18 | 3 | 1 | | | | | | | 22 | 73 |
| | | | | | 3 | 2 | 7 | 3 | | 7 | 2 | 6 | 11 | | 11 | 4 | | | | | | | | 15 | 74 |
| | 1 | | 1 | | 3 | 4 | 4 | 5 | 8 | | | | 8 | 2 | 10 | 2 | 1 | 2 | | | | 1 | | 16 | 75 |

## CLASSIFICATION OF DEATHS

| | Cause of death. | Ages. Under 1. M. | Under 1. F. | 1 and under 5. M. | 1 and under 5. F. | 5 and under 10. M. | 5 and under 10. F. | 10 and under 20. M. | 10 and under 20. F. | 20 and under 50. M. | 20 and under 50. F. | 50 and under 80. M. | 50 and under 80. F. | 80 and under 100. M | 80 and under 100. F. | 100 & over. M | 100 & over. F. | Age unknown. M | Age unknown. F. | Nativities. Born in State. | New England. | Middle. | South. | Southwest. | Northwest. |
|---|---|---|---|---|---|---|---|---|---|---|---|---|---|---|---|---|---|---|---|---|---|---|---|---|---|
| 1 | Leprosy | | | | | | | | | 1 | | | | | | | | | | | | | | 1 | |
| 2 | Lightning | | | | | 1 | | 1 | | 4 | 1 | | | | | | | | | 3 | | | 3 | 1 | |
| 3 | Liver, disease of | 3 | 1 | 1 | | 1 | 2 | 3 | 5 | 9 | 8 | 5 | 1 | | | | | | | 17 | 1 | 1 | 14 | 3 | 1 |
| 4 | Lockjaw | 28 | 32 | 7 | 2 | 1 | 1 | 3 | | 4 | 2 | | | | | | | | | 76 | | | 2 | | |
| 5 | Lungs, disease of | 3 | | 2 | 1 | | 4 | 1 | | 11 | 5 | 2 | 1 | | | | | | | 18 | | 2 | 8 | 1 | 1 |
| 6 | Malformation | 2 | 1 | 1 | | | | | | | | | | | | | | | | 4 | | | | | |
| 7 | Marasmus | 2 | 2 | 3 | 2 | 1 | 1 | | | 1 | 1 | | | | | | | | | 11 | | 1 | | | |
| 8 | Measles | 7 | 6 | 6 | 5 | | 1 | 4 | | 3 | 3 | 3 | 2 | | | | | | | 29 | | | 9 | | |
| 9 | Menses, excess of | | | | | | | | | | 1 | | | | | | | | | 1 | | | | | |
| 10 | Menses, suppress'n of | | | | | | | | 1 | | 2 | | | | | | | | | 1 | | | 2 | | |
| 11 | Mortification | | | | | | 1 | 1 | | 4 | | 2 | | | | | | | | 2 | | 1 | 3 | 1 | |
| 12 | Mumps | 1 | 1 | | 3 | 1 | | | | | | | | | | | | | | 6 | | | | | |
| 13 | Murder | | | | | 1 | | 1 | | 8 | | | 1 | | | | | | | 8 | | | 3 | | |
| 14 | Neuralgia | | | | | | | | 1 | | | 1 | 1 | | | | | | | 1 | | | 2 | | |
| 15 | Old age | | | | | | | | | 1 | | 26 | 37 | 46 | 40 | 16 | 10 | | | 39 | | 4 | 107 | 2 | |
| 16 | Paralysis | | 2 | 1 | | 2 | 1 | 1 | 1 | 5 | 3 | 11 | 10 | 3 | 3 | | | | | 12 | 2 | 1 | 22 | 1 | |
| 17 | Pleurisy | | 3 | | | | 4 | 6 | 6 | 14 | 4 | 12 | 5 | | | | | | | 26 | | | 24 | 3 | |
| 18 | Pneumonia | 47 | 35 | 43 | 44 | 14 | 20 | 54 | 32 | 108 | 71 | 56 | 27 | 5 | 1 | | | | 1 | 340 | 3 | 1 | 169 | 20 | 2 |
| 19 | Poison | 2 | | 1 | 3 | 3 | 3 | 1 | | 1 | 2 | | 1 | | | | | | | 17 | | | | | |
| 20 | Premature birth | 4 | 3 | | | | | | | | | | | | | | | | | 7 | | | | | |
| 21 | Quinsy | 2 | 1 | 6 | 2 | | 2 | | 1 | 3 | 4 | | 1 | | | | | | | 17 | | | 4 | 1 | |
| 22 | Rheumatism | 1 | | | | | 1 | 1 | 3 | 3 | 5 | 8 | 5 | | 1 | | | | | 6 | | 2 | 15 | 1 | |
| 23 | Rickets | | | 2 | 1 | | | | | | | | | | | | | | | 3 | | | | | |
| 24 | Salivation, effects of | | | 1 | 1 | | | | | | | 1 | | | | | | | | 2 | | | 1 | | |
| 25 | Scrofula | 1 | 4 | 5 | 9 | 3 | 3 | 6 | 1 | 2 | 7 | 1 | 2 | | | | | | | 35 | | | 9 | | |
| 26 | Scurvy | | | 1 | | | | | | 1 | | | | | | | | | | 1 | | | | | |
| 27 | Small pox | | | | | 1 | | | | 2 | 1 | | | | | | | | | 2 | | | 1 | | |
| 28 | Spine, disease of | 1 | 1 | 1 | | | | 2 | | | 2 | 1 | | | | | | | | 5 | | | 2 | 1 | |
| 29 | Still born | 4 | 3 | | | | | | | | | | | | | | | | | 7 | | | | | |
| 30 | Suffocation | 39 | 46 | 12 | 7 | 2 | | 2 | 1 | 2 | | | | | | | | | | 110 | | | | | 1 |
| 31 | Suicide | | | | | | | 1 | | 2 | 1 | 2 | | | | | | | | 1 | | 1 | 4 | | |
| 32 | Sun, stroke of | | | | | | | | | 1 | 1 | | | | | | | | | 1 | | | | | |
| 33 | Syphilis | | | | 1 | | | | | | | | | | | | | | | 1 | | | | | |
| 34 | Teething | 26 | 23 | 37 | 46 | | | | | 1 | | | | | | | | | | 132 | | | | 1 | |
| 35 | Tetanus | 1 | | | | | | 2 | 1 | 2 | | | | | | | | | | 3 | | | 1 | | |
| 36 | Tetter | | | | | | | | | 1 | | | | | | | | | | 1 | | | | | |
| 37 | Throat, disease of | | | 1 | 3 | 5 | | 2 | 2 | 2 | 5 | | | | | | | | | 11 | | | 6 | 1 | 1 |
| 38 | Thrush | 5 | 14 | 4 | 2 | | | | | | | | | | | | | | | 25 | | | | | |
| 39 | Tumor | 1 | | 2 | | 2 | | | | | 1 | 2 | | | | | | | | 6 | | | 1 | | |
| 40 | Ulcer | | | 1 | | | 1 | | | 1 | 1 | 1 | 1 | | | | | | | 3 | | | 2 | | |
| 41 | Uterus, disease of | | | | | | | | | | 8 | | 5 | | | | | | | 3 | | | 9 | | 1 |
| 42 | Venereal | | | | | | | | | | | 1 | | | | | | | | 1 | | | | | |
| 43 | White swelling | 1 | | | | | | 2 | | | 1 | | | | | | | | | 3 | | | 1 | | |
| 44 | Worms | 18 | 11 | 75 | 91 | 19 | 32 | 4 | 3 | | | 1 | | | | | | | | 246 | | | 6 | 1 | |
| 45 | Unknown | 362 | 335 | 163 | 162 | 49 | 36 | 74 | 47 | 125 | 213 | 88 | 86 | 12 | 5 | | | 7 | 4 | 1355 | 5 | 7 | 299 | 40 | 9 |
| | Total | 1082 | 942 | 1090 | 968 | 373 | 363 | 515 | 444 | 1065 | 1074 | 580 | 410 | 84 | 63 | 16 | 10 | 7 | 5 | 6379 | 53 | 64 | 1971 | 224 | 54 |

## CLASSIFICATION OF DEATHS

| | Cause of death. | Under 1. M. | Under 1. F. | 1 and under 5. M. | 1 and under 5. F. | 5 and under 10. M. | 5 and under 10. F. | 10 and under 20. M. | 10 and under 20. F. | 20 and under 50. M. | 20 and under 50. F. | 50 and under 80. M. | 50 and under 80. F. | 80 and under 100. M | 80 and under 100. F. | 100 & over. M | 100 & over. F. | Age unknown. M | Age unknown. F. | Born in State. | New England. | Middle. | South. | Southwest. | Northwest. |
|---|---|---|---|---|---|---|---|---|---|---|---|---|---|---|---|---|---|---|---|---|---|---|---|---|---|
| 1 | Abscess | 1 | | | | | | 1 | | | | 1 | | | | | | | | 1 | | | | 1 | 1 |
| 2 | Accident, not specif'd | 3 | 1 | 4 | 1 | 4 | 2 | 8 | 2 | 8 | 1 | 2 | | | | | | | | 20 | | 2 | 3 | 6 | 4 |
| 3 | ....do ..burned | | | 5 | 3 | 2 | 2 | 1 | 2 | 1 | 1 | | | | | | | | | 11 | | | 2 | 3 | 1 |
| 4 | ....do...drowned | | | 3 | | 1 | 1 | 3 | 3 | 9 | | | | | | | | | | 6 | | | 5 | 4 | 3 |
| 5 | ....do...scalded | | 1 | 3 | 1 | | | | | | | | | | | | | | | 4 | | | | 1 | |
| 6 | ....do...shot | | | | | | | 3 | | 2 | | 2 | | | | | | | | | | | 1 | 4 | 1 |
| 7 | Apoplexy | | | 1 | | | | 1 | | 2 | 1 | | 5 | | | | | | | 3 | | | 6 | 1 | |
| 8 | Asthma | | | | | | | | | | 1 | 1 | 1 | | | | | | | | | | 2 | 1 | |
| 9 | Bowels, disease of | | 1 | 3 | 1 | | | 2 | 1 | | 1 | 2 | | | | | | | | 3 | | | 4 | 4 | |
| 10 | Brain.......do | | | | | 1 | | | | | | | | | | | | | | 1 | | | | | |
| 11 | Bronchitis | | 3 | 1 | 1 | | | | | 2 | 4 | | | 1 | | | | | | 5 | | | 3 | 1 | 3 |
| 12 | Cancer | | | | | | | | 1 | 2 | 4 | | 1 | | | | 1 | | | 1 | | | 4 | 4 | |
| 13 | Catarrh | 2 | 4 | | | 1 | 1 | | 7 | 3 | 6 | | 1 | | | | | | | 9 | | | 2 | 11 | 2 |
| 14 | Chicken pox | | | | 1 | | | | | | | | | | | | | | | 1 | | | | | |
| 15 | Child birth | | | | | | | | 6 | | 38 | | | | | | | | | 10 | | 1 | 11 | 17 | 4 |
| 16 | Cholera | 4 | 1 | 16 | 18 | 11 | 12 | 14 | 21 | 70 | 53 | 15 | 10 | | | | | | | 78 | | 3 | 61 | 63 | 31 |
| 17 | ....do..infantum | 4 | 5 | 3 | 2 | | | | | | | | | | | | | | | 13 | | | | 1 | |
| 18 | ....do..morbus | | | 4 | 3 | 1 | 1 | 2 | 1 | 3 | 3 | 4 | | | | | | | | 8 | | | 4 | 5 | 4 |
| 19 | Colic | 1 | 1 | 1 | | | 1 | | | 6 | 1 | 1 | 2 | | | | | | | 8 | | | 3 | 3 | |
| 20 | Congestion | | | 1 | | | 1 | 2 | | | 1 | | | | | | | | | 3 | | | | 1 | 1 |
| 21 | ....do...of brain | | 1 | 1 | 3 | 2 | | 1 | 2 | 2 | 2 | 2 | | | | | | | | 6 | | | 6 | 4 | |

## IN THE STATE OF ALABAMA—Continued.

| Nativities: California and Territories. | Ireland. | Germany. | Other foreign countries. | Unknown. | Season of decease: Spring. | Summer. | Autumn. | Winter. | Duration of sickness: Under 1 week. | 1 week and under 1 month. | 1 month and under 3 months. | 3 months and over. | Whites: Males. | Females. | Total. | Colored: Slaves: Black M. | Black F. | Mulatto M. | Mulatto F. | Free: Black M. | Black F. | Mul. M | Mul. F. | Aggregate deaths. | |
|---|---|---|---|---|---|---|---|---|---|---|---|---|---|---|---|---|---|---|---|---|---|---|---|---|---|
| | | | | | | 1 | | | | | | 1 | | | | 1 | | | | | | | | 1 | 1 |
| | | | | | 1 | 4 | 2 | | 3 | | | | | 1 | 1 | 6 | | | | | | | | 7 | 2 |
| | | 1 | 1 | | 12 | 9 | 10 | 8 | 5 | 8 | 5 | 21 | 18 | 16 | 34 | 4 | 1 | | | | | | | 39 | 3 |
| | | | 2 | | 18 | 19 | 18 | 21 | 66 | 13 | | | 11 | 4 | 15 | 31 | 32 | 1 | | | | | 1 | 80 | 4 |
| | | | | | 9 | 6 | 8 | 7 | 9 | 7 | 4 | 8 | 11 | 7 | 18 | 7 | 4 | 1 | | | | | | 30 | 5 |
| | | | | | 1 | 2 | 1 | | 2 | 1 | | | 3 | | 3 | | 1 | | | | | | | 4 | 6 |
| | | 1 | | | 3 | 3 | 3 | 4 | 5 | 1 | 2 | 3 | 3 | 3 | 6 | 3 | 3 | | | | | 1 | | 13 | 7 |
| | | | | 2 | 14 | 18 | 3 | 5 | 9 | 20 | 4 | 5 | 9 | 4 | 13 | 14 | 12 | | 1 | | | | | 40 | 8 |
| | | | | | | | 1 | | | 1 | | | | 1 | 1 | | | | | | | | | 1 | 9 |
| | | | | | | | 3 | | 1 | | 1 | 1 | | 2 | 2 | | 1 | | | | | | | 3 | 10 |
| | 1 | | | | 1 | 2 | 4 | 1 | 1 | 5 | 1 | 1 | 6 | 1 | 7 | 1 | | | | | | | | 8 | 11 |
| | | | | | 4 | | 2 | | 2 | 2 | | | | | | 2 | 4 | | | | | | | 6 | 12 |
| | | | | | 7 | 2 | 1 | 1 | 5 | | | | 5 | | 5 | 5 | 1 | | | | | | | 11 | 13 |
| | | | | | 2 | 1 | | | 1 | | 1 | 1 | 1 | 1 | 2 | | 1 | | | | | | | 3 | 14 |
| | 4 | 1 | 11 | 8 | 38 | 48 | 49 | 39 | 28 | 16 | 11 | 37 | 33 | 40 | 73 | 53 | 43 | 3 | 2 | | | | 2 | 176 | 15 |
| | 1 | | 3 | 1 | 10 | 16 | 9 | 8 | 8 | 10 | 6 | 17 | 19 | 15 | 34 | 4 | 5 | | | | | | | 43 | 16 |
| | | | | 1 | 19 | 11 | 8 | 14 | 17 | 27 | 4 | 2 | 22 | 13 | 35 | 9 | 9 | | | 1 | | | | 54 | 17 |
| | 2 | 1 | 4 | 16 | 218 | 107 | 94 | 134 | 129 | 352 | 43 | 25 | 156 | 98 | 254 | 164 | 128 | 6 | 4 | 1 | 1 | | | 558 | 18 |
| | | | | | 1 | 8 | 4 | 4 | 9 | 4 | 2 | 2 | 3 | 4 | 7 | 4 | 5 | 1 | | | | | | 17 | 19 |
| | | | | | 2 | 3 | 2 | | 2 | | | | 4 | 1 | 5 | | 2 | | | | | | | 7 | 20 |
| | | | | | 5 | 5 | 7 | 5 | 14 | 8 | | | 10 | 7 | 17 | 1 | 4 | | | | | | | 22 | 21 |
| | 1 | | 2 | 1 | 10 | 5 | 5 | 2 | 2 | 4 | 1 | 20 | 5 | 6 | 11 | 6 | 9 | | | 2 | | | | 28 | 22 |
| | | | | | | 2 | 1 | | | | 1 | 2 | | | | 2 | 1 | | | | | | | 3 | 23 |
| | | | | | | | 1 | 2 | | 2 | | 1 | 2 | 1 | 3 | | | | | | | | | 3 | 24 |
| | | | | | 8 | 13 | 12 | 10 | 3 | 9 | 4 | 26 | 4 | 7 | 11 | 12 | 19 | 2 | | | | | | 44 | 25 |
| | | | | 1 | | | 2 | | 1 | | | 1 | 2 | | 2 | | | | | | | | | 2 | 26 |
| | 1 | | | | 3 | 1 | | | | 4 | | | 1 | | 1 | 2 | 1 | | | | | | | 4 | 27 |
| | | | | | 2 | 3 | | 3 | 1 | 3 | | 3 | 1 | | 1 | 4 | 3 | | | | | | | 8 | 28 |
| | | | | | 1 | 3 | 1 | 2 | | | | | 3 | 3 | 6 | 1 | | | | | | | | 7 | 29 |
| | | | | | 38 | 16 | 27 | 24 | 70 | | | | 3 | 3 | 6 | 52 | 50 | 1 | 1 | 1 | | | | 111 | 30 |
| | | | | | 1 | 1 | 2 | 2 | 3 | | | | 5 | 1 | 6 | | | | | | | | | 6 | 31 |
| | | | | 1 | | | 2 | | 2 | | | | 1 | | 1 | | | | | | | | 1 | 2 | 32 |
| | | | | | | | | 1 | | | | | | 1 | 1 | | | | | | | | | 1 | 33 |
| | | | | | 28 | 41 | 46 | 11 | 31 | 46 | 17 | 13 | 14 | 13 | 27 | 49 | 52 | 1 | 4 | | | | | 133 | 34 |
| | 1 | | 1 | | 4 | | | 2 | 5 | 1 | | | 2 | 1 | 3 | 3 | | | | | | | | 6 | 35 |
| | | | | | 1 | | | | | | 1 | | | | | 1 | | | | | | | | 1 | 36 |
| | | | 1 | | 3 | 9 | 1 | 5 | 9 | 9 | 1 | | 6 | 7 | 13 | 4 | 3 | | | | | | | 20 | 37 |
| | | | | | 7 | 5 | 9 | 3 | 10 | 7 | 6 | | 5 | 8 | 13 | 4 | 8 | | | | | | | 25 | 38 |
| | | | | 1 | 4 | 2 | 2 | | 1 | 2 | 1 | 4 | 2 | | 2 | 5 | 1 | | | | | | | 8 | 39 |
| | | | 1 | | 1 | 2 | 2 | 1 | | | | 6 | | 1 | 1 | 2 | 2 | 1 | | | | | | 6 | 40 |
| | | | | | 4 | 3 | 4 | 2 | 1 | 4 | 3 | 4 | | 1 | 1 | | 12 | | | | | | | 13 | 41 |
| | | | | | | | 1 | | | | | 1 | | | | 1 | | | | | | | | 1 | 42 |
| | | | | | | 2 | 2 | | 2 | | 1 | 1 | 1 | 1 | 2 | 2 | | | | | | | | 4 | 43 |
| | 1 | | | | 48 | 51 | 107 | 37 | 98 | 97 | 24 | 17 | 33 | 35 | 68 | 77 | 97 | 7 | 5 | | | | | 254 | 44 |
| | 15 | 2 | 13 | 23 | 411 | 410 | 517 | 338 | 697 | 306 | 134 | 340 | 406 | 365 | 771 | 451 | 504 | 19 | 16 | 2 | 1 | 2 | 2 | 1768 | 45 |
| .... | 111 | 24 | 106 | 105 | 2084 | 2229 | 2852 | 1686 | 3089 | 2905 | 824 | 1432 | 2386 | 1946 | 4332 | 2287 | 2208 | 116 | 100 | 12 | 5 | 11 | 20 | 9091 | |

## IN THE STATE OF ARKANSAS.

| Nativities: California and Territories. | Ireland. | Germany. | Other foreign countries. | Unknown. | Season of decease: Spring. | Summer. | Autumn. | Winter. | Duration of sickness: Under 1 week. | 1 week and under 1 month. | 1 month and under 3 months. | 3 months and over. | Whites: Males. | Females. | Total. | Colored: Slaves: Black M. | Black F. | Mulatto M. | Mulatto F. | Free: Black M. | Black F. | Mul. M | Mul. F. | Aggregate deaths. | |
|---|---|---|---|---|---|---|---|---|---|---|---|---|---|---|---|---|---|---|---|---|---|---|---|---|---|
| | | | | | 2 | 1 | | | | 1 | | 2 | 3 | | 3 | | | | | | | | | 3 | 1 |
| | | | 1 | | 9 | 10 | 8 | 9 | 21 | 5 | | | 23 | 5 | 28 | 6 | 2 | | | | | | | 36 | 2 |
| | | | | | 10 | 1 | 2 | 4 | 6 | 7 | 2 | 1 | 3 | 5 | 8 | 6 | 3 | | | | | | | 17 | 3 |
| | | | | 2 | 6 | 9 | 3 | 2 | 8 | | | | 6 | 2 | 8 | 7 | 2 | 3 | | | | | | 20 | 4 |
| | | | | | 1 | 2 | 1 | 1 | 2 | 3 | | | 3 | 2 | 5 | | | | | | | | | 5 | 5 |
| | | | | 1 | 2 | 2 | 2 | 1 | 3 | | | 1 | 7 | | 7 | | | | | | | | | 7 | 6 |
| | | | | | 2 | 4 | | 4 | 10 | | | | 3 | 3 | 6 | 1 | 3 | | | | | | | 10 | 7 |
| | | | | | 2 | 1 | | | 1 | | | 2 | 1 | 2 | 3 | | | | | | | | | 3 | 8 |
| | | | | | 1 | 2 | 7 | 1 | 4 | 5 | 1 | | 5 | 2 | 7 | 1 | 2 | 1 | | | | | | 11 | 9 |
| | | | | | | | 1 | | | | | 1 | 1 | | 1 | | | | | | | | | 1 | 10 |
| | | | | | 2 | | 6 | 4 | 2 | 3 | 2 | 5 | 4 | 8 | 12 | | | | | | | | | 12 | 11 |
| | | | | | 4 | 2 | | 3 | | | 1 | 8 | 2 | 5 | 7 | | 2 | | | | | | | 9 | 12 |
| | | 1 | | | 6 | 4 | 8 | 7 | 12 | 10 | 2 | 1 | 5 | 13 | 18 | 1 | 6 | | | | | | | 25 | 13 |
| | | | | | | | 1 | | | 1 | | | | 1 | 1 | | | | | | | | | 1 | 14 |
| | | | | 1 | 15 | 11 | 10 | 8 | 20 | 21 | 3 | | | 32 | 32 | | 11 | | 1 | | | | | 44 | 15 |
| | | | | 9 | 54 | 121 | 16 | 53 | 226 | 16 | | | 53 | 37 | 90 | 69 | 71 | 8 | 7 | | | | | 245 | 16 |
| | | | | | | 3 | 6 | 5 | 6 | 8 | | | 7 | 7 | 14 | | | | | | | | | 14 | 17 |
| | | 1 | | | 4 | 4 | 11 | 3 | 17 | 4 | | 1 | 10 | 4 | 14 | 3 | 3 | 1 | 1 | | | | | 22 | 18 |
| | | | | | 3 | 3 | 2 | 6 | 9 | 4 | | | 6 | 2 | 8 | 3 | 3 | | | | | | | 14 | 19 |
| | | | | | | | 5 | | 3 | 2 | | | 3 | 2 | 5 | | | | | | | | | 5 | 20 |
| | | | | | 1 | 8 | 5 | 1 | 11 | 5 | | | 5 | 7 | 12 | 3 | 1 | | | | | | | 16 | 21 |

CLASSIFICATION OF DEATHS

| | Cause of death. | Ages. | | | | | | | | | | | | | | | | | | Nativities. | | | | | |
|---|---|---|---|---|---|---|---|---|---|---|---|---|---|---|---|---|---|---|---|---|---|---|---|---|---|
| | | Under 1. | | 1 and under 5. | | 5 and under 10. | | 10 and under 20. | | 20 and under 50. | | 50 and under 80. | | 80 and under 100. | | 100 & over. | | Age unknown. | | Born in State. | New England. | Middle. | South. | Southwest. | Northwest. |
| | | M. | F. | M. | F. | M. | F. | M. | F. | M. | F. | M. | F. | M | F. | M | F. | M | F. | | | | | | |
| 1 | Consumption | ... | ... | ... | 1 | 1 | ... | 3 | 6 | 55 | 45 | 13 | 8 | ... | ... | ... | ... | ... | ... | 21 | 2 | 1 | 42 | 36 | 18 |
| 2 | Convulsions | 3 | 4 | 6 | 4 | ... | 1 | 1 | 3 | 2 | 2 | 1 | ... | ... | ... | ... | ... | ... | ... | 18 | ... | ... | 4 | 4 | 1 |
| 3 | Croup | 57 | 38 | 23 | 27 | 1 | 2 | ... | ... | ... | ... | ... | ... | ... | ... | ... | ... | ... | ... | 140 | ... | ... | ... | 6 | 2 |
| 4 | Debility | 2 | 3 | 1 | ... | ... | ... | ... | ... | ... | ... | ... | ... | ... | ... | ... | ... | ... | ... | 6 | ... | ... | ... | ... | ... |
| 5 | Diabetes | ... | ... | 1 | ... | ... | ... | ... | ... | 1 | ... | ... | ... | ... | ... | ... | ... | ... | ... | ... | ... | ... | 1 | ... | 1 |
| 6 | Diarrhœa | 4 | 4 | 6 | 7 | 2 | 4 | 2 | 2 | 8 | 3 | 3 | 2 | ... | ... | ... | ... | ... | ... | 18 | ... | ... | 9 | 15 | 4 |
| 7 | Dropsy | 3 | 1 | 5 | 2 | 6 | 2 | 6 | 5 | 19 | 17 | 11 | 5 | 2 | ... | ... | ... | ... | ... | 28 | 1 | 4 | 21 | 21 | 6 |
| 8 | Dysentery | 4 | 6 | 12 | 15 | 1 | 3 | 1 | 1 | 8 | 3 | 3 | 1 | ... | ... | ... | ... | ... | ... | 34 | ... | ... | 5 | 15 | 3 |
| 9 | Dyspepsia | ... | ... | ... | ... | ... | ... | ... | ... | 1 | ... | 1 | ... | ... | ... | ... | ... | ... | ... | ... | ... | 1 | 1 | ... | ... |
| 10 | Epilepsy | ... | ... | ... | ... | ... | ... | ... | ... | 4 | ... | ... | ... | ... | ... | ... | ... | ... | ... | ... | ... | 1 | 1 | 2 | ... |
| 11 | Erysipelas | 1 | ... | 3 | 2 | 2 | 2 | 3 | ... | 1 | 4 | 2 | ... | ... | ... | ... | ... | ... | ... | 11 | ... | ... | 3 | 3 | 3 |
| 12 | Fever, not specified | 8 | 17 | 38 | 31 | 13 | 24 | 16 | 18 | 53 | 37 | 11 | 13 | ... | ... | ... | ... | ... | ... | 125 | ... | 3 | 36 | 73 | 28 |
| 13 | ..do .bilious | 1 | 2 | 5 | 2 | 6 | 5 | 2 | 4 | 6 | 4 | 1 | 2 | ... | ... | ... | ... | ... | ... | 12 | ... | ... | 9 | 16 | 2 |
| 14 | ..do..brain | 2 | 1 | 2 | 1 | 1 | ... | 1 | ... | ... | ... | ... | ... | ... | ... | ... | ... | ... | ... | 5 | ... | ... | 1 | 1 | ... |
| 15 | ..do..congestion | 6 | 3 | 17 | 11 | 13 | 12 | 8 | 13 | 22 | 12 | 8 | 3 | ... | ... | ... | ... | ... | ... | 49 | 1 | 1 | 30 | 34 | 11 |
| 16 | ..do..intermittent | ... | 3 | 6 | 3 | 5 | 2 | 2 | ... | 1 | 6 | 1 | ... | ... | ... | ... | ... | ... | ... | 11 | ... | 1 | 2 | 12 | 3 |
| 17 | ..do..puerperal | ... | ... | ... | ... | ... | ... | ... | 4 | ... | 12 | ... | ... | ... | ... | ... | ... | ... | ... | 2 | ... | ... | 5 | 6 | 3 |
| 18 | ..do..scarlet | 8 | 2 | 20 | 20 | 21 | 16 | 2 | 6 | 1 | 2 | ... | ... | ... | ... | ... | ... | ... | ... | 75 | ... | ... | 5 | 13 | 5 |
| 19 | ..do..typhus | 1 | ... | 5 | 3 | 3 | 1 | 6 | 3 | 9 | 5 | 3 | ... | ... | ... | ... | ... | ... | ... | 16 | ... | ... | 7 | 8 | 7 |
| 20 | ..do..winter | 1 | ... | 1 | 3 | 3 | 1 | 5 | 5 | 9 | 8 | 2 | 2 | ... | ... | ... | ... | ... | ... | 14 | ... | ... | 7 | 12 | 7 |
| 21 | Frozen | ... | ... | ... | ... | 1 | ... | 1 | ... | 3 | ... | 2 | ... | ... | ... | ... | ... | ... | ... | 1 | ... | ... | 3 | 1 | ... |
| 22 | Gravel | 1 | ... | 1 | ... | ... | ... | ... | ... | ... | ... | ... | 1 | ... | ... | ... | ... | ... | ... | 2 | ... | ... | 1 | ... | ... |
| 23 | Heart, disease of | ... | ... | 1 | ... | ... | 1 | 1 | ... | 1 | 1 | ... | 1 | ... | ... | ... | ... | ... | ... | 3 | ... | ... | 1 | 2 | ... |
| 24 | Hemorrhage | ... | ... | ... | 1 | ... | ... | ... | ... | 2 | 1 | ... | ... | ... | ... | ... | ... | ... | ... | 1 | 1 | ... | 2 | ... | ... |
| 25 | Hernia | ... | ... | ... | 1 | ... | ... | ... | ... | ... | 1 | 1 | ... | ... | ... | ... | ... | ... | ... | 1 | ... | 1 | ... | ... | 1 |
| 26 | Hives | 22 | 14 | 4 | 4 | ... | ... | ... | ... | ... | ... | ... | ... | ... | ... | ... | ... | ... | ... | 43 | ... | ... | ... | 1 | ... |
| 27 | Hooping cough | 12 | 10 | 11 | 13 | 1 | 5 | 1 | 1 | ... | 1 | ... | ... | ... | ... | ... | ... | ... | ... | 45 | ... | ... | ... | 8 | 2 |
| 28 | Hydrocephalus | 3 | ... | 1 | 1 | ... | ... | ... | ... | ... | ... | ... | ... | ... | ... | ... | ... | ... | ... | 5 | ... | ... | ... | ... | ... |
| 29 | Inflamt'n, not specf'd | 1 | 1 | ... | ... | 1 | ... | ... | ... | 2 | ... | ... | 1 | ... | ... | ... | ... | ... | ... | 3 | ... | ... | 1 | 1 | ... |
| 30 | ....do....bowels | 3 | 5 | 9 | 5 | ... | 1 | 2 | 2 | 6 | 3 | 2 | ... | ... | ... | ... | ... | ... | ... | 22 | ... | 2 | 7 | 6 | ... |
| 31 | ....do....brain | 4 | 6 | 7 | 5 | 6 | 6 | 4 | 7 | 6 | 8 | 1 | 1 | ... | ... | ... | ... | ... | ... | 40 | ... | 1 | 6 | 14 | ... |
| 32 | ....do....stomach | ... | ... | ... | ... | ... | ... | 1 | ... | 1 | 1 | ... | ... | ... | ... | ... | ... | ... | ... | 1 | ... | ... | 1 | 1 | ... |
| 33 | Intemperance | ... | ... | ... | ... | ... | ... | ... | ... | 6 | ... | ... | ... | ... | ... | ... | ... | ... | ... | ... | ... | 1 | 1 | 2 | ... |
| 34 | Jaundice | ... | ... | 1 | 1 | ... | ... | ... | ... | 3 | ... | ... | ... | ... | ... | ... | ... | ... | ... | 2 | ... | ... | ... | 3 | ... |
| 35 | Killed | ... | ... | ... | ... | ... | ... | ... | ... | 3 | ... | ... | ... | ... | ... | ... | ... | ... | ... | ... | ... | ... | 2 | ... | ... |
| 36 | Liver, disease of | ... | 1 | ... | 1 | 1 | 1 | 2 | ... | 7 | 13 | 3 | 2 | ... | ... | ... | ... | ... | ... | 5 | ... | ... | 11 | 7 | 4 |
| 37 | Lungs....do | 1 | ... | 2 | ... | ... | ... | ... | 1 | 2 | 1 | ... | ... | ... | ... | ... | ... | ... | ... | 3 | ... | ... | ... | 2 | 1 |
| 38 | Measles | 2 | 2 | 1 | 2 | 1 | ... | ... | ... | 2 | 2 | ... | ... | ... | ... | ... | ... | ... | ... | 7 | ... | ... | ... | 3 | 2 |
| 39 | Menses, excess of | ... | ... | ... | ... | ... | ... | ... | ... | ... | 1 | ... | ... | ... | ... | ... | ... | ... | ... | 1 | ... | ... | ... | ... | ... |
| 40 | Mortification | ... | ... | ... | ... | ... | ... | 1 | ... | 1 | ... | ... | ... | 1 | ... | ... | ... | ... | ... | 1 | ... | ... | 2 | ... | ... |
| 41 | Murder | ... | ... | ... | ... | ... | ... | ... | ... | 7 | ... | 4 | ... | ... | ... | ... | ... | ... | ... | ... | ... | ... | 5 | 3 | ... |
| 42 | Old age | ... | ... | ... | ... | ... | ... | ... | ... | ... | ... | 13 | 6 | 10 | 5 | 2 | 3 | ... | ... | ... | 1 | 1 | 25 | 2 | 2 |
| 43 | Paralysis | ... | ... | ... | 1 | 1 | ... | 1 | 1 | 4 | 1 | 1 | 1 | ... | ... | ... | ... | ... | ... | 3 | ... | ... | 2 | 3 | 1 |
| 44 | Piles | ... | ... | ... | ... | ... | ... | ... | ... | ... | ... | 1 | ... | ... | ... | ... | ... | ... | ... | ... | ... | ... | 1 | ... | ... |
| 45 | Pleurisy | ... | ... | ... | ... | ... | ... | 4 | 2 | 5 | 4 | 6 | ... | ... | ... | ... | ... | ... | ... | 4 | ... | 1 | 6 | 5 | 5 |
| 46 | Pneumonia | 7 | 3 | 9 | 6 | 7 | 2 | 17 | 20 | 52 | 35 | 16 | 11 | 1 | 1 | ... | ... | ... | ... | 58 | 1 | 5 | 40 | 52 | 21 |
| 47 | Poison | ... | ... | 2 | 2 | ... | 1 | 1 | ... | 1 | 1 | ... | ... | ... | ... | ... | ... | ... | ... | 6 | ... | ... | ... | 1 | 1 |
| 48 | Prematurity of birth | 1 | ... | ... | ... | ... | ... | ... | ... | ... | ... | ... | ... | ... | ... | ... | ... | ... | ... | 1 | ... | ... | ... | ... | ... |
| 49 | Quinsy | 1 | ... | 1 | 1 | ... | ... | 1 | 1 | 1 | ... | ... | ... | ... | ... | ... | ... | ... | ... | 5 | ... | ... | ... | ... | 1 |
| 50 | Rheumatism | ... | ... | ... | ... | ... | ... | 1 | ... | 4 | ... | 2 | ... | ... | ... | ... | ... | ... | ... | ... | ... | ... | 4 | 3 | ... |
| 51 | Scrofula | 1 | ... | ... | 2 | ... | ... | ... | ... | 1 | ... | ... | ... | ... | ... | ... | ... | ... | ... | 3 | ... | ... | ... | 1 | ... |
| 52 | Scurvy | ... | ... | ... | ... | ... | ... | ... | ... | 2 | ... | ... | ... | ... | ... | ... | ... | ... | ... | ... | ... | ... | 2 | ... | ... |
| 53 | Small pox | 3 | 2 | 2 | 2 | 1 | ... | 2 | 1 | 11 | 4 | 4 | 1 | ... | ... | ... | ... | ... | ... | 8 | ... | ... | 6 | 8 | 9 |
| 54 | Spine, disease of | ... | ... | 1 | ... | ... | ... | ... | 1 | 1 | ... | ... | ... | ... | ... | ... | ... | ... | ... | 1 | ... | 1 | ... | ... | 1 |
| 55 | Still-born | 3 | 4 | ... | ... | ... | ... | ... | ... | ... | ... | ... | ... | ... | ... | ... | ... | ... | ... | 7 | ... | ... | ... | ... | ... |
| 56 | Suffocation | 5 | 6 | ... | 1 | ... | ... | ... | ... | ... | ... | ... | ... | ... | ... | ... | ... | ... | ... | 11 | ... | ... | 1 | ... | ... |
| 57 | Teething | 3 | 5 | 6 | 1 | ... | ... | ... | ... | ... | ... | ... | ... | ... | ... | ... | ... | ... | ... | 14 | ... | ... | ... | 1 | ... |
| 58 | Tetanus | ... | ... | ... | ... | ... | ... | 1 | ... | ... | ... | ... | ... | ... | ... | ... | ... | ... | ... | ... | ... | ... | ... | 1 | ... |
| 59 | Throat, disease of | ... | ... | ... | ... | ... | ... | 2 | ... | ... | 1 | ... | ... | ... | ... | ... | ... | ... | ... | ... | ... | ... | ... | 3 | ... |
| 60 | Thrush | 2 | 3 | 2 | ... | ... | ... | ... | ... | ... | ... | ... | ... | ... | ... | ... | ... | ... | ... | 6 | ... | ... | ... | 1 | ... |
| 61 | Ulcer | ... | ... | 1 | ... | ... | ... | ... | ... | ... | ... | ... | ... | ... | ... | ... | ... | ... | ... | 1 | ... | ... | ... | ... | ... |
| 62 | Uterus, disease of | ... | ... | ... | ... | ... | ... | ... | ... | ... | 1 | ... | ... | ... | ... | ... | ... | ... | ... | ... | ... | ... | 1 | ... | ... |
| 63 | White swelling | ... | ... | ... | ... | 1 | 1 | ... | 1 | ... | ... | ... | ... | ... | ... | ... | ... | ... | ... | 1 | ... | ... | ... | 1 | 1 |
| 64 | Worms | 7 | 6 | 50 | 40 | 14 | 12 | ... | 1 | 1 | ... | ... | ... | ... | ... | ... | ... | ... | ... | 111 | ... | 2 | 1 | 15 | 2 |
| 65 | Unknown | 85 | 74 | 52 | 40 | 23 | 7 | 21 | 20 | 56 | 57 | 27 | 13 | ... | 1 | ... | ... | ... | ... | 300 | ... | 4 | 57 | 70 | 31 |
| | Total | 283 | 244 | 361 | 296 | 159 | 133 | 160 | 175 | 501 | 414 | 173 | 94 | 15 | 7 | 2 | 4 | ... | ... | 1502 | 7 | 37 | 495 | 633 | 244 |

## IN THE STATE OF ARKANSAS—Continued.

| Nativities: California and Territories. | Nativities: Ireland. | Nativities: Germany. | Nativities: Other foreign countries. | Nativities: Unknown. | Season of decease: Spring. | Season of decease: Summer. | Season of decease: Autumn. | Season of decease: Winter. | Duration of sickness: Under 1 week. | Duration of sickness: 1 week and under 1 month. | Duration of sickness: 1 month and under 3 months. | Duration of sickness: 3 months and over. | Whites: Males. | Whites: Females. | Whites: Total. | Colored: Slaves: Black: M. | Colored: Slaves: Black: F. | Colored: Slaves: Mulatto: M. | Colored: Slaves: Mulatto: F. | Colored: Free: Black: M. | Colored: Free: Black: F. | Colored: Free: Mul.: M | Colored: Free: Mul.: F. | Aggregate deaths. | |
|---|---|---|---|---|---|---|---|---|---|---|---|---|---|---|---|---|---|---|---|---|---|---|---|---|---|
| 1 | | | 3 | 8 | 47 | 27 | 30 | 28 | 2 | 7 | 18 | 102 | 61 | 49 | 110 | 11 | 10 | | 1 | | | | | 132 | 1 |
| | | | | | 6 | 7 | 9 | 5 | 21 | 4 | | 2 | 8 | 8 | 16 | 4 | 5 | 1 | 1 | | | | | 27 | 2 |
| | | | | | 39 | 29 | 48 | 32 | 117 | 28 | 1 | | 66 | 51 | 117 | 12 | 12 | 3 | 4 | | | | | 148 | 3 |
| | | | | | | 2 | 4 | | 4 | 1 | | 1 | | | | 2 | 3 | 1 | | | | | | 6 | 4 |
| | | | | | 1 | | | 1 | | 2 | | | 2 | | 2 | | | | | | | | | 2 | 5 |
| | | | | 1 | 11 | 14 | 13 | 9 | 17 | 16 | 7 | 7 | 20 | 19 | 39 | 3 | 3 | 2 | | | | | | 47 | 6 |
| | 1 | | | 2 | 23 | 26 | 14 | 21 | 1 | 13 | 15 | 53 | 35 | 23 | 58 | 16 | 8 | 1 | 1 | | | | | 84 | 7 |
| | | | 1 | | 2 | 13 | 37 | 6 | 12 | 40 | 6 | | 26 | 27 | 53 | 3 | 2 | | | | | | | 58 | 8 |
| | | | | | 1 | | 1 | | | | | 2 | 2 | | 2 | | | | | | | | | 2 | 9 |
| | | | | | 2 | | 2 | | 1 | | 1 | 1 | 2 | | 2 | 1 | | 1 | | | | | | 4 | 10 |
| | | | | | 5 | 2 | 11 | 2 | 6 | 11 | 1 | 2 | 11 | 6 | 17 | | 2 | 1 | | | | | | 20 | 11 |
| | 2 | 1 | 1 | 10 | 40 | 68 | 137 | 33 | 101 | 149 | 20 | 7 | 101 | 117 | 218 | 29 | 20 | 7 | 2 | | | 2 | 1 | 279 | 12 |
| | | 1 | | | 1 | 9 | 29 | 1 | 11 | 26 | 3 | | 20 | 17 | 37 | | 2 | 1 | | | | | | 40 | 13 |
| | 1 | | | | 1 | 3 | 3 | 1 | 4 | 4 | | | 5 | 2 | 7 | 1 | | | | | | | | 8 | 14 |
| | | 1 | | 1 | 10 | 21 | 80 | 17 | 90 | 86 | | 1 | 59 | 46 | 105 | 13 | 8 | 2 | | | | | | 128 | 15 |
| | | | | | 3 | 6 | 15 | 5 | 10 | 11 | 8 | | 14 | 14 | 28 | 1 | | | | | | | | 29 | 16 |
| | | | | | 8 | 4 | 2 | 2 | 7 | 4 | 3 | 2 | | 11 | 11 | | 3 | | 2 | | | | | 16 | 17 |
| | | | | | 88 | 21 | 19 | 20 | 43 | 53 | 1 | 1 | 45 | 34 | 79 | 7 | 11 | | 1 | | | | | 98 | 18 |
| | | | | 1 | 10 | 4 | 15 | 10 | 3 | 24 | 12 | | 25 | 10 | 35 | 2 | 2 | | | | | | | 39 | 19 |
| | | | | | 17 | 2 | 3 | 18 | 9 | 27 | 4 | | 19 | 18 | 37 | 1 | | 1 | 1 | | | | | 40 | 20 |
| | | 1 | | 1 | 2 | | | 5 | 4 | | 2 | | 4 | | 4 | 3 | | | | | | | | 7 | 21 |
| | | | | | 1 | 1 | | 1 | 2 | | | 1 | 2 | 1 | 3 | | | | | | | | | 3 | 22 |
| | | | | | 3 | 2 | 1 | | 1 | 5 | | | 1 | 1 | 2 | 2 | 2 | | | | | | | 6 | 23 |
| | | | | | 1 | 1 | | 2 | 4 | | | | 2 | 2 | 4 | | | | | | | | | 4 | 24 |
| | | | | | | 1 | 1 | 1 | 3 | | | | | 1 | 1 | 1 | 1 | | | | | | | 3 | 25 |
| | | | | | 12 | 8 | 13 | 8 | 30 | 14 | | | 24 | 17 | 41 | 2 | 1 | | | | | | | 44 | 26 |
| | | | | | 5 | 11 | 16 | 21 | 6 | 28 | 21 | | 7 | 10 | 17 | 15 | 16 | 3 | 4 | | | | | 55 | 27 |
| | | | | | | 1 | 4 | | 1 | 3 | | 1 | 3 | 1 | 4 | 1 | | | | | | | | 5 | 28 |
| | | | | 1 | 2 | 3 | 1 | | 5 | 1 | | | 1 | 2 | 3 | 3 | | | | | | | | 6 | 29 |
| | | | | 1 | 6 | 15 | 11 | 6 | 13 | 20 | 3 | 2 | 18 | 13 | 31 | 4 | 3 | | | | | | | 38 | 30 |
| | | | | | 12 | 18 | 26 | 5 | 34 | 25 | | 2 | 25 | 26 | 51 | 3 | 5 | | 2 | | | | | 61 | 31 |
| | | | | | | 2 | | 1 | 1 | | 1 | 1 | 2 | 1 | 3 | | | | | | | | | 3 | 32 |
| | 2 | | | | 3 | | 1 | 2 | 1 | 4 | 1 | | 6 | | 6 | | | | | | | | | 6 | 33 |
| | | | | | | 1 | 2 | 2 | | 5 | | | 4 | 1 | 5 | | | | | | | | | 5 | 34 |
| | | | | 1 | 1 | 2 | | | 2 | | | | 3 | | 3 | | | | | | | | | 3 | 35 |
| | | 2 | | 2 | 8 | 10 | 9 | 4 | 3 | 9 | 7 | 11 | 10 | 15 | 25 | 3 | 2 | | 1 | | | | | 31 | 36 |
| | | | | 1 | 2 | 2 | 2 | 1 | | 3 | 1 | 3 | 4 | 2 | 6 | 1 | | | | | | | | 7 | 37 |
| | | | | | 2 | 4 | 4 | 2 | 3 | 7 | 1 | 1 | 5 | 5 | 10 | 1 | 1 | | | | | | | 12 | 38 |
| | | | | | 1 | | | | | | | 1 | | | | | 1 | | | | | | | 1 | 39 |
| | | | | | | 1 | 1 | 1 | | 2 | | 1 | 3 | | 3 | | | | | | | | | 3 | 40 |
| | | | | 3 | | 3 | 7 | 1 | 2 | | | | 10 | | 10 | | | 1 | | | | | | 11 | 41 |
| | | | 4 | 4 | 18 | 7 | 6 | 8 | 9 | 6 | 4 | 6 | 12 | 9 | 21 | 13 | 4 | | 1 | | | | | 39 | 42 |
| | | 1 | | 1 | 3 | 3 | 5 | | 3 | 3 | 1 | 4 | 6 | 4 | 10 | 1 | | | | | | | | 11 | 43 |
| | | | | | | | 1 | | 1 | | | | 1 | | 1 | | | | | | | | | 1 | 44 |
| | | | | | 10 | 6 | 1 | 4 | 9 | 11 | 1 | | 11 | 4 | 15 | 3 | 2 | 1 | | | | | | 21 | 45 |
| | | 3 | | 7 | 82 | 19 | 25 | 61 | 48 | 110 | 14 | 9 | 84 | 56 | 140 | 23 | 21 | 2 | 1 | | | | | 187 | 46 |
| | | | | | 2 | 4 | 2 | | 5 | 2 | | 1 | 4 | 1 | 5 | | 3 | | | | | | | 8 | 47 |
| | | | | | | 1 | | | 1 | | | | 1 | | 1 | | | | | | | | | 1 | 48 |
| | | | | | 1 | 1 | | 4 | 5 | 1 | | | 1 | 1 | 2 | 2 | 1 | 1 | | | | | | 6 | 49 |
| | | | | | 4 | 1 | 1 | 1 | | 2 | 2 | 3 | 6 | | 6 | | | 1 | | | | | | 7 | 50 |
| | | | | | 1 | 1 | 1 | 1 | | 1 | 1 | 2 | | | | 1 | 2 | 1 | | | | | | 4 | 51 |
| | | | | | 2 | | | | | | | 2 | 1 | | 1 | | | 1 | | | | | | 2 | 52 |
| | | | | 2 | 20 | 4 | 1 | 8 | 2 | 26 | 5 | | 23 | 7 | 30 | | 3 | | | | | | | 33 | 53 |
| | | | | | 2 | | 1 | | | 1 | 1 | 1 | 1 | 1 | 2 | 1 | | | | | | | | 3 | 54 |
| | | | | | 1 | 2 | 1 | 3 | 1 | | | | 3 | 4 | 7 | | | | | | | | | 7 | 55 |
| | | | | | 5 | | 4 | 2 | 10 | | | | | 1 | 1 | 4 | 5 | 1 | 1 | | | | | 12 | 56 |
| | | | | | 4 | 4 | 3 | 4 | 3 | 11 | 1 | | 4 | 5 | 9 | 5 | | | 1 | | | | | 15 | 57 |
| | | | | | 1 | | | | | | 1 | | | | | 1 | | | | | | | | 1 | 58 |
| | | | | | | 2 | | 1 | 1 | 1 | 1 | | 2 | 1 | 3 | | | | | | | | | 3 | 59 |
| | | | | | 2 | | 3 | 2 | 2 | 4 | 1 | | 3 | 2 | 5 | 1 | 1 | | | | | | | 7 | 60 |
| | | | | | 1 | | | | | | | 1 | 1 | | 1 | | | | | | | | | 1 | 61 |
| | | | | | | 1 | | | | | 1 | | | 1 | 1 | | | | | | | | | 1 | 62 |
| | | | | | 2 | 1 | | | | 1 | | 2 | | 1 | 1 | 1 | 1 | | | | | | | 3 | 63 |
| | | | | | 24 | 25 | 70 | 10 | 65 | 52 | 12 | 1 | 45 | 38 | 83 | 22 | 20 | 5 | 1 | | | | | 131 | 64 |
| | 1 | 1 | | 12 | 121 | 104 | 145 | 89 | 219 | 122 | 38 | 71 | 187 | 131 | 318 | 67 | 72 | 8 | 9 | 1 | | 1 | | 476 | 65 |
| 1 | 7 | 3 | 10 | 72 | 756 | 718 | 935 | 584 | 1319 | 1081 | 232 | 330 | 1201 | 956 | 2157 | 390 | 367 | 59 | 43 | 1 | | 3 | 1 | 3021 | |

## CLASSIFICATION OF DEATHS

| | Cause of death. | AGES. | | | | | | | | | | | | | | | | | | NATIVITIES. | | | | | |
|---|---|---|---|---|---|---|---|---|---|---|---|---|---|---|---|---|---|---|---|---|---|---|---|---|---|
| | | Under 1. | | 1 and under 5. | | 5 and under 10. | | 10 and under 20. | | 20 and under 50. | | 50 and under 80. | | 80 and under 100. | | 100 & over. | | Age unknown. | | Born in State. | New England. | Middle. | South. | Southwest. | Northwest. |
| | | M. | F. | M. | F. | M. | F. | M. | F. | M. | F. | M. | F. | M | F. | M | F. | M | F. | | | | | | |
| 1 | Abscess | | | | | | | | | 1 | | | | | | | | | | | | 1 | | | |
| 2 | Accident, not specif'd | | | | | | | | | 3 | | | | 1 | | | | 1 | | 1 | | 1 | | | 1 |
| 3 | ....do...burned | | | | | | | | | 1 | | 1 | | | | | | | | | | | | | 1 |
| 4 | ....do...drowned | | | | | 1 | | 1 | | 2 | | | | | | | | | | 2 | | | | | 1 |
| 5 | ....do...shot | | | | | | | | | 8 | | | | | | | | | | 1 | | | | | 2 |
| 6 | Apoplexy | | | | | | | | | | | 1 | | | | | | | | 1 | | | | | |
| 7 | Asthma | | | 1 | | | | | | | | 1 | | | | | | | | 1 | | | | | |
| 8 | Cholera | 1 | | 1 | | 1 | | 18 | 3 | 337 | 13 | 26 | 2 | 2 | | | | | | 2 | 78 | 70 | 30 | 21 | 128 |
| 9 | ...do..infantum | | | | 1 | | | | | | | | | | | | | | | | | | | | |
| 10 | Congestion | | | | | | | | | 1 | | | | | | | | | | | | | | 1 | |
| 11 | Consumption | | | | 1 | | | | | 5 | 3 | | | | | | | | | 3 | 1 | 2 | | | 2 |
| 12 | Convulsions | | | | | | | | | 1 | | | | | | | | | | | | | | 1 | |
| 13 | Croup | | 1 | | | | | | | | | | | | | | | | | 1 | | | | | |
| 14 | Diarrhœa | | | 2 | 1 | | 1 | 4 | 1 | 81 | 1 | 8 | 1 | | | | | | | 1 | 19 | 14 | 1 | 4 | 49 |
| 15 | Dropsy | | | | | | | | | 3 | | | | | | | | | | 1 | | 1 | | | 1 |
| 16 | Dysentery | | | 1 | 1 | | | 1 | 1 | 47 | 1 | 2 | | | | | | | | 10 | 11 | 4 | 2 | 5 | 13 |
| 17 | Erysipelas | | | | | | | | | 4 | | | | | | | | | | | | | 1 | | 3 |
| 18 | Fever, not specified | 2 | 1 | 1 | 6 | 1 | 1 | 3 | 2 | 55 | 4 | 3 | | | | | | 2 | | 14 | 12 | 8 | 3 | 3 | 34 |
| 19 | ..do..congestive | | | | | | | | | | 1 | | | | | | | | | | | 1 | | | |
| 20 | ..do..typhus | | | | | | | 1 | | 9 | 1 | | | | | | | | | | 2 | 2 | | 1 | 1 |
| 21 | Head, disease of | | 1 | | | | | | | | | | | | | | | | | | | | | | 1 |
| 22 | Hemorrhage | | | | | | | | | 1 | | | | | | | | | | | 1 | | | | |
| 23 | Inflamt'n, not spcif'd | 1 | | | | | | | | | | | | | | | | | | 1 | | | | | |
| 24 | ....do....bowels | | | | | | | | | 2 | | | | | | | | | | | 1 | | | | 1 |
| 25 | ....do....brain | | | 1 | | | | | | 1 | | | | | | | | | | 1 | | | | 1 | |
| 26 | Intemperance | | | | | | | | | 1 | | 1 | | | | | | | | 1 | | | 1 | | |
| 27 | Killed | | | | | | | | | 3 | | | | | | | | | 1 | | 2 | | | 1 | |
| 28 | Liver, disease of | | | | | | | | | 1 | | | | | | | | | | | | | 1 | | |
| 29 | Mania-a-potu | | | | | | | | | 6 | | | | | | | | | | 1 | | 1 | | | |
| 30 | Measles | | 1 | 1 | | | | | | | | | | | | | | | | 2 | | | | | |
| 31 | Mortification | | | | | | | | | | 1 | | | | | | | | | 1 | | | | | |
| 32 | Murder | | | | | | | | | 13 | | | | | | | | | | | 2 | 1 | | 2 | 2 |
| 33 | Old age | | | | | | | | | | | | | | 2 | | | | | | | | | | |
| 34 | Paralysis | | | | | | | | | 1 | 1 | | | | | | | | | | 1 | | | | |
| 35 | Pneumonia | | | | | | | 1 | | 2 | 1 | | | | | | | | | | | 2 | 1 | | 1 |
| 36 | Scrofula | | | | | | | | | 1 | | | | | | | | | | | | | | | 1 |
| 37 | Scurvy | | | | | | | | | 1 | | | | | | | | | | | | 1 | | | |
| 38 | Spine, disease of | | | 1 | | | | | | | | | | | | | | | | 1 | | | | | |
| 39 | Teething | | 1 | | | | | | | | | | | | | | | | | 1 | | | | | |
| 40 | Ulcer | | | | | | | | | 1 | | | | | | | | | | | | | | | 1 |
| 41 | Worms | | 1 | | | | | 1 | | | | | | | | | | | | 1 | | | | | 1 |
| 42 | Unknown | 12 | 14 | 6 | 13 | 2 | 4 | 10 | 9 | 49 | 6 | 18 | 3 | 1 | | | | 9 | 4 | 109 | 6 | 6 | 3 | 2 | 19 |
| | Total | 16 | 20 | 15 | 23 | 5 | 6 | 40 | 16 | 641 | 33 | 61 | 6 | 4 | 2 | | | 12 | 5 | 157 | 136 | 115 | 43 | 42 | 263 |

## CLASSIFICATION OF DEATHS

| | | | | | | | | | | | | | | | | | | | | | | | | | |
|---|---|---|---|---|---|---|---|---|---|---|---|---|---|---|---|---|---|---|---|---|---|---|---|---|---|
| 1 | Accident, not specif'd | 1 | | 1 | | 1 | 2 | | | 8 | | | 1 | | 1 | | | | | 7 | | 1 | 1 | | |
| 2 | ....do....burned | 1 | | | | 1 | 3 | | 2 | 2 | 1 | | | | | | | | | 6 | | 3 | 1 | | |
| 3 | ....do....drowned | | | | | | | 3 | | 2 | | | | | | | | | | 4 | | | | | |
| 4 | ....do ...railroad | | | | | | | 1 | | | | | | | | | | | | 1 | | | | | |
| 5 | Apoplexy | | | | | | | | | | 2 | | 1 | | | | | | | | | 2 | | | |
| 6 | Asthma | | | | | | | | | | | 2 | 1 | | | | | | | | 1 | 1 | 1 | | |
| 7 | Bowels, disease of | 3 | | 2 | 2 | | | | | | | 1 | 1 | | | | | | | 5 | 1 | 2 | | | |
| 8 | Brain.....do | | | | | | | 2 | | | | | | | | | | | | 2 | | | | | |
| 9 | Bronchitis | | | | | | | | | | 1 | | | | | | | | | | | | | | |
| 10 | Cancer | | | | | | | | | 1 | | | 1 | | | | | | | | | 1 | | | |
| 11 | Carbuncle | | | | | | | | | | 1 | | | | | | | | | | | 1 | | | |
| 12 | Catarrh | 7 | | | 1 | | | | | 2 | | 1 | 1 | | | | | | | 8 | | 3 | 1 | | |
| 13 | Child birth | | | | | | | | 2 | | 7 | | | | | | | | | 6 | | 2 | 1 | | |
| 14 | Cholera | 1 | | | | 2 | | 1 | 1 | 12 | 8 | 4 | 2 | | 1 | | | | | 11 | | 9 | 1 | | |
| 15 | ....do...infantum | 5 | 8 | 7 | 5 | | | | | | | | | | | | | | | 24 | 1 | | | | |
| 16 | ....do...morbus | | | | | | | 2 | | | 2 | | | | | | | | | 2 | | 1 | 1 | | |
| 17 | Congestion, bowels | | 1 | | | | | | | | | | | | | | | | | 1 | | | | | |
| 18 | ....do.....brain | | | | 1 | | | 2 | | 2 | 1 | 1 | | | | | | | | 3 | | | 1 | | |
| 19 | ....do.....lungs | | | | | | | | | | | | 1 | | | | | | | | | | | | |
| 20 | Consumption | 2 | 2 | 8 | 8 | 2 | 3 | 6 | 11 | 26 | 45 | 11 | 10 | 1 | | | | | | 60 | 3 | 46 | 17 | | |
| 21 | Convulsions | 3 | 2 | 3 | 1 | 1 | | 1 | | | | | | | | | | | | 8 | | 2 | 1 | | |
| 22 | Croup | 3 | 2 | 4 | | | 3 | | | | | | | | | | | | | 11 | | 1 | | | |
| 23 | Diarrhœa | 4 | 2 | 2 | 4 | 2 | 1 | 3 | | 4 | 2 | 4 | 1 | | | | | | | 20 | | 4 | 1 | | |
| 24 | Dropsy | | 1 | 1 | 1 | 4 | 1 | 1 | 1 | 2 | 4 | 5 | 4 | | | | | | | 9 | 1 | 12 | 1 | | |

## IN THE STATE OF CALIFORNIA.

| NATIVITIES. | | | | | SEASON OF DECEASE. | | | | DURATION OF SICKNESS. | | | | WHITES. | | | COLORED. | | | | | | | | | |
|---|---|---|---|---|---|---|---|---|---|---|---|---|---|---|---|---|---|---|---|---|---|---|---|---|---|
| | | | | | | | | | | | | | | | | Slaves. | | | | Free. | | | | | |
| | | | | | | | | | | | | | | | | Black. | | Mulatto. | | Black. | | Mul. | | | |
| California and Territories. | Ireland. | Germany. | Other foreign countries. | Unknown. | Spring. | Summer. | Autumn. | Winter. | Under 1 week. | 1 week and under 1 month. | 1 month and under 3 months. | 3 months and over. | Males. | Females. | Total. | M. | F. | M. | F. | M. | F. | M | F. | Aggregate deaths. | |
| | | | | | | | 1 | | | 1 | | | 1 | | 1 | | | | | | | | | 1 | 1 |
| | | | 2 | | | | 3 | | | | | | 5 | | 5 | | | | | | | | | 5 | 2 |
| | | | | 1 | | | 1 | 1 | | | | | 2 | | 2 | | | | | | | | | 2 | 3 |
| | | | | 1 | 1 | 1 | 1 | 1 | | | | | 4 | | 4 | | | | | | | | | 4 | 4 |
| | | | 5 | | | 2 | 5 | | | | | | 8 | | 8 | | | | | | | | | 8 | 5 |
| | | | | | | | 1 | | | | | | 1 | | 1 | | | | | | | | | 1 | 6 |
| | | | 1 | | 1 | | 1 | | | | | 2 | 2 | | 2 | | | | | | | | | 2 | 7 |
| 4 | 17 | 2 | 40 | 12 | | 1 | 206 | 194 | 10 | 3 | | | 382 | 18 | 400 | 1 | | 3 | | | | | | 404 | 8 |
| | | | | 1 | | | | 1 | | | | | | 1 | 1 | | | | | | | | | 1 | 9 |
| | | | | | | | | 1 | | 1 | | | 1 | | 1 | | | | | | | | | 1 | 10 |
| | | | | 1 | 1 | 2 | 4 | 2 | | 4 | | 4 | 5 | 4 | 9 | | | | | | | | | 9 | 11 |
| | | | | | | 1 | | | | | | 1 | 1 | | 1 | | | | | | | | | 1 | 12 |
| | | | | | 1 | | | | | | | | | 1 | 1 | | | | | | | | | 1 | 13 |
| | 2 | | 8 | 2 | 3 | 9 | 55 | 31 | 2 | 11 | 9 | 4 | 92 | 4 | 96 | 1 | | 2 | 1 | | | | | 100 | 14 |
| | | | | | 1 | 1 | | 1 | | | 1 | 1 | 2 | | 2 | 1 | | | | | | | | 3 | 15 |
| | 1 | 6 | | 2 | 4 | 16 | 15 | 18 | 9 | 21 | 1 | 1 | 48 | 3 | 51 | | | | | 2 | | 1 | | 54 | 16 |
| | | | | | | | 1 | 3 | | | | | 4 | | 4 | | | | | | | | | 4 | 17 |
| 2 | 1 | | 3 | 1 | 10 | 10 | 30 | 26 | 1 | 18 | 2 | 1 | 67 | 13 | 80 | | | | | | 1 | | | 81 | 18 |
| | | | | | 1 | | | | | | | | | 1 | 1 | | | | | | | | | 1 | 19 |
| | 1 | 1 | 3 | | | 2 | 6 | 3 | | 10 | | | 10 | 1 | 11 | | | | | | | | | 11 | 20 |
| | | | | | | | 1 | | | | | | | 1 | 1 | | | | | | | | | 1 | 21 |
| | | | | | | | | 1 | | 1 | | | 1 | | 1 | | | | | | | | | 1 | 22 |
| | | | | | | 1 | | | | | | | 1 | | 1 | | | | | | | | | 1 | 23 |
| | | | | | | | 1 | 1 | | | | | 2 | | 2 | | | | | | | | | 2 | 24 |
| | | | | | | 1 | 1 | | | 2 | | | 2 | | 2 | | | | | | | | | 2 | 25 |
| | | | | | | | 2 | | | 1 | 1 | | 2 | | 2 | | | | | | | | | 2 | 26 |
| | 1 | | | | | | 1 | 2 | | 2 | | | 3 | 1 | 4 | | | | | | | | | 4 | 27 |
| | | | | | | | 1 | | | | | | 1 | | 1 | | | | | | | | | 1 | 28 |
| | 2 | | 2 | | 2 | | 4 | | 2 | 1 | | | 6 | | 6 | | | | | | | | | 6 | 29 |
| | | | | | | | 2 | | | 1 | 1 | | 1 | 1 | 2 | | | | | | | | | 2 | 30 |
| | | | | | | 1 | | | | | 1 | | | 1 | 1 | | | | | | | | | 1 | 31 |
| | | | 4 | 2 | | 8 | 3 | | | 5 | | | 13 | | 13 | | | | | | | | | 13 | 32 |
| | | | 2 | | | | 2 | | | | | | | 2 | 2 | | | | | | | | | 2 | 33 |
| | | | | 1 | | | 1 | 1 | 1 | 1 | | | 1 | 1 | 2 | | | | | | | | | 2 | 34 |
| | | | | | 2 | | 2 | | 1 | 1 | | | 3 | 1 | 4 | | | | | | | | | 4 | 35 |
| | | | | | | | 1 | | | | | | 1 | | 1 | | | | | | | | | 1 | 36 |
| | | | | | | | | 1 | | | | | 1 | | 1 | | | | | | | | | 1 | 37 |
| | | | | | | | | 1 | | 1 | | | 1 | | 1 | | | | | | | | | 1 | 38 |
| | | | | | 1 | | | | | | | | | 1 | 1 | | | | | | | | | 1 | 39 |
| | | | | | 1 | | | | | 1 | | | 1 | | 1 | | | | | | | | | 1 | 40 |
| | | | | | | | | 2 | | 1 | | | 1 | 1 | 2 | | | | | | | | | 2 | 41 |
| | | | 12 | 3 | 25 | 36 | 65 | 31 | 2 | 3 | 1 | 1 | 107 | 53 | 160 | | | | | | | | | 160 | 42 |
| 6 | 25 | 9 | 82 | 27 | 54 | 92 | 417 | 322 | 28 | 90 | 17 | 15 | 783 | 109 | 892 | 3 | | 5 | 1 | 2 | 1 | 1 | | 905 | |

## IN THE DISTRICT OF COLUMBIA.

| California and Territories. | Ireland. | Germany. | Other foreign countries. | Unknown. | Spring. | Summer. | Autumn. | Winter. | Under 1 week. | 1 week and under 1 month. | 1 month and under 3 months. | 3 months and over. | Males. | Females. | Total. | Slaves Black M. | Slaves Black F. | Slaves Mulatto M. | Slaves Mulatto F. | Free Black M. | Free Black F. | Free Mul. M | Free Mul. F. | Aggregate deaths. | |
|---|---|---|---|---|---|---|---|---|---|---|---|---|---|---|---|---|---|---|---|---|---|---|---|---|---|
| | 1 | | | | 5 | 1 | 3 | 1 | 4 | 1 | | 2 | 5 | 4 | 9 | 1 | | | | | | | | 10 | 1 |
| | | | | | 4 | 1 | | 5 | 5 | | | | | 2 | 2 | 1 | | | | 3 | 4 | | | 10 | 2 |
| | 1 | | | | | 4 | 1 | | | | | | 4 | | 4 | | | | | 1 | | | | 5 | 3 |
| | | | | | | | 1 | | 1 | | | | | | | | | | | | | 1 | | 1 | 4 |
| | | | | 1 | 2 | | | 1 | 3 | | | | | 1 | 1 | | | | | | 2 | | | 3 | 5 |
| | | | | | 2 | 1 | | | | | | 3 | 2 | 1 | 3 | | | | | | | | | 3 | 6 |
| | 1 | | | | 3 | 1 | 4 | 1 | 4 | 4 | | 1 | 3 | 3 | 6 | | | 1 | | 2 | | | | 9 | 7 |
| | | | | | 1 | 1 | | | 1 | | | | 2 | | 2 | | | | | | | | | 2 | 8 |
| | | | 1 | | 1 | | | | | 1 | | | | 1 | 1 | | | | | | | | | 1 | 9 |
| | 1 | | | | | 1 | | 1 | | | | 2 | | 1 | 1 | | | | | | | 1 | | 2 | 10 |
| | | | | | 1 | | | | | | | 1 | | 1 | 1 | | | | | | | | | 1 | 11 |
| | | | | | 7 | 2 | 2 | 1 | 4 | 3 | 3 | 2 | 7 | | 7 | 1 | | | | 1 | 2 | 1 | | 12 | 12 |
| | | | | | 2 | 3 | 2 | 2 | 4 | 4 | | | | 9 | 9 | | | | | | | | | 9 | 13 |
| | 4 | 1 | 1 | | 3 | 19 | 5 | | 12 | 14 | | | 11 | 5 | 16 | 2 | | 1 | | 6 | 2 | | | 27 | 14 |
| | | | | | | 11 | 12 | | 4 | 13 | 2 | 6 | 9 | 12 | 21 | | | | | 1 | 1 | 2 | | 25 | 15 |
| | | | | | 1 | 2 | 1 | | 2 | 2 | | | 1 | 2 | 3 | | | | | 1 | | | | 4 | 16 |
| | | | | | | 1 | | | | 1 | | | | 1 | 1 | | | | | | | | | 1 | 17 |
| | | 1 | 2 | | 4 | 3 | | | 4 | 3 | | | 4 | 1 | 5 | 1 | | | | | 1 | | | 7 | 18 |
| | 1 | | | | 1 | | | | | 1 | | | | 1 | 1 | | | | | | | | | 1 | 19 |
| | 6 | 2 | 1 | | 42 | 41 | 25 | 24 | 4 | 17 | 12 | 97 | 43 | 52 | 95 | 3 | 2 | 1 | 1 | 7 | 19 | 2 | 5 | 135 | 20 |
| | | | | | 5 | 1 | 3 | 2 | 8 | 1 | 1 | 1 | 6 | 1 | 7 | 1 | 1 | | | 1 | 1 | | | 11 | 21 |
| | | | | | 4 | 3 | | 4 | 7 | 4 | 1 | | 6 | 4 | 10 | | 1 | | | 1 | | | | 12 | 22 |
| | 2 | | 2 | | 4 | 14 | 11 | | 4 | 22 | 1 | 2 | 15 | 8 | 23 | | | | | 3 | | 1 | 2 | 29 | 23 |
| | 1 | 1 | | | 7 | 5 | 8 | 3 | 2 | 6 | 2 | 13 | 11 | 4 | 15 | | 5 | | | 2 | 2 | | 1 | 25 | 24 |

## CLASSIFICATION OF DEATHS

| | Cause of death. | Ages. Under 1. M. | Under 1. F. | 1 and under 5. M. | 1 and under 5. F. | 5 and under 10. M. | 5 and under 10. F. | 10 and under 20. M. | 10 and under 20. F. | 20 and under 50. M. | 20 and under 50. F. | 50 and under 80. M. | 50 and under 80. F. | 80 and under 100. M | 80 and under 100. F. | 100 & over. M | 100 & over. F. | Age unknown. M | Age unknown. F. | Nativities. Born in State. | New England. | Middle. | South. | Southwest. | Northwest. |
|---|---|---|---|---|---|---|---|---|---|---|---|---|---|---|---|---|---|---|---|---|---|---|---|---|---|
| 1 | Dysentery | 2 | 6 | 15 | 10 | 2 | 3 | 2 | | 2 | 8 | 2 | | | | 1 | | | | 42 | 1 | 7 | 1 | | |
| 2 | Dyspepsia | | | | | | | | | | 1 | 1 | | | | | | | | | | 1 | 1 | | |
| 3 | Erysipelas | | 1 | | 1 | | | | | 1 | 2 | 2 | 1 | | | | | | | 2 | | 1 | 3 | | |
| 4 | Fever, not specified | 4 | 2 | 1 | 1 | | | | | 1 | | 1 | | | | | | | | 9 | | | | | |
| 5 | ....do...bilious | | | 1 | | | 2 | 1 | 2 | | 1 | | 2 | 1 | | | | | | 5 | | 4 | 1 | | |
| 6 | ....do...brain | 2 | 1 | 4 | 4 | 2 | 2 | 1 | 3 | 3 | | | | | | | | | | 18 | 1 | 3 | | | |
| 7 | ....do...catarrhal | 4 | 2 | 1 | 1 | 1 | | | | 1 | | | | | | | | | | 9 | | | 1 | | |
| 8 | ....do...congestive | | | | | 1 | | | | | | | | | | | | | | | | | | | 1 |
| 9 | ....do...scarlet | | 1 | 11 | 16 | 6 | 5 | | 3 | | 1 | | | | | | | | | 36 | | 6 | | | |
| 10 | ....do...typhus | 1 | | 1 | | | | | 1 | 4 | 3 | | | | | | | | | 6 | | 2 | 2 | | |
| 11 | Gravel | | | | | | | | | | | 1 | 1 | | | | | | | | | | | | 1 |
| 12 | Heart, disease of | 1 | | | 1 | 1 | | | | 1 | 2 | 2 | 4 | | | | | | | 6 | | 4 | 1 | | |
| 13 | Hooping cough | 2 | 5 | 8 | 4 | | 1 | | | | | | | | | | | | | 16 | | 2 | 2 | | |
| 14 | Hydrocephalus | 3 | 4 | 9 | 4 | 1 | 2 | 2 | 1 | | | | 1 | | | | | | | 22 | | 4 | 1 | | |
| 15 | Inflammation, bowels | 1 | | | | | | | 1 | | 2 | | | | | | | | | 2 | | 1 | | | |
| 16 | ......do......brain | 1 | 1 | 1 | 1 | | | | 1 | 1 | 1 | | | | | | | | | 4 | | 3 | | | |
| 17 | Intemperance | | | | | | | | | 4 | | 1 | 1 | | | | | | | 3 | | 2 | | | |
| 18 | Lockjaw | | | | | | | | | 1 | | | | | | | | | | 1 | | | | | |
| 19 | Lungs, disease of | 1 | | | | | | | | 2 | | | | 1 | | | | | | 4 | | | | | |
| 20 | Measles | | | | 1 | | | | | | | | | | | | | | | | | | 1 | | |
| 21 | Mumps | | | | | | | | | 1 | | | | | | | | | | 1 | | | | | |
| 22 | Neuralgia | | | | | | 1 | | | | | | | | | | | | | 1 | | | | | |
| 23 | Old age | | | | | | | | | | 1 | 6 | 12 | 3 | 6 | | 1 | | | 6 | | 18 | 3 | | |
| 24 | Paralysis | | | | | 1 | | | | | | 3 | 1 | | 3 | | | | | 1 | | 6 | 1 | | |
| 25 | Peritonitis | | | | | | | | | 1 | | | | | | | | | | 1 | | | | | |
| 26 | Piles | | | | | | | | | | 1 | | | | | | | | | | | 1 | | | |
| 27 | Pleurisy | | | 1 | | | | 2 | 1 | 3 | 1 | 3 | 1 | | | | | | | 5 | | 6 | 1 | | |
| 28 | Pneumonia | 3 | | 4 | 4 | | | | | 2 | | | 1 | | | | | | | 10 | 2 | 1 | | | |
| 29 | Poison | | | | | | | | 1 | | | | | | | | | | | 1 | | | | | |
| 30 | Prematurity of birth | 1 | | | | | | | | | | | | | | | | | | 1 | | | | | |
| 31 | Quinsy | | | 1 | | | | | | | | | | 1 | | | | | | 1 | | 1 | | | |
| 32 | Rheumatism | | | | | | | | | 2 | | 1 | 1 | | | | | | | | | 1 | 2 | | |
| 33 | Scrofula | | | | 2 | | 1 | | | 1 | | | | | | | | | | | | 1 | 2 | | |
| 34 | Small pox | 3 | 2 | | 3 | | 1 | | 2 | 12 | 7 | 1 | | | | | | | | 13 | | 12 | | | |
| 35 | Spine, disease of | 1 | | | | | | | | 1 | | | | | | | | | | 1 | | | | | 1 |
| 36 | Summer complaint | | 1 | | 1 | 1 | | | | | | | | | | | | | | 3 | | | | | |
| 37 | Teething | 6 | 4 | 4 | 5 | | | | | | | | | | | | | | | 19 | | | | | |
| 38 | Throat, disease of | | | 1 | | | | | | 1 | 1 | | | | | | | | | 3 | | | | | |
| 39 | Thrush | | 4 | | | | | | 1 | | | | | | | | | | | 2 | | | | | |
| 40 | Tumor | | | | | | | | | 1 | | | 1 | | | | | | | | | 1 | 1 | | |
| 41 | Uterus, disease of | | | | | | | | | | 2 | | | | | | | | | 1 | | | | | |
| 42 | White swelling | | | | | | | 1 | | | 1 | | | | | | | | | 1 | | | 1 | | |
| 43 | Unknown | 17 | 21 | 8 | 5 | 1 | 4 | 3 | 3 | 9 | 10 | 7 | 13 | 2 | | | | | | 67 | | 18 | 9 | 3 | |
| | Total | 83 | 70 | 99 | 87 | 30 | 35 | 34 | 37 | 111 | 114 | 60 | 64 | 9 | 11 | 1 | 1 | | | 511 | 11 | 197 | 62 | 3 | 3 |

## CLASSIFICATION OF DEATHS

| | Cause of death. | Under 1. M. | Under 1. F. | 1 and under 5. M. | 1 and under 5. F. | 5 and under 10. M. | 5 and under 10. F. | 10 and under 20. M. | 10 and under 20. F. | 20 and under 50. M. | 20 and under 50. F. | 50 and under 80. M. | 50 and under 80. F. | 80 and under 100. M | 80 and under 100. F. | 100 & over. M | 100 & over. F. | Age unknown. M | Age unknown. F. | Born in State. | New England. | Middle. | South. | Southwest. | Northwest. |
|---|---|---|---|---|---|---|---|---|---|---|---|---|---|---|---|---|---|---|---|---|---|---|---|---|---|
| 1 | Abscess | | 1 | | 1 | 2 | | | | 1 | | 1 | 1 | | | | | | | 6 | 1 | | | | |
| 2 | Accident, not specif'd | 4 | 3 | 6 | 1 | 4 | | 12 | | 20 | 3 | 14 | 7 | 2 | 3 | | | 1 | | 58 | 4 | 7 | | | |
| 3 | ....do...burned | 1 | | 2 | 2 | | 3 | | 1 | | 2 | | | | | | | | | 10 | | | | | |
| 4 | ....do...drowned | | | 3 | 1 | 10 | 2 | 18 | 6 | 17 | 2 | 5 | 1 | | | | | 1 | | 49 | 4 | 2 | | | |
| 5 | ....do...scalded | | | 2 | 2 | | | | | | | | | | | | | | | 3 | | | | | |
| 6 | ....do...explosion | | | | | | | | | 1 | | | | | | | | | | 1 | | | | | |
| 7 | ....do...railroad | | | | | | 1 | 2 | | 6 | | 1 | | | | | | 1 | | 8 | 1 | | | 1 | |
| 8 | Apoplexy | | | | | | | | | 8 | 6 | 15 | 22 | 4 | 1 | | | | | 52 | 2 | | | | |
| 9 | Asthma | | | | | | | | | | | 1 | 3 | 1 | | | | | | 3 | | | | | |
| 10 | Bladder, disease of | | | | | | | | | 1 | | | | | | | | | | 1 | | | | | |
| 11 | Bowels......do | 7 | 9 | 10 | 9 | 2 | | | 3 | 6 | 6 | 5 | 2 | | | | | | | 53 | 1 | 3 | | | 1 |
| 12 | Brain ......do | 9 | 5 | 8 | 6 | 5 | 7 | 6 | 2 | 6 | 10 | 5 | 2 | | | | | | | 71 | | | | | |
| 13 | Bronchitis | | | 2 | 1 | | | | | 1 | 1 | | | | | | | | | 4 | | | | | |
| 14 | Cancer | 1 | | 2 | | | | | | 5 | 6 | 12 | 25 | 2 | 2 | | | | 1 | 48 | 4 | 1 | | | |
| 15 | Childbirth | | | | | | | | 1 | | 37 | | | | | | | | 1 | 30 | 1 | | | | |
| 16 | Cholera | 2 | 1 | 5 | 3 | 2 | 1 | 3 | 1 | 18 | 7 | 11 | 5 | | | | | 1 | | 35 | 3 | 4 | | | |
| 17 | ...do..infantum | 19 | 15 | 33 | 18 | | | | | | | | | | | | | | | 81 | 2 | 1 | | | |
| 18 | ...do..morbus | 1 | | 3 | 4 | 1 | 1 | | 3 | 4 | 3 | 4 | 1 | 1 | | 1 | | | | 22 | 1 | 3 | | | |
| 19 | Chorea | | | | 1 | | | | | 1 | | | 1 | | | | | | | 3 | | | | | |
| 20 | Cholic | 1 | | 1 | | 1 | 1 | 1 | | 5 | 1 | 3 | 3 | | 1 | | | | | 17 | | 1 | | | |
| 21 | Consumption | 19 | 16 | 22 | 12 | 4 | 5 | 30 | 50 | 190 | 284 | 150 | 157 | 10 | 16 | | | 2 | 1 | 822 | 47 | 22 | 2 | | 3 |
| 22 | Convulsions | 34 | 27 | 13 | 15 | 1 | 2 | 3 | 5 | 21 | 15 | 23 | 14 | 6 | 7 | | | | 1 | 169 | 11 | 1 | | | |
| 23 | Croup | 12 | 16 | 28 | 32 | 8 | 7 | 4 | | | 1 | | | | 1 | | | | 1 | 104 | 1 | 4 | | | |
| 24 | Debility | 9 | 7 | 4 | 1 | | 1 | | | | 2 | 6 | 3 | 1 | 2 | | | | | 36 | | | | | |

## IN THE DISTRICT OF COLUMBIA—Continued.

| Nativities. California and Territories. | Nativities. Ireland. | Nativities. Germany. | Nativities. Other foreign countries. | Nativities. Unknown. | Season of decease. Spring. | Season of decease. Summer. | Season of decease. Autumn. | Season of decease. Winter. | Duration of sickness. Under 1 week. | Duration of sickness. 1 week and under 1 month. | Duration of sickness. 1 month and under 3 months. | Duration of sickness. 3 months and over. | Whites. Males. | Whites. Females. | Whites. Total. | Colored. Slaves. Black. M. | Colored. Slaves. Black. F. | Colored. Slaves. Mulatto. M. | Colored. Slaves. Mulatto. F. | Colored. Free. Black. M. | Colored. Free. Black. F. | Colored. Free. Mul. M | Colored. Free. Mul. F. | Aggregate deaths. | |
|---|---|---|---|---|---|---|---|---|---|---|---|---|---|---|---|---|---|---|---|---|---|---|---|---|---|
| .... | 2 | .. | .... | ... | 8 | 21 | 18 | 6 | 11 | 28 | 8 | 6 | 24 | 22 | 46 | .... | .... | .... | .... | 2 | 4 | .. | 1 | 53 | 1 |
| .... | ... | .. | .... | ... | 1 | .... | .... | 1 | 1 | .... | .... | 1 | 1 | 1 | 2 | .... | .... | .... | .... | ... | ... | .. | .. | 2 | 2 |
| .... | 1 | .. | 1 | ... | 3 | 5 | .... | .... | .... | 7 | .... | 1 | 2 | 3 | 5 | .... | 1 | .... | .... | ... | 1 | 1 | .. | 8 | 3 |
| .... | ... | .. | 1 | ... | 3 | 4 | 2 | 1 | 6 | 3 | .... | 1 | 6 | 3 | 9 | 1 | .... | .... | .... | ... | ... | .. | .. | 10 | 4 |
| .... | ... | .. | .... | ... | 3 | 5 | 2 | .... | 2 | 6 | .... | 2 | 1 | 6 | 7 | .... | .... | .... | .... | 2 | 1 | .. | .. | 10 | 5 |
| .... | ... | .. | .... | ... | 6 | 7 | 3 | 5 | 8 | 11 | 1 | 1 | 7 | 8 | 15 | 2 | .... | .... | .... | 2 | 1 | 1 | 1 | 22 | 6 |
| .... | ... | .. | .... | ... | 4 | 2 | 2 | 2 | 6 | 3 | .... | 1 | 4 | 1 | 5 | .... | 1 | 1 | .... | 1 | 1 | 1 | .. | 10 | 7 |
| .... | ... | .. | .... | ... | .... | .... | 1 | .... | 1 | .... | .... | .... | .... | .... | .... | .... | .... | 1 | .... | ... | ... | .. | .. | 1 | 8 |
| .... | ... | .. | 1 | ... | 16 | 5 | 9 | 11 | 14 | 24 | 2 | 3 | 16 | 21 | 37 | 1 | 1 | .... | .... | ... | 3 | .. | 1 | 43 | 9 |
| .... | ... | .. | .... | ... | 2 | 3 | 3 | 2 | 1 | 8 | .... | .... | 5 | 4 | 9 | .... | .... | .... | .... | 1 | ... | .. | .. | 10 | 10 |
| .... | ... | .. | 1 | ... | .... | 1 | 1 | .... | .... | .... | .... | 2 | 1 | 1 | 2 | .... | .... | .... | .... | ... | ... | .. | .. | 2 | 11 |
| .... | 1 | .. | .... | ... | 2 | 4 | 2 | 4 | 6 | 1 | 1 | 4 | 4 | 3 | 7 | .... | 2 | .... | 1 | ... | ... | 1 | 1 | 12 | 12 |
| .... | ... | .. | .... | ... | 9 | 4 | 2 | 4 | 1 | 8 | 8 | 3 | 7 | 7 | 14 | .... | .... | 1 | .... | ... | 3 | 2 | .. | 20 | 13 |
| .... | ... | .. | .... | ... | 8 | 7 | 5 | 6 | 3 | 21 | 3 | .... | 10 | 10 | 20 | .... | .... | 1 | .... | 2 | 1 | 2 | 1 | 27 | 14 |
| .... | ... | 1 | .... | ... | 3 | 1 | .... | .... | 1 | 3 | .... | .... | .... | 2 | 2 | .... | 1 | .... | .... | 1 | ... | .. | .. | 4 | 15 |
| .... | ... | .. | .... | ... | 3 | 4 | .... | .... | 3 | 4 | .... | .... | 1 | 2 | 3 | 1 | 1 | .... | .... | 1 | 1 | .. | .. | 7 | 16 |
| .... | ... | .. | .... | 1 | 1 | 3 | 1 | 1 | 2 | 2 | .... | 2 | 4 | .... | 4 | .... | .... | .... | .... | 1 | 1 | .. | .. | 6 | 17 |
| .... | ... | .. | .... | ... | .... | .... | .... | 1 | .... | .... | 1 | .... | .... | .... | .... | .... | .... | .... | .... | 1 | ... | .. | .. | 1 | 18 |
| .... | ... | .. | .... | ... | 1 | 1 | 1 | 1 | 1 | 2 | .... | .... | 3 | .... | 3 | .... | .... | 1 | .... | ... | ... | .. | .. | 4 | 19 |
| .... | ... | .. | .... | ... | .... | .... | 1 | .... | .... | 1 | .... | .... | .... | 1 | 1 | .... | .... | .... | .... | ... | ... | .. | .. | 1 | 20 |
| .... | ... | .. | .... | ... | .... | 1 | .... | .... | 1 | .... | .... | .... | .... | .... | .... | .... | .... | .... | .... | 1 | ... | .. | .. | 1 | 21 |
| .... | ... | .. | .... | ... | .... | .... | 1 | .... | .... | 1 | .... | .... | .... | 1 | 1 | .... | .... | .... | .... | ... | ... | .. | .. | 1 | 22 |
| .... | 2 | .. | .... | ... | 6 | 8 | 8 | 7 | 3 | 5 | 5 | 13 | 6 | 12 | 18 | 2 | 1 | .... | 1 | 1 | 5 | .. | 1 | 29 | 23 |
| .... | ... | .. | .... | ... | 4 | 2 | .... | 2 | 3 | 2 | .... | 3 | 2 | 1 | 3 | 1 | .... | .... | .... | 1 | 2 | .. | 1 | 8 | 24 |
| .... | ... | .. | .... | ... | .... | .... | .... | 1 | 1 | .... | .... | .... | 1 | .... | 1 | .... | .... | .... | .... | ... | ... | .. | .. | 1 | 25 |
| .... | ... | .. | .... | ... | .... | 1 | .... | .... | .... | .... | .... | 1 | .... | .... | .... | .... | .... | .... | .... | ... | 1 | .. | .. | 1 | 26 |
| .... | ... | .. | .... | ... | 2 | .... | 3 | 6 | 1 | 9 | 1 | 1 | 4 | 3 | 7 | .... | .... | .... | .... | 4 | ... | 1 | .. | 12 | 27 |
| .... | 1 | .. | .... | ... | 8 | 1 | 2 | 2 | 1 | 11 | 1 | 1 | 9 | 4 | 13 | .... | .... | .... | .... | ... | ... | .. | 1 | 14 | 28 |
| .... | ... | .. | .... | ... | 1 | .... | .... | .... | .... | 1 | .... | .... | .... | .... | .... | .... | .... | .... | .... | ... | 1 | .. | .. | 1 | 29 |
| .... | ... | .. | .... | ... | .... | .... | 1 | .... | .... | .... | .... | .... | 1 | .... | 1 | .... | .... | .... | .... | ... | ... | .. | .. | 1 | 30 |
| .... | ... | .. | .... | ... | 1 | 1 | .... | .... | 1 | 1 | .... | .... | 2 | .... | 2 | .... | .... | .... | .... | ... | ... | .. | .. | 2 | 31 |
| .... | ... | .. | .... | 1 | 1 | .... | 1 | 2 | .... | 1 | .... | 3 | 2 | .... | 2 | .... | .... | .... | .... | 1 | 1 | .. | .. | 4 | 32 |
| .... | ... | 1 | .... | ... | 1 | 1 | .... | 2 | 1 | 3 | .... | .... | .... | 3 | 3 | 1 | .... | .... | .... | ... | ... | .. | .. | 4 | 33 |
| .... | ... | .. | .... | 6 | 9 | 2 | 7 | 11 | 2 | 29 | .... | .... | 2 | 1 | 3 | 1 | 4 | .... | .... | 9 | 8 | 4 | 2 | 31 | 34 |
| .... | ... | .. | .... | ... | .... | 1 | 1 | .... | .... | .... | .... | 2 | 1 | .... | 1 | .... | .... | .... | .... | 1 | ... | .. | .. | 2 | 35 |
| .... | ... | .. | .... | ... | .... | 3 | .... | .... | 2 | .... | .... | 1 | 1 | .... | 1 | .... | .... | .... | .... | ... | 2 | .. | .. | 3 | 36 |
| .... | ... | .. | .... | ... | 2 | 7 | 7 | 3 | 3 | 11 | 3 | 2 | 8 | 6 | 14 | .... | .... | .... | .... | ... | 2 | 2 | 1 | 19 | 37 |
| .... | ... | .. | .... | ... | 1 | .... | .... | 2 | .... | 1 | .... | 2 | 2 | 1 | 3 | .... | .... | .... | .... | ... | ... | .. | .. | 3 | 38 |
| .... | ... | .. | .... | ... | .... | .... | 1 | 1 | .... | 1 | 1 | .... | .... | 1 | 1 | .... | .... | .... | .... | ... | 1 | .. | .. | 2 | 39 |
| .... | ... | .. | .... | ... | 1 | .... | 1 | .... | .... | .... | 1 | 1 | .... | .... | .... | .... | .... | .... | .... | 1 | ... | .. | 1 | 2 | 40 |
| .... | ... | .. | 1 | ... | 1 | .... | .... | 1 | .... | 1 | ... | 1 | .... | 1 | 1 | .... | .... | .... | .... | ... | 1 | .. | .. | 2 | 41 |
| .... | ... | .. | .... | ... | .... | .... | 1 | .... | .... | .... | .... | 2 | 1 | 1 | 2 | .... | .... | .... | .... | ... | ... | .. | .. | 2 | 42 |
| .... | 1 | 3 | 2 | ... | 26 | 33 | 24 | 16 | 38 | 30 | 8 | 13 | 33 | 37 | 70 | 1 | 3 | .... | 2 | 9 | 9 | 4 | 5 | 103 | 43 |
| .... | 26 | 10 | 14 | 9 | 236 | 253 | 189 | 146 | 197 | 336 | 66 | 203 | 300 | 281 | 581 | 21 | 24 | 8 | 5 | 71 | 84 | 27 | 25 | 846 | |

## IN THE STATE OF CONNECTICUT.

| Nativities. California and Territories. | Nativities. Ireland. | Nativities. Germany. | Nativities. Other foreign countries. | Nativities. Unknown. | Season of decease. Spring. | Season of decease. Summer. | Season of decease. Autumn. | Season of decease. Winter. | Duration of sickness. Under 1 week. | Duration of sickness. 1 week and under 1 month. | Duration of sickness. 1 month and under 3 months. | Duration of sickness. 3 months and over. | Whites. Males. | Whites. Females. | Whites. Total. | Colored. Slaves. Black. M. | Colored. Slaves. Black. F. | Colored. Slaves. Mulatto. M. | Colored. Slaves. Mulatto. F. | Colored. Free. Black. M. | Colored. Free. Black. F. | Colored. Free. Mul. M | Colored. Free. Mul. F. | Aggregate deaths. | |
|---|---|---|---|---|---|---|---|---|---|---|---|---|---|---|---|---|---|---|---|---|---|---|---|---|---|
| .... | ... | .. | .... | ... | 2 | 2 | 3 | .... | .... | 1 | 1 | 4 | 4 | 3 | 7 | .... | .... | .... | .... | ... | ... | .. | .. | 7 | 1 |
| .... | 7 | .. | 4 | ... | 15 | 17 | 31 | 14 | 25 | 9 | .... | 6 | 68 | 16 | 79 | .... | .... | .... | .... | ... | ... | .. | 1 | 80 | 2 |
| .... | 1 | .. | .... | ... | 2 | .... | 2 | 7 | 9 | 1 | 1 | .... | 3 | 7 | 10 | .... | .... | .... | .... | ... | 1 | .. | .. | 11 | 3 |
| .... | 8 | .. | 3 | ... | 10 | 38 | 13 | 5 | 66 | .... | .... | .... | 52 | 11 | 63 | .... | .... | .... | .... | 2 | 1 | .. | .. | 66 | 4 |
| .... | ... | .. | 1 | ... | .... | 1 | 1 | 2 | 1 | 2 | .... | .... | 2 | 2 | 4 | .... | .... | .... | .... | ... | ... | .. | .. | 4 | 5 |
| .... | ... | .. | .... | ... | .... | 1 | .... | .... | 1 | .... | .... | .... | 1 | .... | 1 | .... | .... | .... | .... | ... | ... | .. | .. | 1 | 6 |
| .... | 1 | .. | .... | ... | 2 | 3 | 2 | 4 | 5 | 1 | .... | .... | 10 | 1 | 11 | .... | .... | .... | .... | ... | ... | .. | .. | 11 | 7 |
| .... | 2 | .. | .... | ... | 13 | 12 | 19 | 12 | 25 | 5 | 2 | 4 | 27 | 27 | 54 | .... | .... | .... | .... | ... | 2 | .. | .. | 56 | 8 |
| .... | 1 | 1 | .... | ... | 3 | .... | .... | 2 | 1 | 1 | 1 | 2 | 2 | 3 | 5 | .... | .... | .... | .... | ... | ... | .. | .. | 5 | 9 |
| .... | ... | .. | .... | ... | .... | .... | .... | 1 | .... | 1 | .... | .... | 1 | .... | 1 | .... | .... | .... | .... | ... | ... | .. | .. | 1 | 10 |
| .... | ... | .. | 1 | ... | 11 | 16 | 27 | 5 | 22 | 25 | 2 | 3 | 30 | 29 | 59 | .... | .... | .... | .... | ... | ... | .. | .. | 59 | 11 |
| .... | ... | .. | .... | ... | 19 | 17 | 19 | 16 | 20 | 27 | 7 | 3 | 38 | 32 | 70 | .... | .... | .... | .... | ... | 1 | .. | .. | 71 | 12 |
| .... | ... | .. | 1 | ... | 4 | 1 | .... | .... | 2 | 1 | .... | 1 | 3 | 2 | 5 | .... | .... | .... | .... | ... | ... | .. | .. | 5 | 13 |
| .... | 1 | .. | 2 | ... | 12 | 15 | 14 | 15 | 2 | 2 | 5 | 35 | 21 | 35 | 56 | .... | .... | .... | .... | ... | ... | .. | .. | 56 | 14 |
| .... | 4 | 2 | 2 | ... | 12 | 14 | 10 | 3 | 12 | 14 | .... | .... | .... | 38 | 38 | .... | .... | .... | .... | ... | 1 | .. | .. | 39 | 15 |
| .... | 14 | .. | 4 | ... | 1 | 21 | 35 | 3 | 29 | 6 | 2 | .... | 42 | 18 | 60 | .... | .... | .... | .... | ... | ... | .. | .. | 60 | 16 |
| .... | 1 | .. | .... | ... | 2 | 10 | 70 | 3 | 35 | 17 | 2 | 2 | 52 | 32 | 84 | .... | .... | .... | .... | ... | ... | .. | 1 | 85 | 17 |
| .... | 1 | .. | .... | ... | .... | 6 | 17 | 2 | 12 | 2 | 2 | 1 | 15 | 12 | 27 | .... | .... | .... | .... | ... | ... | .. | .. | 27 | 18 |
| .... | ... | .. | .... | ... | .... | 2 | 1 | .... | 3 | .... | .... | .... | 1 | 2 | 3 | .... | .... | .... | .... | ... | ... | .. | .. | 3 | 19 |
| .... | ... | .. | .... | ... | 5 | 5 | 8 | ... | 9 | 3 | .... | .... | 11 | 6 | 17 | .... | .... | .... | .... | 1 | ... | .. | .. | 18 | 20 |
| .... | 51 | 2 | 19 | ... | 268 | 224 | 244 | 232 | 27 | 57 | 77 | 513 | 409 | 525 | 934 | .... | .... | .... | .... | 15 | 13 | 3 | 3 | 968 | 21 |
| .... | 5 | .. | 1 | ... | 58 | 51 | 40 | 38 | 49 | 24 | 11 | 17 | 100 | 86 | 186 | .... | .... | .... | .... | 1 | ... | .. | .. | 187 | 22 |
| .... | ... | .. | 1 | ... | 32 | 14 | 34 | 30 | 70 | 20 | 1 | 4 | 52 | 56 | 108 | .... | .... | .... | .... | ... | 2 | .. | .. | 110 | 23 |
| .... | ... | .. | .... | ... | 9 | 8 | 10 | 9 | 3 | 3 | 3 | 11 | 19 | 16 | 35 | .... | .... | .... | .... | 1 | ... | .. | .. | 36 | 24 |

## CLASSIFICATION OF DEATHS

| | Cause of death. | AGES. Under 1. M. | F. | 1 and under 5. M. | F. | 5 and under 10. M. | F. | 10 and under 20. M. | F. | 20 and under 50. M. | F. | 50 and under 80. M. | F. | 80 and under 100. M. | F. | 100 & over. M | F. | Age unknown. M | F. | NATIVITIES. Born in State. | New England. | Middle. | South. | Southwest. | Northwest. |
|---|---|---|---|---|---|---|---|---|---|---|---|---|---|---|---|---|---|---|---|---|---|---|---|---|---|
| 1 | Diabetes | 1 | | | | 1 | | 1 | 1 | 2 | 1 | 1 | | | | | | | | 8 | | | | | |
| 2 | Diarrhœa | 2 | 3 | | 3 | | | | 1 | 9 | 3 | 3 | 2 | 2 | 2 | | | | | 24 | 3 | 1 | | | |
| 3 | Dropsy | 19 | 11 | 21 | 12 | 12 | 2 | 3 | 1 | 13 | 23 | 47 | 38 | 11 | 12 | | | 3 | 1 | 206 | 10 | 2 | | | |
| 4 | Dysentery | 58 | 42 | 149 | 128 | 58 | 46 | 30 | 33 | 103 | 118 | 76 | 103 | 11 | 8 | | | 1 | 1 | 882 | 22 | 15 | 3 | | 4 |
| 5 | Dyspepsia | | | | | | | | 2 | 2 | 2 | 2 | | | | | | | | 6 | | | | 2 | |
| 6 | Erysipelas | 3 | 2 | 4 | 4 | 3 | | 2 | 4 | 11 | 15 | 17 | 10 | 2 | 2 | | | | | 70 | 4 | 1 | | 1 | |
| 7 | Fever, not specified | 8 | 6 | 20 | 12 | 10 | 3 | 11 | 6 | 41 | 51 | 30 | 20 | 4 | 1 | | | | | 188 | 12 | 1 | | | |
| 8 | ..do..bilious | | | 1 | 1 | 1 | 2 | 3 | 2 | 9 | 12 | 7 | 3 | | 1 | | | 1 | | 39 | 3 | | | | |
| 9 | ..do..brain | 3 | | 8 | 3 | 3 | | 1 | | 11 | 7 | 2 | 1 | | | | | | | 35 | 1 | 1 | | | 1 |
| 10 | ..do..catarrhal | 2 | | 1 | 3 | | | | | 1 | | | 1 | | | | | | | 8 | | | | | |
| 11 | ..do..congestive | 1 | | | 1 | | | 1 | | 1 | | 1 | | | | | | | | 5 | | | | | |
| 12 | ..do..scarlet | 11 | 5 | 18 | 25 | 10 | 10 | 4 | 4 | | 4 | | | | | | | | | 80 | 3 | 3 | | | 1 |
| 13 | ..do..typhoid | 3 | 2 | | 2 | 1 | 5 | 12 | 15 | 35 | 39 | 18 | 18 | | | | | 1 | | 131 | 6 | 2 | | | |
| 14 | ..do..yellow | | | | | | | 1 | | 3 | | | | | | | | | | 3 | | | | | |
| 15 | Fracture | | | | | | | | 1 | 2 | 1 | | 2 | | | | | | | 3 | | | | | 2 |
| 16 | Frozen | | | | | | | | | 2 | 1 | 2 | 1 | | | | | | | 6 | | | | | |
| 17 | Gout | | | | | | | 1 | | | | 5 | | | | | | | | 4 | 1 | | | 1 | |
| 18 | Gravel | | | | | | | | | 2 | | 3 | | 3 | | | | | | 8 | | | | | |
| 19 | Head, disease of | 1 | 3 | | | | | | | | | 2 | | | | | | | | 5 | | | | | |
| 20 | Heart....do | 8 | 10 | 5 | 4 | 4 | | 3 | 1 | 7 | 11 | 27 | 20 | 1 | 5 | | | | | 92 | 3 | 3 | | | |
| 21 | Hemorrhage | | 1 | | | | | | 1 | 1 | 3 | 3 | | | | | | | | 8 | 1 | | | | |
| 22 | Hernia | 1 | 1 | | | | | | | | 2 | 2 | 1 | | | | | | | 5 | 1 | 1 | | | |
| 23 | Hip, disease of | | | 1 | 1 | 2 | | | 1 | | | | | | | | | 1 | | 6 | | | | | |
| 24 | Hooping cough | 7 | 16 | 8 | 12 | 1 | 2 | | | | 2 | | | | | | | | | 45 | 1 | | | | |
| 25 | Hydrocephalus | 4 | 1 | 3 | 3 | 1 | | 1 | | | | | | | | | | | | 11 | | | | | 1 |
| 26 | Inflammation | 9 | 3 | 8 | | 1 | | 2 | 3 | 3 | 10 | 7 | 5 | 4 | 1 | | | | | 49 | 2 | 2 | | | |
| 27 | .....do.....bowels | 3 | | 2 | 5 | 1 | | 4 | | 2 | 4 | 6 | 1 | | 3 | | | | | 27 | 2 | | | | |
| 28 | .....do.....brain | 1 | 1 | 1 | 5 | 1 | 1 | 4 | 2 | 4 | 3 | | | | | | | | | 21 | 1 | 1 | | | |
| 29 | .....do.....stomach | | | | | | | | | | | 1 | 1 | | | | | | | 2 | | | | | |
| 30 | Influenza | 2 | | | 1 | | | 1 | | | | 1 | 1 | 2 | 1 | | | | | 8 | 1 | | | | |
| 31 | Insanity | | | | | | | | | 5 | 1 | 2 | | 1 | | | | | | 3 | 2 | 1 | | 1 | |
| 32 | Intemperance | | | | | | | 1 | | 5 | | 6 | | | | | | 1 | | 11 | | | | | |
| 33 | Jaundice | 1 | 1 | | | | | | 1 | 2 | | 2 | 2 | 2 | | | | | | 9 | 2 | | | | |
| 34 | Kidneys, disease of | | | 1 | 1 | | | | 1 | | | 2 | 2 | 2 | | | | | | 9 | | | | | |
| 35 | Killed | | | 1 | | | | 1 | | 3 | | | | | | | | | | 2 | | | | | |
| 36 | Lightning | | | 1 | 2 | | | 2 | | | 1 | | | | | | | | | 6 | | | | | |
| 37 | Liver, disease of | 2 | 1 | | | | 2 | | 1 | 5 | 6 | 6 | 3 | | | | | | | 22 | 3 | | | | |
| 38 | Lockjaw | 1 | | | | | | | 1 | 2 | | 2 | | | | | | | | 3 | 3 | | | | |
| 39 | Lungs, disease of | 4 | 3 | 4 | 6 | | 2 | | 1 | 4 | 1 | 8 | 5 | 3 | 2 | | | 1 | 1 | 45 | | | | | |
| 40 | Malformation | | | 2 | | 1 | | | | 1 | | | | | | | | | | 4 | | | | | |
| 41 | Marasmus | 4 | | 2 | | | | | | 2 | 1 | 1 | 3 | | 1 | | | | | 13 | | | | | |
| 42 | Mania-a-potu | | | | | | | | | 7 | 1 | 6 | | | | | | | | 9 | 1 | | | | |
| 43 | Measles | 1 | 3 | 6 | 9 | 6 | 2 | | 2 | 1 | 2 | | | | | | | | | 29 | | | | | |
| 44 | Mortification | | | | | | | | | 1 | | 3 | | 1 | | | | | | 3 | 1 | 1 | | | |
| 45 | Mumps | | | | 1 | 1 | | | | | | | | | | | | | | 2 | | | | | |
| 46 | Murder | | | | | | | | | 1 | | 1 | | | | | | | | 2 | | | | | |
| 47 | Neuralgia | | | | | | | | | 2 | 1 | 2 | 1 | 1 | | | | | | 7 | | | | | |
| 48 | Old age | | | | | | | | | | | 34 | 56 | 93 | 162 | 1 | | 4 | 6 | 332 | 13 | 7 | 1 | | |
| 49 | Paralysis | 2 | | | | | | | 1 | 3 | 6 | 21 | 24 | 13 | 13 | | | | | 73 | 5 | 1 | | | |
| 50 | Pleurisy | | 1 | | 1 | | | | | 7 | 8 | 4 | 7 | | 1 | 1 | | | | 24 | 4 | | | | |
| 51 | Pneumonia | 27 | 17 | 16 | 24 | 7 | 3 | 5 | 2 | 24 | 18 | 38 | 39 | 5 | 5 | | | | | 206 | 13 | 2 | | | |
| 52 | Piles | | | | | | | | | | 1 | | | | | | | | | 1 | | | | | |
| 53 | Poison | | | 2 | | | | 1 | 1 | | | 1 | | | | | | | | 5 | | | | | |
| 54 | Putrid sore throat | | | | 2 | | | 2 | | | | 1 | | | | | | | | 5 | | | | | |
| 55 | Quinsy | | | | | | | 1 | 1 | | | | | | | | | | | 2 | | | | | |
| 56 | Rheumatism | | | 1 | 1 | | | | | 2 | | 7 | 4 | 1 | 2 | | | | | 16 | 1 | | | | |
| 57 | Salivation, effects of | | | | | | | | | 1 | | | | | | | | | | | | | 1 | | |
| 58 | Scrofula | 1 | 2 | 3 | | 2 | | | 4 | 1 | 10 | 4 | 1 | 1 | | | | | | 25 | 2 | 1 | | | |
| 59 | Small pox | | 1 | 1 | 1 | | 2 | | 2 | 5 | 2 | 2 | 1 | | | | | | | 12 | 2 | 1 | 1 | | |
| 60 | Spine, disease of | 1 | 2 | 1 | 1 | 1 | | 1 | | 1 | 5 | 1 | 1 | | | | | | | 15 | | | | | |
| 61 | Still born | 5 | 2 | | | | | | | | | | | | | | | | | 7 | | | | | |
| 62 | Stomach, disease of | | 1 | 2 | 1 | | | 1 | | | 1 | 1 | | | | | | | | 6 | | | | | |
| 63 | Suffocation | 1 | | | 2 | 2 | | | | | | | | | | | | | | 5 | | | | | |
| 64 | Summer complaint | | | | 1 | | | | | | | 1 | | | | | | | | 2 | | | | | |
| 65 | Suicide | | | | | | | | | 7 | 4 | 3 | 2 | | | | | | | 13 | 2 | | | | |
| 66 | Sun, stroke of | | | | | | | | | 1 | | | | | 1 | | | | | 2 | | | | | |
| 67 | Teething | 5 | 5 | 5 | 6 | | | | | | | | | | | | | 1 | | 21 | 1 | | | | |
| 68 | Tumor | | | | | | | | 1 | 2 | 1 | 1 | | | 1 | | | | | 6 | | | | | |
| 69 | Ulcer | 1 | | | | | | | | | | 1 | 2 | | | | | | | 3 | | | | | |
| 70 | Uterus, disease of | | | | | | | | | | 1 | | 1 | | | | | | | 2 | | | | | |
| 71 | Venereal | | 1 | | | | | | | 1 | | | | | | | | | | 2 | | | | | |
| 72 | Worms | | | 1 | 2 | | | | | | | | | | | | | | | 3 | | | | | |
| 73 | Unknown | 60 | 69 | 43 | 24 | 7 | 6 | 8 | 19 | 44 | 42 | 37 | 55 | 7 | 18 | | | 40 | 31 | 460 | 9 | 7 | 4 | | |
| | Total | 382 | 316 | 486 | 419 | 177 | 119 | 187 | 188 | 715 | 811 | 717 | 684 | 197 | 275 | 3 | .. | 60 | 45 | 5098 | 224 | 103 | 12 | 6 | 13 |

IN THE STATE OF CONNECTICUT—Continued.

| NATIVITIES. | | | | | SEASON OF DECEASE. | | | | DURATION OF SICKNESS. | | | | WHITES. | | | COLORED. | | | | | | | | | |
|---|---|---|---|---|---|---|---|---|---|---|---|---|---|---|---|---|---|---|---|---|---|---|---|---|---|
| | | | | | | | | | | | | | | | | Slaves. | | | | Free. | | | | | |
| | | | | | | | | | | | | | | | | Black. | | Mulatto. | | Black. | | Mul. | | | |
| California and Territories. | Ireland. | Germany. | Other foreign countries. | Unknown. | Spring. | Summer. | Autumn. | Winter. | Under 1 week. | 1 week and under 1 month. | 1 month and under 3 months. | 3 months and over. | Males. | Females. | Total. | M. | F. | M. | F. | M. | F. | M | F. | Aggregate deaths. | |
| .... | ... | .. | .... | ... | 4 | 1 | 1 | 2 | .... | 4 | .... | 2 | 6 | 2 | 8 | .... | .... | .... | .... | .... | ... | .. | .. | 8 | 1 |
| .... | 2 | .. | .... | ... | 2 | 5 | 19 | 1 | 3 | 4 | 3 | 5 | 15 | 13 | 28 | .... | .... | .... | .... | 1 | 1 | .. | .. | 30 | 2 |
| .... | 8 | .. | 3 | ... | 53 | 66 | 66 | 44 | 34 | 57 | 27 | 74 | 127 | 95 | 222 | .... | .... | .... | .... | ... | 4 | 2 | 1 | 229 | 3 |
| .... | 32 | .. | 7 | ... | 37 | 74 | 778 | 61 | 187 | 338 | 66 | 31 | 483 | 472 | 955 | .... | .... | .... | .... | 3 | 7 | .. | .. | 965 | 4 |
| .... | ... | .. | .... | ... | 2 | 2 | 2 | 2 | .... | .... | .... | 6 | 4 | 4 | 8 | .... | .... | .... | .... | ... | ... | .. | .. | 8 | 5 |
| .... | 2 | .. | 1 | ... | 31 | 23 | 13 | 12 | 26 | 25 | 8 | 3 | 41 | 35 | 76 | .... | .... | .... | .... | 1 | 1 | .. | 1 | 79 | 6 |
| .... | 14 | .. | 8 | ... | 71 | 34 | 68 | 49 | 27 | 131 | 46 | .... | 122 | 99 | 221 | .... | .... | .... | .... | 1 | ... | 1 | .. | 223 | 7 |
| .... | 1 | .. | .... | ... | 11 | 9 | 18 | 5 | 5 | 21 | 11 | .... | 22 | 21 | 43 | .... | .... | .... | .... | ... | ... | .. | .. | 43 | 8 |
| .... | 1 | .. | .... | ... | 15 | 10 | 9 | 5 | 9 | 17 | 5 | 4 | 28 | 11 | 39 | .... | .... | .... | .... | ... | ... | .. | .. | 39 | 9 |
| .... | ... | .. | .... | ... | 4 | 1 | 1 | 2 | .... | .... | .... | .... | 4 | 3 | 7 | .... | .... | .... | .... | ... | 1 | .. | .. | 8 | 10 |
| .... | ... | .. | .... | ... | 1 | 1 | 1 | 2 | 3 | 2 | .... | .... | 4 | 1 | 5 | .... | .... | .... | .... | ... | ... | .. | .. | 5 | 11 |
| .... | 3 | .. | 1 | ... | 32 | 21 | 13 | 23 | 32 | 42 | 6 | 4 | 43 | 47 | 90 | .... | .... | .... | .... | ... | 1 | .. | .. | 91 | 12 |
| .... | 11 | .. | 1 | ... | 25 | 32 | 63 | 30 | 19 | 79 | 27 | 3 | 70 | 79 | 149 | .... | .... | .... | .... | ... | 2 | .. | .. | 151 | 13 |
| .... | ... | .. | 1 | ... | 3 | 1 | .... | .... | 2 | 1 | .... | .... | 4 | .... | 4 | .... | .... | .... | .... | ... | ... | .. | .. | 4 | 14 |
| .... | 1 | .. | .... | ... | 1 | 2 | 1 | 2 | 1 | 1 | 1 | 2 | 2 | 4 | 6 | .... | .... | .... | .... | ... | ... | .. | .. | 6 | 15 |
| .... | ... | .. | .... | ... | 4 | .... | .... | 2 | .... | .... | .... | 1 | 2 | 2 | 4 | .... | .... | .... | .... | 1 | ... | 1 | .. | 6 | 16 |
| .... | ... | .. | .... | ... | .... | 3 | 1 | 2 | 2 | 1 | 1 | .... | 6 | .... | 6 | .... | .... | .... | .... | ... | ... | .. | .. | 6 | 17 |
| .... | ... | .. | .... | ... | 3 | 1 | 1 | 2 | 1 | 3 | .... | 3 | 8 | .... | 8 | .... | .... | .... | .... | ... | ... | .. | .. | 8 | 18 |
| .... | ... | .. | 1 | ... | 3 | 2 | .... | 1 | 1 | 1 | 3 | .... | 3 | 3 | 6 | .... | .... | .... | .... | ... | ... | .. | .. | 6 | 19 |
| .... | 4 | .. | 4 | ... | 33 | 30 | 24 | 18 | 33 | 21 | 9 | 18 | 53 | 51 | 104 | .... | .... | .... | .... | ... | ... | 2 | .. | 106 | 20 |
| .... | ... | .. | .... | ... | 5 | 2 | 1 | 1 | 5 | 1 | 1 | .... | 4 | 5 | 9 | .... | .... | .... | .... | ... | ... | .. | .. | 9 | 21 |
| .... | ... | .. | .... | ... | 3 | 2 | 2 | .... | 2 | 3 | 1 | .... | 3 | 4 | 7 | .... | .... | .... | .... | ... | ... | .. | .. | 7 | 22 |
| .... | ... | .. | .... | ... | .... | 1 | 3 | 2 | 1 | 1 | .... | .... | 4 | 1 | 5 | .... | .... | .... | .... | ... | 1 | .. | .. | 6 | 23 |
| .... | 1 | .. | 1 | ... | 17 | 10 | 11 | 10 | 5 | 25 | 6 | 5 | 16 | 31 | 47 | .... | .... | .... | .... | ... | 1 | .. | .. | 48 | 24 |
| .... | 1 | .. | .... | ... | 7 | 3 | 1 | 2 | .... | 1 | .... | .... | 9 | 4 | 13 | .... | .... | .... | .... | ... | ... | .. | .. | 13 | 25 |
| .... | 1 | .. | 2 | ... | 17 | 10 | 16 | 11 | 22 | 21 | 3 | 1 | 35 | 21 | 56 | .... | .... | .... | .... | ... | ... | .. | .. | 56 | 26 |
| .... | 2 | .. | .... | ... | 8 | 6 | 10 | 7 | 14 | 7 | 1 | 1 | 18 | 12 | 30 | .... | .... | .... | .... | ... | 1 | .. | .. | 31 | 27 |
| .... | ... | .. | .... | ... | 9 | 5 | 3 | 6 | 7 | 10 | 1 | .... | 9 | 12 | 21 | .... | .... | .... | .... | 2 | ... | .. | .. | 23 | 28 |
| .... | ... | .. | .... | ... | .... | 1 | 1 | .... | 1 | 1 | .... | .... | 1 | 1 | 2 | .... | .... | .... | .... | ... | ... | .. | .. | 2 | 29 |
| .... | ... | .. | .... | ... | 4 | 1 | 1 | 3 | 1 | 4 | .... | 1 | 5 | 3 | 8 | .... | .... | .... | .... | 1 | ... | .. | .. | 9 | 30 |
| 1 | 1 | .. | .... | ... | 5 | 2 | 1 | 1 | 1 | 1 | .... | 5 | 8 | 1 | 9 | .... | .... | .... | .... | ... | ... | .. | .. | 9 | 31 |
| .... | 1 | . | 1 | ... | 1 | 6 | 2 | 4 | 3 | ... | .... | .... | 11 | .... | 11 | .... | .... | .... | .... | 2 | ... | .. | .. | 13 | 32 |
| .... | ... | .. | .... | ... | 2 | 3 | 4 | 2 | 1 | 3 | 4 | 2 | 7 | 4 | 11 | .... | .... | .... | .... | ... | ... | .. | .. | 11 | 33 |
| .... | ... | .. | .... | ... | 5 | 2 | 1 | 1 | .... | 1 | 2 | 2 | 5 | 3 | 8 | .... | .... | .... | .... | ... | 1 | .. | .. | 9 | 34 |
| .... | 2 | .. | 1 | ... | .... | 1 | 2 | 2 | 2 | ... | 1 | .... | 5 | .... | 5 | .... | .... | .... | .... | ... | ... | .. | .. | 5 | 35 |
| .... | ... | .. | .... | ... | .... | 1 | 4 | .... | 3 | 1 | 1 | .... | 3 | 3 | 6 | .... | .... | .... | .... | ... | ... | .. | .. | 6 | 36 |
| .... | ... | .. | 1 | ... | 10 | 7 | 6 | 3 | 3 | 4 | 3 | 10 | 13 | 12 | 25 | .... | .... | .... | .... | ... | 1 | .. | .. | 26 | 37 |
| .... | ... | .. | .... | ... | 3 | 1 | 1 | 1 | 2 | 2 | .... | .... | 5 | 1 | 6 | .... | .... | .... | .... | ... | ... | .. | .. | 6 | 38 |
| .... | ... | .. | .... | ... | 20 | 6 | 8 | 11 | 7 | 23 | 1 | 3 | 24 | 19 | 43 | .... | .... | .... | .... | ... | 2 | .. | .. | 45 | 39 |
| .... | ... | .. | .... | ... | .... | 2 | .... | 2 | .... | .... | .... | .... | 4 | .... | 4 | .... | .... | .... | .... | ... | ... | .. | .. | 4 | 40 |
| .... | 1 | .. | .... | ... | 8 | 3 | 1 | 2 | .... | 1 | 1 | 2 | 8 | 5 | 13 | .... | .... | .... | .... | 1 | ... | .. | .. | 14 | 41 |
| .... | 2 | .. | 2 | ... | .... | 3 | 5 | .... | 4 | 2 | 1 | .... | 13 | 1 | 14 | .... | .... | .... | .... | ... | ... | .. | .. | 14 | 42 |
| .... | 2 | .. | 1 | ... | 10 | 8 | 13 | 1 | 7 | 21 | .... | .... | 14 | 18 | 32 | .... | .... | .... | .... | ... | ... | .. | .. | 32 | 43 |
| .... | ... | .. | .... | ... | 2 | .... | 3 | .... | .... | 2 | .... | 2 | 3 | .... | 3 | .... | .... | .... | .... | 1 | ... | 1 | .. | 5 | 44 |
| .... | ... | .. | .... | ... | 1 | 1 | .... | .... | 1 | 1 | .... | .... | 1 | 1 | 2 | .... | .... | .... | .... | ... | ... | .. | .. | 2 | 45 |
| .... | ... | .. | .... | ... | 1 | 1 | .... | .... | 1 | .... | .... | .... | 2 | .... | 2 | .... | .... | .... | .... | ... | ... | .. | .. | 2 | 46 |
| .... | ... | .. | .... | ... | 2 | 2 | 3 | .... | 1 | .... | .... | 3 | 5 | 2 | 7 | .... | .... | .... | .... | ... | ... | .. | .. | 7 | 47 |
| .... | ... | .. | 3 | ... | 122 | 65 | 84 | 81 | 24 | 45 | 11 | 56 | 131 | 220 | 351 | .... | .... | .... | .... | 1 | 2 | .. | 2 | 356 | 48 |
| .... | 1 | .. | 3 | ... | 27 | 14 | 21 | 20 | 22 | 18 | 7 | 20 | 39 | 44 | 83 | .... | .... | .... | .... | ... | ... | .. | .. | 83 | 49 |
| .... | 2 | .. | .... | ... | 12 | 4 | 9 | 5 | 12 | 8 | 1 | 3 | 12 | 18 | 30 | .... | .... | .... | .... | ... | ... | .. | .. | 30 | 50 |
| ... | 7 | 2 | .... | ... | 108 | 43 | 25 | 53 | 73 | 114 | 13 | 6 | 117 | 106 | 223 | .... | .... | .... | .... | 4 | 1 | 1 | 1 | 230 | 51 |
| .... | ... | .. | .... | ... | .... | .... | .... | 1 | .... | .... | ... | 1 | .... | 1 | 1 | .... | .... | .... | .... | ... | ... | .. | .. | 1 | 52 |
| .... | ... | .. | .... | ... | .... | 1 | 2 | 2 | 2 | .... | ... | 1 | 4 | 1 | 5 | .... | .... | .... | .... | ... | ... | .. | .. | 5 | 53 |
| .... | ... | .. | .... | ... | 2 | 1 | 2 | .... | 1 | 3 | .... | 1 | 3 | 2 | 5 | .... | .... | .... | .... | ... | ... | .. | .. | 5 | 54 |
| .... | ... | .. | .... | ... | .... | 1 | 1 | .... | .... | 2 | .... | .... | 1 | 1 | 2 | .... | .... | .... | .... | ... | ... | .. | .. | 2 | 55 |
| .... | ... | .. | 1 | ... | 7 | 3 | 5 | 3 | 3 | 6 | 1 | 4 | 10 | 7 | 17 | .... | .... | .... | .... | ... | ... | 1 | .. | 18 | 56 |
| .... | ... | .. | .... | ... | .... | .... | .... | 1 | .... | 1 | .... | .... | 1 | .... | 1 | .... | .... | .... | .... | ... | ... | .. | .. | 1 | 57 |
| .... | 1 | .. | .... | ... | 6 | 9 | 5 | 9 | 2 | 4 | 8 | 16 | 11 | 17 | 28 | .... | .... | .... | .... | ... | ... | 1 | .. | 29 | 58 |
| .... | 1 | .. | .... | ... | .... | 10 | 3 | 4 | 2 | 12 | 1 | .... | 8 | 9 | 17 | .... | .... | .... | .... | ... | ... | .. | .. | 17 | 59 |
| .... | ... | .. | .... | ... | 2 | 4 | 4 | 5 | 2 | 3 | 1 | 6 | 6 | 9 | 15 | .... | .... | .... | .... | ... | ... | .. | .. | 15 | 60 |
| .... | ... | .. | .... | ... | 2 | 4 | 1 | .... | .... | .... | .... | .... | 5 | 2 | 7 | .... | .... | .... | .... | ... | ... | .. | .. | 7 | 61 |
| .... | 1 | .. | .... | ... | 1 | 2 | 2 | .... | 1 | 4 | .... | 1 | 4 | 3 | 7 | .... | .... | .... | .... | ... | ... | .. | .. | 7 | 62 |
| .... | ... | .. | .... | ... | 3 | .... | .... | 2 | .... | .... | .... | .... | 3 | 2 | 5 | .... | .... | .... | .... | ... | ... | .. | .. | 5 | 63 |
| .... | ... | .. | .... | ... | 1 | .... | .... | 1 | .... | 1 | .... | 1 | 1 | 1 | 2 | .... | .... | .... | .... | ... | ... | .. | .. | 2 | 64 |
| .... | 1 | .. | .... | ... | 5 | 3 | 7 | 1 | .... | .... | .... | .... | 9 | 6 | 15 | .... | .... | .... | .... | 1 | ... | .. | .. | 16 | 65 |
| .... | ... | .. | .... | ... | 1 | 1 | .... | .... | .... | .... | .... | .... | 1 | 1 | 2 | .... | .... | .... | .... | ... | ... | .. | .. | 2 | 66 |
| .... | ... | .. | .... | ... | 5 | 5 | 8 | 4 | 5 | 7 | 2 | 1 | 11 | 11 | 22 | .... | .... | .... | .... | ... | ... | .. | .. | 22 | 67 |
| .... | ... | .. | .... | ... | 1 | 1 | 1 | 3 | .... | 1 | 2 | 1 | 3 | 2 | 5 | .... | .... | .... | .... | ... | 1 | .. | .. | 6 | 68 |
| .... | 1 | .. | .... | ... | .... | 2 | 2 | .... | 2 | .... | 2 | .... | 2 | 2 | 4 | .... | .... | .... | .... | ... | ... | .. | .. | 4 | 69 |
| .... | ... | .. | .... | ... | 2 | .... | .... | .... | 1 | .... | 1 | .... | .... | 2 | 2 | .... | .... | .... | .... | ... | ... | .. | .. | 2 | 70 |
| .... | ... | .. | .... | ... | 1 | .... | .... | 1 | .... | .... | .. | 1 | 1 | 1 | 2 | .... | .... | .... | .... | ... | ... | .. | .. | 2 | 71 |
| .... | ... | .. | .... | ... | 1 | 1 | 1 | .... | 1 | 1 | .... | .... | 1 | 2 | 3 | .... | .... | .... | .... | ... | ... | .. | .. | 3 | 72 |
| .... | 22 | .. | 8 | ... | 126 | 100 | 162 | 90 | 90 | 52 | 22 | 30 | 241 | 259 | 500 | ... | .... | .... | .... | 6 | 3 | .. | 1 | 510 | 73 |
| 1 | 227 | 7 | 90 | ... | 1390 | 1162 | 2127 | 1026 | 1150 | 1388 | 429 | 947 | 2865 | 2794 | 5659 | ... | .... | .... | .... | 46 | 52 | 13 | 11 | 5781 | |

## CLASSIFICATION OF DEATHS

| | Cause of death. | AGES. Under 1. M. | Under 1. F. | 1 and under 5. M. | 1 and under 5. F. | 5 and under 10. M. | 5 and under 10. F. | 10 and under 20. M. | 10 and under 20. F. | 20 and under 50. M. | 20 and under 50. F. | 50 and under 80. M. | 50 and under 80. F. | 80 and under 100. M | 80 and under 100. F. | 100 & over. M | 100 & over. F. | Age unknown. M | Age unknown. F. | NATIVITIES. Born in State. | New England. | Middle. | South. | Southwest. | Northeast. |
|---|---|---|---|---|---|---|---|---|---|---|---|---|---|---|---|---|---|---|---|---|---|---|---|---|---|
| 1 | Accident, not specif'd | | | 1 | 2 | 1 | | 2 | | 1 | | 2 | | | 1 | | | | | 8 | | 2 | | | |
| 2 | ....do....burned... | | | 1 | 1 | | 1 | | | 1 | 1 | | | | | | | | | 4 | | | | | |
| 3 | ....do....drowned. | 1 | | | 1 | | | 2 | | 5 | | | | | | | | | | 8 | | 1 | | | |
| 4 | ....do....railroad.. | | | | | | | | | 1 | | | | | | | | | | 1 | | | | | |
| 5 | Aneurism | | | | | | | | | 1 | | | | | | | | | | 1 | | | | | |
| 6 | Apoplexy | | | | | | | | | | 2 | 3 | 2 | | | | | | | 5 | | 1 | | | |
| 7 | Asthma | | | | | | | | | | | 1 | | | | | | | | 1 | | | | | |
| 8 | Bowels, disease of... | 1 | 1 | | 1 | | | | | | | 1 | | | | | | | | 3 | | | | | |
| 9 | Brain.....do | | | 1 | | | | | | | | | | | | | | | | 1 | | | | | |
| 10 | Cancer | | | 1 | | | | | | | | 2 | | | | | | | | 3 | | | | | |
| 11 | Catarrh | 3 | 5 | 5 | 2 | | | | 1 | 1 | | 2 | 2 | | 1 | | | | | 19 | | | 1 | | |
| 12 | Child birth | | | | | | | | 2 | | 8 | | | | | | | | | 9 | | | | | |
| 13 | Cholera | | | 1 | 2 | 1 | 1 | 1 | 3 | 18 | 29 | 17 | 20 | 4 | | | | | | 74 | | 7 | | | |
| 14 | ....do....infantum.. | 3 | 2 | 1 | 2 | | | | | | | | | | | | | | | 8 | | | | | |
| 15 | ....do....morbus.... | | | | 1 | | 1 | | | 1 | 1 | 1 | 1 | | | | | | | 3 | | 2 | | | |
| 16 | Chorea | | | | | | | | | | | | 1 | | | | | | | 1 | | | | | |
| 17 | Colic | | 2 | 1 | | | | | | 4 | | 1 | 1 | | 1 | | | | | 10 | | | | | |
| 18 | Congest'n, not spec'd | | | 2 | | | 1 | | 1 | | | 1 | | | | | | | | 5 | | | | | |
| 19 | ....do....brain.... | | | 1 | | | 2 | 2 | 1 | 2 | | | 1 | | | | | | | 6 | | 1 | | | |
| 20 | ....do....lungs | | | | | | | | | | 1 | | | | | | | | | | | | | | |
| 21 | Consumption | 1 | 2 | 1 | 5 | | 1 | 4 | 6 | 28 | 34 | 19 | 15 | 1 | 1 | | | | | 94 | | 19 | | | 1 |
| 22 | Convulsions | 2 | 5 | 6 | 3 | 1 | | 1 | 2 | 2 | 1 | 1 | | | | | | | | 22 | | 1 | | | |
| 23 | Cramp | | | | | | | | | | 1 | | | | | | | | | 1 | | | | | |
| 24 | Croup | 8 | 9 | 4 | 6 | | 1 | | | | | | | | | | | | | 28 | | | | | |
| 25 | Debility | | 3 | | | | | | | 1 | | 1 | | | | | | | | 5 | | | | | |
| 26 | Diarrhœa | 4 | 4 | 5 | 4 | 1 | | | | 1 | 1 | | 3 | | | | | | | 20 | | 3 | | | |
| 27 | Dropsy | 1 | 2 | 1 | 2 | 4 | | 4 | 5 | 7 | 5 | 12 | 6 | | 1 | | | | | 37 | | 9 | 1 | | |
| 28 | Dysentery | 8 | 11 | 14 | 10 | 7 | 2 | 2 | 1 | 2 | 3 | 5 | 3 | | | | | | | 59 | | 4 | | | 1 |
| 29 | Dyspepsia | | | | | | | | | 1 | 2 | 1 | 2 | | | | | | | 5 | | 1 | | | |
| 30 | Erysipelas | | 2 | | | | 1 | | | 1 | 5 | 1 | 2 | 1 | | | | | | 8 | | 3 | | | |
| 31 | Fever, not specified.. | 2 | 2 | 3 | 1 | 1 | 1 | | 2 | | 1 | | | | | | | | | 13 | | | | | |
| 32 | ...do..bilious | 3 | 3 | 5 | 9 | 3 | 2 | 2 | 8 | 10 | 8 | 5 | 4 | | 1 | | | | | 53 | | 6 | | | |
| 33 | ...do..brain | 2 | 5 | 3 | 3 | | 1 | 2 | 2 | 7 | 1 | | | | | | | | | 22 | | 3 | | | |
| 34 | ...do..catarrhal | | 1 | 3 | | | | | | | | | | | | | | | | 4 | | | | | |
| 35 | ...do..congestive | | | | | | | 1 | | | 1 | | | | | | | | | 2 | | | | | |
| 36 | ...do..intermittent. | 1 | | | 1 | 2 | | 1 | | | | | | | | | | | | 5 | | | | | |
| 37 | ...do..remittent | 1 | | | 1 | | 1 | | | | 1 | | | | | | | | | 4 | | | | | |
| 38 | ...do..scarlet | 1 | | 6 | 5 | 2 | 3 | | 1 | | 1 | | | | | | | | | 13 | | 6 | | | |
| 39 | ...do..typhus | 1 | | 2 | 3 | | 1 | 6 | 5 | 11 | 6 | 3 | 3 | | | | | | | 25 | | 12 | | | |
| 40 | ...do..yellow | | | | | | | | | 1 | | | | | | | | | | | | | | | |
| 41 | Gravel | | | 1 | | | | | | | | | | | | | | | | 1 | | | | | |
| 42 | Head, disease of | 3 | | 2 | 1 | | | | | | | | | | | | | | | 6 | | | | | |
| 43 | Heart | 1 | | | | 1 | | | | | 1 | 1 | | | | | | | | 3 | | | | | |
| 44 | Hemorrhage | | | 1 | | | | | 1 | 1 | | | | | | | | | | 3 | | | | | |
| 45 | Hernia ...do | 1 | | | | | | 1 | | | | 2 | | | | | | | | 3 | | 1 | | | |
| 46 | Hives | | 2 | | | | | | | | | | | | | | | | | 2 | | | | | |
| 47 | Hooping cough | 7 | 5 | 8 | 11 | | 1 | | | 2 | | | | | | | | | | 33 | | 1 | | | |
| 48 | Hydrocephalus | 1 | 1 | 3 | | | | | | | | | | | | | | | | 5 | | | | | |
| 49 | Inflamat'n, not spec'd | 2 | 1 | 1 | | | | 2 | 1 | 1 | 1 | | 1 | | | | | | | 8 | | 2 | | | |
| 50 | ....do....bowels | 3 | 1 | | | 1 | 1 | 1 | | | | | | | | | | | | 7 | | | | | |
| 51 | ....do....brain | 5 | 3 | 6 | 2 | 1 | | 1 | 1 | 1 | | 1 | | | | | | | | 18 | | 3 | | | |
| 52 | Insanity | | | | | | | | | 1 | | | | | | | | | | 1 | | | | | |
| 53 | Intemperance | | | | | | | | | 3 | | 5 | 1 | | | | | | | 9 | | | | | |
| 54 | Jaundice | | 2 | | 1 | | | | | | 1 | | | | | | | | | 3 | | 1 | | | |
| 55 | Killed | | | | | | | 1 | | 3 | | | | | | | | | | 4 | | | | | |
| 56 | Liver, disease of | | | 1 | | | | | 2 | 2 | | 1 | 1 | | | | | | | 7 | | | | | |
| 57 | Lungs....do | 4 | 1 | 1 | 1 | | | | | | | 2 | 1 | | | | | | | 8 | | 2 | | | |
| 58 | Mania-a-potu | | | | | | | | | 1 | | 1 | | | | | | | | | | 2 | | | |
| 59 | Marasmus | 1 | | | | | | | | | | | | | | | | | | 1 | | | | | |
| 60 | Measles | 3 | 3 | 5 | 7 | 3 | | 2 | | | 1 | | | | | | | | | 22 | | 1 | | | |
| 61 | Mortification | | | 1 | | 2 | | | | | 1 | | | | | | | | | 4 | | | | | |
| 62 | Mumps | | | | | | | | 1 | | | | | | | | | | | 1 | | | | | |
| 63 | Old age | | | | | | | | | | | 4 | 4 | 6 | 12 | 2 | | | | 17 | | 7 | | | |
| 64 | Paralysis | | | | | | | | | 1 | | 7 | 1 | | | | | | | 5 | | 2 | | | |
| 65 | Pleurisy | | 1 | | | 1 | | 2 | | 4 | 2 | 7 | | | | | | | | 13 | | 3 | | | |
| 66 | Pneumonia | | | 1 | 3 | | | | | | 1 | 2 | 2 | | | | | | | 7 | | 2 | | | |
| 67 | Quinsey | 1 | 1 | | | | | | | 1 | | 2 | | 1 | | | | | | 6 | | | | | |
| 68 | Rheumatism | | | | | | | | | | | 2 | | | | | | | | 2 | | | | | |
| 69 | Scrofula | | | | | 1 | | | 1 | | 1 | 1 | | | | | | | | 4 | | | | | |
| 70 | Scurvy | | | | | | | | | 1 | | | | | | | | | | 1 | | | | | |
| 71 | Small pox | 1 | | | | | | | | | 1 | | | | | | | | | 2 | | | | | |
| 72 | Spine, disease of | 1 | 1 | | | 2 | | | 1 | | | | 1 | | | | | | | 5 | | 1 | | | |
| 73 | Stomach....do | 1 | | | | | | | | | | 1 | | | | | | | | 1 | | | | | |
| 74 | Suffocation | 1 | | | | | | | | | | | | | | | | | | 1 | | | | | |
| 75 | Suicide | | | | | | | 1 | | | | | | | | | | | | 1 | | | | | |

## THE STATE OF DELAWARE.

| Nativities: Ireland | Nativities: Germany | Nativities: Other foreign countries | Nativities: Unknown | Season: Spring | Season: Summer | Season: Autumn | Season: Winter | Duration: Under 1 week | Duration: 1 week and under 1 month | Duration: 1 month and under 3 months | Duration: 3 months and over | Whites: Males | Whites: Females | Whites: Total | Colored Slaves Black M. | Colored Slaves Black F. | Colored Slaves Mulatto M. | Colored Slaves Mulatto F. | Colored Free Black M. | Colored Free Black F. | Colored Free Mul. M | Colored Free Mul. F. | Aggregate deaths. | |
|---|---|---|---|---|---|---|---|---|---|---|---|---|---|---|---|---|---|---|---|---|---|---|---|---|
| | | | | | 4 | 3 | 3 | 4 | 2 | | | 6 | 3 | 9 | | | | | 1 | | | | 10 | 1 |
| 1 | | | | 3 | | | 2 | 4 | | | | | 3 | 3 | | | | | 2 | | | | 5 | 2 |
| | | | | | 2 | 2 | 5 | 7 | | | | 3 | 1 | 4 | 1 | | 1 | | 1 | | 2 | | 9 | 3 |
| | | | | 1 | | | | 1 | | | | 1 | | 1 | | | | | | | | | 1 | 4 |
| | | | | | | 1 | | 1 | | | | 1 | | 1 | | | | | | | | | 1 | 5 |
| 1 | | | | 1 | 1 | 2 | 3 | 7 | | | | 3 | 4 | 7 | | | | | | | | | 7 | 6 |
| | | | | 1 | | | | | 1 | | | 1 | | 1 | | | | | | | | | 1 | 7 |
| 1 | | | | | | 3 | 1 | 2 | 1 | 1 | | 2 | 2 | 4 | | | | | | | | | 4 | 8 |
| | | | | | 1 | | | 1 | | | | 1 | | 1 | | | | | | | | | 1 | 9 |
| | | | | 1 | | | 2 | | 1 | 1 | 1 | 3 | | 3 | | | | | | | | | 3 | 10 |
| 1 | | 1 | | 9 | 6 | 1 | 6 | 6 | 11 | 3 | 2 | 9 | 9 | 18 | | | | | 2 | 2 | | | 22 | 11 |
| | | 1 | | | 3 | 3 | 4 | 4 | 2 | 1 | | | 8 | 8 | | | | | | 2 | | | 10 | 12 |
| 10 | 3 | 2 | 1 | 2 | 78 | 17 | | 34 | 2 | | | 26 | 37 | 63 | | | | | 15 | 16 | 1 | 2 | 97 | 13 |
| | | | | 1 | 2 | 3 | 2 | 6 | 1 | 1 | | 4 | 4 | 8 | | | | | | | | | 8 | 14 |
| | | 1 | | | 4 | 2 | | 5 | 1 | | | 1 | 3 | 4 | | | | | 1 | 1 | | | 6 | 15 |
| | | | | 1 | | | | | | | | | | | | | | | | 1 | | | 1 | 16 |
| | | | | 5 | 4 | 1 | | 3 | 4 | | | 1 | | 1 | | | | | 4 | 3 | 1 | 1 | 10 | 17 |
| | | | | 2 | 2 | 1 | | 3 | 2 | | | 3 | 1 | 4 | | 1 | | | | | | | 5 | 18 |
| | | 2 | | 3 | 2 | 1 | 3 | 6 | 2 | | 1 | 4 | 4 | 8 | | | | | 1 | | | | 9 | 19 |
| 1 | | | | | | | 1 | | 1 | | | | 1 | 1 | | | | | | | | | 1 | 20 |
| 3 | | | 1 | 37 | 27 | 29 | 25 | 4 | 12 | 16 | 81 | 42 | 54 | 96 | 1 | | | | 11 | 9 | | 1 | 118 | 21 |
| | | 1 | | 8 | 8 | 4 | 4 | 16 | 3 | 1 | 1 | 10 | 9 | 19 | | | | | 3 | 2 | | | 24 | 22 |
| | | | | | | 1 | | 1 | | | | | 1 | 1 | | | | | | | | | 1 | 23 |
| | | | | 10 | 5 | 7 | 6 | 20 | 6 | 2 | | 8 | 8 | 16 | | | | | 3 | 7 | 1 | 1 | 28 | 24 |
| | | | | 1 | 2 | | 2 | 1 | 2 | 1 | 1 | 2 | 3 | 5 | | | | | | | | | 5 | 25 |
| | | | | 1 | 10 | 10 | 2 | 5 | 10 | 4 | 4 | 11 | 11 | 22 | | 1 | | | | | | | 23 | 26 |
| | 1 | 2 | | 9 | 19 | 10 | 12 | 6 | 9 | 8 | 26 | 24 | 14 | 38 | 1 | 1 | | | 4 | 6 | | | 50 | 27 |
| 3 | | 1 | | 3 | 22 | 36 | 7 | 22 | 40 | 5 | 1 | 30 | 26 | 56 | 1 | | | | 4 | 4 | 3 | | 68 | 28 |
| | | | | 3 | 2 | 1 | | 2 | | 1 | 3 | 2 | 4 | 6 | | | | | | | | | 6 | 29 |
| 1 | | 1 | | 3 | 3 | 4 | 3 | 3 | 9 | 1 | | 3 | 10 | 13 | | | | | | | | | 13 | 30 |
| | | | | 1 | 2 | 9 | 1 | 1 | 10 | 1 | | 5 | 6 | 11 | | 1 | | | 1 | | | | 13 | 31 |
| 2 | 1 | 1 | | 4 | 12 | 41 | 6 | 18 | 36 | 8 | | 26 | 33 | 59 | | | | | 1 | 1 | 1 | 1 | 63 | 32 |
| 1 | | | | 6 | 7 | 6 | 7 | 9 | 17 | | | 13 | 12 | 25 | | | | | 1 | | | | 26 | 33 |
| | | | | 2 | 1 | 1 | | 2 | 2 | | | 3 | 1 | 4 | | | | | | | | | 4 | 34 |
| | | | | | | 2 | | 1 | 1 | | | 1 | 1 | 2 | | | | | | | | | 2 | 35 |
| | | | | 1 | | 3 | 1 | 2 | 3 | | | 3 | 1 | 4 | 1 | | | | | | | | 5 | 36 |
| | | | | 1 | | 1 | 2 | 1 | 1 | 2 | | 1 | 2 | 3 | | | | | | | | 1 | 4 | 37 |
| | | | | 8 | 3 | 1 | 7 | 9 | 7 | 3 | | 9 | 10 | 19 | | | | | | | | | 19 | 38 |
| | 3 | 1 | | 4 | 5 | 27 | 5 | 6 | 26 | 7 | 1 | 18 | 13 | 31 | | | | | 5 | 5 | | | 41 | 39 |
| 1 | | | | | | 1 | | | 1 | | | 1 | | 1 | | | | | | | | | 1 | 40 |
| | | | | 1 | | | | 1 | | | | | | | | | | | 1 | | | | 1 | 41 |
| | | | | 3 | 1 | | 2 | 2 | 3 | 1 | | 3 | 1 | 4 | | | | | 2 | | | | 6 | 42 |
| | | 1 | | | 2 | 2 | | 2 | 2 | | | 3 | 1 | 4 | | | | | | | | | 4 | 43 |
| | | | | 2 | 1 | | | | 1 | 1 | 1 | 2 | 1 | 3 | | | | | | | | | 3 | 44 |
| | | | | | 1 | 1 | 2 | 2 | | 1 | 1 | 3 | | 3 | | | | | 1 | | | | 4 | 45 |
| | | | | 1 | 1 | | | 2 | | | | | 1 | 1 | | | | | | 1 | | | 2 | 46 |
| | | | | 6 | 7 | 11 | 10 | 7 | 21 | 4 | 2 | 11 | 9 | 20 | 1 | 1 | | | 4 | 6 | 1 | 1 | 34 | 47 |
| | | | | | 1 | 3 | 1 | 1 | 4 | | | 4 | 1 | 5 | | | | | | | | | 5 | 48 |
| | | | | 5 | 3 | 1 | 1 | 4 | 5 | 1 | | 6 | 4 | 10 | | | | | | | | | 10 | 49 |
| | | | | 1 | 1 | 3 | 2 | 3 | 2 | 1 | | 3 | 1 | 4 | | | | | 2 | 1 | | | 7 | 50 |
| | | | | 5 | 7 | 4 | 5 | 7 | 12 | 2 | | 11 | 5 | 16 | 1 | 1 | | | 1 | | 2 | | 21 | 51 |
| | | | | | | | 1 | | | | | 1 | | 1 | | | | | | | | | 1 | 52 |
| | | | | 3 | 4 | | 2 | 2 | 1 | | 1 | 4 | | 4 | | | | | 4 | 1 | | | 9 | 53 |
| | | | | 1 | | 2 | 1 | | 2 | 1 | 1 | | 3 | 3 | | | | | | 1 | | | 4 | 54 |
| | | | | 1 | 1 | 1 | 1 | | | | | 3 | | 3 | | | | | 1 | | | | 4 | 55 |
| | | | | 1 | 2 | 3 | 1 | 1 | | 2 | 4 | 2 | 2 | 4 | | | | | 2 | 1 | | | 7 | 56 |
| | | | | 2 | 4 | 3 | 1 | 1 | 4 | 2 | 1 | 6 | 3 | 9 | | | | | 1 | | | | 10 | 57 |
| | | | | | 1 | | 1 | 1 | 1 | | | 1 | | 1 | | | | | 1 | | | | 2 | 58 |
| | | | | | | 1 | | | | | | 1 | | 1 | | | | | | | | | 1 | 59 |
| 1 | | | | 10 | 8 | 4 | 2 | 2 | 6 | 4 | 2 | 12 | 11 | 23 | | | | | 1 | | | | 24 | 60 |
| | | | | | 1 | 3 | | 1 | 1 | 1 | 1 | 3 | 1 | 4 | | | | | | | | | 4 | 61 |
| | | | | 1 | | | | | 1 | | | | 1 | 1 | | | | | | | | | 1 | 62 |
| 3 | | 1 | | 5 | 8 | 6 | 9 | 2 | 2 | 1 | 8 | 6 | 13 | 19 | | | | | 5 | 3 | 1 | | 28 | 63 |
| 2 | | | | 5 | 2 | 1 | 1 | 4 | 1 | | 4 | 8 | 1 | 9 | | | | | | | | | 9 | 64 |
| 1 | | | | 12 | 3 | 1 | 1 | 5 | 9 | 1 | | 12 | 3 | 15 | | | | | | | 2 | | 17 | 65 |
| | | | | 3 | 4 | 1 | 1 | 2 | 6 | 1 | | 3 | 5 | 8 | | | | | | 1 | | | 9 | 66 |
| | | | | 3 | 2 | 1 | | 5 | 1 | | | 4 | 1 | 5 | | | | | 1 | | | | 6 | 67 |
| | | | | | 1 | | 1 | | | | | | | | | | | | 2 | | | | 2 | 68 |
| | | | | 2 | 1 | 1 | | | 2 | | 1 | 1 | 1 | 2 | | | | 1 | 1 | | | | 4 | 69 |
| | | | | | | | 1 | | | | 1 | 1 | | 1 | | | | | | | | | 1 | 70 |
| | | | | 1 | | 1 | | 1 | 1 | | | 2 | | 2 | | | | | | | | | 2 | 71 |
| | | | | 3 | 2 | 1 | | 2 | 2 | 1 | 1 | 2 | 3 | 5 | | | | | 1 | | | | 6 | 72 |
| | | 1 | | 1 | | 1 | | | 1 | 1 | | 2 | | 2 | | | | | | | | | 2 | 73 |
| | | | | 1 | | | | | | | | | | | | | | | 1 | | | | 1 | 74 |
| | | | | | 1 | | | | | | | 1 | | 1 | | | | | | | | | 1 | 75 |

CLASSIFICATION OF DEATHS

| | Cause of death. | AGES. Under 1. | | 1 and under 5. | | 5 and under 10. | | 10 and under 20. | | 20 and under 50. | | 50 and under 80. | | 80 and under 100. | | 100 & over. | | Age unknown. | | NATIVITIES. Born in State. | New England. | Middle. | South. | Southwest. | Northwest. |
|---|---|---|---|---|---|---|---|---|---|---|---|---|---|---|---|---|---|---|---|---|---|---|---|---|---|
| | | M. | F. | M. | F. | M. | F. | M. | F. | M. | F. | M. | F. | M | F. | M | F. | M | F. | | | | | | |
| 1 | Summer complaint | 2 | 1 | 3 | 1 | | | | | | | | | | | | | | | 7 | | | | | |
| 2 | Teething | 4 | 2 | 5 | 3 | | | | | | | | | | | | | | | 14 | | | | | |
| 3 | Tetanus | | | | 1 | | | | | | | | | | | | | | | 1 | | | | | |
| 4 | Throat, disease of | | 1 | | | | | | | 1 | | | | | | | | | | 1 | | 1 | | | |
| 5 | Thrush | 1 | | | | | | | | | | | | | | | | | | 1 | | | | | |
| 6 | Tumor | | | | | | | | | | | | 1 | | | | | | | 1 | | | | | |
| 7 | Worms | 1 | | 1 | | | 2 | | | | | | | | | | | | | 4 | | | | | |
| 8 | Unknown | 39 | 35 | 22 | 8 | 8 | 4 | 3 | 5 | 18 | 19 | 19 | 21 | | 1 | | | | | 180 | 1 | 12 | 2 | | |
| | | 126 | 120 | 130 | 104 | 43 | 28 | 44 | 53 | 149 | 141 | 137 | 100 | 13 | 19 | 2 | | | | 1013 | 1 | 122 | 4 | | 2 |

CLASSIFICATION OF DEATHS

| | Cause of death. | Under 1. M. | Under 1. F. | 1 and under 5. M. | 1 and under 5. F. | 5 and under 10. M. | 5 and under 10. F. | 10 and under 20. M. | 10 and under 20. F. | 20 and under 50. M. | 20 and under 50. F. | 50 and under 80. M. | 50 and under 80. F. | 80 and under 100. M | 80 and under 100. F. | 100 & over. M | 100 & over. F. | Age unknown. M | Age unknown. F. | Born in State. | New England. | Middle. | South. | Southwest. | Northwest. |
|---|---|---|---|---|---|---|---|---|---|---|---|---|---|---|---|---|---|---|---|---|---|---|---|---|---|
| 1 | Abscess | | | | | | | | | 2 | | | | | | | | | | | | 1 | 1 | | |
| 2 | Accident, not specf'd | 1 | 2 | 3 | 1 | 2 | | 8 | 1 | 4 | | | | 1 | | | | | | 16 | | 1 | 6 | | |
| 3 | ....do...burned | | | 2 | 5 | | 3 | | 5 | | | | 1 | | | | | | | 14 | | | 2 | | |
| 4 | ....do...drowned | | | 1 | | 3 | | 5 | | 3 | 2 | 3 | | | | | | | | 9 | | 1 | 4 | | |
| 5 | ....do...shot | | | | | | | | | 1 | | | | | | | | | | | | | | | |
| 6 | Apoplexy | | | | | | | | 1 | | | | 2 | 1 | | | | | | 1 | | 1 | 1 | | |
| 7 | Asthma | | | | | | | | | 2 | | 1 | 1 | | | | | | | | | | 4 | | |
| 8 | Bowels, disease of | 1 | | 3 | 5 | | | | | 1 | | | | | | | | | | 9 | | | 1 | | |
| 9 | Brain ......do | | | 1 | | | | | | 1 | | | | | | | | | | 1 | 1 | | | | |
| 10 | Bronchitis | | | | 1 | | | 1 | | 2 | 1 | | 1 | | | | | | | 3 | | | 3 | | |
| 11 | Cancer | | | | | | | | | 1 | | | 1 | | | | | | | | | | 2 | | |
| 12 | Catarrh | 2 | | | | | | | | | | 1 | 1 | | | | | | | 3 | | | 1 | | |
| 13 | Child birth | | | | | | | | 5 | | 13 | | | | | | | | | 6 | | | 9 | 1 | |
| 14 | Cholera | 3 | 4 | 10 | 6 | | | 1 | 1 | 1 | | | | | | | | | | 24 | | | 2 | | |
| 15 | ...do...infantum | | 5 | 2 | 3 | | | | | | | | | | | | | | | 9 | | | | 1 | |
| 16 | ...do...morbus | | | | | | | | 1 | | | | | | | | | | | | | 1 | | | |
| 17 | Colic | 1 | 1 | | | | | | | 2 | | 1 | 1 | 1 | | | | | | 2 | | 1 | 8 | | |
| 18 | Conges'n, not specf'd | | | | | | | | 1 | | | | | | | | | | | | | | | 1 | |
| 19 | ....do...bowels | | | | | | | | | 1 | | | | | | | | | | | | | 1 | | |
| 20 | ....do...brain | | | | | | | | | 1 | | | | | | | | | | | | | 1 | | |
| 21 | Consumption | | 1 | 1 | 2 | 1 | | 1 | 3 | 13 | 14 | 3 | 4 | | | | | | | 22 | | 2 | 16 | 2 | |
| 22 | Convulsions | 1 | 1 | 1 | 4 | | | | | 1 | 1 | | | | | | | | | 9 | | | | | |
| 23 | Cramp | | | | | | | | | | | 1 | | | | | | | | | | | 1 | | |
| 24 | Croup | 7 | 4 | 5 | 3 | 2 | | | | | | | | | | | | | | 18 | | 1 | 2 | | |
| 25 | Debility | 1 | | | | | | | | | | | 1 | | | | | | | 1 | | | 1 | | |
| 26 | Diabetes | | | | | | | | | | | 1 | | | | | | | | | | 1 | | | |
| 27 | Diarrhœa | 1 | 2 | 10 | 6 | | | 1 | 1 | 6 | 2 | 1 | 1 | | | | | | | 19 | | 2 | 8 | | |
| 28 | Dropsy | 2 | | 2 | 4 | 6 | 6 | 13 | 4 | 8 | 8 | 10 | 3 | | 1 | | | | | 24 | | | 33 | 2 | |
| 29 | Dysentery | 1 | 1 | 5 | 6 | 1 | | | | 4 | 2 | 1 | | | | | | | | 13 | 1 | 1 | 2 | | |
| 30 | Dyspepsia | | | | | | | | | 1 | | | | | | | | | | | | | 1 | | |
| 31 | Eruption | | 2 | | | | | | | | | | | | | | | | | 2 | | | | | |
| 32 | Erysipelas | | 1 | | | | | | | 1 | 1 | | | | | | | | | 1 | | | 1 | | |
| 33 | Fever, not specified | 11 | 8 | 14 | 13 | 4 | 6 | 6 | 7 | 10 | 15 | 3 | 4 | | | | | | | 58 | 2 | | 35 | | |
| 34 | ..do..bilious | 1 | | 1 | 1 | | 2 | 3 | | 3 | 1 | | | | | | | | | 6 | | | 5 | 1 | |
| 35 | ..do..brain | 1 | 1 | 1 | 2 | 4 | 1 | 1 | | 2 | 2 | | 2 | | 1 | | | | | 13 | | | 5 | | |
| 36 | ..do..congestive | | 1 | 5 | 2 | | 2 | 1 | 3 | 1 | 4 | 1 | 1 | | | | | | | 13 | | | 5 | 1 | |
| 37 | ..do..inflammatory | | | 1 | | | 1 | | | | 1 | | | | | | | | | 1 | | | 2 | | |
| 38 | ..do..intermittent | | | 1 | | 1 | | | | 1 | | | | | | | | | | 1 | | | 2 | | |
| 39 | ..do..puerperal | | | | | | | | 1 | | 2 | | | | | | | | | | | | 3 | | |
| 40 | ..do..typhus | | | 1 | | 1 | | | 3 | 2 | 1 | | 1 | | | | | | | 2 | | 1 | 6 | | |
| 41 | ..do..yellow | | | | | | | | | 3 | | | | | | | | | | | | 1 | | | |
| 42 | Frozen | | | | | | | | | | | 1 | | | | | | | | | | | 1 | | |
| 43 | Gravel | | | | | | | 1 | | | | 1 | | | | | | | | 2 | | | | | |
| 44 | Heart, disease of | | | | 1 | 1 | | | | 2 | | 3 | 1 | | | | | | | 1 | | | 5 | | 1 |
| 45 | Heat | | | | | | | | | 1 | | | | | | | | | | | | | 1 | | |
| 46 | Hernia | | | | | | | | | 1 | | 2 | | | | | | | | | | | 2 | | |
| 47 | Hives | 1 | 1 | 1 | 2 | | | | | | | | | | | | | | | 5 | | | | | |
| 48 | Hooping cough | 2 | 5 | 4 | 6 | 1 | 3 | | | | 1 | | | | | | | | | 20 | | | 1 | | |
| 49 | Inflammation | 2 | 2 | | 5 | 1 | | | | 5 | 1 | 2 | 1 | | 1 | | | | | 11 | | | 9 | | |
| 50 | ....do....bowels | 1 | | 7 | 1 | 1 | 1 | | | 4 | | | | 1 | | | | | | 10 | | | 2 | 1 | |
| 51 | ....do....brain | | | | | 1 | | | | | 3 | | | | | | | | | 1 | | | 1 | | |
| 52 | ....do....stomach | 1 | | | | | | | | | | | | | | | | | | 1 | | | | | |
| 53 | Influenza | 3 | | | | | 2 | | | 1 | 3 | | | | | | | | | 5 | | | 4 | | |
| 54 | Insanity | | | | | | | | | | | | 1 | | | | | | | | | | 1 | | |
| 55 | Intemperance | | | | | | | | | 4 | | 1 | | | | | | | | | | 2 | 2 | | |
| 56 | Lightning | | | | | | | | | 1 | | | | | | | | | | | | | 1 | | |
| 57 | Liver, disease of | | | | 1 | | 1 | 1 | 1 | 2 | 2 | 1 | | | | | | | | 3 | | | 4 | 2 | |
| 58 | Lockjaw | | 5 | | 1 | 1 | 1 | 1 | | | 1 | | | | | | | | | 9 | | | 1 | | |

## IN THE STATE OF DELAWARE—Continued.

| NATIVITIES. | | | | | SEASON OF DECEASE. | | | | DURATION OF SICKNESS. | | | | WHITES. | | | COLORED. | | | | | | | | | |
|---|---|---|---|---|---|---|---|---|---|---|---|---|---|---|---|---|---|---|---|---|---|---|---|---|---|
| | | | | | | | | | | | | | | | | Slaves. | | | | Free. | | | | | |
| | | | | | | | | | | | | | | | | Black. | | Mulatto. | | Black. | | Mul. | | | |
| California and Territories. | Ireland. | Germany. | Other foreign countries. | Uknown. | Spring. | Summer. | Autumn. | Winter. | Under 1 week. | 1 week and under 1 month. | 1 month and under 3 months. | 3 months and over. | Males. | Females. | Total. | M. | F. | M. | F. | M. | F. | M | F. | Aggregate deaths. | |
| | | | | | | 3 | 4 | | 1 | 3 | 3 | | 5 | 2 | 7 | | | | | | | | | 7 | 1 |
| | | | | | 4 | 5 | 4 | 1 | 4 | 5 | 4 | 1 | 8 | 3 | 11 | | | | | 1 | 2 | | | 14 | 2 |
| | | | | | | | 1 | | 1 | | | | | 1 | 1 | | | | | | | | | 1 | 3 |
| | | | | | 1 | | 1 | | | 1 | | 1 | 1 | 1 | 2 | | | | | | | | | 2 | 4 |
| | | | | | | | 1 | | | | 1 | | 1 | | 1 | | | | | | | | | 1 | 5 |
| | | | | | | | | 1 | 1 | | | | | 1 | 1 | | | | | | | | | 1 | 6 |
| | | | | | 1 | 1 | | 2 | 1 | 1 | 1 | 1 | 1 | 2 | 3 | | | | | 1 | | | | 4 | 7 |
| | 5 | | 2 | | 56 | 64 | 44 | 36 | 75 | 32 | 16 | 30 | 76 | 71 | 147 | 4 | 1 | 1 | | 25 | 21 | 3 | | 202 | 8 |
| .... | 38 | 8 | 19 | 2 | 273 | 380 | 345 | 209 | 366 | 359 | 118 | 186 | 494 | 452 | 946 | 11 | 7 | 2 | 1 | 119 | 97 | 18 | 8 | 1209 | |

## IN THE STATE OF FLORIDA.

| California and Territories. | Ireland. | Germany. | Other foreign countries. | Uknown. | Spring. | Summer. | Autumn. | Winter. | Under 1 week. | 1 week and under 1 month. | 1 month and under 3 months. | 3 months and over. | Males. | Females. | Total. | Slaves Black M. | Slaves Black F. | Slaves Mulatto M. | Slaves Mulatto F. | Free Black M. | Free Black F. | Free Mul. M | Free Mul. F. | Aggregate deaths. | |
|---|---|---|---|---|---|---|---|---|---|---|---|---|---|---|---|---|---|---|---|---|---|---|---|---|---|
| | | | | | | | 1 | 1 | | | | 2 | 2 | | 2 | | | | | | | | | 2 | 1 |
| | | | | | 5 | 6 | 4 | 7 | 19 | 8 | | | 7 | | 7 | 10 | 4 | 2 | | | | | | 23 | 2 |
| | | | | | 8 | 2 | | 6 | 10 | 3 | 1 | 2 | 1 | 3 | 4 | 1 | 9 | | 2 | | | | | 16 | 3 |
| | 1 | | 1 | 1 | 2 | 11 | 1 | 1 | 13 | | | | 7 | | 7 | 5 | 2 | 2 | | 1 | | | | 17 | 4 |
| | | | | 1 | | 1 | | | 1 | | | | | | | 1 | | | | | | | | 1 | 5 |
| | | | 1 | | 1 | | 1 | 2 | 4 | | | | | 1 | 1 | 1 | 1 | | 1 | | | | | 4 | 6 |
| | | | | | 2 | 1 | | 1 | | | 4 | | 2 | 1 | 3 | 1 | | | | | | | | 4 | 7 |
| | | | | | 2 | 1 | 4 | 2 | 2 | 7 | 1 | | 1 | 1 | 2 | 3 | 2 | 1 | 1 | | | | 1 | 10 | 8 |
| | | | | | | | 2 | | | 1 | 1 | | 2 | | 2 | | | | | | | | | 2 | 9 |
| | | | | | 2 | 2 | 2 | | | 2 | 2 | 2 | 1 | 2 | 3 | 1 | 1 | | 1 | | | | | 6 | 10 |
| | | | | | | | 2 | | | | | 2 | | | | 1 | 1 | | | | | | | 2 | 11 |
| | | | | | 3 | 1 | | | 2 | 2 | | | 1 | | 1 | 2 | 1 | | | | | | | 4 | 12 |
| | | | 1 | 1 | 3 | 8 | 5 | 7 | 11 | 4 | | | | 11 | 11 | | 6 | | 1 | | | | | 18 | 13 |
| | | | | | 7 | 10 | 7 | 2 | 12 | 12 | 2 | | 3 | 2 | 5 | 12 | 6 | | 3 | | | | | 26 | 14 |
| | | | | | 1 | 4 | 5 | | 2 | 5 | 3 | | | 2 | 2 | 2 | 6 | | | | | | | 10 | 15 |
| | | | | | | 1 | | | | 1 | | | 1 | | 1 | | | | | | | | | 1 | 16 |
| | | | 1 | | 1 | 4 | 1 | 1 | 5 | 2 | | | 3 | | 3 | 2 | 1 | | | | | | 1 | 7 | 17 |
| | | | | | | | | 1 | 1 | | | | | 1 | 1 | | | | | | | | | 1 | 18 |
| | | | | | | | 1 | | 1 | | | | | | | 1 | | | | | | | | 1 | 19 |
| | | | | | 1 | | | | 1 | | | | | | | | | 1 | | | | | | 1 | 20 |
| | | | 1 | | 15 | 10 | 13 | 5 | 5 | 4 | 5 | 29 | 15 | 9 | 24 | 3 | 14 | 1 | 1 | | | | | 43 | 21 |
| | | | | | 1 | 4 | 1 | 2 | 6 | 3 | | | | 3 | 3 | 3 | 2 | | | | | | 1 | 9 | 22 |
| | | | | | | | 1 | | | 1 | | | | | | 1 | | | | | | | | 1 | 23 |
| | | | | | 5 | 5 | 7 | 4 | 18 | 2 | | 1 | 8 | 4 | 12 | 6 | 3 | | | | | | | 21 | 24 |
| | | | | | | 1 | 1 | | 1 | | | 1 | 1 | 1 | 2 | | | | | | | | | 2 | 25 |
| | | | | | | 1 | | | 1 | | | | 1 | | 1 | | | | | | | | | 1 | 26 |
| | 1 | 1 | | | 2 | 12 | 11 | 6 | 8 | 14 | 3 | 6 | 14 | 9 | 23 | 5 | 1 | | 2 | | | | | 31 | 27 |
| | 1 | 1 | 5 | 1 | 21 | 17 | 15 | 14 | 4 | 9 | 23 | 31 | 24 | 11 | 35 | 14 | 13 | 2 | 2 | | | 1 | | 67 | 28 |
| | 1 | 1 | 2 | | 2 | 4 | 9 | 6 | | 3 | 12 | 5 | 7 | 7 | 14 | 5 | 2 | | | | | | | 21 | 29 |
| | | | | | | | 1 | | | | | 1 | 1 | | 1 | | | | | | | | | 1 | 30 |
| | | | | | | 2 | | | 2 | | | | | 2 | 2 | | | | | | | | | 2 | 31 |
| | | 1 | | | | 2 | 1 | | 1 | 2 | | | 1 | 1 | 2 | | | | 1 | | | | | 3 | 32 |
| | 2 | | 3 | 1 | 20 | 29 | 37 | 15 | 31 | 57 | 11 | 2 | 31 | 38 | 69 | 15 | 15 | 2 | | | | | | 101 | 33 |
| | | | | | 1 | 3 | 5 | 3 | 4 | 6 | 1 | 1 | 4 | 3 | 7 | 4 | 1 | | | | | | | 12 | 34 |
| | | | | | 3 | 5 | 6 | 4 | 10 | 4 | 4 | | 4 | 4 | 8 | 4 | 3 | 1 | 2 | | | | | 18 | 35 |
| | | | 1 | 1 | 1 | 7 | 9 | 4 | 15 | 5 | 1 | | 5 | 8 | 13 | 2 | 4 | 1 | 1 | | | | | 21 | 36 |
| | | | | | 1 | 1 | 1 | | | 3 | | | 1 | 2 | 3 | | | | | | | | | 3 | 37 |
| | | | | | | | 2 | 1 | 1 | | 1 | 1 | 2 | | 2 | 1 | | | | | | | | 3 | 38 |
| | | | | | | | 2 | 1 | | 3 | | | | 3 | 3 | | | | | | | | | 3 | 39 |
| | | | | | 4 | 2 | 2 | 1 | 1 | 7 | 1 | | 4 | 1 | 5 | | 4 | | | | | | | 9 | 40 |
| | 1 | 1 | | | | | 3 | | 3 | | | | 3 | | 3 | | | | | | | | | 3 | 41 |
| | | | | | | | | 1 | 1 | | | | | | | 1 | | | | | | | | 1 | 42 |
| | | | | | | | 2 | | | | 1 | 1 | | | | 2 | | | | | | | | 2 | 43 |
| | | | 1 | | 2 | 3 | 1 | 2 | 3 | 2 | 1 | 2 | 4 | | 4 | 2 | 2 | | | | | | | 8 | 44 |
| | | | | | 1 | | | | | 1 | | | 1 | | 1 | | | | | | | | | 1 | 45 |
| | | | 1 | | 1 | 2 | | | 1 | 1 | 1 | | | | | 3 | | | | | | | | 3 | 46 |
| | | | | | 2 | 2 | | 1 | 1 | 2 | 2 | | 1 | 1 | 2 | 1 | 2 | | | | | | | 5 | 47 |
| | | | 1 | | 6 | 5 | 6 | 5 | 4 | 11 | 6 | 1 | 3 | 7 | 10 | 4 | 7 | | 1 | | | | | 22 | 48 |
| | | | | | 7 | 3 | 4 | 4 | 7 | 9 | 3 | 1 | 6 | 4 | 10 | 4 | 4 | | 1 | | | | 1 | 20 | 49 |
| | 3 | | | | 4 | 7 | 4 | 1 | 4 | 6 | 2 | 4 | 8 | 1 | 9 | 4 | 1 | 1 | | | | 1 | | 16 | 50 |
| | | | | 2 | 1 | 1 | 1 | 1 | 1 | 2 | 1 | | 1 | 1 | 2 | | 2 | | | | | | | 4 | 51 |
| | | | | | 1 | | | | | 1 | | | 1 | | 1 | | | | | | | | | 1 | 52 |
| | | | | | 4 | | 1 | 4 | 4 | 5 | | | 1 | 2 | 3 | 2 | 3 | 1 | | | | | | 9 | 53 |
| | | | | | | | 1 | | | | 1 | | | | | | 1 | | | | | | | 1 | 54 |
| | 1 | | | | 2 | 2 | | 1 | | 4 | | | 5 | | 5 | | | | | | | | | 5 | 55 |
| | | | | | | 1 | | | | | | | | | | 1 | | | | | | | | 1 | 56 |
| | | | | | 4 | 1 | 1 | 3 | 1 | 1 | 3 | 4 | 3 | 3 | 6 | 1 | 2 | | | | | | | 9 | 57 |
| | | | | | 1 | 3 | 4 | 2 | 8 | 2 | | | | 1 | 1 | 1 | 4 | 1 | 2 | | | | 1 | 10 | 58 |

## CLASSIFICATION OF DEATHS.

| | Cause of death. | Under 1. M. | Under 1. F. | 1 and under 5. M. | 1 and under 5. F. | 5 and under 10. M. | 5 and under 10. F. | 10 and under 20. M. | 10 and under 20. F. | 20 and under 50. M. | 20 and under 50. F. | 50 and under 80. M. | 50 and under 80. F. | 80 and under 100. M | 80 and under 100. F. | 100 & over. M | 100 & over. F. | Age unknown. M | Age unknown. F. | Born in State. | N. England States. | Middle States. | Southern States. | Southwest'n States. | Northwest'n States. |
|---|---|---|---|---|---|---|---|---|---|---|---|---|---|---|---|---|---|---|---|---|---|---|---|---|---|
| 1 | Lungs, disease of | | | | | | | | | 1 | 1 | | | | | | | | | | | | 2 | | |
| 2 | Measles | 1 | | 4 | | | | | | | | | | | | | | | | 5 | | | | | |
| 3 | Murder | | | | | | | | | 5 | | 1 | | | | | | | | 1 | | | 4 | 1 | |
| 4 | Neuralgia | | | | | | | 1 | | | | | | | | | | | | | | | | 1 | |
| 5 | Old age | | | | | | | | | | | 5 | 6 | 7 | 7 | | | | | 2 | | 1 | 16 | 1 | |
| 6 | Paralysis | | | | | | | 1 | | | | | | | | | | | | | | | 1 | | |
| 7 | Piles | | | | | | | | | | | 1 | | | | | | | | | | | 1 | | |
| 8 | Pleurisy | | | 1 | | | | | 1 | 7 | 2 | 2 | 1 | | | | | | | 4 | | | 6 | | |
| 9 | Pneumonia | 1 | | 2 | 4 | 2 | 1 | 4 | 2 | 4 | 6 | 3 | 2 | | | | | | | 11 | | | 17 | 1 | |
| 10 | Poison | | | 1 | | 1 | | | | | | | | | | | | | | 2 | | | | | |
| 11 | Quinsy | 1 | | | 1 | | | | | | | | 1 | | | | | | | 2 | | | 1 | | |
| 12 | Rheumatism | | | | | | | | | 1 | | 1 | | | | | | | | 2 | | | 1 | | |
| 13 | Scrofula | | | 1 | 1 | | 1 | | | | | | 1 | | | | | | | 4 | | | | | |
| 14 | Stillborn | 2 | | | | | | | | | | | | | | | | | | 2 | | | | | |
| 15 | Suffocation | 1 | | | | | | | | | | | | | | | | | | 1 | | | | | |
| 16 | Suicide | | | | | | | | | | | 1 | | | | | | | | | | | 1 | | |
| 17 | Sun, stroke of | | | | | | | | | 1 | | | | | | | | | | | | | | 1 | |
| 18 | Teething | 4 | 4 | 6 | 10 | | | | | | | | | | | | | | | 22 | | | 2 | | |
| 19 | Throat, disease of | | | | 1 | | | | | | | | | | | | | | | 1 | | | | | |
| 20 | Thrush | 1 | | | | | | | | | | | | | | | | | | 1 | | | | | |
| 21 | White swelling | | | | | | | 1 | | | | | | | | | | | | | | | 1 | | |
| 22 | Worms | 6 | 1 | 21 | 9 | | 3 | | | | | | | | | | | | | 36 | | | 4 | | |
| 23 | Unknown | 20 | 16 | 15 | 11 | 3 | 3 | 3 | 3 | 10 | 12 | 7 | 6 | | | | | 4 | | 75 | | 1 | 30 | 2 | |
| | Total | 81 | 68 | 133 | 118 | 37 | 38 | 53 | 43 | 129 | 102 | 59 | 45 | 11 | 10 | | | 4 | | 537 | 4 | 19 | 291 | 19 | 1 |

## CLASSIFICATION OF DEATHS IN SOUTHERN

*Embracing the following counties: Appling, Baker, Bryan, Bullock, Camden, Chatham, Clinch, Lowndes, McIntosh, Macon, Marion, Montgomery, Muscogee, Pulaski,*

| | Cause of death. | Under 1. M. | Under 1. F. | 1 and under 5. M. | 1 and under 5. F. | 5 and under 10. M. | 5 and under 10. F. | 10 and under 20. M. | 10 and under 20. F. | 20 and under 50. M. | 20 and under 50. F. | 50 and under 80. M. | 50 and under 80. F. | 80 and under 100. M | 80 and under 100. F. | 100 & over. M | 100 & over. F. | Age unknown. M | Age unknown. F. | Born in State. | N. England States. | Middle States. | Southern States. | Southwest'n States. | Northwest'n States. |
|---|---|---|---|---|---|---|---|---|---|---|---|---|---|---|---|---|---|---|---|---|---|---|---|---|---|
| 1 | Abscess | | | | | | 1 | | 2 | | 2 | 3 | | | | | | | | 5 | | 1 | 2 | | |
| 2 | Accident, not specif'd | 6 | 12 | 7 | 11 | 6 | 12 | 8 | 3 | 13 | 5 | 5 | | | | | | | | 77 | 1 | | 8 | | |
| 3 | ....do...burned | 1 | 4 | 18 | 9 | 5 | 3 | | 2 | | 1 | 1 | 1 | | 1 | | | | | 45 | | | 1 | | |
| 4 | ....do...drowned | | | | 2 | 4 | | 4 | 1 | 7 | 4 | 1 | | 1 | | | | | | 22 | | | 1 | | |
| 5 | ....do...shot | | | | | 1 | | 1 | | 2 | | | | | | | | | | 3 | | | 1 | | |
| 6 | Apoplexy | 1 | | 1 | | | | 1 | | 2 | 1 | 3 | 4 | | | | | | | 11 | | | 2 | | |
| 7 | Asthma | 1 | | | | | | | | 3 | 1 | 4 | 3 | 1 | | | | | | 6 | | | 2 | | |
| 8 | Bowels, disease of | 6 | 5 | 9 | 13 | | | 4 | 1 | 1 | 2 | 5 | 3 | 2 | | | | | | 47 | | 1 | 3 | | |
| 9 | Brain......do | 1 | 3 | 2 | 3 | | | 4 | 1 | 1 | 3 | | 1 | | | | | | | 17 | | | 2 | | |
| 10 | Bronchitis | 3 | | 1 | | | | 1 | | 1 | 3 | 2 | 1 | | | | | | | 10 | | | 2 | | |
| 11 | Cancer | | | | | | | | | 3 | 7 | 1 | 6 | 1 | 1 | | | | | 12 | 1 | | 5 | | |
| 12 | Catarrh | 8 | 5 | 1 | 4 | | | | | 2 | 3 | 2 | | | | | | | | 24 | | | 1 | | |
| 13 | Chicken pox | 1 | | | | | | | | | 1 | | | | | | | | | 2 | | | | | |
| 14 | Childbirth | | | | | | | | 16 | | 47 | | 1 | | | | | | | 48 | | | 15 | | |
| 15 | Cholera | | | | 2 | | | | | 5 | 2 | 2 | 2 | | | | | | | 13 | | | | | |
| 16 | ...do...infantum | 3 | 2 | 1 | | | | | | | | | | | | | | | | 6 | | | | | |
| 17 | ...do...morbus | 2 | | 2 | 5 | 1 | 1 | 1 | 1 | 2 | | | | | | | | | | 13 | | | 2 | | |
| 18 | Colic | 1 | 1 | 3 | | | 1 | 2 | 2 | 5 | 2 | 11 | 9 | 1 | | | | | | 28 | | | 8 | 1 | |
| 19 | Congestion, not spe'd | 2 | 1 | 5 | 7 | 2 | 3 | 5 | 2 | 1 | | 2 | | | | | | | | 28 | | | 1 | | |
| 20 | .....do....brain | | | 2 | | | 1 | | 1 | | 2 | | | | | | | | | 6 | | | | | |
| 21 | Consumption | | 2 | | | | 1 | 3 | 7 | 29 | 25 | 9 | 11 | | | | | | | 49 | 2 | 2 | 24 | | |
| 22 | Convulsions | 5 | 7 | 5 | 3 | 2 | 2 | 4 | 2 | 4 | 3 | 1 | 1 | | | | | | | 38 | | | 1 | | |
| 23 | Cramp | 1 | | | | | | | | | | | | | | | | | | 1 | | | | | |
| 24 | Croup | 7 | 10 | 13 | 12 | 4 | 4 | 1 | | | | | | | | | | | | 51 | | | | | |
| 25 | Debility | | 1 | | 2 | | | | | | | 1 | 2 | 1 | | | | | | 5 | | | | 1 | |
| 26 | Diabetes | | | | | | | | | 1 | | | | | | | | | | 1 | | | | | |
| 27 | Diarrhœa | 4 | 9 | 13 | 11 | 4 | 2 | 1 | 1 | 2 | 2 | | 3 | | | | | | | 48 | | 3 | | | |
| 28 | Dirt eating | | | | | | | | | | 1 | | | | | | | | | 1 | | | | | |
| 29 | Dropsy | 5 | 2 | 8 | 11 | 13 | 4 | 12 | 15 | 17 | 36 | 43 | 22 | 7 | 5 | | | | | 146 | | 2 | 37 | | |
| 30 | Dysentery | 5 | 3 | 7 | 12 | 2 | 1 | 3 | | 5 | 1 | 4 | 4 | | | | | | | 40 | | | 3 | | |
| 31 | Dyspepsia | | | | | | | | | 1 | | 1 | | | | | | | | 2 | | | | | |
| 32 | Epilepsy | | | | | | | | | 1 | | | | | | | | | | 1 | | | | | |
| 33 | Erysipelas | 1 | 2 | 2 | 3 | | | | | 8 | 5 | 4 | 1 | | | | | | | 17 | 1 | 1 | 5 | | |
| 34 | Fever, not specified | 16 | 15 | 29 | 31 | 16 | 15 | 12 | 18 | 40 | 25 | 16 | 12 | 1 | | | | | | 206 | 2 | | 24 | | |
| 35 | ..do..bilious | | 1 | 1 | 2 | 2 | 5 | 7 | 5 | 7 | 3 | 1 | 1 | | | | | | | 27 | 2 | 3 | | | |
| 36 | ..do..brain | | 2 | | | | 1 | | 3 | 2 | | | | | | | | | | 5 | | 2 | | | |
| 37 | ..do..congestive | 1 | | 1 | 4 | 1 | | | 1 | 9 | 1 | | | | | | | | | 10 | | 1 | 1 | | |
| 38 | ..do. inflammatory | | | | 1 | | 2 | | | | 2 | | | | | | | | | 5 | | | | | |
| 39 | ..do..intermittent | | | | | 1 | | | | | | | | | | | | | | 1 | | | | | |
| 40 | ..do..remittent | | | | | | | | | 1 | | | | | | | | | | 1 | | | | | |

## N THE STATE OF FLORIDA—Continued.

| Nativities: California and Territories | Nativities: Ireland | Nativities: Germany | Nativities: Other foreign countries | Nativities: Unknown | Season of decease: Spring | Season of decease: Summer | Season of decease: Autumn | Season of decease: Winter | Duration of sickness: Under 1 week | Duration of sickness: 1 week and under 1 month | Duration of sickness: 1 month and under 3 months | Duration of sickness: 3 months and over | Whites: Males | Whites: Females | Whites: Total | Colored: Slaves: Black: M. | Colored: Slaves: Black: F. | Colored: Slaves: Mulatto: M. | Colored: Slaves: Mulatto: F. | Colored: Free: Black: M. | Colored: Free: Black: F. | Colored: Free: Mul.: M | Colored: Free: Mul.: F. | Aggregate deaths | |
|---|---|---|---|---|---|---|---|---|---|---|---|---|---|---|---|---|---|---|---|---|---|---|---|---|---|
| | | | | | 1 | | | | | 1 | | 1 | | | | 1 | 1 | | | | | | | 2 | 1 |
| | | | | | | 4 | | 1 | | 3 | 1 | | 3 | | 3 | 2 | | | | | | | | 5 | 2 |
| | | | | | | 3 | 1 | 2 | 6 | | | | 4 | | 4 | 2 | | | | | | | | 6 | 3 |
| | | | | | | 1 | | | | 1 | | | 1 | | 1 | | | | | | | | | 1 | 4 |
| | | | 3 | 2 | 9 | 8 | 4 | 4 | 9 | 3 | 1 | 9 | 3 | 6 | 9 | 9 | 4 | | 1 | | 2 | | | 25 | 5 |
| | | | | | | 1 | | | 1 | | | | 1 | | 1 | | | | | | | | | 1 | 6 |
| | | | | | 1 | | | | | | | 1 | 1 | | 1 | | | | | | | | | 1 | 7 |
| | 1 | | 2 | 1 | 7 | 2 | | 4 | 4 | 7 | 3 | | 6 | 2 | 8 | 3 | 2 | 1 | | | | | | 14 | 8 |
| | | | 2 | | 15 | 8 | 2 | 6 | 13 | 15 | 1 | 2 | 8 | 7 | 15 | 8 | 7 | | 3 | | | | | 31 | 9 |
| | | | | | 1 | | 1 | | 2 | | | | | | | 2 | | | | | | | | 2 | 10 |
| | | | | | 1 | | 1 | 1 | 2 | 1 | | | | 2 | 2 | 1 | | | | | | | | 3 | 11 |
| | | | | 1 | | | 1 | 1 | 1 | | | 1 | 2 | | 2 | | | | | | | | | 2 | 12 |
| | | | | | 1 | 2 | 1 | | | | | 4 | 1 | 1 | 2 | | 2 | | | | | | | 4 | 13 |
| | | | | | | | 1 | | 2 | | | | 2 | | 2 | | | | | | | | | 2 | 14 |
| | | | | | 1 | | | | 1 | | | | | | | 1 | | | | | | | | 1 | 15 |
| | | | | | | | | 1 | 1 | | | | 1 | | 1 | | | | | | | | | 1 | 16 |
| | | | | | | 1 | | | | 1 | | | 1 | | 1 | | | | | | | | | 1 | 17 |
| | | | | | 6 | 4 | 8 | 5 | 5 | 6 | 11 | | 4 | 5 | 9 | 5 | 7 | 1 | 2 | | | | | 24 | 18 |
| | | | | | | 1 | | | | 1 | | | | 1 | 1 | | | | | | | | | 1 | 19 |
| | | | | | | 1 | | | | 1 | | | | | | 1 | | | | | | | | 1 | 20 |
| | | | | | | | 1 | | | 1 | | | 1 | | 1 | | | | | | | | | 1 | 21 |
| | | | | | 5 | 13 | 17 | 5 | 16 | 17 | 3 | 2 | 11 | 4 | 15 | 15 | 7 | 1 | 2 | | | | | 40 | 22 |
| | | | 4 | 1 | 28 | 22 | 20 | 22 | 39 | 25 | 12 | 10 | 36 | 27 | 63 | 22 | 19 | 4 | 2 | | 2 | | 1 | 118 | 23 |
| .... | 12 | 5 | 30 | 13 | 226 | 253 | 246 | 174 | 332 | 295 | 129 | 129 | 277 | 205 | 482 | 204 | 179 | 23 | 30 | 1 | 4 | 2 | 6 | 931 | |

## SECTION OF THE STATE OF GEORGIA.

*Decatur, Dooly, Early, Effingham, Emanuel, Glynn, Houston, Irwin, Lawrens, Lee, Liberty, Randolph, Scrivner, Stewart, Sumter, Tatnall, Telfair, Thomas, Ware, Wayne.*

| Nativities: California and Territories | Nativities: Ireland | Nativities: Germany | Nativities: Other foreign countries | Nativities: Unknown | Season of decease: Spring | Season of decease: Summer | Season of decease: Autumn | Season of decease: Winter | Duration of sickness: Under 1 week | Duration of sickness: 1 week and under 1 month | Duration of sickness: 1 month and under 3 months | Duration of sickness: 3 months and over | Whites: Males | Whites: Females | Whites: Total | Colored: Slaves: Black: M. | Colored: Slaves: Black: F. | Colored: Slaves: Mulatto: M. | Colored: Slaves: Mulatto: F. | Colored: Free: Black: M. | Colored: Free: Black: F. | Colored: Free: Mul.: M | Colored: Free: Mul.: F. | Aggregate deaths | |
|---|---|---|---|---|---|---|---|---|---|---|---|---|---|---|---|---|---|---|---|---|---|---|---|---|---|
| | | | | | 1 | 3 | 3 | 1 | 1 | 2 | 2 | 3 | 3 | 3 | 6 | | 1 | | 1 | | | | | 8 | 1 |
| | 1 | | 1 | | 33 | 10 | 16 | 27 | 75 | 9 | | 2 | 20 | 9 | 29 | 24 | 33 | 1 | 1 | | | | | 88 | 2 |
| | | | | | 17 | 5 | 3 | 20 | 34 | 9 | 1 | 1 | 4 | 5 | 9 | 21 | 16 | | | | | | | 46 | 3 |
| | 1 | | | | 5 | 5 | 3 | 11 | 24 | | | | 4 | | 4 | 12 | 7 | 1 | | | | | | 24 | 4 |
| | | | | | 1 | 1 | 1 | 1 | 4 | | | | 4 | | 4 | | | | | | | | | 4 | 5 |
| | | | | | 6 | 3 | 2 | 2 | 13 | | | | 3 | 2 | 5 | 5 | 3 | | | | | | | 13 | 6 |
| | 2 | | 3 | | 5 | 2 | 1 | 5 | 2 | 3 | 2 | 6 | 5 | 3 | 8 | 4 | 1 | | | | | | | 13 | 7 |
| | | | | | 14 | 9 | 20 | 8 | 22 | 17 | 6 | 5 | 16 | 5 | 21 | 10 | 18 | 1 | 1 | | | | | 51 | 8 |
| | | | | | 6 | 5 | 5 | 3 | 12 | 7 | | | 6 | 6 | 12 | 2 | 5 | | | | | | | 19 | 9 |
| | | | | | 3 | 4 | 3 | 2 | 1 | 5 | 1 | 5 | 3 | 2 | 5 | 5 | 2 | | | | | | | 12 | 10 |
| | | | 1 | | 8 | 5 | 5 | 1 | | 1 | | 18 | 3 | 11 | 14 | 1 | 2 | | | 1 | | | 1 | 19 | 11 |
| | | | | | 9 | | 2 | 14 | 9 | 8 | 4 | 1 | 2 | 3 | 5 | 11 | 9 | | | | | | | 25 | 12 |
| | | | | | | 1 | 1 | | | 2 | | | 1 | 1 | 2 | | | | | | | | | 2 | 13 |
| | 1 | | | | 18 | 14 | 11 | 21 | 37 | 20 | 6 | 1 | | 36 | 36 | | 27 | | 1 | | | | | 64 | 14 |
| | | | | | 1 | 7 | 5 | | 12 | 1 | | | | 1 | 1 | 7 | 4 | | 1 | | | | | 13 | 15 |
| | | | | | | 3 | 1 | 2 | 2 | 3 | 1 | | 3 | 1 | 4 | | 1 | 1 | | | | | | 6 | 16 |
| | | | | | 2 | 4 | 5 | 4 | 10 | 5 | | | 7 | 4 | 11 | 1 | 3 | | | | | | | 15 | 17 |
| | 1 | | | | 8 | 11 | 8 | 10 | 13 | 10 | 3 | 11 | 16 | 9 | 25 | 7 | 6 | | | | | | | 38 | 18 |
| | 1 | | | | 3 | 6 | 18 | 3 | 27 | 2 | 1 | | 11 | 7 | 18 | 6 | 6 | | | | | | | 30 | 19 |
| | | | | | 1 | 3 | 1 | 1 | 5 | 1 | | | 1 | 3 | 4 | 1 | 1 | | | | | | | 6 | 20 |
| | 6 | 2 | 1 | 1 | 25 | 23 | 18 | 21 | | 6 | 12 | 69 | 28 | 23 | 51 | 12 | 19 | | 4 | | | 1 | | 87 | 21 |
| | | | | | 8 | 11 | 9 | 11 | 32 | 6 | | 1 | 10 | 7 | 17 | 11 | 11 | | | | | | | 39 | 22 |
| | | | | | 1 | | | | 1 | | | | 1 | | 1 | | | | | | | | | 1 | 23 |
| | | | | | 11 | 7 | 17 | 16 | 37 | 10 | 2 | 1 | 18 | 19 | 37 | 6 | 6 | 1 | 1 | | | | | 51 | 24 |
| | | | 1 | | 3 | 1 | 1 | 2 | 2 | | 2 | 3 | | 2 | 2 | 1 | 3 | | | | 1 | | | 7 | 25 |
| | | | | | | 1 | | | | 1 | | | | | | 1 | | | | | | | | 1 | 26 |
| | | | 1 | | 10 | 17 | 15 | 10 | 13 | 31 | 6 | 2 | 9 | 15 | 24 | 14 | 11 | | 2 | | | 1 | | 52 | 27 |
| | | | | | 1 | | | | | | | 1 | | | | | 1 | | | | | | | 1 | 28 |
| | 3 | | 6 | 6 | 58 | 48 | 56 | 38 | 15 | 31 | 39 | 110 | 58 | 37 | 95 | 45 | 53 | 2 | 4 | | 1 | | | 200 | 29 |
| | 2 | 1 | 1 | | 9 | 20 | 11 | 7 | 17 | 23 | 2 | 5 | 13 | 10 | 23 | 12 | 11 | 1 | | | | | | 47 | 30 |
| | | | | | | 1 | | 1 | | | | 2 | 2 | | 2 | | | | | | | | | 2 | 31 |
| | | | | | | 1 | | | 1 | | | | 1 | | 1 | | | | | | | | | 1 | 32 |
| | 1 | 1 | | | 13 | 3 | 4 | 6 | 3 | 20 | 1 | 2 | 14 | 7 | 21 | 1 | 3 | | 1 | | | | | 26 | 33 |
| | 10 | | 4 | | 23 | 54 | 135 | 34 | 72 | 138 | 28 | 8 | 76 | 68 | 144 | 51 | 44 | 2 | 4 | | | 1 | | 246 | 34 |
| | 1 | | 2 | | 1 | 1 | 26 | 4 | 16 | 18 | 1 | | 14 | 12 | 26 | 3 | 5 | 1 | | | | | | 35 | 35 |
| | 1 | | | | 1 | 4 | 3 | | 6 | 2 | | | 2 | 3 | 5 | | 1 | | 2 | | | | | 8 | 36 |
| | 5 | | 1 | | 1 | 5 | 5 | 7 | 6 | 12 | | | 8 | 3 | 11 | 4 | 2 | | 1 | | | | | 18 | 37 |
| | | | | | 1 | 1 | 3 | | 2 | 2 | 1 | | | 8 | 8 | | 2 | | | | | | | 5 | 38 |
| | | | | | | | 1 | | 1 | | | | | | | 1 | | | | | | | | 1 | 39 |
| | | | | | | | 1 | | | 1 | | | 1 | | 1 | | | | | | | | | 1 | 40 |

## CLASSIFICATION OF DEATHS IN SOUTHERN

| | Cause of Death. | AGES. Under 1. | | 1 and under 5. | | 5 and under 10. | | 10 and under 20. | | 20 and under 50. | | 50 and under 80. | | 80 and under 100. | | 100 & over. | | Age unknown. | | NATIVITIES. Born in State. | N. England States. | Middle States. | Southern States. | Southwest'n States. | Northwest'n States. |
|---|---|---|---|---|---|---|---|---|---|---|---|---|---|---|---|---|---|---|---|---|---|---|---|---|---|
| | | M. | F. | M. | F. | M. | F. | M. | F. | M. | F. | M. | F. | M | F. | M | F. | M | F. | | | | | | |
| 1 | Fever, scarlet | 4 | 2 | 11 | 7 | 5 | 9 | 6 | 6 | 1 | | | | | | | | | | 47 | | | 2 | | |
| 2 | ..do..typhus | 6 | 4 | 6 | 3 | 6 | 6 | 9 | 8 | 16 | 13 | 3 | 2 | | | | | | | 69 | | | 12 | | |
| 3 | ..do..yellow | | | | 1 | | | | | | | | | | | | | | | 1 | | | | | |
| 4 | Gout | | | | | | | | | | | 1 | | | | | | | | | | | 1 | | |
| 5 | Gravel | 1 | | | | | | | | 1 | | 1 | | 1 | | | | | | 2 | | | 2 | | |
| 6 | Heart, disease of | 1 | | | | 1 | | 1 | | 1 | | | 2 | | | | | | | 4 | | | 2 | | |
| 7 | Hemorrhage | 1 | 2 | 3 | | | | 2 | | | 2 | | | | | | | | | 10 | | | | | |
| 8 | Hernia | | | | | | | | | 1 | | 2 | 1 | | | | | | | 4 | | | | | |
| 9 | Hives | 12 | 8 | 4 | | | | | | | | | | | | | | | | 23 | | | 1 | | |
| 10 | Hooping cough | 11 | 22 | 20 | 18 | 4 | 1 | 2 | 1 | | | | | | | | | | | 79 | | | | | |
| 11 | Inflamat'n, not spec'd | 4 | | 2 | 3 | 1 | 1 | 3 | | 3 | 6 | 2 | 2 | | | | | | | 26 | | | 1 | | |
| 12 | ....do....bowels | 2 | 2 | 2 | 2 | | 1 | | 1 | 3 | 2 | 4 | | | | | | | | 16 | | | 2 | | |
| 13 | ....do....brain | 1 | 6 | 3 | 3 | 1 | | 1 | 2 | 1 | 2 | | 1 | | | | | | | 19 | | | 2 | | |
| 14 | ....do....stomach | | | | | 1 | | | | | | | | | | | | | | 1 | | | | | |
| 15 | Influenza | | 3 | | | | | | | 1 | | 1 | | | | | | | | 4 | | | 1 | | |
| 16 | Insanity | | | | | | | | | 1 | | | | | | | | | | 1 | | | | | |
| 17 | Intemperance | | | | | | | | | 11 | | 5 | | | | | | | | 8 | | | 4 | | |
| 18 | Killed | | | | | | | | | 5 | | | | | | | | | | 3 | | | 2 | | |
| 19 | Lightning | | | | | 1 | 1 | 2 | 1 | 1 | 1 | | | | | | | | | 5 | | | 2 | | |
| 20 | Liver, disease of | | | | | | 1 | | | 6 | 3 | 1 | 3 | | | | | | | 9 | 1 | | 2 | | |
| 21 | Lockjaw | 9 | 8 | | | | | 1 | | 1 | | | | | | | | | | 19 | | | | | |
| 22 | Lungs, disease of | 1 | | 1 | 1 | | | | | 5 | 7 | 4 | 2 | | | | | | | 18 | | | 2 | | |
| 23 | Malformation | | 2 | | | | | | | | | | | | | | | | | 2 | | | | | |
| 24 | Mania-a-potu | | | | | | | | | 2 | | 2 | | | | | | | | 1 | | | 3 | | |
| 25 | Marasmus | | | | 1 | | | | | | | | | | | | | | | 1 | | | | | |
| 26 | Measles | | 4 | 3 | | | 1 | 1 | | | | | | | | | | | | 9 | | | | | |
| 27 | Mortification | | | | | | | 2 | | | 1 | | | | | | | | | 3 | | | | | |
| 28 | Murder | 1 | 1 | 1 | | | | | | 3 | | | | | | | | | | 5 | | | 1 | | |
| 29 | Neuralgia | | | | 1 | | | | | 1 | | | 1 | | | | | | | 3 | | | | | |
| 30 | Old age | | | | | | | | | | 1 | 14 | 28 | 23 | 26 | | | | | 55 | 1 | 1 | 21 | | |
| 31 | Paralysis | | | | | | | 2 | | | 1 | 4 | 2 | 1 | | | | | | 4 | | | 4 | | |
| 32 | Pleurisy | | | 1 | | | | 3 | 1 | 9 | 5 | 10 | 1 | | | | | | | 26 | | 1 | 2 | | |
| 33 | Pneumonia | 8 | 6 | 8 | 6 | 3 | 2 | 16 | 19 | 29 | 24 | 23 | 10 | 1 | | | | | | 116 | | 1 | 35 | | |
| 34 | Poison | | 1 | 1 | | 1 | 2 | 1 | 1 | 1 | 1 | | | | | | | | | 9 | | | | | |
| 35 | Premature birth | 1 | | | | | | | | | | | | | | | | | | 1 | | | | | |
| 36 | Quinsy | | 2 | 2 | | 2 | | | | 1 | 1 | | 1 | 1 | | | | | | 9 | | | 1 | | |
| 37 | Rheumatism | | | | | | 1 | | | | 2 | 3 | 1 | | | | | | | 5 | | | 2 | | |
| 38 | Scrofula | 1 | 1 | | 2 | 1 | | 1 | 2 | 6 | 5 | 1 | 2 | | | | | | | 19 | | | 3 | | |
| 39 | Spine, disease of | | | 1 | | 1 | | | | | 1 | | | | | | | | | 3 | | | | | |
| 40 | Stillborn | 1 | | | | | | | | | | | | | | | | | | 1 | | | | | |
| 41 | Stomach, disease of | | | | | | | | | | | | 1 | | | | | | | 1 | | | | | |
| 42 | Suffocation | 9 | 8 | 2 | 2 | | | | | | | | | | | | | | | 21 | | | | | |
| 43 | Suicide | | | | | | | | 2 | 1 | | 3 | | | | | | | | 4 | | | 2 | | |
| 44 | Teething | 15 | 8 | 21 | 12 | | 1 | | | | | | | | | | | | | 57 | | | | | |
| 45 | Tetanus | | | | | | | | | 1 | | | | | | | | | | 1 | | | | | |
| 46 | Throat, disease of | 1 | | 5 | 4 | | 1 | | | | 1 | 1 | | | | | | | | 12 | | | 1 | | |
| 47 | Thrush | | 3 | 2 | | | | | | | | | | | | | | | | 5 | | | | | |
| 48 | Ulcer | 1 | | 1 | | | | | 1 | 2 | 1 | | 1 | | | | | | | 5 | | | 1 | | |
| 49 | Uterus, disease of | | | | | | | | 2 | | 1 | | | | | | | | | 3 | | | | | |
| 50 | Venereal | | | | | | | | | | 1 | | | | | | | | | 1 | | | | | |
| 51 | Worms | 6 | 8 | 27 | 24 | 4 | 12 | 2 | 1 | | | | | | | | | | | 83 | | | 1 | | |
| 52 | Unknown | 101 | 85 | 60 | 33 | 16 | 9 | 21 | 12 | 54 | 47 | 31 | 22 | 11 | 6 | .. | .. | 1 | 1 | 449 | 2 | 3 | 31 | | |
| | Total | 279 | 273 | 318 | 271 | 112 | 108 | 150 | 144 | 343 | 319 | 238 | 171 | 52 | 40 | .. | .. | 1 | 1 | 2360 | 13 | 22 | 297 | 2 | .. |

## CLASSIFICATION OF DEATHS IN NORTHERN

*Embracing the following counties : Campbell, Carroll, Cass, Chalooga, Cherokee, Clark, Cobb, Hall, Jackson, Lincoln, Lumpkin, Madison, Morgan, Murray, Newton,*

| | | | | | | | | | | | | | | | | | | | | | | | | | |
|---|---|---|---|---|---|---|---|---|---|---|---|---|---|---|---|---|---|---|---|---|---|---|---|---|---|
| 1 | Abscess | | 1 | | 1 | 1 | | 1 | | 2 | | 1 | | | | | | | | 6 | | | 1 | | |
| 2 | Accident not specif'd | 8 | 7 | 7 | 5 | 4 | 2 | 5 | 2 | 8 | 2 | | | | | | | | | 46 | | | 2 | 1 | 1 |
| 3 | ...do...burned | 1 | 1 | 11 | 8 | 1 | 4 | 3 | 3 | 3 | 2 | | | | | | | | | 34 | | | 3 | | |
| 4 | ...do...drowned | | | 2 | 1 | | 1 | 2 | 2 | 3 | | | | | | | | | | 11 | | | | | |
| 5 | ...do...shot | | | | | | | | | 3 | | 1 | | | | | | | | 3 | | | 1 | | |
| 6 | Apoplexy | 1 | 1 | | 1 | | | | | 7 | 4 | 3 | 5 | | | | | | | 16 | | | 5 | 1 | |
| 7 | Asthma | | | | | | | | | | 1 | 4 | 1 | 1 | | | | | | | | | 7 | | |
| 8 | Bladder, disease of | | | | | | | | | | | 1 | | | | | | | | 1 | | | | | |
| 9 | Bowels.....do | 10 | 3 | 10 | 6 | | 1 | | 1 | 2 | 1 | 1 | 1 | 1 | | | | | | 35 | | | 2 | | |
| 10 | Bronchitis | | | | 1 | | | | | | | 1 | | | | | | | | 1 | | | 1 | | |
| 11 | Cancer | | 1 | | | 1 | | | | 1 | 3 | 4 | 7 | 1 | | | | | | 9 | | | 9 | | |

SECTION OF THE STATE OF GEORGIA—Continued.

| NATIVITIES. | | | | | SEASON OF DECEASE. | | | | DURATION OF SICKNESS. | | | | WHITES. | | | COLORED. | | | | | | | | | |
|---|---|---|---|---|---|---|---|---|---|---|---|---|---|---|---|---|---|---|---|---|---|---|---|---|---|
| | | | | | | | | | | | | | | | | Slaves. | | | | Free. | | | | | |
| | | | | | | | | | | | | | | | | Black. | | Mulatto. | | Black. | | Mul. | | | |
| California and Territories. | Ireland. | Germany. | Other foreign countries. | Unknown. | Spring. | Summer. | Autumn. | Winter. | Under 1 week. | 1 week and under 1 month. | 1 month and under 3 months. | 3 months and over. | Males. | Females. | Total. | M. | F. | M. | F. | M. | F. | M | F. | Aggregate deaths. | |
| | 2 | | | | 19 | 17 | 10 | 5 | 26 | 18 | 6 | 1 | 10 | 16 | 26 | 16 | 8 | | | 1 | | | | 51 | 1 |
| | | 1 | | | 15 | 23 | 26 | 18 | 13 | 61 | 6 | 2 | 27 | 23 | 50 | 19 | 13 | | | | | | | 82 | 2 |
| | | | | | | | 1 | | | 1 | | | | 1 | 1 | | | | | | | | | 1 | 3 |
| | | | | | | | | 1 | | 1 | | | 1 | | 1 | | | | | | | | | 1 | 4 |
| | | | | | 2 | | 1 | 1 | | 2 | | 2 | 3 | | 3 | 1 | | | | | | | | 4 | 5 |
| | | | | | 4 | | 2 | | 3 | 1 | 1 | 1 | 1 | 1 | 2 | 3 | 1 | | | | | | | 6 | 6 |
| | | | | | 4 | 3 | 2 | 1 | 8 | 1 | 1 | | 1 | 1 | 2 | 5 | 3 | | | | | | | 10 | 7 |
| | | | | | | 1 | 3 | | 1 | 1 | | 2 | | | | 3 | 1 | | | | | | | 4 | 8 |
| | | | | | 10 | 4 | 6 | 4 | 17 | 5 | | 1 | 14 | 7 | 21 | 2 | 1 | | | | | | | 24 | 9 |
| | | | | | 16 | 28 | 30 | 5 | 18 | 39 | 19 | 3 | 12 | 12 | 24 | 21 | 30 | 3 | | | | 1 | | 79 | 10 |
| | | | | | 6 | 5 | 13 | 3 | 11 | 14 | 2 | | 12 | 8 | 20 | 3 | 4 | | | | | | | 27 | 11 |
| | | | | 1 | 5 | 6 | 6 | 2 | 6 | 9 | 3 | 1 | 6 | 5 | 11 | 5 | 3 | | | | | | | 19 | 12 |
| | | | | | 5 | 7 | 6 | 3 | 11 | 9 | 1 | | 5 | 10 | 15 | 2 | 4 | | | | | | | 21 | 13 |
| | | | | | | | 1 | | | 1 | | | 1 | | 1 | | | | | | | | | 1 | 14 |
| | | | | | 2 | | | 3 | 3 | 2 | | | 2 | | 2 | | 3 | | | | | | | 5 | 15 |
| | | | | | 1 | | | | | | | 1 | | | | 1 | | | | | | | | 1 | 16 |
| | 4 | | | | 6 | 4 | 1 | 5 | 10 | 4 | 1 | 1 | 9 | | 9 | 3 | | 2 | | | | 2 | | 16 | 17 |
| | | | | | | 2 | 1 | 2 | 4 | 1 | | | 4 | | 4 | 1 | | | | | | | | 5 | 18 |
| | | | | | | 5 | 2 | | 6 | 1 | | | 4 | 3 | 7 | | | | | | | | | 7 | 19 |
| | 2 | | | | 4 | 4 | 2 | 4 | 2 | 3 | 2 | 7 | 7 | 6 | 13 | | 1 | | | | | | | 14 | 20 |
| | | | | | 1 | 8 | 9 | 1 | 17 | 2 | | | 1 | | 1 | 9 | 8 | 1 | | | | | | 19 | 21 |
| | 1 | | | | 7 | 10 | 3 | 1 | 7 | 7 | 5 | 2 | 7 | 5 | 12 | 4 | 4 | | | | | | 1 | 21 | 22 |
| | | | | | | | 2 | | 1 | | 1 | | | 2 | 2 | | | | | | | | | 2 | 23 |
| | | | | | 1 | | | 3 | 1 | 1 | 1 | 1 | 3 | | 3 | 1 | | | | | | | | 4 | 24 |
| | | | | | | | 1 | | | | | 1 | | | | | 1 | | | | | | | 1 | 25 |
| | | | | | 2 | 1 | 3 | 3 | 2 | 3 | 2 | 2 | | 2 | 2 | 3 | 3 | 1 | | | | | | 9 | 26 |
| | | | | | | | 3 | | | 2 | 1 | | 2 | 1 | 3 | | | | | | | | | 3 | 27 |
| | | | | | 2 | 1 | 1 | 2 | 5 | 1 | | | 4 | | 4 | | 1 | 1 | | | | | | 6 | 28 |
| | | | | | | 1 | 1 | 1 | | 2 | 1 | | | 2 | 2 | 1 | | | | | | | | 3 | 29 |
| | | 1 | 13 | | 30 | 18 | 21 | 22 | 61 | 10 | 4 | 16 | 7 | 20 | 27 | 29 | 33 | 1 | | | 1 | | 1 | 92 | 30 |
| | | | 1 | 1 | 3 | 4 | 2 | 1 | 3 | 1 | 1 | 5 | 6 | | 6 | 1 | 3 | | | | | | | 10 | 31 |
| | 1 | | | | 11 | 1 | 2 | 16 | 8 | 20 | 1 | 1 | 6 | 2 | 8 | 17 | 5 | | | | | | | 30 | 32 |
| | | | 3 | | 72 | 25 | 17 | 41 | 68 | 75 | 12 | | 36 | 20 | 56 | 50 | 46 | 2 | 1 | | | | | 155 | 33 |
| | | | | | 1 | 5 | 1 | 2 | 3 | 5 | 1 | | 2 | 1 | 3 | 2 | 4 | | | | | | | 9 | 34 |
| | | | | | 1 | | | | 1 | | | | 1 | | 1 | | | | | | | | | 1 | 35 |
| | | | | | 4 | | 3 | 3 | 5 | 4 | | 1 | 3 | 1 | 4 | 3 | 2 | | | | | | 1 | 10 | 36 |
| | | | | | 1 | 2 | 3 | 1 | | 3 | 2 | 2 | 2 | | 2 | 1 | 3 | | 1 | | | | | 7 | 37 |
| | | | | | 7 | 6 | 3 | 6 | 2 | 2 | 3 | 15 | 6 | 6 | 12 | 4 | 5 | | 1 | | | | | 22 | 38 |
| | | | | | 2 | 1 | | | 1 | | | 2 | | | | 2 | 1 | | | | | | | 3 | 39 |
| | | | | | | | 1 | | 1 | | | | | | | 1 | | | | | | | | 1 | 40 |
| | | | | | | 1 | | | | | | 1 | | | | | 1 | | | | | | | 1 | 41 |
| | | | | | 4 | 6 | 1 | 10 | 21 | | | | 1 | 2 | 3 | 10 | 8 | | | | | | | 21 | 42 |
| | | | | | 2 | 3 | | 1 | 6 | | | | 4 | | 4 | | 2 | | | | | | | 6 | 43 |
| | | | | | 11 | 15 | 22 | 9 | 17 | 21 | 11 | 8 | 6 | 6 | 12 | 30 | 15 | | | | | | | 57 | 44 |
| | | | | | | | | 1 | 1 | | | | | | | 1 | | | | | | | | 1 | 45 |
| | | | | | 3 | 2 | 1 | 7 | 5 | 7 | | 1 | 4 | 3 | 7 | 3 | 3 | | | | | | | 13 | 46 |
| | | | | | 1 | 1 | 3 | | | 2 | 3 | | | 2 | 2 | 2 | 1 | | | | | | | 5 | 47 |
| | | | 1 | | 1 | 3 | 3 | | 1 | 3 | 1 | 2 | 1 | 3 | 4 | 3 | | | | | | | | 7 | 48 |
| | | | | | | 2 | 1 | | 2 | | 1 | | | | | | 2 | | 1 | | | | | 3 | 49 |
| | | | | | | | | 1 | | | | 1 | | 1 | 1 | | | | | | | | | 1 | 50 |
| | | | | | 17 | 29 | 26 | 12 | 42 | 31 | 8 | 3 | | 14 | 14 | 39 | 28 | | 3 | | | | | 84 | 51 |
| | 13 | 2 | 10 | | 148 | 114 | 132 | 116 | 273 | 122 | 44 | 71 | 148 | 89 | 237 | 133 | 121 | 10 | 3 | 3 | | 1 | 2 | 510 | 52 |
| | 59 | 8 | 50 | 9 | 738 | 667 | 797 | 610 | 1220 | 905 | 266 | 414 | 736 | 595 | 1331 | 713 | 689 | 32 | 34 | 5 | 3 | 7 | 6 | 2820 | |

## SECTION OF THE STATE OF GEORGIA.

*Dade, DeKalb, Elbert, Forsythe, Floyd, Franklin, Gilmer, Gordon, Greene, Gwinnett, Habersham Oglethorpe, Paulding, Rabun, Taliaferro, Union, Walker, Walton, Wilkes.*

| | | | | | | | | | | | | | | | | | | | | | | | | | |
|---|---|---|---|---|---|---|---|---|---|---|---|---|---|---|---|---|---|---|---|---|---|---|---|---|---|
| | | | | | 1 | 2 | 3 | 1 | 2 | 2 | | 3 | 3 | 1 | 4 | 2 | 1 | | | | | | | 7 | 1 |
| | | | | | 18 | 11 | 9 | 10 | 42 | 3 | 1 | 2 | 16 | 6 | 22 | 15 | 12 | 1 | | | | | | 50 | 2 |
| | | | | | 12 | 8 | 5 | 12 | 23 | 9 | 4 | 1 | 10 | 10 | 20 | 9 | 8 | | | | | | | 37 | 3 |
| | | | | | 2 | 7 | 1 | 1 | 11 | | | | | | | 7 | 3 | | 1 | | | | | 11 | 4 |
| | | | | | 1 | 2 | | 1 | 3 | | | 1 | 3 | | 3 | 1 | | | | | | | | 4 | 5 |
| | | | | | 4 | 5 | 7 | 5 | 21 | | | 1 | 8 | 9 | 17 | 3 | 2 | | | | | | | 22 | 6 |
| | | | | | 5 | 2 | | | | 1 | 1 | 5 | | | | 5 | 2 | | | | | | | 7 | 7 |
| | | | | | | 1 | | | | | | 1 | 1 | | 1 | | | | | | | | | 1 | 8 |
| | | | | | 6 | 14 | 12 | 5 | 11 | 20 | 4 | 2 | 11 | 7 | 18 | 13 | 5 | | 1 | | | | | 37 | 9 |
| | | | | | 1 | | | 1 | 1 | | | 1 | 1 | | 1 | | | | 1 | | | | | 2 | 10 |
| | | | | | 5 | 7 | 3 | 3 | 3 | 3 | | 12 | 7 | 10 | 17 | | 1 | | | | | | | 18 | 11 |

## CLASSIFICATION OF DEATHS IN NORTHERN

| | Cause of death. | AGES. Under 1. M. | Under 1. F. | 1 and under 5. M. | 1 and under 5. F. | 5 and under 10. M. | 5 and under 10. F. | 10 and under 20. M. | 10 and under 20. F. | 20 and under 50. M. | 20 and under 50. F. | 50 and under 80. M. | 50 and under 80. F. | 80 and under 100. M | 80 and under 100. F. | 100 & over. M | 100 & over. F. | Age unknown. M | Age unknown. F. | NATIVITIES. Born in State. | N. England States. | Middle States. | Southern States. | Southwest'n States. | Northwest'n States. |
|---|---|---|---|---|---|---|---|---|---|---|---|---|---|---|---|---|---|---|---|---|---|---|---|---|---|
| 1 | Catarrh | 12 | 9 | 11 | 8 | | | 1 | 1 | | 1 | 2 | 3 | 1 | | | | | | 47 | | | 2 | | |
| 2 | Chicken pox | | | 2 | | | | | | | | | | | | | | | | 2 | | | | | |
| 3 | Child birth | | | | | | | | 9 | | 48 | | | | | | | | | 38 | | | 19 | | |
| 4 | Cholera | | | 1 | | | | | | | | 1 | | | | | | | | 2 | | | | | |
| 5 | ...do..infantum | 10 | 5 | 5 | 3 | 1 | | 1 | | | | | | | | | | | | 23 | | | 2 | | |
| 6 | ...do..morbus | 1 | 1 | 3 | 3 | | 1 | | | | 1 | 2 | 3 | 1 | | | | | | 13 | | | 2 | 1 | |
| 7 | Colic | 2 | 3 | 3 | 2 | | | 1 | | 2 | 4 | 7 | 6 | 2 | | | | | | 17 | | | 14 | 1 | |
| 8 | Congestion | | | 1 | 2 | 1 | | 2 | | 3 | 2 | 1 | 1 | 1 | 1 | | | | | 8 | | 1 | 4 | | |
| 9 | Consumption | 1 | 2 | 1 | 2 | | | 5 | 6 | 22 | 30 | 7 | 11 | 1 | | | | 1 | 1 | 59 | | | 30 | | |
| 10 | Convulsions | 7 | 1 | 2 | 2 | 1 | | 4 | 5 | 4 | 9 | 3 | 8 | 1 | | | | | | 39 | | 1 | 7 | | |
| 11 | Cramp | | | | | | | | | 1 | 1 | | | | | | | | | 1 | | | 1 | | |
| 12 | Croup | 60 | 52 | 37 | 25 | 2 | 6 | | | | 1 | 4 | 1 | 2 | 1 | | | | | 182 | | | 4 | 4 | |
| 13 | Debility | | | | | 1 | | | | | | | 1 | | | | | | | 2 | | | | | |
| 14 | Diabetes | | | | | | 1 | | | | | 2 | | | | | | | | 1 | | | 2 | | |
| 15 | Diarrhœa | 5 | 4 | 11 | 6 | | | 6 | | 3 | 2 | 4 | 5 | | | | | | | 36 | | | 9 | | |
| 16 | Dirt eating | | | 1 | | | | | 1 | | | | | | | | | | | 2 | | | | | |
| 17 | Dropsy | 6 | 8 | 10 | 6 | 8 | 6 | 10 | 14 | 15 | 29 | 30 | 40 | 5 | 7 | | | | | 121 | | 2 | 66 | | |
| 18 | Dysentery | 6 | 3 | 8 | 6 | 2 | 1 | 1 | 1 | 4 | 4 | 1 | 1 | 1 | 2 | | | | | 35 | | | 6 | | |
| 19 | Dyspepsia | | | | | 1 | | | | 7 | 3 | 2 | 1 | 1 | | | | | | 10 | | | 4 | 1 | |
| 20 | Epilepsy | | | | | | | | | 1 | | | | | | | | | | 1 | | | | | |
| 21 | Erysipelas | 1 | 1 | 2 | 1 | 1 | | 1 | | | 3 | 2 | 3 | | | | | | | 9 | | | 6 | | |
| 22 | Executed | | | | | | | | | 1 | | | | | | | | | | | | | 1 | | |
| 23 | Fever, not specified | 13 | 7 | 15 | 20 | 13 | 9 | 26 | 31 | 37 | 32 | 11 | 7 | 1 | 1 | | | | | 175 | | 1 | 39 | 6 | |
| 24 | ..do..bilious | | | 2 | | | 1 | 1 | 2 | 6 | 8 | 2 | | | 1 | | | | | 18 | | | 2 | 3 | |
| 25 | ..do..brain | 1 | | 1 | | | | | 1 | 1 | 1 | | | | | | | | | 5 | | | | | |
| 26 | ..do..congestive | | | 2 | | 1 | | 2 | 1 | 5 | 2 | | 1 | | | | | | | 13 | | | 1 | | |
| 27 | ..do..inflammatory | | 1 | | | | | 1 | | 1 | | | | | | | | | | 2 | | | 1 | | |
| 28 | ..do..intermittent | 1 | | 1 | 1 | 1 | | 1 | | 1 | | | | | | | | | | 6 | | | | | |
| 29 | ..do..puerperal | | | | | | | | | | 2 | | | | | | | | | 1 | | | 1 | | |
| 30 | ..do..remittent | 1 | | | | | | | | | | | | | | | | | | 1 | | | | | |
| 31 | ..do..scarlet | 6 | 2 | 7 | 1 | 2 | 1 | | 1 | | | | | | | | | | | 20 | | | | | |
| 32 | ..do..typhus | 1 | 4 | 8 | 9 | 2 | 6 | 28 | 32 | 42 | 33 | 9 | 6 | | | | | | | 154 | | | 23 | 3 | |
| 33 | ..do..winter | | | | | | 1 | 1 | | | | | | | | | | | | 2 | | | | | |
| 34 | Frozen | | | | | | | | | 1 | | 1 | | | | | | | | 1 | | | 1 | | |
| 35 | Gout | | | | | | | | | | 1 | | | | | | | | | 1 | | | | | |
| 36 | Gravel | | | 1 | 1 | | | | | 2 | | 2 | | 1 | | | | | | 2 | | | 4 | 1 | |
| 37 | Heart, disease of | 1 | 1 | 1 | | | | 1 | | 1 | 1 | 2 | 2 | | | | | | | 8 | | | 2 | | |
| 38 | Heat | | | | | | | | | | | 1 | | | | | | | | | | | 1 | | |
| 39 | Hemorrhage | | | 1 | | | | | 1 | 1 | 2 | 1 | 1 | | | | | | | 6 | | 1 | | | |
| 40 | Hernia | | | | | | | 1 | | 1 | 1 | | | | | | | | | 2 | | | 1 | | |
| 41 | Hip, disease of | | | 1 | 1 | | | | | | | | | | | | | | | 2 | | | | | |
| 42 | Hives | 24 | 27 | 7 | 2 | | | | | | | | | | | | | | | 59 | | | | 1 | |
| 43 | Hooping cough | 30 | 25 | 29 | 36 | | 2 | 2 | 1 | | 1 | | | | | | | | | 124 | | | 1 | 1 | |
| 44 | Hydrophobia | | | | | | | | 1 | | | | | | | | | | | 1 | | | | | |
| 45 | Inflammation | 2 | 2 | 1 | 3 | 2 | | 3 | 4 | 1 | 7 | 3 | 1 | 1 | | | | | | 23 | | | 7 | | |
| 46 | ....do....bowels | 3 | 6 | 1 | 2 | 2 | 1 | 1 | 5 | 1 | 2 | 2 | 1 | | | | | | | 19 | | 1 | 7 | | |
| 47 | ...do....brain | 6 | 3 | 7 | 4 | 1 | 1 | 4 | | 3 | 2 | 4 | | | | | | | | 28 | | | 5 | | 1 |
| 48 | Influenza | | 2 | | 2 | | | 2 | | | | | 1 | | | | | | | 6 | | | 1 | | |
| 49 | Insanity | | | | | | | | | | | | 1 | | | | | | | 1 | | | | | |
| 50 | Intemperance | | | | | | | | | 4 | | 4 | | 2 | | | | | | 2 | | | 7 | | |
| 51 | Jaundice | | 2 | | 2 | | | | | | 1 | | | | | | | | | 5 | | | | | |
| 52 | Kidneys, disease of | | | | | | | | | 1 | | | | | | | | | | 1 | | | | | |
| 53 | Killed | | | | | 1 | | | | 2 | | | | 1 | | | | | | 3 | | | 1 | | |
| 54 | Lightning | | | | | | | 1 | 1 | | | | | | | | | | | 2 | | | | | |
| 55 | Liver, disease of | | | 1 | 2 | | | 1 | | 4 | 1 | 4 | 5 | | | | | | | 9 | | | 9 | | |
| 56 | Lockjaw | | 1 | | 1 | | | | | | | | | | | | | | | 1 | | | 1 | | |
| 57 | Lungs, disease of | 2 | 2 | | 1 | | | | | | 1 | 2 | 1 | | 1 | | | | | 6 | | 1 | 4 | | |
| 58 | Malformation | | 1 | | | | | | | | | | | | | | | | | 1 | | | | | |
| 59 | Measles | 1 | 3 | 7 | 7 | | 1 | 2 | 2 | 1 | 4 | | | | | | | | | 27 | | | 1 | | |
| 60 | Mortification | | 1 | | | | | | | 1 | 1 | 1 | | 1 | | | | | | 3 | | | 2 | | |
| 61 | Murder | | | | | | | | | 2 | | | | | | | | | | 1 | | | 1 | | |
| 62 | Neuralgia | | | | | | | | | | | 1 | 1 | | | | | | | | | 1 | 1 | | |
| 63 | Old age | | | | | | | | | | | 9 | 19 | 26 | 15 | | 1 | | | 19 | | 3 | 43 | | |
| 64 | Paralysis | 1 | | | | 1 | | | | 1 | 2 | 7 | 8 | | 4 | | | | | 11 | | | 12 | | |
| 65 | Piles | | | | | | | | | 1 | | 2 | | | | | | | | 2 | | | 1 | | |
| 66 | Pleurisy | | | | 1 | 2 | | 1 | 3 | 3 | 3 | 2 | 1 | | | | | | | 12 | | | 4 | | |
| 67 | Pneumonia | 21 | 17 | 20 | 23 | 10 | 5 | 15 | 14 | 46 | 28 | 17 | 12 | | | | | | | 190 | 1 | 2 | 34 | | |
| 68 | Poison | | 1 | 3 | | | | | | | 2 | | | | | | | | | 5 | | | 1 | | |
| 69 | Premature birth | 3 | 4 | | | | | | | | | | | | | | | | | 7 | | | | | |
| 70 | Quinsy | 2 | 3 | | 1 | | | 1 | | 1 | 1 | | 1 | | | | | | | 7 | | | 3 | | |
| 71 | Rheumatism | | | | | | 2 | | | 1 | 1 | 2 | 1 | | | | | | | 4 | | | 3 | | |
| 72 | Rickets | | | 1 | 1 | | | | | | | | | | | | | | | 2 | | | | | |
| 73 | Scrofula | | | 1 | 1 | 2 | | 2 | 1 | 3 | 1 | | 1 | | | | | | | 9 | | | 3 | | |
| 74 | Spine, disease of | | 1 | 1 | | 1 | 1 | 1 | | | | | | | | | | | | 4 | | | 1 | | |
| 75 | Stillborn | 12 | 6 | | | | | | | | | | | | | | | | | 18 | | | | | |

## SECTION OF THE STATE OF GEORGIA—Continued.

| NATIVITIES. | | | | | SEASON OF DECEASE. | | | | DURATION OF SICKNESS. | | | | WHITES. | | | COLORED. | | | | | | | | | |
|---|---|---|---|---|---|---|---|---|---|---|---|---|---|---|---|---|---|---|---|---|---|---|---|---|---|
| | | | | | | | | | | | | | | | | Slaves. | | | | Free. | | | | | |
| | | | | | | | | | | | | | | | | Black. | | Mulatto. | | Black. | | Mul. | | | |
| California and Territories. | Ireland. | Germany. | Other foreign countries. | Unknown. | Spring. | Summer. | Autumn. | Winter. | Under 1 week. | 1 week and under 1 month. | 1 month and under 3 months. | 3 months and over. | Males. | Females. | Total. | M. | F. | M. | F. | M. | F. | M | F. | Aggregate deaths. | |
| | | | | | 19 | 10 | 7 | 13 | 29 | 6 | 9 | 4 | 4 | 2 | 6 | 22 | 19 | 1 | 1 | | | | | 49 | 1 |
| | | | | | | | 1 | 1 | | | 1 | 1 | 2 | | 2 | | | | | | | | | 2 | 2 |
| | | | | | 24 | 14 | 11 | 8 | 30 | 24 | 2 | 1 | | 40 | 40 | | 17 | | | | | | | 57 | 3 |
| | | | | | | 2 | | | | 2 | | | 2 | | 2 | | | | | | | | | 2 | 4 |
| | | | | | 4 | 9 | 9 | 3 | 13 | 8 | 3 | 1 | 13 | 5 | 18 | 4 | 2 | | 1 | | | | | 25 | 5 |
| | | | | | 2 | 3 | 7 | 4 | 10 | 5 | | 1 | 6 | 6 | 12 | | 3 | | | 1 | | | | 16 | 6 |
| | | | | | 6 | 11 | 8 | 4 | 16 | 6 | 3 | 7 | 10 | 10 | 20 | 7 | 4 | | 1 | | | | | 32 | 7 |
| | 2 | | | | 1 | 3 | 8 | 2 | 6 | 7 | | 1 | 5 | 4 | 9 | 4 | 2 | | | | | | | 15 | 8 |
| | 1 | | | | 26 | 15 | 20 | 29 | 8 | 4 | 9 | 69 | 28 | 30 | 58 | 9 | 22 | | | 1 | | | | 90 | 9 |
| | | | | | 5 | 14 | 18 | 7 | 23 | 10 | 5 | 6 | 10 | 14 | 24 | 11 | 11 | | | 1 | | | | 47 | 10 |
| | | | | | | | 2 | | 2 | | | | 1 | | 1 | | 1 | | | | | | | 2 | 11 |
| | | | | 1 | 56 | 39 | 34 | 54 | 113 | 57 | 12 | 3 | 72 | 53 | 125 | 33 | 30 | | 3 | | | | | 191 | 12 |
| | | | | | 1 | | 1 | | | | 1 | 1 | 1 | 1 | 2 | | | | | | | | | 2 | 13 |
| | | | | | 1 | | 1 | 1 | 2 | | | 1 | 2 | 1 | 3 | | | | | | | | | 3 | 14 |
| | 1 | | | | 4 | 18 | 18 | 6 | 11 | 19 | 8 | 8 | 20 | 13 | 33 | 8 | 4 | 1 | | | | | | 46 | 15 |
| | | | | | | 1 | 1 | | | 1 | | 1 | | | | 1 | 1 | | | | | | | 2 | 16 |
| | | 1 | | 4 | 50 | 54 | 44 | 45 | 22 | 25 | 36 | 111 | 51 | 58 | 109 | 32 | 49 | 1 | 3 | | | | | 194 | 17 |
| | | | | | 10 | 16 | 9 | 2 | 7 | 18 | 4 | 8 | 19 | 13 | 32 | 3 | 5 | 1 | | | | | | 41 | 18 |
| | | | | | 2 | 4 | 5 | 3 | | | | 15 | 11 | 3 | 14 | | 1 | | | | | | | 15 | 19 |
| | | | | | | | 1 | | | | 1 | | 1 | | 1 | | | | | | | | | 1 | 20 |
| | | | | | 5 | 7 | 1 | 2 | 2 | 7 | 2 | 3 | 5 | 7 | 12 | 2 | | | 1 | | | | | 15 | 21 |
| | | | | | | 1 | | | 1 | | | | | | | 1 | | | | | | | | 1 | 22 |
| | | | 1 | 1 | 45 | 46 | 102 | 29 | 45 | 139 | 33 | 6 | 81 | 16 | 97 | 32 | 88 | 3 | 3 | | | | | 223 | 23 |
| | | | | | 1 | 5 | 11 | 2 | 2 | 14 | 2 | 1 | 6 | 8 | 14 | 5 | 4 | | | | | | | 23 | 24 |
| | | | | | | 4 | 1 | | 2 | 3 | | | 2 | | 2 | 1 | 2 | | | | | | | 5 | 25 |
| | | | | | 1 | 3 | 9 | 1 | 9 | 4 | 1 | | 8 | 2 | 10 | 2 | 2 | | | | | | | 14 | 26 |
| | | | | | 2 | | 1 | | 2 | | 1 | | 2 | | 2 | | 1 | | | | | | | 3 | 27 |
| | | | | | | 1 | 3 | 2 | 4 | 1 | 1 | | 3 | 1 | 4 | 2 | | | | | | | | 6 | 28 |
| | | | | | 1 | | 1 | | 1 | | | 1 | | 2 | 2 | | | | | | | | | 2 | 29 |
| | | | | | | 1 | | | | 1 | | | | | | 1 | | | | | | | | 1 | 30 |
| | | | | | 9 | 1 | | 10 | 13 | 6 | 1 | | 8 | | 8 | 7 | 5 | | | | | | | 20 | 31 |
| | | | | | 31 | 37 | 82 | 30 | 16 | 132 | 30 | 2 | 52 | 38 | 90 | 33 | 50 | 3 | 1 | 2 | 1 | | | 180 | 32 |
| | | | | | 1 | | | 1 | 1 | 1 | | | 1 | 1 | 2 | | | | | | | | | 2 | 33 |
| | | | | | 1 | | | 1 | 1 | | | 1 | 2 | | 2 | | | | | | | | | 2 | 34 |
| | | | | | | | | 1 | | 1 | | | | 1 | 1 | | | | | | | | | 1 | 35 |
| | | | | | 3 | 1 | | 3 | 1 | 1 | | 3 | 3 | 1 | 4 | 3 | | | | | | | | 7 | 36 |
| | | | | | 4 | 1 | 4 | 1 | 3 | 1 | | 6 | 2 | 3 | 5 | 4 | 1 | | | | | | | 10 | 37 |
| | | | | | | | | 1 | 1 | | | | | | | 1 | | | | | | | | 1 | 38 |
| | | | | | 2 | 1 | 2 | 2 | 2 | 3 | | 2 | 2 | | 2 | 1 | 4 | | | | | | | 7 | 39 |
| | | | | | 2 | | | 1 | 1 | 2 | | | 1 | | 1 | 1 | 1 | | | | | | | 3 | 40 |
| | | | | | | | 1 | | 1 | 1 | | | | | | 1 | | | 1 | | | | | 2 | 41 |
| | | | | | 16 | 20 | 16 | 8 | 43 | 14 | 1 | 2 | 26 | 23 | 49 | 5 | 5 | | 1 | | | | | 60 | 42 |
| | | | | | 88 | 37 | 30 | 20 | 26 | 78 | 18 | 4 | 13 | 18 | 31 | 46 | 46 | 2 | 1 | | | | | 126 | 43 |
| | | | | | 1 | | | | | | | 1 | | | | | 1 | | | | | | | 1 | 44 |
| | | | | | 9 | 11 | 5 | 5 | 12 | 11 | 4 | 3 | 8 | 8 | 16 | 5 | 9 | | | | | | | 30 | 45 |
| | | | | | 9 | 4 | 7 | 7 | 12 | 12 | 2 | 1 | 4 | 9 | 13 | 6 | 6 | | 2 | | | | | 27 | 46 |
| | 1 | | | | 8 | 10 | 7 | 10 | 9 | 19 | 5 | 2 | 16 | 6 | 22 | 9 | 4 | | | | | | | 35 | 47 |
| | | | | | 3 | | 2 | 2 | 4 | 3 | | | 1 | 2 | 3 | 1 | 3 | | | | | | | 7 | 48 |
| | | | | | | 1 | | | | | | 1 | | 1 | 1 | | | | | | | | | 1 | 49 |
| | | | | 1 | 4 | | 5 | 1 | 6 | 3 | | 1 | 9 | | 9 | 1 | | | | | | | | 10 | 50 |
| | | | | | | | 1 | 4 | 2 | 2 | 1 | | | 5 | 5 | | | | | | | | | 5 | 51 |
| | | | | | | 1 | | | | | | 1 | 1 | | 1 | | | | | | | | | 1 | 52 |
| | | | | | | 2 | 1 | 1 | 2 | | 1 | 1 | 2 | | 2 | 2 | | | | | | | | 4 | 53 |
| | | | | | | 1 | 1 | | 2 | | | | 1 | 1 | 2 | | | | | | | | | 2 | 54 |
| | | | | | 3 | 7 | 6 | 2 | | 6 | 4 | 6 | 10 | 5 | 15 | | 3 | | | | | | | 18 | 55 |
| | | | | | | | | 2 | 1 | | 1 | | | | | | 2 | | | | | | | 2 | 56 |
| | | | | | 1 | 2 | 6 | 2 | 3 | 5 | 1 | 2 | 4 | 6 | 10 | | 1 | | | | | | | 11 | 57 |
| | | | | | 1 | | | | | | | 1 | | | | | 1 | | | | | | | 1 | 58 |
| | | | | | 5 | 20 | 2 | 1 | | 21 | 5 | 1 | 4 | 8 | 12 | 7 | 9 | | | | | | | 28 | 59 |
| | | | | | 1 | | 2 | 2 | 2 | 3 | | | 2 | 2 | 4 | 1 | | | | | | | | 5 | 60 |
| | | | | | 1 | | | 1 | 2 | | | | 2 | | 2 | | | | | | | | | 2 | 61 |
| | | | | | | | | 2 | | | 1 | 1 | 1 | 1 | 2 | | | | | | | | | 2 | 62 |
| | 2 | | 2 | 1 | 20 | 20 | 14 | 16 | 40 | 12 | 5 | 13 | 22 | 23 | 45 | 13 | 12 | | | | | | | 70 | 63 |
| | | | | 1 | 9 | 5 | 4 | 5 | 6 | 6 | 4 | 7 | 7 | 11 | 18 | 3 | 3 | | | | | | | 24 | 64 |
| | | | | | 2 | | 1 | | | 1 | 1 | 1 | 2 | | 2 | 1 | | | | | | | | 3 | 65 |
| | | | | | 8 | 2 | 1 | 5 | 10 | 5 | 1 | | 6 | 5 | 11 | 2 | 3 | | | | | | | 16 | 66 |
| | | | | 1 | 94 | 49 | 28 | 57 | 71 | 136 | 17 | 3 | 58 | 45 | 103 | 67 | 52 | 3 | 2 | 1 | | | | 228 | 67 |
| | | | | | 1 | 4 | 1 | | 4 | 2 | | | 1 | 2 | 3 | 2 | 1 | | | | | | | 6 | 68 |
| | | | | | 1 | 2 | 3 | 1 | 6 | 1 | | | 2 | 2 | 4 | | 1 | 1 | 1 | | | | | 7 | 69 |
| | | | | | 4 | 1 | 3 | 1 | 6 | 4 | | | 2 | 4 | 6 | 2 | 2 | | | | | | | 10 | 70 |
| | | | | | 1 | 4 | 2 | | | 3 | 2 | 2 | 2 | 1 | 3 | 1 | 3 | | | | | | | 7 | 71 |
| | | | | | | 1 | | 1 | | 2 | | | | | | 1 | 1 | | | | | | | 2 | 72 |
| | | | | | 2 | 4 | 3 | 3 | 2 | 1 | 1 | 3 | 5 | 2 | 7 | 3 | 2 | | | | | | | 12 | 73 |
| | | | | | 1 | 2 | 2 | | | 1 | 1 | 3 | 2 | 2 | 4 | 1 | | | | | | | | 5 | 74 |
| | | | | | 4 | 1 | 4 | 9 | 17 | 1 | | | 7 | 3 | 10 | 4 | 3 | 1 | | | | | | 18 | 75 |

## CLASSIFICATION OF DEATHS IN NORTHERN

| | Cause of death. | Ages. Under 1. M. | Under 1. F. | 1 and under 5. M. | 1 and under 5. F. | 5 and under 10. M. | 5 and under 10. F. | 10 and under 20. M. | 10 and under 20. F. | 20 and under 50. M. | 20 and under 50. F. | 50 and under 80. M. | 50 and under 80. F. | 80 and under 100. M | 80 and under 100. F. | 100 & over. M | 100 & over. F. | Age unknown. M | Age unknown. F. | Nativities. Born in State. | N. England States. | Middle States. | Southern States. | Southwest'n States. | Northwest'n States. |
|---|---|---|---|---|---|---|---|---|---|---|---|---|---|---|---|---|---|---|---|---|---|---|---|---|---|
| 1 | Suffocation | 13 | 8 | 3 | 2 | | | | | 1 | | | | | | | | | | 26 | | | 1 | | |
| 2 | Suicide | | | | | | | | 1 | | | 2 | | | | | | | | 1 | | | 2 | | |
| 3 | Syphilis | | | | | | | | 1 | | | | | | | | | | | 1 | | | | | |
| 4 | Teething | 5 | 8 | 16 | 10 | | | | | | | | | | | | | | | 39 | | | | | |
| 5 | Throat, disease of | | | 1 | 1 | 1 | | 1 | | | 1 | | | | | | | | | 5 | | | | | |
| 6 | Thrush | 4 | 2 | 2 | 1 | | | | | | | | | | | | | | | 9 | | | | | |
| 7 | Tumor | | | | 1 | | | | | | | 1 | 1 | | | | | | | 3 | | | | | |
| 8 | Ulcer | | | | | | | | | | 1 | | | | | | | | | 1 | | | | | |
| 9 | Uterus, disease of | | | | | | | | 1 | | 5 | | | | | | | | | 1 | | | 4 | 1 | |
| 10 | Venereal | | | | | | | | | | | 1 | | | | | | | | 1 | | | | | |
| 11 | White swelling | | | 1 | | 1 | | | | | | 1 | | | | | | | | 3 | | | | | |
| 12 | Worms | 7 | 4 | 27 | 18 | 2 | 3 | | | 2 | 1 | | | | | | | | | 64 | | | | | |
| 13 | Unknown | 161 | 98 | 57 | 70 | 11 | 11 | 21 | 20 | 27 | 56 | 33 | 44 | 3 | 6 | .. | 1 | 6 | 3 | 538 | .. | 3 | 76 | 4 | 1 |
| | Total | 452 | 345 | 354 | 314 | 81 | 68 | 163 | 169 | 297 | 356 | 211 | 215 | 55 | 39 | .. | 2 | 7 | 4 | 2533 | 1 | 17 | 522 | 29 | 3 |

## CLASSIFICATION OF DEATHS IN MIDDLE

*Embracing the following counties : Baldwin, Bibb, Butts, Burke, Columbia, Coweta, Crawford, Putnam, Richmond, Talbot, Troup, Twiggs,*

| | Cause of death. | Under 1. M. | Under 1. F. | 1 and under 5. M. | 1 and under 5. F. | 5 and under 10. M. | 5 and under 10. F. | 10 and under 20. M. | 10 and under 20. F. | 20 and under 50. M. | 20 and under 50. F. | 50 and under 80. M. | 50 and under 80. F. | 80 and under 100. M | 80 and under 100. F. | 100 & over. M | 100 & over. F. | Age unknown. M | Age unknown. F. | Born in State. | N. England States. | Middle States. | Southern States. | Southwest'n States. | Northwest'n States. |
|---|---|---|---|---|---|---|---|---|---|---|---|---|---|---|---|---|---|---|---|---|---|---|---|---|---|
| 1 | Abscess | | | | | | | | | 1 | | 2 | | | | | | | | 3 | | | | | |
| 2 | Accident, not specif'd | 22 | 17 | 12 | 6 | 10 | 2 | 10 | 6 | 24 | 7 | 4 | 3 | | | | | | | 115 | | 1 | 5 | | |
| 3 | ....do...burned | | 3 | 4 | 13 | 6 | 11 | 1 | 4 | | 2 | | | | 1 | | | | 1 | 44 | | | 1 | | |
| 4 | ....do...drowned | | | 1 | 2 | 2 | | 4 | 2 | 4 | | | | | | | | 1 | | 15 | | | | | |
| 5 | ....do...shot | | | | | | | | | 4 | | | | | 1 | | | | | 5 | | | | | |
| 6 | Apoplexy | 1 | | 1 | 1 | | | 1 | 1 | 3 | 5 | 3 | 5 | | | | | | | 18 | | | 3 | | |
| 7 | Asthma | | | | | | | 2 | | 1 | 1 | 2 | 4 | 1 | | | | | | 5 | | | 5 | | |
| 8 | Bladder, disease of | | | | | 1 | | | | | | 2 | | | | | | | | 2 | | | 1 | | |
| 9 | Bowels.......do | 8 | 12 | 8 | 14 | | 1 | 1 | | 1 | 1 | | 1 | | | | | | | 46 | | | 1 | | |
| 10 | Brain.......do. | 4 | 3 | | | 1 | 1 | | 3 | 1 | 1 | 2 | | | | | | | | 16 | | | | | |
| 11 | Bronchitis | 1 | | 2 | 1 | | | | | 2 | 1 | | 1 | | | | | | | 7 | | | 1 | | |
| 12 | Cancer | | | 1 | | 1 | | | 1 | 1 | 5 | 6 | 7 | | | | | 1 | | 16 | | | 6 | | |
| 13 | Catarrh | 21 | 14 | 12 | 2 | 2 | | | 2 | 1 | 4 | 3 | 1 | | | | | | | 58 | | | 2 | | |
| 14 | Childbirth | | | | | | | | 13 | | 43 | | | | | | | | | 49 | | 1 | 6 | | |
| 15 | Cholera | | | | | 1 | | | | 1 | | | | | | | | | | 2 | | | | | |
| 16 | ...do..infantum | 13 | 9 | 6 | 14 | | 2 | | | | | | | | | | | | | 40 | | 2 | 2 | | |
| 17 | ...do..morbus | 2 | 1 | 3 | 2 | 1 | | 1 | 1 | | 2 | 1 | | | | | | 1 | | 14 | | | 1 | | |
| 18 | Colic | 2 | | 1 | | | | | 1 | 3 | 5 | 5 | 4 | 2 | 1 | | | | | 14 | 1 | 1 | 7 | | |
| 19 | Congest'n, not specf'd | 2 | 1 | 2 | 4 | | 2 | 3 | 3 | 6 | 4 | 1 | | | | | | | | 25 | | | 3 | | |
| 20 | ....do....brain | 1 | | | | | | | 1 | | | | | | | | | | | 2 | | | | | |
| 21 | Consumption | | | 2 | 2 | 1 | 1 | 3 | 10 | 21 | 42 | 12 | 8 | | | | | | | 65 | | 3 | 30 | | 1 |
| 22 | Convulsions | 5 | 4 | 9 | 7 | 2 | 1 | 2 | 2 | 5 | 2 | 1 | 3 | | | | | 1 | 2 | 44 | | | 2 | | |
| 23 | Cramp | | | | | | | | | | | 1 | | | | | | | | 1 | | | | | |
| 24 | Croup | 26 | 21 | 28 | 14 | 7 | 2 | 2 | 1 | 1 | | | | | | | | | | 98 | | 1 | 2 | | |
| 25 | Debility | | 2 | | 1 | | | 1 | | | | | | | | | | | | 4 | | | | | |
| 26 | Diabetes | | | 1 | | | | | | | 1 | | | | | | | | | 2 | | | | | |
| 27 | Diarrhœa | 13 | 20 | 16 | 17 | 2 | 1 | 1 | 2 | 7 | 4 | 3 | 4 | .. | 1 | 1 | | | | 83 | | | 7 | | |
| 28 | Dropsy | 2 | 3 | 9 | 9 | 4 | 2 | 8 | 7 | 23 | 31 | 27 | 35 | 5 | 2 | | | | | 129 | | | 46 | | |
| 29 | Dysentery | 3 | 3 | 7 | 9 | 2 | | | 1 | 6 | 4 | 2 | 1 | 2 | | | | | | 37 | | | 3 | | |
| 30 | Dyspepsia | | | | | | | | 1 | 4 | 1 | 5 | 3 | | | | | | | 6 | | | 6 | | |
| 31 | Epilepsy | 2 | | 1 | | | | | | 2 | 1 | | 1 | | | | | | | 6 | | | 1 | | |
| 32 | Erysipelas | 1 | 1 | 2 | 2 | | | | 3 | | 1 | 2 | | | | | | | | 10 | | | 2 | | |
| 33 | Executed | | | | | | | | | | | 1 | | | | | | | | | | | 1 | | |
| 34 | Fever, not specified | 20 | 15 | 31 | 25 | 15 | 8 | 16 | 22 | 28 | 30 | 7 | 6 | 1 | | | | | | 207 | | | 16 | | |
| 35 | ..do..bilious | 2 | 2 | 8 | 5 | 2 | 3 | 2 | 6 | 8 | 4 | 3 | 1 | | | | | | | 43 | | 2 | 1 | | |
| 36 | ..do..brain | 3 | 2 | 4 | 3 | 2 | 2 | 4 | 2 | 5 | 1 | | 1 | | | | | | | 24 | | | 5 | | |
| 37 | ..do..congestive | 1 | | 2 | 3 | 4 | 4 | 2 | 3 | 7 | 3 | | | | | | | | | 22 | | 1 | 6 | | |
| 38 | ..do..inflammatory | | | 1 | | | | 1 | 1 | | 2 | | | | | | | | | 5 | | | | | |
| 39 | ..do..intermittent | | 2 | | | | | | 1 | | | | | | | | | | | 3 | | | | | |
| 40 | ..do..puerperal | | | | | | | | 1 | | 5 | | | | | | | | | 6 | | | | | |
| 41 | ..do..remittent | | | | 1 | 1 | | 1 | | 4 | | 1 | | | | | | | | 7 | 1 | | | | |
| 42 | ..do..scarlet | 6 | 3 | 34 | 31 | 18 | 13 | 6 | 11 | 8 | 5 | | 1 | | | | | | | 124 | | | 5 | 2 | |
| 43 | ..do..typhus | 7 | 6 | 10 | 14 | 11 | 7 | 41 | 38 | 82 | 49 | 15 | 9 | | | | | 2 | 4 | 265 | | 1 | 26 | | |
| 44 | ..do..winter | | | | | | | | | | | | | | | | | | | | | | | | |
| 45 | Gravel | | | | | | | | | | 1 | 5 | | | | | | | | 2 | | 1 | 3 | | |
| 46 | Heart, disease of | | | | | | | 1 | | 3 | 4 | 6 | 2 | | | | | 1 | | 11 | | 1 | 5 | | |
| 47 | Hemorrhage | | | | 1 | | | 1 | 2 | | 1 | | | 1 | | | | | | 6 | | | | | |
| 48 | Hernia | | | | | | | | | 1 | 2 | 1 | 1 | | | | | | | 5 | | | | | |
| 49 | Hives | 12 | 15 | 3 | 3 | | | | | | | | | | | | | | | 33 | | | | | |
| 50 | Hooping cough | 26 | 49 | 34 | 49 | 5 | 3 | 2 | 1 | 4 | 2 | 1 | 2 | | | | | 2 | | 176 | | | 4 | | |

## ECTION OF THE STATE OF GEORGIA—Continued.

| ritories. | NATIVITIES. Ireland. | Germany. | Other foreign countries. | Unknown. | SEASON OF DECEASE. Spring. | Summer. | Autumn. | Winter. | DURATION OF SICKNESS. Under 1 week. | 1 week and under 1 month. | 1 month and under 3 months. | 3 months and over. | WHITES. Males. | Females. | Total. | COLORED. Slaves. Black. M. | Slaves. Black. F. | Slaves. Mulatto. M. | Slaves. Mulatto. F. | Free. Black. M. | Free. Black. F. | Free. Mul. M | Free. Mul. F. | Aggregate deaths. | |
|---|---|---|---|---|---|---|---|---|---|---|---|---|---|---|---|---|---|---|---|---|---|---|---|---|---|
| | | | | | 9 | 11 | 2 | 5 | 27 | | | | 1 | | 1 | 16 | 10 | | | | | | | 27 | 1 |
| | | | | | 1 | 1 | | 1 | 2 | 1 | | | 2 | 1 | 3 | | | | | | | | | 3 | 2 |
| | | | | | 1 | | | | 1 | | | | | 1 | 1 | | | | | | | | | 1 | 3 |
| | | | | | 4 | 19 | 9 | 7 | 4 | 29 | 1 | 5 | 6 | 5 | 11 | 14 | 11 | 1 | 2 | | | | | 39 | 4 |
| | | | | | 1 | | 2 | 2 | 3 | 2 | | | 3 | 2 | 5 | | | | | | | | | 5 | 5 |
| | | | | | 2 | 3 | 2 | 1 | 4 | 3 | | 2 | 2 | 2 | 4 | 4 | 1 | | | | | | | 9 | 6 |
| | | | | | 1 | | 2 | | | 1 | 1 | 1 | 1 | 2 | 3 | | | | | | | | | 3 | 7 |
| | | | | | 1 | | | | | | | | | | | | 1 | | | | | | | 1 | 8 |
| | | | | | 1 | 1 | 3 | 1 | 1 | 2 | | 3 | | 4 | 4 | | 2 | | | | | | | 6 | 9 |
| | | | | | | | 1 | | | | | 1 | 1 | | 1 | | | | | | | | | 1 | 10 |
| | | | | | 2 | 1 | | | | | | 3 | 1 | | 1 | 2 | | | | | | | | 3 | 11 |
| | | | | | 20 | 23 | 11 | 10 | 23 | 25 | 10 | 6 | 12 | 10 | 22 | 24 | 15 | 2 | 1 | | | | | 64 | 12 |
| | | | 4 | 2 | 167 | 157 | 153 | 143 | 278 | 163 | 47 | 101 | 145 | 133 | 278 | 163 | 166 | 11 | 9 | | | | 1 | 628 | 13 |
| ... | 7 | 1 | 7 | 12 | 831 | 808 | 805 | 646 | 1148 | 1125 | 310 | 480 | 890 | 731 | 1621 | 692 | 742 | 32 | 37 | 6 | 1 | .. | 1 | 3132 | |

## ECTION OF THE STATE OF GEORGIA.

*ayette, Hancock, Harris, Heard, Henry, Jasper, Jefferson, Jones, Meriwether, Monroe, Pike, Ipson, Warren, Washington, Wilkinson.*

| ritories. | Ireland. | Germany. | Other foreign countries. | Unknown. | Spring. | Summer. | Autumn. | Winter. | Under 1 week. | 1 week and under 1 month. | 1 month and under 3 months. | 3 months and over. | Males. | Females. | Total. | Slaves. Black. M. | Slaves. Black. F. | Slaves. Mulatto. M. | Slaves. Mulatto. F. | Free. Black. M. | Free. Black. F. | Free. Mul. M | Free. Mul. F. | Aggregate deaths. | |
|---|---|---|---|---|---|---|---|---|---|---|---|---|---|---|---|---|---|---|---|---|---|---|---|---|---|
| | | | | | 1 | | | 2 | | 1 | | 2 | 1 | | 1 | 2 | | | | | | | | 3 | 1 |
| | 1 | | 1 | | 40 | 22 | 25 | 35 | 31 | 11 | 1 | 2 | 26 | 4 | 30 | 52 | 36 | 4 | 1 | | | | | 123 | 2 |
| | | | 1 | | 19 | 8 | 5 | 12 | 27 | 6 | 2 | | 4 | 6 | 10 | 6 | 27 | 1 | 2 | | | | | 46 | 3 |
| | | | 1 | | 4 | 5 | 4 | 3 | 8 | | | | 7 | 2 | 9 | 5 | 2 | | | | | | | 16 | 4 |
| | | | | | 2 | 1 | | 2 | 3 | 2 | | | 4 | 1 | 5 | | | | | | | | | 5 | 5 |
| | | | | | 4 | 7 | 1 | 8 | 18 | 2 | | | 7 | 6 | 13 | 2 | 5 | | 1 | | | | | 21 | 6 |
| | | | 1 | | 5 | 2 | 2 | 2 | 5 | 1 | 1 | 4 | 3 | 3 | 6 | 3 | 2 | | | | | | | 11 | 7 |
| | | | | | | 2 | | 1 | 1 | 2 | | | 1 | | 1 | 2 | | | | | | | | 3 | 8 |
| | | | | | 5 | 21 | 14 | 7 | 24 | 18 | 2 | 3 | 6 | 6 | 12 | 12 | 22 | | 1 | | | | | 47 | 9 |
| | | | | | 3 | 4 | 5 | 4 | 9 | 7 | | | 3 | 2 | 5 | 5 | 6 | | | | | | | 16 | 10 |
| | | | | | 2 | | 2 | 4 | 4 | 3 | | 1 | 3 | 1 | 4 | 2 | 2 | | | | | | | 8 | 11 |
| | | | 1 | | 8 | 3 | 8 | 3 | 2 | 4 | 3 | 13 | 6 | 7 | 13 | 3 | 5 | | 1 | 1 | | | | 23 | 12 |
| | | | 2 | | 20 | 12 | 11 | 19 | 23 | 25 | 6 | 8 | 10 | 7 | 17 | 28 | 10 | 1 | | | | | | 62 | 13 |
| | | | | | 14 | 15 | 14 | 13 | 41 | 11 | 2 | 1 | | 28 | 28 | | 28 | | | | | | | 56 | 14 |
| | | | | | 1 | 1 | | | 1 | 1 | | | 2 | | 2 | | | | | | | | | 2 | 15 |
| | | | | | 7 | 22 | 10 | 5 | 17 | 19 | 3 | 5 | 12 | 12 | 24 | 7 | 11 | | 2 | | | | | 44 | 16 |
| | | | | | 1 | 9 | 5 | | 10 | 3 | 2 | | 6 | 4 | 10 | 3 | 2 | | | | | | | 15 | 17 |
| | | | 1 | | 3 | 9 | 3 | 7 | 18 | 2 | 1 | 2 | 7 | 4 | 11 | 6 | 7 | | | | | | | 24 | 18 |
| | | | | | 7 | 7 | 10 | 4 | 15 | 8 | 2 | 2 | 9 | 5 | 14 | 5 | 9 | | | | | | | 28 | 19 |
| | | | | | 1 | | 1 | | 2 | | | | | | | 1 | 1 | | | | | | | 2 | 20 |
| | 1 | 1 | 1 | | 28 | 22 | 27 | 25 | 4 | 5 | 8 | 80 | 20 | 34 | 54 | 15 | 26 | | 1 | 2 | 1 | 2 | 1 | 102 | 21 |
| | | | | | 16 | 12 | 9 | 8 | 33 | 7 | 2 | 4 | 4 | 9 | 13 | 20 | 10 | 1 | 2 | | | | | 46 | 22 |
| | | | | | | | | 1 | 1 | | | | | | | 1 | | | | | | | | 1 | 23 |
| | | | 1 | | 26 | 23 | 31 | 22 | 82 | 13 | 5 | 1 | 31 | 15 | 46 | 33 | 22 | | 1 | | | | | 102 | 24 |
| | | | | | 3 | 1 | | | 2 | 1 | | 1 | | 2 | 2 | 1 | 1 | | | | | | | 4 | 25 |
| | | | | | | | 2 | | 1 | | 1 | | | | | 1 | 1 | | | | | | | 2 | 26 |
| | 1 | | | 1 | 9 | 38 | 38 | 7 | 20 | 34 | 25 | 13 | 20 | 27 | 47 | 19 | 22 | 4 | | | | | | 92 | 27 |
| | | | 2 | | 41 | 44 | 41 | 50 | 11 | 31 | 50 | 85 | 52 | 38 | 90 | 35 | 49 | 1 | 1 | | | | 1 | 177 | 28 |
| | | | | | 8 | 11 | 14 | 7 | | 28 | 6 | 6 | 7 | 3 | 10 | 13 | 12 | 2 | 3 | | | | | 40 | 29 |
| | | | 2 | | 4 | 3 | 5 | 2 | | 2 | 3 | 9 | 7 | 4 | 11 | 2 | 1 | | | | | | | 14 | 30 |
| | | | | | 2 | 2 | 1 | 2 | 4 | 1 | | 2 | 3 | 2 | 5 | 2 | | | | | | | | 7 | 31 |
| | | | | | 3 | 2 | 2 | 5 | 6 | 5 | 1 | | 5 | 4 | 9 | | 3 | | | | | | | 12 | 32 |
| | | | | | | | 1 | | 1 | | | | 1 | | 1 | | | | | | | | | 1 | 33 |
| | 1 | | | | 32 | 61 | 102 | 28 | 72 | 127 | 18 | 7 | 58 | 42 | 100 | 57 | 63 | 2 | 1 | 1 | | | | 224 | 34 |
| | | | | | 5 | 11 | 24 | 6 | 8 | 34 | 4 | | 13 | 10 | 23 | 12 | 10 | | 1 | | | | | 46 | 35 |
| | | | | | 7 | 9 | 8 | 5 | 17 | 9 | 2 | 1 | 14 | 8 | 22 | 4 | 3 | | | | | | | 29 | 36 |
| | | | | | 6 | 5 | 14 | 4 | 14 | 14 | | 1 | 10 | 6 | 16 | 6 | 6 | | 1 | | | | | 29 | 37 |
| | | | | | 2 | | 3 | | 2 | 3 | | | 1 | 2 | 3 | 1 | 1 | | | | | | | 5 | 38 |
| | | | | | 1 | 2 | | | 1 | 1 | 1 | | | 2 | 2 | | 1 | | | | | | | 3 | 39 |
| | | | | | 3 | 1 | 1 | 1 | | 5 | 1 | | | 2 | 2 | | 4 | | | | | | | 6 | 40 |
| | | | | | | 3 | 3 | 1 | | 7 | 1 | | 5 | | 5 | 2 | 1 | | | | | | | 8 | 41 |
| | | | | | 62 | 38 | 21 | 9 | 62 | 61 | 5 | 1 | 35 | 40 | 75 | 29 | 19 | 3 | 5 | | | | | 131 | 42 |
| | 1 | 1 | 1 | | 52 | 66 | 113 | 62 | 32 | 205 | 42 | 13 | 85 | 62 | 147 | 78 | 65 | 5 | | | | | | 295 | 43 |
| | | | | | | | | | | | | | | | | | | | | | | | | | 44 |
| | | | | | 2 | 1 | 2 | 1 | | 1 | 1 | 4 | 3 | 1 | 4 | 2 | | | | | | | | 6 | 45 |
| | | | | | 4 | 6 | 5 | 2 | 4 | 4 | 2 | 6 | 9 | 4 | 13 | 2 | 2 | | | | | | | 17 | 46 |
| | | | | | 3 | | 1 | 2 | 1 | 3 | | 2 | 1 | | 1 | 1 | 4 | | | | | | | 6 | 47 |
| | | | | | | 1 | 3 | 1 | 2 | 2 | 1 | | | | | 2 | 3 | | | | | | | 5 | 48 |
| | | | | | 7 | 12 | 8 | 6 | 24 | 5 | 3 | 1 | 9 | 13 | 22 | 6 | 5 | | | | | | | 33 | 49 |
| | | | | | 35 | 53 | 58 | 33 | 32 | 92 | 46 | 9 | 10 | 26 | 36 | 63 | 78 | 1 | 2 | | | | | 180 | 50 |

## CLASSIFICATION OF DEATHS IN MIDDLE

| | Cause of death. | Ages. Under 1. M. | F. | 1 and under 5. M. | F. | 5 and under 10. M. | F. | 10 and under 20. M. | F. | 20 and under 50. M. | F. | 50 and under 80. M. | F. | 80 and under 100. M | F. | 100 & over. M | F. | Age unknown. M | F. | Nativities. Born in State. | N. England States. | Middle States. | Southern States. | Southwest'n States. | Northeast'n States. |
|---|---|---|---|---|---|---|---|---|---|---|---|---|---|---|---|---|---|---|---|---|---|---|---|---|---|
| 1 | Inflammation | 5 | 3 | 6 | 3 | 1 | | 3 | 3 | 1 | 5 | 1 | 2 | 1 | | | | 1 | | 32 | | | 3 | | |
| 2 | .....do.....bowels | 6 | 9 | 10 | 6 | 4 | 1 | 1 | 2 | 8 | 7 | 1 | 3 | | | | | | | 52 | | | 5 | | |
| 3 | .....do.....brain | 6 | 3 | 5 | 4 | | 2 | 4 | 5 | 2 | 2 | 1 | | | | | | | | 33 | | | 1 | | |
| 4 | .....do.....stomach | | | | 1 | | | | | | | | | | | | | | | 1 | | | | | |
| 5 | Influenza | | | | 2 | | 2 | 1 | | | | 1 | | | | | | | | 5 | | 1 | | | |
| 6 | Insanity | | | | | | | | | 1 | | | | | | | | | | 1 | | | | | |
| 7 | Intemperance | | | | | | | | | 4 | | 2 | | | | | | | | 4 | | | 2 | | |
| 8 | Jaundice | | 1 | | | 1 | 1 | | | | | 2 | 2 | | | | | | | 5 | | | 2 | | |
| 9 | Kidneys, disease of | | | | | | | | | 1 | | 1 | 1 | | | | | | | 1 | | | 2 | | |
| 10 | Killed | | | | | | | 1 | 1 | 1 | | | | | | | | | | 3 | | | | | |
| 11 | Lightning | | | | | | | | | 1 | | | | | | | | | | 1 | | | | | |
| 12 | Liver, disease of | 2 | | | | | | 5 | 1 | 5 | 5 | 4 | 2 | | | | | | | 17 | 1 | | 6 | | |
| 13 | Lockjaw | 1 | | | | | | 1 | | | | | | | | | | | | 2 | | | | | |
| 14 | Lungs, disease of | 2 | 1 | 2 | | | | | | 4 | | | 1 | 1 | | | | | | 9 | | | 2 | | |
| 15 | Malformation | 2 | | | | | | | | | | | | | | | | | | 2 | | | | | |
| 16 | Marasmus | | | | 2 | | | | | | | 1 | | | | | | | | 2 | | | 1 | | |
| 17 | Measles | 4 | 3 | 9 | 8 | 1 | 3 | 1 | 1 | 2 | 3 | | | | | | | 1 | 1 | 31 | | | 6 | | |
| 18 | Mortification | | | | | | | | | | 1 | | 1 | | | | | | | 2 | | | | | |
| 19 | Murder | | | | 1 | | | | | 11 | | | | | | | | | | 10 | 1 | | 1 | | |
| 20 | Neuralgia | | | | | | | | | | | | | | | | | | | | | | | | |
| 21 | Old age | | | | | | | | | | | 13 | 18 | 24 | 29 | 1 | | | 1 | 41 | 1 | 3 | 32 | | |
| 22 | Paralysis | | | | | | | | | | 4 | 14 | 9 | 3 | 2 | | | | | 5 | | 1 | 24 | | |
| 23 | Pleurisy | 4 | | 3 | 1 | | | 2 | 4 | 9 | 4 | 3 | 1 | | | | | | | 27 | | | 4 | | |
| 24 | Pneumonia | 23 | 22 | 28 | 18 | 9 | 6 | 22 | 18 | 38 | 36 | 26 | 16 | 5 | 1 | | | | | 224 | | | 40 | | |
| 25 | Poison | 1 | 1 | 1 | | 1 | | 2 | | 1 | | | | | | | | | | 6 | | | 1 | | |
| 26 | Quinsy | 1 | 2 | 5 | 4 | | 4 | 2 | | 1 | 2 | 1 | 2 | | | | | | | 19 | | | 5 | | |
| 27 | Rheumatism | | 1 | | | | 1 | 4 | 1 | 2 | 1 | 5 | 4 | | 1 | | | | | 15 | 1 | | 4 | | |
| 28 | Scrofula | | 1 | 3 | 4 | 1 | 4 | 3 | 3 | 4 | 10 | 9 | 13 | | 1 | | | | | 41 | 1 | | 14 | | |
| 29 | Spine, disease of | | | | | | | | | 1 | | | | | | | | | | 1 | | | | | |
| 30 | Stillborn | 4 | 6 | | | | | | | | | | | | | | | | | 10 | | | | | |
| 31 | Suffocation | 16 | 21 | 2 | 2 | | | | | | | | | | | | | | | 41 | | | | | |
| 32 | Suicide | | | | | | | | | 4 | | 1 | | | | | | | | 4 | | | 1 | | |
| 33 | Sun, stroke of | | | | | | | | | 1 | | | | | | | | | | | | | | | |
| 34 | Teething | 10 | 5 | 30 | 21 | 1 | 1 | | | | | | | | | | | 1 | | 69 | | | | | |
| 35 | Throat, disease of | 1 | 3 | 6 | 5 | 4 | 2 | 1 | 5 | 2 | 2 | | 2 | | | | | | | 31 | | | 2 | | |
| 36 | Thrush | 4 | 5 | 5 | 1 | 1 | | | | | | | | | | | | | | 16 | | | | | |
| 37 | Tumor | | 2 | 1 | | | 1 | | 1 | 2 | 1 | 1 | 2 | | | | | | | 11 | | | | | |
| 38 | Ulcer | | | | | | | 1 | | | | 2 | 1 | | | | | | | 4 | | | | | |
| 39 | Uterus, disease of | | | | | | | | | | 4 | | 1 | | | | | | | 4 | | | 1 | | |
| 40 | Venereal | 1 | 1 | | | | | | | | | | 1 | | | | | | | 3 | | | | | |
| 41 | White swelling | 1 | | | | | | 2 | | 1 | 1 | | | | | | | | | 4 | | | 1 | | |
| 42 | Worms | 4 | 3 | 34 | 33 | 14 | 3 | 3 | 5 | 2 | | | | 1 | | | | | | 99 | | | 2 | | |
| 43 | Unknown | 154 | 132 | 96 | 64 | 18 | 17 | 19 | 19 | 38 | 66 | 33 | 29 | 6 | 3 | | | 15 | 8 | 648 | 1 | 1 | 58 | | |
| | Total | 458 | 433 | 501 | 435 | 157 | 114 | 195 | 222 | 414 | 431 | 256 | 215 | 53 | 43 | 2 | | 27 | 17 | 3456 | 8 | 21 | 435 | 2 | 1 |

## CLASSIFICATION OF DEATHS IN

| | Cause of death. | Under 1. M. | F. | 1 and under 5. M. | F. | 5 and under 10. M. | F. | 10 and under 20. M. | F. | 20 and under 50. M. | F. | 50 and under 80. M. | F. | 80 and under 100. M | F. | 100 & over. M | F. | Age unknown. M | F. | Born in State. | N. England States. | Middle States. | Southern States. | Southwest'n States. | Northeast'n States. |
|---|---|---|---|---|---|---|---|---|---|---|---|---|---|---|---|---|---|---|---|---|---|---|---|---|---|
| 1 | Abscess | | 1 | | 1 | 1 | 1 | 1 | 2 | 3 | 2 | 6 | | | | | | | | 14 | | 1 | 3 | | |
| 2 | Accident, not specif'd | 36 | 36 | 26 | 22 | 20 | 16 | 23 | 11 | 45 | 14 | 9 | 3 | | | | | | | 238 | 1 | 1 | 15 | 1 | 1 |
| 3 | ....do...burned | 2 | 8 | 33 | 30 | 12 | 18 | 4 | 9 | 3 | 5 | 1 | 1 | | 2 | | | | 1 | 123 | | | 5 | | |
| 4 | ....do...drowned | | | 3 | 5 | 6 | 1 | 10 | 5 | 14 | 4 | 1 | | 1 | | | | 1 | | 48 | | | 1 | | |
| 5 | ....do...shot | | | | | 1 | | 1 | | 9 | | 1 | | | 1 | | | | | 11 | | | 2 | | |
| 6 | Apoplexy | 3 | 1 | 2 | 2 | | | 2 | 1 | 12 | 10 | 9 | 14 | | | | | | | 45 | | | 10 | 1 | |
| 7 | Asthma | 1 | | | | | | 2 | | 4 | 3 | 10 | 8 | 3 | | | | | | 11 | | | 14 | | |
| 8 | Bladder, disease of | | | | | 1 | | | | | | 3 | | | | | | | | 3 | | | 1 | | |
| 9 | Bowels......do | 24 | 20 | 27 | 33 | | 2 | 5 | 2 | 4 | 4 | 6 | 5 | 3 | | | | | | 128 | | 1 | 6 | | |
| 10 | Brain ......do | 5 | 6 | 2 | 3 | 1 | 1 | 4 | 4 | 2 | 4 | 2 | 1 | | | | | | | 33 | | | 2 | | |
| 11 | Bronchitis | 4 | | 3 | 2 | | | 1 | | 3 | 4 | 3 | 2 | | | | | | | 18 | | | 4 | | |
| 12 | Cancer | | 1 | 1 | | 2 | | | 1 | 5 | 15 | 11 | 20 | 2 | 1 | | | 1 | | 37 | 1 | | 20 | | |
| 13 | Catarrh | 41 | 28 | 24 | 14 | 2 | | 1 | 3 | 3 | 8 | 7 | 4 | 1 | | | | | | 129 | | | 5 | | |
| 14 | Chicken pox | 1 | | 2 | | | | | | | 1 | | | | | | | | | 4 | | | | | |
| 15 | Childbirth | | | | | | | | 38 | | 138 | | 1 | | | | | | | 135 | | 1 | 40 | | |
| 16 | Cholera | | | 1 | 2 | 1 | | | | 6 | 2 | 3 | 2 | | | | | | | 17 | | | | | |
| 17 | ...do..infantum | 26 | 16 | 12 | 17 | 1 | 2 | 1 | | | | | | | | | | | | 69 | | 2 | 4 | | |
| 18 | ...do..morbus | 5 | 2 | 8 | 10 | 2 | 2 | 2 | 2 | 2 | 3 | 3 | 3 | 1 | | | | 1 | | 40 | | | 5 | 1 | |
| 19 | Colic | 5 | 4 | 7 | 2 | | 1 | 3 | 3 | 10 | 11 | 23 | 19 | 5 | 1 | | | | | 59 | 1 | 1 | 29 | 2 | |
| 20 | Congest'n, not spec'd | 4 | 2 | 8 | 13 | 3 | 5 | 10 | 5 | 10 | 6 | 4 | 1 | 1 | 1 | | | | | 61 | | 1 | 8 | | |
| 21 | ....do....brain | 1 | | 2 | | | 1 | | 2 | | 2 | | | | | | | | | 8 | | | | | |
| 22 | Consumption | 1 | 4 | 3 | 4 | 1 | 2 | 11 | 23 | 72 | 97 | 28 | 30 | 1 | | | | 1 | 1 | 173 | 2 | 5 | 84 | | 1 |
| 23 | Convulsions | 17 | 12 | 16 | 12 | 5 | 3 | 10 | 9 | 13 | 14 | 5 | 12 | 1 | | | | 1 | 2 | 121 | | 1 | 10 | | |

## SECTION OF THE STATE OF GEORGIA—Continued.

| NATIVITIES. | | | | | SEASON OF DECEASE. | | | | DURATION OF SICKNESS. | | | | WHITES. | | | COLORED. | | | | | | | | | |
|---|---|---|---|---|---|---|---|---|---|---|---|---|---|---|---|---|---|---|---|---|---|---|---|---|---|
| | | | | | | | | | | | | | | | | Slaves. | | | | Free. | | | | | |
| | | | | | | | | | | | | | | | | Black. | | Mulatto. | | Black. | | Mul. | | | |
| California and Territories. | Ireland. | Germany. | Other foreign countries. | Unknown. | Spring. | Summer. | Autumn. | Winter. | Under 1 week. | 1 week and under 1 month. | 1 month and under 3 months. | 3 months and over. | Males. | Females. | Total. | M. | F. | M. | F. | M. | F. | M | F. | Aggregate deaths. | |
| .... | ... | .. | .... | ... | 8 | 7 | 10 | 6 | 11 | 16 | 3 | 1 | 9 | 12 | 21 | 10 | 4 | .... | .... | ... | ... | .. | .. | 35 | 1 |
| .... | 1 | .. | .... | ... | 7 | 17 | 21 | 13 | 22 | 27 | 6 | 3 | 16 | 13 | 29 | 11 | 15 | 3 | .... | ... | ... | .. | .. | 58 | 2 |
| .... | ... | .. | .... | ... | 8 | 12 | 8 | 4 | 23 | 8 | .... | .... | 11 | 8 | 19 | 5 | 6 | 2 | 2 | ... | ... | .. | .. | 34 | 3 |
| .... | ... | .. | .... | ... | .... | .... | .... | 1 | 1 | .... | .... | .... | .... | 1 | 1 | .... | .... | .... | .... | ... | ... | .. | .. | 1 | 4 |
| .... | ... | .. | .... | ... | .... | 1 | 3 | 1 | 1 | 3 | 1 | .... | 1 | 2 | 3 | 1 | 2 | .... | .... | ... | ... | .. | .. | 6 | 5 |
| .... | ... | .. | .... | ... | .... | .... | 1 | .... | .... | .... | .... | 1 | 1 | .... | 1 | .... | .... | .... | .... | ... | ... | .. | .. | 1 | 6 |
| .... | ... | .. | .... | ... | 1 | 1 | .... | 4 | 3 | 1 | 1 | 1 | 5 | .... | 5 | 1 | .... | .... | .... | ... | ... | .. | .. | 6 | 7 |
| .... | ... | .. | .... | ... | 1 | 3 | 2 | 1 | 2 | 4 | 1 | .... | 3 | 3 | 6 | .... | 1 | .... | .... | ... | ... | .. | .. | 7 | 8 |
| .... | ... | .. | .... | ... | 1 | 1 | .... | 1 | .... | 1 | 2 | .... | .... | 1 | 1 | 1 | .... | 1 | .... | ... | ... | .. | .. | 3 | 9 |
| .... | ... | .. | .... | ... | 2 | .... | .... | 1 | 3 | .... | .... | .... | .... | .... | .... | 1 | 1 | 1 | .... | ... | ... | .. | .. | 3 | 10 |
| .... | ... | .. | .... | ... | 1 | .... | .... | .... | 1 | .... | .... | .... | .... | .... | .... | 1 | .... | .... | .... | ... | ... | .. | .. | 1 | 11 |
| .... | ... | .. | .... | ... | 4 | 6 | 5 | 9 | 2 | 5 | 9 | 8 | 11 | 6 | 17 | 4 | 2 | 1 | .... | ... | ... | .. | .. | 24 | 12 |
| .... | ... | .. | .... | ... | 1 | .... | .... | 1 | 1 | 1 | .... | .... | .... | .... | .... | 2 | .... | .... | .... | ... | ... | .. | .. | 2 | 13 |
| .... | ... | .. | .... | ... | 2 | 4 | 2 | 3 | 4 | 4 | 2 | 1 | 4 | 1 | 5 | 5 | 1 | .... | .... | ... | ... | .. | .. | 11 | 14 |
| .... | ... | .. | .... | ... | .... | .... | .... | 2 | .... | 1 | .... | 1 | .... | .... | .... | 2 | .... | .... | .... | ... | ... | .. | .. | 2 | 15 |
| .... | ... | .. | .... | ... | 1 | 2 | .... | .... | 1 | .... | .... | 2 | .... | 1 | 1 | 1 | 1 | .... | .... | ... | ... | .. | .. | 3 | 16 |
| .... | ... | .. | .... | ... | 9 | 20 | 5 | 3 | 4 | 23 | 6 | 3 | 7 | 7 | 14 | 9 | 12 | 2 | .... | ... | ... | .. | .. | 37 | 17 |
| .... | ... | .. | .... | ... | 1 | 1 | .... | .... | 2 | .... | .... | .... | .... | 1 | 1 | .... | 1 | .... | .... | ... | ... | .. | .. | 2 | 18 |
| .... | ... | .. | .... | ... | 5 | 2 | 3 | 2 | 8 | 3 | 1 | .... | 8 | .... | 8 | 3 | 1 | .... | .... | ... | ... | .. | .. | 12 | 19 |
| .... | ... | .. | .... | ... | .... | .... | .... | .... | .... | .... | .... | .... | .... | .... | .... | .... | .... | .... | .... | ... | ... | .. | .. | ... | 20 |
| .... | 1 | .. | 6 | 2 | 23 | 25 | 25 | 13 | 55 | 13 | 3 | 15 | 13 | 15 | 28 | 23 | 33 | 2 | .... | ... | ... | .. | .. | 86 | 21 |
| .... | ... | .. | 2 | ... | 3 | 9 | 10 | 10 | 7 | 6 | 3 | 16 | 16 | 10 | 26 | 1 | 5 | .... | .... | ... | ... | .. | .. | 32 | 22 |
| .... | ... | .. | .... | ... | 7 | 7 | 4 | 6 | 12 | 15 | 2 | 2 | 2 | 3 | 5 | 18 | 7 | .... | .... | 1 | ... | .. | .. | 31 | 23 |
| .... | ... | 1 | 3 | ... | 124 | 46 | 29 | 67 | 98 | 143 | 22 | 5 | 56 | 43 | 99 | 87 | 71 | 8 | 3 | ... | ... | .. | .. | 268 | 24 |
| .... | ... | .. | .... | ... | .... | 3 | 3 | 1 | 6 | .... | .... | 1 | 2 | .... | 2 | 4 | 1 | .... | .... | ... | ... | .. | .. | 7 | 25 |
| .... | ... | .. | .... | ... | 8 | 3 | 4 | 9 | 12 | 8 | 3 | 1 | 7 | 8 | 15 | 3 | 6 | .... | .... | ... | ... | .. | .. | 24 | 26 |
| .... | ... | .. | .... | ... | 8 | 4 | 3 | 5 | ... | 7 | 4 | 9 | 5 | 5 | 10 | 5 | 4 | 1 | .... | ... | ... | .. | .. | 20 | 27 |
| .... | ... | .. | .... | ... | 11 | 22 | 16 | 7 | 3 | 11 | 4 | 38 | 9 | 12 | 21 | 10 | 23 | 1 | 1 | ... | ... | .. | .. | 56 | 28 |
| .... | ... | .. | .... | ... | .... | 1 | .... | .... | .... | 1 | .... | .... | .... | .... | .... | 1 | .... | .... | .... | ... | ... | .. | .. | 1 | 29 |
| .... | ... | .. | .... | ... | 4 | 3 | 1 | 2 | 10 | .... | .... | .... | 4 | 1 | 5 | .... | 5 | .... | .... | ... | ... | .. | .. | 10 | 30 |
| .... | ... | .. | .... | ... | 14 | 7 | 11 | 9 | 40 | .... | 1 | .... | 5 | .... | 5 | 13 | 23 | .... | .... | ... | ... | .. | .. | 41 | 31 |
| .... | ... | .. | .... | ... | 2 | 1 | 1 | 1 | 5 | .... | .... | .... | 5 | .... | 5 | .... | .... | .... | .... | ... | ... | .. | .. | 5 | 32 |
| .... | 1 | .. | .... | ... | .... | 1 | .... | .... | 1 | .... | .... | .... | 1 | .... | 1 | .... | .... | .... | .... | ... | ... | .. | .. | 1 | 33 |
| .... | ... | .. | .... | ... | 5 | 21 | 35 | 8 | 25 | 26 | 14 | 4 | 10 | 3 | 13 | 31 | 23 | 1 | 1 | ... | ... | .. | .. | 69 | 34 |
| .... | ... | .. | .... | ... | 6 | 6 | 11 | 10 | 10 | 23 | .... | .... | 7 | 9 | 16 | 7 | 10 | .... | .... | ... | ... | .. | .. | 33 | 35 |
| .... | ... | .. | .... | ... | 7 | 3 | 6 | .... | 5 | 8 | 2 | 1 | 1 | 2 | 3 | 9 | 4 | .... | .... | ... | ... | .. | .. | 16 | 36 |
| .... | ... | .. | .... | ... | 1 | 3 | 4 | 3 | 1 | .... | .... | 9 | 1 | 4 | 5 | 3 | 2 | .... | 1 | ... | ... | .. | .. | 11 | 37 |
| .... | ... | .. | .... | ... | .... | 4 | .... | .... | .... | 1 | 2 | 1 | 1 | .... | 1 | 2 | 1 | .... | .... | ... | ... | .. | .. | 4 | 38 |
| .... | ... | .. | .... | ... | 1 | 3 | .... | 1 | .... | 2 | .... | 3 | .... | 3 | 3 | .... | 2 | .... | .... | ... | ... | .. | .. | 5 | 39 |
| .... | ... | .. | .... | ... | 1 | 1 | 1 | .... | 1 | .... | .... | 2 | .... | .... | .... | 1 | 2 | .... | .... | ... | ... | .. | .. | 3 | 40 |
| .... | ... | .. | .... | ... | .... | 5 | .... | .... | .... | 1 | 2 | 2 | 2 | .... | 2 | 2 | 1 | .... | .... | ... | ... | .. | .. | 5 | 41 |
| .... | ... | .. | 1 | ... | 24 | 30 | 35 | 13 | 50 | 40 | 10 | 2 | 10 | 8 | 18 | 43 | 35 | 5 | 1 | ... | ... | .. | .. | 102 | 42 |
| .... | 3 | .. | 6 | ... | 181 | 198 | 174 | 157 | 383 | 181 | 61 | 61 | 133 | 106 | 239 | 238 | 229 | 6 | 3 | 2 | ... | .. | .. | 717 | 43 |
| .... | 11 | 3 | 33 | 3 | 990 | 1060 | 1090 | 795 | 1508 | 1409 | 418 | 482 | 886 | 742 | 1628 | 1109 | 1127 | 59 | 38 | 7 | 1 | 2 | 2 | 3973 | |

## THE STATE OF GEORGIA—AGGREGATE.

| | | | | | | | | | | | | | | | | | | | | | | | | | |
|---|---|---|---|---|---|---|---|---|---|---|---|---|---|---|---|---|---|---|---|---|---|---|---|---|---|
| .... | ... | .. | .... | ... | 3 | 5 | 6 | 4 | 3 | 5 | 2 | 8 | 7 | 4 | 11 | 4 | 2 | .... | 1 | ... | ... | .. | .. | 18 | 1 |
| .... | 2 | .. | 2 | ... | 91 | 43 | 50 | 72 | 148 | 23 | 2 | 6 | 62 | 19 | 81 | 91 | 81 | 6 | 2 | ... | ... | .. | .. | 261 | 2 |
| .... | ... | .. | 1 | ... | 48 | 21 | 13 | 44 | 84 | 24 | 7 | 2 | 18 | 21 | 39 | 36 | 51 | 1 | 2 | ... | ... | .. | .. | 129 | 3 |
| .... | 1 | .. | 1 | ... | 11 | 17 | 8 | 15 | 43 | .... | .... | .... | 11 | 2 | 13 | 24 | 12 | 1 | 1 | ... | ... | .. | .. | 51 | 4 |
| .... | ... | .. | .... | ... | 4 | 4 | 1 | 4 | 10 | 2 | .... | 1 | 11 | 1 | 12 | 1 | .... | .... | .... | ... | ... | .. | .. | 13 | 5 |
| .... | ... | .. | .... | ... | 14 | 15 | 10 | 15 | 52 | 2 | .... | 1 | 18 | 17 | 35 | 10 | 10 | .... | 1 | ... | ... | .. | .. | 56 | 6 |
| ... | 2 | .. | 4 | ... | 15 | 6 | 3 | 7 | 7 | 5 | 4 | 15 | 8 | 6 | 14 | 12 | 5 | .... | .... | ... | ... | .. | .. | 31 | 7 |
| .... | ... | .. | .... | ... | .... | 3 | .... | 1 | 1 | 2 | .... | 1 | 2 | .... | 2 | 2 | .... | .... | .... | ... | ... | .. | .. | 4 | 8 |
| .... | ... | .. | .... | ... | 25 | 44 | 46 | 20 | 57 | 55 | 12 | 10 | 33 | 18 | 51 | 35 | 45 | 1 | 3 | ... | ... | .. | .. | 135 | 9 |
| .... | ... | .. | .... | ... | 9 | 9 | 10 | 7 | 21 | 14 | .... | .... | 9 | 8 | 17 | 7 | 11 | .... | .... | ... | ... | .. | .. | 35 | 10 |
| .... | ... | .. | .... | ... | 6 | 4 | 5 | 7 | 6 | 8 | 1 | 7 | 7 | 3 | 10 | 7 | 4 | .... | 1 | ... | ... | .. | .. | 22 | 11 |
| .... | ... | .. | 2 | ... | 21 | 15 | 16 | 7 | 5 | 8 | 3 | 43 | 16 | 28 | 44 | 4 | 8 | .... | 1 | 2 | ... | .. | 1 | 60 | 12 |
| .... | ... | .. | 2 | ... | 48 | 22 | 20 | 46 | 61 | 39 | 19 | 13 | 16 | 12 | 28 | 61 | 44 | 2 | 1 | ... | ... | .. | .. | 136 | 13 |
| .... | ... | .. | .... | ... | .... | 1 | 2 | 1 | ... | 2 | 1 | 1 | 3 | 1 | 4 | .... | .... | .... | .... | ... | ... | .. | .. | 4 | 14 |
| .... | 1 | .. | .... | ... | 56 | 43 | 36 | 42 | 108 | 55 | 10 | 3 | .... | 104 | 104 | .... | 72 | .... | 1 | ... | ... | .. | .. | 177 | 15 |
| .... | ... | .. | .... | ... | 2 | 10 | 5 | .... | 13 | 4 | .... | .... | 4 | 1 | 5 | 7 | 4 | .... | 1 | ... | ... | .. | .. | 17 | 16 |
| .... | ... | .. | .... | ... | 11 | 34 | 20 | 10 | 32 | 30 | 7 | 6 | 28 | 18 | 46 | 11 | 14 | 1 | 3 | ... | ... | .. | .. | 75 | 17 |
| .... | ... | .. | .... | ... | 5 | 16 | 17 | 8 | 30 | 13 | 2 | 1 | 19 | 14 | 33 | 4 | 8 | .... | .... | 1 | ... | .. | .. | 46 | 18 |
| .... | 1 | .. | 1 | ... | 17 | 31 | 19 | 21 | 47 | 18 | 7 | 20 | 33 | 23 | 56 | 20 | 17 | .... | 1 | ... | ... | .. | .. | 94 | 19 |
| .... | 3 | .. | .... | ... | 11 | 16 | 36 | 9 | 48 | 17 | 3 | 3 | 25 | 16 | 41 | 15 | 17 | .... | .... | ... | ... | .. | .. | 73 | 20 |
| .... | ... | .. | .... | ... | 2 | 3 | 2 | 1 | 7 | 1 | .... | .... | 1 | 3 | 4 | 2 | 2 | .... | .... | ... | ... | .. | .. | 8 | 21 |
| .... | 8 | 3 | 2 | 1 | 79 | 60 | 65 | 75 | 12 | 15 | 29 | 218 | 76 | 87 | 163 | 36 | 67 | .... | 5 | 3 | 1 | 3 | 1 | 279 | 22 |
| .... | ... | .. | .... | ... | 29 | 37 | 36 | 26 | 88 | 23 | 7 | 11 | 24 | 30 | 54 | 42 | 32 | 1 | 2 | 1 | ... | .. | .. | 132 | 23 |

CLASSIFICATION OF DEATHS IN

| | Cause of death. | AGES. | | | | | | | | | | | | | | | | | | NATIVITIES. | | | | | |
|---|---|---|---|---|---|---|---|---|---|---|---|---|---|---|---|---|---|---|---|---|---|---|---|---|---|
| | | Under 1. | | 1 and under 5. | | 5 and under 10. | | 10 and under 20. | | 20 and under 50. | | 50 and under 80. | | 80 and under 100. | | 100 & over. | | Age unknown. | | Born in State. | N. England States. | Middle States. | Southern States. | Southwest'n States. | Northwest'n States. |
| | | M. | F. | M. | F. | M. | F. | M. | F. | M. | F. | M. | F. | M | F. | M | F. | M | F. | | | | | | |
| 1 | Cramp | 1 | | | | | | | | 1 | 1 | 1 | | | | | | | | 3 | | | 1 | | |
| 2 | Croup | 93 | 83 | 78 | 51 | 13 | 12 | 3 | 1 | 1 | 1 | 4 | 1 | 2 | 1 | | | | | 331 | | 1 | 6 | 4 | |
| 3 | Debility | | 3 | | 3 | 1 | | 1 | | | | 1 | 3 | | 1 | | | | | 11 | | | | 1 | |
| 4 | Diabetes | | | 1 | | | 1 | | | 1 | 1 | 2 | | | | | | | | 4 | | | 2 | | |
| 5 | Diarrhœa | 22 | 33 | 40 | 34 | 6 | 3 | 8 | 3 | 12 | 8 | 7 | 12 | | 1 | 1 | | | | 167 | | 3 | 16 | | |
| 6 | Dirt eating | | | 1 | | | | | 1 | | 1 | | | | | | | | | 3 | | | | | |
| 7 | Dropsy | 13 | 13 | 27 | 26 | 25 | 12 | 30 | 36 | 55 | 96 | 110 | 97 | 17 | 14 | | | | | 396 | | 4 | 149 | | |
| 8 | Dysentery | 14 | 9 | 22 | 27 | 6 | 2 | 4 | 2 | 15 | 9 | 7 | 6 | 3 | 2 | | | | | 112 | | | 12 | | |
| 9 | Dyspepsia | | | | | 1 | | | 1 | 12 | 4 | 8 | 4 | 1 | | | | | | 18 | | | 10 | 1 | |
| 10 | Epilepsy | 2 | | 1 | | | | | | 4 | 1 | | 1 | | | | | | | 8 | | | 1 | | |
| 11 | Erysipelas | 3 | 4 | 6 | 6 | 1 | | 1 | 3 | 8 | 9 | 8 | 4 | | | | | | | 36 | 1 | 1 | 13 | | |
| 12 | Executed | | | | | | | | | 1 | | 1 | | | | | | | | | | | 2 | | |
| 13 | Fever, not specified | 49 | 37 | 75 | 76 | 44 | 32 | 54 | 71 | 105 | 87 | 34 | 25 | 3 | 1 | | | | | 588 | 2 | 1 | 79 | 6 | |
| 14 | ..do..bilious | 2 | 3 | 11 | 7 | 4 | 9 | 10 | 13 | 21 | 15 | 6 | 2 | | 1 | | | | | 88 | 2 | 5 | 3 | 3 | |
| 15 | ..do..brain | 4 | 4 | 5 | 3 | 2 | 3 | 4 | 6 | 8 | 2 | | 1 | | | | | | | 34 | | 2 | 5 | | |
| 16 | ..do..congestive | 2 | | 5 | 7 | 6 | 4 | 4 | 5 | 21 | 6 | | 1 | | | | | | | 45 | | 2 | 8 | | |
| 17 | ..do..inflammatory | | 1 | 1 | 1 | | 2 | 2 | 1 | 1 | 4 | | | | | | | | | 12 | | | 1 | | |
| 18 | ..do..intermittent | 1 | 2 | 1 | 1 | 2 | | 1 | 1 | 1 | | | | | | | | | | 10 | | | | | |
| 19 | ..do..puerperal | | | | | | | | 1 | | 7 | | | | | | | | | 7 | | | 1 | | |
| 20 | ..do..remittent | 1 | | | 1 | 1 | | 1 | | 5 | | 1 | | | | | | | | 9 | 1 | | | | |
| 21 | ..do..scarlet | 16 | 7 | 52 | 39 | 25 | 23 | 12 | 13 | 4 | 5 | | 1 | | | | | | | 191 | | | 7 | 2 | |
| 22 | ..do..typhus | 14 | 14 | 24 | 26 | 19 | 19 | 78 | 78 | 140 | 95 | 27 | 17 | | | | | 2 | 4 | 488 | | 1 | 61 | 3 | |
| 23 | ..do..winter | | | | | | 1 | 1 | | | | | | | | | | | | 2 | | | | | |
| 24 | .do..yellow | | | | 1 | | | | | | | | | | | | | | | 1 | | | | | |
| 25 | Frozen | | | | | | | | | 1 | | 1 | | | | | | | | 1 | | | 1 | | |
| 26 | Gout | | | | | | | | | | 1 | 1 | | | | | | | | 1 | | | 1 | | |
| 27 | Gravel | 1 | | 1 | 1 | | | | | 3 | 1 | 8 | | 2 | | | | | | 6 | | 1 | 9 | 1 | |
| 28 | Heart, disease of | 2 | 1 | 1 | | 1 | | 3 | | 5 | 5 | 8 | 6 | | | | | 1 | | 23 | | 1 | 9 | | |
| 29 | Heat | | | | | | | | | | | 1 | | | | | | | | | | | 1 | | |
| 30 | Hemorrhage | 1 | 2 | 4 | 1 | | | 3 | 3 | 1 | 5 | 1 | 1 | 1 | | | | | | 22 | | 1 | | | |
| 31 | Hernia | | | | | | | 1 | | 3 | 3 | 3 | 2 | | | | | | | 11 | | | 1 | | |
| 32 | Hip, disease of | | | 1 | 1 | | | | | | | | | | | | | | | 2 | | | | | |
| 33 | Hives | 48 | 50 | 14 | 5 | | | | | | | | | | | | | | | 115 | | | 1 | 1 | |
| 34 | Hooping cough | 67 | 96 | 83 | 103 | 9 | 6 | 6 | 3 | 4 | 3 | 1 | 2 | | | | | 2 | | 379 | | | 5 | 1 | |
| 35 | Hydrophobia | | | | | | | | 1 | | | | | | | | | | | 1 | | | | | |
| 36 | Inflamt'n, not specf'd | 11 | 5 | 9 | 9 | 4 | 1 | 9 | 7 | 5 | 18 | 6 | 5 | 2 | | | | 1 | | 81 | | | 11 | | |
| 37 | ....do....bowels | 11 | 17 | 13 | 10 | 6 | 3 | 2 | 8 | 12 | 11 | 7 | 4 | | | | | | | 88 | | 1 | 14 | | |
| 38 | ....do....brain | 13 | 12 | 15 | 11 | 2 | 3 | 9 | 7 | 6 | 6 | 5 | 1 | | | | | | | 80 | | | 8 | | 1 |
| 39 | ....do....stomach | | | | 1 | 1 | | | | | | | | | | | | | | 2 | | | | | |
| 40 | Influenza | | 5 | | 4 | | 2 | 3 | | 1 | | 2 | 1 | | | | | | | 15 | | | 3 | | |
| 41 | Insanity | | | | | | | | | 2 | | | 1 | | | | | | | 3 | | | | | |
| 42 | Intemperance | | | | | | | | | 19 | | 11 | | 2 | | | | | | 14 | | | 13 | | |
| 43 | Jaundice | | 3 | | 2 | 1 | 1 | | | | 1 | 2 | 2 | | | | | | | 10 | | | 2 | | |
| 44 | Kidneys, disease of | | | | | | | | | 2 | | 1 | 1 | | | | | | | 2 | | | 2 | | |
| 45 | Killed | | | | | 1 | | 1 | 1 | 8 | | | | 1 | | | | | | 9 | | | 3 | | |
| 46 | Lightning | | | | | 1 | 1 | 3 | 2 | 2 | 1 | | | | | | | | | 8 | | | 2 | | |
| 47 | Liver, disease of | 2 | | 1 | 2 | | 1 | 6 | 1 | 15 | 9 | 9 | 10 | | | | | | | 35 | 2 | | 17 | | |
| 48 | Lockjaw | 10 | 9 | | 1 | | | 2 | | 1 | | | | | | | | | | 22 | | | 1 | | |
| 49 | Lungs, disease of | 5 | 3 | 3 | 2 | | | | | 9 | 8 | 6 | 5 | 1 | 1 | | | | | 33 | | 1 | 8 | | |
| 50 | Malformation | 2 | 3 | | | | | | | | | | | | | | | | | 5 | | | | | |
| 51 | Mania-a-potu | | | | | | | | | 2 | | 2 | | | | | | | | 1 | | | 3 | | |
| 52 | Marasmus | | | | 3 | | | | | | | 1 | | | | | | | | 3 | | | 1 | | |
| 53 | Measles | 5 | 10 | 19 | 15 | 1 | 5 | 4 | 3 | 3 | 7 | | | | | | | 1 | 1 | 67 | | | 7 | | |
| 54 | Mortification | | 1 | | | | | 2 | | 1 | 3 | 1 | 1 | 1 | | | | | | 8 | | | 2 | | |
| 55 | Murder | 3 | 2 | 1 | 1 | | | | | 16 | | | | | | | | | | 19 | 1 | | 3 | | |
| 56 | Neuralgia | | | | 1 | | | | | 1 | | 1 | 2 | | | | | | | 3 | | 1 | 1 | | |
| 57 | Old age | | | | | | | | | | 1 | 36 | 65 | 73 | 70 | 1 | 1 | | 1 | 115 | 2 | 7 | 96 | | |
| 58 | Paralysis | 1 | | | | 1 | | 2 | | 1 | 7 | 25 | 19 | 4 | 6 | | | | | 20 | | 1 | 40 | | |
| 59 | Piles | | | | | | | | | 1 | | 2 | | | | | | | | 2 | | | 1 | | |
| 60 | Pleurisy | 4 | | 4 | 2 | 2 | | 6 | 8 | 21 | 12 | 15 | 3 | | | | | | | 65 | | 1 | 10 | | |
| 61 | Pneumonia | 52 | 45 | 56 | 47 | 22 | 13 | 53 | 51 | 113 | 88 | 66 | 38 | 6 | 1 | | | | | 530 | 1 | 3 | 109 | | |
| 62 | Poison | 1 | 3 | 5 | | 2 | 2 | 3 | 1 | 2 | 3 | | | | | | | | | 20 | | | 2 | | |
| 63 | Prematurity of birth | 4 | 4 | | | | | | | | | | | | | | | | | 8 | | | | | |
| 64 | Quinsy | 3 | 7 | 7 | 5 | 2 | 4 | 3 | | 3 | 4 | 1 | 4 | 1 | | | | | | 35 | | | 9 | | |
| 65 | Rheumatism | | 1 | | | | 4 | 4 | 1 | 3 | 4 | 10 | 6 | | 1 | | | | | 24 | 1 | | 9 | | |
| 66 | Rickets | | | 1 | 1 | | | | | | | | | | | | | | | 2 | | | | | |
| 67 | Scrofula | 1 | 2 | 4 | 7 | 4 | 4 | 6 | 6 | 13 | 16 | 10 | 16 | | 1 | | | | | 68 | 1 | | 20 | | |
| 68 | Spine, disease of | | 1 | 2 | | 2 | 1 | 1 | | 1 | 1 | | | | | | | | | 8 | | | 1 | | |
| 69 | Stillborn | 17 | 12 | | | | | | | | | | | | | | | | | 29 | | | | | |
| 70 | Stomach, disease of | | | | | | | | | | | | 1 | | | | | | | 1 | | | | | |
| 71 | Suffocation | 38 | 37 | 7 | 6 | | | | | 1 | | | | | | | | | | 88 | | | 1 | | |
| 72 | Suicide | | | | | | | | 3 | 5 | | 6 | | | | | | | | 9 | | | 5 | | |
| 73 | Sun stroke | | | | | | | | | 1 | | | | | | | | | | | | | | | |
| 74 | Syphilis | | | | | | | | 1 | | | | | | | | | | | 1 | | | | | |
| 75 | Teething | 30 | 21 | 67 | 43 | 1 | 2 | | | | | | | | | | | 1 | | 165 | | | | | |

THE STATE OF GEORGIA—AGGREGATE—Continued.

| Nativities: California and Territories. | Nativities: Ireland. | Nativities: Germany. | Nativities: Other foreign countries. | Nativities: Unknown. | Season of decease: Spring. | Season of decease: Summer. | Season of decease: Autumn. | Season of decease: Winter. | Duration of sickness: Under 1 week. | Duration of sickness: 1 week and under 1 month. | Duration of sickness: 1 month and under 3 months. | Duration of sickness: 3 months and over. | Whites: Males. | Whites: Females. | Whites: Total. | Colored: Slaves: Black: M. | Colored: Slaves: Black: F. | Colored: Slaves: Mulatto: M. | Colored: Slaves: Mulatto: F. | Colored: Free: Black: M. | Colored: Free: Black: F. | Colored: Free: Mul.: M | Colored: Free: Mul.: F. | Aggregate deaths. | |
|---|---|---|---|---|---|---|---|---|---|---|---|---|---|---|---|---|---|---|---|---|---|---|---|---|---|
| | | | | | 1 | | 2 | 1 | 4 | | | | 2 | | 2 | 1 | 1 | | | | | | | 4 | 1 |
| | | | 1 | 1 | 93 | 69 | 82 | 92 | 232 | 81 | 19 | 5 | 121 | 87 | 208 | 72 | 58 | 1 | 5 | | | | | 344 | 2 |
| | | | 1 | | 7 | 2 | 2 | 2 | 4 | 1 | 3 | 5 | 1 | 5 | 6 | 2 | 4 | | | | 1 | | | 13 | 3 |
| | | | | | 1 | | 3 | 1 | 3 | 1 | 1 | 1 | 2 | 1 | 3 | 2 | 1 | | | | | | | 6 | 4 |
| | 2 | | 1 | 1 | 23 | 73 | 71 | 23 | 44 | 84 | 39 | 23 | 49 | 55 | 104 | 41 | 37 | 5 | 2 | | | 1 | | 190 | 5 |
| | | | | | 1 | 1 | 1 | | | 1 | | 2 | | | | 1 | 2 | | | | | | | 3 | 6 |
| | 3 | 1 | 8 | 10 | 149 | 146 | 141 | 133 | 48 | 87 | 125 | 306 | 161 | 133 | 294 | 112 | 151 | 4 | 8 | | 1 | | 1 | 571 | 7 |
| | 2 | 1 | 1 | | 27 | 47 | 34 | 16 | 24 | 69 | 12 | 19 | 39 | 26 | 65 | 28 | 28 | 4 | 3 | | | | | 128 | 8 |
| | | | 2 | | 6 | 8 | 10 | 6 | | 2 | 3 | 26 | 20 | 7 | 27 | 2 | 2 | | | | | | | 31 | 9 |
| | | | | | 2 | 3 | 2 | 2 | 5 | 1 | 1 | 2 | 5 | 2 | 7 | 2 | | | | | | | | 9 | 10 |
| | 1 | 1 | | | 21 | 12 | 7 | 13 | 11 | 32 | 4 | 5 | 24 | 18 | 42 | 3 | 6 | | 2 | | | | | 53 | 11 |
| | | | | | | 1 | 1 | | 2 | | | | 1 | | 1 | 1 | | | | | | | | 2 | 12 |
| | 11 | | 5 | 1 | 100 | 161 | 339 | 91 | 189 | 404 | 79 | 21 | 215 | 126 | 341 | 140 | 195 | 7 | 8 | 1 | | 1 | | 693 | 13 |
| | 1 | | 2 | | 7 | 17 | 61 | 12 | 26 | 66 | 7 | 1 | 33 | 30 | 63 | 20 | 19 | 1 | 1 | | | | | 104 | 14 |
| | 1 | | | | 8 | 17 | 12 | 5 | 25 | 14 | 2 | 1 | 18 | 11 | 29 | 5 | 6 | | 2 | | | | | 42 | 15 |
| | 5 | | 1 | | 8 | 13 | 28 | 12 | 29 | 30 | 1 | 1 | 26 | 11 | 37 | 12 | 10 | | 2 | | | | | 61 | 16 |
| | | | | | 5 | 1 | 7 | | 6 | 5 | 2 | | 3 | 5 | 8 | 1 | 4 | | | | | | | 13 | 17 |
| | | | | | 1 | 3 | 4 | 2 | 6 | 2 | 2 | | 3 | 3 | 6 | 3 | 1 | | | | | | | 10 | 18 |
| | | | | | 4 | 1 | 2 | 1 | 1 | 5 | 1 | 1 | | 4 | 4 | | 4 | | | | | | | 8 | 19 |
| | | | | | | 4 | 4 | 1 | | 9 | 1 | | 6 | | 6 | 3 | 1 | | | | | | | 10 | 20 |
| | 2 | | | | 90 | 56 | 31 | 24 | 101 | 85 | 12 | 2 | 53 | 56 | 109 | 52 | 32 | 3 | 5 | 1 | | | | 202 | 21 |
| | 1 | 2 | 1 | | 98 | 126 | 221 | 110 | 61 | 398 | 78 | 17 | 164 | 123 | 287 | 130 | 128 | 8 | 1 | 2 | 1 | | | 557 | 22 |
| | | | | | 1 | | | 1 | 1 | 1 | | | 1 | 1 | 2 | | | | | | | | | 2 | 23 |
| | | | | | | | 1 | | | 1 | | | | 1 | 1 | | | | | | | | | 1 | 24 |
| | | | | | 1 | | | 1 | 1 | | | 1 | 2 | | 2 | | | | | | | | | 2 | 25 |
| | | | | | | | | 2 | | 2 | | | 1 | 1 | 2 | | | | | | | | | 2 | 26 |
| | | | | | 7 | 2 | 3 | 5 | 1 | 4 | 1 | 9 | 9 | 2 | 11 | 6 | | | | | | | | 17 | 27 |
| | | | | | 12 | 7 | 11 | 3 | 10 | 6 | 3 | 13 | 12 | 8 | 20 | 9 | 4 | | | | | | | 33 | 28 |
| | | | | | | | | 1 | 1 | | | | | | | 1 | | | | | | | | 1 | 29 |
| | | | | | 9 | 4 | 5 | 5 | 11 | 7 | 1 | 4 | 4 | 1 | 5 | 7 | 11 | | | | | | | 23 | 30 |
| | | | | | 2 | 2 | 6 | 2 | 4 | 6 | | 2 | 1 | | 1 | 6 | 5 | | | | | | | 12 | 31 |
| | | | | | | | 1 | | 1 | 1 | | | | | | 1 | | | 1 | | | | | 2 | 32 |
| | | | | | 33 | 36 | 30 | 18 | 84 | 24 | 4 | 4 | 49 | 43 | 92 | 13 | 11 | | 1 | | | | | 117 | 33 |
| | | | | | 89 | 118 | 118 | 58 | 76 | 209 | 83 | 16 | 35 | 56 | 91 | 130 | 154 | 6 | 3 | | | 1 | | 385 | 34 |
| | | | | | 1 | | | | | | | 1 | | | | | 1 | | | | | | | 1 | 35 |
| | | | | | 23 | 23 | 28 | 14 | 34 | 41 | 9 | 4 | 29 | 28 | 57 | 18 | 17 | | | | | | | 92 | 36 |
| | 1 | | | | 21 | 27 | 34 | 22 | 40 | 48 | 11 | 5 | 26 | 27 | 53 | 22 | 24 | 3 | 2 | | | | | 104 | 37 |
| | 1 | | | | 21 | 29 | 21 | 17 | 43 | 36 | 6 | 2 | 32 | 24 | 56 | 16 | 14 | 2 | 2 | | | | | 90 | 38 |
| | | | | | | | 1 | 1 | 1 | 1 | | | 1 | 1 | 2 | | | | | | | | | 2 | 39 |
| | | | | | 5 | 1 | 5 | 6 | 8 | 8 | 1 | | 4 | 4 | 8 | 2 | 8 | | | | | | | 18 | 40 |
| | | | | | 1 | 1 | 1 | | | | | 3 | 1 | 1 | 2 | 1 | | | | | | | | 3 | 41 |
| | 4 | | | 1 | 11 | 5 | 6 | 10 | 19 | 8 | 2 | 3 | 23 | | 23 | 5 | | 2 | | | | 2 | | 32 | 42 |
| | | | | | 1 | 3 | 3 | 5 | 4 | 6 | 2 | | 3 | 8 | 11 | | 1 | | | | | | | 12 | 43 |
| | | | | | 1 | 2 | | 1 | | 1 | 2 | 1 | 1 | 1 | 2 | 1 | | 1 | | | | | | 4 | 44 |
| | | | | | 2 | 4 | 2 | 4 | 9 | 1 | 1 | 1 | 6 | | 6 | 4 | 1 | 1 | | | | | | 12 | 45 |
| | | | | | 1 | 6 | 3 | | 9 | 1 | | | 5 | 4 | 9 | 1 | | | | | | | | 10 | 46 |
| | 2 | | | | 11 | 17 | 13 | 15 | 4 | 14 | 15 | 21 | 28 | 17 | 45 | 4 | 6 | 1 | | | | | | 56 | 47 |
| | | | | | 2 | 8 | 9 | 4 | 19 | 3 | 1 | | 1 | | 1 | 11 | 10 | 1 | | | | | | 23 | 48 |
| | 1 | | | | 10 | 16 | 11 | 6 | 14 | 16 | 8 | 5 | 15 | 12 | 27 | 9 | 6 | | | | | | 1 | 43 | 49 |
| | | | | | 1 | | 2 | 2 | 1 | 1 | 1 | 2 | | 2 | 2 | 2 | 1 | | | | | | | 5 | 50 |
| | | | | | 1 | | | 3 | 1 | 1 | 1 | 1 | 3 | | 3 | 1 | | | | | | | | 4 | 51 |
| | | | | | 1 | 2 | 1 | | 1 | | | 3 | | 1 | 1 | 1 | 2 | | | | | | | 4 | 52 |
| | | | | | 16 | 41 | 10 | 7 | 6 | 47 | 13 | 6 | 11 | 17 | 28 | 19 | 24 | 3 | | | | | | 74 | 53 |
| | | | | | 2 | 1 | 5 | 2 | 4 | 5 | 1 | | 4 | 4 | 8 | 1 | 1 | | | | | | | 10 | 54 |
| | | | | | 9 | 4 | 5 | 5 | 17 | 5 | 1 | | 14 | | 14 | 5 | 3 | 1 | | | | | | 23 | 55 |
| | | | | | | 1 | 1 | 3 | | 2 | 2 | 1 | 1 | 3 | 4 | 1 | | | | | | | | 5 | 56 |
| | 3 | 1 | 21 | 8 | 73 | 63 | 60 | 51 | 156 | 35 | 12 | 44 | 42 | 58 | 100 | 65 | 78 | 3 | | | 1 | | 1 | 248 | 57 |
| | | | 3 | 2 | 15 | 18 | 16 | 16 | 16 | 13 | 8 | 28 | 29 | 21 | 50 | 5 | 11 | | | | | | | 66 | 58 |
| | | | | | 2 | | 1 | | | 1 | 1 | 1 | 2 | | 2 | 1 | | | | | | | | 3 | 59 |
| | 1 | | | | 26 | 10 | 7 | 27 | 30 | 40 | 4 | 3 | 14 | 10 | 24 | 37 | 15 | | | 1 | | | | 77 | 60 |
| | | 1 | 6 | 1 | 290 | 120 | 74 | 165 | 237 | 354 | 51 | 8 | 150 | 108 | 258 | 204 | 169 | 13 | 6 | 1 | | | | 651 | 61 |
| | | | | | 2 | 12 | 5 | 3 | 13 | 7 | 1 | 1 | 5 | 3 | 8 | 8 | 6 | | | | | | | 22 | 62 |
| | | | | | 2 | 2 | 3 | 1 | 7 | 1 | | | 3 | 2 | 5 | | 1 | 1 | 1 | | | | | 8 | 63 |
| | | | | | 16 | 4 | 10 | 13 | 23 | 16 | 3 | 2 | 12 | 13 | 25 | 8 | 10 | | | | | | 1 | 44 | 64 |
| | | | | | 10 | 10 | 8 | 6 | | 13 | 8 | 13 | 9 | 6 | 15 | 7 | 10 | 1 | 1 | | | | | 34 | 65 |
| | | | | | | 1 | | 1 | | 2 | | | | | | 1 | 1 | | | | | | | 2 | 66 |
| | | | | 1 | 20 | 32 | 22 | 16 | 7 | 14 | 8 | 61 | 20 | 20 | 40 | 17 | 30 | 1 | 2 | | | | 1 | 90 | 67 |
| | | | | | 3 | 4 | 2 | | 1 | 2 | 1 | 5 | 2 | 2 | 4 | 4 | 1 | | | | | | | 9 | 68 |
| | | | | | 8 | 4 | 6 | 11 | 28 | 1 | | | 11 | 4 | 15 | 5 | 8 | 1 | | | | | | 29 | 69 |
| | | | | | | 1 | | | | | | 1 | | | | | 1 | | | | | | | 1 | 70 |
| | | | | | 27 | 24 | 14 | 24 | 88 | | 1 | | 7 | 2 | 9 | 39 | 41 | | | | | | | 89 | 71 |
| | | | | | 5 | 5 | 1 | 3 | 13 | 1 | | | 11 | 1 | 12 | | 2 | | | | | | | 14 | 72 |
| | 1 | | | | | 1 | | | 1 | | | | 1 | | 1 | | | | | | | | | 1 | 73 |
| | | | | | 1 | | | | 1 | | | | | 1 | 1 | | | | | | | | | 1 | 74 |
| | | | | | 20 | 55 | 66 | 24 | 46 | 76 | 26 | 17 | 22 | 14 | 36 | 75 | 49 | 2 | 3 | | | | | 165 | 75 |

## CLASSIFICATION OF DEATHS IN

| | Cause of death. | Ages. Under 1. M. | F. | 1 and under 5. M. | F. | 5 and under 10. M. | F. | 10 and under 20. M. | F. | 20 and under 50. M. | F. | 50 and under 80. M. | F. | 80 and under 100. M | F. | 100 & over. M | F. | Age unknown. M | F. | Nativities. Born in State. | N. England States. | Middle States. | Southern States. | Southwest'n States. | Northwest'n States. |
|---|---|---|---|---|---|---|---|---|---|---|---|---|---|---|---|---|---|---|---|---|---|---|---|---|---|
| 1 | Tetanus | | | | | | | | | 1 | | | | | | | | | | 1 | | | | | |
| 2 | Throat, disease of | 2 | 3 | 12 | 10 | 5 | 3 | 2 | 5 | 2 | 4 | 1 | 2 | | | | | | | 48 | | | 3 | | |
| 3 | Thrush | 8 | 10 | 9 | 2 | 1 | | | | | | | | | | | | | | 30 | | | | | |
| 4 | Tumor | | 2 | 1 | 1 | | 1 | | 1 | 2 | 1 | 2 | 3 | | | | | | | 14 | | | | | |
| 5 | Ulcer | 1 | | 1 | | | | 1 | 1 | 2 | 2 | 2 | 2 | | | | | | | 10 | | | 1 | | |
| 6 | Uterus, disease of | | | | | | | | 3 | | 10 | | 1 | | | | | | | 8 | | | 5 | 1 | |
| 7 | Venereal | 1 | 1 | | | | | | | | 1 | 1 | 1 | | | | | | | 5 | | | | | |
| 8 | White swelling | 1 | | 1 | | 1 | | 2 | | 1 | 1 | 1 | | | | | | | | 7 | | | 1 | | |
| 9 | Worms | 17 | 15 | 88 | 75 | 20 | 18 | 5 | 6 | 4 | 1 | | | 1 | | | | | | 246 | | | 3 | | |
| 10 | Unknown | 414 | 314 | 213 | 167 | 45 | 37 | 61 | 51 | 119 | 169 | 97 | 95 | 20 | 15 | | 1 | 22 | 12 | 1632 | 3 | 8 | 164 | 4 | 1 |
| | Total | 1189 | 1051 | 1173 | 1020 | 350 | 290 | 508 | 535 | 1054 | 1106 | 705 | 601 | 160 | 122 | 2 | 2 | 35 | 22 | 8349 | 22 | 60 | 1254 | 33 | 4 |

## CLASSIFICATION OF DEATHS IN NORTHERN

*Embracing the following counties: Boone, Bureau, Carroll, Cook, De Kalb, Dupage, Grundy, McHenry, Marshall, Mercer, Ogle, Peoria, Putnam, Rock Island,*

| | Cause of death. | Under 1. M. | F. | 1 and under 5. M. | F. | 5 and under 10. M. | F. | 10 and under 20. M. | F. | 20 and under 50. M. | F. | 50 and under 80. M. | F. | 80 and under 100. M | F. | 100 & over. M | F. | Age unknown. M | F. | Born in State. | N. England States. | Middle States. | Southern States. | Southwest'n States. | Northwest'n States. |
|---|---|---|---|---|---|---|---|---|---|---|---|---|---|---|---|---|---|---|---|---|---|---|---|---|---|
| 1 | Abscess | | | | | | | 1 | | 1 | | | | | | | | | | | 1 | | | | |
| 2 | Accident, not specfi'd | 2 | 2 | 6 | 6 | 1 | 2 | 11 | 2 | 25 | 3 | 6 | 1 | | | | | | | 22 | 6 | 11 | 1 | 1 | 8 |
| 3 | ....do....burned | | | 3 | 3 | 1 | 1 | | | | | | | | | | | | | 3 | 4 | | | | |
| 4 | ....do....drowned | | 1 | 2 | 2 | 1 | | 5 | 3 | 13 | 1 | | | | | | | | | 5 | 5 | 8 | | | |
| 5 | Scalded | | | 1 | 1 | | | | | | | | | | | | | | | 2 | | | | | |
| 6 | Apoplexy | | | 2 | | | | | | 3 | 1 | 7 | 2 | 1 | | | | | | 1 | 4 | 5 | 1 | 1 | 1 |
| 7 | Asthma | | | | | | 1 | | | | | | 1 | | | | | | | 1 | | | | | |
| 8 | Bowels, disease of | 4 | 5 | 5 | 7 | 1 | 2 | | 5 | 3 | 4 | | 1 | | | | | | | 21 | 4 | 6 | 1 | | 2 |
| 9 | Brain ....do | 13 | 8 | 15 | 13 | 3 | 7 | 4 | 4 | 10 | 11 | | 1 | | | | | | | 54 | 6 | 11 | 1 | | 7 |
| 10 | Bronchitis | 3 | | 2 | 3 | | | | | 3 | | 1 | | | | | | | | 10 | 1 | | | | |
| 11 | Cancer | | | 1 | | | | 1 | | 3 | 3 | 3 | 2 | | | | | | | 1 | 2 | 6 | | | 2 |
| 12 | Canker | 1 | 2 | 2 | 2 | | | 1 | | | | | | | | | | | | 7 | 1 | | | | |
| 13 | Catarrh | 3 | 3 | 1 | 3 | 1 | | | | | | 1 | | | | | | | | 8 | | 4 | | | |
| 14 | Chicken pox | | 1 | | | | | | | | | | | | | | | | | | 1 | | | | |
| 15 | Child birth | | | | | | | | 3 | | 36 | | 1 | | | | | | | 1 | 5 | 7 | | 1 | 9 |
| 16 | Cholera* | 30 | 20 | 68 | 53 | 32 | 28 | 46 | 38 | 246 | 131 | 57 | 37 | 3 | | | | | 1 | 301 | 39 | 138 | 7 | 5 | 28 |
| 17 | ....do....infantum | 18 | 5 | 10 | 11 | | | | | | | | | | | | | | | 41 | 1 | | 1 | | 1 |
| 18 | ....do....morbus | 1 | | 3 | 1 | 1 | 1 | 2 | | 7 | 2 | 6 | 1 | | | | | | | 6 | 2 | 11 | 1 | | 2 |
| 19 | Colic | 1 | | | | | | | | 3 | 1 | 2 | | | | | | | | 1 | 2 | 2 | | | 1 |
| 20 | Consumption | 16 | 9 | 21 | 19 | 5 | 1 | 19 | 30 | 101 | 119 | 39 | 31 | 2 | | | | 1 | 1 | 87 | 63 | 129 | 15 | 5 | 32 |
| 21 | Convulsions | 24 | 14 | 14 | 6 | | 2 | | 6 | 2 | 5 | 1 | | | | | | | | 56 | 1 | 5 | 1 | | 7 |
| 22 | Congestion | | 1 | 1 | | 1 | 1 | 1 | 2 | 1 | 1 | 1 | | | | | | | | 3 | | 3 | 1 | | 2 |
| 23 | Cramp | 1 | 1 | | | | | | | | | | | | | | | | | 2 | | | | | |
| 24 | Croup | 36 | 22 | 40 | 33 | 8 | 6 | | 1 | | | | | | | | | | | 123 | 2 | 11 | 1 | | 8 |
| 25 | Debility | 12 | 13 | 1 | 1 | | | | | | | | | | | | | | | 25 | | | | | 1 |
| 26 | Diabetes | 4 | 3 | 6 | 1 | 1 | | | 1 | 3 | 1 | | 1 | | | | | | | 11 | 1 | 2 | | | 8 |
| 27 | Diarrhœa | 10 | 11 | 29 | 15 | 2 | | 3 | 2 | 6 | 9 | 5 | 3 | | | | | | | 60 | 6 | 12 | | 1 | 4 |
| 28 | Dropsy | | 2 | 5 | 4 | 2 | 2 | 2 | | 2 | 14 | 9 | 4 | | | | | | | 13 | 7 | 14 | | | 7 |
| 29 | Dysentery | 47 | 29 | 62 | 47 | 5 | 6 | 4 | 1 | 7 | 8 | 3 | 5 | | | | | | | 163 | 4 | 24 | 1 | 1 | 20 |
| 30 | Epilepsy | | | | | | | | 1 | | | | | | | | | | | | 1 | | | | |
| 31 | Erysipelas | 5 | 4 | 5 | 3 | 2 | 3 | 1 | 4 | 13 | 9 | 5 | 7 | | | | | | | 20 | 6 | 14 | 5 | | 8 |
| 32 | Eyes, disease of | | | | | | | | 1 | | | | | | | | | | | | | 1 | | | |
| 33 | Fever, not specified | 10 | 8 | 10 | 17 | 10 | 7 | 7 | 12 | 22 | 19 | 8 | 3 | 1 | | | | | 2 | 56 | 12 | 29 | 2 | 1 | 1[illegible] |
| 34 | ..do..bilious | 1 | 1 | 3 | 5 | 1 | 5 | 2 | 1 | 14 | 2 | 3 | 1 | | | | | | | 13 | 1 | 10 | | | 4 |
| 35 | ..do..brain | 6 | 5 | 4 | 6 | 3 | 2 | 1 | 1 | 3 | 1 | | 2 | | | | | | | 22 | 1 | 3 | | | 1 |
| 36 | ..do..congestive | | 2 | 4 | 1 | 8 | 3 | 7 | 4 | 10 | 14 | 4 | 3 | | | | | | | 11 | 2 | 23 | 4 | | 1[illegible] |
| 37 | ..do..inflammatory | | | | | | | | | 2 | | | | | | | | | | 1 | | 1 | | | |
| 38 | ..do..intermittent | 2 | 3 | | 7 | 2 | 2 | | 1 | 2 | 3 | 1 | 1 | 1 | | | | | | 15 | 1 | 4 | | | |
| 39 | ..do..puerperal | | | | | | | | 1 | | 10 | | | | | | | | | 1 | | 4 | | | |
| 40 | ..do..scarlet | 11 | 8 | 40 | 29 | 14 | 4 | | 3 | | 1 | | 2 | | | | | | | 94 | | 7 | | | |
| 41 | ..do..ship | | | 2 | 1 | 1 | | 1 | 1 | 1 | 2 | 1 | 2 | | | | | | | 6 | | | | | |
| 42 | ..do..typhus | 2 | 1 | 6 | 6 | 10 | 12 | 23 | 13 | 26 | 18 | 14 | 5 | | | | | | | 24 | 19 | 42 | 2 | 2 | 3 |
| 43 | ..do..winter | | | 1 | | 1 | | 1 | | 2 | 1 | 1 | 1 | | | | | | | 2 | 1 | 1 | | | |
| 44 | ..do..yellow | | | | | | | | 1 | | | | | | | | | | | | | | | | |
| 45 | Gout | | | | | | | | | | | 1 | | | | | | | | | | 1 | | | |
| 46 | Gravel | | | | | | | | | | | 4 | | 1 | | | | | | 1 | 2 | 1 | | | |
| 47 | Head, disease of | 1 | 1 | | 2 | | | | | 1 | | | | | | | | | | 3 | 1 | | | | |
| 48 | Heart....do | 2 | 3 | | | | 1 | | 1 | 4 | 5 | 5 | 1 | 1 | | | | | | 6 | 2 | 9 | 1 | | |
| 49 | Hemorrhage | 1 | | | 2 | 1 | | | 1 | 2 | | | | | | | | | | 3 | | 1 | 1 | | |
| 50 | Hernia | | | | | | | | | 2 | | | | | | | | | | | | | | | |
| 51 | Hip, disease of | 1 | | | | | | | | 1 | | | | | | | | | | 2 | | | | | |
| 52 | Hives | 2 | 1 | | | | | | | | | | | | | | | | | 3 | | | | | |

[* 116 white—age and sex not given—included in total whites and aggregate.

## E STATE OF GEORGIA—AGGREGATE—Continued.

| NATIVITIES. Ireland. | Germany. | Other foreign countries. | Unknown. | SEASON OF DECEASE. Spring. | Summer. | Autumn. | Winter. | DURATION OF SICKNESS. Under 1 week. | 1 week and under 1 month. | 1 month and under 3 months. | 3 months and over. | WHITES. Males. | Females. | Total. | COLORED. Slaves. Black. M. | Slaves. Black. F. | Slaves. Mulatto. M. | Slaves. Mulatto. F. | Free. Black. M. | Free. Black. F. | Free. Mul. M | Free. Mul. F. | Aggregate deaths. | |
|---|---|---|---|---|---|---|---|---|---|---|---|---|---|---|---|---|---|---|---|---|---|---|---|---|
| | | | | | | | 1 | 1 | | | | | | | 1 | | | | | | | | 1 | 1 |
| | | | | 10 | 8 | 14 | 19 | 18 | 32 | | 1 | 14 | 14 | 28 | 10 | 13 | | | | | | | 51 | 2 |
| | | | | 10 | 7 | 11 | 1 | 9 | 13 | 5 | 3 | 3 | 6 | 9 | 15 | 6 | | | | | | | 30 | 3 |
| | | | | 2 | 3 | 6 | 3 | 1 | 1 | 1 | 10 | 2 | 6 | 8 | 3 | 2 | | 1 | | | | | 14 | 4 |
| | | 1 | | 2 | 7 | 3 | | 1 | 4 | 3 | 3 | 2 | 3 | 5 | 5 | 2 | | | | | | | 12 | 5 |
| | | | | 2 | 6 | 4 | 2 | 3 | 4 | 1 | 6 | | 7 | 7 | | 6 | | 1 | | | | | 14 | 6 |
| | | | | 1 | 1 | 2 | 1 | 1 | | | 4 | 1 | 1 | 2 | 1 | 2 | | | | | | | 5 | 7 |
| | | | | 2 | 6 | | | | 1 | 2 | 5 | 3 | | 3 | 4 | 1 | | | | | | | 8 | 8 |
| | | 1 | | 61 | 82 | 72 | 35 | 115 | 96 | 28 | 11 | 22 | 32 | 54 | 106 | 78 | 7 | 5 | | | | | 250 | 9 |
| 16 | 2 | 20 | 2 | 495 | 469 | 458 | 416 | 932 | 464 | 153 | 233 | 426 | 328 | 754 | 532 | 515 | 27 | 15 | 5 | | 1 | 3 | 1852 | 10 |
| 77 | 12 | 90 | 24 | 2559 | 2535 | 2692 | 2051 | 3876 | 3439 | 994 | 1376 | 2512 | 2068 | 4580 | 2514 | 2558 | 123 | 109 | 18 | 5 | 9 | 9 | 9925 | |

## CTION OF THE STATE OF ILLINOIS.

*nderson, Henry, Iroquois, Jo Daviess, Kane, Kendall, Knox, Lake, Lasalle, Lee, Livingston, rk, Stephenson, Warren, Whitesides, Will, Winnebago, Woodford.*

| | Ireland. | Germany. | Other foreign countries. | Unknown. | Spring. | Summer. | Autumn. | Winter. | Under 1 week. | 1 week and under 1 month. | 1 month and under 3 months. | 3 months and over. | Males. | Females. | Total. | Slaves. Black. M. | Slaves. Black. F. | Slaves. Mulatto. M. | Slaves. Mulatto. F. | Free. Black. M. | Free. Black. F. | Free. Mul. M | Free. Mul. F. | Aggregate deaths. | |
|---|---|---|---|---|---|---|---|---|---|---|---|---|---|---|---|---|---|---|---|---|---|---|---|---|---|
| | 1 | | | | | 2 | | | | 2 | | | 2 | | 2 | | | | | | | | | 2 | 1 |
| | 9 | 4 | 5 | | 12 | 13 | 24 | 15 | 47 | 9 | 5 | 2 | 51 | 16 | 67 | | | | | | | | | 67 | 2 |
| | | | 1 | | 1 | 3 | 2 | 2 | 5 | 2 | 1 | | 4 | 4 | 8 | | | | | | | | | 8 | 3 |
| | 2 | | 8 | | 5 | 8 | 6 | 9 | 28 | | | | 21 | 7 | 28 | | | | | | | | | 28 | 4 |
| | | | | | 1 | 1 | | | | 1 | | 1 | 1 | 1 | 2 | | | | | | | | | 2 | 5 |
| | 2 | | 1 | | 5 | 6 | 3 | 2 | 12 | 2 | | | 12 | 3 | 15 | | | | | 1 | | | | 16 | 6 |
| | 1 | | | | | | 2 | | | 1 | | 1 | | 2 | 2 | | | | | | | | | 2 | 7 |
| | | | 1 | 2 | 3 | 6 | 21 | 7 | 17 | 18 | 2 | | 13 | 24 | 37 | | | | | | | | | 37 | 8 |
| | 5 | 1 | 4 | | 22 | 19 | 27 | 19 | 38 | 31 | 11 | 2 | 45 | 44 | 89 | | | | | | | | | 89 | 9 |
| | 1 | | | | 3 | 6 | 1 | 2 | 4 | 4 | 1 | 3 | 9 | 3 | 12 | | | | | | | | | 12 | 10 |
| | 1 | | 1 | | 5 | 3 | 1 | 4 | | 1 | 2 | 9 | 8 | 5 | 13 | | | | | | | | | 13 | 11 |
| | | | | | 1 | 1 | 4 | 2 | 1 | 5 | 1 | | 4 | 4 | 8 | | | | | | | | | 8 | 12 |
| | | | | | 6 | 1 | 3 | 2 | 4 | 5 | 1 | | 6 | 6 | 12 | | | | | | | | | 12 | 13 |
| | | | | | | 1 | | | | 1 | | | | 1 | 1 | | | | | | | | | 1 | 14 |
| | 8 | 2 | 6 | 1 | 18 | 10 | 5 | 7 | 25 | 9 | 2 | | | 40 | 40 | | | | | | | | | 40 | 15 |
| | 103 | 102 | 180 | 3 | 20 | 317 | 550 | 8 | 708 | 72 | 2 | | 481 | 308 | 905 | | | | | 1 | | | | 906 | 16 |
| | | | | | 6 | 8 | 25 | 4 | 18 | 19 | 4 | | 28 | 16 | 44 | | | | | | | | | 44 | 17 |
| | 1 | | 2 | | 2 | 6 | 16 | | 15 | 10 | | | 18 | 5 | 23 | | | | | 2 | | | | 25 | 18 |
| | | | 1 | | 1 | 2 | 2 | 2 | 4 | 3 | | | 6 | 1 | 7 | | | | | | | | | 7 | 19 |
| 1 | 23 | 17 | 38 | 4 | 128 | 111 | 85 | 84 | 23 | 62 | 62 | 249 | 203 | 207 | 410 | | | | | 1 | 3 | | | 414 | 20 |
| | | | 4 | | 26 | 15 | 21 | 12 | 56 | 11 | 2 | 1 | 41 | 33 | 74 | | | | | | | | | 74 | 21 |
| | | | 1 | | 2 | 2 | 4 | 2 | 5 | 5 | | | 5 | 5 | 10 | | | | | | | | | 10 | 22 |
| | | | | | 1 | | | 1 | 2 | | | | 1 | 1 | 2 | | | | | | | | | 2 | 23 |
| | | | 1 | | 55 | 24 | 28 | 39 | 120 | 24 | 2 | | 84 | 62 | 146 | | | | | | | | | 146 | 24 |
| | | | 1 | | 9 | 8 | 5 | 5 | 14 | 4 | 3 | 2 | 13 | 14 | 27 | | | | | | | | | 27 | 25 |
| | | | 4 | | 4 | 4 | 13 | | 6 | 11 | 2 | 2 | 14 | 7 | 21 | | | | | | | | | 21 | 26 |
| | 8 | 1 | 3 | | 3 | 22 | 64 | 6 | 26 | 51 | 9 | 5 | 55 | 40 | 95 | | | | | | | | | 95 | 27 |
| | | 1 | 4 | | 12 | 14 | 13 | 5 | 7 | 9 | 10 | 17 | 20 | 26 | 46 | | | | | | | | | 46 | 28 |
| | 3 | 2 | 6 | | 15 | 20 | 161 | 19 | 75 | 109 | 24 | 7 | 128 | 95 | 223 | | | | | | | | 1 | 224 | 29 |
| | | | | | | | | 1 | | | | | | 1 | 1 | | | | | | | | | 1 | 30 |
| | 2 | 1 | 3 | 2 | 15 | 8 | 11 | 27 | 18 | 39 | 3 | | 31 | 30 | 61 | | | | | | | | | 61 | 31 |
| | | | | | | 1 | | | | 1 | | | | 1 | 1 | | | | | | | | | 1 | 32 |
| | 6 | 3 | 10 | 2 | 31 | 25 | 37 | 31 | 28 | 88 | 19 | 1 | 68 | 68 | 136 | | | | | | | | | 136 | 33 |
| | 4 | 4 | 3 | | 2 | 9 | 18 | 10 | 6 | 24 | 5 | 3 | 24 | 15 | 39 | | | | | | | | | 39 | 34 |
| | 3 | 2 | 2 | | 11 | 9 | 11 | 3 | 20 | 13 | 1 | | 17 | 17 | 34 | | | | | | | | | 34 | 35 |
| | | | 2 | | 15 | 11 | 24 | 5 | 28 | 17 | 3 | 7 | 26 | 27 | 53 | | | | | | | 2 | | 55 | 36 |
| | | | | | | 1 | 1 | | 2 | | | | 2 | | 2 | | | | | | | | | 2 | 37 |
| | 4 | 1 | | | 3 | 4 | 12 | 6 | 5 | 11 | 8 | 1 | 7 | 18 | 25 | | | | | | | | | 25 | 38 |
| | | 1 | 1 | | 2 | 3 | 3 | 3 | 4 | 7 | | | | 11 | 11 | | | | | | | | | 11 | 39 |
| | 2 | 2 | 2 | | 43 | 19 | 20 | 29 | 52 | 53 | 6 | | 65 | 47 | 112 | | | | | | | | | 112 | 40 |
| | 3 | | 3 | | | 8 | 4 | | 4 | 6 | 2 | | 6 | 6 | 12 | | | | | | | | | 12 | 41 |
| | 2 | | 11 | 1 | 36 | 16 | 44 | 40 | 12 | 100 | 24 | | 81 | 55 | 136 | | | | | | | | | 136 | 42 |
| | | 2 | | 1 | 6 | | | 2 | | 7 | 1 | | 5 | 2 | 7 | | | | | | | 1 | | 8 | 43 |
| | 1 | | | | | | | 1 | | | | | | 1 | 1 | | | | | | | | | 1 | 44 |
| | | | | | | | | 1 | | | 1 | | 1 | | 1 | | | | | | | | | 1 | 45 |
| | 1 | | | | 2 | 2 | | 1 | 1 | 4 | | | 5 | | 5 | | | | | | | | | 5 | 46 |
| | | | | | 1 | 2 | | 2 | | 4 | | 1 | 2 | 3 | 5 | | | | | | | | | 5 | 47 |
| | 2 | 1 | 2 | | 7 | 5 | 4 | 7 | 5 | 7 | 1 | 10 | 12 | 11 | 23 | | | | | | | | | 23 | 48 |
| | | | | | | 1 | 3 | 3 | 2 | 5 | | | 4 | 3 | 7 | | | | | | | | | 7 | 49 |
| | 1 | | 1 | | | | 1 | 1 | 1 | | | 1 | 2 | | 2 | | | | | | | | | 2 | 50 |
| | | | | | 1 | | 1 | | 1 | | | | 2 | | 2 | | | | | | | | | 2 | 51 |
| | | | | | 1 | | 1 | 1 | 2 | | | | 2 | 1 | 3 | | | | | | | | | 3 | 52 |

## CLASSIFICATION OF DEATHS IN NORTHERN

| | Cause of death. | AGES. Under 1. M. | Under 1. F. | 1 and under 5. M. | 1 and under 5. F. | 5 and under 10. M. | 5 and under 10. F. | 10 and under 20. M. | 10 and under 20. F. | 20 and under 50. M. | 20 and under 50. F. | 50 and under 80. M. | 50 and under 80. F. | 80 and under 100. M | 80 and under 100. F. | 100 & over. M | 100 & over. F. | Age unknown. M | Age unknown. F. | NATIVITIES. Born in State. | N. England States. | Middle States. | Southern States. | Southwest'n States. | Northwest'n States. |
|---|---|---|---|---|---|---|---|---|---|---|---|---|---|---|---|---|---|---|---|---|---|---|---|---|---|
| 1 | Hooping cough | 21 | 21 | 15 | 23 | 3 | 5 | | 1 | | | | | | | | | 1 | | 76 | | 5 | | | 2 |
| 2 | Hydrocephalus | 7 | 2 | 3 | 5 | 1 | | | 1 | 1 | | | | | | | | | | 17 | | 1 | | | 1 |
| 3 | Inflamat'n, not spe'd. | 9 | 7 | 6 | 7 | 2 | | 1 | 2 | 3 | 2 | 3 | 2 | | | | | | | 25 | 1 | 8 | | 1 | 2 |
| 4 | ...do......bowels.. | 5 | 5 | 4 | 6 | | 1 | 2 | 3 | 2 | 5 | 1 | | | | | | | | 21 | | 8 | | | 3 |
| 5 | ....do......brain.... | 9 | 5 | 11 | 11 | 1 | 5 | 8 | 2 | 2 | | 3 | 2 | | | | | | | 40 | 5 | 9 | | | 3 |
| 6 | ....do.......stomach. | | | 1 | | | | | | | 1 | | | | | | | | | | | 1 | | | 1 |
| 7 | Influenza | 1 | 2 | 1 | 1 | | | | | | | | | | | | | | | 5 | | | | | |
| 8 | Insanity | | | | | | | | 1 | | | | 1 | | | | | | | | 1 | 1 | | | |
| 9 | Intemperance | | | | | | | | | 2 | | 3 | | | | | | | | | 1 | 1 | 1 | | 1 |
| 10 | Jaundice | 3 | 3 | | | | | | 1 | 1 | 3 | 3 | 3 | | | | | | | 5 | 2 | 5 | | | 2 |
| 11 | Kidneys, disease of.. | | | | | | | | | | | 1 | | | | | | | | | | | 1 | | |
| 12 | Killed | | | | | | | | 1 | 2 | | | | | | | | | | 1 | | 1 | | | |
| 13 | Lightning | | | | | | | | | 1 | 2 | | | | | | | | | | | 1 | | | 1 |
| 14 | Liver, disease of | 3 | 1 | 2 | 3 | | | | 1 | 10 | 5 | 4 | 1 | | | | | | | 9 | 4 | 7 | 2 | | 4 |
| 15 | Lockjaw | | | 1 | | | | | | | | | | | | | | | | 1 | | | | | |
| 16 | Lungs, disease of | 9 | 5 | 3 | 2 | 2 | 2 | 3 | | 5 | 3 | 2 | | | | | | | | 22 | 3 | 3 | 1 | | 3 |
| 17 | Measles | 1 | 8 | 14 | 8 | 2 | | 3 | 1 | 5 | 2 | | | | | | | | | 32 | | 7 | | | 3 |
| 18 | Milk sickness | | | | | 1 | | | | 1 | 1 | | | | | | | | | 1 | | 1 | | | 1 |
| 19 | Mortification | | | | | | | | | | | | 1 | | | | | | | 1 | | | | | |
| 20 | Mumps | 1 | | | | | | | | | | | | | | | | | | 1 | | | | | |
| 21 | Murder | | | 1 | | | | | | | | | | | | | | | | 1 | | | | | |
| 22 | Old age | | | | | | | | | | | 10 | 8 | 6 | 7 | | | | | | 6 | 10 | 2 | | |
| 23 | Paralysis | | | | | | | | | 2 | 3 | 5 | 7 | | 1 | | | | | 1 | 4 | 9 | 2 | | 1 |
| 24 | Pleurisy | 1 | | | | | | | | 3 | 1 | 4 | | | | | | | | 1 | 2 | 1 | | | 1 |
| 25 | Pneumonia | 36 | 16 | 40 | 28 | 5 | 3 | 8 | 6 | 27 | 25 | 20 | 18 | 3 | | | | | | 109 | 28 | 33 | 11 | 2 | 30 |
| 26 | Poison | | | | | 4 | | 1 | 2 | | 2 | | | | | | | | | 4 | | 2 | | | 3 |
| 27 | Premature birth | | 1 | | | | | | | | | | | | | | | | | 1 | | | | | |
| 28 | Quinsy | 1 | | | 1 | 1 | 1 | | | 2 | | 1 | | | | | | | | 2 | | 3 | | | 2 |
| 29 | Rheumatism | | 1 | | 1 | 2 | | 2 | 3 | 1 | 1 | 4 | 2 | | | | | | | 4 | 2 | 5 | | 1 | |
| 30 | Rickets | | 1 | | 1 | | | | | | | | | | | | | | | 2 | | | | | |
| 31 | Scrofula | 1 | | 2 | | | 1 | 2 | 3 | 3 | 2 | | 1 | | | | | | | 6 | 2 | 1 | | | 2 |
| 32 | Small pox | 4 | 2 | 5 | 1 | 1 | 5 | 2 | 1 | S | 4 | | | | | | | | | 17 | 2 | 4 | 1 | 1 | 5 |
| 33 | Spine, disease of | | | | 2 | 1 | | 1 | | 1 | 2 | | 1 | | | | | | | 3 | | 3 | 1 | 1 | |
| 34 | Stomach.. do | | | 1 | 1 | | | 1 | | | | | | | | | | | | 2 | | | | | 1 |
| 35 | Suffocation | | | | | | | | | 2 | | | | | | | | | | | 1 | 1 | | | |
| 36 | Suicide | | | | | | | | | 2 | 1 | 3 | | | | | | | | | 2 | 1 | | 1 | |
| 37 | Summer complaint | 2 | 1 | 2 | 2 | | | | | | | | | | | | | | | 7 | | | | | |
| 38 | Sun stroke | | | | | | | | | 3 | | 2 | | | | | | | | 1 | | | | | |
| 39 | Teething | 2 | 3 | 4 | 5 | | | | | | | | | | | | | | | 10 | 2 | | | | 1 |
| 40 | Throat, disease of | | 2 | | 3 | | 1 | | 1 | 2 | | | | | | | | | | 4 | | 2 | 1 | | 2 |
| 41 | Thrush | 1 | 3 | | | | | | | | | | | | | | | | | 3 | | 1 | | | |
| 42 | Tumor | 1 | | | | | | | | | | | | | | | | | | 1 | | | | | |
| 43 | Ulcer | | | | | | | | | | | 1 | | | | | | | | | | 1 | | | |
| 44 | White swelling | | | | | 1 | | | | | | | | | | | | | | 1 | | | | | |
| 45 | Worms | | 4 | 2 | 5 | 4 | 1 | | | | | | | | | | | | | 9 | | 2 | 1 | | 1 |
| 46 | Unknown | 108 | 86 | 69 | 51 | 8 | 11 | 13 | 10 | 43 | 56 | 22 | 14 | 1 | | | | 3 | 3 | 331 | 17 | 47 | 12 | 3 | 32 |
| | Total* | 496 | 368 | 562 | 477 | 152 | 135 | 190 | 184 | 678 | 556 | 280 | 180 | 19 | 9 | | | 5 | 7 | 2088 | 302 | 745 | 83 | 28 | 340 |

* 14 "unknown" and 130 "total"—age and sex not given—included in total white and aggregate.

## CLASSIFICATION OF DEATHS IN MIDDLE

*Embracing the following counties: Adams, Brown, Calhoun, Cass, Champaign, Christian, Clark, McLean, Macon, Macoupin, Mason, Menard, Montgomery, Morgan, Moultrie,*

| | Cause of death. | Under 1. M. | Under 1. F. | 1 and under 5. M. | 1 and under 5. F. | 5 and under 10. M. | 5 and under 10. F. | 10 and under 20. M. | 10 and under 20. F. | 20 and under 50. M. | 20 and under 50. F. | 50 and under 80. M. | 50 and under 80. F. | 80 and under 100. M | 80 and under 100. F. | 100 & over. M | 100 & over. F. | Age unknown. M | Age unknown. F. | Born in State. | N. England States. | Middle States. | Southern States. | Southwest'n States. | Northwest'n States. |
|---|---|---|---|---|---|---|---|---|---|---|---|---|---|---|---|---|---|---|---|---|---|---|---|---|---|
| 1 | Abscess | | 1 | 1 | | | | | | 1 | | | 1 | | | | | | | 2 | | 1 | | | 1 |
| 2 | Accident, not specif'd | 1 | 1 | 6 | 4 | 6 | 3 | 8 | 1 | 14 | 1 | 7 | 1 | 1 | | | | | 2 | 26 | 4 | 5 | 3 | 1 | 12 |
| 3 | ....do ..burned | 1 | | 3 | 1 | | | | | | 2 | | 1 | | | | | | | 6 | | | | | 2 |
| 4 | ....do...drowned | | | 4 | | 3 | | 1 | | 7 | | 1 | | | | | | | | 9 | | | | 1 | 4 |
| 5 | ....do...scalded | | | | 1 | | | | | | | | | | | | | | | | | | | | 1 |
| 6 | ....do...expl. steam | | | 1 | | | | | | | 1 | | | | | | | | | 1 | | | | | |
| 7 | Apoplexy | | | | 1 | | | 2 | | | 5 | 3 | 3 | 1 | 2 | | | | | 4 | 4 | 2 | 2 | | 3 |
| 8 | Asthma | | | | | | | | | 1 | | | 1 | | | | | | | 1 | | | | | 1 |
| 9 | Bowels, disease of | 1 | 2 | 1 | 3 | | | | | | 1 | | | | | | | | | 7 | | | | | |
| 10 | Brain.......do | 15 | 7 | 7 | 9 | 2 | 1 | 4 | 3 | 1 | 6 | | | | | | | | | 42 | 1 | 4 | 1 | 1 | 6 |
| 11 | Bronchitis | | 4 | 2 | 2 | | 1 | | 1 | 2 | 3 | | 1 | | | | | | | 9 | | 1 | 2 | | 3 |
| 12 | Cancer | | | | | | | | | 3 | 5 | 2 | 5 | 2 | | | | | | 2 | 2 | 5 | 4 | | 2 |
| 13 | Canker | 1 | 1 | | | | 2 | | | | | | | | | | | | | 4 | | | | | |
| 14 | Catarrh | 3 | 1 | | 3 | | 1 | | 1 | 1 | 1 | 1 | | | 1 | | | | | 8 | | 1 | | | 4 |
| 15 | Child birth | | | | | | | | 6 | | 38 | | 1 | | | | | | | 11 | | 5 | 6 | 1 | 17 |

SECTION OF THE STATE OF ILLINOIS—Continued.

| Nativities: California and Territories. | Nativities: Ireland. | Nativities: Germany. | Nativities: Other foreign countries. | Nativities: Unknown. | Season of decease: Spring. | Season of decease: Summer. | Season of decease: Autumn. | Season of decease: Winter. | Duration of sickness: Under 1 week. | Duration of sickness: 1 week and under 1 month. | Duration of sickness: 1 month and under 3 months. | Duration of sickness: 3 months and over. | Whites: Males. | Whites: Females. | Whites: Total. | Colored: Slaves: Black: M. | Colored: Slaves: Black: F. | Colored: Slaves: Mulatto: M. | Colored: Slaves: Mulatto: F. | Colored: Free: Black: M. | Colored: Free: Black: F. | Colored: Free: Mul.: M | Colored: Free: Mul.: F. | Aggregate deaths. | |
|---|---|---|---|---|---|---|---|---|---|---|---|---|---|---|---|---|---|---|---|---|---|---|---|---|---|
| .... | 4 | 2 | 4 | ... | 24 | 28 | 25 | 12 | 11 | 50 | 23 | 3 | 40 | 50 | 90 | .... | .... | .... | .... | ... | ... | .. | .. | 90 | 1 |
| .... | 1 | .. | .... | ... | 6 | 3 | 5 | 5 | 3 | 11 | 5 | 1 | 12 | 8 | 20 | .... | .... | .... | .... | ... | ... | .. | .. | 20 | 2 |
| .... | 3 | .. | 4 | ... | 16 | 10 | 12 | 6 | 18 | 21 | 2 | 1 | 23 | 20 | 43 | .... | .... | .... | .... | ... | ... | 1 | .. | 44 | 3 |
| .... | ... | 1 | 1 | ... | 6 | 9 | 11 | 7 | 18 | 11 | 2 | .... | 14 | 20 | 34 | .... | .... | .... | .... | ... | ... | .. | .. | 34 | 4 |
| .... | ... | .. | 2 | ... | 15 | 12 | 19 | 13 | 21 | 33 | 2 | 1 | 34 | 25 | 59 | .... | .... | .... | .... | ... | ... | .. | .. | 59 | 5 |
| .... | ... | .. | .... | ... | .... | 1 | 1 | .... | .... | 2 | .... | .... | 1 | 1 | 2 | .... | .... | .... | .... | ... | ... | .. | .. | 2 | 6 |
| .... | ... | .. | .... | ... | 3 | .... | .... | 2 | 3 | 2 | .... | .... | 2 | 3 | 5 | .... | .... | .... | .... | ... | ... | .. | .. | 5 | 7 |
| .... | ... | .. | .... | ... | 1 | 1 | .... | .... | .... | .... | .... | 2 | .... | 2 | 2 | .... | .... | .... | .... | ... | ... | .. | .. | 2 | 8 |
| .... | 1 | .. | .... | ... | 1 | 1 | .... | 3 | 1 | .... | .... | 4 | 5 | .... | 5 | .... | .... | .... | .... | ... | ... | .. | .. | 5 | 9 |
| .... | 2 | .. | 1 | ... | 7 | 4 | 3 | 3 | 5 | 3 | 1 | 7 | 7 | 10 | 17 | .... | .... | .... | .... | ... | ... | .. | .. | 17 | 10 |
| .... | ... | .. | .... | ... | .... | ... | .... | 1 | .... | ... | .... | 1 | 1 | .... | 1 | .... | .... | .... | .... | ... | ... | .. | .. | 1 | 11 |
| .... | ... | .. | 1 | ... | 1 | 1 | 1 | .... | 3 | .... | .... | .... | 2 | 1 | 3 | .... | .... | .... | .... | ... | ... | .. | .. | 3 | 12 |
| .... | ... | .. | 1 | ... | 1 | 1 | 1 | .... | 3 | .... | ... | ... | 1 | 2 | 3 | .... | .... | .... | .... | ... | ... | .. | .. | 3 | 13 |
| .... | 3 | .. | 1 | ... | 10 | 7 | 8 | 4 | 2 | 12 | 5 | 11 | 19 | 11 | 30 | .... | .... | .... | .... | ... | ... | .. | .. | 30 | 14 |
| .... | ... | .. | .... | ... | .... | 1 | .... | .... | 1 | .... | .... | .... | 1 | .... | 1 | .... | .... | .... | .... | ... | ... | .. | .. | 1 | 15 |
| .... | 3 | 1 | ... | ... | 19 | 4 | 8 | 5 | 20 | 14 | 1 | .... | 24 | 12 | 36 | .... | .... | .... | .... | ... | ... | .. | .. | 36 | 16 |
| .... | ... | .. | 1 | 1 | 13 | 22 | 8 | 1 | 5 | 29 | 9 | 1 | 25 | 19 | 44 | .... | .... | .... | .... | ... | ... | .. | .. | 44 | 17 |
| .... | ... | .. | .... | ... | .... | .... | 3 | ... | 1 | 2 | .... | .... | 2 | 1 | 3 | .... | .... | .... | .... | ... | ... | .. | .. | 3 | 18 |
| .... | ... | .. | .... | ... | .... | 1 | .... | .... | .... | 1 | .... | .... | .... | 1 | 1 | .... | .... | .... | .... | ... | ... | .. | .. | 1 | 19 |
| .... | ... | .. | .... | ... | 1 | .... | .... | .... | .... | 1 | .... | .... | 1 | .... | 1 | .... | .... | .... | .... | ... | ... | .. | .. | 1 | 20 |
| .... | ... | .. | .... | ... | .... | .... | 1 | .... | .... | .... | .... | .... | 1 | .... | 1 | .... | .... | .... | .... | ... | ... | .. | .. | 1 | 21 |
| .... | 7 | 1 | 5 | ... | 7 | 12 | 8 | 4 | 8 | 6 | 1 | 13 | 16 | 15 | 31 | .... | .... | .... | .... | ... | ... | .. | .. | 31 | 22 |
| .... | ... | .. | 1 | ... | 4 | 7 | 4 | 3 | 7 | 3 | 2 | 6 | 7 | 11 | 18 | .... | .... | .... | .... | ... | ... | .. | .. | 18 | 23 |
| .... | 4 | .. | .... | ... | 2 | 4 | 2 | 1 | 4 | 5 | .... | .... | 8 | 1 | 9 | .... | .... | .... | .... | ... | ... | .. | .. | 9 | 24 |
| .... | 5 | 4 | 11 | 2 | 133 | 47 | 24 | 30 | 66 | 152 | 12 | 5 | 136 | 96 | 232 | .... | .... | .... | .... | 3 | ... | .. | .. | 235 | 25 |
| .... | ... | .. | .... | ... | .... | 5 | 1 | 1 | 6 | 3 | .... | .... | 5 | 4 | 9 | .... | .... | .... | .... | ... | ... | .. | .. | 9 | 26 |
| .... | ... | .. | .... | ... | 2 | .... | 1 | .... | .... | 1 | .... | .... | .... | 1 | 1 | .... | .... | .... | .... | ... | ... | .. | .. | 1 | 27 |
| .... | ... | .. | .... | ... | 3 | .... | 2 | 2 | 1 | 6 | .... | .... | 5 | 2 | 7 | .... | .... | .... | .... | ... | ... | .. | .. | 7 | 28 |
| .... | ... | 4 | 1 | ... | 8 | 6 | 1 | 1 | 1 | 5 | .... | 10 | 9 | 8 | 17 | .... | .... | .... | .... | ... | ... | .. | .. | 17 | 29 |
| .... | ... | .. | .... | ... | .... | 1 | 1 | .... | 1 | .... | .... | 1 | ... | 2 | 2 | .... | .... | .... | .... | ... | ... | .. | .. | 2 | 30 |
| .... | ... | .. | 4 | ... | 5 | 3 | 3 | 3 | .... | 5 | 2 | 8 | 8 | 7 | 15 | .... | .... | .... | .... | ... | ... | .. | .. | 15 | 31 |
| .... | ... | .. | 2 | 1 | 16 | 5 | .... | 12 | 3 | 30 | .... | .... | 20 | 13 | 33 | .... | .... | .... | .... | ... | ... | .. | .. | 33 | 32 |
| .... | ... | .. | .... | ... | 3 | .... | 4 | 1 | .... | .... | .... | 8 | 3 | 5 | 8 | .... | .... | .... | .... | ... | ... | .. | .. | 8 | 33 |
| .... | ... | .. | .... | ... | 2 | .... | .... | 1 | 1 | 2 | .... | .... | 2 | 1 | 3 | .... | .... | .... | .... | ... | ... | .. | .. | 3 | 34 |
| .... | ... | .. | .... | ... | .... | .... | 2 | .... | 2 | .... | .... | .... | 2 | .... | 2 | .... | .... | .... | .... | ... | ... | .. | .. | 2 | 35 |
| .... | 1 | .. | 1 | ... | 2 | 1 | 2 | 1 | 6 | .... | .... | .... | 5 | 1 | 6 | .... | .... | .... | .... | ... | ... | .. | .. | 6 | 36 |
| .... | ... | .. | .... | ... | .... | 1 | 6 | .... | 1 | 3 | 2 | 1 | 4 | 3 | 7 | .... | .... | .... | .... | ... | ... | .. | .. | 7 | 37 |
| .... | 2 | 1 | 1 | ... | .... | 4 | 1 | .... | 5 | .... | .... | .... | 5 | .... | 5 | .... | .... | .... | .... | ... | ... | .. | .. | 5 | 38 |
| .... | 1 | .. | .... | ... | 2 | 3 | 8 | .... | 2 | 4 | 6 | .... | 6 | 8 | 14 | .... | .... | .... | .... | ... | ... | .. | .. | 14 | 39 |
| .... | ... | .. | .... | ... | 2 | 3 | 2 | 2 | 2 | 5 | 1 | .... | 2 | 7 | 9 | .... | .... | .... | .... | ... | ... | .. | .. | 9 | 40 |
| .... | ... | .. | .... | ... | .... | 2 | 2 | .... | .... | 3 | 1 | .... | 1 | 3 | 4 | .... | .... | .... | .... | ... | ... | .. | .. | 4 | 41 |
| .... | ... | .. | .... | ... | .... | .... | 1 | .... | .... | 1 | .... | .... | 1 | .... | 1 | .... | .... | .... | .... | ... | ... | .. | .. | 1 | 42 |
| .... | ... | .. | .... | ... | .... | .... | .... | .... | .... | .... | .... | 1 | 1 | .... | 1 | .... | .... | .... | .... | ... | ... | .. | .. | 1 | 43 |
| .... | ... | .. | .... | ... | .... | .... | .... | 1 | .... | .... | .... | 1 | 1 | .... | 1 | .... | .... | .... | .... | ... | ... | .. | .. | 1 | 44 |
| .... | 2 | .. | 1 | ... | 1 | 4 | 8 | 3 | 7 | 3 | 1 | 1 | 6 | 10 | 16 | .... | .... | .... | .... | ... | ... | .. | .. | 16 | 45 |
| .... | 21 | 17 | 27 | 5 | 116 | 110 | 142 | 36 | 164 | 131 | 35 | 60 | 267 | 229 | 510 | .... | .... | .... | .... | ... | ... | .. | 2 | 512 | 46 |
| 1 | 256 | 178 | 382 | 25 | 973 | 1081 | 1612 | 596 | 1853 | 1427 | 333 | 472 | 2870 | 1910 | 4410 | .... | .... | .... | .... | 8 | 8 | 4 | 3 | 4428 | |

SECTION OF THE STATE OF ILLINOIS.

*Coles, Cumberland, Dewitt, Edgar, Fulton, Greene, Hancock, Jersey, Logan, McDonough, Marquitte, Piatt, Pike, Schuyler, Scott, Shelby, Tazwell, Vermillion.*

| California and Territories. | Ireland. | Germany. | Other foreign countries. | Unknown. | Spring. | Summer. | Autumn. | Winter. | Under 1 week. | 1 week and under 1 month. | 1 month and under 3 months. | 3 months and over. | Males. | Females. | Total. | Slaves Black M. | Slaves Black F. | Slaves Mulatto M. | Slaves Mulatto F. | Free Black M. | Free Black F. | Free Mul. M | Free Mul. F. | Aggregate deaths. | |
|---|---|---|---|---|---|---|---|---|---|---|---|---|---|---|---|---|---|---|---|---|---|---|---|---|---|
| .... | ... | ... | .... | .. | 2 | 2 | .... | .... | 1 | 1 | 1 | 1 | 2 | 2 | 4 | .... | .... | .... | .... | .... | .... | .. | .. | 4 | 1 |
| .... | 1 | 3 | .... | 1 | 10 | 14 | 12 | 15 | 36 | 7 | .... | 6 | 43 | 13 | 56 | .... | .... | .... | .... | .... | .... | .. | .. | 56 | 2 |
| .... | ... | ... | .... | .. | 5 | .... | .... | 3 | 5 | 1 | 1 | .... | 4 | 4 | 8 | .... | .... | .... | .... | .... | .... | .. | .. | 8 | 3 |
| .... | 2 | ... | .... | .. | 3 | 5 | 5 | 3 | 12 | .... | .... | .... | 16 | .... | 16 | .... | .... | .... | .... | .... | .... | .. | .. | 16 | 4 |
| .... | ... | ... | .... | .. | 1 | .... | .... | .... | .... | 1 | .... | .... | .... | 1 | 1 | .... | .... | .... | .... | .... | .... | .. | .. | 1 | 5 |
| .... | 1 | ... | .... | .. | .... | .... | .... | 2 | 2 | .... | .... | .... | 1 | 1 | 2 | .... | .... | .... | .... | .... | .... | .. | .. | 2 | 6 |
| .... | ... | 1 | 1 | .. | 5 | .... | 8 | 4 | 16 | .... | 1 | .... | 6 | 11 | 17 | .... | .... | .... | .... | .... | .... | .. | .. | 17 | 7 |
| .... | ... | ... | .... | .. | .... | 2 | .... | .... | .... | 2 | .... | .... | 1 | 1 | 2 | .... | .... | .... | .... | .... | .... | .. | .. | 2 | 8 |
| .... | ... | ... | 1 | .. | .... | .... | 7 | 1 | 1 | 3 | 2 | 2 | 2 | 6 | 8 | .... | .... | .... | .... | .... | .... | .. | .. | 8 | 9 |
| .... | ... | ... | .... | .. | 17 | 9 | 20 | 9 | 17 | 34 | 3 | 1 | 29 | 26 | 55 | .... | .... | .... | .... | .... | .... | .. | .. | 55 | 10 |
| .... | ... | ... | 1 | .. | 9 | 8 | 3 | 1 | 2 | 4 | 1 | 8 | 4 | 12 | 16 | .... | .... | .... | .... | .... | .... | .. | .. | 16 | 11 |
| .... | 1 | ... | 1 | .. | 5 | 5 | 5 | 2 | 2 | 2 | 2 | 9 | 7 | 10 | 17 | .... | .... | .... | .... | .... | .... | .. | .. | 17 | 12 |
| .... | ... | ... | ... | .. | 1 | .... | 2 | 1 | 2 | 2 | .... | .... | 1 | 8 | 4 | .... | .... | .... | .... | .... | .... | .. | .. | 4 | 13 |
| .... | ... | ... | .... | .. | 3 | 3 | 5 | 2 | 7 | 3 | 2 | 1 | 5 | 7 | 12 | .... | .... | .... | .... | .... | 1 | .. | .. | 13 | 14 |
| ... | ... | 2 | 2 | 1 | 13 | 12 | 10 | 10 | 27 | 16 | 1 | .... | .... | 45 | 45 | .... | .... | .... | .... | .... | .... | .. | .. | 45 | 15 |

## CLASSIFICATION OF DEATHS IN MIDDLE

| | Cause of death. | Ages. Under 1. M. | Under 1. F. | 1 and under 5. M. | 1 and under 5. F. | 5 and under 10. M. | 5 and under 10. F. | 10 and under 20. M. | 10 and under 20. F. | 20 and under 50. M. | 20 and under 50. F. | 50 and under 80. M. | 50 and under 80. F. | 80 and under 100. M | 80 and under 100. F. | 100 & over. M | 100 & over. F. | Age unknown. M | Age unknown. F. | Nativities. Born in State. | N. England States. | Middle States. | Southern States. | Southwest'n States. | Northwest'n States. |
|---|---|---|---|---|---|---|---|---|---|---|---|---|---|---|---|---|---|---|---|---|---|---|---|---|---|
| 1 | Cholera | 8 | 9 | 18 | 32 | 14 | 17 | 25 | 17 | 120 | 71 | 46 | 21 | | | | | | | 87 | 8 | 48 | 32 | 20 | 68 |
| 2 | ....do..infantum | 22 | 8 | 13 | 11 | 2 | | 1 | | 1 | | 1 | | | | | | | | 53 | | 2 | 1 | | 3 |
| 3 | ....do..morbus | 2 | | 1 | 2 | 1 | | 1 | | 3 | 2 | 1 | 1 | | | | | | | 7 | | 2 | | 1 | 3 |
| 4 | Colic | 1 | 2 | 1 | | | | | | 4 | | | | | | | | | | 4 | | | | 1 | 3 |
| 5 | Congestion | | | | 2 | | | | | 1 | 2 | | | | | | | | | 3 | | 1 | | | 1 |
| 6 | Consumption | 5 | 3 | 6 | 5 | 1 | 2 | 13 | 20 | 78 | 68 | 46 | 18 | | | | | | | 75 | 10 | 37 | 34 | 7 | 79 |
| 7 | Convulsions | 13 | 4 | 6 | 6 | 1 | 2 | 1 | 4 | 3 | 2 | | | | | | | | | 32 | 1 | 2 | 1 | 1 | 4 |
| 8 | Cramp | 2 | | | 1 | | | | | | 2 | | 1 | 1 | | | | | | 3 | | | 1 | | 1 |
| 9 | Croup | 47 | 22 | 39 | 41 | 8 | 6 | 2 | | | 2 | | | | | | | | | 145 | 2 | 5 | | 5 | 10 |
| 10 | Debility | 3 | 2 | | 1 | | | | | | | 1 | 2 | | | | | | | 6 | | | 1 | 1 | |
| 11 | Diarrhœa | 28 | 14 | 23 | 12 | 1 | | 1 | 2 | 8 | 3 | 2 | 1 | 1 | | | | | | 76 | 2 | 3 | 5 | 4 | 4 |
| 12 | Dropsy | 4 | 4 | 6 | 3 | 1 | 2 | 3 | 3 | 4 | 10 | 5 | 6 | | 3 | | | | | 23 | 2 | 7 | 5 | | 13 |
| 13 | Dysentery | 18 | 15 | 34 | 27 | 3 | 1 | 1 | 4 | 5 | 7 | 2 | 3 | | | | | | | 89 | 1 | 9 | 4 | | 15 |
| 14 | Dyspepsia | | | | | | | | | 2 | 3 | 4 | 1 | | | | | | | | | 4 | 6 | | |
| 15 | Epilepsy | | | | 1 | | | | | 1 | | 3 | | | | | | | | 1 | 1 | 1 | 1 | | |
| 16 | Erysipelas | 8 | 8 | 4 | 6 | 3 | | 3 | 3 | 7 | 6 | 2 | 3 | | | | | | | 31 | 4 | 2 | 4 | 2 | 9 |
| 17 | Fever, not specified | 11 | 16 | 16 | 15 | 8 | 12 | 17 | 15 | 29 | 24 | 8 | 14 | 1 | 1 | | | | | 86 | 7 | 18 | 10 | 12 | 42 |
| 18 | ..do..bilious | 4 | 1 | 2 | 4 | 1 | 1 | 3 | 4 | 12 | 7 | 2 | 2 | 1 | | | | | | 16 | | 4 | 7 | 1 | 12 |
| 19 | ..do..brain | 6 | 4 | 8 | 4 | 6 | 1 | 3 | 2 | 1 | 1 | 1 | | | | | | | | 26 | | 3 | | 1 | 4 |
| 20 | ..do..congestive | 1 | 6 | 11 | 5 | 6 | 4 | 12 | 10 | 17 | 8 | 5 | 6 | | | | | | | 37 | 3 | 9 | 5 | 3 | 27 |
| 21 | ..do..inflammatory | | | 1 | | | | | | | | | | | | | | | | | | | | | |
| 22 | ..do..intermittent | 4 | 5 | 1 | 2 | | 2 | 2 | 1 | 5 | 2 | 2 | 2 | | | | | | | 13 | | 2 | 4 | 2 | 4 |
| 23 | ..do..puerperal | | | | | | | | | | 12 | | 1 | | | | | | | 4 | | | 3 | 4 | 2 |
| 24 | ..do..scarlet | 7 | 4 | 18 | 15 | 9 | 7 | 2 | 8 | 2 | 2 | 2 | 3 | | | | | | | 55 | 1 | 3 | 3 | | 15 |
| 25 | ..do..ship | | 1 | | | | 1 | | 2 | 1 | | | | | | | | | | 1 | | | | | 1 |
| 26 | ..do..typhus | | 2 | 5 | 5 | 5 | 5 | 13 | 11 | 14 | 8 | 5 | 5 | | 1 | | | | | 40 | | 8 | 9 | 3 | 17 |
| 27 | ..do..winter | | 2 | 3 | 2 | 1 | 2 | 4 | 1 | 12 | 5 | 2 | | | | | | | | 8 | | 3 | 5 | 3 | 15 |
| 28 | ..do..yellow | | | | 1 | | | | | | | | | | | | | | | 1 | | | | | |
| 29 | Gravel | | | | | | | | | | | 5 | | 1 | | | | | | | | 2 | 2 | 2 | |
| 30 | Head, disease of | | 1 | 1 | | | | | | | | | | | | | | | | 1 | | | | 1 | |
| 31 | Heart ...do | 1 | | | | | | | 1 | 2 | 1 | | | | | | | | | 1 | | 3 | | | 1 |
| 32 | Hemorrhage | | | 2 | | | 1 | 1 | 1 | | 1 | | 1 | | | | | | | 5 | | | | | 2 |
| 33 | Hives | 2 | 4 | 1 | | | | | | 1 | | | | | | | | | | 7 | 1 | | | | |
| 34 | Hooping cough | 9 | 16 | 14 | 19 | 1 | 5 | 1 | 1 | | 1 | | | | | | | | | 59 | | 1 | | 1 | 5 |
| 35 | Hydrocephalus | 2 | 1 | 2 | 2 | 1 | | 1 | 1 | | | | | | | | | | | 8 | | | | | 1 |
| 36 | Inflammation | | 2 | 1 | 2 | | | | 1 | 2 | 1 | 1 | | | | | | | | 7 | | 1 | | 1 | 1 |
| 37 | Influenza | 1 | | | | | | | | | | | | | | | | | | | | | | | |
| 38 | Intemperance | | | | | | | | | 3 | 1 | 1 | | | | | | | | | | | 1 | | 2 |
| 39 | Jaundice | 1 | 1 | | | | | | | 1 | | | | | | | | | | 2 | | 1 | | | |
| 40 | Kidneys, disease of | | | | | | | | | 1 | | | 1 | | | | | | | 1 | | 1 | | | |
| 41 | Killed | | | | | | | | | | | 1 | | | | | | | | | | | | 1 | |
| 42 | Lightning | | | | | | | | 1 | 2 | | | | | | | | | | 1 | | | | | 2 |
| 43 | Liver, disease of | 3 | 2 | 1 | 1 | | | 1 | | 8 | 6 | 5 | 3 | | | | | | | 11 | 1 | 3 | 5 | 1 | 8 |
| 44 | Lungs ...do | 2 | 1 | 3 | 2 | 1 | | 1 | 1 | 5 | 6 | 2 | 1 | | | | | | | 13 | 1 | 3 | 2 | 1 | 5 |
| 45 | Measles | 7 | 3 | 10 | 8 | 2 | 4 | 1 | 1 | 1 | 2 | | | | | | | | | 28 | 1 | 2 | 1 | | 6 |
| 46 | Milk sickness | | | | | 1 | | 1 | 1 | | 1 | | | | | | | | | | | | | | 4 |
| 47 | Mortification | | 1 | | | | | | | | | | | | | | | | | 1 | | | | | |
| 48 | Mumps | | 1 | | | 1 | | 2 | | 1 | | | | | | | | | | 3 | | | | | 2 |
| 49 | Murder | | | | | | | | | 1 | | | | | | | | | | 1 | | | | | |
| 50 | Neuralgia | | | | | | | 1 | | 3 | 1 | 1 | | | | | | | | 1 | | 2 | 1 | | 2 |
| 51 | Old age | | | | | | | | | | | 7 | 19 | 7 | 7 | 1 | | | | 5 | 6 | 6 | 10 | | 5 |
| 52 | Paralysis | | | 1 | | | 1 | | | 2 | 3 | 8 | 2 | 1 | | | | | | 2 | 1 | 4 | 5 | 1 | 3 |
| 53 | Pleurisy | 2 | 2 | 2 | | | 1 | | 1 | 5 | | 5 | 1 | | | | | | | 7 | | 1 | 2 | 4 | 4 |
| 54 | Pneumonia | 23 | 14 | 25 | 23 | 6 | 6 | 10 | 12 | 56 | 24 | 24 | 13 | | | | | | | 116 | 5 | 26 | 15 | 11 | 49 |
| 55 | Poison | | | | | 1 | 2 | 1 | | 2 | 1 | 1 | | | | | | | | 4 | | 1 | | | 3 |
| 56 | Quinsy | 1 | 1 | 1 | 2 | 1 | | | | 1 | 1 | | | | | | | | | 6 | | | | 1 | |
| 57 | Rheumatism | 1 | | | | | | 4 | 1 | 1 | 1 | 1 | | | | | | | | 4 | | 2 | 1 | | 2 |
| 58 | Scrofula | | 1 | 2 | 2 | 2 | | 1 | 1 | 3 | 2 | 1 | | | | | | | | 9 | | 1 | 1 | 1 | 3 |
| 59 | Small pox | 2 | 3 | 1 | 2 | 2 | 3 | | | 8 | 1 | | | | | | | | | 14 | 1 | | 1 | 2 | 4 |
| 60 | Spine, disease of | | | 1 | 1 | | | 1 | 1 | | | | | | | | | | | 2 | | | | | 2 |
| 61 | Stillborn | 1 | 3 | | | | | | | | | | | | | | | | | 4 | | | | | |
| 62 | Suicide | | | | | | | | | 2 | 1 | | | | | | | | | | | 1 | | | 2 |
| 63 | Summer complaint | 5 | 5 | 5 | 7 | | | | | | | | | | | | | | | 22 | | | | | |
| 64 | Teething | 4 | 5 | 5 | 6 | | | | | | | | | | | | | | | 15 | | | | | 2 |
| 65 | Tetanus | | | | | 1 | | | | | | | | | | | | | | 1 | | | | | |
| 66 | Throat, disease of | 1 | | | | 1 | | | | | | | | | | | | | | 1 | | | | | 1 |
| 67 | Thrush | 4 | 1 | | | | | | | | | | | | | | | | | 5 | | | | | |
| 68 | Ulcer | | | | 1 | | | | | | | | | | | | | | | 1 | | | | | |
| 69 | White swelling | 1 | | | | | | | | 1 | 1 | | | | | | | | | 1 | | | | 2 | |
| 70 | Worms | | 2 | 7 | 10 | | 5 | 1 | 1 | | | | | | | | | | | 21 | | | 1 | 3 | |
| 71 | Unknown | 119 | 100 | 65 | 47 | 22 | 15 | 25 | 24 | 72 | 86 | 44 | 43 | 1 | 2 | | | | 1 | 479 | 12 | 31 | 33 | 26 | 62 |
| | Total | 408 | 319 | 391 | 362 | 122 | 116 | 175 | 169 | 544 | 452 | 261 | 188 | 18 | 17 | 1 | | | 3 | 1923 | 82 | 289 | 240 | 134 | 591 |

## SECTION OF THE STATE OF ILLINOIS—Continued.

| NATIVITIES. | | | | | SEASON OF DECEASE. | | | | DURATION OF SICKNESS. | | | | WHITES. | | | COLORED. | | | | | | | | | |
|---|---|---|---|---|---|---|---|---|---|---|---|---|---|---|---|---|---|---|---|---|---|---|---|---|---|
| | | | | | | | | | | | | | | | | Slaves. | | | | Free. | | | | | |
| | | | | | | | | | | | | | | | | Black. | | Mulatto. | | Black. | | Mul. | | | |
| California and Territories. | Ireland. | Germany. | Other foreign countries. | Unknown. | Spring. | Summer. | Autumn. | Winter. | Under 1 week. | 1 week and under 1 month. | 1 month and under 3 months. | 3 months and over. | Males. | Females. | Total. | M. | F. | M. | F. | M. | F. | M | F. | Aggregate deaths. | |
| | 14 | 97 | 20 | 4 | 34 | 255 | 100 | 9 | 256 | 30 | 2 | 1 | 226 | 166 | 392 | | | | | 5 | 1 | | | 398 | 1 |
| | | | | | 3 | 17 | 35 | 1 | 24 | 29 | | | 40 | 19 | 59 | | | | | | | | | 59 | 2 |
| | | | | 1 | 2 | 3 | 7 | 2 | 11 | 8 | | | 9 | 5 | 14 | | | | | | | | | 14 | 3 |
| | | | | | 4 | 3 | | 1 | 7 | 1 | | | 6 | 2 | 8 | | | | | | | | | 8 | 4 |
| | | | | | 1 | 1 | 2 | 1 | 4 | 1 | | | 1 | 4 | 5 | | | | | | | | | 5 | 5 |
| 4 | 5 | 2 | 9 | 3 | 90 | 50 | 53 | 48 | 9 | 21 | 18 | 113 | 149 | 116 | 265 | | | | | | | | | 265 | 6 |
| | | | 1 | | 9 | 15 | 11 | 7 | 28 | 8 | 3 | 2 | 24 | 18 | 42 | | | | | | | | | 42 | 7 |
| | | 2 | | | 3 | 2 | 1 | 1 | 6 | | | 1 | 3 | 4 | 7 | | | | | | | | | 7 | 8 |
| | | | | | 40 | 21 | 54 | 42 | 77 | 37 | | | 96 | 71 | 167 | | | | | | | | | 167 | 9 |
| | | | 1 | | 3 | 2 | 4 | | 2 | 2 | 3 | 2 | 4 | 5 | 9 | | | | | | | | | 9 | 10 |
| | 1 | | 1 | | 7 | 23 | 61 | 5 | 23 | 33 | 18 | 10 | 64 | 32 | 96 | | | | | | | | | 96 | 11 |
| | 1 | 1 | 2 | | 13 | 11 | 21 | 9 | 5 | 15 | 11 | 14 | 23 | 31 | 54 | | | | | | | | | 54 | 12 |
| | | 1 | 1 | | 3 | 17 | 93 | 7 | 46 | 56 | 13 | | 63 | 57 | 120 | | | | | | | | | 120 | 13 |
| | | | | | 1 | 5 | 1 | 3 | 2 | | 3 | 3 | 6 | 4 | 10 | | | | | | | | | 10 | 14 |
| | | | 1 | | 1 | 1 | 2 | 1 | 1 | 2 | | 1 | 4 | 1 | 5 | | | | | | | | | 5 | 15 |
| | 1 | | | | 16 | 13 | 9 | 11 | 17 | 26 | 1 | 2 | 27 | 26 | 53 | | | | | | | | | 53 | 16 |
| | 3 | 3 | 6 | | 48 | 41 | 72 | 26 | 55 | 99 | 20 | 11 | 90 | 97 | 187 | | | | | | | | | 187 | 17 |
| | | 2 | 2 | | 7 | 10 | 19 | 7 | 8 | 25 | 8 | | 25 | 19 | 44 | | | | | | | | | 44 | 18 |
| | | | | | 14 | 8 | 8 | | 14 | 17 | 2 | 1 | 21 | 12 | 33 | | | | | | | 1 | | 34 | 19 |
| | 2 | | 4 | 1 | 23 | 18 | 33 | 16 | 59 | 26 | 4 | | 52 | 39 | 91 | | | | | | | | | 91 | 20 |
| | | | 1 | | | | 1 | | 1 | | | | 1 | | 1 | | | | | | | | | 1 | 21 |
| | | | 2 | 1 | 4 | 4 | 15 | 5 | 8 | 12 | 6 | 2 | 14 | 14 | 28 | | | | | | | | | 28 | 22 |
| | | | | | 4 | 3 | 3 | 3 | 3 | 9 | | | | 13 | 13 | | | | | | | | | 13 | 23 |
| | | | | 2 | 14 | 24 | 20 | 20 | 34 | 42 | | | 40 | 39 | 79 | | | | | | | | | 79 | 24 |
| | 2 | 1 | | | 4 | 1 | | | 1 | 3 | 1 | | 1 | 4 | 4 | | | | | | | | | 5 | 25 |
| | | 1 | 1 | | 21 | 10 | 29 | 17 | 7 | 59 | 9 | 2 | 42 | 37 | 79 | | | | | | | | | 79 | 26 |
| | | | | | 22 | 2 | | 10 | 8 | 26 | | | 22 | 12 | 34 | | | | | | | | | 34 | 27 |
| | | | | | | | | | | | | | | 1 | 1 | | | | | | | | | 1 | 28 |
| | | | | | | 3 | 2 | 1 | 3 | | | 2 | 6 | | 6 | | | | | | | | | 6 | 29 |
| | | | | | | | 1 | 1 | | 2 | | | 1 | 1 | 2 | | | | | | | | | 2 | 30 |
| | | | | | 2 | 1 | 2 | | | 1 | 1 | 3 | 3 | 2 | 5 | | | | | | | | | 5 | 31 |
| | | | | | 1 | 3 | 3 | | 4 | | | 1 | 3 | 4 | 7 | | | | | | | | | 7 | 32 |
| | | | | | 4 | | 1 | 3 | 5 | 3 | | | 4 | 4 | 8 | | | | | | | | | 8 | 33 |
| | | | 1 | | 16 | 19 | 17 | 12 | 12 | 33 | 9 | 9 | 25 | 42 | 67 | | | | | | | | | 67 | 34 |
| | | | 1 | | 4 | 2 | 2 | 2 | 1 | 8 | 1 | | 6 | 4 | 10 | | | | | | | | | 10 | 35 |
| | | | | | | 5 | 4 | 1 | 4 | 3 | | 3 | 4 | 6 | 10 | | | | | | | | | 10 | 36 |
| | | | 1 | | | 1 | | | 1 | | | | 1 | | 1 | | | | | | | | | 1 | 37 |
| | 1 | | 1 | | 2 | 2 | 1 | | 2 | 1 | | 2 | 4 | 1 | 5 | | | | | | | | | 5 | 38 |
| | | | | | 2 | | 1 | | | 2 | | | 2 | | 2 | | | | | | 1 | | | 3 | 39 |
| | | | | | | 1 | 1 | | 1 | | | | 1 | 1 | 2 | | | | | | | | | 2 | 40 |
| | | | | | | | | 1 | 1 | | | | 1 | | 1 | | | | | | | | | 1 | 41 |
| | | | | | | 1 | 2 | | 3 | | | | 2 | 1 | 3 | | | | | | | | | 3 | 42 |
| | 1 | | | | 11 | 9 | 6 | 4 | 2 | 8 | 9 | 11 | 18 | 12 | 30 | | | | | | | | | 30 | 43 |
| | | | | | 6 | 7 | 4 | 8 | 4 | 12 | 1 | 3 | 14 | 11 | 25 | | | | | | | | | 25 | 44 |
| | | | 1 | | 6 | 29 | 1 | | 1 | 28 | 3 | | 21 | 18 | 39 | | | | | | | | | 39 | 45 |
| | | | | | | | 4 | | 4 | | | | 2 | 2 | 4 | | | | | | | | | 4 | 46 |
| | | | | | | | 1 | | 1 | | | | | 1 | 1 | | | | | | | | | 1 | 47 |
| | | | | | 5 | | | | | 5 | | | 4 | 1 | 5 | | | | | | | | | 5 | 48 |
| | | | | | | | 1 | | 1 | | | | 1 | | 1 | | | | | | | | | 1 | 49 |
| | | | | | 1 | 3 | 2 | | 1 | 2 | | 2 | 5 | 1 | 6 | | | | | | | | | 6 | 50 |
| | 3 | 2 | 4 | | 10 | 10 | 7 | 13 | 12 | 8 | 2 | 7 | 15 | 25 | 40 | | | | | | 1 | | | 41 | 51 |
| | 1 | | 1 | | 6 | 5 | 2 | 5 | 2 | 7 | 1 | 6 | 12 | 6 | 18 | | | | | | | | | 18 | 52 |
| | 1 | | | | 8 | 5 | 2 | 4 | 8 | 9 | | 1 | 14 | 5 | 19 | | | | | | | | | 19 | 53 |
| | 4 | 3 | 4 | 3 | 79 | 53 | 26 | 51 | 43 | 158 | 15 | 3 | 141 | 92 | 233 | | | | | 3 | | | | 236 | 54 |
| | | | | | 3 | 1 | 3 | 1 | 3 | 4 | | 1 | 5 | 3 | 8 | | | | | | | | | 8 | 55 |
| | | 1 | | | 2 | 1 | 1 | 3 | 6 | 1 | | | 4 | 4 | 8 | | | | | | | | | 8 | 56 |
| | | | | | 3 | 4 | | 2 | 1 | 4 | 1 | 3 | 7 | 1 | 8 | | | | | | 1 | | | 9 | 57 |
| | | | | | 4 | 7 | 4 | | 1 | | 4 | 6 | 9 | 6 | 15 | | | | | | | | | 15 | 58 |
| | | | | | 4 | 4 | 5 | 9 | 1 | 20 | | 1 | 13 | 9 | 22 | | | | | | | | | 22 | 59 |
| | | | | | 1 | 1 | | 2 | | 1 | | 1 | 2 | 2 | 4 | | | | | | | | | 4 | 60 |
| | | | | | 3 | | 1 | | | | | | 1 | 3 | 4 | | | | | | | | | 4 | 61 |
| | | | | | 1 | 2 | | | 2 | | | | 2 | 1 | 3 | | | | | | | | | 3 | 62 |
| | | | | | | 6 | 7 | | 6 | 7 | 6 | 3 | 10 | 12 | 22 | | | | | | | | | 22 | 63 |
| | 1 | 1 | 1 | | | 8 | 10 | 2 | 7 | 9 | 3 | 1 | 9 | 11 | 20 | | | | | | | | | 20 | 64 |
| | | | | | | 1 | | | | 1 | | | 1 | | 1 | | | | | | | | | 1 | 65 |
| | | | | | | | 1 | 1 | 2 | | | | 2 | | 2 | | | | | | | | | 2 | 66 |
| | | | | | | | 4 | 1 | 3 | 1 | 1 | | 4 | 1 | 5 | | | | | | | | | 5 | 67 |
| | | | | | | | | | | 1 | | | | 1 | 1 | | | | | | | | | 1 | 68 |
| | | | | | 1 | 1 | 1 | | | 1 | 1 | 1 | 2 | 1 | 3 | | | | | | | | | 3 | 69 |
| | | 1 | | | 4 | 5 | 11 | 5 | 11 | 10 | 2 | 3 | 8 | 18 | 26 | | | | | | | | | 26 | 70 |
| | 5 | 3 | 9 | 6 | 120 | 120 | 148 | 109 | 161 | 132 | 36 | 86 | 348 | 316 | 664 | | | | | | 1 | | 1 | 666 | 71 |
| 4 | 51 | 127 | 82 | 23 | 774 | 935 | 1020 | 546 | 1166 | 1140 | 227 | 352 | 1911 | 1619 | 3530 | ... | .... | ... | .... | 8 | 6 | 1 | 1 | 3546 | |

## CLASSIFICATION OF DEATHS IN SOUTHERN

*Embracing the following counties: Bond, Clay, Clinton, Crawford, Edwards, Effingham, Fay Madison, Massac, Marion, Monroe, Perry, Pope, Pulaski, Randolph, Richland, St.*

| | Cause of death. | AGES. | | | | | | | | | | | | | | | | | | NATIVITIES. | | | | | |
|---|---|---|---|---|---|---|---|---|---|---|---|---|---|---|---|---|---|---|---|---|---|---|---|---|---|
| | | Under 1. | | 1 and under 5. | | 5 and under 10. | | 10 and under 20. | | 20 and under 50. | | 50 and under 80. | | 80 and under 100. | | 100 & over. | | Age unknown. | | Born in State. | N. England States. | Middle States. | Southern States. | Southwest'n States. | Northwest'n States. |
| | | M. | F. | M. | F. | M. | F. | M. | F. | M. | F. | M. | F. | M | F | M | F. | M | F. | | | | | | |
| 1 | Abscess | | | | | 1 | 1 | 1 | | | | | | | | | | | | 3 | | | | | |
| 2 | Accident, not specif'd | | 4 | 5 | | 3 | 1 | 7 | | 5 | 1 | 4 | 2 | | | | | | | 17 | | 3 | 5 | | 4 |
| 3 | ....do....burned | 1 | | 3 | 2 | | 3 | | | 2 | 2 | | | | | | | | | 9 | | | | 1 | 2 |
| 4 | ....do....drowned | | | 2 | | 1 | | 1 | | 7 | 1 | 3 | | | | | | | | 5 | 2 | | 1 | 1 | 2 |
| 5 | ....do....scalded | 1 | | | | 1 | | | | | | | | | | | | | | 2 | | | | | |
| 6 | Apoplexy | | | | | | | | | 3 | | 3 | 1 | | | | | | | | | 2 | 2 | 2 | |
| 7 | Asthma | | | | | | | | | | 1 | 1 | 2 | | | | | | | | | | 2 | 1 | |
| 8 | Bowels, disease of | 2 | 7 | 5 | 6 | | 1 | 1 | 2 | | 1 | | | | | | | | | 23 | | 1 | | | 1 |
| 9 | Brain....do | 12 | 8 | 10 | 10 | 3 | 2 | 2 | 1 | 3 | 3 | | | | | | | | | 42 | 1 | 2 | | | [illegible] |
| 10 | Bronchitis | | | 4 | 1 | | | 1 | | 3 | 2 | 1 | 2 | | | | | | | 7 | 1 | 1 | 2 | | 1 |
| 11 | Cancer | | | 1 | | | | | 1 | 1 | 3 | 1 | 1 | | | | | | | 2 | 1 | | 4 | 1 | |
| 12 | Canker | | | | 1 | | | | | | | | | | | | | | | 1 | | | | | |
| 13 | Catarrh | | 1 | 1 | 4 | | | 2 | 4 | | 2 | | 1 | | | | | 1 | | 7 | | | 2 | 3 | [illegible] |
| 14 | Childbirth | | | | | | | | 4 | | 28 | | | | | | | | | 10 | | 1 | 1 | 1 | [illegible] |
| 15 | Cholera | 17 | 31 | 58 | 52 | 26 | 34 | 47 | 35 | 185 | 134 | 69 | 52 | 12 | 1 | 2 | | | | 226 | 16 | 31 | 34 | 43 | [illegible] |
| 16 | ....do....infantum | 10 | 8 | 10 | 7 | 1 | | 1 | 1 | | | | | | | | | | | 36 | | | | 1 | [illegible] |
| 17 | ....do....morbus | 1 | 2 | 3 | 6 | 3 | | | 1 | 4 | 2 | | 1 | | | | | | | 14 | | 1 | 1 | 3 | [illegible] |
| 18 | Chorea | | | | | | | | 1 | 2 | 1 | | | | | | | | | 1 | 1 | | | 2 | |
| 19 | Colic | 1 | 2 | | 1 | | | | | 4 | 2 | 2 | 1 | | | | | | | 3 | | 5 | 1 | 1 | |
| 20 | Consumption | | 2 | 6 | 5 | | 2 | 4 | 10 | 61 | 57 | 25 | 13 | | | | | | 2 | 50 | 8 | 13 | 25 | 29 | [illegible] |
| 21 | Convulsions | 8 | 7 | 4 | 6 | | 1 | 3 | 1 | 5 | 3 | 1 | | | | | | | | 31 | | 1 | | 1 | [illegible] |
| 22 | Cramp | | | | 2 | | | 1 | 1 | | | | | | | | | | | 2 | | | | | 1 |
| 23 | Croup | 44 | 40 | 34 | 31 | 6 | 6 | 1 | | 1 | 1 | | | | | | | | | 143 | | 2 | 2 | 3 | [illegible] |
| 24 | Debility | 1 | 6 | 1 | | | | | | | 2 | 1 | 2 | | | | | | | 8 | 1 | 2 | | 1 | |
| 25 | Diarrhœa | 18 | 16 | 20 | 18 | 1 | | | | 11 | 9 | 3 | 2 | | | | | | | 69 | 1 | 3 | 4 | 7 | [illegible] |
| 26 | Dropsy | 2 | 3 | 1 | 5 | 8 | 4 | 3 | 5 | 20 | 14 | 9 | 7 | 1 | | | | | | 32 | 1 | 2 | 16 | 9 | |
| 27 | Dysentery | 24 | 15 | 22 | 30 | 3 | | 2 | | 5 | 3 | 2 | 1 | | | | | | | 89 | | 2 | 3 | 1 | |
| 28 | Dyspepsia | | | | | | | | | 4 | | | 1 | | | | | | | 2 | | | 3 | | |
| 29 | Epilepsy | | | | 1 | | | | | | | | | | | | | | | 1 | | | | | |
| 30 | Erysipelas | 7 | 4 | 1 | 5 | 1 | 1 | 4 | 3 | 9 | 14 | 1 | 3 | 1 | | | | | | 21 | 2 | 2 | 9 | 6 | 1 |
| 31 | Fever, not specified | 22 | 25 | 26 | 26 | 14 | 11 | 13 | 20 | 54 | 44 | 21 | 15 | | | | | 1 | | 176 | 2 | 18 | 26 | 17 | 4 |
| 32 | ...do..bilious | 2 | 3 | 3 | 5 | 1 | 1 | 2 | 6 | 9 | 8 | 6 | | | | | | | | 20 | | 1 | 6 | 5 | |
| 33 | ...do..brain | 1 | | 3 | 2 | | | | | | | | | | | | | | | 5 | | | 1 | | |
| 34 | ...do..congestive | 4 | 9 | 4 | 5 | 3 | 4 | 14 | 15 | 13 | 16 | 5 | 3 | | 1 | | | | | 53 | 1 | 4 | 11 | 5 | 1 |
| 35 | ...do..inflammatory | | | | | 1 | | | | 1 | 1 | | | | | | | | | 1 | | | | 1 | |
| 36 | ...do..intermittent | 2 | 3 | 10 | 7 | 1 | 3 | 1 | 4 | 5 | 4 | 1 | 3 | | | | | | | 26 | | 2 | 4 | 4 | |
| 37 | ...do..puerperal | | | | | | | | 3 | | 15 | | | | | | | | | 4 | | 1 | 1 | 3 | |
| 38 | ...do..remittent | | | | | 1 | 1 | 2 | 1 | | 5 | | | | | | | | | 3 | | | | 1 | |
| 39 | ...do..scarlet | | 3 | 2 | 5 | 4 | 3 | 1 | 1 | | | | | | | | | | | 17 | | | | | |
| 40 | ...do..ship | | | | | | | 1 | | 1 | | | | | | | | | | 1 | | | | | |
| 41 | ...do..typhus | | | 2 | 3 | 5 | 3 | 8 | 5 | 18 | 8 | 4 | 3 | | | | | | | 16 | 3 | 5 | 7 | 12 | 1 |
| 42 | ...do..winter | 2 | | | 4 | 3 | 3 | 5 | 4 | 17 | 16 | 13 | 2 | | | | | | 1 | 32 | | 2 | 8 | 12 | 1 |
| 43 | ...do..yellow | | | | | | | | | | | | 1 | | | | | | | 1 | | | | | |
| 44 | Gravel | | | | | | | | | 1 | | 3 | | | | | | | | 2 | | | 2 | | |
| 45 | Head, disease of | 1 | 1 | | 2 | | | | | | | | | | | | | 1 | | 4 | | | | | |
| 46 | Heart....do | | | 2 | 1 | | | | | | 1 | | | | | | | | | 2 | | | | | |
| 47 | Heat | | | | | | | 1 | | | | | | | | | | | | 1 | | | | | |
| 48 | Hemorrhage | | | | | 1 | | 1 | | 1 | 1 | 1 | | | | | | | | | | | 1 | | |
| 49 | Hernia | | | | | | | | | | | 1 | | | | | | | | | | | 1 | | |
| 50 | Hives | 25 | 13 | 4 | 6 | | | | | | | | | | | | | | | 47 | | | | 1 | |
| 51 | Hooping cough | 13 | 7 | 6 | 6 | | 2 | | | | | | | | | | | | | 28 | | 1 | | 1 | |
| 52 | Hydrocephalus | 1 | | 1 | | | | | | | | | | | | | | | | 2 | | | | | |
| 53 | Hydrophobia | | | | | | | 1 | | | | | | | | | | | | 1 | | | | | |
| 54 | Inflamat'n, not spec'd | 2 | | 4 | 2 | 1 | | 2 | | 2 | 2 | 3 | | | | | | | | 12 | | 1 | 2 | | |
| 55 | ....do....bowels | 1 | 1 | | 4 | | | | | 2 | 1 | | 1 | | | | | | | 6 | | | | 3 | |
| 56 | ....do....brain | 11 | 3 | 13 | 7 | 3 | 5 | 6 | 5 | 4 | 5 | 2 | | | | | | | | 50 | 1 | 1 | 3 | 3 | |
| 57 | ....do....stomach | 1 | | | | | | | | 1 | | | | | | | | | | | | 1 | | | |
| 58 | Influenza | | | | | 1 | | | | 1 | | | | | | | | | | 1 | | | 1 | | |
| 59 | Intemperance | | | | | | | | | 2 | | 1 | | | | | | | | | | 1 | 1 | | |
| 60 | Jaundice | 1 | | 1 | 4 | | 1 | | | 1 | | | | | | | | | | 7 | | | | | |
| 61 | Kidneys, disease of | | | | | | 1 | 1 | | | | | | | | | | | | 1 | | | | 1 | |
| 62 | Killed | | | 1 | | 1 | | 4 | | 1 | | 1 | | | | | | | | 7 | | | | | |
| 63 | Lightning | | | | | | | 1 | | 1 | 1 | | | | | | | | | 1 | | | | 1 | |
| 64 | Liver, disease of | | 1 | 2 | 1 | 1 | 1 | 1 | 1 | 9 | 3 | 2 | 2 | | | | | | | 12 | | 1 | 5 | 2 | |
| 65 | Lungs...do | 4 | 3 | 3 | 2 | | 2 | 1 | | 7 | 4 | | 2 | | | | | | | 18 | | | 2 | 1 | |
| 66 | Mania-a-potu | | | | | | | | | 5 | | | | | | | | | | | | 3 | 1 | | |
| 67 | Measles | 2 | 1 | 7 | 5 | 2 | 1 | 2 | | 5 | 2 | | | | | | | | | 18 | | 4 | 1 | 3 | |
| 68 | Menses, suppress'n of | | | | | | | | 1 | | 1 | | | | | | | | | | | | 1 | 1 | |
| 69 | Milk sickness | | | | | | | | 1 | 3 | 2 | 1 | | | | | | | | 2 | | | 3 | 1 | |
| 70 | Mortification | | 1 | | | | | | | | | 1 | | | | | | | | 1 | | | 1 | | |
| 71 | Mumps | | | | | | | | 1 | 1 | | | | | | | | | | | | 1 | | | |
| 72 | Murder | | | | | | | | | 4 | | 1 | | | | | | | | | | 2 | 1 | | |

SECTION OF THE STATE OF ILLINOIS.

*ette, Franklin, Gallatin, Hamilton, Hardin, Jackson, Jasper, Jefferson, Johnson, Lawrence, Clair, Saline, Sangamon, Union, Wabash, Washington, Wayne, White, Williamson.*

| NATIVITIES. | | | | | SEASON OF DECEASE. | | | | DURATION OF SICKNESS. | | | | WHITES. | | | COLORED. | | | | | | | | | |
|---|---|---|---|---|---|---|---|---|---|---|---|---|---|---|---|---|---|---|---|---|---|---|---|---|---|
| | | | | | | | | | | | | | | | | Slaves. | | | | Free. | | | | | |
| | | | | | | | | | | | | | | | | Black. | | Mulatto. | | Black. | | Mul. | | | |
| California and Territories. | Ireland. | Germany. | Other foreign countries. | Unknown. | Spring. | Summer. | Autumn. | Winter. | Under 1 week. | 1 week and under 1 month. | 1 month and under 3 months. | 3 months and over. | Males. | Females. | Total. | M. | F. | M. | F. | M. | F. | M | F. | Aggregate deaths. | |
| | | | | | | 1 | 1 | 1 | 2 | 1 | | | 2 | 1 | 3 | | | | | | | | | 3 | 1 |
| | 2 | | 1 | | 10 | 7 | 10 | 5 | 16 | 8 | 3 | 1 | 24 | 8 | 32 | | | | | | | | | 32 | 2 |
| | | 1 | | | 6 | 1 | 2 | 4 | 10 | 1 | | 2 | 6 | 7 | 13 | | | | | | | | | 13 | 3 |
| | 2 | 2 | | | 4 | 6 | 1 | 4 | 9 | 1 | | | 14 | 1 | 15 | | | | | | | | | 15 | 4 |
| | | | | | 1 | | | 1 | 1 | 1 | | | 2 | | 2 | | | | | | | | | 2 | 5 |
| | | | 1 | | 2 | 3 | 1 | 1 | 4 | | | 2 | 6 | 1 | 7 | | | | | | | | | 7 | 6 |
| | | | 1 | | 1 | | 3 | | 2 | 1 | | 1 | 1 | 3 | 4 | | | | | | | | | 4 | 7 |
| | | | | | 2 | 6 | 12 | 5 | 12 | 9 | 2 | 1 | 8 | 17 | 25 | | | | | | | | | 25 | 8 |
| | | 2 | 1 | | 15 | 16 | 16 | 7 | 28 | 21 | 5 | | 30 | 24 | 54 | | | | | | | | | 54 | 9 |
| 1 | | | 1 | | 3 | 5 | 3 | 2 | 2 | 3 | 2 | 5 | 9 | 5 | 14 | | | | | | | | | 14 | 10 |
| | | | | | 3 | 1 | 2 | 2 | | 1 | 2 | 5 | 3 | 5 | 8 | | | | | | | | | 8 | 11 |
| | | | | | | | | 1 | | | 1 | | | 1 | 1 | | | | | | | | | 1 | 12 |
| | | 1 | | | 5 | 3 | 5 | 3 | 3 | 5 | 2 | 3 | 4 | 11 | 15 | | | | | | 1 | | | 16 | 13 |
| | 4 | 3 | 2 | | 7 | 10 | 7 | 8 | 14 | 12 | 3 | 2 | | 32 | 32 | | | | | | | | | 32 | 14 |
| 1 | 15 | 216 | 87 | 18 | 23 | 585 | 139 | 8 | 622 | 71 | 1 | | 410 | 339 | 749 | | | | | 4 | | 2 | | 755 | 15 |
| | | | | | 1 | 15 | 19 | 3 | 17 | 17 | 2 | 1 | 22 | 16 | 38 | | | | | | | | | 38 | 16 |
| | | 1 | | | 1 | 7 | 15 | | 10 | 8 | 1 | 1 | 11 | 12 | 23 | | | | | | | | | 23 | 17 |
| | | | | | | 3 | 1 | | 3 | 1 | | | 2 | 2 | 4 | | | | | | | | | 4 | 18 |
| | | 2 | 1 | | 3 | 4 | 3 | 3 | 8 | 5 | | | 7 | 6 | 13 | | | | | | | | | 13 | 19 |
| 1 | 2 | 10 | 12 | | 63 | 47 | 37 | 39 | 5 | 30 | 34 | 96 | 92 | 89 | 181 | | | | | 3 | 1 | 1 | 1 | 187 | 20 |
| | 1 | | | 1 | 19 | 4 | 10 | 6 | 20 | 11 | 2 | 4 | 21 | 18 | 39 | | | | | | | | | 39 | 21 |
| | | 1 | | | 2 | 1 | 1 | | 3 | 1 | | | 1 | 3 | 4 | | | | | | | | | 4 | 22 |
| | | 2 | | | 39 | 35 | 61 | 29 | 126 | 32 | 4 | | 85 | 78 | 163 | | | | | 1 | | | | 164 | 23 |
| | | | | | 1 | 3 | 2 | 7 | | 3 | 3 | 4 | 2 | 10 | 12 | | | | | 1 | | | | 13 | 24 |
| | 2 | 1 | 2 | 1 | 8 | 37 | 46 | 6 | 28 | 51 | 11 | 8 | 53 | 45 | 98 | | | | | | | | | 98 | 25 |
| | 3 | 9 | 2 | 1 | 22 | 21 | 18 | 19 | 5 | 22 | 16 | 33 | 42 | 38 | 80 | | | | | 2 | | | | 82 | 26 |
| | | 3 | 1 | | 2 | 30 | 69 | 6 | 23 | 63 | 17 | 4 | 58 | 49 | 107 | | | | | | | | | 107 | 27 |
| | | | | | 3 | | 2 | | | 1 | 2 | 2 | 4 | 1 | 5 | | | | | | | | | 5 | 28 |
| | | | | | | | | 1 | 1 | | | | | 1 | 1 | | | | | | | | | 1 | 29 |
| | 1 | | 2 | | 14 | 15 | 11 | 14 | 12 | 32 | 7 | 3 | 24 | 30 | 54 | | | | | | | | | 54 | 30 |
| | 3 | 6 | 2 | 1 | 60 | 55 | 120 | 57 | 66 | 152 | 35 | 3 | 151 | 141 | 292 | | | | | | | | | 292 | 31 |
| | 2 | 4 | 3 | | 4 | 14 | 19 | 7 | 11 | 31 | 4 | | 23 | 23 | 46 | | | | | | | | | 46 | 32 |
| | | | | | 1 | | 3 | 2 | 2 | 3 | | 1 | 4 | 2 | 6 | | | | | | | | | 6 | 33 |
| | 1 | 2 | 1 | 1 | 17 | 16 | 37 | 25 | 65 | 26 | 2 | 2 | 42 | 51 | 93 | | | | | 1 | 1 | | 1 | 96 | 34 |
| | | | | | 3 | | | | 1 | 2 | | | 2 | 1 | 3 | | | | | | | | | 3 | 35 |
| | | 1 | | | 6 | 23 | 7 | | 14 | 19 | 6 | 5 | 20 | 24 | 44 | | | | | | | | | 44 | 36 |
| | | | | | 6 | 3 | 3 | 6 | 9 | 8 | 1 | | | 18 | 18 | | | | | | | | | 18 | 37 |
| | | 1 | 3 | | 4 | 1 | 3 | 2 | 4 | 5 | 1 | | 3 | 7 | 10 | | | | | | | | | 10 | 38 |
| | | | | | 6 | 7 | 5 | 1 | 5 | 13 | 1 | | 7 | 12 | 19 | | | | | | | | | 19 | 39 |
| | 1 | | | | 1 | | 1 | | 2 | | | | 2 | | 2 | | | | | | | | | 2 | 40 |
| | 1 | | | | 18 | 14 | 9 | 18 | 10 | 40 | 1 | 2 | 36 | 22 | 58 | | | | | 1 | | | | 59 | 41 |
| | | 2 | 2 | 1 | 40 | 7 | 9 | 14 | 19 | 48 | 1 | 2 | 39 | 29 | 68 | | | | | | 1 | 1 | | 70 | 42 |
| | | | | | 1 | | | | 1 | | | | | 1 | 1 | | | | | | | | | 1 | 43 |
| | | | | | 1 | 1 | 1 | 1 | 1 | | | 3 | 4 | | 4 | | | | | | | | | 4 | 44 |
| | | | | 1 | 2 | 1 | 1 | 1 | 2 | 2 | 1 | | 2 | 3 | 5 | | | | | | | | | 5 | 45 |
| | | | | | | 3 | | 1 | 2 | 2 | | | 2 | 2 | 4 | | | | | | | | | 4 | 46 |
| | | | | | | 1 | | | | | | | 1 | | 1 | | | | | | | | | 1 | 47 |
| | | 2 | | | 1 | 3 | 1 | | 2 | 2 | 1 | | 4 | 1 | 5 | | | | | | | | | 5 | 48 |
| | | | | | | | | 1 | 1 | | | | 1 | | 1 | | | | | | | | | 1 | 49 |
| | | | | | 11 | 7 | 17 | 9 | 32 | 13 | | | 29 | 19 | 48 | | | | | | | | | 48 | 50 |
| | | | | | 4 | 14 | 8 | 8 | 3 | 19 | 9 | 1 | 18 | 15 | 33 | | | | | 1 | | | | 34 | 51 |
| | | | | | | 1 | | 1 | 1 | 1 | | | 2 | | 2 | | | | | | | | | 2 | 52 |
| | | | | | 1 | | | | 1 | | | | 1 | | 1 | | | | | | | | | 1 | 53 |
| | | 1 | | | 4 | 3 | 7 | 4 | 9 | 6 | 2 | 1 | 14 | 4 | 18 | | | | | | | | | 18 | 54 |
| | 1 | | | | 1 | 5 | 2 | 1 | 1 | 6 | | 1 | 2 | 7 | 9 | | | | | | | 1 | | 10 | 55 |
| | | | 1 | | 25 | 16 | 17 | 6 | 33 | 27 | 4 | | 39 | 25 | 64 | | | | | | | | | 64 | 56 |
| | | | | | | | 1 | 1 | 1 | 1 | | | 2 | | 2 | | | | | | | | | 2 | 57 |
| | | | | | 1 | 1 | | | | 1 | 1 | | 1 | | 1 | | | | | | | 1 | | 2 | 58 |
| | | | | | 1 | 1 | | 1 | 1 | | 1 | | 3 | | 3 | | | | | | | | | 3 | 59 |
| | | | | | 1 | | 2 | 5 | 2 | 4 | | 1 | 3 | 5 | 8 | | | | | | | | | 8 | 60 |
| | | | | | | | | 2 | 1 | 1 | | | 1 | 1 | 2 | | | | | | | | | 2 | 61 |
| | | | | | 2 | | 4 | 2 | 4 | 2 | 1 | | 8 | | 8 | | | | | | | | | 8 | 62 |
| | | | | | | 1 | 1 | 1 | 2 | | 1 | | 2 | 1 | 3 | | | | | | | | | 3 | 63 |
| | | | 1 | | 5 | 8 | 5 | 6 | 2 | 7 | 6 | 9 | 15 | 9 | 24 | | | | | | | | | 24 | 64 |
| | | 1 | 2 | | 10 | 5 | 6 | 7 | 9 | 12 | 5 | 2 | 15 | 13 | 28 | | | | | | | | | 28 | 65 |
| | | | | | 2 | 2 | | 1 | 4 | 1 | | | 5 | | 5 | | | | | | | | | 5 | 66 |
| | 1 | | | | 7 | 20 | | | 5 | 17 | 3 | 2 | 17 | 9 | 26 | | | | | | | 1 | | 27 | 67 |
| | | | | | | | 1 | 1 | | | | | | 2 | 2 | | | | | | | | | 2 | 68 |
| | | | | | 1 | 1 | 3 | 2 | 2 | 5 | | | 4 | 3 | 7 | | | | | | | | | 7 | 69 |
| | | | | | | 2 | | | 1 | 1 | | | 1 | 1 | 2 | | | | | | | | | 2 | 70 |
| | | | | | 2 | | | | | 2 | | | 1 | 1 | 2 | | | | | | | | | 2 | 71 |
| | 1 | | | | 1 | 3 | | 1 | 4 | 1 | | | 4 | | 4 | | | | | 1 | | | | 5 | 72 |

## CLASSIFICATION OF DEATHS IN SOUTHERN

| | Cause of death. | AGES. Under 1. | | 1 and under 5. | | 5 and under 10. | | 10 and under 20. | | 20 and under 50. | | 50 and under 80. | | 80 and under 100. | | 100 & over. | | Age unknown. | | NATIVITIES. Born in State. | N. England States. | Middle States. | Southern States. | Southwest'n States. | Northwest'n States. |
|---|---|---|---|---|---|---|---|---|---|---|---|---|---|---|---|---|---|---|---|---|---|---|---|---|---|
| | | M. | F. | M. | F. | M. | F. | M. | F. | M. | F. | M. | F. | M | F. | M | F. | M | F. | | | | | | |
| 1 | Neuralgia | | | | | | | | | 1 | | | | | | | | | | | | | | 1 | |
| 2 | Old age | | | | | | | | | | | 9 | 15 | 8 | 3 | | | | | | 6 | 9 | 10 | 1 | 4 |
| 3 | Paralysis | | | | 1 | | 1 | | 2 | 1 | 3 | 3 | 2 | | 1 | | | | | 5 | | 3 | 3 | 1 | 1 |
| 4 | Pleurisy | 1 | | 1 | 2 | | | 8 | 7 | 7 | 7 | 3 | 3 | | | | | | | 24 | | 3 | 4 | 4 | 2 |
| 5 | Pneumonia | 6 | 6 | 8 | 16 | 4 | 5 | 18 | 6 | 53 | 23 | 19 | 9 | 1 | 1 | | | | 1 | 72 | 2 | 14 | 29 | 17 | 33 |
| 6 | Poison | | | | | | | 1 | 1 | | | 1 | | | | | | | | | 1 | | | | 2 |
| 7 | Quinsy | 1 | 2 | 1 | 2 | 1 | | | | 1 | 1 | 1 | | | | | | | | 7 | | | 2 | | 1 |
| 8 | Rheumatism | | | 1 | 1 | | | 2 | 2 | 1 | 1 | 2 | | | | | | | | 5 | | | 2 | | 2 |
| 9 | Scrofula | | | 1 | 1 | | 1 | 2 | | | 2 | 1 | | | | | | | | 4 | 1 | | 1 | | 2 |
| 10 | Small pox | | | 2 | | | | 3 | | 3 | 1 | 1 | | | | | | | | 3 | | | 3 | 1 | 2 |
| 11 | Spine, disease of | 1 | | 1 | | 2 | | | | | 1 | | | | | | | | | 3 | | | | 1 | 1 |
| 12 | Stomach....do | | | | | | | | | | 1 | | | | | | | | | 1 | | | | | |
| 13 | Suicide | | | | | | | | | 2 | | | | | | | | | | | | 1 | | 1 | |
| 14 | Summer complaint | | 1 | | | | | | | | | | | | | | | | | 1 | | | | | |
| 15 | Sun stroke | | | | | | | 1 | | | | | | | | | | | | 1 | | | | | |
| 16 | Teething | 3 | 2 | | 2 | | | | | | | | | | | | | | | 6 | | | | 1 | |
| 17 | Throat, disease of | | 1 | | 1 | | | | | | 1 | | | | | | | | | 2 | | | 1 | | |
| 18 | Thrush | 1 | 6 | | 2 | | | | | | | | | | | | | | | 9 | | | | | |
| 19 | Tumor | | 1 | | 1 | | | | | 1 | | | | | | | | | | 2 | | 1 | | | |
| 20 | Ulcer | | | | 3 | 1 | | | | 2 | | 1 | 1 | | | | | | | 4 | 1 | 1 | 1 | | 1 |
| 21 | Uterus, disease of | | | | | | | | 2 | | 4 | | | | | | | | | 2 | 1 | | 1 | | 1 |
| 22 | White swelling | | | | | | | 1 | | | | | | | | | | | | 1 | | | | | |
| 23 | Worms | 1 | 1 | 11 | 12 | 5 | 3 | | | | | | | | | | | 1 | 1 | 31 | | | 1 | | 3 |
| 24 | Unknown | 90 | 94 | 50 | 48 | 25 | 20 | 29 | 20 | 88 | 62 | 39 | 18 | 3 | 2 | | | 3 | | 388 | 7 | 15 | 42 | 32 | 42 |
| | Total | 348 | 344 | 361 | 382 | 139 | 128 | 214 | 178 | 664 | 533 | 273 | 172 | 26 | 9 | 2 | .. | 7 | 5 | 2005 | 61 | 170 | 307 | 255 | 428 |

## CLASSIFICATION OF DEATHS

| | Cause of death. | Under 1. M. | Under 1. F. | 1 and under 5. M. | F. | 5 and under 10. M. | F. | 10 and under 20. M. | F. | 20 and under 50. M. | F. | 50 and under 80. M. | F. | 80 and under 100. M | F. | 100 & over. M | F. | Age unknown. M | F. | Born in State. | N. England States. | Middle States. | Southern States. | Southwest'n States. | Northwest'n States. |
|---|---|---|---|---|---|---|---|---|---|---|---|---|---|---|---|---|---|---|---|---|---|---|---|---|---|
| 1 | Abscess | | 1 | 1 | | 1 | 1 | 2 | | 2 | | | 1 | | | | | | | 5 | 1 | 1 | | | 1 |
| 2 | Accident, not specif'd | 3 | 7 | 17 | 10 | 10 | 6 | 26 | 3 | 44 | 5 | 17 | 4 | 1 | | | | | 2 | 65 | 10 | 19 | 9 | 2 | 24 |
| 3 | ....do...burned | 2 | | 9 | 6 | 1 | 4 | | | 2 | 4 | | 1 | | | | | | | 18 | 4 | | | 1 | 4 |
| 4 | ....do...drowned | | 1 | 8 | 2 | 5 | | 7 | 3 | 27 | 2 | 4 | | | | | | | | 19 | 7 | 8 | 1 | 2 | 6 |
| 5 | ....do...scalded | 1 | | 1 | 2 | 1 | | | | | | | | | | | | | | 4 | | | | | 1 |
| 6 | ....do...expl. steam | | | 1 | | | | | | | 1 | | | | | | | | | 1 | | | | | |
| 7 | Apoplexy | | | 2 | 1 | | | 2 | | 6 | 6 | 13 | 6 | 2 | 2 | | | | | 5 | 8 | 9 | 5 | 3 | 4 |
| 8 | Asthma | | | | | | 1 | | | 1 | 1 | 1 | 4 | | | | | | | 2 | | | 2 | 1 | 1 |
| 9 | Bowels, disease of | 7 | 14 | 11 | 16 | 1 | 3 | 1 | 7 | 3 | 6 | | 1 | | | | | | | 51 | 4 | 7 | 1 | | 3 |
| 10 | Brain.....do | 40 | 23 | 32 | 32 | 8 | 10 | 10 | 8 | 14 | 20 | | 1 | | | | | | | 138 | 8 | 17 | 2 | 1 | 19 |
| 11 | Bronchitis | 3 | 4 | 8 | 6 | | 1 | 1 | 1 | 8 | 5 | 2 | 3 | | | | | | | 26 | 2 | 2 | 4 | | 4 |
| 12 | Cancer | | | 2 | | | | 1 | 1 | 7 | 11 | 6 | 8 | 2 | | | | | | 5 | 5 | 11 | 8 | 1 | 4 |
| 13 | Canker | 2 | 3 | 2 | 3 | | 2 | 1 | | | | | | | | | | | | 12 | 1 | | | | |
| 14 | Catarrh | 6 | 5 | 2 | 10 | 1 | 1 | 2 | 5 | 1 | 3 | 2 | 1 | | 1 | | | 1 | | 23 | | 5 | 2 | 3 | 7 |
| 15 | Chicken pox | | 1 | | | | | | | | | | | | | | | | | | 1 | | | | |
| 16 | Childbirth | | | | | | | | 13 | | 102 | | 2 | | | | | | | 22 | 5 | 13 | 7 | 3 | 36 |
| 17 | Cholera* | 55 | 60 | 144 | 137 | 72 | 79 | 118 | 90 | 551 | 336 | 172 | 110 | 15 | 1 | 2 | | | 1 | 614 | 63 | 217 | 73 | 68 | 164 |
| 18 | ....do...infantum | 50 | 21 | 33 | 29 | 3 | | 2 | 1 | 1 | | 1 | | | | | | | | 130 | 21 | 2 | 2 | 1 | 5 |
| 19 | ....do...morbus | 4 | 2 | 7 | 9 | 5 | 1 | 3 | 1 | 14 | 6 | 7 | 3 | | | | | | | 27 | 2 | 14 | 2 | 4 | 8 |
| 20 | Chorea | | | | | | | | 1 | 2 | 1 | | | | | | | | | 1 | 1 | | | 2 | |
| 21 | Colic | 3 | 4 | 1 | 1 | | | | | 11 | 3 | 4 | 1 | | | | | | | 8 | 2 | 7 | 1 | 2 | 4 |
| 22 | Congestion | | 1 | 1 | 2 | 1 | 1 | 1 | 2 | 2 | 3 | 1 | | | | | | | | 6 | | 4 | 1 | | 3 |
| 23 | Consumption | 21 | 14 | 33 | 29 | 6 | 5 | 36 | 60 | 240 | 244 | 110 | 62 | 2 | | | | 1 | 3 | 212 | 81 | 179 | 74 | 41 | 148 |
| 24 | Convulsions | 45 | 25 | 24 | 18 | 1 | 5 | 4 | 11 | 10 | 10 | 2 | | | | | | | | 119 | 2 | 8 | 2 | 2 | 15 |
| 25 | Cramp | 3 | 1 | | 3 | | | 1 | 1 | | 2 | | 1 | 1 | | | | | | 7 | | | 1 | | 2 |
| 26 | Croup | 127 | 84 | 113 | 105 | 22 | 18 | 3 | 1 | 1 | 3 | | | | | | | | | 411 | 4 | 18 | 3 | 8 | 30 |
| 27 | Debility | 16 | 21 | 2 | 2 | | | | | | 2 | 2 | 4 | | | | | | | 39 | 1 | 2 | 1 | 2 | 2 |
| 28 | Diabetes | 4 | 3 | 6 | 1 | 1 | | | 1 | 3 | 1 | | 1 | | | | | | | 11 | 1 | 2 | | | 3 |
| 29 | Diarrhœa | 56 | 41 | 72 | 45 | 4 | | 4 | 4 | 25 | 21 | 10 | 6 | 1 | | | | | | 205 | 9 | 18 | 9 | 12 | 16 |
| 30 | Dropsy | 6 | 9 | 12 | 12 | 11 | 8 | 8 | 8 | 26 | 38 | 23 | 17 | 1 | 3 | | | | | 68 | 10 | 23 | 21 | 9 | 27 |
| 31 | Dysentery | 89 | 59 | 118 | 104 | 11 | 7 | 7 | 5 | 17 | 18 | 7 | 9 | | | | | | | 341 | 5 | 35 | 8 | 2 | 43 |
| 32 | Dyspepsia | | | | | | | | | 6 | 3 | 4 | 2 | | | | | | | 2 | | 4 | 9 | | |
| 33 | Epilepsy | | | | 2 | | | | 1 | 1 | | 3 | | | | | | | | 2 | 2 | 1 | 1 | | |
| 34 | Erysipelas | 20 | 16 | 10 | 14 | 6 | 4 | 8 | 10 | 29 | 29 | 8 | 18 | 1 | | | | | | 72 | 12 | 18 | 18 | 8 | 28 |
| 35 | Eye, disease of | | | | | | | | 1 | | | | | | | | | | | | | 1 | | | |
| 36 | Fever, not specified | 43 | 49 | 52 | 58 | 32 | 30 | 37 | 47 | 105 | 87 | 37 | 32 | 2 | 1 | | | 1 | 2 | 318 | 21 | 65 | 38 | 30 | 98 |
| 37 | ..do..bilious | 7 | 5 | 8 | 14 | 3 | 7 | 7 | 11 | 35 | 17 | 11 | 3 | 1 | | | | | | 49 | 1 | 15 | 13 | 6 | 21 |
| 38 | ..do..brain | 13 | 9 | 15 | 12 | 6 | 3 | 4 | 3 | 4 | 2 | 1 | 2 | | | | | | | 53 | 1 | 6 | 1 | 1 | 5 |
| 39 | ..do..congestive | 5 | 17 | 19 | 11 | 12 | 11 | 33 | 29 | 40 | 38 | 14 | 12 | | 1 | | | | | 101 | 6 | 36 | 20 | 8 | 57 |
| 40 | ..do..inflammation | | | 1 | | 1 | | | | 3 | 1 | | | | | | | | | 2 | | 1 | | 1 | 1 |
| 41 | ..do..intermittent | 8 | 11 | 11 | 16 | 3 | 7 | 3 | 6 | 12 | 9 | 4 | 6 | | 1 | | | | | 54 | 1 | 8 | 8 | 6 | 11 |
| 42 | ..do..puerperal | | | | | | | | 4 | | 37 | | 1 | | | | | | | 9 | | 5 | 4 | 7 | 15 |

* 116 unknown—age and sex not given—included in total and aggregate.

## SECTION OF THE STATE OF ILLINOIS—Continued.

| NATIVITIES. California and Territories. | Ireland. | Germany. | Other foreign countries. | Unknown. | SEASON OF DECEASE. Spring. | Summer. | Autumn. | Winter. | DURATION OF SICKNESS. Under 1 week. | 1 week and under 1 month. | 1 month and under 3 months. | 3 months and over. | WHITES. Males. | Females. | Total. | COLORED. Slaves. Black. M. | F. | Mulatto. M. | F. | Free. Black. M. | F. | Mul. M | F. | Aggregate deaths. | |
|---|---|---|---|---|---|---|---|---|---|---|---|---|---|---|---|---|---|---|---|---|---|---|---|---|---|
| | | | | | | | 1 | | | | 1 | | 1 | | 1 | | | | | | | | | 1 | 1 |
| | 1 | 2 | 2 | | 7 | 5 | 12 | 11 | 10 | 6 | 6 | | 15 | 18 | 33 | | | | | | | 2 | | 35 | 2 |
| | 1 | | | | 3 | 3 | 2 | 6 | 9 | 3 | 1 | 1 | 4 | 9 | 13 | | | | | | | | 1 | 14 | 3 |
| | | | 1 | 1 | 17 | 8 | 5 | 7 | 17 | 20 | 1 | | 20 | 19 | 39 | | | | | | | | | 39 | 4 |
| | 1 | 3 | 3 | 2 | 63 | 36 | 22 | 55 | 47 | 104 | 10 | 3 | 108 | 67 | 175 | | | | | | | 1 | | 176 | 5 |
| | | | | | | | 1 | 2 | 3 | | | | 2 | 1 | 3 | | | | | | | | | 3 | 6 |
| | | | | | 2 | 3 | 4 | 1 | 7 | 3 | | | 5 | 5 | 10 | | | | | | | | | 10 | 7 |
| | | 1 | | | 3 | 2 | 1 | 4 | 1 | 6 | | 3 | 6 | 4 | 10 | | | | | | | | | 10 | 8 |
| | | | | | 3 | 2 | 1 | 2 | | 2 | 1 | 3 | 4 | 4 | 8 | | | | | | | | | 8 | 9 |
| | | 1 | | | 4 | 2 | 1 | 3 | 2 | 7 | | 1 | 9 | 1 | 10 | | | | | | | | | 10 | 10 |
| | | | | | 1 | 3 | 1 | | 2 | 1 | 2 | | 4 | 1 | 5 | | | | | | | | | 5 | 11 |
| | | | | | 1 | | | | 1 | | | | | 1 | 1 | | | | | | | | | 1 | 12 |
| | | | | | 1 | 1 | | | 2 | | | | 2 | | 2 | | | | | | | | | 2 | 13 |
| | | | | | | | 1 | | | 1 | | | | 1 | 1 | | | | | | | | | 1 | 14 |
| | | | | | | 1 | | | 1 | | | | 1 | | 1 | | | | | | | | | 1 | 15 |
| | | | | | | 3 | 4 | | 3 | 3 | | 1 | 3 | 4 | 7 | | | | | | | | | 7 | 16 |
| | | | | | 2 | | 1 | | 1 | 1 | 1 | | | 3 | 3 | | | | | | | | | 3 | 17 |
| | | | | | 1 | 1 | 4 | 3 | 4 | 3 | 1 | 1 | 1 | 8 | 9 | | | | | | | | | 9 | 18 |
| | | | | | 1 | 1 | 1 | | | 1 | 1 | | 1 | 2 | 3 | | | | | | | | | 3 | 19 |
| | | | | | 1 | 1 | 5 | 1 | | 3 | 4 | | 4 | 4 | 8 | | | | | | | | | 8 | 20 |
| | | 1 | | | | 1 | 1 | 4 | 1 | 4 | | 1 | | 6 | 6 | | | | | | | | | 6 | 21 |
| | | | | | | 1 | | | | | | 1 | 1 | | 1 | | | | | | | | | 1 | 22 |
| | | | | | 5 | 11 | 16 | 3 | 15 | 18 | 1 | | 18 | 17 | 35 | | | | | | | | | 35 | 23 |
| 7 | 9 | 35 | 9 | 5 | 120 | 127 | 143 | 118 | 188 | 160 | 47 | 62 | 324 | 260 | 584 | | | | | 1 | 3 | 2 | 1 | 591 | 24 |
| 10 | 55 | 317 | 144 | 33 | 745 | 1317 | 1017 | 600 | 1635 | 1239 | 290 | 290 | 2006 | 1740 | 3746 | ... | ... | ... | ... | 16 | 7 | 12 | 4 | 3785 | |

## IN THE STATE OF ILLINOIS—AGGREGATE.

| California and Territories. | Ireland. | Germany. | Other foreign countries. | Unknown. | Spring. | Summer. | Autumn. | Winter. | Under 1 week. | 1 week and under 1 month. | 1 month and under 3 months. | 3 months and over. | Males. | Females. | Total. | Slaves. Black. M. | F. | Mulatto. M. | F. | Free. Black. M. | F. | Mul. M | F. | Aggregate deaths. | |
|---|---|---|---|---|---|---|---|---|---|---|---|---|---|---|---|---|---|---|---|---|---|---|---|---|---|
| | 1 | | | | 2 | 5 | 1 | 1 | 3 | 4 | 1 | 1 | 6 | 3 | 9 | | | | | | | | | 9 | 1 |
| | 12 | 7 | 6 | 1 | 32 | 34 | 46 | 35 | 99 | 24 | 8 | 9 | 118 | 37 | 155 | | | | | | | | | 155 | 2 |
| | | 1 | 1 | | 12 | 4 | 4 | 9 | 20 | 4 | 2 | 2 | 14 | 15 | 29 | | | | | | | | | 29 | 3 |
| | 6 | 2 | 8 | | 12 | 19 | 12 | 16 | 48 | | | | 51 | 8 | 59 | | | | | | | | | 59 | 4 |
| | | | | | 3 | 1 | | 1 | 1 | 3 | | 1 | 3 | 2 | 5 | | | | | | | | | 5 | 5 |
| | 1 | | | | | | | 2 | 2 | | | | 1 | 1 | 2 | | | | | | | | | 2 | 6 |
| | 2 | 1 | 3 | | 12 | 9 | 12 | 7 | 32 | 2 | 1 | 2 | 24 | 15 | 39 | | | | | 1 | | | | 40 | 7 |
| | 1 | | 1 | | 1 | 2 | 5 | | 2 | 4 | | 2 | 2 | 6 | 8 | | | | | | | | | 8 | 8 |
| | | | 2 | 2 | 5 | 12 | 40 | 13 | 30 | 30 | 6 | 3 | 23 | 47 | 70 | | | | | | | | | 70 | 9 |
| | 5 | 3 | 5 | | 54 | 44 | 63 | 35 | 83 | 86 | 19 | 3 | 104 | 94 | 198 | | | | | | | | | 198 | 10 |
| 1 | 1 | | 2 | | 15 | 14 | 7 | 5 | 8 | 11 | 4 | 16 | 22 | 20 | 42 | | | | | | | | | 42 | 11 |
| | 2 | | 2 | | 13 | 9 | 8 | 8 | 2 | 4 | 6 | 23 | 18 | 20 | 38 | | | | | | | | | 38 | 12 |
| | | | | | 2 | 1 | 6 | 4 | 3 | 7 | 2 | | 5 | 8 | 13 | | | | | | | | | 13 | 13 |
| | | 1 | | | 14 | 7 | 18 | 7 | 14 | 13 | 5 | 4 | 15 | 24 | 39 | | | | | | 2 | | | 41 | 14 |
| | | | | | | 1 | | | | 1 | | | | 1 | 1 | | | | | | | | | 1 | 15 |
| | 12 | 7 | 10 | 2 | 38 | 32 | 22 | 25 | 66 | 37 | 6 | 2 | | 117 | 117 | | | | | | | | | 117 | 16 |
| 1 | 132 | 415 | 287 | 25 | 77 | 1157 | 789 | 25 | 1586 | 173 | 5 | 1 | 1117 | 813 | 2046 | | | | | 10 | 1 | 2 | | 2059 | 17 |
| | | | | | 10 | 40 | 79 | 8 | 59 | 65 | 6 | 1 | 90 | 51 | 141 | | | | | | | | | 141 | 18 |
| | 1 | 1 | 2 | 1 | 5 | 16 | 38 | 2 | 36 | 21 | 1 | 1 | 38 | 22 | 60 | | | | | 2 | | | | 62 | 19 |
| | | | | | | 3 | 1 | | 3 | 1 | | | 2 | 2 | 4 | | | | | | | | | 4 | 20 |
| | | 2 | 2 | | 8 | 9 | 5 | 6 | 19 | 9 | | | 19 | 9 | 28 | | | | | | | | | 28 | 21 |
| | | | 1 | | 3 | 3 | 6 | 3 | 9 | 6 | | | 6 | 9 | 15 | | | | | | | | | 15 | 22 |
| 6 | 30 | 29 | 59 | 7 | 281 | 208 | 175 | 171 | 37 | 113 | 109 | 458 | 444 | 412 | 856 | | | | | 4 | 4 | 1 | 1 | 866 | 23 |
| | 1 | | 5 | 1 | 54 | 34 | 42 | 25 | 104 | 30 | 7 | 7 | 86 | 69 | 155 | | | | | | | | | 155 | 24 |
| | | 3 | | | 6 | 3 | 2 | 2 | 11 | 1 | | 1 | 5 | 8 | 13 | | | | | | | | | 13 | 25 |
| | | 2 | 1 | | 134 | 80 | 142 | 110 | 323 | 93 | 6 | | 265 | 211 | 476 | | | | | 1 | | | | 477 | 26 |
| | | | 2 | | 13 | 13 | 11 | 12 | 16 | 9 | 9 | 8 | 19 | 29 | 48 | | | | | 1 | | | | 49 | 27 |
| | | | 4 | | 4 | 4 | 13 | | 6 | 11 | 2 | 2 | 14 | 7 | 31 | | | | | | | | | 21 | 28 |
| | 11 | 2 | 6 | 1 | 18 | 82 | 171 | 17 | 77 | 135 | 38 | 23 | 172 | 117 | 289 | | | | | | | | | 289 | 29 |
| | 4 | 11 | 8 | 1 | 47 | 46 | 52 | 33 | 17 | 46 | 37 | 64 | 85 | 95 | 180 | | | | | 2 | | | | 182 | 30 |
| | 3 | 6 | 8 | | 20 | 67 | 323 | 32 | 144 | 228 | 54 | 11 | 249 | 201 | 450 | | | | | | | | 1 | 451 | 31 |
| | | | | | 4 | 5 | 3 | 3 | 2 | 1 | 5 | 5 | 10 | 5 | 15 | | | | | | | | | 15 | 32 |
| | | | 1 | | 1 | 1 | 2 | 3 | 2 | 2 | | 1 | 4 | 3 | 7 | | | | | | | | | 7 | 33 |
| | 4 | 1 | 5 | 2 | 45 | 36 | 31 | 52 | 47 | 97 | 11 | 5 | 82 | 86 | 168 | | | | | | | | | 168 | 34 |
| | | | | | | 1 | | | | 1 | | | | 1 | 1 | | | | | | | | | 1 | 35 |
| | 12 | 12 | 18 | 3 | 139 | 121 | 229 | 114 | 149 | 339 | 74 | 15 | 309 | 306 | 615 | | | | | | | | | 615 | 36 |
| | 6 | 10 | 8 | | 13 | 33 | 56 | 24 | 25 | 80 | 17 | 3 | 72 | 57 | 127 | | | | | | | | | 129 | 37 |
| | 3 | 2 | 2 | | 26 | 17 | 22 | 5 | 36 | 33 | 8 | 2 | 42 | 31 | 73 | | | | | | | 1 | | 74 | 38 |
| | 3 | 2 | 7 | 2 | 55 | 45 | 94 | 46 | 152 | 69 | 9 | 9 | 120 | 117 | 237 | | | | | 1 | 1 | 2 | 1 | 242 | 39 |
| | | | 1 | | 3 | 1 | 2 | | 4 | 2 | | | 5 | 1 | 6 | | | | | | | | | 6 | 40 |
| | 4 | 2 | 2 | 1 | 13 | 31 | 34 | 11 | 27 | 42 | 20 | 8 | 41 | 56 | 97 | | | | | | | | | 97 | 41 |
| | | 1 | 1 | | 12 | 9 | 9 | 12 | 16 | 24 | 1 | | | 42 | 42 | | | | | | | | | 42 | 42 |

## CLASSIFICATION OF DEATHS

| | Cause of death. | Ages. | | | | | | | | | | | | | | | | | | Nativities. | | | | | |
|---|---|---|---|---|---|---|---|---|---|---|---|---|---|---|---|---|---|---|---|---|---|---|---|---|---|
| | | Under 1. | | 1 and under 5. | | 5 and under 10. | | 10 and under 20. | | 20 and under 50. | | 50 and under 80. | | 80 and under 100. | | 100 & over. | | Age unknown. | | Born in State. | N. England States. | Middle States. | Southern States. | Southwest'n States. | Northwest'n States. |
| | | M. | F. | M. | F. | M. | F. | M. | F. | M. | F. | M. | F. | M | F. | M | F. | M | F. | | | | | | |
| 1 | Fever, remittent | | | | | 1 | 1 | 2 | 1 | | 5 | | | | | | | | | 8 | | | | 1 | 2 |
| 2 | ..do..scarlet | 18 | 15 | 60 | 49 | 27 | 14 | 3 | 12 | 2 | 3 | 2 | 5 | | | | | | | 166 | 1 | 10 | 3 | | 22 |
| 3 | ..do..ship | | 1 | 2 | 1 | 1 | 1 | 2 | 3 | 3 | 2 | 1 | 2 | | | | | | | 8 | | | | | 1 |
| 4 | ..do..typhus | 2 | 3 | 13 | 14 | 20 | 20 | 44 | 29 | 58 | 34 | 23 | 13 | | 1 | | | | | 80 | 22 | 55 | 18 | 17 | 65 |
| 5 | ..do..winter | 2 | 2 | 4 | 6 | 5 | 5 | 10 | 5 | 31 | 22 | 16 | 3 | | | | | | 1 | 42 | 1 | 6 | 13 | 15 | 27 |
| 6 | ..do..yellow | | | | 1 | | | | 1 | | | | 1 | | | | | | | 2 | | | | | |
| 7 | Gout | | | | | | | | | | | 1 | | | | | | | | | | 1 | | | |
| 8 | Gravel | | | | | | | | | 1 | | 12 | | 2 | | | | | | 3 | 2 | 3 | 4 | 2 | |
| 9 | Head, disease of | 2 | 3 | 1 | 4 | | | | | 1 | | | | | | | | 1 | | 8 | 1 | | | 1 | 1 |
| 10 | Heart....do | 3 | 3 | 2 | 1 | | 1 | | 2 | 6 | 7 | 5 | 1 | 1 | | | | | | 9 | 2 | 12 | 1 | | 3 |
| 11 | Heat | | | | | | | 1 | | | | | | | | | | | | 1 | | | | | |
| 12 | Hemorrhage | 1 | | 2 | 2 | 2 | 1 | 2 | 2 | 3 | 2 | 1 | 1 | | | | | | | 8 | | 1 | 2 | | 6 |
| 13 | Hernia | | | | | | | | | 2 | | 1 | | | | | | | | | | | 1 | | |
| 14 | Hip, disease of | 1 | | | | | | | | 1 | | | | | | | | | | 2 | | | | | |
| 15 | Hives | 29 | 18 | 5 | 6 | | | | | 1 | | | | | | | | | | 57 | 1 | | | 1 | |
| 16 | Hooping cough | 43 | 44 | 35 | 48 | 4 | 12 | 1 | 2 | | 1 | | | | | | | 1 | | 163 | | 7 | | 2 | 11 |
| 17 | Hydrocephalus | 10 | 3 | 6 | 7 | 2 | | 1 | 2 | 1 | | | | | | | | | | 27 | | 1 | | | 2 |
| 18 | Hydrophophia | | | | | | | 1 | | | | | | | | | | | | 1 | | | | | |
| 19 | Inflamt'n, not specf'd | 11 | 9 | 11 | 11 | 3 | | 3 | 3 | 7 | 5 | 7 | 2 | | | | | | | 44 | 1 | 10 | 2 | 2 | 5 |
| 20 | ....do....bowels | 6 | 6 | 4 | 10 | | 1 | 2 | 3 | 4 | 6 | 1 | 1 | | | | | | | 27 | | 8 | | 3 | 3 |
| 21 | ....do....brain | 20 | 8 | 24 | 18 | 4 | 10 | 14 | 7 | 6 | 5 | 5 | 2 | | | | | | | 90 | 6 | 10 | 3 | 3 | 8 |
| 22 | ....do....stomach | 1 | | 1 | | | | | | 1 | 1 | | | | | | | | | | | 2 | | | 2 |
| 23 | Influenza | 2 | 2 | 1 | 1 | 1 | | | | 1 | | | | | | | | | | 6 | | | 1 | | |
| 24 | Insanity | | | | | | | | 1 | | | | 1 | | | | | | | | 1 | 1 | | | |
| 25 | Intemperance | | | | | | | | | 7 | 1 | 5 | | | | | | | | | 1 | 2 | 3 | | |
| 26 | Jaundice | 5 | 4 | 1 | 4 | | 1 | | 1 | 3 | 3 | 3 | 3 | | | | | | | 14 | 2 | 6 | | | 3 |
| 27 | Kidneys, disease of | | | | | | 1 | 1 | | 1 | | 1 | 1 | | | | | | | 2 | | 1 | 1 | 1 | |
| 28 | Killed | | | 1 | | 1 | | 4 | 1 | 3 | | 2 | | | | | | | | 8 | | 1 | | 1 | 1 |
| 29 | Lightning | | | | | | | 1 | 1 | 4 | 3 | | | | | | | | | 2 | | 1 | | 1 | 4 |
| 30 | Liver, disease of | 6 | 4 | 5 | 5 | 1 | 1 | 2 | 2 | 27 | 14 | 11 | 6 | | | | | | | 32 | 5 | 11 | 12 | 3 | 15 |
| 31 | Lockjaw | | | 1 | | | | | | | | | | | | | | | | 1 | | | | | |
| 32 | Lungs, disease of | 15 | 9 | 9 | 6 | 3 | 4 | 5 | 1 | 17 | 13 | 4 | 3 | | | | | | | 53 | 4 | 6 | 5 | 2 | 12 |
| 33 | Mania-a-potu | | | | | | | | | 5 | | | | | | | | | | | | 3 | 1 | | 1 |
| 34 | Measles | 10 | 12 | 31 | 21 | 6 | 5 | 6 | 2 | 11 | 6 | | | | | | | | | 78 | 1 | 13 | 2 | 3 | 9 |
| 35 | Menses, suppress'n of | | | | | | | | 1 | | 1 | | | | | | | | | | | | 1 | 1 | |
| 36 | Milk sickness | | | | | 2 | | 1 | 2 | 4 | 4 | 1 | | | | | | | | 3 | | 1 | 3 | 1 | 6 |
| 37 | Mortification | | 2 | | | | | | | | | 1 | 1 | | | | | | | 3 | | | 1 | | |
| 38 | Mumps | 1 | 1 | | | 1 | | 2 | 1 | 2 | | | | | | | | | | 4 | | 1 | | | 3 |
| 39 | Murder | | | 1 | | | | | | 5 | | 1 | | | | | | | | 2 | | 2 | 1 | | 1 |
| 40 | Neuralgia | | | | | | | 1 | | 4 | 1 | 1 | | | | | | | | 1 | | 2 | 1 | 1 | 2 |
| 41 | Old age | | | | | | | | | | | 26 | 42 | 21 | 17 | 1 | | | | 5 | 18 | 25 | 22 | 1 | 9 |
| 42 | Paralysis | | | 1 | 1 | | 2 | | 2 | 5 | 9 | 16 | 11 | 1 | 2 | | | | | 8 | 5 | 16 | 10 | 2 | 5 |
| 43 | Pleurisy | 4 | 2 | 3 | 2 | | 1 | 8 | 8 | 15 | 8 | 12 | 4 | | | | | | | 32 | 2 | 5 | 6 | 8 | 7 |
| 44 | Pneumonia | 65 | 36 | 73 | 67 | 15 | 14 | 36 | 24 | 136 | 72 | 63 | 40 | 4 | 1 | | | | 1 | 277 | 35 | 73 | 55 | 30 | 112 |
| 45 | Poison | | | | | 5 | 2 | 3 | 3 | 2 | 3 | 2 | | | | | | | | 8 | 1 | 3 | | | 8 |
| 46 | Prematurity of birth | | 1 | | | | | | | | | | | | | | | | | 1 | | | | | |
| 47 | Quinsy | 3 | 3 | 2 | 5 | 3 | 1 | | | 4 | 2 | 2 | | | | | | | | 15 | | 3 | 2 | 1 | 3 |
| 48 | Rheumatism | 1 | 1 | 1 | 2 | 2 | | 8 | 6 | 3 | 3 | 7 | 2 | | | | | | | 13 | 2 | 7 | 3 | 1 | 4 |
| 49 | Rickets | | 1 | | 1 | | | | | | | | | | | | | | | 2 | | | | | |
| 50 | Scrofula | 1 | 1 | 5 | 3 | 2 | 2 | 5 | 4 | 6 | 6 | 2 | 1 | | | | | | | 19 | 3 | 2 | 2 | 1 | 7 |
| 51 | Small pox | 6 | 5 | 8 | 3 | 3 | 8 | 5 | 1 | 19 | 6 | 1 | | | | | | | | 34 | 3 | 4 | 5 | 4 | 11 |
| 52 | Spine, disease of | 1 | | 2 | 3 | 3 | | 2 | 1 | 1 | 3 | | 1 | | | | | | | 8 | | 3 | 1 | 2 | 3 |
| 53 | Stillborn | 1 | 3 | | | | | | | | | | | | | | | | | 4 | | | | | |
| 54 | Stomach, disease of | | | 1 | 1 | | | 1 | | | 1 | | | | | | | | | 3 | | | | | 1 |
| 55 | Suffocation | | | | | | | | | 2 | | | | | | | | | | | 1 | 1 | | | |
| 56 | Suicide | | | | | | | | | 6 | 2 | 3 | | | | | | | | | 2 | 3 | | 2 | 2 |
| 57 | Summer complaint | 7 | 7 | 7 | 9 | | | | | | | | | | | | | | | 30 | | | | | |
| 58 | Sun stroke | | | | | | | 1 | | 3 | | 2 | | | | | | | | 2 | | | | | |
| 59 | Teething | 9 | 10 | 9 | 13 | | | | | | | | | | | | | | | 31 | 2 | | | 1 | 3 |
| 60 | Tetanus | | | | | 1 | | | | | | | | | | | | | | 1 | | | | | |
| 61 | Throat, disease of | 1 | 3 | | 4 | 1 | 1 | | 1 | 2 | 1 | | | | | | | | | 7 | | 2 | 2 | | 3 |
| 62 | Thrush | 6 | 10 | | 2 | | | | | | | | | | | | | | | 17 | | 1 | | | |
| 63 | Tumor | 1 | 1 | | 1 | | | | | 1 | | | | | | | | | | 3 | | 1 | | | |
| 64 | Ulcer | | | | 4 | 1 | | | | 2 | | 2 | 1 | | | | | | | 5 | 1 | 2 | 1 | | 1 |
| 65 | Uterus, disease of | | | | | | | | 2 | | 4 | | | | | | | | | 2 | 1 | | 1 | | 1 |
| 66 | White swelling | 1 | | | | 1 | | 1 | | 1 | 1 | | | | | | | | | 3 | | | | 2 | |
| 67 | Worms | 1 | 7 | 20 | 27 | 9 | 9 | 1 | 1 | | | | | | | | | 1 | 1 | 61 | | 2 | 3 | 3 | 4 |
| 68 | Unknown* | 317 | 280 | 184 | 146 | 55 | 46 | 67 | 54 | 203 | 204 | 105 | 75 | 5 | 4 | | | 6 | 4 | 1198 | 36 | 93 | 87 | 61 | 136 |
| | Total* | 1252 | 1031 | 1314 | 1221 | 413 | 379 | 579 | 531 | 1886 | 1541 | 814 | 540 | 63 | 35 | 3 | . | 12 | 15 | 6016 | 445 | 1204 | 630 | 417 | 1359 |

*14 "unknown," and 130 "total"—sex not given—included in total and aggregate.

## IN THE STATE OF ILLINOIS—AGGREGATE—Continued.

| NATIVITIES. | | | | | SEASON OF DECEASE. | | | | DURATION OF SICKNESS. | | | | WHITES. | | | COLORED. | | | | | | | | | |
|---|---|---|---|---|---|---|---|---|---|---|---|---|---|---|---|---|---|---|---|---|---|---|---|---|---|
| | | | | | | | | | | | | | | | | Slaves. | | | | Free. | | | | | |
| | | | | | | | | | | | | | | | | Black. | | Mulatto. | | Black. | | Mul. | | | |
| California and Territories. | Ireland. | Germany. | Other foreign countries. | Unknown. | Spring. | Summer. | Autumn. | Winter. | Under 1 week. | 1 week and under 1 month. | 1 month and under 3 months. | 3 months and over. | Males. | Females. | Total. | M. | F. | M. | F. | M. | F. | M | F. | Aggregate deaths. | |
| | | 1 | 3 | | 4 | 1 | 3 | 2 | 4 | 5 | 1 | | 3 | 7 | 10 | | | | | | | | | 10 | 1 |
| | 2 | 2 | 2 | 2 | 63 | 50 | 45 | 50 | 91 | 108 | 7 | | 112 | 98 | 210 | | | | | | | | | 210 | 2 |
| | 6 | 1 | 3 | | 5 | 9 | 5 | | 7 | 9 | 3 | | 9 | 10 | 19 | | | | | | | | | 19 | 3 |
| | 8 | 1 | 12 | 1 | 75 | 40 | 82 | 75 | 29 | 199 | 40 | 4 | 159 | 114 | 273 | | | | | 1 | | | | 274 | 4 |
| | | 4 | 2 | 2 | 68 | 9 | 9 | 26 | 27 | 81 | 2 | 2 | 66 | 43 | 109 | | | | | | 1 | 2 | | 112 | 5 |
| | 1 | | | | 1 | | | 1 | 1 | | | | | 3 | 3 | | | | | | | | | 3 | 6 |
| | | | | | | | | 1 | | | 1 | | 1 | | 1 | | | | | | | | | 1 | 7 |
| | 1 | | | | 3 | 6 | 3 | 3 | 5 | 4 | | 5 | 15 | | 15 | | | | | | | | | 15 | 8 |
| | | | | 1 | 3 | 3 | 2 | 4 | 2 | 8 | 1 | 1 | 5 | 7 | 12 | | | | | | | | | 12 | 9 |
| | 2 | 1 | 2 | | 9 | 9 | 6 | 8 | 7 | 10 | 2 | 13 | 17 | 15 | 32 | | | | | | | | | 32 | 10 |
| | | | | | | 1 | | | | | | | 1 | | 1 | | | | | | | | | 1 | 11 |
| | | 2 | | | 2 | 7 | 7 | 3 | 8 | 7 | 1 | 1 | 11 | 8 | 19 | | | | | | | | | 19 | 12 |
| | 1 | | 1 | | | | 1 | 2 | 2 | | | 1 | 3 | | 3 | | | | | | | | | 3 | 13 |
| | | | | | 1 | | 1 | | 1 | | | | 2 | | 2 | | | | | | | | | 2 | 14 |
| | | | | | 16 | 7 | 19 | 13 | 39 | 16 | | | 35 | 24 | 59 | | | | | | | | | 59 | 15 |
| | 1 | 2 | 5 | | 44 | 61 | 50 | 32 | 26 | 102 | 41 | 13 | 83 | 107 | 190 | | | | | 1 | | | | 191 | 16 |
| | 1 | | 1 | | 10 | 6 | 7 | 8 | 5 | 20 | 6 | 1 | 20 | 12 | 32 | | | | | | | | | 32 | 17 |
| | | | | | 1 | | | | 1 | | | | 1 | | 1 | | | | | | | | | 1 | 18 |
| | 3 | 1 | 4 | | 20 | 18 | 23 | 11 | 31 | 30 | 4 | 5 | 41 | 30 | 71 | | | | | | | 1 | | 72 | 19 |
| | 1 | 1 | 1 | | 7 | 14 | 13 | 8 | 19 | 17 | 2 | 1 | 16 | 27 | 43 | | | | | | | 1 | | 44 | 20 |
| | | | 3 | | 40 | 28 | 36 | 19 | 54 | 60 | 6 | 1 | 73 | 50 | 123 | | | | | | | | | 123 | 21 |
| | | | | | | 1 | 2 | 1 | 1 | 3 | | | 3 | 1 | 4 | | | | | | | | | 4 | 22 |
| | | | 1 | | 4 | 2 | | 2 | 4 | 3 | 1 | | 4 | 3 | 7 | | | | | | | 1 | | 8 | 23 |
| | | | | | 1 | 1 | | | | | | 2 | | 2 | 2 | | | | | | | | | 2 | 24 |
| | 2 | | 1 | | 4 | 4 | 1 | 4 | 4 | 1 | 1 | 6 | 12 | 1 | 13 | | | | | | | | | 13 | 25 |
| | 2 | | 1 | | 10 | 4 | 6 | 8 | 7 | 9 | 1 | 8 | 12 | 15 | 27 | | | | | | 1 | | | 28 | 26 |
| | | | | | | 1 | 1 | 3 | 2 | 1 | | 1 | 3 | 2 | 5 | | | | | | | | | 5 | 27 |
| | | | 1 | | 3 | 1 | 5 | 3 | 8 | 2 | 1 | | 11 | 1 | 12 | | | | | | | | | 12 | 28 |
| | | | 1 | | 1 | 3 | 4 | 1 | 8 | | 1 | | 5 | 4 | 9 | | | | | | | | | 9 | 29 |
| | 4 | | 2 | | 26 | 24 | 19 | 14 | 6 | 27 | 20 | 31 | 52 | 32 | 84 | | | | | | | | | 84 | 30 |
| | | | | | | 1 | | | 1 | | | | 1 | | 1 | | | | | | | | | 1 | 31 |
| | 3 | 2 | 2 | | 35 | 16 | 18 | 20 | 33 | 38 | 7 | 5 | 53 | 36 | 89 | | | | | | | | | 89 | 32 |
| | | | | | 2 | 2 | | 1 | 4 | 1 | | | 5 | | 5 | | | | | | | | | 5 | 33 |
| | 1 | | 2 | 1 | 26 | 71 | 9 | 1 | 11 | 74 | 15 | 3 | 63 | 46 | 109 | | | | | | | 1 | | 110 | 34 |
| | | | | | | | 1 | 1 | | | | | | 2 | 2 | | | | | | | | | 2 | 35 |
| | | | | | 1 | 1 | 10 | 2 | 7 | 7 | | | 8 | 6 | 14 | | | | | | | | | 14 | 36 |
| | | | | | | 3 | 1 | | 2 | 2 | | | 1 | 3 | 4 | | | | | | | | | 4 | 37 |
| | | | | | 8 | | | | | 8 | | | 6 | 2 | 8 | | | | | | | | | 8 | 38 |
| | 1 | | | | 1 | 3 | 2 | 1 | 5 | 1 | | | 6 | | 6 | | | | | 1 | | | | 7 | 39 |
| | | | | | 1 | 3 | 3 | | 1 | 2 | 1 | 2 | 6 | 1 | 7 | | | | | | | | | 7 | 40 |
| | 11 | 5 | 11 | | 24 | 27 | 27 | 28 | 30 | 20 | 9 | 20 | 46 | 58 | 104 | | | | | | 1 | 2 | | 107 | 41 |
| | 2 | | 2 | | 13 | 15 | 8 | 14 | 18 | 13 | 4 | 13 | 23 | 26 | 49 | | | | | | | | 1 | 50 | 42 |
| | 5 | | 1 | 1 | 27 | 17 | 9 | 12 | 29 | 34 | 1 | 1 | 42 | 25 | 67 | | | | | | | | | 67 | 43 |
| | 10 | 10 | 18 | 7 | 275 | 136 | 72 | 136 | 156 | 414 | 37 | 11 | 385 | 255 | 640 | | | | | 6 | | 1 | | 647 | 44 |
| | | | | | 5 | 6 | 5 | 4 | 12 | 7 | | 1 | 12 | 8 | 20 | | | | | | | | | 20 | 45 |
| | | | | | | | 1 | | | 1 | | | | 1 | 1 | | | | | | | | | 1 | 46 |
| | | 1 | | | 7 | 4 | 7 | 6 | 14 | 10 | | | 14 | 11 | 25 | | | | | | | | | 25 | 47 |
| | | 5 | 1 | | 14 | 12 | 2 | 7 | 3 | 15 | 1 | 16 | 22 | 13 | 35 | | | | | | 1 | | | 36 | 48 |
| | | | | | | 1 | 1 | | 1 | | | 1 | | 2 | 2 | | | | | | | | | 2 | 49 |
| | | | 4 | | 12 | 12 | 8 | 5 | 1 | 7 | 7 | 17 | 21 | 17 | 38 | | | | | | | | | 38 | 50 |
| | | 1 | 2 | 1 | 24 | 11 | 6 | 24 | 6 | 57 | | 2 | 42 | 23 | 65 | | | | | | | | | 65 | 51 |
| | | | | | 5 | 4 | 5 | 3 | 2 | 2 | 2 | 9 | 9 | 8 | 17 | | | | | | | | | 17 | 52 |
| | | | | | 3 | | 1 | | | | | | 1 | 3 | 4 | | | | | | | | | 4 | 53 |
| | | | | | 3 | | | 1 | 2 | 2 | | | 2 | 2 | 4 | | | | | | | | | 4 | 54 |
| | | | | | | | 2 | | 2 | | | | 2 | | 2 | | | | | | | | | 2 | 55 |
| | 1 | | 1 | | 4 | 4 | 2 | 1 | 10 | | | | 9 | 2 | 11 | | | | | | | | | 11 | 56 |
| | | | | | | 7 | 14 | | 7 | 11 | 8 | 4 | 14 | 16 | 30 | | | | | | | | | 30 | 57 |
| | 2 | 1 | 1 | | | 5 | 1 | | 6 | | | | 6 | | 6 | | | | | | | | | 6 | 58 |
| | 2 | 1 | 1 | | 2 | 14 | 22 | 2 | 12 | 16 | 9 | 2 | 18 | 23 | 41 | | | | | | | | | 41 | 59 |
| | | | | | | 1 | | | | 1 | | | 1 | | 1 | | | | | | | | | 1 | 60 |
| | | | | | 4 | 3 | 4 | 3 | 5 | 6 | 2 | | 4 | 10 | 14 | | | | | | | | | 14 | 61 |
| | | | | | 1 | 3 | 10 | 4 | 7 | 7 | 3 | 1 | 6 | 12 | 18 | | | | | | | | | 18 | 62 |
| | | | | | 1 | 1 | 2 | | | 2 | 1 | | 2 | 2 | 4 | | | | | | | | | 4 | 63 |
| | | | | | 1 | 1 | 5 | 1 | | 4 | 4 | 1 | 5 | 5 | 10 | | | | | | | | | 10 | 64 |
| | | 1 | | | | 1 | 1 | 4 | 1 | 4 | | 1 | | 6 | 6 | | | | | | | | | 6 | 65 |
| | | | | | 1 | 2 | 1 | 1 | | 1 | 1 | 3 | 4 | 1 | 5 | | | | | | | | | 5 | 66 |
| | 2 | 1 | 1 | | 10 | 20 | 35 | 11 | 33 | 31 | 4 | 4 | 32 | 45 | 77 | | | | | | | | | 77 | 67 |
| 7 | 35 | 55 | 45 | 16 | 355 | 357 | 434 | 263 | 513 | 425 | 118 | 208 | 939 | 805 | 1758 | | | | | 1 | 4 | 2 | 4 | 1769 | 68 |
| 15 | 362 | 622 | 608 | 81 | 2492 | 3333 | 3649 | 1742 | 4654 | 3806 | 850 | 1114 | 6287 | 5269 | 11686 | | | | | 32 | 16 | 17 | 8 | 11759 | |

## CLASSIFICATION OF DEATHS

| | Cause of death. | Ages. | | | | | | | | | | | | | | | | | | Nativities. | | | | | |
|---|---|---|---|---|---|---|---|---|---|---|---|---|---|---|---|---|---|---|---|---|---|---|---|---|---|
| | | Under 1. | | 1 and under 6. | | 5 and under 10. | | 10 and under 20. | | 20 and under 50. | | 50 and under 80. | | 80 and under 100. | | 100 & over. | | Age unknown. | | Born in State. | N. England States. | Middle States. | Southern States. | Southwest'n States. | Northwest'n States. |
| | | M. | F. | M. | F. | M. | F. | M. | F. | M. | F. | M. | F. | M | F. | M | F. | M | F. | | | | | | |
| 1 | Abscess | 3 | | 1 | | | | 1 | | | 3 | | 2 | | | | | | | 7 | | | 2 | | |
| 2 | Accident, not specif'd | | 5 | 16 | 3 | 13 | 2 | 23 | 2 | 38 | 5 | 20 | 4 | 2 | | | | | 1 | 64 | 2 | 26 | 12 | 1 | 14 |
| 3 | ...do...burned | 4 | 2 | 12 | 16 | 1 | 9 | 3 | 3 | 5 | 1 | 1 | 1 | | | | | | | 40 | | 8 | 2 | | 7 |
| 4 | ...do...drowned | | 1 | 17 | 6 | 4 | 1 | 15 | 1 | 25 | 3 | 3 | 1 | | | | | | | 43 | 1 | 9 | 6 | | 12 |
| 5 | ...do...scalded | 2 | | 11 | 4 | 1 | | | | | | | | | | | | | | 15 | | 1 | 1 | | 1 |
| 6 | ...do...expl. steam | | | | | | | | | 1 | | | | | | | | | | 1 | | | | | |
| 7 | Amputation | | | | | | | | | | 1 | | | | | | | | | | | | | | 1 |
| 8 | Apoplexy | | 1 | | | | 3 | 1 | 1 | 6 | 11 | 11 | 8 | | | | | | | 7 | 2 | 7 | 10 | 1 | 9 |
| 9 | Asthma | | | 1 | 1 | | | | | 1 | | 2 | 3 | | | | | | | 3 | | 2 | 1 | | 2 |
| 10 | Bowels, disease of | | | | | | | | | 2 | 1 | | | | | | | | | | | | 1 | | 2 |
| 11 | Bronchitis | 5 | 3 | 2 | 7 | | 2 | 2 | 1 | 9 | 8 | 6 | 3 | | 1 | | | | | 29 | | 6 | 7 | | 7 |
| 12 | Cancer | 1 | 1 | 2 | 2 | | | 1 | | 4 | 8 | 9 | 18 | 2 | 1 | | | | | 13 | 1 | 11 | 7 | 2 | 10 |
| 13 | Catarrh | | 1 | | | | | | 1 | | 1 | | 1 | | | | | | | 2 | | | 1 | | 1 |
| 14 | Chicken pox | | | | 1 | | | | | | | | | | | | | | | 1 | | | | | |
| 15 | Childbirth | | | | | | | | 7 | | 86 | | 1 | | | | | | | 27 | 4 | 14 | 6 | 1 | 28 |
| 16 | Chlorosis | | | | | | | | | | 2 | | | | | | | | | | | 1 | 1 | | |
| 17 | Cholera | 38 | 30 | 100 | 96 | 61 | 62 | 85 | 68 | 407 | 236 | 145 | 82 | 6 | 1 | | | 1 | | 580 | 25 | 173 | 79 | 13 | 182 |
| 18 | ...do..infantum | 34 | 29 | 47 | 41 | 4 | 1 | | | | | | | | | | | | | 148 | | 3 | 1 | | 4 |
| 19 | ...do..morbus | 7 | 5 | 8 | 9 | 3 | 1 | 4 | 3 | 13 | 5 | 3 | 6 | | | | | | | 45 | 1 | 10 | 1 | 2 | 5 |
| 20 | Chorea | | | | | 1 | | | 1 | | 1 | | | | | | | | | 2 | | | 1 | | |
| 21 | Colic | 1 | 1 | 1 | | | 1 | 2 | 2 | 6 | 5 | 5 | 5 | 1 | | | | | | 11 | 1 | 2 | 10 | | 4 |
| 22 | Consumption | 17 | 17 | 21 | 22 | 7 | 7 | 45 | 88 | 303 | 372 | 86 | 78 | 4 | 2 | | | | 1 | 380 | 26 | 174 | 146 | 24 | 266 |
| 23 | Convulsions | 42 | 43 | 20 | 24 | 2 | 7 | 5 | 5 | 11 | 12 | 6 | 5 | | | | | | | 140 | | 9 | 8 | 4 | 19 |
| 24 | Croup | 133 | 90 | 111 | 114 | 30 | 14 | 3 | 1 | 3 | 4 | 1 | | | | | | 1 | | 458 | | 21 | 4 | | 18 |
| 25 | Diabetes | | | 1 | | | | 2 | | 3 | | | | | | | | | | 4 | 1 | | | 1 | |
| 26 | Diarrhœa | 51 | 38 | 52 | 37 | 4 | 1 | 3 | | 20 | 17 | 9 | 9 | 1 | | | | | | 180 | 4 | 12 | 8 | 1 | 31 |
| 27 | Dropsy | 11 | 6 | 19 | 20 | 10 | 9 | 18 | 17 | 38 | 51 | 44 | 42 | 7 | 3 | | | | | 113 | 5 | 56 | 44 | 9 | 47 |
| 28 | Dysentery | 126 | 106 | 301 | 245 | 84 | 80 | 56 | 48 | 76 | 71 | 37 | 39 | 1 | 6 | | | 2 | 1 | 987 | 15 | 66 | 49 | 6 | 120 |
| 29 | Dyspepsia | | 1 | | | | | | | 7 | 4 | 6 | 2 | | | | | | | 2 | | 3 | 8 | 1 | 5 |
| 30 | Epilepsy | 1 | | | 1 | | | 1 | | 1 | 4 | 1 | 1 | 2 | 1 | | | | | 7 | 1 | 2 | 2 | | 1 |
| 31 | Erysipelas | 18 | 21 | 24 | 10 | 6 | 6 | 20 | 7 | 16 | 24 | 19 | 8 | | 1 | | | | | 96 | 3 | 16 | 33 | | 25 |
| 32 | Fever, not specified | 30 | 32 | 59 | 51 | 31 | 29 | 45 | 65 | 130 | 100 | 36 | 22 | 1 | 3 | | | | | 332 | 8 | 51 | 64 | 11 | 122 |
| 33 | ..do..bilious | 3 | 5 | 16 | 8 | 6 | 5 | 8 | 6 | 35 | 21 | 6 | 3 | 2 | | | | | | 64 | | 16 | 5 | 2 | 17 |
| 34 | ..do..brain | 10 | 4 | 9 | 5 | 2 | 5 | 4 | 3 | 4 | 3 | | | 1 | | | | | | 33 | 1 | 5 | 2 | | 7 |
| 35 | ..do..congestive | 9 | 7 | 22 | 20 | 15 | 9 | 20 | 21 | 50 | 28 | 20 | 8 | 1 | | | | 1 | | 125 | 1 | 24 | 22 | 4 | 42 |
| 36 | ..do..inflammatory | | | | | | | 2 | 1 | 1 | | | | | | | | | | 1 | | 1 | | | 2 |
| 37 | ..do..intermittent | 11 | 6 | 6 | 7 | 3 | 1 | 4 | 2 | 5 | 2 | 8 | 2 | 1 | 2 | | | | | 35 | | 5 | 8 | 1 | 8 |
| 38 | ..do..puerperal | | | | | | | | 4 | | 31 | | | | | | | | | 11 | 1 | 3 | 5 | | 10 |
| 39 | ..do..remittent | | 1 | | | | | 1 | | | | | | 1 | | | | | | 2 | | 1 | | | |
| 40 | ..do..scarlet | 30 | 24 | 115 | 124 | 36 | 44 | 14 | 18 | 5 | 4 | 1 | 1 | | | | | | | 349 | | 7 | 5 | 1 | 51 |
| 41 | ..do..typhus | 7 | 4 | 22 | 9 | 18 | 16 | 45 | 42 | 121 | 60 | 19 | 19 | 2 | | | | | | 177 | 10 | 50 | 49 | 3 | 85 |
| 42 | ..do..winter | 2 | 1 | | 3 | 4 | 1 | 4 | 4 | 4 | 6 | 6 | | | | | | | | 23 | 1 | 1 | 3 | 1 | 7 |
| 43 | ..do..yellow | | | | | | | | | 3 | | | | | | | | | | | | 1 | 1 | | 1 |
| 44 | Fistula | | | | | | | | | | 1 | | | | | | | | | | | | 1 | | |
| 45 | Fracture | | | | | 1 | | | | 1 | 1 | | 1 | | | | | | | 1 | | 1 | | 1 | 1 |
| 46 | Frozen | | | | | | | | | 1 | | 2 | | | | | | | | | | | 3 | | |
| 47 | Gravel | | 1 | | 1 | 1 | | 1 | | 4 | 1 | 10 | 5 | 3 | | | | | | 6 | 2 | 8 | 3 | | 3 |
| 48 | Heart, disease of | | 2 | 1 | | 2 | 4 | | 2 | 5 | 10 | 5 | 4 | 2 | | | | | | 15 | 2 | 8 | 5 | 1 | 5 |
| 49 | Hemorrhage | 2 | | | 1 | 1 | 1 | 1 | | 8 | 4 | 4 | | | 1 | | | | | 9 | | 4 | 3 | | 6 |
| 50 | Hernia | 2 | 1 | | | | | | | 1 | 1 | | | 1 | | | | | | 2 | | | 1 | | 1 |
| 51 | Hives | 19 | 8 | 8 | 6 | | | | | | 1 | | | | | | | | | 37 | | 3 | | 1 | 1 |
| 52 | Hooping cough | 37 | 36 | 29 | 65 | 6 | 3 | 1 | 5 | 1 | 2 | | 1 | | | | | | | 162 | | 7 | 2 | | 13 |
| 53 | Hydrocephalus | 6 | 12 | 9 | 6 | | | 1 | | 1 | 1 | | 1 | | | | | | | 32 | 1 | 2 | | | 2 |
| 54 | Inflamat'n, bowels | 18 | 9 | 13 | 21 | 4 | 1 | 3 | 3 | 14 | 10 | 4 | 3 | 1 | | | | | | 73 | 3 | 11 | 3 | 1 | 11 |
| 55 | .....do....brain | 82 | 54 | 73 | 79 | 32 | 24 | 32 | 34 | 30 | 17 | 14 | 1 | 2 | | | | | | 381 | 3 | 20 | 14 | 2 | 51 |
| 56 | .....do....stomach | 4 | 1 | | | 1 | | | | 5 | 5 | | 2 | | | | | | | 5 | | 2 | | | 11 |
| 57 | Influenza | 2 | 4 | 2 | 4 | | 2 | 2 | | 2 | 3 | 2 | 5 | 1 | | | | | | 16 | 1 | 4 | 4 | 1 | 2 |
| 58 | Insanity | | | | | | | 1 | | 1 | | 1 | | | | | | | | 1 | | | 1 | | |
| 59 | Intemperance | | | | | | | | | 3 | | 3 | | | | | | | | | | 4 | 1 | | 1 |
| 60 | Jaundice | 2 | 2 | | 7 | 3 | 1 | | | 3 | | 2 | 3 | | | | | | | 15 | | 2 | 3 | | 2 |
| 61 | Kidneys, disease of | | | | | | | 1 | | 1 | | 6 | 1 | | | | | | | 1 | 1 | 3 | | | 3 |
| 62 | Killed | | | 1 | | | 1 | 6 | | 6 | | 3 | | | | | | | | 6 | | 1 | 1 | | 7 |
| 63 | Leprosy | | | 1 | | | | | | | 1 | | | | | | | | | 1 | | | | | 1 |
| 64 | Lightning | | | | | | | 1 | | | | 1 | | | | | | | | | | | | | 1 |
| 65 | Liver, disease of | 8 | 4 | 13 | 2 | 1 | 1 | 1 | 6 | 22 | 29 | 9 | 9 | | 1 | | | | | 43 | 2 | 18 | 12 | 2 | 21 |
| 66 | Lockjaw | | | | | | | 2 | | | | | | | | | | | | | | | | | 1 |
| 67 | Malformation | 1 | 2 | | 1 | | | | | | | | | | | | | | | 4 | | | | | |
| 68 | Mania-a-potu | | | | | | | | | 8 | | 2 | | | | | | | | 5 | | 1 | 2 | | 1 |
| 69 | Measles | 16 | 17 | 36 | 41 | 8 | 10 | 4 | 10 | 10 | 9 | 1 | 1 | | | | | | | 117 | 4 | 6 | 5 | | 27 |
| 70 | Milk sickness | 1 | | 4 | 2 | 1 | 3 | 6 | 1 | 11 | 11 | 2 | 1 | | | | | | | 23 | 2 | 1 | 2 | 1 | 8 |
| 71 | Mortification | | | | | | | | | | 1 | | | | | | | | | | | | | | |
| 72 | Mumps | 1 | | | 1 | | | 1 | | | 3 | | | | | | | | | 2 | 1 | 2 | | | 1 |
| 73 | Murder | | | | | | | | | 5 | | 1 | | | | | | | | | | | 2 | 1 | 2 |
| 74 | Neuralgia | 1 | | 1 | | 2 | 1 | 1 | 1 | 3 | 3 | 1 | 2 | | | | | | | 7 | | 4 | | 1 | 3 |
| 75 | Old age | | | | | | | | | 1 | | 36 | 46 | 54 | 45 | | | | | 19 | 17 | 58 | 55 | 2 | 6 |

IN THE STATE OF INDIANA.

| NATIVITIES. | | | | | SEASON OF DECEASE. | | | | DURATION OF SICKNESS. | | | | WHITES. | | | COLORED. | | | | | | | | | |
|---|---|---|---|---|---|---|---|---|---|---|---|---|---|---|---|---|---|---|---|---|---|---|---|---|---|
| | | | | | | | | | | | | | | | | Slaves. | | | | Free. | | | | | |
| | | | | | | | | | | | | | | | | Black. | | Mulatto. | | Black. | | Mul. | | | |
| California and Territories. | Ireland. | Germany. | Other foreign countries. | Unknown. | Spring. | Summer. | Autumn. | Winter. | Under 1 week. | 1 week and under 1 month. | 1 month and under 3 months. | 3 months and over. | Males. | Females. | Total. | M. | F. | M. | F. | M. | F. | M | F. | Aggregate deaths. | |
| | | 1 | | | 5 | | 3 | 2 | 2 | 3 | 3 | 1 | 5 | 5 | 10 | | | | | | | | | 10 | 1 |
| | 4 | 8 | 3 | | 42 | 23 | 41 | 28 | 26 | 18 | 6 | 2 | 112 | 22 | 134 | | | | | | | | | 134 | 2 |
| | 1 | | | | 20 | 11 | 10 | 16 | 23 | 15 | 2 | | 25 | 32 | 57 | | | | | | | 1 | | 58 | 3 |
| | 2 | 4 | | | 21 | 29 | 12 | 14 | 4 | 1 | | | 63 | 13 | 76 | | | | | 1 | | | | 77 | 4 |
| | | | | | 9 | 2 | 2 | 5 | 9 | 7 | | | 13 | 4 | 17 | | | | | 1 | | | | 18 | 5 |
| | | | | | | 1 | | | | | | | 1 | | 1 | | | | | | | | | 1 | 6 |
| | | | | | 1 | | | | | 1 | | | | 1 | 1 | | | | | | | | | 1 | 7 |
| | 1 | 4 | 1 | | 15 | 12 | 9 | 6 | 18 | 4 | | | 18 | 24 | 42 | | | | | | | | | 42 | 8 |
| | | | | | 2 | 2 | 2 | 1 | | | 1 | 3 | 4 | 4 | 8 | | | | | | | | | 8 | 9 |
| | | | | | | 1 | 2 | | | 1 | 2 | | 2 | 1 | 3 | | | | | | | | | 3 | 10 |
| | | | | | 15 | 8 | 14 | 11 | 12 | 9 | 7 | 11 | 24 | 25 | 49 | | | | | | | | | 49 | 11 |
| | 2 | 1 | 2 | | 10 | 12 | 12 | 13 | 2 | 5 | 5 | 19 | 19 | 30 | 49 | | | | | | | | | 49 | 12 |
| | | | | | | 1 | 2 | 1 | 1 | 2 | 1 | | | 4 | 4 | | | | | | | | | 4 | 13 |
| | | | | | 1 | | | | | 1 | | | | 1 | 1 | | | | | | | | | 1 | 14 |
| | 7 | 5 | 2 | | 23 | 20 | 28 | 23 | 38 | 30 | 11 | 3 | | 94 | 94 | | | | | | | | | 94 | 15 |
| | | | | | 1 | | 1 | | 1 | | 1 | | | 2 | 2 | | | | | | | | | 2 | 16 |
| | 118 | 197 | 51 | | 43 | 890 | 422 | 25 | 1192 | 137 | 11 | 3 | 838 | 566 | 1404 | | 1 | | | 3 | 6 | 2 | 2 | 1418 | 17 |
| | | | | | 4 | 51 | 85 | 10 | 59 | 59 | 19 | 6 | 84 | 70 | 154 | | 1 | | | | | 1 | | 156 | 18 |
| | 1 | 1 | 1 | | 2 | 23 | 32 | 1 | 39 | 19 | | | 38 | 29 | 67 | | | | | | | | | 67 | 19 |
| | | | | | 1 | 1 | 1 | | | 2 | | | 1 | 2 | 3 | | | | | | | | | 3 | 20 |
| | 1 | | 1 | | 9 | 8 | 8 | 5 | 24 | 5 | | | 16 | 14 | 30 | | | | | | | | | 30 | 21 |
| | 19 | 17 | 18 | | 285 | 300 | 277 | 200 | 44 | 97 | 116 | 489 | 477 | 580 | 1057 | | | | | 4 | 4 | 2 | 3 | 1070 | 22 |
| | | 2 | | | 51 | 41 | 51 | 36 | 94 | 38 | 6 | 5 | 84 | 96 | 180 | | | | | 1 | | 1 | | 182 | 23 |
| | 3 | | 1 | | 124 | 88 | 153 | 135 | 393 | 71 | 5 | 6 | 281 | 222 | 503 | | | | | 1 | 1 | | | 505 | 24 |
| | | | | | 1 | 2 | 3 | | | 3 | 1 | 1 | 6 | | 6 | | | | | | | | | 6 | 25 |
| | 1 | | 5 | | 14 | 72 | 141 | 11 | 58 | 108 | 41 | 16 | 139 | 100 | 239 | | | | | 1 | 1 | | 1 | 242 | 26 |
| | 6 | 9 | 6 | | 77 | 79 | 66 | 67 | 40 | 53 | 45 | 99 | 146 | 146 | 292 | | | | | | 2 | 1 | | 295 | 27 |
| | 9 | 19 | 8 | | 55 | 248 | 911 | 58 | 320 | 789 | 99 | 11 | 683 | 592 | 1275 | | | | | | 4 | | | 1279 | 28 |
| | | 1 | | | 2 | 7 | 7 | 4 | 1 | 6 | | 6 | 13 | 7 | 20 | | | | | | | | | 20 | 29 |
| | | | | | 5 | 2 | 2 | 4 | 1 | 6 | | 4 | 6 | 7 | 13 | | | | | | | | | 13 | 30 |
| | | 3 | 4 | | 57 | 52 | 37 | 34 | 63 | 86 | 12 | 10 | 103 | 77 | 180 | | | | | | | | | 180 | 31 |
| | 13 | 15 | 17 | 1 | 144 | 146 | 231 | 105 | 116 | 403 | 79 | 13 | 328 | 302 | 630 | | | | | 3 | | 1 | | 634 | 32 |
| | 6 | 9 | 5 | | 12 | 45 | 52 | 13 | 25 | 80 | 13 | | 76 | 48 | 124 | | | | | | | | | 124 | 33 |
| | | 2 | | | 18 | 13 | 13 | 6 | 21 | 20 | 6 | 1 | 30 | 20 | 50 | | | | | | | | | 50 | 34 |
| | 4 | 5 | 4 | | 60 | 38 | 85 | 43 | 104 | 96 | 14 | 3 | 137 | 92 | 229 | | | | | 1 | 1 | | | 231 | 35 |
| | | | | | | | 4 | | 1 | 3 | | | 3 | 1 | 4 | | | | | | | | | 4 | 36 |
| | | 2 | 1 | | 9 | 10 | 35 | 6 | 11 | 33 | 8 | 3 | 38 | 22 | 60 | | | | | | | | | 60 | 37 |
| | | 5 | | | 11 | 12 | 4 | 8 | 9 | 19 | 5 | | | 35 | 35 | | | | | | | | | 35 | 38 |
| | | | | | | | 1 | 2 | 1 | 2 | | | 2 | 1 | 3 | | | | | | | | | 3 | 39 |
| | | 1 | 2 | | 127 | 90 | 85 | 112 | 180 | 199 | 21 | 1 | 201 | 215 | 416 | | | | | | | | | 416 | 40 |
| | 3 | 3 | 4 | | 119 | 54 | 101 | 101 | 60 | 251 | 50 | 10 | 234 | 150 | 384 | | | | | | | | | 384 | 41 |
| | | | 2 | | 17 | 5 | 1 | 13 | 7 | 28 | 1 | | 20 | 18 | 38 | | | | | | | | | 38 | 42 |
| | | | | | 1 | | 1 | 1 | 1 | 2 | | | 3 | | 3 | | | | | | | | | 3 | 43 |
| | | | | | | | | 1 | | | | | | 1 | 1 | | | | | | | | | 1 | 44 |
| | | | | | | 3 | | | 1 | | 2 | | 2 | 2 | 4 | | | | | | | | | 4 | 45 |
| | | | | | | | | 3 | 1 | | | | 2 | | 2 | | | | | 1 | | | | 3 | 46 |
| | 1 | 1 | 2 | 1 | 7 | 8 | 5 | 7 | 3 | 14 | 4 | 4 | 19 | 8 | 27 | | | | | | | | | 27 | 47 |
| | 1 | | | | 12 | 8 | 6 | 11 | 5 | 10 | 7 | 4 | 15 | 22 | 37 | | | | | | | | | 37 | 48 |
| | | 1 | | | 9 | 4 | 5 | 5 | 9 | 3 | 5 | 1 | 16 | 7 | 23 | | | | | | | | | 23 | 49 |
| | | 1 | 1 | | 5 | | | 1 | 1 | 1 | 1 | 1 | 4 | 2 | 6 | | | | | | | | | 6 | 50 |
| | | | | | 14 | 4 | 12 | 9 | 29 | 8 | 1 | 1 | 27 | 15 | 42 | | | | | | | | | 42 | 51 |
| | | 1 | 1 | | 41 | 70 | 55 | 20 | 29 | 98 | 43 | 5 | 73 | 111 | 184 | | | | | | | 1 | 1 | 186 | 52 |
| | | | | | 13 | 8 | 10 | 6 | 6 | 20 | 8 | 1 | 17 | 19 | 36 | | | | | | 1 | | | 37 | 53 |
| | 1 | | 1 | | 26 | 23 | 36 | 13 | 31 | 48 | 10 | 5 | 57 | 47 | 104 | | | | | | | | | 104 | 54 |
| | | 3 | | | 123 | 112 | 151 | 84 | 201 | 216 | 29 | 6 | 263 | 209 | 472 | | | | | 1 | | 1 | | 474 | 55 |
| | | | | | 6 | 4 | 5 | 2 | 10 | 8 | | | 10 | 8 | 18 | | | | | | | | | 18 | 56 |
| | 1 | | | | 9 | 4 | 8 | 8 | 12 | 11 | 3 | 2 | 11 | 18 | 29 | | | | | | | | | 29 | 57 |
| | | | 1 | | | 2 | 1 | | | 1 | 1 | 1 | 3 | | 3 | | | | | | | | | 3 | 58 |
| | | | | | 3 | 1 | 1 | 1 | 2 | 1 | | 1 | 6 | | 6 | | | | | | | | | 6 | 59 |
| | | | 1 | | 10 | 3 | 4 | 6 | 4 | 6 | 3 | 5 | 10 | 13 | 23 | | | | | | | | | 23 | 60 |
| | | | 1 | | 5 | 3 | | 1 | | 3 | 2 | 2 | 8 | 1 | 9 | | | | | | | | | 9 | 61 |
| | 1 | | 1 | | 5 | 7 | 4 | 1 | 1 | 1 | | | 16 | 1 | 17 | | | | | | | | | 17 | 62 |
| | | | | | 1 | 1 | | | | | | | 1 | 1 | 2 | | | | | | | | | 2 | 63 |
| | | 1 | | | | 2 | | | | | | | 2 | | 2 | | | | | | | | | 2 | 64 |
| | 1 | 3 | 4 | | 29 | 29 | 33 | 13 | 13 | 27 | 24 | 21 | 54 | 52 | 106 | | | | | | | | | 106 | 65 |
| | | | 1 | | 1 | | | 1 | 1 | 1 | | | 2 | | 2 | | | | | | | | | 2 | 66 |
| | | | | | 1 | 2 | | 1 | 3 | | | 1 | 1 | 3 | 4 | | | | | | | | | 4 | 67 |
| | 1 | | | | 6 | 2 | 2 | | 3 | 1 | | 1 | 10 | | 10 | | | | | | | | | 10 | 68 |
| | 1 | 2 | 1 | | 43 | 63 | 31 | 22 | 29 | 105 | 14 | 4 | 75 | 87 | 162 | | | | | | | | 1 | 163 | 69 |
| | 1 | 2 | 3 | | 3 | 10 | 16 | 12 | 15 | 24 | 2 | | 25 | 18 | 43 | | | | | | | | | 43 | 70 |
| | | 1 | | | | | | 1 | 1 | | | | | 1 | 1 | | | | | | | | | 1 | 71 |
| | | | | | 3 | | | 1 | 3 | 2 | | | 2 | 4 | 6 | | | | | | | | | 6 | 72 |
| | | | 1 | | 2 | 2 | | 2 | 1 | | | | 6 | | 6 | | | | | | | | | 6 | 73 |
| | 1 | | | | 1 | 9 | 2 | 4 | 3 | 4 | 4 | 3 | 9 | 7 | 16 | | | | | | | | | 16 | 74 |
| | 6 | 8 | 10 | 1 | 58 | 40 | 44 | 34 | 27 | 37 | 13 | 13 | 90 | 90 | 180 | | | | | 1 | 1 | | | 182 | 75 |

## CLASSIFICATION OF DEATHS

| | Cause of death. | AGES. Under 1. M. | Under 1. F. | 1 and under 5. M. | 1 and under 5. F. | 5 and under 10. M. | 5 and under 10. F. | 10 and under 20. M. | 10 and under 20. F. | 20 and under 50. M. | 20 and under 50. F. | 50 and under 80. M. | 50 and under 80. F. | 80 and under 100. M | 80 and under 100. F. | 100 & over. M | 100 & over. F. | Age unknown. M | Age unknown. F. | NATIVITIES. Born in State. | N. England States. | Middle States. | Southern States. | Southwest'n States. | Northwest'n States. |
|---|---|---|---|---|---|---|---|---|---|---|---|---|---|---|---|---|---|---|---|---|---|---|---|---|---|
| 1 | Paralysis | .... | 1 | 1 | .. | .. | .. | .. | 1 | 8 | 9 | 22 | 20 | 4 | 6 | .. | .. | .. | .. | 9 | 6 | 20 | 18 | 1 | 1 |
| 2 | Peritonitis | .... | .. | .. | .. | .. | .. | .. | .. | .. | 1 | .. | .. | .. | .. | .. | .. | .. | .. | 1 | .. | .. | .. | .. | .. |
| 3 | Piles | .... | .. | .. | 1 | .. | .. | .. | .. | 2 | .. | 1 | .. | .. | .. | .. | .. | .. | .. | 1 | .. | .. | 1 | 1 | .. |
| 4 | Pleurisy | 5 | .. | 2 | 2 | 3 | 2 | 2 | 4 | 9 | 5 | 6 | 3 | .. | 1 | .. | .. | .. | .. | 16 | 3 | 7 | 6 | .. | |
| 5 | Pneumonia | 47 | 39 | 69 | 45 | 15 | 24 | 31 | 25 | 122 | 75 | 67 | 34 | 4 | 4 | .. | .. | .. | .. | 299 | 19 | 80 | 72 | 8 | 10 |
| 6 | Poison | 1 | 1 | 2 | .. | 1 | 1 | 1 | .. | 3 | 3 | .. | 1 | .. | .. | .. | .. | .. | .. | 6 | .. | 2 | .. | .. | |
| 7 | Prematurity of birth | 3 | .. | .. | .. | .. | .. | .. | .. | .. | .. | .. | .. | .. | .. | .. | .. | .. | .. | 3 | .. | .. | .. | .. | .. |
| 8 | Quinsy | 4 | .. | 9 | 8 | 6 | 7 | 1 | 1 | 4 | 4 | 3 | .. | .. | .. | .. | .. | .. | .. | 34 | .. | 3 | 2 | .. | |
| 9 | Rheumatism | 2 | .. | .. | .. | 2 | .. | 4 | 4 | 1 | 4 | 12 | 3 | .. | .. | .. | .. | .. | .. | 15 | 1 | 9 | 3 | .. | |
| 10 | Rickets | 1 | .. | .. | 2 | .. | .. | 1 | 1 | .. | .. | .. | .. | 1 | .. | .. | .. | .. | .. | 5 | .. | .. | .. | .. | |
| 11 | Salivation, effects of | .... | .. | .. | .. | .. | .. | .. | .. | .. | 1 | .. | .. | .. | .. | .. | .. | .. | .. | .. | .. | .. | 1 | .. | .. |
| 12 | Scrofula | 10 | 5 | 12 | 12 | 2 | 5 | 7 | 3 | 8 | 3 | 2 | 1 | 1 | .. | .. | .. | .. | .. | 54 | .. | 4 | 4 | 2 | |
| 13 | Small pox | 11 | 7 | 21 | 9 | 6 | 2 | 12 | 9 | 42 | 7 | 11 | 3 | .. | .. | .. | .. | .. | .. | 74 | 7 | 10 | 11 | 2 | 2 |
| 14 | Spine, disease of | 2 | 1 | 1 | .. | 3 | 1 | 4 | 2 | 1 | 1 | 3 | 1 | .. | .. | .. | .. | .. | .. | 14 | .. | 3 | 1 | .. | |
| 15 | Spleen....do | .... | .. | .. | .. | .. | .. | .. | .. | 1 | .. | .. | .. | .. | .. | .. | .. | .. | .. | .. | .. | 1 | .. | .. | .. |
| 16 | Stillborn | 22 | 11 | .. | .. | .. | .. | .. | .. | .. | .. | .. | .. | .. | .. | .. | .. | .. | .. | 33 | .. | .. | .. | .. | .. |
| 17 | Suffocation | .... | .. | 1 | .. | .. | 1 | .. | .. | .. | .. | 1 | .. | .. | .. | .. | .. | .. | .. | 2 | .. | 1 | .. | .. | .. |
| 18 | Suicide | .... | .. | .. | .. | .. | .. | 1 | .. | 9 | 1 | 5 | .. | .. | .. | .. | .. | .. | .. | 5 | .. | 5 | 1 | .. | .. |
| 19 | Sun stroke | .... | .. | .. | .. | .. | .. | .. | .. | .. | .. | 1 | .. | .. | .. | .. | .. | .. | .. | .. | .. | .. | 1 | .. | .. |
| 20 | Syphilis | .... | .. | .. | .. | .. | .. | .. | .. | 1 | .. | .. | .. | .. | .. | .. | .. | .. | .. | .. | .. | 1 | .. | .. | .. |
| 21 | Teething | 9 | 3 | 6 | 4 | .. | .. | .. | .. | .. | .. | .. | .. | .. | .. | .. | .. | .. | .. | 19 | .. | .. | .. | .. | .. |
| 22 | Tetanus | .... | .. | .. | .. | .. | .. | .. | 1 | .. | .. | .. | .. | .. | .. | .. | .. | .. | .. | 1 | .. | .. | .. | .. | .. |
| 23 | Tetter | .... | 2 | .. | .. | .. | .. | .. | .. | .. | .. | .. | .. | .. | .. | .. | .. | .. | .. | 2 | .. | .. | .. | .. | .. |
| 24 | Throat, disease of | .... | .. | 1 | .. | .. | .. | .. | .. | .. | .. | .. | .. | .. | .. | .. | .. | .. | .. | 1 | .. | .. | .. | .. | .. |
| 25 | Thrush | 12 | 7 | 1 | 3 | .. | .. | .. | .. | .. | 1 | .. | .. | .. | .. | .. | .. | .. | .. | 22 | .. | .. | .. | .. | .. |
| 26 | Tumor | 1 | 1 | .. | .. | .. | .. | .. | .. | 1 | .. | 2 | 2 | .. | .. | .. | .. | .. | .. | 2 | .. | 2 | 1 | .. | .. |
| 27 | Ulcer | 5 | 4 | 4 | .. | .. | 2 | .. | 3 | 2 | 2 | 1 | 1 | 1 | .. | .. | .. | .. | .. | 17 | .. | 2 | 1 | .. | .. |
| 28 | Uterus, disease of | .... | .. | .. | .. | .. | .. | .. | .. | .. | 5 | .. | 1 | .. | .. | .. | .. | .. | .. | 2 | .. | 2 | 1 | .. | .. |
| 29 | Venereal | .... | .. | .. | .. | .. | .. | .. | .. | .. | .. | 2 | .. | .. | .. | .. | .. | .. | .. | .. | .. | 1 | 1 | .. | .. |
| 30 | White swelling | .... | .. | 2 | .. | 1 | 1 | 4 | .. | 4 | .. | .. | .. | .. | .. | .. | .. | .. | .. | 8 | .. | .. | 1 | .. | .. |
| 31 | Worms | 4 | 4 | 20 | 32 | 4 | 10 | .. | 1 | 1 | .. | .. | .. | .. | .. | .. | .. | .. | .. | 69 | . | .. | 1 | 1 | |
| 32 | Unknown | 399 | 299 | 184 | 148 | 53 | 56 | 60 | 60 | 138 | 201 | 120 | 74 | 6 | 13 | .. | .. | 12 | 5 | 1273 | 26 | 134 | 120 | 18 | 2 |
| | Total | 1336 | 1023 | 1543 | 1389 | 505 | 480 | 630 | 599 | 1857 | 1628 | 878 | 607 | 116 | 92 | .. | .. | 17 | 8 | 7527 | 215 | 1254 | 985 | 136 | |

## CLASSIFICATION OF DEATH

| | Cause of death. | Under 1. M. | Under 1. F. | 1 and under 5. M. | 1 and under 5. F. | 5 and under 10. M. | 5 and under 10. F. | 10 and under 20. M. | 10 and under 20. F. | 20 and under 50. M. | 20 and under 50. F. | 50 and under 80. M. | 50 and under 80. F. | 80 and under 100. M | 80 and under 100. F. | 100 & over. M | 100 & over. F. | Age unknown. M | Age unknown. F. | Born in State. | N. England States. | Middle States. | Southern States. | Southwest'n States. |
|---|---|---|---|---|---|---|---|---|---|---|---|---|---|---|---|---|---|---|---|---|---|---|---|---|
| 1 | Abscess | .... | .. | .. | 1 | .. | .. | .. | .. | .. | .. | .. | 1 | .. | .. | .. | .. | .. | .. | 2 | .. | .. | .. | .. |
| 2 | Accident, not specif'd | .... | 1 | 5 | 1 | 4 | 2 | 5 | .. | 15 | 3 | 2 | .. | 1 | .. | .. | .. | .. | .. | 10 | 1 | 12 | 2 | .. |
| 3 | ....do....burned | .... | .. | 6 | 1 | .. | 2 | .. | .. | .. | .. | .. | .. | .. | .. | .. | .. | .. | .. | 6 | .. | .. | .. | .. |
| 4 | ....do....drowned | .... | 1 | 3 | 1 | .. | .. | 4 | 1 | 5 | 3 | 1 | .. | .. | .. | .. | .. | .. | .. | .... | .. | 8 | 2 | .. |
| 5 | ....do....scalded | .... | .. | 4 | 3 | 1 | 1 | .. | .. | .. | .. | .. | .. | .. | .. | .. | .. | .. | .. | 8 | .. | 1 | .. | .. |
| 6 | Apoplexy | .... | .. | 1 | .. | .. | .. | 1 | .. | 2 | .. | 2 | .. | .. | .. | .. | .. | .. | .. | .. | .. | .. | 2 | .. |
| 7 | Asthma | 1 | .. | .. | .. | .. | .. | .. | .. | .. | 1 | .. | 1 | .. | .. | .. | .. | .. | .. | 1 | .. | 1 | .. | .. |
| 8 | Bowels, disease of | 2 | 3 | 5 | 4 | 2 | .. | .. | .. | 6 | 2 | 1 | .. | .. | .. | .. | .. | 1 | .. | 16 | .. | 3 | 1 | 1 |
| 9 | Brain..... do | 8 | 5 | 10 | 10 | 6 | 4 | 3 | 3 | 7 | 5 | 2 | .. | .. | .. | .. | .. | .. | .. | 33 | 1 | 7 | 3 | 3 |
| 10 | Bronchitis | 1 | .. | .. | 3 | .. | 1 | .. | .. | 2 | .. | .. | .. | .. | .. | .. | .. | .. | .. | 4 | .. | 2 | .. | .. |
| 11 | Cancer | .... | .. | .. | .. | .. | .. | .. | .. | 2 | 1 | 2 | 1 | .. | .. | .. | .. | .. | .. | .. | .. | 3 | 2 | .. |
| 12 | Catarrh | 4 | 6 | .. | 3 | 2 | .. | .. | .. | .. | .. | .. | .. | .. | .. | .. | .. | .. | .. | 14 | .. | .. | .. | .. |
| 13 | Childbirth | .... | .. | .. | .. | .. | .. | .. | 1 | .. | 16 | .. | .. | .. | .. | .. | .. | .. | .. | 4 | .. | 2 | .. | 3 |
| 14 | Cholera | 3 | 5 | 10 | 10 | 5 | 5 | 2 | 4 | 51 | 23 | 14 | 2 | .. | .. | .. | .. | .. | .. | 33 | 4 | 27 | 6 | 2 |
| 15 | ...do..infantum | 4 | 2 | 10 | 9 | 2 | 1 | .. | .. | .. | .. | .. | .. | .. | .. | .. | .. | .. | .. | 23 | .. | .. | .. | .. |
| 16 | ...do..morbus | .... | 1 | .. | .. | .. | .. | 2 | .. | 4 | 1 | 2 | .. | .. | .. | .. | .. | .. | .. | 1 | 1 | 3 | 1 | .. |
| 17 | Chorea | .... | .. | .. | .. | .. | .. | .. | 1 | .. | .. | .. | .. | .. | .. | .. | .. | .. | .. | .. | .. | .. | .. | .. |
| 18 | Colic | 1 | 1 | .. | .. | .. | .. | .. | .. | 1 | .. | 1 | .. | .. | .. | .. | .. | 1 | .. | 4 | .. | 1 | .. | .. |
| 19 | Consumption | 5 | 4 | 3 | 10 | 3 | .. | 4 | 13 | 37 | 57 | 14 | 9 | .. | .. | .. | .. | .. | .. | 34 | 7 | 29 | 16 | 5 |
| 20 | Convulsions | 8 | 5 | 5 | 1 | 1 | .. | 2 | 1 | 2 | 1 | 1 | .. | .. | .. | .. | .. | .. | .. | 16 | 1 | 2 | .. | .. |
| 21 | Croup | 31 | 27 | 18 | 17 | 2 | 2 | .. | .. | .. | .. | .. | .. | .. | .. | .. | .. | .. | .. | 79 | .. | 1 | .. | 1 |
| 22 | Debility | 1 | 2 | .. | 1 | .. | .. | .. | .. | .. | .. | .. | .. | .. | .. | .. | .. | .. | .. | 4 | .. | .. | .. | .. |
| 23 | Diabetes | .... | .. | .. | .. | 1 | .. | .. | .. | .. | .. | 1 | .. | .. | .. | .. | .. | .. | .. | .. | .. | 1 | .. | .. |
| 24 | Diarrhœa | 19 | 15 | 30 | 26 | 6 | 1 | .. | 1 | 3 | 4 | 3 | 2 | .. | .. | .. | .. | .. | .. | 86 | 1 | 3 | .. | 1 |
| 25 | Dropsy | 1 | 1 | 5 | 1 | 3 | .. | 2 | 3 | 2 | 7 | 6 | 3 | .. | 1 | .. | .. | .. | .. | 9 | .. | 3 | 3 | 2 |
| 26 | Dysentery | 10 | 7 | 16 | 18 | .. | 2 | .. | .. | 5 | 4 | 3 | 2 | .. | .. | .. | .. | .. | .. | 47 | .. | 5 | .. | 1 |
| 27 | Dyspepsia | .... | .. | 1 | .. | .. | .. | .. | .. | 3 | 2 | 1 | .. | .. | .. | .. | .. | .. | .. | 1 | 1 | .. | 2 | .. |
| 28 | Erysipelas | .... | 2 | 3 | 1 | 2 | 1 | 5 | 3 | 1 | 1 | .. | .. | .. | .. | .. | .. | .. | .. | 11 | .. | 1 | .. | .. |
| 29 | Fever, not specified | 9 | 12 | 20 | 15 | 5 | 7 | 9 | 12 | 24 | 27 | 13 | 8 | .. | .. | .. | .. | .. | .. | 57 | 2 | 10 | 10 | 8 |
| 30 | ..do..bilious | .... | 1 | 1 | 2 | 3 | .. | 1 | 1 | 8 | 3 | 3 | .. | .. | .. | .. | .. | .. | .. | .... | 1 | 1 | 3 | .. |
| 31 | ..do..brain | 7 | .. | 7 | 3 | 1 | .. | 4 | 2 | 1 | 1 | 1 | 1 | .. | .. | .. | .. | .. | .. | 17 | .. | 1 | 1 | 1 |
| 32 | ..do..congestive | 3 | 5 | 4 | 2 | 3 | 4 | 3 | 2 | 10 | 7 | 3 | 3 | .. | .. | .. | .. | .. | .. | 14 | 2 | 4 | 4 | 7 |
| 33 | ..do..inflammatory | .... | .. | 1 | .. | 1 | .. | .. | .. | .. | 1 | .. | .. | .. | .. | .. | .. | .. | .. | 1 | .. | 1 | .. | .. |

## IN THE STATE OF INDIANA—Continued.

| Nativities: California and Territories. | Nativities: Ireland. | Nativities: Germany. | Nativities: Other foreign countries. | Nativities: Unknown. | Season of decease: Spring. | Season of decease: Summer. | Season of decease: Autumn. | Season of decease: Winter. | Duration of sickness: Under 1 week. | Duration of sickness: 1 week and under 1 month. | Duration of sickness: 1 month and under 3 months. | Duration of sickness: 3 months and over. | Whites: Males. | Whites: Females. | Whites: Total. | Colored: Slaves: Black M. | Colored: Slaves: Black F. | Colored: Slaves: Mulatto M. | Colored: Slaves: Mulatto F. | Colored: Free: Black M. | Colored: Free: Black F. | Colored: Free: Mul. M | Colored: Free: Mul. F. | Aggregate deaths. | |
|---|---|---|---|---|---|---|---|---|---|---|---|---|---|---|---|---|---|---|---|---|---|---|---|---|---|
| | 2 | 2 | 2 | | 28 | 13 | 13 | 17 | 26 | 22 | 2 | 11 | 35 | 37 | 72 | | | | | | | | | 72 | 1 |
| | | | | | 1 | | | | 1 | | | | | 1 | 1 | | | | | | | | | 1 | 2 |
| | | | | | 1 | 1 | 1 | 1 | | 1 | | 1 | 3 | 1 | 4 | | | | | | | | | 4 | 3 |
| | 1 | 2 | | | 16 | 7 | 13 | 7 | 13 | 23 | 5 | | 25 | 16 | 41 | | | | | 2 | 1 | | | 44 | 4 |
| | 4 | 5 | 6 | | 250 | 136 | 79 | 131 | 160 | 341 | 64 | 16 | 353 | 242 | 595 | | | | | 1 | 2 | 1 | 2 | 601 | 5 |
| | 3 | | | | | 7 | 3 | 4 | 9 | 4 | 1 | | 8 | 6 | 14 | | | | | | | | | 14 | 6 |
| | | | | | | | 1 | 2 | 2 | | | | 3 | | 3 | | | | | | | | | 3 | 7 |
| | | | 1 | | 7 | 8 | 16 | 15 | 18 | 23 | 1 | | 27 | 20 | 47 | | | | | | | | | 47 | 8 |
| | | 1 | 1 | | 8 | 7 | 4 | 13 | 7 | 9 | 6 | 7 | 21 | 11 | 32 | | | | | | | | | 32 | 9 |
| | | | | | 3 | 2 | 1 | | 2 | | | 3 | 3 | 3 | 6 | | | | | | | | | 6 | 10 |
| | | | | | | 1 | | | | | 1 | | | 1 | 1 | | | | | | | | | 1 | 11 |
| | | | | | 25 | 15 | 17 | 14 | 12 | 14 | 7 | 17 | 40 | 29 | 69 | | | | | 2 | | | | 71 | 12 |
| | | 9 | 2 | | 51 | 15 | 13 | 60 | 16 | 111 | 3 | 1 | 102 | 36 | 138 | | | | | 1 | | | 1 | 140 | 13 |
| | | | | | 3 | 5 | 10 | 2 | 3 | 6 | 3 | 4 | 14 | 6 | 20 | | | | | | | | | 20 | 14 |
| | | | | | | 1 | | | | | | 1 | 1 | | 1 | | | | | | | | | 1 | 15 |
| | | | | | 10 | 10 | 10 | 3 | | | | | 21 | 10 | 31 | | | | | | 1 | 1 | | 33 | 16 |
| | | | | | 1 | | 1 | 1 | 1 | | | | 2 | 1 | 3 | | | | | | | | | 3 | 17 |
| | 1 | | 1 | | 4 | 6 | 3 | 3 | 2 | 1 | 1 | | 15 | 1 | 16 | | | | | | | | | 16 | 18 |
| | | | | | | | 1 | | | 1 | | | 1 | | 1 | | | | | | | | | 1 | 19 |
| | | | | | | 1 | | | | | | 1 | 1 | | 1 | | | | | | | | | 1 | 20 |
| | | | | | 3 | 8 | 4 | 7 | 8 | 7 | 5 | 1 | 15 | 7 | 22 | | | | | | | | | 22 | 21 |
| | | | | | | | 1 | | 1 | | | | | 1 | 1 | | | | | | | | | 1 | 22 |
| | | | | | | | 2 | | | 1 | 1 | | | 2 | 2 | | | | | | | | | 2 | 23 |
| | | | | | | | 1 | | | 1 | | | 1 | | 1 | | | | | | | | | 1 | 24 |
| | | | | | 5 | 8 | 10 | | 1 | 12 | 4 | 3 | 13 | 11 | 24 | | | | | | | | | 24 | 25 |
| | | | | | 3 | 2 | 2 | | 2 | 1 | 1 | 2 | 4 | 3 | 7 | | | | | | | | | 7 | 26 |
| | 1 | 1 | 1 | | 6 | 4 | 8 | 7 | 7 | 7 | 3 | 6 | 12 | 12 | 24 | | | | | 1 | | | | 25 | 27 |
| | | | | | 1 | 2 | 1 | 2 | 1 | 1 | 1 | 2 | | 6 | 6 | | | | | | | | | 6 | 28 |
| | | | | | 1 | | | 1 | | 1 | | 1 | 2 | | 2 | | | | | | | | | 2 | 29 |
| | | | 1 | | 4 | 1 | 4 | 3 | 1 | 3 | 2 | 4 | 11 | 1 | 12 | | | | | | | | | 12 | 30 |
| | | | | | 23 | 18 | 29 | 6 | 35 | 27 | 7 | 2 | 29 | 47 | 76 | | | | | | | | | 76 | 31 |
| | 16 | 14 | 19 | | 462 | 437 | 540 | 350 | 602 | 492 | 172 | 175 | 963 | 851 | 1814 | | | | | 4 | 2 | 5 | 3 | 1828 | 32 |
| | 245 | 372 | 201 | 3 | 2765 | 3540 | 4166 | 2039 | 4374 | 4471 | 1057 | 1066 | 6834 | 5783 | 12617 | | 2 | | | 30 | 27 | 18 | 14 | 12708 | |

## IN THE STATE OF IOWA.

| California and Territories. | Ireland. | Germany. | Other foreign countries. | Unknown. | Spring. | Summer. | Autumn. | Winter. | Under 1 week. | 1 week and under 1 month. | 1 month and under 3 months. | 3 months and over. | Males. | Females. | Total. | Slaves Black M. | Slaves Black F. | Slaves Mulatto M. | Slaves Mulatto F. | Free Black M. | Free Black F. | Free Mul. M | Free Mul. F. | Aggregate deaths. | |
|---|---|---|---|---|---|---|---|---|---|---|---|---|---|---|---|---|---|---|---|---|---|---|---|---|---|
| | | | | | | | | 2 | 1 | | | 1 | | 2 | 2 | | | | | | | | | 2 | 1 |
| | 1 | 3 | | | 6 | 13 | 12 | 8 | 27 | 4 | 1 | 1 | 32 | 7 | 39 | | | | | | | | | 39 | 2 |
| | | 1 | | | 4 | | 3 | 1 | 5 | | | | 6 | 3 | 9 | | | | | | | | | 9 | 3 |
| | 2 | | 2 | | 7 | 8 | 4 | | 19 | | | | 13 | 6 | 19 | | | | | | | | | 19 | 4 |
| | | | | | 2 | 4 | 2 | 1 | 9 | | | | 5 | 4 | 9 | | | | | | | | | 9 | 5 |
| | 1 | | 1 | | 1 | | 1 | 4 | 6 | | | | 6 | | 6 | | | | | | | | | 6 | 6 |
| | | | | | 2 | | | 1 | 3 | | | | 1 | 2 | 3 | | | | | | | | | 3 | 7 |
| | 2 | | | | 3 | 10 | 9 | 3 | 13 | 9 | 2 | | 16 | 9 | 25 | | | | | 1 | | | | 26 | 8 |
| | | | | | 18 | 17 | 14 | 11 | 29 | 25 | 3 | 1 | 35 | 27 | 62 | | | | | 1 | | | | 63 | 9 |
| | | 1 | | | 3 | 1 | 1 | 2 | 1 | 5 | | 1 | 3 | 4 | 7 | | | | | | | | | 7 | 10 |
| | | | | | 1 | 1 | 3 | 1 | 1 | 1 | | 4 | 4 | 2 | 6 | | | | | | | | | 6 | 11 |
| | | | | | 2 | 2 | 5 | 5 | 3 | 8 | 1 | | 6 | 9 | 15 | | | | | | | | | 15 | 12 |
| | 1 | 1 | | | 6 | 7 | 2 | 2 | 11 | 5 | | | | 17 | 17 | | | | | | | | | 17 | 13 |
| | 2 | 21 | 13 | 2 | 15 | 86 | 25 | 2 | 118 | 7 | | | 83 | 46 | 129 | | | | | 2 | 3 | | | 134 | 14 |
| | | | | | 3 | 6 | 15 | 2 | 13 | 7 | 6 | | 16 | 12 | 28 | | | | | | | | | 28 | 15 |
| | | 2 | | 1 | 2 | 3 | 4 | 1 | 5 | 5 | | | 5 | 1 | 6 | | | | | 3 | 1 | | | 10 | 16 |
| | | | | | 1 | | | | 1 | | | | | 1 | 1 | | | | | | | | | 1 | 17 |
| | | | | | 1 | | 1 | 3 | 3 | 1 | | | 4 | 1 | 5 | | | | | | | | | 5 | 18 |
| | 9 | 4 | 5 | | 43 | 44 | 42 | 30 | 12 | 24 | 20 | 102 | 66 | 93 | 159 | | | | | | | | | 159 | 19 |
| | | 2 | | | 9 | 6 | 8 | 4 | 20 | 5 | | 1 | 19 | 8 | 27 | | | | | | | | | 27 | 20 |
| | | | 2 | | 33 | 14 | 25 | 25 | 70 | 17 | 1 | 1 | 51 | 46 | 97 | | | | | | | | | 97 | 21 |
| | | | | | 1 | | 3 | | 3 | | 1 | | 1 | 3 | 4 | | | | | | | | | 4 | 22 |
| | | | | | 1 | | 1 | | 1 | | | 1 | 2 | | 2 | | | | | | | | | 2 | 23 |
| | 1 | 1 | 5 | | 6 | 26 | 67 | 10 | 34 | 65 | 7 | 8 | 61 | 49 | 110 | | | | | | | | | 110 | 24 |
| | 4 | 1 | 3 | | 14 | 8 | 7 | 6 | 3 | 12 | 4 | 16 | 19 | 16 | 35 | | | | | | | | | 35 | 25 |
| | 4 | | 1 | | 4 | 8 | 49 | 5 | 17 | 38 | 7 | | 33 | 33 | 66 | | | | | 1 | | | | 67 | 26 |
| | | | 1 | | 1 | 2 | 2 | 2 | | | 1 | 5 | 5 | 2 | 7 | | | | | | | | | 7 | 27 |
| | | | | | 4 | 5 | 2 | 6 | 5 | 12 | | | 11 | 8 | 19 | | | | | | | | | 19 | 28 |
| | 1 | 8 | 13 | 3 | 38 | 29 | 54 | 32 | 38 | 83 | 19 | 5 | 80 | 75 | 155 | | | | | | 1 | | | 156 | 29 |
| | 3 | 1 | 1 | | 3 | 7 | 13 | | 8 | 14 | | | 16 | 7 | 23 | | | | | | | | | 23 | 30 |
| | | | 1 | | 9 | 7 | 11 | 1 | 11 | 15 | 1 | | 21 | 7 | 28 | | | | | | | | | 28 | 31 |
| | 2 | 1 | 1 | | 10 | 11 | 15 | 11 | 31 | 11 | 1 | | 26 | 23 | 49 | | | | | | | | | 49 | 32 |
| | | | | | 1 | | 2 | | | 3 | | | 2 | 1 | 3 | | | | | | | | | 3 | 33 |

## CLASSIFICATION OF DEATHS

| | Cause of death. | Ages. Under 1. M. | Under 1. F. | 1 and under 5. M. | 1 and under 5. F. | 5 and under 10. M. | 5 and under 10. F. | 10 and under 20. M. | 10 and under 20. F. | 20 and under 50. M. | 20 and under 50. F. | 50 and under 80. M. | 50 and under 80. F. | 80 and under 100. M | 80 and under 100. F. | 100 & over. M | 100 & over. F. | Age unknown. M | Age unknown. F. | Nativities. Born in State. | N. England States. | Middle States. | Southern States. | Southwest'n States. | Northwest'n States. |
|---|---|---|---|---|---|---|---|---|---|---|---|---|---|---|---|---|---|---|---|---|---|---|---|---|---|
| 1 | Fever, intermittent.. | 5 | 2 | 3 | 5 | | | 1 | 1 | 2 | | | 1 | | | | | | | 14 | | 3 | | 1 | 2 |
| 2 | ..do..puerperal..... | | | | | | | | 1 | | 7 | | | | | | | | | 1 | 1 | 2 | | | 2 |
| 3 | ..do..scarlet ....... | 2 | 2 | 8 | 7 | 9 | 3 | 3 | 7 | | 1 | | | | | | | | | 26 | | 4 | 1 | | 11 |
| 4 | ..do..ship ........ | | | 1 | | | | | | | | | | | | | | | | | | | | | |
| 5 | ..do..typhus ....... | | | 2 | 1 | 2 | 1 | 4 | 3 | 11 | 2 | 4 | | | | | | | | 3 | 1 | 4 | 5 | | 11 |
| 6 | ..do..winter ........ | | 1 | 1 | 2 | 1 | | 1 | 1 | 2 | | 1 | 1 | | | | | | | 3 | 1 | 1 | | 1 | 4 |
| 7 | Head, disease of..... | 2 | 1 | | 1 | | 2 | 1 | | | | | | | | | | | | 4 | | 1 | | | 2 |
| 8 | Heart....do ........ | | | 1 | | | | 1 | | | | 1 | | | | | | | | 1 | | 1 | | | 1 |
| 9 | Hemorrhage......... | | | | | | | | | 1 | | | | | | | | | | | | 1 | | | |
| 10 | Hives............. | 2 | 4 | 1 | | | 1 | | | | | | | | | | | | | 7 | | | | | 1 |
| 11 | Hooping cough...... | 11 | 16 | 10 | 15 | | 3 | 1 | 1 | 1 | | | | | | | | | | 50 | | | 1 | | 5 |
| 12 | Hydrocephalus...... | 2 | | 1 | 1 | | | | | | | | | | | | | | | 4 | | | | | |
| 13 | Inflamt'n, not spcif'd | 9 | 1 | 2 | 2 | | | | | | 2 | 1 | | | | | | | | 10 | | 1 | | | |
| 14 | Intemperance........ | | | | | | | | | 7 | | | | | | | | | | 2 | 1 | 1 | 1 | | |
| 15 | Jaundice .......... | | | | | | | | | 1 | | | | | | | | | | | | | | | 1 |
| 16 | Kidneys, disease of.. | | | | | | | | | 1 | | 1 | | | | | | | | 1 | | | | | 1 |
| 17 | Killed ........... | | | | | | | 2 | | 4 | | | | | | | | | | 1 | | | 2 | | 2 |
| 18 | Liver, disease of .... | 2 | | 2 | | | | | | 2 | 4 | 1 | 3 | | | | | | | 8 | | | | 1 | 5 |
| 19 | Lockjaw........... | | | | | | | | | | 1 | | | | | | | | | | | | | 1 | |
| 20 | Lungs, disease of.... | 4 | 1 | 2 | 2 | | 1 | 2 | 3 | 3 | 3 | 2 | 2 | | | | | | | 6 | | 6 | 1 | | 8 |
| 21 | Measles ........... | 3 | 4 | 17 | 14 | 4 | 2 | 1 | 1 | 1 | 4 | | | | | | | | | 27 | | 3 | 4 | | 14 |
| 22 | Mortification ....... | | | | | | 1 | | | | | | | | | | | | | | | | | | 1 |
| 23 | Mumps .......... | | | | | | | | | 1 | | | | | | | | | | | | | | | 1 |
| 24 | Neuralgia ......... | 1 | | | | 1 | | | | | 1 | 1 | 1 | | | | | | | 1 | | 1 | 2 | | 1 |
| 25 | Old age........ .. | | | | | | | | | | | 4 | 2 | 4 | 3 | | | | | 3 | | 4 | 2 | | 2 |
| 26 | Paralysis .......... | | | | | | | | | 1 | | 4 | | | | | | | | | | 1 | 3 | | |
| 27 | Peritonitis ......... | | | | 1 | | | | | | | | | | | | | | | 1 | | | | | |
| 28 | Pleurisy .......... | | 1 | | 1 | 1 | 1 | | 1 | 3 | 2 | | 1 | | | | | | | 6 | 2 | 2 | | | 1 |
| 29 | P neumonia ........ | 10 | 16 | 19 | 17 | 7 | 2 | 6 | 7 | 32 | 14 | 10 | 6 | | | | | | | 62 | 3 | 18 | 12 | 6 | 37 |
| 30 | Poison ........... | | 1 | 2 | | 1 | | | | 1 | 1 | | | | | | | | | 4 | 1 | | | | 1 |
| 31 | Premature birth .... | 1 | | | | | | | | | | | | | | | | | | 1 | | | | | |
| 32 | Quinsy ............ | 1 | | | | | | | 1 | | | 1 | | | | | | | | | | 1 | 1 | | 1 |
| 33 | Rheumatism ....... | | | | | 2 | | | 1 | 1 | | 1 | | 1 | | | | | | | | 2 | | | 4 |
| 34 | Scrofula .......... | 2 | 2 | 2 | 2 | | 1 | | 1 | 1 | 1 | 1 | | | | | | | | 3 | | 2 | 1 | 1 | 6 |
| 35 | Scurvy ............ | | | | | | | | | 3 | | | | | | | | | | 3 | | | | | |
| 36 | Small pox .. ....... | 3 | 4 | 3 | 3 | | 2 | 3 | 1 | 13 | | 3 | 1 | | | | | | | 15 | 3 | 2 | 4 | | 8 |
| 37 | Stillborn........... | | 1 | | | | | | | | | | | | | | | | | 1 | | | | | |
| 38 | Stomach, disease of.. | | | 1 | 3 | | | | | | 1 | 1 | | | | | | | | 3 | 2 | | | | 1 |
| 39 | Suicide ............ | | | | | | | | 1 | 2 | 1 | 1 | | | | | | | | 2 | | | 1 | | 1 |
| 40 | Throat, disease of... | 2 | 1 | | 1 | | | | 2 | 1 | | | | | | | | | | 3 | | 1 | | | 3 |
| 41 | Thrush ..... ....... | | | | 1 | | | | | | | | | | | | | | | 1 | | | | | |
| 42 | Ulcer ............. | 2 | 1 | 1 | | | | | | | 1 | | | | | | | | | 4 | | 1 | | | |
| 43 | Uterus, disease of... | | | | | | | | | | 1 | | | | | | | | | | | | 1 | | |
| 44 | Worms ........... | | | 5 | 2 | | | | | | | | | | | | | | | 6 | | | 1 | | |
| 45 | Unknown........... | 61 | 51 | 28 | 18 | 6 | 5 | 10 | 6 | 27 | 29 | 11 | 5 | 1 | | | | | | 152 | 2 | 14 | 12 | 5 | 55 |
| | Total.......... | 243 | 216 | 280 | 242 | 87 | 58 | 83 | 87 | 313 | 246 | 125 | 51 | 7 | 4 | ... | ... | 2 | ... | 974 | 39 | 209 | 113 | 51 | 466 |

## CLASSIFICATION OF DEATHS

| | Cause of death. | Under 1. M. | Under 1. F. | 1 and under 5. M. | 1 and under 5. F. | 5 and under 10. M. | 5 and under 10. F. | 10 and under 20. M. | 10 and under 20. F. | 20 and under 50. M. | 20 and under 50. F. | 50 and under 80. M. | 50 and under 80. F. | 80 and under 100. M | 80 and under 100. F. | 100 & over. M | 100 & over. F. | Age unknown. M | Age unknown. F. | Born in State. | N. England States. | Middle States. | Southern States. | Southwest'n States. | Northwest'n States. |
|---|---|---|---|---|---|---|---|---|---|---|---|---|---|---|---|---|---|---|---|---|---|---|---|---|---|
| 1 | Abscess ............ | | | 2 | | | | 1 | | 6 | | 1 | 1 | | | | | | | 5 | 1 | | 2 | 1 | 2 |
| 2 | Accident, not specf'd | 44 | 40 | 52 | 42 | 29 | 18 | 51 | 15 | 95 | 13 | 19 | 7 | 2 | 3 | | | 1 | | 342 | 4 | 9 | 37 | 10 | 8 |
| 3 | ....do...burned.... | 1 | | 1 | 5 | | 1 | | 1 | 1 | | | | | 1 | | | | | 11 | | | | | |
| 4 | ....do...drowned .. | | | 1 | | | | 2 | 2 | 2 | 1 | 3 | | | | | | | | 7 | | | 3 | | 1 |
| 5 | ....do...shot ...... | | | | | 1 | | | | 1 | | | | | | | | | | 2 | | | | | |
| 6 | Apoplexy .......... | | | | | | | 2 | 2 | 17 | 10 | 19 | 24 | 1 | | 2 | | | | 41 | | 7 | 22 | | |
| 7 | Asthma ........ .. | | 1 | 1 | 1 | | 1 | | | 1 | 2 | 3 | 4 | 1 | | | | 1 | | 7 | | 2 | 7 | | |
| 8 | Bladder, disease of.. | | | | | | | | | | | | | 1 | | | | | | | | | 1 | | |
| 9 | Bowels......do..... | 14 | 11 | 10 | 6 | 1 | | 2 | | 7 | 4 | 1 | 2 | 1 | | | | | | 48 | | 1 | 5 | 1 | 2 |
| 10 | Brain ......do..... | 5 | 5 | 8 | 7 | 1 | | 2 | 1 | 2 | | 2 | | | | | | | | 30 | | | 2 | 1 | |
| 11 | Bronchitis .......... | 4 | 4 | 5 | 4 | 2 | | 2 | 2 | 10 | 5 | 6 | 1 | 1 | 1 | | | | | 34 | 1 | 3 | 8 | 1 | |
| 12 | Cancer .... ........ | | | 2 | 1 | | 1 | 1 | 3 | 8 | 13 | 12 | 18 | 4 | 4 | | | | | 26 | | 7 | 30 | 2 | [illegible] |
| 13 | Carbuncle .......... | | | | | | | | | 1 | | 2 | | 1 | | | | | | 1 | | 2 | 1 | | |
| 14 | Catarrh ............ | 24 | 19 | 21 | 18 | 3 | 4 | 7 | 18 | 16 | 12 | 12 | 5 | 3 | 3 | | | | 1 | 134 | 2 | 4 | 16 | 1 | |
| 15 | Chicken pox........ | | | | 1 | | | | | | | | | | | | | | | 1 | | | | | |
| 16 | Childbirth .......... | | | | | | | | 7 | | 88 | | | | | | | | 1 | 76 | | 2 | 9 | 6 | |
| 17 | Chlorosis .......... | | | | | | | | 1 | | 1 | | | | | | | | | 2 | | | | | |
| 18 | Cholera ........... | 55 | 49 | 155 | 119 | 75 | 48 | 103 | 95 | 623 | 326 | 191 | 134 | 13 | 16 | | | 14 | 14 | 1330 | 11 | 94 | 200 | 40 | 7 |
| 19 | ...do...infantum... | 35 | 30 | 45 | 50 | 2 | 1 | | | | | | | | | | | | | 160 | | | 1 | | |
| 20 | ...do...morbus .... | 4 | 3 | 8 | 5 | | 1 | 2 | 1 | 8 | 8 | 4 | | 1 | | | | | | 28 | 1 | 4 | 10 | 1 | |
| 21 | Chorea ........... | | | | | | | | 1 | | 1 | | | | | | | | | 2 | | | | | |

THE STATE OF IOWA—Continued.

| Nativities: Ireland. | Nativities: Germany. | Nativities: Other foreign countries. | Nativities: Unknown. | Season of decease: Spring. | Season of decease: Summer. | Season of decease: Autumn. | Season of decease: Winter. | Duration of sickness: Under 1 week. | Duration of sickness: 1 week and under 1 month. | Duration of sickness: 1 month and under 3 months. | Duration of sickness: 3 months and over. | Whites: Males. | Whites: Females. | Whites: Total. | Colored: Slaves: Black: M. | Colored: Slaves: Black: F. | Colored: Slaves: Mulatto: M. | Colored: Slaves: Mulatto: F. | Colored: Free: Black: M. | Colored: Free: Black: F. | Colored: Free: Mul.: M | Colored: Free: Mul.: F. | Aggregate deaths. | |
|---|---|---|---|---|---|---|---|---|---|---|---|---|---|---|---|---|---|---|---|---|---|---|---|---|
| | | | | 7 | 2 | 10 | | 5 | 12 | | 1 | 11 | 9 | 20 | | | | | | | | | 20 | 1 |
| 1 | | | 1 | 1 | 3 | | 4 | 3 | 4 | 1 | | | 8 | 8 | | | | | | | | | 8 | 2 |
| | | | | 15 | 8 | 7 | 12 | 18 | 23 | 1 | | 22 | 20 | 42 | | | | | | | | | 42 | 3 |
| | 1 | | | | 1 | | | | 1 | | | 1 | | 1 | | | | | | | | | 1 | 4 |
| 1 | | 4 | 1 | 4 | 9 | 12 | 4 | 6 | 19 | 4 | | 23 | 7 | 30 | | | | | | | | | 30 | 5 |
| | | | 1 | 8 | | 1 | 2 | | 9 | 1 | | 6 | 5 | 11 | | | | | | | | | 11 | 6 |
| | | | | 4 | 3 | | | 3 | 3 | | | 3 | 4 | 7 | | | | | | | | | 7 | 7 |
| | | | | 2 | | | 1 | | 1 | 1 | 1 | 3 | | 3 | | | | | | | | | 3 | 8 |
| | | | | 1 | | | | 1 | | | | 1 | | 1 | | | | | | | | | 1 | 9 |
| | | | | 3 | 3 | | 2 | 7 | 1 | | | 3 | 5 | 8 | | | | | | | | | 8 | 10 |
| 1 | | 1 | | 13 | 10 | 21 | 13 | 11 | 31 | 10 | | 23 | 35 | 58 | | | | | | | | | 58 | 11 |
| | | | | 2 | 1 | | 1 | 1 | 2 | | 1 | 3 | 1 | 4 | | | | | | | | | 4 | 12 |
| | | 1 | | 4 | 2 | 10 | 1 | 4 | 10 | | | 12 | 5 | 17 | | | | | | | | | 17 | 13 |
| | | 1 | 1 | 2 | 3 | | 2 | 3 | | 2 | | 7 | | 7 | | | | | | | | | 7 | 14 |
| | | | | | | 1 | | 1 | | | | 1 | | 1 | | | | | | | | | 1 | 15 |
| | | | | 1 | | | 1 | | | 2 | | 2 | | 2 | | | | | | | | | 2 | 16 |
| | | 1 | | 2 | 2 | 2 | | 5 | 1 | | | 6 | | 6 | | | | | | | | | 6 | 17 |
| | | | | 4 | 4 | 5 | 1 | | 5 | 1 | 5 | 7 | 7 | 14 | | | | | | | | | 14 | 18 |
| | | | | | 1 | | | | 1 | | | | 1 | 1 | | | | | | | | | 1 | 19 |
| 2 | 1 | 1 | | 7 | 9 | 5 | 3 | 4 | 16 | 3 | 1 | 13 | 12 | 25 | | | | | | | | | 25 | 20 |
| 1 | | 2 | | 20 | 21 | 8 | 1 | 7 | 35 | 4 | 3 | 26 | 25 | 51 | | | | | | | | | 51 | 21 |
| | | | | 1 | | | | 1 | | | | | 1 | 1 | | | | | | | | | 1 | 22 |
| | | | | | | 1 | | | 1 | | | 1 | | 1 | | | | | | | | | 1 | 23 |
| | | | | 3 | | 1 | 1 | 2 | 2 | | 1 | 3 | 2 | 5 | | | | | | | | | 5 | 24 |
| | 1 | 1 | | 5 | 5 | | 3 | 1 | 8 | 1 | | 8 | 5 | 13 | | | | | | | | | 13 | 25 |
| | 1 | | | 4 | | | 1 | 1 | | 1 | 2 | 5 | | 5 | | | | | | | | | 5 | 26 |
| | | | | | | 1 | | | | | | | 1 | 1 | | | | | | | | | 1 | 27 |
| | | | | 2 | 2 | 1 | 5 | 3 | 7 | | | 4 | 7 | 11 | | | | | | | | | 11 | 28 |
| 2 | 1 | 4 | | 59 | 24 | 24 | 39 | 31 | 91 | 13 | 6 | 84 | 61 | 145 | | | | | | | | 1 | 146 | 29 |
| | | | | 2 | 3 | | 1 | 3 | 3 | | | 4 | 2 | 6 | | | | | | | | | 6 | 30 |
| | | | | | | | 1 | | | | | 1 | | 1 | | | | | | | | | 1 | 31 |
| | | | | 1 | | 1 | 1 | 2 | 1 | | | 2 | 1 | 3 | | | | | | | | | 3 | 32 |
| | | | | 3 | 1 | 1 | 1 | 1 | 1 | 1 | 3 | 5 | 1 | 6 | | | | | | | | | 6 | 33 |
| | | | | 2 | 3 | 5 | 3 | 6 | 5 | 1 | 1 | 6 | 7 | 13 | | | | | | | | | 13 | 34 |
| | | | | | 3 | | | | 1 | 1 | 1 | 3 | | 3 | | | | | | | | | 3 | 35 |
| | | 1 | 3 | 10 | 11 | 9 | 6 | 7 | 17 | 4 | 6 | 24 | 11 | 35 | | | | | 1 | | | | 36 | 36 |
| | | | | | | 1 | | | | | | | 1 | 1 | | | | | | | | | 1 | 37 |
| | | | | | 1 | 2 | 3 | 2 | 2 | 1 | 1 | 2 | 4 | 6 | | | | | | | | | 6 | 38 |
| 1 | | | | | 1 | 3 | 1 | 5 | | | | 3 | 2 | 5 | | | | | | | | | 5 | 39 |
| | | | | 1 | 2 | | 4 | 3 | 4 | | | 3 | 4 | 7 | | | | | | | | | 7 | 40 |
| | | | | | | 1 | | | 1 | | | | 1 | 1 | | | | | | | | | 1 | 41 |
| | | | | 1 | 1 | 2 | 1 | | 2 | 2 | 1 | 3 | 2 | 5 | | | | | | | | | 5 | 42 |
| | | | | 1 | | | | 1 | | | | | 1 | 1 | | | | | | | | | 1 | 43 |
| | | | | 2 | 1 | 3 | 1 | 4 | 2 | 1 | | 5 | 2 | 7 | | | | | | | | | 7 | 44 |
| 1 | 7 | 10 | | 72 | 61 | 65 | 55 | 97 | 57 | 19 | 46 | 143 | 113 | 256 | | | | | 1 | 1 | | | 258 | 45 |
| 43 | 59 | 76 | 13 | 523 | 526 | 605 | 356 | 770 | 755 | 150 | 222 | 1130 | 897 | 2027 | | | | | 10 | 6 | | 1 | 2044 | |

THE STATE OF KENTUCKY.

| Ireland. | Germany. | Other foreign countries. | Unknown. | Spring. | Summer. | Autumn. | Winter. | Under 1 week. | 1 week and under 1 month. | 1 month and under 3 months. | 3 months and over. | Males. | Females. | Total. | Slaves: Black: M. | Slaves: Black: F. | Slaves: Mulatto: M. | Slaves: Mulatto: F. | Free: Black: M. | Free: Black: F. | Free: Mul.: M | Free: Mul.: F. | Aggregate deaths. | |
|---|---|---|---|---|---|---|---|---|---|---|---|---|---|---|---|---|---|---|---|---|---|---|---|---|
| | | | | | 5 | | 6 | 2 | 2 | 1 | 4 | 9 | 1 | 10 | | | | | | | 1 | | 11 | 1 |
| 3 | 12 | 3 | 3 | 120 | 112 | 87 | 105 | 249 | 54 | 17 | 12 | 198 | 73 | 271 | 90 | 61 | 5 | 4 | | | | | 431 | 2 |
| | | | | 5 | 2 | 1 | 2 | 7 | 2 | 2 | | 1 | 4 | 5 | 2 | 3 | | 1 | | | | | 11 | 3 |
| | | | | 1 | 7 | | 3 | 11 | | | | 6 | 3 | 9 | 2 | | | | | | | | 11 | 4 |
| | | | | | 1 | 1 | | 1 | | | | 2 | | 2 | | | | | | | | | 2 | 5 |
| 3 | 2 | 2 | | 27 | 18 | 14 | 18 | 45 | 9 | 4 | 7 | 30 | 26 | 56 | 9 | 10 | 2 | | | | | | 77 | 6 |
| | | | | 5 | 4 | 4 | 3 | 2 | 4 | 2 | 8 | 5 | 5 | 10 | 2 | 4 | | | | | | | 16 | 7 |
| | | | | | 1 | | | | 1 | | | | | | 1 | | | | | | | | 1 | 8 |
| | | 1 | 1 | 11 | 23 | 16 | 9 | 17 | 20 | 8 | 14 | 23 | 16 | 39 | 12 | 6 | | 1 | 1 | | | | 59 | 9 |
| | | | | 11 | 7 | 5 | 9 | 9 | 19 | 3 | 1 | 14 | 10 | 24 | 4 | 3 | 2 | | | | | | 33 | 10 |
| | | | | 17 | 12 | 9 | 9 | 7 | 6 | 8 | 25 | 21 | 16 | 37 | 8 | | 1 | 1 | | | | | 47 | 11 |
| | | 1 | | 23 | 18 | 14 | 12 | 2 | 8 | 6 | 47 | 23 | 33 | 56 | 3 | 6 | 1 | 1 | | | | | 67 | 12 |
| | | | | 1 | | 3 | | | 2 | 1 | 1 | 3 | | 3 | 1 | | | | | | | | 4 | 13 |
| | 3 | 1 | 2 | 58 | 43 | 32 | 28 | 42 | 66 | 25 | 28 | 40 | 47 | 87 | 44 | 29 | 1 | 4 | 1 | | | | 166 | 14 |
| | | | | | | 1 | | | 1 | | | | 1 | 1 | | | | | | | | | 1 | 15 |
| 1 | | 1 | | 26 | 28 | 23 | 19 | 44 | 35 | 5 | 4 | | 75 | 75 | | 17 | | 4 | | | | | 96 | 16 |
| | | | | | 2 | | | | 1 | 1 | | | | | | 2 | | | | | | | 2 | 17 |
| 68 | 118 | 70 | 21 | 97 | 1259 | 611 | 44 | 1607 | 191 | 23 | 7 | 881 | 539 | 1420 | 310 | 221 | 28 | 34 | 5 | 5 | 5 | 2 | 2030 | 18 |
| | | | | 11 | 75 | 71 | 5 | 65 | 60 | 27 | 6 | 68 | 67 | 135 | 9 | 10 | 5 | 4 | | | | | 163 | 19 |
| | 1 | | | 4 | 22 | 12 | 7 | 22 | 21 | 1 | | 24 | 18 | 37 | 2 | 4 | 1 | 1 | | | | | 45 | 20 |
| | | | | 1 | 1 | | | | 2 | | | | 1 | 1 | | 1 | | | | | | | 2 | 21 |

## CLASSIFICATION OF DEATHS

| | Cause of death. | AGES. | | | | | | | | | | | | | | | | | | NATIVITIES. | | | | | |
|---|---|---|---|---|---|---|---|---|---|---|---|---|---|---|---|---|---|---|---|---|---|---|---|---|---|
| | | Under 1. | | 1 and under 5. | | 5 and under 10. | | 10 and under 20. | | 20 and under 50. | | 50 and under 80. | | 80 and under 100. | | 100 & over. | | Age unknown. | | Born in State. | N. England States. | Middle States. | Southern States. | Southwest'n States. | Northwest'n States. |
| | | M. | F. | M. | F. | M. | F. | M. | F. | M. | F. | M. | F. | M | F. | M | F. | M | F. | | | | | | |
| 1 | Colic | 1 | | | | 1 | | 1 | 2 | 6 | 6 | 5 | 1 | | | | | | | 13 | | 2 | 7 | | |
| 2 | Congestion | | 1 | | | | | 1 | 2 | 2 | 1 | 1 | 2 | | | | | | | 6 | | | 2 | 1 | |
| 3 | ....do...brain | 1 | 2 | 2 | 4 | | | 1 | 1 | 2 | 2 | 1 | 1 | | | | | | | 15 | | | 1 | | 1 |
| 4 | Consumption | 20 | 18 | 29 | 41 | 12 | 24 | 59 | 125 | 327 | 428 | 95 | 98 | 4 | 4 | | 1 | 1 | 2 | 940 | 7 | 60 | 180 | 22 | 30 |
| 5 | Convulsions | 32 | 26 | 12 | 19 | 9 | 2 | 9 | 3 | 6 | 14 | 3 | 2 | | | | | 1 | | 120 | 1 | 3 | 8 | 3 | 3 |
| 6 | Cramp | 2 | 1 | 1 | 2 | 1 | 1 | 1 | | 2 | | | | | 1 | | | | | 9 | | | 2 | 1 | |
| 7 | Croup | 171 | 141 | 126 | 127 | 14 | 14 | 2 | 3 | | 2 | | 2 | | | | | 5 | 6 | 593 | | | 4 | 4 | 9 |
| 8 | Debility | 18 | 10 | 1 | 3 | 2 | | | | 1 | | | | | | | | | | 34 | 1 | | | | |
| 9 | Diabetes | | | | | | | 1 | | 2 | | 2 | 1 | 2 | | | | | | 5 | 1 | | 2 | | |
| 10 | Diarrhœa | 25 | 17 | 28 | 30 | 7 | 3 | 4 | 3 | 41 | 16 | 18 | 9 | 1 | 1 | | | 2 | 1 | 132 | | 11 | 28 | 14 | 2 |
| 11 | Dirt eating | | | 1 | | 3 | | | | | | | | | | | | | | 4 | | | | | |
| 12 | Dropsy | 13 | 14 | 21 | 20 | 15 | 13 | 26 | 27 | 43 | 85 | 93 | 66 | 12 | 10 | | | | | 270 | | 37 | 115 | 19 | 4 |
| 13 | Dysentery | 61 | 57 | 164 | 140 | 77 | 56 | 58 | 53 | 54 | 87 | 35 | 43 | 2 | 7 | | | 1 | | 748 | | 26 | 59 | 14 | 29 |
| 14 | Dyspepsia | | | | | | | 1 | 1 | 12 | 13 | 13 | 9 | 1 | | | | | | 24 | 1 | 4 | 19 | 2 | |
| 15 | Epilepsy | | 1 | 1 | | | | 6 | 3 | 13 | 4 | 4 | 3 | | | | | 1 | | 26 | | 1 | 3 | 3 | 1 |
| 16 | Erysipelas | 9 | 6 | 10 | 5 | 2 | 6 | 7 | 3 | 8 | 15 | 10 | 4 | 4 | 2 | | | | | 61 | | 4 | 20 | 4 | 1 |
| 17 | Executed | | | | | | | | | | | 1 | | | | | | | | 1 | | | | | |
| 18 | Fever, not specified | 44 | 31 | 100 | 84 | 49 | 43 | 80 | 119 | 157 | 149 | 47 | 24 | 4 | 5 | | | | | 774 | 1 | 22 | 81 | 24 | 11 |
| 19 | ..do..bilious | 5 | 3 | 9 | 4 | 1 | 3 | 9 | 5 | 27 | 14 | 5 | 5 | | | | | | 1 | 54 | | 4 | 16 | 3 | 4 |
| 20 | ..do..brain | 17 | 12 | 11 | 12 | 5 | 2 | 1 | 2 | 5 | 2 | 2 | | | | | | | | 61 | | 2 | 8 | 2 | 1 |
| 21 | ..do..catarrhal | | 1 | | | | 1 | | | | | | 1 | | | | | | | 2 | | 1 | | | |
| 22 | ..do..congestive | 2 | | 1 | 6 | 3 | 3 | 13 | 6 | 23 | 16 | 5 | 7 | 1 | | | | | | 57 | 1 | 3 | 10 | 8 | 3 |
| 23 | ..do..inflammatory | | | | | | | 1 | | | 1 | | | | | | | | | 2 | | | | | |
| 24 | ..do..intermittent | 1 | 1 | 1 | 5 | 2 | 1 | 1 | 3 | 4 | 2 | 1 | 3 | | | | | | | 11 | | | 7 | 1 | 2 |
| 25 | ..do..puerperal | | | | | | | | 4 | | 28 | | | | | | | | | 26 | | | 2 | 2 | |
| 26 | ..do..remittent | | | 1 | | | | | | 1 | | | | | | | | | | 1 | | | | 1 | |
| 27 | ..do..scarlet | 8 | 14 | 59 | 66 | 21 | 32 | 3 | 11 | 2 | 5 | | | | | | | | | 207 | | | 5 | 4 | 2 |
| 28 | ..do..typhus | 6 | 9 | 34 | 24 | 28 | 37 | 114 | 101 | 233 | 149 | 46 | 33 | | | | | | | 644 | 2 | 17 | 99 | 16 | 13 |
| 29 | ..do..winter | | 2 | 3 | 1 | 2 | | 1 | 2 | 11 | 6 | 6 | 4 | | | | | | | 20 | | 1 | 8 | 3 | 3 |
| 30 | Fistula | | | | | | | | | 1 | | 1 | | 1 | | | | | | 1 | | 1 | 1 | | |
| 31 | Fracture | | | | | 1 | | | | | | | | | | | | | | | | | | | |
| 32 | Frozen | | | | | | 1 | | | 1 | | 3 | | | | | | | | 4 | | | 1 | | |
| 33 | Gout | | | | | | | | | 1 | | | | | | | | | | | | | 1 | | |
| 34 | Gravel | | | 3 | | | 1 | 1 | | 1 | | 20 | 1 | 6 | | | | | | 11 | | 5 | 16 | | |
| 35 | Heart, disease of | 2 | 3 | 2 | 2 | 1 | 2 | 6 | 2 | 10 | 10 | 10 | 16 | 2 | | | | | | 39 | 1 | 5 | 18 | 2 | 1 |
| 36 | Hemorrhage | | 1 | 2 | | 2 | 4 | 1 | 1 | 1 | 4 | 1 | 4 | | | | | | | 11 | | 1 | 5 | | 3 |
| 37 | Hernia | 1 | 2 | 1 | | 1 | | 2 | | | 1 | 3 | | 1 | | | | | | 10 | | | 2 | | |
| 38 | Hives | 42 | 28 | 11 | 6 | 1 | 3 | 1 | 1 | | | | | | | | | | | 88 | | | | 1 | 4 |
| 39 | Hooping cough | 29 | 34 | 45 | 56 | 12 | 10 | | 5 | 2 | | | | | | | | | | 183 | | 3 | 1 | 2 | 3 |
| 40 | Hydrocephalus | 13 | 11 | 7 | 20 | 2 | | | 2 | | | 1 | 1 | | | | | | | 52 | | | 3 | 1 | |
| 41 | Inflamt'n, not specf'd | 7 | 3 | 5 | 4 | | 1 | 1 | 5 | 7 | 5 | 2 | 4 | | 3 | | | | | 30 | 1 | | 12 | 2 | 2 |
| 42 | ....do....bowels | 16 | 12 | 20 | 15 | 5 | 2 | 5 | 8 | 14 | 10 | 13 | 12 | 1 | | | | | | 103 | | 6 | 12 | 2 | 6 |
| 43 | ....do....brain | 51 | 39 | 56 | 40 | 10 | 7 | 13 | 14 | 12 | 8 | 10 | 2 | | | | | | | 234 | 1 | 4 | 10 | 3 | 7 |
| 44 | ....do....stomach | 3 | 1 | 2 | 1 | | | 1 | 1 | 7 | 4 | | 8 | | 1 | | | | | 16 | | 1 | 11 | | 1 |
| 45 | Influenza | 6 | 4 | 4 | 3 | | | | 1 | 1 | 1 | | | | | | | | | 19 | | | 1 | | |
| 46 | Insanity | | | | | | | 1 | | | 2 | | | | | | | 3 | | 3 | | | | | |
| 47 | Intemperance | | | | | | | 1 | | 9 | | 4 | | | | | | | | 7 | | | 4 | 1 | |
| 48 | Jaundice | 4 | 3 | 2 | 1 | 1 | 2 | 1 | | 1 | 1 | 3 | 3 | | | | | | 1 | 16 | | 2 | 4 | | |
| 49 | Kidneys, disease of | | | | 1 | | | | | 1 | 2 | 4 | | | | | | | | 3 | | 2 | 3 | | |
| 50 | Killed | 1 | 1 | | | 2 | | 1 | | 14 | | 1 | | | | | | | | 18 | | | 2 | | |
| 51 | Leprosy | 1 | | | | | | | | | | 1 | | | | | | | | 2 | | | | | |
| 52 | Lightning | | | | | | | | | | 1 | | | | | | | | | 1 | | | | | |
| 53 | Liver, disease of | 3 | 2 | 12 | 2 | 2 | 2 | 2 | 1 | 14 | 16 | 9 | 8 | | 1 | | | | | 49 | 1 | 3 | 15 | 2 | 1 |
| 54 | Lockjaw | 5 | 4 | 2 | 1 | 4 | 2 | 9 | 2 | 4 | 3 | 1 | 1 | | | | | | | 35 | | | 1 | 1 | |
| 55 | Lungs, disease of | 3 | 3 | 6 | 7 | 1 | 1 | 2 | 1 | 9 | 7 | 5 | 3 | 2 | | | | 1 | | 42 | | 4 | 5 | | |
| 56 | Malformation | 1 | | | | | | | | | | | | | | | | | | 1 | | | | | |
| 57 | Mania-a-potu | | | | | | | | | 16 | 2 | 8 | | | | | | 2 | 1 | 15 | | 4 | 2 | | 2 |
| 58 | Marasmus | 2 | 2 | 3 | | 1 | 4 | 1 | 4 | | | 2 | | | | | | | | 19 | | | | | |
| 59 | Measles | 11 | 10 | 32 | 22 | 4 | 8 | 5 | 9 | 13 | 6 | | 1 | | | | | 1 | | 103 | | 1 | 6 | 2 | 8 |
| 60 | Menses, suppres'n of | | | | | | | | | | 2 | | | | | | | | | 1 | | 1 | | | |
| 61 | Milk sickness | | | | | | 3 | | | | 5 | | | | | | | | | 6 | | | 2 | | |
| 62 | Mortification | 1 | 1 | | 1 | | | | | | | 1 | 2 | | | | | | | 4 | | 2 | | | |
| 63 | Mumps | | 1 | 2 | | | | 1 | | | 1 | | | | | | | | | 5 | | | | | |
| 64 | Murder | | | | | 1 | | | | 14 | 2 | 1 | 1 | | | | | | | 14 | 2 | | | 1 | |
| 65 | Neuralgia | | | 2 | | 1 | | | | 3 | 2 | 7 | 4 | 2 | | | | | | 13 | | 1 | 5 | 1 | 1 |
| 66 | Old age | | | | | | | | | | | 40 | 78 | 88 | 87 | 6 | 7 | | | 35 | 1 | 50 | 210 | | |
| 67 | Paralysis | | 1 | | 1 | | | 3 | | 4 | 9 | 30 | 25 | 9 | 9 | | | | | 29 | 1 | 24 | 35 | 1 | |
| 68 | Piles | | | 1 | | | | | | | | | 1 | | | | | | | 1 | | | 1 | | |
| 69 | Pleurisy | 5 | 2 | 5 | 5 | 1 | | 5 | 7 | 15 | 4 | 10 | 4 | 1 | | | | | | 40 | | 3 | 12 | 2 | 3 |
| 70 | Pneumonia | 28 | 18 | 47 | 45 | 14 | 5 | 22 | 17 | 79 | 52 | 56 | 37 | 4 | 5 | | | | | 304 | | 11 | 85 | 13 | 6 |
| 71 | Poison | | 2 | 2 | 3 | 1 | 1 | 2 | 2 | 5 | 5 | 3 | | | | | | | | 20 | | | 4 | 1 | |
| 72 | Putrid sore throat | | | 1 | 1 | | 1 | 1 | 1 | | | | | | | | | | | 4 | | | 1 | | |
| 73 | Quinsy | 3 | 1 | 6 | 8 | | 2 | | | | 1 | | | | | | | | | 20 | | | | | |
| 74 | Rheumatism | | | 2 | | 2 | 1 | 5 | 5 | 5 | 4 | 10 | 9 | 1 | | | | | | 26 | | 2 | 7 | 1 | 3 |
| 75 | Rickets | 1 | 1 | 2 | | | | | | | | | | | | | | | | 4 | | | | | |

## N THE STATE OF KENTUCKY—Continued.

| NATIVITIES. — ritories. | Ireland. | Germany. | Other foreign countries. | Unknown. | SEASON OF DECEASE. — Spring. | Summer. | Autumn. | Winter. | DURATION OF SICKNESS. — Under 1 week. | 1 week and under 1 month. | 1 month and under 3 months. | 3 months and over. | WHITES. — Males. | Females. | Total. | COLORED. Slaves. Black. M. | Slaves. Black. F. | Slaves. Mulatto. M. | Slaves. Mulatto. F. | Free. Black. M. | Free. Black. F. | Free. Mul. M | Free. Mul. F. | Aggregate deaths. | |
|---|---|---|---|---|---|---|---|---|---|---|---|---|---|---|---|---|---|---|---|---|---|---|---|---|---|
| | | | 1 | | 5 | 9 | 5 | 4 | 14 | 7 | | 1 | 9 | 5 | 14 | 4 | 3 | 1 | 1 | | | | | 23 | 1 |
| | | | | 1 | 1 | 1 | 5 | 1 | 2 | 6 | | | 2 | 5 | 7 | 2 | 1 | | | | | | | 10 | 2 |
| | | | | | 4 | 6 | 4 | 3 | 7 | 6 | 2 | 1 | 5 | 7 | 12 | | 2 | 2 | 1 | | | | | 17 | 3 |
| | 19 | 14 | 11 | 5 | 397 | 359 | 300 | 228 | 42 | 82 | 171 | 936 | 387 | 490 | 877 | 146 | 229 | 10 | 16 | 2 | 4 | 2 | 2 | 1288 | 4 |
| | | | | | 44 | 41 | 35 | 17 | 77 | 26 | 8 | 14 | 43 | 48 | 91 | 21 | 16 | 8 | 2 | | | | | 138 | 5 |
| | | | | | | 3 | 5 | 4 | 11 | 1 | | | 5 | 4 | 9 | 2 | 1 | | | | | | | 12 | 6 |
| | 3 | | | | 185 | 138 | 153 | 128 | 413 | 150 | 11 | 6 | 226 | 221 | 447 | 87 | 66 | 4 | 5 | 1 | | | 3 | 613 | 7 |
| | | | | | 10 | 8 | 10 | 5 | 15 | 4 | 2 | 3 | 20 | 6 | 26 | 1 | 4 | 1 | 1 | | | | 2 | 35 | 8 |
| | | | | | 4 | 3 | | 1 | 1 | 5 | | 2 | 6 | 1 | 7 | 1 | | | | | | | | 8 | 9 |
| | 6 | 9 | 1 | 3 | 28 | 85 | 63 | 28 | 32 | 59 | 20 | 72 | 107 | 67 | 174 | 17 | 12 | 2 | 1 | | | | | 206 | 10 |
| | | | | | 1 | 3 | | | | | | 1 | | | | 4 | | | | | | | | 4 | 11 |
| | 5 | 1 | 6 | 1 | 111 | 160 | 94 | 93 | 23 | 75 | 95 | 244 | 152 | 148 | 300 | 64 | 80 | 6 | 6 | 1 | 1 | | | 458 | 12 |
| | 12 | 2 | 3 | 2 | 43 | 282 | 490 | 38 | 168 | 563 | 111 | 38 | 364 | 360 | 724 | 77 | 76 | 10 | 7 | 1 | | | | 895 | 13 |
| | | | | | 17 | 11 | 8 | 14 | 1 | 5 | 3 | 39 | 26 | 22 | 48 | 1 | 1 | | | | | | | 50 | 14 |
| | | | 2 | | 10 | 11 | 5 | 10 | 12 | 3 | 1 | 9 | 19 | 6 | 25 | 6 | 5 | | | | | | | 36 | 15 |
| | | 1 | | | 27 | 25 | 15 | 24 | 27 | 48 | 11 | 4 | 39 | 31 | 70 | 6 | 8 | 4 | 1 | 1 | 1 | | | 91 | 16 |
| | | | | | | | 1 | | 1 | | | | | | | 1 | | | | | | | | 1 | 17 |
| | 4 | 10 | 6 | 3 | 230 | 240 | 315 | 135 | 138 | 557 | 169 | 53 | 345 | 323 | 668 | 123 | 113 | 13 | 14 | | 4 | | 1 | 936 | 18 |
| | 3 | 5 | 1 | 1 | 16 | 32 | 24 | 18 | 14 | 52 | 10 | 5 | 49 | 32 | 81 | 7 | 3 | | | | | | | 91 | 19 |
| | | 1 | | 1 | 19 | 22 | 23 | 7 | 21 | 39 | 5 | 6 | 30 | 25 | 55 | 9 | 5 | 2 | | | | | | 71 | 20 |
| | | | | | 2 | | | 1 | 1 | 1 | | 1 | | 1 | 1 | | 2 | | | | | | | 3 | 21 |
| | 2 | | 1 | 1 | 12 | 20 | 43 | 11 | 36 | 38 | 8 | 3 | 39 | 30 | 69 | 8 | 8 | 1 | | | | | | 86 | 22 |
| | | | | | 1 | | | 1 | | 1 | | 1 | | 1 | 1 | 1 | | | | | | | | 2 | 23 |
| | 1 | 1 | 2 | | 3 | 4 | 11 | 7 | 3 | 11 | 2 | 8 | 10 | 10 | 20 | | 5 | | | | | | | 25 | 24 |
| | | 1 | | 1 | 7 | 5 | 11 | 9 | 8 | 17 | 4 | 3 | | 27 | 27 | | 5 | | | | | | | 32 | 25 |
| | | | | | | 1 | 1 | | | 1 | 1 | | 2 | | 2 | | | | | | | | | 2 | 26 |
| | 3 | | | | 45 | 54 | 64 | 55 | 91 | 107 | 12 | 8 | 82 | 109 | 191 | 11 | 15 | | 4 | | | | | 221 | 27 |
| | 11 | 5 | 4 | 3 | 229 | 187 | 225 | 166 | 67 | 561 | 144 | 40 | 319 | 235 | 554 | 130 | 101 | 10 | 17 | 1 | | 1 | | 814 | 28 |
| | | | | 3 | 21 | 4 | 4 | 9 | 7 | 24 | 3 | 3 | 16 | 11 | 27 | 7 | 4 | | | | | | | 38 | 29 |
| | | | | | 2 | 1 | | | | 1 | | 2 | 2 | | 2 | 1 | | | | | | | | 3 | 30 |
| | | | 1 | | | 1 | | | 1 | | | | 1 | | 1 | | | | | | | | | 1 | 31 |
| | | | | | 2 | | | 3 | 3 | | | | 1 | | 1 | 2 | 1 | | | 1 | | | | 5 | 32 |
| | | | | | | | 1 | | | | | 1 | | | | 1 | | | | | | | | 1 | 33 |
| | 1 | | | | 8 | 13 | 3 | 9 | 2 | 13 | 5 | 11 | 30 | 2 | 32 | 1 | | | | | | | | 33 | 34 |
| | 1 | 1 | | | 27 | 16 | 14 | 11 | 20 | 18 | 6 | 19 | 28 | 22 | 50 | 5 | 10 | | 3 | | | | | 68 | 35 |
| | | | 1 | | 8 | 5 | 5 | 2 | 13 | 5 | 1 | 2 | 6 | 10 | 16 | | 3 | 1 | 1 | | | | | 21 | 36 |
| | | | | | 5 | 3 | 1 | 3 | 7 | 4 | 1 | | 3 | 1 | 4 | 6 | 2 | | | | | | | 12 | 37 |
| | | | | | 34 | 17 | 25 | 17 | 59 | 27 | 4 | 8 | 52 | 34 | 86 | 3 | 4 | | | | | | | 93 | 38 |
| | 1 | | | | 38 | 61 | 52 | 34 | 21 | 94 | 49 | 18 | 46 | 63 | 109 | 39 | 36 | 3 | 5 | | 1 | | | 193 | 39 |
| | | | 1 | | 15 | 16 | 13 | 11 | 7 | 22 | 11 | 15 | 15 | 24 | 39 | 7 | 9 | 1 | 1 | | | | | 57 | 40 |
| | | | | | 11 | 11 | 13 | 10 | 12 | 18 | 7 | 8 | 13 | 24 | 37 | 9 | 1 | | | | | | | 47 | 41 |
| | 2 | | 2 | | 46 | 34 | 30 | 20 | 43 | 67 | 8 | 12 | 56 | 44 | 100 | 13 | 15 | 5 | | | | | | 133 | 42 |
| | 1 | 2 | | | 60 | 70 | 74 | 51 | 88 | 122 | 22 | 13 | 123 | 84 | 207 | 27 | 23 | 2 | 3 | | | | | 262 | 43 |
| | | | 1 | | 9 | 8 | 10 | 3 | 9 | 13 | 3 | 4 | 8 | 15 | 23 | 4 | 2 | 1 | | | | | | 30 | 44 |
| | | | | | 6 | 2 | 4 | 8 | 8 | 8 | 3 | 1 | 3 | 5 | 8 | 7 | 3 | 1 | | | 1 | | | 20 | 45 |
| | 1 | 2 | | | | 3 | 1 | 2 | | | | 2 | 3 | 1 | 4 | 1 | 1 | | | | | | | 6 | 46 |
| | 2 | | | | 5 | 3 | 8 | 3 | 7 | 3 | 2 | 1 | 12 | | 12 | 2 | | | | | | | | 14 | 47 |
| | | | | | 2 | 4 | 7 | 9 | 2 | 9 | 1 | 5 | 11 | 8 | 19 | 1 | 2 | | | | | | | 22 | 48 |
| | | | | | 3 | 2 | 2 | 1 | | 3 | 2 | 2 | 5 | 1 | 6 | | 2 | | | | | | | 8 | 49 |
| | | | | | 7 | 7 | 1 | 5 | 13 | 4 | | | 13 | | 13 | 6 | 1 | | | | | | | 20 | 50 |
| | | | | | 1 | | 1 | | | 1 | | 1 | 2 | | 2 | | | | | | | | | 2 | 51 |
| | | | | | | 1 | | | 1 | | | | | | | | 1 | | | | | | | 1 | 52 |
| | 3 | | | | 11 | 30 | 22 | 11 | 7 | 18 | 12 | 34 | 30 | 25 | 55 | 11 | 7 | 1 | | | | | | 74 | 53 |
| | | 1 | | | 10 | 7 | 14 | 7 | 28 | 9 | 1 | | 12 | 6 | 18 | 13 | 7 | | | | | | | 38 | 54 |
| | | | | | 20 | 17 | 6 | 8 | 10 | 15 | 9 | 13 | 18 | 13 | 31 | 10 | 8 | 1 | 1 | | | | | 51 | 55 |
| | | | | | | | 1 | | 1 | | | | | | | 1 | | | | | | | | 1 | 56 |
| | 4 | 1 | 1 | | 7 | 7 | 8 | 7 | 9 | 5 | 1 | 3 | 23 | 1 | 24 | 1 | 1 | 1 | | 1 | 1 | | | 29 | 57 |
| | | | | | 7 | 3 | 7 | 2 | 3 | | 3 | 12 | 5 | 2 | 7 | 4 | 7 | | 1 | | | | | 19 | 58 |
| | | | 1 | 1 | 42 | 50 | 19 | 9 | 22 | 74 | 13 | 10 | 50 | 40 | 90 | 14 | 12 | 2 | 3 | | 1 | | | 122 | 59 |
| | | | | | 1 | 1 | | | | 1 | | 1 | | 1 | 1 | | 1 | | | | | | | 2 | 60 |
| | | | | | 2 | 1 | 2 | 3 | 2 | 4 | 2 | | | 8 | 8 | | | | | | | | | 8 | 61 |
| | | | | | 1 | 4 | | 1 | 2 | 1 | 1 | 2 | 2 | 3 | 5 | | 1 | | | | | | | 6 | 62 |
| | | | | | 1 | 1 | 1 | 2 | 2 | 3 | | | 2 | 1 | 3 | 1 | 1 | | | | | | | 5 | 63 |
| | | 1 | | 1 | 3 | 10 | 8 | 3 | 11 | 1 | | | 10 | 2 | 12 | 6 | 1 | | | | | | | 19 | 64 |
| | | | | | 4 | 8 | 7 | 2 | 1 | 7 | | 12 | 13 | 6 | 19 | 2 | | | | | | | | 21 | 65 |
| | 3 | 1 | 4 | 2 | 97 | 96 | 46 | 64 | 68 | 52 | 26 | 65 | 92 | 116 | 208 | 38 | 53 | 2 | 1 | 2 | 1 | | 1 | 306 | 66 |
| | 1 | | | | 30 | 19 | 19 | 21 | 22 | 21 | 11 | 30 | 38 | 33 | 71 | 6 | 12 | 1 | | 1 | | | | 91 | 67 |
| | | | | | 2 | | | | 1 | | | 1 | 1 | 1 | 2 | | | | | | | | | 2 | 68 |
| | 2 | | 1 | 1 | 19 | 18 | 15 | 11 | 18 | 30 | 11 | 1 | 30 | 17 | 47 | 12 | 5 | | | | | | | 64 | 69 |
| | 4 | 2 | 8 | 1 | 172 | 101 | 53 | 101 | 74 | 247 | 51 | 49 | 160 | 107 | 267 | 79 | 67 | 10 | 4 | 1 | | | 1 | 429 | 70 |
| | 1 | | | | 10 | 7 | 5 | 4 | 10 | 4 | 3 | 8 | 4 | 3 | 7 | 8 | 9 | | 1 | 1 | | | | 26 | 71 |
| | | | | | | | 1 | 4 | 5 | | | | | 1 | 1 | 2 | 2 | | | | | | | 5 | 72 |
| | | 1 | | | 5 | 5 | 7 | 4 | 5 | 13 | 2 | | 6 | 9 | 15 | 8 | 3 | | | | | | | 21 | 73 |
| | 2 | 2 | 1 | | 11 | 12 | 13 | 8 | 3 | 9 | 4 | 26 | 21 | 13 | 34 | 4 | 4 | | 1 | | 1 | | | 44 | 74 |
| | | | | | 1 | 1 | 1 | 1 | | | 1 | 3 | | | | 3 | 1 | | | | | | | 4 | 75 |

## CLASSIFICATION OF DEATHS IN

| | Cause of death. | Ages. Under 1. M. | Under 1. F. | 1 and under 5. M. | 1 and under 5. F. | 5 and under 10. M. | 5 and under 10. F. | 10 and under 20. M. | 10 and under 20. F. | 20 and under 50. M. | 20 and under 50. F. | 50 and under 80. M. | 50 and under 80. F. | 80 and under 100. M | 80 and under 100. F. | 100 & over. M | 100 & over. F. | Age unknown. M | Age unknown. F. | Nativities. Born in State. | N. England States. | Middle States. | Southern States. | Southwest'n States. | Northeast'n States. |
|---|---|---|---|---|---|---|---|---|---|---|---|---|---|---|---|---|---|---|---|---|---|---|---|---|---|
| 1 | Salivation, effects of. | | | | | | | | 1 | | | | 1 | | | | | | | 2 | | | | | |
| 2 | Scrofula | 8 | 7 | 19 | 22 | 11 | 4 | 13 | 28 | 16 | 19 | 6 | 10 | 2 | | | | | | 143 | | 3 | 14 | 2 | |
| 3 | Small pox | 14 | 9 | 15 | 11 | 12 | 5 | 10 | 7 | 41 | 11 | 11 | 4 | | | | | | | 110 | | 7 | 14 | 2 | 9 |
| 4 | Spine, disease of | 3 | 1 | 4 | 2 | 1 | 2 | 1 | | 5 | 1 | | | 1 | | | | | | 14 | | | 3 | 1 | 3 |
| 5 | Spleen....do | | | | | | | | 1 | | | | 1 | | | | | | | 2 | | | | | |
| 6 | Stillborn | 9 | 8 | | | | | | | | | | | | | | | | | 17 | | | | | |
| 7 | Stomach, disease of | | | | | | | | | | 1 | | | | | | | | | 1 | | | | | |
| 8 | Suffocation | 2 | 1 | 2 | | | | | | | | | | | | | | | | 5 | | | | | |
| 9 | Suicide | | | | | | | | | 13 | 3 | 4 | | | | | | | | 17 | | | 2 | | 1 |
| 10 | Summer complaint | 5 | 2 | 14 | 10 | | | 1 | | | | | | | | | | | | 25 | | 2 | | | 5 |
| 11 | Teething | 10 | 4 | 20 | 16 | | | | | | | | | | | | | | | 42 | 1 | 2 | 1 | 3 | 1 |
| 12 | Tetter | | | | | | | | | | | | 1 | | | | | | | | | 1 | | | |
| 13 | Throat, disease of | | | 5 | 8 | 2 | 2 | | 2 | | | | | | | | | | | 17 | | | 2 | | |
| 14 | Thrush | 6 | 8 | | 3 | | | | | | | | | | | | | | | 16 | | | | | 1 |
| 15 | Tumor | | | 1 | 1 | | | 1 | | 3 | | | 1 | | 2 | | | | | 6 | | 1 | 2 | | |
| 16 | Ulcer | 1 | 1 | 1 | 1 | | | | | 2 | | 3 | | | | | | | | 6 | | | 2 | | |
| 17 | Uterus, disease of | | | | | | | | 1 | | 7 | | 1 | | | | | | | 8 | | | 1 | | |
| 18 | Venereal | | | | | | | | | 2 | | | | | | | | | | 1 | | | 1 | | |
| 19 | White swelling | | | 2 | | | 1 | 2 | 1 | 2 | 1 | 1 | | | | | | | | 8 | | | 2 | | |
| 20 | Worms | 4 | 7 | 35 | 39 | 9 | 16 | 1 | 2 | | 1 | | | | | | | | | 105 | | | 6 | 2 | |
| 21 | Unknown | 516 | 419 | 259 | 226 | 50 | 45 | 81 | 92 | 140 | 217 | 160 | 174 | 29 | 22 | 1 | | 12 | 6 | 1959 | 1 | 66 | 302 | 50 | 27 |
| | Total | 1439 | 1186 | 1588 | 1436 | 523 | 454 | 778 | 852 | 2277 | 1960 | 1113 | 932 | 210 | 188 | 9 | 8 | 46 | 34 | 11292 | 45 | 551 | 1885 | 314 | 315 |

## CLASSIFICATION OF DEATHS IN NORTHERN

*Embracing the parishes of Avoyelles, Bienville, Bossier, Caddo, Caldwell, Carroll, Catahoula, Rapides, Sabine,*

| | Cause of death. | Under 1. M. | Under 1. F. | 1 and under 5. M. | 1 and under 5. F. | 5 and under 10. M. | 5 and under 10. F. | 10 and under 20. M. | 10 and under 20. F. | 20 and under 50. M. | 20 and under 50. F. | 50 and under 80. M. | 50 and under 80. F. | 80 and under 100. M | 80 and under 100. F. | 100 & over. M | 100 & over. F. | Age unknown. M | Age unknown. F. | Born in State. | N. England States. | Middle States. | Southern States. | Southwest'n States. | Northeast'n States. |
|---|---|---|---|---|---|---|---|---|---|---|---|---|---|---|---|---|---|---|---|---|---|---|---|---|---|
| 1 | Accident, not specif'd | 1 | 4 | 3 | 3 | 4 | 4 | 5 | 4 | 14 | 8 | 4 | 3 | | | | | | | 33 | 1 | 6 | 14 | 2 | |
| 2 | ....do ..burned | 2 | | 5 | 8 | 2 | 7 | 2 | 2 | 2 | 3 | 1 | | | | | | | | 26 | | | 1 | 6 | 1 |
| 3 | ....do...drowned | | | 3 | 5 | 4 | 4 | 8 | 2 | 28 | 7 | 5 | | | | | | | | 36 | 1 | 4 | 6 | 7 | 10 |
| 4 | ....do...scalded | | | | 2 | | | | | | | | | | | | | | | 2 | | | | | |
| 5 | Apoplexy | 1 | | | | 1 | | 1 | 2 | 3 | 4 | 1 | 4 | | | | | | | 10 | | | 3 | 2 | 2 |
| 6 | Asthma | | | | | | | 2 | | | 1 | 1 | 2 | | | | | | | 1 | | | 3 | 1 | 1 |
| 7 | Bladder, disease of | | | | | | | | | 1 | | | | | | | | | | | | | 1 | | |
| 8 | Bowels ....do | | | | | | 1 | | 1 | | | 2 | | | | | | | | 3 | | | | | |
| 9 | Brain.......do | | | | | 1 | | 1 | 2 | 1 | 1 | | | | | | | | | 4 | | | 1 | 1 | |
| 10 | Bronchitis | | 1 | 1 | | | | 1 | | 3 | 3 | 1 | 1 | | | | | | | 7 | | 1 | 2 | | 1 |
| 11 | Cancer | | | | | | | | | 2 | 5 | 1 | 1 | | | | | | | 4 | | | 1 | | 1 |
| 12 | Catarrh | 2 | 6 | 2 | 3 | 2 | | 1 | 2 | 11 | 1 | 3 | | | | | | | | 26 | | | 4 | 3 | |
| 13 | Childbirth | | | | | | | | 5 | | 30 | | 2 | | | | | | | 20 | | | 4 | 8 | 3 |
| 14 | Cholera | 13 | 10 | 87 | 75 | 29 | 24 | 54 | 49 | 212 | 145 | 50 | 32 | 2 | 3 | | | 22 | 8 | 444 | 1 | 17 | 136 | 140 | 60 |
| 15 | ...do...infantum | | | 4 | 6 | 1 | 1 | | | | | | | | | | | | | 11 | | | | 1 | |
| 16 | ...do...morbus | | | | | | | 1 | 1 | 1 | | 1 | | | | | | | | 3 | | | 1 | | |
| 17 | Colic | 1 | | | | | | 1 | | 1 | 1 | | | | | | | | | 2 | | | 1 | | 1 |
| 18 | Congestion of brain | 1 | 1 | | 4 | 1 | 2 | 1 | | 2 | 1 | | | | | | | | | 8 | | 1 | | 4 | |
| 19 | Consumption | 3 | 1 | 2 | 6 | 3 | 4 | 2 | 6 | 35 | 43 | 9 | 6 | | | | | | | 53 | | 4 | 30 | 17 | 14 |
| 20 | Convulsions | 3 | 6 | 11 | 7 | 2 | | | 2 | 1 | 1 | | | | | | | | | 28 | | | | 5 | |
| 21 | Croup | 28 | 15 | 18 | 12 | 1 | | | 1 | | | | | | | | | | | 65 | | | 3 | 6 | 1 |
| 22 | Debility | | | | 1 | | | | | | | | | | | | | | | 1 | | | | | |
| 23 | Diabetes | | | | | | 1 | | | | | | | | | | | | | 1 | | | | | |
| 24 | Diarrhœa | 6 | 1 | 9 | 15 | | 1 | 5 | 1 | 18 | 4 | 6 | 4 | 2 | | | | | | 45 | | 1 | 13 | 7 | 3 |
| 25 | Dirt eating | 1 | | | | | 1 | 2 | 2 | 14 | 9 | 3 | | | | | | | | 32 | | | | | |
| 26 | Dropsy | 2 | 1 | 9 | 5 | 4 | 4 | 14 | 5 | 34 | 27 | 19 | 9 | 2 | | | | | | 62 | 1 | 8 | 38 | 11 | 10 |
| 27 | Dysentery | | | 1 | 3 | | | | | 3 | | | 1 | | | | | | | 5 | | | 1 | | 2 |
| 28 | Dyspepsia | | | | | | | | | 1 | | | | | | | | | | 1 | | | | | |
| 29 | Epilepsy | | 1 | 1 | 1 | 2 | 1 | 1 | 4 | 2 | | 2 | 2 | | | | | | | 9 | | 1 | 3 | 4 | |
| 30 | Erysipelas | 1 | | 3 | 1 | | | | | 1 | | | | | | | | | | 6 | | | | | |
| 31 | Executed | | | | | | | | | 1 | | | | | | | | | | | | | | 1 | |
| 32 | Eye, disease of | | | 1 | | 1 | | | | | | | | | | | | | | 2 | | | | | |
| 33 | Fever, not specified | 27 | 16 | 56 | 54 | 22 | 28 | 11 | 11 | 20 | 42 | 11 | 7 | | 1 | | | | | 243 | | 2 | 19 | 30 | 9 |
| 34 | ..do..bilious | 2 | | 7 | 3 | 5 | 4 | 3 | 1 | 3 | 3 | 1 | | | 1 | | | | | 21 | | | 3 | 8 | 1 |
| 35 | ..do..congestive | 2 | 2 | 17 | 11 | 15 | 13 | 9 | 6 | 13 | 8 | 5 | 3 | | | | | | | 62 | | | 15 | 24 | 1 |
| 36 | ..do..intermittent | | 1 | 4 | 3 | 1 | 1 | 2 | | | | | | | | | | | | 11 | | | 1 | | |
| 37 | ..do..puerperal | | | | | | | | 1 | | 11 | | | | | | | | | 3 | | | 5 | | 3 |
| 38 | ..do..remittent | | | | | 1 | 1 | | 1 | 1 | | | | | | | | | | 2 | | | | 2 | |
| 39 | ..do..scarlet | 1 | | 2 | 8 | 5 | 4 | 3 | 3 | | | | | | | | | | | 16 | | | 2 | 8 | |
| 40 | ..do..typhus | | | 8 | 4 | 2 | 4 | 9 | 9 | 15 | 11 | 1 | 2 | | | | | | | 31 | | | 10 | 16 | 7 |
| 41 | ..do..yellow | | 1 | | | | 1 | | | 2 | | | | | | | | | | 1 | | | 1 | 2 | |

## …IE STATE OF KENTUCKY—Continued.

| NATIVITIES. | | | | | SEASON OF DECEASE. | | | | DURATION OF SICKNESS. | | | | WHITES. | | | COLORED. | | | | | | | | | |
|---|---|---|---|---|---|---|---|---|---|---|---|---|---|---|---|---|---|---|---|---|---|---|---|---|
| | | | | | | | | | | | | | | | | Slaves. | | | | Free. | | | | | |
| | | | | | | | | | | | | | | | | Black. | | Mulatto. | | Black. | | Mul. | | | |
| …tories. | Ireland. | Germany. | Other foreign countries. | Unknown. | Spring. | Summer. | Autumn. | Winter. | Under 1 week. | 1 week and under 1 month. | 1 month and under 3 months. | 3 months and over. | Males. | Females. | Total. | M. | F. | M. | F. | M. | F. | M | F. | Aggregate deaths. | |
| | | | | | | | | 2 | | 1 | 1 | | | 2 | 2 | | | | | | | | | 2 | 1 |
| | | | 1 | 2 | 50 | 45 | 33 | 36 | 12 | 17 | 22 | 109 | 30 | 20 | 50 | 42 | 61 | 3 | 7 | | 1 | | 1 | 165 | 2 |
| | 3 | 4 | 1 | | 39 | 32 | 12 | 65 | 13 | 129 | 3 | 3 | 80 | 40 | 120 | 23 | 6 | | 1 | | | | | 150 | 3 |
| | | | | | 5 | 4 | 7 | 5 | 1 | 6 | 5 | 8 | 10 | 4 | 14 | 5 | 1 | | 1 | | | | | 21 | 4 |
| | | | | | | | 2 | | | | | 2 | | 1 | 1 | | 1 | | | | | | | 2 | 5 |
| | | | | | 4 | 5 | 3 | 4 | | | | | 7 | 6 | 13 | | 2 | 2 | | | | | | 17 | 6 |
| | | | | | | 1 | | | | | | 1 | | | | | | | 1 | | | | | 1 | 7 |
| | | | | | 1 | 2 | 2 | | 5 | | | | 1 | | 1 | 3 | 1 | | | | | | | 5 | 8 |
| | | | | | 4 | 5 | 6 | 4 | 15 | | | | 12 | 3 | 15 | 5 | | | | | | | | 20 | 9 |
| | | | | | 1 | 11 | 19 | | 1 | 10 | 10 | 6 | 18 | 12 | 30 | 2 | | | | | | | | 32 | 10 |
| | | | | | 9 | 20 | 16 | 5 | 7 | 30 | 5 | 7 | 21 | 16 | 37 | 8 | 4 | 1 | | | | | | 50 | 11 |
| | | | | | | | | 1 | | 1 | | | | 1 | 1 | | | | | | | | | 1 | 12 |
| | | | | | 2 | 3 | 4 | 10 | 11 | 8 | | | 5 | 8 | 13 | 2 | 4 | | | | | | | 19 | 13 |
| | | | | | 3 | 3 | 10 | | 1 | 13 | | 3 | 5 | 10 | 15 | 1 | | | 1 | | | | | 17 | 14 |
| | | | | | 1 | 3 | 4 | 1 | | | 1 | 5 | 4 | 3 | 7 | 1 | 1 | | | | | | | 9 | 15 |
| | 1 | | | | 3 | 4 | 2 | | | 4 | | 4 | 2 | 2 | 4 | 4 | | | | 1 | | | | 9 | 16 |
| | | | | | 1 | 2 | 5 | 1 | 1 | 1 | 1 | 6 | | 3 | 3 | | 6 | | | | | | | 9 | 17 |
| | | | | | 1 | | | 1 | | 1 | | | 1 | | 1 | 1 | | | | | | | | 2 | 18 |
| | | | | | 3 | 2 | 2 | 3 | 2 | 2 | 2 | 4 | 5 | 3 | 8 | 2 | | | | | | | | 10 | 19 |
| | | | 1 | | 26 | 41 | 22 | 25 | 49 | 49 | 4 | 7 | 26 | 37 | 63 | 22 | 27 | 1 | 1 | | | | | 114 | 20 |
| | 16 | 18 | 7 | 12 | 648 | 729 | 583 | 495 | 863 | 601 | 226 | 473 | 907 | 835 | 1742 | 243 | 268 | 43 | 29 | 53 | 56 | 11 | 13 | 2458 | 21 |
| .. | 193 | 222 | 144 | 72 | 3436 | 4942 | 4060 | 2424 | 4965 | 4772 | 1483 | 2693 | 5734 | 4907 | 10641 | 1952 | 1842 | 202 | 197 | 75 | 78 | 20 | 26 | 15083 | |

## …ECTION OF THE STATE OF LOUISIANA.

*…laiborne, Concordia, De Soto, Franklin, Jackson, Madison, Morehouse, Natchitoches, Ouachita, …ensas, and Union.*

| …tories. | Ireland. | Germany. | Other foreign countries. | Unknown. | Spring. | Summer. | Autumn. | Winter. | Under 1 week. | 1 week and under 1 month. | 1 month and under 3 months. | 3 months and over. | Males. | Females. | Total. | Slaves Black M. | Slaves Black F. | Slaves Mulatto M. | Slaves Mulatto F. | Free Black M. | Free Black F. | Free Mul. M | Free Mul. F. | Aggregate deaths. | |
|---|---|---|---|---|---|---|---|---|---|---|---|---|---|---|---|---|---|---|---|---|---|---|---|---|---|
| | | | 1 | | 19 | 11 | 11 | 15 | 48 | 2 | 1 | | 5 | 3 | 8 | 24 | 23 | 2 | | | | | | 57 | 1 |
| | | | | | 9 | 8 | 6 | 11 | 19 | 13 | | 1 | 3 | 5 | 8 | 11 | 13 | | 2 | | | | | 34 | 2 |
| | 2 | | | | 21 | 27 | 9 | 9 | 61 | | | | 9 | 4 | 13 | 36 | 14 | 3 | | | | | | 66 | 3 |
| | | | | | 1 | 1 | | | 2 | | | | | | | | 2 | | | | | | | 2 | 4 |
| | | | | | 5 | 6 | 2 | 4 | 13 | 1 | | 1 | 1 | 1 | 2 | 5 | 8 | 1 | 1 | | | | | 17 | 5 |
| | | | | | 4 | | | 2 | 1 | 2 | | 3 | 2 | 3 | 5 | 1 | | | | | | | | 6 | 6 |
| | | | | | 1 | | | | | 1 | | | 1 | | 1 | | | | | | | | | 1 | 7 |
| | | | 1 | | 2 | 1 | 1 | | 2 | 1 | | 1 | | 1 | 1 | 2 | 1 | | | | | | | 4 | 8 |
| | | | | | 2 | 1 | 2 | 1 | | 2 | 1 | 1 | 1 | | 1 | 2 | 3 | | | | | | | 6 | 9 |
| | | | | | 4 | 1 | 4 | 2 | 4 | 1 | 1 | 5 | | 4 | 4 | 4 | 1 | 2 | | | | | | 11 | 10 |
| | | | 1 | 2 | 2 | 3 | 2 | 2 | | | 1 | 8 | 2 | 3 | 5 | 1 | 3 | | | | | | | 9 | 11 |
| | | | | | 10 | 5 | 4 | 14 | 21 | 9 | 2 | | 7 | 3 | 10 | 13 | 9 | 1 | | | | | | 33 | 12 |
| | | | 1 | 1 | 10 | 7 | 8 | 11 | 18 | 15 | 1 | | | 15 | 15 | | 20 | | 2 | | | | | 37 | 13 |
| | 3 | 1 | 7 | 6 | 189 | 371 | 72 | 183 | 664 | 54 | 1 | | 81 | 32 | 113 | 372 | 300 | 16 | 13 | | 1 | | | 815 | 14 |
| | | | | | 3 | 2 | 6 | 1 | 3 | 5 | 3 | | | 3 | 3 | 4 | 3 | 1 | 1 | | | | | 12 | 15 |
| | | | | | | 3 | 1 | | 3 | | | | 1 | | 1 | 2 | 1 | | | | | | | 4 | 16 |
| | | | | | | 2 | 1 | 1 | 4 | | | | 1 | | 1 | 2 | 1 | | | | | | | 4 | 17 |
| | | | | | 2 | 7 | 3 | 1 | 5 | 4 | 1 | | 5 | 6 | 11 | | 2 | | | | | | | 13 | 18 |
| | | | 1 | 1 | 44 | 30 | 23 | 20 | 4 | 6 | 7 | 97 | 27 | 27 | 54 | 22 | 35 | 5 | 4 | | | | | 120 | 19 |
| | | | | | 6 | 11 | 10 | 6 | 32 | | | | 6 | 6 | 12 | 10 | 10 | 1 | | | | | | 33 | 20 |
| | | | | | 25 | 19 | 13 | 18 | 53 | 8 | 2 | 4 | 11 | 5 | 16 | 32 | 20 | 4 | 2 | | | | 1 | 75 | 21 |
| | | | | | | | | 1 | | | | | | | | | 1 | | | | | | | 1 | 22 |
| | | | | | | | 1 | | 1 | | | | | 1 | 1 | | | | | | | | | 1 | 23 |
| | | 1 | 2 | | 10 | 17 | 30 | 15 | 21 | 24 | 7 | 20 | 21 | 7 | 28 | 21 | 18 | 4 | 1 | | | | | 72 | 24 |
| | | | | | 8 | 11 | 8 | 5 | 3 | 2 | 2 | 21 | | | | 18 | 11 | 2 | 1 | | | | | 32 | 25 |
| | | | 3 | 2 | 31 | 29 | 39 | 35 | 3 | 7 | 17 | 92 | 31 | 15 | 46 | 48 | 33 | 5 | 3 | | | | | 135 | 26 |
| | | | | | 1 | 2 | 5 | | | 3 | 1 | 1 | 1 | | 1 | 3 | 4 | | | | | | | 8 | 27 |
| | | | | | | 1 | | | | | | 1 | 1 | | 1 | | | | | | | | | 1 | 28 |
| | | | | | 5 | 6 | 3 | 3 | 10 | 2 | | 5 | 2 | 2 | 4 | 6 | 6 | | 1 | | | | | 17 | 29 |
| | | | | | 4 | 1 | | 1 | 2 | 2 | | 2 | 4 | 1 | 5 | 1 | | | | | | | | 6 | 30 |
| | | | | | | | 1 | | 1 | | | | | | | 1 | | | | | | | | 1 | 31 |
| | | | | | | | 2 | | 1 | | | 1 | 1 | | 1 | | | 1 | | | | | | 2 | 32 |
| | 2 | | | 1 | 30 | 86 | 150 | 40 | 130 | 131 | 24 | 5 | 65 | 76 | 141 | 73 | 74 | 9 | 8 | | | | 1 | 306 | 33 |
| | | | | | 1 | 10 | 21 | 1 | 8 | 21 | 2 | 2 | 13 | 8 | 21 | 8 | 4 | | | | | | | 33 | 34 |
| | | | 1 | 1 | 7 | 23 | 69 | 5 | 80 | 18 | 1 | 5 | 61 | 43 | 104 | | | | | | | | | 104 | 35 |
| | | | | | 2 | 1 | 6 | 3 | 8 | | 2 | 2 | 4 | 2 | 6 | 3 | 3 | | | | | | | 12 | 36 |
| | | 1 | | | 3 | 3 | 2 | 4 | 5 | 6 | 1 | | | 9 | 9 | | 3 | | | | | | | 12 | 37 |
| | | | | | 1 | 1 | 2 | | 1 | 3 | | | 1 | 1 | 2 | 1 | 1 | | | | | | | 4 | 38 |
| | | | | | 3 | 3 | 2 | 17 | 9 | 15 | 1 | | 5 | 5 | 10 | 6 | 10 | | | | | | | 26 | 39 |
| | | | | 1 | 19 | 22 | 13 | 11 | 9 | 46 | 9 | 1 | 20 | 13 | 33 | 14 | 17 | 1 | | | | | | 65 | 40 |
| | | | | | 1 | | 3 | | 1 | 2 | 1 | | 2 | 1 | 3 | | 1 | | | | | | | 4 | 41 |

## CLASSIFICATION OF DEATHS IN NORTHERN

| | Cause of death. | Under 1. M. | Under 1. F. | 1 and under 5. M. | 1 and under 5. F. | 5 and under 10. M. | 5 and under 10. F. | 10 and under 20. M. | 10 and under 20. F. | 20 and under 50. M. | 20 and under 50. F. | 50 and under 80. M. | 50 and under 80. F. | 80 and under 100. M | 80 and under 100. F. | 100 & over. M | 100 & over. F | Age unknown. M | Age unknown. F. | Born in State. | N. England States. | Middle States. | Southern States. | Southwest'n States. | Northwest'n States. |
|---|---|---|---|---|---|---|---|---|---|---|---|---|---|---|---|---|---|---|---|---|---|---|---|---|---|
| 1 | Fracture | | | | | | | | | | | 1 | | | | | | | | | | | 1 | | |
| 2 | Gravel | | | | 1 | | | | | 3 | | 1 | | | | | | | | 4 | | | 1 | | |
| 3 | Heart, disease of | | | | 1 | | | 1 | | | 3 | 2 | 2 | | | | | | | 3 | | | 5 | | 1 |
| 4 | Hemorrhage | 1 | 1 | | | | | 1 | 1 | 8 | 4 | 4 | | | | | | | | 7 | | | 4 | 6 | 2 |
| 5 | Hernia | | | | | | | | | | | 1 | | | | | | | | | | | | 1 | |
| 6 | Hives | 8 | 2 | | 2 | | | | | | | | | | | | | | | 12 | | | | | |
| 7 | Hooping cough | 14 | 7 | 17 | 15 | 4 | 8 | 1 | 2 | 1 | | | | | | | | | | 65 | | | | 4 | |
| 8 | Hydrocephalus | | | 1 | | | | | | | | | | | | | | | | 1 | | | | | |
| 9 | Inflamat'n, not spec'd | | 2 | | 1 | | | | 1 | 6 | 6 | 1 | 2 | | | | | | | 11 | | | 2 | 3 | 2 |
| 10 | ....do....bowels | 5 | 3 | 5 | 6 | 2 | 2 | 3 | 2 | 4 | 6 | | 2 | | | | | | | 25 | 1 | 1 | 7 | 5 | |
| 11 | ....do....brain | 3 | 3 | 12 | 14 | 2 | 6 | 8 | 2 | 9 | 7 | 3 | 1 | | | | | | | 48 | | 1 | 5 | 12 | 2 |
| 12 | ....do....stomach | | | 1 | 1 | | 1 | | | 2 | 1 | 1 | | | | | | | | 3 | | | 2 | 1 | |
| 13 | Influenza | 1 | | 1 | 1 | | | | | 1 | | | | | | | | | | 3 | | 1 | | | |
| 14 | Intemperance | | | | | | | | | 1 | | 1 | | | | | | | | 1 | | | 1 | | |
| 15 | Jaundice | | | | 1 | | 2 | | 1 | 1 | | | | | | | | | | 3 | | | 2 | | |
| 16 | Kidneys, disease of | 1 | | | | | | 1 | | 1 | | | | | | | | | | 1 | | | | 2 | |
| 17 | Killed | | | | | | | 2 | | 15 | 1 | 2 | | | | | | | | 7 | | | 5 | 5 | 3 |
| 18 | Leprosy | | | | | | | | | | 1 | | | | | | | | | | | | | | 1 |
| 19 | Lightning | | | | | | | | | 1 | | | | | | | | | | 1 | | | | | |
| 20 | Liver, disease of | | | | 1 | 2 | | | | 4 | 1 | 2 | 2 | | | | | | | 4 | | | 4 | 2 | 2 |
| 21 | Lockjaw | 13 | 16 | 1 | 6 | 2 | | | | 2 | 1 | | | | | | | | | 40 | | | | | |
| 22 | Lungs, disease of | | | 1 | 1 | | | | | 1 | 3 | 1 | | | | | | | | 5 | | | | 1 | |
| 23 | Marasmus | | 1 | | | | | | | | | | | | | | | | | 1 | | | | | |
| 24 | Measles | 1 | | 6 | 1 | | 1 | 1 | | 1 | | | | | | | | | | 7 | | | 1 | 3 | |
| 25 | Menses, suppress'n of | | | | | | | | 1 | | 1 | | | | | | | | | 1 | | | | 1 | |
| 26 | Murder | | | | | | | | | 2 | | | | | | | | | | 2 | | | | | |
| 27 | Neuralgia | | | | | | | | | 2 | | 1 | | | | | | | | 1 | | | 1 | 1 | |
| 28 | Old age | | | | | | | | | | | 6 | 9 | 7 | 14 | 5 | 4 | | | 21 | 1 | 4 | 15 | 1 | |
| 29 | Paralysis | | | 1 | | | | 1 | 1 | 2 | | 1 | | | | | | | | 3 | | | 2 | 1 | |
| 30 | Pleurisy | | | 2 | 1 | 1 | | 5 | 2 | 10 | 4 | 5 | 4 | | | | | | | 22 | | | 3 | 5 | 3 |
| 31 | Pneumonia | 7 | 3 | 17 | 5 | 5 | 7 | 13 | 8 | 54 | 24 | 22 | 7 | 1 | 1 | | | | | 80 | 1 | 11 | 44 | 21 | 14 |
| 32 | Poison | | 1 | | | | 1 | | | 4 | | 1 | | | | | | | | 3 | | | 2 | 2 | |
| 33 | Quinsy | | 1 | 1 | | 1 | | 1 | | 2 | | 1 | | | | | | | | 3 | | | 3 | 1 | |
| 34 | Rheumatism | | | | | | 1 | | 1 | 2 | 1 | | 2 | | | | | | | 3 | | | 4 | | |
| 35 | Rickets | | 1 | 1 | 1 | | | 1 | | | | | | | | | | | | 3 | | | | 1 | |
| 36 | Salivation, effects of | | | | | | 1 | | | 1 | | | 1 | | | | | | | 1 | | | 1 | 1 | |
| 37 | Scrofula | 2 | | 4 | 1 | | 1 | 1 | | 1 | | 1 | | | | | | | | 8 | | | 3 | | |
| 38 | Scurvy | | | | | | | | | | | 1 | | | | | | | | | | | | | 1 |
| 39 | Small pox | | | | 3 | | | | | 3 | 1 | | | | | | | | | 3 | | | 1 | 3 | |
| 40 | Spine, disease of | | | | | | | | | 1 | | | | | | | | | | 1 | | | | | |
| 41 | Stillborn | | 1 | | | | | | | | | | | | | | | | | 1 | | | | | |
| 42 | Stomach, disease of | | | | | 1 | | | | | | | | | | | | | | 1 | | | | | |
| 43 | Suffocation | 13 | 7 | 2 | 1 | | | | | | | | | | | | | | | 22 | | | | 1 | |
| 44 | Suicide | | | | | | | | | 2 | 1 | 1 | | | | | | | | 3 | | | 1 | | |
| 45 | Teething | 6 | 1 | 7 | 9 | | | | | | | | | | | | | | | 23 | | | | | |
| 46 | Tetanus | 2 | 2 | | | 1 | | | | 1 | | | | | | | | | | 6 | | | | | |
| 47 | Throat, disease of | 1 | 1 | | | 1 | | | | | | | | | | | | | | 3 | | | | | |
| 48 | Thrush | 3 | | | 2 | | | | | | | | | | | | | | | 5 | | | | | |
| 49 | Ulcer | | | | | 1 | | | | 2 | | 1 | | | | | | | | 1 | | | 2 | | 1 |
| 50 | Uterus, disease of | | | | | | | | | | 3 | | | | | | | | | 2 | | | 1 | | |
| 51 | Venereal | | | 1 | 1 | | | | | 1 | 2 | | | | | | | | | 4 | | | | 1 | |
| 52 | Worms | 5 | 12 | 53 | 50 | 7 | 10 | 1 | | 2 | | 1 | | | | | | | | 128 | | | 5 | 6 | 1 |
| 53 | Unknown | 121 | 84 | 62 | 51 | 15 | 13 | 17 | 15 | 58 | 71 | 18 | 22 | 3 | | | | 10 | 8 | 467 | | 4 | 32 | 39 | 17 |
| | Total | 304 | 216 | 450 | 417 | 154 | 165 | 197 | 160 | 655 | 512 | 207 | 133 | 17 | 20 | 5 | 4 | 32 | 16 | 2413 | 7 | 67 | 432 | 446 | 181 |

## CLASSIFICATION OF DEATHS IN SOUTHERN

*Embracing the following parishes : Ascension, Assumption, Calcassieu, East Baton Rouge, Eas St. Charles, St. Helena, St. James, St. John Baptist, St. Landry, St. Martins, St. Marys*

| | Cause of death. | Under 1. M. | Under 1. F. | 1 and under 5. M. | 1 and under 5. F. | 5 and under 10. M. | 5 and under 10. F. | 10 and under 20. M. | 10 and under 20. F. | 20 and under 50. M. | 20 and under 50. F. | 50 and under 80. M. | 50 and under 80. F. | 80 and under 100. M | 80 and under 100. F. | 100 & over. M | 100 & over. F | Age unknown. M | Age unknown. F. | Born in State. | N. England States. | Middle States. | Southern States. | Southwest'n States. | Northwest'n States. |
|---|---|---|---|---|---|---|---|---|---|---|---|---|---|---|---|---|---|---|---|---|---|---|---|---|---|
| 1 | Abscess | | | | | | | | | 1 | | 1 | 1 | | | | | | | | | | 1 | | |
| 2 | Accident, not specfi'd | 4 | 6 | 7 | 4 | 3 | 3 | 2 | 1 | 19 | 3 | 7 | 2 | | | | | | | 45 | | 5 | 6 | 2 | |
| 3 | ....do....burned | 1 | | 7 | 6 | 3 | 5 | | 4 | | 3 | | | | | | | | | 29 | | | | | |
| 4 | ....do....drowned | | | 5 | 1 | 4 | | 9 | 1 | 39 | 5 | 7 | 1 | | | | | | | 46 | | 2 | 13 | 3 | |
| 5 | ....do....scalded | | | | 1 | | | 1 | | 2 | | | | | | | | | | 3 | | | 1 | | |
| 6 | Apoplexy | | | | | | | | 2 | 10 | 3 | 6 | 5 | | 1 | | | | | 17 | | 2 | 4 | 1 | |
| 7 | Asthma | | | 1 | 2 | | | | 1 | 2 | 2 | 1 | | | | | | | | 6 | | | 2 | | |
| 8 | Bladder, disease of | 1 | | | | | | | 1 | | | | | 1 | | | | | | 2 | | | | | |
| 9 | Bowels......do | | | | | | | 1 | | 1 | 1 | 1 | 1 | | | | | | | 2 | | | 3 | | |
| 10 | Brain......do | 1 | | | | 1 | | | 1 | 2 | | | | | | | | | | 3 | | | | | |

## ECTION OF THE STATE OF LOUISIANA—Continued.

| California and Territories. | Ireland. | Germany. | Other foreign countries. | Unknown. | Spring. | Summer. | Autumn. | Winter. | Under 1 week. | 1 week and under 1 month. | 1 month and under 3 months. | 3 months and over. | Whites: Males. | Whites: Females. | Whites: Total. | Colored, Slaves, Black: M. | Colored, Slaves, Black: F. | Colored, Slaves, Mulatto: M. | Colored, Slaves, Mulatto: F. | Colored, Free, Black: M. | Colored, Free, Black: F. | Colored, Free, Mul.: M | Colored, Free, Mul.: F. | Aggregate deaths. | |
|---|---|---|---|---|---|---|---|---|---|---|---|---|---|---|---|---|---|---|---|---|---|---|---|---|---|
| | | | | | | 1 | | | | 1 | | | 1 | | 1 | | | | | | | | | 1 | 1 |
| | | | | | | 2 | 1 | 2 | | 1 | 1 | 3 | 1 | 1 | 2 | 2 | | 1 | | | | | | 5 | 2 |
| | | | | | 3 | | 3 | 3 | 4 | | 1 | 2 | | 2 | 2 | 3 | 4 | | | | | | | 9 | 3 |
| | | | 1 | | 4 | 4 | 8 | 9 | 12 | 4 | 1 | 1 | 3 | 4 | 7 | 10 | 1 | 1 | 1 | | | | | 20 | 4 |
| | | | | | 1 | | | | | | | | | | | 1 | | | | | | | | 1 | 5 |
| | | | | | 5 | 1 | 3 | 3 | 8 | 4 | | | 7 | 4 | 11 | 1 | | | | | | | | 12 | 6 |
| | | | | | 19 | 29 | 7 | 14 | 12 | 40 | 14 | 1 | 10 | 8 | 18 | 25 | 22 | 2 | 2 | | | | | 69 | 7 |
| | | | | | | | | 1 | | | | 1 | 1 | | 1 | | | | | | | | | 1 | 8 |
| | | | 1 | | 5 | 2 | 7 | 5 | 8 | 7 | 3 | 1 | 4 | 4 | 8 | 3 | 7 | | 1 | | | | | 19 | 9 |
| | | 1 | | | 10 | 9 | 11 | 9 | 17 | 11 | | 9 | 11 | 6 | 17 | 8 | 13 | | 2 | | | | | 40 | 10 |
| | | | 2 | | 19 | 26 | 16 | 9 | 38 | 22 | 2 | 7 | 20 | 21 | 41 | 15 | 11 | 2 | 1 | | | | | 70 | 11 |
| | 1 | | | | 1 | 1 | 5 | | 4 | 2 | 1 | | 3 | 1 | 4 | 1 | 1 | | 1 | | | | | 7 | 12 |
| | | | | | 1 | 1 | | 2 | 1 | 3 | | | 1 | | 1 | 2 | 1 | | | | | | | 4 | 13 |
| | | | | | | 1 | 1 | | | | | 1 | 1 | | 1 | | | | | | | 1 | | 2 | 14 |
| | | | | | 2 | | | 3 | 1 | 2 | | 2 | | 2 | 2 | 1 | 2 | | | | | | | 5 | 15 |
| | | | | | 1 | | 1 | 1 | | 3 | | | 1 | | 1 | 2 | | | | | | | | 3 | 16 |
| | | | | | 6 | 5 | 4 | 5 | 14 | | | | 17 | | 17 | 2 | | | 1 | | | | | 20 | 17 |
| | | | | | | | | 1 | | | | 1 | | | | | | | 1 | | | | | 1 | 18 |
| | | | | | 1 | | | | 1 | | | | | | | 1 | | | | | | | | 1 | 19 |
| | | | | | 3 | 2 | 5 | 2 | 1 | 2 | 3 | 5 | 6 | 3 | 9 | 2 | | | 1 | | | | | 12 | 20 |
| | 1 | | | | 8 | 12 | 13 | 8 | 17 | 4 | | 1 | 1 | 5 | 6 | 15 | 16 | 1 | 2 | | | 1 | | 41 | 21 |
| | | | 1 | | 2 | 1 | 2 | 2 | | 1 | | 3 | 2 | 3 | 5 | 1 | 1 | | | | | | | 7 | 22 |
| | | | | | | 1 | | | | | | 1 | | 1 | 1 | | | | | | | | | 1 | 23 |
| | | | | | 2 | 7 | 1 | 1 | 6 | 4 | 1 | | 4 | | 4 | 5 | 2 | | | | | | | 11 | 24 |
| | | | | | | | 1 | 1 | | 1 | | 1 | | 1 | 1 | | 1 | | | | | | | 2 | 25 |
| | | | | | 1 | 1 | | | | | | | 1 | | 1 | 1 | | | | | | | | 2 | 26 |
| | | | | | | | | 3 | 1 | 2 | | | 2 | | 2 | 1 | | | | | | | | 3 | 27 |
| | | | 1 | 2 | 9 | 11 | 10 | 13 | 6 | 4 | 2 | 4 | 2 | 7 | 9 | 15 | 17 | | 2 | | 1 | 1 | | 45 | 28 |
| | | | | | 2 | 1 | 2 | 1 | 2 | 3 | | 1 | 3 | 1 | 4 | 2 | | | | | | | | 6 | 29 |
| | | | 1 | | 14 | 5 | 2 | 13 | 8 | 21 | 2 | 2 | 10 | 4 | 14 | 12 | 6 | 1 | 1 | | | | | 34 | 30 |
| | 1 | | 1 | 1 | 73 | 15 | 40 | 46 | 55 | 90 | 10 | 9 | 59 | 29 | 88 | 53 | 23 | 7 | 3 | | | | | 174 | 31 |
| | | | | | 2 | 1 | 4 | | 4 | 1 | | 1 | 1 | 1 | 2 | 4 | 1 | | | | | | | 7 | 32 |
| | | | | | 2 | | 2 | 3 | 5 | 2 | | | 5 | 1 | 6 | 1 | | | | | | | | 7 | 33 |
| | | | | | 2 | 1 | 1 | 3 | | 3 | | 4 | 1 | 3 | 4 | 1 | 2 | | | | | | | 7 | 34 |
| | | | | | | 3 | | 1 | | 1 | | 3 | | 1 | 1 | 2 | 1 | | | | | | | 4 | 35 |
| | | | | | | 2 | 1 | | 1 | 1 | 1 | | 1 | | 1 | | 1 | | 1 | | | | | 3 | 36 |
| | | | | | 4 | 5 | 2 | | 2 | 2 | 1 | 6 | 3 | | 3 | 6 | 2 | | | | | | | 11 | 37 |
| | | | | | | 1 | | | | 1 | | | 1 | | 1 | | | | | | | | | 1 | 38 |
| | | | | | 2 | 3 | 1 | 1 | 1 | 4 | 1 | | 2 | 2 | 4 | 1 | 1 | | 1 | | | | | 7 | 39 |
| | | | | | | 1 | | | | 1 | | | | | | | | | 1 | | | | | 1 | 40 |
| | | | | | | 1 | | | | | | | | 1 | 1 | | | | | | | | | 1 | 41 |
| | | | | | | | 1 | | | 1 | | | 1 | | 1 | | | | | | | | | 1 | 42 |
| | | | | | 7 | 6 | 3 | 7 | 17 | | | | 2 | | 2 | 11 | 7 | 2 | 1 | | | | | 23 | 43 |
| | | | | | 1 | 2 | | 1 | 3 | | | | | | | 3 | 1 | | | | | | | 4 | 44 |
| | | | | | 7 | 5 | 7 | 4 | 5 | 8 | 3 | 1 | | 1 | 1 | 11 | 8 | 2 | | | 1 | | | 23 | 45 |
| | | | | | 1 | 3 | 1 | 1 | 6 | | | | | | | 4 | 2 | | | | | | | 6 | 46 |
| | | | | | 1 | 1 | 1 | | | 2 | | | 1 | | 1 | 1 | 1 | | | | | | | 3 | 47 |
| | | | | | 1 | 1 | 1 | 2 | | 4 | | 1 | 2 | 1 | 3 | 1 | 1 | | | | | | | 5 | 48 |
| | | | | | | 2 | 1 | 1 | | 2 | | 2 | 3 | | 3 | 1 | | | | | | | | 4 | 49 |
| | | | | | 2 | | 1 | | | | 1 | 1 | | | | | 2 | | 1 | | | | | 3 | 50 |
| | | | | | | 4 | | 1 | | | 1 | 4 | | | | 2 | 3 | | | | | | | 5 | 51 |
| | | | 1 | | 30 | 40 | 50 | 18 | 84 | 40 | 5 | 10 | 10 | 10 | 20 | 56 | 59 | 3 | 3 | | | | | 141 | 52 |
| | | 1 | 2 | 6 | 131 | 127 | 164 | 116 | 277 | 69 | 32 | 101 | 66 | 54 | 120 | 221 | 198 | 17 | 11 | | | | 1 | 568 | 53 |
| | 10 | 5 | 29 | 24 | 869 | 1080 | 914 | 758 | 1871 | 782 | 175 | 469 | 665 | 487 | 1152 | 1256 | 1074 | 97 | 76 | | 3 | 3 | 3 | 3664 | |

## SECTION OF THE STATE OF LOUISIANA.

*Feliciana, Iberville, Lafayette, Lafourche, Livingston, Plaquemines, Point Coupee, St. Bernard, St. Tammany, Terre Bonne, Vermillion, Washington, West Baton Rouge, West Feliciana.*

| California and Territories. | Ireland. | Germany. | Other foreign countries. | Unknown. | Spring. | Summer. | Autumn. | Winter. | Under 1 week. | 1 week and under 1 month. | 1 month and under 3 months. | 3 months and over. | Whites: Males. | Whites: Females. | Whites: Total. | Colored, Slaves, Black: M. | Colored, Slaves, Black: F. | Colored, Slaves, Mulatto: M. | Colored, Slaves, Mulatto: F. | Colored, Free, Black: M. | Colored, Free, Black: F. | Colored, Free, Mul.: M | Colored, Free, Mul.: F. | Aggregate deaths. | |
|---|---|---|---|---|---|---|---|---|---|---|---|---|---|---|---|---|---|---|---|---|---|---|---|---|---|
| | | | | | | 1 | | 2 | | 2 | | 1 | 1 | | 1 | 1 | 1 | | | | | | | 3 | 1 |
| | | | 1 | | 19 | 15 | 16 | 11 | 46 | 8 | 1 | 3 | 9 | 6 | 15 | 33 | 12 | | 1 | | | | | 61 | 2 |
| | | | | | 9 | 8 | 7 | 10 | 18 | 1 | | | 4 | 2 | 6 | 6 | 14 | 1 | 2 | | | | | 29 | 3 |
| | 1 | 1 | 3 | | 19 | 19 | 17 | 16 | 72 | | | | 16 | 2 | 18 | 47 | 5 | 1 | | | | | 1 | 72 | 4 |
| | | | | | | 1 | 1 | 2 | 2 | 1 | 1 | | 1 | | 1 | 1 | 1 | 1 | | | | | | 4 | 5 |
| | 1 | | 1 | | 10 | 6 | 8 | 3 | 25 | 1 | | | 7 | 3 | 10 | 9 | 7 | | | | | | 1 | 27 | 6 |
| | | | 1 | | 1 | 2 | | 5 | 2 | 2 | | 4 | 1 | 1 | 2 | 3 | 3 | | 1 | | | | | 9 | 7 |
| | | | 1 | | 1 | | 1 | | 1 | | | 2 | 1 | | 1 | | 1 | | | | 1 | | | 3 | 8 |
| | | | | | 1 | 3 | 1 | | 2 | 2 | | 1 | 1 | | 1 | 2 | 2 | | | | | | | 5 | 9 |
| | 1 | | 1 | | 2 | | 2 | 1 | 2 | 2 | | 1 | 3 | 1 | 4 | 1 | | | | | | | | 5 | 10 |

## CLASSIFICATION OF DEATHS IN SOUTHERN

| | Cause of death. | AGE. | | | | | | | | | | | | | | | | | | NATIVITIES. | | | | | |
|---|---|---|---|---|---|---|---|---|---|---|---|---|---|---|---|---|---|---|---|---|---|---|---|---|---|
| | | Under 1. | | 1 and under 5. | | 5 and under 10. | | 10 and under 20. | | 20 and under 50. | | 50 and under 80. | | 80 and under 100. | | 100 & over. | | Age unknown. | | Born in State. | N. England States. | Middle States. | Southern States. | Southwest'n States. | Northwest'n States. |
| | | M. | F. | M. | F. | M. | F. | M. | F. | M. | F. | M. | F. | M | F. | M | F. | M | F. | | | | | | |
| 1 | Bronchitis | | | | 1 | 1 | | | | 1 | 1 | 1 | 1 | | | | | | | 5 | | | | 1 | |
| 2 | Cancer | | | | | | | | 1 | 2 | 6 | 3 | | | | | | | | 7 | | | 3 | 1 | |
| 3 | Catarrh | 7 | 8 | 4 | 1 | | 2 | | 2 | 3 | 4 | 6 | 2 | | 1 | | | | | 34 | | 1 | 1 | 1 | |
| 4 | Childbirth | | | | | | | | 7 | | 38 | | | | | | | | | 37 | | 1 | 1 | 2 | 3 |
| 5 | Cholera | 9 | 9 | 84 | 86 | 67 | 37 | 91 | 73 | 422 | 198 | 79 | 46 | 4 | | | | | | 898 | 2 | 29 | 174 | 42 | 31 |
| 6 | ....do....infantum | 3 | 1 | 1 | 3 | | | | | | | | | | | | | | | 8 | | | | | |
| 7 | ....do....morbus | | | | | | | | | 1 | | | 1 | | | | | | | | | | 1 | | |
| 8 | Chorea | | | | | | | | | | | | 1 | | | | | | | | | | | 1 | |
| 9 | Colic | 1 | | | 1 | | | | | 1 | | 2 | 1 | | | | | | | 4 | | | 1 | 1 | |
| 10 | Congestion, brain | 1 | | 1 | | 1 | | 1 | 1 | 2 | | | | | | | | | | 6 | | | | 1 | |
| 11 | Consumption | | | 2 | 3 | 2 | | 6 | 8 | 52 | 55 | 12 | 15 | 8 | 1 | | | | | 103 | | 3 | 24 | 10 | 10 |
| 12 | Convulsions | 14 | 3 | 14 | 14 | 2 | 7 | | | 5 | 2 | 1 | 1 | | | | | | | 59 | | | 1 | 1 | 1 |
| 13 | Croup | 8 | 4 | 11 | 10 | 2 | | 1 | | | | | | | | | | | | 35 | | | | 1 | |
| 14 | Debility | 1 | | | | | | | | | | | | | | | | | | 1 | | | | | |
| 15 | Diarrhœa | 7 | 4 | 8 | 9 | | | | 2 | 11 | 7 | 9 | 1 | | | | | | | 45 | 1 | 1 | 3 | | 1 |
| 16 | Dirt eating | | | | | | | 3 | 1 | 6 | 10 | 1 | 1 | | | | | | | 14 | | 1 | 3 | 2 | 2 |
| 17 | Dropsy | 1 | | 11 | 5 | 7 | 2 | 8 | 3 | 22 | 24 | 12 | 12 | 2 | | | | | | 78 | 1 | 1 | 14 | 8 | 1 |
| 18 | Dysentery | 1 | 5 | 8 | 8 | 8 | | 3 | 5 | 20 | 11 | 4 | 2 | | | | | | | 54 | 2 | | 8 | 2 | 5 |
| 19 | Dyspepsia | | | | | | | | | | 1 | | | 1 | | | | | | 1 | | 1 | | | |
| 20 | Epilepsy | | | 1 | 1 | 4 | 2 | 2 | 1 | 2 | 3 | 2 | | | | | | | | 14 | | 1 | 1 | | |
| 21 | Erysipelas | | | | | | | | | 1 | 2 | | | | | | | | | 2 | | | | | |
| 22 | Executed | | | | | | | | | | | | | 1 | | | | | | 1 | | | | | |
| 23 | Fever, not specified | 21 | 20 | 36 | 55 | 21 | 15 | 18 | 22 | 64 | 41 | 12 | 13 | 3 | 3 | 1 | | | | 305 | | 4 | 19 | 4 | 8 |
| 24 | ..do..bilious | | | 2 | 1 | 2 | 1 | | | 3 | 4 | 1 | | | | | 1 | | | 10 | | 1 | 1 | 1 | 1 |
| 25 | ..do..congestive | 2 | 1 | 7 | 3 | 7 | 2 | 2 | 1 | 8 | 4 | 1 | 2 | | | | | | | 33 | | 1 | 4 | 1 | 1 |
| 26 | ..do..intermittent | | | | | | | | | | | | | | | | | | | 1 | | | | | |
| 27 | ..do..puerperal | | | | | | | | | | 1 | | | | | | | | | 1 | | | | | |
| 28 | ..do..scarlet | 3 | 1 | 4 | 4 | | 2 | 1 | 1 | 1 | | | | | | | | | | 15 | | | 1 | | 1 |
| 29 | ..do..typhus | | | 1 | | | 1 | 3 | 6 | 17 | 6 | 5 | 3 | | | | | | | 35 | 2 | | 4 | 1 | |
| 30 | ..do..yellow | | | | | | | 1 | | 2 | | | | | | | | | | 2 | | | | 1 | |
| 31 | Fistula | | | | | | | | | 1 | | | | | | | | | | 1 | | | | | |
| 32 | Fracture | | | | | | | 1 | | 1 | | | | | | | | | | 1 | | | 1 | | |
| 33 | Gout | | | | | | | | | | | 1 | 1 | | | | | | | 2 | | | | | |
| 34 | Heart, disease of | | 1 | | | | 2 | | | 7 | 7 | 1 | 4 | | | | | | | 18 | | 2 | 3 | 2 | 1 |
| 35 | Hemorrhage | | | | | | | | | 2 | 1 | 1 | 1 | | | | | | | 4 | | | | | 1 |
| 36 | Hernia | | | | | | | | 1 | 1 | 1 | 2 | | | | | | | | 4 | | | 1 | | |
| 37 | Hooping cough | 15 | 27 | 15 | 21 | 7 | 4 | 1 | 1 | | | | | | | | | | | 91 | | | | | |
| 38 | Hydrocephalus | 1 | 2 | 2 | 1 | | | | | | | | | | | | | | | 6 | | | | | |
| 39 | Inflamat'n, not spe'd. | | 1 | | | 2 | | 2 | 2 | 4 | 1 | 1 | 1 | | | | | | | 12 | | | | | |
| 40 | .....do....bowels | 2 | 1 | 4 | 5 | 2 | | | | 1 | 2 | | | 1 | | | | | | 16 | | 1 | | | 1 |
| 41 | .....do....brain | 3 | 2 | 4 | 5 | 3 | 2 | 4 | 1 | 8 | 4 | 1 | | | | | | | | 29 | | 1 | 5 | 2 | |
| 42 | .....do....stomach. | | | | | | | | | 1 | 1 | | 1 | | | | | | | 1 | | | | | 1 |
| 43 | Influenza | | 1 | | 2 | 1 | | | | 1 | 1 | 1 | 1 | | | | | | | 5 | | | 1 | 2 | |
| 44 | Insanity | | | | | | | | | | 1 | 1 | | | | | | | | 2 | | | | | |
| 45 | Intemperance | | | | | | | | | | | 2 | | | | | | | | | | 1 | | | |
| 46 | Jaundice | | | | | | | | | 1 | | | | | | | | | | 1 | | | | | |
| 47 | Killed | 1 | | | | | | 1 | | 10 | | 2 | | | | | | | | 8 | 2 | 1 | 1 | | 1 |
| 48 | Leprosy | | | | | | | | | | 1 | | | | | | | | | 1 | | | | | |
| 49 | Lightning | | | | | | | 1 | 1 | | 1 | | | | | | | | | 3 | | | | | |
| 50 | Liver, disease of | | | 1 | | 1 | | | | 11 | 3 | | | | | | | | | 8 | | 1 | 3 | 1 | 1 |
| 51 | Lockjaw | 17 | 20 | 2 | 1 | 2 | 2 | 2 | 1 | 3 | 2 | | | | | | | | | 51 | | | 1 | | |
| 52 | Lungs, disease of | | | | | | | | | 2 | | 2 | | | | | | | | 2 | | | | | |
| 53 | Mania-a-potu | | | | | | | 1 | | 4 | | 2 | | | | | | | | 2 | | 1 | | | |
| 54 | Marasmus | | | 1 | | 1 | | | | 1 | | | | | | | | | | 3 | | | | | |
| 55 | Measles | | | 5 | 3 | 1 | | 2 | | | | | | | | | | | | 11 | | | | | |
| 56 | Mortification | | | | | | | | | 1 | 1 | | | | | | | | | 1 | | | 1 | | |
| 57 | Murder | | | | | | | | | 5 | | | | | | | | | | 3 | | | | | |
| 58 | Old age | | | | | | | | | | | 16 | 10 | 24 | 22 | 5 | 7 | | | 44 | | 4 | 17 | | |
| 59 | Paralysis | | | | | | | 1 | | | | 5 | 1 | | 1 | | 1 | | | 3 | | | 3 | 2 | |
| 60 | Piles | | | | | | | | | | 1 | | 1 | | | | | | | 1 | 1 | | | | |
| 61 | Pleurisy | 1 | | 2 | 2 | | 2 | 2 | 1 | 22 | 12 | 5 | 4 | | | | | | | 39 | | 2 | 10 | | |
| 62 | Pneumonia | 9 | 3 | 5 | 2 | 3 | 1 | 2 | 4 | 16 | 16 | 8 | 1 | 1 | | | | | | 55 | 1 | 3 | 3 | 5 | 2 |
| 63 | Poison | | | | 1 | | | | 1 | 2 | 1 | | | | | | | | | 4 | | | 1 | | |
| 64 | Quinsy | | | | | | 1 | | | | | 1 | | | | | | | | 1 | | | 1 | | |
| 65 | Rheumatism | | | | | | | | | 5 | | 3 | 2 | | | | | | | 7 | | | 2 | 1 | |
| 66 | Scrofula | | 1 | 1 | 2 | 1 | | 1 | | 2 | 2 | 1 | | | | | | | | 8 | | | 1 | 2 | |
| 67 | Scurvy | | | | | | | | | | 1 | | 1 | | | | | | | 1 | | | | | |
| 68 | Skin, disease of | 1 | 3 | | 1 | | | | | | | | | | | | | | | 5 | | | | | |
| 69 | Small pox | | 1 | 1 | | | | 1 | 2 | 3 | 4 | | | | | | | | | 12 | | | | | |
| 70 | Stillborn | 6 | 8 | | | | | | | | | | | | | | | | | 14 | | | | | |
| 71 | Stomach, disease of | | 1 | | | | | | | | | 1 | | | | | | | | 2 | | | | | |
| 72 | Suffocation | 8 | 5 | | | | | | | 1 | | | | | | | | | | 14 | | | | | |
| 73 | Suicide | | | | | | | | | 1 | | 1 | | | | | | | | | | | 2 | | |
| 74 | Sun stroke | | | | | 1 | | 1 | | 2 | | | | | | | | 1 | | 1 | | 1 | | | |
| 75 | Syphilis | | | | 1 | | | | 2 | 1 | 1 | 2 | | | | | | | | 5 | | | 2 | | |

SECTION OF THE STATE OF LOUISIANA—Continued.

| NATIVITIES. | | | | | SEASON OF DECEASE. | | | | DURATION OF SICKNESS. | | | | WHITES. | | | COLORED. | | | | | | | | | |
|---|---|---|---|---|---|---|---|---|---|---|---|---|---|---|---|---|---|---|---|---|---|---|---|---|---|
| | | | | | | | | | | | | | | | | Slaves. | | | | Free. | | | | | |
| | | | | | | | | | | | | | | | | Black. | | Mulatto. | | Black. | | Mul. | | | |
| California and Territories. | Ireland. | Germany. | Other foreign countries. | Unknown. | Spring. | Summer. | Autumn. | Winter. | Under 1 week. | 1 week and under 1 month. | 1 month and under 3 months. | 3 months and over. | Males. | Females. | Total. | M. | F. | M. | F. | M. | F. | M | F. | Aggregate deaths. | |
| | | | | | 4 | | 1 | 1 | 1 | 2 | 1 | 2 | 3 | 1 | 4 | | 2 | | | | | | | 6 | 1 |
| | | 1 | | | 4 | 4 | 2 | 2 | | | 1 | 8 | 1 | 4 | 5 | 4 | 2 | | | | | | 1 | 12 | 2 |
| | | 1 | 2 | | 14 | 3 | 7 | 16 | 9 | 21 | 8 | 1 | 2 | 4 | 6 | 16 | 15 | 2 | 1 | | | | | 40 | 3 |
| | 1 | | | | 12 | 8 | 12 | 13 | 21 | 19 | 4 | | | 27 | 27 | | 16 | | 1 | | | | 1 | 45 | 4 |
| | 5 | 8 | 16 | | 222 | 622 | 180 | 175 | 1091 | 54 | 3 | | 123 | 88 | 211 | 601 | 339 | 27 | 18 | 2 | 3 | 3 | 1 | 1205 | 5 |
| | | | | | 2 | 4 | 2 | | 4 | 2 | 2 | | 1 | 1 | 2 | 3 | 2 | | 1 | | | | | 8 | 6 |
| | | | 1 | | 1 | | 1 | | 2 | | | | 1 | | 1 | | 1 | | | | | | | 2 | 7 |
| | | | | | | 1 | | | | | | 1 | | | | | 1 | | | | | | | 1 | 8 |
| | | | | | | 2 | 1 | 3 | 5 | | | | 3 | 1 | 4 | 1 | 1 | | | | | | | 6 | 9 |
| | | | | | 1 | 2 | 3 | 1 | 6 | | 1 | | 4 | 1 | 5 | 2 | | | | | | | | 7 | 10 |
| | 3 | 3 | 3 | | 42 | 37 | 47 | 33 | 4 | 5 | 17 | 120 | 43 | 35 | 78 | 33 | 45 | 1 | 1 | | | | 1 | 159 | 11 |
| | | | 1 | | 17 | 13 | 17 | 15 | 53 | 7 | 1 | | 14 | 13 | 27 | 18 | 14 | 2 | | | | 2 | | 63 | 12 |
| | | | | | 14 | 8 | 6 | 8 | 27 | 9 | | | 11 | 8 | 19 | 11 | 6 | | | | | | | 36 | 13 |
| | | | | | | | | 1 | 1 | | | | | | | 1 | | | | | | | | 1 | 14 |
| | 1 | 1 | 5 | | 11 | 14 | 23 | 10 | 7 | 17 | 12 | 22 | 15 | 5 | 20 | 19 | 13 | 1 | 4 | | | | 1 | 58 | 15 |
| | | | | | 4 | 10 | 7 | 1 | 1 | 1 | | 16 | | | | 9 | 12 | 1 | | | | | | 22 | 16 |
| | 1 | 2 | 3 | | 17 | 32 | 30 | 30 | 2 | 11 | 33 | 53 | 19 | 9 | 28 | 42 | 34 | 1 | 2 | 1 | | | 1 | 109 | 17 |
| | 1 | 1 | 2 | | 18 | 27 | 16 | 14 | 10 | 42 | 6 | 17 | 22 | 10 | 32 | 20 | 19 | 2 | 2 | | | | | 75 | 18 |
| | | | | | | | 1 | 1 | | | | 2 | 1 | 1 | 2 | | | | | | | | | 2 | 19 |
| | | 1 | 1 | | 3 | 5 | 4 | 6 | 13 | 2 | | 2 | 5 | 4 | 9 | 6 | 3 | | | | | | | 18 | 20 |
| | | | | 1 | | 1 | | 2 | | | 2 | 1 | | 2 | 2 | 1 | | | | | | | | 3 | 21 |
| | | | | | | | 1 | | 1 | | | | | | | 1 | | | | | | | | 1 | 22 |
| | 1 | 3 | 1 | | 56 | 102 | 151 | 36 | 74 | 134 | 19 | 6 | 58 | 57 | 115 | 98 | 90 | 15 | 16 | | | 5 | 6 | 345 | 23 |
| | 1 | | | | 2 | 2 | 8 | 3 | 5 | 8 | 2 | | 7 | 5 | 12 | 1 | 1 | | | | | | 1 | 15 | 24 |
| | | | | | 3 | 11 | 22 | 4 | 19 | 21 | | | 15 | 8 | 23 | 12 | 4 | | 1 | | | | | 40 | 25 |
| | 1 | | | | | | 2 | | | 2 | | | 2 | | 2 | | | | | | | | | 2 | 26 |
| | | | | | | | | 1 | | 1 | | | | | | | 1 | | | | | | | 1 | 27 |
| | | | | | 7 | 1 | 4 | 5 | 9 | 5 | 2 | | 3 | 8 | 11 | 6 | | | | | | | | 17 | 28 |
| | | | | | 12 | 13 | 14 | 3 | 5 | 30 | 5 | 2 | 11 | 10 | 21 | 15 | 6 | | | | | | | 42 | 29 |
| | | | | | | 1 | | 2 | 1 | 2 | | | 3 | | 3 | | | | | | | | | 3 | 30 |
| | | | | | 1 | | | | | | | 1 | 1 | | 1 | | | | | | | | | 1 | 31 |
| | | | | | | 1 | 1 | | | | | 1 | 2 | | 2 | | | | | | | | | 2 | 32 |
| | | | | | | | 1 | 1 | | 2 | | | 1 | 1 | 2 | | | | | | | | | 2 | 33 |
| | | | 1 | | 9 | 6 | 3 | 4 | 5 | 5 | 3 | 7 | 2 | 3 | 5 | 6 | 10 | | 1 | | | | | 22 | 34 |
| | | | | | 1 | 1 | 2 | 1 | 2 | 1 | 1 | 1 | 1 | | 1 | 2 | 2 | | | | | | | 5 | 35 |
| | | | | | 2 | | 2 | 1 | 1 | 1 | 1 | 2 | | | | 3 | 2 | | | | | | | 5 | 36 |
| | | | | | 24 | 32 | 22 | 13 | 12 | 53 | 21 | 4 | 11 | 16 | 27 | 25 | 35 | 2 | | | 2 | | | 91 | 37 |
| | | | | | 1 | 1 | 1 | 3 | 1 | 1 | 1 | 3 | | 1 | 1 | 3 | 1 | | 1 | | | | | 6 | 38 |
| | 1 | | 1 | | 3 | 4 | 5 | 2 | 3 | 5 | | 1 | 3 | 2 | 5 | 5 | 3 | | | | | 1 | | 14 | 39 |
| | | | | | 5 | 6 | 2 | 5 | 5 | 9 | 1 | 3 | 4 | 3 | 7 | 5 | 4 | 1 | 1 | | | | | 18 | 40 |
| | | | | | 11 | 6 | 15 | 5 | 29 | 6 | 2 | | 13 | 7 | 20 | 8 | 6 | 2 | 1 | | | | | 37 | 41 |
| | | 1 | | | | | 2 | 1 | | 1 | 1 | 1 | | 1 | 1 | 1 | 1 | | | | | | | 3 | 42 |
| | | | | | 2 | 1 | 2 | 3 | 4 | 3 | 1 | | | | | 3 | 5 | | | | | | | 8 | 43 |
| | | | | | 2 | | | | | | | 2 | | | | 1 | 1 | | | | | | | 2 | 44 |
| | | | 1 | | 1 | | | 1 | | | 1 | 1 | 2 | | 2 | | | | | | | | | 2 | 45 |
| | | | | | | | | 1 | | 1 | | | | | | 1 | | | | | | | | 1 | 46 |
| | | 1 | | | 1 | 4 | 4 | 5 | 11 | 2 | 1 | | 6 | | 6 | 8 | | | | | | | | 14 | 47 |
| | | | | | 1 | | | | | | | 1 | | | | | 1 | | | | | | | 1 | 48 |
| | | | | | | 2 | 1 | | 3 | | | | 1 | | 1 | | 2 | | | | | | | 3 | 49 |
| | | 2 | | | 6 | 2 | 5 | 3 | 3 | 3 | 2 | 7 | 8 | 2 | 10 | 3 | 1 | 2 | | | | | | 16 | 50 |
| | | | | | 17 | 15 | 7 | 13 | 38 | 9 | | | 3 | 3 | 6 | 22 | 23 | 1 | | | | | | 52 | 51 |
| | 1 | | 1 | | 1 | 1 | | 2 | 1 | | 1 | 2 | 3 | | 3 | 1 | | | | | | | | 4 | 52 |
| | 2 | 1 | 1 | | 1 | 1 | 4 | 1 | 4 | 2 | | 1 | 7 | | 7 | | | | | | | | | 7 | 53 |
| | | | | | | 1 | 2 | | | | | 3 | 1 | | 1 | 2 | | | | | | | | 3 | 54 |
| | | | | | 4 | 4 | 2 | 1 | 5 | 5 | | 1 | | 1 | 1 | 6 | 1 | 2 | 1 | | | | | 11 | 55 |
| | | | | | | | 1 | 1 | 1 | | | 1 | | | | 1 | | | 1 | | | | | 2 | 56 |
| | 1 | | 1 | | 1 | 3 | | 1 | 4 | | | | 3 | | 3 | 1 | | | | | | 1 | | 5 | 57 |
| | | | 19 | | 27 | 17 | 20 | 20 | 8 | 11 | 6 | 5 | 5 | 4 | 9 | 38 | 31 | 1 | 1 | 1 | 1 | | 2 | 84 | 58 |
| | | | 1 | | 1 | 3 | 2 | 3 | 1 | 2 | 1 | 5 | 2 | 1 | 3 | 4 | 2 | | | | | | | 9 | 59 |
| | | | | | | 1 | | 1 | 1 | | | 1 | | 2 | 2 | | | | | | | | | 2 | 60 |
| | | 1 | 1 | | 20 | 7 | 8 | 18 | 15 | 30 | 3 | 2 | 12 | 4 | 16 | 18 | 15 | 1 | 1 | | 1 | 1 | | 53 | 61 |
| | | | 1 | 1 | 28 | 14 | 10 | 19 | 13 | 40 | 6 | 9 | 13 | 5 | 18 | 28 | 21 | 3 | 1 | | | | | 71 | 62 |
| | | | | | 1 | 2 | | 2 | 5 | | | | | | | 2 | 2 | | 1 | | | | | 5 | 63 |
| | | | | | | | 1 | 1 | 1 | 1 | | | 1 | 1 | 2 | | | | | | | | | 2 | 64 |
| | | | | | 2 | 3 | 1 | 4 | | 2 | | 7 | 3 | | 3 | 5 | 2 | | | | | | | 10 | 65 |
| | | | | | | 8 | 1 | 2 | 1 | | 4 | 6 | 1 | | 1 | 5 | 5 | | | | | | | 11 | 66 |
| | 1 | | | | | | | 2 | | | | 2 | | 2 | 2 | | | | | | | | | 2 | 67 |
| | | | | | 1 | 3 | 1 | | 2 | 2 | 1 | | 1 | 1 | 2 | | 3 | | | | | | | 5 | 68 |
| | | | | | 5 | 6 | 1 | | 1 | 10 | 1 | | 1 | 1 | 2 | 4 | 6 | | | | | | | 12 | 69 |
| | | | | | 2 | 5 | 5 | 2 | 14 | | | | 1 | 2 | 3 | 5 | 5 | | | | | | 1 | 14 | 70 |
| | | | | | 1 | | | 1 | | | | 2 | | | | 1 | 1 | | | | | | | 2 | 71 |
| | | | | | 6 | 4 | 1 | 3 | 14 | | | | 1 | 1 | 2 | 5 | 4 | 3 | | | | | | 14 | 72 |
| | | | | | 2 | | | | 2 | | | | 2 | | 2 | | | | | | | | | 2 | 73 |
| | 2 | | 1 | | | 4 | 1 | | 3 | 2 | | | 4 | | 4 | 1 | | | | | | | | 5 | 74 |
| | | | | | 4 | | 1 | 2 | | | 1 | 6 | 1 | | 1 | 2 | 4 | | | | | | | 7 | 75 |

## CLASSIFICATION OF DEATHS IN SOUTHERN

| | Cause of death. | Under 1. M. | Under 1. F. | 1 and under 5. M. | 1 and under 5. F. | 5 and under 10. M. | 5 and under 10. F. | 10 and under 20. M. | 10 and under 20. F. | 20 and under 50. M. | 20 and under 50. F. | 50 and under 80. M. | 50 and under 80. F. | 80 and under 100. M | 80 and under 100. F. | 100 & over. M | 100 & over. F. | Age unknown. M | Age unknown. F. | Born in State. | N. England States. | Middle States. | Southern States. | Southwest'n States. | Northwest'n States. |
|---|---|---|---|---|---|---|---|---|---|---|---|---|---|---|---|---|---|---|---|---|---|---|---|---|---|
| 1 | Teething | 8 | 12 | 26 | 5 | 1 | | | | | | | | | | | | | | 52 | | | | | |
| 2 | Throat, disease of | 1 | 1 | | | | | | | | 2 | | | | | | | | | 3 | | | | | |
| 3 | Uterus.....do | | | | | | | | | | 1 | | 1 | | | | | | | 2 | | | | | |
| 4 | Worms | 4 | 4 | 50 | 43 | 12 | 15 | 1 | 2 | | | | 1 | | | | | | | 127 | | | 4 | | |
| 5 | Unknown | 47 | 40 | 64 | 57 | 15 | 12 | 18 | 38 | 122 | 75 | 57 | 31 | 3 | 1 | 1 | | | | 495 | | 7 | 39 | 14 | 10 |
| | Total | 210 | 196 | 398 | 371 | 188 | 120 | 195 | 202 | 966 | 578 | 291 | 174 | 44 | 30 | 7 | 9 | 1 | .. | 3139 | 12 | 79 | 396 | 119 | 89 |

## CLASSIFICATION OF DEATHS IN CITY SECTION, EMBRACING THE PAR

| | Cause of death. | Under 1. M. | Under 1. F. | 1 and under 5. M. | 1 and under 5. F. | 5 and under 10. M. | 5 and under 10. F. | 10 and under 20. M. | 10 and under 20. F. | 20 and under 50. M. | 20 and under 50. F. | 50 and under 80. M. | 50 and under 80. F. | 80 and under 100. M | 80 and under 100. F. | 100 & over. M | 100 & over. F. | Age unknown. M | Age unknown. F. | Born in State. | N. England States. | Middle States. | Southern States. | Southwest'n States. | Northwest'n States. |
|---|---|---|---|---|---|---|---|---|---|---|---|---|---|---|---|---|---|---|---|---|---|---|---|---|---|
| 1 | Abscess | | | | | | | | | 3 | | | | | | | | | | | | | | | 1 |
| 2 | Accident, not specif'd | 1 | 2 | | 1 | 2 | 1 | 4 | | 22 | 1 | 6 | | | | | | | | 16 | 1 | 1 | 8 | | |
| 3 | ....do...burned | | 1 | 2 | 1 | | 4 | | 2 | 1 | 1 | 1 | 1 | | | | | | | 7 | | 1 | 1 | | 2 |
| 4 | ....do...drowned | | | | | 2 | 1 | 4 | | 16 | | 2 | 1 | | | | | | | 8 | | | 2 | | 1 |
| 5 | ....do...scalded | | | | | | | | | 4 | | | | | | | | | | | | | | | |
| 6 | ....do...expl. steam | | | | | | | | | 11 | | | | | | | | | | | | 6 | 1 | | |
| 7 | ....do...shot | | | | | | | | | 1 | | | | | | | | | | | | | | | |
| 8 | ....do...railroad | | | | | | | | | | 1 | | | | | | | | | 1 | | | | | |
| 9 | Amputation | | | | | | | | | 3 | | | | | | | | | | | | | | | 1 |
| 10 | Aneurism | | | | | | | | | 1 | | | | | | | | | | | | | | | |
| 11 | Apoplexy | | | | | | | | | 16 | 6 | 7 | 6 | | | | | | | 13 | 2 | 1 | 2 | | |
| 12 | Asthma | | 1 | | | | | | | 2 | | 1 | | | 2 | | | | | 2 | | | 1 | | |
| 13 | Bladder, disease of | | | | | | | 1 | | 2 | | | | | | | | | | | | | | | |
| 14 | Bowels.......do | 5 | 1 | 3 | | | | 2 | 1 | 3 | | | 1 | | | | | | | 9 | | | | 1 | |
| 15 | Brain........do | 1 | | | | | | 1 | | 1 | 3 | 2 | | | | | | | | 1 | | | | | |
| 16 | Bronchitis | | | | | | | | | 7 | 3 | | | | | | | | | | | 1 | 1 | | |
| 17 | Cancer | | | | | | | | 1 | 2 | 3 | 2 | 3 | | | | | | | 4 | | | | 1 | |
| 18 | Catarrh | 3 | 1 | 1 | | | | | | 4 | | | 2 | | | | | | | 7 | | | 1 | | |
| 19 | Childbirth | | | | | | | | 3 | | 21 | | | | | | | | | 5 | | 1 | 4 | 1 | |
| 20 | Cholera | 11 | 13 | 50 | 30 | 27 | 22 | 50 | 29 | 427 | 169 | 66 | 26 | | | | | | | 195 | 11 | 45 | 63 | 18 | 22 |
| 21 | ...do..infantum | 2 | 2 | | 3 | | | | | | | | | | | | | | | 6 | | | | | |
| 22 | ...do..morbus | | | | 1 | | | 1 | | | | 1 | | | | | | | | 2 | | | | | |
| 23 | Colic | 1 | | 1 | 1 | | | | | 5 | | | 1 | | | | | | | 3 | 1 | 1 | 1 | | |
| 24 | Congest'n, not specf'd | | | | | | 1 | | 1 | | | | | | | | | | | 1 | | | 1 | | |
| 25 | ....do....bowels | | | | | | | | | 1 | | | | | | | | | | 1 | | | | | |
| 26 | ....do....brain | 1 | 3 | | 2 | | | 1 | 1 | 13 | 1 | 4 | | | | | | | | 8 | | 2 | 2 | | |
| 27 | ....do....lungs | 1 | | | 1 | | | | | | 2 | | | | | | | | | 2 | | | 1 | | |
| 28 | Consumption | 1 | 1 | 7 | 5 | 3 | 2 | 14 | 13 | 198 | 83 | 23 | 11 | | | | | 1 | | 66 | 11 | 20 | 31 | 6 | 9 |
| 29 | Convulsions | 21 | 16 | 16 | 7 | 3 | | | 1 | 4 | 1 | | | | | | | | | 61 | | 2 | | 1 | 1 |
| 30 | Cramp | | 1 | 1 | 2 | | | | | | | | | | | | | | | 4 | | | | | |
| 31 | Croup | 6 | 6 | 12 | 6 | 1 | | | | | | | | | | | | | | 27 | 2 | 1 | | | |
| 32 | Debility | 4 | 3 | 2 | 1 | 1 | | 1 | | 7 | 3 | 1 | | | | | | | | 10 | 1 | 1 | | | |
| 33 | Diarrhœa | | 4 | 4 | 3 | 2 | 2 | 5 | 1 | 107 | 21 | 9 | 8 | | | | | | | 17 | 4 | 4 | 6 | 1 | 2 |
| 34 | Dropsy | 1 | 1 | 2 | | | 1 | 1 | | 42 | 9 | 7 | 10 | 1 | | | | | | 14 | 3 | 8 | | | |
| 35 | Dysentery | 4 | 4 | 12 | 4 | 2 | 1 | 4 | 3 | 82 | 14 | 8 | 4 | | | | | | 1 | 32 | 1 | 5 | 4 | 1 | 2 |
| 36 | Dyspepsia | | | | | | | | | 1 | | | 1 | | | | | | | | | | 1 | | |
| 37 | Epilepsy | | | | | | | 1 | | 5 | 3 | 1 | | | | | | | | 1 | | 1 | 1 | | |
| 38 | Erysipelas | | | | | | | | | 1 | 1 | | | | | | | | | | | | | | |
| 39 | Fever, not specified | 6 | 3 | 5 | 6 | 1 | 3 | 4 | 5 | 36 | 11 | 7 | 10 | | | | | | | 39 | | 3 | 4 | 1 | 1 |
| 40 | ..do..brain | 7 | 8 | 10 | 16 | 5 | 4 | 1 | 2 | 8 | 2 | 1 | | | | | | | | 52 | | 1 | 1 | 1 | |
| 41 | ..do..bilious | | | 1 | | 1 | | | 2 | 8 | 2 | 1 | | | | | | | | 1 | | | 1 | | |
| 42 | ..do..congestive | | | 2 | | 1 | | 2 | 1 | 28 | 7 | 1 | | | | | | | | 6 | 2 | 2 | 1 | | |
| 43 | ..do..intermittent | 1 | | 2 | 1 | | | 2 | 1 | 3 | 1 | 1 | | | | | | | | 5 | | | | | |
| 44 | ..do..puerperal | | | | | | | | | | 5 | | | | | | | | | | | | | | |
| 45 | ..do..remittent | | | | | | | | | 11 | | | | | | | | | | | 2 | 1 | 1 | | 1 |
| 46 | ..do..scarlet | 2 | 1 | 6 | 5 | 9 | 1 | 4 | 3 | 1 | 3 | | | | | | | | | 28 | | 1 | 2 | 1 | |
| 47 | ..do..ship | | | | 2 | | | | 1 | 6 | 7 | 1 | | | | | | | | | | | 1 | | |
| 48 | ..do..typhus | 1 | 1 | 1 | 2 | | 2 | 12 | 6 | 120 | 29 | 5 | 4 | | | | | | | 14 | 1 | 4 | 1 | | 2 |
| 49 | ..do..yellow | 1 | | | | | 1 | 38 | 13 | 439 | 55 | 20 | 1 | | | | | | | 2 | 15 | 17 | 7 | 2 | 6 |
| 50 | Fracture | | | | | | | | | 10 | 1 | 3 | | | | | | | | | | | | | |
| 51 | Gout | | | | | | | | | 2 | 1 | 2 | | | | | | | | 1 | | | 1 | | |
| 52 | Heart, disease of | | | | | | | | | 12 | 4 | 2 | | | | | | | | 5 | 1 | 1 | | | |
| 53 | Heat | | | | | | | 1 | | | | | 1 | | | | | | | 1 | | | | | |
| 54 | Hemorrhage | | | | 1 | | | | | 2 | 2 | | | | | | | | | 2 | | | 1 | | |
| 55 | Hooping cough | 1 | 5 | 3 | 5 | 1 | 1 | | | | | | | | | | | | | 13 | | | | | |
| 56 | Hydrocephalus | | 2 | 1 | 1 | | | | | 1 | | | | | | | | | | 4 | | | | | |
| 57 | Hydrophobia | | | 1 | | | | | | | | | | | | | | | | 1 | | | | | |
| 58 | Inflamat'n, not spe'd | 2 | 2 | 1 | | 1 | 1 | | | 2 | 1 | | 1 | | | | | | | 7 | | 2 | | | |
| 59 | ....do....bowels | 2 | 2 | 7 | 5 | 1 | | | 1 | 21 | 3 | 3 | 2 | | | | | | | 20 | | 1 | 3 | 2 | |
| 60 | ...do....brain | 1 | | 3 | 1 | | | 1 | | 10 | 2 | 1 | | | | | | | | 5 | 2 | | 2 | 1 | |
| 61 | ....do....stomach | | 1 | | | | | | | 2 | 1 | | | | | | | | | 1 | | | | | |

ECTION OF THE STATE OF LOUISIANA—Continued.

| NATIVITIES. | | | | | SEASON OF DECEASE. | | | | DURATION OF SICKNESS. | | | | WHITES. | | | COLORED. Slaves. Black. | | Mulatto. | | Free. Black. | | Mul. | | | |
|---|---|---|---|---|---|---|---|---|---|---|---|---|---|---|---|---|---|---|---|---|---|---|---|---|---|
| ritories. | Ireland. | Germany. | Other foreign countries. | Unknown. | Spring. | Summer. | Autumn. | Winter. | Under 1 week. | 1 week and under 1 month. | 1 month and under 3 months. | 3 months and over. | Males. | Females. | Total. | M. | F. | M. | F. | M. | F. | M | F. | Aggregate deaths. | |
| ... | ... | ... | ... | .. | 8 | 15 | 14 | 15 | 8 | 17 | 18 | 4 | 8 | 1 | 9 | 24 | 15 | 3 | 1 | ... | ... | ... | .. | 52 | 1 |
| ... | ... | ... | 1 | .. | 2 | 1 | ... | 1 | 1 | 2 | 1 | ... | ... | 1 | 1 | 1 | 2 | ... | ... | ... | ... | ... | .. | 4 | 2 |
| ... | ... | ... | ... | .. | ... | 1 | 1 | ... | ... | ... | ... | 2 | ... | ... | ... | ... | 2 | ... | ... | ... | ... | ... | .. | 2 | 3 |
| ... | ... | ... | 1 | .. | 41 | 33 | 36 | 22 | 70 | 36 | 5 | 3 | 5 | 12 | 17 | 58 | 47 | 4 | 5 | ... | ... | ... | 1 | 132 | 4 |
| ... | 3 | 3 | 10 | .. | 136 | 172 | 139 | 120 | 138 | 82 | 33 | 125 | 82 | 76 | 158 | 233 | 164 | 12 | 9 | ... | 1 | .. | 4 | 581 | 5 |
| ... | 29 | 31 | 84 | 2 | 909 | 1363 | 942 | 742 | 1971 | 760 | 288 | 487 | 626 | 471 | 1097 | 1564 | 1102 | 92 | 76 | 5 | 8 | 13 | 23 | 3980 | |

SHES OF JEFFERSON AND ORLEANS, STATE OF LOUISIANA.

| ritories. | Ireland. | Germany. | Other foreign countries. | Unknown. | Spring. | Summer. | Autumn. | Winter. | Under 1 week. | 1 week and under 1 month. | 1 month and under 3 months. | 3 months and over. | Males. | Females. | Total. | Slaves Black M. | Slaves Black F. | Slaves Mulatto M. | Slaves Mulatto F. | Free Black M. | Free Black F. | Free Mul. M | Free Mul. F. | Aggregate deaths. | |
|---|---|---|---|---|---|---|---|---|---|---|---|---|---|---|---|---|---|---|---|---|---|---|---|---|---|
| ... | 1 | 1 | ... | .. | ... | 1 | 1 | 1 | ... | 1 | ... | ... | 3 | ... | 3 | ... | ... | ... | ... | ... | ... | ... | .. | 3 | 1 |
| ... | 3 | 4 | 7 | .. | 8 | 13 | 4 | 15 | 21 | 8 | ... | 1 | 23 | 2 | 25 | 8 | 1 | 1 | 1 | 2 | ... | 1 | 1 | 40 | 2 |
| ... | 1 | 1 | ... | 1 | 5 | ... | 1 | 8 | 6 | 1 | 1 | ... | 2 | 6 | 8 | 1 | 2 | ... | 1 | 1 | ... | .. | 1 | 14 | 3 |
| ... | 6 | 4 | 5 | .. | 6 | 10 | 6 | 4 | ... | ... | ... | ... | 16 | 2 | 18 | 8 | ... | ... | ... | ... | ... | ... | .. | 26 | 4 |
| ... | 2 | ... | ... | 2 | 1 | ... | ... | 3 | ... | ... | ... | ... | 4 | ... | 4 | ... | ... | ... | ... | ... | ... | ... | .. | 4 | 5 |
| ... | 1 | 2 | 1 | .. | 2 | ... | 2 | 7 | 1 | 1 | ... | ... | 10 | ... | 10 | 1 | ... | ... | ... | ... | ... | ... | .. | 11 | 6 |
| ... | ... | ... | 1 | .. | 1 | ... | ... | ... | ... | ... | ... | ... | 1 | ... | 1 | ... | ... | ... | ... | ... | ... | ... | .. | 1 | 7 |
| ... | ... | ... | ... | .. | ... | ... | 1 | ... | 1 | ... | ... | ... | ... | 1 | 1 | ... | ... | ... | ... | ... | ... | ... | .. | 1 | 8 |
| ... | ... | 1 | 1 | .. | ... | 1 | ... | 2 | ... | ... | ... | ... | 3 | ... | 3 | ... | ... | ... | ... | ... | ... | ... | .. | 3 | 9 |
| ... | ... | ... | 1 | .. | ... | 1 | ... | ... | ... | ... | ... | ... | 1 | ... | 1 | ... | ... | ... | ... | ... | ... | ... | .. | 1 | 10 |
| ... | ... | 5 | 11 | 1 | 11 | 14 | 6 | 4 | 22 | 1 | 1 | 1 | 17 | 3 | 20 | 2 | 2 | ... | 1 | 2 | 1 | 2 | 5 | 35 | 11 |
| ... | ... | 1 | 2 | .. | ... | 3 | 2 | 1 | 1 | ... | ... | 4 | 3 | 2 | 5 | ... | ... | ... | ... | ... | 1 | .. | .. | 6 | 12 |
| ... | 2 | 1 | ... | .. | 1 | 2 | ... | ... | ... | ... | ... | ... | 3 | ... | 3 | ... | ... | ... | ... | ... | ... | ... | .. | 3 | 13 |
| ... | 5 | ... | 1 | .. | 2 | 10 | 1 | 3 | 6 | 5 | 3 | ... | 13 | 2 | 15 | ... | ... | ... | 1 | ... | ... | ... | .. | 16 | 14 |
| ... | 1 | ... | 3 | 3 | 2 | 2 | 3 | 1 | 2 | ... | ... | 1 | 4 | 3 | 7 | 1 | ... | ... | ... | ... | ... | ... | .. | 8 | 15 |
| ... | 4 | ... | 4 | .. | 7 | 1 | 1 | 1 | ... | 1 | ... | ... | 7 | 2 | 9 | ... | 1 | ... | ... | ... | ... | ... | .. | 10 | 16 |
| ... | 2 | 3 | 1 | .. | 4 | 1 | 3 | 2 | 1 | ... | ... | 9 | 4 | 5 | 9 | ... | 1 | ... | ... | ... | ... | ... | 1 | 11 | 17 |
| ... | 1 | ... | 1 | 1 | 2 | 4 | 2 | 3 | 3 | 3 | 1 | 4 | 3 | 2 | 5 | 3 | ... | ... | ... | ... | 1 | 2 | .. | 11 | 18 |
| ... | 3 | 5 | 3 | 2 | 1 | 6 | 8 | 9 | 9 | 8 | 2 | 2 | ... | 13 | 13 | ... | 8 | ... | 1 | ... | ... | .. | 2 | 24 | 19 |
| ... | 315 | 96 | 124 | 31 | 324 | 291 | 54 | 244 | 441 | 44 | 2 | 1 | 533 | 218 | 751 | 72 | 48 | 19 | 14 | ... | ... | 7 | 9 | 920 | 20 |
| ... | ... | 1 | ... | .. | 1 | 3 | 1 | 2 | 1 | 4 | ... | 2 | 1 | 5 | 6 | 1 | ... | ... | ... | ... | ... | ... | .. | 7 | 21 |
| ... | ... | ... | 1 | .. | 1 | 2 | ... | ... | 2 | 1 | ... | ... | 2 | ... | 2 | ... | 1 | ... | ... | ... | ... | ... | .. | 3 | 22 |
| ... | ... | 2 | ... | 1 | ... | 4 | 3 | 2 | 5 | 2 | ... | ... | 6 | 2 | 8 | 1 | ... | ... | ... | ... | ... | ... | .. | 9 | 23 |
| ... | ... | ... | ... | .. | 1 | 1 | ... | ... | ... | 1 | ... | 1 | ... | 1 | 1 | ... | ... | ... | 1 | ... | ... | ... | .. | 2 | 24 |
| ... | ... | ... | ... | .. | ... | ... | 1 | ... | 1 | ... | ... | ... | ... | ... | ... | 1 | ... | ... | ... | ... | ... | ... | .. | 1 | 25 |
| ... | 5 | 1 | 5 | 3 | 6 | 5 | 6 | 9 | 8 | 4 | 1 | ... | 16 | 7 | 23 | 2 | ... | ... | ... | 1 | ... | ... | .. | 26 | 26 |
| ... | ... | 1 | ... | .. | 2 | 2 | ... | ... | 2 | 1 | ... | ... | 1 | 2 | 3 | ... | ... | ... | 1 | ... | ... | ... | .. | 4 | 27 |
| ... | 108 | 36 | 69 | 6 | 88 | 90 | 86 | 98 | 4 | 14 | 19 | 184 | 225 | 75 | 300 | 11 | 30 | 4 | 2 | 2 | 3 | 5 | 5 | 362 | 28 |
| ... | 1 | 2 | ... | 1 | 23 | 14 | 18 | 12 | 48 | 14 | 4 | 1 | 36 | 21 | 57 | 3 | 2 | 3 | 1 | ... | ... | 2 | 1 | 69 | 29 |
| ... | ... | ... | ... | .. | 2 | 1 | ... | 1 | 3 | ... | ... | ... | 1 | 2 | 3 | ... | 1 | ... | ... | ... | ... | ... | .. | 4 | 30 |
| ... | ... | 1 | ... | .. | 8 | 11 | 7 | 5 | 25 | 6 | ... | ... | 17 | 9 | 26 | 2 | 3 | ... | ... | ... | ... | ... | .. | 31 | 31 |
| ... | 5 | 2 | 4 | .. | 4 | 6 | 6 | 7 | 1 | 2 | 4 | 6 | 15 | 6 | 21 | ... | ... | ... | ... | ... | ... | 1 | 1 | 23 | 32 |
| ... | 79 | 21 | 26 | 6 | 40 | 39 | 41 | 44 | 4 | 20 | 4 | 10 | 121 | 36 | 157 | 5 | 2 | ... | ... | ... | 1 | 1 | .. | 166 | 33 |
| ... | 25 | 10 | 12 | 3 | 29 | 14 | 14 | 18 | ... | 7 | 8 | 19 | 44 | 17 | 61 | 7 | 2 | ... | 1 | 2 | ... | 1 | 1 | 75 | 34 |
| ... | 60 | 13 | 24 | 1 | 27 | 32 | 37 | 47 | 11 | 15 | 11 | 18 | 102 | 27 | 129 | 8 | 4 | ... | ... | ... | ... | 2 | .. | 143 | 35 |
| ... | ... | ... | 1 | .. | ... | ... | 2 | ... | 1 | 1 | ... | ... | ... | 1 | 1 | 1 | ... | ... | ... | ... | ... | ... | .. | 2 | 36 |
| ... | 1 | 1 | 5 | .. | 2 | 2 | 6 | ... | 1 | ... | 1 | 1 | 7 | 2 | 9 | ... | ... | ... | 1 | ... | ... | ... | .. | 10 | 37 |
| ... | 2 | ... | ... | .. | 1 | 1 | ... | ... | ... | 1 | ... | ... | 1 | 1 | 2 | ... | ... | ... | ... | ... | ... | ... | .. | 2 | 38 |
| ... | 24 | 10 | 13 | 2 | 21 | 24 | 36 | 14 | 32 | 43 | 13 | 5 | 48 | 31 | 79 | 6 | 4 | ... | ... | 5 | 3 | .. | .. | 97 | 39 |
| ... | 2 | 2 | 5 | .. | 15 | 23 | 14 | 12 | 29 | 33 | 2 | ... | 27 | 25 | 52 | 1 | 2 | 2 | ... | ... | ... | 2 | 5 | 64 | 40 |
| ... | 7 | 4 | 2 | .. | 2 | 6 | 7 | ... | 2 | 11 | 1 | ... | 10 | 4 | 14 | 1 | ... | ... | ... | ... | ... | ... | .. | 15 | 41 |
| ... | 19 | 4 | 4 | 4 | 4 | 8 | 20 | 10 | 4 | 7 | 1 | ... | 33 | 5 | 38 | ... | ... | 1 | ... | ... | ... | .. | 3 | 42 | 42 |
| ... | 4 | ... | 3 | .. | 3 | 4 | 4 | 1 | 4 | 3 | ... | 3 | 8 | 3 | 11 | ... | ... | ... | ... | ... | ... | 1 | .. | 12 | 43 |
| ... | 2 | 2 | 1 | .. | 1 | 1 | 3 | ... | ... | ... | ... | ... | ... | 5 | 5 | ... | ... | ... | ... | ... | ... | ... | .. | 5 | 44 |
| ... | 5 | 1 | ... | .. | 1 | 2 | 6 | 2 | ... | 1 | ... | ... | 11 | ... | 11 | ... | ... | ... | ... | ... | ... | ... | .. | 11 | 45 |
| ... | 1 | 2 | ... | .. | 3 | 25 | 1 | 6 | 23 | 9 | 2 | 1 | 12 | 8 | 20 | 9 | 3 | ... | 2 | 1 | ... | ... | .. | 35 | 46 |
| ... | 13 | 1 | 2 | .. | 9 | 2 | ... | 6 | 9 | 7 | 1 | ... | 7 | 9 | 16 | ... | 1 | ... | ... | ... | ... | ... | .. | 17 | 47 |
| ... | 125 | 13 | 23 | .. | 55 | 42 | 32 | 54 | 8 | 12 | 3 | ... | 135 | 42 | 177 | 2 | 1 | ... | ... | ... | ... | 2 | 1 | 183 | 48 |
| ... | 247 | 117 | 142 | 13 | 1 | 12 | 449 | 101 | 34 | 45 | 2 | ... | 497 | 70 | 567 | ... | ... | 1 | ... | ... | ... | ... | .. | 568 | 49 |
| ... | 4 | 4 | 1 | 5 | 2 | 2 | 5 | 5 | ... | ... | ... | ... | 10 | 1 | 11 | 3 | ... | ... | ... | ... | ... | ... | .. | 14 | 50 |
| ... | ... | ... | 3 | .. | 1 | 1 | 3 | ... | ... | 1 | ... | 4 | 3 | ... | 3 | ... | 1 | ... | ... | ... | ... | 1 | .. | 5 | 51 |
| ... | 5 | 1 | 5 | .. | 4 | 6 | 4 | 4 | 3 | 2 | 1 | 3 | 11 | 3 | 14 | 2 | ... | ... | ... | ... | ... | 1 | 1 | 18 | 52 |
| ... | ... | 1 | ... | .. | 1 | 1 | ... | ... | 1 | 1 | ... | ... | 1 | ... | 1 | ... | ... | ... | ... | ... | ... | ... | 1 | 2 | 53 |
| ... | 2 | ... | ... | .. | 3 | .. | 2 | ... | 2 | 1 | ... | ... | 2 | 2 | 4 | ... | 1 | ... | ... | ... | ... | ... | .. | 5 | 54 |
| ... | 1 | 2 | ... | .. | 6 | 7 | 2 | 1 | 2 | 6 | 5 | 3 | 4 | 10 | 14 | 1 | 1 | ... | ... | ... | ... | ... | .. | 16 | 55 |
| ... | ... | ... | 1 | .. | ... | 3 | 1 | ... | 2 | 1 | ... | ... | 2 | 3 | 5 | ... | ... | ... | ... | ... | ... | ... | .. | 5 | 56 |
| ... | ... | ... | ... | .. | ... | 1 | ... | ... | 1 | ... | ... | ... | ... | ... | ... | ... | ... | ... | ... | ... | ... | 1 | .. | 1 | 57 |
| ... | 1 | 1 | ... | .. | 2 | 4 | 3 | 1 | 3 | 5 | ... | ... | 6 | 3 | 9 | ... | 1 | ... | ... | ... | ... | ... | 1 | 11 | 58 |
| ... | 14 | 1 | 4 | 2 | 5 | 15 | 16 | 11 | 10 | 9 | 7 | 4 | 27 | 13 | 40 | 4 | ... | 1 | ... | ... | ... | 2 | .. | 47 | 59 |
| ... | 6 | 1 | 2 | .. | 7 | 4 | 5 | 3 | 4 | 1 | 1 | 1 | 14 | 3 | 17 | 1 | ... | 1 | ... | ... | ... | ... | .. | 19 | 60 |
| ... | 3 | ... | ... | .. | 2 | 2 | ... | ... | ... | 1 | ... | ... | 2 | 2 | 4 | ... | ... | ... | ... | ... | ... | ... | .. | 4 | 61 |

## CLASSIFICATION OF DEATHS IN CITY

| | Cause of Death. | AGES. | | | | | | | | | | | | | | | | | | NATIVITIES. | | | | | |
|---|---|---|---|---|---|---|---|---|---|---|---|---|---|---|---|---|---|---|---|---|---|---|---|---|---|
| | | Under 1. | | 1 and under 5. | | 5 and under 10. | | 10 and under 20. | | 20 and under 50. | | 50 and under 80. | | 80 and under 100. | | 100 & over. | | Age unknown. | | Born in State. | N. England States. | Middle States. | Southern States. | Southwest'n States. | Northwest'n States. |
| | | M. | F. | M. | F. | M. | F. | M. | F. | M. | F. | M. | F. | M | F. | M | F. | M | F. | | | | | | |
| 1 | Influenza | 2 | | | | | | | | | 1 | | | | | | | | | 2 | | | | | |
| 2 | Insanity | | | | | | | | | 1 | 2 | | | | | | | | | 1 | | | | 1 | |
| 3 | Intemperance | | | | | | | | | 5 | 2 | 1 | 1 | | | | | | | 1 | | 2 | 3 | | |
| 4 | Jaundice | | | | | | | | | 7 | | 4 | | | | | | | | 1 | 1 | | | | |
| 5 | Kidneys, disease of | | | | | | | | | 1 | | | 1 | | | | | | | | | | | | |
| 6 | Killed | | | | | | | | 1 | 5 | | | | | | | | | | | | 1 | | | 2 |
| 7 | Leprosy | | | | | | | | | 2 | | | | | | | | | | | | | | | |
| 8 | Lightning | | | | | | | | | 1 | | | | | | | | | | | | | 1 | | |
| 9 | Liver, disease of | | | | | | | | | 14 | 2 | 5 | | | | | | | | 1 | | 3 | | | |
| 10 | Lockjaw | 52 | 33 | 3 | 2 | 1 | 3 | 2 | 1 | 8 | | 1 | 1 | | | | | | | 96 | | | 3 | | |
| 11 | Mania-a-potu | | | | | | | | | 40 | 6 | 3 | | | | | | | | 2 | | 4 | 2 | | 3 |
| 12 | Marasmus | | | 2 | | 1 | | | | 4 | 1 | | | | | | | | | 2 | | 1 | 1 | | 1 |
| 13 | Measles | 2 | 2 | 12 | 15 | 2 | | | 4 | | 1 | | | | | | | | | 30 | | 2 | | | |
| 14 | Mortification | | | | | | 1 | | | 4 | 1 | | | | | | | | | | | | | 1 | |
| 15 | Mumps | 2 | | | | 1 | | | 1 | | | | | | | | | | | 2 | | 1 | | | |
| 16 | Murder | | | | | | | | | 2 | | | | | | | | | | | | 1 | 1 | | |
| 17 | Old age | | | | | | | | | | | 12 | 8 | 9 | 10 | 1 | 1 | | | 18 | | | 3 | | |
| 18 | Paralysis | | | | | | | 1 | | 3 | 1 | 1 | 3 | 1 | | | | | | 1 | | | 2 | | |
| 19 | Peritonitis | | | | | | | | 1 | 5 | 3 | | | | | | | | | 1 | | | 1 | | |
| 20 | Pleurisy | | | | | | | | 1 | 6 | 1 | 3 | | | | | | | | 3 | | | 3 | 1 | |
| 21 | Pneumonia | | 1 | 1 | 1 | | | | | 13 | 5 | | 1 | | | | | 1 | | 4 | | | 2 | 2 | 1 |
| 22 | Poison | | | | 1 | | | | | 1 | | | | | | | | | | 1 | | | | | |
| 23 | Rheumatism | | | | 1 | | | | | 8 | 2 | 4 | 1 | | | | | | | 2 | 1 | | 1 | | |
| 24 | Scrofula | | | | | 1 | | | | 3 | 1 | | | | | | | | | 2 | | | | | |
| 25 | Scurvy | | | | | | 1 | | | | | | | | | | | | | 1 | | | | | |
| 26 | Small pox | | | 2 | 4 | 2 | | 1 | | 22 | 7 | | | | | | | | | 13 | 2 | 1 | 9 | | 1 |
| 27 | Spine, disease of | | | | | | | | | 1 | | | | | | | | | | | | | 1 | | |
| 28 | Stomach..do | | | | 1 | | | | | 2 | | | | | | | | | | 2 | | | | | |
| 29 | Suffocated | 1 | | | | | | | | | | | | | | | | | | 1 | | | | | |
| 30 | Suicide | | | | | | | | | 4 | | | | | | | | | | | | | 1 | | |
| 31 | Summer complaint | 1 | | | | | | | | | | | | | | | | | | 1 | | | | | |
| 32 | Sun, stroke of | | | | 1 | | | | | 14 | 1 | 1 | 1 | | | | | | | 1 | | | 1 | | |
| 33 | Syphilis | | | | | | | | 1 | 3 | 2 | | 1 | | | | | | | 1 | | 2 | | | 1 |
| 34 | Teething | 21 | 21 | 26 | 35 | | | | | | | | | | | | | | | 99 | | 1 | | 1 | 1 |
| 35 | Tetanus | | | | | | | 1 | 1 | 5 | 1 | 1 | | | | | | | | 1 | | | 1 | 1 | |
| 36 | Throat, disease of | 1 | | | | | 1 | | | 1 | 2 | | | | | | | | | 3 | | | | | |
| 37 | Thrush | | 1 | | | | | | | | | | | | | | | | | 1 | | | | | |
| 38 | Tumor | | | 1 | 1 | | | 1 | | | | | | | | | | | | 3 | | | | | |
| 39 | Ulcer | | | | | | | | | 3 | 1 | | | | | | | | | | | | | | 1 |
| 40 | Uterus, disease of | | | | | | | | | | 3 | | 1 | | | | | | | | | | | | |
| 41 | Venereal | | | | | | | | | 1 | 2 | 1 | | | | | | | | 2 | | | 2 | | |
| 42 | White swelling | | | | | | | | | | | 1 | | | | | | | | | | | | | |
| 43 | Worms | | | 1 | 8 | 3 | 2 | | | | | | | | | | | | | 12 | | | | | |
| 44 | Unknown | 26 | 21 | 18 | 22 | 8 | 6 | 12 | 10 | 175 | 61 | 36 | 18 | 1 | 2 | | | 2 | | 135 | 7 | 18 | 18 | 3 | 7 |
| | Total | 195 | 164 | 222 | 205 | 82 | 62 | 173 | 112 | 2078 | 592 | 263 | 131 | 12 | 14 | 1 | 1 | 4 | 1 | 1176 | 71 | 171 | 214 | 48 | 69 |

## CLASSIFICATION OF DEATHS IN

| | Cause of Death. | Under 1. M. | Under 1. F. | 1 and under 5. M. | 1 and under 5. F. | 5 and under 10. M. | 5 and under 10. F. | 10 and under 20. M. | 10 and under 20. F. | 20 and under 50. M. | 20 and under 50. F. | 50 and under 80. M. | 50 and under 80. F. | 80 and under 100. M | 80 and under 100. F. | 100 & over. M | 100 & over. F. | Age unknown. M | Age unknown. F. | Born in State. | N. England States. | Middle States. | Southern States. | Southwest'n States. | Northwest'n States. |
|---|---|---|---|---|---|---|---|---|---|---|---|---|---|---|---|---|---|---|---|---|---|---|---|---|---|
| 1 | Abscess | | | | | | | | | 4 | | 1 | 1 | | | | | | | 2 | | | 1 | | 1 |
| 2 | Accident not specif'd | 6 | 12 | 10 | 8 | 9 | 8 | 11 | 5 | 55 | 12 | 17 | 5 | | | | | | | 94 | 2 | 12 | 28 | 4 | 2 |
| 3 | ...do...burned | 3 | 1 | 14 | 15 | 5 | 16 | 2 | 8 | 3 | 7 | 2 | 1 | | | | | | | 62 | | 1 | 2 | 6 | 8 |
| 4 | ...do...drowned | | | 8 | 6 | 10 | 5 | 21 | 3 | 83 | 12 | 14 | 2 | | | | | | | 90 | 1 | 6 | 21 | 10 | 14 |
| 5 | ...do...expl. steam | | | | | | | | | 11 | | | | | | | | | | | | 6 | 1 | | |
| 6 | ...do...railroad | | | | | | | | | | 1 | | | | | | | | | 1 | | | | | |
| 7 | ...do...scalded | | | | 3 | | | 1 | | 6 | | | | | | | | | | 5 | | | 1 | | |
| 8 | ...do...shot | | | | | | | | | 1 | | | | | | | | | | | | | | | |
| 9 | Amputation | | | | | | | | | 3 | | | | | | | | | | | | | | | 1 |
| 10 | Aneurism | | | | | | | | | 1 | | | | | | | | | | | | | | | |
| 11 | Apoplexy | 1 | | | | 1 | | 1 | 4 | 29 | 13 | 14 | 15 | | 1 | | | | | 40 | 2 | 3 | 9 | 3 | 3 |
| 12 | Asthma | | 1 | 1 | 2 | | | 2 | 1 | 4 | 3 | 3 | 2 | | 2 | | | | | 9 | | | 6 | 1 | 1 |
| 13 | Bladder, disease of | 1 | | | | | | 1 | 1 | 3 | | | | 1 | | | | | | 2 | | | 1 | | |
| 14 | Bowels.....do | 5 | 1 | 3 | | | 1 | 3 | 2 | 4 | 1 | 3 | 2 | | | | | | | 14 | | | 3 | 1 | |
| 15 | Brain...... do | 2 | | | | 2 | | 2 | 3 | 4 | 4 | 2 | | | | | | | | 8 | | | 1 | 1 | |
| 16 | Bronchitis | | 1 | 1 | 1 | 1 | | 1 | | 11 | 7 | 2 | 2 | | | | | | | 12 | | 2 | 3 | 1 | 1 |
| 17 | Cancer | | | | | | | | 2 | 6 | 14 | 6 | 4 | | | | | | | 15 | | | 4 | 2 | 1 |
| 18 | Catarrh | 12 | 15 | 7 | 4 | 2 | 2 | 1 | 4 | 18 | 5 | 9 | 4 | | 1 | | | | | 67 | | 1 | 6 | 4 | |
| 19 | Childbirth | | | | | | | | 15 | | 89 | | 2 | | | | | | | 62 | | 2 | 9 | 11 | 6 |
| 20 | Cholera | 33 | 32 | 221 | 191 | 123 | 83 | 195 | 151 | 1061 | 512 | 195 | 104 | 6 | 3 | | | 22 | 8 | 1537 | 14 | 91 | 373 | 200 | 113 |
| 21 | ...do..infantum | 5 | 3 | 5 | 12 | 1 | 1 | | | | | | | | | | | | | 25 | | | | 1 | |
| 22 | ...do..morbus | | | | 1 | | | 2 | 1 | 2 | | 2 | 1 | | | | | | | 5 | | | 2 | | |

# ECTION OF THE STATE OF LOUISIANA—Continued.

| Nativities: ...ritories. | Nativities: Ireland. | Nativities: Germany. | Nativities: Other foreign countries. | Nativities: Unknown. | Season of decease: Spring. | Season of decease: Summer. | Season of decease: Autumn. | Season of decease: Winter. | Duration of sickness: Under 1 week. | Duration of sickness: 1 week and under 1 month. | Duration of sickness: 1 month and under 3 months. | Duration of sickness: 3 months and over. | Whites: Males. | Whites: Females. | Whites: Total. | Colored: Slaves: Black: M. | Colored: Slaves: Black: F. | Colored: Slaves: Mulatto: M. | Colored: Slaves: Mulatto: F. | Colored: Free: Black: M. | Colored: Free: Black: F. | Colored: Free: Mul.: M | Colored: Free: Mul.: F. | Aggregate deaths. | |
|---|---|---|---|---|---|---|---|---|---|---|---|---|---|---|---|---|---|---|---|---|---|---|---|---|---|
| | | | 1 | | 2 | | | 1 | 3 | | | | | 1 | 1 | 2 | | | | | | | | 3 | 1 |
| | | 1 | | | | 1 | 1 | 1 | 1 | 1 | | 1 | 1 | | 1 | | 2 | | | | | | | 3 | 2 |
| | 1 | 1 | 1 | | | 3 | 2 | 4 | 1 | 4 | 2 | 1 | 2 | 1 | 3 | 4 | 2 | | | | | | | 9 | 3 |
| | 4 | | 5 | | 5 | 4 | | 2 | | 1 | 1 | | 11 | | 11 | | | | | | | | | 11 | 4 |
| | 1 | 1 | | | 1 | | 1 | | | | | | 1 | 1 | 2 | | | | | | | | | 2 | 5 |
| | 1 | 1 | 1 | | 3 | 1 | | 2 | 3 | 2 | | | 5 | 1 | 6 | | | | | | | | | 6 | 6 |
| | | 1 | 1 | | 2 | | | | | | | | 2 | | 2 | | | | | | | | | 2 | 7 |
| | | | | | | | 1 | | | | | | | | | | | 1 | | | | | | 1 | 8 |
| | 4 | 4 | 8 | 1 | 6 | 2 | 7 | 6 | 2 | 2 | 1 | 3 | 19 | 2 | 21 | | | | | | | | | 21 | 9 |
| | 5 | 1 | 2 | | 24 | 22 | 29 | 31 | 92 | 12 | 1 | | 53 | 36 | 89 | 12 | 1 | | | | | 2 | 3 | 107 | 10 |
| | 22 | 2 | 7 | 7 | 19 | 11 | 7 | 12 | 6 | 1 | | | 38 | 6 | 44 | 5 | | | | | | | | 49 | 11 |
| | 2 | | | 1 | 1 | 2 | 3 | 2 | 3 | | 1 | | 7 | | 7 | | 1 | | | | | | | 8 | 12 |
| | 4 | | 2 | | 15 | 21 | 1 | 1 | 6 | 25 | 5 | 1 | 15 | 14 | 29 | 1 | 7 | | | | 1 | | | 38 | 13 |
| | 3 | 1 | 1 | | | 2 | 3 | 1 | | | 1 | | 4 | 1 | 5 | | 1 | | | | | | | 6 | 14 |
| | | 1 | | | 1 | 1 | 1 | 1 | 3 | 1 | | | 1 | 1 | 2 | 1 | | | | | | 1 | | 4 | 15 |
| | | | | | 1 | 1 | | | 2 | | | | 1 | | 1 | 1 | | | | | | | | 2 | 16 |
| | 4 | 1 | 13 | 2 | 13 | 12 | 7 | 9 | 3 | 4 | 4 | 12 | 17 | 12 | 29 | 1 | 3 | 2 | 3 | 1 | | 1 | 1 | 41 | 17 |
| | 3 | | 4 | | 2 | 4 | 3 | 1 | | 2 | | 6 | 4 | 4 | 8 | 2 | | | | | | | | 10 | 18 |
| | 3 | 1 | 3 | | 2 | 2 | 4 | 1 | 1 | | | | 5 | 3 | 8 | | | | | | | | 1 | 9 | 19 |
| | 1 | | 3 | | 3 | 2 | 4 | 2 | 2 | 3 | 3 | | 4 | 1 | 5 | 4 | 1 | | | | | 1 | | 11 | 20 |
| | 11 | 1 | 2 | | 11 | 3 | 2 | 7 | 1 | 6 | 1 | 1 | 13 | 8 | 21 | 2 | | | | | | | | 23 | 21 |
| | 1 | | | | 1 | | | 1 | | 1 | | | 1 | 1 | 2 | | | | | | | | | 2 | 22 |
| | 4 | 1 | 6 | 1 | 2 | 5 | 6 | 3 | | 1 | 2 | 10 | 9 | | 9 | 1 | 3 | | | | | 2 | 1 | 16 | 23 |
| | 2 | | | 1 | 1 | 1 | 2 | 1 | | 1 | 1 | | 2 | 1 | 3 | 1 | | 1 | | | | | | 5 | 24 |
| | | | | | | 1 | | | | | 1 | | | 1 | 1 | | | | | | | | | 1 | 25 |
| | 3 | 4 | 1 | 4 | 11 | 10 | 4 | 12 | 1 | 24 | | 1 | 17 | 6 | 23 | 6 | 8 | 2 | 1 | 1 | | 1 | 1 | 38 | 26 |
| | | | | | | 1 | | | | 1 | | | | | | 1 | | | | | | | | 1 | 27 |
| | | | 1 | | | 1 | 1 | 1 | 3 | | | | | 1 | 1 | 1 | | | | | | 1 | | 3 | 28 |
| | | | | | | | 1 | | | | | | | | | 1 | | | | | | | | 1 | 29 |
| | | | 2 | 1 | | 2 | | 2 | | | | | 3 | | 3 | 1 | | | | | | | | 4 | 30 |
| | | | | | | 1 | | | | | | | | | | 1 | | | | | | | | 1 | 31 |
| | 8 | 4 | 3 | 1 | 1 | 5 | 12 | | 13 | 2 | | | 14 | 2 | 16 | | 1 | 1 | | | | | | 18 | 32 |
| | 1 | | 2 | | 4 | | 2 | 1 | | | | | 3 | 3 | 6 | | | | | | | | 1 | 7 | 33 |
| | | 1 | | | 21 | 38 | 28 | 16 | 31 | 33 | 19 | 20 | 36 | 46 | 82 | 8 | 4 | 2 | 2 | | | 1 | 4 | 103 | 34 |
| | 4 | | 1 | 1 | 2 | 1 | | 6 | 2 | | | | 5 | 2 | 7 | 2 | | | | | | | | 9 | 35 |
| | 1 | | | 1 | | 2 | 1 | 2 | 1 | 1 | | 1 | 2 | 1 | 3 | | | | 1 | | 1 | | | 5 | 36 |
| | | | | | | | | 1 | | 1 | | | | 1 | 1 | | | | | | | | | 1 | 37 |
| | | | | | | | | 3 | | | 1 | 2 | | 1 | 1 | 1 | | 1 | | | | | | 3 | 38 |
| | | | 3 | | 1 | | 1 | 2 | | | | | 3 | 1 | 4 | | | | | | | | | 4 | 39 |
| | 2 | 1 | 1 | | | 4 | | | | | | 1 | | 4 | 4 | | | | | | | | | 4 | 40 |
| | | | | | 3 | | | 1 | | | | 4 | | | | 2 | 2 | | | | | | | 4 | 41 |
| | | | 1 | | 1 | | | | | | | 1 | | | | | | | | | | 1 | | 1 | 42 |
| | | 1 | 1 | | 6 | 6 | 1 | 1 | 6 | 4 | 3 | 1 | 2 | 6 | 8 | 2 | 3 | | 1 | | | | | 14 | 43 |
| | 73 | 57 | 90 | 10 | 81 | 108 | 126 | 98 | 54 | 24 | 9 | 49 | 251 | 106 | 357 | 12 | 14 | 3 | 3 | 4 | 3 | 8 | 14 | 418 | 44 |
| | 1286 | 468 | 690 | 119 | 1006 | 1062 | 1197 | 1014 | 1044 | 522 | 157 | 354 | 2666 | 992 | 3658 | 243 | 171 | 46 | 39 | 22 | 15 | 53 | 65 | 4312 | |

# HE STATE OF LOUISIANA—AGGREGATE.

| Nativities: ...ritories. | Nativities: Ireland. | Nativities: Germany. | Nativities: Other foreign countries. | Nativities: Unknown. | Season of decease: Spring. | Season of decease: Summer. | Season of decease: Autumn. | Season of decease: Winter. | Duration of sickness: Under 1 week. | Duration of sickness: 1 week and under 1 month. | Duration of sickness: 1 month and under 3 months. | Duration of sickness: 3 months and over. | Whites: Males. | Whites: Females. | Whites: Total. | Colored: Slaves: Black: M. | Colored: Slaves: Black: F. | Colored: Slaves: Mulatto: M. | Colored: Slaves: Mulatto: F. | Colored: Free: Black: M. | Colored: Free: Black: F. | Colored: Free: Mul.: M | Colored: Free: Mul.: F. | Aggregate deaths. | |
|---|---|---|---|---|---|---|---|---|---|---|---|---|---|---|---|---|---|---|---|---|---|---|---|---|---|
| | 1 | 1 | | | | 2 | 1 | 3 | | 3 | | 1 | 4 | | 4 | 1 | 1 | | | | | | | 6 | 1 |
| | 3 | 4 | 9 | | 46 | 39 | 31 | 41 | 115 | 18 | 2 | 4 | 37 | 11 | 48 | 65 | 36 | 3 | 2 | 2 | | 1 | 1 | 158 | 2 |
| | 1 | 1 | | 1 | 23 | 11 | 14 | 29 | 43 | 15 | 1 | 1 | 9 | 13 | 22 | 18 | 29 | 1 | 5 | 1 | | | 1 | 77 | 3 |
| | 9 | 5 | 8 | | 46 | 56 | 32 | 29 | 133 | | | | 41 | 8 | 49 | 91 | 19 | 4 | | | | | 1 | 164 | 4 |
| | 1 | 2 | 1 | | 2 | | 2 | 7 | 1 | 1 | | | 10 | | 10 | 1 | | | | | | | | 11 | 5 |
| | | | | | | | 1 | | 1 | | | | | 1 | 1 | | | | | | | | | 1 | 6 |
| | 2 | | | 2 | 2 | 2 | 1 | 5 | 4 | 1 | 1 | | 5 | | 5 | 1 | 3 | 1 | | | | | | 10 | 7 |
| | | | 1 | | 1 | | | | | | | | 1 | | 1 | | | | | | | | | 1 | 8 |
| | | 1 | 1 | | | 1 | | 2 | | | | | 3 | | 3 | | | | | | | | | 3 | 9 |
| | | | 1 | | | 1 | | | | | | | 1 | | 1 | | | | | | | | | 1 | 10 |
| | 1 | 5 | 12 | 1 | 26 | 26 | 16 | 11 | 60 | 8 | 1 | 2 | 25 | 7 | 32 | 16 | 17 | 1 | 2 | 2 | 1 | 2 | 6 | 79 | 11 |
| | | 1 | 3 | | 5 | 5 | 2 | 8 | 4 | 4 | | 11 | 6 | 6 | 12 | 4 | 3 | | 1 | | 1 | | | 21 | 12 |
| | 2 | 1 | 1 | | 3 | 2 | 1 | | 1 | 1 | | 2 | 5 | | 5 | | 1 | | | 1 | | | | 7 | 13 |
| | 5 | | 2 | | 5 | 14 | 8 | 3 | 10 | 8 | 3 | 2 | 14 | 3 | 17 | 4 | 3 | | 1 | | | | | 25 | 14 |
| | 2 | | 4 | 3 | 6 | 3 | 7 | 3 | 4 | 4 | 1 | 3 | 8 | 4 | 12 | 4 | 3 | | | | | | | 19 | 15 |
| | 4 | | 4 | | 15 | 2 | 6 | 4 | 5 | 4 | 2 | 7 | 10 | 7 | 17 | 4 | 4 | 2 | | | | | | 27 | 16 |
| | 2 | 4 | 2 | 2 | 10 | 8 | 7 | 6 | 1 | | 2 | 25 | 7 | 12 | 19 | 5 | 6 | | | | | | 2 | 32 | 17 |
| | 1 | 1 | 3 | 1 | 26 | 12 | 13 | 33 | 33 | 33 | 11 | 5 | 12 | 9 | 21 | 32 | 24 | 3 | 1 | | 1 | 2 | | 84 | 18 |
| | 4 | 5 | 4 | 3 | 23 | 21 | 28 | 33 | 48 | 42 | 7 | 2 | | 55 | 55 | | 44 | | 4 | | | | 3 | 106 | 19 |
| | 323 | 105 | 147 | 37 | 735 | 1284 | 306 | 602 | 2196 | 152 | 6 | 1 | 737 | 338 | 1075 | 1045 | 687 | 62 | 45 | 2 | 4 | 10 | 10 | 2940 | 20 |
| | | 1 | | | 6 | 9 | 9 | 3 | 8 | 11 | 5 | 2 | 2 | 9 | 11 | 8 | 5 | 1 | 2 | | | | | 27 | 21 |
| | | | 2 | | 2 | 5 | 2 | | 7 | 1 | | | 4 | | 4 | 2 | 3 | | | | | | | 9 | 22 |

## CLASSIFICATION OF DEATHS IN

| | Cause of death. | AGES. | | | | | | | | | | | | | | | | | | NATIVITIES. | | | | | |
|---|---|---|---|---|---|---|---|---|---|---|---|---|---|---|---|---|---|---|---|---|---|---|---|---|---|
| | | Under 1. | | 1 and under 5. | | 5 and under 10. | | 10 and under 20. | | 20 and under 50. | | 50 and under 80. | | 80 and under 100. | | 100 & over. | | Age unknown. | | Born in State. | N. England States. | Middle States. | Southern States. | Southwest'n States. | Northwest'n States. |
| | | M. | F. | M. | F. | M. | F. | M. | F. | M. | F. | M. | F. | M | F. | M | F. | M | F. | | | | | | |
| 1 | Chorea | | | | | | | | | | | | 1 | | | | | | | | | | | 1 | |
| 2 | Colic | 3 | | 1 | 2 | | | 1 | | 7 | 1 | 2 | 2 | | | | | | | 9 | 1 | 1 | 3 | 1 | 1 |
| 3 | Congestion, not spe'd | | | | | | 1 | | 1 | | | | | | | | | | | 1 | | | 1 | | |
| 4 | ....do.....bowels | | | | | | | | | 1 | | | | | | | | | | 1 | | | | | |
| 5 | ....do.....brain | 3 | 4 | 1 | 6 | 2 | 2 | 3 | 2 | 17 | 2 | 4 | | | | | | | | 22 | | 3 | 2 | 5 | |
| 6 | ....do.....lungs | 1 | | | 1 | | | | | | 2 | | | | | | | | | 2 | | | 1 | | |
| 7 | Consumption | 4 | 2 | 11 | 14 | 8 | 6 | 22 | 27 | 285 | 181 | 44 | 32 | 3 | 1 | | | 1 | | 222 | 11 | 27 | 85 | 33 | 33 |
| 8 | Convulsions | 33 | 25 | 41 | 28 | 7 | 7 | | 3 | 10 | 4 | 1 | 1 | | | | | | | 148 | | 2 | 1 | 7 | 2 |
| 9 | Cramp | | 1 | 1 | 2 | | | | | | | | | | | | | | | 4 | | | | | |
| 10 | Croup | 42 | 25 | 41 | 28 | 4 | | 1 | 1 | | | | | | | | | | | 127 | 2 | 1 | 3 | 7 | 1 |
| 11 | Debility | 5 | 3 | 2 | 2 | 1 | | 1 | | 7 | 3 | 1 | | | | | | | | 12 | 1 | 1 | | | |
| 12 | Diabetes | | | | | | 1 | | | | | | | | | | | | | 1 | | | | | |
| 13 | Diarrhœa | 13 | 9 | 21 | 27 | 2 | 3 | 10 | 4 | 136 | 32 | 24 | 13 | 2 | | | | | | 107 | 5 | 6 | 22 | 8 | 6 |
| 14 | Dirt eating | 1 | | | | | 1 | 5 | 3 | 20 | 19 | 4 | 1 | | | | | | | 46 | | 1 | 3 | 2 | 2 |
| 15 | Dropsy | 4 | 2 | 22 | 10 | 11 | 7 | 23 | 8 | 98 | 60 | 38 | 31 | 5 | | | | | | 154 | 5 | 17 | 52 | 19 | 11 |
| 16 | Dysentery | 5 | 9 | 21 | 15 | 10 | 1 | 7 | 8 | 105 | 25 | 12 | 7 | | | | | | 1 | 91 | 3 | 5 | 13 | 3 | 9 |
| 17 | Dyspepsia | | | | | | | | | 2 | 1 | | 1 | 1 | | | | | | 2 | | 1 | 1 | | |
| 18 | Epilepsy | | 1 | 2 | 2 | 6 | 3 | 4 | 5 | 9 | 6 | 5 | 2 | | | | | | | 24 | | 3 | 5 | 4 | |
| 19 | Erysipelas | 1 | | 3 | 1 | | | | | 3 | 3 | | | | | | | | | 8 | | | | | |
| 20 | Executed | | | | | | | | | 1 | | | | 1 | | | | | | 1 | | | | 1 | |
| 21 | Eye, disease of | | | 1 | | 1 | | | | | | | | | | | | | | 2 | | | | | |
| 22 | Fever, not specified | 54 | 39 | 97 | 115 | 44 | 46 | 33 | 38 | 120 | 94 | 30 | 30 | 3 | 4 | 1 | | | | 587 | | 9 | 42 | 35 | 18 |
| 23 | ..do..brain | 7 | 8 | 10 | 16 | 5 | 4 | 1 | 2 | 8 | 2 | 1 | | | | | | | | 52 | | 1 | 1 | 1 | |
| 24 | ..do..bilious | 2 | | 10 | 4 | 8 | 5 | 3 | 3 | 14 | 9 | 3 | | | 1 | | 1 | | | 32 | | 1 | 5 | 9 | 2 |
| 25 | ..do..congestive | 4 | 3 | 26 | 14 | 23 | 15 | 13 | 8 | 49 | 19 | 7 | 5 | | | | | | | 101 | 2 | 3 | 20 | 25 | 2 |
| 26 | ..do..intermittent | 1 | 1 | 6 | 4 | 1 | 1 | 4 | 1 | 5 | 1 | 1 | | | | | | | | 17 | | | 1 | | |
| 27 | ..do..puerperal | | | | | | | | 1 | | 17 | | | | | | | | | 4 | | | 5 | | 3 |
| 28 | ..do..remittent | | | | | 1 | 1 | | 1 | 12 | | | | | | | | | | 2 | 2 | 1 | 1 | 2 | 1 |
| 29 | ..do..scarlet | 6 | 2 | 12 | 17 | 14 | 7 | 8 | 7 | 2 | 3 | | | | | | | | | 59 | | 1 | 5 | 9 | 1 |
| 30 | ..do..ship | | | | 2 | | | | 1 | 6 | 7 | 1 | | | | | | | | | | | 1 | | |
| 31 | ..do..typhus | 1 | 1 | 10 | 6 | 2 | 7 | 24 | 21 | 152 | 46 | 11 | 9 | | | | | | | 80 | 3 | 4 | 15 | 17 | 9 |
| 32 | ..do..yellow | 1 | 1 | | | | 2 | 39 | 13 | 443 | 55 | 20 | 1 | | | | | | | 5 | 15 | 17 | 8 | 5 | 6 |
| 33 | Fistula | | | | | | | | | 1 | | | | | | | | | | 1 | | | | | |
| 34 | Fracture | | | | | | | 1 | | 11 | 1 | 4 | | | | | | | | 1 | | | 2 | | |
| 35 | Gout | | | | | | | | | 2 | 1 | 3 | 1 | | | | | | | 3 | | | 1 | | |
| 36 | Gravel | | | | 1 | | | | | 3 | | 1 | | | | | | | | 4 | | | 1 | | |
| 37 | Heart, disease of | | 1 | | 1 | | 2 | 1 | | 19 | 14 | 5 | 6 | | | | | | | 21 | 1 | 3 | 8 | 2 | 2 |
| 38 | Heat | | | | | | | 1 | | | | | 1 | | | | | | | 1 | | | | | |
| 39 | Hemorrhage | 1 | 1 | | 1 | | | 1 | 1 | 12 | 7 | 5 | 1 | | | | | | | 13 | | | 5 | 6 | 8 |
| 40 | Hernia | | | | | | | | 1 | 1 | 1 | 3 | | | | | | | | 4 | | | 1 | 1 | |
| 41 | Hives | 8 | 2 | | 2 | | | | | | | | | | | | | | | 12 | | | | | |
| 42 | Hooping cough | 30 | 39 | 35 | 41 | 12 | 13 | 2 | 3 | 1 | | | | | | | | | | 169 | | | | 1 | |
| 43 | Hydrocephalus | 1 | 4 | 4 | 2 | | | | | 1 | | | | | | | | | | 11 | | | | | |
| 44 | Hydrophobia | | | 1 | | | | | | | | | | | | | | | | 1 | | | | | |
| 45 | Inflamt'n, not specf'd | 2 | 5 | 1 | 1 | 3 | 1 | 2 | 3 | 12 | 8 | 2 | 4 | | | | | | | 30 | | 2 | 2 | 3 | [illegible] |
| 46 | ....do....bowels | 9 | 6 | 16 | 16 | 5 | 2 | 3 | 3 | 26 | 11 | 3 | 4 | 1 | | | | | | 61 | 1 | 3 | 10 | 7 | [illegible] |
| 47 | ....do....brain | 7 | 5 | 19 | 20 | 5 | 8 | 13 | 3 | 27 | 13 | 5 | 1 | | | | | | | 82 | 2 | 2 | 12 | 15 | [illegible] |
| 48 | ....do....stomach | | 1 | 1 | 1 | | 1 | | | 5 | 3 | 1 | 1 | | | | | | | 5 | | | 2 | 1 | [illegible] |
| 49 | Influenza | 3 | 1 | 1 | 3 | 1 | | | | 2 | 2 | 1 | 1 | | | | | | | 10 | | 1 | 1 | 2 | |
| 50 | Insanity | | | | | | | | | 1 | 3 | 1 | | | | | | | | 3 | | | | 1 | |
| 51 | Intemperance | | | | | | | | | 6 | 2 | 4 | 1 | | | | | | | 2 | | 3 | 4 | | |
| 52 | Jaundice | | | | 1 | | 2 | | 1 | 9 | | 4 | | | | | | | | 5 | 1 | | 2 | | |
| 53 | Kidneys, disease of | 1 | | | | | | 1 | | 2 | | | 1 | | | | | | | 1 | | | | 2 | |
| 54 | Killed | 1 | | | | | | 3 | 1 | 30 | 1 | 4 | | | | | | | | 15 | 2 | 2 | 6 | 5 | |
| 55 | Leprosy | | | | | | | | | 2 | 2 | | | | | | | | | 1 | | | | | |
| 56 | Lightning | | | | | | | 1 | 1 | 2 | 1 | | | | | | | | | 4 | | | 1 | | |
| 57 | Liver, disease of | | | 1 | 1 | 3 | | | | 29 | 6 | 7 | 2 | | | | | | | 13 | | 4 | 7 | 3 | |
| 58 | Lockjaw | 82 | 69 | 6 | 9 | 5 | 5 | 4 | 2 | 13 | 3 | 1 | 1 | | | | | | | 187 | | | 4 | | |
| 59 | Lungs, disease of | | | 1 | 1 | | | | | 3 | 3 | 3 | | | | | | | | 7 | | | | | |
| 60 | Mania-a-potu | | | | | | | 1 | | 44 | 6 | 5 | | | | | | | | 4 | | 5 | 2 | | |
| 61 | Marasmus | | 1 | 3 | | 2 | | | | 5 | 1 | | | | | | | | | 6 | | 1 | 1 | | |
| 62 | Measles | 3 | 2 | 23 | 19 | 3 | 1 | 3 | 4 | 1 | 1 | | | | | | | | | 48 | | 2 | 1 | 3 | |
| 63 | Menses, suppress'n of | | | | | | | | 1 | | 1 | | | | | | | | | 1 | | | | 1 | |
| 64 | Mortification | | | | | | 1 | | | 5 | 2 | | | | | | | | | 1 | | | 1 | 1 | |
| 65 | Mumps | 2 | | | | 1 | | | 1 | | | | | | | | | | | 2 | | 1 | | | |
| 66 | Murder | | | | | | | | | 9 | | | | | | | | | | 5 | | 1 | 1 | | |
| 67 | Neuralgia | | | | | | | | | 2 | 1 | 1 | | | | | | | | 1 | | | 1 | 1 | |
| 68 | Old age | | | | | | | | | | | 34 | 27 | 40 | 46 | 11 | 12 | | | 83 | 1 | 8 | 35 | 1 | |
| 69 | Paralysis | | | | | | | 3 | 1 | 5 | 1 | 7 | 4 | 1 | 1 | | 1 | | | 7 | | | 7 | 3 | |
| 70 | Peritonitis | | | | | | | | 1 | 5 | 3 | | | | | | | | | 1 | | | 1 | | |
| 71 | Piles | | | | | | | | | | 1 | | 1 | | | | | | | 1 | 1 | | | | |
| 72 | Pleurisy | 1 | | 4 | 3 | 1 | 2 | 7 | 4 | 38 | 17 | 13 | 8 | | | | | | | 64 | | 2 | 16 | 6 | |
| 73 | Pneumonia | 16 | 7 | 23 | 8 | 8 | 8 | 15 | 12 | 83 | 45 | 30 | 9 | 2 | 1 | | | 1 | | 130 | 2 | 14 | 49 | 28 | [illegible] |
| 74 | Poison | | 1 | | 2 | | 1 | | 1 | 7 | 1 | 1 | | | | | | | | 8 | | | 3 | 2 | |
| 75 | Quinsy | | 1 | 1 | | 1 | 1 | 1 | | 2 | | 2 | | | | | | | | 4 | | | 4 | 1 | |

# THE STATE OF LOUISIANA—AGGREGATE—Continued.

| Nativities: California and Territories. | Nativities: Ireland. | Nativities: Germany. | Nativities: Other foreign countries. | Nativities: Unknown. | Season of decease: Spring. | Season of decease: Summer. | Season of decease: Autumn. | Season of decease: Winter. | Duration of sickness: Under 1 week. | Duration of sickness: 1 week and under 1 month. | Duration of sickness: 1 month and under 3 months. | Duration of sickness: 3 months and over. | Whites: Males. | Whites: Females. | Whites: Total. | Colored: Slaves: Black: M. | Colored: Slaves: Black: F. | Colored: Slaves: Mulatto: M. | Colored: Slaves: Mulatto: F. | Colored: Free: Black: M. | Colored: Free: Black: F. | Colored: Free: Mul.: M | Colored: Free: Mul.: F. | Aggregate deaths. | |
|---|---|---|---|---|---|---|---|---|---|---|---|---|---|---|---|---|---|---|---|---|---|---|---|---|---|
| | | | | | | 1 | | | | | | 1 | | | | | 1 | | | | | | | 1 | 1 |
| | | 2 | | 1 | | 8 | 5 | 6 | 14 | 2 | | | 10 | 3 | 13 | 4 | 2 | | | | | | | 19 | 2 |
| | | | | | | 1 | | | | 1 | | 1 | | 1 | 1 | | | | 1 | | | | | 2 | 3 |
| | | | | | | | 1 | | 1 | | | | | | | 1 | | | | | | | | 1 | 4 |
| | 5 | 1 | 5 | 3 | 9 | 14 | 12 | 11 | 19 | 8 | 3 | | 25 | 14 | 39 | 4 | 2 | | | 1 | | | | 46 | 5 |
| | | 1 | | | 2 | 2 | | | 2 | 1 | | | 1 | 2 | 3 | | | | 1 | | | | | 4 | 6 |
| | 111 | 39 | 73 | 7 | 174 | 157 | 156 | 151 | 12 | 25 | 43 | 351 | 295 | 137 | 432 | 66 | 110 | 10 | 7 | 2 | 3 | 5 | 6 | 641 | 7 |
| | 1 | 2 | 1 | 1 | 46 | 38 | 45 | 33 | 133 | 21 | 5 | 1 | 56 | 40 | 96 | 31 | 26 | 6 | 1 | | | 4 | 1 | 165 | 8 |
| | | | | | 2 | 1 | | 1 | 3 | | | | 1 | 2 | 3 | | 1 | | | | | | | 4 | 9 |
| | | 1 | | | 47 | 38 | 26 | 31 | 105 | 23 | 2 | 4 | 39 | 22 | 61 | 45 | 29 | 4 | 2 | | | | 1 | 142 | 10 |
| | 5 | 2 | 4 | | 4 | 6 | 6 | 9 | 2 | 2 | 4 | 6 | 15 | 6 | 21 | 1 | 1 | | | | | 1 | 1 | 25 | 11 |
| | | | | | | | 1 | | 1 | | | | | 1 | 1 | | | | | | | | | 1 | 12 |
| | 80 | 28 | 33 | 6 | 61 | 70 | 94 | 69 | 32 | 61 | 23 | 52 | 157 | 48 | 205 | 45 | 33 | 5 | 5 | | 1 | 1 | 1 | 296 | 13 |
| | | | | | 12 | 21 | 15 | 6 | 4 | 3 | 2 | 37 | | | | 27 | 23 | 3 | 1 | | | | | 54 | 14 |
| | 26 | 12 | 18 | 5 | 77 | 75 | 83 | 83 | 5 | 25 | 58 | 164 | 94 | 41 | 135 | 97 | 69 | 6 | 6 | 8 | | 1 | 2 | 319 | 15 |
| | 61 | 14 | 26 | 1 | 46 | 61 | 58 | 61 | 21 | 60 | 18 | 36 | 125 | 37 | 162 | 31 | 27 | 2 | 2 | | | 2 | | 226 | 16 |
| | | | 1 | | | 1 | 3 | 1 | 1 | 1 | | 3 | 2 | 2 | 4 | 1 | | | | | | | | 5 | 17 |
| | 1 | 2 | 6 | | 10 | 13 | 13 | 9 | 24 | 4 | 1 | 8 | 14 | 8 | 22 | 12 | 9 | | 2 | | | | | 45 | 18 |
| | 2 | | | 1 | 5 | 3 | | 3 | 2 | 3 | 2 | 3 | 5 | 4 | 9 | 2 | | | | | | | | 11 | 19 |
| | | | | | | | 2 | | 2 | | | | | | | 2 | | | | | | | | 2 | 20 |
| | | | | | | | 2 | | 1 | | | 1 | 1 | | 1 | | | 1 | | | | | | 2 | 21 |
| | 27 | 13 | 14 | 3 | 107 | 212 | 337 | 90 | 236 | 308 | 56 | 16 | 171 | 164 | 335 | 177 | 168 | 24 | 24 | 5 | 3 | 5 | 7 | 748 | 22 |
| | 2 | 2 | 5 | | 15 | 23 | 14 | 12 | 29 | 33 | 2 | | 27 | 25 | 52 | 1 | 2 | 2 | | | | 2 | 5 | 64 | 23 |
| | 8 | 4 | 2 | | 5 | 18 | 36 | 4 | 15 | 40 | 5 | 2 | 30 | 17 | 47 | 10 | 5 | | | | | | 1 | 63 | 24 |
| | 19 | 4 | 5 | 5 | 14 | 42 | 111 | 19 | 103 | 46 | 2 | 5 | 109 | 56 | 165 | 12 | 4 | 1 | 1 | | | | 3 | 186 | 25 |
| | 5 | | 3 | | 5 | 5 | 12 | 4 | 12 | 5 | 2 | 5 | 14 | 5 | 19 | 3 | 3 | | | | | 1 | | 26 | 26 |
| | 2 | 3 | 1 | | 4 | 4 | 5 | 5 | 5 | 7 | 1 | | | 14 | 14 | | 4 | | | | | | | 18 | 27 |
| | 5 | 1 | | | 2 | 3 | 8 | 2 | 1 | 4 | | | 12 | 1 | 13 | 1 | 1 | | | | | | | 15 | 28 |
| | 1 | 2 | | | 13 | 29 | 7 | 28 | 41 | 29 | 5 | 1 | 20 | 21 | 41 | 21 | 13 | | 2 | 1 | | | | 78 | 29 |
| | 13 | 1 | 2 | | 9 | 2 | | 6 | 9 | 7 | 1 | | 7 | 9 | 16 | | 1 | | | | | | | 17 | 30 |
| | 125 | 13 | 23 | 1 | 86 | 77 | 59 | 68 | 22 | 88 | 17 | 3 | 166 | 65 | 231 | 31 | 24 | 1 | | | | 2 | 1 | 290 | 31 |
| | 247 | 117 | 142 | 13 | 2 | 13 | 452 | 103 | 36 | 49 | 3 | | 502 | 71 | 573 | | 1 | 1 | | | | | | 575 | 32 |
| | | | | | 1 | | | | | | | 1 | 1 | | 1 | | | | | | | | | 1 | 33 |
| | 4 | 4 | 1 | 5 | 2 | 4 | 6 | 5 | | 1 | | 1 | 13 | 1 | 14 | 3 | | | | | | | | 17 | 34 |
| | | | 3 | | 1 | 1 | 4 | 1 | | 3 | | 4 | 4 | 1 | 5 | | 1 | | | | | 1 | | 7 | 35 |
| | | | | | | 2 | 1 | 2 | | 1 | 1 | 3 | 1 | 1 | 2 | 2 | | 1 | | | | | | 5 | 36 |
| | 5 | 1 | 6 | | 16 | 12 | 10 | 11 | 12 | 7 | 5 | 12 | 13 | 8 | 21 | 11 | 14 | | 1 | | | 1 | 1 | 49 | 37 |
| | | 1 | | | 1 | 1 | | | 1 | 1 | | | 1 | | 1 | | | | | | | | 1 | 2 | 38 |
| | 2 | | 1 | | 8 | 5 | 7 | 10 | 16 | 6 | 2 | 2 | 6 | 6 | 12 | 12 | 4 | 1 | 1 | | | | | 30 | 39 |
| | | | | | 3 | | 2 | 1 | 1 | 1 | 1 | 2 | | | | 4 | 2 | | | | | | | 6 | 40 |
| | | | | | 5 | 1 | 3 | 3 | 8 | 4 | | | 7 | 4 | 11 | 1 | | | | | | | | 12 | 41 |
| | 1 | 2 | | | 49 | 68 | 31 | 28 | 26 | 99 | 40 | 8 | 25 | 34 | 59 | 51 | 58 | 4 | 2 | | 2 | | | 176 | 42 |
| | | | 1 | | 1 | 4 | 2 | 4 | 3 | 2 | 1 | 4 | 3 | 4 | 7 | 3 | 1 | | 1 | | | | | 12 | 43 |
| | | | | | | 1 | | | 1 | | | | | | | | | | | | | 1 | | 1 | 44 |
| | 2 | 1 | 2 | | 10 | 10 | 15 | 8 | 14 | 17 | 3 | 2 | 13 | 9 | 22 | 8 | 11 | | 1 | | | 1 | 1 | 44 | 45 |
| | 14 | 2 | 4 | 2 | 20 | 30 | 29 | 25 | 32 | 29 | 8 | 16 | 42 | 22 | 64 | 17 | 17 | 2 | 3 | | | 2 | | 105 | 46 |
| | 6 | 1 | 4 | | 37 | 36 | 36 | 17 | 71 | 29 | 5 | 8 | 47 | 31 | 78 | 24 | 17 | 5 | 2 | | | | | 126 | 47 |
| | 4 | 1 | | | 3 | 3 | 7 | 1 | 4 | 4 | 2 | 1 | 5 | 4 | 9 | 2 | 2 | | 1 | | | | | 14 | 48 |
| | | | 1 | | 5 | 2 | 2 | 6 | 8 | 6 | 1 | | 1 | 1 | 2 | 7 | 6 | | | | | | | 15 | 49 |
| | | 1 | | | 2 | 1 | 1 | 1 | 1 | 1 | | 3 | 1 | | 1 | 1 | 3 | | | | | | | 5 | 50 |
| | 1 | 1 | 2 | | 1 | 4 | 3 | 5 | 1 | 4 | 3 | 3 | 5 | 1 | 6 | 4 | 2 | | | | | 1 | | 13 | 51 |
| | 4 | | 5 | | 7 | 4 | | 6 | 1 | 4 | 1 | 2 | 11 | 2 | 13 | 2 | 2 | | | | | | | 17 | 52 |
| | 1 | 1 | | | 2 | | 2 | 1 | | 3 | | | 2 | 1 | 3 | 2 | | | | | | | | 5 | 53 |
| | 1 | 2 | 1 | | 10 | 10 | 8 | 12 | 28 | 4 | 1 | | 28 | 1 | 29 | 10 | | | 1 | | | | | 40 | 54 |
| | | 1 | 1 | | 3 | | | 1 | | | | 2 | 2 | | 2 | | 1 | | 1 | | | | | 4 | 55 |
| | | | | | | 3 | 2 | | 4 | | | | 1 | | 1 | 1 | 2 | 1 | | | | | | 5 | 56 |
| | 4 | 6 | 8 | 1 | 15 | 6 | 17 | 11 | 6 | 8 | 6 | 15 | 33 | 7 | 40 | 5 | 1 | 2 | 1 | | | | | 49 | 57 |
| | 6 | 1 | 2 | | 49 | 49 | 49 | 52 | 147 | 23 | 1 | 1 | 57 | 44 | 101 | 49 | 40 | 2 | 2 | | | 3 | 3 | 200 | 58 |
| | 1 | | 2 | | 3 | 2 | 2 | 4 | 1 | 4 | 1 | 5 | 5 | 3 | 8 | 2 | 1 | | | | | | | 11 | 59 |
| | 24 | 3 | 8 | 7 | 20 | 12 | 11 | 13 | 10 | 3 | | 1 | 45 | 6 | 51 | 5 | | | | | | | | 56 | 60 |
| | 2 | | | 1 | 1 | 4 | 5 | 2 | 3 | | 1 | 4 | 8 | 1 | 9 | 2 | 1 | | | | | | | 12 | 61 |
| | 4 | | 2 | | 21 | 32 | 4 | 3 | 17 | 34 | 6 | 2 | 19 | 15 | 34 | 12 | 10 | 2 | 1 | | 1 | | | 60 | 62 |
| | | | | | | | 1 | 1 | | 1 | | 1 | | 1 | 1 | | 1 | | | | | | | 2 | 63 |
| | 8 | 1 | 1 | | | 2 | 4 | 2 | 1 | | 1 | 1 | 4 | 1 | 5 | 1 | 1 | | 1 | | | | | 8 | 64 |
| | | 1 | | | 1 | 1 | 1 | 1 | 3 | 1 | | | 1 | 1 | 2 | 1 | | | | | | 1 | | 4 | 65 |
| | 1 | | 1 | | 3 | 5 | | 1 | 6 | | | | 5 | | 5 | 3 | | | | | | 1 | | 9 | 66 |
| | | | | | | | | 3 | 1 | 2 | | | 2 | | 2 | 1 | | | | | | | | 3 | 67 |
| | 4 | 1 | 33 | 4 | 49 | 40 | 37 | 42 | 17 | 19 | 12 | 21 | 24 | 23 | 47 | 54 | 51 | 3 | 6 | 2 | 2 | 2 | 3 | 170 | 68 |
| | 3 | | 5 | | 5 | 8 | 7 | 5 | 3 | 7 | 1 | 12 | 9 | 6 | 15 | 8 | 2 | | | | | | | 25 | 69 |
| | 3 | 1 | 3 | | 2 | 2 | 4 | 1 | 1 | | | | 5 | 3 | 8 | | | | | | | | 1 | 9 | 70 |
| | | | | | | 1 | | 1 | 1 | | | 1 | | 2 | 2 | | | | | | | | | 2 | 71 |
| | 1 | 1 | 5 | | 37 | 14 | 14 | 33 | 25 | 54 | 8 | 4 | 26 | 9 | 35 | 34 | 22 | 2 | 2 | | 1 | 2 | | 98 | 72 |
| | 12 | 1 | 4 | 2 | 112 | 32 | 52 | 72 | 69 | 136 | 17 | 19 | 85 | 42 | 127 | 83 | 44 | 10 | 4 | | | | | 268 | 73 |
| | 1 | | | | 4 | 3 | 4 | 3 | 9 | 2 | | 1 | 2 | 2 | 4 | 6 | 3 | | 1 | | | | | 14 | 74 |
| | | | | | 2 | | 3 | 4 | 6 | 3 | | | 6 | 2 | 8 | 1 | | | | | | | | 9 | 75 |

## CLASSIFICATION OF DEATHS IN

| | Cause of death. | Ages. | | | | | | | | | | | | | | | | | | Nativities. | | | | | |
|---|---|---|---|---|---|---|---|---|---|---|---|---|---|---|---|---|---|---|---|---|---|---|---|---|---|
| | | Under 1. | | 1 and under 5. | | 5 and under 10. | | 10 and under 20. | | 20 and under 50. | | 50 and under 80. | | 80 and under 100. | | 100 & over. | | Age unknown. | | Born in State. | N. England States. | Middle States. | Southern States. | Southwest'n States. | Northwest'n States. |
| | | M. | F. | M. | F. | M. | F. | M. | F. | M. | F. | M. | F. | M | F. | M | F. | M | F. | | | | | | |
| 1 | Rheumatism | | | | 1 | | 1 | | 1 | 15 | 3 | 7 | 5 | | | | | | | 12 | 1 | | 7 | 1 | |
| 2 | Rickets | | 1 | 1 | 1 | | | 1 | | | | | | | | | | | | 3 | | | | 1 | |
| 3 | Salivation, effects of | | | | | | 1 | | | 1 | | | 1 | | | | | | | 1 | | | 1 | 1 | |
| 4 | Scrofula | 2 | 1 | 5 | 3 | 2 | 1 | 2 | | 6 | 3 | 2 | | | | | | | | 18 | | | 4 | 2 | |
| 5 | Scurvy | | | | | | 1 | | | | 1 | 1 | 1 | | | | | | | 2 | | | | | 1 |
| 6 | Skin, disease of | 1 | 3 | | 1 | | | | | | | | | | | | | | | 5 | | | | | |
| 7 | Small pox | | 1 | 3 | 7 | 2 | | 2 | 2 | 28 | 12 | | | | | | | | | 28 | 2 | 1 | 10 | 3 | 1 |
| 8 | Spine, disease of | | | | | | | | | 1 | 1 | | | | | | | | | 1 | | | 1 | | |
| 9 | Stillborn | 6 | 9 | | | | | | | | | | | | | | | | | 15 | | | | | |
| 10 | Stomach, disease of | | 1 | | 1 | 1 | | | | 2 | | 1 | | | | | | | | 5 | | | | | |
| 11 | Suffocation | 22 | 12 | 2 | 1 | | | | | 1 | | | | | | | | | | 37 | | | | 1 | |
| 12 | Suicide | | | | | | | | | 7 | 1 | 2 | | | | | | | | 3 | | | 4 | | |
| 13 | Summer complaint | 1 | | | | | | | | | | | | | | | | | | 1 | | | | | |
| 14 | Sun stroke | | | | 1 | 1 | | 1 | | 16 | 1 | 1 | 1 | | | | | 1 | | 2 | | 1 | 1 | | |
| 15 | Syphilis | | | | 1 | | | | 3 | 4 | 3 | 2 | 1 | | | | | | | 6 | | 2 | 2 | | 1 |
| 16 | Teething | 35 | 34 | 59 | 49 | 1 | | | | | | | | | | | | | | 174 | | 1 | | 1 | 1 |
| 17 | Tetanus | 2 | 2 | | | 1 | | 1 | 1 | 6 | 1 | 1 | | | | | | | | 7 | | | 1 | 1 | |
| 18 | Throat, disease of | 3 | 2 | | | 1 | 1 | | | 1 | 4 | | | | | | | | | 9 | | | | | |
| 19 | Thrush | 3 | 1 | | 2 | | | | | | | | | | | | | | | 6 | | | | | |
| 20 | Tumor | | | 1 | 1 | | | 1 | | | | | | | | | | | | 3 | | | | | |
| 21 | Ulcer | | | | | 1 | | | | 5 | 1 | 1 | | | | | | | | 1 | | | 2 | | 2 |
| 22 | Uterus, disease of | | | | | | | | | | 7 | | 2 | | | | | | | 4 | | | 1 | | |
| 23 | Venereal | | | 1 | 1 | | | | | 2 | 4 | 1 | | | | | | | | 6 | | | 2 | 1 | |
| 24 | White swelling | | | | | | | | | | | 1 | | | | | | | | | | | | | |
| 25 | Worms | 9 | 16 | 105 | 101 | 22 | 27 | 2 | 2 | 2 | | 1 | 1 | | | | | | | 267 | | | 9 | 6 | 1 |
| 26 | Unknown | 194 | 145 | 144 | 130 | 38 | 31 | 47 | 63 | 355 | 207 | 111 | 71 | 7 | 3 | 1 | | 12 | 8 | 1097 | 7 | 29 | 89 | 56 | 34 |
| | Total | 709 | 576 | 1070 | 993 | 424 | 347 | 565 | 474 | 3699 | 1682 | 761 | 438 | 73 | 64 | 13 | 14 | 37 | 17 | 6728 | 90 | 317 | 1092 | 613 | 339 |

## CLASSIFICATION OF DEATHS IN NORTHERN

*Embracing the following counties: Aroostook, Franklin,*

| | Cause of death. | Under 1 M. | Under 1 F. | 1–5 M. | 1–5 F. | 5–10 M. | 5–10 F. | 10–20 M. | 10–20 F. | 20–50 M. | 20–50 F. | 50–80 M. | 50–80 F. | 80–100 M | 80–100 F. | 100 & over M | 100 & over F. | Age unknown M | Age unknown F. | Born in State. | N. England States. | Middle States. | Southern States. | Southwest'n States. | Northwest'n States. |
|---|---|---|---|---|---|---|---|---|---|---|---|---|---|---|---|---|---|---|---|---|---|---|---|---|---|
| 1 | Abscess | | | 1 | | 1 | | | | | | | 2 | | | | | | | 3 | 1 | | | | |
| 2 | Accident, not specif'd | | | 3 | 1 | 3 | 1 | 5 | 2 | 10 | | 1 | | | 2 | | | 1 | | 21 | 3 | | | | |
| 3 | ....do...burned | 1 | | 1 | 3 | | | | | | 1 | | | | | | | | | 5 | | | | | |
| 4 | ....do...drowned | | | 2 | 1 | 4 | | 4 | 2 | 7 | | 2 | | | | | | | | 21 | 1 | | | | |
| 5 | ....do...scalded | | 1 | 1 | 1 | | 1 | | | | | | | | | | | | | 4 | | | | | |
| 6 | ....do...suffocated | | | | | | 1 | | | | | | | | | | | | | 1 | | | | | |
| 7 | Apoplexy | | | | | | | | | | | 3 | 2 | 1 | 1 | | | | | 4 | 2 | | | | |
| 8 | Asthma | | | | | | | | | | | | | | 1 | | | | | | 1 | | | | |
| 9 | Bowels, disease of | 1 | | 2 | 4 | | | 2 | 2 | 1 | 1 | 1 | 1 | | | | | | | 15 | | | | | |
| 10 | Bronchitis | | | | | | | | | | 1 | | | | | | | | | 1 | | | | | |
| 11 | Cancer | | | | | | | | | 1 | 10 | 7 | 6 | 1 | | | | | | 16 | 8 | | | | |
| 12 | Canker rash | 3 | 1 | 15 | 14 | 6 | 1 | 1 | 3 | | | | | | | | | | | 44 | | | | | |
| 13 | Catarrh | | 1 | | | | | | | | | | | | | | | | | 1 | | | | | |
| 14 | Chicken pox | | 1 | 1 | | | | | | | | | | | | | | | | 2 | | | | | |
| 15 | Childbirth | | | | | | | | | | 12 | | | | | | | | | 8 | 1 | | | | |
| 16 | Cholera | 1 | 1 | 11 | 9 | 4 | 9 | 5 | 6 | 53 | 23 | 12 | 3 | 1 | | | | | | 92 | 7 | 2 | | | |
| 17 | ...do..infantum | 2 | 1 | 1 | 1 | | | | | | | | | | | | | | | 5 | | | | | |
| 18 | ...do..morbus | 4 | 4 | 18 | 16 | 7 | 5 | | 2 | 3 | 3 | | 2 | | 1 | | | | | 58 | 3 | 1 | | | |
| 19 | Colic | | | | | | 1 | | | 2 | 1 | 1 | | | | | | | | 5 | | | | | |
| 20 | Consumption | 6 | 5 | 7 | 11 | 3 | 3 | 16 | 40 | 99 | 146 | 49 | 48 | 6 | 6 | | | | | 394 | 40 | 1 | | | |
| 21 | Convulsions | 6 | 2 | 4 | 3 | 1 | | 2 | 2 | 1 | 1 | 2 | 3 | | 1 | | | | | 25 | 3 | | | | |
| 22 | Cramp | | | | | | | | | | 1 | | 1 | | | | | | | 2 | | | | | |
| 23 | Croup | 2 | 5 | 13 | 14 | 2 | 3 | 1 | 3 | | | | | | | | | | | 42 | | | | | |
| 24 | Debility | | | 2 | | | | | | | 1 | 1 | | | | | | | | 4 | | | | | |
| 25 | Diabetes | | | | | | | | | | 1 | | | | | | | | | 1 | | | | | |
| 26 | Diarrhœa | 1 | 2 | 7 | 8 | 2 | 1 | 2 | | 3 | 3 | 1 | | | | | | | | 26 | 1 | | | | |
| 27 | Dropsy | 1 | 3 | 8 | 7 | 5 | 3 | 2 | 4 | 2 | 12 | 12 | 9 | 1 | 2 | | | 1 | | 61 | 11 | | | | |
| 28 | Dysentery | 17 | 4 | 37 | 30 | 10 | 5 | 7 | 4 | 7 | 6 | 9 | 3 | | 1 | | | | | 132 | 5 | | | | |
| 29 | Dyspepsia | | | | | | | | | | | 1 | | | | | | | | | 1 | | | | |
| 30 | Erysipelas | 5 | 4 | | 1 | 1 | 2 | 1 | 1 | 3 | 6 | 6 | 3 | | 2 | | | | | 28 | 6 | | | | |
| 31 | Fever, not specified | 1 | 4 | 12 | 9 | 7 | 3 | 8 | 11 | 18 | 12 | 7 | 2 | 1 | 1 | | | | | 87 | 4 | | | | |
| 32 | ..do..bilious | | | | 1 | | | | | | 1 | 2 | 1 | | | | | | | 3 | 2 | | | | |
| 33 | ..do..brain | 3 | 2 | 10 | 5 | 2 | 1 | 3 | 2 | 1 | 8 | 2 | | | | | | | | 38 | 1 | | | | |
| 34 | ..do..inflammatory | | | | 1 | | | | | | | | | | | | | | | 1 | | | | | |
| 35 | ..do..puerperal | | | | | | | | | | 4 | | | | | | | | | 4 | | | | | |
| 36 | ..do..remittent | | | | | | | 1 | | | | | | | | | | | | 1 | | | | | |
| 37 | ..do..scarlet | 1 | 2 | 22 | 17 | 12 | 9 | 3 | | 1 | 1 | | | | | | | | | 68 | | | | | |

## STATE OF LOUISIANA—AGGREGATE—Continued.

| ATIVITIES. | | | | SEASON OF DECEASE. | | | | DURATION OF SICKNESS. | | | | WHITES. | | | COLORED. | | | | | | | | | |
|---|---|---|---|---|---|---|---|---|---|---|---|---|---|---|---|---|---|---|---|---|---|---|---|---|
| | | | | | | | | | | | | | | | Slaves. | | | | Free. | | | | | |
| | | | | | | | | | | | | | | | Black. | | Mulatto. | | Black. | | Mul. | | | |
| Ireland. | Germany. | Other foreign countries. | Unknown. | Spring. | Summer. | Autumn. | Winter. | Under 1 week. | 1 week and under 1 month. | 1 month and under 3 months. | 3 months and over. | Males. | Females. | Total. | M. | F. | M. | F. | M. | F. | M | F. | Aggregate deaths. | |
| 4 | 1 | 6 | 1 | 6 | 9 | 8 | 10 | .... | 6 | 2 | 21 | 13 | 3 | 16 | 7 | 7 | .... | .... | ... | ... | 2 | 1 | 33 | 1 |
| ... | .. | .... | ... | .... | 3 | .... | 1 | .... | 1 | .... | 3 | .... | 1 | 1 | 2 | 1 | .... | .... | ... | ... | .. | .. | 4 | 2 |
| ... | .. | .... | ... | .... | 2 | 1 | .... | 1 | 1 | 1 | .... | 1 | .... | 1 | .... | 1 | .... | 1 | ... | ... | .. | .. | 3 | 3 |
| 2 | .. | .... | 1 | 5 | 14 | 5 | 3 | 3 | 3 | 6 | 12 | 6 | 1 | 7 | 12 | 7 | 1 | .... | ... | ... | .. | .. | 27 | 4 |
| 1 | .. | .... | ... | .... | 2 | .... | 2 | .... | 1 | 1 | 2 | 1 | 3 | 4 | .... | .... | .... | .... | ... | ... | .. | .. | 4 | 5 |
| ... | .. | .... | ... | 1 | 3 | 1 | .... | 2 | 2 | 1 | .... | 1 | 1 | 2 | .... | 3 | .... | .... | ... | ... | .. | .. | 5 | 6 |
| 3 | 4 | 1 | 4 | 18 | 19 | 6 | 13 | 3 | 38 | 2 | 1 | 20 | 9 | 29 | 11 | 10 | 2 | 2 | 1 | ... | 1 | 1 | 57 | 7 |
| ... | .. | .... | ... | .... | 2 | .... | .... | .... | 2 | .... | .... | .... | .... | .... | 1 | 1 | .... | .... | ... | ... | .. | .. | 2 | 8 |
| ... | .. | .... | ... | 2 | 6 | 5 | 2 | 14 | .... | .... | .... | 1 | 3 | 4 | 5 | 5 | .... | .... | ... | ... | .. | 1 | 15 | 9 |
| ... | .. | 1 | ... | 1 | 1 | 2 | 2 | 3 | 1 | .... | 2 | 1 | 1 | 2 | 2 | 1 | .... | .... | ... | ... | 1 | .. | 6 | 10 |
| ... | .. | .... | ... | 13 | 10 | 5 | 10 | 31 | .... | .... | .... | 3 | 1 | 4 | 17 | 11 | 5 | 1 | ... | ... | .. | .. | 38 | 11 |
| ... | .. | 2 | 1 | 3 | 4 | .... | 3 | 5 | .... | .... | .... | 5 | ... | 5 | 4 | 1 | .... | .... | ... | ... | .. | .. | 10 | 12 |
| ... | .. | .... | ... | .... | 1 | .... | .... | .... | .... | .... | .... | .... | .... | .... | 1 | .... | .... | .... | ... | ... | .. | .. | 1 | 13 |
| 10 | 4 | 4 | 1 | 1 | 9 | 13 | .... | 16 | 4 | .... | .... | 18 | 2 | 20 | 1 | 1 | 1 | .... | ... | ... | .. | .. | 23 | 14 |
| 1 | .. | 2 | ... | 8 | .... | 3 | 3 | .... | .... | 1 | 6 | 4 | 3 | 7 | 2 | 4 | .... | .... | ... | ... | .. | 1 | 14 | 15 |
| ... | 1 | .... | ... | 36 | 58 | 49 | 35 | 44 | 58 | 40 | 25 | 44 | 48 | 92 | 43 | 27 | 7 | 3 | ... | 1 | 1 | 4 | 178 | 16 |
| 4 | .. | 1 | 1 | 3 | 4 | 1 | 7 | 8 | .... | .... | .... | 5 | 2 | 7 | 6 | 2 | .... | .... | ... | ... | .. | .. | 15 | 17 |
| 1 | .. | 1 | 1 | 3 | 4 | 2 | 3 | 2 | 5 | 1 | 1 | 3 | 2 | 5 | 2 | 3 | .... | 1 | ... | 1 | .. | .. | 12 | 18 |
| ... | .. | .... | ... | 1 | 1 | 1 | 3 | .... | 5 | .... | 1 | 2 | 2 | 4 | 1 | 1 | .... | .... | ... | ... | .. | .. | 6 | 19 |
| ... | .. | .... | ... | .... | .... | .... | 8 | .... | .... | 1 | 2 | .... | 1 | 1 | 1 | .... | 1 | .... | ... | ... | .. | .. | 8 | 20 |
| ... | .. | 3 | ... | 1 | 2 | 2 | 8 | .... | 2 | .... | 2 | 6 | 1 | 7 | 1 | .... | .... | .... | ... | ... | .. | .. | 8 | 21 |
| 2 | 1 | 1 | ... | 2 | 5 | 2 | .... | .... | .... | 1 | 4 | .... | 4 | 4 | .... | 4 | .... | 1 | ... | ... | .. | .. | 9 | 22 |
| ... | .. | .... | ... | 3 | 4 | .... | 2 | .... | .... | 1 | 8 | .... | .... | .... | 4 | 5 | .... | .... | ... | ... | .. | .. | 9 | 23 |
| ... | .. | 1 | ... | 1 | .... | .... | .... | .... | .... | .... | 1 | .... | .... | .... | .... | .... | .... | .... | ... | ... | 1 | .. | 1 | 24 |
| ... | 1 | 3 | ... | 77 | 79 | 87 | 41 | 160 | 80 | 13 | 14 | 17 | 28 | 45 | 116 | 109 | 7 | 9 | ... | ... | .. | 1 | 287 | 25 |
| 76 | 61 | 102 | 16 | 348 | 407 | 429 | 329 | 469 | 175 | 74 | 275 | 399 | 236 | 635 | 466 | 376 | 32 | 23 | 4 | 4 | 8 | 19 | 1567 | 26 |
| 1825 | 504 | 803 | 145 | 2784 | 3505 | 3053 | 2514 | 4886 | 2064 | 570 | 1810 | 3957 | 1950 | 5907 | 3063 | 2947 | 285 | 191 | 27 | 26 | 69 | 91 | 11956 | |

## TION OF THE STATE OF MAINE.

*ord, Penobscot, Piscataquis, and Somerset.*

| Ireland. | Germany. | Other foreign countries. | Unknown. | Spring. | Summer. | Autumn. | Winter. | Under 1 week. | 1 week and under 1 month. | 1 month and under 3 months. | 3 months and over. | Males. | Females. | Total. | Slaves Black M. | Slaves Black F. | Slaves Mulatto M. | Slaves Mulatto F. | Free Black M. | Free Black F. | Free Mul. M | Free Mul. F. | Aggregate deaths. | |
|---|---|---|---|---|---|---|---|---|---|---|---|---|---|---|---|---|---|---|---|---|---|---|---|---|
| ... | .. | .... | ... | 1 | 2 | .... | 1 | .... | 2 | .... | 2 | 2 | 2 | 4 | .... | .... | .... | .... | ... | ... | .. | .. | 4 | 1 |
| 2 | 1 | 2 | ... | 14 | 5 | 4 | 5 | 21 | 1 | 2 | .... | 23 | 6 | 29 | .... | .... | .... | .... | ... | ... | .. | .. | 29 | 2 |
| ... | .. | 1 | ... | 1 | 2 | 1 | 2 | 4 | 1 | .... | .... | 2 | 4 | 6 | .... | .... | .... | .... | ... | ... | .. | .. | 6 | 3 |
| ... | .. | .... | ... | 2 | 10 | 6 | 4 | 8 | .... | .... | .... | 19 | 3 | 22 | .... | .... | .... | .... | ... | ... | .. | .. | 22 | 4 |
| ... | .. | .... | ... | 2 | .... | 1 | 1 | 3 | 1 | .... | .... | 1 | 3 | 4 | .... | .... | .... | .... | ... | ... | .. | .. | 4 | 5 |
| ... | .. | .... | ... | .... | .... | 1 | .... | 1 | .... | .... | .... | .... | 1 | 1 | .... | .... | .... | .... | ... | ... | .. | .. | 1 | 6 |
| 1 | .. | .... | ... | .... | 1 | 4 | 2 | 6 | .... | .... | .... | 4 | 3 | 7 | .... | .... | .... | .... | ... | ... | .. | .. | 7 | 7 |
| ... | .. | .... | ... | .... | .... | 1 | .... | .... | .... | .... | 1 | .... | 1 | 1 | .... | .... | .... | .... | ... | ... | .. | .. | 1 | 8 |
| ... | .. | .... | ... | 2 | 2 | 6 | 5 | 6 | 7 | 1 | 1 | 7 | 8 | 15 | .... | .... | .... | .... | ... | ... | .. | .. | 15 | 9 |
| ... | .. | .... | ... | 1 | .... | .... | .... | 1 | .... | .... | .... | .... | 1 | 1 | .... | .... | .... | .... | ... | ... | .. | .. | 1 | 10 |
| ... | .. | 1 | ... | 4 | 8 | 9 | 4 | 1 | .... | 2 | 19 | 9 | 16 | 25 | .... | .... | .... | .... | ... | ... | .. | .. | 25 | 11 |
| ... | .. | .... | ... | 21 | 12 | 6 | 5 | 17 | 21 | 5 | .... | 25 | 19 | 44 | .... | .... | .... | .... | ... | ... | .. | .. | 44 | 12 |
| ... | .. | .... | ... | 1 | .... | .... | .... | 1 | .... | .... | .... | .... | 1 | 1 | .... | .... | .... | .... | ... | ... | .. | .. | 1 | 13 |
| ... | .. | .... | ... | .... | .... | 1 | 1 | .... | 2 | .... | .... | 1 | 1 | 2 | .... | .... | .... | .... | ... | ... | .. | .. | 2 | 14 |
| ... | .. | 3 | ... | 5 | 6 | .... | 1 | 7 | 4 | .... | .... | .... | 12 | 12 | .... | .... | .... | .... | ... | ... | .. | .. | 12 | 15 |
| 33 | .. | 4 | ... | 3 | 6 | 127 | 2 | 127 | 10 | .... | .... | 87 | 51 | 138 | .... | .... | .... | .... | ... | ... | .. | .. | 138 | 16 |
| ... | .. | .... | ... | 1 | 3 | 1 | .... | 5 | .... | .... | .... | 3 | 2 | 5 | .... | .... | .... | .... | ... | ... | .. | .. | 5 | 17 |
| ... | .. | 3 | ... | 3 | 7 | 52 | 3 | 34 | 28 | 2 | 1 | 32 | 33 | 65 | .... | .... | .... | .... | ... | ... | .. | .. | 65 | 18 |
| ... | .. | .... | ... | 1 | .... | 4 | .... | 5 | .... | .... | .... | 3 | 2 | 5 | .... | .... | .... | .... | ... | ... | .. | .. | 5 | 19 |
| 4 | .. | 4 | 2 | 137 | 131 | 97 | 80 | 7 | 34 | 39 | 360 | 186 | 259 | 445 | .... | .... | .... | .... | ... | ... | .. | .. | 445 | 20 |
| ... | .. | .... | ... | 6 | 6 | 10 | 6 | 16 | 4 | 2 | 5 | 16 | 12 | 28 | .... | .... | .... | .... | ... | ... | .. | .. | 28 | 21 |
| ... | .. | .... | ... | .... | .... | 1 | 1 | 2 | .... | .... | .... | .... | 2 | 2 | .... | .... | .... | .... | ... | ... | .. | .. | 2 | 22 |
| ... | .. | 1 | ... | 11 | 10 | 10 | 11 | 30 | 11 | 2 | .... | 18 | 25 | 43 | .... | .... | .... | .... | ... | ... | .. | .. | 43 | 23 |
| ... | .. | .... | ... | .... | 2 | 2 | .... | 1 | 2 | .... | 1 | 3 | 1 | 4 | .... | .... | .... | .... | ... | ... | .. | .. | 4 | 24 |
| ... | .. | .... | ... | .... | 1 | .... | .... | .... | .... | .... | 1 | .... | 1 | 1 | .... | .... | .... | .... | ... | ... | .. | .. | 1 | 25 |
| ... | .. | 3 | ... | 3 | 2 | 24 | 1 | 15 | 11 | 2 | .... | 16 | 14 | 30 | .... | .... | .... | .... | ... | ... | .. | .. | 30 | 26 |
| ... | .. | .... | ... | 23 | 26 | 15 | 8 | 5 | 17 | 10 | 38 | 32 | 40 | 72 | .... | .... | .... | .... | ... | ... | .. | .. | 72 | 27 |
| 2 | .. | 1 | ... | 3 | 11 | 114 | 12 | 41 | 91 | 8 | .... | 87 | 53 | 140 | .... | .... | .... | .... | ... | ... | .. | .. | 140 | 28 |
| ... | .. | .... | ... | .... | 1 | .... | .... | .... | .... | .... | 1 | 1 | ... | 1 | .... | .... | .... | .... | ... | ... | .. | .. | 1 | 29 |
| ... | .. | 1 | ... | 17 | 4 | 4 | 10 | 7 | 23 | 4 | .... | 16 | 19 | 35 | .... | .... | .... | .... | ... | ... | .. | .. | 35 | 30 |
| 2 | .. | 2 | 1 | 29 | 26 | 17 | 24 | 27 | 59 | 8 | 2 | 54 | 42 | 96 | .... | .... | .... | .... | ... | ... | .. | .. | 96 | 31 |
| ... | .. | .... | ... | 3 | 2 | .... | .... | .... | 2 | 1 | 2 | 2 | 3 | 5 | .... | .... | .... | .... | ... | ... | .. | .. | 5 | 32 |
| ... | .. | .... | ... | 12 | 8 | 11 | 8 | 10 | 22 | 3 | 3 | 21 | 18 | 39 | .... | .... | .... | .... | ... | ... | .. | .. | 39 | 33 |
| ... | .. | .... | ... | .... | 1 | .... | .... | 1 | .... | .... | .... | .... | 1 | 1 | .... | .... | .... | .... | ... | ... | .. | .. | 1 | 34 |
| ... | .. | .... | ... | 2 | 1 | .... | 1 | 3 | 1 | .... | .... | .... | 4 | 4 | .... | .... | .... | .... | ... | ... | .. | .. | 4 | 35 |
| ... | .. | .... | ... | .... | 1 | .... | .... | .... | 1 | .... | .... | 1 | .... | 1 | .... | .... | .... | .... | ... | ... | .. | .. | 1 | 36 |
| ... | .. | .... | ... | 22 | 16 | 13 | 17 | 32 | 31 | 4 | 1 | 39 | 29 | 68 | .... | .... | .... | .... | ... | ... | .. | .. | 68 | 37 |

## CLASSIFICATION OF DEATHS IN SOUTHERN

| | Cause of death. | Ages: Under 1. M. | Under 1. F. | 1 and under 5. M. | 1 and under 5. F. | 5 and under 10. M. | 5 and under 10. F. | 10 and under 20. M. | 10 and under 20. F. | 20 and under 50. M. | 20 and under 50. F. | 50 and under 80. M. | 50 and under 80. F. | 80 and under 100. M | 80 and under 100. F. | 100 & over. M | 100 & over. F. | Age unknown. M | Age unknown. F. | Nativities: Born in State. | N. England States. | Middle States. | Southern States. | Southwest'n States. | Northwest'n States. |
|---|---|---|---|---|---|---|---|---|---|---|---|---|---|---|---|---|---|---|---|---|---|---|---|---|---|
| 1 | Fever, typhoid | | | 1 | 4 | 3 | 3 | 5 | 7 | 12 | 18 | 6 | 5 | | | | | | | 56 | 5 | | | | |
| 2 | Gravel | | | | | | | 1 | | | 1 | 7 | | | | | | | | 4 | 5 | | | | |
| 3 | Heart, disease of | 1 | | 1 | 1 | | 2 | | 3 | 2 | 6 | 2 | | | | | | | | 16 | 2 | | | | |
| 4 | Hemorrhage | | | | | | | | | 1 | 1 | 1 | | | | | | | | 3 | | | | | |
| 5 | Hernia | | | | | | | | 1 | | | 1 | 1 | 1 | | | | | | 2 | 1 | | | | |
| 6 | Hip, disease of | | | | | | | | 1 | | | | 1 | | | | | | | 1 | 1 | | | | |
| 7 | Hooping cough | 9 | 7 | 10 | 12 | 1 | 1 | | | | | | | | | | | | | 40 | | | | | |
| 8 | Hydrocephalus | 2 | 1 | 7 | 4 | 1 | 1 | | | | 2 | | | | | | | | | 18 | | | | | |
| 9 | Inflamat'n, not spec'd | | | | | | | | 1 | | | 1 | | | | | | | | 1 | 1 | | | | |
| 10 | ....do.....bowels | 4 | | 6 | 2 | | 1 | 1 | 2 | 2 | 1 | 3 | 1 | | | | | | | 19 | 4 | | | | |
| 11 | ....do.....brain | 2 | 1 | | | | | | | | | 1 | | | | | | | | 4 | | | | | |
| 12 | Influenza | 4 | 1 | 2 | | | | | | | | 1 | | | | | | | | 8 | | | | | |
| 13 | Intemperance | | | | | | | | | 1 | | 1 | | | | | | | | | 2 | | | | |
| 14 | Jaundice | | | 1 | | | | | | | | | 3 | | | | | | | 2 | 2 | | | | |
| 15 | Kidneys, disease of | | | | | | | | | 2 | 1 | 2 | | | | | | | | 3 | 2 | | | | |
| 16 | Liver ......do | | | | 1 | 1 | | | | | 1 | 4 | 3 | | | | | | | 7 | 3 | | | | |
| 17 | Lungs......do | 1 | | | | | | | | | | 1 | | | | | | | | 1 | | | | | |
| 18 | Measles | 3 | | 2 | 2 | | | 2 | | 1 | 1 | | | | | | | | | 10 | | | | | |
| 19 | Mumps | 1 | | 1 | | | | | | | | | | | | | | | | 2 | | | | | |
| 20 | Neuralgia | | | | | | | | | | | | 1 | | | | | | | | 1 | | | | |
| 21 | Old age | | | | | | | | | | | 9 | 11 | 23 | 22 | | | | | 28 | 35 | | | | |
| 22 | Paralysis | | | | | | | | | 1 | | 4 | 4 | 2 | 1 | | | | | 9 | 3 | | | | |
| 23 | Pleurisy | | | | | | | | | 1 | | | 1 | | | | | | | 1 | 1 | | | | |
| 24 | Pneumonia | 10 | 6 | 11 | 7 | | | 2 | 2 | 3 | 5 | 8 | 5 | | | | | | | 54 | 4 | | | | |
| 25 | Quinsy | 1 | | | | | 1 | | | | | | | | | | | | | 2 | | | | | |
| 26 | Rheumatism | | | | | | | | | 1 | | | 1 | | | | | | | 1 | 1 | | | | |
| 27 | Scrofula | | 1 | 7 | 2 | 2 | | 1 | 1 | | 3 | | | | | | | | | 17 | | | | | |
| 28 | Spine, disease of | | | | 1 | | | | | 1 | 1 | 1 | | | | | | | | 4 | | | | | |
| 29 | Stillborn | 1 | | | | | | | | | | | | | | | | | | 1 | | | | | |
| 30 | Suicide | | | 2 | | | | | 2 | 4 | 2 | | | | | | | | | 10 | | | | | |
| 31 | Syphilis | | | | | | | | | 1 | | | | | | | | | | | | | | | |
| 32 | Throat, disease of | | | 1 | | 3 | 1 | 2 | 1 | | | | | | 1 | | | | | 8 | 1 | | | | |
| 33 | Thrush | | | | | | 1 | | | | | | | | | | | | | | 1 | | | | |
| 34 | Tumor | | | 1 | | | | | | | 1 | 1 | 1 | | | | | | | 4 | | | | | |
| 35 | Ulcer | 1 | 5 | 2 | 4 | | 1 | | | | | | 1 | | | | | | | 13 | 1 | | | | |
| 36 | White swelling | | | | 1 | | | | | | | | | | | | | | | 1 | | | | | |
| 37 | Worms | | | 1 | 2 | | | | | | | | | | | | | | | 3 | | | | | |
| 38 | Unknown | 24 | 16 | 16 | 23 | 3 | 13 | 6 | 5 | 18 | 23 | 22 | 14 | 4 | 3 | | | | 2 | 159 | 20 | | | | |
| | Total | 119 | 81 | 250 | 223 | 84 | 74 | 83 | 110 | 263 | 322 | 195 | 139 | 41 | 45 | .. | .. | 2 | 2 | 1735 | 197 | 4 | .. | .. | .. |

## CLASSIFICATION OF DEATHS IN SOUTHERN

*Embracing the following counties: Cumberland, Hancock,*

| | Cause of death. | Under 1. M. | Under 1. F. | 1 and under 5. M. | 1 and under 5. F. | 5 and under 10. M. | 5 and under 10. F. | 10 and under 20. M. | 10 and under 20. F. | 20 and under 50. M. | 20 and under 50. F. | 50 and under 80. M. | 50 and under 80. F. | 80 and under 100. M | 80 and under 100. F. | 100 & over. M | 100 & over. F. | Age unknown. M | Age unknown. F. | Born in State. | N. England States. | Middle States. | Southern States. | Southwest'n States. | Northwest'n States. |
|---|---|---|---|---|---|---|---|---|---|---|---|---|---|---|---|---|---|---|---|---|---|---|---|---|---|
| 1 | Abscess | | | | | | 1 | | | 1 | 2 | 2 | 1 | | | | | | | 6 | 1 | | | | |
| 2 | Accident, not specif'd | | 3 | 4 | 1 | 7 | 4 | 15 | | 35 | 1 | 5 | 1 | 3 | | | | | | 65 | 5 | 1 | | 1 | |
| 3 | ....do...burned | | | 2 | 4 | 1 | | | 1 | | | | 1 | | | | | | | 9 | | | | | |
| 4 | ....do...drowned | | 1 | 3 | 1 | 11 | | 25 | 3 | 47 | 4 | 3 | 1 | | | | | | | 88 | 6 | | | | |
| 5 | ....do...scalded | | | 3 | | | | | | | | | | | | | | | | 3 | | | | | |
| 6 | ....do...railroad | | | | | | | 1 | | | | | | | | | | | | | | | | | |
| 7 | Apoplexy | | | | | | | | | 3 | 2 | 13 | 11 | 2 | | | | | | 22 | 7 | | | | |
| 8 | Asthma | | | | | | | | 1 | 1 | | 1 | 2 | | 2 | | | | | 6 | 1 | | | | |
| 9 | Bladder, disease of | | | | | | | | | | 1 | 1 | | | | | | | | 1 | 1 | | | | |
| 10 | Bowels.....do | 14 | 8 | 28 | 16 | 4 | 5 | 3 | 1 | 1 | 6 | 2 | 7 | | | | | | | 91 | 1 | | | | |
| 11 | Brain ......do | 2 | 1 | 2 | 2 | 1 | | 1 | 1 | | | 1 | | | | | | | | 10 | 1 | | | | |
| 12 | Bronchitis | 1 | | 1 | 1 | | | 2 | | 4 | | 2 | | | | | | | | 10 | | | | | |
| 13 | Cancer | | 2 | | 2 | 1 | 1 | 1 | | 1 | 9 | 11 | 14 | 2 | 6 | | | | | 38 | 8 | | | | |
| 14 | Canker rash | 2 | 1 | 5 | 1 | 3 | 3 | 2 | | | | | | | | | | | | 17 | | | | | |
| 15 | Catarrh | 4 | 2 | 1 | | | | | | | 1 | | | | | | | | | 8 | | | | | |
| 16 | Chicken pox | | 1 | | 1 | | | | | | | | | | | | | | | 1 | | | | | |
| 17 | Childbirth | | | | | | | | 2 | | 34 | | | | | | | | | 34 | 1 | | | | |
| 18 | Cholera | 1 | 8 | 8 | 4 | 3 | 1 | 4 | 5 | 22 | 5 | 4 | 5 | 1 | 2 | | | | | 61 | | 1 | | | |
| 19 | ...do...infantum | 23 | 14 | 4 | 5 | 1 | | | | | | | | | | | | | | 46 | 1 | | | | |
| 20 | ...do...morbus | 4 | 1 | 13 | 10 | 1 | 2 | | 3 | 6 | 6 | 5 | 4 | 3 | | | | | | 52 | 2 | | | | |
| 21 | Chorea | | | | | | | | 1 | | | | | | | | | | | 1 | | | | | |
| 22 | Colic | 1 | | | 1 | 1 | | | | 3 | 4 | 4 | 4 | 1 | | | | | | 17 | 1 | | | | |
| 23 | Congestion of brain | | | 1 | 1 | | | | | | | | | | | | | | | 2 | | | | | |
| 24 | .....do.......lungs | 1 | | | 1 | | | | | | | 1 | | | | | | | | 2 | | | | | |
| 25 | Consumption | 22 | 22 | 27 | 29 | 6 | 19 | 26 | 110 | 246 | 408 | 147 | 170 | 9 | 15 | | | | 1 | 1131 | 78 | 2 | 2 | 1 | |
| 26 | Convulsions | 17 | 19 | 14 | 15 | 2 | 1 | 3 | 1 | 10 | 8 | 5 | 3 | | 2 | | | | | 95 | 3 | | | | |
| 27 | Cramp | | | | | | | | | 1 | | 1 | | | | | | | | 1 | | | | | |

## SECTION OF THE STATE OF MAINE—Continued.

| NATIVITIES. | | | | | SEASON OF DECEASE. | | | | DURATION OF SICKNESS. | | | | WHITES. | | | COLORED. | | | | | | | | | |
|---|---|---|---|---|---|---|---|---|---|---|---|---|---|---|---|---|---|---|---|---|---|---|---|---|---|
| | | | | | | | | | | | | | | | | Slaves. | | | | Free. | | | | | |
| | | | | | | | | | | | | | | | | Black. | | Mulatto. | | Black. | | Mul. | | | |
| California and Territories. | Ireland. | Germany. | Other foreign countries. | Unknown. | Spring. | Summer. | Autumn. | Winter. | Under 1 week. | 1 week and under 1 month. | 1 month and under 3 months. | 3 months and over. | Males. | Females. | Total. | M. | F. | M. | F. | M. | F. | M | F. | Aggregate deaths. | |
| | 1 | | 2 | | 12 | 19 | 24 | 9 | 9 | 44 | 9 | 1 | 27 | 37 | 64 | | | | | | | | | 64 | 1 |
| | | | | | 4 | 1 | 3 | 1 | 2 | 2 | 3 | 2 | 8 | 1 | 9 | | | | | | | | | 9 | 2 |
| | | | | | 7 | 3 | 6 | 2 | 5 | 3 | 4 | 6 | 6 | 12 | 18 | | | | | | | | | 18 | 3 |
| | | | | | | | 2 | 1 | 1 | | | 2 | 2 | 1 | 3 | | | | | | | | | 3 | 4 |
| | | | 1 | | 1 | | 2 | 1 | | 2 | | 2 | 2 | 2 | 4 | | | | | | | | | 4 | 5 |
| | | | | | | | 2 | | | 1 | | 1 | | 2 | 2 | | | | | | | | | 2 | 6 |
| | | | | | 18 | 6 | 7 | 9 | 5 | 22 | 10 | 3 | 19 | 19 | 38 | | | | | | 1 | 1 | | 40 | 7 |
| | | | | | 7 | 3 | 2 | 6 | 1 | 9 | 6 | 2 | 10 | 8 | 18 | | | | | | | | | 18 | 8 |
| | | | | | | | | 2 | 2 | | | | 1 | 1 | 2 | | | | | | | | | 2 | 9 |
| | | | | | 6 | 8 | 7 | 2 | 13 | 8 | 2 | | 16 | 7 | 23 | | | | | | | | | 23 | 10 |
| | | | | | 2 | 1 | 1 | | 3 | 1 | | | 3 | 1 | 4 | | | | | | | | | 4 | 11 |
| | | | | | 4 | 2 | | 2 | 5 | 3 | | | 7 | 1 | 8 | | | | | | | | | 8 | 12 |
| | | | | | 1 | | 1 | | | 1 | | 1 | 2 | | 2 | | | | | | | | | 2 | 13 |
| | | | | | 1 | 1 | 1 | 1 | 1 | 1 | 1 | 1 | 1 | 3 | 4 | | | | | | | | | 4 | 14 |
| | | | | | 2 | | | 3 | 1 | 1 | 1 | 2 | 4 | 1 | 5 | | | | | | | | | 5 | 15 |
| | | | | | 2 | 3 | 3 | 2 | | 3 | 2 | 5 | 5 | 5 | 10 | | | | | | | | | 10 | 16 |
| | 1 | | | | 1 | 1 | | | | 1 | | 1 | 2 | | 2 | | | | | | | | | 2 | 17 |
| | | | 1 | | | 6 | 2 | 3 | 2 | 7 | 2 | | 8 | 3 | 11 | | | | | | | | | 11 | 18 |
| | | | | | 1 | | 1 | | | 2 | | | 2 | | 2 | | | | | | | | | 2 | 19 |
| | | | | | | | 1 | | | | | 1 | | 1 | 1 | | | | | | | | | 1 | 20 |
| | | | 2 | | 21 | 19 | 11 | 13 | 10 | 13 | 6 | 15 | 32 | 33 | 65 | | | | | | | | | 65 | 21 |
| | | | | | 6 | 1 | 3 | 2 | 5 | 1 | | 6 | 7 | 5 | 12 | | | | | | | | | 12 | 22 |
| | | | | | 2 | | | | 1 | 1 | | | 1 | 1 | 2 | | | | | | | | | 2 | 23 |
| | | | 1 | | 29 | 12 | 5 | 13 | 15 | 40 | 3 | 1 | 34 | 25 | 59 | | | | | | | | | 59 | 24 |
| | | | | | | | | 2 | 1 | 1 | | | 1 | 1 | 2 | | | | | | | | | 2 | 25 |
| | | | | | | 1 | 1 | | | 1 | | 1 | 1 | 1 | 2 | | | | | | | | | 2 | 26 |
| | | | | | 3 | 3 | 5 | 6 | 2 | 2 | 2 | 11 | 10 | 7 | 17 | | | | | | | | | 17 | 27 |
| | | | | | | 1 | 3 | | 1 | | 1 | 2 | 2 | 2 | 4 | | | | | | | | | 4 | 28 |
| | | | | | | | | 1 | | | | | 1 | | 1 | | | | | | | | | 1 | 29 |
| | | | | | 2 | 8 | | | 3 | | | | 6 | 10 | 10 | | | | | | | | | 10 | 30 |
| | 1 | | | | | 1 | | | | | | 1 | 1 | | 1 | | | | | | | | | 1 | 31 |
| | | | | | | 1 | 5 | 3 | 3 | 6 | | | 6 | 3 | 9 | | | | | | | | | 9 | 32 |
| | | | | | | 1 | | | | | | 1 | | 1 | 1 | | | | | | | | | 1 | 33 |
| | | | | | 1 | 1 | 1 | 1 | | | 1 | 3 | 2 | 2 | 4 | | | | | | | | | 4 | 34 |
| | | | | | 2 | 2 | 6 | 4 | 6 | 6 | | 2 | 3 | 11 | 14 | | | | | | | | | 14 | 35 |
| | | | | | | 1 | | | | 1 | | | | 1 | 1 | | | | | | | | | 1 | 36 |
| | | | | | 1 | 1 | | 1 | 3 | | | | 1 | 2 | 3 | | | | | | | | | 3 | 37 |
| | 9 | | 3 | 1 | 49 | 49 | 47 | 46 | 78 | 35 | 12 | 53 | 93 | 99 | 192 | | | | | | | | | 192 | 38 |
| | 56 | 1 | 36 | 4 | 515 | 469 | 694 | 351 | 622 | 604 | 160 | 564 | 1036 | 995 | 2031 | | | | | | 1 | 1 | | 2033 | |

## SECTION OF THE STATE OF MAINE.

*Kennebeck, Lincoln, Waldo, Washington, and York.*

| California and Territories. | Ireland. | Germany. | Other foreign countries. | Unknown. | Spring. | Summer. | Autumn. | Winter. | Under 1 week. | 1 week and under 1 month. | 1 month and under 3 months. | 3 months and over. | Males. | Females. | Total. | Slaves Black M. | Slaves Black F. | Slaves Mulatto M. | Slaves Mulatto F. | Free Black M. | Free Black F. | Free Mul. M | Free Mul. F. | Aggregate deaths. | |
|---|---|---|---|---|---|---|---|---|---|---|---|---|---|---|---|---|---|---|---|---|---|---|---|---|---|
| | | | | | 1 | | 2 | 4 | 1 | 2 | 2 | 2 | 3 | 4 | 7 | | | | | | | | | 7 | 1 |
| | 5 | | 2 | | 21 | 10 | 24 | 23 | 39 | 3 | | 1 | 67 | 9 | 76 | | | | | 2 | 1 | | | 79 | 2 |
| | | | | | 1 | 5 | 1 | 2 | 3 | | | | 3 | 6 | 9 | | | | | | | | | 9 | 3 |
| | | | 3 | 2 | 24 | 31 | 24 | 17 | 21 | | | | 89 | 10 | 99 | | | | | | | | | 99 | 4 |
| | | | | | 1 | | 2 | | 1 | 1 | | | 3 | | 3 | | | | | | | | | 3 | 5 |
| | 1 | | | | | | 1 | | 1 | | | | 1 | | 1 | | | | | | | | | 1 | 6 |
| | | | 2 | | 15 | 4 | 5 | 6 | 23 | 2 | | 1 | 18 | 12 | 30 | | | | | | | | 1 | 31 | 7 |
| | | | | | 5 | 1 | 1 | | 1 | 3 | | 3 | 2 | 5 | 7 | | | | | | | | | 7 | 8 |
| | | | | | | | 1 | 1 | | 1 | | 1 | 1 | 1 | 2 | | | | | | | | | 2 | 9 |
| | | | 3 | | 9 | 11 | 68 | 7 | 29 | 37 | 4 | 2 | 52 | 42 | 94 | | | | | | | | 1 | 95 | 10 |
| | | | | | 4 | 1 | 3 | 3 | 1 | 5 | 1 | | 6 | 4 | 10 | | | | | 1 | | | | 11 | 11 |
| | | | 1 | | 2 | 3 | 2 | 4 | | 3 | 2 | 6 | 10 | 1 | 11 | | | | | | | | | 11 | 12 |
| | 2 | | 1 | 1 | 12 | 7 | 11 | 19 | 1 | 6 | 6 | 32 | 16 | 34 | 50 | | | | | | | | | 50 | 13 |
| | | | | | 3 | 6 | 4 | 4 | 8 | 7 | 2 | | 12 | 5 | 17 | | | | | | | | | 17 | 14 |
| | | | | | 5 | 1 | | 2 | 6 | 1 | 1 | | 5 | 3 | 8 | | | | | | | | | 8 | 15 |
| | | | 1 | | 1 | 1 | | | 1 | 1 | | | | 2 | 2 | | | | | | | | | 2 | 16 |
| | 1 | | | | 8 | 13 | 6 | 9 | 22 | 8 | 2 | 1 | | 36 | 36 | | | | | | | | | 36 | 17 |
| | 4 | | | 2 | 5 | 15 | 45 | 1 | 48 | 14 | | 1 | 42 | 25 | 67 | | | | | | | 1 | | 68 | 18 |
| | | | | | 8 | 10 | 23 | 6 | 13 | 15 | 4 | 1 | 28 | 19 | 47 | | | | | | | | | 47 | 19 |
| | 1 | | 1 | 2 | 3 | 7 | 45 | 2 | 28 | 14 | 3 | 1 | 32 | 26 | 58 | | | | | | | | | 58 | 20 |
| | | | | | | | 1 | | | | | 1 | | 1 | 1 | | | | | | | | | 1 | 21 |
| | | | | 1 | 5 | 4 | 4 | 6 | 15 | 3 | | | 10 | 8 | 18 | | | | | | | | 1 | 19 | 22 |
| | | | | | 1 | 1 | | | | 1 | 1 | | 1 | 1 | 2 | | | | | | | | | 2 | 23 |
| | | | 1 | | | 2 | 1 | | 1 | | | | 2 | 1 | 3 | | | | | | | | | 3 | 24 |
| | 20 | | 19 | 9 | 350 | 330 | 340 | 236 | 29 | 86 | 154 | 895 | 480 | 770 | 1250 | | | | | 8 | 4 | | | 1257 | 25 |
| | | | 2 | | 29 | 29 | 23 | 19 | 63 | 15 | 1 | 12 | 51 | 48 | 99 | | | | | | | | 1 | 100 | 26 |
| | 1 | | | | | | | 2 | 1 | | | | 2 | | 2 | | | | | | | | | 2 | 27 |

## CLASSIFICATION OF DEATHS IN SOUTHERN

| | Cause of death. | AGES. Under 1. | | 1 and under 5. | | 5 and under 10. | | 10 and under 20. | | 20 and under 50. | | 50 and under 80. | | 80 and under 100. | | 100 & over. | | Age unknown. | | NATIVITIES. Born in State. | N. England States. | Middle States. | Southern States. | Southwest'n States. | Northwest'n States. |
|---|---|---|---|---|---|---|---|---|---|---|---|---|---|---|---|---|---|---|---|---|---|---|---|---|---|
| | | M. | F. | M. | F. | M. | F. | M. | F. | M. | F. | M. | F. | M | F. | M | F. | M | F. | | | | | | |
| 1 | Croup | 19 | 16 | 41 | 32 | 10 | 12 | 1 | | 1 | | | | | | | | | | 129 | | 1 | | | |
| 2 | Debility | 4 | 1 | | 1 | | | 1 | | 1 | | 5 | 3 | | | | | | | 14 | 1 | | | | |
| 3 | Diabetes | | | | | | | | | | | 1 | | | | | | | | | 1 | | | | |
| 4 | Diarrhœa | 16 | 10 | 24 | 33 | 6 | 2 | 5 | 2 | 13 | 7 | 4 | 5 | | | | | | | 120 | 4 | | | | |
| 5 | Dropsy | 14 | 11 | 32 | 12 | 7 | 5 | 2 | 5 | 8 | 28 | 35 | 39 | 13 | 4 | | | | | 181 | 22 | | | | |
| 6 | Dysentery | 24 | 25 | 88 | 68 | 18 | 21 | 19 | 13 | 29 | 19 | 14 | 27 | 1 | 3 | | | | | 344 | 15 | | | | 1. |
| 7 | Dyspepsia | 1 | 1 | | | | | | | | 2 | 4 | 1 | | | | | | | 9 | | | | | |
| 8 | Epilepsy | | | | | | | | | 2 | | 2 | | | 2 | | | | | 5 | 1 | | | | |
| 9 | Erysipelas | 7 | 2 | 2 | 3 | | 2 | 1 | 5 | 8 | 9 | 6 | 8 | | | | | | | 46 | 6 | | | | |
| 10 | Fever, not specified | 10 | 17 | 30 | 21 | 9 | 11 | 25 | 31 | 44 | 35 | 19 | 14 | | 1 | | | | | 246 | 9 | | | | |
| 11 | ..do..bilious | 1 | | 4 | | | | 1 | 3 | 3 | 4 | 3 | 3 | 4 | | | | | | 24 | 2 | | | | |
| 12 | ..do..brain | 9 | 8 | 14 | 11 | 4 | 3 | 11 | 13 | 8 | 7 | 1 | 2 | 1 | | | | | | 83 | 5 | 1 | | | |
| 13 | ..do..inflammatory | | | | | | | | 1 | | | | 1 | | | | | | | 2 | | | | | |
| 14 | ..do..intermittent | | | | | | | 1 | | 1 | | | | | | | | | | 1 | | | | | |
| 15 | ..do..puerperal | | | | | | | | 1 | | 5 | | | | | | | | | 5 | | | | | |
| 16 | ..do..scarlet | 10 | 18 | 71 | 60 | 29 | 41 | 15 | 11 | 1 | 2 | 1 | 3 | | | | | | | 249 | 8 | 1 | | | |
| 17 | ..do..ship | 1 | | 1 | | | | | 2 | 3 | | | | | | | | | | 6 | | | | | |
| 18 | ..do..typhus | 4 | 1 | 9 | 5 | 7 | 5 | 28 | 34 | 44 | 43 | 19 | 17 | 1 | | | | 1 | | 206 | 6 | | | | |
| 19 | ..do..yellow | | | | | | | | | 2 | | | | | | | | | | 1 | | 1 | | | |
| 20 | Fracture | | | | | | | | | 1 | | | 1 | | | | | | | 1 | 1 | | | | |
| 21 | Gout | | | | | | | 1 | | | | 1 | | | | | | | | 1 | 1 | | | | |
| 22 | Gravel | | | 1 | | | | | | | | 10 | 1 | | | | | | | 10 | 1 | | | | |
| 23 | Head, disease of | 4 | | 1 | 1 | 1 | | | | 1 | | | | | | | | | | 8 | | | | | |
| 24 | Heart....do | 1 | 2 | 1 | 1 | 1 | | 1 | 6 | 8 | 5 | 22 | 4 | 4 | 2 | | | | | 49 | 9 | | | | |
| 25 | Heat | | | | | | | | | | | | 1 | | | | | | | 1 | | | | | |
| 26 | Hemorrhage | | | | | 1 | 1 | | | | 1 | | 1 | | | | | | | 4 | | | | | |
| 27 | Hernia | | | | 1 | | | | | 2 | | | | 1 | | | | | | 3 | | | | | |
| 28 | Hip, disease of | | | | | | | | | 1 | | | | | | | | | | 1 | | | | | |
| 29 | Hives | 1 | | | | | | | | | | | | | | | | | | 1 | | | | | |
| 30 | Hooping cough | 16 | 17 | 22 | 25 | | 6 | 1 | 1 | | | | | | | | | | | 85 | 2 | | | | |
| 31 | Hydrocephalus | 7 | 8 | 10 | 8 | 2 | 1 | 3 | 2 | | 2 | | | | | | | | | 42 | 1 | | | | |
| 32 | Inflamat'n, not spe'd. | 1 | 3 | 3 | 4 | 1 | | | 2 | 2 | 2 | 3 | 1 | | | | | | | 17 | 3 | 1 | | | |
| 33 | ....do......brain | 1 | 2 | 4 | 2 | 1 | | 1 | 2 | 3 | | | 1 | | | | | | | 17 | | | | | |
| 34 | ...do......bowels | 2 | 2 | 5 | 2 | 2 | | 2 | 4 | 5 | 1 | 6 | | | | | | | | 25 | 5 | | | | |
| 35 | ....do......stomach | | | | | | | | | 1 | | | | | | | | | | 1 | | | | | |
| 36 | Influenza | 2 | 2 | 1 | | 1 | | | | | | 1 | | 1 | 1 | | | | | 9 | | | | | |
| 37 | Insanity | | | | | | | | | 2 | 1 | 2 | | | | | | | | 5 | | | | | |
| 38 | Intemperance | | | | | | | | | | 2 | 4 | | | | | | | | 4 | | | | | |
| 39 | Jaundice | | 1 | | | | | | | 1 | 1 | 6 | 2 | | | | | | | 8 | 1 | | | | |
| 40 | Kidneys, disease of | | | | | | | | | 1 | | 3 | 1 | | | | | | | 4 | | | | | |
| 41 | Killed | | | | | | 1 | | | 1 | | | | | | | | | | 2 | | | | | |
| 42 | Lightning | | | | | | | | | | | 1 | | | | | | | | 1 | | | | | |
| 43 | Liver, disease of | 2 | 1 | 4 | | | | | 1 | 4 | 2 | 8 | 2 | | | | | | | 18 | 4 | | | | |
| 44 | Lockjaw | | | | | | | 1 | | | | | | | | | | | | 1 | | | | | |
| 45 | Lungs, disease of | | | | | | 1 | | | 1 | 1 | | | | | | | | | 2 | | | | | |
| 46 | Measles | 2 | 9 | 19 | 17 | 3 | 4 | 2 | 3 | | 4 | | 2 | | | | | | | 64 | | | | | |
| 47 | Mortification | | | | | | | | | | | 1 | 2 | 2 | | | | | | 5 | | | | | |
| 48 | Mumps | | 1 | | | | | | | | 1 | | | | | | | | | 2 | | | | | |
| 49 | Neuralgia | | | | | | | 1 | 1 | | | | 1 | | | | | | | 3 | | | | | |
| 50 | Old age | | | | | | | | | 1 | 1 | 28 | 39 | 84 | 92 | | | | | 175 | 54 | | | | 1 |
| 51 | Paralysis | | | | | | | 1 | 2 | 6 | 2 | 21 | 16 | 7 | 8 | | | | | 53 | 9 | | | | |
| 52 | Pleurisy | | | | | | | | | 4 | 1 | 1 | 3 | | | | | | | 7 | 2 | | | | |
| 53 | Pneumonia | 27 | 15 | 27 | 28 | 5 | 4 | 3 | 4 | 11 | 13 | 13 | 10 | 1 | 3 | | | | | 150 | 7 | 1 | | | |
| 54 | Poison | | 1 | | 2 | 1 | | | | 1 | | | | | | | | | | 5 | | | | | |
| 55 | Quinsy | 2 | 2 | 5 | 2 | 1 | 1 | | | | | | | | | | | | | 13 | | | | | |
| 56 | Rheumatism | | | | 1 | 1 | 1 | 2 | | | 1 | 3 | 3 | 2 | | | | | | 12 | 2 | | | | |
| 57 | Rickets | | | 1 | | | | | | | | | | | | | | | | 1 | | | | | |
| 58 | Scrofula | 2 | 2 | 2 | 3 | 2 | 1 | 3 | 2 | 4 | 6 | 3 | 5 | | | | | | | 34 | | | | | |
| 59 | Small pox | | | 2 | 1 | | 1 | 4 | | 13 | 1 | 4 | 2 | 1 | | | | | | 25 | 2 | 1 | | | |
| 60 | Spine, disease of | | | 1 | | | | | 1 | 1 | 4 | | 3 | 1 | | | | | | 11 | | | | | |
| 61 | Suffocation | | | | 2 | | | | | | | | | | | | | | | 2 | | | | | |
| 62 | Suicide | | | | | | | 1 | | 7 | 3 | 4 | 1 | | | | | | | 15 | 1 | | | | |
| 63 | Summer complaint | | 1 | 4 | 2 | | | | | | | | 1 | | | | | | | 8 | | | | | |
| 64 | Sun, stroke of | | | | | | | 1 | | 1 | | | | | | | | | | 2 | | | | | |
| 65 | Teething | 6 | 2 | 6 | 3 | | | | | | | | | | | | | | | 15 | | | | | |
| 66 | Throat, disease of | 5 | 5 | 15 | 20 | 7 | 8 | 7 | 1 | 3 | 3 | 2 | 3 | | 1 | | | | | 74 | 4 | | | | |
| 67 | Tumor | | | | | | | 1 | | 1 | 4 | 3 | 1 | | | | | | | 8 | 2 | | | | |
| 68 | Ulcer | | | | | 6 | 4 | 6 | 3 | 2 | | 3 | 3 | | | | | 1 | | 24 | 3 | | | | |
| 69 | Venereal | | | | | | | | | 1 | | | | | | | | | | 1 | | | | | |
| 70 | White swelling | | | | | | | | 1 | | | | | | | | | | | 1 | | | | | |
| 71 | Worms | | | 8 | 4 | | | | | | | | | | | | | | | 12 | | | | | |
| 72 | Unknown | 70 | 57 | 51 | 63 | 6 | 14 | 15 | 13 | 58 | 50 | 48 | 41 | 15 | 7 | | | 1 | | 456 | 32 | 1 | | | |
| | Total | 363 | 331 | 625 | 530 | 174 | 187 | 259 | 304 | 607 | 734 | 523 | 499 | 169 | 151 | .. | .. | 3 | 1 | 3933 | 236 | 19 | 2 | 4 | |

SECTION OF THE STATE OF MAINE—Continued.

| NATIVITIES. | | | | | SEASON OF DECEASE. | | | | DURATION OF SICKNESS. | | | | WHITES. | | | COLORED. | | | | | | | | | |
|---|---|---|---|---|---|---|---|---|---|---|---|---|---|---|---|---|---|---|---|---|---|---|---|---|---|
| | | | | | | | | | | | | | | | | Slaves. | | | | Free. | | | | | |
| | | | | | | | | | | | | | | | | Black. | | Mulatto. | | Black. | | Mul. | | | |
| California and Territories. | Ireland. | Germany. | Other foreign countries. | Unknown. | Spring. | Summer. | Autumn. | Winter. | Under 1 week. | 1 week and under 1 month. | 1 month and under 3 months. | 3 months and over. | Males. | Females. | Total. | M. | F. | M. | F. | M. | F. | M | F. | Aggregate deaths. | |
| | | | 1 | 1 | 45 | 17 | 33 | 36 | 93 | 19 | | 1 | 72 | 58 | 130 | | | | | | 2 | | | 132 | 1 |
| | 1 | | | | | 11 | 3 | 2 | 4 | 3 | 2 | 6 | 11 | 5 | 16 | | | | | | | | | 16 | 2 |
| | | | | | | 1 | | | | | | 1 | 1 | | 1 | | | | | | | | | 1 | 3 |
| | | | 3 | | 6 | 16 | 95 | 7 | 31 | 52 | 15 | 11 | 68 | 59 | 127 | | | | | | | | | 127 | 4 |
| | 3 | | 5 | 4 | 45 | 61 | 59 | 47 | 36 | 45 | 31 | 85 | 111 | 104 | 215 | | | | | | | | | 215 | 5 |
| | 4 | | 4 | 1 | 12 | 22 | 312 | 18 | 119 | 176 | 31 | 11 | 193 | 175 | 368 | | | | | | 1 | | | 369 | 6 |
| | | | | | 2 | 3 | 3 | | | 2 | 2 | 5 | 5 | 4 | 9 | | | | | | | | | 9 | 7 |
| | | | | | 1 | 2 | 1 | 2 | 2 | 1 | | 3 | 4 | 2 | 6 | | | | | | | | | 6 | 8 |
| | | | 1 | | 18 | 19 | 8 | 8 | 16 | 26 | 3 | 6 | 24 | 29 | 53 | | | | | | | | | 53 | 9 |
| | 3 | | 9 | | 69 | 41 | 85 | 70 | 48 | 152 | 49 | 18 | 137 | 130 | 267 | | | | | | | | | 267 | 10 |
| | | | | | 5 | 7 | 8 | 6 | 8 | 12 | 4 | 2 | 16 | 10 | 26 | | | | | | | | | 26 | 11 |
| | 1 | | 2 | | 19 | 29 | 30 | 14 | 21 | 54 | 11 | 2 | 48 | 44 | 92 | | | | | | | | | 92 | 12 |
| | | | | | 1 | | 1 | | | 2 | | | | 2 | 2 | | | | | | | | | 2 | 13 |
| | 1 | | | | | | 2 | | | | | 1 | 2 | | 2 | | | | | | | | | 2 | 14 |
| | 1 | | | | | 2 | 2 | 2 | 1 | 4 | 1 | | | 6 | 6 | | | | | | | | | 6 | 15 |
| | | | 4 | | 98 | 71 | 54 | 39 | 117 | 110 | 20 | 6 | 127 | 135 | 262 | | | | | | | | | 262 | 16 |
| | | | 1 | | 1 | 2 | 2 | 2 | 1 | 4 | 2 | | 5 | 2 | 7 | | | | | | | | | 7 | 17 |
| | | | 5 | 1 | 33 | 38 | 91 | 56 | 34 | 128 | 39 | 4 | 112 | 104 | 216 | | | | | 1 | | | 1 | 218 | 18 |
| | | | | | | | | 1 | 1 | | | | 2 | | 2 | | | | | | | | | 2 | 19 |
| | | | | | | 1 | 1 | | | | 1 | 1 | 1 | 1 | 2 | | | | | | | | | 2 | 20 |
| | | | | | | | | 2 | | | 1 | 1 | 2 | | 2 | | | | | | | | | 2 | 21 |
| | | | 1 | | 3 | 1 | 4 | 4 | 1 | 1 | 2 | 7 | 11 | 1 | 12 | | | | | | | | | 12 | 22 |
| | | | | | 3 | 3 | 1 | 1 | 2 | 3 | 2 | 1 | 7 | 1 | 8 | | | | | | | | | 8 | 23 |
| | | | | | 20 | 15 | 13 | 10 | 20 | 17 | 4 | 14 | 38 | 20 | 58 | | | | | | | | | 58 | 24 |
| | | | | | | 1 | | | 1 | | | | | 1 | 1 | | | | | | | | | 1 | 25 |
| | | | | | 1 | 2 | | 1 | 2 | 1 | 1 | | 1 | 3 | 4 | | | | | | | | | 4 | 26 |
| | | | 1 | | 1 | | 2 | 1 | 3 | | | 1 | 2 | 1 | 3 | | | | | 1 | | | | 4 | 27 |
| | | | | | | | | 1 | | | | 1 | 1 | | 1 | | | | | | | | | 1 | 28 |
| | | | | | | 1 | | | 1 | | | | 1 | | 1 | | | | | | | | | 1 | 29 |
| | | | 1 | | 37 | 18 | 21 | 11 | 14 | 45 | 18 | 3 | 39 | 49 | 88 | | | | | | | | | 88 | 30 |
| | | | | | 4 | 16 | 9 | 18 | 6 | 23 | 8 | 3 | 22 | 20 | 42 | | | | | | 1 | | | 43 | 31 |
| | | | 1 | | 5 | 10 | 5 | 2 | 8 | 8 | 2 | 3 | 10 | 12 | 22 | | | | | | | | | 22 | 32 |
| | | | | | 6 | 3 | 3 | 5 | 6 | 6 | 1 | 3 | 10 | 7 | 17 | | | | | | | | | 17 | 33 |
| | | | 1 | | 4 | 6 | 16 | 5 | 16 | 11 | 1 | 2 | 22 | 9 | 31 | | | | | | | | | 31 | 34 |
| | | | | | 1 | | | | | 1 | | | 1 | | 1 | | | | | | | | | 1 | 35 |
| | | | | | 2 | 2 | 1 | 4 | 6 | 2 | | 1 | 6 | 3 | 9 | | | | | | | | | 9 | 36 |
| | | | | | 3 | | 1 | 1 | | 2 | | 3 | 4 | 1 | 5 | | | | | | | | | 5 | 37 |
| | 2 | | | | 1 | 1 | 1 | 3 | 1 | 1 | 1 | 2 | 4 | 2 | 6 | | | | | | | | | 6 | 38 |
| | | | 1 | 1 | 2 | 4 | 8 | 2 | | 4 | 2 | 4 | 7 | 4 | 11 | | | | | | | | | 11 | 39 |
| | | | 1 | | | 2 | 2 | 1 | | 2 | | 3 | 4 | 1 | 5 | | | | | | | | | 5 | 40 |
| | | | | | | 1 | 1 | | 2 | | | | 1 | 1 | 2 | | | | | | | | | 2 | 41 |
| | | | | | | 1 | | | 1 | | | | 1 | | 1 | | | | | | | | | 1 | 42 |
| | 1 | | 1 | | 2 | 5 | 13 | 4 | 3 | 5 | 9 | 5 | 18 | 6 | 24 | | | | | | | | | 24 | 43 |
| | | | | | | | 1 | | 1 | | | | 1 | | 1 | | | | | | | | | 1 | 44 |
| | 1 | | | | | 1 | 2 | | | 1 | 1 | 1 | 1 | 2 | 3 | | | | | | | | | 3 | 45 |
| | | | 1 | | 10 | 24 | 26 | 5 | 17 | 29 | 13 | 5 | 26 | 38 | 64 | | | | | | | | 1 | 65 | 46 |
| | | | | | 2 | 1 | | 1 | 1 | 1 | 1 | 1 | 3 | 2 | 5 | | | | | | | | | 5 | 47 |
| | | | | | 1 | 1 | | | 1 | | | 1 | | 2 | 2 | | | | | | | | | 2 | 48 |
| | | | | | 1 | | 2 | | | 1 | | 2 | 1 | 2 | 3 | | | | | | | | | 3 | 49 |
| | 9 | | 2 | 4 | 74 | 66 | 56 | 46 | 41 | 37 | 15 | 55 | 113 | 132 | 245 | | | | | | | | | 245 | 50 |
| | | | 1 | | 15 | 21 | 13 | 13 | 13 | 15 | 5 | 30 | 35 | 28 | 63 | | | | | | | | | 63 | 51 |
| | | | | | 5 | 3 | 1 | | 1 | 7 | | 1 | 5 | 4 | 9 | | | | | | | | | 9 | 52 |
| | 4 | | 2 | | 81 | 34 | 19 | 29 | 38 | 99 | 13 | 4 | 87 | 75 | 162 | | | | | | 2 | | | 164 | 53 |
| | | | | | 1 | | 1 | 3 | 3 | 1 | | | 2 | 3 | 5 | | | | | | | | | 5 | 54 |
| | | | | | 5 | | 3 | 5 | 5 | 8 | | | 8 | 5 | 13 | | | | | | | | | 13 | 55 |
| | | | | | 8 | 2 | 3 | 1 | | 2 | 3 | 8 | 8 | 6 | 14 | | | | | | | | | 14 | 56 |
| | | | | | | | 1 | | | | | 1 | 1 | | 1 | | | | | | | | | 1 | 57 |
| | | | | 1 | 13 | 9 | 8 | 5 | 3 | 8 | 7 | 14 | 15 | 19 | 34 | | | | | 1 | | | | 35 | 58 |
| | | | | 1 | 14 | 6 | 4 | 4 | 4 | 19 | | | 24 | 5 | 29 | | | | | | | | | 29 | 59 |
| | | | | | 3 | 4 | 3 | 1 | 1 | 1 | 1 | 8 | 3 | 8 | 11 | | | | | | | | | 11 | 60 |
| | | | | | 1 | 1 | | | 1 | | | | | 2 | 2 | | | | | | | | | 2 | 61 |
| | | | | | 2 | 7 | 5 | 2 | 3 | | | | 12 | 4 | 16 | | | | | | | | | 16 | 62 |
| | | | | | | | 8 | | 3 | 4 | 1 | | 4 | 4 | 8 | | | | | | | | | 8 | 63 |
| | | | | | | 1 | 1 | | 1 | | | 1 | 2 | | 2 | | | | | | | | | 2 | 64 |
| | | | 2 | | 2 | 6 | 9 | | 2 | 9 | 4 | 1 | 12 | 5 | 17 | | | | | | | | | 17 | 65 |
| | | | 2 | | 30 | 20 | 11 | 18 | 33 | 43 | 1 | | 39 | 41 | 80 | | | | | | | | | 80 | 66 |
| | | | | | 5 | | 2 | 3 | | 2 | 2 | 6 | 5 | 5 | 10 | | | | | | | | | 10 | 67 |
| | | | 1 | | 8 | 8 | | 12 | | 9 | 13 | 6 | 18 | 10 | 28 | | | | | | | | | 28 | 68 |
| | | | | | | | 1 | | | | 1 | | 1 | | 1 | | | | | | | | | 1 | 69 |
| | | | | | 1 | | | | | | | 1 | | 1 | 1 | | | | | | | | | 1 | 70 |
| | | | | | 3 | 3 | 1 | 5 | 5 | 4 | 1 | 1 | 8 | 4 | 12 | | | | | | | | | 12 | 71 |
| | 6 | | 14 | 2 | 119 | 130 | 171 | 76 | 132 | 104 | 28 | 71 | 259 | 246 | 505 | | | | | 2 | 1 | 3 | | 511 | 72 |
| | 72 | | 164 | 33 | 1367 | 1275 | 1675 | 933 | 1840 | 1554 | 553 | 1393 | 2780 | 2723 | 5518 | | | | | 11 | 12 | 4 | 6 | 5551 | |

## CLASSIFICATION OF DEATHS IN

| | Cause of death. | AGES. | | | | | | | | | | | | | | | | | | NATIVITIES. | | | | | |
|---|---|---|---|---|---|---|---|---|---|---|---|---|---|---|---|---|---|---|---|---|---|---|---|---|---|
| | | Under 1. | | 1 and under 6. | | 5 and under 10. | | 10 and under 20. | | 20 and under 50. | | 50 and under 80. | | 80 and under 100. | | 100 & over. | | Age unknown. | | Born in State. | N. England States. | Middle States. | Southern States. | Southwest'n States. | Northwest'n States. |
| | | M. | F. | M. | F. | M. | F. | M. | F. | M. | F. | M. | F. | M | F. | M | F. | M | F. | | | | | | |
| 1 | Abscess | | | 1 | | 1 | 1 | | | 1 | 2 | 2 | 3 | | | | | | | 9 | 2 | | | | |
| 2 | Accident, not specif'd | | 3 | 7 | 2 | 10 | 5 | 20 | 2 | 45 | 1 | 6 | 1 | 3 | 2 | | | 1 | | 86 | 8 | 1 | | 1 | |
| 3 | ...do...burned | 1 | | 3 | 7 | 1 | | | 1 | | 1 | | 1 | | | | | | | 14 | | | | | |
| 4 | ....do...drowned | | 1 | 5 | 2 | 15 | | 29 | 5 | 54 | 4 | 5 | 1 | | | | | | | 109 | 7 | | | | |
| 5 | ....do...scalded | | 1 | 4 | 1 | | 1 | | | | | | | | | | | | | 7 | | | | | |
| 6 | ....do...railroad | | | | | | | 1 | | | | | | | | | | | | | | | | | |
| 7 | Apoplexy | | | | | | | | | 3 | 2 | 16 | 13 | 3 | 1 | | | | | 26 | 9 | | | | |
| 8 | Asthma | | | | | | | | 1 | 1 | | 1 | 2 | | 3 | | | | | 6 | 2 | | | | |
| 9 | Bladder, disease of | | | | | | | | | | 1 | 1 | | | | | | | | 1 | 1 | | | | |
| 10 | Bowels,......do | 15 | 8 | 30 | 20 | 4 | 5 | 5 | 3 | 2 | 7 | 3 | 8 | | | | | | | 106 | 1 | | | | |
| 11 | Brain,.........do | 2 | 1 | 2 | 2 | 1 | | 1 | 1 | | | 1 | | | | | | | | 10 | 1 | | | | |
| 12 | Bronchitis | 1 | | 1 | 1 | | | 2 | | 4 | 1 | 2 | | | | | | | | 11 | | | | | |
| 13 | Cancer | | 2 | | 2 | 1 | 1 | 1 | | 2 | 19 | 18 | 20 | 3 | 6 | | | | | 54 | 16 | | | | |
| 14 | Canker rash | 5 | 2 | 20 | 15 | 9 | 4 | 3 | 3 | | | | | | | | | | | 61 | | | | | |
| 15 | Catarrh | 4 | 3 | 1 | | | | | | | 1 | | | | | | | | | 9 | | | | | |
| 16 | Chicken pox | | 2 | 1 | 1 | | | | | | | | | | | | | | | 3 | | | | | |
| 17 | Childbirth | | | | | | | | 2 | | 46 | | | | | | | | | 42 | 2 | | | | |
| 18 | Cholera | 2 | 4 | 19 | 13 | 7 | 10 | 9 | 11 | 75 | 28 | 16 | 8 | 2 | 2 | | | | | 153 | 7 | 3 | | | |
| 19 | ...do..infantum | 25 | 15 | 5 | 6 | 1 | | | | | | | | | | | | | | 51 | 1 | | | | |
| 20 | ...do..morbus | 8 | 5 | 31 | 26 | 8 | 7 | | 5 | 9 | 9 | 5 | 6 | 3 | 1 | | | | | 110 | 5 | 1 | | | |
| 21 | Chorea | | | | | | | | 1 | | | | | | | | | | | 1 | | | | | |
| 22 | Colic | 1 | | | 1 | 1 | 1 | | | 5 | 5 | 5 | 4 | 1 | | | | | | 22 | 1 | | | | |
| 23 | Congestion of brain | | | 1 | 1 | | | | | | | | | | | | | | | 2 | | | | | |
| 24 | ....do.......lungs | 1 | | | 1 | | | | | | | 1 | | | | | | | | 2 | | | | | |
| 25 | Consumption | 28 | 27 | 34 | 40 | 9 | 22 | 42 | 150 | 345 | 554 | 196 | 218 | 15 | 21 | | | | 1 | 1525 | 113 | 8 | 2 | 1 | |
| 26 | Convulsions | 23 | 21 | 18 | 18 | 3 | 1 | 5 | 3 | 11 | 9 | 7 | 6 | | 3 | | | | | 120 | 6 | | | | |
| 27 | Cramp | | | | | | | | | 1 | 1 | 1 | 1 | | | | | | | 3 | | | | | |
| 28 | Croup | 21 | 21 | 54 | 46 | 12 | 15 | 2 | 3 | 1 | | | | | | | | | | 171 | | 1 | | | |
| 29 | Debility | 4 | 1 | 2 | 1 | | | 1 | | 1 | 1 | 6 | 3 | | | | | | | 18 | 1 | | | | |
| 30 | Diabetes | | | | | | | | | | 1 | 1 | | | | | | | | 1 | 1 | | | | |
| 31 | Diarrhœa | 17 | 12 | 31 | 41 | 8 | 3 | 7 | 2 | 16 | 10 | 5 | 5 | | | | | | | 146 | 5 | | | | |
| 32 | Dropsy | 15 | 14 | 40 | 19 | 12 | 8 | 4 | 9 | 10 | 40 | 47 | 48 | 14 | 6 | | | 1 | | 242 | 33 | | | | |
| 33 | Dysentery | 41 | 29 | 125 | 98 | 28 | 26 | 26 | 17 | 36 | 25 | 23 | 30 | 1 | 4 | | | | | 476 | 20 | | | 1 | |
| 34 | Dyspepsia | 1 | 1 | | | | | | | | 2 | 5 | 1 | | | | | | | 9 | 1 | | | | |
| 35 | Epilepsy | | | | | | | | | 2 | | 2 | | | 2 | | | | | 5 | 1 | | | | |
| 36 | Erysipelas | 12 | 6 | 2 | 4 | 1 | 4 | 2 | 6 | 11 | 15 | 12 | 11 | | 2 | | | | | 74 | 12 | | | | |
| 37 | Fever, not specified | 11 | 21 | 42 | 30 | 16 | 14 | 33 | 42 | 62 | 47 | 26 | 16 | 1 | 2 | | | | | 333 | 13 | | | | |
| 38 | ..do..bilious | 1 | | 4 | 1 | | | 1 | 3 | 3 | 5 | 5 | 4 | 4 | | | | | | 27 | 4 | | | | |
| 39 | ..do..brain | 12 | 10 | 24 | 16 | 6 | 4 | 14 | 15 | 9 | 15 | 3 | 2 | 1 | | | | | | 121 | 6 | 1 | | | |
| 40 | ..do..inflammatory | | | | 1 | | | | 1 | | | | 1 | | | | | | | 3 | | | | | |
| 41 | ..do..intermittent | | | | | | | 1 | | 1 | | | | | | | | | | 1 | | | | | |
| 42 | ..do..puerperal | | | | | | | | 1 | | 9 | | | | | | | | | 9 | | | | | |
| 43 | ..do..remittent | | | | | | | 1 | | | | | | | | | | | | 1 | | | | | |
| 44 | ..do..scarlet | 11 | 20 | 93 | 77 | 41 | 50 | 18 | 11 | 2 | 3 | 1 | 3 | | | | | | | 317 | 8 | 1 | | | |
| 45 | ..do..ship | 1 | | 1 | | | | | 2 | 3 | | | | | | | | | | 6 | | | | | |
| 46 | ..do..typhus | 4 | 1 | 10 | 9 | 10 | 8 | 33 | 41 | 56 | 61 | 25 | 22 | 1 | | | | 1 | | 262 | 11 | | | | |
| 47 | ..do..yellow | | | | | | | | | 2 | | | | | | | | | | 1 | | 1 | | | |
| 48 | Fracture | | | | | | | | | 1 | | | 1 | | | | | | | 1 | 1 | | | | |
| 49 | Gout | | | | | | | 1 | | | | 1 | | | | | | | | 1 | 1 | | | | |
| 50 | Gravel | | | 1 | | | | 1 | | | 1 | 17 | 1 | | | | | | | 14 | 6 | | | | |
| 51 | Head, disease of | 4 | | 1 | 1 | 1 | | | | 1 | | | | | | | | | | 8 | | | | | |
| 52 | Heart,.....do | 2 | 2 | 2 | 2 | 1 | 2 | 1 | 9 | 10 | 11 | 24 | 4 | 4 | 2 | | | | | 65 | 11 | | | | |
| 53 | Heat | | | | | | | | | | | | 1 | | | | | | | 1 | | | | | |
| 54 | Hemorrhage | | | | | 1 | 1 | | | 1 | 2 | 1 | 1 | | | | | | | 7 | | | | | |
| 55 | Hernia | | | | 1 | | | | 1 | 2 | | 1 | 1 | 2 | | | | | | 5 | 1 | | | | |
| 56 | Hip, disease of | | | | | | | | 1 | 1 | | | 1 | | | | | | | 2 | 1 | | | | |
| 57 | Hives | 1 | | | | | | | | | | | | | | | | | | 1 | | | | | |
| 58 | Hooping cough | 25 | 24 | 32 | 37 | 1 | 7 | 1 | 1 | | | | | | | | | | | 125 | 2 | | | | |
| 59 | Hydrocephalus | 9 | 9 | 17 | 12 | 3 | 2 | 3 | 2 | | 4 | | | | | | | | | 60 | 1 | | | | |
| 60 | Inflammation | 1 | 3 | 3 | 4 | 1 | | | 3 | 2 | 2 | 4 | 1 | | | | | | | 18 | 4 | 1 | | | |
| 61 | ....do....bowels | 6 | 2 | 11 | 4 | 2 | 1 | 3 | 6 | 7 | 2 | 9 | 1 | | | | | | | 44 | 9 | | | | |
| 62 | ....do....brain | 3 | 3 | 4 | 2 | 1 | | 1 | 2 | 3 | | 1 | 1 | | | | | | | 21 | | | | | |
| 63 | ....do....stomach | | | | | | | | | 1 | | | | | | | | | | 1 | | | | | |
| 64 | Influenza | 6 | 3 | 3 | | 1 | | | | | | 2 | | 1 | 1 | | | | | 17 | | | | | |
| 65 | Insanity | | | | | | | | | 2 | 1 | 2 | | | | | | | | 5 | | | | | |
| 66 | Intemperance | | | | | | | | | 1 | 2 | 5 | | | | | | | | 4 | 2 | | | | |
| 67 | Jaundice | | 1 | 1 | | | | | | 1 | 1 | 6 | 5 | | | | | | | 10 | 3 | | | | |
| 68 | Kidneys, disease of | | | | | | | | | 3 | 1 | 5 | 1 | | | | | | | 7 | 2 | | | | |
| 69 | Killed | | | | | | 1 | | | 1 | | | | | | | | | | 2 | | | | | |
| 70 | Lightning | | | | | | | | | | | 1 | | | | | | | | 1 | | | | | |
| 71 | Liver, disease of | 2 | 1 | 4 | 1 | 1 | | | 1 | 4 | 8 | 12 | 5 | | | | | | | 25 | 7 | | | | |
| 72 | Lockjaw | | | | | | | 1 | | | | | | | | | | | | 1 | | | | | |
| 73 | Lungs, disease of | 1 | | | | | 1 | | | 1 | 1 | 1 | | | | | | | | 3 | | | | | |
| 74 | Measles | 5 | 9 | 21 | 19 | 3 | 4 | 4 | 3 | 1 | 5 | | 2 | | | | | | | 74 | | | | | |
| 75 | Mortification | | | | | | | | | | | 1 | 2 | 2 | | | | | | 5 | | | | | |

## THE STATE OF MAINE—AGGREGATE.

| Nativities: California and Territories. | Nativities: Ireland. | Nativities: Germany. | Nativities: Other foreign countries. | Nativities: Unknown. | Season of decease: Spring. | Season of decease: Summer. | Season of decease: Autumn. | Season of decease: Winter. | Duration of sickness: Under 1 week. | Duration of sickness: 1 week and under 1 month. | Duration of sickness: 1 month and under 3 months. | Duration of sickness: 3 months and over. | Whites: Males. | Whites: Females. | Whites: Total. | Colored: Slaves: Black: M. | Colored: Slaves: Black: F. | Colored: Slaves: Mulatto: M. | Colored: Slaves: Mulatto: F. | Colored: Free: Black: M. | Colored: Free: Black: F. | Colored: Free: Mul.: M | Colored: Free: Mul.: F. | Aggregate deaths. | |
|---|---|---|---|---|---|---|---|---|---|---|---|---|---|---|---|---|---|---|---|---|---|---|---|---|---|
| | | | | | 2 | 2 | 2 | 5 | 1 | 4 | 2 | 4 | 5 | 6 | 11 | | | | | | | | | 11 | 1 |
| | 7 | 1 | 4 | | 35 | 15 | 28 | 28 | 60 | 4 | 2 | 1 | 90 | 15 | 105 | | | | | 2 | 1 | | | 108 | 2 |
| | | | 1 | | 2 | 7 | 2 | 4 | 7 | 1 | | | 5 | 10 | 15 | | | | | | | | | 15 | 3 |
| | | | 3 | 2 | 26 | 41 | 30 | 21 | 29 | | | | 108 | 13 | 121 | | | | | | | | | 121 | 4 |
| | | | | | 8 | | 3 | 1 | 4 | 2 | | | 4 | 3 | 7 | | | | | | | | | 7 | 5 |
| | 1 | | | | | | 1 | | 1 | | | | 1 | | 1 | | | | | | | | | 1 | 6 |
| | 1 | | 2 | | 15 | 5 | 9 | 8 | 29 | 2 | | 1 | 22 | 15 | 37 | | | | | | | | 1 | 38 | 7 |
| | | | | | 5 | 1 | 2 | | 1 | 3 | | 4 | 2 | 6 | 8 | | | | | | | | | 8 | 8 |
| | | | | | | | 1 | 1 | | 1 | | 1 | 1 | 1 | 2 | | | | | | | | | 2 | 9 |
| | | | 3 | | 11 | 13 | 74 | 12 | 35 | 44 | 5 | 3 | 59 | 50 | 109 | | | | | | | | 1 | 110 | 10 |
| | | | | | 4 | 1 | 3 | 3 | 1 | 5 | 1 | | 6 | 4 | 10 | | | | | 1 | | | | 11 | 11 |
| | | | 1 | | 3 | 3 | 2 | 4 | 1 | 3 | 2 | 6 | 10 | 2 | 12 | | | | | | | | | 12 | 12 |
| | 2 | | 2 | 1 | 16 | 15 | 20 | 23 | 2 | 6 | 8 | 51 | 25 | 50 | 75 | | | | | | | | | 75 | 13 |
| | | | | | 24 | 18 | 10 | 9 | 25 | 28 | 7 | | 37 | 24 | 61 | | | | | | | | | 61 | 14 |
| | | | | | 6 | 1 | | 2 | 7 | 1 | 1 | | 5 | 4 | 9 | | | | | | | | | 9 | 15 |
| | | | 1 | | 1 | 1 | 1 | 1 | 1 | 3 | | | 1 | 3 | 4 | | | | | | | | | 4 | 16 |
| | 1 | | 3 | | 13 | 19 | 6 | 10 | 29 | 12 | 2 | 1 | | 48 | 48 | | | | | | | | | 48 | 17 |
| | 37 | | 4 | 2 | 8 | 21 | 172 | 3 | 175 | 24 | | 1 | 129 | 76 | 205 | | | | | | | 1 | | 206 | 18 |
| | | | | | 9 | 13 | 24 | 6 | 18 | 15 | 4 | 1 | 31 | 21 | 52 | | | | | | | | | 52 | 19 |
| | 1 | | 4 | 2 | 6 | 14 | 97 | 5 | 62 | 42 | 5 | 2 | 64 | 59 | 123 | | | | | | | | | 123 | 20 |
| | | | | | | | 1 | | | | | 1 | | 1 | 1 | | | | | | | | | 1 | 21 |
| | | | | 1 | 6 | 4 | 8 | 6 | 20 | 3 | | | 13 | 10 | 23 | | | | | | | | 1 | 24 | 22 |
| | | | | | 1 | 1 | | | | 1 | 1 | | 1 | 1 | 2 | | | | | | | | | 2 | 23 |
| | | | 1 | | | 2 | 1 | | 1 | | | | 2 | 1 | 3 | | | | | | | | | 3 | 24 |
| | 24 | | 23 | 11 | 487 | 461 | 437 | 816 | 36 | 120 | 193 | 1255 | 666 | 1029 | 1695 | | | | | 3 | 4 | | | 1702 | 25 |
| | | | 2 | | 35 | 35 | 33 | 25 | 79 | 19 | 3 | 17 | 67 | 60 | 127 | | | | | | | | 1 | 128 | 26 |
| | 1 | | | | | | 1 | 3 | 3 | | | | 2 | 2 | 4 | | | | | | | | | 4 | 27 |
| | | | 2 | 1 | 56 | 27 | 43 | 47 | 123 | 30 | 2 | 1 | 90 | 83 | 173 | | | | | | 2 | | | 175 | 28 |
| | 1 | | | | | 13 | 5 | 2 | 5 | 5 | 2 | 7 | 14 | 6 | 20 | | | | | | | | | 20 | 29 |
| | | | | | | 2 | | | | | | 2 | 1 | 1 | 2 | | | | | | | | | 2 | 30 |
| | | | 6 | | 9 | 18 | 119 | 8 | 46 | 63 | 17 | 11 | 84 | 73 | 157 | | | | | | | | | 157 | 31 |
| | 3 | | 5 | 4 | 68 | 87 | 74 | 55 | 41 | 62 | 41 | 123 | 143 | 144 | 287 | | | | | | | | | 287 | 32 |
| | 6 | | 5 | 1 | 15 | 33 | 426 | 30 | 160 | 267 | 39 | 11 | 280 | 228 | 508 | | | | | | 1 | | | 509 | 33 |
| | | | | | 2 | 4 | 3 | | | 2 | 2 | 6 | 6 | 4 | 10 | | | | | | | | | 10 | 34 |
| | | | | | 1 | 2 | 1 | 2 | 2 | 1 | | 3 | 4 | 2 | 6 | | | | | | | | | 6 | 35 |
| | | | 2 | | 35 | 23 | 12 | 18 | 23 | 49 | 7 | 6 | 40 | 48 | 88 | | | | | | | | | 88 | 36 |
| | 5 | | 11 | 1 | 98 | 67 | 102 | 94 | 75 | 211 | 57 | 15 | 191 | 172 | 363 | | | | | | | | | 363 | 37 |
| | | | | | 8 | 9 | 8 | 6 | 8 | 14 | 5 | 4 | 18 | 13 | 31 | | | | | | | | | 31 | 38 |
| | 1 | | 2 | | 31 | 37 | 41 | 22 | 31 | 76 | 14 | 5 | 69 | 62 | 131 | | | | | | | | | 131 | 39 |
| | | | | | 1 | 1 | 1 | | 1 | 2 | | | | 3 | 3 | | | | | | | | | 3 | 40 |
| | 1 | | | | | | 2 | | | | | 1 | 2 | | 2 | | | | | | | | | 2 | 41 |
| | 1 | | | | 2 | 3 | 2 | 3 | 4 | 5 | 1 | | | 10 | 10 | | | | | | | | | 10 | 42 |
| | | | | | | 1 | | | | 1 | | | 1 | | 1 | | | | | | | | | 1 | 43 |
| | | | 4 | | 120 | 87 | 67 | 56 | 149 | 141 | 24 | 7 | 166 | 164 | 330 | | | | | | | | | 330 | 44 |
| | | | 1 | | 1 | 2 | 2 | 2 | 1 | 4 | 2 | | 5 | 2 | 7 | | | | | | | | | 7 | 45 |
| | 1 | | 7 | 1 | 45 | 57 | 115 | 65 | 43 | 172 | 48 | 5 | 139 | 141 | 280 | | | | | 1 | | | 1 | 282 | 46 |
| | | | | | | | | 1 | 1 | | | | 2 | | 2 | | | | | | | | | 2 | 47 |
| | | | | | | 1 | 1 | | | | 1 | 1 | 1 | 1 | 2 | | | | | | | | | 2 | 48 |
| | | | | | | | | 2 | | | 1 | 1 | 2 | | 2 | | | | | | | | | 2 | 49 |
| | | | 1 | | 7 | 2 | 7 | 5 | 3 | 3 | 5 | 9 | 19 | 2 | 21 | | | | | | | | | 21 | 50 |
| | | | | | 3 | 3 | 1 | 1 | 2 | 3 | 2 | 1 | 7 | 1 | 8 | | | | | | | | | 8 | 51 |
| | | | | | 27 | 18 | 19 | 12 | 25 | 20 | 8 | 20 | 44 | 32 | 76 | | | | | | | | | 76 | 52 |
| | | | | | | 1 | | | 1 | | | | | 1 | 1 | | | | | | | | | 1 | 53 |
| | | | | | 1 | 2 | 2 | 2 | 3 | 1 | 1 | 2 | 3 | 4 | 7 | | | | | | | | | 7 | 54 |
| | | | 2 | | 2 | | 4 | 2 | 3 | 2 | | 3 | 4 | 3 | 7 | | | | | 1 | | | | 8 | 55 |
| | | | | | | | 2 | 1 | | 1 | | 2 | 1 | 2 | 3 | | | | | | | | | 3 | 56 |
| | | | | | | 1 | | | 1 | | | | 1 | | 1 | | | | | | | | | 1 | 57 |
| | | | 1 | | 55 | 24 | 28 | 20 | 19 | 67 | 28 | 6 | 58 | 68 | 126 | | | | | | 1 | 1 | | 128 | 58 |
| | | | | | 11 | 19 | 11 | 19 | 7 | 32 | 14 | 5 | 32 | 28 | 60 | | | | | | 1 | | | 61 | 59 |
| | | | 1 | | 5 | 10 | 5 | 4 | 10 | 8 | 2 | 3 | 11 | 13 | 24 | | | | | | | | | 24 | 60 |
| | | | 1 | | 10 | 14 | 23 | 7 | 29 | 19 | 3 | 2 | 38 | 16 | 54 | | | | | | | | | 54 | 61 |
| | | | | | 8 | 4 | 4 | 5 | 9 | 7 | 1 | 3 | 13 | 8 | 21 | | | | | | | | | 21 | 62 |
| | | | | | 1 | | | | | 1 | | | 1 | | 1 | | | | | | | | | 1 | 63 |
| | | | | | 6 | 4 | 1 | 6 | 11 | 5 | | 1 | 13 | 4 | 17 | | | | | | | | | 17 | 64 |
| | | | | | 3 | | 1 | 1 | | 2 | | 3 | 4 | 1 | 5 | | | | | | | | | 5 | 65 |
| | 2 | | | | 2 | 1 | 2 | 3 | 1 | 2 | 1 | 3 | 6 | 2 | 8 | | | | | | | | | 8 | 66 |
| | | | 1 | 1 | 3 | 5 | 4 | 3 | 1 | 5 | 3 | 5 | 8 | 7 | 15 | | | | | | | | | 15 | 67 |
| | | | 1 | | 2 | 2 | 2 | 4 | 1 | 3 | 1 | 5 | 8 | 2 | 10 | | | | | | | | | 10 | 68 |
| | | | | | | 1 | 1 | | 2 | | | | 1 | 1 | 2 | | | | | | | | | 2 | 69 |
| | | | | | | 1 | | | 1 | | | | 1 | | 1 | | | | | | | | | 1 | 70 |
| | 1 | | 1 | | 4 | 8 | 16 | 6 | 3 | 8 | 11 | 10 | 23 | 11 | 34 | | | | | | | | | 34 | 71 |
| | | | | | | | 1 | | 1 | | | | 1 | | 1 | | | | | | | | | 1 | 72 |
| | 2 | | | | 1 | 2 | 2 | | | 2 | 1 | 2 | 3 | 2 | 5 | | | | | | | | | 5 | 73 |
| | | | 2 | | 10 | 30 | 28 | 8 | 19 | 36 | 15 | 5 | 34 | 41 | 75 | | | | | | | | 1 | 76 | 74 |
| | | | | | 2 | 1 | | 1 | 1 | 1 | 1 | 1 | 3 | 2 | 5 | | | | | | | | | 5 | 75 |

## CLASSIFICATION OF DEATHS IN

| | Cause of death. | AGES. | | | | | | | | | | | | | | | | | | NATIVITIES. | | | | | |
|---|---|---|---|---|---|---|---|---|---|---|---|---|---|---|---|---|---|---|---|---|---|---|---|---|---|
| | | Under 1. | | 1 and under 5. | | 5 and under 10. | | 10 and under 20. | | 20 and under 50. | | 50 and under 80. | | 80 and under 100. | | 100 & over. | | Age unknown. | | Born in State. | N. England States. | Middle States. | Southern States. | Southwest'n States. | Northwest'n States. |
| | | M. | F. | M. | F. | M. | F. | M. | F. | M. | F. | M. | F. | M. | F. | M | F. | M | F. | | | | | | |
| 1 | Mumps | 1 | 1 | 1 | | | | | | | 1 | | | | | | | | | 4 | | | | | |
| 2 | Neuralgia | | | | | | | 1 | 1 | | | | 2 | | | | | | | 3 | 1 | | | | |
| 3 | Old age | | | | | | | | | 1 | 1 | 37 | 50 | 107 | 114 | | | | | 203 | 89 | | | 1 | |
| 4 | Paralysis | | | | | | | 1 | 2 | 7 | 2 | 25 | 20 | 9 | 9 | | | | | 62 | 12 | | | | |
| 5 | Pleurisy | | | | | | | | | 5 | 1 | 1 | 4 | | | | | | | 8 | 3 | | | | |
| 6 | Pneumonia | 37 | 21 | 38 | 35 | 5 | 4 | 5 | 6 | 14 | 18 | 21 | 15 | 1 | 3 | | | | | 204 | 11 | 1 | | | |
| 7 | Poison | | 1 | | 2 | 1 | | | | 1 | | | | | | | | | | 5 | | | | | |
| 8 | Quinsy | 3 | 2 | 5 | 2 | 1 | 2 | | | | | | | | | | | | | 15 | | | | | |
| 9 | Rheumatism | | | | 1 | 1 | 1 | 2 | | 1 | 1 | 3 | 4 | 2 | | | | | | 13 | 3 | | | | |
| 10 | Rickets | | | 1 | | | | | | | | | | | | | | | | 1 | | | | | |
| 11 | Scrofula | 2 | 3 | 9 | 5 | 4 | 1 | 4 | 3 | 4 | 9 | 3 | 5 | | | | | | | 51 | | | | | |
| 12 | Small pox | | | 2 | 1 | | 1 | 4 | | 13 | 1 | 4 | 2 | 1 | | | | | | 25 | 2 | 1 | | | |
| 13 | Spine, disease of | | | 1 | 1 | | | | 1 | 2 | 5 | 1 | 3 | 1 | | | | | | 15 | | | | | |
| 14 | Suffocation | | | | 2 | | 1 | | | | | | | | | | | | | 3 | | | | | |
| 15 | Suicide | | | 2 | | | | 1 | 2 | 11 | 5 | 4 | 1 | | | | | | | 25 | 1 | | | | |
| 16 | Summer complaint | | 1 | 4 | 2 | | | | | | | | 1 | | | | | | | 8 | | | | | |
| 17 | Sun, stroke of | | | | | | | 1 | | 1 | | | | | | | | | | 2 | | | | | |
| 18 | Syphilis | | | | | | | | | 1 | | | | | | | | | | | | | | | |
| 19 | Teething, | 6 | 2 | 6 | 3 | | | | | | | | | | | | | | | 15 | | | | | |
| 20 | Throat, disease of | 5 | 5 | 16 | 20 | 10 | 9 | 9 | 2 | 3 | 3 | 2 | 3 | | 2 | | | | | 82 | 5 | | | | |
| 21 | Thrush | | | | | | 1 | | | | | | | | | | | | | | 1 | | | | |
| 22 | Tumor | | | 1 | | | | 1 | | 1 | 5 | 4 | 2 | | | | | | | 12 | 2 | | | | |
| 23 | Ulcer | 1 | 5 | 2 | 4 | 6 | 5 | 6 | 3 | 2 | | 3 | 4 | | | | | 1 | | 37 | 4 | | | | |
| 24 | Venereal | | | | | | | | | 1 | | | | | | | | | | 1 | | | | | |
| 25 | White swelling | | | | 1 | | | | 1 | | | | | | | | | | | 2 | | | | | |
| 26 | Worms | | | 9 | 6 | | | | | | | | | | | | | | | 15 | | | | | |
| 27 | Unknown | 95 | 73 | 67 | 83 | 9 | 27 | 21 | 23 | 76 | 73 | 70 | 55 | 19 | 10 | | | 1 | 2 | 616 | 52 | 1 | | | |
| | Total | 482 | 402 | 875 | 753 | 258 | 261 | 333 | 414 | 960 | 1086 | 718 | 637 | 201 | 196 | | | 5 | 3 | 6721 | 535 | 16 | 2 | 4 | |

## CLASSIFICATION OF DEATHS IN

| | | | | | | | | | | | | | | | | | | | | | | | | | |
|---|---|---|---|---|---|---|---|---|---|---|---|---|---|---|---|---|---|---|---|---|---|---|---|---|---|
| 1 | Abscess | | | | | | | | | 4 | 1 | | | | | | | | | 5 | | | | | |
| 2 | Accident, not specif'd | 29 | 12 | 6 | 4 | 7 | 6 | 17 | | 24 | 1 | 10 | 1 | | 3 | | | | | 103 | | 1 | | | |
| 3 | ....do...burned | 3 | 4 | 9 | 18 | 2 | 8 | 1 | 6 | 2 | 4 | 2 | 3 | | | | | | | 62 | | | | | |
| 4 | ....do...drowned | | | 2 | 4 | 8 | | 10 | | 29 | 2 | 4 | | | | | | | | 37 | | 4 | 1 | | |
| 5 | ... do...scalded | 1 | | 5 | 4 | | | | | 1 | | | | | | | | | | 10 | | | 1 | | |
| 6 | ....do...railroad | | | | | | | | | 1 | | | | | | | | | | | | | | | |
| 7 | Apoplexy | | | | | | | | 2 | 11 | 5 | 24 | 15 | 3 | | | | | | 52 | | 2 | | | |
| 8 | Asthma | | 1 | | | | | | | 2 | 1 | 4 | 4 | | | | | | | 10 | 1 | | | | |
| 9 | Bladder, disease of | | | | | | | | | | | 1 | | | | | | | | 1 | | | | | |
| 10 | Bowels......do | 1 | 2 | 1 | | | | 1 | | 1 | 1 | 1 | | | | | | | | 6 | | | | | |
| 11 | Brain ......do | 18 | 12 | 13 | 15 | 2 | 6 | 2 | 2 | | 2 | 2 | | | 1 | | | | | 75 | | | | | |
| 12 | Bronchitis | 1 | | 1 | 2 | 1 | 3 | | | 6 | 3 | 3 | 2 | | | | | | | 20 | | | | | |
| 13 | Cancer | | | | 1 | | | 2 | 1 | 4 | 12 | 5 | 18 | 2 | 1 | | 1 | | | 39 | | 1 | | | |
| 14 | Catarrh | 12 | 19 | 12 | 15 | 3 | 5 | 5 | 7 | 10 | 5 | 4 | 4 | | 1 | | | | | 93 | 1 | 1 | | | |
| 15 | Chicken pox | | 2 | 1 | 1 | | | | | 1 | | | 1 | | | | | | | 6 | | | | | |
| 16 | Childbirth | | | | | | | | 9 | | 86 | | | | | | | | | 75 | | 4 | 2 | | |
| 17 | Cholera | 2 | 1 | 6 | 1 | 3 | 2 | 8 | 8 | 48 | 33 | 35 | 14 | 3 | 2 | | | | | 109 | 3 | 5 | 1 | | 1 |
| 18 | ....do..infantum | 45 | 38 | 42 | 40 | 1 | | | | | | | | | | | | | | 160 | | 2 | 1 | | |
| 19 | ....do..morbus | | | 1 | 1 | | 1 | 1 | 4 | 4 | 7 | 3 | 5 | 2 | | | | | | 24 | | 1 | 1 | | |
| 20 | Chorea | | | | | | | | 2 | | | | | | | | | | | 2 | | | | | |
| 21 | Colic | 4 | 1 | 1 | 1 | | 1 | 1 | | 8 | 2 | 4 | | | | | | | | 17 | | 2 | 1 | | |
| 22 | Congestion of brain | 3 | 1 | 5 | 2 | 1 | | 2 | | 3 | 3 | 2 | | 1 | | | | | | 21 | | 2 | | | |
| 23 | .....do......lungs | 2 | | 1 | | | 1 | 1 | | | 1 | | 4 | | | | | | | 9 | 1 | | | | |
| 24 | Consumption | 37 | 27 | 31 | 44 | 23 | 14 | 45 | 73 | 262 | 326 | 112 | 90 | 7 | 7 | | | 3 | | 931 | 3 | 53 | 20 | 1 | |
| 25 | Convulsions | 72 | 60 | 12 | 20 | 3 | 3 | 2 | 3 | 7 | 4 | 1 | 1 | | | | | | | 186 | | 1 | | | |
| 26 | Cramp | 3 | 4 | 3 | 1 | 1 | | 2 | | 4 | 1 | 2 | 1 | | | | | | | 17 | | | | | |
| 27 | Croup | 37 | 41 | 59 | 61 | 9 | 11 | | 3 | | 1 | | | | | | | | | 215 | | 2 | 2 | | |
| 28 | Debility | 6 | 10 | 1 | 1 | 1 | | | | | 2 | 2 | | | | | | | | 23 | | | | | |
| 29 | Diabetes | | | | | | | 1 | | 1 | | | | | | | | | | 2 | | | | | |
| 30 | Diarrhœa | 22 | 16 | 21 | 18 | 9 | 2 | 3 | 3 | 18 | 17 | 9 | 14 | 2 | 2 | | | 1 | 1 | 138 | 1 | 4 | 1 | | |
| 31 | Dropsy | 3 | 3 | 27 | 17 | 12 | 14 | 13 | 10 | 43 | 48 | 55 | 53 | 9 | 3 | | 1 | | 1 | 272 | 3 | 11 | 3 | | |
| 32 | Dysentery | 58 | 52 | 119 | 94 | 38 | 40 | 33 | 27 | 44 | 42 | 21 | 25 | 3 | 6 | | | 3 | 2 | 555 | 2 | 15 | 3 | 1 | 1 |
| 33 | Dyspepsia | | | | | | | 1 | | 4 | 10 | 7 | 8 | | | | | | | 22 | 1 | 2 | | | |
| 34 | Epilepsy | 1 | 2 | 1 | 1 | 1 | 3 | 2 | 5 | 6 | 6 | 1 | 3 | | | | | | | 28 | | 2 | | | |
| 35 | Erysipelas | 8 | 7 | 1 | 2 | | 2 | 4 | 4 | 10 | 4 | 11 | 9 | 1 | | | | | | 52 | | 2 | 1 | | |
| 36 | Fever, not specified | 16 | 19 | 12 | 15 | 9 | 8 | 8 | 4 | 21 | 13 | 10 | 2 | | | | | 2 | | 132 | | 2 | 1 | | |
| 37 | ..do..bilious | 9 | 13 | 39 | 21 | 10 | 17 | 21 | 13 | 43 | 30 | 32 | 12 | 1 | 3 | | | | | 242 | | 6 | 4 | | |
| 38 | ..do..catarrhal | 21 | 19 | 25 | 22 | 3 | 5 | 1 | 3 | 3 | | 1 | | | | | | | | 101 | | | 1 | | |
| 39 | ..do..congestive | | 2 | 3 | 1 | 2 | 1 | 1 | 3 | 14 | 10 | 4 | 2 | | 1 | | | | | 39 | | 2 | | | |

## THE STATE OF MAINE—AGGREGATE—Continued.

| Nativities: California and Territories. | Nativities: Ireland. | Nativities: Germany. | Nativities: Other foreign countries. | Nativities: Unknown. | Season of decease: Spring. | Season of decease: Summer. | Season of decease: Autumn. | Season of decease: Winter. | Duration of sickness: Under 1 week. | Duration of sickness: 1 week and under 1 month. | Duration of sickness: 1 month and under 3 months. | Duration of sickness: 3 months and over. | Whites: Males. | Whites: Females. | Whites: Total. | Colored: Slaves: Black: M. | Colored: Slaves: Black: F. | Colored: Slaves: Mulatto: M. | Colored: Slaves: Mulatto: F. | Colored: Free: Black: M. | Colored: Free: Black: F. | Colored: Free: Mul.: M | Colored: Free: Mul.: F. | Aggregate deaths. | |
|---|---|---|---|---|---|---|---|---|---|---|---|---|---|---|---|---|---|---|---|---|---|---|---|---|---|
| | | | | | 2 | 1 | 1 | | 1 | 2 | | 1 | 2 | 2 | 4 | | | | | | | | | 4 | 1 |
| | | | | | 1 | | 3 | | | 1 | | 3 | 1 | 3 | 4 | | | | | | | | | 4 | 2 |
| | 9 | | 4 | 4 | 95 | 85 | 67 | 59 | 51 | 50 | 21 | 70 | 145 | 165 | 310 | | | | | | | | | 310 | 3 |
| | | | 1 | | 21 | 22 | 16 | 15 | 18 | 16 | 5 | 36 | 42 | 33 | 75 | | | | | | | | | 75 | 4 |
| | | | | | 7 | 3 | 1 | | 2 | 8 | | 1 | 6 | 5 | 11 | | | | | | | | | 11 | 5 |
| | 4 | | 3 | | 110 | 46 | 24 | 42 | 53 | 139 | 16 | 5 | 121 | 100 | 221 | | | | | | 2 | | | 223 | 6 |
| | | | | | 1 | | 1 | 3 | 3 | 1 | | | 2 | 3 | 5 | | | | | | | | | 5 | 7 |
| | | | | | 5 | | 3 | 7 | 6 | 9 | | | 9 | 6 | 15 | | | | | | | | | 15 | 8 |
| | | | | | 8 | 3 | 4 | 1 | | 3 | 3 | 9 | 9 | 7 | 16 | | | | | | | | | 16 | 9 |
| | | | | | | | 1 | | | | | 1 | 1 | | 1 | | | | | | | | | 1 | 10 |
| | | | | 1 | 16 | 12 | 13 | 11 | 5 | 10 | 9 | 25 | 25 | 26 | 51 | | | | | 1 | | | | 52 | 11 |
| | | | | 1 | 14 | 6 | 4 | 4 | 4 | 19 | | | 24 | 5 | 29 | | | | | | | | | 29 | 12 |
| | | | | | 3 | 5 | 6 | 1 | 2 | 1 | 2 | 10 | 5 | 10 | 15 | | | | | | | | | 15 | 13 |
| | | | | | 1 | 1 | 1 | | 2 | | | | | 3 | 3 | | | | | | | | | 3 | 14 |
| | | | | | 4 | 15 | 5 | 2 | 6 | | | | 18 | 8 | 26 | | | | | | | | | 26 | 15 |
| | | | | | | | 8 | | 3 | 4 | 1 | | 4 | 4 | 8 | | | | | | | | | 8 | 16 |
| | | | | | | 1 | 1 | | 1 | | | 1 | 2 | | 2 | | | | | | | | | 2 | 17 |
| | 1 | | | | | 1 | | | | | | 1 | 1 | | 1 | | | | | | | | | 1 | 18 |
| | | | 2 | | 2 | 6 | 9 | | 2 | 9 | 4 | 1 | 12 | 5 | 17 | | | | | | | | | 17 | 19 |
| | | | 2 | | 30 | 21 | 16 | 21 | 36 | 49 | 1 | | 45 | 44 | 89 | | | | | | | | | 89 | 20 |
| | | | | | | 1 | | | | | | 1 | | 1 | 1 | | | | | | | | | 1 | 21 |
| | | | | | 6 | 1 | 3 | 4 | | 2 | 3 | 9 | 7 | 7 | 14 | | | | | | | | | 14 | 22 |
| | | | 1 | | 10 | 10 | 6 | 16 | | 18 | 13 | 8 | 21 | 21 | 42 | | | | | | | | | 42 | 23 |
| | | | | | | | 1 | | | | 1 | | 1 | | 1 | | | | | | | | | 1 | 24 |
| | | | | | 1 | 1 | | | | 1 | | 1 | | 2 | 2 | | | | | | | | | 2 | 25 |
| | | | | | 4 | 4 | 1 | 6 | 8 | 4 | 1 | 1 | 9 | 6 | 15 | | | | | | | | | 15 | 26 |
| | 15 | | 17 | 3 | 168 | 179 | 218 | 123 | 266 | 138 | 40 | 124 | 353 | 345 | 698 | | | | | 2 | 1 | 3 | | 704 | 27 |
| | 128 | 1 | 140 | 87 | 1882 | 1744 | 2569 | 1834 | 1962 | 2158 | 716 | 1957 | 3816 | 3733 | 7549 | | | | | 11 | 13 | 5 | 6 | 7584 | |

## THE STATE OF MARYLAND.

| Nativities: California and Territories. | Nativities: Ireland. | Nativities: Germany. | Nativities: Other foreign countries. | Nativities: Unknown. | Season of decease: Spring. | Season of decease: Summer. | Season of decease: Autumn. | Season of decease: Winter. | Duration of sickness: Under 1 week. | Duration of sickness: 1 week and under 1 month. | Duration of sickness: 1 month and under 3 months. | Duration of sickness: 3 months and over. | Whites: Males. | Whites: Females. | Whites: Total. | Colored: Slaves: Black: M. | Colored: Slaves: Black: F. | Colored: Slaves: Mulatto: M. | Colored: Slaves: Mulatto: F. | Colored: Free: Black: M. | Colored: Free: Black: F. | Colored: Free: Mul.: M | Colored: Free: Mul.: F. | Aggregate deaths. | |
|---|---|---|---|---|---|---|---|---|---|---|---|---|---|---|---|---|---|---|---|---|---|---|---|---|---|
| | | | | | 2 | | | 3 | | 1 | | 3 | 4 | | 4 | | | | | | 1 | | | 5 | 1 |
| | 5 | 6 | 5 | | 33 | 36 | 30 | 21 | 88 | 18 | 7 | 3 | 55 | 14 | 69 | 19 | 6 | | 1 | 19 | 5 | | 1 | 120 | 2 |
| | | | | | 26 | 7 | 11 | 18 | 37 | 11 | 3 | 1 | 7 | 14 | 21 | 9 | 20 | | 1 | 2 | 8 | 1 | | 62 | 3 |
| | 3 | 14 | | | 9 | 22 | 16 | 11 | 56 | | | | 43 | 4 | 47 | 4 | | 1 | | 5 | 2 | | | 59 | 4 |
| | | | | | 2 | 3 | 1 | 5 | 5 | 5 | 1 | | 6 | 3 | 9 | | | | | 1 | | | 1 | 11 | 5 |
| | 1 | | | | 1 | | | | 1 | | | | 1 | | 1 | | | | | | | | | 1 | 6 |
| | 3 | 1 | 2 | | 15 | 12 | 18 | 14 | 38 | 9 | 3 | 4 | 28 | 18 | 46 | 6 | 3 | | | 4 | 1 | | | 60 | 7 |
| | | 1 | | | 4 | 1 | 4 | 3 | 3 | 1 | | 8 | 2 | 4 | 6 | 3 | 1 | | | 1 | 1 | | | 12 | 8 |
| | | | | | | 1 | | | | 1 | | | | | | 1 | | | | | | | | 1 | 9 |
| | 2 | | | | | 1 | 3 | 4 | 2 | 2 | | 3 | 4 | 3 | 7 | | | | | 1 | | | | 8 | 10 |
| | | | | | 17 | 22 | 19 | 15 | 27 | 33 | 7 | 4 | 30 | 31 | 61 | 1 | | | | 6 | 6 | | 1 | 75 | 11 |
| | 2 | | | | 5 | 6 | 4 | 5 | 3 | 6 | 3 | 8 | 11 | 7 | 18 | 1 | 2 | | | | 1 | | | 22 | 12 |
| | 4 | 2 | 1 | | 11 | 11 | 13 | 11 | 1 | 7 | 4 | 31 | 9 | 27 | 36 | 3 | 2 | | 2 | 1 | 3 | | | 47 | 13 |
| | 3 | 4 | | | 38 | 19 | 18 | 25 | 19 | 45 | 14 | 12 | 23 | 29 | 52 | 6 | 11 | 1 | 3 | 15 | 12 | 1 | 1 | 102 | 14 |
| | | | | | 2 | 2 | 1 | 1 | | 3 | 1 | 1 | 2 | 2 | 4 | | 1 | | | | 1 | | | 6 | 15 |
| | 2 | 11 | 1 | | 22 | 28 | 24 | 21 | 47 | 40 | 2 | 1 | | 64 | 64 | | 14 | | 4 | | 10 | | 3 | 95 | 16 |
| | 19 | 20 | 8 | | 1 | 125 | 34 | 4 | 154 | 6 | 2 | 1 | 81 | 41 | 122 | 4 | | | | 19 | 19 | 1 | 1 | 166 | 17 |
| | 2 | 1 | | | 6 | 93 | 60 | 7 | 59 | 67 | 21 | 16 | 78 | 70 | 148 | 3 | 5 | 1 | 1 | 5 | 1 | 1 | 1 | 166 | 18 |
| | 1 | 2 | | | 4 | 14 | 8 | 3 | 20 | 6 | 1 | 2 | 7 | 13 | 20 | | 4 | | | 3 | 1 | 1 | | 29 | 19 |
| | | | | | 1 | | 1 | | | 2 | | | | 2 | 2 | | | | | | | | | 2 | 20 |
| | 1 | 1 | 1 | | 5 | 6 | 7 | 5 | 15 | 6 | 2 | | 11 | 3 | 14 | 3 | 1 | 2 | 1 | 2 | | | | 23 | 21 |
| | | | | | 5 | 6 | 7 | 4 | 13 | 8 | | | 16 | 5 | 21 | 1 | | | | | 1 | | | 23 | 22 |
| | | | | | 4 | 2 | 2 | 2 | 6 | 3 | 1 | | 4 | 6 | 10 | | | | | | | | | 10 | 23 |
| | 36 | 43 | 14 | | 317 | 286 | 253 | 228 | 28 | 121 | 139 | 750 | 377 | 415 | 792 | 50 | 61 | 9 | 8 | 69 | 76 | 15 | 21 | 1101 | 24 |
| | | | 1 | | 54 | 51 | 35 | 44 | 127 | 31 | 6 | 9 | 51 | 57 | 108 | 28 | 17 | 2 | | 15 | 15 | 1 | 2 | 188 | 25 |
| | 1 | 3 | 1 | | 4 | 8 | 4 | 6 | 19 | 2 | | | 11 | 7 | 18 | 3 | | | | 1 | | | | 22 | 26 |
| | | 2 | 1 | | 67 | 33 | 44 | 74 | 149 | 55 | 4 | 6 | 84 | 88 | 172 | 12 | 19 | | 1 | 7 | 5 | 2 | 4 | 222 | 27 |
| | | | | | 5 | 10 | 3 | 5 | 6 | 5 | 6 | 3 | 6 | 10 | 16 | 3 | 8 | | | 1 | | | | 23 | 28 |
| | | | | | 1 | | | | | | 1 | | 2 | | 2 | | | | | | | | | 2 | 29 |
| | 6 | 4 | 4 | | 5 | 57 | 75 | 15 | 43 | 74 | 22 | 10 | 68 | 56 | 124 | 9 | 4 | 1 | | 4 | 8 | 3 | 5 | 158 | 30 |
| | 8 | 10 | 5 | | 70 | 88 | 84 | 66 | 11 | 58 | 33 | 185 | 87 | 88 | 175 | 33 | 34 | 1 | | 36 | 25 | 5 | 3 | 312 | 31 |
| | 17 | 10 | 3 | | 40 | 180 | 339 | 42 | 137 | 353 | 60 | 30 | 244 | 240 | 484 | 45 | 33 | 3 | 3 | 21 | 10 | 6 | 2 | 607 | 32 |
| | | | | | 6 | 5 | 8 | 6 | 1 | 6 | 1 | 17 | 9 | 10 | 19 | | 1 | | | 1 | 2 | 2 | | 25 | 33 |
| | 1 | 1 | | | 9 | 5 | 11 | 6 | 16 | 5 | 2 | 6 | 9 | 12 | 21 | 1 | 7 | | | 1 | 1 | 1 | | 32 | 34 |
| | 4 | 1 | 3 | | 23 | 26 | 5 | 6 | 15 | 31 | 8 | 3 | 32 | 27 | 59 | 2 | | | | | 1 | 1 | | 63 | 35 |
| | 3 | | 1 | | 39 | 36 | 43 | 21 | 33 | 95 | 9 | 2 | 62 | 44 | 106 | 9 | 7 | | | 7 | 5 | | 5 | 139 | 36 |
| | 8 | 2 | 1 | 1 | 33 | 56 | 136 | 30 | 51 | 157 | 22 | 16 | 114 | 79 | 193 | 22 | 17 | | 1 | 15 | 10 | 4 | 2 | 264 | 37 |
| | 1 | | | | 56 | 19 | 11 | 16 | 17 | 65 | 14 | 5 | 46 | 45 | 91 | 2 | | | | 6 | 4 | | | 103 | 38 |
| | 2 | | | | 6 | 14 | 16 | 8 | 12 | 28 | 2 | 1 | 15 | 16 | 31 | 3 | 2 | 1 | 1 | 3 | | 2 | 1 | 44 | 39 |

CLASSIFICATION OF DEATHS IN

| | Cause of death. | AGES. | | | | | | | | | | | | | | | | | | NATIVITIES. | | | | | |
|---|---|---|---|---|---|---|---|---|---|---|---|---|---|---|---|---|---|---|---|---|---|---|---|---|---|
| | | Under 1. | | 1 and under 5. | | 5 and under 10. | | 10 and under 20. | | 20 and under 50. | | 50 and under 80. | | 80 and under 100. | | 100 & over. | | Age unknown. | | Born in State. | N. England States. | Middle States. | Southern States. | Southwest'n States. | Northwest'n States. |
| | | M. | F. | M. | F. | M. | F. | M. | F. | M. | F. | M. | F. | M | F. | M | F. | M | F. | | | | | | |
| 1 | Fever, intermittent | 2 | 2 | 2 | 2 | | | | 2 | 4 | 2 | 1 | 2 | | | | | | | 14 | | | 1 | | |
| 2 | ..do..puerperal | | | | | | | | | | 11 | | | | | | | | | 9 | | | | | |
| 3 | ..do..scarlet | 30 | 25 | 161 | 132 | 75 | 66 | 23 | 36 | 7 | 4 | 1 | 1 | | | | | | | 542 | 1 | 10 | | | 3 |
| 4 | ..do..ship | 1 | | | | | | | | 4 | 1 | 1 | 1 | | | | | | | 4 | | | | | |
| 5 | ..do..typhus | 7 | 5 | 20 | 19 | 16 | 3 | 37 | 45 | 91 | 61 | 25 | 25 | 2 | 1 | | | 2 | 1 | 302 | 2 | 17 | 6 | | 1 |
| 6 | ..do..yellow | | | | | | | 1 | | 3 | 1 | 1 | | | | | | | | 4 | | | | | |
| 7 | Fistula | | | | | | | | | | 1 | | | | | | | | | | | | 1 | | |
| 8 | Fracture | | | | | | | | | | | 2 | | | | | | | | 2 | | | | | |
| 9 | Frozen | | | | | | | | | 4 | | | | | | | | | | 4 | | | | | |
| 10 | Gout | | | | | | | | | | | 1 | | 1 | | | | | | 2 | | | | | |
| 11 | Gravel | | | | | | | | | 1 | | 4 | 1 | 1 | | | | | | 5 | | | | | |
| 12 | Heart, disease of | 5 | 6 | 3 | 2 | 2 | 4 | 3 | 6 | 21 | 24 | 29 | 23 | 1 | | | | | | 105 | 2 | 8 | | | 1 |
| 13 | Heat | | | | | | | | | 1 | | | | | | | | | | | | | | | |
| 14 | Hemorrhage | | | | 1 | | | 1 | 3 | 5 | 4 | 3 | 1 | | | | | | | 16 | | 1 | | | 1 |
| 15 | Hernia | | | | 1 | | | | | 4 | | 2 | | 1 | | | | | | 6 | | | | | |
| 16 | Hip, disease of | 1 | | | | 2 | | | | | | | | | | | | | | 3 | | | | | |
| 17 | Hives | | 1 | | | | | | | | | | | | | | | | | 1 | | | | | |
| 18 | Hooping cough | 27 | 24 | 36 | 40 | 7 | 7 | 1 | | | | | | | | | | | | 138 | | 1 | 2 | | |
| 19 | Hydrocephalus | 26 | 21 | 21 | 25 | 4 | 3 | 1 | | 1 | | | | | | | | | | 96 | 1 | 2 | 1 | | |
| 20 | Hydrophophia | | | 1 | | | | | | | | | | | | | | | | 1 | | | | | |
| 21 | Inflammation | 9 | 3 | 3 | 4 | 1 | 1 | 2 | 2 | 3 | 4 | 5 | | | | | | | | 37 | | | | | |
| 22 | ....do....bowels | 10 | 7 | 12 | 10 | 8 | 1 | 5 | 5 | 13 | 7 | 8 | | 1 | | | | | | 76 | | 1 | 1 | | 1 |
| 23 | ....do....brain | 34 | 28 | 39 | 25 | 14 | 8 | 14 | 6 | 25 | 9 | 4 | 4 | | 1 | | | | | 192 | 1 | 3 | 2 | | 2 |
| 24 | ....do....stomach | 1 | 1 | 1 | 1 | | 2 | 1 | | 4 | 3 | 3 | | | | | | | | 15 | | 1 | | | |
| 25 | Influenza | | | | | | | | | 1 | | | 1 | 1 | | | | | | 9 | | | | | |
| 26 | Insanity | | | | | | | | 1 | 3 | 2 | 4 | 1 | | | | | | | 3 | | 1 | | | |
| 27 | Intemperance | | | | | | | | | 8 | 1 | 7 | 1 | | | | | | | 15 | | | | | |
| 28 | Jaundice | 2 | 2 | 2 | 1 | | | | | | | 3 | 2 | | | | | | | 11 | | 1 | | | |
| 29 | Kidneys, disease of | | 1 | | | | | | 1 | 6 | 1 | 1 | 2 | | | | | | | 11 | | | | | |
| 30 | Killed | | | | | 2 | | 3 | | 4 | | 1 | | | | | | | | 8 | | 1 | | | |
| 31 | Liver, disease of | 6 | 7 | 5 | 1 | | 1 | 3 | 3 | 18 | 10 | 6 | 2 | | | | | | | 54 | 2 | 2 | 1 | | |
| 32 | Lockjaw | 1 | | | 1 | 1 | | 1 | | 8 | 1 | 2 | 1 | | | | | | | 14 | | 1 | | | |
| 33 | Lungs, disease of | 5 | 4 | 7 | 6 | 1 | 3 | 1 | 2 | 8 | 7 | 6 | 1 | 1 | | | | | | 46 | | 8 | | | |
| 34 | Malformation | 1 | | | | | | | | | | | | | | | | | | 1 | | | | | |
| 35 | Mania-a-potu | | | | | | | | | 15 | | 4 | | | | | | 1 | | 16 | | 1 | | | |
| 36 | Marasmus | 3 | 3 | | | | | | | | | | | | | | | | | 6 | | | | | |
| 37 | Measles | 8 | 4 | 18 | 13 | 5 | 2 | 2 | 4 | | 2 | | 1 | | | | | | | 55 | | 2 | | | |
| 38 | Mortification | | | | | | | | | | | 1 | 2 | | | | | | | 3 | | | | | |
| 39 | Mumps | | | | 1 | | | | | 1 | | | | | | | | | | 2 | | | | | |
| 40 | Murder | | | | | | | | | 3 | | | | | | | | | | 3 | | | | | |
| 41 | Neuralgia | | 1 | 1 | | | | | | 2 | 2 | 1 | | | | | | | | 7 | | | | | |
| 42 | Old age | | | | | | | | | | | 34 | 77 | 68 | 79 | 9 | 11 | | | 221 | | 18 | 4 | | |
| 43 | Paralysis | 2 | | | | | | | | 6 | 12 | 36 | 38 | 5 | 6 | | | | | 88 | | 6 | 2 | | |
| 44 | Pleurisy | 4 | 6 | 7 | | 3 | 3 | 12 | 7 | 54 | 28 | 53 | 31 | 2 | 3 | | | | | 185 | | 8 | 2 | | |
| 45 | Pneumonia | 12 | 10 | 17 | 9 | 4 | 4 | 3 | 1 | 35 | 15 | 17 | 20 | 2 | | | | | | 129 | 2 | 7 | 1 | | |
| 46 | Poison | | 1 | | | 1 | | | | | | 1 | | | | | | | | 3 | | | | | |
| 47 | Prematurity of birth | 5 | 4 | | | | | | | | | | | | | | | | | 9 | | | | | |
| 48 | Putrid sore throat | | | | | 2 | | | | | | | | | | | | | | 2 | | | | | |
| 49 | Quinsy | 2 | 1 | 1 | 1 | | | | 1 | | 1 | | | | 1 | | | | | 7 | | | | | |
| 50 | Rheumatism | | | 1 | | 2 | 1 | 4 | 3 | 8 | 8 | 6 | 7 | | 1 | | | | | 35 | 1 | | 1 | | |
| 51 | Rickets | | | 1 | | | | | | | | | | | | | | | | 1 | | | | | |
| 52 | Scrofula | 2 | 1 | 8 | 4 | 2 | 1 | 1 | 6 | 4 | 3 | 3 | | | | | | | | 33 | | 1 | | | |
| 53 | Scurvy | | | | | | | | | | | 1 | | | | | | | | 1 | | | | | |
| 54 | Small pox | 15 | 9 | 22 | 21 | 4 | 7 | 4 | 9 | 34 | 14 | 5 | | | | | | | | 122 | 2 | 3 | 4 | | |
| 55 | Spine, disease of | 1 | 3 | 1 | 2 | 2 | 1 | 3 | 2 | 2 | 2 | 2 | 2 | | | | | | | 19 | | 2 | 2 | | |
| 56 | Stillborn | 10 | 7 | | | | | | | | | | | | | | | | | 17 | | | | | |
| 57 | Suffocation | 8 | 4 | 5 | 1 | 1 | | | | 1 | 1 | 1 | | | | | | | | 20 | | | | | |
| 58 | Suicide | | | | | | | | 2 | 3 | | 4 | | | | | | | | 6 | | | 1 | | |
| 59 | Summer complaint | 41 | 40 | 39 | 29 | 1 | 1 | 1 | 1 | | | | | | | | | | | 151 | | 1 | | | |
| 60 | Sun, stroke of | | | | | | | 1 | | 6 | | | | | | | | | | 2 | | | | | |
| 61 | Teething | 25 | 11 | 27 | 17 | | 1 | | | | | | | | | | | | | 79 | | 2 | | | |
| 62 | Tetanus | | 1 | | | | | | | 2 | | | | | | | | | | 3 | | | | | |
| 63 | Tetter | 1 | 1 | | | | | | | | | | | | | | | | | 1 | | | 1 | | |
| 64 | Throat, disease of | 1 | 1 | 2 | 2 | | 2 | 1 | 1 | 3 | 2 | 3 | | 2 | | | | | | 19 | | | | | |
| 65 | Thrush | 6 | 5 | 2 | 4 | | | | | | | | | | | | | | | 17 | | | | | |
| 66 | Tumor | 1 | | 1 | | | | | | 1 | | 1 | 2 | | | | | | | 3 | | | 1 | | |
| 67 | Ulcer | 1 | | | | | | | | | | 1 | | | | | | | | 2 | | | | | |
| 68 | Uterus, disease of | | | | | | | | | | 2 | | 1 | | | | | | | 2 | | | | | |
| 69 | Venereal | | | | | | | | | 2 | | | | | | | | | | 1 | | | | | |
| 70 | White swelling | | | 1 | | | | | | 1 | | 1 | | | | | | | | 3 | | | | | |
| 71 | Worms | 1 | 4 | 20 | 20 | 6 | 7 | | 2 | | | | | | | | | | | 60 | | | | | |
| 72 | Unknown | 296 | 246 | 163 | 139 | 49 | 39 | 59 | 53 | 189 | 188 | 168 | 128 | 12 | 20 | .. | 4 | 2 | 3 | 1627 | .. | 27 | 17 | ... | 1 |
| | Total | 1027 | 867 | 1110 | 961 | 364 | 321 | 376 | 396 | 1258 | 1117 | 835 | 664 | 134 | 142 | 9 | 17 | 14 | 8 | 3599 | 30 | 258 | 95 | 2 | 13 |

## THE STATE OF MARYLAND—Continued.

| Nativities: California and Territories. | Ireland. | Germany. | Other foreign countries. | Unknown. | Season of decease: Spring. | Summer. | Autumn. | Winter. | Duration of sickness: Under 1 week. | 1 week and under 1 month. | 1 month and under 3 months. | 3 months and over. | Whites: Males. | Females. | Total. | Colored: Slaves: Black: M. | F. | Mulatto: M. | F. | Free: Black: M. | F. | Mul: M | F. | Aggregate deaths. | |
|---|---|---|---|---|---|---|---|---|---|---|---|---|---|---|---|---|---|---|---|---|---|---|---|---|---|
| ... | 2 | 2 | ... | ... | 4 | 5 | 8 | 2 | 5 | 9 | 3 | 1 | 6 | 9 | 15 | 1 | 1 | ... | ... | 2 | ... | ... | ... | 19 | 1 |
| ... | 1 | 1 | ... | ... | 3 | 4 | 1 | 3 | 4 | 5 | 2 | ... | ... | 8 | 8 | ... | 3 | ... | ... | ... | ... | ... | ... | 11 | 2 |
| ... | 1 | 3 | 1 | ... | 199 | 123 | 95 | 143 | 227 | 288 | 30 | 6 | 242 | 202 | 444 | 32 | 35 | 9 | 5 | 6 | 15 | 8 | 7 | 561 | 3 |
| ... | 8 | 1 | ... | ... | 1 | 7 | ... | ... | 2 | 4 | 2 | ... | 3 | 2 | 5 | ... | ... | ... | ... | 2 | ... | 1 | ... | 8 | 4 |
| ... | 13 | 14 | 5 | ... | 87 | 74 | 105 | 81 | 52 | 231 | 45 | 20 | 149 | 107 | 256 | 18 | 22 | 2 | 2 | 23 | 25 | 8 | 4 | 360 | 5 |
| ... | ... | 1 | 1 | ... | 2 | 2 | 1 | 1 | 2 | 3 | ... | 1 | 5 | 1 | 6 | ... | ... | ... | ... | ... | ... | ... | ... | 6 | 6 |
| ... | ... | ... | ... | ... | 1 | ... | ... | ... | ... | ... | 1 | ... | ... | 1 | 1 | ... | ... | ... | ... | ... | ... | ... | ... | 1 | 7 |
| ... | ... | ... | ... | ... | ... | 2 | ... | ... | ... | ... | ... | ... | ... | ... | ... | 1 | ... | ... | ... | ... | ... | 1 | ... | 2 | 8 |
| ... | ... | ... | ... | ... | 1 | ... | ... | 3 | 4 | ... | ... | ... | 3 | ... | 3 | 1 | ... | ... | ... | ... | ... | ... | ... | 4 | 9 |
| ... | ... | ... | ... | ... | 1 | ... | 1 | ... | ... | ... | ... | 2 | 2 | ... | 2 | ... | ... | ... | ... | ... | ... | ... | ... | 2 | 10 |
| ... | ... | 2 | ... | ... | 3 | ... | ... | 4 | 2 | ... | 1 | 4 | 4 | 1 | 5 | 2 | ... | ... | ... | ... | ... | ... | ... | 7 | 11 |
| ... | 7 | 2 | 4 | ... | 33 | 38 | 30 | 25 | 45 | 29 | 14 | 36 | 47 | 52 | 99 | 6 | 2 | 1 | 1 | 6 | 10 | 4 | ... | 129 | 12 |
| ... | 1 | ... | ... | ... | ... | 1 | ... | ... | 1 | ... | ... | ... | 1 | ... | 1 | ... | ... | ... | ... | ... | ... | ... | ... | 1 | 13 |
| ... | ... | ... | ... | ... | 5 | 5 | 6 | 2 | 9 | 6 | 2 | 1 | 8 | 9 | 17 | ... | ... | ... | ... | 1 | ... | ... | ... | 18 | 14 |
| ... | ... | 2 | ... | ... | 1 | 6 | 1 | ... | 5 | 2 | ... | ... | 4 | 1 | 5 | 2 | ... | ... | ... | 1 | ... | ... | ... | 8 | 15 |
| ... | ... | ... | ... | ... | 1 | 1 | 1 | ... | ... | 1 | ... | 2 | 1 | ... | 1 | ... | ... | ... | ... | 1 | ... | 1 | ... | 3 | 16 |
| ... | ... | ... | ... | ... | ... | ... | 1 | ... | ... | ... | 1 | ... | ... | 1 | 1 | ... | ... | ... | ... | ... | ... | ... | ... | 1 | 17 |
| ... | ... | 1 | ... | ... | 41 | 36 | 36 | 28 | 12 | 78 | 30 | 13 | 44 | 40 | 84 | 16 | 21 | 1 | ... | 8 | 8 | 2 | 2 | 142 | 18 |
| ... | 2 | ... | ... | ... | 20 | 39 | 26 | 17 | 23 | 49 | 13 | 13 | 43 | 43 | 86 | 2 | 2 | ... | ... | 6 | 4 | 2 | ... | 102 | 19 |
| ... | ... | ... | ... | ... | 1 | ... | ... | ... | ... | 1 | ... | ... | 1 | ... | 1 | ... | ... | ... | ... | ... | ... | ... | ... | 1 | 20 |
| ... | ... | ... | ... | ... | 11 | 10 | 11 | 4 | 8 | 21 | 3 | 4 | 18 | 10 | 28 | 2 | 3 | 1 | ... | 2 | 1 | ... | ... | 37 | 21 |
| ... | 2 | 4 | 2 | ... | 19 | 34 | 22 | 12 | 28 | 46 | 5 | 6 | 47 | 26 | 73 | 5 | 2 | ... | 1 | 4 | 1 | 1 | ... | 87 | 22 |
| ... | 4 | 6 | 2 | ... | 45 | 69 | 58 | 39 | 71 | 98 | 23 | 12 | 104 | 69 | 173 | 11 | 6 | 1 | 1 | 13 | 5 | 1 | ... | 211 | 23 |
| ... | 1 | ... | ... | ... | 6 | 4 | 2 | 4 | 7 | 4 | 2 | 1 | 5 | 5 | 10 | 3 | 2 | ... | ... | 2 | ... | ... | ... | 17 | 24 |
| ... | ... | ... | ... | ... | 1 | 1 | ... | 1 | 2 | 1 | ... | ... | 1 | 1 | 2 | ... | ... | ... | ... | 1 | ... | ... | ... | 3 | 25 |
| ... | ... | ... | 1 | ... | 1 | 5 | 2 | 3 | 1 | 3 | 1 | 6 | 3 | 2 | 5 | 2 | ... | ... | ... | 2 | 2 | ... | ... | 11 | 26 |
| ... | 2 | ... | ... | ... | 4 | 8 | 2 | 3 | 9 | 4 | 1 | 1 | 13 | 2 | 15 | ... | ... | ... | ... | 2 | ... | ... | ... | 17 | 27 |
| ... | ... | ... | ... | ... | 1 | 5 | 6 | ... | ... | 6 | 3 | 3 | 7 | 4 | 11 | ... | ... | ... | ... | ... | 1 | ... | ... | 12 | 28 |
| ... | 1 | ... | ... | ... | 1 | 2 | 3 | 6 | 3 | 3 | 1 | 5 | 7 | 4 | 11 | ... | ... | ... | ... | ... | 1 | ... | ... | 12 | 29 |
| ... | ... | 1 | ... | ... | 1 | 3 | 2 | 4 | 7 | 2 | ... | ... | 8 | ... | 8 | ... | ... | ... | ... | 2 | ... | ... | ... | 10 | 30 |
| ... | 2 | ... | 1 | ... | 20 | 17 | 14 | 11 | 4 | 19 | 11 | 25 | 32 | 17 | 49 | 2 | 1 | ... | ... | 3 | 5 | 1 | 1 | 62 | 31 |
| ... | ... | 1 | ... | ... | 1 | 8 | 6 | 1 | 6 | 8 | ... | 1 | 7 | ... | 7 | 1 | 2 | ... | 1 | 5 | ... | ... | ... | 16 | 32 |
| ... | 1 | 2 | ... | ... | 20 | 14 | 5 | 12 | 5 | 19 | 7 | 16 | 21 | 16 | 37 | 4 | 1 | ... | ... | 1 | 3 | 3 | 3 | 52 | 33 |
| ... | ... | ... | ... | ... | ... | 1 | ... | ... | ... | ... | ... | 1 | 1 | ... | 1 | ... | ... | ... | ... | ... | ... | ... | ... | 1 | 34 |
| ... | 3 | ... | ... | ... | 3 | 4 | 5 | 5 | 9 | 4 | 1 | 2 | 18 | ... | 18 | ... | ... | ... | ... | 1 | ... | 1 | ... | 20 | 35 |
| ... | ... | ... | ... | ... | 3 | 3 | ... | ... | 1 | ... | 1 | ... | 3 | 3 | 6 | ... | ... | ... | ... | ... | ... | ... | ... | 6 | 36 |
| ... | ... | 2 | ... | ... | 16 | 24 | 16 | 3 | 6 | 44 | 5 | 3 | 25 | 20 | 45 | 6 | 5 | ... | ... | 2 | 1 | ... | ... | 59 | 37 |
| ... | ... | ... | ... | ... | 1 | 1 | ... | 1 | ... | 2 | ... | 1 | 1 | 1 | 2 | ... | ... | ... | ... | ... | 1 | ... | ... | 3 | 38 |
| ... | ... | ... | ... | ... | 1 | ... | ... | 1 | ... | 2 | ... | ... | ... | 1 | 1 | 1 | ... | ... | ... | ... | ... | ... | ... | 2 | 39 |
| ... | ... | ... | ... | ... | 1 | ... | 1 | 1 | 2 | ... | ... | ... | 2 | ... | 2 | 1 | ... | ... | ... | ... | ... | ... | ... | 3 | 40 |
| ... | ... | ... | ... | ... | 3 | 1 | 2 | 1 | 1 | 4 | 1 | 1 | 4 | 1 | 5 | ... | 1 | ... | 1 | ... | ... | ... | ... | 7 | 41 |
| ... | 14 | 14 | 5 | 3 | 79 | 78 | 62 | 61 | 37 | 47 | 22 | 75 | 57 | 106 | 163 | 32 | 33 | 4 | 4 | 16 | 24 | 2 | ... | 278 | 42 |
| ... | 3 | 3 | 3 | ... | 39 | 25 | 18 | 23 | 30 | 25 | 10 | 34 | 43 | 47 | 90 | 3 | 1 | ... | ... | 3 | 5 | ... | 3 | 105 | 43 |
| ... | 9 | 5 | 4 | ... | 97 | 32 | 25 | 59 | 59 | 123 | 18 | 5 | 88 | 55 | 143 | 32 | 15 | 2 | ... | 12 | 6 | 1 | 2 | 213 | 44 |
| ... | 9 | 1 | ... | ... | 65 | 37 | 17 | 26 | 43 | 72 | 12 | 12 | 68 | 49 | 117 | 10 | 5 | ... | ... | 9 | 5 | 3 | ... | 149 | 45 |
| ... | ... | ... | ... | ... | ... | 1 | 2 | ... | 1 | 1 | 1 | ... | 1 | 1 | 2 | ... | ... | ... | ... | 1 | ... | ... | ... | 3 | 46 |
| ... | ... | ... | ... | ... | 1 | ... | 3 | 5 | ... | ... | ... | ... | 5 | 2 | 7 | ... | ... | ... | ... | ... | 2 | ... | ... | 9 | 47 |
| ... | ... | ... | ... | ... | ... | ... | 2 | ... | 2 | ... | ... | ... | 2 | ... | 2 | ... | ... | ... | ... | ... | ... | ... | ... | 2 | 48 |
| ... | ... | ... | 1 | ... | 2 | 1 | 1 | 4 | 3 | 4 | ... | ... | 1 | 3 | 4 | 2 | ... | ... | ... | ... | 2 | ... | ... | 8 | 49 |
| ... | 2 | 1 | 1 | ... | 9 | 10 | 11 | 9 | 5 | 7 | 5 | 22 | 12 | 16 | 28 | 4 | 3 | ... | ... | 4 | 1 | 1 | ... | 41 | 50 |
| ... | ... | ... | ... | ... | ... | ... | ... | 1 | 1 | ... | ... | ... | ... | ... | ... | 1 | ... | ... | ... | ... | ... | ... | ... | 1 | 51 |
| ... | ... | 1 | ... | ... | 6 | 14 | 9 | 6 | 1 | 5 | 6 | 23 | 10 | 7 | 17 | 7 | 5 | ... | ... | 2 | 3 | 1 | ... | 25 | 52 |
| ... | ... | ... | ... | ... | 1 | ... | ... | ... | ... | ... | ... | 1 | 1 | ... | 1 | ... | ... | ... | ... | ... | ... | ... | ... | 1 | 53 |
| ... | 5 | 7 | 1 | ... | 51 | 32 | 19 | 39 | 8 | 115 | 7 | 1 | 51 | 51 | 102 | 2 | 2 | ... | ... | 26 | 6 | 5 | 1 | 144 | 54 |
| ... | ... | ... | ... | ... | 3 | 11 | 1 | 8 | 1 | 6 | 4 | 11 | 7 | 10 | 17 | 2 | ... | ... | ... | 2 | 1 | ... | 1 | 23 | 55 |
| ... | ... | ... | ... | ... | 4 | 3 | 1 | 3 | ... | ... | ... | ... | 9 | 5 | 14 | ... | 2 | ... | ... | 1 | ... | ... | ... | 17 | 56 |
| ... | ... | 1 | 1 | ... | 9 | 4 | 5 | 4 | 19 | ... | ... | ... | 7 | 3 | 10 | 9 | 3 | ... | ... | ... | ... | ... | ... | 22 | 57 |
| ... | ... | 1 | 1 | ... | 2 | 4 | 2 | 1 | 7 | 1 | ... | ... | 7 | ... | 7 | ... | 2 | ... | ... | ... | ... | ... | ... | 9 | 58 |
| ... | ... | 1 | ... | ... | 5 | 80 | 57 | 5 | 31 | 65 | 26 | 24 | 70 | 63 | 133 | 2 | 2 | ... | 1 | 9 | 3 | 1 | 2 | 153 | 59 |
| ... | 4 | 1 | ... | ... | ... | 7 | ... | ... | 6 | 1 | ... | ... | 5 | ... | 5 | ... | ... | ... | ... | 2 | ... | ... | ... | 7 | 60 |
| ... | ... | ... | ... | ... | 13 | 35 | 18 | 13 | 18 | 38 | 11 | 8 | 35 | 21 | 56 | 5 | 1 | ... | ... | 12 | 5 | ... | 2 | 81 | 61 |
| ... | ... | ... | ... | ... | 1 | 1 | 1 | ... | 1 | 2 | ... | ... | ... | ... | ... | 1 | 1 | 1 | ... | ... | ... | ... | ... | 3 | 62 |
| ... | ... | ... | ... | ... | 1 | 1 | ... | ... | 2 | ... | ... | ... | 1 | 1 | 2 | ... | ... | ... | ... | ... | ... | ... | ... | 2 | 63 |
| ... | ... | ... | 1 | ... | 5 | 3 | 5 | 7 | 9 | 6 | 2 | 2 | 9 | 7 | 16 | ... | 1 | ... | ... | 2 | ... | 1 | ... | 20 | 64 |
| ... | ... | ... | ... | ... | 2 | 6 | 8 | ... | 2 | 7 | 6 | 2 | 5 | 6 | 11 | 1 | ... | ... | ... | 1 | 2 | 1 | 1 | 17 | 65 |
| ... | ... | ... | ... | ... | 2 | 1 | 1 | 2 | ... | 2 | 1 | 3 | 3 | 1 | 4 | ... | ... | ... | ... | 1 | 1 | ... | ... | 6 | 66 |
| ... | ... | ... | ... | ... | 1 | ... | 1 | ... | ... | 2 | ... | ... | 2 | ... | 2 | ... | ... | ... | ... | ... | ... | ... | ... | 2 | 67 |
| ... | 1 | ... | ... | ... | 1 | 1 | ... | 1 | ... | ... | ... | 3 | ... | 3 | 3 | ... | ... | ... | ... | ... | ... | ... | ... | 3 | 68 |
| ... | 1 | ... | ... | ... | ... | ... | 1 | 1 | ... | ... | ... | 1 | 1 | ... | 1 | 1 | ... | ... | ... | ... | ... | ... | ... | 2 | 69 |
| ... | ... | ... | ... | ... | 1 | ... | 1 | 1 | ... | ... | 1 | 2 | 1 | ... | 1 | 1 | ... | ... | ... | ... | ... | 1 | ... | 3 | 70 |
| ... | ... | ... | ... | ... | 16 | 18 | 12 | 13 | 26 | 20 | 7 | 7 | 11 | 15 | 26 | 11 | 15 | 1 | ... | 4 | 3 | ... | ... | 60 | 71 |
| ... | 41 | 29 | 15 | 1 | 458 | 482 | 461 | 309 | 547 | 327 | 114 | 375 | 589 | 495 | 1084 | 202 | 197 | 9 | 9 | 122 | 107 | 16 | 12 | 1758 | 72 |
| ... | 270 | 248 | 102 | 4 | 2385 | 2730 | 2561 | 1777 | 2681 | 3238 | 863 | 1939 | 3630 | 3180 | 6810 | 733 | 672 | 54 | 53 | 596 | 494 | 114 | 95 | 9621 | |

## CLASSIFICATION OF DEATHS IN NORTHEASTERN

*Embracing the following counties:*

| | Cause of death. | AGES. | | | | | | | | | | | | | | | | | | NATIVITIES. | | | | | |
|---|---|---|---|---|---|---|---|---|---|---|---|---|---|---|---|---|---|---|---|---|---|---|---|---|---|
| | | Under 1. | | 1 and under 5. | | 5 and under 10. | | 10 and under 20. | | 20 and under 50. | | 50 and under 80. | | 80 and under 100. | | 100 & over. | | Age unknown. | | Born in State. | N. England States. | Middle States. | Southern States. | Southwest'n States. | Northwest'n States. |
| | | M. | F. | M. | F. | M. | F. | M. | F. | M. | F. | M. | F. | M | F. | M | F. | M | F. | | | | | | |
| 1 | Abscess | 2 | | | | 1 | | | | 2 | 2 | 2 | | | | | | | | 7 | 1 | | | | |
| 2 | Accident, not specf'd | 1 | | 1 | 3 | | 1 | 2 | 1 | 24 | 1 | 5 | 4 | 1 | | | | | | 39 | 2 | 2 | | | |
| 3 | ....do...burned | | | 2 | 4 | | | | 1 | | | | 1 | | | | | | | 7 | | | | | |
| 4 | ....do...drowned | | | 7 | 2 | 7 | | 6 | 3 | 13 | 1 | 1 | | | | | | 1 | | 30 | 4 | | | | |
| 5 | ....do...scalded | | | 5 | 1 | | | | | | | | | | | | | | | 5 | 1 | | | | |
| 6 | ....do...shot | | | | | | | | | 1 | | | | | | | | | | 1 | | | | | |
| 7 | ....do...railroad | | | | | 1 | | | | 7 | | 1 | | | | | | | | 5 | | | | | |
| 8 | Apoplexy | | | | | | | | | 4 | 4 | 14 | 7 | 3 | | | | | | 27 | | | 1 | | |
| 9 | Asthma | | | | | | | | | | | 2 | 2 | | | | | | | | 2 | | | | |
| 10 | Bladder, disease of | | | | | | | | | | | 1 | | | | | | | | | 1 | | | | |
| 11 | Bowels......do | 9 | 9 | 16 | 13 | 1 | | | 5 | 4 | 2 | 2 | 3 | | | | | | | 54 | 3 | | | | |
| 12 | Brain ......do | 10 | 9 | 15 | 10 | 3 | 3 | 2 | 3 | 6 | 8 | 3 | 1 | | | | | | | 59 | 8 | 1 | | | |
| 13 | Bronchitis | 2 | | 1 | | | | | | 3 | 2 | 2 | 1 | | | | | | | 7 | 2 | 1 | | | |
| 14 | Cancer | 1 | 1 | | 1 | | | 1 | | | 6 | 11 | 10 | 1 | 3 | | | | | 35 | | | | | |
| 15 | Carbuncle | | | | | | | | | 1 | | | | | | | | | | 1 | | | | | |
| 16 | Catarrh | 4 | | | 2 | | | 1 | | 1 | | 1 | | | | | | | | 8 | | | | | |
| 17 | Chicken pox | | 1 | | | | | | | | | | | | | | | | | 1 | | | | | |
| 18 | Childbirth | | | | | | | | 3 | | 41 | | | | | | | | | 27 | 2 | 1 | | | |
| 19 | Cholera | 1 | | 11 | 7 | 3 | 4 | 11 | 13 | 71 | 60 | 26 | 13 | 1 | 2 | | | 1 | | 88 | 21 | 2 | | | |
| 20 | ...do...infantum | 34 | 30 | 14 | 31 | 2 | 1 | 1 | | | | | | | | | | | | 113 | | | | | |
| 21 | ...do...morbus | 1 | 1 | 3 | 2 | 1 | 2 | | 2 | 6 | 5 | 6 | 2 | 1 | 1 | | | | | 24 | 2 | 2 | | | |
| 22 | Chorea | | | | | | | | | | 1 | | | | | | | | | 1 | | | | | |
| 23 | Colic | | | | | | 1 | | 1 | 2 | | 2 | | | | | | | | 5 | | 1 | | | |
| 24 | Congestion | | | | | 1 | | | | 1 | | | | | | | | | | 2 | | | | | |
| 25 | ....do...brain | 1 | | 1 | | | | | | 2 | | | | | | | | | | 3 | 1 | | | | |
| 26 | Consumption | 30 | 20 | 22 | 25 | 3 | 11 | 34 | 79 | 205 | 312 | 139 | 110 | 8 | 6 | | | 1 | 3 | 780 | 109 | 7 | 1 | | |
| 27 | Convulsions | 26 | 9 | 19 | 16 | | 3 | 2 | 3 | 4 | 3 | 2 | 5 | | | | | | | 84 | 4 | | | | |
| 28 | Cramp | | | | 1 | | | | | 1 | 1 | | | 1 | | | | | | 4 | | | | | |
| 29 | Croup | 12 | 3 | 23 | 29 | 4 | 2 | 1 | | | 2 | | | | | | | | 1 | 72 | 4 | 1 | | | |
| 30 | Debility | 11 | 9 | 1 | 2 | 1 | 1 | | 1 | | | 1 | 4 | 2 | | | | | 2 | 35 | | | | | |
| 31 | Diabetes | | | | 1 | | | | | | | 1 | | | | | | | | 2 | | | | | |
| 32 | Diarrhœa | 8 | 5 | 9 | 5 | | 1 | 1 | 1 | 6 | 3 | 11 | 1 | | | | | | | 44 | 2 | 1 | | | |
| 33 | Dropsy | 30 | 22 | 38 | 43 | 13 | 10 | 2 | 4 | 11 | 15 | 33 | 30 | 7 | 3 | | | | | 240 | 8 | | | | |
| 34 | Dysentery | 56 | 39 | 140 | 114 | 27 | 39 | 10 | 19 | 42 | 46 | 27 | 57 | 4 | 6 | | | 2 | 1 | 537 | 48 | 4 | | | 3 |
| 35 | Dyspepsia | | | | | | | | | | 2 | 1 | 1 | | | | | | | 4 | | | | | |
| 36 | Epilepsy | | | | | | | | | 3 | | 1 | | | | | | | | 3 | | 1 | | | |
| 37 | Erysipelas | 2 | 4 | 1 | | | | | 2 | 13 | 6 | 7 | 4 | 1 | 1 | | | | | 32 | 3 | | | | |
| 38 | Fever, not specified | 7 | 6 | 20 | 11 | 10 | 5 | 12 | 15 | 31 | 13 | 8 | 13 | 1 | 1 | | | | | 144 | 7 | 1 | | | |
| 39 | ..do..bilious | | | | 2 | | 1 | 1 | | | 1 | 1 | | | | | | | | 5 | | | | | |
| 40 | ..do..brain | 1 | 5 | 1 | 2 | 2 | | | 3 | 4 | 1 | 1 | 1 | 1 | | | | | | 20 | | | | | |
| 41 | ..do..inflammatory | | | | | | | | | | | | 1 | | | | | | | | 1 | | | | |
| 42 | ..do..intermittent | | | | | | | | | | | | | | | | | | | | | | | | |
| 43 | ..do..puerperal | | | | | | | | 5 | | 26 | | | | | | | | | 14 | 4 | | | | |
| 44 | ..do..remittent | | | | | | | | | | | 1 | | | | | | | | 1 | | | | | |
| 45 | ..do..scarlet | 11 | 8 | 67 | 87 | 28 | 24 | 4 | 10 | 2 | 2 | 1 | | | | | | | | 223 | 6 | 1 | | 1 | 2 |
| 46 | ..do..ship | | | | | | | | 1 | 1 | | | | | | | | | | | | | | | |
| 47 | ..do..typhus | 2 | 1 | 5 | 11 | 7 | 3 | 11 | 33 | 30 | 28 | 5 | 7 | | | | | | | 97 | 29 | 1 | | 1 | |
| 48 | ..do..yellow | | | | | | | | | 1 | | | | | | | | | | 1 | | | | | |
| 49 | Gout | | | | | | | | | | | 1 | | | | | | | | 1 | | | | | |
| 50 | Gravel | | 1 | | | | | | | | | 5 | 1 | 2 | | | | | | 9 | | | | | |
| 51 | Head, disease of | 2 | 1 | | 1 | | | | | 1 | | 1 | | | | | | | | 4 | | | 1 | | |
| 52 | Heart....do | 9 | 8 | 2 | 1 | 5 | 1 | 2 | 7 | 13 | 18 | 24 | 17 | 3 | 3 | | | | | 96 | 2 | | | | |
| 53 | Heat | 2 | | 1 | | | | | | 8 | 2 | 1 | | | | | | 1 | | 5 | | | | | |
| 54 | Hemorrhage | 3 | | | 1 | | | | 1 | 2 | 4 | 2 | | | | | | | | 10 | 2 | | | | |
| 55 | Hernia | | | | | | | | | | | 1 | 1 | | | | | | | 2 | | | | | |
| 56 | Hip, disease of | | | | | | | | | | | 1 | | | | | | | | 1 | | | | | |
| 57 | Hooping cough | 11 | 14 | 12 | 12 | 1 | 1 | | | | | | 1 | 1 | 1 | | | | | 51 | | | | | |
| 58 | Hydrocephalus | 1 | 3 | 3 | 1 | | | | | 1 | | 1 | | | | | | | | 9 | 1 | | | | |
| 59 | Inflamt'n, not specf'd | 6 | 5 | 4 | 1 | | | 3 | 4 | 5 | 6 | | 3 | | | | | | | 33 | 2 | 1 | | | |
| 60 | ....do....bowels | 5 | 4 | 5 | 4 | 1 | 1 | 4 | 1 | 8 | 17 | 6 | 3 | | | | | | | 44 | 8 | 3 | | | |
| 61 | ....do....brain | | | 1 | | | 1 | 1 | 1 | 1 | | | | | | | | | | 3 | 1 | | | | |
| 62 | Influenza | 3 | 2 | 2 | | 1 | | | | | 1 | 3 | 2 | 1 | 1 | | | | | 15 | | | | | |
| 63 | Insanity | | | | | | | | | 7 | 5 | 10 | 9 | | 1 | | | | | 27 | 3 | 1 | | | |
| 64 | Intemperance | | | | | | | | | 12 | 2 | 4 | | | | | | | | 9 | 2 | | | | |
| 65 | Jaundice | | | | | | | | | 2 | | | 1 | | | | | | | 1 | 1 | | | | |
| 66 | Kidneys, disease of | 1 | | | | | | | | 2 | | 1 | | | | | | | | 3 | | | | | |
| 67 | Liver.......do | 2 | 1 | | | | | | | 1 | 3 | 3 | 9 | | | | | | | 16 | 3 | | | | |
| 68 | Lockjaw | | | | | | | 1 | | 2 | | | | | | | | | | 2 | 1 | | | | |
| 69 | Lungs, disease of | 4 | 6 | 8 | 12 | 1 | 3 | | 3 | 2 | 5 | 3 | 4 | 1 | | | | | | 46 | 3 | | | | 1 |
| 70 | Malformation | 2 | | | | | | | | | | | | | | | | | | 1 | | | | | |
| 71 | Measles | | 8 | 5 | 13 | 3 | 1 | 1 | | 1 | 3 | | | | | | | | | 27 | 1 | | | | |
| 72 | Mortification | 12 | 13 | 8 | 5 | | 1 | | | 2 | 4 | 1 | 3 | | 1 | | | | | 48 | 2 | | | | |

# ECTION OF THE STATE OF MASSACHUSETTS.

*ssex and Middlesex.*

| NATIVITIES. | | | | | SEASON OF DECEASE. | | | | DURATION OF SICKNESS. | | | | WHITES. | | | COLORED. | | | | | | | | | |
|---|---|---|---|---|---|---|---|---|---|---|---|---|---|---|---|---|---|---|---|---|---|---|---|---|---|
| | | | | | | | | | | | | | | | | Slaves. | | | | Free. | | | | | |
| | | | | | | | | | | | | | | | | Black. | | Mulatto. | | Black. | | Mul. | | | |
| California and Territories. | Ireland. | Germany. | Other foreign countries. | Unknown. | Spring. | Summer. | Autumn. | Winter. | Under 1 week. | 1 week and under 1 month. | 1 month and under 3 months. | 3 months and over. | Males. | Females. | Total. | M. | F. | M. | F. | M. | F. | M | F. | Aggregate deaths. | |
| | 1 | | | | 1 | 3 | 1 | 4 | 2 | | | 4 | 7 | 2 | 9 | | | | | | | | | 9 | 1 |
| | 1 | | | | 21 | 3 | 15 | 5 | 1 | 8 | 2 | | 34 | 10 | 44 | | | | | | | | | 44 | 2 |
| | 1 | | | | 4 | 1 | | 3 | 2 | | 1 | | 2 | 6 | 8 | | | | | | | | | 8 | 3 |
| | 7 | | | | 4 | 21 | 11 | 5 | 4 | | | | 35 | 6 | 41 | | | | | | | | | 41 | 4 |
| | | | | | 2 | | 2 | 2 | 2 | 1 | | | 5 | 1 | 6 | | | | | | | | | 6 | 5 |
| | | | | | | | | 1 | | | | | 1 | | 1 | | | | | | | | | 1 | 6 |
| | 4 | | | | 1 | 1 | 4 | 3 | | | | | 9 | | 9 | | | | | | | | | 9 | 7 |
| | 4 | | | | 9 | 10 | 6 | 7 | 6 | 3 | | | 21 | 11 | 32 | | | | | | | | | 32 | 8 |
| | | | 2 | | 1 | 1 | 2 | | | | | 3 | 2 | 2 | 4 | | | | | | | | | 4 | 9 |
| | | | | | | | 1 | | | | | | 1 | | 1 | | | | | | | | | 1 | 10 |
| | 5 | | 2 | | 10 | 17 | 29 | 8 | 8 | 17 | 2 | 3 | 32 | 32 | 64 | | | | | | | | | 64 | 11 |
| | 3 | | 2 | | 13 | 23 | 24 | 13 | 7 | 18 | 4 | | 38 | 33 | 71 | | | | | | | 1 | 1 | 73 | 12 |
| | 1 | | | | 6 | 1 | 4 | | | 1 | | 3 | 8 | 3 | 11 | | | | | | | | | 11 | 13 |
| | | | | | 7 | 11 | 4 | 13 | 1 | 1 | 1 | 19 | 14 | 21 | 35 | | | | | | | | | 35 | 14 |
| | | | | | 1 | | | | | | | | 1 | | 1 | | | | | | | | | 1 | 15 |
| | | | 1 | | 4 | 1 | 2 | 2 | 1 | 5 | | 1 | 7 | 2 | 9 | | | | | | | | | 9 | 16 |
| | | | | | 1 | | | | | 1 | | | | 1 | 1 | | | | | | | | | 1 | 17 |
| | 11 | 1 | 2 | | 19 | 8 | 9 | 8 | 15 | 8 | 3 | 1 | | 44 | 44 | | | | | | | | | 44 | 18 |
| | 108 | 1 | 9 | | 2 | 16 | 198 | 8 | 47 | 6 | 1 | | 125 | 99 | 224 | | | | | | | | | 224 | 19 |
| | | | | | 1 | 13 | 97 | 2 | 34 | 28 | 2 | 3 | 51 | 62 | 113 | | | | | | | | | 113 | 20 |
| | 2 | | 3 | | 2 | 12 | 19 | | 9 | 7 | | | 18 | 15 | 33 | | | | | | | | | 33 | 21 |
| | | | | | | | | 1 | | | | | | 1 | 1 | | | | | | | | | 1 | 22 |
| | | | | | 3 | | 1 | 2 | 4 | | | | 4 | 2 | 6 | | | | | | | | | 6 | 23 |
| | | | | | 1 | | | 1 | 1 | | | | 2 | | 2 | | | | | | | | | 2 | 24 |
| | | | | | | 1 | 1 | 2 | | 2 | | | 4 | | 4 | | | | | | | | | 4 | 25 |
| | 78 | 1 | 32 | | 243 | 231 | 291 | 230 | 19 | 22 | 57 | 704 | 441 | 562 | 1003 | | | | | 1 | 3 | | 1 | 1008 | 26 |
| | 4 | | | | 24 | 27 | 17 | 20 | 16 | 10 | 2 | 6 | 52 | 38 | 90 | | | | | 1 | | | 1 | 92 | 27 |
| | | | | | | 1 | 2 | 1 | 1 | | | | 2 | 2 | 4 | | | | | | | | | 4 | 28 |
| | | | | | 16 | 6 | 28 | 26 | 28 | 8 | | | 40 | 37 | 77 | | | | | | | | | 77 | 29 |
| | | | | | 8 | 5 | 16 | 6 | | 1 | | 5 | 16 | 19 | 35 | | | | | | | | | 35 | 30 |
| | | | | | | 1 | 1 | | | 1 | | 1 | 1 | 1 | 2 | | | | | | | | | 2 | 31 |
| | 4 | | | | 3 | 8 | 28 | 12 | 3 | 9 | 5 | 4 | 35 | 16 | 51 | | | | | | | | | 51 | 32 |
| | 5 | | 8 | | 49 | 65 | 73 | 60 | 15 | 58 | 28 | 36 | 133 | 126 | 259 | | | | | 1 | | | 1 | 261 | 33 |
| | 25 | | 12 | | 12 | 73 | 490 | 44 | 87 | 244 | 44 | 23 | 308 | 318 | 626 | | | | | | | | 3 | 629 | 34 |
| | | | | | 2 | 1 | 1 | | | | | 1 | 1 | 3 | 4 | | | | | | | | | 4 | 35 |
| | | | | | 1 | 1 | 1 | 1 | | | | | 4 | | 4 | | | | | | | | | 4 | 36 |
| | 5 | | 1 | | 17 | 10 | 7 | 7 | 2 | 13 | | 3 | 24 | 17 | 41 | | | | | | | | | 41 | 37 |
| | 4 | | 2 | | 35 | 31 | 59 | 33 | 26 | 78 | 16 | 7 | 88 | 69 | 157 | | | | | | | 1 | | 158 | 38 |
| | | | 1 | | | 1 | 4 | 1 | | 4 | 1 | | 2 | 4 | 6 | | | | | | | | | 6 | 39 |
| | 1 | | 1 | | 11 | 1 | 5 | 5 | 2 | 11 | 1 | | 10 | 12 | 22 | | | | | | | | | 22 | 40 |
| | | | | | | | | 1 | | | 1 | | | 1 | 1 | | | | | | | | | 1 | 41 |
| | | | | | | | | | | | | | | | | | | | | | | | | | 42 |
| | 13 | | | | 10 | 2 | 8 | 11 | 3 | 3 | | 2 | | 31 | 31 | | | | | | | | | 31 | 43 |
| | | | | | 1 | | | | | | | | 1 | | 1 | | | | | | | | | 1 | 44 |
| | 4 | | 1 | 6 | 47 | 72 | 78 | 47 | 44 | 72 | 12 | 2 | 113 | 131 | 244 | | | | | | | | | 244 | 45 |
| | 2 | | | | | 1 | | 1 | 1 | | | | 1 | 1 | 2 | | | | | | | | | 2 | 46 |
| | 11 | | 4 | | 28 | 13 | 53 | 48 | 3 | 43 | 21 | 1 | 60 | 82 | 142 | | | | | | 1 | | | 143 | 47 |
| | | | | | 1 | | | | | | 1 | | 1 | | 1 | | | | | | | | | 1 | 48 |
| | | | | | | | | 1 | | | | | 1 | | 1 | | | | | | | | | 1 | 49 |
| | | | | | 5 | 3 | | 1 | | 2 | 1 | 4 | 7 | 2 | 9 | | | | | | | | | 9 | 50 |
| | 1 | | | | 2 | 2 | 2 | | 1 | 2 | | | 4 | 2 | 6 | | | | | | | | | 6 | 51 |
| | 10 | | 5 | | 25 | 22 | 34 | 32 | 13 | 13 | 13 | 18 | 58 | 54 | 112 | | | | | | 1 | | | 113 | 52 |
| | 9 | | 1 | | 1 | 11 | 1 | 2 | 1 | | | | 13 | 2 | 15 | | | | | | | | | 15 | 53 |
| | 1 | | | | 5 | 3 | 2 | 3 | 2 | 3 | 1 | | 7 | 6 | 13 | | | | | | | | | 13 | 54 |
| | | | | | | | 1 | 1 | 2 | | | | 1 | 1 | 2 | | | | | | | | | 2 | 55 |
| | | | | | 1 | | | | | | | 1 | 1 | | 1 | | | | | | | | | 1 | 56 |
| | 1 | | 2 | | 22 | 9 | 10 | 13 | 7 | 2 | 15 | 8 | 25 | 29 | 54 | | | | | | | | | 54 | 57 |
| | | | | | 3 | 1 | 4 | 2 | 1 | 6 | 1 | | 6 | 4 | 10 | | | | | | | | | 10 | 58 |
| | | | 1 | | 16 | 8 | 5 | 7 | 4 | 8 | | 1 | 18 | 19 | 37 | | | | | | | | | 37 | 59 |
| | 2 | | 2 | | 15 | 12 | 22 | 10 | 14 | 13 | 7 | 5 | 29 | 30 | 59 | | | | | | | | | 59 | 60 |
| | 1 | | | | 1 | 2 | 1 | 1 | 2 | 2 | | | 3 | 2 | 5 | | | | | | | | | 5 | 61 |
| | 1 | | | | 9 | | 2 | 5 | 4 | 5 | | 1 | 10 | 6 | 16 | | | | | | | | | 16 | 62 |
| | | | 1 | | 10 | 10 | 5 | 7 | 1 | | 3 | 11 | 16 | 15 | 31 | | | | | 1 | | | | 32 | 63 |
| | 6 | | 1 | | 6 | 6 | 4 | 2 | 2 | 1 | | | 16 | 2 | 18 | | | | | | | | | 18 | 64 |
| | 1 | | | | 1 | | 1 | 1 | | | | 1 | 2 | 1 | 3 | | | | | | | | | 3 | 65 |
| | | | 1 | | | 2 | 1 | 1 | | | 1 | 2 | 4 | | 4 | | | | | | | | | 4 | 66 |
| | | | | | 4 | 3 | 5 | 7 | | 1 | 4 | 6 | 6 | 13 | 19 | | | | | | | | | 19 | 67 |
| | | | | | | 1 | 1 | 1 | 1 | | | | 3 | | 3 | | | | | | | | | 3 | 68 |
| | | 2 | | | 30 | 12 | 4 | 6 | 6 | 1 | 3 | 3 | 18 | 33 | 51 | | | | | 1 | | | | 52 | 69 |
| | 1 | | | | | | 1 | 1 | 1 | | | | 2 | | 2 | | | | | | | | | 2 | 70 |
| | 2 | | | | 5 | 14 | 8 | 3 | 4 | 13 | 1 | 2 | 10 | 20 | 30 | | | | | | | | | 30 | 71 |
| | | | | | 6 | 6 | 29 | 9 | 6 | 13 | 3 | 5 | 22 | 27 | 49 | | | | | | | 1 | | 50 | 72 |

## CLASSIFICATION OF DEATHS IN NORTHEASTER[N]

| | Cause of death. | AGES. | | | | | | | | | | | | | | | | | | NATIVITIES. | | | | |
|---|---|---|---|---|---|---|---|---|---|---|---|---|---|---|---|---|---|---|---|---|---|---|---|---|
| | | Under 1. | | 1 and under 5. | | 5 and under 10. | | 10 and under 20. | | 20 and under 50. | | 50 and under 80. | | 80 and under 100. | | 100 & over. | | Age unknown. | | Born in the State. | N. England States. | Middle States. | Southern States. | Southwest'n States. |
| | | M. | F. | M. | F. | M. | F. | M. | F. | M. | F. | M. | F. | M | F. | M | F. | M | F. | | | | | |
| 1 | Mumps | 1 | | | | | | | | | | | | | | | | | | 1 | | | | |
| 2 | Murder | | | | | | | | | 1 | | | | | | | | | | 1 | | | | |
| 3 | Neuralgia | | | | | | 1 | | | 1 | 1 | | 1 | | | | | | | 3 | | | | |
| 4 | Old age | | | | | | | | | | | 29 | 44 | 58 | 98 | | | | | 209 | 7 | | | |
| 5 | Paralysis | | | | | | | | | 5 | 6 | 28 | 19 | 3 | 11 | | | | | 67 | 4 | | | |
| 6 | Pleurisy | | | | | | | | | 3 | 3 | 1 | | | | | | | | 4 | 1 | | | |
| 7 | Pneumonia | 22 | 14 | 20 | 20 | 3 | 1 | 2 | 1 | 10 | 4 | 17 | 13 | 1 | 2 | | | | | 116 | 4 | | 1 | |
| 8 | Poison | | | | 2 | | 1 | | | 3 | 1 | | | | | | | | | 7 | 1 | | | |
| 9 | Prematurity of birth | | | | | | | | | | | | | | | | | | | | | | | |
| 10 | Quinsy | | | | | | | | | 1 | | | | | | | | | | 1 | | | | |
| 11 | Rash | 1 | | | 1 | | | | | | | | | | | | | | | 2 | | | | |
| 12 | Rheumatism | | | | 1 | | | 1 | | 4 | 1 | 1 | 3 | | | | | | | 8 | | | | |
| 13 | Scrofula | 3 | 3 | 6 | 3 | 1 | 1 | | 1 | 3 | 4 | 2 | 1 | | 1 | | | | | 27 | 1 | | | |
| 14 | Small pox | 1 | 3 | 8 | 1 | 1 | | 1 | 4 | 17 | 7 | 5 | 3 | | | | | | | 41 | 5 | | | |
| 15 | Spine, disease of | | 1 | 1 | | 1 | | 2 | 1 | | 1 | 1 | 1 | | | | | | | 9 | | | | |
| 16 | Spleen....do | | | | | | | | | | | | | | | | | | | | | | | |
| 17 | Stillborn | 13 | 8 | | | | | | | | | | | | | | | | | 21 | | | | |
| 18 | Stomach, disease of | | | | | | | | | | 1 | 2 | 2 | | | | | | | 2 | 1 | | | 1 |
| 19 | Suffocation | | | 1 | | | | | | | | 1 | | | | | | | | 2 | | | | |
| 20 | Suicide | | | | | | | | | 11 | 2 | 4 | | | | | | | | 12 | 3 | | | |
| 21 | Sun stroke | | | | | | 1 | | | 5 | | | | | | | | | | 1 | 2 | | | |
| 22 | Teething | 13 | 11 | 9 | 13 | 1 | | | | | | | | | | | | | | 45 | 2 | | | |
| 23 | Throat, disease of | 2 | | 1 | 1 | | 3 | | 1 | | | 1 | 1 | | | | | | | 8 | 2 | | | |
| 24 | Tumor | | | 1 | | | | | | | 3 | 3 | 1 | 1 | | | | | | 8 | 1 | | | |
| 25 | Ulcer | | 1 | 1 | 1 | | | | | 2 | 1 | 2 | 1 | 1 | | | | | | 9 | | | | |
| 26 | Unknown | 90 | 55 | 12 | 10 | 9 | 5 | 6 | 5 | 40 | 28 | 27 | 17 | 2 | 3 | | | 4 | | 270 | 11 | | 1 | |
| | Total | 471 | 339 | 533 | 529 | 143 | 134 | 126 | 238 | 678 | 732 | 511 | 439 | 106 | 145 | | | 10 | 7 | 4228 | 352 | 32 | 5 | 3 |

## CLASSIFICATION OF DEATHS IN WESTE[RN]

*Embracing the following counties: Berksh[ire]*

| | Cause of death. | Under 1 M. | Under 1 F. | 1–5 M. | 1–5 F. | 5–10 M. | 5–10 F. | 10–20 M. | 10–20 F. | 20–50 M. | 20–50 F. | 50–80 M. | 50–80 F. | 80–100 M | 80–100 F. | 100 & over M | 100 & over F. | Age unknown M | Age unknown F. | Born in the State. | N. England States. | Middle States. | Southern States. | Southwest'n States. |
|---|---|---|---|---|---|---|---|---|---|---|---|---|---|---|---|---|---|---|---|---|---|---|---|---|
| 1 | Abscess | 1 | | 2 | 1 | 1 | | | | 5 | 2 | 4 | | | | | | | | 12 | 1 | 2 | | |
| 2 | Accident, not specif'd | 2 | 3 | 5 | | 4 | 1 | 4 | | 19 | 2 | 11 | 2 | | 1 | | | | | 41 | 3 | 1 | | |
| 3 | ....do....burned | | | 1 | 4 | | 1 | | | | 1 | | 2 | | | | | | | 9 | | | | |
| 4 | ....do....drowned | 1 | | 11 | 1 | 5 | | 3 | 3 | 9 | 3 | 1 | | | | | | | | 26 | 4 | 2 | | |
| 5 | ....do....scalded | | 1 | 6 | 2 | 1 | | | | 1 | | | | | | | | | | 10 | | | | |
| 6 | ....do....explosion | | | | | | | 1 | | | | | | | | | | | | 1 | | | | |
| 7 | ....do....machin'ry | | | | | | | | | 1 | | | | | | | | | | | | | | |
| 8 | ....d5....shot | | | | | | | | | 1 | | | | | | | | | | | | | | |
| 9 | ....do....railroad | | | | | | | 2 | | | | | | | | | | | | 1 | | | | |
| 10 | Amputation | | | | | | | | | 1 | | | | | | | | | | 1 | | | | |
| 11 | Apoplexy | | | | | | | 1 | | 3 | 2 | 12 | 9 | 2 | 1 | | | | | 25 | 5 | | | |
| 12 | Asthma | | | | | | | | | | | 4 | 2 | 3 | | | | | | 8 | 1 | | | |
| 13 | Bladder, disease of | | | | | | | | | | | 1 | | | | | | | | 1 | | | | |
| 14 | Bowels....do | 8 | 7 | 5 | 7 | 2 | 2 | | | 2 | 7 | 2 | 1 | | | | | | | 38 | 4 | 1 | | |
| 15 | Brain......do | 11 | 4 | 9 | 16 | 5 | 1 | 4 | 3 | 7 | 8 | 4 | 5 | 1 | 1 | | | | | 71 | 3 | | | |
| 16 | Bronchitis | 2 | 3 | 2 | 1 | | 2 | | | 1 | 1 | | 1 | | 1 | | | | | 13 | 1 | | | |
| 17 | Cancer | | | 1 | 1 | 1 | 1 | | 1 | 2 | 13 | 12 | 19 | 2 | 4 | | | | | 51 | 6 | | | |
| 18 | Chicken pox | | 1 | | | | | | | | | | | | | | | | | 1 | | | | |
| 19 | Childbirth | | | | | | | | 2 | | 40 | | | | | | | | | 21 | 2 | | | |
| 20 | Cholera | 4 | 3 | 5 | 5 | 3 | 10 | 1 | 6 | 38 | 31 | 21 | 1 | | | | | 1 | | 71 | 5 | 1 | | |
| 21 | ....do....infantum | 23 | 19 | 29 | 29 | | | 1 | | | | | | | | | | | | 94 | 5 | | | |
| 22 | ....do....morbus | 1 | 1 | 3 | 1 | | 3 | | 1 | 2 | 5 | 2 | 1 | | | | | | | 18 | 1 | 1 | | |
| 23 | Chorea | | | | | | | | | | 1 | | | | | | | | | 1 | | | | |
| 24 | Colic | | | | | | | | 1 | 1 | 4 | 2 | 5 | | | | | | | 12 | 1 | | | |
| 25 | Congestion | | | | 1 | | | | | 1 | 1 | | | | 1 | | | | | 3 | | | | |
| 26 | ....do.....brain | 2 | 2 | 2 | 2 | 1 | 1 | | | 1 | | | | | | | | | | 9 | 1 | | | |
| 27 | Consumption | 40 | 24 | 30 | 13 | 5 | 10 | 32 | 61 | 189 | 277 | 105 | 105 | 13 | 11 | | | 1 | | 750 | 90 | 17 | 1 | |
| 28 | Convulsions | 26 | 21 | 11 | 12 | 4 | 3 | 1 | 1 | 5 | 1 | 10 | 8 | 2 | 4 | | | 2 | | 100 | 4 | 2 | | |
| 29 | Cramp | | 1 | | 1 | | 1 | | | | 2 | | | | | | | | | 5 | | | | |
| 30 | Croup | 15 | 11 | 27 | 29 | 4 | 6 | 1 | | | | | | | | | | | | 88 | 3 | | | |
| 31 | Debility | 8 | | 1 | | | | | | 1 | 4 | 4 | 2 | 1 | 2 | | | | | 17 | 1 | | | |
| 32 | Diabetes | | | | 1 | | 2 | 1 | | 3 | | 2 | | 1 | 1 | | | | | 10 | 1 | | | |
| 33 | Diarrhœa | 5 | 3 | 6 | 4 | | 1 | | 2 | 2 | 6 | 1 | 4 | 2 | | | | | | 31 | 2 | 2 | | |
| 34 | Dropsy | 9 | 11 | 15 | 21 | 7 | 4 | 4 | 5 | 6 | 21 | 35 | 30 | | 13 | | | | | 159 | 10 | 5 | | |
| 35 | Dysentery | 92 | 74 | 253 | 174 | 52 | 57 | 17 | 26 | 51 | 58 | 47 | 68 | 11 | 16 | | | | | 883 | 51 | 16 | | |
| 36 | Dyspepsia | | | | | | | | | | 2 | | 1 | | 1 | | | | | 4 | | | | |
| 37 | Epilepsy | | | | | | | | | 3 | 2 | | 1 | | | | | | | 5 | 1 | | | |
| 38 | Erysipelas | 1 | 4 | 1 | 2 | 1 | | | 1 | 4 | 11 | 2 | 7 | 2 | 1 | | | | | 27 | 7 | | | |

## SECTION OF THE STATE OF MASSACHUSETTS—Continued.

| NATIVITIES. California and Territories. | NATIVITIES. Ireland. | NATIVITIES. Germany. | NATIVITIES. Other foreign countries. | NATIVITIES. Unknown. | SEASON OF DECEASE. Spring. | SEASON OF DECEASE. Summer. | SEASON OF DECEASE. Autumn. | SEASON OF DECEASE. Winter. | DURATION OF SICKNESS. Under 1 week. | DURATION OF SICKNESS. 1 week and under 1 month. | DURATION OF SICKNESS. 1 month and under 3 months. | DURATION OF SICKNESS. 3 months and over. | WHITES. Males. | WHITES. Females. | WHITES. Total. | COLORED. Slaves. Black. M. | COLORED. Slaves. Black. F. | COLORED. Slaves. Mulatto. M. | COLORED. Slaves. Mulatto. F. | COLORED. Free. Black. M. | COLORED. Free. Black. F. | COLORED. Free. Mul. M | COLORED. Free. Mul. F. | Aggregate deaths. | |
|---|---|---|---|---|---|---|---|---|---|---|---|---|---|---|---|---|---|---|---|---|---|---|---|---|---|
| .... | .. | .. | .... | ... | 1 | .... | .... | .... | .... | 1 | .... | .... | 1 | ... | 1 | .... | .... | .... | .... | ... | ... | .. | .. | 1 | 1 |
| .... | .. | .. | .... | ... | .... | .... | .... | 1 | .... | .... | .... | .... | 1 | .... | 1 | .... | .... | .... | .... | ... | ... | .. | .. | 1 | 2 |
| .... | 1 | .. | .... | ... | 1 | .... | 2 | 1 | .... | 3 | .... | .... | 1 | 3 | 4 | .... | .... | .... | .... | ... | ... | .. | .. | 4 | 3 |
| .... | 9 | .. | 4 | ... | 60 | 46 | 64 | 59 | 7 | 16 | 14 | 28 | 87 | 141 | 228 | .... | .... | .... | .... | ... | 1 | .. | .. | 229 | 4 |
| .... | .. | .. | 1 | ... | 15 | 19 | 17 | 21 | 6 | 11 | 6 | 14 | 36 | 35 | 71 | .... | .... | .... | .... | ... | 1 | .. | .. | 72 | 5 |
| .... | 1 | .. | 1 | ... | 3 | .... | 1 | 3 | 1 | 1 | 1 | 1 | 4 | 3 | 7 | .... | .... | .... | .... | ... | ... | .. | .. | 7 | 6 |
| .... | 5 | .. | 4 | ... | 50 | 28 | 16 | 35 | 14 | 49 | 14 | 5 | 75 | 55 | 130 | .... | .... | .... | .... | ... | ... | .. | .. | 130 | 7 |
| .... | .. | .. | .... | ... | 3 | 1 | 2 | 2 | 2 | 4 | .... | .... | 3 | 5 | 8 | .... | .... | .... | .... | ... | ... | .. | .. | 8 | 8 |
| .... | .. | .. | .... | ... | .... | .... | .... | .... | .... | .... | .... | .... | .... | .... | .... | .... | .... | .... | .... | ... | ... | .. | .. | ... | 9 |
| .... | .. | .. | .... | ... | 1 | .... | .... | .... | .... | .... | .... | .... | 1 | .... | 1 | .... | .... | .... | .... | ... | ... | .. | .. | 1 | 10 |
| .... | .. | .. | .... | ... | .... | 1 | .... | 1 | 1 | .... | .... | .... | 1 | 1 | 2 | .... | .... | .... | .... | ... | ... | .. | .. | 2 | 11 |
| .... | 2 | .. | 1 | ... | 5 | 2 | 2 | 2 | .... | 3 | 1 | 1 | 6 | 5 | 11 | .... | .... | .... | .... | ... | ... | .. | .. | 11 | 12 |
| .... | 1 | .. | .... | ... | 7 | 8 | 10 | 4 | 1 | 5 | 1 | 10 | 15 | 14 | 29 | .... | .... | .... | .... | ... | ... | .. | .. | 29 | 13 |
| .... | 3 | .. | 2 | ... | 29 | 13 | 4 | 5 | 2 | 25 | .... | ... | 33 | 18 | 51 | .... | .... | .... | .... | ... | ... | .. | .. | 51 | 14 |
| .... | .. | .. | .... | ... | 6 | 1 | 1 | 1 | .... | .... | .... | 3 | 5 | 4 | 9 | .... | .... | .... | .... | ... | ... | .. | .. | 9 | 15 |
| .... | .. | .. | .... | ... | .... | .... | .... | .... | .... | .... | .... | .... | .... | .... | .... | .... | .... | .... | .... | ... | ... | .. | .. | ... | 16 |
| .... | .. | .. | .... | ... | 3 | 3 | 6 | 9 | .... | .... | .... | .... | 13 | 8 | 21 | .... | .... | .... | .... | ... | ... | .. | .. | 21 | 17 |
| .... | 1 | .. | .... | ... | 1 | 2 | 1 | 1 | .... | .... | .... | 1 | 2 | 3 | 5 | .... | .... | .... | .... | ... | ... | .. | .. | 5 | 18 |
| .... | .. | .. | .... | ... | .... | .... | 1 | 1 | .... | .... | .... | .... | 2 | .... | 2 | .... | .... | .... | .... | ... | ... | .. | .. | 2 | 19 |
| .... | 1 | .. | 1 | ... | 2 | 3 | 7 | 5 | .... | .... | 1 | .... | 15 | 2 | 17 | .... | .... | .... | .... | ... | ... | .. | .. | 17 | 20 |
| .... | 3 | .. | .... | ... | .... | 4 | 2 | .... | .... | 1 | .... | .... | 5 | 1 | 6 | .... | .... | .... | .... | ... | ... | .. | .. | 6 | 21 |
| .... | .. | .. | .... | ... | 10 | 10 | 20 | 7 | .... | 5 | 2 | 10 | 23 | 23 | 46 | .... | .... | .... | .... | ... | ... | .. | 1 | 47 | 22 |
| .... | .. | .. | .... | ... | 1 | 5 | 3 | 1 | 1 | 5 | .... | 1 | 4 | 6 | 10 | .... | .... | .... | .... | ... | ... | .. | .. | 10 | 23 |
| .... | .. | .. | .... | ... | 5 | 3 | .... | 1 | .... | 1 | .... | 6 | 5 | 4 | 9 | .... | .... | .... | .... | ... | ... | .. | .. | 9 | 24 |
| .... | 1 | .. | .... | ... | 1 | 4 | 2 | 3 | 1 | 3 | .... | 2 | 6 | 4 | 10 | .... | .... | .... | .... | ... | ... | .. | .. | 10 | 25 |
| .... | 28 | .. | 3 | ... | 76 | 80 | 102 | 55 | 45 | 37 | 18 | 21 | 191 | 121 | 312 | .... | .... | .... | .... | ... | 1 | .. | .. | 313 | 26 |
| ... | 391 | 5 | 114 | 6 | 1063 | 1053 | 1998 | 978 | 584 | 940 | 316 | 1003 | 2571 | 2547 | 5118 | .... | .... | .... | .... | 5 | 8 | 3 | 8 | 5142 | |

## SECTION OF THE STATE OF MASSACHUSETTS.

*Franklin, Hampden, Hampshire, and Worcester.*

| California and Territories. | Ireland. | Germany. | Other foreign countries. | Unknown. | Spring. | Summer. | Autumn. | Winter. | Under 1 week. | 1 week and under 1 month. | 1 month and under 3 months. | 3 months and over. | Males. | Females. | Total. | Slaves Black M. | Slaves Black F. | Slaves Mulatto M. | Slaves Mulatto F. | Free Black M. | Free Black F. | Free Mul. M | Free Mul. F. | Aggregate deaths. | |
|---|---|---|---|---|---|---|---|---|---|---|---|---|---|---|---|---|---|---|---|---|---|---|---|---|---|
| .... | 1 | .. | .... | ... | 3 | 5 | 5 | 3 | 5 | 1 | 1 | 2 | 13 | 3 | 16 | .... | .... | .... | .... | ... | ... | .. | .. | 16 | 1 |
| .... | 8 | .. | 1 | ... | 8 | 19 | 17 | 10 | 17 | 7 | 2 | 1 | 44 | 9 | 53 | .... | .... | .... | .... | 1 | ... | .. | .. | 54 | 2 |
| .... | .. | .. | .... | ... | 3 | 1 | .... | 3 | 3 | 2 | .... | .... | 1 | 8 | 9 | .... | .... | .... | .... | ... | ... | .. | .. | 9 | 3 |
| .... | 5 | .. | .... | ... | 4 | 8 | 19 | 6 | 13 | .... | .... | .... | 30 | 7 | 37 | .... | .... | .... | .... | ... | ... | .. | .. | 37 | 4 |
| .... | .. | .. | 1 | ... | 2 | 2 | 5 | 2 | 6 | 1 | .... | .... | 8 | 3 | 11 | .... | .... | .... | .... | ... | ... | .. | .. | 11 | 5 |
| .... | .. | .. | .... | ... | .... | .... | .... | 1 | .... | .... | .... | .... | 1 | .... | 1 | .... | .... | .... | .... | ... | ... | .. | .. | 1 | 6 |
| .... | 1 | .. | .... | ... | 1 | .... | .... | .... | 1 | .... | .... | .... | 1 | .... | 1 | .... | .... | .... | .... | ... | ... | .. | .. | 1 | 7 |
| .... | 1 | .. | .... | ... | .... | .... | 1 | .... | .... | .... | .... | .... | 1 | .... | 1 | .... | .... | .... | .... | ... | ... | .. | .. | 1 | 8 |
| .... | 1 | .. | .... | ... | 1 | 1 | .... | .... | 1 | .... | .... | .... | 2 | .... | 2 | .... | .... | .... | .... | ... | ... | .. | .. | 2 | 9 |
| .... | .. | .. | .... | ... | .... | .... | 1 | .... | .... | .... | .... | .... | 1 | .... | 1 | .... | .... | .... | .... | ... | ... | .. | .. | 1 | 10 |
| .... | .. | .. | .... | ... | 7 | 8 | 5 | 10 | 13 | 4 | .... | 4 | 18 | 12 | 30 | .... | .... | .... | .... | ... | ... | .. | .. | 30 | 11 |
| .... | .. | .. | .... | ... | 3 | 2 | 2 | 2 | 4 | 2 | 1 | 2 | 7 | 2 | 9 | .... | .... | .... | .... | ... | ... | .. | .. | 9 | 12 |
| .... | .. | .. | .... | ... | .... | .... | .... | 1 | .... | .... | 1 | .... | 1 | .... | 1 | .... | .... | .... | .... | ... | ... | .. | .. | 1 | 13 |
| .... | .. | .. | .... | ... | 6 | 6 | 27 | 4 | 10 | 13 | 10 | 1 | 19 | 24 | 43 | .... | .... | .... | .... | ... | ... | .. | .. | 43 | 14 |
| .... | 3 | .. | 2 | ... | 22 | 20 | 15 | 22 | 22 | 32 | 3 | 11 | 41 | 38 | 79 | .... | .... | .... | .... | ... | ... | .. | .. | 79 | 15 |
| .... | .. | .. | .... | ... | 6 | .... | 3 | 4 | 4 | 4 | 2 | 1 | 5 | 9 | 14 | .... | .... | .... | .... | ... | ... | .. | .. | 14 | 16 |
| .... | .. | .. | .... | ... | 20 | 15 | 11 | 11 | 2 | 4 | 7 | 33 | 18 | 38 | 56 | .... | .... | .... | .... | ... | 1 | .. | .. | 57 | 17 |
| .... | .. | .. | .... | ... | .... | 1 | .... | .... | .... | 1 | .... | .... | .... | 1 | 1 | .... | .... | .... | .... | ... | ... | .. | .. | 1 | 18 |
| .... | 8 | .. | 11 | ... | 15 | 11 | 6 | 10 | 19 | 8 | 1 | .... | .... | 42 | 42 | .... | .... | .... | .... | ... | ... | .. | .. | 42 | 19 |
| .... | 46 | .. | 5 | ... | 2 | 29 | 98 | .... | 78 | 27 | 2 | .... | 73 | 56 | 129 | .... | .... | .... | .... | ... | ... | .. | .. | 129 | 20 |
| .... | 2 | .. | .... | ... | 4 | 20 | 71 | 5 | 49 | 41 | 5 | 2 | 53 | 49 | 102 | .... | .... | .... | .... | ... | ... | .. | .. | 101 | 21 |
| .... | .. | .. | .... | ... | 3 | 1 | 14 | .... | 12 | 5 | .... | .... | 8 | 11 | 19 | .... | .... | .... | .... | ... | ... | .. | .. | 20 | 22 |
| .... | .. | .. | .... | ... | .... | .... | 1 | .... | .... | .... | .... | .... | .... | 1 | 1 | .... | .... | .... | .... | ... | ... | .. | .. | 1 | 23 |
| .... | .. | .. | .... | ... | 5 | 3 | 2 | 3 | 5 | 3 | 1 | 1 | 3 | 10 | 13 | .... | .... | .... | .... | ... | ... | .. | .. | 13 | 24 |
| .... | 1 | .. | .... | ... | 3 | 1 | .... | .... | 1 | .... | .... | .... | 1 | 3 | 4 | .... | .... | .... | .... | ... | ... | .. | .. | 4 | 25 |
| .... | .. | .. | .... | ... | 2 | 4 | 3 | 1 | 4 | 5 | 1 | .... | 6 | 5 | 11 | .... | .... | .... | .... | ... | ... | .. | .. | 11 | 26 |
| .... | 44 | 1 | 13 | ... | 231 | 220 | 266 | 199 | 40 | 58 | 120 | 543 | 406 | 495 | 901 | .... | .... | .... | .... | 8 | 6 | 1 | .. | 916 | 27 |
| .... | 2 | .. | 3 | ... | 26 | 24 | 28 | 22 | 48 | 21 | 6 | 5 | 61 | 50 | 111 | .... | .... | .... | .... | ... | ... | .. | .. | 111 | 28 |
| .... | .. | .. | .... | ... | 1 | 1 | 1 | 2 | 1 | 2 | .... | 2 | .... | 5 | 5 | .... | .... | .... | .... | ... | ... | .. | .. | 5 | 29 |
| .... | 1 | .. | .... | ... | 26 | 17 | 20 | 29 | 55 | 21 | 1 | 1 | 44 | 45 | 89 | .... | .... | .... | .... | 3 | ... | .. | 1 | 93 | 30 |
| .... | .. | .. | .... | ... | 4 | 6 | 4 | 4 | .... | 6 | 1 | 6 | 9 | 8 | 17 | .... | .... | .... | .... | ... | ... | 1 | .. | 18 | 31 |
| .... | .. | .. | .... | ... | 4 | 2 | 1 | 4 | 1 | 5 | .... | 5 | 7 | 4 | 11 | .... | .... | .... | .... | ... | ... | .. | .. | 11 | 32 |
| .... | 1 | .. | .... | ... | 8 | 5 | 24 | 4 | 6 | 16 | 7 | 1 | 16 | 20 | 36 | .... | .... | .... | .... | ... | ... | .. | .. | 36 | 33 |
| .... | 6 | .. | 1 | ... | 39 | 48 | 51 | 43 | 26 | 59 | 25 | 55 | 75 | 105 | 180 | .... | .... | .... | .... | ... | ... | 1 | .. | 181 | 34 |
| 1 | 31 | 1 | 12 | ... | 16 | 75 | 877 | 24 | 262 | 503 | 66 | 21 | 521 | 472 | 993 | .... | .... | .... | .... | 1 | 1 | 1 | .. | 996 | 35 |
| .... | .. | .. | .... | ... | 1 | .... | .... | 3 | .... | 1 | .... | 2 | .... | 4 | 4 | .... | .... | .... | .... | ... | ... | .. | .. | 4 | 36 |
| .... | .. | .. | .... | ... | 2 | 2 | 1 | 1 | 1 | 1 | 2 | 2 | 3 | 3 | 6 | .... | .... | .... | .... | ... | ... | .. | .. | 6 | 37 |
| .... | 3 | .. | .... | ... | 18 | 6 | 6 | 7 | 5 | 24 | 4 | 3 | 11 | 26 | 37 | .... | .... | .... | .... | ... | ... | .. | .. | 37 | 38 |

## CLASSIFICATION OF DEATHS IN WESTERN

| | Cause of death. | AGES. Under 1. M. | Under 1. F. | 1 and under 5. M. | 1 and under 5. F. | 5 and under 10. M. | 5 and under 10. F. | 10 and under 20. M. | 10 and under 20. F. | 20 and under 50. M. | 20 and under 50. F. | 50 and under 80. M. | 50 and under 80. F. | 80 and under 100. M. | 80 and under 100. F. | 100 & over. M | 100 & over. F. | Age unknown. M | Age unknown. F. | NATIVITIES. Born in State. | N. England States. | Middle States. | Southern States. | Southwest'n States. | Northwest'n States. |
|---|---|---|---|---|---|---|---|---|---|---|---|---|---|---|---|---|---|---|---|---|---|---|---|---|---|
| 1 | Fever, not specified.. | 7 | 4 | 9 | 8 | 7 | 6 | 12 | 10 | 33 | 32 | 20 | 13 | 8 | 2 | | | | | 137 | 13 | 4 | | | |
| 2 | ...do..bilious ...... | | | | 3 | 1 | | | 2 | 5 | 3 | 7 | 4 | | | | | | | 18 | 4 | 1 | | | |
| 3 | ...do..brain ........ | 5 | | 7 | 8 | 2 | | 6 | 2 | 2 | 4 | | 1 | | | | | | | 35 | 1 | | | | |
| 4 | ...do..inflammatory | | | | | | | | 1 | | | | | | | | | | | 1 | | | | | |
| 5 | ...do..puerperal.... | | | | | | | | | | 2 | | | | | | | | | 2 | | | | | |
| 6 | ...do..scarlet....... | 1 | 4 | 21 | 30 | 21 | 20 | 3 | 6 | | 1 | | | | | | | 1 | | 98 | 7 | 2 | | | |
| 7 | ...do..ship.......... | | | | | | 1 | 2 | | 2 | 1 | | | | | | | | | 2 | | | | | |
| 8 | ...do..typhus....... | 2 | 1 | 6 | 6 | 6 | 2 | 16 | 33 | 43 | 35 | 20 | 19 | 1 | | | | | | 150 | 26 | 6 | 1 | | |
| 9 | ...do..yellow....... | | | | | | | 1 | | | | | | | | | | | | 1 | | | | | |
| 10 | Gout ............... | | | | | | | | | | | 1 | | | | | | | | 1 | | | | | |
| 11 | Gravel ............. | | | | | | | | | | | 3 | 1 | 1 | | | | | | 5 | | | | | |
| 12 | Head, disease of..... | 1 | 1 | 1 | 1 | | | | | | | | | | | | | | | 4 | | | | | |
| 13 | Heart....do......... | 2 | 3 | 1 | 3 | 6 | | 1 | 1 | 3 | 17 | 22 | 10 | 6 | 2 | | | | | 60 | 11 | 1 | | | |
| 14 | Heat ............... | | | | | | | 1 | | 2 | | 1 | | 2 | | | | | | 3 | | | | | |
| 15 | Hemorrhage.......... | | 1 | 2 | | | | 1 | 1 | 2 | | 2 | 2 | | | | | | | 9 | 2 | | | | |
| 16 | Hernia.............. | | | | | | | | | | 1 | | 1 | | | | | | | 2 | | | | | |
| 17 | Hooping cough...... | 12 | 16 | 13 | 7 | 3 | 1 | | | | | | | | | | | | 1 | 50 | 1 | 1 | | | |
| 18 | Inflammation....... | 2 | 2 | 3 | 7 | 1 | 1 | 1 | 3 | 2 | 11 | 2 | 2 | 1 | 1 | | | | | 31 | 5 | 1 | | | |
| 19 | ....do... . bowels.. | 8 | 1 | 3 | 2 | 2 | | 3 | 5 | 3 | 6 | 3 | 1 | | | | | | | 33 | 1 | | | | |
| 20 | ....do.......stomach | | | | | | | | 1 | | 2 | | 1 | | | | | | | 4 | | | | | |
| 21 | Influenza .......... | 2 | 1 | 1 | | | | | | | | 1 | | | 1 | | | | | 6 | | | | | |
| 22 | Intemperance....... | | | | | | | | | 8 | | 2 | 2 | 1 | 1 | | | | | 12 | 1 | | | | |
| 23 | Insanity............ | | | | | | | | | 3 | 1 | 2 | 2 | | | | | | | 7 | 1 | | | | |
| 24 | Jaundice .......... | | | | | | | | | | | | 2 | 1 | | | | | | 2 | 1 | | | | |
| 25 | Kidneys, disease of.. | | | | | | | | | 1 | | | | | | | | | | 1 | | | | | |
| 26 | Killed ............. | | | | | | | | | 2 | | | | | | | | | | 1 | | | | | |
| 27 | Liver, disease of..... | 2 | 1 | | | 1 | | | 1 | 1 | 5 | 9 | 5 | | 1 | | | | | 24 | 2 | | | | |
| 28 | Lockjaw............ | | | | | 1 | | 1 | | | | | | | | | | | | 2 | | | | | |
| 29 | Lungs, disease of.... | 13 | 4 | 5 | 8 | 1 | 2 | 2 | | 6 | 4 | 6 | 8 | | 2 | | | | | 50 | 6 | 2 | | | |
| 30 | Malformation........ | 3 | 1 | | | | | | | | | | | | | | | | | 4 | | | | | |
| 31 | Measles............. | 4 | 3 | 13 | 14 | 1 | 3 | 1 | 2 | 2 | 4 | | | | | | | | | 45 | 2 | | | | |
| 32 | Mortification........ | 6 | 2 | 2 | 1 | | 1 | 1 | | | 4 | 6 | 2 | 2 | 4 | | | | | 29 | 2 | | | | |
| 33 | Mumps............. | | | | 1 | | | | | | | | | | | | | | | 1 | | | | | |
| 34 | Old age............ | | | | | | | | | | | 24 | 28 | 104 | 97 | 1 | 2 | | | 222 | 23 | 3 | | | |
| 35 | Paralysis........... | | | 1 | | 1 | | | | 3 | 3 | 23 | 22 | 14 | 11 | | | | | 69 | 6 | 1 | 1 | | |
| 36 | Peritonitis.......... | | | | | 1 | | | | 1 | | | | | | | | | | | 1 | | | | |
| 37 | Pleurisy ........... | | 1 | 1 | | | | | | 2 | | 8 | 2 | 1 | 1 | | | | | 12 | 3 | | | | |
| 38 | Pneumonia ......... | 21 | 20 | 14 | 17 | 4 | 4 | 4 | 3 | 7 | 4 | 11 | 16 | 8 | 5 | | | | | 129 | 5 | 2 | | | |
| 39 | Poison............. | 1 | 1 | | | | | 1 | 1 | | | 1 | 1 | | | | | | | 6 | | | | | |
| 40 | Prematurity of birth. | 4 | 1 | | | | | | | | | | | | | | | | | 5 | | | | | |
| 41 | Quinsy ........... | | | 2 | | 1 | | | | 1 | | | | | | | | | | 3 | | | | | |
| 42 | Rash .............. | 9 | 2 | 26 | 28 | 10 | 12 | 1 | 3 | | 1 | | | | | | | | | 85 | 2 | 1 | | | 1 |
| 43 | Rheumatism ........ | | | | | | 1 | | 1 | 2 | 2 | 6 | 1 | | 1 | | | | | 11 | 2 | | | | |
| 44 | Rickets............ | | | 2 | | | | | | | | | | | | | | | | 2 | | | | | |
| 45 | Scrofula........... | 1 | 1 | 2 | 3 | | 2 | 1 | 1 | 2 | 1 | 1 | | | | | | | | 14 | 1 | | | | |
| 46 | Small pox.......... | 4 | 2 | 2 | 1 | 1 | 2 | 3 | 2 | 6 | 3 | 1 | 1 | | 1 | | | | | 24 | 4 | 1 | | | |
| 47 | Spine, disease of..... | 4 | 1 | 1 | | | | 1 | 1 | 1 | 2 | 1 | | | | | | | | 12 | | | | | |
| 48 | Spleen...do ....... | | | | | | | 1 | | | | | | | | | | | | 1 | | | | | |
| 49 | Stillborn .......... | 1 | 1 | | | | | | | | | | | | | | | | | 2 | | | | | |
| 50 | Stomach, disease of.. | | 1 | | | | 1 | | | | | 4 | 1 | | | | | | | 5 | 2 | | | | |
| 51 | Suicide ........... | | | | | | | | | 7 | 5 | 4 | | | | | | | | 14 | | 1 | | | |
| 52 | Summer complaint.. | 1 | 1 | 1 | 1 | | | | | | | | | | | | | | | 4 | | | | | |
| 53 | Sun, stroke of....... | | | | | | | | | 3 | | 1 | | | | | | | | 1 | | | | | |
| 54 | Teething........... | 5 | 7 | 8 | 5 | 1 | | | | | | | | | | | | | | 25 | | | | | 1 |
| 55 | Throat, disease of ... | 5 | | 1 | 4 | 1 | 2 | 1 | | | | | | | | | | | 1 | 14 | | | | | |
| 56 | Thrush ............ | | | | | | | | | | 1 | | | | | | | | | 1 | | | | | |
| 57 | Tumor............. | 1 | 1 | | | | | 1 | | | 1 | 2 | 4 | 1 | | | | | | 10 | 1 | | | | |
| 58 | Ulcer.............. | | 1 | 1 | | 2 | | | | | 2 | | | | | | | | | 4 | 2 | | | | |
| 59 | Uterus, disease of ... | | | | | | | | | | 1 | | | | | | | | | 1 | | | | | |
| 60 | Worms ............ | | 1 | 2 | 1 | | | | | | | | | | | | | | | 4 | | | | | |
| 61 | Unknown........... | 54 | 55 | 25 | 16 | 12 | 7 | 4 | 9 | 32 | 32 | 27 | 31 | 7 | 9 | | | 12 | 6 | 283 | 12 | 4 | | | |
| | Total........... | 428 | 385 | 601 | 563 | 188 | 174 | 148 | 202 | 547 | 606 | 508 | 457 | 195 | 137 | 1 | 2 | 16 | 8 | 4415 | 336 | 51 | 3 | 2 | 4 |

## CLASSIFICATION OF DEATHS IN SOUTHEASTERN

*Embracing the following counties: Barnstable,*

| | Cause of death. | Under 1. M. | Under 1. F. | 1 and under 5. M. | 1 and under 5. F. | 5 and under 10. M. | 5 and under 10. F. | 10 and under 20. M. | 10 and under 20. F. | 20 and under 50. M. | 20 and under 50. F. | 50 and under 80. M. | 50 and under 80. F. | 80 and under 100. M. | 80 and under 100. F. | 100 & over. M | 100 & over. F. | Age unknown. M | Age unknown. F. | Born in State. | N. England States. | Middle States. | Southern States. | Southwest'n States. | Northwest'n States. |
|---|---|---|---|---|---|---|---|---|---|---|---|---|---|---|---|---|---|---|---|---|---|---|---|---|---|
| 1 | Abscess....... ..... | | 1 | | | | | | | | | | | | | | | | | 1 | | | | | |
| 2 | Accident, not specif'd | 1 | | 4 | | 1 | 1 | 2 | 4 | 11 | 2 | 3 | 1 | | 3 | | | | | 29 | 2 | | | 3 | |
| 3 | ....do...burned..... | 1 | | 3 | 2 | 1 | | 1 | | 1 | | | 2 | | | | | | | 9 | | | | | |
| 4 | ....do...drowned... | | | 2 | | 7 | | 6 | 7 | 25 | 4 | 3 | | | | | | 2 | | 43 | 1 | 2 | 1 | | |

## SECTION OF THE STATE OF MASSACHUSETTS—Continued.

| NATIVITIES. | | | | | SEASON OF DECEASE. | | | | DURATION OF SICKNESS. | | | | WHITES. | | | COLORED. | | | | | | | | | |
|---|---|---|---|---|---|---|---|---|---|---|---|---|---|---|---|---|---|---|---|---|---|---|---|---|---|
| | | | | | | | | | | | | | | | | Slaves. | | | | Free. | | | | | |
| | | | | | | | | | | | | | | | | Black. | | Mulatto. | | Black. | | Mul. | | | |
| California and Territories. | Ireland. | Germany. | Other foreign countries. | Unknown. | Spring. | Summer. | Autumn. | Winter. | Under 1 week. | 1 week and under 1 month. | 1 month and under 3 months. | 3 months and over. | Males. | Females. | Total. | M. | F. | M. | F. | M. | F. | M | F. | Aggregate deaths. | |
| .... | 12 | .. | 5 | ... | 46 | 39 | 41 | 44 | 24 | 102 | 32 | 6 | 96 | 74 | 170 | .... | .... | .... | .... | .... | .... | 1 | .. | 171 | 1 |
| .... | .... | .. | 2 | ... | 4 | 5 | 6 | 10 | 7 | 15 | .... | 1 | 13 | 12 | 25 | .... | .... | .... | .... | .... | .... | .. | .. | 25 | 2 |
| .... | 1 | .. | .... | ... | 7 | 7 | 15 | 8 | 11 | 21 | 2 | 3 | 22 | 15 | 37 | .... | .... | .... | .... | .... | .... | .. | .. | 37 | 3 |
| .... | .... | .. | .... | ... | .... | .... | 1 | .... | .... | 1 | .... | .... | .... | 1 | 1 | .... | .... | .... | .... | .... | .... | .. | .. | 1 | 4 |
| .... | .... | .. | .... | ... | .... | .... | 2 | .... | 1 | 1 | .... | .... | .... | 2 | 2 | .... | .... | .... | .... | .... | .... | .. | .. | 2 | 5 |
| .... | 1 | .. | .... | ... | 43 | 25 | 12 | 28 | 50 | 47 | 5 | 1 | 47 | 61 | 108 | .... | .... | .... | .... | .... | .... | .. | .. | 108 | 6 |
| .... | 4 | .. | .... | ... | .... | 3 | .... | 3 | 1 | 1 | 1 | 1 | 4 | 2 | 6 | .... | .... | .... | .... | .... | .... | .. | .. | 6 | 7 |
| .... | 4 | .. | 3 | ... | 29 | 24 | 93 | 44 | 16 | 117 | 31 | 2 | 94 | 95 | 189 | .... | .... | .... | .... | .... | .... | 1 | .. | 190 | 8 |
| .... | .... | .. | .... | ... | 1 | .... | .... | .... | 1 | .. | .... | .... | 1 | .... | 1 | .... | .... | .... | .... | .... | .... | .. | .. | 1 | 9 |
| .... | .... | .. | .... | ... | .... | .... | 1 | .... | .... | .... | 1 | .... | 1 | .... | 1 | .... | .... | .... | .... | .... | .... | .. | .. | 1 | 10 |
| .... | .... | .. | .... | ... | 3 | 1 | 1 | .... | .... | 2 | 1 | 2 | 4 | 1 | 5 | .... | .... | .... | .... | .... | .... | .. | .. | 5 | 11 |
| .... | .... | .. | .... | ... | 1 | 1 | 2 | .... | .... | 2 | 1 | .... | 2 | 2 | 4 | .... | .... | .... | .... | .... | .... | .. | .. | 4 | 12 |
| .... | 2 | .. | 3 | ... | 17 | 21 | 15 | 24 | 23 | 15 | 7 | 16 | 41 | 36 | 77 | .... | .... | .... | .... | .... | .... | .. | .. | 77 | 13 |
| .... | 3 | .. | .... | ... | 4 | 1 | 1 | .... | 2 | 1 | .... | 1 | 6 | .... | 6 | .... | .... | .... | .... | .... | .... | .. | .. | 6 | 14 |
| .... | .... | .. | .... | ... | 3 | 3 | 2 | 3 | 5 | 1 | 2 | 1 | 7 | 4 | 11 | .... | .... | .... | .... | .... | .... | .. | .. | 11 | 15 |
| .... | .... | .. | .... | ... | 1 | .... | .... | 1 | .... | 1 | 1 | .... | .... | 2 | 2 | .... | .... | .... | .... | .... | .... | .. | .. | 2 | 16 |
| .... | 1 | .. | .... | ... | 15 | 19 | 7 | 12 | 4 | 25 | 14 | 3 | 28 | 25 | 53 | .... | .... | .... | .... | .... | .... | .. | .. | 53 | 17 |
| .... | 2 | .. | 1 | ... | 11 | 13 | 7 | 9 | 15 | 17 | 2 | 1 | 13 | 27 | 40 | .... | .... | .... | .... | .... | .... | .. | .. | 40 | 18 |
| .... | 2 | .. | 1 | ... | 10 | 9 | 14 | 4 | 16 | 14 | 6 | 1 | 22 | 15 | 37 | .... | .... | .... | .... | .... | .... | .. | .. | 37 | 19 |
| .... | .... | .. | .... | ... | 2 | 1 | 1 | .... | 1 | 1 | 1 | .... | .. | 3 | 3 | .... | .... | .... | .... | .... | .... | 1 | .. | 4 | 20 |
| .... | .... | .. | .... | ... | 3 | 2 | 1 | .... | 3 | 2 | 1 | .... | 4 | 2 | 6 | .... | .... | .... | .... | .... | .... | .. | .. | 6 | 21 |
| .... | 1 | .. | .... | ... | .... | 1 | 7 | 4 | 4 | 1 | 2 | 1 | 11 | 3 | 14 | .... | .... | .... | .... | .... | .... | .. | .. | 14 | 22 |
| .... | .... | .. | .... | ... | .... | 4 | 1 | 3 | .... | 2 | 1 | 2 | 5 | 3 | 8 | .... | .... | .... | .... | .... | .... | .. | .. | 8 | 23 |
| .... | .... | .. | .... | ... | .... | .... | 3 | .... | .... | .... | 2 | 1 | 1 | 2 | 3 | .... | .... | .... | .... | .... | .... | .. | .. | 3 | 24 |
| .... | .... | .. | .... | ... | .... | 1 | .... | .... | .... | .... | .... | 1 | 1 | ... | 1 | .... | .... | .... | .... | .... | .... | .. | .. | 1 | 25 |
| .... | 1 | .. | .... | ... | .... | 2 | .... | .... | 1 | .... | .... | .... | 2 | .... | 2 | .... | .... | .... | .... | .... | .... | .. | .. | 2 | 26 |
| .... | .... | .. | .... | ... | 7 | 5 | 8 | 4 | 1 | 6 | 8 | 7 | 12 | 13 | 25 | .... | .... | .... | .... | 1 | .... | .. | .. | 26 | 27 |
| .... | .... | .. | .... | ... | .... | .... | 2 | .... | 1 | 1 | .... | .... | 2 | .... | 2 | .... | .... | .... | .... | .... | .... | .. | .. | 2 | 28 |
| .... | 1 | .. | 2 | ... | 25 | 13 | 5 | 18 | 14 | 28 | 5 | 7 | 31 | 28 | 59 | .... | .... | .... | .... | 2 | .... | .. | .. | 61 | 29 |
| .... | .... | .. | .... | ... | 2 | 2 | .... | .... | .... | .... | .... | 1 | 3 | 1 | 4 | .... | .... | .... | .... | .... | .... | .. | .. | 4 | 30 |
| .... | .... | .. | .... | ... | 9 | 19 | 17 | 1 | 8 | 24 | 7 | 1 | 21 | 25 | 46 | .... | .... | .... | .... | .... | 1 | .. | .. | 47 | 31 |
| .... | .... | .. | .... | ... | 6 | 3 | 13 | 8 | 9 | 10 | 3 | 3 | 17 | 14 | 31 | .... | .... | .... | .... | .... | .... | .. | .. | 31 | 32 |
| .... | .... | .. | .... | ... | 1 | .... | .... | .... | .... | 1 | .... | .... | .... | 1 | 1 | .... | .... | .... | .... | .... | .... | .. | .. | 1 | 33 |
| .... | 4 | .. | 4 | ... | 75 | 49 | 64 | 68 | 21 | 60 | 24 | 62 | 127 | 126 | 253 | .... | .... | .... | .... | 2 | 1 | .. | .. | 256 | 34 |
| .... | .... | .. | 1 | ... | 18 | 22 | 21 | 17 | 17 | 19 | 6 | 18 | 42 | 36 | 78 | .... | .... | .... | .... | .... | .... | .. | .. | 78 | 35 |
| .... | 1 | .. | .... | ... | .... | .... | .... | 2 | .... | 2 | .... | .... | 2 | .... | 2 | .... | .... | .... | .... | .... | .... | .. | .. | 2 | 36 |
| .... | 1 | .. | .... | ... | 9 | 1 | 2 | 4 | 4 | 7 | 2 | 2 | 12 | 4 | 16 | .... | .... | .... | .... | .... | .... | .. | .. | 16 | 37 |
| .... | 1 | .. | 1 | ... | 117 | 24 | 16 | 20 | 34 | 78 | 8 | .... | 69 | 69 | 138 | .... | .... | .... | .... | .... | .... | .. | .. | 138 | 38 |
| .... | .... | .. | .... | ... | 2 | 1 | .... | 3 | 2 | 1 | 2 | .... | 3 | 3 | 6 | .... | .... | .... | .... | .... | .... | .. | .. | 6 | 39 |
| .... | .... | .. | .... | ... | 2 | 1 | 1 | 1 | 1 | 1 | .... | .... | 4 | 1 | 5 | .... | .... | .... | .... | .... | .... | .. | .. | 5 | 40 |
| .... | 1 | .. | .... | ... | 1 | 2 | 1 | .... | 1 | 3 | .... | .... | 4 | .... | 4 | .... | .... | .... | .... | .... | .... | .. | .. | 4 | 41 |
| .... | 3 | .. | .... | ... | 32 | 31 | 10 | 19 | 29 | 46 | 5 | 3 | 46 | 46 | 92 | .... | .... | .... | .... | .... | .... | .. | .. | 92 | 42 |
| .... | 1 | .. | .... | ... | 7 | 3 | 1 | 3 | 1 | 6 | 3 | 4 | 8 | 6 | 14 | .... | .... | .... | .... | .... | .... | .. | .. | 14 | 43 |
| .... | .... | .. | .... | ... | 1 | .... | .... | 1 | .... | .... | .... | 1 | 2 | .... | 2 | .... | .... | .... | .... | .... | .... | .. | .. | 2 | 44 |
| .... | .... | .. | .... | ... | 4 | 5 | 3 | 3 | 3 | 1 | 1 | 9 | 7 | 8 | 15 | .... | .... | .... | .... | .... | .... | .. | .. | 15 | 45 |
| .... | .... | .. | .... | ... | 8 | 8 | 7 | 2 | 4 | 22 | 2 | .... | 17 | 12 | 29 | .... | .... | .... | .... | .... | .... | .. | .. | 29 | 46 |
| .... | .... | .. | .... | ... | 3 | 4 | 4 | 1 | 2 | 1 | 1 | 7 | 8 | 4 | 12 | .... | .... | .... | .... | .... | .... | .. | .. | 12 | 47 |
| .... | .... | .. | .... | ... | .... | 1 | .... | .... | .... | .... | .... | 1 | 1 | .... | 1 | .... | .... | .... | .... | .... | .... | .. | .. | 1 | 48 |
| .... | .... | .. | .... | ... | 1 | 1 | .... | .... | .... | .... | .... | .... | 1 | 1 | 2 | .... | .... | .... | .... | .... | .... | .. | .. | 2 | 49 |
| .... | .... | .. | .... | ... | 2 | 2 | 2 | 1 | .... | 4 | 2 | 1 | 4 | 3 | 7 | .... | .... | .... | .... | .... | .... | .. | .. | 7 | 50 |
| .... | .... | .. | 1 | ... | 5 | 4 | 4 | 3 | 2 | 1 | .... | .... | 11 | 5 | 16 | .... | .... | .... | .... | .... | .... | .. | .. | 16 | 51 |
| .... | .... | .. | .... | ... | 1 | .... | 3 | .... | .... | 1 | 2 | .... | 2 | 2 | 4 | .... | .... | .... | .... | .... | .... | .. | .. | 4 | 52 |
| .... | 3 | .. | .... | ... | .... | 4 | .... | .... | 2 | .... | .... | .... | 4 | .... | 4 | .... | .... | .... | .... | .... | .... | .. | .. | 4 | 53 |
| .... | .... | .. | .... | ... | 6 | 4 | 13 | 3 | 8 | 14 | 1 | .... | 14 | 12 | 26 | .... | .... | .... | .... | .... | .... | .. | .. | 26 | 54 |
| .... | .... | 1 | .... | ... | 2 | 1 | 4 | 4 | 4 | 9 | .... | .... | 8 | 7 | 15 | .... | .... | .... | .... | .... | .... | .. | .. | 15 | 55 |
| .... | .... | .. | .... | ... | .... | 1 | .... | .... | .... | 1 | .... | .... | .... | 1 | 1 | .... | .... | .... | .... | .... | .... | .. | .. | 1 | 56 |
| .... | .... | .. | .... | ... | 4 | 3 | 2 | 2 | 2 | 3 | 1 | 5 | 5 | 6 | 11 | .... | .... | .... | .... | .... | .... | .. | .. | 11 | 57 |
| .... | .... | .. | .... | ... | .... | 1 | 3 | 2 | 1 | 1 | 1 | 1 | 3 | 3 | 6 | .... | .... | .... | .... | .... | .... | .. | .. | 6 | 58 |
| .... | .... | .. | .... | ... | .... | .... | 1 | .... | .... | .... | .... | .... | .... | 1 | 1 | .... | .... | .... | .... | .... | .... | .. | .. | 1 | 59 |
| .... | .... | .. | .... | ... | 1 | .... | 2 | 1 | 1 | 2 | .... | .... | 2 | 2 | 4 | .... | .... | .... | .... | .... | .... | .. | .. | 4 | 60 |
| .... | 26 | .. | 8 | ... | 76 | 85 | 111 | 66 | 22 | 13 | 14 | 1 | 171 | 164 | 335 | .... | .... | .... | .... | 2 | 1 | .. | .. | 338 | 61 |
| 1 | 241 | 3 | 81 | ... | 1073 | 1045 | 2143 | 894 | 1093 | 1631 | 481 | 882 | 2596 | 2559 | 5155 | .... | .... | .... | .... | 20 | 34 | 4 | 1 | 5194 | |

## SECTION OF THE STATE OF MASSACHUSETTS.

*Bristol, Dukes, Nantucket, Norfolk, and Plymouth.*

| California and Territories. | Ireland. | Germany. | Other foreign countries. | Unknown. | Spring. | Summer. | Autumn. | Winter. | Under 1 week. | 1 week and under 1 month. | 1 month and under 3 months. | 3 months and over. | Males. | Females. | Total. | Slaves Black M. | Slaves Black F. | Slaves Mulatto M. | Slaves Mulatto F. | Free Black M. | Free Black F. | Free Mul. M | Free Mul. F. | Aggregate deaths. | |
|---|---|---|---|---|---|---|---|---|---|---|---|---|---|---|---|---|---|---|---|---|---|---|---|---|---|
| .... | .... | .. | .... | ... | .... | .... | .... | 1 | .... | 1 | .... | .... | .... | [illegible] | 1 | .... | .... | .... | .... | .... | .... | .. | .. | 1 | 1 |
| .... | 2 | .. | 2 | ... | [illegible] | 15 | 7 | 6 | 9 | .... | 1 | [illegible] | [illegible] | [illegible] | [illegible] | .... | .... | .... | .... | [illegible] | .... | .. | .. | [illegible] | 2 |
| .... | 1 | .. | 1 | ... | 1 | 3 | 2 | 4 | 2 | [illegible] | .... | .... | [illegible] | [illegible] | 11 | .... | .... | .... | .... | .... | .... | .. | .. | 11 | 3 |
| .... | 6 | .. | 3 | ... | 17 | 7 | 13 | 12 | [illegible] | [illegible] | [illegible] | [illegible] | [illegible] | [illegible] | [illegible] | .... | .... | .... | .... | .... | .... | .. | .. | [illegible] | [illegible] |

## CLASSIFICATION OF DEATHS IN SOUTHEASTERN

| | Cause of death. | AGES. | | | | | | | | | | | | | | | | | | NATIVITIES. | | | | | |
|---|---|---|---|---|---|---|---|---|---|---|---|---|---|---|---|---|---|---|---|---|---|---|---|---|---|
| | | Under 1. | | 1 and under 5. | | 5 and under 10. | | 10 and under 20. | | 20 and under 50. | | 50 and under 80. | | 80 and under 100. | | 100 & over. | | Age unknown. | | Born in State. | N. England States. | Middle States. | Southern States. | Southwest'n States. | Northwest'n States. |
| | | M. | F. | M. | F. | M. | F. | M. | F. | M. | F. | M. | F. | M | F. | M | F. | M | F. | | | | | | |
| 1 | Accident, shot | | | | | | | | | 1 | | | | | | | | | | 1 | | | | | |
| 2 | ....do...railroad | | | | | | | | | 1 | | 1 | | | | | | | | 2 | | | | | |
| 3 | Apoplexy | | | 1 | | | | | | 1 | 2 | | 1 | | | | | | | 4 | | | | | |
| 4 | Asthma | | | | | | | | | | | | | | | | | 1 | | 1 | | | | | |
| 5 | Bladder, disease of | | | | | | | | | | | | | | | | | | | | | | | | |
| 6 | Bowels.....do | 15 | 9 | 11 | 10 | | | 1 | 1 | 2 | 4 | 1 | 3 | | | | | | | 50 | 1 | 2 | | | |
| 7 | Brain.......do | 5 | 3 | 8 | 5 | 2 | 3 | | | 3 | | 2 | | | | | | | | 29 | 1 | | | | |
| 8 | Bronchitis | 1 | | | 3 | | 1 | | | | | | 1 | | | | | | | 8 | | | | | |
| 9 | Cancer | 1 | 1 | | | 1 | | | | 2 | 7 | 13 | 16 | 3 | 1 | | | | | 40 | 3 | | | | |
| 10 | Catarrh | | 1 | 1 | | | | | | | | | | | | | | | | 2 | | | | | |
| 11 | Chicken pox | | 1 | | 1 | | | | | | | | | | | | | | | 2 | | | | | |
| 12 | Childbirth | | | | | | | | 3 | | 28 | | 1 | | | | | | | 22 | 1 | | | 1 | |
| 13 | Cholera | | 1 | 2 | 3 | 2 | | 3 | 13 | 32 | 15 | 11 | 7 | | | | | 2 | | 55 | 6 | 2 | | | |
| 14 | ....do..infantum | 21 | 16 | 15 | 15 | | | | | 1 | | | | | | | | | | 66 | | 2 | | | |
| 15 | ....do..morbus | 3 | 4 | 1 | 3 | 2 | | 1 | | 2 | 1 | 6 | 4 | 2 | 2 | | | 1 | | 32 | | | | | |
| 16 | Colic | | | | | | | 1 | | 2 | 5 | 1 | 2 | 1 | | | | | | 11 | | | | | |
| 17 | Congestion | | | | | | | | | | | | | | | | | | | | | | | | |
| 18 | ....do....brain | | 1 | 4 | 1 | | | | | | | | 2 | | | | | | | 8 | | | | | |
| 19 | Consumption | 30 | 23 | 29 | 22 | 3 | 3 | 13 | 59 | 154 | 234 | 108 | 113 | 8 | 17 | | | 2 | 1 | 711 | 34 | 2 | 2 | 8 | |
| 20 | Convulsions | 15 | 8 | 14 | 27 | 2 | 1 | 1 | | 3 | 8 | 8 | 4 | 1 | 4 | | | 1 | | 91 | 2 | | | | |
| 21 | Cramp | | | | | | | 1 | | | | | | | | | | | | | | | | | |
| 22 | Croup | 16 | 10 | 30 | 21 | 5 | 6 | 2 | 4 | 2 | 4 | 6 | 1 | | | | | | | 100 | 2 | 3 | | | |
| 23 | Debility | 8 | 10 | 1 | 2 | | | | 2 | 2 | 2 | 2 | 1 | | | | | 1 | | 30 | | | | | |
| 24 | Diabetes | | | | | 1 | | | | 1 | 1 | | | | 1 | | | | | 4 | | | | | |
| 25 | Diarrhœa | 4 | 4 | 9 | 4 | 1 | | 1 | | 3 | 3 | 2 | 2 | 1 | 1 | | | | | 32 | 1 | 1 | | | |
| 26 | Dropsy | 13 | 9 | 19 | 12 | 3 | 1 | 4 | 5 | 10 | 18 | 29 | 21 | 2 | 6 | | | | 1 | 136 | 9 | 1 | 1 | | |
| 27 | Dysentery | 40 | 36 | 130 | 61 | 19 | 15 | 11 | 9 | 45 | 35 | 26 | 41 | 6 | 9 | | | 4 | 3 | 457 | 12 | 1 | | 3 | 1 |
| 28 | Dyspepsia | | | | | | | | | | | 2 | 2 | | | | | | | 4 | | | | | |
| 29 | Epilepsy | | | | | | | | 1 | | 2 | 1 | | | | | | | | 4 | | | | | |
| 30 | Erysipelas | 4 | 4 | | 1 | | 1 | 1 | 1 | 5 | | 4 | 6 | | | | | | | 24 | 1 | | | | |
| 31 | Fever, not specified | 4 | 1 | 9 | 11 | 5 | 1 | 7 | 6 | 28 | 17 | 8 | 8 | 1 | | | | 4 | | 87 | 4 | 1 | | 5 | |
| 32 | ..do..bilious | | 2 | 1 | 9 | 2 | 1 | 2 | 2 | 6 | 7 | 1 | 4 | 1 | 1 | | | | | 37 | | | | | |
| 33 | ..do..brain | 7 | 9 | 11 | 13 | 8 | 3 | 3 | 2 | 4 | 1 | 1 | | | | | | | | 60 | 2 | | | | |
| 34 | ..do..puerperal | | | | | | | | 1 | | | 1 | | | | | | | | 2 | | | | | |
| 35 | ..do..scarlet | 1 | 1 | 16 | 30 | 11 | 13 | 2 | 2 | 1 | 1 | | 1 | | | | | 1 | | 74 | | 2 | | | |
| 36 | ..do..ship | | | | | | | | | 1 | 3 | | | 1 | | | | | | 2 | | | | | |
| 37 | ..do..typhus | 1 | 1 | 5 | 2 | 5 | 1 | 11 | 10 | 27 | 16 | 7 | 6 | 2 | 1 | | | | | 83 | 4 | 1 | 1 | | |
| 38 | ..do..yellow | | | | | | | | | 6 | | 1 | | | | | | | | 6 | 1 | | | | |
| 39 | Gout | | | | | | | | | | | 1 | | | | | | | | 1 | | | | | |
| 40 | Gravel | | | | | | | | | 2 | | 4 | 1 | 2 | | | | | | 9 | | | | | |
| 41 | Head, disease of | 1 | | 1 | 2 | | | | | | | | | | | | | | | 4 | | | | | |
| 42 | Heart ...do | 1 | 3 | 1 | 1 | 2 | | 1 | 5 | 12 | 18 | 11 | 11 | 3 | | | | 1 | | 65 | 1 | | | | |
| 43 | Heat | | | | | | | 1 | | 4 | | 3 | 1 | | | | | | | 1 | | | | | |
| 44 | Hemorrhage | 1 | | | | | | | 1 | | 1 | | | 1 | | | | | | 4 | | | | | |
| 45 | Hernia | | | | | | | | | | | 1 | | | | | | | | | | | | | |
| 46 | Hip, disease of | | | | | | 1 | | | | | | | | | | | | | 1 | | | | | |
| 47 | Hooping cough | 20 | 24 | 13 | 20 | | 1 | | | 1 | | | | | | | | | | 76 | 1 | 1 | | | |
| 48 | Inflammation | 2 | 1 | 1 | 1 | | 1 | | 2 | 2 | 5 | | | | | | | | | 14 | | | 1 | | |
| 49 | ....do......bowels | 5 | 4 | 5 | 6 | | 2 | 1 | 1 | 3 | 9 | 2 | 2 | | 1 | | | | | 40 | 1 | | | | |
| 50 | ....do......brain | 1 | 1 | 4 | 5 | | | | | 4 | | | | | | | | 1 | | 15 | | | | | |
| 51 | Influenza | 2 | 1 | 1 | | | 1 | | | | | 1 | 2 | 2 | 1 | | | | | 10 | | 1 | | | |
| 52 | Insanity | | | | | | | | | 2 | | 3 | 1 | | | | | | | 6 | | | | | |
| 53 | Intemperance | | | | | | | | | 1 | | 7 | | | | | | 1 | | 7 | | | | | |
| 54 | Jaundice | | | 2 | | | | | | 2 | | 1 | 1 | | | | | | | 6 | | | | | |
| 55 | Kidneys, disease of | | | | | | | | | | | 1 | 1 | 1 | | | | | | 3 | | | | | |
| 56 | Liver ......do | | | | | | 1 | | | 2 | 5 | 4 | 6 | | | | | | | 16 | 1 | | | 1 | |
| 57 | Lockjaw | | | | | | | | | | | 1 | | | | | | | | 1 | | | | | |
| 58 | Lungs, disease of | 5 | | | 4 | 2 | | | | 6 | 2 | 6 | 2 | | 1 | | | | | 23 | 4 | | | 1 | |
| 59 | Malformation | 2 | | | | | | | | | | | | | | | | | | 2 | | | | | |
| 60 | Measles | 3 | 3 | 4 | 7 | | 1 | | 1 | | | | | | | | | | | 18 | | | | | |
| 61 | Mortification | 9 | 4 | 1 | 2 | | | | | | 4 | 3 | 3 | | | | | | | 26 | | | | | |
| 62 | Neuralgia | | | | | | | | | | | | 1 | | | | | | | 1 | | | | | |
| 63 | Old age | | | | | | | | | | | 24 | 32 | 65 | 86 | | | 2 | | 191 | 8 | | 1 | 3 | |
| 64 | Paralysis | | | 1 | 1 | | | | | 7 | 5 | 17 | 13 | 3 | 4 | | | | | 44 | 4 | 1 | | | |
| 65 | Piles | | | | | | | | | | | 1 | | | | | | | | 1 | | | | | |
| 66 | Pleurisy | | | 1 | | | | | | 2 | | 3 | 3 | 1 | | | | 1 | | 11 | | | | | |
| 67 | Pneumonia | 12 | 18 | 24 | 15 | 3 | 1 | 1 | 1 | 9 | 6 | 10 | 7 | 2 | | | | | | 102 | 1 | 1 | | | |
| 68 | Poison | 1 | | | | 1 | | | | 1 | | | | | | | | | | 3 | | | | | |
| 69 | Quinsy | 1 | | 2 | 1 | | | | | | | | 1 | | | | | | | 5 | | | | | |
| 70 | Rash | 2 | 1 | 5 | 3 | | 1 | | 1 | | | | | | | | | | | 13 | | | | | |
| 71 | Rheumatism | | | | | | | 1 | | | 1 | 4 | | | | | | | | 6 | | | | | |
| 72 | Scrofula | 2 | | 1 | 2 | | | 1 | | 2 | 2 | 2 | | | | | | 1 | | 10 | 1 | | | | |
| 73 | Small pox | 1 | 2 | 1 | 3 | 2 | 1 | 2 | | 5 | 2 | 2 | 1 | | | | | | | 16 | 3 | | | | |
| 74 | Spine, disease of | | 1 | | 2 | | | | | 2 | | 1 | 1 | | | | | | | 5 | 2 | | | | |
| 75 | Spleen....do | | | | | | | | | 1 | | | | | | | | | | | | | | | |

## SECTION OF THE STATE OF MASSACHUSETTS—Continued.

| NATIVITIES. California and Territories. | NATIVITIES. Ireland. | NATIVITIES. Germany. | NATIVITIES. Other foreign countries. | NATIVITIES. Unknown. | SEASON OF DECEASE. Spring. | SEASON OF DECEASE. Summer. | SEASON OF DECEASE. Autumn. | SEASON OF DECEASE. Winter. | DURATION OF SICKNESS. Under 1 week. | DURATION OF SICKNESS. 1 week and under 1 month. | DURATION OF SICKNESS. 1 month and under 3 months. | DURATION OF SICKNESS. 3 months and over. | WHITES. Males. | WHITES. Females. | WHITES. Total. | COLORED. Slaves. Black. M. | COLORED. Slaves. Black. F. | COLORED. Slaves. Mulatto. M. | COLORED. Slaves. Mulatto. F. | COLORED. Free. Black. M. | COLORED. Free. Black. F. | COLORED. Free. Mul. M | COLORED. Free. Mul. F. | Aggregate deaths. | |
|---|---|---|---|---|---|---|---|---|---|---|---|---|---|---|---|---|---|---|---|---|---|---|---|---|---|
| | | | | | | | | 1 | | 1 | | | 1 | | 1 | | | | | | | | | 1 | 1 |
| | | | | | | | 2 | | | | | | 2 | | 2 | | | | | | | | | 2 | 2 |
| | 1 | | | | 1 | | 1 | | 1 | | | | 2 | 3 | 5 | | | | | | | | | 5 | 3 |
| | | | | | | | | | | 1 | | | 1 | | 1 | | | | | | | | | 1 | 4 |
| | | | | | | | | | | | | | | | | | | | | | | | | | 5 |
| | 4 | | | | 4 | 13 | 32 | 8 | 15 | 11 | 4 | | 30 | 27 | 57 | | | | | | | | | 57 | 6 |
| | 1 | | | | 7 | 10 | 5 | 9 | 3 | 10 | 2 | 4 | 20 | 11 | 31 | | | | | | | | | 31 | 7 |
| | | | | | 2 | | 2 | 2 | 2 | | 1 | | 1 | 5 | 6 | | | | | | | | | 6 | 8 |
| | 2 | | | | 17 | 11 | 8 | 9 | 1 | 3 | 4 | 25 | 20 | 25 | 45 | | | | | | | | | 45 | 9 |
| | | | | | | | 1 | 1 | 2 | | | | 1 | 1 | 2 | | | | | | | | | 2 | 10 |
| | | | | | 1 | | 1 | | | 1 | 1 | | | 2 | 2 | | | | | | | | | 2 | 11 |
| | 5 | 1 | 2 | | 8 | 7 | 14 | 3 | 10 | 12 | 1 | | | 31 | 31 | | | | | | | | 1 | 32 | 12 |
| | 22 | | 6 | | 2 | 12 | 74 | 2 | 71 | 5 | 1 | | 52 | 38 | 90 | | | | | | 1 | | | 91 | 13 |
| | | | | | 1 | 10 | 50 | 5 | 19 | 32 | 5 | 2 | 37 | 31 | 68 | | | | | | | | | 68 | 14 |
| | | | | | | 7 | 23 | | 13 | 6 | 1 | | 18 | 14 | 32 | | | | | | | | | 32 | 15 |
| | 1 | | | | 2 | | 7 | 3 | 7 | 4 | | | 5 | 7 | 12 | | | | | | | | | 12 | 16 |
| | | | | | | | | | | | | | | | | | | | | | | | | | 17 |
| | | | | | 5 | 1 | | 2 | 1 | 3 | | 1 | 4 | 4 | 8 | | | | | | | | | 8 | 18 |
| | 48 | 2 | 17 | | 204 | 201 | 212 | 192 | 37 | 35 | 81 | 447 | 343 | 470 | 813 | | | | | 4 | 2 | | | 819 | 19 |
| | 4 | | | | 33 | 21 | 23 | 20 | 39 | 8 | 2 | 3 | 45 | 52 | 97 | | | | | | | | | 97 | 20 |
| | 1 | | 1 | | | 1 | | | 1 | | | | 1 | | 1 | | | | | | | | | 1 | 21 |
| | 2 | | | | 26 | 18 | 29 | 27 | 51 | 14 | 4 | 3 | 59 | 45 | 104 | | | | | 2 | 1 | | | 107 | 22 |
| | 1 | | | | 1 | 11 | 15 | 4 | | | 2 | 4 | 14 | 17 | 31 | | | | | | | | | 31 | 23 |
| | | | | | 1 | 1 | 1 | 1 | | 1 | | 1 | 2 | 2 | 4 | | | | | | | | | 4 | 24 |
| | | | 1 | | 3 | 6 | 26 | | 6 | 5 | 4 | 8 | 21 | 14 | 35 | | | | | | | | | 35 | 25 |
| | 2 | | 4 | | 37 | 36 | 37 | 42 | 16 | 37 | 17 | 46 | 79 | 71 | 150 | | | | | 1 | 2 | | | 153 | 26 |
| | 9 | | 7 | | 23 | 48 | 373 | 42 | 101 | 280 | 36 | 11 | 281 | 208 | 489 | | | | | | 1 | | | 490 | 27 |
| | | | | | 1 | 1 | 1 | 1 | | | 1 | 1 | 2 | 2 | 4 | | | | | | | | | 4 | 28 |
| | | | | | 2 | | 1 | 1 | | | | | 1 | 3 | 4 | | | | | | | | | 4 | 29 |
| | 1 | | 1 | | 10 | 7 | 7 | 3 | 4 | 17 | 1 | 2 | 14 | 13 | 27 | | | | | | | | | 27 | 30 |
| | 11 | | 2 | | 30 | 30 | 30 | 17 | 13 | 79 | 15 | 3 | 65 | 41 | 106 | | | | | 1 | 3 | | | 110 | 31 |
| | 2 | | | | 7 | 4 | 9 | 4 | 6 | 6 | 1 | 2 | 13 | 26 | 39 | | | | | | | | | 39 | 32 |
| | | | | | 14 | 20 | 21 | 7 | 19 | 29 | 7 | 2 | 34 | 28 | 62 | | | | | | | | | 62 | 33 |
| | | | | | 1 | | 1 | | | | | | | 2 | 2 | | | | | | | | | 2 | 34 |
| | 1 | | 3 | | 19 | 35 | 12 | 14 | 20 | 31 | 3 | | 32 | 48 | 80 | | | | | | | | | 80 | 35 |
| | 3 | | | | 1 | 3 | | 1 | 4 | | | | 2 | 3 | 5 | | | | | | | | | 5 | 36 |
| | 5 | | 1 | | 12 | 12 | 43 | 28 | 3 | 61 | 12 | 3 | 58 | 37 | 95 | | | | | | | | | 95 | 37 |
| | | | | | 2 | 1 | 2 | 1 | 3 | 3 | | | 7 | | 7 | | | | | | | | | 7 | 38 |
| | | | | | | | 1 | | | | | 1 | 1 | | 1 | | | | | | | | | 1 | 39 |
| | | | | | 7 | | | 2 | 1 | | | 5 | 8 | 1 | 9 | | | | | | | | | 9 | 40 |
| | | | | | 1 | 1 | 1 | 1 | | 2 | 1 | | 2 | 2 | 4 | | | | | | | | | 4 | 41 |
| | 3 | | 1 | | 21 | 11 | 23 | 14 | 16 | 10 | 7 | 6 | 32 | 38 | 70 | | | | | | | | | 70 | 42 |
| | 7 | 1 | | | 1 | 6 | 2 | | 1 | | | | 8 | 1 | 9 | | | | | | | | | 9 | 43 |
| | | | | | | 4 | | | 2 | | | | 2 | 2 | 4 | | | | | | | | | 4 | 44 |
| | | | 1 | | 1 | | | | 1 | | | | 1 | | 1 | | | | | | | | | 1 | 45 |
| | | | | | | | 1 | | | | | 1 | | 1 | 1 | | | | | | | | | 1 | 46 |
| | 1 | | | | 15 | 14 | 44 | 6 | 12 | 34 | 18 | | 34 | 45 | 79 | | | | | | | | | 79 | 47 |
| | | | | | 1 | 4 | 5 | 5 | 7 | 7 | 1 | | 5 | 9 | 14 | | | | | | | | 1 | 15 | 48 |
| | | | | | 6 | 6 | 23 | 6 | 12 | 16 | 4 | | 16 | 25 | 41 | | | | | | | | | 41 | 49 |
| | 1 | | | | 5 | 4 | 2 | 5 | 2 | 10 | | | 10 | 6 | 16 | | | | | | | | | 16 | 50 |
| | | | | | 7 | 1 | 1 | 2 | 3 | 8 | | | 6 | 5 | 11 | | | | | | | | | 11 | 51 |
| | | | | | | 1 | 1 | | | | | 1 | 5 | 1 | 6 | | | | | | | | | 6 | 52 |
| | 2 | | | | 1 | 4 | 2 | 2 | 2 | 3 | | 1 | 9 | | 9 | | | | | | | | | 9 | 53 |
| | | | | | | | 4 | 2 | | 2 | | | 5 | 1 | 6 | | | | | | | | | 6 | 54 |
| | | | | | | 2 | | 1 | | | 1 | 2 | 2 | 1 | 3 | | | | | | | | | 3 | 55 |
| | | | | | 8 | 5 | 2 | 8 | 4 | 2 | 2 | 7 | 6 | 12 | 18 | | | | | | | | | 18 | 56 |
| | | | | | 1 | | | | | | | 1 | 1 | | 1 | | | | | | | | | 1 | 57 |
| | | | | | 6 | 10 | 5 | 7 | 11 | 5 | 3 | 2 | 19 | 9 | 28 | | | | | | | | | 28 | 58 |
| | | | | | 1 | | | 1 | | | | | 2 | | 2 | | | | | | | | | 2 | 59 |
| | 1 | | | | 2 | 9 | 8 | | 2 | 6 | 3 | | 7 | 12 | 19 | | | | | | | | | 19 | 60 |
| | | | | | 3 | 7 | 11 | 5 | 3 | 9 | 3 | 4 | 13 | 13 | 26 | | | | | | | | | 26 | 61 |
| | | | | | 1 | | | | | 1 | | | | 1 | 1 | | | | | | | | | 1 | 62 |
| | 4 | 1 | | | 40 | 49 | 60 | 60 | 13 | 25 | 11 | 33 | 91 | 116 | 207 | | | | | | | 2 | | 209 | 63 |
| | 2 | | | | 14 | 12 | 11 | 13 | 8 | 14 | 2 | 13 | 28 | 23 | 51 | | | | | | | | | 51 | 64 |
| | | | | | | | | 1 | | | | 1 | 1 | | 1 | | | | | | | | | 1 | 65 |
| | | | | | 4 | 1 | | 5 | 3 | 4 | 2 | | 8 | 3 | 11 | | | | | | | | | 11 | 66 |
| | 5 | | | | 40 | 24 | 11 | 31 | 17 | 65 | 8 | 1 | 61 | 48 | 109 | | | | | | | | | 109 | 67 |
| | | | | | 3 | | | | 3 | | | | 3 | | 3 | | | | | | | | | 3 | 68 |
| | | | | | 3 | | | 2 | 1 | | 4 | | 3 | 2 | 5 | | | | | | | | | 5 | 69 |
| | | | | | 3 | 6 | 2 | 2 | 2 | 8 | 2 | | 7 | 6 | 13 | | | | | | | | | 13 | 70 |
| | | | | | 3 | 1 | | 2 | 1 | 1 | | 3 | 5 | 1 | 6 | | | | | | | | | 6 | 71 |
| | 1 | | 1 | | 2 | 3 | 3 | 4 | | 4 | 2 | 4 | 9 | 4 | 13 | | | | | | | | | 13 | 72 |
| | 1 | 1 | 1 | | 5 | 8 | 2 | 4 | 2 | 13 | | | 13 | 9 | 22 | | | | | | | | | 22 | 73 |
| | | | | | 1 | 1 | 3 | 2 | | 2 | 1 | 3 | 3 | 4 | 7 | | | | | | | | | 7 | 74 |
| | 1 | | | | | | | 1 | | | 1 | | 1 | | 1 | | | | | | | | | 1 | 75 |

## CLASSIFICATION OF DEATHS IN SOUTHEASTERN

| | Cause of death. | AGES. | | | | | | | | | | | | | | | | | | NATIVITIES. | | | | | |
|---|---|---|---|---|---|---|---|---|---|---|---|---|---|---|---|---|---|---|---|---|---|---|---|---|---|
| | | Under 1. | | 1 and under 5. | | 5 and under 10. | | 10 and under 20. | | 20 and under 50. | | 50 and under 80. | | 80 and under 100. | | 100 & over. | | Age unknown. | | Born in State. | N. England States. | Middle States. | Southern States. | Southwest'n States. | Northwest'n States. |
| | | M. | F. | M. | F. | M. | F. | M. | F. | M. | F. | M. | F. | M | F. | M | F. | M | F. | | | | | | |
| 1 | Stillborn | .... | 1 | .... | ... | ... | ... | ... | ... | .... | .... | ... | ... | .. | .. | .. | .. | .. | .. | 1 | .. | ... | ... | ... | ... |
| 2 | Stomach, disease of | .... | ... | .... | ... | ... | ... | ... | ... | .... | .... | ... | 1 | .. | .. | .. | .. | .. | .. | 1 | .. | ... | ... | ... | ... |
| 3 | Suffocation | .... | ... | .... | ... | ... | ... | ... | ... | .... | .... | 1 | ... | .. | .. | .. | .. | .. | .. | 1 | .. | ... | ... | ... | ... |
| 4 | Summer complaint | .... | ... | 1 | ... | ... | ... | ... | ... | 1 | .... | ... | ... | .. | .. | .. | .. | .. | .. | 2 | .. | ... | ... | ... | ... |
| 5 | Suicide | .... | ... | .... | ... | ... | ... | ... | ... | 3 | 2 | 4 | 1 | .. | .. | .. | .. | .. | .. | 9 | .. | ... | ... | ... | ... |
| 6 | Sun, stroke of | .... | ... | .... | ... | ... | ... | ... | ... | 4 | 2 | ... | ... | .. | .. | .. | .. | .. | .. | ... | .. | ... | ... | ... | ... |
| 7 | Syphilis | .... | ... | .... | ... | ... | ... | ... | ... | 1 | .... | ... | ... | .. | .. | .. | .. | .. | .. | 1 | .. | ... | ... | ... | ... |
| 8 | Teething | 12 | 7 | 13 | 12 | ... | ... | ... | ... | .... | .... | ... | ... | .. | .. | .. | .. | .. | .. | 43 | .. | ... | ... | ... | ... |
| 9 | Throat, disease of | 4 | 1 | 5 | 6 | 3 | 4 | 1 | 2 | 2 | 3 | 1 | 2 | .. | .. | .. | .. | .. | .. | 33 | .. | ... | ... | ... | ... |
| 10 | Tumor | .... | ... | .... | ... | ... | ... | ... | ... | ... | 3 | ... | ... | .. | .. | .. | .. | .. | .. | 2 | .. | ... | ... | ... | ... |
| 11 | Ulcer | 1 | 1 | 2 | 2 | ... | ... | ... | ... | .... | 5 | ... | 1 | .. | .. | .. | .. | .. | .. | 10 | 2 | ... | ... | ... | ... |
| 12 | Worms | .... | ... | 2 | 3 | ... | ... | ... | ... | .... | .... | ... | ... | .. | .. | .. | .. | .. | .. | 5 | .. | ... | ... | ... | ... |
| 13 | Unknown | 65 | 52 | 25 | 23 | 5 | ... | 8 | 3 | 40 | 36 | 49 | 51 | 10 | 11 | .. | .. | 7 | 3 | 865 | 4 | ... | ... | ... | ... |
| | Total | 344 | 281 | 442 | 379 | 99 | 66 | 91 | 149 | 503 | 531 | 421 | 396 | 119 | 147 | .. | 3 | 33 | 8 | 3586 | 120 | 24 | 7 | 20 | 1 |

## CLASSIFICATION OF DEATHS IN SUFFOLK

| | | | | | | | | | | | | | | | | | | | | | | | | | |
|---|---|---|---|---|---|---|---|---|---|---|---|---|---|---|---|---|---|---|---|---|---|---|---|---|---|
| 1 | Abscess | .... | ... | .... | ... | ... | ... | ... | ... | 4 | .... | ... | ... | .. | .. | .. | .. | .. | .. | 1 | .. | ... | ... | ... | ... |
| 2 | Accident, not specif'd | .... | ... | 7 | 2 | 2 | ... | 5 | 1 | 22 | 4 | 5 | 7 | .. | 1 | .. | .. | 2 | .. | 85 | 3 | ... | ... | ... | ... |
| 3 | ....do ..burned | ... | 1 | 4 | 1 | ... | 3 | ... | ... | 2 | 1 | 1 | 1 | .. | .. | .. | .. | .. | .. | .... | .. | ... | ... | ... | ... |
| 4 | ....do...drowned | 1 | ... | .... | 3 | 4 | 1 | 3 | 2 | 17 | .... | 2 | ... | .. | .. | .. | .. | 1 | 1 | 23 | 1 | ... | ... | ... | ... |
| 5 | ....do...scalded | .... | ... | 5 | 2 | ... | ... | 1 | ... | .... | 1 | ... | ... | .. | .. | .. | .. | .. | .. | 6 | .. | ... | ... | ... | ... |
| 6 | ....do...shot | .... | ... | .... | ... | ... | ... | ... | ... | 1 | .... | ... | ... | .. | .. | .. | .. | .. | .. | .... | .. | ... | ... | ... | ... |
| 7 | Apoplexy | .... | ... | .... | ... | ... | ... | 1 | 1 | 4 | 3 | 6 | 2 | 1 | .. | .. | .. | .. | .. | 8 | 3 | ... | ... | ... | ... |
| 8 | Asthma | .... | ... | .... | ... | ... | ... | ... | ... | 3 | 1 | ... | 1 | .. | .. | .. | .. | .. | .. | 2 | 1 | ... | ... | ... | ... |
| 9 | Bladder, disease of | .... | ... | .... | ... | ... | ... | ... | ... | .... | .... | ... | ... | 1 | .. | .. | .. | .. | .. | 1 | .. | ... | ... | ... | ... |
| 10 | Bowels ....do | 20 | 15 | 84 | 79 | 13 | 9 | 2 | 6 | 13 | 22 | 8 | 6 | .. | .. | .. | .. | .. | .. | 222 | 12 | ... | 1 | ... | ... |
| 11 | Brain........do | 8 | 1 | 25 | 32 | 5 | 9 | 8 | 1 | 13 | 14 | 8 | 2 | .. | 1 | .. | .. | .. | .. | 93 | 10 | ... | ... | ... | ... |
| 12 | Bronchitis | .... | 1 | 2 | 1 | ... | ... | 1 | ... | 3 | .... | ... | ... | .. | 1 | .. | .. | .. | .. | 5 | 2 | ... | ... | ... | ... |
| 13 | Cancer | 1 | ... | .... | 2 | ... | ... | ... | 1 | 5 | 7 | 8 | 3 | .. | .. | .. | .. | .. | .. | 13 | 6 | ... | ... | ... | ... |
| 14 | Canker | .... | ... | .... | 1 | ... | ... | ... | ... | .... | .... | ... | ... | .. | .. | .. | .. | .. | .. | 1 | .. | ... | ... | ... | ... |
| 15 | Chicken pox | .... | ... | .... | 1 | ... | ... | ... | ... | .... | .... | ... | ... | .. | .. | .. | .. | .. | .. | 1 | .. | ... | ... | ... | ... |
| 16 | Childbirth | .... | ... | .... | ... | ... | ... | ... | 2 | .... | 50 | ... | ... | .. | .. | .. | .. | .. | .. | 4 | 3 | ... | ... | ... | ... |
| 17 | Cholera | 3 | 2 | 27 | 24 | 23 | 14 | 21 | 22 | 234 | 181 | 51 | 28 | 1 | 2 | .. | .. | 2 | 3 | 157 | 32 | 9 | 3 | ... | ... |
| 18 | ...do...infantum | 4 | 4 | 13 | 22 | 5 | ... | ... | ... | .... | .... | ... | ... | .. | .. | .. | .. | 2 | .. | 43 | 1 | ... | ... | ... | 1 |
| 19 | ...do...morbus | 2 | ... | 5 | 4 | 1 | 3 | ... | 1 | 12 | 6 | 6 | 1 | .. | .. | .. | .. | .. | .. | 23 | 2 | ... | ... | ... | ... |
| 20 | Chorea | .... | ... | .... | 1 | ... | ... | ... | ... | .... | .... | ... | ... | .. | .. | .. | .. | .. | .. | .... | .. | ... | ... | ... | ... |
| 21 | Congestion | .... | ... | .... | ... | ... | ... | ... | ... | .... | 1 | ... | ... | .. | .. | .. | .. | .. | .. | .... | .. | ... | ... | ... | ... |
| 22 | ....do....brain | .... | ... | 3 | ... | ... | ... | ... | ... | 3 | 2 | ... | ... | .. | .. | .. | .. | .. | .. | 4 | .. | ... | ... | ... | ... |
| 23 | Consumption | 10 | 10 | 68 | 22 | 8 | 5 | 21 | 32 | 188 | 208 | 61 | 48 | .. | .. | .. | .. | .. | 2 | 303 | 70 | 12 | 8 | ... | ... |
| 24 | Convulsions | 14 | 14 | 24 | 17 | 1 | 1 | ... | 1 | 3 | 3 | 4 | 1 | .. | .. | .. | .. | 2 | .. | 68 | 2 | 1 | ... | ... | 1 |
| 25 | Cramp | .... | ... | .... | 1 | ... | ... | ... | ... | .... | 1 | ... | ... | .. | .. | .. | .. | .. | .. | 1 | .. | ... | ... | ... | ... |
| 26 | Croup | 5 | 5 | 28 | 15 | 3 | 2 | ... | 1 | 1 | 2 | ... | ... | .. | .. | .. | .. | .. | .. | 55 | 1 | 1 | ... | ... | ... |
| 27 | Debility | 4 | 3 | .... | 2 | 1 | ... | 1 | 1 | 1 | 6 | 2 | 9 | 1 | .. | .. | .. | .. | .. | 21 | 4 | ... | ... | ... | ... |
| 28 | Diabetes | .... | ... | .... | ... | ... | ... | ... | ... | 3 | .... | ... | 1 | .. | .. | .. | .. | .. | .. | 2 | 1 | ... | 1 | ... | ... |
| 29 | Diarrhœa | 6 | 4 | 12 | 9 | 4 | 2 | 2 | 4 | 23 | 27 | 8 | 13 | .. | .. | .. | .. | 1 | .. | 53 | 1 | ... | ... | ... | ... |
| 30 | Dropsy | 8 | 2 | 76 | 58 | 9 | 9 | 4 | 2 | 16 | 9 | 9 | 14 | .. | 1 | .. | .. | .. | .. | 157 | 17 | 2 | ... | ... | ... |
| 31 | Dysentery | 20 | 5 | 69 | 39 | 25 | 12 | 4 | 14 | 46 | 32 | 23 | 31 | .. | .. | .. | .. | 2 | .. | 214 | 18 | 3 | 1 | ... | ... |
| 32 | Epilepsy | .... | ... | .... | ... | ... | ... | ... | ... | 2 | 1 | ... | 1 | .. | .. | .. | .. | .. | .. | 2 | .. | ... | ... | ... | ... |
| 33 | Erysipelas | 5 | 5 | .... | 3 | 2 | ... | 3 | 7 | 17 | 10 | 10 | 6 | .. | .. | .. | .. | .. | .. | 36 | 13 | ... | ... | ... | ... |
| 34 | Fever, not specified | .... | ... | 3 | 5 | 2 | ... | 3 | 4 | 14 | 13 | 2 | 4 | .. | .. | .. | .. | .. | .. | 25 | 5 | ... | ... | ... | ... |
| 35 | ..do..bilious | .... | ... | .... | ... | ... | 1 | ... | 1 | .... | 2 | ... | ... | .. | .. | .. | .. | .. | .. | 1 | .. | ... | ... | ... | ... |
| 36 | ..do..brain | 2 | ... | 1 | ... | 2 | ... | ... | 1 | 2 | .... | ... | ... | .. | .. | .. | .. | .. | .. | 6 | 2 | ... | ... | ... | ... |
| 37 | ..do..intermittent | .... | ... | .... | ... | ... | ... | ... | ... | 1 | .... | ... | ... | .. | .. | .. | .. | .. | .. | .... | .. | 1 | ... | ... | ... |
| 38 | ..do..puerperal | .... | ... | .... | ... | ... | ... | ... | ... | .... | 3 | ... | ... | .. | .. | .. | .. | .. | .. | .... | 2 | ... | ... | ... | ... |
| 39 | ..do..scarlet | 2 | 3 | 47 | 41 | 25 | 13 | 3 | 2 | 2 | 1 | ... | ... | .. | .. | .. | .. | .. | .. | 120 | 2 | 3 | ... | ... | ... |
| 40 | ..do..ship | .... | ... | .... | ... | ... | ... | ... | ... | 1 | 5 | ... | ... | .. | .. | .. | .. | .. | .. | 1 | .. | ... | ... | ... | ... |
| 41 | ..do..typhus | .... | 1 | 6 | 8 | 4 | 3 | 5 | 13 | 37 | 39 | 4 | 4 | 1 | .. | .. | .. | .. | .. | 52 | 17 | 1 | ... | ... | ... |
| 42 | Gout | .... | ... | .... | ... | ... | ... | ... | ... | .... | .... | 2 | ... | .. | .. | .. | .. | .. | .. | 1 | .. | 1 | ... | ... | ... |
| 43 | Heart, disease of | 3 | 1 | 3 | ... | 1 | 1 | 3 | 4 | 25 | 9 | 16 | 9 | .. | .. | .. | .. | .. | .. | 37 | 14 | 1 | 1 | ... | ... |
| 44 | Heat | .... | ... | 1 | ... | ... | ... | ... | ... | 12 | .... | 1 | ... | .. | .. | .. | .. | .. | .. | .... | .. | ... | ... | ... | ... |
| 45 | Hemorrhage | .... | 2 | .... | 1 | ... | ... | ... | 2 | 5 | 2 | ... | 1 | .. | .. | .. | .. | .. | .. | 8 | 2 | ... | ... | ... | ... |
| 46 | Hernia | .... | ... | .... | ... | ... | ... | ... | ... | .... | 2 | ... | ... | .. | .. | .. | .. | .. | .. | 1 | .. | ... | ... | ... | ... |
| 47 | Hip, disease of | .... | ... | 1 | ... | 1 | ... | 1 | ... | 1 | .... | ... | ... | .. | .. | .. | .. | .. | .. | 2 | .. | ... | ... | ... | ... |
| 48 | Hooping cough | 3 | 5 | 19 | 18 | 1 | 7 | ... | ... | .... | .... | ... | ... | .. | .. | .. | .. | .. | 1 | 51 | 1 | ... | ... | ... | ... |
| 49 | Inflammation | 3 | 3 | 7 | 14 | 2 | 2 | 3 | 2 | 12 | 9 | 4 | 3 | .. | .. | .. | .. | .. | .. | 34 | 2 | 1 | 1 | ... | ... |
| 50 | .....do....stomach | .... | ... | .... | ... | ... | ... | ... | ... | 1 | 1 | 1 | ... | .. | .. | .. | .. | .. | .. | 1 | 1 | ... | ... | ... | ... |
| 51 | Influenza | 1 | ... | .... | ... | ... | ... | ... | ... | .... | 1 | ... | 1 | .. | .. | .. | .. | .. | .. | 3 | .. | ... | ... | ... | ... |
| 52 | Insanity | .... | ... | .... | ... | ... | ... | ... | ... | .... | .... | ... | ... | .. | .. | .. | .. | .. | .. | .... | .. | ... | ... | ... | ... |
| 53 | Intemperance | .... | ... | .... | ... | ... | ... | ... | ... | 5 | 5 | 4 | ... | .. | .. | .. | .. | .. | .. | 4 | 1 | ... | 1 | ... | ... |

SECTION OF THE STATE OF MASSACHUSETTS—Continued.

| NATIVITIES. California and Territories. | NATIVITIES. Ireland. | NATIVITIES. Germany. | NATIVITIES. Other foreign countries. | NATIVITIES. Unknown. | SEASON OF DECEASE. Spring. | SEASON OF DECEASE. Summer. | SEASON OF DECEASE. Autumn. | SEASON OF DECEASE. Winter. | DURATION OF SICKNESS. Under 1 week. | DURATION OF SICKNESS. 1 week and under 1 month. | DURATION OF SICKNESS. 1 month and under 3 months. | DURATION OF SICKNESS. 3 months and over. | WHITES. Males. | WHITES. Females. | WHITES. Total. | COLORED. Slaves. Black. M. | COLORED. Slaves. Black. F. | COLORED. Slaves. Mulatto. M. | COLORED. Slaves. Mulatto. F. | COLORED. Free. Black. M. | COLORED. Free. Black. F. | COLORED. Free. Mul. M | COLORED. Free. Mul. F. | Aggregate deaths. | |
|---|---|---|---|---|---|---|---|---|---|---|---|---|---|---|---|---|---|---|---|---|---|---|---|---|---|
| | | | | | | | | 1 | | | | | | 1 | 1 | | | | | | | | | 1 | 1 |
| | | | | | | | | 1 | | | 1 | | | 1 | 1 | | | | | | | | | 1 | 2 |
| | | | | | 1 | | | | 1 | | | | 1 | | 1 | | | | | | | | | 1 | 3 |
| | | | | | 1 | 1 | | | | | | 1 | 2 | | 2 | | | | | | | | | 2 | 4 |
| | 1 | | | | 4 | 2 | 3 | 1 | | | | 1 | 7 | 3 | 10 | | | | | | | | | 10 | 5 |
| | 6 | | | | | 6 | | | 2 | | | | 4 | 2 | 6 | | | | | | | | | 6 | 6 |
| | | | | | 1 | | | | 1 | | | | 1 | | 1 | | | | | | | | | 1 | 7 |
| | 1 | | | | 8 | 9 | 22 | 5 | 5 | 19 | 6 | | 25 | 19 | 44 | | | | | | | | | 44 | 8 |
| | 1 | | | | 7 | 4 | 12 | 11 | 10 | 17 | 2 | 2 | 15 | 18 | 33 | | | | | 1 | | | | 34 | 9 |
| | 1 | | | | 1 | 1 | 1 | | | | 1 | 2 | | 3 | 3 | | | | | | | | | 3 | 10 |
| | | | | | 1 | 5 | 3 | 3 | 1 | 5 | | 5 | 3 | 9 | 12 | | | | | | | | | 12 | 11 |
| | | | | | 5 | | | | 2 | 1 | 2 | | 2 | 3 | 5 | | | | | | | | | 5 | 12 |
| | 14 | 2 | 3 | | 110 | 94 | 100 | 84 | 92 | 52 | 29 | 37 | 206 | 174 | 380 | | | | | 3 | 3 | | 2 | 388 | 13 |
| | 188 | 8 | 58 | | 850 | 868 | 1459 | 763 | 722 | 1044 | 325 | 706 | 2038 | 1942 | 3980 | | | | | 13 | 15 | | 4 | 4012 | |

COUNTY, IN THE STATE OF MASSACHUSETTS.

| California and Territories. | Ireland. | Germany. | Other foreign countries. | Unknown. | Spring. | Summer. | Autumn. | Winter. | Under 1 week. | 1 week and under 1 month. | 1 month and under 3 months. | 3 months and over. | Males. | Females. | Total. | Slaves. Black. M. | Slaves. Black. F. | Slaves. Mulatto. M. | Slaves. Mulatto. F. | Free. Black. M. | Free. Black. F. | Free. Mul. M | Free. Mul. F. | Aggregate deaths. | |
|---|---|---|---|---|---|---|---|---|---|---|---|---|---|---|---|---|---|---|---|---|---|---|---|---|---|
| | 1 | | 2 | | 1 | | 1 | 2 | | | 1 | | 4 | | 4 | | | | | | | | | 4 | 1 |
| | 19 | | 1 | | 9 | 15 | 19 | 11 | 5 | | | | 43 | 15 | 58 | | | | | | | | | 58 | 2 |
| | 14 | | | | 6 | 4 | 2 | 2 | 8 | | | | 7 | 7 | 14 | | | | | | | | | 14 | 3 |
| | 6 | | 5 | | 2 | 20 | 5 | 4 | | | | | 28 | 7 | 35 | | | | | | | | | 35 | 4 |
| | 1 | | 2 | | 1 | | 3 | 4 | 1 | | | | 6 | 3 | 9 | | | | | | | | | 9 | 5 |
| | | | 1 | | | | | 1 | | | | | 1 | | 1 | | | | | | | | | 1 | 6 |
| | 6 | | 1 | | 1 | | | | | | | | 12 | 6 | 18 | | | | | | | | | 18 | 7 |
| | 1 | | | | 2 | 1 | 1 | | | 1 | | | 3 | 1 | 4 | | | | | | | | | 4 | 8 |
| | | | | | 1 | | | | | | 1 | | 1 | | 1 | | | | | | | | | 1 | 9 |
| | 28 | | 9 | | 24 | 36 | 186 | 24 | 101 | 158 | 1 | 1 | 135 | 136 | 271 | | | | | | 1 | | | 272 | 10 |
| | 11 | | 3 | | 39 | 26 | 23 | 28 | 63 | 48 | | 1 | 55 | 59 | 114 | | | | | 2 | 1 | | | 117 | 11 |
| | 2 | | | | 2 | 3 | | 4 | | 8 | | | 6 | 3 | 9 | | | | | | | | | 9 | 12 |
| | 7 | | 1 | | 1 | 3 | | 4 | | 3 | | 4 | 14 | 13 | 27 | | | | | | | | | 27 | 13 |
| | | | | | | | | 1 | | | | | | 1 | 1 | | | | | | | | | 1 | 14 |
| | | | | | 1 | | | | | 1 | | | | 1 | 1 | | | | | | | | | 1 | 15 |
| | 42 | | 3 | | 14 | 12 | 9 | 17 | 48 | 2 | 1 | | | 52 | 52 | | | | | | | | | 52 | 16 |
| | 387 | | 50 | | | 52 | 585 | | 636 | 2 | | | 360 | 270 | 630 | | | | | 2 | 6 | | | 638 | 17 |
| | 1 | | 4 | | | 7 | 42 | 1 | 19 | 27 | 4 | | 24 | 26 | 50 | | | | | | | | | 50 | 18 |
| | 14 | | 2 | | 14 | 24 | | 3 | 19 | 22 | | | 25 | 15 | 40 | | | | | 1 | | | | 41 | 19 |
| | 1 | | | | | 1 | | | 1 | | | | | 1 | 1 | | | | | | | | | 1 | 20 |
| | | | 1 | | | 1 | | | | 1 | | | | 1 | 1 | | | | | | | | | 1 | 21 |
| | 4 | | | | 5 | | 1 | 2 | 7 | 1 | | | 5 | 2 | 7 | | | | | 1 | | | | 8 | 22 |
| | 241 | 1 | 48 | | 165 | 180 | 146 | 144 | 6 | 51 | 34 | 437 | 352 | 321 | 673 | | | | | 4 | 6 | | | 683 | 23 |
| | 11 | | 2 | | 44 | 1 | 25 | 15 | 75 | 1 | | | 48 | 36 | 84 | | | | | | 1 | | | 85 | 24 |
| | 1 | | | | | 2 | | | 2 | | | | | 2 | 2 | | | | | | | | | 2 | 25 |
| | 4 | | 1 | | 17 | 4 | 12 | 29 | 58 | 4 | | | 37 | 25 | 62 | | | | | | | | | 62 | 26 |
| | 4 | | 2 | | 7 | 10 | 9 | 5 | 3 | 4 | 4 | 15 | 10 | 21 | 31 | | | | | | | | | 31 | 27 |
| | | | | | 1 | 2 | 1 | | | | 1 | 1 | 3 | 1 | 4 | | | | | | | | | 4 | 28 |
| | 54 | | 5 | 2 | 5 | 17 | 88 | 5 | 52 | 61 | 1 | | 55 | 59 | 114 | | | | | 1 | | | | 115 | 29 |
| | 31 | | 9 | 1 | 54 | 53 | 62 | 48 | 38 | 91 | 16 | 27 | 121 | 94 | 215 | | | | | 1 | 1 | | | 217 | 30 |
| | 66 | | 19 | 1 | 8 | 23 | 193 | 98 | 139 | 176 | 4 | 1 | 186 | 133 | 319 | | | | | 3 | | | | 322 | 31 |
| | 1 | | 1 | | | 2 | | 2 | 1 | 2 | | | 2 | 2 | 4 | | | | | | | | | 4 | 32 |
| | 13 | | 6 | | 27 | 14 | 6 | 20 | 11 | 52 | 1 | | 37 | 31 | 68 | | | | | | | | | 68 | 33 |
| | 16 | | 4 | | 23 | 5 | 9 | 13 | 13 | 37 | | | 24 | 26 | 50 | | | | | | | | | 50 | 34 |
| | 2 | | 1 | | 2 | 1 | 1 | | | 4 | | | | 4 | 4 | | | | | | | | | 4 | 35 |
| | | | | | 1 | | 6 | 1 | 5 | 3 | | | 7 | 1 | 8 | | | | | | | | | 8 | 36 |
| | | | | | | | 1 | | | 1 | | | 1 | | 1 | | | | | | | | | 1 | 37 |
| | 1 | | | | 1 | 1 | 1 | | 1 | | 1 | | | 3 | 3 | | | | | | | | | 3 | 38 |
| | 8 | | 6 | | 17 | 60 | 26 | 36 | 72 | 66 | | 1 | 79 | 60 | 139 | | | | | | | | | 139 | 39 |
| | 5 | | | | 1 | | 4 | 1 | | 4 | 1 | 1 | 1 | 5 | 6 | | | | | | | | | 6 | 40 |
| | 44 | | 11 | | 18 | 26 | 47 | 34 | 46 | 75 | 1 | 2 | 57 | 67 | 124 | | | | | | 1 | | | 125 | 41 |
| | | | | | 1 | 1 | | | | | | 1 | 2 | | 2 | | | | | | | | | 2 | 42 |
| | 18 | 1 | 3 | | 12 | 28 | 11 | 23 | 23 | 25 | 1 | | 50 | 24 | 74 | | | | | 1 | | | | 75 | 43 |
| | 14 | | | | | 14 | | | | | | | 14 | | 14 | | | | | | | | | 14 | 44 |
| | 2 | | 1 | | 1 | 7 | 4 | 1 | 6 | 1 | | | 5 | 7 | 12 | | | | | 1 | | | | 13 | 45 |
| | 1 | | | | | | | 2 | 1 | | | | | 2 | 2 | | | | | | | | | 2 | 46 |
| | 2 | | | | 1 | | 2 | 1 | | | 1 | 2 | 4 | | 4 | | | | | | | | | 4 | 47 |
| | 1 | | 1 | | 24 | 13 | 10 | 7 | 2 | 1 | 45 | 4 | 22 | 31 | 53 | | | | | 1 | | | | 54 | 48 |
| | 25 | | 1 | | 1 | 41 | 19 | 3 | 19 | 43 | 1 | | 31 | 33 | 64 | | | | | | | | | 64 | 49 |
| | | | 1 | | 1 | 2 | | | | | 1 | | 2 | 1 | 3 | | | | | | | | | 3 | 50 |
| | | | | | 2 | | | 1 | 3 | | | | 1 | 2 | 3 | | | | | | | | | 3 | 51 |
| | | | | | | | | | | | | | | | | | | | | | | | | | 52 |
| | 6 | | 2 | | 3 | 5 | 1 | 5 | 2 | 1 | 1 | | 8 | 5 | 13 | | | | | 1 | | | | 14 | 53 |

CLASSIFICATION OF DEATHS IN SUFFOLK

| | Cause of death. | AGE. Under 1. | | 1 and under 5. | | 5 and under 10. | | 10 and under 20. | | 20 and under 50. | | 50 and under 80. | | 80 and under 100. | | 100 & over. | | Age unknown. | | NATIVITIES. Born in State. | N. England States. | Middle States. | Southern States. | Southwest'n States. | Northeast'n States. |
|---|---|---|---|---|---|---|---|---|---|---|---|---|---|---|---|---|---|---|---|---|---|---|---|---|---|
| | | M. | F. | M. | F. | M. | F. | M. | F. | M. | F. | M. | F. | M | F. | M | F. | M | F. | | | | | | |
| 1 | Jaundice | | | | | | | 1 | | | | | | | | | | | | | | | | | |
| 2 | Kidneys, disease of | | | | | | | 1 | | | 1 | 1 | 2 | | | | | | | 4 | | | | | |
| 3 | Liver ......do | | | | | | | 1 | | 9 | 4 | 3 | 3 | | | | | | | 8 | 3 | | | | |
| 4 | Lungs......do | 2 | 2 | 20 | 17 | 6 | 1 | 1 | 2 | 16 | 17 | 5 | 7 | 2 | | | | | | 56 | 7 | 1 | 1 | | |
| 5 | Mania-a-potu | | | | | | | | | 8 | 1 | | | | | | | | | 7 | 1 | | | | |
| 6 | Marasmus | 13 | 11 | 18 | 10 | 3 | 1 | | 2 | 1 | 1 | 1 | | | | | | | | 53 | | | | | |
| 7 | Measles | 1 | | | 11 | 5 | 1 | 1 | 2 | 1 | | | | | | | | | | 18 | | | | | |
| 8 | Mortification | 2 | | 1 | 1 | | | | | 1 | | 2 | 1 | | | | | | | 5 | 1 | | | | |
| 9 | Murder | | | | | | | | | | | 1 | | | | | | | | 1 | | | | | |
| 10 | Neuralgia | | | | | | | | | | 2 | | | | | | | | | | | | | | |
| 11 | Old age | | | | | | | | | | | 17 | 21 | 26 | 33 | 1 | | | | 56 | 9 | 2 | 1 | | |
| 12 | Paralysis | | | | | | | | | 4 | 3 | 12 | 11 | | 1 | | | | | 18 | 7 | 1 | | | |
| 13 | Pleurisy | | | | 1 | | | 1 | 2 | 7 | 5 | 1 | 3 | | | | | 1 | | 10 | 2 | | | | |
| 14 | Pneumonia | 10 | 12 | 53 | 42 | 11 | 2 | 4 | 2 | 16 | 10 | 2 | 8 | | | | | | | 127 | 6 | 5 | | | |
| 15 | Poison | | | | 1 | | | | | 1 | | | | | | | | | | 2 | | | | | |
| 16 | Quinsy | 1 | | 1 | | | | | | | | | | | | | | | | 2 | | | | | |
| 17 | Rheumatism | | | | | | | 2 | | 5 | 1 | | 1 | | | | | | | 3 | 1 | | 1 | | |
| 18 | Scrofula | | 1 | 5 | 3 | 1 | | | 2 | | 1 | 1 | | | | | | | | 12 | | | | | |
| 19 | Small pox | 6 | 2 | 20 | 22 | 3 | 4 | 10 | 6 | 33 | 15 | 3 | 1 | | | | | | | 67 | 19 | 7 | | 1 | 1 |
| 20 | Spine, disease of | | | | | | | 1 | 4 | 2 | 2 | | 1 | | | | | | 1 | 7 | | 1 | 1 | | |
| 21 | Stomach...do | | 1 | 2 | | | | | | | 2 | 1 | 2 | | | | | | | 6 | | | | | |
| 22 | Suffocation | | 1 | | 1 | | | | | 2 | 2 | 1 | | | | | | | | 2 | 1 | | | | |
| 23 | Suicide | | | | | | | | | 6 | 5 | 1 | | | | | | 1 | | 3 | 2 | 1 | 1 | | |
| 24 | Sun, stroke of | | | | | | | | | 2 | | | | | | | | | | | | | | | |
| 25 | Syphilis | 1 | | | | | | | | | 1 | | | | | | | | | 2 | | | | | |
| 26 | Teething | 9 | 5 | 69 | 81 | 2 | | | | | | | | | | | | | | 157 | 3 | | | | |
| 27 | Throat, disease of | | 1 | 1 | 2 | | 1 | | 1 | | 1 | | 2 | | | | | | | 5 | 1 | | | | |
| 28 | Tumor | | | | | | | | 1 | 2 | 9 | 4 | 3 | | | | | | | 9 | 3 | | | | |
| 29 | Ulcer | 8 | 6 | 5 | 3 | 1 | 1 | 3 | | 2 | | 1 | 2 | | | | | | | 24 | 4 | 2 | | | |
| 30 | Worms | | | 1 | 5 | 1 | 1 | | | | | | | | | | | | | 6 | 1 | | | | |
| 31 | Unknown | 169 | 150 | 42 | 23 | 7 | 2 | 6 | 3 | 31 | 20 | 4 | 11 | 1 | 1 | | | 43 | 21 | 464 | 10 | 2 | 1 | 1 | |
| | Total | 342 | 279 | 778 | 651 | 184 | 111 | 127 | 155 | 908 | 786 | 297 | 276 | 34 | 41 | 1 | .. | 57 | 29 | 3035 | 333 | 58 | 23 | 2 | 3 |

CLASSIFICATION OF DEATHS IN

| | Cause of death. | Under 1. M. | Under 1. F. | 1 and under 5. M. | F. | 5 and under 10. M. | F. | 10 and under 20. M. | F. | 20 and under 50. M. | F. | 50 and under 80. M. | F. | 80 and under 100. M | F. | 100 & over. M | F. | Age unknown. M | F. | Born in State. | N. England States. | Middle States. | Southern States. | Southwest'n States. | Northeast'n States. |
|---|---|---|---|---|---|---|---|---|---|---|---|---|---|---|---|---|---|---|---|---|---|---|---|---|---|
| 1 | Abscess | 3 | 1 | 2 | 1 | 2 | | | | 11 | 4 | 6 | | | | | | | | 21 | 2 | 2 | | | |
| 2 | Accident, not specfi'd | 4 | 3 | 17 | 5 | 7 | 3 | 13 | 6 | 76 | 9 | 29 | 14 | 1 | 5 | | | 2 | | 144 | 10 | 3 | | 3 | |
| 3 | ....do...burned | 1 | 1 | 10 | 11 | 1 | 4 | 1 | 1 | 3 | 2 | 1 | 6 | | | | | | | 25 | | | | | |
| 4 | ....do...drowned | 2 | | 20 | 6 | 23 | 1 | 18 | 15 | 64 | 8 | 7 | | | | | | 4 | 1 | 122 | 10 | 4 | 1 | | |
| 5 | ....do.. scalded | | 1 | 16 | 5 | 1 | | 1 | | 1 | 1 | | | | | | | | | 21 | 1 | | | | |
| 6 | ....do...explosion | | | | | | | 1 | | | | | | | | | | | | 1 | | | | | |
| 7 | ....do...machinery | | | | | | | | | 1 | | | | | | | | | | | | | | | |
| 8 | ....do...gunshot | | | | | | | | | 4 | | | | | | | | | | 2 | | | | | |
| 9 | ....do...railroad | | | | | 1 | | 2 | | 8 | | 2 | | | | | | | | 8 | | | | | |
| 10 | Amputation | | | | | | | | | 1 | | | | | | | | | | 1 | | | | | |
| 11 | Apoplexy | | | 1 | | | | 2 | 1 | 12 | 11 | 32 | 19 | 6 | 1 | | | | | 64 | 8 | | 1 | | |
| 12 | Asthma | | | | | | | | | 3 | | 6 | 5 | 3 | | | | 1 | | 11 | 4 | | | | |
| 13 | Bladder, disease of | | | | | | | | | | | 2 | | 1 | | | | | | 2 | 1 | | | | |
| 14 | Bowels......do | 52 | 40 | 116 | 109 | 16 | 11 | 3 | 12 | 21 | 35 | 8 | 13 | | | | | | | 364 | 20 | 3 | 1 | | |
| 15 | Brain ......do | 29 | 17 | 57 | 63 | 15 | 16 | 14 | 7 | 29 | 30 | 12 | 8 | 1 | 2 | | | | | 252 | 22 | 1 | | | |
| 16 | Bronchitis | 5 | 4 | 5 | 5 | | 3 | 1 | | 7 | 3 | 2 | 3 | | 2 | | | | | 31 | 5 | 1 | | | |
| 17 | Cancer | 3 | 2 | 1 | 4 | 2 | 1 | 1 | 2 | 9 | 33 | 44 | 48 | 6 | 8 | | | | | 139 | 15 | | | | |
| 18 | Canker | | | | 1 | | | | | | | | | | | | | | | 1 | | | | | |
| 19 | Carbuncle | | | | | | | | | 1 | | | | | | | | | | 1 | | | | | |
| 20 | Catarrh | 4 | 1 | 1 | 2 | | | 1 | | 1 | | 1 | | | | | | | | 10 | | | | | |
| 21 | Chicken pox | | 3 | | 2 | | | | | | | | | | | | | | | 5 | | | | | |
| 22 | Childbirth | | | | | | | | 10 | | 159 | | 1 | | | | | | | 74 | 8 | 1 | | | |
| 23 | Cholera | 8 | 6 | 45 | 39 | 31 | 28 | 36 | 54 | 375 | 287 | 109 | 49 | 2 | 4 | | | 6 | 3 | 371 | 64 | 14 | 3 | 1 | |
| 24 | ....do....infantum | 82 | 69 | 71 | 97 | 7 | 1 | 2 | | | | | | | | | | 2 | | 314 | 6 | 3 | | | 1 |
| 25 | ....do....morbus | 7 | 6 | 12 | 10 | 4 | 8 | 1 | 4 | 23 | 17 | 20 | 8 | 3 | 3 | | | 1 | | 99 | 5 | 2 | | | |
| 26 | Chorea | | | | 1 | | | | | | 2 | | | | | | | | | 2 | | | | | |
| 27 | Colic | | | | | | 1 | 1 | 2 | 15 | 9 | 5 | 7 | 1 | | | | | | 28 | 1 | 1 | | | |
| 28 | Congestion, not spe'd | | | | 1 | 1 | | | | 2 | 2 | | | | 1 | | | | | 5 | | | | | |
| 29 | ....do.....brain | 3 | 3 | 10 | 3 | 1 | 1 | | | 6 | 2 | | 2 | | | | | | | 24 | 2 | | | | 1 |
| 30 | Consumption | 110 | 77 | 149 | 82 | 19 | 29 | 100 | 231 | 736 | 1031 | 413 | 376 | 29 | 34 | | | 4 | 6 | 2548 | 300 | 38 | 10 | 3 | |
| 31 | Convulsions | 81 | 52 | 68 | 72 | 7 | 8 | 4 | 5 | 15 | 15 | 24 | 18 | 3 | 8 | | | 5 | | 339 | 15 | 3 | | | 1 |
| 32 | Cramp | | 1 | | 3 | | 1 | 1 | | 1 | 4 | | | 1 | | | | | | 10 | | | | | |
| 33 | Croup | 48 | 29 | 108 | 94 | 16 | 16 | 4 | 5 | 3 | 8 | 6 | 1 | | | | | | 1 | 315 | 10 | 5 | | 1 | |
| 34 | Debility | 26 | 22 | 3 | 6 | 2 | 1 | 1 | 4 | 4 | 12 | 9 | 16 | 4 | 2 | | | 1 | 2 | 103 | 5 | | | | |
| 35 | Diabetes | | | | 2 | 1 | 2 | 1 | | 7 | 1 | 3 | 1 | 1 | 2 | | | | | 18 | 2 | | 1 | | |

COUNTY, IN THE STATE OF MASSACHUSETTS—Continued.

| NATIVITIES. | | | | | SEASON OF DECEASE. | | | | DURATION OF SICKNESS. | | | | WHITES. | | | COLORED. | | | | | | | | | |
|---|---|---|---|---|---|---|---|---|---|---|---|---|---|---|---|---|---|---|---|---|---|---|---|---|---|
| | | | | | | | | | | | | | | | | Slaves. | | | | Free. | | | | | |
| | | | | | | | | | | | | | | | | Black. | | Mulatto. | | Black. | | Mul. | | | |
| California and Territories. | Ireland. | Germany. | Other foreign countries. | Unknown. | Spring. | Summer. | Autumn. | Winter. | Under 1 week. | 1 week and under 1 month. | 1 month and under 3 months. | 3 months and over. | Males. | Females. | Total. | M. | F. | M. | F. | M. | F. | M | F. | Aggregate deaths. | |
| | 1 | | | | | | 1 | | | | | 1 | 1 | | 1 | | | | | | | | | 1 | 1 |
| | 1 | | | | | | 3 | 2 | | | | | 2 | 3 | 5 | | | | | | | | | 5 | 2 |
| | 5 | 1 | 3 | | 5 | 5 | 6 | 4 | 1 | 9 | 2 | 4 | 13 | 7 | 20 | | | | | | | | | 20 | 3 |
| | 27 | | 6 | | 40 | 12 | 7 | 38 | 22 | 63 | 5 | 1 | 51 | 45 | 96 | | | | | 1 | 1 | | | 98 | 4 |
| | 1 | | | | | 1 | 4 | 4 | 3 | | | | 8 | 1 | 9 | | | | | | | | | 9 | 5 |
| | 5 | | 2 | 1 | 4 | 23 | 27 | 7 | 4 | 15 | 28 | 12 | 36 | 25 | 61 | | | | | | | | | 61 | 6 |
| | 1 | | 3 | | 4 | 12 | 3 | 3 | 8 | 14 | | | 8 | 14 | 22 | | | | | | | | | 22 | 7 |
| | 2 | | | | 2 | 3 | 2 | 1 | 4 | 1 | 1 | | 6 | 2 | 8 | | | | | | | | | 8 | 8 |
| | | | | | | | | 1 | | | | | 1 | | 1 | | | | | | | | | 1 | 9 |
| | 1 | | 1 | | | | | 2 | | | | 2 | | 2 | 2 | | | | | | | | | 2 | 10 |
| | 22 | | 8 | | 24 | 26 | 30 | 18 | 2 | 2 | 2 | | 42 | 53 | 95 | | | | | 2 | 1 | | | 98 | 11 |
| | 3 | | 2 | | 11 | 6 | 9 | 5 | 4 | 4 | 1 | 1 | 16 | 15 | 31 | | | | | | | | | 31 | 12 |
| | 7 | | 1 | 1 | 2 | 7 | 5 | 7 | | 9 | 2 | | 10 | 9 | 19 | | | | | | 2 | | | 21 | 13 |
| | 29 | 1 | 4 | | 67 | 25 | 20 | 50 | 55 | 114 | 1 | | 94 | 76 | 170 | | | | | 2 | | | | 172 | 14 |
| | | | | | 2 | | | | 1 | | | | 1 | 1 | 2 | | | | | | | | | 2 | 15 |
| | | | | | 1 | | 1 | | 2 | | | | 2 | | 2 | | | | | | | | | 2 | 16 |
| | 3 | | 1 | | 1 | 6 | | 2 | 1 | 1 | | 7 | 6 | 2 | 8 | | | | | 1 | | | | 9 | 17 |
| | 2 | | | | 3 | 1 | 4 | 6 | | | | 5 | 7 | 7 | 14 | | | | | | | | | 14 | 18 |
| | 22 | | 12 | 1 | 73 | 36 | 1 | 20 | 60 | 68 | | 1 | 75 | 50 | 125 | | | | | 5 | | | | 130 | 19 |
| | 2 | | | | 3 | 2 | 3 | 3 | | | | 8 | 3 | 8 | 11 | | | | | | | | | 11 | 20 |
| | 2 | | | | 1 | | | 7 | | 2 | 1 | 2 | 3 | 5 | 8 | | | | | | | | | 8 | 21 |
| | 4 | | | | 2 | 1 | 2 | 2 | | | | | 3 | 4 | 7 | | | | | | | | | 7 | 22 |
| | 8 | 1 | 2 | | 3 | 4 | 5 | 1 | 1 | | | | 8 | 4 | 12 | | | | | | 1 | | | 13 | 23 |
| | 2 | | | | | 2 | | | | | | | 2 | | 2 | | | | | | | | | 2 | 24 |
| | | | | | | 1 | 1 | | 1 | 1 | | | 1 | 1 | 2 | | | | | | | | | 2 | 25 |
| | 3 | | 3 | | 30 | 19 | 90 | 26 | 8 | 135 | 23 | 2 | 80 | 86 | 166 | | | | | | | | | 166 | 26 |
| | 3 | | | | 3 | 2 | | 4 | 1 | 5 | 1 | | 1 | 8 | 9 | | | | | | | | | 9 | 27 |
| | 6 | | 1 | | 4 | 5 | 4 | 2 | | | 6 | 7 | 6 | 13 | 19 | | | | | | | | | 19 | 28 |
| | 2 | | | | 6 | 5 | 19 | 2 | 2 | 14 | 3 | 2 | 20 | 12 | 32 | | | | | | | | | 32 | 29 |
| | 1 | | | | 4 | 1 | 1 | 2 | | 1 | | | 2 | 6 | 8 | | | | | | | | | 8 | 30 |
| | 44 | 1 | 9 | 2 | 104 | 76 | 231 | 122 | 50 | 284 | 24 | 12 | 301 | 231 | 532 | | | | | 2 | | | | 534 | 31 |
| | 1320 | 6 | 267 | 9 | 959 | 998 | 2040 | 943 | 1716 | 1714 | 222 | 565 | 2704 | 2298 | 5002 | | | | | 32 | 22 | | | 5056 | |

THE STATE OF MASSACHUSETTS—AGGREGATE.

| California and Territories. | Ireland. | Germany. | Other foreign countries. | Unknown. | Spring. | Summer. | Autumn. | Winter. | Under 1 week. | 1 week and under 1 month. | 1 month and under 3 months. | 3 months and over. | Males. | Females. | Total. | Slaves Black M. | Slaves Black F. | Slaves Mulatto M. | Slaves Mulatto F. | Free Black M. | Free Black F. | Free Mul. M | Free Mul. F. | Aggregate deaths. | |
|---|---|---|---|---|---|---|---|---|---|---|---|---|---|---|---|---|---|---|---|---|---|---|---|---|---|
| | 3 | | 2 | | 5 | 8 | 7 | 10 | 7 | 2 | 2 | 6 | 24 | 6 | 30 | | | | | | | | | 30 | 1 |
| | 30 | | 4 | | 48 | 52 | 58 | 32 | 32 | 15 | 5 | 2 | 147 | 45 | 192 | | | | | 2 | | | | 194 | 2 |
| | 16 | | 1 | | 14 | 9 | 4 | 12 | 15 | 5 | 1 | | 17 | 25 | 42 | | | | | | | | | 42 | 3 |
| | 24 | | 8 | | 27 | 56 | 53 | 27 | 169 | | | | 138 | 31 | 169 | | | | | | | | | 169 | 4 |
| | 1 | | 3 | | 5 | 2 | 10 | 8 | 9 | 2 | | | 19 | 7 | 26 | | | | | | | | | 26 | 5 |
| | | | | | | | | 1 | | | | | 1 | | 1 | | | | | | | | | 1 | 6 |
| | 1 | | | | 1 | | | | 1 | | | | 1 | | 1 | | | | | | | | | 1 | 7 |
| | 1 | | 1 | | | | 1 | 3 | | 1 | | | 4 | | 4 | | | | | | | | | 4 | 8 |
| | 5 | | | | 2 | 2 | 6 | 3 | 1 | | | | 13 | | 13 | | | | | | | | | 13 | 9 |
| | | | | | | | 1 | | | | | | 1 | | 1 | | | | | | | | | 1 | 10 |
| | 11 | | 1 | | 18 | 18 | 12 | 17 | 20 | 7 | | 4 | 53 | 32 | 85 | | | | | | | | | 85 | 11 |
| | 1 | | 2 | | 6 | 4 | 5 | 2 | 4 | 4 | 1 | 5 | 13 | 5 | 18 | | | | | | | | | 18 | 12 |
| | | | | | 1 | | 1 | 1 | | | 2 | | 3 | 9 | 3 | | | | | | | | | 8 | 13 |
| | 37 | | 11 | | 44 | 72 | 274 | 44 | 134 | 199 | 17 | 5 | 216 | 219 | 435 | | | | | | 1 | | | 436 | 14 |
| | 18 | | 7 | | 81 | 79 | 67 | 63 | 95 | 108 | 9 | 16 | 154 | 141 | 295 | | | | | 2 | 1 | 1 | 1 | 300 | 15 |
| | 3 | | | | 16 | 4 | 9 | 10 | 6 | 8 | 3 | 4 | 20 | 20 | 40 | | | | | | | | | 40 | 16 |
| | 9 | | 1 | | 45 | 40 | 23 | 37 | 4 | 11 | 12 | 81 | 66 | 97 | 163 | | | | | | 1 | | | 164 | 17 |
| | | | | | | | | 1 | | | | | | 1 | 1 | | | | | | | | | 1 | 18 |
| | | | | | 1 | | | | | | | | 1 | | 1 | | | | | | | | | 1 | 19 |
| | | | 1 | | 4 | 1 | 3 | 3 | 3 | 5 | | 1 | 8 | 3 | 11 | | | | | | | | | 11 | 20 |
| | | | | | 3 | 1 | 1 | | | 4 | 1 | | | 5 | 5 | | | | | | | | | 5 | 21 |
| | 66 | 2 | 18 | | 56 | 38 | 38 | 38 | 92 | 30 | 6 | 1 | | 169 | 169 | | | | | | | | 1 | 170 | 22 |
| | 558 | 1 | 70 | | 6 | 109 | 955 | 10 | 832 | 40 | 4 | | 610 | 463 | 1073 | | | | | 2 | 7 | | | 1082 | 23 |
| | 3 | | 4 | | 6 | 50 | 260 | 13 | 121 | 128 | 16 | 7 | 164 | 167 | 331 | | | | | | | | | 331 | 24 |
| | 16 | | 5 | | 19 | 44 | 56 | 3 | 53 | 40 | 1 | | 70 | 51 | 126 | | | | | 1 | | | | 127 | 25 |
| | 1 | | | | | 1 | 1 | 1 | 1 | | | | | 3 | 3 | | | | | | | | | 3 | 26 |
| | 1 | | | | 10 | 3 | 10 | 8 | 16 | 7 | 1 | 1 | 12 | 19 | 31 | | | | | | | | | 31 | 27 |
| | 1 | | 1 | | 4 | 2 | | 1 | 2 | 1 | | | 3 | 4 | 7 | | | | | | | | | 7 | 28 |
| | 4 | | | | 12 | 6 | 5 | 7 | 12 | 11 | 1 | 1 | 19 | 11 | 30 | | | | | 1 | | | | 31 | 29 |
| | 412 | 5 | 110 | | 835 | 836 | 913 | 767 | 108 | 160 | 294 | 2111 | 1542 | 1848 | 3390 | | | | | 17 | 17 | 1 | 1 | 3426 | 30 |
| | 22 | | 5 | | 127 | 73 | 107 | 77 | 181 | 46 | 8 | 16 | 206 | 176 | 382 | | | | | 1 | 1 | | 1 | 385 | 31 |
| | 2 | | | | 1 | 5 | 3 | 3 | 5 | 2 | | 2 | 3 | 9 | 12 | | | | | | | | | 12 | 32 |
| | 7 | | 1 | | 85 | 45 | 89 | 111 | 192 | 47 | 5 | 4 | 180 | 152 | 332 | | | | | 5 | 1 | | 1 | 339 | 33 |
| | 5 | | 2 | | 20 | 32 | 44 | 19 | 3 | 11 | 7 | 30 | 49 | 65 | 114 | | | | | | | 1 | | 115 | 34 |
| | | | | | 6 | 6 | 4 | 5 | 1 | 7 | 1 | 8 | 13 | 8 | 21 | | | | | | | | | 21 | 35 |

## CLASSIFICATION OF DEATHS IN

| | Cause of death. | AGES. | | | | | | | | | | | | | | | | | | NATIVITIES. | | | | | |
|---|---|---|---|---|---|---|---|---|---|---|---|---|---|---|---|---|---|---|---|---|---|---|---|---|---|
| | | Under 1. | | 1 and under 5. | | 5 and under 10. | | 10 and under 20. | | 20 and under 50. | | 50 and under 80. | | 80 and under 100. | | 100 & over. | | Age unknown. | | Born in State. | N. England States. | Middle States. | Southern States. | Southwest'n States. | Northwest'n States. |
| | | M. | F. | M. | F. | M. | F. | M. | F. | M. | F. | M. | F. | M. | F. | M | F. | M | F. | | | | | | |
| 1 | Diarrhœa | 23 | 16 | 86 | 22 | 5 | 4 | 4 | 7 | 34 | 39 | 22 | 20 | 3 | 1 | | | 1 | | 160 | 6 | 4 | | | |
| 2 | Dropsy | 60 | 44 | 148 | 134 | 32 | 24 | 14 | 16 | 43 | 63 | 106 | 95 | 9 | 23 | | | | 1 | 692 | 44 | 8 | 1 | | |
| 3 | Dysentery | 208 | 154 | 592 | 388 | 123 | 123 | 42 | 68 | 184 | 171 | 123 | 197 | 21 | 31 | | | 8 | 4 | 2091 | 129 | 24 | 1 | 3 | 5 |
| 4 | Dyspepsia | | | | | | | | | | 4 | 3 | 4 | | 1 | | | | | 12 | | | | | |
| 5 | Epilepsy | | | | | | | | 1 | 8 | 5 | 2 | 2 | | | | | | | 14 | 1 | 1 | | | |
| 6 | Erysipelas | 12 | 17 | 2 | 6 | 3 | 1 | 4 | 11 | 39 | 27 | 23 | 23 | 3 | 2 | | | | | 119 | 24 | | | | |
| 7 | Fever, not specified | 18 | 11 | 41 | 35 | 24 | 12 | 34 | 35 | 106 | 80 | 38 | 38 | 10 | 3 | | | 4 | | 393 | 29 | 6 | | 5 | |
| 8 | ..do..bilious | | 2 | 1 | 14 | 3 | 3 | 3 | 5 | 11 | 13 | 9 | 8 | 1 | 1 | | | | | 61 | 4 | 1 | | | |
| 9 | ..do..brain | 15 | 14 | 20 | 23 | 14 | 3 | 9 | 8 | 12 | 6 | 2 | 2 | 1 | | | | | | 121 | 5 | | | | |
| 10 | ..do..inflammatory | | | | | | | | 1 | | | | 1 | | | | | | | 1 | 1 | | | | |
| 11 | ..do..intermittent | | | | | | | | | 1 | | | | | | | | | | | | 1 | | | |
| 12 | ..do..puerperal | | | | | | | | 6 | | 32 | | | | | | | | | 18 | 6 | | | | |
| 13 | ..do..remittent | | | | | | | | | | | 1 | | | | | | | | 1 | | | | | |
| 14 | ..do..scarlet | 15 | 16 | 151 | 188 | 85 | 70 | 12 | 20 | 5 | 5 | 1 | 1 | | | | | 2 | | 515 | 15 | 8 | | 1 | |
| 15 | ..do..ship | | | | | | 1 | 2 | 1 | 5 | 9 | | | 1 | | | | | | 5 | | | | | |
| 16 | ..do..typhus | 5 | 4 | 22 | 27 | 22 | 9 | 43 | 89 | 137 | 118 | 36 | 36 | 4 | 1 | | | | | 382 | 76 | 9 | 2 | 1 | |
| 17 | ..do..yellow | | | | | | | 1 | | 7 | | 1 | | | | | | | | 8 | 1 | | | | |
| 18 | Gout | | | | | | | | | | | 5 | | | | | | | | 4 | | 1 | | | |
| 19 | Gravel | | 1 | | | | | | | 2 | | 12 | 3 | 5 | | | | | | 23 | | | | | |
| 20 | Head, disease of | 4 | 2 | 2 | 4 | | | | | 1 | | 1 | | | | | | | | 12 | | | 1 | | |
| 21 | Heart....do | 15 | 15 | 7 | 5 | 14 | 2 | 7 | 17 | 53 | 62 | 73 | 47 | 12 | 5 | | | 1 | | 258 | 28 | 2 | 1 | | |
| 22 | Heat | 2 | | 3 | | | | 2 | | 26 | 2 | 6 | 1 | 2 | | | | 1 | | 9 | | | | | |
| 23 | Hemorrhage | 4 | 3 | 2 | 2 | | | 1 | 5 | 9 | 7 | 4 | 3 | 1 | | | | | | 31 | 6 | | | | |
| 24 | Hernia | | | | | | | | | | 3 | 2 | 2 | | | | | | | 5 | | | | | |
| 25 | Hip, disease of | | | 1 | | 1 | 1 | 1 | | 1 | | 1 | | | | | | | | 4 | | | | | |
| 26 | Hooping cough | 46 | 59 | 57 | 57 | 5 | 10 | | | 1 | | | 1 | 1 | 1 | | | | 2 | 228 | 3 | 2 | | | |
| 27 | Hydrocephalus | 1 | 3 | 3 | 1 | | | | | 1 | | 1 | | | | | | | | 9 | 1 | | | | |
| 28 | Inflammation | 13 | 11 | 15 | 23 | 3 | 4 | 7 | 11 | 22 | 31 | 6 | 8 | 1 | 1 | | | | | 112 | 9 | 3 | 2 | | |
| 29 | ....do......bowels | 18 | 9 | 13 | 12 | 3 | 3 | 8 | 7 | 14 | 32 | 11 | 6 | | 1 | | | | | 117 | 10 | 3 | | | |
| 30 | ....do......brain | 1 | 1 | 5 | 5 | | 1 | 1 | 1 | 5 | | | | | | | | 1 | | 18 | 1 | | | | |
| 31 | ....do......stomach | | | | | | | | 1 | 1 | 3 | 1 | 1 | | | | | | | 5 | 1 | | | | |
| 32 | Influenza | 8 | 4 | 4 | | 1 | 1 | | | | 2 | 5 | 5 | 3 | 3 | | | | | 34 | | 1 | | | |
| 33 | Insanity | | | | | | | | | 12 | 6 | 15 | 12 | | 1 | | | | | 40 | 4 | 1 | | | |
| 34 | Intemperance | | | | | | | | | 26 | 7 | 17 | 2 | 1 | 1 | | | 1 | | 32 | 4 | | 1 | | |
| 35 | Jaundice | | | 2 | | | | 1 | | 5 | | 1 | 4 | 1 | | | | | | 10 | 2 | | | | |
| 36 | Kidneys, disease of | 1 | | | | | | 1 | | 2 | 1 | 3 | 3 | 1 | | | | | | 10 | | | | | |
| 37 | Killed | | | | | | | | | 2 | | | | | | | | | | 1 | | | | | |
| 38 | Liver, disease of | 4 | 2 | | | 1 | 1 | 1 | 1 | 13 | 17 | 19 | 23 | | 1 | | | | | 64 | 9 | | | 1 | |
| 39 | Lockjaw | | | | | 1 | | 2 | | 2 | | 1 | | | | | | | | 5 | 1 | | | | |
| 40 | Lungs, disease of | 24 | 12 | 33 | 41 | 10 | 6 | 3 | 5 | 30 | 28 | 20 | 21 | 3 | 3 | | | | | 175 | 20 | 3 | 1 | 1 | |
| 41 | Malformation | 7 | 1 | | | | | | | | | | | | | | | | | 7 | | | | | |
| 42 | Mania-a-potu | | | | | | | | | 8 | 1 | | | | | | | | | 7 | 1 | | | | |
| 43 | Marasmus | 13 | 11 | 18 | 10 | 3 | 1 | | 2 | 1 | 1 | 1 | | | | | | | | 53 | | | | | |
| 44 | Measles | 8 | 9 | 22 | 45 | 9 | 6 | 3 | 5 | 4 | 7 | | | | | | | | | 108 | 3 | | | | |
| 45 | Mortification | 29 | 19 | 12 | 9 | | 2 | 1 | | 3 | 12 | 12 | 9 | 2 | | | | | | 108 | 5 | | | | |
| 46 | Mumps | 1 | | | 1 | | | | | | | | | | | | | | | 2 | | | | | |
| 47 | Murder | | | | | | | | | 1 | | 1 | | | | | | | | 2 | | | | | |
| 48 | Neuralgia | | | | | | 1 | | | 1 | 3 | | 2 | | | | | | | 4 | | | | | |
| 49 | Old age | | | | | | | | | | | 94 | 125 | 253 | 314 | 2 | 2 | 2 | | 678 | 47 | 5 | 2 | 3 | |
| 50 | Paralysis | | | 2 | 1 | 1 | | | | 19 | 17 | 80 | 65 | 20 | 27 | | | | | 198 | 21 | 3 | 1 | | |
| 51 | Peritonitis | | | | | 1 | | | | 1 | | | | | | | | | | | 1 | | | | |
| 52 | Piles | | | | | | | | | | | 1 | | | | | | | | 1 | | | | | |
| 53 | Pleurisy | | 1 | 2 | 1 | | | 1 | 2 | 14 | 8 | 13 | 8 | 2 | 1 | | | 2 | | 37 | 6 | | | | |
| 54 | Pneumonia | 65 | 64 | 111 | 94 | 21 | 8 | 11 | 7 | 42 | 24 | 40 | 44 | 11 | 7 | | | | | 475 | 15 | 8 | 3 | 1 | |
| 55 | Poison | 2 | 1 | | 4 | 1 | 1 | 1 | 1 | 5 | 1 | 1 | 1 | | | | | | | 17 | 2 | | | | |
| 56 | Prematurity of birth | 4 | 1 | | | | | | | | | | | | | | | | | 5 | | | | | |
| 57 | Quinsy | 2 | | 5 | 1 | 1 | | | | 2 | | | 1 | | | | | | | 11 | | | | | |
| 58 | Rash | 12 | 3 | 31 | 32 | 10 | 13 | 1 | 4 | | | | 1 | | | | | | | 100 | 2 | 1 | | | |
| 59 | Rheumatism | | | | 1 | | 1 | 4 | 1 | 11 | 5 | 11 | 5 | | 1 | | | | | 28 | 3 | | 1 | | |
| 60 | Rickets | | | 2 | | | | | | | | | | | | | | | | 2 | | | | | |
| 61 | Scrofula | 6 | 5 | 14 | 11 | 2 | 3 | 2 | 4 | 7 | 8 | 7 | 1 | | 1 | | | | | 63 | 3 | | | | |
| 62 | Small pox | 12 | 9 | 31 | 27 | 7 | 7 | 16 | 12 | 66 | 27 | 11 | 6 | | 1 | | | | | 148 | 31 | 8 | | 1 | |
| 63 | Spine, disease of | 4 | 3 | 2 | 2 | 1 | | 4 | 6 | 5 | 5 | 3 | 3 | | | | | | 1 | 33 | 2 | 1 | 1 | | |
| 64 | Spleen....do | | | | | | | 1 | | 1 | | | | | | | | | | 1 | | | | | |
| 65 | Stillborn | 14 | 10 | | | | | | | | | | | | | | | | | 24 | | | | | |
| 66 | Stomach, disease of | | 2 | 2 | | | 1 | | | | 3 | 7 | 6 | | | | | | | 14 | 3 | | | 1 | |
| 67 | Suffocation | | 1 | 1 | 1 | | | | | 2 | 2 | 3 | | | | | | | | 5 | 1 | | | | |
| 68 | Suicide | | | | | | | | | 27 | 14 | 13 | 1 | | | | | 1 | | 38 | 5 | 2 | 1 | | |
| 69 | Summer complaint | 1 | 1 | 2 | 1 | | | | | 1 | | | | | | | | | | 6 | | | | | |
| 70 | Sun, stroke of | | | | | | 1 | | | 14 | 2 | 1 | | | | | | | | 2 | 2 | | | | |
| 71 | Syphilis | 1 | | | | | | | | 1 | 1 | | | | | | | | | 3 | | | | | |
| 72 | Teething | 39 | 30 | 99 | 111 | 4 | | | | | | | | | | | | | | 270 | 5 | | | | |
| 73 | Throat, disease of | 11 | 2 | 8 | 13 | 4 | 10 | 2 | 4 | 2 | 4 | 2 | 5 | | | | | | 1 | 69 | 8 | | | | |
| 74 | Thrush | | | | | | | | | | 1 | | | | | | | | | 1 | | | | | |
| 75 | Tumor | | 1 | 2 | | | | 1 | 1 | 2 | 16 | 9 | 8 | 2 | | | | | | 29 | 5 | | | | |

## THE STATE OF MASSACHUSETTS—AGGREGATE—Continued.

| Nativities: California and Territories. | Nativities: Ireland. | Nativities: Germany. | Nativities: Other foreign countries. | Nativities: Unknown. | Season of decease: Spring. | Season of decease: Summer. | Season of decease: Autumn. | Season of decease: Winter. | Duration of sickness: Under 1 week. | Duration of sickness: 1 week and under 1 month. | Duration of sickness: 1 month and under 3 months. | Duration of sickness: 3 months and over. | Whites: Males. | Whites: Females. | Whites: Total. | Colored: Slaves: Black: M. | Colored: Slaves: Black: F. | Colored: Slaves: Mulatto: M. | Colored: Slaves: Mulatto: F. | Colored: Free: Black: M. | Colored: Free: Black: F. | Colored: Free: Mul.: M | Colored: Free: Mul.: F. | Aggregate deaths. | |
|---|---|---|---|---|---|---|---|---|---|---|---|---|---|---|---|---|---|---|---|---|---|---|---|---|---|
| | 59 | | 6 | 2 | 14 | 86 | 166 | 21 | 67 | 91 | 17 | 18 | 127 | 109 | 236 | | | | | 1 | | | | 237 | 1 |
| | 44 | | 22 | 1 | 179 | 202 | 223 | 193 | 95 | 245 | 86 | 164 | 408 | 396 | 804 | | | | | 3 | 3 | 1 | 1 | 812 | 2 |
| 1 | 131 | 1 | 50 | 1 | 59 | 219 | 1933 | 208 | 589 | 1203 | 150 | 56 | 1296 | 1131 | 2427 | | | | | 4 | 2 | 1 | 3 | 2437 | 3 |
| | | | | | 4 | 2 | 2 | 4 | | 1 | 1 | 4 | 3 | 9 | 12 | | | | | | | | | 12 | 4 |
| | 1 | | 1 | | 5 | 5 | 3 | 5 | 2 | 3 | 2 | 2 | 10 | 8 | 18 | | | | | | | | | 18 | 5 |
| | 22 | | 8 | | 72 | 37 | 26 | 37 | 22 | 106 | 6 | 8 | 86 | 87 | 173 | | | | | | | | | 173 | 6 |
| | 43 | | 13 | | 134 | 105 | 139 | 107 | 76 | 296 | 63 | 16 | 273 | 210 | 483 | | | | | 1 | 4 | 1 | | 489 | 7 |
| | 4 | | 4 | | 13 | 11 | 20 | 15 | 13 | 29 | 2 | 3 | 28 | 46 | 74 | | | | | | | | | 74 | 8 |
| | 2 | | 1 | | 33 | 28 | 47 | 21 | 37 | 64 | 10 | 5 | 73 | 56 | 129 | | | | | | | | | 129 | 9 |
| | | | | | | | 1 | 1 | | 1 | 1 | | | 2 | 2 | | | | | | | | | 2 | 10 |
| | | | | | | | 1 | | | 1 | | | 1 | | 1 | | | | | | | | | 1 | 11 |
| | 14 | | | | 12 | 3 | 12 | 11 | 5 | 4 | 1 | 2 | | 38 | 38 | | | | | | | | | 38 | 12 |
| | | | | | 1 | | | | | | | | 1 | | 1 | | | | | | | | | 1 | 13 |
| | 14 | | 10 | 6 | 126 | 192 | 128 | 125 | 186 | 216 | 20 | 4 | 271 | 300 | 571 | | | | | | | | | 571 | 14 |
| | 14 | | | | 2 | 7 | 4 | 6 | 6 | 5 | 2 | 2 | 8 | 11 | 19 | | | | | | | | | 19 | 15 |
| | 64 | | 19 | | 87 | 75 | 236 | 154 | 68 | 296 | 65 | 8 | 269 | 281 | 550 | | | | | | 3 | | | 553 | 16 |
| | | | | | 4 | 1 | 2 | 1 | 4 | 3 | 1 | | 9 | | 9 | | | | | | | | | 9 | 17 |
| | | | | | 1 | 1 | 2 | 1 | | | 1 | 2 | 5 | | 5 | | | | | | | | | 5 | 18 |
| | | | | | 15 | 4 | 1 | 3 | 1 | 4 | 2 | 11 | 19 | 4 | 23 | | | | | | | | | 23 | 19 |
| | 1 | | | | 4 | 4 | 5 | 1 | 1 | 6 | 2 | | 8 | 6 | 14 | | | | | | | | | 14 | 20 |
| | 33 | 1 | 12 | | 75 | 82 | 88 | 93 | 80 | 63 | 28 | 40 | 181 | 152 | 333 | | | | | 1 | 1 | | | 335 | 21 |
| | 33 | 2 | 1 | | 6 | 32 | 4 | 2 | 4 | 1 | 1 | 1 | 42 | 3 | 45 | | | | | | | | | 45 | 22 |
| | 3 | | 1 | | 9 | 17 | 8 | 7 | 15 | 5 | 3 | 1 | 21 | 19 | 40 | | | | | 1 | | | | 41 | 23 |
| | 1 | | 1 | | 2 | | 4 | 1 | 4 | | 1 | 1 | 2 | 5 | 7 | | | | | | | | | 7 | 24 |
| | 2 | | | | 2 | | 3 | 1 | | | 1 | 4 | 5 | 1 | 6 | | | | | | | | | 6 | 25 |
| | 4 | | 3 | | 76 | 55 | 71 | 38 | 25 | 62 | 92 | 15 | 109 | 130 | 239 | | | | | 1 | | | | 240 | 26 |
| | | | | | 3 | 1 | 4 | 2 | 1 | 6 | 1 | | 6 | 4 | 10 | | | | | | | | | 10 | 27 |
| | 27 | | 8 | | 29 | 66 | 36 | 24 | 45 | 75 | 4 | 2 | 67 | 88 | 155 | | | | | | | | 1 | 156 | 28 |
| | 4 | | 3 | | 31 | 27 | 59 | 20 | 42 | 43 | 17 | 6 | 67 | 70 | 137 | | | | | | | | | 137 | 29 |
| | 2 | | | | 6 | 6 | 3 | 6 | 4 | 12 | | | 13 | 8 | 21 | | | | | | | | | 21 | 30 |
| | | | 1 | | 3 | 3 | 1 | | 1 | 1 | 2 | | 2 | 4 | 6 | | | | | | 1 | | | 7 | 31 |
| | 1 | | | | 21 | 3 | 4 | 8 | 13 | 15 | 1 | 1 | 21 | 15 | 36 | | | | | | | | | 36 | 32 |
| | | | 1 | | 10 | 15 | 7 | 10 | 1 | 2 | 4 | 14 | 26 | 19 | 45 | | | | | 1 | | | | 46 | 33 |
| | 15 | | 3 | | 10 | 16 | 14 | 13 | 10 | 6 | 3 | 2 | 44 | 10 | 54 | | | | | 1 | | | | 55 | 34 |
| | 2 | | | | 1 | 1 | 9 | 3 | | 2 | 2 | 4 | 10 | 4 | 14 | | | | | | | | | 14 | 35 |
| | 1 | | 1 | | | 4 | 4 | 4 | | | 2 | 4 | 8 | 4 | 12 | | | | | | | | | 12 | 36 |
| | 1 | | | | | 2 | | | 1 | | | | 2 | | 2 | | | | | | | | | 2 | 37 |
| | 5 | 1 | 3 | | 24 | 18 | 21 | 18 | 6 | 18 | 16 | 24 | 37 | 45 | 82 | | | | | 1 | | | | 83 | 38 |
| | | | | | 1 | 1 | 3 | 1 | 2 | 1 | | 1 | 6 | | 6 | | | | | | | | | 6 | 39 |
| | 28 | 2 | 8 | | 101 | 47 | 21 | 69 | 53 | 97 | 16 | 18 | 119 | 115 | 234 | | | | | 4 | 1 | | | 239 | 40 |
| | 1 | | | | 3 | 2 | 1 | 2 | 1 | | | 1 | 7 | 1 | 8 | | | | | | | | | 8 | 41 |
| | 1 | | | | | 1 | 4 | 4 | 3 | | | | 8 | 1 | 9 | | | | | | | | | 9 | 42 |
| | 5 | | 2 | 1 | 4 | 23 | 27 | 7 | 4 | 15 | 28 | 12 | 36 | 25 | 61 | | | | | | | | | 61 | 43 |
| | 4 | | 3 | | 20 | 54 | 86 | 7 | 22 | 57 | 11 | 3 | 46 | 71 | 117 | | | | | | 1 | | | 118 | 44 |
| | 2 | | | | 17 | 19 | 55 | 23 | 22 | 33 | 10 | 12 | 58 | 56 | 114 | | | | | | | 1 | | 115 | 45 |
| | | | | | 2 | | | | | 2 | | | 1 | 1 | 2 | | | | | | | | | 2 | 46 |
| | | | | | | | | 2 | | | | | 2 | | 2 | | | | | | | | | 2 | 47 |
| | 2 | | 1 | | 2 | | 2 | 3 | | 4 | | 2 | 1 | 6 | 7 | | | | | | | | | 7 | 48 |
| | 39 | 1 | 17 | | 199 | 170 | 218 | 205 | 43 | 103 | 51 | 123 | 347 | 436 | 783 | | | | | 4 | 5 | | | 792 | 49 |
| | 5 | | 4 | | 58 | 59 | 58 | 56 | 35 | 48 | 15 | 46 | 122 | 109 | 231 | | | | | | 1 | | | 232 | 50 |
| | 1 | | | | | | | 2 | | 2 | | | 2 | | 2 | | | | | | | | | 2 | 51 |
| | | | | | | | | 1 | | | | 1 | 1 | | 1 | | | | | | | | | 1 | 52 |
| | 9 | | 2 | 1 | 18 | 9 | 8 | 19 | 8 | 21 | 7 | 3 | 34 | 19 | 53 | | | | | | 2 | | | 55 | 53 |
| | 38 | 1 | 8 | | 242 | 97 | 61 | 145 | 106 | 306 | 31 | 24 | 299 | 248 | 547 | | | | | 2 | | | | 549 | 54 |
| | | | | | 10 | 2 | 2 | 5 | 8 | 5 | 2 | | 10 | 9 | 19 | | | | | | | | | 19 | 55 |
| | | | | | 2 | 1 | 1 | 1 | 1 | 1 | | | 4 | 1 | 5 | | | | | | | | | 5 | 56 |
| | 1 | | | | 6 | 2 | 2 | 2 | 4 | 3 | 4 | | 10 | 2 | 12 | | | | | | | | | 12 | 57 |
| | 3 | | | | 35 | 38 | 12 | 22 | 32 | 54 | 7 | 3 | 54 | 53 | 107 | | | | | | | | | 107 | 58 |
| | 6 | | 2 | | 16 | 12 | 3 | 9 | 3 | 11 | 4 | 15 | 25 | 14 | 39 | | | | | 1 | | | | 40 | 59 |
| | | | | | 1 | | | 1 | | | | 1 | 2 | | 2 | | | | | | | | | 2 | 60 |
| | 4 | | 1 | | 16 | 17 | 20 | 17 | 4 | 10 | 4 | 28 | 38 | 33 | 71 | | | | | | | | | 71 | 61 |
| | 26 | 1 | 15 | 1 | 115 | 65 | 14 | 31 | 68 | 128 | 2 | 1 | 138 | 89 | 227 | | | | | 5 | | | | 232 | 62 |
| | 2 | | | | 13 | 8 | 11 | 7 | 2 | 3 | 2 | 21 | 19 | 20 | 39 | | | | | | | | | 39 | 63 |
| | 1 | | | | | 1 | | 1 | | | 1 | 1 | 2 | | 2 | | | | | | | | | 2 | 64 |
| | | | | | 4 | 4 | 6 | 10 | | | | | 14 | 10 | 24 | | | | | | | | | 24 | 65 |
| | 3 | | | | 4 | 4 | 3 | 10 | | 6 | 4 | 4 | 9 | 12 | 21 | | | | | | | | | 21 | 66 |
| | 4 | | | | 3 | 1 | 3 | 3 | 10 | | | | 6 | 4 | 10 | | | | | | | | | 10 | 67 |
| | 5 | 1 | 4 | | 14 | 13 | 19 | 10 | 3 | 1 | 1 | 1 | 41 | 14 | 55 | | | | | | 1 | | | 56 | 68 |
| | | | | | 2 | 1 | 3 | | | 1 | 2 | 1 | 4 | 2 | 6 | | | | | | | | | 6 | 69 |
| | 14 | | | | | 16 | 2 | | 4 | 1 | | | 15 | 3 | 18 | | | | | | | | | 18 | 70 |
| | | | | | 1 | 1 | 1 | | 2 | 1 | | | 2 | 1 | 3 | | | | | | | | | 3 | 71 |
| | 4 | | 3 | | 54 | 42 | 145 | 41 | 16 | 173 | 32 | 12 | 142 | 140 | 282 | | | | | | | | 1 | 283 | 72 |
| | 4 | | 1 | | 13 | 12 | 19 | 20 | 16 | 36 | 3 | 3 | 28 | 39 | 67 | | | | | 1 | | | | 68 | 73 |
| | | | | | | 1 | | | | 1 | | | | 1 | 1 | | | | | | | | | 1 | 74 |
| | 7 | | 1 | | 14 | 12 | 7 | 5 | 2 | 4 | 8 | 20 | 16 | 26 | 42 | | | | | | | | | 42 | 75 |

CLASSIFICATION OF DEATHS IN

| | Cause of Death. | Ages. Under 1. M. | Under 1. F. | 1 and under 5. M. | 1 and under 5. F. | 5 and under 10. M. | 5 and under 10. F. | 10 and under 20. M. | 10 and under 20. F. | 20 and under 50. M. | 20 and under 50. F. | 50 and under 80. M. | 50 and under 80. F. | 80 and under 100. M. | 80 and under 100. F. | 100 & over. M | 100 & over. F. | Age unknown. M | Age unknown. F. | Nativities. Born in State. | N. England States. | Middle States. | Southern States. | Southwest'n States. | Northwest'n States. |
|---|---|---|---|---|---|---|---|---|---|---|---|---|---|---|---|---|---|---|---|---|---|---|---|---|---|
| 1 | Ulcer | 9 | 9 | 9 | 6 | 3 | 1 | 3 | | 4 | 8 | 3 | 4 | 1 | | | | | | 47 | 8 | 2 | | | |
| 2 | Uterus, disease of | | | | | | | | | | 1 | | | | | | | | | 1 | | | | | |
| 3 | Worms | | 1 | 5 | 9 | 1 | 1 | | | | | | | | | | | | | 15 | 1 | | | | |
| 4 | Unknown | 378 | 312 | 104 | 72 | 33 | 14 | 24 | 20 | 143 | 116 | 107 | 109 | 20 | 21 | | 3 | 66 | 30 | 1387 | 37 | 6 | 2 | | |
| | Total | 1584 | 1234 | 2355 | 2063 | 609 | 485 | 487 | 744 | 2636 | 2745 | 1732 | 1568 | 457 | 530 | 2 | 5 | 116 | 52 | 15264 | 116 | 195 | 36 | 27 | 14 |

CLASSIFICATION OF DEATHS IN

| | Cause of Death. | Under 1. M. | Under 1. F. | 1 and under 5. M. | 1 and under 5. F. | 5 and under 10. M. | 5 and under 10. F. | 10 and under 20. M. | 10 and under 20. F. | 20 and under 50. M. | 20 and under 50. F. | 50 and under 80. M. | 50 and under 80. F. | 80 and under 100. M. | 80 and under 100. F. | 100 & over. M | 100 & over. F. | Age unknown. M | Age unknown. F. | Born in State. | N. England States. | Middle States. | Southern States. | Southwest'n States. | Northwest'n States. |
|---|---|---|---|---|---|---|---|---|---|---|---|---|---|---|---|---|---|---|---|---|---|---|---|---|---|
| 1 | Abscess | | | | | 1 | 1 | 1 | | 1 | | | 1 | 1 | | | | | | 2 | 1 | 1 | | | 1 |
| 2 | Accident, not specif'd | 1 | 5 | 10 | 3 | 5 | | 8 | | 32 | | 11 | 1 | | | | | | | 22 | 6 | 20 | 3 | | 3 |
| 3 | ....do...burned | 1 | 1 | 9 | 2 | | | | 1 | | | | 1 | 1 | | | | | | 11 | 1 | 2 | | | 1 |
| 4 | ....do...drowned | | | 9 | 2 | 5 | | 1 | | 16 | | 3 | | | | | | | | 14 | 6 | 4 | 1 | | 2 |
| 5 | ....do...scalded | 1 | | 8 | 4 | | | | | | | | | | | | | | | 12 | | 1 | | | |
| 6 | ....do...expl. steam | | | | | | | | | 1 | | | | | | | | | | | 1 | | | | |
| 7 | Apoplexy | | | | | | | | 1 | 4 | 2 | 9 | 6 | | | | | | | 5 | 11 | 6 | | | |
| 8 | Asthma | | | | | | | | | | | 2 | | | | | | | | | | 1 | | | |
| 9 | Bowels, disease of | 2 | 2 | 1 | | 1 | | | | 2 | | 2 | | | | | | | | 4 | | 3 | | | |
| 10 | Brain .......do | 2 | 4 | 1 | 3 | | | | | 2 | | 1 | 1 | | | | | | | 8 | 1 | 2 | | | |
| 11 | Bronchitis | 2 | | 1 | | 1 | 1 | 1 | | 1 | 1 | | | | | | | | | 3 | | 4 | | | |
| 12 | Cancer | 1 | 2 | | | | | | | | 7 | 2 | 7 | | | | | | | 5 | 4 | 4 | | | |
| 13 | Catarrh | 3 | 3 | 2 | 2 | | | | | | 1 | | | | | | | | | 10 | | 1 | | | |
| 14 | Childbirth | | | | | | | | 4 | | 60 | | 1 | | | | | | 1 | 9 | 6 | 38 | | | |
| 15 | Cholera | 4 | 6 | 8 | 8 | 9 | | 7 | 8 | 47 | 18 | 17 | 4 | 2 | 1 | | | | 1 | 40 | 2 | 22 | | 1 | 6 |
| 16 | ...do..infantum | 1 | 3 | 6 | 2 | 1 | | | | | | | | | | | | | | 7 | | 1 | | | 1 |
| 17 | ...do..morbus | 2 | 1 | 4 | 5 | | 2 | | 1 | 6 | 4 | 8 | 7 | | | | | | | 10 | 7 | 9 | | 1 | 3 |
| 18 | Colic | | | | | 1 | | | 1 | 3 | | | | 1 | | | | | | 1 | | 4 | | | |
| 19 | Congest'n, not specf'd | 5 | 6 | 6 | 4 | 4 | 3 | 2 | 1 | 9 | 2 | 3 | 1 | 1 | | | | | | 27 | 2 | 15 | 1 | | 2 |
| 20 | ....do....bowels | | | | | 1 | 1 | | | 2 | | | | | | | | | | 2 | | 1 | | | |
| 21 | ....do....brain | 5 | 4 | 7 | 9 | 2 | | 11 | 7 | 7 | 9 | 1 | | | | | | | | 37 | 5 | 17 | | | 2 |
| 22 | ....do....lungs | 1 | 2 | 2 | 1 | | | 1 | | 2 | 2 | 3 | 3 | | | | | | | 5 | 4 | 8 | | | |
| 23 | Consumption | 15 | 18 | 20 | 14 | 6 | 5 | 18 | 47 | 151 | 224 | 74 | 64 | | | | | 1 | | 119 | 127 | 278 | 11 | 1 | 27 |
| 24 | Convulsions | 39 | 32 | 17 | 21 | 7 | | 1 | 2 | 2 | 4 | 5 | 4 | | | | | | | 109 | 1 | 10 | | | 4 |
| 25 | Cramp | 1 | | | 1 | | | | | 1 | | | | | | | | | | 2 | | 1 | | | |
| 26 | Croup | 17 | 10 | 39 | 30 | 4 | 2 | | | | | | | | | | | | | 91 | 1 | 5 | | | 3 |
| 27 | Debility | 10 | 3 | | | | | | | 1 | 1 | | 5 | | 1 | | | | | 12 | 2 | 4 | | | |
| 28 | Diabetes | | | | | 2 | | 2 | | 3 | | 2 | | | | | | | | 3 | 3 | 3 | | | |
| 29 | Diarrhœa | 18 | 16 | 21 | 18 | 5 | 4 | 1 | 4 | 12 | 5 | 7 | 3 | | 1 | | | | | 83 | 8 | 16 | | | 5 |
| 30 | Dropsy | 10 | 10 | 14 | 12 | 6 | 2 | 2 | 6 | 12 | 40 | 17 | 20 | | | | | | | 60 | 23 | 53 | | | 4 |
| 31 | Dysentery | 34 | 17 | 66 | 63 | 14 | 11 | 11 | 8 | 13 | 18 | 11 | 11 | | 1 | | | 1 | 1 | 204 | 8 | 43 | 1 | | 6 |
| 32 | Dyspepsia | | | | | | | | | 1 | 2 | 1 | 1 | | | | | | | | 3 | 1 | | | |
| 33 | Epilepsy | | | | 1 | | 1 | | | | | | | | | | | | | 2 | | | | | |
| 34 | Erysipelas | 8 | 5 | 9 | 8 | 5 | 4 | 1 | 2 | 7 | 7 | 5 | | 1 | | | | | | 38 | 4 | 15 | 1 | | 3 |
| 35 | Fever, not specified | 15 | 19 | 26 | 23 | 9 | 16 | 12 | 20 | 33 | 17 | 23 | 14 | 2 | 1 | | | 1 | | 104 | 23 | 57 | 1 | | 11 |
| 36 | ..do..bilious | 3 | 8 | 7 | 9 | 1 | 1 | 1 | 3 | 10 | 6 | 8 | 2 | | | | | | | 24 | 3 | 12 | 1 | | 3 |
| 37 | ..do..brain | 9 | 5 | 12 | 8 | 10 | 8 | 9 | 5 | 12 | 8 | 2 | 1 | | | | | | | 52 | 6 | 27 | | | 2 |
| 38 | ..do..congestive | 5 | 1 | 6 | 4 | 5 | 7 | 4 | 3 | 15 | 8 | 7 | 3 | | | | | | | 27 | 10 | 24 | | | 1 |
| 39 | ..do..inflammatory | | | | 1 | | 1 | | 1 | | 1 | 1 | | | | | | | | 2 | 1 | 2 | | | |
| 40 | ..do..intermittent | 3 | 6 | 5 | 6 | | 2 | 8 | 1 | 3 | 5 | 1 | 4 | 2 | 1 | | | | | 24 | 4 | 6 | | | 3 |
| 41 | ..do..puerperal | | | | | | | | 1 | | 7 | | | | | | | | | | 1 | 6 | | | |
| 42 | ..do..scarlet | 4 | 2 | 11 | 14 | 9 | 4 | 5 | 4 | 1 | | | | | | | | | | 43 | | 8 | | | 3 |
| 43 | ..do..ship | | | | | | | 1 | | 1 | | 1 | | | | | | | | 1 | | 1 | | | |
| 44 | ..do..typhus | | | | 3 | 1 | | 6 | 8 | 19 | 8 | 5 | 5 | | | | | | | 16 | 10 | 18 | 4 | | 3 |
| 45 | Fistula | | | | | | | | | | | | 1 | | | | | | | | 1 | | | | |
| 46 | Gravel | | 1 | | | | | | | | | 5 | 1 | 2 | | | | | | 1 | 1 | 4 | | | |
| 47 | Head, disease of | | 1 | | 1 | 1 | 3 | | 1 | 5 | | 1 | | | | | | | | 9 | 3 | | | | 1 |
| 48 | Heart....do | 2 | | 1 | | | | 3 | 7 | 1 | 6 | 6 | 4 | | | | | | | 8 | 6 | 13 | | | |
| 49 | Heat | | | | | | | | | | | 1 | | | | | | | | | | 1 | | | |
| 50 | Hemorrhage | | 1 | 1 | 1 | | | 1 | | 3 | 3 | 5 | | | | | | | | 2 | 3 | 5 | | | 1 |
| 51 | Hernia | | | | | | | | | 1 | | | | | | | | | | 1 | | 1 | | | |
| 52 | Hip, disease of | | | 1 | | | | | | | | 1 | | | | | | | | | 1 | | | | |
| 53 | Hooping cough | 16 | 18 | 10 | 25 | 2 | 2 | | | | | | | | | | | | | 66 | | 2 | | | 4 |
| 54 | Hydrocephalus | 7 | 7 | 7 | 7 | 1 | | 1 | 3 | | 2 | | | | | | | | | 28 | 1 | 5 | | | 1 |
| 55 | Hydrophobia | | | | | | | | | 1 | | | | | | | | | | | 1 | | | | |
| 56 | Inflamat'n, not spec'd | 18 | 19 | 15 | 18 | 8 | 3 | 11 | 5 | 15 | 13 | 9 | 3 | 1 | 2 | | | 1 | | 83 | 5 | 41 | | | 4 |
| 57 | ....do.....bowels | 6 | 3 | 7 | 9 | 2 | 2 | 3 | 3 | 5 | 2 | | 2 | | | | | | | 28 | 1 | 9 | 1 | | 1 |
| 58 | ....do.....brain | 17 | 8 | 18 | 5 | 6 | 5 | 5 | 3 | 5 | 8 | 3 | | | | | | | | 51 | 5 | 15 | 1 | | 7 |
| 59 | ....do.....stomach | | | | | | | | | 2 | | | | | | | | | | 1 | | 1 | | | |
| 60 | Influenza | 1 | | | 2 | | | | | | | | 1 | | | | | | | 3 | 1 | | | | |
| 61 | Insanity | | | | | | | 1 | | | | | 1 | | 1 | | | | | 1 | 1 | 1 | | | |

## THE STATE OF MASSACHUSETTS—AGGREGATE—Continued.

| NATIVITIES. | | | | | SEASON OF DECEASE. | | | | DURATION OF SICKNESS. | | | | WHITES. | | | COLORED. | | | | | | | | | |
|---|---|---|---|---|---|---|---|---|---|---|---|---|---|---|---|---|---|---|---|---|---|---|---|---|---|
| | | | | | | | | | | | | | | | | Slaves. | | | | Free. | | | | | |
| | | | | | | | | | | | | | | | | Black. | | Mulatto. | | Black. | | Mul. | | | |
| California and Territories. | Ireland. | Germany. | Other foreign countries. | Unknown. | Spring. | Summer. | Autumn. | Winter. | Under 1 week. | 1 week and under 1 month. | 1 month and under 8 months. | 8 months and over. | Males. | Females. | Total. | M. | F. | M. | F. | M. | F. | M | F. | Aggregate deaths. | |
| | 8 | | | | 8 | 15 | 24 | 11 | 5 | 23 | 4 | 10 | 32 | 28 | 60 | | | | | | | | | 60 | 1 |
| | | | | | | | 1 | | | | | | | 1 | 1 | | | | | | | | | 1 | 2 |
| | 1 | | | | 10 | 1 | 3 | 3 | 8 | 4 | 2 | | 6 | 11 | 17 | | | | | | | | | 17 | 3 |
| | 112 | 8 | 23 | 2 | 866 | 885 | 544 | 327 | 209 | 336 | 85 | 70 | 868 | 690 | 1558 | | | | | 7 | 5 | | 2 | 1572 | 4 |
| 1 | 2140 | 22 | 520 | 15 | 3945 | 3964 | 7645 | 3588 | 4244 | 5326 | 1343 | 3156 | 9901 | 9354 | 19255 | | | | | 70 | 59 | 7 | 13 | 19404 | |

## THE STATE OF MICHIGAN.

| Cal. | Ireland. | Germany. | Other. | Unknown. | Spring. | Summer. | Autumn. | Winter. | Under 1 week. | 1 week–1 month. | 1–8 months. | 8 months and over. | Males. | Females. | Total. | Sl. Bl. M. | Sl. Bl. F. | Sl. Mul. M. | Sl. Mul. F. | Fr. Bl. M. | Fr. Bl. F. | Fr. Mul. M | Fr. Mul. F. | Aggregate deaths. | |
|---|---|---|---|---|---|---|---|---|---|---|---|---|---|---|---|---|---|---|---|---|---|---|---|---|---|
| | 1 | | | | 2 | 2 | 1 | 1 | 1 | | 1 | 4 | 4 | 2 | 6 | | | | | | | | | 6 | 1 |
| | 5 | 4 | 18 | | 22 | 22 | 18 | 14 | 55 | 13 | 2 | 8 | 67 | 9 | 76 | | | | | | | | | 76 | 2 |
| | 1 | | | | 8 | 6 | 2 | 5 | 10 | 1 | 1 | | 11 | 5 | 16 | | | | | | | | | 16 | 3 |
| | 4 | 3 | 2 | | 8 | 11 | 9 | 11 | 86 | | | | 82 | 2 | 84 | | | | | 1 | | 1 | | 86 | 4 |
| | | | | | 3 | 3 | 3 | 3 | 7 | 1 | | | 9 | 4 | 13 | | | | | | | | | 13 | 5 |
| | | | | | 1 | | | | 1 | | | | 1 | | 1 | | | | | | | | | 1 | 6 |
| | | | | | 7 | 5 | 5 | 5 | 20 | 2 | | | 13 | 9 | 22 | | | | | | | | | 22 | 7 |
| | 1 | | | | | 1 | 1 | | | | 2 | | 2 | | 2 | | | | | | | | | 2 | 8 |
| | | | 1 | 2 | 5 | 2 | 2 | 1 | 5 | 5 | | | 8 | 2 | 10 | | | | | | | | | 10 | 9 |
| | 1 | | 1 | 1 | 3 | 5 | 5 | 1 | 6 | 5 | 3 | | 6 | 8 | 14 | | | | | | | | | 14 | 10 |
| | | | 1 | | 1 | 3 | 3 | 1 | | 5 | 1 | 2 | 6 | 2 | 8 | | | | | | | | | 8 | 11 |
| | 1 | | 4 | 1 | 2 | 10 | 5 | 2 | 1 | 7 | 2 | 8 | 3 | 16 | 19 | | | | | | | | | 19 | 12 |
| | | | | | 3 | 8 | | 5 | 3 | 7 | 1 | | 5 | 6 | 11 | | | | | | | | | 11 | 13 |
| | 3 | 4 | 6 | | 16 | 15 | 17 | 12 | 8 | 33 | 1 | 1 | | 66 | 66 | | | | | | | | | 66 | 14 |
| | 30 | 14 | 23 | 2 | 2 | 72 | 68 | 1 | 126 | 12 | | | 91 | 46 | 137 | | | | | 3 | | | | 140 | 15 |
| | | | 4 | | | 6 | 5 | 2 | 4 | 7 | 1 | 1 | 8 | 5 | 13 | | | | | | | | | 13 | 16 |
| | 2 | 4 | 4 | | 4 | 15 | 18 | 3 | 32 | 6 | 2 | | 20 | 20 | 40 | | | | | | | | | 40 | 17 |
| | 1 | | | | 1 | 3 | | 2 | 6 | | | | 5 | 1 | 6 | | | | | | | | | 6 | 18 |
| | | | | | 16 | 7 | 17 | 5 | 25 | 20 | | 2 | 28 | 17 | 45 | | | | | 2 | | | | 47 | 19 |
| | 1 | | | | | | 2 | 1 | | | 2 | 1 | 3 | 1 | 4 | | | | | | | | | 4 | 20 |
| | | | 1 | | 11 | 9 | 22 | 18 | 36 | 23 | 1 | 1 | 33 | 29 | 62 | | | | | | | | | 62 | 21 |
| | | | | | 5 | 6 | 2 | 4 | 7 | 9 | | 1 | 9 | 8 | 17 | | | | | | | | | 17 | 22 |
| | 29 | 13 | 51 | 1 | 174 | 164 | 160 | 150 | 23 | 89 | 99 | 423 | 281 | 369 | 650 | | | | | 4 | 2 | | 1 | 657 | 23 |
| | 2 | 1 | 6 | 1 | 42 | 18 | 45 | 26 | 104 | 19 | 1 | 8 | 71 | 62 | 133 | | | | | | 1 | | | 134 | 24 |
| | | | | | | 1 | 1 | 1 | 3 | | | | 2 | 1 | 3 | | | | | | | | | 3 | 25 |
| | | | 2 | | 34 | 20 | 19 | 29 | 79 | 21 | 1 | | 60 | 42 | 102 | | | | | | | | | 102 | 26 |
| | | | 2 | 1 | 5 | 7 | 5 | 4 | 8 | 5 | 2 | 6 | 10 | 10 | 20 | | | | | | | 1 | | 21 | 27 |
| | | | | | 2 | 2 | 2 | 3 | | 4 | 1 | 4 | 9 | | 9 | | | | | | | | | 9 | 28 |
| | 1 | 1 | 1 | | 14 | 17 | 61 | 18 | 36 | 53 | 10 | 12 | 64 | 50 | 114 | | | | | | | | 1 | 115 | 29 |
| | 2 | 2 | 6 | 1 | 40 | 41 | 32 | 37 | 13 | 48 | 29 | 58 | 60 | 89 | 149 | | | | | | 1 | 1 | | 151 | 30 |
| | 4 | 2 | 11 | 1 | 14 | 85 | 194 | 29 | 74 | 179 | 14 | 2 | 150 | 130 | 280 | | | | | | | | | 280 | 31 |
| 2 | | | 1 | | | 2 | 2 | 1 | 1 | | | 4 | 2 | 3 | 5 | | | | | | | | | 5 | 32 |
| | | | | | 2 | | | | 2 | | | | | 2 | 2 | | | | | | | | | 2 | 33 |
| | 1 | | | | 17 | 15 | 16 | 14 | 13 | 36 | 6 | 6 | 36 | 26 | 62 | | | | | | | | | 62 | 34 |
| | 12 | 5 | 17 | 1 | 44 | 36 | 118 | 32 | 57 | 127 | 35 | 6 | 120 | 109 | 229 | | | | | 1 | 1 | | | 231 | 35 |
| | | 2 | 14 | | 7 | 14 | 30 | 8 | 16 | 35 | 6 | 2 | 29 | 29 | 58 | | | | | | | 1 | | 59 | 36 |
| | 1 | | 1 | | 28 | 20 | 23 | 17 | 50 | 34 | 2 | 1 | 54 | 35 | 89 | | | | | | | | | 89 | 37 |
| | 1 | | 5 | | 18 | 15 | 26 | 13 | 22 | 42 | 2 | 2 | 42 | 26 | 68 | | | | | | | | | 68 | 38 |
| | | | | | | 2 | 1 | 2 | 1 | 3 | | | 1 | 4 | 5 | | | | | | | | | 5 | 39 |
| | | | 5 | | 4 | 8 | 22 | 8 | 9 | 23 | 5 | 2 | 17 | 25 | 42 | | | | | | | | | 42 | 40 |
| | | | 1 | | 5 | | 1 | 2 | 2 | 6 | | | | 8 | 8 | | | | | | | | | 8 | 41 |
| | | | | | 21 | 7 | 13 | 12 | 16 | 32 | 2 | | 29 | 24 | 53 | | | | | 1 | | | | 54 | 42 |
| | 1 | | | | 1 | 1 | 1 | | | 2 | 1 | | 3 | | 3 | | | | | | | | | 3 | 43 |
| | 2 | | 2 | | 9 | 15 | 18 | 12 | 7 | 34 | 11 | 2 | 31 | 24 | 55 | | | | | | | | | 55 | 44 |
| | | | | | 1 | | | | | | | 1 | | 1 | 1 | | | | | | | | | 1 | 45 |
| | 3 | | | | 5 | | 4 | | 1 | 5 | 1 | 2 | 7 | 2 | 9 | | | | | | | | | 9 | 46 |
| | | | | | 4 | 5 | 2 | 2 | 8 | 5 | | | 7 | 6 | 13 | | | | | | | | | 13 | 47 |
| | 2 | | 1 | | 9 | 4 | 9 | 7 | 7 | 9 | 6 | 7 | 13 | 17 | 30 | | | | | | | | | 30 | 48 |
| | | | | | | 1 | | | 1 | | | | 1 | | 1 | | | | | | | | | 1 | 49 |
| | 1 | | 8 | | 6 | 8 | 2 | 4 | 11 | 4 | | | 10 | 5 | 15 | | | | | | | | | 15 | 50 |
| | | | | | | | 1 | | 1 | 1 | | | 2 | | 2 | | | | | | | | | 2 | 51 |
| | | | | | | 1 | | | | 1 | | | 1 | | 1 | | | | | | | | | 1 | 52 |
| | | | 1 | | 17 | 17 | 29 | 8 | 13 | 42 | 16 | 2 | 27 | 44 | 71 | | | | | 1 | | | 1 | 73 | 53 |
| | | | | | 14 | 7 | 6 | 8 | 9 | 18 | 5 | 3 | 16 | 18 | 34 | | | | | | 1 | | | 35 | 54 |
| | | | | | | | | 1 | 1 | | | | 1 | | 1 | | | | | | | | | 1 | 55 |
| | 3 | | 5 | | 36 | 36 | 38 | 32 | 49 | 74 | 9 | 6 | 75 | 61 | 136 | | | | | 3 | 2 | | | 141 | 56 |
| | 1 | 1 | 2 | | 12 | 9 | 15 | 8 | 12 | 23 | 1 | 3 | 23 | 21 | 44 | | | | | | | | | 44 | 57 |
| | | 1 | 2 | 1 | 25 | 15 | 22 | 21 | 36 | 33 | 7 | 2 | 54 | 28 | 82 | | | | | | 1 | | | 83 | 58 |
| | | | | | 1 | 1 | | | | 2 | | | 2 | | 2 | | | | | | | | | 2 | 59 |
| | | | | | 2 | | 2 | | 1 | 3 | | | 1 | 3 | 4 | | | | | | | | | 4 | 60 |
| | | | | | | 1 | | 2 | | | | 3 | 1 | 2 | 3 | | | | | | | | | 3 | 61 |

## CLASSIFICATION OF DEATHS IN

| | Cause of death. | AGES. | | | | | | | | | | | | | | | | | | NATIVITIES. | | | | | |
|---|---|---|---|---|---|---|---|---|---|---|---|---|---|---|---|---|---|---|---|---|---|---|---|---|---|
| | | Under 1. | | 1 and under 5. | | 5 and under 10. | | 10 and under 20. | | 20 and under 50. | | 50 and under 80. | | 80 and under 100. | | 100 & over. | | Age unknown. | | Born in State. | N. England States. | Middle States. | Southern States. | Southwest'n States. | Northwest'n States. |
| | | M. | F. | M. | F. | M. | F. | M. | F. | M. | F. | M. | F. | M | F. | M | F. | M | F | | | | | | |
| 1 | Intemperance | .... | .. | .... | .... | .... | .... | .... | .... | 1 | .... | 7 | ... | 2 | 1 | .. | .. | .. | .. | 3 | 1 | 4 | ... | ... | .. |
| 2 | Jaundice | .... | 2 | 1 | 2 | 2 | 1 | .... | .... | .... | .... | .... | 1 | .. | .. | .. | .. | .. | .. | 8 | 1 | ... | ... | ... | .. |
| 3 | Kidneys, disease of | .... | 1 | .... | 1 | 1 | .... | .... | .... | .... | 1 | 3 | ... | .. | .. | .. | .. | .. | .. | 3 | 1 | 1 | ... | ... | .. |
| 4 | Killed | .... | ... | 2 | 2 | 2 | 1 | 2 | .... | .... | .... | 8 | 1 | 1 | .. | .. | .. | .. | .. | 6 | 1 | 8 | ... | ... | 2 |
| 5 | Liver, disease of | 1 | ... | 2 | 1 | 1 | 1 | 2 | ... | 6 | 5 | 6 | 3 | .. | .. | .. | .. | .. | | 7 | 2 | 18 | ... | ... | .. |
| 6 | Lockjaw | .... | .... | .... | .... | .... | .... | .... | .... | .... | .... | 1 | ... | .. | .. | .. | .. | .. | .. | ... | ... | 1 | ... | ... | .. |
| 7 | Lungs, disease of | 6 | 2 | 2 | 1 | 1 | ... | 2 | 1 | 6 | 2 | 5 | ... | .. | .. | .. | .. | .. | .. | 13 | 2 | 9 | ... | ... | .. |
| 8 | Mania-a-potu | .... | .... | .... | .... | .... | .... | .... | .... | 1 | .... | ... | ... | .. | .. | .. | .. | .. | .. | ... | ... | ... | ... | ... | .. |
| 9 | Measles | 9 | 2 | 15 | 14 | 2 | 2 | ... | 1 | 2 | 2 | ... | ... | .. | .. | .. | .. | .. | .. | 37 | ... | 6 | ... | ... | .. |
| 10 | Mortification | .... | .... | 1 | ... | 1 | .... | .... | 1 | .... | .... | ... | ... | .. | .. | .. | .. | .. | .. | 3 | ... | ... | ... | ... | .. |
| 11 | Mumps | .... | .... | 1 | 1 | .... | .... | .... | .... | .... | .... | ... | ... | .. | .. | .. | .. | .. | .. | 2 | ... | ... | ... | ... | .. |
| 12 | Neuralgia | .... | .... | .... | .... | .... | .... | 1 | ... | .... | .... | ... | ... | .. | .. | .. | .. | .. | .. | 1 | ... | ... | ... | ... | .. |
| 13 | Old age | .... | .... | .... | .... | .... | .... | .... | .... | .... | .... | 31 | 81 | 26 | 19 | .. | 2 | .. | | 7 | 32 | 43 | ... | ... | .. |
| 14 | Paralysis | 1 | ... | 1 | .... | .... | .... | .... | 1 | 3 | 3 | 6 | 7 | 1 | .. | .. | .. | .. | .. | 3 | 6 | 11 | ... | ... | .. |
| 15 | Peritonitis | .... | .... | .... | .... | .... | .... | .... | .... | .... | 1 | ... | ... | .. | .. | .. | .. | .. | .. | ... | ... | 1 | ... | ... | .. |
| 16 | Pleurisy | .... | .... | .... | .... | .... | .... | .... | .... | 6 | 2 | 5 | 5 | 1 | .. | .. | .. | .. | .. | 2 | 6 | 8 | ... | ... | .. |
| 17 | Pneumonia | 52 | 30 | 32 | 31 | 8 | 9 | 11 | 11 | 62 | 24 | 41 | 15 | .. | .. | .. | .. | .. | .. | 159 | 39 | 34 | 6 | ... | 9 |
| 18 | Poison | 1 | 2 | 1 | 1 | 1 | ... | 2 | .... | .... | 1 | ... | 1 | .. | .. | .. | .. | .. | .. | 8 | ... | ... | ... | ... | .. |
| 19 | Quinsy | .... | .... | 2 | 2 | .... | .... | .... | .... | .... | 1 | 1 | ... | .. | .. | .. | .. | .. | .. | 5 | ... | ... | ... | ... | .. |
| 20 | Rheumatism | .... | .... | 1 | ... | 2 | 1 | 4 | 1 | 2 | 1 | 1 | 2 | .. | .. | .. | .. | .. | .. | 5 | 5 | 5 | ... | ... | .. |
| 21 | Scrofula | 8 | ... | 8 | 3 | 2 | 8 | 4 | 8 | 5 | 2 | 8 | ... | .. | .. | .. | .. | .. | .. | 15 | 3 | 10 | ... | ... | .. |
| 22 | Scurvy | .... | .... | .... | 1 | .... | .... | .... | .... | .... | .... | ... | ... | .. | .. | .. | .. | .. | .. | ... | ... | ... | ... | ... | .. |
| 23 | Small pox | 2 | 2 | 5 | 2 | 2 | 8 | 4 | 1 | 2 | 3 | ... | ... | .. | .. | .. | .. | .. | .. | 15 | ... | 4 | ... | ... | 2 |
| 24 | Spine, disease of | 1 | 2 | 1 | 1 | .... | .... | .... | .... | .... | 2 | 2 | ... | .. | .. | .. | .. | .. | .. | 3 | ... | 4 | ... | ... | 2 |
| 25 | Spleen....do | .... | .... | .... | 1 | .... | .... | .... | .... | .... | .... | ... | ... | .. | .. | .. | .. | .. | .. | 1 | ... | ... | ... | ... | .. |
| 26 | Stillborn | .... | 4 | .... | .... | .... | .... | .... | .... | .... | .... | ... | ... | .. | .. | .. | .. | .. | .. | 4 | ... | ... | ... | ... | .. |
| 27 | Stomach, disease of | .... | .... | .... | .... | .... | .... | .... | .... | .... | 1 | ... | ... | .. | .. | .. | .. | .. | .. | 1 | ... | ... | ... | ... | .. |
| 28 | Suffocation | .... | .... | 1 | .... | .... | .... | .... | .... | .... | .... | ... | ... | .. | .. | .. | .. | .. | .. | 1 | ... | ... | ... | ... | .. |
| 29 | Suicide | .... | .... | .... | .... | .... | .... | 1 | ... | 4 | 2 | 1 | 1 | .. | .. | .. | .. | .. | .. | ... | ... | 5 | ... | ... | .. |
| 30 | Summer complaint | .... | 2 | 1 | 1 | .... | .... | .... | .... | .... | .... | ... | ... | .. | .. | .. | .. | .. | .. | 4 | ... | ... | ... | ... | .. |
| 31 | Sun, stroke of | .... | .... | .... | .... | .... | .... | 1 | .... | .... | .... | ... | ... | .. | .. | .. | .. | .. | .. | ... | ... | ... | ... | ... | .. |
| 32 | Teething | 6 | 3 | 2 | 8 | .... | .... | .... | .... | .... | .... | ... | ... | .. | .. | .. | .. | .. | .. | 18 | ... | ... | ... | ... | .. |
| 33 | Throat, disease of | 1 | ... | 1 | 3 | 2 | .... | .... | .... | .... | .... | ... | ... | .. | .. | .. | .. | .. | .. | 7 | ... | ... | ... | ... | .. |
| 34 | Thrush | 3 | ... | .... | .... | .... | .... | .... | .... | .... | .... | ... | ... | .. | .. | .. | .. | .. | .. | 3 | ... | ... | ... | ... | .. |
| 35 | Ulcer | 8 | 8 | 2 | 8 | 1 | ... | 2 | 1 | 1 | 1 | ... | ... | .. | .. | .. | .. | .. | .. | 15 | ... | 3 | ... | ... | 1 |
| 36 | White swelling | .... | .... | .... | .... | .... | .... | 1 | .... | .... | .... | ... | ... | .. | .. | .. | .. | .. | .. | ... | ... | 1 | ... | ... | .. |
| 37 | Worms | .... | 1 | 10 | 7 | 1 | 2 | .... | .... | .... | 1 | ... | ... | .. | .. | .. | .. | .. | .. | 17 | ... | 2 | ... | ... | .. |
| 38 | Unknown | 100 | 83 | 32 | 33 | 7 | 11 | 14 | 13 | 37 | 52 | 38 | 17 | 1 | .. | .. | .. | 8 | 2 | 313 | 30 | 77 | 3 | ... | 6 |
| | Total | 478 | 863 | 506 | 473 | 171 | 125 | 180 | 195 | 603 | 608 | 421 | 267 | 46 | 29 | .. | 2 | 7 | 5 | 2221 | 454 | 1157 | 85 | 8 | 140 |

## CLASSIFICATION OF DEATHS IN NORTHWEST

*Embracing the following counties : Bolivar, Carroll, Coahoma, Desoto, Holmes, Lafa*

| | | | | | | | | | | | | | | | | | | | | | | | | | |
|---|---|---|---|---|---|---|---|---|---|---|---|---|---|---|---|---|---|---|---|---|---|---|---|---|---|
| 1 | Abscess | .... | .... | .... | .... | .... | .... | .... | .... | 1 | .... | ... | ... | .. | .. | .. | .. | .. | .. | ... | ... | ... | ... | 1 | ... |
| 2 | Accident not specif'd | 5 | 3 | 3 | 2 | 5 | .. | 4 | 2 | 3 | 2 | ... | 1 | .. | .. | .. | .. | .. | .. | 19 | ... | ... | 4 | 5 | 1 |
| 3 | ...do...burned | 2 | 4 | 6 | 7 | 2 | 7 | 1 | 5 | .... | .... | ... | ... | .. | .. | .. | .. | .. | .. | 30 | ... | ... | 1 | 1 | 1 |
| 4 | ...do...drowned | .... | ... | 1 | ... | ... | 2 | 5 | 1 | 12 | 3 | 1 | ... | .. | .. | .. | .. | .. | .. | 11 | .. | 1 | 5 | 4 | 1 |
| 5 | ...do...scalded | .... | 1 | 1 | ... | .... | .... | .... | .... | .... | .... | ... | ... | .. | .. | .. | .. | .. | .. | 2 | ... | ... | ... | ... | ... |
| 6 | ...do...shot | .... | .... | .... | .... | .... | .... | .... | .... | 4 | .... | ... | ... | .. | .. | .. | .. | .. | .. | 2 | ... | ... | 2 | ... | ... |
| 7 | Aneurism | .... | .... | .... | .... | .... | .... | .... | 1 | .... | .... | ... | ... | .. | .. | .. | .. | .. | .. | ... | ... | ... | 1 | ... | ... |
| 8 | Apoplexy | .... | .... | .... | .... | .... | .... | .... | 2 | 2 | 8 | 2 | ... | .. | .. | .. | .. | .. | .. | ... | ... | ... | 5 | 8 | 1 |
| 9 | Asthma | 1 | ... | 1 | ... | .... | .... | .... | .... | .... | 1 | 1 | ... | .. | .. | .. | .. | .. | .. | 3 | ... | ... | ... | 1 | ... |
| 10 | Black tongue | .... | .... | 1 | ... | .... | .... | .... | .... | .... | .... | 1 | ... | .. | .. | .. | .. | .. | .. | 1 | ... | ... | ... | ... | ... |
| 11 | Bowels disease of | 8 | 9 | 6 | 9 | 1 | ... | ... | 1 | 1 | 1 | ... | ... | .. | .. | .. | .. | .. | .. | 38 | ... | ... | 2 | 1 | ... |
| 12 | Brain......do | 1 | 5 | .... | 1 | .... | .... | .... | .... | .... | .... | ... | ... | .. | .. | .. | .. | .. | .. | 7 | ... | ... | ... | ... | ... |
| 13 | Bronchitis | 2 | 1 | .... | 1 | 1 | ... | ... | ... | 2 | .... | ... | ... | .. | 1 | .. | .. | .. | .. | 5 | ... | ... | 3 | 1 | ... |
| 14 | Cancer | .... | .... | .... | .... | .... | .... | .... | .... | .... | .... | 1 | 1 | .. | .. | .. | .. | .. | .. | 1 | ... | ... | 1 | ... | ... |
| 15 | Catarrh | 13 | 6 | 6 | 5 | ... | 8 | ... | ... | 1 | 4 | 1 | ... | .. | .. | .. | .. | .. | .. | 85 | ... | ... | 2 | 2 | ... |
| 16 | Childbirth | .... | .... | .... | .... | .... | .... | .... | 5 | ... | 19 | ... | ... | .. | .. | .. | .. | .. | .. | 10 | ... | ... | 10 | 3 | 1 |
| 17 | Cholera | 2 | 2 | 26 | 24 | 8 | 10 | 16 | 11 | 73 | 17 | 14 | 7 | .. | .. | .. | .. | .. | .. | 118 | .. | 2 | 46 | 40 | 19 |
| 18 | ...do..infantum | 5 | 9 | 4 | 6 | 1 | ... | .... | .... | .... | .... | ... | ... | .. | .. | .. | .. | .. | .. | 24 | ... | ... | ... | 1 | ... |
| 19 | ...do..morbus | .... | ... | 1 | 2 | 1 | ... | 1 | ... | 2 | 1 | ... | 1 | .. | .. | .. | .. | .. | .. | 7 | ... | ... | 1 | 1 | ... |
| 20 | Colic | .... | .... | 1 | .... | .... | .... | 1 | ... | .... | 1 | ... | ... | .. | .. | .. | .. | .. | .. | 3 | ... | ... | ... | ... | ... |
| 21 | Congestion | .... | 1 | 6 | 2 | 2 | ... | 1 | 4 | 3 | 1 | ... | ... | .. | 1 | .. | .. | .. | .. | 16 | ... | ... | 2 | 2 | ... |
| 22 | ....do.....brain | 1 | 2 | .... | 4 | 4 | 1 | 2 | ... | 3 | 1 | 2 | ... | .. | .. | .. | .. | .. | .. | 10 | ... | ... | 5 | 4 | ... |
| 23 | ....do.....lungs | .... | .... | 2 | 1 | ... | 1 | ... | ... | 1 | 1 | ... | ... | .. | .. | .. | .. | .. | .. | 4 | ... | ... | 1 | 1 | ... |
| 24 | Consumption | 2 | 8 | 2 | 1 | ... | 8 | 3 | 5 | 22 | 30 | 3 | 8 | .. | 1 | .. | .. | .. | .. | 25 | .. | 8 | 32 | 18 | 4 |
| 25 | Convulsions | 9 | 4 | 8 | 4 | 1 | 2 | 1 | 3 | 3 | 4 | ... | ... | .. | .. | .. | .. | .. | .. | 25 | ... | ... | 4 | 3 | 1 |
| 26 | Cramp | .... | .... | .... | .... | .... | .... | .... | .... | .... | .... | ... | ... | .. | .. | .. | .. | .. | .. | 1 | ... | ... | ... | ... | ... |
| 27 | Croup | 58 | 39 | 20 | 25 | 1 | 1 | ... | ... | .... | .... | ... | ... | .. | .. | .. | .. | .. | .. | 136 | ... | ... | 1 | 1 | ... |
| 28 | Debility | 1 | 5 | 2 | 4 | ... | 1 | ... | ... | .... | .... | 4 | ... | .. | .. | .. | .. | .. | .. | 14 | ... | ... | 2 | 1 | ... |
| 29 | Diabetes | .... | .... | .... | .... | .... | .... | 1 | ... | 1 | .... | ... | ... | .. | .. | .. | .. | .. | .. | ... | ... | ... | ... | 2 | ... |

## HE STATE OF MICHIGAN—Continued.

| ritories. (Nativities) | Ireland. | Germany. | Other foreign countries. | Unknown. | Spring. (Season of decease) | Summer. | Autumn. | Winter. | Under 1 week. (Duration of sickness) | 1 week and under 1 month. | 1 month and under 3 months. | 3 months and over. | Males. (Whites) | Females. | Total. | Colored, Slaves, Black, M. | Slaves, Black, F. | Slaves, Mulatto, M. | Slaves, Mulatto, F. | Free, Black, M. | Free, Black, F. | Free, Mul., M. | Free, Mul., F. | Aggregate deaths. | |
|---|---|---|---|---|---|---|---|---|---|---|---|---|---|---|---|---|---|---|---|---|---|---|---|---|---|
| | 2 | | 1 | | 2 | | 6 | 2 | 5 | 2 | | 4 | 10 | 1 | 11 | | | | | | | | | 11 | 1 |
| | | | | | 5 | 2 | | 2 | 4 | 2 | | 3 | 3 | 6 | 9 | | | | | | | | | 9 | 2 |
| | | 1 | 1 | | 1 | 3 | 2 | 1 | | 2 | 1 | 4 | 4 | 3 | 7 | | | | | | | | | 7 | 3 |
| | 2 | | | | 7 | 3 | 5 | 4 | 18 | 1 | | | 15 | 4 | 19 | | | | | | | | | 19 | 4 |
| | | | 1 | | 6 | 8 | 7 | 7 | 6 | 10 | 8 | 3 | 18 | 10 | 28 | | | | | | | | | 28 | 5 |
| | | | | | | 1 | | | 1 | | | | 1 | | 1 | | | | | | | | | 1 | 6 |
| | 2 | | 1 | 1 | 12 | 6 | 2 | 8 | 8 | 16 | 2 | 1 | 22 | 6 | 28 | | | | | | | | | 28 | 7 |
| | | | | 1 | | 1 | | | 1 | | | | 1 | | 1 | | | | | | | | | 1 | 8 |
| | 4 | 1 | 1 | | 6 | 26 | 16 | | 16 | 28 | 2 | 1 | 28 | 21 | 49 | | | | | | | | | 49 | 9 |
| | | | | | | 2 | | 1 | 1 | | 2 | | 2 | 1 | 3 | | | | | | | | | 3 | 10 |
| | | | | | 2 | | | | 1 | 1 | | | 1 | 1 | 2 | | | | | | | | | 2 | 11 |
| | | | | | | | 1 | | | 1 | | | 1 | | 1 | | | | | | | | | 1 | 12 |
| | 8 | 1 | 18 | | 25 | 22 | 34 | 25 | 20 | 24 | 8 | 52 | 57 | 52 | 109 | | | | | | | | | 109 | 13 |
| | 2 | | 1 | | 8 | 4 | 8 | 3 | 3 | 7 | 1 | 10 | 12 | 11 | 23 | | | | | | | | | 23 | 14 |
| | | | | | | 1 | | | | | | 1 | | 1 | 1 | | | | | | | | | 1 | 15 |
| | 1 | | 2 | | 7 | 7 | 2 | 3 | 6 | 11 | 2 | | 12 | 7 | 19 | | | | | | | | | 19 | 16 |
| | 10 | 4 | 14 | 1 | 151 | 59 | 43 | 67 | 86 | 199 | 20 | 14 | 205 | 118 | 323 | | | | | 1 | 1 | | 1 | 326 | 17 |
| | 1 | | | 1 | 4 | 2 | 3 | | 8 | | 1 | | 5 | 5 | 10 | | | | | | | | | 10 | 18 |
| | 1 | | | | 2 | 1 | 2 | 1 | 2 | 4 | | | 3 | 3 | 6 | | | | | | | | | 6 | 19 |
| | | | | | 3 | 8 | 2 | 1 | 3 | 4 | 1 | 5 | 10 | 5 | 15 | | | | | | | | | 15 | 20 |
| | 1 | 2 | | | 10 | 6 | 6 | 7 | | 9 | 2 | 18 | 20 | 11 | 31 | | | | | | | | | 31 | 21 |
| | | | 1 | | | 1 | | | | 1 | | | | 1 | 1 | | | | | | | | | 1 | 22 |
| | | 3 | 1 | 1 | 8 | 3 | 5 | 8 | 2 | 19 | 2 | 1 | 15 | 11 | 26 | | | | | | | | | 26 | 23 |
| | | | | | 3 | 2 | 3 | 1 | 2 | 3 | 2 | 2 | 4 | 5 | 9 | | | | | | | | | 9 | 24 |
| | | | | | | | 1 | | | | | 1 | | 1 | 1 | | | | | | | | | 1 | 25 |
| | | | | | 1 | | 3 | | | | | | | 4 | 4 | | | | | | | | | 4 | 26 |
| | | | | | | | 1 | | | 1 | | | | 1 | 1 | | | | | | | | | 1 | 27 |
| | | | | | | | | | 1 | | | | 1 | | 1 | | | | | | | | | 1 | 28 |
| | 1 | | 3 | | 3 | 3 | 2 | 1 | 9 | | | | 6 | 3 | 9 | | | | | | | | | 9 | 29 |
| | | | | | | | 4 | | | 1 | | | 1 | 3 | 4 | | | | | | | | | 4 | 30 |
| | | 1 | | | | | 1 | | 1 | | | | 1 | | 1 | | | | | | | | | 1 | 31 |
| | | 1 | | | 5 | 11 | 2 | 1 | 6 | 7 | 6 | | 8 | 11 | 19 | | | | | | | | | 19 | 32 |
| | | | | | 5 | 1 | 1 | | 4 | 3 | | | 4 | 3 | 7 | | | | | | | | | 7 | 33 |
| | | | | | | | | 3 | | 3 | | | 3 | | 3 | | | | | | | | | 3 | 34 |
| | 1 | | 2 | | 6 | 2 | 9 | 5 | 7 | 8 | 3 | 4 | 9 | 13 | 22 | | | | | | | | | 22 | 35 |
| | | | | | 1 | | | | | | | 1 | 1 | | 1 | | | | | | | | | 1 | 36 |
| | 1 | 1 | 1 | | 4 | 8 | 10 | | 14 | 4 | 3 | 1 | 11 | 11 | 22 | | | | | | | | | 22 | 37 |
| | 6 | 2 | 6 | | 112 | 105 | 134 | 78 | 205 | 102 | 26 | 72 | 230 | 211 | 441 | | | | | 2 | | | | 443 | 38 |
| | 160 | 74 | 253 | 18 | 1117 | 1047 | 1425 | 832 | 1584 | 1651 | 384 | 789 | 2400 | 2078 | 4478 | | | | | 19 | 10 | 4 | 4 | 4515 | |

## ECTION OF THE STATE OF MISSISSIPPI.

*ette, Marshall, Panola, Sunflower, Tallahatchie, Tunica, Washington, and Yalabusha.*

| ritories. | Ireland. | Germany. | Other foreign countries. | Unknown. | Spring. | Summer. | Autumn. | Winter. | Under 1 week. | 1 week and under 1 month. | 1 month and under 3 months. | 3 months and over. | Males. | Females. | Total. | Slaves, Black, M. | Slaves, Black, F. | Slaves, Mulatto, M. | Slaves, Mulatto, F. | Free, Black, M. | Free, Black, F. | Free, Mul., M. | Free, Mul., F. | Aggregate deaths. | |
|---|---|---|---|---|---|---|---|---|---|---|---|---|---|---|---|---|---|---|---|---|---|---|---|---|---|
| | | | | | | | | 1 | | 1 | | | 1 | | 1 | | | | | | | | | 1 | 1 |
| | | 1 | | | 6 | 11 | 6 | 7 | 17 | 2 | 1 | | 5 | 2 | 7 | 14 | 8 | 1 | | | | | | 30 | 2 |
| | | | | 1 | 13 | 4 | 6 | 9 | 24 | 4 | 3 | 1 | | 4 | 4 | 9 | 19 | 2 | | | | | | 34 | 3 |
| | | | | 3 | 6 | 9 | 5 | 5 | 25 | | | | 5 | | 5 | 13 | 6 | 1 | | | | | | 25 | 4 |
| | | | | | | | 2 | | 2 | | | | 1 | | 1 | | 1 | | | | | | | 2 | 5 |
| | | | | | 1 | 1 | 2 | | 1 | | | | | | | 4 | | | | | | | | 4 | 6 |
| | | | | | 1 | | | | | | | 1 | | | | | 1 | | | | | | | 1 | 7 |
| | | | | | 4 | 4 | 1 | | 8 | | | | 1 | | 1 | 3 | 5 | | | | | | | 9 | 8 |
| | | | | | 2 | 2 | | | 1 | 1 | | 2 | | | | 2 | 1 | 1 | | | | | | 4 | 9 |
| | 1 | | | | | | 2 | | | 1 | | | 2 | | 2 | | | | | | | | | 2 | 10 |
| | | | | | 2 | 14 | 13 | 6 | 11 | 15 | 4 | 3 | 4 | 7 | 11 | 10 | 13 | 2 | | | | | | 36 | 11 |
| | | | | | 1 | 2 | 4 | | 2 | 1 | 1 | | | 1 | 1 | 1 | | | | | | | | 7 | 12 |
| | | | | | 1 | 3 | 2 | 2 | | 2 | 4 | 1 | 4 | 2 | 6 | 1 | 1 | | | | | | | 8 | 13 |
| | | | | | | 1 | 1 | | | | 1 | 1 | | 1 | 1 | 1 | | | | | | | | 2 | 14 |
| | | | | | 8 | 7 | 9 | 8 | 6 | 15 | 2 | 8 | 9 | 6 | 15 | 9 | 11 | 3 | 1 | | | | | 39 | 15 |
| | | | | | 6 | 6 | 9 | 3 | 9 | 4 | | | 9 | 7 | 7 | | 17 | | | | | | | 24 | 16 |
| | | | | 15 | 41 | 159 | 14 | 26 | 226 | 11 | | | 31 | 10 | 41 | 104 | 89 | 4 | 11 | | | | | 249 | 17 |
| | | | | | 3 | 8 | 8 | 6 | 10 | 7 | 2 | 1 | 6 | 9 | 15 | 4 | 6 | | | | | | | 25 | 18 |
| | | | | | 4 | 3 | 1 | 1 | 4 | 1 | | | 2 | 2 | 4 | 3 | 2 | | | | | | | 9 | 19 |
| | | | | | | 1 | 1 | 1 | 3 | | | | | | | 1 | 1 | 1 | | | | | | 3 | 20 |
| | | | | 1 | 5 | 4 | 8 | 1 | 11 | 3 | | 1 | 5 | 6 | 11 | 7 | 3 | | | | | | | 21 | 21 |
| | | | | | 1 | 6 | 9 | 3 | 11 | 2 | | | 6 | 5 | 11 | 4 | 3 | 1 | | | | | | 19 | 22 |
| | | | | | | 4 | 1 | 1 | 3 | 1 | | | 2 | 3 | 5 | 1 | | | | | | | | 6 | 23 |
| | | | | 1 | 33 | 17 | 22 | 11 | 7 | 4 | 17 | 46 | 16 | 29 | 45 | 15 | 20 | 1 | 2 | | | | | 83 | 24 |
| | | | | | 8 | 6 | 13 | 6 | 15 | 7 | | 3 | 3 | 6 | 9 | 13 | 9 | 1 | 1 | | | | | 33 | 25 |
| | | | | | | | | 1 | 1 | | | | | | | 1 | | | | | | | | 1 | 26 |
| | | | | | 40 | 26 | 41 | 31 | 73 | 36 | 2 | 2 | 23 | 25 | 48 | 46 | 39 | 4 | 1 | | | | | 138 | 27 |
| | | | | | 4 | 4 | 6 | 3 | | | 1 | 2 | 4 | 1 | 5 | 3 | 9 | | | | | | | 17 | 28 |
| | | | | | | | | 2 | | 1 | 1 | | 2 | | 2 | | | | | | | | | 2 | 29 |

## CLASSIFICATION OF DEATHS IN NORTHWEST

| | Cause of death. | AGES. Under 1. | | 1 and under 5. | | 5 and under 10. | | 10 and under 20. | | 20 and under 50. | | 50 and under 80. | | 80 and under 100. | | 100 & over. | | Age unknown. | | NATIVITIES. Born in State. | N. England States. | Middle States. | Southern States. | Southwest'n States. | Northwest'n States. |
|---|---|---|---|---|---|---|---|---|---|---|---|---|---|---|---|---|---|---|---|---|---|---|---|---|---|
| | | M. | F. | M. | F. | M. | F. | M. | F. | M. | F. | M. | F. | M | F. | M | F. | M | F. | | | | | | |
| 1 | Diarrhœa | 4 | 14 | 24 | 14 | ... | 2 | 1 | 1 | 7 | 4 | 3 | 2 | .. | 1 | .. | .. | .. | .. | 63 | .. | ... | 7 | 4 | ... |
| 2 | Dropsy | 1 | 1 | 2 | 7 | 2 | 1 | 5 | 8 | 14 | 26 | 11 | 10 | .. | .. | .. | 1 | .. | .. | 38 | .. | 2 | 26 | 17 | 5 |
| 3 | Dysentery | 1 | 2 | 13 | 7 | ... | 2 | 2 | 1 | 2 | ... | ... | 1 | .. | .. | .. | .. | .. | .. | 26 | .. | ... | 3 | 1 | 1 |
| 4 | Dyspepsia | ... | ... | ... | ... | ... | ... | 1 | ... | ... | 3 | 2 | ... | .. | .. | .. | .. | .. | .. | ... | .. | 1 | 3 | 1 | ... |
| 5 | Epilepsy | 3 | 2 | ... | 1 | ... | ... | 1 | ... | ... | ... | 1 | ... | .. | .. | .. | .. | .. | .. | 6 | .. | ... | 2 | ... | ... |
| 6 | Erysipelas | ... | 1 | 2 | 3 | ... | ... | ... | ... | 2 | 4 | ... | ... | .. | .. | .. | .. | .. | .. | 7 | .. | ... | 5 | ... | ... |
| 7 | Executed | ... | ... | ... | ... | ... | ... | ... | ... | 1 | ... | ... | ... | .. | .. | .. | .. | .. | .. | ... | .. | ... | ... | 1 | ... |
| 8 | Fever, not specified. | 3 | 3 | 19 | 15 | 14 | 5 | 8 | 8 | 11 | 19 | 4 | 2 | .. | .. | .. | .. | .. | .. | 65 | .. | ... | 30 | 13 | 1 |
| 9 | ..do..bilious | ... | 1 | 3 | 2 | 1 | ... | 4 | 1 | 6 | 3 | 1 | 2 | .. | .. | .. | .. | .. | .. | 8 | .. | ... | 3 | 10 | 2 |
| 10 | ..do..catarrhal | 1 | 1 | ... | ... | ... | ... | ... | ... | 1 | 1 | ... | ... | .. | .. | .. | .. | .. | .. | 4 | .. | ... | ... | ... | ... |
| 11 | ..do..congestive | 1 | 2 | 7 | 9 | 5 | 2 | 10 | 9 | 10 | 6 | 1 | 2 | .. | .. | .. | .. | .. | .. | 42 | .. | 1 | 3 | 13 | 4 |
| 12 | ..do..inflammatory. | 1 | ... | 1 | ... | ... | ... | ... | 1 | 1 | ... | ... | ... | .. | .. | .. | .. | .. | .. | 2 | .. | ... | 1 | 1 | ... |
| 13 | ..do..intermittent | 2 | ... | 3 | 1 | ... | 1 | ... | ... | 1 | 3 | 3 | 2 | .. | .. | .. | .. | .. | .. | 11 | .. | ... | 5 | ... | ... |
| 14 | ..do..puerperal | ... | ... | ... | ... | ... | ... | ... | 1 | ... | 9 | ... | ... | .. | .. | .. | .. | .. | .. | 1 | .. | . | 6 | 3 | ... |
| 15 | ..do..scarlet | 5 | 3 | 10 | 8 | 5 | 6 | 3 | 9 | ... | 2 | ... | ... | .. | .. | .. | .. | .. | .. | 39 | .. | ... | 4 | 7 | ... |
| 16 | ..do..typhus | 5 | ... | 4 | 4 | 3 | 6 | 8 | 15 | 12 | 7 | 4 | ... | .. | .. | .. | .. | .. | .. | 31 | .. | ... | 17 | 16 | 2 |
| 17 | ..do..winter | 1 | ... | ... | 2 | ... | 1 | 1 | ... | 1 | 1 | ... | ... | .. | .. | .. | .. | .. | .. | 6 | .. | ... | ... | 1 | ... |
| 18 | Fluor albus | ... | ... | ... | ... | ... | ... | ... | ... | ... | 2 | ... | ... | .. | .. | .. | .. | .. | .. | ... | .. | ... | 1 | ... | 1 |
| 19 | Fracture | ... | 1 | ... | ... | ... | ... | ... | ... | 1 | ... | ... | ... | .. | .. | .. | .. | .. | .. | 1 | .. | ... | ... | ... | ... |
| 20 | Gravel | ... | ... | ... | ... | ... | ... | ... | ... | ... | ... | 2 | ... | .. | .. | .. | .. | .. | .. | ... | .. | ... | 2 | ... | ... |
| 21 | Head, disease of | ... | ... | ... | ... | ... | 1 | ... | ... | ... | ... | ... | ... | .. | .. | .. | .. | .. | .. | ... | .. | ... | ... | 1 | ... |
| 22 | Heart....do | 1 | ... | ... | ... | ... | ... | 1 | 2 | 2 | 1 | 2 | ... | .. | .. | .. | .. | .. | .. | 3 | .. | ... | 3 | 2 | 1 |
| 23 | Heat | ... | ... | ... | ... | ... | ... | ... | ... | ... | ... | ... | ... | .. | 1 | .. | .. | .. | .. | ... | .. | ... | 1 | ... | ... |
| 24 | Hemorrhage | ... | ... | ... | ... | ... | ... | ... | ... | 2 | 2 | ... | 1 | .. | .. | .. | .. | .. | .. | 1 | .. | ... | 2 | 2 | ... |
| 25 | Hernia | ... | ... | ... | ... | ... | ... | ... | ... | 3 | ... | ... | ... | .. | .. | .. | .. | .. | .. | 1 | .. | ... | 2 | ... | ... |
| 26 | Hives | 6 | 8 | ... | 1 | 1 | ... | ... | ... | ... | ... | ... | ... | .. | .. | .. | .. | .. | .. | 16 | .. | ... | ... | ... | ... |
| 27 | Hooping cough | 13 | 22 | 21 | 20 | 2 | 3 | 1 | 2 | 1 | ... | ... | ... | .. | .. | .. | .. | .. | .. | 85 | .. | ... | ... | ... | ... |
| 28 | Hydrocephalus | 2 | 2 | ... | 1 | ... | ... | ... | ... | ... | 1 | ... | ... | .. | .. | .. | .. | .. | .. | 4 | .. | ... | 1 | 1 | ... |
| 29 | Inflammation | 1 | 1 | 1 | 1 | ... | 1 | ... | ... | ... | 3 | ... | ... | .. | .. | .. | .. | .. | .. | 6 | .. | 1 | 1 | ... | ... |
| 30 | .....do....bowels | 8 | 6 | 6 | 7 | 2 | ... | 2 | ... | 2 | 3 | 3 | ... | .. | .. | .. | .. | .. | .. | 32 | .. | ... | 6 | 1 | ... |
| 31 | .....do....brain | 9 | 9 | 6 | 5 | 2 | 2 | 4 | 3 | 4 | 2 | ... | ... | .. | .. | .. | .. | .. | .. | 35 | .. | 1 | 7 | 3 | ... |
| 32 | .....do....stomach. | 1 | ... | ... | 2 | ... | ... | ... | 1 | ... | 2 | ... | ... | .. | .. | .. | .. | .. | .. | 4 | .. | ... | 1 | ... | 1 |
| 33 | Jaundice | ... | ... | ... | 2 | ... | ... | ... | ... | ... | ... | ... | ... | .. | .. | .. | .. | .. | .. | 2 | .. | ... | ... | ... | ... |
| 34 | Kidneys, disease of | ... | ... | ... | ... | ... | ... | ... | ... | 1 | ... | ... | ... | .. | .. | .. | .. | .. | .. | 1 | .. | ... | ... | ... | ... |
| 35 | Killed | ... | ... | ... | ... | 1 | ... | 1 | ... | 7 | ... | 1 | ... | .. | .. | .. | .. | .. | .. | 2 | .. | ... | 4 | 1 | 2 |
| 36 | Lightning | ... | ... | ... | ... | ... | ... | ... | ... | ... | 1 | ... | ... | .. | .. | .. | .. | .. | .. | ... | .. | ... | 1 | ... | ... |
| 37 | Liver, disease of | ... | 1 | ... | ... | 1 | ... | ... | 1 | 1 | 4 | 1 | ... | .. | .. | .. | .. | .. | .. | 2 | .. | ... | 1 | 6 | ... |
| 38 | Lockjaw | 2 | 1 | ... | ... | ... | ... | 1 | ... | 1 | ... | ... | ... | .. | .. | .. | .. | .. | .. | 4 | .. | ... | 1 | ... | ... |
| 39 | Lungs, disease of | 1 | ... | ... | ... | ... | ... | ... | ... | 1 | ... | 2 | ... | .. | .. | .. | .. | .. | .. | 3 | .. | ... | 1 | ... | ... |
| 40 | Malformation | ... | ... | 1 | ... | ... | ... | ... | ... | ... | ... | ... | ... | .. | .. | .. | .. | .. | .. | 1 | .. | ... | ... | ... | ... |
| 41 | Measles | 2 | 3 | 5 | 3 | 1 | ... | 1 | ... | ... | 1 | ... | ... | .. | .. | .. | .. | .. | .. | 16 | .. | ... | ... | ... | ... |
| 42 | Menses, suppress'n of | ... | ... | ... | ... | ... | ... | ... | 2 | ... | ... | ... | ... | .. | .. | .. | .. | .. | .. | 1 | .. | ... | 1 | ... | ... |
| 43 | Mortification | ... | ... | ... | ... | ... | 1 | ... | 1 | ... | ... | ... | ... | .. | .. | .. | .. | .. | .. | 1 | .. | ... | 1 | ... | ... |
| 44 | Mumps | ... | ... | ... | ... | ... | ... | ... | ... | ... | ... | ... | ... | .. | .. | .. | .. | 1 | .. | 1 | .. | ... | ... | ... | ... |
| 45 | Murder | ... | ... | ... | ... | ... | ... | ... | ... | 1 | ... | 1 | ... | .. | .. | .. | .. | .. | .. | ... | .. | ... | 1 | 1 | ... |
| 46 | Neuralgia | ... | ... | ... | ... | ... | ... | ... | ... | 1 | ... | ... | 1 | .. | .. | .. | .. | .. | .. | ... | .. | ... | 1 | 1 | ... |
| 47 | Old age | ... | ... | ... | ... | ... | ... | ... | ... | ... | ... | 8 | 8 | 5 | 8 | 2 | 2 | .. | .. | 9 | .. | 1 | 20 | 1 | 1 |
| 48 | Paralysis | 1 | ... | ... | ... | ... | ... | ... | ... | ... | ... | 2 | 3 | .. | .. | .. | .. | .. | .. | 1 | .. | ... | 3 | ... | 1 |
| 49 | Piles | ... | ... | ... | ... | ... | ... | ... | ... | ... | 1 | ... | ... | .. | .. | .. | .. | .. | .. | ... | .. | ... | ... | 1 | ... |
| 50 | Pleurisy | ... | ... | 1 | 1 | ... | 1 | ... | 1 | 4 | ... | 1 | 2 | .. | .. | .. | .. | .. | .. | 10 | .. | ... | 1 | ... | ... |
| 51 | Pneumonia | 9 | 13 | 15 | 12 | 10 | 4 | 6 | 9 | 35 | 21 | 13 | 7 | .. | .. | .. | .. | .. | .. | 77 | 1 | ... | 41 | 24 | 6 |
| 52 | Poison | 1 | 1 | 2 | ... | 1 | ... | 3 | 1 | ... | ... | ... | ... | .. | .. | .. | .. | .. | .. | 8 | .. | ... | 1 | ... | ... |
| 53 | Prematurity of birth. | 1 | 2 | ... | ... | ... | ... | ... | ... | ... | ... | ... | ... | .. | .. | .. | .. | .. | .. | 3 | .. | ... | ... | ... | ... |
| 54 | Rheumatism | ... | ... | ... | ... | 2 | ... | 1 | 1 | 1 | ... | 1 | ... | .. | .. | .. | .. | .. | .. | 4 | .. | ... | 1 | 1 | ... |
| 55 | Rickets | ... | ... | 1 | ... | ... | ... | ... | ... | ... | ... | ... | ... | .. | .. | .. | .. | .. | .. | 1 | .. | ... | ... | ... | ... |
| 56 | Scrofula | 1 | 2 | 2 | ... | 1 | 3 | 1 | 2 | 2 | 3 | ... | ... | .. | .. | .. | .. | .. | .. | 8 | .. | 1 | 5 | 2 | 1 |
| 57 | Small pox | ... | ... | ... | ... | ... | 1 | ... | ... | 1 | ... | ... | ... | .. | .. | .. | .. | .. | .. | 1 | .. | ... | 1 | ... | ... |
| 58 | Spine, disease of | ... | ... | ... | 3 | ... | ... | 1 | ... | 1 | 1 | ... | ... | .. | .. | .. | .. | .. | .. | 5 | .. | ... | ... | 1 | ... |
| 59 | Stillborn | 7 | 1 | ... | ... | ... | ... | ... | ... | ... | ... | ... | ... | .. | .. | .. | .. | .. | .. | 8 | .. | ... | ... | ... | ... |
| 60 | Stomach, disease of | ... | ... | ... | ... | ... | ... | 1 | ... | ... | ... | ... | ... | .. | .. | .. | .. | .. | .. | ... | .. | ... | 1 | ... | ... |
| 61 | Suffocated | 23 | 25 | 2 | 2 | ... | ... | ... | ... | ... | ... | ... | ... | .. | .. | .. | .. | .. | .. | 50 | .. | ... | ... | 1 | 1 |
| 62 | Suicide | ... | ... | ... | ... | ... | ... | ... | ... | 1 | ... | ... | ... | .. | .. | .. | .. | .. | .. | ... | .. | ... | ... | ... | ... |
| 63 | Syphilis | 2 | ... | ... | ... | ... | ... | ... | ... | ... | ... | ... | ... | .. | .. | .. | .. | .. | .. | 2 | .. | ... | ... | ... | ... |
| 64 | Teething | 4 | 1 | 16 | 13 | ... | ... | ... | ... | ... | ... | ... | ... | .. | .. | .. | .. | .. | .. | 32 | .. | ... | 1 | 1 | ... |
| 65 | Tetanus | ... | ... | ... | ... | ... | ... | ... | 1 | 1 | ... | ... | ... | .. | .. | .. | .. | .. | .. | 1 | .. | ... | ... | ... | 1 |
| 66 | Throat, disease of | ... | 1 | 2 | 1 | 1 | 1 | 1 | 2 | 1 | 1 | ... | ... | .. | .. | .. | .. | .. | .. | 7 | .. | ... | ... | 4 | ... |
| 67 | Thrush | 1 | 3 | 1 | ... | ... | ... | ... | ... | ... | 1 | ... | ... | .. | .. | .. | .. | .. | .. | 5 | .. | ... | ... | 1 | ... |
| 68 | Tumor | 1 | ... | ... | ... | ... | 2 | ... | ... | ... | ... | ... | ... | .. | .. | .. | .. | .. | .. | 3 | .. | ... | ... | ... | ... |
| 69 | Ulcer | 1 | ... | 1 | ... | ... | ... | ... | ... | ... | 2 | ... | 1 | .. | .. | .. | .. | .. | .. | 2 | .. | ... | 1 | 1 | ... |
| 70 | Uterus, disease of | ... | ... | ... | 1 | ... | ... | ... | ... | ... | 3 | ... | ... | .. | .. | .. | .. | .. | .. | 2 | .. | ... | 2 | ... | ... |
| 71 | Venereal | ... | ... | ... | ... | ... | ... | ... | 1 | ... | ... | 1 | ... | 1 | .. | .. | .. | .. | .. | 2 | .. | ... | 1 | ... | ... |
| 72 | Worms | 6 | 11 | 36 | 36 | 10 | 6 | ... | ... | 3 | 1 | ... | ... | .. | .. | .. | .. | .. | .. | 104 | .. | ... | 2 | 1 | 1 |
| 73 | Unknown | 62 | 61 | 27 | 23 | 8 | 4 | 9 | 6 | 19 | 19 | 6 | 6 | .. | 1 | .. | .. | 1 | .. | 196 | .. | ... | 20 | 26 | 5 |
| | Total | 298 | 299 | 326 | 305 | 100 | 87 | 114 | 129 | 299 | 282 | 105 | 68 | 6 | 14 | 2 | 3 | 2 | .. | 1654 | 1 | 14 | 384 | 268 | 66 |

## SECTION OF THE STATE OF MISSISSIPPI—Continued.

| Nativities: California and Territories | Nativities: Ireland | Nativities: Germany | Nativities: Other foreign countries | Nativities: Unknown | Season of decease: Spring | Season of decease: Summer | Season of decease: Autumn | Season of decease: Winter | Duration of sickness: Under 1 week | Duration of sickness: 1 week and under 1 month | Duration of sickness: 1 month and under 3 months | Duration of sickness: 3 months and over | Whites: Males | Whites: Females | Whites: Total | Colored: Slaves: Black M. | Colored: Slaves: Black F. | Colored: Slaves: Mulatto M. | Colored: Slaves: Mulatto F. | Colored: Free: Black M. | Colored: Free: Black F. | Colored: Free: Mul. M | Colored: Free: Mul. F. | Aggregate deaths | |
|---|---|---|---|---|---|---|---|---|---|---|---|---|---|---|---|---|---|---|---|---|---|---|---|---|---|
| | | | | 3 | 15 | 23 | 29 | 10 | 16 | 24 | 9 | 12 | 12 | 16 | 28 | 26 | 19 | 1 | 3 | | | | | 77 | 1 |
| | | | | 1 | 25 | 26 | 18 | 19 | 8 | 2 | 15 | 49 | 5 | 10 | 15 | 29 | 43 | | 1 | 1 | | | | 89 | 2 |
| | | | | | 5 | 14 | 10 | 2 | 4 | 17 | 2 | | 8 | 7 | 15 | 10 | 6 | | | | | | | 31 | 3 |
| | | | | 1 | | 2 | 2 | 2 | | | 4 | 1 | 2 | 3 | 5 | 1 | | | | | | | | 6 | 4 |
| | | | | | 1 | 2 | 4 | 1 | 1 | | | 1 | 3 | 1 | 4 | 2 | 2 | | | | | | | 8 | 5 |
| | | | | | 3 | 5 | 3 | 1 | 3 | 6 | 1 | | 1 | 5 | 6 | 3 | 3 | | | | | | | 12 | 6 |
| | | | | | 1 | | | | 1 | | | | | | | | | 1 | | | | | | 1 | 7 |
| | | | | 2 | 14 | 33 | 45 | 19 | 32 | 56 | 8 | 3 | 16 | 21 | 37 | 42 | 27 | 1 | 3 | | | | 1 | 111 | 8 |
| | | | | 1 | 4 | 8 | 11 | 1 | 9 | 13 | 1 | | 8 | 5 | 13 | 6 | 4 | 1 | | | | | | 24 | 9 |
| | | | | | | 3 | | 1 | 2 | | 1 | | 2 | | 2 | | 2 | | | | | | | 4 | 10 |
| | | | | 1 | 15 | 16 | 29 | 4 | 29 | 12 | 1 | | 16 | 8 | 24 | 18 | 21 | | | | 1 | | | 64 | 11 |
| | | | | | | 2 | | 2 | 1 | 2 | | 1 | 2 | | 2 | 1 | 1 | | | | | | | 4 | 12 |
| | | | | | 7 | 3 | 4 | 1 | 6 | 3 | 3 | 1 | 3 | 3 | 6 | 6 | 3 | | 1 | | | | | 16 | 13 |
| | | | | | 4 | 3 | 3 | | 3 | 5 | 1 | | | 6 | 6 | | 4 | | | | | | | 10 | 14 |
| | | | | 1 | 22 | 20 | 4 | 5 | 25 | 18 | 3 | 3 | 15 | 16 | 31 | 8 | 12 | | | | | | | 51 | 15 |
| | | | | 2 | 16 | 15 | 27 | 10 | 7 | 45 | 11 | 1 | 23 | 19 | 42 | 12 | 12 | 1 | 1 | | | | | 68 | 16 |
| | | | | | 3 | | | 4 | | 6 | 1 | | 1 | 2 | 3 | 2 | 2 | | | | | | | 7 | 17 |
| | | | | | 1 | | | 1 | | | 1 | 1 | | 1 | 1 | | 1 | | | | | | | 2 | 18 |
| | | | | 1 | | 2 | | | | 2 | | | | | | 1 | 1 | | | | | | | 2 | 19 |
| | | | | | | | 1 | 1 | | 1 | | 1 | 2 | | 2 | | | | | | | | | 2 | 20 |
| | | | | | 1 | | | | | 1 | | | | | | | | | 1 | | | | | 1 | 21 |
| | | | | | 4 | 3 | 1 | 1 | 3 | | 2 | 4 | 1 | 1 | 2 | 5 | 2 | | | | | | | 9 | 22 |
| | | | | | | | 1 | | | | | | | | | | 1 | | | | | | | 1 | 23 |
| | | | | | 1 | 2 | 1 | 1 | 1 | 2 | | | 1 | 2 | 3 | 1 | 1 | | | | | | | 5 | 24 |
| | | | | | 1 | 1 | | 1 | 2 | 1 | | | | | | 3 | | | | | | | | 3 | 25 |
| | | | | | 4 | 6 | 4 | 2 | 7 | 3 | 1 | | 4 | 4 | 8 | 3 | 5 | | | | | | | 16 | 26 |
| | | | | | 43 | 18 | 14 | 10 | 7 | 17 | 6 | 2 | 8 | 10 | 18 | 29 | 37 | | | 1 | | | | 85 | 27 |
| | | | | | | 4 | 2 | | | 1 | 2 | 3 | 2 | 2 | 4 | | 2 | | | | | | | 6 | 28 |
| | | | | | 4 | 1 | 3 | | 4 | 3 | | | | 2 | 2 | 2 | 3 | | 1 | | | | | 8 | 29 |
| | | | | | 4 | 20 | 12 | 3 | 11 | 18 | 2 | 3 | 10 | 8 | 18 | 13 | 6 | | 2 | | | | | 39 | 30 |
| | | | | | 6 | 15 | 21 | 4 | 15 | 23 | 1 | 2 | 16 | 11 | 27 | 9 | 10 | | | | | | | 46 | 31 |
| | | | | | | 3 | 3 | | 1 | 1 | 1 | 1 | | 4 | 4 | 1 | 1 | | | | | | | 6 | 32 |
| | | | | | 1 | | | 1 | | 1 | | 1 | | 2 | 2 | | | | | | | | | 2 | 33 |
| | | | | | | 1 | | | | 1 | | | | | | 1 | | | | | | | | 1 | 34 |
| | | | | 1 | 2 | 5 | 3 | | 6 | | | | 3 | | 3 | 7 | | | | | | | | 10 | 35 |
| | | | | | | | 1 | | 1 | | | | | | | | 1 | | | | | | | 1 | 36 |
| | | | | | 4 | 4 | | 1 | 1 | 3 | 1 | 4 | 2 | 3 | 5 | 1 | 3 | | | | | | | 9 | 37 |
| | | | | | 2 | 1 | | 2 | 2 | 2 | | | 1 | | 1 | 3 | 1 | | | | | | | 5 | 38 |
| | | | | | 2 | 1 | 1 | | | | 1 | 1 | 1 | | 1 | 2 | | 1 | | | | | | 4 | 39 |
| | | | | | | | 1 | | | | | 1 | | | | 1 | | | | | | | | 1 | 40 |
| | | | | | 7 | 6 | 2 | 1 | 3 | 5 | | | | 1 | 1 | 9 | 6 | | | | | | | 16 | 41 |
| | | | | | 1 | 1 | | | | 1 | | 1 | | 1 | 1 | | 1 | | | | | | | 2 | 42 |
| | | | | | 1 | | | 1 | | 1 | | | | 1 | 1 | | 1 | | | | | | | 2 | 43 |
| | | | | | | | | | | 1 | | | 1 | | 1 | | | | | | | | | 1 | 44 |
| | | | | | | | | 2 | 2 | | | | 1 | | 1 | 1 | | | | | | | | 2 | 45 |
| | | | | | | 2 | | | | 1 | | 1 | | 1 | 1 | 1 | | | | | | | | 2 | 46 |
| | | | 1 | | 7 | 9 | 11 | 6 | 5 | 5 | 3 | 7 | 2 | 11 | 13 | 13 | 6 | | | | 1 | | | 33 | 47 |
| | | | | 1 | 1 | 3 | 1 | 1 | 1 | 2 | | 3 | | 2 | 2 | 3 | 1 | | | | | | | 6 | 48 |
| | | | | | | | 1 | | 1 | | | | | 1 | 1 | | | | | | | | | 1 | 49 |
| | | | | | 6 | 2 | | 2 | | 8 | | | | 1 | 1 | 6 | 4 | | | | | | | 11 | 50 |
| | | | | 5 | 53 | 29 | 26 | 45 | 21 | 75 | 14 | 9 | 30 | 25 | 55 | 56 | 40 | 2 | 1 | | | | | 154 | 51 |
| | | | | | 2 | 2 | 5 | | 5 | 2 | | | 4 | 1 | 5 | 3 | 1 | | | | | | | 9 | 52 |
| | | | | | 1 | 1 | 1 | | | | | | 1 | | 1 | | 2 | | | | | | | 3 | 53 |
| | | | | | 2 | | 1 | 3 | 1 | 1 | | 1 | 1 | | 1 | 3 | 1 | 1 | | | | | | 6 | 54 |
| | | | | | | | 1 | | | | | 1 | | | | 1 | | | | | | | | 1 | 55 |
| | | | | | 7 | 5 | 4 | 1 | | 1 | 3 | 11 | 1 | | 1 | 6 | 10 | | | | | | | 17 | 56 |
| | | | | | 2 | | | | | 2 | | | | 1 | 1 | 1 | | | | | | | | 2 | 57 |
| | | | | | 2 | 2 | 1 | 1 | | | | 3 | | 2 | 2 | 2 | 2 | | | | | | | 6 | 58 |
| | | | | | | 3 | 4 | 1 | | | | | 2 | | 2 | 5 | | | 1 | | | | | 8 | 59 |
| | | | | | 1 | | | | 1 | | | | 1 | | 1 | | | | | | | | | 1 | 60 |
| | | | | | 12 | 17 | 5 | 18 | 52 | | | | | | | 24 | 24 | 1 | 3 | | | | | 52 | 61 |
| | 1 | | | | 1 | | | | | | | | 1 | | 1 | | | | | | | | | 1 | 62 |
| | | | | | | | 1 | 1 | | | 1 | | | | | 2 | | | | | | | | 2 | 63 |
| | | | | | 8 | 13 | 12 | 1 | 8 | 13 | 9 | | 7 | 4 | 11 | 12 | 10 | 1 | | | | | | 34 | 64 |
| | | | | | | | 2 | | | 2 | | | | | | 1 | 1 | | | | | | | 2 | 65 |
| | | | | | 2 | 1 | 2 | 6 | 2 | 8 | | 2 | 2 | 4 | 6 | 3 | 2 | | | | | | | 11 | 66 |
| | | | | | | 1 | 3 | 2 | 1 | 1 | | 1 | | 1 | 1 | 2 | 3 | | | | | | | 6 | 67 |
| | | | | | 1 | 1 | 1 | | | 1 | 1 | | 1 | | 1 | | 2 | | | | | | | 3 | 68 |
| | | | | 1 | 1 | 2 | 1 | 1 | | 1 | 2 | 2 | | 2 | 2 | 2 | 1 | | | | | | | 5 | 69 |
| | | | | | 1 | | 3 | | | | | 2 | | | | | 4 | | | | | | | 4 | 70 |
| | | | | | 1 | 1 | 1 | | 1 | 1 | | | | | | 2 | 1 | | | | | | | 3 | 71 |
| | | | | 1 | 17 | 34 | 36 | 14 | 43 | 26 | 8 | 1 | 10 | 8 | 18 | 42 | 46 | 8 | | | | | | 109 | 72 |
| | | | | 5 | 64 | 81 | 63 | 38 | 118 | 56 | 11 | 39 | 46 | 34 | 80 | 79 | 84 | 7 | 2 | | | | | 252 | 73 |
| ... | 2 | 1 | 1 | 48 | 606 | 780 | 632 | 389 | 946 | 617 | 171 | 247 | 411 | 399 | 810 | 796 | 749 | 43 | 36 | 2 | 2 | .. | 1 | 2439 | |

## CLASSIFICATION OF DEATHS IN NORTHEASTERN

*Embracing the following counties: Chickasaw, Choctaw, Itawamba,*

| | Cause of death. | AGES. Under 1. | | 1 and under 5. | | 5 and under 10. | | 10 and under 20. | | 20 and under 50. | | 50 and under 80. | | 80 and under 100. | | 100 & over. | | Age unknown. | | NATIVITIES. Born in State. | N. England States. | Middle States. | Southern States. | Southwest'n States. | Northwest'n States. |
|---|---|---|---|---|---|---|---|---|---|---|---|---|---|---|---|---|---|---|---|---|---|---|---|---|---|
| | | M. | F. | M. | F. | M. | F. | M. | F. | M. | F. | M. | F. | M | F. | M | F | M | F. | | | | | | |
| 1 | Abscess | | | | | | | | | 2 | | | | | | | | | | 1 | | | 1 | | |
| 2 | Accident, not specif'd | 5 | 5 | 6 | 4 | 1 | 3 | 7 | 1 | 6 | 1 | 2 | | | | | | | | 80 | | | 7 | 3 | |
| 3 | ....do....burned | 1 | 1 | 8 | 5 | | 2 | 1 | 2 | | 2 | | | | | | | | | 19 | | | 2 | | |
| 4 | ....do....drowned | | | 1 | | | | 4 | | 3 | | 1 | | | | | | | | 5 | | | 2 | 1 | 1 |
| 5 | ....do....shot | | | | | | | | | 3 | | | | | | | | | | 2 | | | | 1 | |
| 6 | Apoplexy | | | | | | | 1 | | 2 | | 1 | 1 | | | | | | | 2 | | | 3 | | |
| 7 | Bladder, disease of | | | | | | | | 1 | | | | | | | | | | | | | | | 1 | |
| 8 | Bowels.....do | 3 | 1 | 7 | 2 | 1 | | | 1 | 1 | 1 | 1 | | | | | | | | 16 | | | 1 | | |
| 9 | Bronchitis | | | | | 1 | | 1 | | 1 | 1 | 2 | 1 | | | | | | | 2 | | | 3 | 2 | |
| 10 | Cancer | | | | | | | | | | 1 | 1 | 2 | | | | | | | 1 | | 1 | 2 | | |
| 11 | Carbuncle | | | | | | | | | 1 | | 1 | | | | | | | | | | | 2 | | |
| 12 | Catarrh | 2 | 8 | 2 | 4 | | 1 | | 1 | 3 | 5 | 1 | | | | | 1 | | | 22 | | | 6 | | |
| 13 | Chicken pox | | | 1 | | | | | | | | | | | | | | | | 1 | | | | | |
| 14 | Childbirth | | | | | | | | 1 | | 9 | | | | | | | | | 2 | | | 5 | 2 | |
| 15 | Cholera | | | 1 | 2 | | | 3 | 1 | 7 | 3 | 2 | | | | | | | | 6 | | | 6 | 6 | |
| 16 | ...do..infantum | 3 | 6 | 4 | 8 | | | | | | | | | | | | | | | 21 | | | | | |
| 17 | ...do..morbus | | | 4 | | | 1 | 1 | | 2 | 1 | | | 1 | | | | | | 7 | | | 1 | 2 | |
| 18 | Chlorosis | | | | | | | | 1 | | | | | | | | | | | | | | | 1 | |
| 19 | Colic | | | | | | | | | | | 1 | | | | | | | | | | | 1 | | |
| 20 | Congestion | 1 | 1 | 2 | 1 | | 1 | 1 | | 2 | 1 | | | | | | | | | 6 | | | 8 | 1 | |
| 21 | ..do..brain | 2 | | 2 | 2 | 2 | | | | 3 | | 1 | | | | | | | | 9 | | | 2 | | |
| 22 | ..do..lungs | 1 | | 1 | | 2 | | 1 | | | | 1 | | | | | | | | 4 | | | 1 | 1 | |
| 23 | ..do..stomach | | | | | | | | 1 | | | | | | | | | | | | | | | 1 | |
| 24 | Consumption | | | 1 | 2 | | | 5 | 4 | 17 | 17 | 10 | 3 | 1 | | | | | | 10 | | 2 | 26 | 14 | 2 |
| 25 | Convulsions | 8 | 8 | 8 | 7 | 1 | | 2 | 2 | 4 | 5 | | | | 1 | | | | | 25 | | | 7 | 3 | |
| 26 | Croup | 24 | 17 | 15 | 13 | 1 | 2 | | 1 | | | | | | | | | | | 71 | | | | 2 | |
| 27 | Diarrhœa | 4 | 6 | 9 | 11 | 4 | | 1 | | 2 | 3 | 1 | 3 | | 1 | | | | | 33 | | | 7 | 4 | 1 |
| 28 | Dirt eating | | | | | | | | 1 | | | | | | | | | | | 1 | | | | | |
| 29 | Dropsy | 3 | 1 | 2 | 2 | 3 | 4 | 6 | 5 | 8 | 19 | 10 | 4 | | 3 | | | | | 36 | | | 20 | 9 | 1 |
| 30 | Dysentery | 11 | 6 | 11 | 12 | 5 | 1 | 3 | 2 | 8 | 5 | 5 | | | | | | | | 48 | | | 14 | 7 | |
| 31 | Dyspepsia | | | | | | | | 1 | 2 | 2 | 3 | 2 | | | | | | | 4 | | 1 | 3 | 2 | |
| 32 | Epilepsy | | | | | | | | 1 | | 1 | | | | | | | | | | | | 1 | 1 | |
| 33 | Erysipelas | | | 2 | | | 1 | | | | 3 | | 1 | | | | | | | 3 | | | 1 | 1 | 2 |
| 34 | Executed | | | | | | | | | 1 | | | | | | | | | | | | | 1 | | |
| 35 | Fever, not specified | 13 | 8 | 13 | 21 | 11 | 12 | 14 | 17 | 28 | 27 | 13 | 10 | | | | | | | 95 | | | 55 | 35 | 1 |
| 36 | ..do .bilious | | | | | | 1 | 1 | 1 | 4 | 1 | 1 | | | | | | | | 1 | | | 5 | 3 | |
| 37 | ..do..brain | | | | 1 | 1 | 1 | | 1 | | | | | | | | | | | 3 | | | 1 | | |
| 38 | ..do..congestive | 1 | 3 | 8 | 7 | 11 | 6 | 7 | 6 | 10 | 8 | 3 | 2 | | | | | | | 36 | | | 21 | 14 | |
| 39 | ..do..inflammatory | | | | | | | | | | 1 | | | | | | | | | 1 | | | | | |
| 40 | ..do..intermittent | 2 | | 1 | 1 | 1 | 2 | 1 | 1 | 3 | | | 1 | | | | | | | 8 | | | 4 | 1 | |
| 41 | ..do..puerperal | | | | | | | | 2 | | 2 | | | | | | | | | 1 | | | 1 | 2 | |
| 42 | ..do..scarlet | 2 | 1 | 11 | 6 | 3 | 2 | 3 | 1 | 1 | 1 | | | | | | | | | 29 | | | 1 | 1 | |
| 43 | ..do..typhus | 1 | 1 | 4 | 3 | | 2 | 4 | 10 | 8 | 8 | 5 | 4 | | | | | | | 19 | | | 23 | 8 | |
| 44 | ..do..winter | | | | | | | | | 1 | | 1 | | | | | | | | 2 | | | | | |
| 45 | Frozen | | | | | | | | | 1 | | | | | | | | | | 1 | | | | | |
| 46 | Gravel | | | 1 | | | | | | | | 3 | | 1 | | | | | | 1 | | | 3 | | |
| 47 | Head, disease of | | | | | | | | | 1 | | | 1 | | | | | | | 1 | | | 1 | | |
| 48 | Heart....do | | | 1 | | | | 2 | | 1 | | 1 | | | | | | | | 2 | | | 2 | 1 | |
| 49 | Hemorrhage | | | 1 | | | | | | 1 | 1 | | | | | | | | | 2 | | | 1 | | |
| 50 | Hernia | | | | | | | | | 1 | | | | | | | | | | | | | 1 | | |
| 51 | Hives | 6 | 7 | 2 | | | | | | | | | | | | | | | | 15 | | | | | |
| 52 | Hooping cough | 14 | 13 | 10 | 14 | 2 | 1 | | 2 | | 1 | | | | | | | | | 52 | | | 3 | 2 | |
| 53 | Hydrocephalus | | 1 | 1 | | | | | | | | | | | | | | | | 1 | | | | 1 | |
| 54 | inflammation | 1 | 1 | | 1 | | | | 1 | 2 | 1 | 1 | | | | | | | | 4 | | | 3 | 1 | |
| 55 | .....do....bowels | | 1 | 3 | 1 | | | | | 1 | | | | | | | | | | 5 | | | 1 | | |
| 56 | .....do....brain | 3 | 2 | 6 | 6 | 4 | 1 | 2 | 1 | 3 | 4 | | 2 | | | | | | | 24 | | | 5 | 5 | |
| 57 | .....do....stomach | | | | | | | | 1 | | 2 | 1 | | | | | | | | | | | 1 | 2 | |
| 58 | Intemperance | | | | | | | | | | | 1 | | | | | | | | | | | 1 | | |
| 59 | Jaundice | 1 | | | 1 | 1 | | | 1 | | | | | | | | | | | 2 | | | 1 | 1 | |
| 60 | Kidneys, disease of | | | 1 | | | 1 | | | | | | | | | | | | | 2 | | | | | |
| 61 | Killed | | | | | 1 | | 1 | | 3 | 1 | 1 | | | | | | | | 3 | | | 3 | | |
| 62 | Lightning | | | | | | | 1 | 2 | | | | | | | | | | | 1 | | | | 1 | 1 |
| 63 | Liver, disease of | 1 | | | | | | | | 1 | 1 | 2 | | | | | | | | 3 | | | 2 | | |
| 64 | Lockjaw | | | | | | | | 1 | | | | | | | | | | | 1 | | | | | |
| 65 | Lungs, disease of | | | 1 | | | | | | | | | | | | | | | | 1 | | | | | |
| 66 | Malformation | | | | 2 | | | | | | | | | | | | | | | 2 | | | | | |
| 67 | Measles | 1 | | | 1 | | | | | | | | | | | | | | | 2 | | | | | |
| 68 | Mortification | | | 1 | 1 | | | | | | | | | | | | | | | 2 | | | | | |
| 69 | Mumps | | | | | | | | | 1 | | | | | | | | | | 1 | | | | | |
| 70 | Murder | | | | | | | | | | | 1 | | | | | | | | | | | | | |
| 71 | Neuralgia | | | | | | | 1 | | | | | 1 | | | | | | | | | | 1 | 1 | |
| 72 | Old age | | | | | | | | | | | 7 | 5 | 7 | 3 | | 1 | | | 5 | | | 15 | 2 | |
| 73 | Paralysis | | | | 1 | 1 | | | | 2 | 1 | 2 | 2 | | | | | | | 1 | | 1 | 4 | 2 | 1 |

## ECTION OF THE STATE OF MISSISSIPPI.

*owndes, Monroe, Oktibbeha, Pontotoc, Tippah, and Tishemingo.*

| NATIVITIES. | | | | | SEASON OF DECEASE. | | | | DURATION OF SICKNESS. | | | | WHITES. | | | COLORED. | | | | | | | | Aggregate deaths. | |
|---|---|---|---|---|---|---|---|---|---|---|---|---|---|---|---|---|---|---|---|---|---|---|---|---|---|
| | | | | | | | | | | | | | | | | Slaves. | | | | Free. | | | | | |
| | | | | | | | | | | | | | | | | Black. | | Mulatto. | | Black. | | Mul. | | | |
| California and Territories. | Ireland. | Germany. | Other foreign countries. | Unknown. | Spring. | Summer. | Autumn. | Winter. | Under 1 week. | 1 week and under 1 month. | 1 month and under 3 months. | 3 months and over. | Males. | Females. | Total. | M. | F. | M. | F. | M. | F. | M | F. | | |
| | | | | | | | 1 | 1 | | | 1 | 1 | | | | 1 | | 1 | | | | | | 2 | 1 |
| | | | | 1 | 7 | 5 | 16 | 12 | 30 | 5 | 1 | | 12 | 1 | 13 | 14 | 12 | 1 | 1 | | | | | 41 | 2 |
| | | | | 1 | 12 | 3 | 1 | 5 | 11 | 10 | 1 | | 5 | 3 | 8 | 5 | 8 | | 1 | | | | | 22 | 3 |
| | | | | | 2 | 3 | 2 | 2 | 9 | | | | 4 | | 4 | 5 | | | | | | | | 9 | 4 |
| | | | | | | | 2 | 1 | 3 | | | | 2 | | 2 | 1 | | | | | | | | 3 | 5 |
| | | | | | 1 | 2 | 1 | 1 | 3 | 1 | | 1 | 2 | 1 | 3 | 2 | | | | | | | | 5 | 6 |
| | | | | | | 1 | | | | 1 | | | | 1 | 1 | | | | | | | | | 1 | 7 |
| | | | | | | 7 | 7 | 3 | 2 | 9 | 3 | 3 | 2 | 1 | 3 | 10 | 4 | | | | | | | 17 | 8 |
| | | | | | 3 | 1 | 1 | 1 | 1 | 1 | 1 | 4 | 3 | 1 | 4 | 2 | 1 | | | | | | | 7 | 9 |
| | | | | | 3 | 1 | | | | | | 4 | 1 | 3 | 4 | | | | | | | | | 4 | 10 |
| | | | | | 1 | | | 1 | | 1 | | 1 | 2 | | 2 | | | | | | | | | 2 | 11 |
| | | | | | 12 | 4 | 5 | 5 | 9 | 13 | 1 | 4 | 3 | 3 | 6 | 5 | 15 | | 2 | | | | | 28 | 12 |
| | | | | | | | | 1 | | | 1 | | 1 | | 1 | | | | | | | | | 1 | 13 |
| | | | | 1 | 2 | 1 | 4 | 3 | 7 | 3 | | | | 6 | 6 | | 4 | | | | | | | 10 | 14 |
| | | | | 1 | | 13 | 3 | 3 | 7 | 10 | 2 | | 10 | 4 | 14 | 2 | 1 | 1 | 1 | | | | | 19 | 15 |
| | | | | | 1 | 7 | 11 | 1 | 15 | 5 | 1 | | 2 | 6 | 8 | 5 | 8 | | | | | | | 21 | 16 |
| | | | | | | 4 | 5 | 1 | 6 | 3 | 1 | | 4 | 1 | 5 | 3 | 1 | 1 | | | | | | 10 | 17 |
| | | | | | 1 | | | | | | | 1 | | | | | 1 | | | | | | | 1 | 18 |
| | | | | | 1 | | | | | | | | | | | 1 | | | | | | | | 1 | 19 |
| | | | | | 1 | 4 | 4 | 1 | 7 | 2 | | | 3 | 1 | 4 | 3 | 3 | | | | | | | 10 | 20 |
| | | | | 1 | | 5 | 7 | | 10 | 2 | | | 5 | 1 | 6 | 5 | 1 | | | | | | | 12 | 21 |
| | | | | | 1 | | 4 | 1 | | 6 | | | 5 | | 5 | 1 | | | | | | | | 6 | 22 |
| | | | | | 1 | | | | 1 | | | | | 1 | 1 | | | | | | | | | 1 | 23 |
| | | | | 6 | 9 | 20 | 17 | 14 | | 2 | 8 | 50 | 24 | 15 | 39 | 9 | 10 | 1 | 1 | | | | | 60 | 24 |
| | | | | 1 | 13 | 6 | 12 | 5 | 24 | 6 | | 6 | 8 | 5 | 13 | 10 | 11 | | 2 | | | | | 36 | 25 |
| | | | | | 23 | 15 | 16 | 18 | 53 | 18 | | 2 | 16 | 18 | 34 | 23 | 14 | 1 | 1 | | | | | 73 | 26 |
| | | | | | 4 | 20 | 17 | 2 | 13 | 22 | 4 | 5 | 11 | 14 | 25 | 9 | 10 | 1 | | | | | | 45 | 27 |
| | | | | | | 1 | | | | | | 1 | | | | | 1 | | | | | | | 1 | 28 |
| | 1 | | 1 | 2 | 14 | 19 | 23 | 11 | | 6 | 12 | 50 | 14 | 14 | 28 | 17 | 22 | 1 | 2 | | | | | 70 | 29 |
| | | | | | 5 | 39 | 21 | 4 | 21 | 40 | 5 | 3 | 26 | 22 | 48 | 16 | 4 | 1 | | | | | | 69 | 30 |
| | | | | | 1 | 2 | 6 | 1 | | 1 | 1 | 7 | 4 | 4 | 8 | 1 | 1 | | | | | | | 10 | 31 |
| | | | | | | 2 | | | | 1 | | | | 1 | 1 | | 1 | | | | | | | 2 | 32 |
| | | | | | 2 | 1 | 2 | 2 | 1 | 5 | 1 | | 1 | 5 | 6 | | | 1 | | | | | | 7 | 33 |
| | | | | | 1 | | | | 1 | | | | 1 | | 1 | | | | | | | | | 1 | 34 |
| | | | | 1 | 36 | 38 | 88 | 22 | 46 | 109 | 24 | 7 | 71 | 74 | 145 | 21 | 20 | | 1 | | | | | 187 | 35 |
| | | | | | 1 | 1 | 6 | 1 | 2 | 3 | 4 | | 3 | 2 | 5 | 3 | 1 | | | | | | | 9 | 36 |
| | | | | | | 1 | 3 | | | 3 | 1 | | 1 | | 1 | | 3 | | | | | | | 4 | 37 |
| | | | | 1 | | 7 | 58 | 6 | 44 | 8 | 1 | 1 | 19 | 15 | 34 | 19 | 15 | 2 | 2 | | | | | 72 | 38 |
| | | | | | | | 1 | | 1 | | | | | | | | 1 | | | | | | | 1 | 39 |
| | | | | | 1 | 1 | 7 | 4 | 6 | 3 | | 4 | 3 | 2 | 5 | 5 | 3 | | | | | | | 13 | 40 |
| | | | | | 1 | | 1 | 2 | 2 | 2 | | | | 2 | 2 | | 2 | | | | | | | 4 | 41 |
| | | | | | 16 | 7 | 7 | | 16 | 11 | 2 | | 10 | 7 | 17 | 10 | 4 | | | | | | | 31 | 42 |
| | | | | | 13 | 13 | 18 | 6 | 2 | 33 | 12 | | 17 | 14 | 31 | 5 | 13 | | 1 | | | | | 50 | 43 |
| | | | | | 1 | | | 1 | 1 | 1 | | | | | | 2 | | | | | | | | 2 | 44 |
| | | | | | | | | 1 | | 1 | | | | | | 1 | | | | | | | | 1 | 45 |
| | | | 1 | | 2 | 1 | | 2 | | 2 | | 3 | 2 | | 2 | 3 | | | | | | | | 5 | 46 |
| | | | | | 1 | 1 | | | | 1 | | 1 | | | | 1 | 1 | | | | | | | 2 | 47 |
| | | | | | | 1 | 4 | | | | 1 | 4 | 2 | | 2 | 3 | | | | | | | | 5 | 48 |
| | | | | | 1 | | 2 | | 2 | | 1 | | | 1 | 1 | 2 | | | | | | | | 3 | 49 |
| | | | | | | | | 1 | | 1 | | | 1 | | 1 | | | | | | | | | 1 | 50 |
| | | | | | 3 | 2 | 8 | 2 | 11 | 4 | | | 7 | 6 | 13 | 1 | 1 | | | | | | | 15 | 51 |
| | | | | | 13 | 17 | 18 | 7 | 5 | 28 | 18 | 3 | 10 | 5 | 15 | 14 | 23 | 2 | 3 | | | | | 57 | 52 |
| | | | | | | 1 | 1 | | | 1 | | 1 | | 1 | 1 | | | | | 1 | | | | 2 | 53 |
| | | | | | 3 | 4 | | 1 | 2 | 5 | | 1 | 3 | 2 | 5 | 1 | 1 | | 1 | | | | | 8 | 54 |
| | | | | | | 1 | 3 | 2 | 4 | 1 | | 1 | 1 | 2 | 3 | 3 | | | | | | | | 6 | 55 |
| | | | | | 8 | 8 | 17 | 5 | 17 | 16 | 1 | | 8 | 9 | 17 | 8 | 7 | 2 | | | | | | 34 | 56 |
| | | 1 | | | 1 | | 1 | 2 | | 1 | 1 | 2 | 1 | 3 | 4 | | | | | | | | | 4 | 57 |
| | | | | | | 1 | | | | | 1 | | 1 | | 1 | | | | | | | | | 1 | 58 |
| | | | | | 2 | 1 | | 1 | | 3 | | 1 | 2 | 2 | 4 | | | | | | | | | 4 | 59 |
| | | | | | | | 2 | | | | | 2 | 1 | 1 | 2 | | | | | | | | | 2 | 60 |
| | | | | 1 | 2 | | 4 | 1 | 4 | 3 | | | 3 | | 3 | 3 | 1 | | | | | | | 7 | 61 |
| | | | | | | 3 | | | 3 | | | | | | | 1 | 2 | | | | | | | 3 | 62 |
| | | | | | 1 | 2 | | 2 | | | 2 | 3 | 3 | | 3 | 1 | 1 | | | | | | | 5 | 63 |
| | | | | | | | | 1 | 1 | | | | | | | | 1 | | | | | | | 1 | 64 |
| | | | | | | | 1 | | | | | 1 | | | | | | 1 | | | | | | 1 | 65 |
| | | | | | | 1 | | 1 | | 1 | | 1 | | | | | 2 | | | | | | | 2 | 66 |
| | | | | | 1 | | 1 | | 1 | | | 1 | | | | 1 | 1 | | | | | | | 2 | 67 |
| | | | | | 1 | | | 1 | 1 | 1 | | | 1 | 1 | 2 | | | | | | | | | 2 | 68 |
| | | | | | | 1 | | | 1 | | | | | | | 1 | | | | | | | | 1 | 69 |
| | 1 | | | | | | 1 | | | 1 | | | 1 | | 1 | | | | | | | | | 1 | 70 |
| | | | | | 1 | 1 | | | | 1 | | 1 | 1 | 1 | 2 | | | | | | | | | 2 | 71 |
| | | | 1 | | 6 | 5 | 6 | 6 | 1 | 4 | 1 | 12 | 7 | 4 | 11 | 7 | 5 | | | | | | | 23 | 72 |
| | | | | | 5 | 1 | 3 | | | 1 | | 7 | 4 | 4 | 8 | 1 | | | | | | | | 9 | 73 |

## CLASSIFICATION OF DEATHS IN NORTHEASTERN

| | Cause of death. | Ages. Under 1. | | 1 and under 5. | | 5 and under 10. | | 10 and under 20. | | 20 and under 50. | | 50 and under 80. | | 80 and under 100. | | 100 & over. | | Age unknown. | | Nativities. Born in State. | N. England States. | Middle States. | Southern States. | Southwest'n States. | Northwest'n States. |
|---|---|---|---|---|---|---|---|---|---|---|---|---|---|---|---|---|---|---|---|---|---|---|---|---|---|
| | | M. | F. | M. | F. | M. | F. | M. | F. | M. | F. | M. | F. | M | F. | M | F | M | F. | | | | | | |
| 1 | Pleurisy | .... | ... | 1 | ... | ... | ... | ... | 2 | 3 | .... | 1 | 1 | .. | .. | .. | .. | .. | .. | 2 | .. | 1 | 2 | 2 | ... |
| 2 | Pneumonia | 5 | 3 | 7 | 5 | 1 | 3 | 8 | 3 | 14 | 5 | 13 | 6 | .. | .. | .. | .. | .. | .. | 42 | .. | ... | 20 | 7 | ... |
| 3 | Prematurity of birth | .... | 4 | .... | ... | ... | ... | ... | ... | .... | .... | ... | ... | .. | .. | .. | .. | .. | .. | 4 | .. | ... | ... | ... | ... |
| 4 | Poison | .... | ... | .... | 1 | ... | ... | ... | ... | .... | .... | ... | ... | .. | .. | .. | .. | .. | .. | ... | .. | ... | ... | 1 | ... |
| 5 | Quinsy | .... | ... | .... | ... | ... | ... | ... | ... | .... | .... | ... | 2 | .. | .. | .. | .. | .. | .. | 1 | .. | ... | 1 | ... | ... |
| 6 | Rheumatism | .... | ... | .... | 1 | ... | 1 | ... | 1 | .... | 2 | 2 | ... | .. | .. | .. | .. | .. | .. | 3 | .. | ... | 2 | 1 | ... |
| 7 | Scrofula | 2 | ... | 3 | ... | ... | ... | 1 | ... | 3 | 1 | ... | ... | .. | .. | .. | .. | .. | .. | 8 | .. | ... | 1 | ... | ... |
| 8 | Small pox | .... | ... | 1 | 2 | ... | ... | ... | ... | 1 | 1 | 1 | ... | .. | .. | .. | .. | .. | .. | 3 | .. | ... | ... | 2 | ... |
| 9 | Spine, disease of | .... | ... | .... | 1 | ... | ... | ... | ... | .... | .... | ... | ... | .. | .. | .. | .. | .. | .. | ... | .. | ... | ... | 1 | ... |
| 10 | Suffocation | 8 | 12 | 3 | 1 | 1 | ... | ... | 1 | .... | .... | ... | ... | .. | .. | .. | .. | .. | .. | 26 | .. | ... | ... | ... | ... |
| 11 | Teething | 1 | 2 | 6 | 10 | ... | ... | ... | ... | .... | .... | ... | ... | .. | .. | .. | .. | .. | .. | 19 | .. | ... | ... | ... | ... |
| 12 | Throat, disease of | .... | 1 | 2 | ... | ... | ... | ... | 2 | 2 | 2 | ... | ... | .. | .. | .. | .. | .. | .. | 6 | .. | ... | 3 | ... | ... |
| 13 | Thrush | 1 | ... | 1 | ... | ... | ... | ... | ... | .... | .... | ... | ... | .. | .. | .. | .. | .. | .. | 2 | .. | ... | ... | ... | ... |
| 14 | Uterus, disease of | .... | ... | .... | ... | ... | ... | ... | ... | .... | 2 | ... | ... | .. | .. | .. | .. | .. | .. | 2 | .. | ... | ... | ... | ... |
| 15 | Worms | .... | 1 | 10 | 12 | 4 | 5 | ... | 1 | 1 | .... | ... | ... | .. | .. | .. | .. | .. | .. | 28 | .. | ... | 1 | 5 | ... |
| 16 | Unknown | 45 | 44 | 25 | 31 | 12 | 2 | 12 | 8 | 13 | 44 | 17 | 9 | 1 | 2 | .. | .. | .. | .. | 187 | .. | ... | 43 | 22 | 3 |
| | Total | 176 | 160 | 206 | 206 | 75 | 56 | 95 | 93 | 187 | 97 | 121 | 63 | 11 | 10 | .. | 2 | .. | .. | 1049 | .. | 6 | 360 | 189 | 13 |

## CLASSIFICATION OF DEATHS IN MIDDLE, EASTERN

*Embracing the following counties : Attala, Clark, Jasper, Kemper,*

| | Cause of death. | Under 1. M. | Under 1. F. | 1 and under 5. M. | 1 and under 5. F. | 5 and under 10. M. | 5 and under 10. F. | 10 and under 20. M. | 10 and under 20. F. | 20 and under 50. M. | 20 and under 50. F. | 50 and under 80. M. | 50 and under 80. F. | 80 and under 100. M | 80 and under 100. F. | 100 & over. M | 100 & over. F | Age unknown. M | Age unknown. F. | Born in State. | N. England States. | Middle States. | Southern States. | Southwest'n States. | Northwest'n States. |
|---|---|---|---|---|---|---|---|---|---|---|---|---|---|---|---|---|---|---|---|---|---|---|---|---|---|
| 1 | Abscess | .... | ... | .... | ... | ... | ... | 1 | 1 | 1 | .... | ... | 2 | .. | .. | .. | .. | .. | .. | ... | .. | ... | 3 | 2 | ... |
| 2 | Accident, not specif'd | 1 | 4 | 4 | 4 | ... | ... | ... | 1 | .... | .... | 1 | ... | .. | .. | .. | .. | .. | .. | 13 | .. | ... | 1 | 1 | ... |
| 3 | ....do...burned | 2 | 1 | 4 | 3 | ... | 1 | ... | 1 | .... | 2 | ... | ... | .. | .. | .. | .. | .. | .. | 12 | .. | ... | 2 | ... | ... |
| 4 | ....do...drowned | .... | ... | 2 | ... | 1 | ... | 2 | ... | 2 | 3 | ... | ... | .. | .. | .. | .. | .. | .. | 6 | .. | ... | 3 | 1 | ... |
| 5 | ....do...shot | .... | ... | .... | ... | ... | ... | 1 | ... | 1 | .... | ... | ... | .. | .. | .. | .. | .. | .. | 1 | .. | ... | ... | 1 | ... |
| 6 | Apoplexy | .... | 1 | .... | ... | ... | ... | 1 | ... | 2 | 1 | ... | ... | 1 | .. | .. | .. | .. | .. | 3 | .. | ... | 2 | ... | ... |
| 7 | Asthma | .... | ... | .... | ... | ... | ... | ... | ... | .... | .... | 2 | ... | .. | .. | .. | .. | .. | .. | ... | .. | ... | 2 | ... | ... |
| 8 | Bowels, disease of | .... | ... | .... | ... | ... | ... | ... | ... | .... | 1 | ... | ... | .. | .. | .. | .. | .. | .. | 1 | .. | ... | ... | ... | ... |
| 9 | Brain......do | 1 | 1 | 1 | ... | ... | ... | ... | 1 | 3 | .... | ... | ... | .. | .. | .. | .. | .. | .. | 4 | .. | ... | 2 | 1 | ... |
| 10 | Bronchitis | .... | ... | .... | ... | ... | ... | ... | ... | .... | .... | 1 | ... | .. | .. | .. | .. | .. | .. | ... | .. | ... | 1 | ... | ... |
| 11 | Cancer | .... | ... | .... | ... | ... | ... | ... | ... | .... | .... | 1 | ... | .. | .. | .. | .. | .. | .. | ... | .. | ... | 1 | ... | ... |
| 12 | Catarrh | 2 | 1 | .... | 3 | ... | ... | 2 | ... | 1 | 9 | 1 | ... | .. | 1 | .. | .. | .. | .. | 8 | .. | ... | 10 | 2 | ... |
| 13 | Childbed | .... | ... | .... | ... | ... | ... | ... | 3 | .... | 7 | ... | ... | .. | .. | .. | .. | .. | .. | 2 | .. | ... | 6 | 1 | ... |
| 14 | Cholera | .... | ... | .... | 1 | ... | ... | 2 | ... | 6 | 1 | ... | ... | .. | .. | .. | .. | .. | .. | 3 | .. | ... | 4 | 2 | 1 |
| 15 | ...do..infantum | 2 | 1 | 2 | 4 | 1 | ... | ... | ... | .... | .... | ... | ... | .. | .. | .. | .. | .. | .. | 10 | .. | ... | ... | ... | ... |
| 16 | ...do..morbus | .... | ... | .... | 2 | ... | ... | ... | 1 | 1 | 1 | ... | 1 | .. | .. | .. | .. | .. | .. | 2 | .. | ... | 3 | 1 | ... |
| 17 | Colic | 2 | ... | .... | 1 | ... | ... | ... | 1 | .... | 2 | ... | ... | .. | .. | .. | .. | .. | .. | 2 | .. | ... | 3 | ... | ... |
| 18 | Congestion | .... | ... | 1 | ... | ... | ... | ... | ... | .... | .... | ... | ... | .. | .. | .. | .. | .. | .. | 1 | .. | ... | ... | ... | ... |
| 19 | Consumption | .... | ... | 1 | 2 | ... | ... | 6 | 1 | 9 | 14 | 3 | 1 | .. | .. | .. | .. | .. | 1 | 16 | .. | ... | 12 | 8 | 1 |
| 20 | Convulsions | 8 | 5 | 4 | 4 | ... | 1 | ... | 1 | 2 | 2 | 1 | ... | .. | .. | .. | .. | .. | .. | 20 | .. | ... | 4 | 2 | ... |
| 21 | Croup | 19 | 15 | 23 | 13 | 1 | ... | 1 | 2 | .... | .... | ... | ... | .. | .. | .. | .. | .. | .. | 71 | .. | ... | 2 | 1 | ... |
| 22 | Debility | .... | 1 | .... | 1 | ... | ... | ... | ... | .... | .... | ... | ... | .. | .. | .. | .. | .. | .. | 2 | .. | ... | ... | ... | ... |
| 23 | Diabetes | .... | ... | .... | ... | ... | 1 | ... | ... | .... | .... | ... | ... | .. | .. | .. | .. | .. | .. | 1 | .. | ... | ... | ... | ... |
| 24 | Diarrhœa | 1 | 1 | 6 | 4 | ... | ... | ... | ... | 3 | 2 | 3 | 2 | .. | .. | .. | .. | .. | .. | 12 | .. | ... | 8 | 2 | ... |
| 25 | Dropsy | 1 | ... | 2 | 1 | 2 | ... | 1 | 3 | 3 | 5 | 8 | 2 | .. | .. | .. | .. | .. | .. | 8 | .. | ... | 12 | 6 | ... |
| 26 | Dysentery | 8 | 6 | 10 | 17 | 4 | ... | 4 | 3 | 2 | 1 | 2 | ... | .. | .. | .. | .. | .. | .. | 48 | .. | ... | 6 | 3 | ... |
| 27 | Dyspepsia | .... | ... | .... | ... | ... | ... | ... | ... | 3 | .... | 2 | ... | .. | .. | .. | .. | .. | .. | ... | .. | ... | 5 | ... | ... |
| 28 | Epilepsy | .... | ... | 1 | ... | ... | 1 | ... | ... | .... | 1 | ... | 1 | .. | .. | .. | .. | .. | .. | 3 | .. | ... | 1 | ... | ... |
| 29 | Erysipelas | .... | ... | .... | 1 | 1 | ... | ... | ... | .... | 1 | ... | ... | .. | .. | .. | .. | .. | .. | 2 | .. | ... | 1 | ... | ... |
| 30 | Fever, not specified | 9 | 2 | 23 | 29 | 17 | 13 | 12 | 13 | 35 | 24 | 8 | 6 | .. | 1 | 1 | .. | .. | .. | 107 | .. | ... | 53 | 25 | 2 |
| 31 | ..do..bilious | 1 | ... | 2 | 2 | 2 | 1 | 3 | 2 | 1 | 2 | ... | 2 | .. | .. | .. | .. | .. | .. | 10 | .. | 1 | 3 | 4 | ... |
| 32 | ..do..catarrhal | .... | ... | .... | ... | ... | ... | ... | ... | .... | .... | 1 | ... | .. | .. | .. | .. | .. | .. | ... | .. | ... | 1 | ... | ... |
| 33 | ..do..congestive | .... | 1 | 2 | 3 | 2 | 1 | 2 | 1 | 4 | 5 | 1 | 4 | .. | .. | .. | .. | .. | .. | 13 | .. | ... | 8 | 5 | ... |
| 34 | ..do..intermittent | 2 | 1 | 2 | 1 | 1 | 1 | 1 | ... | .... | .... | ... | ... | .. | .. | .. | .. | .. | .. | 8 | .. | ... | 1 | ... | ... |
| 35 | ..do..puerperal | .... | ... | .... | ... | ... | ... | ... | ... | .... | 4 | ... | ... | .. | .. | .. | .. | .. | .. | 1 | .. | ... | 2 | 1 | ... |
| 36 | ..do..remittent | .... | ... | 1 | ... | ... | ... | ... | 1 | 1 | .... | ... | ... | .. | .. | .. | .. | .. | .. | 2 | .. | ... | 1 | ... | ... |
| 37 | ..do..scarlet | 2 | 4 | 19 | 22 | 6 | 8 | 2 | 8 | .... | .... | ... | ... | .. | .. | .. | .. | .. | .. | 63 | .. | ... | 3 | 5 | ... |
| 38 | ..do..typhus | 4 | 2 | 3 | 2 | 4 | 3 | 8 | 11 | 14 | 8 | 5 | 2 | .. | .. | .. | .. | .. | .. | 25 | .. | 1 | 26 | 13 | .. |
| 39 | Gravel | .... | ... | .... | ... | ... | ... | ... | ... | .... | .... | 1 | ... | .. | .. | .. | .. | .. | .. | ... | .. | ... | ... | ... | ... |
| 40 | Head, disease of | .... | ... | .... | ... | ... | ... | ... | 1 | .... | .... | ... | ... | .. | .. | .. | .. | .. | .. | ... | .. | ... | 1 | ... | ... |
| 41 | Heart....do | 1 | ... | .... | ... | ... | ... | 1 | ... | .... | .... | 2 | 1 | .. | .. | .. | .. | .. | .. | 2 | .. | ... | 3 | ... | ... |
| 42 | Heat | .... | ... | .... | ... | ... | ... | ... | 1 | .... | .... | ... | ... | .. | .. | .. | .. | .. | .. | 1 | .. | ... | ... | ... | ... |
| 43 | Hemorrhage | .... | ... | .... | ... | ... | ... | ... | ... | 1 | 1 | ... | ... | .. | .. | .. | .. | .. | .. | 1 | .. | ... | 1 | ... | ... |
| 44 | Hernia | .... | ... | .... | ... | ... | ... | ... | ... | 1 | .... | ... | ... | .. | .. | .. | .. | .. | .. | ... | .. | ... | ... | 1 | ... |
| 45 | Hives | 4 | 3 | .... | 1 | ... | 1 | ... | ... | .... | .... | ... | ... | .. | .. | .. | .. | .. | .. | 9 | .. | ... | ... | ... | ... |
| 46 | Hooping cough | 3 | 5 | 8 | 5 | 2 | ... | 1 | 1 | .... | .... | ... | ... | .. | .. | .. | .. | .. | .. | 23 | .. | ... | ... | 2 | ... |
| 47 | Inflammation | 1 | ... | 1 | 2 | 1 | ... | ... | 1 | 1 | 1 | 1 | ... | .. | .. | .. | .. | .. | .. | 6 | .. | ... | 2 | ... | ... |
| 48 | ....do....bowels | 3 | ... | 5 | 1 | ... | 1 | 1 | ... | .... | 2 | 1 | ... | .. | 1 | .. | .. | .. | .. | 12 | .. | ... | 2 | 1 | ... |

ECTION OF THE STATE OF MISSISSIPPI—Continued.

| California and Territories | Ireland | Germany | Other foreign countries | Unknown | Spring | Summer | Autumn | Winter | Under 1 week | 1 week and under 1 month | 1 month and under 3 months | 3 months and over | Whites: Males | Whites: Females | Whites: Total | Slaves, Black: M. | Slaves, Black: F. | Slaves, Mulatto: M. | Slaves, Mulatto: F. | Free, Black: M. | Free, Black: F. | Free, Mul.: M | Free, Mul.: F. | Aggregate deaths. | |
|---|---|---|---|---|---|---|---|---|---|---|---|---|---|---|---|---|---|---|---|---|---|---|---|---|---|
| | 1 | | | | | 3 | 1 | 4 | 2 | 4 | 1 | 1 | 1 | 3 | 4 | 3 | | 1 | | | | | | 8 | 1 |
| | 1 | | | 3 | 25 | 12 | 13 | 23 | 22 | 42 | 5 | 8 | 19 | 14 | 33 | 28 | 11 | 1 | | | | | | 73 | 2 |
| | | | | | | | 1 | 3 | 3 | 1 | | | | 1 | 1 | | 1 | | 2 | | | | | 4 | 3 |
| | | | | | 1 | | | | 1 | | | | | 1 | 1 | | | | | | | | | 1 | 4 |
| | | | | | 1 | | 1 | | 1 | | 1 | | | 1 | 1 | | 1 | | | | | | | 2 | 5 |
| | | | | 1 | 2 | 1 | 1 | 3 | 1 | 1 | | 5 | 1 | 3 | 4 | 1 | 2 | | | | | | | 7 | 6 |
| | | | | 1 | 2 | 2 | 5 | 1 | | 1 | | 9 | 3 | | 3 | 6 | 1 | | | | | | | 10 | 7 |
| | | | 1 | | 4 | 1 | 1 | | | 6 | | | 2 | 3 | 5 | 1 | | | | | | | | 6 | 8 |
| | | | | | | 1 | | | | | | 1 | | | | | 1 | | | | | | | 1 | 9 |
| | | | | | 7 | 1 | 6 | 12 | 26 | | | | | | | 10 | 14 | 2 | | | | | | 26 | 10 |
| | | | | | 1 | 6 | 9 | 3 | 3 | 7 | 3 | 5 | 3 | 4 | 7 | 4 | 7 | | 1 | | | | | 19 | 11 |
| | | | | | 1 | 2 | 3 | 3 | 3 | 4 | | 2 | 3 | 1 | 4 | 1 | 4 | | | | | | | 9 | 12 |
| | | | | | | 2 | | | | 1 | 1 | | 2 | | 2 | | | | | | | | | 2 | 13 |
| | | | | | 1 | | | 1 | | 1 | | | | | | | 2 | | | | | | | 2 | 14 |
| | | | | | 9 | 10 | 12 | 3 | 15 | 15 | 1 | 1 | 7 | 5 | 12 | 8 | 12 | | 2 | | | | | 34 | 15 |
| 1 | | | 1 | 8 | 66 | 62 | 74 | 52 | 125 | 52 | 23 | 47 | 39 | 61 | 100 | 78 | 76 | 6 | 3 | 1 | | 1 | | 265 | 16 |
| 1 | 4 | 1 | 5 | 30 | 356 | 409 | 576 | 286 | 611 | 555 | 149 | 274 | 434 | 387 | 821 | 407 | 373 | 27 | 27 | 2 | | 1 | | 1658 | |

SECTION, OF THE STATE OF MISSISSIPPI.

*Lauderdale, Leake, Neshoba, Newton, Noxubee, Scott, Smith, and Winston.*

| California and Territories | Ireland | Germany | Other foreign countries | Unknown | Spring | Summer | Autumn | Winter | Under 1 week | 1 week and under 1 month | 1 month and under 3 months | 3 months and over | Whites: Males | Whites: Females | Whites: Total | Slaves, Black: M. | Slaves, Black: F. | Slaves, Mulatto: M. | Slaves, Mulatto: F. | Free, Black: M. | Free, Black: F. | Free, Mul.: M | Free, Mul.: F. | Aggregate deaths. | |
|---|---|---|---|---|---|---|---|---|---|---|---|---|---|---|---|---|---|---|---|---|---|---|---|---|---|
| | | | | | | 1 | 3 | 1 | | | 4 | 1 | 2 | 2 | 4 | | 1 | | | | | | | 5 | 1 |
| | | | | | 6 | 4 | 3 | 1 | 9 | | | | 3 | 2 | 5 | 3 | 7 | | | | | | | 15 | 2 |
| | | | | | 6 | 3 | 1 | 4 | 13 | 1 | | | 1 | 3 | 4 | 5 | 4 | | 1 | | | | | 14 | 3 |
| | | | | | 2 | 4 | 3 | 1 | 10 | | | | | | | 6 | 3 | 1 | | | | | | 10 | 4 |
| | | | | | 1 | | 1 | | 2 | | | | 2 | | 2 | | | | | | | | | 2 | 5 |
| | | | | 1 | 1 | 2 | 2 | 1 | 2 | | | | 2 | 1 | 3 | 2 | 1 | | | | | | | 6 | 6 |
| | | | | | | | | 2 | | 1 | 1 | | 2 | | 2 | | | | | | | | | 2 | 7 |
| | | | | | | | 1 | | 1 | | | | | | | | 1 | | | | | | | 1 | 8 |
| | | | | | | | 5 | 2 | 4 | 3 | | | 3 | 2 | 5 | 2 | | | | | | | | 7 | 9 |
| | | | | | | 1 | | | | | | | 1 | | 1 | | | | | | | | | 1 | 10 |
| | | | | | | | | 1 | | | | 1 | 1 | | 1 | | | | | | | | | 1 | 11 |
| | | | | | 5 | 2 | 8 | 4 | 4 | 8 | 4 | 2 | | 1 | 1 | 5 | 12 | | 1 | 1 | | | | 20 | 12 |
| | | | | 1 | 3 | | 6 | 1 | 7 | 3 | | | | 5 | 5 | | 3 | | 2 | | | | | 10 | 13 |
| | | | | | 3 | 1 | 1 | 4 | 9 | | | | 5 | 2 | 7 | 3 | | | | | | | | 10 | 14 |
| | | | | | 1 | 4 | 2 | 3 | 6 | 2 | | | 5 | 2 | 7 | | 3 | | | | | | | 10 | 15 |
| | | | | | 1 | 3 | 2 | | 4 | 2 | | | 1 | 1 | 2 | | 4 | | | | | | | 6 | 16 |
| | | | | 1 | 1 | 1 | 4 | | 5 | | | | 1 | | 1 | 1 | 3 | | 1 | | | | | 6 | 17 |
| | | | | | | | 1 | | | | | | 1 | | 1 | | | | | | | | | 1 | 18 |
| | | | | 1 | 12 | 13 | 4 | 9 | | 1 | 4 | 33 | 7 | 12 | 19 | 12 | 7 | | | | | | | 38 | 19 |
| | | | | 2 | 9 | 6 | 10 | 3 | 20 | 5 | | 1 | 5 | 3 | 8 | 9 | 9 | 1 | 1 | | | | | 28 | 20 |
| | | | | | 20 | 17 | 25 | 12 | 60 | 10 | 2 | | 22 | 17 | 39 | 21 | 11 | 1 | 2 | | | | | 74 | 21 |
| | | | | | | 1 | 1 | | | | | 2 | | 1 | 1 | | 1 | | | | | | | 2 | 22 |
| | | | | | 1 | | | | 1 | | | | | 1 | 1 | | | | | | | | | 1 | 23 |
| | | | | | 3 | 9 | 9 | 1 | 5 | 11 | 3 | 1 | 7 | 5 | 12 | 5 | 4 | 1 | | | | | | 22 | 24 |
| | | | | 2 | 5 | 15 | 3 | 5 | | 4 | 4 | 20 | 7 | 6 | 13 | 9 | 5 | 1 | | | | | | 28 | 25 |
| | | | | | 7 | 28 | 20 | 2 | 17 | 37 | 1 | | 13 | 15 | 28 | 14 | 8 | 3 | 4 | | | | | 57 | 26 |
| | | | | | 1 | | 2 | 2 | | 1 | 1 | 3 | 5 | | 5 | | | | | | | | | 5 | 27 |
| | | | | | 3 | 1 | | | 1 | | | 3 | | 1 | 1 | 1 | 2 | | | | | | | 4 | 28 |
| | | | | | 2 | | | 1 | 2 | 1 | | | | 2 | 2 | 1 | | | | | | | | 3 | 29 |
| | | | | 6 | 25 | 39 | 108 | 20 | 42 | 129 | 16 | 2 | 52 | 50 | 102 | 51 | 36 | 2 | 2 | | | | | 193 | 30 |
| | | | | | | 1 | 16 | 1 | 6 | 11 | | 1 | 7 | 5 | 12 | 2 | 4 | | | | | | | 18 | 31 |
| | | | | | | | 1 | | 1 | | | | 1 | | 1 | | | | | | | | | 1 | 32 |
| | | | | | 1 | 2 | 21 | 1 | 17 | 8 | | | 9 | 11 | 20 | 2 | 4 | | | | | | | 26 | 33 |
| | | | | | 2 | | 7 | | 8 | 1 | | | 1 | 2 | 3 | 4 | 1 | 1 | | | | | | 9 | 34 |
| | | | | | | 1 | 2 | 1 | 1 | 3 | | | | 4 | 4 | | | | | | | | | 4 | 35 |
| | | | | | 1 | | 2 | | | 3 | | | 1 | 1 | 2 | 1 | | | | | | | | 3 | 36 |
| | | | | | 27 | 13 | 18 | 13 | 31 | 35 | 5 | | 29 | 37 | 66 | | 5 | | | | | | | 71 | 37 |
| | | | | 1 | 4 | 9 | 43 | 10 | 6 | 42 | 13 | 3 | 31 | 23 | 54 | 7 | 5 | | | | | | | 66 | 38 |
| | | | | 1 | | | 1 | | | | 1 | | | | | 1 | | | | | | | | 1 | 39 |
| | | | | | | | 1 | | 1 | | | | | 1 | 1 | | | | | | | | | 1 | 40 |
| | | | | | | | 2 | 3 | 2 | | 1 | 2 | 4 | | 4 | | 1 | | | | | | | 5 | 41 |
| | | | | | | | 1 | | 1 | | | | | | | | 1 | | | | | | | 1 | 42 |
| | | | | | | 2 | | | | 2 | | | 1 | 1 | 2 | | | | | | | | | 2 | 43 |
| | | | | | | 1 | | | | | | 1 | | | | 1 | | | | | | | | 1 | 44 |
| | | | | | 4 | 3 | 1 | 1 | 7 | 2 | | | 4 | 3 | 7 | | 2 | | | | | | | 9 | 45 |
| | | | | | 3 | 8 | 9 | 4 | 3 | 13 | 2 | 7 | 7 | 5 | 12 | 7 | 6 | | | | | | | 25 | 46 |
| | | | 1 | | 2 | 1 | 5 | 1 | 4 | 4 | 1 | | 4 | 4 | 8 | 1 | | | | | | | | 9 | 47 |
| | | | | | | 9 | 4 | 2 | 7 | 5 | | 3 | 8 | 3 | 11 | 2 | 2 | | | | | | | 15 | 48 |

## CLASSIFICATION OF DEATHS IN MIDDLE, EASTERN,

| | Cause of death. | AGES. Under 1. | | 1 and under 5. | | 5 and under 10. | | 10 and under 20. | | 20 and under 50. | | 50 and under 80. | | 80 and under 100. | | 100 & over. | | Age unknown. | | NATIVITIES. Born in State. | N. England States. | Middle States. | Southern States. | Southwest'n States. | Northwest'n States. |
|---|---|---|---|---|---|---|---|---|---|---|---|---|---|---|---|---|---|---|---|---|---|---|---|---|---|
| | | M. | F. | M. | F. | M. | F. | M. | F. | M. | F. | M. | F. | M | F. | M | F. | M | F. | | | | | | |
| 1 | Inflamta'n, brain | 1 | .. | 2 | 3 | 1 | 1 | 1 | .. | .. | 2 | .. | .. | .. | .. | .. | .. | .. | .. | 8 | .. | .. | 1 | 2 | .. |
| 2 | ....do....stomach. | .. | 1 | .. | .. | .. | .. | .. | .. | 1 | 1 | .. | .. | .. | .. | .. | .. | .. | .. | 3 | .. | .. | .. | .. | .. |
| 3 | Intemperance | .. | .. | .. | .. | .. | .. | .. | .. | 2 | .. | .. | .. | .. | .. | .. | .. | .. | .. | .. | .. | .. | 1 | .. | .. |
| 4 | Jaundice | .. | .. | .. | 1 | 1 | .. | .. | .. | .. | .. | .. | .. | .. | .. | .. | .. | .. | .. | 2 | .. | .. | .. | .. | .. |
| 5 | Kidneys, disease of. | .. | .. | .. | .. | .. | .. | .. | .. | 1 | .. | .. | .. | .. | .. | .. | .. | .. | .. | .. | .. | .. | 1 | .. | .. |
| 6 | Killed | .. | .. | .. | .. | .. | .. | 1 | .. | 2 | .. | .. | .. | .. | .. | .. | .. | .. | .. | .. | .. | .. | 3 | .. | .. |
| 7 | Liver, disease of. | .. | .. | 1 | .. | .. | .. | 1 | 1 | .. | 1 | 1 | .. | .. | .. | .. | .. | .. | .. | 3 | .. | .. | 1 | 1 | .. |
| 8 | Lockjaw | 1 | .. | .. | .. | .. | .. | .. | .. | .. | .. | .. | .. | .. | .. | .. | .. | .. | .. | 1 | .. | .. | .. | .. | .. |
| 9 | Lungs, disease of. | 1 | .. | .. | .. | .. | .. | .. | .. | .. | .. | 2 | .. | .. | .. | .. | .. | .. | .. | 1 | .. | .. | 2 | .. | .. |
| 10 | Measles | .. | .. | .. | 2 | .. | .. | .. | .. | .. | 1 | .. | .. | .. | .. | .. | .. | .. | .. | 2 | .. | .. | .. | 1 | .. |
| 11 | Menses, suppress'n of | .. | .. | .. | .. | .. | .. | .. | .. | .. | 1 | .. | .. | .. | .. | .. | .. | .. | .. | .. | .. | .. | 1 | .. | .. |
| 12 | Neuralgia | .. | .. | .. | .. | .. | .. | .. | .. | .. | .. | 1 | .. | .. | .. | .. | .. | .. | .. | .. | .. | .. | 1 | .. | .. |
| 13 | Old age | .. | .. | .. | .. | .. | .. | .. | .. | .. | .. | 1 | 4 | .. | 5 | 4 | 3 | .. | .. | 1 | .. | 1 | 11 | .. | .. |
| 14 | Paralysis | .. | .. | .. | .. | .. | .. | .. | .. | .. | .. | .. | .. | .. | 1 | .. | .. | .. | .. | .. | .. | .. | 1 | .. | .. |
| 15 | Pleurisy | .. | .. | .. | .. | .. | .. | .. | .. | .. | .. | 1 | 1 | .. | .. | .. | .. | .. | .. | .. | .. | .. | 2 | .. | .. |
| 16 | Pneumonia | 7 | 3 | 6 | 1 | 1 | .. | 5 | 3 | 11 | 5 | 2 | 2 | .. | 2 | .. | .. | .. | .. | 25 | .. | .. | 16 | 7 | .. |
| 17 | Poison | 1 | .. | .. | .. | .. | .. | .. | .. | .. | .. | .. | .. | .. | .. | .. | .. | .. | .. | 1 | .. | .. | .. | .. | .. |
| 18 | Quinsy | .. | .. | 1 | .. | .. | .. | .. | 1 | .. | .. | .. | .. | .. | .. | .. | .. | .. | .. | 1 | .. | .. | 1 | .. | .. |
| 19 | Rheumatism | .. | .. | .. | .. | .. | .. | .. | .. | 1 | .. | .. | 1 | 1 | .. | .. | .. | .. | .. | .. | .. | .. | 2 | 1 | .. |
| 20 | Rickets | .. | .. | 1 | .. | .. | .. | .. | .. | .. | .. | .. | .. | .. | .. | .. | .. | .. | .. | 1 | .. | .. | .. | .. | .. |
| 21 | Salivation, effects of. | .. | .. | .. | .. | .. | .. | .. | .. | 1 | .. | .. | .. | .. | .. | .. | .. | .. | .. | .. | .. | .. | 1 | .. | .. |
| 22 | Scrofula | .. | .. | 2 | .. | .. | .. | .. | 1 | .. | .. | .. | 1 | .. | .. | .. | .. | .. | .. | 2 | .. | .. | 1 | 1 | .. |
| 23 | Suffocation | 3 | 5 | 1 | 4 | .. | .. | .. | .. | .. | .. | .. | .. | .. | .. | .. | .. | .. | .. | 13 | .. | .. | .. | .. | .. |
| 24 | Syphilis | .. | 1 | .. | .. | .. | .. | .. | .. | .. | .. | .. | .. | .. | .. | .. | .. | .. | .. | 1 | .. | .. | .. | .. | .. |
| 25 | Teething | .. | .. | .. | 1 | .. | .. | .. | .. | .. | .. | .. | .. | .. | .. | .. | .. | .. | .. | 1 | .. | .. | .. | .. | .. |
| 26 | Thrush | 1 | 1 | .. | .. | .. | .. | .. | .. | .. | .. | .. | .. | .. | .. | .. | .. | .. | .. | 2 | .. | .. | .. | .. | .. |
| 27 | Tumor | .. | .. | .. | .. | .. | .. | .. | .. | .. | 1 | .. | .. | .. | .. | .. | .. | .. | .. | .. | .. | .. | 1 | .. | .. |
| 28 | Ulcer | .. | .. | .. | .. | .. | .. | .. | 1 | .. | .. | .. | .. | .. | .. | .. | .. | .. | .. | .. | .. | .. | 1 | .. | .. |
| 29 | Uterus, disease of. | .. | .. | .. | .. | .. | .. | .. | .. | .. | 1 | .. | 1 | .. | .. | .. | .. | .. | .. | 1 | .. | .. | 1 | .. | .. |
| 30 | Venereal | .. | .. | .. | .. | .. | .. | .. | .. | .. | 1 | .. | .. | .. | .. | .. | .. | .. | .. | .. | .. | .. | .. | 1 | .. |
| 31 | Worms | 6 | 3 | 14 | 19 | 6 | 5 | .. | 1 | 1 | .. | .. | 1 | .. | .. | .. | .. | .. | .. | 52 | .. | .. | 2 | 1 | 1 |
| 32 | Unknown | 46 | 28 | 22 | 14 | 7 | 8 | 8 | 7 | 16 | 15 | 11 | 12 | 1 | 1 | .. | .. | .. | 2 | 128 | .. | .. | 40 | 16 | 2 |
| | Total | 144 | 97 | 177 | 174 | 61 | 47 | 63 | 74 | 133 | 129 | 64 | 47 | 3 | 12 | 5 | 3 | .. | 3 | 783 | .. | 3 | 292 | 122 | 7 |

## CLASSIFICATION OF DEATHS IN SOUTHWESTERN

*Embracing the following counties: Adams, Amite, Claiborn, Copiah, Franklin, Hinds, Issa*

| | | | | | | | | | | | | | | | | | | | | | | | | | |
|---|---|---|---|---|---|---|---|---|---|---|---|---|---|---|---|---|---|---|---|---|---|---|---|---|---|
| 1 | Abscess | .. | .. | .. | .. | .. | .. | .. | .. | .. | 1 | .. | .. | .. | .. | .. | .. | .. | .. | 1 | .. | .. | .. | .. | .. |
| 2 | Accident, not specfi'd | 5 | 6 | 7 | 7 | .. | 3 | 4 | 3 | 16 | 6 | 3 | 2 | .. | .. | .. | .. | .. | .. | 40 | .. | 2 | 14 | 2 | 2 |
| 3 | ....do....burned | .. | 2 | 7 | 5 | 3 | 4 | 1 | 1 | 1 | 1 | .. | .. | 1 | .. | .. | .. | .. | .. | 26 | .. | .. | .. | .. | .. |
| 4 | ....do....drowned | .. | .. | 5 | .. | 3 | 2 | .. | 2 | 15 | 4 | 1 | .. | .. | .. | .. | .. | .. | .. | 24 | .. | 1 | .. | .. | 3 |
| 5 | ....do....scalded | .. | 1 | 1 | .. | .. | .. | .. | .. | .. | .. | .. | .. | .. | .. | .. | .. | .. | .. | 2 | .. | .. | .. | .. | .. |
| 6 | ....do....shot | .. | .. | .. | .. | .. | .. | 3 | .. | 4 | .. | .. | .. | .. | .. | .. | .. | .. | .. | 5 | .. | .. | 2 | .. | .. |
| 7 | Amputation | .. | .. | .. | .. | .. | .. | 1 | .. | 1 | 1 | .. | .. | .. | .. | .. | .. | .. | .. | 1 | .. | .. | 2 | .. | .. |
| 8 | Apoplexy | .. | .. | .. | .. | .. | .. | .. | 1 | 4 | 3 | 5 | 4 | .. | .. | .. | .. | 1 | .. | 5 | .. | 1 | 9 | 2 | .. |
| 9 | Asthma | .. | .. | .. | .. | .. | .. | .. | 1 | .. | 1 | .. | .. | .. | .. | .. | .. | .. | .. | 2 | .. | .. | .. | .. | .. |
| 10 | Black tongue | .. | .. | .. | .. | 6 | .. | .. | .. | 5 | .. | .. | .. | .. | .. | .. | .. | .. | .. | 11 | .. | .. | .. | .. | .. |
| 11 | Bladder, disease of | .. | .. | .. | .. | .. | .. | .. | .. | .. | .. | 1 | .. | .. | .. | .. | .. | .. | .. | .. | .. | .. | .. | .. | .. |
| 12 | Bowels....do | 1 | 3 | 7 | 1 | .. | 1 | .. | .. | 1 | 2 | .. | .. | .. | .. | .. | .. | .. | .. | 14 | .. | .. | .. | .. | .. |
| 13 | Brain......do | .. | 1 | .. | .. | .. | .. | .. | .. | 1 | .. | 1 | .. | .. | .. | .. | .. | .. | .. | 1 | .. | .. | 1 | .. | .. |
| 14 | Bronchitis | 1 | 2 | .. | .. | .. | .. | .. | .. | 1 | .. | .. | .. | .. | .. | .. | .. | .. | .. | 3 | .. | 1 | .. | .. | .. |
| 15 | Cancer | .. | .. | .. | .. | .. | .. | .. | .. | .. | .. | .. | 4 | .. | 1 | .. | .. | .. | .. | 1 | .. | 1 | 2 | .. | .. |
| 16 | Canker | .. | .. | .. | .. | .. | .. | 1 | .. | .. | .. | .. | .. | .. | .. | .. | .. | .. | .. | 1 | .. | .. | .. | .. | .. |
| 17 | Catarrh | 4 | 3 | 5 | 3 | 1 | 1 | 1 | 1 | .. | 2 | .. | .. | 1 | .. | .. | .. | .. | .. | 19 | .. | .. | 2 | .. | .. |
| 18 | Childbirth | .. | .. | .. | .. | .. | .. | .. | 5 | .. | 26 | .. | .. | .. | .. | .. | .. | .. | .. | 16 | .. | 1 | 10 | 3 | .. |
| 19 | Cholera | 4 | 3 | 23 | 15 | 14 | 14 | 29 | 16 | 99 | 66 | 18 | 8 | .. | .. | .. | .. | 3 | 1 | 186 | .. | 5 | 65 | 16 | 29 |
| 20 | ....do....infantum | 8 | 11 | 12 | 16 | .. | 1 | .. | .. | .. | .. | .. | .. | .. | .. | .. | .. | .. | .. | 47 | .. | .. | .. | 1 | .. |
| 21 | ....do....morbus | .. | .. | 2 | .. | .. | .. | .. | .. | 1 | .. | 1 | .. | .. | .. | .. | .. | .. | .. | 3 | .. | .. | 1 | .. | .. |
| 22 | Chorea | .. | .. | .. | .. | .. | .. | 1 | .. | .. | .. | .. | .. | .. | .. | .. | .. | .. | .. | .. | .. | .. | 1 | .. | .. |
| 23 | Colic | .. | .. | .. | 1 | .. | .. | 1 | .. | 2 | 2 | 3 | .. | 1 | .. | .. | .. | .. | .. | 5 | .. | .. | 3 | .. | 1 |
| 24 | Congestion | .. | .. | 1 | 2 | .. | .. | 1 | 1 | 2 | .. | .. | .. | .. | .. | .. | .. | .. | .. | 5 | .. | .. | 1 | .. | .. |
| 25 | ....do...bowels | 1 | .. | .. | .. | .. | .. | .. | .. | .. | .. | .. | .. | .. | .. | .. | .. | .. | .. | 1 | .. | .. | .. | .. | .. |
| 26 | ....do...brain | 2 | .. | 3 | 2 | 1 | 1 | 3 | 3 | 5 | 1 | 1 | 1 | .. | .. | .. | .. | .. | .. | 16 | .. | .. | 2 | 2 | .. |
| 27 | ....do...lungs | .. | .. | .. | .. | 1 | .. | .. | 1 | .. | .. | .. | .. | .. | .. | .. | .. | .. | .. | 1 | .. | .. | .. | .. | 1 |
| 28 | Consumption | 1 | .. | 2 | 2 | .. | .. | 7 | 12 | 43 | 47 | 6 | 6 | 1 | 1 | .. | .. | .. | .. | 61 | 1 | 3 | 30 | 14 | 6 |
| 29 | Convulsions | 15 | 7 | 5 | 9 | 5 | 2 | 1 | 1 | 1 | 2 | 2 | 1 | .. | 1 | .. | .. | .. | .. | 45 | .. | 1 | 4 | 2 | .. |
| 30 | Cramp | .. | .. | .. | .. | 1 | .. | .. | .. | 1 | 1 | .. | .. | .. | .. | .. | .. | .. | .. | 2 | .. | .. | .. | .. | .. |
| 31 | Croup | 36 | 25 | 25 | 18 | 2 | 1 | .. | .. | .. | .. | .. | .. | .. | .. | .. | .. | .. | .. | 105 | .. | .. | 2 | .. | .. |
| 32 | Debility | 5 | 1 | 2 | 4 | 1 | .. | .. | .. | 4 | 1 | 1 | 2 | 1 | 1 | .. | .. | 1 | .. | 16 | .. | .. | 3 | 1 | .. |

SECTION OF THE STATE OF MISSISSIPPI—Continued.

| NATIVITIES. California and Territories. | Ireland. | Germany. | Other foreign countries. | Unknown. | SEASON OF DECEASE. Spring. | Summer. | Autumn. | Winter. | DURATION OF SICKNESS. Under 1 week. | 1 week and under 1 month. | 1 month and under 3 months. | 3 months and over. | WHITES. Males. | Females. | Total. | COLORED. Slaves. Black. M. | Slaves. Black. F. | Slaves. Mulatto. M. | Slaves. Mulatto. F. | Free. Black. M. | Free. Black. F. | Free. Mul. M | Free. Mul. F. | Aggregate deaths. | |
|---|---|---|---|---|---|---|---|---|---|---|---|---|---|---|---|---|---|---|---|---|---|---|---|---|---|
| ... | ... | .. | ... | ... | 1 | 2 | 7 | 1 | 7 | 4 | ... | ... | 3 | 5 | 8 | 1 | 1 | 1 | ... | ... | ... | .. | .. | 11 | 1 |
| ... | ... | .. | ... | ... | 1 | 1 | ... | 1 | 1 | 2 | ... | ... | 1 | 2 | 3 | ... | ... | ... | ... | ... | ... | .. | .. | 3 | 2 |
| ... | 1 | .. | ... | ... | ... | ... | ... | 2 | 2 | ... | ... | ... | 2 | ... | 2 | ... | ... | ... | ... | ... | ... | .. | .. | 2 | 3 |
| ... | ... | .. | ... | ... | ... | ... | 2 | ... | 1 | ... | ... | 1 | 1 | 1 | 2 | ... | ... | ... | ... | ... | ... | .. | .. | 2 | 4 |
| ... | ... | .. | ... | ... | ... | ... | 1 | ... | ... | 1 | ... | ... | 1 | ... | 1 | ... | ... | ... | ... | ... | ... | .. | .. | 1 | 5 |
| ... | ... | .. | ... | ... | ... | ... | 1 | 2 | 2 | ... | ... | ... | ... | ... | ... | 3 | ... | ... | ... | ... | ... | .. | .. | 3 | 6 |
| ... | ... | .. | ... | ... | 3 | ... | 1 | 1 | 1 | ... | ... | 4 | 2 | 2 | 4 | 1 | ... | ... | ... | ... | ... | .. | .. | 5 | 7 |
| ... | ... | .. | ... | ... | ... | 1 | ... | ... | 1 | ... | ... | ... | ... | ... | ... | 1 | ... | ... | ... | ... | ... | .. | .. | 1 | 8 |
| ... | ... | .. | ... | ... | 2 | ... | ... | 1 | ... | ... | 1 | 2 | 3 | ... | 3 | ... | ... | ... | ... | ... | ... | .. | .. | 3 | 9 |
| ... | ... | .. | ... | ... | 3 | ... | ... | ... | 1 | 2 | ... | ... | ... | ... | ... | ... | 3 | ... | ... | ... | ... | .. | .. | 3 | 10 |
| ... | ... | .. | ... | ... | ... | 1 | ... | ... | ... | ... | 1 | ... | ... | ... | ... | ... | 1 | ... | ... | ... | ... | .. | .. | 1 | 11 |
| ... | ... | .. | ... | ... | ... | ... | 1 | ... | ... | ... | ... | 1 | 1 | ... | 1 | ... | ... | ... | ... | ... | ... | .. | .. | 1 | 12 |
| ... | ... | .. | 3 | 1 | 4 | 6 | 3 | 3 | 2 | 2 | 1 | 4 | 1 | 7 | 8 | 4 | 5 | ... | ... | ... | ... | .. | .. | 17 | 13 |
| ... | ... | .. | ... | ... | 1 | ... | ... | ... | ... | 1 | ... | ... | ... | 1 | 1 | ... | ... | ... | ... | ... | ... | .. | .. | 1 | 14 |
| ... | ... | .. | ... | ... | ... | 1 | ... | 1 | ... | ... | 1 | ... | ... | 1 | 1 | 1 | ... | ... | ... | ... | ... | .. | .. | 2 | 15 |
| ... | ... | .. | ... | ... | 16 | 11 | 13 | 8 | 10 | 31 | 7 | ... | 16 | 9 | 25 | 15 | 7 | ... | ... | 1 | ... | .. | .. | 48 | 16 |
| ... | ... | .. | ... | ... | ... | ... | 1 | ... | ... | 1 | ... | ... | 1 | ... | 1 | ... | ... | ... | ... | ... | ... | .. | .. | 1 | 17 |
| ... | ... | .. | ... | ... | ... | ... | ... | 2 | ... | 2 | ... | ... | ... | 1 | 1 | 1 | ... | ... | ... | ... | ... | .. | .. | 2 | 18 |
| ... | ... | .. | ... | ... | 1 | 1 | ... | 1 | ... | 1 | ... | 2 | 2 | 1 | 3 | ... | ... | ... | ... | ... | ... | .. | .. | 3 | 19 |
| ... | ... | .. | ... | ... | ... | 1 | ... | ... | ... | ... | ... | 1 | ... | ... | ... | 1 | ... | ... | ... | ... | ... | .. | .. | 1 | 20 |
| ... | ... | .. | ... | ... | 1 | ... | ... | ... | ... | 1 | ... | ... | 1 | ... | 1 | ... | ... | ... | ... | ... | ... | .. | .. | 1 | 21 |
| ... | ... | .. | ... | ... | ... | 2 | 1 | 1 | ... | ... | ... | 3 | ... | 1 | 1 | 2 | 1 | ... | ... | ... | ... | .. | .. | 4 | 22 |
| ... | ... | .. | ... | ... | 2 | 6 | 5 | ... | 13 | ... | ... | ... | ... | 3 | 3 | 4 | 6 | ... | ... | ... | ... | .. | .. | 13 | 23 |
| ... | ... | .. | ... | ... | ... | 1 | ... | ... | ... | ... | ... | 1 | ... | ... | ... | ... | ... | ... | 1 | ... | ... | .. | .. | 1 | 24 |
| ... | ... | .. | ... | ... | 1 | ... | ... | ... | ... | ... | ... | 1 | ... | ... | ... | ... | 1 | ... | ... | ... | ... | .. | .. | 1 | 25 |
| ... | ... | .. | ... | ... | ... | 1 | 1 | ... | 1 | 1 | ... | ... | 1 | 1 | 2 | ... | ... | ... | ... | ... | ... | .. | .. | 2 | 26 |
| ... | ... | .. | ... | ... | ... | 1 | ... | ... | ... | ... | ... | 1 | ... | 1 | 1 | ... | ... | ... | ... | ... | ... | .. | .. | 1 | 27 |
| ... | ... | .. | ... | ... | ... | ... | 1 | ... | ... | ... | 1 | ... | ... | 1 | 1 | ... | ... | ... | ... | ... | ... | .. | .. | 1 | 28 |
| ... | ... | .. | ... | ... | ... | 1 | 1 | ... | 1 | ... | ... | 1 | ... | 1 | 1 | ... | 1 | ... | ... | ... | ... | .. | .. | 2 | 29 |
| ... | ... | .. | ... | ... | ... | ... | 1 | ... | ... | ... | ... | 1 | ... | ... | ... | ... | 1 | ... | ... | ... | ... | .. | .. | 1 | 30 |
| ... | ... | .. | ... | ... | 10 | 15 | 23 | 7 | 23 | 31 | 2 | ... | 15 | 12 | 27 | 10 | 11 | 1 | 6 | ... | ... | 1 | .. | 6 | 31 |
| ... | ... | .. | ... | 7 | 39 | 39 | 82 | 27 | 94 | 23 | 9 | 30 | 46 | 41 | 87 | 60 | 45 | ... | 1 | ... | ... | .. | .. | 193 | 32 |
| ... | 1 | .. | 4 | 24 | 247 | 296 | 504 | 175 | 479 | 452 | 85 | 139 | 352 | 325 | 677 | 282 | 239 | 13 | 22 | 2 | .. | 1 | .. | 1236 | |

SECTION OF THE STATE OF MISSISSIPPI.

*quena, Jefferson, Lawrence, Madison, Pike, Rankin, Simpson, Warren, Wilkinson, and Yazoo.*

| California and Territories | Ireland | Germany | Other foreign countries | Unknown | Spring | Summer | Autumn | Winter | Under 1 week | 1 week and under 1 month | 1 month and under 3 months | 3 months and over | Males | Females | Total | Slaves Black M. | Slaves Black F. | Slaves Mulatto M. | Slaves Mulatto F. | Free Black M. | Free Black F. | Free Mul. M | Free Mul. F. | Aggregate deaths | |
|---|---|---|---|---|---|---|---|---|---|---|---|---|---|---|---|---|---|---|---|---|---|---|---|---|---|
| ... | ... | .. | ... | ... | ... | 1 | ... | ... | ... | ... | ... | 1 | 1 | ... | 1 | ... | ... | ... | ... | ... | ... | .. | .. | 1 | 1 |
| ... | 1 | .. | ... | 1 | 17 | 16 | 12 | 17 | 46 | 5 | 2 | 1 | 8 | 3 | 11 | 23 | 23 | 4 | 1 | ... | ... | .. | .. | 62 | 2 |
| ... | ... | .. | ... | ... | 5 | 3 | 4 | 9 | 12 | 1 | 3 | ... | 4 | 5 | 9 | 9 | 8 | ... | ... | ... | ... | .. | .. | 26 | 3 |
| ... | 1 | .. | ... | 3 | 8 | 13 | 5 | 6 | 32 | ... | ... | ... | 5 | ... | 5 | 17 | 8 | 2 | ... | ... | ... | .. | .. | 32 | 4 |
| ... | ... | .. | ... | ... | 1 | 1 | ... | ... | 1 | ... | ... | ... | ... | ... | ... | 1 | 1 | ... | ... | ... | ... | .. | .. | 2 | 5 |
| ... | ... | .. | ... | ... | 4 | 1 | 1 | 1 | 6 | ... | ... | ... | 2 | ... | 2 | 4 | ... | 1 | ... | ... | ... | .. | .. | 7 | 6 |
| ... | ... | .. | ... | ... | 1 | ... | 1 | 1 | 2 | 1 | ... | ... | ... | ... | ... | 2 | 1 | ... | ... | ... | ... | .. | .. | 3 | 7 |
| ... | ... | .. | ... | ... | 3 | 2 | 5 | 8 | 12 | 1 | 1 | ... | 5 | 3 | 8 | 5 | 5 | ... | ... | ... | ... | .. | .. | 18 | 8 |
| ... | 1 | .. | ... | ... | ... | ... | 1 | 1 | ... | ... | ... | 1 | ... | ... | ... | ... | 2 | ... | ... | ... | ... | .. | .. | 2 | 9 |
| ... | ... | .. | ... | ... | ... | 5 | 6 | ... | 11 | ... | ... | ... | ... | ... | ... | 11 | ... | ... | ... | ... | ... | .. | .. | 11 | 10 |
| ... | ... | .. | ... | 1 | ... | 1 | ... | ... | ... | ... | ... | ... | 1 | ... | 1 | ... | ... | ... | ... | ... | ... | .. | .. | 1 | 11 |
| ... | ... | .. | ... | 2 | 2 | 4 | 9 | ... | 2 | 5 | 1 | 1 | 6 | 4 | 10 | 2 | 3 | ... | ... | ... | ... | 1 | .. | 16 | 12 |
| ... | ... | .. | ... | 1 | 2 | ... | ... | 1 | ... | ... | 1 | ... | ... | 1 | 1 | 2 | ... | ... | ... | ... | ... | .. | .. | 3 | 13 |
| ... | ... | .. | ... | ... | 3 | ... | ... | 1 | ... | 2 | 1 | 1 | 1 | ... | 1 | 1 | 2 | ... | ... | ... | ... | .. | .. | 4 | 14 |
| ... | ... | .. | ... | 1 | 2 | 2 | ... | 1 | ... | ... | ... | 4 | ... | 1 | 1 | ... | 4 | ... | ... | ... | ... | .. | .. | 5 | 15 |
| ... | ... | .. | ... | ... | 1 | ... | ... | ... | ... | 1 | ... | ... | 1 | ... | 1 | ... | ... | ... | ... | ... | ... | .. | .. | 1 | 16 |
| ... | 1 | .. | ... | ... | 10 | 2 | 3 | 7 | 9 | 11 | 2 | ... | 3 | 2 | 5 | 9 | 8 | ... | ... | ... | ... | .. | .. | 22 | 17 |
| ... | ... | 1 | ... | ... | 8 | 9 | 5 | 9 | 22 | 7 | 1 | 1 | ... | 12 | 12 | ... | 18 | ... | 1 | ... | ... | .. | .. | 31 | 18 |
| ... | 1 | 1 | 1 | 9 | 138 | 142 | 11 | 21 | 258 | 11 | 1 | 1 | 34 | 7 | 41 | 147 | 112 | 9 | 4 | ... | ... | .. | .. | 313 | 19 |
| ... | ... | .. | ... | ... | 9 | 23 | 6 | 3 | 26 | 5 | 1 | 1 | 6 | 7 | 13 | 14 | 19 | ... | 2 | ... | ... | .. | .. | 48 | 20 |
| ... | ... | .. | ... | ... | 1 | 1 | ... | 2 | 2 | 1 | ... | ... | 1 | ... | 1 | 2 | ... | 1 | ... | ... | ... | .. | .. | 4 | 21 |
| ... | ... | .. | ... | ... | ... | 1 | ... | ... | 1 | ... | ... | ... | ... | ... | ... | 1 | ... | ... | ... | ... | ... | .. | .. | 1 | 22 |
| ... | ... | 1 | ... | ... | ... | 4 | 6 | ... | 6 | 1 | ... | 1 | 4 | ... | 4 | 3 | 3 | ... | ... | ... | ... | .. | .. | 10 | 23 |
| ... | ... | .. | ... | 1 | ... | 1 | 5 | 1 | 5 | 2 | ... | ... | 1 | 1 | 2 | 2 | 2 | 1 | ... | ... | ... | .. | .. | 7 | 24 |
| ... | ... | .. | ... | ... | ... | 1 | ... | ... | 1 | ... | ... | ... | ... | ... | ... | 1 | ... | ... | ... | ... | ... | .. | .. | 1 | 25 |
| ... | ... | .. | 1 | 2 | 6 | 8 | 10 | 3 | 11 | 6 | ... | ... | 6 | 2 | 8 | 8 | 5 | 1 | 1 | ... | ... | .. | .. | 23 | 26 |
| ... | ... | .. | ... | ... | 1 | ... | 1 | ... | ... | 1 | ... | ... | 1 | ... | 1 | ... | 1 | ... | ... | ... | ... | .. | .. | 2 | 27 |
| ... | 2 | 3 | 1 | 7 | 32 | 25 | 39 | 31 | 1 | 1 | 8 | 89 | 31 | 29 | 60 | 28 | 33 | 1 | 6 | ... | ... | .. | .. | 128 | 28 |
| ... | ... | .. | ... | ... | 14 | 14 | 16 | 7 | 25 | 2 | 3 | 3 | 6 | 4 | 10 | 21 | 18 | 2 | 1 | ... | ... | .. | .. | 52 | 29 |
| ... | ... | 1 | ... | ... | 1 | ... | 2 | ... | 1 | 1 | ... | ... | ... | 1 | 1 | 1 | ... | 1 | ... | ... | ... | .. | .. | 3 | 30 |
| ... | ... | .. | ... | ... | 31 | 15 | 25 | 33 | 87 | 10 | ... | ... | 11 | 9 | 20 | 48 | 34 | 4 | 1 | ... | ... | .. | .. | 107 | 31 |
| ... | 1 | .. | 1 | 2 | 3 | 5 | 10 | 5 | ... | 2 | ... | 4 | 7 | 2 | 9 | 8 | 7 | ... | ... | ... | ... | .. | .. | 24 | 32 |

## CLASSIFICATION OF DEATHS IN SOUTHWESTERN

| | Cause of death. | Ages. Under 1. | | 1 and under 5. | | 5 and under 10. | | 10 and under 20. | | 20 and under 50. | | 50 and under 80. | | 80 and under 100. | | 100 & over. | | Age unknown. | | Nativities. Born in State. | N. England States. | Middle States. | Southern States. | Southwest'n States. | Northwest'n States. |
|---|---|---|---|---|---|---|---|---|---|---|---|---|---|---|---|---|---|---|---|---|---|---|---|---|---|
| | | M. | F. | M. | F. | M. | F. | M. | F. | M. | F. | M. | F. | M. | F. | M. | F. | M. | F. | | | | | | |
| 1 | Diabetes | | | | 1 | | | | | | | | | | | | | | | 1 | | | | | |
| 2 | Diarrhœa | 5 | 8 | 14 | 15 | 1 | | 2 | | 23 | 6 | 4 | 4 | | 1 | | | | | 56 | | 2 | 15 | 3 | 2 |
| 3 | Dirt eating | | | | | | | | | | 1 | | | | | | | | | 1 | | | | | |
| 4 | Dropsy | | 1 | 9 | 6 | 3 | 2 | 5 | 1 | 24 | 26 | 13 | 13 | | | | | | | 60 | | 3 | 26 | 4 | 2 |
| 5 | Dysentery | 6 | 6 | 6 | 9 | 1 | 2 | 3 | 2 | 9 | 6 | 1 | 2 | | 1 | | | 1 | | 40 | | | 8 | 1 | 2 |
| 6 | Dyspepsia | | | | | | | | 1 | 3 | 1 | 4 | 1 | | | | | | | 4 | | | 4 | 2 | |
| 7 | Epilepsy | | | | | | | | | 3 | | | | | | | | | | | | 1 | 1 | | |
| 8 | Erysipelas | 2 | 2 | | 1 | | | | | 1 | 2 | | | | | | | | | 6 | | | | 1 | 1 |
| 9 | Executed | | | | | | | | | 1 | | | | | | | | | | | | | 1 | | |
| 10 | Fever, not specified | 36 | 17 | 45 | 41 | 16 | 9 | 13 | 12 | 20 | 16 | 10 | 5 | 2 | 1 | | | 1 | | 207 | | 3 | 19 | 6 | 2 |
| 11 | ..do..bilious | 2 | 1 | 6 | 4 | 3 | 3 | 1 | | 6 | 2 | 1 | | | | | | | | 24 | | | 3 | | 1 |
| 12 | ..do..brain | | 2 | 5 | 1 | 1 | | | 1 | 1 | 1 | | 1 | | | | | | | 9 | | | 3 | 1 | |
| 13 | ..do..catarrhal | | | 2 | 1 | | | | 1 | | 1 | | | | | | | | | 5 | | | | | |
| 14 | ..do..congestive | 4 | 1 | 10 | 9 | 5 | 12 | 7 | 9 | 24 | 8 | 2 | 2 | | | | | 1 | | 71 | | 1 | 15 | 3 | |
| 15 | ..do. inflammatory | 1 | | | | | | | | | | | | | | | | | | 1 | | | | | |
| 16 | ..do..intermittent | | | | | | 2 | | 1 | 1 | | 1 | | | | | | | | 3 | | | 1 | | |
| 17 | ..do..puerperal | | | | | | | | | | 7 | | | | | | | | | 2 | | 2 | 2 | 1 | |
| 18 | ..do..scarlet | 4 | 2 | 8 | 7 | 6 | 8 | 3 | 2 | 2 | 1 | | | | | | | | | 40 | | | 2 | | 1 |
| 19 | ..do..typhus | | 1 | 6 | 6 | 7 | 2 | 9 | 3 | 11 | 20 | 2 | 5 | | 1 | | | | | 41 | | | 11 | 10 | 5 |
| 20 | ..do..yellow | | | | | 1 | | | | | 1 | | | | | | | | | 1 | | | 1 | | |
| 21 | Frozen | | | | | | | | | 1 | | | | | | | | | | 1 | | | | | |
| 22 | Gravel | | | | | | | | | | | 2 | | | | | | | | | | | 2 | | |
| 23 | Heart, disease of | | | 1 | | 3 | | 2 | | 3 | 8 | 1 | 2 | | | | | | 2 | 11 | | 1 | 5 | 3 | |
| 24 | Hemorrhage | | | | | | 1 | | | 2 | | 3 | | | | | | | | 3 | | | 3 | | |
| 25 | Hernia | 1 | 1 | | | | | 1 | | 2 | 2 | | | | | | | | | 4 | | | | 1 | 1 |
| 26 | Hives | 3 | 5 | | 1 | | | | | | | | | | | | | | | 9 | | | | | |
| 27 | Hooping cough | 13 | 6 | 29 | 16 | | | 4 | 1 | 1 | 2 | | | | | | | | | 71 | | | 1 | | |
| 28 | Hydrocephalus | 3 | | 4 | | | | | | 1 | | | | | | | | | | 7 | | | | 1 | |
| 29 | Inflammation | 3 | 1 | 3 | 1 | 1 | 1 | | | 1 | 3 | | | | | | | | | 12 | | | 2 | | |
| 30 | ...do......bowels | 8 | 4 | 12 | 8 | 4 | 4 | | 3 | 7 | 8 | 2 | 1 | | | | | | | 49 | | | 7 | 1 | 4 |
| 31 | ....do......brain | 5 | 2 | 10 | 7 | 3 | 3 | 5 | 7 | 4 | 2 | 2 | 1 | | | | | | | 44 | | | 2 | 1 | 2 |
| 32 | ....do......stomach | | | | | | 1 | | 1 | | 1 | | | | | | | | | 2 | | | | | 1 |
| 33 | Insanity | | | | | | 1 | 1 | | 1 | | 1 | | | | | | 1 | | 3 | | | | 1 | |
| 34 | Intemperance | | | | | | | | | 7 | | 2 | | | | | | 1 | | 5 | | | 1 | | |
| 35 | Killed | 1 | | | | | | | | 3 | | | 1 | | | | | | | 2 | | | 2 | 1 | |
| 36 | Lightning | | | | | | | | | 1 | 2 | | | | | | | | | 2 | | | 1 | | |
| 37 | Liver, disease of | 2 | | | 1 | | | 1 | | 4 | 4 | 3 | | | | | | 1 | | 8 | | 1 | 4 | 2 | |
| 38 | Lockjaw | 6 | 5 | 1 | 3 | 1 | | 2 | | 3 | 1 | 1 | | | | | | | | 21 | | | | | |
| 39 | Lungs, disease of | | | | 1 | | | | | 1 | 3 | | 3 | | | | | | | 2 | | | 4 | | 2 |
| 40 | Malformation | | | 1 | | | | | | | | | | | | | | | | 1 | | | | | |
| 41 | Marasmus | 2 | | 1 | 2 | | | | | | | | | | | | | | | 5 | | | | | |
| 42 | Measles | | | 8 | 6 | | 1 | | 2 | 3 | 3 | 1 | | | | | | | | 22 | | | 1 | | |
| 43 | Menses, suppres'n of | | | | | | | | | | 1 | | | | | | | | | | | | 1 | | |
| 44 | Murder | | | | | | | | | 2 | | | | | | | | 1 | | | | | 2 | | |
| 45 | Neuralgia | | | | | | | | | 1 | | | 1 | | | | | | | | | | 2 | | |
| 46 | Old age | | | | | | | | | | | 8 | 7 | 8 | 11 | 4 | 5 | | | 11 | | 4 | 16 | | |
| 47 | Paralysis | | | | | | | | | 2 | 2 | 5 | 3 | | 1 | | | | | 3 | | | 6 | | 1 |
| 48 | Piles | | | 1 | | | | | | | 1 | 1 | | | | | | | | 1 | | | 2 | | |
| 49 | Pleurisy | | | 1 | | | | 1 | | 5 | | 1 | 2 | | | | | | | 5 | | | 3 | 1 | |
| 50 | Pneumonia | 10 | 10 | 27 | 22 | 5 | 9 | 15 | 16 | 51 | 34 | 13 | 13 | | | | 1 | 1 | | 149 | | 2 | 51 | 13 | |
| 51 | Poison | | | 3 | | 1 | | | | 1 | 1 | | | | | | | | | 4 | | | 1 | 1 | |
| 52 | Quinsy | 1 | | 1 | 1 | | | | | 1 | 1 | 1 | | | | | | | | 5 | | | | | |
| 53 | Rheumatism | | | | | | | | | 1 | 1 | 1 | | | | | | | | 1 | | | 2 | | |
| 54 | Salivation, effects of | | | | | 1 | | | | 1 | | | | | | | | | | | | | 1 | 1 | |
| 55 | Scrofula | 3 | 1 | 5 | 1 | | | 2 | 1 | 1 | 4 | | | | | | | | | 16 | | | | | |
| 56 | Small pox | | | 1 | 1 | | | | | 1 | | | 1 | | | | | | | 3 | | | | | 1 |
| 57 | Spine, disease of | 1 | | 2 | | 1 | | | 1 | 1 | | | | | | | | 2 | | 7 | | | 1 | | |
| 58 | Stillborn | 2 | | | | | | | | | | | | | | | | | | 2 | | | | | |
| 59 | Stomach, disease of | | | | | | | | | | 3 | 2 | | | | | | | | 3 | | | 1 | | |
| 60 | Suffocation | 17 | 22 | 5 | 4 | | | | | | | | | | | | | | | 48 | | | | | |
| 61 | Suicide | | | | | | | | | 1 | | | | | | | | | | | | | | | |
| 62 | Sun, stroke of | | | | | | | | | 1 | | | 1 | | | | | | | 2 | | | | | |
| 63 | Syphilis | | 1 | | 1 | | | | | 1 | 1 | | 1 | | | | | | | 5 | | | | | |
| 64 | Teething | 5 | 8 | 15 | 14 | | | | | | | | | | | | | | | 40 | | | 1 | 1 | |
| 65 | Tetanus | 9 | 8 | 5 | | 1 | | | | 1 | 2 | | | | | | | 1 | | 26 | | | | | |
| 66 | Throat, disease of | 2 | | 1 | 1 | 2 | | | | | | | | | | | | | | 4 | | 1 | 1 | | |
| 67 | Thrush | | 1 | | 2 | | | | | | | | | | | | | | | 2 | | | | 1 | |
| 68 | Tumor | | | | | | 1 | | | 1 | | | | | | | | | | 1 | | | 1 | | |
| 69 | Uterus, disease of | | | | | | | | | | 2 | | 1 | | | | | | | 2 | | | | | |
| 70 | Venereal | | | | | | | | | | 1 | 1 | | | | | | | | 1 | | | 1 | | |
| 71 | Worms | 9 | 6 | 29 | 34 | 2 | 5 | 1 | 1 | | | | | | | | | | | 82 | | | 4 | | 1 |
| 72 | Unknown | 113 | 104 | 33 | 39 | 4 | 5 | 5 | 5 | 22 | 31 | 14 | 6 | | 3 | | 1 | 4 | 3 | 346 | | 2 | 24 | 6 | 2 |
| | Total | 362 | 291 | 417 | 352 | 111 | 102 | 137 | 119 | 476 | 390 | 146 | 105 | 15 | 23 | 4 | 7 | 20 | 6 | 2296 | 1 | 39 | 422 | 110 | 73 |

ECTION OF THE STATE OF MISSISSIPPI—Continued.

| NATIVITIES. | | | | | SEASON OF DECEASE. | | | | DURATION OF SICKNESS. | | | | WHITES. | | | COLORED. | | | | | | | | | |
|---|---|---|---|---|---|---|---|---|---|---|---|---|---|---|---|---|---|---|---|---|---|---|---|---|---|
| | | | | | | | | | | | | | | | | Slaves. | | | | Free. | | | | | |
| | | | | | | | | | | | | | | | | Black. | | Mulatto. | | Black. | | Mul. | | | |
| ritories. | Ireland. | Germany. | Other foreign countries. | Unknown. | Spring. | Summer. | Autumn. | Winter. | Under 1 week. | 1 week and under 1 month. | 1 month and under 3 months. | 3 months and over. | Males. | Females. | Total. | M. | F. | M. | F. | M. | F. | M | F. | Aggregate deaths. | |
| | | | | | | | | 1 | | 1 | | | | 1 | 1 | | | | | | | | | 1 | 1 |
| | | | | 5 | 18 | 23 | 28 | 13 | 6 | 21 | 14 | 34 | 21 | 9 | 31 | 21 | 22 | 6 | 3 | | | 1 | | 83 | 2 |
| | | | | | | 1 | | | | | | | | | | | 1 | | | | | | | 1 | 3 |
| | | 1 | | 7 | 24 | 22 | 31 | 26 | 2 | 3 | 11 | 69 | 14 | 13 | 27 | 39 | 34 | 1 | 2 | | | | | 103 | 4 |
| | 2 | | | 2 | 3 | 32 | 9 | 5 | 6 | 22 | 2 | 1 | 8 | 12 | 20 | 18 | 16 | 1 | | | | | | 55 | 5 |
| | | | | | 5 | | 2 | 3 | | 1 | | 9 | 7 | 2 | 9 | | 1 | | | | | | | 10 | 6 |
| | | | | 1 | 1 | | 1 | 1 | 2 | | | | 2 | | 2 | 1 | | | | | | | | 3 | 7 |
| | | | | | 4 | 2 | 1 | 1 | 1 | 5 | | | 2 | 3 | 5 | 1 | 2 | | | | | | | 8 | 8 |
| | | | | | | 1 | | | 1 | | | | | | | 1 | | | | | | | | 1 | 9 |
| | 3 | | | 4 | 49 | 58 | 106 | 24 | 87 | 73 | 11 | 3 | 33 | 24 | 57 | 108 | 73 | 2 | 4 | | | | | 244 | 10 |
| | | | | 1 | 1 | 5 | 20 | 2 | 4 | 20 | 1 | | 13 | 3 | 16 | 6 | 6 | | 1 | | | | | 29 | 11 |
| | | | | | 2 | 5 | 4 | 2 | 7 | 3 | | | 5 | 2 | 7 | 2 | 4 | | | | | | | 13 | 12 |
| | | | | | | | 2 | 3 | 2 | 3 | | | | | | 2 | 3 | | | | | | | 5 | 13 |
| | 1 | | 1 | 2 | 4 | 19 | 60 | 10 | 49 | 28 | 2 | 1 | 21 | 21 | 42 | 31 | 16 | 1 | 4 | | | | | 94 | 14 |
| | | | | | | 1 | | | 1 | | | | | | | 1 | | | | | | | | 1 | 15 |
| | | | | 1 | | | 3 | 2 | 2 | 2 | | | 2 | 2 | 4 | | | | 1 | | | | | 5 | 16 |
| | | | | | 1 | | 3 | 3 | 2 | 2 | 2 | 1 | | 2 | 2 | | 5 | | | | | | | 7 | 17 |
| | | | | | 9 | 9 | 14 | 11 | 20 | 17 | 5 | | 17 | 14 | 31 | 6 | 5 | | 1 | | | | | 43 | 18 |
| | 1 | 1 | | 4 | 20 | 12 | 23 | 15 | 8 | 48 | 7 | | 8 | 12 | 20 | 27 | 25 | | 1 | | | | | 73 | 19 |
| | | | | | | | 2 | | | 1 | | | 1 | 1 | 2 | | | | | | | | | 2 | 20 |
| | | | | | 1 | | | | | | | | | | | 1 | | | | | | | | 1 | 21 |
| | | | | | | | 2 | | | | | 1 | 1 | | 1 | 1 | | | | | | | | 2 | 22 |
| | 1 | | 1 | | 9 | 4 | | 6 | 2 | 2 | 2 | 7 | 3 | 6 | 9 | 7 | 6 | | | | | | | 22 | 23 |
| | | | | | 2 | 3 | 1 | | 3 | | | 2 | 2 | 1 | 3 | 3 | | | | | | | | 6 | 24 |
| | | | | 1 | 3 | | 2 | 1 | 2 | 1 | | | 1 | 2 | 3 | 3 | 1 | | | | | | | 7 | 25 |
| | | | | | 2 | 2 | 2 | 3 | 4 | 2 | 1 | | 1 | 3 | 4 | 2 | 3 | | | | | | | 9 | 26 |
| | | | | | 4 | 49 | 14 | 5 | 33 | 30 | 3 | | 2 | 1 | 3 | 45 | 23 | | 1 | | | | | 72 | 27 |
| | | | | | 1 | 4 | 1 | 2 | 2 | 2 | | 2 | 4 | | 4 | 4 | | | | | | | | 8 | 28 |
| | | | | | 2 | 5 | 4 | 3 | 7 | 1 | 2 | | 5 | 2 | 7 | 3 | 3 | | 1 | | | | | 14 | 29 |
| | | | | | 11 | 31 | 14 | 5 | 27 | 30 | 4 | | 12 | 10 | 22 | 18 | 17 | 3 | 1 | | | | | 61 | 30 |
| | | | 2 | | 9 | 14 | 20 | 8 | 24 | 19 | 1 | | 19 | 7 | 26 | 9 | 14 | | 1 | | | 1 | | 51 | 31 |
| | | | | | 1 | 1 | | 1 | 1 | 2 | | | | 2 | 2 | | 1 | | | | | | | 3 | 32 |
| | | | | 1 | 1 | 2 | 2 | | | | | 3 | 1 | | 1 | 2 | 1 | 1 | | | | | | 5 | 33 |
| | 1 | | | 3 | 3 | 1 | 5 | 1 | 1 | 1 | 1 | | 5 | | 5 | 5 | | | | | | | | 10 | 34 |
| | | | | | 2 | 1 | 2 | | 5 | | | | 2 | | 2 | 2 | 1 | | | | | | | 5 | 35 |
| | | | | | | 1 | 1 | | 3 | | | | | 1 | 1 | 1 | 1 | | | | | | | 3 | 36 |
| | | | | 1 | 4 | 3 | 6 | 3 | | 3 | 1 | 7 | 8 | 2 | 10 | 3 | 3 | | | | | | | 16 | 37 |
| | 1 | | | 1 | 6 | 5 | 5 | 7 | 17 | 5 | | | 2 | 1 | 3 | 12 | 8 | | | | | | | 23 | 38 |
| | | | | | 7 | 1 | | | 1 | | | 3 | | 5 | 5 | 1 | 2 | | | | | | | 8 | 39 |
| | | | | | | 1 | | | | 1 | | | | | | 1 | | | | | | | | 1 | 40 |
| | | | | | | 1 | 2 | 2 | | 1 | | 1 | 1 | | 1 | 2 | 2 | | | | | | | 5 | 41 |
| | 1 | | | | 13 | 9 | 1 | 1 | 1 | 10 | | | 5 | 4 | 9 | 7 | 8 | | | | | | | 24 | 42 |
| | | | | | | 1 | | | | | 1 | | | | | | 1 | | | | | | | 1 | 43 |
| | 1 | | | | | 1 | 1 | 1 | 2 | | | | 2 | | 2 | | | 1 | | | | | | 3 | 44 |
| | | | | | 1 | | 1 | | | 1 | | 1 | | 1 | 1 | 1 | | | | | | | | 2 | 45 |
| | 1 | | 4 | 7 | 14 | 6 | 9 | 13 | 3 | 1 | | 14 | 2 | 3 | 5 | 18 | 18 | | 1 | | 1 | | | 43 | 46 |
| | 1 | 1 | 1 | | 6 | 2 | 3 | 2 | 3 | 2 | | 5 | 3 | 5 | 8 | 4 | 1 | | | | | | | 13 | 47 |
| | | | | | | 3 | | | 2 | | | 1 | 1 | | 1 | 1 | 1 | | | | | | | 3 | 48 |
| | | | | 1 | 7 | | 1 | 2 | 1 | 7 | | | 3 | | 3 | 5 | 2 | | | | | | | 10 | 49 |
| 1 | 2 | | 2 | 7 | 110 | 22 | 33 | 59 | 82 | 96 | 10 | 7 | 23 | 17 | 40 | 95 | 83 | 4 | 5 | | | | | 227 | 50 |
| | | | | | 1 | 1 | 2 | 2 | 3 | 1 | | | 2 | | 2 | 3 | 1 | | | | | | | 6 | 51 |
| | | 1 | | | 2 | 2 | | 2 | 3 | 1 | | | 2 | 2 | 4 | 2 | | | | | | | | 6 | 52 |
| | | | | | 1 | 1 | 1 | | | | | 2 | 1 | | 1 | 1 | 1 | | | | | | | 3 | 53 |
| | | | | | | 2 | | | 1 | | 1 | | 1 | | 1 | 1 | | | | | | | | 2 | 54 |
| | | | | 2 | 3 | 2 | 7 | 6 | 2 | 4 | 4 | 6 | 1 | 2 | 3 | 10 | 5 | | | | | | | 18 | 55 |
| | | | | | 1 | 1 | 2 | | | 2 | | | 1 | 1 | 2 | 1 | 1 | | | | | | | 4 | 56 |
| | | | | | 1 | 1 | 4 | 2 | | 1 | 1 | 2 | 3 | | 3 | 3 | 1 | 1 | | | | | | 8 | 57 |
| | | | | | 1 | | 1 | | | | | | | | | 2 | | | | | | | | 2 | 58 |
| | | | 1 | | 1 | 1 | 2 | 1 | | | | 1 | 2 | 3 | 5 | | | | | | | | | 5 | 59 |
| | | | | | 16 | 10 | 10 | 10 | 48 | | | | | 1 | 1 | 18 | 23 | 4 | 2 | | | | | 48 | 60 |
| | 1 | | | | | | 1 | | 1 | | | | 1 | | 1 | | | | | | | | | 1 | 61 |
| | | | | | | | 2 | | 2 | | | | | | | | 1 | 1 | | | | | | 2 | 62 |
| | | | | | | 3 | 2 | | | | 1 | 3 | | | | 1 | 3 | | 1 | | | | | 5 | 63 |
| | | | | | 4 | 17 | 16 | 4 | 5 | 14 | 7 | 4 | 4 | 6 | 10 | 16 | 15 | | 1 | | | | | 42 | 64 |
| | | | | 1 | 5 | 8 | 3 | 7 | 8 | 4 | | | 1 | | 1 | 11 | 10 | 5 | | | | | | 27 | 65 |
| | | | | | 1 | | 4 | 1 | | 3 | | | 4 | | 4 | 1 | 1 | | | | | | | 6 | 66 |
| | | | | | | | 2 | 1 | 2 | 1 | | | | 1 | 1 | | 1 | | 1 | | | | | 3 | 67 |
| | | | | | | | 1 | 1 | | | | 2 | | 1 | 1 | 1 | | | | | | | | 2 | 68 |
| | | 1 | | | 3 | | | | | 1 | | 2 | | 1 | 1 | | 2 | | | | | | | 3 | 69 |
| | | | | | 1 | | 1 | | | | | | | | | 1 | | | 1 | | | | | 2 | 70 |
| | | | | | 15 | 23 | 40 | 9 | 39 | 33 | 1 | 6 | 2 | 6 | 8 | 38 | 39 | 1 | 1 | | | | | 87 | 71 |
| | | | 4 | 8 | 92 | 91 | 98 | 88 | 127 | 81 | 12 | 49 | 52 | 40 | 92 | 136 | 148 | 5 | 9 | 1 | | 1 | | 392 | 72 |
| 1 | 25 | 12 | 20 | 90 | 811 | 821 | 823 | 549 | 1244 | 640 | 133 | 358 | 483 | 352 | 835 | 1136 | 982 | 64 | 60 | 1 | 1 | 4 | .. | 3083 | |

## CLASSIFICATION OF DEATHS IN SOUTHEASTERN

*Embracing the following counties: Covington, Greene, Hancock,*

| | Cause of death. | AGES. | | | | | | | | | | | | | | | | | | NATIVITIES. | | | | | |
|---|---|---|---|---|---|---|---|---|---|---|---|---|---|---|---|---|---|---|---|---|---|---|---|---|---|
| | | Under 1. | | 1 and under 5. | | 5 and under 10. | | 10 and under 20. | | 20 and under 50. | | 50 and under 80. | | 80 and under 100. | | 100 & over. | | Age unknown. | | Born in State. | N. England States. | Middle States. | Southern States. | Southwest'n States. | Northwest'n States. |
| | | M. | F. | M. | F. | M. | F. | M. | F. | M. | F. | M. | F. | M | F. | M | F. | M | F. | | | | | | |
| 1 | Accident, not specif'd | 1 | 1 | 1 | | 1 | | | | 5 | 1 | 1 | | | | | | | | 7 | | | 2 | | |
| 2 | ...do...burned | | | 1 | | | 2 | | | | | | | | | | | | | 3 | | | | | |
| 3 | ...do...drowned | | | 1 | 1 | | | | 1 | 3 | 2 | 1 | | 1 | | | | | | 2 | 1 | | 3 | | |
| 4 | ...do...shot | | | | | | | | | | | | | | | | | 1 | | 1 | | | | | |
| 5 | Apoplexy | 1 | | | | | | | 1 | | 2 | 1 | | 1 | | | | | | 2 | | | | 1 | |
| 6 | Cancer | | | | | | | | | 1 | 2 | | | | | | | | | | | | 2 | 1 | |
| 7 | Catarrh | 1 | | | | | 1 | | | | | | | | | | | | | 2 | | | | | |
| 8 | Childbirth | | | | | | | | 5 | | 5 | | | | | | | | | 4 | | | 2 | 3 | |
| 9 | Cholera | | | 2 | | | | | | 2 | | 1 | | | | | | | | 3 | | 1 | | 1 | |
| 10 | ...do..infantum | 2 | 2 | 3 | 2 | 1 | | | | | | | | | | | | | | 8 | | | 1 | 1 | |
| 11 | ...do..morbus | | | | | | | | | 1 | | | | | | | | | | 1 | | | | | |
| 12 | Congestion of brain | | | 1 | | | | | | | | | | | | | | | | 1 | | | | | |
| 13 | Consumption | 1 | | 1 | | 1 | | 1 | | 6 | 8 | 3 | 1 | | 1 | | | | | 8 | | 2 | 8 | 2 | 1 |
| 14 | Convulsions | | | 2 | | 1 | | | | | | | | | | | | | | 1 | | | | | |
| 15 | Croup | 5 | 1 | | | | | | | | | | | | | | | | | 6 | | | | | |
| 16 | Debility | | | | 1 | | | | | | | | | | | | | | | | | | | 1 | |
| 17 | Diabetes | | | | | | | | | | | | | | 1 | | | | | | | | 1 | | |
| 18 | Diarrhœa | 1 | 1 | 1 | 2 | | | | 2 | 4 | 1 | 2 | 1 | | | | | | | 9 | | | 4 | | 1 |
| 19 | Dirt eating | | | | | | | | 1 | | | | | | | | | | | | | | | 1 | |
| 20 | Dropsy | | | 1 | 1 | 1 | | 1 | 1 | | 1 | 4 | 2 | | | | | | | 6 | | | 4 | 1 | |
| 21 | Dysentery | 1 | | | 1 | | | | | 1 | | 1 | | 1 | | | | | | 3 | | | | 1 | |
| 22 | Dyspepsia | | | | | | | | | 1 | | | 1 | | | | | | | | | | 2 | | |
| 23 | Fever, not specified | 1 | | 1 | 2 | 4 | | 1 | 1 | 3 | 7 | 1 | | 1 | 1 | | | | | 13 | | | 6 | 1 | |
| 24 | ..do..bilious | | | | | | | | 1 | | | | | | | | | | | 1 | | | | | |
| 25 | ..do..brain | | | | | | | 1 | | | | | | | | | | | | 1 | | | | | |
| 26 | ..do..congestive | | | | | | | | | 1 | 1 | 1 | 1 | | | | | | | 1 | | | 2 | | |
| 27 | ..do..intermittent | | | | | | | | | | 1 | | | | | | | | | 1 | | | | | |
| 28 | ..do..puerperal | | | | | | | | | | 2 | | | | | | | | | 1 | | | | 1 | |
| 29 | ..do..scarlet | | 1 | 3 | 1 | 1 | 2 | | | | | | | | | | | | | 8 | | | | | |
| 30 | Heart, disease of | | | | | | | 1 | | 1 | | | | | 1 | | | | | 1 | | | 2 | | |
| 31 | Hemorrhage | | | | | | | | | 1 | 1 | | | | | | | | | | | | 1 | | |
| 32 | Hives | 3 | 3 | 1 | 1 | | | | | | | | | | | | | | | 8 | | | | | |
| 33 | Hooping cough | | 1 | 1 | 1 | | | | | | | | | | | | | | | 3 | | | | | |
| 34 | Inflammation, bowels | | | | | | | | | | | 1 | | | | | | | | | | | | | |
| 35 | ....do........brain | | | | | | | 1 | | | | | | | | | | | | 1 | | | | | |
| 36 | Jaundice | | 1 | | | | | | | | | | | | | | | | | 1 | | | | | |
| 37 | Killed | | | | | | | 1 | | 1 | | | | | | | | | | 2 | | | | | |
| 38 | Liver, disease of | | | | | | | | | 3 | | | | | | | | | | 2 | | 1 | | | |
| 39 | Lockjaw | | 1 | | | | | | | | | | | | | | | | | 1 | | | | | |
| 40 | Measles | | | | | | | | | | 1 | | | | | | | | | 1 | | | | | |
| 41 | Mortification | | | 1 | | | | 1 | | | | | | | | | | | | 1 | | | 1 | | |
| 42 | Murder | | | | | | | | | 1 | | | | | | | | | | 1 | | | | | |
| 43 | Old age | | | | | | | | | | | 1 | 1 | 6 | 2 | | | | | 1 | | | 8 | | |
| 44 | Paralysis | | | | 1 | | | | | | | 1 | | | | | | | | 1 | | | 1 | | |
| 45 | Pleurisy | | | | | | | 1 | | | 2 | 1 | | | | | | | | 3 | | | 1 | | |
| 46 | Pneumonia | | | | | | | | | 2 | 1 | 2 | 2 | | | | | | | 2 | | | 5 | | |
| 47 | Poison | | | | | | | 1 | | | 1 | | | | | | | | | 2 | | | | | |
| 48 | Rheumatism | | | 1 | | | | | | 2 | | | | | | | | | | 2 | | 1 | | | |
| 49 | Scrofula | | | | | | | | | 1 | 1 | | | | | | | | | | | 1 | | 1 | |
| 50 | Suffocation | 3 | 1 | 1 | | | 1 | | | | | | | | | | | | | 6 | | | | | |
| 51 | Suicide | | | | | | | | | 1 | 1 | | | | | | | | | | | 1 | | | |
| 52 | White swelling | | | | | | | | | | | 1 | | | | | | | | 1 | | | | | |
| 53 | Worms | | 2 | 5 | 4 | | | | 1 | | | | | | | | | | | 11 | | | | 1 | |
| 54 | Unknown | 7 | 5 | 5 | 5 | 2 | 1 | 3 | 4 | 5 | 5 | 3 | 5 | | 3 | | | | | 37 | | | 8 | 7 | |
| | Total | 27 | 20 | 33 | 23 | 12 | 7 | 13 | 18 | 46 | 46 | 26 | 14 | 10 | 9 | .. | .. | 1 | .. | 181 | 1 | 7 | 64 | 26 | 2 |

## CLASSIFICATION OF DEATHS IN

| | Cause of death. | Under 1 M. | Under 1 F. | 1–5 M. | 1–5 F. | 5–10 M. | 5–10 F. | 10–20 M. | 10–20 F. | 20–50 M. | 20–50 F. | 50–80 M. | 50–80 F. | 80–100 M | 80–100 F. | 100 & over M | 100 & over F. | Age unknown M | Age unknown F. | Born in State. | N. England States. | Middle States. | Southern States. | Southwest'n States. | Northwest'n States. |
|---|---|---|---|---|---|---|---|---|---|---|---|---|---|---|---|---|---|---|---|---|---|---|---|---|---|
| 1 | Abscess | | | | | | | 1 | 1 | 4 | 1 | | 2 | | | | | | | 2 | | | 4 | 3 | |
| 2 | Accident, not specf'd | 17 | 19 | 21 | 17 | 7 | 6 | 15 | 7 | 30 | 10 | 7 | 8 | | | | | | | 109 | | 2 | 28 | 11 | 3 |
| 3 | ....do...burned | 5 | 8 | 26 | 20 | 5 | 16 | 3 | 9 | 1 | 5 | | | 1 | | | | | | 90 | | | 5 | 1 | 1 |
| 4 | ....do...drowned | | | 10 | 1 | 4 | 4 | 11 | 4 | 35 | 12 | 4 | | 1 | | | | | | 48 | 1 | 2 | 13 | 6 | 5 |
| 5 | ....do...scalded | | 2 | 2 | | | | | | | | | | | | | | | | 4 | | | | | |
| 6 | ....do...shot | | | | | | | 4 | | 12 | | | | | | | | 1 | | 11 | | | 4 | 2 | |
| 7 | Amputation | | | | | | | 1 | | 1 | 1 | | | | | | | | | 1 | | | 1 | | |
| 8 | Anneurism | | | | | | | | 1 | | | | | | | | | | | | | | 1 | | |
| 9 | Apoplexy | 1 | 1 | | | | | 2 | 4 | 10 | 9 | 9 | 5 | 2 | | | | 1 | | 12 | | 1 | 19 | 6 | 1 |
| 10 | Asthma | 1 | | 1 | | | | | 1 | | 2 | 3 | | | | | | | | 5 | | | 2 | 1 | |

## SECTION OF THE STATE OF MISSISSIPPI.

*Harrison, Jackson, Jones, Marion, Perry, and Wayne.*

| NATIVITIES. | | | | | SEASON OF DECEASE. | | | | DURATION OF SICKNESS. | | | | WHITES. | | | COLORED. | | | | | | | | | |
|---|---|---|---|---|---|---|---|---|---|---|---|---|---|---|---|---|---|---|---|---|---|---|---|---|---|
| | | | | | | | | | | | | | | | | Slaves. | | | | Free. | | | | | |
| | | | | | | | | | | | | | | | | Black. | | Mulatto. | | Black. | | Mul. | | | |
| California and Territories. | Ireland. | Germany. | Other foreign countries. | Unknown. | Spring. | Summer. | Autumn. | Winter. | Under 1 week. | 1 week and under 1 month. | 1 month and under 3 months. | 3 months and over. | Males. | Females. | Total. | M. | F. | M. | F. | M. | F. | M | F. | Aggregate deaths. | |
| | | | 2 | | 5 | 2 | 2 | 2 | 9 | | | | 6 | 1 | 7 | 3 | 1 | | | | | | | 11 | 1 |
| | | | | | 1 | | | 2 | 3 | | | | | 1 | 1 | 1 | 1 | | | | | | | 3 | 2 |
| | | | 3 | 1 | | 1 | 7 | 2 | 10 | | | | 4 | 2 | 6 | 2 | 1 | | 1 | | | | | 10 | 3 |
| | | | | | 1 | | | | 1 | | | | 1 | | 1 | | | | | | | | | 1 | 4 |
| | | | 3 | | 2 | 3 | 1 | | 5 | | | | 3 | 2 | 5 | | 1 | | | | | | | 6 | 5 |
| | | | | | | 2 | 1 | | | | | 3 | 1 | 2 | 3 | | | | | | | | | 3 | 6 |
| | | | | | | | | 2 | 1 | | | | 1 | 1 | 2 | | | | | | | | | 2 | 7 |
| | | 1 | | | 2 | 3 | 5 | | 5 | 2 | 1 | | | 6 | 6 | | 3 | | 1 | | | | | 10 | 8 |
| | | | | | 1 | 2 | | 2 | 5 | | | | 5 | | 5 | | | | | | | | | 5 | 9 |
| | | | | | 3 | 1 | 5 | 1 | 5 | 4 | 1 | | 4 | 3 | 7 | 2 | 1 | | | | | | | 10 | 10 |
| | | | | | | | 1 | | 1 | | | | 1 | | 1 | | | | | | | | | 1 | 11 |
| | | | | | | | | 1 | 1 | | | | | | | 1 | | | | | | | | 1 | 12 |
| | | | 2 | | 2 | 5 | 13 | 3 | 1 | 1 | 2 | 18 | 11 | 7 | 18 | 2 | 3 | | | | | | | 23 | 13 |
| | | | | | | 2 | | 1 | 1 | 2 | | | 3 | | 3 | | | | | | | | | 3 | 14 |
| | | | | | 2 | 3 | | 1 | 3 | 2 | | 1 | 2 | | 2 | 3 | 1 | | | | | | | 6 | 15 |
| | | | | | 1 | | | | | | | 1 | | | | | | | 1 | | | | | 1 | 16 |
| | | | | | | | 1 | | | | | 1 | | 1 | 1 | | | | | | | | | 1 | 17 |
| | | | 1 | | 1 | 3 | 7 | 4 | 2 | 5 | 1 | 7 | 7 | 2 | 9 | 1 | 5 | | | | | | | 15 | 18 |
| | | | | | | | 1 | | | | | 1 | | 1 | 1 | | | | | | | | | 1 | 19 |
| | | | | 1 | 2 | 4 | 3 | 3 | | 2 | 3 | 7 | 4 | 4 | 8 | 3 | 1 | | | | | | | 12 | 20 |
| | | | | 1 | | 1 | 4 | | | 2 | 1 | 2 | 3 | 1 | 4 | 1 | | | | | | | | 5 | 21 |
| | | | | | 1 | | | 1 | | | | 2 | 1 | 1 | 2 | | | | | | | | | 2 | 22 |
| | 1 | | | 2 | 4 | 1 | 15 | 3 | 6 | 13 | 3 | | 11 | 9 | 20 | 1 | 1 | | | | 1 | | | 23 | 23 |
| | | | | | | 1 | | | | 1 | | | | 1 | 1 | | | | | | | | | 1 | 24 |
| | | | | | | 1 | | | 1 | | | | | | | | | 1 | | | | | | 1 | 25 |
| | | 1 | | | | | 4 | | 2 | 1 | | | 2 | 1 | 3 | | 1 | | | | | | | 4 | 26 |
| | | | | | | | 1 | | | 1 | | | | 1 | 1 | | | | | | | | | 1 | 27 |
| | | | | | 1 | | | 1 | | 2 | | | | 2 | 2 | | | | | | | | | 2 | 28 |
| | | | | | 2 | 2 | | 4 | 2 | 5 | | 1 | 4 | 3 | 7 | | 1 | | | | | | | 8 | 29 |
| | | | | | | 2 | 1 | | | 1 | | 2 | 1 | | 1 | 1 | 1 | | | | | | | 3 | 30 |
| | | | | 1 | | 1 | 1 | | | | 1 | 1 | 1 | | 1 | | 1 | | | | | | | 2 | 31 |
| | | | | | 3 | 1 | 3 | 1 | 6 | 1 | | | 4 | 2 | 6 | | 2 | | | | | | | 8 | 32 |
| | | | | | 1 | 2 | | | | 2 | 1 | | | | | 1 | 2 | | | | | | | 3 | 33 |
| | | | 1 | | | | | 1 | | | | 1 | 1 | | 1 | | | | | | | | | 1 | 34 |
| | | | | | | | | 1 | | 1 | | | 1 | | 1 | | | | | | | | | 1 | 35 |
| | | | | | | | | 1 | | | | | | | | | 1 | | | | | | | 1 | 36 |
| | | | | | | | 1 | 1 | 1 | | 1 | | 2 | | 2 | | | | | | | | | 2 | 37 |
| | | | | | | 2 | 1 | | | | 1 | 2 | 3 | | 3 | | | | | | | | | 3 | 38 |
| | | | | | 1 | | | | 1 | | | | | 1 | 1 | | | | | | | | | 1 | 39 |
| | | | | | | 1 | | | | 1 | | | | 1 | 1 | | | | | | | | | 1 | 40 |
| | | | | | 1 | | | 1 | | 1 | 1 | | 1 | | 1 | 1 | | | | | | | | 2 | 41 |
| | | | | | | | 1 | | 1 | | | | 1 | | 1 | | | | | | | | | 1 | 42 |
| | | | 1 | | 4 | 1 | 1 | 4 | 1 | | | 8 | 5 | 1 | 6 | 2 | 2 | | | | | | | 10 | 43 |
| | | | | | 1 | | | 1 | 1 | | | 1 | 1 | 1 | 2 | | | | | | | | | 2 | 44 |
| | | | | | 3 | | 1 | | 2 | 1 | 1 | | | | | 2 | 2 | | | | | | | 4 | 45 |
| | | | | | 5 | | 2 | | 1 | 6 | | | 3 | 1 | 4 | 1 | 2 | | | | | | | 7 | 46 |
| | | | | | | 1 | 1 | | 2 | | | | 1 | | 1 | | 1 | | | | | | | 2 | 47 |
| | | | | | | | | 3 | | 1 | | 2 | 1 | | 1 | 2 | | | | | | | | 3 | 48 |
| | | | | | | 1 | 1 | | | | 1 | 1 | | 1 | 1 | 1 | | | | | | | | 2 | 49 |
| | | | | | 4 | | 2 | | 6 | | | | | 2 | 2 | 4 | | | | | | | | 6 | 50 |
| | | | 1 | | 1 | 1 | | | 2 | | | | 1 | 1 | 2 | | | | | | | | | 2 | 51 |
| | | | | | | | 1 | | | | 1 | | 1 | | 1 | | | | | | | | | 1 | 52 |
| | | | | | 2 | 4 | 5 | 1 | 5 | 3 | | 4 | 1 | 6 | 7 | 4 | 1 | | | | | | | 12 | 53 |
| | | | 1 | | 12 | 11 | 17 | 13 | 14 | 11 | 7 | 20 | 19 | 17 | 36 | 5 | 10 | | | | | 1 | 1 | 53 | 54 |
| ... | 1 | 2 | 15 | 6 | 69 | 65 | 110 | 61 | 107 | 72 | 27 | 86 | 122 | 86 | 208 | 44 | 46 | 1 | 3 | ... | 1 | 1 | 1 | 305 | |

## THE STATE OF MISSISSIPPI—AGGREGATE.

| California and Territories. | Ireland. | Germany. | Other foreign countries. | Unknown. | Spring. | Summer. | Autumn. | Winter. | Under 1 week. | 1 week and under 1 month. | 1 month and under 3 months. | 3 months and over. | Males. | Females. | Total. | Slaves Black M. | Slaves Black F. | Slaves Mulatto M. | Slaves Mulatto F. | Free Black M. | Free Black F. | Free Mul. M | Free Mul. F. | Aggregate deaths. | |
|---|---|---|---|---|---|---|---|---|---|---|---|---|---|---|---|---|---|---|---|---|---|---|---|---|---|
| | | | | | | 2 | 4 | 3 | ... | 1 | 5 | 3 | 3 | 3 | 6 | 1 | 1 | 1 | | | | | | 9 | 1 |
| | 1 | 1 | 2 | 2 | 41 | 38 | 39 | 39 | 111 | 12 | 4 | 1 | 34 | 9 | 43 | 57 | 51 | 6 | 2 | | | | | 159 | 2 |
| | | | | 2 | 37 | 13 | 12 | 29 | 63 | 16 | 7 | 1 | 10 | 16 | 26 | 29 | 40 | 2 | 2 | | | | | 99 | 3 |
| | 1 | | 3 | 7 | 18 | 30 | 22 | 16 | 86 | | | | 18 | 2 | 20 | 43 | 18 | 4 | 1 | | | | | 86 | 4 |
| | | | | | 1 | 1 | 2 | | 3 | | | | 1 | | 1 | 1 | 2 | | | | | | | 4 | 5 |
| | | | | | 7 | 2 | 6 | 2 | 13 | | | | 7 | | 7 | 9 | | 1 | | | | | | 17 | 6 |
| | | | | | 1 | | 1 | 1 | 2 | 1 | | | | | | 2 | 1 | | | | | | | 3 | 7 |
| | | | | | 1 | | | | | | | 1 | | | | | 1 | | | | | | | 1 | 8 |
| | 1 | | 3 | 1 | 11 | 13 | 10 | 10 | 30 | 2 | 1 | 1 | 13 | 7 | 20 | 12 | 12 | | | | | | | 44 | 9 |
| | | | | | 2 | 2 | 1 | 3 | 1 | 2 | 1 | 3 | 2 | | 2 | 2 | 3 | 1 | | | | | | 8 | 10 |

## CLASSIFICATION OF DEATHS IN

| | Cause of death. | AGES. | | | | | | | | | | | | | | | | | | NATIVITIES. | | | | | |
|---|---|---|---|---|---|---|---|---|---|---|---|---|---|---|---|---|---|---|---|---|---|---|---|---|---|
| | | Under 1. | | 1 and under 5. | | 5 and under 10. | | 10 and under 20. | | 20 and under 50. | | 50 and under 80. | | 80 and under 100. | | 100 & over. | | Age unknown. | | Born in State. | N. England States. | Middle States. | Southern States. | Southwest'n States. | Northwest'n States. |
| | | M. | F. | M. | F. | M. | F. | M. | F. | M. | F. | M. | F. | M | F. | M | F. | M | F. | | | | | | |
| 1 | Black tongue | | | 1 | | 6 | | | | 5 | | 1 | | | | | | | | 12 | | | | | |
| 2 | Bladder, disease of | | | | | | | | 1 | | | 1 | | | | | | | | | | | | 1 | |
| 3 | Bowels......do | 12 | 13 | 20 | 12 | 2 | 1 | | 2 | 2 | 5 | 1 | | | | | | | | 64 | | | 3 | 1 | |
| 4 | Brain ......do | 2 | 7 | 1 | 1 | | | | 1 | 4 | | 1 | | | | | | | | 12 | | | 3 | 1 | |
| 5 | Bronchitis | 3 | 3 | | 1 | 2 | | 1 | | 4 | 1 | 3 | 1 | | 1 | | | | | 10 | | 1 | 6 | 3 | |
| 6 | Cancer | | | | | | | | | 1 | 3 | 3 | 7 | | 1 | | | | | 3 | | 2 | 8 | 1 | |
| 7 | Canker | | | | | | | 1 | | | | | | | | | | | | 1 | | | | | |
| 8 | Carbuncle | | | | | | | | | 1 | | 1 | | | | | | | | | | | 2 | | |
| 9 | Catarrh | 22 | 18 | 13 | 15 | 1 | 6 | 3 | 2 | 5 | 20 | 3 | | 1 | 1 | | 1 | | | 86 | | | 20 | 4 | |
| 10 | Chicken pox | | | 1 | | | | | | | | | | | | | | | | 1 | | | | | |
| 11 | Childbirth | | | | | | | | 19 | | 66 | | | | | | | | | 34 | | 1 | 33 | 12 | 1 |
| 12 | Chlorosis | | | | | | | | 1 | | | | | | | | | | | | | | | 1 | |
| 13 | Cholera | 6 | 5 | 52 | 42 | 22 | 24 | 50 | 28 | 187 | 117 | 35 | 15 | | | | | 3 | 1 | 316 | | 8 | 121 | 65 | 49 |
| 14 | ...do...infantum | 20 | 29 | 25 | 36 | 3 | 1 | | | | | | | | | | | | | 110 | | | 1 | 3 | |
| 15 | ...do...morbus | | | 7 | 4 | 1 | 1 | 2 | 1 | 7 | 3 | 1 | 2 | 1 | | | | | | 20 | | | 6 | 4 | |
| 16 | Chorea | | | | | | | 1 | | | | | | | | | | | | | | | 1 | | |
| 17 | Colic | 2 | | 1 | 2 | | | 2 | 1 | 2 | 5 | 4 | | 1 | | | | | | 10 | | | 7 | | 1 |
| 18 | Congestion | 1 | 2 | 10 | 5 | 2 | 1 | 3 | 6 | 7 | 2 | | | | 1 | | | | | 28 | | | 6 | 4 | |
| 19 | ....do...bowels | 1 | | | | | | | | | | | | | | | | | | 1 | | | | | |
| 20 | ....do...brain | 5 | 2 | 6 | 8 | 7 | 2 | 5 | 3 | 10 | 2 | 4 | 1 | | | | | | | 36 | | | 9 | 6 | |
| 21 | ....do...lungs | 1 | | 3 | 1 | 3 | 1 | 1 | 1 | 1 | 1 | 1 | | | | | | | | 9 | | | 2 | 2 | 1 |
| 22 | Consumption | 4 | 8 | 7 | 7 | 1 | 3 | 22 | 22 | 97 | 116 | 25 | 19 | 2 | 3 | | | | 1 | 120 | 1 | 10 | 108 | 56 | 14 |
| 23 | Convulsions | 40 | 19 | 17 | 24 | 8 | 5 | 4 | 6 | 10 | 13 | 3 | 1 | | 2 | | | | | 116 | | 1 | 19 | 12 | 1 |
| 24 | Cramp | | | | | 1 | | | | 1 | 1 | 1 | | | | | | | | 3 | | | | | |
| 25 | Croup | 137 | 37 | 88 | 69 | 5 | 4 | 1 | 3 | | | | | | | | | | | 389 | | | 5 | 4 | |
| 26 | Debility | 6 | 7 | 4 | 10 | 1 | 1 | | | 4 | 1 | 5 | 2 | 1 | 1 | | | 1 | | 32 | | | 5 | 3 | |
| 27 | Diabetes | | | | 1 | | 1 | 1 | | 1 | | | | | 1 | | | | | 2 | | | 1 | 2 | |
| 28 | Diarrhœa | 15 | 30 | 54 | 46 | 5 | 2 | 4 | 3 | 39 | 16 | 13 | 12 | | 3 | | | | | 173 | | 2 | 41 | 13 | 4 |
| 29 | Dirt eating | | | | | | | | 2 | | 1 | | | | | | | | | 2 | | | | 1 | |
| 30 | Dropsy | 5 | 3 | 16 | 17 | 11 | 7 | 18 | 18 | 49 | 77 | 46 | 31 | | 3 | | 1 | | | 148 | | 5 | 88 | 37 | 8 |
| 31 | Dysentery | 27 | 20 | 40 | 46 | 10 | 5 | 12 | 8 | 22 | 12 | 9 | 3 | 1 | 1 | | | 1 | | 165 | | | 31 | 13 | 3 |
| 32 | Dyspepsia | | | | | | | 1 | 2 | 9 | 6 | 11 | 4 | | | | | | | 8 | | 2 | 17 | 5 | |
| 33 | Epilepsy | 3 | 2 | 1 | 1 | | 1 | 1 | 1 | 3 | 2 | 1 | 1 | | | | | | | 9 | | 1 | 5 | 1 | |
| 34 | Erysipelas | 2 | 3 | 4 | 5 | 1 | 1 | | | 3 | 10 | | 1 | | | | | | | 18 | | | 7 | 2 | 3 |
| 35 | Executed | | | | | | | | | 3 | | | | | | | | | | | | | 2 | 1 | |
| 36 | Fever, not specified | 62 | 30 | 101 | 108 | 62 | 39 | 48 | 51 | 97 | 93 | 86 | 23 | 3 | 3 | 1 | | 1 | | 487 | | 3 | 163 | 80 | 6 |
| 37 | ..do..bilious | 3 | 2 | 11 | 8 | 6 | 5 | 9 | 5 | 17 | 8 | 3 | 4 | | | | | | | 44 | | 1 | 14 | 17 | 8 |
| 38 | ..do..brain | | 2 | 5 | 2 | 2 | 1 | 1 | 2 | 1 | 1 | | 1 | | | | | | | 13 | | | 4 | 1 | |
| 39 | ..do..catarrhal | 1 | 1 | 2 | 1 | | | | 1 | 1 | 2 | 1 | | | | | | | | 9 | | | 1 | | |
| 40 | ..do..congestive | 6 | 7 | 27 | 28 | 23 | 21 | 26 | 25 | 49 | 28 | 8 | 11 | | | | | 1 | | 163 | | 2 | 49 | 35 | 4 |
| 41 | ..do..inflammatory | 2 | | 1 | | | | | 1 | 1 | 1 | | | | | | | | | 4 | | | 1 | 1 | |
| 42 | ..do..intermittent | 6 | 1 | 6 | 3 | 2 | 6 | 2 | 2 | 5 | 4 | 4 | 3 | | | | | | | 31 | | | 11 | 1 | |
| 43 | ..do..puerperal | | | | | | | | 3 | | 24 | | | | | | | | | 6 | | 2 | 11 | 8 | |
| 44 | ..do..remittent | | | 1 | | | | | 1 | 1 | | | | | | | | | | 2 | | | 1 | | |
| 45 | ..do..scarlet | 13 | 11 | 51 | 44 | 21 | 26 | 11 | 20 | 3 | 4 | | | | | | | | | 179 | | | 10 | 13 | 1 |
| 46 | ..do..typhus | 10 | 4 | 17 | 15 | 14 | 13 | 29 | 39 | 45 | 43 | 16 | 11 | | 1 | | | | | 116 | | 1 | 79 | 47 | 7 |
| 47 | ..do..winter | 1 | | | 2 | | 1 | 1 | | 2 | 1 | 1 | | | | | | | | 8 | | | | 1 | |
| 48 | ..do..yellow | | | | | 1 | | | | | 1 | | | | | | | | | 1 | | | 1 | | |
| 49 | Fluor albus | | | | | | | | | | 1 | | | | | | | | | | | | 1 | | 1 |
| 50 | Fracture | | 1 | | | | | | | 1 | | | | | | | | | | 1 | | | | | |
| 51 | Frozen | | | | | | | | | 2 | | | | | | | | | | 2 | | | | | |
| 52 | Gravel | | | 1 | | | | | | | | 8 | | 1 | | | | | | 1 | | | 7 | | |
| 53 | Head, disease of | | | | | | 1 | | 1 | 1 | | | 1 | | | | | | | 1 | | | 2 | 1 | |
| 54 | Heart....do | 2 | | 2 | | 8 | | 7 | 2 | 7 | 9 | 6 | 3 | | 1 | | | | 2 | 19 | | 1 | 15 | 6 | 1 |
| 55 | Heat | | | | | | | | 1 | | | | | | 1 | | | | | 1 | | | 1 | | |
| 56 | Hemorrhage | | | 1 | | | 1 | | | 7 | 5 | 3 | 1 | | | | | | | 7 | | | 8 | 2 | |
| 57 | Hernia | 1 | 1 | | | | | 1 | | 7 | 2 | | | | | | | | | 5 | | | 3 | 2 | 1 |
| 58 | Hives | 22 | 26 | 3 | 4 | 1 | 1 | | | | | | | | | | | | | 57 | | | | | |
| 59 | Hooping cough | 43 | 47 | 69 | 56 | 6 | 4 | 6 | 6 | 2 | 3 | | | | | | | | | 234 | | | 4 | 4 | |
| 60 | Hydrocephalus | 5 | 3 | 5 | 1 | | | | | 1 | 1 | | | | | | | | | 12 | | | 1 | 3 | |
| 61 | Inflammation | 6 | 3 | 5 | 5 | 2 | 2 | | 2 | 4 | 9 | 2 | | | | | | | | 28 | | 1 | 8 | 2 | |
| 62 | ....do....bowels | 19 | 11 | 26 | 17 | 6 | 5 | 3 | 3 | 10 | 13 | 7 | 1 | | 1 | | | | | 98 | | | 16 | 3 | 4 |
| 63 | ....do....brain | 18 | 13 | 24 | 21 | 10 | 7 | 13 | 11 | 11 | 10 | 2 | 3 | | | | | | | 112 | | 1 | 15 | 11 | 2 |
| 64 | ....do....stomach | 1 | 1 | | 2 | | 1 | | 3 | 1 | 6 | 1 | | | | | | | | 9 | | | 2 | 2 | 2 |
| 65 | Insanity | | | | | | 1 | 1 | | 1 | | 1 | | | | | | 1 | | 3 | | | | 1 | |
| 66 | Intemperance | | | | | | | | | 9 | | 3 | | | | | | 1 | | 5 | | | 3 | | |
| 67 | Jaundice | 1 | 1 | | 4 | 2 | | | 1 | | | | | | | | | | | 8 | | | 1 | | |
| 68 | Kidneys, disease of | | | 1 | | | 1 | | | 2 | | | | | | | | | | 8 | | | 1 | | |
| 69 | Killed | 1 | | | | 2 | | 4 | | 16 | 1 | 2 | 1 | | | | | | | 9 | | | 12 | 2 | 2 |
| 70 | Lightning | | | | | | | 1 | 2 | 1 | 8 | | | | | | | | | 3 | | | 2 | 1 | 1 |
| 71 | Liver, disease of | 3 | 1 | 1 | 1 | 1 | | 2 | 2 | 9 | 10 | 7 | | | | | | 1 | | 18 | | 2 | 8 | 9 | |
| 72 | Lockjaw | 9 | 7 | 1 | 3 | 1 | | 3 | 1 | 4 | 1 | 1 | | | | | | | | 28 | | | 1 | | |
| 73 | Lungs, disease of | 2 | | 1 | 1 | | | | | 2 | 3 | 4 | 3 | | | | | | | 7 | | | 7 | | 2 |
| 74 | Malformation | | | 2 | 2 | | | | | | | | | | | | | | | 4 | | | | | |
| 75 | Marasmus | 2 | | 1 | 2 | | | | | | | | | | | | | | | 5 | | | | | |

THE STATE OF MISSISSIPPI—AGGREGATE—Continued.

| Nativities: California and Territories. | Nativities: Ireland. | Nativities: Germany. | Nativities: Other foreign countries. | Nativities: Unknown. | Season of decease: Spring. | Season of decease: Summer. | Season of decease: Autumn. | Season of decease: Winter. | Duration of sickness: Under 1 week. | Duration of sickness: 1 week and under 1 month. | Duration of sickness: 1 month and under 3 months. | Duration of sickness: 3 months and over. | Whites: Males. | Whites: Females. | Whites: Total. | Colored: Slaves: Black: M. | Colored: Slaves: Black: F. | Colored: Slaves: Mulatto: M. | Colored: Slaves: Mulatto: F. | Colored: Free: Black: M. | Colored: Free: Black: F. | Colored: Free: Mul.: M | Colored: Free: Mul.: F. | Aggregate deaths. | |
|---|---|---|---|---|---|---|---|---|---|---|---|---|---|---|---|---|---|---|---|---|---|---|---|---|---|
| | 1 | | | | | 5 | 8 | | 11 | 1 | | | 2 | | 2 | 11 | | | | | | | | 13 | 1 |
| | | | | 1 | | 2 | | | | 1 | | | 1 | 1 | 2 | | | | | | | | | 2 | 2 |
| | | | | 2 | 4 | 25 | 30 | 9 | 16 | 29 | 8 | 7 | 12 | 12 | 24 | 22 | 21 | 2 | | | | 1 | | 70 | 3 |
| | | | | 1 | 3 | 2 | 9 | 3 | 6 | 4 | 2 | | 3 | 4 | 7 | 5 | 5 | | | | | | | 17 | 4 |
| | | | | | 7 | 5 | 3 | 4 | 1 | 5 | 6 | 6 | 9 | 3 | 12 | 4 | 4 | | | | | | | 20 | 5 |
| | | | | 1 | 5 | 6 | 2 | 2 | | | 1 | 13 | 3 | 7 | 10 | 1 | 4 | | | | | | | 15 | 6 |
| | | | | | 1 | | | | | 1 | | | 1 | | 1 | | | | | | | | | 1 | 7 |
| | | | | | 1 | | | 1 | | 1 | | 1 | 2 | | 2 | | | | | | | | | 2 | 8 |
| | 1 | | | | 35 | 15 | 25 | 26 | 29 | 37 | 9 | 9 | 16 | 13 | 29 | 28 | 46 | 3 | 4 | 1 | | | | 111 | 9 |
| | | | | | | | | 1 | | | 1 | | 1 | | 1 | | | | | | | | | 1 | 10 |
| | | 2 | | 2 | 21 | 19 | 29 | 16 | 50 | 19 | 2 | 1 | | 36 | 36 | | 45 | | 4 | | | | | 85 | 11 |
| | | | | | 1 | | | | | | | 1 | | | | | 1 | | | | | | | 1 | 12 |
| | 1 | 1 | 1 | 25 | 183 | 317 | 29 | 56 | 505 | 32 | 3 | 1 | 85 | 23 | 108 | 256 | 193 | 14 | 16 | | | | | 587 | 13 |
| | | | | | 17 | 43 | 32 | 14 | 62 | 23 | 5 | 2 | 23 | 27 | 50 | 25 | 37 | | 2 | | | | | 114 | 14 |
| | | | | | 6 | 11 | 9 | 4 | 17 | 7 | 1 | | 9 | 4 | 13 | 8 | 7 | 2 | | | | | | 30 | 15 |
| | | | | | | 1 | | | 1 | | | | | | | 1 | | | | | | | | 1 | 16 |
| | | 1 | | 1 | 2 | 6 | 11 | 1 | 14 | 1 | | 1 | 5 | | 5 | 6 | 7 | 1 | 1 | | | | | 20 | 17 |
| | | | | 2 | 7 | 9 | 18 | 3 | 24 | 7 | | 1 | 10 | 9 | 19 | 12 | 8 | 1 | | | | | | 40 | 18 |
| | | | | | | 1 | | | 1 | | | | | | | 1 | | | | | | | | 1 | 19 |
| | | | 1 | 3 | 7 | 14 | 26 | 7 | 33 | 10 | | | 17 | 8 | 25 | 18 | 9 | 2 | 1 | | | | | 55 | 20 |
| | | | | | 2 | 4 | 6 | 2 | 3 | 8 | | | 8 | 3 | 11 | 2 | 1 | | | | | | | 14 | 21 |
| | 2 | 3 | 3 | 15 | 88 | 80 | 95 | 68 | 9 | 9 | 39 | 236 | 89 | 92 | 181 | 66 | 73 | 3 | 9 | | | | | 332 | 22 |
| | | | | 3 | 44 | 34 | 51 | 22 | 85 | 22 | 3 | 13 | 25 | 18 | 43 | 53 | 47 | 4 | 5 | | | | | 152 | 23 |
| | | 1 | | | 1 | | 2 | 1 | 2 | 1 | | | | 1 | 1 | 2 | | 1 | | | | | | 4 | 24 |
| | | | | | 116 | 76 | 107 | 95 | 276 | 76 | 4 | 5 | 74 | 69 | 143 | 141 | 99 | 10 | 5 | | | | | 398 | 25 |
| | 1 | | 1 | 2 | 8 | 10 | 17 | 8 | | 2 | 1 | 9 | 11 | 4 | 15 | 11 | 17 | | 1 | | | | | 44 | 26 |
| | | | | | 1 | | 1 | 3 | 1 | 2 | 1 | 1 | 2 | 3 | 5 | | | | | | | | | 5 | 27 |
| | | | 1 | 8 | 41 | 78 | 90 | 30 | 42 | 83 | 31 | 59 | 68 | 46 | 114 | 52 | 60 | 9 | 6 | | | 1 | | 242 | 28 |
| | | | | | | 2 | 1 | | | | | 2 | | 1 | 1 | | 2 | | | | | | | 3 | 29 |
| | 1 | 1 | 1 | 13 | 70 | 86 | 78 | 64 | 10 | 17 | 45 | 195 | 44 | 47 | 91 | 97 | 105 | 8 | 5 | 1 | | | | 302 | 30 |
| | 2 | | | 3 | 20 | 114 | 64 | 13 | 48 | 118 | 11 | 6 | 58 | 57 | 115 | 59 | 34 | 5 | 4 | | | | | 217 | 31 |
| | | | | 1 | 8 | 4 | 12 | 9 | | 3 | 6 | 22 | 19 | 10 | 29 | 2 | 2 | | | | | | | 33 | 32 |
| | | | | 1 | 5 | 5 | 5 | 2 | 4 | 1 | | 4 | 5 | 3 | 8 | 4 | 5 | | | | | | | 17 | 33 |
| | | | | | 11 | 8 | 6 | 5 | 7 | 17 | 2 | | 4 | 15 | 19 | 5 | 5 | 1 | | | | | | 30 | 34 |
| | | | | | 2 | 1 | | | 3 | | | | 1 | | 1 | 1 | | 1 | | | | | | 3 | 35 |
| | 4 | | | 15 | 128 | 169 | 362 | 88 | 213 | 380 | 62 | 15 | 183 | 178 | 361 | 223 | 157 | 5 | 10 | | 1 | | 1 | 758 | 36 |
| | | | | 2 | 6 | 16 | 53 | 5 | 21 | 48 | 6 | 1 | 31 | 16 | 47 | 17 | 15 | 1 | 1 | | | | | 81 | 37 |
| | | | | | 2 | 7 | 7 | 2 | 8 | 6 | 1 | | 6 | 2 | 8 | 2 | 7 | 1 | | | | | | 18 | 38 |
| | | | | | | 3 | 3 | 4 | 5 | 3 | 1 | | 3 | | 3 | 2 | 5 | | | | | | | 10 | 39 |
| | 1 | 1 | 1 | 4 | 20 | 44 | 172 | 21 | 141 | 57 | 4 | 2 | 62 | 60 | 123 | 70 | 53 | 7 | 6 | | 1 | | | 260 | 40 |
| | | | | | | 3 | 1 | 2 | 3 | 2 | | 1 | 2 | | 2 | 2 | 2 | | | | | | | 6 | 41 |
| | | | | 1 | 10 | 4 | 22 | 7 | 22 | 10 | 3 | 5 | 9 | 10 | 19 | 15 | 7 | 1 | 2 | | | | | 44 | 42 |
| | | | | | 7 | 4 | 9 | 7 | 8 | 14 | 3 | 1 | | 16 | 16 | | 11 | | | | | | | 27 | 43 |
| | | | | | 1 | | 2 | | | 3 | | | 1 | 1 | 2 | 1 | | | | | | | | 3 | 44 |
| | | | | 1 | 76 | 51 | 43 | 33 | 94 | 86 | 15 | 4 | 75 | 77 | 152 | 24 | 27 | | 1 | | | | | 204 | 45 |
| | 1 | 1 | | 7 | 53 | 49 | 111 | 41 | 23 | 168 | 43 | 4 | 79 | 68 | 147 | 51 | 55 | 1 | 3 | | | | | 257 | 46 |
| | | | | | 4 | | | 5 | 1 | 7 | 1 | | 1 | 2 | 3 | 4 | 2 | | | | | | | 9 | 47 |
| | | | | | | | 2 | | | 1 | | | 1 | 1 | 2 | | | | | | | | | 2 | 48 |
| | | | | | 1 | | | 1 | | | 1 | 1 | | 1 | 1 | | 1 | | | | | | | 2 | 49 |
| | | | | 1 | | 2 | | | | 2 | | | | | | 1 | 1 | | | | | | | 2 | 50 |
| | | | | | 1 | | | 1 | | 1 | | | | | | 2 | | | | | | | | 2 | 51 |
| | | | 1 | 1 | 2 | 1 | 4 | 3 | | 3 | 1 | 5 | 5 | | 5 | 5 | | | | | | | | 10 | 52 |
| | | | | | 2 | 1 | 1 | | 1 | 2 | | 1 | | 1 | 1 | 1 | 1 | | 1 | | | | | 4 | 53 |
| | 1 | | 1 | | 13 | 10 | 8 | 10 | 7 | 3 | 6 | 19 | 11 | 7 | 18 | 16 | 10 | | | | | | | 44 | 54 |
| | | | | | | | 2 | | 1 | | | | | | | | 2 | | | | | | | 2 | 55 |
| | | | | 1 | 4 | 8 | 5 | 1 | 6 | 4 | 2 | 3 | 5 | 5 | 10 | 6 | 2 | | | | | | | 18 | 56 |
| | | | | 1 | 4 | 2 | 2 | 3 | 4 | 3 | | 1 | 2 | 2 | 4 | 7 | 1 | | | | | | | 12 | 57 |
| | | | | | 16 | 14 | 18 | 9 | 35 | 12 | 2 | | 20 | 18 | 38 | 6 | 13 | | | | | | | 57 | 58 |
| | | | | | 64 | 94 | 55 | 26 | 48 | 90 | 30 | 12 | 27 | 21 | 48 | 96 | 91 | 2 | 4 | 1 | | | | 242 | 59 |
| | | | | | 1 | 9 | 4 | 2 | 2 | 4 | 2 | 6 | 6 | 3 | 9 | 4 | 2 | | | 1 | | | | 16 | 60 |
| | | | 1 | | 11 | 11 | 12 | 6 | 17 | 13 | 3 | 2 | 12 | 11 | 23 | 7 | 7 | | 3 | | | | | 40 | 61 |
| | | | 1 | | 15 | 61 | 33 | 13 | 49 | 54 | 6 | 8 | 32 | 23 | 55 | 36 | 25 | 3 | 3 | | | | | 122 | 62 |
| | | | 2 | | 19 | 39 | 65 | 19 | 63 | 63 | 3 | 2 | 49 | 30 | 79 | 27 | 32 | 1 | 3 | | | 1 | | 143 | 63 |
| | | 1 | | | 3 | 5 | 4 | 4 | 3 | 6 | 2 | 3 | 2 | 11 | 13 | 1 | 2 | | | | | | | 16 | 64 |
| | | | | 1 | 1 | 2 | 2 | | | | | 3 | 1 | | 1 | 2 | 1 | 1 | | | | | | 5 | 65 |
| | 2 | | | 3 | 3 | 2 | 5 | 3 | 3 | 1 | 2 | | 8 | | 8 | 5 | | | | | | | | 13 | 66 |
| | | | | | 3 | 1 | 2 | 3 | 1 | 4 | | 3 | 3 | 5 | 8 | | 1 | | | | | | | 9 | 67 |
| | | | | | | 1 | 3 | | | 2 | | 2 | 2 | 1 | 3 | 1 | | | | | | | | 4 | 68 |
| | | | | 2 | 6 | 6 | 11 | 4 | 18 | 8 | 1 | | 10 | | 10 | 15 | 2 | | | | | | | 27 | 69 |
| | | | | | | 4 | 2 | | 7 | | | | | 1 | 1 | 2 | 4 | | | | | | | 7 | 70 |
| | | | | 1 | 12 | 11 | 8 | 7 | 2 | 6 | 6 | 19 | 18 | 7 | 25 | 6 | 7 | | | | | | | 33 | 71 |
| | 1 | | | 1 | 9 | 7 | 5 | 10 | 22 | 7 | | | 3 | 2 | 5 | 16 | 10 | | | | | | | 31 | 72 |
| | | | | | 11 | 2 | 2 | 1 | 1 | 1 | 1 | 7 | 4 | 5 | 9 | 3 | 2 | 2 | | | | | | 16 | 73 |
| | | | | | | 2 | 1 | 1 | | 2 | | 2 | | | | 2 | 2 | | | | | | | 4 | 74 |
| | | | | | | 1 | 2 | 2 | | 1 | | 1 | 1 | | 1 | 2 | 2 | | | | | | | 5 | 75 |

## CLASSIFICATION OF DEATHS IN

| | Cause of death. | AGES. | | | | | | | | | | | | | | | | | | NATIVITIES. | | | | | |
|---|---|---|---|---|---|---|---|---|---|---|---|---|---|---|---|---|---|---|---|---|---|---|---|---|---|
| | | Under 1. | | 1 and under 5. | | 5 and under 10. | | 10 and under 20. | | 20 and under 50. | | 50 and under 80. | | 80 and under 100. | | 100 & over. | | Age unknown. | | Born in State. | N. England States. | Middle States. | Southern States. | Southwest'n States. | Northwest'n States. |
| | | M. | F. | M. | F. | M. | F. | M. | F. | M. | F. | M. | F. | M | F. | M | F. | M | F. | | | | | | |
| 1 | Measles | 3 | 3 | 13 | 12 | 1 | 1 | 1 | 2 | 8 | 6 | 1 | | | | | | | | 43 | | | 1 | 1 | |
| 2 | Menses, suppress'n of | | | | | | | | 2 | | 2 | | | | | | | | | 1 | | | 3 | | |
| 3 | Mortification | | | 2 | 1 | | 1 | 1 | 1 | | | | | | | | | | | 4 | | | 2 | | |
| 4 | Mumps | | | | | | | | | 1 | | | | | | | | 1 | | 2 | | | | | |
| 5 | Murder | | | | | | | | | 4 | | 2 | | | | | | 1 | | 1 | | | 3 | 1 | |
| 6 | Neuralgia | | | | | | | 1 | | 2 | | 1 | 3 | | | | | | | | | | 5 | 2 | |
| 7 | Old age | | | | | | | | | | | 25 | 25 | 26 | 29 | 10 | 11 | | | 27 | | 6 | 70 | 3 | 1 |
| 8 | Paralysis | 1 | | | 2 | 1 | | | | 4 | 3 | 10 | 8 | | 2 | | | | | 6 | | 1 | 15 | 2 | 3 |
| 9 | Piles | | | 1 | | | | | | | 2 | 1 | | | | | | | | 1 | | | 2 | 1 | |
| 10 | Pleurisy | | | 3 | 1 | | 1 | 2 | 3 | 12 | 2 | 5 | 6 | | | | | | | 20 | | 1 | 9 | 3 | |
| 11 | Pneumonia | 31 | 29 | 55 | 40 | 17 | 16 | 34 | 31 | 113 | 66 | 43 | 30 | | 2 | | 1 | 1 | | 295 | 1 | 2 | 133 | 51 | 6 |
| 12 | Poison | 2 | 1 | 5 | 1 | 2 | | 4 | 1 | 1 | 2 | | | | | | | | | 15 | | | 2 | 2 | |
| 13 | Prematurity of birth. | 1 | 6 | | | | | | | | | | | | | | | | | 7 | | | | | |
| 14 | Quinsy | 1 | | 3 | 1 | | | 1 | 1 | 2 | 1 | 1 | 2 | | | | | | | 10 | | | 2 | | |
| 15 | Rheumatism | | | 1 | 1 | 2 | 1 | 1 | 2 | 5 | 3 | 4 | 1 | 1 | | | | | | 10 | | 1 | 7 | 3 | |
| 16 | Rickets | | | 2 | | | | | | | | | | | | | | | | 2 | | | | | |
| 17 | Salivation, effects of. | | | | | 1 | | | | 2 | | | | | | | | | | | | | 2 | 1 | |
| 18 | Scrofula | 6 | 3 | 12 | 1 | 1 | 3 | 4 | 4 | 7 | 9 | | 1 | | | | | | | 34 | | 2 | 7 | 4 | 1 |
| 19 | Small pox | | | 2 | 3 | | 1 | | | 3 | 1 | 1 | 1 | | | | | | | 7 | | | 1 | 2 | 1 |
| 20 | Spine, disease of | 1 | | 2 | 4 | 1 | | 1 | 1 | 2 | 1 | | | | | | | 2 | | 12 | | | 1 | 2 | |
| 21 | Stillborn | 9 | 1 | | | | | | | | | | | | | | | | | 10 | | | | | |
| 22 | Stomach, disease of | | | | | | | 1 | | | 3 | 2 | | | | | | | | 3 | | | 2 | | |
| 23 | Suffocation | 54 | 65 | 12 | 11 | 1 | 1 | | 1 | | | | | | | | | | | 143 | | | | 1 | 1 |
| 24 | Suicide | | | | | | | | | 3 | 1 | | | | | | | | | | | 1 | | | |
| 25 | Sun, stroke of | | | | | | | | | 1 | | | 1 | | | | | | | 2 | | | | | |
| 26 | Syphilis | 2 | 2 | | 1 | | | | | 1 | 1 | | 1 | | | | | | | 8 | | | | | |
| 27 | Teething | 10 | 11 | 37 | 38 | | | | | | | | | | | | | | | 92 | | | 2 | 2 | |
| 28 | Tetanus | 9 | 8 | 5 | | 1 | | | 1 | 2 | 2 | | | | | | | 1 | | 27 | | | | | 1 |
| 29 | Throat, disease of | 2 | 2 | 4 | 2 | 3 | 1 | | 4 | 2 | 3 | | | | | | | | | 14 | | 1 | 4 | 4 | |
| 30 | Thrush | 3 | 5 | 2 | 2 | | | | | | | | | | | | | | | 11 | | | | 1 | |
| 31 | Tumor | 1 | | | | | 3 | | | 1 | 1 | | | | | | | | | 4 | | | 2 | | |
| 32 | Ulcer | 1 | | 1 | | | | | 1 | | 2 | | 1 | | | | | | | 2 | | | 2 | 1 | |
| 33 | Uterus, disease of | | | | 1 | | | | | | 8 | | 2 | | | | | | | 7 | | | 3 | | |
| 34 | Venereal | | | | | | | | 1 | | 2 | 2 | | 1 | | | | | | 3 | | | 2 | 1 | |
| 35 | White swelling | | | | | | | | | | | 1 | | | | | | | | 1 | | | | | |
| 36 | Worms | 21 | 23 | 94 | 105 | 22 | 21 | 1 | 4 | 5 | 1 | | 1 | | | | | | | 277 | | | 9 | 8 | 3 |
| 37 | Unknown | 273 | 242 | 112 | 112 | 33 | 20 | 32 | 30 | 75 | 114 | 51 | 38 | 2 | 10 | | 1 | 5 | 5 | 893 | | 2 | 135 | 78 | 12 |
| | Total | 1007 | 867 | 1159 | 1060 | 359 | 299 | 422 | 433 | 1141 | 1044 | 462 | 297 | 45 | 68 | 11 | 15 | 23 | 9 | 5957 | 3 | 69 | 1522 | 715 | 161 |

## CLASSIFICATION OF DEATHS IN

| | | | | | | | | | | | | | | | | | | | | | | | | | |
|---|---|---|---|---|---|---|---|---|---|---|---|---|---|---|---|---|---|---|---|---|---|---|---|---|---|
| 1 | Abscess | | 1 | | 1 | | | 1 | | 2 | 2 | | | | | | | | | 5 | | | 1 | 1 | |
| 2 | Accident, not specif'd | 7 | 12 | 16 | 5 | 8 | 4 | 14 | | 38 | 4 | 9 | 4 | 1 | | | | | | 68 | | 4 | 21 | 3 | 18 |
| 3 | ....do...burned | 4 | 4 | 5 | 13 | | 2 | | 3 | 4 | 3 | 1 | | | | | | | | 28 | | 2 | | | 4 |
| 4 | ....do...drowned | 3 | | 7 | 8 | 2 | 2 | 17 | 3 | 27 | 1 | 5 | 1 | | | | | | | 29 | | 2 | 11 | 3 | 12 |
| 5 | ....do...scalded | | | 6 | 1 | | 1 | 1 | | 1 | | | | | | | | | | 7 | | 1 | | 1 | 1 |
| 6 | ....do...shot | | | | | | | 1 | | 6 | | | | | | | | | | 2 | | 4 | 1 | | |
| 7 | Apoplexy | | | | | | | 3 | | 5 | 2 | 3 | 2 | | | | | | | 3 | | 3 | 3 | 1 | 1 |
| 8 | Asthma | | 1 | 1 | | | | | | 1 | | 5 | 1 | 1 | | | | | | 2 | | | 7 | | 1 |
| 9 | Atrophy | | | | | | 1 | | 1 | 1 | 5 | 4 | 7 | | | | | | | 7 | | 1 | 5 | 2 | 2 |
| 10 | Bladder, disease of | | | | | | | | | | | 1 | | | | | | | | | | | 1 | | |
| 11 | Bowels......do | 5 | 3 | 3 | 3 | | | | 1 | 4 | 2 | 1 | | | | | | | | 12 | | 1 | 2 | | 1 |
| 12 | Brain ......do | 4 | 2 | 11 | 9 | 1 | 4 | 1 | 1 | 2 | 1 | 1 | 1 | | | | | | | 31 | | | | 1 | 5 |
| 13 | Bronchitis | 5 | 4 | 3 | 4 | | 1 | | 3 | 8 | 10 | 2 | 2 | | | | | | | 22 | | | 5 | 1 | 11 |
| 14 | Cancer | 2 | 1 | | | | | 1 | | 4 | 4 | 7 | 5 | | 1 | | | | | 5 | | 3 | 9 | 3 | 3 |
| 15 | Catarrh | 8 | 7 | 6 | 6 | 3 | 1 | 1 | 7 | 6 | 21 | 4 | 5 | | | | | | | 39 | | 1 | 11 | 6 | 11 |
| 16 | Chicken pox | 1 | 1 | | 1 | | | | | | | | | | | | | | | 3 | | | | | |
| 17 | Childbirth | | | | | | | | 10 | | 105 | | | | | | | | | 38 | 1 | 1 | 17 | 19 | 22 |
| 18 | Cholera | 99 | 105 | 284 | 260 | 143 | 149 | 200 | 186 | 1158 | 654 | 164 | 174 | 2 | 5 | 2 | | 4 | | 1069 | 39 | 142 | 155 | 99 | 256 |
| 19 | ....do..infantum | 21 | 16 | 21 | 22 | 3 | | | | | | | | | | | | | | 80 | | | | 1 | 1 |
| 20 | ....do..morbus | 4 | 1 | | 3 | | | 2 | | 4 | 5 | 3 | 5 | 1 | | | | | | 10 | | 1 | 9 | 1 | 6 |
| 21 | Chorea | | | | | | | | | | | | | | | | | | | | | | | | |
| 22 | Colic | | 1 | 2 | 3 | 1 | | 1 | | 7 | 3 | 4 | 5 | | | | | | | 9 | 2 | 1 | 6 | 2 | 6 |
| 23 | Congestion | | | | | | | 2 | 1 | 4 | 3 | | | | | | | | | 4 | | | | 3 | 3 |
| 24 | ....do....brain | 13 | 13 | 18 | 8 | 9 | 2 | 5 | 7 | 8 | 7 | 2 | | | | | | | | 75 | | 1 | 5 | 3 | 5 |
| 25 | Consumption | 12 | 6 | 18 | 28 | 9 | 12 | 26 | 57 | 215 | 196 | 33 | 34 | 2 | | | | | | 218 | 8 | 28 | 106 | 40 | 147 |
| 26 | Convulsions | 29 | 30 | 18 | 16 | 5 | 2 | 6 | 5 | 13 | 9 | 3 | 1 | | | | | | | 99 | | 2 | 5 | 5 | 3 |
| 27 | Cramp | 12 | 20 | 12 | 12 | | | | | | | | | | | | | | | 50 | | | | | |
| 28 | Cranium, fracture of. | | | | | | | | | 1 | | | | | | | | | | | | | | | |
| 29 | Croup | 121 | 82 | 107 | 88 | 17 | 14 | 2 | | | | | | 1 | | | | | | 402 | | | 4 | 6 | 14 |

## THE STATE OF MISSISSIPPI—AGGREGATE—Continued.

| NATIVITIES. | | | | | SEASON OF DECEASE. | | | | DURATION OF SICKNESS. | | | | WHITES. | | | COLORED. | | | | | | | | | |
|---|---|---|---|---|---|---|---|---|---|---|---|---|---|---|---|---|---|---|---|---|---|---|---|---|---|
| | | | | | | | | | | | | | | | | Slaves. | | | | Free. | | | | | |
| | | | | | | | | | | | | | | | | Black. | | Mulatto. | | Black. | | Mul. | | | |
| California and Territories. | Ireland. | Germany. | Other foreign countries. | Unknown. | Spring. | Summer. | Autumn. | Winter. | Under 1 week. | 1 week and under 1 month. | 1 month and under 3 months. | 3 months and over. | Males. | Females. | Total. | M. | F. | M. | F. | M. | F. | M | F. | Aggregate deaths. | |
| .... | 1 | .. | .... | .... | 24 | 16 | 4 | 2 | 6 | 18 | .... | 1 | 5 | 6 | 11 | 17 | 18 | .... | .... | .... | .... | .. | .. | 46 | 1 |
| .... | .... | .. | .... | .... | 1 | 3 | .... | .... | .... | 1 | 2 | 1 | .... | 1 | 1 | .... | 3 | .... | .... | .... | .... | .. | .. | 4 | 2 |
| .... | .... | .. | .... | .... | 3 | .... | .... | 3 | 1 | 3 | 1 | .... | 2 | 2 | 4 | 1 | 1 | .... | .... | .... | .... | .. | .. | 6 | 3 |
| .... | .... | .. | .... | .... | .... | 1 | .... | .... | 1 | 1 | .... | .... | 1 | .... | 1 | 1 | .... | .... | .... | .... | .... | .. | .. | 2 | 4 |
| .... | 2 | .. | .... | .... | .... | 1 | 3 | 3 | 5 | 1 | .... | .... | 5 | .... | 5 | 1 | .... | 1 | .... | .... | .... | .. | .. | 7 | 5 |
| .... | .... | .. | .... | .... | 2 | 3 | 2 | .... | .... | 3 | .... | 4 | 2 | 3 | 5 | 2 | .... | .... | .... | .... | .... | .. | .. | 7 | 6 |
| .... | 1 | .. | 10 | 8 | 35 | 27 | 30 | 32 | 12 | 12 | 5 | 45 | 17 | 26 | 43 | 44 | 36 | .... | 1 | .... | 2 | .. | .. | 126 | 7 |
| .... | 1 | 1 | 1 | 1 | 14 | 6 | 7 | 4 | 5 | 6 | .... | 16 | 8 | 13 | 21 | 8 | 2 | .... | .... | .... | .... | .. | .. | 31 | 8 |
| .... | .... | .. | .... | .... | .... | 3 | 1 | .... | 3 | .... | .... | 1 | 1 | 1 | 2 | 1 | 1 | .... | .... | .... | .... | .. | .. | 4 | 9 |
| .... | 1 | .. | .... | 1 | 16 | 6 | 3 | 9 | 5 | 20 | 3 | 1 | 4 | 5 | 9 | 17 | 8 | 1 | .... | .... | .... | .. | .. | 35 | 10 |
| 1 | 3 | .. | 2 | 15 | 209 | 74 | 87 | 135 | 136 | 250 | 36 | 19 | 91 | 66 | 157 | 195 | 143 | 7 | 6 | 1 | .... | .. | .. | 509 | 11 |
| .... | .... | .. | .... | .... | 4 | 4 | 9 | 2 | 11 | 4 | .... | .... | 8 | 2 | 10 | 6 | 3 | .... | .... | .... | .... | .. | .. | 19 | 12 |
| .... | .... | .. | .... | .... | 1 | 1 | 2 | 3 | 3 | 1 | .... | .... | 1 | 1 | 2 | .... | 3 | .... | 2 | .... | .... | .. | .. | 7 | 13 |
| .... | .... | 1 | .... | .... | 3 | 2 | 2 | 6 | 4 | 3 | 1 | .... | 4 | 4 | 8 | 4 | 1 | .... | .... | .... | .... | .. | .. | 13 | 14 |
| .... | .... | .. | .... | 1 | 6 | 3 | 3 | 10 | 2 | 4 | .... | 12 | 6 | 4 | 10 | 7 | 4 | 1 | .... | .... | .... | .. | .. | 22 | 15 |
| .... | .... | .. | .... | .... | .... | 1 | 1 | .... | .... | .... | .... | 2 | .... | .... | .... | 2 | .... | .... | .... | .... | .... | .. | .. | 2 | 16 |
| .... | .... | .. | .... | .... | 1 | 2 | .... | .... | 1 | 1 | 1 | .... | 2 | .... | 2 | 1 | .... | .... | .... | .... | .... | .. | .. | 3 | 17 |
| .... | .... | .. | .... | 3 | 12 | 12 | 18 | 9 | 2 | 6 | 8 | 30 | 5 | 4 | 9 | 25 | 17 | .... | .... | .... | .... | .. | .. | 51 | 18 |
| .... | .... | .. | 1 | .... | 7 | 2 | 3 | .... | .... | 10 | .... | .... | 3 | 5 | 8 | 3 | 1 | .... | .... | .... | .... | .. | .. | 12 | 19 |
| .... | .... | .. | .... | .... | 3 | 4 | 5 | 3 | .... | 1 | 1 | 6 | 3 | 2 | 5 | 5 | 4 | 1 | .... | .... | .... | .. | .. | 15 | 20 |
| .... | .... | .. | .... | .... | 1 | 3 | 5 | 1 | .... | .... | .... | .... | 2 | .... | 2 | 7 | .... | .... | 1 | .... | .... | .. | .. | 10 | 21 |
| .... | .... | .. | 1 | .... | 2 | 1 | 2 | 1 | 1 | .... | .... | 1 | 3 | 3 | 6 | .... | .... | .... | .... | .... | .... | .. | .. | 6 | 22 |
| .... | .... | .. | .... | .... | 41 | 34 | 28 | 40 | 145 | .... | .... | .... | .... | 6 | 6 | 60 | 67 | 7 | 5 | .... | .... | .. | .. | 145 | 23 |
| .... | 2 | .. | 1 | .... | 2 | 1 | 1 | .... | 4 | .... | .... | .... | 3 | 1 | 4 | .... | .... | .... | .... | .... | .... | .. | .. | 4 | 24 |
| .... | .... | .. | .... | .... | .... | .... | 2 | .... | 2 | .... | .... | .... | .... | .... | .... | .... | 1 | 1 | .... | .... | .... | .. | .. | 2 | 25 |
| .... | .... | .. | .... | .... | .... | 4 | 3 | 1 | .... | .... | 2 | 4 | .... | .... | .... | 3 | 3 | .... | 2 | .... | .... | .. | .. | 8 | 26 |
| .... | .... | .. | .... | .... | 13 | 37 | 37 | 8 | 16 | 34 | 19 | 10 | 14 | 14 | 28 | 32 | 33 | 1 | 2 | .... | .... | .. | .. | 96 | 27 |
| .... | .... | .. | .... | 1 | 5 | 8 | 5 | 7 | 8 | 6 | .... | .... | 1 | .... | 1 | 12 | 11 | 5 | .... | .... | .... | .. | .. | 29 | 28 |
| .... | .... | .. | .... | .... | 4 | 3 | 8 | 8 | 5 | 10 | .... | 4 | 7 | 5 | 12 | 4 | 7 | .... | .... | .... | .... | .. | .. | 23 | 29 |
| .... | .... | .. | .... | .... | .... | 4 | 6 | 2 | 4 | 4 | 1 | .... | 3 | 2 | 5 | 2 | 4 | .... | 1 | .... | .... | .. | .. | 12 | 30 |
| .... | .... | .. | .... | .... | 1 | 2 | 2 | 1 | .... | 1 | 1 | 3 | 1 | 2 | 3 | 1 | 2 | .... | .... | .... | .... | .. | .. | 6 | 31 |
| .... | .... | .. | .... | 1 | 1 | 2 | 2 | 1 | .... | 1 | 3 | 2 | .... | 3 | 3 | 2 | 1 | .... | .... | .... | .... | .. | .. | 6 | 32 |
| .... | .... | 1 | .... | .... | 5 | 1 | 4 | 1 | 1 | 2 | .... | 5 | .... | 2 | 2 | .... | 9 | .... | .... | .... | .... | .. | .. | 11 | 33 |
| .... | .... | .. | .... | .... | 2 | 1 | 3 | .... | 1 | 1 | .... | 1 | .... | .... | .... | 3 | 2 | .... | 1 | .... | .... | .. | .. | 6 | 34 |
| .... | .... | .. | .... | .... | .... | .... | 1 | .... | .... | .... | 1 | .... | 1 | .... | 1 | .... | .... | .... | .... | .... | .... | .. | .. | 1 | 35 |
| .... | .... | .. | .... | 1 | 53 | 86 | 116 | 34 | 125 | 108 | 12 | 12 | 35 | 37 | 72 | 102 | 109 | 5 | 9 | .... | .... | 1 | .. | 298 | 36 |
| 1 | .... | .. | 6 | 28 | 274 | 283 | 334 | 218 | 478 | 173 | 61 | 186 | 195 | 191 | 386 | 368 | 367 | 15 | 13 | 2 | .... | 3 | 1 | 1155 | 37 |
| 2 | 33 | 16 | 45 | 198 | 2089 | 2371 | 2645 | 1460 | 3385 | 2338 | 564 | 1104 | 1802 | 1549 | 3351 | 2665 | 238 | 148 | 148 | 7 | 4 | 7 | 2 | 8721 | |

## THE STATE OF MISSOURI.

| California and Territories. | Ireland. | Germany. | Other foreign countries. | Unknown. | Spring. | Summer. | Autumn. | Winter. | Under 1 week. | 1 week and under 1 month. | 1 month and under 3 months. | 3 months and over. | Males. | Females. | Total. | Slaves Black M. | Slaves Black F. | Slaves Mulatto M. | Slaves Mulatto F. | Free Black M. | Free Black F. | Free Mul. M | Free Mul. F. | Aggregate deaths. | |
|---|---|---|---|---|---|---|---|---|---|---|---|---|---|---|---|---|---|---|---|---|---|---|---|---|---|
| .... | .... | .... | .... | .. | 2 | 2 | 2 | 1 | .. | 2 | 1 | 2 | 3 | 3 | 6 | .... | 1 | .... | .... | .... | .... | .. | .. | 7 | 1 |
| .... | 4 | 4 | .... | .. | 15 | 34 | 20 | 23 | 83 | 14 | 6 | 10 | 78 | 15 | 93 | 12 | 12 | 1 | 1 | 2 | 1 | .. | .. | 122 | 2 |
| .... | 2 | 3 | .... | .. | 4 | 11 | 13 | 9 | 28 | 6 | 2 | 2 | 7 | 17 | 24 | 5 | 5 | 1 | 2 | 1 | 1 | .. | .. | 39 | 3 |
| .... | 5 | 10 | 4 | .. | 18 | 39 | 12 | 7 | 76 | .... | .... | .... | 46 | 12 | 58 | 12 | 3 | 2 | .... | .... | .... | 1 | .. | 76 | 4 |
| .... | .... | .... | .... | .. | 3 | 3 | 4 | .... | 8 | 2 | .... | .... | 6 | 1 | 7 | 1 | 1 | 1 | .... | .... | .... | .. | .. | 10 | 5 |
| .... | .... | .... | .... | .. | 1 | 1 | 2 | 3 | 7 | .... | .... | .... | 7 | .... | 7 | .... | .... | .... | .... | .... | .... | .. | .. | 7 | 6 |
| .... | 1 | 1 | 2 | .. | 2 | 6 | 3 | 4 | 12 | 2 | .... | 1 | 10 | 2 | 12 | 1 | 2 | .... | .... | .... | .... | .. | .. | 15 | 7 |
| .... | .... | .... | .... | .. | 2 | 3 | 3 | 2 | 4 | 2 | 1 | 3 | 7 | 2 | 9 | .... | .... | .... | .... | 1 | .... | .. | .. | 10 | 8 |
| .... | .... | 1 | 1 | .. | 6 | 3 | 2 | 8 | 13 | 2 | .... | 2 | 5 | 12 | 17 | .... | 2 | .... | .... | .... | .... | .. | .. | 19 | 9 |
| .... | .... | .... | .... | .. | .... | .... | 1 | .... | .... | 1 | .... | .... | 1 | .... | 1 | .... | .... | .... | .... | .... | .... | .. | .. | 1 | 10 |
| .... | .... | 4 | 2 | .. | 3 | 8 | 9 | 2 | 6 | 9 | 2 | 5 | 12 | 9 | 21 | 1 | .... | .... | .... | .... | .... | .. | .. | 22 | 11 |
| .... | 1 | .... | .... | .. | 10 | 10 | 9 | 8 | 12 | 19 | 2 | 3 | 15 | 15 | 30 | 5 | 2 | .... | .... | .... | .... | .. | 1 | 38 | 12 |
| 1 | .... | .... | 1 | .. | 7 | 18 | 13 | 3 | 7 | 15 | 9 | 10 | 16 | 20 | 36 | 2 | 4 | .... | .... | .... | .... | .. | .. | 42 | 13 |
| .... | 2 | 2 | .... | .. | 11 | 7 | 5 | 3 | .... | 5 | 1 | 19 | 14 | 10 | 24 | .... | 1 | .... | .... | .... | .... | .. | .. | 26 | 14 |
| 1 | 3 | 1 | 2 | .. | 34 | 13 | 9 | 16 | 21 | 32 | 11 | 11 | 20 | 38 | 58 | 7 | 6 | 1 | 1 | .... | 2 | .. | .. | 75 | 15 |
| .... | .... | .... | .... | .. | 1 | 2 | .... | .... | 2 | 1 | .... | .... | 1 | 2 | 3 | .... | .... | .... | .... | .... | .... | .. | .. | 3 | 16 |
| .... | 2 | 13 | 2 | .. | 38 | 27 | 27 | 22 | 71 | 36 | 6 | 2 | .... | 95 | 95 | .... | 18 | .... | 1 | .... | .... | .. | 1 | 115 | 17 |
| .... | 406 | 1042 | 375 | 6 | .... | 3108 | 481 | .... | 3341 | 248 | .... | .... | 1945 | 1445 | 3390 | 90 | 67 | 13 | 13 | 6 | 5 | 2 | 3 | 3589 | 18 |
| .... | .... | .... | .... | .. | .... | 33 | 42 | .... | 37 | 46 | .... | .... | 45 | 31 | 76 | .... | 5 | .... | 2 | .... | .... | .. | .. | 83 | 19 |
| .... | .... | .... | 1 | .. | 5 | 12 | 10 | .... | 17 | 11 | .... | .... | 11 | 13 | 24 | 3 | 1 | .... | .... | .... | .... | .. | .. | 28 | 20 |
| .... | .... | .... | .... | .. | .... | .... | .... | .... | .... | .... | .... | .... | .... | .... | .... | .... | .... | .... | .... | .... | .... | .. | .. | .... | 21 |
| .... | .... | 1 | .... | .. | 9 | 4 | 9 | 4 | 14 | 8 | 1 | 1 | 13 | 9 | 22 | 1 | 3 | 1 | .... | .... | .... | .. | .. | 27 | 22 |
| .... | .... | .... | .... | .. | 2 | 2 | 4 | 2 | 6 | 3 | .... | 1 | 4 | 4 | 8 | 1 | .... | 1 | .... | .... | .... | .. | .. | 10 | 23 |
| .... | 1 | 2 | .... | .. | 31 | 18 | 28 | 14 | 46 | 34 | 7 | 4 | 48 | 32 | 80 | 4 | 5 | 3 | .... | .... | .... | .. | .. | 92 | 24 |
| .... | 35 | 32 | 33 | 1 | 194 | 193 | 159 | 102 | 26 | 94 | 69 | 424 | 277 | 268 | 545 | 31 | 57 | 7 | 8 | .... | .... | .. | .. | 648 | 25 |
| .... | 4 | 8 | 11 | .. | 30 | 35 | 46 | 26 | 93 | 31 | 4 | 9 | 60 | 58 | 118 | 11 | 4 | 2 | .... | 1 | 1 | .. | .. | 137 | 26 |
| .... | .... | 6 | .... | .. | 10 | 32 | 8 | 6 | 49 | 5 | 2 | .... | 24 | 32 | 56 | .... | .... | .... | .... | .... | .... | .. | .. | 56 | 27 |
| .... | .... | 1 | .... | .. | .... | 1 | .... | .... | 1 | .... | .... | .... | 1 | .... | 1 | .... | .... | .... | .... | .... | .... | .. | .. | 1 | 28 |
| .... | 2 | 2 | 1 | .. | 158 | 89 | 116 | 48 | 400 | 11 | .... | .... | 201 | 146 | 347 | 41 | 35 | 5 | 3 | .... | .... | .. | .. | 431 | 29 |

## CLASSIFICATION OF DEATHS IN

| | Cause of death. | Under 1. | | 1 and under 5. | | 5 and under 10. | | 10 and under 20. | | 20 and under 50. | | 50 and under 80. | | 80 and under 100. | | 100 & over. | | Age unknown. | | Born in the State. | N. England States. | Middle States. | Southern States. | Southwest'n States. | Northwest'n States. |
|---|---|---|---|---|---|---|---|---|---|---|---|---|---|---|---|---|---|---|---|---|---|---|---|---|---|
| | | M. | F. | M. | F. | M. | F. | M. | F. | M. | F. | M. | F. | M | F. | M | F. | M | F. | | | | | | |
| 1 | Debility | 12 | 15 | | 1 | | 1 | 1 | | 1 | 2 | | | | | 1 | | | | 30 | | 1 | 3 | | |
| 2 | Diabetes | | | | | | | | | 1 | | | | | | | | | | | | | | 1 | |
| 3 | Diarrhœa | 21 | 21 | 41 | 39 | 4 | 1 | 7 | 6 | 64 | 15 | 10 | 3 | 1 | | | | | | 150 | | 5 | 13 | 10 | 25 |
| 4 | Dirt eating | | | | | | 1 | | | | | | | | | | | | | 1 | | | | | |
| 5 | Dropsy | 7 | 5 | 11 | 6 | 13 | 10 | 9 | 7 | 28 | 45 | 33 | 18 | 4 | | | | | 1 | 73 | 2 | 7 | 47 | 24 | 28 |
| 6 | Dysentery | 20 | 22 | 52 | 54 | 9 | 6 | 9 | 4 | 25 | 26 | 4 | 5 | 1 | | | | 1 | | 154 | 3 | 8 | 14 | 4 | 19 |
| 7 | Dyspepsia | | 1 | 1 | | | | | 1 | 5 | 2 | 7 | 4 | | | | | | | 3 | | | 6 | 2 | 7 |
| 8 | Epilepsy | 1 | | 1 | | | 1 | 1 | | 1 | 4 | 1 | | | | | | | | 4 | | 1 | 2 | | 3 |
| 9 | Erysipelas | 7 | 11 | 9 | 11 | 5 | 4 | 5 | 15 | 17 | 5 | 11 | 1 | | | | | | | 60 | | 6 | 14 | 3 | 11 |
| 10 | Fever, not specified | 31 | 22 | 70 | 52 | 30 | 15 | 47 | 45 | 122 | 100 | 45 | 19 | 1 | 2 | | | | | 297 | | 19 | 61 | 46 | 108 |
| 11 | ..do..bilious | 2 | 4 | 16 | 14 | 3 | 2 | 11 | 7 | 41 | 23 | 13 | 8 | | | | | | | 52 | | 4 | 22 | 7 | 17 |
| 12 | ..do..brain | 9 | 4 | 4 | 7 | 2 | 2 | 1 | 1 | 2 | | | | | | | | | | 25 | | 1 | 1 | 2 | |
| 13 | ..do..congestive | 1 | 8 | 11 | 12 | 9 | 8 | 16 | 12 | 48 | 26 | 14 | 5 | | | | | | | 72 | 1 | 9 | 25 | 12 | 41 |
| 14 | ..do..inflammatory | | | 2 | 1 | 2 | | 3 | 1 | 1 | 1 | 1 | | | | | | | | 1 | | | 1 | 5 | 5 |
| 15 | ..do..intermittent | 9 | 11 | 13 | 8 | 1 | 2 | 3 | 3 | 6 | 7 | 2 | 1 | | | | | | | 43 | 1 | | 2 | 3 | 8 |
| 16 | ..do..puerperal | | | | | | | | 5 | | 24 | | 1 | | | | | | | 7 | | 2 | 5 | 4 | 11 |
| 17 | ..do..remittent | | | | 1 | | 1 | | | | | | | | | | | | | 2 | | | | | |
| 18 | ..do..scarlet | 5 | 7 | 20 | 21 | 6 | 14 | 3 | 8 | 5 | 2 | | | | | | | | | 74 | 1 | 1 | 1 | 5 | 9 |
| 19 | ..do .typhus | 5 | 5 | 28 | 19 | 25 | 13 | 53 | 43 | 158 | 72 | 26 | 10 | | | | | | | 182 | 2 | 11 | 53 | 44 | 86 |
| 20 | ..do..yellow | | | | | | | | | 2 | 2 | | | | | | | | | | | 2 | 1 | | |
| 21 | Fracture | | | | | | | | | 1 | | | | | | | | | | | | | 1 | | |
| 22 | Frozen | 1 | | | | | | | | 3 | | | | | | | | | | 2 | | | | | 2 |
| 23 | Gout | 3 | | | 1 | | | | | 1 | | | | | | | | | | 4 | | | | | |
| 24 | Gravel | | | 1 | | | | | | | 1 | 7 | | 1 | | | | | | | | 2 | 5 | 2 | 1 |
| 25 | Heart, disease of | 1 | 1 | | | 2 | 1 | 2 | 4 | 7 | 8 | 9 | 2 | | | | | | | 10 | | 6 | 8 | 1 | 4 |
| 26 | Hemorrhage | | | | | 1 | | 1 | 1 | 4 | 4 | 1 | | 2 | | | | | | 3 | | 1 | 4 | 1 | 1 |
| 27 | Hernia | | 1 | | | | | | | 2 | 2 | 1 | | | | | | | | 1 | | | | 2 | 3 |
| 28 | Hives | 16 | 14 | 3 | 4 | | | | | | | | | | | | | | | 35 | | | | 1 | 1 |
| 29 | Hooping cough | 26 | 32 | 37 | 43 | 5 | 4 | | 1 | | 3 | 1 | | | | | | | | 137 | | 1 | 1 | 6 | |
| 30 | Hydrocephalus | 6 | 3 | 7 | 7 | 3 | | | 1 | 2 | | | 1 | | | | | | | 19 | | | 1 | 1 | 6 |
| 31 | Inflammation | 3 | 5 | 9 | 6 | 1 | 2 | 3 | | 6 | 6 | 5 | | | | | | | | 26 | | 2 | 8 | 3 | 4 |
| 32 | ....do....bowels | 13 | 11 | 16 | 12 | 4 | 9 | 5 | 3 | 11 | 9 | 2 | | | | | | | | 74 | 1 | 3 | 3 | 2 | 9 |
| 33 | ....do....brain | 26 | 24 | 39 | 27 | 15 | 10 | 15 | 13 | 19 | 9 | 6 | 2 | | | | | | | 133 | | 5 | 11 | 7 | 28 |
| 34 | ....do....stomach | | | | 1 | | | 1 | | | 5 | | | | | | | | | 3 | | 1 | 3 | | |
| 35 | Influenza | 1 | 1 | | 1 | 1 | 1 | | 2 | 1 | 2 | | 1 | | | | | | | 6 | | | 2 | 1 | 1 |
| 36 | Insanity | | | | | | | | | 1 | | | | | | | | | | | | | | | 1 |
| 37 | Intemperance | | | | | | | | | 5 | | 3 | | | | | | | | 2 | | 1 | 2 | 2 | |
| 38 | Jaundice | | 2 | 2 | 1 | | | | 1 | 4 | | 3 | 3 | | | | | | | 7 | | | 2 | | 4 |
| 39 | Kidneys, disease of | | | | | | | | | 2 | 1 | | | | | | | | | | | 1 | | | 2 |
| 40 | Killed | 1 | | | 1 | 1 | 2 | 6 | | 15 | 1 | 5 | | | | | | | | 10 | | 2 | 5 | 1 | 8 |
| 41 | Lightning | | | | | | 1 | 2 | 1 | 1 | 1 | | | | | | | | | 3 | | | 2 | | 1 |
| 42 | Liver, disease of | 3 | 1 | 3 | 1 | | 1 | 4 | 5 | 15 | 16 | 8 | 6 | 1 | | | | 1 | | 15 | | 4 | 18 | 3 | 15 |
| 43 | Lockjaw | | 2 | | 1 | | 2 | 2 | 1 | 2 | 2 | | | | | | | | | 7 | | | 1 | 1 | 3 |
| 44 | Lungs, disease of | 10 | 6 | 10 | 11 | 4 | 8 | 4 | 4 | 20 | 7 | 7 | 5 | 2 | | | | | | 51 | 1 | 5 | 16 | 2 | 17 |
| 45 | Mania-a-potu | | | | | | | 1 | | 11 | | 1 | | | | | | | | | | | 2 | | 1 |
| 46 | Measles | 12 | 11 | 35 | 51 | 14 | 11 | 8 | 10 | 14 | 14 | | | | | | | | | 128 | | 1 | 5 | 10 | 27 |
| 47 | Marasmus | 1 | 2 | 1 | | | | | | | | | | | | | | | | 4 | | | | | |
| 48 | Mortification | | | | 1 | | | | | 2 | 1 | | | | | | | | | | | | 1 | | 3 |
| 49 | Mumps | 1 | 1 | | 2 | | | | 1 | 1 | | | | | | | | | | 5 | | | 1 | | |
| 50 | Murder | 1 | | | | | | 1 | 1 | 3 | | | | | | | | | | 3 | | | 1 | | 2 |
| 51 | Neuralgia | | | | | 1 | 1 | 2 | | 1 | 1 | 1 | | | | | | | | 3 | | | 1 | | 3 |
| 52 | Nerves, disease of | | | 2 | | 3 | | 1 | 1 | 3 | 1 | | 1 | | | | | | | 1 | | | 3 | | 1 |
| 53 | Old age | | | | | | | | | | 1 | 21 | 25 | 21 | 30 | 1 | 1 | | 1 | 19 | 1 | 10 | 42 | 6 | 3 |
| 54 | Paralysis | | | | 2 | 1 | | 2 | 1 | 7 | 3 | 10 | 11 | 1 | | | | | | 9 | | 4 | 10 | 3 | 8 |
| 55 | Phrenitis | 3 | 2 | | 1 | | | | | 1 | | | | | | | | | | 7 | | | | | |
| 56 | Piles | | | | | | | | | 1 | 1 | 3 | | | | | | | | | | | 3 | | 1 |
| 57 | Pleurisy | 2 | 4 | 5 | 3 | 1 | 5 | 3 | 3 | 12 | 10 | 5 | 5 | | | | 1 | | | 22 | | 2 | 10 | 3 | 18 |
| 58 | Pneumonia | 20 | 15 | 31 | 29 | 11 | 9 | 24 | 28 | 96 | 49 | 44 | 18 | 3 | 1 | | | | | 154 | 4 | 17 | 59 | 42 | 70 |
| 59 | Poison | 2 | 1 | 1 | 3 | 1 | 1 | | 1 | 2 | | | 1 | | | | | | | 7 | | | 1 | | 3 |
| 60 | Prematurity of birth | | 3 | | | | | | | | | | | | | | | | | 3 | | | | | |
| 61 | Quinsy | | | 1 | 3 | 1 | | 1 | 2 | 5 | 3 | 3 | | | | | | | | 8 | | 2 | 4 | 1 | 2 |
| 62 | Rheumatism | | | | | | 1 | 6 | 1 | 15 | 1 | 6 | 1 | | | | | | | 5 | | | 5 | 3 | 8 |
| 63 | Rickets | | | 1 | 1 | | | | | | | | | | | | | | | 2 | | | | | |
| 64 | Salivation, effects of | | | | | 2 | | | | 1 | 1 | | 1 | | | | | | | | | 1 | 2 | 1 | |
| 65 | Scrofula | 2 | 1 | 10 | 2 | 11 | 2 | 3 | 9 | 5 | 9 | 2 | 4 | | | | | | | 41 | | | 8 | 1 | 9 |
| 66 | Scurvy | | | | | 1 | | 1 | 1 | 12 | 1 | 2 | | | | | | | | 8 | 1 | 3 | 2 | 1 | 2 |
| 67 | Small pox | 1 | 4 | 5 | 4 | 1 | 3 | 5 | 4 | 20 | 5 | 5 | | | | | | | | 21 | 2 | 2 | 6 | 2 | 15 |
| 68 | Spine, disease of | 3 | 1 | 3 | 1 | 1 | 3 | 1 | 4 | 2 | 1 | 2 | | | | | | | | 13 | 1 | 2 | 2 | | 3 |
| 69 | Stillborn | 5 | 2 | | | | | | | | | | | | | | | | | 7 | | | | | |
| 70 | Stomach, disease of | 1 | | 2 | 2 | 1 | 1 | | 3 | 3 | 2 | 2 | 2 | | | | | | | 10 | | 1 | 3 | 4 | |
| 71 | Suffocation | 4 | | 1 | 6 | | | | | 4 | | | 1 | | | | | 3 | | 15 | | | 1 | | 1 |
| 72 | Suicide | | | | | | | 2 | | 7 | 1 | 1 | | | | | | | | 4 | | 1 | 2 | | 3 |
| 73 | Summer complaint | 23 | 19 | 31 | 40 | 3 | 1 | 1 | | 3 | | 1 | | | | | | | | 102 | | 2 | 1 | 2 | 2 |
| 74 | Sun, stroke of | | | 1 | | 1 | | | | 8 | 1 | | | | | | | | | 1 | | | | | |
| 75 | Teething | 19 | 24 | 41 | 39 | 3 | 1 | | | | | | | | | | | | | 106 | | 3 | | 1 | 3 |

THE STATE OF MISSOURI—Continued.

| NATIVITIES. | | | | | SEASON OF DECEASE. | | | | DURATION OF SICKNESS. | | | | WHITES. | | | COLORED. | | | | | | | | | |
|---|---|---|---|---|---|---|---|---|---|---|---|---|---|---|---|---|---|---|---|---|---|---|---|---|---|
| | | | | | | | | | | | | | | | | Slaves. | | | | Free. | | | | | |
| | | | | | | | | | | | | | | | | Black. | | Mulatto. | | Bl'k. | | Mul. | | | |
| California and Territories. | Ireland. | Germany. | Other foreign countries. | Unknown. | Spring. | Summer. | Autumn. | Winter. | Under 1 week. | 1 week and under 1 month. | 1 month and under 3 months. | 3 months and over. | Males. | Females. | Total. | M. | F. | M. | F. | M. | F. | M | | Aggregate deaths. | |
| | | 1 | | 1 | 4 | 17 | 9 | 6 | 22 | 6 | 3 | 5 | 13 | 13 | 26 | 2 | 5 | | | 1 | 1 | 1 | | 36 | 1 |
| | | | | | | | 1 | | 1 | | | | 1 | | 1 | | | | | | | | | 1 | 2 |
| | 11 | 12 | 7 | | 22 | 72 | 105 | 32 | 62 | 88 | 23 | 60 | 139 | 79 | 218 | 7 | 5 | 2 | 1 | | | | | 233 | 3 |
| | | | | | 1 | | | | | | | | | | | | 1 | | | | | | | 1 | 4 |
| | 1 | 13 | 2 | | 55 | 58 | 49 | 34 | 9 | 31 | 48 | 102 | 87 | 79 | 166 | 14 | 11 | 2 | 1 | 1 | 1 | 1 | | 199 | 5 |
| | 13 | 16 | 7 | | 24 | 62 | 118 | 29 | 76 | 112 | 17 | 23 | 118 | 111 | 229 | 3 | 6 | | | | | | | 238 | 6 |
| | 1 | | 2 | | 7 | 4 | 3 | 6 | 2 | 1 | 2 | 15 | 12 | 8 | 20 | | | | | 1 | | | | 21 | 7 |
| | | | | | 3 | 3 | | 3 | 3 | 2 | 1 | 4 | 5 | 5 | 10 | | | | | | | | | 10 | 8 |
| | 3 | 4 | | | 27 | 18 | 34 | 21 | 23 | 51 | 7 | 17 | 52 | 43 | 95 | 1 | 4 | | | 1 | | | | 101 | 9 |
| | 13 | 42 | 14 | 1 | 106 | 146 | 200 | 113 | 143 | 368 | 66 | 20 | 313 | 224 | 537 | 29 | 29 | 3 | 2 | 1 | 1 | | | 601 | 10 |
| 2 | 9 | 25 | 6 | | 19 | 41 | 68 | 15 | 23 | 97 | 13 | 8 | 81 | 52 | 133 | 5 | 5 | | | | | | 1 | 144 | 11 |
| 1 | 2 | | | | 4 | 12 | 11 | 5 | 8 | 18 | 3 | 3 | 17 | 13 | 30 | 1 | | | | | | | 1 | 32 | 12 |
| | 3 | 4 | 2 | 1 | 32 | 28 | 79 | 30 | 92 | 62 | 3 | 9 | 90 | 65 | 155 | 7 | 5 | 1 | 1 | 1 | | | | 170 | 13 |
| | | | | | | 3 | 7 | 2 | 3 | 7 | 2 | | 8 | 3 | 11 | 1 | | | | | | | | 12 | 14 |
| | 3 | 3 | 3 | | 11 | 13 | 29 | 13 | 16 | 35 | 9 | 6 | 33 | 30 | 63 | 1 | 1 | | 1 | | | | | 66 | 15 |
| | | 1 | | | 12 | 5 | 4 | 9 | 6 | 18 | 2 | 3 | | 30 | 30 | | | | | | | | | 30 | 16 |
| | | | | | | | 2 | | 1 | 1 | | | | 2 | 2 | | | | | | | | | 2 | 17 |
| | | | | | 19 | 19 | 29 | 24 | 32 | 55 | 2 | 1 | 35 | 44 | 79 | 4 | 8 | | | | | | | 91 | 18 |
| | 37 | 24 | 14 | 4 | 146 | 84 | 99 | 124 | 84 | 175 | 33 | 64 | 271 | 139 | 410 | 20 | 21 | 2 | 1 | 2 | 1 | | | 457 | 19 |
| | | 1 | | | | 1 | 2 | 1 | 2 | 2 | | | 2 | 2 | 4 | | | | | | | | | 4 | 20 |
| | | | | | 1 | | | | | 1 | | | 1 | | 1 | | | | | | | | | 1 | 21 |
| | | | | | 2 | | | | 3 | | | | 3 | | 3 | 1 | | | | | | | | 4 | 22 |
| | | 1 | | | 2 | 1 | 1 | 1 | 3 | 1 | | 1 | 4 | 1 | 5 | | | | | | | | | 5 | 23 |
| | | | | | 2 | 4 | 4 | | 4 | 3 | 2 | 1 | 9 | 1 | 10 | | | | | | | | | 10 | 24 |
| | 2 | 3 | 3 | | 9 | 13 | 10 | 4 | 9 | 10 | 3 | 13 | 16 | 14 | 30 | 4 | 2 | 1 | | | | | | 37 | 25 |
| | 1 | 2 | 1 | | 1 | 5 | 6 | 2 | 5 | 7 | | 1 | 8 | 4 | 12 | 1 | 1 | | | | | | | 14 | 26 |
| | | | | | 2 | | 2 | 2 | 1 | 3 | 2 | | 3 | | 3 | | 2 | | 1 | | | | | 6 | 27 |
| | | | | | 11 | 9 | 6 | 11 | 28 | 7 | 1 | 1 | 18 | 15 | 33 | 1 | 3 | | | | | | | 37 | 28 |
| | 2 | 1 | 4 | | 31 | 44 | 60 | 16 | 25 | 97 | 24 | 6 | 55 | 66 | 121 | 12 | 14 | 2 | 3 | | | | | 152 | 29 |
| | 2 | 1 | | | 2 | 13 | 8 | 7 | 7 | 14 | 4 | 3 | 18 | 12 | 30 | | | | | | | | | 30 | 30 |
| | 1 | 2 | | | 8 | 15 | 17 | 6 | 19 | 21 | 4 | | 26 | 17 | 43 | 1 | 2 | | | | | | | 46 | 31 |
| | | 3 | | | 14 | 27 | 39 | 14 | 31 | 45 | 6 | 10 | 47 | 39 | 86 | 3 | 5 | 1 | | | | | | 95 | 32 |
| | 3 | 9 | 7 | 2 | 55 | 51 | 55 | 33 | 91 | 89 | 9 | 15 | 103 | 69 | 172 | 13 | 15 | 2 | | 1 | 1 | 1 | | 205 | 33 |
| | | | | | | | 5 | 1 | | 4 | 1 | 1 | 1 | 6 | 7 | | | | | | | | | 7 | 34 |
| | 1 | | | | 4 | 4 | | 2 | 2 | 8 | | | 2 | 8 | 5 | 1 | 4 | | 1 | | | | | 11 | 35 |
| | | | | | | | | 1 | 1 | | | | 1 | | 1 | | | | | | | | | 1 | 36 |
| | 1 | | | | 4 | 3 | | 1 | 3 | 2 | | 2 | 6 | | 6 | 2 | | | | | | | | 8 | 37 |
| | 2 | | 1 | | 3 | 3 | 6 | 4 | 2 | 6 | 2 | 6 | 8 | 6 | 14 | 1 | 1 | | | | | | | 16 | 38 |
| | | | | | | 3 | | | | | 1 | 2 | 2 | 1 | 3 | | | | | | | | | 3 | 39 |
| | 1 | 4 | 1 | | 8 | 8 | 7 | 9 | 28 | 1 | | 3 | 26 | 4 | 30 | 2 | | | | | | | | 32 | 40 |
| | | | | | 1 | 4 | 1 | | 6 | | | | 2 | 3 | 5 | 1 | | | | | | | | 6 | 41 |
| | 4 | 3 | 3 | | 16 | 24 | 15 | 10 | 6 | 12 | 12 | 35 | 31 | 27 | 58 | 3 | 3 | | | | | 1 | | 65 | 42 |
| | | | | | 5 | 1 | 5 | | 6 | 6 | | | 1 | 5 | 6 | 2 | 2 | 1 | 1 | | | | | 12 | 43 |
| | 4 | 2 | | | 36 | 26 | 18 | 18 | 28 | 36 | 11 | 18 | 47 | 29 | 76 | 8 | 11 | 1 | | 1 | 1 | | | 98 | 44 |
| | 5 | 4 | 1 | | 2 | 7 | 4 | | 8 | 2 | | 3 | 13 | | 13 | | | | | | | | | 13 | 45 |
| 1 | 4 | 1 | 3 | | 53 | 87 | 16 | 24 | 36 | 125 | 8 | 10 | 70 | 83 | 153 | 11 | 9 | 2 | 5 | | | | | 180 | 46 |
| | | | | | | 3 | | 1 | 3 | 1 | | | 1 | 2 | 3 | 1 | | | | | | | | 4 | 47 |
| | | | | | | 2 | 1 | 1 | 1 | 1 | 1 | 1 | 2 | 2 | 4 | | | | | | | | | 4 | 48 |
| | | | | | | 3 | 1 | 2 | 4 | 2 | | | 2 | 3 | 5 | | 1 | | | | | | | 6 | 49 |
| | | | | | 1 | | 2 | 3 | 5 | | | | 4 | 1 | 5 | 1 | | | | | | | | 6 | 50 |
| | | | | | 2 | 1 | 2 | 2 | | 6 | | 1 | 5 | 1 | 6 | | 1 | | | | | | | 7 | 51 |
| | | 7 | | | 1 | 2 | 8 | 1 | 2 | 8 | 2 | | 8 | 3 | 11 | 1 | | | | | | | | 12 | 52 |
| | 6 | 11 | 2 | 1 | 29 | 28 | 25 | 19 | 17 | 29 | 8 | 39 | 37 | 43 | 80 | 6 | 14 | | 1 | | | | | 101 | 53 |
| | 1 | 3 | | | 11 | 7 | 12 | 8 | 11 | 8 | 2 | 17 | 19 | 15 | 34 | 2 | 2 | | | | | | | 38 | 54 |
| | | | | | | 2 | 3 | 2 | 1 | 5 | 1 | | 4 | 3 | 7 | | | | | | | | | 7 | 55 |
| | 1 | | | | 1 | 1 | 3 | | | 2 | | 3 | 4 | 1 | 5 | | | | | | | | | 5 | 56 |
| | | 2 | 2 | | 24 | 11 | 10 | 14 | 15 | 40 | 3 | | 24 | 25 | 49 | 3 | 6 | 1 | | | | | | 59 | 57 |
| 3 | 4 | 20 | 5 | | 159 | 73 | 42 | 104 | 91 | 238 | 30 | 18 | 198 | 129 | 327 | 27 | 19 | 3 | 1 | 1 | | | | 378 | 58 |
| | | 1 | 1 | | 4 | 2 | 5 | 2 | 8 | 3 | | 1 | 6 | 6 | 12 | | 1 | | | | | | | 13 | 59 |
| | | | | | | 2 | 1 | | 3 | | | | | 3 | 3 | | | | | | | | | 3 | 60 |
| | 1 | | 1 | | 5 | 3 | 3 | 7 | 11 | 6 | 2 | | 10 | 8 | 18 | 1 | | | | | | | | 19 | 61 |
| | 4 | 2 | 4 | | 11 | 4 | 7 | 9 | 3 | 9 | 3 | 16 | 26 | 4 | 30 | | | | | | | 1 | | 31 | 62 |
| | | | | | 1 | | | 1 | 1 | | 1 | | | 1 | 1 | 1 | | | | | | | | 2 | 63 |
| | | | | | | 1 | 2 | 2 | | 2 | 1 | 2 | 3 | 2 | 5 | | | | | | | | | 5 | 64 |
| | | 1 | | | 12 | 19 | 19 | 10 | 2 | 10 | 7 | 41 | 17 | 12 | 29 | 15 | 13 | 1 | 2 | | | | | 60 | 65 |
| | | | 1 | | 2 | 3 | 4 | 7 | | 10 | 4 | 1 | 14 | 1 | 15 | 2 | 1 | | | | | | | 18 | 66 |
| | | 9 | | | 17 | 22 | 9 | 9 | 8 | 49 | | | 32 | 16 | 48 | 3 | 2 | 2 | 2 | | | | | 57 | 67 |
| | | 1 | | | 5 | 4 | 8 | 5 | 1 | 7 | 6 | 8 | 11 | 8 | 19 | 1 | 2 | | | | | | | 22 | 68 |
| | | | | | 2 | 1 | 2 | 2 | | | | | 5 | 2 | 7 | | | | | | | | | 7 | 69 |
| | 1 | | | | 5 | 7 | 1 | 6 | 6 | 8 | 4 | 1 | 9 | 9 | 18 | | 1 | | | | | | | 19 | 70 |
| | 2 | | | | 2 | 11 | 2 | 4 | 19 | | | | 4 | 4 | 8 | 8 | 3 | | | | | | | 19 | 71 |
| | | 1 | | | | 5 | 4 | 2 | 9 | | | 2 | 9 | 1 | 10 | 1 | | | | | | | | 11 | 72 |
| | 2 | 6 | 5 | | 6 | 82 | 34 | | 32 | 55 | 8 | 24 | 62 | 59 | 121 | | | | | | | | 1 | 122 | 73 |
| | 4 | 3 | 3 | | | 7 | 4 | | 10 | 1 | | | 10 | 1 | 11 | | | | | | | | | 11 | 74 |
| | 3 | 8 | 3 | | 10 | 74 | 34 | 9 | 37 | 42 | 19 | 29 | 59 | 62 | 121 | 4 | 1 | | 1 | | | | | 127 | 57 |

## CLASSIFICATION OF DEATHS IN

| | Cause of death. | Ages. Under 1. M. | Under 1. F. | 1 and under 5. M. | 1 and under 5. F. | 5 and under 10. M. | 5 and under 10. F. | 10 and under 20. M. | 10 and under 20. F. | 20 and under 50. M. | 20 and under 50. F. | 50 and under 80. M. | 50 and under 80. F. | 80 and under 100. M | 80 and under 100. F. | 100 & over. M | 100 & over. F. | Age unknown. M | Age unknown. F. | Nativities. Born in State. | N. England States. | Middle States. | Southern States. | Southwest'n States. | Northwest'n States. |
|---|---|---|---|---|---|---|---|---|---|---|---|---|---|---|---|---|---|---|---|---|---|---|---|---|---|
| 1 | Tetter | | | | | | | | | 1 | | | | | | | | | | 1 | | | | | |
| 2 | Throat, disease of | 1 | | 3 | 2 | 2 | 1 | | | 1 | 3 | | 2 | | | | | | | 8 | | | 1 | 1 | 2 |
| 3 | Thrush | 3 | 3 | 3 | 3 | | | | | | | | | | | | | | | 12 | | | | | |
| 4 | Tumor | | | | 1 | | 1 | | | | 2 | | | | | | | | | 1 | | 1 | | | 2 |
| 5 | Ulcer | | | | 1 | | | | | 1 | | 2 | | | | | | | | 1 | | | | | |
| 6 | Uterus, disease of | | | | | | | | | | 3 | | 1 | | | | | | | 1 | | | 2 | | |
| 7 | Venereal | | 4 | 3 | 1 | | 1 | | | 2 | | | | | | | | | | 10 | | | | | 1 |
| 8 | White swelling | | | | 1 | | | | 1 | | | 1 | | | | | | | | 2 | | | | | 1 |
| 9 | Worms | 2 | 4 | 29 | 30 | 11 | 6 | 3 | 1 | 1 | | | 1 | | | | | | | 76 | | | 1 | 4 | 7 |
| 10 | Unknown | 343 | 254 | 145 | 137 | 37 | 25 | 48 | 45 | 234 | 181 | 121 | 71 | 3 | 6 | | | 32 | 26 | 1057 | 3 | 24 | 109 | 51 | 288 |
| | Total | 1039 | 904 | 1298 | 1220 | 454 | 390 | 611 | 597 | 2647 | 1765 | 710 | 487 | 50 | 45 | 4 | 2 | 41 | 23 | 5951 | 74 | 385 | 1037 | 546 | 1481 |

## CLASSIFICATION OF DEATHS IN

| | Cause of death. | Under 1. M. | Under 1. F. | 1 and under 5. M. | 1 and under 5. F. | 5 and under 10. M. | 5 and under 10. F. | 10 and under 20. M. | 10 and under 20. F. | 20 and under 50. M. | 20 and under 50. F. | 50 and under 80. M. | 50 and under 80. F. | 80 and under 100. M | 80 and under 100. F. | 100 & over. M | 100 & over. F. | Age unknown. M | Age unknown. F. | Born in State. | N. England States. | Middle States. | Southern States. | Southwest'n States. | Northwest'n States. |
|---|---|---|---|---|---|---|---|---|---|---|---|---|---|---|---|---|---|---|---|---|---|---|---|---|---|
| 1 | Abscess | 2 | | 2 | | | | | 1 | 2 | | 1 | 1 | | | | | | | 6 | 2 | | | | |
| 2 | Accident, not specif'd | 1 | | | 1 | 2 | 2 | 6 | | 22 | 1 | 4 | 3 | | 1 | | | | | 27 | 3 | 1 | | | |
| 3 | ....do...burned | | | 2 | 2 | | | | | 1 | | | 1 | | | | | | | 5 | 1 | | | | |
| 4 | ....do...drowned | | | | 1 | 2 | 1 | 14 | | 12 | 1 | 8 | 2 | | | | | | | 29 | 6 | 1 | 1 | | |
| 5 | ....do...scalded | 2 | 1 | 1 | 1 | | | | | 1 | | | | | | | | | | 5 | 1 | | | | |
| 6 | Apoplexy | | | | | | | | 2 | 3 | 1 | 8 | 11 | 1 | | | | | | 24 | 2 | | | | |
| 7 | Asthma | | | | | | | | | | | | 2 | 1 | 2 | | | | | 4 | 1 | | | | |
| 8 | Bladder, disease of | | | | | | | | | 1 | 1 | | | | | | | | | 2 | | | | | |
| 9 | Bowels.....do | 7 | 7 | 14 | 9 | 1 | 2 | 3 | | 4 | 4 | 1 | 3 | | | | | | | 44 | 7 | | | | |
| 10 | Brain.....do | 3 | 3 | 5 | 4 | | | | 1 | | 1 | | | | | | | | | 15 | 2 | | | | |
| 11 | Bronchitis | | | | | | | | | | 1 | | | 1 | | | | | | 2 | | | | | |
| 12 | Cancer | | | | | | 2 | 3 | 3 | 2 | 4 | 10 | 13 | 1 | 4 | | | | | 37 | 4 | | | | |
| 13 | Catarrh | 1 | | 2 | | | | | | | | 2 | | | | | | | | 4 | 1 | | | | |
| 14 | Chicken pox | 1 | | | | | | | | | | | | | | | | | | 1 | | | | | |
| 15 | Childbirth | | | | | | | | 2 | | 24 | | | | | | | | | 17 | 7 | 1 | | | |
| 16 | Cholera | | 2 | 2 | 2 | | 3 | 1 | 2 | 10 | 9 | 8 | 7 | | 1 | | | | | 30 | 7 | 1 | | | |
| 17 | ....do..infantum | 16 | 12 | 10 | 8 | | 1 | | | | | | | | | | | | | 46 | 1 | | | | |
| 18 | ....do..morbus | | | 4 | 1 | | 1 | 2 | 2 | 3 | 3 | 2 | 6 | | 1 | | | | | 23 | 1 | | | | |
| 19 | Chorea | | | | | | | | 1 | 1 | 1 | | | | | | | | | 3 | | | | | |
| 20 | Colic | | | | | | 1 | 1 | | 1 | | 3 | 3 | | | | | | | 8 | | | | | |
| 21 | Congestion of brain | 1 | 1 | 3 | | 2 | 2 | 1 | 4 | 2 | 2 | | 1 | | | | | | | 15 | 4 | | | | |
| 22 | Consumption | 14 | 14 | 13 | 13 | 6 | 1 | 20 | 79 | 178 | 310 | 121 | 132 | 8 | 15 | | | | | 766 | 128 | 3 | | | |
| 23 | Convulsions | 12 | 11 | 8 | 4 | 1 | | 1 | 1 | 1 | 1 | | 2 | 1 | | | | | | 41 | 2 | | | | |
| 24 | Croup | 16 | 6 | 26 | 14 | 4 | 7 | | 1 | 1 | | | | | | | | | | 70 | 5 | | | | |
| 25 | Debility | | | | 1 | | | | | | 1 | 1 | | | | | | | | 3 | | | | | |
| 26 | Diabetes | | | | | 1 | | | | 2 | | 2 | 1 | | | | | | | 4 | 2 | | | | |
| 27 | Diarrhœa | 8 | 5 | 13 | 8 | 1 | 2 | 1 | | 4 | 2 | 1 | 2 | 1 | 1 | | | | | 48 | 1 | | | | |
| 28 | Dropsy | 5 | 7 | 5 | 13 | 5 | 3 | 3 | 5 | 9 | 24 | 23 | 34 | 13 | 12 | | | | | 130 | 26 | | | | |
| 29 | Dysentery | 36 | 28 | 137 | 110 | 26 | 47 | 27 | 22 | 33 | 42 | 21 | 39 | 3 | 7 | | | | | 509 | 45 | 2 | | | |
| 30 | Dyspepsia | | | | | | | | | 1 | 1 | | 1 | | | | | | | 3 | | | | | |
| 31 | Epilepsy | 1 | 2 | 1 | 1 | 1 | 1 | 2 | 1 | 7 | 5 | 5 | 2 | | 2 | | | | | 28 | 3 | | | | |
| 32 | Erysipelas | 2 | 5 | 2 | 1 | | | | 2 | 4 | 14 | 12 | 5 | 2 | 6 | | | | | 43 | 11 | | | | |
| 33 | Fever, not specified | 16 | 7 | 14 | 19 | 8 | 9 | 11 | 36 | 31 | 35 | 36 | 32 | 4 | 4 | | | | | 283 | 25 | 1 | | | |
| 34 | ..do..bilious | 1 | | 1 | 2 | 1 | 1 | 2 | 1 | 1 | | 2 | 1 | | | | | | | 13 | | | | | |
| 35 | ..do..brain | 4 | 3 | 4 | 2 | 1 | 1 | 3 | 2 | 11 | 4 | 1 | | | | | | | | 30 | 5 | | | | |
| 36 | ..do..congestive | | | | | | | | | | 1 | 2 | | | | | | | | 3 | | | | | |
| 37 | ..do..puerperal | | | | | | | | | | 3 | | | | | | | | | 1 | 2 | | | | |
| 38 | ..do..scarlet | 19 | 9 | 59 | 66 | 19 | 17 | 4 | 5 | 1 | 4 | 1 | | | 1 | | | | | 192 | 12 | | | | |
| 39 | ..do..typhus | 1 | 1 | | 2 | 3 | 6 | 11 | 20 | 29 | 22 | 15 | 9 | 2 | 2 | | | 1 | | 102 | 21 | | | | |
| 40 | Fracture | | | | | | | 2 | | | | | 1 | | 1 | | | | | 4 | | | | | |
| 41 | Frozen | | | | | | | | | 1 | | | | | | | | | | 1 | | | | | |
| 42 | Gravel | | | | | | | | | | | 4 | | 7 | | | | | | 6 | 4 | | | | |
| 43 | Heart, disease of | 8 | 1 | 2 | 2 | 3 | 2 | 2 | 2 | 12 | 13 | 19 | 13 | 4 | 1 | | | | | 71 | 15 | | | | |
| 44 | Hemorrhage | | 1 | | | 1 | | | 1 | 1 | | | | | | | | | | 3 | 1 | | | | |
| 45 | Hernia | | | | | | | | | | 1 | 4 | | | | | | | | 3 | 2 | | | | |
| 46 | Hip, disease of | | | | | | | | 1 | | | 1 | | | | | | | | | 2 | | | | |
| 47 | Hooping cough | 1 | 2 | 4 | 3 | | | | | 1 | 1 | | | | | | | | | 11 | 1 | | | | |
| 48 | Hydrocephalus | 4 | 4 | 4 | 5 | 2 | 3 | 1 | 1 | | | 1 | | | | | | | | 21 | 4 | | | | |
| 49 | Hydrophophia | | | | | | | | 1 | | | | | | | | | | | 1 | | | | | |
| 50 | Inflammation | 2 | | 4 | 3 | 1 | | 1 | 1 | 2 | 3 | 2 | 1 | | | | | | | 18 | 1 | | | | |
| 51 | ....do......bowels | 3 | | 2 | 1 | 2 | | 4 | 8 | 1 | 5 | 2 | | | | | | | | 22 | 1 | | | | |
| 52 | ....do......brain | | | 1 | 1 | | 2 | | 1 | | | | | | | | | | | 3 | 2 | | | | |
| 53 | Influenza | 1 | 1 | 1 | 4 | | | 1 | | 1 | | | 2 | 4 | 3 | | | | | 14 | 4 | | | | |
| 54 | Insanity | | | | | | | | | 2 | 1 | 1 | 4 | | | | | | | 8 | | | | | |
| 55 | Intemperance | | | | | | | | | 2 | | 2 | | | | | | | | 3 | 1 | | | | |
| 56 | Jaundice | 1 | | | | | | | | | 2 | | 1 | | | | | | | 4 | | | | | |

## E STATE OF MISSOURI—Continued.

| | Nativities. Ireland. | Germany. | Other foreign countries. | Unknown. | Season of decease. Spring. | Summer. | Autumn. | Winter. | Duration of sickness. Under 1 week. | 1 week and under 1 month. | 1 month and under 3 months. | 3 months and over. | Whites. Males. | Females. | Total. | Colored. Slaves. Black. M. | F. | Mulatto. M. | F. | Free. Black M. | F. | Mul. M | F. | Aggregate deaths. | |
|---|---|---|---|---|---|---|---|---|---|---|---|---|---|---|---|---|---|---|---|---|---|---|---|---|---|
| | | | | | | 1 | | | 1 | | | | 1 | | 1 | | | | | | | | | 1 | 1 |
| | 2 | 1 | | | 4 | 1 | 4 | 6 | 6 | 6 | | 3 | 6 | 8 | 14 | | 1 | | | | | | | 15 | 2 |
| | | | | | 2 | 3 | 4 | 3 | 3 | 6 | 1 | 2 | 5 | 5 | 10 | 1 | 1 | | | | | | | 12 | 3 |
| | | | | | 1 | 1 | | 2 | 1 | | 1 | 2 | | 3 | 3 | | 1 | | | | | | | 4 | 4 |
| | 2 | 1 | | | 1 | | 2 | 1 | 1 | | 2 | 1 | 3 | 1 | 4 | | | | | | | | | 4 | 5 |
| | | 1 | | | 3 | | 1 | | | 3 | | 1 | | 3 | 3 | | | | | | 1 | | | 4 | 6 |
| | | | | | 2 | 5 | 1 | 2 | 2 | 6 | | 2 | 5 | 6 | 11 | | | | | | | | | 11 | 7 |
| | | | | | 1 | | 2 | | | | 1 | 2 | 1 | 2 | 3 | | | | | | | | | 3 | 8 |
| | | | | | 24 | 19 | 30 | 15 | 33 | 39 | 10 | 6 | 39 | 36 | 75 | 5 | 3 | 2 | 3 | | | | | 88 | 9 |
| 1 | 53 | 124 | 42 | 6 | 422 | 360 | 379 | 300 | 540 | 368 | 88 | 387 | 825 | 599 | 1424 | 144 | 127 | 20 | 16 | 4 | 3 | | | 1708 | 10 |
| | 683 | 1517 | 585 | 23 | 2160 | 5422 | 2842 | 1507 | 6227 | 3238 | 653 | 1539 | 6145 | 4728 | 10873 | 587 | 608 | 87 | 75 | 26 | 20 | 8 | 8 | 12292 | |

## HE STATE OF NEW HAMPSHIRE.

| | Ireland. | Germany. | Other foreign countries. | Unknown. | Spring. | Summer. | Autumn. | Winter. | Under 1 week. | 1 week and under 1 month. | 1 month and under 3 months. | 3 months and over. | Males. | Females. | Total. | Slaves Black M. | F. | Mulatto M. | F. | Free Black M. | F. | Mul. M | F. | Aggregate deaths. | |
|---|---|---|---|---|---|---|---|---|---|---|---|---|---|---|---|---|---|---|---|---|---|---|---|---|---|
| | 1 | | | | 1 | 4 | | 4 | 3 | 4 | 1 | 1 | 7 | 2 | 9 | | | | | | | | | 9 | 1 |
| | 10 | | 2 | | 12 | 8 | 10 | 13 | 33 | 8 | | | 35 | 8 | 43 | | | | | | | | | 43 | 2 |
| | | | | | 2 | 1 | 2 | 1 | 4 | | | 1 | 3 | 3 | 6 | | | | | | | | | 6 | 3 |
| | 8 | | 1 | | 7 | 17 | 7 | 8 | 41 | | | | 36 | 5 | 41 | | | | | | | | | 41 | 4 |
| | | | | | 1 | 1 | 2 | 2 | 5 | 1 | | | 4 | 2 | 6 | | | | | | | | | 6 | 5 |
| | | | | | 6 | 7 | 8 | 5 | 22 | 2 | | 1 | 12 | 14 | 26 | | | | | | | | | 26 | 6 |
| | | | | | 1 | 2 | 1 | 1 | 3 | | 1 | 1 | 1 | 4 | 5 | | | | | | | | | 5 | 7 |
| | | | | | | 1 | | 1 | | 1 | | 1 | 1 | 1 | 2 | | | | | | | | | 2 | 8 |
| | 2 | | 2 | | 10 | 33 | 12 | | 7 | 43 | 4 | 1 | 30 | 25 | 55 | | | | | | | | | 55 | 9 |
| | | | | | 3 | 3 | 9 | 2 | 10 | 6 | 1 | | 8 | 9 | 17 | | | | | | | | | 17 | 10 |
| | | | | | 2 | | | | | | | 2 | 1 | 1 | 2 | | | | | | | | | 2 | 11 |
| | | | 1 | | 9 | 10 | 9 | 12 | | 2 | 1 | 33 | 16 | 26 | 42 | | | | | | | | | 42 | 12 |
| | | | | | 3 | 2 | | | 1 | 4 | | | 5 | | 5 | | | | | | | | | 5 | 13 |
| | | | | | | | 1 | | 1 | | | | 1 | | 1 | | | | | | | | | 1 | 14 |
| | 1 | | | | 10 | 9 | 4 | 3 | 17 | 6 | | 1 | | 26 | 26 | | | | | | | | | 26 | 15 |
| | 8 | | 1 | | | 6 | 41 | | 43 | 4 | | | 21 | 26 | 47 | | | | | | | | | 47 | 16 |
| | | | | | 1 | 3 | 43 | | 23 | 19 | 3 | | 26 | 21 | 47 | | | | | | | | | 47 | 17 |
| | 1 | | | | 1 | 5 | 18 | 1 | 13 | 12 | | | 11 | 14 | 25 | | | | | | | | | 25 | 18 |
| | | | | | 1 | 1 | 1 | | | | 1 | 2 | 1 | 2 | 3 | | | | | | | | | 3 | 19 |
| | 1 | | | | 1 | | 6 | 2 | 9 | | | | 5 | 4 | 9 | | | | | | | | | 9 | 20 |
| | | | | | 10 | 4 | 3 | 2 | 5 | 12 | 2 | | 9 | 10 | 19 | | | | | | | | | 19 | 21 |
| | 19 | | 8 | | 248 | 266 | 221 | 189 | 17 | 65 | 81 | 758 | 358 | 563 | 921 | | | | | 2 | | | 1 | 924 | 22 |
| | | | | | 13 | 10 | 13 | 7 | 34 | 7 | 1 | | 24 | 19 | 43 | | | | | | | | | 43 | 23 |
| | | | | | 29 | 16 | 9 | 21 | 55 | 18 | 2 | | 47 | 28 | 75 | | | | | | | | | 75 | 24 |
| | | | | | | | 1 | 2 | | | | 3 | 1 | 2 | 3 | | | | | | | | | 3 | 25 |
| | | | | | 1 | 1 | 3 | 1 | | 1 | 2 | 3 | 5 | 1 | 6 | | | | | | | | | 6 | 26 |
| | | | | | 2 | 9 | 33 | 5 | 13 | 28 | 6 | 2 | 29 | 20 | 49 | | | | | | | | | 49 | 27 |
| | 3 | | 2 | | 49 | 39 | 39 | 34 | 9 | 33 | 30 | 87 | 63 | 98 | 161 | | | | | | | | | 161 | 28 |
| | 16 | | 6 | | 10 | 52 | 484 | 31 | 153 | 384 | 29 | 10 | 283 | 295 | 578 | | | | | | | | | 578 | 29 |
| | | | | | | 1 | 2 | | | 1 | | 2 | 1 | 2 | 3 | | | | | | | | | 3 | 30 |
| | | | | | 8 | 9 | 4 | 10 | 22 | 4 | 1 | 2 | 17 | 14 | 31 | | | | | | | | | 31 | 31 |
| | 1 | | | | 21 | 11 | 7 | 16 | 11 | 37 | 4 | 3 | 22 | 33 | 55 | | | | | | | | | 55 | 32 |
| | 3 | | | | 70 | 47 | 79 | 63 | 39 | 168 | 40 | 11 | 120 | 142 | 262 | | | | | | | | | 262 | 33 |
| | | | | | 4 | 5 | 3 | 1 | 4 | 8 | 1 | | 8 | 5 | 13 | | | | | | | | | 13 | 34 |
| | 1 | | | | 12 | 3 | 13 | 8 | 8 | 24 | 2 | | 24 | 12 | 36 | | | | | | | | | 36 | 35 |
| | | | | | 1 | 1 | 1 | | | | 2 | 1 | 2 | 1 | 3 | | | | | | | | | 3 | 36 |
| | | | | | | 2 | 1 | | 1 | 1 | 1 | | | 3 | 3 | | | | | | | | | 3 | 37 |
| | 1 | | | | 68 | 49 | 48 | 40 | 103 | 84 | 15 | 3 | 103 | 102 | 205 | | | | | | | | | 205 | 38 |
| | 1 | | | | 22 | 19 | 45 | 38 | 12 | 90 | 21 | 1 | 62 | 62 | 124 | | | | | | | | | 124 | 39 |
| | | | | | 1 | | 1 | 2 | | 1 | 1 | 1 | 2 | 2 | 4 | | | | | | | | | 4 | 40 |
| | | | | | 1 | | | | | | | | 1 | | 1 | | | | | | | | | 1 | 41 |
| | | | | 1 | 3 | 2 | 2 | 4 | 1 | 3 | 2 | 4 | 11 | | 11 | | | | | | | | | 11 | 42 |
| | | | 3 | | 23 | 28 | 21 | 17 | 31 | 22 | 15 | 20 | 50 | 38 | 88 | | | | | | | | 1 | 89 | 43 |
| | | | | | 1 | 2 | 1 | | 2 | 2 | | | 2 | 2 | 4 | | | | | | | | | 4 | 44 |
| | | | | | 2 | | 2 | 1 | 5 | | | | 4 | 1 | 5 | | | | | | | | | 5 | 45 |
| | | | | | | 1 | | 1 | | | 1 | 1 | 1 | 1 | 2 | | | | | | | | | 2 | 46 |
| | | | | | 6 | 1 | 5 | | 2 | 7 | 1 | 1 | 6 | 6 | 12 | | | | | | | | | 12 | 47 |
| | | | | | 5 | 12 | 5 | 3 | 4 | 16 | 4 | 1 | 12 | 12 | 24 | | | | | | | | 1 | 25 | 48 |
| | | | | | | 1 | | | 1 | | | | | 1 | 1 | | | | | | | | | 1 | 49 |
| | 1 | | | | 3 | 6 | 5 | 6 | 11 | 7 | 1 | 1 | 12 | 8 | 20 | | | | | | | | | 20 | 50 |
| | | | | | 8 | 8 | 4 | 3 | 6 | 15 | 2 | | 14 | 9 | 23 | | | | | | | | | 23 | 51 |
| | | | | | 2 | 2 | 1 | | 1 | 4 | | | 1 | 4 | 5 | | | | | | | | | 5 | 52 |
| | | | | | 9 | 3 | 3 | 8 | 8 | 8 | 1 | | 8 | 10 | 18 | | | | | | | | | 18 | 53 |
| | | | | | 2 | 2 | 1 | 2 | | | 1 | 4 | 3 | 5 | 8 | | | | | | | | | 8 | 54 |
| | | | | | | 1 | 2 | 1 | | 1 | | 2 | 4 | | 4 | | | | | | | | | 4 | 55 |
| | | | | | 1 | 2 | 1 | | 2 | 1 | 1 | | 1 | 3 | 4 | | | | | | | | | 4 | 56 |

## CLASSIFICATION OF DEATHS IN

| | Cause of death. | Ages: Under 1. | | 1 and under 6. | | 5 and under 10. | | 10 and under 20. | | 20 and under 50. | | 50 and under 80. | | 80 and under 100. | | 100 & over. | | Age unknown. | | Nativities: Born in State. | N. England States. | Middle States. | Southern States. | Southwest'n States. | Northwest'n States. |
|---|---|---|---|---|---|---|---|---|---|---|---|---|---|---|---|---|---|---|---|---|---|---|---|---|---|
| | | M. | F. | M. | F. | M. | F. | M. | F. | M. | F. | M. | F. | M. | F. | M | F. | M | F. | | | | | | |
| 1 | Kidneys, disease of.. | | | | | | | | | | | 2 | | | | | | | | 1 | 1 | | | | |
| 2 | Killed | | | | | | | | | 2 | | 1 | | | | | | | | 3 | | | | | |
| 3 | Liver, disease of | | | 1 | | | | | | 4 | 4 | 11 | 3 | | | | | | | 16 | 5 | | | | |
| 4 | Lockjaw | | | | | | 1 | | 1 | | | | | | | | | | | 1 | | | | | |
| 5 | Lungs, disease of | 1 | 1 | | 4 | | | | | 1 | | | 2 | | 1 | | | | | 11 | | | | | |
| 6 | Mania-a-potu | | | | | | | | | 1 | | 1 | | | | | | | | 2 | | | | | |
| 7 | Marasmus | 2 | | | | | | | | | 1 | | | | | | | | | 2 | 1 | | | | |
| 8 | Measles | 1 | 2 | 6 | 10 | 1 | | | 1 | 3 | 3 | | | | | | | | | 24 | 2 | | | | |
| 9 | Mortification | 1 | | | | | 1 | | | | | 4 | 1 | | | | | | | 6 | 1 | | | | |
| 10 | Neuralgia | | | | | | 1 | | 1 | 2 | | 4 | 1 | | | | | | | 7 | 2 | | | | |
| 11 | Old age | | | | | | | | | | | 35 | 36 | 87 | 119 | | 2 | | | 194 | 78 | 1 | | | |
| 12 | Paralysis | | | 1 | 1 | | | | | 4 | 2 | 27 | 29 | 11 | 12 | | | | | 71 | 15 | | | | |
| 13 | Pleurisy | | | | | | | | | 1 | 1 | | 4 | | 1 | | | | | 5 | 2 | | | | |
| 14 | Pneumonia | 19 | 11 | 16 | 10 | 1 | 1 | 2 | 4 | 5 | 6 | 17 | 12 | 4 | 7 | | | | | 97 | 14 | | | | |
| 15 | Poison | | | | | | | | | | 1 | | | | | | | | | | 1 | | | | |
| 16 | Quinsy | 1 | | | 2 | | | | | | | | | | | | | | | 3 | | | | | |
| 17 | Rheumatism | | | | | 1 | | 1 | 1 | 1 | 1 | 6 | 1 | 1 | 1 | | | | | 8 | 6 | | | | |
| 18 | Rickets | | | 1 | | | | | | | | | | | | | | | | 1 | | | | | |
| 19 | Scrofula | 4 | 4 | 3 | 3 | | 1 | 1 | 2 | 1 | 3 | 5 | 6 | 1 | 1 | | | | | 31 | 1 | | | | |
| 20 | Small pox | 5 | 2 | 3 | 2 | 2 | 1 | 2 | | 9 | 3 | 6 | 6 | | 1 | | | | | 35 | 6 | | | | |
| 21 | Spine, disease of | | 2 | | | 3 | | | 1 | | 3 | 1 | | | | | | | | 9 | 1 | | | | |
| 22 | Stomach..do | | | | | | | | | | | | | | 1 | | | | | 1 | | | | | |
| 23 | Suffocation | | | 1 | 1 | | | | | | | | 1 | | | | | | | 3 | | | | | |
| 24 | Suicide | | | | | | | | | 10 | 6 | 12 | 1 | | | | | | | 23 | 6 | | | | |
| 25 | Sun, stroke of | | | | | | | | | 4 | | | | | | | | | | | 1 | | | | |
| 26 | Teething | 3 | 1 | 4 | 4 | | | | | | | | | | | | | | | 11 | 1 | | | | |
| 27 | Throat, disease of | 1 | 3 | 3 | 5 | | 3 | 2 | | 2 | | 1 | | | | | | | | 18 | 2 | | | | |
| 28 | Tumor | | | | | | | | | 2 | 4 | 3 | 8 | | | | | | | 12 | 3 | 1 | | | |
| 29 | Ulcer | | | 1 | | | | | | | | | | | | | | | | 1 | | | | | |
| 30 | Uterus, disease of | | | | | | | | | | 1 | | | | | | | | | 1 | | | | | |
| 31 | White swelling | | | | | | | | | 1 | | | | | | | | | | 1 | | | | | |
| 32 | Worms | | 1 | 1 | 1 | 1 | 1 | | | | | | | | | | | | | 5 | | | | | |
| 33 | Unknown | 25 | 30 | 14 | 9 | 3 | 5 | 4 | 7 | 12 | 16 | 30 | 21 | 4 | 6 | | | 1 | 1 | 181 | 19 | 1 | | | |
| | Total | 272 | 191 | 401 | 356 | 105 | 132 | 139 | 222 | 466 | 608 | 492 | 467 | 161 | 214 | .. | 2 | 2 | 1 | 3543 | 544 | 13 | 1 | .. | .. |

## CLASSIFICATION OF DEATHS IN NORTHERN

*Embracing the following counties: Bergen, Essex, Hudson, Hunterdon,*

| | Cause of death. | Under 1 M. | Under 1 F. | 1 and under 6 M. | 1 and under 6 F. | 5 and under 10 M. | 5 and under 10 F. | 10 and under 20 M. | 10 and under 20 F. | 20 and under 50 M. | 20 and under 50 F. | 50 and under 80 M. | 50 and under 80 F. | 80 and under 100 M. | 80 and under 100 F. | 100 & over M. | 100 & over F. | Age unknown M. | Age unknown F. | Born in State. | N. England States. | Middle States. | Southern States. | Southwest'n States. | Northwest'n States. |
|---|---|---|---|---|---|---|---|---|---|---|---|---|---|---|---|---|---|---|---|---|---|---|---|---|---|
| 1 | Abscess | | | | | | | | | | 1 | 2 | 1 | | | | | | | 3 | 1 | | | | |
| 2 | Accident, not specif'd | 2 | 3 | 8 | 4 | 4 | 4 | 6 | | 24 | 2 | 11 | 2 | 1 | 1 | | | | | 50 | | 6 | 1 | | |
| 3 | ....do...burned | | | | | | | 1 | | | | | | | | | | | | 1 | | | | | |
| 4 | ....do...drowned | | | 3 | 2 | 7 | 2 | 4 | | 16 | | | | | | | | | | 23 | | 3 | | | |
| 5 | Apoplexy | | | | | | | | | 9 | 9 | 12 | 9 | 2 | 1 | | | | | 36 | 4 | 1 | | | |
| 6 | Asthma | 1 | | | 1 | | | 1 | | | | 2 | 1 | 2 | | | | | | 5 | | | | | |
| 7 | Bladder, disease of | | | | | | | | | 1 | | 2 | 1 | | | | | | | 3 | | 1 | | | |
| 8 | Bowels.....do | 7 | 3 | 3 | 3 | 1 | | | 1 | 2 | | 3 | | 1 | | | | | | 19 | | 1 | | | |
| 9 | Brain ......do | 1 | 8 | 3 | | | 1 | 1 | 2 | 2 | | 5 | 1 | | | | | | | 18 | 1 | 2 | | | |
| 10 | Bronchitis | 1 | | | | 1 | | | 1 | 2 | | 8 | | | | | | | | 7 | | | | | |
| 11 | Cancer | | | | | | | | | 1 | 4 | 6 | 7 | | | | | | | 16 | 1 | | | | |
| 12 | Carbuncle | | | | | | | | | 1 | | | | | | | | | | | | 1 | | | |
| 13 | Catarrh | 1 | 2 | | | | | | | | 1 | | | | | | | | | 4 | | | | | |
| 14 | Childbirth | | | | | | | | | | 29 | | | | | | | | | 20 | | 2 | | | |
| 15 | Cholera | 16 | 6 | 28 | 32 | 17 | 12 | 25 | 13 | 146 | 88 | 50 | 39 | 1 | | | | | | 276 | 5 | 42 | | | |
| 16 | ...do...infantum | 27 | 12 | 15 | 15 | | | | | | | | | | | | | | | 67 | | 1 | | | |
| 17 | ...do...morbus | 3 | | 1 | | 1 | | | | 1 | 1 | 2 | 1 | | 1 | | | | | 10 | | 1 | | | |
| 18 | Chorea | | | | | | | | | 1 | | | | | | | | | | 1 | | | | | |
| 19 | Colic | | 2 | | | | | | | 2 | | 2 | 2 | | | | | | | 7 | | | | | |
| 20 | Congestion, brain | 1 | 1 | 4 | 4 | | 2 | 2 | | 2 | 1 | 2 | 1 | | | | | | | 18 | | | | | |
| 21 | ....do......lungs | | | | | | | | | 1 | | | | | | | | | | 1 | | | | | |
| 22 | Consumption | 20 | 27 | 10 | 20 | 7 | 6 | 21 | 37 | 139 | 152 | 100 | 63 | 4 | 2 | | | 1 | | 476 | 8 | 47 | 1 | 1 | |
| 23 | Convulsions | 27 | 17 | 20 | 15 | 3 | 3 | 1 | | 4 | 3 | 1 | 4 | | 1 | | | | | 94 | | 3 | | | |
| 24 | Cramp | | | | | | | | | | | 1 | | | | | | | | 1 | | | | | |
| 25 | Croup | 18 | 16 | 36 | 48 | 11 | 8 | 1 | | | | | | | | | | | | 127 | 1 | 7 | | | |
| 26 | D bility | 2 | | | | | | | | 1 | | | | | | | | | | 2 | | 1 | | | |
| 27 | Diarrhœa | 14 | 10 | 11 | 9 | 2 | 1 | 2 | 1 | 5 | 1 | 7 | 10 | | 3 | | | | | 55 | 3 | 10 | | | |
| 28 | Dropsy | 10 | 6 | 14 | 9 | 4 | 5 | 5 | 2 | 13 | 24 | 31 | 35 | 7 | 5 | | | | | 145 | 2 | 6 | 1 | | |
| 29 | Dysentery | 35 | 19 | 71 | 80 | 13 | 10 | 23 | 9 | 22 | 28 | 18 | 23 | 1 | 5 | | | | | 298 | 2 | 27 | 2 | | |
| 30 | Dyspepsia | | | | | | | | | | | 2 | 2 | | | | | | | 3 | | | | | |
| 31 | Epilepsy | 1 | | 1 | | | | 2 | | | | 1 | | | | | | | | 5 | | | | | |

TATE OF NEW HAMPSHIRE—Continued.

| Nativities: ritories. | Ireland. | Germany. | Other foreign countries. | Unknown. | Season of decease: Spring. | Summer. | Autumn. | Winter. | Duration of sickness: Under 1 week. | 1 week and under 1 month. | 1 month and under 3 months. | 3 months and over. | Whites: Males. | Females. | Total. | Colored: Slaves: Black M. | Slaves: Black F. | Slaves: Mulatto M. | Slaves: Mulatto F. | Free: Black M. | Free: Black F. | Free: Mul. M | Free: Mul. F. | Aggregate deaths. | |
|---|---|---|---|---|---|---|---|---|---|---|---|---|---|---|---|---|---|---|---|---|---|---|---|---|---|
| | | | | | | 1 | | 1 | | | | 2 | 2 | | 2 | | | | | | | | | 2 | 1 |
| | | | | | 2 | | 1 | | | | | | 3 | | 3 | | | | | | | | | 3 | 2 |
| | 1 | | 1 | | 6 | 5 | 5 | 6 | 2 | 5 | 4 | 11 | 16 | 7 | 23 | | | | | | | | | 23 | 3 |
| | 1 | | | | | 2 | | | 2 | | | | | 2 | 2 | | | | | | | | | 2 | 4 |
| | | | | | 7 | | 3 | 1 | 4 | 4 | 1 | 2 | 2 | 9 | 11 | | | | | | | | | 11 | 5 |
| | | | | | 1 | | | 1 | | 2 | | | 2 | | 2 | | | | | | | | | 2 | 6 |
| | | | | | 1 | | 2 | | | 1 | | 2 | 2 | 1 | 3 | | | | | | | | | 3 | 7 |
| | 1 | | | | 2 | 18 | 6 | 1 | 4 | 19 | 2 | 2 | 11 | 16 | 27 | | | | | | | | | 27 | 8 |
| | | | | | 1 | 4 | 1 | 1 | 2 | 2 | | 3 | 5 | 2 | 7 | | | | | | | | | 7 | 9 |
| | | | | | | 3 | 4 | 2 | 1 | 3 | 2 | 3 | 6 | 3 | 9 | | | | | | | | | 9 | 10 |
| | 3 | | 2 | 1 | 84 | 71 | 60 | 60 | 36 | 31 | 12 | 64 | 122 | 157 | 279 | | | | | | | | | 279 | 11 |
| | 1 | | | | 29 | 20 | 24 | 13 | 29 | 28 | 8 | 17 | 43 | 44 | 87 | | | | | | | | | 87 | 12 |
| | | | | | 4 | 1 | 2 | | 5 | | 2 | | 1 | 6 | 7 | | | | | | | | | 7 | 13 |
| | 1 | | 3 | | 57 | 20 | 16 | 22 | 24 | 78 | 12 | 1 | 64 | 51 | 115 | | | | | | | | | 115 | 14 |
| | | | | | 1 | | | | 1 | | | | | 1 | 1 | | | | | | | | | 1 | 15 |
| | | | | | | | | 3 | 3 | | | | 1 | 2 | 3 | | | | | | | | | 3 | 16 |
| | | | | | 3 | 5 | 1 | 5 | 1 | 3 | 3 | 7 | 10 | 4 | 14 | | | | | | | | | 14 | 17 |
| | | | | | 1 | | | | | | | 1 | 1 | | 1 | | | | | | | | | 1 | 18 |
| | 1 | | 1 | 1 | 11 | 10 | 8 | 6 | 3 | 6 | 2 | 21 | 15 | 20 | 35 | | | | | | | | | 35 | 19 |
| | | | 1 | | 15 | 7 | 9 | 11 | 12 | 29 | 1 | | 27 | 15 | 42 | | | | | | | | | 42 | 20 |
| | | | | | 2 | 5 | 1 | 2 | 1 | 2 | 2 | 5 | 4 | 6 | 10 | | | | | | | | | 10 | 21 |
| | | | | | | | | 1 | | | 1 | | | 1 | 1 | | | | | | | | | 1 | 22 |
| | | | | | 1 | 2 | | | 3 | | | | 1 | 2 | 3 | | | | | | | | | 3 | 23 |
| | | | | | 8 | 7 | 4 | 9 | 16 | | 1 | 1 | 22 | 7 | 29 | | | | | | | | | 29 | 24 |
| | 3 | | | | | 4 | | | 4 | | | | 4 | | 4 | | | | | | | | | 4 | 25 |
| | | | | | 2 | 3 | 6 | 1 | 1 | 7 | 3 | 1 | 7 | 5 | 12 | | | | | | | | | 12 | 26 |
| | | | | | 12 | 4 | 2 | 2 | 8 | 7 | 4 | 1 | 9 | 11 | 20 | | | | | | | | | 20 | 27 |
| | 1 | | | | 4 | 5 | 2 | 6 | | 3 | 3 | 11 | 5 | 12 | 17 | | | | | | | | | 17 | 28 |
| | | | | | | | 1 | | 1 | | | | 1 | | 1 | | | | | | | | | 1 | 29 |
| | | | | | | 1 | | | | 1 | | | | 1 | 1 | | | | | | | | | 1 | 30 |
| | | | | | 1 | | | | | | | 1 | 1 | | 1 | | | | | | | | | 1 | 31 |
| | | | | | | 3 | | 2 | 4 | | 1 | | 2 | 3 | 5 | | | | | | | | | 5 | 32 |
| | 4 | | 3 | | 52 | 61 | 64 | 30 | 100 | 39 | 9 | 39 | 112 | 95 | 207 | | | | | 1 | | | | 208 | 33 |
| | 90 | | 87 | 3 | 1013 | 990 | 1459 | 752 | 1058 | 1429 | 355 | 1160 | 2035 | 2190 | 4225 | | | | | 3 | | | 3 | 4231 | |

SECTION OF THE STATE OF NEW JERSEY.

*Mercer, Middlesex, Morris, Passaic, Somerset, Sussex, and Warren.*

| Nativities: ritories. | Ireland. | Germany. | Other foreign countries. | Unknown. | Spring. | Summer. | Autumn. | Winter. | Under 1 week. | 1 week and under 1 month. | 1 month and under 3 months. | 3 months and over. | Males. | Females. | Total. | Slaves: Black M. | Slaves: Black F. | Slaves: Mulatto M. | Slaves: Mulatto F. | Free: Black M. | Free: Black F. | Free: Mul. M | Free: Mul. F. | Aggregate deaths. | |
|---|---|---|---|---|---|---|---|---|---|---|---|---|---|---|---|---|---|---|---|---|---|---|---|---|---|
| | | | | | | | 2 | 1 | | 4 | | | 2 | 2 | 4 | | | | | | | | | 4 | 1 |
| | 12 | 2 | 1 | | 26 | 17 | 16 | 13 | 53 | 12 | 2 | 5 | 54 | 15 | 69 | | | | | 2 | | | 1 | 72 | 2 |
| | | | | | | | | 1 | 1 | | | | 1 | | 1 | | | | | | | | | 1 | 3 |
| | 8 | | | | 4 | 17 | 12 | 1 | 34 | | | | 29 | 4 | 33 | | | | | 1 | | | | 34 | 4 |
| | | 1 | | | 13 | 13 | 5 | 11 | 36 | 2 | 1 | | 22 | 17 | 39 | | | | | 1 | 2 | | | 42 | 5 |
| | | | 3 | | 3 | 2 | | 3 | 2 | 2 | | 4 | 6 | 2 | 8 | | | | | | | | | 8 | 6 |
| | | | | | 2 | 1 | | 1 | 1 | 1 | | 2 | 3 | 1 | 4 | | | | | | | | | 4 | 7 |
| | 3 | | 1 | | 5 | 6 | 10 | 3 | 8 | 7 | 6 | 3 | 17 | 6 | 23 | | | | | | 1 | | | 24 | 8 |
| | 2 | | 1 | | 8 | 7 | 3 | 6 | 7 | 12 | 1 | 4 | 12 | 12 | 24 | | | | | | | | | 24 | 9 |
| | 1 | | | | 2 | | 4 | 2 | 1 | 1 | 2 | 4 | 7 | 1 | 8 | | | | | | | | | 8 | 10 |
| | 1 | | | | 3 | 9 | 2 | 4 | | 2 | 2 | 14 | 7 | 11 | 18 | | | | | | | | | 18 | 11 |
| | | | | | | | 1 | | | 1 | | | 1 | | 1 | | | | | | | | | 1 | 12 |
| | | | | | 3 | | 1 | | | 2 | 1 | 1 | 1 | 3 | 4 | | | | | | | | | 4 | 13 |
| | 5 | 2 | | | 11 | 7 | 6 | 3 | 16 | 6 | 2 | 2 | | 29 | 29 | | | | | | | | | 29 | 14 |
| | 102 | 14 | 32 | 2 | 7 | 198 | 265 | 3 | 432 | 39 | 2 | | 271 | 179 | 450 | | 1 | | | 8 | 9 | 4 | 1 | 478 | 15 |
| | | | 1 | | 2 | 12 | 52 | 3 | 37 | 25 | 3 | 3 | 42 | 27 | 69 | | | | | | | | | 69 | 16 |
| | | | | | | 5 | 6 | | 9 | 2 | | | 8 | 3 | 11 | | | | | | | | | 11 | 17 |
| | | | | | 1 | | | | | | | 1 | 1 | | 1 | | | | | | | | | 1 | 18 |
| | | 1 | | | 2 | 1 | 1 | 4 | 5 | 2 | | 1 | 4 | 4 | 8 | | | | | | | | | 8 | 19 |
| | | | 1 | | 4 | 6 | 8 | 1 | 4 | 12 | 1 | 1 | 10 | 9 | 19 | | | | | | | | | 19 | 20 |
| | | | | | | | | 1 | 1 | | | | 1 | | 1 | | | | | | | | | 1 | 21 |
| | 37 | 10 | 24 | 5 | 151 | 152 | 158 | 146 | 18 | 78 | 62 | 405 | 283 | 275 | 558 | 4 | | | | 13 | 30 | 2 | 2 | 609 | 22 |
| | 2 | | | | 34 | 20 | 32 | 12 | 68 | 22 | 3 | 1 | 53 | 43 | 96 | | | | | 2 | | 1 | | 99 | 23 |
| | | | | | | 1 | | | 1 | | | | 1 | | 1 | | | | | | | | | 1 | 24 |
| | 1 | 1 | 1 | | 31 | 26 | 31 | 50 | 96 | 36 | 2 | 1 | 65 | 71 | 136 | | | | | 1 | 1 | | | 138 | 25 |
| | | | | | | 2 | | 1 | 2 | 1 | | | 3 | | 3 | | | | | | | | | 3 | 26 |
| | 3 | 1 | 4 | | 7 | 26 | 36 | 4 | 18 | 29 | 7 | 15 | 37 | 34 | 71 | | | | | 3 | | 1 | 1 | 76 | 27 |
| | 5 | 2 | 9 | | 53 | 31 | 41 | 45 | 20 | 29 | 23 | 81 | 76 | 82 | 158 | | | | | 8 | 4 | | | 170 | 28 |
| | 19 | 5 | 3 | 1 | 8 | 41 | 269 | 39 | 82 | 196 | 22 | 4 | 180 | 174 | 354 | | | | | 3 | | | | 357 | 29 |
| | 1 | | | | | 1 | 3 | | | | | 4 | 2 | 2 | 4 | | | | | | | | | 4 | 30 |
| | | | | | 1 | | 2 | 1 | | | | 2 | 5 | | 5 | | | | | | | | | 5 | 31 |

CLASSIFICATION OF DEATHS IN NORTHERN

| No. | Cause of death. | AGES. Under 1. M. | F. | 1 and under 5. M. | F. | 5 and under 10. M. | F. | 10 and under 20. M. | F. | 20 and under 50. M. | F. | 50 and under 80. M. | F. | 80 and under 100. M | F. | 100 & over. M | F. | Age unknown. M | F. | NATIVITIES. Born in State. | N. England States. | Middle States. | Southern States. | Southwest'n States. | Northwest'n States. |
|---|---|---|---|---|---|---|---|---|---|---|---|---|---|---|---|---|---|---|---|---|---|---|---|---|---|
| 1 | Erysipelas | 6 | 4 | 3 | 5 | 1 | 2 | 1 | 1 | .. | 5 | 5 | 6 | 1 | 1 | .. | .. | .. | .. | 35 | .. | 3 | .. | .. | .. |
| 2 | Executed | .. | .. | .. | .. | .. | .. | .. | .. | 1 | .. | .. | .. | .. | .. | .. | .. | .. | .. | .. | .. | .. | .. | .. | .. |
| 3 | Fever, not specified | 5 | 4 | 10 | 6 | 2 | 1 | 5 | 9 | 26 | 16 | 11 | 9 | 2 | .. | .. | .. | .. | .. | 106 | .. | .. | .. | .. | .. |
| 4 | ..do..bilious | .. | .. | .. | .. | .. | .. | 1 | .. | 6 | 4 | 4 | 6 | .. | 1 | .. | .. | .. | .. | 15 | .. | 1 | .. | .. | .. |
| 5 | ..do..brain | 3 | 3 | 4 | 3 | 4 | 1 | .. | .. | 9 | 4 | .. | .. | .. | .. | .. | .. | .. | .. | 31 | .. | .. | .. | .. | .. |
| 6 | ..do..catarrhal | 1 | .. | .. | .. | .. | .. | .. | .. | .. | .. | .. | .. | .. | .. | .. | .. | .. | .. | 1 | .. | .. | .. | .. | .. |
| 7 | ..do..congestive | .. | .. | 1 | .. | .. | .. | 2 | 2 | 10 | 5 | 2 | 2 | .. | .. | .. | .. | .. | .. | 23 | .. | 1 | .. | .. | .. |
| 8 | ..do..intermittent | .. | .. | 1 | 1 | .. | 1 | .. | 1 | .. | 1 | .. | 1 | .. | .. | .. | .. | .. | .. | 3 | .. | 1 | .. | .. | .. |
| 9 | ..do..remittent | .. | .. | 1 | .. | .. | .. | 1 | 1 | 2 | .. | .. | .. | .. | .. | .. | .. | .. | .. | 2 | .. | 1 | .. | .. | .. |
| 10 | ..do..scarlet | 4 | 2 | 29 | 17 | 10 | 14 | 2 | 3 | .. | 1 | .. | 1 | .. | .. | .. | .. | .. | .. | 77 | .. | 4 | .. | .. | .. |
| 11 | ..do..ship | .. | 1 | .. | 3 | .. | 1 | .. | .. | 1 | .. | .. | .. | .. | .. | .. | .. | .. | .. | 4 | .. | .. | .. | .. | .. |
| 12 | ..do..typhus | .. | .. | 2 | 1 | .. | 1 | 10 | 4 | 21 | 10 | 6 | 8 | 1 | 1 | .. | .. | .. | .. | 45 | 3 | 6 | .. | .. | .. |
| 13 | ..do..yellow | .. | .. | .. | .. | .. | .. | .. | .. | 1 | .. | .. | .. | .. | .. | .. | .. | .. | .. | .. | .. | 1 | .. | .. | .. |
| 14 | Frozen | .. | .. | .. | .. | .. | .. | .. | .. | 1 | .. | 1 | .. | .. | .. | .. | .. | .. | .. | 1 | .. | 1 | .. | .. | .. |
| 15 | Gout | .. | .. | .. | .. | .. | .. | .. | .. | 1 | .. | 1 | .. | .. | .. | .. | .. | .. | .. | 2 | .. | .. | .. | .. | .. |
| 16 | Gravel | .. | .. | .. | .. | .. | .. | .. | .. | .. | .. | 4 | .. | 1 | .. | .. | .. | .. | .. | 4 | .. | .. | .. | .. | .. |
| 17 | Head, disease of | .. | .. | 1 | .. | 1 | .. | .. | .. | .. | .. | .. | .. | .. | .. | .. | .. | .. | .. | 2 | .. | .. | .. | .. | .. |
| 18 | Heart....do | 5 | 3 | .. | .. | .. | .. | 5 | .. | 3 | 5 | 11 | 16 | 1 | .. | .. | .. | .. | .. | 37 | 1 | 5 | .. | .. | .. |
| 19 | Hemorrhage | .. | .. | 1 | .. | .. | .. | 1 | 1 | 7 | 1 | 1 | 2 | .. | .. | .. | .. | .. | .. | 10 | 1 | 1 | .. | .. | .. |
| 20 | Hernia | 1 | .. | .. | .. | .. | .. | .. | .. | .. | .. | 1 | .. | 1 | .. | .. | .. | .. | .. | 2 | .. | .. | .. | .. | .. |
| 21 | Hives | .. | .. | .. | .. | 1 | .. | .. | .. | .. | .. | .. | .. | .. | .. | .. | .. | .. | .. | 1 | .. | .. | .. | .. | .. |
| 22 | Hooping cough | 9 | 8 | 3 | 18 | 1 | 2 | .. | .. | .. | .. | .. | .. | .. | .. | .. | .. | .. | .. | 36 | 3 | 2 | .. | .. | .. |
| 23 | Hydrocephalus | 15 | 12 | 24 | 20 | 3 | 1 | 1 | 1 | 2 | .. | .. | .. | .. | .. | .. | .. | .. | .. | 71 | 1 | 4 | .. | .. | .. |
| 24 | Hydrophobia | .. | .. | .. | .. | .. | .. | .. | .. | .. | .. | 1 | .. | .. | .. | .. | .. | .. | .. | 1 | .. | .. | .. | .. | .. |
| 25 | Inflamt'n, not specf'd | 14 | 9 | 9 | 4 | 3 | 2 | 3 | 4 | 4 | 5 | 3 | 2 | .. | .. | .. | .. | .. | .. | 56 | .. | 3 | .. | .. | .. |
| 26 | ....do.....bowels | 8 | 7 | 11 | 8 | 2 | 1 | 6 | 1 | 6 | 5 | 14 | 7 | .. | .. | .. | .. | 1 | .. | 68 | .. | 1 | .. | .. | .. |
| 27 | ....do......brain | 9 | 4 | 9 | 6 | 4 | 2 | 1 | 5 | 6 | 5 | .. | 2 | .. | .. | .. | .. | .. | .. | 47 | .. | 2 | .. | .. | .. |
| 28 | ....do.......stomach | .. | .. | .. | 1 | .. | .. | .. | .. | .. | .. | .. | .. | .. | .. | .. | .. | .. | .. | 1 | .. | .. | .. | .. | .. |
| 29 | Influenza | .. | 1 | .. | .. | .. | .. | .. | .. | .. | .. | .. | .. | 2 | .. | .. | .. | .. | .. | 3 | .. | .. | .. | .. | .. |
| 30 | Insanity | .. | .. | .. | .. | .. | .. | .. | .. | 2 | .. | 2 | 1 | .. | .. | .. | .. | .. | .. | 4 | .. | .. | .. | .. | .. |
| 31 | Intemperance | .. | .. | .. | .. | .. | .. | .. | .. | 7 | .. | 7 | .. | 1 | .. | .. | .. | .. | .. | 10 | .. | .. | .. | .. | .. |
| 32 | Jaundice | .. | 1 | 1 | .. | .. | .. | .. | .. | 2 | .. | 1 | 3 | .. | .. | .. | .. | .. | .. | 7 | .. | .. | .. | .. | .. |
| 33 | Kidneys, disease of | .. | .. | .. | .. | .. | .. | .. | .. | .. | 1 | 2 | .. | 1 | .. | .. | .. | .. | .. | 2 | .. | 1 | .. | .. | .. |
| 34 | Killed | .. | .. | .. | .. | .. | .. | 1 | .. | 6 | .. | .. | .. | .. | .. | .. | .. | .. | .. | 4 | .. | 2 | .. | .. | .. |
| 35 | Leprosy | .. | .. | .. | .. | .. | .. | .. | .. | 1 | .. | .. | .. | .. | .. | .. | .. | .. | .. | .. | .. | .. | .. | .. | .. |
| 36 | Lightning | .. | .. | 1 | .. | .. | .. | .. | .. | .. | .. | .. | .. | .. | .. | .. | .. | .. | .. | 1 | .. | .. | .. | .. | .. |
| 37 | Liver, disease of | .. | 2 | .. | 1 | 1 | .. | .. | 1 | 7 | 2 | 2 | 2 | .. | .. | .. | .. | .. | .. | 15 | .. | .. | .. | .. | .. |
| 38 | Lockjaw | .. | .. | .. | .. | .. | .. | 2 | .. | .. | .. | .. | .. | .. | .. | .. | .. | .. | .. | 2 | .. | .. | .. | .. | .. |
| 39 | Lungs, disease of | 3 | 2 | .. | 3 | 1 | .. | .. | .. | .. | 1 | 1 | .. | .. | .. | .. | .. | .. | .. | 10 | .. | .. | .. | .. | .. |
| 40 | Mania-a-potu | .. | .. | .. | .. | .. | .. | .. | .. | 1 | .. | 1 | .. | .. | .. | .. | .. | .. | .. | 2 | .. | .. | .. | .. | .. |
| 41 | Measles | .. | 1 | 4 | 8 | 1 | .. | 1 | 2 | .. | 1 | .. | .. | .. | .. | .. | .. | .. | .. | 11 | 1 | 2 | .. | .. | .. |
| 42 | Mortification | .. | .. | .. | .. | .. | .. | .. | .. | .. | .. | 1 | 1 | 1 | 1 | .. | .. | .. | .. | 3 | .. | .. | .. | .. | .. |
| 43 | Mumps | .. | .. | 2 | .. | .. | 1 | .. | 1 | .. | .. | .. | .. | .. | .. | .. | .. | .. | .. | 3 | .. | 1 | .. | .. | .. |
| 44 | Murder | .. | .. | .. | .. | .. | .. | .. | .. | .. | .. | 1 | 1 | .. | .. | .. | .. | .. | .. | 2 | .. | .. | .. | .. | .. |
| 45 | Neuralgia | .. | .. | .. | .. | .. | .. | .. | 1 | 2 | .. | .. | 1 | .. | 1 | .. | .. | .. | .. | 4 | .. | 1 | .. | .. | .. |
| 46 | Old age | .. | .. | .. | .. | .. | .. | .. | .. | .. | 1 | 26 | 30 | 53 | 56 | .. | .. | .. | .. | 131 | 4 | 12 | 2 | .. | .. |
| 47 | Paralysis | .. | .. | .. | .. | .. | .. | .. | .. | 5 | 2 | 17 | 13 | 6 | 10 | .. | .. | .. | .. | 42 | .. | 4 | 2 | .. | .. |
| 48 | Peritonitis | .. | .. | 1 | .. | .. | .. | .. | .. | .. | .. | .. | .. | .. | .. | .. | .. | .. | .. | 1 | .. | .. | .. | .. | .. |
| 49 | Piles | .. | .. | .. | 1 | .. | .. | .. | .. | .. | .. | .. | .. | .. | .. | .. | .. | .. | .. | 1 | .. | .. | .. | .. | .. |
| 50 | Pleurisy | .. | 1 | .. | 1 | .. | .. | .. | 1 | 1 | 5 | 3 | 4 | 3 | .. | .. | .. | .. | .. | 13 | .. | 2 | .. | .. | .. |
| 51 | Pneumonia | 20 | 10 | 20 | 16 | 1 | 1 | 1 | .. | 11 | 3 | 15 | 5 | .. | 1 | .. | .. | .. | .. | 87 | .. | 5 | .. | .. | .. |
| 52 | Poison | .. | .. | .. | 1 | .. | .. | .. | .. | .. | 1 | .. | .. | .. | .. | .. | .. | .. | .. | 2 | .. | .. | .. | .. | .. |
| 53 | Prematurity of birth | 1 | 2 | .. | .. | .. | .. | .. | .. | .. | .. | .. | .. | .. | .. | .. | .. | .. | .. | 3 | .. | .. | .. | .. | .. |
| 54 | Quinsy | .. | .. | .. | .. | .. | .. | .. | .. | 1 | 1 | .. | .. | .. | .. | .. | .. | .. | .. | 2 | .. | .. | .. | .. | .. |
| 55 | Rheumatism | .. | 1 | .. | .. | 1 | 1 | 1 | .. | 3 | .. | 4 | 1 | .. | .. | .. | .. | .. | .. | 8 | 1 | .. | .. | .. | .. |
| 56 | Scrofula | .. | 1 | 2 | 1 | .. | .. | 2 | 3 | 1 | .. | 1 | .. | .. | .. | .. | .. | .. | .. | 9 | 1 | .. | .. | .. | 1 |
| 57 | Scurvy | .. | .. | .. | .. | .. | .. | .. | .. | 1 | .. | .. | .. | .. | .. | .. | .. | .. | .. | 1 | .. | .. | .. | .. | .. |
| 58 | Small pox | 2 | 4 | 9 | 1 | 5 | 2 | 1 | 2 | 7 | 5 | 2 | .. | .. | .. | .. | .. | .. | .. | 32 | .. | 4 | .. | .. | .. |
| 59 | Spine, disease of | 1 | .. | 4 | .. | 1 | .. | 1 | 1 | 3 | 5 | 1 | 1 | .. | .. | .. | .. | .. | .. | 17 | .. | 1 | .. | .. | .. |
| 60 | Stillborn | 3 | 1 | .. | .. | .. | .. | .. | .. | .. | .. | .. | .. | .. | .. | .. | .. | .. | .. | 4 | .. | .. | .. | .. | .. |
| 61 | Suicide | .. | .. | .. | .. | .. | .. | .. | .. | 2 | 1 | 1 | .. | .. | .. | .. | .. | .. | .. | 1 | 1 | 2 | .. | .. | .. |
| 62 | Summer complaint | 4 | 5 | 6 | 4 | 1 | 2 | .. | .. | .. | .. | .. | .. | .. | .. | .. | .. | .. | .. | 20 | .. | 2 | .. | .. | .. |
| 63 | Sun, stroke of | .. | .. | .. | .. | .. | .. | .. | .. | 3 | 1 | 1 | .. | .. | .. | .. | .. | .. | .. | 1 | .. | .. | .. | .. | .. |
| 64 | Teething | 5 | 3 | 9 | 8 | .. | .. | .. | .. | .. | .. | .. | .. | .. | .. | .. | .. | .. | .. | 22 | .. | 2 | .. | .. | .. |
| 65 | Tetanus | .. | 1 | .. | .. | .. | .. | .. | .. | .. | .. | .. | .. | .. | .. | .. | .. | .. | .. | .. | .. | .. | .. | .. | .. |
| 66 | Throat, disease of | 5 | .. | 2 | 3 | 1 | .. | 1 | 1 | .. | 1 | 1 | .. | .. | .. | .. | .. | .. | .. | 12 | .. | 1 | .. | .. | .. |
| 67 | Thrush | 7 | 12 | .. | 1 | .. | .. | .. | .. | .. | .. | .. | .. | .. | .. | .. | .. | .. | .. | 19 | .. | 1 | .. | .. | .. |
| 68 | Tumor | .. | .. | 1 | .. | .. | .. | .. | .. | .. | 1 | .. | .. | .. | .. | .. | .. | .. | .. | 2 | .. | .. | .. | .. | .. |
| 69 | Ulcer | .. | .. | 1 | .. | .. | .. | 1 | .. | 1 | .. | .. | 1 | .. | .. | .. | .. | .. | .. | 2 | .. | 1 | .. | .. | .. |
| 70 | Uterus, disease of | .. | .. | .. | .. | .. | .. | .. | .. | .. | 3 | .. | 1 | .. | .. | .. | .. | .. | .. | 3 | .. | 1 | .. | .. | .. |
| 71 | Worms | .. | .. | 2 | 3 | 1 | .. | .. | .. | .. | .. | .. | .. | .. | .. | .. | .. | .. | .. | 4 | .. | 1 | .. | .. | .. |
| 72 | Unknown | 67 | 68 | 18 | 23 | 18 | 10 | 12 | 6 | 35 | 34 | 48 | 29 | 7 | 3 | .. | .. | 1 | 1 | 341 | 2 | 8 | .. | .. | .. |
| | Total | 385 | 305 | 420 | 410 | 135 | 100 | 158 | 118 | 603 | 480 | 466 | 358 | 100 | 94 | .. | .. | 3 | 1 | 3335 | 47 | 253 | 9 | 1 | 1 |

SECTION OF THE STATE OF NEW JERSEY—Continued.

| NATIVITIES. | | | | | SEASON OF DECEASE. | | | | DURATION OF SICKNESS. | | | | WHITES. | | | COLORED. | | | | | | | | | |
|---|---|---|---|---|---|---|---|---|---|---|---|---|---|---|---|---|---|---|---|---|---|---|---|---|---|
| | | | | | | | | | | | | | | | | Slaves. | | | | Free. | | | | | |
| | | | | | | | | | | | | | | | | Black. | | Mulatto. | | Black. | | Mul. | | | |
| California and Territories. | Ireland. | Germany. | Other foreign countries. | Unknown. | Spring. | Summer. | Autumn. | Winter. | Under 1 week. | 1 week and under 1 month. | 1 month and under 3 months. | 3 months and over. | Males. | Females. | Total. | M. | F. | M. | F. | M. | F. | M | F. | Aggregate deaths. | |
| ... | 1 | .. | 2 | ... | 20 | 10 | 9 | 2 | 11 | 18 | 5 | 5 | 16 | 22 | 38 | ... | ... | ... | ... | 1 | 2 | .. | .. | 41 | 1 |
| ... | ... | .. | 1 | ... | 1 | ... | ... | ... | 1 | ... | ... | ... | 1 | ... | 1 | ... | ... | ... | ... | ... | ... | .. | .. | 1 | 2 |
| ... | ... | .. | ... | ... | 26 | 22 | 36 | 22 | 11 | 85 | 3 | 3 | 60 | 44 | 104 | ... | ... | ... | ... | 1 | ... | .. | 1 | 106 | 3 |
| ... | 4 | .. | 2 | ... | 7 | 4 | 7 | 4 | 5 | 11 | 2 | 1 | 11 | 11 | 22 | ... | ... | ... | ... | ... | ... | .. | .. | 22 | 4 |
| ... | ... | .. | ... | ... | 6 | 7 | 11 | 7 | 5 | 24 | 2 | ... | 20 | 10 | 30 | ... | ... | ... | ... | ... | 1 | .. | .. | 31 | 5 |
| ... | ... | .. | ... | ... | 1 | ... | ... | ... | 1 | ... | ... | ... | 1 | ... | 1 | ... | ... | ... | ... | ... | ... | .. | .. | 1 | 6 |
| ... | ... | .. | ... | ... | 5 | 9 | 6 | 4 | 2 | 20 | 2 | ... | 13 | 8 | 21 | ... | ... | ... | ... | 2 | 1 | .. | .. | 24 | 7 |
| ... | 2 | .. | ... | ... | 1 | 1 | 3 | 1 | 1 | 3 | 1 | 1 | 1 | 5 | 6 | ... | ... | ... | ... | ... | ... | .. | .. | 6 | 8 |
| ... | 1 | .. | 1 | ... | ... | .. | 5 | ... | 1 | 4 | ... | ... | 4 | ... | 4 | ... | ... | ... | ... | ... | 1 | .. | .. | 5 | 9 |
| ... | ... | .. | 2 | ... | 34 | 25 | 10 | 14 | 43 | 33 | 3 | ... | 45 | 38 | 83 | ... | ... | ... | ... | ... | ... | .. | .. | 83 | 10 |
| ... | 2 | .. | ... | ... | 2 | 2 | 2 | ... | 4 | 1 | ... | 1 | 1 | 5 | 6 | ... | ... | ... | ... | ... | ... | .. | .. | 6 | 11 |
| ... | 7 | .. | 3 | 1 | 16 | 13 | 21 | 15 | 9 | 44 | 9 | 1 | 38 | 25 | 63 | ... | ... | ... | ... | 2 | ... | .. | .. | 65 | 12 |
| ... | ... | .. | ... | ... | ... | ... | 1 | ... | 1 | ... | ... | ... | 1 | ... | 1 | ... | ... | ... | ... | ... | ... | .. | .. | 1 | 13 |
| ... | ... | .. | ... | ... | 2 | ... | ... | ... | ... | ... | ... | ... | 1 | ... | 1 | ... | ... | ... | ... | 1 | ... | .. | .. | 2 | 14 |
| ... | ... | .. | ... | ... | 1 | 1 | ... | ... | ... | ... | ... | 1 | 2 | ... | 2 | ... | ... | ... | ... | ... | ... | .. | .. | 2 | 15 |
| ... | ... | .. | 1 | ... | 2 | 2 | ... | 1 | 1 | 2 | 1 | 1 | 5 | ... | 5 | ... | ... | ... | ... | ... | ... | .. | .. | 5 | 16 |
| ... | ... | .. | ... | ... | ... | 2 | ... | ... | ... | 2 | ... | ... | 2 | ... | 2 | ... | ... | ... | ... | ... | ... | .. | .. | 2 | 17 |
| ... | 2 | .. | 4 | ... | 13 | 11 | 10 | 15 | 18 | 14 | 2 | 9 | 23 | 24 | 47 | ... | ... | ... | ... | 2 | ... | .. | .. | 49 | 18 |
| ... | ... | .. | 1 | 1 | 2 | 4 | 4 | 4 | 4 | 7 | 1 | 2 | 10 | 4 | 14 | ... | ... | ... | ... | ... | ... | .. | .. | 14 | 19 |
| ... | 1 | .. | ... | ... | 1 | 1 | 1 | ... | 1 | ... | ... | 2 | 3 | ... | 3 | ... | ... | ... | ... | ... | ... | .. | .. | 3 | 20 |
| ... | ... | .. | ... | ... | ... | ... | ... | 1 | 1 | ... | ... | ... | 1 | ... | 1 | ... | ... | ... | ... | ... | ... | .. | .. | 1 | 21 |
| ... | ... | .. | ... | ... | 18 | 13 | 4 | 6 | 5 | 20 | 8 | 6 | 11 | 27 | 38 | ... | ... | ... | ... | 2 | 1 | .. | .. | 41 | 22 |
| ... | 1 | .. | 2 | ... | 25 | 10 | 26 | 18 | 6 | 56 | 7 | 8 | 45 | 32 | 77 | ... | ... | ... | ... | ... | 2 | .. | .. | 79 | 23 |
| ... | ... | .. | ... | ... | 1 | ... | ... | ... | 1 | ... | ... | ... | 1 | ... | 1 | ... | ... | ... | ... | ... | ... | .. | .. | 1 | 24 |
| ... | 1 | .. | 2 | ... | 27 | 13 | 13 | 8 | 21 | 30 | 5 | 2 | 35 | 25 | 60 | ... | ... | ... | ... | 1 | 1 | .. | .. | 62 | 25 |
| ... | 4 | 1 | 3 | ... | 25 | 13 | 27 | 12 | 26 | 39 | 5 | 5 | 47 | 28 | 75 | ... | ... | ... | ... | 1 | 1 | .. | .. | 77 | 26 |
| ... | 1 | 1 | 2 | ... | 13 | 22 | 11 | 7 | 14 | 32 | 2 | 2 | 28 | 22 | 50 | ... | ... | ... | ... | 1 | 2 | .. | .. | 53 | 27 |
| ... | ... | .. | ... | ... | 1 | ... | ... | ... | ... | ... | ... | ... | ... | 1 | 1 | ... | ... | ... | ... | ... | ... | .. | .. | 1 | 28 |
| ... | ... | .. | ... | ... | 3 | ... | ... | ... | 2 | 1 | ... | ... | 2 | 1 | 3 | ... | ... | ... | ... | ... | ... | .. | .. | 3 | 29 |
| ... | 1 | .. | ... | ... | 2 | 1 | ... | 2 | ... | 1 | ... | 2 | 4 | 1 | 5 | ... | ... | ... | ... | ... | ... | .. | .. | 5 | 30 |
| ... | 1 | .. | 3 | 1 | 3 | 2 | 4 | 6 | 4 | ... | 1 | 3 | 14 | ... | 14 | ... | ... | ... | ... | 1 | ... | .. | .. | 15 | 31 |
| ... | ... | 1 | ... | ... | 2 | 1 | 3 | 2 | 2 | 1 | 1 | 4 | 4 | 4 | 8 | ... | ... | ... | ... | ... | ... | .. | .. | 8 | 32 |
| ... | 1 | .. | ... | ... | 2 | 1 | ... | 1 | ... | 3 | ... | 1 | 3 | 1 | 4 | ... | ... | ... | ... | ... | ... | .. | .. | 4 | 33 |
| ... | ... | .. | 1 | ... | 3 | 1 | 1 | 2 | 7 | ... | ... | ... | 7 | ... | 7 | ... | ... | ... | ... | ... | ... | .. | .. | 7 | 34 |
| ... | ... | .. | 1 | ... | ... | ... | 1 | ... | ... | ... | ... | 1 | 1 | ... | 1 | ... | ... | ... | ... | ... | ... | .. | .. | 1 | 35 |
| ... | ... | .. | ... | ... | ... | ... | 1 | ... | 1 | ... | ... | ... | 1 | ... | 1 | ... | ... | ... | ... | ... | ... | .. | .. | 1 | 36 |
| ... | 2 | .. | 1 | ... | 6 | 3 | 6 | 3 | ... | 5 | 6 | 5 | 10 | 7 | 17 | ... | ... | ... | ... | ... | 1 | .. | .. | 18 | 37 |
| ... | ... | .. | ... | ... | ... | 1 | 1 | ... | ... | 1 | ... | 1 | 2 | ... | 2 | ... | ... | ... | ... | ... | ... | .. | .. | 2 | 38 |
| ... | ... | .. | 1 | ... | 6 | ... | ... | 5 | 5 | 4 | ... | 2 | 5 | 6 | 11 | ... | ... | ... | ... | ... | ... | .. | .. | 11 | 39 |
| ... | ... | .. | ... | ... | 1 | 1 | ... | ... | 1 | 1 | ... | ... | 2 | ... | 2 | ... | ... | ... | ... | ... | ... | .. | .. | 2 | 40 |
| ... | 3 | .. | 1 | ... | 1 | 12 | 3 | 2 | 3 | 10 | 3 | 2 | 6 | 11 | 17 | ... | ... | ... | ... | ... | 1 | .. | .. | 18 | 41 |
| ... | ... | .. | 1 | ... | 2 | ... | 2 | ... | ... | ... | 3 | 1 | 2 | 2 | 4 | ... | ... | ... | ... | ... | ... | .. | .. | 4 | 42 |
| ... | ... | .. | ... | ... | 2 | 1 | 1 | ... | ... | 3 | 1 | ... | 2 | 2 | 4 | ... | ... | ... | ... | ... | ... | .. | .. | 4 | 43 |
| ... | ... | .. | ... | ... | ... | ... | ... | 2 | 2 | ... | ... | ... | 1 | 1 | 2 | ... | ... | ... | ... | ... | ... | .. | .. | 2 | 44 |
| ... | ... | .. | ... | ... | ... | 1 | 1 | 3 | ... | 3 | 1 | 1 | 2 | 3 | 5 | ... | ... | ... | ... | ... | ... | .. | .. | 5 | 45 |
| ... | 8 | 3 | 4 | 2 | 43 | 46 | 44 | 33 | 25 | 21 | 9 | 32 | 73 | 82 | 155 | 4 | 2 | ... | ... | 2 | 3 | .. | .. | 166 | 46 |
| ... | ... | 1 | 4 | ... | 15 | 9 | 9 | 20 | 15 | 14 | 7 | 15 | 28 | 23 | 51 | ... | 1 | ... | ... | ... | 1 | .. | .. | 53 | 47 |
| ... | ... | .. | ... | ... | ... | 1 | ... | ... | ... | ... | ... | 1 | 1 | ... | 1 | ... | ... | ... | ... | ... | ... | .. | .. | 1 | 48 |
| ... | ... | .. | ... | ... | ... | 1 | ... | ... | ... | ... | ... | 1 | ... | 1 | 1 | ... | ... | ... | ... | ... | ... | .. | .. | 1 | 49 |
| ... | 3 | .. | 1 | ... | 9 | 2 | 3 | 5 | 5 | 11 | 1 | ... | 7 | 12 | 19 | ... | ... | ... | ... | ... | ... | .. | .. | 19 | 50 |
| ... | 9 | .. | 3 | ... | 44 | 17 | 19 | 24 | 18 | 67 | 6 | 13 | 64 | 34 | 98 | ... | ... | ... | ... | 4 | 2 | .. | .. | 104 | 51 |
| ... | ... | .. | ... | ... | 1 | 1 | ... | ... | 1 | 1 | ... | ... | ... | 2 | 2 | ... | ... | ... | ... | ... | ... | .. | .. | 2 | 52 |
| ... | ... | .. | ... | ... | 2 | 1 | ... | ... | ... | 1 | ... | ... | 1 | 2 | 3 | ... | ... | ... | ... | ... | ... | .. | .. | 3 | 53 |
| ... | ... | .. | ... | ... | ... | 1 | 1 | ... | ... | 1 | ... | 1 | 1 | 1 | 2 | ... | ... | ... | ... | ... | ... | .. | .. | 2 | 54 |
| ... | 2 | .. | 1 | ... | 3 | 4 | 2 | 3 | ... | 4 | 3 | 5 | 9 | 3 | 12 | ... | ... | ... | ... | ... | ... | .. | .. | 12 | 55 |
| ... | ... | .. | ... | ... | 4 | 3 | 3 | 1 | ... | 3 | ... | 8 | 6 | 5 | 11 | ... | ... | ... | ... | ... | ... | .. | .. | 11 | 56 |
| ... | ... | .. | ... | ... | ... | ... | 1 | ... | ... | ... | 1 | ... | 1 | ... | 1 | ... | ... | ... | ... | ... | ... | .. | .. | 1 | 57 |
| ... | 1 | .. | 3 | ... | 10 | 11 | 5 | 13 | 7 | 31 | 1 | ... | 23 | 14 | 37 | ... | ... | ... | ... | 2 | ... | 1 | .. | 40 | 58 |
| ... | ... | .. | ... | ... | 7 | 4 | 5 | 2 | ... | 4 | 3 | 10 | 10 | 7 | 17 | ... | ... | ... | ... | 1 | ... | .. | .. | 18 | 59 |
| ... | ... | .. | ... | ... | 2 | 1 | 1 | ... | ... | ... | ... | ... | 3 | 1 | 4 | ... | ... | ... | ... | ... | ... | .. | .. | 4 | 60 |
| ... | ... | .. | ... | ... | 2 | ... | ... | 2 | 2 | ... | ... | ... | 3 | 1 | 4 | ... | ... | ... | ... | ... | ... | .. | .. | 4 | 61 |
| ... | ... | .. | ... | ... | 2 | 6 | 14 | ... | 6 | 7 | 2 | 3 | 11 | 11 | 22 | ... | ... | ... | ... | ... | ... | .. | .. | 22 | 62 |
| ... | 4 | .. | ... | ... | ... | 4 | ... | 1 | 3 | 1 | ... | ... | 4 | 1 | 5 | ... | ... | ... | ... | ... | ... | .. | .. | 5 | 63 |
| ... | 1 | .. | ... | ... | 5 | 4 | 14 | 2 | 4 | 11 | 5 | 1 | 13 | 11 | 24 | ... | ... | ... | ... | 1 | ... | .. | .. | 25 | 64 |
| ... | ... | 1 | ... | ... | ... | 1 | ... | ... | ... | 1 | ... | ... | ... | 1 | 1 | ... | ... | ... | ... | ... | ... | .. | .. | 1 | 65 |
| ... | 1 | .. | 1 | ... | 4 | 4 | 4 | 3 | 3 | 10 | 1 | ... | 10 | 4 | 14 | ... | ... | ... | ... | ... | 1 | .. | .. | 15 | 66 |
| ... | ... | .. | ... | ... | 4 | 4 | 11 | 1 | 8 | 11 | ... | ... | 7 | 13 | 20 | ... | ... | ... | ... | ... | ... | .. | .. | 20 | 67 |
| ... | ... | .. | ... | ... | ... | ... | ... | 2 | ... | 1 | ... | 1 | 1 | 1 | 2 | ... | ... | ... | ... | ... | ... | .. | .. | 2 | 68 |
| ... | 1 | .. | ... | ... | 1 | 2 | 1 | ... | 1 | ... | 1 | 2 | 3 | 1 | 4 | ... | ... | ... | ... | ... | ... | .. | .. | 4 | 69 |
| ... | ... | .. | ... | ... | ... | 1 | 3 | ... | ... | 3 | ... | 1 | ... | 4 | 4 | ... | ... | ... | ... | ... | ... | .. | .. | 4 | 70 |
| ... | 1 | .. | ... | ... | 2 | 3 | 1 | ... | 3 | 3 | ... | ... | 3 | 3 | 6 | ... | ... | ... | ... | ... | ... | .. | .. | 6 | 71 |
| ... | 16 | .. | 5 | 8 | 110 | 97 | 97 | 69 | 128 | 58 | 47 | 53 | 197 | 168 | 365 | ... | 1 | ... | ... | 9 | 5 | .. | .. | 380 | 72 |
| ... | 284 | 47 | 138 | 21 | 934 | 1039 | 1423 | 709 | 1401 | 1263 | 303 | 779 | 2177 | 1782 | 3959 | 8 | 5 | ... | ... | 76 | 73 | 9 | 6 | 4136 | |

## CLASSIFICATION OF DEATHS IN SOUTHERN

*Embracing the following counties: Atlantic, Burlington, Camden,*

| | Cause of death. | AGE. | | | | | | | | | | | | | | | | | | NATIVITIES. | | | | | |
|---|---|---|---|---|---|---|---|---|---|---|---|---|---|---|---|---|---|---|---|---|---|---|---|---|---|
| | | Under 1. | | 1 and under 5. | | 5 and under 10. | | 10 and under 20. | | 20 and under 50. | | 50 and under 80. | | 80 and under 100. | | 100 & over. | | Age unknown. | | Born in State. | N. England States. | Middle States. | Southern States. | Southwest'n States. | Northeast'n States. |
| | | M. | F. | M. | F. | M. | F. | M. | F. | M. | F. | M. | F. | M | F. | M | F. | M | F. | | | | | | |
| 1 | Abscess | | 1 | 1 | 2 | | | 1 | 1 | | | | 1 | | | | | | | 7 | | | | | |
| 2 | Accident, not spec'd. | 1 | | 2 | 3 | 3 | 3 | 6 | 1 | 15 | 1 | 3 | 1 | | | | | | | 27 | | 5 | 1 | | |
| 3 | ....do.. burned | | | | | 1 | | | | | | | | | | | | | | | | 1 | | | |
| 4 | ....do...drowned | | | 2 | | | | 8 | | 5 | 1 | 1 | | | | | | | | 16 | | 1 | | | |
| 5 | ....do...scalded | | | | 1 | | | | | | | | | | | | | | | 1 | | | | | |
| 6 | Apoplexy | | | | 1 | | | | 1 | 4 | 3 | 2 | 3 | 1 | | | | | | 10 | 1 | 1 | 1 | | |
| 7 | Asthma | | | | | | | | | | | 1 | | 1 | | | | | | 2 | | | | | |
| 8 | Bowels, disease of | 1 | 3 | 2 | | | | | | 1 | | 1 | | | | | | | | 7 | | 1 | | | |
| 9 | Brain, ......do | 1 | 2 | | | | 3 | | | | | | | | | | | | | 6 | | | | | |
| 10 | Bronchitis | | 1 | | | | 1 | | 1 | | | | 1 | | | | | | 1 | 5 | | | | | |
| 11 | Cancer | | | | | 1 | | | | 1 | 1 | 4 | 6 | 1 | | | | | | 13 | | | | | |
| 12 | Catarrh | 6 | 2 | 9 | 5 | | 1 | | | | 1 | 1 | 1 | | | | | | | 25 | | 1 | | | |
| 13 | Chicken pox | | | | 1 | | | | | | | | | | | | | | | 1 | | | | | |
| 14 | Childbirth | | | | | | | | | | 19 | | | | | | | | | 19 | | | | | |
| 15 | Cholera | 7 | 6 | 14 | 10 | 7 | 5 | 11 | 12 | 50 | 27 | 25 | 29 | 3 | 3 | | | 2 | 2 | 184 | 2 | 19 | 2 | | |
| 16 | ....do...infantum | 13 | 12 | 6 | 5 | | | | | | | | | | | | | | | 35 | | 1 | | | |
| 17 | ....do...morbus | 2 | 1 | 2 | 1 | | | | 1 | | 2 | | 2 | 1 | 1 | | | | | 11 | | 2 | | | |
| 18 | Chorea | | | | | | | | 1 | | | | | | | | | | | 1 | | | | | |
| 19 | Colic | | | | | | | | | | | 1 | | | | | | | | 1 | | | | | |
| 20 | Congestion of brain | | | | | 1 | | | | | | | | | | | | | | 1 | | | | | |
| 21 | Consumption | 10 | 12 | 11 | 7 | 1 | 2 | 12 | 17 | 72 | 70 | 41 | 44 | 4 | | | | 1 | 2 | 267 | | 26 | 1 | | |
| 22 | Convulsions | 8 | 15 | 7 | 5 | 1 | 3 | 1 | | 8 | | 3 | 4 | 1 | | | | | | 51 | | 4 | | | 1 |
| 23 | Cramp | | | 1 | 2 | | | | | | | | | | | | | | | 3 | | | | | |
| 24 | Croup | 5 | 4 | 22 | 13 | 3 | 5 | | 1 | | | | | | | | | | | 45 | | 7 | | | |
| 25 | Debility | 2 | 1 | | | | | | | | | 1 | | | | | | | | 3 | | | | | |
| 26 | Diarrhœa | 9 | 5 | 6 | 5 | 3 | | 1 | 2 | 1 | 1 | 1 | 2 | 1 | | | | | | 35 | | 1 | | | |
| 27 | Dropsy | 3 | 2 | 3 | 3 | 1 | 1 | 1 | 4 | 10 | 17 | 12 | 13 | 5 | 3 | | | | 1 | 69 | | 7 | | | |
| 28 | Dysentery | 12 | 26 | 53 | 42 | 14 | 15 | 7 | 3 | 15 | 15 | 7 | 21 | 1 | 1 | | | 1 | | 216 | 1 | 11 | | 1 | |
| 29 | Dyspepsia | 2 | | 2 | 4 | | | 1 | 1 | | 4 | 1 | 2 | | | | | | | 17 | | | | | |
| 30 | Epilepsy | | | | | | | 1 | | | | | 1 | | 1 | | | | | 3 | | | | | |
| 31 | Erysipelas | | 1 | 1 | | | | 1 | 1 | | 2 | | | 1 | | | | | | 6 | | | | | |
| 32 | Eyes, disease of | | | | | | | | | | | | 1 | | | | | | | 1 | | | | | |
| 33 | Fever, not specified | 5 | 1 | 6 | 2 | 3 | | 7 | 5 | 10 | 9 | 4 | 2 | 2 | | | | 1 | | 52 | | 2 | | | |
| 34 | ..do. bilious | 2 | 1 | 3 | 1 | 3 | 3 | 2 | 4 | 13 | 2 | 2 | 1 | | 1 | | | | | 25 | | 7 | | | |
| 35 | ..do..brain | 9 | 2 | 4 | 2 | 2 | | 5 | 1 | 8 | 3 | | 2 | | | | | | | 32 | | 1 | | | |
| 36 | ..do..catarrhal | 4 | | 10 | 5 | 2 | 2 | | | | | | | | | | | | | 20 | | 3 | | | |
| 37 | ..do..congestive | | | | 1 | | | | | | 1 | | | | | | | | | 2 | | | | | |
| 38 | ..do..intermittent | | | | | | | | | 1 | | | | | | | | | | | | | | | |
| 39 | ..do..puerperal | | | | | | | | | | 6 | | | | | | | | | 5 | | 1 | | | |
| 40 | ..do..remittent | | | | 1 | | 1 | | | 2 | | | 1 | | | | | | | 5 | | | | | |
| 41 | ..do..scarlet | 1 | 1 | 13 | 8 | 6 | 6 | 1 | 2 | | | | | | | | | | | 34 | | 4 | | | |
| 42 | ..do..ship | | | | | | | | 1 | | | | | | | | | | | 1 | | | | | |
| 43 | ..do..typhus | | 1 | 2 | 2 | 3 | 1 | 1 | 7 | 13 | 6 | 5 | 1 | | | | | | | 35 | | 4 | | | |
| 44 | Gout | | | | | | | | | | | 1 | | | 1 | | | | | 2 | | | | | |
| 45 | Gravel | | | | | | | | | | | 1 | | 1 | | | | | | 2 | | | | | |
| 46 | Heart, disease of | | 1 | 1 | 1 | | 1 | 2 | 2 | 4 | 3 | 3 | 5 | | | | | | | 21 | | 1 | | 1 | |
| 47 | Hemorrhage | 1 | | | | | | | | 4 | 3 | | | | | | | | | 6 | | 1 | | | |
| 48 | Hernia | 1 | | | | | | | | | | | | | | | | | | 1 | | | | | |
| 49 | Hives | | | | 1 | | | | | | 1 | | | | | | | | | 2 | | | | | |
| 50 | Hooping cough | 15 | 7 | 12 | 9 | 1 | 2 | 1 | | | | | | | | | | | | 45 | | 1 | | | 1 |
| 51 | Hydrocephalus | 5 | 3 | 6 | 2 | 3 | | 1 | | | | | | | | | | | | 20 | | | | | |
| 52 | Inflamt'n, not specf'd | 6 | 3 | 5 | 3 | | 2 | 1 | 1 | 2 | | 3 | 3 | | | | | | | 27 | | 1 | | | |
| 53 | .....do....bowels | 2 | 3 | 3 | 8 | 2 | 1 | | | 2 | 1 | 2 | 1 | | | | | | | 23 | | 1 | | | |
| 54 | .....do....brain | 5 | 6 | 8 | 11 | 2 | 2 | 2 | | 5 | | 3 | | | | | | | | 38 | | 6 | | | |
| 55 | Influenza | | 2 | | 2 | | | | | | | | | | 1 | | | | | 5 | | | | | |
| 56 | Insanity | | | | | | | | | 2 | 1 | 2 | | | | | | | | 5 | | | | | |
| 57 | Intemperance | | | | | | | | | 5 | | 5 | | | | | | | | 9 | | | | | |
| 58 | Jaundice | | | | | | 1 | | | | | | | 1 | | | | | | 2 | | | | | |
| 59 | Kidneys, disease of | | 1 | | | | | | | | | 1 | | | | | | | | 1 | | 1 | | | |
| 60 | Killed | | | | | | | 1 | | 3 | | | | | | | | | | 1 | | 2 | | | |
| 61 | Liver, disease of | 1 | 2 | 2 | | | | 1 | 1 | 4 | 3 | 3 | 2 | | | | | | | 17 | | 1 | | | |
| 62 | Lockjaw | | | | | | | | | 2 | | 1 | | | | | | | | 2 | | | | | |
| 63 | Lungs, disease of | | 1 | 1 | 2 | | | | | | | | | | | | | | | 3 | | 1 | | | |
| 64 | Mania-a-potu | | | | | | | | | 1 | | 2 | | | | | | | | 2 | | | | | |
| 65 | Measles | 6 | 1 | 10 | 4 | | | | 2 | 1 | 5 | | | | | | | | | 29 | | | | | |
| 66 | Mortification | | 1 | | | | | | | | | | | | | | | | | 1 | | | | | |
| 67 | Mumps | | | | | | | 1 | | | | | | | | | | | | 1 | | | | | |
| 68 | Murder | | | | | | | | | 1 | | | | | | | | 1 | | 1 | | 1 | | | |
| 69 | Neuralgia | | | | | | 1 | | | | | | | | | | | | | 1 | | | | | |
| 70 | Old age | | | | | | | | | | | 16 | 17 | 34 | 37 | | | | 2 | 93 | 2 | 8 | | | |
| 71 | Paralysis | | | | | | | 1 | | 1 | | 6 | 2 | 5 | 5 | | | | 1 | 17 | | 3 | | | |
| 72 | Piles | | | | | | | | | | | | 1 | | | | | | | 1 | | | | | |
| 73 | Pleurisy | | 1 | | 1 | | | 1 | | 6 | | 5 | 5 | 1 | 2 | | | 1 | | 20 | 1 | | | | |

## ECTION OF THE STATE OF NEW JERSEY.

*pe May, Cumberland, Gloucester, Monmouth, Ocean, and Salem.*

| NATIVITIES. | | | | | SEASON OF DECEASE. | | | | DURATION OF SICKNESS. | | | | WHITES. | | | COLORED. | | | | | | | | | |
|---|---|---|---|---|---|---|---|---|---|---|---|---|---|---|---|---|---|---|---|---|---|---|---|---|---|
| | | | | | | | | | | | | | | | | Slaves. | | | | Free. | | | | | |
| | | | | | | | | | | | | | | | | Black. | | Mulatto. | | Black. | | Mul. | | | |
| ritories. | Ireland. | Germany. | Other foreign countries. | Unknown. | Spring. | Summer. | Autumn. | Winter. | Under 1 week. | 1 week and under 1 month. | 1 month and under 3 months. | 3 months and over. | Males. | Females. | Total. | M. | F. | M. | F. | M. | F. | M | F. | Aggregate deaths. | |
| | | | | | 3 | 3 | 1 | | 1 | 2 | 3 | | 2 | 5 | 7 | | | | | | | | | 7 | 1 |
| | 8 | | 8 | | 14 | 9 | 5 | 10 | 22 | 4 | 1 | 2 | 29 | 8 | 37 | | | | | 1 | 1 | | | 39 | 2 |
| | | | | | | | | 1 | 1 | | | | 1 | | 1 | | | | | | | | | 1 | 3 |
| | | | | | 3 | 7 | 5 | 2 | 17 | | | | 16 | 1 | 17 | | | | | | | | | 17 | 4 |
| | | | | | 1 | | | | 1 | | | | | 1 | 1 | | | | | | | | | 1 | 5 |
| | | 1 | 1 | | 7 | 4 | 2 | 2 | 12 | | | 1 | 6 | 8 | 14 | | | | | 1 | | | | 15 | 6 |
| | | | | | | 1 | | 1 | | 1 | | 1 | 2 | | 2 | | | | | | | | | 2 | 7 |
| | | | | | 1 | 5 | 1 | 1 | | 5 | | 1 | 5 | 3 | 8 | | | | | | | | | 8 | 8 |
| | | | | | 3 | | 2 | 1 | 1 | 2 | 2 | | 1 | 5 | 6 | | | | | | | | | 6 | 9 |
| | | | | | 1 | 1 | 2 | | 1 | | 1 | | | 5 | 5 | | | | | | | | | 5 | 10 |
| | 1 | | | | 2 | 3 | 7 | 2 | | | 1 | 10 | 6 | 7 | 13 | | | | | 1 | | | | 14 | 11 |
| | | | | | 10 | 5 | 3 | 8 | 9 | 12 | | 1 | 15 | 9 | 24 | | | | | 1 | 1 | | | 26 | 12 |
| | | | | | | | | 1 | | 1 | | | | 1 | 1 | | | | | | | | | 1 | 13 |
| | | | | | 5 | 9 | 5 | | 6 | 7 | 1 | | | 19 | 19 | | | | | | | | | 19 | 14 |
| | | 2 | 4 | | 2 | 157 | 53 | | 137 | 23 | 2 | | 117 | 89 | 206 | | | | | 2 | 5 | | | 213 | 15 |
| | | | | | | 17 | 18 | 1 | 9 | 16 | 5 | | 18 | 17 | 35 | | | | | 1 | | | | 36 | 16 |
| | | | | | 2 | 8 | 3 | | 8 | 2 | 1 | | 5 | 8 | 13 | | | | | | | | | 13 | 17 |
| | | | | | | 1 | | | | 1 | | | | 1 | 1 | | | | | | | | | 1 | 18 |
| | | | | | | 1 | | | | | | | 1 | | 1 | | | | | | | | | 1 | 19 |
| | | | | | | 1 | | | | 1 | | | 1 | | 1 | | | | | | | | | 1 | 20 |
| | 4 | 1 | 5 | 2 | 95 | 74 | 80 | 56 | 4 | 34 | 36 | 160 | 141 | 145 | 286 | | | | | 5 | 9 | 6 | | 306 | 21 |
| | | | | | 16 | 18 | 11 | 10 | 24 | 10 | 2 | 5 | 29 | 25 | 54 | | | | | | 2 | | | 56 | 22 |
| | | | | | 1 | | | 2 | 3 | | | | 1 | 2 | 3 | | | | | | | | | 3 | 23 |
| | 1 | | | | 15 | 7 | 9 | 22 | 39 | 10 | 1 | | 30 | 22 | 52 | | | | | | 1 | | | 53 | 24 |
| | | | 1 | | | 3 | | 1 | | 1 | | 1 | 3 | 1 | 4 | | | | | | | | | 4 | 25 |
| | 1 | | | | 2 | 8 | 27 | | 10 | 14 | 6 | | 22 | 14 | 36 | | | | | | 1 | | | 37 | 26 |
| | | | 2 | 1 | 21 | 23 | 21 | 14 | 5 | 15 | 11 | 36 | 29 | 42 | 71 | | | | | 4 | 2 | 2 | | 79 | 27 |
| | 3 | | 1 | | 10 | 48 | 160 | 15 | 73 | 132 | 20 | 2 | 108 | 121 | 229 | | | | | 2 | 1 | | 1 | 233 | 28 |
| | | | | | 1 | 1 | 12 | | | | 6 | 7 | 6 | 11 | 17 | | | | | | | | | 17 | 29 |
| | | | | | | 2 | 1 | | 1 | | | 1 | 1 | 2 | 3 | | | | | | | | | 3 | 30 |
| | | | 1 | | 1 | 4 | 1 | 1 | 4 | 3 | | | 3 | 4 | 7 | | | | | | | | | 7 | 31 |
| | | | | | | | | | | | | | | 1 | 1 | | | | | | | | | 1 | 32 |
| | 2 | 1 | | | 16 | 10 | 20 | 11 | 3 | 41 | 7 | 1 | 37 | 19 | 56 | | | | | 1 | | | | 57 | 33 |
| | 2 | 2 | 2 | | 7 | 6 | 17 | 8 | 5 | 23 | 5 | | 23 | 13 | 36 | | | | | | | 2 | | 38 | 34 |
| | | | | | 7 | 10 | 13 | 3 | 11 | 15 | 2 | 1 | 22 | 9 | 31 | | | | | 1 | 1 | | | 33 | 35 |
| | | | | | 12 | 2 | 3 | 6 | 4 | 15 | 1 | | 14 | 7 | 21 | | | | | 2 | | | | 23 | 36 |
| | | | | | | 1 | | 1 | 1 | 1 | | | | 2 | 2 | | | | | | | | | 2 | 37 |
| | 1 | | | | | 1 | | | | 1 | | | 1 | | 1 | | | | | | | | | 1 | 38 |
| | | | | | 2 | 3 | 1 | | | 5 | | | | 6 | 6 | | | | | | | | | 6 | 39 |
| | | | | | | 1 | 4 | | | 5 | | | 2 | 3 | 5 | | | | | | | | | 5 | 40 |
| | | | | | 12 | 15 | 4 | 7 | 12 | 17 | 3 | | 20 | 16 | 36 | | | | | 1 | 1 | | | 38 | 41 |
| | | | | | | | 1 | | 1 | | | | | 1 | 1 | | | | | | | | | 1 | 42 |
| | 2 | 1 | | | 9 | 11 | 15 | 7 | 8 | 26 | 6 | | 20 | 17 | 37 | | | | | 3 | | 1 | 1 | 42 | 43 |
| | | | | | 1 | | | 1 | | | 1 | 1 | 1 | 1 | 2 | | | | | | | | | 2 | 44 |
| | | | | | 2 | | | | | 2 | | | 2 | | 2 | | | | | | | | | 2 | 45 |
| | | | | | 5 | 3 | 5 | 10 | 10 | 5 | 1 | 6 | 10 | 13 | 23 | | | | | | | | | 23 | 46 |
| | 1 | | | | | 3 | 4 | 1 | 4 | | 1 | 1 | 4 | 3 | 7 | | | | | | | 1 | | 8 | 47 |
| | | | | | | | 1 | | | 1 | | | 1 | | 1 | | | | | | | | | 1 | 48 |
| | | | | | 1 | 1 | | | 1 | 1 | | | | 1 | 1 | | | | | | 1 | | | 2 | 49 |
| | | | | | 11 | 16 | 17 | 3 | 1 | 33 | 4 | 2 | 27 | 16 | 43 | | | | | 1 | 1 | 1 | 1 | 47 | 50 |
| | | | | | 4 | 6 | 9 | | 4 | 7 | 5 | 2 | 15 | 5 | 20 | | | | | | | | | 20 | 51 |
| 1 | | | | | 13 | 7 | 6 | 3 | 8 | 12 | 7 | | 16 | 12 | 28 | | | | | 1 | | | | 29 | 52 |
| | 1 | | | | 4 | 5 | 10 | 5 | 3 | 12 | 5 | 2 | 11 | 14 | 25 | | | | | | | | | 25 | 53 |
| | | | | | 12 | 12 | 14 | 6 | 12 | 22 | 6 | | 23 | 19 | 42 | | | | | 2 | | | | 44 | 54 |
| | | | | | 2 | 2 | 1 | | | 4 | 1 | | | 5 | 5 | | | | | | | | | 5 | 55 |
| | | | | | | | 2 | 3 | | 1 | | 1 | 4 | 1 | 5 | | | | | | | | | 5 | 56 |
| | | | 1 | | 2 | 3 | 4 | 1 | 2 | 2 | | 1 | 10 | | 10 | | | | | | | | | 10 | 57 |
| | | | | | 1 | 1 | | | | 2 | | | 1 | 1 | 2 | | | | | | | | | 2 | 58 |
| | | | | | 1 | | 1 | | | 1 | 1 | | | 1 | 1 | | | | | 1 | | | | 2 | 59 |
| | | 1 | | | 1 | 1 | 1 | 1 | 3 | | 1 | | 4 | | 4 | | | | | | | | | 4 | 60 |
| | 1 | | | | 5 | 8 | 5 | 1 | 3 | 5 | 6 | 5 | 10 | 8 | 18 | | | | | 1 | | | | 19 | 61 |
| | 1 | | | | | | 2 | 1 | 2 | 1 | | | 3 | | 3 | | | | | | | | | 3 | 62 |
| | | | | | 2 | | 2 | | 3 | 1 | | | 1 | 3 | 4 | | | | | | | | | 4 | 63 |
| | | | 1 | | 2 | | 1 | | 1 | 1 | | 1 | 3 | | 3 | | | | | | | | | 3 | 64 |
| | | | | | 17 | 9 | 3 | | 4 | 19 | 2 | | 17 | 12 | 29 | | | | | | | | | 29 | 65 |
| | | | | | | | 1 | | 1 | | | | | | | | | | | | 1 | | | 1 | 66 |
| | | | | | | 1 | | | | | 1 | | 1 | | 1 | | | | | | | | | 1 | 67 |
| | | | | | | 1 | | 1 | 2 | | | | 1 | | 1 | | | | | 1 | | | | 2 | 68 |
| | | | | | | | | 1 | | 1 | | | | 1 | 1 | | | | | | | | | 1 | 69 |
| | 2 | | 1 | | 27 | 27 | 30 | 22 | 11 | 12 | 4 | 12 | 44 | 50 | 94 | | | | | 6 | 5 | | 1 | 106 | 70 |
| | 1 | | | | 3 | 9 | 4 | 4 | 7 | 4 | 1 | 4 | 13 | 8 | 21 | | | | | | | | | 21 | 71 |
| | | | | | 1 | | | | | | | 1 | | 1 | 1 | | | | | | | | | 1 | 72 |
| | | 1 | 1 | | 9 | 2 | 3 | 9 | 5 | 15 | | | 14 | 9 | 23 | | | | | | | | | 23 | 73 |

## CLASSIFICATION OF DEATHS IN SOUTHERN

| | Cause of death. | Ages. | | | | | | | | | | | | | | | | | | Nativities. | | | | | |
|---|---|---|---|---|---|---|---|---|---|---|---|---|---|---|---|---|---|---|---|---|---|---|---|---|---|
| | | Under 1. | | 1 and under 5. | | 5 and under 10. | | 10 and under 20. | | 20 and under 50. | | 50 and under 80. | | 80 and under 100. | | 100 & over. | | Age unknown. | | Born in State. | N. England States. | Middle States. | Southern States. | Southwest'n States. | Northwest'n States. |
| | | M. | F. | M. | F. | M. | F. | M. | F. | M. | F. | M. | F. | M | F. | M | F. | M | F. | | | | | | |
| 1 | Pneumonia | 4 | 5 | 1 | 2 | 1 | 1 | 1 | ... | 1 | 3 | 2 | 2 | 1 | 1 | ... | ... | ... | ... | 24 | ... | 1 | ... | ... | ... |
| 2 | Poisoned | ... | ... | 3 | ... | ... | ... | ... | ... | ... | 1 | ... | 1 | ... | ... | ... | ... | ... | ... | 4 | ... | 1 | ... | ... | ... |
| 3 | Quinsy | ... | ... | ... | ... | ... | ... | ... | ... | 1 | ... | ... | ... | ... | ... | ... | ... | ... | ... | 1 | ... | ... | ... | ... | ... |
| 4 | Rheumatism | ... | ... | ... | ... | 1 | ... | 1 | ... | 2 | 1 | 1 | 4 | ... | ... | ... | ... | ... | ... | 10 | ... | ... | ... | ... | ... |
| 5 | Scrofula | 3 | 3 | 2 | 4 | ... | 1 | 1 | 2 | 1 | 3 | ... | ... | 1 | 1 | ... | ... | ... | 1 | 21 | ... | 2 | ... | ... | ... |
| 6 | Small pox | ... | ... | 1 | ... | 1 | 1 | ... | ... | ... | ... | 1 | ... | ... | ... | ... | ... | ... | ... | 3 | ... | ... | ... | ... | ... |
| 7 | Spine, disease of | ... | ... | 1 | ... | ... | 2 | 1 | 2 | 1 | 2 | ... | 1 | ... | ... | ... | ... | ... | ... | 9 | ... | 1 | ... | ... | ... |
| 8 | Suicide | ... | ... | ... | ... | ... | ... | 1 | ... | 1 | ... | 2 | ... | ... | ... | ... | ... | ... | ... | 2 | ... | 2 | ... | ... | ... |
| 9 | Summer complaint | 5 | 4 | 5 | 6 | ... | 1 | ... | ... | ... | ... | ... | ... | ... | ... | ... | ... | ... | ... | 20 | ... | 1 | ... | ... | ... |
| 10 | Sun, stroke of | ... | ... | ... | ... | ... | ... | ... | ... | ... | ... | 1 | ... | ... | ... | ... | ... | ... | ... | 1 | ... | ... | ... | ... | ... |
| 11 | Teething | ... | 2 | 1 | 4 | ... | ... | ... | ... | ... | ... | ... | ... | ... | ... | ... | ... | ... | ... | 6 | ... | ... | ... | ... | ... |
| 12 | Throat, disease of | ... | ... | 2 | ... | ... | 1 | ... | 1 | ... | ... | ... | ... | ... | ... | ... | ... | ... | ... | 4 | ... | ... | ... | ... | ... |
| 13 | Tumor | ... | ... | ... | ... | ... | ... | ... | ... | 1 | 1 | ... | ... | ... | ... | ... | ... | ... | ... | 2 | ... | ... | ... | ... | ... |
| 14 | Ulcer | ... | ... | ... | ... | ... | ... | ... | ... | ... | 1 | ... | ... | ... | ... | ... | ... | ... | ... | ... | ... | 1 | ... | ... | ... |
| 15 | White swelling | ... | ... | ... | ... | ... | ... | ... | ... | ... | 1 | ... | ... | ... | ... | ... | ... | ... | ... | 1 | ... | ... | ... | ... | ... |
| 16 | Worms | ... | ... | 3 | 2 | 2 | ... | ... | ... | ... | ... | ... | ... | ... | ... | ... | ... | ... | ... | 6 | ... | 1 | ... | ... | ... |
| 17 | Unknown | 46 | 35 | 33 | 22 | 7 | 6 | 5 | 3 | 25 | 38 | 38 | 20 | 2 | 1 | ... | ... | 4 | 2 | 266 | 1 | 10 | ... | ... | 1 |
| | Total | 203 | 181 | 282 | 216 | 75 | 75 | 89 | 81 | 300 | 259 | 215 | 203 | 68 | 59 | ... | ... | 11 | 12 | 2077 | 7 | 159 | 5 | 2 | 3 |

## CLASSIFICATION OF DEATHS IN

| | Cause of death. | Under 1. M. | Under 1. F. | 1 and under 5. M. | 1 and under 5. F. | 5 and under 10. M. | 5 and under 10. F. | 10 and under 20. M. | 10 and under 20. F. | 20 and under 50. M. | 20 and under 50. F. | 50 and under 80. M. | 50 and under 80. F. | 80 and under 100. M | 80 and under 100. F. | 100 & over. M | 100 & over. F. | Age unknown. M | Age unknown. F. | Born in State. | N. England States. | Middle States. | Southern States. | Southwest'n States. | Northwest'n States. |
|---|---|---|---|---|---|---|---|---|---|---|---|---|---|---|---|---|---|---|---|---|---|---|---|---|---|
| 1 | Abscess | ... | 1 | 1 | 2 | ... | ... | 1 | 1 | ... | 1 | 2 | 2 | ... | ... | ... | ... | ... | ... | 10 | 1 | ... | ... | ... | ... |
| 2 | Accident, not specif'd | 3 | 3 | 10 | 7 | 7 | 7 | 12 | 1 | 39 | 3 | 14 | 3 | 1 | 1 | ... | ... | ... | ... | 77 | ... | 11 | 2 | ... | ... |
| 3 | ....do....burned | ... | ... | ... | ... | 1 | ... | 1 | ... | ... | ... | ... | ... | ... | ... | ... | ... | ... | ... | 1 | ... | 1 | ... | ... | ... |
| 4 | ....do....drowned | ... | ... | 5 | 2 | 7 | 2 | 12 | ... | 21 | 1 | 1 | ... | ... | ... | ... | ... | ... | ... | 39 | ... | 4 | ... | ... | ... |
| 5 | ....do.. .scalded | ... | ... | ... | 1 | ... | ... | ... | ... | ... | ... | ... | ... | ... | ... | ... | ... | ... | ... | 1 | ... | ... | ... | ... | ... |
| 6 | Apoplexy | ... | ... | ... | 1 | ... | ... | ... | 1 | 18 | 12 | 14 | 12 | 3 | 1 | ... | ... | ... | ... | 46 | 5 | 2 | 1 | ... | ... |
| 7 | Asthma | 1 | ... | ... | 1 | ... | ... | 1 | ... | ... | ... | 3 | 1 | 3 | ... | ... | ... | ... | ... | 7 | ... | ... | ... | ... | ... |
| 8 | Bladder, disease of | ... | ... | ... | ... | ... | ... | ... | ... | 1 | ... | 2 | 1 | ... | ... | ... | ... | ... | ... | 3 | ... | 1 | ... | ... | ... |
| 9 | Bowels.....do | 8 | 6 | 5 | 3 | 1 | ... | ... | 1 | 3 | ... | 4 | ... | 1 | ... | ... | ... | ... | ... | 26 | ... | 2 | ... | ... | ... |
| 10 | Brain......do | 2 | 10 | 3 | ... | ... | 4 | 1 | 2 | 2 | ... | 5 | 1 | ... | ... | ... | ... | ... | ... | 24 | 1 | 2 | ... | ... | ... |
| 11 | Bronchitis | 1 | 1 | ... | ... | 1 | 1 | ... | 2 | 2 | ... | 3 | 1 | ... | ... | ... | ... | ... | 1 | 12 | ... | ... | ... | ... | ... |
| 12 | Cancer | ... | ... | ... | ... | 1 | ... | ... | ... | 2 | 5 | 10 | 13 | 1 | ... | ... | ... | ... | ... | 29 | 1 | ... | ... | ... | ... |
| 13 | Carbuncle | ... | ... | ... | ... | ... | ... | ... | ... | 1 | ... | ... | ... | ... | ... | ... | ... | ... | ... | ... | ... | 1 | ... | ... | ... |
| 14 | Catarrh | 7 | 4 | 9 | 5 | ... | 1 | ... | ... | ... | 2 | 1 | 1 | ... | ... | ... | ... | ... | ... | 29 | ... | 1 | ... | ... | ... |
| 15 | Chicken pox | ... | ... | ... | 1 | ... | ... | ... | ... | ... | ... | ... | ... | ... | ... | ... | ... | ... | ... | 1 | ... | ... | ... | ... | ... |
| 16 | Childbirth | ... | ... | ... | ... | ... | ... | ... | ... | ... | 48 | ... | ... | ... | ... | ... | ... | ... | ... | 89 | ... | 2 | ... | ... | ... |
| 17 | Cholera | 23 | 12 | 42 | 42 | 24 | 17 | 36 | 25 | 196 | 115 | 75 | 68 | 4 | 3 | ... | ... | 2 | 2 | 460 | 7 | 61 | 2 | ... | ... |
| 18 | ...do..infantum | 40 | 24 | 21 | 20 | ... | ... | ... | ... | ... | ... | ... | ... | ... | ... | ... | ... | ... | ... | 102 | ... | 2 | ... | ... | ... |
| 19 | ...do..morbus | 5 | 1 | 3 | 1 | 1 | ... | ... | 1 | 1 | 3 | 2 | 3 | 1 | 2 | ... | ... | ... | ... | 21 | ... | 3 | ... | ... | ... |
| 20 | Chorea | ... | ... | ... | ... | ... | ... | ... | 1 | 1 | ... | ... | ... | ... | ... | ... | ... | ... | ... | 2 | ... | ... | ... | ... | ... |
| 21 | Colic | ... | 2 | ... | ... | ... | ... | ... | ... | 2 | ... | 3 | 2 | ... | ... | ... | ... | ... | ... | 8 | ... | ... | ... | ... | ... |
| 22 | Congestion of brain | 1 | 1 | 4 | 4 | 1 | 2 | 2 | ... | 1 | 1 | 2 | 1 | ... | ... | ... | ... | ... | ... | 19 | ... | ... | ... | ... | ... |
| 23 | ....do......lungs | ... | ... | ... | ... | ... | ... | ... | ... | 1 | ... | ... | ... | ... | ... | ... | ... | ... | ... | 1 | ... | ... | ... | ... | ... |
| 24 | Consumption | 30 | 39 | 21 | 27 | 8 | 8 | 33 | 54 | 211 | 222 | 141 | 107 | 8 | 2 | ... | ... | 2 | 2 | 743 | 8 | 73 | 2 | 1 | ... |
| 25 | Convulsions | 35 | 32 | 27 | 20 | 4 | 6 | 2 | ... | 12 | 3 | 4 | 8 | 1 | 1 | ... | ... | ... | ... | 145 | ... | 7 | ... | ... | 1 |
| 26 | Cramp | ... | ... | 1 | 2 | ... | ... | ... | ... | ... | ... | 1 | ... | ... | ... | ... | ... | ... | ... | 4 | ... | ... | ... | ... | ... |
| 27 | Croup | 23 | 20 | 58 | 61 | 14 | 13 | 1 | 1 | ... | ... | ... | ... | ... | ... | ... | ... | ... | ... | 172 | 1 | 14 | ... | ... | ... |
| 28 | Debility | 4 | 1 | ... | ... | ... | ... | ... | ... | 1 | ... | 1 | ... | ... | ... | ... | ... | ... | ... | 5 | ... | 1 | ... | ... | ... |
| 29 | Diarrhœa | 23 | 15 | 17 | 14 | 5 | 1 | 3 | 3 | 6 | 2 | 8 | 12 | 1 | 3 | ... | ... | ... | ... | 90 | 3 | 11 | ... | ... | ... |
| 30 | Dropsy | 13 | 8 | 17 | 12 | 5 | 6 | 6 | 6 | 23 | 41 | 43 | 48 | 12 | 8 | ... | ... | ... | 1 | 214 | 2 | 13 | 1 | ... | ... |
| 31 | Dysentery | 47 | 45 | 124 | 122 | 27 | 25 | 30 | 12 | 37 | 43 | 25 | 44 | 2 | 6 | ... | ... | 1 | ... | 514 | 3 | 38 | 2 | 1 | ... |
| 32 | Dyspepsia | 2 | ... | 2 | 4 | ... | ... | 1 | 1 | ... | 4 | 3 | 4 | ... | ... | ... | ... | ... | ... | 20 | ... | ... | ... | ... | ... |
| 33 | Epilepsy | 1 | ... | 1 | ... | ... | ... | 3 | ... | ... | ... | 1 | 1 | ... | 1 | ... | ... | ... | ... | 8 | ... | ... | ... | ... | ... |
| 34 | Erysipelas | 6 | 5 | 4 | 5 | 1 | 2 | 2 | 2 | ... | 7 | 5 | 6 | 2 | 1 | ... | ... | ... | ... | 41 | ... | 3 | ... | ... | ... |
| 35 | Executed | ... | ... | ... | ... | ... | ... | ... | ... | 1 | ... | ... | ... | ... | ... | ... | ... | ... | ... | ... | ... | ... | ... | ... | ... |
| 36 | Eyes, disease of | ... | ... | ... | ... | ... | ... | ... | ... | ... | ... | ... | 1 | ... | ... | ... | ... | ... | ... | 1 | ... | ... | ... | ... | ... |
| 37 | Fever, not specified | 10 | 5 | 16 | 8 | 5 | 1 | 12 | 14 | 36 | 25 | 15 | 11 | 4 | ... | ... | ... | 1 | ... | 158 | ... | 2 | ... | ... | ... |
| 38 | ..do..bilious | 2 | 1 | 3 | 1 | 3 | 3 | 3 | 4 | 19 | 6 | 6 | 7 | ... | 2 | ... | ... | ... | ... | 40 | ... | 8 | ... | ... | ... |
| 39 | ..do..brain | 12 | 5 | 8 | 5 | 6 | 1 | 5 | 1 | 12 | 7 | ... | 2 | ... | ... | ... | ... | ... | ... | 63 | ... | 1 | ... | ... | ... |
| 40 | ..do..catarrhal | 5 | ... | 10 | 5 | 2 | 2 | ... | ... | ... | ... | ... | ... | ... | ... | ... | ... | ... | ... | 21 | ... | 3 | ... | ... | ... |
| 41 | ..do..congestive | ... | ... | 1 | 1 | ... | ... | 2 | 2 | 10 | 6 | 2 | 2 | ... | ... | ... | ... | ... | ... | 25 | ... | 1 | ... | ... | ... |
| 42 | ..do..intermittent | ... | ... | 1 | 1 | ... | 1 | ... | 1 | 1 | 1 | ... | 1 | ... | ... | ... | ... | ... | ... | 3 | ... | 1 | ... | ... | ... |
| 43 | ..do..puerperal | ... | ... | ... | ... | ... | ... | ... | ... | ... | 6 | ... | ... | ... | ... | ... | ... | ... | ... | 5 | ... | 1 | ... | ... | ... |
| 44 | ..do..remittent | ... | ... | 1 | 1 | ... | 1 | 1 | 1 | 4 | ... | ... | 1 | ... | ... | ... | ... | ... | ... | 7 | ... | 1 | ... | ... | ... |
| 45 | ..do..scarlet | 5 | 3 | 42 | 25 | 16 | 20 | 3 | 5 | ... | 1 | ... | 1 | ... | ... | ... | ... | ... | ... | 111 | ... | 8 | ... | ... | ... |
| 46 | ..do..ship | ... | 1 | ... | 3 | ... | 1 | ... | 1 | 1 | ... | ... | ... | ... | ... | ... | ... | ... | ... | 5 | ... | ... | ... | ... | ... |
| 47 | ..do..typhus | ... | 1 | 4 | 3 | 3 | 2 | 11 | 11 | 34 | 16 | 11 | 9 | 1 | 1 | ... | ... | ... | ... | 80 | 3 | 10 | ... | ... | ... |
| 48 | ..do..yellow | ... | ... | ... | ... | ... | ... | ... | ... | 1 | ... | ... | ... | ... | ... | ... | ... | ... | ... | ... | ... | 1 | ... | ... | ... |

SECTION OF THE STATE OF NEW JERSEY—Continued.

| NATIVITIES. | | | | | SEASON OF DECEASE. | | | | DURATION OF SICKNESS. | | | | WHITES. | | | COLORED. | | | | | | | | | |
|---|---|---|---|---|---|---|---|---|---|---|---|---|---|---|---|---|---|---|---|---|---|---|---|---|---|
| | | | | | | | | | | | | | | | | Slaves. | | | | Free. | | | | | |
| | | | | | | | | | | | | | | | | Black. | | Mulatto. | | Black. | | Mul. | | | |
| California and Territories. | Ireland. | Germany. | Other foreign countries. | Unknown. | Spring. | Summer. | Autumn. | Winter. | Under 1 week. | 1 week and under 1 month. | 1 month and under 3 months. | 3 months and over. | Males. | Females. | Total. | M. | F. | M. | F. | M. | F. | M | F. | Aggregate deaths. | |
| | | | | | 14 | 5 | | 6 | 8 | 13 | 1 | 2 | 11 | 12 | 23 | | | | | | 1 | | 1 | 25 | 1 |
| | | | | | 1 | 2 | 2 | | 5 | | | | 2 | 2 | 4 | | | | | 1 | | | | 5 | 2 |
| | | | | | 1 | | | | | 1 | | | 1 | | 1 | | | | | | | | | 1 | 3 |
| | | | | | 3 | 1 | 3 | 3 | 2 | 2 | 1 | 5 | 5 | 4 | 9 | | | | | | 1 | | | 10 | 4 |
| | | | | | 11 | 3 | 5 | 3 | 1 | 3 | 4 | 11 | 6 | 14 | 20 | | | | | 2 | 1 | | | 28 | 5 |
| | 1 | | | | | 1 | | 3 | | 4 | | | 3 | 1 | 4 | | | | | | | | | 4 | 6 |
| | | | | | 5 | 1 | 1 | 3 | | 5 | | 5 | 3 | 7 | 10 | | | | | | | | | 10 | 7 |
| | | | | | | 2 | 1 | 1 | 3 | | | | 4 | | 4 | | | | | | | | | 4 | 8 |
| | | | | | | 11 | 7 | 2 | 6 | 9 | 3 | | 10 | 11 | 21 | | | | | | | | | 21 | 9 |
| | | | | | | 1 | | | 1 | | | | 1 | | 1 | | | | | | | | | 1 | 10 |
| | 1 | | | | | 5 | 1 | 1 | 2 | 4 | | | 1 | 6 | 7 | | | | | | | | | 7 | 11 |
| | | | | | 1 | 1 | 1 | 1 | 2 | 2 | | | 2 | 1 | 3 | | | | | | 1 | | | 4 | 12 |
| | | | | | 1 | | | 1 | 1 | | | 1 | | 1 | 1 | | | | | | | 1 | | 2 | 13 |
| | | | | | | 1 | | | | | | | | 1 | 1 | | | | | | | | | 1 | 14 |
| | | | | | 1 | | | | | 1 | | | | 1 | 1 | | | | | | | | | 1 | 15 |
| | | | | | 5 | 1 | 1 | | 1 | 4 | 1 | | 4 | 2 | 6 | | | | | 1 | | | | 7 | 16 |
| | 4 | 1 | 2 | 2 | 79 | 79 | 85 | 37 | 72 | 43 | 12 | 15 | 145 | 119 | 264 | | | | | 14 | 7 | 1 | 1 | 287 | 17 |
| 1 | 33 | 11 | 26 | 5 | 529 | 711 | 740 | 328 | 624 | 700 | 192 | 308 | 1171 | 1036 | 2207 | | | | | 57 | 44 | 15 | 6 | 2329 | |

THE STATE OF NEW JERSEY—AGGREGATE.

| California and Territories. | Ireland. | Germany. | Other foreign countries. | Unknown. | Spring. | Summer. | Autumn. | Winter. | Under 1 week. | 1 week and under 1 month. | 1 month and under 3 months. | 3 months and over. | Males. | Females. | Total. | Slaves Black M. | Slaves Black F. | Slaves Mulatto M. | Slaves Mulatto F. | Free Black M. | Free Black F. | Free Mul. M | Free Mul. F. | Aggregate deaths. | |
|---|---|---|---|---|---|---|---|---|---|---|---|---|---|---|---|---|---|---|---|---|---|---|---|---|---|
| | | | | | 3 | 3 | 3 | 1 | 1 | 6 | 3 | | 4 | 7 | 11 | | | | | | | | | 11 | 1 |
| | 15 | 2 | 4 | | 40 | 26 | 21 | 23 | 75 | 16 | 3 | 7 | 83 | 23 | 106 | | | | | 3 | 1 | | 1 | 111 | 2 |
| | | | | | | | | 2 | 2 | | | | 2 | | 2 | | | | | | | | | 2 | 3 |
| | 8 | | | | 7 | 24 | 17 | 3 | 51 | | | | 45 | 5 | 50 | | | | | 1 | | | | 51 | 4 |
| | | | | | 1 | | | | 1 | | | | | 1 | 1 | | | | | | | | | 1 | 5 |
| | | 2 | 1 | | 20 | 17 | 7 | 13 | 48 | 2 | 1 | 1 | 28 | 25 | 53 | | | | | 2 | 2 | | | 57 | 6 |
| | | | 3 | | 3 | 3 | | 4 | 2 | 3 | | 5 | 8 | 2 | 10 | | | | | | | | | 10 | 7 |
| | | | | | 2 | 1 | | 1 | 1 | 1 | | 2 | 3 | 1 | 4 | | | | | | | | | 4 | 8 |
| | 3 | | 1 | | 6 | 11 | 11 | 4 | 8 | 12 | 6 | 4 | 22 | 9 | 31 | | | | | | 1 | | | 32 | 9 |
| | 2 | | 1 | | 11 | 7 | 5 | 7 | 8 | 14 | 3 | 4 | 18 | 17 | 30 | | | | | | | | | 30 | 10 |
| | 1 | | | | 3 | 1 | 6 | 2 | 2 | 1 | 3 | 4 | 7 | 6 | 13 | | | | | | | | | 13 | 11 |
| | 2 | | | | 5 | 12 | 9 | 6 | | 2 | 3 | 24 | 13 | 18 | 31 | | | | | 1 | | | | 32 | 12 |
| | | | | | | | 1 | | | 1 | | | 1 | | 1 | | | | | | | | | 1 | 13 |
| | | | | | 13 | 5 | 4 | 8 | 9 | 14 | 1 | 2 | 16 | 12 | 28 | | | | | 1 | 1 | | | 30 | 14 |
| | | | | | | | | 1 | | 1 | | | | 1 | 1 | | | | | | | | | 1 | 15 |
| | 5 | 2 | | | 16 | 16 | 11 | 3 | 22 | 18 | 3 | 2 | | 48 | 48 | | | | | | | | | 48 | 16 |
| | 102 | 16 | 36 | 2 | 9 | 355 | 318 | 3 | 569 | 62 | 4 | | 388 | 268 | 656 | | 1 | | | 10 | 14 | 4 | 1 | 686 | 17 |
| | | | 1 | | 2 | 29 | 70 | 4 | 46 | 41 | 8 | 3 | 60 | 44 | 104 | | | | | 1 | | | | 105 | 18 |
| | | | | | 2 | 13 | 9 | | 17 | 4 | 1 | | 13 | 11 | 24 | | | | | | | | | 24 | 19 |
| | | | | | 1 | 1 | | | | 1 | | 1 | 1 | 1 | 2 | | | | | | | | | 2 | 20 |
| | | 1 | | | 2 | 2 | 1 | 4 | 5 | 2 | | 1 | 5 | 4 | 9 | | | | | | | | | 9 | 21 |
| | | | 1 | | 4 | 7 | 8 | 1 | 4 | 13 | 1 | 1 | 11 | 9 | 20 | | | | | | | | | 20 | 22 |
| | | | | | | | | 1 | 1 | | | | 1 | | 1 | | | | | | | | | 1 | 23 |
| | 41 | 11 | 29 | 7 | 246 | 226 | 238 | 202 | 22 | 112 | 98 | 565 | 424 | 420 | 844 | 4 | | | | 18 | 39 | 8 | 2 | 915 | 24 |
| | 2 | | | | 50 | 38 | 43 | 22 | 92 | 32 | 5 | 6 | 82 | 68 | 150 | | | | | 2 | 2 | 1 | | 155 | 25 |
| | | | | | 1 | 1 | | 2 | 4 | | | | 2 | 2 | 4 | | | | | | | | | 4 | 26 |
| | 2 | 1 | 1 | | 46 | 33 | 40 | 72 | 135 | 46 | 3 | 1 | 95 | 93 | 188 | | | | | 1 | 2 | | | 191 | 27 |
| | | | 1 | | | 5 | | 2 | 2 | 2 | | 1 | 6 | 1 | 7 | | | | | | | | | 7 | 28 |
| | 4 | 1 | 4 | | 9 | 34 | 63 | 4 | 28 | 43 | 13 | 15 | 59 | 48 | 107 | | | | | 3 | 1 | 1 | 1 | 113 | 29 |
| | 5 | 2 | 11 | 1 | 74 | 54 | 62 | 59 | 25 | 44 | 34 | 117 | 105 | 124 | 229 | | | | | 12 | 6 | 2 | | 249 | 30 |
| | 22 | 5 | 4 | 1 | 18 | 89 | 429 | 54 | 155 | 328 | 42 | 6 | 288 | 295 | 583 | | | | | 5 | 1 | | 1 | 590 | 31 |
| | 1 | | | | 1 | 2 | 15 | | | | 6 | 11 | 8 | 13 | 21 | | | | | | | | | 21 | 32 |
| | | | | | 1 | 2 | 3 | 1 | 1 | | | 3 | 6 | 2 | 8 | | | | | | | | | 8 | 33 |
| | 1 | | 3 | | 21 | 14 | 10 | 3 | 15 | 21 | 5 | 5 | 19 | 26 | 45 | | | | | 1 | 2 | | | 48 | 34 |
| | | | 1 | | 1 | | | | 1 | | | | 1 | | 1 | | | | | | | | | 1 | 35 |
| | | | | | | | | | | | | | | 1 | 1 | | | | | | | | | 1 | 36 |
| | 2 | 1 | | | 42 | 32 | 56 | 33 | 14 | 126 | 10 | 4 | 97 | 63 | 160 | | | | | 2 | | | 1 | 168 | 37 |
| | 6 | 2 | 4 | | 14 | 10 | 24 | 12 | 10 | 34 | 7 | 1 | 34 | 24 | 58 | | | | | | | 2 | | 60 | 38 |
| | | | | | 18 | 17 | 24 | 10 | 16 | 39 | 4 | 1 | 42 | 19 | 61 | | | | | 1 | 2 | | | 64 | 39 |
| | | | | | 13 | 2 | 3 | 6 | 5 | 15 | 1 | | 15 | 7 | 22 | | | | | 2 | | | | 24 | 40 |
| | | | | | 5 | 10 | 6 | 5 | 3 | 21 | 2 | | 13 | 10 | 23 | | | | | 2 | 1 | | | 26 | 41 |
| | 3 | | | | 1 | 2 | 3 | 1 | 1 | 4 | 1 | 1 | 2 | 5 | 7 | | | | | | | | | 7 | 42 |
| | | | | | 2 | 3 | 1 | | | 5 | | | | 6 | 6 | | | | | | | | | 6 | 43 |
| | 1 | | 1 | | | 1 | 9 | | 1 | 9 | | | 6 | 3 | 9 | | | | | | 1 | | | 10 | 44 |
| | | | 2 | | 46 | 40 | 14 | 21 | 55 | 50 | 6 | | 65 | 54 | 119 | | | | | 1 | 1 | | | 121 | 45 |
| | 2 | | | | 2 | 2 | 3 | | 5 | 1 | | 1 | 1 | 6 | 7 | | | | | | | | | 7 | 46 |
| | 9 | 1 | 3 | 1 | 25 | 24 | 36 | 22 | 17 | 70 | 15 | 1 | 58 | 42 | 100 | | | | | 5 | | 1 | 1 | 107 | 47 |
| | | | | | | | 1 | | 1 | | | | 1 | | 1 | | | | | | | | | 1 | 48 |

## CLASSIFICATION OF DEATHS IN

| | Cause of death. | AGES. | | | | | | | | | | | | | | | | | | NATIVITIES. | | | | | |
|---|---|---|---|---|---|---|---|---|---|---|---|---|---|---|---|---|---|---|---|---|---|---|---|---|---|
| | | Under 1. | | 1 and under 5. | | 5 and under 10. | | 10 and under 20. | | 20 and under 50. | | 50 and under 80. | | 80 and under 100. | | 100 & over. | | Age unknown. | | Born in State. | N. England States. | Middle States. | Southern States. | Southwest'n States. | Northwest'n States. |
| | | M. | F. | M. | F. | M. | F. | M. | F. | M. | F. | M. | F. | M | F. | M | F. | M | F. | | | | | | |
| 1 | Frozen | | | | | | | | | 1 | | 1 | | | | | | | | 1 | | 1 | | | |
| 2 | Gout | | | | | | | | | 1 | | 2 | | | 1 | | | | | 4 | | | | | |
| 3 | Gravel | | | | | | | | | | | 5 | | 2 | | | | | | 6 | | | | | |
| 4 | Head, disease of | | | 1 | | 1 | | | | | | | | | | | | | | 2 | | | | | |
| 5 | Heart....do | 5 | 4 | 1 | 1 | | 1 | 7 | 2 | 7 | 8 | 14 | 21 | 1 | | | | | | 58 | 1 | 6 | | 1 | |
| 6 | Hemorrhage | 1 | | 1 | | | | 1 | 1 | 11 | 4 | 1 | 2 | | | | | | | 16 | 1 | 2 | | | |
| 7 | Hernia | 2 | | | | | | | | | | 1 | | 1 | | | | | | 3 | | | | | |
| 8 | Hives | | | | 1 | 1 | | | | | 1 | | | | | | | | | 3 | | | | | |
| 9 | Hooping cough | 24 | 15 | 15 | 27 | 2 | 4 | 1 | | | | | | | | | | | | 81 | 3 | 3 | | | 1 |
| 10 | Hydrocephalus | 20 | 15 | 30 | 22 | 6 | 1 | 2 | 1 | 2 | | | | | | | | | | 91 | 1 | 4 | | | |
| 11 | Hydrophobia | | | | | | | | | | | 1 | | | | | | | | 1 | | | | | |
| 12 | Inflamat'n, not spec'd | 20 | 12 | 14 | 7 | 3 | 4 | 4 | 5 | 6 | 5 | 6 | 5 | | | | | | | 83 | | 4 | | | |
| 13 | ....do.....bowels | 10 | 10 | 14 | 16 | 4 | 2 | 6 | 1 | 8 | 6 | 16 | 8 | | | | | 1 | | 91 | | 2 | | | |
| 14 | ....do.....brain | 14 | 10 | 17 | 17 | 6 | 4 | 3 | 5 | 11 | 5 | 3 | 2 | | | | | | | 85 | | 8 | | | |
| 15 | ....do.....stomach | | | | 1 | | | | | | | | | | | | | | | 1 | | | | | |
| 16 | Influenza | | 3 | | 2 | | | | | | | | | 2 | 1 | | | | | 8 | | | | | |
| 17 | Insanity | | | | | | | | | 4 | 1 | 4 | 1 | | | | | | | 9 | | | | | |
| 18 | Intemperance | | | | | | | | | 12 | | 12 | | 1 | | | | | | 19 | | | | | |
| 19 | Jaundice | | 1 | 1 | | | 1 | | | 2 | | 1 | 3 | 1 | | | | | | 9 | | | | | |
| 20 | Kidneys, disease of | | 1 | | | | | | | | 1 | 3 | | 1 | | | | | | 3 | | 2 | | | |
| 21 | Killed | | | | | | | 2 | | 9 | | | | | | | | | | 5 | | 4 | | | |
| 22 | Leprosy | | | | | | | | | 1 | | | | | | | | | | | | | | | |
| 23 | Lightning | | | 1 | | | | | | | | | | | | | | | | 1 | | | | | |
| 24 | Liver, disease of | 1 | 4 | 2 | 1 | 1 | | 1 | 2 | 11 | 5 | 5 | 4 | | | | | | | 32 | | 1 | | | |
| 25 | Lockjaw | | | | | | | 2 | | 2 | | 1 | | | | | | | | 4 | | | | | |
| 26 | Lungs, disease of | 3 | 3 | 1 | 5 | 1 | | | | | 1 | 1 | | | | | | | | 13 | | 1 | | | |
| 27 | Mania-a-potu | | | | | | | | | 2 | | 3 | | | | | | | | 4 | | | | | |
| 28 | Measles | 6 | 2 | 14 | 12 | 1 | | 1 | 4 | 1 | 6 | | | | | | | | | 40 | 1 | 2 | | | |
| 29 | Mortification | | 1 | | | | | | | | | 1 | 1 | 1 | 1 | | | | | 4 | | | | | |
| 30 | Mumps | | | 2 | | | 1 | 1 | 1 | | | | | | | | | | | 4 | | 1 | | | |
| 31 | Murder | | | | | | | | | 1 | | 1 | 1 | | | | | 1 | | 3 | | 1 | | | |
| 32 | Neuralgia | | | | | | 1 | | 1 | 2 | | | 1 | | 1 | | | | | 5 | | 1 | | | |
| 33 | Old age | | | | | | | | | | 1 | 42 | 47 | 87 | 93 | | | | 2 | 224 | 6 | 20 | 2 | | |
| 34 | Paralysis | | | | | | | 1 | | 6 | 2 | 23 | 15 | 11 | 15 | | | | 1 | 59 | | 7 | 2 | | |
| 35 | Peritonitis | | | 1 | | | | | | | | | | | | | | | | 1 | | | | | |
| 36 | Piles | | | | 1 | | | | | | | | 1 | | | | | | | 2 | | | | | |
| 37 | Pleurisy | | 2 | | 2 | | | 1 | 1 | 7 | 5 | 8 | 9 | 4 | 2 | | | 1 | | 33 | | 3 | | | |
| 38 | Pneumonia | 24 | 15 | 21 | 18 | 2 | 2 | 2 | | 12 | 6 | 17 | 7 | 1 | 2 | | | | | 111 | | 6 | | | |
| 39 | Poison | | | 3 | 1 | | | | | | 2 | | 1 | | | | | | | 6 | | 1 | | | |
| 40 | Prematurity of birth | 1 | 2 | | | | | | | | | | | | | | | | | 3 | | | | | |
| 41 | Quinsy | | | | | | | | | 2 | 1 | | | | | | | | | 3 | | | | | |
| 42 | Rheumatism | | 1 | | | 2 | 1 | 2 | | 5 | 1 | 5 | 5 | | | | | | | 18 | 1 | | | | |
| 43 | Scrofula | 3 | 4 | 4 | 5 | | 1 | 3 | 5 | 2 | 3 | 1 | | 1 | 1 | | | | 1 | 30 | 1 | 2 | | | 1 |
| 44 | Scurvy | | | | | | | | | 1 | | | | | | | | | | 1 | | | | | |
| 45 | Small pox | 2 | 4 | 10 | 1 | 6 | 3 | 1 | 2 | 7 | 5 | 3 | | | | | | | | 35 | | 4 | | | |
| 46 | Spine, disease of | 1 | | 5 | | 1 | 2 | 2 | 3 | 4 | 7 | 1 | 2 | | | | | | | 26 | | 2 | | | |
| 47 | Stillborn | 3 | 1 | | | | | | | | | | | | | | | | | 4 | | | | | |
| 48 | Suicide | | | | | | | 1 | | 3 | 1 | 3 | | | | | | | | 3 | 1 | 4 | | | |
| 49 | Summer complaint | 9 | 9 | 11 | 10 | 1 | 3 | | | | | | | | | | | | | 40 | | 3 | | | |
| 50 | Sun, stroke of | | | | | | | | | 3 | 1 | 2 | | | | | | | | 2 | | | | | |
| 51 | Teething | 5 | 5 | 10 | 12 | | | | | | | | | | | | | | | 28 | | 2 | | | |
| 52 | Tetanus | | 1 | | | | | | | | | | | | | | | | | | | | | | |
| 53 | Throat, disease of | 5 | | 4 | 3 | 1 | 1 | 1 | 2 | | 1 | 1 | | | | | | | | 16 | | 1 | | | |
| 54 | Thrush | 7 | 12 | | 1 | | | | | | | | | | | | | | | 19 | | 1 | | | |
| 55 | Tumor | | | 1 | | | | | | 1 | 2 | | | | | | | | | 4 | | | | | |
| 56 | Ulcer | | | 1 | | | | 1 | | 1 | 1 | | 1 | | | | | | | 2 | | 2 | | | |
| 57 | Uterus, disease of | | | | | | | | | | 3 | | 1 | | | | | | | 3 | | 1 | | | |
| 58 | White swelling | | | | | | | | | | 1 | | | | | | | | | 1 | | | | | |
| 59 | Worms | | | 5 | 5 | 3 | | | | | | | | | | | | | | 10 | | 2 | | | |
| 60 | Unknown | 113 | 103 | 51 | 45 | 25 | 16 | 17 | 9 | 60 | 72 | 86 | 49 | 9 | 4 | | | 5 | 3 | 607 | 3 | 18 | | | 1 |
| | Total | 588 | 486 | 702 | 626 | 210 | 175 | 247 | 199 | 903 | 739 | 681 | 561 | 168 | 153 | | | 14 | 13 | 5412 | 54 | 412 | 14 | 3 | 4 |

## CLASSIFICATION OF DEATHS IN NORTHERN AND

*Embracing the following counties: Cayuga, Chatauque, Clinton, Erie, Essex, Franklin,*

| | | | | | | | | | | | | | | | | | | | | | | | | | |
|---|---|---|---|---|---|---|---|---|---|---|---|---|---|---|---|---|---|---|---|---|---|---|---|---|---|
| 1 | Abscess | | | 1 | | | | | | 2 | 2 | 1 | 1 | | | | | | | 4 | 2 | | | | |
| 2 | Accident not specif'd | 2 | 1 | 15 | 2 | 6 | 4 | 18 | | 42 | 3 | 14 | 4 | 1 | | | | | | 70 | 13 | 3 | | | |
| 3 | ...do...burned | | | 3 | 7 | 3 | 6 | | | | | 1 | 2 | | 1 | | | | | 18 | | 2 | | | |
| 4 | ...do...drowned | 1 | | 5 | 1 | 17 | 4 | 9 | | 28 | 3 | 3 | 1 | | | | | | | 36 | 8 | | | | |

## IE STATE OF NEW JERSEY—AGGREGATE—Continued.

| NATIVITIES. ritories. | Ireland. | Germany. | Other foreign countries. | Unknown. | SEASON OF DECEASE. Spring. | Summer. | Autumn. | Winter. | DURATION OF SICKNESS. Under 1 week. | 1 week and under 1 month. | 1 month and under 3 months. | 3 months and over. | WHITES. Males. | Females. | Total. | COLORED. Slaves. Black. M. | F. | Mulatto. M. | F. | Free. Black. M. | F. | Mul. M | F. | Aggregate deaths. | |
|---|---|---|---|---|---|---|---|---|---|---|---|---|---|---|---|---|---|---|---|---|---|---|---|---|---|
| | | | | | 2 | | | | | | | | 1 | | 1 | | | | | 1 | | | | 2 | 1 |
| | | | | | 2 | 1 | | 1 | | | 1 | 3 | 3 | 1 | 4 | | | | | | | | | 4 | 2 |
| | | | 1 | | 4 | 2 | | 1 | 1 | 4 | 1 | 1 | 7 | | 7 | | | | | | | | | 7 | 3 |
| | | | | | | 2 | | | | 2 | | | 2 | | 2 | | | | | | | | | 2 | 4 |
| | 2 | | 4 | | 18 | 14 | 15 | 25 | 28 | 19 | 3 | 15 | 33 | 37 | 70 | | | | | 2 | | | | 72 | 5 |
| | 1 | | 1 | 1 | 2 | 7 | 8 | 5 | 8 | 7 | 2 | 3 | 14 | 7 | 21 | | | | | | | 1 | | 22 | 6 |
| | 1 | | | | 1 | 1 | 2 | | 1 | 1 | | 2 | 4 | | 4 | | | | | | | | | 4 | 7 |
| | | | | | 1 | 1 | | 1 | 2 | 1 | | | 1 | 1 | 2 | | | | | | 1 | | | 3 | 8 |
| | | | | | 29 | 29 | 21 | 9 | 6 | 53 | 12 | 8 | 38 | 43 | 81 | | | | | 3 | 2 | 1 | 1 | 88 | 9 |
| | 1 | | 2 | | 29 | 16 | 35 | 18 | 10 | 63 | 12 | 10 | 60 | 37 | 97 | | | | | | 2 | | | 99 | 10 |
| | | | | | 1 | | | | 1 | | | | 1 | | 1 | | | | | | | | | 1 | 11 |
| 1 | 1 | | 2 | | 40 | 20 | 19 | 11 | 29 | 42 | 12 | 2 | 51 | 37 | 88 | | | | | 2 | 1 | | | 91 | 12 |
| | 5 | 1 | 3 | | 29 | 18 | 37 | 17 | 29 | 51 | 10 | 7 | 58 | 42 | 100 | | | | | 1 | 1 | | | 102 | 13 |
| | 1 | 1 | 2 | | 25 | 34 | 25 | 13 | 26 | 54 | 8 | 2 | 51 | 41 | 92 | | | | | 3 | 2 | | | 97 | 14 |
| | | | | | 1 | | | | | | | | | 1 | 1 | | | | | | | | | 1 | 15 |
| | | | | | 5 | 2 | 1 | | 2 | 5 | 1 | | 2 | 6 | 8 | | | | | | | | | 8 | 16 |
| | 1 | | | | 2 | 1 | 2 | 5 | | 2 | | 3 | 8 | 2 | 10 | | | | | | | | | 10 | 17 |
| | 1 | | 4 | 1 | 5 | 5 | 8 | 7 | 6 | 2 | 1 | 4 | 24 | | 24 | | | | | 1 | | | | 25 | 18 |
| | | 1 | | | 3 | 2 | 3 | 2 | 2 | 3 | 1 | 4 | 5 | 5 | 10 | | | | | | | | | 10 | 19 |
| | 1 | | | | 3 | 1 | 1 | 1 | | 4 | 1 | 1 | 3 | 2 | 5 | | | | | 1 | | | | 6 | 20 |
| | | 1 | 1 | | 4 | 2 | 2 | 3 | 10 | | 1 | | 11 | | 11 | | | | | | | | | 11 | 21 |
| | | | 1 | | | | 1 | | | | | 1 | 1 | | 1 | | | | | | | | | 1 | 22 |
| | | | | | | | 1 | | 1 | | | | 1 | | 1 | | | | | | | | | 1 | 23 |
| | 3 | | 1 | | 11 | 11 | 11 | 4 | 3 | 10 | 12 | 10 | 20 | 15 | 35 | | | | | 1 | 1 | | | 37 | 24 |
| | 1 | | | | | 1 | 3 | 1 | 2 | 2 | | 1 | 5 | | 5 | | | | | | | | | 5 | 25 |
| | | | 1 | | 8 | | 2 | 5 | 8 | 5 | | 2 | 6 | 9 | 15 | | | | | | | | | 15 | 26 |
| | | | 1 | | 3 | 1 | 1 | | 2 | 2 | | 1 | 5 | | 5 | | | | | | | | | 5 | 27 |
| | 3 | | 1 | | 18 | 21 | 6 | 2 | 7 | 29 | 5 | 2 | 23 | 23 | 46 | | | | | | 1 | | | 47 | 28 |
| | | | 1 | | 2 | | 3 | | 1 | | 3 | 1 | 2 | 2 | 4 | | | | | | 1 | | | 5 | 29 |
| | | | | | 2 | 2 | 1 | | | 3 | 2 | | 3 | 2 | 5 | | | | | | | | | 5 | 30 |
| | | | | | | 1 | | 3 | 4 | | | | 2 | 1 | 3 | | | | | 1 | | | | 4 | 31 |
| | | | | | | 1 | 1 | 4 | | 4 | 1 | 1 | 2 | 4 | 6 | | | | | | | | | 6 | 32 |
| | 10 | 3 | 5 | 2 | 70 | 73 | 74 | 55 | 36 | 33 | 13 | 44 | 117 | 132 | 249 | 4 | 2 | | | 8 | 8 | | 1 | 272 | 33 |
| | 1 | 1 | 4 | | 18 | 18 | 13 | 24 | 22 | 18 | 8 | 19 | 41 | 31 | 72 | | 1 | | | | 1 | | | 74 | 34 |
| | | | | | | 1 | | | | | | 1 | 1 | | 1 | | | | | | | | | 1 | 35 |
| | | | | | 1 | 1 | | | | | | 2 | | 2 | 2 | | | | | | | | | 2 | 36 |
| | 3 | 1 | 2 | | 18 | 4 | 6 | 14 | 10 | 26 | 1 | | 21 | 21 | 42 | | | | | | | | | 42 | 37 |
| | 9 | | 3 | | 58 | 22 | 19 | 30 | 26 | 78 | 7 | 15 | 75 | 46 | 121 | | | | | 4 | 3 | | 1 | 129 | 38 |
| | | | | | 2 | 3 | 2 | | 6 | 1 | | | 2 | 4 | 6 | | | | | 1 | | | | 7 | 39 |
| | | | | | 2 | 1 | | | | 1 | | | 1 | 2 | 3 | | | | | | | | | 3 | 40 |
| | | | | | 1 | 1 | 1 | | | 2 | | 1 | 2 | 1 | 3 | | | | | | | | | 3 | 41 |
| | 2 | | 1 | | 6 | 5 | 5 | 6 | 2 | 6 | 4 | 10 | 14 | 7 | 21 | | | | | | 1 | | | 22 | 42 |
| | | | | | 15 | 6 | 8 | 4 | 1 | 6 | 4 | 19 | 12 | 19 | 31 | | | | | 2 | 1 | | | 34 | 43 |
| | | | | | | | 1 | | | | 1 | | 1 | | 1 | | | | | | | | | 1 | 44 |
| | 2 | | 3 | | 10 | 12 | 5 | 16 | 7 | 35 | 1 | | 26 | 15 | 41 | | | | | 2 | | 1 | | 44 | 45 |
| | | | | | 12 | 5 | 6 | 5 | | 9 | 3 | 15 | 13 | 14 | 27 | | | | | 1 | | | | 28 | 46 |
| | | | | | 2 | 1 | 1 | | | | | | 3 | 1 | 4 | | | | | | | | | 4 | 47 |
| | | | | | 2 | 2 | 1 | 3 | 5 | | | | 7 | 1 | 8 | | | | | | | | | 8 | 48 |
| | | | | | 2 | 17 | 21 | 2 | 12 | 16 | 5 | 3 | 21 | 22 | 43 | | | | | | | | | 43 | 49 |
| | 4 | | | | | 5 | | 1 | 4 | 1 | | | 5 | 1 | 6 | | | | | | | | | 6 | 50 |
| | 2 | | | | 5 | 9 | 15 | 3 | 6 | 15 | 5 | 1 | 14 | 17 | 31 | | | | | 1 | | | | 32 | 51 |
| | | 1 | | | | 1 | | | | 1 | | | | 1 | 1 | | | | | | | | | 1 | 52 |
| | 1 | | 1 | | 5 | 5 | 5 | 4 | 5 | 12 | 1 | | 12 | 5 | 17 | | | | | | 2 | | | 19 | 53 |
| | | | | | 4 | 4 | 11 | 1 | 8 | 11 | | | 7 | 13 | 20 | | | | | | | | | 20 | 54 |
| | | | | | 1 | | | 3 | 1 | 1 | | 2 | 1 | 2 | 3 | | | | | | | 1 | | 4 | 55 |
| | 1 | | | | 1 | 3 | 1 | | 1 | | 1 | 2 | 3 | 2 | 5 | | | | | | | | | 5 | 56 |
| | | | | | | 1 | 3 | | | 3 | | 1 | | 4 | 4 | | | | | | | | | 4 | 57 |
| | | | | | 1 | | | | | 1 | | | | 1 | 1 | | | | | | | | | 1 | 58 |
| | 1 | | | | 7 | 4 | 2 | | 4 | 7 | 1 | | 7 | 5 | 12 | | | | | 1 | | | | 13 | 59 |
| | 20 | 1 | 7 | 10 | 189 | 176 | 182 | 106 | 200 | 101 | 59 | 68 | 342 | 287 | 629 | | 1 | | | 23 | 12 | 1 | 1 | 667 | 60 |
| 1 | 317 | 58 | 164 | 26 | 1463 | 1750 | 2175 | 1037 | 2025 | 1963 | 495 | 1087 | 3348 | 2818 | 6166 | 8 | 5 | .... | .... | 133 | 117 | 24 | 12 | 6465 | |

## LAKE SECTION OF THE STATE OF NEW YORK.

*Gennesee, Jefferson, Monroe, Niagara, Orleans, Oswego, St. Lawrence, and Wayne.*

| | Ireland. | Germany. | Other foreign countries. | Unknown. | Spring. | Summer. | Autumn. | Winter. | Under 1 week. | 1 week and under 1 month. | 1 month and under 3 months. | 3 months and over. | Males. | Females. | Total. | Slaves Black M. | F. | Mulatto M. | F. | Free Black M. | F. | Mul. M | F. | Aggregate deaths. | |
|---|---|---|---|---|---|---|---|---|---|---|---|---|---|---|---|---|---|---|---|---|---|---|---|---|---|
| | 1 | | | | 2 | 1 | 2 | 2 | 2 | 2 | 1 | 2 | 4 | 3 | 7 | | | | | | | | | 7 | 1 |
| | 11 | 7 | 7 | 1 | 30 | 34 | 20 | 28 | 72 | 9 | 6 | 2 | 97 | 14 | 111 | | | | | 1 | | | | 112 | 2 |
| | | 1 | 2 | | 11 | 4 | 1 | 5 | 15 | 3 | 1 | 1 | 7 | 16 | 93 | | | | | | | | | 23 | 3 |
| | 19 | 3 | 6 | | 11 | 29 | 23 | 7 | 72 | | | | 63 | 9 | 72 | | | | | | | | | 72 | 4 |

## CLASSIFICATION OF DEATHS IN NORTHERN AND LAKE

| | Cause of Death. | AGES. Under 1. | | 1 and under 5. | | 5 and under 10. | | 10 and under 20. | | 20 and under 50. | | 50 and under 80. | | 80 and under 100. | | 100 & over. | | Age unknown. | | NATIVITIES. Born in State. | N. England States. | Middle States. | Southern States. | Southwest'n States. | Northwest'n States. |
|---|---|---|---|---|---|---|---|---|---|---|---|---|---|---|---|---|---|---|---|---|---|---|---|---|---|
| | | M. | F. | M. | F. | M. | F. | M. | F. | M. | F. | M. | F. | M. | F. | M | F. | M | F. | | | | | | |
| 1 | Accident, shot | ... | ... | ... | ... | ... | ... | ... | 1 | ... | ... | ... | ... | ... | ... | ... | ... | ... | ... | 1 | ... | ... | ... | ... | ... |
| 2 | ...do.....scalded | 1 | ... | 9 | 10 | 1 | ... | 1 | ... | 2 | ... | ... | ... | ... | ... | ... | ... | ... | ... | 19 | 1 | ... | ... | ... | ... |
| 3 | ...do.....railroad | ... | ... | ... | 1 | ... | ... | ... | ... | 1 | ... | 1 | ... | ... | ... | ... | ... | ... | ... | 2 | 1 | ... | ... | ... | ... |
| 4 | Apoplexy | ... | 1 | ... | ... | ... | ... | 1 | 1 | 9 | ... | 30 | 16 | 4 | 2 | ... | ... | ... | ... | 26 | 31 | 3 | ... | ... | ... |
| 5 | Asthma | 2 | ... | ... | ... | ... | ... | ... | ... | 1 | ... | 4 | 1 | 1 | ... | ... | ... | ... | ... | 3 | ... | ... | ... | ... | ... |
| 6 | Bowels disease of | 3 | 5 | 15 | 7 | 3 | 3 | 6 | 3 | 3 | 4 | 2 | 1 | ... | ... | ... | ... | ... | ... | 48 | 1 | 1 | ... | ... | 1 |
| 7 | Brain...... do | ... | ... | 2 | 3 | ... | 1 | 1 | 1 | ... | ... | 1 | ... | ... | ... | ... | ... | ... | ... | 7 | 1 | ... | ... | ... | ... |
| 8 | Bronchitis | ... | 1 | ... | ... | ... | ... | ... | 1 | 2 | 2 | 1 | ... | ... | ... | ... | ... | ... | ... | 6 | 1 | ... | ... | ... | ... |
| 9 | Cancer | 3 | 2 | 4 | 1 | 2 | ... | 1 | 2 | 6 | 7 | 14 | 17 | 4 | 1 | ... | ... | 1 | ... | 36 | 20 | ... | ... | ... | ... |
| 10 | Canker | 1 | 3 | ... | 1 | 2 | 1 | ... | ... | 1 | 3 | ... | 1 | ... | ... | ... | ... | ... | ... | 9 | 1 | ... | ... | ... | ... |
| 11 | ...do..rash | ... | 4 | 4 | 11 | 5 | 3 | 3 | 1 | ... | ... | ... | ... | ... | ... | ... | ... | ... | ... | 25 | 1 | ... | ... | ... | ... |
| 12 | Catarrh | 2 | 11 | 3 | 4 | ... | ... | 2 | 1 | 1 | 1 | 2 | 1 | 1 | 1 | ... | ... | ... | ... | 20 | 5 | 1 | ... | ... | 1 |
| 13 | Chicken pox | ... | 1 | ... | 1 | ... | ... | ... | ... | ... | ... | ... | ... | ... | ... | ... | ... | ... | ... | ... | 1 | 1 | ... | ... | ... |
| 14 | Childbirth | ... | ... | ... | ... | ... | ... | ... | 7 | ... | 67 | ... | 1 | ... | ... | ... | ... | ... | ... | 35 | 4 | 4 | ... | ... | 1 |
| 15 | Cholera | 21 | 17 | 81 | 60 | 48 | 40 | 41 | 37 | 236 | 184 | 65 | 42 | 4 | 3 | ... | ... | 57 | 52 | 362 | 37 | 13 | 4 | ... | 7 |
| 16 | ...do..infantum | 7 | 10 | 14 | 12 | 1 | ... | ... | ... | ... | ... | ... | ... | ... | ... | ... | ... | ... | ... | 44 | ... | ... | ... | ... | ... |
| 17 | ...do..morbus | ... | ... | 8 | 6 | 2 | 1 | ... | 3 | 6 | 3 | 8 | 3 | ... | ... | ... | ... | ... | ... | 25 | 3 | 1 | ... | ... | ... |
| 18 | Chorea | ... | 1 | ... | ... | ... | ... | ... | ... | ... | ... | ... | ... | ... | ... | ... | ... | ... | ... | 1 | ... | ... | ... | ... | ... |
| 19 | Colic | 1 | 1 | ... | 2 | 1 | ... | 2 | 2 | 7 | 4 | 2 | 2 | 1 | 2 | ... | ... | ... | ... | 17 | 3 | ... | ... | ... | ... |
| 20 | Congestion | 2 | 1 | 1 | 3 | 2 | ... | 1 | ... | 3 | ... | ... | 1 | ... | 1 | ... | ... | ... | ... | 11 | 3 | ... | ... | ... | ... |
| 21 | ....do....bowels | ... | 1 | ... | ... | ... | 1 | ... | 1 | ... | ... | ... | 1 | ... | ... | ... | ... | ... | ... | 3 | 1 | ... | ... | ... | ... |
| 22 | ....do....brain | 2 | 1 | 5 | 9 | 1 | 2 | 5 | 6 | 6 | 6 | 2 | 1 | ... | ... | ... | ... | ... | ... | 35 | 5 | 1 | ... | ... | ... |
| 23 | ....do....lungs | 1 | 3 | 4 | 1 | ... | 1 | ... | 4 | 2 | 1 | 1 | 6 | 1 | ... | ... | ... | ... | ... | 18 | 5 | ... | ... | ... | ... |
| 24 | ....do....stomach | ... | ... | ... | ... | ... | ... | 1 | ... | ... | ... | ... | ... | ... | ... | ... | ... | ... | ... | 1 | ... | ... | ... | ... | ... |
| 25 | Consumption | 26 | 25 | 51 | 48 | 11 | 13 | 46 | 115 | 347 | 457 | 153 | 161 | 15 | 7 | ... | ... | 1 | 1 | 970 | 246 | 20 | 3 | 1 | 6 |
| 26 | Convulsions | 75 | 61 | 39 | 22 | 2 | 2 | 5 | 5 | 7 | 20 | 7 | 13 | 2 | 2 | ... | ... | ... | ... | 233 | 8 | 2 | ... | ... | 1 |
| 27 | Croup | 34 | 14 | 70 | 73 | 17 | 14 | ... | ... | ... | ... | ... | ... | ... | ... | ... | ... | ... | ... | 202 | 4 | ... | ... | 1 | 1 |
| 28 | Debility | 1 | 1 | ... | 1 | ... | 2 | 1 | ... | 2 | ... | ... | 1 | ... | ... | ... | ... | ... | ... | 8 | ... | ... | ... | ... | ... |
| 29 | Diabetes | ... | ... | ... | ... | ... | ... | 3 | 2 | 3 | 1 | 3 | ... | ... | ... | ... | ... | ... | ... | 7 | 2 | ... | ... | ... | 1 |
| 30 | Diarrhœa | 21 | 9 | 32 | 41 | 6 | 8 | 2 | 6 | 9 | 10 | 9 | 6 | 1 | 1 | ... | ... | 1 | ... | 139 | 6 | 3 | ... | ... | ... |
| 31 | Dropsy | 10 | 19 | 21 | 13 | 7 | 6 | 5 | 12 | 19 | 45 | 38 | 51 | 7 | 5 | ... | ... | 1 | ... | 172 | 60 | 4 | ... | ... | 1 |
| 32 | Dysentery | 57 | 43 | 132 | 105 | 32 | 24 | 20 | 14 | 44 | 41 | 27 | 30 | 7 | 5 | ... | ... | ... | ... | 464 | 45 | 1 | 1 | ... | 2 |
| 33 | Dyspepsia | ... | ... | ... | 1 | ... | ... | ... | ... | 2 | 1 | 3 | 1 | ... | ... | ... | ... | ... | ... | 4 | 3 | ... | ... | ... | ... |
| 34 | Epilepsy | ... | ... | ... | ... | ... | ... | ... | ... | ... | 1 | ... | ... | 1 | ... | ... | ... | ... | ... | 1 | ... | ... | ... | ... | ... |
| 35 | Erysipelas | 11 | 5 | 5 | 10 | 2 | 2 | 1 | 4 | 9 | 16 | 8 | 18 | 1 | 1 | ... | ... | ... | ... | 68 | 17 | 4 | 1 | ... | 1 |
| 36 | Fever, not specified | 14 | 4 | 13 | 12 | 5 | 8 | 13 | 14 | 33 | 31 | 16 | 11 | 1 | 1 | ... | ... | ... | ... | 116 | 21 | 2 | ... | 1 | ... |
| 37 | ..do..bilious | 2 | ... | 4 | 2 | 4 | 1 | 3 | 5 | 16 | 8 | 10 | 3 | 2 | ... | ... | ... | ... | ... | 41 | 6 | 2 | ... | ... | ... |
| 38 | ..do..brain | 9 | 4 | 15 | 9 | 12 | 6 | 8 | 9 | 8 | 6 | 4 | ... | ... | ... | ... | ... | 6 | 2 | 90 | 5 | ... | ... | ... | ... |
| 39 | ..do..congestive | ... | ... | ... | 1 | 4 | 1 | 7 | 3 | 6 | 4 | 3 | 2 | ... | ... | ... | ... | 1 | ... | 28 | 2 | ... | ... | ... | ... |
| 40 | ..do..inflammatory | ... | ... | 1 | ... | 1 | 1 | ... | ... | ... | 2 | ... | ... | ... | ... | ... | ... | ... | ... | 4 | ... | ... | ... | ... | ... |
| 41 | ..do..intermittent | ... | 1 | 1 | ... | 1 | ... | 1 | ... | 2 | 5 | 4 | 3 | ... | ... | ... | ... | ... | ... | 14 | 2 | ... | ... | ... | ... |
| 42 | ..do..puerperal | ... | ... | ... | ... | ... | ... | ... | ... | ... | 9 | ... | ... | ... | ... | ... | ... | ... | ... | 4 | ... | ... | ... | ... | ... |
| 43 | ..do..remittent | 1 | ... | 1 | 1 | ... | ... | ... | ... | ... | 2 | ... | 1 | ... | ... | ... | ... | ... | ... | 5 | ... | ... | ... | ... | ... |
| 44 | ..do..scarlet | 14 | 14 | 77 | 49 | 23 | 39 | 14 | 13 | 8 | 4 | 1 | ... | ... | ... | ... | ... | ... | ... | 234 | 4 | 4 | ... | ... | 2 |
| 45 | ..do..ship | ... | ... | 1 | 1 | ... | ... | ... | ... | 3 | 1 | 1 | ... | 2 | 1 | ... | ... | ... | ... | 4 | ... | ... | ... | ... | ... |
| 46 | ..do..typhus | ... | 1 | 2 | 1 | 5 | 4 | 19 | 21 | 33 | 26 | 18 | 4 | ... | ... | ... | ... | ... | ... | 99 | 17 | 4 | ... | ... | ... |
| 47 | ..do..yellow | ... | ... | 1 | 1 | ... | ... | ... | ... | 1 | ... | ... | ... | ... | ... | ... | ... | ... | ... | 3 | ... | ... | ... | ... | ... |
| 48 | Fracture | ... | ... | ... | ... | ... | ... | ... | ... | ... | 1 | ... | ... | ... | ... | ... | ... | ... | ... | 1 | ... | ... | ... | ... | ... |
| 49 | Frozen | ... | ... | ... | ... | ... | ... | ... | ... | 2 | ... | 2 | ... | ... | ... | ... | ... | ... | ... | ... | 1 | ... | ... | ... | ... |
| 50 | Gravel | ... | ... | ... | ... | ... | ... | 1 | ... | 1 | ... | 9 | 1 | 1 | ... | ... | ... | ... | ... | 4 | 2 | 1 | ... | 1 | ... |
| 51 | Head, disease of | 1 | 1 | 1 | ... | 1 | ... | ... | ... | 2 | ... | ... | ... | ... | ... | ... | ... | ... | ... | 4 | 1 | ... | ... | ... | ... |
| 52 | Heart....do | 5 | 3 | ... | 4 | ... | 1 | 9 | 2 | 14 | 14 | 19 | 16 | 1 | 1 | ... | ... | ... | ... | 50 | 16 | 3 | ... | 1 | ... |
| 53 | Heat | ... | ... | ... | ... | ... | ... | ... | ... | 1 | 1 | 1 | ... | ... | ... | ... | ... | ... | ... | 1 | ... | ... | ... | ... | ... |
| 54 | Hemorrhage | 2 | 2 | ... | ... | ... | ... | 2 | 1 | 5 | 6 | 2 | 1 | ... | ... | ... | ... | ... | ... | 13 | 1 | 1 | ... | ... | ... |
| 55 | Hernia | ... | ... | ... | ... | 1 | ... | ... | ... | 1 | ... | 3 | ... | 1 | ... | ... | ... | ... | ... | 3 | 1 | 1 | ... | ... | 1 |
| 56 | Hip, disease of | ... | ... | ... | ... | 1 | ... | 2 | ... | ... | ... | ... | 1 | ... | ... | ... | ... | ... | ... | 2 | 1 | ... | ... | ... | ... |
| 57 | Hives | ... | ... | ... | ... | ... | 1 | ... | ... | ... | ... | ... | ... | ... | ... | ... | ... | ... | ... | 1 | ... | ... | ... | ... | ... |
| 58 | Hooping cough | 33 | 28 | 41 | 51 | 1 | 6 | 1 | 1 | ... | ... | ... | ... | ... | ... | ... | ... | 1 | ... | 152 | 2 | 1 | ... | ... | ... |
| 59 | Hydrocephalus | 28 | 21 | 33 | 14 | 7 | 3 | 3 | 5 | 5 | 5 | 4 | 1 | ... | ... | ... | ... | ... | ... | 116 | 4 | 1 | ... | ... | 1 |
| 60 | Inflammation | 36 | 22 | 23 | 22 | 8 | 10 | 11 | 14 | 18 | 31 | 15 | 10 | 4 | ... | ... | ... | 1 | ... | 177 | 21 | 4 | ... | ... | 1 |
| 61 | ....do......bowels | 10 | 9 | 6 | 6 | 3 | 3 | 8 | 6 | 10 | 9 | 7 | 2 | ... | ... | ... | ... | ... | ... | 62 | 8 | 1 | ... | ... | 2 |
| 62 | ....do......brain | 13 | 13 | 23 | 20 | 5 | 4 | 8 | 8 | 8 | 8 | 3 | 2 | ... | ... | ... | ... | ... | ... | 92 | 6 | 1 | 1 | ... | ... |
| 63 | ....do......head | 4 | 1 | 1 | ... | ... | ... | 1 | ... | 2 | 1 | ... | ... | ... | ... | ... | ... | ... | ... | 9 | 1 | ... | ... | ... | ... |
| 64 | ....do......stomach | ... | 1 | ... | 1 | ... | ... | ... | 1 | ... | 3 | 1 | ... | ... | ... | ... | ... | ... | ... | 6 | 1 | ... | ... | ... | ... |
| 65 | Insanity | ... | ... | ... | ... | ... | ... | 1 | ... | 3 | 6 | 1 | 3 | ... | ... | ... | ... | ... | ... | 6 | 3 | ... | ... | ... | ... |
| 66 | Intemperance | ... | ... | ... | ... | ... | ... | ... | ... | 3 | ... | 4 | ... | ... | ... | ... | ... | ... | ... | 1 | 1 | ... | ... | ... | ... |
| 67 | Jaundice | 1 | ... | 1 | ... | ... | ... | ... | ... | 3 | 1 | 1 | 2 | ... | ... | ... | ... | ... | ... | 6 | 3 | ... | ... | ... | ... |
| 68 | Kidneys, disease of | ... | ... | 1 | ... | ... | ... | ... | 1 | 2 | 1 | 4 | ... | ... | ... | ... | ... | ... | ... | 7 | 2 | ... | ... | ... | ... |
| 69 | Killed | ... | ... | 1 | ... | 1 | ... | 2 | ... | 12 | ... | 4 | ... | 1 | ... | ... | ... | ... | ... | 13 | 3 | ... | ... | ... | ... |
| 70 | Liver, disease of | ... | ... | 3 | 4 | ... | 1 | 3 | 1 | 8 | 7 | 13 | 8 | ... | ... | ... | ... | ... | ... | 25 | 11 | 2 | ... | ... | ... |
| 71 | Lockjaw | ... | ... | ... | ... | ... | ... | ... | ... | ... | 1 | ... | ... | ... | ... | ... | ... | ... | ... | ... | ... | ... | ... | ... | ... |
| 72 | Lungs, disease of | 1 | ... | 1 | ... | ... | ... | ... | ... | ... | 6 | 3 | 1 | ... | ... | ... | ... | ... | ... | 8 | 1 | ... | ... | ... | ... |
| 73 | Mania-a-potu | ... | ... | ... | ... | ... | ... | ... | ... | 10 | ... | 4 | 1 | ... | ... | ... | ... | ... | ... | 5 | 2 | ... | ... | ... | ... |
| 74 | Marasmus | 1 | ... | ... | ... | ... | ... | ... | ... | ... | 1 | ... | ... | ... | ... | ... | ... | ... | ... | 1 | ... | ... | ... | ... | ... |
| 75 | Measles | 6 | 4 | 24 | 38 | 7 | 12 | ... | 5 | 9 | 7 | 1 | ... | ... | ... | ... | ... | ... | ... | 68 | 2 | 1 | ... | ... | 1 |

TION OF THE STATE OF NEW YORK—Continued.

| NATIVITIES. | | | | SEASON OF DECEASE. | | | | DURATION OF SICKNESS. | | | | WHITES. | | | COLORED. | | | | | | | | Aggregate deaths. | |
|---|---|---|---|---|---|---|---|---|---|---|---|---|---|---|---|---|---|---|---|---|---|---|---|---|
| | | | | | | | | | | | | | | | Slaves. | | | | Free. | | | | | |
| | | | | | | | | | | | | | | | Black. | | Mulatto. | | Black. | | Mul. | | | |
| Ireland. | Germany. | Other foreign countries. | Unknown. | Spring. | Summer. | Autumn. | Winter. | Under 1 week. | 1 week and under 1 month. | 1 month and under 3 months. | 3 months and over. | Males. | Females. | Total. | M. | F. | M. | F. | M. | F. | M | F. | | |
| | | | | | 1 | | | 1 | | | | | 1 | 1 | | | | | | | | | 1 | 1 |
| | 1 | 3 | | 9 | 5 | 4 | 6 | 18 | 8 | 1 | | 14 | 10 | 24 | | | | | | | | | 24 | 2 |
| | | | | 1 | 1 | | 1 | 2 | | | | 2 | 1 | 3 | | | | | | | | | 3 | 3 |
| 3 | | 1 | | 19 | 9 | 21 | 15 | 44 | 9 | 2 | 5 | 44 | 20 | 64 | | | | | | | | | 64 | 4 |
| | 1 | 5 | | 3 | 1 | | 5 | 1 | 1 | | 5 | 8 | 1 | 9 | | | | | | | | | 9 | 5 |
| 2 | | 2 | | 11 | 8 | 32 | 4 | 22 | 23 | 6 | 2 | 32 | 23 | 55 | | | | | | | | | 55 | 6 |
| | | 1 | | 2 | 2 | 1 | 4 | 2 | 3 | 2 | 2 | 4 | 5 | 9 | | | | | | | | | 9 | 7 |
| | | | | 1 | 1 | 3 | 2 | | 2 | 2 | 3 | 3 | 4 | 7 | | | | | | | | | 7 | 8 |
| 1 | 1 | 6 | 1 | 28 | 13 | 12 | 12 | 7 | 12 | 3 | 41 | 35 | 30 | 65 | | | | | | | | | 65 | 9 |
| 1 | | 2 | | 2 | 6 | 5 | | 3 | 4 | 4 | 2 | 4 | 9 | 13 | | | | | | | | | 13 | 10 |
| | | 4 | 1 | 14 | 5 | 2 | 8 | 15 | 13 | 1 | | 12 | 19 | 31 | | | | | | | | | 31 | 11 |
| 1 | | 2 | | 10 | 6 | 8 | 5 | 14 | 13 | 1 | 1 | 11 | 19 | 30 | | | | | | | | | 30 | 12 |
| | | | | | 1 | | 1 | | 1 | | 1 | | 2 | 2 | | | | | | | | | 2 | 13 |
| 11 | 12 | 8 | | 23 | 16 | 17 | 19 | 35 | 25 | 7 | | | 75 | 75 | | | | | | | | | 75 | 14 |
| 166 | 260 | 82 | 7 | 12 | 814 | 598 | 12 | 710 | 86 | 6 | 8 | 541 | 381 | 922 | | | | | 7 | 3 | 5 | 1 | 938 | 15 |
| | | | | 1 | 12 | 29 | 2 | 33 | 9 | | | 22 | 22 | 44 | | | | | | | | | 44 | 16 |
| 6 | 2 | 3 | | 1 | 6 | 28 | 5 | 25 | 12 | 3 | | 24 | 16 | 40 | | | | | | | | | 40 | 17 |
| | | | | | | 1 | | | | | | | 1 | 1 | | | | | | | | | 1 | 18 |
| 2 | | 4 | 1 | 4 | 12 | 9 | 1 | 19 | 5 | 1 | | 14 | 13 | 27 | | | | | | | | | 27 | 19 |
| | | 1 | | 6 | 4 | 3 | 2 | 9 | 5 | 1 | | 9 | 6 | 15 | | | | | | | | | 15 | 20 |
| | | | | 2 | 1 | 1 | | 4 | | | | | 4 | 4 | | | | | | | | | 4 | 21 |
| 2 | | 8 | | 14 | 11 | 10 | 11 | 20 | 21 | 2 | 3 | 21 | 25 | 46 | | | | | | | | | 46 | 22 |
| 1 | | 1 | | 5 | 8 | 6 | 6 | 16 | 7 | 2 | | 9 | 15 | 24 | | | | | | 1 | | | 25 | 23 |
| | | | | | | 1 | | | 1 | | | 1 | | 1 | | | | | | | | | 1 | 24 |
| 85 | 38 | 102 | 6 | 471 | 383 | 823 | 300 | 47 | 122 | 170 | 1076 | 644 | 821 | 1465 | | | | | 5 | 6 | 1 | | 1477 | 25 |
| 5 | 3 | 9 | 1 | 71 | 68 | 73 | 46 | 171 | 35 | 18 | 29 | 136 | 125 | 261 | | | | | 1 | | | | 262 | 26 |
| 7 | 1 | 6 | | 79 | 34 | 49 | 60 | 155 | 54 | 3 | 4 | 121 | 101 | 222 | | | | | | | | | 222 | 27 |
| 1 | | | | 1 | 4 | 3 | 1 | 2 | 2 | | 4 | 4 | 5 | 9 | | | | | | | | | 9 | 28 |
| 1 | | 1 | | 5 | 3 | 2 | 2 | 1 | 4 | 3 | 4 | 9 | 3 | 12 | | | | | | | | | 12 | 29 |
| 5 | 4 | 5 | | 11 | 21 | 116 | 13 | 70 | 70 | 8 | 11 | 81 | 81 | 162 | | | | | | | | | 162 | 30 |
| 7 | 3 | 10 | 2 | 78 | 77 | 53 | 48 | 16 | 75 | 43 | 120 | 108 | 150 | 258 | | | | | | 1 | | | 259 | 31 |
| 25 | 16 | 26 | 1 | 23 | 61 | 456 | 40 | 166 | 326 | 41 | 16 | 318 | 262 | 580 | | | | | 1 | | | | 581 | 32 |
| 1 | | | | 1 | 2 | 3 | 2 | | | 2 | 4 | 5 | 3 | 8 | | | | | | | | | 8 | 33 |
| | | 1 | | | | 1 | 1 | | | | 2 | 1 | 1 | 2 | | | | | | | | | 2 | 34 |
| | | 2 | | 28 | 29 | 16 | 20 | 22 | 56 | 7 | 8 | 36 | 56 | 92 | | | | | 1 | | | | 93 | 35 |
| 16 | 5 | 14 | | 36 | 40 | 69 | 30 | 40 | 92 | 30 | 7 | 94 | 80 | 174 | | | | | 1 | 1 | | | 176 | 36 |
| 2 | 6 | 3 | | 15 | 7 | 29 | 9 | 13 | 35 | 7 | 4 | 41 | 19 | 60 | | | | | | | | | 60 | 37 |
| 1 | | 2 | | 39 | 22 | 18 | 17 | 40 | 37 | 11 | 5 | 62 | 36 | 98 | | | | | | | | | 98 | 38 |
| 1 | 1 | | | 12 | 11 | 6 | 3 | 5 | 22 | 4 | | 21 | 11 | 32 | | | | | | | | | 32 | 39 |
| 1 | | | | 4 | | | 1 | 1 | 4 | | | 2 | 3 | 5 | | | | | | | | | 5 | 40 |
| | | 2 | | 7 | 3 | 6 | 2 | 3 | 8 | 4 | 3 | 9 | 9 | 18 | | | | | | | | | 18 | 41 |
| 2 | | 3 | | 2 | 2 | 2 | 3 | | 7 | 1 | | | 9 | 9 | | | | | | | | | 9 | 42 |
| | | 1 | | 2 | 2 | 2 | | 3 | 3 | | | 2 | 4 | 6 | | | | | | | | | 6 | 43 |
| 6 | 1 | 5 | | 98 | 64 | 49 | 45 | 121 | 117 | 16 | 2 | 137 | 119 | 256 | | | | | | | | | 256 | 44 |
| 5 | 1 | | | 3 | 3 | 1 | 3 | 5 | 4 | 1 | | 7 | 2 | 9 | | | | | | 1 | | | 10 | 45 |
| 3 | 10 | 6 | | 43 | 21 | 35 | 40 | 8 | 93 | 28 | 5 | 82 | 57 | 139 | | | | | | | | | 139 | 46 |
| | | | | 1 | | 2 | | 2 | | 1 | | 2 | 1 | 3 | | | | | | | | | 3 | 47 |
| | | | | | | | 1 | 1 | | | | | 1 | 1 | | | | | | | | | 1 | 48 |
| 2 | | 1 | | 3 | | | 1 | 3 | | | 1 | 4 | | 4 | | | | | | | | | 4 | 49 |
| 1 | 1 | 3 | | 5 | 1 | 3 | 4 | 3 | 5 | 1 | 4 | 12 | 1 | 13 | | | | | | | | | 13 | 50 |
| | | 1 | | 1 | 2 | 2 | 1 | 1 | 4 | 1 | | 5 | 1 | 6 | | | | | | | | | 6 | 51 |
| 7 | | 12 | | 24 | 20 | 23 | 22 | 30 | 19 | 10 | 28 | 48 | 41 | 89 | | | | | | | | | 89 | 52 |
| 1 | | 1 | | 1 | 2 | | | 2 | 1 | | | 2 | 1 | 3 | | | | | | | | | 3 | 53 |
| 4 | 1 | | 1 | 5 | 7 | 7 | 2 | 9 | 8 | 1 | 1 | 11 | 10 | 21 | | | | | | | | | 21 | 54 |
| | | | | | 5 | 1 | | | 2 | 1 | 3 | 5 | | 5 | | | | | 1 | | | | 6 | 55 |
| | | 1 | | 1 | | 3 | | | | 1 | 3 | 3 | 1 | 4 | | | | | | | | | 4 | 56 |
| | | | | 1 | | | | | 1 | | | | 1 | 1 | | | | | | | | | 1 | 57 |
| 2 | 2 | 4 | | 34 | 39 | 62 | 27 | 14 | 91 | 41 | 12 | 77 | 86 | 163 | | | | | | | | | 163 | 58 |
| 2 | | 5 | | 36 | 28 | 36 | 24 | 26 | 62 | 20 | 12 | 79 | 49 | 128 | | | | | 1 | | | | 129 | 59 |
| 4 | 4 | 13 | 1 | 78 | 59 | 46 | 41 | 92 | 102 | 17 | 9 | 116 | 109 | 225 | | | | | | | | | 225 | 60 |
| 1 | 2 | 2 | 1 | 25 | 19 | 16 | 19 | 31 | 39 | 5 | 3 | 44 | 35 | 79 | | | | | | | | | 79 | 61 |
| 6 | 3 | 6 | | 46 | 22 | 32 | 15 | 41 | 61 | 7 | 4 | 60 | 54 | 114 | | | | | | | | 1 | 115 | 62 |
| | | | | 2 | 3 | 5 | | 3 | 5 | 2 | | 8 | 2 | 10 | | | | | | | | | 10 | 63 |
| | | | | 3 | | 3 | 1 | 2 | 2 | | 3 | 1 | 6 | 7 | | | | | | | | | 7 | 64 |
| 4 | 1 | | | 2 | 4 | 3 | 5 | 1 | 4 | | 7 | 5 | 9 | 14 | | | | | | | | | 14 | 65 |
| 2 | 1 | 2 | | 1 | 3 | 3 | | 1 | 2 | 2 | | 7 | | 7 | | | | | | | | | 7 | 66 |
| | | | | 3 | 3 | 2 | 1 | 1 | 2 | 1 | 4 | 6 | 3 | 9 | | | | | | | | | 9 | 67 |
| | | | | 3 | 2 | 3 | 1 | 1 | 4 | | 4 | 7 | 2 | 9 | | | | | | | | | 9 | 68 |
| 1 | 1 | 3 | | 7 | 3 | 9 | 2 | 18 | 1 | | 1 | 20 | | 20 | | | | | 1 | | | | 21 | 69 |
| 4 | | 6 | | 8 | 11 | 17 | 12 | 6 | 16 | 7 | 15 | 27 | 21 | 48 | | | | | | | | | 48 | 70 |
| | | 1 | | 1 | | | | | 1 | | | | 1 | 1 | | | | | | | | | 1 | 71 |
| 3 | | | | 4 | 2 | 4 | 1 | 1 | 2 | 3 | 4 | 5 | 7 | 12 | | | | | | | | | 12 | 72 |
| 3 | 1 | 4 | | 2 | 6 | 4 | 3 | 4 | 6 | | 1 | 14 | 1 | 15 | | | | | | | | | 15 | 73 |
| | | 1 | | | 1 | 1 | | | | 1 | 1 | 1 | 1 | 2 | | | | | | | | | 2 | 74 |
| 18 | 15 | 6 | 2 | 35 | 35 | 18 | 25 | 18 | 71 | 7 | 3 | 46 | 66 | 112 | | | | | 1 | | | | 113 | 75 |

CLASSIFICATION OF DEATHS IN NORTHERN AND

| | Cause of death. | AGES. | | | | | | | | | | | | | | | | | | NATIVITIES. | | | | | |
|---|---|---|---|---|---|---|---|---|---|---|---|---|---|---|---|---|---|---|---|---|---|---|---|---|---|
| | | Under 1. | | 1 and under 5. | | 5 and under 10. | | 10 and under 20. | | 20 and under 50. | | 50 and under 80. | | 80 and under 100. | | 100 & over. | | Age unknown. | | Born in State. | N. England States. | Middle States. | Southern States. | Southwest'n States. | Northwest'n States. |
| | | M. | F. | M. | F. | M. | F. | M. | F. | M. | F. | M. | F. | M. | F. | M | F. | M | F. | | | | | | |
| 1 | Mortification | ... | ... | ... | ... | 1 | ... | ... | ... | 1 | ... | ... | ... | 2 | ... | .. | .. | .. | .. | 2 | 1 | 1 | .. | .. | .. |
| 2 | Mumps | 1 | ... | 2 | 2 | 1 | 1 | 3 | ... | ... | ... | ... | ... | ... | ... | .. | .. | .. | .. | 9 | ... | ... | .. | .. | .. |
| 3 | Murder | ... | ... | ... | ... | ... | ... | ... | ... | 2 | ... | ... | ... | ... | ... | .. | .. | .. | .. | 2 | ... | ... | .. | .. | .. |
| 4 | Neuralgia | ... | ... | ... | ... | ... | ... | 1 | 2 | 3 | 2 | 1 | 2 | ... | ... | .. | .. | .. | .. | 6 | 3 | 1 | .. | .. | .. |
| 5 | Old age | ... | ... | ... | ... | ... | ... | ... | ... | ... | 2 | 52 | 60 | 108 | 10 | 1 | .. | 2 | .. | 72 | 140 | 17 | 2 | .. | .. |
| 6 | Paralysis | 1 | ... | 1 | 2 | ... | 1 | 2 | ... | 6 | 5 | 22 | 36 | 7 | 11 | .. | .. | .. | .. | 42 | 39 | 7 | 1 | .. | .. |
| 7 | Peritonitis | ... | ... | ... | ... | 1 | ... | ... | ... | ... | ... | ... | ... | ... | ... | .. | .. | .. | .. | 1 | ... | ... | .. | .. | .. |
| 8 | Piles | ... | ... | ... | ... | ... | ... | ... | ... | ... | ... | 1 | ... | ... | ... | .. | .. | .. | .. | ... | ... | 1 | .. | .. | .. |
| 9 | Pleurisy | ... | ... | ... | ... | ... | 1 | 2 | ... | 12 | 3 | 2 | 4 | ... | ... | .. | .. | .. | .. | 16 | 5 | ... | .. | .. | .. |
| 10 | Pneumonia | 61 | 36 | 48 | 37 | 9 | 5 | 6 | 8 | 28 | 29 | 23 | 17 | 3 | 4 | .. | .. | .. | .. | 242 | 27 | 6 | .. | 2 | 1 |
| 11 | Poison | 2 | ... | 3 | 1 | ... | 2 | ... | ... | ... | 2 | ... | ... | ... | ... | .. | .. | .. | .. | 9 | ... | ... | .. | .. | .. |
| 12 | Quinsy | 2 | 1 | 1 | 2 | ... | 2 | ... | ... | 1 | ... | ... | 1 | ... | ... | .. | .. | .. | .. | 10 | ... | ... | .. | .. | .. |
| 13 | Rheumatism | ... | ... | ... | 1 | 1 | ... | 3 | 1 | 3 | 2 | 5 | 8 | ... | ... | .. | .. | .. | .. | 12 | 1 | ... | .. | .. | .. |
| 14 | Rickets | ... | ... | 1 | ... | ... | ... | ... | ... | ... | ... | ... | ... | ... | ... | .. | .. | .. | .. | 1 | ... | ... | .. | .. | .. |
| 15 | Scrofula | 3 | 1 | 4 | 6 | 1 | 1 | 4 | 4 | 4 | 4 | 1 | 2 | 2 | ... | .. | .. | .. | .. | 27 | 6 | 1 | .. | .. | .. |
| 16 | Scurvy | ... | ... | ... | ... | ... | ... | ... | ... | ... | 1 | 1 | 1 | ... | ... | .. | .. | .. | .. | 1 | ... | 1 | .. | .. | .. |
| 17 | Small pox | 3 | 5 | 6 | 5 | 5 | 4 | 8 | 6 | 8 | 6 | 2 | ... | ... | ... | .. | .. | .. | .. | 44 | 4 | ... | .. | .. | .. |
| 18 | Spine, disease of | 1 | 1 | 2 | 5 | ... | ... | 2 | 2 | 3 | 4 | 1 | ... | ... | ... | .. | .. | .. | .. | 16 | 2 | ... | .. | .. | .. |
| 19 | Stillborn | 4 | 6 | ... | ... | ... | ... | ... | ... | ... | ... | ... | ... | ... | ... | .. | .. | .. | .. | 10 | ... | ... | .. | .. | .. |
| 20 | Stomach, disease of | ... | 1 | ... | ... | 1 | ... | ... | 1 | ... | 2 | 2 | ... | ... | ... | .. | .. | .. | .. | 3 | 2 | 1 | .. | .. | .. |
| 21 | Suffocation | 2 | ... | ... | 1 | ... | 1 | ... | ... | 1 | ... | 1 | ... | ... | ... | .. | .. | .. | .. | 5 | 1 | ... | .. | .. | .. |
| 22 | Suicide | ... | ... | ... | ... | ... | ... | 2 | ... | 9 | 6 | 4 | ... | ... | ... | .. | .. | .. | .. | 10 | 8 | 1 | .. | .. | .. |
| 23 | Summer complaint | 10 | 8 | 16 | 8 | 2 | 4 | ... | 3 | 1 | ... | ... | 1 | 1 | ... | .. | .. | 4 | 2 | 56 | 2 | 1 | .. | .. | .. |
| 24 | Sun, stroke of | ... | ... | ... | 1 | ... | ... | ... | ... | 3 | ... | 1 | ... | ... | ... | .. | .. | .. | .. | ... | 1 | ... | .. | .. | .. |
| 25 | Teething | 10 | 10 | 12 | 16 | ... | ... | ... | ... | ... | ... | ... | ... | ... | ... | .. | .. | .. | .. | 42 | 1 | ... | .. | .. | .. |
| 26 | Tetter | ... | ... | ... | 1 | ... | ... | ... | ... | ... | ... | ... | 1 | ... | ... | .. | .. | .. | .. | 1 | ... | ... | .. | .. | .. |
| 27 | Throat, disease of | 2 | ... | 2 | 4 | ... | ... | 1 | 1 | 1 | 1 | ... | ... | ... | ... | .. | .. | .. | .. | 10 | 2 | ... | .. | .. | .. |
| 28 | Thrush | ... | 1 | 3 | ... | ... | 1 | ... | ... | ... | 4 | ... | ... | ... | ... | .. | .. | .. | .. | 9 | ... | ... | .. | .. | .. |
| 29 | Tumor | 1 | ... | ... | 1 | ... | ... | ... | 1 | 1 | 5 | 1 | 1 | ... | ... | .. | .. | .. | .. | 7 | 4 | ... | .. | .. | .. |
| 30 | Ulcer | 4 | 6 | ... | ... | ... | ... | 1 | 1 | 3 | ... | 1 | 1 | ... | ... | .. | .. | .. | .. | 16 | ... | ... | .. | .. | 1 |
| 31 | Uterus, disease of | ... | ... | ... | ... | ... | ... | ... | ... | ... | 1 | ... | ... | ... | ... | .. | .. | .. | .. | 1 | ... | ... | .. | .. | .. |
| 32 | Venereal | ... | ... | ... | ... | 1 | ... | ... | ... | 1 | ... | 1 | ... | ... | ... | .. | .. | .. | .. | 3 | ... | ... | .. | .. | .. |
| 33 | Worms | 1 | 2 | 17 | 16 | 4 | 2 | ... | 1 | ... | ... | ... | ... | ... | ... | .. | .. | .. | .. | 39 | ... | ... | .. | .. | .. |
| 34 | Unknown | 173 | 141 | 91 | 84 | 19 | 27 | 23 | 33 | 112 | 122 | 86 | 75 | 8 | 10 | .. | .. | 7 | 5 | 722 | 83 | 14 | .. | .. | 4 |
| | Total | 746 | 589 | 1008 | 886 | 307 | 291 | 350 | 403 | 1237 | 1231 | 766 | 661 | 195 | 130 | 1 | .. | 83 | 62 | 6071 | 1022 | 145 | 13 | 7 | 27 |

CLASSIFICATION OF DEATHS IN EASTERN

*Embracing Albany, Columbia, Dutchess, Greene, Kings, Orange, Putnam, Queen's, Rennsel-*

| | Cause of death. | Under 1. M. | Under 1. F. | 1 and under 5. M. | 1 and under 5. F. | 5 and under 10. M. | 5 and under 10. F. | 10 and under 20. M. | 10 and under 20. F. | 20 and under 50. M. | 20 and under 50. F. | 50 and under 80. M. | 50 and under 80. F. | 80 and under 100. M. | 80 and under 100. F. | 100 & over. M | 100 & over. F. | Age unknown. M | Age unknown. F. | Born in State. | N. England States. | Middle States. | Southern States. | Southwest'n States. | Northwest'n States. |
|---|---|---|---|---|---|---|---|---|---|---|---|---|---|---|---|---|---|---|---|---|---|---|---|---|---|
| 1 | Abscess | ... | ... | ... | ... | 1 | ... | ... | ... | 3 | 3 | 2 | 1 | 1 | ... | .. | .. | .. | .. | 3 | 1 | 2 | .. | .. | .. |
| 2 | Accident, not specfi'd | 6 | 5 | 7 | 5 | 11 | 4 | 16 | 2 | 57 | 2 | 14 | 6 | 3 | 3 | .. | .. | .. | .. | 80 | 11 | 4 | .. | .. | .. |
| 3 | ....do...burned | 1 | 2 | 11 | 10 | 2 | 6 | ... | 3 | ... | 2 | ... | 1 | ... | ... | .. | .. | .. | .. | 33 | 1 | ... | .. | .. | .. |
| 4 | ....do...drowned | ... | ... | 19 | 2 | 21 | 4 | 33 | 3 | 47 | ... | 6 | ... | 1 | ... | .. | .. | .. | .. | 99 | 5 | 3 | 1 | .. | .. |
| 5 | ....do...scalded | 1 | 3 | 5 | ... | 2 | ... | 1 | ... | 3 | ... | ... | ... | ... | ... | .. | .. | .. | .. | 13 | ... | ... | .. | .. | .. |
| 6 | ....do...exp'n ste'm | ... | ... | ... | ... | ... | ... | 1 | ... | 3 | ... | ... | ... | ... | ... | .. | .. | .. | .. | 1 | 1 | 1 | .. | .. | .. |
| 7 | ....do...machinery | ... | ... | ... | ... | ... | ... | ... | ... | 1 | ... | ... | ... | ... | ... | .. | .. | .. | .. | ... | ... | ... | .. | .. | .. |
| 8 | ....do...shot | ... | ... | ... | ... | ... | ... | 1 | ... | 2 | ... | ... | ... | ... | ... | .. | .. | .. | .. | 2 | 1 | ... | .. | .. | .. |
| 9 | ....do...railroad | ... | ... | ... | ... | ... | ... | ... | ... | 8 | ... | 1 | ... | ... | ... | .. | .. | .. | .. | 1 | 1 | ... | .. | .. | .. |
| 10 | Apoplexy | ... | 1 | ... | ... | ... | ... | ... | ... | 14 | 10 | 40 | 35 | 6 | 4 | .. | .. | .. | .. | 83 | 10 | 1 | .. | .. | 1 |
| 11 | Asthma | 1 | ... | ... | 1 | ... | ... | ... | ... | 1 | 1 | 5 | 2 | ... | 1 | .. | .. | .. | .. | 8 | ... | ... | .. | .. | .. |
| 12 | Bladder, disease of | ... | ... | ... | ... | ... | ... | 2 | ... | ... | ... | ... | ... | 1 | ... | .. | .. | .. | .. | 2 | ... | ... | .. | .. | .. |
| 13 | Bowels.....do | 6 | 4 | 4 | 5 | 1 | 1 | 4 | 1 | 8 | ... | 1 | 3 | ... | ... | .. | .. | .. | .. | 24 | 4 | ... | .. | .. | .. |
| 14 | Brain.......do | 6 | 3 | 6 | 4 | 3 | 1 | 2 | 1 | 4 | 1 | 2 | ... | ... | ... | .. | .. | .. | .. | 28 | 1 | ... | .. | .. | .. |
| 15 | Bronchitis | 3 | 2 | 1 | 3 | ... | 1 | 2 | 1 | 2 | 3 | 4 | 1 | ... | ... | .. | .. | .. | .. | 21 | ... | ... | .. | .. | .. |
| 16 | Cancer | 2 | ... | 1 | 1 | ... | ... | ... | 1 | 7 | 17 | 6 | 24 | 4 | 6 | .. | .. | .. | .. | 52 | 8 | 1 | .. | .. | .. |
| 17 | Canker | 1 | 3 | ... | 1 | ... | ... | ... | ... | ... | ... | ... | ... | ... | ... | .. | .. | .. | .. | 4 | 1 | ... | .. | .. | .. |
| 18 | ..do..rash | ... | ... | 2 | 1 | ... | ... | ... | ... | ... | ... | ... | ... | ... | ... | .. | .. | .. | .. | 3 | ... | ... | .. | .. | .. |
| 19 | Carbuncle | ... | ... | ... | ... | ... | ... | ... | 1 | ... | ... | ... | ... | ... | ... | .. | .. | .. | .. | 1 | ... | ... | .. | .. | .. |
| 20 | Catarrh | 14 | 8 | 8 | 11 | 1 | 1 | 2 | 2 | 5 | 3 | 8 | 6 | 2 | 2 | .. | .. | .. | .. | 59 | 3 | ... | .. | .. | .. |
| 21 | Chicken pox | 1 | 1 | ... | ... | ... | ... | ... | ... | ... | ... | ... | ... | ... | ... | .. | .. | .. | .. | 2 | ... | ... | .. | .. | .. |
| 22 | Childbirth | ... | ... | ... | ... | ... | ... | ... | 2 | ... | 78 | ... | 1 | ... | ... | .. | .. | .. | .. | 58 | 1 | 1 | .. | .. | .. |
| 23 | Cholera | 66 | 49 | 157 | 120 | 67 | 81 | 84 | 91 | 553 | 328 | 182 | 123 | 21 | 9 | 1 | .. | 14 | 4 | 1054 | 40 | 22 | 5 | .. | 3 |
| 24 | ....do....infantum | 26 | 25 | 17 | 32 | 3 | 2 | ... | ... | ... | ... | ... | ... | ... | ... | .. | .. | .. | .. | 101 | 1 | 1 | .. | .. | .. |
| 25 | ....do....morbus | 1 | 1 | 14 | 5 | 6 | 3 | 6 | 2 | 10 | 11 | 6 | 5 | ... | 1 | .. | .. | .. | .. | 60 | 2 | ... | .. | .. | .. |
| 26 | Chorea | ... | ... | ... | ... | ... | ... | ... | 1 | ... | 1 | ... | ... | ... | ... | .. | .. | .. | .. | 2 | ... | ... | .. | .. | .. |
| 27 | Colic | 4 | ... | 1 | 1 | 1 | ... | 2 | 1 | 6 | 4 | 6 | 5 | ... | ... | .. | .. | .. | .. | 25 | 1 | 1 | .. | .. | .. |
| 28 | Congestion | 3 | 2 | 2 | 1 | ... | 1 | ... | 1 | 1 | 3 | 1 | 1 | ... | ... | .. | .. | .. | .. | 14 | 1 | ... | .. | .. | .. |
| 29 | ....do.....bowels | ... | ... | ... | ... | ... | ... | ... | ... | ... | ... | 1 | ... | ... | ... | .. | .. | .. | .. | ... | ... | 1 | .. | .. | .. |
| 30 | ....do.....brain | 16 | 5 | 26 | 15 | 5 | 5 | 10 | 2 | 11 | 6 | 3 | 4 | ... | ... | .. | .. | .. | .. | 97 | 2 | 3 | .. | .. | .. |

## LAKE SECTION OF THE STATE OF NEW YORK—Continued.

| Nativities: California and Territories. | Ireland. | Germany. | Other foreign countries. | Unknown. | Season of decease: Spring. | Summer. | Autumn. | Winter. | Duration of sickness: Under 1 week. | 1 week and under 1 month. | 1 month and under 3 months. | 3 months and over. | Whites: Males. | Females. | Total. | Colored: Slaves: Black. M. | F. | Mulatto. M. | F. | Free: Black. M. | F. | Mul. M | F. | Aggregate deaths. | |
|---|---|---|---|---|---|---|---|---|---|---|---|---|---|---|---|---|---|---|---|---|---|---|---|---|---|
| | | | | | 1 | | 1 | 2 | 2 | | 1 | 1 | 4 | | 4 | | | | | | | | | 4 | 1 |
| | 1 | | | | 6 | 1 | 2 | 1 | 3 | 7 | | | 7 | 3 | 10 | | | | | | | | | 10 | 2 |
| | | | | | | | | 2 | 2 | | | | 2 | | 2 | | | | | | | | | 2 | 3 |
| | 1 | | | | 4 | 3 | 1 | 3 | 2 | 3 | 1 | 5 | 5 | 6 | 11 | | | | | | | | | 11 | 4 |
| | 13 | 17 | 30 | 4 | 65 | 86 | 80 | 64 | 44 | 62 | 19 | 58 | 162 | 132 | 294 | | | | | 1 | | | | 295 | 5 |
| | 1 | 1 | 3 | | 25 | 22 | 25 | 20 | 26 | 25 | 10 | 29 | 39 | 55 | 94 | | | | | | | | | 94 | 6 |
| | | | | | | | 1 | | 1 | | | | 1 | | 1 | | | | | | | | | 1 | 7 |
| | | | | | | | | 1 | | | | 1 | 1 | | 1 | | | | | | | | | 1 | 8 |
| | 2 | | 1 | | 7 | 7 | | 9 | 8 | 14 | 1 | | 16 | 8 | 24 | | | | | | | | | 24 | 9 |
| | 9 | 5 | 13 | | 149 | 42 | 45 | 68 | 85 | 171 | 30 | 13 | 177 | 123 | 300 | | | | | 1 | 4 | | | 305 | 10 |
| | 1 | | | | 3 | 2 | 4 | 1 | 7 | 1 | | | 5 | 5 | 10 | | | | | | | | | 10 | 11 |
| | | | | | 2 | 2 | 2 | 4 | 4 | 5 | 1 | | 4 | 5 | 9 | | | | | | 1 | | | 10 | 12 |
| | | | 6 | | 5 | 5 | 6 | 3 | 2 | 4 | 2 | 10 | 12 | 7 | 19 | | | | | | | | | 19 | 13 |
| | | | | | 1 | | | | | | | 1 | 1 | | 1 | | | | | | | | | 1 | 14 |
| | | 1 | 2 | | 7 | 15 | 10 | 5 | 1 | 8 | 5 | 23 | 19 | 17 | 36 | | | | | | 1 | | | 37 | 15 |
| | | | 1 | | | 2 | | 1 | | 1 | 1 | 1 | 1 | 2 | 3 | | | | | | | | | 3 | 16 |
| | 4 | 1 | 5 | | 11 | 22 | 14 | 11 | 10 | 47 | 1 | | 31 | 26 | 57 | | | | | | | 1 | | 58 | 17 |
| | | | 3 | | 4 | 5 | 6 | 6 | 1 | 3 | 6 | 8 | 9 | 12 | 21 | | | | | | | | | 21 | 18 |
| | | | | | 3 | 4 | 2 | 1 | | | | | 4 | 6 | 10 | | | | | | | | | 10 | 19 |
| | 1 | | | | 1 | 4 | | 2 | 2 | | 1 | 4 | 3 | 4 | 7 | | | | | | | | | 7 | 20 |
| | | | | | | 4 | | 2 | 6 | | | | 4 | 2 | 6 | | | | | | | | | 6 | 21 |
| | 1 | | 1 | | 3 | 6 | 5 | 6 | 12 | 2 | | | 15 | 6 | 21 | | | | | | | | | 21 | 22 |
| | | | 1 | | 2 | 9 | 46 | 3 | 15 | 41 | 2 | 1 | 34 | 26 | 60 | | | | | | | | | 60 | 23 |
| | 1 | 2 | 1 | | | 3 | 1 | 1 | 4 | | 1 | | 4 | 1 | 5 | | | | | | | | | 5 | 24 |
| | | 2 | 2 | 1 | 9 | 12 | 20 | 7 | 15 | 22 | 8 | 1 | 22 | 26 | 48 | | | | | | | | | 48 | 25 |
| | | 1 | | | 1 | 1 | | | | 1 | | 1 | | 2 | 2 | | | | | | | | | 2 | 26 |
| | | | | | 2 | 4 | 2 | 4 | 4 | 4 | | 4 | 6 | 6 | 12 | | | | | | | | | 12 | 27 |
| | | | | | | 3 | 6 | | | 3 | 4 | 2 | 3 | 6 | 9 | | | | | | | | | 9 | 28 |
| | | | | | 4 | 1 | 4 | 2 | | | 1 | 10 | 3 | 8 | 11 | | | | | | | | | 11 | 29 |
| | | | | | 5 | 2 | 5 | 4 | 5 | 10 | 1 | 1 | 9 | 8 | 17 | | | | | | | | | 17 | 30 |
| | | | | | 1 | | | | | 1 | | | | 1 | 1 | | | | | | | | | 1 | 31 |
| | | | | | 1 | 2 | | | | | | 3 | 3 | | 3 | | | | | | | | | 3 | 32 |
| | 1 | | 3 | | 10 | 5 | 18 | 10 | 25 | 10 | 6 | 2 | 22 | 21 | 43 | | | | | | | | | 43 | 33 |
| | 55 | 43 | 62 | 33 | 254 | 252 | 273 | 224 | 309 | 182 | 81 | 210 | 517 | 493 | 1010 | | | | | 1 | 3 | 1 | 1 | 1016 | 34 |
| 1 | 557 | 482 | 547 | 64 | 2169 | 2172 | 3033 | 1524 | 2956 | 2573 | 756 | 1894 | 4661 | 4228 | 8889 | | | | | 24 | 22 | 8 | 3 | 8946 | |

## C TION OF THE STATE OF NEW YORK.

*laer, Richmond, Rockland, Saratoga, Suffolk, Ulster, Warren, Washington and Westchester.*

| Nativities: California and Territories. | Ireland. | Germany. | Other foreign countries. | Unknown. | Season of decease: Spring. | Summer. | Autumn. | Winter. | Duration of sickness: Under 1 week. | 1 week and under 1 month. | 1 month and under 3 months. | 3 months and over. | Whites: Males. | Females. | Total. | Colored: Slaves: Black. M. | F. | Mulatto. M. | F. | Free: Black. M. | F. | Mul. M | F. | Aggregate deaths. | |
|---|---|---|---|---|---|---|---|---|---|---|---|---|---|---|---|---|---|---|---|---|---|---|---|---|---|
| | 1 | | 4 | | 3 | 4 | 2 | 2 | 2 | | | 7 | 7 | 4 | 11 | | | | | | | | | 11 | 1 |
| | 29 | 5 | 12 | | 37 | 41 | 28 | 35 | 70 | 29 | 9 | 5 | 108 | 26 | 134 | | | | | 5 | 1 | 1 | | 141 | 2 |
| | 3 | | 1 | | 12 | 4 | 8 | 13 | 23 | 5 | 2 | | 14 | 21 | 35 | | | | | | 2 | | 1 | 38 | 3 |
| | 16 | 2 | 9 | 1 | 18 | 65 | 88 | 14 | 136 | | | | 123 | 9 | 132 | | | | | 3 | | 1 | | 136 | 4 |
| | 2 | | | | 2 | 3 | 5 | 5 | 9 | 2 | | | 12 | 3 | 15 | | | | | | | | | 15 | 5 |
| | 1 | | | | 4 | | | | 4 | | | | 4 | | 4 | | | | | | | | | 4 | 6 |
| | 1 | | | | 1 | | | | | | | | 1 | | 1 | | | | | | | | | 1 | 7 |
| | | | | | 2 | | 1 | | 1 | 1 | | | 3 | | 3 | | | | | | | | | 3 | 8 |
| | 7 | | | | 1 | 3 | 4 | 1 | 4 | | | | 9 | | 9 | | | | | | | | | 9 | 9 |
| | 10 | | 5 | | 36 | 27 | 17 | 30 | 75 | 15 | 1 | 4 | 59 | 49 | 108 | | | | | 1 | 1 | | | 110 | 10 |
| | 3 | | 1 | | 5 | 1 | 1 | 4 | 4 | 6 | | 2 | 7 | 5 | 12 | | | | | | | | | 12 | 11 |
| | | | 1 | | 2 | | | 1 | | 1 | | 1 | 3 | | 3 | | | | | | | | | 3 | 12 |
| | 6 | 2 | 2 | | 10 | 11 | 12 | 5 | 11 | 13 | 10 | 1 | 24 | 14 | 38 | | | | | | | | | 38 | 13 |
| | 3 | | 1 | | 11 | 6 | 8 | 8 | 10 | 17 | 2 | 3 | 23 | 9 | 32 | | | | | | 1 | | | 33 | 14 |
| | 1 | | 1 | | 6 | 4 | 5 | 8 | 6 | 7 | 2 | 8 | 12 | 11 | 23 | | | | | | | | | 23 | 15 |
| | 4 | | 3 | 1 | 23 | 19 | 14 | 13 | 1 | 8 | 5 | 53 | 20 | 49 | 69 | | | | | | | | | 69 | 16 |
| | | | | | | 1 | 3 | 1 | 3 | 1 | 1 | | 1 | 4 | 5 | | | | | | | | | 5 | 17 |
| | | | | | 2 | | | 1 | 1 | 2 | | | 2 | 1 | 3 | | | | | | | | | 3 | 18 |
| | | | | | | | 1 | | | 1 | | | | 1 | 1 | | | | | | | | | 1 | 19 |
| | 5 | 2 | 4 | | 28 | 13 | 15 | 17 | 17 | 40 | 6 | 4 | 39 | 33 | 72 | | | | | 1 | | | | 73 | 20 |
| | | | | | | 1 | 1 | | 1 | | | | 1 | 1 | 2 | | | | | | | | | 2 | 21 |
| | 11 | 6 | 4 | | 26 | 25 | 15 | 14 | 44 | 20 | 5 | 1 | | 81 | 81 | | | | | | | | | 81 | 22 |
| | 583 | 87 | 131 | 25 | 16 | 784 | 1103 | 47 | 1559 | 190 | 84 | 19 | 1115 | 781 | 1896 | | | | | 24 | 24 | 6 | | 1950 | 23 |
| | 1 | | 1 | | 7 | 32 | 65 | 1 | 57 | 35 | 8 | 4 | 45 | 59 | 104 | | | | | 1 | | | | 105 | 24 |
| | 4 | | 5 | | 5 | 26 | 37 | 3 | 35 | 32 | 1 | 2 | 48 | 27 | 70 | | | | | | 1 | | | 71 | 25 |
| | | | | | 1 | 1 | | | | 1 | | 1 | | 2 | 2 | | | | | | | | | 2 | 26 |
| | 3 | | 1 | | 10 | 9 | 6 | 6 | 24 | 7 | | | 20 | 11 | 31 | | | | | | | | | 31 | 27 |
| | | | 1 | | 3 | 4 | 3 | 6 | 5 | 11 | | | 7 | 9 | 16 | | | | | | | | | 16 | 28 |
| | | | | | | | 1 | | 1 | | | | 1 | | 1 | | | | | | | | | 1 | 29 |
| | 5 | | 1 | | 25 | 25 | 28 | 30 | 40 | 50 | 13 | 5 | 71 | 36 | 107 | | | | | | 1 | | | 108 | 30 |

## CLASSIFICATION OF DEATHS IN EASTERN

| | Cause of death. | AGES. | | | | | | | | | | | | | | | | | | NATIVITIES. | | | | | |
|---|---|---|---|---|---|---|---|---|---|---|---|---|---|---|---|---|---|---|---|---|---|---|---|---|---|
| | | Under 1. | | 1 and under 5. | | 5 and under 10. | | 10 and under 20. | | 20 and under 50. | | 50 and under 80. | | 80 and under 100. | | 100 & over. | | Age unknown. | | Born in State. | N. England States. | Middle States. | Southern States. | Southwest'n States. | Northwest'n States. |
| | | M. | F. | M. | F. | M. | F. | M. | F. | M. | F. | M. | F. | M. | F. | M | F. | M | F. | | | | | | |
| 1 | Congestion of lungs | 8 | 8 | 3 | 3 | | | | 1 | 3 | 4 | 4 | 3 | | | | | | | 22 | 5 | 2 | | | |
| 2 | Consumption | 67 | 55 | 76 | 70 | 21 | 36 | 70 | 123 | 496 | 505 | 242 | 183 | 21 | 13 | | | 1 | | 1493 | 122 | 27 | 3 | | 5 |
| 3 | Convulsions | 114 | 73 | 38 | 59 | 6 | 8 | 8 | 6 | 12 | 21 | 8 | 6 | 3 | 3 | | | 1 | | 339 | 10 | 2 | | | |
| 4 | Croup | 65 | 41 | 111 | 80 | 15 | 23 | 1 | 2 | | | 1 | | | | | | 1 | | 320 | 4 | 2 | | | |
| 5 | Debility | 12 | 9 | 4 | 8 | | 1 | 1 | 2 | 8 | 8 | 9 | 9 | | 1 | | | | | 48 | 2 | | | | |
| 6 | Diabetes | | | | | | | 1 | | 1 | | | | | | | | | | 2 | | | | | |
| 7 | Diarrhœa | 35 | 25 | 49 | 50 | 10 | 4 | 8 | 5 | 28 | 15 | 20 | 18 | 3 | 5 | | | | | 214 | 6 | 3 | | | |
| 8 | Dropsy | 19 | 26 | 44 | 36 | 9 | 12 | 7 | 19 | 41 | 52 | 75 | 86 | 16 | 12 | | | | | 374 | 22 | 4 | 1 | | |
| 9 | Dysentery | 124 | 96 | 254 | 236 | 74 | 61 | 33 | 35 | 138 | 122 | 58 | 82 | 6 | 12 | | | | | 1125 | 30 | 11 | 2 | | 1 |
| 10 | Dyspepsia | | | | | | | | | 3 | 2 | 4 | 4 | | | | | | | 11 | 1 | | | | |
| 11 | Epilepsy | | | | | | | | | 4 | | 1 | | | | | | | | 2 | 1 | | | | |
| 12 | Erysipelas | 11 | 10 | 6 | 6 | 1 | 1 | 1 | 4 | 6 | 12 | 7 | 10 | | 5 | | | | | 68 | 5 | | | | |
| 13 | Executed | | | | | | | | | | | | | | | | | | | 1 | | | | | |
| 14 | Eye, disease of | | | | | | | 1 | | | | | | | | | | | | | | | | | |
| 15 | Fever, not specified | 11 | 2 | 16 | 11 | 8 | 7 | 8 | 13 | 41 | 40 | 23 | 14 | 3 | 1 | | | | | 131 | 13 | 1 | 1 | | 2 |
| 16 | ..do..bilious | 2 | 3 | 4 | 6 | 10 | 3 | 10 | 10 | 37 | 12 | 8 | 11 | 1 | | | | 1 | | 90 | 5 | | 1 | | |
| 17 | ..do..brain | 8 | 10 | 15 | 18 | 5 | 1 | 8 | 3 | 15 | 10 | 2 | 8 | 1 | | | | | | 95 | 1 | 3 | | | |
| 18 | ..do..catarrhal | | | | | | | | | 1 | 1 | | | | | | | | | | | | | | |
| 19 | ..do..congestive | | | | | | | 1 | | | 1 | 1 | | | | | | | | 3 | | | | | |
| 20 | ..do..inflammatory | | | | 2 | | | | | 1 | | | | | | | | | | 3 | | | | | |
| 21 | ..do..intermittent | | 1 | | 2 | 1 | | | 2 | 2 | | | | | | | | | | 6 | | | | | |
| 22 | ..do..puerperal | | | | | | | | | | 5 | | | | | | | | | 3 | | | | | |
| 23 | ..do..remittent | | | | 1 | | | 1 | 2 | 6 | 4 | 2 | | | | | | | | 13 | 1 | | | | |
| 24 | ..do..scarlet | 10 | 8 | 54 | 53 | 24 | 37 | 3 | 10 | 2 | 1 | | 1 | 1 | | | | | | 193 | 1 | 4 | | | |
| 25 | ..do..ship | | | 1 | 2 | 1 | | 4 | 5 | 15 | 7 | 3 | 1 | | | | | | | 2 | 1 | | | | |
| 26 | ..do..typhus | 2 | 4 | 4 | 5 | 10 | 10 | 26 | 25 | 156 | 72 | 32 | 14 | | 2 | | | | | 135 | 11 | 5 | 2 | | |
| 27 | ..do..yellow | | | | | | | 1 | | 7 | | | | | | | | | | 5 | | | | | |
| 28 | Fistula | | | | | | | | | | | | 1 | | | | | | | 1 | | | | | |
| 29 | Fracture | | | | | 1 | | | | | | | | | | | | | | 1 | | | | | |
| 30 | Frozen | | | | 1 | | | | | 2 | | 2 | | | | | | | | 4 | 1 | | | | |
| 31 | Gout | | | | | | | | | | | 1 | | | | | | | | | | | | | |
| 32 | Gravel | | | | | | | | | 2 | | 7 | 1 | 5 | | | | | | 11 | 2 | | | | |
| 33 | Head, disease of | 3 | 1 | 3 | 2 | | | | 1 | 2 | | | 2 | | | | | | | 12 | 1 | | | | |
| 34 | Heart....do | 12 | 6 | 4 | 3 | 2 | 5 | 6 | 13 | 34 | 21 | 35 | 24 | 3 | 2 | | | | | 118 | 16 | 7 | 2 | | |
| 35 | Heat | | | | | | | 3 | 1 | 5 | | | | | | | | | | 5 | | | | | |
| 36 | Hemorrhage | 5 | 2 | 3 | 1 | 1 | | | | 16 | 4 | 6 | | | | | | | | 30 | 1 | 2 | | | |
| 37 | Hernia | | | | 1 | | | | | 1 | 3 | | 1 | | | | | | | 2 | 1 | 1 | | | |
| 38 | Hip, disease of | | | 2 | | | | 1 | | | | | | | | | | | | 2 | | | | | |
| 39 | Hives | 4 | | 1 | 1 | 1 | | | | | | | | | | | | | | 7 | | | | | |
| 40 | Hooping cough | 48 | 39 | 49 | 63 | 4 | 5 | 1 | 1 | 1 | | | | | | | | | | 199 | | 3 | | | 1 |
| 41 | Hydrocephalus | 22 | 17 | 41 | 25 | 9 | 4 | 2 | 4 | 3 | 2 | 3 | 1 | | | | | | | 122 | 1 | 1 | | | |
| 42 | Hydrophobia | | | | | 1 | | | | 1 | | | | | | | | | | 1 | | | | | |
| 43 | Inflammation | 40 | 33 | 45 | 25 | 3 | 11 | 10 | 7 | 21 | 23 | 16 | 11 | 6 | 3 | | | | | 217 | 16 | 2 | | | |
| 44 | .....do....bowels | 15 | 14 | 21 | 23 | 5 | 6 | 5 | 5 | 14 | 14 | 11 | 4 | 1 | | | | 1 | | 116 | 8 | | | | |
| 45 | .....do....brain | 30 | 23 | 39 | 27 | 11 | 10 | 10 | 7 | 15 | 6 | 8 | 2 | | | | | | | 172 | 3 | 2 | | | |
| 46 | .....do....head | 3 | 1 | 3 | 3 | 1 | | 1 | 1 | | | | | | | | | | | 12 | 1 | | | | |
| 47 | .....do....stomach | | 1 | | | | 1 | | | 1 | 1 | | 2 | | | | | | | 6 | | | | | |
| 48 | Insanity | | | | | | | | | 7 | 4 | 4 | 5 | | | | | | | 11 | 1 | 2 | | | |
| 49 | Intemperance | | | | | | | 1 | | 9 | 2 | 4 | 1 | | | | | | | 13 | | 1 | | | |
| 50 | Jaundice | 6 | 3 | 2 | 1 | | | 1 | | 1 | 1 | 3 | 3 | | | | | | | 16 | 2 | | | | |
| 51 | Kidneys, disease of | | | 1 | | | | 1 | | 1 | 2 | 9 | 1 | 1 | | | | | | 11 | 4 | | | | |
| 52 | Killed | | | 1 | | 2 | | 2 | | 16 | | 2 | | | 2 | | | | | 17 | 1 | | | | |
| 53 | Lightning | | | | | | | | | 1 | | 1 | | | | | | | | 1 | | | | | |
| 54 | Limb, fracture of | | | | | | | | | 2 | | | 1 | | | | | | | 2 | | | | | |
| 55 | Liver, disease of | 1 | 1 | 2 | 4 | 1 | 1 | 2 | 1 | 14 | 9 | 18 | 26 | 1 | | | | | | 62 | 8 | | | | |
| 56 | Lockjaw | | | | | 1 | 1 | 4 | 1 | 3 | | 1 | | | | | | | | 11 | | | | | |
| 57 | Lungs, disease of | | 1 | 2 | 3 | 1 | | | 2 | 3 | 1 | 3 | 3 | | | | | | | 12 | 1 | | | | |
| 58 | Malformation | 1 | 2 | | | | | | | | | | | | | | | | | 3 | | | | | |
| 59 | Mania-a-potu | | | | | | | 1 | | 17 | | 4 | | | | | | | | 12 | 1 | 3 | | | |
| 60 | Marasmus | 5 | 6 | 8 | 5 | 1 | 1 | 1 | | 1 | | 4 | | 1 | | | | | | 23 | 1 | | | | |
| 61 | Measles | 14 | 12 | 49 | 41 | 6 | 11 | 2 | 9 | 4 | 6 | | 2 | | | | | | | 131 | 2 | 1 | | | 1 |
| 62 | Mortification | | | | | | | | | 3 | | 7 | 1 | 1 | | | | | | 7 | | | | | |
| 63 | Mumps | | | 1 | | 2 | | 2 | 1 | 3 | | 1 | | | | | | | | 9 | 1 | | | | |
| 64 | Murder | | | | | | | | | 1 | | | | | | | | | | 1 | | | | | |
| 65 | Neuralgia | | | | | | | | 1 | 3 | | | 6 | | | | | | | 5 | 2 | | | | |
| 66 | Old age | | | | | | | | | 1 | 1 | 70 | 93 | 130 | 159 | 2 | 8 | | 1 | 298 | 82 | 11 | 1 | | |
| 67 | Paralysis | | | 3 | 2 | 1 | 4 | 1 | 1 | 13 | 6 | 44 | 47 | 14 | 19 | | | | | 121 | 14 | 2 | 1 | | |
| 68 | Piles | | | | | | | | | 2 | | 1 | | 1 | | | | | | 3 | 1 | | | | |
| 69 | Pleurisy | | 1 | | 2 | | | 1 | 1 | 11 | 6 | 6 | 13 | 2 | 2 | | | | | 35 | 1 | | | | |
| 70 | Pneumonia | 56 | 53 | 79 | 57 | 13 | 17 | 6 | 5 | 56 | 26 | 28 | 20 | 1 | 6 | | | 1 | 1 | 346 | 19 | 3 | 3 | | 1 |
| 71 | Poison | 2 | | 5 | 2 | 1 | 2 | | | | 1 | 3 | 1 | | | | | | | 15 | 1 | | | | |
| 72 | Premature birth | 1 | | | | | | | | | | | | | | | | | | 1 | | | | | |
| 73 | Quinsy | 2 | 2 | 1 | | | | | | 3 | | 1 | 2 | | | | | | | 8 | 1 | | | | |
| 74 | Rheumatism | 4 | 3 | 5 | 4 | 2 | | 3 | 1 | 7 | 10 | 11 | 6 | 1 | | | | | | 40 | 2 | 1 | | | |
| 75 | Rickets | 1 | | | | | | | | | | | | | | | | | | 1 | | | | | |

CTION OF THE STATE OF NEW YORK—Continued.

| NATIVITIES. | | | | | SEASON OF DECEASE. | | | | DURATION OF SICKNESS. | | | | WHITES. | | | COLORED. | | | | | | | | | |
|---|---|---|---|---|---|---|---|---|---|---|---|---|---|---|---|---|---|---|---|---|---|---|---|---|---|
| | | | | | | | | | | | | | | | | Slaves. | | | | Free. | | | | | |
| | | | | | | | | | | | | | | | | Black. | | Mulatto. | | Black. | | Mul. | | | |
| ritories. | Ireland. | Germany. | Other foreign countries. | Unknown. | Spring. | Summer. | Autumn. | Winter. | Under 1 week. | 1 week and under 1 month. | 1 month and under 3 months. | 3 months and over. | Males. | Females. | Total. | M. | F. | M. | F. | M. | F. | M | F. | Aggregate deaths. | |
| .. | 1 | | 2 | | 13 | 8 | 5 | 6 | 13 | 13 | 3 | 3 | 18 | 14 | 32 | | | | | | | | | 32 | 1 |
| .. | 221 | 20 | 84 | 4 | 564 | 514 | 469 | 428 | 55 | 240 | 254 | 1277 | 942 | 946 | 1888 | | | | | 46 | 38 | 6 | 1 | 1979 | 2 |
| .. | 9 | 4 | 2 | | 108 | 87 | 93 | 77 | 258 | 58 | 12 | 17 | 186 | 172 | 358 | | | | | 4 | 4 | | | 366 | 3 |
| .. | 5 | 1 | 7 | 1 | 109 | 38 | 80 | 109 | 242 | 75 | 2 | 1 | 191 | 142 | 333 | | | | | 2 | 4 | 1 | | 340 | 4 |
| .. | 19 | 1 | 2 | | 17 | 12 | 23 | 19 | 15 | 10 | 11 | 29 | 32 | 38 | 70 | | | | | 2 | | | | 72 | 5 |
| ... | | | | | | | 1 | 1 | 1 | | | 1 | 2 | | 2 | | | | | | | | | 2 | 6 |
| ... | 38 | 3 | 11 | | 25 | 55 | 157 | 37 | 73 | 125 | 32 | 19 | 151 | 122 | 273 | | | | | 1 | | 1 | | 275 | 7 |
| ... | 32 | 5 | 15 | 1 | 126 | 110 | 111 | 106 | 57 | 183 | 74 | 172 | 202 | 228 | 430 | | | | | 8 | 14 | 1 | 1 | 454 | 8 |
| ... | 112 | 10 | 37 | 3 | 73 | 158 | 964 | 134 | 345 | 773 | 122 | 45 | 678 | 632 | 1310 | | | | | 7 | 11 | 2 | 1 | 1331 | 9 |
| ... | | | 1 | | 4 | 4 | 3 | 2 | | 2 | 3 | 8 | 7 | 5 | 12 | | | | | | | | 1 | 13 | 10 |
| ... | 2 | | | | 3 | | 1 | 1 | | 2 | | | 4 | | 4 | | | | | 1 | | | | 5 | 11 |
| ... | 3 | 1 | 3 | | 33 | 19 | 14 | 14 | 17 | 50 | 8 | 3 | 32 | 48 | 80 | | | | | | | | | 80 | 12 |
| ... | | | | | | | | 1 | 1 | | | | 1 | | 1 | | | | | | | | | 1 | 13 |
| ... | 1 | | | | | | | 1 | | | | 1 | 1 | | 1 | | | | | | | | | 1 | 14 |
| ... | 26 | 7 | 16 | 1 | 60 | 34 | 66 | 38 | 33 | 118 | 29 | 9 | 108 | 85 | 193 | | | | | 2 | 3 | | | 198 | 15 |
| ... | 15 | 2 | 5 | | 18 | 28 | 42 | 30 | 25 | 72 | 15 | 4 | 70 | 45 | 115 | | | | | 3 | | | | 118 | 16 |
| ... | 3 | | 2 | | 30 | 26 | 29 | 19 | 33 | 60 | 7 | 3 | 51 | 48 | 99 | | | | | 3 | 1 | | 1 | 104 | 17 |
| ... | 1 | | 1 | | | | 2 | | 1 | 1 | | | 1 | 1 | 2 | | | | | | | | | 2 | 18 |
| ... | | | | | | 1 | 1 | 1 | 2 | 1 | | | 2 | 1 | 3 | | | | | | | | | 3 | 19 |
| ... | | | | | 1 | | 2 | | | 3 | | | 1 | 2 | 3 | | | | | | | | | 3 | 20 |
| ... | 1 | | 1 | | 1 | 2 | 3 | 2 | 1 | 6 | 1 | | 3 | 5 | 8 | | | | | | | | | 8 | 21 |
| ... | 2 | | | | 2 | | 1 | 2 | 2 | 2 | 1 | | | 5 | 5 | | | | | | | | | 5 | 22 |
| ... | 2 | | | | 1 | 5 | 6 | 4 | 1 | 12 | 1 | | 9 | 7 | 16 | | | | | | | | | 16 | 23 |
| ... | 2 | | 4 | | 73 | 66 | 27 | 87 | 82 | 99 | 14 | 5 | 90 | 110 | 200 | | | | | 4 | | | | 204 | 24 |
| .. | 30 | | 6 | | 7 | 15 | 10 | 7 | 6 | 19 | | 2 | 24 | 15 | 39 | | | | | | | | | 39 | 25 |
| ... | 172 | 16 | 20 | 1 | 101 | 87 | 91 | 82 | 70 | 201 | 55 | 14 | 227 | 129 | 356 | | | | | 2 | 2 | 1 | 1 | 362 | 26 |
| ... | 2 | | 1 | | 2 | 1 | 2 | 3 | 3 | 3 | | | 8 | | 8 | | | | | | | | | 8 | 27 |
| ... | | | | | 1 | | | | | | | 1 | | 1 | 1 | | | | | | | | | 1 | 28 |
| ... | | | | | | | 1 | | | | | | 1 | | 1 | | | | | | | | | 1 | 29 |
| ... | | | | | 2 | | | 3 | 2 | | | | 4 | 1 | 5 | | | | | | | | | 5 | 30 |
| ... | | | 1 | | | | 1 | | | | | 1 | 1 | | 1 | | | | | | | | | 1 | 31 |
| ... | 1 | | | 1 | 5 | 5 | 2 | 3 | 1 | 8 | 1 | 5 | 14 | 1 | 15 | | | | | | | | | 15 | 32 |
| ... | 1 | | | | 3 | 2 | 4 | 5 | 5 | 5 | | 4 | 8 | 6 | 14 | | | | | | | | | 14 | 33 |
| ... | 12 | 2 | 13 | | 43 | 42 | 42 | 43 | 58 | 40 | 19 | 41 | 89 | 71 | 160 | | | | | 6 | 3 | 1 | | 170 | 34 |
| ... | 3 | | 1 | | | 9 | | | 6 | 1 | | | 8 | 1 | 9 | | | | | | | | | 9 | 35 |
| ... | 3 | | 2 | | 11 | 9 | 15 | 3 | 18 | 5 | 3 | 6 | 29 | 7 | 36 | | | | | 2 | | | | 38 | 36 |
| ... | | | 2 | | 2 | 1 | 1 | 2 | | 5 | 1 | | 1 | 5 | 6 | | | | | | | | | 6 | 37 |
| ... | | | 1 | | 2 | 1 | | | | | 1 | 2 | 3 | | 3 | | | | | | | | | 3 | 38 |
| ... | | | | | 2 | 3 | 1 | 1 | 6 | 1 | | | 6 | 1 | 7 | | | | | | | | | 7 | 39 |
| ... | 6 | 1 | 1 | | 71 | 50 | 49 | 41 | 34 | 110 | 47 | 17 | 99 | 101 | 200 | | | | | 4 | 7 | | | 211 | 40 |
| ... | 5 | | 4 | | 35 | 34 | 42 | 20 | 22 | 85 | 12 | 10 | 79 | 52 | 131 | | | | | 1 | 1 | | | 133 | 41 |
| ... | 1 | | | | | 2 | | | 1 | 1 | | | 2 | | 2 | | | | | | | | | 2 | 42 |
| ... | 14 | 1 | 4 | | 86 | 57 | 45 | 62 | 85 | 121 | 18 | 19 | 140 | 111 | 251 | | | | | 1 | 2 | | | 254 | 43 |
| ... | 8 | 3 | 4 | | 36 | 30 | 50 | 22 | 39 | 78 | 14 | 6 | 73 | 63 | 136 | | | | | | 2 | | 1 | 139 | 44 |
| ... | 8 | 1 | 2 | | 45 | 50 | 53 | 38 | 58 | 93 | 17 | 10 | 111 | 73 | 184 | | | | | 2 | 2 | | | 188 | 45 |
| ... | | | | | 5 | 3 | 4 | 1 | 5 | 8 | | | 8 | 4 | 12 | | | | | | 1 | | | 13 | 46 |
| ... | | | | | | 2 | 1 | 3 | 1 | 4 | | 1 | 1 | 5 | 6 | | | | | | | | | 6 | 47 |
| ... | 3 | 1 | 1 | 1 | 9 | 2 | 7 | 2 | 1 | 3 | 2 | 9 | 11 | 9 | 20 | | | | | | | | | 20 | 48 |
| ... | 3 | | | | 4 | 3 | 7 | 3 | 7 | | 1 | 5 | 12 | 2 | 14 | | | | | 2 | 1 | | | 17 | 49 |
| ... | 2 | | 1 | | 8 | 4 | 5 | 4 | 8 | 6 | 3 | 3 | 12 | 8 | 20 | | | | | 1 | | | | 21 | 50 |
| ... | | | 1 | | 7 | 1 | 6 | 2 | | 6 | 2 | 7 | 13 | 3 | 16 | | | | | | | | | 16 | 51 |
| ... | 5 | 1 | 1 | | 4 | 12 | 5 | 3 | 17 | 1 | | 1 | 22 | 2 | 24 | | | | | 1 | | | | 25 | 52 |
| ... | 1 | | | | | 1 | 1 | | 2 | | | | 2 | | 2 | | | | | | | | | 2 | 53 |
| ... | 1 | | | | 1 | 1 | 1 | | | 1 | | 1 | 2 | 1 | 3 | | | | | | | | | 3 | 54 |
| ... | 8 | | 3 | | 24 | 22 | 23 | 12 | 14 | 18 | 12 | 35 | 39 | 40 | 79 | | | | | | 2 | | | 81 | 55 |
| ... | | | | | 2 | 6 | 2 | 1 | 6 | 5 | | | 8 | 2 | 10 | | | | | 1 | | | | 11 | 56 |
| ... | 4 | | 2 | | 6 | 7 | 3 | 3 | 5 | 4 | 2 | 8 | 9 | 10 | 19 | | | | | | | | | 19 | 57 |
| ... | | | | | | 1 | 1 | 1 | 1 | 1 | | 1 | | 1 | 1 | | | | | 1 | 1 | | | 3 | 58 |
| ... | 2 | 2 | 2 | | 7 | 8 | 4 | 3 | 14 | 5 | 1 | | 22 | | 22 | | | | | | | | | 22 | 59 |
| ... | 9 | | | | 5 | 10 | 14 | 4 | 3 | 5 | 5 | 16 | 21 | 12 | 33 | | | | | | | | | 33 | 60 |
| ... | 19 | | 2 | | 39 | 63 | 40 | 14 | 27 | 99 | 19 | 9 | 74 | 80 | 154 | | | | | 1 | 1 | | | 156 | 61 |
| ... | 3 | 1 | 1 | | 3 | 2 | 5 | 2 | 2 | 4 | 3 | 2 | 11 | 1 | 12 | | | | | | | | | 12 | 62 |
| ... | | | | | 4 | 5 | 1 | | 1 | 7 | 1 | | 9 | 1 | 10 | | | | | | | | | 10 | 63 |
| ... | | | | | 1 | | | | | | | | 1 | | 1 | | | | | | | | | 1 | 64 |
| ... | 2 | | 1 | | 3 | | 3 | 4 | 1 | 1 | 2 | 4 | 3 | 7 | 10 | | | | | | | | | 10 | 65 |
| ... | 35 | 5 | 20 | 13 | 343 | 118 | 112 | 92 | 69 | 74 | 81 | 84 | 198 | 251 | 449 | | | | | 4 | 10 | 1 | 1 | 465 | 66 |
| ... | 9 | | 8 | | 42 | 50 | 40 | 22 | 30 | 41 | 18 | 61 | 76 | 76 | 152 | | | | | | 3 | | | 155 | 67 |
| ... | | | | | 1 | 2 | 1 | | 1 | | 2 | 1 | 3 | | 3 | | | | | | | 1 | | 4 | 68 |
| ... | 6 | | 3 | | 15 | 17 | 6 | 6 | 17 | 21 | 4 | 3 | 19 | 23 | 42 | | | | | | 1 | 1 | 1 | 45 | 69 |
| ... | 42 | 4 | 7 | | 182 | 82 | 57 | 103 | 116 | 230 | 52 | 17 | 233 | 178 | 411 | | | | | 5 | 5 | 2 | 2 | 425 | 70 |
| ... | 3 | | | | 2 | 6 | 8 | 3 | 12 | 3 | | 1 | 18 | 6 | 19 | | | | | | | | | 19 | 71 |
| ... | | | | | | | | 1 | | 1 | | | 1 | | 1 | | | | | | | | | 1 | 72 |
| ... | 1 | 1 | | | 5 | 4 | 2 | | 5 | 5 | 1 | | 7 | 4 | 11 | | | | | | | | | 11 | 73 |
| ... | 9 | 4 | 1 | | 12 | 12 | 23 | 10 | 8 | 21 | 10 | 17 | 32 | 22 | 54 | | | | | 1 | 1 | | 1 | 57 | 74 |
| ... | | | | | 1 | | | | | | 1 | | 1 | | 1 | | | | | | | | | 1 | 75 |

## CLASSIFICATION OF DEATHS IN EASTERN

| | Cause of death. | AGES. Under 1. M. | Under 1. F. | 1 and under 5. M. | 1 and under 5. F. | 5 and under 10. M. | 5 and under 10. F. | 10 and under 20. M. | 10 and under 20. F. | 20 and under 50. M. | 20 and under 50. F. | 50 and under 80. M. | 50 and under 80. F. | 80 and under 100. M. | 80 and under 100. F. | 100 & over. M | 100 & over. F. | Age unknown. M | Age unknown. F. | NATIVITIES. Born in State. | N. England States. | Middle States. | Southern States. | Southwest'n States. | Northwest'n States. |
|---|---|---|---|---|---|---|---|---|---|---|---|---|---|---|---|---|---|---|---|---|---|---|---|---|---|
| 1 | Salivation, effects of. | | | | | | | | | | 1 | | | | | | | | | 1 | | | | | |
| 2 | Scrofula | 1 | 1 | 7 | 5 | | 1 | 5 | 6 | 10 | 6 | 3 | 3 | 1 | | | | | | 40 | 4 | | 1 | | 1 |
| 3 | Scurvy | | | | | | | | | 1 | | | | | | | | | | 1 | | | | | |
| 4 | Small pox | 7 | 7 | 8 | 11 | 4 | 4 | 7 | 4 | 25 | 5 | 3 | 2 | | 1 | | | | 1 | 58 | 2 | | | 1 | |
| 5 | Spine, disease of | 6 | 6 | 1 | | 1 | 1 | | | 4 | 1 | 2 | 2 | | | | | | | 21 | | | 1 | | |
| 6 | Stillborn | 9 | 6 | | | | | | | | | | | | | | | | | 15 | | | | | |
| 7 | Stomach, disease of | | | | | | | | | | 1 | 2 | | | | | | | | 2 | 1 | | | | |
| 8 | Suffocation | | 3 | 1 | 2 | 1 | | | | | | | | | | | | | | 7 | | | | | |
| 9 | Suicide | | | | | | | | | 13 | 2 | 7 | | 3 | | | | | | 15 | 1 | | | | |
| 10 | Summer complaint | 7 | 10 | 8 | 10 | 4 | | 2 | 1 | 1 | 2 | 2 | 1 | | | | | | | 44 | 2 | | | | |
| 11 | Sun, stroke of | | | | 1 | | | | 1 | 9 | | | | | | | | | | 4 | | | | | |
| 12 | Syphilis | | | | | | | | | 1 | | | | | | | | | | 1 | | | | | |
| 13 | Teething | 25 | 32 | 41 | 41 | 1 | 1 | | | | | | | | | | | | | 128 | 2 | 2 | 2 | | |
| 14 | Tetanus | | | | | | | | | 2 | | | | | | | | | | 1 | | | | | |
| 15 | Throat, disease of | 1 | 1 | 5 | 3 | 3 | 2 | 1 | 1 | 1 | 3 | 1 | 1 | 1 | | | | | | 20 | 1 | | | | |
| 16 | Thrush | 3 | 3 | 1 | 1 | | | | | | 1 | | | | | | | | | 9 | | | | | |
| 17 | Tumor | 1 | | | | | | | 1 | 3 | 6 | 3 | 2 | | | | | | | 10 | | | | | |
| 18 | Ulcer | | | 1 | 1 | 1 | | 1 | 1 | 1 | | | | | | | | | | 4 | | | | | |
| 19 | Uterus, disease of | | | | | | | | | | | | 1 | | | | | | | 1 | | | | | |
| 20 | Venereal | | | | | | | | | | | | 1 | | | | | | | 1 | | | | | |
| 21 | White swelling | | | | 1 | | | | 1 | | | | 1 | | | | | | | 3 | | | | | |
| 22 | Worms | 1 | 3 | 16 | 7 | 3 | 1 | 2 | 1 | | | | | | | | | | | 28 | 1 | | | | |
| 23 | Unknown | 185 | 162 | 98 | 78 | 34 | 33 | 38 | 49 | 207 | 156 | 140 | 76 | 15 | 9 | | | 48 | 48 | 938 | 34 | 11 | 3 | | |
| | Total | 1167 | 935 | 1517 | 1324 | 441 | 441 | 482 | 511 | 2349 | 1700 | 1266 | 1038 | 282 | 283 | 3 | 8 | 68 | 55 | 10283 | 581 | 160 | 30 | 1 | 16 |

## CLASSIFICATION OF DEATHS IN CENTRA

*Embracing the following counties: Alleghany, Broome, Cataraugus, Chemung, Chenango, Cou Onondaga, Ontario, Otsego, Schenectady, Schoharie, Senec*

| | Cause of death. | Under 1. M. | Under 1. F. | 1 and under 5. M. | 1 and under 5. F. | 5 and under 10. M. | 5 and under 10. F. | 10 and under 20. M. | 10 and under 20. F. | 20 and under 50. M. | 20 and under 50. F. | 50 and under 80. M. | 50 and under 80. F. | 80 and under 100. M. | 80 and under 100. F. | 100 & over. M | 100 & over. F. | Age unknown. M | Age unknown. F. | Born in State. | N. England States. | Middle States. | Southern States. | Southwest'n States. |
|---|---|---|---|---|---|---|---|---|---|---|---|---|---|---|---|---|---|---|---|---|---|---|---|---|
| 1 | Abscess | 1 | | | 1 | | | 1 | 1 | 5 | 2 | | | 1 | | | | | | 10 | 2 | | | |
| 2 | Accident, not specif'd | 6 | 3 | 8 | 10 | 9 | 8 | 20 | 3 | 59 | 3 | 27 | 6 | 3 | | | | | | 116 | 23 | 2 | | |
| 3 | ....do ..burned | 2 | | 10 | 8 | | 2 | | | 2 | 1 | | | 1 | | | | | | 24 | 1 | | | |
| 4 | ....do...drowned | | | 16 | 4 | 19 | 3 | 7 | 6 | 13 | 3 | 4 | | | | | | | | 57 | 3 | | | |
| 5 | ....do...scalded | 3 | 1 | 11 | 12 | | 2 | | | | | | | | | | | | | 27 | | | | |
| 6 | ....do...shot | | | | | | | 1 | | 1 | | | | | | | | | | 1 | | | | |
| 7 | ....do...railroad | | | | | 1 | | 3 | 1 | 4 | | | | | | | | | | 7 | | | | |
| 8 | Aneurism | | | | | | | | | 1 | | | | | | | | | | 1 | | | | |
| 9 | Apoplexy | | | | | | | | | 14 | 13 | 35 | 24 | 8 | 7 | | | 2 | | 52 | 33 | 6 | | |
| 10 | Asthma | | | 2 | | | | | | | 2 | 1 | 2 | | 1 | | | | | 5 | | | 1 | |
| 11 | Bowels, disease of | 4 | 2 | 7 | 5 | | 1 | | 1 | 3 | 2 | | 3 | | 1 | | | | | 24 | 1 | 2 | | |
| 12 | Brain........do | 5 | 3 | 4 | 2 | 2 | 1 | 3 | 1 | 4 | 1 | 3 | 1 | | | | | | | 26 | 3 | | | |
| 13 | Bronchitis | 2 | | 5 | 2 | 2 | | 2 | 1 | 1 | 4 | 7 | 2 | | | | | | | 22 | 5 | 1 | | |
| 14 | Cancer | | 1 | 1 | 1 | 1 | | | | 5 | 13 | 20 | 29 | 8 | 2 | | | | | 43 | 28 | 2 | | |
| 15 | Canker | 1 | 2 | 3 | | | 1 | | | | | | | | | | | | | 7 | | | | |
| 16 | ..do...rash | 4 | | 10 | 5 | 3 | | 1 | 2 | | | | | | | | | | | 25 | | | | |
| 17 | Catarrh | 9 | 6 | | 3 | | | 1 | | 1 | | 2 | 2 | 2 | 1 | | | | | 20 | 4 | 1 | | |
| 18 | Chicken pox | 2 | | | 1 | | | | | | | | | | | | | | | 3 | | | | |
| 19 | Childbirth | | | | | | | | 4 | | 88 | | | | | | | | | 68 | 6 | 5 | | |
| 20 | Cholera | 8 | 8 | 16 | 17 | 6 | 7 | 3 | 1 | 56 | 29 | 31 | 9 | 1 | | | | | | 124 | 18 | 9 | | 1 |
| 21 | ...do...infantum | 11 | 6 | 15 | 8 | 1 | | | | | | | | | | | | | | 39 | | | | |
| 22 | ...do...morbus | 1 | 1 | 9 | 5 | 1 | 3 | 4 | | 13 | 5 | 5 | 4 | 2 | 1 | | | | | 42 | 5 | 1 | | |
| 23 | Chorea | | | | | | | | 2 | 1 | 1 | | 1 | | | | | | | 5 | | | | |
| 24 | Colic | 2 | 1 | 1 | 1 | 2 | 1 | 4 | 1 | 8 | 5 | 10 | 4 | 1 | | | | 1 | | 27 | 9 | 1 | | |
| 25 | Congestion | 2 | 1 | 4 | 5 | 2 | | 3 | | 3 | 3 | 4 | 3 | | | | | | | 27 | 2 | | | |
| 26 | ....do....bowels | | | 1 | | | | | | 1 | | | | | | | | | | 2 | | | | |
| 27 | ....do....brain | 3 | 4 | 8 | 8 | 3 | 4 | 6 | 3 | 11 | 4 | 3 | 2 | 2 | | | | | | 51 | 5 | 1 | | |
| 28 | ....do....lungs | | 1 | 2 | 1 | | | 1 | 1 | 1 | | 2 | 4 | | 1 | | | | | 9 | 4 | 1 | | |
| 29 | Consumption | 88 | 80 | 53 | 58 | 14 | 16 | 57 | 154 | 441 | 554 | 240 | 217 | 24 | 19 | 1 | | | | 1458 | 237 | 69 | 3 | 2 |
| 30 | Convulsions | 91 | 72 | 31 | 32 | 3 | 5 | | 3 | 14 | 11 | 11 | 7 | 2 | | | | 1 | | 257 | 7 | 3 | | |
| 31 | Croup | 60 | 15 | 97 | 77 | 23 | 17 | 2 | | 1 | | 1 | | | | | | | | 279 | 1 | 4 | | |
| 32 | Debility | 5 | 3 | 1 | | | | | | 1 | 4 | 1 | 2 | | | | | | | 15 | 1 | | | |
| 33 | Diabetes | | | 2 | | | | 3 | 1 | 4 | 2 | 5 | 1 | 4 | | | | | | 15 | 4 | 2 | | |
| 34 | Diarrhœa | 27 | 16 | 54 | 53 | 7 | 3 | 7 | 4 | 10 | 15 | 18 | 17 | 8 | 2 | | | | | 199 | 26 | 4 | | |
| 35 | Dropsy | 18 | 24 | 44 | 87 | 18 | 12 | 14 | 17 | 24 | 80 | 99 | 102 | 14 | 18 | | | | | 357 | 92 | 28 | 2 | |
| 36 | Dysentery | 46 | 62 | 251 | 233 | 66 | 54 | 18 | 40 | 64 | 82 | 57 | 43 | 7 | 6 | | | | | 895 | 49 | 13 | | |
| 37 | Dyspepsia | | | | | | | | | 4 | 2 | 5 | 2 | | | | | | | 7 | 2 | 3 | | |
| 38 | Epilepsy | | 1 | | | 1 | | 1 | | 3 | 3 | | 2 | | | | | | | 11 | | | | |
| 39 | Erysipelas | 11 | 7 | 10 | 7 | 7 | 3 | 6 | 4 | 10 | 18 | 10 | 12 | 5 | 1 | | | | | 78 | 22 | 2 | | |

## ECTION OF THE STATE OF NEW YORK—Continued.

| Nativities: ...ritories. | Nativities: Ireland. | Nativities: Germany. | Nativities: Other foreign countries. | Nativities: Unknown. | Season of decease: Spring. | Season of decease: Summer. | Season of decease: Autumn. | Season of decease: Winter. | Duration of sickness: Under 1 week. | Duration of sickness: 1 week and under 1 month. | Duration of sickness: 1 month and under 3 months. | Duration of sickness: 3 months and over. | Whites: Males. | Whites: Females. | Whites: Total. | Colored: Slaves: Black: M. | Colored: Slaves: Black: F. | Colored: Slaves: Mulatto: M. | Colored: Slaves: Mulatto: F. | Colored: Free: Black: M. | Colored: Free: Black: F. | Colored: Free: Mul.: M | Colored: Free: Mul.: F. | Aggregate deaths. | |
|---|---|---|---|---|---|---|---|---|---|---|---|---|---|---|---|---|---|---|---|---|---|---|---|---|---|
| | | | | | | | 1 | | | | | 1 | | 1 | 1 | | | | | | | | | 1 | 1 |
| | 3 | | | | 13 | 13 | 13 | 9 | 2 | 12 | 2 | 28 | 27 | 22 | 49 | | | | | | | | | 49 | 2 |
| | | | | | | 1 | | | | | | 1 | 1 | | 1 | | | | | | | | | 1 | 3 |
| | 17 | 7 | 4 | 1 | 26 | 33 | 7 | 24 | 15 | 58 | 6 | 2 | 51 | 36 | 87 | | | | | 3 | | | | 90 | 4 |
| | 2 | | | | 6 | 5 | 9 | 4 | 1 | 8 | 2 | 9 | 13 | 10 | 23 | | | | | 1 | | | | 24 | 5 |
| | | | | | 2 | 7 | 5 | 1 | | | | | 9 | 6 | 15 | | | | | | | | | 15 | 6 |
| | | | | | 1 | | 1 | 1 | 1 | 1 | | 1 | 2 | 1 | 3 | | | | | | | | | 3 | 7 |
| | | | | | 1 | 1 | 1 | 4 | 7 | | | | 2 | 5 | 7 | | | | | | | | | 7 | 8 |
| | 3 | 1 | 4 | 1 | 6 | 10 | 5 | 3 | 11 | 1 | | | 22 | 2 | 24 | | | | | 1 | | | | 25 | 9 |
| | 2 | | | | 1 | 11 | 30 | 6 | 5 | 33 | 5 | 5 | 24 | 24 | 48 | | | | | | | | | 48 | 10 |
| | 7 | | | | | 9 | 2 | | 10 | | | | 9 | 2 | 11 | | | | | | | | | 11 | 11 |
| | | | | | | | 1 | | | | | 1 | 1 | | 1 | | | | | | | | | 1 | 12 |
| | 3 | 2 | 2 | | 22 | 37 | 63 | 19 | 32 | 64 | 30 | 15 | 64 | 72 | 136 | | | | | 3 | 1 | | 1 | 141 | 13 |
| | 1 | | | | 1 | | | 1 | 2 | | | | 2 | | 2 | | | | | | | | | 2 | 14 |
| | 1 | | 2 | | 10 | 1 | 4 | 7 | 10 | 12 | | 1 | 13 | 11 | 24 | | | | | | | | | 24 | 15 |
| | | | | | 3 | 2 | 3 | 1 | 4 | 2 | 3 | | 4 | 5 | 9 | | | | | | | | | 9 | 16 |
| | 4 | 1 | 1 | | 3 | 6 | 3 | 4 | | 6 | | 8 | 7 | 8 | 15 | | | | | | 1 | | | 16 | 17 |
| | 1 | | 1 | | 2 | | 2 | 2 | | 4 | 1 | | 4 | 2 | 6 | | | | | | | | | 6 | 18 |
| | | | | | 1 | | | | | | | 1 | | 1 | 1 | | | | | | | | | 1 | 19 |
| | | | | | 1 | | | | | | | 1 | | 1 | 1 | | | | | | | | | 1 | 20 |
| | | | | | 1 | 1 | | 1 | | | 2 | 1 | | 3 | 3 | | | | | | | | | 3 | 21 |
| | 2 | | 3 | | 7 | 7 | 13 | 7 | 13 | 13 | 6 | 1 | 22 | 12 | 34 | | | | | | | | | 34 | 22 |
| | 248 | 14 | 62 | 71 | 315 | 409 | 335 | 263 | 333 | 198 | 74 | 165 | 737 | 594 | 1331 | | | | | 27 | 21 | 1 | 1 | 1381 | 23 |
| | 1921 | 266 | 576 | 126 | 2968 | 3671 | 4810 | 2325 | 4633 | 4111 | 1179 | 2382 | 7360 | 6106 | 13466 | | | | | 188 | 174 | 27 | 15 | 13870 | |

## SECTION OF THE STATE OF NEW YORK.

*andt, Delaware, Fulton, Hamilton, Herkimer, Lewis, Livingston, Madison, Montgomery, Oneida, Steuben, Sullivan, Tioga, Tompkins, Wyoming, and Yates.*

| Nativities: ...ritories. | Nativities: Ireland. | Nativities: Germany. | Nativities: Other foreign countries. | Nativities: Unknown. | Season of decease: Spring. | Season of decease: Summer. | Season of decease: Autumn. | Season of decease: Winter. | Duration of sickness: Under 1 week. | Duration of sickness: 1 week and under 1 month. | Duration of sickness: 1 month and under 3 months. | Duration of sickness: 3 months and over. | Whites: Males. | Whites: Females. | Whites: Total. | Colored: Slaves: Black: M. | Colored: Slaves: Black: F. | Colored: Slaves: Mulatto: M. | Colored: Slaves: Mulatto: F. | Colored: Free: Black: M. | Colored: Free: Black: F. | Colored: Free: Mul.: M | Colored: Free: Mul.: F. | Aggregate deaths. | |
|---|---|---|---|---|---|---|---|---|---|---|---|---|---|---|---|---|---|---|---|---|---|---|---|---|---|
| | | | | | | 5 | 4 | 3 | 1 | 2 | 2 | 6 | 8 | 4 | 12 | | | | | | | | | 12 | 1 |
| | 16 | 3 | 4 | | 43 | 49 | 39 | 32 | 90 | 28 | 8 | 7 | 131 | 33 | 164 | | | | | | | 1 | | 165 | 2 |
| | | | 1 | | 10 | 6 | 3 | 7 | 22 | 3 | | | 15 | 11 | 26 | | | | | | | | | 26 | 3 |
| | 10 | | 4 | | 8 | 41 | 16 | 8 | 75 | | | | 58 | 16 | 74 | | | | | 1 | | | | 75 | 4 |
| | | | 1 | | 8 | 9 | 5 | 7 | 20 | 6 | | | 14 | 15 | 29 | | | | | | | | | 29 | 5 |
| | 1 | | | | | | 2 | | 2 | | | | 2 | | 2 | | | | | | | | | 2 | 6 |
| | 2 | | | | 3 | 2 | 3 | 1 | 1 | | 1 | 1 | 8 | 1 | 9 | | | | | | | | | 9 | 7 |
| | | | | | 1 | | | | | | | 1 | 1 | | 1 | | | | | | | | | 1 | 8 |
| | 2 | | 9 | 1 | 35 | 26 | 25 | 17 | 68 | 8 | 2 | 7 | 58 | 44 | 102 | | | | | | | 1 | | 103 | 9 |
| | 1 | | 1 | | 4 | | 2 | 2 | 1 | 4 | | 3 | 3 | 4 | 7 | | | | | | 1 | | | 8 | 10 |
| | 2 | | | | 4 | 5 | 14 | 5 | 8 | 13 | 4 | 3 | 14 | 15 | 29 | | | | | | | | | 29 | 11 |
| | 1 | | | | 13 | 9 | 3 | 5 | 7 | 17 | 3 | 3 | 21 | 9 | 30 | | | | | | | | | 30 | 12 |
| | | | | | 13 | 9 | 4 | 2 | 7 | 7 | | 12 | 19 | 9 | 28 | | | | | | | | | 28 | 13 |
| | 4 | | 3 | 1 | 22 | 23 | 24 | 12 | 5 | 5 | 9 | 58 | 35 | 46 | 81 | | | | | | | | | 81 | 14 |
| | | | | | 4 | 1 | 2 | | 1 | 5 | 1 | | 4 | 3 | 7 | | | | | | | | | 7 | 15 |
| | | | | | 7 | 6 | 5 | 7 | 11 | 12 | 2 | | 18 | 7 | 25 | | | | | | | | | 25 | 16 |
| | | | 1 | | 14 | 3 | 2 | 8 | 11 | 15 | 1 | | 15 | 12 | 27 | | | | | | | | | 27 | 17 |
| | | | | | 1 | 1 | 1 | | 1 | 1 | | 1 | 2 | 1 | 3 | | | | | | | | | 3 | 18 |
| | 3 | 2 | 2 | 1 | 26 | 30 | 15 | 16 | 32 | 39 | 7 | 2 | | 87 | 87 | | | | | | | | | 87 | 19 |
| | 19 | 5 | 12 | 2 | 1 | 66 | 118 | 6 | 164 | 19 | 2 | | 121 | 71 | 192 | | | | | | | | | 192 | 20 |
| | | | 1 | | 1 | 4 | 33 | 3 | 24 | 15 | 2 | | 27 | 14 | 41 | | | | | | | | | 41 | 21 |
| | 3 | | 2 | 1 | 3 | 13 | 33 | 5 | 34 | 15 | 2 | 1 | 35 | 19 | 54 | | | | | | | | | 54 | 22 |
| | | | | | | 3 | 1 | 1 | | | 1 | 1 | 1 | 4 | 5 | | | | | | | | | 5 | 23 |
| | 2 | | 3 | | 12 | 9 | 11 | 10 | 30 | 10 | | 2 | 29 | 13 | 42 | | | | | | | | | 42 | 24 |
| | | 1 | | | 8 | 8 | 6 | 8 | 11 | 14 | 2 | 3 | 18 | 12 | 30 | | | | | | | | | 30 | 25 |
| | | | | | 1 | | | 1 | 2 | | | | 2 | | 2 | | | | | | | | | 2 | 26 |
| | | | 3 | | 19 | 15 | 12 | 15 | 26 | 30 | 4 | | 36 | 25 | 61 | | | | | | | | | 61 | 27 |
| | | | | | 7 | 1 | 2 | 4 | 3 | 7 | 3 | 1 | 6 | 8 | 14 | | | | | | | | | 14 | 28 |
| | 61 | 18 | 55 | 6 | 589 | 464 | 490 | 372 | 63 | 199 | 270 | 1322 | 860 | 1038 | 1898 | | | | | 8 | 10 | | | 1916 | 29 |
| | 4 | 3 | 7 | 2 | 94 | 80 | 60 | 49 | 184 | 61 | 10 | 10 | 151 | 127 | 278 | | | | | 1 | 3 | 1 | | 283 | 30 |
| | 5 | | 2 | | 99 | 59 | 55 | 76 | 207 | 68 | 6 | 4 | 183 | 109 | 292 | | | | | | | 1 | | 293 | 31 |
| | 1 | | | | 2 | 4 | 3 | 8 | 2 | 5 | 5 | 5 | 8 | 9 | 17 | | | | | | | | | 17 | 32 |
| | 1 | | | | 7 | 1 | 4 | 10 | 2 | 5 | 2 | 13 | 18 | 4 | 22 | | | | | | | | | 22 | 33 |
| | 1 | 1 | 9 | | 14 | 28 | 175 | 24 | 70 | 134 | 18 | 18 | 131 | 110 | 241 | | | | | | | | | 241 | 34 |
| | 19 | 4 | 15 | 3 | 126 | 147 | 127 | 121 | 59 | 152 | 85 | 220 | 226 | 287 | 513 | | | | | 4 | 3 | 1 | | 521 | 35 |
| | 42 | 10 | 17 | 2 | 43 | 87 | 829 | 66 | 340 | 585 | 59 | 27 | 507 | 515 | 1022 | | | | | 2 | 8 | | 2 | 1029 | 36 |
| | 1 | | | | 1 | 4 | 4 | 4 | | 3 | 2 | 7 | 9 | 4 | 13 | | | | | | | | | 13 | 37 |
| | | | | | 2 | 3 | 3 | 3 | 8 | 1 | | 2 | 5 | 6 | 11 | | | | | | | | | 11 | 38 |
| | 1 | 2 | 1 | 5 | 34 | 22 | 20 | 35 | 20 | 72 | 13 | 5 | 59 | 52 | 111 | | | | | | | | | 111 | 39 |

CLASSIFICATION OF DEATHS IN CENTRA

| | Cause of death. | AGES. | | | | | | | | | | | | | | | | | | NATIVITIES. | | | | |
|---|---|---|---|---|---|---|---|---|---|---|---|---|---|---|---|---|---|---|---|---|---|---|---|---|
| | | Under 1. | | 1 and under 5. | | 5 and under 10. | | 10 and under 20. | | 20 and under 50. | | 50 and under 80. | | 80 and under 100. | | 100 & over. | | Age unknown. | | Born in the State. | N. England States. | Middle States. | Southern States. | Southwest'n States. |
| | | M. | F. | M. | F. | M. | F. | M. | F. | M. | F. | M. | F. | M. | F. | M | F. | M | F. | | | | | |
| 1 | Fever, not specified | 8 | 6 | 28 | 24 | 11 | 14 | 25 | 27 | 56 | 22 | 21 | 11 | 3 | 1 | | | | 1 | 208 | 19 | 4 | | |
| 2 | ..do..bilious | 2 | 1 | 5 | 6 | 4 | 5 | 9 | 12 | 29 | 18 | 16 | 3 | | 2 | | | | | 92 | 9 | 2 | | |
| 3 | ..do..brain | 9 | 12 | 16 | 12 | 7 | 12 | 18 | 21 | 21 | 8 | 7 | 2 | | | | | | 1 | 127 | 7 | 3 | | |
| 4 | ..do..congestive | 2 | | 2 | 3 | 2 | 3 | 1 | 2 | 5 | 3 | 3 | | | | | | | 1 | 24 | 1 | 2 | | |
| 5 | ..do..inflammatory | | | 1 | | 1 | | | | 1 | 1 | | 1 | | | | | | | 4 | 1 | | | |
| 6 | ..do..intermittent | | 1 | | 3 | | 2 | 1 | | 4 | 1 | 1 | 3 | | | | | | | 14 | 2 | | | |
| 7 | ..do..puerperal | | | | | | | | | | 12 | | | | | | | | | 11 | | | | |
| 8 | ..do..remittent | | | 1 | 1 | | | | 1 | | | | | | | | | | | 2 | | | | |
| 9 | ..do..scarlet | 17 | 12 | 114 | 112 | 60 | 48 | 12 | 15 | 7 | 3 | 1 | | | | | | | | 387 | 3 | 2 | | |
| 10 | ..do..ship | | 1 | 2 | 5 | 1 | 1 | 2 | | 5 | 1 | | | | | | | | | 4 | | | | |
| 11 | ..do..typhoid | 2 | | 8 | 11 | 2 | 6 | 36 | 27 | 73 | 40 | 24 | 17 | | | | | | | 200 | 28 | 8 | | |
| 12 | ..do..yellow | | | | | | | | | 2 | | | 1 | | | | | | | 1 | 1 | 1 | | |
| 13 | Fracture | | | | | 1 | | | | | | 1 | | | | | | | | 1 | | | | |
| 14 | Frozen | | | | | | | | | | | 2 | | | | | | | | | | | | |
| 15 | Gravel | | | | | | | | | 3 | 1 | 21 | 2 | 4 | | | | | | 14 | 13 | 3 | | |
| 16 | Head, disease of | 3 | 4 | 2 | 2 | 1 | 1 | 1 | 1 | | 2 | 2 | 1 | | | | | | | 17 | 1 | 1 | | |
| 17 | Heart....do | 4 | 3 | 1 | 3 | 1 | 3 | 8 | 4 | 23 | 14 | 33 | 20 | 1 | 3 | | | | | 78 | 32 | 4 | | |
| 18 | Heat | | | | | | | | | | | 1 | | | | | | | | | 1 | | | |
| 19 | Hemorrhage | | | 1 | | | | | 1 | 5 | 3 | 2 | 1 | 1 | | | | | | 6 | 5 | 1 | | |
| 20 | Hernia | | | | | | | | | 3 | 1 | 3 | 1 | | 1 | | | | | 4 | 1 | 1 | | |
| 21 | Hip, disease of | | | 1 | | 1 | 1 | 1 | 1 | 1 | 1 | | | | | | | | | 7 | | | | |
| 22 | Hooping cough | 26 | 29 | 26 | 36 | 5 | 5 | | 1 | | 1 | 1 | | | | | | | | 126 | | 1 | | |
| 23 | Hydrocephalus | 28 | 19 | 34 | 21 | 6 | 4 | 2 | 3 | 1 | 5 | 3 | 1 | | | | | | | 122 | 1 | 3 | | |
| 24 | Inflammation | 48 | 33 | 44 | 39 | 10 | 9 | 9 | 10 | 20 | 41 | 21 | 22 | 4 | 1 | | | | | 263 | 26 | 8 | | |
| 25 | ....do....bowels | 14 | 7 | 18 | 21 | 9 | 5 | 7 | 11 | 16 | 16 | 4 | 7 | 1 | | | | | | 120 | 9 | 1 | | |
| 26 | ....do....brain | 27 | 19 | 49 | 29 | 8 | 10 | 21 | 13 | 12 | 10 | 9 | | | | | | | | 197 | 3 | 1 | | |
| 27 | ....do....head | 2 | 2 | 3 | 1 | 1 | | | 1 | 1 | | | | | | | | | | 10 | | 1 | | |
| 28 | ....do....stomach | 1 | | | | 1 | | 2 | | | 1 | 2 | 1 | | | | | | | 5 | 2 | 1 | | |
| 29 | Insanity | | | | | | | | | 5 | 6 | 5 | 9 | | | | | | | 18 | 5 | | | |
| 30 | Intemperance | | | | | | | | | 12 | 2 | 18 | | | | | | | | 22 | 5 | 1 | | |
| 31 | Jaundice | | 1 | 2 | 1 | | | | | 3 | 7 | 3 | 3 | 2 | | | | | | 16 | 2 | | | |
| 32 | Kidneys, disease of | | | | | | | | 1 | 3 | 1 | 8 | 3 | 3 | | | | | | 7 | 10 | 2 | | |
| 33 | Killed | | | | 2 | | | 4 | | 5 | 2 | 4 | 1 | 1 | | | | | | 15 | 2 | 1 | | |
| 34 | Lightning | | | | | | | | | 1 | | | | | | | | | | | | | | |
| 35 | Liver, disease of | 1 | 4 | 3 | | | 1 | 1 | 2 | 7 | 17 | 15 | 14 | 1 | | | | | | 44 | 13 | 2 | | |
| 36 | Lockjaw | | | | | 1 | 1 | | | | | | | | | | | | | 1 | | | | |
| 37 | Lungs, disease of | 5 | 3 | 3 | | 1 | 1 | | | 1 | 3 | 4 | 3 | | | | | | | 22 | 1 | | | |
| 38 | Mania-a-potu | | | | | | | | | 9 | 1 | 5 | 1 | | | | | | | 13 | 2 | | | |
| 39 | Marasmus | 1 | | 3 | 1 | | | 1 | | 1 | 1 | | 1 | | | | | | | 8 | 1 | | | |
| 40 | Measles | 6 | 4 | 24 | 16 | 5 | 7 | 2 | 2 | 2 | 5 | | | | | | | | | 61 | 1 | | | |
| 41 | Mortification | | | | | 1 | | | | 1 | | 1 | 1 | 3 | | | | | | 4 | 3 | | | |
| 42 | Mumps | | | 2 | 3 | | | | 3 | 3 | 1 | | | 1 | | | | | | 11 | | 1 | | |
| 43 | Murder | | | | | | | | 1 | 2 | | | | | | | | | | 2 | | | | |
| 44 | Neuralgia | | | | | 1 | | | | 2 | 7 | 3 | 1 | | 1 | | | 1 | | 14 | 1 | | | |
| 45 | Old age | | | | | | | | | | 2 | 75 | 75 | 183 | 182 | 2 | 1 | | 1 | 182 | 239 | 40 | | |
| 46 | Paralysis | | | | 1 | | | 1 | 1 | 6 | 4 | 45 | 40 | 13 | 12 | | | | | 48 | 50 | 8 | | |
| 47 | Peritonitis | | | | | | | | | 1 | | | | | | | | | | 1 | | | | |
| 48 | Piles | | | | | | | | | | | 2 | 2 | | | | | | | 2 | 1 | | | |
| 49 | Pleurisy | 3 | 1 | 1 | 1 | 1 | | 1 | 1 | 9 | 4 | 9 | 3 | | 1 | | | | | 19 | 10 | 2 | | |
| 50 | Pneumonia | 69 | 52 | 50 | 32 | 2 | 10 | 5 | 5 | 36 | 20 | 34 | 19 | 6 | 3 | | | | | 273 | 42 | 10 | | |
| 51 | Poison | 1 | | 1 | 1 | 1 | | 1 | 1 | 1 | | 1 | | | | | | | | 7 | 1 | | | |
| 52 | Putrid sore throat | 1 | | | | | 2 | 2 | | | | | | | | | | | | 5 | | | | |
| 53 | Quinsy | 1 | | 3 | 4 | 1 | | 1 | 2 | 1 | 3 | 1 | | | | | | | | 13 | 1 | | | |
| 54 | Rheumatism | | 1 | 2 | 1 | 3 | 2 | 5 | 3 | 1 | 4 | 14 | 5 | 1 | 1 | | | | | 30 | 4 | 3 | | |
| 55 | Rickets | 2 | | | | | | | | | | | | | | | | | | 2 | | | | |
| 56 | Scrofula | 8 | 5 | 5 | 7 | 2 | 3 | 3 | 6 | 6 | 7 | 5 | 2 | | 1 | | | | | 48 | 9 | | | |
| 57 | Small pox | | 1 | 2 | 1 | 1 | 2 | 1 | 1 | 6 | | 2 | 2 | | | | | 1 | | 14 | 3 | | | |
| 58 | Spine, disease of | | 2 | 2 | 2 | 1 | | 6 | 5 | 3 | 8 | 3 | | | 1 | | | | | 28 | 3 | 1 | | |
| 59 | Stillborn | 12 | 11 | | | | | | | | | | | | | | | | | 23 | | | | |
| 60 | Stomach, disease of | | 1 | | | | | | | 1 | 2 | 3 | | | | | | | | 3 | 2 | | | |
| 61 | Suffocation | 1 | 1 | 3 | | | | | | 1 | 1 | | | | | | | | | 5 | | | | |
| 62 | Suicide | | | | | | | | 2 | 13 | 7 | 9 | 1 | | | | | | | 21 | 6 | 1 | | |
| 63 | Summer complaint | 11 | 9 | 11 | 12 | 2 | 4 | 1 | 1 | | | 1 | 1 | | | | | | | 52 | | | | |
| 64 | Sun, stroke of | | | | | | 1 | | | | | | | | | | | | | | | | | |
| 65 | Syphilis | | | | | | | | 1 | | 1 | | | | | | | | | | | | | |
| 66 | Teething | 5 | 3 | 6 | 7 | | | | | | | | | | | | | | | 19 | | | | |
| 67 | Tetanus | | | | | | 1 | | | | | | 1 | | | | | | | 2 | | | | |
| 68 | Tetter | | | | | | 1 | | | | | | | | | | | | | 1 | | | | |
| 69 | Throat, disease of | | 2 | 1 | 1 | | 2 | | | 1 | | 3 | 1 | | | | | | | 10 | 1 | | | |
| 70 | Thrush | 2 | | | 1 | | | 1 | | | 5 | | 1 | | | | | | | 7 | 1 | 2 | | |
| 71 | Tumor | 2 | 2 | | 1 | 1 | | | | 4 | 7 | 5 | 6 | | 2 | | | | | 28 | 2 | 3 | | |
| 72 | Ulcer | 4 | 3 | 2 | 2 | 1 | | | | 1 | 3 | 2 | 4 | | | | | | | 19 | 2 | | | |
| 73 | Venereal | | | | | | | | | 1 | | | 1 | | | | | | | 2 | | | | |

SECTION OF THE STATE OF NEW YORK—Continued.

| NATIVITIES. California and Territories. | NATIVITIES. Ireland. | NATIVITIES. Germany. | NATIVITIES. Other foreign countries. | NATIVITIES. Unknown. | SEASON OF DECEASE. Spring. | SEASON OF DECEASE. Summer. | SEASON OF DECEASE. Autumn. | SEASON OF DECEASE. Winter. | DURATION OF SICKNESS. Under 1 week. | DURATION OF SICKNESS. 1 week and under 1 month. | DURATION OF SICKNESS. 1 month and under 3 months. | DURATION OF SICKNESS. 3 months and over. | WHITES. Males. | WHITES. Females. | WHITES. Total. | COLORED. Slaves. Black. M. | COLORED. Slaves. Black. F. | COLORED. Slaves. Mulatto. M. | COLORED. Slaves. Mulatto. F. | COLORED. Free. Black. M. | COLORED. Free. Black. F. | COLORED. Free. Mul. M | COLORED. Free. Mul. F. | Aggregate deaths. | |
|---|---|---|---|---|---|---|---|---|---|---|---|---|---|---|---|---|---|---|---|---|---|---|---|---|---|
| | 18 | 3 | 9 | 1 | 72 | 50 | 82 | 54 | 42 | 148 | 56 | 10 | 150 | 106 | 256 | | | | | 1 | | 1 | | 258 | 1 |
| | 4 | 2 | 3 | | 22 | 24 | 37 | 29 | 21 | 66 | 22 | 1 | 64 | 42 | 111 | | | | | 1 | | | | 112 | 2 |
| | 2 | 2 | 5 | | 57 | 33 | 36 | 20 | 50 | 71 | 20 | 5 | 78 | 68 | 146 | | | | | | | | | 146 | 3 |
| | | | | | 11 | 3 | 9 | 4 | 8 | 14 | 4 | 1 | 15 | 12 | 27 | | | | | | | | | 27 | 4 |
| | | | | | | | 2 | 3 | 1 | 4 | | | 3 | 2 | 5 | | | | | | | | | 5 | 5 |
| | | | | | 1 | 4 | 8 | 3 | 1 | 8 | 5 | 2 | 6 | 10 | 16 | | | | | | | | | 16 | 6 |
| | | | 1 | | 5 | 2 | 2 | 3 | 2 | 7 | 2 | 1 | | 12 | 12 | | | | | | | | | 12 | 7 |
| | 1 | | | | 1 | 1 | | 1 | | 3 | | | 1 | 2 | 3 | | | | | | | | | 3 | 8 |
| | 2 | 1 | 6 | | 145 | 89 | 87 | 80 | 167 | 202 | 29 | 1 | 211 | 190 | 401 | | | | | | | | | 401 | 9 |
| | 14 | | | | 7 | 5 | 3 | 3 | 5 | 7 | 3 | | 10 | 8 | 18 | | | | | | | | | 18 | 10 |
| | 3 | 2 | 4 | | 65 | 34 | 65 | 80 | 21 | 171 | 40 | 6 | 145 | 101 | 246 | | | | | | | | | 246 | 11 |
| | | | | | 1 | 1 | | 1 | 1 | 2 | | | 2 | 1 | 3 | | | | | | | | | 3 | 12 |
| | 1 | | | | 1 | | 1 | | 2 | | | | 2 | | 2 | | | | | | | | | 2 | 13 |
| | 1 | | | 1 | | 1 | | 1 | 1 | | | | 2 | | 2 | | | | | | | | | 2 | 14 |
| | | | | 1 | 7 | 9 | 9 | 6 | 2 | 12 | 1 | 15 | 28 | 3 | 31 | | | | | | | | | 31 | 15 |
| | | | 1 | | 7 | 4 | 4 | 5 | 2 | 11 | 3 | 3 | 9 | 11 | 20 | | | | | | | | | 20 | 16 |
| | 7 | | 5 | | 41 | 34 | 22 | 24 | 27 | 38 | 11 | 42 | 71 | 50 | 121 | | | | | | | | | 121 | 17 |
| | | | | | | 1 | | | | 1 | | | 1 | | 1 | | | | | | | | | 1 | 18 |
| | 1 | 1 | | | 1 | 5 | 2 | 6 | 3 | 7 | 3 | | 8 | 5 | 13 | | | | | 1 | | | | 14 | 19 |
| | 1 | | 2 | | 1 | 2 | 3 | 3 | 4 | 2 | 1 | 1 | 6 | 3 | 9 | | | | | | | | | 9 | 20 |
| | | | | | 4 | | 2 | 1 | | 1 | | 5 | 4 | 3 | 7 | | | | | | | | | 7 | 21 |
| | 2 | | 1 | | 33 | 32 | 35 | 30 | 20 | 76 | 25 | 9 | 58 | 69 | 127 | | | | | | 3 | | | 130 | 22 |
| | 1 | | | | 39 | 33 | 31 | 24 | 22 | 80 | 19 | 6 | 74 | 53 | 127 | | | | | | | | | 127 | 23 |
| | 3 | 2 | 9 | | 92 | 73 | 81 | 65 | 100 | 170 | 27 | 9 | 154 | 151 | 305 | | | | | 2 | 4 | | | 311 | 24 |
| | 3 | 1 | 1 | | 44 | 23 | 32 | 36 | 52 | 71 | 9 | 3 | 67 | 66 | 133 | | | | | 2 | 1 | | | 136 | 25 |
| | 3 | | 3 | | 62 | 40 | 51 | 54 | 70 | 105 | 17 | 5 | 124 | 81 | 205 | | | | | 1 | | 1 | | 207 | 26 |
| | | | | | 6 | 1 | 1 | 3 | 5 | 6 | | | 7 | 4 | 11 | | | | | | | | | 11 | 27 |
| | | | | | 3 | 3 | 2 | | 1 | 1 | 1 | 4 | 6 | 2 | 8 | | | | | | | | | 8 | 28 |
| | 1 | | 1 | | 9 | 10 | 2 | 4 | | 6 | 1 | 12 | 10 | 15 | 25 | | | | | | | | | 25 | 29 |
| | 2 | | 2 | | 6 | 12 | 6 | 8 | 8 | 7 | 4 | 3 | 30 | 1 | 31 | | | | | | 1 | | | 32 | 30 |
| | | 2 | 1 | 1 | 4 | 9 | 4 | 5 | 2 | 7 | 7 | 6 | 9 | 12 | 21 | | | | | 1 | | | | 22 | 31 |
| | | | | | 8 | 5 | 3 | 3 | 3 | 5 | 4 | 6 | 14 | 5 | 19 | | | | | | | | | 19 | 32 |
| | 1 | | | | 5 | 4 | 4 | 6 | 14 | 2 | | | 14 | 5 | 19 | | | | | | | | | 19 | 33 |
| | | 1 | | | | 1 | | | 1 | | | | 1 | | 1 | | | | | | | | | 1 | 34 |
| | 2 | | 5 | | 16 | 23 | 14 | 12 | 6 | 16 | 15 | 28 | 7 28 | 37 | 65 | | | | | | 1 | | | 66 | 35 |
| | | | 1 | | | 1 | 1 | | 2 | | | | 1 | 1 | 2 | | | | | | | | | 2 | 36 |
| | | | 1 | | 6 | 8 | 5 | 5 | 6 | 12 | 1 | 5 | 12 | 10 | 22 | | | | | 2 | | | | 24 | 37 |
| | | | | | 2 | 3 | 3 | 1 | | | 1 | 7 | 6 | 2 | 8 | | | | | | 1 | | | 9 | 38 |
| | 1 | | | | 8 | | 6 | 2 | 6 | 5 | 1 | 1 | 14 | 1 | 15 | | | | | | 1 | | | 16 | 39 |
| | 6 | 1 | 4 | | 21 | 28 | 16 | 7 | 14 | 43 | 11 | 5 | 38 | 34 | 72 | | | | | 1 | | | | 73 | 40 |
| | | | | | 4 | 1 | 2 | | | 1 | 3 | 3 | 6 | 1 | 7 | | | | | | | | | 7 | 41 |
| | | | 1 | | 6 | 4 | | 3 | 2 | 10 | 1 | | 6 | 7 | 13 | | | | | | | | | 13 | 42 |
| | 1 | | | | 1 | 1 | | 1 | | 1 | | | 2 | 1 | 3 | | | | | | | | | 3 | 43 |
| | | | 1 | | 7 | 2 | 3 | 4 | | 3 | | 13 | 7 | 9 | 16 | | | | | | | | | 16 | 44 |
| | 12 | 4 | 32 | 11 | 173 | 110 | 108 | 117 | 91 | 100 | 41 | 104 | 259 | 258 | 517 | | | | | 1 | 3 | | | 521 | 45 |
| | 6 | | 10 | 1 | 26 | 34 | 31 | 31 | 33 | 30 | 12 | 45 | 65 | 58 | 123 | | | | | | | | | 123 | 46 |
| | | | | | | | | 1 | | 1 | | | 1 | | 1 | | | | | | | | | 1 | 47 |
| | | | 1 | | 2 | | 1 | 1 | | 1 | | 3 | 2 | 2 | 4 | | | | | | | | | 4 | 48 |
| | 2 | 1 | 1 | | 12 | 11 | 5 | 7 | 11 | 21 | 1 | 2 | 23 | 11 | 34 | | | | | 1 | | | | 35 | 49 |
| | 4 | 1 | 10 | 1 | 179 | 62 | 43 | 59 | 99 | 203 | 28 | 11 | 199 | 139 | 338 | | | | | 2 | 2 | 1 | | 343 | 50 |
| | | | | | 2 | 3 | 2 | 1 | 6 | 1 | 1 | | 6 | 2 | 8 | | | | | | | | | 8 | 51 |
| | | | | | 2 | 2 | 1 | | 2 | 3 | | | 3 | 2 | 5 | | | | | | | | | 5 | 52 |
| | 1 | | 1 | | 3 | 6 | 7 | 1 | 7 | 10 | | | 8 | 9 | 17 | | | | | | | | | 17 | 53 |
| | 1 | 1 | 3 | 1 | 16 | 10 | 9 | 8 | 4 | 12 | 5 | 20 | 26 | 17 | 43 | | | | | | | | | 43 | 54 |
| | | | | | | | 1 | 1 | 1 | | 1 | | 2 | | 2 | | | | | | | | | 2 | 55 |
| | 3 | | | | 13 | 15 | 19 | 13 | 5 | 14 | 11 | 30 | 28 | 31 | 59 | | | | | 1 | | | | 60 | 56 |
| | 2 | | 1 | | 9 | 2 | 4 | 5 | 2 | 17 | 1 | | 13 | 7 | 20 | | | | | | | | | 20 | 57 |
| | | | 1 | | 16 | 6 | 7 | 4 | 3 | 7 | 5 | 17 | 15 | 18 | 33 | | | | | | | | | 33 | 58 |
| | | | | | 5 | 6 | 5 | 6 | | | | | 12 | 11 | 23 | | | | | | | | | 23 | 59 |
| | 1 | | 1 | | 1 | 3 | 2 | 1 | 1 | 1 | 2 | 3 | 4 | 3 | 7 | | | | | | | | | 7 | 60 |
| | 1 | | 1 | | 3 | | 2 | 2 | 7 | | | | 5 | 2 | 7 | | | | | | | | | 7 | 61 |
| | 1 | 1 | 1 | 1 | 11 | 14 | 3 | 4 | 18 | 2 | | | 22 | 10 | 32 | | | | | | | | | 32 | 62 |
| | 1 | | | | 1 | 5 | 44 | 3 | 20 | 31 | 2 | | 26 | 27 | 53 | | | | | | | | | 53 | 63 |
| | 1 | | | | | 1 | | | 1 | | | | | 1 | 1 | | | | | | | | | 1 | 64 |
| | | | | 2 | | 1 | | 1 | | | | 2 | | 2 | 2 | | | | | | | | | 2 | 65 |
| | | 1 | 1 | | 4 | 8 | 5 | 4 | 7 | 7 | 4 | 1 | 10 | 9 | 19 | | | | | | | 1 | 1 | 21 | 66 |
| | | | | | | 1 | 1 | | 1 | | 1 | | | 2 | 2 | | | | | | | | | 2 | 67 |
| | | | | | 1 | | | | | | | 1 | | 1 | 1 | | | | | | | | | 1 | 68 |
| | | | | | 3 | 2 | 4 | 2 | 6 | 4 | | 1 | 5 | 6 | 11 | | | | | | | | | 11 | 69 |
| | | | | | | 5 | 2 | 3 | 2 | 4 | 3 | 1 | 3 | 7 | 10 | | | | | | | | | 10 | 70 |
| | | | 2 | | 15 | 5 | 6 | 4 | 2 | 6 | 6 | 15 | 12 | 18 | 30 | | | | | | | | | 30 | 71 |
| | | 1 | | | 6 | 5 | 7 | 4 | 5 | 6 | 4 | 6 | 10 | 12 | 22 | | | | | | | | | 22 | 72 |
| | | | | | | 1 | 1 | | | | 1 | 1 | 1 | 1 | 2 | | | | | | | | | 2 | 73 |

CLASSIFICATION OF DEATHS IN CENTRAL

| | Cause of death. | AGES. Under 1. | | 1 and under 5. | | 5 and under 10. | | 10 and under 20. | | 20 and under 50. | | 50 and under 80. | | 80 and under 100. | | 100 & over. | | Age unknown. | | NATIVITIES. Born in State. | N. England States. | Middle States. | Southern States. | Southwest'n States. | Northwest'n States. |
|---|---|---|---|---|---|---|---|---|---|---|---|---|---|---|---|---|---|---|---|---|---|---|---|---|---|
| | | M. | F. | M. | F. | M. | F. | M. | F. | M. | F. | M. | F. | M. | F. | M | F. | M | F. | | | | | | |
| 1 | White swelling | | | | | | | | 1 | 2 | 1 | | | | | | | | | 3 | | 1 | | | |
| 2 | Worms | 3 | 2 | 24 | 26 | 2 | 2 | | | | | | | | | | | | | 58 | | | | | |
| 3 | Unknown | 174 | 147 | 82 | 72 | 24 | 21 | 21 | 32 | 99 | 99 | 124 | 82 | 13 | 18 | | | 10 | 5 | 818 | 100 | 26 | 1 | | |
| | Total | 867 | 674 | 1264 | 1120 | 374 | 333 | 380 | 473 | 1321 | 1381 | 1183 | 878 | 334 | 290 | 3 | 1 | 16 | 9 | 8465 | 1281 | 312 | 7 | 3 | 27 |

CLASSIFICATION OF DEATHS IN

| | Cause of death. | Under 1. M. | Under 1. F. | 1 and under 5. M. | 1 and under 5. F. | 5 and under 10. M. | 5 and under 10. F. | 10 and under 20. M. | 10 and under 20. F. | 20 and under 50. M. | 20 and under 50. F. | 50 and under 80. M. | 50 and under 80. F. | 80 and under 100. M. | 80 and under 100. F. | 100 & over. M | 100 & over. F. | Age unknown. M | Age unknown. F. | Born in State. | N. England States. | Middle States. | Southern States. | Southwest'n States. | Northwest'n States. |
|---|---|---|---|---|---|---|---|---|---|---|---|---|---|---|---|---|---|---|---|---|---|---|---|---|---|
| 1 | Abscess | 2 | 1 | 1 | 1 | | 1 | 3 | 3 | 10 | 6 | 4 | 4 | | | | | | | 12 | 1 | 1 | 2 | | |
| 2 | Accident, not specif'd | 1 | 1 | 6 | 5 | 10 | 7 | 19 | 2 | 84 | 8 | 9 | 1 | | | | | | | 74 | 2 | 4 | | | |
| 3 | ....do...burned | 1 | 1 | 3 | 6 | 1 | 7 | 4 | 2 | 9 | 8 | | 2 | | | | | | | 31 | 2 | 1 | | | |
| 4 | ....do...drowned | | | 1 | | 8 | | 8 | 1 | 34 | 1 | 1 | | | | | | | | 18 | 3 | 1 | 1 | | |
| 5 | ....do...scalded | | | 2 | 1 | 1 | | 1 | | 1 | | | | | | | | | | 4 | | | | | |
| 6 | ....do...shot | | | | | | | | | 1 | | 1 | | | | | | | | 1 | | | | | |
| 7 | Amputation | | | | | | | | | 1 | | | | | 1 | | | | | | 2 | | | | |
| 8 | Aneurism | | | | | | | | | 2 | | 1 | | | | | | | | 1 | 1 | | | | |
| 9 | Apoplexy | | | | 1 | 1 | | 2 | 2 | 23 | 13 | 23 | 7 | 2 | 1 | | | 3 | 1 | 23 | 4 | 8 | 4 | | |
| 10 | Asthma | 1 | 1 | 1 | 2 | | 1 | | | 4 | 1 | 6 | 2 | 1 | 1 | | | | | 10 | 1 | | | | |
| 11 | Bladder, disease of | | | | | | | | | 2 | | 3 | | | | | | | | 2 | | | | | |
| 12 | Bowels, ......do | 13 | 25 | 14 | 11 | 3 | 2 | 2 | 1 | 8 | 5 | 4 | 3 | | | | | 1 | | 75 | 1 | 1 | 1 | | |
| 13 | Brain .......do. | 3 | 1 | 12 | 8 | 1 | 1 | 1 | 1 | 9 | 1 | | 1 | | | | | | | 32 | | 1 | | | |
| 14 | Bronchitis | 4 | 1 | 9 | 5 | 5 | | | 1 | 10 | 4 | 9 | 2 | | | | | 1 | | 35 | 1 | 2 | | | |
| 15 | Cancer | | 1 | 4 | 1 | | 2 | 3 | 1 | 2 | 11 | 7 | 8 | 1 | 1 | | | | | 25 | 3 | 1 | 1 | | |
| 16 | Carbuncle | | | | | | | | | 1 | | 1 | | | | | | | | | | | | | |
| 17 | Catarrh | 3 | 5 | 1 | | | | | | 2 | | 1 | | | | | | | | 10 | | | | | |
| 18 | Chicken pox | | 1 | | 1 | | | | | | | | | | | | | | | 2 | | | | | |
| 19 | Childbirth | | | | | | | | 4 | | 67 | | | | | | | | | 20 | 2 | 3 | | | |
| 20 | Cholera | 68 | 51 | 166 | 190 | 120 | 90 | 92 | 106 | 763 | 653 | 238 | 163 | 7 | 7 | | | 9 | 19 | 1028 | 39 | 111 | 39 | 1 | |
| 21 | ...do..infantum | 52 | 52 | 90 | 57 | 2 | 3 | 1 | | | | | | | | | | | | 242 | 1 | 1 | | 2 | 1 |
| 22 | ...do..morbus | | 2 | 2 | | 3 | | 1 | | 9 | 7 | 4 | 4 | | 1 | | | | | 8 | 2 | 2 | | | |
| 23 | Colic | 3 | | | | 1 | | | 1 | 6 | 3 | 3 | 1 | | | | | | | 8 | 1 | | | | |
| 24 | Congestion | 3 | 2 | 1 | 2 | | 2 | 1 | 1 | 1 | 6 | | 3 | | | | | | | 10 | 1 | | | | |
| 25 | ....do....bowels | | 1 | 2 | 1 | 2 | | | | 4 | 3 | | | | | | | | | 8 | | 1 | 1 | | |
| 26 | ....do....brain | 11 | 7 | 19 | 17 | 8 | 8 | 3 | 3 | 19 | 10 | 4 | 3 | | | | | 1 | | 79 | 3 | 1 | 1 | | |
| 27 | ....do....lungs | 5 | 1 | 3 | 6 | 6 | 3 | 1 | | 9 | 1 | 1 | 2 | 2 | | | | | | 31 | 1 | 2 | | | |
| 28 | Consumption | 26 | 22 | 71 | 58 | 19 | 14 | 55 | 51 | 475 | 358 | 99 | 66 | | 4 | | | | 1 | 610 | 34 | 53 | 13 | 1 | 1 |
| 29 | Convulsions | 81 | 79 | 50 | 50 | 8 | 6 | 4 | 3 | 10 | 10 | 3 | 2 | | | | | 2 | 2 | 275 | 1 | 9 | 1 | | |
| 30 | Cramp | 2 | 1 | 4 | 4 | 2 | | | | 4 | 1 | | | | | | | | | 13 | | 1 | | | |
| 31 | Croup | 34 | 26 | 69 | 43 | 6 | 9 | | 2 | 3 | 1 | | | | | | | | | 178 | 2 | 3 | 3 | | |
| 32 | Debility | 14 | 19 | 17 | 11 | 5 | 1 | 3 | 2 | 19 | 24 | 9 | 20 | 3 | 1 | | | | 1 | 86 | 3 | 2 | | | |
| 33 | Diabetes | 1 | 2 | | 1 | | | | | 5 | 8 | 4 | 2 | | | | | 1 | | 7 | 1 | 1 | | | |
| 34 | Diarrhœa | 25 | 33 | 61 | 66 | 15 | 16 | 8 | 14 | 64 | 44 | 23 | 21 | | 2 | | | 1 | | 269 | 12 | 6 | 2 | | |
| 35 | Dropsy | 18 | 17 | 43 | 32 | 12 | 7 | 8 | 4 | 43 | 36 | 19 | 20 | | 3 | | | | | 168 | 8 | 12 | 3 | | |
| 36 | Dysentery | 62 | 59 | 122 | 118 | 25 | 30 | 24 | 23 | 123 | 85 | 33 | 42 | 2 | | | | 1 | 1 | 513 | 13 | 15 | 4 | | 1 |
| 37 | Dyspepsia | 1 | | | | | | | | 2 | 2 | | | | | | | | | 3 | 1 | | | | |
| 38 | Epilepsy | | | | | | | 1 | | 6 | 6 | 2 | 2 | | | | | | | 5 | | 2 | | | |
| 39 | Erysipelas | 5 | 10 | 5 | 6 | 1 | 2 | 7 | 3 | 17 | 16 | 7 | 6 | | 1 | | | | | 49 | 6 | 5 | 2 | | |
| 40 | Executed | | | | | | | | | 1 | | | | | | | | | | | | | | | |
| 41 | Eye, disease of | | | | | | | 1 | | | | | | | | | | | | | | 1 | | | |
| 42 | Fever, not specified | 8 | 4 | 20 | 11 | 10 | 6 | 6 | 7 | 45 | 27 | 10 | 11 | | 2 | | | | | 70 | 6 | 1 | 1 | | 2 |
| 43 | ..do..bilious | 1 | | 3 | 16 | | | 1 | 1 | 10 | 3 | 5 | | | | | | | | 26 | | 4 | | | |
| 44 | ..do..brain | 8 | 6 | 15 | 9 | 11 | 1 | 2 | 1 | 8 | 4 | 1 | 1 | | | | | | | 54 | 2 | | | | |
| 45 | ..do..congestive | | | | 3 | | | | | 5 | 2 | | 1 | | | | | | | 4 | | 1 | | | |
| 46 | ..do..inflammatory | | | | | | | | | | | 1 | | | | | | | | | | | | | |
| 47 | ..do..intermittent | | | 2 | 1 | 1 | | | 1 | 5 | 3 | | 1 | | | | | | | 11 | | | | | |
| 48 | ..do..puerperal | | | | | | | | | | 10 | | | | | | | | | | | 1 | | | |
| 49 | ..do..remittent | | | 3 | | | 1 | 2 | | 6 | 2 | 1 | | | | | | | | 8 | 1 | 2 | 2 | | |
| 50 | ..do..scarlet | 4 | 8 | 51 | 51 | 19 | 20 | 3 | 3 | 1 | 5 | 1 | | 1 | | | | | | 123 | 1 | 3 | 1 | | |
| 51 | ..do..ship | | | 2 | 1 | 2 | 1 | 1 | 2 | 4 | 2 | 2 | 1 | | | | | | | 1 | | | | | |
| 52 | ..do..typhus | | 5 | 4 | 7 | 9 | 2 | 16 | 12 | 122 | 81 | 20 | 12 | | | | | | | 148 | 8 | 7 | | | |
| 53 | .do..yellow | | | | | | | | | 2 | | | | | | | | | | 1 | 1 | | | | |
| 54 | Fistula | | | | | | | | | 1 | 1 | | | | | | | | | 1 | | | | | |
| 55 | Fracture | | | | | | | 7 | | 59 | 4 | 6 | | | | | | 1 | | 13 | 5 | 1 | | | |
| 56 | Gout | | | | | | | | | 1 | 1 | 1 | 1 | | | | | | | 2 | | | | | |
| 57 | Gravel | 2 | | | | | | | | | | | | | | | | | | 1 | 1 | | | | |
| 58 | Head, disease of | | 1 | 2 | | 1 | | 1 | | 2 | | 2 | | | | | | | | 5 | | | | | |
| 59 | Heart....do | 2 | 6 | 7 | 3 | 11 | 5 | 6 | 8 | 51 | 22 | 22 | 20 | 1 | 1 | | | | | 94 | 7 | 12 | 4 | 1 | |
| 60 | Heat | | | | | | | | | 1 | | 1 | | | | | | | | | | | | | |
| 61 | Hemorrhage | 1 | | 3 | | 2 | | 5 | 2 | 6 | 3 | 2 | 2 | | | | | | | 13 | 2 | 1 | 1 | | |
| 62 | Hernia | | | | | | | 1 | | 4 | | | | | | | | | | 1 | 1 | | 1 | | |

## SECTION OF THE STATE OF NEW YORK—Continued.

| Nativities: California and Territories. | Nativities: Ireland. | Nativities: Germany. | Nativities: Other foreign countries. | Nativities: Unknown. | Season of decease: Spring. | Season of decease: Summer. | Season of decease: Autumn. | Season of decease: Winter. | Duration of sickness: Under 1 week. | Duration of sickness: 1 week and under 1 month. | Duration of sickness: 1 month and under 3 months. | Duration of sickness: 3 months and over. | Whites: Males. | Whites: Females. | Whites: Total. | Colored: Slaves: Black: M. | Colored: Slaves: Black: F. | Colored: Slaves: Mulatto: M. | Colored: Slaves: Mulatto: F. | Colored: Free: Black: M. | Colored: Free: Black: F. | Colored: Free: Mul.: M | Colored: Free: Mul.: F. | Aggregate deaths. | |
|---|---|---|---|---|---|---|---|---|---|---|---|---|---|---|---|---|---|---|---|---|---|---|---|---|---|
| .... | ... | ... | .... | ... | ... | 1 | 1 | 2 | .... | 1 | .... | 3 | 2 | 2 | 4 | .... | .... | .... | .... | .... | .... | .... | .. | 4 | 1 |
| .... | ... | 1 | .... | ... | 22 | 9 | 17 | 11 | 35 | 20 | 2 | .... | 29 | 30 | 59 | .... | .... | .... | .... | .. | .... | .. | .. | 59 | 2 |
| .... | 33 | 12 | 25 | 8 | 307 | 240 | 239 | 201 | 345 | 212 | 79 | 152 | 544 | 470 | 1014 | .... | .... | .... | .... | 2 | 4 | 1 | 2 | 1023 | 3 |
| ... | 352 | 90 | 311 | 53 | 2942 | 2430 | 3408 | 2050 | 3011 | 3676 | 1083 | 2381 | 5697 | 5113 | 10810 | .... | .... | .... | .... | 35 | 41 | 10 | 5 | 10,901 | |

## NEW YORK CITY, STATE OF NEW YORK.

| Cal. & Ter. | Ireland. | Germany. | Other foreign countries. | Unknown. | Spring. | Summer. | Autumn. | Winter. | Under 1 week. | 1 week and under 1 month. | 1 month and under 3 months. | 3 months and over. | Males. | Females. | Total. | Slaves Black M. | Slaves Black F. | Slaves Mulatto M. | Slaves Mulatto F. | Free Black M. | Free Black F. | Free Mul. M | Free Mul. F. | Aggregate deaths. | |
|---|---|---|---|---|---|---|---|---|---|---|---|---|---|---|---|---|---|---|---|---|---|---|---|---|---|
| .... | 16 | 2 | 1 | 1 | 12 | 7 | 9 | 8 | 2 | 7 | 6 | 10 | 20 | 16 | 36 | .... | .... | .... | .... | .. | .. | .. | .. | 36 | 1 |
| .... | 53 | 9 | 11 | .. | 47 | 35 | 39 | 23 | 94 | 15 | 5 | 2 | 127 | 24 | 151 | .... | .... | .... | .... | 1 | .. | 1 | .. | 153 | 2 |
| .... | 7 | 2 | 1 | .. | 12 | 12 | 11 | 9 | 17 | 6 | .... | 1 | 18 | 26 | 44 | .... | .... | .... | .... | .. | .. | .. | .. | 44 | 3 |
| .... | 17 | 5 | 9 | .. | 5 | 20 | 21 | 8 | 54 | .... | .... | .... | 51 | 2 | 53 | .... | .... | .... | .... | 1 | .. | .. | .. | 54 | 4 |
| .... | 2 | ... | .... | .. | 2 | 2 | 2 | .... | 4 | 1 | .... | .... | 5 | 1 | 6 | .... | .... | .... | .... | .. | .. | .. | .. | 6 | 5 |
| .... | .... | 1 | .... | .. | .... | 1 | 1 | .... | .... | .... | .... | .... | 2 | .... | 2 | .... | .... | .... | .... | .. | .. | .. | .. | 2 | 6 |
| .... | .... | ... | .... | .. | 2 | .... | .... | .... | .... | .... | 1 | .... | 1 | 1 | 2 | .... | .... | .... | .... | .. | .. | .. | .. | 2 | 7 |
| .... | 1 | ... | ... | .. | 1 | .... | 2 | .... | 1 | .... | .... | 1 | 2 | .... | 2 | .... | .... | .... | .... | 1 | .. | .. | .. | 3 | 8 |
| .... | 18 | 7 | 13 | 2 | 25 | 25 | 15 | 14 | 40 | 6 | 3 | 1 | 52 | 21 | 73 | .... | .... | .... | ... | 2 | 2 | .. | 2 | 79 | 9 |
| .... | 6 | ... | 4 | .. | 2 | 2 | 3 | 14 | 2 | 5 | 4 | 7 | 13 | 8 | 21 | .... | .... | .... | .... | .. | .. | .. | .. | 21 | 10 |
| .... | 2 | ... | 1 | .. | 2 | 1 | 1 | 1 | 1 | 1 | .... | .... | 5 | .... | 5 | .... | .... | .... | .... | .. | .. | .. | .. | 5 | 11 |
| .... | 8 | ... | 6 | .. | 12 | 20 | 40 | 16 | 14 | 28 | 8 | 5 | 45 | 47 | 92 | .... | .... | .... | .... | .. | .. | .. | .. | 92 | 12 |
| .... | 3 | 1 | 2 | .. | 9 | 9 | 12 | 9 | 6 | 4 | .... | 2 | 26 | 13 | 39 | .... | .... | .... | .... | .. | .. | .. | .. | 39 | 13 |
| .... | 9 | 1 | 8 | .. | 10 | 10 | 10 | 18 | 2 | 6 | 6 | 6 | 38 | 13 | 51 | .... | .... | .... | .... | .. | .. | .. | .. | 51 | 14 |
| .... | 12 | ... | .... | .. | 6 | 11 | 12 | 13 | 4 | 4 | 8 | 14 | 17 | 24 | 41 | .... | .... | .... | .... | .. | 1 | .. | .. | 42 | 15 |
| .... | .... | 2 | .... | .. | 1 | .... | 1 | .... | .... | 1 | 1 | .... | 2 | .... | 2 | .... | .... | .... | .... | .. | .. | .. | .. | 2 | 16 |
| .... | 1 | ... | 1 | .. | 8 | 2 | 1 | 1 | 6 | 4 | 1 | .... | 7 | 5 | 12 | .... | .... | .... | .... | .. | .. | .. | .. | 12 | 17 |
| .... | .... | ... | .... | .. | .... | .... | 2 | .... | .... | 2 | .... | .... | .... | 2 | 2 | .... | .... | .... | .... | .. | .. | .. | .. | 2 | 18 |
| .... | 30 | 13 | 3 | .. | 26 | 23 | 13 | 9 | 41 | 18 | 1 | .... | .... | 69 | 69 | .... | .... | .... | .... | .. | 1 | .. | 1 | 71 | 19 |
| .... | 1086 | 205 | 203 | 20 | 65 | 1566 | 953 | 51 | 1573 | 255 | 11 | 12 | 1425 | 1247 | 2672 | .... | .... | .... | .... | 29 | 28 | 9 | 4 | 2742 | 20 |
| .... | 4 | 2 | 4 | .. | 14 | 90 | 132 | 11 | 82 | 54 | 22 | 5 | 142 | 111 | 253 | .... | .... | .... | .... | 3 | 1 | .. | .. | 257 | 21 |
| .... | 16 | 1 | 4 | .. | 1 | 22 | 8 | 2 | 9 | 7 | .... | 1 | 19 | 14 | 33 | .... | .... | .... | .... | .. | .. | .. | .. | 33 | 22 |
| .... | 7 | 1 | 1 | .. | 4 | 7 | 4 | 2 | 8 | 5 | 1 | .... | 13 | 5 | 18 | .... | .... | .... | .... | .. | .. | .. | .. | 18 | 23 |
| .... | 6 | 1 | 4 | .. | 7 | 5 | 6 | 4 | 7 | 8 | 1 | 2 | 6 | 16 | 22 | .... | .... | .... | .... | .. | .. | .. | .. | 22 | 24 |
| .... | 2 | 1 | .... | .. | 5 | 3 | 3 | 2 | 8 | 4 | 1 | .... | 8 | 5 | 13 | .... | .... | .... | .... | .. | .. | .. | .. | 13 | 25 |
| .... | 15 | 1 | 12 | 1 | 27 | 49 | 22 | 15 | 46 | 30 | 7 | 1 | 64 | 48 | 112 | .... | .... | .... | .... | 1 | .. | .. | .. | 113 | 26 |
| .... | 2 | ... | 4 | .. | 13 | 9 | 7 | 11 | 18 | 9 | 1 | 1 | 27 | 13 | 40 | .... | .... | .... | .... | .. | .. | .. | .. | 40 | 27 |
| .... | 436 | 46 | 123 | 2 | 333 | 385 | 329 | 264 | 35 | 114 | 158 | 598 | 724 | 547 | 1271 | .... | .... | .... | .... | 21 | 26 | .. | 1 | 1319 | 28 |
| .... | 12 | 4 | 8 | .. | 66 | 106 | 68 | 67 | 159 | 65 | 7 | 3 | 156 | 151 | 307 | .... | .... | .... | .... | 2 | 1 | .. | .. | 310 | 29 |
| .... | 3 | 1 | .... | .. | 8 | 2 | 4 | 4 | 7 | 6 | 2 | 2 | 12 | 6 | 18 | .... | .... | .... | .... | .. | .. | .. | .. | 18 | 30 |
| .... | 2 | 2 | 3 | .. | 57 | 44 | 28 | 64 | 131 | 50 | 1 | .... | 112 | 81 | 193 | .... | .... | .... | .... | .. | .. | .. | .. | 193 | 31 |
| .... | 38 | 5 | 14 | 1 | 35 | 40 | 51 | 20 | 27 | 31 | 25 | 28 | 70 | 78 | 148 | .... | .... | .... | .... | .. | 1 | .. | .. | 149 | 32 |
| .... | 7 | 7 | 1 | .. | 3 | 11 | 7 | 3 | 2 | 1 | .... | 3 | 10 | 11 | 21 | .... | .... | .... | .... | 1 | 2 | .. | .. | 24 | 33 |
| .... | 77 | 9 | 16 | 2 | 45 | 118 | 172 | 38 | 46 | 107 | 40 | 23 | 195 | 191 | 386 | .... | .... | .... | .... | 2 | 5 | .. | .. | 393 | 34 |
| .... | 44 | 8 | 19 | .. | 65 | 59 | 79 | 52 | 32 | 82 | 32 | 77 | 140 | 116 | 256 | .... | .... | .... | .... | 3 | 3 | .. | .. | 262 | 35 |
| .... | 136 | 27 | 40 | 1 | 56 | 183 | 431 | 80 | 137 | 283 | 71 | 28 | 392 | 355 | 747 | .... | .... | .... | .... | .. | 3 | . | .. | 750 | 36 |
| .... | .... | ... | 1 | .. | 2 | .... | 1 | 3 | .... | 1 | 1 | 1 | 3 | 2 | 5 | .... | .... | .... | .... | .. | .. | .. | .. | 5 | 37 |
| .... | 5 | 1 | 4 | .. | 4 | 7 | 3 | 3 | 4 | .... | .... | 3 | 9 | 8 | 17 | .... | .... | .... | .... | .. | .. | .. | .. | 17 | 38 |
| .... | 17 | 1 | 6 | .. | 27 | 28 | 14 | 16 | 16 | 31 | 5 | 3 | 42 | 40 | 82 | .... | .... | .... | .... | .. | 1 | .. | 3 | 86 | 39 |
| ... | 1 | ... | .... | .. | .... | 1 | .... | ... | 1 | .... | .... | .... | 1 | .... | 1 | .... | .... | .... | .... | .. | .. | .. | .. | 1 | 40 |
| .... | .... | ... | .... | .. | .... | .... | .... | 1 | .... | .... | .... | .... | 1 | .... | 1 | .... | .... | .... | .... | .. | .. | .. | .. | 1 | 41 |
| .... | 56 | 16 | 14 | 1 | 39 | 56 | 45 | 27 | 40 | 62 | 14 | 8 | 98 | 67 | 165 | .... | .... | .... | .... | 1 | 1 | .. | .. | 167 | 42 |
| .... | 6 | 3 | 1 | .. | 3 | 8 | 20 | 5 | 5 | 13 | 5 | 2 | 20 | 20 | 40 | .... | .... | .... | .... | .. | .. | .. | .. | 40 | 43 |
| .... | 8 | 2 | 1 | .. | 11 | 30 | 11 | 15 | 14 | 28 | 7 | 2 | 44 | 22 | 66 | .... | .... | .... | .... | 1 | .. | .. | .. | 67 | 44 |
| .... | 5 | 1 | .... | .. | 1 | 4 | 5 | 1 | 2 | 3 | .... | .... | 5 | 6 | 11 | .... | .... | .... | .... | .. | .. | .. | .. | 11 | 45 |
| .... | 1 | ... | .... | .. | .... | .... | .... | 1 | .... | .... | .... | .... | 1 | .... | 1 | .... | .... | .... | .... | .. | .. | .. | .. | 1 | 46 |
| .... | 1 | 1 | 1 | .. | 7 | .... | 7 | .... | 1 | 9 | .... | .... | 8 | 6 | 14 | .... | .... | .... | .... | .. | .. | .. | .. | 14 | 47 |
| .... | 7 | 2 | .... | .. | 5 | 2 | .... | 3 | 4 | 4 | 1 | 1 | .... | 10 | 10 | .... | .... | .... | .... | .. | .. | .. | .. | 10 | 48 |
| .... | 1 | 1 | .... | .. | .... | 5 | 5 | 5 | .... | 7 | 1 | 1 | 12 | 3 | 15 | .... | .... | .... | .... | .. | .. | .. | .. | 15 | 49 |
| .... | 26 | 2 | 11 | .. | 61 | 48 | 27 | 31 | 48 | 62 | 11 | 1 | 80 | 86 | 166 | .... | .... | .... | .... | .. | .. | .. | 1 | 167 | 50 |
| .... | 16 | 1 | .... | .. | 9 | 5 | 3 | 1 | 8 | 7 | 1 | .... | 11 | 7 | 18 | .... | .... | .... | .... | .. | .. | .. | .. | 18 | 51 |
| .... | 98 | 18 | 10 | 1 | 93 | 77 | 64 | 56 | 29 | 60 | 15 | 5 | 168 | 119 | 287 | .... | .... | .... | .... | 3 | .. | .. | .. | 290 | 52 |
| .... | .... | ... | .... | .. | 1 | 1 | .... | .... | 1 | .... | .... | .... | 2 | ... | 2 | .... | .... | .... | .... | .. | .. | .. | .. | 2 | 53 |
| .... | .... | 1 | .... | .. | ... | 2 | .... | .... | .... | .... | 1 | .... | 1 | 1 | 2 | .... | .... | .... | .... | .. | .. | .. | .. | 2 | 54 |
| .... | 44 | 5 | 8 | 1 | 18 | 17 | 23 | 19 | .... | .... | .... | .... | 73 | 4 | 77 | .... | .... | .... | .... | .. | .. | .. | .. | 77 | 55 |
| .... | 1 | ... | .... | 1 | 1 | 1 | 1 | 1 | .... | .... | .... | .... | 2 | 2 | 4 | .... | .... | .... | .... | .. | .. | .. | .. | 4 | 56 |
| .... | .... | ... | .... | .. | .... | 1 | .... | 1 | .... | 1 | 1 | .... | 2 | .... | 2 | .... | .... | .... | .... | .. | .. | .. | .. | 2 | 57 |
| .... | 3 | 1 | .... | .. | 3 | 1 | 3 | 2 | .... | 5 | 2 | 2 | 8 | 1 | 9 | .... | .... | .... | .... | .. | .. | .. | .. | 9 | 58 |
| .... | 33 | 7 | 7 | .. | 41 | 56 | 36 | 29 | 45 | 24 | 23 | 29 | 99 | 62 | 161 | .... | .... | .... | .... | 1 | 3 | .. | .. | 165 | 59 |
| .... | 2 | ... | .... | .. | .... | 1 | 1 | ... | 1 | .... | .... | .... | 2 | .... | 2 | .... | .... | .... | .... | .. | .. | .. | .. | 2 | 60 |
| .... | 2 | 3 | 3 | 1 | 5 | 4 | 7 | 10 | 4 | 5 | .... | .... | 19 | 7 | 26 | .... | .... | .... | .... | .. | .. | .. | .. | 26 | 61 |
| .... | 2 | ... | .... | .. | .... | 3 | .... | 2 | .... | .... | .... | 1 | 4 | .... | 4 | .... | .... | .... | .... | 1 | .. | .. | .. | 5 | 62 |

CLASSIFICATION OF DEATHS IN

| | Cause of death. | AGES. | | | | | | | | | | | | | | | | | | NATIVITIES. | | | | | |
|---|---|---|---|---|---|---|---|---|---|---|---|---|---|---|---|---|---|---|---|---|---|---|---|---|---|
| | | Under 1. | | 1 and under 5. | | 5 and under 10. | | 10 and under 20. | | 20 and under 50. | | 50 and under 80. | | 80 and under 100. | | 100 & over. | | Age unknown. | | Born in State. | N. England States. | Middle States. | Southern States. | Southwest'n States. | Northwest'n States. |
| | | M. | F. | M. | F. | M. | F. | M. | F. | M. | F. | M. | F. | M | F. | M | F. | M | F. | | | | | | |
| 1 | Hip, disease of | | | 2 | | 1 | | | | | | | | | | | | | | 3 | | | | | |
| 2 | Hives | 1 | | 2 | 2 | | | | | | | | | | | | | | | 5 | | | | | |
| 3 | Hooping cough | 25 | 21 | 38 | 38 | 10 | 6 | 2 | 1 | | 1 | | 2 | | | | | | 1 | 129 | 1 | | 1 | | |
| 4 | Hydrocephalus | 46 | 30 | 85 | 69 | 11 | 12 | 3 | 1 | 8 | 2 | 3 | 1 | | | | | | | 240 | 1 | 6 | 2 | | |
| 5 | Hydrophobia | | | | | | | | | | 1 | | | | | | | | | | | | | | |
| 6 | Inflammation | 23 | 27 | 26 | 21 | 5 | 2 | 1 | 1 | 9 | 11 | 3 | 2 | | | | | | | 100 | 1 | 3 | | | |
| 7 | ....do....bowels | 24 | 13 | 17 | 16 | 11 | 5 | 4 | 3 | 22 | 18 | 8 | 5 | | 1 | | | | | 101 | 3 | 5 | | 2 | |
| 8 | ....do....brain | 9 | 6 | 21 | 19 | 7 | 2 | 1 | 5 | 10 | 5 | 4 | 2 | 1 | | | | | | 74 | | | 2 | | |
| 9 | ....do....stomach | | 1 | | 1 | 1 | 1 | | 2 | 4 | 6 | 3 | | | | | | | | 7 | | | | | |
| 10 | Insanity | | | | | | | | | 4 | 2 | | | | | | | | | 4 | | | | | |
| 11 | Intemperance | | | | | | | | | 8 | 13 | 2 | | | | | | | | 14 | | 1 | | | |
| 12 | Jaundice | 8 | 1 | | 3 | 2 | | | | 1 | 1 | | 1 | | | | | | | 8 | | | | | |
| 13 | Kidneys, disease of | | | 1 | | | 1 | 1 | | 5 | | 1 | | | | | | | | 3 | | 1 | | | |
| 14 | Killed | | | 1 | 1 | 2 | | 3 | | 13 | | 2 | | | | | | | | 6 | 1 | 1 | 1 | | |
| 15 | Liver, disease of | | 1 | | 2 | | | 3 | | 15 | 15 | 5 | 8 | | | | | | | 15 | 1 | 1 | | | |
| 16 | Lockjaw | | | | | | | | | 3 | | | | | | | | | | 1 | | | | | |
| 17 | Lungs, disease of | 2 | 3 | 2 | 1 | 2 | | | | 6 | 6 | 1 | 5 | | 1 | | | | | 17 | 1 | 2 | | | |
| 18 | Malformation | 2 | 2 | | | | | | | | | | | | | | | | | 4 | | | | | |
| 19 | Mania-a-potu | | | | | | | | 1 | 38 | 12 | 4 | | | | | | | | 10 | 1 | 1 | | | 1 |
| 20 | Marasmus | 23 | 73 | 26 | 29 | 3 | 5 | 1 | 2 | 1 | 6 | 6 | 1 | | | | | | | 164 | 3 | | | | |
| 21 | Measles | 10 | 14 | 45 | 48 | 13 | 20 | 3 | 5 | 2 | 1 | | | | | | | 1 | 1 | 140 | 1 | 3 | | | |
| 22 | Mortification | | | 4 | 2 | | | 3 | | 8 | 6 | | 1 | 1 | | | | | | 11 | 1 | | | | |
| 23 | Neuralgia | | | | | | 1 | | | 2 | 2 | | 2 | | | | | | | 3 | | 1 | | | |
| 24 | Old age | | | | | | | | | | | 19 | 28 | 20 | 45 | | | | | 35 | 7 | 5 | 4 | | |
| 25 | Paralysis | | | | | 1 | 1 | | | 7 | 7 | 24 | 18 | 1 | | | | | | 24 | 2 | 2 | 1 | | |
| 26 | Peritonitis | | | | | | | 1 | 1 | 2 | | 1 | | | | | | | | 2 | | | 1 | | |
| 27 | Piles | | | | | | | | | 1 | | | | | | | | | | | | | | | |
| 28 | Pleurisy | 1 | | | 1 | | | 1 | | 18 | 5 | 5 | 1 | | | | | | | 8 | 3 | 2 | | | |
| 29 | Pneumonia | 44 | 48 | 54 | 55 | 15 | 17 | 6 | 6 | 69 | 42 | 24 | 4 | 1 | 2 | | | | 1 | 278 | 8 | 2 | 4 | 1 | |
| 30 | Poison | | | | | | | | | | | | 1 | | | | | | | | | | | | |
| 31 | Prematurity of birth | | 4 | | | | | | | | | | | | | | | | | 4 | | | | | |
| 32 | Quinsy | | | 1 | 1 | 1 | | | | 1 | | 1 | | | | | | | | 3 | | | | | |
| 33 | Rheumatism | | | 1 | 1 | 2 | | 2 | 1 | 3 | 8 | 1 | 3 | | | | | | | 6 | | 2 | | | |
| 34 | Salivation, effects of | | | | | | | | | | 1 | | | | | | | | | | | | | | |
| 35 | Scrofula | 1 | 3 | 4 | 7 | 3 | 2 | 2 | 3 | 3 | 3 | | | | | | | | | 26 | | 2 | | | |
| 36 | Small pox | 19 | 12 | 20 | 25 | 9 | 6 | 2 | 2 | 11 | | | | | | | | | 1 | 81 | 3 | 1 | | | |
| 37 | Spine, disease of | 2 | 1 | 1 | | 1 | | 4 | 1 | 4 | 1 | 2 | 1 | | | | | | | 10 | 2 | | | | |
| 38 | Stillborn | 2 | 1 | | | | | | | | | | | | | | | | | 3 | | | | | |
| 39 | Stomach, disease of | | | | | | | | | | 1 | | | | | | | | | | | | | | |
| 40 | Suffocation | | | | | | | | | | 1 | | | | | | | | | | | | | | |
| 41 | Suicide | | | | | | | | 1 | 5 | 5 | 5 | | | | | | | | 5 | 1 | | | | |
| 42 | Summer complaint | 8 | 15 | 15 | 19 | | 2 | | | | 2 | | | | | | | | | 52 | 1 | 1 | | | |
| 43 | Sun, stroke of | | | 1 | 1 | 1 | 1 | 1 | 1 | 11 | 1 | 8 | 1 | | | | | 1 | 1 | 8 | | | | | |
| 44 | Syphilis | 1 | | | | | | 1 | 1 | 5 | 5 | | 1 | | | | | | | 8 | 1 | 1 | | | |
| 45 | Teething | 36 | 36 | 72 | 78 | | 1 | | | | | | | | | | | | | 202 | 2 | 4 | | | |
| 46 | Tetanus | | 1 | | | | | 1 | | | | | | | | | | | | 1 | | | | | |
| 47 | Throat, disease of | 2 | 4 | 7 | 6 | 1 | 4 | | 1 | 7 | 1 | 1 | 3 | | | | | | | 26 | | 2 | | | |
| 48 | Thrush | 1 | 4 | 12 | 11 | 6 | 10 | | | | 1 | 1 | | | | | | | | 45 | | | | | |
| 49 | Tumor | | | | | 1 | | | 4 | 5 | 4 | 1 | 5 | | | | | | | 11 | 1 | 1 | | | 1 |
| 50 | Ulcer | | | | 1 | | | | 1 | 1 | | 2 | | | | | | | | 2 | 1 | | | | |
| 51 | Uterus, disease of | | | | | | | | | | 6 | | | | | | | | | 4 | | | | | |
| 52 | Venereal | | | | | | | | | 1 | | | | | | | | | | 1 | | | | | |
| 53 | White swelling | | | | | | | 1 | | | | | | | | | | | | | | 1 | | | |
| 54 | Worms | | 1 | 3 | 5 | 1 | 2 | | | | 1 | | | | | | | | | 10 | | | | | |
| 55 | Unknown | 68 | 71 | 49 | 35 | 13 | 15 | 16 | 33 | 100 | 124 | 61 | 51 | 2 | 3 | | | 1 | 1 | 436 | 13 | 17 | 5 | | 4 |
| | Total | 823 | 845 | 1401 | 1304 | 454 | 364 | 369 | 345 | 2532 | 1896 | 787 | 584 | 46 | 78 | | | 24 | 31 | 6895 | 247 | 352 | 109 | 8 | 11 |

CLASSIFICATION OF DEATHS IN

| | Cause of death. | Under 1. M. | Under 1. F. | 1 and under 5. M. | 1 and under 5. F. | 5 and under 10. M. | 5 and under 10. F. | 10 and under 20. M. | 10 and under 20. F. | 20 and under 50. M. | 20 and under 50. F. | 50 and under 80. M. | 50 and under 80. F. | 80 and under 100. M | 80 and under 100. F. | 100 & over. M | 100 & over. F. | Age unknown. M | Age unknown. F. | Born in State. | N. England States. | Middle States. | Southern States. | Southwest'n States. | Northwest'n States. |
|---|---|---|---|---|---|---|---|---|---|---|---|---|---|---|---|---|---|---|---|---|---|---|---|---|---|
| 1 | Abscess | 3 | 1 | 2 | 2 | 1 | 1 | 4 | 4 | 20 | 13 | 7 | 6 | 2 | | | | | | 29 | 6 | 3 | 2 | | |
| 2 | Accident, not specif'd | 15 | 10 | 36 | 22 | 36 | 23 | 73 | 7 | 242 | 16 | 64 | 17 | 7 | 3 | | | | | 340 | 49 | 13 | | | 1 |
| 3 | ....do...burned | 4 | 3 | 27 | 31 | 6 | 21 | 4 | 5 | 11 | 11 | 1 | 5 | 1 | 1 | | | | | 106 | 4 | 3 | | | |
| 4 | ....do...drowned | 1 | | 41 | 7 | 65 | 11 | 57 | 10 | 122 | 7 | 14 | 1 | 1 | | | | | | 210 | 19 | 4 | 2 | | 1 |
| 5 | ....do...scalded | 5 | 4 | 27 | 23 | 4 | 2 | 3 | | 6 | | | | | | | | | | 63 | 1 | | | | 1 |
| 6 | ....do...expl. steam | | | | | | | 1 | | 3 | | | | | | | | | | 1 | 1 | 1 | | | |
| 7 | ....do...machin'ry | | | | | | | | | 1 | | | | | | | | | | | | | | | |
| 8 | ....do...railroad | | | | 1 | 1 | | 3 | 1 | 13 | | 2 | | | | | | | | 10 | 2 | | | | |
| 9 | ....do...shot | | | | | | | 2 | 1 | 4 | | 1 | | | | | | | | 5 | 1 | | | | |
| 10 | Amputation | | | | | | | | | 1 | | | | | 1 | | | | | | 2 | | | | |

## NEW YORK CITY, STATE OF NEW YORK—Continued.

| NATIVITIES. | | | | | SEASON OF DECEASE. | | | | DURATION OF SICKNESS. | | | | WHITES. | | | COLORED. | | | | | | | | | |
|---|---|---|---|---|---|---|---|---|---|---|---|---|---|---|---|---|---|---|---|---|---|---|---|---|---|
| | | | | | | | | | | | | | | | | Slaves. | | | | Free. | | | | | |
| | | | | | | | | | | | | | | | | Black. | | Mulatto. | | Bl'ck. | | Mul. | | | |
| California and Territories. | Ireland. | Germany. | Other foreign countries. | Unknown. | Spring. | Summer. | Autumn. | Winter. | Under 1 week. | 1 week and under 1 month. | 1 month and under 3 months. | 3 months and over. | Males. | Females. | Total. | M. | F. | M. | F. | M. | F. | M | F. | Aggregate deaths. | |
| | | | | | 1 | 1 | | 1 | | | | 3 | 3 | | 3 | | | | | | | | | 3 | 1 |
| | | | | | 1 | | 3 | 1 | 3 | 1 | | 1 | 3 | 1 | 4 | | | | | | 1 | | | 5 | 2 |
| | 8 | | 3 | 3 | 31 | 36 | 41 | 34 | 13 | 50 | 24 | 23 | 71 | 69 | 140 | | | | | 4 | 1 | | | 145 | 3 |
| | 13 | 3 | 6 | | 41 | 88 | 75 | 56 | 62 | 123 | 24 | 16 | 154 | 115 | 269 | | | | | 2 | | | | 271 | 4 |
| | | 1 | | | | | | 1 | | | | | | 1 | 1 | | | | | | | | | 1 | 5 |
| | 20 | 2 | 5 | | 34 | 35 | 30 | 23 | 34 | 66 | 14 | 4 | 64 | 62 | 126 | | | | | 2 | 1 | 1 | 1 | 131 | 6 |
| | 27 | 3 | 6 | | 35 | 36 | 45 | 31 | 39 | 55 | 9 | 2 | 84 | 60 | 144 | | | | | 2 | 1 | | | 147 | 7 |
| | 9 | 2 | 5 | | 19 | 37 | 22 | 14 | 23 | 45 | 4 | 2 | 52 | 37 | 89 | | | | | 1 | 1 | | 1 | 92 | 8 |
| | 9 | 1 | 2 | | 2 | 8 | 6 | 2 | 2 | 3 | | 2 | 8 | 10 | 18 | | | | | | 1 | | | 19 | 9 |
| | | 2 | | | 3 | 2 | | 1 | 1 | 3 | | 2 | 4 | 2 | 6 | | | | | | | | | 6 | 10 |
| | 3 | 1 | 2 | 2 | 5 | 7 | 7 | 4 | | | | | 10 | 13 | 23 | | | | | | | | | 23 | 11 |
| | 6 | 1 | 2 | | 6 | 2 | 7 | 2 | 6 | 5 | 1 | 1 | 11 | 6 | 17 | | | | | | | | | 17 | 12 |
| | 2 | 1 | 2 | | 3 | 2 | 2 | 2 | | 1 | 1 | 4 | 8 | 1 | 9 | | | | | | | | | 9 | 13 |
| | 8 | 3 | 2 | | 5 | 3 | 10 | 2 | 21 | | | | 20 | 1 | 21 | | | | | 1 | | | | 22 | 14 |
| | 25 | 2 | 5 | | 10 | 10 | 18 | 11 | 2 | 15 | 9 | 11 | 23 | 26 | 49 | | | | | | | | | 49 | 15 |
| | 2 | | | | 1 | | | 2 | 2 | 1 | | | 3 | | 3 | | | | | | | | | 3 | 16 |
| | 6 | 1 | 2 | | 6 | 3 | 10 | 10 | 3 | 1 | 1 | | 13 | 16 | 29 | | | | | | | | | 29 | 17 |
| | | | | | | 4 | | | | | | 1 | 2 | 2 | 4 | | | | | | | | | 4 | 18 |
| | 33 | 2 | 4 | 3 | 11 | 21 | 13 | 10 | 12 | 7 | | 2 | 42 | 13 | 55 | | | | | | | | | 55 | 19 |
| | 5 | 1 | 2 | 1 | 38 | 48 | 60 | 30 | 4 | 10 | 14 | 15 | 60 | 116 | 176 | | | | | | | | | 176 | 20 |
| | 13 | 2 | 4 | | 35 | 64 | 24 | 38 | 24 | 57 | 17 | 1 | 74 | 89 | 163 | | | | | | | | | 163 | 21 |
| | 9 | 1 | 3 | | 4 | 7 | 12 | 2 | 5 | 3 | | 2 | 16 | 9 | 25 | | | | | | | | | 25 | 22 |
| | 2 | | 1 | | 3 | 1 | 2 | 1 | | 2 | | 3 | 2 | 5 | 7 | | | | | | | | | 7 | 23 |
| | 30 | 12 | 17 | 2 | 20 | 43 | 25 | 24 | 18 | 14 | 4 | 28 | 37 | 70 | 107 | | | | | 1 | 2 | 1 | 1 | 112 | 24 |
| | 13 | 3 | 12 | 2 | 11 | 15 | 15 | 13 | 12 | 9 | 3 | 18 | 32 | 25 | 57 | | | | | | | 1 | 1 | 59 | 25 |
| | | 1 | 1 | | 2 | | 2 | 1 | | | | 1 | 3 | 1 | 4 | | | | | | | 1 | | 5 | 26 |
| | | 1 | | | | | 1 | | | | | | 1 | | 1 | | | | | | | | | 1 | 27 |
| | 15 | 2 | 2 | | 7 | 10 | 7 | 8 | 6 | 12 | | 3 | 23 | 7 | 30 | | | | | 2 | | | | 32 | 28 |
| | 72 | 8 | 12 | 3 | 113 | 83 | 67 | 99 | 57 | 94 | 35 | 15 | 211 | 174 | 385 | | | | | 1 | 1 | 1 | | 388 | 29 |
| | | | 1 | | | 1 | | | | | | | | 1 | 1 | | | | | | | | | 1 | 30 |
| | | | | | 2 | | | 2 | | | | | | 4 | 4 | | | | | | | | | 4 | 31 |
| | | | 2 | | 2 | | 1 | 2 | 2 | 2 | 1 | | 4 | 1 | 5 | | | | | | | | | 5 | 32 |
| | 9 | 1 | 3 | 1 | 6 | 11 | 2 | 3 | 2 | 7 | 3 | 6 | 9 | 13 | 22 | | | | | | | | | 22 | 33 |
| | | | 1 | | | 1 | | | | 1 | | | | 1 | 1 | | | | | | | | | 1 | 34 |
| | 3 | | | | 8 | 11 | 8 | 4 | 1 | | 4 | 11 | 13 | 15 | 28 | | | | | | 3 | | | 31 | 35 |
| | 16 | 3 | 3 | | 14 | 45 | 22 | 26 | 12 | 70 | 11 | 3 | 59 | 46 | 105 | | | | | 2 | | | | 107 | 36 |
| | 4 | | 2 | | 4 | 6 | 4 | 4 | 2 | 2 | 2 | 8 | 13 | 4 | 17 | | | | | | | 1 | | 18 | 37 |
| | | | | | | 3 | | | | | | | 2 | 1 | 3 | | | | | | | | | 3 | 38 |
| | 1 | | | | | | 1 | | | | | | | 1 | 1 | | | | | | | | | 1 | 39 |
| | 1 | | | | | | 1 | | 1 | | | | | 1 | 1 | | | | | | | | | 1 | 40 |
| | 7 | 1 | 2 | | 3 | 6 | 4 | 3 | 7 | | 1 | | 10 | 6 | 16 | | | | | | | | | 16 | 41 |
| | 3 | 2 | 2 | | 7 | 28 | 25 | | 15 | 22 | 17 | 6 | 23 | 38 | 61 | | | | | | | | | 61 | 42 |
| | 12 | 2 | 2 | | | 16 | 8 | | 18 | 1 | | | 18 | 6 | 24 | | | | | | | | | 24 | 43 |
| | 3 | | 1 | | 4 | 4 | 5 | 1 | | | | 2 | 5 | 5 | 10 | | | | | 2 | 2 | | | 14 | 44 |
| | 10 | 3 | 2 | | 35 | 80 | 77 | 28 | 48 | 107 | 30 | 21 | 107 | 114 | 221 | | | | | | 1 | 1 | | 223 | 45 |
| | | 1 | | | | 1 | | 1 | 1 | | | | 1 | 1 | 2 | | | | | | | | | 2 | 46 |
| | 8 | | | 1 | 15 | 7 | 8 | 7 | 7 | 11 | 2 | 1 | 18 | 19 | 37 | | | | | | | | | 37 | 47 |
| | 1 | | | | 4 | 6 | 14 | 12 | 3 | 2 | 2 | 2 | 20 | 26 | 46 | | | | | | | | | 46 | 48 |
| | 5 | | 1 | | 7 | 5 | 2 | 6 | 3 | 3 | 5 | 1 | 6 | 12 | 18 | | | | | | 1 | 1 | | 20 | 49 |
| | 2 | | | | 1 | 2 | 1 | 1 | 1 | 1 | 1 | | 3 | 2 | 5 | | | | | | | | | 5 | 50 |
| | 1 | 1 | | | 1 | 3 | | | | | 1 | | | 6 | 6 | | | | | | | | | 6 | 51 |
| | | | | | | 1 | | | | | | | 1 | | 1 | | | | | | | | | 1 | 52 |
| | | | | | 1 | | | | | | | 1 | 1 | | 1 | | | | | | | | | 1 | 53 |
| | 1 | | 2 | | 5 | 1 | 4 | 3 | 3 | 8 | 2 | 3 | 4 | 9 | 13 | | | | | | | | | 13 | 54 |
| | 112 | 26 | 26 | 2 | 139 | 130 | 126 | 113 | 134 | 82 | 42 | 69 | 297 | 313 | 610 | | | | | 10 | 15 | 3 | 3 | 641 | 55 |
| | 2942 | 526 | 728 | 65 | 2022 | 4171 | 3592 | 1703 | 3447 | 2432 | 791 | 1186 | 6311 | 5318 | 11629 | | | | | 104 | 110 | 21 | 19 | 11883 | |

## THE STATE OF NEW YORK—AGGREGATE.

| California and Territories. | Ireland. | Germany. | Other foreign countries. | Unknown. | Spring. | Summer. | Autumn. | Winter. | Under 1 week. | 1 week and under 1 month. | 1 month and under 3 months. | 3 months and over. | Males. | Females. | Total. | Slaves Black M. | Slaves Black F. | Slaves Mulatto M. | Slaves Mulatto F. | Free Bl'ck M. | Free Bl'ck F. | Free Mul. M | Free Mul. F. | Aggregate deaths. | |
|---|---|---|---|---|---|---|---|---|---|---|---|---|---|---|---|---|---|---|---|---|---|---|---|---|---|
| | 18 | 2 | 5 | 1 | 17 | 17 | 17 | 15 | 7 | 11 | 9 | 2[illegible] | 39 | 27 | 66 | | | | | | | | | 66 | 1 |
| | 109 | 24 | 34 | 1 | 157 | 159 | 126 | 118 | 326 | 81 | 28 | 1[illegible] | 463 | 97 | 560 | | | | | 7 | 1 | 3 | | 571 | 2 |
| | 10 | 3 | 5 | | 45 | 26 | 23 | 34 | 77 | 17 | 3 | [illegible] | 54 | 74 | 128 | | | | | | 2 | | 1 | 131 | 3 |
| | 62 | 10 | 28 | 1 | 42 | 155 | 98 | 37 | 337 | | | | 295 | 36 | 331 | | | | | 5 | | 1 | | 337 | 4 |
| | 4 | 1 | 4 | | 21 | 19 | 16 | 18 | 51 | 12 | 1 | | 45 | 29 | 74 | | | | | | | | | 74 | 5 |
| | 1 | | | | 4 | | | | 4 | | | | 4 | | 4 | | | | | | | | | 4 | 6 |
| | 1 | | | | 1 | | | | | | | | 1 | | 1 | | | | | | | | | 1 | 7 |
| | 9 | | | | 5 | 6 | 7 | 3 | 7 | | 1 | 1 | 19 | 2 | 21 | | | | | | | | | 21 | 8 |
| | 1 | 1 | | | 2 | 2 | 4 | | 4 | 1 | | | 7 | 1 | 8 | | | | | | | | | 8 | 9 |
| | | | | | 2 | | | | | | 1 | | 1 | 1 | 2 | | | | | | | | | 2 | 10 |

CLASSIFICATION OF DEATHS IN

| | Cause of death. | AGES. | | | | | | | | | | | | | | | | | | NATIVITIES. | | | | | |
|---|---|---|---|---|---|---|---|---|---|---|---|---|---|---|---|---|---|---|---|---|---|---|---|---|---|
| | | Under 1. | | 1 and under 5. | | 5 and under 10. | | 10 and under 20. | | 20 and under 50. | | 50 and under 80. | | 80 and under 100. | | 100 & over. | | Age unknown. | | Born in State. | N. England States. | Middle States. | Southern States. | Southwest'n States. | Northwest'n States. |
| | | M. | F. | M. | F. | M. | F. | M. | F. | M. | F. | M. | F. | M. | F. | M. | F. | M. | F. | | | | | | |
| 1 | Aneurism | | | | | | | | | 3 | | 1 | | | | | | | | 2 | 1 | | | | |
| 2 | Apoplexy | | 2 | | 1 | 1 | | 3 | 3 | 60 | 36 | 128 | 82 | 20 | 14 | | | 5 | 1 | 184 | 73 | 18 | 4 | | 1 |
| 3 | Asthma | 4 | 1 | 3 | 3 | | 1 | | | 6 | 4 | 16 | 7 | 2 | 3 | | | | | 26 | 1 | | 1 | | |
| 4 | Bladder, disease of | | | | | | | 2 | | 2 | | 3 | | 1 | | | | | | 4 | | | | | |
| 5 | Bowels.....do | 26 | 36 | 40 | 28 | 7 | 7 | 12 | 6 | 22 | 11 | 7 | 10 | | 1 | | | 1 | | 171 | 7 | 4 | 1 | | 1 |
| 6 | Brain.......do | 14 | 7 | 24 | 17 | 6 | 4 | 7 | 4 | 17 | 8 | 6 | 2 | | | | | | | 93 | 5 | 1 | | | |
| 7 | Bronchitis | 9 | 4 | 15 | 10 | 7 | 1 | 4 | 4 | 15 | 13 | 21 | 5 | | | | | 1 | | 84 | 7 | 3 | | | |
| 8 | Cancer | 5 | 4 | 10 | 4 | 3 | 2 | 4 | 4 | 20 | 48 | 47 | 78 | 17 | 10 | | | 1 | | 156 | 59 | 4 | 1 | | |
| 9 | Canker | 3 | 8 | 3 | 2 | 2 | 2 | | | 1 | 3 | | 1 | | | | | | | 20 | 2 | | | | |
| 10 | ...do..rash | 4 | 4 | 16 | 17 | 8 | 3 | 4 | 3 | | | | | | | | | | | 53 | 1 | | | | |
| 11 | Carbuncle | | | | | | | | 1 | 1 | | 1 | | | | | | | | 1 | | | | | |
| 12 | Catarrh | 28 | 30 | 12 | 18 | 1 | 1 | 5 | 3 | 9 | 4 | 13 | 9 | 5 | 4 | | | | | 109 | 12 | 2 | | | 2 |
| 13 | Chicken pox | 3 | 3 | | 3 | | | | | | | | | | | | | | | 7 | 1 | 1 | | | |
| 14 | Childbirth | | | | | | | | 17 | | 295 | | 2 | | | | | | | 181 | 13 | 13 | | | 1 |
| 15 | Cholera | 163 | 125 | 420 | 387 | 241 | 218 | 220 | 235 | 1608 | 1144 | 516 | 337 | 33 | 19 | 1 | | 80 | 75 | 2568 | 134 | 155 | 48 | 2 | 12 |
| 16 | ....do..infantum | 96 | 93 | 136 | 109 | 7 | 5 | 1 | | | | | | | | | | | | 426 | 2 | 2 | | 2 | 2 |
| 17 | ....do..morbus | 2 | 4 | 33 | 16 | 12 | 7 | 11 | 5 | 38 | 26 | 23 | 16 | 2 | 3 | | | | | 135 | 12 | 4 | | | |
| 18 | Chorea | | 1 | | | | | | 3 | 1 | 2 | | 1 | | | | | | | 8 | | | | | |
| 19 | Colic | 10 | 2 | 2 | 4 | 5 | 1 | 8 | 5 | 27 | 16 | 21 | 12 | 2 | 2 | | | 1 | | 77 | 14 | 2 | | | |
| 20 | Congestion | 10 | 6 | 8 | 11 | 4 | 3 | 6 | 2 | 8 | 12 | 5 | 8 | | 1 | | | | | 63 | 7 | | | | |
| 21 | ....do...bowels | | 2 | 3 | 1 | 2 | 1 | | 1 | 5 | 3 | 1 | 1 | | | | | | | 13 | 1 | 2 | 1 | | |
| 22 | ....do...brain | 32 | 17 | 58 | 49 | 17 | 19 | 24 | 14 | 47 | 26 | 12 | 10 | 2 | | | | 1 | | 262 | 15 | 6 | 1 | | 1 |
| 23 | ....do...lungs | 14 | 8 | 12 | 11 | 6 | 4 | 2 | 6 | 15 | 6 | 8 | 15 | 3 | 1 | | | | | 80 | 15 | 5 | | | |
| 24 | Consumption | 157 | 132 | 251 | 234 | 65 | 79 | 228 | 443 | 1759 | 1874 | 734 | 627 | 60 | 43 | 1 | | 2 | 2 | 4531 | 639 | 169 | 22 | 4 | 19 |
| 25 | Convulsions | 361 | 285 | 158 | 163 | 19 | 21 | 17 | 17 | 43 | 62 | 29 | 28 | 7 | 5 | | | 4 | 2 | 1104 | 26 | 16 | 1 | | 1 |
| 26 | Cramp | 2 | 1 | 4 | 4 | 2 | | | | 4 | 1 | | | | | | | | | 13 | | 1 | | | |
| 27 | Croup | 193 | 96 | 347 | 273 | 61 | 63 | 3 | 4 | 4 | 1 | 2 | | | | | | 1 | | 979 | 11 | 9 | 3 | 1 | 3 |
| 28 | Debility | 32 | 32 | 22 | 20 | 5 | 4 | 5 | 4 | 30 | 36 | 19 | 32 | 3 | 2 | | | | 1 | 157 | 6 | 2 | | | |
| 29 | Diabetes | 1 | 2 | 2 | 1 | | | 7 | 3 | 13 | 11 | 12 | 3 | 4 | | | | 1 | | 31 | 7 | 3 | | | 1 |
| 30 | Diarrhœa | 108 | 83 | 196 | 210 | 38 | 31 | 25 | 29 | 111 | 84 | 70 | 62 | 12 | 10 | | | 2 | | 821 | 50 | 16 | 2 | | 1 |
| 31 | Dropsy | 65 | 86 | 152 | 118 | 46 | 37 | 34 | 52 | 127 | 213 | 231 | 259 | 37 | 38 | | | 1 | | 1071 | 182 | 48 | 6 | | 2 |
| 32 | Dysentery | 289 | 260 | 759 | 692 | 197 | 169 | 95 | 112 | 369 | 330 | 175 | 197 | 22 | 23 | | | 1 | 1 | 2997 | 137 | 40 | 7 | | 5 |
| 33 | Dyspepsia | 1 | | | 1 | | | | | 11 | 7 | 12 | 7 | | | | | | | 25 | 7 | 3 | | | |
| 34 | Epilepsy | | 1 | | | 1 | | 2 | | 13 | 10 | 3 | 4 | 1 | | | | | | 19 | 1 | 2 | | | |
| 35 | Erysipelas | 38 | 32 | 26 | 29 | 11 | 8 | 15 | 15 | 42 | 62 | 32 | 46 | 6 | 8 | | | | | 263 | 50 | 11 | 3 | | 1 |
| 36 | Executed | | | | | | | | | 1 | | 1 | | | | | | | | 1 | | | | | |
| 37 | Eye, disease of | | | | | | | 2 | | | | | | | | | | | | | | 1 | | | |
| 38 | Fever, not specified | 41 | 16 | 77 | 58 | 34 | 35 | 52 | 61 | 175 | 120 | 70 | 47 | 7 | 5 | | | | 1 | 529 | 59 | 8 | 2 | 1 | 5 |
| 39 | ..do..bilious | 7 | 4 | 16 | 30 | 18 | 9 | 23 | 28 | 92 | 41 | 39 | 17 | 3 | 2 | | | 1 | | 249 | 20 | 8 | 1 | | |
| 40 | ..do..brain | 34 | 32 | 61 | 48 | 35 | 20 | 36 | 34 | 52 | 28 | 14 | 11 | 1 | | | | 6 | 3 | 366 | 15 | 6 | | | |
| 41 | ..do..catarrhal | | | | | | | | | 1 | 1 | | | | | | | | | | | | | | |
| 42 | ..do..congestive | 2 | | 2 | 7 | 6 | 4 | 9 | 5 | 16 | 10 | 7 | 3 | | | | | 1 | 1 | 59 | 3 | 3 | | | |
| 43 | ..do..inflammatory | | | 2 | 2 | 2 | 1 | | | 2 | 3 | 1 | 1 | | | | | | | 11 | 1 | | | | |
| 44 | ..do..intermittent | | 3 | 3 | 6 | 3 | 2 | 2 | 3 | 13 | 9 | 5 | 7 | | | | | | | 45 | 4 | | | | |
| 45 | ..do..puerperal | | | | | | | | | | 36 | | | | | | | | | 18 | | 1 | | | |
| 46 | ..do..remittent | 1 | | 5 | 3 | | 1 | 3 | 3 | 12 | 8 | 3 | 1 | | | | | | | 28 | 2 | 2 | 2 | | |
| 47 | ..do..scarlet | 45 | 42 | 296 | 265 | 126 | 144 | 32 | 41 | 18 | 13 | 3 | 1 | 2 | | | | | | 937 | 9 | 13 | 1 | | 2 |
| 48 | ..do..ship | | 1 | 6 | 9 | 4 | 2 | 7 | 7 | 27 | 11 | 6 | 2 | 1 | 1 | | | | | 11 | 1 | | | | |
| 49 | ..do..typhus | 4 | 10 | 18 | 24 | 26 | 22 | 97 | 85 | 389 | 219 | 94 | 47 | | 2 | | | | | 582 | 64 | 24 | 2 | | 1 |
| 50 | ..do..yellow | | | 1 | 1 | | | 1 | | 12 | | | 1 | | | | | | | 10 | 2 | 1 | | | |
| 51 | Fistula | | | | | | | | | 1 | 1 | | 1 | | | | | | | 2 | | | | | |
| 52 | Fracture | | | | | 2 | | 7 | | 61 | 5 | 7 | 1 | | | | | 1 | | 18 | 5 | 1 | | | |
| 53 | Frozen | | | | 1 | | | | | 4 | | 6 | | | | | | | | 4 | 2 | | | | |
| 54 | Gout | | | | | | | | | 1 | 1 | 2 | 1 | | | | | | | 2 | | | | | |
| 55 | Gravel | 2 | | | | | | 1 | | 6 | 1 | 37 | 4 | 10 | | | | | | 30 | 18 | 4 | | 1 | |
| 56 | Head, disease of | 7 | 7 | 8 | 4 | 3 | 1 | 2 | 2 | 6 | 2 | 4 | 3 | | | | | | | 38 | 3 | 1 | | | |
| 57 | Heart....do | 23 | 18 | 12 | 13 | 14 | 14 | 29 | 27 | 122 | 71 | 109 | 80 | 6 | 7 | | | | | 335 | 71 | 26 | 6 | 2 | |
| 58 | Heat | | | | | | | 3 | 1 | 7 | 1 | 3 | | | | | | | | 6 | 1 | | | | |
| 59 | Hemorrhage | 8 | 4 | 7 | 1 | 3 | | 7 | 4 | 32 | 16 | 12 | 4 | 1 | | | | | | 62 | 9 | 5 | 1 | | |
| 60 | Hernia | | | | 1 | 1 | | 1 | | 9 | 4 | 6 | 2 | 1 | 1 | | | | | 10 | 4 | 3 | 1 | | 1 |
| 61 | Hip, disease of | | | 5 | | 3 | 1 | 4 | 1 | 1 | 1 | | 1 | | | | | | | 14 | 1 | | | | |
| 62 | Hives | 5 | | 3 | 3 | 1 | 1 | | | | | | | | | | | | | 13 | | | | | |
| 63 | Hooping cough | 132 | 117 | 154 | 188 | 20 | 22 | 4 | 4 | 1 | 2 | 1 | 2 | | | | | 1 | 1 | 606 | 8 | 5 | 1 | | 1 |
| 64 | Hydrocephalus | 124 | 87 | 193 | 129 | 33 | 23 | 10 | 13 | 17 | 14 | 13 | 4 | | | | | | | 600 | 7 | 11 | 2 | | 1 |
| 65 | Hydrophophia | | | | | 1 | | | | 1 | 1 | | | | | | | | | 1 | | | | | |
| 66 | Inflammation | 147 | 115 | 138 | 107 | 26 | 32 | 31 | 32 | 68 | 106 | 55 | 45 | 14 | 4 | | | 1 | | 757 | 64 | 17 | | | 1 |
| 67 | ....do......bowels | 63 | 43 | 62 | 66 | 28 | 19 | 24 | 25 | 62 | 57 | 30 | 18 | 2 | 1 | | | 1 | | 399 | 28 | 7 | | 2 | 3 |
| 68 | ....do......brain | 79 | 61 | 132 | 95 | 31 | 26 | 40 | 33 | 45 | 29 | 24 | 6 | 1 | | | | | | 535 | 12 | 4 | 3 | | |
| 69 | ....do......head | 9 | 4 | 7 | 4 | 2 | | 2 | 2 | 3 | 1 | | | | | | | | | 31 | 2 | 1 | | | |
| 70 | ....do......stomach | 1 | 3 | | 2 | 2 | 2 | 2 | 3 | 5 | 11 | 6 | 3 | | | | | | | 24 | 3 | 1 | | | |
| 71 | Insanity | | | | | | | 1 | | 19 | 18 | 10 | 17 | | | | | | | 39 | 9 | 2 | | | |
| 72 | Intemperance | | | | | | | 1 | | 32 | 17 | 28 | 1 | | | | | | | 50 | 6 | 3 | | | |
| 73 | Jaundice | 15 | 5 | 5 | 5 | 2 | | 1 | | 8 | 10 | 7 | 9 | 2 | | | | | | 46 | 7 | | | | |
| 74 | Kidneys, disease of | | | 3 | | | 1 | 2 | 2 | 11 | 4 | 22 | 4 | 4 | | | | | | 28 | 16 | 3 | | | |
| 75 | Killed | | | 3 | 3 | 5 | | 11 | | 46 | 2 | 12 | 1 | 2 | 2 | | | | | 51 | 7 | 2 | 1 | | |

## THE STATE OF NEW YORK—AGGREGATE—Continued.

| NATIVITIES. | | | | | SEASON OF DECEASE. | | | | DURATION OF SICKNESS. | | | | WHITES. | | | COLORED. | | | | | | | | | |
|---|---|---|---|---|---|---|---|---|---|---|---|---|---|---|---|---|---|---|---|---|---|---|---|---|---|
| | | | | | | | | | | | | | | | | Slaves. | | | | Free. | | | | | |
| | | | | | | | | | | | | | | | | Black. | | Mulatto. | | Black | | Mul. | | | |
| California and Territories. | Ireland. | Germany. | Other foreign countries. | Unknown. | Spring. | Summer. | Autumn. | Winter. | Under 1 week. | 1 week and under 1 month. | 1 month and under 3 months. | 3 months and over. | Males. | Females. | Total. | M. | F. | M. | F. | M. | F. | M | F. | Aggregate deaths. | |
| ... | 1 | ... | ... | .. | 2 | ... | 2 | ... | 1 | ... | ... | 2 | 3 | ... | 3 | ... | ... | ... | ... | 1 | .. | .. | .. | 4 | 1 |
| ... | 33 | 7 | 28 | 3 | 115 | 87 | 78 | 76 | 227 | 38 | 8 | 17 | 213 | 134 | 347 | ... | ... | ... | ... | 3 | 3 | 1 | 2 | 356 | 2 |
| ... | 10 | 1 | 11 | .. | 14 | 4 | 6 | 25 | 8 | 16 | 4 | 17 | 31 | 18 | 49 | ... | ... | ... | ... | ... | 1 | .. | .. | 50 | 3 |
| ... | 2 | ... | 2 | .. | 4 | 1 | 1 | 2 | 1 | 2 | ... | 1 | 8 | ... | 8 | ... | ... | ... | ... | ... | .. | .. | .. | 8 | 4 |
| ... | 18 | 2 | 10 | .. | 37 | 44 | 98 | 30 | 55 | 77 | 28 | 11 | 115 | 99 | 214 | ... | ... | ... | ... | ... | .. | .. | .. | 214 | 5 |
| ... | 7 | 1 | 4 | .. | 35 | 26 | 24 | 26 | 25 | 41 | 7 | 10 | 74 | 36 | 110 | ... | ... | ... | ... | ... | 1 | .. | .. | 111 | 6 |
| ... | 10 | 1 | 4 | .. | 30 | 24 | 22 | 30 | 15 | 22 | 10 | 29 | 72 | 37 | 109 | ... | ... | ... | ... | ... | .. | .. | .. | 109 | 7 |
| ... | 21 | 1 | 12 | 3 | 79 | 66 | 62 | 50 | 17 | 29 | 20 | 166 | 107 | 149 | 256 | ... | ... | ... | ... | ... | 1 | .. | .. | 257 | 8 |
| ... | 1 | ... | 2 | .. | 6 | 8 | 10 | 1 | 7 | 10 | 6 | 2 | 9 | 16 | 25 | ... | ... | ... | ... | ... | .. | .. | .. | 25 | 9 |
| ... | ... | ... | 4 | 1 | 23 | 11 | 7 | 16 | 27 | 27 | 3 | ... | 32 | 27 | 59 | ... | ... | ... | ... | ... | .. | .. | .. | 59 | 10 |
| ... | ... | 2 | ... | .. | 1 | ... | 2 | ... | ... | 2 | 1 | ... | 2 | 1 | 3 | ... | ... | ... | ... | ... | .. | .. | .. | 3 | 11 |
| ... | 7 | 2 | 8 | .. | 60 | 24 | 26 | 31 | 48 | 72 | 9 | 5 | 72 | 69 | 141 | ... | ... | ... | ... | 1 | .. | .. | .. | 142 | 12 |
| ... | ... | ... | ... | .. | 1 | 3 | 4 | 1 | 2 | 4 | ... | 2 | 3 | 6 | 9 | ... | ... | ... | ... | ... | .. | .. | .. | 9 | 13 |
| ... | 55 | 33 | 17 | 1 | 101 | 94 | 60 | 58 | 152 | 102 | 20 | 3 | ... | 312 | 312 | ... | ... | ... | ... | ... | 1 | .. | 1 | 314 | 14 |
| ... | 1854 | 557 | 428 | 64 | 94 | 2730 | 2772 | 116 | 4006 | 550 | 53 | 89 | 3202 | 2480 | 5682 | ... | ... | ... | ... | 60 | 55 | 20 | 5 | 5822 | 15 |
| ... | 5 | 2 | 6 | .. | 23 | 138 | 259 | 17 | 196 | 113 | 32 | 9 | 236 | 206 | 442 | ... | ... | ... | ... | 4 | 1 | .. | .. | 447 | 16 |
| ... | 29 | 3 | 14 | 1 | 10 | 67 | 106 | 15 | 103 | 66 | 6 | 4 | 121 | 76 | 197 | ... | ... | ... | ... | ... | 1 | .. | .. | 198 | 17 |
| ... | ... | ... | ... | .. | 1 | 4 | 2 | 1 | ... | 1 | 1 | 2 | 1 | 7 | 8 | ... | ... | ... | ... | ... | .. | .. | .. | 8 | 18 |
| ... | 14 | 1 | 9 | 1 | 30 | 37 | 30 | 19 | 81 | 27 | 2 | 2 | 76 | 42 | 118 | ... | ... | ... | ... | ... | .. | .. | .. | 118 | 19 |
| ... | 6 | 2 | 6 | .. | 24 | 21 | 19 | 20 | 32 | 39 | 4 | 5 | 41 | 43 | 84 | ... | ... | ... | ... | ... | .. | .. | .. | 84 | 20 |
| ... | 2 | 1 | ... | .. | 8 | 4 | 5 | 3 | 15 | 4 | 1 | ... | 11 | 9 | 20 | ... | ... | ... | ... | ... | .. | .. | .. | 20 | 21 |
| ... | 22 | 1 | 19 | 1 | 85 | 100 | 72 | 71 | 132 | 131 | 26 | 9 | 192 | 134 | 326 | ... | ... | ... | ... | 1 | 1 | .. | .. | 328 | 22 |
| ... | 4 | ... | 7 | .. | 38 | 26 | 20 | 27 | 50 | 36 | 9 | 5 | 60 | 50 | 110 | ... | ... | ... | ... | ... | 1 | .. | .. | 111 | 23 |
| ... | 803 | 122 | 364 | 18 | 1957 | 1746 | 1611 | 1364 | 200 | 675 | 852 | 4273 | 3170 | 3352 | 6522 | ... | ... | ... | ... | 80 | 80 | 7 | 2 | 6691 | 24 |
| ... | 30 | 14 | 26 | 3 | 339 | 341 | 294 | 239 | 772 | 219 | 42 | 59 | 629 | 575 | 1204 | ... | ... | ... | ... | 8 | 8 | 1 | .. | 1221 | 25 |
| ... | 3 | 1 | ... | .. | 8 | 2 | 4 | 4 | 7 | 6 | 2 | 2 | 12 | 6 | 18 | ... | ... | ... | ... | ... | .. | .. | .. | 18 | 26 |
| ... | 19 | 4 | 18 | 1 | 344 | 175 | 212 | 309 | 735 | 247 | 12 | 9 | 607 | 433 | 1040 | ... | ... | ... | ... | 2 | 4 | 2 | .. | 1048 | 27 |
| ... | 59 | 6 | 16 | 1 | 55 | 60 | 80 | 48 | 46 | 48 | 41 | 66 | 114 | 130 | 244 | ... | ... | ... | ... | 2 | 1 | .. | .. | 247 | 28 |
| ... | 9 | 7 | 2 | .. | 15 | 15 | 14 | 16 | 6 | 10 | 5 | 21 | 39 | 18 | 57 | ... | ... | ... | ... | 1 | 2 | .. | .. | 60 | 29 |
| ... | 121 | 17 | 41 | 2 | 95 | 222 | 620 | 112 | 259 | 436 | 98 | 71 | 558 | 504 | 1062 | ... | ... | ... | ... | 3 | 5 | 1 | .. | 1071 | 30 |
| ... | 102 | 20 | 59 | 6 | 395 | 393 | 370 | 327 | 155 | 442 | 234 | 589 | 676 | 781 | 1457 | ... | ... | ... | ... | 15 | 21 | 2 | 1 | 1496 | 31 |
| ... | 315 | 63 | 120 | 7 | 195 | 489 | 2680 | 320 | 988 | 1967 | 293 | 116 | 1895 | 1764 | 3659 | ... | ... | ... | ... | 10 | 17 | 2 | 3 | 3691 | 32 |
| ... | 2 | ... | 2 | .. | 8 | 10 | 11 | 10 | ... | 6 | 8 | 20 | 24 | 14 | 38 | ... | ... | ... | ... | ... | .. | .. | 1 | 39 | 33 |
| ... | 7 | 1 | 5 | .. | 9 | 10 | 8 | 8 | 12 | 3 | ... | 7 | 19 | 15 | 34 | ... | ... | ... | ... | 1 | .. | .. | .. | 35 | 34 |
| ... | 21 | 4 | 12 | 5 | 122 | 98 | 64 | 85 | 75 | 209 | 33 | 19 | 169 | 196 | 365 | ... | ... | ... | ... | 1 | 1 | .. | 3 | 370 | 35 |
| ... | 1 | ... | ... | .. | ... | 1 | ... | 1 | 2 | ... | ... | ... | 2 | ... | 2 | ... | ... | ... | ... | ... | .. | .. | .. | 2 | 36 |
| ... | 1 | ... | ... | .. | ... | ... | ... | 2 | ... | ... | ... | 1 | 2 | ... | 2 | ... | ... | ... | ... | ... | .. | .. | .. | 2 | 37 |
| 1 | 116 | 31 | 53 | 3 | 207 | 180 | 262 | 149 | 155 | 420 | 129 | 34 | 450 | 338 | 788 | ... | ... | ... | ... | 5 | 5 | 1 | .. | 799 | 38 |
| ... | 27 | 13 | 12 | .. | 58 | 67 | 128 | 73 | 64 | 186 | 49 | 11 | 195 | 131 | 326 | ... | ... | ... | ... | 4 | .. | .. | .. | 330 | 39 |
| ... | 14 | 4 | 10 | .. | 137 | 111 | 94 | 71 | 137 | 196 | 45 | 15 | 235 | 174 | 409 | ... | ... | ... | ... | 4 | 1 | .. | 1 | 415 | 40 |
| ... | 1 | ... | 1 | .. | ... | ... | 2 | ... | 1 | 1 | ... | ... | 1 | 1 | 2 | ... | ... | ... | ... | ... | .. | .. | .. | 2 | 41 |
| ... | 6 | 2 | ... | .. | 24 | 19 | 21 | 9 | 17 | 40 | 8 | 1 | 43 | 30 | 73 | ... | ... | ... | ... | ... | .. | .. | .. | 73 | 42 |
| ... | 2 | ... | ... | .. | 5 | ... | 4 | 5 | 2 | 11 | ... | ... | 7 | 7 | 14 | ... | ... | ... | ... | ... | .. | .. | .. | 14 | 43 |
| ... | 2 | 1 | 4 | .. | 16 | 9 | 24 | 7 | 6 | 31 | 10 | 5 | 26 | 30 | 56 | ... | ... | ... | ... | ... | .. | .. | .. | 56 | 44 |
| ... | 11 | 2 | 4 | .. | 14 | 6 | 5 | 11 | 8 | 20 | 5 | 2 | ... | 36 | 36 | ... | ... | ... | ... | ... | .. | .. | .. | 36 | 45 |
| ... | 4 | 1 | 1 | .. | 4 | 13 | 13 | 10 | 4 | 25 | 2 | 1 | 24 | 16 | 40 | ... | ... | ... | ... | ... | .. | .. | .. | 40 | 46 |
| ... | 36 | 4 | 26 | .. | 377 | 267 | 190 | 193 | 418 | 480 | 70 | 9 | 518 | 505 | 1023 | ... | ... | ... | ... | 4 | .. | .. | 1 | 1028 | 47 |
| ... | 65 | 2 | 6 | .. | 26 | 28 | 17 | 14 | 24 | 37 | 5 | 2 | 52 | 32 | 84 | ... | ... | ... | ... | ... | 1 | .. | .. | 85 | 48 |
| ... | 276 | 46 | 40 | 2 | 302 | 219 | 255 | 258 | 128 | 525 | 138 | 30 | 622 | 406 | 1028 | ... | ... | ... | ... | 5 | 2 | 1 | 1 | 1037 | 49 |
| ... | 2 | ... | 1 | .. | 5 | 3 | 4 | 4 | 7 | 5 | 1 | ... | 14 | 2 | 16 | ... | ... | ... | ... | ... | .. | .. | .. | 16 | 50 |
| ... | ... | 1 | ... | .. | 1 | 2 | ... | ... | ... | ... | 1 | 1 | 1 | 2 | 3 | ... | ... | ... | ... | ... | .. | .. | .. | 3 | 51 |
| ... | 46 | 5 | 8 | 1 | 20 | 18 | 26 | 20 | 3 | 1 | ... | 1 | 78 | 6 | 84 | ... | ... | ... | ... | ... | .. | .. | .. | 84 | 52 |
| ... | 3 | ... | 1 | 1 | 5 | 1 | ... | 5 | 6 | ... | ... | 1 | 10 | 1 | 11 | ... | ... | ... | ... | ... | .. | .. | .. | 11 | 53 |
| ... | 1 | ... | 1 | 1 | 1 | 1 | 2 | 1 | ... | ... | ... | 1 | 3 | 2 | 5 | ... | ... | ... | ... | ... | .. | .. | .. | 5 | 54 |
| ... | 2 | 1 | 3 | 2 | 17 | 16 | 14 | 14 | 6 | 26 | 4 | 24 | 56 | 5 | 61 | ... | ... | ... | ... | ... | .. | .. | .. | 61 | 55 |
| ... | 4 | 1 | 2 | .. | 14 | 9 | 13 | 13 | 8 | 25 | 6 | 9 | 30 | 19 | 49 | ... | ... | ... | ... | ... | .. | .. | .. | 49 | 56 |
| ... | 59 | 9 | 87 | .. | 149 | 152 | 123 | 118 | 160 | 121 | 63 | 140 | 307 | 224 | 531 | ... | ... | ... | ... | 7 | 6 | 1 | .. | 545 | 57 |
| ... | 6 | ... | 2 | .. | 1 | 13 | 1 | ... | 9 | 3 | ... | ... | 13 | 2 | 15 | ... | ... | ... | ... | ... | .. | .. | .. | 15 | 58 |
| ... | 10 | 5 | 5 | 2 | 22 | 25 | 31 | 21 | 34 | 25 | 7 | 7 | 67 | 29 | 96 | ... | ... | ... | ... | 3 | .. | .. | .. | 99 | 59 |
| ... | 3 | ... | 4 | .. | 3 | 11 | 5 | 7 | 4 | 9 | 3 | 5 | 16 | 8 | 24 | ... | ... | ... | ... | 2 | .. | .. | .. | 26 | 60 |
| ... | ... | ... | 2 | .. | 8 | 2 | 5 | 2 | ... | 1 | 2 | 13 | 13 | 4 | 17 | ... | ... | ... | ... | ... | .. | .. | .. | 17 | 61 |
| ... | ... | ... | ... | .. | 4 | 3 | 4 | 2 | 9 | 3 | ... | 1 | 9 | 3 | 12 | ... | ... | ... | ... | ... | 1 | .. | .. | 13 | 62 |
| ... | 18 | 3 | 9 | 3 | 169 | 157 | 187 | 132 | 81 | 327 | 137 | 61 | 305 | 325 | 630 | ... | ... | ... | ... | 8 | 11 | .. | .. | 649 | 63 |
| ... | 21 | 3 | 15 | .. | 151 | 183 | 184 | 124 | 132 | 350 | 75 | 44 | 386 | 269 | 655 | ... | ... | ... | ... | 4 | 1 | .. | .. | 660 | 64 |
| ... | 1 | 1 | ... | .. | ... | 2 | ... | 1 | 1 | 1 | ... | ... | 2 | 1 | 3 | ... | ... | ... | ... | ... | .. | .. | .. | 3 | 65 |
| ... | 41 | 9 | 31 | 1 | 290 | 224 | 202 | 191 | 311 | 459 | 76 | 41 | 474 | 433 | 907 | ... | ... | ... | ... | 5 | 7 | 1 | 1 | 921 | 66 |
| ... | 39 | 9 | 13 | 1 | 140 | 108 | 143 | 108 | 161 | 243 | 37 | 14 | 268 | 224 | 492 | ... | ... | ... | ... | 4 | 4 | .. | 1 | 501 | 67 |
| ... | 26 | 6 | 16 | .. | 172 | 149 | 158 | 121 | 19[illegible] | 304 | 45 | 21 | 347 | 245 | 592 | ... | ... | ... | ... | 4 | 3 | 1 | 2 | 602 | 68 |
| ... | ... | ... | ... | .. | 13 | 7 | 10 | 4 | 13 | 19 | 2 | ... | 23 | 10 | 33 | ... | ... | ... | ... | ... | 1 | .. | .. | 34 | 69 |
| ... | 9 | 1 | 2 | .. | 8 | 13 | 12 | 6 | 6 | 10 | 1 | 10 | 16 | 23 | 39 | ... | ... | ... | ... | ... | 1 | .. | .. | 40 | 70 |
| ... | 8 | 4 | 2 | 1 | 23 | 18 | 12 | 12 | 3 | 16 | 3 | 30 | 30 | 35 | 65 | ... | ... | ... | ... | ... | .. | .. | .. | 65 | 71 |
| ... | 10 | 2 | 6 | 2 | 16 | 25 | 23 | 15 | 16 | 9 | 7 | 8 | 59 | 16 | 75 | ... | ... | ... | ... | 2 | 2 | .. | .. | 79 | 72 |
| ... | 8 | 3 | 4 | 1 | 21 | 18 | 18 | 12 | 17 | 20 | 12 | 14 | 38 | 29 | 67 | ... | ... | ... | ... | 2 | .. | .. | .. | 69 | 73 |
| ... | 2 | 1 | 3 | .. | 21 | 10 | 14 | 8 | 4 | 16 | 7 | 21 | 42 | 11 | 53 | ... | ... | ... | ... | ... | .. | .. | .. | 53 | 74 |
| ... | 15 | 5 | 6 | .. | 21 | 22 | 28 | 13 | 70 | 4 | ... | 2 | 76 | 8 | 84 | ... | ... | ... | ... | 3 | .. | .. | .. | 87 | 75 |

## CLASSIFICATION OF DEATHS IN

| | Cause of death. | Ages. | | | | | | | | | | | | | | | | | | Nativities. | | | | | |
|---|---|---|---|---|---|---|---|---|---|---|---|---|---|---|---|---|---|---|---|---|---|---|---|---|---|
| | | Under 1. | | 1 and under 5. | | 5 and under 10. | | 10 and under 20. | | 20 and under 50. | | 50 and under 80. | | 80 and under 100. | | 100 & over. | | Age unknown. | | Born in State. | N. England States. | Middle States. | Southern States. | Southwest'n States. | Northwest'n States. |
| | | M. | F. | M. | F. | M. | F. | M. | F. | M. | F. | M. | F. | M. | F. | M | F. | M | F. | | | | | | |
| 1 | Lightning | ... | ... | ... | ... | ... | ... | ... | ... | 2 | ... | 1 | ... | ... | ... | .. | .. | .. | .. | 1 | ... | ... | .. | .. | .. |
| 2 | Liver, disease of | 2 | 6 | 8 | 10 | 1 | 3 | 9 | 4 | 44 | 48 | 51 | 56 | 2 | ... | .. | .. | .. | .. | 146 | 33 | 5 | .. | .. | .. |
| 3 | Lockjaw | ... | ... | ... | ... | 2 | 2 | 4 | 1 | 6 | 1 | 1 | ... | ... | ... | .. | .. | .. | .. | 13 | ... | ... | .. | .. | .. |
| 4 | Lungs, disease of | 8 | 7 | 8 | 4 | 4 | 1 | ... | 2 | 10 | 16 | 11 | 12 | ... | 1 | .. | .. | .. | .. | 59 | 4 | 2 | .. | .. | .. |
| 5 | Malformation | 3 | 4 | ... | ... | ... | ... | ... | ... | ... | ... | ... | ... | ... | ... | .. | .. | .. | .. | 7 | ... | ... | .. | .. | .. |
| 6 | Mania-a-potu | ... | ... | ... | ... | ... | ... | 1 | 1 | 74 | 13 | 17 | 2 | ... | ... | .. | .. | .. | .. | 40 | 6 | 4 | .. | .. | 1 |
| 7 | Marasmus | 30 | 79 | 37 | 35 | 4 | 6 | 3 | 2 | 3 | 8 | 10 | 2 | 1 | ... | .. | .. | .. | .. | 196 | 5 | ... | .. | .. | .. |
| 8 | Measles | 36 | 34 | 142 | 143 | 31 | 50 | 7 | 21 | 17 | 19 | 1 | 2 | ... | ... | .. | .. | 1 | 1 | 400 | 6 | 5 | .. | .. | 2 |
| 9 | Mortification | ... | ... | 4 | 2 | 2 | ... | 3 | ... | 13 | 6 | 8 | 3 | 7 | ... | .. | .. | .. | .. | 24 | 5 | 1 | .. | .. | .. |
| 10 | Mumps | 1 | ... | 5 | 5 | 3 | 1 | 5 | 4 | 6 | 1 | 1 | ... | 1 | ... | .. | .. | .. | .. | 29 | 1 | 1 | .. | .. | .. |
| 11 | Murder | ... | ... | ... | ... | ... | ... | ... | 1 | 5 | ... | ... | ... | ... | ... | .. | .. | .. | .. | 5 | ... | ... | .. | .. | .. |
| 12 | Neuralgia | ... | ... | ... | ... | 1 | 1 | 1 | 3 | 10 | 11 | 4 | 11 | ... | 1 | .. | .. | 1 | .. | 28 | 6 | 2 | .. | .. | .. |
| 13 | Old age | ... | ... | ... | ... | ... | ... | ... | ... | 1 | 5 | 216 | 256 | 441 | 456 | 5 | 9 | 2 | 2 | 587 | 468 | 73 | 7 | .. | 1 |
| 14 | Paralysis | 1 | ... | 4 | 5 | 2 | 6 | 4 | 2 | 32 | 22 | 135 | 141 | 35 | 42 | .. | .. | .. | .. | 235 | 105 | 19 | 3 | .. | .. |
| 15 | Peritonitis | ... | ... | ... | ... | 1 | ... | 1 | 1 | 3 | ... | 1 | ... | ... | ... | .. | .. | .. | .. | 4 | ... | ... | 1 | .. | .. |
| 16 | Piles | ... | ... | ... | ... | ... | ... | ... | ... | 3 | ... | 4 | 2 | 1 | ... | .. | .. | .. | .. | 5 | 2 | 1 | .. | .. | .. |
| 17 | Pleurisy | 4 | 2 | 1 | 4 | 1 | 1 | 5 | 2 | 50 | 18 | 22 | 21 | 2 | 3 | .. | .. | .. | .. | 78 | 19 | 4 | .. | .. | .. |
| 18 | Pneumonia | 230 | 189 | 231 | 181 | 39 | 49 | 23 | 24 | 189 | 108 | 109 | 60 | 11 | 15 | .. | .. | 1 | 2 | 1139 | 96 | 21 | 7 | 3 | 4 |
| 19 | Poison | 5 | ... | 9 | 4 | 2 | 4 | 1 | 1 | 3 | 3 | 4 | 2 | ... | ... | .. | .. | .. | .. | 31 | 2 | ... | .. | .. | .. |
| 20 | Prematurity of birth | 1 | 4 | ... | ... | ... | ... | ... | ... | ... | ... | ... | ... | ... | ... | .. | .. | .. | .. | 5 | ... | ... | .. | .. | .. |
| 21 | Putrid sore throat | 1 | ... | ... | ... | ... | 2 | 2 | ... | ... | ... | ... | ... | ... | ... | .. | .. | .. | .. | 5 | ... | ... | .. | .. | .. |
| 22 | Quinsy | 5 | 3 | 6 | 7 | 2 | 2 | 1 | 2 | 6 | 3 | 3 | 3 | ... | ... | .. | .. | .. | .. | 34 | 2 | ... | .. | .. | 1 |
| 23 | Rheumatism | 4 | 4 | 8 | 7 | 8 | 2 | 13 | 6 | 14 | 24 | 31 | 17 | 2 | 1 | .. | .. | .. | .. | 88 | 7 | 6 | .. | .. | .. |
| 24 | Rickets | 3 | ... | 1 | ... | ... | ... | ... | ... | ... | ... | ... | ... | ... | ... | .. | .. | .. | .. | 4 | ... | ... | .. | .. | .. |
| 25 | Salivation, effects of | ... | ... | ... | ... | ... | ... | ... | ... | ... | 2 | ... | ... | ... | ... | .. | .. | .. | .. | 1 | ... | ... | .. | .. | .. |
| 26 | Scrofula | 13 | 10 | 20 | 25 | 6 | 7 | 14 | 19 | 23 | 20 | 9 | 7 | 3 | 1 | .. | .. | .. | .. | 141 | 19 | 3 | 1 | .. | 1 |
| 27 | Scurvy | ... | ... | ... | ... | ... | ... | ... | ... | 1 | 1 | 1 | 1 | ... | ... | .. | .. | .. | .. | 2 | .. | 1 | .. | .. | .. |
| 28 | Small pox | 29 | 25 | 36 | 43 | 19 | 16 | 18 | 13 | 50 | 11 | 7 | 4 | ... | 1 | .. | .. | 1 | 2 | 197 | 12 | 1 | .. | 1 | .. |
| 29 | Spine, disease of | 9 | 10 | 6 | 7 | 3 | 1 | 12 | 8 | 14 | 14 | 8 | 3 | ... | 1 | .. | .. | .. | .. | 75 | 7 | 1 | 1 | . | .. |
| 30 | Stillborn | 27 | 24 | ... | ... | ... | ... | ... | ... | ... | ... | ... | ... | ... | ... | .. | .. | .. | .. | 51 | ... | ... | .. | .. | .. |
| 31 | Stomach, disease of | ... | 2 | ... | ... | 1 | ... | ... | 1 | 1 | 6 | 7 | ... | ... | ... | .. | .. | .. | .. | 8 | 5 | 1 | .. | .. | .. |
| 32 | Suffocation | 3 | 4 | 4 | 3 | 1 | 1 | ... | ... | 2 | 2 | 1 | ... | ... | ... | .. | .. | .. | .. | 17 | 1 | ... | .. | .. | .. |
| 33 | Suicide | ... | ... | ... | ... | ... | ... | 2 | 3 | 40 | 20 | 25 | 1 | 3 | ... | .. | .. | .. | .. | 51 | 16 | 2 | .. | .. | .. |
| 34 | Summer complaint | 36 | 42 | 50 | 49 | 8 | 10 | 3 | 5 | 2 | 4 | 3 | 3 | 1 | ... | .. | .. | 4 | 2 | 204 | 5 | 2 | .. | .. | .. |
| 35 | Sun, stroke of | ... | ... | 1 | 3 | 1 | 2 | 1 | 2 | 23 | 1 | 4 | 1 | ... | ... | .. | .. | 1 | 1 | 12 | 1 | ... | .. | .. | .. |
| 36 | Syphilis | 1 | ... | ... | ... | ... | ... | 1 | 2 | 6 | 6 | ... | 1 | ... | ... | .. | .. | .. | .. | 9 | 1 | 1 | .. | .. | .. |
| 37 | Teething | 76 | 81 | 131 | 142 | 1 | 2 | ... | ... | ... | ... | ... | ... | ... | ... | .. | .. | .. | .. | 391 | 5 | 6 | 2 | .. | .. |
| 38 | Tetanus | ... | 1 | ... | ... | ... | 1 | 1 | ... | 2 | ... | ... | 1 | ... | ... | .. | .. | .. | .. | 4 | ... | ... | .. | .. | .. |
| 39 | Tetter | ... | ... | ... | 1 | ... | 1 | ... | ... | ... | ... | ... | 1 | ... | ... | .. | .. | .. | .. | 2 | ... | ... | .. | .. | .. |
| 40 | Throat, disease of | 5 | 7 | 15 | 14 | 4 | 8 | 2 | 3 | 10 | 5 | 5 | 5 | 1 | ... | .. | .. | .. | .. | 66 | 4 | 2 | .. | .. | .. |
| 41 | Thrush | 6 | 8 | 16 | 13 | 6 | 11 | 1 | ... | ... | 11 | 1 | 1 | ... | ... | .. | .. | .. | .. | 70 | 1 | 2 | .. | .. | .. |
| 42 | Tumor | 4 | 2 | ... | 2 | 2 | ... | ... | 6 | 13 | 22 | 10 | 14 | ... | 2 | .. | .. | .. | .. | 51 | 7 | 4 | .. | .. | 1 |
| 43 | Ulcer | 8 | 9 | 3 | 4 | 2 | ... | 2 | 3 | 6 | 3 | 5 | 5 | ... | ... | .. | .. | .. | .. | 41 | 3 | ... | .. | .. | 1 |
| 44 | Uterus, disease of | ... | ... | ... | ... | ... | ... | ... | ... | ... | 7 | ... | 1 | ... | ... | .. | .. | .. | .. | 6 | ... | ... | .. | .. | .. |
| 45 | Venereal | ... | ... | ... | ... | 1 | ... | ... | ... | 3 | ... | 1 | 2 | ... | ... | .. | .. | .. | .. | 7 | ... | ... | .. | .. | .. |
| 46 | White swelling | ... | ... | ... | 1 | ... | ... | 1 | 2 | 2 | 1 | ... | 1 | ... | ... | .. | .. | .. | .. | 6 | ... | 2 | .. | .. | .. |
| 47 | Worms | 5 | 8 | 60 | 54 | 10 | 7 | 2 | 2 | ... | 1 | ... | ... | ... | ... | .. | .. | .. | .. | 135 | 1 | ... | .. | .. | .. |
| 48 | Unknown | 600 | 521 | 320 | 269 | 90 | 101 | 100 | 147 | 518 | 501 | 411 | 284 | 38 | 40 | .. | .. | 66 | 59 | 2918 | 230 | 68 | 9 | .. | 8 |
| | Total | 3603 | 3048 | 5190 | 4634 | 1576 | 1429 | 1581 | 1732 | 7439 | 6208 | 4002 | 3161 | 857 | 787 | 7 | 9 | 191 | 157 | 3164 | 3131 | 969 | 159 | 19 | 91 |

## CLASSIFICATION OF DEATHS IN EASTERN SECTION

*Embracing the following counties: Beaufort, Bertie, Brunswick, Camden, Carteret, Craven, Hanover, Onslow, Pasquotank, Perquimans,*

| | Cause of death. | Under 1. M. | Under 1. F. | 1–5 M. | 1–5 F. | 5–10 M. | 5–10 F. | 10–20 M. | 10–20 F. | 20–50 M. | 20–50 F. | 50–80 M. | 50–80 F. | 80–100 M. | 80–100 F. | 100 & over M | 100 & over F. | Age unknown M | Age unknown F. | Born in State. | N. England States. | Middle States. | Southern States. | Southwest'n States. | Northwest'n States. |
|---|---|---|---|---|---|---|---|---|---|---|---|---|---|---|---|---|---|---|---|---|---|---|---|---|---|
| 1 | Abscess | ... | ... | ... | ... | ... | ... | ... | ... | ... | ... | ... | ... | ... | ... | .. | .. | .. | .. | ... | .. | ... | ... | ... | ... |
| 2 | Accident, not specfi'd | 6 | 9 | 2 | 5 | 3 | 2 | ... | 1 | 11 | ... | 5 | ... | ... | ... | .. | .. | .. | .. | 40 | .. | ... | 4 | ... | ... |
| 3 | ....do....burned | ... | ... | 2 | 16 | 5 | 9 | ... | 2 | 1 | 1 | 1 | ... | ... | ... | .. | .. | .. | .. | 37 | .. | ... | ... | ... | ... |
| 4 | ....do....drowned | ... | ... | 6 | ... | ... | ... | 5 | ... | 17 | ... | 2 | 1 | ... | ... | 1 | .. | 1 | .. | 32 | .. | 1 | ... | ... | ... |
| 5 | ....do....shot | ... | ... | ... | ... | ... | ... | ... | ... | 1 | ... | ... | ... | ... | ... | .. | .. | .. | .. | 1 | .. | ... | ... | ... | ... |
| 6 | Apoplexy | ... | ... | 1 | ... | ... | ... | 2 | ... | 5 | 3 | 7 | 5 | 2 | ... | .. | .. | .. | .. | 24 | .. | ... | ... | ... | ... |
| 7 | Asthma | ... | ... | ... | ... | ... | ... | ... | ... | ... | ... | 1 | ... | ... | 1 | .. | .. | .. | .. | 1 | .. | 1 | ... | ... | ... |
| 8 | Black tongue | ... | 1 | ... | ... | ... | ... | 1 | 1 | 1 | 2 | 1 | ... | ... | ... | .. | .. | .. | .. | 7 | .. | ... | ... | ... | ... |
| 9 | Bowels, disease of | 12 | 12 | 13 | 12 | 1 | 1 | 1 | ... | 4 | 1 | 1 | 2 | 1 | ... | .. | .. | .. | .. | 60 | .. | ... | ... | ... | ... |
| 10 | Brain......do | ... | 1 | ... | ... | 1 | ... | ... | ... | 1 | ... | ... | 1 | ... | ... | .. | .. | .. | .. | 4 | .. | ... | ... | ... | ... |
| 11 | Bronchitis | ... | ... | ... | ... | ... | ... | ... | ... | 1 | ... | ... | ... | ... | ... | .. | .. | .. | .. | 1 | .. | ... | ... | ... | ... |
| 12 | Cancer | ... | ... | 1 | ... | ... | ... | ... | ... | 2 | 8 | 3 | 4 | ... | ... | .. | .. | .. | .. | 17 | .. | 1 | ... | ... | ... |
| 13 | Catarrh | 6 | 6 | 1 | 1 | ... | ... | 1 | 1 | 1 | 1 | 1 | 1 | ... | ... | .. | .. | .. | .. | 20 | .. | ... | ... | ... | ... |
| 14 | Childbirth | ... | ... | ... | ... | ... | ... | ... | 5 | ... | 52 | ... | ... | ... | ... | .. | .. | .. | .. | 56 | .. | 1 | ... | ... | ... |

## THE STATE OF NEW YORK—AGGREGATE—Continued.

| NATIVITIES. | | | | | SEASON OF DECEASE. | | | | DURATION OF SICKNESS. | | | | WHITES. | | | COLORED. | | | | | | | | | |
|---|---|---|---|---|---|---|---|---|---|---|---|---|---|---|---|---|---|---|---|---|---|---|---|---|---|
| | | | | | | | | | | | | | | | | Slaves. | | | | Free. | | | | | |
| | | | | | | | | | | | | | | | | Black. | | Mulatto. | | Black. | | Mul. | | | |
| California and Territories. | Ireland. | Germany. | Other foreign countries. | Unknown. | Spring. | Summer. | Autumn. | Winter. | Under 1 week. | 1 week and under 1 month. | 1 month and under 3 months. | 3 months and over. | Males. | Females. | Total. | M. | F. | M. | F. | M. | F. | M | F. | Aggregate deaths. | |
| | 1 | 1 | | | | 2 | 1 | | 3 | | | | 3 | | 3 | | | | | | | | | 3 | 1 |
| | 39 | 2 | 19 | | 58 | 66 | 72 | 47 | 28 | 65 | 43 | 89 | 117 | 124 | 241 | | | | | | 3 | | | 244 | 2 |
| | 2 | | 2 | | 4 | 7 | 3 | 3 | 10 | 7 | | | 12 | 4 | 16 | | | | | 1 | | | | 17 | 3 |
| | 13 | 1 | 5 | | 22 | 20 | 22 | 19 | 15 | 19 | 7 | 17 | 39 | 43 | 82 | | | | | 2 | | | | 84 | 4 |
| | | | | | | 5 | 1 | 1 | 1 | 1 | | 2 | 2 | 3 | 5 | | | | | 1 | 1 | | | 7 | 5 |
| | 39 | 5 | 10 | 3 | 28 | 35 | 27 | 18 | 36 | 23 | 2 | 4 | 92 | 15 | 107 | | | | | | 1 | | | 108 | 6 |
| | 14 | 1 | 3 | 1 | 45 | 62 | 78 | 35 | 7 | 15 | 21 | 39 | 88 | 131 | 219 | | | | | | 1 | | | 220 | 7 |
| | 56 | 18 | 16 | 2 | 130 | 190 | 98 | 84 | 83 | 270 | 54 | 18 | 232 | 269 | 501 | | | | | 3 | 1 | | | 505 | 8 |
| | 12 | 2 | 4 | | 12 | 10 | 20 | 6 | 9 | 8 | 7 | 8 | 37 | 11 | 48 | | | | | | | | | 48 | 9 |
| | 1 | | 1 | | 16 | 10 | 3 | 4 | 6 | 24 | 2 | | 22 | 11 | 33 | | | | | | | | | 33 | 10 |
| | 1 | | | | 2 | 1 | | 3 | 2 | 1 | | | 5 | 1 | 6 | | | | | | | | | 6 | 11 |
| | 5 | | 3 | | 17 | 6 | 9 | 12 | 3 | 9 | 3 | 25 | 17 | 27 | 44 | | | | | | | | | 44 | 12 |
| | 90 | 38 | 99 | 30 | 401 | 357 | 325 | 297 | 222 | 250 | 95 | 274 | 656 | 711 | 1367 | | | | | 7 | 15 | 2 | 2 | 1393 | 13 |
| | 29 | 4 | 33 | 3 | 104 | 121 | 111 | 86 | 101 | 105 | 43 | 153 | 212 | 214 | 426 | | | | | | 3 | 1 | 1 | 431 | 14 |
| | | 1 | 1 | | 2 | | 3 | 2 | 1 | 1 | | 1 | 5 | 1 | 6 | | | | | | | 1 | | 7 | 15 |
| | | 1 | 1 | | 3 | 2 | 3 | 2 | 1 | 1 | 2 | 5 | 7 | 2 | 9 | | | | | | | 1 | | 10 | 16 |
| | 25 | 3 | 7 | | 41 | 45 | 18 | 30 | 42 | 68 | 6 | 8 | 81 | 49 | 130 | | | | | 3 | 1 | 1 | 1 | 136 | 17 |
| | 127 | 18 | 42 | 4 | 623 | 269 | 212 | 329 | 357 | 698 | 145 | 56 | 820 | 614 | 1434 | | | | | 9 | 12 | 4 | 2 | 1461 | 18 |
| | 4 | | 1 | | 7 | 12 | 14 | 5 | 25 | 5 | 1 | 1 | 24 | 14 | 38 | | | | | | | | | 38 | 19 |
| | | | | | 2 | | | 3 | | 1 | | | 1 | 4 | 5 | | | | | | | | | 5 | 20 |
| | | | | | 2 | 2 | 1 | | 2 | 3 | | | 3 | 2 | 5 | | | | | | | | | 5 | 21 |
| | 2 | 1 | 3 | | 12 | 12 | 12 | 7 | 18 | 22 | 3 | | 23 | 19 | 42 | | | | | | 1 | | | 43 | 22 |
| | 19 | 6 | 13 | 2 | 39 | 38 | 40 | 24 | 16 | 44 | 20 | 53 | 79 | 59 | 138 | | | | | 1 | 1 | | 1 | 141 | 23 |
| | | | | | 2 | | 1 | 1 | 1 | | 2 | 1 | 4 | | 4 | | | | | | | | | 4 | 24 |
| | | | 1 | | | 1 | 1 | | | 1 | | 1 | | 2 | 2 | | | | | | | | | 2 | 25 |
| | 9 | 1 | 2 | | 41 | 54 | 50 | 31 | 9 | 34 | 22 | 92 | 87 | 85 | 172 | | | | | 1 | 4 | | | 177 | 26 |
| | | | 1 | | | 3 | | 1 | | 1 | 1 | 2 | 2 | 2 | 4 | | | | | | | | | 4 | 27 |
| | 39 | 11 | 13 | 1 | 60 | 102 | 47 | 66 | 39 | 192 | 19 | 5 | 154 | 115 | 269 | | | | | 5 | | 1 | | 276 | 28 |
| | 6 | | 6 | | 30 | 22 | 26 | 18 | 7 | 20 | 15 | 42 | 50 | 44 | 94 | | | | | 1 | | 1 | | 96 | 29 |
| | | | | | 10 | 20 | 12 | 8 | | | | | 27 | 24 | 51 | | | | | | | | | 51 | 30 |
| | 3 | | 1 | | 3 | 7 | 4 | 4 | 4 | 2 | 3 | 8 | 9 | 9 | 18 | | | | | | | | | 18 | 31 |
| | 2 | | 1 | | 4 | 5 | 4 | 8 | 21 | | | | 11 | 10 | 21 | | | | | | | | | 21 | 32 |
| | 12 | 3 | 8 | 2 | 23 | 36 | 17 | 16 | 48 | 5 | 1 | | 69 | 24 | 93 | | | | | 1 | | | | 94 | 33 |
| | 6 | 2 | 3 | | 11 | 53 | 145 | 12 | 55 | 127 | 26 | 12 | 107 | 115 | 222 | | | | | | | | | 222 | 34 |
| | 21 | 4 | 3 | | | 29 | 11 | 1 | 33 | 1 | 1 | | 31 | 10 | 41 | | | | | | | | | 41 | 35 |
| | 3 | | 1 | 2 | 4 | 5 | 6 | 2 | | | | 5 | 6 | 7 | 13 | | | | | 2 | 2 | | | 17 | 36 |
| | 13 | 8 | 7 | 1 | 71 | 137 | 165 | 58 | 102 | 200 | 72 | 38 | 203 | 221 | 424 | | | | | 3 | 2 | 2 | 2 | 433 | 37 |
| | 1 | 1 | | | 1 | 2 | 1 | 2 | 4 | | 1 | | 3 | 3 | 6 | | | | | | | | | 6 | 38 |
| | | 1 | | | 2 | 1 | | | | 1 | | 2 | | 3 | 3 | | | | | | | | | 3 | 39 |
| | 9 | | 2 | 1 | 30 | 14 | 18 | 20 | 27 | 31 | 2 | 7 | 42 | 42 | 84 | | | | | | | | | 84 | 40 |
| | 1 | | | | 7 | 16 | 25 | 16 | 9 | 11 | 12 | 5 | 30 | 44 | 74 | | | | | | | | | 74 | 41 |
| | 9 | 1 | 4 | | 29 | 17 | 15 | 16 | 5 | 15 | 12 | 34 | 28 | 46 | 74 | | | | | | 2 | 1 | | 77 | 42 |
| | 3 | 1 | 1 | | 14 | 10 | 15 | 11 | 11 | 21 | 7 | 7 | 26 | 24 | 50 | | | | | | | | | 50 | 43 |
| | 1 | 1 | | | 3 | 3 | | | | 1 | 1 | 1 | | 8 | 8 | | | | | | | | | 8 | 44 |
| | | | | | 2 | 4 | 1 | | | | 1 | 5 | 5 | 2 | 7 | | | | | | | | | 7 | 45 |
| | | | | | 2 | 2 | 1 | 3 | | 1 | 2 | 5 | 3 | 5 | 8 | | | | | | | | | 8 | 46 |
| | 4 | 1 | 8 | | 44 | 22 | 52 | 31 | 76 | 46 | 16 | 6 | 77 | 72 | 149 | | | | | | | | | 149 | 47 |
| | 448 | 95 | 175 | 114 | 1014 | 1031 | 973 | 801 | 1121 | 674 | 276 | 596 | 2097 | 1872 | 3969 | | | | | 40 | 43 | 6 | 7 | 4065 | 48 |
| 1 | 5772 | 1324 | 2162 | 308 | 10101 | 12444 | 14843 | 7602 | 14047 | 12792 | 3809 | 7843 | 24029 | 20765 | 44794 | | | | | 351 | 347 | 66 | 42 | 45600 | |

## OF THE STATE OF NORTH CAROLINA.

*Currituck, Chowan, Duplin, Gates, Greene, Hertford, Hyde, Jones, Lenoir, Martin, New Pitt, Tazewell, and Washington.*

| California and Territories. | Ireland. | Germany. | Other foreign countries. | Unknown. | Spring. | Summer. | Autumn. | Winter. | Under 1 week. | 1 week and under 1 month. | 1 month and under 3 months. | 3 months and over. | Males. | Females. | Total. | Slaves Black M. | Slaves Black F. | Slaves Mulatto M. | Slaves Mulatto F. | Free Black M. | Free Black F. | Free Mul. M | Free Mul. F. | Aggregate deaths. | |
|---|---|---|---|---|---|---|---|---|---|---|---|---|---|---|---|---|---|---|---|---|---|---|---|---|---|
| | | | | | | | | | | | | | | | | | | | | | | | | | 1 |
| | | | | | 17 | 10 | 3 | 14 | 26 | 3 | | 1 | 12 | 3 | 15 | 14 | 14 | | | 1 | | | | 44 | 2 |
| | | | | | 20 | 5 | 1 | 11 | | | | | 1 | 3 | 4 | 8 | 23 | | 1 | | | | 1 | 37 | 3 |
| | | | | | 8 | 14 | 6 | 4 | 33 | | | | 13 | 1 | 14 | 16 | | | | 1 | | 2 | | 33 | 4 |
| | | | | | | 1 | | | 1 | | | | | | | 1 | | | | | | | | 1 | 5 |
| | | | 1 | | 8 | 9 | 2 | 6 | 15 | 4 | | 1 | 8 | 3 | 11 | 8 | 4 | 1 | 1 | | | | | 25 | 6 |
| | | | | | 2 | | | | 1 | | | 1 | | | | 1 | 1 | | | | | | | 2 | 7 |
| | | | | | | | | | | | | | 2 | 4 | 6 | | | | | | | 1 | | 7 | 8 |
| | | 1 | | | 4 | 27 | 17 | 13 | 9 | 23 | 17 | 10 | 19 | 12 | 31 | 14 | 15 | | 1 | | | | | 61 | 9 |
| | | | | | | 1 | 2 | 1 | | 2 | 1 | 1 | 1 | 1 | 2 | | 1 | | | 1 | | | | 4 | 10 |
| | | | | | | | 1 | | | 1 | | | | | | 1 | | | | | | | | 1 | 11 |
| | | | | | 3 | 6 | 7 | 2 | 2 | 2 | 3 | 10 | 5 | 3 | 8 | 1 | 9 | | | | | | | 18 | 12 |
| | | | | | 8 | 2 | 5 | 5 | 5 | 13 | 2 | | 5 | 4 | 9 | 5 | 6 | | | | | | | 20 | 13 |
| | | | | | 14 | 11 | 17 | 15 | 24 | 20 | 2 | 1 | | 39 | 39 | | 17 | | 1 | | | | | 57 | 14 |

## CLASSIFICATION OF DEATHS IN EASTERN SECTION

| | Cause of death. | AGES. Under 1. | | 1 and under 5. | | 5 and under 10. | | 10 and under 20. | | 20 and under 50. | | 50 and under 80. | | 80 and under 100. | | 100 & over. | | Age unknown. | | NATIVITIES. Born in State. | N. England States. | Middle States. | Southern States. | Southwest'n States. | Northwest'n States. |
|---|---|---|---|---|---|---|---|---|---|---|---|---|---|---|---|---|---|---|---|---|---|---|---|---|---|
| | | M. | F. | M. | F. | M. | F. | M. | F. | M. | F. | M. | F. | M | F. | M | F. | M | F. | | | | | | |
| 1 | Cholera | | | 1 | 2 | | 1 | 2 | 1 | 8 | 4 | 4 | 3 | | | | | | | 25 | | | 1 | | |
| 2 | ....do....infantum | | 1 | | 1 | | | | | | | | | | | | | | | 2 | | | | | |
| 3 | ....do....morbus | | | | | 1 | | | | | | | | | | | | | | 1 | | | | | |
| 4 | Chorea | | | | | | | | | | | | | | 1 | | | | | 1 | | | | | |
| 5 | Colic | 5 | 1 | 3 | 2 | | | 1 | 2 | 7 | 2 | 4 | 1 | 1 | | | | | | 28 | | | 1 | | |
| 6 | Congestion | | | | | | | | | | 1 | | | | | | | | | 1 | | | | | |
| 7 | ....do...brain | | | | | 1 | 1 | 1 | | 2 | 1 | | | | | | | | | 6 | | | | | |
| 8 | Consumption | | 1 | | 2 | 2 | 5 | 5 | 8 | 38 | 50 | 23 | 23 | 2 | 6 | | | | | 159 | | | 5 | | |
| 9 | Convulsions | 7 | 4 | 4 | 2 | 2 | | 1 | 2 | 3 | 1 | 3 | 2 | | | | | | | 30 | | | | | |
| 10 | Cramp | 2 | | 2 | 1 | | | | 1 | | 1 | 1 | | | | | | | | 8 | | | | | |
| 11 | Croup | 7 | 4 | 6 | 15 | 1 | | 1 | | 1 | | | | | | | | | | 35 | | | | | |
| 12 | Debility | | | | | | | | | | 1 | | | | | | | | | 1 | | | | | |
| 13 | Diarrhœa | 3 | 6 | 9 | 7 | | 1 | | | 4 | 2 | | 1 | | | | | | | 32 | | | 1 | | |
| 14 | Dropsy | 1 | 2 | 10 | 9 | 14 | 13 | 31 | 12 | 15 | 25 | 26 | 13 | 5 | 4 | | | 1 | | 178 | | | 3 | | |
| 15 | Dysentery | 6 | 5 | 8 | 10 | 2 | 2 | | 2 | 4 | 2 | | 2 | | | | | | | 43 | | | | | |
| 16 | Dyspepsia | | | | | | | | | | 4 | | 1 | 1 | | | | | | 6 | | | | | |
| 17 | Eating dirt | | | | | 1 | | | | | | | | | | | | | | 1 | | | | | |
| 18 | Erysipelas | 1 | 2 | 1 | | 2 | 1 | 5 | 1 | 8 | 8 | 5 | 5 | | | | | | | 39 | | | | | |
| 19 | Fever, not specified | 12 | 13 | 23 | 17 | 3 | 4 | 4 | 6 | 5 | 11 | | 3 | 1 | | | | | | 101 | | | 1 | | |
| 20 | ..do..bilious | 8 | 8 | 28 | 15 | 10 | 6 | 8 | 13 | 21 | 23 | 4 | 11 | 2 | 2 | | | | | 153 | 1 | | 5 | | |
| 21 | ..do..brain | 2 | 8 | 5 | 3 | 3 | 2 | 2 | 2 | 4 | 1 | | 1 | | | | | | | 27 | | | | | |
| 22 | ..do..catarrhal | 3 | 7 | 3 | 1 | 1 | 3 | 2 | | 1 | 4 | 1 | 1 | | 1 | | | | | 26 | | 1 | 1 | | |
| 23 | ..do..congestive | | 1 | 3 | 2 | 1 | 5 | 3 | 2 | 2 | 2 | 3 | 3 | | | | | | | 24 | 1 | | 1 | | |
| 24 | ..do..intermittent | | 1 | 1 | 1 | | | | | | | 1 | | | | | | | | 4 | | | | | |
| 25 | ..do..puerperal | | | | | | | | | | 4 | | | | | | | | | 4 | | | | | |
| 26 | ..do..scarlet | | | 2 | 1 | | 1 | | | | | | | | | | | | | 4 | | | | | |
| 27 | ..do..typhus | 2 | 2 | 3 | 2 | 7 | 6 | 3 | 8 | 13 | 5 | 6 | | | | | | | | 56 | | | 1 | | |
| 28 | Gout | | | | | | | | | | | 1 | | | | | | | | 1 | | | | | |
| 29 | Gravel | | | 2 | | | | | | | | 2 | | | | 1 | | | | 5 | | | | | |
| 30 | Heart, disease of | | | | | | | 1 | 1 | 2 | | 2 | 1 | | | | | | | 6 | | 1 | | | |
| 31 | Hemorrhage | 1 | | | | | | | | 5 | 5 | 1 | 1 | | | | | | | .12 | | | 1 | | |
| 32 | Hernia | 2 | | | | | | | | | | 1 | 2 | | | | | | | 5 | | | | | |
| 33 | Hooping cough | 14 | 26 | 27 | 19 | 1 | 5 | 2 | 1 | | | | 1 | | | | | | | 96 | | | | | |
| 34 | Hydrocephalus | 1 | | | 1 | | | | | 1 | | | | | | | | | | 3 | | | | | |
| 35 | Hydrophobia | | | | | | | | | | | | 1 | | | | | | | 1 | | | | | |
| 36 | Inflammation | 1 | 3 | | 1 | 1 | | 2 | | 3 | 4 | 2 | 1 | | | | | | | 17 | | | 1 | | |
| 37 | ....do.....bowels | 2 | 1 | 3 | 1 | | | 5 | 3 | 4 | 3 | 2 | 3 | | | | | | | 26 | | | 1 | | |
| 38 | ....do.....brain | 2 | 2 | 5 | 6 | 1 | 3 | 5 | 2 | 5 | 5 | 2 | 2 | | | | | | | 37 | | | 2 | | |
| 39 | ....do.....stomach | | 1 | 1 | | | | | | 1 | 1 | | | | | | | | | 4 | | | | | |
| 40 | Insanity | | | | | | | | | | 1 | | | 1 | | | | | | 2 | | | | | |
| 41 | Intemperance | | | | | | | | | 3 | | 1 | | | | | | | | 4 | | | | | |
| 42 | Jaundice | | 1 | | 1 | | | 1 | | | | | | | | | | | | 3 | | | | | |
| 43 | Kidneys, disease of | | | | | | | | | | | | 1 | | | | | | | 1 | | | | | |
| 44 | Killed | 2 | 1 | 2 | 1 | | | 3 | | 2 | | 1 | | | | | | | | 12 | | | | | |
| 45 | Lightning | | | | | | | 1 | | 1 | | | | | | | | | | 2 | | | | | |
| 46 | Liver, disease of | | | | | | | | 1 | 7 | 7 | 6 | 3 | | | | | | | 21 | | | 2 | | |
| 47 | Lockjaw | 2 | 2 | | | | | | | | 1 | | | | | | | | | 5 | | | | | |
| 48 | Lungs, disease of | | | 1 | | | 1 | | | 1 | | | 1 | | | | | | | 4 | | | | | |
| 49 | Malformation | | 1 | | | | | | | | | | | | | | | | | 1 | | | | | |
| 50 | Measles | 5 | | 6 | 7 | 4 | 1 | 4 | 1 | 5 | 2 | 1 | 1 | | | | | | | 37 | | | | | |
| 51 | Marasmus | | 1 | 1 | | | | | | | | | | | | | | | | 2 | | | | | |
| 52 | Mortification | | | | | | | 1 | | 2 | 2 | 2 | 1 | | | | | | | 8 | | | | | |
| 53 | Mumps | | | | | | | | | | 1 | | | | | | | | | 1 | | | | | |
| 54 | Murder | | | | | | | | | 3 | | | | | | | | | | 3 | | | | | |
| 55 | Neuralgia | 1 | | | | | | | | 1 | 1 | | | | | | | | | 3 | | | | | |
| 56 | Old age | | | | | | | | | | | 19 | 24 | 22 | 38 | 5 | 3 | | | 107 | | | 3 | | |
| 57 | Paralysis | | | | | | | 1 | | 1 | 4 | 8 | 2 | | | | | | | 16 | | | | | |
| 58 | Pleurisy | 1 | 2 | 3 | 2 | 2 | | 9 | 5 | 25 | 18 | 16 | 7 | 2 | | | | | | 89 | | 1 | 2 | | |
| 59 | Pneumonia | 6 | 2 | 10 | 8 | 3 | 6 | 13 | 7 | 31 | 19 | 19 | 9 | 1 | 1 | | | | | 125 | | | 1 | | |
| 60 | Poison | | | 1 | | | 2 | | | | 1 | | | | | | | | | 4 | | | | | |
| 61 | Piles | | | 1 | | | | | | | | | | | | | | | | 1 | | | | | |
| 62 | Prematurity of birth | 1 | 1 | | | | | | | | | | | | | | | | | 3 | | | | | |
| 63 | Quinsy | 1 | 1 | 2 | 3 | 3 | 1 | | | 3 | 4 | 3 | | | | | | | | 20 | | | 1 | | |
| 64 | Rheumatism | | | | | | | 1 | | 3 | 1 | 2 | 1 | | | | | | | 7 | | 1 | | | |
| 65 | Scrofula | | 1 | 1 | | 1 | | | | 2 | | 2 | | | | | | | | 6 | | | 1 | | |
| 66 | Small pox | | 2 | | | 2 | | 2 | 2 | 7 | 3 | 6 | 2 | 1 | | | | | | 27 | | | | | |
| 67 | Spine, disease of | | | | | | 1 | 1 | 1 | | 2 | | 1 | | | | | | | 6 | | | | | |
| 68 | Suffocation | 8 | 13 | 3 | 2 | | | | | | | | | | | | | | | 26 | | | | | |
| 69 | Suicide | | | | | | | | | 2 | | | | | | | | | | 1 | 1 | | | | |
| 70 | Summer complaint | | | 2 | 1 | | | | | | | | | | | | | | | 3 | | | | | |
| 71 | Sun, stroke of | | | | | | | | 1 | 1 | | | | | | | | | | 2 | | | | | |
| 72 | Teething | 1 | | 5 | 2 | | | | | | | | | | | | | | | 8 | | | | | |
| 73 | Throat, disease of | | | 2 | | | | | 1 | | 1 | 1 | | | | | | | | 5 | | | | | |
| 74 | Thrush | 8 | 8 | | 1 | | | | | | | | | | | | | | | 7 | | | | | |
| 75 | Tumor | | | | | | | | | | | 1 | | | | | | | | 1 | | | | | |

SECTION OF THE STATE OF NORTH CAROLINA—Continued.

| NATIVITIES. | | | | | SEASON OF DECEASE. | | | | DURATION OF SICKNESS. | | | | WHITES. | | | COLORED. | | | | | | | | | |
|---|---|---|---|---|---|---|---|---|---|---|---|---|---|---|---|---|---|---|---|---|---|---|---|---|---|
| | | | | | | | | | | | | | | | | Slaves. | | | | Free. | | | | | |
| | | | | | | | | | | | | | | | | Black. | | Mulatto. | | Black. | | Mul. | | | |
| California and Territories. | Ireland. | Germany. | Other foreign countries. | Unknown. | Spring. | Summer. | Autumn. | Winter. | Under 1 week. | 1 week and under 1 month. | 1 month and under 3 months. | 3 months and over. | Males. | Females. | Total. | M. | F. | M. | F. | M. | F. | M | F. | Aggregate deaths. | |
| | | | | | 1 | 12 | 11 | 2 | 24 | 2 | | | 7 | 7 | 14 | 8 | 3 | | | | | | 1 | 26 | 1 |
| | | | | | | | 2 | | | 2 | | | | 1 | 1 | | 1 | | | | | | | 2 | 2 |
| | | | | | | | | 1 | | | | | 1 | | 1 | | | | | | | | | 1 | 3 |
| | | | | | | | | | | | | | | | | | 1 | | | | | | | 1 | 4 |
| | | | | | 8 | 7 | 9 | 5 | 16 | 6 | 1 | | 11 | 2 | 13 | 9 | 5 | 1 | | | 1 | | | 29 | 5 |
| | | | | | | 1 | | | 1 | | | | | | | | 1 | | | | | | | 1 | 6 |
| | | | | | | | 2 | 4 | 3 | 2 | | 1 | 3 | 1 | 4 | | | | 1 | 1 | | | | 6 | 7 |
| | | | 1 | | 47 | 46 | 42 | 28 | 4 | 9 | 16 | 116 | 58 | 65 | 133 | 9 | 27 | | 1 | 2 | 1 | 1 | 1 | 165 | 8 |
| | | | 1 | | 10 | 5 | 9 | 7 | 21 | 4 | | 3 | 11 | 2 | 13 | 8 | 7 | | | | | 1 | 2 | 31 | 9 |
| | | | | | 3 | 1 | 2 | 2 | 3 | 4 | | | 3 | 1 | 4 | 1 | 2 | 1 | | | | | | 8 | 10 |
| | | | | | 8 | 5 | 6 | 15 | 21 | 8 | 4 | 1 | 8 | 7 | 15 | 8 | 12 | | | | | | | 35 | 11 |
| | | | | | | | 1 | | | | | | | 1 | 1 | | | | | | | | | 1 | 12 |
| | | | | | 2 | 15 | 13 | 3 | 5 | 14 | 5 | 6 | 10 | 12 | 22 | 6 | 5 | | | | | | | 33 | 13 |
| | | | | | 53 | 48 | 36 | 42 | 2 | 27 | 30 | 106 | 62 | 47 | 109 | 33 | 24 | 4 | 3 | 2 | 2 | 2 | 2 | 181 | 14 |
| | | | | | 4 | 19 | 19 | 1 | 3 | 26 | 9 | 2 | 7 | 13 | 20 | 11 | 8 | | | 2 | 2 | | | 43 | 15 |
| | | | | | | 3 | 2 | 1 | | 1 | 1 | 4 | | 4 | 4 | 1 | 1 | | | | | | | 6 | 16 |
| | | | | | | | | 1 | | | | 1 | 1 | | 1 | | | | | | | | | 1 | 17 |
| | | | | | 16 | 5 | 6 | 11 | 8 | 17 | 3 | 2 | 16 | 11 | 27 | 5 | 5 | | | 1 | | | 1 | 39 | 18 |
| | | | | | 8 | 29 | 39 | 17 | 26 | 55 | 8 | 2 | 20 | 30 | 50 | 26 | 22 | 1 | 1 | | | 1 | 1 | 102 | 19 |
| | | | | | 13 | 36 | 89 | 20 | 31 | 99 | 15 | 13 | 46 | 56 | 102 | 26 | 15 | | 2 | 6 | 2 | 3 | 3 | 159 | 20 |
| | | | 1 | | 5 | 7 | 12 | 8 | 14 | 11 | 1 | 1 | 8 | 8 | 16 | 7 | 4 | 1 | | | | | | 28 | 21 |
| | | | | | 14 | 7 | 2 | 5 | 8 | 8 | 3 | 2 | 6 | 6 | 12 | 4 | 9 | 1 | 2 | | | | | 28 | 22 |
| | | | 1 | | 7 | 4 | 12 | 8 | 15 | 11 | | | 9 | 13 | 22 | 3 | 2 | | | | | | | 27 | 23 |
| | | | | | 1 | 2 | | 1 | | 3 | | 1 | 2 | | 2 | | 2 | | | | | | | 4 | 24 |
| | | | | | 2 | 1 | | 1 | | 2 | 2 | | | 2 | 2 | | 2 | | | | | | | 4 | 25 |
| | | | | | 1 | 3 | | | 2 | | | 2 | | 2 | 2 | 2 | | | | | | | | 4 | 26 |
| | | | | | 5 | 17 | 27 | 8 | 2 | 36 | 7 | 2 | 18 | 10 | 28 | 15 | 12 | | | 1 | 1 | | | 57 | 27 |
| | | | | | 1 | | | | | | | 1 | 1 | | 1 | | | | | | | | | 1 | 28 |
| | | | | | 2 | 3 | | | 1 | 2 | 1 | 1 | 3 | | 3 | 2 | | | | | | | | 5 | 29 |
| | | | | | 3 | 3 | 1 | | 2 | 1 | 1 | 2 | 3 | 2 | 5 | 2 | | | | | | | | 7 | 30 |
| | | | | | 5 | 2 | 4 | 2 | 1 | 5 | 1 | 1 | 3 | 2 | 5 | 3 | 3 | | 1 | 1 | | | | 13 | 31 |
| | | | | | | 2 | 2 | 1 | | 3 | 1 | | 2 | 1 | 3 | 1 | 1 | | | | | | | 5 | 32 |
| | | | | | 34 | 24 | 16 | 22 | 16 | 44 | 16 | 6 | 8 | 16 | 24 | 34 | 35 | 1 | | | 1 | 1 | | 96 | 33 |
| | | | | | 1 | | 1 | 1 | | 2 | 1 | | 1 | 1 | 2 | 1 | | | | | | | | 3 | 34 |
| | | | | | | | 1 | | | | | | | | | | 1 | | | | | | | 1 | 35 |
| | | | | | 7 | 3 | 4 | 4 | 7 | 6 | 2 | | 6 | 5 | 11 | 3 | 4 | | | | | | | 18 | 36 |
| | | | | | 9 | 10 | 4 | 4 | 12 | 7 | 5 | | 10 | 6 | 16 | 6 | 4 | | 1 | | | | | 27 | 37 |
| | 1 | | | | 13 | 10 | 8 | 9 | 18 | 19 | 2 | | 14 | 15 | 29 | 6 | 2 | | 1 | | | | 2 | 38 | 38 |
| | | | | | 1 | 1 | 2 | | 3 | 1 | | | 1 | 1 | 2 | 1 | 1 | | | | | | | 4 | 39 |
| | | | | | | | | 1 | | | | 1 | | | | 1 | 1 | | | | | | | 2 | 40 |
| | | | | | 2 | 1 | 1 | | 1 | | 1 | | 4 | | 4 | | | | | | | | | 4 | 41 |
| | | | | | 1 | | 1 | 1 | 1 | | 1 | 1 | | 2 | 2 | 1 | | | | | | | | 3 | 42 |
| | | | | | 1 | | | | | | | 1 | | | | | 1 | | | | | | | 1 | 43 |
| | | | | | 2 | 4 | 1 | 5 | | | | | 4 | | 4 | 5 | 2 | | | | | 1 | | 12 | 44 |
| | | | | | | 2 | | | 2 | | | | | | | 2 | | | | | | | | 2 | 45 |
| | 1 | | | | 7 | 8 | 3 | 6 | 2 | 8 | 4 | 10 | 11 | 9 | 20 | 2 | 2 | | | | | | | 24 | 46 |
| | | | | | 1 | 2 | 2 | | 4 | 1 | | | | 2 | 2 | 1 | | 1 | | | 1 | | | 5 | 47 |
| | | | | | 1 | | 3 | | | 3 | | | 1 | | 1 | 1 | 2 | | | | | | | 4 | 48 |
| | | | | | 1 | | | | | | | | | 1 | 1 | | | | | | | | | 1 | 49 |
| | | | | | 8 | 5 | 13 | 10 | 9 | 23 | 1 | 2 | 14 | 8 | 22 | 9 | 4 | | | | | 2 | | 37 | 50 |
| | | | | | | | 2 | | | | | 2 | 1 | 1 | 2 | | | | | | | | | 2 | 51 |
| | | | | | 3 | 2 | 1 | 2 | 3 | 5 | | | 5 | 3 | 8 | | | | | | | | | 8 | 52 |
| | | | | | | | | 1 | | 1 | | | | | | | 1 | | | | | | | 1 | 53 |
| | | | | | 1 | | 1 | 1 | 2 | | | | 2 | | 2 | | | | | | | 1 | | 3 | 54 |
| | | | | | 1 | | 1 | 1 | | 1 | 1 | 1 | 2 | 1 | 3 | | | | | | | | | 3 | 55 |
| | | | 1 | | 34 | 30 | 20 | 23 | 13 | 14 | 5 | 17 | 6 | 23 | 29 | 36 | 37 | | 2 | 3 | 1 | 1 | 2 | 111 | 56 |
| | | | | | 7 | 2 | 4 | 3 | 2 | 3 | | 10 | 6 | 2 | 8 | 3 | 2 | 1 | 2 | | | | | 16 | 57 |
| | | | | | 47 | 12 | 12 | 21 | 26 | 51 | 9 | 3 | 33 | 22 | 55 | 24 | 10 | | | | 1 | 2 | | 92 | 58 |
| | 1 | | 1 | | 57 | 22 | 14 | 34 | 40 | 74 | 6 | 2 | 51 | 27 | 78 | 28 | 17 | 2 | | 1 | 1 | 1 | | 128 | 59 |
| | | | | | | 2 | 2 | | 3 | 1 | | | 1 | 1 | 2 | | 2 | | | | | | | 4 | 60 |
| | | | | | | | | 1 | | | | | | | | 1 | | | | | | | | 1 | 61 |
| | | | | | 1 | | 2 | | 1 | 1 | | | 1 | 1 | 2 | | 1 | | | | | | | 3 | 62 |
| | | | | | 4 | 5 | 2 | 10 | 14 | 7 | | | 8 | 5 | 13 | 4 | 4 | | | | | | | 21 | 63 |
| | | | | | 1 | 2 | 3 | 2 | 1 | | | 7 | 6 | 1 | 7 | | 1 | | | | | | | 8 | 64 |
| | | | | | 2 | 1 | | 4 | 1 | | 1 | 3 | 4 | | 4 | 2 | 1 | | | | | | | 7 | 65 |
| | | | | | 24 | 3 | | | 4 | 21 | | 1 | 13 | 6 | 19 | 5 | 3 | | | | | | | 27 | 66 |
| | | | | | 2 | 2 | 2 | | | 3 | 1 | 1 | 1 | 2 | 3 | | 3 | | | | | | | 6 | 67 |
| | | | | | 8 | 7 | 7 | 4 | 26 | | | | 1 | 2 | 3 | 10 | 13 | | | | | | | 26 | 68 |
| | | | | | | 1 | 1 | | | | | | 2 | | 2 | | | | | | | | | 2 | 69 |
| | | | | | | 1 | 2 | | | | | | | | | 2 | 1 | | | | | | | 3 | 70 |
| | | | | | | 2 | | | 2 | | | | | | | 1 | 1 | | | | | | | 2 | 71 |
| | | | | | | 5 | 3 | | | 5 | 2 | | 4 | 1 | 5 | 2 | 1 | | | | | | | 8 | 72 |
| | | | | | 1 | 2 | 1 | 1 | | 3 | 1 | 1 | | 1 | 1 | 3 | 1 | | | | | | | 5 | 73 |
| | | | | | 1 | 4 | 2 | | 1 | 3 | 3 | | 2 | 3 | 5 | 1 | 1 | | | | | | | 7 | 74 |
| | | | | | | 1 | | | | | | 1 | 1 | | 1 | | | | | | | | | 1 | 75 |

## CLASSIFICATION OF DEATHS IN EASTERN

| | Cause of death. | AGES. | | | | | | | | | | | | | | | | | | NATIVITIES. | | | | | |
|---|---|---|---|---|---|---|---|---|---|---|---|---|---|---|---|---|---|---|---|---|---|---|---|---|---|
| | | Under 1. | | 1 and under 5. | | 5 and under 10. | | 10 and under 20. | | 20 and under 50. | | 50 and under 80. | | 80 and under 100. | | 100 & over. | | Age unknown. | | Born in State. | N. England States. | Middle States. | Southern States. | Southwest'n States. | Northwest'n States. |
| | | M. | F. | M. | F. | M. | F. | M. | F. | M. | F. | M. | F. | M | F. | M | F. | M | F. | | | | | | |
| 1 | Ulcer | | | | | | | | | 1 | | | | | | | | | 1 | 2 | | | | | |
| 2 | Uterus, disease of | | | | | | | | | | 1 | | | | | | | | | 1 | | | | | |
| 3 | Venereal | | | | | | | | | | 1 | | | | | | | | | 1 | | | | | |
| 4 | Worms | 1 | 4 | 24 | 22 | 3 | 5 | 1 | 1 | | | | | | 1 | | | | | 61 | | 1 | | | |
| 5 | Unknown | 124 | 110 | 54 | 58 | 11 | 17 | 31 | 29 | 67 | 77 | 58 | 53 | 9 | 1 | 1 | | 1 | | 684 | | 2 | 6 | 3 | |
| | Total | 262 | 269 | 294 | 258 | 93 | 105 | 163 | 126 | 370 | 385 | 262 | 200 | 51 | 56 | 8 | 3 | 3 | 1 | 2830 | 3 | 11 | 48 | 3 | .. |

## CLASSIFICATION OF DEATHS IN WESTERN

*Embracing the following counties: Alexander, Ashe, Buncombe, Burke, Caldwell, Catawba, Rutherford, Surry, Wa-*

| | Cause of death. | Under 1 M. | Under 1 F. | 1–5 M. | 1–5 F. | 5–10 M. | 5–10 F. | 10–20 M. | 10–20 F. | 20–50 M. | 20–50 F. | 50–80 M. | 50–80 F. | 80–100 M | 80–100 F. | 100 & over M | 100 & over F. | Age unknown M | Age unknown F. | Born in State. | N. England States. | Middle States. | Southern States. | Southwest'n States. | Northwest'n States. |
|---|---|---|---|---|---|---|---|---|---|---|---|---|---|---|---|---|---|---|---|---|---|---|---|---|---|
| 1 | Accident, not specif'd | 2 | | | 3 | 1 | | 5 | | 8 | | 4 | 1 | | 1 | | | | | 24 | | | | 1 | |
| 2 | ....do...burned | | | 3 | 5 | | 2 | | 2 | 1 | 1 | | 1 | | | | | | | 13 | | | 2 | | |
| 3 | ....do...drowned | | 1 | 3 | 1 | | | 3 | 1 | 5 | 1 | | | | | | | | | 14 | | | 1 | | |
| 4 | ....do...scalded | | | | 1 | | 1 | | | | | | | | | | | | | 2 | | | | | |
| 5 | Apoplexy | | | | | | | | | 1 | 1 | 3 | 4 | | 1 | | | | | 8 | | | 2 | | |
| 6 | Asthma | | | 1 | | | | | | | | | | | | | | | | 1 | | | | | |
| 7 | Bowels, disease of | | | | 2 | 1 | | | | | | | | | | | | | | 3 | | | | | |
| 8 | Brain ......do | 2 | | | | | 1 | | | | | 2 | | | | | | | | 3 | | 2 | | | |
| 9 | Bronchitis | 1 | | | | | | | 1 | | | | | | | | | | | 1 | | | 1 | | |
| 10 | Cancer | | | | 1 | | | | | | 3 | 5 | 5 | | 1 | | | | | 12 | | 1 | 1 | | |
| 11 | Catarrh | 1 | 2 | 5 | | | 2 | 2 | | 1 | 5 | 1 | | | | | | | | 19 | | | | | |
| 12 | Childbirth | | | | | | | | 1 | | 16 | | | | | | | | | 17 | | | | | |
| 13 | Cholera infantum | 3 | 3 | 1 | 2 | | | | | | | | | | | | | | | 9 | | | | | |
| 14 | ...do...morbus | 2 | 1 | 1 | | | 1 | | | 2 | | | 2 | | | | | | | 9 | | | | | |
| 15 | Colic | | | | | | 1 | | | | | 4 | 3 | | | | | | | 7 | | | 1 | | |
| 16 | Congestion | | | | | | | | | | 1 | | | | | | | | | 1 | | | | | |
| 17 | Consumption | 1 | | 1 | | | 1 | 3 | 3 | 10 | 16 | 6 | 6 | 1 | 3 | | | | | 40 | | 2 | 7 | | |
| 18 | Convulsions | 1 | 1 | 3 | 1 | | | 1 | | 1 | 1 | 3 | | | | | | | | 12 | | | | | |
| 19 | Croup | 38 | 32 | 13 | 18 | 1 | 4 | | | | | | | | | | | | | 106 | | | | | |
| 20 | Debility | | | | | | | | | | | 1 | 1 | 4 | | | 1 | | | 2 | | 1 | 4 | | |
| 21 | Diabetes | | | | | | | | | | 1 | | | | | | | | | | | | 1 | | |
| 22 | Diarrhœa | 2 | 1 | 4 | 3 | 1 | 1 | | | 1 | | 3 | 1 | | | | | | | 13 | 1 | 1 | 2 | | |
| 23 | Dropsy | 2 | | 1 | 1 | 4 | 6 | 11 | 7 | 7 | 24 | 26 | 24 | 6 | 9 | 1 | | | | 102 | | 6 | 16 | | |
| 24 | Dysentery | 2 | 3 | 3 | 1 | | | | | | | | 1 | 2 | 1 | | | | | 11 | | | 1 | | |
| 25 | Dyspepsia | | | | | | 1 | 1 | | 1 | | 5 | | | | | | | | 8 | | | | | |
| 26 | Epilepsy | | | 1 | | | | | | | 1 | | | 1 | | | | | | 3 | | | | | |
| 27 | Erysipelas | 3 | 6 | | 1 | | | | | | | | | | | | | | | 10 | | | | | |
| 28 | Fever, not specified | 3 | 5 | 9 | 8 | 7 | 7 | 9 | 22 | 30 | 43 | 7 | 10 | | | | | | | 155 | 1 | | 2 | 1 | 1 |
| 29 | ..do..bilious | | | | | | 1 | 1 | 2 | 2 | 2 | 1 | | | | | | | | 9 | | | | | |
| 30 | ..do..brain | | | 2 | | | | 1 | | | 1 | | | | | | | | | 3 | | | 1 | | |
| 31 | ..do..catarrhal | | | 1 | | | | | | | | | | | | | | | | 1 | | | | | |
| 32 | ..do..congestive | | | | | | | | | 1 | 1 | | | | | | | | | 1 | | | | | |
| 33 | ..do..intermittent | | | 1 | | | | | | 1 | | | 1 | | | | | | | 3 | | | | | |
| 34 | ..do..puerperal | | | | | | | | | | 8 | | | | | | | | | 7 | | | 1 | | |
| 35 | ..do..scarlet | | | | | | | | | | 1 | | | | | | | | | 1 | | | | | |
| 36 | ..do..typhoid | | 1 | 1 | | 3 | 2 | 7 | 8 | 25 | 18 | 4 | 4 | 1 | | | | | 1 | 75 | | | | | |
| 37 | Gravel | | | | | | | | | | 1 | 7 | | 1 | | | | | | 6 | | 2 | 1 | | |
| 38 | Heart, disease of | | | | | | | 1 | | | | 3 | 1 | | | | | | | 5 | | | | | |
| 39 | Heat | | | | | | | | | 2 | | | | | | | | | | 2 | | | | | |
| 40 | Hemorrhage | | | | | | | 1 | | | 1 | 1 | 1 | | | | | | | 4 | | | | | |
| 41 | Hernia | | | | | | | | | | | 1 | | | | | | | | 2 | | | | | |
| 42 | Hip, disease of | | | | | | | | | | | | | | | | | | | | | | | | |
| 43 | Hives | 21 | 12 | 2 | 4 | | | | | | | | | | | | | | | 39 | | | | | |
| 44 | Hooping cough | 10 | 3 | 10 | 12 | 1 | 1 | | | | | | | | | | | | | 37 | | | | | |
| 45 | Hydrocephalus | | | 3 | | | | | | | | | | | | | | | | 3 | | | | | |
| 46 | Inflammation | 1 | 1 | 1 | | 1 | | | | | 2 | 1 | 1 | | | | | | | 8 | | | | | |
| 47 | ....do....bowels | 1 | 1 | 1 | 1 | 2 | | 1 | | 1 | | 1 | | | | | | | | 9 | | | | | |
| 48 | ....do....brain | | 1 | | 1 | | | 2 | 1 | 1 | 1 | 2 | | | | | | | | 9 | | | | | |
| 49 | ....do....stomach | | | | | 1 | | | | | | | | | | | | | | 1 | | | | | |
| 50 | Insanity | | | | | | | | | 1 | | | | | | | | | | 1 | | | | | |
| 51 | Intemperance | | | | | | | | | 2 | | 2 | | | | | | | | 4 | | | | | |
| 52 | Jaundice | | | | 1 | | | | | | | | | | | | | | | 1 | | | | | |
| 53 | Kidneys, disease of | | | | | | | | | | | 1 | | 1 | | | | | | 2 | | | | | |
| 54 | Killed | | | | | | | | | 1 | | | | | | | | | | 1 | | | | | |
| 55 | Lightning | | | | | 1 | | | | | | | | | | | | | | 1 | | | | | |
| 56 | Liver, disease of | 1 | | | | 2 | 1 | | 2 | 2 | 5 | 1 | 1 | | | | | | | 13 | | | 2 | | |
| 57 | Lungs....do | | | | | | | | | 2 | 2 | 1 | 2 | | | | | | | 5 | | | 2 | | |
| 58 | Malformation | | 1 | 1 | | | | | | | | | | | | | | | | 2 | | | | | |

SECTION OF THE STATE OF NORTH CAROLINA—Continued.

| NATIVITIES. California and Territories. | Ireland. | Germany. | Other foreign countries. | Unknown. | SEASON OF DECEASE. Spring. | Summer. | Autumn. | Winter. | DURATION OF SICKNESS. Under 1 week. | 1 week and under 1 month. | 1 month and under 3 months. | 3 months and over. | WHITES. Males. | Females. | Total. | COLORED. Slaves. Black. M. | Slaves. Black. F. | Slaves. Mulatto. M. | Slaves. Mulatto. F. | Free. Black. M. | Free. Black. F. | Free. Mul. M | Free. Mul. F. | Aggregate deaths. | |
|---|---|---|---|---|---|---|---|---|---|---|---|---|---|---|---|---|---|---|---|---|---|---|---|---|---|
| | | | | | | 2 | | | 1 | | | 1 | | 1 | 1 | 1 | | | | | | | | 2 | 1 |
| | | | | | | | | 1 | 1 | | | | | | | | 1 | | | | | | | 1 | 2 |
| | | | | | | | | 1 | | | | 1 | | 1 | 1 | | | | | | | | | 1 | 3 |
| | | | | | 9 | 18 | 27 | 7 | 22 | 18 | 9 | 7 | 7 | 5 | 12 | 20 | 26 | 1 | 2 | | | 1 | | 62 | 4 |
| | 2 | | 1 | 1 | 184 | 176 | 172 | 138 | 197 | 136 | 62 | 154 | 174 | 178 | 352 | 163 | 149 | 8 | 8 | 5 | 4 | 6 | 6 | 699 | 5 |
| ... | 5 | 1 | 111 | 1 | 779 | 741 | 750 | 573 | 764 | 887 | 267 | 527 | 790 | 732 | 1522 | 638 | 599 | 24 | 31 | 28 | 18 | 27 | 22 | 2909 | |

SECTION OF THE STATE OF NORTH CAROLINA.

*Cherokee, Cleveland, Gaston, Haywood, Henderson, Iredell, Lincoln, McDowell, Macon, tauga, Wilkes, Yancy.*

| California and Territories. | Ireland. | Germany. | Other foreign countries. | Unknown. | Spring. | Summer. | Autumn. | Winter. | Under 1 week. | 1 week and under 1 month. | 1 month and under 3 months. | 3 months and over. | Males. | Females. | Total. | Slaves Black M. | Slaves Black F. | Slaves Mulatto M. | Slaves Mulatto F. | Free Black M. | Free Black F. | Free Mul. M | Free Mul. F. | Aggregate deaths. | |
|---|---|---|---|---|---|---|---|---|---|---|---|---|---|---|---|---|---|---|---|---|---|---|---|---|---|
| | | | | | 5 | 10 | 4 | 6 | 10 | 2 | 1 | 2 | 16 | 4 | 20 | 2 | 1 | 2 | | | | | | 25 | 1 |
| | | | | | 6 | 5 | | 4 | 6 | 5 | 3 | | 3 | 6 | 9 | 1 | 5 | | | | | | | 15 | 2 |
| | | | | | 2 | 10 | 1 | 1 | 15 | | | | 4 | 3 | 7 | 6 | | 1 | | | | | 1 | 15 | 3 |
| | | | | | | 1 | 1 | | 1 | 1 | | | | 2 | 2 | | | | | | | | | 2 | 4 |
| | | | | | 2 | 2 | 1 | 5 | 8 | 1 | | 1 | 4 | 4 | 8 | | 2 | | | | | | | 10 | 5 |
| | | | | | 1 | | | | | | | 1 | | | | 1 | | | | | | | | 1 | 6 |
| | | | | | 1 | | 2 | | 2 | | | 1 | 1 | 2 | 3 | | | | | | | | | 3 | 7 |
| | | | | | 2 | 1 | | 2 | | 2 | 1 | 2 | 3 | | 3 | 1 | 1 | | | | | | | 5 | 8 |
| | | | | | 1 | 1 | | | | 2 | | | | 1 | 1 | 1 | | | | | | | | 2 | 9 |
| | | | 1 | | 7 | 2 | 1 | 4 | | | 1 | 13 | 4 | 10 | 14 | 1 | | | | | | | | 15 | 10 |
| | | | | | 7 | 1 | 2 | 9 | 4 | 9 | 4 | 2 | 8 | 9 | 17 | 2 | | | | | | | | 19 | 11 |
| | | | | | 6 | 4 | | 6 | 12 | 2 | 2 | | | 13 | 13 | | 3 | | | | | | 1 | 17 | 12 |
| | | | | | | 5 | 2 | 2 | 1 | 2 | 1 | 1 | 4 | 5 | 9 | | | | | | | | | 9 | 13 |
| | | | | | 1 | 5 | 2 | 1 | 7 | 2 | | | 5 | 4 | 9 | | | | | | | | | 9 | 14 |
| | | | | | 1 | 3 | 3 | 1 | 6 | 1 | 1 | | 4 | 3 | 7 | | 1 | | | | | | | 8 | 15 |
| | | | | | | | 1 | | 1 | | | | | 1 | 1 | | | | | | | | | 1 | 16 |
| | 1 | | 1 | | 12 | 15 | 13 | 11 | 1 | 1 | 8 | 36 | 18 | 25 | 43 | 3 | 4 | | | 1 | | | | 51 | 17 |
| | | | | | 4 | 6 | 1 | 1 | 7 | 2 | 2 | | 5 | 2 | 7 | 4 | 1 | | | | | | | 12 | 18 |
| | | | | | 28 | 16 | 33 | 27 | 65 | 33 | 4 | | 35 | 42 | 77 | 17 | 9 | | 2 | | | | 1 | 106 | 19 |
| | | | | | 2 | 2 | 1 | 2 | 1 | 3 | | 2 | 4 | 2 | 6 | 1 | | | | | | | | 7 | 20 |
| | | | | | | | | 1 | | | | 1 | | 1 | 1 | | | | | | | | | 1 | 21 |
| | | | | | 1 | 5 | 7 | 4 | 3 | 6 | 4 | 4 | 9 | 4 | 13 | 2 | 2 | | | | | | | 17 | 22 |
| | 2 | | 1 | 1 | 34 | 42 | 25 | 26 | 4 | 14 | 28 | 73 | 51 | 58 | 109 | 6 | 12 | | | | 1 | | | 128 | 23 |
| | | | | 1 | 1 | 8 | 1 | 2 | 3 | 7 | 1 | 1 | 6 | 6 | 12 | 1 | | | | | | | | 13 | 24 |
| | | | | | 1 | 4 | 2 | 1 | | 1 | 2 | 5 | 7 | | 7 | | | | | | 1 | | | 8 | 25 |
| | | | | | 1 | | 2 | | 3 | | | | 2 | 1 | 3 | | | | | | | | | 3 | 26 |
| | | | | | 4 | 2 | 1 | 3 | 4 | 4 | 1 | | 3 | 6 | 9 | | 1 | | | | | | | 10 | 27 |
| | | | | | 24 | 38 | 71 | 27 | 22 | 93 | 34 | 9 | 50 | 65 | 115 | 15 | 28 | | 2 | | | | | 160 | 28 |
| | | | | | | 3 | 4 | 2 | 1 | 5 | 2 | 1 | 4 | 4 | 8 | | 1 | | | | | | | 9 | 29 |
| | | | | | | 1 | 2 | 1 | | 3 | | 1 | 2 | 1 | 3 | 1 | | | | | | | | 4 | 30 |
| | | | | | | | | 1 | | 1 | | | 1 | | 1 | | | | | | | | | 1 | 31 |
| | | | | | 1 | 1 | | | | 1 | 1 | | 1 | 1 | 2 | | | | | | | | | 2 | 32 |
| | | | | | | | 2 | 1 | | 3 | | | 2 | 1 | 3 | | | | | | | | | 3 | 33 |
| | | | | | 4 | 1 | | 3 | 1 | | | | | 5 | 5 | | 3 | | | | | | | 8 | 34 |
| | | | | | | | | 1 | | 1 | | | | | | | 1 | | | | | | | 1 | 35 |
| | | | | | 21 | 7 | 20 | 26 | 4 | 46 | 18 | 6 | 26 | 22 | 48 | 15 | 10 | | 2 | | | | | 75 | 36 |
| | | | | | 3 | 3 | 2 | 1 | 1 | 2 | 1 | 4 | 8 | 1 | 8 | | | | | | | | | 9 | 37 |
| | | | | | | | 3 | 2 | | | 1 | 4 | 1 | | 1 | 3 | 1 | | | | | | | 5 | 38 |
| | | | | | 1 | 1 | | | | 1 | | | 2 | | 2 | | | | | | | | | 2 | 39 |
| | | | | | 1 | 2 | | 1 | 2 | 2 | | | 1 | 1 | 2 | 1 | 1 | | | | | | | 4 | 40 |
| | | | | | | 2 | | | | 1 | | | 1 | | 1 | 1 | | | | | | | | 2 | 41 |
| | | | | | | | | | | | | | | | | | | | | | | | | | 42 |
| | | | | | 4 | 8 | 10 | 17 | 27 | 10 | 1 | | 20 | 16 | 36 | 3 | | | | | | | | 39 | 43 |
| | | | | | 11 | 10 | 7 | 9 | 5 | 22 | 9 | | 13 | 7 | 20 | 6 | 8 | 2 | 1 | | | | | 37 | 44 |
| | | | | | 1 | 1 | 1 | | 1 | | 1 | | 1 | | 1 | 2 | | | | | | | | 3 | 45 |
| | | | | | 4 | 1 | 1 | 2 | 1 | 6 | 1 | | 2 | 3 | 5 | 2 | 1 | | | | | | | 8 | 46 |
| | | | | | 1 | 4 | 2 | 2 | 3 | 4 | 1 | | 6 | 1 | 7 | 1 | 1 | | | | | | | 9 | 47 |
| | | | | | 2 | 3 | 2 | 2 | 7 | 2 | | | 4 | 3 | 7 | 1 | 1 | | | | | | | 9 | 48 |
| | | | | | 1 | | | | | 1 | | | 1 | | 1 | | | | | | | | | 1 | 49 |
| | | | | | 1 | | | | | | | 1 | 1 | | 1 | | | | | | | | | 1 | 50 |
| | | | | | 3 | | | | | 3 | | 1 | 4 | | 4 | | | | | | | | | 4 | 51 |
| | | | | | | | | 1 | 1 | | | | | | | | 1 | | | | | | | 1 | 52 |
| | | | | | | | | 2 | | 1 | | 1 | 2 | | 2 | | | | | | | | | 2 | 53 |
| | | | | | 1 | | | | 1 | | | | 1 | | 1 | | | | | | | | | 1 | 54 |
| | | | | | | 1 | | | 1 | | | | 1 | | 1 | | | | | | | | | 1 | 55 |
| | | | | | 6 | 2 | 5 | 2 | 3 | 2 | 8 | 2 | 5 | 8 | 13 | 1 | 1 | | | | | | | 15 | 56 |
| | | | | | 2 | 1 | 3 | 1 | | | 2 | 3 | 2 | 4 | 6 | 1 | | | | | | | | 7 | 57 |
| | | | | | 1 | 1 | | | 1 | 1 | | | | 1 | 1 | 1 | | | | | | | | 2 | 58 |

## CLASSIFICATION OF DEATHS IN WESTERN

| | Cause of death. | Ages. Under 1. M. | F. | 1 and under 5. M. | F. | 5 and under 10. M. | F. | 10 and under 20. M. | F. | 20 and under 50. M. | F. | 50 and under 80. M. | F. | 80 and under 100. M | F. | 100 & over. M | F. | Age unknown. M | F. | Nativities. Born in State. | N. England States. | Middle States. | Southern States. | Southwest'n States. | Northwest'n States. |
|---|---|---|---|---|---|---|---|---|---|---|---|---|---|---|---|---|---|---|---|---|---|---|---|---|---|
| 1 | Measles | 3 | 5 | 6 | 2 | 1 | 2 | ... | ... | 2 | 2 | ... | ... | .. | .. | .. | .. | .. | .. | 22 | .. | ... | 1 | ... | ... |
| 2 | Milk sickness | ... | ... | ... | ... | ... | ... | ... | ... | 2 | 1 | ... | ... | .. | .. | .. | .. | .. | .. | 3 | .. | ... | ... | ... | ... |
| 3 | Mortification | ... | ... | ... | ... | ... | ... | ... | ... | ... | ... | ... | 1 | .. | .. | .. | .. | .. | .. | 1 | .. | ... | ... | ... | ... |
| 4 | Mumps | ... | ... | ... | ... | ... | 1 | 1 | ... | ... | ... | ... | ... | .. | .. | .. | .. | .. | .. | 2 | .. | ... | ... | ... | ... |
| 5 | Murder | ... | ... | ... | ... | ... | ... | ... | ... | 1 | ... | ... | ... | .. | .. | .. | .. | .. | .. | 1 | .. | ... | ... | ... | ... |
| 6 | Neuralgia | ... | ... | ... | ... | ... | ... | ... | ... | ... | 1 | ... | ... | .. | .. | .. | .. | .. | .. | 1 | .. | ... | ... | ... | ... |
| 7 | Old age | ... | ... | ... | ... | ... | ... | ... | ... | ... | ... | 6 | 6 | 19 | 28 | 3 | 3 | .. | .. | 41 | .. | 4 | 15 | ... | ... |
| 8 | Paralysis | ... | ... | ... | ... | ... | ... | ... | 1 | 3 | ... | 8 | 5 | 2 | 1 | .. | .. | .. | .. | 16 | .. | 1 | 3 | ... | ... |
| 9 | Pleurisy | ... | ... | ... | ... | ... | ... | 2 | 1 | 3 | 1 | ... | 1 | .. | .. | .. | .. | .. | .. | 7 | .. | ... | ... | ... | ... |
| 10 | Pneumonia | 2 | 3 | 7 | 5 | 4 | 3 | 13 | 4 | 12 | 10 | 5 | 3 | 1 | 1 | .. | .. | .. | .. | 66 | .. | ... | 6 | 1 | ... |
| 11 | Poison | ... | ... | ... | ... | ... | ... | ... | ... | 2 | 1 | ... | ... | .. | .. | .. | .. | .. | .. | 3 | .. | ... | ... | ... | ... |
| 12 | Prematurity of birth | 5 | 3 | ... | ... | ... | ... | ... | ... | ... | ... | ... | ... | .. | .. | .. | .. | .. | .. | 8 | .. | ... | ... | ... | ... |
| 13 | Quinsy | ... | ... | 2 | 1 | ... | 4 | ... | ... | ... | ... | ... | 1 | .. | .. | .. | .. | .. | .. | 8 | .. | ... | ... | ... | ... |
| 14 | Rheumatism | ... | ... | ... | ... | 1 | ... | 1 | ... | 3 | ... | 1 | ... | 1 | 1 | .. | .. | .. | .. | 7 | .. | 1 | ... | ... | ... |
| 15 | Rickets | 1 | ... | ... | ... | ... | ... | ... | ... | ... | ... | ... | ... | .. | .. | .. | .. | .. | .. | 1 | .. | ... | ... | ... | ... |
| 16 | Scrofula | ... | ... | ... | ... | ... | ... | 2 | ... | 1 | ... | 1 | 2 | .. | .. | .. | .. | .. | .. | 6 | .. | ... | ... | ... | ... |
| 17 | Stillborn | 4 | 4 | ... | ... | ... | ... | ... | ... | ... | ... | ... | ... | .. | .. | .. | .. | .. | .. | 8 | .. | ... | ... | ... | ... |
| 18 | Suffocation | 2 | 2 | ... | ... | ... | ... | ... | ... | ... | ... | ... | 1 | .. | .. | .. | .. | .. | .. | 5 | .. | ... | ... | ... | ... |
| 19 | Suicide | ... | ... | ... | ... | ... | ... | ... | 3 | 4 | ... | 1 | ... | .. | .. | .. | .. | .. | .. | 7 | .. | ... | 1 | ... | ... |
| 20 | Teething | 1 | 1 | 3 | 4 | ... | ... | ... | ... | ... | ... | ... | ... | .. | .. | .. | .. | .. | .. | 9 | .. | ... | ... | ... | ... |
| 21 | Throat, disease of | ... | ... | 1 | ... | ... | 4 | 1 | ... | ... | ... | ... | 1 | .. | .. | .. | .. | .. | .. | 6 | .. | ... | 1 | ... | ... |
| 22 | Thrush | ... | 1 | ... | ... | ... | ... | ... | ... | ... | ... | ... | ... | .. | .. | .. | .. | .. | .. | 1 | .. | ... | ... | ... | ... |
| 23 | Tumor | ... | 1 | ... | ... | ... | ... | ... | 1 | ... | ... | ... | 1 | .. | .. | .. | .. | .. | .. | 2 | .. | ... | 1 | ... | ... |
| 24 | Ulcer | 1 | 1 | ... | ... | ... | ... | ... | ... | ... | 1 | ... | 1 | .. | .. | .. | .. | .. | .. | 4 | .. | ... | ... | ... | ... |
| 25 | Uterus, disease of | ... | ... | ... | ... | ... | ... | ... | 1 | ... | 3 | ... | 2 | .. | .. | .. | .. | .. | .. | 4 | .. | ... | 2 | ... | ... |
| 26 | Venereal | ... | ... | ... | ... | ... | ... | ... | ... | 1 | 1 | ... | ... | .. | .. | .. | .. | .. | .. | 2 | .. | ... | ... | ... | ... |
| 27 | Worms | ... | 2 | 5 | 6 | 1 | 1 | ... | ... | ... | ... | ... | ... | .. | .. | .. | .. | .. | .. | 15 | .. | ... | ... | ... | ... |
| 28 | Unknown | 57 | 54 | 24 | 20 | 5 | 15 | 19 | 13 | 19 | 28 | 9 | 25 | 4 | 3 | 1 | 2 | .. | .. | 278 | .. | 2 | 13 | ... | ... |
| | Total | 173 | 152 | 120 | 105 | 38 | 63 | 88 | 74 | 162 | 206 | 127 | 120 | 43 | 50 | 5 | 6 | .. | 1 | 1394 | 2 | 23 | 91 | 8 | 1 |

## CLASSIFICATION OF DEATHS IN NORTHERN, MIDDLE

*Embracing the following counties: Alamance, Casswell, Chatham, Davidson, Davie, Edgecombe, Rockingham, Rowan*

| | Cause of death. | Under 1. M. | F. | 1 and under 5. M. | F. | 5 and under 10. M. | F. | 10 and under 20. M. | F. | 20 and under 50. M. | F. | 50 and under 80. M. | F. | 80 and under 100. M | F. | 100 & over. M | F. | Age unknown. M | F. | Born in State. | N. England States. | Middle States. | Southern States. | Southwest'n States. | Northwest'n States. |
|---|---|---|---|---|---|---|---|---|---|---|---|---|---|---|---|---|---|---|---|---|---|---|---|---|---|
| 1 | Abscess | ... | 1 | ... | ... | ... | ... | ... | ... | ... | ... | ... | ... | .. | .. | .. | .. | .. | .. | 1 | .. | ... | ... | ... | ... |
| 2 | Accident, not specif'd | 3 | 1 | 5 | 7 | 5 | ... | 5 | 1 | 12 | 1 | 2 | 2 | 1 | 1 | .. | .. | .. | .. | 44 | .. | ... | 1 | ... | ... |
| 3 | ....do...burned | 2 | 3 | 10 | 13 | 7 | 10 | 1 | 3 | 4 | 6 | 3 | 2 | .. | .. | .. | .. | .. | .. | 59 | 5 | ... | ... | ... | ... |
| 4 | ....do...drowned | ... | ... | 1 | 1 | ... | ... | 5 | ... | 5 | ... | 1 | ... | 1 | .. | .. | .. | .. | .. | 14 | .. | ... | ... | ... | ... |
| 5 | ....do...scalded | ... | ... | ... | ... | ... | ... | ... | ... | ... | ... | 1 | ... | .. | .. | .. | .. | .. | .. | 1 | .. | ... | ... | ... | ... |
| 6 | ....do...shot | ... | ... | ... | ... | ... | 1 | ... | ... | ... | ... | ... | ... | .. | .. | .. | .. | .. | .. | 1 | .. | ... | ... | ... | ... |
| 7 | Amputation | ... | ... | ... | ... | ... | ... | ... | ... | ... | ... | 1 | ... | .. | .. | .. | .. | .. | .. | 1 | .. | ... | ... | ... | ... |
| 8 | Apoplexy | ... | 1 | ... | ... | 1 | ... | ... | ... | 3 | 2 | 10 | 8 | .. | .. | .. | .. | .. | .. | 21 | .. | ... | 4 | ... | ... |
| 9 | Bowels, disease of | 4 | ... | 6 | 4 | 1 | ... | 1 | ... | 5 | 2 | ... | 1 | .. | .. | .. | .. | 1 | .. | 22 | .. | ... | 3 | ... | ... |
| 10 | Brain ......do | 1 | 1 | 1 | ... | 3 | ... | 1 | ... | 3 | 3 | ... | 2 | .. | .. | .. | .. | .. | .. | 14 | .. | ... | 1 | ... | ... |
| 11 | Bronchitis | ... | 2 | 1 | 4 | ... | ... | 1 | 1 | 4 | 1 | ... | ... | .. | .. | .. | .. | .. | .. | 14 | .. | ... | ... | ... | ... |
| 12 | Cancer | 1 | ... | ... | ... | ... | ... | ... | ... | ... | 8 | 8 | 16 | 1 | .. | .. | .. | .. | .. | 28 | .. | 1 | 5 | ... | ... |
| 13 | Catarrh | 3 | 5 | 4 | 6 | 2 | ... | 2 | 1 | 4 | 5 | 2 | 1 | .. | 3 | .. | .. | .. | .. | 36 | .. | 1 | 1 | ... | ... |
| 14 | Childbirth | ... | ... | ... | ... | ... | ... | ... | 4 | ... | 46 | ... | ... | .. | .. | .. | .. | .. | .. | 47 | .. | ... | 3 | ... | ... |
| 15 | Cholera | ... | 1 | 1 | 2 | ... | ... | 1 | ... | 2 | ... | ... | ... | .. | .. | .. | .. | .. | .. | 7 | .. | ... | ... | ... | ... |
| 16 | ...do...infantum | 20 | 14 | 16 | 7 | ... | 1 | ... | ... | ... | ... | ... | ... | .. | .. | .. | .. | .. | .. | 58 | .. | ... | ... | ... | ... |
| 17 | ...do...morbus | ... | 1 | 2 | 2 | ... | 1 | 2 | ... | 1 | 2 | 1 | 1 | .. | .. | .. | .. | .. | .. | 13 | .. | ... | ... | ... | ... |
| 18 | Chorea | ... | ... | ... | ... | ... | ... | ... | 1 | ... | ... | ... | ... | .. | .. | .. | .. | .. | .. | 1 | .. | ... | ... | ... | ... |
| 19 | Colic | 5 | 2 | ... | 3 | ... | ... | 1 | 1 | 3 | 3 | 2 | 2 | 1 | .. | .. | .. | .. | .. | 20 | .. | ... | 3 | ... | ... |
| 20 | Congestion | ... | ... | ... | ... | ... | ... | ... | ... | 1 | 2 | ... | ... | .. | .. | .. | .. | .. | .. | 3 | .. | ... | ... | ... | ... |
| 21 | ....do.....brain | ... | ... | 1 | 2 | ... | ... | 1 | 1 | 1 | 2 | ... | ... | .. | .. | .. | .. | .. | .. | 8 | .. | ... | ... | ... | ... |
| 22 | Consumption | 2 | 4 | 2 | 4 | 2 | 6 | 8 | 31 | 54 | 88 | 28 | 29 | 2 | 5 | .. | .. | .. | .. | 244 | .. | 2 | 18 | ... | ... |
| 23 | Convulsions | 12 | 15 | 5 | 2 | 2 | 1 | 2 | 5 | 1 | 7 | 2 | 3 | .. | 1 | .. | .. | .. | .. | 56 | .. | ... | 1 | 1 | ... |
| 24 | Croup | 34 | 26 | 32 | 27 | 4 | 5 | 2 | ... | 1 | ... | ... | ... | .. | .. | .. | .. | .. | .. | 130 | .. | ... | 1 | ... | ... |
| 25 | D bility | ... | ... | 3 | 1 | ... | ... | ... | ... | ... | ... | 2 | 2 | .. | 1 | .. | .. | .. | .. | 9 | .. | ... | ... | ... | ... |
| 26 | Diarrhœa | 11 | 15 | 19 | 7 | ... | 2 | 2 | 4 | 3 | 4 | 6 | 1 | 1 | .. | .. | .. | .. | .. | 71 | .. | 1 | 2 | ... | ... |
| 27 | Dropsy | 3 | 1 | 15 | 9 | 11 | 14 | 26 | 7 | 47 | 37 | 64 | 49 | 9 | 4 | .. | .. | .. | 1 | 269 | .. | 2 | 24 | ... | ... |
| 28 | Dysentery | 5 | 4 | 13 | 8 | 1 | ... | 3 | ... | 1 | 2 | ... | 3 | 1 | .. | .. | .. | .. | .. | 39 | .. | 1 | 1 | ... | ... |
| 29 | Dyspepsia | ... | ... | ... | ... | ... | ... | ... | ... | 3 | 3 | 5 | 3 | 1 | .. | .. | .. | .. | .. | 12 | .. | 2 | 1 | ... | ... |
| 30 | Epilepsy | ... | ... | ... | ... | ... | ... | ... | ... | ... | ... | 1 | ... | .. | .. | .. | .. | .. | .. | 1 | .. | ... | ... | ... | ... |
| 31 | Erysipelas | 3 | 1 | 1 | ... | ... | ... | 1 | 2 | 2 | 5 | 1 | ... | .. | .. | .. | .. | .. | .. | 15 | .. | ... | 1 | ... | ... |
| 32 | Fever, not specified | 2 | 4 | 6 | 7 | 1 | 3 | 8 | 10 | 21 | 10 | 7 | 2 | 1 | 2 | .. | .. | .. | .. | 74 | .. | ... | 10 | ... | ... |
| 33 | ..do..bilious | 3 | ... | 5 | 10 | 4 | 2 | 5 | 5 | 4 | 8 | 9 | 8 | 1 | 2 | .. | .. | .. | .. | 63 | .. | ... | 3 | ... | ... |
| 34 | ..do..brain | ... | ... | ... | ... | ... | ... | 1 | ... | 1 | ... | ... | ... | .. | .. | .. | .. | .. | .. | 2 | .. | ... | ... | ... | ... |
| 35 | ..do..catarrhal | 1 | ... | 2 | ... | 1 | ... | ... | 1 | ... | 1 | 1 | 2 | 1 | .. | .. | .. | .. | .. | 8 | .. | ... | 2 | ... | ... |

## [S]ECTION OF THE STATE OF NORTH CAROLINA—Continued.

| NATIVITIES: California and Territories | NATIVITIES: Ireland | NATIVITIES: Germany | NATIVITIES: Other foreign countries | NATIVITIES: Unknown | SEASON OF DECEASE: Spring | SEASON OF DECEASE: Summer | SEASON OF DECEASE: Autumn | SEASON OF DECEASE: Winter | DURATION OF SICKNESS: Under 1 week | DURATION OF SICKNESS: 1 week and under 1 month | DURATION OF SICKNESS: 1 month and under 3 months | DURATION OF SICKNESS: 3 months and over | WHITES: Males | WHITES: Females | WHITES: Total | COLORED: Slaves, Black, M. | COLORED: Slaves, Black, F. | COLORED: Slaves, Mulatto, M. | COLORED: Slaves, Mulatto, F. | COLORED: Free, Black, M. | COLORED: Free, Black, F. | COLORED: Free, Mul., M | COLORED: Free, Mul., F. | Aggregate deaths. | |
|---|---|---|---|---|---|---|---|---|---|---|---|---|---|---|---|---|---|---|---|---|---|---|---|---|---|
| | | | | | 9 | 2 | 7 | 5 | 9 | 13 | 1 | | 10 | 6 | 16 | 2 | 4 | | | | 1 | | | 23 | 1 |
| | | | | | 2 | 1 | | | 1 | 2 | | 1 | 2 | 1 | 3 | | | | | | | | | 3 | 2 |
| | | | | | | 1 | | | | | | | | 1 | 1 | | | | | | | | | 1 | 3 |
| | | | | | | 2 | | | 1 | 1 | | | 1 | 1 | 2 | | | | | | | | | 2 | 4 |
| | | | | | | | | 1 | | | | | 1 | | 1 | | | | | | | | | 1 | 5 |
| | | | | | | | 1 | | | | | 1 | | | | | 1 | | | | | | | 1 | 6 |
| | 1 | 1 | 3 | | 19 | 16 | 17 | 13 | 11 | 8 | 8 | 15 | 22 | 29 | 51 | 5 | 5 | | | 1 | 3 | | | 65 | 7 |
| | | | | | 7 | 5 | 4 | 4 | 5 | 6 | 2 | 5 | 13 | 7 | 20 | | | | | | | | | 20 | 8 |
| | | | 1 | | 2 | 1 | 1 | 4 | 1 | 4 | 2 | 1 | 3 | 2 | 5 | 2 | 1 | | | | | | | 8 | 9 |
| | | | | | 29 | 14 | 11 | 18 | 20 | 45 | 5 | 2 | 42 | 25 | 67 | | 4 | | | | | | | 73 | 10 |
| | | | | | | | 3 | | | 3 | | | 1 | 1 | 2 | | | | | 1 | | | | 3 | 11 |
| | | | | | 3 | 4 | | 1 | 7 | 1 | | | 2 | 1 | 3 | 3 | 2 | | | | | | | 8 | 12 |
| | | | | | 1 | | 2 | 5 | 1 | 3 | 4 | | 2 | 6 | 8 | | | | | | | | | 8 | 13 |
| | | | | | 2 | 4 | | 2 | 1 | 1 | | 6 | 4 | 1 | 5 | 3 | | | | | | | | 8 | 14 |
| | | | | | | 1 | | | | | | 1 | 1 | | 1 | | | | | | | | | 1 | 15 |
| | | | | | 3 | 1 | 2 | | | 1 | | 5 | 3 | 2 | 5 | 1 | | | | | | | | 6 | 16 |
| | | | | | 3 | 3 | 1 | 1 | | | | | 4 | 4 | 8 | | | | | | | | | 8 | 17 |
| | | | | | 3 | 1 | 1 | | 5 | | | | | 2 | 2 | 2 | 1 | | | | | | | 5 | 18 |
| | | | | | 4 | 3 | | 1 | 6 | | | | 4 | 3 | 7 | 1 | | | | | | | | 8 | 19 |
| | | | | | 2 | 5 | 2 | | 2 | 3 | 2 | 1 | 2 | 2 | 4 | 2 | 3 | | | | | | | 9 | 20 |
| | | | | | 1 | 1 | 3 | 2 | 3 | 4 | | | 2 | 3 | 5 | | 2 | | | | | | | 7 | 21 |
| | | | | | 1 | | | | | | | 1 | | 1 | 1 | | | | | | | | | 1 | 22 |
| | | | | | 1 | 1 | | 1 | 1 | | 1 | 1 | | 2 | 2 | | 1 | | | | | | | 3 | 23 |
| | | | | | 2 | | 1 | 1 | 2 | 1 | | 1 | | 2 | 2 | 1 | | | | | 1 | | | 4 | 24 |
| | | | | | 1 | | 2 | 2 | 2 | 1 | | 3 | | 5 | 5 | | 1 | | | | | | | 6 | 25 |
| | | | | | | 1 | 1 | | | | 1 | 1 | | | | 1 | 1 | | | | | | | 2 | 26 |
| | | | | | 1 | 6 | 6 | 2 | 6 | 8 | 1 | | 5 | 6 | 11 | 1 | 2 | | | | | | 1 | 15 | 27 |
| | | 2 | | 3 | 87 | 87 | 57 | 64 | 101 | 66 | 33 | 51 | 112 | 122 | 234 | 25 | 37 | | 1 | 1 | | | | 298 | 28 |
| | 4 | 3 | 7 | 5 | 406 | 401 | 363 | 351 | 431 | 482 | 204 | 274 | 593 | 593 | 1186 | 154 | 165 | 5 | 8 | 4 | 7 | | 4 | 1533 | |

## SECTION OF THE STATE OF NORTH CAROLINA.

*Forsyth, Franklin, Granville, Guilford, Halifax, Nash, Northampton, Orange, Randolph, Stokes, and Wake.*

| NATIVITIES: California and Territories | NATIVITIES: Ireland | NATIVITIES: Germany | NATIVITIES: Other foreign countries | NATIVITIES: Unknown | SEASON OF DECEASE: Spring | SEASON OF DECEASE: Summer | SEASON OF DECEASE: Autumn | SEASON OF DECEASE: Winter | DURATION OF SICKNESS: Under 1 week | DURATION OF SICKNESS: 1 week and under 1 month | DURATION OF SICKNESS: 1 month and under 3 months | DURATION OF SICKNESS: 3 months and over | WHITES: Males | WHITES: Females | WHITES: Total | COLORED: Slaves, Black, M. | COLORED: Slaves, Black, F. | COLORED: Slaves, Mulatto, M. | COLORED: Slaves, Mulatto, F. | COLORED: Free, Black, M. | COLORED: Free, Black, F. | COLORED: Free, Mul., M | COLORED: Free, Mul., F. | Aggregate deaths. | |
|---|---|---|---|---|---|---|---|---|---|---|---|---|---|---|---|---|---|---|---|---|---|---|---|---|---|
| | | | | | | | 1 | | | | | | | 1 | 1 | | | | | | | | | 1 | 1 |
| | | | | 1 | 11 | 16 | 5 | 14 | 24 | 6 | 2 | 4 | 13 | 4 | 17 | 18 | 9 | 1 | | | | 1 | | 46 | 2 |
| | | | | | 25 | 8 | 6 | 16 | 32 | 12 | 2 | 2 | 10 | 8 | 18 | 12 | 25 | 4 | 3 | | 1 | 1 | | 64 | 3 |
| | | | | | 5 | 9 | | | 14 | | | | 3 | | 3 | 6 | | | | | 1 | 4 | | 14 | 4 |
| | | | | | | | | | | | | | | | | 1 | | | | | | | | 1 | 5 |
| | | | | | 1 | | | | 1 | | | | | | | | 1 | | | | | | | 1 | 6 |
| | | | | | | | 1 | | | | 1 | | 1 | | 1 | | | | | | | | | 1 | 7 |
| | | | | | 4 | 7 | 6 | 8 | 15 | 8 | 1 | 1 | 7 | 8 | 15 | 7 | 3 | | | | | | | 25 | 8 |
| | | | | | 9 | 9 | 2 | 5 | 5 | 8 | 4 | 8 | 8 | 2 | 10 | 9 | 5 | 1 | | | | | | 25 | 9 |
| | | | | | 5 | 3 | 4 | 3 | 5 | 3 | | 5 | 4 | 4 | 8 | 3 | 2 | 2 | | | | | | 15 | 10 |
| | | | | | 5 | 3 | 2 | 3 | 3 | 2 | 1 | 7 | 4 | 3 | 7 | 2 | 5 | | | | | | | 14 | 11 |
| | | | | | 7 | 10 | 7 | 10 | | 2 | 2 | 27 | 9 | 16 | 25 | 1 | 8 | | | | | | | 84 | 12 |
| | | | | | 10 | 7 | 10 | 9 | 7 | 22 | 5 | 4 | 4 | 7 | 11 | 13 | 14 | | 1 | | | | | 38 | 13 |
| | | | | | 14 | 11 | 15 | 10 | 22 | 8 | 4 | 2 | | 35 | 35 | | 14 | | 1 | | | | | 50 | 14 |
| | | | | | 2 | 3 | 1 | | 5 | 2 | | | 2 | | 2 | 2 | 3 | | | | | | | 7 | 15 |
| | | | | | 7 | 25 | 18 | 8 | 18 | 27 | 7 | 4 | 12 | 4 | 16 | 20 | 17 | 2 | | 1 | | 1 | 1 | 58 | 16 |
| | | | | | 2 | 9 | 1 | | 6 | 4 | 1 | 1 | 4 | 5 | 9 | 2 | 2 | | | | | | | 13 | 17 |
| | | | | | | 1 | | | | 1 | | | | 1 | 1 | | | | | | | | | 1 | 18 |
| | | | | | 9 | 9 | 4 | | 13 | 7 | | 2 | 9 | 2 | 11 | 2 | 6 | 1 | 2 | | | | | 23 | 19 |
| | | | | | | | 3 | | 1 | 2 | | | | 2 | 2 | | | | | | | 1 | | 3 | 20 |
| | | | | | 3 | 3 | | 2 | 3 | 4 | | 1 | 2 | 1 | 3 | 1 | 3 | | 1 | | | | | 8 | 21 |
| | | | 1 | | 84 | 78 | 48 | 47 | 13 | 7 | 30 | 186 | 53 | 93 | 146 | 41 | 59 | 1 | 7 | | 3 | 3 | 5 | 265 | 22 |
| | | | | | 20 | 14 | 14 | 9 | 32 | 13 | 1 | 8 | 11 | 17 | 28 | 13 | 14 | | 2 | | 1 | | | 58 | 23 |
| | | | | | 41 | 32 | 26 | 32 | 33 | 30 | 5 | 4 | 35 | 21 | 56 | 34 | 33 | 3 | 2 | | 1 | 1 | 1 | 131 | 24 |
| | | | | | 6 | 1 | 1 | 1 | 2 | | | 3 | 3 | 2 | 5 | 2 | 2 | | | | | | | 9 | 25 |
| | 1 | | | | 10 | 30 | 23 | 3 | 12 | 40 | 6 | 13 | 21 | 16 | 37 | 15 | 12 | 3 | 3 | | | 3 | 2 | 75 | 26 |
| | | | 1 | 1 | 81 | 91 | 64 | 61 | 13 | 25 | 28 | 211 | 120 | 71 | 191 | 48 | 43 | 2 | 4 | 1 | 3 | 4 | 1 | 297 | 27 |
| | | | | | 3 | 21 | 15 | 2 | 4 | 35 | 2 | | 21 | 9 | 30 | 3 | 7 | | | | 1 | | | 41 | 28 |
| | | | | | 8 | 4 | 2 | 1 | 1 | | 1 | 12 | 8 | 5 | 13 | 1 | 1 | | | | | | | 15 | 29 |
| | | | | | | 1 | | | | 1 | | | 1 | | 1 | | | | | | | | | 1 | 30 |
| | | | | | 3 | 6 | 3 | 4 | 3 | 11 | | 1 | 5 | 5 | 10 | 3 | 3 | | | | | | | 16 | 31 |
| | | | | | 16 | 23 | 31 | 13 | 14 | 50 | 12 | 6 | 33 | 18 | 51 | 12 | 15 | 1 | 5 | | | | | 84 | 32 |
| | | | | | 4 | 19 | 31 | 10 | 13 | 43 | 6 | 1 | 18 | 23 | 41 | 11 | 9 | | 2 | 1 | | 1 | 1 | 66 | 33 |
| | | | | | | 2 | | | 1 | | | 1 | | | | 1 | | 1 | | | | | | 2 | 34 |
| | | | | | | 7 | | 3 | | 8 | 1 | 1 | 4 | 3 | 7 | 1 | 1 | | | | | 1 | | 10 | 35 |

## CLASSIFICATION OF DEATHS IN NORTHERN MIDDLE

| | Cause of death. | AGE. Under 1. M. | F. | 1 and under 5. M. | F. | 5 and under 10. M. | F. | 10 and under 20. M. | F. | 20 and under 50. M. | F. | 50 and under 80. M. | F. | 80 and under 100. M | F. | 100 & over. M | F. | Age unknown. M | F. | NATIVITIES. Born in State. | N. England States. | Middle States. | Southern States. | Southwest'n States. | Northeast'n States. |
|---|---|---|---|---|---|---|---|---|---|---|---|---|---|---|---|---|---|---|---|---|---|---|---|---|---|
| 1 | Fever, congestive | | 1 | 3 | | 2 | 2 | 2 | 6 | 11 | 11 | 3 | 5 | | 1 | | | | | 41 | | | 6 | | |
| 2 | ..do..intermittent | 2 | 4 | 1 | 3 | 1 | 1 | | 1 | 2 | 4 | 2 | 6 | 1 | | | | | | 28 | | | | | |
| 3 | ..do..puerperal | | | | | | | | | | 8 | | | | | | | | | 7 | | 1 | | | |
| 4 | ..do..remittent | | | | | | | 1 | 1 | 2 | | | | | | | | | | 4 | | | | | |
| 5 | ..do..scarlet | 2 | 1 | 1 | 5 | | 1 | | 1 | | 1 | | | | | | | | | 12 | | | | | |
| 6 | ..do..typhoid | | | 4 | 4 | 3 | 4 | 14 | 9 | 24 | 16 | 6 | 3 | | | | | | | 81 | | | 6 | | |
| 7 | ..do..winter | | | | | | | | | | | | | | 1 | | | | | 1 | | | | | |
| 8 | Gravel | | | 1 | | | | | | 1 | 1 | 17 | 1 | 4 | | | | | | 23 | | 1 | 1 | | |
| 9 | Heart, disease of | | 1 | 1 | 1 | | 2 | | 1 | 5 | 1 | 1 | 1 | | | | | | | 13 | | | 1 | | |
| 10 | Hemorrhage | | | 1 | | | | 1 | 1 | 5 | 2 | | | | | | | | | 10 | | | | | |
| 11 | Hernia | | | | | | | 1 | | | | | | 1 | | | | | | 2 | | | | | |
| 12 | Hives | 5 | 1 | | | | | | | | | | | | | | | | | 6 | | | | | |
| 13 | Hooping cough | 4 | 18 | 12 | 10 | 2 | | | | | | | | | | | | | | 41 | | | | | |
| 14 | Hydrocephalus | 2 | 1 | 2 | | | 2 | | | | | | | | | | | | | 7 | | | | | |
| 15 | Inflammation | 2 | 1 | 2 | 2 | 1 | 1 | | | 2 | | 1 | 1 | | | | | | | 12 | | 1 | | | |
| 16 | ...do......bowels | 5 | 2 | 1 | 3 | 1 | 1 | 1 | 2 | 5 | 2 | 2 | | | | | | | | 23 | | | 2 | | |
| 17 | ....do......brain | 8 | 2 | 6 | 1 | 1 | 3 | 1 | 4 | 3 | 5 | | | | | | | | | 32 | | | | 2 | |
| 18 | ....do......stomach | 1 | | | | | | | | 1 | 2 | 2 | | | | | | | | 6 | | | | | |
| 19 | Insanity | | | | | | | | | 1 | | 2 | | | | | | | | 2 | | | 1 | | |
| 20 | Intemperance | | | | | | | | | 7 | | 4 | 1 | | | | | | | 11 | | | 1 | | |
| 21 | Jaundice | 2 | | | | | 1 | | | 1 | | 1 | 3 | | | | | | | 8 | | | | | |
| 22 | Kidneys, disease of | | | | | | | | | | 1 | 3 | 1 | 2 | | | | | | 7 | | | | | |
| 23 | Killed | | | | | | | | | 1 | | 1 | | | | | | | | 2 | | | | | |
| 24 | Lightning | | | | | | | | | | 1 | | | | | | | | | 1 | | | | | |
| 25 | Liver, disease of | 1 | | 2 | | | | 4 | 1 | 1 | 6 | 4 | 5 | | | | | | | 22 | 1 | | | 1 | |
| 26 | Lockjaw | 2 | | | 1 | | | | | 1 | | 1 | | | | | | | | 5 | | | | | |
| 27 | Lungs, disease of | | 1 | 1 | | | | 1 | | 1 | 2 | 3 | 6 | | | | | | | 14 | | | 1 | | |
| 28 | Malformation | | 4 | 1 | | | | | | | | | | | | | | | | 5 | | | | | |
| 29 | Mania-a-potu | | | | | | | | | 1 | | | | | | | | | | 1 | | | | | |
| 30 | Marasmus | | | | | | | | 1 | | | | | | | | | | | 1 | | | | | |
| 31 | Measles | 5 | 1 | 12 | 8 | 1 | 1 | 3 | | 2 | 3 | | 2 | | | | | | | 38 | | | | | |
| 32 | Mercury, effects of | | | | | | | 1 | | | | | | | | | | | | 1 | | | | | |
| 33 | Mortification | | | | | | | | | | | | 1 | | | | | | | 1 | | | | | |
| 34 | Mumps | | | | | | | 1 | | | | | | | | | | | | 1 | | | | | |
| 35 | Murder | | | | | | | | | 2 | | | | | | | | | | 2 | | | | | |
| 36 | Neuralgia | | | | | 1 | | 1 | | | 1 | | 2 | | | | | | | 5 | | | | | |
| 37 | Old age | | | | | | | | | | | 24 | 30 | 50 | 58 | 5 | 13 | | | 130 | | 9 | 37 | | |
| 38 | Paralysis | | | 1 | 1 | | | 1 | 2 | 5 | 5 | 11 | 16 | 4 | 4 | | | | 1 | 44 | | 2 | 5 | | |
| 39 | Pleurisy | 1 | | 5 | 1 | | | 2 | 3 | 13 | 4 | 3 | 6 | 1 | | | | 1 | | 35 | | | 2 | 1 | |
| 40 | Pneumonia | 12 | 6 | 21 | 19 | 7 | 8 | 35 | 23 | 87 | 52 | 44 | 32 | 6 | 6 | 1 | | | | 330 | | | 27 | | |
| 41 | Poison | | | | 1 | 1 | | 1 | 1 | 3 | | 1 | 1 | | | | | | | 8 | | | 1 | | |
| 42 | Quinsy | | | 1 | 2 | 1 | 1 | | | 2 | 1 | 1 | 1 | | | | | | | 10 | | | | | |
| 43 | Rheumatism | | | | | 2 | | 4 | 1 | 3 | 1 | 5 | 7 | 1 | | | | | | 19 | | | 4 | | |
| 44 | Rickets | | | 1 | 1 | | | | | | | | | | | | | | | 2 | | | | | |
| 45 | Scrofula | 2 | 1 | 7 | 6 | 1 | 2 | 7 | | 4 | 3 | 3 | | | | | | | | 34 | | | 2 | | |
| 46 | Small pox | | | | | | | 1 | | | 1 | | | | | | | | | 2 | | | | | |
| 47 | Spine, disease of | 2 | 1 | | | | 1 | 2 | | 1 | | | | | | | | | | 7 | | | | | |
| 48 | Spleen... do | | 2 | | | | | | | | 1 | | | | | | | | | 3 | | | | | |
| 49 | Stillborn | 6 | 4 | | | | | | | | | | | | | | | | | 10 | | | | | |
| 50 | Stomach, disease of | | | | | | | | | | | | | | | | | | | | | | | | |
| 51 | Suffocation | 17 | 28 | 5 | 1 | | | | | | | 1 | | | | | | | | 47 | | | | | |
| 52 | Suicide | | | | | | | | | 4 | | 1 | | | | | | | | 4 | | 1 | | | |
| 53 | Syphilis | | | | | | | | | | 1 | | | | | | | | | 1 | | | | | |
| 54 | Teething | 4 | 2 | 5 | 6 | | | | | | | | | | | | | | | 16 | | | 1 | | |
| 55 | Tetanus | | | | | | | | | 1 | | | | | | | | | | 1 | | | | | |
| 56 | Throat, disease of | 1 | 1 | | 1 | | 1 | | | 1 | | | 1 | | | | | | | 6 | | | | | |
| 57 | Thrush | 1 | 3 | 1 | 1 | | | | | | | | | | | | | | | 6 | | | | | |
| 58 | Ulcer | | | | | | | | | 1 | 1 | 2 | | | | | | | | 3 | | | | | |
| 59 | Uterus, disease of | | | | | | | | | | 4 | | 1 | | | | | | | 4 | | | 1 | | |
| 60 | Venereal | | | | | | | | 1 | 1 | 2 | 1 | | | | | | | | 5 | | | | | |
| 61 | White swelling | | | | | 1 | | 1 | 1 | 1 | | | | | | | | | | 4 | | | | | |
| 62 | Worms | 2 | 4 | 20 | 25 | 1 | 4 | 2 | 1 | | | | | | | | | | | 59 | | | | | |
| 63 | Unknown | 199 | 122 | 106 | 90 | 25 | 21 | 24 | 36 | 41 | 105 | 70 | 78 | 11 | 11 | | | 1 | | 910 | | 4 | 24 | | |
| | Total | 403 | 304 | 375 | 319 | 97 | 103 | 191 | 175 | 433 | 496 | 377 | 348 | 102 | 100 | 6 | 13 | 3 | 2 | 3582 | 6 | 29 | 208 | 5 | ... |

## CLASSIFICATION OF DEATHS IN SOUTHERN MIDDLE

*Embracing the following counties : Anson, Bladen, Cabarras, Columbus, Cumberland, Johnson,*

| | | | | | | | | | | | | | | | | | | | | | | | | | |
|---|---|---|---|---|---|---|---|---|---|---|---|---|---|---|---|---|---|---|---|---|---|---|---|---|---|
| 1 | Abscess | 1 | | | | | | | | 1 | | | | | | | | | | 2 | | | | | |
| 2 | Accident, not specf'd | 4 | 6 | 2 | 2 | 1 | 1 | 4 | 2 | 3 | 1 | 1 | | 3 | 1 | 1 | | | | 31 | | | 1 | | |

## [S]ECTION OF THE STATE OF NORTH CAROLINA—Continued.

| NATIVITIES. | | | | | SEASON OF DECEASE. | | | | DURATION OF SICKNESS. | | | | WHITES. | | | COLORED. | | | | | | | | | |
|---|---|---|---|---|---|---|---|---|---|---|---|---|---|---|---|---|---|---|---|---|---|---|---|---|---|
| | | | | | | | | | | | | | | | | Slaves. | | | | Free. | | | | | |
| | | | | | | | | | | | | | | | | Black. | | Mulatto. | | Black. | | Mul. | | | |
| [Ter]ritories. | Ireland. | Germany. | Other foreign countries. | Unknown. | Spring. | Summer. | Autumn. | Winter. | Under 1 week. | 1 week and under 1 month. | 1 month and under 3 months. | 3 months and over. | Males. | Females. | Total. | M. | F. | M. | F. | M. | F. | M | F. | Aggregate deaths. | |
| ... | ... | ... | ... | ... | 7 | 8 | 25 | 7 | 20 | 25 | 2 | ... | 12 | 16 | 28 | 6 | 10 | 1 | ... | 1 | ... | 1 | ... | 47 | 1 |
| ... | ... | ... | ... | ... | 4 | 6 | 12 | 5 | 2 | 9 | 5 | 11 | 7 | 14 | 21 | 2 | 4 | ... | ... | ... | 1 | ... | ... | 28 | 2 |
| ... | ... | ... | ... | ... | 2 | 4 | ... | 2 | 1 | 7 | ... | ... | ... | 8 | 8 | ... | ... | ... | ... | ... | ... | ... | ... | 8 | 3 |
| ... | ... | ... | ... | ... | ... | ... | 1 | 3 | ... | 2 | 2 | ... | 2 | ... | 2 | 1 | 1 | ... | ... | ... | ... | ... | ... | 4 | 4 |
| ... | ... | ... | ... | ... | 4 | 2 | 2 | 4 | 2 | 8 | ... | 2 | 2 | 7 | 9 | 1 | 2 | ... | ... | ... | ... | ... | ... | 12 | 5 |
| ... | ... | ... | ... | ... | 18 | 16 | 35 | 18 | 8 | 43 | 29 | 4 | 25 | 23 | 48 | 24 | 10 | ... | ... | 1 | 1 | 1 | 2 | 87 | 6 |
| ... | ... | ... | ... | ... | ... | ... | ... | ... | 1 | ... | ... | ... | ... | ... | ... | ... | 1 | ... | ... | ... | ... | ... | ... | 1 | 7 |
| ... | ... | ... | ... | ... | 6 | 9 | 6 | 3 | 2 | 9 | 1 | 12 | 14 | 1 | 15 | 7 | 1 | ... | ... | 1 | ... | 1 | ... | 25 | 8 |
| ... | ... | ... | ... | ... | 7 | 2 | ... | 5 | 4 | ... | 2 | 8 | 5 | 4 | 9 | 2 | 3 | ... | ... | ... | ... | ... | ... | 14 | 9 |
| ... | ... | ... | ... | ... | 4 | 4 | 1 | 1 | ... | 4 | 1 | 4 | 6 | ... | 6 | 1 | 3 | ... | ... | ... | ... | ... | ... | 10 | 10 |
| ... | ... | ... | ... | ... | ... | 1 | ... | 1 | ... | 2 | ... | ... | 1 | ... | 1 | 1 | ... | ... | ... | ... | ... | ... | ... | 2 | 11 |
| ... | ... | ... | ... | ... | 2 | 1 | 2 | 1 | 3 | 2 | ... | ... | 4 | ... | 4 | 1 | 1 | ... | ... | ... | ... | ... | ... | 6 | 12 |
| ... | ... | ... | ... | ... | 7 | 19 | 10 | 5 | 3 | 24 | 11 | 1 | 7 | 4 | 11 | 8 | 11 | ... | 3 | 3 | 3 | ... | 2 | 41 | 13 |
| ... | ... | ... | ... | ... | ... | 3 | 2 | 2 | 1 | 4 | 1 | 1 | 2 | 2 | 4 | 2 | 1 | ... | ... | ... | ... | ... | ... | 7 | 14 |
| ... | ... | ... | ... | ... | 3 | 7 | 2 | 1 | 2 | 3 | 2 | 1 | 1 | 2 | 3 | 6 | 3 | 1 | ... | ... | ... | ... | ... | 13 | 15 |
| ... | ... | ... | ... | ... | 5 | 9 | 10 | 1 | 11 | 8 | 3 | 3 | 8 | 6 | 14 | 6 | 4 | 1 | ... | ... | ... | ... | ... | 25 | 16 |
| ... | ... | ... | ... | ... | 12 | 11 | 5 | 6 | 14 | 15 | ... | 4 | 14 | 8 | 22 | 5 | 6 | ... | 1 | ... | ... | ... | ... | 34 | 17 |
| ... | ... | ... | ... | ... | 5 | ... | ... | 1 | 2 | 2 | 1 | 1 | 2 | ... | 2 | 2 | 2 | ... | ... | ... | ... | ... | ... | 6 | 18 |
| ... | ... | ... | ... | ... | 1 | 1 | ... | 1 | ... | 2 | ... | ... | 1 | ... | 1 | 2 | ... | ... | ... | ... | ... | ... | ... | 3 | 19 |
| ... | ... | ... | ... | ... | 3 | 3 | 2 | 4 | 2 | 4 | 3 | 2 | 11 | 1 | 12 | ... | ... | ... | ... | ... | ... | ... | ... | 12 | 20 |
| ... | ... | ... | ... | ... | 2 | 2 | 1 | 3 | 1 | 3 | 1 | 3 | 4 | 4 | 8 | ... | ... | ... | ... | ... | ... | ... | ... | 8 | 21 |
| ... | ... | ... | ... | ... | 2 | 3 | ... | 2 | ... | ... | 3 | 3 | 2 | 2 | 4 | 3 | ... | ... | ... | ... | ... | ... | ... | 7 | 22 |
| ... | ... | ... | ... | ... | ... | ... | 2 | ... | 1 | ... | ... | ... | 2 | ... | 2 | ... | ... | ... | ... | ... | ... | ... | ... | 2 | 23 |
| ... | ... | ... | ... | ... | ... | ... | 1 | ... | 1 | ... | ... | ... | ... | 1 | 1 | ... | ... | ... | ... | ... | ... | ... | ... | 1 | 24 |
| ... | ... | ... | ... | ... | 3 | 9 | 7 | 5 | 1 | 6 | 2 | 14 | 9 | 10 | 19 | 3 | 2 | ... | ... | ... | ... | ... | ... | 24 | 25 |
| ... | ... | ... | ... | ... | 2 | ... | 1 | 2 | 1 | 3 | ... | ... | 1 | ... | 1 | 3 | 1 | ... | ... | ... | ... | ... | ... | 5 | 26 |
| ... | ... | ... | ... | ... | 6 | 2 | 4 | 3 | 4 | 5 | 1 | 4 | 1 | 5 | 6 | 5 | 3 | ... | ... | ... | ... | ... | 1 | 15 | 27 |
| ... | ... | ... | ... | ... | 1 | 2 | 2 | ... | ... | 1 | 1 | 1 | ... | 1 | 1 | 1 | 3 | ... | ... | ... | ... | ... | ... | 5 | 28 |
| ... | ... | ... | ... | ... | 1 | ... | ... | ... | ... | 1 | ... | ... | 1 | ... | 1 | ... | ... | ... | ... | ... | ... | ... | ... | 1 | 29 |
| ... | ... | ... | ... | ... | ... | 1 | ... | ... | ... | ... | ... | 1 | ... | ... | ... | ... | 1 | ... | ... | ... | ... | ... | ... | 1 | 30 |
| ... | ... | ... | ... | ... | 11 | 15 | 7 | 5 | 7 | 20 | 7 | 3 | 10 | 8 | 18 | 13 | 4 | ... | 2 | ... | ... | ... | 1 | 38 | 31 |
| ... | ... | ... | ... | ... | 1 | ... | ... | ... | ... | ... | 1 | ... | 1 | ... | 1 | ... | ... | ... | ... | ... | ... | ... | ... | 1 | 32 |
| ... | ... | ... | ... | ... | ... | ... | ... | 1 | ... | ... | ... | 1 | ... | 1 | 1 | ... | ... | ... | ... | ... | ... | ... | ... | 1 | 33 |
| ... | ... | ... | ... | ... | 1 | ... | ... | ... | ... | ... | 1 | ... | 1 | ... | 1 | ... | ... | ... | ... | ... | ... | ... | ... | 1 | 34 |
| ... | ... | ... | ... | ... | ... | ... | ... | 2 | 2 | ... | ... | ... | 2 | ... | 2 | ... | ... | ... | ... | ... | ... | ... | ... | 2 | 35 |
| ... | ... | ... | ... | ... | 1 | 3 | ... | 1 | ... | 1 | 1 | 3 | 2 | 2 | 4 | ... | ... | ... | ... | ... | ... | ... | 1 | 5 | 36 |
| ... | ... | ... | 2 | 2 | 53 | 50 | 42 | 35 | 21 | 29 | 7 | 26 | 29 | 40 | 69 | 44 | 58 | 3 | 2 | 3 | 8 | ... | 8 | 180 | 37 |
| ... | ... | ... | ... | ... | 16 | 15 | 12 | 8 | 14 | 10 | 2 | 23 | 20 | 21 | 41 | 2 | 8 | ... | ... | ... | ... | ... | ... | 51 | 38 |
| ... | ... | ... | ... | 2 | 16 | 9 | 6 | 9 | 12 | 21 | 4 | 3 | 14 | 8 | 22 | 10 | 6 | ... | ... | 1 | ... | 1 | ... | 40 | 39 |
| 1 | ... | ... | ... | 1 | 176 | 63 | 37 | 80 | 83 | 215 | 23 | 16 | 101 | 79 | 180 | 103 | 60 | 3 | 6 | 3 | ... | 3 | 1 | 359 | 40 |
| ... | ... | ... | ... | ... | 1 | 3 | 4 | 1 | 1 | 3 | 4 | 1 | 2 | ... | 2 | 3 | 2 | ... | 1 | ... | ... | 1 | ... | 9 | 41 |
| ... | ... | ... | ... | ... | ... | 3 | 2 | 4 | 5 | 4 | 1 | ... | 3 | 4 | 7 | 2 | 1 | ... | ... | ... | ... | ... | ... | 10 | 42 |
| ... | ... | ... | ... | 1 | 2 | 6 | 8 | 8 | 5 | 5 | 2 | 11 | 9 | 7 | 16 | 4 | 1 | 1 | 1 | 1 | ... | ... | ... | 24 | 43 |
| ... | ... | ... | ... | ... | 2 | ... | ... | ... | 1 | 1 | ... | ... | ... | ... | ... | 1 | 1 | ... | ... | ... | ... | ... | ... | 2 | 44 |
| ... | ... | ... | ... | ... | 14 | 10 | 8 | 4 | ... | 4 | 4 | 25 | 5 | 1 | 6 | 18 | 11 | ... | ... | ... | ... | 1 | ... | 36 | 45 |
| ... | ... | ... | ... | ... | ... | 1 | ... | 1 | 2 | ... | ... | ... | ... | 1 | 1 | 1 | ... | ... | ... | ... | ... | ... | ... | 2 | 46 |
| ... | ... | ... | ... | ... | 2 | 3 | ... | 2 | 1 | 1 | ... | 3 | 2 | 1 | 3 | 2 | 1 | 1 | ... | ... | ... | ... | ... | 7 | 47 |
| ... | ... | ... | ... | ... | ... | 1 | 1 | 1 | ... | ... | ... | 2 | ... | 2 | 2 | ... | 1 | ... | ... | ... | ... | ... | ... | 3 | 48 |
| ... | ... | ... | ... | ... | 3 | 4 | 3 | ... | ... | ... | ... | ... | 5 | 3 | 8 | 1 | 1 | ... | ... | ... | ... | ... | ... | 10 | 49 |
| ... | ... | ... | ... | ... | ... | ... | ... | ... | ... | ... | ... | ... | ... | ... | ... | ... | ... | ... | ... | ... | ... | ... | ... | ... | 50 |
| ... | ... | ... | ... | ... | 12 | 13 | 9 | 12 | 47 | ... | ... | ... | 5 | ... | 5 | 16 | 20 | 1 | 1 | 1 | 2 | ... | 1 | 47 | 51 |
| ... | ... | ... | ... | ... | 2 | 2 | ... | 1 | 4 | ... | ... | ... | 5 | ... | 5 | ... | ... | ... | ... | ... | ... | ... | ... | 5 | 52 |
| ... | ... | ... | ... | ... | ... | ... | 1 | ... | ... | ... | ... | 1 | ... | ... | ... | ... | 1 | ... | ... | ... | ... | ... | ... | 1 | 53 |
| ... | ... | ... | ... | ... | 6 | 2 | 5 | 3 | 5 | 10 | 1 | ... | 1 | 4 | 5 | 7 | 3 | 1 | 1 | ... | ... | ... | ... | 17 | 54 |
| ... | ... | ... | ... | ... | 1 | ... | ... | ... | ... | 1 | ... | ... | ... | ... | ... | 1 | ... | ... | ... | ... | ... | ... | ... | 1 | 55 |
| ... | ... | ... | ... | ... | ... | 1 | 1 | 4 | 1 | 2 | 1 | ... | 1 | 3 | 4 | ... | 1 | 1 | ... | ... | ... | ... | ... | 6 | 56 |
| ... | ... | ... | ... | ... | ... | 2 | 2 | 2 | 3 | 1 | 2 | ... | 1 | 2 | 3 | 1 | 1 | ... | ... | ... | ... | ... | 1 | 6 | 57 |
| ... | ... | ... | ... | 1 | ... | 2 | 2 | ... | ... | 1 | 2 | 1 | 2 | 1 | 3 | 1 | ... | ... | ... | ... | ... | ... | ... | 4 | 58 |
| ... | ... | ... | ... | ... | 2 | 2 | 1 | ... | ... | ... | 1 | 3 | ... | 2 | 2 | ... | 2 | ... | ... | ... | 1 | ... | ... | 5 | 59 |
| ... | ... | ... | ... | ... | 2 | 1 | 1 | 1 | 1 | 1 | ... | 3 | ... | 1 | 1 | 1 | 1 | 1 | ... | ... | 1 | ... | ... | 5 | 60 |
| ... | ... | ... | ... | ... | ... | 1 | 1 | 2 | ... | 1 | 1 | 2 | 1 | 1 | 2 | 1 | ... | ... | ... | ... | ... | 1 | ... | 4 | 61 |
| ... | ... | ... | ... | ... | 13 | 19 | 11 | 16 | 18 | 24 | 5 | 11 | 5 | 12 | 17 | 15 | 22 | 2 | ... | 1 | ... | 2 | ... | 59 | 62 |
| ... | ... | ... | ... | 2 | 263 | 301 | 205 | 171 | 366 | 188 | 91 | 223 | 230 | 180 | 410 | 218 | 241 | 17 | 18 | 5 | 8 | 7 | 16 | 940 | 63 |
| 1 | 1 | .. | 4 | 11 | 1102 | 1114 | 846 | 735 | 1047 | 1116 | 354 | 946 | 1026 | 888 | 1914 | 841 | 831 | 56 | 69 | 24 | 32 | 40 | 40 | 3847 | |

## SECTION OF THE STATE OF NORTH CAROLINA.

*Mecklenburg, Montgomery, Moore, Richmond, Robeson, Sampson, Stanley, Union, and Wayne.*

| | | | | | | | | | | | | | | | | | | | | | | | | | |
|---|---|---|---|---|---|---|---|---|---|---|---|---|---|---|---|---|---|---|---|---|---|---|---|---|---|
| ... | ... | .. | ... | ... | 1 | 1 | ... | ... | ... | 1 | ... | 1 | 1 | ... | 1 | 1 | ... | ... | ... | ... | ... | .. | .. | 2 | 1 |
| ... | ... | .. | 1 | 1 | 8 | 7 | 7 | 9 | 25 | 3 | ... | ... | 7 | 6 | 13 | 12 | 7 | ... | ... | ... | ... | .. | .. | 32 | 2 |

## CLASSIFICATION OF DEATHS IN SOUTHERN MIDDLE

| | Cause of death. | AGES. | | | | | | | | | | | | | | | | | | NATIVITIES. | | | | | |
|---|---|---|---|---|---|---|---|---|---|---|---|---|---|---|---|---|---|---|---|---|---|---|---|---|---|
| | | Under 1. | | 1 and under 5. | | 5 and under 10. | | 10 and under 20. | | 20 and under 50. | | 50 and under 80. | | 80 and under 100. | | 100 & over. | | Age unknown. | | Born in State. | N. England States. | Middle States. | Southern States. | Southwest'n States. | Northwest'n States. |
| | | M. | F. | M. | F. | M. | F. | M. | F. | M. | F. | M. | F. | M | F. | M | F. | M | F. | | | | | | |
| 1 | Accident, burned | 8 | 8 | 8 | 3 | 4 | 10 | | 6 | 1 | | 1 | 1 | 1 | | | | | | 41 | | | | | |
| 2 | ....do...drowned | | | | | 2 | | 2 | | 5 | | | 1 | | | | | | | 10 | | | | | |
| 3 | ....do...scalded | | | 1 | | | | | | | | | | | | | | | | 1 | | | | | |
| 4 | ....do...gunshot | | | | | | | | | 3 | | | | | | | | | | 3 | | | | | |
| 5 | Apoplexy | | | | | | | 1 | | 2 | 1 | 2 | | | | | | | | 6 | | | | | |
| 6 | Asthma | | | | | | | | | | | | | | 1 | | | | | | | | | | |
| 7 | Black tongue | | | 1 | | | | | | | | | | | | | | | | 1 | | | | | |
| 8 | Bowels, disease of | 1 | 3 | 3 | | | | | | | | | | | | | | | | 7 | | | | | |
| 9 | Brain .....do | 2 | | 1 | 1 | | | | | | | | | | | | | | | 4 | | | | | |
| 10 | Bronchitis | 1 | | 2 | 2 | | | | | 1 | 2 | | | | | | | | | 8 | | | | | |
| 11 | Cancer | | | | | | 2 | | | | 3 | 2 | 4 | | 1 | | | | | 12 | | | | | |
| 12 | Catarrh | 3 | 2 | 3 | 1 | | | 2 | | 3 | 3 | 1 | 2 | | | | | | | 19 | | | | | |
| 13 | Childbirth | | | | | | | | 3 | | 21 | | | | | | | | | 23 | | | 1 | | |
| 14 | Cholera | | | | | | 1 | | 1 | 1 | | | | | | | | | | 3 | | | | | |
| 15 | ...do..infantum | | | 2 | 3 | | | | | | | | | | | | | | | 4 | | | 1 | | |
| 16 | ...do..morbus | 1 | | 1 | 4 | 1 | | | | | 2 | 1 | | | | | | | | 10 | | | | | |
| 17 | Colic | 2 | | | | | | 2 | | 3 | 2 | 3 | 1 | | | | | | | 11 | | | | | |
| 18 | Congestion of brain | 1 | | | | | | | | | | | | | | | | | | 1 | | | | | |
| 19 | Consumption | | | 1 | | | | 2 | 3 | 22 | 27 | 12 | 12 | 2 | | | | | | 70 | | 1 | 4 | 1 | |
| 20 | Convulsions | 9 | 4 | 3 | | 1 | 2 | 2 | 2 | 1 | 1 | 4 | | | | | | | | 29 | | | | | |
| 21 | Croup | 14 | 17 | 11 | 6 | 1 | 3 | | | | | | | | | | | | | 52 | | | | | |
| 22 | Debility | | | | | | | | | | | | | 1 | | | | | | 1 | | | | | |
| 23 | Diabetes | | | | | | | | | 1 | | 1 | | | | | | | | 2 | | | | | |
| 24 | Diarrhœa | 4 | 4 | 6 | 2 | | | 1 | | 3 | 1 | 1 | | | | | | | | 22 | | | | | |
| 25 | Dropsy | | | 3 | 4 | 5 | 5 | 10 | 6 | 20 | 19 | 15 | 22 | 2 | 7 | | | | | 108 | 2 | 1 | 4 | | |
| 26 | Dysentery | 1 | 1 | 1 | 2 | 1 | 1 | 2 | | | | | 2 | | | | | | | 11 | | | | | |
| 27 | Dyspepsia | | | | | | 1 | | | 1 | | 1 | 1 | | | | | | | 4 | | | | | |
| 28 | Eating dirt | | | | | | | | | | | | | | | | | | | | | | | | |
| 29 | Erysipelas | 1 | | 1 | | | | | | 1 | | | 1 | | | | | | | 4 | | | | | |
| 30 | Executed, hung | | | | | | | | | 1 | | | | | | | | | | 1 | | | | | |
| 31 | Fever, not specified | 2 | 3 | 20 | 6 | 6 | 6 | 10 | 19 | 29 | 20 | 9 | 6 | 2 | | | | | | 137 | | 1 | | | |
| 32 | ..do..bilious | | | 1 | 2 | 4 | 2 | 2 | 3 | 7 | 5 | 3 | 5 | | | | | | | 34 | | | | | |
| 33 | ..do..brain | | | | | | | | | | 3 | | | | | | | | | 3 | | | | | |
| 34 | ..do..catarrhal | 1 | | | | | | | | | | | | | | | | | | 1 | | | | | |
| 35 | ..do..congestive | | | 2 | 1 | 1 | 1 | | | 1 | | | 1 | | | | | | | 7 | | | | | |
| 36 | ..do. inflammatory | | | | 1 | | | | | | | | | | | | | | | 1 | | | | | |
| 37 | ..do..intermittent | 2 | 1 | | | | | | | | 1 | 1 | 1 | | | | | | | 6 | | | | | |
| 38 | ..do..puerperal | | | | | | | | | | 5 | | | | | | | | | 5 | | | | | |
| 39 | ..do..scarlet | | 1 | 1 | | | 1 | | 1 | | | | | | | | | | | 4 | | | | | |
| 40 | ..do..typhoid | | 1 | 4 | 3 | 2 | 4 | 17 | 13 | 28 | 29 | 6 | 4 | 1 | 1 | | | | | 109 | | 1 | 2 | | |
| 41 | ..do..yellow | | | | | | | | | 1 | | | | | | | | | | 1 | | | | | |
| 42 | Gravel | | | | | | | | | | | 3 | | | | | | 1 | | 4 | | | | | |
| 43 | Heart, disease of | | | | | | 1 | | | | | | 1 | | | | | | | 2 | | | | | |
| 44 | Hemorrhage | | | | | | | | | | 1 | | | | | | | | | 1 | | | | | |
| 45 | Hernia | | | | | | | | | 2 | 1 | | | 1 | | | | | | 4 | | | | | |
| 46 | Hip, disease of | | | | | | | | | | | | | | | | | | | | | | | | |
| 47 | Hives | 3 | 4 | | | | | | | | | | | | | | | | | 6 | | | | 1 | |
| 48 | Hooping cough | 9 | 13 | 9 | 16 | 1 | 4 | 1 | | | | | | | | | | | | 53 | | | | | |
| 49 | Inflammation | 2 | | 1 | 1 | 1 | | 2 | 1 | 4 | 2 | | | | | | | | | 14 | | | | | |
| 50 | .....do.....bowels | 4 | | 1 | | 1 | | 2 | | 3 | 2 | 2 | 2 | | | | | | | 17 | | | | | |
| 51 | .....do.....brain | 2 | 2 | 4 | 2 | | | | | 3 | | | | | | | | | | 12 | | | 1 | | |
| 52 | .....do.....stomach | | 1 | | | | | | | | | | | | | | | | | 1 | | | | | |
| 53 | Intemperance | | | | | | | | | 2 | | 1 | | | | | | | | 2 | | | 1 | | |
| 54 | Insanity | | | | | | | | | | | 1 | | | | | | | | 1 | | | | | |
| 55 | Jaundice | | | | | | | | | 1 | 1 | | | | | | | | | 2 | | | | | |
| 56 | Kidneys, disease of | | | | | | | | | | | 2 | 1 | 1 | | | | | | 5 | | | | | |
| 57 | Lightning | | | | | | | | | 1 | | | | | | | | | | 1 | | | 1 | | |
| 58 | Liver, disease of | 1 | 1 | | 2 | | | 1 | 3 | 4 | 2 | 3 | 3 | | | | | | | 16 | | | 2 | 1 | |
| 59 | Lockjaw | | | | | | | 1 | | | 1 | | | | | | | | | 2 | | | | | |
| 60 | Lungs, disease of | | | | | | | | | 1 | 1 | | | | | | | | | 1 | | | 1 | | |
| 61 | Malformation | 1 | | 1 | | | | | | | | | | | | | | | | 2 | | | | | |
| 62 | Measles | | | 5 | 4 | | | 2 | 1 | 1 | 1 | | | | | | | | | 14 | | | | | |
| 63 | Mortification | | | | | | | | | | 2 | | | | | | | | | 1 | | | 1 | | |
| 64 | Murder | | | | | | | | | 2 | | | | | | | | | | 2 | | | | | |
| 65 | Neuralgia | | | | | | | | | 2 | 1 | | | | | | | | | 2 | | | 1 | | |
| 66 | Old age | | | | | | | | | | | 5 | 12 | 16 | 17 | 1 | 2 | | | 33 | | 1 | 11 | | |
| 67 | Paralysis | | | | | | | 1 | | 4 | 1 | 3 | 5 | 1 | | | | | | 14 | | | | | |
| 68 | Pleurisy | 1 | | 2 | | 2 | | 4 | 2 | 2 | 3 | 1 | 2 | | | | | | | 19 | | | | | |
| 69 | Pneumonia | 2 | 2 | 5 | 3 | 4 | 1 | 15 | 6 | 23 | 18 | 9 | 15 | | 1 | | | | | 101 | | | 3 | | |
| 70 | Poison | 1 | | 4 | | 2 | | 1 | 1 | 2 | 2 | | | | | | | | | 13 | | | | | |
| 71 | Prematurity of birth | 1 | | | | | | | | | | | | | | | | | | 1 | | | | | |
| 72 | Quinsy | | | | | | | | 1 | 1 | 2 | | 1 | | | | | | | 5 | | | | | |
| 73 | Rheumatism | | | | | | | 1 | | | 1 | 2 | 2 | | | | | | | 4 | | | 2 | | |
| 74 | Rickets | | | 1 | | | | | | | 1 | | | | | | | | | 2 | | | | | |
| 75 | Scrofula | 1 | 1 | 1 | 2 | | | | | | | | 1 | | | | | | | 6 | | | | | |

## SECTION OF THE STATE OF NORTH CAROLINA—Continued.

| Nativities: California and Territories. | Ireland. | Germany. | Other foreign countries. | Unknown. | Season of decease: Spring. | Summer. | Autumn. | Winter. | Duration of sickness: Under 1 week. | 1 week and under 1 month. | 1 month and under 3 months. | 3 months and over. | Whites: Males. | Females. | Total. | Colored: Slaves: Black: M. | F. | Mulatto: M. | F. | Free: Black: M. | F. | Mul. M | F. | Aggregate deaths. | |
|---|---|---|---|---|---|---|---|---|---|---|---|---|---|---|---|---|---|---|---|---|---|---|---|---|---|
| | | | | | 13 | 5 | 8 | 15 | 25 | 10 | 1 | 1 | 7 | 3 | 10 | 11 | 18 | | 1 | | | | 1 | 41 | 1 |
| | | | | | 4 | 2 | 2 | 2 | 10 | | | | | | | 7 | 1 | | | | | 2 | | 10 | 2 |
| | | | | | 1 | | | | 1 | | | | 1 | | 1 | | | | | | | | | 1 | 3 |
| | | | | | 1 | | 1 | | 3 | | | | 2 | | 2 | | | | | | | 1 | | 3 | 4 |
| | | | | | 1 | 1 | 3 | 1 | | | | | 4 | | 4 | 1 | 1 | | | | | | | 6 | 5 |
| | | | 1 | | 1 | | | | | | | | | 1 | 1 | | | | | | | | | 1 | 6 |
| | | | | | | | 1 | | | 1 | | | 1 | | 1 | | | | | | | | | 1 | 7 |
| | | | | | 1 | 4 | | 2 | 1 | 4 | 1 | 1 | 1 | 2 | 3 | 2 | 1 | 1 | | | | | | 7 | 8 |
| | | | | | 1 | | 1 | 2 | 1 | 1 | 1 | 1 | 1 | | 1 | 2 | 1 | | | | | | | 4 | 9 |
| | | | | | 3 | 1 | 2 | 2 | | 3 | 2 | 3 | 2 | 2 | 4 | 2 | 2 | | | | | | | 8 | 10 |
| | | | | | 3 | 4 | 3 | 2 | | | | 12 | 2 | 7 | 9 | | 2 | | | | | | 1 | 12 | 11 |
| | | | 1 | | 3 | 4 | 5 | 7 | 4 | 11 | 3 | | 5 | 3 | 8 | 7 | 4 | | 1 | | | | | 20 | 12 |
| | | | | | 5 | 5 | 4 | 9 | 18 | 3 | 1 | | | 16 | 16 | | 8 | | | | | | | 24 | 13 |
| | | | | | | 1 | 1 | | 2 | | | 1 | | 1 | 1 | 1 | | | 1 | | | | | 3 | 14 |
| | | | | | | 2 | 2 | 1 | | 4 | | 1 | 1 | 3 | 4 | 1 | | | | | | | | 5 | 15 |
| | | | | | 3 | 4 | 1 | 2 | 3 | 7 | | | 3 | 5 | 8 | 1 | | | 1 | | | | | 10 | 16 |
| | 1 | | 1 | | 7 | 1 | 3 | 2 | 8 | 4 | | 1 | 7 | 2 | 9 | 2 | 1 | | | | | 1 | | 13 | 17 |
| | | | | | | | 1 | | 1 | | | | 1 | | 1 | | | | | | | | | 1 | 18 |
| | | | 5 | | 21 | 20 | 18 | 22 | | 2 | 16 | 61 | 28 | 30 | 58 | 9 | 10 | 1 | 1 | | 1 | 1 | | 81 | 19 |
| | | | | | 8 | 6 | 5 | 10 | 14 | 7 | 1 | 5 | 10 | 5 | 15 | 10 | 3 | | | | 1 | | | 29 | 20 |
| | | | | | 13 | 8 | 16 | 13 | 39 | 9 | | 3 | 13 | 12 | 25 | 13 | 13 | | | | 1 | | | 52 | 21 |
| | | | | | 1 | | | | | | | 1 | | | | 1 | | | | | | | | 1 | 22 |
| | | | | | | | 2 | | | 1 | | 1 | 1 | | 1 | 1 | | | | | | | | 2 | 23 |
| | | | | | 2 | 13 | 4 | 3 | 6 | 10 | 3 | 3 | 11 | 3 | 14 | 4 | 3 | | | | | | 1 | 22 | 24 |
| | | | 2 | 1 | 39 | 27 | 24 | 27 | 2 | 9 | 23 | 81 | 31 | 39 | 70 | 21 | 23 | 2 | 1 | 1 | | | | 118 | 25 |
| | | | | | 4 | 4 | 1 | 2 | 3 | 6 | 1 | 1 | 1 | 3 | 4 | 4 | 3 | | | | | | | 11 | 26 |
| | | | | | 1 | 2 | 1 | | | | | 4 | 1 | 1 | 2 | 1 | 1 | | | | | | | 4 | 27 |
| | | | | | | | | | | | | | | | | | | | | | | | | .... | 28 |
| | | | | | 2 | 1 | 1 | | | 2 | | | 2 | 1 | 3 | 1 | | | | | | | | 4 | 29 |
| | | | | | 1 | | | | 1 | | | | 1 | | 1 | | | | | | | | | 1 | 30 |
| | | | | | 18 | 21 | 51 | 39 | 18 | 98 | 20 | 2 | 46 | 29 | 75 | 30 | 29 | | 2 | 1 | | 1 | | 188 | 31 |
| | | | | | 4 | 7 | 20 | 3 | 7 | 21 | 6 | | 14 | 11 | 25 | 1 | 6 | | | 1 | | 1 | | 34 | 32 |
| | | | | | 1 | | | 2 | 2 | | | 1 | | 2 | 2 | | 1 | | | | | | | 3 | 33 |
| | | | | | | | | 1 | | 1 | | | 1 | | 1 | | | | | | | | | 1 | 34 |
| | | | | | 1 | 1 | 4 | 1 | 4 | 3 | | | 2 | 2 | 4 | 2 | 1 | | | | | | | 7 | 35 |
| | | | | | | | 1 | | | 1 | | | | | | | 1 | | | | | | | 1 | 36 |
| | | | | | 2 | 1 | 1 | 2 | 1 | 2 | 1 | 2 | 2 | 3 | 5 | 1 | | | | | | | | 6 | 37 |
| | | | | | 1 | 2 | 1 | 1 | 2 | 2 | | | | 3 | 3 | | 2 | | | | | | | 5 | 38 |
| | | | | | | | 1 | 3 | | 3 | 1 | | | | | 1 | 3 | | | | | | | 4 | 39 |
| | | | 1 | | 23 | 28 | 42 | 20 | 12 | 81 | 18 | 2 | 37 | 37 | 74 | 18 | 17 | 2 | | 1 | 1 | | | 118 | 40 |
| | | | | | | | 1 | | | 1 | | | 1 | | 1 | | | | | | | | | 1 | 41 |
| | | | | | | 1 | 2 | 1 | 1 | 1 | | 2 | 3 | | 3 | 1 | | | | | | | | 4 | 42 |
| | | | | | 1 | | | 1 | | 1 | | 1 | | 2 | 2 | | | | | | | | | 2 | 43 |
| | | | | | | | 1 | | | 1 | | | | 1 | 1 | | | | | | | | | 1 | 44 |
| | | | | | 2 | | 2 | | | 2 | | 2 | 2 | 1 | 3 | 1 | | | | | | | | 4 | 45 |
| | | | | | | | | | | | | | | | | | | | | | | | | .... | 46 |
| | | | | | 3 | | 1 | 3 | 3 | 1 | | 1 | 2 | 4 | 6 | 1 | | | | | | | | 7 | 47 |
| | | | | | 26 | 12 | 7 | 8 | 7 | 35 | 7 | 3 | 8 | 9 | 17 | 12 | 23 | | | | | 1 | | 53 | 48 |
| | | | | | 6 | 6 | 1 | 1 | 9 | 5 | | | 6 | 2 | 8 | 3 | 2 | 1 | | | | | | 14 | 49 |
| | | | | | 6 | 8 | 2 | 1 | 5 | 7 | 1 | 4 | 9 | 3 | 12 | 4 | 1 | | | | | | | 17 | 50 |
| | | | | | 2 | 3 | 6 | 2 | 8 | 4 | | 1 | 6 | 3 | 9 | 3 | 1 | | | | | | | 13 | 51 |
| | | | | | | 1 | | | 1 | | | | | 1 | 1 | | | | | | | | | 1 | 52 |
| | | | | | | 2 | 1 | | 1 | 1 | | 1 | 3 | | 3 | | | | | | | | | 3 | 53 |
| | | | | | | | | 1 | 1 | | | | | | | 1 | | | | | | | | 1 | 54 |
| | | | | | 1 | | | 1 | | 1 | 1 | | 1 | 1 | 2 | | | | | | | | | 2 | 55 |
| | | | | | 1 | | 2 | 2 | 1 | 1 | 1 | 2 | 2 | 2 | 4 | 1 | | | | | | | | 5 | 56 |
| | | | | | | 1 | | | | | | | | 1 | | 1 | | | | | | | | 1 | 57 |
| | | | | | 6 | 6 | 2 | 5 | 1 | 7 | 6 | 4 | 7 | 9 | 16 | 1 | 3 | | | | | | | 19 | 58 |
| | | | | | | 1 | 1 | | | 2 | | | 1 | | 1 | | 1 | | | | | | | 2 | 59 |
| | | | | | 2 | | | | | 2 | | | | | | 1 | 1 | | | | | | | 2 | 60 |
| | | | | | 1 | | | 1 | 1 | | | | | | | 2 | | | | | | | | 2 | 61 |
| | | | | | 2 | 9 | 3 | | 1 | 8 | 4 | | 1 | 2 | 3 | 6 | 4 | | | | | 1 | | 14 | 62 |
| | | | | | 1 | | | 1 | 2 | | | | | 1 | 1 | | 1 | | | | | | | 2 | 63 |
| | | | | | | 2 | | | | | | | 1 | | 1 | 1 | | | | | | | | 2 | 64 |
| | | | | | | | | 3 | | | | 1 | 2 | 1 | 3 | | | | | | | | | 3 | 65 |
| | 1 | | 7 | | 13 | 10 | 17 | 13 | 5 | 6 | 5 | 12 | 14 | 13 | 27 | 8 | 14 | | | | | 1 | 3 | 53 | 66 |
| | | | 1 | | 6 | 2 | 2 | 5 | 2 | 6 | 2 | 5 | 6 | 4 | 10 | 3 | 2 | | | | | | | 15 | 67 |
| | | | | | 9 | 1 | 4 | 5 | 5 | 10 | 3 | 1 | 8 | 4 | 12 | 4 | 2 | | | | | | 1 | 19 | 68 |
| | | | | | 47 | 16 | 13 | 27 | 21 | 70 | 12 | 1 | 30 | 34 | 64 | 27 | 9 | | | | | 1 | 3 | 104 | 69 |
| | | | | | 6 | 8 | 2 | 2 | 5 | 5 | 2 | | 1 | | 1 | 9 | 3 | | | | | | | 13 | 70 |
| | | | | | | | 1 | | | | | | | | | 1 | | | | | | | | 1 | 71 |
| | | | | | 2 | 1 | 1 | 1 | 5 | | | | | 3 | 3 | 1 | 1 | | | | | | | 5 | 72 |
| | | | | | 3 | | | 2 | | 3 | | 6 | 2 | 1 | 3 | | 2 | 1 | | | | | | 6 | 73 |
| | | | | | | 2 | | | | | | 1 | | 1 | 1 | 1 | | | | | | | | 2 | 74 |
| | | | | | 1 | 3 | | 2 | 1 | | 4 | 1 | 1 | 3 | 4 | 1 | 1 | | | | | | | 6 | 75 |

## CLASSIFICATION OF DEATHS IN SOUTHERN MIDDLE

| | Cause of death. | Ages. | | | | | | | | | | | | | | | | | | Nativities. | | | | | |
|---|---|---|---|---|---|---|---|---|---|---|---|---|---|---|---|---|---|---|---|---|---|---|---|---|---|
| | | Under 1. | | 1 and under 5. | | 5 and under 10. | | 10 and under 20. | | 20 and under 50. | | 50 and under 80. | | 80 and under 100. | | 100 & over. | | Age unknown. | | Born in State. | N. England States. | Middle States. | Southern States. | Southwest'n States. | Northwest'n States. |
| | | M. | F. | M. | F. | M. | F. | M. | F. | M. | F. | M. | F. | M | F. | M | F. | M | F. | | | | | | |
| 1 | Small pox | | | | | 1 | | | | 1 | | | 1 | | | | | | | 3 | | | | | |
| 2 | Spine, disease of | 1 | 1 | 1 | | | | | | 1 | | | | | | | | | | 3 | | | | | |
| 3 | Stillborn | 1 | 1 | | | | | | | | | | | | | | | | | 2 | | | | | |
| 4 | Suffocation | 12 | 15 | | 1 | | | | | | | | | | | | | | | 28 | | | | | |
| 5 | Summer complaint | 1 | | | 2 | | | | | | | | | | | | | | | 3 | | | | | |
| 6 | Suicide | | | | | | | | | 2 | 2 | | | | | | | | | 4 | | | | | |
| 7 | Teething | 1 | | 3 | 1 | | | | | | | | | | | | | | | 5 | | | | | |
| 8 | Throat, disease of | 6 | 4 | 23 | 24 | 9 | 9 | 3 | 4 | 2 | 4 | | | | | | | | | 88 | | | | | |
| 9 | Thrush | 2 | 4 | | | | | | | | | | | | | | | | | 6 | | | | | |
| 10 | Tumor | | 1 | | | | | | | | 1 | | 1 | | | | | | | 2 | | | 1 | | |
| 11 | Ulcer | | | | | | | | | 1 | 1 | | | | | | | | | 2 | | | | | |
| 12 | Uterus, disease of | | | | | | | | | | 2 | | | | | | | | | 2 | | | 1 | | |
| 13 | White swelling | | | | | | | | | | | | 1 | | | | | | | 1 | | | | | |
| 14 | Worms | 2 | 1 | 10 | 6 | 3 | 3 | 5 | | | | | | | | | | | | 30 | | | | | |
| 15 | Unknown | 101 | 82 | 46 | 32 | 9 | 4 | 7 | 25 | 23 | 46 | 46 | 23 | 8 | 5 | | | | | 445 | 1 | 2 | 3 | | |
| | Total | 207 | 178 | 195 | 139 | 62 | 62 | 103 | 103 | 227 | 245 | 142 | 135 | 39 | 34 | 2 | 2 | 1 | .. | 1795 | 3 | 7 | 40 | 2 | .. |

## CLASSIFICATION OF DEATHS IN THE

| | | | | | | | | | | | | | | | | | | | | | | | | | |
|---|---|---|---|---|---|---|---|---|---|---|---|---|---|---|---|---|---|---|---|---|---|---|---|---|---|
| 1 | Abscess | 1 | 1 | | | | | | | 1 | | | | | | | | | | 3 | | | | | |
| 2 | Accident, not specif'd | 15 | 16 | 9 | 17 | 10 | 3 | 14 | 4 | 33 | 2 | 12 | 3 | 4 | 3 | 1 | | | | 138 | | | 5 | 1 | |
| 3 | ....do...burned | 5 | 6 | 23 | 37 | 16 | 31 | 1 | 13 | 7 | 8 | 5 | 4 | 1 | | | | | | 150 | 2 | | 3 | | |
| 4 | ....do...drowned | | 1 | 10 | 2 | 2 | | 15 | 1 | 32 | 1 | 3 | 2 | 1 | | 1 | | 1 | | 70 | | 1 | 1 | | |
| 5 | ... do...scalded | | | 1 | 1 | | 1 | | | | | 1 | | | | | | | | 4 | | | | | |
| 6 | ....do...shot | | | | | | 1 | | | 5 | | | | | | | | | | 6 | | | | | |
| 7 | Amputation | | | | | | | | | | | 1 | | | | | | | | 1 | | | | | |
| 8 | Apoplexy | | 1 | 1 | | 1 | | 3 | 1 | 11 | 7 | 22 | 17 | 2 | 1 | | | | | 60 | | | 6 | | |
| 9 | Asthma | | | 1 | | | | | | | | 1 | | | 2 | | | | | 2 | | 1 | | | |
| 10 | Black tongue | | 1 | 1 | | | | 1 | 1 | 1 | 2 | 1 | | | | | | | | 8 | | | | | |
| 11 | Bowels, disease of | 17 | 15 | 22 | 18 | 4 | 1 | 2 | | 9 | 3 | 1 | 3 | 1 | | | | 1 | | 93 | | | 3 | | |
| 12 | Brain ......do | 2 | 1 | 1 | 1 | 3 | 1 | 1 | | 1 | 3 | | 3 | | | | | | | 16 | | | 1 | | |
| 13 | Bronchitis | 2 | 2 | 3 | 6 | | | 1 | 2 | 6 | 3 | | | | | | | | | 24 | | 1 | | | |
| 14 | Cancer | 1 | 1 | 1 | | | 2 | | | 2 | 22 | 18 | 29 | 1 | 2 | | | | | 69 | | 3 | 6 | | |
| 15 | Catarrh | 13 | 15 | 13 | 8 | 2 | 2 | 7 | 2 | 9 | 14 | 5 | 4 | | 3 | | | | | 94 | | 1 | 1 | | |
| 16 | Childbirth | | | | | | | | 13 | | 137 | | | | | | | | | 145 | | 1 | 4 | | |
| 17 | Cholera | | 1 | 2 | 4 | | 2 | 3 | 2 | 11 | 4 | 4 | 8 | | | | | | | 35 | | | 1 | | |
| 18 | ....do..infantum | 23 | 18 | 19 | 13 | | 1 | | | | | | | | | | | | | 73 | | | 1 | | |
| 19 | ....do..morbus | 3 | 2 | 4 | 6 | 2 | 2 | 2 | | 3 | 4 | 2 | 3 | | | | | | | 33 | | | | | |
| 20 | Chorea | | | | | | | | 1 | | | | | | 1 | | | | | 2 | | | | | |
| 21 | Colic | 12 | 3 | 3 | 5 | | 1 | 4 | 3 | 13 | 7 | 13 | 7 | 2 | | | | | | 66 | | | 5 | | |
| 22 | Congestion | | | | | | | | | 1 | 4 | | | | | | | | | 5 | | | | | |
| 23 | ....do....brain | 1 | | 1 | 2 | 1 | 1 | 2 | 1 | 3 | 3 | | | | | | | | | 15 | | | | | |
| 24 | Consumption | 3 | 5 | 4 | 6 | 4 | 12 | 18 | 45 | 124 | 181 | 69 | 70 | 7 | 14 | | | | | 513 | | 5 | 34 | 1 | |
| 25 | Convulsions | 29 | 24 | 15 | 5 | 5 | 3 | 6 | 9 | 6 | 10 | 12 | 5 | | 1 | | | | | 127 | | | 1 | 1 | |
| 26 | Cramp | 2 | | 2 | 1 | | | | 1 | | 1 | 1 | | | | | | | | 8 | | | | | |
| 27 | Croup | 93 | 79 | 62 | 66 | 7 | 12 | 3 | | 2 | | | | | | | | | | 323 | | | 1 | | |
| 28 | Debility | | | 3 | 1 | | | | | | 1 | 3 | 3 | 5 | 1 | | 1 | | | 13 | | 1 | 4 | | |
| 29 | Diabetes | | | | | | | | | 1 | 1 | 1 | | | | | | | | 2 | | | 1 | | |
| 30 | Diarrhœa | 20 | 26 | 38 | 19 | 1 | 4 | 3 | 4 | 11 | 7 | 10 | 3 | 1 | | | | | | 138 | 1 | 2 | 5 | | |
| 31 | Dirt eating | | | | | 1 | | | | | | | | | | | | | | 1 | | | | | |
| 32 | Dropsy | 6 | 3 | 29 | 23 | 34 | 38 | 78 | 32 | 89 | 105 | 131 | 108 | 21 | 24 | 1 | | 1 | 1 | 657 | 2 | 9 | 47 | | |
| 33 | Dysentery | 14 | 13 | 25 | 21 | 4 | 3 | 5 | 2 | 5 | 4 | | 8 | 3 | 1 | | | | | 104 | | 1 | 2 | | |
| 34 | Dyspepsia | | | | | | 2 | 1 | | 5 | 7 | 11 | 5 | 2 | | | | | | 30 | | 2 | 1 | | |
| 35 | Epilepsy | | | 1 | | | | | | | 1 | 1 | | 1 | | | | | | 4 | | | | | |
| 36 | Erysipelas | 8 | 9 | 3 | 1 | 2 | 1 | 6 | 3 | 11 | 13 | 6 | 6 | | | | | | | 68 | | | 1 | | |
| 37 | Executed | | | | | | | | | 1 | | | | | | | | | | 1 | | | | | |
| 38 | Fever, not specified | 19 | 25 | 58 | 38 | 17 | 20 | 31 | 57 | 85 | 84 | 23 | 21 | 4 | 2 | | | | | 467 | 1 | 1 | 13 | 1 | 1 |
| 39 | ..do..bilious | 11 | 8 | 34 | 27 | 18 | 11 | 16 | 22 | 34 | 38 | 17 | 23 | 3 | 4 | | | | | 257 | 1 | | 8 | | |
| 40 | ..do..brain | 2 | 3 | 7 | 3 | 3 | 2 | 4 | 2 | 5 | 5 | | 1 | | | | | | | 35 | | | 1 | | |
| 41 | ..do..catarrhal | 5 | 7 | 6 | 1 | 2 | 3 | 2 | 1 | 1 | 5 | 2 | 3 | 1 | 1 | | | | | 36 | | 1 | 3 | | |
| 42 | ..do..congestive | | 2 | 8 | 3 | 4 | 8 | 5 | 8 | 15 | 14 | 6 | 9 | | 1 | | | | | 73 | 1 | | 7 | | |
| 43 | ..do..inflammatory | | | | 1 | | | | | | | | | | | | | | | 1 | | | | | |
| 44 | ..do..intermittent | 4 | 6 | 3 | 4 | 1 | 1 | | 1 | 3 | 5 | 4 | 8 | 1 | | | | | | 41 | | | | | |
| 45 | ..do..puerperal | | | | | | | | | | 25 | | | | | | | | | 23 | | 1 | 1 | | |
| 46 | ..do..remittent | | | | | | | 1 | 1 | 2 | | | | | | | | | | 4 | | | | | |
| 47 | ..do..scarlet | 2 | 2 | 4 | 6 | | 3 | | 2 | | 2 | | | | | | | | | 21 | | | | | |
| 48 | ..do..typhus | 2 | 4 | 12 | 9 | 15 | 16 | 41 | 39 | 90 | 68 | 22 | 12 | 2 | 2 | | | | 1 | 322 | | 1 | 9 | | |
| 49 | ..do..yellow | | | | | | | | | 1 | | | | | | | | | | 1 | | | | | |
| 50 | Gout | | | | | | | | | | | 1 | | | | | | | | 1 | | | | | |
| 51 | Gravel | | | 3 | | | | | | 1 | 3 | 29 | 1 | 5 | | 1 | | 1 | | 39 | | 3 | 2 | | |

CTION OF THE STATE OF NORTH CAROLINA—Continued.

| NATIVITIES. | | | | SEASON OF DECEASE. | | | | DURATION OF SICKNESS. | | | | WHITES. | | | COLORED. | | | | | | | | | |
|---|---|---|---|---|---|---|---|---|---|---|---|---|---|---|---|---|---|---|---|---|---|---|---|---|
| | | | | | | | | | | | | | | | Slaves. | | | | Free. | | | | | |
| | | | | | | | | | | | | | | | Black. | | Mulatto. | | Black. | | Mul. | | | |
| Ireland. | Germany. | Other foreign countries. | Unknown. | Spring. | Summer. | Autumn. | Winter. | Under 1 week. | 1 week and under 1 month. | 1 month and under 3 months. | 3 months and over. | Males. | Females. | Total. | M. | F. | M. | F. | M. | F. | M | F. | Aggregate deaths. | |
| | | | | | | | 3 | | 3 | | | 2 | | 2 | | 1 | | | | | | | 3 | 1 |
| | | | | 1 | | 1 | 1 | | 1 | | 1 | 2 | | 2 | 1 | | | | | | | | 3 | 2 |
| | | | | | | 1 | 1 | | | | | 1 | 1 | 2 | | | | | | | | | 2 | 3 |
| | | | | 6 | 5 | 2 | 12 | 28 | | | | | 2 | 2 | 12 | 14 | | | | | | | 28 | 4 |
| | | | | | 2 | 1 | | | 3 | | | | 1 | 1 | 1 | 1 | | | | | | | 3 | 5 |
| | | | | 1 | 1 | 1 | 1 | 2 | | | | 1 | 1 | 2 | 1 | 1 | | | | | | | 4 | 6 |
| | | | | | 3 | 2 | | | | 2 | 1 | 2 | | 2 | 2 | 1 | | | | | | | 5 | 7 |
| | | | | 18 | 6 | 37 | 27 | 31 | 52 | 1 | 4 | 27 | 34 | 61 | 15 | 9 | 1 | 1 | | | | 1 | 88 | 8 |
| | | | | 2 | | 2 | 2 | 1 | 1 | 3 | | 2 | 3 | 5 | | | | 1 | | | | | 6 | 9 |
| | | | | 1 | | 2 | | | | 1 | 2 | | 2 | 2 | | | | | | | | 1 | 3 | 10 |
| | | | | | 2 | | | | | 1 | 1 | 1 | | 1 | | | | | | | | 1 | 2 | 11 |
| | | | | | 1 | 1 | | | | 1 | 1 | | 1 | 1 | | 1 | | | | | | | 2 | 12 |
| | | | | 1 | | | | | | | 1 | | | | | 1 | | | | | | | 1 | 13 |
| | | | | 8 | 7 | 12 | 3 | 9 | 13 | 3 | 5 | 9 | 3 | 12 | 8 | 6 | 2 | 1 | | | 1 | | 30 | 14 |
| | | 4 | 1 | 128 | 122 | 103 | 97 | 189 | 95 | 41 | 81 | 113 | 108 | 211 | 109 | 99 | 3 | 3 | 3 | 1 | 9 | 8 | 457 | 15 |
| 2 | | 24 | 3 | 510 | 422 | 466 | 439 | 545 | 657 | 200 | 342 | 524 | 492 | 1016 | 411 | 366 | 16 | 13 | 7 | 7 | 19 | 21 | 1876 | |

ATE OF NORTH CAROLINA—AGGREGATE.

| Ireland. | Germany. | Other foreign countries. | Unknown. | Spring. | Summer. | Autumn. | Winter. | Under 1 week. | 1 week and under 1 month. | 1 month and under 3 months. | 3 months and over. | Males. | Females. | Total. | Slaves Black M. | Slaves Black F. | Slaves Mulatto M. | Slaves Mulatto F. | Free Black M. | Free Black F. | Free Mul. M | Free Mul. F. | Aggregate deaths. | |
|---|---|---|---|---|---|---|---|---|---|---|---|---|---|---|---|---|---|---|---|---|---|---|---|---|
| | | | | 1 | 1 | 1 | | | 1 | | 1 | 1 | 1 | 2 | 1 | | | | | | | | 3 | 1 |
| | | 1 | 1 | 41 | 42 | 19 | 43 | 84 | 14 | 3 | 7 | 48 | 17 | 65 | 45 | 31 | 3 | | 1 | | 1 | | 146 | 2 |
| | | 1 | 1 | 64 | 23 | 15 | 46 | 63 | 27 | 5 | 3 | 21 | 20 | 41 | 32 | 71 | 5 | 4 | | 1 | 1 | 2 | 157 | 3 |
| | | | | 19 | 35 | 9 | 7 | 72 | | | | 20 | 4 | 24 | 35 | 1 | 1 | | 1 | 1 | 8 | 1 | 72 | 4 |
| | | | | 1 | 1 | 1 | | 2 | 1 | | | 1 | 2 | 3 | 1 | | | | | | | | 4 | 5 |
| | | | | 2 | 2 | 1 | | 6 | | | | 2 | | 2 | 2 | 1 | | | | | 1 | | 6 | 6 |
| | | | | | | 1 | | | | 1 | | 1 | | 1 | | | | | | | | | 1 | 7 |
| | | 1 | | 15 | 20 | 12 | 20 | 38 | 14 | 1 | 3 | 23 | 16 | 39 | 16 | 10 | 1 | 1 | | | | | 67 | 8 |
| | | 1 | | 4 | | | | 1 | | | 1 | | 1 | 1 | 2 | 1 | | | | | | | 4 | 9 |
| | | | | | | 1 | | | 1 | | | 3 | 4 | 7 | | | | | | | 1 | | 8 | 10 |
| | 1 | | | 16 | 40 | 21 | 20 | 17 | 36 | 22 | 20 | 29 | 18 | 47 | 26 | 21 | 2 | 1 | | | | | 97 | 11 |
| | | | | 5 | 3 | 5 | 4 | 4 | 5 | 2 | 4 | 3 | 4 | 7 | 3 | 5 | 2 | | | | | | 17 | 12 |
| | | | | 9 | 5 | 5 | 5 | 3 | 8 | 3 | 10 | 6 | 6 | 12 | 6 | 7 | | | | | | | 25 | 13 |
| | | 1 | | 20 | 22 | 18 | 18 | 2 | 4 | 6 | 62 | 20 | 36 | 56 | 3 | 19 | | | | | | 1 | 79 | 14 |
| | | 1 | | 28 | 14 | 22 | 30 | 20 | 55 | 14 | 6 | 22 | 22 | 44 | 27 | 24 | | 2 | | | | | 97 | 15 |
| | | | | 39 | 31 | 87 | 41 | 78 | 33 | 9 | 3 | | 104 | 104 | | 43 | | 2 | | | | 1 | 150 | 16 |
| | | | | 3 | 16 | 13 | 2 | 31 | 4 | | 1 | 9 | 8 | 17 | 11 | 6 | | 1 | | | | 1 | 36 | 17 |
| | | | | 7 | 32 | 24 | 11 | 19 | 35 | 8 | 6 | 17 | 13 | 30 | 21 | 18 | 2 | | 1 | | 1 | 1 | 74 | 18 |
| | | | | 6 | 18 | 4 | 4 | 16 | 13 | 1 | 1 | 13 | 14 | 27 | 8 | 2 | | 1 | | | | | 33 | 19 |
| | | | | | 1 | | | | 1 | | | | 1 | 1 | | 1 | | | | | | | 2 | 20 |
| 1 | | 1 | | 25 | 20 | 19 | 8 | 43 | 18 | 2 | 3 | 31 | 9 | 40 | 13 | 13 | 2 | 2 | | 2 | 1 | | 73 | 21 |
| | | | | | 1 | 4 | | 3 | 2 | | | | 3 | 3 | | 1 | | | | | 1 | | 5 | 22 |
| | | | | 3 | 3 | 3 | 6 | 7 | 6 | | 2 | 6 | 2 | 8 | 1 | 3 | | 2 | 1 | | | | 15 | 23 |
| 1 | | 8 | | 164 | 154 | 121 | 108 | 18 | 19 | 70 | 399 | 157 | 213 | 370 | 62 | 100 | 2 | 9 | 3 | 5 | 5 | 6 | 562 | 24 |
| | | 1 | | 42 | 31 | 29 | 27 | 74 | 26 | 4 | 16 | 37 | 26 | 63 | 35 | 25 | | 2 | | 2 | 1 | 2 | 130 | 25 |
| | | | | 3 | 1 | 2 | 2 | 3 | 4 | | | 3 | 1 | 4 | 1 | 2 | 1 | | | | | | 8 | 26 |
| | | | | 90 | 61 | 81 | 87 | 208 | 80 | 13 | 8 | 91 | 82 | 173 | 72 | 67 | 3 | 4 | | 2 | 1 | 2 | 324 | 27 |
| | | | | 9 | 3 | 3 | 3 | 3 | 3 | | 6 | 7 | 5 | 12 | 4 | 2 | | | | | | | 18 | 28 |
| | | | | | | 2 | 1 | | 1 | | 2 | 1 | 1 | 2 | 1 | | | | | | | | 3 | 29 |
| 1 | | | | 15 | 63 | 47 | 13 | 26 | 70 | 18 | 26 | 51 | 35 | 86 | 27 | 22 | 3 | 3 | | | 3 | 3 | 147 | 30 |
| | | | | | | | 1 | | | | 1 | 1 | | 1 | | | | | | | | | 1 | 31 |
| 2 | | 4 | 3 | 207 | 208 | 149 | 156 | 21 | 75 | 109 | 471 | 263 | 215 | 478 | 108 | 102 | 9 | 8 | 4 | 6 | 6 | 3 | 724 | 32 |
| | | | 1 | 12 | 52 | 36 | 7 | 13 | 74 | 13 | 4 | 35 | 31 | 66 | 19 | 18 | | | 2 | 3 | | | 108 | 33 |
| | | | | 10 | 13 | 7 | 3 | 1 | 2 | 4 | 25 | 16 | 10 | 26 | 3 | 3 | | | | 1 | | | 33 | 34 |
| | | | | 1 | 1 | 2 | | 3 | 1 | | | 3 | 1 | 4 | | | | | | | | | 4 | 35 |
| | | | | 25 | 14 | 11 | 18 | 15 | 34 | 4 | 3 | 26 | 23 | 49 | 9 | 9 | | | 1 | | | 1 | 69 | 36 |
| | | | | | | 1 | | 1 | | | | 1 | | 1 | | | | | | | | | 1 | 37 |
| | | | | 66 | 111 | 192 | 96 | 70 | 296 | 74 | 19 | 150 | 141 | 291 | 83 | 94 | 2 | 10 | 1 | | 2 | 1 | 484 | 38 |
| | | | | 21 | 65 | 132 | 35 | 52 | 168 | 27 | 15 | 82 | 92 | 174 | 38 | 31 | | 4 | 8 | 2 | 5 | 4 | 266 | 39 |
| | | 1 | | 6 | 10 | 14 | 6 | 17 | 14 | 1 | 4 | 10 | 11 | 21 | 9 | 5 | 2 | | | | | | 37 | 40 |
| | | | | 14 | 14 | 2 | 10 | 8 | 18 | 4 | 3 | 12 | 9 | 21 | 5 | 10 | 1 | 2 | | | 1 | | 40 | 41 |
| | | 2 | | 16 | 14 | 41 | 11 | 39 | 40 | 3 | | 24 | 32 | 56 | 11 | 13 | 1 | | 1 | | 1 | | 83 | 42 |
| | | | | | | 1 | | | 1 | | | | | | | 1 | | | | | | | 1 | 43 |
| | | | | 7 | 9 | 15 | 9 | 3 | 17 | 6 | 14 | 13 | 18 | 31 | 3 | 6 | | | | 1 | | | 41 | 44 |
| | | | | 9 | 8 | 1 | 7 | 4 | 11 | 2 | | | 18 | 18 | | 7 | | | | | | | 25 | 45 |
| | | | | | | 1 | 3 | | 2 | 2 | | 2 | | 2 | 1 | 1 | | | | | | | 4 | 46 |
| | | | | 5 | 5 | 3 | 8 | 4 | 12 | 1 | 4 | 2 | 9 | 11 | 4 | 6 | | | | | | | 21 | 47 |
| | | 3 | | 67 | 68 | 126 | 72 | 27 | 206 | 74 | 14 | 106 | 94 | 200 | 72 | 50 | 2 | 2 | 3 | 3 | 1 | 2 | 335 | 48 |
| | | | | | | 1 | | | 1 | | | 1 | | 1 | | | | | | | | | 1 | 49 |
| | | | | 1 | | | | | | | 1 | 1 | | 1 | | | | | | | | | 1 | 50 |
| | | | | 11 | 16 | 11 | 5 | 5 | 14 | 3 | 21 | 28 | 2 | 30 | 10 | 2 | | | 1 | | 1 | | 44 | 51 |

## CLASSIFICATION OF DEATHS IN THE

| | Cause of Death. | Ages. Under 1. M. | Under 1. F. | 1 and under 5. M. | 1 and under 5. F. | 5 and under 10. M. | 5 and under 10. F. | 10 and under 20. M. | 10 and under 20. F. | 20 and under 50. M. | 20 and under 50. F. | 50 and under 80. M. | 50 and under 80. F. | 80 and under 100. M. | 80 and under 100. F. | 100 & over. M | 100 & over. F. | Age unknown. M | Age unknown. F. | Nativities. Born in State. | N. England States. | Middle States. | Southern States. | Southwest'n States. | Northwest'n States. |
|---|---|---|---|---|---|---|---|---|---|---|---|---|---|---|---|---|---|---|---|---|---|---|---|---|---|
| 1 | Head, disease of | 3 | 1 | 1 | | 1 | | | | 3 | | 2 | | | | | | | | 9 | | 2 | | | |
| 2 | Heart....do | | 1 | 1 | 1 | | 3 | 2 | 2 | 7 | 1 | 6 | 4 | | | | | | | 26 | | 1 | 1 | | |
| 3 | Heat | | | | | | | | | 2 | | | | | | | | | | 2 | | | | | |
| 4 | Hemorrhage | 1 | | 1 | | | | 2 | 1 | 10 | 9 | 2 | 2 | | | | | | | 27 | | | 1 | | |
| 5 | Hernia | 2 | 2 | | | | | 1 | | 2 | 1 | 2 | 2 | 2 | | | | | | 14 | | | | | |
| 6 | Hives | 29 | 17 | 2 | 4 | | | | | | | | | | | | | | | 51 | | | | 1 | |
| 7 | Hooping cough | 37 | 55 | 58 | 57 | 5 | 10 | 3 | 2 | | | | | | | | | | | 227 | | | | | |
| 8 | Hydrocephalus | 3 | 1 | 5 | 1 | | 2 | | | 1 | | | | | | | | | | 13 | | | | | |
| 9 | Hydrophobia | | | | | | | | | | | | 1 | | | | | | | 1 | | | | | |
| 10 | Inflammation | 6 | 5 | 4 | 4 | 4 | 1 | 4 | 1 | 9 | 8 | 4 | 3 | | | | | | | 51 | | 1 | 1 | | |
| 11 | ....do.....bowels | 12 | 4 | 6 | 5 | 4 | 1 | 9 | 5 | 13 | 7 | 7 | 5 | | | | | | | 75 | | | 3 | | |
| 12 | ....do......brain | 12 | 7 | 15 | 10 | 2 | 6 | 8 | 7 | 12 | 11 | 4 | 2 | | | | | | | 90 | | | 5 | | |
| 13 | ....do.......stomach | 1 | 2 | 1 | | 1 | | | | 2 | 3 | 2 | | | | | | | | 12 | | | | | |
| 14 | Insanity | | | | | | | | | 2 | 1 | 3 | | 1 | | | | | | 6 | | | 1 | | |
| 15 | Intemperance | | | | | | | | | 14 | | 8 | 1 | | | | | | | 21 | | | 2 | | |
| 16 | Jaundice | 2 | 1 | | 2 | | 1 | 1 | | 2 | 1 | 1 | 3 | | | | | | | 14 | | | | | |
| 17 | Kidneys, disease of | | | | | | | | | | 1 | 6 | 5 | 4 | | | | | | 16 | | | | | |
| 18 | Killed | 2 | 1 | 2 | 1 | | | 3 | | 4 | | 2 | | | | | | | | 15 | | | | | |
| 19 | Lightning | | | | | 1 | | 1 | | 2 | 1 | | | | | | | | | 4 | | | 1 | | |
| 20 | Liver, disease of | 2 | 1 | 2 | 2 | 2 | 1 | 5 | 7 | 14 | 20 | 14 | 11 | | | | | | | 72 | 1 | | 7 | | |
| 21 | Lockjaw | 4 | 2 | | 1 | | | 1 | | 1 | 2 | 1 | | | | | | | | 12 | | | | | |
| 22 | Lungs, disease of | | 1 | 2 | | | 1 | 1 | | 5 | 5 | 4 | 9 | | | | | | | 24 | | | 4 | | |
| 23 | Malformation | 1 | 6 | 3 | | | | | | | | | | | | | | | | 10 | | | | | |
| 24 | Mania-a-potu | | | | | | | | | 1 | | | | | | | | | | 1 | | | | | |
| 25 | Marasmus | | 1 | 1 | | | | | 1 | | | | | | | | | | | 3 | | | | | |
| 26 | Measles | 13 | 6 | 29 | 21 | 6 | 4 | 9 | 2 | 10 | 8 | 1 | 3 | | | | | | | 111 | | | 1 | | |
| 27 | Mercury, effects of | | | | | | | 1 | | | | | | | | | | | | 1 | | | | | |
| 28 | Milk sickness | | | | | | | | | 2 | 1 | | | | | | | | | 3 | | | | | |
| 29 | Mortification | | | | | | | 1 | | 2 | 4 | 2 | 3 | | | | | | | 11 | | | 1 | | |
| 30 | Mumps | | | | | | 1 | 2 | | | 1 | | | | | | | | | 4 | | | | | |
| 31 | Murder | | | | | | | | | 8 | | | | | | | | | | 8 | | | | | |
| 32 | Neuralgia | 1 | | | | 1 | | 1 | | 3 | 4 | | 2 | | | | | | | 11 | | | 1 | | |
| 33 | Old age | | | | | | | | | | | 54 | 72 | 107 | 141 | 14 | 21 | | | 311 | | 14 | 66 | | |
| 34 | Paralysis | | | 1 | 1 | | | 3 | 3 | 13 | 10 | 30 | 28 | 7 | 5 | | | | 1 | 90 | | 3 | 8 | | |
| 35 | Pleurisy | 3 | 2 | 10 | 3 | 4 | | 17 | 11 | 43 | 26 | 20 | 16 | 3 | | | | 1 | | 150 | | 1 | 4 | 1 | |
| 36 | Pneumonia | 22 | 13 | 43 | 30 | 18 | 18 | 76 | 40 | 153 | 99 | 77 | 57 | 8 | 9 | 1 | | | | 622 | | | 37 | 1 | |
| 37 | Piles | | | 1 | | | | | | | | | | | | | | | | 1 | | | | | |
| 38 | Poison | 1 | | 5 | 1 | 3 | 2 | 2 | 2 | 7 | 4 | 1 | 1 | | | | | | | 28 | | | 1 | | |
| 39 | Prematurity of birth | 7 | 5 | | | | | | | | | | | | | | | | | 12 | | | | | |
| 40 | Quinsy | 1 | 1 | 5 | 6 | 4 | 6 | | 1 | 6 | 7 | 4 | 3 | | | | | | | 43 | | | 1 | | |
| 41 | Rheumatism | | | | | 3 | | 7 | 1 | 9 | 3 | 10 | 10 | 2 | 1 | | | | | 37 | | 2 | 6 | | |
| 42 | Rickets | 1 | | 2 | 1 | | | | | | 1 | | | | | | | | | 5 | | | | | |
| 43 | Scrofula | 3 | 3 | 9 | 8 | 2 | 2 | 9 | | 8 | 4 | 6 | 3 | | | | | | | 54 | | | 3 | | |
| 44 | Small pox | | 2 | | | 3 | | 3 | 2 | 8 | 4 | 6 | 3 | 1 | | | | | | 32 | | | | | |
| 45 | Spine, disease of | 3 | 1 | 1 | | | 2 | 3 | 1 | 2 | 2 | | 1 | | | | | | | 16 | | | | | |
| 46 | Spleen....do | | 1 | | 1 | | | | | | 1 | | | | | | | | | 3 | | | | | |
| 47 | Stillborn | 11 | 9 | | | | | | | | | | | | | | | | | 20 | | | | | |
| 48 | Suffocation | 39 | 53 | 8 | 4 | | | | | | | 1 | 1 | | | | | | | 106 | | | | | |
| 49 | Suicide | | | | | | | | 3 | 12 | 2 | 2 | | | | | | | | 16 | 1 | 1 | 1 | | |
| 50 | Summer complaint | 1 | | 2 | 3 | | | | | | | | | | | | | | | 6 | | | | | |
| 51 | Sun, stroke of | | | | | | | | 1 | 1 | | | | | | | | | | 2 | | | | | |
| 52 | Syphilis | | | | | | | | | | 1 | | | | | | | | | 1 | | | | | |
| 53 | Teething | 7 | 3 | 16 | 13 | | | | | | | | | | | | | | | 38 | | | 1 | | |
| 54 | Tetanus | | | | | | | | | 1 | | | | | | | | | | 1 | | | | | |
| 55 | Throat, disease of | 7 | 5 | 26 | 25 | 9 | 14 | 4 | 5 | 3 | 4 | 1 | 2 | | | | | | | 104 | | | 1 | | |
| 56 | Thrush | 6 | 11 | 1 | 2 | | | | | | | | | | | | | | | 20 | | | | | |
| 57 | Tumor | | 2 | | | | 1 | | 1 | | 1 | 2 | 2 | | | | | | | 7 | | | 2 | | |
| 58 | Ulcer | 1 | 1 | | | | | | | 3 | 3 | 3 | 2 | | | | | | 1 | 13 | | | | | |
| 59 | Uterus, disease of | | | | | | | | 1 | | 10 | | 2 | | | | | | | 11 | | | 2 | | |
| 60 | Venereal | | | | | | | | 1 | 2 | 4 | 3 | | | | | | | | 10 | | | | | |
| 61 | White swelling | | | | | 1 | | 1 | 1 | 1 | | | 1 | | | | | | | 5 | | | | | |
| 62 | Worms | 5 | 11 | 59 | 59 | 8 | 13 | 8 | 2 | | | | | | 1 | | | | | 165 | | 1 | | | |
| 63 | Unknown | 481 | 366 | 230 | 200 | 49 | 56 | 81 | 102 | 149 | 253 | 179 | 178 | 32 | 20 | 2 | 2 | 2 | | 2305 | 4 | 8 | 46 | 3 | |
| | Total | 1045 | 903 | 984 | 821 | 290 | 333 | 545 | 478 | 1192 | 1332 | 908 | 808 | 235 | 240 | 21 | 24 | 7 | 4 | 9601 | 14 | 69 | 336 | 10 | 1 |

## CLASSIFICATION OF DEATHS IN NORTHEASTERN

*Embracing the following counties : Ashland, Ashtabula, Cuyahoga, Geauga, Lake,*

| | | Under 1. M. | Under 1. F. | 1 and under 5. M. | 1 and under 5. F. | 5 and under 10. M. | 5 and under 10. F. | 10 and under 20. M. | 10 and under 20. F. | 20 and under 50. M. | 20 and under 50. F. | 50 and under 80. M. | 50 and under 80. F. | 80 and under 100. M. | 80 and under 100. F. | 100 & over. M | 100 & over. F. | Age unknown. M | Age unknown. F. | Born in State. | N. England States. | Middle States. | Southern States. | Southwest'n States. | Northwest'n States. |
|---|---|---|---|---|---|---|---|---|---|---|---|---|---|---|---|---|---|---|---|---|---|---|---|---|---|
| 1 | Abscess | | | | 1 | | | 1 | | 1 | 1 | | | | | | | | | 2 | | | 1 | | |
| 2 | Accident, not spec'd | | | 3 | | 6 | | 8 | | 18 | 4 | 7 | 6 | 3 | 2 | | | | | 21 | 10 | 14 | 1 | 2 | |

## STATE OF NORTH CAROLINA—AGGREGATE—Continued.

| Nativities: California and Territories. | Nativities: Ireland. | Nativities: Germany. | Nativities: Other foreign countries. | Nativities: Unknown. | Season of decease: Spring. | Season of decease: Summer. | Season of decease: Autumn. | Season of decease: Winter. | Duration of sickness: Under 1 week. | Duration of sickness: 1 week and under 1 month. | Duration of sickness: 1 month and under 3 months. | Duration of sickness: 3 months and over. | Whites: Males. | Whites: Females. | Whites: Total. | Colored: Slaves: Black: M. | Colored: Slaves: Black: F. | Colored: Slaves: Mulatto: M. | Colored: Slaves: Mulatto: F. | Colored: Free: Black: M. | Colored: Free: Black: F. | Colored: Free: Mul.: M | Colored: Free: Mul.: F. | Aggregate deaths. | |
|---|---|---|---|---|---|---|---|---|---|---|---|---|---|---|---|---|---|---|---|---|---|---|---|---|---|
| | | | | | 3 | 2 | 2 | 4 | 2 | 3 | 1 | 5 | 6 | 1 | 7 | 3 | | | | 1 | | | | 11 | 1 |
| | | | | | 11 | 5 | 4 | 8 | 6 | 2 | 4 | 15 | 9 | 8 | 17 | 7 | 4 | | | | | | | 28 | 2 |
| | | | | | 1 | 1 | | | | | 1 | | 2 | | 2 | | | | | | | | | 2 | 3 |
| | | | | | 10 | 8 | 6 | 4 | 3 | 12 | 2 | 5 | 10 | 4 | 14 | 5 | 7 | | 1 | 1 | | | | 28 | 4 |
| | | | | | 3 | 6 | 4 | 1 | 1 | 8 | 1 | 2 | 6 | 3 | 9 | 4 | 1 | | 1 | | | | | 14 | 5 |
| | | | | | 9 | 9 | 13 | 21 | 33 | 13 | 1 | 1 | 26 | 20 | 46 | 5 | 1 | | | | | | | 52 | 6 |
| | | | | | 78 | 65 | 40 | 44 | 31 | 125 | 43 | 10 | 36 | 36 | 72 | 60 | 77 | 3 | 4 | 3 | 5 | 1 | 2 | 227 | 7 |
| | | | | | 2 | 4 | 4 | 3 | 2 | 6 | 3 | 1 | 4 | 3 | 7 | 5 | 1 | | | | | | | 13 | 8 |
| | | | | | | | 1 | | | | | | | | | | 1 | | | | | | | 1 | 9 |
| | | | | | 20 | 17 | 8 | 8 | 19 | 2[illegible] | 5 | 1 | 15 | 12 | 27 | 14 | 10 | 2 | | | | | | 53 | 10 |
| | | | | | 21 | 31 | 18 | 8 | 31 | 26 | 10 | 7 | 33 | 16 | 49 | 17 | 10 | 1 | 1 | | | | | 78 | 11 |
| | 1 | | | | 29 | 27 | 21 | 19 | 47 | 40 | 2 | 5 | 38 | 29 | 67 | 15 | 10 | | 2 | | | | 2 | 96 | 12 |
| | | | | | 7 | 2 | 2 | 1 | 6 | 4 | 1 | 1 | 4 | 2 | 6 | 3 | 3 | | | | | | | 12 | 13 |
| | | | | | 2 | 1 | | 3 | 1 | 2 | | 2 | 2 | | 2 | 4 | 1 | | | | | | | 7 | 14 |
| | | | | | 8 | 6 | 4 | 4 | 4 | 8 | 4 | 4 | 22 | 1 | 23 | | | | | | | | | 23 | 15 |
| | | | | | 4 | 2 | 2 | 6 | 3 | 4 | 3 | 4 | 5 | 7 | 12 | 1 | 1 | | | | | | | 14 | 16 |
| | | | | | 4 | 3 | 2 | 6 | 1 | 2 | 4 | 7 | 6 | 5 | 11 | 4 | 1 | | | | | | | 16 | 17 |
| | | | | | 3 | 4 | 3 | 5 | 2 | | | | 7 | | 7 | 5 | 2 | | | | | | | 15 | 18 |
| | | | | | | 4 | 1 | | 4 | | | | 1 | 1 | 2 | 3 | | | | | | | | 5 | 19 |
| | 1 | | | | 22 | 25 | 17 | 17 | 7 | 22 | 20 | 30 | 32 | 35 | 67 | 7 | 7 | | | | | | | 81 | 20 |
| | | | | | 3 | 3 | 4 | 2 | 5 | 6 | | | 2 | 2 | 4 | 4 | 2 | 1 | | | 1 | | | 12 | 21 |
| | | | | | 11 | 3 | 10 | 4 | 4 | 10 | 3 | 7 | 4 | 9 | 13 | 8 | 6 | | | | | | 1 | 28 | 22 |
| | | | | | 4 | 3 | 2 | 1 | 2 | 2 | 1 | 1 | | 3 | 3 | 4 | 3 | | | | | | | 10 | 23 |
| | | | | | 1 | | | | | 1 | | | 1 | | 1 | | | | | | | | | 1 | 24 |
| | | | | | | 1 | 2 | | | | | 3 | 1 | 1 | 2 | | 1 | | | | | | | 3 | 25 |
| | | | | | 30 | 31 | 30 | 20 | 26 | 64 | 13 | 5 | 35 | 24 | 59 | 30 | 16 | | 2 | | 1 | 3 | 1 | 112 | 26 |
| | | | | | 1 | | | | | | 1 | | | 1 | 1 | | | | | | | | | 1 | 27 |
| | | | | | 2 | 1 | | | 1 | 2 | | | 2 | 1 | 3 | | | | | | | | | 3 | 28 |
| | | | | | 4 | 3 | 1 | 4 | 5 | 5 | | 2 | 5 | 6 | 11 | | 1 | | | | | | | 12 | 29 |
| | | | | | 1 | 2 | | 1 | 1 | 2 | 1 | | 1 | 2 | 3 | | 1 | | | | | | | 4 | 30 |
| | | | | | 1 | 2 | 1 | 4 | 4 | | | | 4 | 2 | 6 | 1 | | | | | | 1 | | 8 | 31 |
| | | | | | 2 | 3 | 2 | 5 | | 2 | 2 | 6 | 6 | 4 | 10 | | 1 | | | | | | 1 | 12 | 32 |
| | 2 | 1 | 13 | 2 | 119 | 106 | 96 | 84 | 50 | 57 | 25 | 70 | 71 | 105 | 176 | 93 | 109 | 3 | 4 | 7 | 8 | 1 | 8 | 409 | 33 |
| | | | 1 | | 36 | 24 | 22 | 20 | 23 | 25 | 6 | 43 | 45 | 34 | 79 | 8 | 12 | 1 | 2 | | | | | 102 | 34 |
| | | | 1 | 2 | 74 | 23 | 23 | 39 | 44 | 86 | 18 | 8 | 58 | 36 | 94 | 40 | 19 | | | 1 | 1 | 3 | 1 | 159 | 35 |
| 1 | 1 | | 1 | 1 | 309 | 115 | 75 | 159 | 164 | 404 | 46 | 21 | 224 | 165 | 389 | 160 | 90 | 5 | 6 | 4 | 1 | 5 | 4 | 664 | 36 |
| | | | | | | | | 1 | | | | | | | | 1 | | | | | | | | 1 | 37 |
| | | | | | 7 | 8 | 11 | 3 | 9 | 12 | 6 | 1 | 5 | 2 | 7 | 12 | 7 | | 1 | 1 | | 1 | | 29 | 38 |
| | | | | | 4 | 4 | 3 | 1 | 8 | 2 | | | 3 | 2 | 5 | 4 | 3 | | | | | | | 12 | 39 |
| | | | | | 7 | 9 | 7 | 20 | 25 | 14 | 5 | | 13 | 18 | 31 | 7 | 6 | | | | | | | 44 | 40 |
| | | | | 1 | 8 | 12 | 11 | 14 | 7 | 9 | 2 | 27 | 21 | 10 | 31 | 7 | 4 | 2 | 1 | 1 | | | | 46 | 41 |
| | | | | | 2 | 3 | | | 1 | 1 | | 2 | 1 | 1 | 2 | 2 | 1 | | | | | | | 5 | 42 |
| | | | | | 20 | 15 | 11 | 11 | 2 | 6 | 9 | 35 | 14 | 7 | 21 | 22 | 13 | | | | | 1 | | 50 | 43 |
| | | | | | 24 | 4 | | 4 | 6 | 24 | | 1 | 15 | 7 | 22 | 6 | 4 | | | | | | | 32 | 44 |
| | | | | | 5 | 5 | 3 | 3 | 1 | 5 | 1 | 5 | 5 | 3 | 8 | 3 | 4 | 1 | | | | | | 16 | 45 |
| | | | | | | 1 | 1 | 1 | | | | 2 | | 2 | 2 | | 1 | | | | | | | 3 | 46 |
| | | | | | 6 | 7 | 5 | 2 | | | | | 10 | 8 | 18 | 1 | 1 | | | | | | | 20 | 47 |
| | | | | | 29 | 26 | 19 | 29 | 106 | | | | 6 | 6 | 12 | 40 | 48 | 1 | 1 | 1 | 2 | | 1 | 106 | 48 |
| | | | | | 7 | 7 | 2 | 3 | 12 | | | | 12 | 4 | 16 | 2 | 1 | | | | | | | 19 | 49 |
| | | | | | | 3 | 3 | | | 3 | | | | 1 | 1 | 3 | 2 | | | | | | | 6 | 50 |
| | | | | | | 2 | | | 2 | | | | | | | 1 | 1 | | | | | | | 2 | 51 |
| | | | | | | | 1 | | | | | 1 | | | | | 1 | | | | | | | 1 | 52 |
| | | | | | 8 | 15 | 12 | 3 | 7 | 18 | 7 | 2 | 9 | 7 | 16 | 13 | 8 | 1 | 1 | | | | | 39 | 53 |
| | | | | | 1 | | | | | 1 | | | | | | 1 | | | | | | | | 1 | 54 |
| | | | | | 20 | 10 | 41 | 34 | 35 | 61 | 3 | 4 | 30 | 40 | 70 | 18 | 13 | 2 | 2 | | | | 1 | 105 | 55 |
| | | | | | 4 | 6 | 6 | 4 | 5 | 5 | 8 | 1 | 5 | 9 | 14 | 2 | 2 | | 1 | | | | 1 | 20 | 56 |
| | | | | | 2 | 3 | 2 | 2 | 1 | 1 | 2 | 5 | 2 | 5 | 7 | | 1 | | | | | | 1 | 9 | 57 |
| | | | | | 2 | 6 | 4 | 2 | 3 | 3 | 3 | 5 | 4 | 5 | 9 | 3 | | | | | 1 | | 1 | 14 | 58 |
| | | | | | 3 | 3 | 4 | 3 | 3 | 1 | 2 | 6 | | 7 | 7 | | 5 | | | | 1 | | | 13 | 59 |
| | | | | | 2 | 3 | 3 | 2 | 1 | 2 | 1 | 6 | 1 | 2 | 3 | 3 | 2 | 1 | | | 1 | | | 10 | 60 |
| | | | | | 1 | 1 | 1 | 2 | | 1 | 1 | 3 | 1 | 1 | 2 | 1 | 1 | | | | | 1 | | 5 | 61 |
| | | | | | 31 | 50 | 56 | 28 | 55 | 63 | 18 | 23 | 26 | 26 | 52 | 44 | 56 | 5 | 3 | 1 | | 4 | 1 | 166 | 62 |
| | 2 | 2 | 5 | 7 | 660 | 682 | 533 | 467 | 849 | 480 | 227 | 506 | 627 | 581 | 1208 | 513 | 524 | 28 | 29 | 14 | 13 | 23 | 30 | 2382 | 63 |
| 1 | 12 | 4 | 47 | 20 | 2797 | 2678 | 2425 | 2097 | 2794 | 3142 | 1025 | 2090 | 2930 | 2706 | 5639 | 2044 | 1961 | 101 | 121 | 63 | 64 | 86 | 87 | 10165 | |

## SECTION OF THE STATE OF OHIO.

*Lorain, Mahoning, Medina, Portage, Stark, Summit, Trumbull and Wayne.*

| | | | | | | | | | | | | | | | | | | | | | | | | | |
|---|---|---|---|---|---|---|---|---|---|---|---|---|---|---|---|---|---|---|---|---|---|---|---|---|---|
| | 1 | | | | | 1 | 2 | 1 | | | 2 | 2 | 2 | 2 | 4 | | | | | | | | | 4 | 1 |
| | 1 | 8 | 4 | 1 | 16 | 16 | 14 | 11 | 34 | 4 | 5 | | 45 | 12 | 57 | | | | | | | | | 57 | 2 |

## CLASSIFICATION OF DEATHS IN NORTHEASTERN

| | Cause of death. | AGES. | | | | | | | | | | | | | | | | | | NATIVITIES. | | | | | |
|---|---|---|---|---|---|---|---|---|---|---|---|---|---|---|---|---|---|---|---|---|---|---|---|---|---|
| | | Under 1. | | 1 and under 5. | | 5 and under 10. | | 10 and under 20. | | 20 and under 50. | | 50 and under 80. | | 80 and under 100. | | 100 & over. | | Age unknown. | | Born in State. | N. England States. | Middle States. | Southern States. | Southwest'n States. | Northwest'n States. |
| | | M. | F. | M. | F. | M. | F. | M. | F. | M. | F. | M. | F. | M | F. | M | F. | M | F. | | | | | | |
| 1 | Accident, burned | ... | ... | 2 | 7 | ... | 1 | ... | ... | 1 | 1 | ... | ... | .. | .. | .. | .. | .. | .. | 8 | .. | 2 | ... | ... | ... |
| 2 | ....do...drowned | ... | ... | 4 | 2 | 5 | ... | 5 | 1 | 6 | ... | 1 | ... | .. | .. | .. | .. | .. | .. | 17 | 1 | 1 | ... | ... | ... |
| 3 | ....do...scalded | ... | ... | 6 | 4 | ... | ... | ... | ... | ... | ... | ... | ... | .. | .. | .. | .. | .. | .. | 9 | .. | ... | ... | ... | ... |
| 4 | ....do...railroad | ... | ... | ... | ... | ... | ... | 1 | ... | 1 | ... | ... | ... | .. | .. | .. | .. | .. | .. | 2 | .. | ... | ... | ... | ... |
| 5 | Apoplexy | ... | ... | ... | ... | ... | ... | 1 | ... | 6 | 2 | 17 | 2 | 1 | .. | .. | .. | .. | .. | 2 | 14 | 10 | ... | ... | ... |
| 6 | Asthma | ... | ... | ... | ... | ... | ... | ... | ... | ... | ... | ... | 1 | .. | .. | .. | .. | .. | .. | ... | 1 | ... | ... | ... | ... |
| 7 | Bowels, disease of | 5 | ... | 4 | 1 | ... | ... | ... | ... | ... | 1 | 1 | ... | .. | .. | .. | .. | .. | .. | 9 | .. | 2 | ... | ... | ... |
| 8 | Brain,......do | 4 | 3 | 7 | 4 | ... | ... | 2 | ... | 1 | 4 | 2 | ... | .. | .. | .. | .. | .. | .. | 22 | 4 | 1 | ... | ... | ... |
| 9 | Bronchitis | 1 | ... | ... | ... | ... | ... | ... | ... | 2 | 1 | ... | ... | .. | .. | .. | .. | .. | .. | 2 | .. | 1 | ... | ... | ... |
| 10 | Cancer | ... | ... | ... | ... | ... | ... | ... | ... | 3 | 4 | 7 | 14 | .. | .. | .. | .. | .. | .. | 3 | 13 | 7 | ... | ... | ... |
| 11 | Canker rash | 1 | 1 | 3 | 2 | 4 | 2 | ... | 1 | ... | ... | ... | ... | .. | .. | .. | .. | .. | .. | 13 | 1 | ... | ... | ... | ... |
| 12 | Catarrh | 5 | 2 | 1 | ... | ... | ... | ... | ... | ... | ... | 1 | ... | 1 | .. | .. | .. | .. | .. | 8 | .. | 1 | ... | ... | ... |
| 13 | Chicken pox | ... | 1 | ... | ... | ... | ... | ... | ... | ... | ... | ... | ... | .. | .. | .. | .. | .. | .. | 1 | .. | ... | ... | ... | ... |
| 14 | Childbirth | ... | ... | ... | ... | ... | ... | ... | 2 | ... | 37 | ... | ... | .. | .. | .. | .. | .. | .. | 9 | 8 | 14 | 1 | ... | ... |
| 15 | Cholera | 3 | 3 | 11 | 9 | 10 | 2 | 3 | 6 | 55 | 34 | 13 | 10 | .. | 2 | .. | .. | .. | .. | 47 | 8 | 21 | 2 | ... | ... |
| 16 | ...do...infantum | 14 | 12 | 1 | 6 | ... | ... | ... | ... | ... | ... | ... | ... | .. | .. | .. | .. | .. | .. | 32 | .. | 1 | ... | ... | ... |
| 17 | ...do...morbus | 1 | ... | 5 | 2 | ... | ... | 1 | ... | 2 | 2 | 3 | 1 | .. | .. | .. | .. | .. | .. | 11 | 2 | 3 | ... | ... | ... |
| 18 | Colic | ... | 2 | ... | 1 | 1 | ... | 1 | ... | 3 | 2 | 1 | ... | 1 | .. | .. | .. | .. | .. | 6 | 1 | 4 | ... | ... | ... |
| 19 | Congestion | 1 | ... | ... | ... | 1 | 1 | 1 | ... | ... | ... | ... | ... | .. | .. | .. | .. | .. | .. | 4 | .. | ... | ... | ... | ... |
| 20 | ....do....brain | 1 | 2 | 3 | 1 | ... | ... | 1 | 3 | 1 | ... | ... | ... | .. | .. | .. | .. | .. | .. | 11 | 1 | ... | ... | ... | ... |
| 21 | ....do....lungs | 1 | ... | 2 | 2 | ... | 1 | ... | ... | ... | ... | 1 | ... | .. | .. | .. | .. | .. | .. | 6 | 1 | ... | ... | ... | ... |
| 22 | Consumption | 12 | 17 | 11 | 9 | 5 | 4 | 25 | 33 | 114 | 159 | 61 | 47 | 5 | 7 | .. | .. | .. | .. | 189 | 89 | 147 | 7 | ... | 2 |
| 23 | Convulsions | 39 | 25 | 15 | 12 | 3 | 1 | 2 | 3 | 3 | 9 | 3 | 1 | .. | .. | .. | .. | .. | .. | 100 | 4 | 7 | ... | ... | ... |
| 24 | Croup | 24 | 15 | 40 | 33 | 13 | 11 | 3 | 1 | ... | ... | ... | ... | .. | .. | .. | .. | .. | .. | 127 | 1 | 7 | ... | ... | 2 |
| 25 | Debility | 3 | 2 | ... | 3 | ... | ... | 1 | 1 | 1 | 1 | 1 | ... | .. | .. | .. | .. | .. | .. | 9 | 1 | 2 | ... | ... | ... |
| 26 | Diabetes | ... | ... | ... | ... | 2 | ... | ... | 2 | ... | ... | 5 | ... | .. | .. | .. | .. | .. | .. | 3 | 4 | 2 | ... | ... | ... |
| 27 | Diarrhœa | 4 | 6 | 6 | 2 | ... | 2 | ... | ... | 2 | 3 | 3 | 1 | .. | .. | .. | .. | .. | .. | 20 | 2 | 3 | ... | ... | ... |
| 28 | Dropsy | 3 | 6 | 6 | 13 | 3 | 5 | 4 | 5 | 15 | 17 | 25 | 32 | 5 | 1 | .. | .. | .. | .. | 59 | 19 | 43 | 4 | 3 | ... |
| 29 | Dysentery | 50 | 30 | 115 | 107 | 33 | 27 | 21 | 15 | 30 | 42 | 18 | 21 | 5 | 5 | .. | .. | .. | .. | 390 | 30 | 58 | 3 | ... | 2 |
| 30 | Dyspepsia | ... | ... | ... | ... | ... | ... | ... | ... | ... | 1 | 5 | 4 | .. | .. | .. | .. | .. | .. | 1 | 3 | 5 | ... | ... | ... |
| 31 | Epilepsy | ... | ... | ... | ... | ... | ... | 2 | ... | 2 | ... | ... | ... | .. | .. | .. | .. | .. | .. | 3 | .. | 1 | ... | ... | ... |
| 32 | Erysipelas | 7 | 6 | 4 | 9 | 4 | 4 | 2 | 13 | 18 | 33 | 16 | 11 | 1 | 3 | .. | .. | .. | .. | 63 | 29 | 26 | 2 | ... | 1 |
| 33 | Fever not, specified | 5 | 3 | 26 | 5 | 9 | 6 | 11 | 12 | 55 | 40 | 18 | 20 | 1 | .. | .. | .. | .. | .. | 111 | 26 | 45 | 1 | 1 | 1 |
| 34 | ..do .bilious | 1 | ... | ... | 1 | ... | ... | ... | 1 | 4 | 7 | 5 | 2 | .. | .. | .. | .. | .. | .. | 10 | 4 | 3 | ... | ... | ... |
| 35 | ..do..brain | 8 | 1 | 7 | 2 | 1 | ... | 1 | ... | 1 | 1 | 1 | 1 | .. | .. | .. | .. | .. | .. | 19 | 2 | ... | ... | ... | ... |
| 36 | ..do..catarrhal | ... | ... | ... | 1 | ... | ... | ... | ... | ... | ... | ... | ... | .. | .. | .. | .. | .. | .. | ... | .. | 1 | ... | ... | ... |
| 37 | ..do..congestive | ... | ... | 2 | 2 | 1 | ... | 1 | 1 | 2 | ... | 1 | ... | .. | .. | .. | .. | .. | .. | 7 | 1 | 2 | ... | ... | ... |
| 38 | ..do..inflammatory | ... | ... | ... | ... | ... | ... | ... | ... | ... | 1 | ... | ... | .. | .. | .. | .. | .. | .. | ... | .. | 1 | ... | ... | ... |
| 39 | ..do..intermittent | 2 | 2 | ... | 2 | 1 | ... | ... | ... | 1 | ... | 4 | 1 | .. | .. | .. | .. | .. | .. | 6 | 2 | 2 | ... | ... | 1 |
| 40 | ..do..puerperal | ... | ... | ... | ... | ... | ... | ... | ... | ... | 4 | ... | ... | .. | .. | .. | .. | .. | .. | 2 | .. | 1 | ... | ... | ... |
| 41 | ..do..scarlet | 7 | 8 | 51 | 33 | 20 | 15 | 7 | 6 | 1 | 2 | ... | ... | .. | .. | .. | .. | .. | .. | 130 | 2 | 7 | ... | 1 | 2 |
| 42 | ..do..typhoid | ... | 1 | 6 | 2 | 2 | 8 | 11 | 12 | 39 | 27 | 7 | 4 | .. | .. | .. | .. | .. | .. | 69 | 3 | 31 | ... | ... | 2 |
| 43 | ..do..winter | ... | ... | ... | ... | ... | ... | ... | ... | 1 | ... | ... | ... | .. | .. | .. | .. | .. | .. | ... | .. | 1 | ... | ... | ... |
| 44 | Fracture | ... | ... | ... | ... | ... | ... | ... | ... | ... | ... | 1 | ... | .. | .. | .. | .. | .. | .. | ... | .. | 1 | ... | ... | ... |
| 45 | Gravel | 1 | ... | ... | 1 | ... | ... | ... | ... | 2 | 1 | 7 | 1 | 2 | .. | .. | .. | .. | .. | 3 | 3 | 6 | ... | ... | ... |
| 46 | Head, disease of | ... | 1 | 1 | 1 | 1 | ... | ... | ... | 2 | ... | ... | ... | .. | .. | .. | .. | .. | .. | 5 | .. | 1 | ... | ... | ... |
| 47 | Heart....do | 2 | 2 | ... | 1 | 1 | 1 | 5 | 2 | 7 | 6 | 5 | 12 | .. | .. | .. | .. | .. | .. | 16 | 13 | 13 | ... | ... | ... |
| 48 | Hemorrhage | ... | ... | ... | ... | 1 | ... | 1 | 1 | 4 | 3 | 2 | ... | .. | 1 | .. | .. | .. | .. | 2 | .. | 7 | ... | 1 | ... |
| 49 | Hernia | ... | ... | ... | ... | ... | ... | ... | ... | ... | ... | 1 | 1 | .. | .. | .. | .. | .. | .. | ... | 1 | 1 | ... | ... | ... |
| 50 | Hives | 1 | ... | 1 | ... | ... | ... | ... | ... | ... | ... | ... | ... | .. | .. | .. | .. | .. | .. | 2 | .. | ... | ... | ... | ... |
| 51 | Hooping cough | 16 | 12 | 19 | 17 | 1 | 3 | ... | ... | ... | ... | ... | ... | .. | .. | .. | .. | .. | .. | 62 | .. | 5 | ... | ... | 1 |
| 52 | Hydrocephalus | 2 | ... | 3 | 3 | 1 | 2 | ... | ... | ... | 1 | ... | ... | .. | .. | .. | .. | .. | .. | 10 | .. | 1 | ... | ... | 1 |
| 53 | Inflammation | 9 | 6 | 13 | 6 | 3 | 2 | 5 | 3 | 3 | 6 | 2 | 2 | .. | .. | .. | .. | .. | .. | 47 | 2 | 7 | ... | ... | ... |
| 54 | ....do......bowels | 4 | 2 | 7 | ... | 3 | 2 | 2 | 2 | 5 | 7 | 6 | 1 | .. | .. | .. | .. | .. | .. | 23 | 4 | 7 | ... | ... | 1 |
| 55 | ....do......brain | 7 | 9 | 5 | 6 | 2 | 3 | 1 | 3 | 4 | 1 | 1 | ... | .. | .. | .. | .. | .. | .. | 37 | .. | 5 | ... | ... | ... |
| 56 | ....do......stomach | ... | ... | 1 | ... | ... | ... | ... | ... | ... | 1 | ... | ... | .. | .. | .. | .. | .. | .. | 1 | .. | 1 | ... | ... | ... |
| 57 | Insanity | ... | ... | ... | ... | ... | ... | ... | ... | ... | 1 | 2 | ... | .. | .. | .. | .. | .. | .. | 1 | 1 | ... | ... | ... | ... |
| 58 | Intemperance | ... | ... | ... | ... | ... | ... | ... | ... | 1 | ... | 1 | ... | .. | .. | .. | .. | .. | .. | ... | .. | 2 | ... | ... | ... |
| 59 | Jaundice | ... | 1 | ... | ... | ... | ... | 1 | ... | 2 | ... | 2 | ... | .. | .. | .. | .. | .. | .. | 2 | .. | 3 | ... | ... | 1 |
| 60 | Killed | ... | ... | 1 | ... | ... | ... | 2 | ... | 1 | ... | ... | 1 | .. | .. | .. | .. | .. | .. | 2 | 1 | ... | ... | ... | 1 |
| 61 | Lightning | ... | ... | ... | ... | ... | ... | 4 | ... | ... | ... | ... | ... | .. | .. | .. | .. | .. | .. | 4 | .. | ... | ... | ... | ... |
| 62 | Liver, disease of | 3 | ... | 1 | 1 | ... | 1 | 1 | 1 | 3 | 3 | 4 | 6 | .. | 1 | .. | .. | .. | .. | 11 | 4 | 7 | 1 | ... | ... |
| 63 | Lockjaw | ... | ... | 1 | ... | ... | ... | ... | ... | ... | ... | ... | ... | .. | .. | .. | .. | .. | .. | 1 | .. | ... | ... | ... | ... |
| 64 | Lungs, disease of | 9 | 6 | 2 | 3 | 4 | 1 | 1 | 1 | 3 | 5 | 8 | 3 | .. | .. | .. | .. | .. | .. | 32 | 5 | 8 | ... | ... | ... |
| 65 | Malformation | 1 | 2 | 1 | ... | 1 | ... | ... | ... | ... | ... | ... | ... | .. | .. | .. | .. | .. | .. | 4 | .. | ... | ... | ... | ... |
| 66 | Mania-a-potu | ... | ... | ... | ... | ... | ... | ... | ... | 4 | ... | 3 | ... | .. | .. | .. | .. | .. | .. | 1 | 2 | 1 | ... | ... | 1 |
| 67 | Measles | 5 | 2 | 12 | 15 | 4 | ... | 2 | 2 | ... | ... | ... | ... | .. | .. | .. | .. | .. | .. | 39 | .. | 2 | ... | ... | 1 |
| 68 | Mortification | ... | ... | ... | ... | ... | ... | ... | ... | ... | ... | ... | 1 | 1 | .. | .. | .. | .. | .. | ... | 1 | 1 | ... | ... | ... |
| 69 | Mumps | ... | ... | 1 | ... | ... | ... | ... | ... | ... | ... | ... | ... | .. | .. | .. | .. | .. | .. | 1 | .. | ... | ... | ... | ... |
| 70 | Murder | ... | ... | ... | ... | ... | ... | ... | ... | 2 | 1 | ... | ... | .. | .. | .. | .. | .. | .. | ... | .. | ... | ... | ... | ... |
| 71 | Neuralgia | ... | ... | ... | 1 | ... | ... | 1 | ... | ... | 1 | ... | 1 | .. | .. | .. | .. | .. | 1 | 3 | 1 | 1 | ... | ... | ... |
| 72 | Old age | ... | ... | ... | ... | ... | ... | ... | ... | ... | ... | 11 | 21 | 28 | 33 | .. | 1 | .. | .. | 10 | 36 | 31 | 3 | ... | ... |
| 73 | Paralysis | ... | ... | ... | 1 | ... | ... | ... | 1 | 3 | 5 | 18 | 11 | 6 | 2 | .. | .. | .. | .. | 4 | 13 | 24 | 2 | ... | ... |
| 74 | Piles | ... | ... | ... | ... | ... | ... | ... | ... | 1 | ... | 1 | ... | .. | .. | .. | .. | .. | .. | ... | .. | 2 | ... | ... | ... |
| 75 | Pleurisy | ... | 1 | ... | 1 | ... | ... | ... | ... | 1 | 4 | 1 | 1 | 1 | 1 | .. | .. | .. | .. | 3 | 2 | 4 | ... | ... | ... |

SECTION OF THE STATE OF OHIO—Continued.

| NATIVITIES. | | | | | SEASON OF DECEASE. | | | | DURATION OF SICKNESS. | | | | WHITES. | | | COLORED. | | | | | | | | Aggregate deaths. | |
|---|---|---|---|---|---|---|---|---|---|---|---|---|---|---|---|---|---|---|---|---|---|---|---|---|---|
| California and Territories. | Ireland. | Germany. | Other foreign countries. | Unknown. | Spring. | Summer. | Autumn. | Winter. | Under 1 week. | 1 week and under 1 month. | 1 month and under 3 months. | 3 months and over. | Males. | Females. | Total. | Slaves. | | | | Free. | | | | | |
| | | | | | | | | | | | | | | | | Black. | | Mulatto. | | Black. | | Mul. | | | |
| | | | | | | | | | | | | | | | | M. | F. | M. | F. | M. | F. | M | F. | | |
| | | 1 | 1 | | 3 | 3 | 2 | 4 | 8 | 3 | | | 3 | 9 | 12 | | | | | | | | | 12 | 1 |
| | | 2 | 2 | 1 | 2 | 12 | 4 | 5 | 24 | | | | 20 | 3 | 23 | | | | | | | 1 | | 24 | 2 |
| | | | 1 | | 3 | 2 | 4 | 1 | 2 | 3 | | 1 | 6 | 4 | 10 | | | | | | | | | 10 | 3 |
| | | | | | | | 2 | | | | | | 2 | | 2 | | | | | | | | | 2 | 4 |
| | | 1 | 2 | | 10 | 11 | 5 | 8 | 16 | 8 | | | 24 | 4 | 28 | | | | | 1 | | | | 29 | 5 |
| | | | | | 1 | | | | | | | 1 | | 1 | 1 | | | | | | | | | 1 | 6 |
| | | | 1 | | 1 | 5 | 5 | 1 | 8 | 9 | | | 9 | 2 | 11 | | | | | | | 1 | | 12 | 7 |
| | | | | | 11 | 4 | 5 | 7 | 12 | 10 | 2 | 1 | 16 | 11 | 27 | | | | | | | | | 27 | 8 |
| | | | | 1 | 2 | | 2 | | | 1 | 1 | 2 | 3 | 1 | 4 | | | | | | | | | 4 | 9 |
| | | | 3 | 2 | 8 | 9 | 5 | 5 | | 1 | 2 | 19 | 10 | 18 | 2[illegible] | | | | | | | | | 28 | 10 |
| | | | | | 6 | 2 | 4 | 2 | 4 | 6 | 2 | 1 | 8 | 6 | 14 | | | | | | | | | 14 | 11 |
| | | 1 | | | 4 | 2 | 3 | 1 | 2 | 6 | 1 | 1 | 8 | 2 | 10 | | | | | | | | | 10 | 12 |
| | | | | | | 1 | | | 1 | | | | | 1 | 1 | | | | | | | | | 1 | 13 |
| | | 4 | 2 | 1 | 9 | 15 | 5 | 8 | 18 | 11 | 2 | 1 | | 38 | 38 | | | | | | 1 | | | 39 | 14 |
| | 32 | 27 | 22 | 2 | 3 | 50 | 103 | 1 | 59 | 14 | | 1 | 95 | 66 | 161 | | | | | | | | | 161 | 15 |
| | | | | | 2 | 11 | 20 | | 18 | 6 | 3 | 2 | 15 | 18 | 33 | | | | | | | | | 33 | 16 |
| | 1 | | | | 1 | 1 | 12 | 3 | 15 | 2 | | | 12 | 5 | 17 | | | | | | | | | 17 | 17 |
| | | 1 | | | 1 | 4 | 3 | 4 | 4 | 8 | | | 7 | 5 | 12 | | | | | | | | | 12 | 18 |
| | | | | | 2 | 2 | | | 2 | 2 | | | 3 | 1 | 4 | | | | | | | | | 4 | 19 |
| | | | | | 4 | 3 | 1 | 4 | 5 | 6 | | | 6 | 6 | 12 | | | | | | | | | 12 | 20 |
| | | | | | 1 | 1 | 2 | 3 | 4 | 3 | | | 4 | 3 | 7 | | | | | | | | | 7 | 21 |
| | 16 | 23 | 28 | 8 | 154 | 133 | 132 | 90 | 12 | 47 | 49 | 363 | 233 | 276 | 509 | | | | | | | | | 509 | 22 |
| | 3 | 1 | 1 | | 36 | 24 | 35 | 21 | 58 | 24 | 2 | 4 | 64 | 51 | 115 | | | | | | | 1 | | 116 | 23 |
| | 1 | 2 | | | 35 | 22 | 34 | 48 | 103 | 27 | 2 | 3 | 80 | 60 | 140 | | | | | | | | | 140 | 24 |
| | 1 | | | | 4 | 5 | 2 | 2 | 1 | 2 | 2 | 5 | 6 | 7 | 13 | | | | | | | | | 13 | 25 |
| | | | | | 2 | 3 | 2 | 2 | 1 | 1 | | 7 | 7 | 2 | 9 | | | | | | | | | 9 | 26 |
| | 2 | | 2 | | 3 | 3 | 21 | 1 | 5 | 18 | 3 | 3 | 15 | 14 | 29 | | | | | | | | | 29 | 27 |
| | 2 | 4 | 6 | | 42 | 37 | 25 | 35 | 14 | 38 | 23 | 54 | 61 | 78 | 139 | | | | | | | | 1 | 140 | 28 |
| | 11 | 7 | 17 | 1 | 13 | 45 | 423 | 25 | 132 | 306 | 18 | 9 | 272 | 247 | 519 | | | | | | | | | 519 | 29 |
| | 1 | | | | 2 | 3 | 2 | 3 | 1 | 1 | 1 | 7 | 5 | 5 | 10 | | | | | | | | | 10 | 30 |
| | | | | | 1 | | 3 | | | 1 | | 3 | 4 | | 4 | | | | | | | | | 4 | 31 |
| | | 2 | 5 | 3 | 47 | 32 | 18 | 34 | 48 | 70 | 5 | 7 | 51 | 77 | 128 | | | | | 1 | 1 | | 1 | 131 | 32 |
| | 5 | 12 | 7 | 2 | 65 | 45 | 63 | 35 | 80 | 124 | 24 | 8 | 125 | 85 | 210 | | | | | | 1 | | | 211 | 33 |
| | 1 | 1 | 2 | | 5 | 2 | 8 | 5 | 1 | 10 | 8 | | 10 | 11 | 21 | | | | | | | | | 21 | 34 |
| | 1 | 1 | 1 | | 9 | 3 | 6 | 6 | 9 | 8 | | 1 | 19 | 5 | 24 | | | | | | | | | 24 | 35 |
| | | | | | 1 | | | | | 1 | | | | 1 | 1 | | | | | | | | | 1 | 36 |
| | | | | | 5 | 3 | 2 | | 4 | 8 | | | 7 | 3 | 10 | | | | | | | | | 10 | 37 |
| | | | | | | | | 1 | | 1 | | | | 1 | 1 | | | | | | | | | 1 | 38 |
| | | | 2 | | 2 | 4 | 6 | 1 | 4 | 5 | | 3 | 8 | 5 | 13 | | | | | | | | | 13 | 39 |
| | 1 | | | | 3 | | 1 | | 3 | | | | | 4 | 4 | | | | | | | | | 4 | 40 |
| | 1 | 2 | 5 | | 54 | 37 | 31 | 27 | 60 | 76 | 6 | | 86 | 64 | 150 | | | | | | | | | 150 | 41 |
| | 2 | 1 | 5 | 1 | 31 | 17 | 43 | 23 | 11 | 76 | 18 | 4 | 65 | 49 | 114 | | | | | | | | | 114 | 42 |
| | | | | | 1 | | | | | 1 | | | 1 | | 1 | | | | | | | | | 1 | 43 |
| | | | | | | 1 | | | 1 | | | | 1 | | 1 | | | | | | | | | 1 | 44 |
| | 1 | | 1 | 1 | 2 | 4 | 5 | 4 | 2 | 2 | 3 | 7 | 12 | 3 | 15 | | | | | | | | | 15 | 45 |
| | | | | | 2 | 2 | 1 | 1 | 2 | 3 | 1 | | 4 | 2 | 6 | | | | | | | | | 6 | 46 |
| | | 2 | | | 11 | 7 | 15 | 11 | 14 | 14 | 7 | 6 | 20 | 24 | 44 | | | | | | | | | 44 | 47 |
| | | 1 | 2 | | 3 | 3 | 3 | 4 | 7 | 2 | 1 | | 8 | 5 | 13 | | | | | | | | | 13 | 48 |
| | | | | | 1 | | 1 | | | 1 | 1 | | 1 | 1 | 2 | | | | | | | | | 2 | 49 |
| | | | | | 1 | 1 | | | | 2 | | | 2 | | 2 | | | | | | | | | 2 | 50 |
| | | | | | 17 | 15 | 23 | 13 | 14 | 30 | 11 | 3 | 36 | 32 | 68 | | | | | | | | | 68 | 51 |
| | | | | | 3 | 4 | 4 | 1 | 1 | 8 | 1 | 2 | 6 | 6 | 12 | | | | | | | | | 12 | 52 |
| | | 1 | 3 | | 23 | 14 | 11 | 11 | 11 | 33 | 2 | 2 | 35 | 25 | 60 | | | | | | | | | 60 | 53 |
| | 4 | 1 | | 1 | 13 | 4 | 12 | 11 | 16 | 18 | 1 | 1 | 27 | 14 | 41 | | | | | | | | | 41 | 54 |
| | | | | | 14 | 10 | 11 | 7 | 12 | 23 | | | 20 | 22 | 42 | | | | | | | | | 42 | 55 |
| | | | | | | 1 | 1 | | 2 | | | | 1 | 1 | 2 | | | | | | | | | 2 | 56 |
| | 1 | | | | 1 | 1 | 1 | | | 2 | | 1 | 2 | 1 | 3 | | | | | | | | | 3 | 57 |
| | | | | | | 2 | | | | 1 | | | 2 | | 2 | | | | | | | | | 2 | 58 |
| | | | | | 1 | 2 | 2 | 1 | 1 | 2 | | 3 | 5 | 1 | 6 | | | | | | | | | 6 | 59 |
| | | 1 | | | 1 | 2 | | 2 | 1 | | 1 | | 4 | 1 | 5 | | | | | | | | | 5 | 60 |
| | | | | | | 2 | 1 | | 3 | | | | 4 | | 4 | | | | | | | | | 4 | 61 |
| | 1 | 1 | | | 9 | 9 | 3 | 4 | 3 | 5 | 4 | 11 | 12 | 13 | 25 | | | | | | | | | 25 | 62 |
| | | | | | | | 1 | | | 1 | | | | | | | | | | 1 | | | | 1 | 63 |
| | 1 | | | | 20 | 7 | 8 | 11 | 11 | 21 | 5 | 7 | 26 | 19 | 45 | | | | | 1 | | | | 46 | 64 |
| | | 1 | | | 3 | 1 | 1 | | 2 | 2 | | 1 | 3 | 2 | 5 | | | | | | | | | 5 | 65 |
| | 1 | 1 | | | 2 | 4 | 1 | | 2 | 4 | | | 7 | | 7 | | | | | | | | | 7 | 66 |
| | | | | | 10 | 16 | 13 | 3 | 9 | 23 | 8 | 1 | 22 | 19 | 41 | | | | | 1 | | | | 42 | 67 |
| | | | | | 1 | | 1 | | | | 1 | 1 | 1 | 1 | 2 | | | | | | | | | 2 | 68 |
| | | | | | 1 | | | | | | 1 | | 1 | | 1 | | | | | | | | | 1 | 69 |
| | 1 | | 1 | 1 | | | 2 | 1 | 1 | 1 | | | 2 | | 2 | | | | | | 1 | | | 3 | 70 |
| | | | | | 2 | 2 | | 1 | | | 1 | 3 | 1 | 3 | 4 | | | | | | 1 | | | 5 | 71 |
| | 5 | 3 | 5 | 1 | 33 | 14 | 19 | 28 | 11 | 19 | 5 | 9 | 37 | 55 | 94 | | | | | | | | | 94 | 72 |
| | 1 | 1 | 2 | | 19 | 4 | 15 | 9 | 16 | 9 | 5 | 14 | 27 | 20 | 47 | | | | | | | | | 47 | 73 |
| | | | | | | 1 | 1 | | | 1 | | 1 | 2 | | 2 | | | | | | | | | 2 | 74 |
| | 1 | | 1 | | 5 | 1 | 3 | 2 | 3 | 5 | | 3 | 3 | 8 | 11 | | | | | | | | | 11 | 75 |

## CLASSIFICATION OF DEATHS IN NORTHEASTERN

| | Cause of death. | AGES. | | | | | | | | | | | | | | | | | | NATIVITIES. | | | | | |
|---|---|---|---|---|---|---|---|---|---|---|---|---|---|---|---|---|---|---|---|---|---|---|---|---|---|
| | | Under 1. | | 1 and under 5. | | 5 and under 10. | | 10 and under 20. | | 20 and under 50. | | 50 and under 80. | | 80 and under 100. | | 100 & over. | | Age unknown. | | Born in State. | N. England States. | Middle States. | Southern States. | Southwest'n States. | Northwest'n States. |
| | | M. | F. | M. | F. | M. | F. | M. | F. | M. | F. | M. | F. | M | F. | M | F. | M | F. | | | | | | |
| 1 | Pneumonia | 2[illegible] | 13 | 17 | 20 | 8 | 5 | 4 | 3 | 17 | 8 | 15 | 12 | 4 | 1 | | | | | 87 | 11 | 33 | 1 | | 1 |
| 2 | Poison | | | | 1 | | | | | | | | | | | | | | | 1 | | | | | |
| 3 | Putrid sore throat | | | | | 2 | | 2 | 1 | | | | | | | | | | | 4 | 1 | | | | |
| 4 | Quinsy | | | | | | | | | 1 | | | | | | | | | | | | | | | |
| 5 | Rheumatism | | | | | | | 3 | 1 | 2 | 1 | 3 | | | | | | | | 4 | 2 | 1 | | 1 | |
| 6 | Rickets | | 1 | | | | | | | | | | | | | | | | | 1 | | | | | |
| 7 | Scrofula | 1 | 2 | 1 | 2 | 1 | | | 1 | | 1 | 1 | | | | | | | | 7 | 1 | 2 | | | |
| 8 | Small pox | 6 | | 2 | 4 | 1 | 6 | | 1 | 12 | 2 | 3 | 2 | 1 | 1 | | | | | 20 | 5 | 8 | 2 | | |
| 9 | Spine, disease of | 1 | | | | 1 | | | | 2 | 1 | 1 | | | | | | | | 3 | 1 | 1 | | | |
| 10 | Stillborn | 1 | | | | | | | | | | | | | | | | | | 1 | | | | | |
| 11 | Stomach, disease of | | | | | | 1 | | | 1 | 2 | 3 | | | | | | | | 1 | 3 | 3 | | | |
| 12 | Suicide | | | | | | | 1 | | 4 | 3 | 2 | | | | | | | | 1 | 3 | 1 | | | |
| 13 | Summer complaint | | 1 | | 1 | | | | | | | | | | | | | | | 2 | | | | | |
| 14 | Teething | | 6 | 3 | 3 | | | | | | | | | | | | | | | 11 | | | | | |
| 15 | Throat, disease of | | | 1 | 1 | | 2 | | 2 | | | | | | | | | | | 5 | | | | | |
| 16 | Thrush | 2 | | 3 | 1 | | | | | | | | | | | | | | | 5 | | | | | |
| 17 | Tumor | | | | | 1 | | 1 | 2 | 1 | 1 | 1 | | | | | | | | 5 | 2 | | | | |
| 18 | Ulcer | | | | 1 | | | | | 1 | 4 | | | | | | | | | 4 | 1 | 1 | | | |
| 19 | Worms | 1 | 1 | 6 | 3 | | | 1 | | | | | | | | | | | | 12 | | | | | |
| 20 | Unknown | 66 | 48 | 10 | 11 | 7 | 7 | 7 | 7 | 25 | 34 | 24 | 16 | 4 | 4 | | | 2 | 1 | 171 | 27 | 41 | 1 | 1 | 1 |
| | Total | 360 | 264 | 453 | 383 | 167 | 121 | 161 | 152 | 508 | 548 | 356 | 271 | 70 | 64 | .. | 1 | 2 | 2 | 2235 | 483 | 709 | 32 | 10 | 22 |

## CLASSIFICATION OF DEATHS IN NORTHWESTERN

*Embracing the following counties: Allen, Crawford, Defiance, Erie, Fulton, Hancock, Henry, Wood, and*

| | | | | | | | | | | | | | | | | | | | | | | | | | |
|---|---|---|---|---|---|---|---|---|---|---|---|---|---|---|---|---|---|---|---|---|---|---|---|---|---|
| 1 | Abscess | | | | | | | | 1 | 1 | | | | | | | | | | 1 | | 1 | | | |
| 2 | Accident, not specif'd | | | 4 | 2 | 4 | | 9 | 1 | 14 | 1 | 2 | | | | | | | | 20 | | 7 | 2 | | |
| 3 | ..do....burned | 1 | | 1 | 2 | 1 | 6 | 1 | | | 1 | | 1 | | | | | | | 12 | 1 | 1 | | | |
| 4 | ...do....drowned | | | | 1 | 1 | 1 | 4 | | 3 | | 2 | | | | | | | | 11 | 1 | 4 | | | |
| 5 | ...do....scalded | 1 | 1 | 1 | 2 | 1 | | | | 1 | | | | | | | | | | 7 | | | | | |
| 6 | ...do....railroad | | | | | | | | | 1 | | 1 | | | | | | | | | | | | | |
| 7 | Apoplexy | | | | | | | 1 | | 2 | 4 | 3 | 2 | | 1 | | | | | 2 | 1 | 7 | 1 | | |
| 8 | Asthma | | | 1 | | | | | | | | 1 | 2 | | | | | | | 2 | | 2 | | | |
| 9 | Bowels disease of | | | 2 | | | | | | 1 | 2 | | | | | | | | | 2 | 1 | 2 | | | |
| 10 | Brain...... do | 2 | 1 | 2 | 1 | | | 1 | | | 1 | | | | | | | | | 6 | | | | | 1 |
| 11 | Bronchitis | 1 | | 1 | 1 | | | | | | 1 | 1 | | | | | | | | 4 | | 1 | | | |
| 12 | Cancer | | | 1 | | 1 | | | | 1 | 2 | 5 | 3 | | | | | | | 2 | 1 | 8 | 1 | | |
| 13 | Canker rash | | | | 1 | | | | | | | | | | | | | | | | | | | | 1 |
| 14 | Catarrh | 1 | 2 | 3 | | | | | 1 | 1 | | | | | | | | | | 7 | | 1 | | | |
| 15 | Chicken pox | | | 1 | | | | | | | | | | | | | | | | 1 | | | | | |
| 16 | Childbirth | | | | | | | | 5 | | 36 | | | | | | | | 1 | 19 | 1 | 16 | | | |
| 17 | Cholera | 10 | 7 | 28 | 22 | 25 | 17 | 43 | 48 | 215 | 83 | 47 | 12 | 4 | 2 | | | | | 185 | 21 | 71 | 4 | | 5 |
| 18 | ...do..in fantum | 4 | 3 | 6 | 1 | | | | | | | | | | | | | | | 13 | 1 | | | | |
| 19 | ...do..morbus | 5 | 2 | 5 | 3 | 1 | | 2 | | 3 | 2 | 2 | | | | | | | | 18 | 1 | 6 | | | |
| 20 | Colic | | 1 | 2 | 1 | 1 | 1 | | | 3 | | 1 | | | | | | | | 5 | | 1 | 1 | | |
| 21 | Congestion of brain | 1 | | | | | | | | 1 | | | | | | | | | | 2 | | | | | |
| 22 | Consumption | 6 | 5 | 4 | 11 | 3 | 3 | 7 | 21 | 79 | 81 | 27 | 31 | | | | | | | 111 | 21 | 116 | 4 | | 2 |
| 23 | Convulsions | 24 | 23 | 20 | 14 | 1 | 2 | | 3 | 6 | 2 | | 1 | | | | | | | 84 | 1 | 5 | 1 | | 3 |
| 24 | Croup | 23 | 16 | 44 | 44 | 14 | 10 | 2 | 2 | 1 | 1 | | | | | | | | | 150 | | 6 | | | |
| 25 | Debility | | | | | | | | | 2 | | 3 | | | | | | | | | 1 | 2 | | | |
| 26 | Diabetes | | | | | | | | | 1 | | 1 | | | | | | | | 1 | | 1 | | | |
| 27 | Diarrhœa | 11 | 10 | 9 | 13 | 1 | 3 | 1 | 2 | 6 | 1 | 5 | 3 | | | | | 1 | | 54 | 1 | 7 | | | |
| 28 | Dropsy | 3 | 6 | 5 | 3 | 5 | 3 | 1 | 1 | 8 | 16 | 10 | 14 | | 1 | | | | | 32 | 9 | 23 | 3 | | 1 |
| 29 | Dysentery | 19 | 13 | 42 | 34 | 19 | 8 | 8 | 4 | 15 | 22 | 14 | 9 | | 3 | | | 2 | | 146 | 8 | 37 | 2 | | 2 |
| 30 | Dyspepsia | | | | | | | | | | 1 | 4 | | | | | | | | 2 | | 3 | | | |
| 31 | Erysipelas | 4 | 3 | 5 | 9 | 1 | 5 | 5 | 6 | 13 | 21 | 7 | 8 | | | | | | | 51 | 4 | 20 | 6 | | |
| 32 | Fever, not specified | 16 | 12 | 34 | 23 | 10 | 17 | 12 | 19 | 37 | 29 | 26 | 13 | 2 | 1 | | | | 1 | 153 | 13 | 47 | 5 | | 2 |
| 33 | ..do..bilious | 1 | 1 | 3 | 2 | | 1 | 2 | 4 | 9 | 9 | 2 | 3 | | | | | | | 17 | 1 | 10 | 1 | | |
| 34 | ..do..brain | 1 | 1 | 8 | 4 | 1 | | 2 | 1 | 4 | 1 | | 1 | | | | | | | 17 | | 6 | | | |
| 35 | ..do..congestive | 3 | 1 | 1 | | 2 | 3 | 2 | 1 | 3 | 1 | 1 | 4 | | | | | | | 17 | | 4 | 1 | | |
| 36 | ..do..inflammatory | | | | | | | | | 1 | | | | | | | | | | | | | | | |
| 37 | ..do..intermittent | 3 | 2 | 3 | 3 | | 2 | 1 | | | 3 | | 2 | 1 | 1 | | | | | 14 | 1 | 4 | | | 2 |
| 38 | ..do..puerperal | | | | | | | | 1 | | 4 | | | | | | | | | 2 | | | | | |
| 39 | ..do..scarlet | 11 | 6 | 44 | 26 | 15 | 17 | 5 | 8 | | 4 | 1 | | | | | | | 1 | 123 | 3 | 6 | 1 | | |
| 40 | ..do..typhoid | 2 | 1 | 5 | 3 | 2 | 6 | 9 | 18 | 41 | 24 | 11 | 6 | | | | | | | 74 | 8 | 34 | 3 | | |
| 41 | ..do..winter | | | | | | | 1 | 2 | 2 | 1 | 3 | | 1 | | | | | | 3 | 1 | 4 | | | |
| 42 | Gravel | | | | | | | | | 1 | | 6 | | | | | | | | | 1 | 5 | 1 | | |
| 43 | Head, disease of | 1 | 1 | | 1 | | | 1 | | 1 | | | | | | | | | | 4 | | 1 | | | |

## SECTION OF THE STATE OF OHIO—Continued.

| Nativities: California and Territories | Nativities: Ireland | Nativities: Germany | Nativities: Other foreign countries | Nativities: Unknown | Season of decease: Spring | Season of decease: Summer | Season of decease: Autumn | Season of decease: Winter | Duration of sickness: Under 1 week | Duration of sickness: 1 week and under 1 month | Duration of sickness: 1 month and under 3 months | Duration of sickness: 3 months and over | Whites: Males | Whites: Females | Whites: Total | Colored: Slaves: Black: M. | Colored: Slaves: Black: F. | Colored: Slaves: Mulatto: M. | Colored: Slaves: Mulatto: F. | Colored: Free: Black: M. | Colored: Free: Black: F. | Colored: Free: Mul.: M | Colored: Free: Mul.: F | Aggregate deaths. | |
|---|---|---|---|---|---|---|---|---|---|---|---|---|---|---|---|---|---|---|---|---|---|---|---|---|---|
| .... | 1 | 5 | 8 | | 69 | 34 | 17 | 25 | 33 | 87 | 13 | 2 | 83 | 60 | 143 | | | | | 1 | 1 | 1 | 1 | 147 | 1 |
| | | | | | | | 1 | | 1 | | | | | 1 | 1 | | | | | | | | | 1 | 2 |
| | | | | | 2 | 1 | 2 | | 1 | 4 | | | 4 | 1 | 5 | | | | | | | | | 5 | 3 |
| | | | 1 | | | 1 | | | 1 | | | | 1 | | 1 | | | | | | | | | 1 | 4 |
| | 1 | 1 | | | 5 | 1 | 1 | 3 | | 6 | 1 | 1 | 8 | 2 | 10 | | | | | | | | | 10 | 5 |
| | | | | | | | 1 | | | 1 | | | | 1 | 1 | | | | | | | | | 1 | 6 |
| | | | | | 3 | 2 | 3 | 2 | | 3 | 2 | 4 | 4 | 6 | 10 | | | | | | | | | 10 | 7 |
| | 1 | 2 | 2 | 1 | 17 | 6 | 4 | 14 | 8 | 28 | 1 | | 24 | 16 | 40 | | | | | 1 | | | | 41 | 8 |
| | | 1 | | | 8 | 1 | 2 | | | 3 | 1 | 1 | 5 | 1 | 6 | | | | | | | | | 6 | 9 |
| | | | | | | 1 | | | | | | | 1 | | 1 | | | | | | | | | 1 | 10 |
| | | | | | | 3 | 1 | 3 | 1 | 3 | 1 | | 4 | 3 | 7 | | | | | | | | | 7 | 11 |
| | | 1 | 2 | 1 | 6 | 1 | 2 | 1 | 2 | | | | 7 | 3 | 10 | | | | | | | | | 10 | 12 |
| | | | | | | 1 | | 1 | 1 | 1 | | | | 2 | 2 | | | | | | | | | 2 | 13 |
| | | 1 | | | 2 | 4 | 4 | 2 | 1 | 3 | 1 | | 3 | 9 | 12 | | | | | | | | | 12 | 14 |
| | | | 1 | | 1 | 3 | | 1 | 2 | 2 | 1 | | 1 | 5 | 6 | | | | | | | | | 6 | 15 |
| | | | 1 | | 1 | 4 | 1 | | 3 | 2 | 1 | | 5 | 1 | 6 | | | | | | | | | 6 | 16 |
| | | | | | 1 | 3 | 3 | | 1 | | 2 | 4 | 4 | 3 | 7 | | | | | | | | | 7 | 17 |
| | | | | | 1 | 1 | 3 | 1 | 2 | | 2 | 2 | 1 | 5 | 6 | | | | | | | | | 6 | 18 |
| | | | | | 9 | | 1 | 2 | 5 | 5 | 1 | | 8 | 4 | 12 | | | | | | | | | 12 | 19 |
| | 7 | 8 | 13 | 3 | 81 | 53 | 78 | 58 | 79 | 47 | 20 | 50 | 144 | 127 | 271 | | | | | | 1 | 1 | | 273 | 20 |
| .... | 110 | 128 | 162 | 82 | 1004 | 827 | 1343 | 661 | 1009 | 1365 | 287 | 653 | 2060 | 1791 | 3851 | .... | .... | .... | .... | 7 | 7 | 5 | 3 | 3878 | |

## SECTION OF THE STATE OF OHIO,

*Huron, Lucas, Ottawa, Paulding, Putnam, Richland, Sandusky, Seneca, Van Wert, Williams, Wyandott.*

| Nativities: California and Territories | Nativities: Ireland | Nativities: Germany | Nativities: Other foreign countries | Nativities: Unknown | Season of decease: Spring | Season of decease: Summer | Season of decease: Autumn | Season of decease: Winter | Duration of sickness: Under 1 week | Duration of sickness: 1 week and under 1 month | Duration of sickness: 1 month and under 3 months | Duration of sickness: 3 months and over | Whites: Males | Whites: Females | Whites: Total | Colored: Slaves: Black: M. | Colored: Slaves: Black: F. | Colored: Slaves: Mulatto: M. | Colored: Slaves: Mulatto: F. | Colored: Free: Black: M. | Colored: Free: Black: F. | Colored: Free: Mul.: M | Colored: Free: Mul.: F | Aggregate deaths. | |
|---|---|---|---|---|---|---|---|---|---|---|---|---|---|---|---|---|---|---|---|---|---|---|---|---|---|
| | | | | | 1 | | | 1 | | 1 | | 1 | 1 | 1 | 2 | | | | | | | | | 2 | 1 |
| | 2 | 5 | 1 | | 10 | 10 | 9 | 8 | 10 | 9 | 1 | 3 | 33 | 4 | 37 | | | | | | | | | 37 | 2 |
| | | | | | 6 | 5 | 2 | 1 | 3 | 3 | 1 | | 4 | 10 | 14 | | | | | | | | | 14 | 3 |
| | 1 | | 1 | | 8 | 6 | 5 | 4 | 18 | | | | 16 | 2 | 18 | | | | | | | | | 18 | 4 |
| | | | | | 3 | 2 | | 2 | 5 | 2 | | | 4 | 3 | 7 | | | | | | | | | 7 | 5 |
| | 2 | | | | | | 2 | | | | | | 2 | | 2 | | | | | | | | | 2 | 6 |
| | 1 | | 1 | | 4 | 2 | 5 | 2 | 10 | | | 1 | 6 | 7 | 13 | | | | | | | | | 13 | 7 |
| | | | | | | | 2 | 2 | 1 | 2 | | 1 | 2 | 2 | 4 | | | | | | | | | 4 | 8 |
| | | | | | 1 | 1 | 3 | | 1 | 1 | 1 | 2 | 3 | 2 | 5 | | | | | | | | | 5 | 9 |
| | | | 1 | | 2 | 2 | 2 | 2 | 4 | 2 | 1 | 1 | 4 | 3 | 7 | | | | | 1 | | | | 8 | 10 |
| | | | | | 1 | 1 | 1 | 2 | 1 | 2 | 1 | 1 | 3 | 2 | 5 | | | | | | | | | 5 | 11 |
| | | 1 | | | 2 | 3 | 6 | 2 | | 3 | 1 | 8 | 8 | 5 | 13 | | | | | | | | | 13 | 12 |
| | | | | | | | 1 | | | 1 | | | | 1 | 1 | | | | | | | | | 1 | 13 |
| | | | | | 4 | 1 | | 3 | 4 | 3 | 1 | | 5 | 3 | 8 | | | | | | | | | 8 | 14 |
| | | | | | | 1 | | | | | | | 1 | | 1 | | | | | | | | | 1 | 15 |
| | 2 | 3 | | 1 | 11 | 13 | 7 | 11 | 23 | 15 | 2 | | | 42 | 42 | | | | | | | | | 42 | 16 |
| | 80 | 109 | 54 | 34 | 3 | 326 | 234 | | 536 | 20 | | | 361 | 184 | 545 | | | | | 6 | 1 | 5 | 6 | 563 | 17 |
| | | | | | | 2 | 11 | 1 | 5 | 9 | | | 10 | 4 | 14 | | | | | | | | | 14 | 18 |
| | | | | | | 5 | 19 | 1 | 14 | 9 | 1 | | 18 | 7 | 25 | | | | | | | | | 25 | 19 |
| | 1 | 1 | | 1 | 2 | 4 | 4 | | 6 | 3 | | 1 | 7 | 3 | 10 | | | | | | | | | 10 | 20 |
| | | | | | | 1 | | 1 | 2 | | | | 2 | | 2 | | | | | | | | | 2 | 21 |
| | 3 | 15 | 3 | 3 | 93 | 65 | 61 | 56 | 13 | 43 | 20 | 195 | 126 | 151 | 277 | | | | | | 1 | | | 278 | 22 |
| | | 1 | 1 | | 29 | 14 | 40 | 12 | 57 | 24 | 3 | 6 | 50 | 44 | 94 | | | | | | | | | 96 | 23 |
| | | 1 | | | 54 | 17 | 44 | 41 | 120 | 29 | 1 | 2 | 84 | 73 | 157 | | | | | | | 1 | 1 | 157 | 24 |
| | 2 | | | | | 2 | 3 | | | 1 | 1 | 3 | 5 | | 5 | | | | | | | | | 5 | 25 |
| | | | | | 1 | | 1 | | | | 1 | 1 | 2 | | 2 | | | | | | | | | 2 | 26 |
| | 1 | 2 | 1 | | 3 | 15 | 43 | 5 | 23 | 33 | 8 | 1 | 34 | 32 | 66 | | | | | | | | | 66 | 27 |
| | 1 | 6 | 1 | | 24 | 17 | 21 | 14 | 12 | 20 | 7 | 37 | 32 | 44 | 76 | | | | | | | | | 76 | 28 |
| | 3 | 4 | 9 | 1 | 9 | 22 | 173 | 7 | 71 | 128 | 11 | 2 | 119 | 93 | 212 | | | | | | | | | 212 | 29 |
| | | | | | 1 | 3 | 1 | | | | | 5 | 4 | 1 | 5 | | | | | | | | | 5 | 30 |
| | 1 | 2 | 3 | | 27 | 18 | 12 | 29 | 34 | 49 | 2 | | 35 | 52 | 87 | | | | | | | | | 87 | 31 |
| | 8 | 18 | 6 | | 77 | 43 | 107 | 25 | 80 | 142 | 15 | 11 | 135 | 114 | 249 | | | | | 1 | 1 | 1 | | 252 | 32 |
| | 1 | 5 | 2 | | 6 | 5 | 20 | 6 | 9 | 23 | 2 | 3 | 17 | 20 | 37 | | | | | | | | | 37 | 33 |
| | | 1 | | | 9 | 3 | 8 | 4 | 10 | 13 | | 1 | 16 | 8 | 24 | | | | | | | | | 24 | 34 |
| | | | | | 4 | 1 | 15 | 1 | 11 | 7 | 2 | 1 | 12 | 10 | 22 | | | | | | | | | 22 | 35 |
| | | 1 | | | 1 | | | | | 1 | | | 1 | | 1 | | | | | | | | | 1 | 36 |
| | | | | | 2 | 6 | 11 | 2 | 10 | 9 | 2 | | 8 | 13 | 21 | | | | | | | | | 21 | 37 |
| | 1 | 2 | | | 1 | 3 | | 1 | 2 | 2 | | | | 5 | 5 | | | | | | | | | 5 | 38 |
| | 1 | 2 | 2 | | 54 | 33 | 26 | 25 | 67 | 63 | 6 | 2 | 76 | 62 | 138 | | | | | | | | | 138 | 39 |
| | | 5 | 4 | | 15 | 15 | 59 | 37 | 14 | 89 | 23 | 2 | 70 | 58 | 128 | | | | | | | | | 128 | 40 |
| | 1 | 1 | | | 4 | 1 | | 5 | 4 | 5 | | 1 | 6 | 3 | 9 | | | | | 1 | | | | 10 | 41 |
| | | | | | 1 | 4 | | 2 | 2 | 1 | | 4 | 7 | | 7 | | | | | | | | | 7 | 42 |
| | | | | | | 1 | 2 | 2 | 3 | 2 | | | 3 | 2 | 5 | | | | | | | | | 5 | 43 |

## CLASSIFICATION OF DEATHS IN NORTHWESTERN

| | Cause of death. | AGES. | | | | | | | | | | | | | | | | | | NATIVITIES. | | | | | |
|---|---|---|---|---|---|---|---|---|---|---|---|---|---|---|---|---|---|---|---|---|---|---|---|---|---|
| | | Under 1. | | 1 and under 5. | | 5 and under 10. | | 10 and under 20. | | 20 and under 50. | | 50 and under 80. | | 80 and under 100. | | 100 & over. | | Age unknown. | | Born in State. | N. England States. | Middle States. | Southern States. | Southwest'n States. | Northwest'n States. |
| | | M. | F. | M. | F. | M. | F. | M. | F. | M. | F. | M. | F. | M | F. | M | F. | M | F. | | | | | | |
| 1 | Heart, disease of | | 1 | 1 | | 1 | | 1 | | 2 | 2 | 2 | 2 | | | | | | | 6 | | 5 | | | |
| 2 | Hemorrhage | | | | 1 | | | | | 4 | 1 | 1 | | | | | | 1 | | 2 | | 5 | | | |
| 3 | Hernia | | | 1 | | | | | | | | 1 | | | | | | | | 1 | | 1 | | | |
| 4 | Hip, disease of | | | | | | | | | 1 | | | | | | | | | | | | 1 | | | |
| 5 | Hives | | 2 | | 1 | 1 | | | | | | | | | | | | | | 3 | | | | | |
| 6 | Hooping cough | 8 | 2 | 14 | 11 | 3 | 3 | | | 1 | | | | | | | | 2 | | 39 | | 4 | | | 1 |
| 7 | Hydrocephalus | 5 | 1 | 1 | 2 | | | | | | | | | | | | | | | 8 | 1 | | | | |
| 8 | Inflammation | 3 | 4 | 4 | 6 | 1 | 1 | 1 | 1 | 2 | 4 | 2 | | 1 | | | | | 1 | 24 | 2 | 3 | | | |
| 9 | .....do....bowels | 6 | 3 | 6 | 3 | 2 | | 4 | 2 | 3 | 3 | 1 | | | | | | | | 23 | 1 | 5 | 1 | | |
| 10 | .....do....brain | 5 | 9 | 5 | 8 | 4 | 5 | 1 | 4 | 10 | 7 | 2 | | | | | | | | 41 | 2 | 9 | | | 2 |
| 11 | Insanity | | | | | | | | | | 1 | 1 | | | | | | | | | 1 | 1 | | | |
| 12 | Intemperance | | | | | | | | | 1 | | | 1 | | | | | | | | | 1 | | | |
| 13 | Jaundice | 1 | | | | | 1 | | | | | | | | | | | | | 2 | | | | | |
| 14 | Kidneys, disease of | | | | | | | | | | 1 | | | | | | | | | 1 | | | | | |
| 15 | Killed | | | 1 | | | | | | 2 | 1 | | | | | | | | | 1 | | 2 | | | |
| 16 | Liver, disease of | 1 | 1 | | | | | | | 5 | 4 | 3 | | | | | | | | 4 | 1 | 6 | 1 | 1 | |
| 17 | Lungs.....do | 3 | | | 1 | 2 | 1 | | | | | 1 | | | 1 | | | | | 6 | 1 | 2 | | | |
| 18 | Mania-a-potu | | | | | | | | | 2 | | | | | | | | | | | | | | | |
| 19 | Marasmus | | | | | | | | | | | | 1 | | | | | | | | | 1 | | | |
| 20 | Measles | 3 | 2 | 11 | 14 | 5 | 2 | 2 | 2 | | 1 | 1 | | | | | | | | 36 | 1 | 2 | 2 | | |
| 21 | Milk sickness | | | | | | | 1 | | | 2 | | | | | | | | | 2 | | 1 | | | |
| 22 | Mumps | 2 | | | | | | | | | | | | | | | | | | 2 | | | | | |
| 23 | Murder | | | | | | | | | | | 1 | | | | | | | | | 1 | | | | |
| 24 | Neuralgia | | | | | | | | | | | 1 | | | | | | | | | | | | | |
| 25 | Old age | | | | | | | | | | 1 | 12 | 19 | 6 | 9 | | | | | 1 | 11 | 24 | 2 | | |
| 26 | Paralysis | | | 1 | | | 1 | | | 2 | 2 | 5 | 3 | | 1 | | | | | 4 | | 5 | 2 | | |
| 27 | Pleurisy | | | 2 | | | | 1 | 1 | 2 | 1 | 4 | 3 | | | | | | | 6 | | 5 | | | |
| 28 | Pneumonia | 13 | 10 | 26 | 18 | 3 | 3 | 13 | 10 | 36 | 23 | 25 | 4 | | | | | 1 | | 113 | 8 | 44 | | | 2 |
| 29 | Poison | | | 2 | | 1 | | | | | | | 1 | | | | | | | 3 | | 1 | | | |
| 30 | Premature birth | 1 | | | | | | | | | | | | | | | | | | 1 | | | | | |
| 31 | Putrid sore throat | | 1 | 1 | 5 | 1 | 2 | | 2 | | | | | | | | | | | 12 | | | | | |
| 32 | Quinsy | | | 3 | 2 | | | | | 1 | 1 | | | | | | | | | 6 | | 1 | | | |
| 33 | Rheumatism | | | | | 1 | | 2 | | 2 | 2 | 3 | | | | | | | | 4 | | 3 | 2 | | |
| 34 | Scrofula | 1 | | 1 | | | | | | 1 | 1 | | 1 | | | | | | | 2 | 1 | 2 | | | |
| 35 | Small pox | 1 | 1 | 1 | 3 | | 1 | 2 | 2 | 7 | 1 | 1 | | | | | | | | 16 | 1 | 1 | 2 | | |
| 36 | Spine, disease of | | | | | | 1 | | | 2 | 1 | | | | | | | | | 1 | | 2 | 1 | | |
| 37 | Stomach....do | | 1 | | | | | 1 | | 2 | | | | | | | | | | 2 | | | 2 | | |
| 38 | Suicide | | | | | | | | | 2 | | 1 | | | | | | | | | | 2 | 1 | | |
| 39 | Summer complaint | 3 | | 1 | | | | | | | | | | | | | | | | 4 | | | | | |
| 40 | Teething | | | 1 | | | | | | | | | | | | | | | | | | 1 | | | |
| 41 | Throat, disease of | 1 | | 2 | 1 | 3 | 2 | | | | | | | | | | | | | 8 | | 1 | | | |
| 42 | Thrush | 1 | | | | | | | | | | | | | | | | | | 1 | | | | | |
| 43 | Tumor | | | | | | | | | | 1 | 1 | | | | | | | | | | 2 | | | |
| 44 | Ulcer | | | | | | | | | | 1 | 1 | | | | | | | | | | | | | 1 |
| 45 | Uterus, disease of | | | | | | | | | | 1 | | | | | | | | | 1 | | | | | |
| 46 | White swelling | | | | | | | | | 1 | | | | | | | | | | 1 | | | | | |
| 47 | Worms | | | 8 | 5 | 2 | 1 | | | | | | | | | | | | | 16 | | | | | |
| 48 | Unknown | 79 | 54 | 27 | 27 | 11 | 8 | 12 | 18 | 30 | 43 | 27 | 22 | 4 | 2 | .. | .. | 3 | 5 | 255 | 18 | 62 | 6 | ... | 3 |
| | Total | 291 | 210 | 405 | 335 | 156 | 137 | 161 | 191 | 598 | 460 | 283 | 172 | 20 | 22 | .. | .. | 10 | 9 | 2032 | 152 | 674 | 59 | 1 | 23 |

## CLASSIFICATION OF DEATHS IN MIDDLE

*Embracing the following counties: Carroll, Columbiana, Coshocton, Fairfield,*

| | Cause of death. | Under 1 M. | Under 1 F. | 1–5 M. | 1–5 F. | 5–10 M. | 5–10 F. | 10–20 M. | 10–20 F. | 20–50 M. | 20–50 F. | 50–80 M. | 50–80 F. | 80–100 M | 80–100 F. | 100+ M | 100+ F. | Unknown M | Unknown F. | Born in State. | N. England States. | Middle States. | Southern States. | Southwest'n States. | Northwest'n States. |
|---|---|---|---|---|---|---|---|---|---|---|---|---|---|---|---|---|---|---|---|---|---|---|---|---|---|
| 1 | Abscess | 1 | | | | | | | | | 1 | 2 | | | | | | | | 2 | | | 1 | | |
| 2 | Accident, not specfi'd | 1 | 1 | 2 | 2 | 6 | 1 | 4 | 1 | 16 | 2 | 10 | 2 | 1 | | | | | | 25 | 3 | 9 | 2 | | |
| 3 | ....do...burned | | 1 | 1 | 1 | .. | 1 | | | | 1 | | | 1 | | | | | | 4 | | 1 | | | |
| 4 | ....do...drowned | | | 4 | 2 | 2 | 2 | 3 | | 7 | | | | | | | | | | 13 | | | | | 2 |
| 5 | ....do...scalded | 2 | | 1 | | | | | | | | | | | | | | | | 3 | | | | | |
| 6 | ....do...shot | | | | | | | | | 1 | | | | | | | | | | | | | | | 1 |
| 7 | Apoplexy | | 1 | | | 1 | | | 1 | 4 | 2 | 5 | 7 | 3 | | | | | | 6 | 2 | 6 | 6 | | |
| 8 | Asthma | | | | 1 | | | | | | | 1 | 2 | 1 | | | | | | 1 | | 4 | | | |
| 9 | Bowels, disease of | 1 | | | | | | 1 | | 1 | 1 | 1 | | | | | | | | 2 | 2 | | | | |
| 10 | Brain.......do | 2 | 2 | 3 | | 1 | | 1 | 1 | 2 | 1 | | | 2 | | | | | | 12 | | 2 | 1 | | |
| 11 | Bronchitis | | 1 | 1 | 2 | | | | 1 | 3 | 1 | 2 | 1 | | | | | | | 9 | | 2 | | | |
| 12 | Cancer | | 1 | | 2 | | | | | 1 | 4 | 8 | 5 | 4 | | | | | | 4 | | 14 | 2 | | |
| 13 | Catarrh | 5 | 4 | 1 | 1 | | 1 | | 2 | 1 | 1 | | 1 | | | | | | | 15 | | 1 | | | |
| 14 | Childbirth | | | | | | | | 1 | | 33 | | | | | | | | | 20 | | 7 | 2 | | |
| 15 | Cholera | 2 | | 2 | 3 | 2 | 2 | 6 | | 23 | 2 | 5 | 2 | | | | | | | 25 | 2 | 14 | | | 1 |
| 16 | ....do....infantum | 14 | 8 | 8 | 7 | | | | | | | | | | | | | | | 36 | | 1 | | | |

## SECTION OF THE STATE OF OHIO—Continued.

| Nativities: California and Territories. | Nativities: Ireland. | Nativities: Germany. | Nativities: Other foreign countries. | Nativities: Unknown. | Season of decease: Spring. | Season of decease: Summer. | Season of decease: Autumn. | Season of decease: Winter. | Duration of sickness: Under 1 week. | Duration of sickness: 1 week and under 1 month. | Duration of sickness: 1 month and under 3 months. | Duration of sickness: 3 months and over. | Whites: Males. | Whites: Females. | Whites: Total. | Colored: Slaves: Black: M. | Colored: Slaves: Black: F. | Colored: Slaves: Mulatto: M. | Colored: Slaves: Mulatto: F. | Colored: Free: Black: M. | Colored: Free: Black: F. | Colored: Free: Mul.: M | Colored: Free: Mul.: F. | Aggregate deaths. | |
|---|---|---|---|---|---|---|---|---|---|---|---|---|---|---|---|---|---|---|---|---|---|---|---|---|---|
| | | 1 | | | 2 | 2 | 4 | 4 | 4 | 2 | 2 | 2 | 7 | 5 | 12 | | | | | | | | | 12 | 1 |
| | | 1 | | | | 2 | 3 | 3 | 5 | 1 | 1 | 1 | 6 | 2 | 8 | | | | | | | | | 8 | 2 |
| | | | | | | 2 | | | 1 | | 1 | | 2 | | 2 | | | | | | | | | 2 | 3 |
| | | | | | 1 | | | | | | | 1 | 1 | | 1 | | | | | | | | | 1 | 4 |
| | | 1 | | | 2 | 2 | | | 3 | | | 1 | 1 | 3 | 4 | | | | | | | | | 4 | 5 |
| | | | | | 9 | 15 | 13 | 6 | 6 | 29 | 4 | 3 | 28 | 16 | 44 | | | | | | | | | 44 | 6 |
| | | | | | 1 | 2 | 3 | 3 | 2 | 6 | 1 | | 6 | 3 | 9 | | | | | | | | | 9 | 7 |
| | 1 | 1 | | | 6 | 8 | 15 | 2 | 10 | 17 | 1 | 2 | 14 | 17 | 31 | | | | | | | | | 31 | 8 |
| | 1 | 1 | 1 | | 11 | 9 | 9 | 4 | 20 | 12 | 1 | | 22 | 11 | 33 | | | | | | | | | 33 | 9 |
| | 3 | 1 | 2 | | 21 | 15 | 16 | 8 | 37 | 18 | 3 | 1 | 27 | 33 | 60 | | | | | | | | | 60 | 10 |
| | | | | | | | 1 | 1 | | | | | 1 | 1 | 2 | | | | | | | | | 2 | 11 |
| | 1 | | | | 1 | | 1 | | | 2 | | | 1 | 1 | 2 | | | | | | | | | 2 | 12 |
| | | | | | | 1 | | 1 | 1 | 1 | | | 1 | 1 | 2 | | | | | | | | | 2 | 13 |
| | | | | | | | 1 | | | 1 | | | | 1 | 1 | | | | | | | | | 1 | 14 |
| | 1 | | | | 2 | 1 | 1 | | 1 | | | | 3 | 1 | 4 | | | | | | | | | 4 | 15 |
| | | 1 | | | 5 | 2 | 3 | 4 | 1 | 7 | 2 | 4 | 9 | 5 | 14 | | | | | | | | | 14 | 16 |
| | | | | | 4 | 3 | 2 | | 4 | 3 | 1 | 1 | 6 | 3 | 9 | | | | | | | | | 9 | 17 |
| | 2 | | | | | | | 2 | 2 | | | | 2 | | 2 | | | | | | | | | 2 | 18 |
| | | | | | | 1 | | | | | | 1 | | 1 | 1 | | | | | | | | | 1 | 19 |
| | | 2 | | | 8 | 12 | 18 | 5 | 13 | 24 | 2 | 3 | 22 | 21 | 43 | | | | | | | | | 43 | 20 |
| | | | | | 1 | 1 | | 1 | 2 | | 1 | | 1 | 2 | 3 | | | | | | | | | 3 | 21 |
| | | | | | 1 | | 1 | | 1 | 1 | | | 2 | | 2 | | | | | | | | | 2 | 22 |
| | | | | | 1 | | | | | | | | 1 | | 1 | | | | | | | | | 1 | 23 |
| | | | 1 | | | 1 | | | | | 1 | | 1 | | 1 | | | | | | | | | 1 | 24 |
| | 5 | 2 | 2 | | 10 | 11 | 24 | 2 | 10 | 9 | 3 | 4 | 18 | 29 | 47 | | | | | | | | | 47 | 25 |
| | | 3 | | 1 | 2 | 3 | 7 | 3 | 5 | 1 | 3 | 4 | 8 | 7 | 15 | | | | | | | | | 15 | 26 |
| | 1 | 1 | 1 | | 6 | 2 | 4 | 2 | 5 | 7 | 1 | 1 | 9 | 5 | 14 | | | | | | | | | 14 | 27 |
| | 4 | 9 | 5 | 1 | 84 | 45 | 24 | 33 | 55 | 108 | 12 | 10 | 118 | 68 | 186 | | | | | | | | | 186 | 28 |
| | | | | | | | 4 | | 2 | 2 | | | 3 | 1 | 4 | | | | | | | | | 4 | 29 |
| | | | | | | | 1 | | 1 | | | | 1 | | 1 | | | | | | | | | 1 | 30 |
| | | | | | 8 | 1 | 2 | 1 | 10 | 2 | | | 2 | 10 | 12 | | | | | | | | | 12 | 31 |
| | | | | | 2 | 1 | 1 | 3 | 4 | 1 | | | 4 | 3 | 7 | | | | | | | | | 7 | 32 |
| | 1 | | | | 5 | 2 | 1 | 2 | | 4 | 3 | 3 | 7 | 2 | 9 | | | | | | | 1 | | 10 | 33 |
| | | | | | 2 | 3 | | | 1 | | 2 | 2 | 3 | 2 | 5 | | | | | | | | | 5 | 34 |
| | | | | | 2 | 1 | 4 | 13 | 4 | 16 | | | 12 | 8 | 20 | | | | | | | | | 20 | 35 |
| | | | | | 3 | 1 | | | | 1 | 1 | 2 | 2 | 2 | 4 | | | | | | | | | 4 | 36 |
| | | | | | 1 | 1 | 2 | | | 3 | | 1 | 3 | 1 | 4 | | | | | | | | | 4 | 37 |
| | | | | | | | 2 | 1 | 3 | | | | 2 | | 2 | | | | | | | 1 | | 3 | 38 |
| | | | | | 1 | 1 | 2 | | 3 | | 1 | | 4 | | 4 | | | | | | | | | 4 | 39 |
| | | | | | 1 | | | | | 1 | | | 1 | | 1 | | | | | | | | | 1 | 40 |
| | | | | | 3 | | 4 | 2 | 2 | 7 | | | 6 | 3 | 9 | | | | | | | | | 9 | 41 |
| | | | | | | | 1 | | | 1 | | | 1 | | 1 | | | | | | | | | 1 | 42 |
| | | | | | 1 | | 1 | | | | 1 | 1 | 1 | 1 | 2 | | | | | | | | | 2 | 43 |
| | | | | 1 | 1 | 1 | | | | | 1 | 1 | 1 | 1 | 2 | | | | | | | | | 2 | 44 |
| | | | | | | | | 1 | | | | 1 | | 1 | 1 | | | | | | | | | 1 | 45 |
| | | | | | 1 | | | | | 1 | | | 1 | | 1 | | | | | | | | | 1 | 46 |
| | | | | | 6 | 4 | 4 | 2 | 9 | 7 | | | 10 | 6 | 16 | | | | | | | | | 16 | 47 |
| | 10 | 9 | 8 | 1 | 102 | 77 | 113 | 74 | 121 | 69 | 11 | 84 | 193 | 178 | 371 | | | | | | 1 | | | 372 | 48 |
| | 142 | 218 | 110 | 44 | 785 | 906 | 1252 | 500 | 1533 | 1133 | 174 | 430 | 1906 | 1525 | 3431 | | | | | 9 | 4 | 9 | 7 | 3460 | |

## EASTERN SECTION OF THE STATE OHIO.

*Guernsey, Harrison, Holmes, Knox, Licking, Muskingum, Perry and Tuscarawas.*

| California and Territories. | Ireland. | Germany. | Other foreign countries. | Unknown. | Spring. | Summer. | Autumn. | Winter. | Under 1 week. | 1 week and under 1 month. | 1 month and under 3 months. | 3 months and over. | Males. | Females. | Total. | Slaves Black M. | Slaves Black F. | Slaves Mulatto M. | Slaves Mulatto F. | Free Black M. | Free Black F. | Free Mul. M | Free Mul. F. | Aggregate deaths. | |
|---|---|---|---|---|---|---|---|---|---|---|---|---|---|---|---|---|---|---|---|---|---|---|---|---|---|
| | 1 | | | | 1 | | 2 | 1 | 2 | 1 | | 1 | 3 | 1 | 4 | | | | | | | | | 4 | 1 |
| | 4 | 2 | 3 | 1 | 11 | 14 | 13 | 10 | 17 | 10 | 1 | 5 | 40 | 9 | 49 | | | | | | | | | 49 | 2 |
| | | 1 | | | 4 | 1 | 1 | | 2 | 4 | | | 2 | 4 | 6 | | | | | | | | | 6 | 3 |
| | 4 | | 1 | | 6 | 7 | 3 | 4 | 20 | | | | 15 | 4 | 19 | | | | | 1 | | | | 20 | 4 |
| | | | | | | | | 3 | 2 | 1 | | | 3 | | 3 | | | | | | | | | 3 | 5 |
| | | | | | 1 | | | | | | | | 1 | | 1 | | | | | | | | | 1 | 6 |
| | 1 | 1 | 1 | 1 | 4 | 5 | 7 | 8 | 10 | 1 | | 1 | 13 | 10 | 23 | | | | | | 1 | | | 24 | 7 |
| | | | | | 1 | 2 | 1 | 1 | 2 | | | 2 | 2 | 3 | 5 | | | | | | | | | 5 | 8 |
| | 1 | | | | 1 | | 4 | | 2 | 1 | 1 | | 4 | 1 | 5 | | | | | | | | | 5 | 9 |
| | | | | | 5 | 6 | 4 | | 4 | 6 | 3 | 1 | 11 | 4 | 15 | | | | | | | | | 15 | 10 |
| | | 1 | | | 3 | 3 | 4 | 2 | 1 | 3 | 1 | 7 | 6 | 6 | 12 | | | | | | | | | 12 | 11 |
| | 4 | | 1 | | 3 | 6 | 7 | 9 | 1 | 3 | | 20 | 13 | 12 | 25 | | | | | | | | | 25 | 12 |
| | | 1 | | | 9 | 1 | 2 | 5 | 7 | 8 | 2 | | 7 | 10 | 17 | | | | | | | | | 17 | 13 |
| | 2 | 3 | | | 12 | 8 | 9 | 5 | 10 | 20 | 2 | | | 34 | 34 | | | | | | | | | 34 | 14 |
| | | 3 | 3 | 1 | 5 | 23 | 20 | 1 | 44 | 1 | | | 40 | 9 | 49 | | | | | | | | | 49 | 15 |
| | | | | | | 14 | 20 | 3 | 20 | 12 | 5 | | 22 | 15 | 37 | | | | | | | | | 37 | 16 |

## CLASSIFICATION OF DEATHS IN MIDDLE

| | Cause of death. | AGES. | | | | | | | | | | | | | | | | | | NATIVITIES. | | | | | |
|---|---|---|---|---|---|---|---|---|---|---|---|---|---|---|---|---|---|---|---|---|---|---|---|---|---|
| | | Under 1. | | 1 and under 5. | | 5 and under 10. | | 10 and under 20. | | 20 and under 50. | | 50 and under 80. | | 80 and under 100. | | 100 & over. | | Age unknown. | | Born in State. | N. England States. | Middle States. | Southern States. | Southwest'n States. | Northwest'n States. |
| | | M. | F. | M. | F. | M. | F. | M. | F. | M. | F. | M. | F. | M | F. | M | F. | M | F. | | | | | | |
| 1 | Cholera morbus | | 4 | 2 | 6 | | 2 | 2 | 1 | 2 | 1 | 3 | 1 | | | | | | | 18 | | 1 | 1 | | |
| 2 | Colic | 2 | | | | | | 1 | | 4 | 4 | 4 | 4 | | | | | | | 6 | | 3 | 4 | | 1 |
| 3 | Congestion | | | 1 | 1 | 1 | | | | 1 | | | 1 | | | | | | | 3 | | | | | |
| 4 | ..do.....brain | | | 1 | 1 | 1 | | | | 1 | 1 | 1 | | | | | | | | 4 | | 2 | | | |
| 5 | Consumption | 5 | 1 | 4 | 6 | 3 | 4 | 19 | 35 | 85 | 141 | 42 | 36 | 3 | 2 | | | | | 216 | 8 | 99 | 19 | | 2 |
| 6 | Convulsions | 18 | 10 | 5 | 9 | | 2 | 1 | 2 | 5 | 9 | 3 | 1 | | | | | | 1 | 53 | 2 | 8 | 1 | | |
| 7 | Croup | 41 | 18 | 60 | 50 | 11 | 14 | 1 | | | 1 | | | | | | | | | 188 | | 3 | | | 3 |
| 8 | Diabetes | | | | | | | | | 1 | 2 | | 1 | | | | | | | 1 | | 3 | | | |
| 9 | Diarrhœa | 9 | 7 | 9 | 5 | 1 | | 3 | | 7 | 2 | 7 | 2 | | 1 | | | | | 37 | 1 | 7 | 2 | | |
| 10 | Dropsy | 3 | 3 | 8 | 1 | 2 | 1 | 3 | 6 | 12 | 24 | 21 | 21 | 4 | 3 | | | | | 49 | 2 | 33 | 15 | | 2 |
| 11 | Dysentery | 56 | 34 | 130 | 101 | 54 | 42 | 37 | 36 | 29 | 36 | 22 | 24 | 4 | 1 | | | | | 502 | 8 | 45 | 15 | | 2 |
| 12 | Dyspepsia | | | | | | | | | | 1 | 6 | 1 | | | | | | | | | 5 | 1 | | |
| 13 | Epilepsy | | | | | | | | | | 2 | 1 | | | | | | | | | | 3 | | | |
| 14 | Erysipelas | 5 | 2 | 3 | 3 | 1 | | 1 | 3 | 3 | 7 | 2 | 4 | 1 | | | | | | 24 | 2 | 7 | | | |
| 15 | Fever, not specified | 9 | 4 | 10 | 23 | 5 | 8 | 12 | 11 | 82 | 31 | 16 | 17 | | 2 | | | | | 110 | 5 | 39 | 2 | 2 | |
| 16 | ..do. bilious | | | 2 | 1 | | | | | 5 | 4 | 1 | | | | | | | | 7 | | 2 | | 2 | |
| 17 | ..do..brain | 2 | 1 | 3 | | 2 | | 1 | | | | | 1 | | | | | | | 9 | | 1 | | | |
| 18 | ..do..catarrhal | 1 | 1 | 1 | | | | | | | | | | | | | | | | 3 | | | | | |
| 19 | ..do..congestive | | | 1 | 1 | | | 1 | | 2 | 1 | 1 | 2 | | | | | | | 4 | | 3 | | | |
| 20 | ..do..inflammatory | 1 | 1 | | | | 1 | | | | 1 | | | | | | | | | 4 | | | | | |
| 21 | ..do..intermittent | 1 | 2 | 1 | 1 | | 1 | | 1 | 2 | 5 | 1 | 1 | | | | | | | 9 | 1 | 5 | | | |
| 22 | ..do..puerperal | | | | | | | | | | 1 | | 1 | | | | | | | 1 | | | 1 | | |
| 23 | ..do..remittent | | | | | | 1 | | 1 | 2 | | | | | | | | | | 4 | | | | | |
| 24 | ..do..scarlet | 18 | 14 | 69 | 72 | 19 | 26 | 5 | 4 | 2 | 1 | 1 | | | | | | 1 | | 227 | | 3 | | | |
| 25 | ..do..ship | | 1 | | | | | | | | | | | | | | | | | | | 1 | | | |
| 26 | ..do..typhus | | 1 | 5 | 1 | | 1 | 10 | 19 | 36 | 19 | 8 | 4 | 3 | | | | | | 63 | 5 | 24 | 7 | 1 | |
| 27 | ..do..winter | 1 | | 1 | | | | 1 | | | | 1 | 1 | | | | | | | 4 | | 1 | | | |
| 28 | Frozen | | | | | | | | | | | 1 | | | | | | | | | | 1 | | | |
| 29 | Gravel | | | | | | | | | 2 | | 5 | | 2 | | | | | | 2 | | 4 | 1 | | |
| 30 | Head, disease of | 2 | 1 | 1 | 2 | | | | | 1 | | | | | | | | | | 5 | | 2 | | | |
| 31 | Heart, ...do | | 1 | | 1 | | | 1 | | 2 | 2 | 5 | 1 | | | | | | | 7 | 4 | 1 | | | |
| 32 | Hemorrhage | | | | | | | | | | | 2 | 1 | | | | | | | | | 2 | 1 | | |
| 33 | Hernia | | | | | | | | | 1 | | 1 | 2 | | | | | | | 2 | | | | | |
| 34 | Hives | 2 | 2 | 1 | 2 | | | | | | | | | | | | | | | 7 | | | | | |
| 35 | Hooping cough | 13 | 11 | 20 | 33 | 3 | 2 | | | | 1 | | | | | | | | | 79 | | 1 | | | 3 |
| 36 | Hydrocephalus | 1 | | 1 | | | | | | | | | | | | | | | | 2 | | | | | |
| 37 | Inflammation | 12 | 8 | 9 | 7 | 1 | 2 | 3 | 2 | 4 | 7 | | 1 | | | | | | | 48 | 1 | 6 | | | |
| 38 | ....do.....bowels | 4 | 4 | 6 | 2 | 1 | 1 | 5 | 2 | 4 | 1 | 2 | | 1 | | | | | | 28 | | 4 | 1 | | |
| 39 | ....do.....brain | 6 | 6 | 11 | 6 | | 1 | 1 | 6 | 2 | 2 | | | | | | | | | 38 | | 2 | | | |
| 40 | Intemperance | | | | | | | | | 1 | | 1 | | | | | | | | | | 2 | | | |
| 41 | Jaundice | 2 | | | 1 | | | | | | | 1 | 1 | | | | | | | 3 | | 2 | | | |
| 42 | Kidneys, disease of | | | | | | | | | | | 1 | | | | | | | | | | 1 | | | |
| 43 | Killed | | | | | | | 1 | | | | 1 | | | | | | | | 1 | | | | | |
| 44 | Lightning | | | | | | | | | 1 | | | | | | | | | | 1 | | | | | |
| 45 | Liver, disease of | 2 | 2 | 1 | 3 | 1 | 2 | 1 | 1 | 2 | 3 | 8 | 3 | | | | | | | 16 | | 10 | 3 | | |
| 46 | Lockjaw | | | | | | | 1 | | | | | | | | | | | | 1 | | | | | |
| 47 | Lungs, disease of | 1 | 2 | 2 | 2 | | 2 | | | 3 | 3 | | | 1 | | | | | | 13 | | 1 | | | |
| 48 | Malformation | 1 | 1 | | 1 | | | | | | | | | | | | | | | 3 | | | | | |
| 49 | Mania-a-potu | | | | | | | | | 4 | | | | | | | | | | 1 | | | | | |
| 50 | Marasmus | 1 | | | | | | | | | | | | | | | | | | 1 | | | | | |
| 51 | Measles | 6 | 2 | 18 | 13 | 4 | 3 | | 6 | 1 | 9 | | | | | | | | | 58 | | 3 | | | |
| 52 | Mortification | | | | | | | | | | | | 1 | | 1 | | | | | 2 | | | | | |
| 53 | Mumps | | | | | | | 1 | | | | | | | | | | | | | | | 1 | | |
| 54 | Neuralgia | | | 2 | | | | | | 2 | 4 | | 2 | | | | | | | 4 | | 2 | 1 | | 1 |
| 55 | Old age | | | | | | | | | | 1 | 16 | 24 | 31 | 33 | 1 | 1 | | | 11 | 7 | 49 | 15 | | 1 |
| 56 | Paralysis | | | 1 | | 1 | | 2 | 1 | | 1 | 16 | 18 | 3 | 2 | 1 | | | | 11 | 1 | 20 | 5 | | |
| 57 | Pleurisy | 1 | | | 1 | | | | 1 | 3 | 2 | 3 | 1 | | | | | | | 6 | | 3 | 2 | | |
| 58 | Pneumonia | 21 | 11 | 16 | 12 | 6 | 3 | 3 | 4 | 24 | 12 | 13 | 5 | 3 | | | | | | 92 | 2 | 18 | 6 | | |
| 59 | Premature birth | | 1 | | | | | | | | | | | | | | | | | 1 | | | | | |
| 60 | Putrid sore throat | | | | 1 | 2 | 2 | | 2 | 1 | | | | | | | | | | 7 | | | | | |
| 61 | Quinsy | | | 1 | | | 1 | | | | | | | | | | | | | 2 | | | | | |
| 62 | Rheumatism | | | | | | | 6 | | 2 | 1 | 4 | 1 | 1 | 1 | | | | | 7 | 1 | 7 | | | |
| 63 | Scrofula | 2 | 8 | 1 | | 1 | | 2 | 5 | 3 | 1 | | | | | | | | | 15 | | 1 | 2 | | |
| 64 | Scurvy | | | | | | | 1 | | 1 | | | | | | | | | | 2 | | | | | |
| 65 | Small pox | | | 1 | 3 | | | | 3 | 4 | 1 | 3 | | | | | | | | 9 | | 4 | 2 | | |
| 66 | Spine, disease of | | | 1 | 1 | | | 1 | 1 | 1 | 1 | | 1 | | | | | | | 5 | | 1 | 1 | | |
| 67 | Stillborn | 4 | | | | | | | | | | | | | | | | | | 4 | | | | | |
| 68 | Stomach, disease of | | | | | | | | | | 1 | 1 | 1 | | | | | | | 2 | | | | | |
| 69 | Suffocation | 1 | 2 | 1 | | | | | | | | 1 | | | | | | | | 4 | 1 | | | | |
| 70 | Suicide | | | | | | | 1 | | | 1 | | | | | | | | | 1 | | | | | 1 |
| 71 | Sun, stroke of | | | | | | | | | 1 | | | | | | | | | | | | | | | 1 |
| 72 | Teething | 2 | 1 | 1 | | | | | | | | | | | | | | | | 4 | | | | | |
| 73 | Throat, disease of | 1 | | 5 | 2 | | | | 2 | | | | 1 | | | | | | | 9 | | 2 | | | |
| 74 | Thrush | 2 | 1 | | 1 | | | | | | | | | | | | | | | 4 | | | | | |
| 75 | Tumor | | | | | | | | | 1 | 1 | 1 | 2 | | | | | | | | 1 | 3 | | | |

EASTERN SECTION OF THE STATE OF OHIO—Continued.

| NATIVITIES. | | | | | SEASON OF DECEASE. | | | | DURATION OF SICKNESS. | | | | WHITES. | | | COLORED. | | | | | | | | | |
|---|---|---|---|---|---|---|---|---|---|---|---|---|---|---|---|---|---|---|---|---|---|---|---|---|---|
| | | | | | | | | | | | | | | | | Slaves. | | | | Free. | | | | | |
| | | | | | | | | | | | | | | | | Black. | | Mulatto. | | Black. | | Mul. | | | |
| California and Territories. | Ireland. | Germany. | Other foreign countries. | Unknown. | Spring. | Summer. | Autumn. | Winter. | Under 1 week. | 1 week and under 1 month. | 1 month and under 3 months. | 3 months and over. | Males. | Females. | Total. | M. | F. | M. | F. | M. | F. | M | F. | Aggregate deaths. | |
| | 4 | | | | | 8 | 15 | 1 | 21 | 3 | | | 9 | 15 | 24 | | | | | | | | | 24 | 1 |
| | 1 | 3 | 1 | | 5 | 5 | 7 | 2 | 13 | 6 | | | 11 | 8 | 19 | | | | | | | | | 19 | 2 |
| | 2 | | | | 1 | 2 | 1 | 1 | 2 | 2 | | 1 | 3 | 2 | 5 | | | | | | | | | 5 | 3 |
| | | | | | 2 | | 3 | 1 | 2 | 3 | | | 4 | 2 | 6 | | | | | | | | | 6 | 4 |
| | 21 | 10 | 11 | | 131 | 112 | 71 | 71 | 13 | 40 | 58 | 267 | 160 | 221 | 381 | | | | | | 3 | 1 | 1 | 386 | 5 |
| | 2 | | | | 20 | 18 | 17 | 11 | 35 | 18 | 1 | 4 | 32 | 34 | 66 | | | | | | | | | 66 | 6 |
| | | | 2 | | 61 | 31 | 56 | 45 | 158 | 32 | 2 | 1 | 112 | 82 | 194 | | | | | 1 | | | 1 | 196 | 7 |
| | | | | | | | 2 | 2 | | | 1 | 3 | 1 | 3 | 4 | | | | | | | | | 4 | 8 |
| | 1 | 4 | | 1 | 5 | 15 | 28 | 5 | 14 | 29 | 7 | 3 | 36 | 17 | 53 | | | | | | | | | 53 | 9 |
| | 4 | 2 | 4 | 1 | 38 | 27 | 29 | 18 | 9 | 26 | 19 | 55 | 52 | 59 | 111 | | | | | | | 1 | | 112 | 10 |
| | 11 | 9 | 12 | 2 | 18 | 71 | 496 | 21 | 146 | 408 | 39 | 3 | 331 | 274 | 605 | | | | | 1 | | | | 606 | 11 |
| | 1 | | 1 | | 1 | 2 | 1 | 4 | | 2 | 2 | 3 | 6 | 2 | 8 | | | | | | | | | 8 | 12 |
| | | | | | 2 | | 1 | | 2 | | | 1 | 1 | 2 | 3 | | | | | | | | | 3 | 13 |
| | 1 | | 1 | | 9 | 6 | 14 | 6 | 8 | 16 | 10 | 1 | 16 | 18 | 34 | | | | | | 1 | | | 35 | 14 |
| | 7 | 8 | 7 | | 48 | 30 | 66 | 35 | 35 | 111 | 24 | 8 | 84 | 96 | 180 | | | | | | | | | 180 | 15 |
| | 1 | | 1 | | 2 | 1 | 9 | 1 | 1 | 11 | 1 | | 8 | 5 | 13 | | | | | | | | | 13 | 16 |
| | | | | | 3 | 3 | 3 | 1 | 2 | 6 | 1 | 1 | 8 | 2 | 10 | | | | | | | | | 10 | 17 |
| | | | | | 2 | 1 | | | | 3 | | | 2 | 1 | 3 | | | | | | | | | 3 | 18 |
| | 2 | | | | | 3 | 5 | 1 | 2 | 6 | 1 | | 5 | 4 | 9 | | | | | | | | | 9 | 19 |
| | | | | | 3 | | 1 | | 1 | 3 | | | 1 | 3 | 4 | | | | | | | | | 4 | 20 |
| | 1 | | | | 4 | 1 | 10 | 1 | 5 | 9 | 2 | | 5 | 11 | 16 | | | | | | | | | 16 | 21 |
| | | | | | 1 | | | 1 | | 1 | 1 | | | 2 | 2 | | | | | | | | | 2 | 22 |
| | | | | | | 1 | 2 | 1 | 1 | 2 | 1 | | 2 | 2 | 4 | | | | | | | | | 4 | 23 |
| | 1 | | 1 | | 72 | 57 | 47 | 56 | 106 | 117 | 7 | 1 | 115 | 117 | 232 | | | | | | | | | 232 | 24 |
| | | | | | | | 1 | | 1 | | | | | 1 | 1 | | | | | | | | | 1 | 25 |
| | 2 | 2 | 2 | 1 | 36 | 16 | 27 | 28 | 7 | 87 | 9 | 2 | 62 | 45 | 107 | | | | | | | | | 107 | 26 |
| | | | | | 3 | | | 2 | | 4 | 1 | | 4 | 1 | 5 | | | | | | | | | 5 | 27 |
| | | | | | | | | 1 | | | | | | | | | | | | 1 | | | | 1 | 28 |
| | | 1 | 1 | | 3 | 1 | 1 | 4 | | 3 | 1 | 5 | 9 | | 9 | | | | | | | | | 9 | 29 |
| | | | | | | 3 | 4 | | 4 | 3 | | | 4 | 2 | 6 | | | | | | 1 | | | 7 | 30 |
| | | 1 | | | 5 | 1 | 6 | 1 | 1 | 5 | 3 | 1 | 8 | 5 | 13 | | | | | | | | | 13 | 31 |
| | | | | | 2 | | 1 | | 1 | 1 | 1 | | 2 | 1 | 3 | | | | | | | | | 3 | 32 |
| | 1 | | 1 | | | 1 | 2 | 1 | 1 | 1 | 1 | 1 | 2 | 2 | 4 | | | | | | | | | 4 | 33 |
| | | | | | 3 | | 3 | 1 | 7 | | | | 3 | 4 | 7 | | | | | | | | | 7 | 34 |
| | | | | | 21 | 30 | 21 | 11 | 9 | 56 | 17 | 1 | 35 | 47 | 82 | | | | | | | 1 | | 83 | 35 |
| | | | | | | 1 | 1 | | 1 | 1 | | | 2 | | 2 | | | | | | | | | 2 | 36 |
| | 1 | | | | 16 | 20 | 17 | 3 | 18 | 28 | 8 | 2 | 29 | 26 | 55 | | | | | | | | 1 | 56 | 37 |
| | | | | | 13 | 8 | 5 | 7 | 11 | 13 | 6 | 3 | 23 | 10 | 33 | | | | | | | | | 33 | 38 |
| | | | 1 | | 11 | 8 | 15 | 7 | 20 | 18 | | 2 | 20 | 20 | 40 | | | | | | 1 | | | 41 | 39 |
| | | | | | 2 | | | | 2 | | | | 2 | | 2 | | | | | | | | | 2 | 40 |
| | | | | | 1 | 1 | | 3 | 1 | 3 | 1 | | 3 | 2 | 5 | | | | | | | | | 5 | 41 |
| | | | | | | | | 1 | | | | 1 | 1 | | 1 | | | | | | | | | 1 | 42 |
| | 1 | | | | 1 | 1 | | | | | | | 2 | | 2 | | | | | | | | | 2 | 43 |
| | | | | | | 1 | | | | | | | 1 | | 1 | | | | | | | | | 1 | 44 |
| | | | | | 6 | 6 | 8 | 9 | 4 | 8 | 7 | 9 | 15 | 14 | 29 | | | | | | | | | 29 | 45 |
| | | | | | | | | 1 | 1 | | | | 1 | | 1 | | | | | | | | | 1 | 46 |
| | 1 | 1 | | | 4 | 6 | 3 | 3 | 1 | 11 | 3 | 1 | 7 | 9 | 16 | | | | | | | | | 16 | 47 |
| | | | | | 2 | | | 1 | 2 | 1 | | | 1 | 2 | 3 | | | | | | | | | 3 | 48 |
| | 1 | 1 | 1 | | | 3 | 1 | | 1 | 1 | | | 4 | | 4 | | | | | | | | | 4 | 49 |
| | | | | | | | 1 | | | 1 | | | 1 | | 1 | | | | | | | | | 1 | 50 |
| | | 1 | | | 24 | 17 | 11 | 9 | 14 | 82 | 12 | 2 | 29 | 33 | 62 | | | | | | | | | 62 | 51 |
| | | | | | 1 | | 1 | | | | 1 | | | 2 | 2 | | | | | | | | | 2 | 52 |
| | | | | | 1 | | | | | 1 | | | | | | | | | | 1 | | | | 1 | 53 |
| | | 2 | | | 2 | 2 | 2 | 4 | 2 | 2 | 1 | 5 | 4 | 6 | 10 | | | | | | | | | 10 | 54 |
| | 12 | 10 | 2 | | 40 | 22 | 25 | 19 | 23 | 18 | 11 | 12 | 48 | 57 | 105 | | | | | | 1 | | 1 | 107 | 55 |
| | 2 | 1 | 1 | | 17 | 7 | 9 | 8 | 8 | 11 | 4 | 15 | 24 | 17 | 41 | | | | | | | | | 41 | 56 |
| | | 1 | | | 5 | 1 | 5 | 1 | 4 | 8 | | | 7 | 5 | 12 | | | | | | | | | 12 | 57 |
| | 6 | 5 | 3 | 1 | 76 | 18 | 14 | 25 | 24 | 89 | 13 | 5 | 84 | 45 | 129 | | | | | 1 | 2 | 1 | | 133 | 58 |
| | | | | | | 1 | | | | 1 | | | | 1 | 1 | | | | | | | | | 1 | 59 |
| | | 1 | | | 1 | 3 | 4 | | 4 | 4 | | | 3 | 5 | 8 | | | | | | | | | 8 | 60 |
| | | | | | | 1 | 1 | | | 2 | | | 1 | 1 | 2 | | | | | | | | | 2 | 61 |
| | 1 | | | | 4 | 5 | 2 | 5 | 4 | 4 | 4 | 4 | 13 | 3 | 16 | | | | | | | | | 16 | 62 |
| | | | | | 2 | 7 | 6 | 3 | 2 | 4 | 3 | 9 | 9 | 9 | 18 | | | | | | | | | 18 | 63 |
| | | | | | | | 1 | 1 | | | 2 | | 2 | | 2 | | | | | | | | | 2 | 64 |
| | | | | | 5 | 4 | 3 | 3 | | 14 | 1 | | 8 | 7 | 15 | | | | | | | | | 15 | 65 |
| | | | | | 2 | 2 | 1 | 2 | 1 | 1 | 2 | 3 | 3 | 4 | 7 | | | | | | | | | 7 | 66 |
| | | | | | | 1 | 2 | 1 | | | | | 4 | | 4 | | | | | | | | | 4 | 67 |
| | 1 | | | | 1 | | 1 | 1 | 1 | 1 | 1 | | 1 | 2 | 3 | | | | | | | | | 3 | 68 |
| | | | | | 1 | 2 | | 2 | 5 | | | | 3 | 2 | 5 | | | | | | | | | 5 | 69 |
| | | | | | 1 | 1 | | | | | | | 1 | 1 | 2 | | | | | | | | | 2 | 70 |
| | | | | | | | 1 | | | 1 | | | 1 | | 1 | | | | | | | | | 1 | 71 |
| | | | | | 2 | 2 | | | 1 | 1 | 2 | | 3 | 1 | 4 | | | | | | | | | 4 | 72 |
| | | | | | 2 | 6 | 1 | 2 | 4 | 6 | | | 6 | 5 | 11 | | | | | | | | | 11 | 73 |
| | | | | | | 1 | 3 | | 1 | 3 | | | 2 | 2 | 4 | | | | | | | | | 4 | 74 |
| | 1 | | | | 3 | 1 | | 1 | 1 | | | 4 | 2 | 3 | 5 | | | | | | | | | 5 | 75 |

## CLASSIFICATION OF DEATHS IN MIDDLE

| | Cause of death. | Ages. Under 1. M. | Under 1. F. | 1 and under 5. M. | 1 and under 5. F. | 5 and under 10. M. | 5 and under 10. F. | 10 and under 20. M. | 10 and under 20. F. | 20 and under 50. M. | 20 and under 50. F. | 50 and under 80. M. | 50 and under 80. F. | 80 and under 100. M | 80 and under 100. F. | 100 & over. M | 100 & over. F. | Age unknown. M | Age unknown. F. | Nativities. Born in State. | N. England States. | Middle States. | Southern States. | Southwest'n States. | Northwest'n States. |
|---|---|---|---|---|---|---|---|---|---|---|---|---|---|---|---|---|---|---|---|---|---|---|---|---|---|
| 1 | Ulcer | | | | | | | | | 1 | | | 1 | | | | | | | | | 1 | | | |
| 2 | Uterus, disease of | | | | | | | | | | 2 | | | | | | | | | | | | 1 | | |
| 3 | Worms | | 1 | 4 | 3 | 1 | 1 | | | | | | | | | | | | | 10 | | | | | |
| 4 | Unknown | 107 | 74 | 50 | 32 | 14 | 13 | 12 | 17 | 34 | 51 | 50 | 49 | 11 | 2 | | | 1 | 1 | 373 | 4 | 79 | 20 | | 1 |
| | Total | 394 | 257 | 493 | 432 | 147 | 143 | 155 | 179 | 396 | 451 | 311 | 254 | 80 | 48 | 2 | 1 | 2 | 2 | 2624 | 65 | 591 | 144 | 5 | 22 |

## CLASSIFICATION OF DEATHS IN MIDDLE

*Embracing the following counties: Auglaize, Champaign, Clark, Darke, Delaware, Franklin,*

| | Cause of death. | Under 1. M. | Under 1. F. | 1 and under 5. M. | 1 and under 5. F. | 5 and under 10. M. | 5 and under 10. F. | 10 and under 20. M. | 10 and under 20. F. | 20 and under 50. M. | 20 and under 50. F. | 50 and under 80. M. | 50 and under 80. F. | 80 and under 100. M | 80 and under 100. F. | 100 & over. M | 100 & over. F. | Age unknown. M | Age unknown. F. | Born in State. | N. England States. | Middle States. | Southern States. | Southwest'n States. | Northwest'n States. |
|---|---|---|---|---|---|---|---|---|---|---|---|---|---|---|---|---|---|---|---|---|---|---|---|---|---|
| 1 | Accident, not specif'd | | | 1 | 1 | 4 | 2 | 7 | | 14 | 2 | 7 | 3 | | | | | | | 20 | 1 | 10 | 4 | | |
| 2 | ....do...burned | | 2 | 4 | 5 | 2 | 2 | | 1 | | | | | | | | | | | 15 | | | 1 | | |
| 3 | ....do...drowned | | | 3 | 4 | 2 | | 1 | 1 | 2 | | | | 1 | | | | | | 11 | | 2 | 1 | | |
| 4 | ....do.. scalded | | | 3 | 3 | 4 | | | | 1 | | | | | | | | | | 10 | | 1 | | | |
| 5 | ....do...shot | | | | | | | 3 | | | | | | | | | | | | 2 | | 1 | | | |
| 6 | ....do...railroad | | | | | | | | | 1 | | | | | | | | | | 1 | | | | | |
| 7 | Apoplexy | | | 1 | | | | 2 | 1 | 1 | 3 | 5 | 5 | | | | | | | 6 | | 9 | 3 | | |
| 8 | Asthma | | | 1 | | | | | | 1 | | 1 | 2 | 1 | | | | | | 2 | | 3 | 1 | | |
| 9 | Bowels, disease of | 2 | 2 | | 2 | 1 | 1 | | | 1 | 1 | 2 | | | | | | | | 9 | 1 | | 1 | | |
| 10 | Brain......do | 7 | 3 | 4 | 2 | | 2 | 1 | 2 | 6 | 4 | | | | | | | | | 25 | | 2 | 3 | | |
| 11 | Bronchitis | | | 1 | 1 | | 1 | | | 8 | 1 | 2 | 1 | 1 | | | | | | 6 | | 2 | | | |
| 12 | Cancer | | | | | | | | | 1 | 1 | 5 | 2 | | | | | | | 2 | | 5 | 1 | | 1 |
| 13 | Canker rash | | 1 | | | | | | | | 1 | | | | | | | | | 2 | | | | | |
| 14 | Catarrh | 2 | 4 | 3 | | | | 1 | 1 | 2 | 2 | 2 | | | | | | | | 14 | 1 | | 1 | | |
| 15 | Childbirth | | | | | | | | 1 | | 24 | | | | | | | | | 15 | | 4 | 4 | | 1 |
| 16 | Cholera | 14 | 14 | 45 | 58 | 55 | 26 | 51 | 55 | 338 | 154 | 112 | 34 | 2 | 3 | | | 1 | 2 | 448 | 22 | 106 | 55 | 3 | 19 |
| 17 | ...do..infantum | 19 | 15 | 8 | 8 | | | | | | | | | | | | | | | 49 | | 1 | | | |
| 18 | ...do..morbus | | | 3 | | 2 | 2 | | | 3 | 3 | 4 | 1 | | | | | | | 8 | | 2 | 2 | | |
| 19 | Chorea | | | | | | | | 1 | | | | | | | | | | | 1 | | | | | |
| 20 | Colic | 2 | | | | | | | | 2 | | 3 | 2 | | | | | | | 3 | 1 | 3 | 2 | | |
| 21 | Congestion | | 1 | 1 | | | | 1 | 1 | 1 | 2 | | | | | | | | | 7 | | | | | |
| 22 | ....do....brain | 1 | | 1 | | | | | 1 | | | | | | | | | | | 2 | | 1 | | | |
| 23 | ....do....lungs | | | | | | | 1 | | | | 1 | | | | | | | | 1 | | 1 | | | |
| 24 | Consumption | 3 | 4 | 3 | 8 | 4 | 1 | 7 | 23 | 86 | 84 | 38 | 24 | 4 | 1 | | | | | 130 | 15 | 79 | 31 | 2 | 5 |
| 25 | Convulsions | 17 | 9 | 7 | 20 | 3 | 1 | 1 | 4 | 3 | 1 | 2 | 1 | | 1 | | | | | 63 | 1 | 2 | 3 | | |
| 26 | Croup | 39 | 24 | 29 | 42 | 10 | 10 | | 1 | | | | | | | | | | | 147 | | 5 | 1 | | |
| 27 | Debility | 2 | 1 | 1 | | | | | | | | | | | | | | | | 4 | | | | | |
| 28 | Diabetes | | | | | 1 | | | | 1 | | 1 | | | | | | | | 2 | | 1 | | | |
| 29 | Diarrhœa | 7 | 5 | 17 | 10 | 1 | 1 | | | 5 | 4 | 11 | 5 | | | | | | | 44 | 3 | 6 | 4 | 1 | 4 |
| 30 | Dropsy | 3 | 3 | 10 | 7 | 4 | 2 | 1 | 2 | 7 | 18 | 13 | 11 | 1 | | | | | | 47 | 4 | 15 | 11 | 2 | |
| 31 | Dysentery | 10 | 14 | 66 | 60 | 16 | 7 | 8 | 7 | 16 | 13 | 8 | 8 | | 1 | | | 1 | | 196 | 2 | 20 | 7 | | 1 |
| 32 | Dyspepsia | | | | | | | | | 3 | 2 | 6 | 2 | | | | | | | 3 | 2 | 1 | 3 | | 1 |
| 33 | Epilepsy | | | | 1 | | | | | | | | | | | | | | | 1 | | | | | |
| 34 | Erysipelas | 7 | 3 | 3 | 4 | | 2 | 3 | 1 | 8 | 8 | | 1 | | | | | | | 30 | 1 | 5 | 2 | | 1 |
| 35 | Fever, not specified | 13 | 16 | 30 | 20 | 15 | 8 | 22 | 21 | 52 | 57 | 27 | 12 | | | | | | | 191 | 2 | 39 | 20 | | 8 |
| 36 | ..do..bilious | | | 4 | 1 | 3 | 1 | 4 | 2 | 14 | 5 | 9 | 3 | | | | | | | 22 | 3 | 13 | 1 | | 1 |
| 37 | ..do..brain | 1 | 1 | 2 | 2 | | | | | | | | | | | | | | | 5 | | | | | |
| 38 | ..do..congestive | | 1 | 2 | 2 | 3 | 1 | 3 | 4 | 7 | 5 | 4 | | 1 | | | | | | 22 | 1 | 5 | 2 | | 1 |
| 39 | ..do..inflammatory | 1 | | | | | | | | 1 | | | | | | | | | | 1 | | 1 | | | |
| 40 | ..do..intermittent | 2 | 1 | 2 | | 1 | 3 | 1 | | 1 | 3 | 2 | 2 | 1 | | | | | | 16 | | 1 | 1 | | |
| 41 | ..do..puerperal | | | | | | | | 1 | | 1 | | | | | | | | | 1 | | 1 | | | |
| 42 | ..do..remittent | 1 | 1 | | | 1 | | 1 | 1 | | 1 | 1 | 1 | | | | | | | 5 | | 1 | | | |
| 43 | ..do..scarlet | 14 | 13 | 99 | 97 | 50 | 46 | 11 | 12 | 2 | 4 | 1 | 2 | | | | | | | 329 | | 9 | 3 | 5 | 1 |
| 44 | ..do..typhus | 1 | 3 | 3 | 4 | 3 | 7 | 7 | 21 | 35 | 21 | 5 | 2 | | | | | | | 78 | 3 | 22 | 6 | | |
| 45 | ..do..winter | | 1 | 1 | 4 | 1 | | 1 | 1 | 6 | 2 | 3 | | | | | | | | 10 | | 5 | 3 | | |
| 46 | Fracture | | | | | | | | | 2 | | | | | | | | | | 2 | | | | | |
| 47 | Gravel | | | | | | | | | 1 | | 3 | | | | | | | | | | 2 | 1 | | 1 |
| 48 | Head, disease of | 1 | 2 | 2 | 3 | 5 | | 2 | 1 | 1 | 1 | 2 | | | | | | 1 | 1 | 21 | | | 1 | | |
| 49 | Heart....do | 1 | | | | 1 | 1 | | 3 | 2 | 2 | 2 | 2 | | | | | | | 8 | 1 | 3 | 2 | | |
| 50 | Hemorrhage | 1 | | | | | | | | 2 | | 1 | 1 | | | | | | | 2 | | 2 | 1 | | |
| 51 | Hernia | | | | | | | | | | 1 | | | | | | | | | | | 1 | | | |
| 52 | Hives | 1 | 1 | | | | | | | | | | | | | | | | | 2 | | | | | |
| 53 | Hooping cough | 19 | 16 | 19 | 21 | | 2 | | 1 | | | | | | | | | 1 | | 79 | | | | | |
| 54 | Hydrocephalus | 2 | 1 | 3 | | | | | | | | | | | | | | | | 6 | | | | | |
| 55 | Inflammation | 7 | 2 | 7 | 6 | 3 | 8 | 4 | 2 | 8 | 5 | 3 | 1 | | | | | | | 45 | 2 | 6 | 3 | | |
| 56 | ....do....bowels | 2 | 4 | 1 | 2 | 1 | 1 | 2 | | 3 | 4 | 2 | | | | | | | | 15 | | 5 | | | |
| 57 | ....do....brain | 6 | 3 | 15 | 9 | 4 | 4 | 2 | | 4 | | 1 | | | | | | | | 43 | | 3 | 1 | | |
| 58 | Insanity | | | | | | | 1 | | 1 | 2 | | | | | | | | | 3 | | | 1 | | |
| 59 | Intemperance | | | | | | | | | 1 | | 3 | | | | | | | | | | 1 | | | 1 |
| 60 | Jaundice | | 1 | 1 | | | | 1 | | | | 1 | 1 | | | | | | | 3 | | 1 | | | |

## EASTERN SECTION OF THE STATE OF OHIO—Continued.

| Nativities: California and Territories | Nativities: Ireland | Nativities: Germany | Nativities: Other foreign countries | Nativities: Unknown | Season of decease: Spring | Season of decease: Summer | Season of decease: Autumn | Season of decease: Winter | Duration of sickness: Under 1 week | Duration of sickness: 1 week and under 1 month | Duration of sickness: 1 month and under 3 months | Duration of sickness: 3 months and over | Whites: Males | Whites: Females | Whites: Total | Colored: Slaves: Black: M. | Colored: Slaves: Black: F. | Colored: Slaves: Mulatto: M. | Colored: Slaves: Mulatto: F. | Colored: Free: Black: M. | Colored: Free: Black: F. | Colored: Free: Mul.: M | Colored: Free: Mul.: F. | Aggregate deaths | |
|---|---|---|---|---|---|---|---|---|---|---|---|---|---|---|---|---|---|---|---|---|---|---|---|---|---|
| | | | 1 | | 2 | | | | | 2 | | | 1 | 1 | 2 | | | | | | | | | 2 | 1 |
| | | 1 | | | | 1 | 1 | | | 1 | 1 | | | 2 | 2 | | | | | | | | | 2 | 2 |
| | | | | | 2 | 3 | 1 | 4 | 3 | 7 | | | 5 | 5 | 10 | | | | | | | | | 10 | 3 |
| | 17 | 15 | 4 | 5 | 163 | 111 | 135 | 103 | 190 | 126 | 46 | 72 | 278 | 235 | 512 | | | | | | 2 | 1 | 2 | 518 | 4 |
| | 124 | 91 | 67 | 14 | 980 | 810 | 1328 | 615 | 1105 | 1509 | 354 | 548 | 1969 | 1749 | 3718 | | | | | 6 | 12 | 5 | 6 | 3747 | |

## WESTERN SECTION OF THE STATE OF OHIO.

*Hardin, Logan, Madison, Marion, Mercer, Miami, Morrow, Pickaway, Shelby, and Union.*

| Nativities: California and Territories | Nativities: Ireland | Nativities: Germany | Nativities: Other foreign countries | Nativities: Unknown | Season of decease: Spring | Season of decease: Summer | Season of decease: Autumn | Season of decease: Winter | Duration of sickness: Under 1 week | Duration of sickness: 1 week and under 1 month | Duration of sickness: 1 month and under 3 months | Duration of sickness: 3 months and over | Whites: Males | Whites: Females | Whites: Total | Colored: Slaves: Black: M. | Colored: Slaves: Black: F. | Colored: Slaves: Mulatto: M. | Colored: Slaves: Mulatto: F. | Colored: Free: Black: M. | Colored: Free: Black: F. | Colored: Free: Mul.: M | Colored: Free: Mul.: F. | Aggregate deaths | |
|---|---|---|---|---|---|---|---|---|---|---|---|---|---|---|---|---|---|---|---|---|---|---|---|---|---|
| | 2 | 2 | 1 | 1 | 11 | 9 | 11 | 10 | 19 | 7 | 2 | 1 | 33 | 8 | 41 | | | | | | | | | 41 | 1 |
| | | | | | 6 | 3 | 4 | 3 | 11 | 2 | 1 | | 6 | 9 | 15 | | | | | | 1 | | | 16 | 2 |
| | | | | | 5 | 6 | 2 | 1 | 14 | | | | 8 | 5 | 13 | | | | | | | 1 | | 14 | 3 |
| | | | | | 3 | 1 | 1 | 4 | 8 | 1 | | | 8 | 3 | 11 | | | | | | | | | 11 | 4 |
| | | | | | | 1 | 1 | 1 | 1 | | | | 3 | | 3 | | | | | | | | | 3 | 5 |
| | | | | | | 1 | | | 1 | | | | 1 | | 1 | | | | | | | | | 1 | 6 |
| | | | | | 3 | 9 | | 5 | 9 | | | | 9 | 9 | 18 | | | | | | | | | 18 | 7 |
| | | | | | 3 | 1 | | 2 | 3 | | 1 | 2 | 4 | 2 | 6 | | | | | | | | | 6 | 8 |
| | | 1 | | | 2 | 4 | 4 | 2 | 4 | 7 | | | 6 | 6 | 12 | | | | | | | | | 12 | 9 |
| | | | 1 | | 8 | 8 | 8 | 7 | 12 | 13 | 2 | 1 | 17 | 13 | 30 | | | | | 1 | | | | 31 | 10 |
| | 1 | 1 | 1 | | 3 | 2 | 4 | 2 | | 7 | 2 | 2 | 7 | 4 | 11 | | | | | | | | | 11 | 11 |
| | | | | | | 4 | 2 | 3 | | 1 | 1 | 6 | 6 | 3 | 9 | | | | | | | | | 9 | 12 |
| | | | | | 1 | | 1 | | | 2 | | | | 2 | 2 | | | | | | | | | 2 | 13 |
| | 1 | | | | 9 | 3 | 3 | 2 | 3 | 11 | 1 | 1 | 10 | 7 | 17 | | | | | | | | | 17 | 14 |
| | | | 1 | | 7 | 6 | 7 | 5 | 11 | 10 | 2 | 1 | | 25 | 25 | | | | | | | | | 25 | 15 |
| | 21 | 287 | 3 | | 7 | 545 | 406 | 6 | 783 | 54 | 5 | 1 | 597 | 336 | 933 | | | | | 15 | 10 | 6 | | 964 | 16 |
| | | | | | 1 | 17 | 31 | 1 | 23 | 18 | 2 | 2 | 27 | 23 | 50 | | | | | | | | | 50 | 17 |
| | 1 | 3 | 2 | | 1 | 6 | 10 | 1 | 9 | 8 | | 1 | 11 | 6 | 17 | | | | | | | 1 | | 18 | 18 |
| | | | | | | 1 | | | | 1 | | | | 1 | 1 | | | | | | | | | 1 | 19 |
| | | | | | 3 | 1 | 1 | 4 | 7 | 2 | | | 7 | 2 | 9 | | | | | | | | | 9 | 20 |
| | | 1 | | | 2 | 1 | 3 | 2 | 5 | 3 | | | 3 | 4 | 7 | | | | | | | 1 | | 8 | 21 |
| | | | | | 2 | | 1 | | 1 | 2 | | | 2 | 1 | 3 | | | | | | | | | 3 | 22 |
| | | | | | 1 | | | 1 | | 2 | | | 2 | | 2 | | | | | | | | | 2 | 23 |
| | 1 | 12 | 15 | | 78 | 77 | 77 | 57 | 5 | 27 | 44 | 195 | 140 | 40 | 280 | | | | | 2 | 2 | 3 | 3 | 290 | 24 |
| | | 1 | | | 23 | 16 | 17 | 14 | 42 | 13 | 3 | 5 | 33 | 37 | 70 | | | | | | | | | 70 | 25 |
| | | 2 | | | 44 | 24 | 58 | 29 | 107 | 34 | 2 | | 77 | 77 | 154 | | | | | | | 1 | | 155 | 26 |
| | | | | | 1 | | 2 | | 1 | 1 | 1 | | 3 | 1 | 4 | | | | | | | | | 4 | 27 |
| | | | | | 1 | | | 2 | | 1 | 1 | 1 | 3 | | 3 | | | | | | | | | 3 | 28 |
| | 1 | 2 | 1 | | 3 | 13 | 42 | 8 | 18 | 27 | 11 | 7 | 41 | 25 | 66 | | | | | | | | | 66 | 29 |
| | | 1 | 2 | | 27 | 20 | 19 | 16 | 8 | 21 | 13 | 34 | 37 | 43 | 80 | | | | | 1 | | 1 | | 82 | 30 |
| | 3 | 3 | 3 | | 6 | 35 | 184 | 9 | 57 | 149 | 14 | 3 | 123 | 107 | 230 | | | | | | 2 | 2 | 1 | 235 | 31 |
| | 2 | | 1 | | 3 | 3 | 3 | 4 | 1 | 1 | 6 | 5 | 9 | 4 | 13 | | | | | | | | | 13 | 32 |
| | | | | | | | | 1 | 1 | | | | | 1 | 1 | | | | | | | | | 1 | 33 |
| | | 1 | | | 13 | 7 | 13 | 7 | 12 | 20 | 5 | 2 | 21 | 19 | 40 | | | | | | | | | 40 | 34 |
| | 5 | 17 | 11 | | 69 | 51 | 124 | 48 | 54 | 189 | 29 | 8 | 157 | 131 | 288 | | | | | 2 | 3 | | | 293 | 35 |
| | 2 | 3 | 1 | | 10 | 6 | 27 | 2 | 6 | 34 | 3 | 2 | 34 | 12 | 46 | | | | | | | | | 46 | 36 |
| | 1 | | | | 3 | 2 | 1 | | 1 | 5 | | | 3 | 3 | 6 | | | | | | | | | 6 | 37 |
| | | | 1 | 1 | 9 | 8 | 11 | 5 | 14 | 16 | 2 | 1 | 20 | 13 | 33 | | | | | | | | | 33 | 38 |
| | | | | | | | 2 | | 1 | 1 | | | 2 | | 2 | | | | | | | | | 2 | 39 |
| | | 1 | | | 3 | 5 | 8 | 3 | 6 | 10 | 2 | 1 | 10 | 9 | 19 | | | | | | | | | 19 | 40 |
| | | | | | 1 | | 1 | | 1 | | 1 | | | 2 | 2 | | | | | | | | | 2 | 41 |
| | | 2 | | | 1 | 3 | 3 | 1 | 3 | 4 | | | 4 | 4 | 8 | | | | | | | | | 8 | 42 |
| | | 4 | | | 99 | 86 | 84 | 81 | 161 | 157 | 17 | | 177 | 174 | 351 | | | | | | | | | 351 | 43 |
| | | 3 | | | 19 | 5 | 63 | 24 | 10 | 86 | 7 | 4 | 54 | 58 | 112 | | | | | | | | | 112 | 44 |
| | 1 | | 1 | | 7 | 5 | 1 | 7 | 5 | 12 | 1 | 1 | 11 | 8 | 19 | | | | | | | 1 | | 20 | 45 |
| | | | | | | 2 | | | | 1 | 1 | | 2 | | 2 | | | | | | | | | 2 | 46 |
| | | | | | 1 | 1 | 1 | 1 | | 2 | 1 | 1 | 4 | | 4 | | | | | | | | | 4 | 47 |
| | | | | | 7 | 6 | 8 | 1 | 5 | 10 | 5 | 1 | 14 | 8 | 22 | | | | | | | | | 22 | 48 |
| | | | | | 3 | 6 | 3 | 2 | 4 | 2 | | 3 | 6 | 8 | 14 | | | | | | | | | 14 | 49 |
| | | | | | 2 | 1 | 2 | | 2 | 2 | 1 | | 4 | 1 | 5 | | | | | | | | | 5 | 50 |
| | | | | | | 1 | | | | 1 | | | | 1 | 1 | | | | | | | | | 1 | 51 |
| | | | | | 1 | | 1 | | 2 | | | | 1 | 1 | 2 | | | | | | | | | 2 | 52 |
| | | | | | 22 | 22 | 26 | 9 | 8 | 45 | 19 | 3 | 38 | 40 | 78 | | | | | 1 | | | | 79 | 53 |
| | | | | | 2 | 1 | 1 | 2 | 2 | 3 | 2 | 1 | 5 | 1 | 6 | | | | | | | | | 6 | 54 |
| | | | | | 18 | 12 | 17 | 9 | 23 | 18 | 4 | 4 | 32 | 24 | 56 | | | | | | | | | 56 | 55 |
| | 1 | 1 | | | 5 | 6 | 8 | 2 | 7 | 11 | 2 | 1 | 11 | 11 | 22 | | | | | | | | | 22 | 56 |
| | 1 | | | | 15 | 11 | 13 | 9 | 18 | 22 | 3 | 4 | 32 | 14 | 46 | | | | | | 1 | | 1 | 48 | 57 |
| | | | | | | | 3 | 1 | | 1 | | 1 | 2 | 2 | 4 | | | | | | | | | 4 | 58 |
| | 2 | | | | 2 | 1 | | 1 | 1 | 1 | | | 4 | | 4 | | | | | | | | | 4 | 59 |
| | | | 1 | | 1 | | 2 | 2 | | 3 | | 2 | 3 | 2 | 5 | | | | | | | | | 5 | 60 |

## CLASSIFICATION OF DEATHS IN MIDDLE

| | Cause of death. | AGES. | | | | | | | | | | | | | | | | | | NATIVITIES. | | | | | |
|---|---|---|---|---|---|---|---|---|---|---|---|---|---|---|---|---|---|---|---|---|---|---|---|---|---|
| | | Under 1. | | 1 and under 5. | | 5 and under 10. | | 10 and under 20. | | 20 and under 50. | | 50 and under 80. | | 80 and under 100. | | 100 & over. | | Age unknown. | | Born in State. | N. England States. | Middle States. | Southern States. | Southwest'n States. | Northwest'n States. |
| | | M. | F. | M. | F. | M. | F. | M. | F. | M. | F. | M. | F. | M | F. | M | F. | M | F. | | | | | | |
| 1 | Kidneys, disease of.. | ... | ... | ... | ... | 1 | ... | ... | ... | ... | ... | 1 | ... | ... | ... | ... | ... | ... | ... | 1 | .. | 1 | ... | ... | ... |
| 2 | Killed | ... | ... | ... | 1 | ... | ... | 1 | ... | 2 | ... | ... | ... | ... | ... | ... | ... | ... | ... | 2 | .. | ... | 1 | ... | ... |
| 3 | Liver, disease of | 1 | 3 | 5 | 2 | ... | 1 | 1 | 2 | 5 | 9 | 3 | ... | ... | ... | ... | ... | ... | ... | 22 | .. | 3 | 1 | ... | 1 |
| 4 | Lockjaw | ... | ... | ... | ... | ... | ... | ... | ... | 1 | ... | ... | ... | ... | ... | ... | ... | ... | ... | 1 | .. | ... | ... | ... | ... |
| 5 | Lungs, disease of | 6 | 3 | 3 | 5 | 3 | ... | 2 | 1 | 3 | 4 | 5 | 3 | .. | 1 | ... | ... | ... | ... | 25 | 1 | 6 | 6 | ... | ... |
| 6 | Mania-a-potu | ... | ... | ... | ... | ... | ... | ... | ... | 1 | ... | ... | ... | ... | ... | ... | ... | ... | ... | ... | .. | ... | ... | ... | ... |
| 7 | Marasmus | 2 | ... | 1 | 1 | ... | 1 | ... | ... | 2 | ... | 1 | ... | ... | ... | ... | ... | ... | ... | 6 | 1 | 1 | ... | ... | ... |
| 8 | Measles | 3 | 2 | 20 | 9 | 2 | 2 | 1 | ... | 2 | 5 | 1 | ... | ... | ... | ... | ... | ... | ... | 42 | .. | 1 | 1 | ... | ... |
| 9 | Milk sickness | ... | ... | ... | ... | ... | 2 | ... | 3 | 2 | 1 | ... | ... | ... | ... | ... | ... | ... | ... | 7 | .. | 1 | ... | ... | ... |
| 10 | Mortification | ... | ... | ... | ... | ... | ... | ... | ... | ... | 1 | ... | ... | 1 | ... | ... | ... | ... | ... | ... | .. | ... | 1 | ... | ... |
| 11 | Mumps | ... | ... | ... | ... | ... | ... | 1 | ... | ... | ... | ... | ... | ... | ... | ... | ... | ... | ... | 1 | .. | ... | ... | ... | ... |
| 12 | Murder | ... | ... | ... | ... | ... | ... | ... | ... | 2 | ... | ... | ... | ... | ... | ... | ... | ... | ... | 1 | .. | ... | ... | ... | ... |
| 13 | Neuralgia | ... | ... | ... | ... | ... | ... | 1 | ... | ... | ... | ... | ... | ... | ... | ... | ... | ... | ... | ... | .. | 1 | ... | ... | ... |
| 14 | Old age | ... | ... | ... | ... | ... | ... | ... | ... | 1 | ... | 16 | 14 | 25 | 24 | 1 | .. | .. | 1 | 11 | 6 | 34 | 21 | 2 | ... |
| 15 | Paralysis | ... | ... | ... | ... | ... | 1 | ... | 1 | 1 | 1 | 7 | 9 | 1 | .. | ... | ... | ... | ... | 2 | 2 | 11 | 4 | ... | ... |
| 16 | Peritonitis | ... | ... | ... | ... | ... | ... | ... | ... | ... | 3 | ... | 1 | ... | ... | ... | ... | ... | ... | 2 | .. | 1 | 1 | ... | ... |
| 17 | Pleurisy | 1 | ... | 1 | ... | ... | ... | 1 | 1 | 5 | 7 | 3 | ... | .. | 1 | ... | ... | ... | ... | 12 | .. | 5 | 1 | ... | ... |
| 18 | Pneumonia | 13 | 6 | 17 | 17 | 6 | 6 | 3 | 8 | 27 | 16 | 18 | 8 | 1 | .. | ... | ... | ... | ... | 98 | 1 | 26 | 11 | ... | 2 |
| 19 | Poison | ... | 1 | ... | 1 | 1 | ... | ... | ... | ... | 1 | ... | ... | ... | ... | ... | ... | ... | ... | 2 | .. | 2 | ... | ... | ... |
| 20 | Putrid sore throat | ... | ... | 1 | 1 | 1 | ... | ... | 2 | ... | ... | ... | ... | ... | ... | ... | ... | ... | ... | 5 | .. | ... | ... | ... | ... |
| 21 | Quinsy | ... | ... | 1 | 1 | 1 | 2 | 1 | 1 | ... | ... | 1 | ... | ... | ... | ... | ... | ... | ... | 6 | .. | 1 | 1 | ... | ... |
| 22 | Rheumatism | 1 | ... | ... | ... | ... | 1 | 2 | ... | 1 | ... | 1 | 4 | ... | ... | ... | ... | ... | ... | 4 | .. | 4 | 2 | ... | ... |
| 23 | Rickets | ... | ... | 1 | ... | ... | ... | ... | ... | ... | ... | ... | ... | ... | ... | ... | ... | ... | ... | 1 | .. | ... | ... | ... | ... |
| 24 | Scrofula | 1 | ... | 1 | ... | 1 | 1 | 2 | 1 | 1 | ... | ... | 1 | ... | ... | ... | ... | ... | ... | 6 | 1 | 1 | ... | ... | 1 |
| 25 | Scurvy | ... | ... | ... | ... | ... | ... | ... | ... | 1 | ... | ... | ... | ... | ... | ... | ... | ... | ... | 1 | .. | ... | ... | ... | ... |
| 26 | Small pox | 8 | 2 | 2 | 2 | 1 | 2 | 5 | 4 | 10 | 3 | 1 | 3 | ... | ... | ... | ... | ... | ... | 31 | .. | 8 | 3 | ... | ... |
| 27 | Spine, disease of | 1 | ... | 1 | ... | ... | ... | ... | 1 | 1 | 1 | 1 | ... | ... | ... | ... | ... | ... | ... | 3 | .. | 1 | ... | ... | 2 |
| 28 | Stomach..do | ... | 1 | 1 | ... | ... | 1 | ... | ... | 1 | ... | 1 | 1 | ... | ... | ... | ... | ... | ... | 4 | 1 | ... | 1 | ... | ... |
| 29 | Suffocation | ... | ... | 1 | ... | ... | ... | 1 | ... | ... | ... | ... | ... | ... | ... | ... | ... | ... | ... | 1 | .. | 1 | ... | ... | ... |
| 30 | Suicide | ... | ... | ... | ... | ... | ... | ... | ... | 3 | ... | ... | ... | ... | ... | ... | ... | ... | ... | ... | .. | 2 | ... | ... | ... |
| 31 | Summer complaint | ... | 2 | 3 | ... | ... | ... | ... | ... | ... | ... | ... | ... | ... | ... | ... | ... | ... | ... | 5 | .. | ... | ... | ... | ... |
| 32 | Teething | ... | 1 | 1 | ... | ... | ... | ... | ... | ... | ... | ... | ... | ... | ... | ... | ... | ... | ... | 2 | .. | ... | ... | ... | ... |
| 33 | Throat, disease of | ... | 1 | 1 | 1 | 2 | 3 | 1 | ... | ... | 1 | ... | ... | ... | ... | ... | ... | ... | ... | 8 | .. | ... | 1 | ... | 1 |
| 34 | Thrush | 1 | 1 | 1 | 1 | ... | ... | ... | ... | ... | ... | ... | ... | ... | ... | ... | ... | ... | ... | 4 | .. | ... | ... | ... | ... |
| 35 | Tumor | ... | ... | ... | ... | ... | ... | ... | ... | ... | 1 | ... | ... | ... | ... | ... | ... | ... | ... | ... | .. | 1 | ... | ... | ... |
| 36 | Ulcer | ... | ... | ... | ... | ... | ... | ... | ... | ... | ... | ... | 1 | ... | ... | ... | ... | ... | ... | ... | .. | ... | ... | ... | ... |
| 37 | White swelling | ... | ... | ... | ... | ... | ... | 1 | ... | 2 | ... | ... | ... | ... | ... | ... | ... | ... | ... | 2 | .. | ... | 1 | ... | ... |
| 38 | Worms | 2 | 1 | 6 | 8 | ... | 1 | ... | ... | ... | ... | ... | ... | ... | ... | ... | ... | ... | ... | 18 | .. | ... | ... | ... | ... |
| 39 | Unknown | 101 | 72 | 45 | 44 | 13 | 13 | 10 | 13 | 56 | 58 | 41 | 34 | 3 | 4 | .. | .. | 8 | 1 | 401 | 9 | 49 | 19 | 1 | 7 |
| | Total | 849 | 269 | 520 | 500 | 232 | 179 | 184 | 216 | 779 | 554 | 394 | 208 | 43 | 36 | 1 | .. | 12 | 5 | 2972 | 38 | 569 | 263 | 16 | 60 |

## CLASSIFICATION OF DEATHS IN SOUTHEASTERN

*Embracing the following counties: Athens, Belmont, Gallia, Hocking, Jackson, Jefferson,*

| | Cause of death. | Under 1. M. | Under 1. F. | 1 and under 5. M. | 1 and under 5. F. | 5 and under 10. M. | 5 and under 10. F. | 10 and under 20. M. | 10 and under 20. F. | 20 and under 50. M. | 20 and under 50. F. | 50 and under 80. M. | 50 and under 80. F. | 80 and under 100. M | 80 and under 100. F. | 100 & over. M | 100 & over. F. | Age unknown. M | Age unknown. F. | Born in State. | N. England States. | Middle States. | Southern States. | Southwest'n States. | Northwest'n States. |
|---|---|---|---|---|---|---|---|---|---|---|---|---|---|---|---|---|---|---|---|---|---|---|---|---|---|
| 1 | Abscess | ... | ... | ... | ... | ... | ... | ... | 1 | 1 | 2 | ... | ... | ... | ... | ... | ... | ... | ... | 3 | .. | 1 | ... | ... | ... |
| 2 | Accident, not specif'd | 1 | ... | 3 | 1 | 5 | 5 | 9 | 1 | 15 | 2 | 4 | 2 | 1 | .. | ... | ... | ... | ... | 34 | 2 | 5 | 6 | ... | ... |
| 3 | ....do...burned | ... | 3 | 1 | 5 | 1 | ... | ... | 1 | 1 | ... | ... | 1 | .. | 1 | ... | ... | ... | ... | 10 | 1 | 1 | 1 | ... | ... |
| 4 | ....do...drowned | 1 | ... | 1 | 2 | 4 | 1 | 6 | 2 | 15 | 1 | 2 | ... | ... | ... | ... | ... | ... | ... | 22 | .. | 5 | 1 | ... | ... |
| 5 | ....do...scalded | 1 | 2 | 6 | 2 | 1 | ... | ... | ... | ... | ... | ... | ... | ... | ... | ... | ... | ... | ... | 12 | .. | ... | ... | ... | ... |
| 6 | Apoplexy | ... | ... | ... | ... | ... | ... | ... | 1 | ... | 3 | 8 | 1 | 2 | .. | ... | ... | ... | ... | 1 | 1 | 8 | 1 | ... | ... |
| 7 | Asthma | ... | ... | ... | ... | ... | 1 | ... | ... | ... | ... | 2 | 3 | .. | ... | ... | ... | ... | ... | 1 | .. | 4 | 1 | ... | ... |
| 8 | Bowels, disease of | 2 | 1 | 2 | 2 | 2 | ... | ... | ... | 2 | ... | ... | 1 | .. | ... | ... | ... | ... | ... | 9 | .. | 2 | ... | ... | ... |
| 9 | Brain.......do | 3 | 5 | 7 | 7 | 5 | ... | ... | ... | 3 | 2 | 2 | ... | ... | ... | ... | ... | ... | ... | 30 | .. | 2 | 2 | ... | ... |
| 10 | Bronchitis | 1 | ... | 2 | 4 | ... | ... | ... | ... | 5 | ... | 2 | ... | ... | ... | ... | ... | ... | ... | 11 | .. | 1 | ... | ... | ... |
| 11 | Cancer | ... | ... | ... | ... | ... | 1 | ... | ... | 1 | 2 | 2 | 6 | .. | ... | ... | ... | ... | ... | 2 | 1 | 4 | 3 | ... | ... |
| 12 | Catarrh | 11 | 11 | 1 | 5 | 1 | 1 | ... | 2 | 5 | 4 | 1 | 2 | 2 | .. | ... | ... | ... | ... | 38 | 1 | 2 | 1 | ... | ... |
| 13 | Chicken pox | ... | ... | 1 | ... | ... | ... | ... | ... | ... | 1 | ... | ... | ... | ... | ... | ... | ... | ... | 1 | .. | ... | ... | ... | ... |
| 14 | Childbirth | ... | ... | ... | ... | ... | ... | ... | 1 | ... | 21 | ... | ... | ... | ... | ... | ... | ... | ... | 14 | 1 | ... | 3 | ... | 1 |
| 15 | Cholera | 6 | 8 | 19 | 14 | 10 | 9 | 17 | 7 | 78 | 33 | 30 | 12 | 1 | .. | ... | ... | 1 | .. | 120 | 3 | 42 | 20 | ... | 11 |
| 16 | ....do...infantum | 9 | 9 | 10 | 6 | ... | ... | ... | ... | ... | ... | ... | ... | ... | ... | ... | ... | ... | ... | 32 | .. | 1 | 1 | ... | ... |
| 17 | ....do...morbus | 1 | ... | 2 | ... | ... | ... | ... | ... | 2 | 1 | 4 | 2 | .. | ... | ... | ... | ... | ... | 5 | .. | 4 | 1 | ... | ... |
| 18 | Colic | 1 | 1 | ... | ... | 2 | ... | ... | ... | 4 | 2 | 3 | 2 | .. | ... | ... | ... | ... | ... | 5 | 1 | 4 | 1 | ... | ... |
| 19 | Congestion | 1 | ... | ... | ... | ... | ... | ... | ... | ... | ... | ... | ... | ... | ... | ... | ... | ... | ... | 1 | .. | ... | ... | ... | ... |
| 20 | ....do....brain | 1 | ... | ... | ... | 1 | ... | ... | ... | ... | ... | ... | ... | ... | ... | ... | ... | ... | ... | 2 | .. | ... | ... | ... | ... |
| 21 | ....do....lungs | ... | 1 | ... | ... | ... | ... | ... | 1 | ... | ... | 1 | ... | ... | ... | ... | ... | ... | ... | 2 | .. | 1 | ... | ... | ... |
| 22 | Consumption | 4 | 4 | 12 | 7 | 2 | 7 | 13 | 26 | 99 | 127 | 37 | 27 | 4 | .. | ... | ... | 2 | .. | 223 | 14 | 76 | 34 | 1 | 4 |
| 23 | Convulsions | 15 | 10 | 7 | 7 | 2 | ... | 1 | ... | ... | 2 | ... | ... | ... | ... | ... | ... | ... | ... | 42 | .. | 2 | ... | ... | ... |
| 24 | Croup | 30 | 32 | 35 | 39 | 11 | 5 | 1 | 1 | ... | ... | 2 | ... | ... | ... | ... | ... | ... | ... | 153 | .. | 2 | ... | ... | ... |
| 25 | Debility | ... | 1 | ... | ... | ... | ... | ... | 1 | ... | ... | ... | ... | ... | ... | ... | ... | ... | ... | 2 | .. | ... | ... | ... | ... |

## WESTERN SECTION OF THE STATE OF OHIO—*Continued.*

| NATIVITIES. | | | | | SEASON OF DECEASE. | | | | DURATION OF SICKNESS. | | | | WHITES. | | | COLORED. | | | | | | | | | |
|---|---|---|---|---|---|---|---|---|---|---|---|---|---|---|---|---|---|---|---|---|---|---|---|---|---|
| | | | | | | | | | | | | | | | | Slaves. | | | | Free. | | | | | |
| | | | | | | | | | | | | | | | | Black. | | Mulatto. | | Black. | | Mul. | | | |
| [...]ritories. | Ireland. | Germany. | Other foreign countries. | Unknown. | Spring. | Summer. | Autumn. | Winter. | Under 1 week. | 1 week and under 1 month. | 1 month and under 3 months. | 3 months and over. | Males. | Females. | Total. | M. | F. | M. | F. | M. | F. | M | F. | Aggregate deaths. | |
| ... | ... | ... | ... | ... | ... | 1 | ... | 1 | ... | 1 | ... | 1 | 2 | ... | 2 | ... | ... | ... | ... | ... | ... | ... | ... | 2 | 1 |
| ... | ... | 1 | ... | ... | ... | ... | 1 | 3 | ... | ... | ... | ... | 3 | 1 | 4 | ... | ... | ... | ... | ... | ... | ... | ... | 4 | 2 |
| ... | 1 | 2 | 1 | 1 | 6 | 6 | 14 | 5 | 5 | 8 | 7 | 9 | 15 | 17 | 32 | ... | ... | ... | ... | ... | ... | ... | ... | 32 | 3 |
| ... | ... | ... | ... | ... | ... | 1 | ... | ... | 1 | ... | ... | ... | 1 | ... | 1 | ... | ... | ... | ... | ... | ... | ... | ... | 1 | 4 |
| ... | ... | 1 | ... | ... | 14 | 10 | 8 | 7 | 4 | 11 | 10 | 11 | 22 | 16 | 38 | ... | ... | ... | ... | ... | 1 | ... | ... | 39 | 5 |
| ... | 1 | ... | ... | ... | ... | ... | 1 | ... | 1 | ... | ... | ... | 1 | ... | 1 | ... | ... | ... | ... | ... | ... | ... | ... | 1 | 6 |
| ... | ... | ... | ... | ... | 1 | 2 | 5 | ... | ... | ... | 4 | 3 | 6 | 2 | 8 | ... | ... | ... | ... | ... | ... | ... | ... | 8 | 7 |
| ... | 2 | ... | 1 | ... | 17 | 15 | 9 | 5 | 7 | 38 | 2 | ... | 29 | 18 | 47 | ... | ... | ... | ... | ... | ... | ... | ... | 47 | 8 |
| ... | ... | ... | ... | ... | ... | 4 | 4 | ... | 1 | 6 | 1 | ... | 2 | 6 | 8 | ... | ... | ... | ... | ... | ... | ... | ... | 8 | 9 |
| ... | ... | ... | 1 | ... | ... | ... | 2 | ... | ... | 2 | ... | ... | 1 | 1 | 2 | ... | ... | ... | ... | ... | ... | ... | ... | 2 | 10 |
| ... | ... | ... | ... | ... | ... | ... | ... | 1 | 1 | ... | ... | ... | 1 | ... | 1 | ... | ... | ... | ... | ... | ... | ... | ... | 1 | 11 |
| ... | ... | 1 | ... | ... | ... | ... | 1 | 1 | 1 | ... | ... | ... | 2 | ... | 2 | ... | ... | ... | ... | ... | ... | ... | ... | 2 | 12 |
| ... | ... | ... | ... | ... | ... | 1 | ... | ... | ... | ... | ... | 1 | 1 | ... | 1 | ... | ... | ... | ... | ... | ... | ... | ... | 1 | 13 |
| ... | 2 | 4 | 2 | ... | 26 | 19 | 19 | 14 | 9 | 16 | 8 | 12 | 41 | 39 | 80 | ... | ... | ... | ... | 2 | ... | ... | ... | 82 | 14 |
| ... | ... | 1 | 1 | ... | 6 | 4 | 6 | 5 | 7 | 9 | ... | 3 | 9 | 12 | 21 | ... | ... | ... | ... | ... | ... | ... | ... | 21 | 15 |
| ... | ... | ... | ... | ... | ... | 1 | 1 | 2 | 3 | 1 | ... | ... | ... | 4 | 4 | ... | ... | ... | ... | ... | ... | ... | ... | 4 | 16 |
| ... | ... | 2 | ... | ... | 5 | 5 | 4 | 6 | 7 | 13 | ... | ... | 10 | 8 | 18 | ... | ... | ... | ... | 1 | 1 | ... | ... | 20 | 17 |
| ... | 1 | 5 | 2 | ... | 72 | 31 | 22 | 21 | 31 | 91 | 12 | 5 | 84 | 60 | 144 | ... | ... | ... | ... | 1 | ... | ... | 1 | 146 | 18 |
| ... | ... | ... | ... | ... | ... | 1 | 1 | 2 | 1 | 1 | ... | ... | 1 | 3 | 4 | ... | ... | ... | ... | ... | ... | ... | ... | 4 | 19 |
| ... | ... | ... | ... | ... | 2 | ... | 1 | 2 | 2 | 3 | ... | ... | 2 | 3 | 5 | ... | ... | ... | ... | ... | ... | ... | ... | 5 | 20 |
| ... | ... | ... | ... | ... | 4 | 2 | ... | 2 | 4 | 2 | 2 | ... | 4 | 4 | 8 | ... | ... | ... | ... | ... | ... | ... | ... | 8 | 21 |
| ... | ... | ... | ... | ... | 2 | 3 | 2 | 3 | 1 | 4 | 1 | 4 | 5 | 5 | 10 | ... | ... | ... | ... | ... | ... | ... | ... | 10 | 22 |
| ... | ... | ... | ... | ... | ... | 1 | ... | ... | ... | ... | 1 | ... | 1 | ... | 1 | ... | ... | ... | ... | ... | ... | ... | ... | 1 | 23 |
| ... | ... | ... | ... | ... | 3 | 2 | 2 | 2 | ... | 3 | 1 | 5 | 6 | 3 | 9 | ... | ... | ... | ... | ... | ... | ... | ... | 9 | 24 |
| ... | ... | ... | ... | ... | ... | ... | ... | 1 | ... | ... | 1 | ... | 1 | ... | 1 | ... | ... | ... | ... | ... | ... | ... | ... | 1 | 25 |
| ... | ... | ... | 1 | ... | 15 | 6 | 3 | 19 | 5 | 37 | 1 | ... | 24 | 16 | 40 | ... | ... | ... | ... | 2 | ... | 1 | ... | 43 | 26 |
| ... | ... | ... | ... | ... | 3 | ... | 3 | ... | 1 | 2 | 2 | 1 | 4 | 2 | 6 | ... | ... | ... | ... | ... | ... | ... | ... | 6 | 27 |
| ... | ... | ... | ... | ... | ... | ... | 4 | 2 | 2 | 3 | 1 | ... | 3 | 3 | 6 | ... | ... | ... | ... | ... | ... | ... | ... | 6 | 28 |
| ... | ... | ... | ... | ... | ... | ... | ... | 2 | 2 | ... | ... | ... | 2 | ... | 2 | ... | ... | ... | ... | ... | ... | ... | ... | 2 | 29 |
| ... | ... | 1 | ... | ... | 2 | 1 | ... | ... | 1 | ... | ... | ... | 3 | ... | 3 | ... | ... | ... | ... | ... | ... | ... | ... | 3 | 30 |
| ... | ... | ... | ... | ... | ... | 1 | 4 | ... | 3 | 2 | ... | ... | 3 | 2 | 5 | ... | ... | ... | ... | ... | ... | ... | ... | 5 | 31 |
| ... | ... | ... | ... | ... | 1 | ... | 1 | ... | 1 | ... | 1 | ... | 1 | 1 | 2 | ... | ... | ... | ... | ... | ... | ... | ... | 2 | 32 |
| ... | ... | ... | ... | ... | ... | 2 | 4 | 4 | 5 | 2 | 1 | ... | 4 | 6 | 10 | ... | ... | ... | ... | ... | ... | ... | ... | 10 | 33 |
| ... | ... | ... | ... | ... | 2 | 2 | ... | ... | 2 | ... | 1 | 1 | 2 | 2 | 4 | ... | ... | ... | ... | ... | ... | ... | ... | 4 | 34 |
| ... | ... | ... | ... | ... | ... | 1 | ... | ... | ... | ... | 1 | ... | ... | 1 | 1 | ... | ... | ... | ... | ... | ... | ... | ... | 1 | 35 |
| ... | 1 | ... | ... | ... | ... | ... | 1 | ... | ... | ... | ... | 1 | ... | 1 | 1 | ... | ... | ... | ... | ... | ... | ... | ... | 1 | 36 |
| ... | ... | ... | ... | ... | 2 | ... | 1 | ... | 1 | ... | 2 | ... | 3 | ... | 3 | ... | ... | ... | ... | ... | ... | ... | ... | 3 | 37 |
| ... | ... | ... | ... | ... | 5 | 2 | 9 | 2 | 8 | 7 | 2 | ... | 8 | 10 | 18 | ... | ... | ... | ... | ... | ... | ... | ... | 18 | 38 |
| ... | 5 | 21 | 8 | 1 | 151 | 130 | 145 | 87 | 161 | 104 | 51 | 103 | 272 | 241 | 513 | ... | ... | ... | ... | 3 | 2 | 2 | 1 | 521 | 39 |
| ... | 59 | 387 | 63 | 4 | 916 | 1319 | 1603 | 618 | 1787 | 1447 | 332 | 468 | 2463 | 1937 | 4400 | ... | ... | ... | ... | 31 | 23 | 20 | 7 | 4481 | |

## [...] SECTION OF THE STATE OF OHIO.

*Lawrence, Meigs, Monroe, Morgan, Pike, Ross, Sciota, Vinton, and Washington.*

| [...]ritories. | Ireland. | Germany. | Other foreign countries. | Unknown. | Spring. | Summer. | Autumn. | Winter. | Under 1 week. | 1 week and under 1 month. | 1 month and under 3 months. | 3 months and over. | Males. | Females. | Total. | Slaves Black M. | Slaves Black F. | Slaves Mulatto M. | Slaves Mulatto F. | Free Black M. | Free Black F. | Free Mul. M | Free Mul. F. | Aggregate deaths. | |
|---|---|---|---|---|---|---|---|---|---|---|---|---|---|---|---|---|---|---|---|---|---|---|---|---|---|
| ... | ... | ... | ... | ... | 1 | 1 | 1 | 1 | 1 | ... | 1 | 2 | 1 | 3 | 4 | ... | ... | ... | ... | ... | ... | ... | ... | 4 | 1 |
| ... | ... | 1 | 1 | ... | 11 | 14 | 17 | 7 | 19 | 6 | 1 | 1 | 38 | 11 | 49 | ... | ... | ... | ... | ... | ... | ... | ... | 49 | 2 |
| ... | ... | 1 | ... | ... | 6 | 3 | 3 | 2 | 2 | 5 | 1 | 3 | 3 | 11 | 14 | ... | ... | ... | ... | ... | ... | ... | ... | 14 | 3 |
| ... | 1 | 2 | 4 | ... | 6 | 17 | 6 | 6 | 35 | ... | ... | ... | 29 | 6 | 35 | ... | ... | ... | ... | ... | ... | ... | ... | 35 | 4 |
| ... | ... | ... | ... | ... | 1 | 3 | 3 | 5 | 9 | 2 | 1 | ... | 8 | 4 | 12 | ... | ... | ... | ... | ... | ... | ... | ... | 12 | 5 |
| ... | 1 | 2 | 1 | ... | 4 | 4 | 4 | 3 | 8 | ... | 1 | 1 | 10 | 5 | 15 | ... | ... | ... | ... | ... | ... | ... | ... | 15 | 6 |
| ... | ... | ... | ... | ... | 1 | 2 | 1 | 2 | ... | 1 | ... | 4 | 2 | 3 | 5 | ... | ... | ... | ... | ... | ... | ... | 1 | 6 | 7 |
| ... | 1 | ... | ... | ... | 2 | 4 | 5 | 1 | 3 | 8 | ... | 1 | 8 | 4 | 12 | ... | ... | ... | ... | ... | ... | ... | ... | 12 | 8 |
| ... | ... | ... | ... | ... | 6 | 11 | 12 | 5 | 14 | 15 | 3 | 2 | 20 | 14 | 34 | ... | ... | ... | ... | ... | ... | ... | ... | 34 | 9 |
| ... | 1 | ... | 1 | ... | 2 | 3 | 5 | 4 | 3 | 6 | 1 | 2 | 10 | 4 | 14 | ... | ... | ... | ... | ... | ... | ... | ... | 14 | 10 |
| ... | 1 | ... | 1 | ... | 4 | 3 | 3 | 2 | 1 | 1 | ... | 9 | 3 | 9 | 12 | ... | ... | ... | ... | ... | ... | ... | ... | 12 | 11 |
| ... | 1 | 2 | 1 | ... | 17 | 7 | 9 | 13 | 14 | 20 | 7 | 2 | 19 | 25 | 44 | ... | ... | ... | ... | ... | ... | 2 | ... | 46 | 12 |
| ... | ... | 1 | ... | ... | ... | ... | 1 | 1 | ... | 1 | ... | 1 | 1 | 1 | 2 | ... | ... | ... | ... | ... | ... | ... | ... | 2 | 13 |
| ... | ... | 2 | 1 | ... | 7 | 7 | 1 | 7 | 15 | 4 | 1 | 1 | ... | 22 | 22 | ... | ... | ... | ... | ... | ... | ... | ... | 22 | 14 |
| ... | 10 | 15 | 24 | ... | 6 | 149 | 79 | 10 | 223 | 17 | ... | ... | 161 | 83 | 244 | ... | ... | ... | ... | 1 | ... | ... | ... | 245 | 15 |
| ... | ... | ... | ... | ... | 1 | 10 | 22 | 1 | 19 | 11 | 3 | ... | 19 | 15 | 34 | ... | ... | ... | ... | ... | ... | ... | ... | 34 | 16 |
| ... | ... | 2 | ... | ... | 1 | 8 | 2 | 1 | 8 | 4 | ... | ... | 9 | 3 | 12 | ... | ... | ... | ... | ... | ... | ... | ... | 12 | 17 |
| ... | 2 | ... | 2 | ... | 4 | 4 | 2 | 5 | 9 | 5 | ... | 1 | 10 | 5 | 15 | ... | ... | ... | ... | ... | ... | ... | ... | 15 | 18 |
| ... | ... | ... | ... | ... | ... | ... | ... | 1 | ... | 1 | ... | ... | 1 | ... | 1 | ... | ... | ... | ... | ... | ... | ... | ... | 1 | 19 |
| ... | ... | ... | ... | ... | 1 | 1 | ... | ... | 1 | 1 | ... | ... | 2 | ... | 2 | ... | ... | ... | ... | ... | ... | ... | ... | 2 | 20 |
| ... | ... | ... | ... | ... | 2 | ... | ... | 1 | ... | 2 | 1 | ... | 1 | 2 | 3 | ... | ... | ... | ... | ... | ... | ... | ... | 3 | 21 |
| ... | 5 | 6 | 7 | 1 | 129 | 92 | 70 | 80 | 14 | 34 | 45 | 265 | 166 | 190 | 356 | ... | ... | ... | ... | 2 | 4 | 5 | 4 | 371 | 22 |
| ... | ... | ... | ... | ... | 13 | 14 | 8 | 9 | 25 | 12 | 2 | 4 | 25 | 19 | 44 | ... | ... | ... | ... | ... | ... | ... | ... | 44 | 23 |
| ... | ... | ... | 1 | ... | 37 | 34 | 47 | 38 | 114 | 22 | 4 | 2 | 78 | 76 | 154 | ... | ... | ... | ... | ... | 1 | 1 | ... | 156 | 24 |
| ... | ... | ... | ... | ... | 1 | ... | ... | 1 | ... | 1 | ... | 1 | ... | 2 | 2 | ... | ... | ... | ... | ... | ... | ... | ... | 2 | 25 |

## CLASSIFICATION OF DEATHS IN SOUTHEASTERN

| | Cause of death. | AGES. | | | | | | | | | | | | | | | | | | NATIVITIES. | | | | | |
|---|---|---|---|---|---|---|---|---|---|---|---|---|---|---|---|---|---|---|---|---|---|---|---|---|---|
| | | Under 1. | | 1 and under 5. | | 5 and under 10. | | 10 and under 20. | | 20 and under 50. | | 50 and under 80. | | 80 and under 100. | | 100 & over. | | Age unknown. | | Born in State. | N. England States. | Middle States. | Southern States. | Southwest'n States. | Northwest'n States. |
| | | M. | F. | M. | F. | M. | F. | M. | F. | M. | F. | M. | F. | M | F. | M | F. | M | F. | | | | | | |
| 1 | Diarrhœa | 5 | 13 | 5 | 13 | 1 | | 1 | 2 | 9 | 3 | 2 | 2 | | | | | | | 48 | 1 | 4 | | | |
| 2 | Dropsy | 4 | 1 | 9 | 5 | 2 | | | 7 | 9 | 15 | 12 | 16 | 1 | 1 | | | | | 34 | 6 | 23 | 9 | | |
| 3 | Dysentery | 26 | 17 | 73 | 54 | 29 | 27 | 17 | 11 | 27 | 15 | 9 | 12 | | | | | | | 273 | 6 | 21 | 7 | 1 | |
| 4 | Dyspepsia | | | | | | | | | 5 | 1 | 2 | 1 | | | | | | | | | 5 | 4 | | |
| 5 | Erysipelas | 8 | 4 | 12 | 4 | 3 | 4 | 2 | 5 | 2 | 6 | 6 | 5 | | 1 | | | | | 48 | | 8 | 4 | | |
| 6 | Fever, not specified | 10 | 7 | 14 | 12 | 4 | 3 | 14 | 15 | 33 | 29 | 6 | 13 | | 1 | | | | | 103 | 3 | 18 | 23 | 1 | 3 |
| 7 | ..do..bilious | 3 | 1 | 3 | 1 | 1 | 1 | 3 | 4 | 6 | 6 | 4 | | | 1 | | | | | 21 | 2 | 3 | 1 | | 1 |
| 8 | ..do..brain | 2 | 1 | 1 | | 1 | | 1 | 1 | | 1 | | | | | | | | | 6 | | 1 | 1 | | |
| 9 | ..do..catarrhal | 4 | 2 | 2 | 3 | | | | | | | | | | | | | | | 11 | | | | | |
| 10 | ..do..congestive | | 1 | | | | | | | 2 | | 5 | | | | | | | | 7 | | 1 | | | |
| 11 | ..do..inflammatory | | 1 | | | | | | | | | | | | | | | | | 1 | | | | | |
| 12 | ..do..intermittent | 1 | 1 | | 1 | 1 | | | | 3 | 1 | 1 | 1 | | | | | | | 6 | | 3 | | | |
| 13 | ..do..puerperal | | | | | | | | 1 | | 1 | | 1 | | | | | | | 2 | | | | | |
| 14 | ..do..scarlet | 7 | 8 | 54 | 53 | 21 | 25 | 10 | 5 | 8 | 3 | 2 | 1 | | | | | | | 187 | 1 | 7 | 1 | | |
| 15 | ..do..ship | | | 1 | | | | | | 2 | | | | | | | | | | 2 | | | | | |
| 16 | ..do..typhus | 1 | | 4 | 1 | 4 | | 11 | 16 | 33 | 16 | 8 | 9 | | | | | | | 63 | 5 | 26 | 3 | 1 | |
| 17 | ..do..winter | | 1 | | | | | 1 | 2 | 4 | 1 | | | 2 | | | | | | 3 | 3 | 4 | 1 | | |
| 18 | Gravel | | | | | | | | | 1 | | 4 | | 1 | | | | | | 2 | 1 | 1 | | | |
| 19 | Head, disease of | 4 | 4 | 1 | | | 2 | | | | | | | | | | | | | 11 | | | | | |
| 20 | Heart....do | 1 | 1 | | 1 | | 1 | 1 | 2 | 3 | 4 | 4 | 2 | 1 | 1 | | | | | 11 | | 7 | 2 | | |
| 21 | Hemorrhage | | 2 | | | | 1 | 1 | | 3 | 2 | 1 | 1 | 1 | | | | | | 8 | | 3 | 1 | | |
| 22 | Hernia | | | | | | | 1 | | | | | | | | | | | | 1 | | | | | |
| 23 | Hives | 1 | 3 | 1 | | | | | | | | | | | | | | | | 5 | | | | | |
| 24 | Hooping cough | 20 | 24 | 27 | 21 | 1 | | | | 1 | 1 | 1 | | | | | | | | 96 | | | | | |
| 25 | Hydrocephalus | 2 | | 2 | 3 | | 2 | | | | | 2 | | | 1 | | | | | 9 | | 2 | 1 | | |
| 26 | Inflammation | 3 | 2 | 4 | 3 | | | | | 2 | 4 | | | | | | | | | 15 | | 1 | 1 | | |
| 27 | .....do.....bowels | 5 | 3 | 1 | 4 | 1 | 1 | 1 | 1 | 2 | 6 | 2 | | | | | | | | 21 | | 4 | | | |
| 28 | .....do.....brain | 15 | 12 | 15 | 11 | 3 | 1 | 2 | 4 | 1 | 1 | | 2 | | | | | | | 64 | | 1 | | | |
| 29 | .....do.....stomach | 1 | | | 1 | 1 | | | 1 | | 1 | | 1 | | | | | | | 4 | | 1 | 1 | | |
| 30 | Insanity | | | | | | | | | 1 | 1 | | | | | | | | | 1 | | 1 | | | |
| 31 | Intemperar | | | | | | | | | 2 | | | | | | | | | | | | 1 | | | |
| 32 | Jaundice | | | | | 1 | 1 | | | | 2 | | | | | | | | | 3 | | | | | |
| 33 | Killed | | | | | | | | | 2 | | | | | | | | | | 1 | | 1 | | | |
| 34 | Lightning | | | | | | | 2 | | | | | | | | | | | | 2 | | | | | |
| 35 | Liver, disease of | 1 | | 2 | 4 | | | | 1 | 2 | 2 | 7 | 4 | | | | | | | 10 | | 7 | 1 | | |
| 36 | Lockjaw | | | | | | 1 | 1 | | | | | | | | | | | | 1 | | 1 | | | |
| 37 | Lungs, disease of | | | 1 | 4 | | 2 | 1 | | 5 | 1 | 1 | | | | | | | | 12 | | 1 | 1 | | |
| 38 | Mania-a-potu | | | | | | | | | | | 1 | | | | | | | | | | 1 | | | |
| 39 | Measles | 4 | 7 | 17 | 19 | 6 | 4 | 5 | 7 | | 5 | | | | | | | | | 67 | | 2 | 5 | | |
| 40 | Mortification | | | | | | | 1 | | | | | | | | | | | | 1 | | | | | |
| 41 | Mumps | 1 | | | | | | | | 1 | 1 | | | | | | | | | 2 | | | | | 1 |
| 42 | Murder | | | | | | | | | | | | 1 | | | | | | | | | 1 | | | |
| 43 | Neuralgia | | | | | | 1 | | | | 1 | | 1 | | | | | | | 2 | | | 1 | | |
| 44 | Old age | | | | | | | | | | | 10 | 15 | 31 | 21 | 1 | | | | | 5 | 44 | 11 | | |
| 45 | Paralysis | | | | 1 | | | | 2 | | 2 | 10 | 11 | 2 | 2 | | | | | 5 | 4 | 12 | 4 | | |
| 46 | Piles | | | | | | | | | | | 1 | | | | | | | | | | 1 | | | |
| 47 | Pleurisy | | 1 | | | 1 | | 1 | | 5 | 2 | 5 | 1 | 1 | | | | | | 2 | 1 | 8 | 3 | | 1 |
| 48 | Pneumonia | 15 | 15 | 15 | 16 | 5 | 2 | 4 | 6 | 12 | 7 | 6 | 5 | 3 | 2 | | | | | 90 | 6 | 7 | 4 | | |
| 49 | Poison | | | | | | | | | | 2 | | | | | | | | | 2 | | | | | |
| 50 | Putrid sore throat | | | 2 | 4 | 4 | 1 | 2 | 1 | 2 | | 1 | 1 | | | | | | | 17 | | | 1 | | |
| 51 | Quinsy | | | | | | | | 1 | | 2 | 1 | 2 | 1 | | | | | | 1 | 1 | 3 | 1 | | |
| 52 | Rheumatism | | | 1 | | | | | 1 | 1 | 2 | 1 | 2 | 1 | | | | | | 2 | 1 | 5 | 1 | | |
| 53 | Salivation, effects of | | | 1 | | | | | | | | | | | | | | | | 1 | | | | | |
| 54 | Scrofula | | 2 | 4 | 4 | 1 | 1 | 2 | 1 | 5 | 4 | | 1 | | | | | | | 16 | 1 | 6 | 1 | 1 | |
| 55 | Scurvy | | | | | | | | | 1 | | | | | | | | | | | | 1 | | | |
| 56 | Small pox | 1 | 1 | 2 | | | 1 | | 1 | 1 | | 3 | | | | | | | | 6 | | 2 | 1 | | |
| 57 | Spine, disease of | 1 | | 1 | | | 1 | 1 | | 3 | | 2 | | | | | | | | 6 | 1 | 1 | | | |
| 58 | Stomach.. do | | | | | | | | | 1 | | | | | | | | | | | | 1 | | | |
| 59 | Suffocation | 1 | 1 | 1 | | | | | | | | | | | | | | | | 3 | | | | | |
| 60 | Suicide | | | | | | | | | 2 | | 3 | | | | | | | | 3 | | | 2 | | |
| 61 | Summer complaint | 1 | | | 1 | | | | | | | | | | | | | | | 2 | | | | | |
| 62 | Teething | | 2 | | 2 | | | | | | | | | | | | | | | 3 | | 1 | | | |
| 63 | Throat, disease of | | | 2 | 2 | 2 | 2 | 2 | 1 | | | | | | | | | | | 11 | | | | | |
| 64 | Thrush | 3 | 2 | 1 | | | | | | | | | | | | | | | | 6 | | | | | |
| 65 | Tumor | | | | 1 | | | 1 | | | | 2 | | | | | | | | 3 | | 1 | | | |
| 66 | Ulcer | | | | | | 1 | | | | 1 | 1 | | | | | | | | 1 | 1 | | 1 | | |
| 67 | White swelling | | | | | | | | 1 | 1 | 1 | | | | | | | | | 2 | | | 1 | | |
| 68 | Worms | | | 7 | 4 | | 2 | | | | 1 | | | | | | | | | 14 | | | | | |
| 69 | Unknown | 70 | 57 | 35 | 29 | 12 | 1 | 11 | 20 | 24 | 46 | 28 | 27 | 7 | 4 | | | 1 | 2 | 263 | 6 | 57 | 31 | | 2 |
| | Total | 809 | 285 | 430 | 333 | 152 | 119 | 147 | 165 | 458 | 403 | 254 | 197 | 62 | 36 | 1 | .. | 4 | 2 | 2398 | 80 | 477 | 206 | 5 | 24 |

## SECTION OF THE STATE OF OHIO—Continued.

| NATIVITIES. | | | | | SEASON OF DECEASE. | | | | DURATION OF SICKNESS. | | | | WHITES. | | | COLORED. | | | | | | | | | |
|---|---|---|---|---|---|---|---|---|---|---|---|---|---|---|---|---|---|---|---|---|---|---|---|---|---|
| | | | | | | | | | | | | | | | | Slaves. | | | | Free. | | | | | |
| | | | | | | | | | | | | | | | | Black. | | Mulatto. | | Black. | | Mul. | | | |
| California and Territories. | Ireland. | Germany. | Other foreign countries. | Unknown. | Spring. | Summer. | Autumn. | Winter. | Under 1 week. | 1 week and under 1 month. | 1 month and under 3 months. | 3 months and over. | Males. | Females. | Total. | M. | F. | M. | F. | M. | F. | M | F. | Aggregate deaths. | |
| | 1 | | 2 | | 6 | 11 | 31 | 7 | 16 | 23 | 9 | 6 | 23 | 32 | 55 | | | | | | | | 1 | 56 | 1 |
| | 1 | 7 | 2 | | 21 | 32 | 19 | 9 | 6 | 22 | 16 | 33 | 37 | 44 | 81 | | | | | | 1 | | | 82 | 2 |
| | 2 | 3 | 4 | | 7 | 53 | 225 | 31 | 111 | 160 | 30 | 3 | 180 | 133 | 313 | | | | | | 3 | 1 | | 317 | 3 |
| | | | | | 3 | 2 | 2 | 2 | 1 | 1 | 1 | 6 | 7 | 2 | 9 | | | | | | | | | 9 | 4 |
| | 1 | | 1 | | 23 | 14 | 15 | 10 | 22 | 28 | 9 | 2 | 33 | 29 | 62 | | | | | | | | | 62 | 5 |
| | 1 | 5 | 3 | 1 | 41 | 40 | 57 | 23 | 26 | 97 | 22 | 3 | 80 | 77 | 157 | | | | | | 3 | 1 | | 161 | 6 |
| | 2 | 2 | 1 | 1 | 7 | 8 | 12 | 7 | 5 | 20 | 9 | | 20 | 14 | 34 | | | | | | | | | 34 | 7 |
| | | | | | 2 | 1 | 3 | 2 | 3 | 5 | | | 4 | 3 | 7 | | | | | 1 | | | | 8 | 8 |
| | | | | | 6 | 2 | 3 | | 6 | 3 | 2 | | 6 | 5 | 11 | | | | | | | | | 11 | 9 |
| | | | | | | 2 | 5 | 1 | 1 | 7 | | | 7 | 1 | 8 | | | | | | | | | 8 | 10 |
| | | | | | | | | 1 | | 1 | | | | 1 | 1 | | | | | | | | | 1 | 11 |
| | | | 1 | | 2 | 1 | 5 | 2 | 3 | 7 | | | 6 | 4 | 10 | | | | | | | | | 10 | 12 |
| | | | 1 | | 1 | | | 2 | 1 | 2 | | | | 3 | 3 | | | | | | | | | 3 | 13 |
| | | 1 | | | 64 | 58 | 29 | 46 | 90 | 91 | 7 | 8 | 101 | 95 | 196 | | | | | | | 1 | | 197 | 14 |
| | 1 | | | | | 3 | | | | 3 | | | 3 | | 3 | | | | | | | | | 3 | 15 |
| | | 1 | 4 | | 28 | 19 | 25 | 31 | 15 | 75 | 12 | 1 | 61 | 42 | 103 | | | | | | | | | 103 | 16 |
| | | | | | 7 | 1 | | 3 | 3 | 8 | | | 5 | 4 | 9 | | | | | 2 | | | | 11 | 17 |
| | 1 | | 1 | | 2 | 1 | 2 | 1 | 3 | | | 2 | 6 | | 6 | | | | | | | | | 6 | 18 |
| | | | | | 6 | 1 | 3 | 1 | 4 | 6 | 1 | | 5 | 6 | 11 | | | | | | | | | 11 | 19 |
| | | 1 | | 1 | 8 | 5 | 3 | 6 | 9 | 5 | 1 | 5 | 9 | 12 | 21 | | | | | 1 | | | | 22 | 20 |
| | | | | | 3 | 3 | 3 | 3 | 5 | 2 | | 2 | 6 | 6 | 12 | | | | | | | | | 12 | 21 |
| | | | | | 1 | | | | 1 | | | | 1 | | 1 | | | | | | | | | 1 | 22 |
| | | | | | 3 | 1 | 1 | | 3 | 2 | | | 2 | 3 | 5 | | | | | | | | | 5 | 23 |
| | | | | | 32 | 24 | 29 | 11 | 16 | 47 | 24 | 4 | 50 | 45 | 95 | | | | | | 1 | | | 96 | 24 |
| | | | | | 1 | 5 | 3 | 3 | 4 | 5 | 2 | 1 | 5 | 6 | 11 | | | | | | | 1 | | 12 | 25 |
| | | | 1 | | 6 | 4 | 7 | 1 | 3 | 10 | | | 8 | 9 | 17 | | | | | | | 1 | | 18 | 26 |
| | 1 | 1 | | | 6 | 4 | 12 | 5 | 12 | 8 | 5 | 2 | 12 | 15 | 27 | | | | | | | | | 27 | 27 |
| | 1 | | | 1 | 20 | 12 | 19 | 16 | 29 | 27 | 6 | 8 | 36 | 30 | 66 | | | | | | | | 1 | 67 | 28 |
| | | | | | 1 | 3 | 1 | 1 | 3 | 1 | 2 | | 2 | 4 | 6 | | | | | | | | | 6 | 29 |
| | | | | | 1 | | 1 | | | | | 1 | 1 | 1 | 2 | | | | | | | | | 2 | 30 |
| | 1 | | | | 2 | | | | | 1 | | 1 | 2 | | 2 | | | | | | | | | 2 | 31 |
| | | | 1 | | | 3 | 1 | | | 2 | 1 | 1 | 1 | 3 | 4 | | | | | | | | | 4 | 32 |
| | | | | | | 1 | 1 | | | | 1 | | 2 | | 2 | | | | | | | | | 2 | 33 |
| | | | | | 1 | 1 | | | 1 | | | | 2 | | 2 | | | | | | | | | 2 | 34 |
| | 5 | | | | 5 | 6 | 8 | 4 | 2 | 4 | 9 | 6 | 12 | 11 | 23 | | | | | | | | | 23 | 35 |
| | | | | | 1 | | 1 | | 1 | 1 | | | 1 | 1 | 2 | | | | | | | | | 2 | 36 |
| | | | 1 | | 3 | 3 | 5 | 4 | 1 | 11 | | 2 | 8 | 7 | 15 | | | | | | | | | 15 | 37 |
| | | | | | | | | 1 | | | | | 1 | | 1 | | | | | | | | | 1 | 38 |
| | | | | | 32 | 17 | 13 | 12 | 16 | 51 | 6 | 1 | 27 | 41 | 68 | | | | | 4 | 1 | 1 | | 74 | 39 |
| | | | | | | | 1 | | | | 1 | | 1 | | 1 | | | | | | | | | 1 | 40 |
| | | | | | 1 | 1 | | 1 | 2 | 1 | | | 2 | 1 | 3 | | | | | | | | | 3 | 41 |
| | | | | | | | 1 | | | | | | | 1 | 1 | | | | | | | | | 1 | 42 |
| | | | | | 1 | 1 | | 1 | | | 1 | 2 | | 3 | 3 | | | | | | | | | 3 | 43 |
| | 10 | 1 | 6 | 1 | 24 | 20 | 17 | 17 | 7 | 15 | 9 | 12 | 42 | 35 | 77 | | | | | | 1 | | | 78 | 44 |
| | 3 | 2 | | | 11 | 4 | 7 | 8 | 3 | 12 | 3 | 10 | 12 | 18 | 30 | | | | | | | | | 30 | 45 |
| | | | | | 1 | | | | | | | 1 | 1 | | 1 | | | | | | | | | 1 | 46 |
| | | | 2 | | 8 | 2 | 3 | 4 | 3 | 12 | | 1 | 13 | 3 | 16 | | | | | | 1 | | | 17 | 47 |
| | 4 | | 1 | 1 | 51 | 19 | 16 | 27 | 29 | 58 | 18 | 5 | 59 | 52 | 111 | | | | | | 1 | 1 | | 113 | 48 |
| | | | | | | 1 | 1 | | 1 | 1 | | | | 2 | 2 | | | | | | | | | 2 | 49 |
| | | | | | 5 | 1 | 7 | 5 | 9 | 9 | | | 10 | 7 | 17 | | | | | 1 | | | | 18 | 50 |
| | 1 | | | | 3 | 1 | | 3 | 1 | 4 | 1 | 1 | 2 | 5 | 7 | | | | | | | | | 7 | 51 |
| | | | | | 4 | 1 | 2 | 2 | | 3 | 1 | 5 | 4 | 5 | 9 | | | | | | | | | 9 | 52 |
| | | | | | | 1 | | | | 1 | | | 1 | | 1 | | | | | | | | | 1 | 53 |
| | | | | | 8 | 5 | 7 | 5 | | 9 | 3 | 13 | 12 | 13 | 25 | | | | | | | | | 25 | 54 |
| | | | | | | | | 1 | | | 1 | | 1 | | 1 | | | | | | | | | 1 | 55 |
| | | | 1 | | 6 | 2 | | 2 | | 9 | 1 | | 7 | 3 | 10 | | | | | | | | | 10 | 56 |
| | 1 | | | | 3 | 3 | 1 | 2 | 3 | 1 | 1 | 4 | 8 | 1 | 9 | | | | | | | | | 9 | 57 |
| | | | | | | 1 | | | 1 | | | | 1 | | 1 | | | | | | | | | 1 | 58 |
| | | | | | | 1 | | 2 | 3 | | | | 2 | 1 | 3 | | | | | | | | | 3 | 59 |
| | | | | | | 2 | 1 | 2 | | | | | 5 | | 5 | | | | | | | | | 5 | 60 |
| | | | | | | 1 | 1 | | 1 | | | | 1 | 1 | 2 | | | | | | | | | 2 | 61 |
| | | | | | 1 | | 2 | 1 | 1 | 3 | | | | 4 | 4 | | | | | | | | | 4 | 62 |
| | | | | | 5 | | 5 | 1 | 3 | 8 | | | 6 | 5 | 11 | | | | | | | | | 11 | 63 |
| | | | | | 1 | 2 | 3 | | | 3 | | 2 | 4 | 2 | 6 | | | | | | | | | 6 | 64 |
| | | | | | 3 | | 1 | | | | | 4 | 3 | 1 | 4 | | | | | | | | | 4 | 65 |
| | | | | | 3 | | | | | | 1 | 2 | 1 | 2 | 3 | | | | | | | | | 3 | 66 |
| | | | | | 2 | 1 | | | | 1 | | 2 | 1 | 2 | 3 | | | | | | | | | 3 | 67 |
| | | | | | 4 | 2 | 8 | | 6 | 5 | | 2 | 5 | 6 | 11 | | | | | 1 | 1 | 1 | | 14 | 68 |
| | 8 | 4 | 3 | | 113 | 78 | 101 | 69 | 114 | 89 | 37 | 80 | 182 | 175 | 357 | | | | | | 6 | 5 | 6 | 374 | 69 |
| | 68 | 62 | 80 | 7 | 873 | 882 | 1030 | 605 | 1146 | 1159 | 325 | 541 | 1782 | 1554 | 3336 | | | | | 13 | 24 | 22 | 12 | 3407 | |

## CLASSIFICATION OF DEATHS IN SOUTH-

*Embracing the following counties: Adams, Brown, Butler, Clermont, Clinton,*

| | Cause of death. | AGES. | | | | | | | | | | | | | | | | | | NATIVITIES. | | | | | |
|---|---|---|---|---|---|---|---|---|---|---|---|---|---|---|---|---|---|---|---|---|---|---|---|---|---|
| | | Under 1. | | 1 and under 5. | | 5 and under 10. | | 10 and under 20. | | 20 and under 50. | | 50 and under 80. | | 80 and under 100. | | 100 & over. | | Age unknown. | | Born in State. | N. England States. | Middle States. | Southern States. | Southwest'n States. | Northwest'n States. |
| | | M. | F. | M. | F. | M. | F. | M. | F. | M. | F. | M. | F. | M | F. | M | F. | M | F. | | | | | | |
| 1 | Abscess | ... | ... | ... | ... | ... | ... | ... | ... | 3 | ... | ... | ... | .. | .. | .. | .. | .. | .. | ... | .. | ... | ... | ... | ... |
| 2 | Accident, not specif'd | ... | ... | 6 | 7 | 4 | 1 | 10 | 2 | 22 | ... | 4 | 1 | .. | .. | .. | .. | .. | .. | 36 | 1 | 4 | 2 | ... | 1 |
| 3 | ....do...burned | ... | ... | ... | 4 | ... | ... | ... | 1 | ... | 2 | ... | ... | .. | .. | .. | .. | .. | .. | 4 | .. | 2 | ... | ... | ... |
| 4 | ....do...drowned | ... | ... | 3 | ... | 8 | 2 | 4 | 1 | 18 | 2 | 2 | ... | .. | .. | .. | .. | .. | .. | 23 | .. | 3 | ... | ... | 2 |
| 5 | ....do...scalded | 1 | ... | 2 | 3 | ... | 1 | ... | ... | 2 | ... | ... | ... | .. | .. | .. | .. | .. | .. | 7 | .. | ... | ... | ... | 2 |
| 6 | ....do...expl. steam | ... | ... | ... | ... | ... | ... | 1 | ... | ... | ... | ... | ... | .. | .. | .. | .. | .. | .. | ... | .. | ... | ... | ... | ... |
| 7 | ....do...railroad | ... | ... | ... | ... | ... | ... | ... | ... | 1 | ... | ... | ... | .. | .. | .. | .. | .. | .. | 1 | .. | ... | ... | ... | ... |
| 8 | Apoplexy | ... | ... | ... | 1 | 1 | ... | ... | ... | 3 | 4 | 11 | 3 | 1 | .. | .. | .. | .. | .. | 2 | 3 | 8 | 3 | 1 | 1 |
| 9 | Asthma | ... | ... | ... | ... | ... | ... | ... | ... | 2 | ... | 1 | 2 | 3 | 1 | .. | .. | .. | .. | 1 | .. | 4 | 2 | ... | ... |
| 10 | Bladder, disease of | ... | ... | ... | ... | ... | ... | 1 | ... | ... | 1 | 2 | ... | .. | .. | .. | .. | .. | .. | ... | .. | 3 | 1 | ... | ... |
| 11 | Bowels, ......do | 5 | 3 | 6 | 2 | ... | ... | 2 | 1 | 1 | 1 | 3 | ... | .. | 1 | .. | .. | .. | .. | 15 | .. | 2 | 1 | ... | ... |
| 12 | Brain ......do. | 4 | 7 | 7 | 3 | 2 | 2 | ... | ... | 5 | 2 | 3 | ... | .. | .. | .. | .. | .. | .. | 26 | .. | ... | 1 | ... | ... |
| 13 | Bronchitis | 1 | 1 | ... | 5 | 1 | ... | ... | 1 | 5 | 3 | 2 | ... | .. | 1 | .. | .. | .. | .. | 11 | .. | 5 | 1 | ... | ... |
| 14 | Cancer | ... | ... | ... | ... | ... | 1 | ... | ... | ... | 1 | 6 | 7 | 1 | .. | .. | .. | .. | .. | 1 | .. | 6 | 5 | ... | 1 |
| 15 | Catarrh | 3 | 1 | 4 | 2 | ... | ... | 1 | 1 | 1 | 2 | 1 | 1 | 1 | 1 | .. | .. | .. | .. | 13 | 1 | 2 | ... | ... | 1 |
| 16 | Childbirth | ... | ... | ... | ... | ... | ... | ... | 2 | ... | 36 | ... | ... | .. | .. | .. | .. | .. | .. | 20 | .. | 5 | 1 | ... | ... |
| 17 | Cholera | 127 | 127 | 346 | 335 | 188 | 153 | 179 | 182 | 974 | 704 | 294 | 198 | 7 | 10 | .. | .. | .. | 2 | 1710 | 39 | 372 | 97 | 7 | 76 |
| 18 | ...do..infantum | 12 | 13 | 20 | 18 | 1 | ... | ... | ... | ... | ... | ... | ... | .. | .. | .. | .. | .. | .. | 63 | .. | 1 | ... | ... | ... |
| 19 | ...do..morbus | 1 | ... | 2 | 1 | 2 | 1 | 1 | 1 | 3 | 1 | ... | 2 | .. | 2 | .. | .. | .. | .. | 6 | 1 | 6 | ... | ... | 1 |
| 20 | Colic | ... | ... | ... | 1 | ... | ... | ... | ... | 3 | 1 | 1 | ... | .. | .. | .. | .. | .. | .. | 2 | .. | ... | 1 | ... | 1 |
| 21 | Congestion | ... | ... | ... | 1 | ... | ... | ... | ... | ... | ... | ... | ... | .. | .. | .. | .. | .. | .. | 1 | .. | ... | ... | ... | ... |
| 22 | ....do....brain | 2 | 1 | 6 | 6 | 1 | 1 | ... | ... | ... | 1 | 2 | ... | .. | .. | .. | .. | .. | .. | 17 | .. | 2 | ... | ... | ... |
| 23 | ....do....lungs | 1 | ... | ... | ... | ... | ... | ... | ... | ... | ... | ... | ... | .. | .. | .. | .. | .. | .. | 1 | .. | ... | ... | ... | ... |
| 24 | Consumption | 12 | 15 | 28 | 30 | 5 | 10 | 26 | 43 | 222 | 219 | 62 | 50 | 2 | .. | .. | .. | .. | .. | 381 | 10 | 131 | 54 | 3 | 19 |
| 25 | Convulsions | 33 | 25 | 24 | 18 | 2 | 6 | 3 | 5 | 9 | 4 | 3 | 1 | 1 | .. | .. | .. | .. | .. | 113 | .. | 8 | 3 | ... | 4 |
| 26 | Croup | 40 | 37 | 61 | 61 | 14 | 10 | 1 | ... | 2 | 1 | ... | ... | .. | .. | .. | .. | .. | .. | 214 | .. | 1 | 1 | 1 | 4 |
| 27 | Debility | 2 | 3 | 2 | 1 | 1 | 1 | ... | ... | 3 | ... | 2 | 1 | .. | .. | .. | .. | .. | .. | 7 | 1 | ... | ... | ... | 1 |
| 28 | Diabetes | ... | ... | ... | ... | ... | ... | ... | ... | 1 | ... | 1 | ... | .. | .. | .. | .. | .. | .. | 1 | .. | ... | 1 | ... | ... |
| 29 | Diarrhœa | 17 | 13 | 14 | 9 | ... | 1 | 2 | 1 | 29 | 12 | 1 | 9 | 5 | 1 | .. | .. | .. | .. | 63 | .. | 13 | 8 | ... | 3 |
| 30 | Dropsy | 4 | 1 | 10 | 5 | 2 | ... | 4 | 5 | 25 | 20 | 26 | 23 | 4 | 3 | .. | .. | .. | .. | 43 | 4 | 35 | 20 | ... | 5 |
| 31 | Dysentery | 57 | 48 | 139 | 112 | 46 | 36 | 24 | 26 | 72 | 48 | 23 | 38 | 1 | 2 | .. | .. | 1 | 1 | 515 | 7 | 56 | 17 | 1 | 16 |
| 32 | Dyspepsia | ... | ... | ... | ... | 1 | ... | ... | ... | 2 | 3 | 1 | 4 | .. | .. | .. | .. | .. | .. | 4 | .. | 4 | 1 | ... | 1 |
| 33 | Epilepsy | ... | ... | 1 | ... | ... | ... | ... | ... | ... | 1 | 1 | ... | .. | .. | .. | .. | .. | .. | 2 | .. | 1 | ... | ... | ... |
| 34 | Erysipelas | 7 | 4 | 2 | 4 | 3 | ... | 5 | 4 | 11 | 7 | 5 | 1 | .. | .. | .. | .. | .. | .. | 33 | .. | 7 | 3 | ... | 3 |
| 35 | Fever, not specified | 26 | 18 | 55 | 53 | 21 | 19 | 19 | 20 | 61 | 48 | 27 | 11 | 1 | 3 | .. | .. | .. | .. | 248 | 1 | 38 | 22 | 1 | 6 |
| 36 | ..do..bilious | 3 | 3 | 4 | 2 | 1 | 2 | 2 | 3 | 17 | 6 | 4 | 3 | .. | .. | .. | .. | .. | .. | 28 | 1 | 4 | 5 | ... | 2 |
| 37 | ..do..brain | 8 | 6 | 7 | 13 | 4 | 4 | ... | 2 | 3 | 3 | ... | ... | .. | .. | .. | .. | .. | .. | 39 | .. | 3 | 1 | ... | 3 |
| 38 | ..do..catarrhal | 1 | 1 | 3 | 1 | 1 | 2 | ... | ... | ... | ... | ... | ... | .. | .. | .. | .. | .. | .. | 8 | .. | 1 | ... | ... | ... |
| 39 | ..do..congestive | 1 | ... | 6 | 3 | ... | 2 | ... | ... | 12 | 2 | 2 | 2 | .. | .. | .. | .. | .. | .. | 22 | .. | 5 | 2 | ... | 1 |
| 40 | ..do..inflammatory | ... | ... | ... | ... | ... | ... | ... | ... | ... | 1 | ... | ... | .. | .. | .. | .. | .. | .. | ... | .. | ... | ... | ... | ... |
| 41 | ..do..intermittent | ... | ... | ... | 1 | 1 | ... | 1 | ... | 3 | 1 | 2 | 1 | .. | .. | .. | .. | 1 | .. | 7 | .. | 2 | 1 | ... | ... |
| 42 | ..do..puerperal | ... | ... | ... | ... | ... | ... | ... | ... | ... | 1 | ... | ... | .. | .. | .. | .. | .. | .. | 1 | .. | ... | ... | ... | ... |
| 43 | ..do..remittent | ... | ... | ... | ... | ... | ... | ... | ... | 2 | 1 | ... | ... | .. | .. | .. | .. | .. | .. | ... | .. | ... | ... | ... | ... |
| 44 | ..do..scarlet | 11 | 12 | 78 | 70 | 20 | 22 | 4 | 10 | 5 | 1 | ... | ... | .. | .. | .. | .. | .. | .. | 216 | .. | 4 | 1 | 1 | 6 |
| 45 | ..do..ship | ... | ... | ... | 1 | 3 | ... | ... | ... | 3 | 3 | 2 | ... | .. | .. | .. | .. | .. | .. | 2 | .. | ... | ... | ... | ... |
| 46 | ..do..typhus | 1 | 3 | 9 | 6 | 4 | 7 | 10 | 25 | 72 | 28 | 11 | 9 | 1 | .. | .. | .. | .. | .. | 100 | 1 | 35 | 7 | 1 | 10 |
| 47 | ..do..winter | ... | ... | 1 | ... | 1 | ... | ... | 2 | 1 | 1 | ... | ... | .. | .. | .. | .. | .. | .. | 6 | .. | ... | ... | ... | ... |
| 48 | ..do..yellow | 1 | ... | ... | ... | ... | ... | ... | ... | 4 | ... | ... | ... | .. | .. | .. | .. | .. | .. | 1 | .. | ... | 1 | ... | ... |
| 49 | Fistula | ... | ... | ... | ... | ... | ... | ... | ... | 1 | ... | 1 | ... | .. | .. | .. | .. | .. | .. | 1 | .. | 1 | ... | ... | ... |
| 50 | Fracture | ... | ... | ... | ... | ... | ... | ... | ... | 1 | ... | ... | 1 | .. | 1 | .. | .. | .. | .. | 2 | .. | 1 | ... | ... | ... |
| 51 | Gravel | ... | ... | ... | ... | 1 | ... | 1 | ... | 1 | 1 | 11 | ... | 2 | .. | .. | .. | .. | .. | 5 | .. | 5 | 3 | ... | 2 |
| 52 | Head, disease of | 6 | 10 | 5 | 4 | 1 | ... | ... | 1 | ... | ... | 1 | ... | .. | .. | .. | .. | .. | .. | 26 | .. | 2 | ... | ... | ... |
| 53 | Heart....do | 2 | 2 | 1 | 2 | ... | 1 | 2 | 5 | 4 | 6 | 4 | 3 | .. | .. | .. | .. | .. | .. | 14 | .. | 6 | 3 | ... | 2 |
| 54 | Hemorrhage | 2 | ... | 1 | ... | ... | ... | ... | 1 | 1 | ... | ... | ... | .. | .. | .. | .. | .. | .. | 4 | 1 | ... | ... | ... | ... |
| 55 | Hernia | ... | ... | ... | 1 | ... | ... | ... | ... | 1 | ... | 2 | ... | .. | .. | .. | .. | .. | .. | 2 | .. | ... | 2 | ... | ... |
| 56 | Hip, disease of | ... | ... | 1 | ... | ... | ... | ... | ... | ... | ... | ... | ... | .. | .. | .. | .. | .. | .. | 1 | .. | ... | ... | ... | ... |
| 57 | Hives | 2 | 2 | ... | 1 | ... | ... | 1 | ... | ... | ... | ... | ... | .. | .. | .. | .. | .. | .. | 6 | .. | ... | ... | ... | ... |
| 58 | Hooping cough | 17 | 18 | 17 | 22 | 1 | 3 | 1 | ... | 1 | ... | ... | ... | .. | .. | .. | .. | .. | .. | 74 | .. | 2 | 1 | ... | ... |
| 59 | Hydrocephalus | 8 | 1 | 3 | 7 | ... | ... | ... | ... | ... | ... | ... | ... | .. | .. | .. | .. | .. | .. | 14 | .. | ... | ... | ... | ... |
| 60 | Inflammation | 5 | 6 | 6 | 4 | 1 | ... | 3 | 3 | 2 | 6 | 3 | ... | .. | .. | .. | .. | .. | .. | 28 | .. | 5 | 2 | ... | 2 |
| 61 | ....do....bowels | 10 | 10 | 11 | 13 | 1 | 2 | 3 | 5 | 6 | 10 | 5 | 1 | .. | .. | .. | .. | .. | .. | 63 | 1 | 2 | 4 | ... | 2 |
| 62 | ....do....brain | 36 | 22 | 35 | 24 | 6 | 5 | 7 | 2 | 9 | 4 | ... | ... | .. | .. | .. | .. | .. | .. | 138 | 1 | 2 | ... | ... | 6 |
| 63 | Insanity | ... | ... | ... | ... | ... | ... | ... | ... | 2 | ... | ... | ... | .. | .. | .. | .. | .. | .. | ... | .. | ... | ... | ... | ... |
| 64 | Intemperance | ... | ... | ... | ... | ... | ... | ... | ... | 2 | ... | ... | ... | .. | .. | .. | .. | .. | .. | 1 | .. | ... | ... | ... | ... |
| 65 | Jaundice | 2 | ... | ... | ... | ... | ... | ... | ... | 2 | 1 | ... | ... | .. | 1 | .. | .. | .. | .. | 3 | .. | ... | ... | ... | ... |
| 66 | Kidneys, disease of | 1 | ... | ... | ... | ... | ... | ... | ... | 1 | ... | 3 | 1 | .. | .. | .. | .. | .. | .. | 1 | .. | 4 | 1 | ... | ... |
| 67 | Killed | ... | ... | 1 | ... | ... | ... | 2 | ... | 14 | ... | 2 | ... | .. | 1 | .. | .. | .. | .. | 7 | .. | 4 | 1 | ... | 1 |
| 68 | Lightning | ... | ... | ... | ... | ... | ... | ... | ... | 2 | ... | ... | ... | .. | .. | .. | .. | .. | .. | 2 | .. | ... | ... | ... | ... |
| 69 | Liver, disease of | 5 | 2 | 5 | 4 | ... | 1 | ... | 5 | 13 | 8 | 4 | 2 | .. | .. | .. | .. | .. | .. | 30 | .. | 7 | 4 | ... | 4 |
| 70 | Lockjaw | 1 | 2 | 1 | ... | 1 | ... | 1 | ... | 1 | ... | ... | ... | .. | .. | .. | .. | .. | .. | 5 | .. | ... | 1 | ... | ... |
| 71 | Lungs, disease of | 1 | ... | 1 | ... | ... | 1 | ... | 1 | 1 | 3 | 1 | ... | .. | .. | .. | .. | .. | .. | 5 | .. | ... | 3 | ... | ... |
| 72 | Malformation | ... | 1 | ... | ... | ... | ... | ... | ... | ... | ... | ... | ... | .. | .. | .. | .. | .. | .. | 1 | .. | ... | ... | ... | ... |
| 73 | Mania-a-potu | ... | ... | ... | ... | ... | ... | ... | ... | 19 | 1 | 3 | ... | .. | 1 | .. | .. | 1 | .. | 3 | .. | 3 | 2 | ... | 1 |

## [W]ESTERN SECTION OF THE STATE OF OHIO.

*[F]ayette, Greene, Hamilton, Highland, Montgomery, Preble, and Warren.*

| NATIVITIES. | | | | | SEASON OF DECEASE. | | | | DURATION OF SICKNESS. | | | | WHITES. | | | COLORED. | | | | | | | | | |
|---|---|---|---|---|---|---|---|---|---|---|---|---|---|---|---|---|---|---|---|---|---|---|---|---|---|
| | | | | | | | | | | | | | | | | Slaves. | | | | Free. | | | | | |
| | | | | | | | | | | | | | | | | Black. | | Mulatto. | | Black | | Mul. | | | |
| [California and Ter]ritories. | Ireland. | Germany. | Other foreign countries. | Unknown. | Spring. | Summer. | Autumn. | Winter. | Under 1 week. | 1 week and under 1 month. | 1 month and under 3 months. | 3 months and over. | Males. | Females. | Total. | M. | F. | M. | F. | M. | F. | M | F. | Aggregate deaths. | |
| | 1 | 2 | | | | 1 | | 2 | | | | | 3 | | 3 | | | | | | | | | 3 | 1 |
| | 6 | 7 | | | 19 | 11 | 16 | 10 | 29 | 6 | 2 | 2 | 46 | 10 | 56 | | | | | | 1 | | | 57 | 2 |
| | | 1 | | | 4 | 1 | | 2 | 4 | | | | | 7 | 7 | | | | | | | | | 7 | 3 |
| | 3 | 6 | 2 | 1 | 7 | 19 | 5 | 9 | 40 | | | | 35 | 5 | 40 | | | | | | | | | 40 | 4 |
| | | | | | 2 | 2 | 3 | 2 | 4 | 2 | 1 | | 4 | 4 | 8 | | | | | 1 | | | | 9 | 5 |
| | | 1 | | | | 1 | | | | 1 | | | 1 | | 1 | | | | | | | | | 1 | 6 |
| | | | | | 1 | | | | | | | | 1 | | 1 | | | | | | | | | 1 | 7 |
| | 1 | 3 | 2 | | 6 | 6 | 5 | 7 | 14 | 4 | | 1 | 16 | 8 | 24 | | | | | | | | | 24 | 8 |
| | 1 | | | 1 | 6 | 2 | 1 | | | 1 | 1 | 5 | 6 | 3 | 9 | | | | | | | | | 9 | 9 |
| | | | | | 2 | | | 2 | 1 | 2 | | 1 | 3 | 1 | 4 | | | | | | | | | 4 | 10 |
| | 4 | 1 | 2 | | 4 | 5 | 11 | 5 | 5 | 7 | 3 | 2 | 17 | 8 | 25 | | | | | | | | | 25 | 11 |
| | 3 | 3 | 2 | | 5 | 12 | 10 | 8 | 11 | 8 | 3 | 3 | 21 | 13 | 34 | | | | | | 1 | | | 35 | 12 |
| | | 1 | 2 | | 8 | 6 | 3 | 3 | 5 | 4 | 2 | 8 | 9 | 11 | 20 | | | | | | | | | 20 | 13 |
| | 1 | 2 | | | 3 | 4 | 5 | 4 | 2 | 1 | 1 | 9 | 7 | 9 | 16 | | | | | | | | | 16 | 14 |
| | 1 | 1 | | | 12 | 2 | 2 | 3 | 7 | 8 | | 4 | 10 | 8 | 18 | | | | | 1 | | | | 19 | 15 |
| | 1 | 10 | 1 | | 9 | 12 | 8 | 9 | 15 | 14 | 2 | 3 | | 38 | 38 | | | | | | | | | 38 | 16 |
| | 225 | 1124 | 137 | 39 | 71 | 3074 | 617 | 56 | 3212 | 232 | 15 | 7 | 2086 | 1687 | 3773 | | | | | 15 | 19 | 14 | 5 | 3826 | 17 |
| | | | | | 4 | 34 | 25 | | 34 | 22 | 3 | 5 | 33 | 31 | 64 | | | | | | | | | 64 | 18 |
| | 1 | 2 | | | 1 | 9 | 7 | | 11 | 5 | | | 9 | 8 | 17 | | | | | | | | | 17 | 19 |
| | | 1 | 1 | | 2 | 2 | 1 | 1 | 3 | 2 | | | 4 | 2 | 6 | | | | | | | | | 6 | 20 |
| | | | | | | | | 1 | | | | | | 1 | 1 | | | | | | | | | 1 | 21 |
| | 1 | | | | 5 | 8 | 5 | 2 | 10 | 8 | 1 | 1 | 11 | 9 | 20 | | | | | | | | | 20 | 22 |
| | | | | | | | | 1 | | 1 | | | 1 | | 1 | | | | | | | | | 1 | 23 |
| | 39 | 67 | 12 | 8 | 222 | 196 | 176 | 130 | 24 | 56 | 62 | 508 | 349 | 361 | 710 | | | | | 6 | 5 | 2 | 1 | 724 | 24 |
| | | 6 | | | 38 | 35 | 38 | 23 | 76 | 37 | 2 | 18 | 72 | 58 | 130 | | | | | 1 | 1 | 2 | | 134 | 25 |
| | 1 | 3 | 2 | | 59 | 32 | 64 | 69 | 161 | 50 | | 2 | 118 | 108 | 226 | | | | | | | | 1 | 227 | 26 |
| | 3 | 2 | 2 | | 6 | 5 | 3 | 2 | | | | 5 | 10 | 6 | 16 | | | | | | | | | 16 | 27 |
| | | | | | | 1 | | 1 | | 1 | | 1 | 2 | | 2 | | | | | | | | | 2 | 28 |
| | 16 | 5 | 7 | | 17 | 31 | 51 | 15 | 21 | 39 | 13 | 23 | 67 | 45 | 112 | | | | | | 1 | 1 | | 114 | 29 |
| | 9 | 13 | 3 | | 39 | 35 | 36 | 21 | 15 | 23 | 8 | 73 | 74 | 56 | 130 | | | | | 1 | | | 1 | 132 | 30 |
| | 22 | 24 | 14 | 2 | 25 | 179 | 428 | 41 | 171 | 401 | 47 | 26 | 356 | 307 | 663 | | | | | 3 | 2 | 4 | 2 | 674 | 31 |
| | | | 1 | | 3 | 3 | 4 | 1 | 1 | 1 | 1 | 8 | 4 | 7 | 11 | | | | | | | | | 11 | 32 |
| | | | | | 2 | | | 1 | 2 | | | 1 | 2 | 1 | 3 | | | | | | | | | 3 | 33 |
| | 4 | 2 | 1 | | 16 | 13 | 18 | 6 | 15 | 26 | 4 | 2 | 33 | 20 | 53 | | | | | | | | | 53 | 34 |
| | 16 | 42 | 5 | 3 | 101 | 105 | 117 | 58 | 110 | 225 | 28 | 6 | 207 | 166 | 373 | | | | | 3 | 4 | | 2 | 382 | 35 |
| | 2 | 6 | 2 | | 14 | 13 | 13 | 8 | 5 | 30 | 13 | | 31 | 19 | 50 | | | | | | | | | 50 | 36 |
| | | 2 | 2 | | 10 | 16 | 14 | 10 | 24 | 23 | 2 | | 21 | 27 | 48 | | | | | | | 1 | 1 | 50 | 37 |
| | | | | | 3 | 4 | | 2 | 2 | 7 | | | 5 | 4 | 9 | | | | | | | | | 9 | 38 |
| | | | | | 4 | 13 | 7 | 6 | 6 | 20 | 4 | | 21 | 8 | 29 | | | | | | | | 1 | 30 | 39 |
| | | | 1 | | 1 | | | | | | | 1 | | 1 | 1 | | | | | | | | | 1 | 40 |
| | | 1 | | | 4 | 4 | 2 | 1 | 1 | 8 | | 1 | 8 | 3 | 11 | | | | | | | | | 11 | 41 |
| | | | | | | | | | | 1 | | | | 1 | 1 | | | | | | | | | 1 | 42 |
| | 1 | 2 | | | | | 3 | | | | | | 2 | 1 | 3 | | | | | | | | | 3 | 43 |
| | 1 | 3 | 1 | | 59 | 74 | 46 | 54 | 100 | 119 | 8 | 3 | 115 | 113 | 228 | | | | | 3 | 2 | | | 233 | 44 |
| | 7 | 3 | | | 9 | 1 | | 2 | 2 | 7 | | | 8 | 4 | 12 | | | | | | | | | 12 | 45 |
| | 16 | 12 | 4 | | 55 | 41 | 56 | 34 | 17 | 110 | 19 | 9 | 105 | 77 | 182 | | | | | 2 | | 1 | 1 | 186 | 46 |
| | | | | | 3 | 1 | | 2 | 1 | 3 | 2 | | 3 | 3 | 6 | | | | | | | | | 6 | 47 |
| | 2 | 1 | | | 1 | 2 | 2 | | 2 | 2 | | | 5 | | 5 | | | | | | | | | 5 | 48 |
| | | | | | 1 | 1 | | | | | | 2 | 2 | | 2 | | | | | | | | | 2 | 49 |
| | | | | | | | 1 | 2 | 1 | 1 | | 1 | 1 | 2 | 3 | | | | | | | | | 3 | 50 |
| | 1 | 1 | | | 8 | 2 | 3 | 4 | 2 | 9 | 2 | 4 | 16 | 1 | 17 | | | | | | | | | 17 | 51 |
| | | | | | 6 | 10 | 9 | 3 | 9 | 14 | 2 | 2 | 13 | 15 | 28 | | | | | | | | | 28 | 52 |
| | 6 | 1 | | | 9 | 10 | 8 | 5 | 8 | 9 | 3 | 7 | 12 | 19 | 31 | | | | | 1 | | | | 32 | 53 |
| | | | | | 3 | | 1 | 1 | 3 | 2 | | | 4 | 1 | 5 | | | | | | | | | 5 | 54 |
| | | | | | 2 | | 1 | 1 | 2 | 1 | | 1 | 3 | 1 | 4 | | | | | | | | | 4 | 55 |
| | | | | | | | 1 | | | 1 | | | 1 | | 1 | | | | | | | | | 1 | 56 |
| | | | | | | 2 | 3 | 1 | 5 | 1 | | | 3 | 3 | 6 | | | | | | | | | 6 | 57 |
| | 2 | 1 | | | 22 | 31 | 18 | 9 | 16 | 45 | 7 | 11 | 34 | 39 | 73 | | | | | 1 | 4 | 2 | | 80 | 58 |
| | | | | | 7 | 4 | 2 | 1 | 3 | 6 | 2 | 3 | 6 | 8 | 14 | | | | | | | | | 14 | 59 |
| | | | 2 | | 13 | 8 | 9 | 9 | 10 | 18 | 2 | 4 | 20 | 18 | 38 | | | | | | | | 1 | 39 | 60 |
| | 2 | 2 | | 1 | 14 | 25 | 24 | 14 | 28 | 35 | 6 | 8 | 35 | 41 | 76 | | | | | | | 1 | | 77 | 61 |
| | 1 | 2 | | | 34 | 37 | 43 | 36 | 52 | 76 | 8 | 6 | 89 | 56 | 145 | | | | | 2 | | 2 | 1 | 150 | 62 |
| | 1 | 1 | | | 1 | 1 | | | | 1 | | | 2 | | 2 | | | | | | | | | 2 | 63 |
| | | | 1 | | | | 2 | | 1 | 1 | | | 2 | | 2 | | | | | | | | | 2 | 64 |
| | 2 | | 1 | | 2 | 2 | 2 | | 1 | 1 | | 2 | 4 | 2 | 6 | | | | | | | | | 6 | 65 |
| | | | | | 1 | 1 | 3 | 1 | 1 | | 4 | 1 | 5 | 1 | 6 | | | | | | | | | 6 | 66 |
| | 3 | 2 | 1 | 1 | 7 | 6 | 5 | 2 | 11 | 1 | | | 19 | 1 | 20 | | | | | | | | | 20 | 67 |
| | | | | | | 2 | | | | | | | 2 | | 2 | | | | | | | | | 2 | 68 |
| | 2 | 2 | | | 10 | 18 | 16 | 5 | 5 | 16 | 7 | 18 | 27 | 22 | 49 | | | | | | | | | 49 | 69 |
| | | 1 | | | 1 | 1 | 2 | 3 | 5 | 2 | | | 5 | 2 | 7 | | | | | | | | | 7 | 70 |
| | 1 | | | | 1 | 5 | 2 | 1 | 1 | 3 | 1 | 4 | 4 | 5 | 9 | | | | | | | | | 9 | 71 |
| | | | | | | 1 | | | | 1 | | | | 1 | 1 | | | | | | | | | 1 | 72 |
| | 9 | 2 | 4 | 1 | 8 | 6 | 7 | 4 | 3 | 3 | 1 | | 23 | 2 | 25 | | | | | | | | | 25 | 73 |

## CLASSIFICATION OF DEATHS IN SOUTH-

| | Cause of death. | Ages. Under 1. M. | Under 1. F. | 1 and under 5. M. | 1 and under 5. F. | 5 and under 10. M. | 5 and under 10. F. | 10 and under 20. M. | 10 and under 20. F. | 20 and under 50. M. | 20 and under 50. F. | 50 and under 80. M. | 50 and under 80. F. | 80 and under 100. M | 80 and under 100. F. | 100 & over. M | 100 & over. F. | Age unknown. M | Age unknown. F. | Nativities. Born in the State. | N. England States. | Middle States. | Southern States. | Southwest'n States. | Northwest'n States. |
|---|---|---|---|---|---|---|---|---|---|---|---|---|---|---|---|---|---|---|---|---|---|---|---|---|---|
| 1 | Marasmus | | | | 2 | | | | | | | | 1 | | | | | | | 1 | | | | | |
| 2 | Measles | 7 | 10 | 30 | 25 | 7 | 7 | 2 | 2 | 1 | 4 | | | | | | | | | 84 | | 3 | 1 | | 2 |
| 3 | Milk sickness | | | | | | 1 | 1 | | | | 1 | | | | | | | | 2 | | | | | |
| 4 | Mortification | | | | | | | 1 | | 1 | | | | | | | | | | 1 | | | | | |
| 5 | Mumps | | | 1 | 1 | | 1 | | | 1 | 1 | | | | | | | | | 4 | | 1 | | | |
| 6 | Murder | | | | | | | | | 2 | | | | | | | | | | 2 | | | | | |
| 7 | Neuralgia | | | 1 | | | 1 | | 1 | 1 | 1 | 1 | 1 | | | | | | | 4 | | | 1 | | 1 |
| 8 | Old age | | | | | | | | | 1 | | 18 | 27 | 25 | 25 | | 2 | | | 7 | 2 | 37 | 31 | | 1 |
| 9 | Paralysis | | | 1 | | | | 1 | | 5 | 4 | 12 | 17 | 2 | | | 1 | | | 7 | | 22 | 7 | | 3 |
| 10 | Peritonitis | | | | | | | | | | 2 | | | | | | | | | 1 | | | | | |
| 11 | Pleurisy | 1 | | 1 | 1 | | | | 1 | 4 | 2 | | 2 | | | | | | | 7 | | 3 | 1 | | 1 |
| 12 | Pneumonia | 24 | 13 | 21 | 26 | 2 | 5 | 8 | 3 | 36 | 12 | 14 | 5 | | 1 | | | | | 106 | 3 | 14 | 10 | | 7 |
| 13 | Poison | | | 1 | 2 | 1 | | | | | 1 | | | | | | | | | 4 | | 1 | | | |
| 14 | Quinsy | | | 5 | 2 | 1 | 1 | | | 1 | | | | | | | | | | 8 | | | | | 1 |
| 15 | Rheumatism | | | 1 | 1 | | | | | 4 | 2 | 2 | 2 | | | | | | | 3 | | 4 | 2 | | 1 |
| 16 | Salivation, effects of | | | | | | | | | | 1 | | | | | | | | | 1 | | | | | |
| 17 | Scrofula | 5 | 3 | 6 | 4 | 1 | 2 | 2 | 1 | 1 | 6 | 1 | 2 | | | | | | | 27 | | 4 | 1 | | 1 |
| 18 | Scurvy | | | | | | | | | 1 | | | | | | | | | | | | | | | |
| 19 | Small pox | 64 | 38 | 63 | 55 | 16 | 9 | 24 | 13 | 100 | 24 | 9 | 5 | 1 | 1 | | | | | 310 | 1 | 22 | 14 | 3 | 11 |
| 20 | Spine, disease of | | 1 | 1 | | 1 | | | 1 | 3 | 3 | | | | | | | | | 5 | | 1 | | | 1 |
| 21 | Starvation | 1 | | | | 1 | | | | | | | | | | | | | | | | | | | |
| 22 | Stillborn | 1 | | | | | | | | | | | | | | | | | | 1 | | | | | |
| 23 | Stomach, disease of | | | | | 1 | | 1 | | | | | | | | | | | | 1 | | | 1 | | |
| 24 | Suffocation | 1 | | 1 | | | | | | | | | | | | | | | | 2 | | | | | |
| 25 | Suicide | | | | | | | 1 | | 1 | 1 | | 1 | | | | | | | 2 | | 1 | | | |
| 26 | Summer complaint | 19 | 10 | 19 | 20 | | 1 | | | | | | | | | | | | | 62 | | | | 1 | 2 |
| 27 | Syphilis | | | | | | | | | | | 1 | | | | | | | | | | | | | |
| 28 | Teething | 8 | 4 | 16 | 10 | | | | | | | | | | | | | | | 34 | | 1 | 1 | | |
| 29 | Throat, disease of | 2 | | 4 | 3 | 1 | 3 | 1 | 2 | 1 | 1 | 1 | | | | | | | | 16 | | 1 | 2 | | |
| 30 | Thrush | | 7 | | 1 | | | | | | | | | | | | | | | 8 | | | | | |
| 31 | Tumor | | | | | | | | | 1 | | | | | | | | | | | | | | | |
| 32 | Ulcer | 1 | | 2 | | | 1 | | | 1 | 1 | 2 | | 1 | | | | | | 5 | 1 | 1 | | | |
| 33 | Uterus, disease of | | | | | | | | | | 1 | | | | | | | | | | | | | | |
| 34 | White swelling | | | | | | | | | 1 | | | | | | | | | | 1 | | | | | |
| 35 | Worms | 1 | 1 | 2 | 10 | 1 | 3 | 2 | | | | | | | | | | | | 18 | | 1 | | | |
| 36 | Unknown | 178 | 155 | 98 | 107 | 11 | 12 | 18 | 19 | 132 | 104 | 79 | 49 | 6 | 7 | | | 5 | | 681 | 16 | 75 | 50 | 2 | 24 |
| | Total | 782 | 660 | 1208 | 1131 | 394 | 344 | 383 | 404 | 1985 | 1383 | 686 | 487 | 65 | 63 | .. | 3 | 8 | 3 | 5864 | 96 | 1009 | 412 | 22 | 246 |

## CLASSIFICATION OF DEATHS IN

| | Cause of death. | Under 1. M. | Under 1. F. | 1 and under 5. M. | 1 and under 5. F. | 5 and under 10. M. | 5 and under 10. F. | 10 and under 20. M. | 10 and under 20. F. | 20 and under 50. M. | 20 and under 50. F. | 50 and under 80. M. | 50 and under 80. F. | 80 and under 100. M | 80 and under 100. F. | 100 & over. M | 100 & over. F. | Age unknown. M | Age unknown. F. | Born in the State. | N. England States. | Middle States. | Southern States. | Southwest'n States. | Northwest'n States. |
|---|---|---|---|---|---|---|---|---|---|---|---|---|---|---|---|---|---|---|---|---|---|---|---|---|---|
| 1 | Abscess | 1 | | | 1 | | | 1 | 2 | 6 | 4 | 2 | | | | | | | | 8 | | 2 | 2 | | |
| 2 | Accident not specif'd | 2 | 1 | 19 | 13 | 29 | 9 | 47 | 5 | 99 | 11 | 34 | 14 | 5 | 2 | | | | | 156 | 17 | 49 | 17 | 2 | 1 |
| 3 | ...do...burned | 1 | 6 | 9 | 24 | 4 | 10 | 1 | 3 | 2 | 5 | | 2 | 1 | 1 | | | | | 53 | 2 | 7 | 2 | | |
| 4 | ...do...drowned | 1 | | 15 | 11 | 28 | 6 | 23 | 5 | 51 | 3 | 7 | | 1 | | | | | | 97 | 2 | 15 | 2 | | 4 |
| 5 | ...do...scalded | 5 | 3 | 19 | 14 | 6 | 1 | | | 4 | | | | | | | | | | 48 | | 1 | | | 2 |
| 6 | ...do...exp'n ste'm | | | | | | | 1 | | | | | | | | | | | | | | | | | |
| 7 | ...do...shot | | | | | | | 3 | | 1 | | | | | | | | | | 2 | | 1 | | | 1 |
| 8 | ...do...railroad | | | | | | | 1 | | 4 | | 1 | | | | | | | | 4 | | | | | |
| 9 | Apoplexy | | 1 | 1 | 1 | 2 | .'. | 4 | 3 | 16 | 18 | 49 | 20 | 7 | 1 | | | | | 19 | 21 | 48 | 14 | 1 | 1 |
| 10 | Asthma | | | 2 | 1 | | 1 | | | 3 | | 6 | 12 | 5 | 1 | | | | | 7 | 1 | 17 | 4 | | |
| 11 | Bladder, disease of | | | | | | | 1 | | | 1 | 2 | | | | | | | | | | 3 | 1 | | |
| 12 | Bowels.....do | 15 | 6 | 14 | 7 | 3 | 1 | 3 | 1 | 6 | 6 | 7 | 1 | | 1 | | | | | 46 | 4 | 8 | 2 | | |
| 13 | Brain......do | 22 | 21 | 30 | 17 | 8 | 4 | 5 | 3 | 17 | 14 | 7 | | 2 | | | | | | 121 | 4 | 7 | 7 | | 1 |
| 14 | Bronchitis | 4 | 2 | 5 | 13 | 1 | 1 | | 2 | 18 | 7 | 9 | 2 | 1 | 1 | | | | | 43 | | 12 | 1 | | |
| 15 | Cancer | | 1 | 1 | 2 | 1 | 3 | | | 7 | 14 | 33 | 37 | 5 | | | | | | 14 | 15 | 44 | 12 | | 2 |
| 16 | Canker rash | 1 | 2 | 3 | 3 | 4 | 2 | | 1 | | 1 | | | | | | | | | 15 | 1 | | | | 1 |
| 17 | Catarrh | 27 | 24 | 13 | 8 | 1 | 2 | 2 | 7 | 10 | 9 | 5 | 4 | 4 | 1 | | | | | 95 | 3 | 7 | 2 | | 1 |
| 18 | Chicken pox | | 1 | 2 | | | | | | | 1 | | | | | | | | | 3 | | | | | |
| 19 | Childbirth | | | | | | | | 12 | | 187 | | | | | | | | 1 | 97 | 10 | 46 | 11 | | 2 |
| 20 | Cholera | 162 | 159 | 451 | 441 | 290 | 209 | 299 | 298 | 1683 | 1010 | 501 | 268 | 14 | 17 | | | 2 | 4 | 2535 | 95 | 626 | 178 | 10 | 112 |
| 21 | ...do...infantum | 72 | 60 | 53 | 46 | 1 | | | | | | | | | | | | | | 225 | 1 | 5 | 1 | | |
| 22 | ...do...morbus | 8 | 6 | 19 | 12 | 5 | 5 | 6 | 2 | 15 | 10 | 16 | 7 | | 2 | | | | | 66 | 4 | 22 | 4 | | 1 |
| 23 | Chorea | | | | | | | | 1 | | | | | | | | | | | 1 | | | | | |
| 24 | Colic | 5 | 4 | 3 | 3 | 4 | 1 | 2 | | 19 | 9 | 13 | 8 | 1 | | | | | | 27 | 3 | 15 | 9 | | 2 |
| 25 | Congestion | 2 | 1 | 3 | 2 | 2 | 1 | 2 | 1 | 2 | 2 | | 1 | | | | | | | 16 | | | | | |
| 26 | .....do.......brain | 6 | 3 | 11 | 8 | 3 | 1 | 1 | 4 | 3 | 2 | 3 | | | | | | | | 38 | 1 | 5 | | | |
| 27 | .....do.......lungs | 2 | 1 | 2 | 2 | | 1 | 1 | 1 | | | 3 | | | | | | | | 10 | 1 | 2 | | | |
| 28 | Consumption | 42 | 46 | 62 | 71 | 22 | 29 | 97 | 181 | 685 | 811 | 267 | 215 | 18 | 10 | | | 2 | | 1250 | 157 | 648 | 149 | 6 | 34 |
| 29 | Convulsions | 146 | 102 | 78 | 80 | 11 | 12 | 8 | 17 | 26 | 27 | 11 | 5 | 1 | 1 | | | | 1 | 455 | 8 | 32 | 8 | | 7 |
| 30 | Croup | 197 | 142 | 269 | 269 | 73 | 60 | 8 | 5 | 3 | 3 | 2 | | | | | | | | 979 | 1 | 24 | 2 | 1 | 9 |

## ESTERN SECTION OF THE STATE OF OHIO—Continued.

| Nativities. Ireland. | Nativities. Germany. | Nativities. Other foreign countries. | Nativities. Unkown. | Season of decease. Spring. | Season of decease. Summer. | Season of decease. Autumn. | Season of decease. Winter. | Duration of sickness. Under 1 week. | Duration of sickness. 1 week and under 1 month. | Duration of sickness. 1 month and under 3 months. | Duration of sickness. 3 months and over. | Whites. Males. | Whites. Females. | Whites. Total. | Colored. Slaves. Black. M. | Colored. Slaves. Black. F. | Colored. Slaves. Mulatto. M. | Colored. Slaves. Mulatto. F. | Colored. Free. Black M. | Colored. Free. Black F. | Colored. Free. Mul. M | Colored. Free. Mul. F. | Aggregate deaths. | |
|---|---|---|---|---|---|---|---|---|---|---|---|---|---|---|---|---|---|---|---|---|---|---|---|---|
| | 2 | | | 2 | | 1 | | | | | 3 | | 3 | 3 | | | | | | | | | 3 | 1 |
| 1 | 4 | | | 20 | 55 | 12 | 7 | 25 | 59 | 7 | 3 | 46 | 47 | 93 | | | | | 1 | 1 | | | 95 | 2 |
| 1 | | | | | 1 | | 2 | 1 | 2 | | | 2 | 1 | 3 | | | | | | | | | 3 | 3 |
| 1 | | | | 1 | 1 | | | | 1 | | | 2 | | 2 | | | | | | | | | 2 | 4 |
| | | | | | 2 | 1 | 2 | | 4 | 1 | | 2 | 3 | 5 | | | | | | | | | 5 | 5 |
| | | | | | | 1 | 1 | 1 | | | | 2 | | 2 | | | | | | | | | 2 | 6 |
| | | 1 | | 1 | 1 | 3 | 2 | 3 | 1 | 1 | 2 | 3 | 4 | 7 | | | | | | | | | 7 | 7 |
| 7 | 10 | 1 | 2 | 36 | 26 | 17 | 19 | 20 | 19 | 5 | 26 | 42 | 53 | 95 | | | | | 2 | 1 | | | 98 | 8 |
| 3 | 1 | | | 12 | 12 | 11 | 8 | 14 | 9 | 2 | 15 | 21 | 21 | 42 | | | | | | 1 | | | 43 | 9 |
| | | 1 | | | | 2 | | | | 1 | | | 2 | 2 | | | | | | | | | 2 | 10 |
| | | | | 3 | 5 | 2 | 2 | 4 | 5 | | 3 | 5 | 6 | 11 | | | | | | | 1 | | 12 | 11 |
| 18 | 9 | 2 | | 77 | 28 | 37 | 28 | 24 | 91 | 11 | 20 | 102 | 63 | 165 | | | | | 3 | 1 | | 1 | 170 | 12 |
| | | | | | 4 | 1 | | 5 | | | | 2 | 3 | 5 | | | | | | | | | 5 | 13 |
| | 1 | | | 2 | 1 | 6 | 1 | 6 | 4 | | | 7 | 3 | 10 | | | | | | | | | 10 | 14 |
| | 1 | 1 | | 1 | 5 | 5 | 1 | 1 | 3 | 1 | 6 | 7 | 5 | 12 | | | | | | | | | 12 | 15 |
| | | | | | | | 1 | | | | 1 | | 1 | 1 | | | | | | | | | 1 | 16 |
| | 1 | | | 7 | 10 | 10 | 7 | 3 | 2 | 4 | 25 | 15 | 18 | 33 | | | | | 1 | | | | 34 | 17 |
| | 1 | | | | | | 1 | | | 1 | | 1 | | 1 | | | | | | | | | 1 | 18 |
| 6 | 43 | 11 | 1 | 122 | 38 | 70 | 191 | 71 | 257 | 7 | 5 | 264 | 140 | 404 | | | | | 9 | 3 | 4 | 2 | 422 | 19 |
| 1 | 1 | 1 | | 4 | | 5 | 1 | 1 | 2 | | 4 | 5 | 5 | 10 | | | | | | | | | 10 | 20 |
| 2 | | | | | | 1 | 1 | 1 | | | | 2 | | 2 | | | | | | | | | 2 | 21 |
| | | | | 1 | | | | | | | | 1 | | 1 | | | | | | | | | 1 | 22 |
| | | | | | | 1 | 1 | 1 | | | 1 | 2 | | 2 | | | | | | | | | 2 | 23 |
| | | | | 1 | | 1 | | 2 | | | | 2 | | 2 | | | | | | | | | 2 | 24 |
| 1 | | | | 2 | | | 2 | 2 | | | | 2 | 2 | 4 | | | | | | | | | 4 | 25 |
| | 3 | 1 | | 1 | 43 | 23 | 1 | 19 | 18 | 6 | 24 | 38 | 31 | 69 | | | | | | | | | 69 | 26 |
| | | | 1 | 1 | | | | | | | | 1 | | 1 | | | | | | | | | 1 | 27 |
| 1 | 1 | | | 4 | 15 | 12 | 7 | 14 | 11 | 7 | 3 | 24 | 14 | 38 | | | | | | | | | 38 | 28 |
| | | | | 5 | 3 | 10 | 1 | 8 | 9 | 1 | 1 | 10 | 9 | 19 | | | | | | | | | 19 | 29 |
| | | | | 2 | 4 | 2 | | 3 | 4 | | 1 | | 8 | 8 | | | | | | | | | 8 | 30 |
| | 1 | | | 1 | | | | | | | | 1 | | 1 | | | | | | | | | 1 | 31 |
| 2 | | | | | 1 | 7 | 1 | | 2 | 1 | 5 | 7 | 2 | 9 | | | | | | | | | 9 | 32 |
| | | | 1 | 1 | | | | | | | | | 1 | 1 | | | | | | | | | 1 | 33 |
| | | | | | 1 | | | | | | 1 | 1 | | 1 | | | | | | | | | 1 | 34 |
| | | | 1 | 6 | 7 | 6 | 1 | 10 | 10 | | | 6 | 14 | 20 | | | | | | | | | 20 | 35 |
| 12 | 83 | 23 | 9 | 239 | 325 | 243 | 155 | 286 | 182 | 35 | 217 | 512 | 442 | 954 | | | | | 7 | 6 | 3 | 5 | 975 | 36 |
| 474 | 1536 | 258 | 72 | 1564 | 4776 | 2454 | 1160 | 4855 | 2459 | 383 | 1178 | 5410 | 4400 | 9810 | | | | | 63 | 53 | 38 | 25 | 9989 | |

## HE STATE OF OHIO—AGGREGATE.

| Nativities. Ireland. | Nativities. Germany. | Nativities. Other foreign countries. | Nativities. Unkown. | Season of decease. Spring. | Season of decease. Summer. | Season of decease. Autumn. | Season of decease. Winter. | Duration of sickness. Under 1 week. | Duration of sickness. 1 week and under 1 month. | Duration of sickness. 1 month and under 3 months. | Duration of sickness. 3 months and over. | Whites. Males. | Whites. Females. | Whites. Total. | Colored. Slaves. Black. M. | Colored. Slaves. Black. F. | Colored. Slaves. Mulatto. M. | Colored. Slaves. Mulatto. F. | Colored. Free. Black M. | Colored. Free. Black F. | Colored. Free. Mul. M | Colored. Free. Mul. F. | Aggregate deaths. | |
|---|---|---|---|---|---|---|---|---|---|---|---|---|---|---|---|---|---|---|---|---|---|---|---|---|
| 3 | 2 | | | 3 | 3 | 5 | 6 | 3 | 2 | 3 | 6 | 10 | 7 | 17 | | | | | | | | | 17 | 1 |
| 15 | 20 | 10 | 3 | 78 | 74 | 80 | 56 | 128 | 42 | 12 | 12 | 235 | 54 | 289 | | | | | | 1 | | | 290 | 2 |
| | 4 | 1 | | 29 | 16 | 12 | 12 | 30 | 17 | 3 | 3 | 18 | 50 | 68 | | | | | | 1 | | | 69 | 3 |
| 9 | 10 | 10 | 2 | 29 | 67 | 25 | 29 | 151 | | | | 123 | 25 | 148 | | | | | 1 | | 2 | | 151 | 4 |
| | | 1 | | 12 | 10 | 11 | 17 | 30 | 11 | 2 | 1 | 33 | 18 | 51 | | | | | 1 | | | | 52 | 5 |
| | 1 | | | | 1 | | | | 1 | | | 1 | | 1 | | | | | | | | | 1 | 6 |
| | | | | 1 | 1 | 1 | 1 | 1 | | | | 4 | | 4 | | | | | | | | | 4 | 7 |
| 2 | | | | 1 | 1 | 4 | | 1 | | | | 6 | | 6 | | | | | | | | | 6 | 8 |
| 4 | 7 | 7 | 1 | 31 | 37 | 26 | 28 | 67 | 8 | 1 | 4 | 78 | 43 | 121 | | | | | 1 | 1 | | | 123 | 9 |
| 1 | | | 1 | 12 | 7 | 5 | 7 | 6 | 4 | 2 | 15 | 16 | 15 | 31 | | | | | | | | | 31 | 10 |
| | | | | 2 | | | 2 | 1 | 2 | | 1 | 3 | 1 | 4 | | | | | | | | | 4 | 11 |
| 6 | 2 | 3 | | 11 | 19 | 32 | 9 | 18 | 33 | 5 | 5 | 47 | 23 | 70 | | | | | | | 1 | | 71 | 12 |
| 3 | 3 | 4 | | 37 | 43 | 41 | 29 | 57 | 54 | 14 | 9 | 89 | 58 | 147 | | | | | 2 | 1 | | | 150 | 13 |
| 2 | 3 | 4 | 1 | 19 | 15 | 19 | 13 | 10 | 23 | 8 | 22 | 38 | 28 | 66 | | | | | | | | | 66 | 14 |
| 6 | 3 | 5 | 2 | 20 | 29 | 28 | 25 | 4 | 10 | 5 | 71 | 47 | 56 | 103 | | | | | | | | | 103 | 15 |
| | | | | 7 | 2 | 6 | 2 | 4 | 9 | 2 | 1 | 8 | 9 | 17 | | | | | | | | | 17 | 16 |
| 3 | 5 | 1 | | 55 | 16 | 19 | 27 | 37 | 56 | 12 | 8 | 59 | 55 | 114 | | | | | 1 | | 2 | | 117 | 17 |
| | 1 | | | | 2 | 1 | 1 | 1 | 1 | | 1 | 2 | 2 | 4 | | | | | | | | | 4 | 18 |
| 5 | 22 | 5 | 2 | 55 | 61 | 37 | 45 | 92 | 74 | 11 | 6 | | 199 | 199 | | | | | | 1 | | | 200 | 19 |
| 368 | 1565 | 243 | 76 | 95 | 4167 | 1459 | 74 | 4857 | 338 | 20 | 9 | 3340 | 2365 | 5705 | | | | | 37 | 30 | 25 | 11 | 5808 | 20 |
| | | | | 8 | 88 | 129 | 6 | 119 | 78 | 16 | 9 | 126 | 106 | 232 | | | | | | | | | 232 | 21 |
| 7 | 7 | 2 | | 4 | 37 | 65 | 7 | 78 | 31 | 1 | 1 | 68 | 44 | 112 | | | | | | | 1 | | 113 | 22 |
| | | | | | 1 | | | | 1 | | | | 1 | 1 | | | | | | | | | 1 | 23 |
| 4 | 6 | 4 | 1 | 17 | 20 | 18 | 16 | 42 | 26 | | 2 | 46 | 25 | 71 | | | | | | | | | 71 | 24 |
| 2 | 1 | | | 5 | 5 | 4 | 5 | 9 | 8 | | 1 | 10 | 8 | 18 | | | | | | | 1 | | 19 | 25 |
| 1 | | | | 14 | 13 | 10 | 8 | 21 | 20 | 1 | 1 | 27 | 18 | 45 | | | | | | | | | 45 | 26 |
| | | | | 4 | 1 | 2 | 6 | 4 | 8 | 1 | | 8 | 5 | 13 | | | | | | | | | 13 | 27 |
| 85 | 133 | 76 | 20 | 807 | 675 | 587 | 484 | 81 | 247 | 278 | 1793 | 1174 | 1339 | 2513 | | | | | 10 | 15 | 11 | 9 | 2558 | 28 |
| 5 | 9 | 2 | | 159 | 121 | 155 | 90 | 293 | 128 | 13 | 41 | 277 | 244 | 521 | | | | | 1 | 1 | 3 | | 526 | 29 |
| 2 | 8 | 5 | | 290 | 160 | 303 | 270 | 763 | 194 | 11 | 10 | 548 | 475 | 1023 | | | | | 1 | 1 | 3 | 3 | 1031 | 30 |

CLASSIFICATION OF DEATHS IN

| | Cause of death. | AGES. | | | | | | | | | | | | | | | | | | NATIVITIES. | | | | | |
|---|---|---|---|---|---|---|---|---|---|---|---|---|---|---|---|---|---|---|---|---|---|---|---|---|---|
| | | Under 1. | | 1 and under 5. | | 5 and under 10. | | 10 and under 20. | | 20 and under 50. | | 50 and under 80. | | 80 and under 100. | | 100 & over. | | Age unknown. | | Born in State. | N. England States. | Middle States. | Southern States. | Southwest'n States. | Northwest'n States. |
| | | M. | F. | M. | F. | M. | F. | M. | F. | M. | F. | M. | F. | M. | F. | M | F. | M | F. | | | | | | |
| 1 | Debility | 7 | 7 | 8 | 4 | 1 | 1 | 1 | 2 | 6 | 1 | 6 | 1 | ... | ... | ... | ... | ... | ... | 22 | 3 | 4 | ... | .. | 1 |
| 2 | Diabetes | ... | ... | ... | ... | 3 | ... | ... | 2 | 4 | 2 | 8 | 1 | ... | ... | ... | ... | ... | ... | 8 | 4 | 7 | 1 | .. | ... |
| 3 | Diarrhœa | 53 | 53 | 60 | 52 | 4 | 7 | 7 | 5 | 58 | 25 | 29 | 22 | 5 | 2 | .. | .. | 1 | .. | 265 | 8 | 40 | 14 | 1 | 7 |
| 4 | Dropsy | 20 | 20 | 48 | 34 | 18 | 11 | 13 | 26 | 76 | 110 | 107 | 117 | 15 | 9 | .. | .. | .. | .. | 264 | 44 | 172 | 62 | 5 | 8 |
| 5 | Dysentery | 218 | 156 | 565 | 468 | 197 | 147 | 115 | 99 | 189 | 176 | 94 | 112 | 10 | 12 | .. | .. | 4 | 1 | 2022 | 61 | 237 | 51 | 2 | 23 |
| 6 | Dyspepsia | ... | ... | ... | ... | 1 | ... | ... | ... | 10 | 9 | 24 | 12 | ... | ... | .. | .. | .. | .. | 10 | 5 | 23 | 9 | .. | 2 |
| 7 | Epilepsy | ... | ... | 1 | 1 | ... | ... | 2 | ... | 2 | 3 | 2 | ... | ... | ... | .. | .. | .. | .. | 6 | ... | 5 | ... | .. | ... |
| 8 | Erysipelas | 38 | 22 | 29 | 33 | 12 | 15 | 18 | 32 | 55 | 82 | 36 | 30 | 2 | 4 | .. | .. | .. | .. | 249 | 36 | 73 | 17 | .. | 5 |
| 9 | Fever, not specified | 79 | 60 | 169 | 136 | 64 | 61 | 90 | 98 | 270 | 234 | 120 | 86 | 4 | 7 | .. | .. | .. | 1 | 916 | 50 | 226 | 73 | 5 | 20 |
| 10 | ..do..bilious | 8 | 5 | 16 | 8 | 5 | 5 | 11 | 14 | 55 | 37 | 25 | 11 | ... | 1 | .. | .. | .. | .. | 105 | 11 | 35 | 8 | 2 | 4 |
| 11 | ..do. brain | 22 | 11 | 28 | 21 | 9 | 4 | 5 | 4 | 8 | 6 | 1 | 8 | ... | ... | .. | .. | .. | .. | 95 | 2 | 11 | 2 | .. | 3 |
| 12 | ..do..catarrhal | 6 | 4 | 6 | 5 | 1 | 2 | ... | ... | ... | ... | ... | ... | ... | ... | .. | .. | .. | .. | 22 | ... | 2 | ... | .. | ... |
| 13 | ..do..congestive | 4 | 3 | 12 | 8 | 6 | 6 | 7 | 6 | 28 | 9 | 14 | 8 | 1 | ... | .. | .. | .. | .. | 79 | 2 | 20 | 5 | .. | 2 |
| 14 | ..do..inflammatory | 2 | 2 | ... | ... | ... | 1 | ... | ... | 2 | 3 | ... | ... | ... | ... | .. | .. | .. | .. | 6 | ... | 2 | ... | .. | ... |
| 15 | ..do..intermittent | 9 | 8 | 6 | 8 | 4 | 6 | 3 | 1 | 10 | 13 | 10 | 8 | 2 | 1 | .. | .. | 1 | .. | 58 | 4 | 17 | 2 | .. | 3 |
| 16 | ..do..puerperal | ... | ... | ... | ... | ... | ... | ... | 3 | ... | 12 | ... | 2 | ... | ... | .. | .. | .. | .. | 9 | ... | 3 | ... | .. | ... |
| 17 | ..do..remittent | 1 | 1 | ... | ... | 1 | 1 | 1 | 2 | 4 | 2 | 1 | 1 | ... | ... | .. | .. | .. | .. | 9 | ... | 1 | ... | .. | ... |
| 18 | ..do..scarlet | 68 | 61 | 395 | 351 | 145 | 151 | 42 | 45 | 18 | 15 | 5 | 3 | ... | ... | .. | .. | 1 | 1 | 1212 | 6 | 36 | 6 | 7 | 9 |
| 19 | ..do..ship | ... | 1 | 1 | 1 | 3 | ... | ... | ... | 5 | 3 | 2 | ... | ... | ... | .. | .. | .. | .. | 4 | ... | 1 | ... | .. | ... |
| 20 | ..do ..typhus | 5 | 9 | 32 | 17 | 15 | 24 | 58 | 111 | 256 | 135 | 50 | 34 | 4 | ... | .. | .. | .. | .. | 447 | 25 | 172 | 26 | 3 | 12 |
| 21 | ..do..winter | 1 | 2 | 3 | 4 | 2 | ... | 4 | 7 | 14 | 5 | 7 | 1 | 3 | ... | .. | .. | .. | .. | 26 | 4 | 15 | 4 | .. | ... |
| 22 | ..do..yellow | 1 | ... | ... | ... | ... | ... | ... | ... | 4 | ... | ... | ... | ... | ... | .. | .. | .. | .. | 1 | ... | ... | 1 | .. | ... |
| 23 | Fistula | ... | ... | ... | ... | ... | ... | ... | ... | 1 | ... | 1 | ... | ... | ... | .. | .. | .. | .. | 1 | ... | 1 | ... | .. | ... |
| 24 | Fracture | ... | ... | ... | ... | ... | ... | ... | ... | 3 | ... | 1 | 1 | ... | 1 | .. | .. | .. | .. | 4 | ... | 2 | ... | .. | ... |
| 25 | Frozen | ... | ... | ... | ... | ... | ... | ... | ... | ... | ... | 1 | ... | ... | ... | .. | .. | .. | .. | ... | ... | 1 | ... | .. | ... |
| 26 | Gravel | 1 | ... | ... | 1 | 1 | ... | 1 | ... | 8 | 2 | 36 | 1 | 7 | ... | .. | .. | .. | .. | 12 | 5 | 23 | 6 | .. | 3 |
| 27 | Head, disease of | 14 | 19 | 10 | 11 | 7 | 2 | 3 | 2 | 5 | 1 | 3 | ... | ... | ... | .. | .. | 1 | 1 | 72 | ... | 7 | ... | .. | ... |
| 28 | Heart....do | 6 | 7 | 2 | 5 | 3 | 4 | 10 | 12 | 20 | 22 | 22 | 22 | 1 | 1 | .. | .. | .. | .. | 62 | 18 | 35 | 7 | .. | 2 |
| 29 | Hemorrhage | 3 | 2 | 1 | 1 | 1 | 1 | 2 | 2 | 14 | 6 | 7 | 3 | 1 | 1 | .. | .. | 1 | .. | 18 | 1 | 19 | 3 | 1 | ... |
| 30 | Hernia | ... | ... | 1 | 1 | ... | ... | 1 | ... | 2 | 1 | 5 | 3 | ... | ... | .. | .. | .. | .. | 6 | 1 | 3 | 2 | .. | ... |
| 31 | Hip, disease of | ... | ... | 1 | ... | ... | ... | ... | ... | 1 | ... | ... | ... | ... | ... | .. | .. | .. | .. | 1 | ... | 1 | ... | .. | ... |
| 32 | Hives | 7 | 10 | 3 | 4 | 1 | ... | 1 | ... | ... | ... | ... | ... | ... | ... | .. | .. | .. | .. | 25 | ... | ... | ... | .. | ... |
| 33 | Hooping cough | 93 | 83 | 116 | 125 | 9 | 13 | 1 | 1 | 3 | 2 | 1 | ... | ... | ... | .. | .. | 3 | .. | 429 | ... | 12 | 1 | .. | 5 |
| 34 | Hydrocephalus | 15 | 3 | 13 | 15 | 1 | 4 | ... | ... | ... | 1 | 2 | ... | ... | 1 | .. | .. | .. | .. | 49 | 1 | 3 | 1 | .. | 1 |
| 35 | Inflammation | 39 | 28 | 43 | 32 | 9 | 13 | 16 | 11 | 21 | 32 | 10 | 4 | 1 | ... | .. | .. | .. | 1 | 207 | 7 | 28 | 6 | .. | 2 |
| 36 | ....do....bowels | 31 | 26 | 32 | 24 | 9 | 7 | 17 | 12 | 23 | 31 | 18 | 2 | 1 | ... | .. | .. | .. | .. | 173 | 6 | 27 | 6 | .. | 3 |
| 37 | ....do....brain | 75 | 61 | 86 | 64 | 19 | 19 | 14 | 19 | 30 | 15 | 4 | 2 | ... | ... | .. | .. | .. | .. | 361 | 8 | 22 | 1 | .. | 8 |
| 38 | ....do....stomach | 1 | ... | 1 | 1 | 1 | ... | ... | 1 | ... | 2 | ... | 1 | ... | ... | .. | .. | .. | .. | 5 | ... | 2 | 1 | .. | ... |
| 39 | Insanity | ... | ... | ... | ... | ... | ... | 1 | ... | 4 | 5 | 3 | ... | ... | ... | .. | .. | .. | .. | 5 | 2 | 3 | ... | .. | ... |
| 40 | Intemperance | ... | ... | ... | ... | ... | ... | ... | ... | 8 | ... | 5 | 1 | ... | ... | .. | .. | .. | .. | 1 | ... | 7 | ... | .. | 1 |
| 41 | Jaundice | 5 | 2 | 1 | 1 | 1 | 2 | 2 | ... | 4 | 3 | 4 | 2 | ... | 1 | .. | .. | .. | .. | 16 | ... | 6 | ... | .. | 1 |
| 42 | Kidneys, disease of | 1 | ... | ... | ... | 1 | ... | ... | ... | 1 | 1 | 5 | 1 | ... | ... | .. | .. | .. | .. | 3 | ... | 6 | 1 | .. | ... |
| 43 | Killed | ... | ... | 3 | 1 | ... | ... | 6 | ... | 21 | 1 | 3 | 1 | ... | 1 | .. | .. | .. | .. | 14 | 1 | 7 | 2 | .. | 2 |
| 44 | Lightning | ... | ... | ... | ... | ... | ... | 6 | ... | 3 | ... | ... | ... | ... | ... | .. | .. | .. | .. | 9 | ... | ... | ... | .. | ... |
| 45 | Liver, disease of | 13 | 8 | 14 | 14 | 1 | 5 | 3 | 10 | 30 | 29 | 29 | 15 | ... | 1 | .. | .. | .. | .. | 93 | 5 | 40 | 11 | 1 | 5 |
| 46 | Lockjaw | 1 | 2 | 2 | ... | 1 | 1 | 3 | ... | 2 | ... | ... | ... | ... | ... | .. | .. | .. | .. | 9 | ... | 1 | 1 | .. | ... |
| 47 | Lungs, disease of | 20 | 11 | 9 | 15 | 9 | 7 | 4 | 3 | 15 | 16 | 16 | 6 | 1 | 2 | .. | .. | .. | .. | 93 | 7 | 18 | 10 | .. | ... |
| 48 | Malformation | 2 | 4 | 1 | 1 | 1 | ... | ... | ... | ... | ... | ... | ... | ... | ... | .. | .. | .. | .. | 8 | ... | ... | ... | .. | ... |
| 49 | Mania-a-potu | ... | ... | ... | ... | ... | ... | ... | ... | 30 | 1 | 7 | ... | ... | 1 | .. | .. | 1 | .. | 5 | 2 | 5 | 2 | .. | 2 |
| 50 | Marasmus | 3 | ... | 1 | 3 | ... | 1 | ... | ... | 2 | ... | 1 | 2 | ... | ... | .. | .. | .. | .. | 8 | 1 | 2 | ... | .. | ... |
| 51 | Measles | 28 | 25 | 108 | 95 | 28 | 18 | 12 | 19 | 4 | 24 | 2 | ... | ... | ... | .. | .. | .. | .. | 326 | 1 | 13 | 9 | .. | 3 |
| 52 | Milk sickness | ... | ... | ... | ... | ... | 3 | 2 | 3 | 2 | 3 | 1 | ... | ... | ... | .. | .. | .. | .. | 11 | ... | 2 | ... | .. | ... |
| 53 | Mortification | ... | ... | ... | ... | ... | ... | 2 | ... | 1 | 1 | ... | 2 | 2 | 1 | . | .. | .. | .. | 4 | 1 | 1 | 1 | .. | ... |
| 54 | Mumps | 3 | ... | 2 | 1 | ... | 1 | 2 | ... | 2 | 2 | ... | ... | ... | ... | .. | .. | .. | .. | 10 | ... | 1 | 1 | .. | 1 |
| 55 | Murder | ... | ... | ... | ... | ... | ... | ... | ... | 6 | 1 | 1 | 1 | ... | ... | .. | .. | .. | .. | 3 | 1 | 1 | ... | .. | ... |
| 56 | Neuralgia | ... | ... | 3 | 1 | ... | 2 | 2 | 1 | 3 | 7 | 2 | 5 | ... | ... | .. | .. | .. | 1 | 13 | 1 | 4 | 3 | .. | 2 |
| 57 | Old age | ... | ... | ... | ... | ... | ... | ... | ... | 2 | 2 | 83 | 120 | 146 | 145 | 3 | 4 | .. | 1 | 40 | 67 | 219 | 83 | 2 | 2 |
| 58 | Paralysis | ... | ... | 3 | 2 | 1 | 2 | 3 | 5 | 11 | 15 | 68 | 64 | 14 | 7 | 1 | 1 | .. | .. | 33 | 20 | 94 | 24 | .. | 3 |
| 59 | Peritonitis | ... | ... | ... | ... | ... | ... | ... | ... | ... | 5 | ... | 1 | ... | ... | .. | .. | .. | .. | 3 | ... | 1 | 1 | .. | ... |
| 60 | Piles | ... | ... | ... | ... | ... | ... | ... | ... | 1 | ... | 2 | ... | ... | ... | .. | .. | .. | .. | ... | ... | 3 | ... | .. | ... |
| 61 | Pleurisy | 3 | 2 | 4 | 3 | 1 | ... | 3 | 4 | 20 | 18 | 16 | 8 | 2 | 2 | .. | .. | .. | .. | 36 | 3 | 28 | 7 | .. | 2 |
| 62 | Pneumonia | 106 | 68 | 112 | 109 | 30 | 24 | 35 | 34 | 152 | 78 | 91 | 39 | 12 | 4 | .. | .. | 1 | .. | 586 | 31 | 142 | 32 | .. | 12 |
| 63 | Poison | ... | 1 | 3 | 4 | 3 | ... | ... | ... | ... | 4 | ... | 1 | ... | ... | .. | .. | .. | .. | 12 | ... | 4 | ... | .. | ... |
| 64 | Prematurity of birth | 1 | 1 | ... | ... | ... | ... | ... | ... | ... | ... | ... | ... | ... | ... | .. | .. | .. | .. | 2 | ... | ... | ... | .. | ... |
| 65 | Putrid sore throat | ... | 1 | 4 | 11 | 10 | 5 | 4 | 8 | 3 | ... | 1 | 1 | ... | ... | .. | .. | .. | .. | 45 | 1 | ... | 1 | .. | ... |
| 66 | Quinsy | ... | ... | 10 | 5 | 2 | 4 | 1 | 2 | 3 | 3 | 2 | 2 | 1 | ... | .. | .. | .. | .. | 23 | 1 | 5 | 2 | .. | 1 |
| 67 | Rheumatism | 1 | ... | 2 | 1 | 1 | 1 | 13 | 2 | 12 | 8 | 14 | 9 | 2 | 1 | .. | .. | .. | .. | 24 | 4 | 24 | 7 | 1 | 1 |
| 68 | Rickets | ... | 1 | 1 | ... | ... | ... | ... | ... | ... | ... | ... | ... | ... | ... | .. | .. | .. | .. | 2 | ... | ... | ... | .. | ... |
| 69 | Salivation, effects of | ... | ... | 1 | ... | ... | ... | ... | ... | ... | 1 | ... | ... | ... | ... | .. | .. | .. | .. | 2 | ... | ... | ... | .. | ... |
| 70 | Scrofula | 10 | 10 | 14 | 10 | 5 | 4 | 8 | 9 | 11 | 13 | 2 | 5 | ... | ... | .. | .. | .. | .. | 73 | 4 | 16 | 4 | 1 | 2 |
| 71 | Scurvy | ... | ... | ... | ... | ... | ... | 1 | ... | 4 | ... | ... | ... | ... | ... | .. | .. | .. | .. | 3 | ... | 1 | ... | .. | ... |
| 72 | Small pox | 80 | 42 | 71 | 67 | 18 | 19 | 31 | 24 | 134 | 31 | 20 | 10 | 2 | 2 | .. | .. | .. | .. | 392 | 7 | 45 | 24 | 3 | 11 |
| 73 | Spine, disease of | 3 | 1 | 4 | 1 | 2 | 2 | 2 | 3 | 12 | 7 | 4 | 1 | ... | ... | .. | .. | .. | .. | 23 | 2 | 7 | 2 | .. | 3 |
| 74 | Starvation | 1 | ... | ... | ... | ... | 1 | ... | ... | ... | ... | ... | ... | ... | ... | .. | .. | .. | .. | ... | ... | ... | ... | .. | ... |
| 75 | Stillborn | 6 | ... | ... | ... | ... | ... | ... | ... | ... | ... | ... | ... | ... | ... | .. | .. | .. | .. | 6 | ... | ... | ... | .. | ... |

## THE STATE OF OHIO—AGGREGATE—Continued.

| NATIVITIES. | | | | | SEASON OF DECEASE. | | | | DURATION OF SICKNESS. | | | | WHITES. | | | COLORED. | | | | | | | | | |
|---|---|---|---|---|---|---|---|---|---|---|---|---|---|---|---|---|---|---|---|---|---|---|---|---|---|
| | | | | | | | | | | | | | | | | Slaves. | | | | Free. | | | | | |
| | | | | | | | | | | | | | | | | Black. | | Mulatto. | | Bl'k. | | Mul. | | | |
| California and Territories. | Ireland. | Germany. | Other foreign countries. | Unknown. | Spring. | Summer. | Autumn. | Winter. | Under 1 week. | 1 week and under 1 month. | 1 month and under 3 months. | 3 months and over. | Males. | Females. | Total. | M. | F. | M. | F. | M | F. | M | F. | Aggregate deaths. | |
| .... | 6 | 2 | 2 | ... | 12 | 12 | 10 | 5 | 2 | 5 | 4 | 14 | 24 | 16 | 40 | | | | | | | | | 40 | 1 |
| .... | | | | | 4 | 4 | 5 | 7 | 1 | 3 | 3 | 13 | 15 | 5 | 20 | | | | | | | | | 20 | 2 |
| .... | 22 | 13 | 13 | 1 | 37 | 88 | 216 | 41 | 97 | 169 | 51 | 43 | 216 | 165 | 381 | | | | | | 1 | 1 | 1 | 384 | 3 |
| .... | 17 | 33 | 18 | 1 | 191 | 168 | 149 | 113 | 64 | 150 | 86 | 286 | 293 | 324 | 617 | | | | | 2 | 1 | 2 | 2 | 624 | 4 |
| .... | 52 | 50 | 59 | 6 | 78 | 405 | 1929 | 134 | 688 | 1552 | 159 | 46 | 1381 | 1161 | 2542 | | | | | 4 | 7 | 7 | 8 | 2568 | 5 |
| .... | 4 | | 3 | | 13 | 16 | 13 | 14 | 4 | 6 | 11 | 34 | 35 | 21 | 56 | | | | | | | | | 56 | 6 |
| .... | | | | | 5 | | 4 | 2 | 5 | 1 | | 5 | 7 | 4 | 11 | | | | | | | | | 11 | 7 |
| .... | 7 | 7 | 11 | 3 | 135 | 90 | 90 | 92 | 139 | 209 | 35 | 14 | 189 | 215 | 404 | | | | | 1 | 2 | | 1 | 408 | 8 |
| .... | 42 | 102 | 39 | 6 | 401 | 314 | 534 | 224 | 335 | 888 | 142 | 44 | 788 | 669 | 1457 | | | | | 6 | 12 | 2 | 2 | 1479 | 9 |
| .... | 9 | 17 | 9 | 1 | 44 | 35 | 89 | 29 | 27 | 128 | 36 | 5 | 120 | 81 | 201 | | | | | | | | | 201 | 10 |
| .... | 2 | 4 | 3 | | 36 | 28 | 35 | 23 | 49 | 60 | 3 | 3 | 71 | 48 | 119 | | | | | 1 | | 1 | 1 | 122 | 11 |
| .... | | | | | 12 | 7 | 3 | 2 | 8 | 14 | 2 | | 13 | 11 | 24 | | | | | | | | | 24 | 12 |
| .... | 2 | | 1 | 1 | 22 | 30 | 45 | 14 | 38 | 59 | 9 | 2 | 72 | 39 | 111 | | | | | | | | 1 | 112 | 13 |
| .... | | 1 | 1 | | 5 | | 3 | 2 | 2 | 7 | | 1 | 4 | 6 | 10 | | | | | | | | | 10 | 14 |
| .... | 1 | 2 | 3 | | 17 | 21 | 42 | 10 | 29 | 48 | 6 | 5 | 45 | 45 | 90 | | | | | | | | | 90 | 15 |
| .... | 2 | 2 | 1 | | 7 | 3 | 2 | 4 | 7 | 6 | 2 | | | 17 | 17 | | | | | | | | | 17 | 16 |
| .... | 1 | 4 | | | 1 | 4 | 8 | 2 | 4 | 6 | 1 | | 8 | 7 | 15 | | | | | | | | | 15 | 17 |
| .... | 4 | 12 | 9 | | 402 | 345 | 263 | 289 | 584 | 623 | 51 | 14 | 670 | 625 | 1295 | | | | | 3 | 2 | 1 | | 1301 | 18 |
| .... | 8 | 3 | | | 9 | 4 | 1 | 2 | 3 | 10 | | | 11 | 5 | 16 | | | | | | | | | 16 | 19 |
| .... | 20 | 24 | 19 | 2 | 184 | 113 | 273 | 177 | 74 | 523 | 88 | 22 | 417 | 329 | 746 | | | | | 2 | | 1 | 1 | 750 | 20 |
| .... | 2 | 1 | 1 | | 25 | 8 | 1 | 19 | 13 | 33 | 4 | 2 | 30 | 19 | 49 | | | | | 3 | | 1 | | 53 | 21 |
| .... | 2 | 1 | | | 1 | 2 | 2 | | 2 | 2 | | | 5 | | 5 | | | | | | | | | 5 | 22 |
| .... | | | | | 1 | 1 | | | | | | 2 | 2 | | 2 | | | | | | | | | 2 | 23 |
| .... | | | | | | 3 | 1 | 2 | 2 | 2 | 1 | 1 | 4 | 2 | 6 | | | | | | | | | 6 | 24 |
| .... | | | | | | | | 1 | | | | | | | | | | | | 1 | | | | 1 | 25 |
| .... | 3 | 2 | 3 | 1 | 17 | 13 | 12 | 16 | 9 | 17 | 7 | 23 | 54 | 4 | 58 | | | | | | | | | 58 | 26 |
| .... | | | | | 21 | 23 | 27 | 8 | 27 | 38 | 9 | 3 | 43 | 35 | 78 | | | | | | 1 | | | 79 | 27 |
| .... | 6 | 6 | | 1 | 38 | 31 | 39 | 29 | 40 | 30 | 16 | 24 | 62 | 73 | 135 | | | | | 2 | | | | 137 | 28 |
| .... | | 2 | 2 | | 13 | 9 | 13 | 11 | 23 | 10 | 4 | 3 | 30 | 16 | 46 | | | | | | | | | 46 | 29 |
| .... | 1 | | 1 | | 4 | 4 | 4 | 2 | 5 | 4 | 3 | 2 | 9 | 5 | 14 | | | | | | | | | 14 | 30 |
| .... | | | | | 1 | | 1 | | | 1 | | 1 | 2 | | 2 | | | | | | | | | 2 | 31 |
| .... | | 1 | | | 10 | 6 | 8 | 2 | 20 | 5 | | 1 | 12 | 14 | 26 | | | | | | | | | 26 | 32 |
| .... | 2 | 1 | | | 123 | 137 | 130 | 59 | 69 | 252 | 82 | 25 | 221 | 219 | 440 | | | | | 2 | 5 | 3 | | 450 | 33 |
| .... | | | | | 14 | 17 | 14 | 10 | 11 | 29 | 8 | 7 | 30 | 24 | 54 | | | | | | | 1 | | 55 | 34 |
| .... | 2 | 2 | 6 | | 82 | 66 | 76 | 35 | 75 | 124 | 17 | 14 | 138 | 119 | 257 | | | | | | | 1 | 2 | 260 | 35 |
| .... | 9 | 6 | 1 | 2 | 62 | 56 | 70 | 43 | 94 | 97 | 21 | 15 | 130 | 102 | 232 | | | | | | | 1 | | 233 | 36 |
| .... | 6 | 3 | 3 | 1 | 115 | 93 | 117 | 83 | 168 | 184 | 20 | 16 | 224 | 175 | 399 | | | | | 2 | 2 | 2 | 3 | 408 | 37 |
| .... | | | | | 1 | 4 | 2 | 1 | 5 | 1 | 2 | | 3 | 5 | 8 | | | | | | | | | 8 | 38 |
| .... | 2 | 1 | | | 3 | 2 | 6 | 2 | | 4 | | 3 | 8 | 5 | 13 | | | | | | | | | 13 | 39 |
| .... | 4 | | 1 | | 7 | 3 | 3 | 1 | 4 | 6 | | 1 | 13 | 1 | 14 | | | | | | | | | 14 | 40 |
| .... | 2 | | 3 | | 5 | 9 | 7 | 7 | 4 | 12 | 2 | 8 | 17 | 11 | 28 | | | | | | | | | 28 | 41 |
| .... | | | | | 1 | 2 | 4 | 3 | 1 | 2 | 4 | 3 | 8 | 2 | 10 | | | | | | | | | 10 | 42 |
| .... | 5 | 4 | 1 | 1 | 11 | 11 | 8 | 7 | 13 | 1 | 2 | | 33 | 4 | 37 | | | | | | | | | 37 | 43 |
| .... | | | | | 1 | 6 | 1 | | 4 | | | | 9 | | 9 | | | | | | | | | 9 | 44 |
| .... | 9 | 6 | 1 | 1 | 41 | 47 | 52 | 31 | 20 | 48 | 36 | 57 | 90 | 82 | 172 | | | | | | | | | 172 | 45 |
| .... | | 1 | | | 2 | 2 | 4 | 4 | 8 | 4 | | | 8 | 3 | 11 | | | | | 1 | | | | 12 | 46 |
| .... | 3 | 2 | 1 | | 46 | 34 | 28 | 26 | 22 | 60 | 20 | 26 | 73 | 59 | 132 | | | | | 1 | 1 | | | 134 | 47 |
| .... | | 1 | | | 5 | 2 | 1 | 1 | 4 | 4 | | 1 | 4 | 5 | 9 | | | | | | | | | 9 | 48 |
| .... | 14 | 4 | 5 | 1 | 10 | 13 | 10 | 7 | 9 | 8 | 1 | | 38 | 2 | 40 | | | | | | | | | 40 | 49 |
| .... | | 2 | | | 3 | 3 | 7 | | | 1 | 4 | 7 | 7 | 6 | 13 | | | | | | | | | 13 | 50 |
| .... | 3 | 7 | 1 | | 111 | 132 | 76 | 41 | 84 | 227 | 37 | 10 | 175 | 179 | 354 | | | | | 6 | 2 | 1 | | 363 | 51 |
| .... | 1 | | | | 1 | 6 | 4 | 3 | 4 | 8 | 2 | | 5 | 9 | 14 | | | | | | | | | 14 | 52 |
| .... | 1 | | 1 | | 3 | 1 | 5 | | | 8 | 3 | 1 | 5 | 4 | 14 | | | | | | | | | 9 | 53 |
| .... | | | | | 4 | 3 | 2 | 4 | 4 | 7 | 2 | | 9 | 4 | 13 | | | | | | | | | 13 | 54 |
| .... | 1 | 1 | 1 | 1 | 1 | | 5 | 3 | 3 | | | | 7 | 1 | 8 | | | | | | 1 | | | 9 | 55 |
| .... | | 2 | 2 | | 6 | 8 | 5 | 8 | 5 | 4 | 5 | 13 | 10 | 16 | 26 | | | | | | 1 | | | 27 | 56 |
| .... | 41 | 30 | 18 | 4 | 169 | 112 | 121 | 99 | 80 | 96 | 41 | 75 | 230 | 268 | 498 | | | | | 4 | 3 | | 1 | 506 | 57 |
| .... | 9 | 9 | 4 | 1 | 67 | 34 | 55 | 41 | 53 | 51 | 17 | 61 | 101 | 95 | 196 | | | | | | 1 | | | 197 | 58 |
| .... | | | 1 | | | 1 | 3 | 2 | 3 | 1 | 1 | | | 6 | 6 | | | | | | | | | 6 | 59 |
| .... | | | | | 1 | 1 | 1 | | | 1 | | 2 | 3 | | 3 | | | | | | | | | 3 | 60 |
| .... | 2 | 4 | 4 | | 32 | 16 | 21 | 17 | 26 | 50 | 1 | 8 | 47 | 35 | 82 | | | | | 1 | 2 | 1 | | 86 | 61 |
| .... | 34 | 33 | 22 | 3 | 429 | 175 | 130 | 159 | 196 | 524 | 79 | 47 | 530 | 348 | 878 | | | | | 6 | 5 | 3 | 3 | 895 | 62 |
| .... | | | | | | 6 | 8 | 2 | 10 | 4 | | | 6 | 10 | 16 | | | | | | | | | 16 | 63 |
| .... | | | | | | 1 | 1 | | 1 | 1 | | | 1 | 1 | 2 | | | | | | | | | 2 | 64 |
| .... | | 1 | | | 18 | 6 | 16 | 8 | 26 | 22 | | | 21 | 26 | 47 | | | | | 1 | | | | 48 | 65 |
| .... | 1 | 1 | 1 | | 11 | 7 | 8 | 9 | 16 | 13 | 3 | 1 | 19 | 16 | 35 | | | | | | | | | 35 | 66 |
| .... | 3 | 2 | 1 | | 21 | 17 | 13 | 16 | 6 | 24 | 11 | 23 | 44 | 22 | 66 | | | | | | | 1 | | 67 | 67 |
| .... | | | | | | 1 | 1 | | | 1 | 1 | | 1 | 1 | 2 | | | | | | | | | 2 | 68 |
| .... | | | | | | 1 | | 1 | | 1 | | 1 | 1 | 1 | 2 | | | | | | | | | 2 | 69 |
| .... | | 1 | | | 25 | 29 | 28 | 19 | 6 | 21 | 15 | 58 | 49 | 51 | 100 | | | | | 1 | | | | 101 | 70 |
| .... | | 1 | | | | | 1 | 4 | | | 5 | | 5 | | 5 | | | | | | | | | 5 | 71 |
| .... | 7 | 45 | 15 | 2 | 167 | 57 | 84 | 242 | 83 | 361 | 11 | 5 | 339 | 190 | 529 | | | | | 12 | 3 | 5 | 2 | 551 | 72 |
| .... | 2 | 2 | 1 | | 18 | 7 | 12 | 5 | 6 | 10 | 7 | 15 | 27 | 15 | 42 | | | | | | | | | 42 | 73 |
| .... | 2 | | | | | | 1 | 1 | 1 | | | | 2 | | 2 | | | | | | | | | 2 | 74 |
| .... | | | | | 1 | 2 | 2 | 1 | | | | | 6 | | 6 | | | | | | | | | 6 | 75 |

## CLASSIFICATION OF DEATHS IN

| | Cause of death. | AGES. | | | | | | | | | | | | | | | | | | NATIVITIES. | | | | | |
|---|---|---|---|---|---|---|---|---|---|---|---|---|---|---|---|---|---|---|---|---|---|---|---|---|---|
| | | Under 1. | | 1 and under 5. | | 5 and under 10. | | 10 and under 20. | | 20 and under 50. | | 50 and under 80. | | 80 and under 100. | | 100 & over. | | Age unknown. | | Born in State. | N. England States. | Middle States. | Southern States. | Southwest'n States. | Northwest'n States. |
| | | M. | F. | M. | F. | M. | F. | M. | F. | M. | F. | M. | F. | M. | F. | M | F. | M | F. | | | | | | |
| 1 | Stomach, disease of | ... | 2 | 1 | ... | 1 | 2 | 2 | ... | 5 | 3 | 5 | 2 | ... | ... | ... | ... | ... | ... | 10 | 4 | 4 | 4 | ... | ... |
| 2 | Suffocation | 3 | 3 | 4 | ... | ... | ... | 1 | ... | ... | ... | 1 | ... | ... | ... | ... | ... | ... | ... | 10 | 1 | 1 | ... | ... | ... |
| 3 | Suicide | ... | ... | ... | ... | ... | ... | 3 | ... | 12 | 5 | 6 | 1 | ... | ... | ... | ... | ... | ... | 8 | 3 | 6 | 3 | .. | 1 |
| 4 | Summer complaint | 23 | 13 | 23 | 22 | ... | 1 | ... | ... | ... | ... | ... | ... | ... | ... | ... | ... | ... | ... | 75 | ... | ... | ... | 1 | 2 |
| 5 | Sun stroke | ... | ... | ... | ... | ... | ... | ... | ... | 1 | ... | ... | ... | ... | ... | ... | ... | ... | ... | ... | ... | ... | ... | ... | 1 |
| 6 | Syphilis | ... | ... | ... | ... | ... | ... | ... | ... | ... | ... | 1 | ... | ... | ... | ... | ... | ... | ... | ... | ... | ... | ... | ... | ... |
| 7 | Teething | 10 | 14 | 22 | 15 | ... | ... | ... | ... | ... | ... | ... | ... | ... | ... | ... | ... | ... | ... | 54 | ... | 3 | 1 | ... | ... |
| 8 | Throat, disease of | 4 | 1 | 15 | 10 | 8 | 12 | 4 | 7 | 1 | 2 | 1 | 1 | ... | ... | ... | ... | ... | ... | 57 | ... | 4 | 3 | ... | 1 |
| 9 | Thrush | 9 | 11 | 5 | 4 | ... | ... | ... | ... | ... | ... | ... | ... | ... | ... | ... | ... | ... | ... | 28 | ... | ... | ... | ... | ... |
| 10 | Tumor | ... | ... | ... | 1 | 1 | ... | 2 | 2 | 3 | 4 | 5 | 2 | ... | ... | ... | ... | ... | ... | 8 | 3 | 7 | ... | ... | ... |
| 11 | Ulcer | 1 | ... | 2 | 1 | ... | 2 | ... | ... | 3 | 7 | 4 | 2 | 1 | ... | ... | ... | ... | ... | 10 | 3 | 3 | 1 | .. | 1 |
| 12 | Uterus, disease of | ... | ... | ... | ... | ... | ... | ... | ... | ... | 4 | ... | ... | ... | ... | ... | ... | ... | ... | 1 | ... | ... | 1 | ... | ... |
| 13 | White swelling | ... | ... | ... | ... | ... | ... | 1 | 1 | 5 | 1 | ... | ... | ... | ... | ... | ... | ... | ... | 6 | ... | ... | 2 | ... | ... |
| 14 | Worms | 4 | 4 | 33 | 33 | 4 | 8 | 3 | ... | ... | 1 | ... | ... | ... | ... | ... | ... | ... | ... | 88 | ... | 1 | ... | ... | ... |
| 15 | Unknown | 596 | 461 | 265 | 249 | 68 | 54 | 70 | 99 | 301 | 336 | 249 | 197 | 35 | 23 | .. | .. | 20 | 10 | 2144 | 80 | 360 | 130 | 4 | 38 |
| | Total | 2485 | 1945 | 3509 | 3164 | 1248 | 1043 | 1191 | 1307 | 4719 | 3794 | 2284 | 1589 | 340 | 269 | 4 | 5 | 38 | 23 | 18125 | 914 | 4029 | 1116 | 59 | 402 |

## CLASSIFICATION OF DEATHS IN EASTERN

*Embracing the following counties: Berks, Bucks, Chester, Delaware, Lancaster,*

| | Cause of death. | Under 1. M. | Under 1. F. | 1 and under 5. M. | 1 and under 5. F. | 5 and under 10. M. | 5 and under 10. F. | 10 and under 20. M. | 10 and under 20. F. | 20 and under 50. M. | 20 and under 50. F. | 50 and under 80. M. | 50 and under 80. F. | 80 and under 100. M. | 80 and under 100. F. | 100 & over. M | 100 & over. F. | Age unknown. M | Age unknown. F. | Born in State. | N. England States. | Middle States. | Southern States. | Southwest'n States. | Northwest'n States. |
|---|---|---|---|---|---|---|---|---|---|---|---|---|---|---|---|---|---|---|---|---|---|---|---|---|---|
| 1 | Abscess | ... | ... | ... | ... | ... | ... | 1 | ... | 1 | 1 | ... | 1 | .. | .. | .. | .. | .. | .. | 3 | ... | 1 | ... | ... | ... |
| 2 | Accident, not specif'd | 2 | 1 | 8 | 1 | 12 | 2 | 12 | 1 | 35 | 1 | 19 | 5 | 2 | 2 | .. | .. | .. | .. | 90 | ... | 1 | ... | ... | ... |
| 3 | ....do...burned | ... | ... | 5 | 7 | ... | 4 | ... | 1 | ... | ... | ... | 1 | .. | 1 | .. | .. | .. | .. | 19 | ... | ... | ... | ... | ... |
| 4 | ....do...drowned | ... | ... | 8 | 4 | 7 | 2 | 9 | 2 | 11 | 2 | 2 | 1 | .. | .. | .. | .. | 2 | .. | 39 | ... | 1 | ... | ... | ... |
| 5 | ....do...scalded | ... | ... | 3 | 2 | ... | ... | ... | ... | ... | ... | ... | ... | .. | .. | .. | .. | .. | .. | 2 | ... | ... | 1 | ... | ... |
| 6 | Apoplexy | 4 | 2 | 4 | 3 | ... | 1 | ... | 2 | 7 | 12 | 36 | 30 | 3 | 5 | .. | .. | .. | .. | 98 | ... | 8 | ... | ... | ... |
| 7 | Asthma | ... | ... | 1 | ... | ... | ... | 1 | 2 | ... | ... | 6 | 3 | 1 | 1 | .. | .. | .. | .. | 13 | ... | ... | ... | ... | ... |
| 8 | Bladder, disease of | ... | ... | ... | ... | ... | ... | ... | ... | ... | ... | 2 | ... | 2 | .. | .. | .. | .. | .. | 3 | ... | ... | ... | ... | ... |
| 9 | Bowels.....do | 2 | 1 | 3 | 2 | ... | ... | 1 | ... | 2 | 1 | ... | ... | 2 | .. | .. | .. | .. | .. | 14 | ... | ... | ... | ... | ... |
| 10 | Brain ......do | 5 | 1 | 3 | 4 | 3 | 3 | ... | 2 | 4 | ... | 3 | 3 | .. | .. | .. | .. | .. | .. | 30 | ... | ... | ... | ... | ... |
| 11 | Bronchitis | 1 | ... | ... | ... | ... | ... | 2 | ... | 1 | 2 | ... | ... | .. | .. | .. | .. | .. | .. | 5 | ... | ... | ... | ... | ... |
| 12 | Cancer | ... | ... | 3 | ... | ... | 2 | 1 | ... | 8 | 6 | 18 | 24 | 5 | 3 | .. | .. | .. | .. | 66 | ... | ... | ... | ... | ... |
| 13 | Carbuncle | ... | ... | ... | ... | ... | ... | ... | ... | 2 | ... | 1 | ... | .. | .. | .. | .. | .. | .. | 3 | ... | ... | ... | ... | ... |
| 14 | Catarrh | 8 | 5 | 4 | 1 | ... | 1 | ... | 1 | ... | 1 | ... | ... | .. | .. | .. | .. | .. | .. | 20 | ... | ... | ... | ... | ... |
| 15 | Childbirth | ... | ... | ... | ... | ... | ... | ... | 3 | ... | 62 | ... | ... | .. | .. | .. | .. | .. | .. | 58 | ... | 1 | 1 | .. | 1 |
| 16 | Cholera | 1 | 5 | 7 | 13 | 9 | 4 | 8 | 4 | 50 | 23 | 10 | 22 | 6 | 2 | .. | .. | .. | .. | 114 | ... | 6 | 6 | .. | ... |
| 17 | ...do...infantum | 14 | 6 | 5 | 6 | ... | ... | ... | ... | ... | ... | ... | ... | .. | .. | .. | .. | .. | .. | 29 | ... | 2 | ... | ... | ... |
| 18 | ...do...morbus | 9 | 6 | 11 | 8 | ... | 3 | 2 | 2 | 11 | 6 | 7 | 5 | 2 | 1 | .. | .. | .. | .. | 66 | ... | 2 | ... | ... | ... |
| 19 | Chorea | ... | 1 | ... | ... | ... | ... | ... | ... | ... | 1 | ... | ... | .. | .. | .. | .. | .. | .. | 2 | ... | ... | ... | ... | ... |
| 20 | Colic | 2 | ... | 1 | 1 | ... | ... | ... | 1 | 3 | 2 | 2 | 2 | .. | .. | .. | .. | .. | .. | 12 | ... | 1 | ... | ... | ... |
| 21 | Congest'n, not specf'd | ... | ... | ... | ... | ... | ... | ... | ... | 1 | ... | ... | ... | .. | .. | .. | .. | .. | .. | 1 | ... | ... | ... | ... | ... |
| 22 | ....do....brain | ... | ... | 1 | ... | ... | ... | 1 | 2 | ... | ... | ... | 1 | .. | .. | .. | .. | .. | .. | 5 | ... | ... | ... | ... | ... |
| 23 | Consumption | 11 | 14 | 23 | 23 | 9 | 6 | 33 | 45 | 214 | 226 | 158 | 109 | 11 | 10 | .. | .. | .. | .. | 792 | ... | 27 | 5 | 1 | 1 |
| 24 | Convulsions | 82 | 65 | 30 | 28 | 4 | 5 | ... | 3 | 9 | 5 | 1 | ... | .. | .. | .. | .. | .. | .. | 229 | ... | 2 | ... | ... | ... |
| 25 | Cramp | 2 | ... | ... | 1 | ... | ... | ... | 1 | 3 | 1 | 4 | 3 | .. | .. | .. | .. | .. | .. | 15 | ... | ... | ... | ... | ... |
| 26 | Croup | 29 | 22 | 67 | 57 | 11 | 6 | 3 | ... | 1 | 1 | ... | ... | .. | .. | .. | .. | .. | .. | 192 | ... | 2 | ... | ... | ... |
| 27 | Debility | 7 | 6 | ... | 1 | ... | ... | ... | ... | ... | ... | ... | ... | .. | .. | .. | .. | .. | .. | 14 | ... | ... | ... | ... | ... |
| 28 | Diabetes | ... | ... | ... | ... | ... | ... | ... | ... | ... | 1 | 1 | 2 | .. | .. | .. | .. | .. | .. | 4 | ... | ... | ... | ... | ... |
| 29 | Diarrhœa | 30 | 13 | 25 | 25 | 3 | 9 | 3 | ... | 4 | 5 | 12 | 5 | 2 | 2 | .. | .. | 1 | .. | 128 | ... | 4 | ... | .. | 1 |
| 30 | Dropsy | 16 | 15 | 23 | 13 | 10 | 3 | 6 | 10 | 25 | 33 | 66 | 61 | 8 | 6 | .. | .. | .. | .. | 261 | ... | 16 | ... | .. | ... |
| 31 | Dysentery | 115 | 93 | 201 | 194 | 68 | 55 | 52 | 40 | 51 | 46 | 25 | 34 | 6 | 7 | .. | .. | 1 | .. | 947 | ... | 7 | ... | 1 | ... |
| 32 | Dyspepsia | 1 | ... | ... | ... | ... | ... | ... | 1 | 4 | 3 | 5 | 4 | 1 | .. | .. | .. | .. | .. | 17 | ... | 1 | ... | ... | ... |
| 33 | Epilepsy | 2 | ... | ... | ... | ... | ... | ... | 2 | 1 | ... | ... | ... | .. | .. | .. | .. | .. | .. | 5 | ... | ... | ... | ... | ... |
| 34 | Erysipelas | 11 | 6 | 2 | 4 | 1 | 1 | 1 | 4 | 1 | 8 | 9 | 9 | .. | 1 | .. | .. | .. | .. | 48 | ... | 2 | 1 | .. | ... |
| 35 | Fever, not specified | 82 | 18 | 30 | 20 | 11 | 5 | 10 | 11 | 39 | 24 | 11 | 12 | 1 | 1 | .. | .. | .. | .. | 216 | ... | 5 | .. | .. | ... |
| 36 | ..do..bilious | 3 | ... | 6 | 5 | 1 | ... | 5 | 3 | 23 | 12 | 9 | 5 | .. | 1 | .. | .. | .. | .. | 66 | ... | 1 | ... | ... | ... |
| 37 | ..do..brain | 9 | 5 | 15 | 19 | 8 | 6 | 8 | 3 | 10 | 3 | ... | ... | .. | .. | .. | .. | .. | .. | 80 | ... | 1 | ... | ... | ... |
| 38 | ..do..catarrhal | 8 | 4 | 13 | 11 | 1 | 1 | ... | ... | 1 | 1 | 3 | 2 | .. | .. | .. | .. | .. | .. | 44 | ... | ... | ... | ... | ... |
| 39 | ..do..congestive | ... | ... | ... | 1 | ... | ... | ... | ... | ... | ... | 1 | ... | .. | .. | .. | .. | .. | .. | 2 | ... | ... | ... | ... | ... |
| 40 | ..do..intermittent | 2 | 3 | 2 | 4 | 2 | 3 | 3 | 1 | 11 | 5 | 1 | 4 | .. | .. | .. | .. | .. | .. | 37 | ... | ... | ... | .. | ... |
| 41 | ..do..puerperal | ... | ... | ... | ... | ... | ... | ... | ... | ... | 10 | ... | ... | .. | .. | .. | .. | .. | .. | 9 | ... | 1 | ... | ... | ... |
| 42 | ..do..remittent | ... | ... | ... | ... | ... | 1 | 1 | 2 | 1 | 1 | ... | ... | .. | .. | .. | .. | .. | .. | 5 | ... | 1 | ... | ... | ... |
| 43 | ..do..scarlet | 38 | 35 | 205 | 180 | 78 | 119 | 11 | 34 | 2 | 2 | ... | 1 | 1 | .. | .. | .. | .. | .. | 690 | ... | 6 | 2 | .. | ... |
| 44 | ..do..ship | ... | ... | ... | ... | 1 | ... | ... | 2 | ... | ... | 1 | 1 | .. | .. | .. | .. | .. | .. | 2 | ... | ... | ... | ... | ... |
| 45 | ..do..typhus | ... | ... | 5 | 5 | 4 | 7 | 14 | 28 | 41 | 31 | 8 | 10 | 1 | .. | .. | .. | .. | .. | 145 | ... | 1 | ... | ... | ... |
| 46 | Fracture | ... | ... | ... | ... | ... | ... | ... | ... | ... | ... | ... | 1 | 1 | .. | .. | .. | .. | .. | 2 | ... | ... | ... | ... | ... |
| 47 | Gout | ... | ... | ... | ... | ... | ... | ... | ... | ... | ... | 1 | ... | .. | .. | .. | .. | .. | .. | 1 | ... | ... | ... | ... | ... |
| 48 | Gravel | ... | ... | ... | ... | ... | ... | ... | ... | ... | ... | 9 | ... | .. | .. | .. | .. | .. | .. | 9 | ... | ... | ... | ... | ... |

## E STATE OF OHIO—AGGREGATE—Continued.

| NATIVITIES. | | | | SEASON OF DECEASE. | | | | DURATION OF SICKNESS. | | | | WHITES. | | | COLORED. | | | | | | | | | |
|---|---|---|---|---|---|---|---|---|---|---|---|---|---|---|---|---|---|---|---|---|---|---|---|---|
| | | | | | | | | | | | | | | | Slaves. | | | | Free. | | | | | |
| | | | | | | | | | | | | | | | Black. | | Mulatto. | | Bl'k. | | Mul. | | | |
| Ireland. | Germany. | Other foreign countries. | Unknown. | Spring. | Summer. | Autumn. | Winter. | Under 1 week. | 1 week and under 1 month. | 1 month and under 3 months. | 3 months and over. | Males. | Females. | Total. | M. | F. | M. | F. | M | F. | M | F. | Aggregate deaths. | |
| 1 | | | | 2 | 5 | 9 | 7 | 6 | 10 | 3 | 2 | 14 | 9 | 23 | | | | | | | | | 23 | 1 |
| | | | | 2 | 3 | 1 | 6 | 12 | | | | 9 | 3 | 12 | | | | | | | | | 12 | 2 |
| 1 | 2 | 2 | 1 | 11 | 5 | 5 | 6 | 8 | | | | 20 | 6 | 26 | | | | | | | 1 | | 27 | 3 |
| | 1 | 1 | | 2 | 47 | 30 | 2 | 27 | 21 | 7 | 24 | 46 | 36 | 82 | | | | | | | | | 82 | 4 |
| | | | | | | 1 | | | 1 | | | 1 | | 1 | | | | | | | | | 1 | 5 |
| | | | 1 | 1 | | | | | | | | 1 | | 1 | | | | | | | | | 1 | 6 |
| 1 | 2 | | | 11 | 21 | 19 | 10 | 18 | 19 | 11 | 3 | 32 | 29 | 61 | | | | | | | | | 61 | 7 |
| | | 1 | | 16 | 14 | 24 | 11 | 24 | 34 | 3 | 1 | 33 | 33 | 66 | | | | | | | | | 66 | 8 |
| | | 1 | | 6 | 13 | 10 | | 9 | 13 | 2 | 4 | 14 | 15 | 29 | | | | | | | | | 29 | 9 |
| 1 | 1 | | | 9 | 5 | 5 | 1 | 2 | | 4 | 13 | 11 | 9 | 20 | | | | | | | | | 20 | 10 |
| 8 | | 1 | 1 | 7 | 3 | 11 | 2 | 2 | 4 | 5 | 11 | 11 | 12 | 23 | | | | | | | | | 23 | 11 |
| | 1 | | 1 | 1 | 1 | 1 | 1 | | 1 | 1 | 1 | | 4 | 4 | | | | | | | | | 4 | 12 |
| | | | | 5 | 2 | 1 | | 1 | 2 | 2 | 3 | 6 | 2 | 8 | | | | | | | | | 8 | 13 |
| | | | 1 | 32 | 18 | 29 | 11 | 41 | 41 | 3 | 2 | 42 | 45 | 87 | | | | | 1 | 1 | 1 | | 90 | 14 |
| 59 | 140 | 59 | 19 | 849 | 774 | 815 | 546 | 951 | 617 | 200 | 606 | 1580 | 1397 | 2977 | | | | | 11 | 18 | 13 | 14 | 3033 | 15 |
| 977 | 2422 | 740 | 173 | 6122 | 9520 | 9010 | 4159 | 11484 | 9072 | 1855 | 3818 | 15590 | 12956 | 28546 | | | | | 129 | 123 | 99 | 60 | 28957 | |

## TION OF THE STATE OF PENNSYLVANIA.

*non, Lehigh, Monroe, Montgomery, Northampton, Pike, and York.*

| Ireland. | Germany. | Other foreign countries. | Unknown. | Spring. | Summer. | Autumn. | Winter. | Under 1 week. | 1 week and under 1 month. | 1 month and under 3 months. | 3 months and over. | Males. | Females. | Total. | Slaves Black M. | Slaves Black F. | Slaves Mulatto M. | Slaves Mulatto F. | Free Bl'k M. | Free Bl'k F. | Free Mul. M. | Free Mul. F. | Aggregate deaths. | |
|---|---|---|---|---|---|---|---|---|---|---|---|---|---|---|---|---|---|---|---|---|---|---|---|---|
| | | | | 1 | 1 | 2 | | 1 | | 2 | 1 | 2 | 2 | 4 | | | | | | | | | 4 | 1 |
| 8 | 2 | 3 | | 26 | 26 | 38 | 14 | 83 | 15 | | 1 | 89 | 14 | 103 | | | | | 1 | | | | 104 | 2 |
| | | | | 5 | 4 | 7 | 3 | 17 | 2 | | | 5 | 14 | 19 | | | | | | | | | 19 | 3 |
| 7 | 2 | 1 | | 10 | 15 | 17 | 7 | 50 | | | | 39 | 10 | 49 | | | | | | | | 1 | 50 | 4 |
| 1 | 1 | | | 2 | 1 | 1 | 1 | 4 | 1 | | | 3 | 2 | 5 | | | | | | | | | 5 | 5 |
| 2 | | 1 | | 35 | 31 | 22 | 21 | 74 | 22 | 2 | 7 | 54 | 55 | 109 | | | | | | | | | 109 | 6 |
| 1 | | 1 | | 7 | 4 | | 4 | | 6 | 1 | 8 | 9 | 6 | 15 | | | | | | | | | 15 | 7 |
| | 1 | | | | 2 | | 2 | | 2 | | 2 | 4 | | 4 | | | | | | | | | 4 | 8 |
| | | | | 2 | 5 | 5 | 2 | 3 | 7 | 3 | 1 | 10 | 4 | 14 | | | | | | | | | 14 | 9 |
| 1 | | | | 11 | 9 | 7 | 4 | 11 | 16 | 1 | 1 | 15 | 12 | 27 | | | | | 3 | 1 | | | 31 | 10 |
| | 1 | | | 2 | 2 | 2 | | | 2 | | 4 | 4 | 2 | 6 | | | | | | | | | 6 | 11 |
| 2 | 2 | | | 16 | 24 | 17 | 13 | | 9 | 13 | 48 | 35 | 35 | 70 | | | | | | | | | 70 | 12 |
| | | | | 2 | 1 | | | | 3 | | | 3 | | 3 | | | | | | | | | 3 | 13 |
| | | 1 | | 13 | 4 | | 4 | 8 | 10 | 2 | 1 | 12 | 8 | 20 | | | | | | 1 | | | 21 | 14 |
| 2 | | 2 | | 22 | 12 | 16 | 15 | 27 | 21 | 4 | 2 | | 64 | 64 | | | | | | | | 1 | 65 | 15 |
| 22 | 6 | 3 | 37 | 4 | 137 | 49 | 4 | 174 | 19 | | 1 | 107 | 66 | 173 | | | | | 12 | 6 | 2 | 1 | 194 | 16 |
| | | | | 1 | 11 | 18 | 1 | 14 | 16 | 1 | | 18 | 11 | 29 | | | | | | | 1 | 1 | 31 | 17 |
| 1 | 3 | 1 | | 4 | 18 | 44 | 7 | 55 | 18 | | | 42 | 31 | 73 | | | | | | | | | 73 | 18 |
| | | | | 1 | 1 | | | | | 1 | 1 | | 2 | 2 | | | | | | | | | 2 | 19 |
| 1 | | | | | 7 | 4 | 3 | 12 | 1 | | 1 | 8 | 6 | 14 | | | | | | | | | 14 | 20 |
| | | | | 1 | | | | | | | 1 | 1 | | 1 | | | | | | | | | 1 | 21 |
| | | | | 2 | 1 | 1 | 1 | 2 | 2 | | 1 | 1 | 3 | 4 | | | | | 1 | | | | 5 | 22 |
| 32 | 16 | 14 | 4 | 289 | 226 | 179 | 198 | 35 | 139 | 126 | 575 | 438 | 412 | 850 | | | | | 12 | 17 | 9 | 4 | 892 | 23 |
| 1 | | | | 76 | 56 | 54 | 45 | 144 | 55 | 10 | 13 | 120 | 101 | 221 | | | | | 4 | 3 | 2 | 2 | 232 | 24 |
| | | | | 5 | 3 | 2 | 5 | 8 | 4 | | 2 | 9 | 6 | 15 | | | | | | | | | 15 | 25 |
| | 1 | 2 | | 62 | 33 | 40 | 62 | 144 | 51 | 1 | | 107 | 84 | 191 | | | | | 4 | 1 | | 1 | 197 | 26 |
| | | | | 4 | 2 | 6 | 2 | 8 | 4 | | 2 | 7 | 7 | 14 | | | | | | | | | 14 | 27 |
| | | | | 1 | 1 | 1 | 1 | | 1 | 1 | 2 | 1 | 3 | 4 | | | | | | | | | 4 | 28 |
| 5 | | 1 | | 9 | 35 | 82 | 12 | 36 | 76 | 14 | 9 | 77 | 56 | 133 | | | | | 3 | 2 | | 1 | 139 | 29 |
| 7 | 8 | 3 | | 89 | 66 | 75 | 64 | 21 | 73 | 53 | 141 | 146 | 134 | 280 | | | | | 7 | 6 | 1 | 1 | 295 | 30 |
| 16 | 11 | 5 | | 43 | 95 | 784 | 64 | 339 | 556 | 59 | 18 | 508 | 465 | 973 | | | | | 8 | 3 | 3 | 1 | 988 | 31 |
| 1 | | | | 2 | 6 | 7 | 4 | | 6 | 2 | 11 | 11 | 8 | 19 | | | | | | | | | 19 | 32 |
| | | | | 1 | 3 | 1 | | 2 | 2 | | 1 | 2 | 2 | 4 | | | | | 1 | | | | 5 | 33 |
| 3 | 3 | 1 | | 20 | 22 | 9 | 7 | 11 | 35 | 9 | 3 | 25 | 30 | 55 | | | | | | 2 | | 1 | 58 | 34 |
| 1 | 2 | 1 | | 69 | 48 | 69 | 36 | 58 | 132 | 21 | 9 | 132 | 91 | 223 | | | | | 1 | | 1 | | 225 | 35 |
| 4 | 2 | | | 12 | 17 | 33 | 11 | 8 | 58 | 5 | 2 | 45 | 26 | 71 | | | | | 2 | | | | 73 | 36 |
| 2 | 1 | 2 | | 22 | 27 | 19 | 18 | 29 | 53 | 3 | 1 | 49 | 36 | 85 | | | | | 1 | | | | 86 | 37 |
| 1 | | | | 25 | 6 | 8 | 6 | 9 | 32 | 2 | 2 | 25 | 19 | 44 | | | | | 1 | | | | 45 | 38 |
| | | | | | 1 | 1 | | | 2 | | | 1 | 1 | 2 | | | | | | | | | 2 | 39 |
| 3 | | 1 | | 11 | 4 | 16 | 10 | 5 | 31 | 5 | | 21 | 18 | 39 | | | | | | 1 | | 1 | 41 | 40 |
| | | | | 4 | 4 | 1 | 1 | 1 | 8 | 1 | | | 10 | 10 | | | | | | | | | 10 | 41 |
| | | | | | 2 | 2 | 2 | 1 | 5 | | | 2 | 4 | 6 | | | | | | | | | 6 | 42 |
| 2 | | 5 | 1 | 332 | 104 | 86 | 159 | 302 | 349 | 27 | 3 | 333 | 365 | 698 | | | | | 1 | 4 | 1 | 2 | 706 | 43 |
| 3 | | | | | 1 | 3 | 1 | | 2 | | | 2 | 3 | 5 | | | | | | | | | 5 | 44 |
| 4 | 1 | 3 | | 36 | 23 | 57 | 38 | 14 | 119 | 17 | 4 | 72 | 81 | 153 | | | | | | | 1 | | 154 | 45 |
| | | | | 1 | 1 | | | | 2 | | | 1 | 1 | 2 | | | | | | | | | 2 | 46 |
| | | | | | | 1 | | 1 | | | | 1 | | 1 | | | | | | | | | 1 | 47 |
| | | | | 3 | 3 | | 3 | | 5 | | 3 | 9 | | 9 | | | | | | | | | 9 | 48 |

## CLASSIFICATION OF DEATHS IN EASTERN

| | Cause of death. | AGES. | | | | | | | | | | | | | | | | | | NATIVITIES. | | | | | |
|---|---|---|---|---|---|---|---|---|---|---|---|---|---|---|---|---|---|---|---|---|---|---|---|---|---|
| | | Under 1. | | 1 and under 5. | | 5 and under 10. | | 10 and under 20. | | 20 and under 50. | | 50 and under 80. | | 80 and under 100. | | 100 & over. | | Age unknown. | | Born in State. | N. England States. | Middle States. | Southern States. | Southwest'n States. | Northwest'n States. |
| | | M. | F. | M. | F. | M. | F. | M. | F. | M. | F. | M. | F. | M | F. | M | F. | M | F. | | | | | | |
| 1 | Heart, disease of.... | 3 | 4 | 2 | 1 | 2 | ... | 4 | 3 | 8 | 5 | 18 | 10 | 1 | .. | .. | .. | .. | 1 | 55 | .. | 2 | ... | ... | ... |
| 2 | Hemorrhage ........ | 1 | ... | ... | ... | ... | ... | 1 | ... | 1 | 2 | 1 | 1 | .. | .. | .. | .. | .. | .. | 7 | .. | ... | ... | ... | ... |
| 3 | Hernia ........ | ... | ... | ... | ... | ... | ... | 2 | ... | 1 | 2 | 3 | ... | 1 | .. | .. | .. | .. | .. | 7 | .. | ... | ... | ... | ... |
| 4 | Hip, disease of...... | ... | ... | ... | ... | ... | ... | 1 | ... | 1 | ... | ... | ... | .. | .. | .. | .. | .. | .. | 2 | .. | ... | ... | ... | ... |
| 5 | Hives ........... | 2 | 1 | 1 | 1 | 1 | 1 | ... | ... | ... | ... | ... | ... | .. | .. | .. | .. | .. | .. | 7 | .. | ... | ... | ... | ... |
| 6 | Hooping cough...... | 7 | 5 | 6 | 9 | 2 | ... | 1 | ... | ... | ... | ... | ... | .. | .. | .. | .. | .. | .. | 28 | .. | ... | ... | ... | ... |
| 7 | Hydrocephalus...... | 7 | 8 | 11 | 5 | 1 | 1 | ... | 1 | ... | ... | ... | ... | .. | .. | .. | .. | .. | .. | 33 | .. | ... | ... | ... | ... |
| 8 | Inflamat'n, not spec'd | 10 | 3 | 10 | 5 | ... | 1 | 2 | 1 | 6 | 5 | 5 | 5 | 1 | 1 | .. | .. | .. | .. | 52 | .. | 1 | ... | ... | ... |
| 9 | ....do....bowels ... | 6 | 4 | 5 | 4 | 2 | 3 | 1 | ... | 8 | 3 | 8 | ... | 1 | .. | .. | .. | .. | .. | 40 | .. | 1 | 1 | ... | ... |
| 10 | ....do....brain .... | 13 | 10 | 19 | 9 | 6 | 6 | 3 | 2 | 4 | 3 | 4 | 1 | .. | .. | .. | .. | .. | .. | 77 | .. | ... | 1 | ... | ... |
| 11 | ....do....stomach.. | ... | ... | 1 | ... | 1 | ... | ... | ... | ... | ... | ... | ... | .. | .. | .. | .. | .. | .. | 1 | .. | ... | ... | ... | ... |
| 12 | Influenza.......... | ... | ... | 1 | ... | ... | ... | ... | ... | ... | ... | 1 | ... | .. | .. | .. | .. | .. | .. | 2 | .. | ... | ... | ... | ... |
| 13 | Insanity.......... | ... | ... | ... | ... | ... | ... | ... | ... | 2 | 3 | 2 | ... | .. | .. | .. | .. | .. | .. | 6 | .. | ... | ... | ... | ... |
| 14 | Intemperance ...... | ... | ... | ... | ... | ... | ... | ... | ... | 1 | ... | 6 | ... | .. | .. | .. | .. | .. | .. | 6 | .. | ... | ... | ... | ... |
| 15 | Jaundice ......... | ... | ... | ... | ... | ... | ... | ... | ... | 1 | ... | 1 | 5 | .. | .. | .. | .. | .. | .. | 7 | .. | ... | ... | ... | ... |
| 16 | Kidneys, disease of.. | ... | ... | ... | ... | ... | ... | ... | 1 | 1 | 3 | 3 | 1 | .. | 1 | .. | .. | .. | .. | 10 | .. | ... | ... | ... | ... |
| 17 | Killed ........... | ... | ... | ... | ... | ... | ... | 1 | ... | 3 | ... | ... | ... | .. | .. | .. | .. | .. | .. | ... | .. | 2 | ... | ... | ... |
| 18 | Liver, disease of..... | 7 | ... | 1 | 3 | ... | ... | 1 | 1 | 2 | 8 | 5 | 9 | 1 | .. | .. | .. | .. | .. | 31 | 1 | 4 | ... | ... | ... |
| 19 | Lockjaw........... | 1 | ... | ... | ... | ... | ... | 1 | ... | 1 | 1 | ... | ... | .. | .. | .. | .. | .. | .. | 3 | .. | ... | ... | ... | ... |
| 20 | Lungs, disease of.... | 1 | 3 | 3 | 3 | 1 | 1 | ... | 1 | 4 | 2 | 5 | 4 | 2 | 1 | .. | .. | .. | .. | 29 | .. | ... | 1 | ... | ... |
| 21 | Malformation ....... | 2 | 1 | ... | ... | ... | ... | ... | ... | ... | ... | ... | ... | .. | .. | .. | .. | .. | .. | 3 | .. | ... | ... | ... | ... |
| 22 | Mania-a-potu....... | ... | ... | ... | ... | ... | ... | ... | ... | 6 | ... | 3 | ... | .. | .. | .. | .. | .. | .. | 7 | .. | ... | ... | ... | ... |
| 23 | Marasmus ......... | 4 | ... | ... | 1 | ... | ... | 3 | ... | 1 | 2 | 1 | ... | .. | .. | .. | .. | .. | .. | 10 | 1 | ... | ... | ... | ... |
| 24 | Measles ........... | 2 | 2 | 9 | 10 | 2 | 2 | 1 | ... | ... | 1 | 1 | ... | .. | .. | .. | .. | .. | .. | 28 | .. | ... | ... | ... | ... |
| 25 | Mortification ....... | 1 | 1 | ... | ... | ... | ... | ... | ... | 1 | 3 | ... | ... | 1 | .. | .. | .. | .. | .. | 7 | .. | ... | ... | ... | ... |
| 26 | Mumps ........... | ... | ... | 1 | ... | ... | ... | ... | 1 | ... | ... | ... | ... | .. | .. | .. | .. | .. | .. | 2 | .. | ... | ... | ... | ... |
| 27 | Murder............ | ... | ... | ... | ... | ... | ... | ... | 1 | 1 | ... | ... | ... | .. | .. | .. | .. | .. | .. | 1 | .. | ... | ... | ... | ... |
| 28 | Neuralgia ......... | ... | ... | ... | ... | ... | ... | ... | 1 | ... | 2 | ... | 1 | .. | .. | .. | .. | .. | .. | 4 | .. | ... | ... | ... | ... |
| 29 | Old age .......... | ... | ... | ... | ... | ... | ... | ... | ... | ... | ... | 36 | 53 | 64 | 91 | 1 | .. | .. | .. | 222 | .. | 4 | ... | ... | ... |
| 30 | Paralysis .......... | 1 | 1 | 1 | 2 | ... | 1 | 6 | 3 | 8 | 3 | 43 | 42 | 13 | 8 | 1 | .. | .. | .. | 123 | .. | 3 | ... | ... | ... |
| 31 | Pleurisy .......... | 1 | 3 | 2 | 4 | ... | 2 | 2 | 3 | 11 | 8 | 12 | 6 | .. | .. | .. | .. | .. | .. | 46 | .. | 4 | ... | ... | ... |
| 32 | Pneumonia ........ | 14 | 13 | 17 | 14 | 3 | 4 | 2 | 7 | 12 | 5 | 9 | 12 | .. | .. | .. | .. | .. | .. | 105 | .. | 2 | ... | ... | ... |
| 33 | Poison............ | ... | ... | 1 | ... | ... | ... | ... | ... | 1 | ... | ... | ... | .. | .. | .. | .. | .. | .. | 2 | .. | ... | ... | ... | ... |
| 34 | Putrid sore throat... | ... | ... | 2 | 2 | 1 | 1 | 1 | 1 | ... | ... | ... | ... | 1 | .. | .. | .. | .. | .. | 9 | .. | ... | ... | ... | ... |
| 35 | Quinsy .......... | 1 | ... | 2 | ... | 1 | ... | ... | 1 | ... | ... | 1 | 1 | .. | .. | .. | .. | .. | .. | 6 | .. | 1 | ... | ... | ... |
| 36 | Rheumatism........ | ... | 1 | 1 | 3 | 2 | 1 | 4 | 6 | 2 | 4 | 7 | 5 | .. | .. | .. | .. | .. | .. | 36 | .. | ... | ... | ... | ... |
| 37 | Rickets........... | ... | 1 | 1 | ... | ... | ... | ... | ... | ... | ... | ... | ... | .. | .. | .. | .. | .. | .. | 2 | .. | ... | ... | ... | ... |
| 38 | Scrofula ......... | 1 | 1 | 5 | 3 | 1 | 5 | 3 | 3 | 1 | 4 | ... | ... | .. | .. | .. | .. | .. | .. | 27 | .. | ... | ... | ... | ... |
| 39 | Small pox.......... | 2 | 6 | 1 | 4 | 2 | 1 | 2 | 2 | 6 | 2 | 3 | 1 | .. | .. | .. | .. | .. | .. | 28 | .. | 1 | ... | ... | ... |
| 40 | Spine, disease of .... | 1 | ... | 2 | ... | 2 | 2 | 1 | 1 | 4 | ... | ... | ... | .. | .. | .. | .. | .. | .. | 12 | .. | ... | ... | ... | ... |
| 41 | Stillborn.......... | 1 | 3 | ... | ... | ... | ... | ... | ... | ... | ... | ... | ... | .. | .. | .. | .. | .. | .. | 4 | .. | ... | ... | ... | ... |
| 42 | Stomach, disease of.. | ... | ... | ... | ... | ... | ... | ... | ... | ... | ... | 1 | ... | .. | .. | .. | .. | .. | .. | 1 | .. | ... | ... | ... | ... |
| 43 | Suffocation ........ | ... | ... | 1 | ... | ... | ... | ... | ... | 1 | ... | ... | ... | .. | .. | .. | .. | .. | .. | 2 | .. | ... | ... | ... | ... |
| 44 | Suicide .......... | ... | ... | ... | ... | ... | ... | ... | ... | 2 | ... | 2 | 2 | .. | .. | .. | .. | .. | .. | 4 | .. | 1 | ... | ... | ... |
| 45 | Summer complaint.. | 7 | 4 | 7 | 8 | 1 | 1 | ... | ... | ... | ... | ... | ... | .. | .. | .. | .. | .. | .. | 27 | .. | ... | ... | ... | ... |
| 46 | Sun, stroke of....... | ... | ... | ... | ... | ... | ... | ... | ... | 2 | ... | ... | ... | .. | .. | .. | .. | .. | .. | ... | .. | ... | ... | ... | ... |
| 47 | Syphilis.......... | ... | ... | ... | ... | ... | ... | ... | ... | ... | 1 | ... | ... | .. | .. | .. | .. | .. | .. | 1 | .. | ... | ... | ... | ... |
| 48 | Teething.......... | 3 | 3 | 3 | 1 | ... | ... | ... | ... | ... | ... | ... | ... | .. | .. | .. | .. | .. | .. | 10 | .. | ... | ... | ... | ... |
| 49 | Throat, disease of.... | 5 | 1 | 5 | 3 | 8 | 5 | 2 | 8 | 2 | 2 | 1 | ... | 1 | .. | .. | .. | .. | .. | 38 | .. | 4 | ... | ... | ... |
| 50 | Thrush............ | 1 | ... | ... | 1 | ... | ... | ... | ... | ... | ... | ... | ... | .. | .. | .. | .. | .. | .. | 2 | .. | ... | ... | ... | ... |
| 51 | Tumor .......... | ... | 1 | ... | ... | ... | ... | ... | 1 | 1 | 3 | ... | 3 | .. | 1 | .. | .. | .. | .. | 9 | .. | ... | ... | ... | ... |
| 52 | Ulcer.......... | ... | ... | ... | ... | ... | ... | 1 | ... | ... | ... | ... | ... | 1 | .. | .. | .. | .. | .. | 2 | .. | ... | ... | ... | ... |
| 53 | Uterus, disease of ... | ... | ... | ... | ... | ... | ... | ... | ... | ... | 1 | ... | ... | .. | .. | .. | .. | .. | .. | 1 | .. | ... | ... | ... | ... |
| 54 | Venereal.......... | ... | ... | ... | ... | ... | ... | ... | ... | ... | ... | 1 | ... | .. | .. | .. | .. | .. | .. | ... | .. | ... | ... | ... | ... |
| 55 | White swelling...... | ... | ... | ... | ... | 2 | ... | 1 | ... | 1 | ... | ... | ... | .. | .. | .. | .. | .. | .. | 4 | .. | ... | ... | ... | ... |
| 56 | Worms .......... | ... | ... | 4 | 2 | ... | 1 | ... | 1 | ... | ... | ... | ... | .. | .. | .. | .. | .. | .. | 6 | .. | ... | ... | ... | ... |
| 57 | Unknown .......... | 173 | 162 | 78 | 59 | 21 | 22 | 27 | 43 | 91 | 76 | 82 | 84 | 14 | 9 | .. | .. | 54 | 25 | 991 | 1 | 12 | 1 | ... | 1 |
| | Total.......... | 724 | 569 | 917 | 800 | 305 | 310 | 262 | 307 | 775 | 692 | 726 | 607 | 157 | 155 | 2 | .. | 58 | 26 | 6747 | 3 | 142 | 20 | 2 | 4 |

## CLASSIFICATION OF DEATHS IN WESTERN

*Embracing the following counties: Alleghany, Armstrong, Beaver, Butler, Cambria, Clarion, Potter, Somersett, Warren, Wash*

| | Cause of death. | Under 1 M. | Under 1 F. | 1–5 M. | 1–5 F. | 5–10 M. | 5–10 F. | 10–20 M. | 10–20 F. | 20–50 M. | 20–50 F. | 50–80 M. | 50–80 F. | 80–100 M | 80–100 F. | 100 & over M | 100 & over F. | Age unknown M | Age unknown F. | Born in State. | N. England States. | Middle States. | Southern States. | Southwest'n States. | Northwest'n States. |
|---|---|---|---|---|---|---|---|---|---|---|---|---|---|---|---|---|---|---|---|---|---|---|---|---|---|
| 1 | Accident, not specif'd | 2 | ... | 8 | 2 | 7 | 2 | 20 | 4 | 23 | 2 | 11 | 1 | 1 | .. | .. | .. | .. | .. | 59 | 1 | 5 | 1 | ... | 5 |
| 2 | ....do...burned.... | 2 | 1 | 7 | 9 | 1 | 6 | ... | 1 | .... | 1 | 1 | ... | .. | .. | .. | .. | .. | .. | 26 | .. | 2 | ... | ... | ... |
| 3 | ....do...drowned... | .... | 1 | 2 | 4 | 4 | 1 | 9 | 1 | 24 | 4 | 5 | ... | .. | .. | .. | .. | .. | .. | 30 | 1 | 4 | 2 | ... | 2 |
| 4 | ....do...scalded .: | .... | 1 | 8 | 7 | 2 | 1 | ... | ... | 1 | 1 | ... | 1 | .. | .. | .. | .. | .. | .. | 21 | .. | ... | ... | ... | ... |
| 5 | Apoplexy.......... | 1 | 1 | 1 | ... | 1 | 1 | 3 | ... | 6 | 7 | 21 | 10 | 3 | .. | .. | .. | .. | .. | 33 | 3 | 3 | 1 | ... | ... |
| 6 | Asthma .... ....... | .... | 2 | ... | ... | ... | ... | ... | ... | 1 | 2 | 3 | 2 | .. | 1 | .. | .. | .. | .. | 7 | .. | ... | ... | ... | ... |

## CTION OF THE STATE OF PENNSYLVANIA—Continued.

| NATIVITIES. | | | | | SEASON OF DECEASE. | | | | DURATION OF SICKNESS. | | | | WHITES. | | | COLORED. | | | | | | | | | |
|---|---|---|---|---|---|---|---|---|---|---|---|---|---|---|---|---|---|---|---|---|---|---|---|---|
| | | | | | | | | | | | | | | | | Slaves. | | | | Free. | | | | | |
| | | | | | | | | | | | | | | | | Black. | | Mulatto. | | Black. | | Mul. | | | |
| ritories. | Ireland. | Germany. | Other foreign countries. | Unknown. | Spring. | Summer. | Autumn. | Winter. | Under 1 week. | 1 week and under 1 month. | 1 month and under 3 months. | 3 months and over. | Males. | Females. | Total. | M. | F. | M. | F. | M. | F. | M | F. | Aggregate deaths. | |
| | 3 | | 2 | | 24 | 16 | 14 | 8 | 17 | 18 | 10 | 17 | 35 | 23 | 58 | | | | | 3 | | | 1 | 62 | 1 |
| | | | | | | 2 | 2 | 3 | 6 | 1 | | | 4 | 3 | 7 | | | | | | | | | 7 | 2 |
| | 1 | | 1 | | 3 | 3 | 3 | | 5 | 2 | | 2 | 7 | 2 | 9 | | | | | | | | | 9 | 3 |
| | | | | | 1 | 1 | | | | 1 | | 1 | 2 | | 2 | | | | | | | | | 2 | 4 |
| | | | | | 1 | 4 | 1 | 1 | 7 | | | | 4 | 2 | 6 | | | | | | 1 | | | 7 | 5 |
| | 1 | | 1 | | 6 | 11 | 7 | 6 | 7 | 14 | 6 | 3 | 16 | 13 | 29 | | | | | | 1 | | | 30 | 6 |
| | | | 1 | | 14 | 6 | 10 | 4 | 13 | 14 | 5 | 1 | 19 | 15 | 34 | | | | | | | | | 34 | 7 |
| | 1 | 1 | | | 21 | 14 | 10 | 10 | 20 | 29 | 2 | 1 | 32 | 20 | 52 | | | | | 2 | | | 1 | 55 | 8 |
| | 1 | | 2 | | 9 | 15 | 10 | 11 | 18 | 17 | 5 | 5 | 30 | 13 | 43 | | | | | 1 | 1 | | | 45 | 9 |
| | | 1 | 1 | | 19 | 28 | 17 | 16 | 33 | 39 | 6 | 2 | 49 | 28 | 77 | | | | | | 3 | | | 80 | 10 |
| | | | 1 | | 1 | 1 | | | | | | | 2 | | 2 | | | | | | | | | 2 | 11 |
| | | | | | 1 | 1 | | | | 2 | | | 2 | | 2 | | | | | | | | | 2 | 12 |
| | 1 | | | | 3 | 2 | 2 | | | 3 | 1 | 3 | 4 | 3 | 7 | | | | | | | | | 7 | 13 |
| | | 1 | | | 2 | 3 | 1 | 1 | 1 | 3 | | 3 | 7 | | 7 | | | | | | | | | 7 | 14 |
| | | | | | 3 | | 3 | 1 | | 1 | 4 | 2 | 2 | 5 | 7 | | | | | | | | | 7 | 15 |
| | | | | | 4 | 2 | 2 | 2 | | 4 | 4 | 2 | 4 | 6 | 10 | | | | | | | | | 10 | 16 |
| | 2 | | | | 1 | 1 | 1 | 1 | 1 | 2 | | | 3 | | 3 | | | | | 1 | | | | 4 | 17 |
| | 1 | | 1 | | 12 | 5 | 15 | 6 | 3 | 13 | 4 | 18 | 17 | 21 | 38 | | | | | | | | | 38 | 18 |
| | | | 1 | | 2 | | 1 | 1 | 2 | 2 | | | 3 | 1 | 4 | | | | | | | | | 4 | 19 |
| | 1 | | | | 16 | 6 | 8 | 1 | 6 | 14 | 2 | 9 | 16 | 13 | 29 | | | | | | 2 | | | 31 | 20 |
| | | | | | 3 | | | | 1 | 1 | | 1 | 2 | 1 | 3 | | | | | | | | | 3 | 21 |
| | 1 | 1 | | | 1 | 2 | 2 | 4 | 5 | 4 | | | 9 | | 9 | | | | | | | | | 9 | 22 |
| | 1 | | | | 6 | | 5 | 1 | | 3 | 4 | 5 | 9 | 3 | 12 | | | | | | | | | 12 | 23 |
| | 2 | | | | 10 | 11 | 7 | 2 | 11 | 16 | 2 | 1 | 15 | 15 | 30 | | | | | | | | | 30 | 24 |
| | | | | | 4 | 1 | 2 | | 2 | 3 | 1 | 1 | 3 | 3 | 6 | | | | | | 1 | | | 7 | 25 |
| | | | | | 2 | | | | | 2 | | | 1 | 1 | 2 | | | | | | | | | 2 | 26 |
| | | 1 | | | | | 1 | 1 | 1 | 1 | | | 1 | 1 | 2 | | | | | | | | | 2 | 27 |
| | | | | | | 3 | 1 | | | 1 | 1 | 2 | | 4 | 4 | | | | | | | | | 4 | 28 |
| | 10 | 4 | 1 | 4 | 78 | 53 | 57 | 57 | 31 | 64 | 19 | 65 | 100 | 142 | 242 | | | | | 1 | 2 | | | 245 | 29 |
| | 2 | 4 | 1 | | 42 | 37 | 24 | 30 | 57 | 30 | 8 | 36 | 73 | 59 | 132 | | | | | | 1 | | | 133 | 30 |
| | 3 | | | 1 | 25 | 9 | 9 | 11 | 20 | 28 | 3 | 3 | 27 | 23 | 50 | | | | | 1 | 3 | | | 54 | 31 |
| | 3 | 1 | 1 | | 68 | 13 | 6 | 24 | 25 | 67 | 6 | 10 | 55 | 55 | 110 | | | | | 2 | | | | 112 | 32 |
| | | | | | 1 | | | 1 | 2 | | | | 2 | | 2 | | | | | | | | | 2 | 33 |
| | | | | | | 3 | 1 | 4 | 2 | 6 | | | 5 | 4 | 9 | | | | | | | | | 9 | 34 |
| | | | | | 2 | 2 | 3 | | 6 | 1 | | | 5 | 2 | 7 | | | | | | | | | 7 | 35 |
| | | | | | 15 | 6 | 9 | 6 | 9 | 12 | 3 | 11 | 16 | 20 | 36 | | | | | | | | | 36 | 36 |
| | | | | | | | 2 | | | | 1 | 1 | 1 | 1 | 2 | | | | | | | | | 2 | 37 |
| | | | | | 6 | 10 | 6 | 4 | 1 | 5 | 2 | 19 | 10 | 15 | 25 | | | | | 1 | 1 | | | 27 | 38 |
| | 3 | | | | 12 | 11 | 3 | 6 | 4 | 25 | 2 | | 16 | 16 | 32 | | | | | | | | | 32 | 39 |
| | 1 | | | | 5 | 3 | 4 | 1 | 1 | 3 | 2 | 7 | 9 | 3 | 12 | | | | | 1 | | | | 13 | 40 |
| | | | | | 1 | 1 | 2 | | | | | | 1 | 3 | 4 | | | | | | | | | 4 | 41 |
| | | | | | | 1 | | | | | 1 | | 1 | | 1 | | | | | | | | | 1 | 42 |
| | | | | | 1 | | 1 | | 2 | | | | 2 | | 2 | | | | | | | | | 2 | 43 |
| | | 1 | | | 2 | 1 | 1 | 2 | 4 | | | | 4 | 2 | 6 | | | | | | | | | 6 | 44 |
| | | | 1 | | 1 | 8 | 16 | 3 | 13 | 7 | 5 | 3 | 15 | 13 | 28 | | | | | | | | | 28 | 45 |
| | | 2 | | | | 2 | | | 2 | | | | 2 | | 2 | | | | | | | | | 2 | 46 |
| | | | | | | 1 | | | | | | 1 | | | | | | | | | 1 | | | 1 | 47 |
| | | | | | 3 | 3 | 3 | 1 | 4 | 3 | 1 | 1 | 6 | 2 | 8 | | | | | | 1 | | 1 | 10 | 48 |
| | | 1 | | | 6 | 6 | 8 | 23 | 13 | 25 | 8 | 2 | 24 | 19 | 43 | | | | | | | | | 43 | 49 |
| | | | | | | | 1 | 1 | 1 | | 1 | | 1 | 1 | 2 | | | | | | | | | 2 | 50 |
| | 1 | | | | 4 | 2 | 3 | 1 | 3 | 2 | 4 | 1 | 1 | 9 | 10 | | | | | | | | | 10 | 51 |
| | | | | | 1 | 1 | | | | 1 | | 1 | 2 | | 2 | | | | | | | | | 2 | 52 |
| | | | | | | 1 | | | | 1 | | | | 1 | 1 | | | | | | | | | 1 | 53 |
| | | | | 1 | | 1 | | | | 1 | | | | | | | | | | 1 | | | | 1 | 54 |
| | | | | | 1 | 1 | 2 | | | 2 | | 2 | 4 | | 4 | | | | | | | | | 4 | 55 |
| | 2 | | | | 2 | 1 | 3 | 2 | 2 | 4 | 1 | | 4 | 4 | 8 | | | | | | | | | 8 | 56 |
| | 27 | 19 | 16 | 42 | 301 | 254 | 239 | 202 | 341 | 219 | 64 | 206 | 520 | 460 | 980 | | | | | 20 | 17 | | 3 | 1020 | 57 |
| 1 | 201 | 100 | 82 | 90 | 2029 | 1674 | 2314 | 1314 | 2413 | 2688 | 572 | 1330 | 3809 | 3360 | 7169 | | | | | 96 | 82 | 21 | 24 | 7392 | |

## ECTION OF THE STATE OF PENNSYLVANIA.

*learfield, Crawford, Elk, Erie, Fayette, Greene, Indiana, Jefferson, Lawrence, McKean, Mercer, ngton, Westmoreland, and Venango.*

| | Ireland. | Germany. | Other foreign countries. | Unknown. | Spring. | Summer. | Autumn. | Winter. | Under 1 week. | 1 week and under 1 month. | 1 month and under 3 months. | 3 months and over. | Males. | Females. | Total. | Slaves Black M. | F. | Mulatto M. | F. | Free Black M. | F. | Mul. M | F. | Aggregate deaths. | |
|---|---|---|---|---|---|---|---|---|---|---|---|---|---|---|---|---|---|---|---|---|---|---|---|---|---|
| | 4 | 6 | 2 | | 32 | 23 | 18 | 10 | 58 | 13 | 2 | 2 | 72 | 11 | 83 | | | | | | | | | 83 | 1 |
| | | 1 | | | 9 | 3 | 6 | 11 | 21 | 2 | 2 | 1 | 10 | 18 | 28 | | | | | 1 | | | | 29 | 2 |
| | 2 | 9 | 5 | | 10 | 24 | 8 | 11 | 55 | | | | 43 | 11 | 54 | | | | | | | 1 | | 55 | 3 |
| | 1 | | | | 3 | 6 | 4 | 8 | 13 | 6 | | | 10 | 10 | 20 | | | | | 1 | 1 | | | 22 | 4 |
| | 7 | 3 | 4 | 1 | 18 | 17 | 12 | 7 | 44 | 5 | 1 | 2 | 36 | 19 | 55 | | | | | | | | | 55 | 5 |
| | 3 | 1 | | | 4 | 2 | 3 | 2 | 2 | 3 | 1 | 4 | 4 | 7 | 11 | | | | | | | | | 11 | 6 |

## CLASSIFICATION OF DEATHS IN MIDDLE

| | Cause of death. | AGES. Under 1. | | 1 and under 5. | | 5 and under 10. | | 10 and under 20. | | 20 and under 50. | | 50 and under 80. | | 80 and under 100. | | 100 & over. | | Age unknown. | | NATIVITIES. Born in State. | N. England States. | Middle States. | Southern States. | Southwest'n States. | Northwest'n States. |
|---|---|---|---|---|---|---|---|---|---|---|---|---|---|---|---|---|---|---|---|---|---|---|---|---|---|
| | | M. | F. | M. | F. | M. | F. | M. | F. | M. | F. | M. | F. | M | F. | M | F. | M | F. | | | | | | |
| 1 | Bladder, disease of | | | | | | | | | 1 | | | | 2 | | | | | | 1 | | 1 | | | |
| 2 | Bowels.....do | 4 | 1 | 3 | 1 | 1 | | 1 | | | 1 | 2 | | | | | | | | 10 | | | | | 1 |
| 3 | Brain.......do | 7 | 2 | 7 | | 2 | 2 | | 1 | 2 | 3 | 1 | 1 | | | | | | | 24 | | | | | 1 |
| 4 | Bronchitis | 2 | 1 | 1 | 4 | 1 | 1 | 2 | 1 | 8 | 3 | 6 | 1 | | | | | | | 21 | | 2 | | | |
| 5 | Cancer | 1 | 1 | | | | | | | 1 | 9 | 10 | 16 | 4 | 1 | | | | | 25 | 2 | 3 | 1 | | |
| 6 | Catarrh | 2 | | 4 | 1 | | | | 1 | | | | | | | | | | | 8 | | | | | |
| 7 | Chicken pox | 1 | | | | | | | | | | | | | | | | | | 1 | | | | | |
| 8 | Childbirth | | | | | | | | 9 | | 77 | | | | | | | | | 62 | 2 | 3 | 2 | | 1 |
| 9 | Cholera | 5 | 3 | 19 | 14 | 11 | 5 | 21 | 9 | 105 | 31 | 24 | 9 | 1 | | | | | 1 | 126 | 2 | 4 | 7 | | 3 |
| 10 | ....do..infantum | 15 | 4 | 8 | 4 | 1 | | | | | | | | | | | | | | 31 | 1 | | | | |
| 11 | ....do..morbus | 5 | 1 | 10 | 6 | 1 | 1 | 1 | 3 | 5 | 2 | 9 | 2 | | | | | | | 37 | 1 | 2 | | | |
| 12 | Colic | 1 | | | 1 | 2 | | | | 4 | | 8 | 2 | | | | | | | 11 | 1 | | | | |
| 13 | Congestion of brain | | | 1 | | | | 1 | | 2 | | | | | | | | | | 4 | | | | | |
| 14 | Consumption | 19 | 15 | 20 | 16 | 7 | 6 | 35 | 57 | 233 | 247 | 107 | 86 | 5 | 1 | | | | 1 | 631 | 26 | 62 | 17 | 1 | 3 |
| 15 | Convulsions | 48 | 41 | 20 | 13 | 2 | 1 | 4 | 3 | 9 | 8 | 3 | 1 | | | | | | | 142 | | 2 | | | 1 |
| 16 | Cramp | | | 1 | | | | | 1 | | 1 | 3 | | | | | | | | 4 | | | | | |
| 17 | Croup | 66 | 52 | 84 | 78 | 13 | 10 | | 2 | | | | | | | | | | | 290 | 1 | 5 | | | 4 |
| 18 | Debility | 3 | 1 | | 1 | 1 | | | 1 | | | | | | | | | | | 6 | | | | | |
| 19 | Diabetes | | | | | | 1 | 1 | | 4 | | 3 | | | | | | | | 7 | | | | | |
| 20 | Diarrhœa | 15 | 9 | 24 | 23 | 4 | 2 | 1 | 3 | 12 | 7 | 5 | 10 | 2 | | | | | | 89 | 1 | 3 | | | |
| 21 | Dropsy | 7 | 4 | 9 | 13 | 4 | 2 | 5 | 6 | 9 | 35 | 54 | 43 | 14 | 4 | | | 3 | | 153 | 4 | 13 | 3 | | 1 |
| 22 | Dysentery | 30 | 26 | 94 | 82 | 25 | 25 | 18 | 12 | 24 | 21 | 22 | 15 | 1 | 3 | | | | 1 | 356 | | 11 | 1 | | 1 |
| 23 | Dyspepsia | | | | | | | 2 | | 7 | 4 | 8 | 3 | | | | | | | 17 | 2 | 1 | | | |
| 24 | Epilepsy | | | | | | | 1 | | 1 | | | 2 | | | | | | | 4 | | | | | |
| 25 | Erysipelas | 11 | 11 | 8 | 4 | 3 | 2 | 5 | 5 | 15 | 22 | 12 | 13 | 1 | | | | | | 102 | 1 | 1 | 1 | | 1 |
| 26 | Executed | | | | | | | | | | 1 | | | | | | | | | 1 | | | | | |
| 27 | Fever, not specified | 10 | 11 | 17 | 22 | 7 | 10 | 14 | 16 | 38 | 36 | 15 | 11 | | 2 | | | | | 173 | 2 | 8 | | | 4 |
| 28 | ..do..bilious | 2 | 1 | 2 | 5 | 9 | 1 | 8 | 6 | 17 | 4 | 7 | 3 | | | | | | | 39 | 1 | 4 | | | 2 |
| 29 | ..do..brain | 9 | 3 | 12 | 4 | 4 | | 2 | 1 | 3 | 4 | 1 | | | | | | | | 39 | | | | | |
| 30 | ..do..catarrhal | 22 | 15 | 25 | 35 | 9 | 4 | | 1 | 2 | 3 | | 1 | | | | | | | 114 | 1 | | 1 | | |
| 31 | ..do..congestive | | 2 | 2 | 1 | 1 | | 1 | 2 | 3 | 3 | 2 | 1 | | | | | | | 14 | | 2 | 1 | | |
| 32 | ..do..intermittent | 1 | 1 | 3 | 1 | 1 | | 1 | 3 | 8 | 1 | 1 | 3 | | | | | | | 22 | | | 1 | | |
| 33 | ..do..puerperal | | | | | | | | 2 | | 23 | | | | | | | | | 23 | | | | | |
| 34 | ..do..remittent | | | | 1 | | | | | 1 | | | | | | | | | | 2 | | | | | |
| 35 | ..do..scarlet | 20 | 16 | 135 | 118 | 55 | 64 | 16 | 23 | 4 | 2 | | | | | | | | | 442 | | 1 | | | 2 |
| 36 | ..do..ship | | | | | | 1 | 5 | 3 | 5 | 3 | 4 | | | | | | | | 14 | 1 | 1 | | | |
| 37 | ..do..typhus | | 2 | 9 | 5 | 9 | 9 | 23 | 28 | 81 | 46 | 22 | 11 | 1 | 2 | | | 1 | | 204 | | 9 | 1 | | 7 |
| 38 | Fistula | | | | | | | | | 1 | | | | | | | | | | | | | | | |
| 39 | Fracture | | | | | | | | | 1 | | 1 | | | | | | | | 1 | | | | | |
| 40 | Frozen | | | | | | | | | | | 2 | | | | | | | | 1 | | | | | |
| 41 | Gravel | | | | | 1 | | | | 2 | | 18 | 1 | 8 | | | | | | 18 | 1 | 4 | | | |
| 42 | Heart, disease of | 5 | 2 | 1 | 4 | 2 | 1 | 2 | 5 | 16 | 13 | 13 | 6 | 1 | 1 | | | | | 49 | 2 | 5 | 2 | | |
| 43 | Hemorrhage | 1 | 1 | 1 | | 1 | | 1 | 1 | 5 | | 2 | 1 | | | | | | | 8 | | | | | |
| 44 | Hernia | | | | | | | | | 1 | | 3 | | | | | | | | 3 | | | 1 | | |
| 45 | Hives | 6 | 4 | 2 | 1 | | | | | | | | | | | | | | | 13 | | | | | |
| 46 | Hooping cough | 29 | 28 | 46 | 32 | 6 | 3 | 1 | 1 | | | | | | | | | | | 140 | | | 1 | | |
| 47 | Hydrocephalus | 10 | 8 | 10 | 9 | 1 | 1 | 3 | 1 | 1 | 1 | | | | | | | | | 39 | | 2 | 1 | | 2 |
| 48 | Inflamat'n, not spec'd | 14 | 8 | 12 | 16 | 3 | 4 | 2 | 2 | 6 | 8 | 7 | 2 | 2 | | | | | | 75 | 2 | 5 | | | |
| 49 | ....do.....bowels | 19 | 13 | 10 | 7 | 2 | 7 | 4 | 1 | 11 | 9 | 4 | 2 | 1 | | | | | | 80 | 1 | 1 | | | |
| 50 | ....do.....brain | 34 | 28 | 27 | 22 | 17 | 7 | 9 | 6 | 8 | 7 | 1 | 5 | | | | | | | 152 | 1 | 9 | 1 | | 2 |
| 51 | ....do.....stomach | 2 | 2 | | 1 | 1 | | 1 | | 4 | 2 | 3 | 2 | | | | | | | 15 | | | | | 1 |
| 52 | Influenza | 1 | | 5 | 2 | 1 | 2 | 1 | 2 | 1 | 2 | | 5 | | | | | | | 21 | 1 | | | | |
| 53 | Insanity | | | | | | | | | 3 | | 1 | | | | | | | | 1 | | 1 | | | |
| 54 | Intemperance | | | | | | | | | 9 | 2 | 1 | | | | | | | | 6 | | 1 | 1 | | |
| 55 | Jaundice | | 1 | 2 | | | 1 | | | 2 | 2 | 3 | 3 | | | | | | | 9 | | | | | |
| 56 | Kidneys, disease of | | | | | | | | | 1 | | 4 | 1 | 1 | | | | | | 4 | | 1 | | | |
| 57 | Killed | | | 1 | | 2 | | 2 | | 2 | | | | 1 | | | | | | 7 | | 1 | | | |
| 58 | Liver, disease of | 5 | 2 | 5 | 2 | 2 | 2 | | 1 | 9 | 9 | 13 | 5 | 3 | | | | | | 43 | 1 | 3 | 1 | | 1 |
| 59 | Lockjaw | | | | | | | 1 | | 2 | | | | | | | | | | 1 | 1 | | | | 1 |
| 60 | Lungs, disease of | 6 | 5 | 6 | 5 | 1 | 1 | 1 | 1 | 11 | 7 | 4 | 2 | 1 | | | | | | 45 | | | 1 | | |
| 61 | Malformation | | 1 | 1 | | | | | | | | | | | | | | | | 2 | | | | | |
| 62 | Mania-a-potu | | | | | | | | | 5 | | 1 | | | | | | | | 3 | | 2 | | | 1 |
| 63 | Marasmus | 6 | 3 | 3 | | | | | 2 | 1 | | 1 | | 1 | 2 | | | | | 17 | | | | | |
| 64 | Measles | 10 | 6 | 24 | 23 | 3 | 12 | 4 | | 2 | 3 | | | | | | | | | 81 | | | | | 1 |
| 65 | Mortification | 1 | 1 | | | 1 | | | | 2 | 1 | 3 | 1 | | | | | | | 9 | | 1 | | | |
| 66 | Mumps | | | | | | | | 1 | 2 | | | | | | | | | | 2 | | | | | |
| 67 | Murder | | | | | | | | | 1 | | | | | | | | | | 1 | | | | | |
| 68 | Neuralgia | | | | 1 | 1 | 2 | | | 5 | 2 | | 3 | | | | | | | 12 | 1 | | | | |
| 69 | Old age | | | | | | | | | | | 41 | 52 | 79 | 65 | 3 | 1 | | | 106 | 7 | 29 | 8 | | |
| 70 | Paralysis | | 1 | | 1 | 1 | | 1 | 2 | 4 | 4 | 34 | 35 | 9 | 6 | | | | | 60 | 2 | 17 | | | |
| 71 | Peritonitis | | | | | 1 | | | | | | | | | | | | | | 1 | | | | | |
| 72 | Piles | | | | | | | | | 1 | | | 1 | | | | | | | 2 | | | | | |
| 73 | Pleurisy | | 1 | 4 | 3 | | | 3 | 3 | 10 | 4 | 7 | 4 | 1 | | | | | 1 | 29 | 1 | 2 | | | |
| 74 | Pneumonia | 31 | 23 | 26 | 18 | 4 | 5 | 6 | 3 | 15 | 6 | 16 | 3 | 1 | 1 | | | | | 142 | 1 | 3 | | | |
| 75 | Poison | | 1 | | | | 2 | 1 | | 1 | | 1 | | | | | | | | 4 | | 1 | | | |

SECTION OF THE STATE OF PENNSYLVANIA—Continued.

| NATIVITIES. | | | | | SEASON OF DECEASE. | | | | DURATION OF SICKNESS. | | | | WHITES. | | | COLORED. | | | | | | | | | |
|---|---|---|---|---|---|---|---|---|---|---|---|---|---|---|---|---|---|---|---|---|---|---|---|---|---|
| | | | | | | | | | | | | | | | | Slaves. | | | | Free. | | | | | |
| | | | | | | | | | | | | | | | | Black. | | Mulatto. | | Black. | | Mul. | | | |
| California and Territories. | Ireland. | Germany. | Other foreign countries. | Unknown. | Spring. | Summer. | Autumn. | Winter. | Under 1 week. | 1 week and under 1 month. | 1 month and under 3 months. | 3 months and over. | Males. | Females. | Total. | M. | F. | M. | F. | M. | F. | M | F. | Aggregate deaths. | |
| ... | 1 | ... | ... | ... | 1 | ... | ... | 2 | ... | 1 | ... | 2 | 3 | ... | 3 | ... | ... | ... | ... | ... | ... | ... | ... | 3 | 1 |
| ... | 2 | ... | 1 | ... | 1 | 5 | 5 | 3 | 2 | 2 | 2 | 6 | 11 | 3 | 14 | ... | ... | ... | ... | ... | ... | ... | ... | 14 | 2 |
| ... | ... | 2 | 1 | ... | 8 | 11 | 5 | 4 | 9 | 14 | 2 | 3 | 19 | 9 | 28 | ... | ... | ... | ... | ... | ... | ... | ... | 28 | 3 |
| ... | 6 | 1 | 1 | ... | 12 | 10 | 5 | 4 | 1 | 6 | 10 | 11 | 20 | 10 | 30 | ... | ... | ... | ... | ... | ... | ... | 1 | 31 | 4 |
| ... | 9 | 2 | 1 | ... | 12 | 16 | 6 | 9 | 2 | 3 | 5 | 31 | 16 | 25 | 41 | ... | ... | ... | ... | ... | 1 | ... | 1 | 43 | 5 |
| ... | ... | ... | ... | ... | 3 | 2 | 2 | 1 | 3 | 3 | ... | 2 | 5 | 2 | 7 | ... | ... | ... | ... | ... | ... | 1 | ... | 8 | 6 |
| ... | ... | ... | ... | ... | ... | ... | 1 | ... | 1 | ... | ... | ... | 1 | ... | 1 | ... | ... | ... | ... | ... | ... | ... | ... | 1 | 7 |
| ... | 7 | 2 | 7 | ... | 37 | 18 | 14 | 15 | 36 | 34 | 4 | ... | ... | 85 | 85 | ... | ... | ... | ... | ... | ... | ... | 1 | 86 | 8 |
| ... | 41 | 44 | 31 | 1 | 6 | 87 | 160 | 6 | 220 | 15 | 2 | ... | 178 | 70 | 248 | ... | ... | ... | ... | 1 | 1 | 7 | 2 | 259 | 9 |
| ... | ... | ... | ... | ... | 2 | 10 | 18 | ... | 17 | 11 | 1 | ... | 24 | 8 | 32 | ... | ... | ... | ... | ... | ... | ... | ... | 32 | 10 |
| ... | 2 | 2 | 2 | ... | 5 | 8 | 31 | 2 | 34 | 10 | 1 | ... | 31 | 15 | 46 | ... | ... | ... | ... | ... | ... | ... | ... | 46 | 11 |
| ... | 2 | 3 | 1 | ... | 5 | 4 | 4 | 5 | 16 | 2 | ... | ... | 15 | 3 | 18 | ... | ... | ... | ... | ... | ... | ... | ... | 18 | 12 |
| ... | ... | ... | ... | ... | 1 | 1 | ... | 2 | 2 | 1 | ... | 1 | 4 | ... | 4 | ... | ... | ... | ... | ... | ... | ... | ... | 4 | 13 |
| ... | 62 | 24 | 27 | 2 | 247 | 260 | 181 | 161 | 26 | 81 | 126 | 550 | 413 | 413 | 826 | ... | ... | ... | ... | 8 | 9 | 5 | 7 | 855 | 14 |
| ... | 2 | 4 | 2 | ... | 56 | 37 | 33 | 26 | 72 | 35 | 8 | 5 | 85 | 66 | 151 | ... | ... | ... | ... | ... | 1 | 1 | ... | 153 | 15 |
| ... | ... | 2 | ... | ... | 2 | 2 | 1 | 1 | 2 | 2 | 1 | ... | 4 | 2 | 6 | ... | ... | ... | ... | ... | ... | ... | ... | 6 | 16 |
| ... | 2 | 3 | ... | ... | 90 | 63 | 68 | 77 | 228 | 56 | 4 | 3 | 161 | 142 | 303 | ... | ... | ... | ... | 1 | ... | 1 | ... | 305 | 17 |
| ... | 1 | ... | ... | ... | 1 | 5 | 1 | ... | ... | 2 | ... | 5 | 4 | 3 | 7 | ... | ... | ... | ... | ... | ... | ... | ... | 7 | 18 |
| ... | 2 | ... | ... | ... | 3 | 2 | 2 | 2 | 3 | 4 | 1 | 1 | 8 | 1 | 9 | ... | ... | ... | ... | ... | ... | ... | ... | 9 | 19 |
| ... | 15 | 4 | 5 | ... | 13 | 32 | 62 | 10 | 29 | 59 | 16 | 7 | 62 | 54 | 116 | ... | ... | ... | ... | ... | ... | 1 | ... | 117 | 20 |
| ... | 26 | 6 | 6 | ... | 60 | 53 | 57 | 41 | 21 | 41 | 39 | 108 | 103 | 106 | 209 | ... | ... | ... | ... | 2 | 1 | ... | ... | 212 | 21 |
| ... | 19 | 7 | 4 | ... | 19 | 42 | 301 | 37 | 128 | 229 | 27 | 6 | 207 | 183 | 390 | ... | ... | ... | ... | 4 | 1 | 3 | 1 | 399 | 22 |
| ... | 2 | ... | 2 | ... | 8 | 7 | 6 | 3 | 1 | 4 | 3 | 16 | 17 | 7 | 24 | ... | ... | ... | ... | ... | ... | ... | ... | 24 | 23 |
| ... | ... | ... | ... | ... | ... | 2 | 1 | 1 | ... | ... | ... | 3 | 2 | 2 | 4 | ... | ... | ... | ... | ... | ... | ... | ... | 4 | 24 |
| ... | 5 | 1 | ... | ... | 38 | 34 | 18 | 21 | 35 | 65 | 4 | 2 | 55 | 57 | 112 | ... | ... | ... | ... | ... | ... | ... | ... | 112 | 25 |
| ... | ... | ... | ... | ... | ... | 1 | ... | ... | 1 | ... | ... | ... | ... | 1 | 1 | ... | ... | ... | ... | ... | ... | ... | ... | 1 | 26 |
| ... | 5 | 13 | 4 | ... | 78 | 36 | 61 | 33 | 42 | 125 | 26 | 12 | 99 | 107 | 206 | ... | ... | ... | ... | ... | ... | 2 | 1 | 209 | 27 |
| ... | 6 | 12 | ... | 1 | 13 | 27 | 16 | 9 | 8 | 46 | 7 | 3 | 44 | 19 | 63 | ... | ... | ... | ... | ... | 1 | 1 | ... | 65 | 28 |
| ... | 3 | ... | 1 | ... | 13 | 10 | 14 | 6 | 15 | 20 | 5 | 2 | 30 | 12 | 42 | ... | ... | ... | ... | ... | ... | 1 | ... | 43 | 29 |
| ... | 1 | ... | ... | ... | 54 | 22 | 18 | 23 | 30 | 74 | 10 | 3 | 58 | 56 | 114 | ... | ... | ... | ... | ... | ... | ... | 3 | 117 | 30 |
| ... | 1 | ... | ... | ... | 5 | 5 | 2 | 6 | 1 | 15 | 1 | 1 | 9 | 9 | 18 | ... | ... | ... | ... | ... | ... | ... | ... | 18 | 31 |
| ... | 2 | ... | ... | ... | 4 | 5 | 10 | 5 | 2 | 15 | 5 | 2 | 15 | 9 | 24 | ... | ... | ... | ... | ... | ... | ... | ... | 24 | 32 |
| ... | ... | ... | 2 | ... | 13 | 8 | 1 | 3 | 6 | 15 | 3 | ... | ... | 25 | 25 | ... | ... | ... | ... | ... | ... | ... | ... | 25 | 33 |
| ... | ... | ... | ... | ... | 1 | ... | ... | 1 | ... | 1 | ... | ... | 1 | 1 | 2 | ... | ... | ... | ... | ... | ... | ... | ... | 2 | 34 |
| ... | 2 | 2 | 4 | ... | 148 | 80 | 99 | 124 | 201 | 224 | 23 | 1 | 229 | 223 | 452 | ... | ... | ... | ... | ... | ... | 1 | ... | 453 | 35 |
| ... | 2 | 2 | 1 | ... | 3 | 4 | 5 | 9 | 1 | 18 | 1 | ... | 14 | 7 | 21 | ... | ... | ... | ... | ... | ... | ... | ... | 21 | 36 |
| ... | 18 | 5 | 3 | 2 | 81 | 44 | 58 | 66 | 19 | 177 | 38 | 11 | 145 | 102 | 247 | ... | ... | ... | ... | 1 | ... | ... | 1 | 249 | 37 |
| ... | 1 | ... | ... | ... | ... | ... | ... | 1 | ... | ... | 1 | ... | 1 | ... | 1 | ... | ... | ... | ... | ... | ... | ... | ... | 1 | 38 |
| ... | ... | 1 | ... | ... | 1 | ... | ... | 1 | ... | 1 | ... | ... | 2 | ... | 2 | ... | ... | ... | ... | ... | ... | ... | ... | 2 | 39 |
| ... | ... | ... | 1 | ... | 1 | ... | ... | 1 | 2 | ... | ... | ... | 2 | ... | 2 | ... | ... | ... | ... | ... | ... | ... | ... | 2 | 40 |
| ... | 6 | ... | 1 | ... | 6 | 9 | 6 | 9 | 2 | 14 | 4 | 10 | 29 | 1 | 30 | ... | ... | ... | ... | ... | ... | ... | ... | 30 | 41 |
| ... | 7 | 3 | 4 | ... | 20 | 23 | 10 | 19 | 20 | 21 | 9 | 16 | 40 | 32 | 72 | ... | ... | ... | ... | ... | ... | ... | ... | 72 | 42 |
| ... | 4 | 2 | ... | ... | 2 | 7 | 4 | 1 | 12 | ... | ... | 1 | 11 | 3 | 14 | ... | ... | ... | ... | ... | ... | ... | ... | 14 | 43 |
| ... | ... | ... | ... | ... | ... | 3 | ... | 1 | 1 | 1 | 1 | 1 | 4 | ... | 4 | ... | ... | ... | ... | ... | ... | ... | ... | 4 | 44 |
| ... | ... | ... | ... | ... | 5 | 4 | 2 | 2 | 8 | 4 | ... | ... | 8 | 5 | 13 | ... | ... | ... | ... | ... | ... | ... | ... | 13 | 45 |
| ... | 1 | 2 | 2 | ... | 44 | 28 | 38 | 36 | 17 | 79 | 27 | 14 | 81 | 63 | 144 | ... | ... | ... | ... | 1 | ... | ... | 1 | 146 | 46 |
| ... | 1 | ... | ... | ... | 13 | 11 | 10 | 11 | 10 | 24 | 7 | 3 | 25 | 20 | 45 | ... | ... | ... | ... | ... | ... | ... | ... | 45 | 47 |
| ... | 2 | ... | 2 | ... | 34 | 20 | 22 | 10 | 20 | 47 | 16 | 3 | 45 | 40 | 85 | ... | ... | ... | ... | ... | ... | ... | ... | 86 | 48 |
| ... | 4 | 3 | ... | 1 | 17 | 24 | 24 | 24 | 39 | 42 | 5 | 2 | 51 | 39 | 90 | ... | ... | ... | ... | ... | ... | ... | ... | 90 | 49 |
| ... | 3 | 2 | 1 | ... | 44 | 44 | 54 | 27 | 60 | 95 | 9 | 3 | 95 | 75 | 170 | ... | ... | ... | ... | 1 | ... | ... | ... | 171 | 50 |
| ... | 1 | 1 | ... | ... | 5 | 5 | 4 | 1 | 4 | 7 | 2 | 2 | 11 | 7 | 18 | ... | ... | ... | ... | ... | ... | ... | ... | 18 | 51 |
| ... | ... | ... | ... | ... | 18 | 4 | 2 | 3 | 11 | 10 | 1 | ... | 9 | 13 | 22 | ... | ... | ... | ... | ... | ... | ... | ... | 22 | 52 |
| ... | 1 | 1 | ... | ... | ... | ... | 3 | 1 | ... | 2 | 1 | ... | 4 | ... | 4 | ... | ... | ... | ... | ... | ... | ... | ... | 4 | 53 |
| ... | 1 | ... | 3 | ... | 6 | ... | 4 | 2 | 5 | 2 | 1 | 1 | 10 | 2 | 12 | ... | ... | ... | ... | ... | ... | ... | ... | 12 | 54 |
| ... | 2 | 2 | 1 | ... | 5 | 1 | 2 | 6 | 2 | 6 | 3 | 2 | 7 | 7 | 14 | ... | ... | ... | ... | ... | ... | ... | ... | 14 | 55 |
| ... | 2 | ... | ... | ... | 1 | 2 | 4 | ... | ... | 2 | ... | 2 | 6 | 1 | 7 | ... | ... | ... | ... | ... | ... | ... | ... | 7 | 56 |
| ... | ... | ... | ... | ... | 2 | 3 | 1 | 2 | 6 | 1 | ... | ... | 8 | ... | 8 | ... | ... | ... | ... | ... | ... | ... | ... | 8 | 57 |
| ... | 4 | 2 | 3 | ... | 15 | 13 | 15 | 14 | 9 | 15 | 8 | 24 | 37 | 20 | 57 | ... | ... | ... | ... | ... | 1 | ... | ... | 58 | 58 |
| ... | ... | ... | ... | ... | 2 | ... | ... | 1 | 3 | ... | ... | ... | 3 | ... | 3 | ... | ... | ... | ... | ... | ... | ... | ... | 3 | 59 |
| ... | 4 | 1 | ... | ... | 18 | 14 | 8 | 10 | 12 | 16 | 6 | 14 | 30 | 21 | 51 | ... | ... | ... | ... | ... | ... | ... | ... | 51 | 60 |
| ... | ... | ... | ... | ... | 1 | ... | ... | 1 | ... | ... | 1 | ... | 1 | 1 | 2 | ... | ... | ... | ... | ... | ... | ... | ... | 2 | 61 |
| ... | ... | ... | ... | ... | 1 | 5 | ... | ... | 2 | 3 | ... | ... | 5 | ... | 5 | ... | ... | ... | ... | 1 | ... | ... | ... | 6 | 62 |
| ... | ... | 2 | ... | ... | 7 | 3 | 6 | 3 | 6 | 7 | 1 | 3 | 12 | 7 | 19 | ... | ... | ... | ... | ... | ... | ... | ... | 19 | 63 |
| ... | 3 | 1 | 1 | ... | 18 | 40 | 24 | 5 | 21 | 44 | 14 | 7 | 43 | 44 | 87 | ... | ... | ... | ... | ... | ... | ... | ... | 87 | 64 |
| ... | ... | ... | ... | ... | 2 | 3 | 4 | 1 | 2 | 4 | ... | 4 | 7 | 3 | 10 | ... | ... | ... | ... | ... | ... | ... | ... | 10 | 65 |
| ... | ... | ... | 1 | ... | ... | 2 | ... | 1 | ... | 2 | ... | ... | 2 | 1 | 3 | ... | ... | ... | ... | ... | ... | ... | ... | 3 | 66 |
| ... | ... | ... | ... | ... | ... | ... | 1 | ... | 1 | ... | ... | ... | 1 | ... | 1 | ... | ... | ... | ... | ... | ... | ... | ... | 1 | 67 |
| ... | 1 | ... | ... | ... | 3 | 2 | 3 | 6 | 2 | 4 | 1 | 7 | 6 | 8 | 14 | ... | ... | ... | ... | ... | ... | ... | ... | 14 | 68 |
| ... | 6 | 15 | 15 | ... | 84 | 57 | 47 | 52 | 37 | 32 | 14 | 38 | 120 | 117 | 237 | ... | ... | ... | ... | 2 | ... | 1 | 1 | 241 | 69 |
| ... | 11 | 4 | 4 | ... | 35 | 26 | 12 | 25 | 30 | 24 | 7 | 36 | 49 | 49 | 98 | ... | ... | ... | ... | ... | ... | ... | ... | 98 | 70 |
| ... | ... | ... | ... | ... | 1 | ... | ... | ... | 1 | ... | ... | ... | 1 | ... | 1 | ... | ... | ... | ... | ... | ... | — | ... | 1 | 71 |
| ... | ... | ... | ... | ... | ... | 1 | 1 | ... | ... | 2 | ... | ... | 1 | 1 | 2 | ... | ... | ... | ... | ... | ... | ... | ... | 2 | 72 |
| ... | 5 | ... | 4 | ... | 12 | 14 | 9 | 6 | 9 | 23 | 7 | 1 | 25 | 16 | 41 | ... | ... | ... | ... | ... | ... | ... | ... | 41 | 73 |
| ... | 5 | 2 | 5 | ... | 69 | 31 | 20 | 38 | 43 | 85 | 16 | 5 | 99 | 58 | 157 | ... | ... | ... | ... | ... | ... | ... | 1 | 158 | 74 |
| ... | 1 | ... | ... | ... | 2 | 2 | 2 | ... | 5 | ... | 1 | ... | 3 | 3 | 6 | ... | ... | ... | ... | ... | ... | ... | ... | 6 | 75 |

## CLASSIFICATION OF DEATHS IN WESTERN

| | Cause of death. | Ages. Under 1. M. | F. | 1 and under 5. M. | F. | 5 and under 10. M. | F. | 10 and under 20. M. | F. | 20 and under 50. M. | F. | 50 and under 80. M. | F. | 80 and under 100. M | F. | 100 & over. M | F. | Age unknown. M | F. | Nativities. Born in State. | N. England States. | Middle States. | Southern States. | Southwest'n States. | Northwest'n States. |
|---|---|---|---|---|---|---|---|---|---|---|---|---|---|---|---|---|---|---|---|---|---|---|---|---|---|
| 1 | Putrid sore throat | .... | ... | 1 | 1 | 1 | 1 | 2 | 2 | .... | .... | .. | .. | .. | .. | .. | .. | .. | .. | 7 | .. | 1 | ... | ... | ... |
| 2 | Quinsy | 1 | ... | 3 | ... | ... | ... | 2 | 1 | 3 | 1 | 1 | .. | .. | .. | .. | .. | .. | .. | 10 | .. | ... | ... | ... | ... |
| 3 | Rheumatism | .... | ... | 1 | 1 | 2 | ... | 1 | 1 | 3 | 2 | 1 | 1 | .. | 1 | .. | .. | .. | .. | 10 | .. | 3 | ... | ... | ... |
| 4 | Rickets | 2 | ... | 1 | ... | ... | ... | 1 | ... | .... | .... | .. | .. | .. | .. | .. | .. | .. | .. | 4 | .. | ... | ... | ... | ... |
| 5 | Scrofula | 2 | 2 | 5 | 3 | ... | 3 | 5 | 2 | 12 | 2 | 3 | 3 | .. | .. | .. | .. | .. | .. | 35 | 1 | 2 | 1 | ... | 1 |
| 6 | Small pox | 6 | 4 | 11 | 9 | 4 | 3 | 7 | 2 | 22 | 3 | 3 | .. | .. | .. | .. | .. | .. | .. | 53 | 2 | 1 | 1 | ... | 2 |
| 7 | Spine, disease of | .... | 2 | 3 | ... | ... | 1 | 1 | 3 | 1 | 3 | ... | 3 | .. | .. | .. | .. | .. | .. | 12 | .. | 2 | ... | ... | 1 |
| 8 | Spleen....do | .... | ... | 2 | ... | ... | ... | ... | ... | 1 | .... | .. | .. | .. | .. | .. | .. | .. | .. | 2 | 1 | ... | ... | ... | ... |
| 9 | Stillborn | 5 | 3 | ... | ... | ... | ... | ... | ... | .... | .... | .. | .. | .. | .. | .. | .. | .. | .. | 8 | .. | ... | ... | ... | ... |
| 10 | Stomach, disease of | .... | ... | ... | 1 | ... | ... | ... | ... | 1 | .... | 3 | .. | .. | .. | .. | .. | .. | .. | 4 | .. | ... | ... | ... | ... |
| 11 | Suffocation | 2 | 4 | 1 | 1 | ... | ... | ... | ... | .... | .... | .. | .. | .. | .. | .. | .. | .. | .. | 6 | .. | 1 | ... | ... | 1 |
| 12 | Suicide | .... | ... | ... | ... | ... | ... | 1 | ... | 3 | 3 | 1 | 1 | .. | .. | .. | .. | .. | .. | 5 | 1 | ... | ... | ... | ... |
| 13 | Summer complaint | 10 | 5 | 24 | 24 | 2 | 1 | ... | ... | .... | .... | .. | .. | .. | .. | .. | .. | .. | .. | 59 | .. | 1 | ... | ... | ... |
| 14 | Sun, stroke of | .... | ... | 1 | ... | ... | ... | ... | ... | .... | .... | 2 | .. | .. | .. | .. | .. | .. | .. | 1 | 1 | ... | ... | ... | ... |
| 15 | Teething | 3 | 9 | 10 | 9 | ... | ... | ... | ... | .... | .... | .. | .. | .. | .. | .. | .. | .. | .. | 31 | .. | ... | ... | ... | ... |
| 16 | Tetter | .... | ... | 1 | ... | ... | ... | ... | ... | .... | .... | 1 | .. | .. | .. | .. | .. | .. | .. | 2 | .. | ... | ... | ... | ... |
| 17 | Throat, disease of | 1 | 5 | 6 | 13 | 6 | 8 | 3 | 5 | .... | 2 | 4 | .. | .. | .. | .. | .. | .. | .. | 49 | .. | 2 | ... | ... | ... |
| 18 | Thrush | 3 | 1 | ... | ... | ... | ... | ... | ... | .... | .... | .. | .. | .. | .. | .. | .. | .. | .. | 4 | .. | ... | ... | ... | ... |
| 19 | Tumor | .... | ... | ... | 1 | ... | ... | ... | ... | .... | 1 | ... | 1 | .. | .. | .. | .. | .. | .. | 3 | .. | ... | ... | ... | ... |
| 20 | Ulcer | .... | 1 | ... | 1 | ... | ... | ... | ... | .... | 1 | 1 | 1 | .. | .. | .. | .. | .. | .. | 4 | .. | 1 | ... | ... | ... |
| 21 | Uterus, disease of | .... | ... | ... | ... | ... | ... | ... | ... | .... | 5 | .. | .. | .. | .. | .. | .. | .. | .. | 4 | .. | ... | ... | ... | ... |
| 22 | White swelling | .... | ... | ... | ... | ... | ... | 1 | ... | .... | .... | 1 | .. | .. | .. | .. | .. | .. | .. | 2 | .. | ... | ... | ... | ... |
| 23 | Worms | .... | 1 | 8 | 6 | ... | ... | ... | ... | .... | .... | .. | .. | .. | .. | .. | .. | .. | .. | 14 | .. | ... | ... | ... | 1 |
| 24 | Unknown | 170 | 118 | 49 | 63 | 25 | 14 | 20 | 20 | 76 | 82 | 73 | 49 | 9 | 6 | .. | .. | 5 | 4 | 665 | 8 | 22 | 6 | 3 | 2 |
| | Total | 696 | 523 | 857 | 755 | 279 | 239 | 287 | 278 | 926 | 802 | 648 | 441 | 153 | 96 | 3 | 1 | 9 | 8 | 5620 | 90 | 276 | 65 | 4 | 56 |

## CLASSIFICATION OF DEATHS IN MIDDLE

*Embracing the following counties: Adams, Bedford, Blair, Bradford, Carbon, Centre Clinton, Mifflin, Montour, Northumberland, Perry, Schuylkill, Sulli-*

| | Cause of death. | Ages. Under 1. M. | F. | 1 and under 5. M. | F. | 5 and under 10. M. | F. | 10 and under 20. M. | F. | 20 and under 50. M. | F. | 50 and under 80. M. | F. | 80 and under 100. M | F. | 100 & over. M | F. | Age unknown. M | F. | Nativities. Born in State. | N. England States. | Middle States. | Southern States. | Southwest'n States. | Northwest'n States. |
|---|---|---|---|---|---|---|---|---|---|---|---|---|---|---|---|---|---|---|---|---|---|---|---|---|---|
| 1 | Abscess | .... | ... | ... | ... | ... | ... | ... | ... | .... | .... | .... | 1 | .. | .. | .. | .. | .. | .. | 1 | .. | ... | ... | ... | ... |
| 2 | Accident, not specf'd | .... | 3 | 8 | 8 | 9 | 3 | 23 | 2 | 61 | 1 | 12 | 4 | 1 | .. | .. | .. | 1 | .. | 88 | 1 | 7 | 2 | ... | ... |
| 3 | ....do...burned | 1 | 1 | 10 | 7 | ... | 2 | ... | 1 | 3 | 3 | 1 | 1 | 1 | .. | .. | .. | .. | .. | 23 | 1 | 2 | ... | ... | ... |
| 4 | ....do...drowned | .... | ... | 7 | 5 | 8 | ... | 7 | 5 | 15 | 3 | 2 | 1 | .. | .. | .. | .. | .. | .. | 38 | 1 | 5 | ... | ... | ... |
| 5 | ....do...scalded | 1 | ... | 8 | 3 | ... | ... | ... | ... | .... | .... | .... | .. | .. | .. | .. | .. | .. | .. | 12 | .. | ... | ... | ... | ... |
| 6 | Apoplexy | .... | 2 | 2 | ... | ... | ... | 1 | ... | 3 | 9 | 19 | 15 | 4 | 2 | .. | .. | .. | .. | 36 | 3 | 9 | 1 | ... | ... |
| 7 | Asthma | 1 | ... | 1 | ... | ... | ... | ... | ... | 2 | .... | 4 | 4 | .. | .. | .. | .. | .. | .. | 6 | .. | 2 | ... | ... | ... |
| 8 | Bowels, disease of | 2 | ... | 1 | 1 | 1 | ... | ... | ... | 2 | .... | 1 | 1 | .. | .. | .. | .. | .. | .. | 9 | .. | ... | ... | ... | ... |
| 9 | Brain......do | 4 | 2 | 2 | 3 | 4 | ... | ... | ... | 2 | 1 | ... | 1 | 1 | .. | .. | .. | .. | .. | 20 | .. | ... | ... | ... | ... |
| 10 | Bronchitis | 2 | 3 | 1 | 3 | ... | 1 | ... | ... | 5 | 2 | 3 | 1 | 1 | 1 | .. | .. | .. | .. | 20 | .. | 2 | ... | ... | ... |
| 11 | Cancer | .... | ... | 1 | ... | ... | ... | ... | ... | 3 | 6 | 13 | 14 | 2 | .. | .. | .. | .. | .. | 28 | 1 | 5 | 1 | ... | ... |
| 12 | Catarrh | 4 | 4 | 4 | 3 | 1 | ... | 1 | 1 | 1 | 2 | 2 | 2 | .. | .. | .. | .. | .. | .. | 24 | .. | ... | ... | ... | ... |
| 13 | Chicken pox | .... | 2 | ... | ... | ... | ... | ... | ... | 1 | .... | .... | .. | .. | .. | .. | .. | .. | .. | 2 | .. | ... | ... | ... | ... |
| 14 | Childbirth | .... | ... | ... | ... | ... | ... | ... | 7 | .... | 115 | ... | 3 | .. | .. | .. | .. | .. | .. | 94 | 2 | 8 | 1 | ... | ... |
| 15 | Cholera | 1 | ... | 3 | 1 | 3 | ... | 7 | ... | 11 | 3 | 4 | .. | .. | .. | .. | .. | .. | .. | 19 | .. | 2 | 1 | ... | ... |
| 16 | ...do..infantum | 18 | 12 | 11 | 15 | 3 | 1 | ... | ... | .... | .... | .... | .. | .. | .. | .. | .. | .. | .. | 59 | .. | 1 | ... | ... | ... |
| 17 | ...do..morbus | 9 | 2 | 7 | 8 | 2 | 1 | 1 | 2 | 12 | 6 | 3 | 5 | 2 | .. | .. | .. | .. | .. | 49 | 1 | 2 | ... | ... | ... |
| 18 | Chorea | .... | ... | ... | ... | ... | ... | ... | 3 | .... | .... | .... | .. | .. | .. | .. | .. | .. | .. | 2 | .. | ... | ... | ... | ... |
| 19 | Colic | 1 | 1 | 2 | ... | 3 | ... | 3 | 1 | 9 | 1 | 9 | 6 | .. | 1 | .. | .. | .. | .. | 29 | 1 | 4 | ... | ... | ... |
| 20 | Congest'n, not spec'd | .... | 1 | ... | 3 | ... | ... | ... | ... | 2 | 1 | .... | .. | .. | .. | .. | .. | .. | .. | 5 | .. | ... | ... | ... | ... |
| 21 | Consumption | 23 | 23 | 25 | 15 | 5 | 11 | 26 | 47 | 203 | 251 | 131 | 92 | 9 | 7 | .. | .. | .. | .. | 681 | 30 | 64 | 1 | ... | ... |
| 22 | Convulsions | 80 | 54 | 27 | 34 | 8 | 4 | 5 | 6 | 8 | 4 | 4 | 2 | 1 | .. | .. | .. | 1 | .. | 223 | .. | 2 | ... | ... | ... |
| 23 | Cramp | .... | ... | 1 | 1 | ... | 1 | ... | ... | 7 | 1 | 3 | 1 | .. | .. | .. | .. | .. | .. | 10 | .. | ... | ... | ... | ... |
| 24 | Croup | 69 | 37 | 96 | 94 | 16 | 18 | 1 | 5 | 1 | 1 | .... | .. | .. | .. | .. | .. | .. | .. | 328 | .. | 4 | ... | ... | ... |
| 25 | D bility | 3 | 9 | ... | ... | ... | ... | ... | ... | .... | .... | .... | .. | .. | .. | .. | .. | .. | .. | 12 | .. | ... | ... | ... | ... |
| 26 | Diabetes | .... | ... | ... | ... | ... | ... | ... | ... | 2 | .... | 2 | .. | .. | .. | .. | .. | .. | .. | 3 | 1 | ... | ... | ... | ... |
| 27 | Diarrhœa | 14 | 22 | 35 | 23 | 6 | 2 | 2 | 5 | 17 | 5 | 9 | 6 | 1 | .. | .. | .. | .. | .. | 124 | 3 | 12 | ... | ... | ... |
| 28 | Dropsy | 12 | 8 | 8 | 11 | 4 | 6 | 2 | 6 | 23 | 30 | 55 | 59 | 6 | 2 | .. | .. | .. | .. | 183 | 8 | 10 | 2 | ... | ... |
| 29 | Dysentery | 64 | 58 | 162 | 145 | 35 | 30 | 27 | 14 | 39 | 31 | 27 | 18 | .. | .. | .. | .. | .. | 1 | 603 | 5 | 16 | 1 | ... | ... |
| 30 | Dyspepsia | .... | ... | ... | ... | ... | ... | ... | ... | 2 | 1 | 10 | 5 | .. | 1 | .. | .. | .. | .. | 15 | .. | 2 | ... | ... | ... |
| 31 | Epilepsy | 3 | 4 | 2 | ... | ... | ... | ... | 1 | .... | 1 | .... | .. | .. | .. | .. | .. | .. | .. | 9 | .. | ... | ... | ... | ... |
| 32 | Erysipelas | 9 | 7 | 3 | 7 | 3 | 1 | 1 | 5 | 11 | 10 | 12 | 9 | .. | 1 | .. | .. | .. | .. | 69 | .. | 6 | 1 | ... | ... |
| 33 | Fever, not specified | 29 | 24 | 62 | 67 | 20 | 15 | 41 | 32 | 81 | 78 | 31 | 23 | 4 | .. | .. | .. | .. | .. | 451 | 3 | 11 | ... | ... | ... |
| 34 | ..do..bilious | 2 | 5 | 4 | 9 | 6 | 2 | 21 | 13 | 37 | 19 | 19 | 7 | .. | 1 | .. | .. | .. | 1 | 117 | 5 | 7 | ... | ... | ... |
| 35 | ..do..brain | 1 | 2 | 5 | 4 | 3 | 5 | 3 | 2 | 3 | 2 | ... | 1 | .. | .. | .. | .. | .. | .. | 29 | .. | 1 | ... | ... | ... |
| 36 | .do..catarrhal | 12 | 6 | 16 | 8 | 1 | 2 | 1 | 1 | .... | 2 | 1 | .. | .. | .. | .. | .. | .. | .. | 50 | .. | ... | ... | ... | ... |
| 37 | ..do..congestive | 1 | 1 | 1 | 2 | ... | ... | ... | 1 | 4 | 3 | 1 | .. | .. | .. | .. | .. | .. | .. | 14 | .. | ... | ... | ... | ... |
| 38 | ..do..intermittent | 2 | 2 | 4 | 4 | 2 | 2 | ... | ... | 5 | 1 | 2 | 1 | 1 | .. | .. | .. | .. | .. | 21 | .. | ... | ... | ... | ... |
| 39 | ..do..puerperal | .... | ... | ... | ... | ... | ... | ... | ... | .... | 10 | .... | .. | .. | .. | .. | .. | .. | .. | 7 | .. | ... | 1 | ... | ... |

## SECTION OF THE STATE OF PENNSYLVANIA—Continued.

| NATIVITIES. | | | | | SEASON OF DECEASE. | | | | DURATION OF SICKNESS. | | | | WHITES. | | | COLORED. | | | | | | | | | |
|---|---|---|---|---|---|---|---|---|---|---|---|---|---|---|---|---|---|---|---|---|---|---|---|---|---|
| | | | | | | | | | | | | | | | | Slaves. | | | | Free. | | | | | |
| | | | | | | | | | | | | | | | | Black. | | Mulatto. | | Black | | Mul. | | | |
| California and Territories. | Ireland. | Germany. | Other foreign countries. | Unknown. | Spring. | Summer. | Autumn. | Winter. | Under 1 week. | 1 week and under 1 month. | 1 month and under 3 months. | 3 months and over. | Males. | Females. | Total. | M. | F. | M. | F. | M. | F. | M | F | Aggregate deaths. | |
| | | | | | 1 | 1 | 4 | 2 | 1 | 5 | 1 | | 4 | 4 | 8 | | | | | | | | | 8 | 1 |
| | 2 | | | | 5 | 1 | 3 | 3 | 4 | 7 | 1 | | 10 | 2 | 12 | | | | | | | | | 12 | 2 |
| | 1 | | | | 5 | 4 | 2 | 3 | 2 | 5 | 2 | 5 | 8 | 6 | 14 | | | | | | | | | 14 | 3 |
| | | | | | 2 | 1 | 1 | | 1 | 1 | | 2 | 4 | | 4 | | | | | | | | | 4 | 4 |
| | 1 | | 1 | | 12 | 12 | 6 | 12 | 4 | 6 | 3 | 28 | 26 | 15 | 41 | | | | | 1 | | | | 42 | 5 |
| | 5 | 5 | 5 | | 27 | 13 | 12 | 22 | 3 | 60 | 4 | 7 | 52 | 21 | 73 | | | | | 1 | | | | 74 | 6 |
| | 2 | | | | 3 | 4 | 4 | 6 | 3 | 4 | | 8 | 5 | 12 | 17 | | | | | | | | | 17 | 7 |
| | | | | | 2 | | 1 | | | | | 3 | 3 | | 3 | | | | | | | | | 3 | 8 |
| | | | | | 2 | 1 | 3 | 2 | | | | | 5 | 3 | 8 | | | | | | | | | 8 | 9 |
| | | | 1 | | 2 | 1 | 2 | | | 4 | 1 | | 4 | 1 | 5 | | | | | | | | | 5 | 10 |
| | | | | | 2 | 2 | 2 | 2 | 8 | | | | 3 | 5 | 8 | | | | | | | | | 8 | 11 |
| | 1 | 1 | 1 | | 3 | 3 | 3 | | 7 | | | | 5 | 4 | 9 | | | | | | | | | 9 | 12 |
| | 2 | 2 | 2 | | 1 | 32 | 32 | 1 | 7 | 24 | 9 | 9 | 36 | 27 | 63 | | | | | | 1 | | 2 | 66 | 13 |
| | 1 | | | | | 2 | 1 | | 3 | | | | 3 | | 3 | | | | | | | | | 3 | 14 |
| | | | | | 7 | 8 | 10 | 6 | 6 | 15 | 8 | 2 | 12 | 18 | 30 | | | | | | | 1 | | 31 | 15 |
| | | | | | | 1 | 1 | | | | | 2 | 2 | | 2 | | | | | | | | | 2 | 16 |
| | 1 | | 1 | | 11 | 8 | 21 | 13 | 17 | 29 | 5 | 2 | 20 | 33 | 53 | | | | | | | | | 53 | 17 |
| | | | | | 1 | 1 | 1 | 1 | | 4 | | | 3 | 1 | 4 | | | | | | | | | 4 | 18 |
| | | | | | 1 | | 1 | 1 | 1 | | | 1 | | 3 | 3 | | | | | | | | | 3 | 19 |
| | | | | | 2 | 1 | 2 | | | 2 | 1 | 2 | 1 | 4 | 5 | | | | | | | | | 5 | 20 |
| | | | 1 | | 2 | 2 | | 1 | 1 | 2 | | 2 | | 5 | 5 | | | | | | | | | 5 | 21 |
| | | | | | 1 | | | 1 | | | | 2 | 1 | | 1 | | | | | 1 | | | | 2 | 22 |
| | | | | | 3 | 8 | 2 | 2 | 9 | 5 | 1 | | 8 | 7 | 15 | | | | | | | | | 15 | 23 |
| | 43 | 15 | 18 | 1 | 251 | 181 | 194 | 138 | 264 | 198 | 60 | 138 | 424 | 352 | 776 | | | | | 2 | 3 | 1 | 1 | 783 | 24 |
| | 453 | 228 | 195 | 9 | 1954 | 1716 | 1967 | 1304 | 2150 | 2429 | 640 | 1213 | 3800 | 3093 | 6893 | | | | | 29 | 21 | 29 | 24 | 6996 | |

## SECTION OF THE STATE OF PENNSYLVANIA.

*Columbia, Cumberland, Dauphin, Franklin, Fulton, Huntingdon, Juniata, Luzerne, Lycoming, van, Susquehanna, Tioga, Union, Wayne, and Wyoming.*

| California and Territories. | Ireland. | Germany. | Other foreign countries. | Unknown. | Spring. | Summer. | Autumn. | Winter. | Under 1 week. | 1 week and under 1 month. | 1 month and under 3 months. | 3 months and over. | Males. | Females. | Total. | Slaves Black M. | Slaves Black F. | Slaves Mulatto M. | Slaves Mulatto F. | Free Black M. | Free Black F. | Free Mul. M | Free Mul. F | Aggregate deaths. | |
|---|---|---|---|---|---|---|---|---|---|---|---|---|---|---|---|---|---|---|---|---|---|---|---|---|---|
| | | | | | | | | 1 | | | | 1 | | 1 | 1 | | | | | | | | | 1 | 1 |
| | 23 | 7 | 8 | | 38 | 36 | 35 | 27 | 107 | 18 | 2 | 4 | 115 | 21 | 136 | | | | | | | | | 136 | 2 |
| | 3 | | 2 | | 11 | 6 | 7 | 7 | 25 | 4 | 1 | | 15 | 15 | 30 | | | | | 1 | | | | 31 | 3 |
| | 5 | 1 | 3 | | 9 | 18 | 11 | 15 | 53 | | | | 39 | 14 | 53 | | | | | | | | | 53 | 4 |
| | | | | | 5 | 2 | 2 | 3 | 6 | 5 | 1 | | 9 | 3 | 12 | | | | | | | | | 12 | 5 |
| | 3 | 3 | 2 | | 18 | 17 | 12 | 10 | 42 | 6 | 2 | 7 | 29 | 28 | 57 | | | | | | | | | 57 | 6 |
| | 2 | 1 | | 1 | 5 | 2 | 1 | 4 | | 5 | 3 | 4 | 8 | 4 | 12 | | | | | | | | | 12 | 7 |
| | | | | | 1 | 1 | 7 | | | 4 | 2 | 3 | 7 | 2 | 9 | | | | | | | | | 9 | 8 |
| | | | | | 4 | 7 | 4 | 5 | 4 | 11 | | 3 | 13 | 7 | 20 | | | | | | | | | 20 | 9 |
| | | | 1 | | 9 | 3 | 8 | 3 | 1 | 10 | 2 | 10 | 12 | 11 | 23 | | | | | | | | | 23 | 10 |
| | 2 | | 2 | | 12 | 12 | 10 | 4 | | 4 | 5 | 27 | 19 | 20 | 39 | | | | | | | | | 39 | 11 |
| | 1 | | | | 14 | 6 | 2 | 3 | 11 | 12 | 1 | 1 | 12 | 12 | 24 | | | | | 1 | | | | 25 | 12 |
| | 1 | | | | | 1 | 1 | 1 | | 3 | | | 1 | 2 | 3 | | | | | | | | | 3 | 13 |
| | 10 | 3 | 7 | | 49 | 29 | 19 | 26 | 55 | 54 | 4 | 1 | | 122 | 122 | | | | | | 2 | | 1 | 125 | 14 |
| | 6 | 3 | 2 | | 1 | 14 | 18 | | 30 | 2 | | | 27 | 4 | 31 | | | | | 1 | | 1 | | 33 | 15 |
| | | | | | 6 | 25 | 22 | 6 | 31 | 24 | 2 | 1 | 32 | 27 | 59 | | | | | | 1 | | | 60 | 16 |
| | 5 | 2 | 1 | | 3 | 19 | 36 | 2 | 36 | 20 | 1 | 2 | 36 | 24 | 60 | | | | | | | | | 60 | 17 |
| | | | | | | 2 | | | | 1 | | 1 | | 2 | 2 | | | | | | | | | 2 | 18 |
| | 2 | | 1 | | 12 | 7 | 10 | 7 | 25 | 10 | 1 | | 27 | 10 | 37 | | | | | | | | | 37 | 19 |
| | 1 | | | | 4 | 1 | 1 | 1 | 3 | 2 | 2 | | 2 | 5 | 7 | | | | | | | | | 7 | 20 |
| | 44 | 16 | 29 | 1 | 289 | 221 | 191 | 167 | 38 | 126 | 143 | 550 | 399 | 428 | 827 | | | | | 19 | 11 | 4 | 7 | 868 | 21 |
| | 5 | 4 | 3 | | 86 | 57 | 45 | 48 | 139 | 57 | 18 | 19 | 133 | 100 | 283 | | | | | | 2 | 1 | 2 | 238 | 22 |
| | 3 | 1 | | 1 | 7 | 3 | 2 | 3 | 12 | 3 | | | 11 | 4 | 15 | | | | | | | | | 15 | 23 |
| | 2 | 2 | 2 | | 115 | 48 | 81 | 94 | 198 | 77 | 4 | 1 | 181 | 154 | 335 | | | | | 2 | | | 1 | 338 | 24 |
| | | | | | 3 | 5 | 2 | 2 | 6 | 2 | 1 | 1 | 3 | 9 | 12 | | | | | | | | | 12 | 25 |
| | | | | | 1 | 2 | 1 | | | 1 | 1 | 2 | 4 | | 4 | | | | | | | | | 4 | 26 |
| | 4 | 2 | 1 | 1 | 11 | 25 | 97 | 14 | 43 | 80 | 13 | 7 | 84 | 62 | 146 | | | | | | 1 | | | 147 | 27 |
| | 14 | 6 | 7 | 1 | 83 | 59 | 50 | 38 | 17 | 46 | 31 | 131 | 110 | 120 | 230 | | | | | | | | 2 | 232 | 28 |
| | 14 | 3 | 8 | | 30 | 100 | 485 | 36 | 199 | 383 | 43 | 24 | 351 | 293 | 644 | | | | | 2 | | 1 | 4 | 651 | 29 |
| | 1 | 1 | | | 5 | 6 | 5 | 3 | | | 2 | 17 | 12 | 7 | 19 | | | | | | | | | 19 | 30 |
| | 2 | | | | 3 | 4 | 2 | 2 | 7 | 2 | | 2 | 5 | 5 | 10 | | | | | | 1 | | | 11 | 31 |
| | 1 | 1 | 1 | | 32 | 16 | 11 | 18 | 21 | 43 | 4 | 7 | 39 | 40 | 79 | | | | | | | | | 79 | 32 |
| | 22 | 7 | 10 | 1 | 194 | 105 | 122 | 86 | 116 | 324 | 53 | 14 | 265 | 233 | 498 | | | | | 3 | 3 | | 3 | 507 | 33 |
| | 6 | 5 | 6 | | 34 | 25 | 61 | 26 | 17 | 113 | 14 | 2 | 89 | 57 | 146 | | | | | | | | | 146 | 34 |
| | | | 1 | | 12 | 9 | 4 | 6 | 10 | 17 | 3 | 1 | 15 | 15 | 30 | | | | | | 1 | | | 31 | 35 |
| | | | | | 35 | 12 | | 3 | 4 | 39 | 5 | 2 | 31 | 18 | 49 | | | | | | | | 1 | 50 | 36 |
| | | | | | 2 | 6 | 2 | 4 | 8 | 2 | 3 | 1 | 7 | 7 | 14 | | | | | | | | | 14 | 37 |
| | 3 | | 1 | | 4 | 5 | 13 | 3 | 10 | 11 | 2 | 2 | 16 | 9 | 25 | | | | | | | | | 25 | 38 |
| | 1 | 1 | | | 5 | 3 | | 2 | 2 | 8 | | | | 9 | 9 | | | | | | | | 1 | 10 | 39 |

## CLASSIFICATION OF DEATHS IN MIDDLE

| | Cause of death. | AGE. Under 1. | | 1 and under 5. | | 5 and under 10. | | 10 and under 20. | | 20 and under 50. | | 50 and under 80. | | 80 and under 100. | | 100 & over. | | Age unknown. | | NATIVITIES. Born in State. | N. England States. | Middle States. | Southern States. | Southwest'n States. | Northeast'n States. |
|---|---|---|---|---|---|---|---|---|---|---|---|---|---|---|---|---|---|---|---|---|---|---|---|---|---|
| | | M. | F. | M. | F. | M. | F. | M. | F. | M. | F. | M. | F. | M | F. | M | F. | M | F. | | | | | | |
| 1 | Fever, remittent | | | | | 1 | | 1 | | | 1 | | | | | | | | | 3 | | | | | |
| 2 | ..do..scarlet | 20 | 28 | 100 | 105 | 48 | 32 | 11 | 16 | 2 | 4 | | | | | | | | | 359 | 1 | 4 | | | |
| 3 | ..do..ship | | | 1 | 1 | 1 | 1 | | | 1 | 1 | | | | | | | | | 2 | | | | | |
| 4 | ..do..typhus | 1 | 2 | 3 | 2 | 5 | 5 | 14 | 19 | 31 | 22 | 12 | 5 | 1 | | | | | | 101 | 1 | 11 | | | |
| 5 | Fracture | | | | | | | | 1 | | 1 | | | | | | | | | 2 | | | | | |
| 6 | Frozen | | | | | | | | | 2 | | 1 | | | | | | | | 1 | | | | | |
| 7 | Gout | | | | | | | | | | | 2 | | | | | | | | 1 | | | | | |
| 8 | Gravel | | | | | | | 1 | | | | 13 | | 6 | | | | | | 14 | 2 | 2 | | | |
| 9 | Heart, disease of | | | 1 | | | 1 | 1 | 2 | 3 | 7 | 7 | 6 | 1 | | | | | | 20 | 2 | 4 | 1 | | |
| 10 | Hemorrhage | | 1 | | | | | 5 | | 4 | 3 | 2 | 1 | | | | | | | 15 | | | | | |
| 11 | Hernia | | | 1 | | 2 | | 1 | | 1 | | | 1 | | | | | | | 5 | 1 | | | | |
| 12 | Hip, disease of | | | | | | | | 1 | 1 | | | | | | | | | | 1 | | 1 | | | |
| 13 | Hives | 8 | | 1 | | | 1 | | | | | | | | | | | | | 10 | | | | | |
| 14 | Hooping cough | 11 | 13 | 5 | 15 | 1 | 4 | 1 | | | | | | | | | | | | 48 | | | 1 | | |
| 15 | Hydrocephalus | 8 | 8 | 16 | 9 | 2 | 1 | 1 | 1 | | | | | | | | | | | 42 | 1 | | | | |
| 16 | Inflamat'n, not spec'd | 16 | 9 | 16 | 16 | 6 | 1 | 3 | 3 | 9 | 8 | 12 | 4 | 3 | 2 | | | | | 99 | 4 | | 1 | | |
| 17 | .....do....bowels | 9 | 10 | 18 | 5 | 6 | 3 | 6 | 3 | 7 | 6 | 6 | 1 | | | | | | | 68 | 1 | 6 | | | |
| 18 | .....do....brain | 22 | 16 | 34 | 17 | 9 | 3 | 9 | 4 | 12 | 7 | | 3 | | | | | | | 128 | 4 | | | | |
| 19 | .....do....stomach | | | | | | | | | | 1 | | | | | | | | | 1 | | | | | |
| 20 | Influenza | | 1 | 3 | 1 | | | | | | | | | 2 | | | | | | 6 | 1 | | | | |
| 21 | Insanity | | | 1 | | | | | | 3 | 3 | 4 | 2 | | | | | | | 7 | | 2 | | | |
| 22 | Intemperance | | | | | | | | | 5 | | 4 | | | | | | 1 | | 6 | | 1 | | | |
| 23 | Jaundice | 1 | 2 | 1 | 1 | | 1 | | | | 2 | 2 | 1 | 1 | | | | | | 10 | | 1 | | | |
| 24 | Kidneys, disease of | 1 | | | 1 | 1 | | 1 | | 1 | | | | | | | | | | 5 | | | | | |
| 25 | Killed | | | | | | | 1 | | 5 | | | | | | | | | | 5 | | | | | |
| 26 | Lightning | | | 1 | | | | 2 | | | | | | | | | | | | 3 | | | | | |
| 27 | Liver, disease of | 5 | 2 | 5 | | | | | | 5 | 12 | 5 | 9 | 1 | | | | | | 37 | 1 | 1 | | | |
| 28 | Lockjaw | | | | | | | | | 2 | 2 | | | | | | | | | 2 | 1 | | | | |
| 29 | Lungs, disease of | 6 | | 1 | 2 | 1 | | 2 | 2 | 2 | 2 | 6 | | | 1 | | | | | 23 | | | | | |
| 30 | Malformation | 1 | 1 | | | | | | | | | | | | | | | | | 2 | | | | | |
| 31 | Mania-a-potu | | | | | | | | | 12 | | 3 | | | | | | | | 10 | | | | | |
| 32 | Marasmus | 4 | 6 | 2 | 3 | | | | 1 | 1 | | 1 | | | | | | 1 | | 18 | | | | | |
| 33 | Measles | 10 | 11 | 26 | 26 | 5 | 6 | 1 | 4 | | 1 | 1 | | | | | | | | 88 | | | | | |
| 34 | Mortification | | 1 | | | | | | | | | 3 | | 1 | 1 | | | | | 4 | | 2 | | | |
| 35 | Mumps | 1 | | 2 | | | | 1 | | | | | | | | | | | | 4 | | | | | |
| 36 | Neuralgia | | | | | | | 1 | | 2 | 1 | 3 | 2 | | | | | | | 8 | | 1 | | | |
| 37 | Old age | | | | | | | | | | | 39 | 52 | 71 | 79 | | | 1 | 1 | 149 | 29 | 30 | 2 | | |
| 38 | Paralysis | | 1 | 1 | 1 | | | | | 7 | 8 | 32 | 48 | 8 | 7 | | | | | 83 | 5 | 16 | | | |
| 39 | Peritonitis | | | | | 1 | | | | | | | | | | | | | | 1 | | | | | |
| 40 | Piles | | | | | | | | | | | 1 | | | | | | | | 1 | | | | | |
| 41 | Pleurisy | 3 | 2 | 3 | 3 | 1 | | 8 | | 22 | 7 | 9 | 11 | 2 | 1 | | | | | 58 | | 2 | 1 | | |
| 42 | Pneumonia | 22 | 23 | 26 | 24 | 4 | 6 | | 1 | 12 | 8 | 7 | 5 | | 1 | | | | | 129 | 2 | 2 | | | |
| 43 | Poison | | | 2 | | | | | | | | | | | | | | | | 2 | | | | | |
| 44 | Putrid sore throat | | | | | | | | 1 | | | | | | | | | | | 1 | | | | | |
| 45 | Quinsy | 1 | | 4 | 4 | 2 | 1 | | 2 | 2 | 3 | 3 | 3 | | | | | | | 22 | | | | | |
| 46 | Rheumatism | | | 1 | | 5 | 3 | 2 | 3 | 3 | | 2 | 3 | | | | | 2 | 1 | 20 | 1 | 3 | | | |
| 47 | Rickets | | 2 | | | 1 | | | 1 | | | | | | | | | | | 3 | | | | | |
| 48 | Salivation, effects of | | | | | | | | | | 1 | | | | | | | | | 1 | | | | | |
| 49 | Scrofula | 2 | | 4 | 3 | 1 | 1 | 3 | 4 | 7 | 2 | 3 | | 1 | | | | | | 24 | 1 | 3 | | | 2 |
| 50 | Small pox | 4 | 2 | 9 | 5 | 6 | 1 | 1 | 2 | 5 | | 2 | | | | | | | | 33 | 1 | 1 | | | |
| 51 | Spine, disease of | | 2 | 1 | 2 | 1 | | 2 | | 1 | 2 | | 2 | | | | | | | 9 | 1 | 2 | | | |
| 52 | Stillborn | 6 | 6 | | | | | | | | | | | | | | | | | 12 | | | | | |
| 53 | Stomach, disease of | | | | | | 1 | | | | | 1 | | | | | | | | 2 | | | | | |
| 54 | Suffocation | 1 | 1 | | | | | | | | | | | | | | | | | 2 | | | | | |
| 55 | Suicide | | | | | | | | | 9 | 2 | | | | | | | | | 7 | | | | | |
| 56 | Summer complaint | 2 | | 5 | 2 | | | | | | | | | | | | | | | 9 | | | | | |
| 57 | Sun, stroke of | | | | | | | 1 | | | | | | | | | | | | | | | | | |
| 58 | Teething | 4 | 3 | 3 | 2 | | | | | | | | | | | | | | | 12 | | | | | |
| 59 | Throat, disease of | 5 | 3 | 6 | 5 | 6 | 4 | 2 | 2 | 2 | 4 | 1 | 3 | | | | | | | 42 | | 1 | | | |
| 60 | Tumor | | 1 | | 1 | | 1 | | 1 | | | 1 | 1 | | | | | | | 5 | | 1 | | | |
| 61 | Ulcer | | | | 1 | | | | | 1 | 1 | 3 | | | | | | | | 6 | | | | | |
| 62 | White swelling | | | | | | | 1 | 1 | 1 | 2 | | | | | | | | | 4 | 1 | | | | |
| 63 | Worms | 1 | 3 | 4 | 7 | 1 | 1 | | | | | | | | | | | | | 13 | | 2 | | | |
| 64 | Unknown | 192 | 136 | 74 | 78 | 23 | 19 | 27 | 18 | 82 | 105 | 77 | 61 | 11 | 4 | .. | .. | 13 | 4 | 822 | 10 | 34 | 1 | | |
| | Total | 735 | 591 | 900 | 825 | 283 | 204 | 283 | 252 | 840 | 832 | 648 | 507 | 143 | 112 | .. | .. | 20 | 8 | 6143 | 137 | 317 | 19 | .. | 10 |

## CLASSIFICATION OF DEATHS IN CITY

*Embracing Philadelphia*

| | Cause of death. | Under 1 M. | F. | 1–5 M. | F. | 5–10 M. | F. | 10–20 M. | F. | 20–50 M. | F. | 50–80 M. | F. | 80–100 M. | F. | 100 & over M. | F. | Age unknown M. | F. | Born in State. | N. England States. | Middle States. | Southern States. | Southwest'n States. | Northeast'n States. |
|---|---|---|---|---|---|---|---|---|---|---|---|---|---|---|---|---|---|---|---|---|---|---|---|---|---|
| 1 | Abscess | | 1 | | 1 | | | | 1 | 2 | | 1 | 2 | | | | | | | 5 | | 1 | | | |
| 2 | Accident, not spec'd. | 2 | | 5 | 1 | 5 | 1 | 6 | 3 | 25 | | 6 | 2 | 1 | 1 | | | | | 27 | 1 | 10 | | | |

## SECTION OF THE STATE OF PENNSYLVANIA—Continued.

| NATIVITIES. California and Territories. | Ireland. | Germany. | Other foreign countries. | Unknown. | SEASON OF DECEASE. Spring. | Summer. | Autumn. | Winter. | DURATION OF SICKNESS. Under 1 week. | 1 week and under 1 month. | 1 month and under 3 months. | 3 months and over. | WHITES. Males. | Females. | Total. | COLORED. Slaves. Black. M. | Slaves. Black. F. | Slaves. Mulatto. M. | Slaves. Mulatto. F. | Free. Black. M. | Free. Black. F. | Free. Mul. M | Free. Mul. F. | Aggregate deaths. | |
|---|---|---|---|---|---|---|---|---|---|---|---|---|---|---|---|---|---|---|---|---|---|---|---|---|---|
| .... | .... | .... | .... | .... | .... | 1 | 2 | .... | 1 | 1 | 1 | .... | 2 | 1 | 3 | .... | .... | .... | .... | .... | .... | .... | .... | 3 | 1 |
| .... | .... | .... | 2 | .... | 175 | 77 | 44 | 70 | 171 | 163 | 24 | 4 | 181 | 184 | 365 | .... | .... | .... | .... | .... | 1 | .... | .... | 366 | 2 |
| .... | 4 | .... | .... | .... | .... | 1 | 3 | 2 | .... | 5 | .... | 1 | 3 | 3 | 6 | .... | .... | .... | .... | .... | .... | .... | .... | 6 | 3 |
| .... | 3 | 2 | 4 | .... | 37 | 17 | 41 | 27 | 13 | 81 | 25 | 1 | 67 | 55 | 122 | .... | .... | .... | .... | .... | .... | .... | .... | 122 | 4 |
| .... | .... | .... | .... | .... | 1 | 1 | .... | .... | .... | 1 | 1 | .... | .... | 2 | 2 | .... | .... | .... | .... | .... | .... | .... | .... | 2 | 5 |
| .... | 2 | .... | .... | .... | 2 | .... | .... | 1 | 3 | .... | .... | .... | 3 | .... | 3 | .... | .... | .... | .... | .... | .... | .... | .... | 3 | 6 |
| .... | .... | .... | 1 | .... | .... | 2 | .... | .... | 1 | .... | .... | 1 | 2 | .... | 2 | .... | .... | .... | .... | .... | .... | .... | .... | 2 | 7 |
| .... | 2 | .... | .... | .... | 6 | 8 | 3 | 3 | 3 | 9 | 3 | 5 | 20 | .... | 20 | .... | .... | .... | .... | .... | .... | .... | .... | 20 | 8 |
| .... | 1 | 1 | .... | .... | 6 | 7 | 4 | 12 | 11 | 4 | 5 | 8 | 12 | 15 | 27 | .... | .... | .... | .... | .... | 1 | 1 | .... | 29 | 9 |
| .... | .... | 1 | .... | .... | 8 | 4 | .... | 4 | 7 | 4 | 1 | 3 | 11 | 5 | 16 | .... | .... | .... | .... | .... | .... | .... | .... | 16 | 10 |
| .... | .... | .... | .... | .... | 1 | 2 | 3 | .... | 1 | 4 | 1 | .... | 4 | 1 | 5 | .... | .... | .... | .... | 1 | .... | .... | .... | 6 | 11 |
| .... | .... | .... | .... | .... | .... | 1 | .... | 1 | .... | .... | .... | 2 | 1 | 1 | 2 | .... | .... | .... | .... | .... | .... | .... | .... | 2 | 12 |
| .... | .... | .... | .... | .... | 6 | 2 | 1 | 1 | 8 | 2 | .... | .... | 9 | 1 | 10 | .... | .... | .... | .... | .... | .... | .... | .... | 10 | 13 |
| .... | 1 | .... | .... | .... | 13 | 19 | 12 | 5 | 3 | 34 | 9 | 4 | 15 | 30 | 45 | .... | .... | .... | .... | 1 | .... | 2 | 2 | 50 | 14 |
| .... | 3 | .... | .... | .... | 10 | 16 | 8 | 10 | 8 | 24 | 8 | 2 | 27 | 18 | 45 | .... | .... | .... | .... | .... | .... | .... | 1 | 46 | 15 |
| .... | 1 | .... | 3 | .... | 45 | 28 | 17 | 17 | 33 | 59 | 7 | 9 | 64 | 43 | 107 | .... | .... | .... | .... | 1 | .... | .... | .... | 108 | 16 |
| .... | 2 | 1 | 1 | 1 | 22 | 20 | 28 | 10 | 35 | 30 | 7 | 5 | 52 | 27 | 79 | .... | .... | .... | .... | .... | 1 | .... | .... | 80 | 17 |
| .... | 3 | .... | 1 | .... | 52 | 22 | 32 | 26 | 61 | 58 | 7 | 4 | 86 | 50 | 136 | .... | .... | .... | .... | .... | .... | .... | .... | 136 | 18 |
| .... | .... | .... | .... | .... | .... | .... | 1 | .... | .... | 1 | .... | .... | .... | 1 | 1 | .... | .... | .... | .... | .... | .... | .... | .... | 1 | 19 |
| .... | .... | .... | .... | .... | 4 | 1 | .... | 2 | 2 | 4 | 1 | .... | 5 | 2 | 7 | .... | .... | .... | .... | .... | .... | .... | .... | 7 | 20 |
| .... | .... | 3 | .... | 1 | 3 | 4 | 1 | 5 | 1 | 2 | .... | 8 | 8 | 5 | 13 | .... | .... | .... | .... | .... | .... | .... | .... | 13 | 21 |
| .... | 2 | .... | .... | 1 | 2 | 4 | 3 | 1 | 6 | 3 | .... | .... | 10 | .... | 10 | .... | .... | .... | .... | .... | .... | .... | .... | 10 | 22 |
| .... | .... | .... | .... | 1 | 5 | 2 | .... | 4 | 4 | 4 | 2 | 2 | 5 | 7 | 12 | .... | .... | .... | .... | .... | .... | .... | .... | 12 | 23 |
| .... | .... | .... | .... | .... | 2 | 1 | 1 | 1 | .... | 2 | 1 | 2 | 4 | 1 | 5 | .... | .... | .... | .... | .... | .... | .... | .... | 5 | 24 |
| .... | 1 | .... | .... | .... | 1 | 2 | 1 | 2 | 2 | 2 | .... | 1 | 5 | .... | 5 | .... | .... | .... | .... | 1 | .... | .... | .... | 6 | 25 |
| .... | .... | .... | .... | .... | .... | 3 | .... | .... | 3 | .... | .... | .... | 3 | .... | 3 | .... | .... | .... | .... | .... | .... | .... | .... | 3 | 26 |
| .... | 4 | 1 | .... | .... | 16 | 8 | 10 | 10 | 4 | 19 | 7 | 13 | 21 | 23 | 44 | .... | .... | .... | .... | .... | .... | .... | .... | 44 | 27 |
| .... | .... | 1 | .... | .... | 2 | 1 | 1 | .... | 3 | 1 | .... | .... | 2 | 2 | 4 | .... | .... | .... | .... | .... | .... | .... | .... | 4 | 28 |
| .... | 2 | .... | .... | .... | 14 | 3 | 4 | 4 | 4 | 11 | 2 | 8 | 18 | 7 | 25 | .... | .... | .... | .... | .... | .... | .... | .... | 25 | 29 |
| .... | .... | .... | .... | .... | 1 | 1 | .... | .... | 1 | .... | .... | .... | 1 | 1 | 2 | .... | .... | .... | .... | .... | .... | .... | .... | 2 | 30 |
| .... | 2 | 2 | 1 | .... | 4 | 3 | 4 | 4 | 8 | 4 | .... | .... | 14 | .... | 14 | .... | .... | .... | .... | 1 | .... | .... | .... | 15 | 31 |
| .... | 1 | .... | .... | .... | 3 | 4 | 6 | 4 | 1 | 5 | 5 | 6 | 9 | 10 | 19 | .... | .... | .... | .... | .... | .... | .... | .... | 19 | 32 |
| .... | 2 | 1 | .... | .... | 36 | 28 | 11 | 21 | 19 | 54 | 8 | 4 | 42 | 48 | 90 | .... | .... | .... | .... | 1 | .... | .... | .... | 91 | 33 |
| .... | .... | .... | .... | .... | .... | 3 | 3 | .... | 1 | 1 | 3 | 1 | 3 | 2 | 5 | .... | .... | .... | .... | .... | .... | 1 | .... | 6 | 34 |
| .... | .... | .... | .... | .... | 3 | .... | .... | 1 | .... | 3 | .... | 1 | 4 | .... | 4 | .... | .... | .... | .... | .... | .... | .... | .... | 4 | 35 |
| .... | .... | .... | .... | .... | 3 | 2 | 2 | 2 | 2 | 1 | .... | 6 | 6 | 3 | 9 | .... | .... | .... | .... | .... | .... | .... | .... | 9 | 36 |
| .... | 22 | 6 | 3 | 2 | 84 | 55 | 45 | 55 | 21 | 54 | 14 | 41 | 110 | 129 | 239 | .... | .... | .... | .... | 1 | 3 | .... | .... | 243 | 37 |
| .... | 4 | 3 | 1 | 1 | 85 | 28 | 38 | 11 | 35 | 31 | 8 | 38 | 47 | 65 | 112 | .... | .... | .... | .... | 1 | .... | .... | .... | 113 | 38 |
| .... | .... | .... | .... | .... | .... | .... | .... | 1 | .... | 1 | .... | .... | 1 | .... | 1 | .... | .... | .... | .... | .... | .... | .... | .... | 1 | 39 |
| .... | .... | .... | .... | .... | .... | .... | 1 | .... | 1 | .... | .... | .... | 1 | .... | 1 | .... | .... | .... | .... | .... | .... | .... | .... | 1 | 40 |
| .... | 3 | 2 | 5 | 1 | 33 | 13 | 10 | 12 | 20 | 44 | 2 | 3 | 44 | 23 | 67 | .... | .... | .... | .... | 2 | .... | 2 | 1 | 72 | 41 |
| .... | 3 | 1 | 2 | .... | 65 | 26 | 23 | 24 | 32 | 85 | 8 | 12 | 67 | 66 | 133 | .... | .... | .... | .... | 3 | 2 | 1 | .... | 139 | 42 |
| .... | .... | .... | .... | .... | 1 | .... | .... | 1 | 2 | .... | .... | .... | 2 | .... | 2 | .... | .... | .... | .... | .... | .... | .... | .... | 2 | 43 |
| .... | .... | .... | .... | .... | .... | 1 | .... | .... | .... | 1 | .... | .... | .... | 1 | 1 | .... | .... | .... | .... | .... | .... | .... | .... | 1 | 44 |
| .... | 1 | .... | 2 | .... | 11 | 4 | 3 | 7 | 9 | 14 | .... | 2 | 12 | 13 | 25 | .... | .... | .... | .... | .... | .... | .... | .... | 25 | 45 |
| .... | .... | .... | 1 | .... | 4 | 7 | 9 | 4 | 2 | 11 | 4 | 7 | 15 | 10 | 25 | .... | .... | .... | .... | .... | .... | .... | .... | 25 | 46 |
| .... | .... | 1 | .... | .... | .... | 2 | 1 | 1 | .... | .... | 1 | 3 | 1 | 3 | 4 | .... | .... | .... | .... | .... | .... | .... | .... | 4 | 47 |
| .... | .... | .... | .... | .... | .... | .... | .... | 1 | .... | .... | 1 | .... | .... | 1 | 1 | .... | .... | .... | .... | .... | .... | .... | .... | 1 | 48 |
| .... | 1 | .... | .... | .... | 13 | 12 | 5 | 1 | .... | 5 | 5 | 20 | 21 | 8 | 29 | .... | .... | .... | .... | .... | 1 | .... | 1 | 31 | 49 |
| .... | 2 | .... | .... | .... | 15 | 9 | 2 | 11 | 6 | 28 | 3 | .... | 26 | 10 | 36 | .... | .... | .... | .... | 1 | .... | .... | .... | 37 | 50 |
| .... | .... | .... | 1 | .... | 4 | 3 | 4 | 2 | 1 | 3 | 2 | 4 | 5 | 8 | 13 | .... | .... | .... | .... | .... | .... | .... | .... | 13 | 51 |
| .... | .... | .... | .... | .... | 6 | 2 | 1 | 3 | .... | .... | .... | .... | 6 | 6 | 12 | .... | .... | .... | .... | .... | .... | .... | .... | 12 | 52 |
| .... | .... | .... | .... | .... | .... | .... | .... | 2 | .... | 1 | .... | 1 | 1 | 1 | 2 | .... | .... | .... | .... | .... | .... | .... | .... | 2 | 53 |
| .... | .... | .... | .... | .... | 1 | .... | .... | 1 | 2 | .... | .... | .... | 1 | 1 | 2 | .... | .... | .... | .... | .... | .... | .... | .... | 2 | 54 |
| .... | 1 | 1 | 1 | 1 | 2 | 4 | 1 | 4 | 8 | 2 | .... | .... | 9 | 2 | 11 | .... | .... | .... | .... | .... | .... | .... | .... | 11 | 55 |
| .... | .... | .... | .... | .... | 1 | 1 | 7 | .... | 1 | 7 | 1 | .... | 7 | 2 | 9 | .... | .... | .... | .... | .... | .... | .... | .... | 9 | 56 |
| .... | 1 | .... | .... | .... | .... | 1 | .... | .... | 1 | .... | .... | .... | 1 | .... | 1 | .... | .... | .... | .... | .... | .... | .... | .... | 1 | 57 |
| .... | .... | .... | .... | .... | 3 | 3 | 3 | 3 | 4 | 7 | 1 | .... | 7 | 5 | 12 | .... | .... | .... | .... | .... | .... | .... | .... | 12 | 58 |
| .... | .... | .... | .... | .... | 12 | 8 | 16 | 7 | 17 | 22 | 3 | 1 | 22 | 21 | 43 | .... | .... | .... | .... | .... | .... | .... | .... | 43 | 59 |
| .... | .... | .... | .... | .... | 1 | .... | 1 | 4 | 1 | 3 | 1 | 1 | 1 | 5 | 6 | .... | .... | .... | .... | .... | .... | .... | .... | 6 | 60 |
| .... | .... | .... | .... | .... | 2 | 1 | 1 | 2 | 2 | 1 | .... | 3 | 4 | 2 | 6 | .... | .... | .... | .... | .... | .... | .... | .... | 6 | 61 |
| .... | .... | .... | .... | .... | .... | 3 | 1 | 1 | 1 | 1 | 1 | 2 | 2 | 3 | 5 | .... | .... | .... | .... | .... | .... | .... | .... | 5 | 62 |
| .... | 2 | .... | .... | .... | 5 | 3 | 5 | 4 | 9 | 4 | 3 | 1 | 6 | 11 | 17 | .... | .... | .... | .... | .... | .... | .... | .... | 17 | 63 |
| .... | 35 | 10 | 9 | 3 | 279 | 227 | 236 | 161 | 361 | 224 | 65 | 162 | 490 | 421 | 911 | .... | .... | .... | .... | 9 | 4 | .... | .... | 924 | 64 |
| .... | 297 | 106 | 136 | 18 | 2212 | 1625 | 2039 | 1253 | 2232 | 2674 | 620 | 1250 | 3736 | 3269 | 7055 | .... | .... | .... | .... | 52 | 35 | 14 | 27 | 7183 | |

## SECTION OF THE STATE OF PENNSYLVANIA.

*city and county.*

| | | | | | | | | | | | | | | | | | | | | | | | | | |
|---|---|---|---|---|---|---|---|---|---|---|---|---|---|---|---|---|---|---|---|---|---|---|---|---|---|
| .... | 2 | .. | .... | .... | 3 | 3 | .... | 2 | .... | 6 | .... | 1 | 3 | 5 | 8 | .... | .... | .... | .... | .... | .... | .... | .... | 8 | 1 |
| .... | 9 | 2 | 9 | .... | 9 | 17 | 18 | 18 | 37 | 6 | 1 | 1 | 50 | 8 | 58 | .... | .... | .... | .... | .... | .... | .... | .... | 58 | 2 |

CLASSIFICATION OF DEATHS IN CITY

| | Cause of death. | AGES. | | | | | | | | | | | | | | | | | | NATIVITIES. | | | | | |
|---|---|---|---|---|---|---|---|---|---|---|---|---|---|---|---|---|---|---|---|---|---|---|---|---|---|
| | | Under 1. M. | Under 1. F. | 1 and under 5. M. | 1 and under 5. F. | 5 and under 10. M. | 5 and under 10. F. | 10 and under 20. M. | 10 and under 20. F. | 20 and under 50. M. | 20 and under 50. F. | 50 and under 80. M. | 50 and under 80. F. | 80 and under 100. M | 80 and under 100. F. | 100 & over. M | 100 & over. F. | Age unknown. M | Age unknown. F. | Born in State. | N. England States. | Middle States. | Southern States. | Southwest'n States. | Northwest'n States. |
| 1 | Accident, burned | | | 3 | 9 | 3 | 2 | 3 | 3 | 8 | 2 | | | | | | | | | 26 | | | 1 | | |
| 2 | ....do...drowned | | | 1 | | 8 | | 14 | | 27 | | 3 | | | | | | | | 34 | | 7 | 1 | | |
| 3 | ....do...scalded | | 1 | 5 | | | 1 | | | | | | | | | | | | | 7 | | | | | |
| 4 | Apoplexy | | | | 2 | 2 | | 1 | 2 | 20 | 4 | 25 | 16 | 2 | | | | | | 41 | 1 | 13 | | 1 | |
| 5 | Asthma | 2 | | | 2 | | | | | 2 | 1 | 1 | 7 | | 1 | | | | | 8 | | 6 | | | |
| 6 | Bowels, disease of | 7 | 11 | 7 | 8 | 1 | 2 | 1 | | 3 | 2 | 4 | 1 | | | | | | | 38 | | 2 | 1 | | |
| 7 | Brain,......do | 12 | 10 | 12 | 7 | 2 | 1 | | 2 | 17 | 2 | 4 | 1 | | | | | | | 64 | | 2 | | | |
| 8 | Bronchitis | 2 | 1 | 1 | 1 | 3 | 1 | | | 2 | 5 | 4 | 3 | | | | | | | 17 | | 2 | 1 | | 1 |
| 9 | Cancer | 2 | | | | | | | | 9 | 6 | 7 | 9 | 1 | 3 | | | | | 20 | | 2 | | | |
| 10 | Carbuncle | | | | | | | 1 | | 1 | | | | | | | | | | 2 | | | | | |
| 11 | Catarrh | 31 | 23 | 19 | 30 | 2 | 1 | | 1 | 3 | 1 | | | 1 | | | | | | 109 | | 2 | | | |
| 12 | Childbirth | | | | | | | | 2 | | 31 | | | | | | | | | 16 | | 2 | 1 | | |
| 13 | Cholera | 11 | 13 | 32 | 24 | 14 | 12 | 39 | 24 | 254 | 182 | 106 | 77 | 2 | 13 | 1 | | 4 | 2 | 405 | 7 | 84 | 14 | 1 | 2 |
| 14 | ...do...infantum | 38 | 37 | 38 | 22 | 1 | 1 | | | | | | | | | | | | | 129 | | 1 | | | |
| 15 | ...do...morbus | 8 | 10 | 6 | 5 | 1 | 2 | 4 | 1 | 13 | 12 | 4 | 1 | | 1 | | | | | 48 | 1 | 10 | | | |
| 16 | Colic | | 2 | | | | | 1 | | 3 | 2 | 1 | 1 | | | | | | | 5 | | 1 | | | |
| 17 | Congest'n, not spec'd | | | | | 1 | | | | | | | | | | | | | | 1 | | | | | |
| 18 | ....do....brain | | 4 | 4 | 3 | 2 | 2 | 3 | | 7 | | 2 | 1 | | | | | | | 19 | 1 | 1 | | | |
| 19 | Consumption | 18 | 21 | 27 | 31 | 7 | 13 | 24 | 38 | 286 | 285 | 77 | 68 | 7 | 1 | | | 1 | 1 | 563 | 13 | 87 | 9 | 1 | 6 |
| 20 | Convulsions | 51 | 34 | 22 | 28 | 4 | 4 | 2 | | 9 | 6 | | 2 | | 1 | | | | | 149 | | 4 | | | |
| 21 | Cramp | | | 1 | | | | | | 2 | | | | | | | | | | 1 | | | | | |
| 22 | Croup | 17 | 14 | 66 | 49 | 7 | 10 | | 1 | | 1 | | 1 | | | | | | | 152 | | 5 | | | 2 |
| 23 | Debility | 17 | 13 | 1 | 2 | | | | | 2 | 4 | 1 | 3 | | | | | | | 37 | | 1 | | | |
| 24 | Diabetes | | | | | | | | | 1 | | | | | | | | | | 1 | | | | | |
| 25 | Diarrhœa | 30 | 28 | 19 | 16 | 8 | 5 | 1 | 3 | 26 | 16 | 5 | 14 | 2 | | | | | | 124 | 1 | 7 | | | |
| 26 | Dropsy | 21 | 14 | 32 | 19 | 7 | 4 | 5 | 6 | 35 | 19 | 28 | 29 | 1 | 4 | | | | | 160 | 2 | 17 | 1 | | |
| 27 | Dysentery | 63 | 72 | 132 | 95 | 27 | 13 | 17 | 8 | 83 | 54 | 35 | 37 | 4 | 5 | | | | | 471 | 3 | 22 | 5 | | 2 |
| 28 | Dyspepsia | | | | | | | | | 1 | | 1 | | | | | | | | | | | | | |
| 29 | Epilepsy | | | 1 | | | | 2 | 2 | 8 | 4 | 1 | | | 1 | | | | | 8 | | 2 | 1 | | |
| 30 | Erysipelas | 3 | 9 | 2 | 2 | | 2 | 1 | | 8 | 4 | 4 | 6 | | 1 | | | | | 32 | 1 | 2 | | | |
| 31 | Fever, not specified | 7 | 6 | 13 | 14 | 2 | 4 | 2 | 5 | 16 | 4 | 1 | | | | | | | | 58 | | 6 | | | |
| 32 | ..do .bilious | 2 | 2 | 7 | 5 | 3 | 4 | 1 | 3 | 14 | 7 | 7 | 5 | 1 | | | | | | 38 | 2 | 5 | | | 1 |
| 33 | ..do..brain | 16 | 20 | 30 | 23 | 11 | 6 | 4 | 3 | 19 | 5 | 4 | | | | | | | | 116 | | 4 | | | 1 |
| 34 | ..do..catarrhal | 3 | 4 | 7 | 8 | | | | | | | | | | | | | | | 22 | | | | | |
| 35 | ..do..congestive | 1 | | | 1 | | | | | | | | 1 | | | | | | | 2 | | 1 | | | |
| 36 | ..do..intermittent | 2 | 1 | 2 | 2 | | | 1 | | 1 | 3 | 2 | | | | | | | | 8 | | 1 | | | |
| 37 | ..do..puerperal | | | | | | | | | | 1 | | | | | | | | | 1 | | | | | |
| 38 | ..do..remittent | | | | | | | 1 | 1 | 1 | | | | | | | | | | 2 | | | | | |
| 39 | ..do..scarlet | 25 | 18 | 159 | 137 | 44 | 48 | 7 | 5 | 3 | 2 | | | | | | | | 1 | 415 | 2 | 12 | | 1 | 1 |
| 40 | ..do..ship | | | | | | | 1 | | 2 | 4 | 3 | | | | | | | | 3 | | | | | |
| 41 | ..do..typhus | 2 | 1 | 9 | 2 | 2 | 5 | 12 | 16 | 69 | 30 | 22 | 11 | 1 | 2 | | | | | 82 | 3 | 28 | 3 | | |
| 42 | Fistula | | | | | | | | | | 1 | | | | | | | | | | | | | | |
| 43 | Fracture | 1 | | 2 | | | | 4 | | 22 | | 1 | | | | | | | | 16 | | 1 | | | |
| 44 | Gout | | | | | | | | | | | 1 | | | | | | | | 1 | | | | | |
| 45 | Gravel | 1 | | | | | | | | 1 | | 2 | | | | | | | | 4 | | | | | |
| 46 | Heart, disease of | 13 | 4 | 10 | 4 | 3 | 7 | 7 | 7 | 39 | 22 | 18 | 21 | 4 | 1 | | | | | 107 | 1 | 17 | 1 | | 1 |
| 47 | Hemorrhage | | | | 1 | | | 1 | 1 | 8 | 3 | 1 | | | | | | | | 8 | 1 | 1 | | | |
| 48 | Hernia | 2 | | | | | | | | 3 | 1 | | | | | | | 1 | | 4 | 1 | | | | |
| 49 | Hip, disease of | | | 1 | | | | | | 2 | 1 | | | | | | | | | 2 | | | | | |
| 50 | Hives | | | 1 | | | | | | | | | | | | | | | | 1 | | | | | |
| 51 | Hooping cough | 11 | 14 | 15 | 17 | 3 | 2 | | | | | | | | | | | | | 58 | | | | | |
| 52 | Hydrocephalus | 19 | 15 | 28 | 24 | 4 | 3 | 1 | | 1 | | | | | | | | | | 88 | | 2 | | | |
| 53 | Hydrophobia | | | | | | | | | 2 | | | | | | | | | | 2 | | | | | |
| 54 | Inflamat'n, not spe'd | 4 | 4 | 3 | | | | 1 | 1 | 1 | 2 | 2 | 1 | | | | | | | 16 | | | | | |
| 55 | ....do......bowels | 10 | 7 | 5 | 2 | 3 | 3 | | | 5 | 5 | 5 | 4 | | | | | | | 37 | | 3 | | | |
| 56 | ....do......brain | 7 | 6 | 17 | 10 | 3 | 1 | 2 | 3 | 13 | 2 | 1 | | | | | | | | 47 | | 2 | | | |
| 57 | ....do......stomach | | | | | | | | | | | | 2 | | | | | | | 1 | | | | | |
| 58 | Insanity | | | | | | | | 2 | 16 | 5 | 2 | 2 | | | | | | | 9 | | 4 | | | |
| 59 | Intemperance | | | | | | | | | 1 | 3 | 1 | | | | | | | | 2 | | | | | |
| 60 | Jaundice | | 3 | | 1 | | | | 1 | 4 | | 2 | 1 | | | | | | | 8 | | | | | |
| 61 | Kidneys, disease of | | | | 1 | 1 | | 2 | | 5 | | 1 | | 1 | | | | | | 7 | | | | | |
| 62 | Killed | | | | | | | 1 | | 1 | | 2 | | | | | | | | 3 | | | | | |
| 63 | Liver, disease of | 4 | 2 | 4 | 3 | | | | | 14 | 6 | 4 | 7 | | | | | | | 23 | 1 | 6 | | | |
| 64 | Lockjaw | | | | | 1 | | 2 | 1 | 3 | | 1 | | | | | | | | 7 | | 1 | | | |
| 65 | Lungs, disease of | 1 | 3 | 6 | 3 | 1 | | 1 | | 4 | 2 | 6 | 2 | | | | | | | 23 | 2 | | 1 | | |
| 66 | Malformation | 3 | | | | | | | | | | | | | | | | | | 3 | | | | | |
| 67 | Mania-a-potu | | | | | | | | | 10 | | 4 | | | | | | | | 7 | | 2 | | | |
| 68 | Marasmus | 10 | 9 | 11 | 13 | 1 | 2 | | | | | 2 | 2 | | | | | | | 40 | | 2 | | | |
| 69 | Measles | 11 | 7 | 35 | 46 | 2 | 4 | 1 | | 1 | 1 | | | | | | | | | 91 | | 5 | | | |
| 70 | Menses, suppres'n of | | | | | | | | | | 1 | | | | | | | | | | | | | | |
| 71 | Mortification | 1 | | | | | | | 1 | 3 | | 3 | | | 1 | | | | | 6 | | | | | |
| 72 | Mumps | 1 | | | | | | | | | | | | | | | | | | 1 | | | | | |
| 73 | Murder | | | | | | | 1 | | 7 | | | 1 | | | | | | | 5 | | 1 | | | |
| 74 | Neuralgia | | | | | | | | | 1 | 1 | | 1 | | | | | | | 1 | | 1 | | | |
| 75 | Old age | | | | | | | | | | | 38 | 60 | 40 | 54 | | | 2 | 5 | 86 | 3 | 29 | 2 | | |

## CTION OF THE STATE OF PENNSYLVANIA—Continued.

| NATIVITIES. Ireland. | NATIVITIES. Germany. | NATIVITIES. Other foreign countries. | NATIVITIES. Unknown. | SEASON OF DECEASE. Spring. | SEASON OF DECEASE. Summer. | SEASON OF DECEASE. Autumn. | SEASON OF DECEASE. Winter. | DURATION OF SICKNESS. Under 1 week. | DURATION OF SICKNESS. 1 week and under 1 month. | DURATION OF SICKNESS. 1 month and under 3 months. | DURATION OF SICKNESS. 3 months and over. | WHITES. Males. | WHITES. Females. | WHITES. Total. | COLORED. Slaves. Black. M. | COLORED. Slaves. Black. F. | COLORED. Slaves. Mulatto. M. | COLORED. Slaves. Mulatto. F. | COLORED. Free. Black. M. | COLORED. Free. Black. F. | COLORED. Free. Mul. M | COLORED. Free. Mul. F. | Aggregate deaths. | |
|---|---|---|---|---|---|---|---|---|---|---|---|---|---|---|---|---|---|---|---|---|---|---|---|---|
| 3 | 3 | | | 10 | 9 | 8 | 6 | 24 | 3 | 3 | | 17 | 15 | 32 | | | | | | 1 | | | 33 | 1 |
| 6 | 1 | 4 | | 9 | 26 | 11 | 6 | 53 | | | | 49 | | 49 | | | | | 2 | | 2 | | 53 | 2 |
| | | | | 1 | 3 | 1 | 2 | 5 | 2 | | | 5 | 2 | 7 | | | | | | | | | 7 | 3 |
| 10 | 2 | 6 | | 12 | 20 | 22 | 20 | 56 | 5 | 2 | 2 | 49 | 24 | 73 | | | | | 1 | | | | 74 | 4 |
| 1 | | 1 | | 6 | 4 | 5 | 1 | 5 | 7 | | 4 | 2 | 11 | 13 | | | | | 3 | | | | 16 | 5 |
| 6 | | | | 5 | 15 | 13 | 10 | 9 | 24 | 4 | 6 | 23 | 24 | 47 | | | | | | | | | 47 | 6 |
| 1 | 1 | 2 | | 23 | 15 | 15 | 17 | 19 | 32 | 12 | 4 | 46 | 23 | 69 | | | | | 1 | | | | 70 | 7 |
| | 1 | 1 | | 7 | 5 | 6 | 4 | 3 | 9 | 2 | 7 | 12 | 10 | 22 | | | | | | | | 1 | 23 | 8 |
| 5 | 4 | 6 | | 14 | 5 | 5 | 9 | 3 | 7 | 1 | 16 | 19 | 18 | 37 | | | | | | | | | 37 | 9 |
| | | | | | 1 | 1 | | 1 | | | 1 | 2 | | 2 | | | | | | | | | 2 | 10 |
| 1 | | | | 48 | 17 | 14 | 31 | 28 | 58 | 18 | 7 | 50 | 52 | 102 | | | | | 6 | 4 | | | 112 | 11 |
| 8 | 4 | 2 | | 8 | 12 | 5 | 8 | 13 | 12 | 3 | | | 32 | 32 | | | | | | | | 1 | 33 | 12 |
| 199 | 49 | 49 | | 9 | 604 | 171 | 19 | 705 | 87 | 8 | 6 | 433 | 321 | 754 | | | | | 30 | 22 | | 4 | 810 | 13 |
| 6 | | 1 | | 11 | 66 | 40 | 17 | 51 | 71 | 11 | 2 | 76 | 57 | 133 | | | | | 1 | 3 | | | 137 | 14 |
| 7 | | 2 | | 7 | 16 | 12 | 4 | 10 | 27 | 2 | | 32 | 28 | 60 | | | | | 4 | 4 | | | 68 | 15 |
| 3 | 1 | | | 4 | 4 | 1 | 1 | 8 | 2 | | | 5 | 5 | 10 | | | | | | | | | 10 | 16 |
| | | | | | 1 | | | | 1 | | | 1 | | 1 | | | | | | | | | 1 | 17 |
| 4 | 3 | | | 6 | 9 | 7 | 6 | 15 | 9 | | 4 | 17 | 9 | 26 | | | | | 1 | 1 | | | 28 | 18 |
| 132 | 38 | 55 | 1 | 217 | 258 | 202 | 163 | 38 | 152 | 119 | 387 | 416 | 423 | 839 | | | | | 27 | 29 | 4 | 6 | 905 | 19 |
| 5 | 1 | 4 | | 46 | 58 | 27 | 28 | 107 | 32 | 10 | 3 | 87 | 72 | 159 | | | | | 1 | 3 | | | 163 | 20 |
| 1 | | 1 | | | 2 | 1 | | 3 | | | | 3 | | 3 | | | | | | | | | 3 | 21 |
| 4 | | 3 | | 38 | 43 | 38 | 46 | 133 | 30 | 2 | | 87 | 75 | 162 | | | | | 3 | 1 | | | 166 | 22 |
| 3 | | 2 | | 11 | 16 | 7 | 9 | 14 | 17 | 2 | 7 | 21 | 22 | 43 | | | | | | | | | 43 | 23 |
| | | | | | 1 | | | | | | | 1 | | 1 | | | | | | | | | 1 | 24 |
| 22 | 10 | 9 | | 18 | 68 | 74 | 12 | 62 | 86 | 14 | 10 | 85 | 74 | 159 | | | | | 6 | 8 | | | 173 | 25 |
| 19 | 13 | 12 | | 60 | 63 | 56 | 45 | 34 | 78 | 35 | 59 | 121 | 89 | 210 | | | | | 5 | 5 | 3 | 1 | 224 | 26 |
| 93 | 18 | 30 | 1 | 49 | 205 | 332 | 57 | 148 | 337 | 70 | 42 | 348 | 274 | 622 | | | | | 12 | 10 | 1 | | 645 | 27 |
| 2 | | | | 2 | | | | | | | 2 | 2 | | 2 | | | | | | | | | 2 | 28 |
| 5 | 1 | 2 | | 3 | 10 | 4 | 2 | 4 | 2 | 1 | 10 | 10 | 7 | 17 | | | | | 2 | | | | 19 | 29 |
| 3 | 2 | 2 | | 14 | 12 | 9 | 7 | 9 | 20 | 7 | 4 | 14 | 24 | 38 | | | | | 4 | | | | 42 | 30 |
| 8 | 1 | 1 | | 20 | 28 | 16 | 9 | 21 | 38 | 12 | 1 | 40 | 32 | 72 | | | | | 1 | 1 | | | 74 | 31 |
| 6 | 5 | 4 | | 7 | 16 | 28 | 10 | 6 | 43 | 10 | 2 | 35 | 25 | 60 | | | | | | 1 | | | 61 | 32 |
| 11 | 4 | 5 | | 27 | 49 | 39 | 26 | 60 | 60 | 13 | 4 | 82 | 54 | 136 | | | | | 2 | 3 | | | 141 | 33 |
| | | | | 5 | 6 | 7 | 4 | 8 | 7 | 1 | 5 | 8 | 9 | 17 | | | | | 2 | 3 | | | 22 | 34 |
| | | | | 1 | 1 | | 1 | 2 | 1 | | | 1 | 2 | 3 | | | | | | | | | 3 | 35 |
| 4 | | 1 | | 2 | 4 | 4 | 4 | 1 | 9 | 3 | 1 | 8 | 5 | 13 | | | | | | | | 1 | 14 | 36 |
| | | | | 1 | | | | | | 1 | | | 1 | 1 | | | | | | | | | 1 | 37 |
| 1 | | | | 1 | 1 | 1 | | | 3 | | | 2 | 1 | 3 | | | | | | | | | 3 | 38 |
| 12 | 2 | 4 | | 188 | 118 | 48 | 94 | 186 | 234 | 19 | 5 | 236 | 208 | 444 | | | | | | 2 | 2 | 1 | 449 | 39 |
| 6 | | 1 | | 4 | 3 | 1 | 2 | | 8 | 1 | | 6 | 4 | 10 | | | | | | | | | 10 | 40 |
| 41 | 19 | 8 | | 40 | 39 | 69 | 36 | 19 | 143 | 21 | 1 | 116 | 64 | 180 | | | | | 1 | 3 | | | 184 | 41 |
| 1 | | | | | | 1 | | | | 1 | | | 1 | 1 | | | | | | | | | 1 | 42 |
| 10 | 1 | 2 | | 5 | 9 | 10 | 6 | 12 | 8 | | 2 | 28 | | 28 | | | | | 2 | | | | 30 | 43 |
| | | | | | 1 | | | | 1 | | | 1 | | 1 | | | | | | | | | 1 | 44 |
| | | | | 1 | 1 | 1 | 1 | 1 | 1 | | 2 | 4 | | 4 | | | | | | | | | 4 | 45 |
| 18 | 6 | 8 | 1 | 44 | 42 | 34 | 37 | 65 | 33 | 17 | 30 | 84 | 60 | 144 | | | | | 9 | 5 | 1 | 1 | 160 | 46 |
| 2 | 1 | 2 | | 2 | 5 | 8 | | 4 | 9 | 2 | | 9 | 4 | 13 | | | | | 1 | 1 | | | 15 | 47 |
| | | 2 | | 3 | | 2 | 2 | 5 | 1 | | | 5 | 1 | 6 | | | | | 1 | | | | 7 | 48 |
| 1 | | 1 | | 1 | 1 | 2 | | 2 | | 1 | | 3 | 1 | 4 | | | | | | | | | 4 | 49 |
| | | | | | 1 | | | 1 | | | | 1 | | 1 | | | | | | | | | 1 | 50 |
| 3 | | 1 | | 22 | 18 | 18 | 2 | 9 | 27 | 12 | 7 | 28 | 30 | 58 | | | | | 1 | 3 | | | 62 | 51 |
| 3 | 2 | | | 29 | 22 | 21 | 23 | 22 | 59 | 7 | 5 | 49 | 41 | 90 | | | | | 3 | 1 | 1 | | 95 | 52 |
| | | | | 1 | | 1 | | 2 | | | | 2 | | 2 | | | | | | | | | 2 | 53 |
| 2 | | 1 | | 7 | 7 | 3 | 2 | 9 | 7 | 1 | 2 | 11 | 8 | 19 | | | | | | | | | 19 | 54 |
| 7 | 1 | 1 | | 7 | 18 | 19 | 5 | 17 | 21 | 6 | 4 | 27 | 21 | 48 | | | | | 1 | | | | 49 | 55 |
| 7 | 1 | 8 | | 14 | 20 | 12 | 19 | 26 | 36 | 2 | | 43 | 20 | 63 | | | | | | 2 | | | 65 | 56 |
| 1 | | | | 1 | | | 1 | | 1 | | 1 | | 2 | 2 | | | | | | | | | 2 | 57 |
| 9 | 3 | 2 | | 5 | 12 | 7 | 3 | 1 | 5 | | 20 | 15 | 8 | 23 | | | | | 3 | 1 | | | 27 | 58 |
| 3 | | | | 2 | | 1 | 2 | 1 | 3 | 1 | | 2 | 3 | 5 | | | | | | | | | 5 | 59 |
| 4 | | | | 2 | 4 | 3 | 3 | | 9 | 2 | 1 | 6 | 6 | 12 | | | | | | | | | 12 | 60 |
| 3 | | 1 | | 1 | 6 | 1 | 3 | 5 | 6 | | | 10 | 1 | 11 | | | | | | | | | 11 | 61 |
| | | 1 | | 2 | 2 | | | 4 | | | | 4 | | 4 | | | | | | | | | 4 | 62 |
| 7 | 2 | 5 | | 13 | 12 | 10 | 8 | 8 | 10 | 10 | 13 | 26 | 18 | 44 | | | | | | | | | 44 | 63 |
| | | | | 3 | 1 | 3 | 1 | 4 | 4 | | | 7 | 1 | 8 | | | | | | | | | 8 | 64 |
| 2 | 1 | | | 13 | 5 | 4 | 7 | 11 | 7 | 2 | 4 | 19 | 10 | 29 | | | | | | | | | 29 | 65 |
| | | | | | 1 | | 2 | 2 | 1 | | | 3 | | 3 | | | | | | | | | 3 | 66 |
| 4 | | 1 | | 3 | 7 | 1 | 3 | 11 | 2 | 1 | | 14 | | 14 | | | | | | | | | 14 | 67 |
| 4 | 1 | 2 | 1 | 9 | 16 | 20 | 5 | 3 | 41 | 2 | 4 | 21 | 25 | 46 | | | | | 3 | 1 | | | 50 | 68 |
| 8 | 2 | 2 | | 45 | 38 | 13 | 10 | 25 | 63 | 11 | 5 | 50 | 57 | 107 | | | | | | 1 | | | 108 | 69 |
| 1 | | | | | | 1 | | | 1 | | | | 1 | 1 | | | | | | | | | 1 | 70 |
| 2 | | 1 | | 1 | 5 | 2 | 1 | 2 | 4 | 1 | 2 | 7 | | 7 | | | | | | 2 | | | 9 | 71 |
| | | | | 1 | | | | | 1 | | | 1 | | 1 | | | | | | | | | 1 | 72 |
| 1 | 1 | 1 | | 1 | 3 | 4 | | 4 | | | | 8 | 1 | 9 | | | | | | | | | 9 | 73 |
| | 1 | | | | 1 | 2 | | 1 | 1 | | 1 | 1 | 2 | 3 | | | | | | | | | 3 | 74 |
| 37 | 18 | 24 | | 44 | 77 | 44 | 34 | 26 | 74 | 23 | 26 | 75 | 111 | 186 | | | | | 5 | 7 | | 1 | 199 | 75 |

## CLASSIFICATION OF DEATHS IN CITY

| | Cause of Death. | Ages. Under 1. M. | Under 1. F. | 1 and under 5. M. | 1 and under 5. F. | 5 and under 10. M. | 5 and under 10. F. | 10 and under 20. M. | 10 and under 20. F. | 20 and under 50. M. | 20 and under 50. F. | 50 and under 80. M. | 50 and under 80. F. | 80 and under 100. M | 80 and under 100. F. | 100 & over. M | 100 & over. F. | Age unknown. M | Age unknown. F. | Nativities. Born in State. | N. England States. | Middle States. | Southern States. | Southwest'n States. | Northwest'n States. |
|---|---|---|---|---|---|---|---|---|---|---|---|---|---|---|---|---|---|---|---|---|---|---|---|---|---|
| 1 | Paralysis | | | 2 | 1 | | 1 | | | 11 | 4 | 10 | 19 | | 4 | | | | 1 | 26 | | 10 | 1 | | |
| 2 | Peritonitis | | | | | | | 1 | | 1 | 2 | | | | | | | | | 2 | | 1 | | | |
| 3 | Piles | | | | | | | | | | 1 | | | | | | | | | | | | | | |
| 4 | Pleurisy | | | | | | | | | 7 | 1 | 4 | 1 | | | | | | | 4 | | 2 | | | |
| 5 | Pneumonia | 10 | 5 | 9 | 11 | 2 | 2 | 1 | 2 | 15 | 4 | 12 | 2 | 1 | | | | | | 53 | | | | | 1 |
| 6 | Poison | | 1 | 1 | | | | | | | | | | | | | | | | 2 | | | | | |
| 7 | Putrid sore throat | | | | 2 | | | | | | | | | | | | | | | 2 | | | | | |
| 8 | Quinsy | | | 3 | | 1 | | 1 | | 1 | | | 2 | | | | | | | 7 | | 1 | | | |
| 9 | Rheumatism | 1 | | | 1 | | 2 | 1 | 3 | 4 | 6 | 5 | 4 | 1 | | | | | | 15 | 1 | 3 | | | |
| 10 | Scrofula | 9 | 16 | 17 | 12 | 2 | 3 | 8 | 1 | 5 | 2 | | | | | | | | | 62 | | 4 | | | |
| 11 | Scurvy | | | | | | | | | 1 | | | | | | | | | | | | | | | |
| 12 | Small pox | 4 | 7 | 12 | 21 | 1 | | 3 | 1 | 6 | 5 | | | | | | | | | 51 | | 2 | | | |
| 13 | Spine, disease of | 3 | 1 | 2 | 1 | 3 | | 8 | 2 | 6 | 2 | 2 | | | | | | 1 | | 19 | | 2 | | | |
| 14 | Stillborn | 4 | 5 | | | | | | | | | | | | | | | | | 9 | | | | | |
| 15 | Stomach, disease of | 1 | | 1 | | | | | | | | 1 | | | | | | | | 3 | | | | | |
| 16 | Suffocation | 2 | 1 | | | | | | | | | | | | | | | | | 3 | | | | | |
| 17 | Suicide | | | | | | | | 1 | 8 | | | | | | | | | | 9 | | | | | |
| 18 | Summer complaint | 9 | 5 | 15 | 7 | | | | | | | | | | | | | | | 35 | | | | | |
| 19 | Sun, stroke of | | | | | | | 2 | | 14 | 3 | 1 | | | | | | | | 7 | | 1 | | | |
| 20 | Syphilis | | | 1 | | | | | | | | | | | | | | | | 1 | | | | | |
| 21 | Teething | 5 | 4 | 12 | 5 | | | | | | | | | | | | | | | 21 | 1 | 3 | | | |
| 22 | Throat, disease of | 4 | | | 1 | | | | | | | 1 | | | | | | | | 6 | | | | | |
| 23 | Tumor | | | 1 | 1 | | | | | 2 | 2 | 1 | 5 | | | | | | | 6 | 1 | 3 | 1 | | |
| 24 | Ulcer | | | 1 | | | | | | 1 | | | | | | | | | | 1 | | | | | |
| 25 | Uterus, disease of | | | | | | | | | | 3 | | | | | | | | | 2 | | | | | |
| 26 | Venereal | | | | | | | | | 5 | 2 | | | | | | | | | 4 | | 1 | | | |
| 27 | White swelling | | | 1 | 1 | | | | | | | | | | | | | | | 2 | | | | | |
| 28 | Worms | | | 2 | 5 | 1 | | | | | | | | | | | | | | 7 | | | | | |
| 29 | Unknown | 94 | 69 | | | 11 | 9 | 13 | 8 | | | | | 2 | 8 | | | | | 366 | 1 | 26 | 1 | 1 | |
| | Total | 638 | 558 | 927 | 780 | 210 | 183 | 206 | 165 | 1296 | 831 | 537 | 455 | 72 | 102 | 1 | .. | 9 | 10 | 4905 | 51 | 486 | 45 | 5 | 18 |

## CLASSIFICATION OF DEATHS IN THE

| | Cause of Death. | Under 1. M. | Under 1. F. | 1 and under 5. M. | 1 and under 5. F. | 5 and under 10. M. | 5 and under 10. F. | 10 and under 20. M. | 10 and under 20. F. | 20 and under 50. M. | 20 and under 50. F. | 50 and under 80. M. | 50 and under 80. F. | 80 and under 100. M | 80 and under 100. F. | 100 & over. M | 100 & over. F. | Age unknown. M | Age unknown. F. | Born in State. | N. England States. | Middle States. | Southern States. | Southwest'n States. | Northwest'n States. |
|---|---|---|---|---|---|---|---|---|---|---|---|---|---|---|---|---|---|---|---|---|---|---|---|---|---|
| 1 | Abscess | | 1 | | 1 | | | 1 | 1 | 3 | 1 | 1 | 4 | | | | | | | 9 | | 2 | | | |
| 2 | Accident, not specfi'd | 6 | 4 | 29 | 12 | 33 | 8 | 61 | 11 | 144 | 4 | 48 | 12 | 5 | 3 | | | 1 | | 264 | 3 | 23 | 3 | | 5 |
| 3 | ....do...burned | 3 | 2 | 25 | 32 | 4 | 14 | 3 | 6 | 11 | 6 | 2 | 2 | 1 | 1 | | | | | 94 | 1 | 4 | 1 | | |
| 4 | ....do...drowned | | 1 | 18 | 13 | 27 | 3 | 39 | 8 | 77 | 9 | 12 | 2 | | | | | 2 | | 141 | 2 | 17 | 3 | | 2 |
| 5 | ....do...scalded | 1 | 2 | 24 | 12 | 2 | 2 | | | 1 | 1 | | 1 | | | | | | | 42 | | | 1 | | |
| 6 | Apoplexy | 5 | 5 | 7 | 5 | 3 | 2 | 5 | 4 | 36 | 32 | 101 | 71 | 12 | 7 | | | | | 208 | 7 | 33 | 2 | 1 | |
| 7 | Asthma | 3 | 2 | 2 | 2 | | | 1 | 2 | 5 | 3 | 14 | 16 | 1 | 3 | | | | | 34 | | 8 | | | |
| 8 | Bladder, disease of | | | | | | | | | 1 | | 2 | | 4 | | | | | | 4 | | 1 | | | |
| 9 | Bowels.....do | 15 | 13 | 14 | 12 | 3 | 2 | 3 | | 7 | 4 | 7 | 2 | 2 | | | | | | 71 | | 2 | 1 | | 1 |
| 10 | Brain........do | 28 | 15 | 24 | 14 | 11 | 6 | | 5 | 25 | 6 | 8 | 6 | 1 | | | | | | 138 | | 2 | | | 1 |
| 11 | Bronchitis | 7 | 5 | 3 | 8 | 4 | 3 | 4 | 1 | 16 | 12 | 13 | 5 | 1 | 1 | | | | | 63 | | 6 | 1 | | 1 |
| 12 | Cancer | 3 | 1 | 4 | | | 2 | 1 | | 21 | 27 | 48 | 63 | 12 | 7 | | | | | 139 | 3 | 10 | 2 | | |
| 13 | Carbuncle | | | | | | | 1 | | 3 | | 1 | | | | | | | | 5 | | | | | |
| 14 | Catarrh | 45 | 32 | 31 | 35 | 3 | 2 | 1 | 4 | 4 | 4 | 2 | 2 | 1 | | | | | | 161 | | 2 | | | |
| 15 | Chicken pox | 1 | 2 | | | | | | | 1 | | | | | | | | | | 3 | | | | | |
| 16 | Childbirth | | | | | | | | 21 | | 235 | | 3 | | | | | | | 230 | 4 | 14 | 5 | | 2 |
| 17 | Cholera | 18 | 21 | 61 | 52 | 37 | 21 | 75 | 37 | 420 | 240 | 174 | 108 | 9 | 15 | 1 | | 4 | 3 | 664 | 9 | 96 | 28 | 1 | 5 |
| 18 | ....do....infantum | 85 | 59 | 62 | 47 | 5 | 2 | | | | | | | | | | | | | 248 | 1 | 4 | | | |
| 19 | ....do....morbus | 31 | 19 | 34 | 27 | 4 | 7 | 8 | 8 | 41 | 26 | 23 | 13 | 4 | 2 | | | | | 200 | 3 | 16 | | | |
| 20 | Chorea | | 1 | | | | | | 2 | | 1 | | | | | | | | | 4 | | | | | |
| 21 | Colic | 4 | 3 | 3 | 2 | 5 | | 4 | 2 | 19 | 5 | 20 | 11 | | 1 | | | | | 57 | 2 | 6 | | | |
| 22 | Congest'n, not specf'd | | 1 | | 3 | 1 | | | | 3 | 1 | | | | | | | | | 7 | | | | | 1 |
| 23 | ...do.....brain | | 4 | 6 | 3 | 2 | 2 | 5 | 2 | 9 | | 2 | 2 | | | | | | | 28 | 1 | 1 | | | |
| 24 | Consumption | 71 | 73 | 95 | 85 | 28 | 36 | 118 | 187 | 936 | 1009 | 473 | 355 | 32 | 19 | | | 1 | 2 | 2667 | 69 | 240 | 32 | 3 | 12 |
| 25 | Convulsions | 261 | 194 | 99 | 103 | 18 | 14 | 11 | 12 | 35 | 23 | 8 | 5 | 1 | 1 | | | 1 | | 743 | | 10 | | | 2 |
| 26 | Cramp | 2 | | 3 | 2 | | 1 | | 2 | 12 | 3 | 10 | 4 | | | | | | | 30 | | | | | |
| 27 | Croup | 181 | 125 | 313 | 278 | 47 | 44 | 4 | 8 | 2 | 3 | | 1 | | | | | | | 962 | 1 | 16 | | | 6 |
| 28 | Debility | 30 | 29 | 1 | 4 | 1 | | | 1 | 2 | 4 | 1 | 3 | | | | | | | 69 | | 1 | | | |
| 29 | Diabetes | | | | | | 1 | 1 | | 7 | 1 | 6 | 2 | | | | | | | 15 | 1 | | | | |
| 30 | Diarrhœa | 89 | 72 | 103 | 87 | 21 | 18 | 7 | 11 | 59 | 33 | 31 | 35 | 7 | 2 | | | 1 | | 465 | 5 | 26 | | | 1 |
| 31 | Dropsy | 56 | 41 | 72 | 56 | 25 | 15 | 18 | 28 | 92 | 117 | 203 | 192 | 29 | 16 | | | 3 | | 757 | 14 | 56 | 6 | | 2 |
| 32 | Dysentery | 272 | 249 | 589 | 516 | 155 | 123 | 114 | 74 | 197 | 152 | 109 | 104 | 11 | 15 | | | 1 | 2 | 2377 | 8 | 56 | 7 | 1 | 4 |
| 33 | Dyspepsia | 1 | | | | | | 2 | 1 | 14 | 8 | 24 | 12 | 1 | 1 | | | | | 49 | 2 | 4 | | | |
| 34 | Epilepsy | 5 | 4 | 3 | | | | 3 | 5 | 10 | 5 | 1 | 2 | | 1 | | | | | 26 | | 2 | 1 | | |
| 35 | Erysipelas | 34 | 33 | 15 | 17 | 7 | 6 | 8 | 14 | 35 | 44 | 37 | 37 | 1 | 3 | | | | | 251 | 2 | 11 | 3 | | 1 |
| 36 | Executed | | | | | | | | | | 1 | | | | | | | | | 1 | | | | | |
| 37 | Fever, not specified | 78 | 59 | 122 | 123 | 40 | 34 | 67 | 64 | 174 | 142 | 58 | 46 | 5 | 3 | | | | | 898 | 5 | 30 | | | 6 |

## SECTION OF THE STATE OF PENNSYLVANIA—Continued.

| NATIVITIES. | | | | | SEASON OF DECEASE. | | | | DURATION OF SICKNESS. | | | | WHITES. | | | COLORED. | | | | | | | | | |
|---|---|---|---|---|---|---|---|---|---|---|---|---|---|---|---|---|---|---|---|---|---|---|---|---|---|
| | | | | | | | | | | | | | | | | Slaves. | | | | Free. | | | | | |
| | | | | | | | | | | | | | | | | Black. | | Mulatto. | | Black. | | Mul. | | | |
| California and Territories. | Ireland. | Germany. | Other foreign countries. | Unknown. | Spring. | Summer. | Autumn. | Winter. | Under 1 week. | 1 week and under 1 month. | 1 month and under 3 months. | 3 months and over. | Males. | Females. | Total. | M. | F. | M. | F. | M. | F. | M. | F. | Aggregate deaths. | |
| .... | 13 | 1 | 2 | .. | 13 | 14 | 16 | 10 | 11 | 16 | 4 | 16 | 23 | 29 | 52 | .... | .... | .... | .... | .. | 1 | .. | .. | 53 | 1 |
| .... | 1 | .. | .... | .. | .... | 2 | 2 | .... | .... | 3 | 1 | .... | 1 | 2 | 3 | .... | .... | .... | .... | 1 | .. | .. | .. | 4 | 2 |
| .... | 1 | .. | .... | .. | 1 | .... | .... | .... | 1 | .... | .... | .... | .... | 1 | 1 | .... | .... | .... | .... | .. | .. | .. | .. | 1 | 3 |
| .... | 4 | 2 | 1 | .. | 7 | 3 | 2 | 1 | 6 | 6 | .... | 1 | 11 | 2 | 13 | .... | .... | .... | .... | .. | .. | .. | .. | 13 | 4 |
| .... | 14 | 4 | 4 | .. | 25 | 19 | 15 | 16 | 24 | 45 | 5 | 2 | 48 | 26 | 74 | .... | .... | .... | .... | 1 | .. | 1 | .. | 76 | 5 |
| .... | .. | .. | .... | .. | .... | 1 | 1 | .... | 2 | .... | .... | .... | 1 | 1 | 2 | .... | .... | .... | .... | .. | .. | .. | .. | 2 | 6 |
| .... | .. | .. | .... | .. | 2 | .... | .... | .... | .... | 1 | 1 | .... | .... | 2 | 2 | .... | .... | .... | .... | .. | .. | .. | .. | 2 | 7 |
| .... | .. | .. | .... | .. | .... | 3 | 4 | 1 | 3 | 3 | .... | .... | 6 | 2 | 8 | .... | .... | .... | .... | .. | .. | .. | .. | 8 | 8 |
| .... | 4 | .. | 3 | 1 | 11 | 9 | 6 | 2 | 5 | 7 | 5 | 9 | 11 | 14 | 25 | .... | .... | .... | .... | 1 | 2 | .. | .. | 28 | 9 |
| .... | 3 | .. | 1 | .. | 13 | 34 | 11 | 12 | 5 | 42 | 6 | 12 | 32 | 31 | 63 | .... | .... | .... | .... | 4 | 3 | .. | .. | 70 | 10 |
| .... | .. | 1 | .... | .. | .... | .... | 1 | .... | .... | 1 | .... | .... | 1 | .... | 1 | .... | .... | .... | .... | .. | .. | .. | .. | 1 | 11 |
| .... | 4 | 2 | 1 | .. | 16 | 24 | 8 | 11 | 6 | 51 | 2 | 1 | 25 | 34 | 59 | .... | .... | .... | .... | 1 | .. | .. | .. | 60 | 12 |
| .... | 4 | .. | 1 | .. | 9 | 7 | 7 | 3 | 3 | 6 | 2 | 10 | 20 | 5 | 25 | .... | .... | .... | .... | .. | 1 | .. | .. | 26 | 13 |
| .... | .. | .. | .... | .. | .... | 4 | .... | 3 | .... | .... | .... | .... | 3 | 5 | 8 | .... | .... | .... | .... | 1 | .. | .. | .. | 9 | 14 |
| .... | .. | .. | .... | .. | 2 | 1 | .... | .... | 1 | 2 | .... | .... | 3 | .... | 3 | .... | .... | .... | .... | .. | .. | .. | .. | 3 | 15 |
| .... | .. | .. | .... | .. | 2 | .... | 1 | .... | 3 | .... | .... | .... | 2 | .... | 2 | .... | .... | .... | .... | .. | .. | .. | 1 | 3 | 16 |
| .... | .. | .. | .... | .. | 4 | 2 | 1 | 2 | 2 | .... | .... | .... | 8 | 1 | 9 | .... | .... | .... | .... | .. | .. | .. | .. | 9 | 17 |
| .... | 1 | .. | .... | .. | 1 | 22 | 13 | .... | 7 | 12 | 9 | 2 | 22 | 11 | 33 | .... | .... | .... | .... | 1 | 1 | 1 | .. | 36 | 18 |
| .... | 8 | 2 | 2 | .. | 2 | 14 | 4 | .... | 16 | 2 | 2 | .... | 17 | 2 | 19 | .... | .... | .... | .... | .. | 1 | .. | .. | 20 | 19 |
| .... | .. | .. | .... | .. | .... | 1 | .... | .... | .... | 1 | .... | .... | 1 | .... | 1 | .... | .... | .... | .... | .. | .. | .. | .. | 1 | 20 |
| .... | 1 | .. | .... | .. | 8 | 9 | 5 | 4 | 11 | 11 | 3 | 1 | 15 | 8 | 23 | .... | .... | .... | .... | .. | 1 | 2 | .. | 26 | 21 |
| .... | .. | .. | .... | .. | 2 | 3 | 1 | .... | 2 | 2 | .... | 2 | 4 | 1 | 5 | .... | .... | .... | .... | 1 | .. | .. | .. | 6 | 22 |
| .... | .. | 2 | .... | .. | 3 | 6 | 2 | 1 | 3 | 3 | 1 | 5 | 4 | 6 | 10 | .... | .... | .... | .... | .. | .. | .. | 2 | 12 | 23 |
| .... | 1 | .. | .... | .. | 1 | 1 | .... | .... | 1 | 1 | .... | .... | 2 | .... | 2 | .... | .... | .... | .... | .. | .. | .. | .. | 2 | 24 |
| .... | .. | .. | 1 | .. | 1 | 1 | 1 | .... | 1 | 2 | .... | .... | .... | 2 | 2 | .... | .... | .... | .... | .. | 1 | .. | .. | 3 | 25 |
| .... | 1 | .. | 1 | .. | 2 | 3 | .... | 2 | 1 | 3 | 2 | 1 | 4 | 1 | 5 | .... | .... | .... | .... | 1 | 1 | .. | .. | 7 | 26 |
| .... | .. | .. | .... | .. | 1 | 1 | .... | .... | .... | .... | .... | 2 | 1 | 1 | 2 | .... | .... | .... | .... | .. | .. | .. | .. | 2 | 27 |
| .... | 1 | .. | .... | .. | 1 | 3 | 2 | 2 | 1 | 5 | 1 | 1 | 2 | 5 | 7 | .... | .... | .... | .... | .. | .. | 1 | .. | 8 | 28 |
| .... | 89 | 12 | 13 | 1 | 99 | 127 | 137 | 90 | 191 | 80 | 36 | 65 | 256 | 181 | 437 | .... | .... | ... | .... | 13 | 8 | 1 | 1 | 460 | 29 |
| .... | 889 | 252 | 323 | 6 | 1454 | 2502 | 1809 | 1071 | 2489 | 2409 | 590 | 853 | 3707 | 2915 | 6622 | .... | .... | .... | .... | 169 | 148 | 20 | 21 | 6980 | |

## STATE OF PENNSYLVANIA—AGGREGATE.

| California and Territories. | Ireland. | Germany. | Other foreign countries. | Unknown. | Spring. | Summer. | Autumn. | Winter. | Under 1 week. | 1 week and under 1 month. | 1 month and under 3 months. | 3 months and over. | Males. | Females. | Total. | Slaves Black M. | Slaves Black F. | Slaves Mulatto M. | Slaves Mulatto F. | Free Black M. | Free Black F. | Free Mul. M. | Free Mul. F. | Aggregate deaths. | |
|---|---|---|---|---|---|---|---|---|---|---|---|---|---|---|---|---|---|---|---|---|---|---|---|---|---|
| .... | 2 | .. | .... | .. | 4 | 4 | 2 | 3 | 1 | 6 | 2 | 3 | 5 | 8 | 13 | .... | .... | .... | .... | .. | .. | .. | .. | 13 | 1 |
| .... | 44 | 17 | 22 | .. | 105 | 102 | 109 | 64 | 285 | 52 | 5 | 8 | 326 | 54 | 380 | .... | .... | .... | .... | 1 | .. | .. | .. | 381 | 2 |
| .... | 6 | 4 | 2 | .. | 35 | 22 | 28 | 27 | 87 | 11 | 6 | 1 | 47 | 62 | 109 | .... | .... | .... | .... | 2 | 1 | .. | .. | 112 | 3 |
| .... | 20 | 13 | 13 | .. | 38 | 83 | 47 | 39 | 211 | .... | .... | .... | 170 | 35 | 205 | .... | .... | .... | .... | 2 | .. | 3 | 1 | 211 | 4 |
| .... | 2 | 1 | .... | .. | 11 | 12 | 8 | 14 | 28 | 14 | 1 | .... | 27 | 17 | 44 | .... | .... | .... | .... | 1 | 1 | .. | .. | 46 | 5 |
| .... | 22 | 8 | 13 | 1 | 83 | 85 | 68 | 58 | 216 | 38 | 7 | 18 | 168 | 126 | 294 | .... | .... | .... | .... | 1 | .. | .. | .. | 295 | 6 |
| .... | 7 | 2 | 2 | 1 | 22 | 12 | 9 | 11 | 7 | 21 | 5 | 20 | 23 | 28 | 51 | .... | .... | .... | .... | 3 | .. | .. | .. | 54 | 7 |
| .... | 1 | 1 | .... | .. | 1 | 2 | .... | 4 | .... | 3 | .... | 4 | 7 | .... | 7 | .... | .... | .... | .... | .. | .. | .. | .. | 7 | 8 |
| .... | 8 | .. | 1 | .. | 9 | 26 | 30 | 15 | 14 | 37 | 11 | 16 | 51 | 33 | 84 | .... | .... | .... | .... | .. | .. | .. | .. | 84 | 9 |
| .... | 2 | 3 | 3 | .. | 46 | 42 | 31 | 30 | 43 | 73 | 15 | 11 | 93 | 51 | 144 | .... | .... | .... | .... | 4 | 1 | .. | .. | 149 | 10 |
| .... | 6 | 3 | 3 | .. | 30 | 20 | 21 | 11 | 5 | 27 | 14 | 32 | 48 | 33 | 81 | .... | .... | .... | .... | .. | .. | .. | 2 | 83 | 11 |
| .... | 18 | 8 | 9 | .. | 54 | 57 | 41 | 35 | 5 | 23 | 24 | 122 | 89 | 98 | 187 | .... | .... | .... | .... | .. | 1 | .. | 1 | 189 | 12 |
| .... | .. | .. | .... | .. | 2 | 2 | 1 | .... | 1 | 3 | .... | 1 | 5 | ... | 5 | .... | .... | .... | .... | .. | .. | .. | .. | 5 | 13 |
| .... | 2 | .. | 1 | .. | 78 | 29 | 18 | 39 | 50 | 83 | 21 | 11 | 79 | 74 | 153 | .... | .... | .... | .... | 7 | 5 | 1 | .. | 166 | 14 |
| .... | 1 | .. | .... | .. | .... | 1 | 2 | 1 | 1 | 3 | .... | .... | 2 | 2 | 4 | .... | .... | .... | .... | .. | .. | .. | .. | 4 | 15 |
| .... | 27 | 9 | 18 | .. | 116 | 71 | 54 | 64 | 131 | 121 | 15 | 3 | .... | 303 | 303 | .... | .... | .... | .... | .. | 2 | .. | 4 | 309 | 16 |
| .... | 268 | 102 | 85 | 38 | 20 | 842 | 398 | 29 | 1129 | 123 | 10 | 7 | 745 | 461 | 1206 | .... | .... | .... | .... | 44 | 29 | 10 | 7 | 1296 | 17 |
| .... | 6 | .. | 1 | .. | 20 | 112 | 98 | 24 | 113 | 122 | 15 | 3 | 150 | 103 | 253 | .... | .... | .... | .... | 1 | 4 | 1 | 1 | 260 | 18 |
| .... | 15 | 7 | 6 | .. | 19 | 61 | 123 | 15 | 135 | 75 | 4 | 2 | 141 | 98 | 239 | .... | .... | .... | .... | 4 | 4 | .. | .. | 247 | 19 |
| .... | .. | .. | .... | .. | 1 | 3 | .... | .... | .... | 1 | 1 | 2 | .... | 4 | 4 | .... | .... | .... | .... | .. | .. | .. | .. | 4 | 20 |
| .... | 8 | 4 | 2 | .. | 21 | 22 | 19 | 16 | 61 | 15 | 1 | 1 | 55 | 24 | 79 | .... | .... | .... | .... | .. | .. | .. | .. | 79 | 21 |
| .... | 1 | .. | .... | .. | 5 | 2 | 1 | 1 | 3 | 3 | 2 | 1 | 4 | 5 | 9 | .... | .... | .... | .... | .. | .. | .. | .. | 9 | 22 |
| .... | 4 | 3 | .... | .. | 9 | 11 | 8 | 9 | 19 | 12 | .... | 6 | 22 | 12 | 34 | .... | .... | .... | .... | 2 | 1 | .. | .. | 37 | 23 |
| .... | 270 | 94 | 125 | 8 | 1042 | 965 | 753 | 689 | 147 | 498 | 514 | 2062 | 1666 | 1676 | 3342 | .... | .... | .... | .... | 66 | 66 | 22 | 24 | 3520 | 24 |
| .... | 13 | 9 | 9 | .. | 264 | 208 | 159 | 147 | 462 | 179 | 46 | 40 | 425 | 339 | 764 | .... | .... | .... | .... | 5 | 9 | 4 | 4 | 786 | 25 |
| .... | 4 | 3 | 1 | 1 | 14 | 10 | 6 | 9 | 25 | 9 | 1 | 2 | 27 | 12 | 39 | .... | .... | .... | .... | .. | .. | .. | .. | 39 | 26 |
| .... | 8 | 6 | 7 | .. | 305 | 187 | 227 | 279 | 703 | 214 | 11 | 4 | 536 | 455 | 991 | .... | .... | .... | .... | 10 | 2 | 1 | 2 | 1006 | 27 |
| .... | 4 | .. | 2 | .. | 19 | 28 | 16 | 13 | 28 | 25 | 3 | 15 | 35 | 41 | 76 | .... | .... | .... | .... | .. | .. | .. | .. | 76 | 28 |
| .... | 2 | .. | .... | .. | 5 | 6 | 4 | 3 | 3 | 6 | 3 | 5 | 14 | 4 | 18 | .... | .... | .... | .... | .. | .. | .. | .. | 18 | 29 |
| .... | 46 | 16 | 16 | 1 | 51 | 160 | 315 | 48 | 170 | 301 | 57 | 33 | 308 | 246 | 554 | .... | .... | .... | .... | 9 | 11 | 1 | 1 | 576 | 30 |
| .... | 66 | 33 | 28 | 1 | 292 | 241 | 238 | 188 | 93 | 238 | 158 | 434 | 480 | 449 | 929 | .... | .... | .... | .... | 14 | 12 | 4 | 4 | 963 | 31 |
| 1 | 142 | 39 | 47 | 1 | 141 | 442 | 1902 | 194 | 814 | 1505 | 199 | 80 | 1414 | 1215 | 2629 | .... | .... | .... | .... | 26 | 14 | 8 | 6 | 2683 | 32 |
| .... | 6 | 1 | 2 | .. | 17 | 19 | 18 | 10 | 1 | 10 | 7 | 46 | 42 | 22 | 64 | .... | .... | .... | .... | .. | .. | .. | .. | 64 | 33 |
| .... | 7 | 1 | 2 | .. | 7 | 19 | 8 | 5 | 13 | 6 | 1 | 16 | 19 | 16 | 35 | .... | .... | .... | .... | 3 | 1 | .. | .. | 39 | 34 |
| .... | 12 | 7 | 4 | .. | 104 | 84 | 47 | 53 | 76 | 163 | 24 | 16 | 133 | 151 | 284 | .... | .... | .... | .... | 4 | 2 | .. | 1 | 291 | 35 |
| .... | .. | .. | .... | .. | .... | 1 | .... | .... | 1 | .... | .... | .... | .... | 1 | 1 | .... | .... | .... | .... | .. | .. | .. | .. | 1 | 36 |
| .... | 36 | 23 | 16 | 1 | 361 | 217 | 268 | 164 | 237 | 619 | 115 | 36 | 536 | 463 | 999 | .... | .... | .... | .... | 5 | 4 | 3 | 4 | 1015 | 37 |

CLASSIFICATION OF DEATHS IN THE

| | Cause of death. | AGES. | | | | | | | | | | | | | | | | | | NATIVITIES. | | | | | |
|---|---|---|---|---|---|---|---|---|---|---|---|---|---|---|---|---|---|---|---|---|---|---|---|---|---|
| | | Under 1. | | 1 and under 5. | | 5 and under 10. | | 10 and under 20. | | 20 and under 50. | | 50 and under 80. | | 80 and under 100. | | 100 & over. | | Age unknown. | | Born in State. | N. England States. | Middle States. | Southern States. | Southwest'n States. | Northwest'n States. |
| | | M. | F. | M. | F. | M. | F. | M. | F. | M. | F. | M. | F. | M. | F. | M | F. | M | F. | | | | | | |
| 1 | Fever, bilious | 9 | 8 | 19 | 24 | 19 | 7 | 35 | 25 | 91 | 42 | 42 | 20 | 1 | 2 | .. | .. | .. | 1 | 260 | 8 | 17 | .. | .. | 3 |
| 2 | ..do..brain | 35 | 30 | 62 | 50 | 26 | 17 | 17 | 9 | 35 | 14 | 5 | 1 | .. | .. | .. | .. | .. | .. | 264 | .. | 6 | .. | .. | 1 |
| 3 | ..do..catarrhal | 45 | 29 | 61 | 62 | 11 | 7 | 1 | 2 | 3 | 6 | 4 | 3 | .. | .. | .. | .. | .. | .. | 230 | 1 | .. | 1 | .. | .. |
| 4 | ..do..congestive | 2 | 3 | 3 | 5 | 1 | .. | 1 | 3 | 7 | 6 | 4 | 2 | .. | .. | .. | .. | .. | .. | 32 | .. | 3 | 1 | .. | .. |
| 5 | ..do..intermittent | 7 | 7 | 11 | 10 | 5 | 5 | 5 | 4 | 25 | 10 | 6 | 8 | 1 | .. | .. | .. | .. | .. | 87 | .. | 1 | 1 | .. | .. |
| 6 | ..do..puerperal | .. | .. | .. | .. | .. | .. | .. | 2 | .. | 44 | .. | .. | .. | .. | .. | .. | .. | .. | 40 | .. | 1 | 1 | .. | .. |
| 7 | ..do..remittent | .. | .. | .. | 1 | 1 | 1 | 3 | 3 | 3 | 2 | .. | .. | .. | .. | .. | .. | .. | .. | 12 | .. | 1 | .. | .. | .. |
| 8 | ..do..scarlet | 103 | 97 | 599 | 540 | 225 | 263 | 45 | 78 | 11 | 10 | .. | 1 | 1 | .. | .. | .. | .. | 1 | 1906 | 3 | 23 | 2 | 1 | 3 |
| 9 | ..do..ship | .. | .. | 1 | 1 | 2 | 2 | 6 | 5 | 8 | 8 | 8 | 1 | .. | .. | .. | .. | .. | .. | 21 | 1 | 1 | .. | .. | .. |
| 10 | ..do..typhus | 3 | 5 | 26 | 14 | 20 | 26 | 63 | 91 | 222 | 129 | 64 | 37 | 4 | 4 | .. | .. | 1 | .. | 532 | 4 | 49 | 4 | .. | 7 |
| 11 | Fistula | .. | .. | .. | .. | .. | .. | .. | .. | 1 | 1 | .. | .. | .. | .. | .. | .. | .. | .. | .. | .. | .. | .. | .. | .. |
| 12 | Fracture | 1 | .. | 2 | .. | .. | .. | 4 | 1 | 23 | 1 | 2 | 1 | 1 | .. | .. | .. | .. | .. | 21 | .. | 1 | .. | .. | .. |
| 13 | Frozen | .. | .. | .. | .. | .. | .. | .. | .. | 2 | .. | 3 | .. | .. | .. | .. | .. | .. | .. | 2 | .. | .. | .. | .. | .. |
| 14 | Gout | .. | .. | .. | .. | .. | .. | .. | .. | .. | .. | 4 | .. | .. | .. | .. | .. | .. | .. | 3 | .. | .. | .. | .. | .. |
| 15 | Gravel | 1 | .. | .. | .. | 1 | .. | 1 | .. | 3 | .. | 42 | 1 | 14 | .. | .. | .. | .. | .. | 45 | 3 | 6 | .. | .. | .. |
| 16 | Heart, disease of | 21 | 10 | 14 | 9 | 7 | 9 | 14 | 17 | 66 | 47 | 56 | 43 | 7 | 2 | .. | .. | .. | 1 | 231 | 5 | 28 | 4 | .. | 1 |
| 17 | Hemorrhage | 2 | 2 | 1 | 1 | 1 | .. | 8 | 2 | 18 | 8 | 6 | 3 | .. | .. | .. | .. | .. | .. | 38 | 1 | 1 | .. | .. | .. |
| 18 | Hernia | 2 | .. | 1 | .. | 2 | .. | 3 | .. | 6 | 3 | 6 | 1 | 1 | .. | .. | .. | 1 | .. | 19 | 2 | .. | 1 | .. | .. |
| 19 | Hip, disease of | .. | .. | 1 | .. | .. | .. | 1 | 1 | 4 | 1 | .. | .. | .. | .. | .. | .. | .. | .. | 5 | .. | 1 | .. | .. | .. |
| 20 | Hives | 16 | 5 | 5 | 2 | 1 | 2 | .. | .. | .. | .. | .. | .. | .. | .. | .. | .. | .. | .. | 31 | .. | .. | .. | .. | .. |
| 21 | Hooping cough | 58 | 60 | 72 | 73 | 12 | 9 | 3 | 1 | .. | .. | .. | .. | .. | .. | .. | .. | .. | .. | 274 | .. | .. | 2 | .. | .. |
| 22 | Hydrocephalus | 44 | 39 | 65 | 47 | 8 | 6 | 5 | 3 | 2 | 1 | .. | .. | .. | .. | .. | .. | .. | .. | 202 | 1 | 4 | 1 | .. | 2 |
| 23 | Hydrophobia | .. | .. | .. | .. | .. | .. | .. | .. | 2 | .. | .. | .. | .. | .. | .. | .. | .. | .. | 2 | .. | .. | .. | .. | .. |
| 24 | Infl'm't'n, not specf'd | 44 | 24 | 41 | 37 | 9 | 6 | 8 | 7 | 22 | 23 | 26 | 12 | 6 | 3 | .. | .. | .. | .. | 242 | 6 | 6 | 1 | .. | .. |
| 25 | ...do......bowels | 44 | 34 | 38 | 18 | 13 | 16 | 11 | 4 | 31 | 23 | 23 | 7 | 2 | .. | .. | .. | .. | .. | 225 | 2 | 11 | 1 | .. | .. |
| 26 | ....do......brain | 76 | 60 | 97 | 58 | 35 | 17 | 23 | 15 | 37 | 19 | 6 | 9 | .. | .. | .. | .. | .. | .. | 404 | 5 | 11 | 2 | .. | 2 |
| 27 | ....do......stomach | 2 | 2 | 1 | 1 | 2 | .. | 1 | .. | 4 | 3 | 3 | 4 | .. | .. | .. | .. | .. | .. | 18 | .. | .. | .. | .. | 1 |
| 28 | Influenza | 1 | 1 | 9 | 3 | 1 | 2 | 1 | 2 | 1 | 2 | 1 | 5 | 2 | .. | .. | .. | .. | .. | 29 | 2 | .. | .. | .. | .. |
| 29 | Insanity | .. | .. | 1 | .. | .. | .. | .. | 2 | 24 | 11 | 9 | 4 | .. | .. | .. | .. | .. | .. | 23 | .. | 7 | .. | .. | .. |
| 30 | Intemperance | .. | .. | .. | .. | .. | .. | .. | 1 | 16 | 5 | 12 | .. | .. | .. | .. | .. | 1 | .. | 20 | .. | 2 | 1 | .. | .. |
| 31 | Jaundice | 1 | 6 | 3 | 2 | .. | 2 | .. | 1 | 7 | 4 | 8 | 10 | 1 | .. | .. | .. | .. | .. | 34 | .. | 1 | .. | .. | .. |
| 32 | Kidneys, disease of | 1 | .. | .. | 2 | 2 | .. | 3 | 1 | 8 | 3 | 8 | 2 | 2 | 1 | .. | .. | .. | .. | 26 | .. | 1 | .. | .. | .. |
| 33 | Killed | .. | .. | 1 | .. | 2 | .. | 5 | .. | 11 | .. | 2 | .. | 1 | .. | .. | .. | .. | .. | 15 | .. | 3 | .. | .. | .. |
| 34 | Lightning | .. | .. | 1 | .. | .. | .. | 2 | .. | .. | .. | .. | .. | .. | .. | .. | .. | .. | .. | 3 | .. | .. | .. | .. | .. |
| 35 | Liver, disease of | 21 | 6 | 15 | 8 | 2 | 2 | 1 | 2 | 30 | 35 | 27 | 30 | 5 | .. | .. | .. | .. | .. | 134 | 4 | 14 | 1 | .. | 1 |
| 36 | Lockjaw | 1 | .. | .. | .. | 1 | .. | 4 | 1 | 8 | 3 | 1 | .. | .. | .. | .. | .. | .. | .. | 13 | 2 | 1 | .. | .. | 1 |
| 37 | Lungs, disease of | 14 | 11 | 16 | 13 | 4 | 2 | 4 | 4 | 21 | 13 | 21 | 8 | 3 | 2 | .. | .. | .. | .. | 120 | 2 | .. | 3 | .. | .. |
| 38 | Malformation | 6 | 3 | 1 | .. | .. | .. | .. | .. | .. | .. | .. | .. | .. | .. | .. | .. | .. | .. | 10 | .. | .. | .. | .. | .. |
| 39 | Mania-a-potu | .. | .. | .. | .. | .. | .. | .. | .. | 33 | .. | 11 | .. | .. | .. | .. | .. | .. | .. | 27 | .. | 4 | .. | .. | 1 |
| 40 | Marasmus | 24 | 18 | 16 | 17 | 1 | 2 | 3 | 3 | 3 | 2 | 5 | 2 | 1 | 2 | .. | .. | 1 | .. | 85 | 1 | 2 | .. | .. | .. |
| 41 | Measles | 33 | 26 | 94 | 105 | 12 | 24 | 7 | 4 | 3 | 6 | 2 | .. | .. | .. | .. | .. | .. | .. | 288 | .. | 5 | .. | .. | 1 |
| 42 | Menses, suppress'n of | .. | .. | .. | .. | .. | .. | .. | .. | .. | 1 | .. | .. | .. | .. | .. | .. | .. | .. | .. | .. | .. | .. | .. | .. |
| 43 | Mortification | 3 | 3 | .. | .. | 1 | .. | .. | 1 | 6 | 4 | 9 | 1 | 2 | 2 | .. | .. | .. | .. | 26 | .. | 3 | .. | .. | .. |
| 44 | Mumps | 2 | .. | 3 | .. | .. | .. | 1 | 2 | 2 | .. | .. | .. | .. | .. | .. | .. | .. | .. | 9 | .. | .. | .. | .. | .. |
| 45 | Murder | .. | .. | .. | .. | .. | .. | 1 | 1 | 9 | .. | .. | 1 | .. | .. | .. | .. | .. | .. | 7 | .. | 1 | .. | .. | .. |
| 46 | Neuralgia | .. | .. | .. | 1 | 1 | 2 | 1 | 1 | 8 | 6 | 3 | 7 | .. | .. | .. | .. | .. | .. | 25 | 1 | 2 | .. | .. | .. |
| 47 | Old age | .. | .. | .. | .. | .. | .. | .. | .. | .. | .. | 154 | 217 | 254 | 289 | 4 | 1 | 3 | 6 | 563 | 39 | 92 | 12 | .. | .. |
| 48 | Paralysis | 1 | 3 | 4 | 5 | 1 | 2 | 7 | 5 | 30 | 19 | 119 | 144 | 30 | 25 | 1 | .. | .. | 1 | 292 | 7 | 46 | 1 | .. | .. |
| 49 | Peritonitis | .. | .. | .. | .. | 2 | .. | 1 | .. | 1 | 2 | .. | .. | .. | .. | .. | .. | .. | .. | 4 | .. | 1 | .. | .. | .. |
| 50 | Piles | .. | .. | .. | .. | .. | .. | .. | .. | 1 | 1 | 1 | 1 | .. | .. | .. | .. | .. | .. | 3 | .. | .. | .. | .. | .. |
| 51 | Pleurisy | 4 | 6 | 9 | 10 | 1 | 2 | 13 | 6 | 50 | 20 | 32 | 22 | 3 | 1 | .. | .. | .. | 1 | 137 | 1 | 10 | 1 | .. | .. |
| 52 | Pneumonia | 77 | 64 | 78 | 67 | 13 | 17 | 9 | 13 | 54 | 23 | 44 | 22 | 2 | 2 | .. | .. | .. | .. | 429 | 3 | 7 | .. | .. | 1 |
| 53 | Poison | .. | 2 | 4 | .. | .. | 2 | 1 | .. | 2 | .. | 1 | .. | .. | .. | .. | .. | .. | .. | 10 | .. | 1 | .. | .. | .. |
| 54 | Putrid sore throat | .. | .. | 3 | 5 | 2 | 2 | 3 | 4 | .. | .. | .. | .. | 1 | .. | .. | .. | .. | .. | 19 | .. | 1 | .. | .. | .. |
| 55 | Quinsy | 3 | .. | 12 | 4 | 4 | 1 | 3 | 4 | 6 | 4 | 5 | 6 | .. | .. | .. | .. | .. | .. | 45 | .. | 2 | .. | .. | .. |
| 56 | Rheumatism | 1 | 1 | 3 | 5 | 9 | 6 | 8 | 13 | 12 | 12 | 15 | 13 | 1 | 1 | .. | .. | 2 | 1 | 81 | 2 | 9 | 1 | .. | .. |
| 57 | Rickets | 2 | 3 | 2 | .. | 1 | .. | 1 | 1 | .. | .. | .. | .. | .. | .. | .. | .. | .. | .. | 9 | .. | .. | .. | .. | .. |
| 58 | Salivation, effects of | .. | .. | .. | .. | .. | .. | .. | .. | .. | 1 | .. | .. | .. | .. | .. | .. | .. | .. | 1 | .. | .. | .. | .. | .. |
| 59 | Scrofula | 14 | 19 | 31 | 21 | 4 | 12 | 14 | 10 | 25 | 10 | 6 | 3 | 1 | .. | .. | .. | .. | .. | 148 | 2 | 9 | 1 | .. | 3 |
| 60 | Scurvy | .. | .. | .. | .. | .. | .. | .. | .. | 1 | .. | .. | .. | .. | .. | .. | .. | .. | .. | .. | .. | .. | .. | .. | .. |
| 61 | Small pox | 16 | 19 | 33 | 39 | 13 | 5 | 13 | 7 | 39 | 10 | 8 | 1 | .. | .. | .. | .. | .. | .. | 165 | 3 | 5 | 1 | .. | 2 |
| 62 | Spine, disease of | 4 | 5 | 8 | 3 | 6 | 3 | 7 | 6 | 12 | 7 | 2 | 5 | .. | .. | .. | .. | 1 | .. | 52 | 1 | 6 | .. | .. | 1 |
| 63 | Spleen... do | .. | .. | 2 | .. | .. | .. | .. | .. | 1 | .. | .. | .. | .. | .. | .. | .. | .. | .. | 2 | 1 | .. | .. | .. | .. |
| 64 | Stillborn | 16 | 17 | .. | .. | .. | .. | .. | .. | .. | .. | .. | .. | .. | .. | .. | .. | .. | .. | 33 | .. | .. | .. | .. | .. |
| 65 | Stomach, disease of | 1 | .. | 1 | 1 | .. | 1 | .. | .. | 1 | .. | 6 | .. | .. | .. | .. | .. | .. | .. | 10 | .. | .. | .. | .. | .. |
| 66 | Suffocation | 5 | 6 | 2 | 1 | .. | .. | .. | .. | 1 | .. | .. | .. | .. | .. | .. | .. | .. | .. | 13 | .. | 1 | .. | .. | 1 |
| 67 | Suicide | .. | .. | .. | .. | .. | .. | 1 | 1 | 22 | 5 | 3 | 3 | .. | .. | .. | .. | .. | .. | 25 | 1 | 1 | .. | .. | .. |
| 68 | Summer complaint | 28 | 14 | 51 | 41 | 3 | 2 | .. | .. | .. | .. | .. | .. | .. | .. | .. | .. | .. | .. | 130 | .. | 1 | .. | .. | .. |
| 69 | Sun, stroke of | .. | .. | 1 | .. | .. | .. | 3 | .. | 16 | 3 | 3 | .. | .. | .. | .. | .. | .. | .. | 8 | 1 | 1 | .. | .. | .. |
| 70 | Syphilis | .. | .. | 1 | .. | .. | .. | .. | .. | .. | 1 | .. | .. | .. | .. | .. | .. | .. | .. | 2 | .. | .. | .. | .. | .. |
| 71 | Teething | 15 | 19 | 28 | 17 | .. | .. | .. | .. | .. | .. | .. | .. | .. | .. | .. | .. | .. | .. | 74 | 1 | 3 | .. | .. | .. |
| 72 | Tetter | .. | .. | 1 | .. | .. | .. | .. | .. | .. | .. | 1 | .. | .. | .. | .. | .. | .. | .. | 2 | .. | .. | .. | .. | .. |
| 73 | Throat, disease of | 15 | 9 | 17 | 22 | 20 | 17 | 7 | 15 | 4 | 8 | 7 | 3 | 1 | .. | .. | .. | .. | .. | 135 | .. | 7 | .. | .. | .. |
| 74 | Thrush | 4 | 1 | .. | 1 | .. | .. | .. | .. | .. | .. | .. | .. | .. | .. | .. | .. | .. | .. | 6 | .. | .. | .. | .. | .. |
| 75 | Tumor | .. | 2 | 1 | 3 | .. | 1 | .. | 2 | 3 | 6 | 2 | 10 | .. | 1 | .. | .. | .. | .. | 23 | 1 | 4 | .. | .. | .. |

STATE OF PENNSYLVANIA—AGGREGATE—Continued.

| Nativities. | | | | | Season of decease. | | | | Duration of sickness. | | | | Whites. | | | Colored. | | | | | | | | Aggregate deaths. | |
|---|---|---|---|---|---|---|---|---|---|---|---|---|---|---|---|---|---|---|---|---|---|---|---|---|---|
| | | | | | | | | | | | | | | | | Slaves. | | | | Free. | | | | | |
| | | | | | | | | | | | | | | | | Black. | | Mulatto. | | Black. | | Mul. | | | |
| California and Territories. | Ireland. | Germany. | Other foreign countries. | Unknown. | Spring. | Summer. | Autumn. | Winter. | Under 1 week. | 1 week and under 1 month. | 1 month and under 3 months. | 3 months and over. | Males. | Females. | Total. | M. | F. | M. | F. | M. | F. | M | F. | | |
| | 22 | 24 | 10 | 1 | 66 | 85 | 138 | 56 | 39 | 260 | 36 | 9 | 213 | 127 | 340 | | | | | 2 | 2 | 1 | | 345 | 1 |
| | 16 | 5 | 9 | | 74 | 95 | 76 | 56 | 114 | 150 | 24 | 8 | 176 | 117 | 293 | | | | | 3 | 4 | 1 | | 301 | 2 |
| | 2 | | | | 119 | 46 | 33 | 36 | 51 | 152 | 18 | 12 | 122 | 102 | 224 | | | | | 3 | 3 | | 4 | 234 | 3 |
| | 1 | | | | 8 | 13 | 5 | 11 | 11 | 20 | 4 | 2 | 18 | 19 | 37 | | | | | | | | | 37 | 4 |
| | 12 | | 3 | | 21 | 18 | 43 | 22 | 18 | 66 | 15 | 5 | 60 | 41 | 101 | | | | | | 1 | | 2 | 104 | 5 |
| | 1 | 1 | 2 | | 23 | 15 | 2 | 6 | 9 | 31 | 5 | | | 45 | 45 | | | | | | | | 1 | 46 | 6 |
| | 1 | | | | 2 | 4 | 5 | 3 | 2 | 10 | 1 | | 7 | 7 | 14 | | | | | | | | | 14 | 7 |
| | 16 | 4 | 15 | 1 | 843 | 379 | 277 | 447 | 860 | 970 | 93 | 13 | 979 | 980 | 1959 | | | | | 1 | 7 | 4 | 3 | 1974 | 8 |
| | 15 | 2 | 2 | | 7 | 9 | 12 | 14 | 1 | 33 | 2 | 1 | 25 | 17 | 42 | | | | | | | | | 42 | 9 |
| | 66 | 27 | 18 | 2 | 194 | 123 | 225 | 167 | 65 | 520 | 101 | 17 | 400 | 302 | 702 | | | | | 2 | 3 | 1 | 1 | 709 | 10 |
| | 2 | | | | | | 1 | 1 | | | 1 | 1 | 1 | 1 | 2 | | | | | | | | | 2 | 11 |
| | 10 | 2 | 2 | | 8 | 11 | 10 | 7 | 12 | 12 | 1 | 2 | 31 | 3 | 34 | | | | | 2 | | | | 36 | 12 |
| | 2 | | 1 | | 3 | | | 2 | 5 | | | | 5 | | 5 | | | | | | | | | 5 | 13 |
| | | | 1 | | | 3 | 1 | | 3 | 1 | | | 4 | | 4 | | | | | | | | | 4 | 14 |
| | 8 | | 1 | | 16 | 21 | 10 | 16 | 6 | 29 | 7 | 20 | 62 | 1 | 63 | | | | | | | | | 63 | 15 |
| | 29 | 10 | 14 | 1 | 94 | 88 | 62 | 76 | 113 | 76 | 41 | 71 | 171 | 130 | 301 | | | | | 12 | 6 | 2 | 2 | 323 | 16 |
| | 6 | 4 | 2 | | 12 | 18 | 14 | 8 | 29 | 14 | 3 | 4 | 35 | 15 | 50 | | | | | 1 | 1 | | | 52 | 17 |
| | 1 | | 3 | | 7 | 8 | 8 | 3 | 12 | 8 | 2 | 3 | 20 | 4 | 24 | | | | | 2 | | | | 26 | 18 |
| | 1 | | 1 | | 2 | 3 | 2 | 1 | 2 | 1 | 1 | 3 | 6 | 2 | 8 | | | | | | | | | 8 | 19 |
| | | | | | 12 | 11 | 4 | 4 | 24 | 6 | | | 22 | 8 | 30 | | | | | | 1 | | | 31 | 20 |
| | 6 | 2 | 4 | | 85 | 76 | 75 | 49 | 36 | 154 | 54 | 28 | 140 | 136 | 276 | | | | | 3 | 4 | 2 | 3 | 288 | 21 |
| | 7 | 2 | 1 | | 66 | 55 | 49 | 48 | 53 | 121 | 27 | 11 | 120 | 94 | 214 | | | | | 3 | 1 | 1 | 1 | 220 | 22 |
| | | | | | 1 | | 1 | | 2 | | | | 2 | | 2 | | | | | | | | | 2 | 23 |
| | 6 | 1 | 6 | | 107 | 69 | 52 | 39 | 82 | 142 | 26 | 15 | 152 | 111 | 263 | | | | | 3 | | 1 | 1 | 268 | 24 |
| | 14 | 5 | 4 | 2 | 55 | 77 | 81 | 50 | 109 | 110 | 23 | 16 | 160 | 100 | 260 | | | | | 2 | 2 | | | 264 | 25 |
| | 13 | 4 | 11 | | 129 | 114 | 115 | 88 | 180 | 228 | 24 | 9 | 273 | 173 | 446 | | | | | 1 | 5 | | | 452 | 26 |
| | 2 | 1 | 1 | | 7 | 6 | 5 | 2 | 4 | 9 | 2 | 3 | 13 | 10 | 23 | | | | | | | | | 23 | 27 |
| | | | | | 18 | 6 | 2 | 5 | 13 | 16 | 2 | | 16 | 15 | 31 | | | | | | | | | 31 | 28 |
| | 11 | 7 | 2 | 1 | 11 | 18 | 13 | 9 | 2 | 12 | 2 | 31 | 31 | 16 | 47 | | | | | 3 | 1 | | | 51 | 29 |
| | 6 | 1 | 3 | 1 | 12 | 7 | 9 | 6 | 13 | 11 | 2 | 4 | 29 | 5 | 34 | | | | | | | | | 34 | 30 |
| | 6 | 2 | 1 | 1 | 15 | 7 | 8 | 14 | 6 | 20 | 11 | 7 | 20 | 25 | 45 | | | | | | | | | 43 | 31 |
| | 5 | | 1 | | 8 | 11 | 8 | 6 | 5 | 14 | 5 | 6 | 24 | 9 | 33 | | | | | | | | | 33 | 32 |
| | 3 | | 1 | | 6 | 8 | 3 | 5 | 13 | 5 | | 1 | 22 | | 22 | | | | | | | | | 22 | 33 |
| | | | | | | 3 | | | 3 | | | | 3 | | 3 | | | | | | | | | 3 | 34 |
| | 16 | 5 | 9 | | 56 | 38 | 50 | 38 | 24 | 57 | 29 | 68 | 101 | 82 | 183 | | | | | | 1 | | | 184 | 35 |
| | | 1 | 1 | | 9 | 2 | 5 | 3 | 12 | 7 | | | 15 | 4 | 19 | | | | | | | | | 19 | 36 |
| | 9 | 2 | | | 61 | 28 | 24 | 22 | 33 | 48 | 12 | 35 | 83 | 51 | 134 | | | | | | 2 | | | 136 | 37 |
| | | | | | 5 | 2 | | 3 | 4 | 2 | 1 | 1 | 7 | 3 | 10 | | | | | | | | | 10 | 38 |
| | 7 | 3 | 2 | | 9 | 17 | 7 | 11 | 26 | 13 | 1 | | 43 | | 43 | | | | | 1 | | | | 44 | 39 |
| | 6 | 3 | 2 | 1 | 25 | 23 | 37 | 13 | 10 | 56 | 12 | 18 | 51 | 45 | 96 | | | | | 3 | 1 | | | 100 | 40 |
| | 15 | 4 | 3 | | 109 | 112 | 55 | 38 | 76 | 177 | 35 | 17 | 150 | 164 | 314 | | | | | 1 | 1 | | | 316 | 41 |
| | 1 | | | | | | 1 | | | 1 | | | | 1 | 1 | | | | | | | | | 1 | 42 |
| | 2 | | 1 | | 7 | 12 | 11 | 2 | 7 | 12 | 5 | 8 | 20 | 8 | 28 | | | | | | 3 | 1 | | 32 | 43 |
| | | | 1 | | 6 | 2 | | 2 | | 8 | | 1 | 8 | 2 | 10 | | | | | | | | | 10 | 44 |
| | 1 | 2 | 1 | | 1 | 3 | 6 | 1 | 6 | 1 | | | 10 | 2 | 12 | | | | | | | | | 12 | 45 |
| | 1 | 1 | | | 6 | 8 | 8 | 8 | 5 | 7 | 2 | 16 | 13 | 17 | 30 | | | | | | | | | 30 | 46 |
| | 180 | 43 | 43 | 6 | 290 | 242 | 193 | 198 | 115 | 224 | 70 | 170 | 402 | 499 | 901 | | | | | 12 | 12 | 1 | 2 | 928 | 47 |
| | 30 | 12 | 8 | 1 | 125 | 105 | 90 | 76 | 133 | 101 | 27 | 126 | 192 | 202 | 394 | | | | | 1 | 2 | | | 397 | 48 |
| | 1 | | | | 1 | 2 | 2 | 1 | 1 | 4 | 1 | | 3 | 2 | 5 | | | | | 1 | | | | 6 | 49 |
| | 1 | | | | 1 | 1 | 2 | | 2 | 2 | | | 2 | 2 | 4 | | | | | | | | | 4 | 50 |
| | 15 | 4 | 10 | 2 | 77 | 39 | 30 | 30 | 55 | 101 | 12 | 8 | 107 | 64 | 171 | | | | | 3 | 3 | 2 | 1 | 180 | 51 |
| | 25 | 8 | 12 | | 227 | 89 | 64 | 102 | 124 | 282 | 35 | 29 | 269 | 205 | 474 | | | | | 6 | 2 | 2 | 1 | 485 | 52 |
| | 1 | | | | 4 | 3 | 3 | 2 | 11 | | 1 | | 8 | 4 | 12 | | | | | | | | | 12 | 53 |
| | | | | | 3 | 5 | 5 | 6 | 3 | 13 | 2 | | 9 | 11 | 20 | | | | | | | | | 20 | 54 |
| | 3 | | 2 | | 18 | 10 | 13 | 11 | 22 | 25 | 1 | 2 | 33 | 19 | 52 | | | | | | | | | 52 | 55 |
| | 5 | | 4 | 1 | 35 | 26 | 26 | 15 | 17 | 35 | 15 | 32 | 50 | 50 | 100 | | | | | 1 | 2 | | | 103 | 56 |
| | | 1 | | | 2 | 3 | 4 | 1 | 1 | 1 | 2 | 6 | 6 | 4 | 10 | | | | | | | | | 10 | 57 |
| | | | | | | | | 1 | | | 1 | | | 1 | 1 | | | | | | | | | 1 | 58 |
| | 5 | | 2 | | 44 | 68 | 28 | 29 | 10 | 58 | 16 | 79 | 89 | 69 | 158 | | | | | 6 | 5 | | 1 | 170 | 59 |
| | | 1 | | | | | 1 | | | 1 | | | 1 | | 1 | | | | | | | | | 1 | 60 |
| | 14 | 7 | 6 | | 70 | 57 | 25 | 50 | 19 | 164 | 11 | 8 | 119 | 81 | 200 | | | | | 3 | | | | 203 | 61 |
| | 7 | | 2 | | 21 | 17 | 19 | 12 | 8 | 16 | 6 | 29 | 39 | 28 | 67 | | | | | 1 | 1 | | | 69 | 62 |
| | | | | | 2 | | 1 | | | | | 3 | 3 | | 3 | | | | | | | | | 3 | 63 |
| | | | | | 9 | 8 | 6 | 8 | | | | | 15 | 17 | 32 | | | | | 1 | | | | 33 | 64 |
| | | | 1 | | 4 | 3 | 2 | 2 | 1 | 7 | 2 | 1 | 9 | 2 | 11 | | | | | | | | | 11 | 65 |
| | | | | | 6 | 2 | 4 | 3 | 15 | | | | 8 | 6 | 14 | | | | | | | | 1 | 15 | 66 |
| | 2 | 3 | 2 | 1 | 11 | 10 | 6 | 8 | 21 | 2 | | | 26 | 9 | 35 | | | | | | | | | 35 | 67 |
| | 3 | 2 | 3 | | 4 | 63 | 68 | 4 | 28 | 50 | 24 | 14 | 80 | 53 | 133 | | | | | 1 | 2 | 1 | 2 | 139 | 68 |
| | 10 | 4 | 2 | | 2 | 19 | 5 | | 22 | 2 | 2 | | 23 | 2 | 25 | | | | | | 1 | | | 26 | 69 |
| | | | | | | 2 | | | | 1 | | 1 | 1 | | 1 | | | | | | 1 | | | 2 | 70 |
| | 1 | | | | 21 | 23 | 21 | 14 | 25 | 36 | 13 | 4 | 40 | 33 | 73 | | | | | | 2 | 3 | 1 | 79 | 71 |
| | | | | | | 1 | 1 | | | | | 2 | 2 | | 2 | | | | | | | | | 2 | 72 |
| | 1 | 1 | 1 | | 31 | 25 | 46 | 43 | 49 | 78 | 11 | 7 | 70 | 74 | 144 | | | | | 1 | | | | 145 | 73 |
| | | | | | 1 | 1 | 2 | 2 | 1 | 4 | 1 | | 4 | 2 | 6 | | | | | | | | | 6 | 74 |
| | 1 | 2 | | | 9 | 8 | 7 | 7 | 8 | 8 | 6 | 8 | 6 | 23 | 29 | | | | | | | | 2 | 31 | 75 |

## CLASSIFICATION OF DEATHS IN THE

| | Cause of death. | Ages. Under 1. M. | Under 1. F. | 1 and under 5. M. | 1 and under 5. F. | 5 and under 10. M. | 5 and under 10. F. | 10 and under 20. M. | 10 and under 20. F. | 20 and under 50. M. | 20 and under 50. F. | 50 and under 80. M. | 50 and under 80. F. | 80 and under 100. M | 80 and under 100. F. | 100 & over. M | 100 & over. F. | Age unknown. M | Age unknown. F. | Nativities. Born in State. | N. England States. | Middle States. | Southern States. | Southwest'n States. | Northwest'n States. |
|---|---|---|---|---|---|---|---|---|---|---|---|---|---|---|---|---|---|---|---|---|---|---|---|---|---|
| 1 | Ulcer........ | .... | 1 | 1 | 2 | ... | ... | 1 | ... | 2 | 2 | 4 | 1 | 1 | .. | .. | .. | .. | .. | 13 | .. | 1 | ... | ... | ... |
| 2 | Uterus, disease of... | .... | .... | .... | .... | ... | ... | ... | ... | .... | 9 | ... | ... | .. | .. | .. | .. | .. | .. | 7 | .. | ... | ... | ... | ... |
| 3 | Venereal......... | .... | .... | .... | .... | ... | ... | ... | ... | 5 | 2 | 1 | ... | .. | .. | .. | .. | .. | .. | 4 | .. | 1 | ... | ... | ... |
| 4 | White swelling..... | .... | .... | 1 | 1 | 2 | ... | 3 | 1 | 2 | 2 | 1 | ... | .. | .. | .. | .. | .. | .. | 12 | 1 | ... | ... | ... | ... |
| 5 | Worms........ | 1 | 4 | 18 | 20 | 2 | 2 | ... | 1 | .... | .... | ... | ... | .. | .. | .. | .. | .. | .. | 40 | .. | 2 | ... | ... | 1 |
| 6 | Unknown.......... | 629 | 485 | 247 | 237 | 80 | 64 | 87 | 89 | 309 | 302 | 276 | 214 | 36 | 27 | .. | .. | 72 | 33 | 2754 | 20 | 94 | 9 | 4 | 3 |
| | Total......... | 2793 | 2241 | 3601 | 3160 | 1077 | 936 | 1038 | 997 | 3837 | 3157 | 2559 | 2010 | 525 | 465 | 6 | 1 | 96 | 52 | 23415 | 281 | 1221 | 149 | 11 | 88 |

## CLASSIFICATION OF DEATHS IN

| | Cause of death. | Under 1. M. | Under 1. F. | 1 and under 5. M. | 1 and under 5. F. | 5 and under 10. M. | 5 and under 10. F. | 10 and under 20. M. | 10 and under 20. F. | 20 and under 50. M. | 20 and under 50. F. | 50 and under 80. M. | 50 and under 80. F. | 80 and under 100. M | 80 and under 100. F. | 100 & over. M | 100 & over. F. | Age unknown. M | Age unknown. F. | Born in State. | N. England States. | Middle States. | Southern States. | Southwest'n States. | Northwest'n States. |
|---|---|---|---|---|---|---|---|---|---|---|---|---|---|---|---|---|---|---|---|---|---|---|---|---|---|
| 1 | Abscess ........ | .... | ... | 1 | ... | ... | ... | ... | ... | 1 | 1 | ... | ... | .. | .. | .. | .. | .. | .. | .... | .. | 2 | ... | ... | ... |
| 2 | Accident, not specif'd | .. | 2 | 2 | 4 | 3 | 2 | 3 | 1 | 12 | 3 | 3 | 3 | 2 | .. | .. | .. | .. | .. | 30 | 2 | ... | ... | ... | ... |
| 3 | ....do...burned.... | .... | .... | .... | .... | ... | ... | ... | ... | 1 | ... | 1 | ... | .. | .. | .. | .. | .. | .. | 2 | .. | ... | ... | ... | ... |
| 4 | ....do...drowned .. | .... | ... | 5 | 2 | 3 | ... | 4 | ... | 18 | 2 | 1 | ... | .. | .. | .. | .. | .. | .. | 23 | 1 | 2 | ... | ... | ... |
| 5 | Apoplexy ........ | .... | .... | .... | .... | ... | ... | ... | 1 | 4 | 3 | 4 | 8 | 1 | .. | .. | .. | .. | .. | 18 | 2 | ... | ... | ... | ... |
| 6 | Asthma.... ...... | 1 | .... | .... | .... | ... | ... | ... | ... | .... | .... | ... | 1 | .. | .. | .. | .. | .. | .. | 2 | .. | ... | ... | ... | ... |
| 7 | Bladder, disease of.. | .... | .... | .... | .... | ... | ... | ... | ... | .... | .... | ... | 1 | .. | .. | .. | .. | .. | .. | 1 | .. | ... | ... | ... | ... |
| 8 | Bowels......do...... | 1 | ... | 1 | 3 | ... | ... | 1 | ... | 2 | .... | ... | ... | .. | .. | .. | .. | .. | .. | 6 | .. | ... | ... | ... | ... |
| 9 | Brain ......do...... | 10 | 7 | 17 | 9 | 8 | 2 | 2 | 2 | 5 | 1 | 2 | 2 | .. | .. | .. | .. | .. | .. | 54 | 7 | 2 | ... | ... | ... |
| 10 | Bronchitis ......... | .... | .... | 3 | .... | ... | ... | ... | ... | .... | .... | ... | 1 | .. | .. | .. | .. | .. | .. | 4 | .. | ... | ... | ... | ... |
| 11 | Cancer........... | .... | .... | .... | .... | 1 | ... | ... | ... | 1 | 4 | 1 | 7 | 1 | 1 | .. | .. | .. | .. | 14 | 1 | ... | ... | ... | ... |
| 12 | Catarrh........... | 1 | .... | .... | 1 | ... | ... | ... | ... | .... | .... | ... | ... | .. | .. | .. | .. | .. | .. | 2 | .. | ... | ... | ... | ... |
| 13 | Childbirth ........ | .... | .... | .... | .... | ... | ... | ... | 2 | .... | 12 | ... | ... | .. | .. | .. | .. | .. | .. | 7 | 4 | ... | ... | ... | ... |
| 14 | Cholera ......... | 4 | 2 | 12 | 11 | 3 | 3 | 1 | 3 | 51 | 37 | 17 | 13 | 1 | .. | .. | .. | .. | 1 | 105 | 3 | ... | ... | ... | ... |
| 15 | ....do..infantum... | 15 | 8 | 18 | 11 | 2 | ... | 1 | 1 | .... | .... | ... | ... | .. | .. | .. | .. | .. | .. | 56 | .. | ... | ... | ... | ... |
| 16 | ....do..morbus..... | .... | 1 | 1 | .... | ... | ... | ... | 2 | 3 | 2 | 3 | 1 | .. | .. | .. | .. | .. | .. | 10 | 2 | ... | ... | ... | ... |
| 17 | Colic .......... | .... | .... | 1 | .... | ... | 1 | 1 | ... | .... | 2 | 1 | 2 | .. | .. | .. | .. | .. | .. | 4 | 2 | 1 | ... | ... | ... |
| 18 | Congest'n, not specf'd | .... | .... | .... | .... | ... | ... | 1 | ... | .... | 1 | 1 | ... | .. | .. | .. | .. | .. | .. | 2 | .. | 1 | ... | ... | ... |
| 19 | ....do....brain..... | .... | 2 | 2 | .... | 2 | ... | 1 | ... | 2 | .... | ... | ... | .. | .. | .. | .. | .. | .. | 6 | 3 | ... | ... | ... | ... |
| 20 | Consumption ....... | 25 | 14 | 3 | 16 | 5 | 1 | 14 | 35 | 88 | 142 | 60 | 54 | 5 | 6 | .. | .. | 2 | .. | 371 | 38 | ... | ... | ... | ... |
| 21 | Convulsions ........ | 7 | 6 | 12 | 5 | 1 | ... | 1 | 2 | 3 | 6 | 6 | 4 | 2 | 1 | .. | .. | .. | .. | 47 | 2 | ... | ... | ... | ... |
| 22 | Croup........... | 4 | 9 | 12 | 12 | 2 | 6 | ... | ... | .... | .... | ... | ... | .. | .. | .. | .. | .. | .. | 39 | 2 | ... | ... | ... | ... |
| 23 | Debility ......... | 6 | 5 | .... | 3 | ... | ... | ... | ... | .... | 1 | ... | ... | .. | .. | .. | .. | .. | .. | 15 | .. | ... | ... | ... | ... |
| 24 | Diabetes.......... | .... | .... | .... | .... | ... | ... | ... | ... | .... | .... | 1 | ... | .. | .. | .. | .. | .. | .. | 1 | .. | ... | ... | ... | ... |
| 25 | Diarrhœa ........ | 5 | 9 | 8 | 6 | ... | ... | 1 | 1 | 3 | 4 | 2 | 3 | 2 | 1 | .. | .. | .. | .. | 38 | 3 | ... | ... | ... | 1 |
| 26 | Dropsy........... | 3 | 3 | 8 | 4 | 2 | 1 | 1 | ... | 12 | 13 | 9 | 21 | .. | .. | .. | .. | .. | 1 | 62 | 6 | 1 | ... | ... | ... |
| 27 | Dysentery......... | 22 | 17 | 61 | 49 | 10 | 6 | 3 | 8 | 23 | 12 | 16 | 14 | 2 | 2 | .. | .. | .. | .. | 217 | 11 | ... | ... | ... | ... |
| 28 | Dyspepsia ........ | .... | .... | .... | .... | ... | ... | ... | ... | .... | .... | ... | 1 | .. | .. | .. | .. | .. | .. | 1 | .. | ... | ... | ... | ... |
| 29 | Epilepsy......... | .... | .... | .... | .... | ... | ... | 1 | ... | 2 | .... | ... | 1 | .. | .. | .. | .. | .. | .. | 4 | .. | ... | ... | ... | ... |
| 30 | Erysipelas ......... | 4 | 3 | .... | .... | ... | ... | ... | ... | 1 | 3 | 1 | 1 | .. | 2 | .. | .. | .. | .. | 14 | .. | ... | ... | ... | ... |
| 31 | Fever, not specified.. | 4 | 5 | 2 | 3 | ... | 1 | 4 | 7 | 6 | 8 | 7 | 6 | .. | 2 | .. | .. | .. | .. | 47 | 3 | 2 | ... | ... | ... |
| 32 | ..do..brain ....... | 1 | 3 | 2 | 5 | 1 | ... | 3 | ... | 5 | 2 | 1 | ... | .. | .. | .. | .. | .. | .. | 23 | .. | ... | ... | ... | ... |
| 33 | ..do..bilious ....... | .... | .... | .... | .... | ... | ... | ... | 2 | 4 | .... | ... | 1 | .. | .. | .. | .. | .. | .. | 5 | 1 | ... | ... | ... | ... |
| 34 | ..do..inflammatory. | .... | .... | .... | .... | ... | ... | ... | ... | .... | 1 | ... | 1 | .. | .. | .. | .. | .. | .. | 2 | .. | ... | ... | ... | ... |
| 35 | ..do..puerperal..... | .... | .... | .... | .... | ... | ... | ... | ... | .... | 1 | ... | ... | .. | .. | .. | .. | .. | .. | .... | .. | ... | ... | ... | ... |
| 36 | ..do..scarlet ....... | 5 | 1 | 20 | 13 | 8 | 4 | 1 | ... | .... | 1 | ... | ... | .. | .. | .. | .. | .. | .. | 51 | 2 | ... | ... | ... | ... |
| 37 | ..do..ship......... | .... | .... | .... | .... | ... | ... | ... | ... | 1 | 1 | ... | ... | .. | .. | .. | .. | .. | .. | 1 | .. | ... | ... | ... | ... |
| 38 | ..do..typhus........ | .... | ... | 4 | 3 | 1 | 1 | 5 | 6 | 12 | 10 | 5 | 2 | .. | .. | .. | .. | .. | .. | 38 | 7 | ... | ... | ... | ... |
| 39 | Heart, disease of.... | 2 | 2 | 1 | .... | ... | ... | 2 | 1 | 3 | 6 | 5 | 8 | 1 | .. | .. | .. | .. | .. | 24 | 3 | 3 | ... | ... | ... |
| 40 | Hemorrhage........ | 2 | 1 | .... | .... | ... | ... | ... | ... | 2 | 1 | ... | ... | .. | .. | .. | .. | .. | .. | 6 | .. | ... | ... | ... | ... |
| 41 | Hip, disease of...... | .... | .... | .... | .... | ... | ... | 2 | ... | .... | .... | 1 | ... | .. | .. | .. | .. | .. | .. | 3 | .. | ... | ... | ... | ... |
| 42 | Hooping cough...... | 3 | 3 | 3 | 4 | ... | ... | ... | ... | .... | .... | ... | ... | .. | .. | .. | .. | .. | .. | 13 | .. | ... | ... | ... | ... |
| 43 | Hydrocephalus...... | .... | .. | 4 | 1 | ... | ... | ... | ... | .... | .... | 1 | ... | .. | .. | .. | .. | .. | .. | 6 | .. | ... | ... | ... | ... |
| 44 | Hydrophobia........ | .... | ... | 1 | ... | 1 | 2 | ... | ... | .... | .... | ... | ... | .. | .. | .. | .. | .. | .. | 4 | .. | ... | ... | ... | ... |
| 45 | Inflamt'n, not specf'd | 1 | 1 | .... | 1 | ... | ... | 2 | ... | .... | 2 | 2 | 1 | .. | .. | .. | .. | .. | .. | 8 | .. | ... | ... | ... | ... |
| 46 | ....do....bowels.... | .... | ... | 2 | 1 | ... | ... | 1 | 1 | .... | 1 | 1 | 1 | .. | .. | .. | .. | .. | .. | 7 | .. | ... | ... | ... | ... |
| 47 | ....do....brain..... | .... | ... | 2 | ... | 1 | ... | 1 | 1 | 1 | 1 | ... | ... | .. | .. | .. | .. | .. | .. | 5 | 1 | ... | ... | ... | ... |
| 48 | Influenza ......... | .... | .... | .... | .... | ... | ... | ... | ... | .... | .... | 1 | ... | .. | .. | .. | .. | .. | .. | 1 | .. | ... | ... | ... | ... |
| 49 | Insanity.......... | .... | .... | .... | .... | ... | ... | ... | ... | 1 | 3 | ... | 1 | 1 | .. | .. | .. | .. | .. | 5 | .. | ... | ... | ... | ... |
| 50 | Intemperance....... | .... | .... | .... | .... | ... | ... | ... | ... | 3 | 1 | 3 | ... | .. | .. | .. | .. | .. | .. | 6 | .. | ... | ... | ... | ... |
| 51 | Jaundice. ......... | .... | .... | .... | .... | ... | ... | ... | ... | .... | .... | ... | 1 | .. | .. | .. | .. | .. | .. | 1 | .. | ... | ... | ... | ... |
| 52 | Liver, disease of..... | 4 | 2 | .... | 1 | ... | 1 | ... | ... | 2 | 3 | 3 | 2 | .. | .. | .. | .. | .. | .. | 12 | 1 | 1 | ... | ... | ... |
| 53 | Lockjaw.......... | .... | .... | .... | .... | 1 | ... | ... | ... | .... | .... | 1 | ... | .. | .. | .. | .. | .. | .. | 2 | .. | ... | ... | ... | ... |
| 54 | Lungs, disease of.... | 4 | 6 | 10 | 3 | ... | 1 | ... | 2 | 3 | 3 | 5 | 7 | .. | .. | .. | .. | .. | .. | 34 | 6 | 1 | ... | ... | ... |
| 55 | Malformation....... | 1 | .... | .... | .... | ... | ... | ... | ... | .... | .... | ... | ... | .. | .. | .. | .. | .. | .. | 1 | .. | ... | ... | ... | ... |
| 56 | Mania-a-potu ...... | .... | .... | .... | .... | ... | ... | ... | ... | 2 | .... | ... | ... | .. | .. | .. | .. | .. | .. | 2 | .. | ... | ... | ... | ... |
| 57 | Marasmus ........ | 4 | 3 | 2 | 2 | ... | ... | ... | 1 | .... | 1 | ... | 2 | .. | .. | .. | .. | .. | .. | 13 | .. | ... | ... | ... | ... |
| 58 | Measles.......... | 2 | ... | 1 | 2 | 2 | ... | ... | 1 | .... | .... | ... | ... | .. | .. | .. | .. | .. | .. | 8 | .. | ... | ... | ... | ... |
| 59 | Mortification ...... | .... | .... | .... | .... | ... | ... | 1 | ... | 1 | .... | 2 | 1 | .. | .. | .. | .. | .. | .. | 5 | .. | ... | ... | ... | ... |

STATE OF PENNSYLVANIA—AGGREGATE—Continued.

| NATIVITIES. | | | | | SEASON OF DECEASE. | | | | DURATION OF SICKNESS. | | | | WHITES. | | | COLORED. | | | | | | | | | |
|---|---|---|---|---|---|---|---|---|---|---|---|---|---|---|---|---|---|---|---|---|---|---|---|---|---|
| | | | | | | | | | | | | | | | | Slaves. | | | | Free. | | | | | |
| | | | | | | | | | | | | | | | | Black. | | Mulatto. | | Black. | | Mul. | | | |
| California and Territories. | Ireland. | Germany. | Other foreign countries. | Unknown. | Spring. | Summer. | Autumn. | Winter. | Under 1 week. | 1 week and under 1 month. | 1 month and under 3 months. | 3 months and over. | Males. | Females. | Total. | M. | F. | M. | F. | M. | F. | M | F. | Aggregate deaths. | |
| | 1 | | | | 6 | 4 | 3 | 2 | 3 | 5 | 1 | 6 | 9 | 6 | 15 | | | | | | | | | 15 | 1 |
| | | | 2 | | 3 | 4 | 1 | 1 | 2 | 5 | | 2 | | 8 | 8 | | | | | | 1 | | | 9 | 2 |
| | 1 | | 1 | 1 | 2 | 4 | | 2 | 1 | 4 | 2 | 1 | 4 | 1 | 5 | | | | | 2 | 1 | | | 8 | 3 |
| | | | | | 3 | 5 | 3 | 2 | 1 | 3 | 1 | 8 | 8 | 4 | 12 | | | | | 1 | | | | 13 | 4 |
| | 5 | | | | 11 | 15 | 12 | 10 | 21 | 18 | 6 | 2 | 20 | 27 | 47 | | | | | | | 1 | | 48 | 5 |
| | 144 | 56 | 56 | 47 | 930 | 789 | 806 | 591 | 1157 | 721 | 225 | 571 | 1690 | 1414 | 3104 | | | | | 44 | 32 | 2 | 5 | 3187 | 6 |
| 1 | 1840 | 686 | 736 | 123 | 7649 | 7517 | 8129 | 4942 | 9284 | 10200 | 2422 | 4646 | 15102 | 12637 | 27739 | | | | | 346 | 286 | 84 | 96 | 28551 | |

THE STATE OF RHODE ISLAND.

| California and Territories. | Ireland. | Germany. | Other foreign countries. | Unknown. | Spring. | Summer. | Autumn. | Winter. | Under 1 week. | 1 week and under 1 month. | 1 month and under 3 months. | 3 months and over. | Males. | Females. | Total. | Slaves Black M. | Slaves Black F. | Slaves Mulatto M. | Slaves Mulatto F. | Free Black M. | Free Black F. | Free Mul. M | Free Mul. F. | Aggregate deaths. | |
|---|---|---|---|---|---|---|---|---|---|---|---|---|---|---|---|---|---|---|---|---|---|---|---|---|---|
| | 1 | | | | 2 | 1 | | | | 1 | 2 | | 2 | 1 | 3 | | | | | | | | | 3 | 1 |
| | 4 | | 4 | | 5 | 16 | 10 | 9 | 11 | 4 | | | 23 | 15 | 38 | | | | | 2 | | | | 40 | 2 |
| | | | | | | 1 | | 1 | 1 | | 1 | | 2 | | 2 | | | | | | | | | 2 | 3 |
| | 4 | 1 | 4 | | 7 | 11 | 10 | 7 | 35 | | | | 31 | 4 | 35 | | | | | | | | | 35 | 4 |
| | 1 | | | | 2 | 5 | 4 | 8 | 13 | | | | 9 | 11 | 20 | | | | | | 1 | | | 21 | 5 |
| | | | | | 1 | | | 1 | | 1 | | 1 | | 1 | 1 | | | | | 1 | | | | 2 | 6 |
| | | | | | 1 | | | | | | | | | 1 | 1 | | | | | | | | | 1 | 7 |
| | 2 | | | | 1 | 3 | 4 | | 2 | 2 | | | 5 | 3 | 8 | | | | | | | | | 8 | 8 |
| | 1 | | 3 | | 14 | 16 | 24 | 13 | 12 | 34 | 4 | 4 | 43 | 22 | 65 | | | | | 1 | 1 | | | 67 | 9 |
| | | | | | 3 | | 1 | | | | | 1 | 3 | 1 | 4 | | | | | | | | | 4 | 10 |
| | | | 1 | | 5 | 3 | 4 | 3 | 1 | 1 | | 9 | 4 | 11 | 15 | | | | | | 1 | | | 16 | 11 |
| | | | | | | 1 | | 1 | 1 | | | | 1 | 1 | 2 | | | | | | | | | 2 | 12 |
| | 2 | | 1 | | 4 | 5 | 1 | 4 | 7 | 2 | 1 | 2 | | 14 | 14 | | | | | | | | | 14 | 13 |
| | 50 | | 1 | | 2 | 25 | 129 | 3 | 57 | 8 | 2 | | 88 | 68 | 156 | | | | | 1 | 1 | | 1 | 159 | 14 |
| | | | | | 2 | 11 | 41 | 2 | 7 | 5 | 3 | 1 | 35 | 19 | 54 | | | | | 1 | 1 | | | 56 | 15 |
| | 1 | | | | 1 | 5 | 6 | 1 | 10 | 2 | | 1 | 5 | 5 | 10 | | | | | 1 | 1 | 1 | | 13 | 16 |
| | 1 | | | | 3 | 2 | 2 | 1 | 6 | 1 | | 1 | 2 | 5 | 7 | | | | | | | 1 | | 8 | 17 |
| | | | | | | 1 | 2 | | | 2 | | 1 | 2 | 1 | 3 | | | | | | | | | 3 | 18 |
| | | | | | 4 | 3 | 2 | | 1 | 2 | | | 7 | 2 | 9 | | | | | | | | | 9 | 19 |
| | 41 | 2 | 16 | 2 | 129 | 115 | 114 | 104 | 14 | 29 | 32 | 290 | 195 | 262 | 457 | | | | | 6 | 6 | 1 | | 470 | 20 |
| | 4 | | 3 | | 16 | 9 | 20 | 11 | 24 | 7 | 1 | 4 | 32 | 24 | 56 | | | | | | | | | 56 | 21 |
| | 3 | | 1 | | 12 | 9 | 6 | 18 | 33 | 7 | 1 | | 18 | 27 | 45 | | | | | | | | | 45 | 22 |
| | | | | | 3 | 4 | 5 | 3 | 4 | 4 | 2 | 2 | 6 | 8 | 14 | | | | | | | | 1 | 15 | 23 |
| | | | | | | | | 1 | | | | | | | | | | | | | | 1 | | 1 | 24 |
| | 3 | | | | | 10 | 29 | 6 | 3 | 9 | | 2 | 20 | 22 | 42 | | | | | 1 | 2 | | | 45 | 25 |
| | 5 | | 4 | | 16 | 22 | 21 | 19 | 7 | 12 | 9 | 27 | 34 | 42 | 76 | | | | | 1 | 1 | | | 78 | 26 |
| | 9 | | 8 | | 11 | 47 | 168 | 19 | 52 | 108 | 24 | 17 | 134 | 106 | 240 | | | | | 3 | 2 | | | 245 | 27 |
| | | | | | | | | 1 | | 1 | | | | 1 | 1 | | | | | | | | | 1 | 28 |
| | | | | | 1 | 1 | 1 | 1 | 1 | | | 1 | 3 | 1 | 4 | | | | | | | | | 4 | 29 |
| | | | 1 | | 4 | 3 | 2 | 6 | 1 | 5 | 3 | 2 | 6 | 9 | 15 | | | | | | | | | 15 | 30 |
| | 1 | | 2 | | 13 | 10 | 19 | 13 | 5 | 30 | 10 | 8 | 23 | 32 | 55 | | | | | | | | | 55 | 31 |
| | | | | | 5 | 6 | 6 | 6 | 4 | 14 | 2 | 2 | 13 | 10 | 23 | | | | | | | | | 23 | 32 |
| | | | | 1 | | 2 | 2 | 3 | | 6 | | | 3 | 3 | 6 | | | | | 1 | | | | 7 | 33 |
| | | | | | 1 | | 1 | | | 1 | | 1 | | 2 | 2 | | | | | | | | | 2 | 34 |
| | 1 | | | | | | | 1 | | | | | | 1 | 1 | | | | | | | | | 1 | 35 |
| | | | | | 20 | 10 | 15 | 8 | 14 | 18 | 2 | 1 | 33 | 19 | 52 | | | | | 1 | | | | 53 | 36 |
| | 1 | | | | 1 | | 1 | | | 1 | | | 1 | 1 | 2 | | | | | | | | | 2 | 37 |
| | 4 | | | | 12 | 6 | 16 | 15 | | 22 | 5 | 4 | 26 | 22 | 48 | | | | | | | 1 | | 49 | 38 |
| | 1 | | | | 7 | 12 | 5 | 7 | 8 | 11 | 2 | 2 | 14 | 14 | 28 | | | | | | 1 | | 2 | 31 | 39 |
| | | | | | | 1 | 1 | 4 | 2 | 2 | | | 4 | 2 | 6 | | | | | | | | | 6 | 40 |
| | | | | | | 2 | | 1 | | | | 3 | 3 | | 3 | | | | | | | | | 3 | 41 |
| | | | | | 2 | 3 | 5 | 3 | 1 | 6 | 1 | 1 | 6 | 7 | 13 | | | | | | | | | 13 | 42 |
| | | | | | 1 | 2 | 1 | 2 | | 1 | | 1 | 4 | 1 | 5 | | | | | | | 1 | | 6 | 43 |
| | | | | | 1 | 1 | | 2 | | | | | 2 | 2 | 4 | | | | | | | | | 4 | 44 |
| | 2 | | | | 2 | 1 | 5 | 2 | 3 | 3 | 1 | 2 | 5 | 5 | 10 | | | | | | | | | 10 | 45 |
| | | | 1 | | 1 | 3 | 4 | | | 3 | 1 | | 4 | 4 | 8 | | | | | | | | | 8 | 46 |
| | 1 | | | | 5 | 2 | | | | 1 | 1 | 2 | 5 | 2 | 7 | | | | | | | | | 7 | 47 |
| | | | | | 1 | | | | | | | | 1 | | 1 | | | | | | | | | 1 | 48 |
| | 1 | | | | 2 | 2 | | 2 | 1 | | 1 | 1 | 2 | 4 | 6 | | | | | | | | | 6 | 49 |
| | 1 | | | | 3 | 1 | 3 | | | 2 | | 1 | 6 | | 6 | | | | | | | | 1 | 7 | 50 |
| | | | | | | | | 1 | | | | 1 | | 1 | 1 | | | | | | | | | 1 | 51 |
| | 3 | | 1 | | 3 | 7 | 1 | 7 | 1 | 4 | 1 | 5 | 9 | 9 | 18 | | | | | | | | | 18 | 52 |
| | | | | | | 1 | | 1 | 2 | | | | 2 | | 2 | | | | | | | | | 2 | 53 |
| | 1 | | 2 | | 20 | 7 | 4 | 13 | 8 | 24 | 1 | 5 | 22 | 18 | 40 | | | | | | 4 | | | 44 | 54 |
| | | | | | | | | 1 | | | | | 1 | | 1 | | | | | | | | | 1 | 55 |
| | | | | | | 1 | 1 | | | | | | 2 | | 2 | | | | | | | | | 2 | 56 |
| | 2 | | | | 2 | 2 | 8 | 3 | | | | 1 | 5 | 9 | 14 | | | | | 1 | | | | 15 | 57 |
| | | | | | 2 | 4 | 2 | | 1 | 3 | 2 | 2 | 5 | 3 | 8 | | | | | | | | | 8 | 58 |
| | | | | | 1 | 3 | 1 | | 2 | 1 | | | 4 | 1 | 5 | | | | | | | | | 5 | 59 |

## CLASSIFICATION OF DEATHS IN THE

| | Cause of death. | AGES. | | | | | | | | | | | | | | | | | | NATIVITIES. | | | | | |
|---|---|---|---|---|---|---|---|---|---|---|---|---|---|---|---|---|---|---|---|---|---|---|---|---|---|
| | | Under 1. | | 1 and under 5. | | 5 and under 10. | | 10 and under 20. | | 20 and under 50. | | 50 and under 80. | | 80 and under 100. | | 100 & over. | | Age unknown. | | Born in State. | N. England States. | Middle States. | Southern States. | Southwest'n States. | Northwest'n States. |
| | | M. | F. | M. | F. | M. | F. | M. | F. | M. | F. | M. | F. | M | F. | M | F. | M | F. | | | | | | |
| 1 | Mumps | | | | 1 | | | 1 | | | | | | | | | | | | 2 | | | | | |
| 2 | Neuralgia | | | 1 | | | | | | | | | | | | | | | | 1 | | | | | |
| 3 | Old age | | | | | | | | | 2 | | 13 | 24 | 18 | 37 | | | 1 | 2 | 83 | 8 | 1 | | | |
| 4 | Paralysis | | | | 1 | | | | | 1 | 2 | 1 | 10 | | 3 | | | | | 16 | 2 | | | | |
| 5 | Peritonitis | | | 1 | | | | | | | | | | | | | | | | 1 | | | | | |
| 6 | Pleurisy | | | | | | | | | 2 | 1 | | | 1 | | | | | | | 1 | | | | |
| 7 | Pneumonia | 4 | 1 | 5 | 3 | 2 | 2 | 1 | 2 | 3 | 3 | 4 | 6 | 1 | | | | | | 32 | 1 | | | | |
| 8 | Poison | 1 | | | | | | | | 1 | | | | | | | | | | 2 | | | | | |
| 9 | Prematurity of birth | 2 | | | | | | | | | | | | | | | | | | 2 | | | | | |
| 10 | Quinsy | | 1 | | 1 | | | | | | | | | | | | | | | 2 | | | | | |
| 11 | Rheumatism | | | | | | 1 | | | | | | | 1 | 1 | | | | | 3 | | | | | |
| 12 | Scrofula | | 1 | 2 | 1 | | | | 1 | | | | | | | | | | | 5 | | | | | |
| 13 | Small pox | 1 | | 1 | 2 | | | | | 2 | 1 | 1 | 1 | 1 | | | | | | 9 | 1 | | | | |
| 14 | Spine, disease of | | | | | 1 | | 1 | | | 1 | 1 | | | | | | | | 3 | 1 | | | | |
| 15 | Stillborn | 12 | 5 | | | | | | | | | | | | | | | | | 17 | | | | | |
| 16 | Stomach, disease of | | | 1 | | | | | | | | | | | | | | | | | | | | | |
| 17 | Suicide | | | | | | | | | 3 | | 3 | | | | | | | | 5 | 1 | | | | |
| 18 | Sun, stroke of | | | | 1 | | | | | 4 | | | | | | | | | | 2 | | | | | |
| 19 | Syphilis | | | | | | | | | | 1 | | | | | | | | | | | | | | |
| 20 | Teething | 4 | 3 | 4 | 1 | | | | | | | | | | | | | | | 10 | 1 | | | | |
| 21 | Throat, disease of | 2 | | | | 1 | 1 | 1 | | | 1 | 1 | | | | | | | | 7 | | | | | |
| 22 | Thrush | 1 | | | | | | | | | | | | | | | | | | 1 | | | | | |
| 23 | Tumor | 1 | 1 | | | 1 | | | | 3 | 1 | | 1 | | | | | | | 6 | 1 | | | | |
| 24 | Ulcer | 4 | | | | | | | | | | 3 | | | | | | | | 6 | | | | | |
| 25 | Worms | | | 2 | | | | | | | | | | | | | | | | 2 | | | | | |
| 26 | Unknown | 40 | 24 | 8 | 13 | 3 | 2 | 3 | 2 | 10 | 15 | 25 | 9 | 1 | 1 | | | 2 | | 138 | 4 | | | | |
| | Total | 213 | 151 | 246 | 199 | 65 | 38 | 65 | 85 | 309 | 321 | 219 | 223 | 41 | 57 | | | 5 | 4 | 1843 | 134 | 17 | | | 1 |

## CLASSIFICATION OF DEATHS IN EASTERN SECTION

*Embracing the following districts : Beaufort, Charleston,*

| | Cause of death. | Under 1. M. | Under 1. F. | 1 and under 5. M. | 1 and under 5. F. | 5 and under 10. M. | 5 and under 10. F. | 10 and under 20. M. | 10 and under 20. F. | 20 and under 50. M. | 20 and under 50. F. | 50 and under 80. M. | 50 and under 80. F. | 80 and under 100. M | 80 and under 100. F. | 100 & over. M | 100 & over. F. | Age unknown. M | Age unknown. F. | Born in State. | N. England States. | Middle States. | Southern States. | Southwest'n States. | Northwest'n States. |
|---|---|---|---|---|---|---|---|---|---|---|---|---|---|---|---|---|---|---|---|---|---|---|---|---|---|
| 1 | Abscess | | | | | | | | 1 | | | | 1 | | | | | | | 2 | | | | | |
| 2 | Accident, not specif'd | 2 | 3 | | 1 | 1 | | 5 | | 6 | 1 | 2 | 2 | | | | | | | 22 | 1 | | | | |
| 3 | ..do....burned | 1 | 2 | | 9 | 1 | 1 | 1 | | | | | 1 | | | | | | | 16 | | | | | |
| 4 | ...do....drowned | | | 2 | | 1 | | 5 | | 12 | | 2 | 1 | | | | | | | 22 | | | 1 | | |
| 5 | Amputation | | | | | | | | | 1 | | 1 | | | | | | | | 2 | | | | | |
| 6 | Apoplexy | 1 | | | | | | | | 10 | 1 | 7 | 6 | | | | | | | 22 | | | 1 | | |
| 7 | Asthma | | | | | 1 | | | | 1 | | 4 | | | | | | | | 6 | | | | | |
| 8 | Bowels disease of | 3 | 2 | 2 | 2 | | 1 | | | 4 | | 1 | 1 | | | | | | | 16 | | | | | |
| 9 | Brain......do | 1 | | | | | | | | | | | | | | | | | | 1 | | | | | |
| 10 | Bronchitis | | 1 | | | | 1 | 1 | | 1 | 2 | 1 | 1 | | | | | | | 8 | | | | | |
| 11 | Cancer | | | | | | | | | 1 | 1 | | 4 | | | | | | | 4 | | | 1 | | |
| 12 | Carbuncle | | | | | | | | | | | | 2 | | | | | | | 2 | | | | | |
| 13 | Catarrh | 1 | 6 | 2 | 3 | | | | | 1 | 1 | | 1 | | | | | | | 15 | | | | | |
| 14 | Childbirth | | | | | | | | 7 | | 41 | | | | | | | | | 47 | | | | | |
| 15 | Cholera | | | | | | | | 1 | 4 | 3 | 1 | | | | | | 33 | 25 | 67 | | | | | |
| 16 | ...do..infantum | 7 | 7 | 12 | 10 | | | | | | | | | | | | | | | 36 | | | | | |
| 17 | ...do..morbus | | | | 4 | 1 | | 1 | | | 1 | | | | | | | | | 6 | | | 1 | | |
| 18 | Colic | 2 | 1 | 1 | | | | | | 4 | 3 | 4 | 2 | | | | | | | 16 | | | 1 | | |
| 19 | Cong'st'n, not specf'd | | | | 2 | | | | 1 | | | | | | | | | | | 3 | | | | | |
| 20 | ....do....bowels | | | | | | | | | 1 | | | | | | | | | | 1 | | | | | |
| 21 | ....do....brain | | 1 | | 1 | | | | | | 1 | 1 | | | | | | | | 2 | | 1 | | | |
| 22 | ....do....lungs | | | | | | | | | | 2 | | | | | | | | | 2 | | | | | |
| 23 | ....do....stomach | | | | | | | | | | | 1 | | | | | | | | 1 | | | | | |
| 24 | Consumption | 1 | | 1 | | 1 | | 2 | 10 | 32 | 29 | 14 | 11 | | 1 | | | | | 89 | 2 | 1 | | | 1 |
| 25 | Convulsions | 2 | 4 | 7 | 18 | | 3 | 4 | 1 | 5 | 8 | 4 | 4 | | | | | | | 59 | | | | | |
| 26 | Croup | 1 | 3 | 6 | 8 | 2 | 1 | | 1 | | | | | | | | | | | 22 | | | | | |
| 27 | Debility | | 1 | | | | | | | | | | | | | | | | | 1 | | | | | |
| 28 | Diarrhœa | | 3 | 6 | 5 | 1 | | | 1 | 3 | 3 | 2 | 3 | | | | | | | 27 | | | | | |
| 29 | Dirt eating | | | | | 1 | | | | | | | | | | | | | | 1 | | | | | |
| 30 | Dropsy | | 3 | 10 | 10 | 7 | 3 | 8 | 2 | 31 | 25 | 43 | 34 | 7 | 4 | 2 | | | | 180 | 1 | 1 | | | |
| 31 | Dysentery | 2 | 1 | 3 | 6 | | | 1 | | 6 | 1 | 1 | 1 | | | | | | | 21 | | | | 1 | |
| 32 | Dyspepsia | | | | 1 | | | | | 1 | | | 2 | | | | | | | 4 | | | | | |
| 33 | Epilepsy | | | | | | | | 1 | | | | 2 | | | | | | | 3 | | | | | |
| 34 | Erysipelas | | | | 1 | | 1 | | | | 1 | | | | | | | | | 3 | | | | | |
| 35 | Fever, not specified | 7 | 10 | 35 | 34 | 13 | 10 | 15 | 8 | 20 | 19 | 20 | 15 | 1 | 2 | | | | | 199 | | 1 | 2 | | |
| 36 | ..do..bilious | | | 2 | | 4 | 3 | 3 | 7 | 1 | 1 | 1 | 2 | | 1 | | | | | 25 | | | | | |
| 37 | ..do..brain | | | | | | | | | | 1 | 1 | | | | | | | | 1 | | | | | |
| 38 | ..do..congestive | | | | 1 | | 1 | | | 1 | | | | | | | | | | 3 | | | | | |

STATE OF RHODE ISLAND—Continued.

| NATIVITIES: California and Territories. | Ireland. | Germany. | Other foreign countries. | Unknown. | SEASON OF DECEASE: Spring. | Summer. | Autumn. | Winter. | DURATION OF SICKNESS: Under 1 week. | 1 week and under 1 month. | 1 month and under 3 months. | 3 months and over. | WHITES: Males. | Females. | Total. | COLORED: Slaves, Black, M. | Slaves, Black, F. | Slaves, Mulatto, M. | Slaves, Mulatto, F. | Free, Black, M. | Free, Black, F. | Free, Mul., M | Free, Mul., F. | Aggregate deaths. | |
|---|---|---|---|---|---|---|---|---|---|---|---|---|---|---|---|---|---|---|---|---|---|---|---|---|---|
| | | | | | 2 | | | | 2 | | | | 1 | 1 | 2 | | | | | | | | | 2 | 1 |
| | | | | | 1 | | | | 1 | | | | 1 | | 1 | | | | | | | | | 1 | 2 |
| | 1 | | 4 | | 24 | 21 | 28 | 24 | 11 | 11 | 6 | 18 | 34 | 61 | 95 | | | | | | 1 | | 1 | 97 | 3 |
| | | | | | 5 | 5 | 4 | 4 | | 3 | 1 | 12 | 2 | 14 | 16 | | | | | | 2 | | | 18 | 4 |
| | | | | | | | 1 | | | | | | 1 | | 1 | | | | | | | | | 1 | 5 |
| | 1 | | 2 | | 3 | 1 | | | | 1 | | 1 | 3 | 1 | 4 | | | | | | | | | 4 | 6 |
| | 4 | | | | 23 | 7 | 4 | 3 | 3 | 11 | 4 | 1 | 19 | 17 | 36 | | | | | 1 | | | | 37 | 7 |
| | | | | | | 1 | 1 | | | 1 | | | 2 | | 2 | | | | | | | | | 2 | 8 |
| | | | | | | 2 | | | | | | | 2 | | 2 | | | | | | | | | 2 | 9 |
| | | | | | 1 | | | 1 | | | 1 | | | 2 | 2 | | | | | | | | | 2 | 10 |
| | | | | | 1 | 1 | 1 | | | | 1 | 2 | 1 | 2 | 3 | | | | | | | | | 3 | 11 |
| | | | | | | 2 | 1 | 2 | | 1 | | 1 | 2 | 2 | 4 | | | | | | 1 | | | 5 | 12 |
| | | | | | 5 | 2 | 2 | 1 | 3 | 5 | | 1 | 6 | 4 | 10 | | | | | | | | | 10 | 13 |
| | | | | | 2 | 1 | 1 | | | 1 | | 3 | 3 | 1 | 4 | | | | | | | | | 4 | 14 |
| | | | | | 4 | 5 | 4 | 4 | | | | | 12 | 5 | 17 | | | | | | | | | 17 | 15 |
| | | | 1 | | | 1 | | | | 1 | | | 1 | | 1 | | | | | | | | | 1 | 16 |
| | | | | | 1 | 4 | 1 | | 2 | | | | 5 | | 5 | | | | | 1 | | | | 6 | 17 |
| | 2 | | 1 | | | 4 | | 1 | 2 | | 1 | 1 | 4 | 1 | 5 | | | | | | | | | 5 | 18 |
| | 1 | | | | 1 | | | | | | | | | 1 | 1 | | | | | | | | | 1 | 19 |
| | | | 1 | | 1 | | 7 | 4 | 1 | 2 | 1 | 1 | 8 | 4 | 12 | | | | | | | | | 12 | 20 |
| | | | | | 2 | 1 | 3 | 1 | | 1 | 1 | 2 | 5 | 2 | 7 | | | | | | | | | 7 | 21 |
| | | | | | | 1 | | | | | | 1 | 1 | | 1 | | | | | | | | | 1 | 22 |
| | | 1 | | | 3 | | 3 | 2 | 2 | | | 3 | 4 | 3 | 7 | | | | | 1 | | | | 8 | 23 |
| | 1 | | | | 2 | 2 | 2 | 1 | 2 | 1 | 2 | | 7 | | 7 | | | | | | | | | 7 | 24 |
| | | | | | | 1 | 1 | | | 1 | 1 | | 2 | | 2 | | | | | | | | | 2 | 25 |
| | 10 | | 6 | | 38 | 40 | 46 | 34 | 39 | 26 | 10 | 21 | 91 | 64 | 155 | | | | | 1 | 1 | | 1 | 158 | 26 |
| ... | 171 | 4 | 68 | 3 | 473 | 520 | 817 | 420 | 428 | 466 | 144 | 477 | 1132 | 1044 | 2176 | ... | ... | ... | ... | 25 | 27 | 6 | 7 | 2241 | |

OF THE STATE OF SOUTH CAROLINA.

*Colleton, Georgetown, Horry, Marion, and Williamsburg.*

| California and Territories. | Ireland. | Germany. | Other foreign countries. | Unknown. | Spring. | Summer. | Autumn. | Winter. | Under 1 week. | 1 week and under 1 month. | 1 month and under 3 months. | 3 months and over. | Males. | Females. | Total. | Slaves, Black, M. | Slaves, Black, F. | Slaves, Mulatto, M. | Slaves, Mulatto, F. | Free, Black, M. | Free, Black, F. | Free, Mul., M | Free, Mul., F. | Aggregate deaths. | |
|---|---|---|---|---|---|---|---|---|---|---|---|---|---|---|---|---|---|---|---|---|---|---|---|---|---|
| | | | | | | 1 | 1 | | | 1 | 1 | | | 1 | 1 | | 1 | | | | | | | 2 | 1 |
| | | | | | 5 | 5 | 5 | 6 | 13 | 1 | | | 5 | 1 | 6 | 10 | 6 | 1 | | | | | | 23 | 2 |
| | | | | | 6 | 4 | 1 | 5 | 7 | 5 | | | | 3 | 3 | 3 | 8 | | 1 | | | | 1 | 16 | 3 |
| | | | | | 5 | 9 | 6 | 3 | 23 | | | | | | | 19 | 1 | 2 | | | | 1 | | 23 | 4 |
| | | | | | 1 | | 1 | | 1 | 1 | | | | | | 2 | | | | | | | | 2 | 5 |
| | 2 | | | | 8 | 8 | 5 | 4 | 21 | 2 | 1 | | 10 | 2 | 12 | 8 | 4 | | 1 | | | | | 25 | 6 |
| | | | | | 3 | 1 | 1 | 1 | 1 | | 2 | 3 | | | | 4 | | 2 | | | | | | 6 | 7 |
| | | | | | 5 | 5 | 3 | 3 | 6 | 6 | 2 | 2 | 1 | 1 | 2 | 9 | 5 | | | | | | | 16 | 8 |
| | | | | | | 1 | | | 1 | | | | | | | 1 | | | | | | | | 1 | 9 |
| | | | | | 2 | 1 | 5 | | 4 | 2 | | 2 | 2 | 3 | 5 | 1 | 2 | | | | | | | 8 | 10 |
| | 1 | | | | 1 | 1 | 1 | 2 | | | 1 | 3 | | 4 | 4 | 1 | 1 | | | | | | | 6 | 11 |
| | | | | | 1 | 1 | | | | 2 | | | | 2 | 2 | | | | | | | | | 2 | 12 |
| | | | | | 4 | 2 | 2 | 7 | 9 | 2 | 2 | 2 | 1 | 4 | 5 | 3 | 7 | | | | | | | 15 | 13 |
| | | 1 | | | 14 | 10 | 15 | 9 | 31 | 10 | 1 | | | 17 | 17 | | 30 | | 1 | | | | | 48 | 14 |
| | | | | | | | 9 | | 9 | | | | | | | 38 | 29 | | | | | | | 67 | 15 |
| | | | | | 6 | 19 | 10 | 1 | 16 | 17 | 3 | | 10 | 8 | 18 | 9 | 9 | | | | | | | 36 | 16 |
| | | | | | 1 | 4 | 2 | | 6 | 1 | | | 1 | | 1 | 1 | 5 | | | | | | | 7 | 17 |
| | | | | | 4 | 7 | 4 | 2 | 15 | 1 | | | 1 | 1 | 2 | 10 | 5 | | | | | | | 17 | 18 |
| | | | | | 1 | | 1 | 1 | 3 | | | | | 3 | 3 | | | | | | | | | 3 | 19 |
| | | | | | | | 1 | | 1 | | | | | | | 1 | | | | | | | | 1 | 20 |
| | 1 | | | | 2 | 1 | | 1 | 2 | 2 | | | 1 | 2 | 3 | | 1 | | | | | | | 4 | 21 |
| | | | | | 1 | | 1 | | 1 | 1 | | | | | | | 2 | | | | | | | 2 | 22 |
| | | | | | 1 | | | | 1 | | | | | | | 1 | | | | | | | | 1 | 23 |
| | 4 | 3 | 2 | | 33 | 24 | 25 | 20 | 4 | 10 | 21 | 67 | 23 | 19 | 42 | 25 | 27 | 2 | 2 | | | 1 | 3 | 102 | 24 |
| | | | 1 | | 17 | 19 | 13 | 9 | 46 | 7 | 1 | 1 | 5 | 7 | 12 | 15 | 30 | 2 | | | | | 1 | 60 | 25 |
| | | | | | 10 | 1 | 6 | 5 | 19 | 1 | 1 | 1 | 2 | 5 | 7 | 5 | 8 | 1 | | | | 1 | | 22 | 26 |
| | | | | | | 1 | | | 1 | | | | | | | | 1 | | | | | | | 1 | 27 |
| | | | | | 8 | 9 | 8 | 2 | 9 | 13 | 2 | 2 | 1 | 2 | 3 | 11 | 10 | | | | 2 | | 1 | 27 | 28 |
| | | | | | 1 | | | | | 1 | | | | | | 1 | | | | | | | | 1 | 29 |
| | 3 | 1 | 3 | | 57 | 52 | 49 | 29 | 22 | 37 | 32 | 81 | 22 | 15 | 37 | 82 | 60 | 2 | 3 | 1 | 1 | 1 | 2 | 189 | 30 |
| | | | | | 2 | 7 | 6 | 5 | 2 | 11 | 3 | 4 | 5 | 2 | 7 | 8 | 6 | | 1 | | | | | 22 | 31 |
| | | | | | | 2 | 1 | 1 | | | 1 | 3 | 1 | 1 | 2 | | 2 | | | | | | | 4 | 32 |
| | | | | | 1 | 1 | | 1 | 1 | | 1 | | | 1 | 1 | | 2 | | | | | | | 3 | 33 |
| | | | | | 1 | | 2 | | 1 | 2 | | | | 1 | 1 | | 2 | | | | | | | 3 | 34 |
| | 3 | | 4 | | 35 | 55 | 94 | 24 | 70 | 119 | 10 | 3 | 46 | 31 | 77 | 61 | 62 | 1 | 2 | | 1 | 3 | 2 | 209 | 35 |
| | | | | | 2 | 5 | 18 | | 8 | 16 | 1 | | 6 | 4 | 10 | 5 | 10 | | | | | | | 25 | 36 |
| | | | 1 | | | | 2 | | 1 | | 1 | | 1 | | 1 | | 1 | | | | | | | 2 | 37 |
| | | | | | | | 2 | 1 | 3 | | | | 1 | 2 | 3 | | | | | | | | | 3 | 38 |

## CLASSIFICATION OF DEATHS IN EASTERN SECTION

| | Cause of death. | AGES. Under 1. M. | F. | 1 and under 5. M. | F. | 5 and under 10. M. | F. | 10 and under 20. M. | F. | 20 and under 50. M. | F. | 50 and under 80. M. | F. | 80 and under 100. M. | F. | 100 & over. M. | F. | Age unknown. M. | F. | NATIVITIES. Born in State. | N. England States. | Middle States. | Southern States. | Southwest'n States. | Northwest'n States. |
|---|---|---|---|---|---|---|---|---|---|---|---|---|---|---|---|---|---|---|---|---|---|---|---|---|---|
| 1 | Fever, intermittent | | | | | | 1 | | | | | | 1 | | | | | | | 2 | | | | | |
| 2 | ..do..puerperal | | | | | | | | | | 1 | | | | | | | | | 1 | | | | | |
| 3 | ..do..scarlet | 3 | | 14 | 8 | 5 | 4 | 3 | 4 | 6 | 4 | 3 | 4 | | | | | | | 56 | | | 1 | | |
| 4 | ..do..typhus | | | 6 | 3 | 4 | 2 | 6 | 3 | 4 | 3 | 4 | 4 | | | | | | | 38 | | | | | |
| 5 | ..do..yellow | | | 1 | 3 | 3 | | 6 | 5 | 66 | 27 | 6 | 5 | | 2 | | | | | 25 | 4 | 9 | 3 | | |
| 6 | Head, disease of | 1 | | 1 | | | | 2 | 1 | | | 1 | | | | | | | | 6 | | | | | |
| 7 | Heart....do | 1 | | | | | | | | 2 | 4 | 1 | 3 | | | | | | | 9 | | 1 | | | |
| 8 | Hemorrhage | | | | | | | | | 5 | | | 1 | | | | | | | 6 | | | | | |
| 9 | Hernia | | | | | | | | | 3 | | 1 | | | | | | | | 4 | | | | | |
| 10 | Hives | | | | 1 | | | | | | | | | | | | | | | 1 | | | | | |
| 11 | Hooping cough | 10 | 14 | 25 | 11 | 2 | 8 | 1 | 3 | | | | | | | | | | | 74 | | | | | |
| 12 | Hydrocephalus | 1 | | 2 | | | | | | | | | | | | | | | | 3 | | | | | |
| 13 | Inflammation | | | | 2 | 1 | | | 1 | 2 | 1 | 1 | 1 | | | | | | | 9 | | | | | |
| 14 | .....do.....bowels | | 1 | 1 | | 1 | 1 | | | 3 | 2 | 1 | 1 | | | | | | | 11 | | | | | |
| 15 | .....do.....brain | 1 | | 1 | | 2 | | | 1 | 2 | 1 | 2 | | | | | | | | 10 | | | | | |
| 16 | .....do.....stomach | | | | | | | | | 2 | 2 | 1 | | | | | | | | 3 | | 1 | | | |
| 17 | Insanity | | | | | | | | | 1 | | 2 | 1 | | | | | | | 2 | 1 | | | | |
| 18 | Leprosy | | | | | | | | | | 1 | | | | | | | | | 1 | | | | | |
| 19 | Lightning | | | | | | | 2 | | | 1 | 1 | | | | | | | | 4 | | | | | |
| 20 | Liver, disease of | | | 1 | | | 1 | | | 6 | 3 | 1 | 3 | | | | | | | 13 | | 1 | | | |
| 21 | Lockjaw | 6 | 5 | 1 | 1 | | | | 1 | 1 | 1 | | | | | | | | | 16 | | | | | |
| 22 | Lungs, disease of | | | | | | | | | | 1 | | 1 | | | | | | | 2 | | | | | |
| 23 | Marasmus | 1 | 2 | 1 | 2 | | | 1 | | 1 | 1 | | | | | | | | | 9 | | | | | |
| 24 | Measles | | | | 2 | | | | | | 3 | | 1 | | | | | | | 6 | | | | | |
| 25 | Menses, excess of | | | | | | | | | | 2 | | 1 | | | | | | | 3 | | | | | |
| 26 | ...do..suppress'n of | | | | | | | | 1 | | | | | | | | | | | 1 | | | | | |
| 27 | Mortification | | | | | | | | | | 1 | | | | | | | | | 1 | | | | | |
| 28 | Murder | | | | | | | | | 1 | | | | | | | | | | 1 | | | | | |
| 29 | Neuralgia | | | | | | | | | | | 1 | | | | | | | | | | | | | |
| 30 | Old age | | | | | | | | | | | 20 | 22 | 38 | 28 | 5 | 4 | | | 98 | | | 1 | | |
| 31 | Paralysis | | | | | | | | | 3 | 1 | 7 | 7 | | 1 | | | | | 14 | | | 2 | | |
| 32 | Pleurisy | | | | | | | 2 | | 4 | 4 | 2 | 4 | | | | | | | 16 | | | | | |
| 33 | Pneumonia | | | 8 | 4 | 7 | 4 | 17 | 11 | 29 | 27 | 20 | 15 | 3 | 1 | | | | | 143 | | 1 | | | |
| 34 | Poison | | | | | | | 1 | | | | | | | | | | | | 1 | | | | | |
| 35 | Putrid sore throat | | | 2 | 1 | 1 | 1 | | | | | | | | | | | | | 5 | | | | | |
| 36 | Quinsy | | | 1 | | | | | | | 2 | | | | | | | | | 3 | | | | | |
| 37 | Rheumatism | | | | | | | 1 | | | 1 | | 2 | | | | | | | 3 | | | 1 | | |
| 38 | Scrofula | | | | 1 | | | | | | 1 | | | | | | | | | 2 | | | | | |
| 39 | Spine, disease of | | | 1 | | 1 | | 1 | | | | 1 | | | | | | | | 3 | | | | | |
| 40 | Suffocation | 4 | 2 | | | | | | | | | | | | | | | | | 6 | | | | | |
| 41 | Teething | 7 | 7 | 29 | 20 | | | | | | | | | | | | | | | 63 | | | | | |
| 42 | Tetanus | | | | | | | 2 | | | | | | | | | | | | 2 | | | | | |
| 43 | Throat, disease of | 1 | 1 | 4 | 6 | 2 | 8 | | 3 | | 1 | 1 | 2 | | | | | | | 29 | | | | | |
| 44 | Thrush | | 3 | | | | | | | | | | | | | | | | | 3 | | | | | |
| 45 | Ulcer | | | | | | | | | | | 3 | 1 | | | | | | | 3 | | | | | |
| 46 | Uterus, disease of | | | | | | | | | | | | 1 | | | | | | | 1 | | | | | |
| 47 | Venereal | | | | | | | | | 1 | | 3 | 2 | | | | | | | 5 | | | | | |
| 48 | Worms | 9 | 5 | 61 | 60 | 13 | 10 | 2 | 3 | | 2 | | | | | | | | | 165 | | | | | |
| 49 | Unknown | 74 | 66 | 10 | 12 | 4 | 8 | 8 | 6 | 12 | 20 | 22 | 9 | 7 | 5 | 1 | | 29 | 18 | 301 | | | 4 | | |
| | Total | 150 | 134 | 259 | 253 | 80 | 73 | 101 | 84 | 300 | 263 | 216 | 183 | 56 | 45 | 8 | 4 | 62 | 43 | 2140 | 9 | 17 | 19 | 1 | 1 |

## CLASSIFICATION OF DEATHS IN NORTHERN

*Embracing the following districts: Chester, Chesterfield, Darlington,*

| | | | | | | | | | | | | | | | | | | | | | | | | | |
|---|---|---|---|---|---|---|---|---|---|---|---|---|---|---|---|---|---|---|---|---|---|---|---|---|---|
| 1 | Abscess | | | | | | | | | 1 | | | | | | | | | | 1 | | | | | |
| 2 | Accident, not specif'd | 4 | 3 | 4 | 1 | 1 | 1 | 4 | 2 | 12 | 1 | 6 | 3 | | | | | | | 37 | | | 3 | | |
| 3 | ....do....burned | 1 | | 4 | 7 | 3 | 11 | 2 | 1 | | 2 | | 1 | 1 | 1 | | | | | 31 | | | 1 | | |
| 4 | ....do....drowned | | | 2 | | | | 1 | | 2 | | | | | | | | | | 5 | | | | | |
| 5 | ....do....scalded | | | 1 | | | | | | | | | | | | | | | | 1 | | | | | |
| 6 | ....do....shot | | | | | | | | | 2 | | | | | | | | | | 2 | | | | | |
| 7 | Apoplexy | | | | | | | | 1 | 2 | 3 | 3 | 3 | | | | | | | 11 | | | 1 | | |
| 8 | Asthma | | | | | 1 | | | | | | 2 | 2 | | | | | | | 5 | | | | | |
| 9 | Bowels, disease of | 4 | 2 | 1 | 2 | | | 1 | 1 | 2 | | 3 | 1 | | 1 | | | | | 18 | | | | | |
| 10 | Brain .....do | | | | | | | | | | 1 | | | | | | | | | 1 | | | | | |
| 11 | Bronchitis | | 1 | 2 | 1 | | | | | 3 | | | | | | | | | | 7 | | | | | |
| 12 | Cancer | | | | | | | | | | 3 | | 4 | | 1 | | | | | 6 | | | 1 | | |
| 13 | Catarrh | 7 | 3 | 1 | 2 | 2 | | | | 1 | 3 | 1 | 4 | | | | | | | 27 | | | 2 | | |
| 14 | Childbirth | | | | | | | | 1 | | 32 | | | | | | | | | 31 | | | 2 | | |
| 15 | Cholera | | | 1 | | | | | | | | | | | | | | | | 1 | | | | | |

OF THE STATE OF SOUTH CAROLINA—Continued.

| NATIVITIES. | | | | | SEASON OF DECEASE. | | | | DURATION OF SICKNESS. | | | | WHITES. | | | COLORED. | | | | | | | | | |
|---|---|---|---|---|---|---|---|---|---|---|---|---|---|---|---|---|---|---|---|---|---|---|---|---|---|
| | | | | | | | | | | | | | | | | Slaves. | | | | Free. | | | | | |
| | | | | | | | | | | | | | | | | Black. | | Mulatto. | | Black. | | Mul. | | | |
| California and Territories. | Ireland. | Germany. | Other foreign countries. | Unknown. | Spring. | Summer. | Autumn. | Winter. | Under 1 week. | 1 week and under 1 month. | 1 month and under 3 months. | 3 months and over. | Males. | Females. | Total. | M. | F. | M. | F. | M. | F. | M | F. | Aggregate deaths. | |
| | | | | | 1 | | 1 | | 1 | 1 | | | | 1 | 1 | | 1 | | | | | | | 2 | 1 |
| | | | | | | 1 | | | 1 | | | | | | | | 1 | | | | | | | 1 | 2 |
| | 1 | | | | 11 | 28 | 13 | 12 | 28 | 22 | 2 | 1 | 12 | 11 | 23 | 22 | 9 | | | | | | 4 | 58 | 3 |
| | | | 1 | | 14 | 11 | 11 | 3 | 11 | 25 | 1 | 2 | 5 | 8 | 13 | 18 | 7 | | | | | 1 | | 39 | 4 |
| | 51 | 16 | 16 | | 1 | | 114 | 7 | 36 | 86 | | | 80 | 39 | 119 | | 2 | 1 | | | | 1 | 1 | 124 | 5 |
| | | | | | 4 | 1 | 1 | | 4 | | | 1 | 2 | | 2 | 3 | 1 | | | | | | | 6 | 6 |
| | | | 1 | | 3 | 3 | 2 | 3 | 4 | 2 | 3 | 2 | 4 | 3 | 7 | | 4 | | | | | | | 11 | 7 |
| | | | | | 2 | 2 | 1 | 1 | 3 | 2 | 1 | | 2 | 1 | 3 | 2 | | | | | | 1 | | 6 | 8 |
| | | | | | 2 | | | 2 | 1 | 1 | | 2 | | | | 4 | | | | | | | | 4 | 9 |
| | | | | | | | 1 | | 1 | | | | | 1 | 1 | | | | | | | | | 1 | 10 |
| | | | | | 21 | 23 | 19 | 10 | 3 | 38 | 9 | 8 | 5 | 2 | 7 | 31 | 31 | 2 | 1 | | 1 | | 1 | 74 | 11 |
| | | | | | | 3 | | | | | | 3 | | | | 3 | | | | | | | | 3 | 12 |
| | | | | | 2 | 4 | 3 | | 3 | 6 | | | | 1 | 1 | 4 | 4 | | | | | | | 9 | 13 |
| | | | | | 1 | 5 | 4 | 1 | 3 | 7 | 1 | | 5 | 1 | 6 | 1 | 4 | | | | | | | 11 | 14 |
| | | | | | 3 | 1 | 3 | 3 | 4 | 5 | 1 | | 3 | 1 | 4 | 5 | 1 | | | | | | | 10 | 15 |
| | | | 1 | | 1 | 1 | 2 | 1 | 1 | 2 | 2 | | 2 | 2 | 4 | 1 | | | | | | | | 5 | 16 |
| | | | 1 | | 1 | 1 | 1 | 1 | 1 | | | 3 | 3 | | 3 | | 1 | | | | | | | 4 | 17 |
| | | | | | 1 | | | | | | | 1 | | | | | 1 | | | | | | | 1 | 18 |
| | | | | | | | 4 | | 2 | | | | | | | 3 | 1 | | | | | | | 4 | 19 |
| | | | 1 | | 4 | 2 | 6 | 3 | 2 | 3 | 3 | 7 | 4 | 5 | 9 | 4 | 2 | | | | | | | 15 | 20 |
| | | | | | 8 | 1 | 6 | | 14 | 1 | | | 1 | | 1 | 7 | 8 | | | | | | | 16 | 21 |
| | | | | | | 1 | 1 | | | | 1 | 1 | | 1 | 1 | | 1 | | | | | | | 2 | 22 |
| | | | | | 1 | 2 | 3 | 3 | 1 | | 3 | 3 | 1 | 2 | 3 | 3 | 3 | | | | | | | 9 | 23 |
| | | | | | 3 | 2 | 1 | | | 3 | | | | 1 | 1 | | 5 | | | | | | | 6 | 24 |
| | | | | | 1 | | 1 | 1 | 3 | | | | | | | | 3 | | | | | | | 3 | 25 |
| | | | | | | 1 | | | | 1 | | | | | | | 1 | | | | | | | 1 | 26 |
| | | | | | | | 1 | | | 1 | | | | | | | 1 | | | | | | | 1 | 27 |
| | | | | | | | 1 | | | | | | 1 | | 1 | | | | | | | | | 1 | 28 |
| | | | 1 | | | | 1 | | | | | 1 | 1 | | 1 | | | | | | | | | 1 | 29 |
| | 1 | | 17 | | 42 | 20 | 21 | 31 | 14 | 20 | 13 | 16 | 3 | 9 | 12 | 58 | 44 | 1 | | | | 1 | 1 | 117 | 30 |
| | 2 | | 1 | | 6 | 5 | 6 | 2 | 5 | 6 | 3 | 5 | 7 | 3 | 10 | 2 | 5 | | | 1 | | | 1 | 19 | 31 |
| | | | | | 5 | | | 11 | 4 | 8 | 2 | 1 | 1 | 1 | 2 | 7 | 7 | | | | | | | 16 | 32 |
| | | | 2 | | 84 | 8 | 13 | 40 | 71 | 70 | 2 | 2 | 9 | 8 | 17 | 72 | 53 | 1 | 1 | | | 2 | | 146 | 33 |
| | | | | | | 1 | | | 1 | | | | | | | 1 | | | | | | | | 1 | 34 |
| | | | | | 1 | | 2 | 2 | 3 | 2 | | | 3 | 2 | 5 | | | | | | | | | 5 | 35 |
| | | | | | | 1 | 2 | | 3 | | | | | 1 | 1 | 1 | 1 | | | | | | | 3 | 36 |
| | | | | | 1 | 2 | | 1 | 1 | | | 2 | | 1 | 1 | 1 | 2 | | | | | | | 4 | 37 |
| | | | | | | 1 | 1 | | | | 1 | 1 | | | | | 2 | | | | | | | 2 | 38 |
| | | | 1 | | 1 | 3 | | | | 1 | 1 | 2 | 1 | | 1 | 3 | | | | | | | | 4 | 39 |
| | | | | | 2 | 1 | | 3 | 6 | | | | | | | 4 | 2 | | | | | | | 6 | 40 |
| | | | | | 12 | 19 | 23 | 9 | 15 | 31 | 3 | 9 | 8 | 4 | 12 | 28 | 23 | | | | | | | 63 | 41 |
| | | | | | | 1 | 1 | | 1 | 1 | | | | | | 2 | | | | | | | | 2 | 42 |
| | | | | | 11 | 5 | 7 | 6 | 14 | 12 | | | 4 | 13 | 17 | 4 | 8 | | | | | | | 29 | 43 |
| | | | | | 1 | 2 | | | 1 | 2 | | | | | | | 3 | | | | | | | 3 | 44 |
| | | | 1 | | 2 | | | 1 | | 2 | | 1 | | | | 3 | 1 | | | | | | | 4 | 45 |
| | | | | | | | | 1 | | | | 1 | | | | | 1 | | | | | | | 1 | 46 |
| | 1 | | | | 2 | 1 | 3 | | | | 1 | 4 | 2 | | 2 | 2 | 1 | | 1 | | | | | 6 | 47 |
| | | | | | 26 | 53 | 66 | 16 | 82 | 66 | 5 | 5 | 8 | 9 | 17 | 76 | 70 | 1 | 1 | | | | | 165 | 48 |
| | 2 | 2 | 2 | | 64 | 45 | 53 | 81 | 78 | 13 | 11 | 27 | 34 | 20 | 54 | 130 | 124 | 2 | | | | 1 | | 311 | 49 |
| .... | 72 | 23 | 57 | .. | 583 | 507 | 699 | 347 | 784 | 711 | 161 | 287 | 356 | 293 | 649 | 839 | 776 | 21 | 15 | 2 | 5 | 14 | 18 | 3889 | |

SECTION OF THE STATE OF SOUTH CAROLINA.

*Fairfield, Kershaw, Lancaster, Richland, Sumter, and York.*

| California and Territories. | Ireland. | Germany. | Other foreign countries. | Unknown. | Spring. | Summer. | Autumn. | Winter. | Under 1 week. | 1 week and under 1 month. | 1 month and under 3 months. | 3 months and over. | Males. | Females. | Total. | Slaves Black M. | Slaves Black F. | Slaves Mulatto M. | Slaves Mulatto F. | Free Black M. | Free Black F. | Free Mul. M | Free Mul. F. | Aggregate deaths. | |
|---|---|---|---|---|---|---|---|---|---|---|---|---|---|---|---|---|---|---|---|---|---|---|---|---|---|
| | | | | | 1 | | | | | 1 | | | | | | 1 | | | | | | | | 1 | 1 |
| | 1 | | 1 | | 16 | 8 | 2 | 14 | 19 | | 2 | 5 | 11 | 3 | 14 | 19 | 7 | 1 | | | 1 | | | 42 | 2 |
| | | | 2 | | 15 | 5 | 4 | 10 | 17 | 3 | 2 | 1 | 3 | 3 | 6 | 8 | 20 | | | | | | | 34 | 3 |
| | | | | | | 3 | 1 | 1 | 5 | | | | 2 | | 2 | 3 | | | | | | | | 5 | 4 |
| | | | | | | | 1 | | | 1 | | | 1 | | 1 | | | | | | | | | 1 | 5 |
| | | | | | 2 | | | | 1 | | | | 2 | | 2 | | | | | | | | | 2 | 6 |
| | | | | | 5 | 3 | 3 | 1 | 9 | 1 | | 2 | 4 | 2 | 6 | 1 | 5 | | | | | | | 12 | 7 |
| | | | | | | 1 | | 4 | 1 | 1 | 1 | 2 | 2 | | 2 | 1 | 2 | | | | | | | 6 | 8 |
| | | | | | 2 | 11 | 4 | 1 | 4 | 8 | 1 | 5 | 7 | 6 | 13 | 3 | 1 | 1 | | | | | | 18 | 9 |
| | | | | | | | 1 | | | | | 1 | | | | | 1 | | | | | | | 1 | 10 |
| | | | | | 1 | 1 | 3 | 2 | | 5 | | 1 | 1 | 1 | 2 | 4 | 1 | | | | | | | 7 | 11 |
| | | | 1 | | 2 | 3 | 2 | 1 | | | | 3 | | 4 | 4 | | 3 | | 1 | | | | | 8 | 12 |
| | | | | | 6 | 10 | 7 | 5 | 6 | 16 | 1 | 5 | 2 | 1 | 3 | 10 | 16 | | | | | | | 29 | 13 |
| | | | | | 10 | 11 | 7 | 5 | 13 | 12 | | 2 | | 14 | 14 | | 19 | | | | | | | 33 | 14 |
| | | | | | | | | 1 | | | | | | | | 1 | | | | | | | | 1 | 15 |

CLASSIFICATION OF DEATHS IN NORTHERN

| | Cause of death. | AGES. | | | | | | | | | | | | | | | | | | NATIVITIES. | | | | | |
|---|---|---|---|---|---|---|---|---|---|---|---|---|---|---|---|---|---|---|---|---|---|---|---|---|---|
| | | Under 1. | | 1 and under 5. | | 5 and under 10. | | 10 and under 20. | | 20 and under 50. | | 50 and under 80. | | 80 and under 100. | | 100 & over. | | Age unknown. | | Born in State. | N. England States. | Middle States. | Southern States. | Southwest'n States. | Northwest'n States. |
| | | M. | F. | M. | F. | M. | F. | M. | F. | M. | F. | M. | F. | M | F. | M | F. | M | F. | | | | | | |
| 1 | Cholera infantum | 1 | 1 | 3 | | | | | | | | | | | | | | | | 5 | | | | | |
| 2 | Colic | 1 | 1 | | | | | | 1 | | 1 | 2 | 2 | 2 | | | | | | 8 | | | 2 | | |
| 3 | Congestion | | | | | | | | | | | | 1 | | | | | | | 1 | | | | | |
| 4 | ....do.....bowels | | | | 1 | | | 1 | | | | | | | | | | | | 2 | | | | | |
| 5 | ....do.....brain | | | | | | | 2 | | | | | | | | | | | | 2 | | | | | |
| 6 | Consumption | | 1 | 1 | 2 | | | 1 | 3 | 14 | 25 | 12 | 12 | 1 | | | | | | 64 | | 1 | 4 | | |
| 7 | Convulsions | 4 | 10 | 4 | 2 | 2 | 1 | 4 | 2 | 2 | 3 | 2 | 1 | | | | | | | 36 | | | 1 | | |
| 8 | Croup | 9 | 15 | 7 | 12 | | 1 | | | | | | | | | | | | | 44 | | | | | |
| 9 | Diarrhœa | 4 | 10 | 7 | 5 | | | 2 | 1 | 3 | 2 | 3 | 1 | | | | | | | 38 | | | | | |
| 10 | Dirt eating | | | | 1 | | | | | | | | | | | | | | | 1 | | | | | |
| 11 | Dropsy | | | 10 | 5 | 6 | 1 | 6 | 5 | 10 | 17 | 17 | 23 | 5 | | | | | | 92 | | 1 | 7 | | |
| 12 | Dysentery | 4 | 2 | 4 | 3 | | | | | 3 | 1 | 3 | 1 | 1 | | | | | | 21 | | | | | |
| 13 | Dyspepsia | | | 1 | | | | | | | 2 | 1 | | | | | | | | 2 | | | 2 | | |
| 14 | Epilepsy | | | | | | | | | 1 | | 1 | | | | | | | | 2 | | | | | |
| 15 | Erysipelas | 1 | | | | | | 1 | | | | | | | | | | | | 2 | | | | | |
| 16 | Fever, not specified | 6 | 5 | 11 | 18 | 5 | 6 | 15 | 16 | 26 | 34 | 6 | 10 | | | | | | | 148 | | 1 | 9 | | |
| 17 | ..do..bilious | 1 | | 7 | 7 | 1 | 4 | 6 | 10 | 10 | 9 | 4 | 3 | | 1 | | | | | 61 | | | 2 | | |
| 18 | ..do..brain | 1 | | 2 | | 1 | 1 | | | 2 | 1 | | | | | | | | | 7 | | | 1 | | |
| 19 | ..do..catarrhal | 1 | | | | | | | | | | | | | | | | | | 1 | | | | | |
| 20 | ..do..congestive | 1 | 1 | 3 | 4 | 1 | 6 | 5 | 4 | 9 | 5 | 3 | 5 | | | | 1 | | | 46 | | | 1 | | |
| 21 | ..do..intermittent | 3 | | 3 | 1 | 1 | 1 | | 1 | 1 | 1 | | 1 | 1 | | | | | | 13 | | | | | |
| 22 | ..do..scarlet | | | 1 | 2 | | | | | | | | | | | | | | | 3 | | | | | |
| 23 | ..do..typhus | 1 | | 3 | 7 | 4 | 1 | 8 | 10 | 18 | 9 | 2 | 3 | | | | | | | 64 | | | 1 | | |
| 24 | Gravel | | | | | | | | | | | 3 | | | | | | | | 1 | | | 2 | | |
| 25 | Head, disease of | 1 | 2 | | | | | | | | | | | | | | | | | 3 | | | | | |
| 26 | Heart,.....do | | | | | 1 | | | | 1 | | 1 | 1 | | | | | | | 3 | | | 1 | | |
| 27 | Hemorrhage | | | | | | 1 | | | | | 1 | | | | | | | | 1 | | | | | |
| 28 | Hernia | | | | | | | | | 2 | | | | | | | | | | 2 | | | | | |
| 29 | Hives | 2 | 1 | | | | | | | | | | | | | | | | | 3 | | | | | |
| 30 | Hooping cough | 17 | 26 | 27 | 19 | 3 | 4 | | 1 | 1 | 2 | | | | | | | | | 100 | | | | | |
| 31 | Hydrocephalus | | 1 | | 1 | | | | | | | | | | | | | | | 2 | | | | | |
| 32 | Inflammation | 3 | 3 | | | 1 | | 1 | | 2 | | | | | | | | | | 10 | | | | | |
| 33 | .....do.....bowels | 5 | 2 | 3 | 1 | 1 | 1 | | | 2 | 4 | | | 1 | | | | | | 18 | | | | | |
| 34 | .....do.....brain | | 3 | 1 | 6 | 1 | | 2 | | | | 1 | 3 | | | | | | | 17 | | | | | |
| 35 | Insanity | | | | | | | | | | | | 1 | | | | | | | | | | | | |
| 36 | Intemperance | | | | | | | | | 3 | | | | | | | | | | 3 | | | | | |
| 37 | Jaundice | | | | | | | | | | 1 | | | | | | | | | 1 | | | | | |
| 38 | Kidneys, disease of | | 1 | | | | | | | | | | | | | | | | | 1 | | | | | |
| 39 | Killed | | | | | 1 | | | | 1 | | 1 | | | | | | | | 2 | | | 1 | | |
| 40 | Lightning | | | | | | | | | | 1 | | | | | | | | | 1 | | | | | |
| 41 | Liver, disease of | | | | 1 | | | 1 | | 2 | 8 | 2 | 2 | | | | | | | 13 | | 1 | 1 | | |
| 42 | Lockjaw | 1 | | | | 1 | | | | | | | | | | | | | | 2 | | | | | |
| 43 | Lungs, disease of | | | 2 | 1 | | | | 3 | | | 1 | | | 1 | | | | | 6 | | | 2 | | |
| 44 | Malformation | 1 | 1 | | 1 | | | | | | | | | | | | | | | 3 | | | | | |
| 45 | Mania-a-potu | | | | | | | | | 2 | | | | | | | | | | | | | 2 | | |
| 46 | Measles | 1 | 2 | 2 | 1 | | | | | | 1 | 1 | | | | | | | | 8 | | | | | |
| 47 | Mortification | | | | | 1 | | | | | | | | | | | | | | 1 | | | | | |
| 48 | Murder | | | | | | | | | 1 | | | | | | | | | | 1 | | | | | |
| 49 | Neuralgia | | | | | | | | | | | 2 | | | | | | | | 2 | | | | | |
| 50 | Old age | | | | | | | | | | | 12 | 15 | 12 | 13 | 3 | 1 | | | 40 | | | 10 | | |
| 51 | Paralysis | | | | | | | | | 2 | | 5 | 5 | | 1 | | | | | 10 | | | 2 | | |
| 52 | Piles | | | | | | | | | | | 1 | | | | | | | | 1 | | | | | |
| 53 | Pleurisy | | | | | | | 3 | | | 2 | 2 | 1 | | 1 | | | | | 9 | | | | | |
| 54 | Pneumonia | 9 | 8 | 12 | 9 | 4 | 5 | 10 | 6 | 23 | 17 | 9 | 9 | | 1 | | | | | 115 | | 1 | 2 | | |
| 55 | Poison | 1 | | | | | | | | 1 | | | | | | | | | | 2 | | | | | |
| 56 | Putrid sore throat | | | | 5 | | 1 | | | 1 | | | | | | | | | | 5 | | | 2 | | |
| 57 | Quinsy | 1 | | 1 | | | | | | | | 1 | | | | | | | | 3 | | | | | |
| 58 | Rheumatism | | | 1 | | | | 1 | | 2 | | 2 | 1 | | | | | | | 7 | | | | | |
| 59 | Rickets | | | 1 | | | | | | | | | | | | | | | | 1 | | | | | |
| 60 | Scrofula | 1 | 1 | 1 | | 1 | 1 | 2 | | 1 | 2 | | | | | | | | | 10 | | | | | |
| 61 | Spine, disease of | | | | | | 1 | | | | | | | | | | | | | 1 | | | | | |
| 62 | Stillborn | 3 | 2 | | | | | | | | | | | | | | | | | 5 | | | | | |
| 63 | Suffocation | 12 | 11 | | 3 | 1 | | | | | | | | | | | | | | 27 | | | | | |
| 64 | Suicide | | | | | | | | | | 1 | 1 | | | | | | | | 1 | | | 1 | | |
| 65 | Teething | 10 | 15 | 14 | 17 | | | | | | | | | | | | | | | 56 | | | | | |
| 66 | Throat, disease of | 2 | 1 | 10 | 3 | 1 | 1 | | 1 | | 1 | | | | | | | | | 20 | | | | | |
| 67 | Thrush | 2 | 2 | 2 | 2 | | | | | | | | | | | | | | | 8 | | | | | |
| 68 | Tumor | | | | | | | | | 1 | | | | | | | | | | 1 | | | | | |
| 69 | Ulcer | | | | | | | | | 1 | | 1 | | | | | | | | 2 | | | | | |
| 70 | Uterus, disease of | | | | | | | | | | 3 | | 1 | | | | | | | 3 | | | 1 | | |
| 71 | Venereal | | | | | | | | | | 1 | 2 | | | | | | | | 2 | | | | | |
| 72 | Worms | 1 | 1 | 12 | 12 | 4 | 3 | | | | | | | | | | | | | 32 | | | 1 | | |
| 73 | Unknown | 63 | 56 | 59 | 24 | 6 | 6 | 9 | 14 | 19 | 32 | 25 | 27 | 2 | 1 | | | | | 319 | | | 8 | | |
| | Total | 190 | 199 | 222 | 139 | 55 | 58 | 88 | 84 | 193 | 231 | 145 | 147 | 25 | 22 | 3 | 2 | .. | .. | 1781 | .. | 5 | 76 | ... | ... |

## SECTION OF THE STATE OF SOUTH CAROLINA—Continued.

| Nativities. | | | | | Season of decease. | | | | Duration of sickness. | | | | Whites. | | | Colored. | | | | | | | | Aggregate deaths. | |
|---|---|---|---|---|---|---|---|---|---|---|---|---|---|---|---|---|---|---|---|---|---|---|---|---|---|
| | | | | | | | | | | | | | | | | Slaves. | | | | Free. | | | | | |
| | | | | | | | | | | | | | | | | Black. | | Mulatto. | | Black | | Mul | | | |
| California and Territories. | Ireland. | Germany. | Other foreign countries. | Unknown. | Spring. | Summer. | Autumn. | Winter. | Under 1 week. | 1 week and under 1 month. | 1 month and under 3 months. | 3 months and over. | Males. | Females. | Total. | M. | F. | M. | F. | M. | F. | M | F. | | |
| | | | | | | 2 | 3 | | 1 | 3 | 1 | | 2 | | 2 | 2 | 1 | | | | | | | 5 | 1 |
| | | | | | 2 | 3 | 4 | 1 | 6 | 4 | | | 2 | 2 | 4 | 3 | 3 | | | | | | | 10 | 2 |
| | | | | | 1 | | | | 1 | | | | | 1 | 1 | | | | | | | | | 1 | 3 |
| | | | | | 2 | | | | 2 | | | | | 1 | 1 | | | 1 | | | | | | 2 | 4 |
| | | | | | | 1 | 1 | | 2 | | | | 1 | | 1 | 1 | | | | | | | | 2 | 5 |
| | 1 | | 2 | | 29 | 17 | 18 | 8 | | 1 | 4 | 63 | 11 | 26 | 37 | 18 | 16 | | | | 1 | | | 72 | 6 |
| | | | | | 9 | 15 | 6 | 6 | 24 | 5 | 1 | 3 | 3 | 5 | 8 | 14 | 14 | | | 1 | | | | 37 | 7 |
| | | | | | 11 | 8 | 14 | 11 | 25 | 16 | 1 | 1 | 6 | 7 | 18 | 10 | 21 | | | | | | | 44 | 8 |
| | | | | | 8 | 17 | 9 | 4 | 5 | 15 | 6 | 6 | 8 | 3 | 11 | 11 | 16 | | | | | | | 38 | 9 |
| | | | | | | | | 1 | | 1 | | | | | | | 1 | | | | | | | 1 | 10 |
| | 2 | | 2 | 1 | 29 | 38 | 21 | 16 | 2 | 5 | 14 | 79 | 26 | 19 | 45 | 27 | 30 | 1 | | | 2 | | | 105 | 11 |
| | 1 | | | | 2 | 11 | 6 | 3 | 3 | 14 | 1 | 3 | 5 | 3 | 8 | 10 | 4 | | | | | | | 22 | 12 |
| | | | | | 1 | 1 | 2 | | 1 | 1 | 1 | 1 | 1 | 1 | 2 | 1 | 1 | | | | | | | 4 | 13 |
| | | | | | | 2 | | | 1 | | 1 | | | | | 2 | | | | | | | | 2 | 14 |
| | | | | | | | 2 | | | 2 | | | 2 | | 2 | | | | | | | | | 2 | 15 |
| | | | | | 20 | 59 | 58 | 20 | 37 | 90 | 11 | 4 | 33 | 39 | 72 | 33 | 48 | 3 | 1 | | | | 1 | 158 | 16 |
| | | | | | 5 | 20 | 35 | 3 | 17 | 34 | 12 | | 4 | 9 | 13 | 24 | 23 | 1 | 1 | | | | 1 | 63 | 17 |
| | | | | | 1 | 2 | 3 | 2 | 2 | 4 | 1 | | 4 | | 4 | 2 | 2 | | | | | | | 8 | 18 |
| | | | | | | 1 | | | | 1 | | | 1 | | 1 | | | | | | | | | 1 | 19 |
| | 1 | | | | 4 | 9 | 32 | 3 | 22 | 18 | 3 | 1 | 9 | 11 | 20 | 13 | 12 | | 1 | | | | 2 | 48 | 20 |
| | 1 | | | | 1 | 3 | 6 | 4 | 4 | 9 | | 1 | 5 | 1 | 6 | 4 | 4 | | | | | | | 14 | 21 |
| | | | | | | 3 | | | 1 | 2 | | | 1 | 2 | 3 | | | | | | | | | 3 | 22 |
| | | | | 1 | 9 | 15 | 23 | 19 | 11 | 40 | 13 | 2 | 11 | 4 | 15 | 25 | 25 | | 1 | | | | | 66 | 23 |
| | | | | | | 1 | | 2 | 1 | 1 | | 1 | 1 | | 1 | 2 | | | | | | | | 3 | 24 |
| | | | | | 1 | 1 | | 1 | 1 | 1 | | 1 | | | | 1 | 2 | | | | | | | 3 | 25 |
| | | | | | 1 | 1 | | 2 | 3 | | 1 | | 1 | 1 | 2 | 2 | | | | | | | | 4 | 26 |
| | 1 | | | | | 1 | 1 | | 2 | | | | 1 | | 1 | | 1 | | | | | | | 2 | 27 |
| | | | | | 1 | | 1 | | 2 | | | | | | | 1 | | | | 1 | | | | 2 | 28 |
| | | | | | | 1 | 2 | | 3 | | | | 1 | 1 | 2 | 1 | | | | | | | | 3 | 29 |
| | | | | | 17 | 30 | 22 | 23 | 11 | 42 | 13 | 9 | 10 | | 10 | 38 | 52 | | | | | | | 100 | 30 |
| | | | | | | 1 | | 1 | | 1 | 1 | | | | | | 2 | | | | | | | 2 | 31 |
| | | | | | 2 | 5 | 3 | | 1 | 3 | 2 | 3 | 4 | 3 | 7 | 3 | | | | | | | | 10 | 32 |
| | 1 | | 1 | | 7 | 9 | 3 | 1 | 5 | 9 | 3 | 3 | 5 | 5 | 10 | 7 | 3 | | | | | | | 20 | 33 |
| | | | | | 4 | 1 | 7 | 5 | 10 | 6 | | 1 | 1 | 7 | 8 | 4 | 5 | | | | | | | 17 | 34 |
| | 1 | | | | | | 1 | | | | | 1 | | 1 | 1 | | | | | | | | | 1 | 35 |
| | | | | | | | 2 | 1 | 2 | | | | 3 | | 3 | | | | | | | | | 3 | 36 |
| | | | | | | 1 | | | | 1 | | | | 1 | 1 | | | | | | | | | 1 | 37 |
| | | | | | | 1 | | | | 1 | | | | | | | 1 | | | | | | | 1 | 38 |
| | | | | | | 2 | | 1 | 3 | | | | 2 | | 2 | 1 | | | | | | | | 3 | 39 |
| | | | | | | 1 | | | 1 | | | | | 1 | 1 | | | | | | | | | 1 | 40 |
| | 1 | | | | 5 | 5 | 3 | 3 | | 3 | 3 | 10 | 4 | 8 | 12 | 1 | 3 | | | | | | | 16 | 41 |
| | | | | | 1 | | | 1 | 2 | | | | | | | 2 | | | | | | | | 2 | 42 |
| | | | | | 1 | 3 | 3 | 1 | 1 | 3 | 2 | 2 | 1 | 1 | 2 | 2 | 3 | | | | 1 | | | 8 | 43 |
| | | | | | 1 | 2 | | | | 1 | | 1 | 1 | | 1 | | 2 | | | | | | | 3 | 44 |
| | | | | | | 1 | 1 | | | 1 | | 1 | 2 | | 2 | | | | | | | | | 2 | 45 |
| | | | | | | 5 | 2 | 1 | 1 | 4 | 2 | 1 | | 1 | 1 | 4 | 3 | | | | | | | 8 | 46 |
| | | | | | | 1 | | | | | | | | | | 1 | | | | | | | | 1 | 47 |
| | | | | | | | | 1 | | | | | 1 | | 1 | | | | | | | | | 1 | 48 |
| | | | | | 1 | 1 | | | | | 1 | 1 | 2 | | 2 | | | | | | | | | 2 | 49 |
| | | | 4 | 2 | 10 | 22 | 13 | 11 | 10 | 4 | | 8 | 6 | 10 | 16 | 21 | 18 | | 1 | | | | | 56 | 50 |
| | | | 1 | | 5 | 5 | 2 | 1 | 6 | 1 | | 6 | 5 | 4 | 9 | 2 | 2 | | | | | | | 13 | 51 |
| | | | | | 1 | | | | | | 1 | | | | | 1 | | | | | | | | 1 | 52 |
| | | | | | 6 | 1 | | 2 | 1 | 6 | 2 | | 2 | 1 | 3 | 3 | 3 | | | | | | | 9 | 53 |
| | 1 | | 3 | | 52 | 26 | 14 | 29 | 29 | 73 | 9 | 7 | 21 | 15 | 36 | 45 | 39 | 1 | 1 | | | | | 122 | 54 |
| | | | | | | 2 | | | 1 | | | | 1 | | 1 | 1 | | | | | | | | 2 | 55 |
| | | | | | 1 | 1 | 1 | 4 | 3 | 4 | | | 1 | 5 | 6 | | 1 | | | | | | | 7 | 56 |
| | | | | | 2 | | | 1 | 1 | 2 | | | 2 | | 2 | 1 | | | | | | | | 3 | 57 |
| | | | | | 2 | | 2 | 3 | 1 | | 3 | 3 | 3 | 1 | 4 | 3 | | | | | | | | 7 | 58 |
| | | | | | | | 1 | | | | | 1 | 1 | | 1 | | | | | | | | | 1 | 59 |
| | | | | | 1 | 3 | 2 | 4 | 1 | 1 | 2 | 6 | | | | 6 | 4 | | | | | | | 10 | 60 |
| | | | | | | | | 1 | | | 1 | | | | | | 1 | | | | | | | 1 | 61 |
| | | | | | | 5 | | | | | | | 1 | | 1 | 2 | 2 | | | | | | | 5 | 62 |
| | | | | | 10 | 6 | 5 | 6 | 27 | | | | | | | 13 | 14 | | | | | | | 27 | 63 |
| | | | | | 1 | | | 1 | | | | | | 1 | 1 | 1 | | | | | | | | 2 | 64 |
| | | | | | 6 | 32 | 11 | 7 | 9 | 22 | 16 | 5 | 1 | 5 | 6 | 21 | 27 | 2 | | | | | | 56 | 65 |
| | | | | | 2 | 8 | 6 | 4 | 6 | 9 | | | 7 | 3 | 10 | 6 | 4 | | | | | | | 20 | 66 |
| | | | | | 3 | 4 | 1 | | 1 | 5 | 1 | 1 | 2 | | 2 | 2 | 3 | | 1 | | | | | 8 | 67 |
| | | | | | 1 | | | | | | | 1 | 1 | | 1 | | | | | | | | | 1 | 68 |
| | | | | | | | 2 | | | 1 | | 1 | 2 | | 2 | | | | | | | | | 2 | 69 |
| | | | | | 3 | 1 | | | | | | 4 | | 2 | 2 | | 2 | | | | | | | 4 | 70 |
| | | | 1 | | | 2 | | 1 | | | | 3 | 2 | | 2 | | 1 | | | | | | | 3 | 71 |
| | | | | | 9 | 12 | 9 | 3 | 12 | 13 | 3 | 4 | 4 | 4 | 8 | 13 | 11 | | 1 | | | | | 33 | 72 |
| | 2 | | 4 | 1 | 80 | 98 | 74 | 52 | 120 | 54 | 17 | 87 | 49 | 38 | 87 | 120 | 117 | 4 | 2 | | 2 | 1 | 1 | 334 | 73 |
| .... | 14 | .. | 22 | 5 | 431 | 585 | 472 | 320 | 519 | 585 | 165 | 368 | 321 | 287 | 608 | 582 | 622 | 15 | 11 | 2 | 7 | 1 | 5 | 1853 | |

## CLASSIFICATION OF DEATHS IN SOUTHERN

*Embracing the following districts : Barnwell, Edgefield,*

| | Cause of death. | AGES. | | | | | | | | | | | | | | | | | | NATIVITIES. | | | | | |
|---|---|---|---|---|---|---|---|---|---|---|---|---|---|---|---|---|---|---|---|---|---|---|---|---|---|
| | | Under 1. | | 1 and under 5. | | 5 and under 10. | | 10 and under 20. | | 20 and under 50. | | 50 and under 80. | | 80 and under 100. | | 100 & over. | | Age unknown. | | Born in State. | N. England States. | Middle States. | Southern States. | Southwest'n States. | Northwest'n States. |
| | | M. | F. | M. | F. | M. | F. | M. | F. | M. | F. | M. | F. | M | F. | M | F. | | | | | | | | |
| 1 | Abscess | | | | | | | | | 1 | | | | | | | | | | 1 | | | | | |
| 2 | Accident, not specif'd | 2 | 2 | 2 | 2 | 2 | 2 | 7 | | 4 | | 1 | 1 | | | | | | | 25 | | | | | |
| 3 | ....do...burned | | 1 | 7 | 7 | 6 | 4 | | 6 | 1 | 1 | | 2 | | | | | | | 35 | | | | | |
| 4 | ....do...drowned | | | 1 | | | | 2 | 2 | 3 | | | | | | | | | | 8 | | | | | |
| 5 | ....do...scalded | | | 1 | | | | | | | | | | | | | | | | 1 | | | | | |
| 6 | ....do...shot | | | | | 1 | | | 1 | 1 | | 1 | | | | | | | | 4 | | | | | |
| 7 | Apoplexy | | | 1 | | | | | | 2 | 3 | 3 | 4 | | 1 | | | | | 12 | 1 | | 1 | | |
| 8 | Asthma | | | | 1 | | | | | | 1 | 4 | 2 | | 1 | | | | | 6 | | | 2 | | |
| 9 | Bowels, disease of | 6 | 2 | 1 | 4 | 1 | 1 | | | | | 1 | | | | | | | | 15 | | | | 1 | |
| 10 | Brain ......do | | | | | | | 1 | 1 | | | | | | | | | | | 2 | | | | | |
| 11 | Bronchitis | | | 2 | 1 | | | | | 1 | 1 | | | | | | | | | 5 | | | | | |
| 12 | Cancer | | | | | | 1 | | | 1 | 1 | 2 | 2 | | | | | | | 5 | | | 1 | | |
| 13 | Catarrh | 5 | 6 | 1 | 5 | | 1 | 1 | 2 | 4 | | 2 | 5 | | 1 | | | | | 29 | 1 | | 1 | | |
| 14 | Childbirth | | | | | | | | 5 | | 22 | | | | | | | | | 26 | | | | | |
| 15 | Chlorosis | | | | | | | | | | 1 | | | | | | | | | 1 | | | | | |
| 16 | Cholera | | | | | | | 1 | | | | | | | | | | | | 1 | | | | | |
| 17 | ...do...infantum | | 5 | 4 | 1 | | | | | | | | | | | | | | | 10 | | | | | |
| 18 | ...do...morbus | | | 2 | | 1 | | | | 1 | | 1 | 2 | | | | | | | 6 | | | | | |
| 19 | Colic | 1 | 1 | 1 | 2 | | | | | 3 | 2 | 2 | 1 | | | | | | | 10 | | | 2 | | |
| 20 | Congestion | | 1 | 1 | | | | | 1 | | | | | | | | | | | 3 | | | | | |
| 21 | ....do....brain | | | | 1 | 1 | 5 | | 1 | 1 | 1 | | | | | | | | | 9 | | | 1 | | |
| 22 | Consumption | 2 | 1 | 2 | 2 | 1 | | 1 | 5 | 4 | 17 | 9 | 7 | | 1 | | | | | 48 | | | 3 | | |
| 23 | Convulsions | 4 | 4 | 5 | 7 | | 1 | 1 | | 1 | 4 | 1 | 1 | | | | | | | 28 | | | 1 | | |
| 24 | Croup | 29 | 18 | 16 | 9 | 1 | 8 | | | | | | | | | | | | | 76 | | | | | |
| 25 | Debility | | 1 | | | | | | | | | | | | | | | | | 1 | | | | | |
| 26 | Diabetes | | | | | | | | | | | 1 | | | | | | | | 1 | | | | | |
| 27 | Diarrhœa | 5 | 2 | 3 | 2 | | | | 1 | 1 | 1 | 2 | 1 | | | | | | | 18 | | | | | |
| 28 | Dirt eating | | | | | 1 | | | | 1 | 1 | | | | | | | | | 3 | | | | | |
| 29 | Dropsy | 1 | | 4 | | 4 | 2 | 3 | 2 | 12 | 19 | 25 | 23 | 6 | 1 | | | | | 92 | | 1 | 7 | | |
| 30 | Dysentery | 3 | 1 | 8 | 4 | | | 1 | | 4 | | | | | 1 | | | | | 21 | | | 1 | | |
| 31 | Dyspepsia | | | | | | | | | 2 | 1 | 3 | 1 | | | | | | | 6 | | | 1 | | |
| 32 | Epilepsy | | | 1 | | | | 1 | 1 | | 3 | 1 | | | | | | | | 7 | | | | | |
| 33 | Erysipelas | | | | 1 | | | 1 | | | | | | | | | | | | 2 | | | | | |
| 34 | Executed | | | | | | | 1 | | 2 | | | | | | | | | | 2 | | | 1 | | |
| 35 | Fever, not specified | 3 | 9 | 8 | 4 | 4 | 2 | 2 | 7 | 4 | 10 | 5 | 2 | | | | | | | 58 | | 1 | 1 | | |
| 36 | ..do..bilious | 6 | 13 | 27 | 24 | 17 | 13 | 13 | 16 | 9 | 20 | 8 | 4 | 1 | | | 1 | | | 168 | | | 2 | 1 | |
| 37 | ..do..brain | | | | | 1 | | 1 | | | | | | | | | | | | 2 | | | | | |
| 38 | ..do..congestive | 1 | | 8 | 3 | 7 | 4 | 5 | 2 | 7 | 5 | | 5 | | | | | | | 44 | | | 3 | | |
| 39 | ..do..intermittent | 2 | 1 | 1 | | | 1 | | | | 5 | | | 1 | | | | | | 10 | | | 1 | | |
| 40 | ..do..puerperal | | | | | | | | 1 | | 4 | | | | | | | | | 5 | | | | | |
| 41 | ..do..remittent | | | 2 | | 1 | 1 | 1 | 1 | 1 | | 1 | | | | | | | | 8 | | | | | |
| 42 | ..do..scarlet | | | | | | | | 2 | | | | | | | | | | | 2 | | | | | |
| 43 | ..do..typhus | | | 3 | 3 | 3 | 2 | 24 | 14 | 27 | 24 | 5 | 3 | | | | | | | 105 | | | 3 | | |
| 44 | Gravel | | | | | | | | | | | 1 | | | | | | | | 1 | | | | | |
| 45 | Head, disease of | 1 | | | | | | | | | | | | | | | | | | 1 | | | | | |
| 46 | Heart....do | | | | | | 1 | | | 1 | 1 | 3 | 2 | | | | | | | 6 | | | 1 | | |
| 47 | Hemorrhage | | | | | | | 1 | | 1 | | 2 | | | | | | | | 3 | | | 1 | | |
| 48 | Hernia | | | | | | | | | 1 | | 1 | | | | | | | | 1 | | | | | |
| 49 | Hives | 3 | 5 | | | | | | | | | | | | | | | | | 8 | | | | | |
| 50 | Hooping cough | 10 | 10 | 11 | 11 | 5 | 1 | | | | | | | | | | | | | 48 | | | | | |
| 51 | Hydrocephalus | | 1 | | | | | | | | | | | | | | | | | 1 | | | | | |
| 52 | Inflammation | | 3 | 1 | 2 | | 1 | 1 | | 7 | 4 | 1 | 1 | | | | | | | 21 | | | | | |
| 53 | .....do.....bowels | 3 | | 3 | 1 | 1 | | | 1 | 1 | 4 | 4 | | | | | | | | 17 | | | 1 | | |
| 54 | .....do.....brain | | 2 | 1 | | 1 | | 1 | 1 | | | 2 | 2 | | | | | | | 8 | | | 2 | | |
| 55 | .....do.....stomach | | | 1 | | | | | | | 1 | 1 | | | | | | | | 2 | | | | | |
| 56 | Jaundice | | 1 | | | | | | 1 | | | | | | | | | | | 2 | | | | | |
| 57 | Kidneys, disease of | | | | | | | | | | | 2 | | | | | | | | 2 | | | | | |
| 58 | Killed | | | | | | | | | 4 | | | | | | | | | | 4 | | | | | |
| 59 | Lightning | | | | | | | | | 1 | | | | | | | | | | 1 | | | | | |
| 60 | Liver, disease of | | | 1 | | | | | | 2 | 4 | 6 | 2 | 1 | | | | | | 15 | | | 1 | | |
| 61 | Lungs.....do | | | 1 | 1 | | | | | 1 | 2 | 2 | | 1 | | | | | | 7 | | | 1 | | |
| 62 | Malformation | 1 | | | | | | | | | | | | | | | | | | 1 | | | | | |
| 63 | Mania-a-potu | | | | | | | | | 1 | | | | | | | | | | 1 | | | | | |
| 64 | Marasmus | | 1 | | | | | | | | | | | | | | | | | 1 | | | | | |
| 65 | Measles | 2 | 7 | 13 | 10 | | 1 | | 2 | 1 | | 1 | | | | | | | | 37 | | | | | |
| 66 | Murder | | | | | | | | | 2 | | | | | | | | | | 2 | | | | | |
| 67 | Neuralgia | | | | | | | | 1 | 1 | | | 2 | | | | | | | 3 | | | 1 | | |
| 68 | Old age | | | | | | | | | | | 6 | 5 | 5 | 7 | 3 | 5 | | | 20 | | | 7 | | |
| 69 | Paralysis | | | | | 1 | | | | 1 | 1 | 6 | 5 | 2 | 1 | | | | | 13 | | 1 | 2 | | 1 |
| 70 | Piles | | | | | | | | | | | 1 | | | | | | | | 1 | | | | | |
| 71 | Pleurisy | 1 | | | | | | | 2 | 1 | 1 | 1 | 3 | | | | | | | 9 | | | | | |
| 72 | Pneumonia | 11 | 17 | 23 | 22 | 7 | 7 | 85 | 20 | 58 | 27 | 21 | 11 | 5 | | | | | | 245 | | | 11 | 1 | |

## SECTION OF THE STATE OF SOUTH CAROLINA.

*Lexington, Newberry, and Orangeburg.*

| NATIVITIES. | | | | | SEASON OF DECEASE. | | | | DURATION OF SICKNESS. | | | | WHITES. | | | COLORED. | | | | | | | | | |
|---|---|---|---|---|---|---|---|---|---|---|---|---|---|---|---|---|---|---|---|---|---|---|---|---|---|
| | | | | | | | | | | | | | | | | Slaves. | | | | Free. | | | | | |
| | | | | | | | | | | | | | | | | Black. | | Mulatto. | | Black. | | Mul. | | | |
| California and Territories. | Ireland. | Germany. | Other foreign countries. | Unknown. | Spring. | Summer. | Autumn. | Winter. | Under 1 week. | 1 week and under 1 month. | 1 month and under 3 months. | 3 months and over. | Males. | Females. | Total. | M. | F. | M. | F. | M. | F. | M | F. | Aggregate deaths. | |
| | | | | | | 1 | | | | | | 1 | | | | 1 | | | | | | | | 1 | 1 |
| | | | | | 7 | 7 | 4 | 7 | 14 | 3 | 2 | | 8 | 2 | 10 | 10 | 4 | | 1 | | | | | 25 | 2 |
| | | | | | 17 | 7 | 4 | 7 | 23 | 5 | 2 | 2 | | 3 | 3 | 13 | 18 | 1 | | | | | | 35 | 3 |
| | | | | | 3 | 2 | 3 | | 8 | | | | 2 | | 2 | 4 | 2 | | | | | | | 8 | 4 |
| | | | | | | | 1 | | 1 | | | | | | | 1 | | | | | | | | 1 | 5 |
| | | | | | 2 | 1 | | 1 | 3 | | | | 1 | | 1 | 1 | 1 | 1 | | | | | | 4 | 6 |
| | | | | | 9 | 1 | 4 | | 12 | | | | 3 | 3 | 6 | 3 | 5 | | | | | | | 14 | 7 |
| | | | 1 | | 3 | 1 | 3 | 2 | | 2 | 5 | 2 | 2 | 2 | 4 | 2 | 3 | | | | | | | 9 | 8 |
| | | | | | | 9 | 6 | 1 | 5 | 6 | 3 | 2 | 4 | 3 | 7 | 4 | 4 | 1 | | | | | | 16 | 9 |
| | | | | | | | 1 | 1 | 2 | | | | 1 | 1 | 2 | | | | | | | | | 2 | 10 |
| | | | | | | 2 | 1 | 2 | | 1 | 1 | 3 | | 1 | 1 | 3 | 1 | | | | | | | 5 | 11 |
| | | | | | 1 | 1 | 1 | 3 | | | 1 | 5 | 1 | 1 | 2 | 1 | 3 | | | | | | | 6 | 12 |
| | | | 2 | | 12 | 7 | 4 | 10 | 9 | 17 | 3 | 1 | 4 | 5 | 9 | 9 | 15 | | | | | | | 33 | 13 |
| | 1 | | | | 5 | 7 | 8 | 7 | 14 | 12 | | | | 11 | 11 | | 15 | | 1 | | | | | 27 | 14 |
| | | | | | | 1 | | | | | | 1 | | | | | 1 | | | | | | | 1 | 15 |
| | | | | | | 1 | | | 1 | | | | 1 | | 1 | | | | | | | | | 1 | 16 |
| | | | | | 1 | 4 | 3 | 2 | 6 | 3 | 1 | | 1 | 2 | 3 | 3 | 4 | | | | | | | 10 | 17 |
| | | | 1 | | | 2 | 5 | | 6 | 1 | | | 1 | 2 | 3 | 4 | | | | | | | | 7 | 18 |
| | 1 | | | | 5 | 2 | 3 | 3 | 11 | 2 | | | 2 | 2 | 4 | 5 | 3 | | 1 | | | | | 13 | 19 |
| | | | | | 2 | | | 1 | 3 | | | | | 1 | 1 | 1 | 1 | | | | | | | 3 | 20 |
| | | | | | 2 | 2 | 3 | 3 | 9 | | | | | 5 | 5 | 2 | 3 | | | | | | | 10 | 21 |
| | 1 | | | | 12 | 13 | 19 | 8 | 3 | 4 | 9 | 36 | 9 | 13 | 22 | 10 | 19 | | 1 | | | | | 52 | 22 |
| | | | | | 10 | 9 | 4 | 6 | 21 | 6 | 1 | | 4 | 4 | 8 | 6 | 13 | 2 | | | | | | 29 | 23 |
| | | | | | 27 | 13 | 13 | 23 | 65 | 9 | 2 | | 12 | 6 | 18 | 34 | 24 | | | | | | | 76 | 24 |
| | | | | | | | | 1 | | | 1 | | | | | | 1 | | | | | | | 1 | 25 |
| | | | | | | 1 | | | | | | 1 | 1 | | 1 | | | | | | | | | 1 | 26 |
| | | | | | 2 | 11 | 3 | 2 | 7 | 5 | 3 | 1 | 1 | 4 | 5 | 9 | 3 | 1 | | | | | | 18 | 27 |
| | | | | | 1 | | 2 | | | 1 | | 2 | | | | 1 | 1 | 1 | | | | | | 3 | 28 |
| | 1 | | 1 | | 39 | 30 | 22 | 11 | 1 | 6 | 15 | 78 | 24 | 14 | 38 | 31 | 33 | | | | | | | 102 | 29 |
| | | | | | 3 | 5 | 12 | 2 | 5 | 12 | 3 | 2 | 6 | 2 | 8 | 9 | 4 | | | | | 1 | | 22 | 30 |
| | | | | | 2 | | 2 | 3 | 1 | 1 | 2 | 3 | 5 | 1 | 6 | | 1 | | | | | | | 7 | 31 |
| | | | | | 1 | 2 | 4 | | 1 | | 1 | 5 | | 2 | 2 | 3 | 1 | | 1 | | | | | 7 | 32 |
| | | | | | | | 1 | 1 | | 2 | | | | | | 1 | 1 | | | | | | | 2 | 33 |
| | | | | | 1 | | 1 | 1 | 3 | | | | | | | 3 | | | | | | | | 3 | 34 |
| | | | | | 7 | 16 | 26 | 11 | 10 | 44 | 4 | 2 | 13 | 12 | 25 | 13 | 22 | | | | | | | 60 | 35 |
| | | | 1 | | 18 | 47 | 87 | 20 | 39 | 96 | 23 | 11 | 34 | 46 | 80 | 45 | 44 | 2 | 1 | | | | | 172 | 36 |
| | | | | | 1 | | 1 | | 1 | 1 | | | | | | 1 | | 1 | | | | | | 2 | 37 |
| | | | | | 1 | 4 | 38 | 4 | 26 | 18 | 3 | | 18 | 8 | 26 | 10 | 11 | | | | | | | 47 | 38 |
| | | | | | | 1 | 5 | 5 | 3 | 7 | | 1 | 2 | 2 | 4 | 2 | 5 | | | | | | | 11 | 39 |
| | | | | | 2 | 1 | 2 | | 1 | 4 | | | | 2 | 2 | | 3 | | | | | | | 5 | 40 |
| | | | | | | | 8 | | 1 | 7 | | | 1 | | 1 | 5 | 2 | | | | | | | 8 | 41 |
| | | | | | 1 | 1 | | | | 2 | | | | 2 | 2 | | | | | | | | | 2 | 42 |
| | | | | | 17 | 20 | 46 | 25 | 5 | 84 | 18 | 1 | 31 | 16 | 47 | 31 | 30 | | | | | | | 108 | 43 |
| | | | | | | | 1 | | | 1 | | | | | | 1 | | | | | | | | 1 | 44 |
| | | | | | | | | 1 | | 1 | | | | | | 1 | | | | | | | | 1 | 45 |
| | | | 1 | | 2 | 3 | 1 | 2 | 4 | 1 | 1 | 1 | 1 | 2 | 3 | 3 | 2 | | | | | | | 8 | 46 |
| | | | | | 1 | | 1 | 2 | | 3 | 1 | | 1 | | 1 | 2 | | | | | | | | 4 | 47 |
| | | | | | | 2 | | | 1 | 1 | | | | | | 2 | | | | | | | | 2 | 48 |
| | | | | | 3 | 2 | 3 | | 7 | 1 | | | 1 | 2 | 3 | 2 | 3 | | | | | | | 8 | 49 |
| | | | | | 10 | 19 | 4 | 5 | 8 | 30 | 9 | 1 | 4 | 3 | 7 | 22 | 19 | | | | | | | 48 | 50 |
| | | | | | 1 | | | | | | | 1 | | | | | 1 | | | | | | | 1 | 51 |
| | | | | | 7 | 4 | 7 | 3 | 8 | 7 | 4 | 2 | 8 | 5 | 13 | 2 | 5 | | | | | | 1 | 21 | 52 |
| | | | | | | 6 | 11 | 1 | 3 | 12 | 2 | 1 | 7 | 5 | 12 | 5 | 1 | | | | | | | 18 | 53 |
| | | | | | 1 | 3 | 4 | 2 | 6 | 2 | 1 | 1 | 2 | 4 | 6 | 3 | 1 | | | | | | | 10 | 54 |
| | | | 1 | | 1 | | 2 | | 1 | 1 | 1 | | | 1 | 1 | 2 | | | | | | | | 3 | 55 |
| | | | | | | | 1 | 1 | | | | 2 | | 1 | 1 | | 1 | | | | | | | 2 | 56 |
| | | | | | 1 | 1 | | | | | | 2 | 2 | | 2 | | | | | | | | | 2 | 57 |
| | | | | | | | 3 | 1 | 4 | | | | | | | 4 | | | | | | | | 4 | 58 |
| | | | | | | 1 | | | 1 | | | | | | | 1 | | | | | | | | 1 | 59 |
| | | | | | 5 | 5 | 3 | 3 | | 5 | 5 | 6 | 6 | 1 | 7 | 3 | 4 | | 1 | | | 1 | | 16 | 60 |
| | | | | | 5 | 1 | 1 | 1 | 1 | 1 | 1 | 4 | 1 | | 1 | 4 | 3 | | | | | | | 8 | 61 |
| | | | | | | 1 | | | | 1 | | | | | | 1 | | | | | | | | 1 | 62 |
| | | | | | | | 1 | | | 1 | | | 1 | | 1 | | | | | | | | | 1 | 63 |
| | | | | | 1 | | | | | 1 | | | | 1 | 1 | | | | | | | | | 1 | 64 |
| | | | | | 6 | 18 | 6 | 7 | 4 | 17 | 10 | 4 | | 1 | 1 | 17 | 19 | | | | | | | 37 | 65 |
| | | | | | 1 | | | 1 | | | | | 1 | | 1 | 1 | | | | | | | | 2 | 66 |
| | | | | | 1 | 1 | | 2 | 2 | | 1 | 1 | 1 | 1 | 2 | | 2 | | | | | | | 4 | 67 |
| | | | 4 | | 10 | 6 | 7 | 8 | 5 | 3 | 4 | 11 | 2 | 8 | 10 | 12 | 9 | | | | | | | 31 | 68 |
| | | | | | 6 | 5 | 3 | 3 | 3 | 4 | 1 | 9 | 5 | 5 | 10 | 5 | 2 | | | | | | | 17 | 70 |
| | | | | | | 1 | | | | 1 | | | | | | 1 | | | | | | | | 1 | 71 |
| | | | | | 4 | | 1 | 4 | 2 | 5 | 1 | 1 | 1 | 3 | 4 | 2 | 3 | | | | | | | 9 | 72 |
| | 1 | | 1 | | 122 | 34 | 37 | 66 | 83 | 158 | 16 | 1 | 68 | 36 | 104 | 86 | 67 | 1 | 1 | | | | | 259 | 73 |

## CLASSIFICATION OF DEATHS IN SOUTHERN

| | Cause of death. | AGES. Under 1. | | 1 and under 5. | | 5 and under 10. | | 10 and under 20. | | 20 and under 50. | | 50 and under 80. | | 80 and under 100. | | 100 & over. | | Age unknown. | | NATIVITIES. Born in State. | N. England States. | Middle States. | Southern States. | Southwest'n States. | Northwest'n States. |
|---|---|---|---|---|---|---|---|---|---|---|---|---|---|---|---|---|---|---|---|---|---|---|---|---|---|
| | | M. | F. | M. | F. | M. | F. | M. | F. | M. | F. | M. | F. | M | F. | M | F. | M | F. | | | | | | |
| 1 | Poison | | | | | 1 | 1 | | | | | | | | | | | | | 2 | | | | | |
| 2 | Quinsy | | | 3 | 3 | 1 | | 2 | 1 | 3 | 2 | 1 | | | | | | | | 16 | | | | | |
| 3 | Rheumatism | | | | | | 1 | 1 | | 1 | | 4 | 2 | | | | | | | 8 | | | 1 | | |
| 4 | Rickets | | | 1 | | | | | | | | | | | | | | | | 1 | | | | | |
| 5 | Scrofula | 1 | | | 2 | | | | | 1 | 2 | | | | | | | | | 6 | | | | | |
| 6 | Scurvy | | | | | | | | | | 1 | | | | | | | | | 1 | | | | | |
| 7 | Spine, disease of | | | 1 | | | | | | | 1 | | | | | | | | | 2 | | | | | |
| 8 | Suffocation | 19 | 7 | 1 | 2 | | | | | | | | | | | | | | | 29 | | | | | |
| 9 | Suicide | | | | | | | | | | | 1 | | | | | | | | 1 | | | | | |
| 10 | Teething | 4 | 4 | 9 | 11 | | | | | | | | | | | | | | | 28 | | | | | |
| 11 | Throat, disease of | | | 1 | 1 | 1 | 1 | 1 | | 1 | | 2 | | | | 1 | | | | 7 | | | | | |
| 12 | Thrush | 4 | | 1 | | | | | | | | | | | | | | | | 5 | | | | | |
| 13 | Tumor | | | 1 | | | | | | | | | | 1 | | | | | | 2 | | | | | |
| 14 | Ulcer | | | 1 | | | | | | 2 | | 1 | 1 | 1 | | | | | | 4 | | | 1 | | |
| 15 | Uterus, disease of | | | | | | | | | | 1 | | | | | | | | | 1 | | | | | |
| 16 | White swelling | | | | | | | 1 | | | | | | | | | | | | 1 | | | | | |
| 17 | Worms | 2 | 2 | 23 | 16 | 1 | 1 | 2 | 1 | | | | | | | | | | | 48 | | | | | |
| 18 | Unknown | 38 | 25 | 26 | 27 | 6 | 8 | 10 | 9 | 18 | 18 | 22 | 15 | 1 | 3 | | | | | 220 | | 2 | | | |
| | Total | 170 | 153 | 235 | 192 | 77 | 66 | 122 | 110 | 202 | 217 | 170 | 117 | 25 | 17 | 4 | 6 | | | 1784 | 2 | 5 | 62 | 8 | 1 |

## CLASSIFICATION OF DEATHS IN WESTERN

*Embracing the following districts: Abbeville, Anderson, Greenville,*

| | Cause of death. | Under 1. M. | Under 1. F. | 1 and under 5. M. | 1 and under 5. F. | 5 and under 10. M. | 5 and under 10. F. | 10 and under 20. M. | 10 and under 20. F. | 20 and under 50. M. | 20 and under 50. F. | 50 and under 80. M. | 50 and under 80. F. | 80 and under 100. M. | 80 and under 100. F. | 100 & over. M. | 100 & over. F. | Age unknown. M. | Age unknown. F. | Born in State. | N. England States. | Middle States. | Southern States. | Southwest'n States. | Northwest'n States. |
|---|---|---|---|---|---|---|---|---|---|---|---|---|---|---|---|---|---|---|---|---|---|---|---|---|---|
| 1 | Accident, not specif'd | 3 | 2 | 4 | 5 | 2 | | 3 | | 9 | | 9 | 1 | | | | | | | 35 | | | 2 | | |
| 2 | ....do...burned | | 2 | 4 | 7 | 2 | 2 | | 3 | | | | | | | | | | | 20 | | | | | |
| 3 | ....do...drowned | | | | | | 1 | 2 | | 2 | | | | | | | | | | 5 | | | | | |
| 4 | ....do...shot | | | | | | | 1 | | | | | | | | | | | | 1 | | | | | |
| 5 | Apoplexy | | | | | | | | | 2 | 2 | 4 | 3 | | 1 | | | | | 9 | | 1 | 2 | | |
| 6 | Asthma | | | | | | | | 1 | 1 | | 2 | | | 1 | | | | | 3 | | | 2 | | |
| 7 | Bowels, disease of | 1 | 1 | 2 | 2 | 1 | | | | | | | | | | | | | | 7 | | | | | |
| 8 | Brain......do | | | | | | | | 2 | | | 1 | | 1 | | | | | | 4 | | | | | |
| 9 | Bronchitis | | 1 | | | 2 | | 1 | | | 1 | 2 | | | | | | | | 5 | 1 | | 1 | | |
| 10 | Cancer | | | | | | | | | 2 | 4 | 4 | 2 | | 2 | | | | | 10 | | | 3 | | |
| 11 | Catarrh | 7 | 11 | 10 | 6 | | | 1 | 1 | 1 | 1 | 1 | 4 | | | | | | | 42 | | | 1 | | |
| 12 | Childbirth | | | | | | | | 1 | | 9 | | | | | | | | | 9 | | | 1 | | |
| 13 | Cholera infantum | 3 | 8 | 1 | 1 | | | | | | | | | | | | | | | 12 | | | 1 | | |
| 14 | ...do,.morbus | | | 2 | | | | | | 2 | 2 | 2 | | | | | | | | 7 | | | | | 1 |
| 15 | Colic | | 2 | | 1 | | | | 1 | 3 | | 2 | 2 | | | | | | | 8 | | | 3 | | |
| 16 | Congestion | 1 | | | 1 | | | | | | | | | | | | | | | 2 | | | | | |
| 17 | ....do....bowels | | | 2 | | | 1 | | 3 | | 2 | | | | | | | | | 8 | | | | | |
| 18 | ....do....brain | 2 | | 6 | 3 | 1 | 2 | 2 | 3 | 2 | | 1 | | | | | | | | 20 | | | | 2 | |
| 19 | Consumption | | | 1 | | | | | 4 | 9 | 18 | 3 | 5 | | 1 | | | | | 32 | 1 | | 7 | | |
| 20 | Convulsions | 8 | 3 | 4 | | 1 | | 1 | | 3 | 1 | 1 | 4 | | 1 | | | | | 25 | | | 1 | | |
| 21 | Croup | 22 | 16 | 10 | 9 | 3 | | | | | | | | | | | | | | 60 | | | | | |
| 22 | Diabetes | | | | | | | 1 | | | | 1 | | | | | | | | 2 | | | | | |
| 23 | Diarrhœa | 6 | 2 | 7 | 14 | 1 | 2 | | | 1 | 3 | 2 | 4 | 3 | 1 | | | | | 39 | | 1 | 5 | | |
| 24 | Dirt eating | | | 1 | | | 1 | 1 | | | | | | | | | | | | 3 | | | | | |
| 25 | Dropsy | | 1 | 2 | 6 | 5 | 1 | 11 | 3 | 13 | 19 | 23 | 24 | 7 | 3 | | 1 | | | 93 | | 1 | 21 | | |
| 26 | Dysentery | 1 | 3 | 5 | 4 | 2 | 1 | 3 | | | 1 | | 1 | | | | | | | 20 | | | 1 | | |
| 27 | Dyspepsia | | | | | | | | | | 2 | 1 | 1 | | | | | | | 4 | | | | | |
| 28 | Epilepsy | | | | | | | | 1 | | | | | | | | | | | 1 | | | | | |
| 29 | Erysipelas | 2 | | | 1 | | | | 1 | | 1 | | | | | | | | | 5 | | | | | |
| 30 | Fever, not specified | 3 | 3 | 6 | 11 | 5 | 14 | 21 | 18 | 19 | 15 | 9 | 4 | | | | | | | 123 | | | 5 | | |
| 31 | ..do..bilious | 1 | 1 | | | 1 | 2 | | 1 | 2 | 3 | 2 | | | | | | | | 13 | | | | | |
| 32 | ..do..brain | 1 | | | | 1 | | 1 | | | | | | | | | | | | 3 | | | | | |
| 33 | ..do..congestive | 1 | 3 | 7 | 7 | 3 | 2 | 7 | 6 | 6 | 7 | 2 | 3 | | 1 | | | | | 53 | | 1 | 1 | | |
| 34 | ..do..inflammatory | | | 1 | | | | 1 | | | 2 | | | | | | | | | 4 | | | | | |
| 35 | ..do..intermittent | 1 | | 1 | | | | | | | | | | | | | | | | 2 | | | | | |
| 36 | ..do..puerperal | | | | | | | | 2 | | 12 | | | | | | | | | 13 | | | 1 | | |
| 37 | ..do..scarlet | | | 4 | 3 | 1 | | 1 | 2 | 1 | | | | | | | | | | 12 | | | | | |
| 38 | ..do..typhus | 2 | | 4 | 4 | 9 | 7 | 24 | 31 | 62 | 31 | 11 | 10 | 1 | 1 | | | | | 187 | | | 10 | | |
| 39 | Gravel | | | | | | | | | | | 4 | | 1 | | | | | | 1 | | | 4 | | |
| 40 | Head, disease of | | | | | 1 | | | | | 1 | | | | | | | | | 2 | | | | | |
| 41 | Heart....do | 1 | 1 | | | | | 1 | 1 | | | 3 | | | | | | | | 7 | | | | | |
| 42 | Hemorrhage | 1 | | | | 1 | | 2 | | | 2 | | | | | | | | | 6 | | | | | |
| 43 | Hernia | | 1 | | | | | | | 1 | 1 | | | | | | | | | 3 | | | | | |
| 44 | Hives | 15 | 10 | 4 | 1 | | | | | | | | | | | | | | | 30 | | | | | |
| 45 | Hooping cough | 12 | 10 | 11 | 13 | | 1 | | | | | | | | | | | | | 46 | | | 1 | | |
| 46 | Hydrocephalus | | 1 | | | | | | | | | | | | | | | | | 1 | | | | | |

## SECTION OF THE STATE OF SOUTH CAROLINA—Continued.

| NATIVITIES. | | | | | SEASON OF DECEASE. | | | | DURATION OF SICKNESS. | | | | WHITES. | | | COLORED. | | | | | | | | | |
|---|---|---|---|---|---|---|---|---|---|---|---|---|---|---|---|---|---|---|---|---|---|---|---|---|---|
| | | | | | | | | | | | | | | | | Slaves. | | | | Free. | | | | | |
| | | | | | | | | | | | | | | | | Black. | | Mulatto. | | Black. | | Mul. | | | |
| California and Territories. | Ireland. | Germany. | Other foreign countries. | Unknown. | Spring. | Summer. | Autumn. | Winter. | Under 1 week. | 1 week and under 1 month. | 1 month and under 3 months. | 3 months and over. | Males. | Females. | Total. | M. | F. | M. | F. | M. | F. | M | F. | Aggregate deaths. | |
| | | | | | 1 | 1 | | | 2 | | | | | | | 1 | 1 | | | | | | | 2 | 1 |
| | | | | | 9 | 1 | 1 | 5 | 14 | 1 | 1 | | 7 | 3 | 10 | 3 | 3 | | | | | | | 16 | 2 |
| | | | | | 4 | 2 | 2 | 1 | | 2 | 2 | 5 | 5 | 1 | 6 | 1 | 2 | | | | | | | 9 | 3 |
| | | | | | | 1 | | | 1 | | | | | | | 1 | | | | | | | | 1 | 4 |
| | | | | | 3 | 1 | 1 | 1 | | 1 | 2 | 3 | | 1 | 1 | 2 | 3 | | | | | | | 6 | 5 |
| | | | | | | 1 | | | | 1 | | | | | | | 1 | | | | | | | 1 | 6 |
| | | | | | 1 | | | 1 | 1 | | | 1 | | | | 1 | 1 | | | | | | | 2 | 7 |
| | | | | | 13 | 7 | 6 | 3 | 29 | | | | 1 | | 1 | 19 | 9 | | | | | | | 29 | 8 |
| | | | | | | | | 1 | 1 | | | | 1 | | 1 | | | | | | | | | 1 | 9 |
| | | | | | 4 | 13 | 9 | 2 | 4 | 12 | 5 | 5 | 2 | 3 | 5 | 11 | 12 | | | | | | | 28 | 10 |
| | | | 2 | | 1 | 3 | 2 | 3 | 3 | 4 | 1 | 1 | 1 | | 1 | 6 | 2 | | | | | | | 9 | 11 |
| | | | | | 2 | 2 | | 1 | | 4 | 1 | | | | | 5 | | | | | | | | 5 | 12 |
| | | | | | | 1 | 1 | | | 1 | | 1 | | | | 2 | | | | | | | | 2 | 13 |
| | | 1 | | | 1 | 1 | 3 | 1 | 1 | 3 | 1 | 1 | 2 | | 2 | 3 | 1 | | | | | | | 6 | 14 |
| | | | | | | | 1 | | | | | 1 | | | | | 1 | | | | | | | 1 | 15 |
| | | | | | | 1 | | | | | 1 | | | | | 1 | | | | | | | | 1 | 16 |
| | | | | | 6 | 11 | 22 | 9 | 23 | 15 | 6 | 3 | 3 | 3 | 6 | 23 | 17 | 2 | | | | | | 48 | 17 |
| | | | 4 | | 59 | 58 | 53 | 56 | 108 | 39 | 21 | 48 | 40 | 42 | 82 | 79 | 61 | 2 | 1 | | | | 1 | 226 | 18 |
| | 5 | 1 | 20 | | 506 | 449 | 558 | 370 | 650 | 701 | 202 | 277 | 367 | 310 | 677 | 621 | 557 | 15 | 9 | | | 2 | 2 | 1883 | |

## SECTION OF THE STATE OF SOUTH CAROLINA.

*Laurens, Pickens, Spartansburg, and Union.*

| California and Territories. | Ireland. | Germany. | Other foreign countries. | Unknown. | Spring. | Summer. | Autumn. | Winter. | Under 1 week. | 1 week and under 1 month. | 1 month and under 3 months. | 3 months and over. | Whites Males. | Whites Females. | Whites Total. | Slaves Black M. | Slaves Black F. | Slaves Mulatto M. | Slaves Mulatto F. | Free Black M. | Free Black F. | Free Mul. M | Free Mul. F. | Aggregate deaths. | |
|---|---|---|---|---|---|---|---|---|---|---|---|---|---|---|---|---|---|---|---|---|---|---|---|---|---|
| | 1 | | | | 17 | 6 | 6 | 8 | 28 | 4 | 3 | 1 | 15 | 4 | 19 | 15 | 4 | | | | | | | 38 | 1 |
| | | | | | 7 | 1 | 2 | 10 | 13 | 5 | | | 1 | 1 | 2 | 5 | 13 | | | | | | | 20 | 2 |
| | | | | | 2 | 3 | | | 5 | | | | 3 | | 3 | 1 | 1 | | | | | | | 5 | 3 |
| | | | | | | | 1 | | 1 | | | | 1 | | 1 | | | | | | | | | 1 | 4 |
| | | | | | 4 | 3 | 3 | 2 | 11 | | | | 3 | 3 | 6 | 3 | 3 | | | | | | | 12 | 5 |
| | | | | | 2 | 1 | 1 | 1 | 3 | | | 2 | 1 | 1 | 2 | 2 | 1 | | | | | | | 5 | 6 |
| | | | | | 1 | 3 | 2 | 1 | 1 | 3 | 2 | 1 | 1 | 1 | 2 | 3 | 2 | | | | | | | 7 | 7 |
| | | | | | | 2 | | 2 | 2 | 1 | | 1 | | 1 | 1 | 2 | 1 | | | | | | | 4 | 8 |
| | | | | | 1 | 4 | 1 | 1 | | 4 | 2 | 1 | 3 | | 3 | 2 | 2 | | | | | | | 7 | 9 |
| | 1 | | | | 6 | 3 | 3 | 2 | | 1 | 2 | 10 | 5 | 4 | 9 | 1 | 3 | | 1 | | | | | 14 | 10 |
| | | | | | 13 | 3 | 8 | 19 | 11 | 21 | 4 | 7 | 4 | 3 | 7 | 15 | 20 | 1 | | | | | | 43 | 11 |
| | | | | | 2 | 3 | | 4 | 8 | 2 | | | | 6 | 6 | | 4 | | | | | | | 10 | 12 |
| | | | | | 4 | 4 | 4 | 1 | 7 | 4 | 2 | | 2 | 3 | 5 | 2 | 6 | | | | | | | 13 | 13 |
| | | | | | 1 | 3 | 3 | 1 | 5 | 3 | | | 3 | 2 | 5 | 1 | | 1 | | 1 | | | | 8 | 14 |
| | | | | | 3 | 4 | | 4 | 9 | 2 | | | 4 | 3 | 7 | 1 | 3 | | | | | | | 11 | 15 |
| | | | | | 1 | | | 1 | | 1 | | | 1 | | 1 | | 1 | | | | | | | 2 | 16 |
| | | | | | 1 | 3 | 1 | 3 | 4 | 4 | | | 1 | 1 | 2 | 1 | 4 | | 1 | | | | | 8 | 17 |
| | | | | | 8 | 4 | 8 | 2 | 16 | 5 | 1 | | 4 | 4 | 8 | 10 | 4 | | | | | | | 22 | 18 |
| | 1 | | | | 8 | 15 | 10 | 8 | 1 | 4 | 6 | 26 | 9 | 17 | 26 | 4 | 8 | | 2 | | 1 | | | 41 | 19 |
| | | | | 1 | 11 | 9 | 5 | 1 | 21 | 4 | 1 | 1 | 7 | 4 | 11 | 10 | 5 | 1 | | | | | | 27 | 20 |
| | | | | | 12 | 17 | 16 | 14 | 45 | 9 | 2 | | 14 | 7 | 21 | 21 | 18 | | | | | | | 60 | 21 |
| | | | | | | | | 2 | 1 | 1 | | | 2 | | 2 | | | | | | | | | 2 | 22 |
| | | | 1 | | 5 | 21 | 11 | 9 | 4 | 25 | 11 | 6 | 10 | 7 | 17 | 10 | 19 | | | | | | | 46 | 23 |
| | | | | | | 2 | | | | 1 | | | 1 | | 1 | 1 | 1 | | | | | | | 3 | 24 |
| | 2 | | 1 | 1 | 24 | 39 | 30 | 26 | 4 | 16 | 20 | 77 | 38 | 22 | 60 | 23 | 36 | | | | | | | 119 | 25 |
| | | | | | 1 | 17 | 3 | | 9 | 7 | 3 | 2 | 6 | 7 | 13 | 5 | 3 | | | | | | | 21 | 26 |
| | | | | | 1 | 2 | 1 | | | | | 4 | 1 | 3 | 4 | | | | | | | | | 4 | 27 |
| | | | | | 1 | | | | | 1 | | | | | | | 1 | | | | | | | 1 | 28 |
| | | | | | 1 | 3 | | 1 | 2 | 2 | 1 | | 1 | 3 | 4 | 1 | | | | | | | | 5 | 29 |
| | | | | | 17 | 36 | 56 | 18 | 18 | 79 | 27 | 4 | 41 | 29 | 70 | 21 | 33 | 1 | 3 | | | | | 128 | 30 |
| | | | | | 1 | 2 | 8 | 2 | 4 | 8 | 1 | | 5 | 4 | 9 | 1 | 3 | | | | | | | 13 | 31 |
| | | | | | | | 1 | 2 | 1 | 2 | | | 2 | | 2 | 1 | | | | | | | | 3 | 32 |
| | | | | | 9 | 10 | 28 | 8 | 35 | 20 | | | 14 | 17 | 31 | 10 | 12 | 1 | | 1 | | | | 55 | 33 |
| | | | | | | | 2 | 2 | 1 | 3 | | | 2 | 1 | 3 | | 1 | | | | | | | 4 | 34 |
| | | | | | | | 2 | | | 1 | 1 | | 2 | | 2 | | | | | | | | | 2 | 35 |
| | | | | | 2 | 7 | 2 | 3 | 5 | 8 | 1 | | | 5 | 5 | | 8 | | | | | | 1 | 14 | 36 |
| | | | | | 1 | 3 | 7 | 1 | 2 | 9 | 1 | | 5 | 4 | 9 | 2 | 1 | | | | | | | 12 | 37 |
| | | | | | 29 | 38 | 88 | 42 | 15 | 157 | 24 | 1 | 55 | 37 | 92 | 54 | 46 | 1 | | 3 | 1 | | | 197 | 38 |
| | | | | | 2 | 2 | | 1 | | 1 | 1 | 2 | 3 | | 3 | 2 | | | | | | | | 5 | 39 |
| | | | | | | | 2 | | 1 | | | 1 | | | | | 1 | 1 | | | | | | 2 | 40 |
| | | | | | 4 | 2 | | 1 | 3 | | 2 | 2 | 3 | 2 | 4 | 2 | | | | | | | | 7 | 41 |
| | | | | | 1 | 3 | 1 | 1 | 3 | 2 | | | 2 | | 2 | 2 | 2 | | | | | | | 6 | 42 |
| | | | | | 1 | 1 | | 1 | 2 | | 1 | | 1 | | 1 | | 2 | | | | | | | 3 | 43 |
| | | | | | 9 | 5 | 6 | 9 | 19 | 8 | 3 | | 14 | 6 | 20 | 5 | 4 | | 1 | | | | | 30 | 44 |
| | | | | | 8 | 18 | 13 | 7 | 2 | 31 | 9 | 4 | 1 | 1 | 2 | 21 | 22 | 1 | 1 | | | | | 47 | 45 |
| | | | | | 1 | | | | | | 1 | | | 1 | 1 | | | | | | | | | 1 | 46 |

## CLASSIFICATION OF DEATHS IN WESTERN

| | Cause of death. | Ages. Under 1. M. | Under 1. F. | 1 and under 5. M. | 1 and under 5. F. | 5 and under 10. M. | 5 and under 10. F. | 10 and under 20. M. | 10 and under 20. F. | 20 and under 50. M. | 20 and under 50. F. | 50 and under 80. M. | 50 and under 80. F. | 80 and under 100. M | 80 and under 100. F. | 100 & over. M | 100 & over. F. | Age unknown. M | Age unknown. F. | Nativities. Born in State. | N. England States. | Middle States. | Southern States. | Southwest'n States. | Northwest'n States. |
|---|---|---|---|---|---|---|---|---|---|---|---|---|---|---|---|---|---|---|---|---|---|---|---|---|---|
| 1 | Inflammation | | | 1 | | | | | | | 1 | | | | | | | | | 2 | | | | | |
| 2 | ....do....bowels | 2 | 1 | 4 | | 1 | | | | 1 | 4 | 2 | 1 | | | | | | | 13 | | | 3 | | |
| 3 | ....do....brain | 1 | | | 1 | 1 | 2 | 1 | | | 2 | 2 | 1 | | | | | | | 9 | | | 1 | 1 | |
| 4 | Jaundice | | | 1 | | 1 | | | | | 2 | | 1 | | | | | | | 4 | | | 1 | | |
| 5 | Killed | | | | | 1 | | | | 1 | | | | | | | | | | 2 | | | | | |
| 6 | Lightning | | | | | 1 | | | 2 | 1 | | | | | | | | | | 4 | | | | | |
| 7 | Liver, disease of | 1 | | 1 | | | | | | 5 | 3 | 1 | 2 | | | | | | | 11 | | | 1 | | |
| 8 | Lockjaw | 1 | | 1 | | | | | | | | | | | | | | | | 2 | | | | | |
| 9 | Lungs, disease of | | | | | | | | | | 2 | | | | | | | | | 1 | | | 1 | | |
| 10 | Malformation | | 1 | 1 | | | | | | | | | | | | | | | | 2 | | | | | |
| 11 | Mania-a-potu | | | | | | | | | 2 | | | | | | | | | | 2 | | | | | |
| 12 | Marasmus | | 1 | | 3 | | | | | | | | | | | | | | | 4 | | | | | |
| 13 | Measles | 2 | 3 | 2 | 1 | 1 | 1 | 5 | 2 | | 1 | | | | | | | | | 18 | | | | | |
| 14 | Menses, suppress'n of | | | | | | | | 1 | | | | | | | | | | | 1 | | | | | |
| 15 | Mortification | 1 | | | | | 1 | | | | | | | | | | | | | 2 | | | | | |
| 16 | Mumps | | | | | | | | 1 | | | | | | | | | | | 1 | | | | | |
| 17 | Murder | | | | | | | | | 2 | | | | | | | | | | 1 | | | 1 | | |
| 18 | Neuralgia | | | | | 1 | | | | | | | | | | | | | | 1 | | | | | |
| 19 | Old age | | | | | | | | | | | 9 | 11 | 17 | 16 | 3 | 3 | | | 19 | | 4 | 20 | | |
| 20 | Paralysis | | | | | | | 1 | | 2 | 3 | 8 | 4 | | 2 | | | | | 14 | | 1 | 4 | | |
| 21 | Piles | | | | | | | | | | | 1 | | | | | | | | 1 | | | | | |
| 22 | Pleurisy | | | | | | | | | 2 | | 1 | 1 | | | | | | | 2 | | | 1 | | |
| 23 | Pneumonia | 25 | 15 | 25 | 19 | 7 | 8 | 10 | 17 | 39 | 13 | 23 | 10 | 2 | 1 | | | | | 199 | | 1 | 10 | | |
| 24 | Poison | | | | | | 1 | 1 | | | | | | | | | | | | 2 | | | | | |
| 25 | Putrid sore throat | | | 1 | 1 | 2 | 1 | 1 | 1 | | | | | | | | | | | 7 | | | | | |
| 26 | Quinsy | 2 | 1 | 1 | | 2 | 1 | | 2 | 3 | 3 | 2 | | | | | | | | 17 | | | | | |
| 27 | Rheumatism | 1 | | 1 | | | | 1 | 2 | 1 | 1 | 1 | 3 | | | | | | | 9 | | | 1 | | |
| 28 | Scrofula | 2 | | | 1 | 1 | | 1 | 2 | 1 | | 1 | 1 | | | | | | | 10 | | | | | |
| 29 | Spine, disease of | | 1 | 1 | | | | 2 | | | 1 | 1 | | | | | | | | 5 | | | 1 | | |
| 30 | Stillborn | 4 | 2 | | | | | | | | | | | | | | | | | 6 | | | | | |
| 31 | Stomach, disease of | 1 | | | | 1 | | | | | 1 | | | | | | | | | 2 | | | 1 | | |
| 32 | Suffocation | 6 | 10 | | | | | | | | | | | | | | | | | 16 | | | | | |
| 33 | Suicide | | | | | | | | | | 1 | | | | | | | | | 1 | | | | | |
| 34 | Teething | 5 | 2 | 6 | 6 | | | | | | | | | | | | | | | 16 | | | | 3 | |
| 35 | Throat, disease of | 1 | | | | | 1 | | | 2 | 1 | | | | | | | | | 5 | | | | | |
| 36 | Thrush | 2 | | | | | | | | | | | | | | | | | | 2 | | | | | |
| 37 | Tumor | | | | 1 | | 1 | | | | 2 | | 1 | | | | | | | 3 | | | 2 | | |
| 38 | Uterus, disease of | | | | | | | | | | 1 | | | | | | | | | 1 | | | | | |
| 39 | Venereal | | | | 1 | | | | | | 1 | 1 | | | | | | | | 3 | | | | | |
| 40 | White swelling | | | | | | | 1 | | 1 | | | | | | | | | | 2 | | | | | |
| 41 | Worms | 1 | 1 | 17 | 15 | 2 | 3 | | | | | | | | | | | | | 39 | | | | | |
| 42 | Unknown | 75 | 58 | 41 | 29 | 7 | 8 | 10 | 7 | 17 | 33 | 25 | 17 | 6 | 3 | | | | | 313 | | 3 | 22 | | |
| | Total | 227 | 178 | 203 | 177 | 71 | 65 | 119 | 122 | 221 | 221 | 168 | 121 | 33 | 34 | 3 | 4 | | | 1771 | 2 | 13 | 143 | 6 | 1 |

## CLASSIFICATION OF DEATHS IN THE

| | Cause of death. | Under 1. M. | Under 1. F. | 1 and under 5. M. | 1 and under 5. F. | 5 and under 10. M. | 5 and under 10. F. | 10 and under 20. M. | 10 and under 20. F. | 20 and under 50. M. | 20 and under 50. F. | 50 and under 80. M. | 50 and under 80. F. | 80 and under 100. M | 80 and under 100. F. | 100 & over. M | 100 & over. F. | Age unknown. M | Age unknown. F. | Born in State. | N. England States. | Middle States. | Southern States. | Southwest'n States. | Northwest'n States. |
|---|---|---|---|---|---|---|---|---|---|---|---|---|---|---|---|---|---|---|---|---|---|---|---|---|---|
| 1 | Abscess | | | | | | | | 1 | 2 | | | 1 | | | | | | | 4 | | | | | |
| 2 | Accident, not specif'd | 11 | 10 | 10 | 9 | 6 | 8 | 19 | 2 | 31 | 2 | 18 | 7 | | | | | | | 119 | 1 | | 5 | | |
| 3 | ...do...burned | 2 | 5 | 15 | 30 | 12 | 18 | 3 | 10 | 1 | 3 | | 4 | 1 | 1 | | | | | 102 | | | 1 | | |
| 4 | ....do...drowned | | | 5 | | 1 | 1 | 10 | 2 | 19 | | 2 | 1 | | | | | | | 40 | | | 1 | | |
| 5 | ....do...scalded | | | 2 | | | | | | | | | | | | | | | | 2 | | | | | |
| 6 | ...do....shot | | | | | 1 | | 1 | 1 | 3 | | 1 | | | | | | | | 7 | | | | | |
| 7 | Amputation | | | | | | | | | 1 | | 1 | | | | | | | | 2 | | | | | |
| 8 | Apoplexy | 1 | | 1 | | | | | 1 | 16 | 9 | 17 | 16 | | 2 | | | | | 54 | 1 | 1 | 5 | | |
| 9 | Asthma | | | | 1 | 2 | | | 1 | 2 | 1 | 12 | 4 | | 2 | | | | | 20 | | | 4 | | |
| 10 | Bowels, disease of | 14 | 7 | 6 | 10 | 2 | 2 | 1 | 1 | 6 | | 5 | 2 | | 1 | | | | | 56 | | | | 1 | |
| 11 | Brain.......do | 1 | | | | | | 1 | 3 | | 1 | 1 | | 1 | | | | | | 8 | | | | | |
| 12 | Bronchitis | | 3 | 4 | 2 | 2 | 1 | 2 | | 5 | 4 | 3 | 1 | | | | | | | 25 | 1 | | 1 | | |
| 13 | Cancer | | | | | | 1 | | | 3 | 9 | 6 | 12 | | 3 | | | | | 25 | | | 6 | | |
| 14 | Carbuncle | | | | | | | | | | | | 2 | | | | | | | 2 | | | | | |
| 15 | Catarrh | 21 | 31 | 14 | 16 | 2 | 1 | 2 | 3 | 7 | 5 | 4 | 14 | | 1 | | | | | 114 | 1 | | 4 | | |
| 16 | Childbirth | | | | | | | | 14 | | 104 | | | | | | | | | 113 | | | 3 | | |
| 17 | Chlorosis | | | | | | | | | | 1 | | | | | | | | | 1 | | | | | |
| 18 | Cholera | | | 1 | | | | 1 | 1 | 4 | 3 | 1 | | | | | | 33 | 25 | 69 | | | | | |
| 19 | ....do...infantum | 11 | 21 | 20 | 12 | | | | | | | | | | | | | | | 63 | | | 1 | | |
| 20 | ....do...morbus | | | 4 | 4 | 2 | | 1 | | 3 | 3 | 3 | 2 | | | | | | | 19 | | | 1 | | 1 |
| 21 | Colic | 4 | 5 | 2 | 3 | | | | 2 | 10 | 6 | 10 | 7 | 2 | | | | | | 42 | | | 8 | | |
| 22 | Congestion | 1 | 1 | 1 | 3 | | | | 2 | | | 1 | 1 | | | | | | | 10 | | | | | |
| 23 | .....do....bowels | | | 2 | 1 | | 1 | 1 | 3 | 1 | 2 | | | | | | | | | 11 | | | | | |
| 24 | .....do....brain | 2 | 1 | 6 | 5 | 2 | 7 | 4 | 4 | 8 | 2 | 2 | | | | | | | | 33 | | 1 | 1 | 2 | |

## CTION OF THE STATE OF SOUTH CAROLINA—Continued.

| | Nativities. | | | | Season of decease. | | | | Duration of sickness. | | | | Whites. | | | Colored. | | | | | | | | | |
|---|---|---|---|---|---|---|---|---|---|---|---|---|---|---|---|---|---|---|---|---|---|---|---|---|---|
| | | | | | | | | | | | | | | | | Slaves. | | | | Free. | | | | | |
| | | | | | | | | | | | | | | | | Black. | | Mulatto. | | Black. | | Mul. | | | |
| | Ireland. | Germany. | Other foreign countries. | Unknown. | Spring. | Summer. | Autumn | Winter. | Under 1 week. | 1 week and under 1 month. | 1 month and under 3 months. | 3 months and over. | Males. | Females. | Total. | M. | F. | M. | F. | M. | F. | M | F. | Aggregate deaths. | |
| | | | | | 1 | | 1 | | 1 | 1 | | | 1 | 1 | 2 | | | | | | | | | 2 | 1 |
| | | | | | 4 | 5 | 4 | 3 | 4 | 8 | 1 | 2 | 5 | 2 | 7 | 5 | 4 | | | | | | | 16 | 2 |
| | | | | | 4 | 2 | 2 | 3 | 3 | 5 | 2 | 1 | 4 | 4 | 6 | 1 | 2 | | | | | | | 11 | 3 |
| | | | | | 1 | 1 | | 3 | 1 | 1 | 1 | 2 | 1 | 3 | 4 | 1 | | | | | | | | 5 | 4 |
| | | | | | 1 | 1 | | | 2 | | | | | | | 1 | | | | | | 1 | | 2 | 5 |
| | | | | | | 4 | | | 2 | | | | | | | 2 | 2 | | | | | | | 4 | 6 |
| | 1 | | | | 2 | 6 | 4 | 1 | | 3 | 2 | 7 | 8 | 4 | 13 | | 1 | | | | | | | 13 | 7 |
| | | | | | 1 | | 1 | | 1 | 1 | | | 1 | | 1 | 1 | | | | | | | | 2 | 8 |
| | | | | | | | 1 | 1 | | | | 2 | | | | | 2 | | | | | | | 2 | 9 |
| | | | | | | 2 | | | | | | | | | | 1 | 1 | | | | | | | 2 | 10 |
| | | | | | | | | 2 | 2 | | | | 2 | | 2 | | | | | | | | | 2 | 11 |
| | | | | | 1 | 1 | 1 | 1 | | | 2 | 2 | | | | | 4 | | | | | | | 4 | 12 |
| | | | | | 5 | 5 | 6 | 2 | 4 | 9 | 5 | | 2 | 2 | 4 | 7 | 6 | | | 1 | | | | 18 | 13 |
| | | | | | | | 1 | | | | | 1 | | | | | 1 | | | | | | | 1 | 14 |
| | | | | | 1 | | 1 | | | 1 | | | 1 | | 1 | | 1 | | | | | | | 2 | 15 |
| | | | | | | 1 | | | | 1 | | | | | | | 1 | | | | | | | 1 | 16 |
| | | | | | | | 1 | 1 | 2 | | | | 2 | | 2 | | | | | | | | | 2 | 17 |
| | | | | | 1 | | | | 1 | | | | 1 | | 1 | | | | | | | | | 1 | 18 |
| | 6 | | 9 | 1 | 12 | 16 | 17 | 14 | 8 | 10 | 6 | 6 | 11 | 21 | 32 | 17 | 9 | 1 | | | | | | 59 | 19 |
| | 1 | | | | 6 | 4 | 5 | 5 | 3 | 5 | 4 | 6 | 9 | 6 | 15 | 2 | 2 | | 1 | | | | | 20 | 20 |
| | | | | | | | 1 | | | 1 | | | | | | 1 | | | | | | | | 1 | 21 |
| | 1 | | | | | 1 | | 3 | 2 | 2 | | | 1 | 1 | 2 | 2 | | | | | | | | 4 | 22 |
| | 1 | | 3 | | 87 | 36 | 26 | 63 | 70 | 131 | 10 | 1 | 49 | 31 | 80 | 81 | 51 | 1 | 1 | | | | | 214 | 23 |
| | | | | | 2 | | | | 2 | | | | | | | 1 | 1 | | | | | | | 2 | 24 |
| | | | | | | | 4 | 3 | 1 | 6 | | | 4 | 3 | 7 | | | | | | | | | 7 | 25 |
| | | | | | 6 | 3 | 5 | 3 | 12 | 4 | 1 | | 6 | 6 | 12 | 4 | 1 | | | | | | | 17 | 26 |
| | 1 | | | | 3 | 2 | 4 | 2 | | 4 | 2 | 5 | 2 | 1 | 3 | 3 | 3 | | 1 | | | | 1 | 11 | 27 |
| | | | | | 1 | 1 | 4 | 4 | | 1 | 3 | 6 | 1 | 1 | 2 | 5 | 3 | | | | | | | 10 | 28 |
| | | | | | 3 | | 2 | 1 | 1 | | 1 | 4 | 3 | 1 | 4 | 1 | 1 | | | | | | | 6 | 29 |
| | | | | | 1 | 4 | 1 | | | | | | 3 | 2 | 5 | 1 | | | | | | | | 6 | 30 |
| | | | | | | | 1 | 2 | 2 | | | 1 | | | | 2 | 1 | | | | | | | 3 | 31 |
| | | | | | 6 | 4 | | 6 | 16 | | | | | | | 6 | 9 | | 1 | | | | | 16 | 32 |
| | | | | | | 1 | | | 1 | | | | | 1 | 1 | | | | | | | | | 1 | 33 |
| | | | | | 5 | 5 | 5 | 4 | 4 | 6 | 5 | 4 | 7 | 4 | 11 | 4 | 4 | | | | | | | 19 | 34 |
| | | | | | 1 | 1 | 2 | 1 | | 5 | | | 2 | 2 | 4 | 1 | | | | | | | | 5 | 35 |
| | | | | | 1 | | | 1 | | 1 | 1 | | | | | 2 | | | | | | | | 2 | 36 |
| | | | | | 1 | 1 | 1 | 2 | | 1 | 1 | 2 | | 3 | 3 | | 2 | | | | | | | 5 | 37 |
| | | | | | 1 | | | | 1 | | | | | | | | 1 | | | | | | | 1 | 38 |
| | | | | | | 2 | 1 | | | 1 | | 2 | 1 | | 1 | | 2 | | | | | | | 3 | 39 |
| | | | | | 1 | 1 | | | | | 1 | | 1 | | 1 | 1 | | | | | | | | 2 | 40 |
| | | | | | 8 | 14 | 13 | 4 | 17 | 15 | 6 | 1 | 3 | 4 | 7 | 16 | 13 | 1 | 1 | | 1 | | | 39 | 41 |
| | 3 | | | | 87 | 89 | 82 | 72 | 151 | 69 | 23 | 66 | 79 | 58 | 137 | 98 | 100 | 3 | 1 | 1 | 1 | | | 341 | 42 |
| | 19 | | 14 | 3 | 476 | 515 | 532 | 428 | 636 | 751 | 209 | 274 | 500 | 375 | 875 | 528 | 526 | 14 | 15 | 7 | 4 | 1 | 2 | 1972 | |

## TATE OF SOUTH CAROLINA—AGGREGATE.

| | Ireland. | Germany. | Other foreign countries. | Unknown. | Spring. | Summer. | Autumn | Winter. | Under 1 week. | 1 week and under 1 month. | 1 month and under 3 months. | 3 months and over. | Males. | Females. | Total. | Slaves Black M. | Slaves Black F. | Slaves Mulatto M. | Slaves Mulatto F. | Free Black M. | Free Black F. | Free Mul. M | Free Mul. F. | Aggregate deaths. | |
|---|---|---|---|---|---|---|---|---|---|---|---|---|---|---|---|---|---|---|---|---|---|---|---|---|---|
| | | | | | 1 | 2 | 1 | | | 2 | 1 | 1 | | 1 | 1 | 2 | 1 | | | | | | | 4 | 1 |
| | 2 | | 1 | | 45 | 26 | 17 | 35 | 74 | 8 | 7 | 6 | 39 | 10 | 49 | 54 | 21 | 2 | 1 | | 1 | | | 128 | 2 |
| | | | 2 | | 45 | 17 | 11 | 32 | 60 | 18 | 4 | 3 | 4 | 10 | 14 | 29 | 59 | 1 | 1 | | | | 1 | 105 | 3 |
| | | | | | 10 | 17 | 10 | 4 | 41 | | | | 7 | | 7 | 27 | 4 | 2 | | | | 1 | | 41 | 4 |
| | | | | | | | 2 | | 1 | 1 | | | 1 | | 1 | 1 | | | | | | | | 2 | 5 |
| | | | | | 4 | 1 | 1 | 1 | 5 | | | | 4 | | 4 | 1 | 1 | 1 | | | | | | 7 | 6 |
| | | | | | 1 | | 1 | | 1 | 1 | | | | | | 2 | | | | | | | | 2 | 7 |
| | 2 | | | | 26 | 15 | 15 | 7 | 53 | 8 | 1 | 2 | 20 | 10 | 30 | 15 | 17 | | 1 | | | | | 63 | 8 |
| | | | 1 | | 8 | 4 | 5 | 8 | 5 | 3 | 8 | 9 | 5 | 3 | 8 | 9 | 6 | 2 | | | | | | 25 | 9 |
| | | | | | 8 | 28 | 15 | 6 | 16 | 23 | 8 | 10 | 13 | 11 | 24 | 19 | 12 | 2 | | | | | | 57 | 10 |
| | | | | | | 3 | 2 | 3 | 5 | 1 | | 2 | 1 | 2 | 3 | 3 | 2 | | | | | | | 8 | 11 |
| | | | | | 4 | 8 | 10 | 5 | 4 | 12 | 3 | 7 | 6 | 5 | 11 | 10 | 6 | | | | | | | 27 | 12 |
| | 2 | | 1 | | 10 | 8 | 7 | 8 | | 1 | 4 | 26 | 6 | 13 | 19 | 3 | 10 | | 2 | | | | | 34 | 13 |
| | | | | | 1 | 1 | | | | 2 | | | | 2 | 2 | | | | | | | | | 2 | 14 |
| | | | 2 | | 35 | 23 | 21 | 41 | 35 | 57 | 10 | 15 | 12 | 13 | 25 | 37 | 58 | 1 | | | | | | 121 | 15 |
| | 1 | 1 | | | 31 | 31 | 30 | 25 | 66 | 36 | 1 | 2 | | 48 | 48 | | 68 | | 2 | | | | | 118 | 16 |
| | | | | | | 1 | | | | | 1 | | | | | | 1 | | | | | | | 1 | 17 |
| | | | | | | 1 | 9 | 1 | 10 | | | | 1 | | 1 | 39 | 29 | | | | | | | 69 | 18 |
| | | | | | 11 | 29 | 20 | 4 | 30 | 27 | 7 | | 15 | 13 | 28 | 16 | 20 | | | | | | | 64 | 19 |
| | | | 1 | | 2 | 9 | 10 | 1 | 17 | 5 | | | 5 | 4 | 9 | 6 | 5 | 1 | | 1 | | | | 22 | 20 |
| | 1 | | | | 14 | 16 | 11 | 10 | 41 | 9 | | | 9 | 8 | 17 | 19 | 14 | | 1 | | | | | 51 | 21 |
| | | | | | 6 | | 1 | 3 | 8 | 1 | | | 1 | 5 | 6 | 2 | 2 | | | | | | | 10 | 22 |
| | | | | | 3 | 3 | 2 | 3 | 7 | 4 | | | 1 | 2 | 3 | 2 | 4 | 1 | 1 | | | | | 11 | 23 |
| | 1 | | | | 12 | 8 | 12 | 6 | 29 | 7 | 1 | | 6 | 11 | 17 | 13 | 8 | | | | | | | 38 | 24 |

CLASSIFICATION OF DEATHS IN THE

| | Cause of death. | Ages. Under 1. M. | Under 1. F. | 1 and under 5. M. | 1 and under 5. F. | 5 and under 10. M. | 5 and under 10. F. | 10 and under 20. M. | 10 and under 20. F. | 20 and under 50. M. | 20 and under 50. F. | 50 and under 80. M. | 50 and under 80. F. | 80 and under 100. M | 80 and under 100. F. | 100 & over. M | 100 & over. F. | Age unknown. M | Age unknown. F. | Nativities. Born in the State. | N. England States. | Middle States. | Southern States. | Southwest'n States. | Northwest'n States. |
|---|---|---|---|---|---|---|---|---|---|---|---|---|---|---|---|---|---|---|---|---|---|---|---|---|---|
| 1 | | | | | | | | | | | | | | | | | | | | | | | | | |
| 2 | Congestion of lungs. | | | | | | | | | | 2 | | | | | | | | | 2 | | | | | |
| 3 | Consumption | 3 | 2 | 5 | 4 | 2 | | 4 | 22 | 59 | 89 | 38 | 35 | 1 | 3 | | | | | 233 | 3 | 2 | 14 | | 1 |
| 4 | Convulsions | 18 | 21 | 20 | 27 | 3 | 5 | 10 | 3 | 11 | 16 | 8 | 10 | | 1 | | | | | 148 | | | 3 | | |
| 5 | Croup | 61 | 52 | 39 | 38 | 6 | 5 | | 1 | | | | | | | | | | | 202 | | | | | |
| 6 | Debility | | 2 | | | | | | | | | | | | | | | | | 2 | | | | | |
| 7 | Diabetes | | | | | | | 1 | | | | 2 | | | | | | | | 3 | | | | | |
| 8 | Diarrhœa | 15 | 17 | 23 | 26 | 2 | 2 | 2 | 3 | 8 | 9 | 9 | 9 | 3 | 1 | | | | | 122 | | 1 | 5 | | |
| 9 | Dirt eating | | | 1 | 1 | 2 | 1 | 1 | | 1 | 1 | | | | | | | | | 8 | | | | | |
| 10 | Dropsy | 1 | 4 | 26 | 21 | 22 | 7 | 28 | 12 | 66 | 80 | 108 | 104 | 25 | 8 | 2 | 1 | | | 457 | 1 | 4 | 35 | | |
| 11 | Dysentery | 10 | 7 | 20 | 17 | 2 | 1 | 5 | | 13 | 3 | 4 | 3 | 1 | 1 | | | | | 83 | | | 2 | 1 | |
| 12 | Dyspepsia | | | 1 | 1 | | | | | 3 | 5 | 5 | 4 | | | | | | | 16 | | | 3 | | |
| | Epilepsy | | | 1 | | | | 1 | 3 | 1 | 3 | 2 | 2 | | | | | | | 13 | | | | | |
| 13 | Erysipelas | 3 | | | 3 | | 1 | 2 | 1 | | 2 | | | | | | | | | 12 | | | | | |
| 14 | Executed | | | | | | | 1 | | 2 | | | | | | | | | | 2 | | | 1 | | |
| 15 | Fever, not specified | 19 | 27 | 60 | 67 | 27 | 32 | 53 | 49 | 69 | 78 | 40 | 31 | 1 | 2 | | | | | 528 | | 3 | 17 | | |
| 16 | ..do..bilious | 8 | 14 | 36 | 31 | 23 | 22 | 22 | 34 | 22 | 33 | 15 | 9 | 1 | 2 | | 1 | | | 267 | | | 4 | 1 | |
| 17 | ..do..brain | 2 | | 2 | | 3 | 1 | 2 | | 2 | 2 | 1 | | | | | | | | 13 | | | 1 | | |
| 18 | ..do..congestive | 3 | 4 | 18 | 15 | 11 | 13 | 17 | 12 | 23 | 17 | 5 | 13 | | 1 | | 1 | | | 146 | | 1 | 5 | | |
| 19 | ..do..inflammatory | | | 1 | | | | 1 | | | 2 | | | | | | | | | 4 | | | | | |
| 20 | ..do..intermittent | 6 | 1 | 5 | 1 | 1 | 3 | | 1 | 1 | 6 | | 2 | 2 | | | | | | 27 | | | 1 | | |
| 21 | ..do..puerperal | | | | | | | | 3 | | 17 | | | | | | | | | 19 | | | 1 | | |
| 22 | ..do..remittent | | | 2 | | 1 | 1 | 1 | 1 | 1 | | 1 | | | | | | | | 8 | | | | | |
| 23 | ..do .scarlet | 8 | | 19 | 13 | 6 | 4 | 4 | 8 | 7 | 4 | 3 | 4 | | | | | | | 73 | | | 1 | | |
| 24 | ..do..typhoid | 8 | | 16 | 17 | 20 | 12 | 62 | 58 | 111 | 67 | 22 | 20 | 1 | 1 | | | | | 394 | | | 14 | | |
| 25 | .do..yellow | | | 1 | 3 | 3 | | 6 | 5 | 66 | 27 | 6 | 5 | | 2 | | | | | 25 | 4 | 9 | 3 | | |
| 26 | Gravel | | | | | | | | | | | 8 | | 1 | | | | | | 3 | | | 6 | | |
| 27 | Head, disease of | 3 | 2 | 1 | | 1 | | 2 | 1 | | 1 | 1 | | | | | | | | 12 | | | | | |
| 28 | Heart....do | 2 | 1 | | | 1 | 1 | 1 | 1 | 4 | 5 | 8 | 6 | | | | | | | 25 | | 1 | 2 | | |
| 29 | Hemorrhage | 1 | | | | 1 | 1 | 8 | | 6 | 2 | 3 | 1 | | | | | | | 16 | | | 1 | | |
| 30 | Hernia | | 1 | | | | | | | 7 | 1 | 2 | | | | | | | | 10 | | | | | |
| 31 | Hives | 20 | 16 | 4 | 2 | | | | | | | | | | | | | | | 42 | | | | | |
| 32 | Hooping cough | 49 | 60 | 74 | 54 | 10 | 14 | 1 | 4 | 1 | 2 | | | | | | | | | 268 | | | 1 | | |
| 33 | Hydrocephalus | 1 | 3 | 2 | 1 | | | | | | | | | | | | | | | 7 | | | | | |
| 34 | Inflammation | 3 | 6 | 2 | 4 | 2 | 1 | 2 | 1 | 11 | 6 | 2 | 2 | | | | | | | 42 | | | | | |
| 35 | ....do....bowels | 10 | 4 | 11 | 2 | 4 | 2 | | 1 | 7 | 14 | 7 | 2 | 1 | | | | | | 59 | | | 4 | | |
| 36 | ....do....brain | 2 | 5 | 3 | 7 | 5 | 2 | 4 | 2 | 2 | 3 | 7 | 6 | | | | | | | 44 | | | 3 | 1 | |
| 37 | ....do....stomach | | | 1 | | | | | | 2 | 3 | 2 | | | | | | | | 5 | | 1 | | | |
| 38 | Insanity | | | | | | | | | 1 | | 2 | 2 | | | | | | | 2 | 1 | | | | |
| 39 | Intemperance | | | | | | | | | 3 | | | | | | | | | | 3 | | | | | |
| 40 | Jaundice | | 1 | 1 | | 1 | | | 1 | | 3 | | 1 | | | | | | | 7 | | | 1 | | |
| 41 | Kidneys, disease of | | 1 | | | | | | | | | 2 | | | | | | | | 3 | | | | | |
| 42 | Killed | | | | | 2 | | | | 6 | | 1 | | | | | | | | 8 | | | 1 | | |
| 43 | Leprosy | | | | | | | | | | 1 | | | | | | | | | 1 | | | | | |
| 44 | Lightning | | | | | 1 | | 2 | 2 | 2 | 2 | 1 | | | | | | | | 10 | | | | | |
| 45 | Liver, disease of | 1 | | 3 | 1 | | 1 | 1 | | 15 | 18 | 10 | 9 | 1 | | | | | | 52 | | 2 | 3 | | |
| 46 | Lockjaw | 8 | 5 | 2 | 1 | 1 | | | 1 | 1 | 1 | | | | | | | | | 20 | | | | | |
| 47 | Lungs, disease of | | | 3 | 2 | | | | 3 | 1 | 5 | 3 | 1 | 1 | 1 | | | | | 16 | | | 4 | | |
| 48 | Malformation | 2 | 2 | 1 | 1 | | | | | | | | | | | | | | | 6 | | | | | |
| 49 | Mania-a-potu | | | | | | | | | 5 | | | | | | | | | | 3 | | | 2 | | |
| 50 | Marasmus | 1 | 4 | 1 | 5 | | | 1 | | 1 | 1 | | | | | | | | | 14 | | | | | |
| 51 | Measles | 5 | 12 | 17 | 14 | 1 | 2 | 5 | 4 | 1 | 5 | 2 | 1 | | | | | | | 69 | | | | | |
| 52 | Menses, excess of | | | | | | | | | | 2 | | 1 | | | | | | | 3 | | | | | |
| 53 | ...do ..suppress'n of | | | | | | | | 2 | | | | | | | | | | | 2 | | | | | |
| 54 | Mortification | 1 | | | | 1 | 1 | | | | 1 | | | | | | | | | 4 | | | | | |
| 55 | Mumps | | | | | | | | 1 | | | | | | | | | | | 1 | | | | | |
| 56 | Murder | | | | | | | | | 6 | | | | | | | | | | 5 | | | 1 | | |
| 57 | Neuralgia | | | | | 1 | | | 1 | 1 | | 3 | 2 | | | | | | | 6 | | | 1 | | |
| 58 | Old age | | | | | | | | | | | 47 | 53 | 72 | 64 | 14 | 13 | | | 177 | | 4 | 38 | | |
| 59 | Paralysis | | | | | 1 | | 1 | | 8 | 5 | 26 | 21 | 2 | 5 | | | | | 51 | | 2 | 10 | | 1 |
| 60 | Piles | | | | | | | | | | | 3 | | | | | | | | 3 | | | | | |
| 61 | Pleurisy | 1 | | | | | | 5 | 2 | 7 | 7 | 6 | 9 | | 1 | | | | | 36 | | | 1 | | |
| 62 | Pneumonia | 45 | 40 | 68 | 54 | 25 | 24 | 72 | 54 | 144 | 84 | 73 | 45 | 10 | 3 | | | | | 702 | | 3 | 23 | 1 | |
| 63 | Poison | 1 | | | | 1 | 2 | 2 | | 1 | | | | | | | | | | 7 | | | | | |
| 64 | Putrid sore throat | | | 3 | 7 | 3 | 3 | 1 | 1 | 1 | | | | | | | | | | 17 | | | 2 | | |
| 65 | Quinsy | 3 | 1 | 6 | 3 | 3 | 1 | 2 | 3 | 6 | 7 | 4 | | | | | | | | 39 | | | | | |
| 66 | Rheumatism | 1 | | 2 | | | 1 | 4 | 2 | 4 | 2 | 7 | 8 | | | | | | | 27 | | | 3 | | |
| 67 | Rickets | | | 2 | | | | | | | | | | | | | | | | 2 | | | | | |
| 68 | Scrofula | 4 | 1 | 1 | 4 | 2 | 1 | 3 | 2 | 3 | 5 | 1 | 1 | | | | | | | 28 | | | | | |
| 69 | Scurvy | | | | | | | | | | 1 | | | | | | | | | 1 | | | | | |
| 70 | Spine, disease of | | 1 | 3 | | 1 | 1 | 3 | | | 2 | 2 | | | | | | | | 11 | | | 1 | | |
| 71 | Stillborn | 7 | 4 | | | | | | | | | | | | | | | | | 11 | | | | | |
| 72 | Stomach, disease of | 1 | | | | 1 | | | | | 1 | | | | | | | | | 2 | | | 1 | | |
| 73 | Suffocation | 41 | 30 | 1 | 5 | 1 | | | | | | | | | | | | | | 78 | | | | | |
| 74 | Suicide | | | | | | | | | | 2 | 2 | | | | | | | | 3 | | | 1 | | |

STATE OF SOUTH CAROLINA—AGGREGATE—Continued.

| NATIVITIES. | | | | | SEASON OF DECEASE. | | | | DURATION OF SICKNESS. | | | | WHITES. | | | COLORED. | | | | | | | | | |
|---|---|---|---|---|---|---|---|---|---|---|---|---|---|---|---|---|---|---|---|---|---|---|---|---|---|
| | | | | | | | | | | | | | | | | Slaves. | | | | Free. | | | | | |
| | | | | | | | | | | | | | | | | Black. | | Mulatto. | | Black. | | Mul. | | | |
| California and Territories. | Ireland. | Germany. | Other foreign countries. | Unknown. | Spring. | Summer. | Autumn. | Winter. | Under 1 week. | 1 week and under 1 month. | 1 month and under 3 months. | 3 months and over. | Males. | Females. | Total. | M. | F. | M. | F. | M. | F. | M | F. | Aggregate deaths. | |
| | | | | | 1 | | 1 | | 1 | 1 | | | | | | | 2 | | | | | | | 2 | 1 |
| | 7 | 3 | 4 | | 82 | 69 | 72 | 44 | 8 | 19 | 40 | 192 | 52 | 75 | 127 | 57 | 70 | 2 | 5 | | 2 | 1 | 3 | 267 | 2 |
| | | | 1 | 1 | 47 | 52 | 28 | 22 | 112 | 22 | 4 | 5 | 19 | 20 | 39 | 45 | 62 | 5 | | 1 | | | 1 | 153 | 3 |
| | | | | | 60 | 39 | 49 | 53 | 154 | 35 | 6 | 2 | 34 | 25 | 59 | 70 | 71 | 1 | | | | 1 | | 202 | 4 |
| | | | | | | 1 | | 1 | 1 | | 1 | | | | | | 2 | | | | | | | 2 | 5 |
| | | | | | | 1 | | 2 | 1 | 1 | | 1 | 3 | | 3 | | | | | | | | | 3 | 6 |
| | | | 1 | | 23 | 58 | 31 | 17 | 25 | 58 | 22 | 15 | 20 | 16 | 36 | 41 | 48 | 1 | | | 2 | | 1 | 129 | 7 |
| | | | | | 2 | 2 | 2 | 1 | | 4 | | 2 | 1 | | 1 | 3 | 3 | 1 | | | | | | 8 | 8 |
| | 8 | 1 | 7 | 2 | 149 | 159 | 122 | 82 | 29 | 64 | 81 | 315 | 110 | 70 | 180 | 163 | 159 | 3 | 3 | 1 | 3 | 1 | 2 | 515 | 9 |
| | 1 | | | | 8 | 40 | 27 | 10 | 19 | 44 | 10 | 11 | 22 | 14 | 36 | 32 | 17 | | 1 | | | 1 | | 87 | 10 |
| | | | | | 4 | 5 | 6 | 4 | 2 | 2 | 4 | 11 | 8 | 6 | 14 | 1 | 4 | | | | | | | 19 | 11 |
| | | | | | 3 | 5 | 4 | 1 | 3 | 1 | 3 | 5 | | 3 | 3 | 5 | 4 | | 1 | | | | | 13 | 12 |
| | | | | | 2 | 3 | 5 | 2 | 3 | 8 | 1 | | 3 | 4 | 7 | 2 | 3 | | | | | | | 12 | 13 |
| | | | | | 1 | | 1 | 1 | 3 | | | | | | | 3 | | | | | | | | 3 | 14 |
| | 3 | | 4 | | 79 | 166 | 234 | 73 | 135 | 332 | 52 | 13 | 133 | 111 | 244 | 128 | 165 | 5 | 6 | | 1 | 3 | 3 | 555 | 15 |
| | | | 1 | | 26 | 74 | 148 | 25 | 68 | 154 | 37 | 11 | 49 | 63 | 112 | 75 | 80 | 3 | 2 | | | | 1 | 273 | 16 |
| | | | 1 | | 2 | 2 | 7 | 4 | 5 | 7 | 2 | | 7 | | 7 | 4 | 3 | 1 | | | | | | 15 | 17 |
| | 1 | | | | 14 | 23 | 100 | 16 | 86 | 56 | 6 | 1 | 42 | 38 | 80 | 33 | 35 | 1 | 1 | 1 | | | 2 | 153 | 18 |
| | | | | | | | 2 | 2 | 1 | 2 | | | 2 | 1 | 3 | | 1 | | | | | | | 4 | 19 |
| | 1 | | | | 2 | 4 | 14 | 9 | 8 | 18 | 1 | 2 | 9 | 4 | 13 | 6 | 10 | | | | | | | 29 | 20 |
| | | | | | 4 | 9 | 4 | 3 | 7 | 12 | 1 | | | 7 | 7 | | 12 | | | | | | 1 | 20 | 21 |
| | | | | | | | 8 | | 1 | 7 | | | 1 | | 1 | 5 | 2 | | | | | | | 8 | 22 |
| | 1 | | | | 13 | 25 | 20 | 13 | 31 | 35 | 3 | 1 | 18 | 19 | 37 | 24 | 10 | | | | | | 4 | 75 | 23 |
| | | | 1 | 1 | 69 | 84 | 168 | 89 | 42 | 306 | 56 | 6 | 102 | 65 | 167 | 128 | 108 | 1 | 1 | 3 | 1 | 1 | | 410 | 24 |
| | 51 | 16 | 16 | | 1 | | 114 | 7 | 36 | 86 | | 2 | 80 | 39 | 119 | | 2 | 1 | | | | 1 | 1 | 124 | 25 |
| | | | | | 2 | 3 | 1 | 3 | 1 | 3 | 1 | 3 | 4 | | 4 | 5 | | | | | | | | 9 | 26 |
| | | | | | 5 | 2 | 3 | 2 | 6 | 2 | | 3 | 2 | | 2 | 5 | 4 | 1 | | | | | | 12 | 27 |
| | | | 2 | | 10 | 9 | 3 | 8 | 14 | 3 | 7 | 5 | 8 | 8 | 16 | 8 | 6 | | | | | | | 30 | 28 |
| | 1 | | | | 4 | 6 | 4 | 4 | 8 | 7 | 2 | | 7 | 1 | 8 | 6 | 3 | | | | | 1 | | 18 | 29 |
| | | | 1 | | 4 | 3 | 1 | 3 | 6 | 2 | 1 | 2 | 1 | | 1 | 7 | 2 | | | 1 | | | | 11 | 30 |
| | | | | | 12 | 8 | 12 | 9 | 30 | 9 | 3 | | 16 | 10 | 26 | 8 | 7 | | 1 | | | | | 42 | 31 |
| | | | | | 56 | 90 | 68 | 45 | 24 | 141 | 45 | 22 | 20 | 6 | 26 | 112 | 124 | 3 | 2 | | 1 | | 1 | 269 | 32 |
| | | | | | 2 | 4 | | 1 | | 1 | 2 | 4 | | 1 | 1 | 3 | 3 | | | | | | | 7 | 33 |
| | | | | | 12 | 13 | 14 | 3 | 13 | 17 | 6 | 5 | 13 | 10 | 23 | 9 | 9 | | | | | | 1 | 42 | 34 |
| | 1 | | 1 | | 12 | 25 | 22 | 6 | 15 | 36 | 7 | 6 | 22 | 13 | 35 | 18 | 12 | | | | | | | 65 | 35 |
| | | | | | 12 | 7 | 16 | 13 | 23 | 18 | 4 | 3 | 10 | 16 | 26 | 13 | 9 | | | | | | | 48 | 36 |
| | | | 2 | | 2 | 1 | 4 | 1 | 2 | 3 | 3 | | 2 | 3 | 5 | 3 | | | | | | | | 8 | 37 |
| | 1 | | 1 | | 1 | 1 | 2 | 1 | 1 | | | 4 | 3 | 1 | 4 | | 1 | | | | | | | 5 | 38 |
| | | | | | | | 2 | 1 | 2 | | | | 3 | | 3 | | | | | | | | | 3 | 39 |
| | | | | | 1 | 2 | 1 | 4 | 1 | 2 | 1 | 4 | 1 | 5 | 6 | 1 | 1 | | | | | | | 8 | 40 |
| | | | | | 1 | 2 | | | | 1 | | 2 | 2 | | 2 | | 1 | | | | | | | 3 | 41 |
| | | | | | 1 | 3 | 3 | 2 | 9 | | | | 2 | | 2 | 6 | | | | | | 1 | | 9 | 42 |
| | | | | | 1 | | | | | | | 1 | | | | | 1 | | | | | | | 1 | 43 |
| | | | | | | 6 | 4 | | 6 | | | | | 1 | 1 | 6 | 3 | | | | | | | 10 | 44 |
| | 2 | | 1 | | 16 | 18 | 16 | 10 | 2 | 14 | 13 | 30 | 22 | 18 | 40 | 8 | 10 | | 1 | | | 1 | | 60 | 45 |
| | | | | | 10 | 1 | 7 | 1 | 17 | 2 | | | 2 | | 2 | 10 | 8 | | | | | | | 20 | 46 |
| | | | | | 6 | 5 | 6 | 3 | 2 | 4 | 4 | 9 | 2 | 2 | 4 | 6 | 9 | | | | 1 | | | 20 | 47 |
| | | | | | 1 | 5 | | | | 2 | | 1 | 1 | | 1 | 2 | 3 | | | | | | | 6 | 48 |
| | | | | | | 1 | 2 | 2 | 2 | 2 | | 1 | 5 | | 5 | | | | | | | | | 5 | 49 |
| | | | | | 3 | 3 | 4 | 4 | 1 | 1 | 5 | 7 | 1 | 3 | 4 | 3 | 7 | | | | | | | 14 | 50 |
| | | | | | 14 | 30 | 15 | 10 | 9 | 33 | 17 | 5 | 2 | 5 | 7 | 28 | 33 | | | 1 | | | | 69 | 51 |
| | | | | | 1 | | 1 | 1 | 3 | | | | | | | | 3 | | | | | | | 3 | 52 |
| | | | | | | 1 | 1 | | | 1 | | 1 | | | | | 2 | | | | | | | 2 | 53 |
| | | | | | 1 | 1 | 2 | | | 2 | | | 1 | | 1 | 1 | 2 | | | | | | | 4 | 54 |
| | | | | | 1 | | | | | 1 | | | | | | | 1 | | | | | | | 1 | 55 |
| | | | | | 1 | | 2 | 3 | 2 | | | | 5 | | 5 | 1 | | | | | | | | 6 | 56 |
| | | | 1 | | 3 | 2 | 1 | 2 | 3 | | 2 | 3 | 5 | 1 | 6 | | 2 | | | | | | | 8 | 57 |
| | 7 | | 34 | 3 | 74 | 64 | 58 | 64 | 37 | 37 | 23 | 41 | 22 | 48 | 70 | 108 | 80 | 2 | 1 | | | 1 | 1 | 263 | 58 |
| | 3 | | 2 | | 23 | 19 | 16 | 11 | 17 | 16 | 8 | 26 | 26 | 18 | 44 | 11 | 11 | | 1 | 1 | | | 1 | 69 | 59 |
| | | | | | 1 | 1 | 1 | | | 2 | 1 | | | | | 3 | | | | | | | | 3 | 60 |
| | 1 | | | | 15 | 2 | 1 | 20 | 9 | 21 | 5 | 2 | 5 | 6 | 11 | 14 | 13 | | | | | | | 38 | 61 |
| | 3 | | 9 | | 345 | 104 | 90 | 198 | 253 | 432 | 37 | 11 | 147 | 90 | 237 | 284 | 210 | 4 | 4 | | | 2 | | 741 | 62 |
| | | | | | 3 | 4 | | | 6 | | | | 1 | | 1 | 4 | 2 | | | | | | | 7 | 63 |
| | | | | | 2 | 1 | 7 | 9 | 7 | 12 | | | 8 | 10 | 18 | | 1 | | | | | | | 19 | 64 |
| | | | | | 17 | 5 | 8 | 9 | 30 | 7 | 2 | | 15 | 10 | 25 | 9 | 5 | | | | | | | 39 | 65 |
| | 1 | | | | 10 | 8 | 6 | 7 | 2 | 6 | 7 | 15 | 10 | 4 | 14 | 8 | 7 | | 1 | | | | 1 | 31 | 66 |
| | | | | | | 1 | 1 | | 1 | | | 1 | 1 | | 1 | 1 | | | | | | | | 2 | 67 |
| | | | | | 5 | 6 | 8 | 9 | 1 | 3 | 8 | 16 | 1 | 2 | 3 | 13 | 12 | | | | | | | 28 | 68 |
| | | | | | | 1 | | | | 1 | | | | | | | 1 | | | | | | | 1 | 69 |
| | | | 1 | | 5 | 3 | 2 | 3 | 2 | 1 | 3 | 7 | 4 | 1 | 5 | 5 | 3 | | | | | | | 13 | 70 |
| | | | | | 1 | 9 | 1 | | | | | | 4 | 2 | 6 | 3 | 2 | | | | | | | 11 | 71 |
| | | | | | | | 1 | 2 | 2 | | 1 | | | | | 2 | 1 | | | | | | | 3 | 72 |
| | | | | | 31 | 18 | 11 | 18 | 78 | | | | 1 | | 1 | 42 | 34 | | 1 | | | | | 78 | 73 |
| | | | | | 1 | 1 | | 2 | 2 | | | | 1 | 2 | 3 | 1 | | | | | | | | 4 | 74 |

## CLASSIFICATION OF DEATHS IN THE

| | Cause of death. | AGES. | | | | | | | | | | | | | | | | | | NATIVITIES. | | | | | |
|---|---|---|---|---|---|---|---|---|---|---|---|---|---|---|---|---|---|---|---|---|---|---|---|---|---|
| | | Under 1. | | 1 and under 5. | | 5 and under 10. | | 10 and under 20. | | 20 and under 50. | | 50 and under 80. | | 80 and under 100. | | 100 & over. | | Age unknown. | | Born in State. | N. England States. | Middle States. | Southern States. | Southwest'n States. | Northwest'n States. |
| | | M. | F. | M. | F. | M. | F. | M. | F. | M. | F. | M. | F. | M | F. | M | F. | M | F. | | | | | | |
| 1 | Teething | 26 | 28 | 58 | 54 | | | | | | | | | | | | | | | 163 | | | | 3 | |
| 2 | Tetanus | | | | | | | 2 | | | | | | | | | | | | 2 | | | | | |
| 3 | Throat, disease of | 4 | 2 | 15 | 10 | 4 | 11 | 1 | 4 | 3 | 3 | 3 | 2 | | | 1 | | | | 61 | | | | | |
| 4 | Thrush | 8 | 5 | 3 | 2 | | | | | | | | | | | | | | | 18 | | | | | |
| 5 | Tumor | | | 1 | 1 | | 1 | | | 1 | 2 | | 1 | 1 | | | | | | 6 | | | 2 | | |
| 6 | Ulcer | | | 1 | | | | | | 3 | | 5 | 2 | 1 | | | | | | 9 | | | 1 | | |
| 7 | Uterus, disease of | | | | | | | | | | 5 | | 2 | | | | | | | 6 | | | 1 | | |
| 8 | Venereal | | | | 1 | | | | | 1 | 2 | 6 | 2 | | | | | | | 10 | | | | | |
| 9 | White swelling | | | | | | | 2 | | 1 | | | | | | | | | | 3 | | | | | |
| 10 | Worms | 13 | 9 | 113 | 103 | 20 | 17 | 4 | 4 | | 2 | | | | | | | | | 284 | | | 1 | | |
| 11 | Unknown | 250 | 205 | 127 | 92 | 23 | 30 | 37 | 36 | 66 | 103 | 94 | 68 | 16 | 12 | 1 | | 29 | 18 | 1153 | | 5 | 34 | | |
| | Total | 737 | 684 | 919 | 811 | 283 | 262 | 430 | 400 | 915 | 932 | 699 | 578 | 145 | 118 | 18 | 16 | 62 | 43 | 7426 | 13 | 40 | 300 | 10 | 3 |

## CLASSIFICATION OF DEATHS IN EASTERN

*Embracing the following counties: Anderson, Blount, Bradly, Campbell, Carter, Clairborne, Monroe, Polk, Roane, Sevier,*

| | | | | | | | | | | | | | | | | | | | | | | | | | |
|---|---|---|---|---|---|---|---|---|---|---|---|---|---|---|---|---|---|---|---|---|---|---|---|---|---|
| 1 | Abscess | | 1 | | | | | | | | | | | | | | | | | 1 | | | | | |
| 2 | Accident not specif'd | 2 | 3 | | 1 | 3 | 2 | 5 | | 8 | 1 | 6 | | 1 | | | | | | 25 | 1 | 5 | | | |
| 3 | ...do...burned | 1 | 1 | 6 | 6 | 2 | 2 | 1 | | | 1 | | | | | | | | | 19 | | | | | 1 |
| 4 | ...do...drowned | | | 5 | 1 | 1 | 2 | 3 | 1 | 4 | 1 | 1 | | | | | | | | 15 | | | 4 | | |
| 5 | ...do...scalded | | 1 | | | | | | | | | | | | | | | | | 1 | | | | | |
| 6 | ...do...shot | | | | | | | | | 1 | | | | | | | | | | 1 | | | | | |
| 7 | Apoplexy | | | | | | | | | | | 4 | | | | | | | | 1 | | 1 | 2 | | |
| 8 | Asthma | | | | | | | | | | | 1 | 2 | 1 | | | | | | 1 | | | 8 | | |
| 9 | Bronchitis | 2 | | 2 | | | | | | 1 | 8 | 1 | | | | | | | | 6 | | 1 | 2 | | |
| 10 | Cancer | | | | | | | | | 1 | 1 | 1 | 4 | 2 | | | | | | 5 | | | 3 | | |
| 11 | Catarrh | | | | | | | | | | 1 | | | | | | | | | 1 | | | | | |
| 12 | Carbuncle | | | | | | | | | | 1 | | | | | | | | | | | | 1 | | |
| 13 | Chicken pox | | | 1 | | 1 | 1 | | | | | | | | | | | | | 3 | | | | | |
| 14 | Childbirth | | | | | | | | 4 | | 14 | | | | | | | | | 14 | | | 4 | | |
| 15 | Cholera | | | | | 1 | | | | 2 | | 1 | | | | | | | | 2 | | | 2 | | |
| 16 | ...do...infantum | 5 | 1 | 4 | 2 | | 1 | | | | | | | | | | | | | 13 | | | | | |
| 17 | ...do...morbus | 4 | 2 | 3 | 3 | 2 | | 2 | 1 | 1 | | 1 | | 1 | | | | | | 16 | | | 2 | | 2 |
| 18 | Colic | | | | 1 | | | | | 2 | 1 | 3 | | | | | | | | 5 | | | 2 | | |
| 19 | Congestion, not spef'd | | | | | | | | 1 | | 1 | | | | | | | | | 1 | | | 1 | | |
| 20 | Consumption | 1 | 2 | 2 | 3 | | 1 | 5 | 4 | 34 | 53 | 7 | 15 | 1 | | | | | | 96 | 1 | 8 | 25 | 2 | 1 |
| 21 | Convulsions | 1 | 5 | 3 | 2 | 1 | | | 2 | 1 | 5 | 1 | 1 | | 1 | | | | | 21 | | | 2 | | |
| 22 | Croup | 48 | 22 | 31 | 22 | 6 | 3 | 1 | 1 | | | | | | | | | | | 143 | | | 1 | | |
| 23 | Diabetes | | | 1 | | | | | | | | 1 | | | | | | | | 1 | | | | | |
| 24 | Diarrhœa | 5 | 5 | 8 | 5 | 1 | 1 | | 1 | 4 | 1 | | 2 | | | | | | | 29 | | | 4 | | |
| 25 | Dropsy | 2 | | 5 | 1 | | 8 | 3 | 4 | 6 | 14 | 13 | 23 | 5 | | | | | | 45 | | 4 | 29 | | |
| 26 | Dysentery | 3 | 2 | 3 | 6 | | 3 | 2 | 1 | 1 | | 1 | 2 | | 1 | | | | | 21 | | | 4 | | |
| 27 | Dyspepsia | | | | | | | | | 4 | 1 | 4 | 2 | | | | | | | 4 | | | 7 | | |
| 28 | Erysipelas | 2 | 3 | | | | | | | | | | | | 1 | | | | | 5 | | 1 | | | |
| 29 | Fever, not specified | 6 | 7 | 15 | 16 | 8 | 9 | 25 | 32 | 58 | 32 | 23 | 8 | | | | | | | 214 | | | 23 | 1 | 1 |
| 30 | ..do..bilious | | | | | 1 | 1 | 4 | 4 | 9 | 1 | 2 | 2 | | | | | | | 22 | | 1 | 1 | | |
| 31 | ..do. brain | | | 1 | 3 | | | 1 | | | | | | | | | | | | 5 | | | | | |
| 32 | ..do..congestive | 1 | | | | | | 2 | 1 | 1 | 4 | 2 | 1 | | | | | | | 10 | | | 1 | | 1 |
| 33 | ..do..intermittent | 2 | | 1 | 2 | | | | 2 | | | 2 | 1 | | | | | | | 7 | | 1 | 2 | | |
| 34 | ..do..puerperal | | | | | | | | | | 6 | | | | | | | | | 5 | | | 1 | | |
| 35 | ..do..scarlet | | | 3 | 2 | 1 | | | | | | | | | | | | | | 6 | | | | | |
| 36 | ..do..typhus | | | 1 | 2 | | 1 | 14 | 13 | 24 | 12 | 3 | 4 | | | | | | | 58 | | 1 | 6 | 8 | |
| 37 | Gravel | 1 | | 1 | | | | | | | | 3 | 1 | 1 | | | | | | 3 | | 1 | 2 | 1 | |
| 38 | Heart, disease of | 1 | | 1 | 1 | | | 1 | | 1 | 1 | 3 | 1 | | | | | | | 6 | | 1 | 3 | | |
| 39 | Hemorrhage | | | | | | | 1 | 1 | 1 | | 1 | | 1 | 1 | | | | | 3 | | 1 | 2 | | |
| 40 | Hives | 14 | 16 | 1 | 2 | | | | | | | | | | | | | | | 32 | | | 1 | | |
| 41 | Hooping cough | 13 | 20 | 12 | 23 | 3 | 5 | 1 | 1 | | | | | | | | | | | 74 | | | 4 | | |
| 42 | Hydrocephalus | 1 | | 1 | 2 | | 1 | | | | | | | | | | | | | 5 | | | | | |
| 43 | Inflammation | | 3 | 1 | | | | 1 | | | | | | | | | | | | 5 | | | | | |
| 44 | ....do....bowels | 3 | 2 | 4 | 2 | | 1 | 2 | 1 | 2 | 1 | 3 | | | | | | | | 20 | | | 1 | | |
| 45 | ....do....brain | 3 | | 2 | 2 | 2 | 1 | 3 | 1 | 2 | 2 | 1 | | | | | | | | 16 | | | 3 | | |
| 46 | ....do....stomach | | | | | | | | | | 1 | | 2 | | | | | | | 2 | | | 1 | | |
| 47 | Intemperance | | | | | | | | | 4 | | 1 | | | | | | | | 5 | | | | | |
| 48 | Jaundice | | 1 | | | | | 1 | | | | 1 | 1 | | | | | | | 3 | | | 1 | | |
| 49 | Kidneys, disease of | | | | | | | | | | | 1 | | | | | | | | 1 | | | | | |
| 50 | Killed | | | | | | | | | 2 | | | | | | | | | | 1 | | | 1 | | |
| 51 | Liver, disease of | 4 | 1 | | 1 | | | 2 | | 4 | 8 | 4 | 2 | 1 | | | | | | 18 | | 1 | 8 | | |
| 52 | Malformation | | 1 | 1 | | | | | | | | | | | | | | | | 2 | | | | | |

## TATE OF SOUTH CAROLINA—AGGREGATE—Continued.

| NATIVITIES. | | | | | SEASON OF DECEASE. | | | | DURATION OF SICKNESS. | | | | WHITES. | | | COLORED. | | | | | | | | | |
|---|---|---|---|---|---|---|---|---|---|---|---|---|---|---|---|---|---|---|---|---|---|---|---|---|---|
| | | | | | | | | | | | | | | | | Slaves. | | | | Free. | | | | | |
| | | | | | | | | | | | | | | | | Black. | | Mulatto. | | Black. | | Mul. | | | |
| ritories. | Ireland. | Germany. | Other foreign countries. | Unknown. | Spring. | Summer. | Autumn. | Winter. | Under 1 week. | 1 week and under 1 month. | 1 month and under 3 months. | 3 months and over. | Males. | Females. | Total. | M. | F. | M. | F. | M. | F. | M | F. | Aggregate deaths. | |
| .. | ... | .. | ... | ... | 27 | 69 | 48 | 22 | 82 | 71 | 34 | 23 | 18 | 16 | 34 | 64 | 66 | 2 | ... | ... | ... | . | .. | 166 | 1 |
| .. | ... | .. | ... | ... | ... | 1 | 1 | ... | 1 | 1 | ... | ... | ... | ... | ... | 2 | ... | ... | ... | ... | ... | .. | .. | 2 | 2 |
| .. | ... | .. | 2 | ... | 15 | 17 | 17 | 14 | 23 | 30 | 1 | 1 | 14 | 18 | 32 | 17 | 14 | ... | ... | ... | ... | .. | .. | 63 | 3 |
| .. | ... | .. | ... | ... | 7 | 8 | 1 | 2 | 2 | 12 | 3 | 1 | 2 | ... | 2 | 9 | 6 | ... | 1 | ... | ... | .. | .. | 18 | 4 |
| .. | ... | .. | ... | ... | 2 | 2 | 2 | 2 | ... | 2 | 1 | 4 | 1 | 3 | 4 | 2 | 2 | ... | ... | ... | ... | .. | .. | 8 | 5 |
| .. | ... | 1 | 1 | ... | 3 | 1 | 5 | 2 | 1 | 6 | 1 | 3 | 4 | ... | 4 | 6 | 2 | ... | ... | ... | ... | .. | .. | 12 | 6 |
| .. | ... | .. | ... | ... | 4 | 1 | 1 | 1 | 1 | ... | ... | 6 | ... | 2 | 2 | ... | 5 | ... | ... | ... | ... | .. | .. | 7 | 7 |
| .. | 1 | .. | 1 | ... | 2 | 5 | 4 | 1 | ... | 1 | 1 | 9 | 5 | ... | 5 | 2 | 4 | ... | 1 | ... | ... | .. | .. | 12 | 8 |
| .. | ... | .. | ... | ... | 1 | 2 | ... | ... | ... | ... | 2 | ... | 1 | ... | 1 | 2 | ... | ... | ... | ... | ... | .. | .. | 3 | 9 |
| .. | ... | .. | ... | ... | 49 | 90 | 110 | 82 | 134 | 109 | 26 | 18 | 18 | 20 | 38 | 128 | 111 | 4 | 3 | ... | 1 | .. | .. | 285 | 10 |
| .. | 7 | 2 | 10 | 1 | 290 | 290 | 262 | 211 | 457 | 175 | 78 | 227 | 202 | 158 | 360 | 427 | 402 | 11 | 4 | 1 | 3 | 2 | 2 | 1212 | 11 |
| .. | 110 | 24 | 118 | 8 | 1997 | 2057 | 2259 | 1465 | 2589 | 2748 | 740 | 1205 | 1544 | 1265 | 2809 | 2570 | 2481 | 65 | 50 | 11 | 16 | 18 | 27 | 8047 | |

## ECTION OF THE STATE OF TENNESSEE.

*ocke, Grainger, Greene, Hancock, Hawkins, Jefferson, Johnson, Knox, McMinn, Meigs, ullivan, and Washington.*

| ritories. | Ireland. | Germany. | Other foreign countries. | Unknown. | Spring. | Summer. | Autumn. | Winter. | Under 1 week. | 1 week and under 1 month. | 1 month and under 3 months. | 3 months and over. | Males. | Females. | Total. | Slaves Black M. | Slaves Black F. | Slaves Mulatto M. | Slaves Mulatto F. | Free Black M. | Free Black F. | Free Mul. M | Free Mul. F. | Aggregate deaths. | |
|---|---|---|---|---|---|---|---|---|---|---|---|---|---|---|---|---|---|---|---|---|---|---|---|---|---|
| ... | ... | .. | ... | ... | 1 | ... | ... | ... | ... | 1 | ... | ... | ... | 1 | 1 | ... | ... | ... | ... | ... | ... | .. | .. | 1 | 1 |
| ... | 1 | .. | ... | ... | 8 | 7 | 9 | 8 | 15 | 6 | 1 | 1 | 22 | 5 | 27 | 1 | 2 | 2 | ... | ... | ... | .. | .. | 32 | 2 |
| ... | ... | .. | ... | ... | 12 | ... | 2 | 4 | 10 | 5 | 1 | ... | 10 | 10 | 20 | ... | ... | ... | ... | ... | ... | .. | .. | 20 | 3 |
| ... | ... | .. | ... | ... | 7 | 6 | 1 | 4 | 19 | ... | ... | ... | 14 | 4 | 18 | ... | ... | ... | ... | ... | ... | .. | 1 | 19 | 4 |
| ... | ... | .. | ... | ... | 1 | ... | ... | ... | 1 | ... | ... | ... | ... | ... | ... | ... | 1 | ... | ... | ... | ... | .. | .. | 1 | 5 |
| ... | ... | .. | ... | ... | ... | 1 | ... | ... | 1 | ... | ... | ... | 1 | ... | 1 | ... | ... | ... | ... | ... | ... | .. | .. | 1 | 6 |
| ... | ... | .. | ... | ... | 2 | ... | 2 | ... | 2 | ... | ... | ... | 2 | ... | 2 | 2 | ... | ... | ... | ... | ... | .. | .. | 4 | 7 |
| ... | ... | .. | ... | ... | 4 | ... | ... | ... | 2 | ... | 1 | ... | 2 | 2 | 4 | ... | ... | ... | ... | ... | ... | .. | .. | 4 | 8 |
| ... | ... | .. | ... | ... | 4 | 1 | 1 | 3 | 2 | ... | 1 | 4 | 4 | 3 | 7 | 1 | ... | 1 | ... | ... | ... | .. | .. | 9 | 9 |
| ... | ... | .. | 1 | ... | 2 | 1 | 4 | 2 | ... | 2 | ... | 2 | 4 | 4 | 8 | ... | 1 | ... | ... | ... | ... | .. | .. | 9 | 10 |
| ... | ... | .. | ... | ... | ... | ... | 1 | ... | ... | ... | ... | 1 | ... | 1 | 1 | ... | ... | ... | ... | ... | ... | .. | .. | 1 | 11 |
| ... | ... | .. | ... | ... | ... | ... | 1 | ... | ... | 1 | ... | ... | ... | 1 | 1 | ... | ... | ... | ... | ... | ... | .. | .. | 1 | 12 |
| ... | ... | .. | ... | ... | ... | 2 | 1 | ... | 2 | 1 | ... | ... | 2 | 1 | 3 | ... | ... | ... | ... | ... | ... | .. | .. | 3 | 13 |
| ... | ... | .. | ... | ... | 7 | 5 | ... | 6 | 13 | 4 | 1 | ... | ... | 16 | 16 | ... | 2 | ... | ... | ... | ... | .. | .. | 18 | 14 |
| ... | ... | .. | ... | ... | ... | 2 | 1 | 1 | 3 | 1 | ... | ... | 4 | ... | 4 | ... | ... | ... | ... | ... | ... | .. | .. | 4 | 15 |
| ... | ... | .. | ... | ... | 1 | 7 | 5 | ... | 7 | 3 | ... | 2 | 9 | 4 | 13 | ... | ... | ... | ... | ... | ... | .. | .. | 13 | 16 |
| ... | ... | .. | ... | ... | 8 | 9 | ... | ... | 4 | 8 | 2 | 2 | 14 | 6 | 20 | ... | ... | ... | ... | ... | ... | .. | .. | 20 | 17 |
| ... | ... | .. | ... | ... | 4 | 2 | ... | 1 | 4 | 3 | ... | ... | 3 | 2 | 5 | 1 | ... | 1 | ... | ... | ... | .. | .. | 7 | 18 |
| ... | ... | .. | ... | ... | 1 | 1 | ... | ... | 1 | 1 | ... | ... | ... | 2 | 2 | ... | ... | ... | ... | ... | ... | .. | .. | 2 | 19 |
| ... | ... | .. | ... | ... | 35 | 41 | 18 | 31 | 5 | 9 | 20 | 61 | 37 | 61 | 98 | 7 | 12 | 3 | 3 | 2 | 1 | 1 | 1 | 128 | 20 |
| ... | ... | .. | ... | ... | 5 | 7 | 2 | 6 | 7 | 4 | 2 | ... | 6 | 15 | 21 | 1 | ... | ... | 1 | ... | ... | .. | .. | 23 | 21 |
| ... | ... | .. | ... | ... | 26 | 25 | 59 | 31 | 100 | 31 | 6 | ... | 76 | 50 | 126 | 8 | 7 | 2 | ... | ... | 1 | .. | .. | 144 | 22 |
| ... | 1 | .. | ... | ... | ... | ... | ... | ... | 1 | 1 | ... | ... | 2 | ... | 2 | ... | ... | ... | ... | ... | ... | .. | .. | 2 | 23 |
| ... | ... | .. | ... | ... | 3 | 13 | 14 | 3 | 3 | 16 | 6 | 6 | 16 | 14 | 30 | 1 | 1 | ... | ... | 1 | ... | .. | .. | 33 | 24 |
| ... | ... | .. | 1 | ... | 20 | 20 | 16 | 20 | 6 | 7 | 13 | 32 | 29 | 41 | 70 | 5 | 3 | ... | 1 | ... | ... | .. | .. | 79 | 25 |
| ... | ... | .. | ... | ... | ... | 12 | 10 | 2 | 4 | 14 | 3 | 2 | 9 | 13 | 22 | 1 | ... | ... | 1 | ... | 1 | .. | .. | 25 | 26 |
| ... | ... | .. | ... | ... | 4 | 1 | 3 | 3 | 1 | ... | 2 | 3 | 8 | 3 | 11 | ... | ... | ... | ... | ... | ... | .. | .. | 11 | 27 |
| ... | ... | .. | ... | ... | 2 | 1 | 1 | 2 | 2 | 4 | ... | ... | 2 | 3 | 5 | ... | 1 | ... | ... | ... | ... | .. | .. | 6 | 28 |
| ... | ... | .. | ... | ... | 65 | 60 | 77 | 37 | 39 | 153 | 40 | 7 | 113 | 88 | 201 | 15 | 14 | 3 | ... | 1 | ... | 3 | 2 | 239 | 29 |
| .. | ... | .. | ... | ... | 4 | 8 | 10 | 2 | 2 | 1 | 20 | ... | 14 | 7 | 21 | 2 | 1 | ... | ... | ... | ... | .. | .. | 24 | 30 |
| ... | ... | .. | ... | ... | 1 | 3 | ... | 1 | 1 | 4 | ... | ... | 2 | 3 | 5 | ... | ... | ... | ... | ... | ... | .. | .. | 5 | 31 |
| ... | ... | .. | ... | ... | 1 | 2 | 7 | 2 | 3 | 8 | ... | 1 | 4 | 5 | 9 | 2 | 1 | ... | ... | ... | ... | .. | .. | 12 | 32 |
| ... | ... | .. | ... | ... | 1 | 3 | 3 | 3 | 2 | 5 | 1 | 1 | 4 | 5 | 9 | 1 | ... | ... | ... | ... | ... | .. | .. | 10 | 33 |
| ... | ... | .. | ... | ... | 1 | 2 | ... | 3 | 1 | 5 | ... | ... | ... | 6 | 6 | ... | ... | ... | ... | ... | ... | .. | .. | 6 | 34 |
| ... | ... | .. | ... | ... | 1 | 1 | 4 | ... | 1 | 4 | ... | ... | 4 | 2 | 6 | ... | ... | ... | ... | ... | ... | .. | .. | 6 | 35 |
| 1 | ... | .. | ... | ... | 17 | 19 | 21 | 17 | 5 | 46 | 17 | 4 | 40 | 27 | 67 | 1 | 5 | 1 | ... | ... | ... | .. | .. | 74 | 36 |
| ... | ... | .. | ... | ... | 1 | 2 | 2 | 2 | ... | 2 | 1 | 3 | 6 | 1 | 7 | ... | ... | ... | ... | ... | ... | .. | .. | 7 | 37 |
| ... | ... | .. | ... | ... | 1 | 5 | 1 | 3 | 3 | 2 | 1 | 2 | 7 | 3 | 10 | ... | ... | ... | ... | ... | ... | .. | .. | 10 | 38 |
| ... | ... | .. | ... | ... | 1 | 3 | 2 | ... | 1 | 1 | 1 | 3 | 4 | ... | 4 | ... | 2 | ... | ... | ... | ... | .. | .. | 6 | 39 |
| ... | ... | .. | ... | ... | 11 | 8 | 5 | 8 | 21 | 9 | 1 | ... | 14 | 17 | 31 | ... | 1 | 1 | ... | ... | ... | .. | .. | 33 | 40 |
| ... | ... | .. | ... | ... | 30 | 23 | 12 | 12 | 5 | 39 | 29 | 4 | 23 | 40 | 63 | 6 | 7 | ... | 2 | ... | ... | .. | .. | 78 | 41 |
| ... | ... | .. | ... | ... | 1 | ... | 1 | 3 | 1 | 3 | ... | 1 | 2 | 3 | 5 | ... | ... | ... | ... | ... | ... | .. | .. | 5 | 42 |
| ... | ... | .. | ... | ... | 1 | 2 | ... | 2 | 1 | 2 | 1 | 1 | 2 | 3 | 5 | ... | ... | ... | ... | ... | ... | .. | .. | 5 | 43 |
| ... | ... | .. | ... | ... | 12 | 3 | 2 | 4 | 8 | 12 | ... | ... | 11 | 5 | 16 | 2 | 2 | 1 | ... | ... | ... | .. | .. | 21 | 44 |
| ... | ... | .. | ... | ... | 9 | 3 | 3 | 4 | 7 | 7 | 1 | 3 | 13 | 6 | 19 | ... | ... | ... | ... | ... | ... | .. | .. | 19 | 45 |
| ... | ... | .. | ... | ... | 1 | 2 | ... | ... | 1 | 1 | 1 | ... | ... | 3 | 3 | ... | ... | ... | ... | ... | ... | .. | .. | 3 | 46 |
| ... | ... | .. | ... | ... | ... | 2 | 2 | 1 | ... | 2 | 1 | ... | 5 | ... | 5 | ... | ... | ... | ... | ... | ... | .. | .. | 5 | 47 |
| ... | ... | .. | ... | ... | ... | ... | 1 | 2 | ... | 1 | 1 | ... | 2 | 2 | 4 | ... | ... | ... | ... | ... | ... | .. | .. | 4 | 48 |
| ... | ... | .. | ... | ... | ... | ... | ... | 1 | ... | ... | ... | ... | 1 | ... | 1 | ... | ... | ... | ... | ... | ... | .. | .. | 1 | 49 |
| ... | ... | .. | ... | ... | ... | ... | 2 | ... | ... | 1 | ... | ... | 2 | ... | 2 | ... | ... | ... | ... | ... | ... | .. | .. | 2 | 50 |
| ... | ... | .. | ... | ... | 5 | 10 | 9 | 3 | 3 | 7 | 3 | 3 | 14 | 10 | 24 | 1 | 2 | ... | ... | ... | ... | .. | .. | 27 | 51 |
| ... | ... | .. | ... | ... | 2 | ... | ... | ... | 1 | ... | ... | 1 | 1 | 1 | 2 | ... | ... | ... | ... | ... | ... | .. | .. | 2 | 52 |

## CLASSIFICATION OF DEATHS IN EASTERN

| | Cause of death. | AGES. Under 1. M. | Under 1. F. | 1 and under 5. M. | 1 and under 5. F. | 5 and under 10. M. | 5 and under 10. F. | 10 and under 20. M. | 10 and under 20. F. | 20 and under 50. M. | 20 and under 50. F. | 50 and under 80. M. | 50 and under 80. F. | 80 and under 100. M | 80 and under 100. F. | 100 & over. M | 100 & over. F. | Age unknown. M | Age unknown. F. | NATIVITIES. Born in State. | N. England States. | Middle States. | Southern States. | Southwest'n States. | Northwest'n States. |
|---|---|---|---|---|---|---|---|---|---|---|---|---|---|---|---|---|---|---|---|---|---|---|---|---|---|
| 1 | Measles | .... | ... | .... | ... | ... | ... | ... | ... | .... | 1 | ... | ... | .. | .. | .. | .. | .. | .. | .... | .. | ... | 1 | ... | ... |
| 2 | Mumps | .... | 1 | 1 | ... | ... | ... | ... | ... | .... | .... | ... | ... | .. | .. | .. | .. | .. | .. | 1 | .. | ... | 1 | ... | ... |
| 3 | Murder | .... | ... | .... | ... | ... | ... | 2 | ... | 1 | .... | ... | ... | .. | .. | .. | .. | .. | .. | 3 | .. | ... | ... | ... | ... |
| 4 | Neuralgia | .... | ... | .... | 1 | 1 | ... | ... | ... | .... | .... | 1 | 1 | .. | .. | .. | .. | .. | .. | 1 | .. | ... | 3 | ... | ... |
| 5 | Old age | .... | ... | .... | ... | ... | ... | ... | ... | .... | .... | 9 | 12 | 21 | 25 | 3 | .. | .. | .. | 17 | .. | 7 | 44 | ... | ... |
| 6 | Paralysis | 1 | ... | .... | ... | 1 | ... | ... | 3 | 1 | 1 | 5 | 8 | .. | 4 | .. | .. | .. | .. | 10 | .. | 3 | 11 | ... | ... |
| 7 | Piles | .... | ... | .... | ... | ... | ... | ... | ... | .... | .... | 2 | ... | .. | .. | .. | .. | .. | .. | ... | .. | ... | 2 | ... | ... |
| 8 | Pleurisy | 1 | ... | .... | ... | ... | 1 | ... | ... | 3 | 1 | ... | 1 | 1 | .. | .. | .. | .. | .. | 5 | .. | ... | 2 | ... | ... |
| 9 | Pneumonia | 2 | 2 | 3 | 9 | 2 | 4 | 5 | 7 | 16 | 10 | 12 | 10 | 2 | 1 | .. | .. | .. | .. | 67 | .. | 7 | 11 | ... | ... |
| 10 | Poison | .... | ... | .... | ... | ... | ... | ... | ... | .... | 1 | 1 | ... | .. | .. | .. | .. | .. | .. | 2 | .. | ... | ... | ... | ... |
| 11 | Prematurity of birth | 1 | 1 | .... | ... | ... | ... | ... | ... | .... | .... | ... | ... | .. | .. | .. | .. | .. | .. | 2 | .. | ... | ... | ... | ... |
| 12 | Quinsy | .... | ... | 3 | 1 | 2 | 1 | ... | 1 | .... | .... | 1 | 1 | .. | .. | .. | .. | .. | .. | 9 | .. | ... | 1 | ... | ... |
| 13 | Rheumatism | .... | ... | .... | ... | ... | ... | 1 | ... | 2 | 1 | 1 | ... | 1 | .. | .. | .. | .. | .. | 3 | .. | ... | 3 | ... | ... |
| 14 | Scrofula | 2 | ... | 3 | 4 | 1 | ... | 1 | 1 | 2 | 2 | ... | 2 | .. | .. | .. | .. | .. | .. | 17 | .. | ... | 1 | ... | ... |
| 15 | Spine, disease of | .... | ... | 1 | ... | ... | ... | 2 | 1 | 2 | .... | ... | 1 | .. | .. | .. | .. | .. | .. | 6 | .. | ... | 1 | ... | ... |
| 16 | Stillborn | 3 | 4 | .... | ... | ... | ... | ... | ... | .... | .... | ... | ... | .. | .. | .. | .. | .. | .. | 7 | .. | ... | ... | ... | ... |
| 17 | Suffocation | .... | 1 | .... | ... | ... | ... | ... | ... | .... | 1 | ... | ... | .. | .. | .. | .. | .. | .. | 2 | .. | ... | ... | ... | ... |
| 18 | Suicide | .... | ... | .... | ... | ... | ... | ... | ... | .... | 1 | 1 | ... | .. | .. | .. | .. | .. | .. | 2 | .. | ... | ... | ... | ... |
| 19 | Teething | .... | 1 | .... | ... | ... | ... | ... | ... | .... | .... | ... | ... | .. | .. | .. | .. | .. | .. | 1 | .. | ... | ... | ... | ... |
| 20 | Throat, disease of | .... | ... | .... | 1 | .. | 1 | 1 | ... | .... | 1 | ... | ... | .. | .. | .. | .. | .. | .. | 3 | .. | ... | 1 | ... | ... |
| 21 | Thrush | .... | 1 | .... | ... | ... | ... | ... | ... | .... | .... | ... | ... | .. | .. | .. | .. | .. | .. | 1 | .. | ... | ... | ... | ... |
| 22 | Ulcer | 1 | ... | 1 | ... | ... | ... | ... | ... | 2 | 1 | 1 | 1 | 1 | 1 | .. | .. | .. | .. | 6 | .. | ... | 3 | ... | ... |
| 23 | Uterus, disease of | .... | ... | .... | ... | ... | ... | ... | 1 | .... | 1 | ... | 1 | .. | .. | .. | .. | .. | .. | 1 | .. | ... | 2 | ... | ... |
| 24 | White swelling | .... | ... | 1 | ... | ... | ... | ... | ... | 1 | .... | ... | ... | .. | .. | .. | .. | .. | .. | 2 | .. | ... | ... | ... | ... |
| 25 | Worms | .... | 1 | 11 | 7 | 3 | 4 | 2 | ... | .... | .... | ... | ... | .. | .. | .. | .. | .. | .. | 25 | .. | ... | 3 | ... | ... |
| 26 | Unknown | 81 | 72 | 27 | 27 | 8 | 6 | 14 | 18 | 26 | 47 | 28 | 29 | 4 | 8 | .. | .. | 3 | 2 | 341 | .. | 7 | 50 | ... | ... |
| | Total | 217 | 193 | 170 | 161 | 51 | 55 | 108 | 108 | 234 | 236 | 158 | 141 | 44 | 43 | 3 | .. | 3 | 2 | 1552 | 2 | 46 | 299 | 12 | 6 |

## CLASSIFICATION OF DEATHS IN WESTERN

*Embracing the following counties : Benton, Carroll, Dyer, Fayette, Gibson, Harden, Hardeman,*

| | Cause of death. | Under 1. M. | Under 1. F. | 1 and under 5. M. | 1 and under 5. F. | 5 and under 10. M. | 5 and under 10. F. | 10 and under 20. M. | 10 and under 20. F. | 20 and under 50. M. | 20 and under 50. F. | 50 and under 80. M. | 50 and under 80. F. | 80 and under 100. M | 80 and under 100. F. | 100 & over. M | 100 & over. F. | Age unknown. M | Age unknown. F. | Born in State. | N. England States. | Middle States. | Southern States. | Southwest'n States. | Northwest'n States. |
|---|---|---|---|---|---|---|---|---|---|---|---|---|---|---|---|---|---|---|---|---|---|---|---|---|---|
| 1 | Abscess | .... | ... | .... | 2 | ... | ... | 3 | 1 | .... | .... | 1 | ... | .. | .. | .. | .. | .. | .. | 5 | .. | ... | 2 | ... | ... |
| 2 | Accident, not specifi'd | 5 | 11 | 3 | 1 | 1 | 6 | 8 | 1 | 17 | 1 | 2 | 3 | 1 | .. | .. | .. | 4 | .. | 45 | .. | 1 | 14 | ... | 2 |
| 3 | ....do...burned | 2 | 4 | 7 | 7 | 2 | 5 | 3 | 2 | 3 | 2 | ... | ... | .. | .. | .. | .. | .. | .. | 31 | .. | ... | 5 | ... | 1 |
| 4 | ....do...drowned | .... | ... | .... | ... | 1 | ... | 8 | 3 | 3 | .... | ... | 1 | .. | .. | .. | .. | .. | .. | 9 | .. | ... | 4 | ... | 1 |
| 5 | ....do.. scalded | 1 | ... | .... | ... | ... | 2 | ... | ... | .... | .... | ... | ... | .. | .. | .. | .. | .. | .. | 3 | .. | ... | ... | ... | ... |
| 6 | ....do...shot | .... | ... | .... | ... | ... | ... | 1 | ... | .... | .... | ... | ... | .. | .. | .. | .. | .. | .. | ... | .. | ... | ... | ... | 1 |
| 7 | Apoplexy | .... | ... | .... | 1 | ... | ... | ... | ... | 2 | 3 | 2 | 3 | 1 | .. | .. | .. | .. | .. | 7 | .. | ... | 5 | ... | ... |
| 8 | Asthma | .... | ... | 1 | 1 | ... | ... | 1 | ... | .... | .... | 1 | ... | .. | .. | .. | .. | .. | .. | 2 | .. | ... | 2 | ... | ... |
| 9 | Bowels, disease of | 1 | 2 | 2 | 2 | 1 | ... | ... | ... | .... | 1 | 1 | 1 | .. | .. | .. | .. | .. | .. | 8 | .. | ... | 3 | ... | ... |
| 10 | Bronchitis | .... | 1 | 6 | 1 | ... | ... | ... | 1 | 1 | 1 | 1 | 1 | .. | .. | .. | .. | .. | .. | 11 | .. | ... | 2 | ... | ... |
| 11 | Cancer | .... | ... | .... | 1 | ... | ... | ... | 1 | .... | 3 | ... | 1 | 1 | .. | .. | .. | .. | .. | 3 | .. | ... | 6 | ... | ... |
| 12 | Catarrh | 2 | 1 | 1 | ... | ... | ... | ... | ... | .... | .... | ... | ... | .. | .. | .. | .. | .. | .. | 4 | .. | ... | ... | ... | ... |
| 13 | Chicken pox | .... | ... | .... | 1 | ... | ... | ... | ... | .... | .... | ... | ... | .. | .. | .. | .. | .. | .. | 1 | .. | ... | ... | ... | ... |
| 14 | Childbirth | .... | ... | .... | ... | ... | ... | ... | 3 | .... | 19 | ... | ... | .. | .. | .. | .. | .. | 1 | 12 | .. | ... | 11 | ... | ... |
| 15 | Cholera | 4 | 3 | 14 | 8 | 3 | 3 | 8 | 12 | 43 | 41 | 17 | 6 | 2 | 1 | .. | .. | 12 | 4 | 114 | 3 | 1 | 42 | ... | 5 |
| 16 | ...do..infantum | 5 | 12 | 9 | 5 | 1 | 2 | ... | ... | .... | .... | ... | ... | .. | .. | .. | .. | .. | .. | 31 | .. | ... | 3 | ... | ... |
| 17 | ...do..morbus | .... | ... | 1 | 2 | ... | ... | ... | 3 | .... | 2 | ... | ... | .. | .. | .. | .. | .. | .. | 4 | .. | ... | 4 | ... | ... |
| 18 | Chorea | .... | 1 | 1 | ... | ... | ... | ... | 1 | 1 | 1 | ... | ... | .. | .. | .. | .. | .. | .. | 5 | .. | ... | ... | ... | ... |
| 19 | Colic | 1 | ... | .... | ... | ... | ... | 1 | ... | 3 | 2 | 1 | 1 | .. | .. | .. | .. | .. | .. | 6 | .. | ... | 3 | ... | ... |
| 20 | Congest'n, not spec'fd | .... | ... | 1 | ... | ... | ... | 1 | ... | 1 | .... | ... | ... | .. | .. | .. | .. | .. | .. | 2 | .. | ... | 1 | ... | ... |
| 21 | ....do ...brain | .... | ... | 1 | ... | ... | ... | ... | ... | .... | .... | ... | ... | .. | .. | .. | .. | .. | .. | 1 | .. | ... | ... | ... | ... |
| 22 | Consumption | 3 | 1 | 4 | 5 | ... | 3 | 12 | 26 | 48 | 65 | 32 | 18 | 1 | 2 | .. | .. | 2 | 1 | 123 | 1 | 1 | 89 | ... | 7 |
| 23 | Convulsions | 14 | 4 | 3 | 2 | 2 | 1 | 5 | 1 | 4 | 1 | ... | ... | .. | .. | .. | .. | .. | .. | 32 | .. | ... | 1 | 3 | .. |
| 24 | Croup | 33 | 40 | 28 | 26 | 5 | 2 | ... | ... | .... | .... | ... | ... | .. | .. | .. | .. | .. | .. | 126 | .. | ... | 6 | ... | 2 |
| 25 | Debility | .... | ... | .... | ... | ... | ... | ... | ... | .... | .... | ... | ... | .. | .. | .. | .. | .. | .. | ... | .. | ... | ... | ... | ... |
| 26 | Diarrhœa | 14 | 24 | 34 | 16 | 3 | 2 | 2 | 3 | 6 | 12 | 7 | 2 | 1 | .. | .. | .. | 11 | .. | 122 | .. | ... | 10 | ... | 1 |
| 27 | Dropsy | 3 | 1 | 11 | 6 | 4 | 2 | 12 | 5 | 10 | 13 | 18 | 13 | 2 | 2 | .. | .. | 3 | 1 | 60 | .. | 2 | 41 | ... | 2 |
| 28 | Dysentery | 2 | 1 | 7 | 6 | ... | 1 | ... | ... | 4 | 1 | ... | 2 | .. | .. | .. | .. | .. | .. | 23 | .. | ... | 1 | ... | ... |
| 29 | Dyspepsia | .... | ... | .... | ... | ... | ... | ... | 1 | 1 | 2 | 3 | ... | .. | .. | .. | .. | .. | .. | 4 | .. | ... | 3 | ... | ... |
| 30 | Epilepsy | 1 | ... | .... | ... | ... | ... | ... | ... | 2 | .. | 1 | ... | .. | .. | .. | .. | .. | .. | 2 | .. | ... | 2 | ... | ... |
| 31 | Erysipelas | 1 | ... | .... | ... | ... | ... | ... | 1 | 1 | 1 | 1 | 1 | .. | .. | .. | .. | .. | .. | 3 | .. | ... | 3 | ... | ... |
| 32 | Fever, not specified | 10 | 6 | 13 | 10 | 13 | 6 | 9 | 5 | 16 | 17 | 6 | 8 | 1 | .. | .. | .. | .. | .. | 72 | 1 | 3 | 31 | ... | 5 |
| 33 | ..do..bilious | 1 | ... | 3 | 5 | ... | 3 | 1 | 1 | 5 | .... | 2 | 1 | .. | .. | .. | .. | .. | .. | 16 | .. | ... | 5 | ... | ... |
| 34 | ..do..brain | .... | 1 | .... | 2 | ... | ... | 1 | 1 | .... | 1 | ... | ... | .. | .. | .. | .. | .. | .. | 5 | .. | ... | 1 | ... | ... |
| 35 | ..do..congestive | 4 | ... | 6 | 5 | 2 | 2 | 6 | 3 | 16 | 10 | 3 | 3 | 1 | 1 | .. | .. | 1 | .. | 41 | 1 | ... | 11 | ... | ... |
| 36 | ..do..intermittent | 3 | 1 | .... | 2 | 1 | ... | ... | 1 | .... | .... | ... | ... | 1 | .. | .. | .. | 3 | .. | 11 | .. | ... | ... | ... | ... |
| 37 | ..do..puerperal | .... | ... | .... | ... | ... | ... | ... | ... | .... | 4 | ... | ... | .. | .. | .. | .. | .. | .. | 4 | .. | ... | ... | ... | ... |
| 38 | ..do..remittent | .... | ... | .... | ... | ... | ... | ... | ... | .... | .... | ... | 1 | .. | .. | .. | .. | .. | .. | ... | .. | ... | 1 | ... | ... |

## SECTION OF THE STATE OF TENNESSEE—Continued.

| NATIVITIES. California and Territories. | NATIVITIES. Ireland. | NATIVITIES. Germany. | NATIVITIES. Other foreign countries. | NATIVITIES. Unknown. | SEASON OF DECEASE. Spring. | SEASON OF DECEASE. Summer. | SEASON OF DECEASE. Autumn. | SEASON OF DECEASE. Winter. | DURATION OF SICKNESS. Under 1 week. | DURATION OF SICKNESS. 1 week and under 1 month. | DURATION OF SICKNESS. 1 month and under 3 months. | DURATION OF SICKNESS. 3 months and over. | WHITES. Males. | WHITES. Females. | WHITES. Total. | COLORED. Slaves. Black. M. | COLORED. Slaves. Black. F. | COLORED. Slaves. Mulatto. M. | COLORED. Slaves. Mulatto. F. | COLORED. Free. Black. M. | COLORED. Free. Black. F. | COLORED. Free. Mul. M | COLORED. Free. Mul. F. | Aggregate deaths. | |
|---|---|---|---|---|---|---|---|---|---|---|---|---|---|---|---|---|---|---|---|---|---|---|---|---|---|
| | | | | | | 1 | | | | | | 1 | | | | | 1 | | | | | | | 1 | 1 |
| | | | | | | 2 | | | | 1 | 1 | | 1 | | 1 | | 1 | | | | | | | 2 | 2 |
| | | | | | 1 | 2 | | | 1 | | 1 | | 2 | | 2 | 1 | | | | | | | | 3 | 3 |
| | | | | | 1 | 1 | 2 | | 2 | 1 | 1 | | 2 | 2 | 4 | | | | | | | | | 4 | 4 |
| | 2 | | | | 18 | 20 | 17 | 15 | 18 | 20 | 17 | 15 | 32 | 34 | 66 | 1 | 2 | | | | 1 | | | 70 | 5 |
| | | | | | 4 | 10 | 5 | 5 | 6 | 6 | 2 | 7 | 8 | 16 | 24 | | | | | | | | | 24 | 6 |
| | | | | | 1 | | 1 | | | 1 | 1 | | 2 | | 2 | | | | | | | | | 2 | 7 |
| | 1 | | | | 2 | 2 | 1 | 3 | 2 | 3 | 2 | | 5 | 3 | 8 | | | | | | | | | 8 | 8 |
| | | | | | 37 | 15 | 7 | 26 | 17 | 43 | 19 | 2 | 36 | 34 | 70 | 6 | 7 | | 1 | | | | 1 | 85 | 9 |
| | | | | | 1 | | 1 | | 1 | | | | 1 | 1 | 2 | | | | | | | | | 2 | 10 |
| | | | | | | 1 | | 1 | | 2 | | | 1 | 1 | 2 | | | | | | | | | 2 | 11 |
| | | | | | 4 | 2 | 1 | 3 | 5 | 4 | | 1 | 5 | 4 | 9 | 1 | | | | | | | | 10 | 12 |
| | | | | | 1 | 2 | 1 | 2 | | 1 | | 2 | 5 | 1 | 6 | | | | | | | | | 6 | 13 |
| | | | | | 5 | 4 | 4 | 5 | 5 | 2 | 3 | 4 | 7 | 6 | 13 | 2 | 1 | | | | | | 2 | 18 | 14 |
| | | | | | 2 | | 2 | 2 | 1 | | 1 | 4 | 4 | 2 | 6 | | | 1 | | | | | | 7 | 15 |
| | | | | | 3 | | 2 | 2 | | | | | 3 | 3 | 6 | | 1 | | | | | | | 7 | 16 |
| | | | | | | 1 | 1 | | 2 | | | | | 2 | 2 | | | | | | | | | 2 | 17 |
| | | | | | | | 1 | 1 | | | | | 1 | 1 | 2 | | | | | | | | | 2 | 18 |
| | | | | | | | | 1 | 1 | | | | | 1 | 1 | | | | | | | | | 1 | 19 |
| | | | | | 1 | | 2 | 1 | | 3 | | | | 3 | 3 | 1 | | | | | | | | 4 | 20 |
| | | | | | | | | 1 | 1 | | | | | 1 | 1 | | | | | | | | | 1 | 21 |
| | | | | | 1 | 2 | 2 | 4 | | 1 | 3 | 2 | 6 | 3 | 9 | | | | | | | | | 9 | 22 |
| | | | | | | 2 | 1 | | | | | | | 3 | 3 | | | | | | | | | 3 | 23 |
| | | | | | | 1 | | 1 | | 2 | | | 2 | | 2 | | | | | | | | | 2 | 24 |
| | | | | | 9 | 6 | 6 | 7 | 14 | 10 | 2 | | 13 | 12 | 25 | 1 | | 1 | | | | 1 | | 28 | 25 |
| | | | 1 | 1 | 93 | 91 | 100 | 86 | 104 | 84 | 36 | 52 | 160 | 176 | 336 | 25 | 28 | 5 | 3 | 1 | | | 2 | 400 | 26 |
| 1 | 5 | .. | 3 | 1 | 507 | 490 | 472 | 403 | 501 | 621 | 267 | 245 | 860 | 808 | 1668 | 96 | 106 | 22 | 12 | 5 | 4 | 5 | 9 | 1927 | |

## SECTION OF THE STATE OF TENNESSEE.

*Haywood, Henderson, Henry, Lauderdale, Madison, McNairy, Obion, Shelby, Tipton, & Weakly.*

| California and Territories. | Ireland. | Germany. | Other foreign countries. | Unknown. | Spring. | Summer. | Autumn. | Winter. | Under 1 week. | 1 week and under 1 month. | 1 month and under 3 months. | 3 months and over. | Males. | Females. | Total. | Slaves Black M. | Slaves Black F. | Slaves Mulatto M. | Slaves Mulatto F. | Free Black M. | Free Black F. | Free Mul. M | Free Mul. F. | Aggregate deaths. | |
|---|---|---|---|---|---|---|---|---|---|---|---|---|---|---|---|---|---|---|---|---|---|---|---|---|---|
| | | | | | 3 | 2 | 2 | | 1 | | 4 | 2 | | 3 | 3 | 4 | | | | | | | | 7 | 1 |
| | 2 | | | | 24 | 11 | 12 | 16 | 22 | 11 | 1 | 1 | 30 | 10 | 40 | 11 | 13 | | | | | | | 64 | 2 |
| | | | | | 16 | 5 | 6 | 10 | 6 | 14 | 5 | 1 | 7 | 10 | 17 | 9 | 9 | 1 | 1 | | | | | 37 | 3 |
| | 2 | | | | 3 | 4 | 4 | 5 | 16 | | | | 6 | 3 | 9 | 2 | 1 | 4 | | | | | | 16 | 4 |
| | | | | | 1 | | 1 | 1 | 1 | | | | 1 | 2 | 3 | | | | | | | | | 3 | 5 |
| | | | | | | 1 | | | | | | | 1 | | 1 | | | | | | | | | 1 | 6 |
| | | | | | 3 | 4 | 3 | 2 | 5 | 1 | | | 1 | 4 | 5 | 4 | 3 | | | | | | | 12 | 7 |
| | | | | | 2 | | 1 | 1 | | 2 | | | 1 | 1 | 2 | 2 | | | | | | | | 4 | 8 |
| | | | | | | 4 | 5 | 2 | 2 | 3 | 4 | 2 | 1 | 4 | 5 | 4 | 2 | | | | | | | 11 | 9 |
| | | | | | 7 | 3 | 1 | 2 | 2 | 5 | | 2 | 3 | 5 | 8 | 4 | | 1 | | | | | | 13 | 10 |
| | | | | | 4 | 2 | 2 | 1 | | | 1 | 5 | 2 | 4 | 6 | 1 | 2 | | | | | | | 9 | 11 |
| | | | | | 3 | | | 1 | 1 | 3 | | | 1 | | 1 | 2 | 1 | | | | | | | 4 | 12 |
| | | | | | | | | 1 | | | 1 | | | 1 | 1 | | | | | | | | | 1 | 13 |
| | | | | | 8 | 5 | 4 | 6 | 11 | 5 | 2 | 3 | | 14 | 14 | | 9 | | | | | | | 23 | 14 |
| | 7 | 6 | 3 | | 23 | 124 | 21 | 13 | 167 | 14 | | | 64 | 51 | 115 | 33 | 27 | 5 | | | | 1 | | 181 | 15 |
| | | | | | 2 | 21 | 6 | 5 | 12 | 10 | 5 | 2 | 13 | 17 | 30 | 2 | 1 | | 1 | | | | | 34 | 16 |
| | | | | | | 2 | 4 | 1 | 2 | 5 | | | 1 | 5 | 6 | | 2 | | | | | | | 8 | 17 |
| | | | | | 1 | 3 | | 1 | 4 | | | 1 | 1 | 1 | 2 | 1 | 2 | | | | | | | 5 | 18 |
| | | | | | 4 | 1 | 2 | 2 | 4 | 1 | | 1 | 3 | | 3 | 3 | 3 | | | | | | | 6 | 19 |
| | | | | | | | 2 | 1 | 2 | | | 1 | 1 | | 1 | 2 | | | | | | | | 3 | 20 |
| | | | | | | | | | | | | | 1 | | 1 | | | | | | | | | 1 | 21 |
| | 1 | | 1 | | 70 | 54 | 54 | 46 | 6 | 9 | 13 | 123 | 70 | 81 | 151 | 30 | 37 | 2 | 3 | | | | | 223 | 22 |
| | 1 | | | | 10 | 11 | 7 | 8 | 18 | 5 | | 4 | 18 | 4 | 22 | 10 | 5 | | | | | | | 37 | 23 |
| | | | | | 33 | 16 | 46 | 39 | 97 | 30 | 6 | 1 | 41 | 41 | 82 | 23 | 26 | 1 | 1 | 1 | | | | 134 | 24 |
| | | | | | | | | | | | | | | | | | | | | | | | | | 25 |
| | 3 | | 1 | | 28 | 38 | 58 | 12 | 19 | 49 | 15 | 10 | 46 | 33 | 79 | 29 | 22 | 3 | 4 | | | | | 137 | 26 |
| | 1 | | | | 37 | 22 | 18 | 29 | 3 | 12 | 19 | 89 | 41 | 23 | 64 | 22 | 19 | | 1 | | | | | 106 | 27 |
| | | | | | 5 | 16 | 8 | | 7 | 11 | 4 | 1 | 10 | 5 | 15 | 3 | 6 | | | | | | | 24 | 28 |
| | | | | | 4 | | 2 | 1 | | | 1 | 5 | 4 | 2 | 6 | | 1 | | | | | | | 7 | 29 |
| | | | | | 1 | 1 | 1 | 1 | 2 | | | 1 | 3 | | 3 | 1 | | | | | | | | 4 | 30 |
| | | | | | 3 | 1 | 1 | 1 | 4 | 1 | | 1 | 2 | 3 | 5 | 1 | | | | | | | | 6 | 31 |
| | 2 | | 1 | | 30 | 30 | 30 | 25 | 20 | 69 | 22 | 14 | 44 | 24 | 68 | 21 | 21 | 3 | 2 | | | | | 115 | 32 |
| | 1 | | | | 5 | 6 | 10 | 1 | 3 | 12 | 6 | 1 | 11 | 6 | 17 | 1 | 4 | | | | | | | 22 | 33 |
| | | | | | 2 | 1 | 1 | 2 | 4 | 2 | | | 1 | 4 | 5 | | 1 | | | | | | | 6 | 34 |
| | 1 | | | | 8 | 19 | 23 | 7 | 40 | 11 | 2 | | 25 | 21 | 46 | 8 | 3 | | | | | | | 57 | 35 |
| | | | 1 | | | 1 | 6 | 5 | 2 | 4 | 2 | 1 | 7 | 1 | 8 | 1 | 3 | | | | | | | 12 | 36 |
| | | | | | | | 3 | 1 | 1 | 2 | | 1 | | 3 | 3 | | 1 | | | | | | | 4 | 37 |
| | | | | | | | 1 | | | 1 | | | | 1 | 1 | | | | | | | | | 1 | 38 |

## CLASSIFICATION OF DEATHS IN WESTERN

| | Cause of death. | AGES. | | | | | | | | | | | | | | | | | | NATIVITIES. | | | | | |
|---|---|---|---|---|---|---|---|---|---|---|---|---|---|---|---|---|---|---|---|---|---|---|---|---|---|
| | | Under 1. | | 1 and under 5. | | 5 and under 10. | | 10 and under 20. | | 20 and under 50. | | 50 and under 80. | | 80 and under 100. | | 100 & over. | | Age unknown. | | Born in State. | N. England States. | Middle States. | Southern States. | Southwest'n States. | Northwest'n States. |
| | | M. | F. | M. | F. | M. | F. | M. | F. | M. | F. | M. | F. | M | F. | M | F. | M | F. | | | | | | |
| 1 | Fever, scarlet | 12 | 3 | 13 | 10 | 4 | 2 | ... | 3 | ... | 1 | | | | | | | | | 47 | | | 1 | | |
| 2 | ..do..typhus | 3 | 2 | 6 | 5 | 9 | 9 | 28 | 41 | 37 | 27 | 8 | 8 | .. | 6 | | | | | 110 | | | 75 | 1 | |
| 3 | Gravel | 1 | | | | | | 1 | | 2 | 1 | 2 | | | | | | | | 3 | | | 4 | | |
| 4 | Head, disease of | | | 1 | | | | | | | | | | | | | | | | | | | 1 | | |
| 5 | Heart....do | 1 | | | | 1 | | | | 1 | | 2 | 1 | .. | 1 | | | | | 5 | | | 2 | | |
| 6 | Hemorrhage | | | | | 1 | | 1 | 2 | 2 | 1 | 1 | 3 | | | | | | | 4 | | | 7 | | |
| 7 | Hives | 10 | 11 | 4 | | | 1 | | | | | | | | | | | | | 25 | | | 1 | | |
| 8 | Hooping cough | 12 | 10 | 20 | 22 | | 5 | 1 | | 1 | | | | | | | | | | 70 | | | 1 | | |
| 9 | Hydrocephalus | 2 | 3 | 1 | 1 | | | | 1 | | | | | | | | | | | 8 | | | | | |
| 10 | Inflam'ation bowels | 4 | 3 | 2 | 1 | 2 | | 2 | 1 | 6 | 2 | | | 1 | | | | | | 19 | | | 3 | | |
| 11 | ..do........brain | 16 | 11 | 16 | 13 | 2 | 5 | 5 | 4 | 6 | 4 | 2 | 1 | | | | | | | 77 | | 1 | 7 | | |
| 12 | ..do........stomach | 1 | 1 | 1 | | | | | | 1 | 2 | | | | | | | | | 4 | | | 2 | | |
| 13 | Insanity | | | | | | | | | | 1 | | | | | | | | | 1 | | | | | |
| 14 | Intemperance | | | | | | | | | 6 | | 5 | | | | | | 5 | | 9 | | | 7 | | |
| 15 | Jaundice | 1 | 3 | | | | | | 1 | | | | | | | | | | | 4 | | | 1 | | |
| 16 | Kidneys, disease of | | | | | | | | | | | | 1 | | | | | | | | | | 1 | | |
| 17 | Killed | | | 1 | | | | 1 | | 1 | | 1 | | | | | | | | 3 | | | 1 | | |
| 18 | Lightning | | | | | | | | | 1 | | | | | | | | | | 1 | | | | | |
| 19 | Liver, disease of | | | | | 1 | | 2 | | 2 | 5 | | 2 | | | | | | | 9 | | | 3 | | |
| 20 | Lockjaw | 1 | 1 | | | | | | | | | | | | | | | | | 2 | | | | | |
| 21 | Lungs, disease of | | 1 | | | | | | | | | | | | | | | | | 1 | | | | | |
| 22 | Malformation | 1 | | | | | | | | | | | | | | | | | | 1 | | | | | |
| 23 | Marasmus | 3 | | | | | | | | | | | | | | | | | | 3 | | | | | |
| 24 | Measles | | | | 1 | | | 1 | | 2 | | | | | | | | | | 2 | | | 1 | | |
| 25 | Murder | | | | | | | | | 1 | | 1 | | | | | | | | 1 | | | 1 | | |
| 26 | Neuralgia | | | | | | | | | | | | | 1 | | | | | | | | | 1 | | |
| 27 | Old age | | | | | | | | | | | 8 | 5 | 11 | 18 | | | | | 3 | | 2 | 34 | | |
| 28 | Paralysis | | | | | | 1 | | | 1 | 2 | 1 | 3 | | | | | | | 2 | | 1 | 4 | | |
| 29 | Pleurisy | 1 | 1 | | 1 | 2 | 1 | 3 | | 4 | 2 | 4 | 4 | | | | | | | 11 | | | 9 | | |
| 30 | Pneumonia | 11 | 18 | 13 | 19 | 4 | 4 | 10 | 5 | 57 | 26 | 17 | 7 | 1 | 2 | .. | .. | 1 | .. | 118 | | 3 | 63 | | |
| 31 | Poison | | | | | | | | | 3 | 2 | | | | | | | | | 3 | | | 2 | | |
| 32 | Prematurity of birth | 1 | | | | | | | | | | | | | | | | | | 1 | | | | | |
| 33 | Quinsy | | | | 2 | | | | | 1 | 1 | | | | | | | | | 3 | | | 1 | | |
| 34 | Rheumatism | | | 1 | | | | | | 4 | 3 | 1 | | | | | | | | 3 | 1 | | 4 | | |
| 35 | Rickets | 1 | | 4 | 3 | | | 1 | | | | | | | | | | | | 9 | | | | | |
| 36 | Scrofula | 2 | 4 | 3 | 4 | 5 | 2 | 3 | 4 | 2 | 3 | 2 | 2 | | | | | | | 28 | | | 6 | | |
| 37 | Small pox | 1 | 1 | | | | | 2 | | 11 | 3 | 3 | 3 | | | | | 7 | 4 | 27 | | | 7 | | |
| 38 | Spine, disease of | 3 | | | | | | | | 1 | 1 | | 1 | | | | | | | 3 | | | 3 | | |
| 39 | Stillborn | | 2 | | | | | | | | | | | | | | | | | 2 | | | | | |
| 40 | Suffocation | 6 | 13 | 6 | | | | | | | | | | | | | | | | 25 | | | | | |
| 41 | Suicide | | | | | | | | | 1 | | | | | | | | 1 | | 2 | | | | | |
| 42 | Sun, stroke of | | | | | | | | | 1 | | | | | | | | | | 1 | | | | | |
| 43 | Teething | 4 | 5 | 9 | 4 | | | | | | | | | | | | | | | 17 | | | 3 | | |
| 44 | Tetanus | 3 | | | | | | | | | | | | | | | | | | 3 | | | | | |
| 45 | Throat, disease of | | | | | 1 | | | 1 | | | | | | | | | | | 2 | | | | | |
| 46 | Thrush | 1 | 6 | 3 | 1 | | | | | | | | | | | | | | | 11 | | | | | |
| 47 | Ulcer | | 1 | | | | | | | 1 | 1 | | 1 | | | | | | | 1 | | | 3 | | |
| 48 | Uterus, disease of | | | | | | | | 2 | | | | 1 | | | | | | | 2 | | | 1 | | |
| 49 | White swelling | 1 | | | | 1 | | | 1 | 2 | 1 | | | | | | | | | 4 | | | 2 | | |
| 50 | Worms | 3 | 3 | 17 | 15 | 2 | 4 | 1 | | | | | | | | | | | | 42 | | | 3 | | |
| 51 | Unknown | 156 | 145 | 59 | 57 | 13 | 7 | 26 | 25 | 55 | 80 | 36 | 19 | 6 | 2 | .. | .. | 3 | .. | 567 | .. | 3 | 96 | 2 | |
| | Total | 372 | 357 | 336 | 276 | 88 | 81 | 170 | 167 | 396 | 372 | 193 | 123 | 32 | 35 | .. | .. | 53 | 11 | 2250 | 7 | 18 | 673 | 6 | |

## CLASSIFICATION OF DEATHS IN EASTERN CENT

*Embracing the following counties: Bledsoe, Cannon, Coffee, De Kalb, Fentress, Grundy,* ... *White,*

| | Cause of death. | Under 1. M. | F. | 1 and under 5. M. | F. | 5 and under 10. M. | F. | 10 and under 20. M. | F. | 20 and under 50. M. | F. | 50 and under 80. M. | F. | 80 and under 100. M | F. | 100 & over. M | F. | Age unknown. M | F. | Born in State. | N. England States. | Middle States. | Southern States. | Southwest'n States. | Northwest'n States. |
|---|---|---|---|---|---|---|---|---|---|---|---|---|---|---|---|---|---|---|---|---|---|---|---|---|---|
| 1 | Abscess | | 2 | | | | | | | | | | | | | | | | | 2 | | | | | |
| 2 | Accident, not specif'd | 4 | 3 | 2 | 3 | 2 | | 5 | 1 | 8 | | 5 | 1 | 1 | | | | | | 28 | | 1 | 6 | | |
| 3 | ....do...burned | 1 | | 5 | 6 | 1 | 1 | | | | 1 | | | | | | | | | 15 | | | | | |
| 4 | ....do...drowned | | | | 1 | | 1 | 3 | 3 | 4 | 1 | 1 | | | | | | | | 11 | | | 2 | | |
| 5 | ....do...scalded | 1 | | 1 | 1 | | | | | | | | | | | | | | | 3 | | | | | |
| 6 | ....do...shot | | | | | | | | | 1 | | | | | | | | | | 1 | | | | | |
| 7 | Apoplexy | | | | | | | | | | 3 | 1 | 3 | 1 | | | | | | 4 | | 1 | 3 | | |
| 8 | Asthma | | | | | | | | | | | | 3 | | | | | | | 2 | | | 1 | | |
| 9 | Bronchitis | | | 1 | | | | | | | | | | | | | | | | 1 | | | | | |
| 10 | Cancer | 2 | | 1 | 1 | | | | | 1 | 2 | 6 | 3 | 1 | | | | | | 11 | | | 5 | | |
| 11 | Catarrh | | | | | | | | | | 1 | | | | 1 | | | | | 2 | | | | | |
| 12 | Carbuncle | | | | | | | 1 | 1 | | | | | | | | | | | 2 | | | | | |
| 13 | Childbirth | | | | | | | | 1 | | 12 | | | | | | | | | 11 | | | 2 | | |
| 14 | Cholera | 8 | 9 | 12 | 19 | 6 | 8 | 9 | 24 | 63 | 48 | 37 | 15 | 1 | 3 | | | | | 198 | | 3 | 53 | | |

## SECTION OF THE STATE OF TENNESSEE—Continued.

| NATIVITIES. | | | | | SEASON OF DECEASE. | | | | DURATION OF SICKNESS. | | | | WHITES. | | | COLORED. | | | | | | | | | |
|---|---|---|---|---|---|---|---|---|---|---|---|---|---|---|---|---|---|---|---|---|---|---|---|---|---|
| | | | | | | | | | | | | | | | | Slaves. | | | | Free. | | | | | |
| | | | | | | | | | | | | | | | | Black. | | Mulatto. | | Black. | | Mul. | | | |
| California and Territories. | Ireland. | Germany. | Other foreign countries. | Unknown. | Spring. | Summer. | Autumn. | Winter. | Under 1 week. | 1 week and under 1 month. | 1 month and under 3 months. | 3 months and over. | Males. | Females. | Total. | M. | F. | M. | F. | M. | F. | M | F. | Aggregate deaths. | |
| … | … | … | … | … | 21 | 6 | 7 | 14 | 16 | 27 | 5 | … | 26 | 14 | 40 | 3 | 5 | … | … | … | … | … | … | 48 | 1 |
| … | 1 | … | … | … | 47 | 34 | 60 | 48 | 24 | 88 | 64 | 10 | 67 | 73 | 140 | 24 | 24 | … | 1 | … | … | … | … | 189 | 2 |
| … | … | … | … | … | … | 2 | 3 | 2 | 1 | 1 | 1 | 2 | 5 | 1 | 6 | 1 | … | … | … | … | … | … | … | 7 | 3 |
| … | … | … | … | … | 1 | … | … | … | … | … | … | … | 1 | … | 1 | … | … | … | … | … | … | … | … | 1 | 4 |
| … | … | … | … | … | 3 | 2 | 1 | 1 | 1 | … | 1 | 2 | 2 | 2 | 4 | 3 | … | … | … | … | … | … | … | 7 | 5 |
| … | … | … | … | … | 7 | 2 | 1 | 1 | 1 | 3 | 3 | 3 | 3 | 4 | 7 | 2 | 2 | … | … | … | … | … | … | 11 | 6 |
| … | … | … | … | … | 8 | 4 | 6 | 5 | 14 | 10 | … | 1 | 11 | 11 | 22 | 3 | 1 | … | … | … | … | … | … | 26 | 7 |
| … | … | … | … | … | 21 | 15 | 18 | 17 | 12 | 30 | 12 | 7 | 9 | 16 | 25 | 25 | 20 | … | 1 | … | … | … | … | 71 | 8 |
| … | … | … | … | … | 2 | 2 | 3 | 1 | 2 | 3 | 1 | 2 | 3 | 4 | 7 | … | 1 | … | … | … | … | … | … | 8 | 9 |
| … | … | … | … | … | 3 | 7 | 10 | 4 | 7 | 13 | 1 | 1 | 11 | 5 | 16 | 6 | 2 | … | … | … | … | … | … | 24 | 10 |
| … | … | … | … | … | 23 | 26 | 24 | 13 | 30 | 42 | 6 | … | 32 | 27 | 59 | 15 | 9 | 1 | 2 | 24 | 3 | … | … | 86 | 11 |
| … | … | … | … | … | 1 | 1 | 1 | 3 | 5 | 1 | … | … | 3 | 3 | 6 | … | … | … | … | … | … | … | … | 6 | 12 |
| … | … | … | … | … | … | … | 1 | … | … | … | … | … | … | … | … | … | 1 | … | … | … | … | … | … | 1 | 13 |
| … | … | … | … | … | 3 | 4 | 4 | 5 | 2 | 2 | … | 4 | 16 | … | 16 | … | … | … | … | … | … | … | … | 16 | 14 |
| … | … | … | … | … | 2 | … | 3 | … | 2 | 3 | … | … | 1 | 4 | 5 | … | … | … | … | … | … | … | … | 5 | 15 |
| … | … | … | … | … | … | 1 | … | … | … | … | … | 1 | … | 1 | 1 | … | … | … | … | … | … | … | … | 1 | 16 |
| … | … | … | … | … | 2 | 1 | 1 | … | 1 | … | … | … | 1 | … | 1 | 3 | … | … | … | … | … | … | … | 4 | 17 |
| … | … | … | … | … | … | … | 1 | … | … | … | … | … | 1 | … | 1 | … | … | … | … | … | … | … | … | 1 | 18 |
| … | … | … | … | … | 2 | 5 | 4 | 1 | … | 2 | 4 | 2 | 4 | 5 | 9 | 1 | 2 | … | … | … | … | … | … | 12 | 19 |
| … | … | … | … | … | … | 1 | 1 | … | 2 | … | … | … | … | 1 | 1 | 1 | … | … | … | … | … | … | … | 2 | 20 |
| … | … | … | … | … | 1 | … | … | … | … | 1 | … | … | … | … | … | … | 1 | … | … | … | … | … | … | 1 | 21 |
| … | … | … | … | … | 1 | … | … | … | … | … | … | … | 1 | … | 1 | … | … | … | … | … | … | … | … | 1 | 22 |
| … | … | … | … | … | 2 | 1 | … | … | … | 1 | 1 | 1 | 1 | … | 1 | 2 | … | … | … | … | … | … | … | 3 | 23 |
| … | … | … | … | … | 1 | 2 | 1 | … | … | … | 2 | 1 | 2 | … | 2 | 1 | 1 | … | … | … | … | … | … | 4 | 24 |
| … | … | … | … | … | 1 | … | 1 | … | … | … | … | … | 2 | … | 2 | … | … | … | … | … | … | … | … | 2 | 25 |
| … | … | … | … | … | … | 1 | … | … | … | 1 | … | … | 1 | … | 1 | … | … | … | … | … | … | … | … | 1 | 26 |
| … | … | … | 3 | … | 9 | 13 | 7 | 13 | 2 | 7 | 2 | 5 | 9 | 13 | 22 | 10 | 10 | … | … | … | … | … | … | 42 | 27 |
| … | … | … | … | … | 2 | 2 | 1 | 3 | 1 | 1 | 1 | 2 | 1 | 5 | 6 | 1 | 1 | … | … | … | … | … | … | 8 | 28 |
| … | … | … | 1 | … | 9 | 6 | 4 | 4 | 6 | 6 | 3 | 6 | 10 | 6 | 16 | 3 | 3 | 1 | … | … | … | … | … | 23 | 29 |
| … | … | … | … | … | 56 | 45 | 23 | 60 | 26 | 135 | 20 | 9 | 63 | 41 | 104 | 47 | 33 | 4 | 2 | … | … | … | … | 190 | 30 |
| … | … | … | … | … | 2 | 1 | 2 | … | 1 | 2 | … | 1 | 2 | … | 2 | 1 | 2 | … | … | … | … | … | … | 5 | 31 |
| … | … | … | … | … | … | 1 | … | … | … | … | … | … | 1 | … | 1 | … | … | … | … | … | … | … | … | 1 | 32 |
| … | … | … | … | … | 1 | … | 1 | 2 | 3 | 1 | … | … | 1 | 1 | 2 | … | 2 | … | … | … | … | … | … | 4 | 33 |
| … | … | … | … | … | 4 | 2 | 2 | 1 | … | 3 | 1 | 4 | 4 | 2 | 6 | 2 | 1 | … | … | … | … | … | … | 9 | 34 |
| … | … | … | … | … | 1 | 6 | 1 | 1 | … | … | 2 | 4 | 4 | … | 4 | 2 | 3 | … | … | … | … | … | … | 9 | 35 |
| … | … | … | … | … | 11 | 10 | 10 | 5 | 1 | 4 | 1 | 14 | 8 | 7 | 15 | 8 | 11 | 1 | 1 | … | … | … | … | 36 | 36 |
| … | … | … | … | … | 20 | 5 | … | 10 | 3 | 28 | 4 | … | 14 | 5 | 19 | 10 | 6 | … | … | … | … | … | … | 35 | 37 |
| … | … | … | … | … | 1 | … | 4 | 1 | 1 | 1 | … | 3 | 2 | 2 | 4 | 2 | … | … | … | … | … | … | … | 6 | 38 |
| … | … | … | … | … | 1 | 1 | … | … | … | … | … | … | … | … | … | … | 2 | … | … | … | … | … | … | 2 | 39 |
| … | … | … | … | … | 8 | 3 | 9 | 5 | 25 | … | … | … | 1 | 3 | 4 | 11 | 10 | … | … | … | … | … | … | 25 | 40 |
| … | … | … | … | … | 2 | … | … | … | … | 1 | … | … | 2 | … | 2 | … | … | … | … | … | … | … | … | 2 | 41 |
| … | … | … | … | … | … | … | 1 | … | … | … | … | … | … | … | … | 1 | … | … | … | … | … | … | … | 1 | 42 |
| … | 1 | … | … | … | 3 | 9 | 7 | 3 | 4 | 5 | 8 | 3 | 8 | 7 | 15 | 5 | 2 | … | … | … | … | … | … | 22 | 43 |
| … | … | … | … | … | 2 | … | … | 1 | 2 | … | … | 1 | 1 | … | 1 | 2 | … | … | … | … | … | … | … | 3 | 44 |
| … | … | … | … | … | … | 1 | 1 | … | 1 | 1 | … | … | 1 | 1 | 2 | … | … | … | … | … | … | … | … | 2 | 45 |
| … | … | … | … | … | 3 | 2 | 3 | 3 | … | 6 | 3 | 1 | 4 | 2 | 6 | … | 4 | … | 1 | … | … | … | … | 11 | 46 |
| … | … | … | … | … | 1 | 2 | 1 | … | … | 2 | … | 2 | 1 | 3 | 4 | … | … | … | … | … | … | … | … | 4 | 47 |
| … | … | … | … | … | … | 2 | … | 1 | 1 | … | … | 1 | … | 1 | 1 | … | 2 | … | … | … | … | … | … | 3 | 48 |
| … | … | … | … | … | 1 | 2 | 2 | 1 | … | 2 | … | 3 | 2 | 1 | 3 | 2 | 1 | … | … | … | … | … | … | 6 | 49 |
| … | … | … | … | … | 10 | 12 | 12 | 11 | 13 | 22 | 5 | 1 | 9 | 13 | 22 | 11 | 8 | 3 | 1 | … | … | … | … | 45 | 50 |
| … | 5 | … | 1 | … | 188 | 151 | 159 | 144 | 125 | 129 | 60 | 64 | 216 | 196 | 412 | 129 | 132 | 8 | 7 | 1 | … | … | … | 689 | 51 |
| … | 28 | 6 | 12 | … | 827 | 801 | 739 | 633 | 809 | 886 | 324 | 374 | 1028 | 867 | 1895 | 571 | 526 | 38 | 29 | 2 | … | 1 | … | 3062 | |

## SECTION OF THE STATE OF TENNESSEE.

*ilton, Jackson, Marion, Morgan, Overton, Rhea, Scott, Smith, Sumner, Van Buren, Warren, Wilson.*

| California and Territories. | Ireland. | Germany. | Other foreign countries. | Unknown. | Spring. | Summer. | Autumn. | Winter. | Under 1 week. | 1 week and under 1 month. | 1 month and under 3 months. | 3 months and over. | Males. | Females. | Total. | Slaves Black M. | Slaves Black F. | Slaves Mulatto M. | Slaves Mulatto F. | Free Black M. | Free Black F. | Free Mul. M | Free Mul. F. | Aggregate deaths. | |
|---|---|---|---|---|---|---|---|---|---|---|---|---|---|---|---|---|---|---|---|---|---|---|---|---|---|
| … | … | … | … | … | 1 | … | … | 1 | 1 | … | … | 1 | … | 2 | 2 | … | … | … | … | … | … | … | … | 2 | 1 |
| … | … | … | … | … | 8 | 6 | 11 | 9 | 11 | 6 | 1 | 1 | 22 | 5 | 27 | 5 | 2 | … | 1 | … | … | … | … | 35 | 2 |
| … | … | … | … | … | 4 | 2 | 6 | 3 | 7 | 5 | … | 2 | 6 | 6 | 12 | 1 | 2 | … | … | … | … | … | … | 15 | 3 |
| … | … | … | … | … | 6 | 4 | 4 | … | 14 | … | … | … | 5 | … | 5 | 3 | 6 | … | … | … | … | … | … | 14 | 4 |
| … | … | … | … | … | … | … | 2 | 1 | … | 2 | … | 1 | 2 | 1 | 3 | … | … | … | … | … | … | … | … | 3 | 5 |
| … | … | … | … | … | … | … | 1 | … | 1 | … | … | … | 1 | … | 1 | … | … | … | … | … | … | … | … | 1 | 6 |
| … | … | … | … | … | 1 | 4 | 1 | 1 | 3 | 1 | 2 | 1 | 1 | 6 | 7 | 1 | … | … | … | … | … | … | … | 8 | 7 |
| … | … | … | … | … | 1 | … | … | 1 | … | 1 | … | 1 | … | 2 | 2 | … | 1 | … | … | … | … | … | … | 3 | 8 |
| … | … | … | … | … | … | 1 | … | … | 1 | … | … | … | 1 | … | 1 | … | … | … | … | … | … | … | … | 1 | 9 |
| … | … | … | … | … | 3 | 3 | 6 | 3 | … | … | 5 | 10 | 11 | 5 | 16 | … | 1 | … | … | … | … | … | … | 17 | 10 |
| … | … | … | … | … | 1 | 1 | … | … | … | 1 | 1 | … | … | 1 | 1 | … | 1 | … | … | … | … | … | … | 2 | 11 |
| … | … | … | … | … | 1 | … | … | 1 | … | … | 1 | 1 | 1 | 1 | 2 | … | … | … | … | … | … | … | … | 2 | 12 |
| … | … | … | … | … | 3 | 4 | 2 | 4 | 7 | 4 | 1 | … | … | 12 | 12 | … | 1 | … | … | … | … | … | … | 13 | 13 |
| … | 1 | … | … | … | 5 | 94 | 154 | 9 | 219 | 15 | 1 | … | 76 | 70 | 146 | 55 | 48 | 2 | 4 | 1 | … | 2 | 4 | 262 | 14 |

## CLASSIFICATION OF DEATHS IN EASTERN CENTRE

| | Cause of Death. | AGES. | | | | | | | | | | | | | | | | | | NATIVITIES. | | | | | |
|---|---|---|---|---|---|---|---|---|---|---|---|---|---|---|---|---|---|---|---|---|---|---|---|---|---|
| | | Under 1. | | 1 and under 5. | | 5 and under 10. | | 10 and under 20. | | 20 and under 50. | | 50 and under 80. | | 80 and under 100. | | 100 & over. | | Age unknown. | | Born in State. | N. England States. | Middle States. | Southern States. | Southwest'n States. | Northwest'n States. |
| | | M. | F. | M. | F. | M. | F. | M. | F. | M. | F. | M. | F. | M | F. | M | F. | M | F. | | | | | | |
| 1 | Cholera infantum | 1 | 4 | 4 | 1 | | 1 | | | | | | | | | | | | | 10 | | | 1 | | |
| 2 | ...do...morbus | 4 | | 1 | 1 | | | 1 | | | 1 | | | | | | | | | 8 | | | | | |
| 3 | Colic | | 1 | | | | | | | 1 | 1 | 2 | 1 | | | | | | | 3 | | | 3 | | |
| 4 | Congestion | | | | | | | 1 | | 1 | | | | | | | | | | 2 | | | | | |
| 5 | Consumption | | 4 | 2 | 5 | 1 | 1 | 9 | 18 | 50 | 64 | 18 | 20 | | | | | | | 144 | | 1 | 44 | | 2 |
| 6 | Convulsions | 2 | 4 | 3 | 2 | 1 | | 3 | 2 | 5 | 1 | | | 1 | | | | | | 21 | | | 2 | | |
| 7 | Cramp | 1 | 1 | | | | | | | | | | | | | | | | | 2 | | | | | |
| 8 | Croup | 39 | 33 | 23 | 28 | 7 | 2 | | | | | | | | | | | | | 131 | | | 1 | | |
| 9 | Diabetes | | | | | | | | | 1 | | 1 | | | | | | | | 2 | | | | | |
| 10 | Diarrhœa | 4 | 5 | 1 | 6 | 2 | | 2 | | 3 | | 3 | 3 | | | | | | | 23 | | | 5 | | |
| 11 | Dirt eating | | | | | 1 | | 1 | | | | | | | | | | | | 2 | | | | | |
| 12 | Dropsy | 2 | 2 | 3 | 5 | 5 | 5 | 12 | 7 | 10 | 20 | 16 | 16 | 4 | 4 | | | | | 64 | | | 42 | | 5 |
| 13 | Dysentery | 7 | 4 | 17 | 18 | 4 | 3 | 4 | 1 | 2 | 11 | 3 | 2 | | | | | | | 68 | | | 8 | | |
| 14 | Dyspepsia | | | | | 1 | | | | | 1 | 3 | 2 | | | | | | | 3 | | 1 | 3 | | |
| 15 | Erysipelas | 1 | 1 | 1 | | | | | 1 | | | | | | | | | | | 3 | | | 1 | | |
| 16 | Executed | | | | | | | | | 1 | | | | | | | | | | 1 | | | | | |
| 17 | Fever, not specified | 7 | 12 | 17 | 23 | 15 | 16 | 30 | 49 | 44 | 50 | 6 | 3 | 1 | 1 | | | | | 241 | | | 28 | | 5 |
| 18 | ..do..bilious | | | | | | | | 1 | 1 | 2 | | | | | | | | | 3 | | | 1 | | |
| 19 | ..do..brain | 1 | 1 | 2 | 1 | | 1 | | | | | | | | | | | | | 6 | | | | | |
| 20 | ..do..congestive | 1 | | 1 | | | | 1 | 3 | 1 | 5 | 1 | 3 | | | | | | | 12 | | | 4 | | |
| 21 | ..do..intermittent | 1 | 1 | 1 | | | 1 | | | | | 1 | | | | | | | | 4 | | | 1 | | |
| 22 | ..do..puerperal | | | | | | | | | | 4 | | | | | | | | | 4 | | | | | |
| 23 | ..do..scarlet | 3 | 3 | 12 | 12 | 6 | 5 | 1 | 2 | 1 | 1 | | | | | | | | | 46 | | | | | |
| 24 | ..do..typhus | 4 | | 5 | 2 | 3 | 4 | 9 | 11 | 20 | 18 | 5 | | | | | | | | 64 | 1 | | 14 | | 2 |
| 25 | ..do..winter | | | 1 | | | | | | | 1 | | | | | | | | | 2 | | | | | |
| 26 | Fracture | | | | | | | | | | | 1 | | | | | | | | | | | 1 | | |
| 27 | Gout | | | | | | | | | | | | 1 | | | | | | | 1 | | | | | |
| 28 | Gravel | | | | | | | 1 | | | | 7 | | 3 | | | | | | 3 | | | 8 | | |
| 29 | Heart, disease of | | | | | | | | | 1 | | | | | | | | | | 1 | | | | | |
| 30 | Hemorrhage | | | | | | | | | 3 | 2 | 2 | | | | | | | | 4 | | | 3 | | |
| 31 | Hives | 21 | 14 | 7 | 5 | | 1 | | | | | | | | | | | | | 48 | | | | | |
| 32 | Hooping cough | 5 | | 2 | 2 | | | | | | | | | | | | | | | 9 | | | | | |
| 33 | Hydrocephalus | 2 | | 1 | | | | 1 | | | | | | | | | | | | 4 | | | | | |
| 34 | Inflamat'n, not spec'd | | 1 | | | | | | | | | | | | | | | | | 1 | | | | | |
| 35 | ....do....brain | 5 | 8 | 5 | 6 | 1 | 1 | | 1 | | 1 | 2 | 1 | | | | | | | 29 | 1 | | 1 | | |
| 36 | ....do....stomach | | | 1 | | | | | | 2 | 1 | 1 | | | | | | | | 3 | | 1 | 1 | | |
| 37 | Influenza | | | | | 1 | | | | | | | | | | | | | | | | | 1 | | |
| 38 | Intemperance | | | | | 1 | | | | 1 | 1 | 2 | | | | | | | | 1 | | | 2 | | 1 |
| 39 | Jaundice | 1 | | | | | | | | | | | | | | | | | | 1 | | | | | |
| 40 | Killed | | | | | | | 1 | | 2 | | | | | | | | | | 3 | | | | | |
| 41 | Liver, disease of | | | | | 1 | | 1 | | 4 | 1 | 1 | 1 | | | | | | | 6 | | | 3 | | |
| 42 | Lockjaw | | | 1 | | | | 1 | | | | | | | | | | | | 2 | | | | | |
| 43 | Measles | | | 3 | | 2 | | | | | 1 | | | | | | | | | 5 | | | 1 | | |
| 44 | Milk sickness | | | | | | 1 | | | 2 | 1 | | | | | | | | | 4 | | | | | |
| 45 | Mumps | | | | | | | | 1 | | | | | | | | | | | 1 | | | | | |
| 46 | Murder | | | | | | | | | | | 2 | | | | | | | | 1 | | | 1 | | |
| 47 | Old age | | | | | | | | | | | 8 | 8 | 18 | 37 | | | | | 8 | 1 | 4 | 58 | | |
| 48 | Paralysis | | | | | | 1 | | 1 | | 4 | 7 | 5 | 1 | 3 | | | | | 7 | 1 | | 13 | | |
| 49 | Piles | | | | | | | | | | | 1 | | | | | | | | | | | 1 | | |
| 50 | Pleurisy | | 1 | 2 | 3 | 1 | | | 2 | 5 | 2 | 3 | 3 | | | | | | | 15 | | | 7 | | |
| 51 | Pneumonia | 2 | 1 | 1 | 1 | 2 | 1 | 5 | 1 | 4 | 4 | 5 | 4 | | | | | | | 25 | | | 6 | | |
| 52 | Poison | | | 1 | | | | | | 2 | 1 | 1 | | | | | | | | 4 | | 1 | | | |
| 53 | Prematurity of birth | 6 | 3 | | | | | | | | | | | | | | | | | 9 | | | | | |
| 54 | Quinsy | 1 | 1 | | 1 | 1 | | | | | 2 | | | | | | | | | 6 | | | | | |
| 55 | Rheumatism | | | | | | 1 | 1 | | 1 | | | 1 | 1 | | | | | | 3 | 1 | | 1 | | |
| 56 | Rickets | | | | 1 | | | | | | | | | | | | | | | 1 | | | | | |
| 57 | Scrofula | 2 | | 7 | | | 1 | 2 | 1 | 1 | 5 | | | | | | | | | 18 | | | 1 | | |
| 58 | Small pox | 1 | | | 1 | 1 | | | 1 | 3 | | | 1 | | | | | | | 6 | | | 2 | | |
| 59 | Spine, disease of | | 1 | 2 | 3 | 1 | 1 | 1 | 2 | 5 | 5 | 2 | 3 | | | | | | | 19 | | | 6 | | 1 |
| 60 | Stillborn | 3 | | | | | | | | | | | | | | | | | | 3 | | | | | |
| 61 | Suffocation | 7 | 1 | 1 | | | | | | | | | | | | | | | | 9 | | | | | |
| 62 | Suicide | | | | | | | 1 | | 1 | | | | | | | | | | 2 | | | | | |
| 63 | Syphilis | | | | | | | | | | 1 | | | | | | | | | 1 | | | | | |
| 64 | Teething | 3 | 3 | 9 | 4 | | | | | | | | | | | | | | | 18 | | | 1 | | |
| 65 | Thrush | 2 | 1 | 1 | | | | | | | | | | | | | | | | 4 | | | | | |
| 66 | Tumor | | | | | | | | | 1 | | | 1 | | | | | | | 1 | | | 1 | | |
| 67 | Ulcer | | | | | | | | | | 1 | | | | | | | | | 1 | | | | | |
| 68 | Uterus, disease of | | | | | | | | | | 1 | | | | | | | | | 1 | | | | | |
| 69 | White swelling | | | | | | | | 1 | | | | | | | | | | | 1 | | | | | |
| 70 | Worms | 2 | 5 | 16 | 12 | 5 | 2 | | 1 | | 1 | | | | | | | | | 42 | | | 2 | | |
| 71 | Unknown | 97 | 102 | 50 | 32 | 16 | 11 | 28 | 33 | 38 | 56 | 40 | 51 | 5 | 5 | | | | | 467 | | 2 | 88 | | 5 |
| | Total | 254 | 232 | 226 | 206 | 88 | 70 | 135 | 170 | 294 | 339 | 194 | 155 | 33 | 54 | | | | | 1953 | 5 | 15 | 439 | | 30 |

ECTION OF THE STATE OF TENNESSEE—Continued.

| NATIVITIES. | | | | | SEASON OF DECEASE. | | | | DURATION OF SICKNESS. | | | | WHITES. | | | COLORED. | | | | | | | | | |
|---|---|---|---|---|---|---|---|---|---|---|---|---|---|---|---|---|---|---|---|---|---|---|---|---|---|
| | | | | | | | | | | | | | | | | Slaves. | | | | Free. | | | | | |
| | | | | | | | | | | | | | | | | Black. | | Mulatto. | | Black. | | Mul. | | | |
| ritories. | Ireland. | Germany. | Other foreign countries. | Unknown | Spring. | Summer. | Autumn. | Winter. | Under 1 week. | 1 week and under 1 month. | 1 month and under 3 months. | 3 months and over. | Males. | Females. | Total. | M. | F. | M. | F. | M. | F. | M | F. | Aggregate deaths. | |
| | | | | | | 2 | 7 | 1 | 4 | 6 | | | 4 | 5 | 9 | 1 | 1 | | | | | | | 11 | 1 |
| | | | | | 1 | 4 | 3 | | 2 | 6 | | | 6 | 2 | 8 | | | | | | | | | 8 | 2 |
| | | | | | 2 | 2 | 1 | 1 | 4 | 2 | | | 3 | 2 | 5 | | 1 | | | | | | | 6 | 3 |
| | | | | | | 2 | | | 1 | 1 | | | 2 | | 2 | | | | | | | | | 2 | 4 |
| | | 1 | | | 58 | 50 | 44 | 40 | 5 | 13 | 33 | 107 | 55 | 87 | 142 | 24 | 19 | | 6 | 1 | | | | 192 | 5 |
| | 1 | | | | 6 | 7 | 4 | 7 | 6 | 2 | 1 | 1 | 12 | 7 | 19 | 3 | 2 | | | | | | | 24 | 6 |
| | | | | | 1 | | | 1 | 2 | | | | 1 | 1 | 2 | | | | | | | | | 2 | 7 |
| | | | | | 33 | 29 | 40 | 29 | 93 | 22 | 9 | 1 | 56 | 51 | 107 | 13 | 11 | | 1 | | | | | 132 | 8 |
| | | | | | | 1 | 1 | | | 1 | | | 2 | | 2 | | | | | | | | | 2 | 9 |
| | | | | 1 | 6 | 8 | 14 | 1 | 6 | 14 | 6 | 3 | 14 | 11 | 25 | 1 | 3 | | | | | | | 29 | 10 |
| | | | | | | 2 | | | 1 | | | 1 | 2 | | 2 | | | | | | | | | 2 | 11 |
| | | | | | 33 | 33 | 24 | 21 | 9 | 11 | 23 | 58 | 43 | 40 | 83 | 8 | 17 | 1 | | | | | 2 | 111 | 12 |
| | | | | | 2 | 32 | 35 | 7 | 8 | 56 | 12 | | 32 | 32 | 64 | 4 | 6 | 1 | 1 | | | | | 76 | 13 |
| | | | | | 2 | 2 | 3 | | | | 3 | 4 | 4 | 3 | 7 | | | | | | | | | 7 | 14 |
| | | | | | 1 | | 3 | | | | 2 | 1 | 2 | 2 | 4 | | | | | | | | | 4 | 15 |
| | | | | | 1 | | | | 1 | | | | 1 | | 1 | | | | | | | | | 1 | 16 |
| | | | | | 63 | 43 | 102 | 58 | 38 | 182 | 47 | 7 | 89 | 118 | 207 | 30 | 33 | 1 | 3 | | | | | 274 | 17 |
| | | | | | | 1 | 3 | | | 2 | 2 | | 1 | 3 | 4 | | | | | | | | | 4 | 18 |
| | | | | | 1 | 4 | 1 | | 1 | 5 | | | 3 | 2 | 5 | | 1 | | | | | | | 6 | 19 |
| | | | | | 5 | 3 | 6 | 2 | 6 | 5 | 1 | | 5 | 10 | 15 | | 1 | | | | | | | 16 | 20 |
| | | | | | 1 | 3 | 1 | | 1 | 1 | 2 | | 3 | 2 | 5 | | | | | | | | | 5 | 21 |
| | | | | | 3 | 1 | | | | 1 | | | | 4 | 4 | | | | | | | | | 4 | 22 |
| | | | | | 10 | 6 | 20 | 10 | 18 | 21 | 4 | 2 | 21 | 20 | 41 | 2 | 3 | | | | | | | 46 | 23 |
| | | | | | 10 | 15 | 35 | 14 | 6 | 57 | 18 | | 29 | 25 | 54 | 16 | 10 | 1 | | | | | | 81 | 24 |
| | | | | | 1 | | 1 | | | | 1 | 1 | 1 | 1 | 2 | | | | | | | | | 2 | 25 |
| | | | | | 1 | | | | | | 1 | | 1 | | 1 | | | | | | | | | 1 | 26 |
| | | | | | 1 | | | | | 1 | | | | | | | 1 | | | | | | | 1 | 27 |
| | | | | | 4 | 3 | 2 | 2 | | 5 | 2 | 3 | 10 | | 10 | 1 | | | | | | | | 11 | 28 |
| | | | | | | | | 1 | | | | 1 | 1 | | 1 | | | | | | | | | 1 | 29 |
| | | | | | 1 | 3 | 1 | 2 | 3 | 1 | | 3 | 1 | 1 | 2 | 4 | 1 | | | | | | | 7 | 30 |
| | | | | | 9 | 12 | 15 | 12 | 32 | 10 | 1 | | 25 | 19 | 44 | 3 | 1 | | | | | | | 48 | 31 |
| | | | | | 3 | 4 | 1 | 1 | | 2 | 6 | | 2 | | 2 | 4 | 1 | 1 | 1 | | | | | 9 | 32 |
| | | | | | | 3 | 1 | | | 4 | | | 2 | | 2 | 2 | | | | | | | | 4 | 33 |
| | | | | | | 1 | | | | 1 | | | | 1 | 1 | | | | | | | | | 1 | 34 |
| | | | | | 5 | 9 | 3 | 11 | 10 | 17 | 3 | | 12 | 17 | 29 | | 1 | 1 | | | | | | 31 | 35 |
| | | | | | 1 | 1 | 3 | | | 3 | | 2 | 2 | 1 | 3 | 2 | | | | 2 | | | | 5 | 36 |
| | | | | | | | | 1 | | 1 | | | 1 | | 1 | | | | | | | | | 1 | 37 |
| | 1 | | | | 2 | 2 | 1 | | 4 | | | 1 | 4 | 1 | 5 | | | | | | | | | 5 | 38 |
| | | | | | | 1 | | | | | | | 1 | | 1 | | | | | | | | | 1 | 39 |
| | | | | | | 1 | | 2 | | | | | 3 | | 3 | | | | | | | | | 3 | 40 |
| | | | | | 3 | 4 | 1 | 1 | 1 | 3 | 2 | 3 | 6 | 2 | 8 | 1 | | | | | | | | 9 | 41 |
| | | | | | 1 | | 1 | | 2 | | | | 1 | | 1 | 1 | | | | | | | | 2 | 42 |
| | | | | | 2 | 1 | | 3 | 1 | | 4 | | 4 | | 4 | 1 | 1 | | | | | | | 6 | 43 |
| | | | | | 1 | 3 | | | 2 | 2 | | | 1 | 2 | 3 | 1 | | | | | | | | 4 | 44 |
| | | | | | | | | | | | | | | 1 | 1 | | | | | | | | | 1 | 45 |
| | | | | | 1 | | 1 | | | | | | 2 | | 2 | | | | | | | | | 2 | 46 |
| | | | | | 17 | 20 | 20 | 14 | 8 | 20 | 7 | 13 | 20 | 36 | 56 | 5 | 9 | 1 | | | | | | 71 | 47 |
| | | | | 1 | 8 | 8 | 2 | 4 | 7 | 1 | 2 | 10 | 7 | 14 | 21 | 1 | | | | | | | | 22 | 48 |
| | | | | | | | | 1 | | | | | 1 | | 1 | | | | | | | | | 1 | 49 |
| | | | | | 4 | 8 | 6 | 4 | 7 | 12 | 3 | | 5 | 6 | 11 | 4 | 5 | 1 | | | | 1 | | 22 | 50 |
| | | | | | 10 | 7 | 7 | 7 | 7 | 21 | 2 | 1 | 17 | 10 | 27 | 2 | 2 | | | | | | | 31 | 51 |
| | | | | | 3 | 1 | | 1 | 2 | 1 | 1 | 1 | 1 | | 1 | 2 | 1 | 1 | | | | | | 5 | 52 |
| | | | | | 1 | 1 | 3 | 4 | | | | | 6 | 3 | 9 | | | | | | | | | 9 | 53 |
| | | | | | 2 | | 1 | 3 | 3 | 3 | | | 2 | 4 | 6 | | | | | | | | | 6 | 54 |
| | | | | | 3 | 1 | | 1 | 1 | | | 4 | 3 | 2 | 5 | | | | | | | | | 5 | 55 |
| | | | | | | 1 | | | 1 | | | | | 1 | 1 | | | | | | | | | 1 | 56 |
| | | | | | 6 | 3 | 7 | 3 | 1 | 4 | 2 | 10 | 5 | | 5 | 6 | 7 | 1 | | | | | | 19 | 57 |
| | | | | | 3 | | | 5 | 2 | 6 | | | 4 | 3 | 7 | 1 | | | | | | | | 8 | 58 |
| | | | | | 20 | 2 | | 3 | 6 | 10 | 3 | 3 | 8 | 15 | 23 | 3 | | | | | | | | 26 | 59 |
| | | | | | 3 | | | | | | | | 2 | | 2 | | | 1 | | | | | | 3 | 60 |
| | | | | | 3 | | 2 | 3 | 9 | | | | 5 | | 5 | 3 | 1 | | | | | | | 9 | 61 |
| | | | | | | 1 | 1 | | | | | | 2 | | 2 | | | | | | | | | 2 | 62 |
| | | | | | | 1 | | | | | | | | | | | 1 | | | | | | | 1 | 63 |
| | | | | | 1 | 8 | 9 | 1 | 6 | 8 | 4 | | 5 | 3 | 8 | 6 | 4 | 1 | | | | | | 19 | 64 |
| | | | | | | | 2 | 2 | 1 | 2 | 1 | | 1 | 1 | 2 | 2 | | | | | | | | 4 | 65 |
| | | | | | 1 | | 1 | | 1 | 1 | | | 1 | 1 | 2 | | | | | | | | | 2 | 66 |
| | | | | | | | 1 | | | 1 | | | | | | | | | | | | | 1 | 1 | 67 |
| | | | | | | 1 | | | | | | | | 1 | 1 | | | | | | | | | 1 | 68 |
| | | | | | | 1 | | | | | 1 | | | 1 | 1 | | | | | | | | | 1 | 69 |
| | | | | | 6 | 13 | 19 | 6 | 19 | 18 | 6 | 1 | 13 | 14 | 27 | 8 | 6 | | 1 | 1 | | 1 | | 44 | 70 |
| | 2 | | | | 142 | 144 | 149 | 102 | 219 | 150 | 81 | 87 | 212 | 205 | 417 | 57 | 75 | 5 | 7 | | | | 3 | 564 | 71 |
| .. | 5 | 1 | ... | 2 | 542 | 638 | 795 | 425 | 331 | 751 | 308 | 347 | 916 | 904 | 1820 | 287 | 287 | 19 | 25 | 3 | ... | 4 | 10 | 2455 | |

## CLASSIFICATION OF DEATHS IN WESTERN CENTRE

*Embracing the following counties: Bedford, Davidson, Decatur, Dickson, Franklin, Giles, Robertson, Rutherford, Stewart,*

| | Cause of death. | AGES. Under 1. | | 1 and under 5. | | 5 and under 10. | | 10 and under 20. | | 20 and under 50. | | 50 and under 80. | | 80 and under 100. | | 100 & over. | | Age unknown. | | NATIVITIES. Born in State. | N. England States. | Middle States. | Southern States. | Southwest'n States. | Northwest'n States. |
|---|---|---|---|---|---|---|---|---|---|---|---|---|---|---|---|---|---|---|---|---|---|---|---|---|---|
| | | M. | F. | M. | F. | M. | F. | M. | F. | M. | F. | M. | F. | M | F. | M | F. | M | F. | | | | | | |
| 1 | Abscess | 1 | 1 | | | | | | | | | 1 | | | | | | | | 1 | | | 1 | | |
| 2 | Accident, not specfi'd | 7 | 5 | 6 | 3 | 6 | 2 | 10 | 2 | 11 | 2 | 5 | 2 | 2 | | | | | | 55 | | | 7 | | 1 |
| 3 | ....do...burned | 3 | 2 | 4 | 11 | 1 | 5 | | 1 | 3 | 3 | | 1 | | | | | | | 32 | | | 1 | | 1 |
| 4 | ....do...drowned | | | 3 | 3 | 2 | 2 | 8 | 1 | 7 | | 2 | 1 | | | | | | | 22 | | | 5 | | 1 |
| 5 | ....do...scalded | | 1 | 2 | 1 | | | | | | | | | | | | | | | 4 | | | | | |
| 6 | ....do...shot | | | | | | | | | 4 | | | | | | | | | | 2 | | | 2 | | |
| 7 | Apoplexy | | | | 1 | | | | 1 | 5 | 10 | 7 | 6 | | | | | | | 15 | | 2 | 9 | | 2 |
| 8 | Asthma | | | 2 | | | | | | 1 | | 1 | | | | | | | | 2 | | | 2 | | |
| 9 | Bowels, disease of | 1 | | 1 | | | | | | | | | | | | | | | | 2 | | | | | |
| 10 | Bronchitis | 2 | 1 | 3 | 2 | | | | 1 | 1 | 4 | 3 | | | | | | | | 15 | | | 1 | | 1 |
| 11 | Cancer | | | | | | | | | 2 | 6 | 8 | 11 | 2 | 3 | | | | | 6 | | | 25 | | 1 |
| 12 | Chicken pox | 1 | | | | | | | | | | | | | | | | | | 1 | | | | | |
| 13 | Childbirth | | | | | | | | 7 | | 39 | | | | | | | | | 35 | | | 10 | | 1 |
| 14 | Cholera | 7 | 7 | 35 | 30 | 19 | 21 | 24 | 34 | 116 | 60 | 28 | 23 | 2 | | | | | | 276 | | 16 | 71 | | 14 |
| 15 | ....do..infantum | 10 | 7 | 9 | 11 | | 1 | | | | | | | | | | | | | 37 | | | 1 | | |
| 16 | ....do..morbus | | 1 | 2 | 1 | | 2 | | | 1 | 4 | 1 | | | | | | | | 9 | | | 2 | | 1 |
| 17 | Colic | | | 2 | | | 1 | | 1 | 6 | 3 | 2 | 3 | 1 | | | | | | 15 | | | 2 | | 2 |
| 18 | Congest'n, not specf'd | | | | 1 | | | | | | | | | | | | | | | 1 | | | | | |
| 19 | Consumption | 5 | 1 | 13 | 10 | 3 | 5 | 16 | 27 | 90 | 104 | 23 | 33 | 3 | 3 | | | | | 240 | | 4 | 79 | | 7 |
| 20 | Convulsions | 7 | 6 | 6 | 2 | 2 | 1 | 2 | | 4 | 7 | 2 | 1 | | | | | | | 34 | | | 5 | | 1 |
| 21 | Croup | 77 | 63 | 45 | 41 | 4 | 10 | | 1 | 1 | | | | | | | | | | 238 | | | 3 | | 1 |
| 22 | Diarrhœa | 10 | 6 | 10 | 8 | 2 | 1 | 1 | | 11 | 5 | 8 | 5 | 1 | | | | | | 53 | | 1 | 12 | | |
| 23 | Dropsy | | 2 | 4 | 5 | 3 | 3 | 14 | 7 | 13 | 33 | 26 | 26 | 2 | 4 | | | | | 75 | | 8 | 52 | | 6 |
| 24 | Dysentery | 4 | 4 | 15 | 11 | 6 | 1 | 1 | | | 4 | 2 | 1 | | | | | | | 42 | | 1 | 5 | | |
| 25 | Dyspepsia | | | | | | | | 1 | 2 | 4 | 3 | 1 | | | | | | | 5 | | | 4 | | 2 |
| 26 | Epilepsy | | | | | | | | | | 1 | | | 1 | | | | | | 1 | | | | | |
| 27 | Erysipelas | 2 | 3 | 3 | 3 | | 1 | 1 | | | 2 | 1 | | | | | | | | 15 | | 1 | | | |
| 28 | Executed | | | | | | | | | 1 | 1 | | | | | | | | | 2 | | | | | |
| 29 | Fever, not specified | 7 | 11 | 20 | 11 | 12 | 7 | 26 | 26 | 43 | 31 | 12 | 5 | | | | | | | 171 | | 1 | 30 | 2 | |
| 30 | ..do..bilious | 3 | 1 | 1 | 2 | 2 | 1 | 1 | 1 | 11 | 5 | 2 | 2 | | | | | | | 23 | | | 9 | | |
| 31 | ..do..brain | | 1 | 2 | | | | | | 1 | | | | | 1 | | | | | 4 | | 1 | | | |
| 32 | ..do..congestive | | 2 | 1 | | 2 | 3 | 2 | 4 | 18 | 8 | 2 | 4 | | | | | | | 35 | | | 8 | | |
| 33 | ..do..intermittent | 2 | | 1 | | 1 | | 2 | | 3 | 2 | 2 | | 1 | 2 | | | | | 11 | | | 5 | | |
| 34 | ..do..puerperal | | | | | | | | 1 | | 3 | | | | | | | | | 4 | | | | | |
| 35 | ..do..scarlet | 3 | 5 | 22 | 10 | 4 | 10 | 3 | 8 | 4 | 3 | | | | | | | | | 69 | | | 3 | | |
| 36 | ..do..typhus | 3 | 4 | 11 | 8 | 11 | 11 | 55 | 39 | 70 | 53 | 11 | 7 | | | | | | | 219 | | 2 | 52 | 1 | |
| 37 | ..do..yellow | | | | | | | | | 1 | | | | | | | | | | 1 | | | | | |
| 38 | Gout | | | | | | | | | | | 1 | | | | | | | | | | | 1 | | |
| 39 | Gravel | | | | | | | | | | | 10 | | 1 | | | | | | | | | 10 | | |
| 40 | Head, disease of | | | | | | | | | | 1 | | | | | | | | | 1 | | | | | |
| 41 | Heart....do | 4 | 1 | | | | 1 | | 1 | 4 | 3 | | 1 | | 1 | | | | | 11 | | | 5 | | |
| 42 | Heat | | | | | | | | | | 1 | | | | | | | | | 1 | | | | | |
| 43 | Hemorrhage | | | | | | | 1 | | 7 | 4 | 1 | 3 | | 1 | | | | | 14 | | | 3 | | |
| 44 | Hernia | | | | | | | | | 1 | | 1 | | | | | | | | | | | 2 | | |
| 45 | Hives | 22 | 20 | 2 | 5 | 1 | | | | | | | | | | | | | | 49 | | | 1 | | |
| 46 | Hooping cough | 16 | 14 | 17 | 15 | 2 | 2 | | | | | | | | | | | | | 66 | | | | | |
| 47 | Hydrocephalus | 3 | 2 | 1 | | | 1 | | | | | | | | | | | | | 7 | | | | | |
| 48 | Inflammation, bowels | 8 | 7 | 9 | 10 | 1 | 2 | 2 | 2 | 8 | 6 | 4 | | | | | | | | 50 | | 1 | 5 | 1 | |
| 49 | ....do.....brain | 24 | 15 | 22 | 14 | 3 | 5 | 3 | 3 | 5 | 6 | 2 | 4 | | | | | | | 96 | | | 10 | | |
| 50 | ....do.....stomach | 1 | | | 1 | | | | | | 4 | 2 | 1 | | 1 | | | | | 5 | | 1 | 4 | | |
| 51 | Influenza | | | 1 | | | | | | | | | | | | | | | | 1 | | | | | |
| 52 | Insanity | | | | | | | | | | 1 | 2 | 1 | | | | | | | 1 | | | 3 | | |
| 53 | Intemperance | | | | | | | | | | | 4 | | | | | | | | 1 | | | 3 | | |
| 54 | Jaundice | | 1 | 1 | | 1 | | | | | | | | | | | | | | 2 | | | 1 | | |
| 55 | Killed | | | | | 1 | | 1 | | 5 | | | | | | | | | | 5 | | | 1 | | |
| 56 | Lightning | | | | | 1 | | | | | | | | | | | | | | 1 | | | | | |
| 57 | Liver, disease of | 2 | | 1 | 1 | | | 1 | | 2 | 5 | 5 | 1 | 1 | | | | | | 11 | | | 6 | | |
| 58 | Lockjaw | 10 | 6 | 1 | 4 | 1 | 4 | | 3 | 2 | 4 | | 1 | | | | | | | 36 | | | | | |
| 59 | Mania-a-potu | | | | | | | | | 2 | | | | | | | | | | 1 | | | 1 | | |
| 60 | Marasmus | 1 | 1 | | | | | | | | | | | | | | | | | 1 | | | 1 | | |
| 61 | Measles | 1 | | 3 | 5 | 2 | 1 | 2 | 4 | 3 | 1 | | | | | | | | | 18 | | | 4 | | |
| 62 | Murder | | | | | | | | | 4 | | 1 | | | | | | | | 3 | | | 1 | | |
| 63 | Neuralgia | | | | | 1 | 1 | | | | | 1 | | | | | | | | 3 | | | | | |
| 64 | Old age | | | | | | | | | 1 | | 16 | 21 | 42 | 47 | 3 | 3 | | | 28 | | 19 | 77 | | |
| 65 | Paralysis | | | | | | | | 1 | 4 | 5 | 12 | 7 | | 3 | | | | | 8 | | 1 | 21 | | |
| 66 | Pleurisy | 1 | 1 | | | 2 | | 1 | | 11 | 2 | 5 | 1 | | | | | | | 18 | | | 6 | | |
| 67 | Pneumonia | 8 | 2 | 15 | 6 | 4 | 2 | 3 | 19 | 22 | 10 | 11 | 9 | | | | | | | 86 | | 6 | 18 | | |
| 68 | Poison | 1 | 1 | 1 | | | | | | 5 | 1 | 1 | | | | | | | | 8 | | | 1 | | |
| 69 | Prematurity of birth | 2 | 2 | | | | | | | | | | | | | | | | | 4 | | | | | |
| 70 | Quinsy | 2 | | 1 | 2 | 1 | 1 | 1 | 1 | 2 | 1 | 1 | | | | | | | | 11 | | | 1 | | |
| 71 | Rheumatism | | | | | 1 | | | 2 | 2 | 2 | 3 | 1 | | | | | | | 6 | | 1 | 4 | | |
| 72 | Scrofula | | 2 | 8 | 5 | 4 | 4 | 4 | 6 | 6 | 3 | 2 | 2 | | | | | | | 40 | | 1 | 4 | | |

SECTION OF THE STATE OF TENNESSEE.

*Hickman, Humphreys, Lawrence, Lewis, Lincoln, Marshall, Maury, Montgomery, Perry, Wayne, and Williamson.*

| Nativities: California and Territories. | Nativities: Ireland. | Nativities: Germany. | Nativities: Other foreign countries. | Nativities: Unknown. | Season of decease: Spring. | Season of decease: Summer. | Season of decease: Autumn. | Season of decease: Winter. | Duration of sickness: Under 1 week. | Duration of sickness: 1 week and under 1 month. | Duration of sickness: 1 month and under 3 months. | Duration of sickness: 3 months and over. | Whites: Males. | Whites: Females. | Whites: Total. | Colored: Slaves: Black: M. | Colored: Slaves: Black: F. | Colored: Slaves: Mulatto: M. | Colored: Slaves: Mulatto: F. | Colored: Free: Black: M. | Colored: Free: Black: F. | Colored: Free: Mul.: M | Colored: Free: Mul.: F. | Aggregate deaths. | |
|---|---|---|---|---|---|---|---|---|---|---|---|---|---|---|---|---|---|---|---|---|---|---|---|---|---|
| | 1 | | | | | 2 | 1 | | 1 | | 1 | 1 | 2 | | 2 | | 1 | | | | | | | 3 | 1 |
| | | | | | 12 | 12 | 19 | 17 | 17 | 8 | 2 | | 30 | 2 | 32 | 16 | 14 | 1 | | | | | | 63 | 2 |
| | | | | | 7 | 2 | 8 | 14 | 11 | 11 | 3 | | 4 | 11 | 15 | 7 | 12 | | | | | | | 34 | 3 |
| | | | 1 | | 4 | 14 | 7 | 4 | 29 | | | | 8 | 6 | 14 | 13 | | 1 | 1 | | | | | 29 | 4 |
| | | | | | | 2 | 1 | 1 | | 4 | | | 1 | 1 | 2 | | 1 | 1 | | | | | | 4 | 5 |
| | | | | | 1 | 1 | 2 | | 1 | | | | 4 | | 4 | | | | | | | | | 4 | 6 |
| | 1 | | 1 | | 11 | 4 | 10 | 5 | 14 | 2 | | | 10 | 9 | 19 | 1 | 9 | 1 | | | | | | 30 | 7 |
| | | | | | 1 | 2 | 1 | | 2 | 1 | | | 2 | | 2 | 2 | | | | | | | | 4 | 8 |
| | | | | | | | 2 | | | 1 | 1 | | 1 | | 1 | 1 | | | | | | | | 2 | 9 |
| | | | | | 3 | 4 | 5 | 5 | | 9 | 2 | 4 | 7 | 6 | 13 | 2 | 2 | | | | | | | 17 | 10 |
| | | | | | 11 | 11 | 6 | 4 | | 1 | 1 | 15 | 10 | 15 | 25 | 2 | 5 | | | | | | | 32 | 11 |
| | | | | | 1 | | | | | 1 | | | | | | 1 | | | | | | | | 1 | 12 |
| | | | | | 17 | 7 | 7 | 13 | 18 | 15 | 4 | | | 36 | 36 | | 9 | | 1 | | | | | 46 | 13 |
| | 10 | 11 | 8 | | 17 | 307 | 33 | 16 | 355 | 43 | 5 | | 163 | 124 | 287 | 54 | 40 | 7 | 6 | 1 | 1 | 6 | 4 | 406 | 14 |
| | | | | | 4 | 17 | 13 | 4 | 14 | 15 | 3 | 3 | 14 | 14 | 28 | 5 | 5 | | | | | | | 38 | 15 |
| | | | | | 1 | 7 | 3 | 1 | 8 | 1 | 2 | | 3 | 3 | 6 | 1 | 4 | | 1 | | | | | 12 | 16 |
| | | | | | 3 | 5 | 7 | 4 | 10 | 7 | 1 | | 5 | 5 | 10 | 6 | 3 | | | | | | | 19 | 17 |
| | | | | | 1 | | | | 1 | | | | | | | | 1 | | | | | | | 1 | 18 |
| | 5 | | 1 | | 108 | 102 | 65 | 61 | 7 | 30 | 53 | 152 | 105 | 124 | 229 | 43 | 56 | 4 | 2 | 1 | 1 | | | 336 | 19 |
| | | | | | 21 | 9 | 2 | 4 | 11 | 6 | 14 | 9 | 19 | 13 | 32 | 4 | 3 | | 1 | | | | | 40 | 20 |
| | | | | | 55 | 51 | 67 | 66 | 159 | 55 | 4 | 5 | 84 | 57 | 141 | 43 | 54 | | 4 | | | | | 242 | 21 |
| | | 1 | 1 | | 6 | 26 | 26 | 10 | 13 | 28 | 8 | 11 | 30 | 17 | 47 | 12 | 8 | 1 | | | | | | 68 | 22 |
| | | | 1 | | 30 | 50 | 30 | 32 | 8 | 16 | 20 | 59 | 40 | 53 | 93 | 21 | 22 | | 5 | 1 | | | | 142 | 23 |
| | | 1 | | | | 28 | 19 | 2 | 14 | 25 | 3 | 5 | 21 | 16 | 37 | 7 | 5 | | | | | | | 49 | 24 |
| | | | | | 4 | 2 | 3 | 2 | 3 | 3 | 1 | 3 | 5 | 5 | 10 | | 1 | | | | | | | 11 | 25 |
| | | | | | 1 | | 1 | | | 1 | | | 1 | 1 | 2 | | | | | | | | | 2 | 26 |
| | | | | | 5 | 4 | 2 | 5 | | 13 | 1 | 1 | 6 | 7 | 13 | 1 | 2 | | | | | | | 16 | 27 |
| | | | | | | 2 | | | 2 | | | | | | | 1 | 1 | | | | | | | 2 | 28 |
| | 3 | | | | 35 | 66 | 75 | 34 | 29 | 135 | 36 | 11 | 91 | 56 | 147 | 28 | 33 | | 2 | | | 1 | | 211 | 29 |
| | | | | | 7 | 10 | 12 | 3 | 3 | 27 | 2 | | 15 | 10 | 25 | 3 | 1 | | | 1 | | 1 | 1 | 32 | 30 |
| | | | | | 1 | 3 | 1 | | | 5 | | | 1 | 1 | 2 | 1 | 1 | 1 | | | | | | 5 | 31 |
| | | | | | 5 | 15 | 21 | 5 | 20 | 22 | 4 | | 22 | 14 | 36 | 3 | 6 | | 1 | | | | | 46 | 32 |
| | | | | | 3 | 2 | 8 | 3 | 4 | 8 | 2 | | 10 | 4 | 14 | 2 | | | | | | | | 16 | 33 |
| | | | | | 2 | 2 | | | 1 | 3 | | | | 2 | 2 | | 2 | | | | | | | 4 | 34 |
| | | | | | 12 | 21 | 18 | 21 | 22 | 41 | 6 | 2 | 28 | 25 | 53 | 8 | 11 | | | | | | | 72 | 35 |
| | 1 | | | | 80 | 60 | 90 | 53 | 20 | 208 | 50 | 5 | 98 | 63 | 161 | 59 | 56 | 3 | 2 | 1 | | | 1 | 283 | 36 |
| | | | | | | | 1 | | 1 | | | | 1 | | 1 | | | | | | | | | 1 | 37 |
| | | | | | 1 | | | | | 1 | | | 1 | | 1 | | | | | | | | | 1 | 38 |
| | | | | | 6 | 2 | 1 | 2 | 1 | 4 | 4 | 2 | 10 | | 10 | 1 | | | | | | | | 11 | 39 |
| | | | | | 1 | | | | | | 1 | | | 1 | 1 | | | | | | | | | 1 | 40 |
| | | | | | 2 | 4 | 2 | 8 | 4 | 5 | 1 | 2 | 7 | 7 | 14 | 1 | 1 | | | | | | | 16 | 41 |
| | | | | | | 1 | | | 1 | | | | | 1 | 1 | | | | | | | | | 1 | 42 |
| | | | | | 3 | 2 | 7 | 5 | 2 | 3 | 3 | 4 | 5 | 3 | 8 | 4 | 5 | | | | | | | 17 | 43 |
| | | | | | 1 | 1 | | | | 1 | | | | | | 2 | | | | | | | | 2 | 44 |
| | | | | | 10 | 4 | 15 | 14 | 31 | 13 | 3 | | 19 | 22 | 41 | 5 | 2 | 1 | | | | | 1 | 50 | 45 |
| | | | | | 6 | 34 | 15 | 11 | 12 | 33 | 14 | 6 | 13 | 12 | 25 | 20 | 17 | 2 | 2 | | | | | 66 | 46 |
| | | | | | 3 | 1 | 1 | 2 | 1 | 3 | 2 | | 3 | 3 | 6 | 1 | | | | | | | | 7 | 47 |
| | 2 | | | | 11 | 19 | 20 | 5 | 12 | 30 | 8 | 3 | 20 | 23 | 43 | 12 | 3 | | 1 | | | | | 59 | 48 |
| | | | | | 28 | 36 | 24 | 17 | 35 | 45 | 13 | 3 | 43 | 33 | 76 | 16 | 13 | | | | | | 1 | 106 | 49 |
| | | | | | 3 | 3 | 3 | 1 | 1 | 7 | 2 | | 2 | 6 | 8 | | 1 | 1 | | | | | | 10 | 50 |
| | | | | | | | 1 | | 1 | | | | | | | 1 | | | | | | | | 1 | 51 |
| | | | | | 1 | | 1 | 2 | | 1 | | 2 | 1 | 2 | 3 | 1 | | | | | | | | 4 | 52 |
| | | | | | 3 | 1 | | | 1 | 1 | 1 | 1 | 4 | | 4 | | | | | | | | | 4 | 53 |
| | | | | | 1 | 1 | 1 | | 1 | | 1 | | 2 | 1 | 3 | | | | | | | | | 3 | 54 |
| | 1 | | | | 3 | 2 | 2 | | 1 | 1 | | | 5 | | 5 | 2 | | | | | | | | 7 | 55 |
| | | | | | 1 | | | | 1 | | | | | | | 1 | | | | | | | | 1 | 56 |
| | | | | | 4 | 9 | 2 | 3 | 2 | 5 | 6 | 6 | 11 | 6 | 17 | 1 | 1 | | | | | | | 19 | 57 |
| | | | | | 5 | 16 | 10 | 5 | 23 | 6 | 1 | 1 | 6 | 5 | 11 | 8 | 16 | | 1 | | | | | 36 | 58 |
| | | | | | | 1 | 1 | | | 2 | | | 2 | | 2 | | | | | | | | | 2 | 59 |
| | | | | | | 1 | | | | 1 | | | | 1 | 1 | 1 | | | | | | | | 2 | 60 |
| | | | | | 5 | 9 | 2 | 6 | | 7 | 1 | 4 | 4 | 5 | 9 | 7 | 6 | | | | | | | 22 | 61 |
| | | | | | 3 | 1 | | 1 | 1 | | | 1 | 3 | | 3 | 1 | | 1 | | | | | | 5 | 62 |
| | | | | | | 1 | 2 | | | 2 | | 1 | | | | 2 | 1 | | | | | | | 3 | 63 |
| | 3 | | 5 | | 37 | 30 | 37 | 25 | 7 | 28 | 12 | 14 | 42 | 43 | 85 | 19 | 28 | 1 | | | | | | 133 | 64 |
| | 1 | | | | 10 | 3 | 8 | 10 | 6 | 9 | 2 | 7 | 14 | 13 | 27 | 2 | 2 | | | | | | 1 | 32 | 65 |
| | | | | | 12 | 4 | 3 | 5 | 6 | 13 | 4 | | 14 | 1 | 15 | 6 | 3 | | | | | | | 24 | 66 |
| | | | | | 46 | 19 | 23 | 23 | 18 | 75 | 9 | 4 | 35 | 28 | 63 | 26 | 17 | 1 | 3 | 1 | | | | 111 | 67 |
| | | | | | 1 | 2 | 2 | 5 | 5 | 3 | 2 | | 4 | | 4 | 4 | 2 | | | | | | | 10 | 68 |
| | | | | | | 2 | | 2 | 1 | | | | 1 | 1 | 2 | 1 | 1 | | | | | | | 4 | 69 |
| | | | | | 3 | 3 | 3 | 4 | 3 | 9 | 1 | | 5 | 4 | 9 | 3 | 1 | | | | | | | 13 | 70 |
| | | | | | 7 | 2 | 2 | | 1 | 4 | 1 | 4 | 4 | 4 | 8 | 2 | 1 | | | | | | | 11 | 71 |
| | | | | | 14 | 11 | 12 | 7 | 1 | 9 | 3 | 14 | 5 | 6 | 11 | 19 | 15 | | 1 | | | | | 46 | 72 |

## CLASSIFICATION OF DEATHS IN WESTERN CENTRE

| | Cause of death. | AGES. Under 1. M. | F. | 1 and under 5. M. | F. | 5 and under 10. M. | F. | 10 and under 20. M. | F. | 20 and under 50. M. | F. | 50 and under 80. M. | F. | 80 and under 100. M | F. | 100 & over. M | F. | Age unknown. M | F. | NATIVITIES. Born in State. | N. England States. | Middle States. | Southern States. | Southwest'n States. | Northwest'n States. |
|---|---|---|---|---|---|---|---|---|---|---|---|---|---|---|---|---|---|---|---|---|---|---|---|---|---|
| 1 | Small pox | | 2 | 1 | 1 | | | 1 | 2 | 6 | 2 | 1 | 2 | | | | | | | 14 | | 1 | 3 | | |
| 2 | Spine, disease of | | | | | | | 1 | | | 1 | | | | | | | | | 1 | | | | | 1 |
| 3 | Spleen... do | | | | | | | | 1 | | | | | | | | | | | 1 | | | | | |
| 4 | Stillborn | 11 | 6 | | | | | | | | | | | | | | | | | 17 | | | | | |
| 5 | Suffocation | 19 | 20 | | 2 | | | | | | | | | | | | | | | 40 | | | 1 | | |
| 6 | Suicide | | | | | | | | | 1 | 1 | 2 | | | | | | | | 2 | | | 2 | | |
| 7 | Teething | 2 | 4 | 12 | 19 | | | | | | | | | | | | | | | 36 | | | | | 1 |
| 8 | Tetanus | 1 | | | | | | 2 | | 3 | | | | | | | | | | 5 | | | 1 | | |
| 9 | Throat, disease of | 2 | | 1 | | 2 | 2 | 1 | 1 | 2 | | 1 | 1 | | | | | | | 11 | | 1 | 1 | | |
| 10 | Thrush | 5 | 2 | 1 | 1 | | | | | | | | | | | | | | | 9 | | | | | |
| 11 | Tumor | 1 | | | | | | | | | | | 1 | | | | | | | 2 | | | | | |
| 12 | Ulcer | | 1 | | | | | | | 1 | 2 | | | | | | | | | 2 | | | 1 | | |
| 13 | Uterus, disease of | | | | | | | | 1 | | 4 | | | | 1 | | | | | 4 | | | 2 | | |
| 14 | White swelling | | | | | | 1 | | 1 | | 1 | 1 | | | | | | | | 1 | | | 2 | 1 | |
| 15 | Worms | 4 | 1 | 20 | 15 | 2 | 2 | 2 | 2 | | | | | | | | | | | 41 | 1 | | 6 | | |
| 16 | Uuknown | 229 | 213 | 120 | 58 | 26 | 27 | 37 | 35 | 56 | 118 | 52 | 59 | 10 | 16 | | | | | 890 | 1 | 7 | 136 | 1 | 11 |
| | Total | 535 | 458 | 461 | 339 | 136 | 144 | 229 | 248 | 595 | 586 | 294 | 248 | 69 | 83 | 3 | 3 | | | 3441 | 2 | 76 | 755 | 6 | 81 |

## CLASSIFICATION OF DEATHS IN THE

| | Cause of death. | Under 1. M. | F. | 1 and under 5. M. | F. | 5 and under 10. M. | F. | 10 and under 20. M. | F. | 20 and under 50. M. | F. | 50 and under 80. M. | F. | 80 and under 100. M | F. | 100 & over. M | F. | Age unknown. M | F. | Born in State. | N. England States. | Middle States. | Southern States. | Southwest'n States. | Northwest'n States. |
|---|---|---|---|---|---|---|---|---|---|---|---|---|---|---|---|---|---|---|---|---|---|---|---|---|---|
| 1 | Abscess | 1 | 4 | | 2 | | | 3 | 1 | | | 2 | | | | | | | | 9 | | | 3 | | |
| 2 | Accident, not specf'd | 18 | 22 | 11 | 8 | 12 | 10 | 28 | 4 | 44 | 4 | 18 | 6 | 5 | | | | 4 | | 154 | 1 | 7 | 27 | | 3 |
| 3 | ....do...burned | 7 | 7 | 22 | 30 | 6 | 13 | 4 | 3 | 6 | 7 | | 1 | | | | | | | 97 | | | 6 | | 3 |
| 4 | ....do...drowned | | | 8 | 5 | 4 | 5 | 22 | 8 | 18 | 2 | 4 | 2 | | | | | | | 57 | | | 15 | | 3 |
| 5 | ....do...scalded | 2 | 2 | 3 | 2 | | 2 | | | | | | | | | | | | | 11 | | | | | |
| 6 | ....do...shot | | | | | | | 1 | | 6 | | | | | | | | | | 4 | | | 2 | | 1 |
| 7 | Apoplexy | | | | 2 | | | | 1 | 7 | 16 | 14 | 12 | 2 | | | | | | 27 | | 4 | 19 | | 2 |
| 8 | Asthma | | | 3 | 1 | | | 1 | | 1 | | 3 | 5 | 1 | | | | | | 7 | | | 8 | | |
| 9 | Bowels, disease of | 2 | 2 | 3 | 2 | 1 | | | | | 1 | 1 | 1 | | | | | | | 10 | | | 3 | | |
| 10 | Bronchitis | 4 | 2 | 12 | 3 | | | | 2 | 3 | 8 | 5 | 1 | | | | | | | 33 | | 1 | 5 | | 1 |
| 11 | Cancer | 2 | | 1 | 2 | | | | 1 | 6 | 12 | 15 | 19 | 6 | 3 | | | | | 25 | | | 39 | | 2 |
| 12 | Carbuncle | | | | | | | 1 | 1 | | 1 | | | | | | | | | 2 | | | 1 | | |
| 13 | Catarrh | 1 | | | | | | 1 | | 3 | 4 | 1 | 1 | | 1 | | | | | 9 | | | 3 | | |
| 14 | Chicken pox | 1 | | 1 | 1 | 1 | 1 | | | | | | | | | | | | | 5 | | | | | |
| 15 | Childbirth | | | | | | | | 15 | | 84 | | | | | | | | 1 | 72 | | | 27 | | 1 |
| 16 | Cholera | 19 | 19 | 61 | 57 | 29 | 32 | 41 | 70 | 224 | 149 | 83 | 44 | 5 | 4 | | | 12 | 4 | 590 | 3 | 20 | 168 | | 26 |
| 17 | ...do..infantum | 21 | 24 | 26 | 19 | 1 | 5 | | | | | | | | | | | | | 91 | | | 5 | | |
| 18 | ...do..morbus | 8 | 3 | 7 | 7 | 2 | 2 | 3 | 4 | 2 | 7 | 2 | | 1 | | | | | | 37 | | | 8 | | 3 |
| 19 | Chorea | | 1 | 1 | | | | | 1 | 1 | 1 | | | | | | | | | 5 | | | | | |
| 20 | Colic | 2 | 2 | 3 | 1 | | 1 | | 1 | 9 | 5 | 7 | 4 | 1 | | | | | | 27 | | | 7 | | 2 |
| 21 | Congestion | | | 1 | 1 | | | 2 | 1 | 2 | 1 | | | | | | | | | 6 | | | 2 | | |
| 22 | ....do....brain | | | 1 | | | | | | | | | | | | | | | | 1 | | | | | |
| 23 | Consumption | 9 | 8 | 21 | 23 | 4 | 10 | 42 | 75 | 222 | 286 | 80 | 86 | 5 | 5 | | | 2 | 1 | 603 | 2 | 9 | 237 | 2 | 17 |
| 24 | Convulsions | 24 | 19 | 15 | 8 | 6 | 2 | 10 | 5 | 14 | 14 | 3 | 2 | 1 | 1 | | | | | 108 | | | 10 | 3 | 1 |
| 25 | Cramp | 1 | 1 | | | | | | | | | | | | | | | | | 2 | | | | | |
| 26 | Croup | 197 | 168 | 127 | 117 | 22 | 17 | 1 | 2 | 1 | | | | | | | | | | 638 | | | 11 | | 3 |
| 27 | Diabetes | | | 1 | | | | | | 1 | | 2 | | | | | | | | 3 | | | | | |
| 28 | Diarrhœa | 33 | 40 | 53 | 35 | 8 | 4 | 5 | 4 | 24 | 18 | 18 | 12 | 2 | | | | 11 | | 227 | | 1 | 31 | | 1 |
| 29 | Dirt eating | | | | | 1 | | 1 | | | | | | | | | | | | 2 | | | | | |
| 30 | Dropsy | 7 | 5 | 23 | 17 | 12 | 13 | 41 | 23 | 39 | 80 | 73 | 78 | 13 | 10 | | | 3 | 1 | 244 | | 14 | 164 | | 13 |
| 31 | Dysentery | 16 | 11 | 42 | 41 | 10 | 8 | 7 | 2 | 7 | 16 | 6 | 7 | | 1 | | | | | 154 | | 1 | 18 | | |
| 32 | Dyspepsia | | | | | 1 | | | 2 | 7 | 8 | 13 | 5 | | | | | | | 16 | | 1 | 17 | | 2 |
| 33 | Epilepsy | 1 | | | | | | | | 2 | 1 | 1 | | 1 | | | | | | 3 | | | 2 | | 1 |
| 34 | Erysipelas | 6 | 7 | 4 | 3 | | 1 | 1 | 2 | 1 | 3 | 2 | 1 | | 1 | | | | | 26 | | 2 | 4 | | |
| 35 | Executed | | | | | | | | | 2 | 1 | | | | | | | | | 3 | | | | | |
| 36 | Fever, not specified | 30 | 36 | 65 | 60 | 48 | 38 | 90 | 112 | 161 | 130 | 47 | 19 | 2 | 1 | | | | | 698 | 1 | 4 | 112 | 3 | 15 |
| 37 | ..do..bilious | 4 | 1 | 4 | 7 | 3 | 5 | 6 | 7 | 26 | 8 | 6 | 5 | | | | | | | 64 | | 1 | 16 | | |
| 38 | ..do..brain | 1 | 3 | 5 | 6 | | 1 | 2 | 1 | 1 | 1 | | | | 1 | | | | | 20 | | 1 | 1 | | |
| 39 | ..do..congestive | 6 | 2 | 8 | 5 | 4 | 5 | 11 | 11 | 30 | 27 | 8 | 11 | 1 | 1 | | | 1 | | 101 | 1 | | 24 | | 4 |
| 40 | ..do..intermittent | 8 | 2 | 3 | 4 | 2 | 1 | 2 | 3 | 3 | 2 | 5 | 1 | 2 | 2 | | | 3 | | 33 | | 1 | 8 | | |
| 41 | ..do..puerperal | | | | | | | | 1 | | 17 | | | | | | | | | 17 | | | 1 | | |
| 42 | ..do..remittent | | | | | | | | | | | | 1 | | | | | | | | | | 1 | | |
| 43 | ..do..scarlet | 18 | 11 | 50 | 34 | 15 | 17 | 4 | 13 | 5 | 5 | | | | | | | | | 168 | | | 4 | | |
| 44 | ..do..typhus | 10 | 6 | 24 | 17 | 23 | 25 | 106 | 104 | 152 | 111 | 27 | 19 | | 6 | | | | | 453 | 1 | 3 | 148 | 10 | 12 |
| 45 | ..do..yellow | | | | | | | | | 1 | | | | | | | | | | 1 | | | | | |
| 46 | Fracture | | | | | | | | | | | 1 | | | | | | | | | | | 1 | | |
| 47 | Gout | | | | | | | | | | | 1 | 1 | | | | | | | 1 | | | 1 | | |
| 48 | Gravel | 2 | | 1 | | | | 2 | | 2 | 1 | 22 | 1 | 5 | | | | | | 9 | | 1 | 24 | 1 | 1 |
| 49 | Head, disease of | | | 1 | | | | | | | 1 | | | | | | | | | 1 | | | 1 | | |
| 50 | Heart....do | 6 | 1 | 1 | 1 | 1 | 1 | 1 | 1 | 7 | 4 | 5 | 3 | | 2 | | | | | 23 | | 1 | 10 | | |

## SECTION OF THE STATE OF TENNESSEE—Continued.

| Nativities: California and Territories. | Ireland. | Germany. | Other foreign countries. | Unknown. | Season of decease: Spring. | Summer. | Autumn. | Winter. | Duration of sickness: Under 1 week. | 1 week and under 1 month. | 1 month and under 3 months. | 3 months and over. | Whites: Males. | Females. | Total. | Colored: Slaves: Black: M. | F. | Mulatto: M. | F. | Free: Black: M. | F. | Mul.: M | F. | Aggregate deaths. | |
|---|---|---|---|---|---|---|---|---|---|---|---|---|---|---|---|---|---|---|---|---|---|---|---|---|---|
| .... | .... | .. | .... | ... | 12 | 4 | .... | 2 | 1 | 16 | 1 | .... | 8 | 7 | 15 | .... | 2 | 1 | .... | ... | ... | .. | .. | 18 | 1 |
| .... | .... | .. | .... | ... | 1 | .... | .... | 1 | .... | 1 | .... | 1 | .... | .... | .... | 1 | 1 | .... | .... | ... | ... | .. | .. | 2 | 2 |
| .... | .... | .. | .... | ... | .... | .... | .... | 1 | .... | .... | .... | 1 | .... | .... | .... | .... | 1 | .... | .... | ... | ... | .. | .. | 1 | 3 |
| .... | .... | .. | .... | ... | 7 | 4 | 1 | 5 | .... | .... | .... | .... | 7 | 2 | 9 | 4 | 1 | .... | 1 | ... | ... | .. | 2 | 17 | 4 |
| .... | .... | .. | .... | ... | 12 | 6 | 7 | 16 | 41 | .... | .... | .... | 3 | 2 | 5 | 14 | 18 | 2 | 2 | ... | ... | .. | .. | 41 | 5 |
| .... | .... | .. | .... | ... | 1 | 1 | 1 | 1 | .... | .... | .... | .... | 2 | 1 | 3 | 1 | .... | .... | .... | ... | ... | .. | .. | 4 | 6 |
| .... | .... | .. | .... | ... | 4 | 16 | 12 | 4 | 7 | 18 | 7 | 2 | 9 | 16 | 25 | 5 | 7 | .... | .... | ... | ... | .. | .. | 37 | 7 |
| .... | .... | .. | .... | ... | 1 | 1 | 2 | 2 | 1 | 4 | .... | .... | 5 | .... | 5 | 1 | .... | .... | .... | ... | ... | .. | .. | 6 | 8 |
| .... | .... | .. | .... | ... | 1 | 5 | 7 | .... | 3 | 7 | .... | 2 | 5 | 2 | 7 | 4 | 2 | .... | .... | ... | ... | .. | .. | 13 | 9 |
| .... | .... | .. | .... | ... | 1 | 4 | 2 | 2 | 4 | 1 | 2 | 1 | 3 | 3 | 6 | 2 | .... | 1 | .... | ... | ... | .. | .. | 9 | 10 |
| .... | .... | .. | .... | ... | 1 | .... | 1 | .... | .... | 1 | .... | .... | 1 | 1 | 2 | .... | .... | .... | .... | ... | ... | .. | .. | 2 | 11 |
| .... | 1 | .. | .... | ... | 1 | 2 | 1 | .... | 1 | 1 | .... | 2 | 1 | 1 | 2 | .... | 2 | .... | .... | ... | ... | .. | .. | 4 | 12 |
| .... | .... | .. | .... | ... | 1 | 4 | 1 | .... | .... | .... | 1 | .... | .... | 3 | 3 | .... | 2 | .... | 1 | ... | ... | .. | .. | 6 | 13 |
| .... | .... | .. | .... | ... | 1 | 1 | .... | 2 | .... | .... | .... | 3 | 1 | 1 | 2 | .... | 2 | .... | .... | ... | ... | .. | .. | 4 | 14 |
| .... | .... | .. | .... | ... | 9 | 16 | 16 | 7 | 22 | 21 | 3 | 2 | 12 | 8 | 20 | 15 | 12 | 1 | .... | ... | ... | .. | .. | 48 | 15 |
| 1 | 5 | .. | 4 | ... | 295 | 250 | 216 | 188 | 265 | 216 | 106 | 103 | 284 | 320 | 604 | 227 | 193 | 15 | 10 | 4 | 1 | .. | 2 | 1056 | 16 |
| 1 | 34 | 13 | 22 | ... | 1048 | 1389 | 1033 | 783 | 1322 | 1352 | 444 | 482 | 1467 | 1298 | 2764 | 790 | 747 | 47 | 48 | 10 | 3 | 8 | 13 | 4431 | |

## STATE OF TENNESSEE—AGGREGATE.

| California and Territories. | Ireland. | Germany. | Other foreign countries. | Unknown. | Spring. | Summer. | Autumn. | Winter. | Under 1 week. | 1 week and under 1 month. | 1 month and under 3 months. | 3 months and over. | Whites: Males. | Females. | Total. | Slaves: Black M. | Black F. | Mulatto M. | Mulatto F. | Free: Black M. | Black F. | Mul. M | Mul. F. | Aggregate deaths. | |
|---|---|---|---|---|---|---|---|---|---|---|---|---|---|---|---|---|---|---|---|---|---|---|---|---|---|
| .... | 1 | .. | .... | ... | 5 | 4 | 3 | 1 | 3 | 1 | 5 | 4 | 2 | 6 | 8 | 4 | 1 | .... | .... | ... | ... | .. | .. | 13 | 1 |
| .... | 2 | .. | .... | ... | 42 | 36 | 51 | 60 | 65 | 31 | 5 | 3 | 104 | 22 | 126 | 33 | 31 | 3 | 1 | ... | ... | .. | .. | 194 | 2 |
| .... | .... | .. | .... | ... | 39 | 9 | 22 | 31 | 34 | 35 | 9 | 3 | 27 | 37 | 64 | 17 | 23 | 1 | 1 | ... | ... | .. | .. | 106 | 3 |
| .... | 2 | .. | 1 | ... | 20 | 28 | 16 | 13 | 78 | .... | .... | .... | 33 | 13 | 46 | 18 | 7 | 5 | 1 | ... | ... | .. | 1 | 78 | 4 |
| .... | .... | .. | .... | ... | 2 | 2 | 4 | 3 | 2 | 6 | .... | 1 | 4 | 4 | 8 | .... | 2 | 1 | .... | ... | ... | .. | .. | 11 | 5 |
| .... | .... | .. | .... | ... | 1 | 3 | 3 | .... | 3 | .... | .... | .... | 7 | .... | 7 | .... | .... | .... | .... | ... | ... | .. | .. | 7 | 6 |
| .... | 1 | .. | 1 | ... | 17 | 12 | 16 | 8 | 24 | 4 | 2 | 1 | 14 | 19 | 33 | 8 | 12 | 1 | .... | ... | ... | .. | .. | 54 | 7 |
| .... | .... | .. | .... | ... | 8 | 2 | 2 | 2 | 4 | 4 | 1 | 1 | 5 | 5 | 10 | 4 | 1 | .... | .... | ... | ... | .. | .. | 15 | 8 |
| .... | .... | .. | .... | ... | .... | 4 | 7 | 2 | 2 | 4 | 5 | 2 | 2 | 4 | 6 | 5 | 2 | .... | .... | ... | ... | .. | .. | 13 | 9 |
| .... | .... | .. | .... | ... | 14 | 9 | 7 | 10 | 5 | 14 | 3 | 10 | 15 | 14 | 29 | 7 | 2 | 2 | .... | ... | ... | .. | .. | 40 | 10 |
| .... | .... | .. | 1 | ... | 20 | 17 | 18 | 10 | .... | 3 | 7 | 32 | 27 | 28 | 55 | 3 | 9 | .... | .... | ... | ... | .. | .. | 67 | 11 |
| .... | .... | .. | .... | ... | 1 | .... | 1 | 1 | .... | 1 | 1 | 1 | 1 | 2 | 3 | .... | .... | .... | .... | ... | ... | .. | .. | 3 | 12 |
| .... | .... | .. | .... | ... | 5 | 2 | 3 | 2 | 4 | 2 | 1 | 2 | 3 | 2 | 5 | 3 | 4 | .... | .... | ... | ... | .. | .. | 12 | 13 |
| .... | .... | .. | .... | ... | 1 | 2 | 1 | 1 | 2 | 2 | 1 | .... | 2 | 2 | 4 | 1 | .... | .... | .... | ... | ... | .. | .. | 5 | 14 |
| .... | .... | .. | .... | ... | 35 | 21 | 13 | 29 | 49 | 28 | 8 | 3 | .... | 78 | 78 | .... | 21 | .... | 1 | ... | ... | .. | .. | 100 | 15 |
| .... | 18 | 17 | 11 | ... | 45 | 527 | 209 | 39 | 744 | 73 | 6 | .... | 307 | 245 | 552 | 142 | 115 | 14 | 10 | 2 | 1 | 9 | 8 | 853 | 16 |
| .... | .... | .. | .... | ... | 7 | 47 | 31 | 10 | 37 | 34 | 8 | 7 | 40 | 40 | 80 | 8 | 7 | .... | 1 | ... | ... | .. | .. | 96 | 17 |
| .... | .... | .. | .... | ... | 10 | 22 | 10 | 2 | 16 | 20 | 4 | 2 | 24 | 16 | 40 | 1 | 6 | .... | 1 | ... | ... | .. | .. | 48 | 18 |
| .... | .... | .. | .... | ... | 1 | 3 | .... | 1 | 4 | .... | .... | 1 | 1 | 1 | 2 | 1 | 2 | .... | .... | ... | ... | .. | .. | 5 | 19 |
| .... | .... | .. | .... | ... | 12 | 9 | 8 | 7 | 19 | 15 | 1 | .... | 12 | 9 | 21 | 9 | 5 | 1 | .... | ... | ... | .. | .. | 36 | 20 |
| .... | .... | .. | .... | ... | 2 | 3 | 2 | 1 | 5 | 2 | .... | 1 | 3 | 2 | 5 | 2 | 1 | .... | .... | ... | ... | .. | .. | 8 | 21 |
| .... | .... | .. | .... | ... | .... | .... | .... | .... | .... | .... | .... | .... | 1 | .... | 1 | .... | .... | .... | .... | ... | ... | .. | .. | 1 | 22 |
| .... | 6 | 1 | 2 | ... | 271 | 247 | 179 | 178 | 23 | 61 | 119 | 443 | 267 | 353 | 620 | 104 | 124 | 9 | 14 | 4 | 2 | 1 | 1 | 879 | 23 |
| .... | 2 | .. | .... | ... | 42 | 34 | 15 | 25 | 42 | 17 | 17 | 14 | 55 | 39 | 94 | 18 | 10 | .... | 2 | ... | ... | .. | .. | 124 | 24 |
| .... | .... | .. | .... | ... | 1 | .... | .... | 1 | 2 | .... | .... | .... | 1 | 1 | 2 | .... | .... | .... | .... | ... | ... | .. | .. | 2 | 25 |
| .... | .... | .. | .... | ... | 147 | 121 | 212 | 165 | 449 | 138 | 25 | 7 | 257 | 199 | 456 | 87 | 98 | 3 | 6 | 1 | 1 | .. | .. | 652 | 26 |
| .... | 1 | .. | .... | ... | .... | 1 | 1 | .... | 1 | 2 | .... | .... | 4 | .... | 4 | .... | .... | .... | .... | ... | ... | .. | .. | 4 | 27 |
| .... | 3 | 1 | 2 | 1 | 43 | 85 | 112 | 26 | 41 | 107 | 35 | 80 | 106 | 75 | 181 | 43 | 34 | 4 | 4 | 1 | ... | .. | .. | 267 | 28 |
| .... | .... | .. | .... | ... | .... | 2 | .... | .... | 1 | .... | .... | 1 | 2 | .... | 2 | .... | .... | .... | .... | ... | ... | .. | .. | 2 | 29 |
| .... | 1 | .. | 2 | ... | 120 | 125 | 88 | 92 | 26 | 46 | 75 | 188 | 153 | 157 | 310 | 56 | 61 | 1 | 7 | 1 | ... | .. | 2 | 438 | 30 |
| .... | .... | 1 | .... | ... | 7 | 88 | 67 | 11 | 33 | 106 | 22 | 8 | 72 | 66 | 138 | 15 | 17 | 1 | 2 | ... | 1 | .. | .. | 174 | 31 |
| .... | .... | .. | .... | ... | 14 | 5 | 11 | 6 | 4 | 3 | 7 | 15 | 21 | 13 | 34 | .... | 2 | .... | .... | ... | ... | .. | .. | 36 | 32 |
| .... | .... | .. | .... | ... | 2 | 1 | 2 | 1 | 2 | 1 | .... | 1 | 4 | 1 | 5 | 1 | .... | .... | .... | ... | ... | .. | .. | 6 | 33 |
| .... | .... | .. | .... | ... | 11 | 6 | 7 | 8 | 6 | 18 | 3 | 3 | 12 | 15 | 27 | 2 | 3 | .... | .... | ... | ... | .. | .. | 32 | 34 |
| .... | .... | .. | .... | ... | 1 | 2 | .... | .... | 3 | .... | .... | .... | 1 | .... | 1 | 1 | 1 | .... | .... | ... | ... | .. | .. | 3 | 35 |
| .... | 5 | .. | 1 | ... | 193 | 199 | 284 | 154 | 126 | 539 | 145 | 29 | 337 | 286 | 623 | 94 | 101 | 7 | 7 | 1 | ... | 4 | 2 | 839 | 36 |
| .... | 1 | .. | .... | ... | 16 | 25 | 35 | 6 | 8 | 42 | 30 | 1 | 41 | 26 | 67 | 6 | 6 | .... | .... | 1 | ... | 1 | 1 | 82 | 37 |
| .... | .... | .. | .... | ... | 5 | 11 | 3 | 3 | 6 | 16 | .... | .... | 7 | 10 | 17 | 1 | 3 | 1 | .... | ... | ... | .. | .. | 22 | 38 |
| .... | 1 | .. | .... | ... | 19 | 39 | 57 | 16 | 69 | 46 | 7 | 1 | 56 | 50 | 106 | 13 | 11 | .... | 1 | ... | ... | .. | .. | 131 | 39 |
| .... | .... | .. | 1 | ... | 5 | 9 | 18 | 11 | 9 | 18 | 7 | 2 | 24 | 12 | 36 | 4 | 3 | .... | .... | ... | ... | .. | .. | 43 | 40 |
| .... | .... | .. | .... | ... | 6 | 5 | 3 | 4 | 3 | 11 | .... | 1 | .... | 15 | 15 | .... | 3 | .... | .... | ... | ... | .. | .. | 18 | 41 |
| .... | .... | .. | .... | ... | .... | .... | 1 | .... | .... | 1 | .... | .... | .... | 1 | 1 | .... | .... | .... | .... | ... | ... | .. | .. | 1 | 42 |
| .... | .... | .. | .... | ... | 44 | 34 | 49 | 45 | 57 | 93 | 15 | 4 | 79 | 61 | 140 | 13 | 19 | .... | .... | ... | ... | .. | .. | 172 | 43 |
| 1 | 2 | .. | .... | ... | 155 | 128 | 208 | 132 | 55 | 400 | 150 | 20 | 236 | 189 | 425 | 100 | 95 | 5 | 3 | 1 | ... | .. | 1 | 630 | 44 |
| .... | .... | .. | .... | ... | .... | .... | 1 | .... | 1 | .... | .... | .... | 1 | .... | 1 | .... | .... | .... | .... | ... | ... | .. | .. | 1 | 45 |
| .... | .... | .. | .... | ... | 1 | .... | .... | .... | .... | .... | 1 | .... | 1 | .... | 1 | .... | .... | .... | .... | ... | ... | .. | .. | 1 | 46 |
| .... | .... | .. | .... | ... | 2 | .... | .... | .... | .... | 2 | .... | .... | 1 | .... | 1 | .... | 1 | .... | .... | ... | ... | .. | .. | 2 | 47 |
| .... | .... | .. | .... | ... | 11 | 9 | 8 | 8 | 2 | 12 | 8 | 10 | 31 | 2 | 33 | 3 | .... | .... | .... | ... | ... | .. | .. | 36 | 48 |
| .... | .... | .. | .... | ... | 2 | .... | .... | .... | .... | .... | 1 | .... | 1 | 1 | 2 | .... | .... | .... | .... | ... | ... | .. | .. | 2 | 49 |
| .... | .... | .. | .... | ... | 6 | 11 | 4 | 13 | 8 | 7 | 8 | 7 | 17 | 12 | 29 | 4 | 1 | .... | .... | ... | ... | .. | .. | 34 | 50 |

## CLASSIFICATION OF DEATHS IN THE

| | Cause of death. | AGE. | | | | | | | | | | | | | | | | | | NATIVITIES. | | | | | |
|---|---|---|---|---|---|---|---|---|---|---|---|---|---|---|---|---|---|---|---|---|---|---|---|---|---|
| | | Under 1. | | 1 and under 5. | | 5 and under 10. | | 10 and under 20. | | 20 and under 50. | | 50 and under 80. | | 80 and under 100. | | 100 & over. | | Age unknown. | | Born in State. | N. England States. | Middle States. | Southern States. | Southwest'n States. | Northeast'n States. |
| | | M. | F. | M. | F. | M. | F. | M. | F. | M. | F. | M. | F. | M | F. | M | F. | M | F. | | | | | | |
| 1 | Heat | | | | | | | | | | 1 | | | | | | | | | 1 | | | | | |
| 2 | Hemorrhage | | | | | 1 | | 3 | 3 | 13 | 7 | 5 | 6 | 1 | 2 | | | | | 25 | | 1 | 15 | | |
| 3 | Hernia | | | | | | | | | 1 | | 1 | | | | | | | | | | | 2 | | |
| 4 | Hives | 67 | 61 | 14 | 12 | 1 | 2 | | | | | | | | | | | | | 154 | | | 3 | | |
| 5 | Hooping cough | 46 | 44 | 51 | 62 | 5 | 12 | 2 | 1 | 1 | | | | | | | | | | 219 | | | 5 | | |
| 6 | Hydrocephalus | 8 | 5 | 4 | 3 | | 2 | 1 | 1 | | | | | | | | | | | 24 | | | | | |
| 7 | Inflammation | | 5 | 2 | 1 | 1 | 1 | 1 | | | | | | | | | | | | 11 | | | | | |
| 8 | .....do....bowels | 15 | 12 | 15 | 13 | 2 | 2 | 6 | 4 | 17 | 10 | 7 | | 1 | | | | | | 89 | | 1 | 9 | 1 | 2 |
| 9 | .....do....brain | 48 | 34 | 45 | 35 | 9 | 12 | 11 | 9 | 13 | 13 | 7 | 6 | | | | | | | 218 | 1 | 1 | 21 | | 1 |
| 10 | .....do....stomach | 2 | | 1 | | | | | | 1 | 7 | 3 | 3 | | 1 | | | | | 9 | | 2 | 7 | | |
| 11 | Influenza | | | 1 | | 1 | | | | | | | | | | | | | | 1 | | | 1 | | |
| 12 | Insanity | | | | | | | | | | 2 | 2 | 1 | | | | | | | 2 | | | 3 | | |
| 13 | Intemperance | | | | | 1 | | | | 11 | 1 | 12 | | | | | | 5 | | 16 | | | 12 | | 1 |
| 14 | Jaundice | 2 | 6 | 1 | | 1 | | 1 | 1 | | | 1 | 1 | | | | | | | 11 | | | 3 | | |
| 15 | Kidneys, disease of | | | | | | | | | | | 1 | 1 | | | | | | | 1 | | | 1 | | |
| 16 | Killed | | | 1 | | 1 | | 3 | | 10 | | 1 | | | | | | | | 12 | | | 3 | | |
| 17 | Lightning | | | | | 1 | | | | 1 | | | | | | | | | | 1 | | | 1 | | |
| 18 | Liver, disease of | 6 | 1 | 1 | 2 | 2 | | 6 | | 12 | 19 | 10 | 6 | 2 | | | | | | 44 | | 1 | 20 | | 2 |
| 19 | Lockjaw | 11 | 7 | 2 | 4 | 1 | 4 | 1 | 3 | 2 | 4 | | 1 | | | | | | | 40 | | | | | |
| 20 | Lungs, disease of | | 1 | | | | | | | | | | | | | | | | | 1 | | | | | |
| 21 | Malformation | 1 | 1 | 1 | | | | | | | | | | | | | | | | 3 | | | | | |
| 22 | Mania-a-potu | | | | | | | | | 2 | | | | | | | | | | 1 | | | 1 | | |
| 23 | Marasmus | 4 | 1 | | | | | | | | | | | | | | | | | 4 | | | 1 | | |
| 24 | Measles | 1 | | 6 | 6 | 4 | 1 | 3 | 4 | 5 | 3 | | | | | | | | | 25 | | | 7 | | 1 |
| 25 | Milk sickness | | | | | | 1 | | | 2 | 1 | | | | | | | | | 4 | | | | | |
| 26 | Mumps | | 1 | 1 | | | | | 1 | | | | | | | | | | | 2 | | | 1 | | |
| 27 | Murder | | | | | | | 2 | | 6 | | 4 | | | | | | | | 8 | | | 3 | | 1 |
| 28 | Neuralgia | | | | 1 | 2 | 1 | | | | | 2 | 1 | 1 | | | | | | 4 | | | 4 | | |
| 29 | Old age | | | | | | | | | 1 | | 41 | 46 | 92 | 127 | 6 | 3 | | | 56 | 1 | 32 | 213 | | 1 |
| 30 | Paralysis | 1 | | | | 1 | 2 | | 5 | 6 | 12 | 25 | 23 | 1 | 10 | | | | | 27 | 1 | 5 | 49 | | 2 |
| 31 | Piles | | | | | | | | | | | 3 | | | | | | | | | | | 3 | | |
| 32 | Pleurisy | 3 | 3 | 2 | 4 | 5 | 2 | 4 | 2 | 23 | 7 | 12 | 9 | 1 | | | | | | 49 | | | 24 | | 2 |
| 33 | Pneumonia | 23 | 18 | 32 | 35 | 12 | 11 | 23 | 32 | 99 | 50 | 45 | 30 | 3 | 3 | | | 1 | | 296 | | 16 | 98 | | 7 |
| 34 | Poison | 1 | 1 | 2 | | | | | | 10 | 5 | 3 | | | | | | | | 17 | | 1 | 3 | | 1 |
| 35 | Prematurity of birth | 10 | 6 | | | | | | | | | | | | | | | | | 16 | | | | | |
| 36 | Quinsy | 3 | 1 | 4 | 6 | 4 | 2 | 1 | 2 | 3 | 4 | 2 | 1 | | | | | | | 29 | | | 3 | | 1 |
| 37 | Rheumatism | | | 1 | | 1 | 1 | 2 | 2 | 9 | 6 | 5 | 2 | 2 | | | | | | 15 | 2 | 1 | 12 | | 1 |
| 38 | Rickets | 1 | | 4 | 4 | | | 1 | | | | | | | | | | | | 10 | | | | | |
| 39 | Scrofula | 6 | 6 | 21 | 13 | 10 | 7 | 10 | 12 | 11 | 13 | 4 | 6 | | | | | | | 103 | | 1 | 12 | | 3 |
| 40 | Small pox | 2 | 3 | 1 | 2 | 1 | | 3 | 3 | 20 | 5 | 4 | 6 | | | | | 7 | 4 | 47 | | 1 | 12 | | 1 |
| 41 | Spine, disease of | 3 | 1 | 3 | 3 | 1 | 1 | 4 | 3 | 8 | 7 | 2 | 5 | | | | | | | 29 | | | 10 | | 2 |
| 42 | Spleen....do | | | | | | | | 1 | | | | | | | | | | | 1 | | | | | |
| 43 | Stillborn | 17 | 12 | | | | | | | | | | | | | | | | | 29 | | | | | |
| 44 | Suffocation | 32 | 34 | 7 | 2 | | | | | | 1 | | | | | | | | | 75 | | | 1 | | |
| 45 | Suicide | | | | | | | 1 | | 3 | 2 | 3 | | | | | | | | 8 | | | 2 | | |
| 46 | Sun, stroke of | | | | | | | | | 1 | | | | | | | | | | 1 | | | | | |
| 47 | Syphilis | | | | | | | | | | 1 | | | | | | | | | 1 | | | | | |
| 48 | Teething | 9 | 13 | 30 | 27 | | | | | | | | | | | | | | | 72 | | | 4 | | 2 |
| 49 | Tetanus | 4 | | | | | | 2 | | 3 | | | | | | | | 1 | | 8 | | | 1 | | |
| 50 | Throat, disease of | 2 | | 1 | 1 | 3 | 3 | 2 | 2 | 2 | 1 | 1 | 1 | | | | | | | 16 | | 1 | 1 | | |
| 51 | Thrush | 8 | 10 | 5 | 2 | | | | | | | | | | | | | | | 25 | | | | | |
| 52 | Tumor | 1 | | | | | | | | 1 | | | 2 | | | | | | | 3 | | | 1 | | |
| 53 | Ulcer | 1 | 2 | 1 | | | | | | 4 | 5 | 1 | 2 | 1 | 1 | | | | | 10 | | | 7 | | |
| 54 | Uterus, disease of | | | | | | | | 4 | | 6 | | 2 | | 1 | | | | | 8 | | | 5 | | |
| 55 | White swelling | 1 | | 1 | | 1 | 1 | | 3 | 3 | 2 | 1 | | | | | | | | 8 | | | 4 | 1 | |
| 56 | Worms | 9 | 10 | 64 | 49 | 12 | 12 | 5 | 3 | | 1 | | | | | | | | | 150 | 1 | | 14 | | |
| 57 | Unknown | 563 | 532 | 256 | 174 | 63 | 51 | 105 | 111 | 175 | 301 | 156 | 158 | 25 | 31 | | | 6 | 2 | 2265 | 1 | 19 | 370 | 3 | 31 |
| | Total | 1378 | 1240 | 1193 | 982 | 363 | 350 | 642 | 693 | 1519 | 1533 | 839 | 667 | 183 | 215 | 6 | 3 | 56 | 13 | 9201 | 16 | 155 | 2166 | 24 | 179 |

## CLASSIFICATION OF DEATHS IN NORTHERN

*Embracing the following counties : Angelina, Bowie, Cass, Collin, Cook, Denton, Fanin, San Augustin, Shelby,*

| | Cause of death. | Under 1 M. | Under 1 F. | 1–5 M. | 1–5 F. | 5–10 M. | 5–10 F. | 10–20 M. | 10–20 F. | 20–50 M. | 20–50 F. | 50–80 M. | 50–80 F. | 80–100 M | 80–100 F. | 100+ M | 100+ F. | Unknown M | Unknown F. | Born in State. | N. England States. | Middle States. | Southern States. | Southwest'n States. | Northeast'n States. |
|---|---|---|---|---|---|---|---|---|---|---|---|---|---|---|---|---|---|---|---|---|---|---|---|---|---|
| 1 | Abscess | | | | | 1 | | | | 1 | 1 | | | | | | | | | | | | 1 | 1 | |
| 2 | Accident, not spec'd | 1 | | 1 | 2 | | | | | 5 | | 3 | | | | | | | | 5 | | | 4 | 3 | |
| 3 | ....do...burned | | 1 | | 6 | | | | | | 1 | | | 1 | | | | | | 6 | | | 2 | 1 | |
| 4 | ....do...drowned | | | 1 | | 1 | | 1 | 1 | 3 | | | | | | | | | | 2 | | | 2 | 2 | 1 |
| 5 | ....do...scalded | | | 1 | | | | | | | | | | | | | | | | 1 | | | | | |

## STATE OF TENNESSEE—AGGREGATE—Continued.

| NATIVITIES. | | | | | SEASON OF DECEASE. | | | | DURATION OF SICKNESS. | | | | WHITES. | | | COLORED. | | | | | | | | | |
|---|---|---|---|---|---|---|---|---|---|---|---|---|---|---|---|---|---|---|---|---|---|---|---|---|---|
| | | | | | | | | | | | | | | | | Slaves. | | | | Free. | | | | | |
| | | | | | | | | | | | | | | | | Black. | | Mulatto. | | Black. | | Mul. | | | |
| California and Territories. | Ireland. | Germany. | Other foreign countries. | Unknown. | Spring. | Summer. | Autumn. | Winter. | Under 1 week. | 1 week and under 1 month. | 1 month and under 3 months. | 3 months and over. | Males. | Females. | Total. | M. | F. | M. | F. | M. | F. | M | F. | Aggregate deaths. | |
| | | | | | | 1 | | | 1 | | | | | 1 | 1 | | | | | | | | | 1 | 1 |
| | | | | | 12 | 10 | 11 | 8 | 7 | 8 | 7 | 13 | 13 | 8 | 21 | 10 | 10 | | | | | | | 41 | 2 |
| | | | | | 1 | 1 | | | | 1 | | | | | | 2 | | | | | | | | 2 | 3 |
| | | | | | 38 | 28 | 41 | 39 | 98 | 42 | 5 | 1 | 69 | 69 | 138 | 11 | 5 | 2 | | | | | 1 | 157 | 4 |
| | | | | | 60 | 76 | 46 | 41 | 29 | 104 | 61 | 17 | 47 | 68 | 115 | 55 | 45 | 3 | 6 | | | | | 224 | 5 |
| | | | | | 4 | 6 | 6 | 8 | 3 | 12 | 4 | 4 | 10 | 10 | 20 | 3 | 1 | | | | | | | 24 | 6 |
| | | | | | 4 | 3 | 3 | 1 | 4 | 7 | | | 2 | 6 | 8 | 2 | 1 | | | | | | | 11 | 7 |
| | 2 | | | | 26 | 29 | 32 | 13 | 27 | 55 | 9 | 4 | 42 | 33 | 75 | 20 | 7 | 1 | 1 | | | | | 104 | 8 |
| | | | | | 65 | 74 | 54 | 45 | 82 | 111 | 23 | 6 | 100 | 83 | 183 | 31 | 23 | 2 | 2 | | | | 1 | 242 | 9 |
| | | | | | 5 | 7 | 3 | 3 | 5 | | 3 | 2 | 6 | 11 | 17 | | | 1 | | | | | | 18 | 10 |
| | | | | | | | 1 | 1 | 1 | 1 | | | 1 | | 1 | 1 | | | | | | | | 2 | 11 |
| | | | | | 1 | | 2 | 2 | | 1 | | 2 | 1 | 2 | 3 | 1 | 1 | | | | | | | 5 | 12 |
| | 1 | | | | 8 | 9 | 7 | 6 | 7 | 5 | 2 | 6 | 29 | 1 | 30 | | | | | | | | | 30 | 13 |
| | | | | | 4 | 2 | 4 | 3 | 3 | 5 | 2 | | 6 | 8 | 14 | | | | | | | | | 14 | 14 |
| | | | | | | 1 | | 1 | | | | 1 | 1 | 1 | 2 | | | | | | | | | 2 | 15 |
| | 1 | | | | 5 | 4 | 5 | 2 | 2 | 2 | | | 11 | | 11 | 5 | | | | | | | | 16 | 16 |
| | | | | | 1 | | 1 | | 2 | | | | 1 | | 1 | 1 | | | | | | | | 2 | 17 |
| | | | | | 14 | 28 | 16 | 8 | 6 | 17 | 15 | 19 | 35 | 23 | 58 | 4 | 5 | | | | | | | 67 | 18 |
| | | | | | 6 | 17 | 12 | 5 | 27 | 6 | 1 | 1 | 7 | 6 | 13 | 10 | 16 | | 1 | | | | | 40 | 19 |
| | | | | | 1 | | | | | 1 | | | | | | | 1 | | | | | | | 1 | 20 |
| | | | | | 3 | | | | 1 | | | 1 | 2 | 1 | 3 | | | | | | | | | 3 | 21 |
| | | | | | | 1 | 1 | | | 2 | | | 2 | | 2 | | | | | | | | | 2 | 22 |
| | | | | | 2 | 2 | | | | 2 | 1 | 1 | 1 | 1 | 2 | 3 | | | | | | | | 5 | 23 |
| | | | | | 8 | 13 | 3 | 9 | 1 | 7 | 7 | 6 | 10 | 5 | 15 | 9 | 9 | | | | | | | 33 | 24 |
| | | | | | 1 | 3 | | | 2 | 2 | | | 1 | 2 | 3 | 1 | | | | | | | | 4 | 25 |
| | | | | | | 2 | | | | 1 | 1 | | 1 | 1 | 2 | | 1 | | | | | | | 3 | 26 |
| | | | | | 6 | 3 | 2 | 1 | 2 | | 1 | 1 | 9 | | 9 | 2 | | 1 | | | | | | 12 | 27 |
| | | | | | 1 | 3 | 4 | | 2 | 4 | 1 | 1 | 3 | 2 | 5 | 2 | 1 | | | | | | | 8 | 28 |
| | 5 | | 8 | | 81 | 83 | 81 | 67 | 35 | 75 | 38 | 47 | 103 | 126 | 229 | 35 | 49 | 2 | | | 1 | | | 316 | 29 |
| | 1 | | | 1 | 24 | 23 | 16 | 22 | 20 | 17 | 7 | 26 | 30 | 48 | 78 | 4 | 3 | | | | | | 1 | 86 | 30 |
| | | | | | 1 | | 1 | 1 | | 1 | 1 | | 3 | | 3 | | | | | | | | | 3 | 31 |
| | 1 | | 1 | | 27 | 20 | 14 | 16 | 21 | 34 | 12 | 6 | 34 | 16 | 50 | 13 | 11 | 2 | | | | 1 | | 77 | 32 |
| | | | | | 149 | 86 | 60 | 116 | 68 | 274 | 50 | 16 | 151 | 113 | 264 | 81 | 59 | 5 | 6 | 1 | | | 1 | 417 | 33 |
| | | | | | 7 | 4 | 5 | 6 | 9 | 6 | 3 | 2 | 8 | 1 | 9 | 7 | 5 | 1 | | | | | | 22 | 34 |
| | | | | | 1 | 5 | 3 | 7 | 1 | 2 | | | 9 | 5 | 14 | 1 | 1 | | | | | | | 16 | 35 |
| | | | | | 10 | 5 | 6 | 12 | 14 | 17 | 1 | 1 | 13 | 13 | 26 | 4 | 3 | | | | | | | 33 | 36 |
| | | | | | 15 | 7 | 5 | 4 | 2 | 8 | 2 | 14 | 16 | 9 | 25 | 4 | 2 | | | | | | | 31 | 37 |
| | | | | | 1 | 7 | 1 | 1 | 1 | | 2 | 4 | 4 | 1 | 5 | 2 | 3 | | | | | | | 10 | 38 |
| | | | | | 36 | 28 | 33 | 20 | 8 | 19 | 9 | 42 | 25 | 19 | 44 | 35 | 34 | 2 | 2 | | | | 2 | 119 | 39 |
| | | | | | 35 | 9 | | 17 | 6 | 50 | 5 | | 26 | 15 | 41 | 11 | 8 | 1 | | | | | | 61 | 40 |
| | | | | | 24 | 2 | 6 | 7 | 8 | 12 | 4 | 11 | 14 | 19 | 33 | 6 | 1 | 1 | | | | | | 41 | 41 |
| | | | | | | | | 1 | | | | 1 | | | | | 1 | | | | | | | 1 | 42 |
| | | | | | 14 | 5 | 3 | 7 | | | | | 12 | 5 | 17 | 4 | 4 | 1 | 1 | | | | 2 | 29 | 43 |
| | | | | | 31 | 10 | 18 | 14 | 76 | | | | 9 | 6 | 15 | 28 | 29 | 2 | 3 | | | | | 76 | 44 |
| | | | | | 3 | 2 | 3 | 2 | | 1 | | | 7 | 2 | 9 | 1 | | | | | | | | 10 | 45 |
| | | | | | | | 1 | | | | | | | | | 1 | | | | | | | | 1 | 46 |
| | | | | | | 1 | | | | | | | | | | | 1 | | | | | | | 1 | 47 |
| | 1 | | | | 8 | 33 | 28 | 9 | 18 | 31 | 19 | 5 | 22 | 27 | 49 | 16 | 13 | 1 | | | | | | 79 | 48 |
| | | | | | 3 | 1 | 2 | 3 | 3 | 4 | | 1 | 6 | | 6 | 3 | | | | | | | | 9 | 49 |
| | 1 | | | | 2 | 6 | 10 | 1 | 4 | 11 | | 2 | 6 | 6 | 12 | 5 | 2 | | | | | | | 19 | 50 |
| | | | | | 4 | 6 | 7 | 8 | 6 | 9 | 6 | 2 | 8 | 7 | 15 | 4 | 4 | 1 | 1 | | | | | 25 | 51 |
| | | | | | 2 | | 2 | | 1 | 2 | | | 2 | 2 | 4 | | | | | | | | | 4 | 52 |
| | 1 | | | | 3 | 6 | 5 | 4 | 1 | 5 | 3 | 6 | 8 | 7 | 15 | | 2 | | | | | | 1 | 18 | 53 |
| | | | | | 1 | 9 | 2 | 1 | 1 | | 1 | 1 | | 8 | 8 | | 4 | | 1 | | | | | 13 | 54 |
| | | | | | 2 | 5 | 2 | 4 | | 4 | 1 | 6 | 5 | 3 | 8 | 2 | 3 | | | | | | | 13 | 55 |
| | | | | | 34 | 47 | 53 | 31 | 68 | 71 | 16 | 4 | 47 | 47 | 94 | 35 | 26 | 5 | 2 | 1 | | 2 | | 165 | 56 |
| 1 | 12 | | 6 | 1 | 719 | 636 | 626 | 529 | 702 | 596 | 283 | 306 | 872 | 897 | 1769 | 438 | 428 | 33 | 27 | 6 | 1 | | 7 | 2709 | 57 |
| 2 | 72 | 20 | 37 | 3 | 2924 | 3318 | 3039 | 2244 | 3462 | 3610 | 1343 | 1448 | 4271 | 3877 | 8148 | 1744 | 1666 | 126 | 114 | 20 | 7 | 18 | 32 | 11875 | |

## SECTION OF THE STATE OF TEXAS.

*Grayson, Harrison, Hopkins, Hunt, Lamar, Nacogdoches, Panola, Red River, Rusk, Sabine, Titus, and Upshur.*

| California and Territories. | Ireland. | Germany. | Other foreign countries. | Unknown. | Spring. | Summer. | Autumn. | Winter. | Under 1 week. | 1 week and under 1 month. | 1 month and under 3 months. | 3 months and over. | Males. | Females. | Total. | Slaves Black M. | Slaves Black F. | Slaves Mulatto M. | Slaves Mulatto F. | Free Black M. | Free Black F. | Free Mul. M | Free Mul. F. | Aggregate deaths. | |
|---|---|---|---|---|---|---|---|---|---|---|---|---|---|---|---|---|---|---|---|---|---|---|---|---|---|
| | | | | 1 | 3 | | | | | | 1 | 2 | 1 | | 1 | 1 | 1 | | | | | | | 3 | 1 |
| | | | | | 8 | | 4 | | 6 | 2 | 1 | | 7 | 1 | 8 | 3 | 1 | | | | | | | 12 | 2 |
| | | | | | 4 | 2 | 2 | 1 | 8 | | | | | 2 | 2 | 1 | 6 | | | | | | | 9 | 3 |
| | | | | | 1 | 4 | | 2 | 7 | | | | 1 | 1 | 2 | 3 | | 2 | | | | | | 7 | 4 |
| | | | | | | | 1 | | 1 | | | | 1 | | 1 | | | | | | | | | 1 | 5 |

## CLASSIFICATION OF DEATHS IN NORTHERN

| | Cause of death. | AGES. | | | | | | | | | | | | | | | | | | NATIVITIES. | | | | | |
|---|---|---|---|---|---|---|---|---|---|---|---|---|---|---|---|---|---|---|---|---|---|---|---|---|---|
| | | Under 1. | | 1 and under 5. | | 5 and under 10. | | 10 and under 20. | | 20 and under 50. | | 50 and under 80. | | 80 and under 100. | | 100 & over. | | Age unknown. | | Born in State. | N. England States. | Middle States. | Southern States. | Southwest'n States. | Northwest'n States. |
| | | M. | F. | M. | F. | M. | F. | M. | F. | M. | F. | M. | F. | M | F. | M | F. | M | F. | | | | | | |
| 1 | Accident, shot | | | | | | | | 1 | 3 | | | | | | | | | | 1 | | | 1 | 2 | |
| 2 | Apoplexy | | | | | | | | 1 | 1 | 2 | | | | | | | | | 2 | | | 1 | | 1 |
| 3 | Asthma | | | | | | | | | | | | 1 | | | | | | | | | | | | |
| 4 | Bowels, disease of | 1 | | 1 | | | | 1 | | | | | | | | | | | | 3 | | | | | |
| 5 | Brain, do | | | 2 | 1 | | | | | | | | | | | | | | | 3 | | | | | |
| 6 | Bronchitis | | | | | | | | | | 1 | 1 | | | | | | | | | | | 1 | 1 | |
| 7 | Cancer | | | | | | | | | 1 | 3 | | | | | | | | | | | | 1 | 3 | |
| 8 | Catarrh | 2 | | | 2 | | 1 | | 1 | 4 | 3 | | 2 | | | | | | | 6 | | 1 | 4 | 2 | 1 |
| 9 | Childbirth | | | | | | | | 3 | | 18 | | | | | | | | | 1 | | | 4 | 9 | 6 |
| 10 | Cholera | 2 | 2 | 10 | 8 | 9 | 2 | 10 | 1 | 14 | 9 | 3 | 1 | | 1 | | | | | 28 | | | 18 | 20 | 1 |
| 11 | ....do..infantum | 1 | | 1 | | | | | | | | | | | | | | | | 2 | | | | | |
| 12 | Colic | | | | | | | | | 2 | 1 | 1 | | | | | | | | | | | 3 | 1 | |
| 13 | Congest'n, not specf'd | | | | | | | 3 | | | 3 | 1 | | | | | | | | | | | | 4 | 1 |
| 14 | ....do....brain | | | 2 | 1 | 1 | 1 | | | 2 | 1 | | | | | | | | | 6 | | | 1 | | 1 |
| 15 | Consumption | | | | | | | | 4 | 20 | 18 | 3 | 4 | 1 | | | | 1 | | 4 | | 1 | 16 | 21 | 6 |
| 16 | Convulsions | 1 | 1 | | 1 | | | 2 | | | | | | | | | | | | 5 | | | | | |
| 17 | Croup | 12 | 12 | 7 | 9 | 1 | | 1 | | | | | | | | | | | | 41 | | | | 1 | |
| 18 | Diarrhœa | 4 | 2 | 4 | 3 | | | | 2 | 1 | 1 | 2 | | | | | | | | 11 | | | 2 | 4 | 1 |
| 19 | Dropsy | 1 | | 4 | 3 | | 1 | 1 | 3 | 7 | 8 | 6 | 1 | | | | | | | 9 | | | 11 | 11 | 2 |
| 20 | Dysentery | | 1 | 1 | 1 | | 1 | 2 | | | | | | | | | | | | 3 | | | | 3 | |
| 21 | Dyspepsia | | | | | | | 1 | | 1 | 1 | 2 | | | | | | | | | | | 3 | 2 | |
| 22 | Erysipelas | | | | 2 | | 1 | | 2 | 1 | 2 | 1 | 1 | | | | | | | 3 | | | 3 | 2 | |
| 23 | Fever, not specified | 6 | 6 | 11 | 9 | 10 | 4 | 10 | 5 | 2 | 9 | 3 | 2 | | | | | | | 37 | | 2 | 12 | 21 | 5 |
| 24 | ..do .bilious | 2 | | 5 | 4 | 2 | 1 | 1 | | 6 | 3 | 2 | 1 | | | | | | | 9 | | | 7 | 7 | 3 |
| 25 | ..do..congestive | 1 | 1 | 11 | 6 | 2 | 6 | 5 | 3 | 6 | 10 | 3 | 1 | | | | | | | 19 | 1 | | 8 | 21 | 5 |
| 26 | ..do..intermittent | 3 | | 4 | 2 | 1 | | 1 | 1 | | 1 | 1 | | | 1 | | | | | 9 | | 1 | | 4 | |
| 27 | ..do..puerperal | | | | | | | | | | 1 | | | | | | | | | | | | 1 | | |
| 28 | ..do..scarlet | 1 | 2 | 9 | 13 | 6 | 4 | 3 | 7 | | | 1 | | | | | | | | 34 | | | 1 | 10 | 1 |
| 29 | ..do..typhus | | | 1 | 2 | 3 | 2 | 1 | 1 | 12 | 7 | 2 | | | | | | | | 6 | | 1 | 3 | 17 | 3 |
| 30 | Heart, disease of | | | | 1 | | | 1 | 1 | 2 | | | | | | | | | | 1 | | | 3 | | |
| 31 | Hemorrhage | | | | | | | 1 | | 1 | | | | | | | | | | 1 | | | 1 | | |
| 32 | Hives | 1 | 7 | 1 | 3 | | | | | | | | | | | | | | | 12 | | | | | |
| 33 | Hooping cough | 5 | 5 | 2 | 4 | | | | | | | | | | | | | | | 16 | | | | | |
| 34 | Hydrocephalus | | | | 1 | | | | | | | | | | | | | | | 1 | | | | | |
| 35 | Inflammation | 1 | 1 | 2 | 2 | 1 | | 2 | 2 | 1 | 2 | 1 | | 1 | | | | | | 6 | | | 4 | 6 | |
| 36 | ...do......bowels | | | 3 | 1 | 1 | | 1 | | 3 | 1 | 2 | | | | | | | | 3 | | | 4 | 3 | 2 |
| 37 | ....do......brain | 1 | 1 | 2 | 6 | 1 | 2 | 3 | 1 | 2 | | | | 1 | | | | | | 5 | | | 4 | 10 | |
| 38 | Jaundice | 1 | | | | 1 | | | | | | | | | | | | | | 2 | | | | | |
| 39 | Killed | | | | | 1 | | | | 3 | | 1 | | | | | | | | | | | 1 | 2 | 1 |
| 40 | Lightning | | | | | | | | | 1 | | | | | | | | | | 1 | | | | | |
| 41 | Liver, disease of | | | | | | 1 | 2 | 1 | 4 | 2 | 3 | 1 | | | | | | | 2 | | | 6 | 3 | 3 |
| 42 | Lockjaw | 1 | | | | | | | | | | | | | | | | | | 1 | | | | | |
| 43 | Lungs, disease of | | | | | | | | | 1 | 1 | 1 | | | | | | | | | | | 1 | | 2 |
| 44 | Malformation | | | 1 | | | | | | | | | | | | | | | | 1 | | | | | |
| 45 | Measles | 3 | | | 1 | | | | | | | | | | | | | | | | | | | 4 | |
| 46 | Menses, excess of | | | | | | | | 1 | | 3 | | 1 | | | | | | | 3 | | | | 1 | 1 |
| 47 | Mortification | | | | | | | | 1 | | | | | | | | | | | 1 | | | | | |
| 48 | Old age | | | | | | | | | | | 2 | 7 | 1 | | 1 | 2 | | | | | 1 | 8 | 2 | |
| 49 | Paralysis | | | | | | 1 | 1 | 1 | | | 3 | | | | | | | | 3 | | | 1 | 2 | |
| 50 | Pleurisy | | | | | | | | | 6 | 1 | 2 | | | | | | | | | | | 3 | 4 | 1 |
| 51 | Pneumonia | 5 | 2 | 6 | 2 | 3 | | 2 | 7 | 19 | 5 | 4 | 1 | 1 | | | | | | 18 | | 1 | 14 | 21 | 6 |
| 52 | Poison | | 1 | | 1 | | | | | 1 | | | 1 | | | | | | | 2 | | | 2 | | |
| 53 | Quinsy | | | | | | | | 1 | 2 | 2 | | | | | | | | | 3 | | | 1 | | |
| 54 | Rheumatism | | | | | | | | | | 2 | 1 | 1 | | | | | | | | | | 3 | 1 | |
| 55 | Rickets | | | 1 | | | | | | | | | | | | | | | | | | | | 1 | |
| 56 | Salivation, effects of | | | | 1 | | | | | | | | | | | | | | | | | | | 1 | |
| 57 | Scrofula | | | | 2 | | | 1 | 2 | | 1 | 1 | | | | | | | | 3 | | | 2 | 1 | |
| 58 | Spine, disease of | | | | | | | | | 1 | | | | | | | | | | | | | | 1 | |
| 59 | Stillborn | 1 | 1 | | | | | | | | | | | | | | | | | 2 | | | | | |
| 60 | Suffocation | 4 | 5 | | | | | | | | | | | | | | | | | 9 | | | | | |
| 61 | Suicide | | | | | | | | | 1 | | | | | | | | | | 1 | | | | | |
| 62 | Sun, stroke of | | | | | | | 1 | | | | | | | | | | | | 1 | | | | | |
| 63 | Teething | | 4 | 3 | 2 | | | | | | | | | | | | | | | 8 | | | | 1 | |
| 64 | Throat, disease of | | | | | 1 | | | | 1 | | | | | | | | | | | | 1 | | 1 | |
| 65 | Thrush | 1 | | 1 | | | | | | | | | | | | | | | | 2 | | | | | |
| 66 | Tumor | | | | | | | | 1 | | 1 | | | | | | | | | | | | | 1 | |
| 67 | Uterus, disease of | | | | | | | | | | 1 | | | | | | | | | 1 | | | | | |
| 68 | Worms | 6 | 1 | 7 | 10 | 2 | 1 | | 1 | | | | | | | | | | | 22 | | | 2 | 3 | 1 |
| 69 | Unknown | 29 | 37 | 23 | 13 | 4 | 1 | 7 | 9 | 14 | 13 | 8 | 7 | | | | | | | 106 | | 3 | 24 | 23 | 7 |
| | Total | 96 | 93 | 128 | 125 | 52 | 30 | 65 | 65 | 155 | 139 | 64 | 33 | 6 | 1 | 1 | 2 | 1 | .. | 488 | 1 | 12 | 194 | 265 | 62 |

## SECTION OF THE STATE OF TEXAS—Continued.

| NATIVITIES. | | | | | SEASON OF DECEASE. | | | | DURATION OF SICKNESS. | | | | WHITES. | | | COLORED. | | | | | | | | | |
|---|---|---|---|---|---|---|---|---|---|---|---|---|---|---|---|---|---|---|---|---|---|---|---|---|---|
| | | | | | | | | | | | | | | | | Slaves. | | | | Free. | | | | | |
| | | | | | | | | | | | | | | | | Black. | | Mulatto. | | Black | | Mul. | | | |
| California and Territories. | Ireland. | Germany. | Other foreign countries. | Unknown. | Spring. | Summer. | Autumn. | Winter. | Under 1 week. | 1 week and under 1 month. | 1 month and under 3 months. | 3 months and over. | Males. | Females. | Total. | M. | F. | M. | F. | M. | F. | M | F | Aggregate deaths. | |
| .... | ... | .. | .... | ... | 1 | .... | 2 | 1 | 3 | 1 | .... | .... | 3 | 1 | 4 | .... | .... | .... | .... | ... | ... | .. | .. | 4 | 1 |
| .... | ... | .. | .... | ... | 1 | 1 | 2 | .... | 3 | .... | .... | .... | 1 | .... | 1 | .... | 3 | .... | .... | ... | ... | .. | .. | 4 | 2 |
| .... | ... | .. | .... | 1 | .... | .... | 1 | .... | 1 | .... | .... | .... | .... | .... | .... | .... | 1 | .... | .... | ... | ... | .. | .. | 1 | 3 |
| .... | ... | .. | .... | ... | 2 | 1 | .... | .... | .... | 2 | 1 | .... | 1 | .... | 1 | 2 | .... | .... | .... | ... | ... | .. | .. | 3 | 4 |
| .... | ... | .. | .... | ... | 1 | 2 | .... | .... | 1 | 1 | .... | 1 | 1 | .... | 1 | 1 | 1 | .... | .... | ... | ... | .. | .. | 3 | 5 |
| .... | ... | .. | .... | ... | 2 | .... | .... | .... | .... | .... | 1 | 1 | 1 | .... | 1 | .... | 1 | .... | .... | ... | ... | .. | .. | 2 | 6 |
| .... | ... | .. | .... | ... | 1 | 1 | .... | 2 | .... | .... | .... | 4 | 1 | 3 | 4 | .... | .... | .... | .... | ... | ... | .. | .. | 4 | 7 |
| .... | ... | .. | .... | 1 | 5 | 1 | 2 | 7 | 3 | 5 | 5 | 1 | 2 | 6 | 8 | 4 | 3 | .... | .... | ... | ... | .. | .. | 15 | 8 |
| .... | ... | .. | .... | 1 | 9 | 2 | 6 | 4 | 13 | 6 | 2 | .... | .... | 18 | 18 | .... | 3 | .... | .... | ... | ... | .. | .. | 21 | 9 |
| .... | ... | .. | .... | 5 | 20 | 7 | 1 | 40 | 43 | 14 | 2 | .... | 33 | 10 | 43 | 14 | 14 | 1 | .... | ... | ... | .. | .. | 72 | 10 |
| .... | ... | .. | .... | ... | .... | 2 | .... | .... | 2 | .... | .... | .... | 2 | .... | 2 | .... | .... | .... | .... | ... | ... | .. | .. | 2 | 11 |
| .... | ... | .. | .... | ... | 1 | .... | 1 | 2 | 2 | 1 | .... | 1 | 1 | 1 | 2 | 2 | .... | .... | .... | ... | ... | .. | .. | 4 | 12 |
| .... | ... | .. | 1 | 1 | 1 | .... | 5 | 1 | 5 | 1 | 1 | .... | 4 | 1 | 5 | .... | 1 | .... | 1 | ... | ... | .. | .. | 7 | 13 |
| .... | ... | .. | .... | ... | 2 | 1 | 4 | 1 | 6 | 2 | .... | .... | 5 | 1 | 6 | .... | 2 | .... | .... | ... | ... | .. | .. | 8 | 14 |
| .... | ... | .. | 1 | 2 | 15 | 12 | 7 | 16 | .... | 4 | 9 | 36 | 21 | 17 | 38 | 4 | 8 | .... | 1 | ... | ... | .. | .. | 51 | 15 |
| .... | ... | .. | .... | ... | 1 | 1 | 2 | 1 | 1 | 1 | 1 | 2 | .... | 2 | 2 | 2 | .... | 1 | .... | ... | ... | .. | .. | 5 | 16 |
| .... | ... | .. | .... | ... | 6 | 11 | 16 | 9 | 34 | 7 | .... | .... | 12 | 14 | 26 | 8 | 7 | 1 | .... | ... | ... | .. | .. | 42 | 17 |
| .... | ... | .. | 1 | ... | 2 | 6 | 8 | 8 | 3 | 10 | 3 | 3 | 7 | 7 | 14 | 4 | 1 | .... | .... | ... | ... | .. | .. | 19 | 18 |
| .... | ... | .. | .... | 2 | 11 | 6 | 7 | 11 | 1 | 6 | 7 | 21 | 14 | 9 | 23 | 5 | 7 | .... | .... | ... | ... | .. | .. | 35 | 19 |
| .... | ... | .. | .... | ... | 1 | 2 | 3 | ... | 3 | 3 | .... | .... | 2 | 3 | 5 | 1 | .... | .... | .... | ... | ... | .. | .. | 6 | 20 |
| .... | ... | .. | .... | ... | 3 | .... | 2 | .... | 2 | .... | .... | 3 | 4 | 1 | 5 | .... | .... | .... | .... | ... | ... | .. | .. | 5 | 21 |
| .... | ... | .. | .... | 2 | 5 | 4 | .... | 1 | 2 | 7 | .... | .... | .... | 4 | 4 | 2 | 4 | .... | .... | ... | ... | .. | .. | 10 | 22 |
| .... | ... | .. | .... | ... | 8 | 17 | 44 | 8 | 28 | 43 | 6 | .... | 30 | 37 | 57 | 11 | 6 | 1 | 2 | ... | ... | 1 | .. | 77 | 23 |
| .... | ... | .. | .... | 1 | 5 | 5 | 15 | 2 | 6 | 18 | 3 | .... | 15 | 9 | 24 | 3 | .... | .... | .... | ... | ... | .. | .. | 27 | 24 |
| .... | ... | .. | .... | 1 | 6 | 10 | 32 | 7 | 36 | 18 | 1 | .... | 21 | 20 | 41 | 7 | 6 | .... | 1 | ... | ... | .. | .. | 55 | 25 |
| .... | ... | .. | .... | ... | 2 | 2 | 5 | 5 | 7 | 4 | 1 | 1 | 8 | 3 | 11 | 2 | 1 | .... | .... | ... | ... | .. | .. | 14 | 26 |
| .... | ... | .. | .... | ... | .... | 1 | .... | .... | .... | 1 | .... | .... | .... | 1 | 1 | .... | .... | .... | .... | ... | ... | .. | .. | 1 | 27 |
| .... | ... | .. | .... | ... | 14 | 10 | 9 | 13 | 18 | 33 | 4 | 1 | 15 | 16 | 31 | 4 | 10 | .... | .... | ... | ... | 1 | .. | 46 | 28 |
| .... | .. | .. | .... | 1 | 12 | 3 | 6 | 10 | 3 | 25 | 1 | 1 | 18 | 11 | 29 | 1 | 1 | .... | .... | ... | ... | .. | .. | 31 | 29 |
| .... | ... | .. | .... | 1 | 2 | 3 | .... | .... | 1 | 1 | .... | 3 | .... | 2 | 2 | 2 | .... | 1 | .... | ... | ... | .. | .. | 5 | 30 |
| .... | ... | .. | .... | ... | .... | 1 | 1 | .... | .... | .... | 1 | 1 | 1 | .... | 1 | 1 | .... | .... | .... | ... | ... | .. | .. | 2 | 31 |
| .... | ... | .. | .... | ... | 1 | 3 | 3 | 5 | 9 | 3 | .... | .... | 1 | 7 | 8 | 1 | 3 | .... | .... | ... | ... | .. | .. | 12 | 32 |
| .... | ... | .. | .... | ... | 8 | 5 | 1 | 2 | 1 | 7 | 5 | 2 | 2 | 4 | 6 | 4 | 3 | 1 | 2 | ... | ... | .. | .. | 16 | 33 |
| .... | ... | .. | .... | ... | .... | 1 | .... | .... | .... | 1 | .... | .... | .... | 1 | 1 | .... | .... | .... | .... | ... | ... | .. | .. | 1 | 34 |
| .... | ... | .. | .... | ... | 2 | 7 | 6 | 1 | 5 | 10 | 1 | .... | 8 | 7 | 15 | 1 | .... | .... | .... | ... | ... | .. | .. | 16 | 35 |
| .... | ... | .. | .... | ... | 5 | 1 | 5 | 1 | 3 | 8 | 1 | .... | 9 | 2 | 11 | 1 | .... | .... | .... | ... | ... | .. | .. | 12 | 36 |
| .... | ... | .. | .... | 1 | 2 | 5 | 10 | 3 | 9 | 6 | 4 | .... | 8 | 9 | 17 | 2 | 1 | .... | .... | ... | ... | .. | .. | 20 | 37 |
| .... | ... | .. | .... | ... | .... | 2 | .... | .... | .... | .... | 2 | .... | 2 | .... | 2 | .... | .... | .... | .... | ... | ... | .. | .. | 2 | 38 |
| .... | ... | .. | .... | 1 | .... | 1 | 3 | 1 | 3 | 1 | .... | .... | 2 | .... | 2 | 2 | .... | 1 | .... | ... | ... | .. | .. | 5 | 39 |
| .... | ... | .. | .... | ... | .... | 1 | .... | .... | .... | .... | .... | .... | .... | .... | .... | 1 | .... | .... | .... | ... | ... | .. | .. | 1 | 40 |
| .... | ... | .. | .... | ... | 3 | 3 | 5 | 3 | 3 | 5 | 1 | 4 | 9 | 5 | 14 | .... | .... | .... | .... | ... | ... | .. | .. | 14 | 41 |
| .... | ... | .. | .... | ... | .... | .... | .... | 1 | 1 | .... | .... | .... | .... | .... | .... | 1 | .... | .... | .... | ... | ... | .. | .. | 1 | 42 |
| .... | ... | .. | .... | ... | 1 | 1 | 1 | .... | .... | 2 | .... | 1 | 2 | 1 | 3 | .... | .... | .... | .... | ... | ... | .. | .. | 3 | 43 |
| .... | ... | .. | .... | ... | .... | .... | 1 | .... | .... | .... | .... | 1 | 1 | .... | 1 | .... | .... | .... | .... | ... | ... | .. | .. | 1 | 44 |
| .... | ... | .. | .... | ... | .... | .... | 3 | 1 | .... | .... | .... | .... | .... | .... | .... | 3 | 1 | .... | .... | ... | ... | .. | .. | 4 | 45 |
| .... | ... | .. | .... | ... | .... | .... | 3 | 2 | .... | 1 | 2 | 2 | .... | 3 | 3 | .... | 2 | .... | .... | ... | ... | .. | .. | 5 | 46 |
| .... | ... | .. | .... | ... | .... | .... | .... | 1 | 1 | .... | .... | .... | .... | 1 | 1 | .... | .... | .... | .... | ... | ... | .. | .. | 1 | 47 |
| .... | ... | .. | 1 | 1 | 3 | 2 | 4 | 4 | 4 | 2 | 1 | 1 | 2 | 6 | 8 | 2 | 3 | .... | .... | ... | ... | .. | .. | 13 | 48 |
| .... | ... | .. | .... | ... | 2 | 1 | 2 | 1 | 1 | 1 | 1 | 3 | 3 | 2 | 5 | 1 | .... | .... | .... | ... | ... | .. | .. | 6 | 49 |
| .... | ... | .. | .... | 1 | 3 | 2 | 2 | 2 | 4 | 5 | ... | .... | 7 | 1 | 8 | 1 | .... | .... | .... | ... | ... | .. | .. | 9 | 50 |
| .... | ... | .. | .... | 2 | 24 | 10 | 7 | 16 | 10 | 40 | 2 | 2 | 31 | 13 | 44 | 9 | 4 | .... | .... | ... | ... | .. | .. | 57 | 51 |
| .... | ... | .. | .... | .. | 1 | 1 | 1 | .... | 3 | .... | .... | 1 | .... | 3 | 3 | 1 | .... | .... | .... | ... | ... | .. | .. | 4 | 52 |
| ... | ... | .. | .... | 1 | 3 | .... | 2 | .... | 4 | 1 | .... | .... | 1 | 2 | 3 | 1 | 1 | .... | .... | ... | ... | .. | .. | 5 | 53 |
| .... | ... | .. | .... | ... | 1 | .... | 2 | 1 | .... | .... | 2 | 1 | 1 | 2 | 3 | .... | 1 | .... | .... | ... | ... | .. | .. | 4 | 54 |
| .... | ... | .. | .... | ... | .... | .... | 1 | .... | .... | .... | .... | 1 | .... | .... | .... | 1 | .... | .... | .... | ... | ... | .. | .. | 1 | 55 |
| .... | ... | .. | .... | ... | .... | .... | 1 | .... | .... | 1 | .... | .... | .... | 1 | 1 | .... | .... | .... | .... | ... | ... | .. | .. | 1 | 56 |
| ... | ... | .. | .... | 1 | .... | 1 | 5 | 1 | .... | 1 | .... | 6 | 1 | 3 | 4 | 1 | 2 | .... | .... | ... | ... | .. | .. | 7 | 57 |
| .... | ... | .. | .... | ... | .... | 1 | .... | .... | 1 | .... | .... | .... | .... | .... | .... | 1 | .... | .... | .... | ... | ... | .. | .. | 1 | 58 |
| .... | ... | .. | .... | ... | 2 | .... | .... | .... | .... | .... | .... | .... | .... | 1 | 1 | 1 | .... | .... | .... | ... | ... | .. | .. | 2 | 59 |
| .... | ... | .. | .... | ... | 3 | 3 | 1 | 2 | 9 | .... | .... | .... | .... | 2 | 2 | 4 | 2 | .... | 1 | ... | ... | .. | .. | 9 | 60 |
| .... | ... | .. | .... | ... | .... | .... | .... | .... | 1 | .... | .... | .... | .... | .... | .... | 1 | .... | .... | .... | ... | ... | .. | .. | 1 | 61 |
| .... | ... | .. | .... | ... | .... | 1 | .... | .... | .... | 1 | .... | .... | 1 | .... | 1 | .... | .... | .... | .... | ... | ... | .. | .. | 1 | 62 |
| .... | ... | .. | .... | ... | .... | 1 | 5 | 3 | 1 | 4 | 4 | .... | .... | 3 | 3 | 3 | 3 | .... | .... | ... | ... | .. | .. | 9 | 63 |
| .... | ... | .. | .... | ... | 1 | 1 | .... | .... | .... | 2 | .... | .... | 2 | .... | 2 | .... | .... | .... | .... | ... | ... | .. | .. | 2 | 64 |
| .... | ... | .. | .... | ... | .... | 1 | .... | 1 | 1 | 1 | .... | .... | 1 | .... | 1 | 1 | .... | .... | .... | ... | ... | .. | .. | 2 | 65 |
| .... | ... | .. | .... | 1 | .... | .... | .... | 2 | .... | .... | .... | 2 | .... | 1 | 1 | .... | 1 | .... | .... | ... | ... | .. | .. | 2 | 66 |
| .... | ... | .. | .... | ... | .... | .... | .... | 1 | .... | .... | .... | .... | .... | .... | .... | .... | 1 | .... | .... | ... | ... | .. | .. | 1 | 67 |
| .... | ... | .. | .... | ... | 4 | 13 | 6 | 4 | 11 | 8 | 2 | 1 | 5 | 6 | 11 | 10 | 6 | .... | 1 | ... | ... | .. | .. | 28 | 68 |
| .... | ... | .. | .... | 2 | 35 | 45 | 45 | 32 | 49 | 59 | 18 | 21 | 30 | 46 | 96 | 32 | 81 | 1 | 3 | ... | ... | 2 | .. | 165 | 69 |
| .... | .. | .. | 4 | 31 | 259 | 231 | 313 | 238 | 383 | 376 | 97 | 131 | 382 | 323 | 705 | 174 | 153 | 10 | 12 | ... | ... | 3 | .. | 1057 | |

## CLASSIFICATION OF DEATHS IN SOUTHERN

*Embracing the following counties: Austin, Brazoria, Calhoun, (Cameron, Star, and Webb,) Liberty, Matagorda, Montgomery, Newton, Neuces, Polk,*

| | Cause of death. | AGES. Under 1. | | 1 and under 5. | | 5 and under 10. | | 10 and under 20. | | 20 and under 50. | | 50 and under 80. | | 80 and under 100. | | 100 & over. | | Age unknown. | | NATIVITIES. Born in State. | N. England States. | Middle States. | Southern States. | Southwest'n States. | Northwest'n States. |
|---|---|---|---|---|---|---|---|---|---|---|---|---|---|---|---|---|---|---|---|---|---|---|---|---|---|
| | | M. | F. | M. | F. | M. | F. | M. | F. | M. | F. | M. | F. | M | F. | M | F. | M | F. | | | | | | |
| 1 | Abscess | ... | ... | ... | ... | ... | ... | ... | ... | 1 | 1 | ... | ... | ... | ... | ... | ... | ... | ... | ... | 1 | ... | ... | ... | ... |
| 2 | Accident, not specif'd | 1 | 2 | ... | ... | 2 | 1 | 1 | ... | 1 | 1 | ... | ... | ... | ... | ... | ... | ... | ... | 8 | ... | 1 | ... | ... | ... |
| 3 | ....do...burned | ... | ... | 2 | 2 | ... | ... | ... | 1 | ... | ... | ... | ... | ... | ... | ... | ... | ... | ... | 4 | ... | ... | ... | 1 | ... |
| 4 | ....do...drowned | ... | ... | ... | 1 | 3 | ... | 2 | 2 | 6 | ... | 2 | ... | ... | ... | ... | ... | ... | ... | 6 | ... | 1 | 4 | 2 | ... |
| 5 | Apoplexy | ... | ... | ... | ... | ... | ... | ... | ... | 2 | 3 | 2 | ... | ... | ... | ... | ... | ... | ... | ... | 1 | 1 | 3 | 1 | ... |
| 6 | Asthma | ... | ... | ... | 1 | ... | ... | ... | ... | ... | ... | ... | ... | ... | ... | ... | ... | ... | ... | 1 | ... | ... | ... | ... | ... |
| 7 | Bronchitis | ... | ... | 1 | ... | ... | ... | ... | ... | ... | ... | ... | ... | ... | ... | ... | ... | ... | ... | 1 | ... | ... | ... | ... | ... |
| 8 | Cancer | ... | ... | ... | ... | ... | ... | ... | ... | ... | ... | ... | 1 | ... | ... | ... | ... | ... | ... | ... | ... | ... | 1 | ... | ... |
| 9 | Catarrh | 1 | ... | 3 | 2 | ... | 1 | ... | ... | 1 | 2 | ... | 1 | ... | ... | ... | ... | ... | ... | 7 | ... | 2 | 2 | ... | ... |
| 10 | Childbirth | ... | ... | ... | ... | ... | ... | ... | 2 | ... | 16 | ... | ... | ... | ... | ... | ... | ... | ... | 3 | ... | ... | 2 | 7 | 1 |
| 11 | Cholera | 1 | 2 | 14 | 12 | 8 | 5 | 10 | 6 | 28 | 22 | 5 | 4 | ... | ... | ... | ... | 5 | 4 | 47 | 1 | 5 | 19 | 32 | 4 |
| 12 | ...do..morbus | ... | ... | 1 | 2 | 1 | ... | 1 | ... | 1 | ... | ... | ... | ... | ... | ... | ... | ... | ... | ... | ... | ... | ... | 6 | ... |
| 13 | Colic | ... | 1 | ... | ... | ... | ... | 1 | ... | 1 | 1 | ... | ... | ... | ... | ... | ... | ... | ... | 1 | ... | ... | 1 | ... | ... |
| 14 | Cong'st'n, not specf'd | 1 | ... | 2 | 2 | 2 | 1 | ... | 1 | 2 | ... | 1 | 1 | ... | ... | ... | ... | ... | ... | 6 | ... | ... | 1 | 2 | 1 |
| 15 | ....do....brain | ... | ... | ... | ... | 3 | ... | 1 | ... | 2 | ... | ... | ... | ... | ... | ... | ... | ... | ... | 3 | ... | 1 | 1 | ... | ... |
| 16 | Consumption | ... | ... | ... | ... | ... | ... | ... | ... | 11 | 2 | 5 | 1 | ... | ... | ... | ... | ... | ... | 1 | 2 | 3 | 5 | 2 | 2 |
| 17 | Convulsions | 2 | 3 | 4 | 7 | ... | ... | ... | ... | ... | 1 | ... | ... | ... | ... | ... | ... | ... | ... | 16 | ... | ... | ... | ... | ... |
| 18 | Croup | 5 | 4 | ... | 4 | ... | ... | ... | ... | ... | ... | ... | ... | ... | ... | ... | ... | ... | ... | 11 | ... | ... | ... | 2 | ... |
| 19 | Diarrhœa | 1 | 1 | ... | 2 | ... | ... | ... | ... | 5 | 1 | 1 | 1 | ... | ... | ... | ... | ... | ... | 4 | ... | ... | ... | 2 | 1 |
| 20 | Dropsy | ... | ... | 1 | ... | 3 | 2 | 4 | ... | 2 | 6 | 4 | ... | ... | 1 | ... | ... | ... | ... | 6 | 1 | ... | 7 | 7 | ... |
| 21 | Dysentery | 2 | ... | ... | ... | ... | ... | 1 | ... | 2 | ... | ... | ... | ... | ... | ... | ... | ... | ... | 2 | ... | ... | 1 | 1 | ... |
| 22 | Dyspepsia | ... | ... | ... | ... | ... | ... | ... | ... | ... | ... | 1 | ... | ... | ... | ... | ... | ... | ... | ... | ... | ... | 1 | ... | ... |
| 23 | Epilepsy | ... | ... | ... | ... | ... | ... | 1 | ... | ... | ... | ... | ... | ... | ... | ... | ... | ... | ... | 1 | ... | ... | ... | ... | ... |
| 24 | Fever, not specified | 10 | 14 | 21 | 15 | 9 | 5 | 13 | 5 | 22 | 18 | 6 | 4 | ... | ... | ... | ... | ... | ... | 71 | ... | 3 | 23 | 14 | 3 |
| 25 | ..do..bilious | ... | ... | 2 | ... | ... | 1 | 1 | ... | ... | 1 | ... | ... | ... | ... | ... | ... | ... | ... | 4 | ... | ... | ... | ... | ... |
| 26 | ..do..brain | ... | ... | ... | ... | 2 | 1 | ... | ... | 1 | ... | ... | ... | ... | ... | ... | ... | ... | ... | 1 | ... | 1 | ... | 2 | ... |
| 27 | ..do..congestive | ... | ... | 1 | 3 | 1 | 2 | 2 | ... | 7 | ... | ... | ... | ... | ... | ... | ... | ... | ... | 8 | 1 | 1 | ... | 3 | ... |
| 28 | ..do..intermittent | ... | ... | ... | ... | 1 | ... | 1 | ... | ... | ... | ... | ... | ... | 1 | ... | ... | ... | ... | ... | ... | ... | 3 | ... | ... |
| 29 | ..do..puerperal | ... | ... | ... | ... | ... | ... | ... | 1 | ... | 2 | ... | ... | ... | ... | ... | ... | ... | ... | 1 | ... | ... | 2 | ... | ... |
| 30 | ..do..scarlet | 1 | 1 | 4 | 5 | 1 | 2 | 2 | 2 | ... | 3 | ... | ... | ... | ... | ... | ... | ... | ... | 14 | ... | ... | 4 | 2 | 1 |
| 31 | ..do..typhus | 1 | 1 | 3 | ... | 1 | ... | 1 | ... | 1 | ... | ... | ... | ... | ... | ... | ... | ... | ... | 5 | ... | ... | 2 | 1 | ... |
| 32 | Heart, disease of | 1 | ... | ... | 1 | ... | ... | ... | 1 | 1 | ... | ... | ... | ... | ... | ... | ... | ... | ... | 3 | ... | ... | 1 | ... | ... |
| 33 | Hemorrhage | ... | 1 | ... | ... | ... | ... | ... | ... | ... | 1 | ... | ... | ... | ... | ... | ... | ... | ... | 1 | ... | ... | ... | 1 | ... |
| 34 | Hernia | ... | ... | ... | ... | ... | ... | ... | ... | ... | ... | 1 | ... | ... | ... | ... | ... | ... | ... | ... | ... | ... | 1 | ... | ... |
| 35 | Hives | 1 | 3 | ... | ... | ... | ... | ... | ... | ... | ... | ... | ... | ... | ... | ... | ... | ... | ... | 4 | ... | ... | ... | ... | ... |
| 36 | Hooping cough | 2 | 3 | 4 | 1 | ... | ... | ... | ... | ... | ... | ... | ... | ... | ... | ... | ... | ... | ... | 10 | ... | ... | ... | ... | ... |
| 37 | Hydrocephalus | 1 | 1 | ... | ... | ... | ... | ... | ... | ... | ... | ... | ... | ... | ... | ... | ... | ... | ... | 2 | ... | ... | ... | ... | ... |
| 38 | Inflamt'n, not specf'd | ... | 1 | ... | ... | 1 | ... | ... | ... | 2 | ... | 1 | ... | ... | ... | ... | ... | ... | ... | 1 | 1 | ... | ... | 2 | ... |
| 39 | ....do....bowels | ... | 2 | ... | 3 | ... | ... | 1 | ... | ... | 1 | ... | ... | ... | ... | ... | ... | ... | ... | 4 | ... | ... | 1 | ... | 1 |
| 40 | ....do....brain | ... | ... | 2 | ... | ... | 1 | 1 | ... | 1 | ... | ... | ... | ... | ... | ... | ... | ... | ... | 3 | ... | ... | ... | 1 | ... |
| 41 | ....do....stomach | ... | ... | ... | 1 | ... | ... | ... | ... | ... | ... | ... | ... | ... | ... | ... | ... | ... | ... | 1 | ... | ... | ... | ... | ... |
| 42 | Intemperance | ... | ... | ... | ... | ... | ... | ... | ... | 1 | ... | ... | ... | ... | ... | ... | ... | ... | ... | ... | ... | ... | ... | ... | ... |
| 43 | Jaundice | ... | ... | 1 | ... | ... | ... | ... | ... | ... | ... | ... | ... | ... | ... | ... | ... | ... | ... | 1 | ... | ... | ... | ... | ... |
| 44 | Killed | ... | ... | ... | ... | ... | ... | 1 | ... | 9 | ... | 1 | ... | ... | ... | ... | ... | ... | ... | ... | ... | 1 | 1 | 2 | 2 |
| 45 | Liver, disease of | ... | ... | ... | ... | ... | ... | ... | ... | 1 | 2 | ... | ... | ... | ... | ... | ... | ... | ... | ... | ... | ... | 1 | ... | ... |
| 46 | Lockjaw | 6 | 8 | ... | 1 | ... | ... | ... | ... | 1 | ... | ... | ... | ... | ... | ... | ... | ... | ... | 15 | ... | ... | ... | ... | ... |
| 47 | Lungs, disease of | ... | ... | ... | ... | ... | ... | ... | ... | ... | 2 | ... | ... | ... | ... | ... | ... | ... | ... | 1 | ... | ... | ... | 1 | ... |
| 48 | Measles | ... | 1 | ... | 1 | ... | ... | ... | ... | 1 | 1 | ... | ... | ... | ... | ... | ... | ... | ... | 2 | ... | 1 | ... | 1 | ... |
| 49 | Murder | ... | ... | ... | ... | ... | ... | 2 | ... | 8 | ... | 1 | ... | ... | ... | ... | ... | ... | ... | 10 | 1 | ... | ... | ... | ... |
| 50 | Old age | ... | ... | ... | ... | ... | ... | ... | ... | ... | ... | 2 | 1 | 2 | 4 | ... | 1 | ... | ... | ... | 1 | 1 | 4 | ... | ... |
| 51 | Paralysis | ... | ... | ... | ... | ... | ... | ... | ... | ... | 1 | ... | 1 | ... | ... | ... | ... | ... | ... | 1 | 1 | ... | ... | ... | ... |
| 52 | Pleurisy | ... | ... | ... | ... | ... | 1 | 2 | ... | 1 | 1 | 1 | ... | ... | ... | ... | ... | ... | ... | 1 | ... | ... | 3 | 1 | 1 |
| 53 | Pneumonia | ... | ... | 4 | 3 | 1 | 2 | 6 | 2 | 12 | 6 | 3 | 2 | ... | ... | ... | ... | ... | ... | 12 | ... | ... | 8 | 10 | 3 |
| 54 | Poison | ... | ... | ... | ... | ... | ... | ... | ... | 3 | ... | ... | ... | ... | ... | ... | ... | ... | ... | ... | ... | ... | ... | 1 | ... |
| 55 | Quinsy | ... | ... | ... | ... | ... | ... | ... | ... | 1 | ... | ... | ... | ... | ... | ... | ... | ... | ... | ... | ... | ... | 1 | ... | ... |
| 56 | Rheumatism | ... | ... | ... | ... | ... | ... | ... | ... | 1 | 1 | 1 | ... | ... | ... | ... | ... | ... | ... | ... | ... | ... | 1 | 1 | ... |
| 57 | Small pox | ... | ... | ... | ... | ... | ... | 1 | ... | 2 | ... | ... | ... | ... | ... | ... | ... | ... | ... | 1 | ... | ... | ... | ... | ... |
| 58 | Stillborn | 1 | 1 | ... | ... | ... | ... | ... | ... | ... | ... | ... | ... | ... | ... | ... | ... | ... | ... | 2 | ... | ... | ... | ... | ... |
| 59 | Suffocation | 8 | 2 | ... | ... | ... | ... | ... | ... | ... | ... | ... | ... | ... | ... | ... | ... | ... | ... | 5 | ... | ... | ... | ... | ... |
| 60 | Suicide | ... | ... | ... | ... | ... | ... | ... | ... | ... | 1 | ... | ... | ... | ... | ... | ... | ... | ... | ... | ... | ... | ... | ... | ... |
| 61 | Teething | ... | ... | 4 | 2 | ... | ... | ... | ... | ... | ... | ... | ... | ... | ... | ... | ... | ... | ... | 4 | ... | ... | ... | 1 | ... |
| 62 | Throat, disease of | ... | ... | ... | ... | ... | ... | ... | ... | 2 | ... | ... | ... | ... | ... | ... | ... | ... | ... | ... | ... | ... | ... | 1 | 1 |
| 63 | Thrush | 1 | ... | 1 | ... | ... | ... | ... | ... | ... | ... | ... | ... | ... | ... | ... | ... | ... | ... | 2 | ... | ... | ... | ... | ... |
| 64 | Tumor | ... | ... | 1 | ... | ... | ... | ... | ... | ... | ... | ... | ... | ... | ... | ... | ... | ... | ... | 1 | ... | ... | ... | ... | ... |
| 65 | Worms | ... | 1 | 5 | 9 | 5 | 1 | ... | ... | ... | ... | ... | ... | ... | ... | ... | ... | ... | ... | 19 | ... | ... | 2 | ... | ... |
| 66 | Unknown* | 22 | 26 | 11 | 8 | 4 | 5 | 3 | 5 | 7 | 11 | 2 | 2 | ... | ... | ... | ... | ... | ... | 88 | 1 | 1 | 7 | 11 | ... |
| | Total | 64 | 79 | 92 | 88 | 48 | 31 | 59 | 28 | 150 | 108 | 40 | 19 | 2 | 6 | .. | 1 | 5 | 4 | 421 | 12 | 23 | 113 | 121 | 21 |

* 48, age and sex not given, but are included in the aggregate.

## ECTION OF THE STATE OF TEXAS.

*olorado, Dewitt, Fort Bend, Galveston, Goliad, Harris, Jackson, Jasper, Jefferson, Lavacca, efugio, San Patricio, Tyler, Victoria, and Wharton.*

| NATIVITIES. | | | | | SEASON OF DECEASE. | | | | DURATION OF SICKNESS. | | | | WHITES. | | | COLORED. | | | | | | | | | |
|---|---|---|---|---|---|---|---|---|---|---|---|---|---|---|---|---|---|---|---|---|---|---|---|---|---|
| | | | | | | | | | | | | | | | | Slaves. | | | | Free. | | | | | |
| | | | | | | | | | | | | | | | | Black. | | Mulatto. | | Black. | | Mul. | | | |
| ritories. | Ireland. | Germany. | Other foreign countries. | Unknown. | Spring. | Summer. | Autumn. | Winter. | Under 1 week. | 1 week and under 1 month. | 1 month and under 3 months. | 3 months and over. | Males. | Females. | Total. | M. | F. | M. | F. | M. | F. | M | F. | Aggregate deaths. | |
| | | | | 1 | 1 | | 1 | | | 1 | | 1 | 1 | 1 | 2 | | | | | | | | | 2 | 1 |
| | | | | | 3 | 4 | 2 | | 2 | 2 | | | 4 | 2 | 6 | 1 | 2 | | | | | | | 9 | 2 |
| | | | | | 2 | 1 | | 2 | 2 | 1 | 1 | | 1 | | 1 | 1 | 3 | | | | | | | 5 | 3 |
| | | | 2 | 1 | 4 | 8 | 3 | 1 | 16 | | | | 7 | 1 | 8 | 6 | 2 | | | | | | | 16 | 4 |
| | | | 1 | | | 2 | 4 | 1 | 6 | 1 | | | 2 | 1 | 3 | 2 | 2 | | | | | | | 7 | 5 |
| | | | | | | | | | 1 | | | | | | | | 1 | | | | | | | 1 | 6 |
| | | | | | | 1 | | | 1 | | | | 1 | | 1 | | | | | | | | | 1 | 7 |
| | | | | | | 1 | | | | | | 1 | | | | | 1 | | | | | | | 1 | 8 |
| | | | | | 1 | | 4 | 6 | 6 | 3 | 1 | 1 | 2 | 2 | 4 | 3 | 4 | | | | | | | 11 | 9 |
| | | 2 | 2 | 1 | 1 | 3 | 6 | 8 | 7 | 8 | | 2 | | 15 | 15 | | 3 | | | | | | | 18 | 10 |
| | 2 | 10 | | 6 | 38 | 24 | 19 | 45 | 116 | 6 | 1 | 2 | 18 | 14 | 32 | 48 | 38 | 5 | 3 | | | | | 126 | 11 |
| | | | | | 6 | | | | 4 | 2 | | | 3 | 1 | 4 | 1 | 1 | | | | | | | 6 | 12 |
| | | 2 | | | | 1 | 2 | 1 | 3 | 1 | | | 2 | 2 | 4 | | | | | | | | | 4 | 13 |
| | | 2 | 1 | | | 4 | 7 | 2 | 8 | 5 | | | 6 | 4 | 10 | 2 | 1 | | | | | | | 13 | 14 |
| | | | 1 | | 1 | 1 | 4 | | 4 | 2 | | | 5 | | 5 | 1 | | | | | | | | 6 | 15 |
| | 1 | | 2 | 1 | 7 | 4 | 4 | 4 | 3 | 2 | 3 | 11 | 14 | 1 | 15 | 2 | 2 | | | | | | | 19 | 16 |
| | | 1 | | | 2 | 4 | 8 | 2 | 11 | 3 | 1 | | 5 | 8 | 13 | 1 | 3 | | | | | | | 17 | 17 |
| | | | | | 4 | 2 | 2 | 5 | 11 | 2 | | | 2 | 4 | 6 | 2 | 4 | 1 | | | | | | 13 | 18 |
| | | 1 | 1 | 3 | 4 | 3 | 3 | 2 | 2 | 6 | 1 | 2 | 7 | 2 | 9 | | 3 | | | | | | | 12 | 19 |
| | | 1 | 1 | | 2 | 6 | 6 | 9 | 1 | 3 | 6 | 11 | 9 | 5 | 14 | 5 | 4 | | | | | | | 23 | 20 |
| | | 1 | | | | 1 | 1 | 3 | 2 | 3 | | | 3 | | 3 | 2 | | | | | | | | 5 | 21 |
| | | | | | | 1 | | | | | 1 | | 1 | | 1 | | | | | | | | | 1 | 22 |
| | | | | | | | 1 | | | | | 1 | 1 | | 1 | | | | | | | | | 1 | 23 |
| | 4 | 14 | 4 | 6 | 26 | 36 | 60 | 18 | 55 | 70 | 8 | 5 | 58 | 30 | 83 | 25 | 29 | 2 | 2 | | | 1 | | 142 | 24 |
| | | 1 | | | | 1 | 4 | | 2 | 3 | | | 1 | 2 | 3 | 2 | | | | | | | | 5 | 25 |
| | | | | | | 1 | 3 | | 2 | 1 | 1 | | 3 | | 3 | | 1 | | | | | | | 4 | 26 |
| | 1 | | 1 | 1 | | 2 | 10 | 4 | 10 | 4 | 1 | | 8 | 4 | 12 | 3 | 1 | | | | | | | 16 | 27 |
| | | | | | 1 | | 1 | | 3 | | | | | | | 2 | 1 | | | | | | | 3 | 28 |
| | | | | | 1 | 2 | | | | 1 | 1 | | | 3 | 3 | | | | | | | | | 3 | 29 |
| | | | | | 9 | 2 | 4 | 6 | 9 | 6 | 5 | | 7 | 8 | 15 | 1 | 4 | | 1 | | | | | 21 | 30 |
| | | | | | 7 | | 1 | | 4 | 3 | 1 | | 2 | 1 | 3 | 5 | | | | | | | | 8 | 31 |
| | | | | | 2 | 1 | 1 | | 1 | 3 | | | 1 | | 1 | 1 | 2 | | | | | | | 4 | 32 |
| | | | | | | 1 | 1 | | 2 | | | | | 2 | 2 | | | | | | | | | 2 | 33 |
| | | | | | | 1 | | | | | | | | | | 1 | | | | | | | | 1 | 34 |
| | | | | | | 1 | 1 | 2 | 4 | | | | 1 | 2 | 3 | | 1 | | | | | | | 4 | 35 |
| | | | | | 4 | 3 | 2 | 1 | 2 | 4 | 2 | | 5 | 2 | 7 | 1 | 2 | | | | | | | 10 | 36 |
| | | | | | | 1 | 1 | | 1 | 1 | | | 1 | 1 | 2 | | | | | | | | | 2 | 37 |
| | | 1 | | | 1 | 1 | 2 | 1 | 2 | 2 | 1 | | 4 | | 4 | | 1 | | | | | | | 5 | 38 |
| | | | 1 | | 1 | 2 | 3 | 1 | 3 | 4 | | | 1 | 5 | 6 | | 1 | | | | | | | 7 | 39 |
| | 1 | | | | | 2 | 3 | | 4 | 1 | | | 3 | 1 | 4 | 1 | | | | | | | | 5 | 40 |
| | | | | | | | | 1 | 1 | | | | | 1 | 1 | | | | | | | | | 1 | 41 |
| | | | 1 | | | | | 1 | | 1 | | | 1 | | 1 | | | | | | | | | 1 | 42 |
| | | | | | | | 1 | | 1 | | | | 1 | | 1 | | | | | | | | | 1 | 43 |
| | | | 8 | 2 | 3 | 6 | 2 | | 3 | 2 | | | 10 | 1 | 10 | 1 | | | | | | | | 11 | 44 |
| | | | 1 | 1 | 1 | | 1 | 1 | | 1 | | 2 | 1 | 1 | 2 | | 1 | | | | | | | 3 | 45 |
| | | | | 1 | 5 | 4 | 4 | 3 | 12 | 4 | | | | | | 7 | 9 | | | | | | | 16 | 46 |
| | | | | | | | 1 | 1 | | | 1 | | | 1 | 1 | | | | 1 | | | | | 2 | 47 |
| | | | | | 2 | 2 | | | 2 | 2 | | | 1 | 1 | 2 | | 2 | | | | | | | 4 | 48 |
| | | | | | 5 | 2 | | 4 | | | | | 11 | | 11 | | | | | | | | | 11 | 49 |
| | | | 1 | 3 | 1 | 2 | 6 | 1 | 3 | 2 | 1 | | 3 | 3 | 6 | 1 | 3 | | | | | | | 10 | 50 |
| | | | | | 2 | | | | 2 | | | | | 2 | 2 | | | | | | | | | 2 | 51 |
| | | | | | | | 2 | 4 | 1 | 5 | | | 2 | 1 | 3 | 1 | 1 | 1 | | | | | | 6 | 52 |
| | 1 | | 1 | 6 | 19 | | 6 | 16 | 14 | 24 | 3 | | 18 | 11 | 29 | 8 | 4 | | | | | | | 41 | 53 |
| | | | 1 | 1 | 2 | | 1 | | 2 | | 1 | | 2 | | 2 | 1 | | | | | | | | 3 | 54 |
| | | | | | | 1 | | | 1 | | | | 1 | | 1 | | | | | | | | | 1 | 55 |
| | 1 | | | | 1 | 1 | | 1 | | 2 | | 1 | 2 | 1 | 3 | | | | | | | | | 3 | 56 |
| | 1 | | | 1 | | 3 | | | 1 | 2 | | | 2 | | 2 | 1 | | | | | | | | 3 | 57 |
| | | | | | 1 | | 1 | | | | | | 1 | 1 | 2 | | | | | | | | | 2 | 58 |
| | | | | | | | | 3 | 5 | | | | 1 | | 1 | 2 | 1 | | 1 | | | | | 5 | 59 |
| | | | 1 | | | 1 | | | 1 | | | | | 1 | 1 | | | | | | | | | 1 | 60 |
| | | 1 | | | 2 | | 3 | 1 | | 2 | 4 | | 1 | 1 | 2 | 3 | 1 | | | | | | | 6 | 61 |
| | | | | | 1 | | | 1 | 1 | 1 | | | 2 | | 2 | | | | | | | | | 2 | 62 |
| | | | | | | | 2 | | | 2 | | | 2 | | 2 | | | | | | | | | 2 | 63 |
| | | | | | | 1 | | | | | 1 | | | | | 1 | | | | | | | | 1 | 64 |
| | | | | | 2 | 5 | 11 | 2 | 14 | 5 | 1 | 1 | 3 | 4 | 7 | 6 | 6 | 1 | 1 | | | | | 21 | 65 |
| | | 1 | 1 | 49 | 24 | 26 | 32 | 20 | 41 | 17 | 11 | 15 | 25 | 32 | 105 | 24 | 23 | | 2 | | | | | 154 | 66 |
| .... | 12 | 38 | 27 | 84 | 199 | 182 | 247 | 184 | 415 | 226 | 58 | 56 | 274 | 185 | 507 | 175 | 168 | 10 | 11 | .. | .. | 1 | .. | 872 | |

## CLASSIFICATION OF DEATHS IN CENTRAL

*Embracing the following counties: Anderson, Bastrop, Bexar, Brazos, Burlson, Caldwell, Henderson, Houston, Kaufman, Leon, Limestone, Medina, Milam, Navarro, Robert-*

| | Cause of death. | AGES. Under 1. | | 1 and under 5. | | 5 and under 10. | | 10 and under 20. | | 20 and under 50. | | 50 and under 80. | | 80 and under 100. | | 100 & over. | | Age unknown. | | NATIVITIES. Born in State. | N. England States. | Middle States. | Southern States. | Southwest'n States. | Northwest'n States. |
|---|---|---|---|---|---|---|---|---|---|---|---|---|---|---|---|---|---|---|---|---|---|---|---|---|---|
| | | M. | F. | M. | F. | M. | F. | M. | F. | M. | F. | M. | F. | M | F. | M | F. | M | F. | | | | | | |
| 1 | Accident, not specif'd | 8 | 5 | 4 | 1 | 1 | | 4 | 2 | 8 | | 4 | 1 | | | | | | | 14 | | 1 | 7 | 5 | 3 |
| 2 | ..do....burned | | 1 | 1 | 1 | | 4 | | 2 | | | | | | | | | | | 7 | | | | | |
| 3 | ...do....drowned | | | | 2 | 2 | 1 | 2 | 1 | 4 | 3 | | | | | | | | | 3 | | 1 | 6 | 2 | 1 |
| 4 | ...do....shot | | | | | | | 1 | | 3 | | | | | | | | | | | | | 2 | 2 | |
| 5 | Apoplexy | | | | | | 1 | 1 | 1 | | | | 1 | | | | | | | 1 | | | 1 | 2 | |
| 6 | Brain, disease of | | | 1 | | | | | | | | | | | | | | | | 1 | | | | | |
| 7 | Bronchitis | | | | | | 1 | | | | | | | | | | | | | | | | | | 1 |
| 8 | Cancer | | | | | | | | | | 1 | | 1 | | | | 1 | | | | | | 2 | | 1 |
| 9 | Catarrh | 1 | 3 | 1 | 1 | | | | 2 | 4 | 3 | 2 | | | | | | | | 6 | | | 5 | 3 | 2 |
| 10 | Chicken pox | | 1 | | | | 1 | | | | | | | | | | | | | 2 | | | | | |
| 11 | Childbirth | | | | | | | | 2 | | 13 | | | | | | | | | 1 | | | 1 | 5 | 4 |
| 12 | Cholera | 1 | | 5 | 9 | 3 | 1 | 4 | 6 | 30 | 12 | 11 | 2 | | | | | | | 18 | | 2 | 15 | 12 | 6 |
| 13 | ....do....infantum | | 4 | 4 | 2 | | | | | | | | | | | | | | | 8 | | | 1 | 1 | |
| 14 | ....do....morbus | | | 1 | 1 | 1 | | | | | 4 | | | | | | | | | 1 | | | 1 | 3 | 2 |
| 15 | Colic | 2 | | | | | | | 1 | | | 2 | 1 | | | | | | | 2 | | | 1 | 1 | |
| 16 | Congest'n, not spec'd | 2 | 1 | 1 | 4 | | 1 | | | 2 | 2 | | | | | | | | | 6 | | 1 | 1 | 3 | 1 |
| 17 | ..do.....brain | | 1 | | 2 | | 1 | | | 1 | | | | | | | | | | 2 | | | | 3 | |
| 18 | Consumption | 1 | | | 1 | 1 | | 1 | 1 | 18 | 6 | 6 | 7 | | | | | | | 3 | 2 | 4 | 11 | 11 | 7 |
| 19 | Convulsions | 4 | 2 | 2 | 2 | 1 | | 1 | 2 | | 2 | | | | | | | | | 12 | | | 1 | 3 | |
| 20 | Croup | 11 | 14 | 2 | 8 | | | | | | | | | | | | | | | 31 | | | | 4 | |
| 21 | Debility | 1 | 1 | | | | | | | | | | | | | | | | | 2 | | | | | |
| 22 | Diarrhœa | 1 | 3 | 1 | 2 | 2 | 2 | | | 2 | 1 | 2 | 1 | | | | | | | 10 | | | 3 | 2 | 1 |
| 23 | Dropsy | | | 2 | 1 | 2 | 2 | 3 | | 3 | 2 | 2 | 1 | | 1 | 1 | | | | 4 | | | 6 | 6 | 4 |
| 24 | Dysentery | 1 | 1 | 2 | | | | | | 3 | 2 | | | 1 | | | | | | 5 | | 1 | | | 1 |
| 25 | Dyspepsia | | | 1 | | | | | | | | | | | | | | | | 1 | | | | | |
| 26 | Erysipelas | 1 | | | 1 | 1 | | 3 | | 2 | 2 | | 2 | | | | | | | 4 | 1 | | 2 | 3 | 2 |
| 27 | Fever, not specified | 3 | 7 | 7 | 10 | 5 | 7 | 8 | 7 | 17 | 12 | 7 | 8 | | 1 | | | | | 35 | | 1 | 14 | 25 | 7 |
| 28 | ..do..bilious | 1 | 1 | 1 | 4 | 1 | | 1 | | 7 | 3 | 8 | | | | | | | | 5 | | | 4 | 5 | 3 |
| 29 | ..do..congestive | 2 | 5 | 4 | 3 | 5 | 4 | 4 | 2 | 9 | 1 | 4 | 3 | 1 | | | | | | 13 | | | 10 | 17 | 4 |
| 30 | ..do..intermittent | 1 | 8 | 5 | 1 | | | 2 | | 1 | 1 | 8 | 1 | | | | | | | 14 | | | 1 | 2 | |
| 31 | ..do..puerperal | | | | | | | | | | 9 | | | | | | | | | | | | 4 | 5 | |
| 32 | ..do..scarlet | 2 | 1 | 5 | 2 | 3 | 5 | | 1 | 2 | 1 | | | | | | | | | 16 | | | 1 | 3 | 2 |
| 33 | ..do..typhus | | | 2 | 4 | 1 | 1 | 1 | 4 | 6 | 5 | | 3 | | | | | | | 9 | | 1 | 6 | 7 | 4 |
| 34 | Gravel | | | | | | | | | | | 2 | | 1 | | | | | | | | | 3 | | |
| 35 | Heart, disease of | | | 1 | | | 1 | | | | | | | | | | | | | | | | 1 | | 1 |
| 36 | Hemorrhage | | | | | | | | | 1 | 1 | 2 | | | | | | | | | 1 | | 2 | 1 | |
| 37 | Hives | 10 | 3 | | | | 1 | | | | | | | | | | | | | 12 | | | | 2 | |
| 38 | Hooping cough | 5 | 5 | 4 | 6 | 1 | | 2 | | | | | | | | | | | | 11 | | | | 10 | 2 |
| 39 | Hydrocephalus | 2 | | 1 | | 1 | | | | | | | | | | | | | | 4 | | | | | |
| 40 | Inflamat'n, not spe'd | | 1 | | | | | 1 | 1 | 1 | 4 | 1 | | | | | | | | 2 | | | 2 | 2 | 2 |
| 41 | ....do.....bowels | | 2 | 2 | | 1 | 1 | | | 1 | 3 | 2 | | | | | | | | 4 | | | 2 | 1 | 2 |
| 42 | ....do......brain | 1 | 2 | 2 | 2 | 1 | 2 | 3 | 1 | 2 | 2 | | | | | | | | | 9 | | | 4 | 2 | 3 |
| 43 | Jaundice | | 1 | | | 1 | 1 | | | 2 | | | | | | | | | | 2 | | | 1 | 1 | |
| 44 | Killed | | | | | | | | | 6 | 1 | | | | | | | | | 1 | | 2 | 1 | 1 | 1 |
| 45 | Liver, disease of | 1 | | | 1 | 2 | 1 | | | 4 | 1 | 2 | | | | | | | | 4 | | | 1 | 4 | 1 |
| 46 | Lockjaw | 1 | | 1 | | | | | | | | | | | | | | | | 2 | | | | | |
| 47 | Lungs, disease of | | | | | 1 | | | | 1 | | | | | | | | | | | | | | 2 | |
| 48 | Malformation | 1 | | | | | | | | | | | | | | | | | | 1 | | | | | |
| 49 | Menses, excess of | | | | | | | | | | 1 | | | | | | | | | | | | 1 | | |
| 50 | Mortification | | | | | | | | | | 1 | | | | | | | | | | | | | | 1 |
| 51 | Murder | | | | | | | 2 | | 6 | | | | | | | | | | 1 | | 2 | | | |
| 52 | Old age | | | | | | | | | | | 4 | 5 | 1 | 1 | | | | | | | 2 | 2 | 1 | |
| 53 | Paralysis | | | | | | | | | | 1 | | | | | | | | | 1 | | | | | |
| 54 | Pleurisy | 1 | 1 | | | | | 1 | 1 | 2 | 1 | | | | | | | | | 3 | | | | 3 | |
| 55 | Pneumonia | 2 | 3 | 8 | 8 | 3 | 1 | 6 | 7 | 26 | 13 | 5 | | | | | | | | 13 | | 1 | 14 | 27 | 14 |
| 56 | Poison | | | | 1 | | | | 1 | 1 | | | | | | | | | | 1 | | | | 2 | |
| 57 | Quinsy | | | 1 | | | | | | | 1 | | | | | | | | | 2 | | | | | |
| 58 | Rheumatism | | | | | | | | | 2 | | | 1 | | | | | | | | | | 2 | | 1 |
| 59 | Scrofula | | | | | | | 1 | | 1 | | | | | | | | | | | | | | | 1 |
| 60 | Small pox | 1 | 2 | 1 | 4 | | 1 | 4 | | 6 | | | | | | | | | | 13 | | | | 3 | |
| 61 | Spine, disease of | | 1 | | | | | | | | | | | | | | | | | 1 | | | | | |
| 62 | Stillborn | 1 | 1 | | | | | | | | | | | | | | | | | 2 | | | | | |
| 63 | Suffocation | 1 | 3 | | | | | | | | | | | | | | | | | 4 | | | | | |
| 64 | Suicide | | | | | | | | | 3 | | | | | | | | | | | | | | | |
| 65 | Sun, stroke of | | | | | | | | | | | 1 | | | | | | | | | | | 1 | | |
| 66 | Teething | 3 | | 2 | 2 | | | | | | | | | | | | | | | 6 | | | | 1 | |
| 67 | Thrush | 3 | | | 1 | | | | | | | | | | | | | | | 3 | | | 1 | | |
| 68 | Tumor | 1 | | | | | | | | | | | 1 | | | | | | | 1 | | | | | |
| 69 | Worms | 1 | 2 | 3 | 4 | 2 | 2 | 1 | | | | | | | | | | | | 8 | | | | 6 | 1 |
| 70 | Unknown | 38 | 28 | 20 | 17 | 5 | 5 | 5 | 11 | 26 | 31 | 10 | 11 | 1 | | | | | | 121 | 1 | 4 | 20 | 27 | 9 |
| | Total | 111 | 114 | 98 | 103 | 47 | 48 | 62 | 56 | 213 | 146 | 75 | 45 | 5 | 3 | 1 | 1 | .. | .. | 463 | 5 | 23 | 164 | 231 | 95 |

## SECTION OF THE STATE OF TEXAS.

*Cherokee, Comal, Dallas, Ellis, Fayette, Gaudalupe, Gillespie, Gonzales, Grimes, Hays, son, Smith, Tarrant, Travis, Van Zandt, Walker, Washington, and Williamson.*

| Nativities: California and Territories. | Nativities: Ireland. | Nativities: Germany. | Nativities: Other foreign countries. | Nativities: Unknown. | Season of decease: Spring. | Season of decease: Summer. | Season of decease: Autumn. | Season of decease: Winter. | Duration of sickness: Under 1 week. | Duration of sickness: 1 week and under 1 month. | Duration of sickness: 1 month and under 3 months. | Duration of sickness: 3 months and over. | Whites: Males. | Whites: Females. | Whites: Total. | Colored: Slaves: Black: M. | Colored: Slaves: Black: F. | Colored: Slaves: Mulatto: M. | Colored: Slaves: Mulatto: F. | Colored: Free: Black: M. | Colored: Free: Black: F. | Colored: Free: Mul.: M | Colored: Free: Mul.: F | Aggregate deaths. | |
|---|---|---|---|---|---|---|---|---|---|---|---|---|---|---|---|---|---|---|---|---|---|---|---|---|---|
| | | 2 | | 1 | 4 | 12 | 7 | 10 | 21 | 5 | 1 | | 19 | 4 | 23 | 5 | 4 | | 1 | | | | | 33 | 1 |
| | | 2 | | | 3 | 2 | 1 | 3 | 6 | | 1 | | 1 | 4 | 5 | | 3 | | 1 | | | | | 9 | 2 |
| | 1 | | | 1 | 8 | 4 | 2 | | 15 | | | | 6 | | 6 | 2 | 6 | | 1 | | | | | 15 | 3 |
| | | | | | 2 | 1 | | 1 | 1 | | | | 4 | | 4 | | | | | | | | | 4 | 4 |
| | | | | | 2 | | 1 | 1 | 4 | | | | | 1 | 1 | | 2 | 1 | | | | | | 4 | 5 |
| | | | | | | | | 1 | | 1 | | | 1 | | 1 | | | | | | | | | 1 | 6 |
| | | | | | | | | 1 | 1 | | | | | 1 | 1 | | | | | | | | | 1 | 7 |
| | | | | | | | 1 | 2 | | | | 3 | | 2 | 2 | | 1 | | | | | | | 3 | 8 |
| | | | | 1 | 7 | 2 | 3 | 5 | 3 | 9 | 4 | 1 | 6 | 5 | 11 | 9 | 3 | | 1 | | | | | 17 | 9 |
| | | | | | | | 2 | | 1 | 1 | | | | 2 | 2 | | | | | | | | | 2 | 10 |
| | | 2 | 2 | | 5 | 3 | 5 | 2 | 11 | 4 | | | | 14 | 14 | | 1 | | | | | | | 15 | 11 |
| | | 27 | 3 | 1 | 2 | 53 | 3 | 26 | 74 | 10 | | | 44 | 22 | 66 | 10 | 7 | | 1 | | | | | 84 | 12 |
| | | | | | 1 | 4 | 2 | 3 | 3 | 4 | 2 | 1 | 4 | 6 | 10 | | | | | | | | | 10 | 13 |
| | | | | | 2 | 3 | 2 | | 4 | 2 | | 1 | 2 | 5 | 7 | | | | | | | | | 7 | 14 |
| | | 1 | 1 | | 1 | 2 | 1 | 2 | 5 | 1 | | | 4 | 2 | 6 | | | | | | | | | 6 | 15 |
| | | | | 1 | | 6 | 4 | 3 | 9 | 3 | | 1 | 4 | 6 | 10 | 1 | 2 | | | | | | | 13 | 16 |
| | | | | | 1 | 1 | 3 | | 3 | 2 | | | 1 | 4 | 5 | | | | | | | | | 5 | 17 |
| | 1 | 2 | | 1 | 10 | 6 | 13 | 13 | 2 | 6 | 1 | 33 | 27 | 15 | 42 | | | | | | | | | 42 | 18 |
| | | | | | 4 | 3 | 3 | 5 | 7 | 5 | | 4 | 7 | 7 | 14 | | 1 | 1 | | | | | | 16 | 19 |
| | | | | | 10 | 7 | 8 | 10 | 32 | 1 | 2 | | 8 | 18 | 26 | 5 | 4 | | | | | | | 35 | 20 |
| | | | | | | 1 | | 1 | 1 | 1 | | | 1 | | 1 | | 1 | | | | | | | 2 | 21 |
| | | 1 | | | 3 | 9 | 3 | 2 | 7 | 9 | 1 | | 8 | 9 | 17 | | | | | | | | | 17 | 22 |
| | | | | | 7 | 5 | 4 | 4 | | 2 | 4 | 14 | 13 | 6 | 19 | | 1 | | | | | | | 20 | 23 |
| | 1 | 1 | | 1 | 2 | 1 | 3 | 4 | 5 | 4 | | 1 | 6 | 1 | 7 | 1 | 2 | | | | | | | 10 | 24 |
| | | | | | | | 1 | | | | | 1 | 1 | | 1 | | | | | | | | | 1 | 25 |
| | | | | | 5 | 3 | 2 | 2 | 5 | 2 | 3 | 2 | 6 | 3 | 9 | 1 | 1 | | 1 | | | | | 12 | 26 |
| | 1 | 4 | 7 | | 13 | 21 | 45 | 15 | 26 | 50 | 11 | 6 | 40 | 39 | 79 | 7 | 8 | | | | | | | 94 | 27 |
| | | 5 | | | | 8 | 13 | 1 | 2 | 18 | 1 | 1 | 13 | 8 | 21 | 1 | | | | | | | | 22 | 28 |
| | | 3 | | | 4 | 5 | 32 | 6 | 28 | 17 | 2 | | 25 | 15 | 40 | 3 | 3 | 1 | | | | | | 47 | 29 |
| | | 2 | 3 | 1 | 1 | 2 | 14 | 6 | 2 | 7 | 7 | 7 | 12 | 11 | 23 | | | | | | | | | 23 | 30 |
| | | | | | 3 | 2 | 1 | 3 | 4 | 5 | | | | 8 | 8 | | 1 | | | | | | | 9 | 31 |
| | | | | | 9 | 6 | 3 | 4 | 14 | 6 | 2 | | 11 | 8 | 19 | 1 | 2 | | | | | | | 22 | 32 |
| | | | | | 8 | 5 | 12 | 2 | 7 | 13 | 4 | 3 | 8 | 16 | 24 | 2 | 1 | | | | | | | 27 | 33 |
| | | | | | 1 | 1 | | 1 | | 3 | | | 3 | | 3 | | | | | | | | | 3 | 34 |
| | | | | | | | 1 | 1 | 1 | | | | | 1 | 1 | 1 | | | | | | | | 2 | 35 |
| | | | | | 1 | 3 | | | 1 | 2 | | 1 | 3 | 1 | 4 | | | | | | | | | 4 | 36 |
| | | | | | 6 | 3 | 3 | 2 | 11 | 2 | | | 9 | 4 | 13 | 1 | | | | | | | | 14 | 37 |
| | | | | | 3 | 3 | 11 | 6 | 4 | 13 | 6 | | 9 | 10 | 19 | 3 | | | 1 | | | | | 23 | 38 |
| | | | | | | 1 | 1 | 2 | 1 | 3 | | | 3 | | 3 | 1 | | | | | | | | 4 | 39 |
| | | 1 | | | 1 | 4 | 4 | | 3 | 6 | | | 3 | 6 | 9 | | | | | | | | | 9 | 40 |
| | | 2 | 1 | | 1 | 4 | 2 | 5 | 5 | 6 | 1 | | 4 | 6 | 10 | 2 | | | | | | | | 12 | 41 |
| | | | | | 3 | 5 | 6 | 4 | 14 | 2 | | 1 | 9 | 9 | 18 | | | | | | | | | 18 | 42 |
| | | | | 1 | 1 | | 1 | 3 | 2 | | 1 | 2 | 2 | 2 | 4 | 1 | | | | | | | | 5 | 43 |
| | | | 1 | | 3 | 2 | 2 | | 2 | | | | 5 | 1 | 6 | 1 | | | | | | | | 7 | 44 |
| | | 1 | 1 | | 4 | 2 | 2 | 4 | | 5 | | 7 | 9 | 3 | 12 | | | | | | | | | 12 | 45 |
| | | | | | | 1 | 1 | | 2 | | | | | | | 2 | | | | | | | | 2 | 46 |
| | | | | | 1 | 1 | | | | 1 | | 1 | 2 | | 2 | | | | | | | | | 2 | 47 |
| | | | | | | | | 1 | 1 | | | | 1 | | 1 | | | | | | | | | 1 | 48 |
| | | | | | | | | 1 | | 1 | | | | 1 | 1 | | | | | | | | | 1 | 49 |
| | | | | | 1 | | | | 1 | | | | | 1 | 1 | | | | | | | | | 1 | 50 |
| | 2 | | 3 | | 1 | 1 | | 6 | | | | | 8 | | 8 | | | | | | | | | 8 | 51 |
| | | 3 | 1 | 2 | 1 | 3 | 5 | 2 | 2 | 2 | | 3 | 3 | 5 | 8 | 2 | 1 | | | | | | | 11 | 52 |
| | | | | | | | 1 | | | 1 | | | | | | | 1 | | | | | | | 1 | 53 |
| | | | 1 | | 2 | 2 | 2 | 1 | 4 | 3 | | | 3 | 3 | 6 | 1 | | | | | | | | 7 | 54 |
| | 1 | | 4 | 3 | 31 | 13 | 11 | 22 | 18 | 46 | 6 | 5 | 40 | 22 | 62 | 10 | 5 | | | | | | | 77 | 55 |
| | | | | | | 2 | | 1 | 1 | 1 | | | | 2 | 2 | 1 | | | | | | | | 3 | 56 |
| | | | | | 1 | 1 | | | 1 | 1 | | | 1 | 1 | 2 | | | | | | | | | 2 | 57 |
| | | | | | 1 | 1 | 1 | | 1 | 1 | 1 | | 2 | 1 | 3 | | | | | | | | | 3 | 58 |
| | | | 1 | | 1 | | | 1 | 1 | 1 | | | 2 | | 2 | | | | | | | | | 2 | 59 |
| | | | 3 | | | 1 | 12 | 6 | 3 | 6 | | | 11 | 7 | 18 | 1 | | | | | | | | 19 | 60 |
| | | | | | | 1 | | | | 1 | | | | 1 | 1 | | | | | | | | | 1 | 61 |
| | | | | | 2 | | | | | | | | 1 | 1 | 2 | | | | | | | | | 2 | 62 |
| | | | | | 1 | 3 | | | 4 | | | | | | | 1 | 3 | | | | | | | 4 | 63 |
| | | | 3 | | | | 3 | | 1 | | | | 3 | | 3 | | | | | | | | | 3 | 64 |
| | | | | | | | 1 | | 1 | | | | | | | 1 | | | | | | | | 1 | 65 |
| | | | | | 1 | 2 | 4 | | 1 | 2 | 2 | 2 | 4 | 2 | 6 | 1 | | | | | | | | 7 | 66 |
| | | | | | 1 | | 1 | 2 | 3 | 1 | | | 3 | | 3 | | | | 1 | | | | | 4 | 67 |
| | | | | 1 | | | 1 | 1 | | | 2 | | 1 | 1 | 2 | | | | | | | | | 2 | 68 |
| | | | | | 2 | 2 | 6 | 5 | 5 | 7 | 1 | 2 | 5 | 8 | 13 | 1 | | 1 | | | | | | 15 | 69 |
| | 1 | 5 | 17 | 3 | 39 | 54 | 58 | 54 | 52 | 20 | 9 | 49 | 99 | 92 | 191 | 6 | 10 | | 1 | | | | | 208 | 70 |
| ... | 8 | 64 | 52 | 18 | 227 | 293 | 334 | 269 | 449 | 325 | 75 | 152 | 530 | 433 | 963 | 78 | 74 | 4 | 9 | ... | ... | ... | ... | 8123 | |

CLASSIFICATION OF DEATHS IN THE

| | Cause of death. | AGES. | | | | | | | | | | | | | | | | | | NATIVITIES. | | | | | |
|---|---|---|---|---|---|---|---|---|---|---|---|---|---|---|---|---|---|---|---|---|---|---|---|---|---|
| | | Under 1. | | 1 and under 5. | | 5 and under 10. | | 10 and under 20. | | 20 and under 50. | | 50 and under 80. | | 80 and under 100. | | 100 & over. | | Age unknown. | | Born in State. | N. England States. | Middle States. | Southern States. | Southwest'n States. | Northwest'n States. |
| | | M. | F. | M. | F. | M. | F. | M. | F. | M. | F. | M. | F. | M | F. | M | F. | M | F. | | | | | | |
| 1 | Abscess | | | | | 1 | | | | 2 | 2 | | | | | | | | | | 1 | | 1 | 1 | |
| 2 | Accident, not specif'd | 5 | 7 | 5 | 3 | 3 | 1 | 5 | 2 | 14 | 1 | 7 | 1 | | | | | | | 27 | | 2 | 11 | 8 | 3 |
| 3 | ....do...burned | | 2 | 3 | 9 | | 4 | | 3 | | 1 | | | 1 | | | | | | 17 | | | 2 | 2 | |
| 4 | ....do...drowned | | | 1 | 3 | 6 | 1 | 5 | 4 | 13 | 3 | 2 | | | | | | | | 11 | | 2 | 12 | 6 | 2 |
| 5 | ....do...scalded | | | 1 | | | | | | | | | | | | | | | | 1 | | | | | |
| 6 | ....do...shot | | | | | | | 1 | 1 | 6 | | | | | | | | | | 1 | | | 3 | 4 | |
| 7 | Apoplexy | | | | | | 1 | 1 | 2 | 3 | 5 | 2 | 1 | | | | | | | 3 | 1 | 1 | 5 | 3 | 1 |
| 8 | Asthma | | | | 1 | | | | | | | | 1 | | | | | | | 1 | | | | | |
| 9 | Bowels, disease of | 1 | | 1 | | | | 1 | | | | | | | | | | | | 3 | | | | | |
| 10 | Brain.......do | | | 3 | 1 | | | | | | | | | | | | | | | 4 | | | | | |
| 11 | Bronchitis | | | 1 | | | 1 | | | | 1 | 1 | | | | | | | | 1 | | | 1 | 1 | 1 |
| 12 | Cancer | | | | | | | | | 1 | 4 | | 2 | | | | 1 | | | | | | 4 | 3 | 1 |
| 13 | Catarrh | 4 | 3 | 4 | 5 | | 2 | | 3 | 9 | 8 | 2 | 3 | | | | | | | 19 | | 3 | 11 | 5 | 3 |
| 14 | Chicken pox | | 1 | | | | 1 | | | | | | | | | | | | | 2 | | | | | |
| 15 | Childbirth | | | | | | | | 7 | | 47 | | | | | | | | | 5 | | | 7 | 21 | 11 |
| 16 | Cholera | 4 | 4 | 29 | 29 | 20 | 8 | 24 | 13 | 72 | 43 | 19 | 7 | | 1 | | | 5 | 4 | 93 | 1 | 7 | 52 | 64 | 11 |
| 17 | ...do...infantum | 1 | 4 | 5 | 2 | | | | | | | | | | | | | | | 10 | | | 1 | 1 | |
| 18 | ...do...morbus | | | 2 | 3 | 2 | | 1 | | 1 | 4 | | | | | | | | | 1 | | | 1 | 9 | 2 |
| 19 | Colic | 2 | 1 | | | | | 1 | 1 | 3 | 2 | 3 | 1 | | | | | | | 3 | | | 5 | 2 | |
| 20 | Congest'n, not spec'd | 3 | 1 | 3 | 6 | 2 | 2 | 3 | 1 | 4 | 5 | 2 | 1 | | | | | | | 12 | | 1 | 2 | 9 | 3 |
| 21 | ....do....brain | | 1 | 2 | 3 | 4 | 2 | 1 | | 5 | 1 | | | | | | | | | 11 | | 1 | 2 | 3 | 1 |
| 22 | Consumption | 1 | | | 1 | 1 | | 1 | 5 | 49 | 26 | 14 | 12 | 1 | | | | 1 | | 8 | 4 | 8 | 32 | 34 | 15 |
| 23 | Convulsions | 7 | 6 | 6 | 10 | 1 | | 3 | 2 | | 8 | | | | | | | | | 33 | | | 1 | 3 | |
| 24 | Croup | 28 | 30 | 9 | 21 | 1 | | 1 | | | | | | | | | | | | 83 | | | | 7 | |
| 25 | Debility | 1 | 1 | | | | | | | | | | | | | | | | | 2 | | | | | |
| 26 | Diarrhœa | 6 | 6 | 5 | 7 | 2 | 2 | | 2 | 8 | 3 | 5 | 2 | | | | | | | 25 | | | 5 | 8 | 3 |
| 27 | Dropsy | 1 | | 7 | 4 | 5 | 5 | 8 | 3 | 12 | 16 | 12 | 2 | | 2 | 1 | | | | 19 | 1 | | 24 | 24 | 6 |
| 28 | Dysentery | 3 | 2 | 3 | 1 | | 1 | 3 | | 5 | 2 | | | 1 | | | | | | 10 | | 1 | 1 | 4 | 1 |
| 29 | Dyspepsia | | | 1 | | | | 1 | | 1 | 1 | 3 | | | | | | | | 1 | | | 4 | 2 | |
| 30 | Epilepsy | | | | | | | 1 | | | | | | | | | | | | 1 | | | | | |
| 31 | Erysipelas | 1 | | | 3 | 1 | 1 | 3 | 2 | 3 | 4 | 1 | 3 | | | | | | | 7 | 1 | | 5 | 5 | 2 |
| 32 | Fever, not specified | 19 | 27 | 39 | 34 | 24 | 16 | 31 | 17 | 41 | 39 | 16 | 9 | | 1 | | | | | 143 | | 6 | 49 | 60 | 15 |
| 33 | ..do..billious | 3 | 1 | 8 | 8 | 3 | 2 | 3 | | 13 | 7 | 5 | 1 | | | | | | | 18 | | | 11 | 12 | 6 |
| 34 | ..do..brain | | | | | 2 | 1 | | | 1 | | | | | | | | | | 1 | | 1 | | 2 | |
| 35 | ..do..congestive | 3 | 6 | 16 | 12 | 8 | 12 | 11 | 5 | 22 | 11 | 7 | 4 | 1 | | | | | | 40 | 2 | 1 | 18 | 41 | 9 |
| 36 | ..do..intermittent | 4 | 8 | 9 | 3 | 2 | | 4 | 1 | 1 | 2 | 4 | 1 | | 1 | | | | | 23 | | 1 | 4 | 6 | |
| 37 | ..do..puerperal | | | | | | | | 1 | | 12 | | | | | | | | | 1 | | | 7 | 5 | |
| 38 | ..do..scarlet | 4 | 4 | 18 | 20 | 10 | 11 | 5 | 10 | 2 | 4 | 1 | | | | | | | | 64 | | | 6 | 15 | 4 |
| 39 | ..do..typhus | 1 | 1 | 6 | 6 | 5 | 3 | 3 | 5 | 19 | 12 | 2 | 3 | | | | | | | 20 | | 2 | 11 | 25 | 7 |
| 40 | Gravel | | | | | | | | | | | 2 | | 1 | | | | | | | | | 3 | | |
| 41 | Heart, disease of | 1 | | 1 | 2 | | 1 | 1 | 2 | 3 | | | | | | | | | | 4 | | | 5 | | 1 |
| 42 | Hemorrhage | | 1 | | | | | 1 | | 2 | 2 | 2 | | | | | | | | 2 | 1 | | 3 | 2 | |
| 43 | Hernia | | | | | | | | | | | 1 | | | | | | | | | | | 1 | | |
| 44 | Hives | 12 | 13 | 1 | 3 | | 1 | | | | | | | | | | | | | 28 | | | | 2 | |
| 45 | Hooping cough | 12 | 13 | 10 | 11 | 1 | | 2 | | | | | | | | | | | | 87 | | | | 10 | 2 |
| 46 | Hydrocephalus | 3 | 1 | 1 | 1 | 1 | | | | | | | | | | | | | | 7 | | | | | |
| 47 | Inflamat'n, not spec'd | 1 | 3 | 2 | 2 | 2 | | 3 | 3 | 4 | 6 | 3 | | 1 | | | | | | 9 | 1 | | 6 | 10 | 2 |
| 48 | ....do....bowels | | 4 | 5 | 4 | 2 | 1 | 2 | | 4 | 5 | 4 | | | | | | | | 11 | | | 7 | 4 | 5 |
| 49 | ....do....brain | 2 | 3 | 6 | 8 | 2 | 5 | 7 | 2 | 5 | 2 | | | 1 | | | | | | 17 | | | 8 | 13 | 3 |
| 50 | ....do....stomach | | | | 1 | | | | | | | | | | | | | | | 1 | | | | | |
| 51 | Intemperance | | | | | | | | | 1 | | | | | | | | | | | | | | | |
| 52 | Jaundice | 1 | 1 | 1 | | 2 | 1 | | | 2 | | | | | | | | | | 5 | | | 1 | 1 | |
| 53 | Killed | | | | | 1 | | 1 | | 18 | 1 | 2 | | | | | | | | 1 | | 3 | 3 | 5 | 4 |
| 54 | Lightning | | | | | | | | | 1 | | | | | | | | | | 1 | | | | | |
| 55 | Liver, disease of | 1 | | | 1 | 2 | 2 | 2 | 1 | 9 | 5 | 5 | 1 | | | | | | | 6 | | | 8 | 7 | 4 |
| 56 | Lockjaw | 8 | 8 | 1 | 1 | | | | | 1 | | | | | | | | | | 18 | | | | | |
| 57 | Lungs, disease of | | | | | 1 | | | | 2 | 3 | 1 | | | | | | | | 1 | | | 1 | 3 | 2 |
| 58 | Malformation | 1 | | 1 | | | | | | | | | | | | | | | | 2 | | | | | |
| 59 | Measles | 3 | 1 | | 2 | | | | | 1 | 1 | | | | | | | | | 2 | | 1 | | 5 | |
| 60 | Menses, excess of | | | | | | | | 1 | | 4 | | 1 | | | | | | | 3 | | | 1 | 1 | 1 |
| 61 | Mortification | | | | | | | | 1 | | 1 | | | | | | | | | 1 | | | | | 1 |
| 62 | Murder | | | | | | | 4 | | 14 | | 1 | | | | | | | | 11 | 1 | 2 | | | |
| 63 | Old age | | | | | | | | | | | 8 | 13 | 4 | 5 | 1 | 3 | | | | 1 | 4 | 14 | 3 | |
| 64 | Paralysis | | | | | | 1 | 1 | 1 | | 2 | 3 | 1 | | | | | | | 5 | 1 | | 1 | 2 | |
| 65 | Pleurisy | 1 | 1 | | | | 1 | 3 | 1 | 9 | 3 | 3 | | | | | | | | 4 | | | 6 | 8 | 2 |
| 66 | Pneumonia | 7 | 5 | 18 | 8 | 7 | 3 | 14 | 16 | 57 | 24 | 12 | 3 | 1 | | | | | | 38 | | 2 | 36 | 58 | 23 |
| 67 | Poison | | 1 | | 2 | | | | 1 | 5 | | | 1 | | | | | | | 3 | | | 2 | 3 | |
| 68 | Quinsy | | | 1 | | | | | 1 | 3 | 3 | | | | | | | | | 5 | | | 2 | | |
| 69 | Rheumatism | | | | | | | | | 3 | 3 | 2 | 2 | | | | | | | | | | 6 | 2 | 1 |
| 70 | Rickets | | | 1 | | | | | | | | | | | | | | | | | | | | 1 | |
| 71 | Salivation, effects of | | | | 1 | | | | | | | | | | | | | | | | | | | 1 | |
| 72 | Scrofula | | | | 2 | | | 2 | 2 | 1 | 1 | 1 | | | | | | | | 3 | | | 2 | 1 | 1 |
| 73 | Small pox | 1 | 2 | 1 | 4 | | 1 | 5 | | 8 | | | | | | | | | | 14 | | | | 3 | |
| 74 | Spine, disease of | | 1 | | | | | | | 1 | | | | | | | | | | 1 | | | | 1 | |
| 75 | Stillborn | 3 | 3 | | | | | | | | | | | | | | | | | 6 | | | | | |

## STATE OF TEXAS—AGGREGATE.

| Nativities: California and Territories. | Nativities: Ireland. | Nativities: Germany. | Nativities: Other foreign countries. | Nativities: Unknown. | Season of decease: Spring. | Season of decease: Summer. | Season of decease: Autumn. | Season of decease: Winter. | Duration of sickness: Under 1 week. | Duration of sickness: 1 week and under 1 month. | Duration of sickness: 1 month and under 3 months. | Duration of sickness: 3 months and over. | Whites: Males. | Whites: Females. | Whites: Total. | Colored: Slaves: Black: M. | Colored: Slaves: Black: F. | Colored: Slaves: Mulatto: M. | Colored: Slaves: Mulatto: F. | Colored: Free: Black: M. | Colored: Free: Black: F. | Colored: Free: Mul: M | Colored: Free: Mul: F. | Aggregate deaths. | |
|---|---|---|---|---|---|---|---|---|---|---|---|---|---|---|---|---|---|---|---|---|---|---|---|---|---|
| ... | ... | ... | ... | 2 | 4 | ... | 1 | ... | ... | 1 | 1 | 3 | 2 | 1 | 3 | 1 | 1 | ... | ... | ... | ... | ... | ... | 5 | 1 |
| ... | ... | 2 | ... | 1 | 15 | 16 | 13 | 10 | 29 | 9 | 2 | ... | 30 | 7 | 37 | 9 | 7 | ... | 1 | ... | ... | ... | ... | 54 | 2 |
| ... | ... | 2 | ... | ... | 9 | 5 | 3 | 6 | 16 | 1 | 2 | ... | 2 | 6 | 8 | 2 | 12 | ... | 1 | ... | ... | ... | ... | 23 | 3 |
| ... | 1 | ... | 2 | 2 | 13 | 16 | 5 | 3 | 38 | ... | ... | ... | 14 | 2 | 16 | 11 | 8 | 2 | 1 | ... | ... | ... | ... | 38 | 4 |
| ... | ... | ... | ... | ... | ... | ... | 1 | ... | 1 | ... | ... | ... | 1 | ... | 1 | ... | ... | ... | ... | ... | ... | ... | ... | 1 | 5 |
| ... | ... | ... | ... | ... | 3 | 1 | 2 | 2 | 4 | 1 | ... | ... | 7 | 1 | 8 | ... | ... | ... | ... | ... | ... | ... | ... | 8 | 6 |
| ... | ... | ... | 1 | ... | 3 | 3 | 7 | 2 | 13 | 1 | ... | ... | 3 | 2 | 5 | 2 | 7 | 1 | ... | ... | ... | ... | ... | 15 | 7 |
| ... | ... | ... | ... | 1 | ... | ... | 1 | ... | 2 | ... | ... | ... | ... | ... | ... | ... | 2 | ... | ... | ... | ... | ... | ... | 2 | 8 |
| ... | ... | ... | ... | ... | 2 | 1 | ... | ... | ... | 2 | 1 | ... | 1 | ... | 1 | 2 | ... | ... | ... | ... | ... | ... | ... | 3 | 9 |
| ... | ... | ... | ... | ... | 1 | 2 | ... | 1 | 1 | 2 | ... | 1 | 2 | ... | 2 | 1 | 1 | ... | ... | ... | ... | ... | ... | 4 | 10 |
| ... | ... | ... | ... | ... | 2 | 1 | ... | 1 | 2 | ... | 1 | 1 | 2 | 1 | 3 | ... | 1 | ... | ... | ... | ... | ... | ... | 4 | 11 |
| ... | ... | ... | ... | ... | 1 | 2 | 1 | 4 | ... | ... | ... | 8 | 1 | 5 | 6 | ... | 2 | ... | ... | ... | ... | ... | ... | 8 | 12 |
| ... | ... | ... | ... | 2 | 13 | 3 | 9 | 18 | 12 | 17 | 10 | 3 | 10 | 13 | 23 | 9 | 10 | ... | 1 | ... | ... | ... | ... | 43 | 13 |
| ... | ... | ... | ... | ... | ... | ... | 2 | ... | 1 | 1 | ... | ... | ... | 2 | 2 | ... | ... | ... | ... | ... | ... | ... | ... | 2 | 14 |
| ... | ... | 4 | 4 | 2 | 15 | 8 | 17 | 14 | 31 | 18 | 2 | 2 | ... | 47 | 47 | ... | 7 | ... | ... | ... | ... | ... | ... | 54 | 15 |
| ... | 2 | 37 | 3 | 12 | 60 | 84 | 23 | 111 | 233 | 30 | 3 | 2 | 95 | 46 | 141 | 72 | 59 | 6 | 4 | ... | ... | ... | ... | 282 | 16 |
| ... | ... | ... | ... | ... | 1 | 6 | 2 | 3 | 5 | 4 | 2 | 1 | 6 | 6 | 12 | ... | ... | ... | ... | ... | ... | ... | ... | 12 | 17 |
| ... | ... | ... | ... | ... | 8 | 3 | 2 | ... | 8 | 4 | ... | 1 | 5 | 6 | 11 | 1 | 1 | ... | ... | ... | ... | ... | ... | 13 | 18 |
| ... | ... | 3 | 1 | ... | 2 | 3 | 4 | 5 | 10 | 3 | ... | 1 | 7 | 5 | 12 | 2 | ... | ... | ... | ... | ... | ... | ... | 14 | 19 |
| ... | ... | 2 | 2 | 2 | 1 | 10 | 16 | 6 | 22 | 9 | 1 | 1 | 14 | 11 | 25 | 3 | 4 | ... | 1 | ... | ... | ... | ... | 33 | 20 |
| ... | ... | ... | 1 | ... | 4 | 3 | 11 | 1 | 13 | 6 | ... | ... | 11 | 5 | 16 | 1 | 2 | ... | ... | ... | ... | ... | ... | 19 | 21 |
| ... | 2 | 2 | 3 | 4 | 32 | 22 | 24 | 33 | 5 | 12 | 13 | 80 | 62 | 33 | 95 | 6 | 10 | ... | 1 | ... | ... | ... | ... | 112 | 22 |
| ... | ... | 1 | ... | ... | 7 | 8 | 13 | 8 | 19 | 9 | 2 | 6 | 12 | 17 | 29 | 3 | 4 | 2 | ... | ... | ... | ... | ... | 38 | 23 |
| ... | ... | ... | ... | ... | 20 | 20 | 26 | 24 | 77 | 10 | 2 | ... | 22 | 36 | 58 | 15 | 15 | 2 | ... | ... | ... | ... | ... | 90 | 24 |
| ... | ... | ... | ... | ... | ... | 1 | ... | 1 | 1 | 1 | ... | ... | 1 | ... | 1 | ... | 1 | ... | ... | ... | ... | ... | ... | 2 | 25 |
| ... | ... | 2 | 2 | 3 | 9 | 18 | 14 | 7 | 12 | 25 | 5 | 5 | 22 | 18 | 40 | 4 | 4 | ... | ... | ... | ... | ... | ... | 48 | 26 |
| ... | ... | 1 | 1 | 2 | 20 | 17 | 17 | 24 | 2 | 11 | 17 | 46 | 36 | 20 | 56 | 10 | 12 | ... | ... | ... | ... | ... | ... | 78 | 27 |
| ... | 1 | 2 | ... | 1 | 8 | 4 | 7 | 7 | 10 | 10 | ... | 1 | 11 | 4 | 15 | 4 | 2 | ... | ... | ... | ... | ... | ... | 21 | 28 |
| ... | ... | ... | ... | ... | 3 | 1 | 3 | ... | 2 | ... | 1 | 4 | 6 | 1 | 7 | ... | ... | ... | ... | ... | ... | ... | ... | 7 | 29 |
| ... | ... | ... | ... | ... | ... | ... | 1 | ... | ... | ... | ... | 1 | 1 | ... | 1 | ... | ... | ... | ... | ... | ... | ... | ... | 1 | 30 |
| ... | ... | ... | ... | 2 | 10 | 7 | 2 | 3 | 7 | 9 | 3 | 2 | 6 | 7 | 13 | 3 | 5 | ... | 1 | ... | ... | ... | ... | 22 | 31 |
| ... | 5 | 18 | 11 | 6 | 47 | 74 | 149 | 41 | 109 | 163 | 25 | 11 | 123 | 96 | 219 | 43 | 43 | 3 | 4 | ... | ... | 1 | ... | 313 | 32 |
| ... | ... | 6 | ... | 1 | 5 | 14 | 32 | 3 | 10 | 39 | 4 | 1 | 29 | 19 | 48 | 6 | ... | ... | ... | ... | ... | ... | ... | 54 | 33 |
| ... | ... | ... | ... | ... | ... | 1 | 3 | ... | 2 | 1 | 1 | ... | 3 | ... | 3 | ... | 1 | ... | ... | ... | ... | ... | ... | 4 | 34 |
| ... | 1 | 3 | 1 | 2 | 10 | 17 | 74 | 17 | 74 | 39 | 4 | ... | 54 | 39 | 93 | 13 | 10 | 1 | 1 | ... | ... | ... | ... | 118 | 35 |
| ... | ... | 2 | 3 | 1 | 4 | 4 | 20 | 11 | 12 | 11 | 8 | 8 | 20 | 14 | 34 | 4 | 2 | ... | ... | ... | ... | ... | ... | 40 | 36 |
| ... | ... | ... | ... | ... | 4 | 5 | 1 | 3 | 4 | 7 | 1 | ... | ... | 12 | 12 | ... | 1 | ... | ... | ... | ... | ... | ... | 13 | 37 |
| ... | ... | ... | ... | ... | 32 | 18 | 16 | 23 | 41 | 35 | 11 | 1 | 33 | 32 | 65 | 6 | 16 | ... | 1 | ... | ... | 1 | ... | 89 | 38 |
| ... | ... | ... | ... | 1 | 27 | 8 | 19 | 12 | 14 | 41 | 6 | 4 | 28 | 28 | 56 | 8 | 2 | ... | ... | ... | ... | ... | ... | 66 | 39 |
| ... | ... | ... | ... | ... | 1 | 1 | ... | 1 | ... | 3 | ... | ... | 3 | ... | 3 | ... | ... | ... | ... | ... | ... | ... | ... | 3 | 40 |
| ... | ... | ... | ... | 1 | 4 | 4 | 2 | 1 | 3 | 4 | ... | 3 | 1 | 3 | 4 | 4 | 2 | 1 | ... | ... | ... | ... | ... | 11 | 41 |
| ... | ... | ... | ... | ... | 1 | 5 | 2 | ... | 3 | 2 | 1 | 2 | 4 | 3 | 7 | 1 | ... | ... | ... | ... | ... | ... | ... | 8 | 42 |
| ... | ... | ... | ... | ... | ... | 1 | ... | ... | ... | ... | ... | ... | ... | ... | ... | 1 | ... | ... | ... | ... | ... | ... | ... | 1 | 43 |
| ... | ... | ... | ... | ... | 7 | 7 | 7 | 9 | 24 | 5 | ... | ... | 11 | 13 | 24 | 2 | 4 | ... | ... | ... | ... | ... | ... | 30 | 44 |
| ... | ... | ... | ... | ... | 15 | 11 | 14 | 9 | 7 | 24 | 13 | 2 | 16 | 16 | 32 | 8 | 5 | 1 | 3 | ... | ... | ... | ... | 49 | 45 |
| ... | ... | ... | ... | ... | ... | 3 | 2 | 2 | 2 | 5 | ... | ... | 4 | 2 | 6 | 1 | ... | ... | ... | ... | ... | ... | ... | 7 | 46 |
| ... | ... | 2 | ... | ... | 4 | 12 | 12 | 2 | 10 | 18 | 2 | ... | 15 | 13 | 28 | 1 | 1 | ... | ... | ... | ... | ... | ... | 30 | 47 |
| ... | ... | 2 | 2 | ... | 7 | 7 | 10 | 7 | 11 | 18 | 2 | ... | 14 | 13 | 27 | 3 | 1 | ... | ... | ... | ... | ... | ... | 31 | 48 |
| ... | 1 | ... | ... | 1 | 5 | 12 | 19 | 7 | 27 | 9 | 4 | 1 | 20 | 19 | 39 | 3 | 1 | ... | ... | ... | ... | ... | ... | 43 | 49 |
| ... | ... | ... | ... | ... | ... | ... | ... | 1 | 1 | ... | ... | ... | ... | 1 | 1 | ... | ... | ... | ... | ... | ... | ... | ... | 1 | 50 |
| ... | ... | ... | 1 | ... | ... | ... | ... | 1 | ... | 1 | ... | ... | 1 | ... | 1 | ... | ... | ... | ... | ... | ... | ... | ... | 1 | 51 |
| ... | ... | ... | ... | 1 | 1 | 2 | 2 | 3 | 3 | ... | 3 | 2 | 5 | 2 | 7 | 1 | ... | ... | ... | ... | ... | ... | ... | 8 | 52 |
| ... | ... | ... | 4 | 3 | 6 | 9 | 7 | 1 | 8 | 3 | ... | ... | 17 | 1 | 18 | 4 | ... | 1 | ... | ... | ... | ... | ... | 23 | 53 |
| ... | ... | ... | ... | ... | ... | 1 | ... | ... | ... | ... | ... | ... | ... | ... | ... | 1 | ... | ... | ... | ... | ... | ... | ... | 1 | 54 |
| ... | ... | 1 | 2 | 1 | 8 | 5 | 8 | 8 | 3 | 11 | 1 | 13 | 19 | 9 | 28 | ... | 1 | ... | ... | ... | ... | ... | ... | 29 | 55 |
| ... | ... | ... | ... | 1 | 5 | 5 | 5 | 4 | 15 | 4 | ... | ... | ... | ... | ... | 10 | 9 | ... | ... | ... | ... | ... | ... | 19 | 56 |
| ... | ... | ... | ... | ... | 2 | 2 | 2 | 1 | ... | 3 | 1 | 2 | 4 | 2 | 6 | ... | ... | ... | 1 | ... | ... | ... | ... | 7 | 57 |
| ... | ... | ... | ... | ... | ... | ... | 1 | 1 | 1 | ... | ... | 1 | 2 | ... | 2 | ... | ... | ... | ... | ... | ... | ... | ... | 2 | 58 |
| ... | ... | ... | ... | ... | 2 | 2 | 3 | 1 | 2 | 2 | ... | ... | 1 | 1 | 2 | 3 | 3 | ... | ... | ... | ... | ... | ... | 8 | 59 |
| ... | ... | ... | ... | ... | ... | ... | 3 | 3 | ... | 2 | 2 | 2 | ... | 4 | 4 | ... | 2 | ... | ... | ... | ... | ... | ... | 6 | 60 |
| ... | ... | ... | ... | ... | 1 | ... | ... | 1 | 2 | ... | ... | ... | ... | 2 | 2 | ... | ... | ... | ... | ... | ... | ... | ... | 2 | 61 |
| ... | 2 | ... | 3 | ... | 6 | 3 | ... | 10 | ... | ... | ... | ... | 19 | ... | 19 | ... | ... | ... | ... | ... | ... | ... | ... | 19 | 62 |
| ... | ... | 3 | 3 | 6 | 5 | 7 | 15 | 7 | 9 | 6 | 2 | 4 | 8 | 14 | 22 | 5 | 7 | ... | ... | ... | ... | ... | ... | 34 | 63 |
| ... | ... | ... | ... | ... | 4 | 1 | 3 | 1 | 3 | 2 | 1 | 3 | 3 | 4 | 7 | 1 | 1 | ... | ... | ... | ... | ... | ... | 9 | 64 |
| ... | ... | ... | 1 | 1 | 5 | 4 | 6 | 7 | 9 | 13 | ... | ... | 12 | 5 | 17 | 3 | 1 | 1 | ... | ... | ... | ... | ... | 22 | 65 |
| ... | 2 | ... | 5 | 11 | 74 | 23 | 24 | 54 | 42 | 110 | 11 | 7 | 89 | 46 | 135 | 27 | 13 | ... | ... | ... | ... | ... | ... | 175 | 66 |
| ... | ... | ... | 1 | 1 | 3 | 3 | 2 | 1 | 6 | 1 | 1 | 1 | 2 | 5 | 7 | 3 | ... | ... | ... | ... | ... | ... | ... | 10 | 67 |
| ... | ... | ... | ... | 1 | 4 | 2 | 2 | ... | 6 | 2 | ... | ... | 3 | 3 | 6 | 1 | 1 | ... | ... | ... | ... | ... | ... | 8 | 68 |
| ... | 1 | ... | ... | ... | 3 | 2 | 3 | 2 | 1 | 3 | 3 | 2 | 5 | 4 | 9 | ... | 1 | ... | ... | ... | ... | ... | ... | 10 | 69 |
| ... | ... | ... | ... | ... | ... | ... | 1 | ... | ... | ... | ... | 1 | ... | ... | ... | 1 | ... | ... | ... | ... | ... | ... | ... | 1 | 70 |
| ... | ... | ... | ... | ... | ... | ... | 1 | ... | ... | 1 | ... | ... | ... | 1 | 1 | ... | ... | ... | ... | ... | ... | ... | ... | 1 | 71 |
| ... | ... | ... | 1 | 1 | 1 | 1 | 5 | 2 | 1 | 2 | ... | 6 | 3 | 3 | 6 | 1 | 2 | ... | ... | ... | ... | ... | ... | 9 | 72 |
| ... | 1 | ... | 3 | 1 | ... | 4 | 12 | 6 | 4 | 8 | ... | ... | 13 | 7 | 20 | 2 | ... | ... | ... | ... | ... | ... | ... | 22 | 73 |
| ... | ... | ... | ... | ... | ... | 2 | ... | ... | 1 | 1 | ... | ... | ... | 1 | 1 | 1 | ... | ... | ... | ... | ... | ... | ... | 2 | 74 |
| ... | ... | ... | ... | ... | 5 | ... | 1 | ... | ... | ... | ... | ... | 2 | 3 | 5 | 1 | ... | ... | ... | ... | ... | ... | ... | 6 | 75 |

## CLASSIFICATION OF DEATHS IN

| | Cause of death. | Ages. Under 1. M. | F. | 1 and under 5. M. | F. | 5 and under 10. M. | F. | 10 and under 20. M. | F. | 20 and under 50. M. | F. | 50 and under 80. M. | F. | 80 and under 100. M. | F. | 100 & over. M. | F. | Age unknown. M. | F. | Nativities. Born in State. | N. England States. | Middle States. | Southern States. | Southwest'n States. | Northwest'n States. |
|---|---|---|---|---|---|---|---|---|---|---|---|---|---|---|---|---|---|---|---|---|---|---|---|---|---|
| 1 | Suffocation | 8 | 10 | ... | ... | ... | ... | ... | ... | ... | ... | ... | ... | ... | ... | ... | ... | ... | ... | 18 | ... | ... | ... | ... | ... |
| 2 | Suicide | ... | ... | ... | ... | ... | ... | ... | ... | 4 | 1 | ... | ... | ... | ... | ... | ... | ... | ... | 1 | ... | ... | ... | ... | ... |
| 3 | Sun, stroke of | ... | ... | ... | ... | ... | ... | 1 | ... | ... | ... | 1 | ... | ... | ... | ... | ... | ... | ... | 1 | ... | ... | 1 | ... | ... |
| 4 | Teething | 3 | 4 | 9 | 6 | ... | ... | ... | ... | ... | ... | ... | ... | ... | ... | ... | ... | ... | ... | 18 | ... | ... | ... | 3 | ... |
| 5 | Throat, disease of | ... | ... | ... | ... | 1 | ... | ... | ... | 3 | ... | ... | ... | ... | ... | ... | ... | ... | ... | ... | ... | 1 | ... | 2 | 1 |
| 6 | Thrush | 5 | ... | 2 | 1 | ... | ... | ... | ... | ... | ... | ... | ... | ... | ... | ... | ... | ... | ... | 7 | ... | ... | 1 | ... | ... |
| 7 | Tumor | 1 | ... | 1 | ... | ... | ... | ... | 1 | ... | 1 | ... | 1 | ... | ... | ... | ... | ... | ... | 2 | ... | ... | ... | 1 | ... |
| 8 | Uterus, disease of | ... | ... | ... | ... | ... | ... | ... | ... | ... | 1 | ... | ... | ... | ... | ... | ... | ... | ... | 1 | ... | ... | ... | ... | ... |
| 9 | Worms | 7 | 4 | 15 | 23 | 9 | 4 | 1 | 1 | ... | ... | ... | ... | ... | ... | ... | ... | ... | ... | 49 | ... | ... | 4 | 9 | 2 |
| 10 | Unknown* | 89 | 91 | 54 | 38 | 13 | 11 | 15 | 25 | 47 | 55 | 20 | 20 | 1 | ... | ... | ... | ... | ... | 310 | 2 | 8 | 51 | 61 | 16 |
| | Total | 272 | 286 | 318 | 316 | 147 | 109 | 186 | 149 | 518 | 393 | 179 | 97 | 13 | 10 | 2 | 4 | 6 | 4 | 1377 | 18 | 58 | 471 | 617 | 178 |

* 48, age and sex not given, but are included in the aggregate.

## CLASSIFICATION OF DEATHS IN

| | Cause of death. | Under 1. M. | F. | 1 and under 5. M. | F. | 5 and under 10. M. | F. | 10 and under 20. M. | F. | 20 and under 50. M. | F. | 50 and under 80. M. | F. | 80 and under 100. M. | F. | 100 & over. M. | F. | Age unknown. M. | F. | Born in State. | N. England States. | Middle States. | Southern States. | Southwest'n States. | Northwest'n States. |
|---|---|---|---|---|---|---|---|---|---|---|---|---|---|---|---|---|---|---|---|---|---|---|---|---|---|
| 1 | Abscess | ... | ... | ... | ... | ... | ... | ... | ... | 1 | 2 | ... | ... | ... | ... | ... | ... | ... | ... | 2 | ... | ... | ... | ... | ... |
| 2 | Accident, not specif'd | ... | ... | 1 | ... | 1 | 1 | 6 | 2 | 17 | 2 | 6 | 2 | .. | 1 | .. | .. | ... | ... | 18 | 8 | ... | ... | ... | 2 |
| 3 | ....do...burned | ... | ... | 2 | 2 | ... | ... | ... | 3 | 1 | 1 | ... | ... | ... | 1 | .. | .. | ... | ... | 8 | 2 | ... | ... | ... | ... |
| 4 | ....do...drowned | ... | ... | 4 | ... | 3 | ... | 5 | 2 | 5 | ... | ... | ... | ... | ... | ... | ... | ... | ... | 16 | 1 | ... | ... | ... | ... |
| 5 | ....do...scalded | ... | ... | 1 | 2 | ... | ... | ... | ... | ... | ... | ... | ... | ... | ... | ... | ... | ... | ... | 3 | ... | ... | ... | ... | ... |
| 6 | Apoplexy | ... | ... | 1 | ... | ... | ... | 1 | 3 | 1 | 2 | 23 | 10 | 8 | 3 | .. | .. | ... | ... | 21 | 26 | 3 | ... | ... | ... |
| 7 | Asthma | ... | ... | ... | ... | ... | ... | ... | ... | 1 | 2 | ... | ... | ... | ... | ... | ... | ... | ... | 2 | 1 | ... | ... | ... | ... |
| 8 | Bowels, disease of | 2 | .. | 3 | 1 | 1 | ... | ... | ... | 5 | ... | 1 | 1 | ... | ... | ... | ... | ... | ... | 11 | 3 | ... | ... | ... | ... |
| 9 | Brain ......do | 2 | 1 | ... | 1 | ... | ... | ... | ... | ... | ... | 1 | ... | ... | ... | ... | ... | ... | ... | 5 | ... | ... | ... | ... | ... |
| 10 | Bronchitis | ... | ... | ... | ... | ... | 1 | ... | ... | 1 | ... | ... | 1 | ... | ... | ... | ... | ... | ... | 2 | 1 | ... | ... | ... | ... |
| 11 | Cancer | ... | ... | ... | 2 | ... | ... | ... | ... | 4 | 8 | 10 | 18 | 7 | 3 | ... | ... | ... | ... | 10 | 40 | 1 | ... | ... | ... |
| 12 | Canker rash | 4 | 7 | 18 | 19 | 13 | 12 | 1 | 1 | ... | 2 | ... | 1 | ... | ... | ... | ... | ... | ... | 75 | 1 | 1 | ... | ... | ... |
| 13 | Catarrh | 4 | 1 | ... | 1 | ... | ... | ... | ... | ... | ... | ... | ... | ... | ... | ... | ... | ... | ... | 6 | ... | ... | ... | ... | ... |
| 14 | Chicken pox | 1 | ... | ... | ... | ... | ... | ... | ... | ... | ... | ... | ... | ... | ... | ... | ... | ... | ... | 1 | ... | ... | ... | ... | ... |
| 15 | Childbirth | ... | ... | ... | ... | ... | ... | ... | 1 | ... | 23 | ... | ... | ... | ... | ... | ... | ... | ... | 16 | 1 | ... | ... | ... | ... |
| 16 | Colera | ... | 2 | 1 | 2 | 1 | 1 | 1 | ... | 10 | 5 | 5 | 2 | .. | 1 | ... | ... | ... | ... | 17 | 7 | 1 | ... | ... | ... |
| 17 | ...do..infantum | 1 | ... | 3 | 2 | ... | ... | ... | ... | ... | ... | ... | ... | ... | ... | ... | ... | ... | ... | 6 | ... | ... | ... | ... | ... |
| 18 | ...do..morbus | ... | 1 | 3 | ... | 3 | 2 | ... | 1 | 3 | ... | 4 | 1 | .. | 2 | ... | ... | ... | ... | 16 | 4 | ... | ... | ... | ... |
| 19 | Chorea | ... | ... | ... | ... | ... | ... | ... | ... | ... | 1 | ... | ... | ... | ... | ... | ... | ... | ... | 1 | ... | ... | ... | ... | ... |
| 20 | Colic | ... | ... | ... | ... | ... | ... | ... | ... | ... | 1 | 5 | 1 | 1 | ... | ... | ... | ... | ... | 4 | 4 | ... | ... | ... | ... |
| 21 | Congestion | ... | ... | 1 | ... | ... | ... | ... | ... | ... | ... | 1 | ... | ... | ... | ... | ... | ... | ... | 1 | 1 | ... | ... | ... | ... |
| 22 | ....do....brain | 1 | ... | 1 | ... | ... | 2 | ... | 1 | ... | 1 | 1 | ... | ... | ... | ... | ... | ... | ... | 5 | 2 | ... | ... | ... | ... |
| 23 | ....do....lungs | ... | ... | ... | ... | ... | ... | ... | ... | ... | 1 | 1 | ... | ... | ... | ... | ... | ... | ... | 1 | 1 | ... | ... | ... | ... |
| 24 | Consumption | 10 | 7 | 16 | 11 | 4 | 3 | 20 | 57 | 144 | 217 | 97 | 133 | 18 | 14 | ... | ... | ... | ... | 554 | 155 | 15 | ... | ... | ... |
| 25 | Convulsions | 13 | 5 | 3 | 1 | 2 | ... | 1 | 1 | 5 | 3 | 3 | 3 | 3 | 2 | ... | ... | ... | ... | 33 | 9 | 1 | ... | ... | ... |
| 26 | Croup | 11 | 7 | 21 | 17 | 1 | 3 | 1 | 2 | ... | 1 | ... | ... | ... | ... | ... | ... | ... | ... | 57 | 5 | ... | ... | ... | ... |
| 27 | Debility | 1 | ... | ... | ... | ... | ... | ... | ... | ... | ... | ... | 1 | ... | ... | ... | ... | ... | ... | 2 | ... | ... | ... | ... | ... |
| 28 | Diabetes | ... | ... | ... | ... | ... | ... | ... | ... | 3 | ... | 2 | ... | ... | ... | ... | ... | ... | ... | 4 | 1 | ... | ... | ... | ... |
| 29 | Diarrhœa | ... | ... | ... | ... | ... | ... | ... | ... | ... | ... | 1 | 1 | ... | ... | ... | ... | ... | ... | 1 | 1 | ... | ... | ... | ... |
| 30 | Dropsy | 5 | 2 | 5 | 9 | 3 | 2 | 3 | 4 | 6 | 13 | 27 | 36 | 6 | 4 | ... | ... | ... | ... | 73 | 43 | 4 | ... | ... | ... |
| 31 | Dysentery | 21 | 9 | 72 | 68 | 16 | 9 | 14 | 19 | 8 | 15 | 13 | 27 | 6 | 3 | ... | ... | ... | ... | 247 | 42 | 5 | ... | ... | ... |
| 32 | Dyspepsia | ... | ... | ... | ... | ... | ... | ... | ... | 1 | 1 | 1 | ... | ... | ... | ... | ... | ... | ... | 3 | ... | ... | ... | ... | ... |
| 33 | Epilepsy | ... | ... | ... | ... | ... | ... | ... | ... | ... | 1 | 1 | ... | ... | ... | ... | ... | ... | ... | 2 | ... | ... | ... | ... | ... |
| 34 | Erysipelas | 4 | 3 | 4 | ... | 1 | ... | ... | 5 | 2 | 2 | 12 | 9 | 1 | 1 | ... | ... | ... | ... | 27 | 17 | ... | ... | ... | ... |
| 35 | Fever, not specified | 14 | 5 | 12 | 12 | 8 | 8 | 11 | 12 | 33 | 32 | 21 | 21 | 3 | 2 | ... | ... | ... | ... | 138 | 42 | 4 | ... | ... | ... |
| 36 | ..do..bilious | 1 | ... | ... | 2 | ... | ... | ... | 2 | 8 | 3 | 3 | 6 | ... | ... | ... | ... | ... | ... | 15 | 3 | ... | ... | ... | ... |
| 37 | ..do..brain | 1 | ... | 2 | 3 | ... | 1 | 1 | 3 | 2 | 4 | 1 | 1 | ... | ... | ... | ... | ... | ... | 14 | 3 | 1 | ... | ... | ... |
| 38 | ..do..congestive | ... | ... | ... | ... | ... | 1 | ... | ... | ... | ... | ... | ... | ... | ... | ... | ... | ... | ... | 1 | ... | ... | ... | ... | ... |
| 39 | ..do..intermittent | ... | ... | 1 | ... | ... | ... | ... | ... | ... | ... | ... | ... | ... | ... | ... | ... | ... | ... | 1 | ... | ... | ... | ... | ... |
| 40 | ..do..puerperal | ... | ... | ... | ... | ... | ... | ... | ... | ... | 3 | ... | ... | ... | ... | ... | ... | ... | ... | 3 | ... | ... | ... | ... | ... |
| 41 | ..do..scarlet | 2 | 4 | 16 | 11 | 7 | 4 | 2 | 2 | 1 | ... | ... | ... | ... | ... | ... | ... | ... | ... | 42 | 4 | 3 | ... | ... | ... |
| 42 | ..do..typhus | 1 | ... | 5 | 3 | ... | 1 | 8 | 14 | 20 | 8 | 8 | 6 | ... | ... | ... | ... | ... | ... | 61 | 8 | 2 | ... | ... | ... |
| 43 | Gravel | ... | ... | ... | ... | ... | ... | ... | ... | ... | ... | 7 | ... | 1 | ... | ... | ... | ... | ... | 2 | 6 | ... | ... | ... | ... |
| 44 | Head, disease of | 2 | 1 | 2 | ... | ... | ... | 1 | ... | ... | ... | 1 | ... | ... | 1 | ... | ... | ... | ... | 5 | 3 | ... | ... | ... | ... |
| 45 | Heart....do | 2 | 1 | 1 | ... | 4 | 1 | 1 | 2 | 3 | 12 | 14 | 16 | 6 | 4 | ... | ... | ... | ... | 37 | 27 | 2 | ... | ... | ... |
| 46 | Heat | ... | ... | ... | ... | ... | ... | ... | ... | 2 | ... | ... | ... | ... | ... | ... | ... | ... | ... | 2 | ... | ... | ... | ... | ... |
| 47 | Hemorrhage | ... | ... | ... | ... | ... | ... | ... | 4 | ... | 2 | ... | 1 | ... | ... | ... | ... | ... | ... | 7 | ... | ... | ... | ... | ... |
| 48 | Hernia | ... | ... | ... | ... | ... | ... | ... | ... | 1 | 1 | 2 | ... | 1 | ... | ... | ... | ... | ... | 1 | 3 | 1 | ... | ... | ... |
| 49 | Hooping cough | 9 | 8 | 7 | 6 | ... | 1 | ... | 1 | 1 | ... | ... | ... | ... | ... | ... | ... | ... | ... | 33 | 3 | ... | ... | ... | ... |
| 50 | Hydrocephalus | 3 | 2 | 2 | 7 | 1 | 4 | ... | 2 | 1 | 2 | ... | ... | ... | ... | ... | ... | ... | ... | 21 | 2 | 1 | ... | ... | ... |
| 51 | Hydrophobia | ... | ... | ... | ... | ... | ... | ... | ... | ... | ... | 2 | ... | ... | ... | ... | ... | ... | ... | 2 | ... | ... | ... | ... | ... |
| 52 | Inflammation | 3 | 1 | 5 | 8 | ... | 2 | 2 | 2 | 5 | 3 | ... | 4 | ... | ... | ... | ... | ... | ... | 30 | 4 | ... | ... | ... | ... |
| 53 | ....do....bowels | 2 | 1 | 2 | 1 | 1 | 1 | 1 | 2 | 3 | 4 | 2 | 3 | ... | ... | ... | ... | ... | ... | 19 | 4 | ... | ... | ... | ... |
| 54 | ....do....brain | 5 | 1 | 8 | 2 | 3 | 2 | 1 | 3 | 5 | 1 | 2 | 2 | ... | ... | ... | ... | ... | ... | 29 | 2 | 2 | ... | ... | ... |

## THE STATE OF TEXAS—AGGREGATE—Continued.

| NATIVITIES. | | | | | SEASON OF DECEASE. | | | | DURATION OF SICKNESS. | | | | WHITES. | | | COLORED. | | | | | | | | | |
|---|---|---|---|---|---|---|---|---|---|---|---|---|---|---|---|---|---|---|---|---|---|---|---|---|---|
| | | | | | | | | | | | | | | | | Slaves. | | | | Free. | | | | | |
| | | | | | | | | | | | | | | | | Black. | | Mulatto. | | Black. | | Mul. | | | |
| California and Territories. | Ireland. | Germany. | Other foreign countries. | Unknown. | Spring. | Summer. | Autumn | Winter. | Under 1 week. | 1 week and under 1 month. | 1 month and under 3 months. | 3 months and over. | Males. | Females. | Total. | M. | F. | M. | F. | M. | F. | M | F. | Aggregate deaths. | |
| | | | | | 4 | 6 | 1 | 5 | 18 | | | | 1 | 2 | 3 | 7 | 6 | | 2 | | | | | 18 | 1 |
| | | | 4 | | | 1 | 3 | | 3 | | | | 3 | 1 | 4 | 1 | | | | | | | | 5 | 2 |
| | | | | | | 1 | 1 | | 1 | 1 | | | 1 | | 1 | 1 | | | | | | | | 2 | 3 |
| | | 1 | | | 3 | 3 | 12 | 4 | 2 | 8 | 10 | 2 | 5 | 6 | 11 | 7 | 4 | | | | | | | 22 | 4 |
| | | | | | 2 | 1 | | 1 | 1 | 3 | | | 4 | | 4 | | | | | | | | | 4 | 5 |
| | | | | | 1 | 1 | 3 | 3 | 4 | 4 | | | 6 | | 6 | 1 | | | 1 | | | | | 8 | 6 |
| | | | | 2 | | 1 | 1 | 3 | | | 3 | 2 | 1 | 2 | 3 | 1 | 1 | | | | | | | 5 | 7 |
| | | | | | | | | 1 | | | | | | | | | 1 | | | | | | | 1 | 8 |
| | | | | | 8 | 20 | 23 | 11 | 30 | 20 | 4 | 4 | 13 | 18 | 31 | 17 | 12 | 2 | 2 | | | | | 64 | 9 |
| | 1 | 6 | 18 | 54 | 98 | 125 | 135 | 106 | 142 | 96 | 38 | 85 | 174 | 170 | 392 | 62 | 64 | 1 | 6 | | | 2 | | 527 | 10 |
| ... | 20 | 102 | 83 | 133 | 685 | 706 | 894 | 691 | 1247 | 927 | 230 | 339 | 1186 | 941 | 2175 | 427 | 395 | 24 | 32 | ... | ... | 4 | .. | 3057 | |

## THE STATE OF VERMONT.

| California and Territories. | Ireland. | Germany. | Other foreign countries. | Unknown. | Spring. | Summer. | Autumn | Winter. | Under 1 week. | 1 week and under 1 month. | 1 month and under 3 months. | 3 months and over. | Males. | Females. | Total. | Slaves Black M. | Slaves Black F. | Slaves Mulatto M. | Slaves Mulatto F. | Free Black M. | Free Black F. | Free Mul. M | Free Mul. F. | Aggregate deaths. | |
|---|---|---|---|---|---|---|---|---|---|---|---|---|---|---|---|---|---|---|---|---|---|---|---|---|---|
| | | | 1 | | | | 2 | 1 | | | | 3 | 1 | 2 | 3 | | | | | | | | | 3 | 1 |
| | 10 | | 1 | | 14 | 5 | 7 | 12 | 35 | 1 | | 2 | 31 | 8 | 39 | | | | | | | | | 39 | 2 |
| | | | | | 2 | 2 | 5 | 1 | 9 | 1 | | | 3 | 7 | 10 | | | | | | | | | 10 | 3 |
| | 1 | | 1 | | | 10 | 5 | 4 | 19 | | | | 17 | 2 | 19 | | | | | | | | | 19 | 4 |
| | | | | | 2 | 1 | | | 3 | | | | 1 | 2 | 3 | | | | | | | | | 3 | 5 |
| | | | 2 | | 22 | 9 | 8 | 13 | 39 | 10 | 1 | 2 | 34 | 18 | 52 | | | | | | | | | 52 | 6 |
| | | | | | 1 | | 1 | 1 | 1 | 1 | | 1 | 1 | 2 | 3 | | | | | | | | | 3 | 7 |
| | | | | | 2 | 1 | 5 | 6 | 6 | 5 | 3 | | 12 | 2 | 14 | | | | | | | | | 14 | 8 |
| | | | | | 2 | 1 | | 2 | | 2 | 1 | 2 | 3 | 2 | 5 | | | | | | | | | 5 | 9 |
| | | | | | 2 | | | 1 | | 2 | | 1 | 1 | 2 | 3 | | | | | | | | | 3 | 10 |
| | 1 | | | | 13 | 11 | 17 | 11 | 1 | 5 | 7 | 36 | 21 | 31 | 52 | | | | | | | | | 52 | 11 |
| | | | 1 | | 33 | 13 | 19 | 13 | 34 | 42 | 2 | | 36 | 42 | 78 | | | | | | | | | 78 | 12 |
| | | | | | 4 | 1 | | 1 | 3 | 3 | | | 4 | 2 | 6 | | | | | | | | | 6 | 13 |
| | | | | | | 1 | | | | 1 | | | 1 | | 1 | | | | | | | | | 1 | 14 |
| | 4 | | 3 | | 10 | 10 | 3 | 1 | 13 | 11 | | | | 24 | 24 | | | | | | | | | 24 | 15 |
| | 4 | | 2 | | 1 | 11 | 19 | | 20 | 11 | | | 18 | 13 | 31 | | | | | | | | | 31 | 16 |
| | | | | | 1 | | 5 | | 5 | | | | 4 | 2 | 6 | | | | | | | | | 6 | 17 |
| | | | | | | 7 | 11 | 2 | 17 | 3 | | | 13 | 7 | 20 | | | | | | | | | 20 | 18 |
| | | | | | 1 | | | | | | | | | 1 | 1 | | | | | | | | | 1 | 19 |
| | | | | | 4 | 1 | 2 | 1 | 4 | 3 | | 1 | 6 | 2 | 8 | | | | | | | | | 8 | 20 |
| | | | | | | 1 | 1 | | | 2 | | | 2 | | 2 | | | | | | | | | 2 | 21 |
| | | | | | 1 | 1 | 5 | | 1 | 5 | | 1 | 3 | 4 | 7 | | | | | | | | | 7 | 22 |
| | | | | | 1 | 1 | | | 1 | 1 | | | 1 | 1 | 2 | | | | | | | | | 2 | 23 |
| | 8 | 1 | 16 | 2 | 224 | 193 | 172 | 148 | 19 | 71 | 102 | 441 | 308 | 442 | 750 | | | | | 1 | | | | 751 | 24 |
| | 1 | | 1 | | 18 | 6 | 7 | 14 | 35 | 7 | 2 | 1 | 30 | 15 | 45 | | | | | | | | | 45 | 25 |
| | 1 | | 1 | | 12 | 4 | 20 | 28 | 47 | 16 | 1 | | 34 | 29 | 63 | | | | | | 1 | | | 64 | 26 |
| | | | | | | 1 | 1 | | | 1 | | 1 | 1 | 1 | 2 | | | | | | | | | 2 | 27 |
| | | | | | | 1 | 3 | 1 | 1 | 1 | | 3 | 5 | | 5 | | | | | | | | | 5 | 28 |
| | | | | | | | 1 | 1 | | 1 | 1 | | 1 | 1 | 2 | | | | | | | | | 2 | 29 |
| | 3 | | 2 | | 40 | 36 | 35 | 13 | 8 | 38 | 23 | 54 | 55 | 69 | 124 | | | | | | | | 1 | 125 | 30 |
| | 4 | | 2 | | 11 | 25 | 252 | 11 | 96 | 99 | 11 | 4 | 150 | 150 | 300 | | | | | | | | | 300 | 31 |
| | | | | | 1 | 1 | | 1 | | 1 | | 2 | 2 | 1 | 3 | | | | | | | | | 3 | 32 |
| | | | | | 2 | | | | 2 | | | | 1 | 1 | 2 | | | | | | | | | 2 | 33 |
| | | | | | 17 | 10 | 9 | 8 | 15 | 23 | 3 | 2 | 24 | 20 | 44 | | | | | | | | | 44 | 34 |
| | 5 | | 3 | | 65 | 38 | 47 | 38 | 36 | 123 | 29 | 5 | 101 | 91 | 192 | | | | | 1 | 1 | | | 194 | 35 |
| | 1 | | 1 | | 8 | 4 | 6 | 2 | 4 | 12 | 3 | 1 | 7 | 13 | 20 | | | | | | | | | 20 | 36 |
| | 1 | | | | 10 | 2 | 4 | 3 | 6 | 11 | | 2 | 7 | 12 | 19 | | | | | | | | | 19 | 37 |
| | | | | | | | | 1 | | 1 | | | | 1 | 1 | | | | | | | | | 1 | 38 |
| | | | | | | 2 | | | | | 1 | | 1 | 1 | 2 | | | | | | | | | 2 | 39 |
| | | | | | 2 | 1 | | | 1 | 2 | | | | 3 | 3 | | | | | | | | | 3 | 40 |
| | | | | | 25 | 12 | 6 | 6 | 20 | 24 | 5 | | 28 | 21 | 49 | | | | | | | | | 49 | 41 |
| | | | 3 | | 21 | 7 | 21 | 25 | 7 | 53 | 14 | | 42 | 32 | 74 | | | | | | | | | 74 | 42 |
| | | | | | 1 | 1 | 4 | 2 | 2 | 3 | | 3 | 8 | | 8 | | | | | | | | | 8 | 43 |
| | | | | | 2 | | 5 | 1 | 5 | 1 | 1 | 1 | 6 | 2 | 8 | | | | | | | | | 8 | 44 |
| | | | 1 | | 17 | 13 | 23 | 14 | 22 | 15 | 8 | 21 | 31 | 36 | 67 | | | | | | | | | 67 | 45 |
| | | | | | | 2 | | | 2 | | | | 2 | | 2 | | | | | | | | | 2 | 46 |
| | | | | | 3 | 2 | 1 | 1 | 5 | 2 | | | | 7 | 7 | | | | | | | | | 7 | 47 |
| | | | | | 1 | | | 4 | 1 | 4 | | | 4 | 1 | 5 | | | | | | | | | 5 | 48 |
| | | | | | 14 | 6 | 5 | 8 | 2 | 24 | 6 | 1 | 17 | 16 | 33 | | | | | | | | | 33 | 49 |
| | | | | | 8 | 4 | 7 | 5 | 3 | 12 | 6 | 3 | 7 | 17 | 24 | | | | | | | | | 24 | 50 |
| | | | | | | | | 2 | 1 | 1 | | | 2 | | 2 | | | | | | | | | 2 | 51 |
| | 1 | | | | 7 | 9 | 11 | 8 | 17 | 17 | | 1 | 14 | 20 | 34 | | | | | 1 | | | | 35 | 52 |
| | | | | | 2 | 9 | 8 | 4 | 9 | 13 | | 1 | 11 | 12 | 23 | | | | | | | | | 23 | 53 |
| | | | 2 | | 11 | 9 | 9 | 6 | 9 | 19 | 4 | 3 | 24 | 11 | 35 | | | | | | | | | 35 | 54 |

## CLASSIFICATION OF DEATHS IN

| | Cause of death. | AGES. Under 1. M. | Under 1. F. | 1 and under 5. M. | 1 and under 5. F. | 5 and under 10. M. | 5 and under 10. F. | 10 and under 20. M. | 10 and under 20. F. | 20 and under 50. M. | 20 and under 50. F. | 50 and under 80. M. | 50 and under 80. F. | 80 and under 100. M | 80 and under 100. F. | 100 & over. M | 100 & over. F. | Age unknown. M | Age unknown. F. | NATIVITIES. Born in State. | N. England States. | Middle States. | Southern States. | Southwest'n States. | Northwest'n States. |
|---|---|---|---|---|---|---|---|---|---|---|---|---|---|---|---|---|---|---|---|---|---|---|---|---|---|
| 1 | Inflamt'n of stomach | | | | | | | | 1 | 1 | 1 | | | | | | | | | 3 | | | | | |
| 2 | Insanity | | | | | | | 1 | | | | 1 | 1 | | | | | | | 2 | 1 | | | | |
| 3 | Intemperance | | | | | | | | | | | 1 | | | | | | | | | 1 | | | | |
| 4 | Jaundice | | | 1 | | | | | | 1 | | | 1 | | | | | | | 2 | 1 | | | | |
| 5 | Kidneys, disease of | | | | | | | | | | | 2 | | 1 | | | | | | | 2 | | | | |
| 6 | Killed | | | | | | | | | | | 1 | | | | | | | | 1 | | | | | |
| 7 | Liver, disease of | 1 | 1 | | | | | | 2 | 2 | 2 | 8 | 5 | | 1 | | | | | 10 | 11 | | | | |
| 8 | Lockjaw | | | | | | | | | | 1 | | | | | | | | | | | | | | |
| 9 | Lungs, disease of | 1 | 3 | 1 | | | | | 1 | | | | 1 | | 1 | | | | | 5 | 3 | | | | |
| 10 | Mania-a-potu | | | | | | | | | 2 | | 2 | | | | | | | | 2 | 1 | | | | |
| 11 | Marasmus | | | | | | | | | 1 | | 4 | 5 | 1 | | | | | | 7 | 3 | | | | |
| 12 | Measles | | 1 | 1 | 4 | | | | 1 | 2 | 2 | 1 | 1 | | | | | | | 11 | 1 | 1 | | | |
| 13 | Neuralgia | | | | | | 1 | | 1 | | | 1 | 1 | | | | | | | 4 | | | | | |
| 14 | Old age | | | | | | | | | | | 25 | 33 | 70 | 80 | 1 | 1 | | | 76 | 126 | 1 | 1 | | |
| 15 | Paralysis | | | | | | | | | 1 | 1 | 21 | 23 | 4 | 7 | | | | | | 50 | 1 | | | |
| 16 | Peritonitis | 1 | | | | | | | | | | | | | | | | | | 1 | | | | | |
| 17 | Pleurisy | | | | | | | 2 | | 2 | | 2 | 3 | | 1 | | | | | 5 | 4 | | | | |
| 18 | Pneumonia | 17 | 9 | 7 | 7 | 2 | 3 | 1 | 1 | 3 | 8 | 11 | 16 | 1 | 7 | | | | | 66 | 22 | 3 | | | |
| 19 | Putrid sore throat | | | 2 | | 1 | 1 | 1 | 1 | | | | | | | | | | | 5 | | | | | |
| 20 | Quinsy | | | 1 | 1 | 1 | | | | | | | | | | | | | | 2 | 1 | | | | |
| 21 | Rheumatism | | | | | | | | | 2 | | 1 | 1 | | | | | | | 3 | | 1 | | | |
| 22 | Scrofula | 2 | 1 | 1 | | 2 | 1 | | 2 | 1 | 1 | 1 | | 1 | | | | | | 11 | 2 | | | | |
| 23 | Small pox | | | 1 | 1 | 1 | | 2 | 2 | 2 | 1 | 2 | | | | | | | | 7 | 3 | | | | |
| 24 | Spine, disease of | | | | | | | | 2 | 2 | 1 | 1 | | | | | | | | 5 | 1 | | | | |
| 25 | Stillborn | 1 | | | | | | | | | | | | | | | | | | 1 | | | | | |
| 26 | Stomach, disease of | | | | | | | | | | 1 | 1 | 1 | | | | | | | 2 | 1 | | | | |
| 27 | Suffocation | | 1 | 1 | | | | | | | | | | | | | | | | 2 | | | | | |
| 28 | Suicide | | | | | | | | | 8 | 1 | 4 | 1 | | | | | | | 7 | 5 | | | | |
| 29 | Teething | | 2 | 8 | 1 | 1 | | | | | | | | | | | | | | 6 | | 1 | | | |
| 30 | Throat, disease of | | | 1 | | 2 | | 1 | 1 | | | 2 | | | | | | | | 5 | 2 | | | | |
| 31 | Thrush | 1 | 2 | | | | | | | | | | | | | | | | | 3 | | | | | |
| 32 | Tumor | | | | | | | | 1 | 1 | 4 | | 4 | | | | | | | 8 | 2 | | | | |
| 33 | Ulcer | | | | | | | | | | | 2 | | | | | | | | | 2 | | | | |
| 34 | White swelling | | | 1 | | | | | | | | | | | | | | | | 1 | | | | | |
| 35 | Worms | | 1 | 3 | 2 | | | | 1 | | | | | | | | | | | 7 | | | | | |
| 36 | Unknown | 30 | 31 | 14 | 9 | 6 | 5 | 6 | 6 | 24 | 32 | 37 | 26 | 6 | 3 | | | 3 | | 171 | 39 | 10 | | | |
| | Total | 179 | 121 | 260 | 218 | 89 | 73 | 95 | 174 | 353 | 435 | 409 | 431 | 145 | 142 | 1 | 1 | 3 | | 2151 | 774 | 65 | 1 | | 5 |

## CLASSIFICATION OF DEATHS IN EASTERN

*Embracing the following counties: Accomac, Alexandria, Caroline, Charles City, Elizabeth and Queen, King George, King William, Lancaster, Loudon, Matthews, Middlesex, Prince William, Princess Anne, Richmond, Southampton, Spottsyl-*

| | Cause of death. | Under 1. M. | Under 1. F. | 1 and under 5. M. | 1 and under 5. F. | 5 and under 10. M. | 5 and under 10. F. | 10 and under 20. M. | 10 and under 20. F. | 20 and under 50. M. | 20 and under 50. F. | 50 and under 80. M. | 50 and under 80. F. | 80 and under 100. M | 80 and under 100. F. | 100 & over. M | 100 & over. F. | Age unknown. M | Age unknown. F. | Born in State. | N. England States. | Middle States. | Southern States. | Southwest'n States. | Northwest'n States. |
|---|---|---|---|---|---|---|---|---|---|---|---|---|---|---|---|---|---|---|---|---|---|---|---|---|---|
| 1 | Abscess | | | 1 | | | | | | 2 | 1 | 1 | | | | | | | | 5 | | | | | |
| 2 | Accident, not specif'd | 15 | 11 | 14 | 10 | 3 | 5 | 5 | 2 | 13 | 4 | 9 | 2 | 2 | 1 | | | | | 94 | 1 | | | | |
| 3 | ....do...burned | | 2 | 16 | 26 | 2 | 6 | 1 | 11 | 3 | 10 | 3 | 4 | | | | | | | 84 | | | | | |
| 4 | ....do...drowned | | | 4 | 4 | 1 | | 11 | 4 | 14 | 1 | 4 | 1 | | | | | | | 39 | | 1 | 1 | | |
| 5 | ....do...shot | | | | | | | | | 1 | 1 | | | | | | | | | 1 | | 1 | | | |
| 6 | Apoplexy | 1 | | | | | | 2 | 2 | 7 | 6 | 19 | 11 | | | | | | | 43 | | | | | |
| 7 | Asthma | | 1 | | | | | | | 5 | 8 | 9 | 10 | | 1 | | | | | 29 | | | | | |
| 8 | Bladder, disease of | | | | | | | | | | | 3 | | | | | | | | 3 | | | | | |
| 9 | Black tongue | | | | | | | | | | 1 | 1 | | | | | | | | 2 | | | | | |
| 10 | Bowels, disease of | 2 | 3 | 3 | 1 | | | 3 | 1 | 1 | | 2 | | | | | | | | 15 | | | | | |
| 11 | Brain.......do | 3 | | 6 | 2 | | | 1 | 3 | 2 | | 1 | | | | | | | | 18 | | | | | |
| 12 | Bronchitis | 1 | | 2 | 1 | | | | 1 | 4 | | 7 | 1 | | | | | | | 16 | | 1 | | | |
| 13 | Cancer | | | | | | | | 1 | 4 | 6 | 4 | 14 | 2 | 1 | | | | 1 | 31 | | 1 | | | |
| 14 | Catarrh | 10 | 4 | 5 | 5 | | 1 | 1 | 2 | 1 | 7 | 5 | 4 | | 1 | | | | | 46 | | | | | |
| 15 | Childbirth | | | | | | | | 13 | | 101 | | | | | | | | | 108 | | 2 | | | |
| 16 | Cholera | 21 | 8 | 34 | 25 | 9 | 14 | 26 | 19 | 140 | 91 | 68 | 58 | 1 | 4 | 1 | | 3 | | 480 | 2 | 10 | 10 | | |
| 17 | ....do...infantum | 28 | 15 | 25 | 17 | | 2 | | | | | | | | | | | | | 87 | | | | | |
| 18 | ....do...morbus | | 1 | | 1 | 1 | | 1 | 3 | 1 | 1 | 2 | 2 | | | | | | | 13 | | | | | |
| 19 | Colic | 1 | 1 | 2 | 1 | 1 | | 2 | | 4 | 2 | 5 | 3 | | 1 | 1 | | | | 24 | | | | | |
| 20 | Congestion | 1 | | | | | 1 | | 1 | | | 1 | | | | | | | | 4 | | | | | |
| 21 | .....do....brain | 1 | | 1 | 2 | 3 | | 4 | 2 | 1 | 3 | 2 | | | | | | | | 18 | | | | | |
| 22 | Consumption | 1 | 7 | 10 | 5 | 8 | 4 | 14 | 34 | 159 | 199 | 72 | 77 | 2 | 7 | | 1 | 1 | 3 | 566 | 4 | 18 | 2 | | |
| 23 | Convulsions | 53 | 35 | 8 | 12 | | 3 | 5 | 2 | 8 | 11 | 2 | 3 | | 1 | | | | | 141 | | 1 | | | |
| 24 | Cramp | | | | | | | 1 | | | 1 | 2 | 1 | | | | | | | 5 | | | | | |
| 25 | Croup | 16 | 13 | 20 | 32 | 2 | 2 | | 1 | 1 | 2 | | | | | | | | | 89 | | | | | |
| 26 | Debility | 1 | | 1 | | 1 | | | | 1 | 2 | | | | | | | | | 6 | | | | | |
| 27 | Diabetes | | | | | | | | 1 | 1 | | | | | | | | | | 2 | | | | | |
| 28 | Diarrhœa | 14 | 15 | 25 | 20 | 4 | 5 | 3 | 4 | 20 | 14 | 15 | 5 | | 1 | | | | | 142 | | 1 | | | |

STATE OF VERMONT—Continued.

| NATIVITIES. California and Territories. | NATIVITIES. Ireland. | NATIVITIES. Germany. | NATIVITIES. Other foreign countries. | NATIVITIES. Unknown. | SEASON OF DECEASE. Spring. | SEASON OF DECEASE. Summer. | SEASON OF DECEASE. Autumn. | SEASON OF DECEASE. Winter. | DURATION OF SICKNESS. Under 1 week. | DURATION OF SICKNESS. 1 week and under 1 month. | DURATION OF SICKNESS. 1 month and under 3 months. | DURATION OF SICKNESS. 3 months and over. | WHITES. Males. | WHITES. Females. | WHITES. Total. | COLORED. Slaves. Black. M. | COLORED. Slaves. Black. F. | COLORED. Slaves. Mulatto. M. | COLORED. Slaves. Mulatto. F. | COLORED. Free. Black. M. | COLORED. Free. Black. F. | COLORED. Free. Mul. M | COLORED. Free. Mul. F. | Aggregate deaths. | |
|---|---|---|---|---|---|---|---|---|---|---|---|---|---|---|---|---|---|---|---|---|---|---|---|---|---|
| .... | .... | .. | .... | .... | .... | 2 | .... | 1 | 2 | .... | 1 | .... | 1 | 2 | 3 | .... | .... | .... | .... | .... | .... | .. | .. | 3 | 1 |
| .... | .... | .. | .... | .... | 1 | .... | .... | 2 | .... | .... | .... | 2 | 2 | 1 | 3 | .... | .... | .... | .... | .... | .... | .. | .. | 3 | 2 |
| .... | .... | .. | .... | .... | 1 | .... | .... | .... | .... | .... | .... | 1 | 1 | .... | 1 | .... | .... | .... | .... | .... | .... | .. | .. | 1 | 3 |
| .... | .... | .. | .... | .... | 1 | .... | 2 | .... | 1 | .... | .... | 2 | 2 | 1 | 3 | .... | .... | .... | .... | .... | .... | .. | .. | 3 | 4 |
| .... | .... | .. | .... | 1 | 2 | .... | 1 | .... | 1 | .... | .... | 1 | 3 | .... | 3 | .... | .... | .... | .... | .... | .... | .. | .. | 3 | 5 |
| .... | .... | .. | .... | .... | .... | .... | 1 | .... | 1 | .... | .... | .... | 1 | .... | 1 | .... | .... | .... | .... | .... | .... | .. | .. | 1 | 6 |
| .... | .... | .. | 1 | .... | 6 | 3 | 7 | 6 | 3 | 6 | 2 | 10 | 11 | 11 | 22 | .... | .... | .... | .... | .... | .... | .. | .. | 22 | 7 |
| .... | 1 | .. | .... | .... | .... | .... | 1 | .... | 1 | .... | .... | .... | .... | 1 | 1 | .... | .... | .... | .... | .... | .... | .. | .. | 1 | 8 |
| .... | .... | .. | .... | .... | 5 | .... | 3 | 1 | 2 | 3 | 1 | 1 | 2 | 6 | 8 | .... | .... | .... | .... | .... | .... | .. | .. | 8 | 9 |
| .... | 1 | .. | .... | .... | 4 | .... | .... | .... | 4 | .... | .... | .... | 4 | .... | 4 | .... | .... | .... | .... | .... | .... | .. | .. | 4 | 10 |
| .... | .... | .. | 1 | .... | 4 | 3 | 3 | 1 | 1 | .... | 6 | 4 | 6 | 5 | 11 | .... | .... | .... | .... | .... | .... | .. | .. | 11 | 11 |
| .... | .... | .. | .... | .... | 5 | 6 | 2 | .... | 6 | 5 | 2 | .... | 4 | 9 | 13 | .... | .... | .... | .... | .... | .... | .. | .. | 13 | 12 |
| .... | .... | .. | .... | .... | 1 | 2 | .... | 1 | .... | 3 | .... | 1 | 1 | 3 | 4 | .... | .... | .... | .... | .... | .... | .. | .. | 4 | 13 |
| .... | 1 | .. | 5 | .... | 64 | 45 | 44 | 57 | 38 | 44 | 25 | 55 | 96 | 114 | 210 | .... | .... | .... | .... | .... | .... | .. | .. | 210 | 14 |
| .... | 3 | .. | 3 | .... | 17 | 16 | 15 | 9 | 20 | 16 | 7 | 12 | 26 | 31 | 57 | .... | .... | .... | .... | .... | .... | .. | .. | 57 | 15 |
| .... | .... | .. | .... | .... | .... | .... | .... | 1 | 1 | .... | .... | .... | 1 | .... | 1 | .... | .... | .... | .... | .... | .... | .. | .. | 1 | 16 |
| .... | 1 | .. | .... | .... | 1 | 3 | 2 | 4 | 3 | 5 | 1 | 1 | 6 | 4 | 10 | .... | .... | .... | .... | .... | .... | .. | .. | 10 | 17 |
| .... | 2 | .. | .... | .... | 42 | 21 | 7 | 23 | 26 | 57 | 7 | 3 | 42 | 51 | 93 | .... | .... | .... | .... | .... | .... | .. | .. | 93 | 18 |
| .... | .... | .. | .... | .... | 1 | 3 | 1 | .... | 1 | 4 | .... | .... | 3 | 2 | 5 | .... | .... | .... | .... | .... | .... | .. | .. | 5 | 19 |
| .... | .... | .. | .... | .... | 1 | .... | 2 | .. | 1 | 2 | .... | .... | 2 | 1 | 3 | .... | .... | .... | .... | .... | .... | .. | .. | 3 | 20 |
| .... | .... | .. | .... | .... | 1 | 2 | 1 | .. | 1 | 1 | 1 | 1 | 3 | 1 | 4 | .... | .... | .... | .... | .... | .... | .. | .. | 4 | 21 |
| .... | .... | .. | .... | .... | 2 | 5 | 4 | 2 | 1 | 3 | 2 | 7 | 8 | 5 | 13 | .... | .... | .... | .... | .... | .... | .. | .. | 13 | 22 |
| .... | .... | .. | 2 | .... | 8 | .... | 2 | 2 | 5 | 6 | 1 | .... | 8 | 4 | 12 | .... | .... | .... | .... | .... | .... | .. | .. | 12 | 23 |
| .... | .... | .. | .... | .... | 1 | 1 | 3 | 1 | .... | .... | .... | 5 | 3 | 3 | 6 | .... | .... | .... | .... | .... | .... | .. | .. | 6 | 24 |
| .... | .... | .. | .... | .... | .... | .... | .... | .... | .... | .... | .... | .... | 1 | .... | 1 | .... | .... | .... | .... | .... | .... | .. | .. | 1 | 25 |
| .... | .... | .. | .... | .... | 2 | .... | 1 | .... | .... | 1 | .... | 2 | 1 | 2 | 3 | .... | .... | .... | .... | .... | .... | .. | .. | 3 | 26 |
| .... | .... | .. | .... | .... | .... | 1 | .... | 1 | 2 | .... | .... | .... | 1 | 1 | 2 | .... | .... | .... | .... | .... | .... | .. | .. | 2 | 27 |
| .... | 1 | .. | 1 | .... | .... | 7 | 5 | 2 | 8 | 1 | .... | 1 | 12 | 2 | 14 | .... | .... | .... | .... | .... | .... | .. | .. | 14 | 28 |
| .... | .... | .. | .... | .... | 1 | 3 | 2 | 1 | 4 | 1 | 2 | .... | 4 | 3 | 7 | .... | .... | .... | .... | .... | .... | .. | .. | 7 | 29 |
| .... | .... | .. | .... | .... | 1 | .... | 3 | 3 | 2 | 3 | 2 | .... | 6 | 1 | 7 | .... | .... | .... | .... | .... | .... | .. | .. | 7 | 30 |
| .... | .... | .. | .... | .... | 1 | .... | 1 | 1 | 3 | .... | .... | .... | 1 | 2 | 3 | .... | .... | .... | .... | .... | .... | .. | .. | 3 | 31 |
| .... | .... | .. | .... | .... | 1 | 3 | 1 | 4 | 1 | 1 | 2 | 6 | 1 | 9 | 10 | .... | .... | .... | .... | .... | .... | .. | .. | 10 | 32 |
| .... | .... | .. | .... | .... | 2 | .... | .... | .... | .... | 2 | .... | .... | 2 | .... | 2 | .... | .... | .... | .... | .... | .... | .. | .. | 2 | 33 |
| .... | .... | .. | .... | .... | 1 | .... | .... | .... | .... | 1 | .... | .... | 1 | .... | 1 | .... | .... | .... | .... | .... | .... | .. | .. | 1 | 34 |
| .... | .... | .. | .... | .... | 1 | 1 | 2 | 3 | 4 | 3 | .... | .... | 3 | 4 | 7 | .... | .... | .... | .... | .... | .... | .. | .. | 7 | 35 |
| .... | 8 | 1 | 4 | 5 | 74 | 60 | 54 | 39 | 75 | 47 | 19 | 33 | 126 | 112 | 238 | .... | .... | .... | .... | .... | .... | .. | .. | 238 | 36 |
| .... | 63 | 2 | 60 | 8 | 890 | 672 | 941 | 590 | 804 | 919 | 315 | 747 | 1531 | 1592 | 3123 | .... | .... | .... | .... | 3 | 2 | .. | 1 | 3129 | |

## SECTION OF THE STATE OF VIRGINIA.

*City, Essex, Fairfax, Fauquier, Gloucester, Hanover, Henrico, Isle of Wight, James City, King Nansemond, New Kent, Norfolk, Northampton, Northumberland, Prince George, vania, Stafford, Surry, Sussex, Warwick, Westmoreland, and York.*

| California and Territories. | Ireland. | Germany. | Other foreign countries. | Unknown. | Spring. | Summer. | Autumn. | Winter. | Under 1 week. | 1 week and under 1 month. | 1 month and under 3 months. | 3 months and over. | Males. | Females. | Total. | Slaves. Black. M. | Slaves. Black. F. | Slaves. Mulatto. M. | Slaves. Mulatto. F. | Free. Black. M. | Free. Black. F. | Free. Mul. M | Free. Mul. F. | Aggregate deaths. | |
|---|---|---|---|---|---|---|---|---|---|---|---|---|---|---|---|---|---|---|---|---|---|---|---|---|---|
| .... | .... | .. | .... | .... | 1 | 3 | 1 | .... | .... | 2 | 1 | 1 | 3 | 1 | 4 | 1 | .... | .... | .... | .... | .... | .. | .. | 5 | 1 |
| .... | 1 | .. | .... | .... | 28 | 29 | 10 | 24 | 69 | 12 | 4 | 2 | 23 | 5 | 28 | 31 | 26 | 3 | 2 | 4 | 1 | .. | 1 | 96 | 2 |
| .... | .... | .. | .... | .... | 31 | 16 | 10 | 27 | 56 | 20 | 4 | 4 | 5 | 15 | 20 | 15 | 35 | .... | 1 | 4 | 7 | 1 | 1 | 84 | 3 |
| .... | 2 | .. | 1 | .... | 13 | 18 | 5 | 8 | 44 | .... | .... | .... | 18 | 6 | 24 | 11 | 3 | 1 | 1 | 2 | .... | 2 | .. | 44 | 4 |
| .... | .... | .. | .... | .... | .... | .... | 2 | .... | .... | .... | 2 | .... | 1 | 1 | 2 | .... | .... | .... | .... | .... | .... | .. | .. | 2 | 5 |
| .... | 2 | .. | 3 | .... | 12 | 10 | 12 | 14 | 40 | 5 | .... | 3 | 13 | 5 | 18 | 13 | 11 | .... | 2 | 2 | 1 | 1 | .. | 48 | 6 |
| .... | .... | .. | .... | .... | 8 | 7 | 3 | 8 | 5 | 5 | 4 | 13 | 6 | 6 | 12 | 7 | 8 | .... | 1 | .... | .... | 1 | .. | 29 | 7 |
| .... | .... | .. | .... | .... | 2 | .... | 1 | .... | .... | 3 | .... | .... | 2 | .... | 2 | 1 | .... | .... | .... | .... | .... | .. | .. | 3 | 8 |
| .... | .... | .. | .... | .... | 1 | .... | .... | 1 | .... | 2 | .... | .... | .... | .... | .... | 1 | 1 | .... | .... | .... | .... | .. | .. | 2 | 9 |
| .... | .... | .. | 1 | .... | 1 | 7 | 6 | 2 | 2 | 6 | 6 | 2 | 8 | 1 | 9 | 3 | 3 | .... | .... | .... | 1 | .. | .. | 16 | 10 |
| .... | .... | .. | .... | .... | 5 | 6 | 2 | 5 | 10 | 7 | .... | 1 | 8 | 2 | 10 | 4 | 2 | 1 | 1 | .... | .... | .. | .. | 18 | 11 |
| .... | .... | .. | .... | .... | 4 | 6 | 1 | 6 | 2 | 12 | 1 | 2 | 8 | 2 | 10 | 6 | 1 | .... | .... | .... | .... | .. | .. | 17 | 12 |
| .... | .... | .. | 1 | .... | 3 | 8 | 11 | 11 | 1 | 3 | 2 | 28 | 6 | 16 | 22 | 4 | 6 | .... | 1 | .... | .... | .. | .. | 33 | 13 |
| .... | .... | .. | .... | .... | 17 | 10 | 7 | 11 | 16 | 25 | 3 | 1 | 5 | 7 | 12 | 15 | 15 | 2 | 1 | .... | 1 | .. | .. | 46 | 14 |
| .... | 1 | 2 | 1 | .... | 25 | 37 | 24 | 26 | 61 | 34 | 7 | 2 | .... | 58 | 58 | .... | 45 | .... | 1 | .... | 4 | .. | 6 | 114 | 15 |
| .... | 2 | 6 | 11 | 1 | 5 | 432 | 80 | 5 | 457 | 42 | 8 | 8 | 134 | 91 | 225 | 134 | 93 | 14 | 6 | 15 | 21 | 6 | 8 | 522 | 16 |
| .... | .... | .. | .... | .... | 4 | 37 | 32 | 2 | 23 | 30 | 15 | 9 | 34 | 21 | 55 | 15 | 11 | 1 | .... | .... | 2 | 3 | .. | 87 | 17 |
| .... | .... | .. | .... | .... | 1 | 6 | 5 | 1 | 6 | 6 | .... | 1 | 1 | 4 | 5 | 2 | 2 | 1 | .... | 1 | 1 | .. | 1 | 13 | 18 |
| .... | .... | .. | .... | .... | 4 | 5 | 10 | 5 | 24 | .... | .... | .... | 6 | 2 | 8 | 8 | 5 | .... | .... | 2 | .... | .. | 1 | 24 | 19 |
| .... | .... | .. | .... | .... | .... | 2 | 1 | 1 | 1 | 2 | .... | .... | 1 | 1 | 2 | 1 | 1 | .... | .... | .... | .... | .. | .. | 4 | 20 |
| .... | .... | .. | 1 | .... | 10 | 1 | 7 | .... | 10 | 7 | 1 | 1 | 3 | 6 | 9 | 8 | 1 | 1 | .... | .... | .... | .. | .. | 19 | 21 |
| .... | 4 | 2 | 8 | .... | 161 | 169 | 161 | 111 | 16 | 61 | 73 | 423 | 174 | 200 | 374 | 72 | 99 | 2 | 12 | 18 | 19 | 1 | 7 | 604 | 22 |
| .... | 1 | .. | .... | .... | 36 | 43 | 37 | 21 | 108 | 21 | 1 | 5 | 23 | 26 | 49 | 44 | 36 | 4 | 3 | 5 | 2 | .. | .. | 143 | 23 |
| .... | .... | .. | .... | .... | 2 | 2 | .... | 1 | 3 | .... | .... | .... | 1 | .... | 1 | 2 | 1 | .... | .... | .... | 1 | .. | .. | 5 | 24 |
| .... | .... | .. | .... | .... | 30 | 15 | 24 | 20 | 61 | 24 | 1 | 2 | 21 | 25 | 46 | 17 | 20 | .... | 3 | 1 | 1 | .. | 1 | 89 | 25 |
| .... | .... | .. | .... | .... | 1 | 5 | .... | .... | 1 | 1 | 3 | 1 | 2 | 1 | 3 | 1 | 1 | 1 | .... | .... | .... | .. | .. | 6 | 26 |
| .... | .... | .. | .... | .... | 1 | 1 | .... | .... | .... | .... | .... | 2 | .... | 1 | 1 | 1 | .... | .... | .... | .... | .... | .. | .. | 2 | 27 |
| .... | .... | 1 | 1 | .... | 17 | 58 | 60 | 10 | 23 | 61 | 26 | 23 | 54 | 35 | 89 | 28 | 24 | 2 | 1 | 2 | 2 | .. | 2 | 145 | 28 |

## CLASSIFICATION OF DEATHS IN EASTERN

| | Cause of death. | AGES. | | | | | | | | | | | | | | | | | | NATIVITIES. | | | | | |
|---|---|---|---|---|---|---|---|---|---|---|---|---|---|---|---|---|---|---|---|---|---|---|---|---|---|
| | | Under 1. | | 1 and under 5. | | 5 and under 10. | | 10 and under 20. | | 20 and under 50. | | 50 and under 80. | | 80 and under 100. | | 100 & over. | | Age unknown. | | Born in State. | N. England States. | Middle States. | Southern States. | Southwest'n States. | Northwest'n States. |
| | | M. | F. | M. | F. | M. | F. | M. | F. | M. | F. | M. | F. | M | F. | M | F | M | F | | | | | | |
| 1 | Dirt eating | | | | | | | 1 | | | | | | | | | | | | 1 | | | | | |
| 2 | Dropsy | 5 | 3 | 17 | 15 | 17 | 18 | 27 | 20 | 29 | 60 | 67 | 49 | 2 | 5 | | | | | 322 | | 5 | 1 | | |
| 3 | Dysentery | 30 | 30 | 47 | 35 | 12 | 5 | 14 | 6 | 16 | 9 | 4 | 17 | | 2 | | | 5 | 1 | 227 | | 3 | 2 | | |
| 4 | Dyspepsia | | | 1 | | 1 | | 1 | | 1 | 5 | 2 | 2 | | | | | | | 13 | | | | | |
| 5 | Epilepsy | | | 1 | | | | 2 | 1 | | | | | | | | | | | 4 | | | | | |
| 6 | Erysipelas | 1 | 3 | 1 | 1 | | 1 | 2 | | 5 | 6 | 2 | | | | | | | | 22 | | | | | |
| 7 | Fever, not specified | 10 | 7 | 8 | 9 | 2 | 8 | 7 | 8 | 19 | 15 | 7 | 4 | | | | | | 1 | 100 | 2 | 1 | | | |
| 8 | ..do..bilious | 11 | 7 | 24 | 32 | 16 | 17 | 12 | 13 | 29 | 22 | 12 | 11 | | 1 | | | 6 | 8 | 211 | | 2 | 2 | | |
| 9 | ..do..brain | 6 | 2 | 8 | 8 | 8 | 2 | 6 | 6 | 5 | 5 | 2 | | | | | | | | 55 | 1 | 1 | 1 | | |
| 10 | ..do..catarrhal | 1 | 1 | 1 | 2 | | 1 | | | 1 | | | | | 1 | | | | | 7 | | 1 | | | |
| 11 | ..do..congestive | | 2 | 7 | 6 | 3 | 4 | 4 | 10 | 2 | 3 | 1 | 3 | | | | | | | 43 | | 1 | 1 | | |
| 12 | ..do..inflammatory | | | | | | | | | | 1 | 1 | 1 | | | | | | | 3 | | | | | |
| 13 | ..do..intermittent | 3 | 1 | 1 | 2 | 1 | 2 | | 1 | 1 | 1 | 4 | | 1 | | | | | | 18 | | | | | |
| 14 | ..do..puerperal | | | | | | | | 2 | | 2 | | | | | | | | | 4 | | | | | |
| 15 | ..do..remittent | | | | | | | 1 | | | | | | | | | | | | 1 | | | | | |
| 16 | ..do .scarlet | 6 | 2 | 32 | 31 | 25 | 33 | 4 | 14 | 2 | 3 | 2 | | | | | | 1 | | 151 | | 2 | | | 1 |
| 17 | ..do..typhus | 2 | 4 | 8 | 6 | 13 | 12 | 20 | 27 | 20 | 28 | 8 | 7 | 1 | | | | | | 152 | 1 | 1 | | | |
| 18 | Frozen | | | | | | | | | | | 1 | | 1 | 1 | | | | | 3 | | | | | |
| 19 | Gout | | | | | | | | | | | 1 | | | | | | | | 1 | | | | | |
| 20 | Gravel | 1 | | | | | | 1 | | | | 7 | 1 | 1 | | | | | | 10 | | 1 | | | |
| 21 | Head, disease of | | | | | | | | 1 | | | 2 | | | | | | | | 3 | | | | | |
| 22 | Heart....do | | 3 | | 1 | 2 | 1 | 4 | 6 | 4 | 8 | 21 | 9 | | | | | | | 56 | 2 | 1 | | | |
| 23 | Heat | | | | | | | 1 | | | | | | | | | | | | | | 1 | | | |
| 24 | Hemorrhage | | | | | | | 1 | | 4 | 5 | 3 | 6 | | | | | | | 18 | | 1 | | | |
| 25 | Hernia | | | | | | | | | 1 | | 1 | | 2 | | | | | | 4 | | | | | |
| 26 | Hooping cough | 14 | 17 | 20 | 30 | 3 | 6 | | | | 1 | | | | | | | | | 90 | | 1 | | | |
| 27 | Hydrocephalus | 1 | 2 | 5 | 3 | 1 | 1 | | 1 | 1 | | 1 | 1 | | | | | | | 16 | | 1 | | | |
| 28 | Hydrophobia | | | | | | | | | | | 1 | | | | | | | | 1 | | | | | |
| 29 | Inflammation | | 3 | 4 | 2 | 1 | 1 | | 3 | | 1 | 1 | 1 | | | | | | | 16 | | | | | 1 |
| 30 | .....do.....bowels | 7 | 4 | 8 | 10 | 3 | 2 | 3 | 3 | 7 | 4 | 6 | 2 | 1 | 1 | | | | | 57 | 2 | 2 | | | |
| 31 | .....do.....brain | 12 | 7 | 10 | 11 | 3 | 9 | 7 | 4 | 6 | 7 | 2 | 1 | | | | | | | 77 | 1 | | | | |
| 32 | .....do.....stomach | | 1 | | | | | | | | 1 | | 1 | | | | | | | 3 | | | | | |
| 33 | Influenza | 1 | | | | | | | 1 | | | | 1 | | | | | | | 3 | | | | | |
| 34 | Insanity | | | | | | | | | | 1 | 1 | 1 | 1 | 1 | | | | | 5 | | | | | |
| 35 | Intemperance | | | | | | | | | 22 | 5 | 10 | 1 | | | | | | | 34 | | 1 | 1 | | |
| 36 | Jaundice | 1 | | 1 | | | | | | 1 | | 1 | 1 | | | | | | | 5 | | | | | |
| 37 | Kidneys, disease of | | | | | | 1 | | | 1 | 1 | 2 | | | | | | | | 5 | | | | | |
| 38 | Killed | | | 1 | | 1 | | 1 | | 3 | | 1 | 1 | | | | | | | 7 | | 1 | | | |
| 39 | Lightning | | | | | | | | | 1 | 1 | 1 | | | | | | | | 3 | | | | | |
| 40 | Liver, disease of | 1 | | | | | 1 | 2 | 2 | 7 | 6 | 5 | 5 | | | | | | 1 | 28 | | 2 | | | |
| 41 | Lockjaw | 4 | 1 | 2 | | 1 | 1 | 1 | 2 | 4 | 1 | | | | | | | | | 17 | | | | | |
| 42 | Lungs, disease of | | | 5 | 2 | | 1 | | 5 | 4 | 4 | 4 | 5 | | | | | | 1 | 29 | | 1 | 1 | | |
| 43 | Malformation | 1 | | | | | | | | | | | | | | | | | | 1 | | | | | |
| 44 | Mania-a-potu | | | | | | | | | 2 | | 2 | | | | | | | | 4 | | | | | |
| 45 | Marasmus | 1 | 2 | | | 1 | | | | | | 1 | | | | | | | | 5 | | | | | |
| 46 | Measles | 5 | 7 | 20 | 17 | 5 | 3 | 4 | 4 | 7 | 4 | 1 | | | | | | | | 76 | | 1 | | | |
| 47 | Mortification | | | | | | | | | | | 1 | | | | | | | | | | | | | |
| 48 | Mumps | | | | | | | | | | 1 | | | | | | | | | 1 | | | | | |
| 49 | Murder | | | 1 | | | | | | 1 | | 2 | 1 | | | | | | | 4 | | 1 | | | |
| 50 | Neuralgia | | | | | | | | | 1 | 1 | | | | | | | | | 2 | | | | | |
| 51 | Old age | | | | | | | | | | | 54 | 51 | 69 | 89 | 11 | 16 | 2 | | 278 | | 7 | | | |
| 52 | Paralysis | 1 | | 1 | | | 1 | | | 5 | 8 | 21 | 2) | 6 | 2 | | | | | 64 | | 1 | | | |
| 53 | Pleurisy | 4 | | 9 | 6 | 5 | 1 | 18 | 11 | 62 | 42 | 34 | 31 | 2 | 4 | | | 2 | 1 | 227 | 1 | 2 | | | |
| 54 | Pneumonia | 8 | 13 | 17 | 12 | 6 | 1 | 8 | 15 | 41 | 28 | 26 | 19 | 2 | 1 | | | | | 192 | 1 | 3 | | | |
| 55 | Poison | 1 | | 2 | 3 | | 1 | | 1 | 1 | 3 | | | | 1 | | | | | 12 | | | | | |
| 56 | Prematurity of birth | | 1 | | | | | | | | | | | | | | | | | 1 | | | | | |
| 57 | Quinsy | | | 1 | | | | | | 3 | | | | | | | | | | 3 | | 1 | | | |
| 58 | Rheumatism | | | 1 | | | 1 | 2 | 2 | 4 | 4 | 7 | 8 | | | | | | 1 | 26 | | 1 | | | 1 |
| 59 | Rickets | | | 1 | | | | | | | | | | | | | | | | 1 | | | | | |
| 60 | Scrofula | 1 | 1 | 6 | 8 | 3 | 8 | 8 | 6 | 12 | 6 | 9 | 3 | 2 | | | | | | 73 | | | | | |
| 61 | Scurvy | | | | | | | 1 | | 1 | 1 | | | | | | | | 1 | 2 | | 1 | 1 | | |
| 62 | Small pox | | 1 | 1 | | | | 1 | 2 | 7 | 5 | 1 | 1 | | 1 | | | | | 19 | | | 1 | | |
| 63 | Spine, disease of | 3 | 2 | 2 | 3 | | | 3 | 1 | 1 | 1 | | 1 | | | | | | | 17 | | | | | |
| 64 | Stillborn | | 2 | | | | | | | | | | | | | | | | | 2 | | | | | |
| 65 | Stomach, disease of | | 1 | | | | | | | | | 3 | 1 | | | | | | | 5 | | | | | |
| 66 | Suffocation | 14 | 15 | 2 | 3 | | | | | | | | | | | | | | | 34 | | | | | |
| 67 | Suicide | | | | | | | | 1 | 3 | 2 | | | 1 | | | | | | 6 | | 1 | | | |
| 68 | Summer complaint | 9 | 5 | 5 | 5 | 1 | 2 | | | | | | | | | | | | 1 | 28 | | | | | |
| 69 | Teething | 10 | 15 | 23 | 17 | | | | | | | | | | | | | | | 65 | | | | | |
| 70 | Throat, disease of | 1 | | 4 | 1 | 1 | 2 | | 2 | 3 | 4 | 3 | 1 | | | | | | | 22 | | | | | |
| 71 | Thrush | 6 | 6 | 5 | 6 | | | | | | | | | | | | | | | 23 | | | | | |
| 72 | Tumor | | | 1 | | | 1 | | | | 2 | | 1 | | | | | | | 5 | | | | | |
| 73 | Ulcer | | | | | | | | | 1 | | | 1 | | | | | | | 2 | | | | | |
| 74 | Uterus, disease of | | | | 4 | | | | | | 6 | | 1 | | | | | | | 11 | | | | | |
| 75 | Venereal | | | | | | | | | 1 | 1 | 2 | | | | | | | | 4 | | | | | |

SECTION OF THE STATE OF VIRGINIA—Continued.

| NATIVITIES. | | | | | SEASON OF DECEASE. | | | | DURATION OF SICKNESS. | | | | WHITES. | | | COLORED. | | | | | | | | | |
|---|---|---|---|---|---|---|---|---|---|---|---|---|---|---|---|---|---|---|---|---|---|---|---|---|---|
| | | | | | | | | | | | | | | | | Slaves. | | | | Free. | | | | | |
| | | | | | | | | | | | | | | | | Black. | | Mulatto. | | Black. | | Mul. | | | |
| California and Territories. | Ireland. | Germany. | Other foreign countries. | Unknown. | Spring. | Summer. | Autumn. | Winter. | Under 1 week. | 1 week and under 1 month. | 1 month and under 3 months. | 3 months and over. | Males. | Females. | Total. | M. | F. | M. | F. | M. | F. | M | F. | Aggregate deaths. | |
| | | | | | | 1 | | | | | | | 1 | | 1 | | | | | | | | | 1 | 1 |
| | 1 | | | | 86 | 97 | 84 | 62 | 18 | 38 | 49 | 207 | 70 | 92 | 162 | 81 | 50 | 2 | 7 | 6 | 11 | 5 | 5 | 329 | 2 |
| | | | 1 | | 25 | 107 | 83 | 16 | 40 | 119 | 25 | 29 | 68 | 58 | 126 | 50 | 39 | 1 | 2 | 7 | 5 | 2 | 1 | 233 | 3 |
| | | | | | 2 | 3 | 4 | 4 | | 2 | 2 | 9 | 3 | 6 | 9 | 3 | | | | | 1 | | | 13 | 4 |
| | | | | | 1 | 1 | 1 | 1 | 4 | | | | | 1 | 1 | 3 | | | | | | | | 4 | 5 |
| | | | | | 3 | 8 | 4 | 7 | 3 | 11 | 4 | 3 | 7 | 10 | 17 | 4 | 1 | | | | | | | 22 | 6 |
| | | | 2 | | 28 | 22 | 38 | 15 | 26 | 63 | 10 | 6 | 26 | 21 | 47 | 23 | 27 | | | 4 | 2 | | 2 | 105 | 7 |
| | 1 | | | | 18 | 37 | 142 | 19 | 56 | 132 | 15 | 7 | 66 | 64 | 130 | 30 | 33 | 7 | 1 | 2 | 6 | 5 | 2 | 216 | 8 |
| | | | | | 15 | 14 | 21 | 7 | 33 | 22 | | 3 | 23 | 17 | 40 | 9 | 6 | 1 | | 1 | | 1 | | 58 | 9 |
| | | | | | 5 | 1 | 1 | 1 | 4 | 4 | | | 2 | 3 | 5 | | 1 | | | | | 1 | 1 | 8 | 10 |
| | | | | | 7 | 6 | 27 | 4 | 22 | 18 | 2 | 2 | 8 | 17 | 25 | 8 | 11 | | | 1 | | | | 45 | 11 |
| | | | | | 1 | 1 | 1 | | 2 | 1 | | | | 1 | 1 | 1 | 1 | | | | | | | 3 | 12 |
| | | | | | 5 | 3 | 8 | 2 | 5 | 6 | 5 | | 4 | 3 | 7 | 7 | 2 | | | | 1 | | 1 | 18 | 13 |
| | | | | | 2 | | | 2 | 3 | 1 | | | | 1 | 1 | | 2 | | 1 | | | | | 4 | 14 |
| | | | | | | | 1 | | | 1 | | | | | | | | | | 1 | | | | 1 | 15 |
| | 1 | | | | 56 | 25 | 17 | 57 | 74 | 70 | 8 | 1 | 48 | 57 | 105 | 21 | 19 | 3 | 4 | | 1 | | 2 | 155 | 16 |
| | 1 | | | 1 | 32 | 39 | 71 | 31 | 20 | 97 | 26 | 8 | 30 | 35 | 65 | 36 | 40 | 2 | 4 | 1 | 5 | 1 | | 156 | 17 |
| | | | | | 1 | | 1 | 1 | 2 | | | | 1 | | 1 | 1 | 1 | | | | | | | 3 | 18 |
| | | | | | | | 1 | | | | 1 | | 1 | | 1 | | | | | | | | | 1 | 19 |
| | | | | | 1 | 4 | 2 | 4 | 1 | 5 | 1 | 3 | 4 | | 4 | 6 | | | | | 1 | | | 11 | 20 |
| | | | | | 2 | | 1 | | 1 | | | 2 | | | | 2 | 1 | | | | | | | 3 | 21 |
| | | | | | 18 | 23 | 10 | 8 | 17 | 10 | 12 | 20 | 17 | 21 | 38 | 14 | 6 | | | | | | 1 | 59 | 22 |
| | | | | | | | 1 | | 1 | | | | 1 | | 1 | | | | | | | | | 1 | 23 |
| | | | | | 4 | 5 | 4 | 6 | 9 | 6 | 1 | 3 | 4 | 2 | 6 | 3 | 8 | | | 1 | | | 1 | 19 | 24 |
| | | | | | 2 | 1 | | 1 | 3 | 1 | | | | | | 4 | | | | | | | | 4 | 25 |
| | | | | | 26 | 22 | 29 | 14 | 12 | 46 | 23 | 10 | 17 | 20 | 37 | 13 | 24 | 2 | 3 | 4 | 6 | 1 | 1 | 91 | 26 |
| | | | | | 4 | 4 | 6 | 3 | 4 | 7 | 4 | 2 | 5 | 7 | 12 | 4 | 1 | | | | | | | 17 | 27 |
| | | | | | | | | 1 | | 1 | | | | | | 1 | | | | | | | | 1 | 28 |
| | | | | | 2 | 9 | 5 | 1 | 3 | 10 | 1 | 3 | 3 | 2 | 5 | 2 | 7 | | 1 | 1 | 1 | | | 17 | 29 |
| | | | | | 8 | 23 | 19 | 9 | 15 | 30 | 10 | 5 | 19 | 14 | 33 | 13 | 8 | 2 | 2 | 1 | | | 2 | 61 | 30 |
| | | 1 | | | 10 | 27 | 25 | 16 | 32 | 28 | 4 | 4 | 25 | 20 | 45 | 11 | 14 | 2 | | | 3 | 2 | 2 | 79 | 31 |
| | | | | | 1 | 1 | 1 | | | 2 | 1 | | | 2 | 2 | | 1 | | | | | | | 3 | 32 |
| | | | | | 1 | 1 | | 1 | | 2 | | 1 | | 1 | 1 | 1 | 1 | | | | | | | 3 | 33 |
| | | | | | | | 3 | 2 | 1 | 2 | 1 | 1 | 1 | 1 | 2 | 1 | 2 | | | | | | | 5 | 34 |
| | | | 1 | 1 | 11 | 5 | 6 | 14 | 8 | 8 | 4 | 8 | 22 | 4 | 26 | 6 | 1 | | | 2 | 1 | 2 | | 38 | 35 |
| | | | | | 2 | 1 | 2 | | | 2 | 2 | 1 | 3 | 1 | 4 | 1 | | | | | | | | 5 | 36 |
| | | | | | | 1 | 3 | 1 | 2 | | 2 | 1 | 3 | 2 | 5 | | | | | | | | | 5 | 37 |
| | | | | | 2 | 1 | 4 | 1 | 7 | | | | 3 | 1 | 4 | 2 | | 1 | | | | 1 | | 8 | 38 |
| | | | | | | 3 | | | 3 | | | | 1 | | 1 | 1 | 1 | | | | | | | 3 | 39 |
| | | | | | 4 | 12 | 9 | 5 | 4 | 8 | 4 | 14 | 13 | 9 | 22 | 1 | 6 | | | | | 1 | | 30 | 40 |
| | | | | | 5 | 4 | 3 | 5 | 10 | 6 | | | | 2 | 2 | 10 | 3 | 2 | | | | | | 17 | 41 |
| | | | | | 18 | 5 | 5 | 3 | 2 | 15 | 8 | 6 | 6 | 12 | 18 | 7 | 6 | | | | | | | 31 | 42 |
| | | | | | 1 | | | | 1 | | | | | | | 1 | | | | | | | | 1 | 43 |
| | | | | | | 3 | 1 | | 3 | 1 | | | 4 | | 4 | | | | | | | | | 4 | 44 |
| | | | | | 1 | 2 | 1 | | | | 1 | 4 | 2 | | 2 | 1 | 1 | | 1 | | | | | 5 | 45 |
| | | | | | 10 | 32 | 26 | 8 | 16 | 38 | 7 | 11 | 26 | 16 | 42 | 13 | 16 | 2 | 1 | 1 | | | 2 | 77 | 46 |
| | | | | 1 | 1 | | | | | | 1 | | 1 | | 1 | | | | | | | | | 1 | 47 |
| | | | | | 1 | | | | | | | 1 | | | | | 1 | | | | | | | 1 | 48 |
| | | | | | 1 | 3 | | 1 | 5 | | | | 1 | | 1 | 2 | | | 1 | 1 | | | | 5 | 49 |
| | | | | | 1 | | 1 | | 1 | | 1 | | 1 | 1 | 2 | | | | | | | | | 2 | 50 |
| | | 1 | 5 | 1 | 83 | 85 | 60 | 60 | 32 | 49 | 14 | 58 | 33 | 42 | 75 | 79 | 96 | 9 | 5 | 11 | 8 | 4 | 5 | 292 | 51 |
| | | | | | 23 | 17 | 13 | 10 | 16 | 12 | 10 | 22 | 19 | 14 | 33 | 12 | 10 | 2 | 2 | 1 | 3 | | 2 | 65 | 52 |
| | | | 2 | | 118 | 28 | 29 | 57 | 59 | 136 | 26 | 11 | 54 | 56 | 110 | 60 | 34 | 7 | 2 | 8 | 4 | 7 | | 232 | 53 |
| | | 1 | 1 | | 76 | 37 | 27 | 53 | 35 | 105 | 22 | 14 | 46 | 30 | 76 | 55 | 50 | 4 | 5 | 2 | 3 | 1 | 2 | 198 | 54 |
| | 1 | | | | 1 | 7 | 5 | | 5 | 1 | 1 | 5 | | 2 | 2 | 3 | 7 | 1 | | | | | | 13 | 55 |
| | | | | | 1 | | | | 1 | | | | | | | | 1 | | | | | | | 1 | 56 |
| | | | | | 1 | 1 | 1 | 1 | 3 | 1 | | | 3 | | 3 | | | 1 | | | | | | 4 | 57 |
| | | 1 | 1 | | 5 | 12 | 5 | 8 | 3 | 5 | | 20 | 5 | 9 | 14 | 8 | 3 | 1 | 2 | | 2 | | | 30 | 58 |
| | | | | | | 1 | | | | | | 1 | | | | 1 | | | | | | | | 1 | 59 |
| | | | | | 24 | 24 | 12 | 12 | | 8 | 10 | 55 | 9 | 4 | 13 | 25 | 25 | 1 | 2 | 4 | | 2 | 1 | 73 | 60 |
| | | | | | 3 | 1 | | | | 3 | | 1 | 2 | 2 | 4 | | | | | | | | | 4 | 61 |
| | | | | | 10 | 7 | 2 | 1 | 7 | 12 | | 1 | 7 | 7 | 14 | 1 | 3 | 1 | | 1 | | | | 20 | 62 |
| | | | | | 5 | 6 | 3 | 3 | 2 | 3 | 1 | 8 | 3 | 5 | 8 | 6 | 2 | | 1 | | | | | 17 | 63 |
| | | | | | 2 | | | | 2 | | | | | | | | 2 | | | | | | | 2 | 64 |
| | | | | | 1 | 1 | 2 | 1 | | 3 | 2 | | 1 | 2 | 3 | 1 | | 1 | | | | | | 5 | 65 |
| | | | | | 7 | 8 | 5 | 7 | 34 | | | | 4 | 4 | 8 | 12 | 14 | | | | | | | 34 | 66 |
| | | | | | 4 | 1 | 1 | 1 | 4 | | | 1 | 3 | 2 | 5 | 1 | | | 1 | | | | | 7 | 67 |
| | | | | | 4 | 5 | 13 | 6 | 4 | 9 | 7 | 6 | 9 | 9 | 18 | 5 | 4 | 1 | | | | | | 28 | 68 |
| | | | | | 9 | 28 | 19 | 6 | 9 | 20 | 18 | 15 | 19 | 16 | 35 | 11 | 11 | 1 | 2 | | 1 | 2 | 2 | 65 | 69 |
| | | | | | 5 | 5 | 8 | 8 | 5 | 13 | 1 | 2 | 6 | 5 | 11 | 5 | 5 | 1 | | | | | | 22 | 70 |
| | | | | | 1 | 4 | 10 | 8 | 2 | 16 | 1 | 4 | 4 | 7 | 11 | 5 | 5 | | | 1 | | 1 | | 23 | 71 |
| | | | | | | 1 | 1 | 3 | | 1 | | 4 | | 2 | 2 | 1 | 2 | | | | | | | 5 | 72 |
| | | | | | | 1 | 1 | | | 1 | 1 | | | | | 1 | 1 | | | | | | | 2 | 73 |
| | | | | | 3 | 2 | 4 | 2 | 1 | 5 | 2 | 3 | | 1 | 1 | | 9 | | 1 | | | | | 11 | 74 |
| | | | | | 3 | 1 | | | | | 1 | 3 | 1 | | 1 | 2 | 1 | | | | | | | 4 | 75 |

## CLASSIFICATION OF DEATHS IN EASTERN

| Cause of death. | AGES. | | | | | | | | | | | | | | | | | | NATIVITIES. | | | | | |
|---|---|---|---|---|---|---|---|---|---|---|---|---|---|---|---|---|---|---|---|---|---|---|---|---|
| | Under 1. | | 1 and under 5. | | 5 and under 10. | | 10 and under 20. | | 20 and under 50. | | 50 and under 80. | | 80 and under 100. | | 100 & over. | | Age unknown. | | Born in State. | N. England States. | Middle States. | Southern States. | Southwest'n States. | Northwest'n States. |
| | M. | F. | M. | F. | M. | F. | M. | F. | M. | F. | M. | F. | M | F. | M | F. | M | F. | | | | | | |
| 1 White swelling...... | ... | ... | ... | ... | ... | ... | ... | ... | ... | ... | 1 | ... | .. | 1 | .. | .. | .. | .. | 2 | .. | ... | ... | ... | ... |
| 2 Worms.............. | 7 | 3 | 24 | 33 | 10 | 7 | 1 | ... | 1 | 1 | ... | ... | .. | .. | .. | .. | .. | .. | 87 | .. | ... | ... | ... | ... |
| 3 Unknown............ | 239 | 235 | 147 | 132 | 39 | 45 | 57 | 70 | 159 | 195 | 155 | 148 | 13 | 18 | 2 | 1 | 5 | 5 | 1136 | 4 | 16 | 3 | ... | ... |
| Total............ | 597 | 525 | 662 | 620 | 219 | 238 | 305 | 359 | 905 | 988 | 744 | 615 | 112 | 147 | 15 | 18 | 25 | 20 | 6876 | 22 | 101 | 27 | ... | 3 |

## CLASSIFICATION OF DEATHS IN SOUTHERN

*Embracing the following counties : Albemarle, Amelia, Amherst, Appomatox, Bedford, Brunswick, Franklin, Goochland, Greene, Greenville, Halifax, Henry, Louisa, Lunenburg, Madison, Meck*

| | | | | | | | | | | | | | | | | | | | | | | | | |
|---|---|---|---|---|---|---|---|---|---|---|---|---|---|---|---|---|---|---|---|---|---|---|---|---|
| 1 Abscess .... ........ | ... | ... | ... | ... | ... | ... | ... | ... | 1 | ... | ... | 1 | .. | .. | .. | .. | .. | .. | 2 | .. | ... | ... | ... | ... |
| 2 Accident, not specif'd | 10 | 14 | 2 | 5 | 5 | 4 | 8 | 3 | 16 | 2 | 11 | 1 | .. | .. | .. | .. | .. | .. | 80 | .. | 1 | ... | ... | ... |
| 3 ....do...burned..... | 4 | 6 | 9 | 19 | 4 | 5 | 2 | 5 | 3 | 4 | 2 | 2 | .. | .. | .. | 1 | .. | .. | 65 | .. | ... | ... | ... | ... |
| 4 ....do...drowned.... | ... | 1 | ... | ... | 2 | 1 | 3 | ... | 7 | 3 | 6 | ... | .. | .. | .. | .. | .. | .. | 23 | .. | ... | ... | ... | ... |
| 5 ....do...scalded .... | ... | ... | ... | 1 | ... | ... | ... | ... | ... | ... | ... | ... | .. | .. | .. | .. | .. | .. | 1 | .. | ... | ... | ... | ... |
| 6 ....do...explosion.. | ... | ... | ... | ... | ... | ... | ... | ... | 1 | ... | ... | ... | .. | .. | .. | .. | .. | .. | 1 | .. | ... | ... | ... | ... |
| 7 ....do...shot .. .... | ... | ... | ... | ... | ... | ... | ... | ... | 1 | ... | ... | ... | .. | .. | .. | .. | .. | .. | 1 | .. | ... | ... | ... | ... |
| 8 Apoplexy........... | ... | ... | ... | ... | ... | ... | 1 | ... | 4 | 3 | 13 | 15 | 1 | 2 | .. | .. | .. | .. | 36 | .. | 2 | ... | ... | ... |
| 9 Asthma............. | 2 | ... | ... | 1 | ... | ... | ... | ... | 1 | 1 | 7 | 8 | 1 | 1 | .. | .. | .. | .. | 22 | .. | ... | ... | ... | ... |
| 10 Bladder, disease of.. | 1 | ... | ... | ... | ... | 1 | 1 | ... | 1 | ... | 1 | ... | 1 | .. | .. | .. | .. | .. | 6 | .. | ... | ... | ... | ... |
| 11 Bowels......do...... | 7 | 1 | 5 | 11 | ... | 2 | 1 | 1 | 1 | 3 | ... | 5 | .. | .. | .. | .. | .. | .. | 37 | .. | ... | ... | ... | ... |
| 12 Brain ......do...... | 2 | 4 | 2 | 2 | 2 | ... | 3 | ... | 3 | 2 | 3 | 1 | .. | .. | .. | .. | .. | .. | 24 | .. | ... | ... | ... | ... |
| 13 Bronchitis .......... | 1 | 2 | 4 | 4 | ... | 1 | 1 | 1 | 5 | 6 | 2 | 1 | 1 | .. | .. | .. | .. | .. | 28 | .. | ... | ... | ... | ... |
| 14 Cancer ............. | ... | ... | 2 | ... | ... | ... | ... | 1 | 3 | 5 | 7 | 20 | 2 | 1 | 1 | 1 | .. | .. | 42 | .. | 1 | ... | ... | ... |
| 15 Carbuncle .......... | ... | ... | ... | ... | ... | ... | ... | ... | 1 | 1 | ... | 1 | .. | .. | .. | .. | .. | .. | 3 | .. | ... | ... | ... | ... |
| 16 Catarrh ............ | 36 | 24 | 33 | 30 | 8 | 4 | ... | 7 | 10 | 13 | 33 | 20 | 2 | 2 | .. | .. | .. | .. | 221 | .. | ... | 1 | ... | ... |
| 17 Childbirth .......... | ... | ... | ... | ... | ... | ... | ... | 14 | ... | 57 | ... | ... | .. | .. | .. | .. | .. | .. | 71 | .. | ... | ... | ... | ... |
| 18 Cholera..... ........ | ... | 3 | 6 | 4 | 3 | 2 | 4 | 4 | 35 | 19 | 16 | 7 | 1 | 1 | .. | .. | .. | .. | 101 | .. | ... | ... | ... | ... |
| 19 ...do...infantum.... | 9 | 9 | 4 | 9 | ... | ... | ... | ... | ... | ... | ... | ... | .. | .. | .. | .. | .. | .. | 31 | .. | ... | ... | ... | ... |
| 20 ...do...morbus..... | 1 | 2 | ... | ... | ... | ... | ... | ... | 1 | ... | 1 | ... | .. | .. | .. | .. | .. | .. | 5 | .. | ... | ... | ... | ... |
| 21 Colic .............. | ... | 1 | 1 | ... | 1 | 2 | ... | ... | 10 | 1 | 5 | 7 | .. | .. | .. | .. | .. | .. | 28 | .. | ... | ... | ... | ... |
| 22 Congestion.......... | 1 | 1 | 2 | ... | 1 | ... | 2 | 2 | 3 | 1 | 1 | ... | .. | .. | .. | .. | .. | .. | 14 | .. | ... | ... | ... | ... |
| 23 ....do....brain..... | 2 | 1 | 2 | 3 | 2 | 3 | 8 | 4 | 3 | 3 | 3 | 1 | .. | .. | .. | .. | .. | .. | 35 | .. | ... | ... | ... | ... |
| 24 Consumption......... | 7 | 7 | 13 | 17 | 2 | 6 | 13 | 45 | 93 | 170 | 40 | 43 | 2 | 2 | .. | .. | .. | .. | 455 | .. | 2 | 1 | ... | ... |
| 25 Convulsions ......... | 26 | 21 | 10 | 14 | 4 | 2 | 4 | 5 | 6 | 10 | 3 | 4 | 1 | .. | .. | .. | .. | .. | 110 | .. | ... | ... | ... | ... |
| 26 Cramp .............. | 1 | ... | 1 | 2 | ... | 1 | ... | ... | ... | ... | ... | ... | .. | .. | .. | .. | .. | .. | 5 | .. | ... | ... | ... | ... |
| 27 Croup............... | 29 | 14 | 27 | 23 | 4 | 1 | ... | ... | ... | ... | ... | ... | .. | .. | .. | .. | .. | .. | 98 | .. | ... | ... | ... | ... |
| 28 Debility............ | 2 | ... | ... | 2 | ... | ... | ... | ... | ... | 3 | 2 | 6 | 1 | .. | .. | .. | .. | .. | 16 | .. | ... | ... | ... | ... |
| 29 Diabetes............ | ... | ... | ... | ... | 1 | ... | ... | ... | 2 | ... | ... | ... | .. | .. | .. | .. | .. | .. | 3 | .. | ... | ... | ... | ... |
| 30 Diarrhœa............ | 18 | 12 | 26 | 22 | 2 | 4 | 3 | 2 | 8 | 5 | 9 | 5 | 1 | 3 | .. | .. | .. | .. | 119 | .. | 1 | ... | ... | ... |
| 31 Dirt eating......... | ... | ... | ... | ... | ... | ... | 1 | ... | 1 | ... | ... | ... | .. | .. | .. | .. | .. | .. | 2 | .. | ... | ... | ... | ... |
| 32 Dropsy.............. | 3 | 4 | 17 | 10 | 5 | 5 | 7 | 11 | 37 | 49 | 88 | 60 | 14 | 3 | .. | 1 | .. | .. | 311 | .. | 2 | 1 | ... | ... |
| 33 Dysentery .......... | 14 | 20 | 18 | 12 | 6 | 1 | 7 | ... | 3 | 2 | 3 | 5 | 2 | .. | .. | .. | .. | .. | 88 | .. | ... | ... | ... | ... |
| 34 Dyspepsia .......... | ... | ... | ... | ... | ... | ... | 1 | ... | 3 | 4 | 2 | 3 | .. | .. | .. | .. | .. | .. | 13 | .. | ... | ... | ... | ... |
| 35 Epilepsy............ | ... | 1 | ... | ... | ... | ... | ... | ... | ... | 1 | ... | ... | .. | .. | .. | .. | .. | .. | 2 | .. | ... | ... | ... | ... |
| 36 Erysipelas ......... | 1 | 2 | ... | 2 | ... | 1 | ... | 2 | 2 | ... | ... | 3 | .. | .. | .. | .. | .. | .. | 12 | .. | ... | 1 | ... | ... |
| 37 Fever, not specified.. | 6 | 8 | 22 | 24 | 13 | 17 | 25 | 23 | 30 | 36 | 11 | 11 | .. | .. | .. | .. | .. | .. | 226 | .. | ... | ... | ... | ... |
| 38 ..do..bilious ....... | 3 | 1 | 1 | 1 | 1 | ... | 3 | 2 | 8 | 11 | 4 | 4 | .. | 1 | .. | .. | .. | .. | 39 | .. | ... | ... | ... | ... |
| 39 ..do..brain......... | ... | ... | ... | ... | ... | ... | 1 | ... | 3 | 1 | ... | ... | .. | .. | .. | .. | .. | .. | 5 | .. | ... | ... | ... | ... |
| 40 ..do..catarrhal..... | 1 | 2 | 1 | 2 | ... | ... | 1 | ... | ... | ... | 1 | 1 | 1 | .. | .. | .. | .. | .. | 10 | .. | ... | ... | ... | ... |
| 41 ..do..congestive ... | 1 | ... | 1 | 1 | ... | 1 | 2 | 2 | 7 | 6 | 2 | 1 | .. | .. | .. | .. | .. | .. | 24 | .. | ... | ... | ... | ... |
| 42 ..do..inflammatory. | ... | ... | ... | ... | ... | ... | ... | ... | ... | ... | ... | 1 | .. | .. | .. | .. | .. | .. | 1 | .. | ... | ... | ... | ... |
| 43 ..do..intermittent .. | ... | 1 | 1 | 2 | 2 | 1 | 3 | ... | 2 | 1 | 3 | 5 | .. | .. | .. | .. | .. | .. | 21 | .. | ... | ... | ... | ... |
| 44 ..do..puerperal .... | ... | ... | ... | ... | ... | ... | ... | ... | ... | 1 | ... | ... | .. | .. | .. | .. | .. | .. | 1 | .. | ... | ... | ... | ... |
| 45 ..do..remittent .... | ... | ... | 1 | ... | ... | ... | ... | ... | ... | ... | ... | ... | .. | .. | .. | .. | .. | .. | 1 | .. | ... | ... | ... | ... |
| 46 ..do..scarlet ....... | 3 | 2 | 8 | 4 | 4 | 4 | 2 | 1 | ... | ... | ... | ... | .. | .. | .. | .. | .. | .. | 28 | .. | ... | ... | ... | ... |
| 47 ..do..typhus ....... | 2 | 2 | 14 | 10 | 13 | 10 | 44 | 53 | 84 | 49 | 22 | 18 | 1 | 1 | .. | .. | .. | .. | 319 | .. | ... | 3 | .. | 1 |
| 48 Fracture ........... | ... | ... | ... | 1 | ... | ... | ... | ... | ... | ... | ... | ... | .. | .. | .. | .. | .. | .. | 1 | .. | ... | ... | ... | ... |
| 49 Frozen ............. | ... | ... | ... | ... | ... | ... | 1 | ... | ... | 1 | 4 | ... | .. | .. | .. | .. | .. | .. | 6 | .. | ... | ... | ... | ... |
| 50 Gout ............... | ... | ... | ... | ... | ... | ... | ... | ... | ... | ... | ... | 1 | .. | .. | .. | .. | .. | .. | 1 | .. | ... | ... | ... | ... |
| 51 Gravel ............. | ... | ... | ... | ... | ... | ... | ... | ... | ... | ... | 9 | ... | 1 | .. | 1 | .. | .. | .. | 10 | .. | 1 | ... | ... | ... |
| 52 Head, disease of.... | ... | 2 | 1 | ... | ... | ... | ... | ... | ... | 2 | ... | 1 | .. | .. | .. | .. | .. | .. | 6 | .. | ... | ... | ... | ... |
| 53 Heart....do......... | 3 | 1 | 2 | 1 | ... | ... | 1 | 1 | 4 | 6 | 5 | 2 | .. | .. | .. | .. | .. | .. | 26 | .. | ... | ... | ... | ... |
| 54 Hemorrhage ......... | 1 | ... | 1 | ... | ... | 2 | 2 | 1 | 6 | 7 | 2 | ... | .. | .. | .. | .. | .. | .. | 22 | .. | ... | ... | ... | ... |
| 55 Hernia ............. | 1 | ... | ... | ... | ... | ... | 1 | ... | 5 | ... | 8 | ... | .. | .. | .. | .. | .. | .. | 15 | .. | ... | ... | ... | ... |
| 56 Hives............... | 1 | 1 | 1 | ... | ... | ... | ... | ... | ... | ... | ... | ... | .. | .. | .. | .. | .. | .. | 3 | .. | ... | ... | ... | ... |
| 57 Hooping cough...... | 1 | 7 | 9 | 6 | ... | 2 | ... | ... | ... | ... | ... | ... | .. | .. | .. | .. | .. | .. | 25 | .. | ... | ... | ... | ... |
| 58 Hydrocephalus...... | 6 | 2 | 4 | 1 | 1 | ... | ... | 1 | ... | ... | ... | ... | .. | .. | .. | .. | .. | .. | 15 | .. | ... | ... | ... | ... |
| 59 Inflammation ....... | ... | ... | 4 | 1 | ... | 2 | 2 | 2 | 3 | 3 | 1 | ... | .. | .. | .. | .. | .. | .. | 17 | .. | ... | ... | ... | 1 |
| 60 .....do.....bowels.. | 7 | 2 | 4 | 4 | 2 | ... | ... | 1 | 7 | 6 | 5 | 5 | .. | .. | .. | .. | .. | .. | 41 | .. | ... | ... | ... | ... |
| 61 .....do.....brain... | 8 | 2 | 8 | 8 | 2 | 4 | 10 | 5 | 7 | 4 | 1 | 1 | .. | .. | .. | .. | .. | .. | 60 | .. | ... | ... | ... | ... |

SECTION OF THE STATE OF VIRGINIA—Continued.

| NATIVITIES. | | | | | SEASON OF DECEASE. | | | | DURATION OF SICKNESS. | | | | WHITES. | | | COLORED. | | | | | | | | | |
|---|---|---|---|---|---|---|---|---|---|---|---|---|---|---|---|---|---|---|---|---|---|---|---|---|---|
| | | | | | | | | | | | | | | | | Slaves. | | | | Free. | | | | | |
| | | | | | | | | | | | | | | | | Black. | | Mulatto. | | Black. | | Mul. | | | |
| California and Territories. | Ireland. | Germany. | Other foreign countries. | Unknown. | Spring. | Summer. | Autumn. | Winter. | Under 1 week. | 1 week and under 1 month. | 1 month and under 3 months. | 3 months and over. | Males. | Females. | Total. | M. | F. | M. | F. | M. | F. | M | F. | Aggregate deaths. | |
| | | | | | | 1 | | 1 | 2 | | | | 1 | | 1 | | 1 | | | | | | | 2 | 1 |
| | | | | | 10 | 28 | 35 | 12 | 34 | 29 | 9 | 7 | 6 | 14 | 20 | 31 | 23 | 3 | 1 | 2 | 4 | 1 | 2 | 87 | 2 |
| | 3 | | 3 | | 426 | 436 | 462 | 293 | 517 | 369 | 135 | 34[illegible] | 361 | 382 | 743 | 341 | 364 | 44 | 28 | 51 | 47 | 19 | 28 | 1665 | 3 |
| .... | 21 | 15 | 44 | 5 | 1672 | 2221 | 1897 | 1206 | 2289 | 2005 | 653 | 1485 | 1696 | 1677 | 3373 | 1563 | 1464 | 138 | 116 | 171 | 180 | 76 | 93 | 7114 | |

SECTION OF THE STATE OF VIRGINIA.

*Buckingham, Campbell, Charlotte, Chesterfield, Culpeper, Cumberland, Dinwiddie, Fluvanna, lenburg, Nelson, Nottoway, Orange, Patrick, Pittsylvania, Powhatan, P. Edward, Rappahannock.*

| California and Territories. | Ireland. | Germany. | Other foreign countries. | Unknown. | Spring. | Summer. | Autumn. | Winter. | Under 1 week. | 1 week and under 1 month. | 1 month and under 3 months. | 3 months and over. | Males. | Females. | Total. | Slaves Black M. | Slaves Black F. | Slaves Mulatto M. | Slaves Mulatto F. | Free Black M. | Free Black F. | Free Mul. M | Free Mul. F. | Aggregate deaths. | |
|---|---|---|---|---|---|---|---|---|---|---|---|---|---|---|---|---|---|---|---|---|---|---|---|---|---|
| | | | | | 1 | | 1 | | | | | | | 1 | 1 | 1 | | | | | | | | 2 | 1 |
| | | | | | 22 | 13 | 26 | 20 | 57 | 8 | 5 | 4 | 18 | 5 | 23 | 32 | 23 | 2 | | | | | 1 | 81 | 2 |
| | 1 | | | | 22 | 10 | 9 | 25 | 42 | 14 | 2 | 4 | 2 | 14 | 15 | 19 | 22 | 2 | 5 | 1 | 1 | | 1 | 66 | 3 |
| | | | | | 3 | 14 | 3 | 1 | 23 | | | | 1 | 3 | 4 | 17 | | | 1 | | | | 1 | 23 | 4 |
| | | | | | | | | | | | | | | | | | 1 | | | | | | | 1 | 5 |
| | | | | | | 1 | | | 1 | | | | | | | 1 | | | | | | | | 1 | 6 |
| | | | | | | | 1 | | | | | | 1 | | 1 | | | | | | | | | 1 | 7 |
| | 1 | | | | 9 | 14 | 7 | 9 | 26 | 3 | 1 | 3 | 10 | 3 | 13 | 9 | 14 | | 3 | | | | | 39 | 8 |
| | | | | | 9 | 4 | 3 | 6 | 2 | 5 | 3 | 11 | 4 | 2 | 6 | 6 | 8 | 1 | 1 | | | | | 22 | 9 |
| | | | | | | 2 | 1 | 3 | 1 | 2 | 2 | 1 | 2 | | 2 | 3 | 1 | | | | | | | 6 | 10 |
| | | | | | 2 | 15 | 11 | 9 | 6 | 14 | 6 | 8 | 6 | 10 | 16 | 7 | 12 | 1 | 1 | | | | | 37 | 11 |
| | | | | | 11 | 5 | 3 | 5 | 9 | 7 | 1 | 4 | 5 | 5 | 10 | 10 | 2 | | 2 | | | | | 24 | 12 |
| | | | 1 | | 10 | 7 | 4 | 8 | 6 | 5 | 3 | 12 | 5 | 4 | 9 | 8 | 10 | | | 1 | | | 1 | 29 | 13 |
| | | | | | 7 | 11 | 10 | 15 | | 2 | 2 | 38 | 13 | 17 | 30 | 2 | 11 | | | | | | | 43 | 14 |
| | | | | | 1 | | | | | | | 1 | | 2 | 2 | 1 | | | | | | | | 3 | 15 |
| | | | | | 90 | 53 | 18 | 46 | 53 | 93 | 23 | 33 | 36 | 12 | 48 | 76 | 83 | 6 | 4 | 4 | 1 | | | 222 | 16 |
| | | | | | 22 | 22 | 13 | 14 | 45 | 16 | 1 | | | 19 | 19 | | 47 | | 5 | | | | | 71 | 17 |
| | 3 | | 1 | | 6 | 81 | 14 | 2 | 79 | 6 | 1 | 1 | 14 | 17 | 31 | 26 | 7 | 2 | | 19 | 12 | 4 | 4 | 105 | 18 |
| | | | | | 2 | 14 | 11 | 2 | 6 | 7 | 3 | 2 | 10 | 12 | 22 | 2 | 6 | 1 | | | | | | 31 | 19 |
| | | | | | | 4 | 1 | | 4 | 1 | | | 1 | 1 | 2 | 2 | 1 | | | | | | | 5 | 20 |
| | | | | | 8 | 8 | 7 | 4 | 19 | 8 | 1 | | 5 | 5 | 10 | 11 | 5 | 1 | | | | | 1 | 28 | 21 |
| | | | | | 3 | 7 | 3 | 1 | 13 | | | | 2 | 1 | 3 | 8 | 3 | | | | | | | 14 | 22 |
| | | | | | 10 | 17 | 4 | 3 | 17 | 10 | 3 | 3 | 9 | 4 | 13 | 10 | 11 | 1 | | | | | | 35 | 23 |
| | 2 | | | | 158 | 119 | 95 | 74 | 8 | 37 | 49 | 325 | 76 | 150 | 226 | 87 | 118 | 3 | 11 | 3 | 5 | 1 | 6 | 460 | 24 |
| | | | | | 81 | 34 | 22 | 22 | 62 | 29 | 2 | 9 | 10 | 20 | 30 | 41 | 33 | 1 | 3 | 1 | | 1 | | 110 | 25 |
| | | | | | 2 | 2 | 1 | | 5 | | | | | | | 2 | 3 | | | | | | | 5 | 26 |
| | | | | | 37 | 19 | 21 | 21 | 58 | 28 | 3 | | 21 | 1 | 22 | 39 | 29 | | 5 | | 3 | | | 98 | 27 |
| | | | | | 2 | 8 | 2 | 4 | | 2 | 4 | 8 | 1 | 8 | 9 | 4 | 3 | | | | | | | 16 | 28 |
| | | | | | | 1 | | 2 | | 1 | | 1 | 2 | | 2 | 1 | | | | | | | | 3 | 29 |
| | | | | | 15 | 57 | 32 | 16 | 22 | 49 | 25 | 22 | 26 | 13 | 39 | 36 | 34 | 3 | 3 | 2 | 1 | | 2 | 120 | 30 |
| | | | | | | 1 | 1 | | | 1 | | 1 | | | | 1 | | 1 | | | | | | 2 | 31 |
| | | | | | 89 | 112 | 71 | 42 | 14 | 38 | 71 | 175 | 61 | 42 | 103 | 99 | 93 | 5 | 3 | 4 | 3 | 2 | 2 | 314 | 32 |
| | | | | | 9 | 45 | 29 | 5 | 16 | 47 | 10 | 8 | 17 | 13 | 30 | 27 | 25 | 3 | 2 | 1 | | | | 88 | 33 |
| | | | | | 2 | 5 | 2 | 4 | | 3 | 3 | 6 | 4 | 6 | 10 | 2 | 2 | | | | | | | 13 | 34 |
| | | | | | 1 | | | 1 | 2 | | | | | | | | 2 | | | | | | | 2 | 35 |
| | | | | | 5 | 5 | 2 | 1 | 6 | 2 | 4 | | 2 | 6 | 8 | 1 | 3 | | 1 | | | | | 13 | 36 |
| | | | | | 59 | 48 | 68 | 49 | 35 | 125 | 38 | 21 | 47 | 57 | 104 | 54 | 55 | 5 | 6 | | | 1 | 1 | 226 | 37 |
| | 1 | | | | 2 | 17 | 16 | 5 | 5 | 18 | 6 | 1 | 4 | 7 | 11 | 14 | 13 | 1 | | 1 | | | | 40 | 38 |
| | | | | | 2 | 2 | | 1 | 1 | 3 | 1 | | | | | 4 | | | 1 | | | | | 5 | 39 |
| | | | | | 4 | 2 | 1 | 3 | 2 | 2 | 3 | 2 | 2 | 1 | 3 | 3 | 4 | | | | | | | 10 | 40 |
| | | | | | 6 | 7 | 7 | 4 | 5 | 12 | 5 | | 4 | 6 | 10 | 8 | 5 | 1 | | | | | | 24 | 41 |
| | | | | | | | | 1 | | 1 | | | | | | | | | 1 | | | | | 1 | 42 |
| | | | | | 7 | 2 | 5 | 6 | 4 | 10 | 3 | 2 | 5 | 4 | 9 | 6 | 4 | | 1 | | 1 | | | 21 | 43 |
| | | | | | | | 1 | | | 1 | | | | 1 | 1 | | | | | | | | | 1 | 44 |
| | | | | | | | 1 | | | | 1 | | | | | 1 | | | | | | | | 1 | 45 |
| | | | | | 8 | 7 | 2 | 11 | 12 | 13 | | 1 | 9 | 5 | 14 | 8 | 5 | | 1 | | | | | 28 | 46 |
| | | | | | 47 | 90 | 125 | 60 | 32 | 204 | 65 | 11 | 57 | 33 | 90 | 116 | 100 | 5 | 9 | 1 | | 1 | 1 | 323 | 47 |
| | | | | | | | | 1 | | 1 | | | | 1 | 1 | | | | | | | | | 1 | 48 |
| | | | | | 2 | | 1 | 3 | 2 | 1 | | | 2 | | 2 | 2 | 1 | 1 | | | | | | 6 | 49 |
| | | | | | | | 1 | | | | | 1 | | 1 | 1 | | | | | | | | | 1 | 50 |
| | | | | | 3 | 2 | 3 | 3 | 1 | 5 | 1 | 4 | 4 | | 4 | 7 | | | | | | | | 11 | 51 |
| | | | | | 2 | | 1 | 2 | 4 | | | 1 | 1 | | 1 | | 5 | | | | | | | 6 | 52 |
| | | | | | 11 | 6 | 5 | 4 | 4 | 1 | 6 | 11 | 7 | 6 | 13 | 7 | 3 | 1 | 2 | | | | | 26 | 53 |
| | | | | | 8 | 7 | 5 | 2 | 6 | 6 | 3 | 7 | 2 | 5 | 7 | 6 | 5 | 2 | | 2 | | | | 22 | 54 |
| | | | | | 4 | 4 | 4 | 3 | 5 | 4 | 3 | 2 | 1 | | 1 | 13 | | 1 | | | | | | 15 | 55 |
| | | | | | | 1 | 1 | 1 | 2 | 1 | | | 1 | 1 | 2 | 1 | | | | | | | | 3 | 56 |
| | | | | | 8 | 7 | 3 | 1 | | 9 | 2 | 6 | 1 | 2 | 3 | 9 | 13 | | | | | | | 25 | 57 |
| | | | | | 4 | 3 | 5 | 3 | 2 | 8 | 1 | 3 | 3 | | 3 | 7 | 4 | 1 | | | | | | 15 | 58 |
| | | | | | 4 | 3 | 6 | 5 | 5 | 8 | 4 | 1 | 3 | 3 | 6 | 7 | 5 | | | | | | | 18 | 59 |
| | | | 2 | | 10 | 18 | 10 | 5 | 10 | 20 | 3 | 7 | 6 | 9 | 15 | 18 | 8 | 1 | 1 | | | | | 43 | 60 |
| | | | | | 16 | 18 | 18 | 8 | 26 | 17 | 7 | 5 | 17 | 10 | 27 | 17 | 13 | 2 | 1 | | | | | 60 | 61 |

## CLASSIFICATION OF DEATHS IN SOUTHERN

| | Cause of death. | AGES. | | | | | | | | | | | | | | | | | | NATIVITIES. | | | | | |
|---|---|---|---|---|---|---|---|---|---|---|---|---|---|---|---|---|---|---|---|---|---|---|---|---|---|
| | | Under 1. | | 1 and under 5. | | 5 and under 10. | | 10 and under 20. | | 20 and under 50. | | 50 and under 80. | | 80 and under 100. | | 100 & over. | | Age unknown. | | Born in State. | N. England States. | Middle States. | Southern States. | Southwest'n States. | Northwest'n States. |
| | | M. | F. | M. | F. | M. | F. | M. | F. | M. | F. | M. | F. | M | F. | M | F. | M | F. | | | | | | |
| 1 | Inflammat'n, stomach | .... | 1 | .... | 1 | .... | .... | .... | .... | .... | 3 | 2 | 2 | .. | .. | .. | .. | .. | .. | 8 | .. | 1 | .... | .... | .. |
| 2 | Influenza | 1 | 1 | 2 | .... | .... | .... | .... | .... | .... | .... | .... | .... | .. | .. | .. | .. | .. | .. | 4 | .. | .... | .... | .... | .. |
| 3 | Insanity | .... | .... | .... | .... | .... | .... | .... | .... | .... | .... | 2 | 1 | .. | 1 | .. | .. | .. | .. | 4 | .. | .... | .... | .... | .. |
| 4 | Intemperance | .... | .... | .... | .... | .... | .... | .... | .... | 11 | 2 | 6 | 2 | 1 | 1 | .. | .. | .. | .. | 22 | .. | .... | .... | .... | .. |
| 5 | Jaundice | 4 | 1 | .... | .... | 1 | 2 | 2 | 1 | 2 | .... | .... | 1 | 1 | .. | .. | .. | .. | .. | 14 | 1 | .... | .... | .... | .. |
| 6 | Kidneys, disease of | .... | .... | 1 | .... | .... | 1 | .... | .... | .... | 2 | 2 | 1 | .. | .. | .. | .. | .. | .. | 7 | .. | .... | .... | .... | .. |
| 7 | Killed | .... | .... | 1 | 1 | .... | 1 | 3 | .... | 3 | .... | 1 | .... | .. | .. | .. | .. | .. | .. | 10 | .. | .... | .... | .... | .. |
| 8 | Lightning | .... | .... | .... | .... | 1 | .... | .... | .... | 2 | .... | 1 | .... | .. | .. | .. | .. | .. | .. | 4 | .. | .... | .... | .... | .. |
| 9 | Liver, disease of | .... | 1 | 2 | 2 | .... | .... | 1 | .... | 8 | 2 | 13 | 3 | .. | .. | .. | .. | .. | .. | 30 | 2 | .... | .... | .... | .. |
| 10 | Lockjaw | .... | 1 | 1 | .... | 2 | 1 | 2 | .... | 1 | .... | .... | .... | .. | .. | .. | .. | .. | .. | 8 | .. | .... | .... | .... | .. |
| 11 | Lungs, disease of | .... | .... | 4 | 4 | 1 | .... | 2 | 2 | 2 | 6 | 3 | 2 | 1 | .. | .. | .. | .. | .. | 26 | .. | 1 | .... | .... | .. |
| 12 | Malformation | 1 | .... | 2 | 1 | .... | .... | .... | .... | .... | .... | .... | .... | .. | .. | .. | .. | .. | .. | 4 | .. | .... | .... | .... | .. |
| 13 | Marasmus | .... | 1 | .... | 1 | .... | .... | .... | .... | 2 | .... | .... | .... | .. | .. | .. | .. | .. | .. | 4 | .. | .... | .... | .... | .. |
| 14 | Measles | 6 | 3 | 7 | 16 | 4 | 3 | 7 | 5 | 6 | 8 | 1 | 6 | .. | .. | .. | .. | .. | .. | 72 | .. | .... | .... | .... | .. |
| 15 | Mortification | .... | .... | .... | 1 | .... | .... | .... | .... | .... | .... | .... | 1 | .. | 1 | .. | .. | .. | .. | 3 | .. | .... | .... | .... | .. |
| 16 | Mumps | 1 | .... | .... | .... | .... | .... | .... | .... | .... | .... | .... | .... | .. | .. | .. | .. | .. | .. | 1 | .. | .... | .... | .... | .. |
| 17 | Murder | .... | .... | .... | .... | .... | .... | 1 | .... | 1 | .... | 2 | .... | 1 | 2 | .. | .. | .. | .. | 7 | .. | .... | .... | .... | .. |
| 18 | Neuralgia | .... | .... | .... | .... | .... | .... | .... | .... | .... | .... | 2 | .... | .. | .. | .. | .. | .. | .. | 2 | .. | .... | .... | .... | .. |
| 19 | Old age | .... | .... | .... | .... | .... | .... | .... | .... | .... | .... | 51 | 63 | 94 | 117 | 7 | 13 | 1 | .. | 334 | .. | 2 | 5 | .... | .. |
| 20 | Paralysis | .... | .... | .... | .... | .... | .... | .... | .... | 4 | 4 | 18 | 17 | 6 | 2 | .. | .. | .. | .. | 50 | .. | 1 | .... | .... | .. |
| 21 | Pleurisy | 2 | 1 | 6 | 1 | 1 | 2 | 6 | 9 | 21 | 11 | 18 | 11 | 2 | .. | .. | .. | .. | .. | 89 | .. | .... | 1 | .... | .. |
| 22 | Pneumonia | 23 | 16 | 30 | 43 | 12 | 10 | 39 | 82 | 112 | 57 | 49 | 34 | 4 | 7 | .. | .. | .. | .. | 464 | .. | 2 | .... | .... | 1 |
| 23 | Poison | 1 | .... | 3 | 5 | 2 | 2 | 1 | 1 | 8 | 7 | 3 | .... | .. | .. | .. | .. | .. | .. | 33 | .. | .... | .... | .... | .. |
| 24 | Quinsy | .... | 1 | .... | .... | 1 | 1 | .... | .... | .... | 1 | 1 | .... | .. | .. | .. | .. | .. | .. | 5 | .. | .... | .... | .... | .. |
| 25 | Rheumatism | .... | 1 | .... | .... | 2 | 3 | 1 | 1 | 2 | 5 | 7 | 7 | 1 | .. | .. | .. | .. | .. | 30 | .. | .... | .... | .... | .. |
| 26 | Rickets | .... | .... | 4 | 1 | .... | .... | .... | .... | .... | .... | .... | .... | .. | .. | .. | .. | .. | .. | 5 | .. | .... | .... | .... | .. |
| 27 | Scrofula | 7 | 3 | 16 | 9 | 5 | 8 | 10 | 11 | 15 | 14 | 6 | 5 | .. | .. | .. | .. | .. | .. | 107 | .. | .... | 2 | .... | .. |
| 28 | Small pox | .... | .... | 1 | 2 | .... | 1 | 1 | .... | 4 | .... | 2 | .... | .. | 2 | .. | .. | .. | .. | 13 | .. | .... | .... | .... | .. |
| 29 | Spasms | 3 | .... | 1 | .... | .... | .... | .... | .... | .... | .... | .... | .... | .. | .. | .. | .. | .. | .. | 4 | .. | .... | .... | .... | .. |
| 30 | Spine, disease of | .... | .... | 1 | 3 | .... | .... | .... | .... | 1 | .... | 1 | 1 | .. | .. | .. | .. | .. | .. | 7 | .. | .... | .... | .... | .. |
| 31 | Stillborn | 2 | 2 | .... | .... | .... | .... | .... | .... | .... | .... | .... | .... | .. | .. | .. | .. | .. | .. | 4 | .. | .... | .... | .... | .. |
| 32 | Stomach, disease of | 1 | 1 | .... | 1 | .... | .... | .... | .... | 1 | 2 | 3 | .... | .. | .. | .. | .. | .. | .. | 9 | .. | .... | .... | .... | .. |
| 33 | Suffocation | 41 | 51 | 13 | 8 | 1 | 1 | .... | .... | .... | .... | 1 | 1 | .. | .. | .. | .. | .. | .. | 117 | .. | .... | .... | .... | .. |
| 34 | Suicide | .... | .... | .... | .... | .... | .... | 1 | .... | 4 | .... | 1 | .... | .. | .. | .. | .. | .. | .. | 6 | .. | .... | .... | .... | .. |
| 35 | Summer complaint | 3 | 1 | 2 | 1 | .... | .... | .... | .... | .... | .... | .... | .... | .. | .. | .. | .. | .. | .. | 7 | .. | .... | .... | .... | .. |
| 36 | Teething | 11 | 10 | 25 | 34 | 2 | .... | .... | .... | .... | .... | .... | .... | .. | .. | .. | .. | .. | .. | 82 | .. | .... | .... | .... | .. |
| 37 | Tetanus | 2 | 2 | 1 | .... | .... | .... | .... | .... | 1 | .... | .... | .... | .. | .. | .. | .. | .. | .. | 6 | .. | .... | .... | .... | .. |
| 38 | Tetter | .... | .... | .... | .... | .... | .... | .... | .... | .... | .... | .... | 1 | .. | .. | .. | .. | .. | .. | 1 | .. | .... | .... | .... | .. |
| 39 | Throat, disease of | 2 | 1 | 2 | .... | 2 | 4 | 2 | 1 | 1 | 6 | .... | 1 | .. | .. | .. | .. | .. | .. | 22 | .. | .... | .... | .... | .. |
| 40 | Thrush | 7 | 5 | 1 | .... | .... | .... | .... | 1 | .... | .... | .... | .... | .. | .. | .. | .. | .. | .. | 14 | .. | .... | .... | .... | .. |
| 41 | Tumor | 4 | .... | .... | .... | 1 | .... | .... | 1 | .... | .... | .... | .... | .. | .. | .. | .. | .. | .. | 6 | .. | .... | .... | .... | .. |
| 42 | Ulcer | .... | .... | .... | .... | .... | .... | .... | .... | 1 | .... | 2 | .... | .. | .. | .. | .. | .. | .. | 3 | .. | .... | .... | .... | .. |
| 43 | Uterus, disease of | .... | .... | .... | .... | .... | .... | .... | .... | .... | 8 | .... | 2 | .. | .. | .. | .. | .. | .. | 10 | .. | .... | .... | .... | .. |
| 44 | Venereal | .... | .... | .... | .... | .... | .... | .... | .... | .... | 2 | .... | .... | .. | .. | .. | .. | .. | .. | 2 | .. | .... | .... | .... | .. |
| 45 | White swelling | .... | .... | .... | .... | .... | .... | 3 | .... | .... | 1 | .... | .... | .. | .. | .. | .. | .. | .. | 4 | .. | .... | .... | .... | .. |
| 46 | Worms | 2 | .... | 32 | 20 | 3 | 2 | .... | .... | .... | 1 | .... | .... | .. | .. | .. | .. | .. | .. | 60 | .. | .... | .... | .... | .. |
| 47 | Unknown | 272 | 265 | 191 | 173 | 27 | 21 | 36 | 48 | 105 | 137 | 119 | 125 | 16 | 19 | .. | .. | 5 | 8 | 1556 | .. | 2 | 1 | .... | .. |
| | Total | 617 | 552 | 611 | 587 | 158 | 152 | 286 | 312 | 749 | 781 | 653 | 557 | 160 | 169 | 9 | 16 | 6 | 3 | 6314 | 3 | 19 | 16 | .. | 3 |

## CLASSIFICATION OF DEATHS IN WESTERN

*Embracing the following counties: Barbour, Boone, Braxton, Brooke, Cabell, Doddridge, Mason, Monongalia, Nicholas, Ohio, Preston, Putnam, Randolph,*

| | Cause of death. | Under 1 M. | Under 1 F. | 1–5 M. | 1–5 F. | 5–10 M. | 5–10 F. | 10–20 M. | 10–20 F. | 20–50 M. | 20–50 F. | 50–80 M. | 50–80 F. | 80–100 M | 80–100 F. | 100 & over M | 100 & over F. | Age unknown M | Age unknown F. | Born in State. | N. England States. | Middle States. | Southern States. | Southwest'n States. | Northwest'n States. |
|---|---|---|---|---|---|---|---|---|---|---|---|---|---|---|---|---|---|---|---|---|---|---|---|---|---|
| 1 | Abscess | .... | 1 | 1 | .. | .... | .... | .... | 1 | 1 | .... | 1 | .. | .. | .. | .. | .. | .. | .. | 4 | .. | .... | .... | .... | .. |
| 2 | Accident, not specif'd | 2 | .... | 2 | 3 | 3 | 1 | 4 | 2 | 8 | .... | 5 | 1 | 2 | .. | .. | .. | .. | .. | 28 | .. | 4 | .... | 1 | .. |
| 3 | ....do....burned | 1 | .... | 2 | 3 | 1 | 1 | .... | .... | 1 | 2 | .... | 1 | .. | .. | .. | .. | .. | .. | 11 | .. | 1 | .... | .... | .. |
| 4 | ....do....drowned | .... | .... | 4 | 2 | 2 | 2 | 3 | 1 | 10 | .... | 2 | .... | .. | .. | .. | .. | .. | .. | 21 | .. | 2 | .... | .... | 2 |
| 5 | ....do....scalded | 1 | 1 | 2 | 4 | .... | .... | .... | .... | .... | .... | .... | .... | .. | .. | .. | .. | .. | .. | 8 | .. | .... | .... | .... | .. |
| 6 | ...do....explosion | .... | .... | .... | .... | .... | .... | 1 | .... | 1 | .... | .... | .... | .. | .. | .. | .. | .. | .. | 1 | .. | .... | .... | .... | .. |
| 7 | ....do....shot | .... | .... | .... | .... | .... | 1 | .... | .... | .... | .... | 1 | .... | .. | .. | .. | .. | .. | .. | 2 | .. | .... | .... | .... | .. |
| 8 | Apoplexy | .... | .... | .... | .... | .... | .... | .... | .... | 1 | .... | 1 | 1 | 2 | .. | .. | .. | .. | .. | 2 | .. | 3 | .... | .... | .. |
| 9 | Asthma | .... | 1 | 1 | .... | .... | .... | .... | .... | .... | .... | 2 | 1 | .. | .. | .. | .. | .. | .. | 2 | 1 | .... | .... | .... | .. |
| 10 | Black tongue | .... | .... | 1 | .... | .... | .... | .... | .... | .... | .... | .... | .... | .. | .. | .. | .. | .. | .. | 1 | .. | .... | .... | .... | .. |
| 11 | Brain, disease of | 1 | 1 | 1 | .... | .... | .... | .... | .... | 3 | .... | .... | .... | .. | .. | .. | .. | .. | .. | 6 | .. | .... | .... | .... | .. |
| 12 | Bronchitis | 1 | .... | 1 | .... | .... | .... | .... | 2 | .... | 3 | 1 | 1 | 1 | .. | .. | .. | .. | .. | 8 | .. | .... | .... | .... | 1 |
| 13 | Cancer | .. | .... | .... | .... | .... | .... | 1 | .... | .... | 2 | 4 | 5 | 1 | .. | .. | .. | .. | .. | 8 | .. | 4 | .... | .... | .. |
| 14 | Catarrh | 4 | 3 | 1 | 4 | 1 | .... | 1 | 2 | 2 | 4 | .... | 4 | .. | 1 | .. | .. | .. | .. | 26 | .. | 1 | .... | .... | .. |
| 15 | Childbirth | .... | .... | .... | .... | .... | .... | .... | 2 | .... | 14 | .... | .... | .. | .. | .. | .. | .. | .. | 12 | .. | 4 | .... | .... | .. |
| 16 | Cholera | 2 | 4 | 7 | 9 | 5 | 9 | 12 | 6 | 62 | 20 | 18 | 7 | 1 | .. | .. | .. | .. | .. | 138 | .. | 9 | 2 | .... | 4 |
| 17 | ...do..infantum | 5 | 8 | 1 | 3 | .... | .... | .... | .... | .... | .... | .... | .... | .. | .. | .. | .. | .. | .. | 17 | .. | .... | .... | .... | .. |
| 18 | ...do..morbus | .... | 1 | 2 | 2 | 1 | .... | .... | 1 | 1 | 1 | 2 | 1 | .. | .. | .. | .. | .. | .. | 12 | .. | .... | .... | .... | .. |

## SECTION OF THE STATE OF VIRGINIA—Continued.

| NATIVITIES. | | | | | SEASON OF DECEASE. | | | | DURATION OF SICKNESS. | | | | WHITES. | | | COLORED. | | | | | | | | | |
|---|---|---|---|---|---|---|---|---|---|---|---|---|---|---|---|---|---|---|---|---|---|---|---|---|---|
| | | | | | | | | | | | | | | | | Slaves. | | | | Free. | | | | | |
| | | | | | | | | | | | | | | | | Black. | | Mulatto. | | Black. | | Mul. | | | |
| California and Territories. | Ireland. | Germany. | Other foreign countries. | Unknown. | Spring. | Summer. | Autumn. | Winter. | Under 1 week. | 1 week and under 1 month. | 1 month and under 3 months. | 3 months and over. | Males. | Females. | Total. | M. | F. | M. | F. | M. | F. | M | F. | Aggregate deaths. | |
| .... | .... | .. | .... | ... | 3 | 4 | 2 | .... | 2 | 1 | 4 | 2 | 1 | 4 | 5 | 1 | 2 | .... | .... | ... | 1 | .. | .. | 9 | 1 |
| .... | .... | .. | .... | ... | 2 | .... | 1 | 1 | 2 | .... | 2 | .... | .... | .... | .... | 3 | .... | .... | 1 | ... | ... | .. | .. | 4 | 2 |
| .... | .... | .. | .... | ... | 1 | 1 | .... | 2 | 1 | .... | 1 | 2 | 2 | .... | 2 | .... | 1 | .... | .... | ... | 1 | .. | .. | 4 | 3 |
| .... | 1 | .. | .... | ... | 4 | 3 | 2 | 11 | 9 | 5 | .... | .... | 15 | 3 | 18 | 3 | .... | 1 | .... | .. | 1 | .. | .. | 23 | 4 |
| .... | .... | .. | .... | ... | 4 | .... | 5 | 6 | 3 | 8 | 1 | 3 | 6 | 4 | 10 | 3 | 1 | 1 | .... | ... | ... | .. | .. | 15 | 5 |
| .... | .... | .. | .... | ... | 3 | 1 | 3 | .... | 1 | 2 | 2 | 2 | 2 | 2 | 4 | 1 | 1 | .... | 1 | ... | ... | .. | .. | 7 | 6 |
| .... | .... | .. | .... | ... | 1 | 1 | 4 | 4 | 9 | .... | 1 | ... | 4 | 1 | 5 | 3 | 1 | .... | .... | ... | ... | 1 | .. | 10 | 7 |
| .... | .... | .. | .... | ... | .... | 3 | 1 | .... | 3 | .... | .... | .... | .... | .... | .... | 4 | .... | .... | .... | ... | ... | .. | .. | 4 | 8 |
| .... | .... | .. | .... | ... | 9 | 9 | 5 | 8 | .... | 4 | 5 | 14 | 15 | 5 | 20 | 9 | 3 | .... | .... | ... | ... | .. | .. | 32 | 9 |
| .... | .... | .. | .... | ... | 1 | 2 | 1 | 4 | 4 | 3 | ... | .... | 1 | .... | 1 | 4 | 2 | 1 | .... | ... | ... | .. | .. | 8 | 10 |
| .... | .... | .. | .... | ... | 7 | 6 | 7 | 7 | 2 | 5 | 9 | 9 | 3 | 4 | 7 | 10 | 9 | .... | .... | ... | ... | .. | 1 | 27 | 11 |
| .... | .... | .. | .... | ... | 1 | 1 | 2 | .... | 1 | 1 | .... | 1 | .... | .... | .... | 3 | 1 | .... | .... | ... | ... | .. | .. | 4 | 12 |
| .... | .... | .. | .... | ... | 1 | 2 | .... | 1 | .... | .... | 1 | 2 | 2 | 1 | 3 | .... | 1 | .... | .... | ... | ... | .. | .. | 4 | 13 |
| .... | .... | | .... | ... | 3 | 27 | 30 | 4 | 2 | 22 | 19 | 7 | 5 | 10 | 15 | 24 | 28 | 2 | 3 | ... | .. | .. | .. | 72 | 14 |
| .... | .... | .. | .... | ... | .... | 2 | .... | 1 | 2 | .... | .... | .... | .... | 1 | 1 | .... | 2 | .... | .... | ... | ... | .. | .. | 3 | 15 |
| .... | .... | .. | .... | ... | 1 | .... | .... | .... | 1 | .... | .... | .... | 1 | .... | 1 | .... | .... | .... | .... | ... | ... | .. | .. | 1 | 16 |
| .... | .... | .. | .... | ... | 1 | 2 | 2 | 2 | 3 | 1 | 1 | 2 | 2 | .... | 2 | 3 | 2 | .... | .... | ... | ... | .. | .. | 7 | 17 |
| .... | .... | .. | .... | ... | 1 | .... | 1 | .... | .... | 1 | 1 | .... | 2 | .... | 2 | .... | .... | .... | .... | ... | ... | .. | .. | 2 | 18 |
| .... | 2 | 1 | 1 | 1 | 113 | 69 | 66 | 98 | 47 | 52 | 29 | 59 | 27 | 68 | 95 | 105 | 114 | 14 | 4 | 4 | 6 | 3 | 1 | 346 | 19 |
| .... | .... | .. | .... | ... | 15 | 11 | 6 | 17 | 11 | 7 | 4 | 24 | 18 | 14 | 32 | 8 | 6 | 1 | 1 | 1 | 1 | .. | 1 | 51 | 20 |
| .... | .... | .. | 1 | ... | 37 | 10 | 22 | 21 | 16 | 52 | 8 | 5 | 13 | 17 | 30 | 40 | 16 | 1 | 2 | 1 | ... | 1 | .. | 91 | 21 |
| .... | 1 | .. | .... | ... | 209 | 98 | 43 | 108 | 112 | 272 | 40 | 32 | 66 | 55 | 121 | 192 | 137 | 5 | 6 | 4 | 1 | 2 | .. | 468 | 22 |
| .... | .... | .. | .... | ... | 8 | 12 | 6 | 7 | 5 | 12 | 5 | 10 | .... | 2 | 2 | 18 | 13 | .... | .... | ... | ... | .. | .. | 33 | 23 |
| .... | .... | .. | .... | ... | 3 | .... | 1 | 1 | 1 | 3 | .... | 1 | .... | 1 | 1 | 2 | 1 | .... | 1 | ... | ... | .. | .. | 5 | 24 |
| .... | .... | .. | .... | ... | 10 | 10 | 2 | 8 | 1 | 10 | 1 | 16 | 5 | 9 | 14 | 8 | 8 | .... | .... | ... | ... | .. | .. | 30 | 25 |
| .... | .... | .. | .... | ... | 2 | .... | 1 | 2 | 1 | .... | 1 | 3 | .... | .... | .... | 4 | 1 | .... | .... | ... | ... | .. | .. | 5 | 26 |
| .... | .... | .. | .... | ... | 33 | 29 | 26 | 21 | 4 | 8 | 19 | 73 | 4 | 4 | 8 | 53 | 42 | 1 | 4 | 1 | ... | .. | .. | 109 | 27 |
| .... | .... | .. | .... | ... | 1 | .... | 6 | 6 | 3 | 8 | .... | 1 | 3 | 2 | 5 | 5 | 2 | .... | 1 | ... | ... | .. | .. | 13 | 28 |
| .... | .... | .. | .... | ... | 1 | 2 | .... | 1 | .... | .... | .... | .... | 1 | .... | 1 | 3 | .... | .... | .... | ... | ... | .. | .. | 4 | 29 |
| .... | .... | .. | .... | ... | 1 | 1 | 1 | 4 | .... | .... | 1 | 6 | 1 | 1 | 2 | 2 | 3 | .... | .... | ... | ... | .. | .. | 7 | 30 |
| .... | .... | .. | .... | ... | 2 | .... | .... | 2 | 4 | .... | .... | .... | .... | .... | .... | 2 | 1 | .... | 1 | ... | ... | .. | .. | 4 | 31 |
| .... | .... | .. | .... | ... | 4 | .... | 4 | 1 | 1 | 2 | .... | 3 | 3 | 3 | 6 | 2 | 1 | .... | .... | ... | ... | .. | .. | 9 | 32 |
| .... | .... | .. | .... | ... | 36 | 30 | 22 | 26 | 117 | .... | .... | .... | 4 | 5 | 9 | 49 | 51 | 3 | 5 | ... | ... | .. | .. | 117 | 33 |
| .... | .... | .. | .... | ... | .... | 1 | 1 | 3 | 4 | .... | .... | .... | 6 | .... | 6 | .... | .... | .... | .... | ... | ... | .. | .. | 6 | 34 |
| .... | .... | .. | .... | ... | .... | 3 | 2 | 2 | .... | 2 | 1 | .... | 3 | .... | 3 | 2 | 2 | .... | .... | ... | ... | .. | .. | 7 | 35 |
| .... | .... | .. | .... | ... | 10 | 30 | 33 | 7 | 11 | 32 | 23 | 14 | 2 | 14 | 16 | 34 | 26 | 1 | 3 | ... | 1 | 1 | .. | 82 | 36 |
| .... | .... | .. | .... | ... | 2 | .... | 2 | 2 | 2 | .... | .... | .... | .... | .... | .... | 4 | 2 | .... | .... | ... | ... | .. | .. | 6 | 37 |
| .... | .... | .. | .... | ... | .... | .... | .... | 1 | .... | .... | .... | .... | .... | .... | .... | .... | 1 | .... | .... | ... | ... | .. | .. | 1 | 38 |
| .... | .... | .. | .... | ... | 5 | 7 | 6 | 4 | 6 | 12 | 3 | 1 | 3 | 7 | 10 | 6 | 6 | .... | .... | ... | ... | .. | .. | 22 | 39 |
| .... | .... | .. | .... | ... | 2 | 6 | 4 | 1 | 3 | 4 | 3 | 3 | 6 | 2 | 8 | 2 | 4 | .... | .... | ... | ... | .. | .. | 14 | 40 |
| .... | .... | .. | .... | ... | 1 | 2 | 2 | 1 | .... | 2 | 1 | 3 | 2 | 1 | 3 | 3 | .... | .... | .... | ... | ... | .. | .. | 6 | 41 |
| .... | .... | .. | .... | ... | .... | 1 | 2 | .... | 1 | .... | 1 | 1 | 2 | .. | 2 | 1 | .... | .... | .... | ... | ... | .. | .. | 3 | 42 |
| .... | .... | .. | .... | ... | 2 | 1 | 5 | 2 | .... | 3 | 2 | 5 | .... | 1 | 1 | .... | 8 | .... | 1 | ... | ... | .. | .. | 10 | 43 |
| .... | .... | .. | .... | ... | .... | .... | .... | .... | .... | .... | .... | 1 | .... | 1 | 1 | .... | 1 | .... | .... | ... | ... | .. | .. | 2 | 44 |
| .... | .... | .. | .... | ... | .... | 2 | 2 | .... | .... | ... | 2 | 2 | 1 | .... | 1 | .... | 1 | 1 | .... | ... | ... | 1 | .. | 4 | 45 |
| .... | .... | .. | .... | ... | 22 | 19 | 9 | 9 | 13 | 20 | 18 | 7 | 5 | 3 | 8 | 31 | 20 | 1 | .... | ... | ... | .. | .. | 60 | 46 |
| .... | ... | 1 | 2 | ... | 441 | 426 | 339 | 308 | 492 | 295 | 116 | 261 | 176 | 235 | 411 | 551 | 493 | 29 | 36 | 8 | 14 | 7 | 13 | 1562 | 47 |
| .... | 12 | 2 | 8 | 1 | 1799 | 1788 | 1396 | 1260 | 1665 | 1757 | 705 | 1341 | 951 | 1028 | 1979 | 2097 | 1868 | 116 | 143 | 59 | 53 | 26 | 37 | 6378 | |

## SECTION OF THE STATE OF VIRGINIA.

*Fayette, Gilmer, Hancock, Harrison, Jackson, Kanawha, Lewis, Logan, Marion, Marshall, Ritchie, Taylor, Tyler, Wayne, Welzel, Wirt, and Wood.*

| California and Territories. | Ireland. | Germany. | Other foreign countries. | Unknown. | Spring. | Summer. | Autumn. | Winter. | Under 1 week. | 1 week and under 1 month. | 1 month and under 3 months. | 3 months and over. | Males. | Females. | Total. | Slaves Black M. | Slaves Black F. | Slaves Mulatto M. | Slaves Mulatto F. | Free Black M. | Free Black F. | Free Mul. M | Free Mul. F. | Aggregate deaths. | |
|---|---|---|---|---|---|---|---|---|---|---|---|---|---|---|---|---|---|---|---|---|---|---|---|---|---|
| .... | .... | .. | 1 | ... | 1 | 1 | .... | 3 | 2 | 2 | 1 | .... | 3 | 2 | 5 | .... | .... | .... | .... | ... | ... | .. | .. | 5 | 1 |
| .... | .... | .. | .... | ... | 10 | 8 | 6 | 7 | 26 | 5 | ... | 2 | 24 | 7 | 31 | 1 | ... | .... | .... | ... | ... | 1 | .. | 33 | 2 |
| .... | .... | .. | .... | ... | 4 | 3 | 1 | 4 | 8 | 3 | ... | 1 | 4 | 6 | 10 | 1 | 1 | .... | .... | ... | ... | .. | .. | 12 | 3 |
| .... | 1 | .. | .... | ... | 8 | 13 | 2 | 3 | 26 | .... | ... | .... | 19 | 5 | 24 | 2 | .... | .... | .... | ... | ... | .. | .. | 26 | 4 |
| .... | .... | .. | .... | ... | 3 | 1 | 4 | .... | 7 | 1 | .... | .... | 3 | 5 | 8 | .... | .... | .... | .... | ... | ... | .. | .. | 8 | 5 |
| .... | 1 | .. | .... | ... | 1 | .... | .... | 1 | 2 | .... | .... | .... | 2 | .... | 2 | .... | .... | .... | .... | ... | ... | .. | .. | 2 | 6 |
| .... | .... | .. | .... | ... | 2 | .... | .... | .... | 1 | 1 | .... | .... | 1 | .... | 1 | .... | 1 | .... | .... | ... | ... | .. | .. | 2 | 7 |
| .... | .... | .. | .... | ... | 2 | 1 | .... | 2 | 4 | 1 | .... | .... | 4 | 1 | 5 | .... | ... | .... | .... | ... | ... | .. | .. | 5 | 8 |
| .... | .... | 1 | 1 | ... | 4 | 1 | .... | .... | 2 | 2 | .... | 1 | 2 | 2 | 4 | 1 | .... | .... | .... | ... | ... | .. | .. | 5 | 9 |
| .... | .... | .. | .... | ... | 1 | ... | .... | .... | 1 | .... | .... | .... | 1 | .... | 1 | .... | .... | .... | .... | ... | ... | .. | .. | 1 | 10 |
| .... | .... | .. | .... | ... | 1 | .... | 2 | 2 | 1 | 4 | .... | .... | 5 | 1 | 6 | .... | .... | .... | .... | ... | ... | .. | .. | 6 | 11 |
| .... | .... | .. | 1 | ... | 4 | 1 | 2 | 3 | .... | 3 | 3 | 3 | 3 | 6 | 9 | 1 | .... | .... | .... | ... | ... | .. | .. | 10 | 12 |
| .... | 1 | .. | .... | ... | 5 | 3 | 3 | 2 | 1 | 2 | 4 | 4 | 6 | 7 | 13 | .... | .... | .... | .... | ... | ... | .. | .. | 13 | 13 |
| .... | .... | .. | .... | ... | 10 | 5 | 4 | 8 | 5 | 12 | 6 | 8 | 5 | 14 | 19 | 3 | 4 | 1 | .... | ... | ... | .. | .. | 27 | 14 |
| .... | .... | .. | .... | ... | 6 | 3 | 5 | 2 | 11 | 5 | .... | .... | .... | 16 | 16 | .... | .... | .... | .... | ... | ... | .. | .. | 16 | 15 |
| .... | .... | 5 | 3 | 1 | 5 | 96 | 57 | 4 | 143 | 19 | .... | ... | 67 | 40 | 107 | 28 | 13 | 9 | 1 | 3 | ... | .. | 1 | 162 | 16 |
| .... | .... | .. | .... | ... | .... | 8 | 6 | 3 | 11 | 3 | 2 | 1 | 6 | 10 | 16 | .... | 1 | .... | .... | ... | ... | .. | .. | 17 | 17 |
| .... | .... | .. | .... | ... | 3 | 2 | 5 | 2 | 8 | 3 | 1 | .... | 6 | 6 | 12 | .... | .... | .... | .... | ... | ... | .. | .. | 12 | 18 |

## CLASSIFICATION OF DEATHS IN WESTERN

| | Cause of death. | AGES. | | | | | | | | | | | | | | | | | | NATIVITIES. | | | | | |
|---|---|---|---|---|---|---|---|---|---|---|---|---|---|---|---|---|---|---|---|---|---|---|---|---|---|
| | | Under 1. | | 1 and under 5. | | 5 and under 10. | | 10 and under 20. | | 20 and under 50. | | 50 and under 80. | | 80 and under 100. | | 100 & over. | | Age unknown. | | Born in State. | N. England States. | Middle States. | Southern States. | Southwest'n States. | Northwest'n States. |
| | | M. | F. | M. | F. | M. | F. | M. | F. | M. | F. | M. | F. | M | F. | M | F. | M | F. | | | | | | |
| 1 | Chorea | .. | .. | .. | .. | .. | 1 | .. | .. | .. | .. | .. | .. | .. | .. | .. | .. | .. | .. | 1 | .. | .. | .. | .. | .. |
| 2 | Colic | .. | .. | 1 | 2 | .. | 1 | 1 | 1 | 5 | 3 | 3 | 3 | .. | .. | .. | .. | .. | .. | 18 | .. | 2 | .. | .. | .. |
| 3 | Congestion of brain | .. | .. | .. | .. | .. | .. | .. | .. | .. | 1 | .. | .. | .. | .. | .. | .. | .. | .. | 1 | .. | .. | .. | .. | .. |
| 4 | Consumption | 3 | 3 | 3 | 5 | .. | .. | 7 | 17 | 54 | 71 | 26 | 19 | 1 | 1 | .. | .. | .. | .. | 158 | 4 | 28 | 1 | .. | 7 |
| 5 | Convulsions | 5 | 6 | 5 | .. | .. | .. | 3 | 1 | 1 | 1 | 2 | 2 | .. | .. | .. | .. | .. | .. | 20 | .. | 3 | .. | .. | .. |
| 6 | Cramp | .. | .. | .. | 1 | .. | .. | .. | .. | .. | .. | .. | .. | .. | .. | .. | .. | .. | .. | 1 | .. | .. | .. | .. | .. |
| 7 | Croup | 25 | 17 | 40 | 19 | 2 | 1 | .. | .. | .. | .. | .. | .. | .. | .. | .. | .. | .. | .. | 96 | .. | 3 | .. | .. | 5 |
| 8 | Diabetes | .. | .. | .. | .. | .. | .. | .. | .. | 1 | .. | .. | .. | .. | .. | .. | .. | .. | .. | 1 | .. | .. | .. | .. | .. |
| 9 | Diarrhœa | 3 | 2 | 1 | 7 | .. | 1 | 1 | .. | .. | 1 | 1 | .. | .. | .. | .. | .. | .. | .. | 14 | .. | 3 | .. | .. | .. |
| 10 | Dropsy | 1 | 3 | 6 | 1 | 5 | .. | 3 | 2 | 4 | 8 | 23 | 13 | 3 | 2 | .. | .. | .. | .. | 55 | .. | 15 | .. | .. | 3 |
| 11 | Dysentery | 10 | 8 | 19 | 21 | 13 | 5 | 7 | 9 | 6 | 12 | 3 | 7 | 1 | .. | .. | .. | .. | .. | 107 | .. | 4 | .. | .. | 8 |
| 12 | Dyspepsia | .. | .. | .. | .. | .. | 2 | .. | .. | 1 | 1 | 6 | .. | .. | .. | .. | .. | .. | .. | 9 | 1 | .. | .. | .. | .. |
| 13 | Epilepsy | .. | .. | 1 | .. | .. | .. | .. | .. | .. | .. | 1 | .. | .. | .. | .. | .. | .. | .. | 2 | .. | .. | .. | .. | .. |
| 14 | Erysipelas | 1 | 2 | 4 | 1 | .. | 1 | 1 | .. | 1 | 2 | 1 | 1 | .. | .. | .. | .. | .. | .. | 13 | .. | 1 | .. | .. | 1 |
| 15 | Fever, not specified | 3 | 2 | 6 | 3 | 1 | 2 | 7 | 11 | 19 | 10 | 7 | 3 | .. | .. | .. | .. | .. | .. | 58 | .. | 8 | .. | .. | 4 |
| 16 | ..do..bilious | .. | 1 | 2 | 1 | 2 | .. | 1 | .. | 8 | 2 | 2 | .. | .. | .. | .. | .. | .. | .. | 15 | .. | 4 | .. | .. | .. |
| 17 | ..do..catarrhal | 2 | 2 | 1 | 1 | .. | .. | .. | .. | .. | .. | .. | .. | .. | .. | .. | .. | .. | .. | 6 | .. | .. | .. | .. | .. |
| 18 | ..do..congestive | .. | .. | 1 | .. | .. | .. | 3 | .. | 2 | .. | 1 | .. | .. | .. | .. | .. | .. | .. | 5 | 1 | .. | .. | .. | 1 |
| 19 | ..do..intermittent | .. | .. | .. | 1 | .. | 1 | .. | 1 | .. | .. | .. | .. | .. | .. | .. | .. | .. | .. | 2 | .. | 1 | .. | .. | .. |
| 20 | ..do..puerperal | .. | .. | .. | .. | .. | .. | .. | .. | .. | 4 | .. | .. | .. | .. | .. | .. | .. | .. | 1 | .. | 1 | .. | .. | 2 |
| 21 | ..do..remittent | .. | .. | .. | .. | .. | .. | .. | .. | .. | 1 | .. | .. | .. | .. | .. | .. | .. | .. | 1 | .. | .. | .. | .. | .. |
| 22 | ..do..scarlet | 12 | 9 | 50 | 46 | 25 | 15 | 6 | 7 | 3 | 2 | .. | .. | .. | .. | .. | .. | .. | .. | 156 | .. | 6 | .. | .. | 8 |
| 23 | ..do..typhus | 1 | .. | 1 | 3 | 3 | 1 | 11 | 8 | 31 | 15 | 3 | 5 | .. | 1 | .. | .. | .. | .. | 76 | 1 | 5 | .. | .. | 1 |
| 24 | ..do..winter | .. | .. | 2 | .. | .. | .. | 2 | 4 | .. | .. | .. | .. | .. | .. | .. | .. | .. | .. | 7 | .. | 1 | .. | .. | .. |
| 25 | Frozen | .. | .. | .. | .. | .. | .. | .. | .. | 1 | .. | .. | .. | .. | .. | .. | .. | .. | .. | 1 | .. | .. | .. | .. | .. |
| 26 | Gravel | .. | .. | .. | .. | .. | .. | .. | .. | .. | 1 | 6 | .. | 1 | .. | .. | .. | .. | .. | 5 | .. | 3 | .. | .. | .. |
| 27 | Head, disease of | .. | .. | 2 | 1 | .. | .. | .. | .. | 2 | .. | .. | 2 | .. | .. | .. | .. | .. | .. | 5 | .. | 1 | .. | .. | 1 |
| 28 | Heart, ....do | 1 | .. | .. | .. | .. | 1 | 1 | 1 | 3 | .. | 1 | .. | .. | .. | .. | .. | .. | .. | 7 | 1 | .. | .. | .. | .. |
| 29 | Hemorrhage | .. | .. | .. | .. | .. | .. | .. | .. | 1 | 5 | .. | .. | .. | .. | .. | .. | .. | .. | 4 | .. | 2 | .. | .. | .. |
| 30 | Hives | 3 | 4 | 1 | .. | .. | .. | .. | .. | .. | .. | .. | .. | .. | .. | .. | .. | .. | .. | 7 | .. | 1 | .. | .. | .. |
| 31 | Hooping cough | 5 | 7 | 12 | 14 | 3 | 4 | .. | .. | .. | .. | .. | .. | .. | .. | .. | .. | .. | .. | 42 | .. | 2 | .. | .. | 1 |
| 32 | Hydrocephalus | 2 | 3 | 1 | .. | .. | 2 | .. | .. | .. | .. | .. | 1 | .. | .. | .. | .. | .. | .. | 8 | .. | .. | .. | .. | 1 |
| 33 | Inflammation | 3 | .. | 3 | 3 | .. | 1 | 2 | .. | 1 | 1 | 2 | .. | .. | .. | .. | .. | .. | .. | 11 | 1 | 4 | .. | .. | .. |
| 34 | .....do.....bowels | 4 | 3 | 5 | 3 | 1 | .. | .. | .. | 5 | 2 | 1 | 1 | .. | .. | .. | .. | .. | .. | 20 | .. | 3 | .. | .. | 1 |
| 35 | .....do.....brain | 12 | 4 | 11 | 7 | .. | 3 | .. | 2 | 3 | 2 | 3 | 1 | .. | .. | .. | .. | .. | .. | 41 | 1 | 2 | .. | .. | 3 |
| 36 | Intemperance | .. | .. | .. | .. | .. | .. | .. | .. | 1 | .. | .. | .. | .. | .. | .. | .. | .. | .. | 1 | .. | .. | .. | .. | .. |
| 37 | Jaundice | .. | .. | .. | .. | .. | .. | .. | 1 | .. | 1 | .. | 1 | .. | 1 | .. | .. | .. | .. | 4 | .. | .. | .. | .. | .. |
| 38 | Kidneys, disease of | .. | .. | .. | .. | .. | .. | .. | .. | .. | .. | 1 | .. | 1 | .. | .. | .. | .. | .. | 2 | .. | .. | .. | .. | .. |
| 39 | Killed | .. | .. | .. | .. | .. | .. | .. | .. | 3 | .. | .. | .. | .. | .. | .. | .. | .. | .. | 2 | .. | .. | .. | .. | 1 |
| 40 | Liver, disease of | .. | .. | .. | 1 | .. | .. | 1 | .. | 3 | 7 | 1 | 1 | .. | .. | .. | .. | .. | .. | 11 | .. | 3 | .. | .. | .. |
| 41 | Lockjaw | .. | .. | .. | .. | .. | .. | .. | 1 | 2 | .. | .. | .. | .. | .. | .. | .. | .. | .. | 2 | 1 | .. | .. | .. | .. |
| 42 | Lungs, disease of | 1 | .. | 1 | .. | 1 | .. | .. | 1 | .. | 4 | 1 | 1 | 1 | .. | .. | .. | .. | .. | 11 | .. | .. | .. | .. | .. |
| 43 | Malformation | .. | 1 | .. | .. | .. | .. | .. | .. | .. | .. | .. | .. | .. | .. | .. | .. | .. | .. | 1 | .. | .. | .. | .. | .. |
| 44 | Measles | 2 | 4 | 13 | 13 | 1 | 3 | 2 | 2 | 2 | 4 | 2 | .. | .. | .. | .. | .. | .. | .. | 39 | .. | 5 | .. | .. | 2 |
| 45 | Mortification | 1 | .. | .. | .. | .. | .. | .. | .. | .. | 1 | .. | .. | .. | .. | .. | .. | .. | .. | 2 | .. | .. | .. | .. | .. |
| 46 | Murder | .. | .. | .. | .. | .. | .. | .. | .. | 1 | .. | .. | .. | .. | .. | .. | .. | .. | .. | 2 | .. | .. | .. | .. | .. |
| 47 | Mania-a-potu | .. | .. | .. | .. | .. | .. | .. | .. | 1 | .. | .. | .. | .. | .. | .. | .. | .. | .. | 1 | .. | .. | .. | .. | .. |
| 48 | Neuralgia | .. | .. | .. | .. | .. | .. | .. | .. | .. | 1 | 2 | 1 | .. | .. | .. | .. | .. | .. | 3 | .. | 1 | .. | .. | .. |
| 49 | Old age | .. | .. | .. | .. | .. | .. | .. | .. | .. | .. | 7 | 14 | 18 | 26 | 1 | 4 | .. | .. | 48 | .. | 20 | .. | .. | .. |
| 50 | Paralysis | .. | .. | .. | .. | .. | .. | .. | .. | 1 | .. | 3 | 9 | 3 | 3 | .. | .. | .. | .. | 11 | .. | 6 | .. | .. | .. |
| 51 | Piles | .. | .. | .. | .. | .. | .. | .. | .. | 1 | .. | .. | .. | .. | .. | .. | .. | .. | .. | 1 | .. | .. | .. | .. | .. |
| 52 | Pleurisy | 1 | .. | 2 | 1 | .. | .. | 1 | .. | 3 | 1 | 1 | 2 | .. | .. | .. | .. | .. | .. | 9 | 1 | 1 | .. | .. | 1 |
| 53 | Pneumonia | 3 | .. | 7 | 8 | 2 | 1 | 1 | 4 | 4 | 4 | 5 | 1 | .. | 2 | .. | .. | .. | .. | 39 | .. | 1 | .. | .. | 1 |
| 54 | Poison | 1 | .. | .. | .. | .. | .. | .. | 1 | .. | .. | .. | .. | .. | .. | .. | .. | .. | .. | 2 | .. | .. | .. | .. | .. |
| 55 | Rheumatism | .. | .. | .. | .. | .. | 1 | .. | .. | 1 | 2 | 1 | 1 | .. | .. | .. | .. | .. | .. | 4 | .. | 1 | .. | .. | .. |
| 56 | Scrofula | 1 | .. | 3 | 1 | .. | .. | .. | 2 | 1 | 1 | 2 | 1 | .. | .. | .. | .. | .. | .. | 10 | .. | 1 | .. | .. | 1 |
| 57 | Small pox | .. | .. | 3 | 1 | .. | .. | 1 | .. | 2 | .. | .. | .. | .. | .. | .. | .. | .. | .. | 5 | .. | .. | .. | .. | 1 |
| 58 | Spine, disease of | 1 | 1 | 3 | 1 | .. | .. | 2 | 1 | .. | 1 | 1 | .. | .. | .. | .. | .. | .. | .. | 9 | .. | 2 | .. | .. | .. |
| 59 | Stillborn | 4 | 3 | .. | .. | .. | .. | .. | .. | .. | .. | .. | .. | .. | .. | .. | .. | .. | .. | 7 | .. | .. | .. | .. | .. |
| 60 | Stomach, disease of | .. | .. | .. | .. | .. | .. | .. | .. | .. | 1 | .. | .. | .. | .. | .. | .. | .. | .. | .. | .. | .. | .. | .. | 1 |
| 61 | Suffocation | 1 | 1 | 1 | 2 | .. | .. | .. | .. | .. | .. | .. | .. | .. | .. | .. | .. | .. | .. | 5 | .. | .. | .. | .. | .. |
| 62 | Suicide | .. | .. | .. | .. | .. | .. | 1 | .. | .. | 1 | .. | .. | 1 | .. | .. | .. | .. | .. | 2 | .. | 1 | .. | .. | .. |
| 63 | Summer complaint | 2 | 2 | 1 | 1 | .. | .. | .. | .. | .. | .. | .. | .. | .. | .. | .. | .. | .. | .. | 6 | .. | .. | .. | .. | .. |
| 64 | Teething | 1 | 1 | 1 | 1 | .. | .. | .. | .. | .. | .. | .. | .. | .. | .. | .. | .. | .. | .. | 4 | .. | .. | .. | .. | .. |
| 65 | Tetter | .. | .. | .. | .. | .. | .. | .. | .. | .. | .. | .. | .. | 1 | .. | .. | .. | .. | .. | 1 | .. | .. | .. | .. | .. |
| 66 | Throat, disease of | 1 | .. | 3 | 2 | 2 | 2 | 2 | 2 | .. | .. | .. | .. | .. | .. | .. | .. | .. | .. | 11 | .. | 3 | .. | .. | .. |
| 67 | Thrush | 2 | 1 | .. | 1 | .. | .. | .. | .. | .. | .. | .. | .. | .. | .. | .. | .. | .. | .. | 4 | .. | .. | .. | .. | .. |
| 68 | Tumor | 1 | .. | .. | .. | .. | .. | .. | .. | .. | 1 | .. | .. | .. | .. | .. | .. | .. | .. | 2 | .. | .. | .. | .. | .. |
| 69 | Ulcer | .. | .. | .. | .. | .. | .. | 1 | .. | 1 | .. | 1 | .. | .. | .. | .. | .. | .. | .. | 2 | .. | .. | .. | .. | .. |
| 70 | White swelling | .. | .. | .. | .. | .. | .. | 1 | .. | 1 | .. | .. | .. | .. | .. | .. | .. | .. | .. | 2 | .. | .. | .. | .. | .. |
| 71 | Worms | 1 | 1 | 4 | 8 | 1 | 1 | .. | .. | .. | .. | .. | .. | .. | .. | .. | .. | .. | .. | 15 | .. | 1 | .. | .. | .. |
| 72 | Unknown | 78 | 54 | 30 | 26 | 11 | .. | 6 | 5 | 16 | 20 | 15 | 13 | 1 | 4 | .. | .. | .. | .. | 260 | .. | 15 | .. | 1 | 1 |
| | Total | 215 | 165 | 276 | 237 | 86 | 64 | 97 | 101 | 287 | 241 | 166 | 125 | 39 | 41 | 1 | 4 | .. | .. | 1816 | 13 | 192 | 3 | 2 | 63 |

SECTION OF THE STATE OF VIRGINIA—Continued.

| NATIVITIES. | | | | | SEASON OF DECEASE. | | | | DURATION OF SICKNESS. | | | | WHITES. | | | COLORED. | | | | | | | | | |
|---|---|---|---|---|---|---|---|---|---|---|---|---|---|---|---|---|---|---|---|---|---|---|---|---|---|
| | | | | | | | | | | | | | | | | Slaves. | | | | Free. | | | | | |
| | | | | | | | | | | | | | | | | Black. | | Mulatto. | | Black. | | Mul. | | | |
| California and Territories. | Ireland. | Germany. | Other foreign countries. | Unknown. | Spring. | Summer. | Autumn. | Winter. | Under 1 week. | 1 week and under 1 month. | 1 month and under 3 months. | 3 months and over. | Males. | Females. | Total. | M. | F. | M. | F. | M. | F. | M | F. | Aggregate deaths. | |
| | | | | | 1 | | | | 1 | | | | | 1 | 1 | | | | | | | | | 1 | 1 |
| | 1 | 1 | 3 | | 7 | 4 | 5 | 4 | 14 | 6 | | | 8 | 9 | 17 | 2 | 1 | | | | | | | 20 | 2 |
| | | | | | 1 | | | | 1 | | | | | 1 | 1 | | | | | | | | | 1 | 3 |
| | 1 | 1 | 4 | | 68 | 55 | 44 | 37 | 7 | 14 | 18 | 148 | 85 | 103 | 188 | 3 | 11 | | 1 | | | | 1 | 204 | 4 |
| | 1 | 1 | 1 | | 8 | 7 | 6 | 5 | 17 | 5 | | 2 | 13 | 9 | 22 | 3 | | | 1 | | | | | 26 | 5 |
| | | | | | | 1 | | | 1 | | | | | 1 | 1 | | | | | | | | | 1 | 6 |
| | | | | | 32 | 19 | 25 | 28 | 87 | 15 | | | 61 | 34 | 95 | 6 | 3 | | | | | | | 104 | 7 |
| | | | | | | | | 1 | | 1 | | | 1 | | 1 | | | | | | | | | 1 | 8 |
| | | | | | 1 | 4 | 7 | 5 | 9 | 5 | 2 | 1 | 6 | 11 | 17 | | | | | | | | | 17 | 9 |
| | | | 1 | | 20 | 22 | 19 | 13 | 1 | 8 | 13 | 46 | 42 | 28 | 70 | 1 | | 1 | | | | 1 | 1 | 74 | 10 |
| | 1 | 1 | | | 7 | 15 | 85 | 14 | 21 | 86 | 4 | 3 | 58 | 61 | 119 | | 1 | | 1 | | | | | 121 | 11 |
| | | | | | 3 | 3 | 3 | 1 | | 1 | | 8 | 7 | 3 | 10 | | | | | | | | | 10 | 12 |
| | | | | | 1 | | 1 | | 1 | | | 1 | 2 | | 2 | | | | | | | | | 2 | 13 |
| | | | | | 5 | | 6 | 4 | 3 | 8 | 3 | 1 | 8 | 7 | 15 | | | | | | | | | 15 | 14 |
| 1 | 1 | | 1 | 1 | 21 | 17 | 10 | 24 | 6 | 45 | 18 | 4 | 40 | 29 | 69 | 1 | 1 | 2 | 1 | | | | | 74 | 15 |
| | | | | | 5 | 4 | 4 | 6 | 2 | 12 | 5 | | 14 | 4 | 18 | 1 | | | | | | | | 19 | 16 |
| | | | | | 2 | 2 | 1 | 1 | 2 | 4 | | | 2 | 3 | 5 | 1 | | | | | | | | 6 | 17 |
| | | | | | 4 | 2 | 1 | | 3 | 3 | 1 | | 6 | | 6 | 1 | | | | | | | | 7 | 18 |
| | | | | | 1 | | 2 | | 1 | 1 | 1 | | | 3 | 3 | | | | | | | | | 3 | 19 |
| | | | | | 4 | | | | 2 | 2 | | | | 4 | 4 | | | | | | | | | 4 | 20 |
| | | | | | | 1 | | | | | 1 | | | 1 | 1 | | | | | | | | | 1 | 21 |
| | 3 | 1 | | 1 | 38 | 20 | 37 | 79 | 88 | 76 | 7 | 2 | 95 | 77 | 172 | 1 | 1 | | 1 | | | | | 175 | 22 |
| | | | | | 35 | 19 | 9 | 20 | 4 | 61 | 15 | 3 | 46 | 28 | 74 | 4 | 2 | | 3 | | | | | 83 | 23 |
| | | | | | 4 | | 1 | 3 | 2 | 6 | | | 4 | 3 | 7 | | 1 | | | | | | | 8 | 24 |
| | | | | | | | | 1 | 1 | | | | 1 | | 1 | | | | | | | | | 1 | 25 |
| | | | | | 3 | 1 | 2 | 2 | 1 | 5 | | 2 | 7 | 1 | 8 | | | | | | | | | 8 | 26 |
| | | | | | 3 | 1 | | 3 | 2 | 3 | 2 | | 4 | 3 | 7 | | | | | | | | | 7 | 27 |
| | | | | | 2 | 2 | 1 | 3 | 1 | 1 | 2 | 4 | 6 | 2 | 8 | | | | | | | | | 8 | 28 |
| | | | | | 2 | 3 | | 1 | 2 | 1 | 1 | 1 | 1 | 4 | 5 | | 1 | | | | | | | 6 | 29 |
| | | | | | 2 | 3 | 1 | 2 | 6 | 2 | | | 4 | 4 | 8 | | | | | | | | | 8 | 30 |
| | | | | | 5 | 22 | 10 | 8 | 4 | 25 | 13 | 3 | 17 | 23 | 40 | 2 | 1 | 1 | | | | | 1 | 45 | 31 |
| | | | | | 4 | 1 | 2 | 2 | 3 | | 5 | 1 | 2 | 6 | 8 | | | 1 | | | | | | 9 | 32 |
| | | | | | 5 | 1 | 4 | 6 | 5 | 9 | 2 | | 11 | 5 | 16 | | | | | | | | | 16 | 33 |
| | | | 1 | | 5 | 10 | 5 | 5 | 11 | 11 | 3 | | 15 | 9 | 24 | 1 | | | | | | | | 25 | 34 |
| | 1 | | | | 13 | 12 | 15 | 8 | 14 | 29 | 5 | | 28 | 19 | 47 | 1 | | | | | | | | 48 | 35 |
| | | | | | 1 | | | | | | | | 1 | | 1 | | | | | | | | | 1 | 36 |
| | | | | | 2 | 1 | | 1 | | 3 | | 1 | | 4 | 4 | | | | | | | | | 4 | 37 |
| | | | | | | | | 2 | | 1 | 1 | | 2 | | 2 | | | | | | | | | 2 | 38 |
| | | | | | 1 | | 1 | 1 | 2 | | 1 | | 3 | | 2 | | | | | | | | | 3 | 39 |
| | | | | | 4 | 2 | 3 | 5 | | 4 | 3 | 5 | 5 | 8 | 13 | | 1 | | | | | | | 14 | 40 |
| | | | | | 1 | 1 | 1 | | 2 | 1 | | | 2 | | 2 | | 1 | | | | | | | 3 | 41 |
| | | | | | 5 | 3 | 1 | 2 | 1 | 3 | 2 | 5 | 3 | 6 | 9 | 2 | | | | | | | | 11 | 42 |
| | | | | | | | | 1 | | 1 | | | | 1 | 1 | | | | | | | | | 1 | 43 |
| | 1 | | 1 | | 10 | 20 | 12 | 6 | 10 | 35 | 1 | 2 | 20 | 23 | 43 | 2 | 3 | | | | | | | 48 | 44 |
| | | | | | | 1 | 1 | | 1 | 1 | | | 1 | 1 | 2 | | | | | | | | | 2 | 45 |
| | | | | | 1 | | | 1 | 2 | | | | 2 | | 2 | | | | | | | | | 2 | 46 |
| | | | | | | | | 1 | 1 | | | | 1 | | 1 | | | | | | | | | 1 | 47 |
| | | | | | 2 | 2 | | | | 3 | | 1 | 2 | 2 | 4 | | | | | | | | | 4 | 48 |
| | 1 | | | 1 | 29 | 8 | 18 | 15 | 12 | 16 | 5 | 14 | 24 | 42 | 66 | 2 | 2 | | | | | | | 70 | 49 |
| | 1 | | | 1 | 5 | 7 | 5 | 2 | 4 | 5 | 4 | 5 | 6 | 11 | 17 | 1 | | | | | | 1 | | 19 | 50 |
| | | | | | 1 | | | | | | | | 1 | | 1 | | | | | | | | | 1 | 51 |
| | | | | | 4 | 1 | 3 | 4 | 4 | 7 | 1 | | 8 | 4 | 12 | | | | | | | | | 12 | 52 |
| | 1 | | | | 16 | 6 | 4 | 16 | 4 | 34 | 2 | 2 | 19 | 17 | 36 | 3 | 3 | | | | | | | 42 | 53 |
| | | | | | 1 | | 1 | | 2 | | | | 1 | 1 | 2 | | | | | | | | | 2 | 54 |
| | | | 1 | | 2 | 3 | 1 | | | 1 | 3 | 2 | 2 | 4 | 6 | | | | | | | | | 6 | 55 |
| | 1 | | | | 2 | 5 | 4 | 1 | | 1 | 4 | 7 | 7 | 5 | 12 | | | | | | | | | 12 | 56 |
| | | | | | 2 | 1 | | 4 | | 6 | 1 | | 5 | 1 | 6 | | | | | | | 1 | | 7 | 57 |
| | | | | | 1 | 6 | 2 | 2 | 3 | 2 | | 4 | 4 | 4 | 8 | 2 | | | | | | 1 | | 11 | 58 |
| | | | | | 4 | | | 3 | | | | | 4 | 3 | 7 | | | | | | | | | 7 | 59 |
| | | | | | | | 1 | | | 1 | | | | 1 | 1 | | | | | | | | | 1 | 60 |
| | | | | | 3 | | 1 | 1 | 5 | | | | 1 | 1 | 2 | | 1 | 2 | | | | | | 5 | 61 |
| | | | | | | 1 | 2 | | 2 | | | | 2 | 1 | 3 | | | | | | | | | 3 | 62 |
| | | | | | | 4 | 2 | | 3 | 3 | | | 3 | 3 | 6 | | | | | | | | | 6 | 63 |
| | | | | | 1 | | 2 | 1 | 2 | 2 | | | 2 | 1 | 3 | | | 1 | | | | | | 4 | 64 |
| | | | | | 1 | | | | | 1 | | | 1 | | 1 | | | | | | | | | 1 | 65 |
| | | | | | 1 | 2 | 6 | 5 | 2 | 11 | | 1 | 8 | 6 | 14 | | | | | | | | | 14 | 66 |
| | | | | | 2 | 1 | | 1 | | 3 | | 1 | 2 | 2 | 4 | | | | | | | | | 4 | 67 |
| | | | | | | | 1 | 1 | | 1 | | 1 | 1 | 1 | 2 | | | | | | | | | 2 | 68 |
| | | | 1 | | 2 | | 1 | | | 2 | | 1 | 3 | | 3 | | | | | | | | | 3 | 69 |
| | | | | | 1 | | | | | | | 2 | 2 | | 2 | | | | | | | | | 2 | 70 |
| | | | | | 4 | 6 | 3 | 3 | 5 | 8 | 3 | | 5 | 7 | 12 | 1 | | 2 | | 1 | | | | 16 | 71 |
| | | | 2 | | 76 | 80 | 68 | 48 | 96 | 65 | 36 | 48 | 145 | 104 | 249 | 12 | | 15 | | | | 2 | 1 | 279 | 72 |
| 1 | 17 | 12 | 21 | 5 | 567 | 553 | 547 | 460 | 745 | 732 | 205 | 347 | 1054 | 889 | 1941 | 91 | 73 | 15 | 10 | 3 | 3 | 4 | 5 | 2145 | |

## CLASSIFICATION OF DEATHS IN MOUNTAIN

*Embracing the following counties: Alleghany, Augusta, Bath, Berkley, Botetourt, Carroll, Lee, Mercer, Monroe, Montgomery, Morgan, Page, Pendleton, Pocahontas, Pulaski, well, Warren, Wash*

| | Cause of death. | AGES. | | | | | | | | | | | | | | | | | | NATIVITIES. | | | | | |
|---|---|---|---|---|---|---|---|---|---|---|---|---|---|---|---|---|---|---|---|---|---|---|---|---|---|
| | | Under 1. | | 1 and under 5. | | 5 and under 10. | | 10 and under 20. | | 20 and under 50. | | 50 and under 80. | | 80 and under 100. | | 100 & over. | | Age unknown. | | Born in State. | N. England States. | Middle States. | Southern States. | Southwest'n States. | Northwest'n States. |
| | | M. | F. | M. | F. | M. | F. | M. | F. | M. | F. | M. | F. | M. | F. | M | F. | M | F. | | | | | | |
| 1 | Abscess | | | | | | | | | 2 | | | | | | | | | | 2 | | | | | |
| 2 | Accident, not specfi'd | 2 | 2 | 9 | 3 | 2 | 1 | 7 | 1 | 15 | 3 | 9 | 3 | 1 | | | | | | 56 | | 1 | | | |
| 3 | ....do...burned | 1 | | 2 | 4 | | 1 | | 1 | 1 | | | | | | | | | | 10 | | | | | |
| 4 | ....do...drowned | | | 2 | 3 | 1 | | 4 | 3 | 8 | 1 | 2 | | | | | | | | 24 | | | | | |
| 5 | ....do.. scalded | | | 6 | 1 | | 1 | | | | | | | | | | | | | 7 | | | | | |
| 6 | ....do...shot | | | | | 1 | | 1 | | | | | | | | | | | | 2 | | | | | |
| 7 | ....do...railroad | | | | | | | 1 | | | | | | | | | | | | 1 | | | | | |
| 8 | Apoplexy | | | | | | | 1 | 1 | 5 | 9 | 8 | 9 | | | | | | | 29 | | 2 | | | |
| 9 | Asthma | | | | | 1 | | | | | 2 | 3 | 3 | | 1 | | | | | 9 | | 1 | | | |
| 10 | Black tongue | | | | | | | | | 1 | | | | | | | | | | 1 | | | | | |
| 11 | Bladder, disease of | | | | | | | | | | 1 | | | | | | | | | 1 | | | | | |
| 12 | Bowels....do | | | 1 | 3 | 1 | 1 | 1 | 2 | 1 | 3 | 2 | | | | | | | | 15 | | | | | |
| 13 | Brain.......do | | | 4 | 1 | 1 | | | 3 | 2 | 2 | 2 | 1 | | | | | | | 16 | | | | | |
| 14 | Bronchitis | | 1 | 4 | 1 | 2 | | | | 4 | 2 | 2 | | | | | | | | 13 | 1 | | 1 | | 1 |
| 15 | Cancer | | | | | | | | | 1 | 3 | 11 | 11 | | | | | | | 23 | | 2 | | | |
| 16 | Catarrh | 9 | 10 | 5 | 6 | | | 1 | 2 | 4 | 6 | 5 | 5 | | 1 | | | | | 52 | 1 | | | | |
| 17 | Chicken pox | | | | | 1 | | | | | | | | | | | | | | 1 | | | | | |
| 18 | Childbirth | | | | | | | | 8 | | 54 | | | | | | | | | 57 | | 3 | 2 | | |
| 19 | Cholera | 1 | | | | | | | | 3 | 1 | | 1 | | | | | | | 6 | | | | | |
| 20 | ...do...infantum | 4 | 8 | 4 | 4 | | | | | | 2 | 1 | | | | | | | | 18 | | | | | |
| 21 | ...do...morbus | 1 | 2 | 2 | 2 | | | 1 | | | | 1 | | | | | | | | 9 | | | | | |
| 22 | Chorea | | | | | | | | 1 | | | | | | | | | | | 1 | | | | | |
| 23 | Colic | | | 1 | | 1 | | 1 | | 4 | | 1 | | | | | | | | 8 | | | | | |
| 24 | Congestion of brain | | 1 | 1 | 1 | | | | 1 | | 2 | | | | | | | | | 6 | | | | | |
| 25 | Consumption | 5 | 4 | 3 | 8 | 2 | 3 | 17 | 26 | 69 | 118 | 32 | 53 | 6 | 2 | | | | | 325 | | 9 | 4 | 5 | |
| 26 | Convulsions | 15 | 8 | 5 | 4 | 1 | | 2 | 1 | 7 | 6 | 3 | 1 | | | | | | | 50 | | 2 | 1 | | |
| 27 | Cramp | 5 | 1 | 2 | 2 | 1 | | | | | | | | | | | | | | 11 | | | | | |
| 28 | Croup | 29 | 22 | 36 | 37 | 9 | 10 | | | | | | | | | | | | | 143 | | | | | |
| 29 | Debility | | | | | | | | | | | | 1 | | 1 | | | | | 2 | | | | | |
| 30 | Diabetes | | | 1 | | | | | | | 1 | 1 | | | | | | | | 2 | | 1 | | | |
| 31 | Diarrhœa | 2 | 1 | 10 | 9 | 3 | 2 | 1 | 1 | 3 | 6 | 1 | 1 | 2 | | | | | | 40 | | 1 | | | |
| 32 | Dropsy | 1 | 2 | 4 | 2 | 5 | 1 | 5 | 12 | 10 | 20 | 41 | 34 | 2 | 1 | 2 | 2 | | | 130 | | 11 | | | |
| 33 | Dysentery | 9 | 7 | 22 | 15 | 5 | 8 | 3 | 5 | 4 | 6 | 9 | 5 | 2 | 1 | | | | | 96 | | 3 | | | |
| 34 | Dyspepsia | | | 1 | 1 | | | | | 3 | | 5 | 1 | 1 | | | | | | 10 | | 2 | | | |
| 35 | Epilepsy | | | | 1 | | | | | | | | 1 | | | | | | | 1 | | 1 | | | |
| 36 | Erysipelas | 2 | 3 | 2 | 1 | 1 | | 1 | 4 | 4 | 2 | 4 | 2 | 1 | | | | | | 26 | | | | | |
| 37 | Fever, not specified | 1 | | 5 | 6 | 3 | 3 | 15 | 16 | 23 | 26 | 7 | 6 | | | | | 1 | 1 | 106 | | 1 | 3 | 4 | |
| 38 | ..do..bilious | | | | 1 | 1 | | 2 | 1 | 4 | 2 | 3 | 3 | | 1 | | | | | 16 | | 2 | | | |
| 39 | ..do. brain | 1 | 1 | 1 | | 1 | | | | | | | | | | | | | | 4 | | | | | |
| 40 | ..do..catarrhal | | 1 | 1 | | | | | 1 | | | | | | | | | | | 3 | | | | | |
| 41 | ..do..congestive | | | | | | | 1 | 1 | 1 | | | | | | | | | | 3 | | | | | |
| 42 | ..do..intermittent | | | | | | | | | 1 | | 1 | | | | | | | | 1 | | | 1 | | |
| 43 | ..do..puerperal | | | | | | | | 2 | | 14 | | | | | | | | | 16 | | | | | |
| 44 | ..do..scarlet | 12 | 4 | 36 | 36 | 31 | 21 | 4 | 15 | 2 | 3 | | 1 | | | | | | | 164 | | 1 | | | |
| 45 | ..do .typhus | 2 | 1 | 6 | 5 | 6 | 4 | 16 | 22 | 45 | 21 | 14 | 6 | 1 | 2 | | | | | 139 | 1 | 6 | 2 | 1 | |
| 46 | ..do..winter | | | | | | | | | | | 1 | | | | | | | | 1 | | | | | |
| 47 | Frozen | | | | | | | | | 1 | | | | | | | | | | 1 | | | | | |
| 48 | Gravel | | | | | | | 3 | | 1 | | 9 | | 4 | | | | | | 13 | 1 | 1 | | 2 | |
| 49 | Head, disease of | 1 | | 1 | | | | | | | 1 | 1 | | | | | | | | 4 | | | | | |
| 50 | Heart....do | 1 | 1 | | | | | | | 1 | 2 | 3 | 1 | 1 | | | | | | 9 | | 1 | | | |
| 51 | Heat | | | | | | | 1 | | | | | 1 | | | | | | | 2 | | | | | |
| 52 | Hemorrhage | | | 1 | | 1 | | | 1 | 1 | 1 | | | | 1 | | | | | 6 | | | | | |
| 53 | Hernia | | | | 1 | | | | | 1 | | | | 1 | | | | | | 3 | | | | | |
| 54 | Hives | 9 | 5 | 2 | 1 | 1 | | | | | | | | | | | | | | 18 | | | | | |
| 55 | Hooping cough | 10 | 7 | 13 | 23 | 2 | | | | | | | | | | | | | | 55 | | | | | |
| 56 | Hydrocephalus | 3 | 1 | 2 | 7 | | | | | 2 | | | 2 | | | | | | | 16 | | 1 | | | |
| 57 | Hydrophobia | | | | 1 | | | | | | 1 | | 1 | | | | | | | 3 | | | | | |
| 58 | Inflammation | | 2 | 2 | 1 | 1 | 1 | | 2 | 1 | 3 | | | | | | | | | 13 | | | | | |
| 59 | .....do....bowels | | 3 | 3 | 3 | 1 | 1 | 1 | | 4 | 4 | 6 | 4 | | | | | | | 30 | | | | | |
| 60 | .....do....brain | 6 | 5 | 3 | 6 | 6 | | 4 | 2 | 2 | 2 | 3 | | | | | | | | 37 | | 1 | | | 1 |
| 61 | .....do....stomach | | | | 1 | | | | | | 2 | 3 | | | | | | | | 5 | | | | 1 | |
| 62 | Influenza | | 1 | 1 | | | | | | | 2 | 1 | | | | | | | | 4 | | 1 | | | |
| 63 | Intemperance | | | | | | | | | 1 | | 2 | | | | | | | | 3 | | | | | |
| 64 | Jaundice | | 2 | | | 1 | | | | 1 | 1 | 1 | 3 | 1 | | | | | | 9 | | 1 | | | |
| 65 | Kidneys, disease of | | | | | | | | | | | 3 | | | | | | | | 2 | | | 1 | | |
| 66 | Killed | | | | | | | 1 | | 1 | | | | | | | | | | 2 | | | | | |
| 67 | Liver, disease of | 1 | 1 | 1 | | | | | 2 | 4 | 10 | 1 | | | | | | | | 2[illegible] | | | | | |
| 68 | Lockjaw | | 1 | | | 1 | | | 1 | | | | | | | | | | | 3 | | | | | |
| 69 | Lungs, disease of | 2 | | 2 | 2 | 1 | | 1 | | 3 | 11 | 8 | 4 | | | | | | | 28 | | | | 1 | |
| 70 | Mania-a-potu | | | | | | | | | 8 | 1 | | | | | | | | | 8 | | | | | |

## ECTION OF THE STATE OF VIRGINIA.

*Clarke, Floyd, Frederick, Giles, Grayson, Greenbrier, Hampshire, Hardy, Highland, Jefferson, Raleigh, Roanoke, Rockbridge, Rockingham, Russell, Scott, Shenandoah, Smyth, Taze- ngton, Wyoming, and Wythe.*

| Nativities: California and Territories. | Nativities: Ireland. | Nativities: Germany. | Nativities: Other foreign countries. | Nativities: Unknown. | Season of decease: Spring. | Season of decease: Summer. | Season of decease: Autumn. | Season of decease: Winter. | Duration of sickness: Under 1 week. | Duration of sickness: 1 week and under 1 month. | Duration of sickness: 1 month and under 3 months. | Duration of sickness: 3 months and over. | Whites: Males. | Whites: Females. | Whites: Total. | Colored: Slaves: Black: M. | Colored: Slaves: Black: F. | Colored: Slaves: Mulatto: M. | Colored: Slaves: Mulatto: F. | Colored: Free: Black: M. | Colored: Free: Black: F. | Colored: Free: Mul.: M | Colored: Free: Mul.: F. | Aggregate deaths. | |
|---|---|---|---|---|---|---|---|---|---|---|---|---|---|---|---|---|---|---|---|---|---|---|---|---|---|
| .... | ... | .. | .... | ... | 1 | 1 | .... | .... | .... | 1 | .... | 1 | 2 | .... | 2 | .... | .... | .... | .... | ... | ... | .. | .. | 2 | 1 |
| .... | 1 | .. | .... | ... | 19 | 15 | 10 | 14 | 44 | 6 | 4 | 2 | 38 | 4 | 42 | 6 | 7 | .... | 1 | ... | 1 | 1 | .. | 58 | 2 |
| .... | ... | .. | .... | ... | 3 | 2 | 1 | 3 | 3 | 4 | 1 | 1 | 2 | 4 | 6 | 2 | 1 | .... | 1 | ... | ... | .. | .. | 10 | 3 |
| .... | ... | .. | .... | ... | 5 | 10 | 7 | 1 | 24 | .... | .... | .... | 14 | 7 | 21 | 1 | .... | 1 | .... | ... | ... | 1 | .. | 24 | 4 |
| .... | 1 | .. | .... | ... | 3 | 1 | 1 | 3 | 6 | 2 | .... | .... | 5 | 2 | 7 | .... | .... | 1 | .... | ... | ... | .. | .. | 8 | 5 |
| .... | ... | .. | .... | ... | 1 | .... | .... | 1 | 2 | .... | .... | .... | 2 | ... | 2 | .... | .... | .... | .... | ... | ... | .. | .. | 2 | 6 |
| .... | ... | .. | .... | ... | .... | .... | .... | 1 | 1 | .... | .... | .... | 1 | .... | 1 | .... | .... | .... | .... | ... | ... | .. | .. | 1 | 7 |
| .... | 1 | .. | 1 | ... | 10 | 10 | 6 | 7 | 20 | 1 | 1 | 1 | 13 | 12 | 25 | .... | 7 | 1 | .... | ... | ... | .. | .. | 33 | 8 |
| .... | ... | .. | .... | ... | .... | 4 | 1 | 5 | 1 | 1 | 1 | 5 | 3 | 4 | 7 | 1 | 2 | .... | .... | ... | ... | .. | .. | 10 | 9 |
| .... | ... | .. | .... | ... | .... | .... | .... | 1 | .... | 1 | .... | .... | 1 | .... | 1 | .... | .... | .... | .... | ... | ... | .. | .. | 1 | 10 |
| .... | ... | .. | .... | ... | 1 | .... | .... | .... | .... | 1 | .... | .... | .... | 1 | 1 | .... | .... | .... | .... | ... | ... | .. | .. | 1 | 11 |
| .... | ... | .. | .... | ... | 4 | 4 | 4 | 3 | 4 | 3 | 3 | 2 | 5 | 7 | 12 | 1 | 2 | .... | .... | ... | ... | .. | .. | 15 | 12 |
| .... | ... | .. | .... | ... | 5 | 3 | 6 | 2 | 4 | 8 | .... | 4 | 6 | 5 | 11 | 3 | 2 | .... | .... | ... | ... | .. | .. | 16 | 13 |
| .... | ... | .. | .... | ... | 4 | 2 | 6 | 4 | 7 | 4 | 2 | 2 | 10 | 4 | 14 | 2 | .... | .... | .... | ... | ... | .. | .. | 16 | 14 |
| .... | 1 | .. | .... | ... | 5 | 9 | 4 | 8 | 5 | 1 | 2 | 14 | 11 | 12 | 23 | 1 | 1 | .... | 1 | ... | ... | .. | .. | 26 | 15 |
| .... | 1 | .. | .... | ... | 29 | 8 | 8 | 9 | 21 | 25 | 4 | 4 | 15 | 19 | 34 | 8 | 9 | .... | 2 | 1 | ... | .. | .. | 54 | 16 |
| .... | ... | .. | .... | ... | 1 | .... | .... | .... | .... | 1 | .... | .... | .... | .... | .... | 1 | .... | .... | .... | ... | ... | .. | .. | 1 | 17 |
| .... | ... | .. | .... | ... | 21 | 12 | 14 | 15 | 27 | 23 | 5 | 2 | .... | 54 | 54 | .... | 5 | .... | 2 | ... | 1 | .. | .. | 62 | 18 |
| .... | ... | .. | .... | ... | 2 | 3 | 1 | .... | 4 | 1 | .... | 1 | 3 | 1 | 4 | 1 | .... | .... | 1 | ... | ... | .. | .. | 6 | 19 |
| .... | ... | .. | .... | ... | 2 | 7 | 8 | 1 | 6 | 10 | .... | .... | 7 | 8 | 15 | 1 | .... | 1 | 1 | ... | ... | .. | .. | *18 | 20 |
| .... | ... | .. | .... | ... | 1 | 4 | 2 | 2 | 6 | 2 | .... | 1 | 3 | 4 | 7 | 2 | .... | .... | .... | ... | ... | .. | .. | 9 | 21 |
| .... | ... | .. | .... | ... | .... | .... | .... | 1 | .... | 1 | .... | .... | .... | 1 | 1 | .... | .... | .... | .... | ... | ... | .. | .. | 1 | 22 |
| .... | ... | .. | .... | ... | 3 | 2 | 1 | 2 | 7 | 1 | .... | .... | 7 | .... | 7 | 1 | .... | .... | .... | ... | ... | .. | .. | 8 | 23 |
| .... | ... | .. | .... | ... | 2 | .... | 2 | 2 | 3 | 2 | .... | 1 | 1 | 4 | 5 | .... | 1 | .... | .... | ... | ... | .. | .. | 6 | 24 |
| .... | 8 | .. | 2 | ... | 111 | 101 | 65 | 66 | 10 | 27 | 47 | 243 | 98 | 159 | 257 | 29 | 45 | 4 | 5 | 1 | 4 | 2 | 1 | 348 | 25 |
| .... | ... | .. | .... | ... | 21 | 14 | 8 | 9 | 26 | 10 | 3 | 9 | 25 | 13 | 38 | 6 | 5 | 1 | 1 | ... | ... | 1 | 1 | 53 | 26 |
| .... | ... | .. | .... | ... | 4 | 2 | 2 | 2 | 9 | 2 | .... | .... | 6 | 2 | 8 | .... | 1 | 1 | .... | 1 | ... | .. | .. | 11 | 27 |
| .... | ... | .. | .... | ... | 55 | 22 | 36 | 30 | 115 | 26 | 2 | .... | 64 | 55 | 119 | 6 | 11 | 4 | 3 | ... | ... | .. | .. | 143 | 28 |
| .... | ... | .. | .... | ... | 2 | .... | .... | .... | .... | .... | 1 | .... | .... | 1 | 1 | .... | 1 | .... | .... | ... | ... | .. | .. | 2 | 29 |
| .... | ... | .. | .... | ... | 2 | .... | 1 | .... | .... | .... | 1 | 2 | 2 | 1 | 3 | .... | .... | .... | .... | ... | ... | .. | .. | 3 | 30 |
| .... | 1 | .. | .... | ... | 5 | 15 | 17 | 5 | 11 | 19 | 7 | 4 | 20 | 19 | 39 | 1 | 1 | 1 | .... | ... | ... | .. | .. | 42 | 31 |
| .... | 1 | 1 | 1 | ... | 45 | 48 | 22 | 29 | 11 | 16 | 27 | 77 | 58 | 51 | 109 | 10 | 17 | 1 | 5 | ... | 1 | 1 | .. | 144 | 32 |
| .... | 2 | .. | .... | ... | 10 | 34 | 49 | 6 | 19 | 67 | 12 | 1 | 45 | 42 | 87 | 9 | 4 | .... | .... | ... | ... | .. | 1 | 101 | 33 |
| .... | ... | .. | .... | ... | 6 | 3 | 2 | 1 | 1 | 2 | .... | 7 | 9 | 2 | 11 | .... | .... | 1 | .... | ... | ... | .. | .. | 12 | 34 |
| .... | ... | .. | .... | ... | .... | 1 | 1 | .... | 1 | 1 | .... | .... | .... | 2 | 2 | .... | .... | .... | .... | ... | ... | .. | .. | 2 | 35 |
| .... | ... | 1 | .... | ... | 13 | 3 | 4 | 7 | 5 | 15 | 5 | 1 | 12 | 10 | 22 | 3 | .... | .... | 2 | ... | ... | .. | .. | 27 | 36 |
| .... | ... | .. | .... | ... | 33 | 22 | 32 | 27 | 14 | 68 | 27 | 4 | 43 | 46 | 89 | 10 | 12 | 2 | 1 | ... | ... | .. | .. | 114 | 37 |
| .... | ... | .. | .... | ... | 4 | 1 | 8 | 5 | 2 | 11 | 5 | .... | 7 | 6 | 13 | 3 | 1 | .... | 1 | ... | ... | .. | .. | 18 | 38 |
| .... | ... | .. | .... | ... | 1 | 2 | .... | 1 | 2 | 1 | 1 | .... | 2 | .... | 2 | 1 | 1 | .... | .... | ... | ... | .. | .. | 4 | 39 |
| .... | ... | .. | .... | ... | 3 | .... | .... | .... | 1 | .... | 1 | 1 | 1 | 2 | 3 | .... | .... | .... | .... | ... | ... | .. | .. | 3 | 40 |
| .... | ... | .. | .... | ... | .... | .... | 2 | 1 | .... | 3 | .... | .... | 1 | .... | 1 | 1 | 1 | .... | .... | ... | ... | .. | .. | 3 | 41 |
| .... | ... | .. | .... | ... | 1 | .... | 1 | .... | .... | 2 | .... | .... | 2 | .... | 2 | .... | .... | .... | .... | ... | ... | .. | .. | 2 | 42 |
| .... | ... | .. | .... | ... | 4 | 7 | 3 | 2 | 2 | 12 | 2 | .... | .... | 13 | 13 | .... | 1 | .... | 2 | ... | ... | .. | .. | 16 | 43 |
| .... | ... | .. | .... | ... | 45 | 28 | 35 | 56 | 86 | 65 | 9 | 2 | 70 | 65 | 135 | 12 | 11 | 3 | 3 | ... | ... | .. | 1 | 165 | 44 |
| .... | ... | .. | 2 | ... | 67 | 20 | 34 | 30 | 15 | 106 | 27 | 3 | 70 | 44 | 114 | 18 | 13 | 1 | 1 | 1 | 3 | .. | .. | 151 | 45 |
| .... | ... | .. | .... | ... | 1 | .... | .... | .... | .... | 1 | .... | .... | 1 | .... | 1 | .... | .... | .... | .... | ... | ... | .. | .. | 1 | 46 |
| .... | ... | .. | .... | ... | .... | 1 | .... | .... | 1 | .... | .... | .... | 1 | .... | 1 | .... | .... | .... | .... | ... | ... | .. | .. | 1 | 47 |
| .... | ... | .. | .... | ... | 5 | 4 | 4 | 4 | 1 | 4 | 3 | 8 | 15 | .... | 15 | 2 | .... | .... | .... | ... | ... | .. | .. | 17 | 48 |
| .... | ... | .. | .... | ... | .... | .... | 2 | 1 | .... | 2 | .... | 1 | 1 | 1 | 2 | 2 | .... | .... | .... | ... | ... | .. | .. | 4 | 49 |
| .... | ... | .. | .... | ... | 4 | 2 | 1 | 3 | 6 | 1 | 1 | 1 | 4 | 1 | 5 | 2 | 3 | .... | .... | ... | ... | .. | .. | 10 | 50 |
| .... | ... | .. | .... | ... | .... | 2 | .... | .... | 2 | .... | .... | .... | 1 | .... | 1 | .... | 1 | .... | .... | ... | ... | .. | .. | 2 | 51 |
| .... | ... | .. | .... | ... | 3 | 1 | 1 | 1 | 1 | 2 | 1 | 1 | 3 | 2 | 5 | .... | 1 | .... | .... | ... | ... | .. | .. | 6 | 52 |
| .... | ... | .. | .... | ... | 1 | .... | .... | 2 | 2 | .... | .... | 1 | 2 | 1 | 3 | .... | .... | .... | .... | ... | ... | .. | .. | 3 | 53 |
| .... | ... | .. | .... | ... | 4 | 4 | 6 | 4 | 9 | 7 | .... | 1 | 12 | 6 | 18 | .... | .... | .... | .... | ... | ... | .. | .. | 18 | 54 |
| .... | ... | .. | .... | ... | 16 | 19 | 14 | 6 | 30 | 12 | 3 | .... | 10 | 20 | 30 | 13 | 8 | 2 | 1 | ... | ... | .. | 1 | 55 | 55 |
| .... | ... | .. | .... | ... | 6 | 4 | 4 | 3 | 1 | 12 | 4 | .... | 7 | 7 | 14 | .... | 1 | .... | 2 | ... | ... | .. | .. | 17 | 56 |
| .... | ... | .. | .... | ... | 1 | 1 | 1 | .... | .... | 1 | 2 | .... | .... | 2 | 2 | .... | 1 | .... | .... | ... | ... | .. | .. | 3 | 57 |
| .... | ... | .. | .... | ... | 2 | 4 | 6 | 1 | 7 | 4 | 2 | .... | 4 | 8 | 12 | .... | .... | .... | 1 | ... | ... | .. | .. | 13 | 58 |
| .... | ... | .. | .... | ... | 5 | 12 | 6 | 7 | 10 | 12 | 2 | 3 | 11 | 12 | 23 | 3 | 2 | .... | 1 | 1 | ... | .. | .. | 30 | 59 |
| .... | ... | .. | .... | ... | 16 | 9 | 5 | 9 | 14 | 24 | 1 | .... | 20 | 15 | 35 | 3 | .... | 1 | .... | ... | ... | .. | .. | 39 | 60 |
| .... | ... | .. | .... | ... | .... | 4 | .... | 2 | 2 | 1 | 1 | 2 | 3 | 2 | 5 | .... | .... | .... | 1 | ... | ... | .. | .. | 6 | 61 |
| .... | ... | .. | .... | ... | 1 | 2 | .... | 1 | 1 | 2 | .... | 2 | 2 | 3 | 5 | .... | .... | .... | .... | ... | ... | .. | .. | 5 | 62 |
| .... | ... | .. | .... | ... | 1 | .... | 1 | 1 | 2 | .... | .... | 1 | 2 | .... | 2 | .... | .... | 1 | .... | ... | ... | .. | .. | 3 | 63 |
| .... | ... | .. | .... | ... | 3 | 1 | 4 | 2 | 1 | 3 | 2 | 1 | 3 | 5 | 8 | 1 | .... | .... | 1 | ... | ... | .. | .. | 10 | 64 |
| .... | ... | .. | .... | ... | .... | .... | 2 | 1 | .... | .... | .... | 1 | 3 | .... | 3 | .... | .... | .... | .... | ... | ... | .. | .. | 3 | 65 |
| .... | ... | .. | .... | ... | .... | .... | .... | 2 | 2 | .... | .... | .... | 2 | .... | 2 | .... | .... | .... | .... | ... | ... | .. | .. | 2 | 66 |
| .... | ... | .. | .... | ... | 8 | 8 | 3 | 1 | 2 | 6 | 3 | 9 | 5 | 13 | 18 | 1 | .... | 1 | .... | ... | ... | .. | .. | 20 | 67 |
| .... | ... | .. | .... | ... | 2 | 1 | .... | .... | 3 | .... | .... | .... | .... | .... | .... | 1 | 2 | .... | .... | ... | ... | .. | .. | 3 | 68 |
| .... | ... | .. | .... | ... | 8 | 12 | 5 | 4 | 5 | 9 | 2 | 12 | 7 | 10 | 17 | 4 | 6 | 1 | 1 | ... | ... | .. | .. | 29 | 69 |
| .... | 1 | .. | .... | ... | 2 | 1 | 1 | .... | .... | 2 | 2 | .... | 3 | 1 | 4 | .... | .... | .... | .... | ... | ... | .. | .. | 4 | 70 |

* 3 adults included erroneously by marshals.

## CLASSIFICATION OF DEATHS IN MOUNTAIN

| | Cause of death. | Ages. Under 1. M. | Under 1. F. | 1 and under 5. M. | 1 and under 5. F. | 5 and under 10. M. | 5 and under 10. F. | 10 and under 20. M. | 10 and under 20. F. | 20 and under 50. M. | 20 and under 50. F. | 50 and under 80. M. | 50 and under 80. F. | 80 and under 100. M. | 80 and under 100. F. | 100 & over. M | 100 & over. F. | Age unknown. M | Age unknown. F. | Nativities. Born in State. | N. England States. | Middle States. | Southern States. | Southwest'n States. | Northwest'n States. |
|---|---|---|---|---|---|---|---|---|---|---|---|---|---|---|---|---|---|---|---|---|---|---|---|---|---|
| 1 | Marasmus | ... | 1 | ... | ... | ... | ... | ... | ... | ... | ... | ... | ... | ... | ... | .. | .. | .. | .. | 1 | .. | ... | ... | ... | .. |
| 2 | Measles | 2 | ... | 6 | 3 | 4 | 1 | 1 | 2 | 2 | 3 | ... | 1 | ... | ... | .. | .. | .. | .. | 25 | .. | ... | ... | ... | .. |
| 3 | Mumps | ... | ... | ... | 1 | 1 | ... | 1 | 1 | 2 | ... | ... | ... | ... | ... | .. | .. | .. | .. | 6 | .. | ... | ... | ... | .. |
| 4 | Murder | ... | ... | ... | ... | ... | ... | 1 | ... | ... | ... | 1 | ... | 1 | ... | .. | .. | .. | .. | 3 | .. | ... | ... | ... | .. |
| 5 | Neuralgia | ... | ... | ... | ... | ... | 1 | ... | ... | 2 | 1 | 1 | ... | ... | ... | .. | .. | .. | .. | 5 | .. | ... | ... | ... | .. |
| 6 | Old age | ... | ... | ... | ... | ... | ... | ... | ... | ... | ... | 28 | 18 | 55 | 50 | 4 | 4 | .. | .. | 130 | .. | 17 | 6 | ... | .. |
| 7 | Paralysis | ... | 1 | ... | ... | 1 | ... | 1 | 1 | 3 | 5 | 23 | 20 | 6 | 7 | .. | .. | .. | .. | 55 | .. | 10 | ... | ... | .. |
| 8 | Peritonitis | ... | ... | ... | ... | ... | ... | ... | ... | ... | 1 | ... | ... | ... | ... | .. | .. | .. | .. | 1 | .. | ... | ... | ... | .. |
| 9 | Piles | ... | ... | ... | ... | ... | ... | ... | ... | ... | ... | 1 | ... | ... | ... | .. | .. | .. | .. | ... | .. | ... | 1 | ... | .. |
| 10 | Pleurisy | ... | 1 | 1 | ... | 1 | 1 | 3 | 1 | 5 | 2 | 6 | 2 | 2 | 1 | .. | .. | .. | .. | 23 | .. | 3 | ... | ... | .. |
| 11 | Pneumonia | 8 | 10 | 16 | 4 | 4 | 4 | 9 | 9 | 21 | 17 | 18 | 15 | 2 | 1 | .. | .. | .. | .. | 132 | .. | 4 | ... | ... | .. |
| 12 | Poison | ... | ... | 1 | ... | ... | ... | ... | ... | ... | ... | ... | 1 | ... | ... | .. | .. | .. | .. | 1 | .. | 1 | ... | ... | .. |
| 13 | Quinsy | ... | ... | ... | ... | 1 | ... | ... | ... | 1 | 3 | ... | 1 | ... | ... | .. | .. | .. | .. | 6 | .. | ... | ... | ... | .. |
| 14 | Rheumatism | ... | ... | ... | 1 | ... | 1 | ... | 1 | 1 | 1 | 3 | 6 | 1 | ... | .. | .. | .. | .. | 14 | .. | ... | 1 | ... | .. |
| 15 | Rickets | ... | ... | 1 | ... | ... | ... | ... | ... | ... | ... | ... | ... | ... | ... | .. | .. | .. | .. | 1 | .. | ... | ... | ... | .. |
| 16 | Scrofula | 2 | 1 | 6 | 1 | 1 | ... | 5 | 7 | 4 | 9 | 4 | 5 | 1 | 1 | .. | .. | .. | .. | 44 | .. | 3 | ... | ... | .. |
| 17 | Small pox | 1 | ... | ... | ... | ... | ... | ... | ... | 2 | ... | 2 | 1 | ... | ... | .. | .. | .. | .. | 6 | .. | ... | ... | ... | .. |
| 18 | Spine, disease of | ... | ... | ... | 1 | ... | ... | ... | ... | 2 | 1 | ... | 1 | ... | ... | .. | .. | .. | .. | 5 | .. | ... | ... | ... | .. |
| 19 | Stillborn | 1 | 1 | ... | ... | ... | ... | ... | ... | ... | ... | ... | ... | ... | ... | .. | .. | .. | .. | 2 | .. | ... | ... | ... | .. |
| 20 | Stomach, disease of | 1 | ... | ... | ... | ... | ... | ... | ... | ... | 1 | ... | 2 | ... | ... | .. | .. | .. | .. | 3 | .. | 1 | ... | ... | .. |
| 21 | Suffocation | 3 | 3 | 1 | ... | ... | ... | ... | ... | ... | ... | ... | ... | ... | ... | .. | .. | .. | .. | 7 | .. | ... | ... | ... | .. |
| 22 | Suicide | ... | ... | ... | ... | ... | ... | ... | ... | 2 | 2 | ... | ... | ... | ... | .. | .. | .. | .. | 4 | .. | ... | ... | ... | .. |
| 23 | Teething | 1 | 1 | 6 | 3 | ... | ... | ... | ... | ... | ... | ... | ... | ... | ... | .. | .. | .. | .. | 11 | .. | ... | ... | ... | .. |
| 24 | Tetanus | ... | ... | ... | ... | ... | ... | 1 | ... | 1 | ... | ... | ... | ... | ... | .. | .. | .. | .. | 2 | .. | ... | ... | ... | .. |
| 25 | Tetter | ... | ... | ... | ... | ... | ... | ... | ... | 1 | ... | ... | ... | ... | ... | .. | .. | .. | .. | 1 | .. | ... | ... | ... | .. |
| 26 | Throat, disease of | 2 | 2 | 9 | 12 | 13 | 15 | 11 | 16 | 2 | 1 | 1 | 1 | ... | ... | .. | .. | .. | .. | 85 | .. | ... | ... | ... | .. |
| 27 | Tumor | ... | ... | 1 | ... | ... | ... | ... | ... | 1 | 1 | ... | ... | ... | ... | .. | .. | .. | .. | 3 | .. | ... | ... | ... | .. |
| 28 | Ulcer | 1 | ... | ... | ... | ... | ... | ... | ... | 1 | ... | ... | ... | ... | ... | .. | .. | .. | .. | 2 | .. | ... | ... | ... | .. |
| 29 | Uterus, disease of | ... | ... | ... | ... | ... | ... | ... | ... | ... | 2 | ... | 1 | ... | ... | .. | .. | .. | .. | 3 | .. | ... | ... | ... | .. |
| 30 | White swelling | ... | ... | ... | ... | ... | ... | ... | ... | ... | 1 | 1 | 2 | ... | ... | .. | .. | .. | .. | 4 | .. | ... | ... | ... | .. |
| 31 | Worms | ... | 2 | 9 | 7 | 3 | 3 | ... | 1 | ... | ... | ... | ... | ... | ... | .. | .. | .. | .. | 25 | .. | ... | ... | ... | .. |
| 32 | Unknown | 136 | 116 | 64 | 59 | 23 | 9 | 14 | 29 | 57 | 68 | 56 | 52 | 12 | 3 | .. | .. | .. | .. | 679 | .. | 10 | 6 | 1 | 1 |
| | Total | 293 | 243 | 328 | 295 | 147 | 93 | 143 | 206 | 364 | 476 | 350 | 293 | 103 | 74 | 6 | 6 | 1 | 1 | 3232 | 5 | 105 | 29 | 15 | 3 |

## CLASSIFICATION OF DEATHS IN THE

| | Cause of death. | Under 1. M. | Under 1. F. | 1 and under 5. M. | 1 and under 5. F. | 5 and under 10. M. | 5 and under 10. F. | 10 and under 20. M. | 10 and under 20. F. | 20 and under 50. M. | 20 and under 50. F. | 50 and under 80. M. | 50 and under 80. F. | 80 and under 100. M. | 80 and under 100. F. | 100 & over. M | 100 & over. F. | Age unknown. M | Age unknown. F. | Born in State. | N. England States. | Middle States. | Southern States. | Southwest'n States. | Northwest'n States. |
|---|---|---|---|---|---|---|---|---|---|---|---|---|---|---|---|---|---|---|---|---|---|---|---|---|---|
| 1 | Abscess | ... | 1 | 2 | ... | ... | ... | ... | 1 | 6 | 1 | 2 | 1 | ... | .. | .. | .. | .. | .. | 13 | .. | ... | ... | ... | .. |
| 2 | Accident not specif'd | 29 | 27 | 27 | 21 | 13 | 11 | 24 | 8 | 52 | 9 | 34 | 7 | 5 | 1 | .. | .. | .. | .. | 258 | 1 | 6 | ... | 1 | .. |
| 3 | ...do...burned | 6 | 8 | 29 | 52 | 7 | 13 | 3 | 17 | 8 | 16 | 5 | 7 | ... | .. | .. | 1 | .. | .. | 170 | .. | 1 | ... | ... | .. |
| 4 | ...do...drowned | ... | 1 | 10 | 9 | 6 | 3 | 21 | 8 | 39 | 5 | 14 | 1 | ... | .. | .. | .. | .. | .. | 107 | .. | 3 | 1 | ... | 2 |
| 5 | ...do...scalded | 1 | 1 | 8 | 6 | ... | 1 | ... | ... | ... | ... | ... | ... | ... | .. | .. | .. | .. | .. | 16 | .. | ... | ... | ... | .. |
| 6 | ...do...explosion | ... | ... | ... | ... | ... | ... | 1 | ... | 2 | ... | ... | ... | ... | .. | .. | .. | .. | .. | 2 | .. | ... | ... | ... | .. |
| 7 | ...do...shot | ... | ... | ... | ... | 1 | 1 | 1 | ... | 2 | 1 | 1 | ... | ... | .. | .. | .. | .. | .. | 6 | .. | 1 | ... | ... | .. |
| 8 | ...do...railroad | ... | ... | ... | ... | ... | ... | 1 | ... | ... | ... | ... | ... | ... | .. | .. | .. | .. | .. | 1 | .. | ... | ... | ... | .. |
| 9 | Apoplexy | 1 | ... | ... | ... | ... | ... | 4 | 3 | 17 | 18 | 41 | 36 | 3 | 2 | .. | .. | .. | .. | 110 | .. | 7 | ... | ... | .. |
| 10 | Asthma | 2 | 2 | 1 | 1 | 1 | ... | ... | ... | 6 | 6 | 21 | 22 | 1 | 3 | .. | .. | .. | .. | 62 | 1 | 1 | ... | ... | .. |
| 11 | Black tongue | ... | ... | 1 | ... | ... | ... | ... | ... | 1 | 1 | 1 | ... | ... | .. | .. | .. | .. | .. | 4 | .. | ... | ... | ... | .. |
| 12 | Bladder, disease of | 1 | ... | ... | ... | ... | 1 | 1 | ... | 1 | 1 | 4 | ... | 1 | .. | .. | .. | .. | .. | 10 | .. | ... | ... | ... | .. |
| 13 | Bowels, ......do | 9 | 4 | 9 | 15 | 1 | 3 | 5 | 4 | 3 | 6 | 5 | 5 | ... | .. | .. | .. | .. | .. | 68 | .. | ... | ... | ... | .. |
| 14 | Brain ......do. | 6 | 5 | 13 | 5 | 3 | ... | 4 | 6 | 10 | 4 | 6 | 2 | ... | .. | .. | .. | .. | .. | 64 | .. | ... | ... | ... | .. |
| 15 | Bronchitis | 3 | 3 | 11 | 6 | 2 | 1 | 1 | 4 | 13 | 11 | 12 | 3 | 2 | .. | .. | .. | .. | .. | 65 | 1 | 1 | 1 | ... | 2 |
| 16 | Cancer | ... | ... | 2 | ... | ... | ... | 1 | 2 | 8 | 16 | 26 | 50 | 5 | 2 | 1 | 1 | .. | 1 | 104 | .. | 8 | ... | ... | .. |
| 17 | Carbuncle | ... | ... | ... | ... | ... | ... | ... | ... | 1 | 1 | ... | 1 | ... | .. | .. | .. | .. | .. | 3 | .. | ... | ... | ... | .. |
| 18 | Catarrh | 59 | 41 | 44 | 45 | 9 | 5 | 3 | 13 | 17 | 30 | 43 | 32 | 2 | 5 | .. | .. | .. | .. | 344 | 1 | 1 | 1 | ... | .. |
| 19 | Chicken pox | ... | ... | ... | ... | 1 | ... | ... | ... | ... | ... | ... | ... | ... | .. | .. | .. | .. | .. | 1 | .. | ... | ... | ... | .. |
| 20 | Childbirth | ... | ... | ... | ... | ... | ... | ... | 37 | ... | 226 | ... | ... | ... | .. | .. | .. | .. | .. | 248 | .. | 9 | 2 | ... | .. |
| 21 | Cholera | 24 | 15 | 47 | 38 | 17 | 25 | 42 | 29 | 240 | 131 | 102 | 78 | 3 | 5 | 1 | .. | 3 | .. | 725 | 2 | 19 | 12 | ... | 4 |
| 22 | ....do..infantum | 46 | 35 | 34 | 33 | ... | 2 | ... | ... | ... | ... | ... | ... | ... | .. | .. | .. | .. | .. | 150 | .. | ... | ... | ... | .. |
| 23 | ....do..morbus | 2 | 6 | 4 | 5 | 2 | ... | 2 | 4 | 3 | 4 | 7 | 3 | ... | .. | .. | .. | .. | .. | 42 | .. | ... | ... | ... | .. |
| 24 | Chorea | ... | ... | ... | ... | ... | 1 | ... | 1 | ... | ... | ... | ... | ... | .. | .. | .. | .. | .. | 2 | .. | ... | ... | ... | .. |
| 25 | Colic | 1 | 2 | 5 | 3 | 3 | 3 | 4 | 1 | 23 | 6 | 14 | 13 | ... | 1 | 1 | .. | .. | .. | 73 | .. | 2 | ... | ... | .. |
| 26 | Congestion | 2 | 1 | 2 | ... | 1 | 1 | 2 | 3 | 3 | 1 | 2 | ... | ... | .. | .. | .. | .. | .. | 18 | .. | ... | ... | ... | .. |
| 27 | ....do....brain | 3 | 2 | 4 | 6 | 5 | 3 | 12 | 7 | 4 | 9 | 5 | 1 | ... | .. | .. | .. | .. | .. | 60 | .. | ... | ... | ... | .. |
| 28 | Consumption | 16 | 21 | 29 | 35 | 12 | 13 | 51 | 122 | 375 | 558 | 164 | 192 | 11 | 12 | .. | 1 | 1 | 3 | 1504 | 8 | 57 | 8 | 5 | 7 |
| 29 | Convulsions | 105 | 73 | 30 | 30 | 5 | 5 | 14 | 9 | 22 | 28 | 10 | 10 | 1 | 1 | .. | .. | .. | .. | 332 | .. | 6 | 1 | ... | .. |
| 30 | Cramp | 6 | 1 | 3 | 5 | 1 | 1 | 1 | ... | ... | 1 | 2 | 1 | ... | .. | .. | .. | .. | .. | 22 | .. | ... | ... | ... | .. |
| 31 | Croup | 99 | 66 | 123 | 111 | 17 | 14 | ... | 1 | 1 | 2 | ... | ... | ... | .. | .. | .. | .. | .. | 426 | .. | 3 | .. | ... | 5 |
| 32 | Debility | 3 | ... | 1 | 2 | 2 | ... | ... | ... | 3 | 5 | 2 | 7 | 1 | 1 | .. | .. | .. | .. | 27 | .. | ... | ... | ... | .. |
| 33 | Diabetes | ... | ... | 1 | ... | 1 | ... | ... | 1 | 4 | 1 | 1 | ... | ... | .. | .. | .. | .. | .. | 8 | .. | 1 | ... | ... | .. |

## SECTION OF THE STATE OF VIRGINIA—Continued.

| NATIVITIES. | | | | | SEASON OF DECEASE. | | | | DURATION OF SICKNESS. | | | | WHITES. | | | COLORED. | | | | | | | | | |
|---|---|---|---|---|---|---|---|---|---|---|---|---|---|---|---|---|---|---|---|---|---|---|---|---|---|
| | | | | | | | | | | | | | | | | Slaves. | | | | Free. | | | | | |
| | | | | | | | | | | | | | | | | Black. | | Mulatto. | | Black. | | Mul. | | | |
| California and Territories. | Ireland. | Germany. | Other foreign countries. | Unknown | Spring. | Summer. | Autumn. | Winter. | Under 1 week. | 1 week and under 1 month. | 1 month and under 3 months. | 3 months and over. | Males. | Females. | Total. | M. | F. | M. | F. | M. | F. | M | F. | Aggregate deaths. | |
| | | | | | | | 1 | | | | | 1 | | | | | 1 | | | | | | | 1 | 1 |
| | | | | | 7 | 8 | 7 | 3 | 4 | 11 | 3 | 5 | 10 | 7 | 17 | 3 | 3 | 2 | | | | | | 25 | 2 |
| | | | | | 2 | | 1 | 3 | 1 | 5 | | | 3 | 2 | 5 | 1 | | | | | | | | 6 | 3 |
| | | | | | 1 | 1 | | 1 | 2 | 1 | | | 3 | | 3 | | | | | | | | | 3 | 4 |
| | | | | | 2 | 3 | | | | 1 | 1 | 2 | 3 | 1 | 4 | | 1 | | | | | | | 5 | 5 |
| | 3 | 2 | | 1 | 67 | 40 | 22 | 30 | 23 | 22 | 10 | 22 | 70 | 57 | 127 | 16 | 13 | 1 | | | 2 | | | 159 | 6 |
| | | 2 | | 1 | 19 | 12 | 17 | 20 | 24 | 18 | 6 | 14 | 30 | 30 | 60 | 3 | 4 | 1 | | | | | | 68 | 7 |
| | | | | | | 1 | | | | | 1 | | | 1 | 1 | | | | | | | | | 1 | 8 |
| | | | | | | | | 1 | | | | 1 | 1 | | 1 | | | | | | | | | 1 | 9 |
| | | | | | 13 | 6 | 2 | 5 | 11 | 10 | 3 | 2 | 17 | 6 | 23 | 1 | 1 | | 1 | | | | | 26 | 10 |
| | 2 | | | | 67 | 22 | 15 | 30 | 22 | 81 | 19 | 10 | 53 | 44 | 97 | 19 | 11 | 2 | 2 | 3 | 3 | 1 | | 138 | 11 |
| | | | | | | | 1 | 1 | 1 | | | 1 | 1 | 1 | 2 | | | | | | | | | 2 | 12 |
| | | | | | 1 | 3 | 2 | | 5 | 1 | | | 2 | 4 | 6 | | | | | | | | | 6 | 13 |
| | | | | | 7 | 3 | 3 | 2 | | 5 | | 9 | 5 | 6 | 11 | | 3 | | 1 | | | | | 15 | 14 |
| | | | | | 1 | | | | | 1 | | | | | | | | 1 | | | | | | 1 | 15 |
| | | | | | 16 | 17 | 6 | 7 | 6 | 7 | 3 | 27 | 17 | 13 | 30 | 6 | 8 | | 3 | | | | | 47 | 16 |
| | | | | | 5 | | | 1 | 1 | 2 | 2 | | | 1 | 1 | 4 | | | | 1 | | | | 6 | 17 |
| | | | | | 2 | 1 | 1 | 1 | 1 | | | 4 | 1 | 2 | 3 | | 1 | 1 | | | | | | 5 | 18 |
| | | | | | 1 | | | 1 | | | | | 1 | 1 | 2 | | | | | | | | | 2 | 19 |
| | | | | | 2 | 1 | 1 | | | 2 | 1 | 1 | | 3 | 3 | 1 | | | | | | | | 4 | 20 |
| | | | | | 5 | 1 | 1 | | 7 | | | | | 1 | 1 | 3 | 2 | 1 | | | | | | 7 | 21 |
| | | | | | | 2 | 2 | | 3 | | | | 2 | 2 | 4 | | | | | | | | | 4 | 22 |
| | | | | | 1 | 6 | 4 | | 5 | 5 | 1 | | 5 | 3 | 8 | 1 | | 1 | 1 | | | | | 11 | 23 |
| | | | | | | 1 | | 1 | | 2 | | | | | | 2 | | | | | | | | 2 | 24 |
| | | | | | | 1 | | | 1 | | | | 1 | | 1 | | | | | | | | | 1 | 25 |
| | | | | | 11 | 20 | 33 | 20 | 22 | 57 | 5 | 1 | 36 | 45 | 81 | 2 | 2 | | | | | | | 85 | 26 |
| | | | | | 1 | 2 | | | | 1 | | 2 | 1 | 1 | 2 | 1 | | | | | | | | 3 | 27 |
| | | | | | 2 | | | | | | 1 | 1 | 2 | | 2 | | | | | | | | | 2 | 28 |
| | | | | | 1 | 1 | 1 | | | 1 | | 2 | | 2 | 2 | | 1 | | | | | | | 3 | 29 |
| | | | | | 3 | 1 | | | | 2 | | 2 | 1 | 2 | 3 | | 1 | | | | | | | 4 | 30 |
| | | | | | 9 | 4 | 7 | 5 | 7 | 14 | 2 | 1 | 9 | 12 | 21 | 2 | | | | | 1 | 1 | | 25 | 31 |
| | 1 | | | | 217 | 173 | 139 | 132 | 231 | 164 | 41 | 101 | 246 | 236 | 482 | 98 | 80 | 9 | 15 | 3 | 4 | 6 | 1 | 698 | 32 |
| .... | 19 | 6 | 6 | 2 | 1106 | 842 | 736 | 682 | 1004 | 1070 | 328 | 647 | 1326 | 1278 | 2604 | 335 | 319 | 48 | 64 | 12 | 20 | 14 | 6 | 3422 | |

## STATE OF VIRGINIA—AGGREGATE.

| California and Territories. | Ireland. | Germany. | Other foreign countries. | Unknown | Spring. | Summer. | Autumn. | Winter. | Under 1 week. | 1 week and under 1 month. | 1 month and under 3 months. | 3 months and over. | Males. | Females. | Total. | Slaves Black M. | Slaves Black F. | Slaves Mulatto M. | Slaves Mulatto F. | Free Black M. | Free Black F. | Free Mul. M | Free Mul. F. | Aggregate deaths. | |
|---|---|---|---|---|---|---|---|---|---|---|---|---|---|---|---|---|---|---|---|---|---|---|---|---|---|
| | | | 1 | | 4 | 5 | 2 | 3 | 2 | 5 | 2 | 2 | 8 | 4 | 12 | 2 | | | | | | | | 14 | 1 |
| | 2 | | | | 79 | 65 | 52 | 65 | 196 | 31 | 13 | 10 | 103 | 21 | 124 | 70 | 56 | 5 | 3 | 4 | 2 | 2 | 2 | 268 | 2 |
| | 1 | | | | 62 | 31 | 21 | 59 | 109 | 41 | 7 | 10 | 13 | 38 | 51 | 37 | 59 | 2 | 7 | 5 | 8 | 1 | 2 | 172 | 3 |
| | 3 | | 1 | | 29 | 55 | 17 | 13 | 117 | | | | 52 | 21 | 73 | 31 | 3 | 2 | 2 | 2 | | 3 | 1 | 117 | 4 |
| | 1 | | | | 6 | 2 | 5 | 3 | 13 | 3 | | | 8 | 7 | 15 | | 1 | 1 | | | | | | 17 | 5 |
| | 1 | | | | 1 | 1 | | 1 | 3 | | | | 2 | | 2 | 1 | | | | | | | | 3 | 6 |
| | | | | | 3 | | 3 | 1 | 3 | 1 | 2 | | 5 | 1 | 6 | | 1 | | | | | | | 7 | 7 |
| | | | | | | | | 1 | 1 | | | | 1 | | 1 | | | | | | | | | 1 | 8 |
| | 4 | | 4 | | 33 | 35 | 25 | 32 | 90 | 10 | 2 | 7 | 40 | 21 | 61 | 22 | 32 | 1 | 5 | 2 | 1 | 1 | | 125 | 9 |
| | | 1 | 1 | | 21 | 16 | 7 | 19 | 10 | 13 | 8 | 30 | 15 | 14 | 29 | 15 | 18 | 1 | 2 | | | 1 | | 66 | 10 |
| | | | | | 2 | | | 2 | 1 | 3 | | | 2 | | 2 | 1 | 1 | | | | | | | 4 | 11 |
| | | | | | 3 | 2 | 2 | 3 | 1 | 6 | 2 | 1 | 4 | 1 | 5 | 4 | 1 | | | | | | | 10 | 12 |
| | | | 1 | | 8 | 26 | 21 | 14 | 12 | 23 | 15 | 13 | 19 | 18 | 37 | 12 | 17 | 1 | 1 | | 1 | | | 69 | 13 |
| | | | | | 22 | 14 | 13 | 14 | 24 | 26 | 1 | 9 | 24 | 13 | 37 | 17 | 6 | 1 | 3 | | | | | 64 | 14 |
| | | | 2 | | 22 | 16 | 13 | 21 | 15 | 24 | 9 | 19 | 26 | 16 | 42 | 17 | 11 | | | 1 | | | 1 | 72 | 15 |
| | 2 | | 1 | | 20 | 31 | 28 | 36 | 7 | 8 | 10 | 79 | 36 | 52 | 88 | 7 | 18 | | 2 | | | | | 115 | 16 |
| | | | | | 1 | | | | | | | 1 | | 2 | 2 | 1 | | | | | | | | 3 | 17 |
| | 1 | | | | 146 | 76 | 37 | 73 | 94 | 155 | 36 | 41 | 61 | 52 | 113 | 102 | 110 | 9 | 7 | 5 | 2 | | | 348 | 18 |
| | | | | | 1 | | | | | 1 | | | | | | 1 | | | | | | | | 1 | 19 |
| | 1 | 2 | 1 | | 74 | 74 | 56 | 57 | 144 | 78 | 13 | 4 | | 147 | 147 | | 97 | | 8 | | 5 | | 6 | 263 | 20 |
| | 5 | 11 | 15 | 2 | 18 | 612 | 152 | 11 | 683 | 68 | 4 | 5 | 218 | 149 | 367 | 189 | 113 | 25 | 8 | 37 | 33 | 10 | 13 | 795 | 21 |
| | | | | | 8 | 66 | 57 | 8 | 46 | 50 | 20 | 12 | 56 | 49 | 105 | 18 | 18 | 3 | 1 | | 2 | 3 | | 150 | 22 |
| | | | | | 5 | 16 | 13 | 5 | 24 | 12 | 1 | 2 | 12 | 17 | 29 | 6 | 3 | 1 | | 1 | 1 | | 1 | 42 | 23 |
| | | | | | 1 | | | 1 | 1 | 1 | | | | 2 | 2 | | | | | | | | | 2 | 24 |
| | 1 | 1 | 3 | | 22 | 19 | 23 | 15 | 64 | 15 | 1 | | 26 | 16 | 42 | 22 | 11 | 1 | | 2 | | | 2 | 80 | 25 |
| | | | | | 3 | 9 | 4 | 2 | 14 | 2 | | | 3 | 2 | 5 | 9 | 4 | | | | | | | 18 | 26 |
| | | | | | 23 | 18 | 13 | 5 | 31 | 19 | 4 | 5 | 13 | 15 | 28 | 18 | 13 | 2 | | | | | | 61 | 27 |
| | 10 | 3 | 14 | | 498 | 444 | 365 | 288 | 41 | 139 | 187 | 1139 | 433 | 612 | 1045 | 191 | 273 | 9 | 29 | 22 | 28 | 4 | 15 | 1616 | 28 |
| | 2 | 1 | 1 | | 102 | 101 | 73 | 59 | 224 | 65 | 6 | 25 | 72 | 69 | 141 | 100 | 76 | 7 | 8 | 6 | 2 | 2 | 1 | 343 | 29 |
| | | | | | 8 | 7 | 3 | 3 | 18 | 2 | | | 7 | 3 | 10 | 4 | 5 | 1 | | 1 | 1 | | | 22 | 30 |
| | | | | | 154 | 75 | 106 | 99 | 321 | 98 | 6 | 2 | 167 | 115 | 282 | 68 | 63 | 4 | 11 | 1 | 4 | | 1 | 434 | 31 |
| | | | | | 5 | 14 | 2 | 6 | 1 | 4 | 8 | 10 | 5 | 10 | 15 | 5 | 5 | 1 | | | | | | 27 | 32 |
| | | | | | 3 | 2 | 1 | 3 | | 2 | 1 | 5 | 5 | 2 | 7 | 2 | | | | | | | | 9 | 33 |

CLASSIFICATION OF DEATHS IN THE

| | Cause of death. | AGES. Under 1. | | 1 and under 5. | | 5 and under 10. | | 10 and under 20. | | 20 and under 50. | | 50 and under 80. | | 80 and under 100. | | 100 & over. | | Age unknown. | | NATIVITIES. Born in State. | N. England States. | Middle States. | Southern States. | Southwest'n States. | Northwest'n States. |
|---|---|---|---|---|---|---|---|---|---|---|---|---|---|---|---|---|---|---|---|---|---|---|---|---|---|
| | | M. | F. | M. | F. | M. | F. | M. | F. | M. | F. | M. | F. | M. | F. | M | F | M | F | | | | | | |
| 1 | Diarrhœa | 37 | 30 | 62 | 58 | 9 | 12 | 8 | 7 | 31 | 26 | 26 | 11 | 3 | 4 | | | | | 315 | | 6 | | | |
| 2 | Dirt eating | | | | | | | 2 | | 1 | | | | | | | | | | 3 | | | | | |
| 3 | Dropsy | 10 | 12 | 44 | 28 | 32 | 19 | 42 | 45 | 80 | 137 | 219 | 156 | 21 | 11 | 2 | 3 | | | 818 | | 33 | 2 | | 3 |
| 4 | Dysentery | 63 | 65 | 101 | 83 | 36 | 19 | 31 | 20 | 29 | 29 | 19 | 34 | 5 | 3 | | | 5 | 1 | 518 | | 10 | 2 | | 8 |
| 5 | Dyspepsia | | | 2 | 1 | 1 | 2 | 2 | | 8 | 10 | 15 | 6 | 1 | | | | | | 45 | 1 | 2 | | | |
| 6 | Epilepsy | | 1 | 2 | 1 | | | 2 | 1 | | 1 | 1 | 1 | | | | | | | 9 | | 1 | | | |
| 7 | Erysipelas | 5 | 10 | 6 | 5 | | 3 | 4 | 6 | 12 | 10 | 7 | 6 | 1 | | | | | | 71 | | 1 | 1 | | 1 |
| 8 | Fever, not specified | 20 | 18 | 41 | 42 | 19 | 30 | 54 | 58 | 91 | 87 | 32 | 24 | | | | | 1 | 2 | 490 | 2 | 10 | 3 | 4 | 4 |
| 9 | ..do..bilious | 14 | 9 | 27 | 35 | 20 | 17 | 18 | 16 | 49 | 37 | 21 | 18 | | 3 | | | 6 | 3 | 281 | | 8 | | 2 | |
| 10 | ..do..brain | 7 | 3 | 9 | 8 | 9 | 2 | 7 | 6 | 8 | 6 | 2 | | | | | | | | 64 | 1 | 1 | 1 | | |
| 11 | ..do..catarrhal | 4 | 6 | 4 | 5 | | 1 | 1 | 1 | 1 | | 1 | 1 | 1 | 1 | | | | | 26 | | 1 | | | |
| 12 | ..do..congestive | 1 | 2 | 9 | 7 | 3 | 5 | 10 | 13 | 12 | 9 | 4 | 4 | | | | | | | 75 | 1 | 1 | 1 | | 1 |
| 13 | ..do..inflammatory | | | | | | | | | | 1 | 1 | 2 | | | | | | | 4 | | | | | |
| 14 | ..do..intermittent | 3 | 2 | 2 | 5 | 3 | 4 | 3 | 2 | 4 | 2 | 8 | 5 | 1 | | | | | | 42 | | 1 | 1 | | |
| 15 | ..do..puerperal | | | | | | | | 4 | | 21 | | | | | | | | | 22 | | 1 | | | 2 |
| 16 | ..do..remittent | | | 1 | | | | 1 | | | 1 | | | | | | | | | 3 | | | | | |
| 17 | ..do..scarlet | 33 | 17 | 126 | 117 | 85 | 73 | 16 | 37 | 7 | 8 | 2 | 1 | | | | | 1 | | 499 | | 9 | | | 9 |
| 18 | ..do..typhus | 8 | 7 | 36 | 29 | 36 | 28 | 94 | 117 | 183 | 114 | 50 | 36 | 3 | 6 | | | | | 717 | 3 | 14 | 5 | 1 | 3 |
| 19 | Fracture | | | | 1 | | | | | | | | | | | | | | | 1 | | | | | |
| 20 | Frozen | | | | | | | 1 | | 2 | 1 | 5 | | 1 | 1 | | | | | 11 | | | | | |
| 21 | Gout | | | | | | | | | | | 1 | 1 | | | | | | | 2 | | | | | |
| 22 | Gravel | 1 | | | | | | 4 | | 1 | 1 | 31 | 1 | 7 | | 1 | | | | 38 | 1 | 6 | | 2 | |
| 23 | Head, disease of | 1 | 2 | 4 | 1 | | | | 1 | 2 | 3 | 3 | 3 | | | | | | | 18 | | 1 | | | 1 |
| 24 | Heart....do | 5 | 5 | 2 | 2 | 2 | 2 | 6 | 8 | 12 | 16 | 30 | 12 | 1 | | | | | | 98 | 3 | 2 | | | |
| 25 | Heat | | | | | | | 2 | | | | | 1 | | | | | | | 2 | | 1 | | | |
| 26 | Hemorrhage | 1 | | 2 | | 1 | 2 | 8 | 2 | 12 | 18 | 5 | 6 | | 1 | | | | | 50 | | 3 | | | |
| 27 | Hernia | 1 | | 1 | 1 | 1 | | 1 | | 7 | | 9 | | 3 | | | | | | 24 | | | | | |
| 28 | Hives | 13 | 10 | 4 | 1 | 1 | | | | | | | | | | | | | | 28 | | 1 | | | |
| 29 | Hooping cough | 30 | 38 | 54 | 73 | 8 | 12 | | | | 1 | | | | | | | | | 212 | | 3 | | | 1 |
| 30 | Hydrocephalus | 12 | 8 | 12 | 11 | 2 | 3 | | 2 | 3 | | 1 | 4 | | | | | | | 55 | | 2 | | | 1 |
| 31 | Hydrophobia | | | | 1 | | | | | | 1 | 1 | 1 | | | | | | | 4 | | | | | |
| 32 | Inflammation | 3 | 5 | 13 | 7 | 2 | 5 | 4 | 7 | 5 | 8 | 4 | 1 | | | | | | | 57 | 1 | 4 | | | 2 |
| 33 | ....do....bowels | 18 | 12 | 20 | 20 | 7 | 3 | 4 | 4 | 23 | 16 | 18 | 12 | 1 | 1 | | | | | 148 | 2 | 5 | | | 1 |
| 34 | ....do....brain | 38 | 18 | 32 | 32 | 11 | 16 | 21 | 13 | 18 | 15 | 9 | 3 | | | | | | | 215 | 2 | 3 | | | 4 |
| 35 | ....do....stomach | | 2 | | 2 | | | | | | 6 | 5 | 3 | | | | | | | 16 | | 1 | | 1 | |
| 36 | Influenza | 2 | 2 | 3 | | | | | 1 | | 2 | 1 | 1 | | | | | | | 11 | | 1 | | | |
| 37 | Insanity | | | | | | | | | | 1 | 3 | 2 | 1 | 1 | | | | | 9 | | | | | |
| 38 | Intemperance | | | | | | | | | 35 | 7 | 18 | 3 | 1 | 1 | | | | | 61 | | 1 | 1 | | |
| 39 | Jaundice | 5 | 3 | 1 | | 2 | 2 | 2 | 2 | 4 | 2 | 2 | 6 | 2 | 1 | | | | | 32 | 1 | 1 | | | |
| 40 | Kidneys, disease of | | | 1 | | | 2 | | | 1 | 3 | 8 | 1 | 1 | | | | | | 16 | | | 1 | | |
| 41 | Killed | | | 2 | 1 | 1 | 1 | 5 | | 10 | | 2 | 1 | | | | | | | 21 | | 1 | | | 1 |
| 42 | Lightning | | | | | 1 | | | | 3 | 1 | 2 | | | | | | | | 7 | | | | | |
| 43 | Liver, disease of | 2 | 2 | 3 | 3 | | 1 | 4 | 4 | 22 | 25 | 20 | 9 | | | | | | 1 | 89 | 2 | 5 | | | |
| 44 | Lockjaw | 4 | 3 | 3 | | 4 | 2 | 3 | 4 | 7 | 1 | | | | | | | | | 30 | 1 | | | | |
| 45 | Lungs, disease of | 3 | 1 | 18 | 11 | 4 | 1 | 3 | 11 | 11 | 27 | 14 | 14 | 2 | | | | | 1 | 114 | | 3 | 1 | 1 | |
| 46 | Malformation | 2 | 1 | 2 | 1 | | | | | | | | | | | | | | | 6 | | | | | |
| 47 | Mania-a-potu | | | | | | | | | 6 | 1 | 2 | | | | | | | | 8 | | | | | |
| 48 | Marasmus | 1 | 4 | | 1 | 1 | | | | 2 | | 1 | | | | | | | | 10 | | | | | |
| 49 | Measles | 15 | 14 | 46 | 49 | 14 | 10 | 14 | 13 | 17 | 19 | 4 | 7 | | | | | | | 212 | | 6 | | | 2 |
| 50 | Mortification | 1 | | | 1 | | | | | | 1 | 1 | 1 | | 1 | | | | | 5 | | | | | |
| 51 | Mumps | 1 | | | 1 | 1 | | 1 | 1 | 2 | 1 | | | | | | | | | 8 | | | | | |
| 52 | Murder | | | 1 | | | | 2 | | 4 | | 5 | 1 | 2 | 2 | | | | | 16 | | 1 | | | |
| 53 | Neuralgia | | | | | | 1 | | | 3 | 3 | 5 | 1 | | | | | | | 12 | | 1 | | | |
| 54 | Old age | | | | | | | | | | | 140 | 146 | 236 | 282 | 23 | 37 | 3 | | 790 | | 46 | 11 | | |
| 55 | Paralysis | 1 | 1 | 1 | | 1 | 1 | 1 | 1 | 13 | 17 | 65 | 66 | 21 | 14 | | | | | 180 | | 18 | | | |
| 56 | Piles | | | | | | | | | 1 | 1 | 1 | | | | | | | | 2 | | | 1 | | |
| 57 | Pleurisy | 7 | 2 | 18 | 8 | 7 | 4 | 28 | 21 | 91 | 56 | 59 | 46 | 6 | 5 | | | 2 | 1 | 348 | 2 | 6 | 1 | | 1 |
| 58 | Pneumonia | 41 | 38 | 59 | 59 | 22 | 15 | 56 | 55 | 173 | 103 | 93 | 67 | 8 | 9 | | | | | 784 | 1 | 8 | | | 1 |
| 59 | Poison | 3 | | 6 | 8 | 2 | 3 | 1 | 3 | 9 | 10 | 3 | 1 | | 1 | | | | | 48 | | 1 | | | |
| 60 | Prematurity of birth | | 1 | | | | | | | | | | | | | | | | | 1 | | | | | |
| 61 | Quinsy | | 1 | 1 | | 2 | 1 | | | 4 | 4 | 1 | 1 | | | | | | | 14 | | 1 | | | |
| 62 | Rheumatism | | 1 | 1 | 1 | 2 | 6 | 3 | 4 | 8 | 12 | 18 | 22 | 2 | | | | | 1 | 74 | | 2 | 1 | | 1 |
| 63 | Rickets | | | 6 | 1 | | | | | | | | | | | | | | | 7 | | | | | |
| 64 | Scrofula | 11 | 5 | 31 | 19 | 9 | 16 | 23 | 26 | 32 | 30 | 21 | 14 | 3 | 1 | | | | | 234 | | 4 | 2 | | 1 |
| 65 | Scurvy | | | | | | | 1 | | 1 | 1 | | | | | | | | 1 | 2 | | 1 | 1 | | |
| 66 | Small pox | 1 | 1 | 5 | 3 | | 1 | 3 | 2 | 15 | 5 | 5 | 2 | | 3 | | | | | 43 | | | 1 | | 1 |
| 67 | Spine, disease of | 4 | 3 | 6 | 8 | | | 5 | 2 | 4 | 3 | 2 | 3 | | | | | | | 38 | | 2 | | | |
| 68 | Stillborn | 7 | 8 | | | | | | | | | | | | | | | | | 15 | | | | | |
| 69 | Stomach, disease of | 2 | 2 | | 1 | | | | | 1 | 4 | 6 | 3 | | | | | | | 17 | | 1 | | | 1 |
| 70 | Suffocation | 56 | 67 | 16 | 13 | 1 | 1 | | | | | 1 | 1 | | | | | | | 156 | | | | | |
| 71 | Suicide | | | | | | | 2 | 1 | 9 | 5 | 1 | | 2 | | | | | | 18 | | 2 | | | |
| 72 | Summer complaint | 14 | 8 | 8 | 7 | 1 | 2 | | | | | | | | | | | | 1 | 41 | | | | | |
| 73 | Teething | 23 | 27 | 55 | 55 | 2 | | | | | | | | | | | | | | 162 | | | | | |
| 74 | Tetanus | 2 | 2 | 1 | | | | 1 | | 2 | | | | | | | | | | 8 | | | | | |
| 75 | Tetter | | | | | | | | | 1 | | | 1 | 1 | | | | | | 3 | | | | | |

STATE OF VIRGINIA—AGGREGATE—Continued.

| NATIVITIES. | | | | | SEASON OF DECEASE. | | | | DURATION OF SICKNESS. | | | | WHITES. | | | COLORED. | | | | | | | | | |
|---|---|---|---|---|---|---|---|---|---|---|---|---|---|---|---|---|---|---|---|---|---|---|---|---|---|
| | | | | | | | | | | | | | | | | Slaves. | | | | Free. | | | | | |
| | | | | | | | | | | | | | | | | Black. | | Mulatto. | | Black. | | Mul. | | | |
| California and Territories. | Ireland. | Germany. | Other foreign countries. | Unknown. | Spring. | Summer. | Autumn. | Winter. | Under 1 week. | 1 week and under 1 month. | 1 month and under 3 months. | 3 months and over. | Males. | Females. | Total. | M. | F. | M. | F. | M. | F. | M | F. | Aggregate deaths. | |
| | 1 | 1 | 1 | | 38 | 134 | 116 | 36 | 65 | 134 | 60 | 56 | 106 | 78 | 184 | 60 | 59 | 6 | 4 | 4 | 3 | | 4 | 324 | 1 |
| | | | | | | 2 | 1 | | | 1 | | 1 | 1 | | 1 | 1 | | 1 | | | | | | 3 | 2 |
| | 2 | 1 | 2 | | 240 | 279 | 196 | 146 | 44 | 100 | 160 | 505 | 231 | 213 | 444 | 191 | 160 | 9 | 15 | 10 | 15 | 9 | 8 | 861 | 3 |
| | 3 | 1 | 1 | | 51 | 201 | 246 | 41 | 96 | 319 | 51 | 41 | 188 | 174 | 362 | 86 | 69 | 4 | 5 | 8 | 5 | 2 | 2 | 543 | 4 |
| | | | | | 13 | 14 | 11 | 10 | 1 | 8 | 5 | 30 | 23 | 17 | 40 | 5 | 1 | 1 | | | 1 | | | 48 | 5 |
| | | | | | 8 | 2 | 3 | 2 | 8 | 1 | | 1 | 2 | 3 | 5 | 3 | 2 | | | | | | | 10 | 6 |
| | | 1 | | | 26 | 15 | 15 | 19 | 17 | 36 | 14 | 5 | 27 | 33 | 60 | 8 | 4 | | 3 | | | | | 75 | 7 |
| 1 | 1 | | 3 | 1 | 141 | 109 | 148 | 115 | 81 | 301 | 93 | 35 | 156 | 153 | 309 | 88 | 95 | 9 | 8 | 4 | 2 | 1 | 3 | 519 | 8 |
| | 2 | | | | 29 | 59 | 170 | 35 | 65 | 173 | 31 | 8 | 91 | 81 | 172 | 48 | 47 | 8 | 2 | 3 | 6 | 5 | 2 | 293 | 9 |
| | | | | | 18 | 18 | 21 | 9 | 36 | 26 | 2 | 3 | 25 | 17 | 42 | 14 | 7 | 1 | 1 | 1 | | 1 | | 67 | 10 |
| | | | | | 14 | 5 | 3 | 5 | 9 | 10 | 4 | 3 | 7 | 9 | 16 | 4 | 5 | | | | | 1 | 1 | 27 | 11 |
| | | | | | 17 | 15 | 37 | 9 | 30 | 36 | 8 | 2 | 19 | 23 | 42 | 18 | 17 | 1 | | 1 | | | | 79 | 12 |
| | | | | | 1 | 1 | 1 | 1 | 2 | 2 | | | | 1 | 1 | 1 | 1 | | 1 | | | | | 4 | 13 |
| | | | | | 14 | 5 | 16 | 8 | 10 | 19 | 9 | 2 | 11 | 10 | 21 | 13 | 6 | | 1 | | 2 | | 1 | 44 | 14 |
| | | | | | 10 | 7 | 4 | 4 | 7 | 16 | 2 | | | 19 | 19 | | 3 | | 3 | | | | | 25 | 15 |
| | | | | | | 1 | 2 | | | 1 | 2 | | | 1 | 1 | 1 | | | | 1 | | | | 3 | 16 |
| | 4 | 1 | | 1 | 147 | 80 | 91 | 203 | 260 | 224 | 24 | 6 | 222 | 204 | 426 | 42 | 36 | 6 | 9 | | 1 | | 3 | 523 | 17 |
| | 1 | | 2 | 1 | 194 | 155 | 243 | 154 | 73 | 497 | 134 | 27 | 219 | 154 | 373 | 176 | 157 | 8 | 17 | 3 | 8 | 4 | 1 | 747 | 18 |
| | | | | | | | | 1 | | 1 | | | | 1 | 1 | | | | | | | | | 1 | 19 |
| | | | | | 3 | 1 | 2 | 5 | 6 | 1 | | | 5 | | 5 | 3 | 2 | 1 | | | | | | 11 | 20 |
| | | | | | | | 2 | | | | 1 | 1 | 1 | 1 | 2 | | | | | | | | | 2 | 21 |
| | | | | | 12 | 11 | 11 | 13 | 4 | 19 | 5 | 17 | 30 | 1 | 31 | 15 | | | | | 1 | | | 47 | 22 |
| | | | | | 7 | 1 | 4 | 6 | 7 | 5 | 2 | 4 | 6 | 4 | 10 | 4 | 6 | | | | | | | 20 | 23 |
| | | | | | 35 | 33 | 17 | 18 | 28 | 13 | 21 | 36 | 34 | 30 | 64 | 23 | 12 | 1 | 2 | | | | 1 | 103 | 24 |
| | | | | | | 2 | 1 | | 3 | | | | 2 | | 2 | | 1 | | | | | | | 3 | 25 |
| | | | | | 17 | 16 | 10 | 10 | 18 | 15 | 6 | 12 | 10 | 13 | 23 | 9 | 15 | 2 | | 3 | | | 1 | 53 | 26 |
| | | | | | 7 | 6 | 5 | 6 | 10 | 5 | 5 | 2 | 5 | 1 | 6 | 17 | | 1 | | | | | | 24 | 27 |
| | | | | | 6 | 8 | 8 | 7 | 17 | 10 | | 1 | 17 | 11 | 28 | 1 | | | | | | | | 29 | 28 |
| | | | | | 55 | 70 | 56 | 29 | 46 | 92 | 41 | 19 | 45 | 65 | 110 | 37 | 46 | 5 | 4 | 4 | 6 | 1 | 3 | 216 | 29 |
| | | | | | 18 | 12 | 17 | 11 | 10 | 27 | 14 | 6 | 17 | 20 | 37 | 11 | 6 | 2 | 2 | | | | | 58 | 30 |
| | | | | | 1 | 1 | 1 | 1 | | 2 | 2 | | | 2 | 2 | 1 | 1 | | | | | | | 4 | 31 |
| | | | | | 13 | 17 | 21 | 13 | 20 | 31 | 9 | 4 | 21 | 18 | 39 | 9 | 12 | | 2 | 1 | 1 | | | 64 | 32 |
| | | | 3 | | 28 | 63 | 40 | 26 | 46 | 73 | 18 | 15 | 51 | 44 | 95 | 35 | 18 | 8 | 4 | 2 | | | 2 | 159 | 33 |
| | 1 | 1 | | | 55 | 66 | 63 | 41 | 86 | 98 | 17 | 9 | 90 | 64 | 154 | 32 | 27 | 5 | 1 | | 3 | 2 | 2 | 226 | 34 |
| | | | | | 4 | 9 | 3 | 2 | 4 | 4 | 6 | 4 | 4 | 8 | 12 | 1 | 3 | | 1 | | 1 | | | 18 | 35 |
| | | | | | 4 | 3 | 2 | 3 | 3 | 4 | 2 | 3 | 2 | 4 | 6 | 4 | 1 | | 1 | | | | | 12 | 36 |
| | | | | | 1 | 1 | 3 | 4 | 2 | 2 | 2 | 3 | 3 | 1 | 4 | 1 | 3 | | | | 1 | | | 9 | 37 |
| | | | 1 | 1 | 17 | 8 | 9 | 26 | 19 | 13 | 4 | 9 | 40 | 7 | 47 | 9 | 1 | 2 | | 2 | 2 | 2 | | 65 | 38 |
| | | | | | 11 | 8 | 11 | 9 | 4 | 16 | 5 | 6 | 12 | 14 | 26 | 5 | 1 | 1 | 1 | | | | | 34 | 39 |
| | | | | | 8 | 2 | 8 | 4 | 3 | 3 | 5 | 4 | 10 | 4 | 14 | 1 | 1 | | 1 | | | | | 17 | 40 |
| | | | | | 4 | 2 | 9 | 8 | 20 | | 2 | | 12 | 2 | 14 | 5 | 1 | 1 | | | | 2 | | 23 | 41 |
| | | | | | | 6 | 1 | | 6 | | | | 1 | | 1 | 5 | 1 | | | | | | | 7 | 42 |
| | | | | | 25 | 31 | 20 | 19 | 6 | 22 | 15 | 42 | 38 | 35 | 73 | 11 | 10 | 1 | | | | 1 | | 96 | 43 |
| | | | | | 9 | 8 | 5 | 9 | 19 | 10 | | | 2 | 3 | 5 | 15 | 8 | 3 | | | | | | 31 | 44 |
| | 1 | | 1 | | 48 | 30 | 23 | 20 | 14 | 47 | 25 | 32 | 30 | 40 | 70 | 23 | 24 | 1 | 1 | 1 | | | 1 | 121 | 45 |
| | | | | | 2 | 1 | 2 | 1 | 2 | 2 | | 1 | | 1 | 1 | 4 | 1 | | | | | | | 6 | 46 |
| | 1 | | | | 2 | 4 | 2 | 1 | 4 | 3 | 2 | | 8 | 1 | 9 | | | | | | | | | 9 | 47 |
| | | | | | 2 | 4 | 2 | 1 | | | 2 | 7 | 4 | 1 | 5 | 1 | 3 | | 1 | | | | | 10 | 48 |
| | 1 | | 1 | | 30 | 87 | 75 | 21 | 32 | 106 | 30 | 25 | 61 | 56 | 117 | 42 | 50 | 6 | 4 | 1 | | | 2 | 222 | 49 |
| | | | | 1 | 1 | 3 | 1 | 1 | 3 | 1 | 1 | | 2 | 2 | 4 | | 2 | | | | | | | 6 | 50 |
| | | | | | 4 | | 1 | 3 | 2 | 5 | | 1 | 4 | 2 | 6 | 1 | 1 | | | | | | | 8 | 51 |
| | | | | | 4 | 6 | 2 | 5 | 12 | 2 | 1 | 2 | 8 | | 8 | 5 | 2 | | 1 | 1 | | | | 17 | 52 |
| | | | | | 6 | 5 | 2 | | 1 | 5 | 3 | 3 | 8 | 4 | 12 | | 1 | | | | | | | 13 | 53 |
| | 6 | 4 | 7 | 3 | 292 | 202 | 166 | 203 | 114 | 139 | 58 | 153 | 154 | 209 | 363 | 202 | 225 | 24 | 9 | 15 | 16 | 7 | 6 | 867 | 54 |
| | 1 | 2 | | 2 | 62 | 47 | 41 | 49 | 55 | 42 | 24 | 65 | 73 | 69 | 142 | 24 | 20 | 4 | 3 | 2 | 5 | | 3 | 203 | 55 |
| | | | | | 1 | 1 | | 1 | | | 1 | 1 | 2 | 1 | 3 | | | | | | | | | 3 | 56 |
| | | | 3 | | 172 | 45 | 56 | 87 | 90 | 205 | 38 | 18 | 92 | 83 | 175 | 101 | 51 | 8 | 5 | 9 | 4 | 8 | | 361 | 57 |
| | 3 | 1 | | | 350 | 155 | 81 | 193 | 169 | 455 | 78 | 56 | 162 | 127 | 289 | 267 | 197 | 11 | 13 | 8 | 7 | 4 | 2 | 798 | 58 |
| | 1 | | | | 10 | 19 | 13 | 8 | 13 | 13 | 6 | 16 | 2 | 6 | 8 | 21 | 20 | 1 | | | | | | 50 | 59 |
| | | | | | 1 | | | | 1 | | | | | | | | 1 | | | | | | | 1 | 60 |
| | | | | | 5 | 4 | 4 | 2 | 9 | 5 | | 1 | 5 | 5 | 10 | 2 | 1 | 1 | 1 | | | | | 15 | 61 |
| | | 2 | 1 | | 24 | 28 | 11 | 18 | 4 | 21 | 4 | 47 | 17 | 28 | 45 | 16 | 14 | 1 | 3 | | 2 | | | 81 | 62 |
| | | | | | 3 | 1 | 1 | 2 | 1 | 1 | 1 | 4 | | | | 5 | 1 | 1 | | | | | | 7 | 63 |
| | | | | | 75 | 75 | 48 | 41 | 10 | 24 | 36 | 162 | 37 | 26 | 63 | 84 | 75 | 2 | 9 | 5 | | 2 | 1 | 241 | 64 |
| | | | | | 3 | 1 | | | | 3 | | 1 | 2 | 2 | 4 | | | | | | | | | 4 | 65 |
| | 1 | | | | 18 | 8 | 8 | 12 | 11 | 28 | 3 | 2 | 15 | 11 | 26 | 10 | 5 | 1 | 1 | 2 | | 1 | | 46 | 66 |
| | | | | | 9 | 14 | 7 | 10 | 6 | 5 | 2 | 22 | 9 | 12 | 21 | 10 | 6 | 1 | 1 | | | 1 | | 40 | 67 |
| | | | | | 9 | | | 6 | | | | | 5 | 4 | 9 | 2 | 3 | | 1 | | | | | 15 | 68 |
| | | | | | 7 | 2 | 8 | 2 | 1 | 8 | 3 | 4 | 4 | 9 | 13 | 4 | 1 | 1 | | | | | | 19 | 69 |
| | | | | | 46 | 38 | 28 | 34 | 156 | | | | 9 | 10 | 19 | 62 | 67 | 3 | 5 | | | | | 156 | 70 |
| | | | | | 4 | 5 | 6 | 4 | 13 | | | 1 | 13 | 5 | 18 | 7 | | | 11 | | | | | 20 | 71 |
| | | | | | 4 | 12 | 17 | 8 | 7 | 14 | 8 | 6 | 15 | 12 | 27 | | 6 | 1 | | | | | | 41 | 72 |
| | | | | | 21 | 64 | 58 | 14 | 27 | 59 | 42 | 29 | 28 | 34 | 62 | 46 | 38 | 3 | 6 | | 2 | 3 | 2 | 162 | 73 |
| | | | | | 2 | 1 | 2 | 3 | 2 | 2 | | | | | | 6 | 2 | | | | | | | 8 | 74 |
| | | | | | 1 | 1 | | 1 | 1 | 1 | | | 2 | | 2 | | 1 | | | | | | | 3 | 75 |

## CLASSIFICATION OF DEATHS IN

| | Cause of Death. | AGES. | | | | | | | | | | | | | | | | | | NATIVITIES. | | | | | |
|---|---|---|---|---|---|---|---|---|---|---|---|---|---|---|---|---|---|---|---|---|---|---|---|---|---|
| | | Under 1. | | 1 and under 5. | | 5 and under 10. | | 10 and under 20. | | 20 and under 50. | | 50 and under 80. | | 80 and under 100. | | 100 & over. | | Age unknown. | | Born in State. | N. England States. | Middle States. | Southern States. | Southwest'n States. | Northwest'n States. |
| | | M. | F. | M. | F. | M. | F. | M. | F. | M. | F. | M. | F. | M | F. | M | F. | M | F | | | | | | |
| 1 | Throat, disease of | 6 | 3 | 18 | 15 | 18 | 23 | 15 | 21 | 6 | 11 | 4 | 3 | | | | | | | 140 | | 8 | | | |
| 2 | Thrush | 15 | 12 | 6 | 7 | | | | 1 | | | | | | | | | | | 41 | | | | | |
| 3 | Tumor | 5 | | 2 | | 1 | 1 | | 1 | 1 | 4 | | 1 | | | | | | | 16 | | | | | |
| 4 | Ulcer | 1 | | | | | | 1 | | 4 | | 3 | 1 | | | | | | | 9 | | | | | |
| 5 | Uterus, disease of | | | | 4 | | | | | | 16 | | 4 | | | | | | | 24 | | | | | |
| 6 | Venereal | | | | | | | | | 1 | 3 | 1 | | | | | | | | 5 | | | | | |
| 7 | White swelling | | | | | | | 4 | | 1 | 2 | 2 | 2 | | 1 | | | | | 12 | | | | | |
| 8 | Worms | 10 | 6 | 69 | 68 | 17 | 13 | 1 | 1 | 1 | 2 | | | | | | | | | 187 | | 1 | | | |
| 9 | Unknown | 725 | 670 | 432 | 390 | 99 | 75 | 113 | 152 | 335 | 420 | 344 | 340 | 42 | 45 | 2 | 1 | 10 | 8 | 4122 | 5 | 44 | 12 | | 2 |
| | Total | 1722 | 1485 | 1877 | 1739 | 610 | 547 | 831 | 978 | 2305 | 2486 | 1913 | 1590 | 414 | 431 | 31 | 44 | 32 | 24 | 18238 | 43 | 417 | 75 | 17 | 72 |

## CLASSIFICATION OF DEATHS IN

| | Cause of Death. | Under 1 M. | Under 1 F. | 1–5 M. | 1–5 F. | 5–10 M. | 5–10 F. | 10–20 M. | 10–20 F. | 20–50 M. | 20–50 F. | 50–80 M. | 50–80 F. | 80–100 M | 80–100 F. | 100 M | 100 F. | Unk. M | Unk. F | Born in State. | N. England States. | Middle States. | Southern States. | Southwest'n States. | Northwest'n States. |
|---|---|---|---|---|---|---|---|---|---|---|---|---|---|---|---|---|---|---|---|---|---|---|---|---|---|
| 1 | Abscess | 1 | | | | | | 1 | | 1 | 1 | | | | | | | | | 2 | | 1 | | | |
| 2 | Accident, not specif'd | 3 | 2 | 4 | 2 | 3 | 2 | 5 | | 22 | 2 | 4 | 1 | | | | | | | 14 | 5 | 14 | | 1 | |
| 3 | ....do...burned | 1 | | 3 | 4 | 2 | | | | | | | | | | | | | | 6 | | 1 | | | 1 |
| 4 | ....do...drowned | | 1 | 7 | 2 | 5 | 2 | 4 | 2 | 8 | 1 | 1 | | | | | | | | 15 | 3 | 3 | | | 4 |
| 5 | ....do...scalded | 2 | | | 1 | | | | | | | | | | | | | | | 2 | 1 | | | | |
| 6 | ....do...shot | | | | | | | | | 4 | | | | | | | | | | | | 1 | | | |
| 7 | Apoplexy | | | | | 1 | | | | 2 | 1 | 4 | | | | | | | | | 1 | 5 | | | |
| 8 | Asthma | 2 | | | | | | | | 1 | | | | | | | | | | 1 | 1 | 1 | | | |
| 9 | Bowels, disease of | 2 | 3 | 2 | | | | | | 1 | | | | | | | | | | 4 | 1 | | | | 1 |
| 10 | Brain,......do | 4 | 6 | 9 | 2 | | | 3 | 3 | | 1 | 2 | 1 | | | | | | | 16 | 2 | 5 | 1 | | 5 |
| 11 | Bronchitis | | | 2 | 2 | 1 | | | | 2 | 2 | 1 | | | | | | | | 3 | 2 | 4 | | | 1 |
| 12 | Cancer | | | 1 | | | | | | 2 | 5 | 2 | 1 | | | | | | | 1 | 2 | 5 | | | |
| 13 | Catarrh | 4 | 2 | 2 | 1 | 1 | | 1 | | 1 | | 1 | | | | | | | | 10 | | 1 | | | 1 |
| 14 | Childbirth | | | | | | | | 4 | | 34 | | 1 | | | | | | | 4 | 1 | 12 | | | 1 |
| 15 | Cholera | 9 | | 22 | 13 | 6 | 7 | 11 | 18 | 79 | 44 | 21 | 2 | | | | | | | 43 | 19 | 38 | 1 | 1 | 8 |
| 16 | ..do..infantum | 2 | 3 | 9 | | | | | | | | | | | | | | | | 9 | | | | | 5 |
| 17 | ...do..morbus | 1 | 4 | 4 | 1 | | | 1 | | 4 | 3 | | | | | | | | | 7 | | 5 | 1 | | 3 |
| 18 | Colic | | | 1 | | | | | | 1 | | 1 | | | | | | | | | | 1 | | | |
| 19 | Cong'st'n, not specf'd | 2 | | 1 | | 1 | | | | 3 | | | | | | | | | | 2 | | 4 | | | 1 |
| 20 | ....do....brain | 3 | 1 | 3 | 2 | 2 | 1 | 1 | | 4 | 1 | 1 | | | | | | | | 10 | 1 | 3 | | | 1 |
| 21 | ....do....lungs | 1 | 2 | 1 | 1 | | | | 1 | | | | | | | | | | | 3 | 1 | 1 | | | 1 |
| 22 | Consumption | 7 | 8 | 9 | 13 | 1 | 4 | 14 | 16 | 78 | 87 | 29 | 23 | 1 | | | | | | 48 | 36 | 87 | 6 | 2 | 24 |
| 23 | Convulsions | 19 | 14 | 11 | 8 | 2 | | | 2 | 1 | 4 | 3 | | | | | | 1 | | 40 | 6 | 5 | | | 3 |
| 24 | Croup | 21 | 17 | 30 | 27 | 8 | 6 | 2 | 2 | | | | | | | | | | | 77 | 5 | 15 | | | 7 |
| 25 | Debility | | 2 | | | | | | 2 | | | | | | | | | | | 3 | | | | | 1 |
| 26 | Diabetes | | | | | | | | | 2 | | | 1 | | | | | | | | | 2 | 1 | | |
| 27 | Diarrhœa | 26 | 28 | 48 | 39 | 2 | 1 | 1 | 2 | 9 | 7 | 2 | 3 | | | | | | | 91 | 8 | 14 | 1 | | 21 |
| 28 | Dropsy | 4 | 7 | 10 | 7 | 2 | 6 | 3 | 1 | 12 | 8 | 4 | 8 | 1 | 1 | | | | | 28 | 11 | 12 | | | 2 |
| 29 | Dysentery | 14 | 15 | 33 | 34 | 1 | 2 | 3 | 5 | 8 | 5 | 3 | 6 | | 1 | | | | | 73 | 11 | 23 | | 1 | 7 |
| 30 | Dyspepsia | | | | | | | | 2 | 2 | | 3 | | | | | | | | | 1 | 3 | 1 | | |
| 31 | Epilepsy | | | | | | | | | 1 | | | | | | | | | | | | 1 | | | |
| 32 | Erysipelas | 2 | 4 | 4 | 4 | 1 | | 1 | 2 | 3 | 1 | 1 | | | | | | | | 11 | 1 | 5 | | | 3 |
| 33 | Fever, not specified | 8 | 5 | 17 | 10 | 6 | 3 | 5 | 5 | 20 | 23 | 13 | 8 | | | | | | | 41 | 6 | 24 | | 1 | 9 |
| 34 | ..do..bilious | 2 | | | 4 | 4 | 3 | 3 | 2 | 16 | 5 | 4 | 4 | | 1 | | | | | 9 | 2 | 11 | 1 | | 2 |
| 35 | ..do..brain | 3 | 3 | 6 | 5 | 4 | | | 3 | 6 | 2 | | | | | | | | | 14 | 1 | 2 | | | 4 |
| 36 | ..do..congestive | 1 | 1 | 1 | | | 1 | 1 | | 7 | 2 | | 1 | | | | | | | 5 | 2 | 3 | | | 1 |
| 37 | ..do..inflammatory | | | | | | | | | | 2 | | | | | | | | | 1 | | | | | 1 |
| 38 | ..do..intermittent | 2 | | | | | | 1 | 2 | | 1 | | | | | | | | | 2 | 2 | 1 | | | |
| 39 | ..do..puerperal | | | | | | | | | | 6 | | 1 | | | | | | | | 1 | 3 | | | |
| 40 | ..do..remittent | | 1 | | | | | | | | | | | | | | | | | 1 | | | | | |
| 41 | ..do..scarlet | 3 | 4 | 26 | 26 | 10 | 11 | 3 | 5 | 4 | 5 | | | | | | | | | 49 | 3 | 17 | 1 | | 9 |
| 42 | ..do..ship | | | 2 | 2 | 1 | 1 | 1 | 1 | 3 | 3 | | | | | | | | | 3 | | | | | |
| 43 | ..do..typhus | 1 | | 3 | 2 | 2 | 6 | 13 | 11 | 31 | 25 | 2 | 1 | | | | | | | 26 | 7 | 33 | 2 | | 7 |
| 44 | Frozen | | | | | | | | | 1 | | 2 | | | | | | | | | | | | | |
| 45 | Gravel | | | | | 1 | | | | | | 1 | | | | | | | | | | | | | |
| 46 | Heart, disease of | 2 | | | | | | 1 | | 1 | 1 | 3 | 4 | | | | | | | 2 | 4 | 5 | | | |
| 47 | Heat | | | | | | | 1 | | 1 | | | | | | | | | | | | | | | |
| 48 | Hemorrhage | 2 | | | | | | | 1 | 1 | 1 | | | | | | | | | 2 | 1 | 1 | | | |
| 49 | Hernia | | | | | | | | | 1 | | 2 | | | | | | | | 1 | | 1 | | | |
| 50 | Hives | 1 | | | | | | | | | | | | | | | | | | 1 | | | | | |
| 51 | Hooping cough | 19 | 25 | 21 | 23 | 3 | 5 | | | | | | | | | | | | | 71 | | 4 | 1 | | 14 |
| 52 | Hydrocephalus | | | 1 | | | | | | | | | | | | | | | | 1 | | | | | |
| 53 | Inflamat'n, not spec'd | 15 | 5 | 7 | 7 | 3 | | 1 | 2 | 4 | 4 | 2 | | | 1 | | | | | 29 | 5 | 8 | 1 | | 3 |
| 54 | .....do....bowels | 11 | 8 | 6 | 5 | 1 | 2 | 2 | 2 | 5 | 6 | 2 | | | | | | | | 30 | 1 | 13 | | | |
| 55 | .....do....brain | 8 | 2 | 12 | 11 | 4 | 4 | 2 | | 7 | 4 | | 1 | | | | | | | 27 | | 13 | | | 11 |
| 56 | Influenza | 1 | | | | | | | | | | | | | | | | | | 1 | | | | | |

THE STATE OF VIRGINIA—AGGREGATE—Continued.

| NATIVITIES. California and Territories. | NATIVITIES. Ireland. | NATIVITIES. Germany. | NATIVITIES. Other foreign countries. | NATIVITIES. Unknown. | SEASON OF DECEASE. Spring. | SEASON OF DECEASE. Summer. | SEASON OF DECEASE. Autumn. | SEASON OF DECEASE. Winter. | DURATION OF SICKNESS. Under 1 week. | DURATION OF SICKNESS. 1 week and under 1 month. | DURATION OF SICKNESS. 1 month and under 3 months. | DURATION OF SICKNESS. 3 months and over. | WHITES. Males. | WHITES. Females. | WHITES. Total. | COLORED. Slaves. Black. M. | COLORED. Slaves. Black. F. | COLORED. Slaves. Mulatto. M. | COLORED. Slaves. Mulatto. F. | COLORED. Free. Black M. | COLORED. Free. Black F. | COLORED. Free. Mul. M | COLORED. Free. Mul. F | Aggregate deaths. | |
|---|---|---|---|---|---|---|---|---|---|---|---|---|---|---|---|---|---|---|---|---|---|---|---|---|---|
| | | | | | 22 | 34 | 48 | 37 | 35 | 93 | 9 | 5 | 53 | 63 | 116 | 13 | 13 | 1 | | | | | | 143 | 1 |
| | | | | | 5 | 11 | 14 | 10 | 5 | 23 | 4 | 8 | 12 | 11 | 23 | 7 | 9 | | | 1 | | 1 | | 41 | 2 |
| | | | | | 2 | 5 | 4 | 5 | | 5 | 1 | 10 | 4 | 5 | 9 | 5 | 2 | | | | | | | 16 | 3 |
| | | | 1 | | 4 | 2 | 4 | | 1 | 3 | 3 | 3 | 7 | | 7 | 2 | 1 | | | | | | | 10 | 4 |
| | | | | | 6 | 4 | 10 | 4 | 1 | 9 | 4 | 10 | | 4 | 4 | | 18 | | 2 | | | | | 24 | 5 |
| | | | | | 2 | 1 | | | | | 1 | 3 | 1 | 1 | 2 | 1 | 2 | | | | | | | 5 | 6 |
| | | | | | 4 | 4 | 2 | 2 | 2 | 2 | 2 | 6 | 5 | 2 | 7 | | 3 | 1 | | | | 1 | | 12 | 7 |
| | | | | | 45 | 57 | 54 | 29 | 59 | 71 | 32 | 16 | 25 | 36 | 61 | 65 | 45 | 4 | 2 | 2 | 5 | 2 | 2 | 188 | 8 |
| | 5 | 1 | 6 | 1 | 1160 | 1115 | 1008 | 780 | 1337 | 892 | 328 | 754 | 924 | 959 | 1883 | 1002 | 953 | 82 | 79 | 62 | 67 | 32 | 43 | 4203 | 9 |
| 1 | 69 | 35 | 79 | 13 | 5144 | 5409 | 4576 | 3608 | 5701 | 5564 | 1891 | 3820 | 5027 | 4870 | 9897 | 4026 | 3724 | 317 | 333 | 245 | 256 | 120 | 141 | 19059 | |

THE STATE OF WISCONSIN.

| California and Territories. | Ireland. | Germany. | Other foreign countries. | Unknown. | Spring. | Summer. | Autumn. | Winter. | Under 1 week. | 1 week and under 1 month. | 1 month and under 3 months. | 3 months and over. | Males. | Females. | Total. | Slaves Black M. | Slaves Black F. | Slaves Mulatto M. | Slaves Mulatto F. | Free Black M. | Free Black F. | Free Mul. M | Free Mul. F | Aggregate deaths. | |
|---|---|---|---|---|---|---|---|---|---|---|---|---|---|---|---|---|---|---|---|---|---|---|---|---|---|
| | | | | 1 | 1 | 2 | 1 | | | | | 4 | 3 | 1 | 4 | | | | | | | | | 4 | 1 |
| | 3 | 3 | 10 | | 12 | 15 | 14 | 8 | 23 | 5 | 3 | 1 | 40 | 9 | 49 | | | | | | | 1 | | 50 | 2 |
| | | 2 | | | 5 | 1 | 1 | 3 | 6 | 3 | | | 6 | 4 | 10 | | | | | | | | | 10 | 3 |
| | 4 | 1 | 3 | | 9 | 12 | 8 | 4 | 33 | | | | 25 | 8 | 33 | | | | | | | | | 33 | 4 |
| | | | | | 1 | | | 2 | 3 | | | | 2 | 1 | 3 | | | | | | | | | 3 | 5 |
| | 1 | | 2 | | 2 | 2 | | | 4 | | | | 4 | | 4 | | | | | | | | | 4 | 6 |
| | | 1 | 1 | | 3 | 2 | 2 | 1 | 5 | 2 | | | 6 | 1 | 7 | | | | | | | 1 | | 8 | 7 |
| | | | | | 1 | | | 2 | 1 | | 2 | | 3 | | 3 | | | | | | | | | 3 | 8 |
| | | | 2 | | | 3 | 4 | 1 | 3 | 1 | 3 | 1 | 5 | 3 | 8 | | | | | | | | | 8 | 9 |
| | 1 | | | 1 | 7 | 8 | 7 | 9 | 11 | 12 | 5 | 2 | 18 | 13 | 31 | | | | | | | | | 31 | 10 |
| | | | | | 6 | | 2 | 2 | 2 | 1 | 1 | 6 | 6 | 4 | 10 | | | | | | | | | 10 | 11 |
| | 2 | | 1 | | 1 | 1 | 7 | 2 | 1 | 1 | 2 | 7 | 5 | 5 | 10 | | | | | | | | 1 | 11 | 12 |
| | | 1 | | | 4 | 3 | 3 | 3 | 3 | 4 | 3 | 2 | 10 | 3 | 13 | | | | | | | | | 13 | 13 |
| 1 | 7 | 3 | 10 | | 17 | 6 | 8 | 8 | 24 | 10 | | 2 | | 38 | 38 | | | | | | | | 1 | 39 | 14 |
| | 25 | 31 | 58 | 8 | 4 | 83 | 139 | 6 | 205 | 18 | 2 | 1 | 146 | 84 | 230 | | | | | | | 2 | | 232 | 15 |
| | | | | | | 4 | 9 | 1 | 8 | 6 | | | 11 | 3 | 14 | | | | | | | | | 14 | 16 |
| | | | 2 | | | 3 | 15 | | 4 | 13 | 1 | | 10 | 8 | 18 | | | | | | | | | 18 | 17 |
| | | | 2 | | 2 | 1 | | | 3 | | | | 3 | | 3 | | | | | | | | | 3 | 18 |
| | | | | | 5 | 1 | 1 | | 4 | 3 | | | 7 | | 7 | | | | | | | | | 7 | 19 |
| | 1 | | 3 | | 6 | 3 | 7 | 2 | 8 | 4 | 1 | 2 | 14 | 5 | 19 | | | | | | | | | 19 | 20 |
| | | | | | 3 | 2 | | 1 | 3 | 3 | | | 2 | 4 | 6 | | | | | | | | | 6 | 21 |
| | 21 | 18 | 43 | 5 | 103 | 62 | 64 | 61 | 10 | 31 | 31 | 193 | 135 | 148 | 283 | | | | | 1 | | 3 | 3 | 290 | 22 |
| | 1 | 4 | 6 | | 19 | 16 | 15 | 15 | 43 | 17 | 3 | 2 | 37 | 28 | 65 | | | | | | | | | 65 | 23 |
| | 1 | 3 | 5 | | 41 | 24 | 18 | 30 | 85 | 22 | 1 | 2 | 61 | 52 | 113 | | | | | | | | | 113 | 24 |
| | | | | | | 3 | | 1 | | | | 3 | | 4 | 4 | | | | | | | | | 4 | 25 |
| | | | | | 2 | | | 1 | 1 | | | 2 | 2 | 1 | 3 | | | | | | | | | 3 | 26 |
| | 7 | 8 | 17 | 1 | 14 | 20 | 117 | 15 | 39 | 91 | 26 | 9 | 88 | 80 | 168 | | | | | | | | | 168 | 27 |
| 1 | 5 | 6 | 7 | 2 | 26 | 9 | 27 | 12 | 9 | 22 | 10 | 32 | 36 | 38 | 74 | | | | | | | | | 74 | 28 |
| | 1 | | 14 | | 6 | 14 | 98 | 12 | 31 | 76 | 15 | 5 | 62 | 68 | 130 | | | | | | | | | 130 | 29 |
| | | | 2 | | 2 | 2 | 2 | 1 | | | | 7 | 5 | 2 | 7 | | | | | | | | | 7 | 30 |
| | | | | | | 1 | | | | 1 | | | 1 | | 1 | | | | | | | | | 1 | 31 |
| | 1 | | 2 | | 5 | 7 | 6 | 5 | 5 | 13 | 3 | 1 | 12 | 11 | 23 | | | | | | | | | 23 | 32 |
| | 5 | 13 | 23 | 1 | 32 | 26 | 37 | 27 | 20 | 70 | 16 | 15 | 69 | 53 | 122 | | | | | | | | 1 | 123 | 33 |
| | 3 | 6 | 14 | | 5 | 5 | 26 | 10 | 9 | 29 | 7 | 2 | 29 | 19 | 48 | | | | | | | | | 48 | 34 |
| | 6 | 2 | 3 | | 7 | 6 | 14 | 5 | 12 | 14 | 6 | | 19 | 13 | 32 | | | | | | | | | 32 | 35 |
| | 3 | | 1 | | 1 | 5 | 6 | 3 | 5 | 7 | 1 | 1 | 10 | 5 | 15 | | | | | | | | | 15 | 36 |
| | | | | | | 1 | | 1 | | | 1 | | | 2 | 2 | | | | | | | | | 2 | 37 |
| | | | 1 | | 2 | | 2 | 2 | | 5 | | 1 | 3 | 3 | 6 | | | | | | | | | 6 | 38 |
| | 1 | | 2 | | 2 | 3 | 2 | | | 4 | 1 | | | 7 | 7 | | | | | | | | | 7 | 39 |
| | | | | | | | | 1 | 1 | | | | | 1 | 1 | | | | | | | | | 1 | 40 |
| | 2 | 3 | 13 | | 34 | 24 | 19 | 19 | 43 | 44 | 8 | | 46 | 51 | 97 | | | | | | | | | 97 | 41 |
| | 7 | 1 | 3 | | 3 | 6 | 2 | 3 | 4 | 6 | 2 | 2 | 7 | 7 | 14 | | | | | | | | | 14 | 42 |
| | 4 | 3 | 13 | 2 | 21 | 9 | 27 | 31 | 10 | 51 | 15 | 6 | 52 | 44 | 96 | | | | | | | | 1 | 97 | 43 |
| | 1 | 1 | 1 | | 2 | | | 1 | 1 | 1 | | | 3 | | 3 | | | | | | | | | 3 | 44 |
| | 1 | | 1 | | | 1 | 1 | | | | | 2 | 2 | | 2 | | | | | | | | | 2 | 45 |
| | | | 1 | | 6 | 3 | 2 | 1 | 4 | 4 | 2 | 2 | 7 | 4 | 11 | | | | | | | | 1 | 12 | 46 |
| | | | 2 | | | 2 | | | 2 | | | | 2 | | 2 | | | | | | | | | 2 | 47 |
| | | | 1 | | 1 | 1 | 1 | 2 | 2 | 3 | | | 3 | 2 | 5 | | | | | | | | | 5 | 48 |
| | 1 | | | | | 2 | | 1 | 3 | | | | 3 | | 3 | | | | | | | | | 3 | 49 |
| | | | | | | | | 1 | 1 | | | | 1 | | 1 | | | | | | | | | 1 | 50 |
| | 1 | | 5 | | 33 | 19 | 27 | 17 | 13 | 56 | 13 | 7 | 43 | 53 | 96 | | | | | | | | | 96 | 51 |
| | | | | | | | | 1 | 1 | | | | 1 | | 1 | | | | | | | | | 1 | 52 |
| | 2 | | 3 | | 19 | 8 | 17 | 7 | 24 | 21 | 4 | 2 | 32 | 19 | 51 | | | | | | | | | 51 | 53 |
| | 1 | | 5 | | 17 | 10 | 17 | 6 | 26 | 21 | 3 | | 27 | 23 | 50 | | | | | | | | | 50 | 54 |
| | | | 4 | | 17 | 11 | 20 | 7 | 13 | 35 | 3 | 3 | 33 | 22 | 55 | | | | | | | | | 55 | 55 |
| | | | | | 1 | | | | 1 | | | | 1 | | 1 | | | | | | | | | 1 | 56 |

CLASSIFICATION OF DEATHS IN

| | Cause of death. | AGE. Under 1. M. | Under 1. F. | 1 and under 5. M. | 1 and under 5. F. | 5 and under 10. M. | 5 and under 10. F. | 10 and under 20. M. | 10 and under 20. F. | 20 and under 50. M. | 20 and under 50. F. | 50 and under 80. M. | 50 and under 80. F. | 80 and under 100. M | 80 and under 100. F. | 100 & over. M | 100 & over. F. | Age unknown. M | Age unknown. F. | NATIVITIES. Born in State. | N. England States. | Middle States. | Southern States. | Southwest'n States. | Northeast'n States. |
|---|---|---|---|---|---|---|---|---|---|---|---|---|---|---|---|---|---|---|---|---|---|---|---|---|---|
| 1 | Insanity | | | | | | | | | 1 | | | | | | | | | | | | | | | |
| 2 | Intemperance | | | | | | | | 1 | 6 | | | | | | | | | | 1 | | | | | |
| 3 | Jaundice | | | 1 | | | 1 | | | | 1 | | 1 | | | | | | | 1 | | 2 | | | |
| 4 | Kidneys, disease of | 2 | | | | | | | | | | | | | | | | | | 2 | | | | | |
| 5 | Liver ......do | 1 | 1 | 2 | 1 | | | | 1 | 3 | 1 | 1 | | | | | | | | 3 | 1 | 3 | 1 | | 2 |
| 6 | Lungs......do | 3 | 3 | 2 | 1 | | 1 | | | 2 | 1 | 1 | | 1 | 1 | | | | | 12 | | 3 | | 1 | |
| 7 | Mania-a-potu | | | | | | | | | | 1 | | | | | | | | | 1 | | | | | |
| 8 | Marasmus | 1 | | | | | 1 | | | | | | 1 | | | | | | | 2 | | | | | |
| 9 | Measles | 3 | 2 | 8 | 9 | 1 | 2 | 1 | 1 | | | | | | | | | | | 19 | 1 | 2 | | | 4 |
| 10 | Mumps | | | | | 1 | | | | | | | | | | | | | | 1 | | | | | |
| 11 | Murder | | | | | | | | | 1 | | | | | | | | | | | | 1 | | | |
| 12 | Neuralgia | 1 | | 2 | | | | | | 1 | | 1 | 2 | | | | | | | 3 | | 1 | 1 | | |
| 13 | Old age | | | | | | | | | | | 14 | 10 | 3 | 2 | | | | | 1 | 7 | 3 | 1 | | |
| 14 | Paralysis | | | | | | | | | 1 | 2 | 2 | 1 | | 1 | | | | | | 8 | 3 | | | |
| 15 | Piles | | | | | | | | | | | | 1 | | | | | | | | 1 | | | | |
| 16 | Pleurisy | | | | | | | 1 | | 4 | | | | | | | | | | 1 | 1 | 1 | | | |
| 17 | Pneumonia | 27 | 22 | 27 | 31 | 5 | 6 | 9 | 2 | 29 | 19 | 11 | 6 | | | | | | | 102 | 16 | 34 | 4 | | 20 |
| 18 | Poison | | | | 1 | | | | 1 | | 1 | | | | | | | | | 1 | 1 | | | | |
| 19 | Prematurity of birth | 1 | 1 | | | | | | | | | | | | | | | | | 2 | | | | | |
| 20 | Quinsy | | 1 | | 1 | | | | | | | | | | | | | | | 2 | | | | | |
| 21 | Rheumatism | | | | | | | 1 | 3 | 4 | 1 | | | | 1 | | | | | | 3 | 4 | | | |
| 22 | Salivation, effects of | | | | | | | | | 1 | | | | | | | | | | 1 | | | | | |
| 23 | Scrofula | 2 | 2 | 4 | | | 2 | 2 | 3 | 1 | 5 | | 1 | | | | | | | 5 | 2 | 7 | | 1 | 4 |
| 24 | Small pox | 2 | 1 | 2 | 1 | | | | | 4 | 1 | 1 | 2 | | | | | | | 2 | 5 | 2 | 1 | | 4 |
| 25 | Spine, disease of | 1 | 1 | 2 | | 1 | 1 | 1 | 2 | 1 | 2 | 1 | | | | | | | | 4 | 1 | 5 | | | |
| 26 | Stomach..do | | | | | | | | 1 | | 1 | 1 | | | | | | | | | 1 | 2 | | | |
| 27 | Suicide | | | | | | | 1 | | 1 | 1 | 2 | | | | | | | | | 1 | | | | 1 |
| 28 | Sun, stroke of | | | | | | | 1 | | | | | | | | | | | | | | | | | |
| 29 | Teething | 4 | 8 | 6 | 11 | | | | | | | | | | | | | | | 14 | 2 | 3 | | | 5 |
| 30 | Throat, disease of | | | 2 | | | | | | | | | | | | | | | | 2 | | | | | |
| 31 | Thrush | | 1 | | | | | | | | | | | | | | | | | | | | | | 1 |
| 32 | Tumor | | | | | | | | | | 1 | | | | | | | | | | | 1 | | | |
| 33 | Ulcer | | | | | | | | | 1 | | | | | | | | | | | 1 | | | | |
| 34 | Uterus, disease of | | | | | | | | | | 1 | | | | | | | | | | | 1 | | | |
| 35 | Venereal | | | | | | | | | 1 | | | | | | | | | | | 1 | | | | |
| 36 | White swelling | | | | | | 1 | | | | | | | | | | | | | | | | | | 1 |
| 37 | Worms | 1 | | 2 | 5 | 1 | 1 | | | | | | | | | | | | | 7 | | 1 | | | 1 |
| 38 | Unknown | 71 | 78 | 48 | 36 | 6 | 7 | 6 | 12 | 24 | 22 | 17 | 7 | | | | | 1 | | 193 | 22 | 34 | 1 | | 18 |
| | Total | 329 | 294 | 426 | 355 | 93 | 90 | 108 | 123 | 445 | 358 | 166 | 99 | 6 | 9 | .. | .. | 2 | .. | 1221 | 224 | 524 | 27 | 8 | 223 |

CLASSIFICATION OF DEATHS IN

| | Cause of death. | Under 1. M. | Under 1. F. | 1 and under 5. M. | 1 and under 5. F. | 5 and under 10. M. | 5 and under 10. F. | 10 and under 20. M. | 10 and under 20. F. | 20 and under 50. M. | 20 and under 50. F. | 50 and under 80. M. | 50 and under 80. F. | 80 and under 100. M | 80 and under 100. F. | 100 & over. M | 100 & over. F. | Age unknown. M | Age unknown. F. | Born in State. | N. England States. | Middle States. | Southern States. | Southwest'n States. | Northeast'n States. |
|---|---|---|---|---|---|---|---|---|---|---|---|---|---|---|---|---|---|---|---|---|---|---|---|---|---|
| 1 | Accident, burned | | | | | | 1 | | | 2 | | | | | | | | | | | | | | | 1 |
| 2 | ....do...shot | | | | | 1 | | | | | | | | | | | | | | | | 1 | | | |
| 3 | Cholera | | | | | | 1 | | | 3 | 1 | | | | | | | | | 1 | | 1 | | | 2 |
| 4 | ....do....infantum | 1 | | | 1 | | | | | | | | | | | | | | | 2 | | | | | |
| 5 | Colic | | | | | | | | | 1 | | | | | | | | | | | | | | | |
| 6 | Consumption | | | | | | | | | 1 | | | | | | | | | | | | | | | 1 |
| 7 | Dropsy | | | | 1 | | | | | | | | | | | | | | | 1 | | | | | |
| 8 | Fever, not specified | | | 1 | | | | | | | | | 1 | | | | | | | 1 | | | | | |
| 9 | ..do..bilious | 1 | | | | | | | | | | | | | | | | | | 1 | | | | | |
| 10 | ..do..brain | 2 | | | | | | | | | | | | | | | | | | 2 | | | | | |
| 11 | ..do..congestive | | | 1 | | | 1 | | | | | | | | | | | | | | | | | | 2 |
| 12 | Inflamat'n, not spe'd | | 1 | | | | | | | | | | | | | | | | | 1 | | | | | |
| 13 | ....do......brain | 1 | | | | | | | | | | | | | | | | | | 1 | | | | | |
| 14 | Lungs, disease of | | | 1 | | | | 1 | | | | | | 1 | | | | | | 1 | | | | | |
| 15 | Teething | | | 1 | 1 | | | | | | | | | | | | | | | | | | | | 2 |
| 16 | Unknown | | | 1 | 1 | 1 | | | | | | | | | | | | | | 1 | 1 | | | | 1 |
| | Total | 5 | 1 | 5 | 4 | 2 | 3 | 1 | ... | 5 | 1 | ... | 1 | 1 | .. | .. | .. | .. | .. | 12 | 1 | 2 | ... | ... | 9 |

THE STATE OF WISCONSIN—Continued.

| Nativities: California and Territories. | Nativities: Ireland. | Nativities: Germany. | Nativities: Other foreign countries. | Nativities: Unknown. | Season of decease: Spring. | Season of decease: Summer. | Season of decease: Autumn. | Season of decease: Winter. | Duration of sickness: Under 1 week. | Duration of sickness: 1 week and under 1 month. | Duration of sickness: 1 month and under 3 months. | Duration of sickness: 3 months and over. | Whites: Males. | Whites: Females. | Whites: Total. | Colored: Slaves: Black: M. | Colored: Slaves: Black: F. | Colored: Slaves: Mulatto: M. | Colored: Slaves: Mulatto: F. | Colored: Free: Black: M. | Colored: Free: Black: F. | Colored: Free: Mul.: M | Colored: Free: Mul.: F. | Aggregate deaths. | |
|---|---|---|---|---|---|---|---|---|---|---|---|---|---|---|---|---|---|---|---|---|---|---|---|---|---|
| .... | 1 | .. | .... | ... | .... | .... | 1 | .... | .... | .... | .... | 1 | 1 | .... | 1 | .... | .... | .... | .... | ... | ... | .. | .. | 1 | 1 |
| .... | 3 | .. | 3 | ... | 1 | 2 | 2 | 2 | 5 | 2 | .... | .... | 6 | 1 | 7 | .... | .... | .... | .... | ... | ... | .. | .. | 7 | 2 |
| .... | 1 | .. | .... | ... | 2 | .... | .... | 2 | 2 | 1 | 1 | .... | 1 | 3 | 4 | .... | .... | .... | .... | ... | ... | .. | .. | 4 | 3 |
| .... | .... | .. | .... | ... | .... | .... | 2 | .... | 1 | 1 | .... | .... | 2 | .... | 2 | .... | .... | .... | .... | ... | ... | .. | .. | 2 | 4 |
| .... | .... | .. | 1 | ... | 1 | 3 | 5 | 2 | 1 | 6 | 2 | 2 | 7 | 4 | 11 | .... | .... | .... | .... | ... | ... | .. | .. | 11 | 5 |
| .... | .... | .. | .... | ... | 5 | 4 | 3 | 4 | 3 | 7 | 2 | 2 | 9 | 7 | 16 | .... | .... | .... | .... | ... | ... | .. | .. | 16 | 6 |
| .... | .... | .. | .... | ... | .... | .... | 1 | .... | .... | .... | .... | .... | .... | 1 | 1 | .... | .... | .... | .... | ... | ... | .. | .. | 1 | 7 |
| .... | 1 | .. | .... | ... | .... | .... | 2 | 1 | .... | .... | .... | 2 | 1 | 2 | 3 | .... | .... | .... | .... | ... | ... | .. | .. | 3 | 8 |
| .... | .... | .. | 1 | ... | 9 | 6 | 9 | 3 | 4 | 11 | 6 | 5 | 13 | 14 | 27 | .... | .... | .... | .... | ... | ... | .. | .. | 27 | 9 |
| .... | .... | .. | .... | ... | 1 | .... | .... | .... | .... | 1 | .... | .... | 1 | .... | 1 | .... | .... | .... | .... | ... | ... | .. | .. | 1 | 10 |
| .... | .... | .. | .... | ... | 1 | .... | .... | .... | .... | .... | .... | .... | 1 | .... | 1 | .... | .... | .... | .... | ... | ... | .. | .. | 1 | 11 |
| .... | .... | 2 | .... | ... | .... | 2 | 4 | 1 | .... | 6 | .... | 1 | 5 | 2 | 7 | .... | .... | .... | .... | ... | ... | .. | .. | 7 | 12 |
| .... | 3 | 4 | 10 | ... | 9 | 7 | 9 | 4 | 3 | 9 | 2 | 4 | 17 | 12 | 29 | .... | .... | .... | .... | ... | ... | .. | .. | 29 | 13 |
| .... | .... | 1 | .... | ... | 3 | 2 | 1 | 1 | ... | 1 | 1 | 4 | 2 | 3 | 5 | .... | .... | .... | .... | ... | ... | 1 | 1 | 7 | 14 |
| .... | .... | .. | .... | ... | .... | 1 | .... | .... | .... | .... | .... | 1 | .... | 1 | 1 | .... | .... | .... | .... | ... | ... | .. | .. | 1 | 15 |
| .... | 2 | .. | .... | ... | 4 | .... | .... | 1 | 1 | 4 | .... | .... | 5 | .... | 5 | .... | .... | .... | .... | ... | ... | .. | .. | 5 | 16 |
| 1 | 8 | 1 | 7 | 1 | 91 | 38 | 21 | 43 | 47 | 115 | 9 | 12 | 107 | 86 | 193 | .... | .... | .... | .... | ... | ... | 1 | .. | 194 | 17 |
| .... | .... | 1 | .... | ... | 1 | 1 | 1 | .... | 2 | .... | .... | .... | .... | 3 | 3 | .... | .... | .... | .... | ... | ... | .. | .. | 3 | 18 |
| .... | .... | .. | .... | ... | .... | .... | .... | .... | .... | 1 | .... | 1 | 1 | 1 | 2 | .... | .... | .... | .... | ... | ... | .. | .. | 2 | 19 |
| .... | .... | .. | .... | ... | 2 | .... | .... | .... | 1 | ... | .... | .... | .... | 2 | 2 | .... | .... | .... | .... | ... | ... | .. | .. | 2 | 20 |
| .... | .... | 2 | 1 | ... | 3 | 2 | 1 | 4 | .... | 7 | .... | 2 | 5 | 5 | 10 | .... | .... | .... | .... | ... | ... | .. | .. | 10 | 21 |
| .... | .... | .. | .... | ... | .... | .... | .... | 1 | .... | .... | .... | .... | 1 | .... | 1 | .... | .... | .... | .... | ... | ... | .. | .. | 1 | 22 |
| .... | .... | 1 | 2 | ... | 8 | 6 | 2 | 6 | 1 | 6 | 3 | 12 | 9 | 13 | 22 | .... | .... | .... | .... | ... | ... | .. | .. | 22 | 23 |
| .... | .... | .. | .... | ... | 6 | 6 | 2 | .... | 4 | 10 | .... | .... | 9 | 5 | 14 | .... | .... | .... | .... | ... | ... | .. | .. | 14 | 24 |
| .... | .... | .. | 2 | 1 | 2 | 3 | 3 | 5 | 3 | 3 | 1 | 6 | 7 | 6 | 13 | .... | .... | .... | .... | ... | ... | .. | .. | 13 | 25 |
| .... | .... | .. | .... | ... | 1 | .... | 1 | 1 | .... | 3 | .... | .... | 1 | 2 | 3 | .... | .... | .... | .... | ... | ... | .. | .. | 3 | 26 |
| .... | .... | 2 | 1 | ... | .... | 2 | 2 | 1 | 2 | .... | .... | .... | 4 | 1 | 5 | .... | .... | .... | .... | ... | ... | .. | .. | 5 | 27 |
| .... | 1 | .. | .... | ... | .... | 1 | .... | .... | 1 | .... | .... | .... | 1 | .... | 1 | .... | .... | .... | .... | ... | ... | .. | .. | 1 | 28 |
| .... | 1 | 1 | 8 | ... | 4 | 9 | 8 | 8 | 6 | 15 | 2 | 6 | 10 | 19 | 29 | .... | .... | .... | .... | ... | ... | .. | .. | 29 | 29 |
| .... | .... | .. | .... | ... | .... | 1 | .... | 1 | .... | 1 | .... | .... | 2 | .... | 2 | .... | .... | .... | .... | ... | ... | .. | .. | 2 | 30 |
| .... | .... | .. | .... | ... | .... | .... | 1 | .... | .... | 1 | .... | .... | .... | 1 | 1 | .... | .... | .... | .... | ... | ... | .. | .. | 1 | 31 |
| .... | .... | .. | .... | ... | .... | 1 | .... | .... | .... | .... | .... | 1 | .... | 1 | 1 | .... | .... | .... | .... | ... | ... | .. | .. | 1 | 32 |
| .... | .... | .. | .... | ... | 1 | .... | .... | .... | 1 | .... | .... | .... | 1 | .... | 1 | .... | .... | .... | .... | ... | ... | .. | .. | 1 | 33 |
| .... | .... | .. | .... | ... | .... | .... | .... | 1 | .... | 1 | .... | .... | .... | 1 | 1 | .... | .... | .... | .... | ... | ... | .. | .. | 1 | 34 |
| .... | .... | .. | .... | ... | .... | 1 | .... | .... | .... | .... | .... | 1 | 1 | .... | 1 | .... | .... | .... | .... | ... | ... | .. | .. | 1 | 35 |
| .... | .... | .. | .... | ... | .... | .... | 1 | .... | .... | .... | .... | 1 | .... | 1 | 1 | .... | .... | .... | .... | ... | ... | .. | .. | 1 | 36 |
| .... | 1 | .. | .... | ... | 3 | .... | 6 | 1 | 7 | 1 | 1 | 1 | 4 | 6 | 10 | .... | .... | .... | .... | ... | ... | .. | .. | 10 | 37 |
| .... | 23 | 10 | 29 | 5 | 100 | 80 | 80 | 62 | 114 | 87 | 24 | 53 | 169 | 161 | 330 | .... | .... | .... | .... | ... | ... | 4 | 1 | 335 | 38 |
| 8 | 164 | 135 | 346 | 28 | 768 | 630 | 963 | 509 | 981 | 1030 | 248 | 445 | 1561 | 1318 | 2879 | .... | .... | .... | .... | 1 | ... | 13 | 10 | 2903 | |

THE TERRITORY OF MINNESOTA.

| California and Territories. | Ireland. | Germany. | Other foreign countries. | Unknown. | Spring. | Summer. | Autumn. | Winter. | Under 1 week. | 1 week and under 1 month. | 1 month and under 3 months. | 3 months and over. | Males. | Females. | Total. | Slaves Black M. | Slaves Black F. | Slaves Mulatto M. | Slaves Mulatto F. | Free Black M. | Free Black F. | Free Mul. M | Free Mul. F. | Aggregate deaths. | |
|---|---|---|---|---|---|---|---|---|---|---|---|---|---|---|---|---|---|---|---|---|---|---|---|---|---|
| .... | ... | .. | .... | ... | 1 | .... | .... | .... | 1 | .... | .... | .... | .... | 1 | 1 | .... | .... | .... | .... | ... | ... | .. | .. | 1 | 1 |
| .... | ... | .. | .... | ... | .... | 1 | .... | .... | 1 | .... | .... | .... | 1 | .... | 1 | .... | .... | .... | .... | ... | ... | .. | .. | 1 | 2 |
| .... | ... | .. | 1 | ... | 1 | 4 | .... | .... | 5 | .... | .... | .... | 3 | 2 | 5 | .... | .... | .... | .... | ... | ... | .. | .. | 5 | 3 |
| .... | ... | .. | .... | ... | .... | 1 | 1 | .... | ... | 2 | .... | .... | 1 | 1 | 2 | .... | .... | .... | .... | ... | ... | .. | .. | 2 | 4 |
| .... | ... | 1 | .... | ... | .... | 1 | .... | .... | .... | 1 | .... | .... | 1 | ... | 1 | .... | .... | .... | .... | ... | ... | .. | .. | 1 | 5 |
| .... | ... | .. | .... | ... | .... | .... | .... | 1 | .... | ... | 1 | .... | 1 | .... | 1 | .... | .... | .... | .... | ... | ... | .. | .. | 1 | 6 |
| .... | ... | .. | .... | ... | .... | .... | 1 | .... | .... | 1 | .... | .... | .... | 1 | 1 | .... | .... | .... | .... | ... | ... | .. | .. | 1 | 7 |
| .... | ... | .. | 1 | ... | 1 | 1 | .... | .... | .... | 2 | .... | .... | 1 | 1 | 2 | .... | .... | .... | .... | ... | ... | .. | .. | 2 | 8 |
| .... | ... | .. | .... | ... | .... | 1 | .... | .... | .... | 1 | .... | .... | 1 | .... | 1 | .... | .... | .... | .... | ... | ... | .. | .. | 1 | 9 |
| .... | ... | .. | .... | ... | .... | .... | .... | 2 | 1 | 1 | .... | .... | 2 | .... | 2 | .... | .... | .... | .... | ... | ... | .. | .. | 2 | 10 |
| .... | ... | .. | .... | ... | .... | .... | 2 | .... | 2 | .... | .... | .... | 1 | 1 | 2 | .... | .... | .... | .... | ... | ... | .. | .. | 2 | 11 |
| .... | ... | .. | .... | ... | 1 | .... | .... | .... | 1 | .... | .... | .... | .... | 1 | 1 | .... | .... | .... | .... | ... | ... | .. | .. | 1 | 12 |
| .... | ... | .. | .... | ... | 1 | .... | .... | .... | .... | 1 | .... | .... | 1 | .... | 1 | .... | .... | .... | .... | ... | ... | .. | .. | 1 | 13 |
| .... | ... | .. | 2 | ... | .... | .... | 1 | 2 | .... | 1 | 1 | .... | 3 | .... | 3 | .... | .... | .... | .... | ... | ... | .. | .. | 3 | 14 |
| .... | ... | .. | .... | ... | .... | .... | 1 | 1 | .... | 2 | .... | .... | 1 | 1 | 2 | .... | .... | .... | .... | ... | ... | .. | .. | 2 | 15 |
| .... | ... | .. | .... | ... | 1 | 1 | 1 | .... | .... | 1 | 1 | .... | 2 | 1 | 3 | .... | .... | .... | .... | ... | ... | .. | .. | 3 | 16 |
| .... | ... | 1 | 4 | ... | 6 | 10 | 7 | 6 | 11 | 13 | 3 | .... | 19 | 10 | 29 | .... | .... | .... | .... | ... | ... | .. | .. | 29 | |

## CLASSIFICATION OF DEATHS IN

| | Cause of death. | Ages. Under 1. M. | F. | 1 and under 5. M. | F. | 5 and under 10. M. | F. | 10 and under 20. M. | F. | 20 and under 50. M. | F. | 50 and under 80. M. | F. | 80 and under 100. M | F | 100 & over. M | F. | Age unknown. M | F. | Nativities. Born in Territory. | N. England States. | Middle States. | Southern States. | Southwest'n States. | Northwest'n States. |
|---|---|---|---|---|---|---|---|---|---|---|---|---|---|---|---|---|---|---|---|---|---|---|---|---|---|
| 1 | Abscess | | 1 | | | | | | | | | | | | | | | | | 1 | | | | | |
| 2 | Accident, not specif'd | | | | | 1 | | | | 4 | | 1 | | | | | | | | 6 | | | | | |
| 3 | ..do....burned | | 1 | 3 | 3 | 3 | | | | | 1 | 1 | | | | | | | | 12 | | | | | |
| 4 | ...do....drowned | | | | | | 1 | 3 | 1 | | | | | | | | | | | 5 | | | | | |
| 5 | Apoplexy | | | | | | | | | | 1 | | | | | | | | | 1 | | | | | |
| 6 | Asthma | | | 1 | 1 | | | | | 1 | | 1 | | | | | | | | 4 | | | | | |
| 7 | Bowels, disease of | | | | | | | 1 | | | 1 | | 3 | | | | | | | 4 | | | | | |
| 8 | Brain.....do | | | | | | | | | | | 1 | | | | | | | | 1 | | | | | |
| 9 | Cancer | | | | | | | 1 | | | | | | | | | | | | 1 | | | | | |
| 10 | Catarrh | | | 1 | | | | | | | | | | | | | | | | 1 | | | | | |
| 11 | Childbirth | | | | | | | | 5 | | 25 | | 1 | | | | | | | 31 | | | | | |
| 12 | Cholera | | | 1 | | 1 | | 1 | 1 | | 1 | 1 | 1 | | | | | | | 7 | | | | | |
| 13 | ..do....morbus | | 1 | | | | | 2 | | | 1 | | | | | | | | | 4 | | | | | |
| 14 | Colic | | | | | | | | 3 | 2 | 3 | 3 | | | | | | | | 11 | | | | | |
| 15 | Congestion of brain | | | | | | | | | | | | | | | | | 1 | | 1 | | | | | |
| 16 | Consumption | | | 1 | 1 | | | | | 2 | | | 1 | | | | | | | 4 | | | 1 | | |
| 17 | Convulsions | | | | | | | | | 1 | | | | | | | | | | 1 | | | | | |
| 18 | Croup | | | | 1 | | | | | | | | | | | | | | | 1 | | | | | |
| 19 | Debility | | 1 | 2 | | | | | | | | | | | | | | | | 3 | | | | | |
| 20 | Diarrhœa | | | 1 | 1 | | | | | 3 | | | | | | | | | | 2 | | | | | |
| 21 | Dropsy | 1 | 3 | 1 | 1 | | | 1 | 2 | 4 | 12 | 7 | 6 | 2 | | | | | | 40 | | | | | |
| 22 | Dysentery | 1 | | 3 | 1 | | | | | 6 | 6 | 2 | | | | | | | | 14 | | | | | 1 |
| 23 | Epilepsy | | | 1 | 1 | 1 | | | | | 2 | | | | | | | | | 4 | | | | | |
| 24 | Erysipelas | 8 | 6 | 7 | 9 | 3 | 6 | 7 | 5 | 11 | 11 | 5 | 4 | | | | | | | 81 | | | | | |
| 25 | Fever, not specified | 7 | 8 | 22 | 26 | 5 | 4 | 10 | 14 | 29 | 27 | 13 | 9 | 2 | 1 | | | | | 172 | | 1 | | | 1 |
| 26 | ..do..brain | 1 | | | | | | | 1 | | 1 | | | | | | | | | 3 | | | | | |
| 27 | ..do..inflammatory | 1 | | | | | | | | | | | | | | | | | | 1 | | | | | |
| 28 | ..do..typhus | | | 5 | 2 | | 8 | | | 2 | | | | | 1 | | | | | 13 | | | | | |
| 29 | Fracture | | | | | | | | | 1 | | | | | | | | | | 1 | | | | | |
| 30 | Frozen | | | | | | | | | 1 | | | | | | | | | | 1 | | | | | |
| 31 | Head, disease of | | | | | | | | 1 | | | | | | 2 | | | | | 3 | | | | | |
| 32 | Heart....do | | | | | | | | | 1 | | 1 | | | | | | | | 2 | | | | | |
| 33 | Hemorrhage | | | | | | | | | 1 | 3 | | | | | | | | | 4 | | | | | |
| 34 | Hernia | | | | | | | | | | | | 1 | | | | | | | 1 | | | | | |
| 35 | Hip, disease of | | | | | | | | 1 | | | | | | | | | | | 1 | | | | | |
| 36 | Hooping cough | 3 | 2 | 4 | 3 | | | | | 1 | | | | | | | | | | 13 | | | | | |
| 37 | Hydrophobia | | | | | 1 | | | | 1 | 1 | | | | | | | | | 3 | | | | | |
| 38 | Inflammation | | | 1 | | | 1 | | | 1 | 3 | 1 | 1 | 1 | | | | | | 8 | | | | | |
| 39 | ...do.......bowels | 1 | | | | | | | | | | 1 | | | | | | | | 2 | | | | | |
| 40 | ....do.......brain | | | 1 | | | | | | 1 | | | | | | | | | | 2 | | | | | |
| 41 | ....do......stomach | | | 1 | | | | | 1 | 1 | | | | | | | | | | 3 | | | | | |
| 42 | Jaundice | | | | | | | | | | | 1 | | | | | | | | 1 | | | | | |
| 43 | Killed | 1 | | | 1 | 2 | 1 | 4 | | 16 | 1 | 2 | | | | | | | | 27 | | | | | |
| 44 | Lightning | | | | | | | 1 | | | | | | | | | | | | 1 | | | | | |
| 45 | Lungs, disease of | | | | | | | | | | | 1 | | | | | | | | 1 | | | | | |
| 46 | Mania-a-potu | | | | | | | | | 1 | | | | | | | | | | | | 1 | | | |
| 47 | Measles | | | 1 | 2 | | | | | | | | | | | | | | | 3 | | | | | |
| 48 | Mumps | 2 | | | 1 | | | | | | | | | | | | | | | 3 | | | | | |
| 49 | Murder | | | | | 1 | | | | 6 | | | | | | | | | | 7 | | | | | |
| 50 | Old age | | | | | | | | | | | 5 | 5 | 8 | 7 | | 1 | | | 26 | | | | | |
| 51 | Onanism | | | | | | | | | 1 | | | | | | | | | | | | | 1 | | |
| 52 | Paralysis | | | | | | 1 | | | | | | | | | | | | | 1 | | | | | |
| 53 | Piles | | | | | | | | | 1 | 1 | 1 | | | | | | | | 3 | | | | | |
| 54 | Pleurisy | 27 | 27 | 17 | 17 | 4 | 4 | 3 | 3 | 6 | 10 | 6 | 10 | 2 | | | | | | 136 | | | | | |
| 55 | Pneumonia | | | | | | | | | | 1 | | 1 | 1 | | | | 1 | | 4 | | | | | |
| 56 | Poison | | | | | | | | | 1 | | | | | | | | | | | | 1 | | | |
| 57 | Prematurity of birth | 2 | 1 | | | | | | | | | | | | | | | | | 3 | | | | | |
| 58 | Quinsy | 1 | 1 | 2 | 3 | | 1 | 1 | 1 | 1 | 3 | | | | | | | | | 14 | | | | | |
| 59 | Rheumatism | | | | 1 | | | | 1 | 2 | 4 | 1 | | | | | | | | 8 | | | 1 | | |
| 60 | Scrofula | | | 6 | 4 | 1 | | 3 | 3 | 12 | 16 | 5 | 3 | 2 | | | | | | 54 | | | | | |
| 61 | Scurvy | | | | 1 | 1 | | | | | 1 | | 1 | | | | | 1 | | 5 | | | | | |
| 62 | Small pox | | | 3 | | | | | | | 1 | | | | | | | | | 4 | | | | | |
| 63 | Stomach, disease of | | | | | | | | | | 2 | | 1 | | | | | | | 3 | | | | | |
| 64 | Suffocation | | | | 1 | 1 | | | | | | | | | | | | | | 2 | | | | | |
| 65 | Syphilis | | | 1 | | | | 1 | | 2 | 6 | | | | | | | | | 10 | | | | | |
| 66 | Teething | | | | 1 | | | | | | | | | | | | | | | 1 | | | | | |
| 67 | Ulcer | | | | | | | | | | 1 | 1 | | | | | | | | 1 | | 1 | | | |
| 68 | Uterus, disease of | | | | | | | | | | 1 | | | | | | | | | 1 | | | | | |
| 69 | Worms | | | | | | | | | | | 1 | | | | | | | | 1 | | | | | |
| 70 | Unknown | 50 | 48 | 35 | 41 | 12 | 8 | 15 | 22 | 35 | 31 | 15 | 14 | 6 | 5 | | | 7 | | 338 | | | | | |
| | Total | 106 | 100 | 121 | 123 | 37 | 30 | 54 | 65 | 151 | 178 | 77 | 64 | 24 | 16 | .. | 1 | 10 | .. | 1131 | .. | 4 | 3 | .. | 2 |

## THE TERRITORY OF NEW MEXICO.

| Nativities: California and Territories. | Nativities: Ireland. | Nativities: Germany. | Nativities: Other foreign countries. | Nativities: Unknown. | Season of decease: Spring. | Season of decease: Summer. | Season of decease: Autumn. | Season of decease: Winter. | Duration of sickness: Under 1 week. | Duration of sickness: 1 week and under 1 month. | Duration of sickness: 1 month and under 3 months. | Duration of sickness: 3 months and over. | Whites: Males. | Whites: Females. | Whites: Total. | Colored: Slaves: Black: M. | Colored: Slaves: Black: F. | Colored: Slaves: Mulatto: M. | Colored: Slaves: Mulatto: F. | Colored: Free: Black: M. | Colored: Free: Black: F. | Colored: Free: Mul.: M | Colored: Free: Mul.: F. | Aggregate deaths. | |
|---|---|---|---|---|---|---|---|---|---|---|---|---|---|---|---|---|---|---|---|---|---|---|---|---|---|
| | | | | | 1 | | | | | 1 | | | | 1 | 1 | | | | | | | | | 1 | 1 |
| | | | | | | 6 | | | 2 | 1 | | | 6 | | 6 | | | | | | | | | 6 | 2 |
| | | | | | 4 | 1 | 3 | 4 | 3 | 5 | | | 7 | 5 | 12 | | | | | | | | | 12 | 3 |
| | | | | | | 1 | 4 | | 5 | | | | 3 | 2 | 5 | | | | | | | | | 5 | 4 |
| | | | | | | | | 1 | | | 1 | | | 1 | 1 | | | | | | | | | 1 | 5 |
| | | | | | | 1 | 1 | 2 | | 1 | 1 | 1 | 3 | 1 | 4 | | | | | | | | | 4 | 6 |
| | | | | | 1 | 1 | 2 | 1 | 2 | 1 | | 1 | 1 | 4 | 5 | | | | | | | | | 5 | 7 |
| | | | | | | | | | | | | | 1 | | 1 | | | | | | | | | 1 | 8 |
| | | | | | | 1 | | | 1 | | | | 1 | | 1 | | | | | | | | | 1 | 9 |
| | | | | | | 1 | | | 1 | | | | 1 | | 1 | | | | | | | | | 1 | 10 |
| | | | | | 7 | 3 | 10 | 7 | 18 | 8 | 3 | | | 31 | 31 | | | | | | | | | 31 | 11 |
| | | | | | 3 | 2 | 1 | 1 | 5 | 2 | | | 4 | 3 | 7 | | | | | | | | | 7 | 12 |
| | | | | | | 1 | 1 | 2 | 2 | 2 | | | 2 | 2 | 4 | | | | | | | | | 4 | 13 |
| | | | | | 3 | 2 | 4 | 2 | 6 | 5 | | | 5 | 6 | 11 | | | | | | | | | 11 | 14 |
| | | | | | | | | 1 | | | | | 1 | | 1 | | | | | | | | | 1 | 15 |
| | | | | | 1 | 1 | 1 | | 1 | | | 2 | 3 | 2 | 5 | | | | | | | | | 5 | 16 |
| | | | | | 1 | | | | | | | | 1 | | 1 | | | | | | | | | 1 | 17 |
| | | | | | 1 | | | | | 1 | | | | 1 | 1 | | | | | | | | | 1 | 18 |
| | | | | | | | 2 | 1 | | | 1 | 1 | 2 | 1 | 3 | | | | | | | | | 3 | 19 |
| | 2 | | 1 | | 1 | 2 | 1 | 1 | | 1 | | 4 | 4 | 1 | 5 | | | | | | | | | 5 | 20 |
| | | | | | 6 | 10 | 10 | 10 | 5 | 1 | 3 | 9 | 16 | 24 | 40 | | | | | | | | | 40 | 21 |
| | | | | | 6 | 1 | 5 | 3 | 3 | 6 | | 6 | 6 | 9 | 15 | | | | | | | | | 15 | 22 |
| | | | | 1 | | | | | 2 | 1 | | | 2 | 3 | 5 | | | | | | | | | 5 | 23 |
| | | | | 1 | 24 | 11 | 10 | 19 | 18 | 43 | 10 | 4 | 41 | 41 | 82 | | | | | | | | | 82 | 24 |
| | | | 3 | | 48 | 44 | 35 | 40 | 31 | 104 | 10 | 14 | 88 | 89 | 177 | | | | | | | | | 177 | 25 |
| | | | | | 1 | 1 | 1 | | | 3 | | | 1 | 2 | 3 | | | | | | | | | 3 | 26 |
| | | | | | | | 1 | | | 1 | | | 1 | | 1 | | | | | | | | | 1 | 27 |
| | | | | | 2 | | | | | 6 | 2 | | 1 | 6 | 13 | | | | | | | | | 13 | 28 |
| | | | | | 1 | | | | 1 | | | | 1 | | 1 | | | | | | | | | 1 | 29 |
| | | | | | | | | 1 | | | | | 1 | | 1 | | | | | | | | | 1 | 30 |
| | | | | | 1 | | | | | | | | | 3 | 3 | | | | | | | | | 3 | 31 |
| | | | | | | | 1 | 1 | | | | 2 | 2 | | 2 | | | | | | | | | 2 | 32 |
| | | | | | | 1 | 1 | | 2 | | 1 | 1 | 1 | 3 | 4 | | | | | | | | | 4 | 33 |
| | | | | | 1 | | | | | | | | | 1 | 1 | | | | | | | | | 1 | 34 |
| | | | | | | | 1 | | | | | | | 1 | 1 | | | | | | | | | 1 | 35 |
| | | | | | | 1 | 3 | 9 | 2 | 7 | 3 | | 8 | 5 | 13 | | | | | | | | | 13 | 36 |
| | | | | | | 1 | | 2 | 2 | 1 | | | 2 | 1 | 3 | | | | | | | | | 3 | 37 |
| | | | | | 1 | | 2 | 2 | | 2 | 5 | 1 | 3 | 5 | 8 | | | | | | | | | 8 | 38 |
| | | | | | 1 | | | 1 | | 1 | | 1 | 2 | | 2 | | | | | | | | | 2 | 39 |
| | | | | | 1 | 1 | | | 2 | | | | 2 | | 2 | | | | | | | | | 2 | 40 |
| | | | | | 1 | | 1 | 1 | 1 | | 1 | 1 | 2 | 1 | 3 | | | | | | | | | 3 | 41 |
| | | | | | | | | 1 | | | | 1 | 1 | | 1 | | | | | | | | | 1 | 42 |
| | | | | 1 | 5 | 7 | 8 | 8 | 1 | | | | 25 | 3 | 28 | | | | | | | | | 28 | 43 |
| | | | | | | 1 | | | | | | | 1 | | 1 | | | | | | | | | 1 | 44 |
| | | | | | | 1 | | | 1 | | | | 1 | | 1 | | | | | | | | | 1 | 45 |
| | | | | | | | 1 | | 1 | | | | 1 | | 1 | | | | | | | | | 1 | 46 |
| | | | | | | 1 | 1 | 1 | | 3 | | | 1 | 2 | 3 | | | | | | | | | 3 | 47 |
| | | | | | | | | 3 | | 2 | 1 | | 2 | 1 | 3 | | | | | | | | | 3 | 48 |
| | | | | | 1 | | 5 | 1 | | | | | 7 | | 7 | | | | | | | | | 7 | 49 |
| | | | | | 5 | 7 | 2 | 9 | 2 | 2 | 12 | 3 | 13 | 13 | 26 | | | | | | | | | 26 | 50 |
| | | | | | | | | 1 | | | | | 1 | | 1 | | | | | | | | | 1 | 51 |
| | | | | | | | | 1 | | | | 1 | | 1 | 1 | | | | | | | | | 1 | 52 |
| | | | | | | 1 | 1 | | | | | | 2 | 1 | 3 | | | | | | | | | 3 | 53 |
| | | | | | 34 | 35 | 27 | 33 | 41 | 70 | 11 | 5 | 65 | 71 | 136 | | | | | | | | | 136 | 54 |
| | | | | | | 1 | | 2 | | 3 | 1 | | 2 | 2 | 4 | | | | | | | | | 4 | 55 |
| | | | | | | | 1 | | 1 | | | | 1 | | 1 | | | | | | | | | 1 | 56 |
| | | | | | 1 | 2 | | | | | | | 2 | 1 | 3 | | | | | | | | | 3 | 57 |
| | | | | | 3 | 6 | 1 | 3 | 4 | 7 | | | 5 | 9 | 14 | | | | | | | | | 14 | 58 |
| | | | | | 4 | | 3 | 2 | | 1 | | 3 | 3 | 6 | 9 | | | | | | | | | 9 | 59 |
| | | | 1 | | 12 | 14 | 13 | 9 | 7 | 7 | 2 | 31 | 29 | 26 | 55 | | | | | | | | | 55 | 60 |
| | | | | | | | | 1 | | | 1 | | 2 | 3 | 5 | | | | | | | | | 5 | 61 |
| | | | | | 2 | 1 | | 1 | 1 | | | 1 | 3 | 1 | 4 | | | | | | | | | 4 | 62 |
| | | | | | 1 | 1 | 1 | | | | 1 | 1 | | 3 | 3 | | | | | | | | | 3 | 63 |
| | | | | | | | | 2 | 2 | | | | 1 | 1 | 2 | | | | | | | | | 2 | 64 |
| | | | | | | | | | | | | | 4 | 6 | 10 | | | | | | | | | 10 | 65 |
| | | | | | | | | 1 | | 1 | | | | 1 | 1 | | | | | | | | | 1 | 66 |
| | | | | | 1 | 1 | | | 1 | | | | 1 | 1 | 2 | | | | | | | | | 2 | 67 |
| | | | | | | 1 | | | | | | 1 | | 1 | 1 | | | | | | | | | 1 | 68 |
| | | | | | | | 1 | | | | | | 1 | | 1 | | | | | | | | | 1 | 69 |
| | | | 3 | 3 | 101 | 61 | 48 | 101 | 72 | 130 | 27 | 20 | 175 | 169 | 344 | | | | | | | | | 344 | 70 |
| ... | 2 | .. | 9 | 6 | 287 | 235 | 214 | 292 | 249 | 430 | 97 | 105 | 580 | 577 | 1157 | ... | ... | ... | ... | ... | ... | .. | .. | 1157 | |

CLASSIFICATION OF DEATHS IN

| | Cause of death. | AGES. | | | | | | | | | | | | | | | | | | NATIVITIES. | | | | | |
|---|---|---|---|---|---|---|---|---|---|---|---|---|---|---|---|---|---|---|---|---|---|---|---|---|---|
| | | Under 1. | | 1 and under 5. | | 5 and under 10. | | 10 and under 20. | | 20 and under 50. | | 50 and under 80. | | 80 and under 100. | | 100 & over. | | Age unknown. | | Born in Territory. | N. England States. | Middle States. | Southern States. | Southwest'n States. | Northwest'n States. |
| | | M. | F. | M. | F. | M. | F. | M. | F. | M. | F. | M. | F. | M | F | M | F. | M | F. | | | | | | |
| 1 | Accident, drowned | | | | | | | 1 | | 1 | | | | | | | | | | | | | 2 | | |
| 2 | Aneurism | | | | | | | | | 1 | | | | | | | | | | | | 1 | | | |
| 3 | Apoplexy | | | | | | | | | | | 1 | | | | | | | | | | | | | |
| 4 | Brain, disease of | 1 | | | | | | | | | | | | | | | | | | 1 | | | | | |
| 5 | Childbirth | | | | | | | | | | 1 | | | | | | | | | | | 1 | | | |
| 6 | Cholera infantum | | | 1 | | | | | | | | | | | | | | | | 1 | | | | | |
| 7 | Consumption | | | | | | | | | 3 | 1 | | 1 | | | | | | | 1 | | 2 | | | 1 |
| 8 | Croup | 1 | | | 1 | | | | | | | | | | | | | | | 2 | | | | | |
| 9 | Diarrhœa | | | 1 | | | | | | | 1 | | 1 | | | | | | | 1 | | 2 | | | |
| 10 | Dropsy | | | | | | | | | | 1 | | | | | | | | | | | | 1 | | |
| 11 | Dysentery | | | | | | | 1 | | 3 | | | | | | | | | | | 2 | 1 | | | 1 |
| 12 | Fever, not specified | | | 1 | | | 1 | | 1 | 3 | | | | | | | | | | 1 | 1 | | | | 4 |
| 13 | ..do..bilious | | | | 1 | | | | | 1 | | | | | | | | | | | | | | | 1 |
| 14 | ..do..typhus | | | 2 | | 2 | | | | | 1 | | | | | | | | | 1 | | | 3 | | 1 |
| 15 | Inflammation, bowels | | | 1 | 1 | | | | | | | | | | | | | | | 2 | | | | | |
| 16 | ....do.....stomach | | | | | | | | | | | 1 | | | | | | | | | | 1 | | | |
| 17 | Murder | | | | | | | | | 1 | | | | | | | | | | | | | | | 1 |
| 18 | Pneumonia | | | | | | | | | | 1 | | | | | | | | | 1 | | | | | |
| 19 | Ulcer | | | | | | | | | 1 | | | | | | | | | | | | 1 | | | |
| 20 | White swelling | 1 | | | | | | | | | | | | | | | | | | 1 | | | | | |
| 21 | Worms | 1 | | | | | | | | | | | | | | | | | | 1 | | | | | |
| 22 | Uuknown | 1 | | 1 | 1 | | | | | | 1 | | | | | | | | | 3 | | | 1 | | |
| | Total | 5 | ... | 7 | 4 | 2 | 1 | 2 | 1 | 14 | 7 | 2 | 2 | .. | .. | .. | .. | .. | .. | 16 | 3 | 9 | 7 | ... | 9 |

CLASSIFICATION OF DEATHS IN

| | Cause of death. | Under 1. M. | Under 1. F. | 1 and under 5. M. | 1 and under 5. F. | 5 and under 10. M. | 5 and under 10. F. | 10 and under 20. M. | 10 and under 20. F. | 20 and under 50. M. | 20 and under 50. F. | 50 and under 80. M. | 50 and under 80. F. | 80 and under 100. M | 80 and under 100. F | 100 & over. M | 100 & over. F. | Age unknown. M | Age unknown. F. | Born in Territory. | N. England States. | Middle States. | Southern States. | Southwest'n States. | Northwest'n States. |
|---|---|---|---|---|---|---|---|---|---|---|---|---|---|---|---|---|---|---|---|---|---|---|---|---|---|
| 1 | Accident, not specfi'd | | | | | 1 | | | | 1 | | | | | | | | | | | | | 1 | | 1 |
| 2 | ....do...drowned | | | | 1 | | | 1 | | | | | | | | | | | | 1 | | | | | 1 |
| 3 | ....do...shot | | | | | | | 1 | | 1 | | | | | | | | | | | | | | | 2 |
| 4 | Canker | 1 | 2 | | 2 | | | 1 | | | 2 | | | | 1 | | | | | 2 | 1 | | 2 | | 4 |
| 5 | Catarrh | | | 2 | | | | | | | | | 1 | | | | | | | | | 2 | 1 | | |
| 6 | Childbirth | | | | | | | | | | 1 | | | | | | | | | | | | | | |
| 7 | Cholera | 2 | | 10 | 10 | 6 | 7 | 4 | 7 | 12 | 19 | 3 | 2 | | | | | | | 3 | 7 | 18 | 2 | 7 | 34 |
| 8 | Colic | | | | | | | 1 | | | | | | | | | | | | | | | | | 1 |
| 9 | Consumption | | | 2 | | | | 1 | | 8 | 1 | 1 | 1 | | | | | | | 4 | 2 | 4 | 1 | | 1 |
| 10 | Convulsions | 1 | 2 | 1 | | 1 | | 1 | | | | 1 | | | | | | | | 4 | | | | | 1 |
| 11 | Croup | 1 | | | | | | | | | | | | | | | | | | 1 | | | | | |
| 12 | Dropsy | | | | | | | | | | | | 3 | | | | | | | 1 | | | | | |
| 13 | Dysentery | | | | | | | | | | | 2 | | | | | | | | | 2 | | | | |
| 14 | Erysipelas | 3 | 1 | 4 | 1 | | | 1 | 4 | 4 | 4 | 4 | 1 | | | | | | | 9 | 4 | 7 | 1 | | 4 |
| 15 | Fever, not specified | | 1 | 3 | 1 | | | 1 | | | 2 | 2 | 1 | | | | | | | 6 | | 2 | 1 | | 2 |
| 16 | ..do..bilious | | | | | | | | | 1 | | 1 | | | | | | | | | | | 1 | 1 | |
| 17 | ..do..congestive | 1 | | | | | | | | | | | | | | | | | | | | | | | 1 |
| 18 | ..do..scarlet | | | 1 | | | | | | | | | | | | | | | | | | | | | |
| 19 | ..do..typhus | | | | | 1 | | | | | | | | | | | | | | | 1 | | | | |
| 20 | Gravel | | | | | | | | | | | 1 | | | | | | | | | | 1 | | | |
| 21 | Hemorrhage | | | | | | | | | 2 | | | | | | | | | | | 1 | | | | |
| 22 | Hives | 1 | 1 | | | | | | | | | | | | | | | | | 2 | | | | | |
| 23 | Hooping cough | | 1 | 1 | 1 | | | | | | | | | | | | | | | 1 | | | | | 2 |
| 24 | Hydrocephalus | 1 | | | 1 | | | | | | 1 | | | | | | | 1 | | 3 | | | | 1 | |
| 25 | Inflammation | | | | 2 | | | 1 | 2 | | | | | | | | | | | 1 | 1 | 1 | | | 2 |
| 26 | .....do..... bowels | | | | | | | | | 1 | | | | | | | | | | | 1 | | | | |
| 27 | Jaundice | | | | | | | | | | 1 | | | | | | | | | | | | | | |
| 28 | Liver, disease of | 1 | | | | | | | | | | | | | | | | | | 1 | | | | | |
| 29 | Measles | 1 | | | 2 | 1 | 1 | | | | 1 | | | | | | | | | 4 | | | 1 | | 1 |
| 30 | Old age | | | | | | | | | | | | 1 | | | | | | | | | 1 | | | |
| 31 | Paralysis | | | | | | | | | | | 1 | | | | | | | | | 1 | | | | |
| 32 | Pleurisy | | | | | | | | | 1 | | 2 | | | | | | | | 2 | | | | | 1 |
| 33 | Pneumonia | 1 | 1 | | 1 | 1 | 1 | | 1 | 3 | 1 | 2 | | | | | | | | 1 | 1 | 2 | 2 | 1 | 4 |
| 34 | Poison | | | 1 | 1 | | | | | | | 1 | | | | | | | | | 1 | | | | 2 |
| 35 | Quinsy | | | | | | | 1 | | | 1 | 1 | | | | | | | | | | | | | 3 |
| 36 | Small pox | | | | 1 | | | | | | | | | | | | | | | | | | | | |
| 37 | Worms | | | 1 | | | | | | | | | | | | | | | | | | | | | 1 |
| 38 | Unknown | 4 | 3 | 1 | 2 | | 1 | 2 | 1 | | | 1 | | | | | | 1 | | 13 | 2 | | | | 1 |
| | Total | 18 | 12 | 27 | 26 | 11 | 10 | 16 | 15 | 34 | 34 | 23 | 10 | .. | 1 | .. | .. | 2 | .. | 59 | 25 | 38 | 13 | 10 | 69 |

## THE TERRITORY OF OREGON.

| Nativities: California and Territories. | Ireland. | Germany. | Other foreign countries. | Unknown. | Season of decease: Spring. | Summer. | Autumn. | Winter. | Duration of sickness: Under 1 week. | 1 week and under 1 month. | 1 month and under 3 months. | 3 months and over. | Whites: Males. | Females. | Total. | Colored: Slaves: Black: M. | F. | Mulatto: M. | F. | Free: Black: M. | F. | Mul. M | F. | Aggregate deaths. | |
|---|---|---|---|---|---|---|---|---|---|---|---|---|---|---|---|---|---|---|---|---|---|---|---|---|---|
| | | | | | | | 1 | 1 | 2 | | | | 2 | | 2 | | | | | | | | | 2 | 1 |
| | | | | | | | 1 | | | 1 | | | 1 | | 1 | | | | | | | | | 1 | 2 |
| | | | 1 | | | | | 1 | | | | 1 | 1 | | 1 | | | | | | | | | 1 | 3 |
| | | | | | | | | | 1 | | | | 1 | | 1 | | | | | | | | | 1 | 4 |
| | | | | | 1 | | | | | 1 | | | | 1 | 1 | | | | | | | | | 1 | 5 |
| | | | | | | | | 1 | | | | | 1 | | 1 | | | | | | | | | 1 | 6 |
| | | | | 1 | 1 | 2 | 1 | 1 | | | 1 | 1 | 3 | 2 | 5 | | | | | | | | | 5 | 7 |
| | | | | | | 1 | 1 | | 2 | | | | 1 | 1 | 2 | | | | | | | | | 2 | 8 |
| | | | | | 1 | 1 | 1 | | 2 | 1 | | | 1 | 2 | 3 | | | | | | | | | 3 | 9 |
| | | | | | | | 1 | | | | | 1 | | 1 | 1 | | | | | | | | | 1 | 10 |
| | | | | | 1 | | | 3 | | | 4 | | 4 | | 4 | | | | | | | | | 4 | 11 |
| | | | | | 2 | | 2 | 2 | 1 | 4 | | 1 | 4 | 2 | 6 | | | | | | | | | 6 | 12 |
| | | | 1 | | 1 | | | 1 | | 2 | | | 1 | 1 | 2 | | | | | | | | | 2 | 13 |
| | | | | | 1 | | | 4 | | 5 | | | 4 | 1 | 5 | | | | | | | | | 5 | 14 |
| | | | | | | | | 2 | | 1 | | | 1 | 1 | 2 | | | | | | | | | 2 | 15 |
| | | | | | 1 | | | | | | | | 1 | | 1 | | | | | | | | | 1 | 16 |
| | | | | | | | | 1 | 1 | | | | 1 | | 1 | | | | | | | | | 1 | 17 |
| | | | | | | | | 1 | 1 | | | | | 1 | 1 | | | | | | | | | 1 | 18 |
| | | | | | | | 1 | | | 1 | | | 1 | | 1 | | | | | | | | | 1 | 19 |
| | | | | | 1 | | | | | 1 | | | 1 | | 1 | | | | | | | | | 1 | 20 |
| | | | | | 1 | | | | | 1 | | | 1 | | 1 | | | | | | | | | 1 | 21 |
| | | | | | 2 | 1 | | 1 | 1 | 1 | | 2 | 2 | 2 | 4 | | | | | | | | | 4 | 22 |
| | | | 2 | 1 | 13 | 5 | 9 | 19 | 11 | 19 | 5 | 6 | 32 | 15 | 47 | | | | | | | | | 47 | |

## THE TERRITORY OF UTAH.

| Nativities: California and Territories. | Ireland. | Germany. | Other foreign countries. | Unknown. | Season of decease: Spring. | Summer. | Autumn. | Winter. | Duration of sickness: Under 1 week. | 1 week and under 1 month. | 1 month and under 3 months. | 3 months and over. | Whites: Males. | Females. | Total. | Colored: Slaves: Black: M. | F. | Mulatto: M. | F. | Free: Black: M. | F. | Mul. M | F. | Aggregate deaths. | |
|---|---|---|---|---|---|---|---|---|---|---|---|---|---|---|---|---|---|---|---|---|---|---|---|---|---|
| | | | | | | 1 | 1 | | | | | | 2 | | 2 | | | | | | | | | 2 | 1 |
| | | | | | | 1 | 1 | | 2 | | | | 1 | 1 | 2 | | | | | | | | | 2 | 2 |
| | | | | | 1 | 1 | | | | | | | 2 | | 2 | | | | | | | | | 2 | 3 |
| | | | | | | 3 | 3 | 3 | | | | | 2 | 7 | 9 | | | | | | | | | 9 | 4 |
| | | | | | 2 | | 1 | | | | | | 2 | 1 | 3 | | | | | | | | | 3 | 5 |
| | | | 1 | | 1 | | | | | | | | | 1 | 1 | | | | | | | | | 1 | 6 |
| 1 | 2 | | 8 | | 6 | 73 | 3 | | | | | | 37 | 45 | 82 | | | | | | | | | 82 | 7 |
| | | | | | | 1 | | | | | | | 1 | | 1 | | | | | | | | | 1 | 8 |
| | | | 2 | | 6 | 2 | 1 | 5 | | | | | 12 | 2 | 14 | | | | | | | | | 14 | 9 |
| | | | 2 | | 3 | | | 4 | | | | | 5 | 2 | 7 | | | | | | | | | 7 | 10 |
| | | | | | | | | 1 | | | | | 1 | | 1 | | | | | | | | | 1 | 11 |
| | | | 2 | | | | 1 | 2 | | | | | | 3 | 3 | | | | | | | | | 3 | 12 |
| | | | | | | | 2 | | | | | | 2 | | 2 | | | | | | | | | 2 | 13 |
| | | | 2 | | 11 | 2 | | 14 | | | | | 16 | 11 | 27 | | | | | | | | | 27 | 14 |
| | | | | | 2 | 1 | 3 | 5 | | | | | 6 | 5 | 11 | | | | | | | | | 11 | 15 |
| | | | | | | | 1 | 1 | | | | | 2 | | 2 | | | | | | | | | 2 | 16 |
| | | | | | 1 | | | | | | | | 1 | | 1 | | | | | | | | | 1 | 17 |
| | | | 1 | | | 1 | | | | | | | 1 | | 1 | | | | | | | | | 1 | 18 |
| | | | | | 1 | | | | | | | | 1 | | 1 | | | | | | | | | 1 | 19 |
| | | | | | | | | 1 | | | | | 1 | | 1 | | | | | | | | | 1 | 20 |
| | | | 1 | | 2 | | | | | | | | 2 | | 2 | | | | | | | | | 2 | 21 |
| | | | | | 1 | | 1 | | | | | | 1 | 1 | 2 | | | | | | | | | 2 | 22 |
| | | | | | | 1 | 1 | 1 | | | | | 1 | 2 | 3 | | | | | | | | | 3 | 23 |
| | | | | | 2 | | 1 | 1 | | | | | 2 | 2 | 4 | | | | | | | | | 4 | 24 |
| | | | | | 3 | | | 2 | | | | | 1 | 4 | 5 | | | | | | | | | 5 | 25 |
| | | | | | | | 1 | | | | | | 1 | | 1 | | | | | | | | | 1 | 26 |
| | | | 1 | | | 1 | | | | | | | | 1 | 1 | | | | | | | | | 1 | 27 |
| | | | | | | | 1 | | | | | | 1 | | 1 | | | | | | | | | 1 | 28 |
| | | | | | 4 | 2 | | | | | | | 2 | 4 | 6 | | | | | | | | | 6 | 29 |
| | | | | | | | | 1 | | | | | | 1 | 1 | | | | | | | | | 1 | 30 |
| | | | | | | | 1 | | | | | | 1 | | 1 | | | | | | | | | 1 | 31 |
| | | | | | | | 1 | 1 | | | | | 3 | | 3 | | | | | | | | | 3 | 32 |
| | | | 1 | | 6 | | | 5 | | | | | 7 | 5 | 12 | | | | | | | | | 12 | 33 |
| | | | | | 1 | | | 2 | | | | | 2 | 1 | 3 | | | | | | | | | 3 | 34 |
| | | | | | | 3 | | | | | | | 2 | 1 | 3 | | | | | | | | | 3 | 35 |
| | | | 1 | | | 1 | | | | | | | | 1 | 1 | | | | | | | | | 1 | 36 |
| | | | | | | | 1 | | | | | | 1 | | 1 | | | | | | | | | 1 | 37 |
| | | | | | 3 | 3 | 5 | 3 | | | | | 9 | 6 | 15 | | | | | | | | | 16 | 38 |
| 1 | 2 | | 22 | | 56 | 97 | 80 | 52 | 2 | | | | 131 | 107 | 238 | | | | | | | | | 239 | |

## CLASSIFICATION OF DEATHS IN SOME OF THE LEADING CITIES OF THE UNITED STATES.

| | Name of city. | AGES. | | | | | | | | | | | | | | | | | | | | NATIVITIES. | | | | | | | | | | | SEASON OF DECEASE. | | | | |
|---|---|---|---|---|---|---|---|---|---|---|---|---|---|---|---|---|---|---|---|---|---|---|---|---|---|---|---|---|---|---|---|---|---|---|---|---|---|
| | | Under 1. | | 1 and under 5. | | 5 and under 10. | | 10 and under 20. | | 20 and under 50. | | 50 and under 80. | | 80 and under 100. | | 100 & over. | | Age unknown. | | Total. | | Born in State. | N. Engl'd States. | Middle States. | Southern States. | S. West'n States. | N. West'n States. | California and Territories. | Ireland. | Germany. | Other foreign countries. | Unknown. | Spring. | Summer. | Autumn. | Winter. | Unknown. |
| | | M. | F. | M. | F. | M. | F. | M. | F. | M. | F. | M. | F. | M. | F. | | F. | M | F. | M. | F. | | | | | | | | | | | | | | | | |
| 1 | Albany, N. Y. | 83 | 71 | 126 | 128 | 51 | 49 | 36 | 53 | 196 | 151 | 96 | 63 | 4 | 15 | .. | .. | 33 | 42 | 618 | 579 | 684 | 24 | 3 | 3 | .... | 1 | .... | 290 | 41 | 87 | 64 | 182 | 361 | 435 | 211 | 8 |
| 2 | Alleghany City, Pa. | 16 | 14 | 24 | 23 | 8 | 5 | 10 | 10 | 24 | 23 | 11 | 5 | 8 | 3 | .. | .. | .. | .. | 96 | 83 | 131 | 1 | 1 | 2 | .... | 4 | .... | 23 | 7 | 10 | .... | 62 | 36 | 40 | 40 | 1 |
| 3 | Alexandria, Va. | 15 | 7 | 11 | 19 | 11 | 10 | 8 | 9 | 12 | 20 | 18 | 14 | .... | 1 | .. | .. | .. | .. | 75 | 80 | 133 | .... | 14 | .... | .... | .... | .... | 6 | .... | 2 | .... | 45 | 44 | 49 | 27 | .... |
| 4 | Augusta, Me. | 7 | 6 | 21 | 21 | 3 | 5 | 6 | 8 | 25 | 19 | 15 | 16 | 1 | 1 | .. | .. | .. | .. | 78 | 76 | 142 | 11 | 1 | .... | .... | .... | .... | .... | .... | .... | .... | 29 | 43 | 55 | 25 | 2 |
| 5 | Baltimore, Md | 428 | 371 | 479 | 416 | 125 | 94 | 128 | 125 | 525 | 410 | 227 | 228 | 29 | 49 | .. | 5 | 11 | 5 | 1152 | 1708 | 3037 | 21 | 123 | 49 | 2 | 2 | .... | 178 | 180 | 61 | 2 | 837 | 1117 | 873 | 742 | 86 |
| 6 | Bangor, Me. | 8 | 8 | 19 | 25 | 7 | 15 | 8 | 7 | 58 | 35 | 15 | 6 | 1 | 2 | .. | .. | .. | 1 | 111 | 99 | 146 | 10 | 2 | .... | .... | .... | .... | 45 | 1 | 6 | .... | 27 | 26 | 135 | 22 | .... |
| 7 | Boston, Mass | 325 | 268 | 748 | 635 | 178 | 109 | 124 | 152 | 786 | 765 | 284 | 270 | 34 | 36 | .. | .. | 57 | 29 | 2643 | 2257 | 2939 | 311 | 50 | 19 | 2 | 2 | .... | 1301 | 7 | 258 | 11 | 922 | 978 | 1973 | 918 | 109 |
| 8 | Brooklyn, N. Y | 261 | 209 | 295 | 267 | 84 | 71 | 59 | 60 | 318 | 205 | 103 | 108 | 5 | 13 | .. | .. | 1 | .. | 1126 | 933 | 1265 | 72 | 67 | 6 | .... | 7 | .... | 402 | 23 | 115 | 2 | 367 | 643 | 730 | 307 | 12 |
| 9 | Buffalo, N. Y. | 92 | 76 | 139 | 137 | 53 | 35 | 47 | 40 | 216 | 154 | 45 | 39 | 4 | 3 | .. | .. | 52 | 48 | 648 | 532 | 595 | 29 | 15 | 3 | .... | 10 | .... | 162 | 246 | 96 | 24 | 146 | 358 | 587 | 88 | 1 |
| 10 | Charleston, S. C. | 14 | 11 | 43 | 46 | 14 | 5 | 15 | 19 | 124 | 58 | 47 | 37 | 5 | 9 | 3 | .. | .. | .. | 265 | 185 | 289 | 8 | 15 | 6 | .... | 1 | .... | 69 | 23 | 39 | .... | 71 | 97 | 220 | 60 | 2 |
| 11 | Chicago, Ill. | 44 | 29 | 50 | 45 | 22 | 22 | 22 | 29 | 112 | 59 | 21 | 8 | 2 | .... | .. | .. | .. | .. | 273 | 192 | 197 | 19 | 42 | .... | 1 | 13 | .... | 62 | 67 | 59 | 5 | 59 | 140 | 232 | 30 | 4 |
| 12 | Cincinnati, Ohio. | 412 | 340 | 608 | 564 | 209 | 153 | 170 | 137 | 1110 | 658 | 258 | 184 | 7 | 9 | .. | .. | 5 | 3 | 2779 | 2052 | 2238 | 47 | 268 | 80 | 16 | 93 | .... | 414 | 1336 | 205 | 34 | 612 | 2841 | 804 | 555 | 19 |
| 13 | Cleveland ..do | 36 | 22 | 46 | 30 | 11 | 7 | 7 | 5 | 53 | 37 | 10 | 9 | 1 | 1 | .. | .. | .. | .. | 164 | 111 | 132 | 9 | 12 | 1 | .... | 1 | .... | 38 | 48 | 30 | 4 | 48 | 58 | 126 | 41 | 2 |
| 14 | Columbus ..do | 11 | 8 | 13 | 26 | 12 | 3 | 7 | 14 | 158 | 32 | 41 | 11 | 3 | 3 | .. | .. | .. | .. | 245 | 97 | 128 | 18 | 70 | 34 | 4 | 10 | ... | 21 | 43 | 12 | 2 | 40 | 193 | 93 | 11 | 5 |
| 15 | Detroit, Mich | 44 | 46 | 61 | 47 | 11 | 5 | 14 | 9 | 68 | 41 | 29 | 16 | 1 | 2 | .. | .. | .. | .. | 228 | 166 | 205 | 18 | 83 | 2 | .... | 11 | 1 | 53 | 29 | 42 | .... | 63 | 156 | 134 | 36 | 5 |
| 16 | Georgetown, D, C | 10 | 11 | 17 | 25 | 9 | 8 | 12 | 6 | 21 | 25 | 15 | 13 | .... | .... | 1 | .. | .. | .. | 85 | 88 | 113 | .... | 42 | 11 | 2 | 1 | .... | 2 | 1 | 1 | .... | 43 | 66 | 37 | 26 | 1 |
| 17 | Lancaster, Pa. | 22 | 19 | 32 | 34 | 12 | 13 | 5 | 7 | 35 | 14 | 16 | 13 | .... | 4 | .. | .. | .. | .. | 122 | 104 | 197 | 1 | 5 | .... | .... | .... | .... | 6 | 15 | 2 | .... | 57 | 49 | 68 | 51 | 1 |
| 18 | Louisville, Ky. | 97 | 80 | 112 | 98 | 42 | 22 | 34 | 30 | 207 | 125 | 70 | 85 | 6 | 6 | .. | .. | 18 | 15 | 586 | 411 | 457 | 11 | 78 | 59 | 15 | 62 | .... | 101 | 168 | 40 | 6 | 235 | 350 | 271 | 141 | ... |
| 19 | Memphis, Tenn | 26 | 20 | 39 | 27 | 6 | 7 | 23 | 24 | 90 | 53 | 23 | 15 | 4 | 1 | .. | .. | 56 | 11 | 267 | 158 | 305 | 3 | 5 | 52 | 1 | 17 | .... | 25 | 6 | 11 | .... | 94 | 163 | 88 | 80 | .... |
| 20 | Mobile, Ala | 68 | 74 | 44 | 43 | 10 | 14 | 19 | 11 | 218 | 95 | 44 | 17 | 2 | 4 | .. | 1 | .. | .. | 405 | 259 | 316 | 37 | 20 | 98 | 4 | 7 | .... | 95 | 19 | 67 | 1 | 127 | 157 | 200 | 180 | .... |
| 21 | Nashville, Tenn | 19 | 15 | 48 | 41 | 16 | 12 | 16 | 23 | 91 | 47 | 19 | 34 | 3 | 1 | .. | .. | .. | .. | 212 | 178 | 252 | 1 | 15 | 64 | .... | 11 | .... | 21 | 10 | 11 | .... | 53 | 263 | 40 | 25 | 4 |
| 22 | Newark, N. J. | 63 | 58 | 62 | 67 | 15 | 9 | 19 | 14 | 82 | 71 | 53 | 43 | 4 | 7 | .. | .. | .. | .. | 298 | 264 | 364 | 15 | 46 | 2 | .... | .... | .... | 82 | 18 | 35 | .... | 132 | 142 | 203 | 85 | .... |
| 23 | N. Orleans, includ'g Jeff. Par | 195 | 164 | 222 | 205 | 82 | 62 | 173 | 112 | 2078 | 592 | 263 | 131 | 12 | 14 | 1 | 1 | 4 | 1 | 3030 | 1282 | 1176 | 71 | 171 | 214 | 48 | 69 | .... | 1286 | 468 | 690 | 119 | 1006 | 1062 | 1197 | 1014 | 33 |
| 24 | New York, N. Y. | 823 | 845 | 1401 | 1304 | 454 | 364 | 369 | 345 | 2532 | 1896 | 787 | 584 | 46 | 78 | .. | .. | 24 | 31 | 6456 | 5447 | 6895 | 247 | 352 | 109 | 8 | 11 | .... | 2942 | 526 | 728 | 65 | 2022 | 4171 | 3592 | 1703 | 395 |
| 25 | Norfolk, Va. | 17 | 16 | 23 | 19 | 13 | 7 | 15 | 21 | 61 | 45 | 44 | 32 | 1 | 9 | .. | .. | .. | .. | 174 | 149 | 288 | 5 | 10 | 8 | .... | .... | .... | 4 | 2 | 11 | .... | 56 | 142 | 85 | 40 | .... |
| 26 | Petersburg, Va. | 14 | 19 | 11 | 9 | 4 | 3 | 5 | 6 | 40 | 38 | 19 | 19 | 3 | 5 | .. | .. | 4 | 3 | 100 | 102 | 183 | 1 | 5 | 1 | .... | .... | .... | 5 | .... | 7 | .... | 32 | 83 | 54 | 33 | .... |
| 27 | Philadelphia, Pa | 688 | 558 | 927 | 780 | 210 | 183 | 206 | 165 | 1296 | 831 | 537 | 455 | 72 | 102 | 1 | .. | 9 | 10 | 3896 | 3084 | 4905 | 51 | 486 | 45 | 5 | 18 | .... | 889 | 252 | 323 | 6 | 1454 | 2502 | 1809 | 1071 | 144 |
| 28 | Pittsburg, Pa | 92 | 83 | 99 | 90 | 35 | 21 | 25 | 21 | 159 | 71 | 60 | 25 | 9 | 5 | .. | .. | 1 | 1 | 483 | 314 | 508 | 9 | 21 | 9 | .... | 6 | .... | 146 | 51 | 52 | .... | 53 | 273 | 337 | 132 | 2 |
| 29 | Portland, Me | 51 | 43 | 83 | 74 | 18 | 17 | 13 | 19 | 90 | 52 | 35 | 33 | 6 | 11 | .. | .. | .. | .. | 296 | 249 | 444 | 24 | 7 | .... | 1 | .... | .... | 28 | ... | 22 | 19 | 97 | 110 | 234 | 104 | .... |
| 30 | Portsmouth, Va. | 22 | 15 | 18 | 13 | .... | 4 | 6 | 11 | 24 | 27 | 12 | 18 | 1 | 6 | .. | .. | .. | .. | 88 | 94 | 168 | 1 | 3 | 2 | .... | .... | .... | 1 | .... | 2 | .... | 22 | 96 | 38 | 20 | 1 |
| 31 | Poughkeepsie, N. Y | 42 | 85 | 58 | 56 | 23 | 26 | 15 | 19 | 142 | 88 | 55 | 34 | 14 | 5 | 1 | .. | .. | .. | 350 | 263 | 466 | 8 | 5 | 1 | .... | .... | ... | 81 | 20 | 31 | 1 | 70 | 146 | 311 | 80 | 6 |
| 32 | Providence, R. I | 86 | 51 | 112 | 86 | 21 | 18 | 25 | 28 | 125 | 143 | 69 | 80 | 10 | 20 | .. | .. | 13 | 6 | 461 | 432 | 707 | 31 | 6 | .... | .... | .... | .... | 125 | 1 | 23 | .... | 153 | 205 | 370 | 165 | .... |
| 33 | Quincy, Ill. | 20 | 16 | 17 | 13 | 14 | 8 | 6 | 3 | 37 | 25 | 7 | 7 | .... | .... | .. | .. | .. | .. | 101 | 72 | 96 | 7 | 15 | 4 | .... | 7 | .... | 12 | 28 | 10 | .... | 20 | 85 | 60 | 8 | .... |
| 34 | Richmond, Va | 29 | 23 | 64 | 46 | 8 | 17 | 12 | 20 | 101 | 69 | 55 | 39 | 3 | 6 | .. | .. | .. | .. | 272 | 220 | 440 | 7 | 12 | 2 | .... | .... | .... | 4 | 10 | 16 | 1 | 95 | 219 | 116 | 62 | .... |
| 35 | St. Louis, Mo | 213 | 218 | 414 | 394 | 140 | 123 | 169 | 149 | 1105 | 560 | 196 | 141 | 5 | 1 | .. | .. | 6 | 2 | 2248 | 1586 | 1354 | 64 | 148 | 82 | 63 | 125 | .... | 654 | 1037 | 300 | 7 | 340 | 2564 | 647 | 218 | 65 |
| 36 | Washington, D. C | 67 | 53 | 74 | 57 | 17 | 23 | 18 | 28 | 80 | 80 | 37 | 47 | 7 | 9 | .. | 1 | 1 | .. | 801 | 298 | 354 | 9 | 131 | 49 | 2 | 1 | .... | 22 | 9 | 13 | 9 | 168 | 166 | 131 | 111 | 23 |
| 37 | Wilmington, Del. | 19 | 17 | 35 | 20 | 6 | 3 | 9 | 12 | 35 | 44 | 40 | 34 | 7 | 5 | .. | .. | .. | .. | 151 | 185 | 212 | .... | 45 | .... | .... | .... | .... | 19 | 4 | 5 | 1 | 62 | 120 | 68 | 36 | .... |
| 38 | Wilmington, N. C. | 15 | 19 | 23 | 11 | 8 | 4 | 10 | 6 | 32 | 15 | 7 | 12 | 1 | .... | .. | .. | .. | .. | 91 | 67 | 142 | 4 | 4 | 4 | .... | .... | .... | 2 | .... | 2 | .... | 45 | 61 | 29 | 23 | .... |

## CLASSIFICATION OF DEATHS IN SOME OF THE LEADING CITIES OF THE UNITED STATES—Continued.

| | Name of city. | DURATION OF SICKNESS. | | | | | OCCUPATIONS. | | | | | | WHITES. | | | COLORED. | | | | | | | | | | | | Aggregate deaths. |
|---|---|---|---|---|---|---|---|---|---|---|---|---|---|---|---|---|---|---|---|---|---|---|---|---|---|---|---|---|
| | | | | | | | | | | | | | | | | Slaves. | | | | | | Free. | | | | | | |
| | | | | | | | | | | | | | | | | Black. | | Mulatto. | | Total. | | Black. | | Mulatto. | | Total. | | |
| | | Under 1 week. | 1 week and under 1 month. | 1 month and under 3 months. | 3 months and over. | Unknown. | Agricultural. | Mechanical. | Labor not specified. | Commercial. | Educational. | Other pursuits. | Males. | Females. | Total. | M. | F. | M. | F. | Blk. | Mul. | M. | F. | M. | F. | Blk. | Mul. | |
| 1 | Albany, N. Y | 399 | 259 | 98 | 159 | 288 | 8 | 49 | 53 | 20 | 10 | 6 | 608 | 575 | 1183 | .... | .... | .... | .... | .... | .... | 9 | 4 | 1 | .... | 13 | 1 | 1197 |
| 2 | Alleghany City, Pa | 52 | 68 | 8 | 39 | 12 | .... | 17 | 9 | .... | 1 | 3 | 95 | 83 | 178 | .... | .... | .... | .... | .... | .... | 1 | .... | .... | .... | 1 | .... | 179 |
| 3 | Alexandria, Va | 62 | 39 | 11 | 33 | 10 | 3 | 9 | 1 | 3 | 1 | 1 | 62 | 63 | 125 | 3 | 8 | 1 | 2 | 11 | 3 | 4 | 1 | 5 | 6 | 5 | 11 | 155 |
| 4 | Augusta, Me | 36 | 41 | 25 | 46 | 6 | 18 | 8 | 4 | 2 | 2 | 2 | 78 | 75 | 153 | .... | .... | .... | .... | .... | .... | .... | .... | .... | 1 | .... | 1 | 154 |
| 5 | Baltimore, Md | 998 | 1286 | 390 | 750 | 231 | 7 | 229 | 211 | 174 | 22 | 2 | 1567 | 1376 | 2943 | 17 | 26 | 6 | 4 | 43 | 10 | 299 | 244 | 68 | 53 | 543 | 116 | 3655 |
| 6 | Bangor, Me | 121 | 46 | 8 | 34 | 1 | 4 | 17 | 10 | 10 | 2 | 2 | 111 | 98 | 209 | .... | .... | .... | .... | .... | .... | .... | 1 | .... | .... | 1 | .... | 210 |
| 7 | Boston, Mass | 1656 | 1652 | 202 | 550 | 840 | 38 | 241 | 284 | 96 | 15 | 8 | 2606 | 2241 | 4847 | .... | .... | .... | .... | .... | .... | 30 | 23 | .... | .... | 53 | .... | 4900 |
| 8 | Brooklyn, N. Y | 885 | 584 | 202 | 321 | 67 | 4 | 128 | 150 | 55 | 32 | 12 | 1096 | 901 | 1997 | .... | .... | .... | .... | .... | .... | 25 | 30 | 5 | 2 | 55 | 7 | 2059 |
| 9 | Buffalo, N. Y | 591 | 238 | 74 | 247 | 30 | 1 | 85 | 112 | 26 | 15 | 7 | 637 | 527 | 1164 | .... | .... | .... | .... | .... | .... | 7 | 4 | 4 | 1 | 11 | 5 | 1180 |
| 10 | Charleston, S. C | 140 | 185 | 55 | 61 | .... | 14 | 38 | 29 | 48 | 6 | .... | 189 | 131 | 320 | 54 | 34 | 11 | 3 | 88 | 14 | 1 | 5 | 10 | 12 | 6 | 22 | 450 |
| 11 | Chicago, Ill | 265 | 91 | 20 | 20 | 69 | 3 | 29 | 37 | 7 | 13 | .... | 272 | 191 | 463 | .... | .... | .... | .... | .... | .... | .... | 1 | 1 | .... | .... | .... | 465 |
| 12 | Cincinnati, Ohio | 2733 | 809 | 114 | 372 | 803 | 14 | 356 | 365 | 114 | 24 | 12 | 2733 | 2022 | 4755 | .... | .... | .... | .... | .... | .... | 21 | 20 | 25 | 10 | 41 | 35 | 4831 |
| 13 | Cleveland ..do | 44 | 44 | 5 | 19 | 163 | 2 | 7 | 27 | 9 | 1 | .... | 163 | 109 | 272 | .... | .... | .... | .... | .... | .... | .... | 2 | 1 | .... | 2 | 1 | 275 |
| 14 | Columbus.. do | 112 | 55 | 15 | 21 | 39 | 45 | 67 | 57 | 15 | 6 | 10 | 222 | 85 | 307 | .... | .... | .... | .... | .... | .... | 21 | 12 | 2 | .... | 33 | 2 | 342 |
| 15 | Detroit, Mich | 152 | 155 | 30 | 48 | 9 | 1 | 25 | 45 | 8 | 7 | 5 | 225 | 161 | 386 | .... | .... | .... | .... | .... | .... | 1 | 3 | 2 | 2 | 4 | 4 | 394 |
| 16 | Georgetown, D. C | 29 | 83 | 11 | 45 | 5 | 1 | 7 | 6 | 7 | 3 | .... | 64 | 66 | 130 | 3 | 4 | .... | .... | 7 | .... | 16 | 17 | 2 | 1 | 33 | 3 | 173 |
| 17 | Lancaster, Pa | 76 | 77 | 23 | 43 | 7 | 3 | 36 | 4 | 5 | 2 | .... | 121 | 99 | 220 | .... | .... | .... | .... | .... | .... | 1 | 2 | .... | 3 | 3 | 3 | 226 |
| 18 | Louisville, Ky | 304 | 205 | 68 | 216 | 204 | 7 | 60 | 54 | 19 | 5 | 37 | 494 | 337 | 831 | 77 | 54 | 11 | 16 | 131 | 27 | 3 | 2 | 1 | 2 | 4 | 4 | 997 |
| 19 | Memphis, Tenn | 196 | 98 | 33 | 30 | 68 | 7 | 17 | 21 | 7 | 4 | 2 | 205 | 112 | 317 | 50 | 40 | 11 | 6 | 90 | 17 | .... | .... | 1 | .... | .... | 1 | 425 |
| 20 | Mobile, Ala | 240 | 151 | 35 | 119 | 119 | 10 | 25 | 105 | 69 | 5 | 4 | 310 | 163 | 473 | 77 | 73 | 9 | 10 | 150 | 19 | .... | .... | 9 | 13 | .... | 22 | 664 |
| 21 | Nashville, Tenn | 206 | 93 | 39 | 33 | 14 | 1 | 25 | 1 | 6 | 4 | .... | 162 | 126 | 288 | 33 | 35 | 7 | 5 | 68 | 12 | 4 | 1 | 6 | 6 | 5 | 12 | 385 |
| 22 | Newark, N. J | 225 | 173 | 37 | 110 | 17 | 8 | 55 | 14 | 21 | 9 | 2 | 295 | 255 | 550 | .... | .... | .... | .... | .... | .... | 1 | 7 | 2 | 2 | 8 | 4 | 562 |
| 23 | New Orleans, including Jeff. parish, La | 1044 | 522 | 157 | 354 | 2235 | 74 | 428 | 1046 | 275 | 39 | 32 | 2666 | 992 | 3658 | 243 | 171 | 46 | 39 | 414 | 85 | 22 | 15 | 53 | 65 | 37 | 118 | 4312 |
| 24 | ew York, N. Y | 3447 | 2432 | 791 | 1186 | 4027 | 81 | 568 | 616 | 131 | 51 | 375 | 6311 | 5318 | 11629 | .... | .... | .... | .... | .... | .... | 104 | 110 | 21 | 19 | 214 | 40 | 11883 |
| 25 | Norfolk, Va | 136 | 63 | 26 | 78 | 20 | .... | 28 | 15 | 17 | 7 | 1 | 102 | 98 | 200 | 54 | 38 | 4 | .... | 92 | 4 | 10 | 11 | 4 | 2 | 21 | 6 | 323 |
| 26 | Petersburg, Va | 44 | 5 | 1 | 10 | 142 | 3 | 12 | .... | 6 | 3 | 2 | 61 | 67 | 128 | 7 | 3 | 2 | 1 | 10 | 3 | 27 | 22 | 3 | 9 | 49 | 12 | 202 |
| 27 | Philadelphia, Pa | 2489 | 2409 | 590 | 853 | 639 | 44 | 691 | 314 | 203 | 42 | 11 | 3707 | 2915 | 6622 | .... | .... | .... | .... | .... | .... | 169 | 148 | 20 | 21 | 317 | 41 | 6980 |
| 28 | Pittsburg, Pa | 217 | 238 | 63 | 98 | 181 | 4 | 46 | 97 | 22 | 10 | 5 | 464 | 297 | 761 | .... | .... | .... | .... | .... | .... | .... | .... | 19 | 17 | .... | 36 | 797 |
| 29 | Portland, Me | 95 | 98 | 33 | 92 | 227 | 1 | 27 | 18 | 46 | 6 | 3 | 285 | 237 | 522 | .... | .... | .... | .... | .... | .... | 9 | 11 | 2 | 1 | 20 | 3 | 545 |
| 30 | Portsmouth, Va | 80 | 42 | 11 | 26 | 18 | 1 | 9 | 10 | 6 | 2 | 1 | 60 | 60 | 120 | 16 | 19 | 4 | 6 | 35 | 10 | 3 | 6 | .... | 3 | 9 | 3 | 177 |
| 31 | Poughksepsie, N. Y | 275 | 155 | 40 | 96 | 47 | 5 | 30 | 44 | 9 | 12 | 1 | 331 | 255 | 586 | .... | .... | .... | .... | .... | .... | 14 | 8 | 5 | .. | 22 | 5 | 613 |
| 32 | Providence, R. I | 109 | 73 | 21 | 56 | 634 | 3 | 17 | 47 | 15 | 3 | 1 | 452 | 416 | 868 | .... | .... | .... | .... | .... | .... | 5 | 10 | 4 | 6 | 15 | 10 | 893 |
| 33 | Quincy, Ill | 116 | 44 | 5 | 8 | .... | 2 | 17 | 12 | 2 | 2 | .... | 94 | 70 | 164 | .... | .... | .... | .... | .... | .... | 5 | 2 | 2 | .... | 7 | 2 | 173 |
| 34 | Richmond, Va | 157 | 156 | 52 | 104 | 23 | 1 | 53 | 3 | 14 | 3 | 7 | 175 | 139 | 314 | 61 | 37 | 13 | 11 | 98 | 24 | 19 | 19 | 4 | 14 | 38 | 18 | 492 |
| 35 | St. Louis, Mo | 2538 | 648 | 88 | 90 | 470 | 11 | 214 | 650 | 68 | 36 | 11 | 2192 | 1535 | 3727 | 17 | 14 | 4 | 3 | 31 | 7 | 22 | 18 | 13 | 16 | 40 | 29 | 3834 |
| 36 | Washington, D. C | 144 | 120 | 49 | 151 | 135 | 1 | 23 | 52 | 11 | 4 | 2 | 217 | 206 | 423 | 15 | 16 | 6 | 4 | 81 | 10 | 46 | 56 | 17 | 16 | 102 | 33 | 599 |
| 37 | Wilmington, Del | .... | .... | .... | .... | .... | 5 | 18 | 2 | 5 | 4 | .... | 117 | 104 | 221 | .... | .... | .... | .... | .... | .... | 34 | 31 | .... | .... | 65 | .... | 286 |
| 38 | Wilmington, N. C | 21 | 46 | 17 | 40 | 34 | .... | 6 | 3 | 7 | 2 | 1 | 48 | 33 | 81 | 35 | 27 | 4 | 4 | 62 | 8 | .... | 1 | 4 | 2 | 1 | 6 | 158 |

# CAUSES OF DEATH,

EMBRACING—

1. *List of diseases which appear in the United States tables (in italics.)*
2. *Terms found upon the returns of the marshals and appearing on the State tables or condensed under other terms, according to the best medical authorities and State reports. This list does not include all of the original terms. Those omitted were condensed in the same manner.*

*Abscess.*—Abortion. *Accident.*—This term has been returned with every conceivable specification.—*Burned, drowned, scalded.* Affection, ague, dumb ague. fever and ague, Amenorrhea, Anasarca, Anæmia. *Aneurism* of the heart, angina, angina maligna, angina pectoris, apthæ. *Apoplexy.*—Apoplectic stroke, apoplectic fit, arachnitis, articulo mortis, in., ascites, asphyxia. *Asthma.*—Atrophy, bed sores, bilious, bilious colic, bite of snake, of rattlesnake, &c., black vomit. *Bladder, disease of.*—"Inflammation of," "Cystitis," &c., bleeding, "from lungs," "from nose," "from stomach," &c., bl eding and bloody piles, blood vessels—broken, rupture of, blue disease, blue sickness. *Bowels, disease of.*—Bowell "complaint," "congestion of," "consumption of," "mortification," &c. *Brain, disease of.*—"Affection of" "atrophy of," "concussion," "compression," "effusion," &c., &c., breast—"affection," "cancer," "disease," "inflammation," "congestion," &c.; breasts—"broken," "sore," "Inflammation," &c.; breach, broken heart. *Bronchitis.*—Bronchia, disease of, "bronchial rupture," bronchocele, bursting of blood vessel, of artery, bursting of bowels, cachexia, cachexy, calculus, calculus in bladder. *Cancer.*—Carcinoma, schinus, cancer of various organs, caries of hip, caries of spine, of backbone, canker, canker rash. *Carbuncle.*—Carditis, casualty, catalepsy, catamenia. *Catarrh.*—Cold. *Cephalitis.*—Inflammation of brain, cerebral disease, change of life, chest, "affection of," "congestion of," "disease of," "inflammation," chilblains, chills, chills and fever, chlorosis, choked. *Cholera—infantum, morbus*—"Asiatic," "bilious," "epidemic," "spasmodic," summer complaint. *Chorea.*—"St. Vitus' dance," "St. Anthony's dance," (?) "chronic," cirrposis, clap. *Colic.*—"Bilious," "cramp," "painters," "pictonum," "ileus," cold, exposure to, cold, cold water drinking, colonic dyspepsia, coma, compression of brain, concussion of brain, congenital disease, congestion of brain, of liver, of lungs, &c., congestive chills. *Consumption.*—"Pulmonary," "of lungs," "of the blood," "phthisis," "tubercular phthisis." "galloping," "hasty," "decline." *Convulsions.*—Spasms, convulsions, puerperal, costiveness, coup de soleil, cramp, "of the stomach." *Croup.*—Cynanche trachealis, curvature of the spine, cutaneous disease, cyanosis, cynanche—maligna, parotidea, tonsillaris, trachealis—black jaundice, blue disease, blue sickness, blue skin, cystitis. *Debility.*—Weakness, decay, decline. *Delirium tremens.*—Mania-a-potu, madness from drink, delirium, dementia, dentition. *Diabetes.*—Diaphragm, inflammation of, diaphragmitis. *Diarrhœa.*—Bowel complaint, purging, chronic diarhœa. *Dirt eating.*—Cachexia, Africanus, negro cachexia, dislocation, difficult labor, drinking, drinking spirits, drinking whiskey, &c., &c., drinking cold water, dropsical. *Dropsy.*—Dropsy, abdominal, of the chest, of the heart, &c., &c., dropsy of head, of brain, &c., drunkenness. *Dysentery.*—Flux, bloody flux, chronic dysentery, dysmenorrhea. *Dyspepsia.*—Dyspeptic, indigestion, dyspnœa, ear, disease of, inflammation of, effects of mercury, of salivation, effusion on the brain, emaciation, empyema, encephalitis, enlargement of the heart, enlargement of the spleen. *Enteritis.*—Inflammation of bowels. *Epilepsy.*—Epileptic fit, falling sickness, epistaxis, eruption, eruptive disease. *Erysipelas.*—St. Anthony's fire, exanthema. *Executed.*—Hung, capitally punished, fainting, fall, felon. *Fever, not otherwise specified,* bilious, brain, catarrhal, childbed, congestive, continued, eruptive, Chagres, gastric, hectic, infantile remittent, inflammatory. *Fever, intermittent,* jail, lung, malignant, milk, mesenteric, nervous, Panama. *Fever, puerperal,* putrid. *Fever, remittent,* rheumatic. *Fever, scarlet,* slow. *Fever, ship,* spotted, synocha, synochus, typhoid. *Fever, typhus,* typhus gravior, worm. *Fever, yellow. Fistula.* Fistula in ano, fits, flooding, fluor albus, flux, found dead. *Fracture.*—Fright, frost, frostbitten. *Frozen.*—Frozen to death, fungus, fungus hematodes, gall stones, gangrene, gastralgia. *Gastritis.*—Gastro enteritis, inflammation of stomach, goitre, gonorrhea. *Gout.*—Gout in the stomach. *Gravel.*—Green sickness, hæmatemesis. *Hemorrhage,* with many specifications, hemorrhage from uterus, hanged. *Heart, disease of,* aneurism of, dilatation of, enlargement of, hypertrophy of, inflammation of, organic affection of, carditis, pericarditis, &c., &c., head, disease of, head, inflammation of, head, congestion of, head, water on, dropsy of. *Heat.*—Excessive, overheated, &c., hemiplegia. *Hemorrhoids.*—hepatitis, h. chronic. *Hernia.*—Strangulated hernia, herpes, hip complaint. *Hip, disease of.*—Hip disease, hives, bold hives. *Hooping cough. Hydrocephalus. Hydrophobia,*—Hydrothorax, hypertrophy, of heart, of liver, &c., hypocondria, hysteria, hysterics, hysteric fits, hysteritis, icturus, ictus solis, iliac passion, ileus, indigestion, infanticide, infantile, infantile disease, infantile complaint. *Inflammation.*—This term is returned with countless specifications of organs and localities. *Influenza.*—Injury, with many specifications. *Insanity.*—Intestines, abscess of, mortification of, stricture of, intussusception of. *Intemperance.*—Intoxication, intussusception. *Jaundice.*—Jaw, tumor of. *Kidneys, disease of,* inflammation of, nephritis, &c., killed, king's evil. *Laryngitis.*—Laudanum, "overdose," "poison by," lead colic, leg, fracture of, leg, mortification of, leg, amputation of. *Leprosy.*—Lethargy, leucorrhea. *Lightning. Liver, disease of.*—Complaint, congestion of, inflammation of, enlargement of, &c. Lost at sea, lockjaw, lues venereal, lumbar abscess. *Lungs, disease of.*—Lungs, inflammation of; lungs, bleeding from; hemorrhage of, &c. Madness, malignant sore throat. *Malformation.*—Mania, mania-a-potu, mania puerpual, manslaughter. *Marasmus. Measles.*—Meningitis, menorrhagia; menstruation, difficult, excessive, suppressed; mesenteric disease, milk leg, miscarriage, milk sickness. *Mortification.*—Mumps. *Murder.*—Necrosis, nephritis, nerves, disease of, nervous affection, nervous disease, nervous fever, nettlerash, neuralgia; obstruction of bladder, of bowels, &c., œdema. *Old age.*—Onanism, operation, ophthalmia, organic disease, overflow of blood, on brain, overlaid; pain, painter's colic, palsy. *Paralysis.*—Paralytic fit. *Paramenia.*—Paraplegia, paronychia, parotitis, pericarditis, peripneumonia, pertussis, phlegmasia dolens, phlegmon, phrenitis, phthisis, piles, plague, spotted; pleura, inflammation of. *Pleurisy.*—Pleuritis. *Pneumonia. Poison.* Pox, premature birth, polypus, polypus in nose, &c., prolapsus uteri, psoriasis, psoas abscess, puerperal fever, convulsions, mania; pulmonary, pulmonary disease, &c., purpura, putrid sore throat, pyrosis. *Quinsy.*—Rachitis, rash, rash fever, red gum, remittent fever, retention of urine, rheumatic fever. *Rheumatism.*—Rheumatism of the heart. *Rickets.*—Ringworm, rose rash, roseola, rubeola, rum, rum-drinking, &c., rupture; salivation, effects of; scald-head, scarletina, sciatica, schirrous tumor, schirrus, scorbutus. *Scrofula.*—Scrofulous tumor. *Scurvy.*—Sea-sickness, senectus, shingles. *Skin, disease of.*—Skin, smothered. *Small pox.* Sore throat, spasms, spinal disease. *Spine, disease of.*—Spitting of blood. *Spleen, disease of.*—Spleenitis, spotted fever, spotted plague, St. Anthony's fire, St. Vitus's dance, starvation. *Stomach, disease of.*—Stomach, inflammation of; stone, stoppage in bowels, strangulation, strangulated hernia, strangury, stricture, stricture of the urethra, sudden. *Suffocation. Suicide.*—Suppression of urine, swelling, synochus. *Syphilis.*—Tabes, tabes mesenterica. *Teething. Tetanus. Throat, disease of.*—Inflammation of. *Thrush.*—Tic douloureux, tongue, inflammation of; tonsils, swelling of; tonsils, inflammation; tonsillitis, toothache, trismus, trismus nascentium, tubercular disease. *Tumor.*—Turn of life, twist in bowels, typhus, typhoid. *Ulcer.*—Ulceration, urine, suppression, retention, stoppage; urticaria, uterine hemorrhage, uterus, disease of; vaccination, varicella, variola, veins, disease of; venereal, vermes, vertigo, violence, vomitting blood, wasting away, water on brain, on head, water on chest, &c., &c; waterbrash, wen, whites, whitlow. *White swelling.*—Windpipe, inflammation of; wind colic, womb, disease of; inflammation, &c., &c. *Worms.*—Worm fever, wound, yellow fever, yellow gum, yellow jaundice.